The **Thomas Guide**®

D0523070

Pacific Northwest
Washington • Oregon • Western Idaho • Southwestern British Columbia

road atlas

TELL US
response form in back
WHAT YOU THINK

CONTENTS

intro

maps

index

⊛ RAND MᶜNALLY

using your road atlas

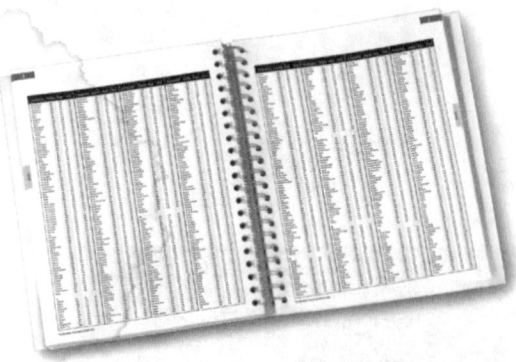

city listings

• The Cities and Communities Index on page F includes all communities large or small. County, page number, and grid location for each are listed.

• Find the community you're looking for in the list, then turn to the page number indicated.

index

• Street listings are separate from points of interest.

• In the street listings, read across for city, state, page number, and grid reference.

• Points of interest include campgrounds, wineries, ski areas, and more.

• The grid reference, a letter-number combination such as D6, tells where on the map to find a listing.

STREET		
City State		Page-Grid
DAVENPORT CREEK RD		
SAN LUIS OBISPO CO CA		271-D6
DAVID AV		
MONTEREY CO CA		337-E4
PACIFIC GROVE CA		337-D5

FEATURE NAME		
City State		Page-Grid
1000 STEPS CO BCH		
PACIFIC COAST HWY, LAGUNA BEACH CA		365-G10
ALISO BEACH		
S COAST HWY, LAGUNA BEACH CA		365-F9
ANCHOR MARINA		
1970 TAYLOR RD, CONTRA COSTA CO CA		174-C2

working with the maps

• The grid is created by combining letters running along the top of the map with numbers running along the side.

• To use a grid reference, follow the numbered row until it crosses the lettered column.

• To find an adjacent map, turn to the map number indicated on map edges.

• The Legend on page A explains symbols and colors.

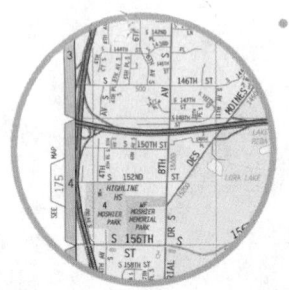

street sign image © PhotoDisc, Inc.

USING FOUR TYPES OF MAPS

PageFinder™ map

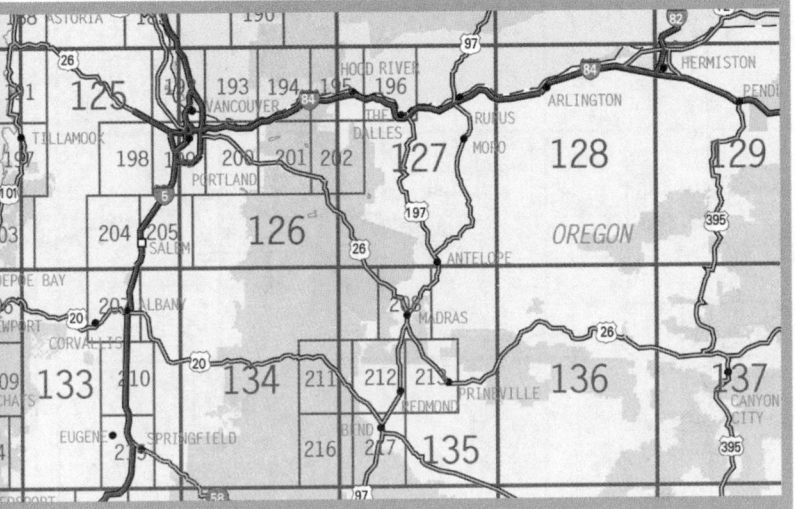

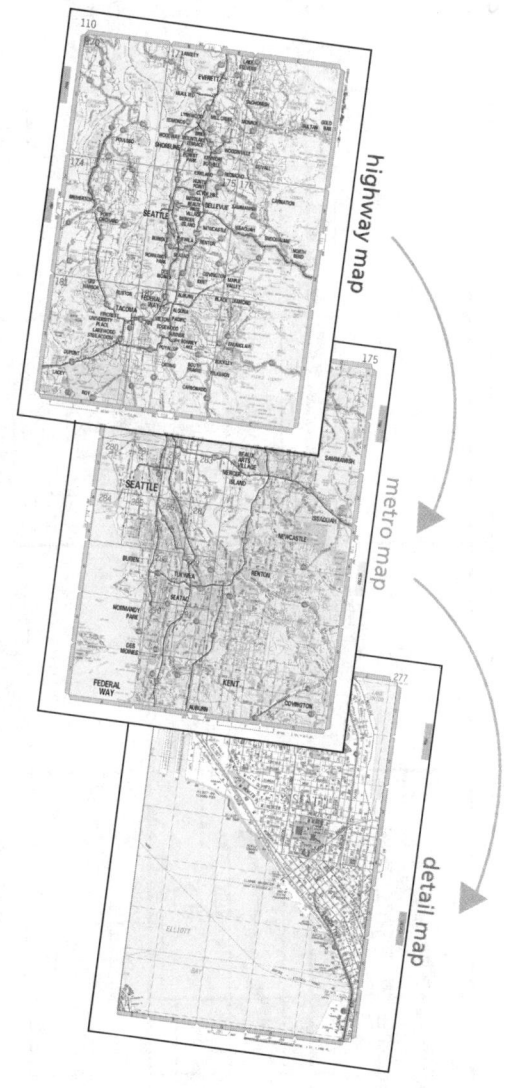

highway map

metro map

detail map

You will find red boxes on many different types of maps in this atlas. Each box indicates an area covered in greater detail on a subsequent page. If your area of interest falls within one of these boxes, turn to the indicated page to view in greater detail.

PageFinder™ map

- The PageFinder™ map provides an overview of the entire area covered in this atlas.
- Use the PageFinder™ map to guide you to the page(s) showing your general area of interest.

highway maps

- Highway maps offer a general view of your area of interest.
- Use Highway maps for long distance planning and navigation.

metro maps

- Metro maps offer greater detail than Highway maps and cover major cities and areas of special interest.
- Use Metro maps for navigation within cities and for locating points of interest.

detail maps

- Detail maps offer street detail as well as multiple points of interest.
- Use Detail maps for local planning and navigation and for locating many points of interest.

INTRO

HWY & METRO PAGES
PAGEFINDER™

128 Highway Page- Small scale area map, shown with a wide border

208 Metro Page- Mid scale area map, shown with a thin border

PageFinder™ Map Scale (1 Inch to 62 Miles)

0 20 40 60 80 Miles

0 60 120 Kilometers

© 2004 Rand McNally Maps®

BRITISH COLUMBIA

CAMPBELL RIVER

92 93 94 95

MERRITT

1

VANCOUVER 157

HOPE

CHILLIWACK

BRITISH COLUMBIA
WASHINGTON
CANADA
USA

VANCOUVER

100 101 102 103 104 105 106 107

ISLAND

VICTORIA 159

BELLINGHAM

160 161

BURLINGTON

OMAK

OKANOGAN

LAKE CHELAN

GRAND COULEE

KETTLE FALLS

COLVILLE

LAKE PEND OREILLE

KOOTENAI

244

162 163 164 165 166 167 168

FORKS

PORT ANGELES

ARLINGTON

EVERETT
SNOHOMISH

169

170 11

REDMOND

SEATTLE

NORTH BEND

237

WATERVILLE

236

238 239
WENATCHEE

DAVENPORT

SPOKANE

POST FALLS

245

COEUR D'ALENE

108 172 109 173 174 176 111 112 113 114 248 115

SHELTON

177 178 179 180 181 182 110

ABERDEEN OLYMPIA TACOMA

MOSES LAKE 242

RITZVILLE

LIBERTY LAKE 247

240 241

CLE ELUM

183 184

RAYMOND

CHEHALIS

ELLENSBURG

212

WASHINGTON

COLFAX

IDAHO

185

MOUNT RAINIER

116 186 117 18 118 119 120 121 122 123

OCEAN

RAYMOND

YAKIMA

RICHLAND

PASCO

WALLA WALLA

POMEROY

DAYTON

LEWISTON

250

188 ASTORIA 190 MOUNT SAINT HELENS MOUNT ADAMS KENNEWICK

LONGVIEW

WASHINGTON
OREGON

GRANGEVILLE

121 125 193 194 195 196 127 128 129 130 131

TILLAMOOK

VANCOUVER

HOOD RIVER

THE DALLES

RUFUS MORO

ARLINGTON

HERMISTON

PENDLETON

LA GRANDE

NEW MEADOWS 251

124 197 198 199 200 201 202 OREGON

PORTLAND

ANTELOPE

203 204 205 126

SALEM

DEPOE BAY

NEWPORT 206 207 ALBANY

CORVALLIS

218 MADRAS

BAKER CITY

COUNCIL 252

132 209 133 210 134 211 212 213 136 137 138 139

YACHATS

EUGENE SPRINGFIELD

PRINEVILLE

REDMOND

CANYON CITY

ONTARIO

PAYETTE

214 21 216 217 135

BEND

BOISE

218 219

REEDSPORT

58

BURNS

HINES

HOMEDALE CALDWELL 253

COOS BAY 220 140 221 141 222 223 142 143 144 145 146 147

BANDON

ROSEBURG

CRATER LAKE

HARNEY LAKE

MALHEUR LAKE

JORDAN VALLEY

224 PORT ORFORD 22 226 227

228 229 230 231 CHILOQUIN

GRANTS PASS MEDFORD

232 148 233 149 234 150 235 151 152 153 154 155

ASHLAND

KLAMATH FALLS

LAKEVIEW

OREGON CALIFORNIA

GOOSE LAKE

OREGON NEVADA

IDAHO NEVADA

CRESCENT CITY YREKA CALIFORNIA NEVADA

CITIES & COMMUNITIES

Community	State	Page	Grid
A			
* ABBOTSFORD	BC	102	B1
Aberdeen	BC	102	B1
* ABERDEEN	WA	178	A7
Aberdeen Gardens	WA	178	B5
Abernethy	OR	317	H1
Abrams	OR	141	C1
Acme	WA	161	C2
Acton	WA	120	C2
Ada	OR	214	B5
* ADAIR VILLAGE	OR	207	B4
* ADAMS	OR	129	C1
Addy	WA	106	A3
Adel	WA	152	B2
Adelaide	WA	175	D1
Adelaide	WA	182	A1
Adna	WA	184	A7
Advance	OR	199	C5
Agassiz	BC	94	C3
Agate Beach	OR	206	B3
Agness	OR	148	B1
Agnew	WA	165	D6
Ahsahka	ID	123	C2
Ahtanum	WA	243	A7
Ainsworth Corner	CA	150	C3
Ainsworth Corner	WA	151	A2
Airlie	OR	207	A2
* AIRWAY HEIGHTS	WA	246	A4
Ajlune	OR	118	A2
Alameda	OR	314	A1
* ALBANY	OR	326	A12
Albee	OR	129	B2
* ALBION	WA	249	A4
Alder	OR	130	C2
Alder	OR	133	A1
Alder	WA	118	B1
Alder Creek	OR	201	A4
Aldergate	WA	128	B1
Alderton	WA	182	C4
Alderwood Manor	WA	171	B5
Alexander Beach	WA	259	D6
Alfalfa	OR	135	B3
Alger	WA	161	B3
Algoma	OR	235	C1
* ALGONA	WA	182	B2
Alicel	OR	130	A2
Alkali Lake	OR	144	B3
Alki	WA	280	B3
Allegany	OR	218	D7
Allentown	WA	286	D7
Allison	WA	182	A4
Allyn	WA	173	D6
Allyn-Grapeview	WA	173	D7
* ALMIRA	WA	237	D7
Almota	WA	122	B1
Aloha	OR	199	A2
Aloha	WA	177	B2
Alpha	WA	118	A2
Alpine	OR	128	C1
Alpine	OR	133	B2
Alsea	OR	133	A2
Alston	OR	189	A4
Altamont	OR	338	H11
Alta Vista	WA	118	B2
Alto	WA	122	A2
Altoona	WA	117	A2
Alvadore	OR	133	B2
Amanda Park	WA	109	A2
Amber	WA	114	B2
Amboy	WA	193	B1
American	OR	210	A3
American Lk Gdns	WA	181	C4
* AMITY	OR	204	B2
* ANACORTES	WA	259	D4
Anatone	WA	122	C3
Anderson	OR	200	B3
Andrews	OR	153	C1
Angle Lake	WA	290	D2
Anlauf	OR	219	B2
* ANMORE	BC	157	A3
Annapolis	WA	271	A13
Annex	OR	139	A2
Annieville	BC	156	D6
* ANTELOPE	OR	127	C3
Antone	OR	136	B2
Apex	OR	129	B1
Apiary	OR	189	B5
Applegate	OR	149	B2
Appleton	WA	196	B3
Appleyard	WA	239	A5
Arago	OR	220	D6
Arbor Heights	WA	284	D4
Arbor Lodge	OR	308	D5
Arbutus	BC	254	D14
Arcadia	WA	180	C3
Archabal	ID	251	C6
Arch Cape	OR	191	A2
Arden	WA	171	A6
Ardenvoir	WA	112	A1
Ardenwald	OR	318	A6
Argay	OR	193	A7
Ariel	OR	118	A3
Arletta	WA	181	B1
* ARLINGTON	OR	128	A1
* ARLINGTON	WA	168	D5
Arlington Heights	OR	312	B7
Arlington Heights	WA	102	C3
Arnold Creek	OR	320	C2
Arock	OR	146	C3
Arrow Head Beach	WA	167	D3
Artondale	WA	181	B1
Asert	OR	200	B1
Ashdale	OR	199	D4
Ashford	WA	118	B1
* ASHLAND	OR	337	D9
Ashwood	OR	135	C1
* ASOTIN	WA	250	B6
Aspen Grove	BC	95	C1
* ASTORIA	OR	300	F5
* ATHENA	OR	129	C1
* ATHOL	ID	245	B2
Atkinson	WA	176	A6
* AUBURN	WA	182	C2
* AUMSVILLE	OR	205	B7
* AURORA	OR	199	B7
Aurora Village	WA	171	A6
Austa	OR	133	A2
Austin	OR	137	C1
Austin	WA	170	D2
Austin Junction	OR	137	C1
Avon	WA	161	A7
Avondale	WA	171	D7
Ayer	WA	121	C2
Azalea	OR	225	C6
Azwell	WA	112	B1
B			
Baby Island Heights	WA	167	D7
Bade	OR	129	C2
Badger Corner	OR	323	E12
Bagdad Junction	WA	237	D4
Bagley Junction	WA	176	C6
Bainbridge Island	WA	174	D2
* BAKER CITY	OR	138	B1
Baker-Langdon	WA	345	E13
Balch	WA	117	B1
Balder	WA	114	C3
Ballard	WA	272	D4
Ballston	OR	204	A3
Bamberton	BC	159	B3
Bamfield	BC	100	A1
Bancroft	OR	140	C3
* BANDON	OR	220	B6
Bangor	WA	170	A7
Barber	ID	253	D3
Barberton	WA	192	D5
Baring	WA	111	A1
Barnesdale	OR	191	B5
Barneston	WA	176	B7
Barnett	OR	128	A2
Barnhart	OR	129	B1
Barton	OR	200	B4
Barton Heights	OR	131	B2
Barview	OR	191	A7
Barview	OR	220	C1
Basin City	WA	121	A2
Basque	OR	154	B1
Bassett Junction	WA	113	A3
Bates	OR	137	C1
Batterson	OR	191	D4
Battin	OR	319	G7
* BATTLE GROUND	WA	192	D3
Bay Center	WA	183	C7
* BAY CITY	OR	191	B7
Bay City	WA	183	B2
Bayne	WA	110	C3
Bayocean	OR	191	A7
Bay Park	OR	333	J13
Bayshore	WA	180	B2
Bayside Gardens	OR	191	B4
Bayview	ID	245	C1
Bayview	OR	328	C2
Bay View	WA	160	D6
Bayview	WA	170	D1
Bay View	WA	181	C2
Bazan Bay	BC	159	B3
Beach Grove	BC	101	C1
Beach Haven	BC	101	C2
Beacon Hill	WA	282	C2
Beacon Hill	WA	303	C3
Bear	ID	131	B3
Beatty	OR	151	A1
Beaumont Wilshire	OR	314	B1
* BEAUX ARTS VLG	WA	175	C3
Beaver	OR	197	C5
Beaver	WA	163	A6
Beavercreek	OR	200	A6
Beaver Homes	OR	189	C6
Beaver Marsh	OR	142	C2
Beaver Springs	OR	189	B5
* BEAVERTON	OR	199	B2
Bedford	WA	117	B1
Beebe	WA	236	D3
Beech Creek	OR	137	A1
Bel Air	OR	199	B2
* BELCARRA	BC	157	A3
Belfair	WA	173	D5
Belknap Springs	OR	134	B2
Bellevue	OR	204	A2
* BELLEVUE	WA	175	C2
Bellfountain	OR	133	B2
* BELLINGHAM	WA	258	G4
Bells Beach	WA	167	D7
* BEND	OR	332	E7
Bendemeer	OR	192	A7
Benewah	ID	115	A3
Benge	WA	122	A1
* BENTON CITY	WA	120	C3
Berkeley	WA	182	A6
Berne	WA	111	B1
Berrydale	WA	182	D1
Berteleda	CA	148	B3
Bertsche Terrace	CA	148	B3
Bethany	OR	192	A7
Bethel	OR	329	F4
Bethel	WA	174	B4
Bethel Gospel Park	OR	205	A3
Beulah	OR	138	A3
Beverly	WA	120	B1
Beverly Beach	OR	206	B2
Beverly Beach	WA	167	D7
Beverly Park	WA	268	D4
Bickleton	WA	120	A3
Biggam	WA	120	C3
Biggs	OR	127	C1
Biggs Junction	OR	127	C1
Biloxi	WA	174	D4
* BINGEN	WA	195	D5
Bingham Springs	OR	130	A1
Birch	WA	110	C3
Birch Bay	WA	158	B4
Birchfield	WA	120	A2
Birchfield	WA	243	C7
Birkenfeld	OR	117	B3
Bissell	OR	200	D6
Bitter Lake	WA	171	A7
Blachly	OR	133	A2
Black Butte Ranch	OR	211	C3
Black Creek	BC	92	A1
* BLACK DIAMOND	WA	110	C3
Black River Jct	WA	289	H2
Blaine	OR	197	D6
* BLAINE	WA	158	A3
Blakeley	WA	129	C1
Blalock	OR	128	A1
Blanchard	ID	107	A3
Blanchard	WA	161	A4
Blewett	WA	238	A5
Bliss Landing	BC	92	B1
Blitzen	OR	153	B1
Blockhouse	WA	127	B1
Blodgett	OR	133	A1
Blooming	OR	198	C2
Blubber Bay	BC	92	B1
Bluecreek	WA	106	A3
Blue Mountain	OR	129	C1
Blue Ridge	WA	171	A7
Blue River	OR	134	A2
Bluestem	WA	114	A2
Bly	OR	151	B1
Blyn	WA	109	C1
* BOARDMAN	OR	128	C1
Boardman Junction	OR	128	C1
Bodie	OR	129	C2
Bogachiel	WA	169	D3
Boise	OR	313	F1
Boise	WA	110	C3
* BOISE	ID	253	D3
Boise Hills Village	ID	253	D2
Boistfort	WA	187	A2
Bolton	OR	199	D4
* BONANZA	OR	151	A2
Bonifer	OR	129	C1
Bonita	OR	199	B3
Bonlow	WA	243	A4
* BONNERS FERRY	ID	107	B2
Bonneville	OR	194	B7
* BONNEY LAKE	WA	182	C4
Bonny Slope	OR	199	B1
Bordeaux	WA	184	A2
Boring	OR	200	B3
Boston Bar	BC	95	A1
Boston Harbor	WA	180	C4
* BOTHELL	WA	171	C6
Boulevard Park	WA	285	J6
Boundary	WA	106	B1
Bourne	OR	138	A1
* BOVILL	ID	123	B1
Bow	WA	161	A4
Bowen Island	BC	93	B3
Bowers Junction	OR	192	A7
Bowmont	OR	147	C1
Bowser	BC	92	B2
Boyd	OR	127	B2
Brackendale	BC	93	C1
Bradwood	OR	117	B3
Brady	WA	179	A7
Brandstrom	WA	168	B3
Braymill	OR	150	C1
Breakers	WA	186	A5
Breidablick	WA	170	B5
Breitenbush Hot Spgs	OR	134	B1
* BREMERTON	WA	270	G10
Bremerton Junction	WA	174	A4
Brentwood Bay	BC	159	C4
Brentwd-Darlington	OR	318	D6
* BREWSTER	WA	104	B3
Briarwood	OR	321	G4
Brickerville	OR	214	D1
Bridal Veil	OR	201	A1
Bridesville	BC	105	A1
Bridge	OR	140	C3
Bridgeport	OR	138	B1
* BRIDGEPORT	WA	112	C1
Bridgeton	OR	309	G2
Bridgeview	OR	233	B5
Bridlemile	OR	316	A2
* BRIER	WA	171	B6
Brighouse	BC	156	B6
Brighton	WA	191	B5
Brightwood	OR	201	B4
Brinnon	WA	109	C1
Bristol	WA	196	A4
Britannia Beach	BC	93	C2
Broadacres	OR	205	B1
Broadbent	OR	140	B3
Broadmoor	BC	156	B7
Brogan	OR	138	C2
Bromart	WA	171	D3
Brookdale	WA	182	A5
Brookfield	WA	117	A2
* BROOKINGS	OR	232	C6
Brooklyn	OR	317	H2
Brooks	OR	205	A3
Brookwild	OR	318	D7
Brothers	OR	135	C3
Brownsboro	OR	149	C1
Brownsmead	OR	117	A3
Browns Point	WA	181	D1
Brownstown	WA	119	C2
* BROWNSVILLE	OR	210	C2
Brush Prairie	WA	193	A4
Bryant	WA	168	D4
Bryn Mawr	WA	175	C4
Buchanan	OR	145	C1
Buck Fork	OR	141	B2

*Indicates City, District or Township

INTRO

Community	State	Page	Grid	Community	State	Page	Grid	Community	State	Page	Grid	Community	State	Page	Grid
* BUCKLEY	WA	182	D4	* CASCADE LOCKS	OR	194	D5	Cicero	WA	102	C3	Concord	OR	321	J7
Buckman	OR	313	H6	Cascade Summit	OR	142	B1	Cinebar	WA	118	A2	Concordia	OR	310	A6
Bucks Corners	OR	129	A1	Cascade Valley	WA	242	C3	City Center	WA	181	C4	* CONCRETE	WA	102	C2
* BUCODA	WA	184	D4	Cascadia	OR	134	A2	* CITY OF CHILLIWCK	BC	94	C3	* CONDON	OR	128	A2
Buell	OR	125	B3	* CASHMERE	WA	238	C2	* CITY OF COLWOOD	BC	159	B7	Conkling Park	ID	248	A5
Buena	WA	120	A2	Casino	BC	106	B1	* CTY OF N VANCVR	BC	254	J4	Conley	OR	130	A2
Buena Vista	OR	207	C2	Casino Corner	WA	268	B5	* CITY OF SURREY	BC	157	B7	* CONNELL	WA	121	B1
Buenna	WA	175	A7	Casland	WA	111	C3	* CITY OF VICTORIA	BC	256	H7	Conway	WA	168	B2
Bull Run	OR	200	D3	* CASTLE ROCK	WA	187	C7	* CITY OF WHT ROCK	BC	158	A2	Cook	WA	195	B5
Bunker Hill	OR	333	J11	Cataldo	ID	115	B2	Clackamas	OR	199	D3	Coolin	ID	107	A2
Burbank	WA	121	B3	Cathcart	WA	171	D5	Clackamas Heights	OR	199	D4	Coombs	BC	92	C3
Burbank Heights	WA	121	A3	Cathedral Park	WA	192	B6	Clallam Bay	WA	163	B3	* COOS BAY	OR	333	D10
* BURIEN	WA	285	F7	* CATHLAMET	WA	117	B3	Claquato	WA	184	B6	Cooston	OR	218	B7
Burley	WA	174	B6	Caufield	BC	156	A3	Clarkes	OR	200	A7	Copalis Beach	WA	177	B4
Burlington	OR	192	A6	Cavalero Corner	WA	171	D1	* CLARK FORK	ID	107	C3	Copalis Crossing	WA	177	C4
* BURLINGTON	WA	260	D7	* CAVE JUNCTION	OR	233	A5	Clarkia	ID	115	C3	Copco	CA	150	A3
* BURNABY	BC	255	H10	Cavelero Beach	WA	167	D5	* CLARKSTON	WA	250	B4	Copeland	ID	107	B1
Burnett	WA	182	D5	Caycuse	BC	100	C1	Clarkston Heights	WA	250	B4	Coppei	WA	122	A3
* BURNS	OR	145	A1	Cayuse	OR	129	C1	Clarksville	ID	245	B5	Copperfield	OR	131	A3
Burns Junction	OR	146	B3	Cecil	OR	128	B1	Clarno	OR	128	A3	Copperville	ID	131	C1
Burnt Woods	OR	133	A1	Cecil	WA	106	C2	* CLATSKANIE	OR	117	B3	* COQUILLE	OR	220	D4
Buroker	WA	122	A3	Cedar	BC	93	A3	Clatsop Station	OR	188	B3	* COQUITLAM	BC	157	A3
Burop	WA	111	A3	Cedardale	BC	254	G4	Clay City	WA	118	B1	Corbett	OR	200	C1
Burr Canyon	WA	121	B2	Cedardale	OR	126	A3	Clayton	WA	114	B1	Corbt-Trwlgr-Lair Hl	OR	317	F4
Burrows	WA	177	C5	Cedar Falls	WA	176	C6	Clearbrook	BC	102	B1	Cordova Bay	BC	159	C5
Burton	WA	174	D6	Cedar Hills	OR	199	B1	Clear Creek	CA	149	A3	* CORNELIUS	OR	198	C1
Busby	WA	249	B6	Cedarhome	WA	168	B3	Clear Creek	OR	125	B1	Cornelius Pass	OR	192	A6
* BUTTE FALLS	OR	150	A1	Cedarhurst	WA	174	D5	Clear Lake	OR	204	D4	Cornell	WA	168	A6
Butter Creek Jct	OR	128	C1	Cedar Mill	OR	199	B1	Clear Lake	WA	161	C6	Cornell Place	WA	129	A1
Butterfield	OR	301	H1	Cedar Mountain	WA	175	D6	Clearview	WA	171	D5	Corner	WA	168	B3
Butteville	OR	199	A6	Cedar Point	OR	220	D4	Clearwater	OR	222	D4	Cornucopia	OR	130	C3
Buxton	OR	125	B1	Cedar Valley	WA	171	B5	* CLE ELUM	WA	240	B2	Coronado Shores	OR	203	A6
B Z Corner	WA	195	D2	Cedarville	WA	117	B1	Clem	OR	128	A2	Cortes Bay	BC	92	B1
				Celilo Village	OR	127	B1	Cleo	OR	220	D2	* CORVALLIS	OR	327	F7
C				Centennial	OR	200	A1	Cleveland	OR	221	A3	* COSMOPOLIS	WA	178	B7
Cabell City	OR	129	C3	Center	OR	314	D5	Cleveland	WA	120	A3	* COTTAGE GROVE	OR	215	B7
Cadboro Bay	BC	257	E4	Center	WA	170	A2	Clifton	OR	117	B3	* COTTONWOOD	ID	123	C3
Calder	ID	115	C2	Centerville	WA	127	B1	Clifton	OR	195	C5	Cottonwood Bay	WA	158	B4
* CALDWELL	ID	147	B1	Central Area	WA	278	C5	Clinton	WA	171	A2	Cottrell	OR	200	C3
Calhounville	WA	121	C3	Central Ferry	WA	122	B1	Clo-oose	BC	100	B2	Cougar	WA	190	A5
Callahan	OR	141	A2	* CENTRALIA	WA	299	E4	Cloquallum	WA	179	C4	* COULEE CITY	WA	113	A2
Cama Beach	WA	167	D6	Central Park	WA	178	C7	Cloverdale	BC	158	B1	* COULEE DAM	WA	237	C2
Camano	WA	167	D5	Central Point	OR	199	C6	Cloverdale	ID	253	B3	* COUNCIL	ID	139	C1
* CAMAS	WA	193	B7	* CENTRAL POINT	OR	336	A6	Cloverdale	OR	197	B7	Country Homes	WA	347	B11
Camas Valley	OR	141	A3	Central Valley	WA	174	B1	Cloverdale	OR	212	D4	County Line	BC	158	D1
* CAMBRIDGE	ID	139	B1	Ceres	WA	117	B2	Cloverdale	WA	189	D6	* COUPEVILLE	WA	167	B4
Camden	WA	106	C3	Chaffee	WA	120	C3	Cloverland	WA	122	C2	* COURTENAY	BC	92	A2
Cameron	ID	123	B1	Chain Hill	WA	184	D2	Clow Corner	OR	204	B6	Courtrock	OR	137	A1
Cameron	WA	106	C3	Chamber	WA	249	B7	Clyde	WA	121	C2	* COVE	OR	130	B2
* CAMPBELL RIVER	BC	92	A1	Chapman	OR	125	C1	* CLYDE HILL	WA	175	C2	Cove	WA	174	D5
Camp Discover	WA	170	A5	Chard	WA	122	B2	Coal Canyon	WA	118	B2	Covello	WA	122	B2
Camp Elkanah	OR	129	C2	Charleston	OR	220	C1	Coal Creek	WA	175	D4	Cove Orchard	OR	198	B4
Camp Grande	WA	167	D4	Charleston	WA	270	G11	Coal Creek	WA	189	B2	* COVINGTON	WA	175	D7
Camp Lagoon	WA	167	D4	Charlestown	OR	129	A1	Coaledo	OR	220	D3	Cowichan Bay	BC	101	B1
Camp Sealth	WA	174	C7	Chattaroy	WA	114	C1	Coalfield	WA	175	D4	Cowiche	WA	119	C1
Camp Sherman	OR	211	C1	* CHATCOLET	ID	248	A6	Coalmont	BC	95	C2	Cowlitz	WA	118	A2
Camp Twelve	OR	206	C3	* CHEHALIS	WA	299	C10	Cobble Hill	BC	159	A1	Crabtree	OR	133	C1
Camp Union	WA	173	D2	Chehalis Junction	WA	299	B14	* COBURG	OR	210	B7	Crab Tree	WA	114	C3
Canaan	OR	189	C7	Chehalis Village	WA	117	B1	Cocolalla	ID	107	A3	* CRAIGMONT	ID	123	B2
Canary	OR	214	B4	* CHELAN	WA	236	D3	* COEUR D'ALENE	ID	355	E11	Crane	OR	145	C2
* CANBY	OR	199	C6	Chelan Falls	WA	236	D4	Cohassett	WA	183	B2	Crates	WA	196	C6
Canby	WA	114	A2	Chelatchie	WA	118	A3	Cokedale	WA	161	D5	Crawfordville	OR	133	C2
Canemah	OR	199	D5	Chemainus	BC	101	A1	Colbert	WA	114	C1	Creosote	WA	174	D2
* CANNON BEACH	OR	188	A7	Chemawa	OR	323	D5	Colburn	ID	107	B2	Crescent	OR	142	C1
Cannon Beach Jct	OR	188	B6	Chemult	OR	142	C2	Colby	WA	271	H13	Crescent Beach	BC	158	A1
* CANYON CITY	OR	137	B2	* CHENEY	WA	246	A7	Colchester	WA	271	H14	* CRESCENT CITY	CA	148	B3
Canyon Park	WA	171	C6	Chenois Creek	WA	177	D6	Cold Springs	OR	129	A1	Crescent Lake	OR	142	B1
* CANYONVILLE	OR	225	C3	Chenoweth	OR	196	C6	Cold Springs Jct	OR	129	A1	Crescent Lake Jct	OR	142	B1
Cape Meares	OR	197	A1	Cherry Grove	OR	198	A2	Coles Corner	WA	111	C1	* CRESTON	WA	113	C1
Capitol Hill	WA	278	C3	Cherry Heights	OR	196	C7	Colestin	OR	234	D7	Creston Kenilworth	OR	318	B2
* CARBONADO	WA	182	D6	Cherry Valley	WA	110	C1	* COLFAX	WA	122	C1	Crestwood	OR	316	A7
Carlsborg	WA	166	A6	Cherryville	OR	201	A4	College Hill	OR	329	J9	* CRESWELL	OR	215	C5
Carlson	WA	118	B1	Chesaw	WA	105	A1	* COLLEGE PLACE	WA	344	G11	Creswell Heights	WA	193	C5
* CARLTON	OR	198	B5	Cheshire	OR	133	B2	Collins	WA	195	A5	Criterion	OR	127	B3
Carlton	WA	104	A3	Chester	WA	350	H14	Collins View	OR	320	D2	Crocker	WA	182	C5
Carnahan	OR	188	B3	* CHEWELAH	WA	106	B3	Colton	OR	126	A3	Crofton	BC	101	B1
Carnation	OR	198	B1	Chico	WA	270	B4	* COLTON	WA	250	A1	Cromwell	WA	181	B2
* CARNATION	WA	176	B1	Chilco	ID	245	A3	Columbia	WA	283	E5	Crosby	WA	173	D3
Carpenterville	OR	232	C2	* CHILLIWACK	BC	102	C1	Columbia Beach	WA	171	A2	Croskey	WA	114	A2
Carrolls	WA	189	C4	* CHILOQUIN	OR	231	D4	* COLUMBIA CITY	OR	192	B1	Cross	WA	174	C6
Carson	OR	131	A3	Chimacum	WA	170	A1	Columbia Gardens	BC	106	B1	Crossing	WA	168	C6
* CARSON	WA	194	D4	Chinook	WA	186	B7	Columbia Heights	WA	302	G2	Crow	OR	133	B3
Carson River Valley	WA	194	D4	Chiwaukum	WA	111	C2	Columbia Vly Gdns	WA	302	G6	Crowfoot	OR	133	C1
Carus	OR	199	D6	* CHRISTINA LAKE	BC	105	C1	* COLVILLE	WA	106	A2	Crown Hill	WA	273	E1
Carver	OR	200	A4	Christmas Valley	OR	143	C2	Colvos	WA	174	D5	Crown Point	OR	220	C2
Cascade	BC	105	C1	Christopher	WA	182	C1	* COMOX	BC	92	A2	Cruzatt	WA	194	A7
* CASCADE	ID	252	D6	Chrome	OR	220	D4	Comstock	OR	219	C1	Crystal Springs	WA	271	C3
Cascade Gorge	OR	150	A1	Chuckanut Village	WA	258	B13	Concomly	OR	205	A2	* CULDESAC	ID	123	B2
Cascade Heights	BC	156	C5	Chumstick	WA	111	C2	* CONCONULLY	WA	104	B2	Cully	OR	310	D7

*Indicates City, District or Township

Community	State	Page	Grid
Culp Creek	OR	141	C1
Cultus Lake	BC	102	C1
* CULVER	OR	208	B7
Cumberland	BC	92	A2
Cumberland	WA	110	C3
Cunningham	WA	121	B1
Cuprum	ID	131	B3
Curiew	WA	105	B1
Currinsville	OR	200	C5
Curtin	OR	219	B1
Curtis	WA	187	A1
Cushman	OR	214	B3
* CUSICK	WA	106	C3
Custer	WA	158	C4
Cutler City	OR	203	A5
D			
Dabob	WA	170	A4
Dahl Pine	OR	127	A3
Dahua	WA	117	A2
Dairy	OR	151	A2
Dale	OR	129	B3
* DALLAS	OR	204	A6
Dallesport	WA	196	C7
* DALTON GARDENS	ID	355	E3
Damascus	OR	200	A3
Danner	OR	146	C3
Dant	OR	127	B3
Danville	WA	105	C1
Danville	WA	175	D7
Darknell	WA	114	C2
Darlington	WA	267	J1
Darlingtonia	CA	148	C3
* DARRINGTON	WA	103	A3
Dartford	WA	346	H5
Dash Point	WA	181	D1
Dash Point	WA	182	A1
* DAVENPORT	WA	114	A2
Davidson	ID	131	B1
Davis	WA	117	B1
Davis Creek	CA	152	A3
Davis Terrace	WA	303	F10
Dawson	OR	133	B2
Day Island	WA	181	C2
Days Creek	OR	225	D2
* DAYTON	OR	198	C7
* DAYTON	WA	122	A2
Dayton	WA	179	D2
* DAYVILLE	OR	136	C2
Deadwood	OR	132	C3
Deady	OR	221	C2
* DEARY	ID	123	B1
Deckerville	WA	179	A2
Deep Cove	BC	156	D3
Deep Cove	BC	159	B2
Deep Creek	ID	107	B2
Deep Creek	WA	114	B2
Deep Harbor	WA	101	C2
Deerhorn	OR	133	C3
Deer Island	OR	189	C7
* DEER PARK	WA	114	B1
Dehlinger	OR	235	D6
Delake	OR	203	A5
Delaney	WA	122	A2
Delano Heights	WA	237	C3
Delena	OR	189	A4
Delkena	WA	106	C3
Dellwood	OR	140	C2
Dellwood	OR	198	B3
Delphi	WA	184	B1
Delta	ID	115	C2
Deming	WA	102	B1
Denio	NV	153	C3
Denison	WA	114	B1
Denman Island	BC	92	B2
Denmark	OR	224	B3
Denneux	OR	199	B2
* DEPOE BAY	OR	203	A7
Deroche	BC	94	C3
De Smet	ID	115	A3
* DES MOINES	WA	290	B5
Deschutes Rvr Wds	OR	217	B4
Detour	OR	198	B1
* DETROIT	OR	134	B1
Dewatto	WA	173	B5
Dewdney	BC	94	B3
Dewey	OR	198	C4
Dewey	WA	259	J14
Dexter	OR	133	C3

Community	State	Page	Grid
Dexter By The Sea	WA	183	B5
Diablo	WA	103	B2
Diamond	OR	145	C3
Diamond	WA	122	B1
Diamond Lake	OR	223	C6
Diamond Lake	WA	106	C3
Diamond Lake Jct	OR	142	C3
Dickey Prairie	OR	126	A3
Dieringer	WA	182	C2
Dillard	OR	221	B7
Dilley	OR	198	B2
Dilworth	WA	174	D5
Disautel	WA	105	A3
Dishman	WA	350	A9
Disque	WA	164	C5
Disston	OR	141	C1
* DIST OF CNTL SNCH	BC	159	C3
* DIST OF DELTA	BC	101	C1
* DIST OF KENT	BC	94	C3
* DIST OF LANGFORD	BC	159	B6
* DIST OF MATSQUI	BC	94	B3
* DIST OF METCHOSN	BC	159	A7
* DIST OF MISSION	BC	94	B3
* DIST OF N SAANICH	BC	159	C2
* DIST OF N VANCVR	BC	254	H2
* DIST OF OAK BAY	BC	257	C7
* DIST OF SAANICH	BC	256	B1
* DIST OF W VANCVR	BC	254	C1
Divide	OR	219	C1
Divide	WA	118	B1
Dixie	WA	122	A3
Dixonville	OR	221	D5
Dockton	WA	174	D7
Dodge	WA	122	B2
Dodson	OR	194	B7
Dole	WA	193	C3
Dollarton	BC	156	D3
Dollers Corner	WA	192	D3
Dolomite	WA	106	A1
* DONALD	OR	199	A7
Donald	WA	120	A2
* DONNELLY	ID	252	D1
Dora	OR	140	C2
Dorena	OR	141	C1
Dorris	CA	150	B3
Dot	WA	128	A1
Doty	WA	117	B1
Douglas	WA	236	D7
Douglas Ridge	OR	200	C5
* DOVER	ID	244	A1
Dover	OR	200	D5
Downing	OR	189	A3
Downs	OR	205	C4
Downs	WA	113	C2
Downtown	OR	313	F6
* DRAIN	OR	219	A3
Drakes Crossing	OR	205	D6
Draperville	OR	207	D4
Drew	OR	141	C3
Drewsey	OR	137	C3
Drift Creek	OR	209	B1
Dryad	WA	117	A3
Dry Creek	WA	121	C3
Dryden	WA	238	B2
Dryland	OR	205	D1
Duckabush	WA	173	C1
Dudley	ID	115	B2
Dudley	WA	240	D3
* DUFUR	OR	127	B2
Dukes Valley	OR	195	C7
* DUNCAN	BC	101	A1
Duncan	WA	246	C7
Duncan Bay	BC	92	A1
Dundarave	BC	254	B2
* DUNDEE	OR	198	C6
Dune	OR	127	B1
* DUNES CITY	OR	214	B4
Dungeness	WA	262	D2
Dunnean	OR	146	A2
Dunthorpe	OR	321	G4
* DUPONT	WA	181	B5
Durham	WA	110	C3
Durkee	OR	138	C1
Duroc	OR	129	C1
Dusty	WA	122	B1
* DUVALL	WA	110	C1
Dynamite	WA	246	B7

Community	State	Page	Grid
E			
Eagle	ID	115	C1
* EAGLE	ID	253	B1
Eagle Creek	OR	200	B4
Eagledale	WA	174	D2
Eagle Harbour	BC	156	A2
* EAGLE POINT	OR	230	D5
Eakin	OR	127	C2
Earl	WA	113	C2
Earlington	WA	289	H3
Earlmont	WA	175	C1
Earls Cove	BC	93	A2
East Aberdeen	WA	17	B7
East Bremerton	WA	270	H6
East Columbia	OR	309	H3
East Farms	WA	352	G7
East Gardener	OR	218	D1
Eastgate	WA	175	D3
* EAST HOPE	ID	244	D2
East Hoquiam	WA	178	A7
East Kamiah	ID	123	C2
East Kittitas	WA	241	D6
East Lind	WA	121	C1
Eastman	WA	122	A3
East Maupin	OR	127	B3
Eastmoreland	OR	318	A5
East Olympia	WA	184	D1
Easton	WA	111	B3
Eastport	ID	107	B1
East Port Orchard	WA	174	C4
East Quilcene	WA	109	C1
Eastside	OR	220	D1
East Sooke	BC	164	D1
Eastsound	WA	101	C2
East Spokane	WA	350	A9
* EAST WENATCHEE	WA	239	A4
East Wntchee Bnch	WA	239	A4
* EATONVILLE	WA	118	B1
Eby	OR	126	A3
* ECHO	OR	129	A1
Echo Beach	ID	115	A1
Echo Dell	OR	200	A5
Eckman Lake	OR	328	G7
Eddyville	ID	248	B1
Eddyville	OR	133	A1
Edgecomb	WA	168	D6
Edgewater	WA	171	B2
Edgewick	WA	176	C6
* EDGEWOOD	WA	182	B3
Edison	WA	161	A4
Edison Station	WA	161	A4
* EDMONDS	WA	171	A5
Edwall	WA	114	A2
Eglon	WA	170	D4
Eightmile	OR	128	B2
Elbe	WA	118	B1
Elberton	WA	114	C3
Eldon	WA	173	B3
* ELECTRIC CITY	WA	237	C3
Elgarose	OR	221	A3
* ELGIN	OR	130	A1
Elgin	WA	174	B7
Eliot	OR	313	G2
Elk	WA	114	C1
Elk City	OR	206	D4
Elkhead	OR	219	C5
Elkhorn	OR	134	A1
Elk Lake	OR	216	A4
* ELK RIVER	ID	123	C1
* ELKTON	OR	141	A1
Elk Valley	CA	233	A7
Ella	OR	128	B1
Ellendale	OR	125	B3
* ELLENSBURG	WA	241	B6
Elliott Avenue	WA	243	A6
Ellisford	WA	104	C1
Ellisport	WA	174	D6
Ellsworth	WA	311	G2
* ELMA	WA	179	B7
* ELMER CITY	WA	237	C2
Elmira	ID	107	B2
Elmira	OR	133	B2
Elmonica	OR	199	A1
Elsie	OR	125	A1
Eltopia	WA	121	A2
Elwood	OR	200	B7
Embro	WA	111	B1
Emerald Heights	OR	300	H4
Emerson	OR	127	B2

Community	State	Page	Grid
Emida	ID	115	B3
* EMMETT	ID	139	C3
Empire	OR	333	C6
Enaville	ID	115	C2
* ENDICOTT	WA	122	B1
Enetai	WA	271	C9
Englewood	OR	333	F12
* ENTERPRISE	OR	130	C2
* ENTIAT	WA	236	A6
* ENUMCLAW	WA	110	C3
Eola Village	OR	204	C1
* EPHRATA	WA	112	C3
Erlands Point	WA	270	D6
Ernies Grove	WA	176	D4
Espanola	WA	114	B2
* ESTACADA	OR	200	C6
Eufaula	WA	189	A2
* EUGENE	OR	330	B6
Eureka	WA	121	C3
Evaline	WA	187	C2
* EVERETT	WA	267	G3
Evergreen	ID	131	C3
Evergreen	OR	321	F6
* EVERSON	WA	102	B1
Ewan	WA	114	B3
Excelsior Beach	ID	115	A1
F			
Factoria	WA	175	C3
Fairbanks	OR	127	B1
Fairchild	WA	114	B2
Fairfax	WA	110	C3
Fairfield	OR	204	D2
* FAIRFIELD	WA	114	C2
Fairholm	WA	164	A6
Fairmont	WA	109	C1
Fairmount	WA	171	A2
Fairoaks	OR	221	D1
Fair Oaks	OR	321	H5
Fairview	OR	128	B2
Fairview	OR	140	B2
Fairview	OR	197	C2
* FAIRVIEW	OR	200	B1
Fairview	WA	270	E3
Fairview Sumach	WA	243	C7
Fairwood	WA	175	D5
Fairwood	WA	346	H7
Falcon Heights	OR	235	C5
Fall City	WA	176	B3
Fall Creek	OR	133	C3
* FALLS CITY	OR	125	A3
Falls View	OR	200	A7
Fanny Bay	BC	92	B2
Fargher Lake	WA	193	A1
Farmington	OR	198	D3
* FARMINGTON	WA	115	A3
Farron	WA	119	C2
Faubion	OR	201	C5
Fauntleroy	WA	284	D3
Fawn	OR	134	A1
Fayetteville	OR	210	A1
* FEDERAL WAY	WA	182	A1
Felida	WA	192	C5
Fenn	ID	123	C3
* FERDINAND	ID	123	B3
* FERNAN LAKE VLG	ID	355	J11
Ferncliff	WA	174	D1
Ferndale	WA	121	C3
* FERNDALE	WA	158	C6
Fern Heath	WA	175	A6
Fern Hill	OR	188	D2
Fernwood	ID	115	B3
Fernwood	WA	173	A7
Fernwood	WA	174	B4
Fields	OR	153	C2
* FIFE	WA	182	A3
Finley	WA	121	A3
Finn Rock	OR	134	A3
* FIRCREST	WA	294	A1
Firdale	WA	117	A1
Firdale	WA	171	A6
Fir Grove	OR	200	A5
Fir Grove	OR	215	A1
First Hill	WA	278	C5
Fir Villa	OR	204	A6
Firwood	OR	200	D4
Fischers Mill	OR	200	B5
Fisher	OR	209	D4
Fisher	WA	193	A7

*Indicates City, District or Township

Community	State	Page	Grid	Community	State	Page	Grid	Community	State	Page	Grid	Community	State	Page	Grid
Fishers Corner	OR	199	D6	Garden Home	OR	199	B2	Graham Point	WA	180	C2	* HARRAH	WA	119	C2
Five Corners	OR	152	A2	Garden Village	BC	156	C5	* GRAND COULEE	WA	237	C3	Harriman	OR	231	A6
Five Corners	WA	192	D5	Gardiner	OR	218	C1	* GRAND FORKS	BC	105	C1	* HARRINGTON	WA	113	C2
Fletcher Bay	WA	174	C1	Gardiner	WA	166	D7	Grand Mound	WA	184	B4	Harris	OR	133	A1
Flett	WA	181	C3	Garfield	OR	200	C6	Grand Ronde	OR	125	A3	* HARRISBURG	OR	210	A5
Flora	OR	122	C3	* GARFIELD	WA	114	C3	Grand Ronde Agncy	OR	125	A3	* HARRISON	ID	248	A4
* FLORENCE	OR	214	B3	Garibaldi	BC	93	C1	* GRANDVIEW	WA	120	B3	* HARRISN HOT SPGS	BC	94	C3
Florence	WA	168	B4	* GARIBALDI	OR	191	B7	* GRANGER	WA	120	A2	Harrison Mills	BC	94	C3
Flynn	OR	133	B1	Garibaldi Highlands	BC	93	C2	* GRANGEVILLE	ID	123	C3	Hartford	WA	110	C1
Foley Springs	OR	134	B2	Garrett	WA	344	E8	* GRANITE	OR	137	C1	Hartland	WA	196	D4
Folkenberg	OR	192	A6	Gasquet	CA	148	C3	* GRANITE FALLS	WA	102	C3	* HARTLINE	WA	113	A2
Foothills	WA	247	A2	* GASTON	OR	198	B3	Grant Park	OR	314	A2	Hartstene	WA	180	D2
Fordair	WA	113	A2	Gas Works	OR	234	B2	* GRANTS PASS	OR	335	D6	Harvard	ID	123	A1
Fords Prairie	WA	299	A2	Gate	WA	184	A3	* GRASS VALLEY	OR	127	C2	Harwood	WA	243	A7
Forest	ID	123	B3	* GATES	OR	134	A1	Gravelford	OR	140	B2	Hatfield	CA	151	A3
Forest	WA	187	D1	Gateway	OR	208	C2	Gravelles	WA	114	A2	Hathaway Mead	OR	197	C2
Forest Beach	WA	173	C6	Gaylord	OR	140	B3	Gray Gables	WA	177	D6	* HATTON	WA	121	B1
Forest Beach	WA	181	B1	Gazley	OR	225	D3	Grayland	WA	183	B3	Hatwai	ID	250	C4
Forest Glade	WA	110	C1	* GEARHART	OR	301	G4	Grays Harbor City	WA	177	D7	* HAUSER	ID	353	B2
* FOREST GROVE	OR	198	B1	Geiger Heights	WA	246	B5	Grays River	WA	117	A2	Hauser	OR	218	B5
Forest Knolls	BC	157	D7	Gem	OR	235	D5	Green	OR	221	B6	Havana	OR	129	B1
Forest Park	OR	192	B7	* GENESEE	ID	250	C1	Green Acres	OR	220	D3	Hawkinsville	CA	149	C3
Forfar	OR	206	B6	Geneva	WA	161	A1	Greenacres	WA	351	E6	Hay	WA	122	A1
* FORKS	WA	169	D1	George	OR	200	D6	Greenbank	WA	167	C6	Hay Creek Ranch	OR	135	B1
Fort Bidwell	CA	152	B3	* GEORGE	WA	112	B3	Greenberry	OR	133	B2	* HAYDEN	ID	245	A5
Fort Dick	CA	148	B3	Georgetown	WA	176	A7	Green Bluff	WA	114	C1	Hayden Island	OR	304	E6
Fort Hill	OR	125	A3	Georgetown	WA	282	A7	Greenburg	OR	199	B3	* HAYDEN LAKE	ID	245	A5
Fort Klamath	OR	231	C1	* GERVAIS	OR	205	B2	Greencreek	ID	123	C3	Hayesville	OR	323	F5
Fort Klamath Jct	OR	231	C1	Getchell	WA	168	D7	* GREEN HORN	OR	137	C1	Hayford	WA	246	A5
Fort Langley	BC	157	D6	Getchell Hill	WA	168	D7	* GREENLEAF	ID	147	B1	Hayhurst	OR	316	A4
Fort Nisqually	WA	181	C1	Gibbon	OR	129	C1	Greenleaf	OR	133	A2	Hazel	WA	102	C3
Fort Rains	WA	194	C6	Gibbon	WA	120	C3	Greenwater	WA	110	A3	Hazeldale	OR	199	A2
Fort Rock	OR	143	B2	Gibson	BC	93	B3	* GREENWOOD	BC	105	B1	Hazel Dell	WA	192	D5
Fort Steilacoom	WA	181	C4	Gifford	ID	123	B2	Greenwood	WA	178	B4	Hazel Green	OR	205	A4
Fort Stevens	OR	188	B2	* GIG HARBOR	WA	181	C1	Greenwood	WA	273	G1	Hazelia	OR	199	C4
Fortune Branch	OR	225	C6	Gilbert	OR	200	A1	Greer	ID	123	C2	Hazelwood	OR	200	A1
Foss	OR	191	C4	Gilberton	WA	271	C1	* GRESHAM	OR	200	B1	Headquarters	WA	189	D1
* FOSSIL	OR	128	A3	Gilchrist	OR	142	C1	Gresham Butte	OR	200	B1	Healy Heights	OR	316	C3
Foster	OR	134	A2	Gillespie Corners	OR	133	B3	Grisdale	WA	109	A2	Heather	OR	142	B1
Foster	WA	289	E2	Gillies Bay	BC	92	C2	Grizzly	OR	213	C1	Heather	WA	183	B4
Foster-Powell	OR	319	E3	Gilmer	OR	195	D2	Gromore	WA	119	C2	Hebo	OR	197	B6
Four Corners	OR	200	B6	Givens Hot Springs	ID	147	B1	Groners Corner	OR	199	A3	Heceta Beach	OR	214	A2
Four Corners	OR	234	C7	Glacier	WA	102	C1	Grosscup	WA	120	C2	Heceta Junction	OR	214	B2
Four Corners	OR	323	F14	* GLADSTONE	OR	199	D4	Grotto	WA	111	A1	Hedges	WA	121	A3
Four Corners	OR	336	E4	Gladtidings	OR	205	D2	Guerrier	WA	187	D1	Heisson	WA	193	A2
Four Corners	WA	110	C1	Glasgow	OR	333	H1	Guler	WA	119	A3	* HELIX	OR	129	B2
Four Corners	WA	118	A1	Gleed	WA	243	A5	Gurdane	OR	129	A2	Helmer	ID	123	B1
Four Corners	WA	170	B5	Glen Acres	WA	174	D5	Gwendolen	OR	128	A2	Helsing Junction	WA	184	A4
Four Corners	WA	263	B13	Glenada	OR	214	B3					Helvetia	OR	192	A7
Four Lakes	WA	176	A5	Glen Avon	OR	126	A3					Hemlock	OR	142	A1
Four Lakes	WA	246	A6	Glenbrook	OR	133	B2	**H**				Hemlock	OR	197	B5
Fourmile	OR	224	B1	Glencoe	OR	125	C1	Hadlock	WA	170	A1	Hemlock Valley	BC	94	C3
Fox	OR	137	A1	Glen Cove	WA	263	A8	Haig	BC	95	A3	Henley	CA	150	A3
Fox Valley	OR	134	A1	Glendale	ID	131	C3	* HAINES	OR	130	A3	Henley	OR	235	D5
Fragaria	WA	174	C5	* GLENDALE	OR	225	A7	Haley	OR	200	B3	Henrici	OR	199	D5
Frances	WA	117	B2	Glendale	WA	171	A3	Halfmoon Bay	BC	93	A2	Henrybro	WA	119	C2
Franklin	OR	133	B2	Glendale Junction	OR	225	B6	Halford	WA	111	A1	* HEPPNER	OR	128	C2
Franklin Camp	BC	100	B1	Glen Echo	OR	199	D4	* HALFWAY	OR	131	A3	Hereford	OR	138	A1
Fraser	BC	156	B5	Gleneden Beach	OR	203	B6	Haller Lake	WA	171	B7	Hermans	OR	126	A3
Fraserview	BC	156	C5	Glenfair	OR	200	A1	* HALSEY	OR	210	B2	* HERMISTON	OR	129	A1
Fredrickson	WA	182	A5	Glengary	OR	221	B6	Hamburg	CA	149	B3	Heron	MT	107	C3
Freedom	WA	114	C2	Glenoma	WA	118	B2	Hamilton	OR	137	A1	Herron	WA	180	D2
Freeland	WA	170	D1	Glen Valley	BC	94	B3	* HAMILTON	WA	102	C2	Hidaway Springs	OR	129	B2
Freeman	WA	247	A6	Glenwood	OR	125	B1	Hamlet	OR	188	D7	High Bridge	WA	110	C1
Fremont	WA	273	J7	Glenwood	OR	188	B3	Hammond	OR	188	B1	Highland	WA	171	A7
Frenchglen	OR	145	B3	Glenwood	OR	330	H8	Hampton	ID	123	A1	Highland	WA	343	C14
* FRIDAY HARBOR	WA	101	C2	Glenwood	WA	119	A3	Hampton	OR	134	A3	Highland Heights	WA	177	B2
Friend	OR	127	A2	Glide	OR	141	B2	Hampton	OR	144	A1	Highlands	ID	253	C2
Frisken Wye	WA	179	A2	Globe	WA	117	A1	Hamricks Corner	OR	205	D1	High Point	WA	176	A4
* FRUITLAND	ID	139	A3	Goble	OR	189	C5	Haney	BC	157	C5	High Rock	WA	110	C1
Fruitland	OR	205	A6	* GOLD BAR	WA	110	C1	Hansville	WA	170	C3	Hilda	WA	117	B1
Fruitvale	ID	131	C3	* GOLD BEACH	OR	228	A5	Happy Camp	CA	149	A3	Hilgard	OR	130	A2
Fruitvale	WA	243	B6	* GOLDENDALE	WA	127	C1	Happy Hollow	OR	203	D1	Hillcrest	WA	113	C3
Fryelands	WA	110	C1	* GOLD HILL	OR	230	A6	* HAPPY VALLEY	OR	199	D3	Hillgrove	WA	179	D6
Fulford Harbour	BC	101	B1	Goldstream	BC	159	A6	Happy Valley	WA	258	E11	Hills	OR	215	D4
Fulton	OR	129	B1	Goodnoe Hills	WA	128	A1	Harbeck-Fruitdale	OR	335	H12	* HILLSBORO	OR	198	D1
				Goodrich	ID	139	B1	Harbor	OR	232	C6	Hillsdale	OR	316	C4
G				Gooseberry	OR	128	B2	Harbor Island	WA	281	H3	Hillsdale	WA	295	J6
Gabriola	BC	93	A3	Goose Hollow	OR	312	D6	Harborton	OR	192	B6	Hillside	OR	312	B5
Galena	OR	137	B1	Goose Prairie	WA	119	A1	Hardman	OR	128	C3	Hillside	WA	243	C3
Galena	WA	111	A1	Gordon River	BC	100	C1	Harlan	OR	133	A1	Hilltop	WA	102	B1
Gales Creek	OR	125	B1	Gorst	WA	174	B4	Harmony	OR	127	C2	Hillview	OR	200	B3
Galiano	BC	101	B1	Goshen	OR	330	H14	Harmony	OR	199	D3	Hillyard	WA	349	E3
Galice	OR	149	A1	Gottville	CA	149	C3	Harmony	WA	118	A2	Hilt	CA	149	C3
Galvin	WA	184	B5	Gould City	WA	122	B2	Harmony Point	OR	199	D3	* HINES	OR	145	A1
Ganges	BC	101	B1	Govan	WA	113	B1	Harney	OR	145	B1	Hinkle	OR	129	A1
Gap	OR	219	D1	Government Camp	OR	202	A6	Harper	OR	138	C3	Hiouchi	CA	148	A3
* GARDEN CITY	ID	253	B2	Grace	WA	171	D6	Harper	WA	174	D4	Hite Center	WA	173	D2
Garden City	WA	179	C6	Graham	WA	182	B6	Harper Junction	OR	138	C3	Hito	OR	199	B7

*Indicates City, District or Township

Community	State	Page	Grid
Hobart	WA	176	A6
Hobsonville	OR	191	B7
Hockinson	WA	193	A4
Hogback	OR	200	A6
Hoko	WA	163	A2
Holbrook	OR	192	A5
Holden Village	WA	103	C3
Holdman	OR	129	B1
Holiday Beach	OR	206	B5
Holland	OR	233	C5
Holland	WA	249	B5
Holley	OR	133	C2
Hollow Hedges	WA	121	A3
Holly	WA	173	C3
Hollybrook	OR	200	A1
Hollyburn	BC	254	E3
Hollywood	OR	314	B3
Hollywood	WA	171	D7
Hollywood Beach	WA	236	A1
Holman	WA	186	A6
Holtzinger	WA	119	C1
Home	WA	181	A2
Home Acres	WA	265	H6
* HOMEDALE	ID	147	A1
Homestead	OR	131	A3
Homestead	OR	316	D2
Home Valley	WA	195	A5
Honeymoon Bay	BC	100	C1
* HOOD RIVER	OR	195	D5
Hoodsport	WA	173	A6
Hoodview	OR	199	B5
Hooper	WA	122	A1
* HOPE	BC	95	A3
* HOPE	ID	244	D2
Hope	OR	138	C3
Hopemere	OR	204	D3
Hopewell	OR	204	C2
Hopington	BC	158	D1
* HOQUIAM	WA	178	A7
Horlick	WA	240	C3
Hornbrook	CA	150	A3
Hornby Island	BC	92	B2
Horse Creek	CA	149	B3
Horseshoe Bay	BC	156	A2
* HORSESHOE BEND	ID	139	C3
Horton	OR	133	A2
Hosford	OR	317	H1
Hoskins	OR	133	A1
Hosley	OR	235	D7
Hot Lake	OR	130	A2
Hot Springs	OR	151	A2
Hoyt	ID	115	C3
* HUBBARD	OR	205	C1
Hubner	WA	111	B3
* HUETTER	ID	354	H7
Hugo	OR	229	B3
Humboldt	OR	309	F6
Humptulips	WA	177	D2
Hunter	WA	105	C3
Hunter Creek	OR	228	A6
Huntingdon	BC	102	B1
* HUNTINGTON	OR	138	C2
Huntington Jct	OR	138	B2
Huntley	WA	114	B3
* HUNTS POINT	WA	175	C1
Huntsville	WA	122	A2
Hurricane Grange	OR	130	C2
Huscroft	BC	107	B1
Huston	ID	147	B1
Husum	WA	195	D3
Hyak	WA	111	A2
Hyland Hills	OR	199	A2
Hylands	WA	110	C1
I			
* IDANHA	OR	134	B1
Idaville	OR	197	B1
Idleyld Park	OR	141	B2
Illahee	WA	177	B6
Illahee	WA	271	C4
Illinois Valley	OR	233	A5
* ILWACO	WA	186	A6
* IMBLER	OR	130	A2
Imnaha	OR	131	A1
Inchelium	WA	105	C3
* INDEPENDENCE	OR	204	B7
* INDEX	WA	110	A1
Indian Beach	OR	167	D5
Indianola	WA	170	D6
Indian Valley	ID	139	C1
Indian Village	WA	160	C4
Inglewood	WA	171	C7
Inglis	OR	117	B3
Innis	WA	171	A6
Interbay	WA	272	D7
Intercity	WA	268	C6
Interlachen	OR	200	B1
Inverness	WA	171	B7
Ioco	BC	157	A3
* IONE	OR	128	B2
* IONE	WA	106	B1
Irby	WA	113	B2
Irondale	WA	263	D13
Irondate	WA	170	A1
Ironside	OR	138	B2
Iron Springs	WA	177	B3
* IRRIGON	OR	128	C1
Irvines Landing	BC	93	A2
Irving	OR	215	A1
Irvington	OR	313	H3
Isadore	OR	219	A6
* ISLAND CITY	OR	130	A2
Island Sch Crossing	WA	168	C5
Island View	WA	342	C7
* ISSAQUAH	WA	175	D3
Izee	OR	137	A3
J			
* JACKSONVILLE	OR	234	A2
Jacktown	OR	198	D3
Jamestown	WA	262	F6
Jamieson	OR	138	C2
Jamison Corner	WA	110	C1
Jasper	OR	215	D3
Jean	OR	199	B4
Jeffers Garden	OR	300	B10
* JEFFERSON	OR	207	D3
Jefferson	WA	114	C2
Jennings Lodge	OR	199	D4
Jerome Prairie	OR	229	A6
Jewell	OR	117	A3
* JOHN DAY	OR	137	B2
Johnson	OR	220	D5
Johnson	WA	249	B7
* JOHNSON CITY	OR	199	D3
Jordan	OR	128	B2
Jordan	OR	134	A1
Jordan	WA	102	C3
Jordan Creek	OR	125	A1
* JORDAN VALLEY	OR	147	A3
Joseph	ID	131	B1
* JOSEPH	OR	130	C2
Jovita	WA	182	B2
Joyce	WA	164	C5
* JULIAETTA	ID	123	B1
Juanita	WA	171	C7
* JUNCTION CITY	OR	210	A6
Junction City	WA	178	B7
Junction Park	WA	118	B1
Juno	OR	197	B1
Juno	WA	114	B3
Juntura	OR	146	A1
K			
* KAHLOTUS	WA	121	C1
Kahneeta Hot Spgs	OR	208	B1
* KALAMA	WA	189	D5
Kamela	OR	129	C2
* KAMIAH	ID	123	C2
Kamilche	WA	180	A4
Kanaka	BC	95	A1
Kanaskat	WA	110	C3
Kangley	WA	176	B7
Keating	OR	130	B3
Keats Island	BC	93	B3
Keechelus	WA	111	A2
Keefers	BC	95	A1
Keelers Corner	WA	171	B4
Keith Lynn	BC	255	D5
* KEIZER	OR	322	H3
* KELLOGG	ID	115	C2
Kellogg	OR	141	A1
Kelly Creek	OR	200	B1
Kellys Korner	WA	181	A7
Kelso	WA	200	C3
* KELSO	WA	303	F10
* KENDRICK	ID	123	B1
* KENMORE	WA	171	B6
Kennedy	WA	111	A3
* KENNEWICK	WA	342	E9
Keno	OR	235	A5
Kent	OR	127	C3
* KENT	WA	291	G5
Kenton	OR	308	D4
Keona	OR	198	B4
Kerby	OR	233	B3
Kerns	OR	313	H5
Kernville	OR	203	A6
Kerrisdale	BC	156	B5
Kerry	OR	117	B3
* KETTLE FALLS	WA	106	A2
Kettle Valley	BC	105	A1
Keuterville	ID	123	B3
Keymes Beach	WA	263	C14
Keyport	WA	170	C7
Keystone	WA	167	C5
Kildonan	BC	100	A1
Killarney	BC	156	C5
Kimberly	OR	136	C1
Kimwood	OR	219	D1
King	OR	309	H7
* KING CITY	OR	125	C2
King Cole	OR	150	B2
Kingsgate	BC	107	B1
Kingsley	OR	127	B2
Kingston	ID	115	B2
Kingston	WA	170	D5
Kings Valley	OR	133	A1
Kinton	OR	199	A3
Kinzua	OR	128	B3
Kiona	WA	120	C3
* KIRKLAND	WA	171	C7
Kishwalks	OR	127	A3
Kitsap Lake	WA	270	A8
Kitson Hot Spring	OR	142	A1
* KITTITAS	WA	241	C6
Kitts Corner	WA	182	B1
Klaber	WA	187	A2
Klamath Agency	OR	231	C3
Klamath Agncy Jct	OR	231	C5
* KLAMATH FALLS	OR	338	C3
Klamath Junction	OR	234	D5
Klamath River	CA	149	C3
Klaus	WA	187	D1
Klickitat	WA	196	D3
Klickitat Springs	WA	196	D3
Klipsan Beach	WA	186	A3
Klondike	OR	127	C1
Knab	WA	118	A2
Knapp	WA	192	C4
Knappa	OR	117	A3
Knappa Junction	OR	117	A3
Kokel Corner	OR	126	A3
Kooskooskie	WA	122	A3
* KOOTENAI	ID	244	A1
Kopiah	WA	184	D6
Kopplein	OR	133	A1
Korea	WA	111	B1
Kosmos	WA	118	B2
Kountze	WA	240	D3
Krain	WA	110	C3
Krewson	OR	219	A2
Kruse	WA	168	C7
* KUNA	ID	253	A5
Kyro	WA	181	A7
L			
Labish Village	OR	323	F2
Lacamas	WA	118	A2
* LA CENTER	WA	192	C1
* LACEY	WA	297	H7
Laclede	ID	107	A3
Lacomb	OR	133	C1
* LA CONNER	WA	167	D1
* LA CROSSE	WA	122	A1
Ladd Hill	OR	199	A6
Ladner	BC	101	C1
Ladysmith	BC	101	A1
* LAFAYETTE	OR	198	B6
La Granda	WA	118	B1
* LA GRANDE	OR	130	A2
Laidlaw	BC	95	A3
Lake	OR	231	C4
Lakebay	WA	181	A2
Lake Cowichan	BC	101	A1
Lakecreek	OR	149	C1
Lakedale	WA	111	B3
* LAKE FOREST PARK	WA	171	B6
Lake Fork	ID	251	D6
Lake Grove	OR	320	B7
Lakeland Village	WA	114	B2
* LAKE OSWEGO	OR	320	B5
Lake Park	WA	181	D5
* LAKESIDE	OR	218	C4
Lakeside	WA	236	C3
* LAKE STEVENS	WA	171	D1
Lakeview	ID	245	D1
* LAKEVIEW	OR	152	A2
Lakeview	WA	181	C4
Lakeview Park	WA	112	C2
Lakewood	OR	321	F6
Lakewood	WA	168	C6
* LAKEWOOD	WA	294	A7
Lakota	WA	182	A1
Lamar	WA	121	C2
Lamona	WA	113	C2
* LAMONT	WA	114	A3
Lancaster	OR	210	A5
Lancaster	WA	114	B3
Landore	ID	131	B3
Landsburg	WA	176	A7
Lang Bay	BC	92	C1
Langdon	WA	345	B12
Langell Valley	OR	151	A3
* LANGLEY	BC	157	C7
* LANGLEY	WA	171	A1
Langlois	OR	224	B2
Langrell	OR	131	A3
Lantzville	BC	93	A3
La Pine	OR	143	A1
La Push	WA	169	A2
* LAPWAI	ID	123	A2
Larchmont	WA	181	D4
Lardo	ID	251	C5
Larimers Corner	WA	171	D4
Lasqueti	BC	92	C2
* LATAH	WA	114	C2
Latham	OR	215	B7
Latourell	OR	200	D1
Laurel	OR	198	D3
Laurel	WA	158	D5
Laurel Grove	OR	220	A7
Laurelhurst	OR	314	B5
Laurelhurst	WA	275	F6
Laurelwood	OR	198	C3
Lavender	WA	111	B3
Lawen	OR	145	B1
Laws Corner	WA	196	A4
Leaburg	OR	133	C3
Leahy	WA	112	C1
* LEAVENWORTH	WA	238	A1
Lebam	WA	117	A1
* LEBANON	OR	133	C1
Lehman Hot Spgs	OR	129	B3
Leland	ID	123	B1
Leland	OR	229	A2
Lemolo	WA	170	B7
Lena	OR	129	A2
Leneve	OR	220	C4
Lenore	ID	123	B2
Lents	OR	319	H4
Lenz	OR	142	C3
Lenz	OR	195	D6
Leona	WA	219	B2
Lester	WA	111	A3
Letha	ID	139	B3
Lewisburg	OR	207	B5
* LEWISTON	ID	250	C4
Lewiston Orchards	ID	250	C5
* LEXINGTON	OR	128	C2
Lexington	WA	303	C3
Libby	OR	333	F14
Liberty	OR	324	F6
Liberty	WA	240	D1
Liberty Lake	WA	247	B4
Lilliwaup	WA	173	A5
Lime	OR	138	C2
Lincoln	OR	150	A2
Lincoln	WA	113	C1
Lincoln Beach	OR	203	A7
* LINCOLN CITY	OR	203	A4
* LIND	WA	121	B1
Lindbergh	OR	189	C4
Lindell Beach	BC	102	C1
Linns Mill	OR	200	A4
Linnton	OR	192	B7

*Indicates City, District or Township

INTRO

Community	State	Page	Grid	Community	State	Page	Grid	Community	State	Page	Grid	Community	State	Page	Grid
Lions Bay	BC	93	C2	Manette	WA	271	B10	Meacham	OR	129	C2	Minnick	WA	122	A3
Lisabuela	WA	174	D6	Manhattan	WA	290	A1	Meacham Corner	OR	125	C1	Mirrormont	WA	176	A5
Lister	BC	107	B1	Manhattan Beach	OR	191	B5	Mead	WA	347	F7	Mission	OR	129	B1
Littell	WA	184	B7	Manitou Beach	WA	174	D1	Meadow Creek	WA	111	A3	Mist	OR	117	B3
Little Albany	OR	209	C2	Manning	OR	125	B1	Meadowdale	WA	171	B4	Mitchell	OR	136	A1
Little Falls	WA	114	A1	Manning	WA	122	C1	Meadowdale	WA	270	H2	Moclips	WA	177	B2
Little Hoquiam	WA	180	C1	* MANSFIELD	WA	112	C1	Meadows	ID	251	B4	Modoc Point	OR	231	D6
Little Oklahoma	WA	165	D7	Manson	WA	236	B2	Meadows	WA	184	B4	Mohler	OR	191	B4
Little River	BC	92	A2	Manson Landing	BC	92	A1	Meaghersville	WA	238	A7	Mohler	WA	113	C2
Littlerock	WA	184	B2	* MANZANITA	OR	191	B4	* MEDFORD	OR	336	D11	Mohrweis	OR	179	D1
Little Shasta	CA	150	A3	Manzanita	WA	174	C1	* MEDICAL LAKE	WA	114	B2	* MOLALLA	OR	126	A3
Little Valley	OR	138	C3	Manzanita	WA	174	D7	Medical Springs	OR	130	B3	Mondovi	WA	114	A1
Lobert Junction	OR	231	D4	Maple Bay	BC	101	B1	Medimont	ID	248	C4	Monitor	OR	205	C2
Lochdale	BC	156	D4	Maple Grove	WA	164	D6	* MEDINA	WA	279	J4	Monitor	WA	238	C3
Lochsloy	WA	102	C3	* MAPLE RIDGE	BC	157	D6	Mehama	OR	134	A1	Monkland	OR	127	C2
Locoda	OR	117	B3	Mapleton	OR	214	D2	* MELBA	ID	147	C1	* MONMOUTH	OR	204	B7
Lofall	WA	170	B5	* MAPLE VALLEY	WA	176	A6	Melbourne	WA	117	A1	Monohon	WA	175	D3
Logan	OR	200	B5	Maplewood	WA	174	C6	Melmont	ID	147	C1	* MONROE	OR	133	B2
Logan Hill	WA	184	D7	Maplewood	WA	175	C5	Melrose	OR	221	A4	* MONROE	WA	110	C1
Logsden	OR	133	A1	Marble Creek	ID	115	C3	Melville	OR	188	C4	Monson Corner	WA	168	B3
London	OR	219	D3	Marblemount	WA	103	A2	Mendota	WA	184	D5	* MONTAGUE	CA	150	A3
Lone Cemetery	ID	248	D3	Marcellus	WA	113	C3	Menlo	WA	117	A1	Montavilla	OR	315	G6
Lone Elder	OR	199	C7	Marcola	OR	210	D7	Menlo Park	WA	181	C3	Montborne	WA	168	C1
Lone Pine	OR	150	C1	Marcus	WA	106	A2	* MERCER ISLAND	WA	283	J2	Monte Cristo	WA	111	A1
Lone Pine	WA	237	C2	Marengo	WA	122	B2	Merideth	WA	175	B7	* MONTESANO	WA	178	D6
* LONEROCK	OR	128	B3	Marial	OR	140	C3	* MERIDIAN	ID	253	A3	Montlake	WA	278	C1
Lone Tree	OR	130	A2	Marietta	WA	158	C7	Merlin	OR	229	A4	Montour	ID	139	C3
* LONG BEACH	WA	186	A5	Marine Drive	WA	270	D8	* MERRILL	OR	150	C2	* MONTROSE	BC	106	B1
Longbranch	WA	181	A3	Marion	WA	133	C1	Merritt	BC	95	C1	* MONUMENT	OR	136	C1
* LONG CREEK	OR	137	A1	Marion Forks	OR	134	C1	Merritt	WA	111	C1	Moody	OR	127	B1
Long Lake	WA	114	A1	Markham	OR	320	B1	Merville	BC	92	A1	Moores Corner	WA	186	A5
Longmire	WA	185	B5	* MARLIN	WA	113	A2	Mesa	ID	139	C1	Moreland	OR	317	H6
Long Tom Station	OR	133	A2	Marmot	OR	201	A4	* MESA	WA	121	A2	Morgan	OR	128	B2
* LONGVIEW	WA	302	F8	Marquam	OR	205	D3	Meskill	WA	117	B1	Morgan Acres	WA	347	D11
Looking Glass	OR	130	B1	Marshall	WA	246	B6	* METALINE	WA	106	B1	* MORO	OR	127	C2
Lookingglass	OR	221	A5	Marshall Park	OR	320	C1	* METALINE FALLS	WA	106	C1	* MORTON	WA	118	B2
Lookout	OR	142	A1	Marshland	OR	117	B3	Metchosin	BC	165	A1	* MOSCOW	ID	249	C5
Loomis	WA	104	C1	* MARSING	ID	147	B1	Methow	WA	104	B3	* MOSES LAKE	WA	242	C3
Loon Lake	WA	106	B3	Martin	WA	111	A3	* METOLIUS	OR	208	C5	* MOSIER	OR	196	A5
Lopez	WA	101	C2	Martindale	WA	121	B3	Metzger	OR	199	B3	* MOSSYROCK	WA	118	A2
Lorane	OR	133	B3	Maryhill	WA	127	C1	Mica	ID	247	D4	Mountaindale	OR	125	C1
Lorella	OR	151	A2	Marylhurst	OR	199	C4	Mica	WA	247	A5	Mountain Home	OR	198	D4
* LOSTINE	OR	130	C2	Marys Corner	WA	187	D2	Michigan Hill	WA	184	A4	Mountain Home	WA	238	A6
Loveland	WA	182	A6	* MARYSVILLE	WA	168	C7	Middle Grove	OR	323	F9	Mountain Home Pk	WA	122	A3
Lowden	WA	121	C3	Mason	WA	114	B2	* MIDDLETON	ID	147	B1	Mountain View	WA	158	C6
* LOWELL	OR	133	C3	Massinger Corner	OR	200	A7	Middleton	OR	199	A5	Mountain View Bch	WA	168	A6
Lowell	WA	265	F7	Matlock	WA	179	B2	Midland	OR	235	B5	* MOUNT ANGEL	OR	205	C3
Lower Highland	OR	200	B7	Matsqui	BC	102	B1	Midland	WA	182	A4	Mount Baker	WA	282	E2
Lower Nicola	BC	95	C1	* MATTAWA	WA	120	B1	* MIDVALE	ID	139	B1	Mount Hebron	CA	150	B3
Loyal Heights	WA	272	D2	* MAUPIN	OR	127	B3	Midway	BC	105	B1	Mount Hood	OR	200	B1
Lucerne	WA	103	C3	Maury	WA	175	A6	Midway	ID	147	B1	Mount Hood	OR	202	C1
Lucile	ID	131	C1	May Creek	WA	175	C4	Midway	OR	125	A3	Mount Hope	OR	126	A3
Lummi Island	WA	160	B1	Mayfield	WA	118	A2	Midway	OR	129	B1	Mount Hope	WA	114	C2
Lund	BC	92	B1	Mayger	OR	189	A2	Midway	OR	198	D3	Mount Idaho	ID	123	C3
Lunnville	OR	198	B4	Maynard	WA	109	C1	Midway	OR	336	A3	* MOUNTLAKE TER	WA	171	B6
Lyle	WA	196	B5	Mayne	BC	101	B1	Midway	WA	181	C1	Mount Pleasant	WA	193	D7
* LYMAN	WA	102	C2	Maytown	WA	184	C2	Midway	WA	290	D7	Mount Scott-Arleta	OR	318	D3
* LYNDEN	WA	158	D4	Mayview	WA	122	C1	Mikkalo	OR	128	A2	Mount Tabor	OR	314	D6
Lynn Creek	BC	255	F1	Mayville	OR	128	A3	Milan	WA	114	C1	* MOUNT VERNON	OR	137	A2
Lynn Valley	BC	255	C1	Maywood	OR	133	B3	Milburn	WA	184	A7	* MOUNT VERNON	WA	260	H12
* LYNNWOOD	WA	171	B5	* MAYWOOD PARK	OR	315	J2	Miles	WA	113	C1	Mount View	WA	150	A2
Lynwood Center	WA	271	F6	Mazame	OR	142	C3	Miles Crossing	OR	300	C10	Mowich	OR	142	C2
* LYONS	OR	134	A1	McBee	OR	129	B1	Mileta Raeco	WA	175	A7	* MOXEE CITY	WA	243	D7
				* MCCALL	ID	251	D5	Mill A	WA	195	B4	* MOYIE SPRINGS	ID	107	B1
M				* MCCLEARY	WA	179	D6	Mill Bay	BC	159	A2	Mud Springs	WA	112	B1
Mabel	OR	133	C2	McCormac	OR	333	J14	* MILL CITY	OR	134	A1	* MUKILTEO	WA	266	D5
* MABTON	WA	120	B3	McCormick	WA	117	B2	* MILL CREEK	WA	171	C4	Mulino	OR	199	D7
Macdoel	CA	150	B3	McCormmach	OR	129	B1	Miller	OR	192	B6	Mulloy	OR	199	B5
Machias	WA	110	C1	McCoy	OR	204	B3	Miller River	WA	111	A1	Multnomah	OR	316	B6
Mack	WA	122	A1	McCoy	WA	114	C3	* MILLERSBURG	OR	326	G2	Mumby	WA	184	B2
Macksburg	OR	199	C7	McCredie Springs	OR	142	B1	Millican	OR	135	B3	Munra	OR	129	B1
Macleay	OR	205	B6	McDermitt	NV	154	B2	Millington	OR	220	D2	Murdock	WA	196	C6
Madison Park	OR	279	F2	McDermitt	OR	154	B2	Mill Park	OR	200	A1	Murnen	WA	117	B1
Madison South	OR	315	G3	McDonald	WA	242	D4	Mill Plain	WA	193	A6	Murphy	ID	147	C2
* MADRAS	OR	208	C5	McEwan	OR	138	A1	Millwood	WA	141	A2	Murphy	OR	229	B7
Madras Station	OR	208	C5	McGuire	ID	353	D7	* MILLWOOD	WA	350	D5	Murrayhill	OR	199	A3
Madrona Beach	WA	167	D4	McKay	OR	129	C2	Milner	BC	157	C7	Murrayville	BC	158	C1
Madrona Park	WA	278	D4	McKee Bridge	OR	149	B2	Milnes Landing	BC	101	A2	Myrick	OR	129	B1
Magnolia Beach	WA	174	D7	McKenna	WA	118	A1	Milo	OR	141	B3	* MYRTLE CREEK	OR	225	C1
Magnolia Bluff	WA	276	D1	McKenzie Bridge	OR	134	B2	* MILTON	WA	182	B2	* MYRTLE POINT	OR	140	B2
Mahan	OR	198	D1	McKinley	OR	140	C2	* MILTON-FREEWTR	WA	121	C3				
Malahat	BC	159	A4	McLeod	OR	149	C1	* MILWAUKIE	OR	318	A7	**N**			
Malaya	WA	239	B5	McLoughlin Heights	WA	306	D6	Milwaukie Heights	OR	321	J4	* NACHES	WA	243	A4
* MALDEN	WA	114	B3	McMicken Heights	WA	288	D6	Mima	WA	184	B3	Naef	OR	199	D4
* MALIN	OR	151	A3	McMillin	WA	182	C5	Minam	OR	130	B1	Nahcotta	WA	186	A2
Malone	WA	179	C7	* MCMINNVILLE	OR	198	A7	Mineral	ID	139	A1	* NAMPA	ID	147	B1
Malott	WA	104	C3	McMurray	WA	168	C2	Mineral	WA	118	B1	* NANAIMO	BC	93	A3
Maltby	WA	171	D5	McNab	OR	128	B2	Minerva	OR	214	C1	Nanoose Bay	BC	92	C3
Manchester	WA	271	H12	McNary	OR	129	A1	Minnehaha	WA	305	J1	* NAPAVINE	WA	187	C1

*Indicates City, District or Township

Community	State	Page	Grid
Naples	ID	107	B2
Napton	OR	147	A1
Narrows	OR	133	C2
Narrows	OR	145	B2
Naselle	WA	186	C5
Nashville	OR	133	A1
Nason Creek	WA	111	C1
Natal	OR	117	B3
National	OR	118	B1
Navy Yard City	WA	270	E11
Naylor	WA	112	C3
Neah Bay	BC	100	B2
Neahkahnie Beach	OR	191	B3
Neawanna Station	OR	301	J6
Necanicum Jct	OR	188	D7
Nedonna Beach	OR	191	B5
Needy	OR	205	D1
* NEHALEM	OR	191	B4
Neilton	WA	109	A2
Nelscott	OR	203	A5
Nelson	WA	240	A2
Nelway	BC	106	C1
Nena	OR	127	B3
Neotsu	OR	203	B4
Neptune Beach	WA	158	B6
Nesika Beach	OR	228	A4
Neskowin	OR	203	B2
* NESPELEM	WA	105	A3
Netarts	OR	197	A2
Newaukum	WA	184	B7
* NEWBERG	OR	198	D5
New Bridge	OR	139	A1
New Brighton	BC	93	B2
* NEWCASTLE	WA	175	C4
New Era	OR	199	C5
Newell	CA	151	A3
Newhalem	WA	103	B2
New Hope	OR	229	B7
New Idaho	OR	152	A2
New Idanha	OR	134	B1
New Kamilche	WA	180	A5
New London	WA	178	A5
Newman Lake	WA	352	F6
* NEW MEADOWS	ID	251	A4
New Pine Creek	CA	152	A3
New Pine Creek	OR	152	A3
* NEW PLYMOUTH	ID	139	B3
* NEWPORT	OR	206	B4
* NEWPORT	WA	106	C3
Newport Heights	OR	206	B4
Newport Hills	WA	175	C3
New Princeton	OR	145	C2
Newton	BC	157	A7
Newton	OR	198	D1
Newton	WA	177	C5
* NEW WESTMNSTR	BC	156	D5
* NEZ PERCE	ID	123	C2
Niagara	OR	134	A1
Nicola	BC	95	C1
Nighthawk	WA	104	C1
Nile	OR	119	B1
Nimrod	OR	134	A3
Nine Mile Falls	WA	246	A2
Ninety One	OR	205	C1
Nippon	WA	111	B1
Nisqually	WA	181	A6
Nisson	WA	178	B4
Nitinat	BC	100	B1
Nolin	OR	129	A1
Nonpareil	OR	141	B2
* NOOKSACK	WA	102	B1
Nksck Slmn Htchry	WA	102	B1
Noon	OR	133	B1
Norgate	BC	254	H5
Norma Beach	WA	171	B4
Norman	WA	168	B4
* NORMANDY PARK	WA	175	A6
North Albany	OR	326	B5
North Beach	OR	214	B5
North Beach	WA	171	A7
North Bend	BC	95	A1
* NORTH BEND	OR	333	F6
* NORTH BEND	WA	176	C4
* NORTH BONNEVLE	WA	194	C6
North Central	OR	200	B1
North City	WA	171	B6
North Cowichan	BC	101	A1
Northeast	OR	200	B1
Northfork	OR	151	B1
North Fork	OR	214	C7
North Gate	WA	171	B7
North Gresham	OR	200	A1
North Howell	OR	205	B4
Northilla	WA	174	D7
N Jct (Davidson)	OR	127	B3
North Lewiston	ID	250	C4
North Olympia	WA	180	D5
* NORTH PLAINS	OR	125	C1
* NORTHPORT	WA	106	A1
* NORTH POWDER	OR	130	B2
North Prosser	WA	120	C3
North Puyallup	WA	182	A3
North Santiam	OR	133	C1
North Scholls	OR	198	D3
North Springfield	OR	330	G2
Northwest	OR	312	C4
Northwest Industrl	OR	312	B2
Norway	OR	220	D6
Norwood	ID	251	C7
Norwood	OR	199	B4
* NOTUS	ID	147	B1
Novelty	WA	110	C1
Nulls Crossing	WA	184	D6
Nye	OR	129	B2
Nyland	WA	110	C1
* NYSSA	OR	139	A3
O			
* OAKESDALE	WA	114	C3
Oak Grove	OR	195	C6
Oak Grove	OR	321	J6
* OAK HARBOR	WA	167	B2
Oak Hills	OR	199	A1
* OAKLAND	OR	219	A7
Oakland	WA	180	B2
Oak Park	OR	323	E9
Oak Park	WA	193	B7
Oak Point	WA	117	B3
* OAKRIDGE	OR	142	A1
Oaks	OR	334	E11
Oak Springs	OR	127	B3
* OAKVILLE	WA	117	B1
OBrien	OR	233	A6
OBrien	WA	291	J5
Ocasta	WA	183	B2
Ocean City	WA	177	B5
Oceanlake	OR	203	A4
Ocean Park	BC	158	D1
Ocean Park	WA	186	A2
* OCEAN SHORES	WA	298	C2
Oceanside	OR	197	A2
Oceanside	WA	186	A4
Odell	OR	195	C7
Odell Lake	OR	142	B1
Odessa	OR	231	B6
* ODESSA	WA	113	B3
Ohop	WA	118	B1
* OKANOGAN	WA	104	C3
Oklahoma Hill	OR	117	B3
Olalla	OR	141	A2
Olalla	WA	174	C6
Old Colton	OR	126	A3
Old Town	OR	219	A7
Oldtown	WA	106	C3
Oldtown-Chinatwn	OR	313	F5
Olene	OR	150	C2
Olex	OR	128	A2
Olga	WA	160	A3
Olney	OR	188	D3
* OLYMPIA	WA	297	C7
Olympic View	WA	170	A7
* OMAK	WA	104	C2
Omens	WA	114	A2
Ona	OR	206	B7
Onalaska	WA	118	A2
* ONAWAY	ID	249	D1
ONeil	OR	213	A4
ONeil Corners	OR	199	C6
* ONTARIO	OR	139	A3
Ontario Heights	OR	139	A3
Opal City	OR	212	D2
Ophir	OR	228	A3
Opportunity	WA	350	H12
Orcas	WA	101	C2
Orchard	WA	193	A6
Orchard Avenue	WA	350	B5
Orchard Heights	WA	271	B14
Orchard Park	WA	349	J6
Orchard View	OR	198	A6
Ordnance	OR	128	C1
Oreana	ID	147	C2
* OREGON CITY	OR	199	D5
Oregon Trunk Jct	OR	127	B1
Orenco	OR	199	A1
Oretown	OR	203	B1
Orient	OR	200	C1
Orient	WA	105	C1
Orilla	WA	289	J7
* OROFINO	ID	123	C2
Orondo	WA	236	A1
* OROVILLE	WA	104	C1
Orrs Corner	OR	204	B6
* ORTING	WA	182	C5
Osborn Corner	WA	171	C4
* OSBURN	ID	115	C2
Osceola	WA	182	D3
Oso	WA	102	C3
* OSOYOOS	BC	104	C1
Ostrander	WA	303	F1
* OTHELLO	WA	121	A1
Otis	OR	203	B3
Otis Junction	OR	203	B3
Otis Orchards	WA	352	B9
Otter Bay	BC	101	B1
Otter Point	BC	101	A2
Otter Rock	OR	206	B2
Outlet Bay	ID	107	A2
Outlook	OR	200	A4
Outlook	WA	120	B2
Overland	OR	220	D3
Overlook	OR	308	C6
Owyhee	ID	253	D6
Owyhee	OR	139	A3
Oxman	OR	138	C1
Oxyoke	OR	229	B3
Oyhut	WA	177	B6
Oyster River	BC	92	A1
Oysterville	OR	206	B5
Oysterville	WA	186	A1
P			
* PACIFIC	WA	182	B2
Pacific Beach	WA	177	B2
Pacific Beach	WA	186	A4
Pacific City	OR	197	A7
Packard	WA	113	C3
Packwood	WA	118	C2
Page	ID	115	C2
* PAISLEY	OR	151	C1
Palmer Junction	OR	130	B1
* PALOUSE	WA	249	B1
Panakanic	WA	196	B1
Pandora	WA	114	C3
Park	WA	161	C2
Parkdale	OR	202	C2
Parker	WA	120	A2
Parkersburg	OR	220	B5
Parkers Mill	OR	128	C3
Parkland	WA	181	D4
Park Place	OR	199	D4
Parkrose	OR	315	J1
Parkrose Heights	OR	315	J3
* PARKSVILLE	BC	92	C3
Parkwater	WA	349	H6
Parkwood	WA	174	C4
Parliament	OR	131	B1
* PARMA	ID	139	A3
Parvin	WA	122	C1
Pasadena Park	WA	350	E3
* PASCO	WA	343	E4
Pataha	WA	122	A2
Pataha	WA	122	B2
* PATEROS	WA	112	B1
Paterson	WA	120	C3
Patrick Creek	CA	148	C3
Paulina	OR	136	B3
* PAYETTE	ID	139	A3
Payette Heights	ID	139	A3
Pearl District	OR	313	E4
Pebble Beach	WA	168	A7
Peck	ID	123	B2
Pedee	OR	133	B1
Pe Ell	WA	117	B2
Pelican City	OR	338	A3
Penawawa	WA	122	B1
Pendair Heights	OR	129	B1
Pender Island	BC	101	B1
* PENDLETON	OR	129	B2
Pend Oreille Village	WA	106	B1
Penn Cove Park	WA	167	B4
Peola	WA	122	C2
Peoria	OR	210	A1
Perrinville	WA	171	B5
Perry	OR	130	A2
Perrydale	OR	204	B3
Peshastin	WA	238	A1
Petersburg	OR	196	D7
Peterson	BC	106	A1
Peyton	WA	122	B1
* PHILOMATH	OR	133	B1
Phoenix	BC	105	B1
* PHOENIX	OR	234	B2
Piedmont	OR	309	F6
Piedmont	WA	164	C6
Pigeon Springs	WA	118	A3
Pilchuck	WA	168	D4
Pillar Rock	WA	117	A2
* PILOT ROCK	OR	129	B2
Pinckney	OR	322	G11
Pine	OR	131	A3
Pine City	OR	128	C1
Pine City	WA	114	B3
Pine Glen	WA	111	B3
Pine Grove	OR	127	A3
Pine Grove	OR	195	D6
* PINEHURST	ID	115	C2
Pinehurst	ID	131	C2
Pinehurst	OR	150	A2
Pinehurst	WA	269	F2
Pine Ridge	ID	131	C3
Pine Ridge	OR	231	D3
Ping	WA	122	B1
Pirtle	OR	207	C5
Pistol River	OR	232	B1
Pitt	WA	196	C3
* PITT MEADOWS	BC	157	B5
Pittsburg	OR	125	B1
Placer	OR	229	C2
Plain	WA	111	C1
Plainview	OR	210	C1
Plainview	OR	212	A6
Plaza	WA	114	C2
Pleasantdale	OR	204	D1
Pleasant Hill	OR	215	D4
Pleasant Hill	WA	189	C1
Pleasant Home	OR	200	C1
Pleasant Valley	OR	197	C4
Pleasant Valley	OR	200	A1
Pleasant Valley	OR	229	B3
Pleasant View	WA	121	C2
* PLUMMER	ID	115	A2
Plush	OR	152	B1
Pluvius	WA	117	B2
Plymouth	WA	121	A3
Pocahontas	OR	138	A1
Pocahontas Bay	WA	106	C3
Pocono	ID	115	C3
Point Roberts	WA	101	C1
Point Terrace	OR	214	D2
Point White	WA	271	F7
Pollock	ID	131	C2
* POMEROY	WA	122	B2
Pomona	WA	243	C4
* PONDERAY	ID	244	A1
Ponderosa Estates	WA	182	C4
Ponders	WA	181	C4
Pondosa	OR	130	B3
Portage	WA	174	D6
* PORT ALBERNI	BC	92	B3
* PORT ANGELES	WA	261	E5
* PORT COQUITLAM	BC	157	B4
Porter	WA	117	B1
Port Gamble	WA	170	C4
Port Hammond	BC	157	C6
Porthill	ID	107	B1
Port Kells	BC	157	B6
* PORTLAND	OR	316	C3
Port Ludlow	WA	170	B3
Port Madison	WA	170	D7
Port Mellon	BC	93	B2
* PORT MOODY	BC	157	A4
* PORT ORCHARD	WA	270	J14
* PORT ORFORD	OR	224	A6
Port Renfrew	BC	100	C2
Portsmouth	OR	308	A3

*Indicates City, District or Township

Community	State	Page	Grid	Community	State	Page	Grid	Community	State	Page	Grid	Community	State	Page	Grid
* PORT TOWNSEND	WA	263	C2	Reed	OR	318	A3	Rosario Beach	WA	259	C14	Satsop	WA	179	A7
Port Washington	BC	101	B1	Reeds Mill	OR	128	C3	Roseberry	ID	252	D1	Saturna	BC	101	C1
Port Williams	WA	262	J8	* REEDSPORT	OR	218	C2	* ROSEBURG	OR	334	H4	Saunders Lake	OR	218	B5
Possession	WA	171	A3	Reedville	OR	199	A2	Rosebush	OR	127	C2	Savary Island	BC	92	B1
Post	OR	136	A2	Rees Corner	WA	171	D4	Rose City Park	OR	314	C4	Saxby	WA	247	B7
* POST FALLS	ID	353	F5	Relief	WA	122	A2	Rosedale	BC	94	C3	* SCAPPOOSE	OR	192	A3
* POTLATCH	ID	249	D1	Remac	BC	106	B1	Rosedale	OR	324	F11	Scenic	WA	111	B1
Potlatch	WA	173	A6	Remote	OR	140	C3	Rosedale	WA	174	B7	Schaefer	WA	113	C3
Potlatch Junction	ID	249	D1	Renfrew Heights	BC	255	E14	Rosehilla	WA	174	D7	Schefflin Corner	OR	125	C1
* POULSBO	WA	170	B7	* RENTON	WA	289	J4	Rose Lake	ID	248	D2	Schneiders Prairie	WA	180	B5
Powell Butte	OR	213	B6	Renton Junction	WA	289	J6	Rose Lodge	OR	203	C4	Scholls	OR	198	D4
Powellhurst	OR	200	A1	* REPUBLIC	WA	105	B2	Rosemont	OR	199	C4	Schoonover	WA	113	C3
* POWELL RIVER	BC	92	C1	Reser	WA	121	C2	Rose Springs	WA	122	B2	Schrag	WA	113	B3
Powell Valley	OR	200	B1	Reston	OR	141	A2	Roseway	OR	315	E2	Schwana	WA	120	B1
Power City	OR	129	A1	* REUBENS	ID	123	B2	Rosewood	OR	199	C4	Schwarder	WA	243	B7
Power House	WA	243	A4	Rex	OR	198	D5	* ROSLYN	WA	240	A1	* SCIO	OR	133	C1
* POWERS	OR	140	B3	Rhinehart	OR	130	A2	* ROSSLAND	BC	106	A1	Scofield	OR	125	B1
Powers	WA	122	A2	Rhodesia Beach	WA	183	C7	Roswell	ID	139	A3	Scott Bar	CA	149	B3
Prahl	OR	199	B6	Rhododendron	OR	201	C5	Rothe	OR	199	D4	* SCOTTS MILLS	OR	205	D4
Prairie Center	WA	167	B4	Rhododendron Pk	WA	182	C4	Round Prairie	OR	221	B7	Scottsburg	OR	140	C1
* PRAIRIE CITY	OR	137	B2	Rice	OR	127	B2	Rowena	OR	196	B6	Scribner	WA	246	B6
Prairie Heights	WA	182	D4	Rice	WA	105	C2	* ROY	WA	181	C7	Seabeck	WA	173	D1
Prairie Ridge	WA	182	C4	Rice Hill	OR	219	A5	* ROYAL CITY	WA	120	C1	Seabold	WA	170	C7
Pratum	OR	205	B5	* RICHLAND	OR	139	A1	Royal Oak	BC	159	C5	Seahurst	WA	175	A5
Preachers Slough	WA	117	A1	* RICHLAND	WA	340	E13	Royston	BC	92	A2	Seal Rock	OR	206	A7
* PRESCOTT	OR	189	C5	* RICHMOND	BC	156	C6	Roy Vadis	OR	125	C1	Seal Rock	WA	109	C1
* PRESCOTT	WA	121	C2	Richmond	OR	136	B1	Roza	WA	243	C3	Searose Beach	OR	209	A5
Preston	WA	176	B4	Richmond	OR	318	B1	Rubicon	ID	131	C3	* SEASIDE	OR	301	E9
Prichard	ID	115	C1	Richmond Beach	WA	171	A6	Ruch	OR	149	B2	* SEATAC	WA	288	C3
Priest Rapids	WA	120	B2	Rickreall	OR	204	B6	Ruff	WA	113	A3	* SEATTLE	WA	273	G3
* PRIEST RIVER	ID	107	A3	* RIDDLE	OR	225	B3	* RUFUS	OR	127	C1	Seattle Heights	WA	171	A5
* PRINCETON	BC	95	C3	* RIDGEFIELD	WA	192	C3	Ruggs	OR	128	C2	Seaview	WA	186	A6
Princeton	ID	123	A1	Rieth	OR	129	B1	Rupple	WA	119	C2	Sechelt	BC	93	A2
Prindle	WA	194	A7	Rifton	WA	121	C2	Rural Dell	OR	205	D2	* SEDRO-WOOLLEY	WA	260	J2
* PRINEVILLE	OR	213	C4	* RIGGINS	ID	131	C2	Russell	OR	133	A1	Seekseequa Jct	OR	208	A4
Prineville Junction	OR	212	D4	Riley	OR	144	C1	Russell Landing	WA	311	F1	Seiad Valley	CA	149	B3
Pringle	OR	324	J1	Riparia	WA	122	A2	* RUSTON	WA	181	D1	Sekiu	WA	163	B2
Proebstel	WA	193	A5	Ripplebrook	OR	126	B3	Rutledge	OR	127	C2	* SELAH	WA	243	B5
Prospect	OR	226	C7	Risbeck	WA	122	C1	Ryderwood	WA	187	B5	Selleck	WA	176	B7
Prosper	OR	220	B5	Ritter	OR	129	A3	Rye Valley	OR	138	C2	Sellwood	OR	317	H5
* PROSSER	WA	120	B3	* RITZVILLE	WA	113	C3	Rykerts	BC	107	B1	Selma	OR	233	B2
Pryor	OR	142	A1	Riverdale	OR	321	G2					* SENECA	OR	137	B3
* PULLMAN	WA	249	B5	River Jordan	BC	100	C2	**S**				* SEQUIM	WA	262	D13
Purdy	WA	174	C6	River Junction	OR	192	B6	Saanichton	BC	159	C3	Service Creek	OR	136	B1
Purrington	WA	122	B1	Riversdale	OR	221	B3	Sabin	OR	313	H1	Seven Mile	WA	246	A2
* PUYALLUP	WA	182	B4	Riverside	ID	123	C2	Safley	OR	219	B2	Seven Oaks	OR	230	C7
				Riverside	OR	146	A1	Saginaw	OR	215	B6	Sexton Mountain	OR	199	A2
Q				Riverside	OR	207	B5	Sagle	ID	244	A3	Seymour	BC	255	J5
Qualicum Beach	BC	92	C3	Riverside	WA	102	C3	Sago	OR	130	B3	Shadowood	OR	199	C4
Quartz Mountain	OR	151	C2	Riverside	WA	104	C2	Sahalee	WA	175	D2	Shady	OR	334	E13
Quatama	OR	199	A1	Riverton	OR	220	C5	Saint Andrews	WA	112	C2	Shady Brook	OR	125	C1
Quathiaski Cove	BC	92	A1	Riverton	WA	289	F1	* SAINT HELENS	OR	192	B2	* SHADY COVE	OR	230	D2
Queen Anne Hill	WA	277	G2	Riverton Heights	WA	288	D3	Saint Joe	ID	115	B2	Shady Pine	OR	235	C1
Queen Borough	BC	156	D6	Riverwood	OR	321	G3	* SAINT JOHN	WA	114	B3	* SHANIKO	OR	127	C3
Queets	WA	172	B3	Roads End	OR	203	A4	Saint Johns	OR	192	B6	Shale City	OR	150	A2
Quilcene	WA	109	C1	Roanoke	WA	283	J1	Saint Joseph	OR	198	B7	Shangri-la Mill	OR	141	C3
Quilchena	BC	95	C1	Roberts	OR	135	C3	Saint Louis	OR	205	A2	Sharps Corner	OR	129	A1
Quinaby	OR	204	D4	Robinette	OR	139	A1	* SAINT MARIES	ID	248	D7	Shawnee	WA	122	C1
Quinault	WA	109	A2	Robinwood	OR	199	C4	St. Martins Hot Spgs	WA	195	A4	Shawnigan Lake	BC	159	A2
Quincy	OR	117	B3	Roche Harbor	WA	101	C2	* SAINT PAUL	OR	198	D7	Sheaville	OR	147	A2
* QUINCY	WA	112	B3	Rochester	WA	184	A3	Saint Urbans	WA	187	C2	Shedd	OR	210	B1
Quines Creek	OR	225	C6	Rockaway Beach	ID	245	B5	* SALEM	OR	325	D5	Shelburn	OR	133	C1
				* ROCKAWAY BEACH	OR	191	B6	Salisbury	OR	138	B1	Shelfler	WA	121	B2
R				Rock Creek	BC	105	A1	Salishan	WA	182	A3	* SHELTON	WA	180	A3
Rafton	OR	192	A6	Rock Creek	OR	128	A2	Salkum	WA	118	A2	Sherar	OR	127	B2
Rahms	WA	114	C2	Rock Creek	OR	130	A3	Salmon	OR	201	B4	* SHERIDAN	OR	125	B3
Rainbow	OR	134	B2	Rock Creek	OR	192	A7	Salmon Beach	WA	181	C1	Sheridan Park	WA	270	H8
* RAINIER	OR	302	F14	Rockdale	WA	111	A1	Salmonberry	OR	125	A1	Sherman	WA	113	B1
* RAINIER	WA	118	A1	Rockford	OR	195	C5	Salmon Creek	WA	192	C5	* SHERWOOD	OR	199	A4
Rainier Beach	WA	287	G3	* ROCKFORD	WA	114	C2	Saltery Bay	BC	92	C1	Sherwood Beach	ID	107	A2
Rainier Valley	WA	282	D6	Rockford Bay	ID	247	D4	Samish Island	WA	160	D4	Shine	WA	170	B4
Rainrock	OR	214	D1	* ROCK ISLAND	WA	239	B5	* SAMMAMISH	WA	175	D2	Shirley	BC	101	A2
Raleigh Hills	OR	199	B2	Rockport	WA	103	A1	Sams Valley	OR	230	B5	Shore Acres	WA	181	C1
Ramapo	WA	164	D6	Rockwood	OR	200	A1	San de Fuca	WA	167	B4	* SHORELINE	WA	171	A6
Ramey	ID	139	A3	Rocky Point	ID	248	B6	Sanders	ID	115	A3	Shorewood	OR	218	B6
Ramsey	ID	245	A3	Rocky Point	OR	231	B5	Sand Hollow	ID	139	B3	Shorewood	WA	285	G7
Rand	OR	149	A1	Rocky Point	WA	270	E7	Sand Hollow	OR	128	C1	Shorewood Beach	WA	181	B2
Randle	WA	118	C2	Rocky Point	WA	303	E4	Sandlake	OR	197	B5	Shortys Corner	OR	200	D4
* RATHDRUM	ID	115	A1	Rodena Beach	WA	167	C4	* SANDPOINT	ID	244	A1	Shrine Beach	WA	236	A1
Ravenna	WA	274	D4	* ROGUE RIVER	OR	229	D6	Sandwick	BC	92	A2	Shutler	OR	128	A1
Ravensdale	WA	176	A7	Rollingbay	WA	174	D1	* SANDY	OR	200	C4	Sidley	BC	105	A1
* RAYMOND	WA	117	A1	Rollins	WA	114	C2	San Marine	OR	328	B14	Sidney	OR	207	C2
* REARDAN	WA	114	A2	Rome	OR	146	C3	Santa	ID	115	B3	Sifton	WA	193	A5
Redd	WA	121	B2	Ronald	WA	240	A1	Santa Clara	OR	215	A1	Sightly	WA	118	A2
Redland	OR	200	A5	Rony	WA	117	B1	Santa Cruz	OR	200	C7	Silcott	WA	250	A4
* REDMOND	OR	212	D5	Roosevelt	WA	110	C1	Santiam Junction	OR	134	C2	* SILETZ	OR	206	C2
* REDMOND	WA	171	D7	Roosevelt	WA	128	A1	Sappho	WA	163	B6	Silica	BC	106	A1
Redondo	WA	175	B7	* ROSALIA	WA	114	C3	Saratoga	WA	167	D7	Siltcoos	OR	214	B5
Redwood	OR	229	B6	Rosario	WA	101	C2	Sardis	BC	94	C3	Silvana	WA	168	C5

*Indicates City, District or Township

INTRO

Community	State	Page	Grid
Silver Beach	WA	102	B1
Silver Brook	WA	118	C2
Silver City	ID	147	B3
Silver Creek	WA	118	A2
Silverdale	WA	174	B1
Silver Falls City	OR	205	D7
Silver Lake	BC	95	A3
Silver Lake	OR	143	B2
Silverlake	WA	187	D7
Silver Sands Beach	ID	115	A1
Silverton	ID	115	C2
* SILVERTON	OR	205	C4
Silvies	OR	137	B3
Similk Beach	WA	160	C7
Simnasho	OR	127	A3
Sims Corner	WA	112	C1
Sisco	WA	168	D6
Sisco Heights	WA	168	D6
Siskiyou	OR	234	D6
* SISTERS	OR	211	D5
Sitkum	OR	140	C2
Siuslaw	OR	132	C3
Six Corners	OR	199	A4
Sixes	OR	224	B4
Six Prong	WA	128	B1
Skamania	WA	194	B7
Skamokawa	WA	117	B2
Skelley	OR	219	A4
Skull Spring	OR	146	B1
* SKYKOMISH	OR	111	A1
Skyway	WA	287	J7
Slate Creek	ID	131	C1
Sliammon	BC	92	B1
Smelter Heights	ID	115	C2
* SMELTERVILLE	ID	115	C2
Smeltz	OR	129	B1
Smith Prairie	WA	167	C4
Smith River	CA	148	B3
Smithville	WA	196	C6
Smokey Point	WA	168	C6
Snake River	WA	121	B2
Snake River Jct	WA	121	B2
Snee Oosh	WA	160	D7
* SNOHOMISH	WA	171	D3
* SNOQUALMIE	WA	176	B4
Snowden	WA	196	A2
Snug Harbor	WA	164	D6
* SOAP LAKE	WA	112	C2
Soda Springs	WA	119	B2
* SODAVILLE	OR	133	C2
Sokulk	WA	114	C3
Somerset West	OR	199	A1
Sooke	BC	101	A2
Sorrento Ridge	OR	199	B3
South Aberdeen	WA	178	B7
South Arm	BC	156	B6
South Bay	WA	180	D5
South Beach	OR	206	B4
South Beach	WA	101	C1
South Beach	WA	174	D3
South Bellingham	WA	258	C10
* SOUTH BEND	WA	183	D6
South Burlingame	OR	316	D6
South Cheney	WA	114	B2
* SOUTH CLE ELUM	WA	240	B2
South Colby	WA	174	C4
South Elma	WA	179	B7
South Highlands	WA	343	C12
South Junction	OR	208	C1
South Lk Oswego	OR	320	E7
* SOUTH PRAIRIE	WA	182	D5
South Slope	BC	156	C5
South Tabor	OR	318	E1
South Tacoma	WA	294	D5
South Union	WA	184	C1
South Wellington	BC	93	A3
Southwest	OR	200	A1
Southwest Hills	OR	316	B1
South Westminster	BC	156	D6
Southwick	ID	123	B1
Southworth	WA	174	D4
Spanaway	WA	181	D5
* SPANGLE	WA	114	C2
Sparks	OR	129	B1
Sparta	OR	130	C3
Spee-bi-dah	WA	168	B3
* SPIRIT LAKE	ID	115	A1
Spitzenberg	OR	125	C1
* SPOKANE	WA	346	B13

Community	State	Page	Grid
Spokane Valley	WA	349	G10
* SPRAGUE	WA	114	A3
Sprague River	OR	151	A1
* SPRAY	OR	136	B1
Spring Beach	WA	174	C7
Springbrook	OR	198	D5
Springbrook	WA	181	D4
Springdale	OR	200	C1
* SPRINGDALE	WA	106	B3
Springfield Jct	OR	331	E6
Spring Glen	WA	175	C5
Spring Lake	OR	235	C5
Springston	ID	248	B4
Spring Valley	WA	114	C2
Spuzzum	BC	95	A2
* SQUAMISH	BC	93	C2
Squaw Canyon	WA	114	C3
Stabler	WA	194	C3
Stafford	OR	199	C4
Staley	WA	249	B6
Stampede	WA	111	A3
* STANFIELD	OR	129	A1
Stanfield Junction	OR	129	A1
* STANWOOD	WA	168	B4
Star	ID	147	C1
* STARBUCK	WA	122	A2
Starkey	ID	131	C3
Starkey	OR	125	C1
Starkey	OR	129	C2
Starlake	WA	175	B7
Startup	WA	110	C1
Starvation Heights	OR	229	D5
State Line Village	ID	352	H9
Stave Falls	BC	94	B3
* STAYTON	OR	133	C1
Steelhead	BC	94	B3
Stehekin	WA	103	C3
* STEILACOOM	WA	181	B4
Stephens	OR	221	B1
Steptoe	WA	114	C3
Stevens	ID	131	C3
* STEVENSON	WA	194	C5
Steveston	BC	156	B7
Stillwater	BC	92	C2
Stillwater	WA	176	B1
Stimson Mill	OR	198	B2
Stoddard	ID	147	C2
Stratford	WA	113	A2
Strawberry	OR	128	C2
Striebels Corner	WA	170	C5
Stronghold	CA	151	A3
Stuck	WA	182	C2
Sturdies Bay	BC	101	B1
Sturgeon	ID	115	A1
* SUBLIMITY	OR	133	C1
Sudden Valley	WA	161	B1
Sullivans Gulch	OR	313	J4
Sulphur Springs	OR	214	D7
* SULTAN	WA	110	C1
* SUMAS	WA	102	B1
Summer Lake	OR	143	C3
* SUMMERVILLE	OR	130	A2
Summit	OR	195	C6
Summit	WA	176	A7
Summit	WA	182	A4
Summits	OR	133	A1
Sumner	OR	140	B2
* SUMNER	WA	182	B3
* SUMPTER	OR	138	A1
Suncrest	BC	156	C5
Sundale	WA	128	A1
Sunderland	OR	310	B4
Sunlight Beach	WA	170	D2
Sunnycrest	OR	198	C5
Sunnydale	WA	175	A5
Sunnydale	WA	184	C3
Sunny Shores	WA	168	B6
Sunny Shores Acres	WA	168	A6
Sunnyside	OR	200	A2
Sunnyside	OR	314	A7
Sunnyside	OR	324	J12
* SUNNYSIDE	WA	120	B2
Sunnyside	WA	121	C3
Sunnyslope	WA	174	A4
Sunnyslope	WA	238	D3
Sunny Valley	OR	229	B2
Sunriver	OR	217	A6
Sunset	BC	156	B5

Community	State	Page	Grid
Sunset	OR	131	A3
Sunset	OR	199	D4
Sunset	WA	114	B3
Sunset Beach	OR	188	B3
Sunset Beach	WA	167	D4
Sunset Beach	WA	173	D6
Sunset Beach	WA	174	D6
Sunset Beach	WA	177	B2
Sunset Beach	WA	181	C3
Suplee	OR	136	C3
Suquamish	WA	170	C7
Surrey Centre	BC	157	B7
Susanville	OR	137	B1
* SUTHERLIN	OR	221	C1
Sutico	WA	117	B1
Sutton	WA	122	A1
Suver Junction	OR	207	B2
Svensen	OR	117	A3
Svensen Junction	OR	117	A3
Swansonville	WA	170	B3
Swedetown	OR	189	A5
Sweeney	ID	115	C2
Sweet	ID	139	C3
* SWEET HOME	OR	134	A2
Sweetwater	ID	123	A2
Swem	WA	117	B1
Swift	WA	122	B1
Swinomish Village	WA	160	D7
Swisshome	OR	132	C3
Sylvan	WA	181	B2
Sylvan Beach	WA	174	D5
Sylvan Highlands	OR	312	A7
Sylvanite	MT	107	C1
T			
Table Rock	OR	230	C6
* TACOMA	WA	292	D5
Taft	OR	203	A5
Tahlequah	WA	181	D1
Taholah	WA	172	B6
Tahuya	WA	173	B7
Takilma	OR	233	B6
Talache	ID	244	B5
Talbot	OR	207	C2
* TALENT	OR	234	B3
Tamarack	ID	131	C3
Tampico	WA	119	C2
* TANGENT	OR	207	C6
Tanner	WA	176	C5
Tasker	WA	119	C1
Taylorville	OR	117	B3
Teanaway	WA	240	C2
* TEKOA	WA	114	C3
Telford	WA	113	C1
Telma	WA	111	C1
Telocaset	OR	130	B3
Templeton	OR	218	C4
* TENINO	WA	184	D3
Tenino Junction	WA	184	D3
Tenmile	OR	141	A2
Tenmile	OR	218	B4
* TENSED	ID	115	A3
Terrace Heights	WA	243	C6
Terrebone	OR	212	D4
Terrys Corner	WA	167	D4
* THE DALLES	OR	196	C7
Thomas	WA	175	B7
Thompson	BC	156	A6
Thompson Place	WA	181	A6
Thorndyke	WA	289	E4
Thorn Hollow	OR	129	C1
Thornton	WA	114	C3
Thorp	WA	241	A4
Thrall	WA	241	B7
Thrashers Corner	WA	171	C5
Three Lakes	WA	110	C1
Three Lynx	OR	126	B3
Three Pines	OR	229	B3
Three Rivers	OR	217	A7
Three Rocks	OR	203	A3
Three Tree Point	WA	175	A5
Thrift	WA	182	B6
Thurston	OR	331	J6
Tide	OR	132	C3
Tidewater	OR	209	C1
Tiernan	WA	214	C2
Tierra Del Mar	OR	197	A6
* TIETON	WA	119	C1
Tietonview Grange	WA	119	C2

Community	State	Page	Grid
* TIGARD	OR	199	B3
* TILLAMOOK	OR	197	B2
Tillamook Junction	OR	125	C1
Tiller	OR	141	C3
Tillicum	BC	256	E5
Tillicum	WA	181	C5
Timber Grove	OR	126	A3
Timberlane	WA	175	D7
Tokeland	WA	183	C5
Tokio	WA	113	C3
Tokul	WA	176	C4
* TOLEDO	OR	206	C4
* TOLEDO	WA	187	D4
Tolovana Park	WA	191	B1
* TONASKET	WA	104	C2
Tongue Point Vlg	OR	188	D1
Tono	WA	184	D4
Top Hat	WA	285	J5
* TOPPENISH	WA	120	A2
Torga	WA	111	A2
Touchet	WA	121	B3
Toutle	WA	118	A2
Town & Country	WA	346	J14
* TWN OF ESQUIMLT	BC	256	C8
* TOWN OF SIDNEY	BC	159	C2
* TWN OF VW ROYAL	BC	256	A4
* TWP OF LANGLY	BC	157	D7
Tracy	OR	200	C6
Tracyton	WA	270	G4
Trail	OR	230	D2
Treharne	OR	125	B1
Trenholm	OR	125	C1
Trent	OR	215	D4
Trentwood	WA	351	A3
Trestle Creek	ID	244	C2
Tri-City	OR	225	C2
Trinity	WA	103	C3
* TROUTDALE	OR	200	B1
Trout Lake	WA	119	A3
* TROY	ID	123	A1
* TROY	MT	107	C2
Troy	OR	122	C3
Trude	WA	176	B7
Tsawwassen	BC	101	C1
* TUALATIN	OR	199	B4
Tucannon	WA	122	A2
* TUKWILA	WA	289	F3
Tulalip	WA	168	B7
Tulalip Shores	WA	168	B7
Tulameen	BC	95	C2
Tulare Beach	WA	168	B6
Tulelake	CA	151	A3
Tulips	WA	177	C5
Tumalo	OR	217	B1
* TUMWATER	WA	296	F9
Tumtum	WA	114	B1
Turkey	WA	166	D7
* TURNER	OR	325	G12
Turner	WA	122	B2
Turner Corner	WA	171	C5
Twickenham	OR	136	A1
Twin Beaches	ID	248	C3
Twin Lakes	WA	182	A1
Twinlow	ID	115	A1
Twin Rocks	OR	191	A6
* TWISP	WA	104	A3
Twomile	OR	220	B7
Tye	WA	111	B1
Tyee	OR	141	A1
Tyee Beach	WA	168	A7
Tygh Valley	OR	127	B2
Tyler	WA	114	B2
Tynehead	BC	157	B6
U			
* UKIAH	OR	129	B3
Umapine	WA	121	C3
* UMATILLA	OR	129	A1
Umli	OR	142	B1
Umpqua	OR	221	A1
Umtanum	WA	243	C2
Uncas	WA	109	C1
Underwood	OR	195	C4
Underwood Heights	WA	195	C4
* UNION	OR	130	B2
Union	WA	173	A7
Union Bay	BC	92	B2
Union Creek	OR	141	A3

*Indicates City, District or Township

INTRO

Community	State	Page	Grid
Union Creek	OR	226	D4
Union Gap	OR	221	C1
* UNION GAP	WA	243	C7
Union Junction	OR	130	B2
Union Mills	OR	126	A3
Union Mills	WA	181	A6
* UNIONTOWN	WA	250	B2
Unionville	OR	204	C2
United Junction	OR	192	B6
* UNITY	OR	138	A2
University	WA	274	C5
* UNV ENDWMT LDS	BC	156	A4
University Park	WA	308	A5
* UNIVERSITY PLACE	WA	294	A4
Upper Farm	OR	206	D2
Upper Highland	OR	200	B7
Upper Mill	WA	110	C3
Upper Preston	WA	176	B4
Upper Soda	OR	134	B2
Usk	WA	106	C3
Ustick	ID	253	B2
Utsalady	WA	167	D3
V			
* VADER	WA	187	C4
Vadis	OR	125	C1
Vail	WA	118	A1
Valby	OR	128	B2
* VALE	OR	138	C3
Valle Vista	OR	192	A7
Valley	WA	106	B3
Valleycliffe	BC	93	C2
Valley Falls	OR	152	A1
Valleyford	WA	246	D6
Valley Junction	OR	125	A3
Van	OR	137	B3
Vananda	BC	92	B2
Van Asselt	WA	286	D1
* VANCOUVER	BC	254	G13
* VANCOUVER	WA	305	F3
Vancouver Junction	WA	192	C5
Van Horn	OR	195	D6
Vantage	WA	120	B1
Van Zandt	WA	102	B1
Vasa Park	WA	175	D3
Vashon	WA	174	D5
Vashon Center	WA	174	D6
Vashon Heights	WA	174	D4
Vaughn	OR	133	A2
Vaughn	WA	174	A7
Vega	WA	181	A4
Venator	OR	146	A2
Venersborg	WA	193	B3
* VENETA	OR	133	B3
Venice	WA	174	C1
Veradale	WA	351	C8
Verboort	OR	125	B1
Vermon	OR	309	J6
* VERNONIA	OR	125	B1
Vesuvius	BC	101	B1
Victoria	BC	156	C5
Vida	OR	134	A2
View Ridge	WA	275	G3
Village Bay	BC	101	B1
Vineland	WA	250	B4
Vinemaple	OR	125	A1
Vinland	WA	170	B6
Vinson	OR	129	A2
Viola	ID	249	C3
Viola	OR	200	B6
Virden	WA	240	D1
Virginia	WA	170	B7
Vision Acres	WA	189	C4
Voltage	OR	145	B2
Voorhies	OR	234	B2
W			
Wabash	WA	182	D2
Waconda	OR	205	A3
Wagner	WA	110	C1
Wagnersburg	WA	239	A1
Wagontire	OR	144	B2
Wahkiacus	WA	196	D3
* WAITSBURG	WA	122	A2
Waitsburg Junction	WA	122	A2
Wakonda Beach	OR	328	B10
Waldale	WA	241	B5
* WALDPORT	OR	328	C7
Walker	OR	215	B6
* WALLACE	ID	115	C2
Wallace	OR	199	B6
* WALLA WALLA	WA	344	E6
Walla Walla East	WA	345	E9
Wallingford	WA	274	A5
* WALLOWA	OR	130	B1
Wallula	WA	121	B3
Walnut Grove	BC	157	C6
Walnut Grove	WA	192	D5
Walters	WA	114	C3
Walters Ferry	ID	147	B2
Walterville	OR	133	C3
Walton	OR	133	A2
Walville	WA	117	B2
Wamic	OR	127	A2
Wanapum Village	WA	120	B1
Waneta	BC	106	B1
Wankers Corner	OR	199	C4
Wapato	OR	198	B3
* WAPATO	WA	120	A2
Wapinitia	OR	127	A3
* WARDEN	WA	121	A1
* WARDNER	ID	115	C2
Warm Beach	WA	168	A5
Warm Springs	OR	208	A3
Warner	OR	140	B3
Warren	OR	192	A2
Warren	WA	181	B1
* WARRENTON	OR	188	B2
Warwick	WA	127	B1
* WASCO	OR	127	C1
Washington Harbor	WA	166	B7
* WASHOUGAL	WA	193	B7
* WASHTUCNA	WA	121	C1
* WATERLOO	OR	133	C1
Waterman	OR	129	C1
Waterman	OR	136	B1
Waterman	WA	271	E9
Waterman Point	WA	271	F8
* WATERVILLE	WA	236	C7
Watseco	OR	191	A6
Waukon	WA	114	A2
Wauna	OR	117	B3
Wauna	WA	174	B6
Wautauga Beach	WA	271	G8
* WAVERLY	WA	114	C2
Wawawai	WA	122	C1
Wayland	OR	129	C1
Wayside	WA	114	B1
Weaver	OR	225	C1
Webster Corners	BC	157	D5
Wecoma Beach	OR	203	A4
Wedderburn	OR	228	A5
Weikel	WA	243	A6
* WEISER	ID	139	A2
Welches	OR	201	C5
Wellington	BC	93	A3
Wellpinit	WA	114	A1
Wells	WA	114	A3
Wemme	OR	201	C5
* WENATCHEE	WA	238	D4
Wenatchee Heights	WA	239	A6
Wendling	OR	133	C2
Wendson	OR	214	C3
West Beach	WA	101	C2
West Blakely	WA	271	H7
West Fairfield	WA	114	C2
* WESTFIR	OR	142	A1
West Fork	WA	105	B2
West Haven	OR	199	B1
Westhaven	WA	298	F11
West Highlands	WA	342	H10
West Kelso	WA	303	B7
West Klamath	OR	235	B4
West Lake	OR	188	B4
Westlake	OR	214	A5
Westlake	WA	242	C3
Westland	OR	129	A1
* WEST LINN	OR	199	C4
Westma	ID	147	C1
Westmond	ID	244	A5
* WESTON	OR	129	C1
Weston	WA	111	A3
West Park	WA	270	D11
West Pastco	WA	342	E5
Westport	OR	117	B3
* WESTPORT	WA	298	G13
West Portland Park	OR	320	A2
* WEST RICHLAND	WA	341	A3
West Salem	OR	322	F12
West Seattle	WA	280	D4
West Side	OR	152	A2
West Slope	OR	199	B2
Westsound	WA	101	C2
West Spokane	WA	348	F8
West Stayton	OR	133	C1
West Union	OR	192	A7
West Valley	WA	243	A6
West Wenatchee	WA	238	D4
Westwood	WA	285	G2
West Woodbury	OR	205	B1
Wetico	WA	118	A1
Wetmore	OR	128	B3
Wetzels Corner	OR	200	B3
Wheatland	OR	204	D3
* WHEELER	OR	191	B4
Wheeler Heights	OR	191	B4
Whelan	WA	249	B4
Whetstone	WA	122	A2
Whiskey Hill	OR	205	C1
* WHISTLER	BC	93	C1
Whiststran	WA	120	C3
White	WA	171	D7
* WHITE BIRD	ID	131	C1
White Center	WA	285	G4
White City	OR	230	D6
Whites	WA	179	C6
* WHITE SALMON	WA	195	D4
Whiteson	OR	204	B1
White Swan	WA	119	C2
Whitewater	OR	126	B3
Whitlow	WA	249	B5
Whitman	WA	121	A3
Whitney	OR	138	A1
Whitney	WA	344	J12
Whittier	WA	111	A3
Whonnock	BC	94	B3
Wickersham	WA	161	C3
Wilbur	OR	221	C2
* WILBUR	WA	113	B1
Wilburton	WA	175	C2
Wilcox	OR	127	C3
Wildcat Lake	WA	174	A2
* WILDER	ID	147	A1
Wilderness	WA	176	A7
Wilderville	OR	229	A7
Wildwood	WA	187	A4
Wildwood Heights	BC	92	B1
Wiley City	WA	243	A7
Wilhoit Springs	OR	126	A3
Wilkes	OR	200	A1
Wilkes East	OR	200	A1
* WILKESON	WA	182	D5
Wilkins	OR	210	B6
Willada	WA	114	B3
Willamette	OR	199	C5
Willamette City	OR	142	A1
* WILLAMINA	OR	125	A3
Willapa	WA	117	A1
Willard	WA	195	B3
Williams	OR	149	B2
Willow Creek	OR	138	C2
Willow Ranch	CA	152	A3
Willows	WA	263	A8
Wilson	WA	316	D5
Wilson	OR	118	A2
Wilson Corner	OR	200	B3
* WILSON CREEK	WA	113	A2
* WILSONVILLE	OR	199	B5
Wimer	OR	229	D4
Winant	OR	206	B5
Winberry	OR	133	C3
Winchester	ID	123	B2
Winchester	OR	221	C3
Winchester	WA	112	C3
Winchester Bay	OR	218	C2
Windermere	WA	275	F5
Windmaster Corner	WA	195	C5
Winema Beach	OR	203	B1
Wingville	OR	130	B3
Winlock	OR	128	B3
* WINLOCK	WA	187	C3
Winona	OR	229	C3
Winona	OR	322	E13
Winona	WA	122	B1
Winslow	WA	271	H2
* WINSTON	OR	221	B6
Winston	OR	118	A2
Winterville	OR	220	B6
* WINTHROP	WA	104	A2
Winton	WA	111	C1
Wishkah	WA	178	B6
Wishram	WA	127	B1
Wishram Heights	WA	127	B1
Witch Hazel	OR	198	D2
Withrow	WA	112	B2
Wocus	OR	338	B1
Wolf Creek	OR	229	B1
Wolf Lodge	ID	248	C1
Wollochet	WA	181	C2
Wonder	OR	149	A1
* WOODBURN	OR	205	B1
Woodfibre	BC	93	C2
* WOODINVILLE	WA	171	D6
Woodland	ID	131	C3
* WOODLAND	WA	189	D7
Woodland Beach	WA	167	D4
Woodland Park	OR	200	A1
Woodland Park	OR	315	J4
Woodland Park	WA	118	A3
Woodlawn	OR	309	H5
Woodmans	WA	170	A1
Woodmont	WA	175	B7
Woodruff	WA	110	C1
Woodruff Mill	WA	196	D2
Woods	OR	197	A7
Woodson	WA	117	B3
Woodstock	OR	318	B4
* WOOD VILLAGE	OR	200	B1
* WOODWAY	WA	171	A6
Worden	OR	235	B7
* WORLEY	ID	115	A2
Wren	OR	133	A1
Wrentham	OR	127	B2
Wye	BC	256	F4
Wyeth	OR	195	A5
Wymer	WA	243	C2
Wynaco	WA	182	C1
Y			
* YACHATS	OR	209	A3
* YACOLT	WA	193	B1
Yaculta	BC	92	A1
* YAKIMA	WA	243	B6
Yale	BC	95	A2
Yale	WA	118	A3
* YAMHILL	OR	198	B5
Yamsay	OR	142	C3
Yankton	OR	192	A1
Yaquina	OR	206	B5
* YARROW POINT	WA	175	C1
* YELM	WA	118	A1
Yennadon	BC	157	D5
Yeomalt	WA	174	D2
Yoakum	OR	129	A1
Yoder	OR	205	D2
Yokeko Point	WA	160	C7
Yoman	WA	181	A3
Yoman Dock	WA	181	B4
* YONCALLA	OR	219	A4
Youbou	BC	100	C1
Young	OR	133	C1
* YREKA	CA	149	C3
Z			
Zena	OR	204	C4
Zenith	WA	290	A7
Zigzag	OR	201	C5
* ZILLAH	WA	120	A2
Zumwalt	OR	131	A1
Zumwalt	WA	122	B2

*Indicates City, District or Township

General Information

Highway Patrol

British Columbia
Washington State   In case of emergency, call 911
Oregon State
Idaho State

Road Conditions

British Columbia   British Columbia Ministry of Transportation and Highways: (205) 387-7788
                         www.th.gov.bc.ca/bchighways/roadreports/roadreports.htm

Washington State   Washington State Department of Transportation: (800) 695-7623
                         http://traffic.wsdot.wa.gov

Oregon State   Salem Online: (503) 588-6161
                         www.oregonlink.com/weather/index.html

Idaho State   Weather Net: (208) 336-6600
                         http://164.165.237.41/RoadReports

Department of Transportation

British Columbia   BC Ministry of Transportation & Highways: (800) 613-9993
                         www.th.gov.bc.ca/bchighways

Washington State   Washington State Department of Transportation: (360) 705-7000
                         www.wsdot.wa.gov

Oregon State   Oregon Department of Transportation:(888) 275-6368
                         www.odot.state.or.us

Idaho State   Idaho State Department of Transportation: (208) 334-8000
                         www.state.id.us/itd

Ferry Crossing

British Columbia   BC Ferries' Corporate Marketing Group: (250) 381-1401
                         www.bcferries.bc.ca

Washington State   Washington State Department of Transportation: (206) 464-6400
                         toll free in state: (888) 808-7977 or/toll free in state: (800) 843-3779
                         www.wsdot.wa.gov/ferries

Crossing the Border

British Columbia   Revenue Canada: (800) 461-9999
                         www.rc.gc.ca

Washington State   U.S. Customs: (206) 553-0770
                         www.customs.ustreas.gov

Weather Conditions

British Columbia   www.cnn.com/WEATHER
Washington State   www.weather.com
Oregon State   www.weather.com
Idaho State   www.weather.com

Visitor's Information

British Columbia   British Columbia Visitor's Information: (250) 356-6363
                         www.sightseeing.com

Washington State   Washington State Tourism Division Info Package: (800) 544-1800
                         www.tourism.wa.gov

Oregon State   Oregon Tourism Commission (800) 547-7842
                         www.traveloregon.com

Idaho State   Idaho Department of Commerce: (208) 334-2631
                         www.idoc.state.id.us

Pacific Northwest National, Provincial & State Park Information

Camping & Lodging Information

British Columbia	Campgrounds of Canada: www.campcanada.com
Washington State	Online Travel Information: www.tourism.wa.gov
Oregon State	Oregon State Parks Reservation Center (800) 452-5687 www.prd.state.or.us/reservation.html
Idaho State	Discover Idaho www.visitid.org

National, Provincial & State Park Information

British Columbia	British Columbia Ministry of Environment Lands & Parks: (800) 689-9025 www.env.gov.bc.ca/bcparks/reserv/campers.htm
Washington State	Washington State Parks & Recreation Commission: www.parks.wa.gov
Oregon State	Oregon State Parks: www.prd.state.or.us
Idaho State	Idaho State Parks: http://www.idoc.state.id.us/irti/stateparks

Selected National, Provincial & State Parks Including Recreation Areas, Forests, and National Monuments

Prov	Park	Page & Grid	Camping	Trailer / RV	Picnicking	Swimming	Fishing	Hiking	Boating	Beach
BC	**National Parks**									
	Pacific Rim National Park	100, A1	●	●	●	●	●	●	●	●
	Provincial Parks									
	Carmanah Pacific Provincial Park	92, B2	●	●	●			●		
	Cathedral Provincial Park	104, A1	●	●	●		●	●		
	Cultus Lake Provincial Park	102, C1	●		●	●	●	●	●	●
	Desolation Sound Provincial Marine Park	92, B1	●			●	●	●		
	Garibaldi Provincial Park	94, A1	●	●	●		●	●		
	Golden Ears Provincial Park	94, B2	●	●	●	●	●	●	●	●
	Manning Provincial Park	95, C3	●	●	●	●	●	●	●	●
	Skagit Valley Provincial Park	103, B1	●	●	●	●	●	●	●	●
	Strathcona Provincial Park	92, A2	●	●	●	●	●	●	●	●
State	**Park**									
WA	**National Parks**									
	Mount Rainier National Park	118, C1	●	●	●		●	●	●	
	North Cascades National Park	103, A1	●	●	●		●	●	●	
	Olympic National Park	109, B1	●	●	●		●	●	●	
	National / State Forests									
	Colville National Forest	105, C2	●	●	●	●	●	●	●	●
	Gifford Pinchot National Forest	118, C2	●	●	●	●	●	●	●	●
	Kaniksu National Forest	106, C2	●	●	●	●	●	●	●	●
	Mount Baker National Forest	103, A2	●	●	●	●	●	●	●	●
	Mount Baker-Snoqualmie National Forest	111, A2	●	●	●	●	●	●	●	●
	Okanogan National Forest	104, B2	●	●	●	●	●	●	●	●
	Olympic National Forest	109, B2	●	●	●	●	●	●	●	●
	Wenatchee National Forest	112, A1	●	●	●	●	●	●	●	●
	Parks / Recreation Areas / Monuments									
	Beacon Rock State Park	194, B6	●	●	●		●		●	●
	Birch Bay State Park	158, B5	●	●	●		●			●
	Bogachiel State Park	169, D3	●	●	●		●			●
	Brooks Memorial State Park	119, C3	●	●	●		●			
	Columbia River Gorge National Scenic Area	200, C1	●	●	●		●	●	●	
	Coulee Dam National Recreation Area	237, D3	●	●	●	●	●	●	●	●
	Fort Canby State Park	186, A6	●	●	●		●		●	●
	Fort Flagler State Park	167, B6	●	●	●		●		●	●
	Fort Worden State Park	167, A6	●	●	●		●		●	●
	Kanaskat-Palmer State Park	110, C3	●	●	●				●	●
	Lake Chelan National Recreation Area	103, C3	●	●	●		●	●	●	
	Larrabee State Park	160, D2	●	●	●		●		●	●
	Millersylvania State Park	184, C2	●	●	●	●	●			
	Mount Saint Helens National Volcanic Monument	190, B1						●		
	Mount Spokane State Park	114, C1	●		●					
	Ocean City State Park	177, B6	●	●	●		●			●
	Pacific Beach State Park	177, B2	●	●	●		●			●
	Potholes State Park	242, C6	●	●	●		●		●	
	Ross Lake National Recreation Area	103, B1	●	●	●		●	●	●	
	Schafer State Park	179, A5	●	●	●		●			●
	Seaquest State Park	187, D7	●	●	●					
	Sequim Bay State Park	166, C7	●	●	●		●		●	
	Sun Lakes State Park	112, C2	●	●	●	●	●		●	
	Twanoh State Park	173, C7	●	●	●	●	●		●	

Selected National, Provincial & State Parks Including Recreation Areas, Forests, and National Monuments

State	Park	Page & Grid	Camping	Trailer / RV	Picnicking	Swimming	Fishing	Hiking	Boating	Beach
WA	**Parks/Recreation Areas/Monuments cont...**									
	Wenberg State Park	168, B6	●	○	●		●		●	○
	Yakima Sportsman State Park	243, C7	●	○	●		○			○
OR	**National Parks**									
	Crater Lake National Park	227, C3	●	○	●			●		
	National/State Forests									
	Clatsop State Forest	191, D2	●	○	●	●	●	●	●	○
	Deschutes National Forest	143, A1	●	○	●	●	●	●	●	○
	Elliott State Forest	140, C1	●	○	●	●	●	●	●	○
	Fremont National Forest	151, C2	●	○	●	●	●	●	●	○
	Malheur National Forest	137, B1	●	○	●	●	●	●	●	○
	McDonald State Forest	207, A5	●	○	●	●	●	●	●	○
	Mount Hood National Forest	202, B2	●	○	●	●	●	●	●	○
	Ochoco National Forest	136, B2	●	○	●	●	●	●	●	○
	Rogue River National Forest	149, B3	●	○	●	●	●	●	●	○
	Santiam State Forest	134, A1	●	○	●	●	●	●	●	○
	Siskiyou National Forest	148, B2	●	○	●	●	●	●	●	○
	Siuslaw National Forest	132, C2	●	○	●	●	●	●	●	○
	Tillamook State Forest	125, A1	●	○	●	●	●	●	●	○
	Umatilla National Forest	129, B3	●	○	●	●	●	●	●	○
	Umpqua National Forest	142, A2	●	○	●	●	●	●	●	○
	Wallowa-Whitman National Forest	138, A1	●	○	●	●	●	●	●	○
	Willamette National Forest	134, B1	●	○	●	●	●	●	●	○
	Winema National Forest	142, C2	●	○	●	●	●	●	●	○
	Parks/Recreation Areas/Monuments									
	Beachside State Park	328, A11	●	○	●		●			
	Beverly Beach State Park	206, B2	●	○	●		●	●		
	Bullards Beach State Park	220, B5	●	○	●		●	●	●	
	Cape Blanco State Park	224, A4	●	○	●		●	●		○
	Cape Lookout State Park	197, A3	●	○	●		●	●		○
	Champoeg State Park	199, A6	●	○	●		●	●	●	
	Collier Memorial State Park	231, D2	●	○	●		●	●		
	Columbia River Gorge National Scenic Area	200, C1	●	○	●		●	●	●	
	Detroit Lake State Park	134, B1	●	○	●	●	●		●	○
	Emigrant Lake County Recreation Area	243, D4								
	Fort Stevens State Park	188, B1	●	○	●		●	●	●	○
	Harris Beach State Park	232, C6	●	○	●		●	●		○
	Hells Canyon National Recreation Area	131, B1	●	○	●		●	●	●	○
	Humbug Mountain State Park	224, B7	●	○	●		●	●		○
	Jessie M Honeyman Memorial State Park	214, B4	●	○	●	●	●	●	●	○
	John Day Fossil Beds National Monument	136, C1			●			●		
	Joseph Stewart State Park	149, C1	●	○	●	●	●	●	●	
	Lake Owyhee State Park	147, A1	●	○	●		●		●	
	Memaloose State Park	196, A5	●	○						
	Milo McIver State Park	200, B6	●	○	●		●	●	●	
	Nehalem Bay State Park	191, B5	●	○	●		●	●	●	○
	Newberry National Volcanic Monument	143, B1						●		
	Oregon Cascades Recreation Area	142, B1	●	○	●	●	●	●	●	○
	Oregon Caves National Monument	149, D5			●			●		
	Oregon Dunes National Recreation Area	214, A5	●		●		●	●		○
	Silver Falls State Park	205, D7	●	○	●		●	●		○
	South Beach State Park	206, B5	●	○	●		●	●		○
	Sunset Bay State Park	220, B1	●	○	●	●	●	●		○
	The Cove Palisades State Park	208, A6	●	○	●	●	●	●	●	○
	Umpqua Lighthouse State Park	218, B2	●	○	●		●	●	●	○
	Valley of the Rogue State Park	229, D6	●	○	●		●	●	●	
	Viento State Park	195, B5	●	○	●					
	Wallowa Lake State Park	130, C2	●	○	●		●	●	●	○
	William M Tugman State Park	218, C3	●	○	●	●	●	●	●	○
ID	**National/State Forest**									
	Coeur d'Alene National Forest	115. B1	●	○	●	●	●	●	●	○
	Kaniksu National Forest	106, C2	●	○	●	●	●	●	●	○
	Nez Perce	131, C1	●	○	●	●	●	●	●	○
	Payette National Forest	131, B3	●	○	●	●	●	●	●	○
	Saint Joe National Forest	115, B3	●	○	●	●	●	●	●	○
	Parks/Recreation Areas/Monuments									
	Farragut State Park	245, C1	●	○	●	●	●	●	●	
	Heyburn State Park	248, A6	●	○	●	●	●	●	●	
CA	**National Parks**									
	Redwood National Park	148, B3	●	○	●		●	●	●	
	National/State Forests									
	Klamath National Forest	149, B3	●	○	●	●	●	●	●	○
	Modoc National Forest	151, B3	●	○	●	●	●	●	●	○
	Siskiyou National Forest	148, B2	●	○	●	●	●	●	●	○
	Six River National Forest	148, C3	●	○	●	●	●	●	●	○
	Parks/Recreation Areas/Monuments									
	Del Norte Coast Redwoods State Park	148, B3	●	○	●		●	●		○
	Lava Beds National Monument	151, A3	●	○	●			●		
	Smith River National Recreation Area	148, C3	●	○	●		●	●	●	○
NV	**National/State Forests**									
	Humboldt National Forest	154, C3	●	○	●		●	●	●	○
MT	**National/State Forests**									
	Kootenai National Forest	107, C1	●	○	●		●	●	●	

© 2004 Thomas Bros. Maps® —N—

A | B | C

CAMPBELL RIVER

ELK FALLS PARK

BLENKIN MEMORIAL PARK

Duncan Bay

Discovery Passage

MARINA ISLAND

MANSON LANDING CAMPGROUND

Manson Landing

Cortes Bay

DESOLATION SOUND

Orange Point

Quathiaski Cove

SMELT BAY CAMPGROUND

Sarah Point

HERNANDO ISLAND

COPELAND ISLANDS MARINE PARK

Bliss Landing

DESOLATION SOUND PROVINCIAL MARINE PARK

OKEOVER ARM CAMPGROUND

MALASPINA PENINSULA

Lund

POWELL LAKE

GOAT ISLAND

GOAT LAKE

POWELL LAKE

WINDSOR LAKE

DODD LAKE

WILLOW POINT

SHELTER POINT

OYSTER BAY

Fransisco Point

MITLENATCH ISLAND NATURE PARK

MARSON PASSAGE

SAVARY ISLAND

Savary Island

BRITISH COLUMBIA

BUNSTER HILLS

SLIAMMOA LAKE

Wildwood Heights

INLAND LAKE

HASLAM LAKE

SMITH RANGE

HORSESHOE LAKE

KUHUSHAN POINT

Oyster River

Black Creek

101

Sliammon

HANWOOD ISLAND

POWELL RIVER HISTORIC MUSEUM

POWELL RIVER

LOIS LAKE

MOUNT TROUBRIDGE

Merville

19

19A

MOUNT WASHINGTON

WOLF LAKE

INLAND ISLAND HWY

LITTLE RIVER-POWELL RIVER FERRY

Blubber Bay

GRILSE POINT

GRIEF POINT

Lang Bay

SALTERY BAY CAMPGROUND

Saltery Bay

KIN BEACH CAMPGROUND

Little River

KYE BAY

COMOX AIRPORT

COURTENAY

Sandwick

FISH HATCHERY

COMOX

COMOX HARBOUR

GARTLEY POINT

Royston

STRATHCONA PROVINCIAL PARK

WOOD MOUNTAIN SKI PARK

Cumberland

COMOX LAKE

Union Bay

SANDY ISLAND PARK

DENMAN ISLAND

Denman Island

FILLONGLEY CAMPGROUND

HORNBY ISLAND

HELLIWELL CAMPGROUND

ST JOHN POINT

Hornby Island

TRIBUNE BAY CAMPGROUND

NORMAN POINT

STRAIT OF GEORGIA

Vananda

FAVADA POINT

Gillies Bay

TEXADA ISLAND

MOUNT DAVIES

SABINE CHANNEL

MOUNT SHEPHERD

HARDY ISLAND

NELSON ISLAND

Stillwater

UPWOOD POINT

LASQUETI ISLAND

Lasqueti

JENKINS ISLAND

YOUNG POINT

SANGSTER ISLAND

TSABLE LAKE

WILLEMAR LAKE

BEAUFORT RANGE

ELSIE LAKE

Fanny Bay

BOYLE POINT

Bowser

19A

PARKSVILLE-LASQUETI FERRY

LOWRY LAKE

GREAT CENTRAL LAKE

ROBERTSON FISH HATCHERY

STAMP FALLS CAMPGROUND

HORNE LAKE CAVES CAMPGROUND

SPIDER LAKE CAMPGROUND

HORNE LAKE

QUALICUM BAY

19

Qualicum Beach

BIG QUALICUM RIVER HATCHERY

LITTLE QUALICUM FALLS CAMPGROUND

CRAIG HERITAGE MUS

PARKSVILLE

RATHTREVOR BEACH CAMPGROUND

BALLENAS ISLAND

SPROAT LAKE CAMPGROUND

TAYLOR ARM CAMPGROUND

CAMERON LAKE

MACMILLAN CAMPGROUND

BUTTERFLY WORLD

INLAND ISLAND HWY

ENGLISHMAN RIVER FALLS CAMPGROUND

19

NAROOSE HARBOUR

SPROAT LAKE

MOUNT ANDERSON

4

MUS

PORT ALBERNI

MOUNT ARROWSMITH PARK

MCLAUGHLIN RIDGE

MOUNT MORIARTY

LABOUR DAY LAKE

MOUNT DE COSMOS

NAHMINT LAKE

ALBERNI INLET

CHINA CREEK PARK

EFFINGHAM INLET

HENDERSON LAKE

HANNAH MOUNTAIN

NANAIMO LAKES

SEE 93 MAP

SEE 100 MAP

0 2.5 5 7.5 10 miles 1 in. = 7.5 mi.

HWY

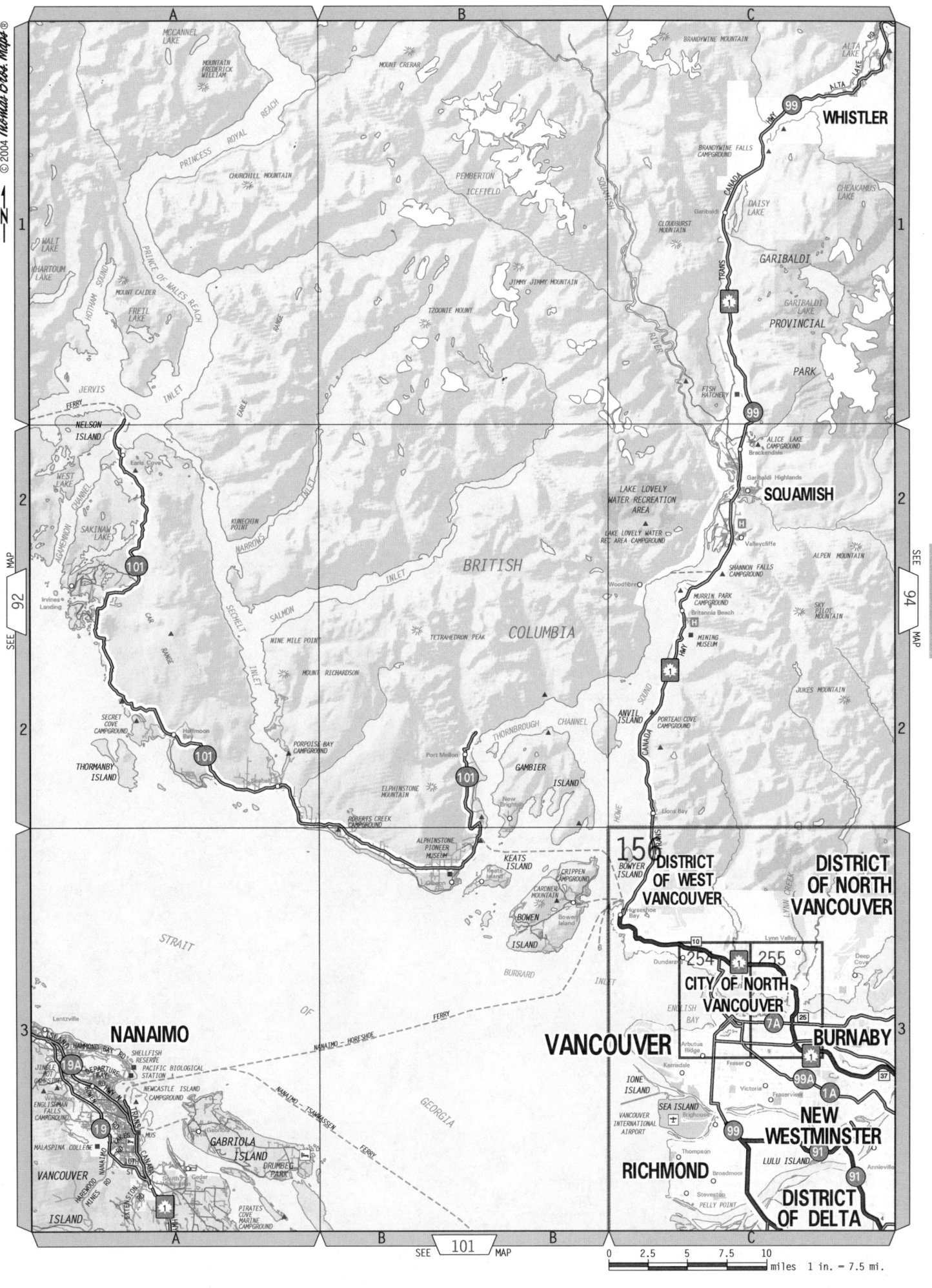

© 2004 Thomas Bros. Maps ®

HWY

SEE 93 MAP

SEE 95 MAP

A **B** **C**

1 1

SUMMER LAKE

WEDGE MOUNTAIN

CHEAKAMUS MOUNTAIN

CHEAKAMUS LAKE

GARIBALDI

MOUNT SIR RICHARD

LILLOOET LAKE

MOUNT PITT

PROVINCIAL

LILLOOET RIVER

COAST

2 2

MANQUAM MOUNTAIN

MESLILLOET MOUNTAIN

MOUNT BONNYCASTLE

PITT

LAKE

PARK

GOLDEN

THOMAS LAKE

EARS

OSPREY MOUNTAIN

PENEPLAIN PEAK

BRITISH COLUMBIA

MOUNT BREAKENRIDGE

MOUNT BREIER

HARRISON LAKE

LONG ISLAND

15

CROKER ISLAND

INDIAN ARM

COQUITLAM LAKE

WIDGEON LAKE

WIDGEON PEAK

GOOSE ISLAND

PROVINCIAL

RAVEN LAKE

PARK

STAVE LAKE

CHEHALIS LAKE

MOUNT JASPER

Hemlock Valley

ECHO ISLAND

BUNTZEN LAKE BELCARRA PARK

COQUITLAM ISLAND

SIWASH ISLAND

MOUNT BLANSHARD

ALOUETTE MOUNTAIN

ALOUETTE LAKE

MOUNT CATHERWOOD

WEAVER CREEK PROV PARK

HEMLOCK VALLEY RD

HEMLOCK SKI AREA

SASQUATCH PROV PARK

BELCARRA

ANMORE

7A

PORT MOODY

COQUITLAM REGIONAL PARK

BURKE MOUNTAIN

COQUITLAM

EUNICE LAKE

LOON LAKE

MAPLE RIDGE

GOLDCREEK CAMPGROUND

ALOUETTE CAMPGROUND

SAYRES LAKE

MOUNT CRICKMER

DISTRICT OF MISSION

DAVIS LAKE PROVINCIAL PARK

DICKSON LAKE

CHEHALIS HATCHERY

MORRIS VALLEY RD

MOUNT AGASSIZ

HARRISON HOT SPRINGS

7

3 3

7

PORT COQUITLAM

PITT RIVER

PITT MEADOWS

Haney DEWDNEY

Yennadon

Webster Corners

WINDY POINT

ROLLEY LAKE

ROLLEY LAKE PROVINCIAL PARK

CANNELL LAKE

HARTLEY RD

STAVE SILVESTER RD

HARRISON RIVER

DISTRICT OF KENT

Harrison Mills

9

KIMBERT RD

7

McCALLUM RD

FRASER

48

Port Hammond

Port Kells

1

1A

Walnut Grove

Fort Langley

7

DEWDNEY TRUNK

BELL ST

WILSON ST

STAVE FALLS RD

Stave Falls

Steelhead

HAYWARD

DERCHE RD

NICOMEN ISLAND

DEWDNEY

7

SKUMALASPH ISLAND

YOUNG RD

VYE RD

McSWEEN RD

McGUIRE RD

CASTLEMAN RD

1

NEVIN RD

CITY OF SURREY

Newton

99A

Surrey Centre

15

LANGLEY

10

58

Milner

Forest Knolls

TOWNSHIP OF LANGLEY

DISTRICT OF MATSQUI

Glen Valley

FRASER RIVER

7TH AV

RIVER

LOUGHEED HWY

FERNDALE AV

GLENMORE AV

HARRIS RD

Matsqui

11

MATSQUI ISLAND

PAGE RD

RIZZO RD

FRASER RIVER

SUMAS MOUNTAIN PROV PARK

CHADSEY LAKE

TRANS CANADA

SOUTH SUMAS RD

LICKMAN RD

VEDDER RD

YALE RD

BAILEY RD

CITY OF CHILLIWACK

BRIDAL VEIL FALLS PROV PARK

1

SEE 102 MAP

0 2.5 5 7.5 10

miles 1 in. = 7.5 mi.

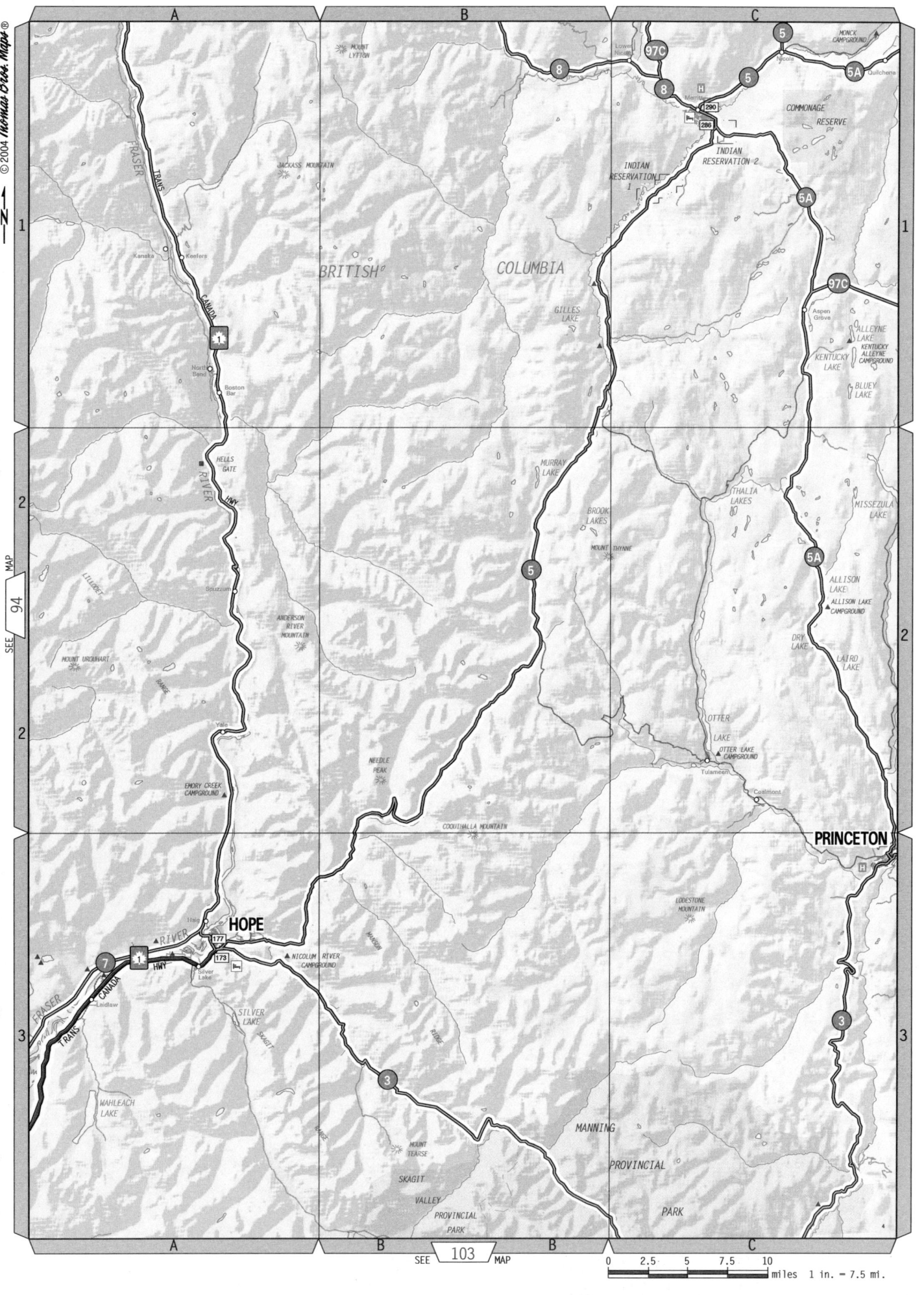

N

A B C

PRINCETON

HOPE

MANNING

PROVINCIAL

PARK

BRITISH COLUMBIA

FRASER RIVER

TRANS CANADA HWY

HELLS GATE

1

2

3

SEE 94 MAP

HWY

SEE 103 MAP

miles 1 in. = 7.5 mi.

0   2.5   5   7.5   10

© 2004 Thomas Bros. Maps ®

—N—

HWY

A   **B**   **B**   **C**

CATARACT LAKE

ALMA RUSSELL ISLAND

SEDALL ISLAND

Kildonan

IMPERIAL EAGLE CHANNEL

FERRY

TZARTUS ISLAND

FLEMING ISLAND

FERRY

SARITA LAKE

SANDFORD ISLAND

DIANA ISLAND

Bamfield

CAPE BEALE

PACHENA BAY

BLACK LAKE

SOMERSET RANGE

PACHENA POINT

TSUSIAT LAKE

SQUALICUM LAKE

HOBITON LAKE

DOOBAH LAKE

SPRISE LAKE

CHEEWHAT LAKE

Clo-oose

NITINAT LAKE

SMOKEHOUSE MOUNTAIN

CARMANAH POINT

CARMANAH PACIFIC PROVINCIAL PARK

GLAD LAKE

MOUNT WALBRAN

Franklin Camp

MOUNT GREY

TUCK LAKE

HEATHER LAKE

Nitinat

McCLURE LAKE

EDINBURGH MOUNTAIN

BRITISH COLUMBIA

FOURTH LAKE

NANAIMO LAKES

HEATHER MOUNTAIN

RHEINHART LAKE

MOUNT LANDALT

MOUNT WHYMPER

COWICHAN

Caycuse

Youbou

LAKE

VANCOUVER ISLAND

TOWNCUT MOUNTAIN

GORDON BAY PROVINCIAL PARK

GORDON BAY PROVINCIAL CAMPGROUND

Honeymoon Bay

Gordon River

HONEYMOON BAY NATURE PARK

LAKEVIEW PARK CAMPGROUND

18 MUS

1   **1**

PACIFIC

RIM

NATIONAL

PARK

CANADA

USA

STRAIT OF JUAN DE FUCA

PORT SAN JUAN

MUSEUM

Port Renfrew

SAN JUAN POINT

LOSS CREEK PROVINCIAL PARK

BRITISH COLUMBIA

WASHINGTON

14

River Jordan

2   **2**

DUNTZE ROCK

TATOOSH ISLAND

CAPE FLATTERY LIGHTHOUSE

ARCHAWAT PEAK

WAADAH ISLAND

Neah Bay

NEAH BAY RD

CLALLAM CO

162

MAKAH

WAATCH PEAK

INDIAN

RESERVATION

SHIPWRECK POINT

CLALLAM

COUNTY

163

PACIFIC

OCEAN

FLATTERY

ROCKS

NATIONAL

WASHBURN HILL

WILDLIFE

OLYMPIC

NATIONAL

REFUGE

WILDLIFE

PARK

OZETTE LAKE

PREACHERS POINT

SNAG PEAK

SEKIU MOUNTAIN

OZETTE RD

HOKO RD

WASHINGTON

NELSON HILL

Hoko

Sekiu

Clallam Bay

RIVER

BLUE CANYON

STOLZENBERGS MOUNTAIN

112

112

113

BURNT MOUNTAIN

BURNT MOUNTAIN RD

OLYMPIC

DICKEY HOKO SUMMIT

Sappho

NATIONAL

101

SOL DUC RIVER

BIGLER MOUNTAIN

SCHUTZ PASS

FOREST

QUILLAYUTE NATIONAL WILDLIFE REFUGE

KAYOSTLA BEACH

DICKEY RIVER WEST FORK

DICKEY RIVER

DICKEY RIVER EAST FORK

GUNDERSON MOUNTAIN

Beaver

SOL DUC

CALAWAH RIDGE

3   **3**

A   **B**   **B**   **C**

0   2.5   5   7.5   10   miles   1 in. = 7.5 mi.

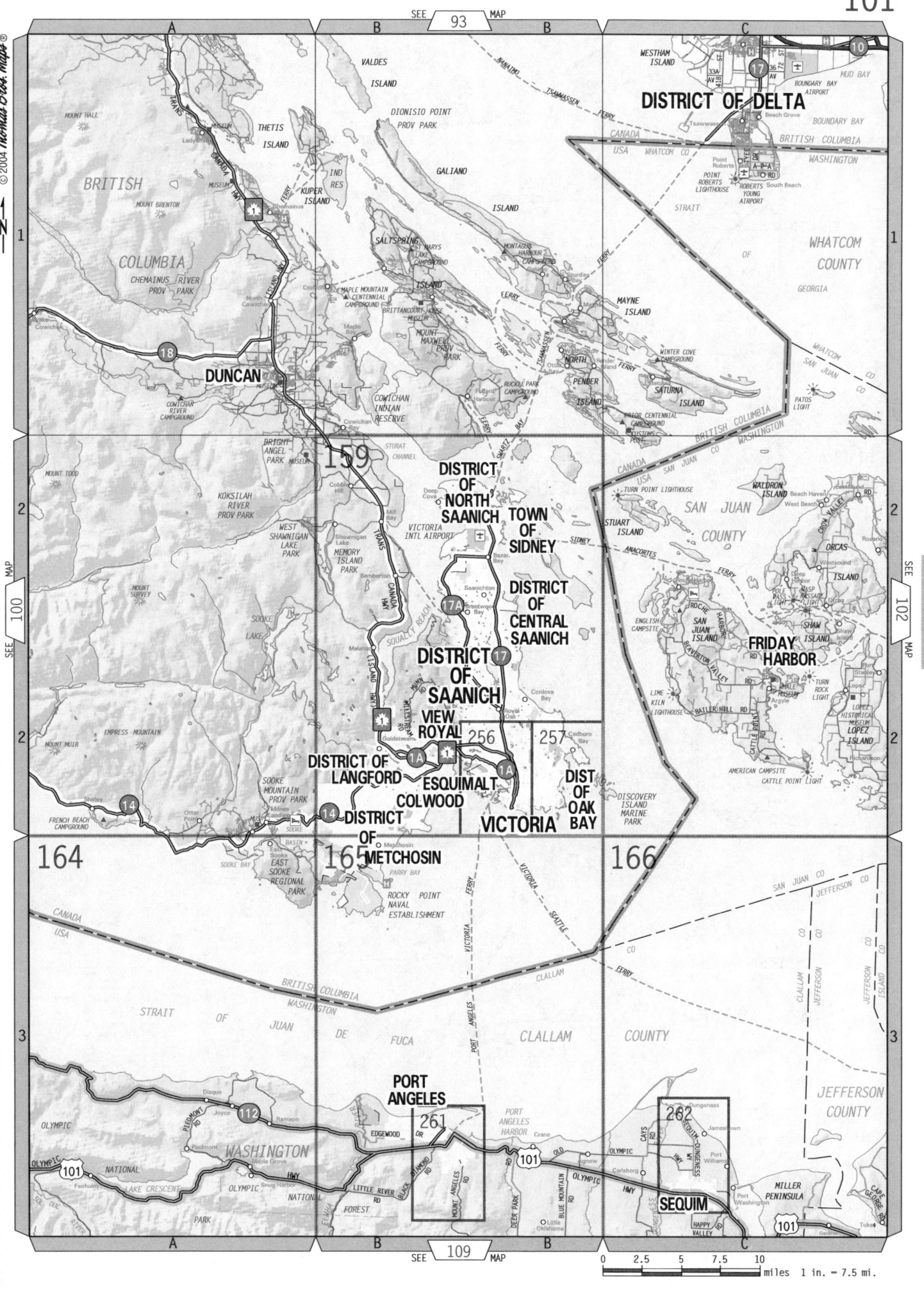

SEE 93 MAP

DISTRICT OF DELTA

WESTHAM ISLAND

BOUNDARY BAY AIRPORT

BOUNDARY BAY

CANADA USA WHATCOM CO

BRITISH COLUMBIA WASHINGTON

Point Roberts

POINT ROBERTS LIGHTHOUSE

ROBERTS YOUNG AIRPORT

South Beach

WHATCOM COUNTY

GEORGIA

BRITISH COLUMBIA

MOUNT HALL

THETIS ISLAND

Ladysmith

BRITISH

COLUMBIA

CHEMAINUS RIVER PROV PARK

MOUNT BRENTON

KUPER ISLAND

IND RES

VALDES ISLAND

DIONISIO POINT PROV PARK

GALIANO ISLAND

SALTSPRING ISLAND

MAPLE MOUNTAIN CENTENNIAL CAMPGROUND

BRITTANCOURT HOUSE MUSEUM

MOUNT MAXWELL PROV PARK

MONTAGUE HARBOUR CAMPGROUND

MAYNE ISLAND

WINTER COVE CAMPGROUND

NORTH PENDER

SATURNA ISLAND

PATOS LIGHT

SAN JUAN CO

WHATCOM CO

18 DUNCAN

COWICHAN RIVER CAMPGROUND

COWICHAN INDIAN RESERVE

RUCKLE PARK CAMPGROUND

Fulford Harbour

SOUTH PENDER ISLAND

PRIOR CENTENNIAL CAMPGROUND CUSTOMS POST

BRITISH COLUMBIA WASHINGTON

159

MOUNT TODD

KOKSILAH RIVER PROV PARK

WEST SHAWNIGAN LAKE PARK

MOUNT SURVEY

MEMORY ISLAND PARK

Shawnigan Lake

Cobble Hill

Mill Bay

Deep Cove

VICTORIA INTL AIRPORT

DISTRICT OF NORTH SAANICH

TOWN OF SIDNEY

DISTRICT OF CENTRAL SAANICH

Saanichton

17A

DISTRICT OF SAANICH

17

VIEW ROYAL

STUART ISLAND

TURN POINT LIGHTHOUSE

WALDRON ISLAND

Beach Haven

West Beach

SAN JUAN COUNTY

ORCAS ISLAND

Westsound

Rosario

SEE 102 MAP

HWY

SOOKE LAKE

MOUNT SURVEY

EMPRESS MOUNTAIN

MOUNT MUIR

SOOKE MOUNTAIN PROV PARK

14 Shirley

Otter Point

14 DISTRICT OF METCHOSIN

SOOKE

DISTRICT OF LANGFORD

ESQUIMALT COLWOOD

256

Goldstream

1A 1

1A

257

Cadboro Bay

Royal Oak

Cordova Bay

DIST OF OAK BAY

DISCOVERY ISLAND MARINE PARK

ROCHE HARBOR

SAN JUAN ISLAND

FRIDAY HARBOR

SHAW ISLAND

BEAVERTON VALLEY

ENGLISH CAMPSITE

LIME KILN LIGHTHOUSE

BAILER HILL RD

CATTLE POINT

AMERICAN CAMPSITE

CATTLE POINT LIGHT

LOPEZ HISTORICAL MUSEUM

LOPEZ ISLAND

Richardson

FRENCH BEACH CAMPGROUND

164

EAST SOOKE REGIONAL PARK

165

Metchosin

Parry Bay

ROCKY POINT NAVAL ESTABLISHMENT

166

SAN JUAN CO

JEFFERSON CO

VICTORIA

VICTORIA

SEATTLE

CLALLAM CO

FERRY

JEFFERSON COUNTY

CANADA USA

BRITISH COLUMBIA WASHINGTON

STRAIT OF JUAN DE FUCA

PORT ANGELES HARBOR

CLALLAM COUNTY

3

OLYMPIC

PIEDMONT RD

Joyce

112

Ramapo

WASHINGTON

PORT ANGELES

261

EDGEWOOD DR

PORT ANGELES HARBOR

Crane

101

Dungeness

Jamestown

262

SEQUIM-DUNGENESS HWY

Port Williams

101 LAKE CRESCENT

Fairholm

OLYMPIC NATIONAL PARK

SOL DUC RIVER

Maple Grove

OLYMPIC NATIONAL FOREST

LITTLE RIVER RD

Snug Harbor

BLACK DIAMOND RD

MOUNT ANGELES RD

Little Oklahoma

DEER PARK RD

OLD OLYMPIC HWY

BLUE MOUNTAIN RD

101

Agnew

Carlsborg

OLYMPIC HWY

Port Washington

MILLER PENINSULA

SEQUIM

HAPPY VALLEY

101

CAPE GEORGE RD

SEE 109 MAP

0   2.5   5   7.5   10

miles   1 in. = 7.5 mi.

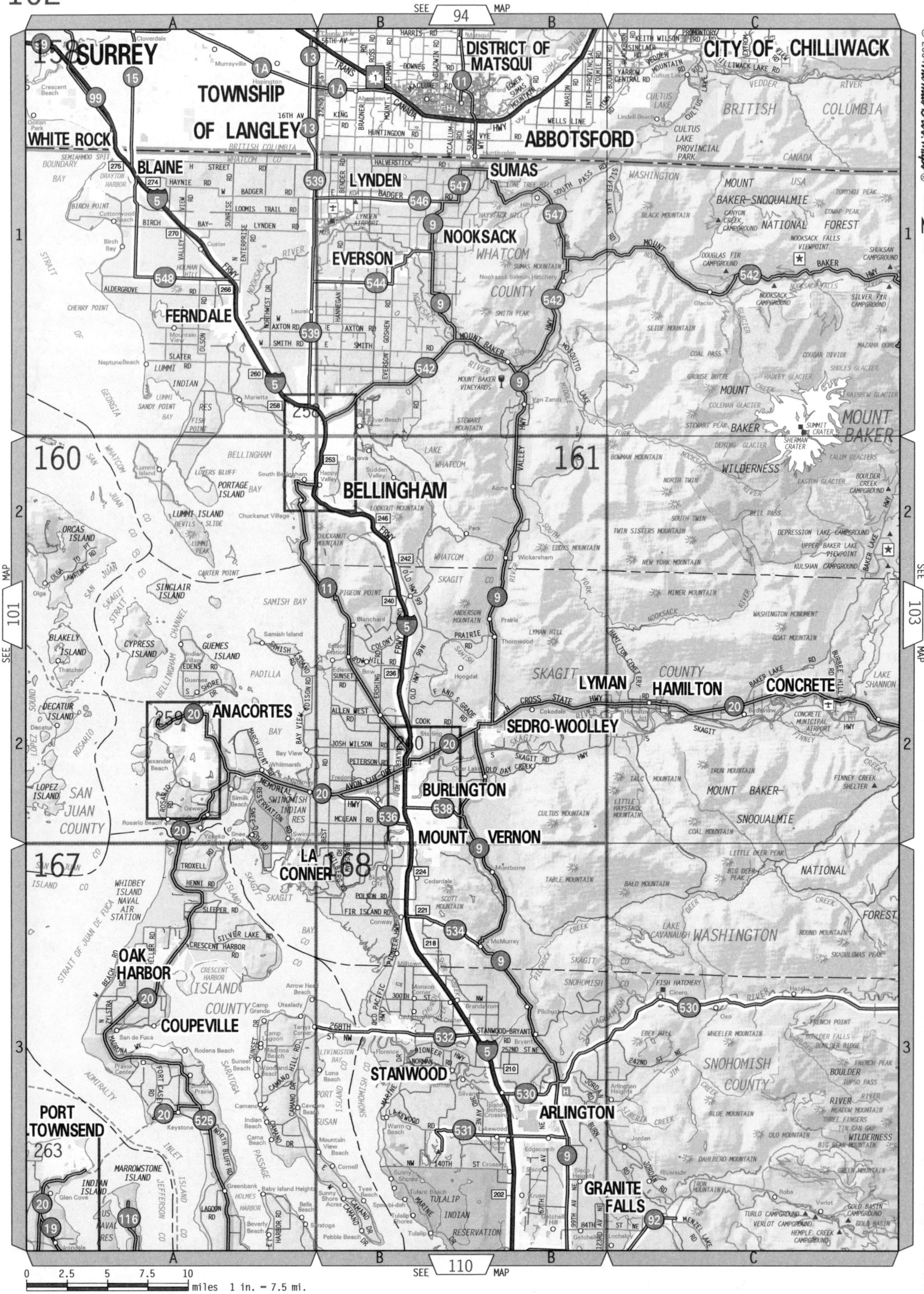

SEE 94 MAP

SURREY
TOWNSHIP OF LANGLEY
WHITE ROCK
BLAINE
FERNDALE

DISTRICT OF MATSQUI
ABBOTSFORD
LYNDEN
SUMAS
EVERSON
NOOKSACK

CITY OF CHILLIWACK
BRITISH COLUMBIA
WASHINGTON USA
MOUNT BAKER-SNOQUALMIE NATIONAL FOREST
MOUNT BAKER
WILDERNESS

WHATCOM COUNTY
BELLINGHAM

SKAGIT COUNTY
ANACORTES
SEDRO-WOOLLEY
BURLINGTON
MOUNT VERNON
LA CONNER
LYMAN
HAMILTON
CONCRETE

OAK HARBOR
COUPEVILLE
PORT TOWNSEND
STANWOOD
ARLINGTON
GRANITE FALLS
SNOHOMISH COUNTY

160   161
HWY SEE 101 MAP
SEE 103 MAP
167   168

SEE 110 MAP

0 2.5 5 7.5 10
miles 1 in. = 7.5 mi.

© 2004 Thomas Bros. Maps

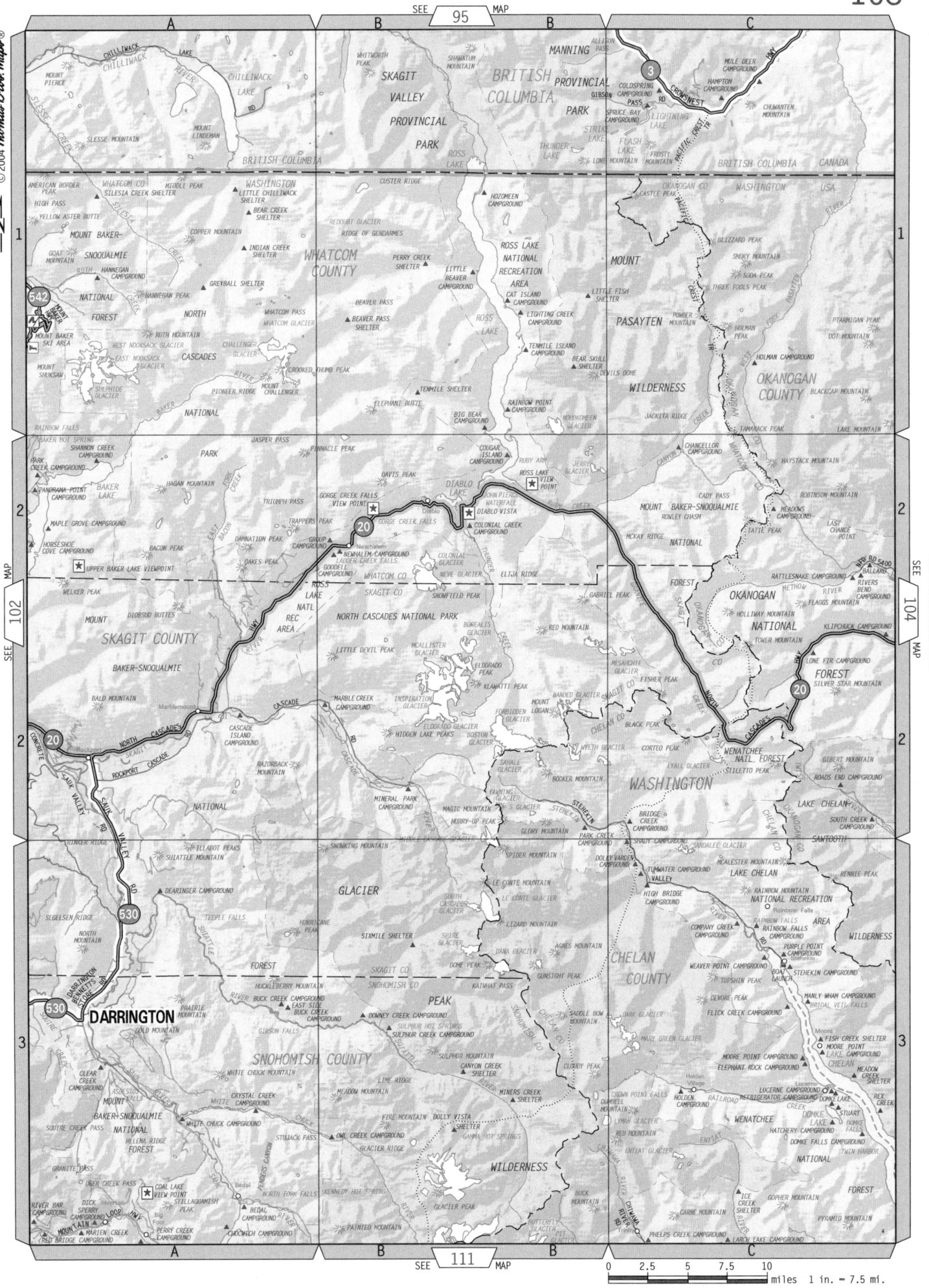

SEE 102 MAP

SEE 104 MAP

HWY

0   2.5   5   7.5   10
miles   1 in. = 7.5 mi.

104

A   B   C

© 2004 Thomas Bros. Maps ®

CATHEDRAL PROVINCIAL PARK

QUINISCOE LAKE
GLACIER LAKE
PYRAMID LAKE
LADYSLIPPER LAKE
LAKEVIEW MOUNTAIN

BRITISH COLUMBIA

SNOWY MOUNTAIN

3

3A
97
OSOYOOS LAKE
OSOYOOS
OKANOGAN INDIAN CAMPING GROUND
DEADMAN LAKE PROVINCIAL PARK
ANARCHIST MOUNTAIN
BLUE LAKE
MOUNT KRUGER
OSOYOOS MUSEUM
3

BRITISH COLUMBIA — CANADA
USA

1

BUNKER HILL
SHEEP MOUNTAIN
OKANOGAN CO. CATHEDRAL PEAK
AMPHITHEATER MOUNTAIN
BALD MOUNTAIN
VAN PEAK
FREDS MOUNTAIN
MIDDLE MOUNTAIN
PASAYTEN
WOLFRAMITE MOUNTAIN
WASHINGTON
APEX MOUNTAIN
SADDLE PEAK
TEAPOT DOME
TOPAZ MOUNTAIN
HAIG MOUNTAIN
ROCK MOUNTAIN
PICK PEAK
WINDY PEAK
HORSESHOE MOUNTAIN
SNOMSHOE MOUNTAIN
JOE MILLS MOUNTAIN
CHOPAKA MOUNTAIN
NIGHTHAWK CUSTOMS
LOOMIS-OROVILLE SIMILKAMEEN
Nighthawk
ELLEMEHAM MOUNTAIN
PALMER MOUNTAIN
CHOPAKA LAKE CAMPGROUND
MOLSON SCHOOL MUSEUM
OSOYOOS LAKE
COPPER MOUNTAIN
OROVILLE
97
OKANOGAN NATIONAL FOREST

DOLLAR WATCH MOUNTAIN
TWO POINT MOUNTAIN
PEEPSIGHT MOUNTAIN
CAL PEAK
WILDERNESS
IRON GATE CAMPGROUND
HICKEY HUMP
CHEWACK FALLS
DAISY CAMPGROUND
LONG SWAMP CAMPGROUND
NORTH FORK NINEMILE CAMPGROUND
SOUTH FORK JUNCTION CAMPGROUND
GRANDVIEW MOUNTAIN
PALMER LAKE
PALMER MOUNTAIN
WANNACUT LAKE
SPECTACLE LAKE CAMPGROUND
Loomis

NANNY GOAT MOUNTAIN
COLEMAN PEAK
KAY PEAK
THIRTYMILE PEAK
THIRTYMILE CAMPGROUND
TILLMAN MOUNTAIN
RATTLESNAKE MOUNTAIN
GOLD HILL
LOOMIS-OROVILLE
Ellisford

PASS BUTTE
BILLY GOAT MOUNTAIN
BURCH MOUNTAIN
OBSTRUCTION PEAK
ANDREWS CREEK CAMPGROUND
THUNDER MOUNTAIN
DOUGLAS MOUNTAIN

2

PISTOL PEAKS
EIGHTMILE PEAK
BIG CRAGGY PEAK
SHERMAN PEAK
BURGETT PEAK
FAREWELL PEAK
NORTH TWENTYMILE PEAK
OKANOGAN COUNTY
AENEAS MOUNTAIN
TWIN PEAKS
CAYUSE MOUNTAIN
TONASKET
20
97

MCLEOD MOUNTAIN
HONEYMOON CAMPGROUND
RUFFED GROUSE CAMPGROUND
OKANOGAN
TIFFANY SPRING CAMPGROUND
ROCK MOUNTAIN
COUGAR MOUNTAIN
BLUE GOAT MOUNTAIN
CARTER MOUNTAIN
PINE CREEK

BALLARD CAMPGROUND
SWEETGRASS BUTTE
CHEWUCH CAMPGROUND
FALLS CREEK FALLS
TIFFANY MOUNTAIN
SALMON MEADOWS CAMPGROUND
MIDDLE MOUNTAIN
FISH LAKE RD
97

GATE CREEK CAMPGROUND
ISLAND MOUNTAIN
NICE CAMPGROUND
CLARK PEAK
FALLS CREEK CAMPGROUND
ALDER CAMPGROUND
KERR CAMPGROUND
ORIOLE CAMPGROUND
SUGARLOAF CAMPGROUNDS
COTTONWOOD CAMPGROUND
20
MCLOUGHLIN FALLS
MAZAMA
EARLY WINTERS CAMPGROUND
FLAT CAMPGROUND
BUCK LAKE CAMPGROUND
RENDEVOUS MOUNTAIN
OLD BALDY
MEMORIAL CAMPGROUND
MINERAL HILL
SALMON FALLS
CONCONULLY
ALBRIGHT CAVE

NORTH GARDNER MOUNTAIN
GARDNER MOUNTAIN
GRIZZLY MOUNTAIN
LEWIS BUTTE
TRIPOD PEAK
BOULDER CREEK
CONGER CREEK RD
WEST FORK
PEACOCK MOUNTAIN
GRANITE MOUNTAIN
SCHALOW MOUNTAIN
RIVERSIDE CUTOFF
20
EAST RIVERSIDE
GREENACRES RD

MILTON MOUNTAIN
LAKE CHELAN-
OKANOGAN
20
SHAFER MUSEUM
WINTHROP NATL FISH HATCHERY
PATTERSON MOUNTAIN
WINTHROP
BLUE BUCK MOUNTAIN
FOREST
BOBCAT MOUNTAIN
ROCK LAKES CAMPGROUND
RUBY HILL
WRIGHT MOUNTAIN
WENATCHEE VALLEY COLLEGE
OMAK
215

POPLAR FLAT CAMPGROUND
METHOW VALLEY STATE AIRPORT
KOA CAMPGROUND
BEAVER CAMPGROUND
BEAR MOUNTAIN
LOUP LOUP CAMPGROUND
BUCK MOUNTAIN
ROCK CREEK CAMPGROUND
LEADER LAKE CAMPGROUND
SAINT MARYS MISSION
155

MYSTERY CAMPGROUND
WAR CREEK CAMPGROUND
TWISP RIVER
TWISP RIVER RD
TWISP
LOUP LOUP SKI AREA
20
SAINT MARYS FARM
20
OKANOGAN

SAWTOOTH
DUCKBILL MOUNTAIN
BLOCK MOUNTAIN
BLACKPINE LAKE CAMPGROUND
MCCLURE MOUNTAIN
TWISP MUNICIPAL AIRPORT
POLE PICK MOUNTAIN
FINLEY MOUNTAIN
COOK MOUNTAIN
COLVILLE

BATTLE MOUNTAIN
OVAL PEAK
GRAY PEAK
SPIRIT MOUNTAIN
NATIONAL
WILDERNESS
OKANOGAN
LIBBY CREEK RD
Chiliton
97
SALT HILL

3

BALDY MOUNTAIN
HOODOO PEAK
FINNEY PEAK
SKIDOKUM MOUNTAIN
OLD MAID MOUNTAIN
MARTIN PEAK
CRATER CREEK CAMPGROUND
FOGGY DEW CAMPGROUND
153
INDIAN

PRINCE CREEK CAMPGROUND
CHELAN COUNTY
WENATCHEE NATIONAL FERRY PEAK
NORTH NAVARRE PEAK
END MOUNTAIN
FOGGY DEW FALLS
HUNGRY MOUNTAIN
Methow
BUCKHORN MOUNTAIN
CRAZY RAPIDS
RESERVATION

UNO PEAK
SOUTH NAVARRE CAMPGROUND
GRAHAM HARBOR CAMPGROUND
SAFETY HARBOR CREEK CAMPGROUND
LAKE CHELAN
SKI PEAK
POISON CREEK CAMPGROUND
FOREST
TENAS MOUNTAIN
BREWSTER
97
LAKE PATEROS
CRANES NW RD
97
173
17
EAGLE RAPIDS
BOX CANYON
LONG RAPIDS
DOUGLAS CO

0 2.5 5 7.5 10 miles 1 in. = 7.5 mi.

SEE 112 MAP

SEE 103 MAP   SEE 105 MAP   HWY

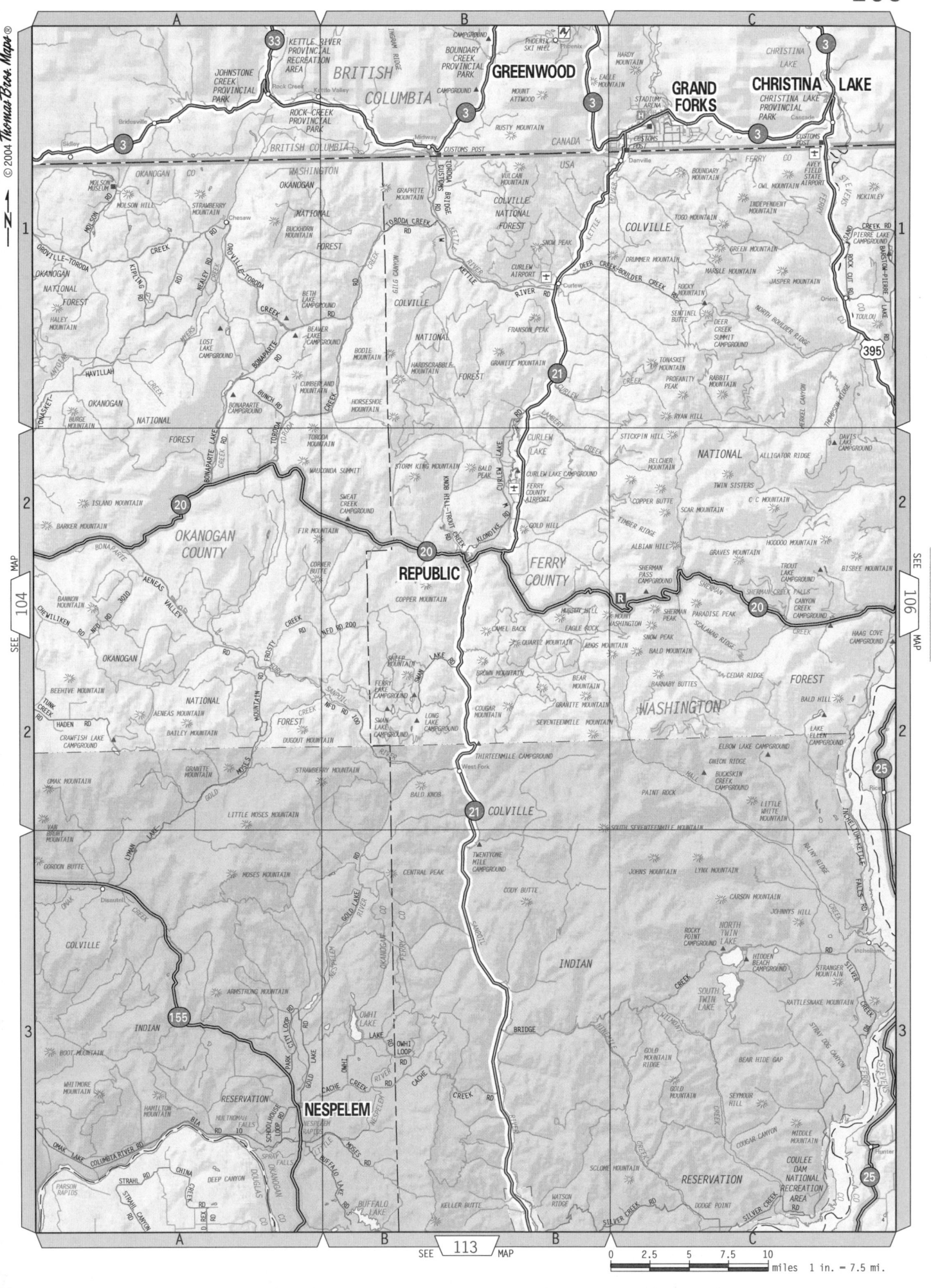

© 2004 Thomas Bros. Maps ®

—N→

A | **B** | **C**

ROSSLAND · MONTROSE · BRITISH COLUMBIA

RED MOUNTAIN SKI AREA · NANCY GREENE RECREATIONAL AREA · BEAVER CREEK PROV PARK · Casino · Columbia Gardens · LOST MOUNTAIN · RIPPLE MOUNTAIN · STAGLEAP PROVINCIAL PARK

MOUNT JELDNESS · BALDY MOUNTAIN · GROUSE RIDGE · LAKE MOUNTAIN · VIOLIN LAKE · PEND OREILLE RIVER · Remac

BRITISH COLUMBIA · Waneta · WASHINGTON MITCHELL MOUNTAIN · Boundary · CANADA · USA · Nelway · BOUNDARY CO · WASHINGTON · IDAHO

1

STEVENS CO · HOPE MOUNTAIN · LEAD PENCIL MOUNTAIN · COLVILLE NATIONAL FOREST · CHURCHILL MOUNTAIN · LAEL FLAT · BELSHAZZAR MOUNTAIN · SHEEP CREEK FALLS · SHEEP CREEK RD · NORTHPORT · FRISCO MOUNTAIN · PEWEE FALLS · CRESCENT LAKE CAMPGROUND · SLUMBER PEAK · SALMO-PRIEST WILDERNESS · GYPSY PEAK · GREEN MOUNTAIN · BOUNDARY CO

BILLY GOAT MOUNTAIN · COUGAR MOUNTAIN · NORTHPORT-FLAT · ABERCROMBIE MOUNTAIN · ELECTRIC POINT · COLVILLE · METALINE FALLS · BLUE BIRD RIDGE · CROWELL MOUNTAIN · THUNDER MOUNTAIN · HUGHES RIDGE VIEW POINT ★

JUMBO MOUNTAIN · LITTLE DALLES · BLACK HAWK MOUNTAIN · Dolomite · STONE MOUNTAIN · BLACK CANYON · METALINE · Pend Oreille Village · HELMER MOUNTAIN · GOLD PEAK · KANIKSU

COULEE DAM NATIONAL RECREATION AREA · FREDERICKSON HILL · BALDY MOUNTAIN · MILL POND CAMPGROUND · SULLIVAN CREEK · SULLIVAN LAKE CAMPGROUND · SULLIVAN LAKE · LASOTA FALLS · GRANITE FALLS · STAGGER INN CAMPGROUND

NORTH GORGE CAMPGROUND · LOOKOUT MOUNTAIN · DEER MOUNTAIN · BOX CANYON DAM VIEW POINT ★ · IONE · EDGEWATER CAMPGROUND · NOISY CREEK CAMPGROUND · COLVILLE NATIONAL · HIGH ROCK MOUNTAIN · DUSTY PEAK

PEND OREILLE COUNTY · TILLICUM PEAK · IDAHO

2

395 · SNAG COVE CAMPGROUND · KETTLE RIVER CAMPGROUND · EVANS HILL CUTOFF · EVANS CAMPGROUND · ONION MOUNTAIN · COLVILLE NATIONAL FOREST · RABBIT MOUNTAIN · ALADDIN MOUNTAIN · SELOOM SEEN MOUNTAIN · IONE MUNI AIRPORT · MOLYBDENITE MOUNTAIN

STEVENS COUNTY · SPION KOP · BOSSBURG · BONANZA HILL · Marcus · FRANKLIN D ROOSEVELT LAKE · ECHO MOUNTAIN · CLUGSTON · DOUGLAS FALLS · MIDDLE FORK MILL CREEK RD · GREEN MOUNTAIN · LAKE THOMAS CAMPGROUND · JOLIFF RD · LAKE LEO CAMPGROUND · GRANITE PEAK · COYOTE HILL · KANIKSU FOREST · PETIT LAKE CAMPGROUND · DIAMOND PEAK · KALISPELL FALLS · NATIONAL

SAINT PAUL'S MISSION · DOUGLASS FALLS · SOUTH FORK MILL CREEK · OLD DOMINION MOUNTAIN · KANIKSU · HANLON MOUNTAIN · HUNGRY MOUNTAIN · FOURTH OF JULY PEAK · GLEASON MOUNTAIN

KETTLE FALLS · OLD KETTLE · LIONS ISLAND · BONANZA LEAD MILL · COLVILLE MOUNTAIN · COLVILLE · FLODELLE CAMPGROUND · COLVILLE MUNI AIRPORT · NORTH BALDY

25 · 20 · COLVILLE-TIGER · LITTLE PEND OREILLE · CRYSTAL FALLS · SCRABBLER MOUNTAIN · PANHANDLE CAMPGROUND · NATIONAL

MINGO MOUNTAIN · 395 · MILL BUTTE · NATIONAL WILDLIFE REFUGE · RUBY MOUNTAIN · RIVER BEND AIRPORT · PELKE RIVER · FOREST · TOLA POINT

BRADBURY CAMPGROUND · CARTER CANYON · NORTH BASIN · BEAR CANYON · BOULDER MOUNTAIN · SULLIVAN POINT · BROWNS LAKE CAMPGROUND · NORTH SKOOKUM CAMPGROUND

DAY MOUNTAIN · RICE-ORIN · FREEMAN HILL · ADDY MOUNTAIN · ROCKY BUTTE · TACOMA PEAK · NATIONAL · SOUTH SKOOKUM LAKE CAMPGROUND

WASHINGTON · BREWER MOUNTAIN · LITTLE CALISPELL PEAK · FOURTH OF JULY MOUNTAIN · KINGS MOUNTAIN

MARBLE SOUTH · VALLEY BASIN · TOWNSEND-SACKMAN RD · COLVILLE · WILSON MOUNTAIN · WINCHESTER PEAK · CUSICK · KALISPEL INDIAN RESERVATION · COOKS MOUNTAIN · FOREST

3

McKERN-SCOTT RD · GOLD HILL · DEADMAN HILL · DUNN MOUNTAIN · DEER ADDY MOUNTAIN · GOLD HILL · EAGLE MOUNTAIN · FORTY NINE DEGREES NORTH SKI AREA · BARTLETTE RD · CALISPELL LAKE · NO NAME PEAK · SKOOKUM MOUNTAIN

25 · ADDY-GIFFORD RD · SUMMIT VALLEY · BLUE CREEK WEST RD · Bluecreek · CHEWELAH · FLOWERY TRAIL · QUARTZITE MOUNTAIN · NATIONAL · NORTH · NEWPORT GEOPHYSICAL OBSERVATORY · NO NAME LAKE CAMPGROUND

QUARTZ MOUNTAIN · CLOVERLEAF BEACH CAMPGROUND · COULEE DAM NATIONAL RECREATION AREA · McKALE CANYON · HEINE · 395 · H · PARKER MOUNTAIN · COTTONWOOD CREEK RD · FOREST · POWER PEAK · BUNNETT CREEK · DELKENA · Usk · DAVIS LAKE · CUBAN HILL · STONE JOHNNY

HUCKLEBERRY MOUNTAIN · NEWTON · HAFER RD · ROUNDTOP MOUNTAIN · NELSON PEAK · BOYER MOUNTAIN · SADDLE MOUNTAIN · 20 · COOKS MOUNTAIN

CEDONIA-ADDY · LESSIG SOUTH FORK RD · WAITTS LAKE · MARBLE · LANE MOUNTAIN · BALD MOUNTAIN · GRANITE MOUNTAIN · BENSON PEAK · LITTLE BLUE GROUSE MOUNTAIN · LITTLE ROUNDTOP · SACHEEN LAKE · NEWPORT · H · 2 · SAND BUTTE VALLEY · Oldtown · SCOTIA VALLEY · 41

STENSGAR MOUNTAIN · LITTLE COYOTE MOUNTAIN · BOUDES HILL · LONG PRAIRIE RD · DEER CREEK RD · GLASSER CREEK RD · GROUSE CREEK · DEER LAKE · BLUE GROUSE MOUNTAIN · LITTLE BLUE GROUSE VALLEY · DIAMOND LAKE · 211 · SCOTIA · LONE MOUNTAIN · SPRING VALLEY

SPRINGDALE-HUNTERS · EMPEY MOUNTAIN · 231 · JUMPOFF JOE MOUNTAIN · LINEKIN HILL · DEER LAKE LOOP · LOON LAKE MOUNTAIN · PEND OREILLE CO · BARE MOUNTAIN · SPOKANE CO

SPRINGDALE · 292 · ADAMS VALLEY · LOON LAKE · Pocahontas Bay · SPOKANE CO

A | **B** | SEE 114 MAP | **B** | **C**

HWY · SEE 105 MAP · SEE 107 MAP

0 2.5 5 7.5 10 miles 1 in. = 7.5 mi.

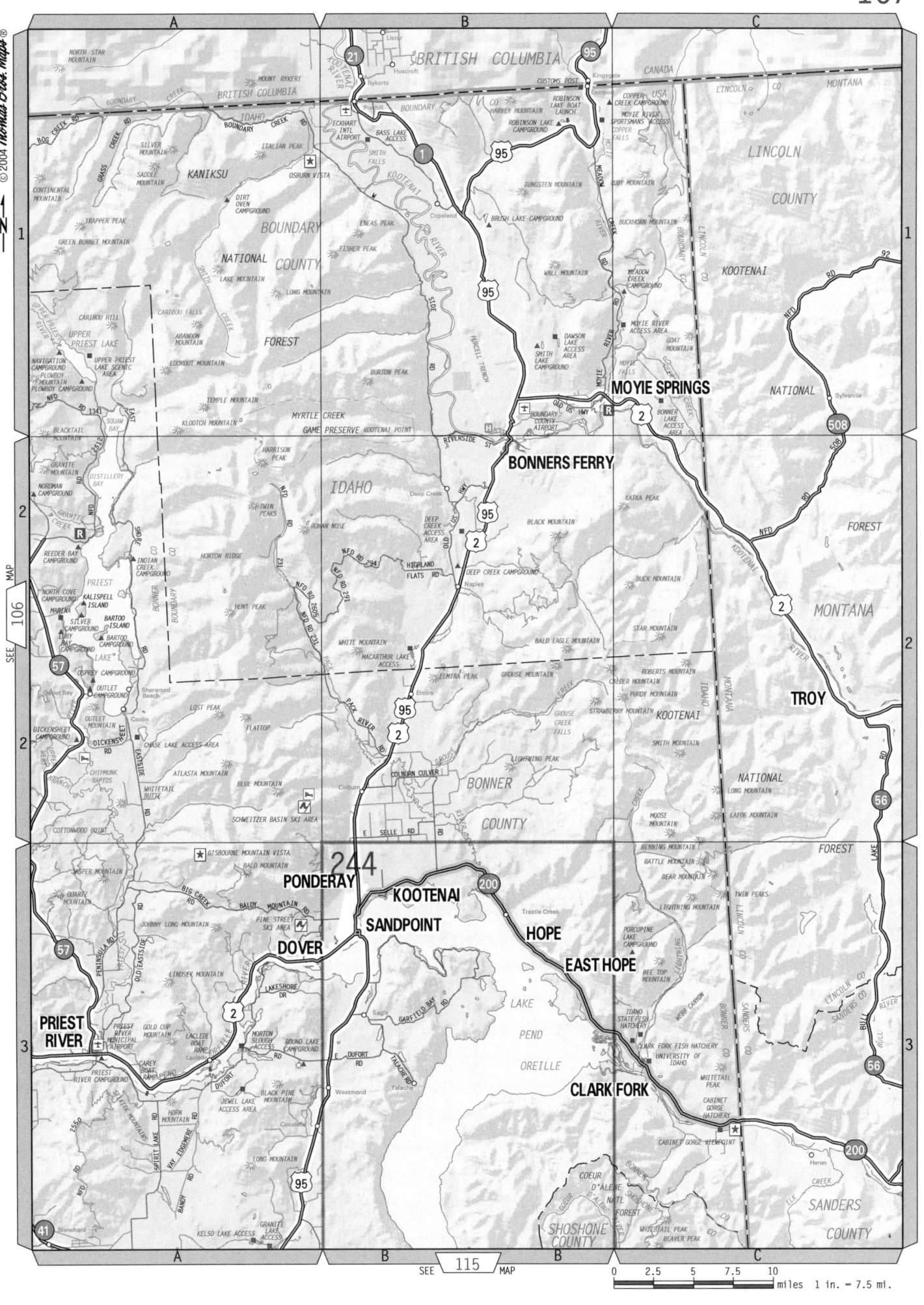

miles 1 in. = 7.5 mi.

SEE 100 MAP

169

QUILLAYUTE RD
RICKEY RIVER
SOL DUC RIVER
PUSH
MORA RD
La Push
LA
CLALLAM CO
JEFFERSON CO

110

FORKS

101

OLYMPIC NATIONAL FOREST
HUNGER MOUNTAIN
SITKUM SHELTER
ELK RIDGE
SITKUM RIVER
RUGGED RIDGE
CLALLAM COUNTY
CALAWAH SHELTER
OLYMPIC
BOGACHIEL SHELTER
NATIONAL PARK
FIFTEENMILE SHELTER
Bogachiel
FLAPJACK SHELTER
BOGACHIEL RIVER

OLYMPIC NATIONAL PARK

SPRUCE MOUNTAIN
GEODETIC HILL
UPPER HOH OX BOW
HOH
MINNIE PETERSON CAMPGROUND
HOH RIVER
WILLOUGHBY CREEK CAMPGROUND
RD
HUELSDONK CAMPGROUND
SOUTH FORK HOH
HUELSDONK RIDGE
CITY
OIL
JEFFERSON COUNTY
OWL CREEK
WASHINGTON
HOH INDIAN RESERVATION

101

COPPER MINE BOTTOM CAMPGROUND
UPPER CLEARWATER CAMPGROUND
YAHOO LAKE CAMPGROUND
CLEARWATER RD

DESTRUCTION ISLAND
BROWNS POINT

PACIFIC

172

CLEARWATER
OLYMPIC NATIONAL FOREST
RIVER
OLYMPIC NATIONAL
Queets
QUEETS RIVER
OLYMPIC NATIONAL PARK
JEFFERSON CO
GRAYS HARBOR CO
FOREST

101

SEE 109 MAP

GRAYS HARBOR COUNTY
QUINAULT
THIMBLE MOUNTAIN
LONE MOUNTAIN
QUINAULT RIVER

WILLOUGHBY ROCK
SPLIT ROCK

INDIAN

OCEAN

Tsholah

RESERVATION

OLYMPIC NATIONAL FOREST

109

177

Moclips
Sunset Beach
Highland Heights
Pacific Beach
Aloha
OCEAN
YELLOW BLUFF
Humptulips
RD
RIVER
COPALIS ROCK
Iron Springs
COPALIS HEAD
COPALIS CROSSING RD

COPALIS BEACH
Copalis Beach
BEACH RD
Copalis Crossing
Newton
Tulips
Ocean City
COPALIS
Burrows

109

115

BURROWS RD
Chenois Creek
Illahee
Oyhut
Gray Gables
Grays Harbor City

OCEAN SHORES

BRECKENRIDGE BLUFF

298

A B SEE 100 MAP B C 1

2

3

A B SEE 116 MAP B C

0 2.5 5 7.5 10 miles 1 in. = 7.5 mi.

© 2004 Thomas Bros. Maps®

—N—

HWY

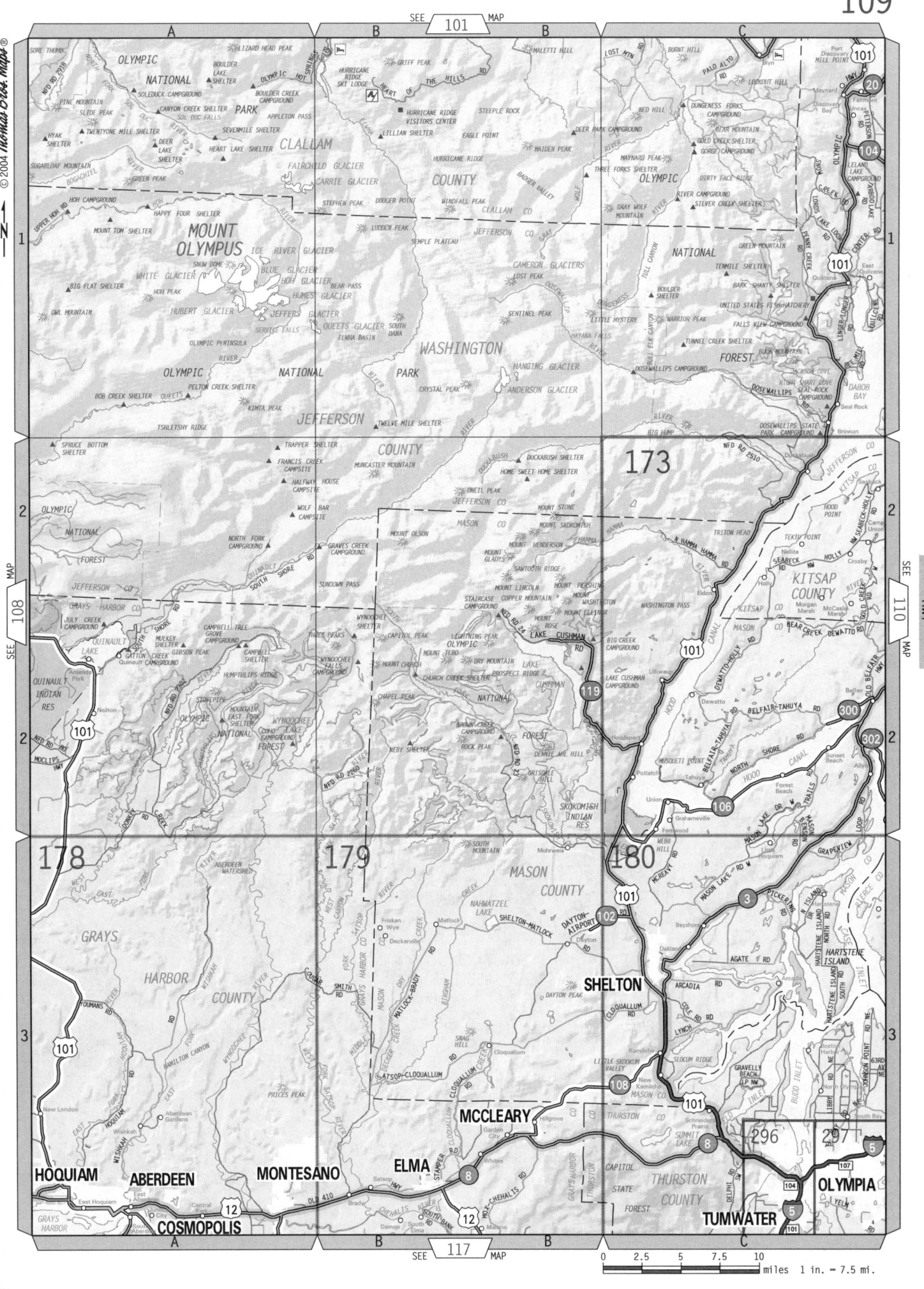

© 2004 Thomas Bros. Maps ®

A | B | B | C

170

21

19

104

JEFFERSON COUNTY

174

3

305

303

3

BREMERTON

166

PORT ORCHARD

3

16

KITSAP COUNTY

302

181

GIG HARBOR

16

TACOMA

292 293

FIRCREST

UNIVERSITY PLACE

294

LAKEWOOD

STEILACOOM

127

124

123

DUPONT

118 119 120

114

LACEY

510

ROY

507

JEFFERSON CO.

525

LANGLEY

17

525

MUKILTEO

264 194

266 267 268 269

192

189

5

EVERETT

529

204

9

LAKE STEVENS

92

2

SNOHOMISH

96

MILL CREEK

LYNNWOOD

99

EDMONDS

181

183

527

MONROE

522

524

203

GOLD BAR

SULTAN

2

SNOHOMISH COUNTY

MOUNT BAKER-SNOQUALMIE NATIONAL FOREST

KING CO.

104

WOODWAY

BRIER

26

MOUNTLAKE TERRACE

405

522

23

WOODINVILLE

DUVALL

SHORELINE

176

LAKE FOREST PARK

174

KENMORE

BOTHELL

20

202

REDMOND

KIRKLAND

272 273 274 275

171

5

HUNTS POINT

18

520

CARNATION

175 **176**

KING COUNTY

276 277 278 279

CLYDE HILL

520

14

MEDINA

BEAUX ARTS VILLAGE

164

12

BELLEVUE

SAMMAMISH

202

280 281 282 283

90

163

10

SEATTLE

162

9

15

ISSAQUAH

284 285 286

7

MERCER ISLAND

NEWCASTLE

17

SNOQUALMIE

NORTH BEND

99

157

509

405

RENTON

4

5

900

18

90

BURIEN

288

156

518

405

154

SEATAC

152

290

NORMANDY PARK

149

67

DES MOINES

147

KENT

169

COVINGTON

MAPLE VALLEY

516

WASHINGTON

MOUNT BAKER-SNOQUALMIE NATIONAL

AUBURN

5

BLACK DIAMOND

FEDERAL WAY

509

142

ALGONA

PACIFIC

169

MILTON

136

5

FIFE

EDGEWOOD

64

ENUMCLAW

7

129

SUMNER

BONNEY LAKE

410

BUCKLEY

410

512

PUYALLUP

162

ORTING

SOUTH PRAIRIE

WILKESON

PIERCE COUNTY

161

CARBONADO

7

165

PIERCE COUNTY

MOUNT BAKER-SNOQUALMIE NATIONAL FOREST

SEE 111 MAP

N

0 2.5 5 7.5 10 miles 1 in. = 7.5 mi.

© 2004 Thomas Bros. Maps®

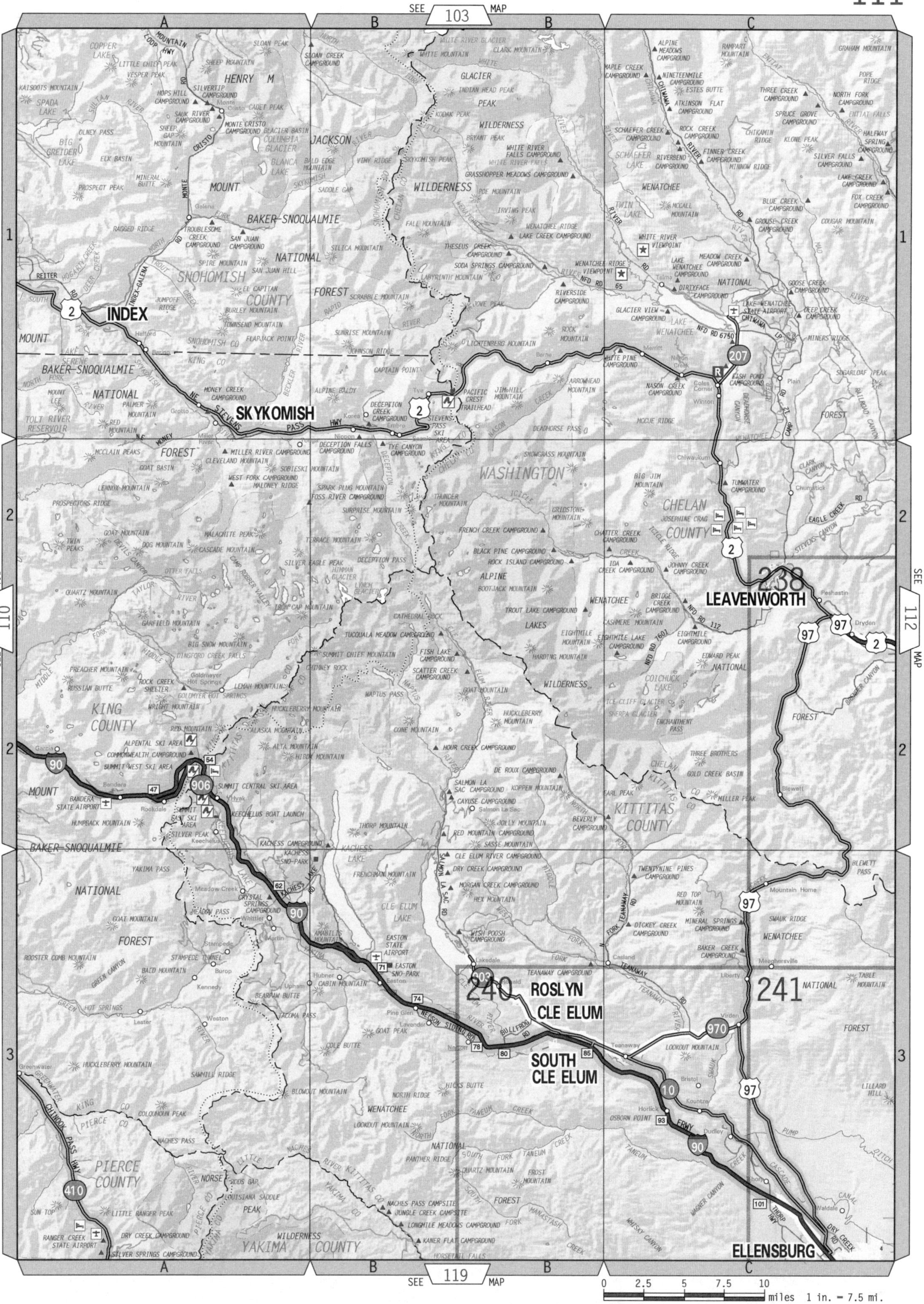

SEE 103 MAP

SEE 110 MAP

SEE 112 MAP

HWY

SEE 119 MAP

WASHINGTON

INDEX

SKYKOMISH

LEAVENWORTH

ROSLYN
CLE ELUM

SOUTH CLE ELUM

ELLENSBURG

HENRY M JACKSON WILDERNESS

GLACIER PEAK WILDERNESS

MOUNT BAKER-SNOQUALMIE NATIONAL FOREST

SNOHOMISH COUNTY

CHELAN COUNTY

WENATCHEE NATIONAL FOREST

ALPINE LAKES WILDERNESS

KING COUNTY

KITTITAS COUNTY

MOUNT BAKER-SNOQUALMIE NATIONAL FOREST

PIERCE COUNTY

YAKIMA COUNTY

238

240

241

207

906

90

2

97

970

410

101

STEVENS PASS

0 2.5 5 7.5 10 miles   1 in. = 7.5 mi.

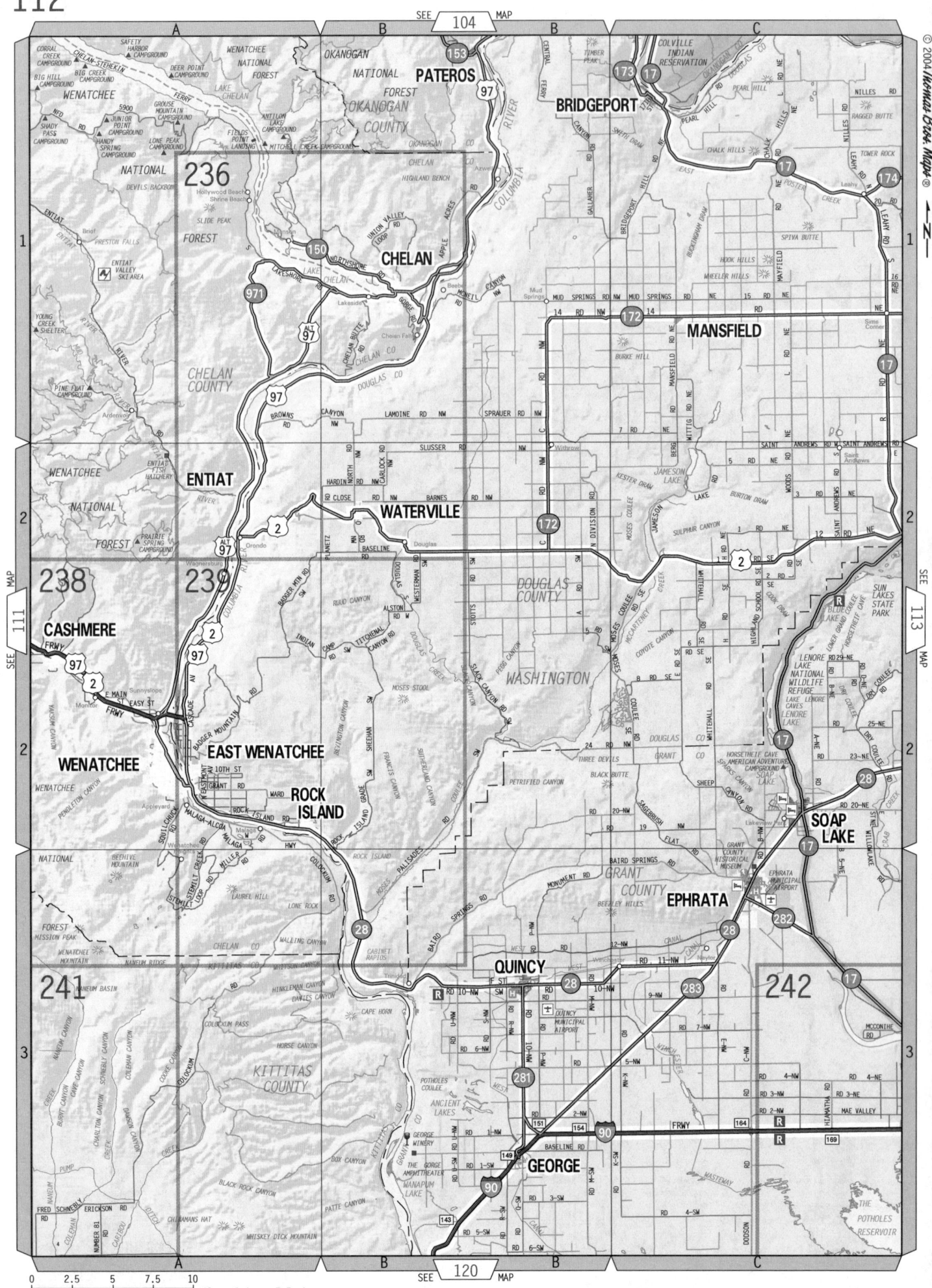

237

ELMER CITY

COULEE DAM

GRAND COULEE

ELECTRIC CITY

OKANOGAN COUNTY

COLVILLE

FERRY COUNTY

INDIAN

STEVENS CO.

SPOKANE INDIAN RESERVATION

DOUGLAS COUNTY

STEAMBOAT ROCK STATE PARK

BANKS LAKE

COULEE DAM NATIONAL RECREATION AREA

FRANKLIN D ROOSEVELT LAKE

COULEE DAM NATIONAL RECREATION AREA

1

WILBUR

CRESTON

ALMIRA

HARTLINE

LINCOLN COUNTY

2

COULEE CITY

SUN LAKES STATE PARK

GRANT COUNTY

WASHINGTON

HWY

HARRINGTON

SUMMER FALLS STATE PARK

WILSON CREEK

MARLIN

ODESSA

ODESSA MUNICIPAL AIRPORT

242

MOSES LAKE

ADAMS COUNTY

RITZVILLE

RITZVILLE MUNICIPAL AIRPORT

3

THE POTHOLES RESERVOIR

0 2.5 5 7.5 10
miles 1 in. = 7.5 mi.

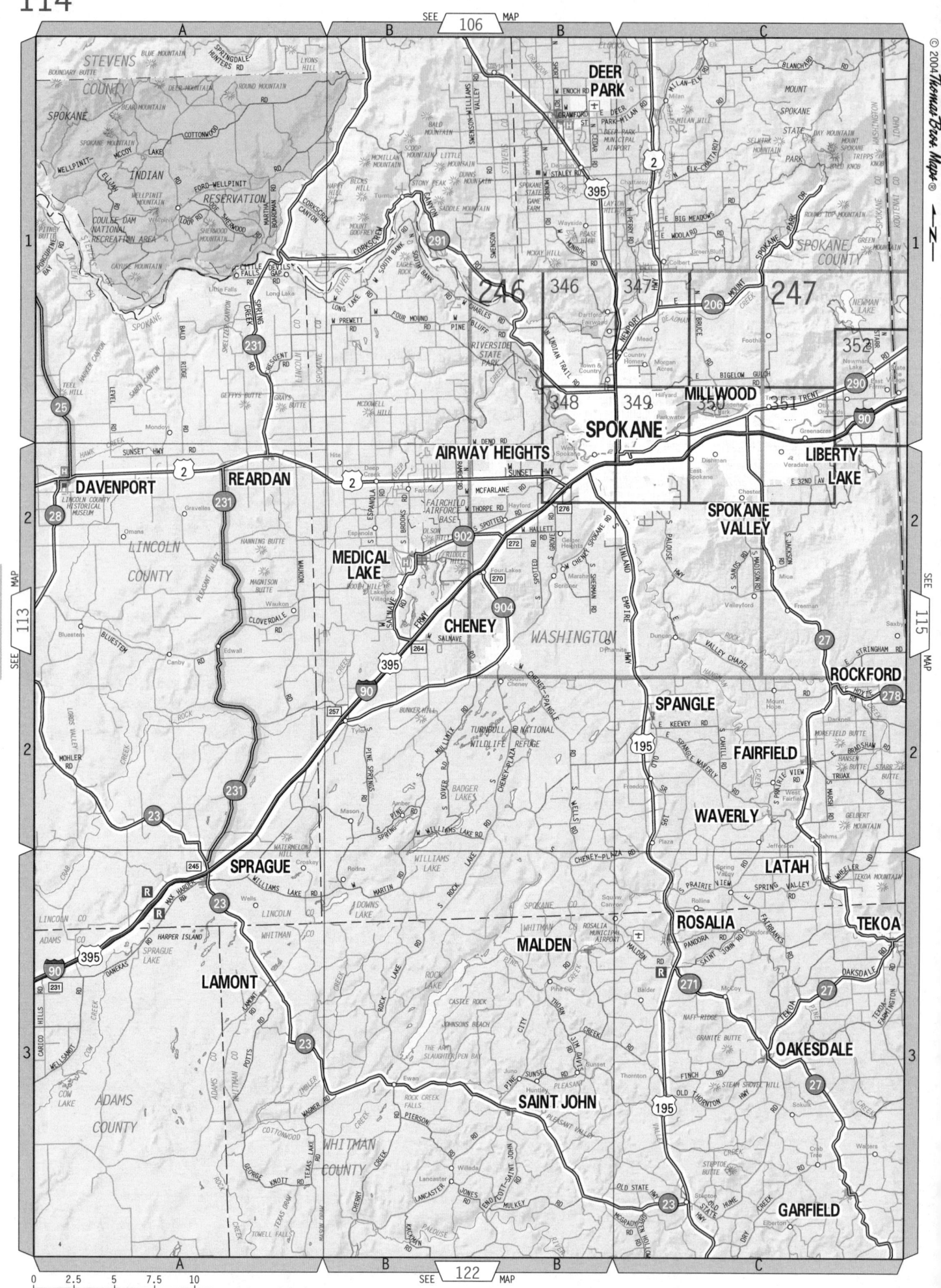

© 2004 Thomas Bros. Maps® ←Z→

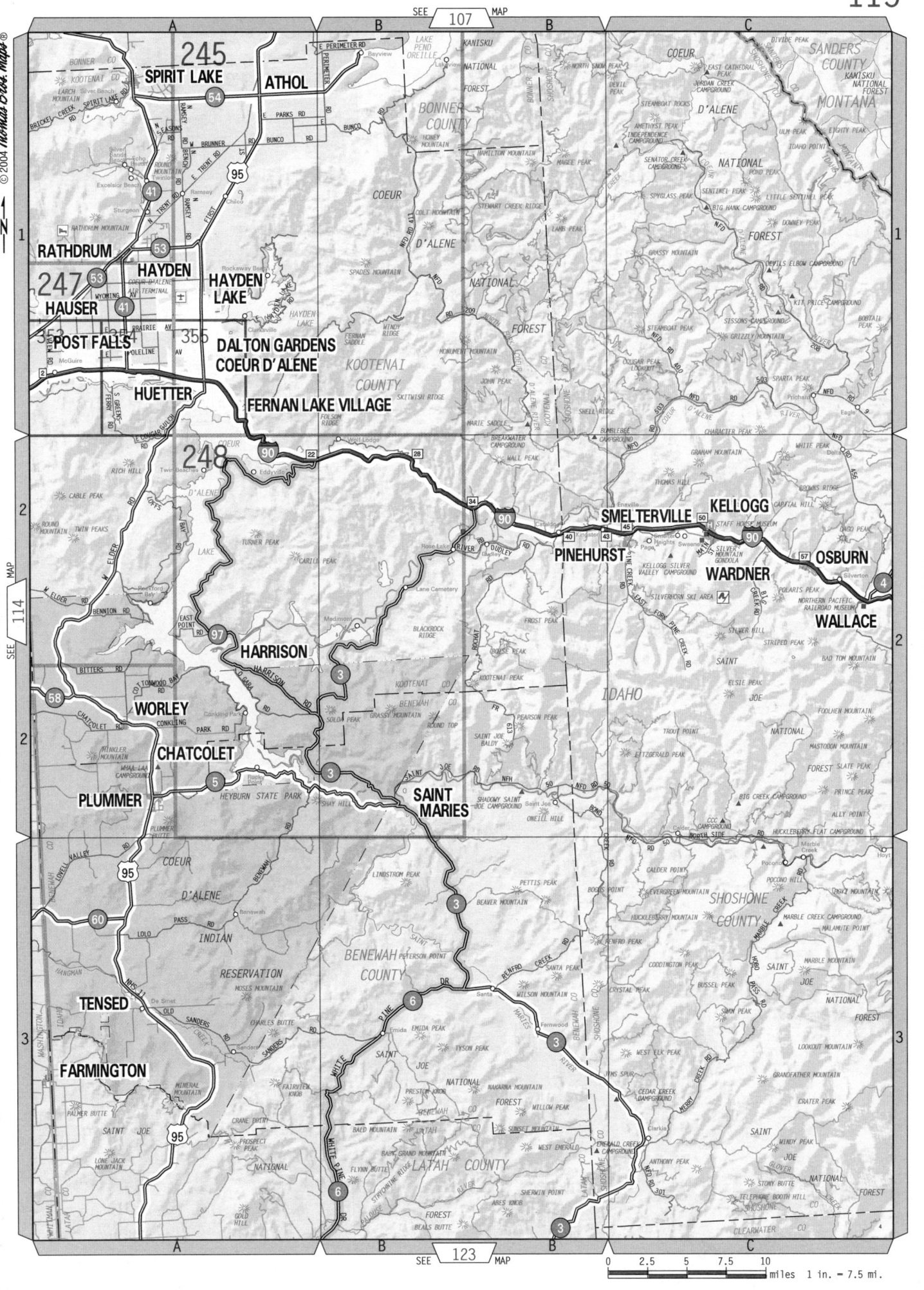

SEE 114 MAP

HWY

0 2.5 5 7.5 10   miles 1 in. = 7.5 mi.

116

A
B
B
C

298

OCEAN
SHORES

183

WESTPORT

105

Westhaven
Cohassett
Bay City
Acosta

GRAYS HARBOR
COUNTY
GRAYS HARBOR CO
PACIFIC CO

Grayland

Heather

WASHINGTON

Dexter
By The Sea

1

TOKELAND RD

105

Tokeland

WILLAPA
BAY

WILLAPA
NATIONAL
WILDLIFE
REFUGE

Bay Center

101

LEADBETTER POINT
STATE PARK

Rhodesia
Beach

PACIFIC

186

Oysterville

2

4TH

Nahcotta

LONG
ISLAND

Ocean
Park

OCEAN

Klipsan
Beach

103

SANDRIDGE RD

WILLAPA
NATIONAL
WILDLIFE
REFUGE

101

Oceanside
Pacific
Beach

Breakers

LONG
BEACH

Mooras Corner

PACIFIC
COUNTY

Seaview
Holm

CHINOOK VALLEY

2

100

STRINGTOWN RD

PACIFIC CO
WASHINGTON

101

Chinook

ROBERT

ILWACO

CLATSOP CO
OREGON

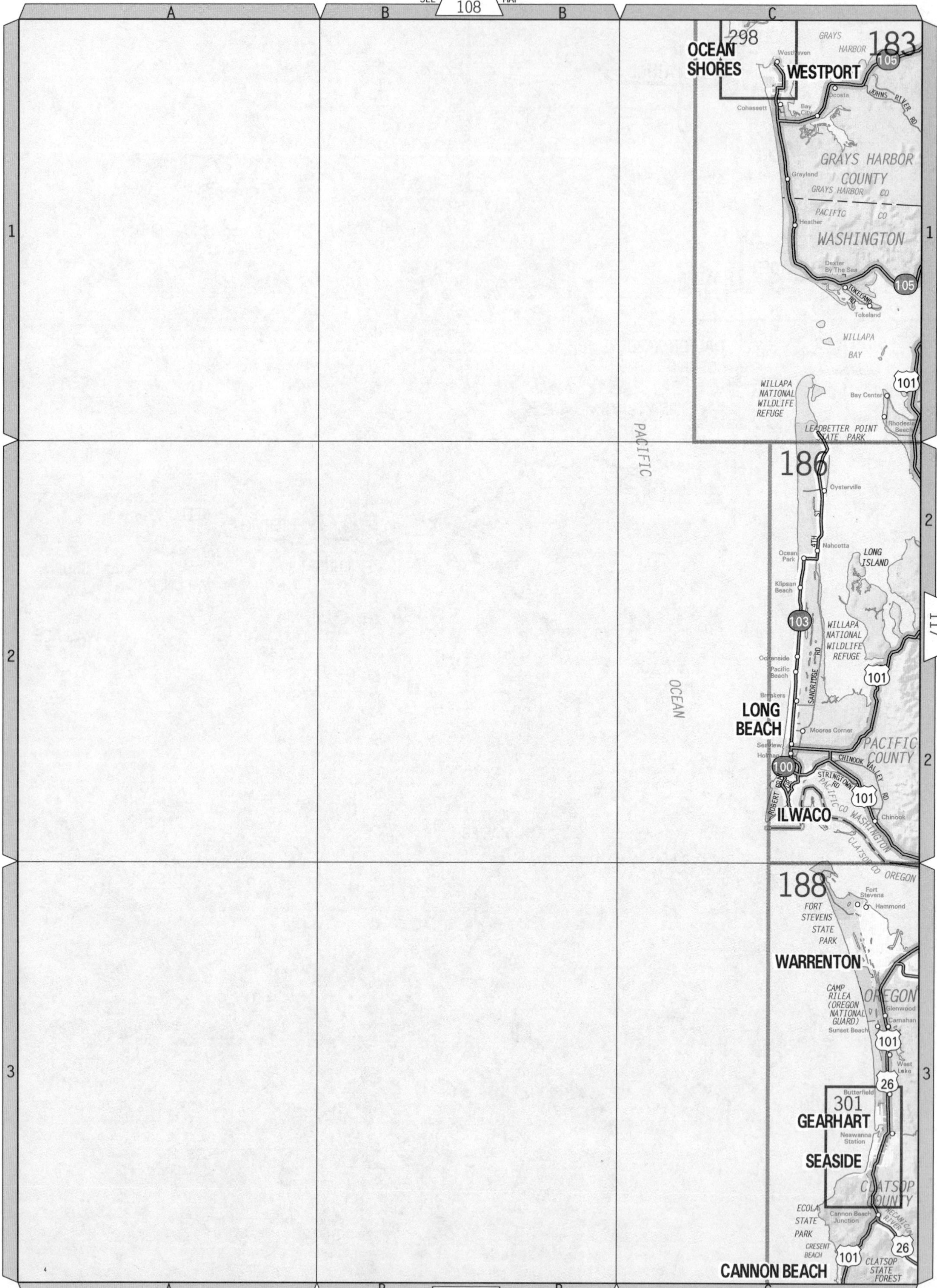

SEE 117 MAP

188

FORT
STEVENS

Fort
Stevens

Hammond

3

FORT
STEVENS
STATE
PARK

WARRENTON

CAMP
RILEA
(OREGON
NATIONAL
GUARD)

OREGON

Glenwood

Camahan

Sunset Beach

101

West
Lake

26

Butterfield

301

GEARHART

Neawanna
Station

SEASIDE

CLATSOP
COUNTY

ECOLA
STATE
PARK

Cannon Beach
Junction

101

CRESENT
BEACH

CANNON BEACH

26

CLATSOP
STATE
FOREST

A
B
B
C

SEE 124 MAP

0 2.5 5 7.5 10 miles 1 in. = 7.5 mi.

© 2004 Thomas Bros. Maps ®

HWY

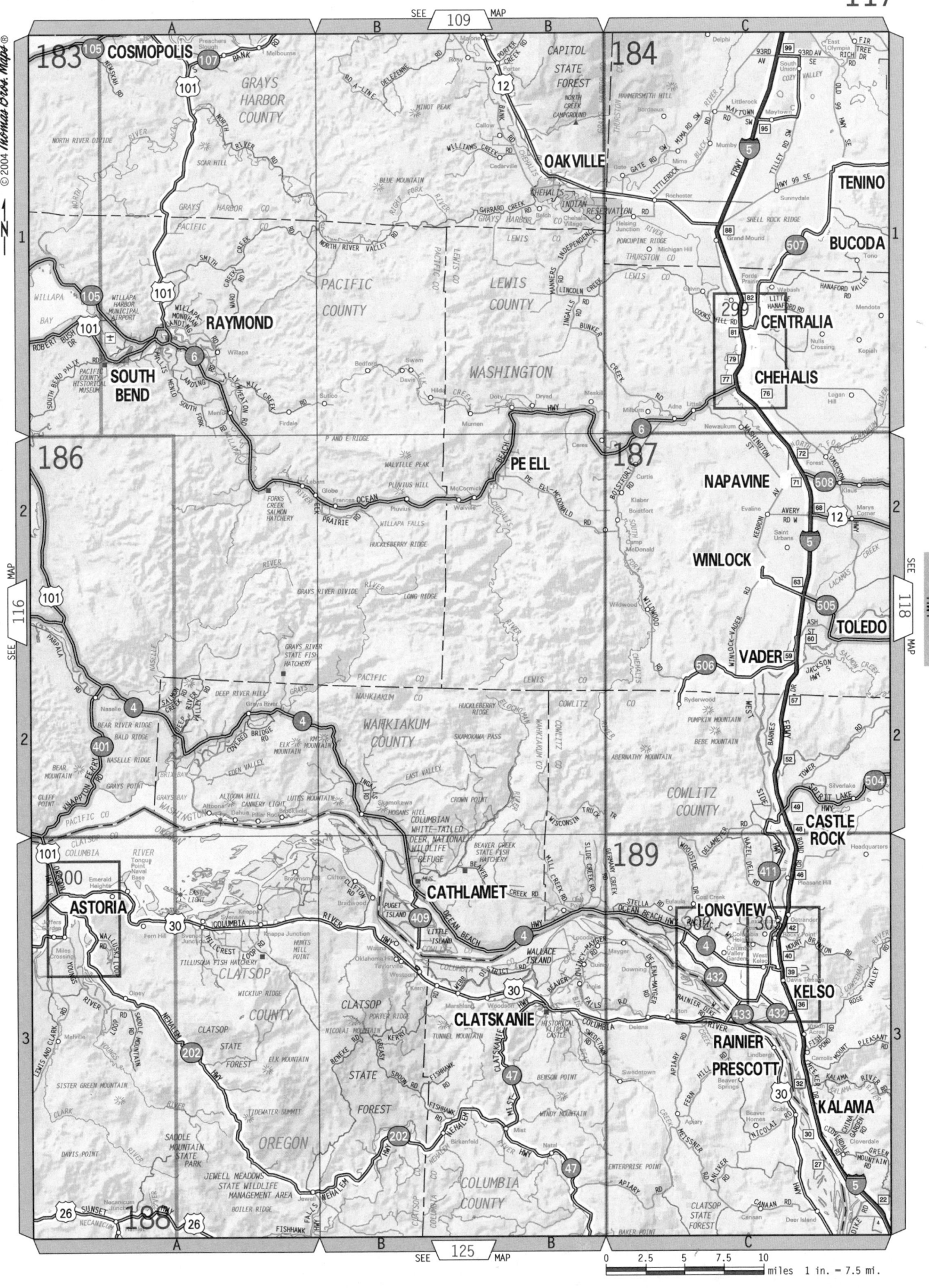

miles 1 in. = 7.5 mi.

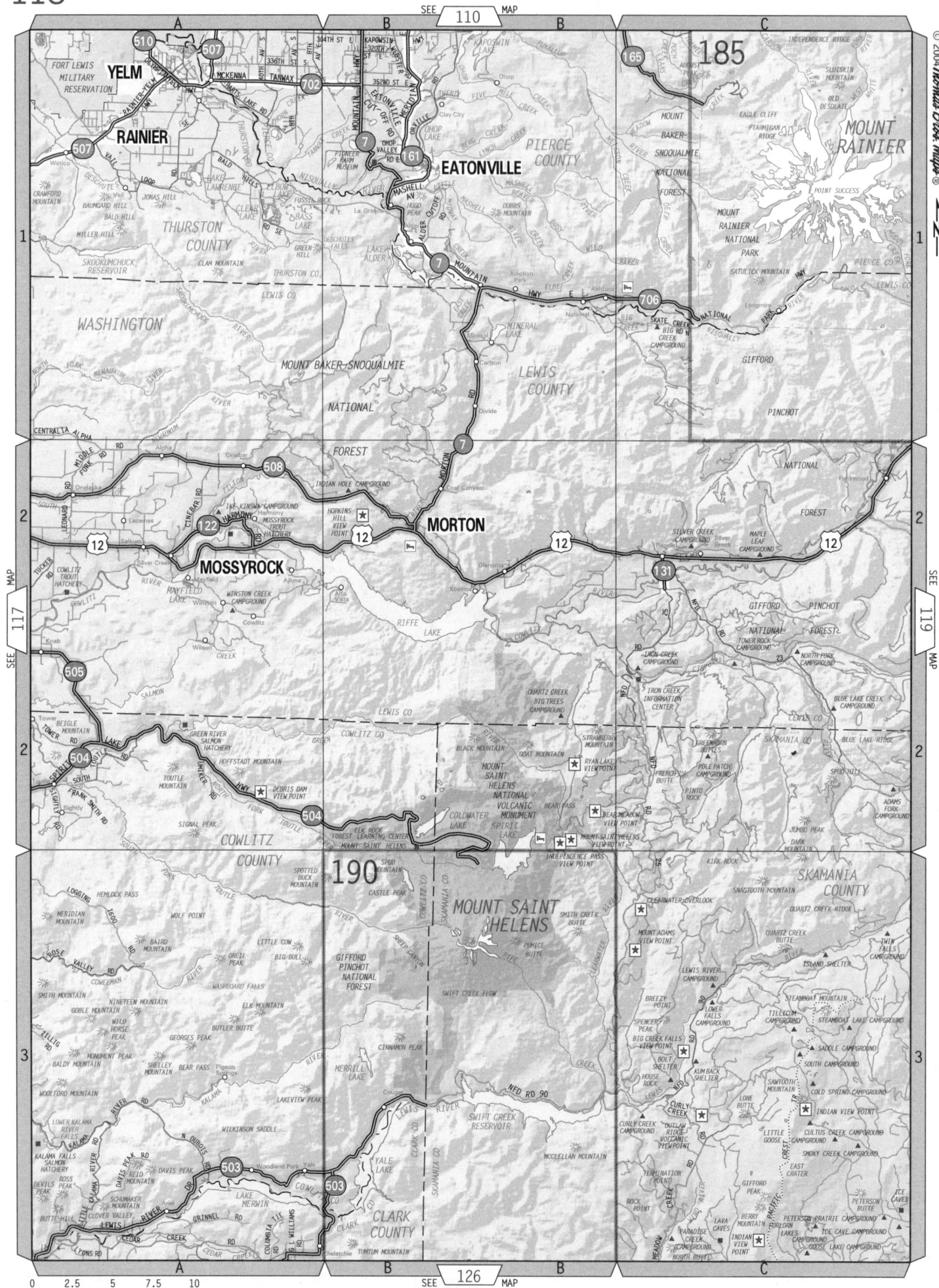

SEE 110 MAP

185

MOUNT RAINIER

MOUNT RAINIER NATIONAL PARK

YELM

RAINIER

EATONVILLE

PIERCE COUNTY

THURSTON COUNTY

WASHINGTON

LEWIS COUNTY

MOUNT BAKER-SNOQUALMIE

NATIONAL

FOREST

GIFFORD

PINCHOT

MORTON

MOSSYROCK

RIFFE LAKE

GIFFORD PINCHOT NATIONAL FOREST

COWLITZ COUNTY

190

MOUNT SAINT HELENS

SKAMANIA COUNTY

0 2.5 5 7.5 10 miles 1 in. = 7.5 mi.

SEE 126 MAP

SEE 117 MAP

SEE 119 MAP

HWY

N↑

185

240

243

24

ELLENSBURG

PIERCE COUNTY

MOUNT RAINIER NATIONAL PARK

410

CRYSTAL MTN SKI RESORT
MARCUS PEAK
NORSE PEAK WILDERNESS
HAYDEN PASS
FIFES PEAKS
BIG CROW BASIN
NORSE PEAK
CEMENT BASIN
LODGEPOLE CAMPGROUND
PLEASANT VALLEY CAMPGROUND
PINE NEEDLE CAMPGROUND
LITTLE NACHES CAMPGROUND
AMERICAN FORKS CAMPGROUND
INDIAN FLAT CAMPGROUND
CEDAR SPRINGS CAMPGROUND
HALFWAY FLAT CAMPGROUND
BOULDER CAVE CAMPGROUND
Cliffdell
SODA SPRINGS CAMPGROUND
COUGAR FLAT CAMPGROUND
Goose Prairie
LINDSAY CAMPGROUND
"WENATCHEE
BALD MOUNTAIN
NATIONAL
FOREST

SUNRISE PARK RD
MATHER MEMORIAL PKWY
CRYSTAL MOUNTAIN BLVD
SUNRISE PARK RD
GOVERNORS RIDGE
MOUNT RAINIER NATIONAL PARK
YAKIMA PEAK
NACHES PEAK
COWLITZ CHIMNEYS
SHRINER PEAK
SOURDOUGH GAP
MORSE CREEK CAMPGROUND
BUMPING LAKE MARINA
BOAT LANDING CAMPGROUND
BUMPING LAKE
BIG BASIN
BUMPING DAM CAMPGROUND
NELSON RIDGE
MINERS RIDGE
CRAG MOUNTAIN
MOUNT BAKER-SNOQUALMIE NATIONAL FOREST
HANGING TREE CAMPGROUND
TIMBERWOLF MOUNTAIN
410

STEVENS CANYON RD
123
Ohanapecosh Hot Springs
SUMMIT CREEK CAMPGROUND
GIFFORD PINCHOT NATIONAL FOREST
CARLTON PASS
BISMARCK PEAK
RATTLESNAKE PEAKS
YAKIMA COUNTY
HORSE RIDGE
BEAR LAKE CAMPGROUND
NACHES
Bonlow
Power House
CLEAR CREEK
SODA SPRINGS CAMPGROUND
MOSQUITO VALLEY
PEAR BUTTE
MCNEIL PEAK
INDIAN
BURNT MOUNTAIN
IRONSTONE MOUNTAIN
HAUSE CREEK CAMPGROUND
Rimrock
WINDY POINT CAMPGROUND
TIETON
NACHES-TIETON RD
Tieton
Holtzinger
COWICHE MILL RD
COWICHE
12
LAVA CREEK FALLS VIEW POINT
SAND LAKE SHELTER
DOG LAKE CAMPGROUND
CRAMER MOUNTAIN
CLEAR CREEK OVERLOOK
INDIAN CREEK CAMPGROUND
RIVER BEND CAMPGROUND
LOST LAKE CAMPGROUND
12
SKEETER SHELTER
WHITE PASS CAMPGROUND
KNUPPENBURG LAKE CAMPGROUND
PIGTAIL PEAK
HOGBACK MOUNTAIN
NORTH CAMPGROUND
PENINSULA CAMPGROUND
SELAH
WHITE PASS SKI AREA
CLEAR LAKE SOUTH CAMPGROUND
LONESOME COVE
TIETON RESERVOIR
TIETON STATE AIRPORT
COWICHE MILL RD
YAKIMA
GOAT ROCKS WILDERNESS
LEWIS COUNTY
HAGER LAKE CAMPGROUND
DANA YELVERTON SHELTER
MCCALL GLACIER
IVES PEAK
CONRAD GLACIER
MEADE GLACIER
CHAMBERS LAKE CAMPGROUND
SOUTH FORK CAMPGROUND
GREY CREEK CAMPGROUND
DOME PEAK
STROBACH MOUNTAIN
PINE MOUNTAIN
Tietonview Grange
Cottonwood Canyon
TIETON DR
NOB HILL BLVD
W WASHINGTON AV
Ahtanum
Harwood
NCLAINE CANYON
AHTANUM MEADOW CAMPGROUND
Soda Springs
Tampico
WALUPT LAKE CAMPGROUND
PETROSS SIDEHILL
CEDAR SWAMP
DIAMOND BUTTE
HUCKLEBERRY SWAMP
FAIRVIEW RIDGE
JENNIES BUTTE
NORTH FORK AHTANUM
TREE PHONES CAMPGROUND
SOUTH FORK AHTANUM
YAKAMA INDIAN RESERVATION
WHITEFOOT CANYON
WAPATO
EVANS RD
PROGRESSIVE
BROWNSTOWN
Brownstown
BRANCH
Rupple
HARRAH
Fulton
SKAMANIA CO
LEWIS CO
CAT CREEK CAMPGROUND
GREEN MOUNTAIN
SPRING CREEK CAMPGROUND
CHAIN OF LAKES CAMPGROUND
OLALLIE LAKE CAMPGROUND
KILLEN CREEK CAMPGROUND
COUNCIL LAKE CAMPGROUND
POTATO HILL
RED BUTTE
BIA RD
GLACIATE BUTTE
CASTILE FALLS
SODA SPRING CAMPGROUND
LOST SPRINGS CAMPGROUND
BIA RD 140
BIA RD 255
ESEP POINT
BULLGROUSE RIDGE
WINDY POINT
JOHNS BUTTE
YESMOWIT CANYON
FORT SIMCOE HISTORICAL STATE PARK
AGENCY
White Swan
FORT
SIGNAL PEAK RD
N WHITE SWAN RD
W WHITE SWAN RD
WESLEY RD
SMITH RD
YOST RD
WASHINGTON
TOPPENISH MOUNTAIN
SATUS PEAK
SIMON BUTTE
DRY CREEK FALLS
LOGY CREEK FALLS
97
MOUNT ADAMS
PINNACLE GLACIER
ADAMS
MOUNT ADAMS
WILDERNESS
SKAMANIA COUNTY
MULLIGAN BUTTE
MCKAYS BUTTE
POLAND BUTTE
OAK HILL
HOG SWAMP
SHEEP BUTTE
STAGMAN BUTTE
LOGY CREEK
BLACK CANYON
CROOKED CREEK FALLS
TIMBERLINE CAMPGROUND
COLD SPRINGS CAMPGROUND
CROFTON BUTTE
MORRISON CREEK CAMPGROUND
HAYSTACK BUTTE
WICKY CREEK SHELTER
SNIPES MOUNTAIN
EDWARD POINT
MCDONALD RIDGE
ISLAND CAMPGROUND
BIRD CREEK CAMPGROUND
KING MOUNTAIN
STOUT CAMPGROUND
BLUE JAY CAMPGROUND
KLOSE BUTTE
HAGERTY BUTTE
TWIN BUTTES
YAKIMA CO
NFD RD 23
3
CHRISTMAS TREE CAVE
141
CHEESE CAVE
BUTTER CAVE
LAVA BRIDGE
GABLEHOUSE MILL
SHEELTZER MILL
GIFFORD PINCHOT NATIONAL FOREST
GROSS MOUNTAIN
RED BUTTE
MEADOW BUTTE
QUIGLEY BUTTE
TROUT LAKE
TROUT LAKE HWY
CEMETERY RD
CANBOY LAKE
NATIONAL WILDLIFE REFUGE
Glenwood
GLENWOOD
GOLDENDALE
KLICKITAT STATE FISH HATCHERY
OUTLET FALLS
OUTLET CREEK CAMPGROUND
YAKAMA INDIAN RESERVATION
KAISER BUTTE
POTATO BUTTE
CASTLE ROCK
SIMCOE MOUNTAIN
INDIAN ROCK
KLICKITAT COUNTY
GRAYBACK MOUNTAIN
WHITE PINE BUTTES
UPPER BOWMAN CAMPSITE
LOWER BOWMAN CAMPSITE
DEVILS CANYON
BROOKS MEMORIAL STATE PARK SKI AREA
BROOKS MEMORIAL STATE PARK
DEVILS POCKET
LONE PINE BUTTE
WILSON CHARLEY CANYON
DEAD CANYON
WILLIS CANYON
SHEEP CANYON
BLACK BUTTE
KLICKITAT CO

HWY

0 2.5 5 7.5 10 miles 1 in. = 7.5 mi.

SEE 112 MAP

24 KITTITAS
242

43

82
97
821

KITTITAS COUNTY

GINKO PETRIFIED FOREST STATE PARK

WANAPUM LAKE
WANAPUM DAM

26
243

ROYAL CITY

MATTAWA

GRANT COUNTY

U S DEPARTMENT OF ENERGY HANFORD SITE

SADDLE MOUNTAIN NATIONAL WILDLIFE REFUGE

COLUMBIA NATIONAL WILDLIFE REFUGE

262

26

24

YAKIMA
33
34
36

MOXEE CITY

UNION GAP

82
12

PRIEST RAPIDS DAM

YAKIMA COUNTY

24

24

240

BENTON COUNTY

U S DEPARTMENT OF ENERGY HANFORD SITE

241

WAPATO
97
50
52
54
22

ZILLAH

TOPPENISH

GRANGER
223
58
82
12
67
69

SUNNYSIDE

22

GRANDVIEW

MABTON

WASHINGTON

WEST RICHLAND
225

BENTON CITY
224
12
82
96

PROSSER
221
82
80
73
75

221

YAKAMA INDIAN RESERVATION

KLICKITAT COUNTY

BENTON CO

JOHN DAY WILDLIFE MANAGEMENT AREA

SEE 128 MAP

© 2004 Thomas Bros. Maps ®

HWY SEE 119 MAP

SEE 121 MAP

0 2.5 5 7.5 10 miles 1 in. = 7.5 mi.

© 2004 Thomas Bros. Maps ®

242

SEE 120 MAP

SEE 122 MAP

HWY

WARDEN

LIND

OTHELLO

HATTON

WASHTUCNA

ADAMS COUNTY

COLUMBIA NATIONAL WILDLIFE REFUGE

CONNELL

KAHLOTUS

MESA

FRANKLIN COUNTY

WALLA WALLA COUNTY

US DEPARTMENT OF ENERGY HANFORD SITE

WASHINGTON

JUNIPER DUNES WILDERNESS

340 **RICHLAND**

PRESCOTT

343 **PASCO**

WEST RICHLAND

KENNEWICK

BENTON COUNTY

344 **WALLA WALLA**

345

COLLEGE PLACE

UMATILLA COUNTY

OREGON

MILTON-FREEWATER

0 2.5 5 7.5 10 miles 1 in. = 7.5 mi.

A | B | B | C

© 2004 Thomas Bros. Maps ® —N→

249

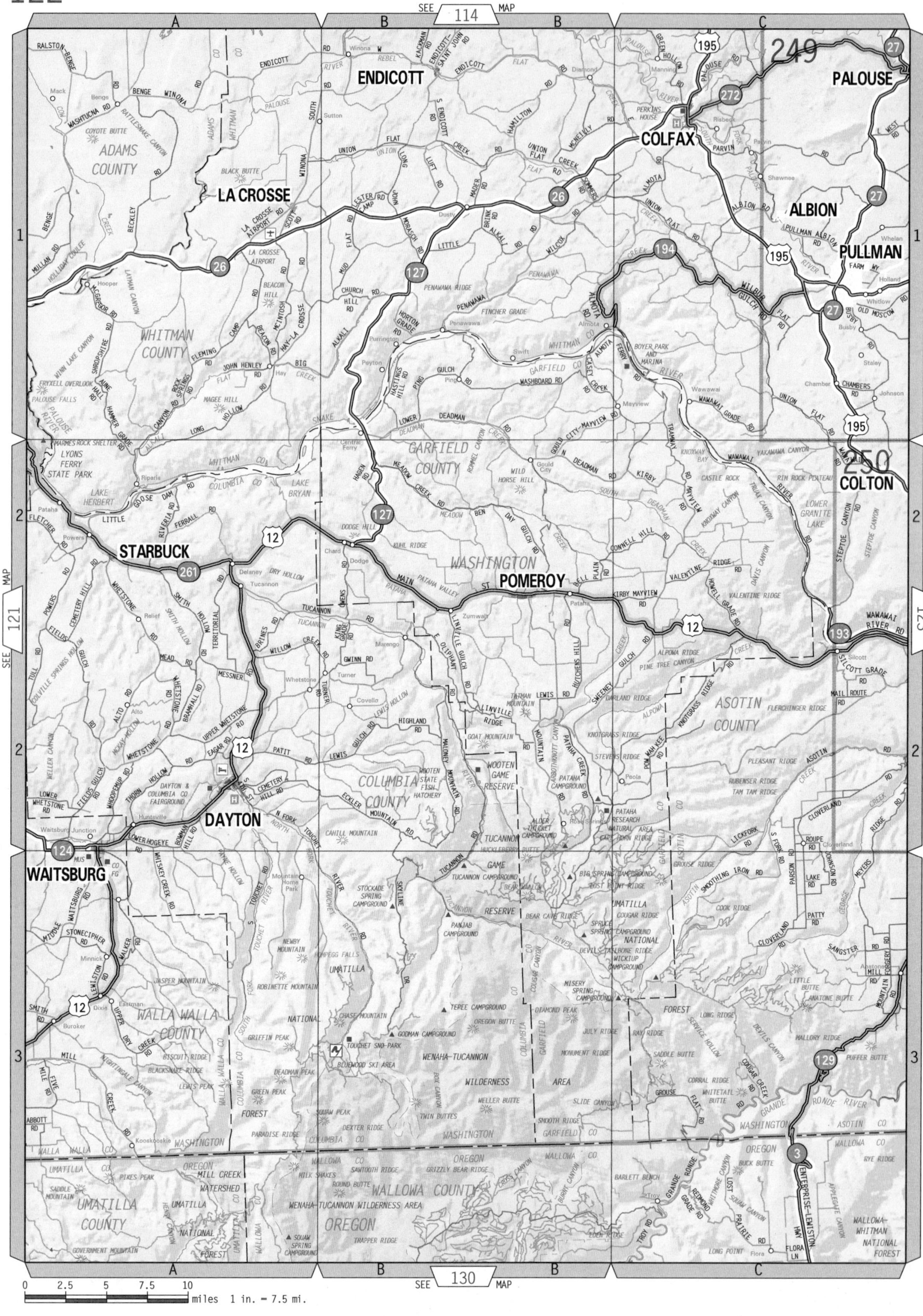

ENDICOTT

PALOUSE

COLFAX

LA CROSSE

ALBION

PULLMAN

ADAMS COUNTY

WHITMAN COUNTY

GARFIELD CO

250
COLTON

1

SEE 121 MAP

HWY

STARBUCK

WASHINGTON

POMEROY

GARFIELD COUNTY

ASOTIN COUNTY

SEE 123 MAP

2

DAYTON

COLUMBIA COUNTY

WOOTEN GAME RESERVE

WAITSBURG

WALLA WALLA COUNTY

UMATILLA NATIONAL FOREST

WENAHA-TUCANNON WILDERNESS AREA

3

UMATILLA COUNTY

OREGON

WALLOWA COUNTY

WALLOWA-WHITMAN NATIONAL FOREST

A | B | B | C

0 2.5 5 7.5 10 miles   1 in. = 7.5 mi.

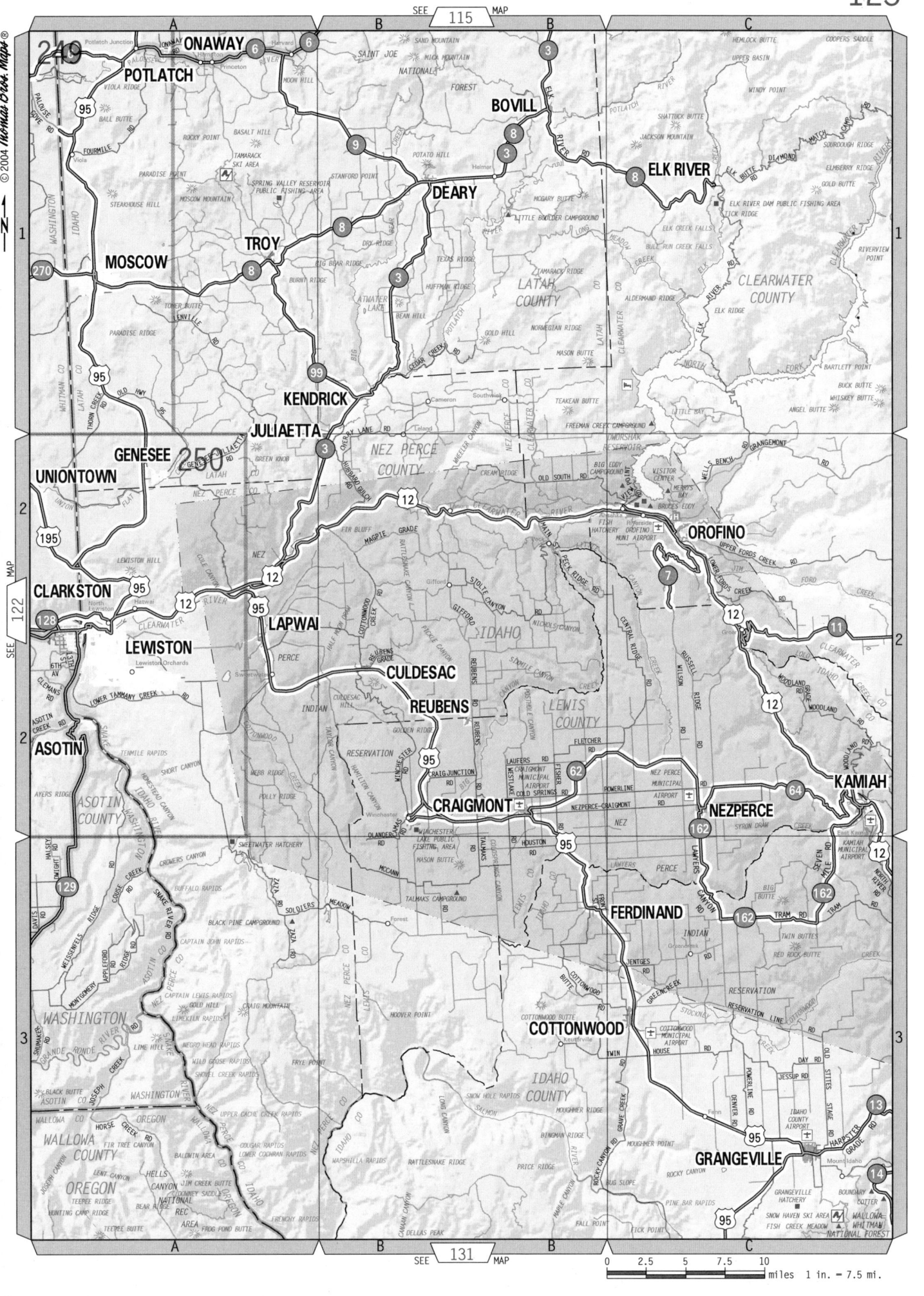

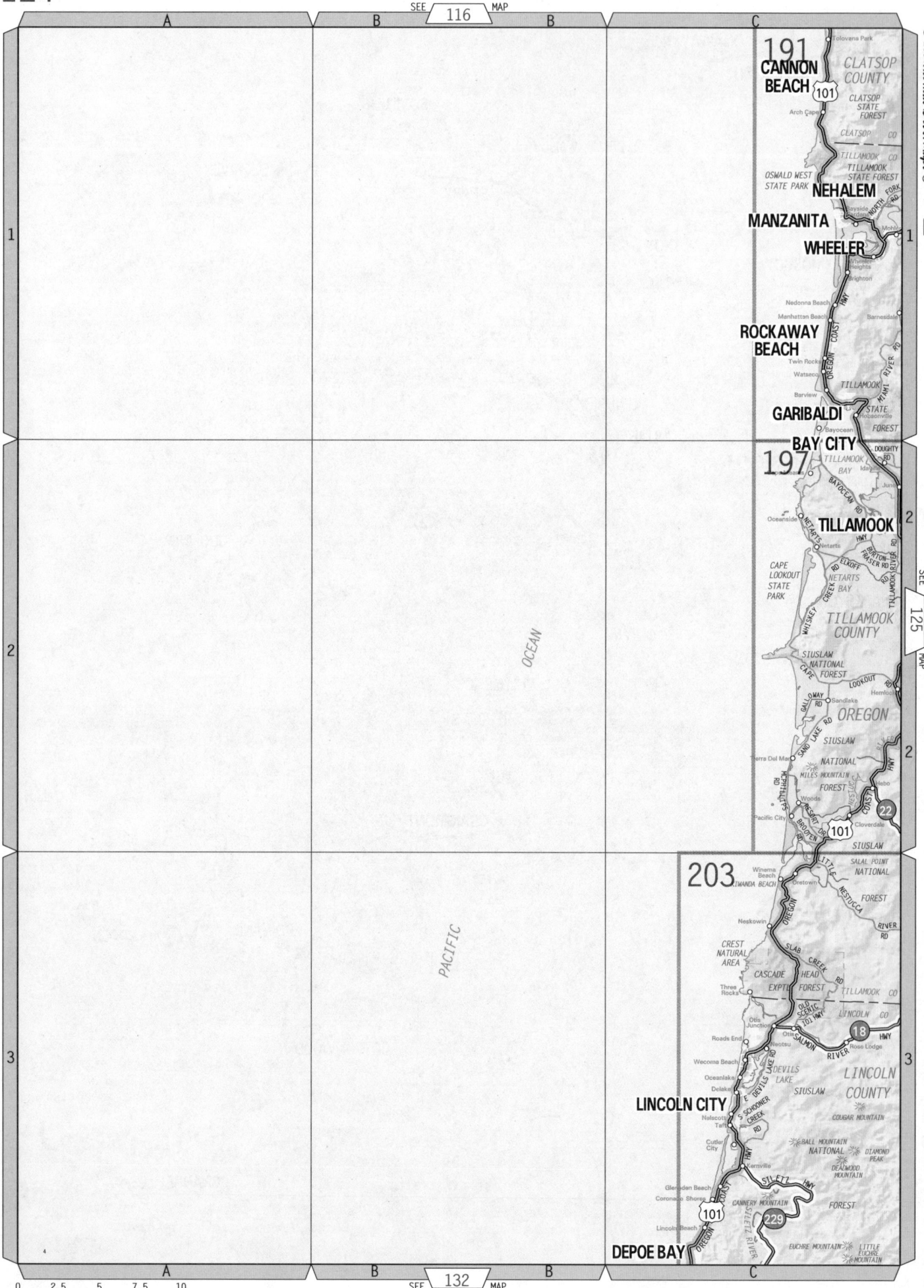

HWY

SEE 125 MAP

191
CANNON BEACH
101
CLATSOP COUNTY
CLATSOP STATE FOREST
Arch Cape
CLATSOP CO
TILLAMOOK CO
TILLAMOOK STATE FOREST
OSWALD WEST STATE PARK
NEHALEM
MANZANITA
WHEELER
Bayside Gardens
NORTH FORK
Mohler
Wheeler Heights
Brighton
Nedonna Beach
Barnesdale
Manhattan Beach
MIAMI RIVER RD
ROCKAWAY BEACH
Twin Rocks
Watseco
OREGON COAST HWY
TILLAMOOK
Barview
Hobsonville
STATE FOREST
Bayocean
GARIBALDI
BAY CITY
Doughty RD
197
TILLAMOOK BAY
Idaville
BAYOCEAN RD
Oceanside
Netarts
TILLAMOOK
Juno
BURTON FRASER RD
TILLAMOOK RIVER
ELKOFF RD
NETARTS HWY
CAPE LOOKOUT STATE PARK
NETARTS BAY
WHISKEY CREEK RD
TILLAMOOK COUNTY
SIUSLAW NATIONAL FOREST
CAPE
GALLOWAY RD
Sandlake
LOOKOUT RD
Hemlock
OREGON
SAND LAKE RD
SIUSLAW
Terra Del Mar
NATIONAL
NESTUCCA HWY
MILES MOUNTAIN
Nebo
FOREST
SANDLAKE RD
Woods
22
Pacific City
OREGON COAST HWY
BROOTEN RD
RESORT DR
101
Cloverdale
SIUSLAW
203
Winama Beach
SALAL POINT NATIONAL
KIWANDA BEACH
Oretown
LITTLE NESTUCCA
FOREST
Neskowin
OREGON COAST HWY
RIVER RD
CREST NATURAL AREA
SLAB CREEK RD
CASCADE HEAD EXPTL FOREST
TILLAMOOK CO
Three Rocks
LINCOLN CO
OLD SCENIC 101 HWY
Otis Junction
SALMON RIVER
18 HWY
Roads End
Neotsu
Rose Lodge
Wecoma Beach
DEVILS LAKE RD
Oceanlake
DEVILS LAKE
SIUSLAW
LINCOLN COUNTY
Delake
E DEVILS LAKE RD
COUGAR MOUNTAIN
LINCOLN CITY
Nelscott
S SCHOONER CREEK RD
Taft
BALL MOUNTAIN NATIONAL
Cutler City
DIAMOND PEAK
Kernville
DEADWOOD MOUNTAIN
Gleneden Beach
Coronado Shores
CANNERY MOUNTAIN
SILETZ HWY
FOREST
101
OREGON COAST HWY
SILETZ RIVER
229
Lincoln Beach
EUCHRE MOUNTAIN
LITTLE EUCHRE MOUNTAIN
DEPOE BAY

PACIFIC

OCEAN

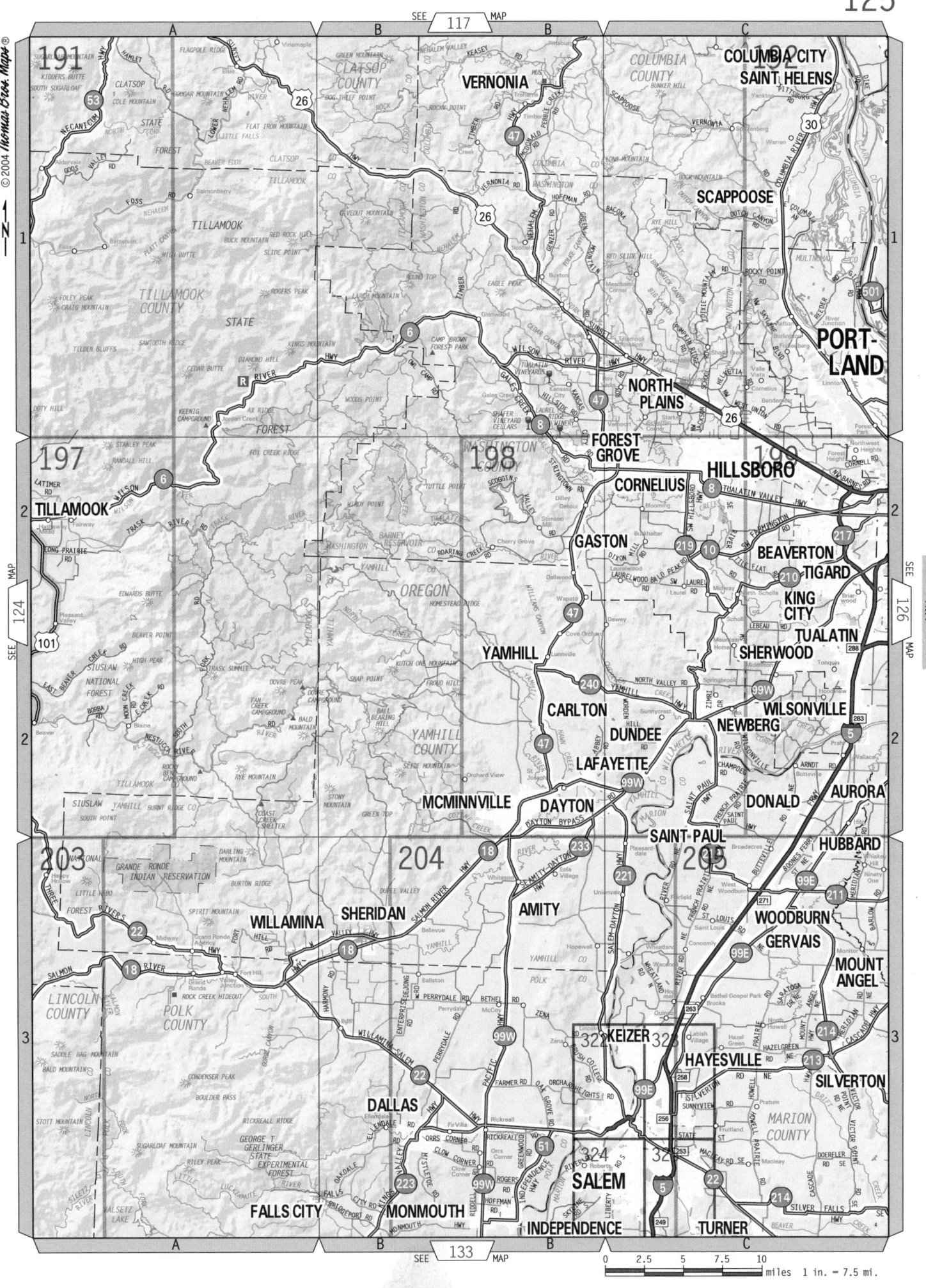

© 2004 Thomas Bros. Maps ®

SEE 117 MAP

SEE 133 MAP

191

197

203

198

204

192

199

205

COLUMBIA CITY
SAINT HELENS

VERNONIA

SCAPPOOSE

PORT-
LAND

NORTH
PLAINS

FOREST
GROVE

HILLSBORO

CORNELIUS

GASTON

BEAVERTON

TIGARD

KING
CITY

TUALATIN

SHERWOOD

YAMHILL

WILSONVILLE

CARLTON

NEWBERG

DUNDEE

DONALD

AURORA

LAFAYETTE

HUBBARD

MCMINNVILLE

DAYTON

SAINT PAUL

WILLAMINA

SHERIDAN

AMITY

WOODBURN

GERVAIS

MOUNT
ANGEL

TILLAMOOK

KEIZER

HAYESVILLE

SILVERTON

DALLAS

SALEM

FALLS CITY

MONMOUTH

INDEPENDENCE

TURNER

0   2.5   5   7.5   10
miles   1 in. = 7.5 mi.

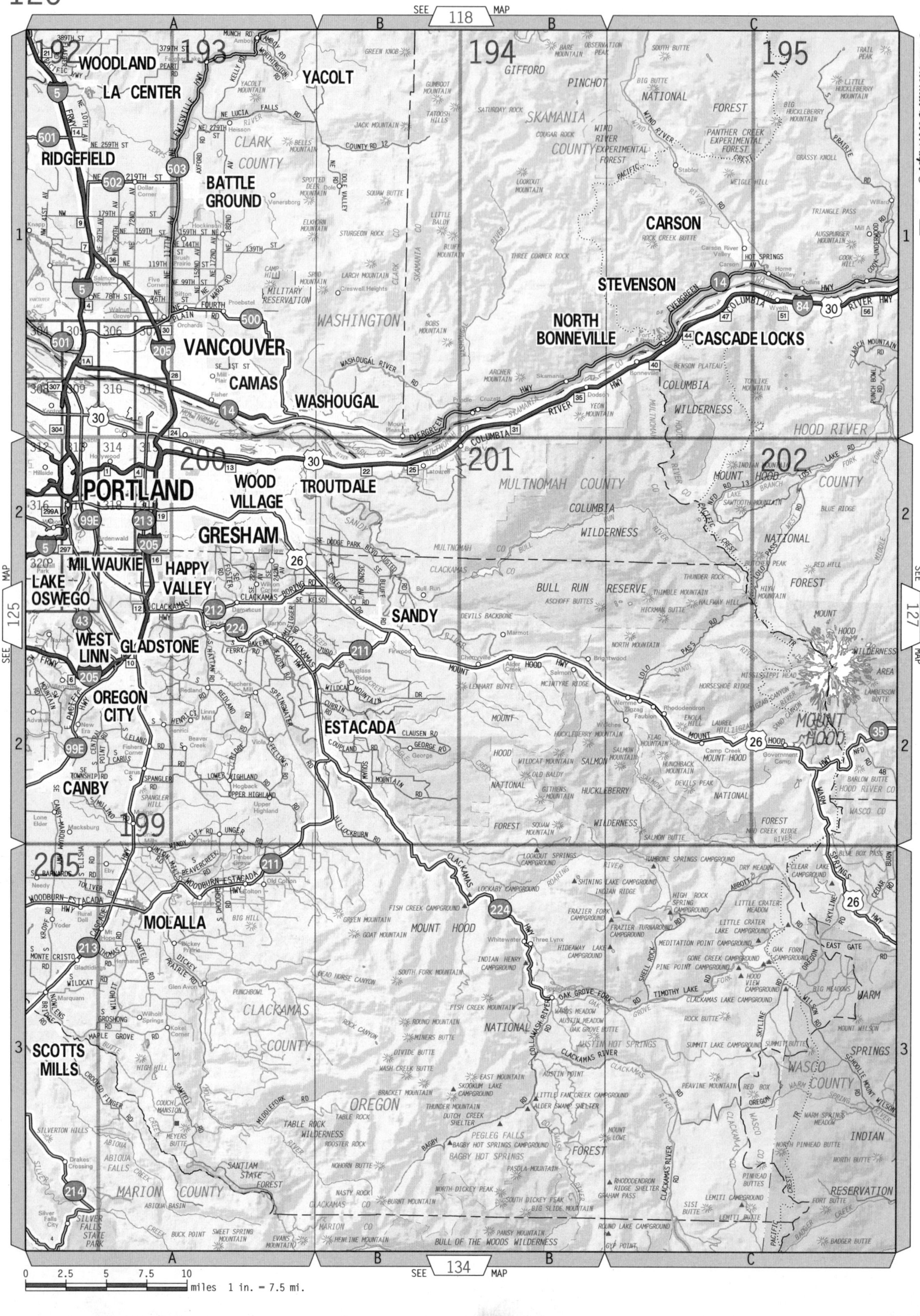

SEE MAP 118

© 2004 Thomas Bros. Maps ® —N—

192 WOODLAND 193 YACOLT 194 GIFFORD PINCHOT 195

LA CENTER

NATIONAL FOREST

501

RIDGEFIELD

502 503

BATTLE GROUND

CLARK COUNTY

SKAMANIA COUNTY

WIND RIVER

CARSON

HOT SPRINGS

1

STEVENSON

WASHINGTON

500

VANCOUVER

CAMAS

WASHOUGAL

NORTH BONNEVILLE

CASCADE LOCKS

14

COLUMBIA WILDERNESS

84 30

HOOD RIVER

205 30

200 201 202

PORTLAND WOOD VILLAGE TROUTDALE

MULTNOMAH COUNTY

COLUMBIA WILDERNESS

MOUNT HOOD

MULTNOMAH CO

CLACKAMAS CO

NATIONAL

2

GRESHAM

26

MILWAUKIE HAPPY VALLEY

FOREST

LAKE OSWEGO

205

212

224

SANDY

WEST LINN GLADSTONE

211

MOUNT HOOD WILDERNESS

OREGON CITY

ESTACADA

MOUNT HOOD

35

26

CANBY

99E

199

BULL RUN RESERVE

WASCO CO

205

211

MOLALLA

213

MOUNT HOOD

NATIONAL

26

EAST GATE

TIMOTHY LAKE

WARM SPRINGS

3

SCOTTS MILLS

CLACKAMAS COUNTY

CLACKAMAS RIVER

WASCO COUNTY

OREGON

NATIONAL FOREST

INDIAN RESERVATION

214

MARION COUNTY

SILVER FALLS STATE PARK

BULL OF THE WOODS WILDERNESS

MARION CO

SEE MAP 134

0 2.5 5 7.5 10 miles 1 in. = 7.5 mi.

SEE MAP 125 SEE MAP 127

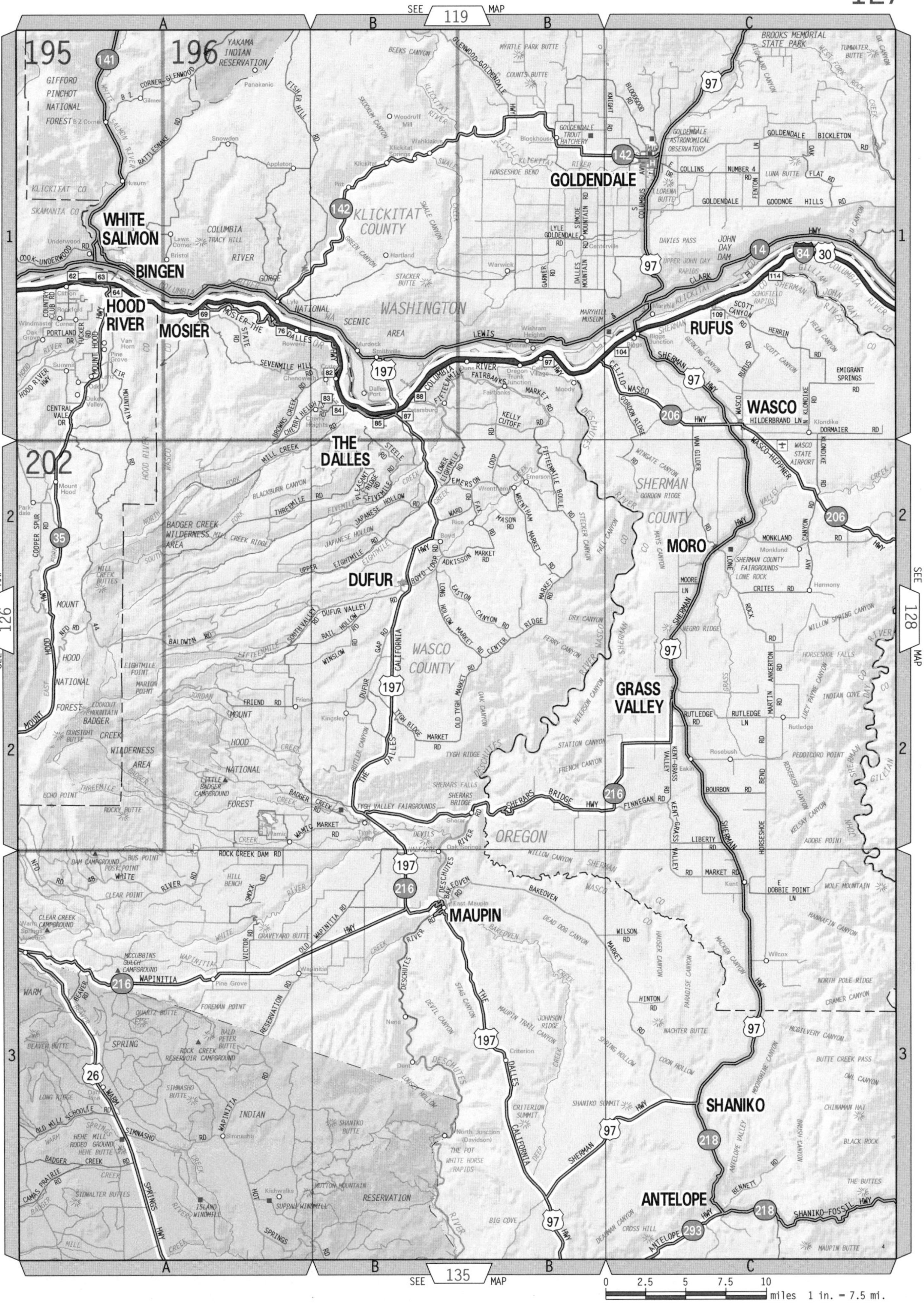

© 2004 Thomas Bros. Maps ®

SEE 119 MAP

195 141 196

GIFFORD PINCHOT NATIONAL FOREST

YAKAMA INDIAN RESERVATION

KLICKITAT CO
SKAMANIA CO

WHITE SALMON

BINGEN

HOOD RIVER

MOSIER

KLICKITAT COUNTY

142

GOLDENDALE

WASHINGTON

97

14 84 30

RUFUS

WASCO

206

202

35

SEE 126 MAP

THE DALLES

DUFUR

WASCO COUNTY

197

MORO

SHERMAN COUNTY

GRASS VALLEY

97

216

SEE 128 MAP

HWY

206

OREGON

MAUPIN

197 216

26

216

WAPINITIA

WARM SPRING

SIMNASHO

WARM SPRINGS INDIAN RESERVATION

97

SHANIKO

218

ANTELOPE

218

293

SEE 135 MAP

0 2.5 5 7.5 10
miles 1 in. = 7.5 mi.

SEE MAP 120

© 2004 Thomas Bros. Maps ® —N—

A B B C

GOLDENDALE
BICKLETON RD
EAST
ALDER
CREEK
SPRING CANYON
SAND
PHINNY HILL
BENTON
COUNTY
UMATILLA
NATIONAL
WILDLIFE
REFUGE
CANOE RIDGE
BLALOCK
ISLANDS
JOHN DAY
WILDLIFE
MANAGEMENT
CHRISTIE RD
WASHINGTON ST
MAIN AV
IRRIGON
730
HWY

WASHINGTON
SCHRANTZ RD
PINE
MIDDLE
BIG HORN CANYON
WHITE DRAW
JUNIPER
GRADE RD
ROOSEVELT
SIX
PRONG
SIX PRONG
RIDGE RD
PETERSON
GOLGOTHA BUTTE
ALDER RIDGE
KLICKITAT
ALDERDALE
Alderdale
QUARRY BUTTE
BOARDMAN IRRIGON
COLUMBIA
WASHINGTON
159
164
Boardman
168
COLUMBIA
PATTERSON
FERRY
OLD OREGON
171
84
30
UMATILLA
ORDNANCE
DEPOT
Ordnance

GLASS CANYON
DOT RD
Dot
KLICKITAT
COUNTY
14
151
KUNZE
SE
WILSON
BOARDMAN

HARRISON RIDGE
ROCK CREEK RD
SAND SPRING RD
OLD LADY CANYON
COLUMBIA
RIVER
HWY
COLUMBIA RIVER HWY
R
THREEMILE CANYON
MORROW
COUNTY
OREGON
BOARDMAN BOMBING RANGE
HOMESTEAD RD
POLE LINE
HOMESTEAD
RD

GOODNOE
STATION
GOLDENDALE
Goodnoe
Hills
GOODNOE
HILLS
147
ARLINGTON
MUNICIPAL
AIRPORT
RHEA
DALREED BUTTE
POVERTY RIDGE
FINLEY BUTTES

LAKE
UMATILLA
Sundale
84
30
HWY 137
ARLINGTON
74
HWY
WILLOW
SIXMILE CANYON
WELL SPRING CANYON
JUNIPER CANYON
Alpine
BUTTER CREEK JUNCTION

TUMWATER FALLS
COLUMBIA
129 RIVER
Blalock
GILLIAM
COUNTY
FOURMILE RD
HORN BUTTE
CECIL
Cecil
BAKER RD
HEPPNER
ELLA RD
JUNIPER
Sand Hollow
CARPENTER BUTTE
PINE CITY
BIG BUTTE
LITTLE BUTTE CREEK

DAY RIVER
BLALOCK CANYON
ALDALE CANYON
Shutler
FOURMILE CANYON RD
FAIRVIEW LN
HICKLAND BUTTE
ELLA BUTTE
Strawberry
207
BOMBING HWY

OLD OREGON TRAIL
MONUMENT
TURNER BUTTE
CEDAR
SPRINGS
WEATHERFORD
HISTORICAL
MONUMENT
DIAMOND BUTTE
Rock Creek
EIGHTMILE CANYON
WILLOW
SQUAW BUTTE
Ella
MILK CANYON

GILLIAM
SHERMAN CO
STARVATION POINT
BIG EDDY
19
BARNETT
Barnett
JOHN DAY
BASE LINE RD
OLEX-MCNAB RD
McNab
74
IONE
Jordan
JORDAN BUTTE
LEXINGTON
AIRPORT
LEXINGTON-ECHO
SMAGGART BUTTES
BELL CANYON

206
MIKKALO RD
Mikkalo
UPPER RD
PATS CANYON
ROCK CREEK RD
Clem
SPRING HOLLOW RD
WOLF HOLLOW
MORROW
RIDGE
KING CANYON
RHEA CREEK
CLARKS CANYON RD
LEXINGTON
BLACKHORSE CANYON
74
207
MORROW
COUNTY
FAIRGROUNDS
74
HWY

WASCO
SIXMILE CANYON
ESAU CANYON
DEVILS BACKBONE
WESTER BUTTE
HAY CREEK BUTTE
Gwendolen
WOLF HOLLOW FALLS
CAYUSE CANYON
UTTS BUTTE
IONE-GOOSEBERRY
BRENNER CANYON
Morgan
FAIRVIEW
FULLER CANYON RD
FULLER CANYON
HEPPNER
206

ELBM CANYON
DEVILS CANYON
ALVILLE LN
FERRY CANYON RD
LAMBERSON CANYON RD
JUNIPER CANYON
BULL BASIN
RICHMOND
TERNVILLE CANYON
HEPPNER HWY
WALLACE CANYON
CONDON STATE AIRPORT
GILLIAM COUNTY FAIRGROUNDS
DALZELL
ART
MCELLIGOTT
RATTLESNAKE GRADE
Valby
ROBINSON CANYON
Gooseberry
Eightmile
206
WASCO
REDDING RD
HEPPNER
Ruggs
207
SOCIAL RIDGE
206
BALSEY CANYON RD
SANFORD RD
FORK RD
GILMAN CANYON
STALTER CANYON
SANFORD CANYON
SIX DOLLAR CANYON

CONDON
WASCO
206
HEPPNER
LONEROCK
BLACK BUTTE
BUTTERMILK CANYON
ROOD HILL
ROCK
HEPPNER-SPRAY
STUCKEY BUTTE
ROAD CANYON
Hardman
WATERFALL CANYON
WARM HILL
GILLIAM CANYON
RHEA

WHISTLE POINT
MELDRUM CANYON
Coyote Butte
CORRAL CANYON
TABLE ROCK
COFFIN CANYON
DEVILS CANYON
BUCKHORN RD
GREINER LN
WEHRLI LN
DAY
QUINN RD
Mayville
LONEROCK
MCPHERSON CANYON
LONE ROCK
VALLEY
COLESOCK CANYON
BUTTERMILK CANYON
BRIDGE CREEK
LITTLE ROUND BUTTE
SHINGLE MILL BUTTE
207
DEADMAN HILL
BURTON HILL
BUCK FALLS
LONE PINE BUTTE
Reeds Mill
SUNFLOWER FLAT
Parkers Mill
Tupper
UMATILLA
COPPLE BUTTE
TEXAS BUTTE
MADISON BUTTE
TUPPER BUTTE
NATIONAL

WHEELER
JOHN DAY RIVER
HARVEY CANYON
CUMMINGS HILL SUMMIT
HOOVER RD
19
WHEELER COUNTY FAIRGROUNDS
BLACK BUTTE
KINZUA LN
Kinzua
LONEROCK
SQUAW BUTTE
LOST VALLEY RD
THE FROG
Wetmore
UMATILLA
COLLINS BUTTE
KINZUA RD
MORROW
RED HILL CO
WESTERN
ROUTE
FOREST

FOSSIL
IRON MOUNTAIN
JOHN DAY FOSSIL BEDS NATIONAL MONUMENT
Clarno
STONE
PRINDLE PEAK
STEIWER PEAKS
BALD MOUNTAIN
218
SHANIKO-FOSSIL
HORSE MOUNTAIN
JOHN DAY HWY
ROWE CREEK RD
WHEELER
COUNTY
Winlock
19
INDIAN MOUNTAIN
FRIZZEL MOUNTAIN
ALDER CREEK
TABLE ROCK
KANILES BASIN
NATIONAL
BIG BACK CANYON
TAMARACK MOUNTAIN
HAPPY JACK RIDGE
207
SPRAY HEPPNER-
UMATILLA
MARIGANT BUTTE
CHINA CAP
GRANT
CO
MILLIGAN STEW CANYON
GRASSE BUTTE
TURNER MOUNTAIN
BONEYARD CANYON
COPPER CANYON

SEE MAP 136

SEE 127 MAP

SEE 129 MAP

HWY

0 2.5 5 7.5 10 miles   1 in. = 7.5 mi.

© 2004 Thomas Bros. Maps®

A | B | C

UMATILLA
82 395 207 730

HERMISTON
STANFIELD

ECHO
207

HELIX

ATHENA **WESTON**
11 204

ADAMS
11

PENDLETON
30 395 202 84 198 199 210 216 209

Pendleton Municipal Airport
Blue Mountain Community College
Pendleton Underground Tours
Umatilla County Historical Museum
Round-Up Hall of Fame
Wildhorse Resort & Casino

UMATILLA INDIAN RESERVATION

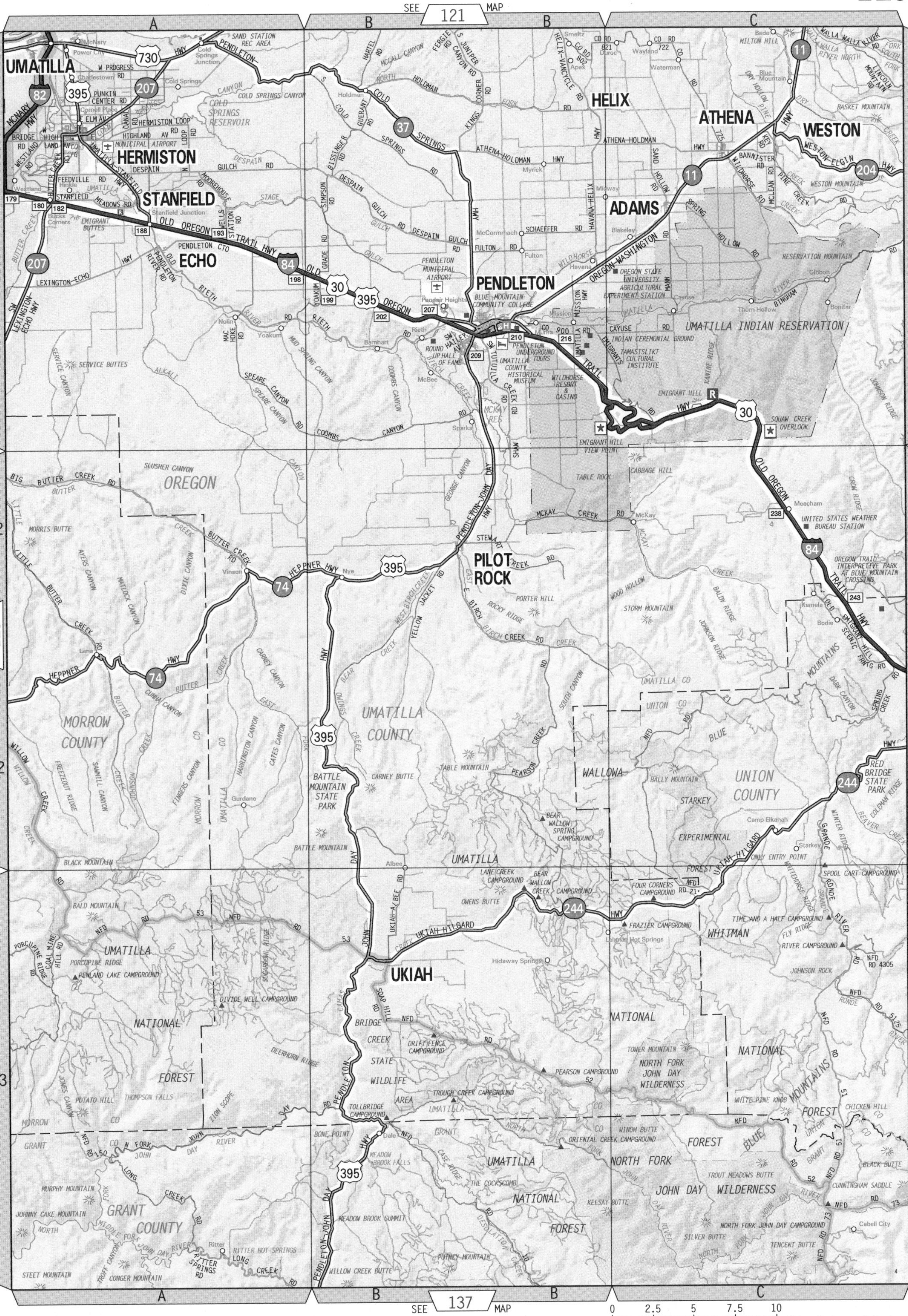

Oregon State University Agricultural Experiment Station
Tamastslikt Cultural Institute
Indian Ceremonial Ground

Emigrant Hill
Squaw Creek Overlook
30 238 84 243

Meacham
Oregon Trail Interpretive Park at Blue Mountain Crossing

OREGON

Heppner Hwy
74 395

PILOT ROCK

MORROW COUNTY

Heppner
74

Battle Mountain State Park

UMATILLA COUNTY

Umatilla Co / Union Co

BLUE

WALLOWA

UNION COUNTY
244 Red Bridge State Park

WHITMAN

395

UKIAH
244

UMATILLA

NATIONAL

FOREST

NATIONAL FOREST

GRANT COUNTY

NATIONAL

FOREST

NORTH FORK JOHN DAY WILDERNESS

BLUE MOUNTAINS

395

0 2.5 5 7.5 10 miles   1 in. = 7.5 mi.

SEE MAP 128
SEE MAP 130

HWY

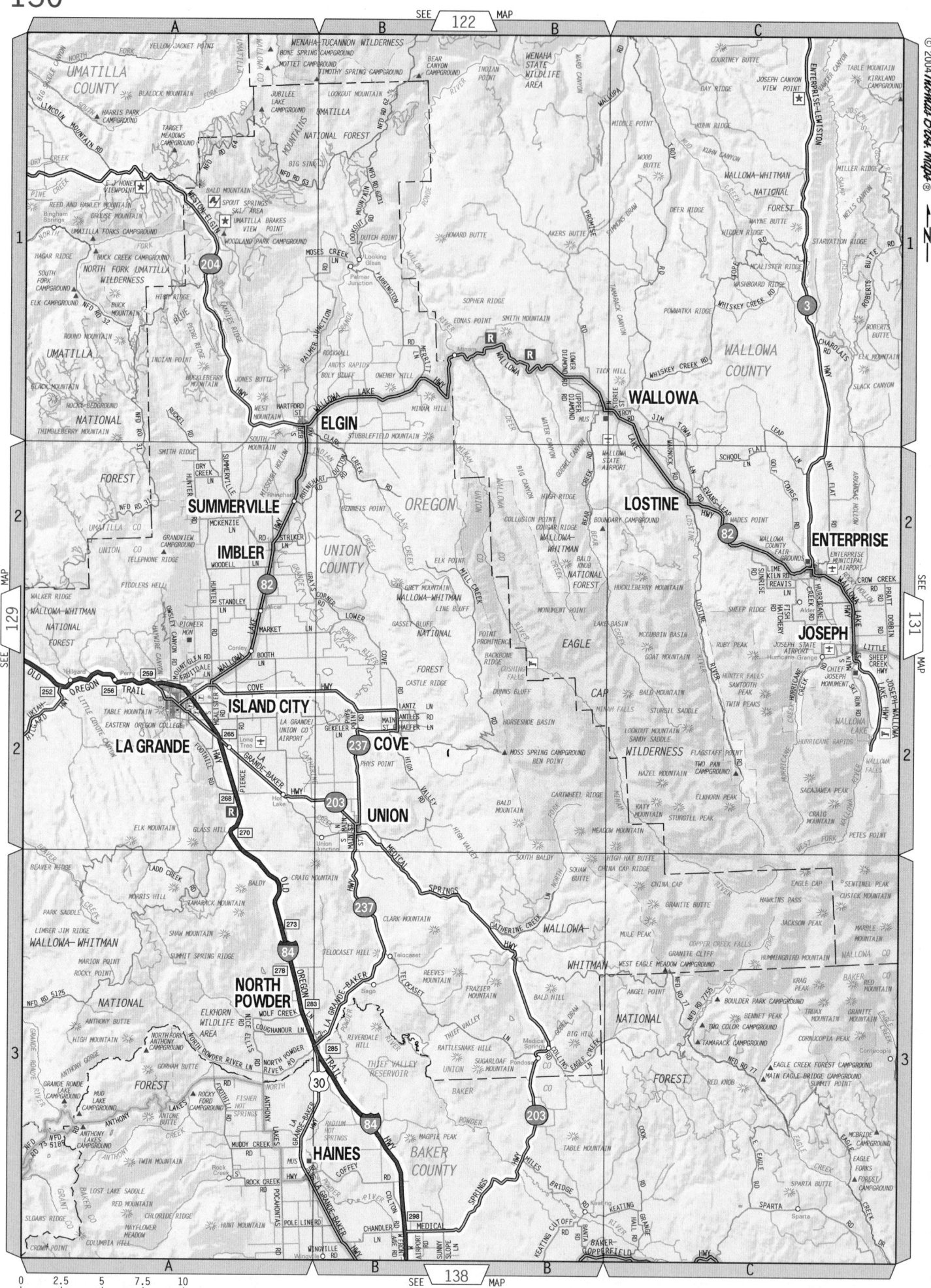

0 2.5 5 7.5 10

miles 1 in. = 7.5 mi.

© 2004 Thomas Bros. Maps ®

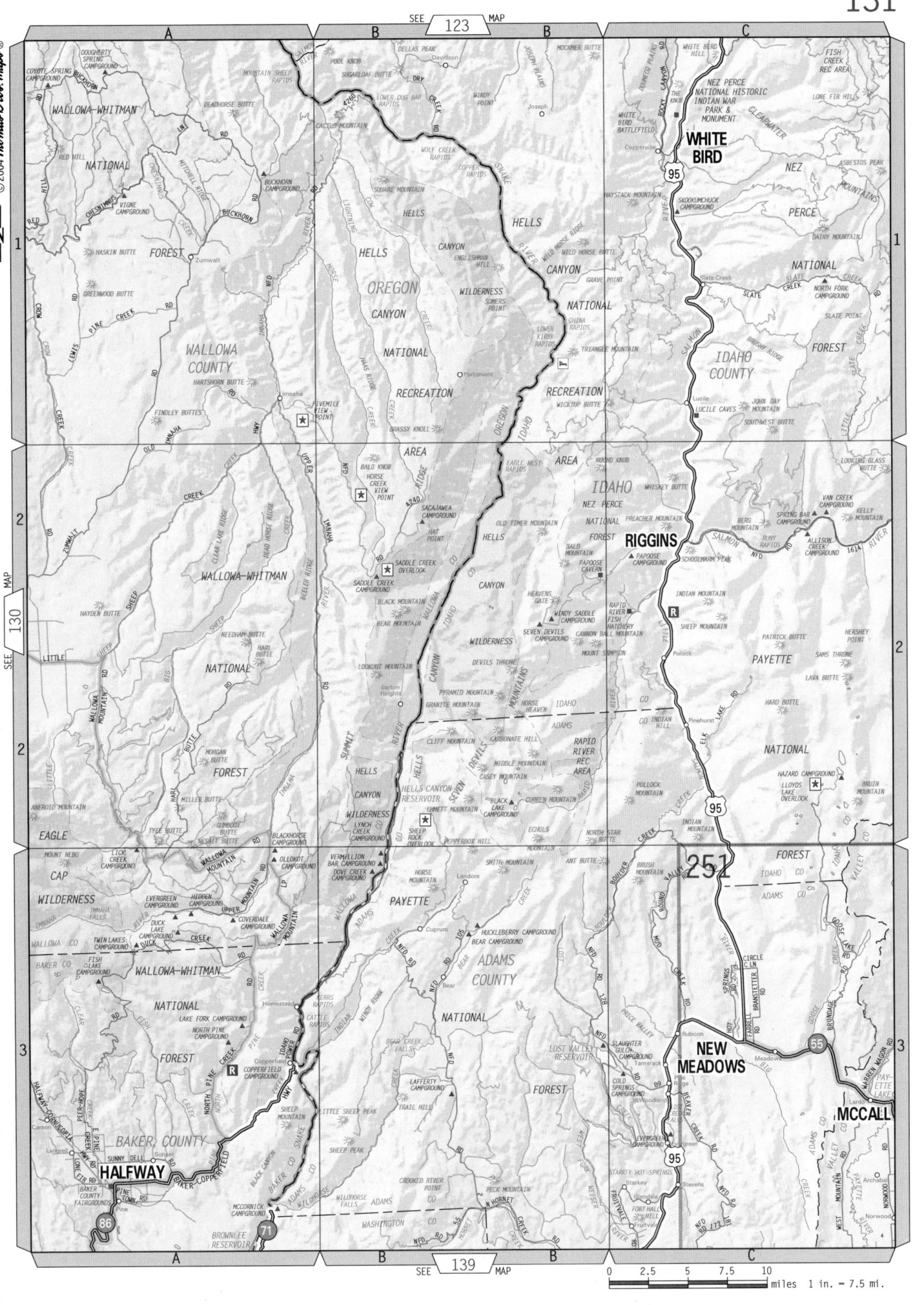

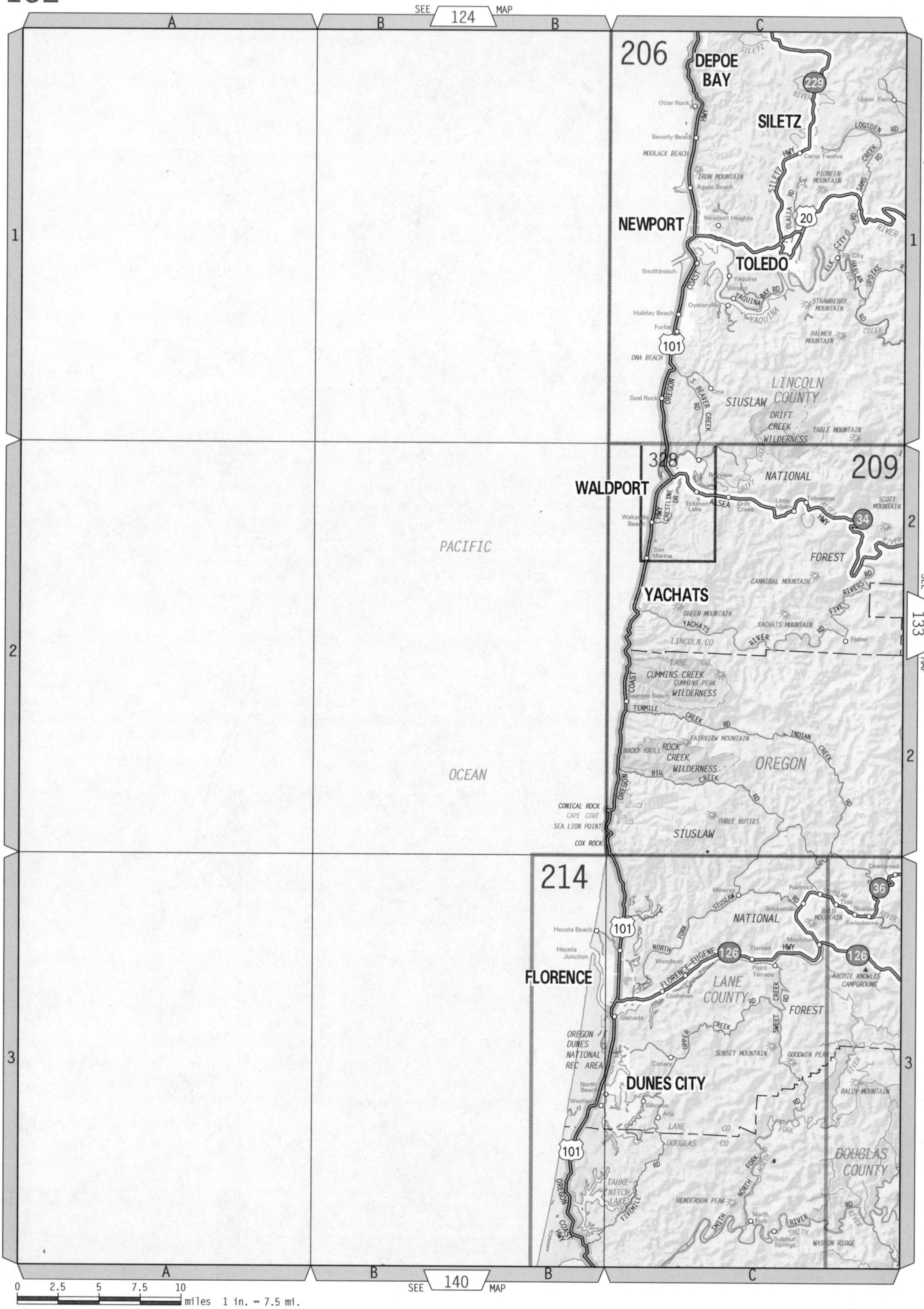

© 2004 Rand McNally ®

—N—

A | B | B | C

206

DEPOE BAY

229

Otter Rock

SILETZ

Beverly Beach

MOOLACK BEACH

IRON MOUNTAIN

Agate Beach

LOGSDEN RD

Camp Twelve

PIONEER MOUNTAIN

NEWPORT

Newport Heights

20

Southbeach

TOLEDO

Yaquina

Winant

YAQUINA

Elk City

Oysterville

STRAWBERRY MOUNTAIN

Holiday Beach

Forfar

101

PALMER MOUNTAIN

ONA BEACH

LINCOLN COUNTY

Seal Rock

Ona

SIUSLAW

DRIFT CREEK WILDERNESS

TABLE MOUNTAIN

328

Bayview

NATIONAL

209

WALDPORT

ALSEA

Eckman Lake

Drift Creek

Tidewater

SCOTT MOUNTAIN

34

Wakonda Beach

San Marine

FOREST

CANNIBAL MOUNTAIN

YACHATS

GREEN MOUNTAIN

YACHATS

YACHATS MOUNTAIN

Fisher

LINCOLN CO.

LANE CO.

CUMMINS CREEK

CUMMINS PEAK WILDERNESS

Searose Beach

TENMILE

FAIRVIEW MOUNTAIN

INDIAN

ROCKY KNOLL

ROCK CREEK WILDERNESS

OREGON

BIG

THREE BUTTES

CONICAL ROCK

CAPE COVE

SEA LION POINT

SIUSLAW

COX ROCK

214

Deadwood

Minerva

Rainrock

36

Heceta Beach

SIUSLAW

NATIONAL

Brickerville

Swisshome

101

Heceta Junction

Wendson

126

Tiernan

Point Terrace

126

Mapleton

ARCHIE KNOWLES CAMPGROUND

FLORENCE

Cushman

LANE COUNTY

FOREST

Glenada

SUNSET MOUNTAIN

GOODWIN PEAK

OREGON DUNES NATIONAL REC AREA

Canary

BALDY MOUNTAIN

North Beach

Westlake

DUNES CITY

Siltcoos

Ada

LANE CO.

DOUGLAS CO.

DOUGLAS COUNTY

101

TAHKE NITCH LAKE

HENDERSON PEAK

North Fork

SMITH RIVER

Sulphur Springs

WASSON RIDGE

PACIFIC

OCEAN

A | B | B | C

0 2.5 5 7.5 10 miles   1 in. = 7.5 mi.

HWY

SEE 125 MAP
SEE 141 MAP
SEE 132 MAP
SEE 134 MAP
A
B
C
1
2
3
207
210
215
326
327
329
330
331
TURNER
AUMSVILLE
SUBLIMITY
STAYTON
MARION COUNTY
POLK COUNTY
JEFFERSON
SCIO
MILLERSBURG
ALBANY
ADAIR VILLAGE
CORVALLIS
PHILOMATH
TANGENT
LEBANON
WATERLOO
SODAVILLE
LINN COUNTY
BROWNSVILLE
SWEET HOME
HALSEY
BENTON COUNTY
LINCOLN COUNTY
MONROE
HARRISBURG
JUNCTION CITY
COBURG
EUGENE
SPRINGFIELD
VENETA
LANE COUNTY
CRESWELL
LOWELL
COTTAGE GROVE
OREGON
DOUGLAS COUNTY
MCDONALD STATE FOREST
PAUL DUNN STATE FOREST
SIUSLAW NATIONAL FOREST
WILLAMETTE NATIONAL FOREST
UMPQUA NATIONAL FOREST
FINLEY NATIONAL WILDLIFE REFUGE
ANKENY NATIONAL WILDLIFE REFUGE
FERN RIDGE LAKE
DEXTER LAKE
DORENA LAKE
MARYS PEAK
0 2.5 5 7.5 10
miles 1 in. = 7.5 mi.

HWY

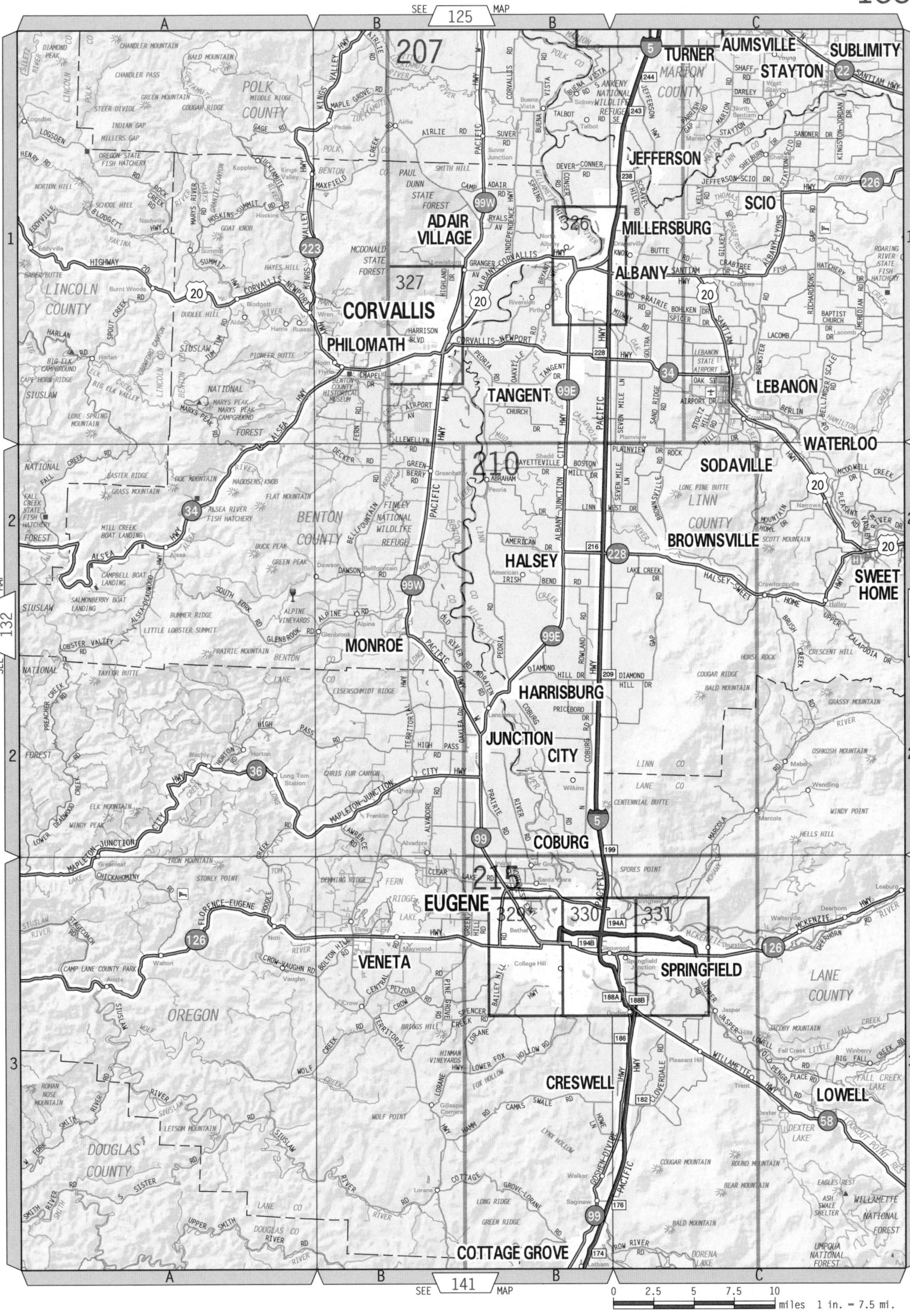

SEE 126 MAP

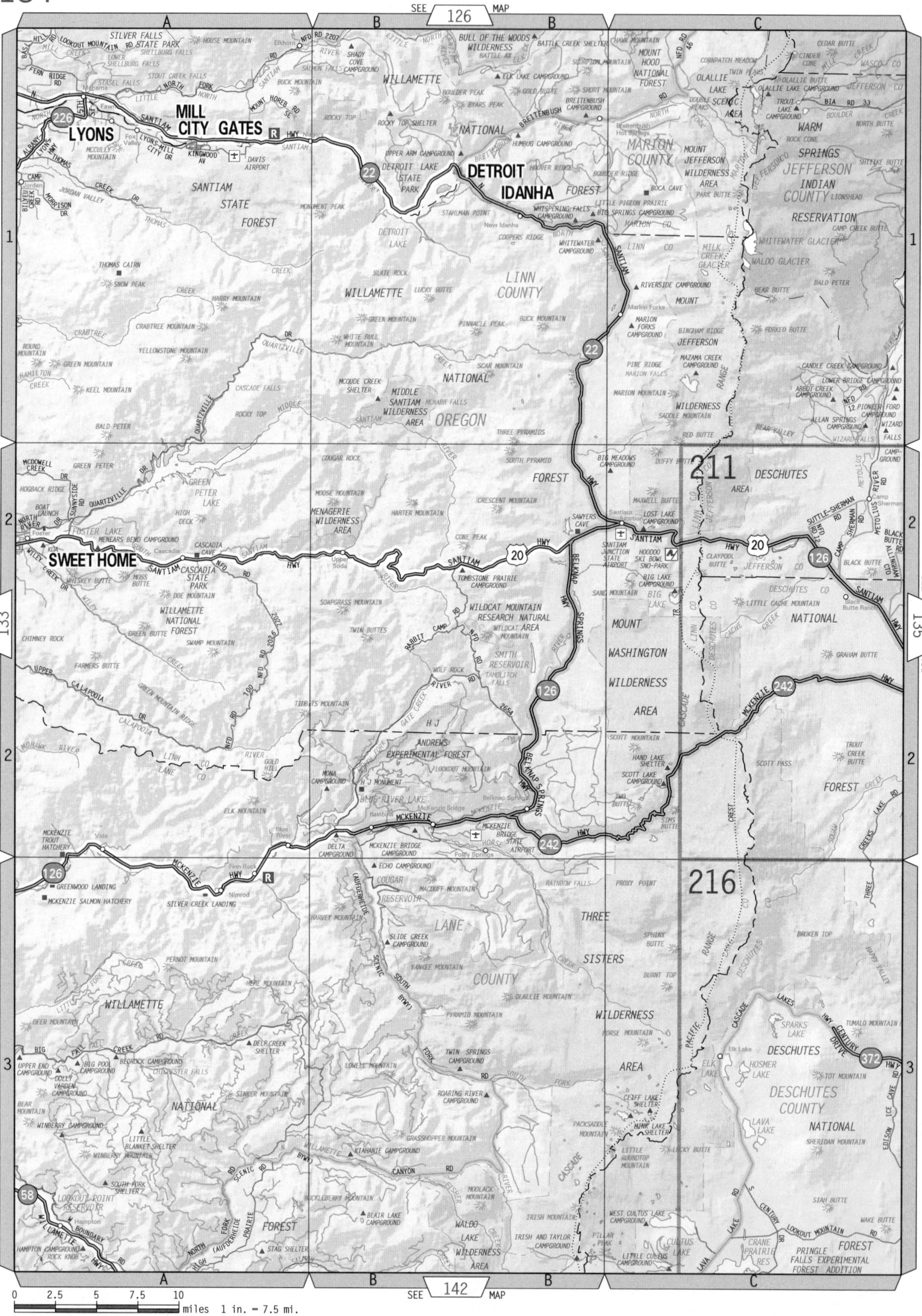

| A | B | C |

© 2004 THOMAS BROS. MAPS ®

LYONS
MILL CITY GATES
DETROIT
IDAHA
SWEET HOME
McKENZIE

SILVER FALLS STATE PARK
SANTIAM STATE FOREST
WILLAMETTE NATIONAL FOREST
BULL OF THE WOODS WILDERNESS
MARION COUNTY
LINN COUNTY
JEFFERSON COUNTY INDIAN RESERVATION
MOUNT HOOD NATIONAL FOREST
OLALLIE LAKE SCENIC AREA
WARM SPRINGS
WHITEWATER GLACIER
WALDO GLACIER
MOUNT JEFFERSON WILDERNESS AREA
MIDDLE SANTIAM WILDERNESS AREA
MENAGERIE WILDERNESS AREA
OREGON
DESCHUTES NATIONAL FOREST
MOUNT WASHINGTON WILDERNESS AREA
THREE SISTERS WILDERNESS AREA
CASCADIA STATE PARK
ANDREWS EXPERIMENTAL FOREST
LANE COUNTY
DESCHUTES COUNTY
DESCHUTES NATIONAL FOREST
WILLAMETTE NATIONAL FOREST
WALDO LAKE WILDERNESS AREA

211
216

SEE 133 MAP
SEE 135 MAP
HWY

SEE 142 MAP

| A | B | C |

0 2.5 5 7.5 10
miles   1 in. = 7.5 mi.

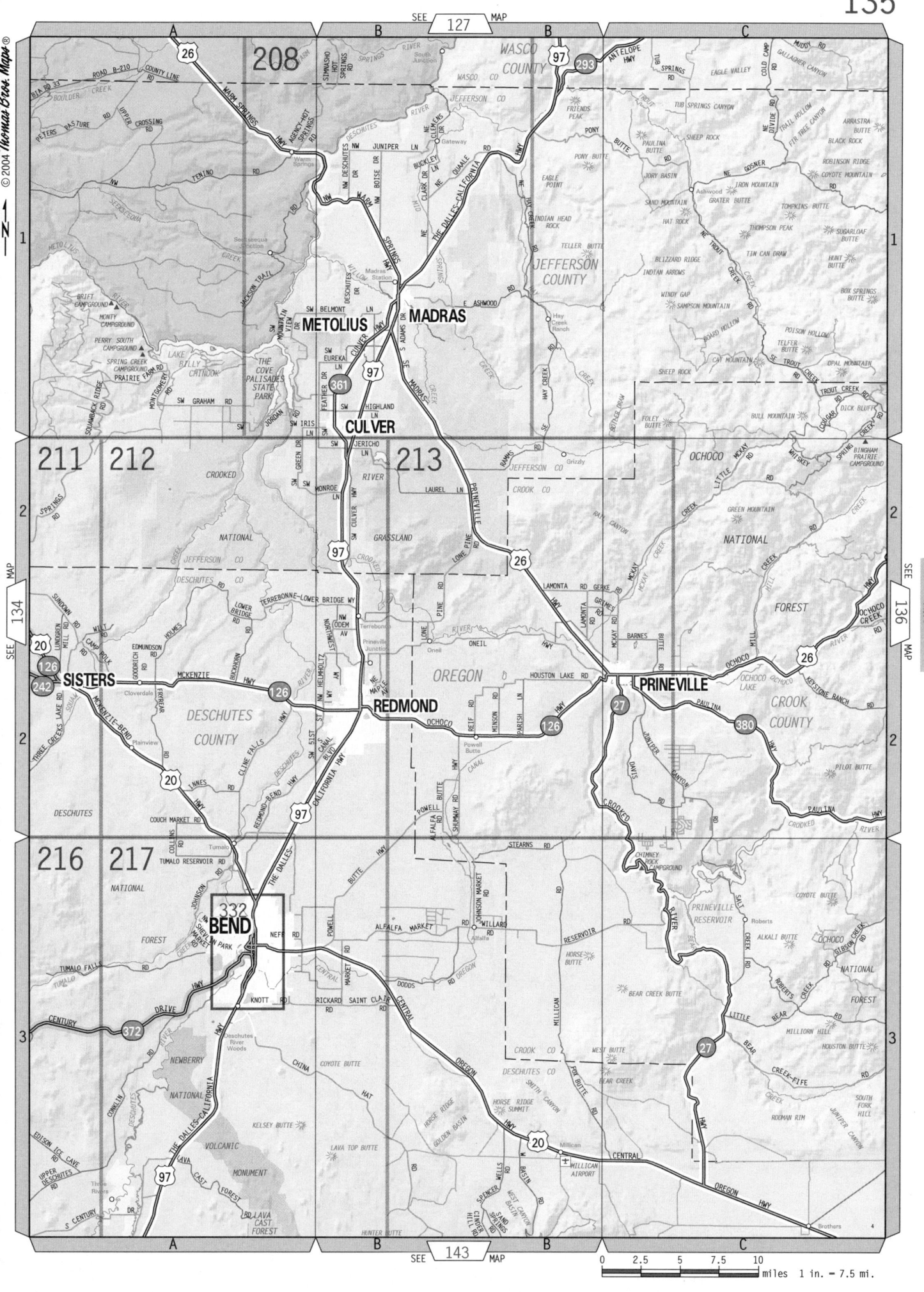

208

211 212 213

216 217

332

SEE 127 MAP

SEE 134 MAP

SEE 136 MAP

HWY

SEE 143 MAP

METOLIUS

MADRAS

CULVER

SISTERS

REDMOND

PRINEVILLE

BEND

WASCO COUNTY

JEFFERSON COUNTY

OCHOCO NATIONAL FOREST

CROOK COUNTY

DESCHUTES COUNTY

OREGON

0 2.5 5 7.5 10 miles 1 in. = 7.5 mi.

—N—

SEE 128 MAP

A | B | B | C

SPRAY

MONUMENT

19 | 207 | 19 | 207 | 19

CURRANT PEAK | SHEEP MOUNTAIN | CORRAL MOUNTAIN | ALDER MOUNTAIN | HARPER MOUNTAIN | MASIKER MOUNTAIN | LITTLE TAMARACK MOUNTAIN | UMATILLA NATIONAL FOREST | FRANKLIN MOUNTAIN

WASCO CO | JENNIES PEAK | SUGARLOAF MOUNTAIN | CROSS WHITE CREEK | HEIDTMANN MOUNTAIN | THORN SPRING BUTTE | RAINS CANYON | CREEK | JACK OF CLUBS

JEFFERSON CO | DRY HOLLOW RD | ROWE | KENTUCKY BUTTE | ABLE MOUNTAIN | SERVICE | SENTINEL PEAK | KIMBERLY-LONG | JOHNSON | PORTUGESE CANYON

WAGNER MOUNTAIN | COYOTE MOUNTAIN | RED ROCK | SQUAW BUTTE | KEYS MOUNTAIN | BUTLER MOUNTAIN | CHINA HAT PEAK | KIMBERLY | FRANKS

DOMOGALLA RIDGE | SAND SPRING BUTTE | CAMEL HUMP | RICHMOND | MOUNT MISERY | GRANT COUNTY

ROSS BUTTE | BRIDGE | JOHN | DAY | HWY | TWICKENHAM | HORSE MOUNTAIN | CREEK-MITCHELL | IRON MOUNTAIN | STEAMBOAT MOUNTAIN | CHINA PEAK

GOSNER RD | BLACK ROCK | RED GAP | PACKSADDLE MOUNTAIN | SISSMOTER | R

HORSE HEAVEN MOUNTAIN | SANDROCK MOUNTAIN | LOCKWOOD CANYON | SUTTON MOUNTAIN | SCOTT BUTTE | BIG BASIN | SUGARLOAF MOUNTAIN | RUDIO MOUNTAIN

HOLE IN WALL ROCK | JOHN DAY FOSSIL BEDS NATIONAL MONUMENT PAINTED HILLS UNIT | TONEY BUTTE | BALDY | MIDDLE MOUNTAIN | 19 | TIMBER BASIN

TOMPKINS PASS | WHEELER | COUNTY | WATERMAN | JOHN DAY FOSSIL BEDS NATIONAL MONUMENT

JEFFERSON COUNTY | SHEEP MOUNTAIN | SAND MOUNTAIN | SARGENT BUTTE | FLOCK MOUNTAIN | JUNIPER BUTTE | PICTURE GORGE

RED ROCK PASS | HUDSPETH MILL | PEGGY BUTTE | KEYES MOUNTAIN

STEPHENSON MOUNTAIN | LAWSON MOUNTAIN | MARSHALL BUTTE | MITCHELL | PARRISH | TABLE ROCK | 26

JEFFERSON CO | BAILEY BUTTE | MITCHELL | OCHOCO | MOUNTAIN | TABLE MOUNTAIN | FRANKS | 26

CROOK CO | BEAR CREEK | BLACK BUTTE | BAILEY BUTTE | DOLLARHIDE RD | HWY | DAYVILLE

GILCHRIST BUTTE | DOVE MOUNTAIN | WHITE BUTTE | JUNIPER BUTTE | COTTONWOOD BASIN | JOHN DAY RIVER

COUGAR BUTTE | OCHOCO | LEWIS BUTTE | RICHARD BUTTE | MOUNT PISGAH | PINE HOLLOW | McNULTY BASIN | VANATA BASIN

OCHOCO AGATE BEDS | R | OCHOCO DIVIDE CAMPGROUND | OLD KELLY MILL | BRIDGE CREEK | CARROL CAMPGROUND | PETERSON POINT | BARNHOUSE CAMPGROUND | ANTONE | DEAD PINE | LITTLE ALDRICH MOUNTAIN

MILL CREEK | F | HWY | OCHOCO DIVIDE RESEARCH AREA CAMPGROUND | WILDWOOD CAMPGROUND | SUMMIT | WILDERNESS | OCHOCO | BADGER | BUCK | SUMMIT | SPANISH PEAK | WINDY POINT | BATTLE CREEK MOUNTAIN | ALDRICH MOUNTAIN

26 | GRANT BUTTE | HAMILTON BUTTE | OCHOCO BUTTE | SLIDE MOUNTAIN | CAMP | SCOTTS CAMPGROUND | NATIONAL | COTTONWOOD CAMPGROUND | BLACK CANYON | PINE TREE CAMPGROUND | MALHEUR NATIONAL FOREST

OCHOCO | HOWARD CREEK | MOUNTAINS | INDIAN BUTTE | LONESOME SPRING CAMPGROUND | WHEELER CO | BEAR SKULL | WILDERNESS | GROUNDHOG KNOLL | JACKASS MOUNTAIN

KOCH BUTTE | WALTON LAKE CAMPGROUND | HOWARD MOUNTAIN | ALLEN CREEK CAMPGROUND | JONES LAVA | CROOK CO | LITTLE SUMMIT CAMPGROUND | WOLF MOUNTAIN

DUNCAN BUTTE | O'NEIL BUTTE | CREEK | BIG SUMMIT PRAIRIE | BLACK MOUNTAIN | TIMOTHY MEADOW | FOREST | MUD SPRING CAMPGROUND

CANYON CREEK CAMPGROUND LOOKOUT MOUNTAIN | ARVID | NELSON | BIG SPRINGS CAMPGROUND | HOLLOW | TAMARACK BUTTE

HAWKINS BUTTE | HOWARD BUTTE | DEEP CREEK CAMPGROUND | BUCK BUTTE | PAULINA | TIMBER MOUNTAIN

SULPHUR SPRING BUTTE | SOUTH POINT | TWIN SPRINGS CAMPGROUND | ROBA BUTTE | BULL | BEAR BUTTE | MALHEUR

SHEEP CREEK BUTTE | NELSON MONUMENT | GRAY | UPPER FALLS | BIG RATTLESNAKE BUTTE | WOLF CREEK CAMPGROUND | SPRING | RAGER | NATIONAL

GEROW BUTTE | LUCKY BUTTE | NELSON | LUTSEY POINT | PINE MOUNTAIN | RUBY BUTTE | MINNEFIE RIDGE | SUGAR CREEK CAMPGROUND RATTLESNAKE BUTTE | POWELL VALLEY RANCH | FRAZIER CAMPGROUND | COUGAR MOUNTAIN

ARVID | PRAIRIE HILL | CABIN BUTTE | JUNIPER BUTTE | FAULKNER BUTTE | MILLS BUTTE | DAHLGREN RIM | POWELL MOUNTAIN | SPUR BUTTE

POLLARD BUTTE | KELLY GAP | JUNIPER CANYON | 4295 | LOWER FALLS | ISADORE BUTTE | BEAVER | PUITT | NORTH | FORK | BIG BALDY | ELLINGSON MILL

JOE BUTTE | POST | TEATERS RD | ROUGH CANYON | RABBIT VALLEY | HIDEBOUND BUTTE | BEAVER | SALEM RIDGE | MUD SPRING BUTTE | FRENCHY BUTTE

PAULINA | 380 | NORTH | FORK | CROOKED | CROOK | COUNTY | X X RIDGE | PAULINA | DORSCHEL BUTTE | ALLYN DRAW | SHELEE BUTTE | LITTLE BALDY

NEWSOME CREEK | HWY | POLK BUTTE | RIVER | HWY | PAULINA | PAULINA | SODA TABLE | SUGARLOAF MOUNTAIN | MORGAN MOUNTAIN

SHERWOOD | WEST SHOTGUN SPRING | MILK BUTTE | RYEGRASS TABLE | FORBES BUTTE | GREEN MOUNTAIN | HARRISON MOUNTAIN

MULE DEER RIDGE | EAST SHOTGUN SPRING | TOWER POINT | MAUPIN BUTTE | ANGELL BUTTE | SUPLEE | SMITH BASIN | SUPLEE | BUSH RANCH | PITT BUTTE

PINE CREEK CAMPGROUND | DRAKE BUTTE | WILEY FLAT CAMPGROUND | HAWK RIM | COLPITTS BUTTE | WEBERG | WINDY RIDGE | SHEEP CREEK BUTTE

KLOOCHMAN CREEK | MAURY | OCHOCO NATIONAL MOUNTAINS FOREST | ARROWWOOD POINT | HOMESTEAD BUTTE | YREKA RIM | WADE BUTTE | IRON MOUNTAIN | SUPLEE HOT SPRING | MALHEUR NATIONAL FOREST

OREGON | TWELVEMILE TABLE | GREAT SANDY DESERT | COFFEE BUTTE | DUCK RIDGE | LITTLE MOWICH MOUNTAIN

ROBERTS | BEAR | CREEK | CAMP | FORK | ORR POINT | GRINDSTONE | TURPIN CANYON | GRANT CO | HARNEY CO | BIG MOWICH MOUNTAIN | UTLEY BUTTE

BEAR | LOGAN BUTTE | STEENS RIDGE | BEAR | SPECKLE BUTTE | THREE BUTTES | HARNEY CO | HOWARD VALLEY | EMIGRANT

CREEK-FIFE | SMOKY BUTTE | SAND HOLLOW | MOON MOUNTAIN | WALKER RIDGE | WHISTLE | CREEK | DELINTMENT LAKE | EMIGRANT CREEK

PRINGLE FLAT | CAMP | FORK | TWELVEMILE | PRICE-TWELVEMILE | MAGPIE BUTTE | OCHOCO | CORRAL RIDGE | DONELLY BUTTE | BEAR CANYON BUTTE

MERRILL | MONTGOMERY RD | DESCHUTES CO | CROOK CO | SOUTH | FORK | SHERMAN RIM | SADDLE BUTTE | HARNEY CO | NATIONAL FOREST | HOWARD RIDGE | HARNEY COUNTY

GRASSY BUTTE | GERRY MOUNTAIN | ANN BUTTE | WILLOW BUTTE | FREEZEOUT RIDGE

KID PEAK | IBEX BUTTE | BRADFORD RIDGE

SEE 144 MAP

SEE 135 MAP

SEE 137 MAP

HWY 135 | HWY 137

0 2.5 5 7.5 10 miles 1 in. = 7.5 mi.

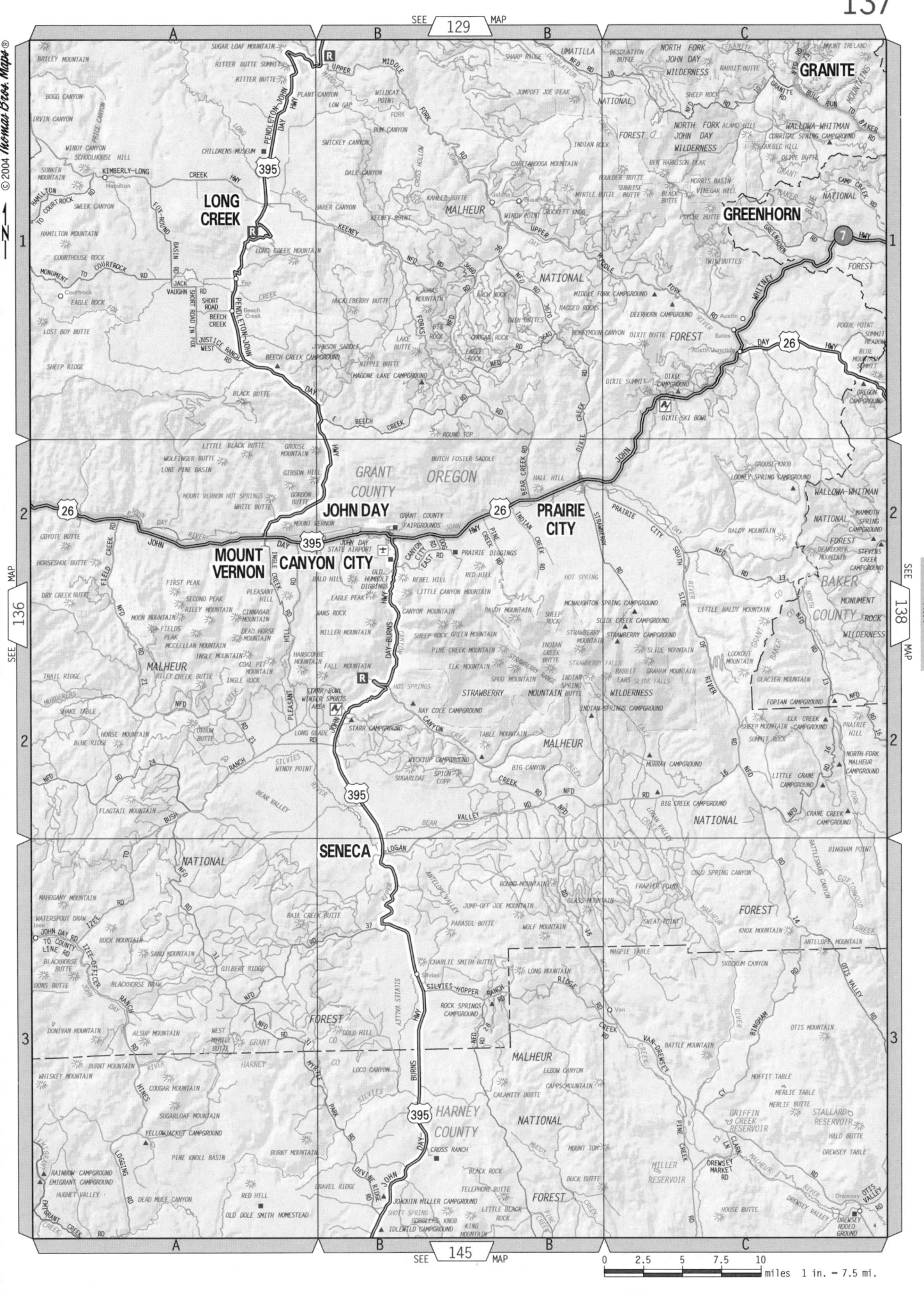

0 2.5 5 7.5 10
miles 1 in. = 7.5 mi.

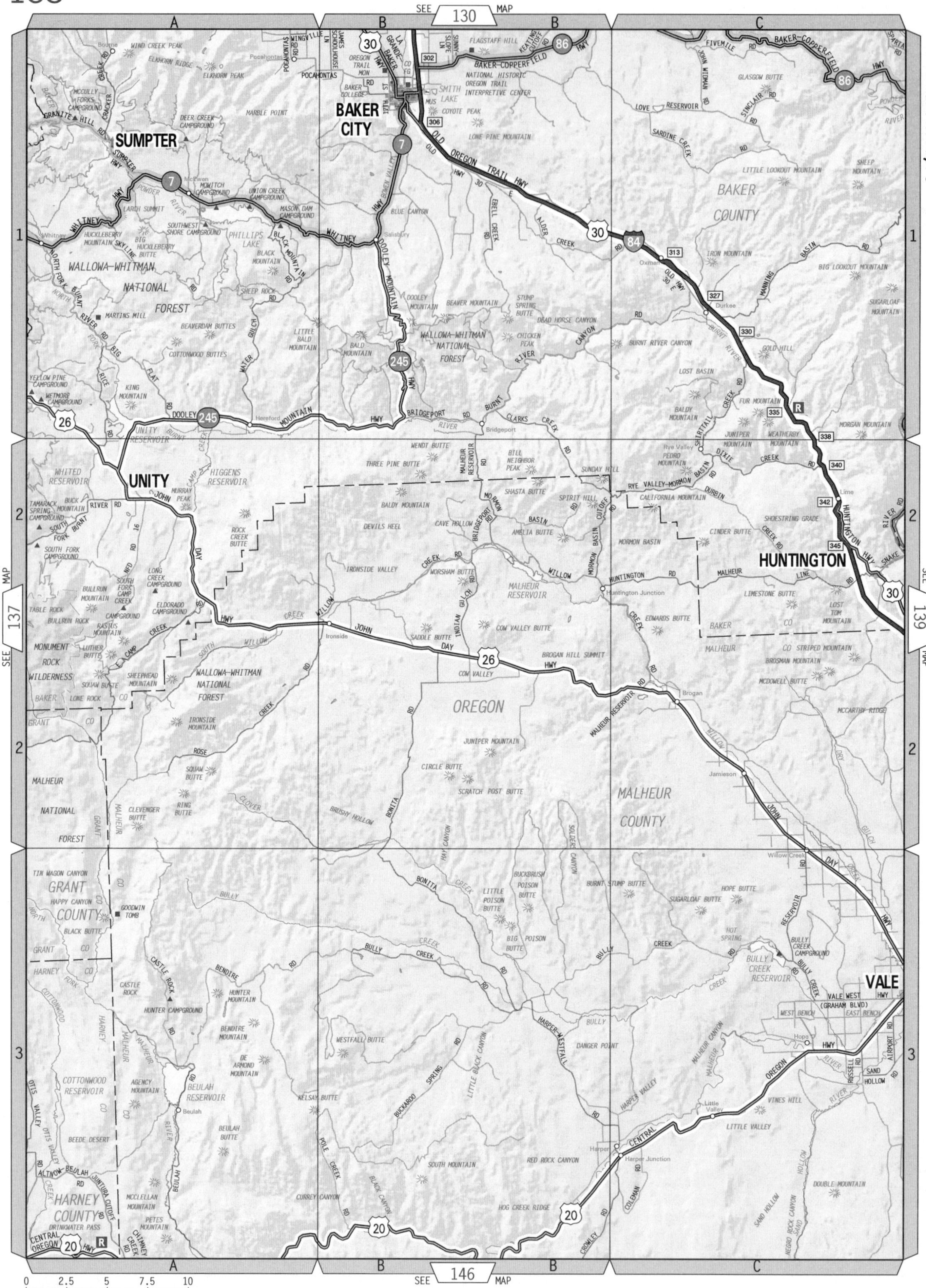

© 2004 Thomas Bros. Maps ® ←N→

SEE 130 MAP

BAKER CITY

SUMPTER

A   B   B   C

SEE 137 MAP HWY

UNITY

HUNTINGTON

VALE

WALLOWA-WHITMAN NATIONAL FOREST

BAKER COUNTY

OREGON

MALHEUR COUNTY

GRANT COUNTY

HARNEY COUNTY

MALHEUR NATIONAL FOREST

MONUMENT ROCK WILDERNESS

SEE 139 MAP

SEE 146 MAP

0 2.5 5 7.5 10 miles 1 in. = 7.5 mi.

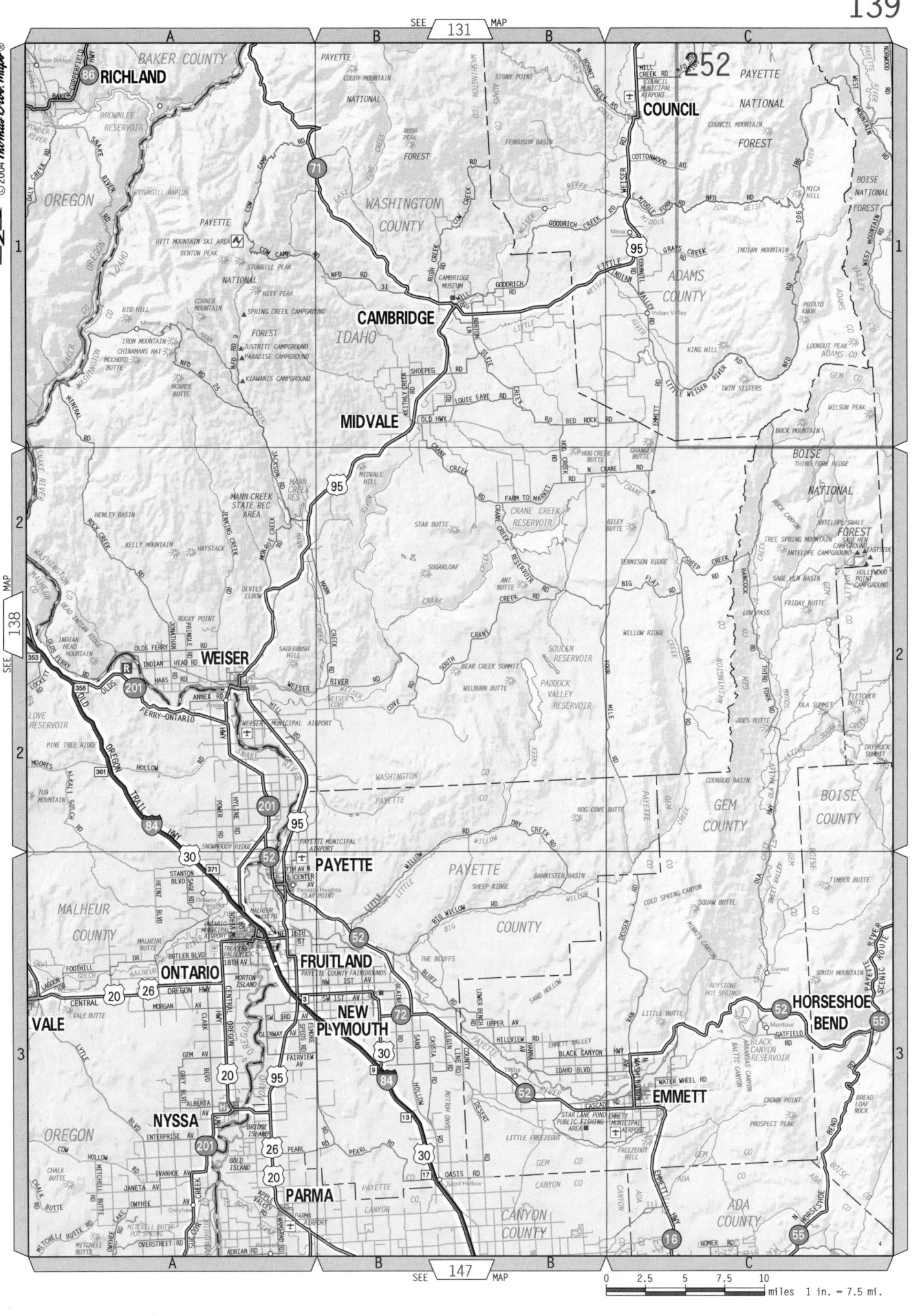

SEE 132 MAP

218

—N—

A | B | B | C

REEDSPORT

101

OREGON DUNES NATIONAL RECREATION AREA

Winchester Bay

East Gardiner

SIUSLAW NATIONAL FOREST

UMPQUA HWY

38

Scottsburg

1

LAKESIDE

OREGON DUNES NATIONAL RECREATION AREA

CLEAR LAKE

SCHOFIELD RD

NORTH LAKE RD

ELLIOTT

STATE

FOREST

DOUGLAS COUNTY

TEN MILE LAKE

LANDING RD

SHUTTERS

Saunders Lake

Hauser

Shorewood

North Bay Dr

OCEAN

DEAR MOUNTAIN

CAMP CREEK RD

LOON LAKE RD

STULLS FALLS

SILVER FALLS

GOLDEN & SILVER FALLS STATE PARK

GOLDEN FALLS

EAST FORK MILLICOMA RIVER

333

NORTH BEND

Glasgow

Coosten

COOS

TAYLOR BUTTE

Allegany

McKEEVER MOUNTAIN

COOS RIDGE

220

COOS BAY

CAPE ARAGO

Charleston

Englewood

Bunker Hill

Bay Park

McCom...

Millington Cleo

LIBBY DR

EAST BAY DR

COOS RIVER RD

COOS RIVER FISH HATCHERY

Delkwood

COOS RIVER

SOUTH FORK COOS RIVER RD

2

Crown Point

SEVEN DEVILS RD

CAPE ARAGO HWY

SOUTH SLOUGH NATIONAL ESTUARY

COOS BAY HWY

CATCHING SLOUGH RD

SUMNER RD

Sumner

SUMNER-FAIRVIEW RD

COQUILLE-FAIRVIEW RD

LAVERNE PARK NORTH FORK RD

NORTH FORK COQUILLE RIVER

OREGON

COOS MOUNTAIN

LAVERNE FALLS

MIDDLE CREEK RD

BURNT RIDGE

MOUNTAIN ACCESS RD

BURNT MOUNTAIN ACCESS RD

101

42

Green Acres

Overland

Coaledo

AGATE BEACH

SEVEN DEVILS RD

BEAVER HILL RD

OREGON COAST HWY

N BANK RD

N BANK RD

Chrome

Cedar Point

COQUILLE-FAIRVIEW RD

Fairview

FAIRVIEW-McKINLEY RD

MIDDLE CREEK FALLS

McKinley

McKINLEY RD

POINT-SITKUM RD

Dora

BREWSTER CANYON

BREWSTER ROCK

MARIA C JACKSON STATE PARK

LOST CREEK FALLS

SITKUM-COUNTY LINE RD

Sitkum

COQUILLE RIVER

BREWSTER VALLEY

BULLARDS BEACH STATE PARK

PACIFIC

N BANK RD

Prosper

Parkersburg

Riverton

SHELLEY RD

RINK PEAK

COQUILLE VALLEY

Johnson

COQUILLE

COQUILLE-BANDON HWY

LEE RD

COOS BAY-ROSEBURG HWY

SHUCK MOUNTAIN

NORWAY

SPLIT MOUNTAIN

42S

BANDON

Winterville

OLD BEACH LOOP RD

N BANK RD

BEAR CREEK RD

ROSA RD

MORRISON RD

MYRTLE POINT TAMPA

Arago

Gravelford

Norway

MYRTLE POINT BRIDGE RD

CAMAS RD

MYRTLE POINT

COOS COUNTY

SCOTT MOUNTAIN

BANDON STATE PARK

Twomile

TWOMILE RANGE

Laurel Grove

Fourmile

MYRTLE POINT

COOS COUNTY FAIRGROUNDS

MYRTLE POINT

COOS

WEST SIDE RD

ANDERSON MOUNTAIN

THOMAS MOUNTAIN

224

NEW RIVER PARK

NORTH FOURMILE RD

CATCHING CREEK RD

SCHNEIDER BUTTE

Broadbent

ROBBINS BUTTE

SAMISON MOUNTAIN

Bridge

COOS BAY-ROSEBURG HWY

SANDY CREEK RD

KENYON MOUNTAIN

42

COOS BAY-ROSEBURG

DOUGLAS COUNTY

3

BUZZARD BUTTE

COAST RD

COTTON BUTTE

BENNETT BUTTE

WHITNEY RD

Warner

WHIDBEY MOUNTAIN

POWERS RD

SOUTH RD

Gaylord

MYRTLE CREEK

ROCK CREEK RD

MYRTLEWOOD CAMPGROUND

ELBOW POINT

Remote

BEAR CREEK CAMPGROUND

ROUND TOP

WATCHES BUTTE

FLORAS CREEK

COOS CO CURRY CO

Bancroft

PYRAMID ROCK

BEN GRANT RIDGE

BONE MOUNTAIN

Langlois

LANGLOIS

FLORAS LAKE RD

FLORAS

Denmark

WHITE MOUNTAIN

CALF RANCH MOUNTAIN

HOOD MOUNTAIN

SUICIDE ROCK

FLORAS LAKE

SUMMIT MOUNTAIN

EIGHTMILE PRAIRIE MOUNTAIN

CURRY COUNTY

BINGHAM MOUNTAIN

POWERS

SISKIYOU NATIONAL FOREST

MOODBY MOUNTAIN

EDEN VALLEY

GOLD MOUNTAIN

101

AIRPORT RD

CAPE BLANCO STATE PARK

CAPE BLANCO HWY

Sixes

SIXES RIVER

COUNTY LINE CANYON

SUGARLOAF MOUNTAIN

POWERS STATE AIRPORT

BOUNDARY CAMPGROUND

SAND ROCK MOUNTAIN

ELK CREEK FALLS

ELK FALLS CREEK

ELK CREEK

COAL CREEK CAMPGROUND

BIG TREE CAMPGROUND

PIONEER CAMPGROUND

EDEN VALLEY CAMPGROUND

DIAMOND PEAK

BLM RD 32

EDEN VALLEY

SADDLE PEAKS

CURRY COUNTY

DOUGLAS CO

ELK WALLOWS

MOON MOUNTAIN

JOHNSON MOUNTAIN

CHINA FLAT CAMPGROUND

SOUTH RD

MYRTLE GROVE CAMPGROUND

EDEN RIDGE

WILD ROGUE WILDERNESS

KELSEY PEAK

GRASSY KNOB

CHINA PEAK

RUSTY BUTTE

ANVIL MOUNTAIN WILDERNESS

BRAY RIDGE

BARKLOW MOUNTAIN CAMPGROUND

DAPHNE GROVE CAMPGROUND

NATIONAL FOREST

SQUAW LAKE CAMPGROUND

FORT LAMERICK

Marial

PORT ORFORD

OREGON COAST HWY

HUMBUG MOUNTAIN STATE PARK

PEARSE PEAK

OAK RIDGE

FATHER MOUNTAIN

MILBURY MOUNTAIN

IRON MOUNTAIN

ELK RIVER RD

COQUILLE RIVER FALLS

ROCK CREEK CAMPGROUND

BALD KNOB

CLAY HILL

ROGUE RIVER

CURRY CO JOSEPHINE CO

A | B | B | C

SEE 148 MAP

HWY

SEE 141 MAP

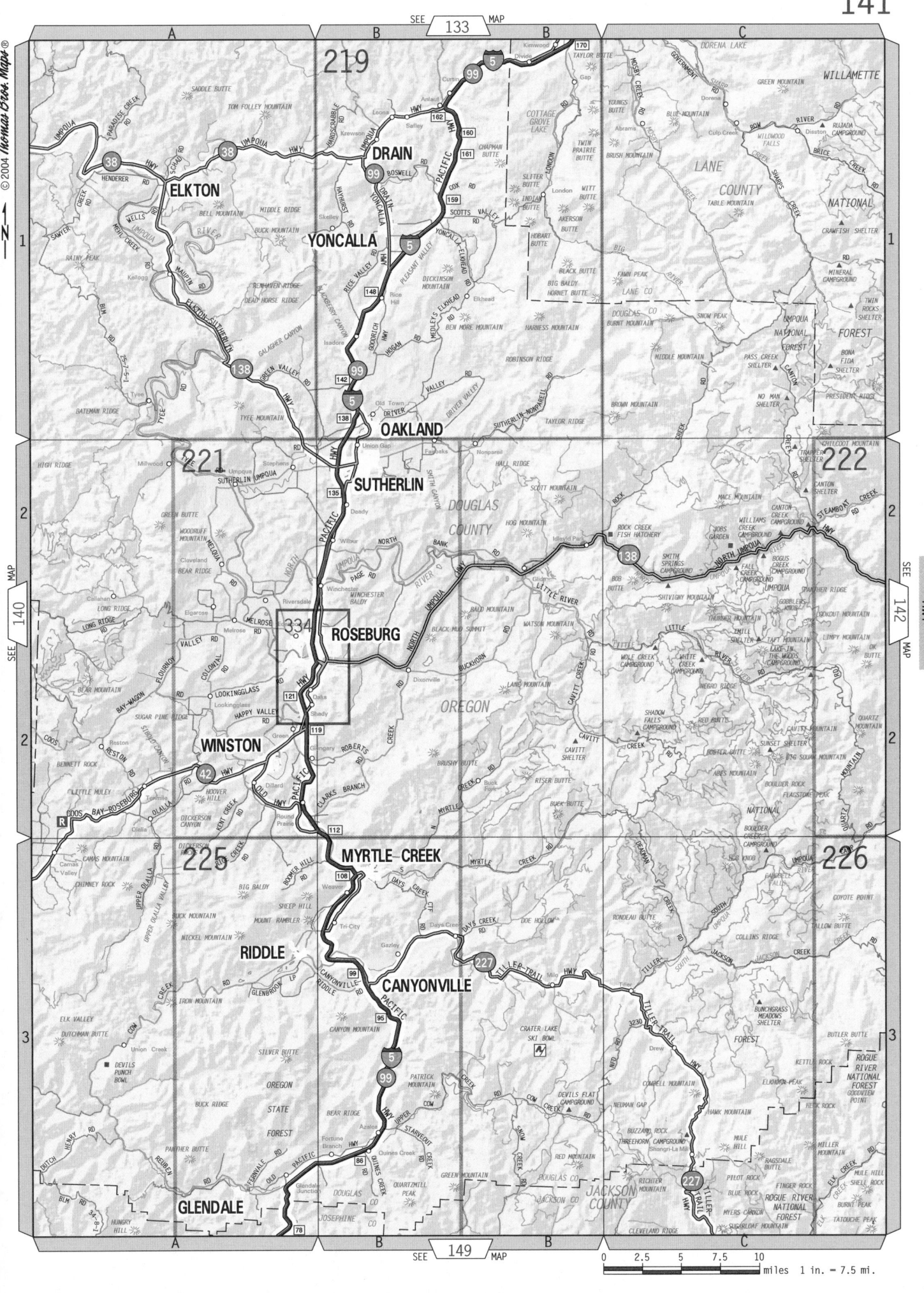

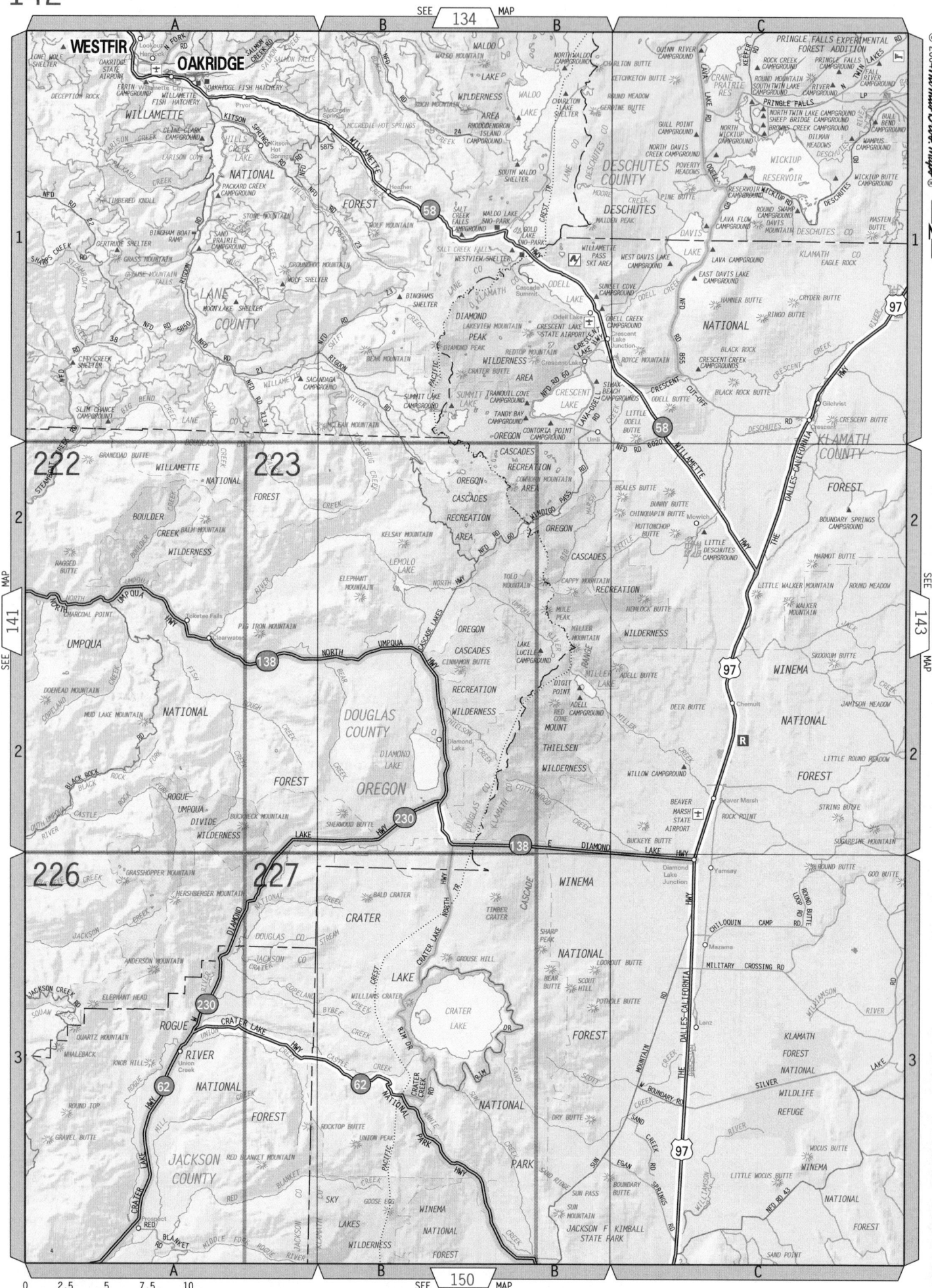

SEE 134 MAP

SEE 141 MAP

SEE 143 MAP

SEE 150 MAP

miles 1 in. = 7.5 mi.

SEE 135 MAP

© 2004 Thomas Bros. Maps®

A | B | B | C

Grid Row 1:

FALL RIVER, LA PINE STATE REC AREA
LA PINE STATE PARK
Three Rivers
DESCHUTES RIVER
HWY 97
PRINGLE FALLS L.P.
DORRANCE MEADOW
BURGESS RD
HUNTINGTON RD
SHAY RD
6TH ST
FINLEY BUTTE RD
La Pine
THE DALLES-CALIFORNIA HWY
PHERVIEW
OGDEN GROUP CAMPGROUND
NORTH COVE CAMPGROUND
PRAIRIE CAMPGROUND
PAULINA-EAST LAKE
PAULINA CREEK CAMPGROUND
ROSLAND CAMPGROUND
SIX MILE SNOWPARK
TEN MILE SNOWPARK
PAULINA LAKE CAMPGROUND
NEWBERRY GROUP CAMPGROUND
PAULINA CAMPGROUND
DEVILS HORN
PAULINA MOUNTAINS
SURVEYORS ICE CAVE
FINLEY BUTTE
SAND FLAT ICE CAVE RD
DESCHUTES CO
KLAMATH CO

LAVA CAST FOREST
NEWBERRY NATIONAL VOLCANIC MONUMENT
KAWAK BUTTE
WARM SPRINGS CAMPGROUND
EAST LAKE
EAST LAKE CAMPGROUND
LITTLE CRATER CAMPGROUND
CHIEF PAULINA MOUNTAIN
NEWBERRY CRATER FR
CHIEF SAND BUTTE
WEASEL BUTTE
TOPSO BUTTE
BOX BUTTE
PILPIL BUTTE
LOMILLO BUTTE
COMPANY BUTTE
CINDER HILL
CINDER HILL CAMPGROUND
HOT SPRINGS CAMPGROUND
GROUND HOG BUTTE
CHINA HAT
CHINA HAT CAMPGROUND
KELLY BUTTE
ROGERS BUTTE
CHINA HILL RD
CINDER HILL RD
SAND SPRINGS
HAT RD
PINE MOUNTAIN OBSERVATORY
PINE RIDGE
PINE RIDGE
HWY 20
DESCHUTES COUNTY
FIRESTONE BASIN
MAHOGANY BUTTE
SAND SPRING CAMPGROUND
LAVACICLE CAVE
ANTELOPE BUTTE
WHISKEY ROCK
QUARTZ MOUNTAIN
WATKINS BUTTE
SOLDIERS CAP
DOG BUTTE
DESCHUTES CO
LAKE CO

Grid Row 2:

HWY 31
FREMONT
IPSOOT BUTTE
SPRING BUTTE
MOFFITT BUTTE
HOOLIGAN HILL
YOUTLKUT BUTTE
GREEN BUTTE
INDIAN BUTTE
NFD RD 22
NFD RD 24
NATIONAL FOREST
POLY TOP BUTTE
WIGTOP BUTTE
SQUAW MOUNTAIN
DERRICK CAVE
HOGBACK BUTTE
TWIN BUTTES
CABIN LAKE CAMPGROUND
QUARTER BUTTE
DEVILS HOLE
TRAIL BUTTE
MILLICAN RD
BUTTE RD

KLAMATH COUNTY
FREMONT
BIG HOLE
MOWICH SPRING BUTTE
STANS MOUNTAIN
CORRAL BUTTE
LOOKOUT POINT
PUMICE BUTTE
SPROATS MEADOW
PARKER BUTTE
WINEMA
STIMSON MEADOW
PARKER MEADOW
TEA TABLE MOUNTAIN
DAVIS FLAT
HIDDEN MEADOW
NATIONAL
BEAR FLAT DRAW
SAGEBRUSH DRAW
BEAR WALLOW
LOCATION BUTTE
ANTELOPE MOUNTAIN
ROCK BUTTE
BEAR FLAT
BEAR BUTTE
MCCARTY MEADOW
WICKIUP BUTTE
MCCARTHY BUTTE
TIMBER BUTTE
BALD MOUNTAIN
WART PEAK
TIMOTHY BUTTE
NFD RD 2516
NFD RD
FORT ROCK CAVE
FORT ROCK STATE MONUMENT
Fort Rock
FORT ROCK
CABIN LAKE RD
CAVES RD
DERRICK RD
FORT ROCK RD
FORT ROCK VALLEY
SPIKE BUTTE
COYOTE BUTTE
CONNLEY HILLS
TUFF BUTTE
PICTURE RD
SILVER LAKE
COUGAR MOUNTAIN
TABLE MOUNTAIN
GREEN MOUNTAIN
EAST GREEN MOUNTAIN
SOUTH GREEN MOUNTAIN
FRAZEE-FREDERICK RD
ICE CAVE
VALLEY-WAGONTIRE RD
CHRISTMAS VALLEY-WAGONTIRE
Christmas Valley
CHRISTMAS VALLEY RD
TABLE ROCK
OLD LAKE RD
LAKE RD
SINK RD
LAKE COUNTY
SAINT PATRICK MOUNTAIN
CHRISTMAS
OREGON

Grid Row 3:

FOREST
DOESKIN BUTTE
BUCKSKIN BUTTE
FIRE BUTTE
DILLON BUTTE
LITTLE YAMSAY MOUNTAIN
SILVER LAKE RD
JACKSON CREEK CAMPGROUND
BLOODY POINT
WILLIAMSON RIVER
BUCK RIDGE
JACKSON RIDGE
YAMSAY MOUNTAIN
WILDHORSE RIDGE
WILLIAMSON RIDGE
NFD RD 49
WINEMA NATIONAL FOREST
WILLIAMSON RIVER RD
HAYSTACK DRAW
HAMBLETON BUTTE
KLAMATH CO
LAKE CO
RODMAN ROCK
MCCARTY BUTTE
BRIDGE CREEK
SILVER CREEK
WEST FORK SILVER CREEK
SILVER CREEK MARSH CAMPGROUND
MAHOGANY MOUNTAIN
HAGER MOUNTAIN
PARTIN BUTTE
ROUND BUTTE
THOMPSON RESERVOIR CAMPGROUND
THOMPSON RESERVOIR
DEER HEAD
FREMONT NATIONAL FOREST
SYCAN MARSH
LONG CREEK
SYCAN RIVER
NFD RD 2988
NFD RD 3142
NFD RD 2863
DEAD INDIAN MOUNTAIN
SILVER LAKE
WINTER RIDGE
CAMPBELL HILL
HUNTER HILL
SUMMER LAKE
Summer Lake
SUMMER LAKE GAME MANAGEMENT AREA
SQUAW BUTTE
CARLON RD
SHUFFIELD RD
ROCKY BUTTE
JUNIPER CANYON
DIABLO PEAK
FOURMILE POINT
DIABLO MOUNTAINS
FIVEMILE POINT
HWY 31

SEE 142 MAP
SEE 144 MAP
HWY
SEE 151 MAP

0 2.5 5 7.5 10
miles 1 in. = 7.5 mi.

A B B C

CROOK COUNTY

BUCK SPRING CAMPGROUND
CHAPIN TABLE
MINERAL CANYON
DONELLY
OCHOCO
NATIONAL
FOREST
SAWMILL CREEK RD
MCCANLIES
EGYPT CANYON
HAMPTON BUTTE
MACKEY BUTTE
OCHOCO NATIONAL FOREST
EGY PT CANYON
MILLER CANYON
MONTGOMERY RD
VAN LAKE
LIZARD CREEK RD
HARMAN RD
BEAR
BUCK CREEK
CREEK-FIFE RD

20

CENTRAL

CROOK CO
DESCHUTES CO
CROOK CO
HARNEY CO

COYOTE ROCK
HAMPTON STATE AIRPORT
Hampton
DESCHUTES COUNTY
BRONCO BUTTE
FREDERICK BUTTE
SCHRAEDER RD
RANCH RD
DESCHUTES
HARNEY
DRY MOUNTAIN
GIBBONS MILL CANYON
SILVER CREEK VALLEY
GUM BOOT CANYON
ROCK QUARRY CANYON RESERVOIR

CORRAL BUTTE
FREDERICK BUTTE
YREKA BUTTE
DESCHUTES CO
LAKE CO
INDIAN BUTTE
HAT BUTTE
CHICKAHOMINY RESERVOIR
SILVER CREEK
SILVER RD
MILLER RD

1

HWY 20

HARDER BUTTE
GLASS BUTTES
MIDNIGHT POINT
CENTRAL
20 OREGON
SHIELDS BUTTE
Riley
HWY
FRAZEE-FREDERICK
PETERS BUTTE
EAST BUTTE
STUDHORSE BUTTE
BUCK BUTTE
LITTLE GLASS BUTTE
JUNIPER RIDGE
CREEK

WEST BUTTE
BENJAMIN CAVES
ROUND TOP BUTTE
SQUAW BUTTE RANGE EXPERIMENT STATION HQ
SQUAW BUTTE EXPERIMENT STATION
395 HWY

ROCKY DRAW
COYOTE RIM

MOONLIGHT BUTTE
LOST FOREST RESEARCH NATURAL AREA
PILOT BUTTE
TIRED HORSE BUTTE
SHEEP MOUNTAIN
EGLI CANYON
SPRING CANYON
ALEC BUTTE
TURPIN CANYON
RANCH-WAGONTIRE
RD

2

WAGONTIRE MOUNTAIN
BIG STICK
BLACK CANYON
RD
BLIZZARD CREEK

ELK MOUNTAIN
RAMS BUTTE
GAP
Wagontire
LITTLE TANK CANYON
IRON MOUNTAIN
CHRISTMAS
VALLEY RD
GOOSE EGG BUTTE

VALLEY-WAGONTIRE
RD
WAGON DRAW
HAPPY CAMP
WILSON RD

2

LAKE COUNTY
HORSE MOUNTAIN
DRY VALLEY
HORSEHEAD MOUNTAIN
DRY VALLEY HWY
SMOKE OUT CANYON
WILSON BUTTE

LITTLE JUNIPER MOUNTAIN
HWY
DRY VALLEY

HARNEY COUNTY

DOUGHNUT MOUNTAIN
ALKALI LAKE STATE AIRPORT
JUNIPER
DRY VALLEY RIM

OREGON
ALKALI BUTTES
LAKE CO
HARNEY CO
LITTLE
DRY VALLEY
LITTLE VALLEY

LAKEVIEW-BURNS
ROCK CAMP DRAW
OPEN DRAW

Alkali Lake
GRAYS BUTTE
JUNIPER MOUNTAIN
BACON
KIT CANYON
MULE TIT

VENATOR BUTTE
395
BACON CAMP RD
THREE STORY RIM
LITTLE STEAMBOAT POINT
OREJANA CANYON

3

SHARP TOP
TWIN BUTTES
JUG MOUNTAIN
R
FLAT

BISCUIT POINT
NASTY
HORSESHOE RIM
BLACK CAP
MULE SPRING RD

COBURN BUTTE
XL RANCH RD
SHELL ROCK CANYON
HARNEY CO
BLUEJOINT LAKE
BLACK RIM

SAWED HORN
FLINT HILLS

A B B C

0 2.5 5 7.5 10 miles   1 in. = 7.5 mi.

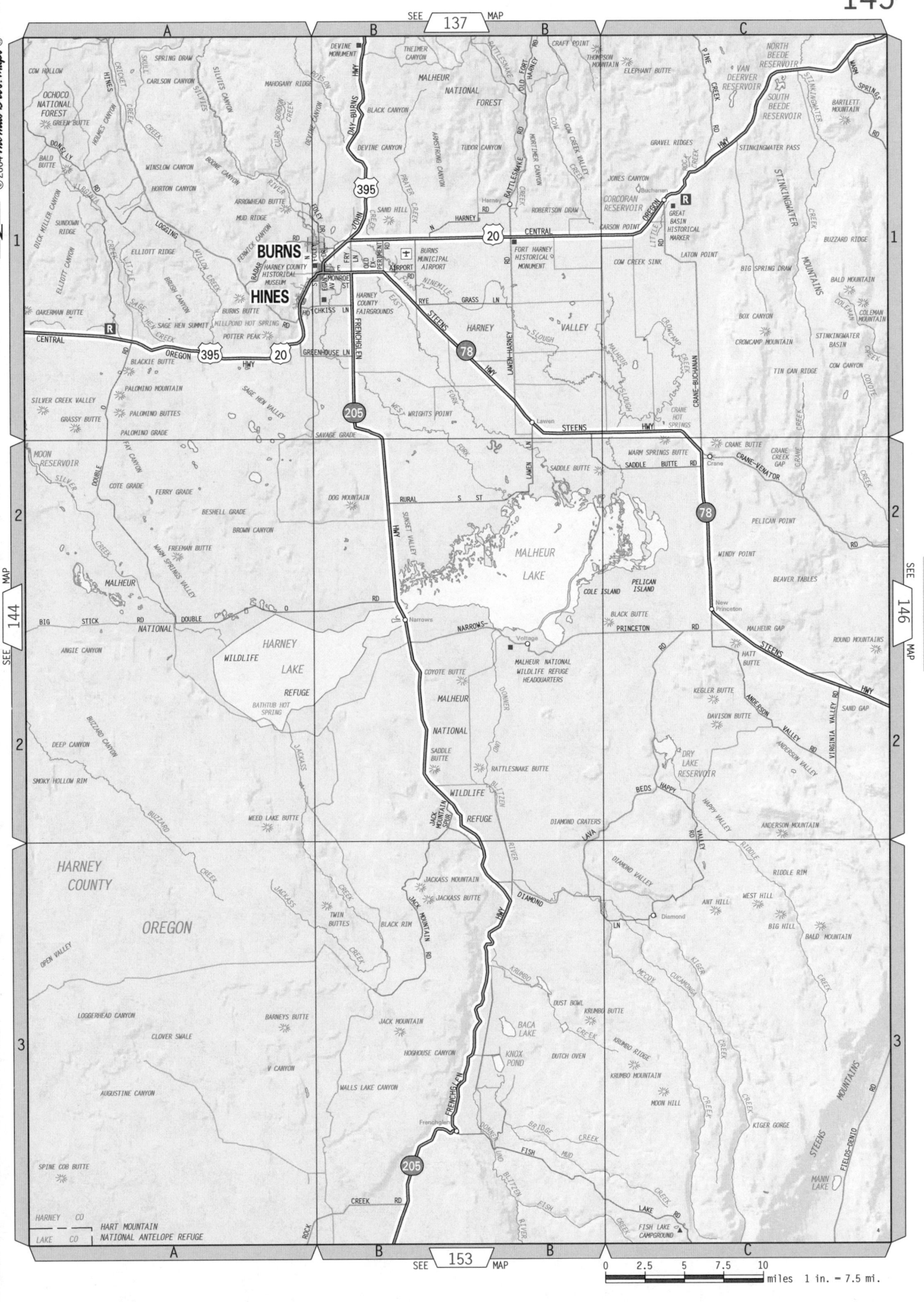

HARNEY COUNTY

MALHEUR COUNTY

OREGON

SEE 145 MAP

SEE 147 MAP

HWY

US 20

HWY 78

US 95

ALTNOW GAP
CAT ROCK
UPTON MOUNTAIN
WARM SPRINGS
RILEY BUTTE
WARM SPRINGS RESERVOIR
TEXACO BASIN
BLACK BUTTE
Juntura
RIVERSIDE
MEEKER MOUNTAIN
TWIN KNOLLS
TABLE TOP
MOSQUITO MOUNTAIN
JUNTURA
RESERVOIR RD
Riverside
GRANITE
COLEMAN
BUCK MOUNTAIN
CRANE CREEK
COYOTE CREEK
LUCE HOT SPRINGS
McEWEN BUTTE
SWAMP
CROWLEY-RIVERSIDE RD
Dunnean
WHISKEY CREEK
VENATOR
SADDLE DRAW
CHINA HILL
Venator
CRANE
HAT BUTTE
BARREN VALLEY
RED MOUNTAIN
MALHEUR CAVE
INDIAN CREEK BUTTE
REEDS BASIN
STEENS HWY
BIG GULCH
DUCK CREEK BUTTE
INDIAN CREEK BUTTES
DOWELL BUTTE
STOCKADE BUTTES
WHITEHORSE MOUNTAIN
STOCKADE MOUNTAIN
SWAMP CREEK BUTTES
STAR MOUNTAIN
TURNBULL MOUNTAIN
MUSTANG BUTTE
WRANGLE BUTTE
SADDLE BUTTE
TURNBULL PEAK
FOLLY FARM
TENCENT LAKE
FIFTEENCENT LAKE
SQUAW FLAT
FIELDS-DENIO
RYEGRASS BUTTE
SMALL BUTTE
IRON
IRON CTO
FARM CTO
SHEEPSHEAD MOUNTAINS
TUDOR LAKE
STONEHOUSE CANYON
COFFIN BUTTE
TABLE MOUNTAIN
MICKEY BASIN
WILDCAT
PALOMINO
RYEGRASS
PALOMINO HILLS
STEENS HWY
SCOTT BUTTE
IRON MOUNTAIN
KIGER
COYOTE TRAP CAVE
MOUNTAIN
TIRE TUBE CAVE
FORTYMILE CAVE
OWYHEE RIVER CAVE
BURNS CAVE
Burns Junction
IDAHO
CLARK CANYON
TIMS PEAK
HUNTER PEAK
JONES BUTTE
MONUMENT PEAK
PRAVA PEAK
HAT TOP
RUFINO BUTTE
RED BUTTE
CUTOFF
SHUMWAY RANCH
MONUMENTAL ROCK
DRY BUTTES
CROWLEY
PIUTE LAKE BED
RINEHART
SACRAMENTO BUTTE
IRON POINT
Skull Spring
COPELAND BUTTE
ANTELOPE FLAT
CEDAR MOUNTAIN
RINEHART RD
RANCH
DRY LAKE
TUB SPRINGS
BOGUS
OWYHEE
ROME STATE AIRPORT
Rome
CREEK STATE HISTORIC MONUMENT
OREGON-NEVADA HWY
NEVADA HWY
HARPER BASIN
SHELL ROCK BUTTE
HOODOO RIDGE
MITCHELL BUTTE
HAYSTACK ROCK
NEGRO ROCK
SOURDOUGH MOUNTAIN
GRASSY MOUNTAIN
FREEZEOUT MOUNTAIN
BURNT MOUNTAIN
NANNYS NIPPLE
DEER BUTTE
BURNT MOUNTAIN
HAMMOND HILL
DRY CREEK BUTTES
IRON MOUNTAIN
SAND HILLS
OWYHEE LAKE
SADDLE BUTTE
OWYHEE RESERVOIR STATE AIRPORT
KNOTTINGHAM BUTTE
MUD
BLACK BUTTE
RED BUTTE
SOUTH TABLE MOUNTAIN
NORTH TABLE MOUNTAIN
ROOSTER COMB
LESLIE GULCH
OWYHEE BREAKS
HOT SPRING
DIAMOND BUTTE
THE TONGUE
MORCOM
DEER BUTTE
JORDAN CRATERS
BLOWOUT RESERVOIR
COFFEEPOT CRATER
BIRCH CREEK
MAHOGANY
BISCUIT BUTTE
CRATER LAKE RD
UPPER COW LAKE
LOWER COW LAKE
CLARKS BUTTE
BOGUS CREEK CAVE
WEST CRATER
LAVA BUTTE
SADDLE BUTTE
THREEMILE HILL
OWYHEE BUTTE
TUCKNESS
OWYHEE AIRSTRIP
LITTLE OWYHEE BUTTE
Arock
GRAHAMS HILL
RATTLESNAKE CAVE
Danner
NEVADA
OREGON
JORDAN CREEK
NEVADA HWY
ROCK CREEK
ROUND MOUNTAIN
ARISTOLA
SKULL
OWYHEE CANYON
LITTLE GRASSY MOUNTAIN
LITTLE GRASSY RESERVOIR
DEAD HORSE BUTTE
INDIAN FORT CREEK
STITZEL RD
BANNER HWY

miles 1 in. = 7.5 mi.

0 2.5 5 7.5 10

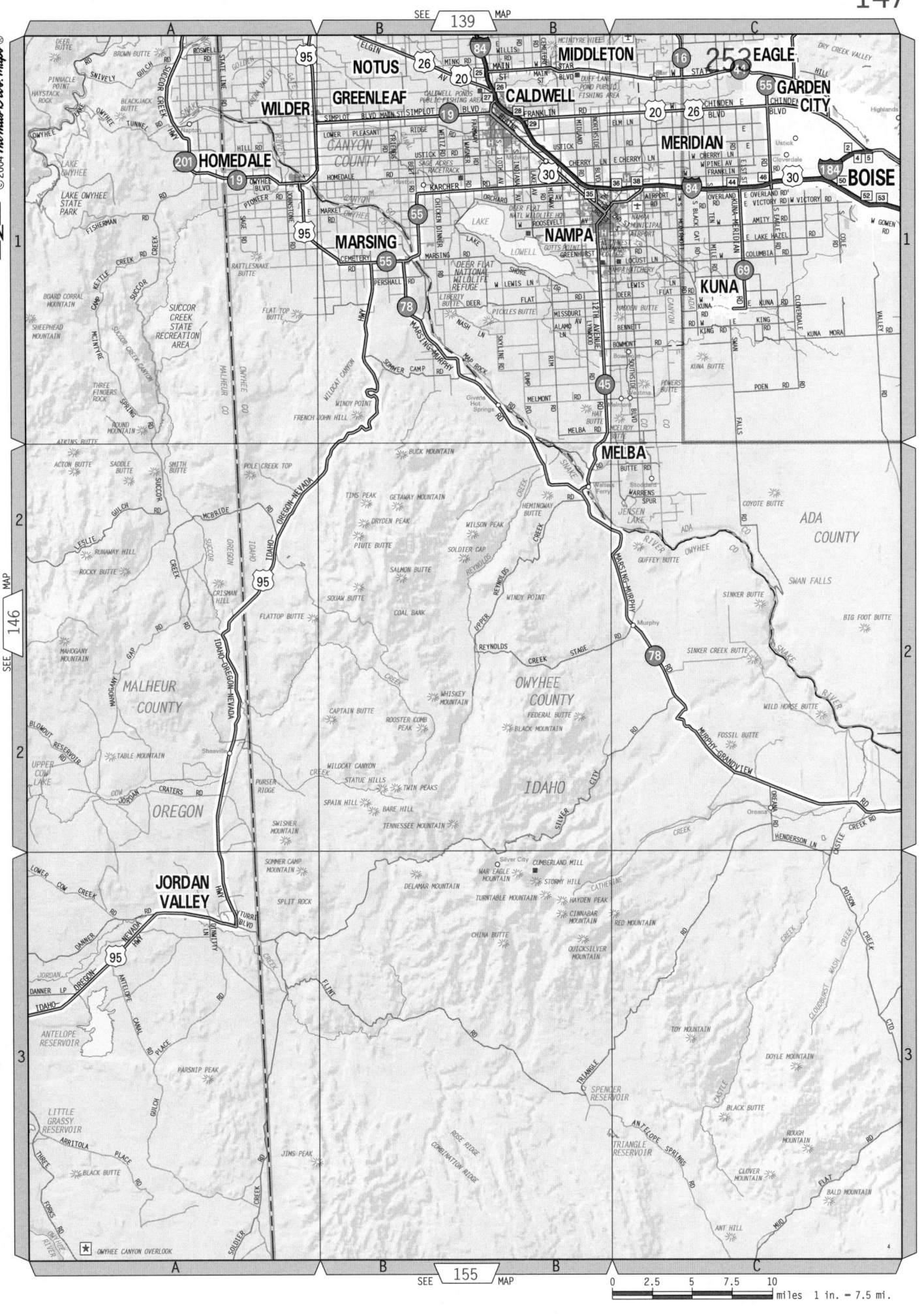

SEE 139 MAP

SEE 146 MAP

SEE 155 MAP

HWY

0 2.5 5 7.5 10
miles 1 in. = 7.5 mi.

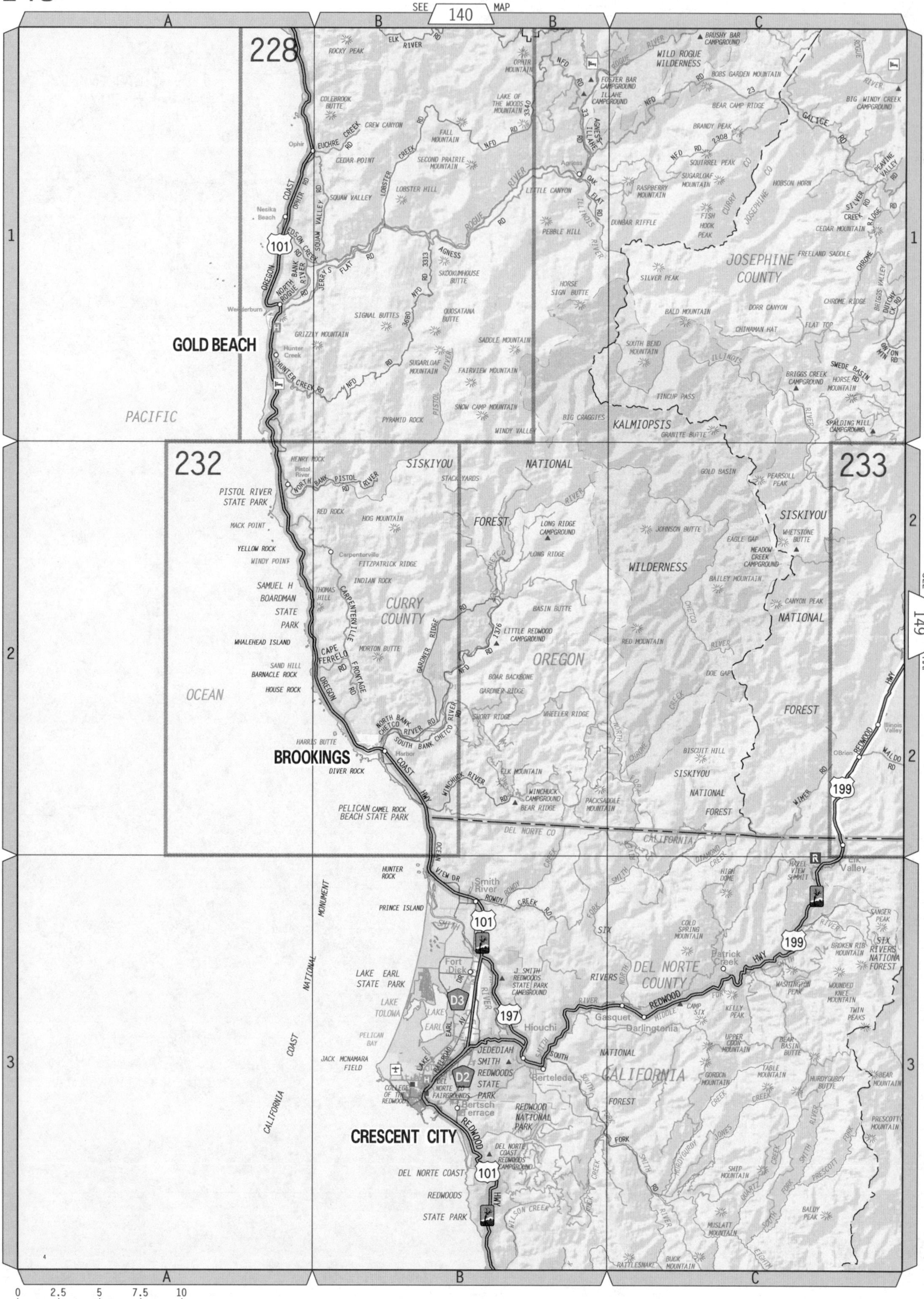

SEE 140 MAP

© 2004 Thomas Bros. Maps ®

—N—

A | B | B | C

228

232

233

GOLD BEACH

BROOKINGS

CRESCENT CITY

PACIFIC

OCEAN

JOSEPHINE COUNTY

CURRY COUNTY

DEL NORTE COUNTY

SISKIYOU NATIONAL FOREST

OREGON

CALIFORNIA

SISKIYOU NATIONAL FOREST

SIX RIVERS NATIONAL FOREST

WILD ROGUE WILDERNESS

KALMIOPSIS WILDERNESS

REDWOOD NATIONAL PARK

JEDEDIAH SMITH REDWOODS STATE PARK

DEL NORTE COAST REDWOODS STATE PARK

PISTOL RIVER STATE PARK

SAMUEL H BOARDMAN STATE PARK

LAKE EARL STATE PARK

DEL NORTE COAST REDWOODS STATE PARK

CALIFORNIA COASTAL NATIONAL MONUMENT

101   197   199

HMY

SEE 149 MAP

0 2.5 5 7.5 10

miles 1 in. = 7.5 mi.

HWY

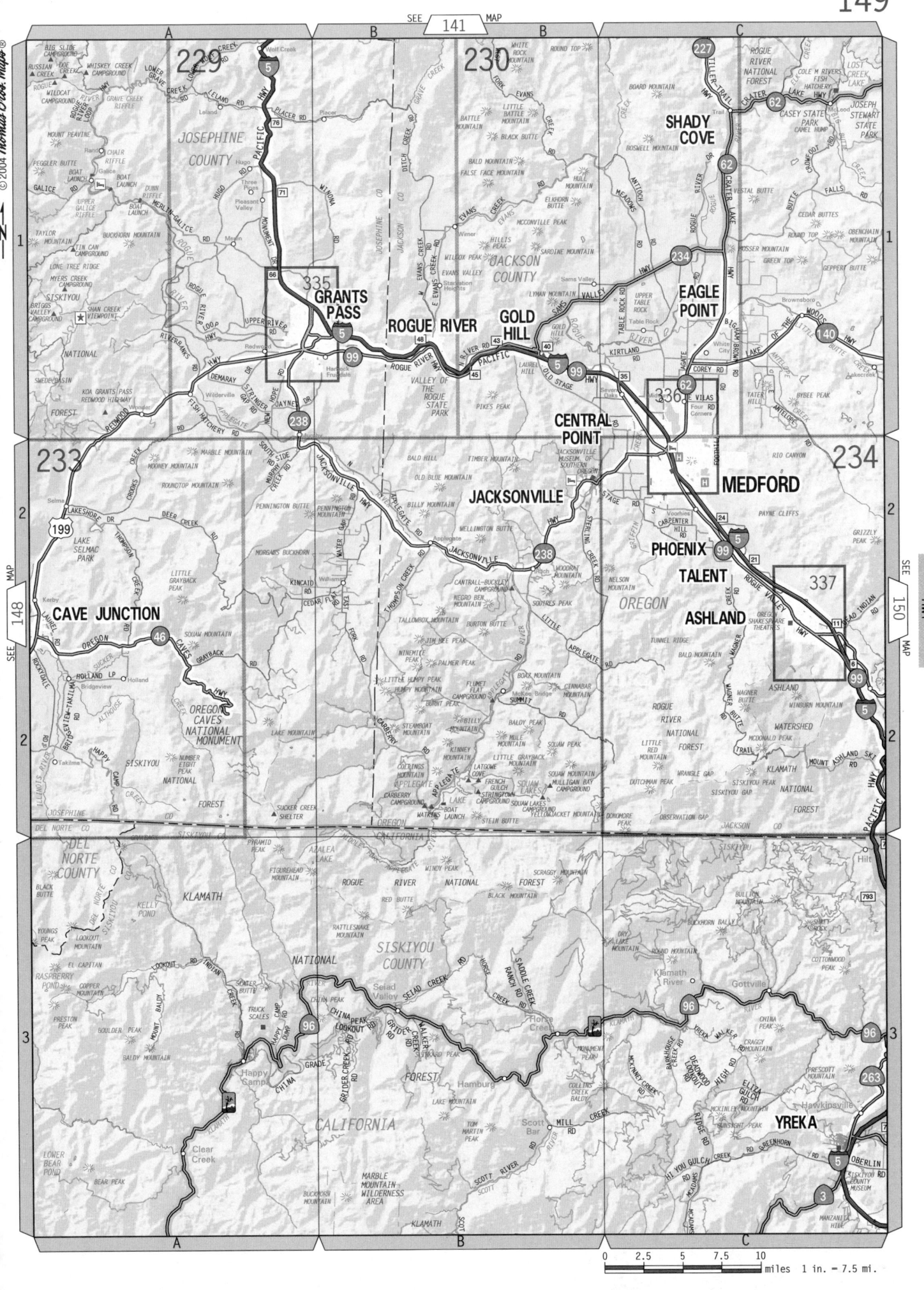

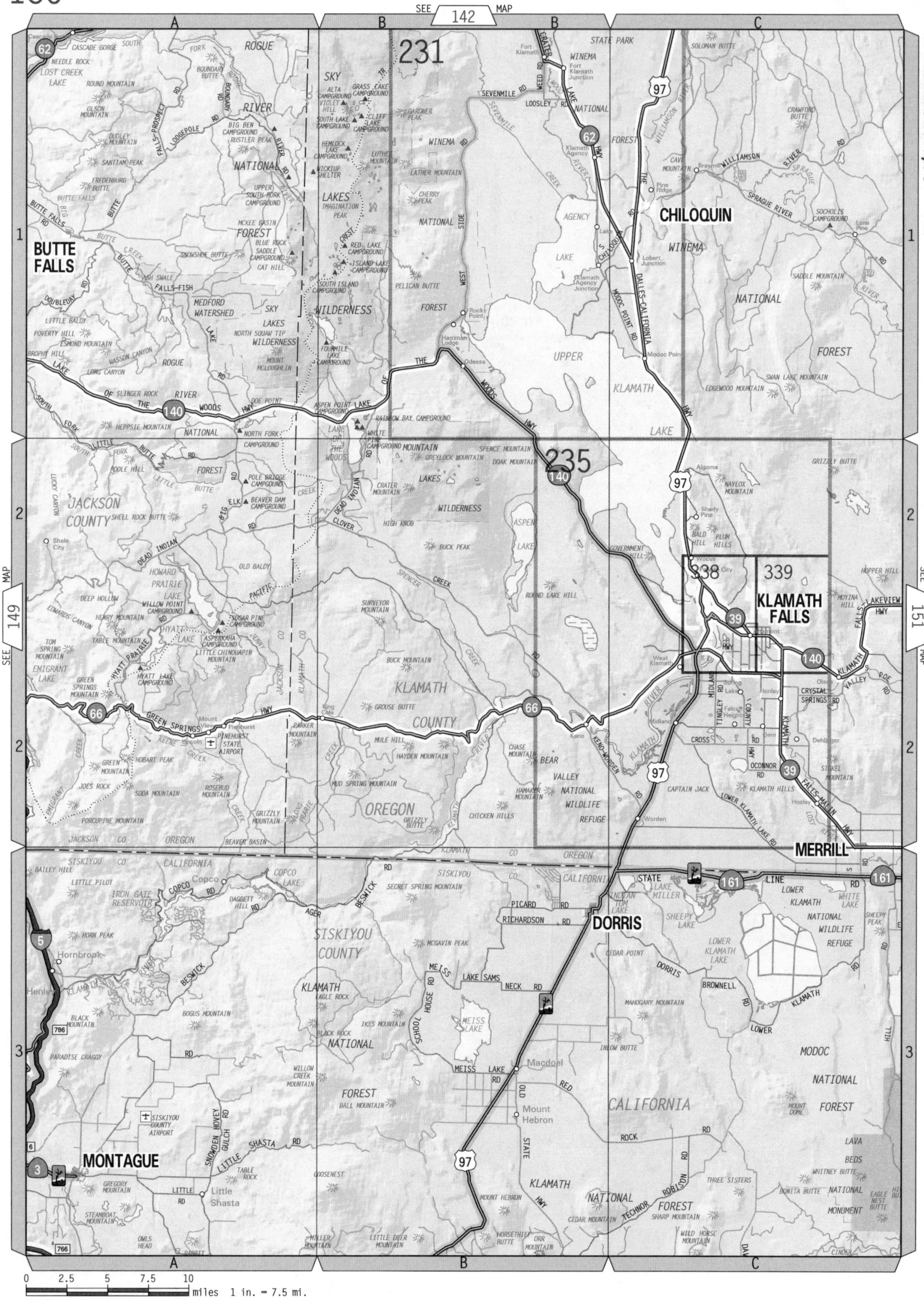

A | B | B | C

231

235

BUTTE FALLS

CHILOQUIN

KLAMATH FALLS

338 | 339

MERRILL

DORRIS

MONTAGUE

ROGUE RIVER NATIONAL FOREST

SKY LAKES WILDERNESS

MEDFORD WATERSHED

JACKSON COUNTY

KLAMATH COUNTY

WINEMA NATIONAL FOREST

UPPER KLAMATH LAKE

OREGON

CALIFORNIA

SISKIYOU COUNTY

KLAMATH NATIONAL FOREST

MODOC NATIONAL FOREST

LOWER KLAMATH NATIONAL WILDLIFE REFUGE

LAVA BEDS NATIONAL MONUMENT

GREEN SPRINGS

0 2.5 5 7.5 10
miles 1 in. = 7.5 mi.

© 2004 Thomas Bros. Maps ®

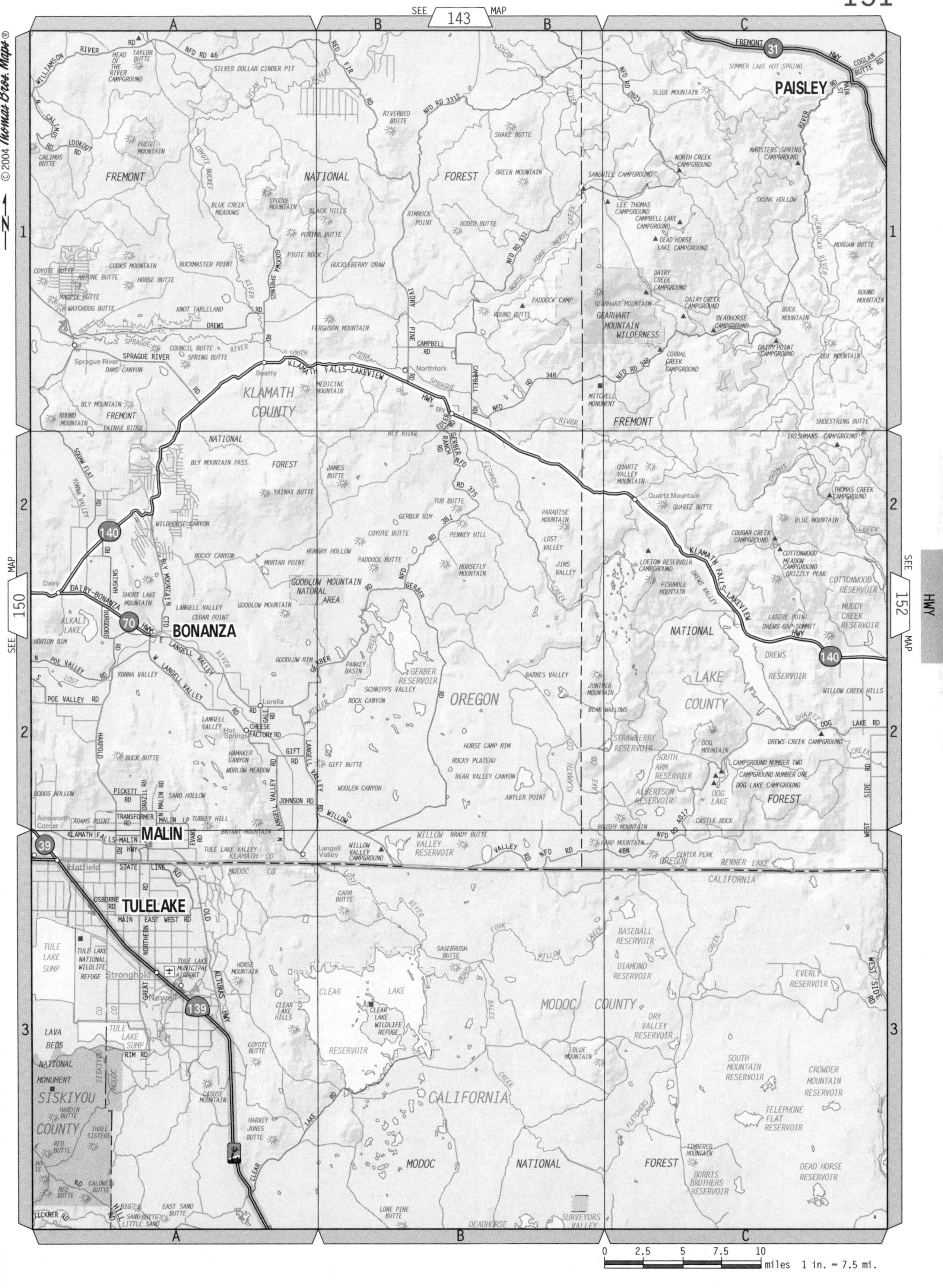

—N→

SEE MAP 143

PAISLEY

FREMONT NATIONAL FOREST

KLAMATH COUNTY

SPRAGUE RIVER

BONANZA

MALIN

TULELAKE

LAKE COUNTY

OREGON

CALIFORNIA

MODOC COUNTY

SISKIYOU COUNTY

LAVA BEDS NATIONAL MONUMENT

TULE LAKE SUMP

TULE LAKE NATIONAL WILDLIFE REFUGE

CLEAR LAKE RESERVOIR

CLEAR LAKE WILDLIFE REFUGE

MODOC NATIONAL FOREST

SEE MAP 150

SEE MAP 152

HWY

0 2.5 5 7.5 10
miles 1 in. = 7.5 mi.

A   B   B   C

© 2004 Thomas Bros. Maps ®

Row 1

COGLAN BUTTE   RED HOUSE RD

COGLAN BUTTES

CHEWAUCAN RIVER

FREMONT HWY

TUCKER HILL

31

395

LAKEVIEW-BURNS HWY

Valley Falls

ABERT RIM HISTORICAL MARKER

LAKE ABERT

LAKE COUNTY OREGON

RABBIT CREEK

HOBACK CREEK

RABBIT HILLS

COYOTE HILLS

BLUEJOINT LAKE

SNYDER CANYON

TURPIN LAKE

STONE CORRAL LAKE

CAMPBELL LAKE

FLAGSTAFF LAKE

FLAGSTAFF RD

MUGWUMP LAKE

SWAMP LAKE

ANDERSON LAKE

HART

HART MOUNTAIN RD

FRENCHGLEN

HART MOUNTAIN NATIONAL ANTELOPE REFUGE STATION

HOT SPRINGS

HOT SPRINGS CAMPGROUND

SOUTH FORK DEGARMO CANYON

WARNER PEAK

HART MOUNTAIN

BLM RD

HART MOUNTAIN NATIONAL ANTELOPE REFUGE

GUANO CREEK

S 1064

FREMONT NATIONAL

CAMPBELL MILL

ABERT RIM VIEW POINT ★

395

HART

Plush

HART LAKE

Row 2

THOMAS RD

GILMORE PEAK

FISK HILL

NORTH WARNER VIEW POINT ★

CROOK PEAK

MCDOWELL PEAK

TWELVEMILE PEAK

LIGHT PEAK

DRAKE PEAK

TWELVEMILE CUTOFF

PLUSH

IRISH HILL

PRIDAY RESERVOIR

CRUMP LAKE

BIG FLAT

CAT BUTTE

HOT SPRINGS

CALDERWOOD RESERVOIR

MUD LAKE RESERVOIR

S 6194

SHIRK LAKE

SEE 151 MAP

HWY

151

New Idaho

Five Corners

FIVE CORNERS RD

THOMAS CREEK RD

FREMONT

WARNER

CAMAS CREEK

WARNER CANYON SKI AREA

MUD CREEK CAMPGROUND

SQUAW BUTTE

OLD PERPETUAL GEYSER

BLACK CAP

KLAMATH FALLS LAKEVIEW

SCHMINCK MEMORIAL MUSEUM

140

LAKEVIEW

HWY AV

STOCK OAK DRIVE RD AV 9TH ST

ROBERTA AV

WEST SIDE RD

BULLTUNNEL HILL RD

DOG LAKE RD

West Side

Lake County Airport

FREMONT NATIONAL FOREST

SAGE HEN BUTTE

CAMAS CREEK

CRUMP RESERVOIR

DEEP CREEK FALLS

140

Adel

WARNER

COLEMAN

CRUMP GEYSER

PELICAN LAKE

FISHER LAKE

WARNER VALLEY

GREASER CANYON

GREASER BASIN

LITTLE JUNIPER MOUNTAIN

R

SEE 153 MAP

RED PEAK

WILLOW CREEK CAMPGROUND ▲

WILLOW POINT

CRANE MOUNTAIN

DEEP CREEK CAMPGROUND

DEEP CREEK

BIG VALLEY

TWENTYMILE CREEK

ROUND MOUNTAIN

BALD HILLS

TWENTYMILE CREEK

HORSE LAKE

COLEMAN VALLEY

GREASER RESERVOIR

BARRY RESERVOIR

HWY

PLUTE RESERVOIR

GUANO VALLEY

BEATYS BUTTE

LANGSLET MONUMENT

R

Row 3

GOOSE LAKE REC AREA

New Pine Creek

LAKE CO

MODOC CO

New Pine Creek

HIGHGRADE

OREGON

CALIFORNIA

STATE LINE CANYON

LAKE CO

OREGON

WASHOE CO

NEVADA

TWIN LAKES

ANTELOPE FLAT

MACY FLAT

CHARLES SHELDON REFUGE

ANTELOPE REFUGE

CATNIP RES

WEST SIDE RD

GOOSE LAKE

STRINGERS ORCHARD

YELLOW MOUNTAIN

HIGHGRADE RD

Willow Ranch

MOUNT VIDA

MODOC COUNTY

BIDWELL MOUNTAIN

TWO BUTTES

COW HEAD LAKE

CALIFORNIA NEVADA

COLEMAN CREEK

MOSQUITO MOUNTAIN

RACETRACK RESERVOIR

CALCUTTA LAKE

CHARLES

SHELDON

MULE MOUNTAIN

WILDLIFE

YELLOW PEAK

REFUGE

CHARLES SHELDON ANTELOPE REFUGE

PAINTED POINT RANGE

395

FANDANGO PEAK

FANDANGO PASS RD

FORT BIDWELL INDIAN RESERVATION

LAKE ANNIE

SURPRISE VALLEY

Fort Bidwell

CALIFORNIA

FEE RESERVOIR

LITTLE MUD LAKE

BIG MUD LAKE

MODOC COUNTY

WASHOE COUNTY

MOSQUITO LAKE

WASHOE COUNTY

ROCK FLAT

COW LAKE

YELLOW CREEK

LONG VALLEY

FISH CREEK

BADGER LAKE

BITNER BUTTE

WEST SIDE RD

SUGAR HILL

MODOC NATIONAL FOREST

GOOSE CREEK

DAVIS CREEK RD

WEST SIDE RD

Davis Creek

BUCK MOUNTAIN

BENTON MEADOW

UPPER ALKALI LAKE

HOLY VALLEY

NEW YEAR LAKE

NEVADA

MIDDLE LAKE

LITTLE BASIN

A   B   B   C

0   2.5   5   7.5   10   miles   1 in. = 7.5 mi.

HWY

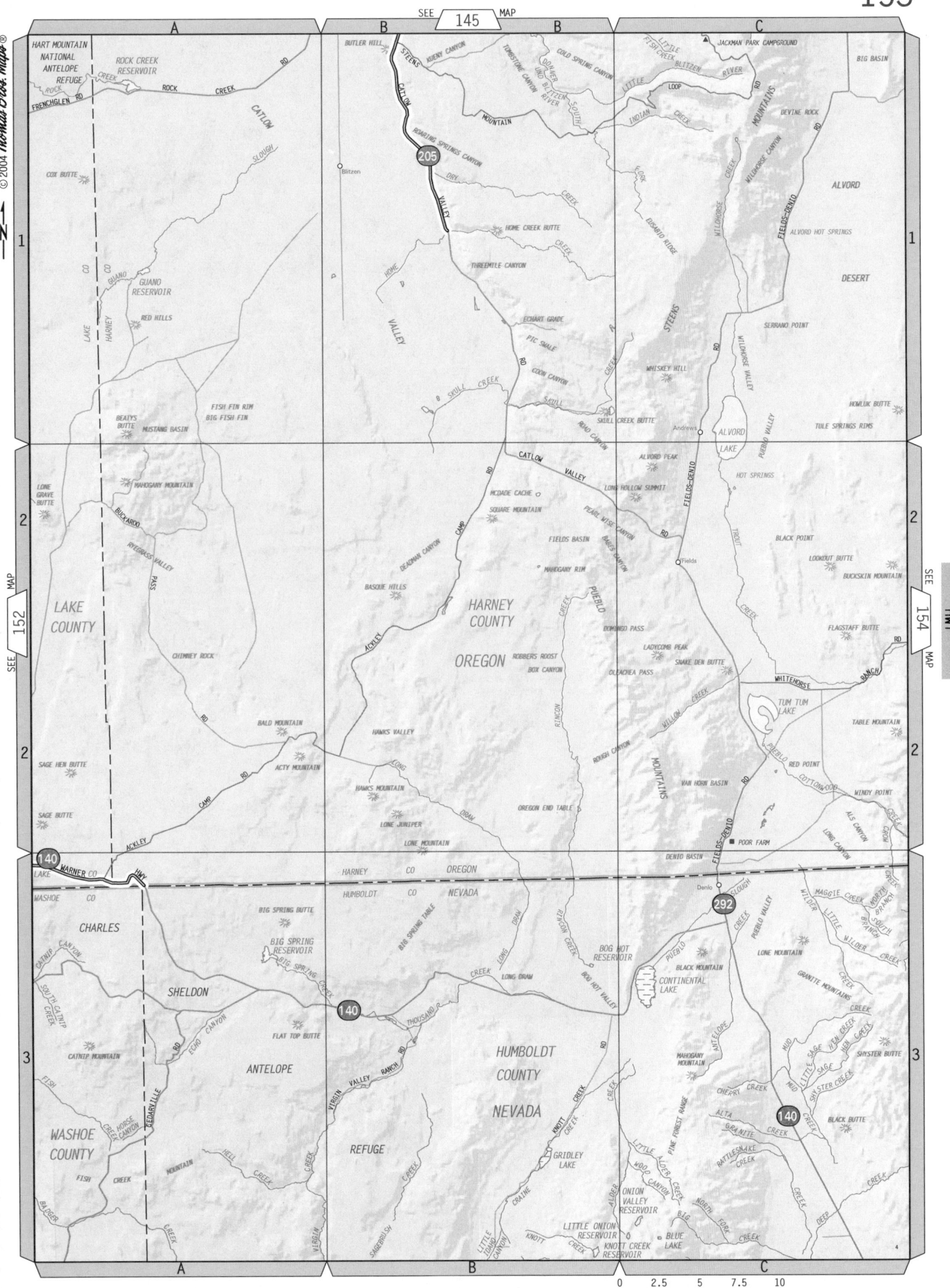

SEE 145 MAP

SEE 152 MAP

SEE 154 MAP

HART MOUNTAIN NATIONAL ANTELOPE REFUGE

ROCK CREEK RESERVOIR

CATLOW

FRENCHGLEN RD
ROCK CREEK RD

COX BUTTE

GUANO RESERVOIR

RED HILLS

LAKE CO
HARNEY CO

GUANO

SLOUGH

BEATYS BUTTE
MUSTANG BASIN

FISH FIN RIM
BIG FISH FIN

Blitzen

BUTLER HILL

STEENS

CATLOW

205

ROARING SPRINGS CANYON

KUENY CANYON

TOMBSTONE CANYON

DONNER UND BLITZEN RIVER

COLD SPRING CANYON

SOUTH

MOUNTAIN

DRY VALLEY

HOME CREEK BUTTE

HOME CREEK

THREEMILE CANYON

HOME VALLEY

ECHART GRADE
PIC SWALE

EDEN CANYON

RD

SKULL CREEK

SKULL

ROAD CANYON

SKULL CREEK BUTTE

JACKMAN PARK CAMPGROUND

LITTLE FISH CREEK

BLITZEN RIVER

BIG BASIN

LOOP

INDIAN CREEK

LITTLE

FORK

ECHARLO RIDGE

STEENS

MOUNTAINS

DEVINE ROCK

ALVORD

ALVORD HOT SPRINGS

FIELDS-DENIO RD

DESERT

WHISKEY HILL

SERRANO POINT

Andrews

ALVORD LAKE

WILDHORSE CANYON

WILDHORSE VALLEY

HOWLUK BUTTE

TULE SPRINGS RIMS

LONE GRAVE BUTTE

MAHOGANY MOUNTAIN

BUCKAROO

RYEGRASS VALLEY

PASS

LAKE COUNTY

CHIMNEY ROCK

SAGE HEN BUTTE

SAGE BUTTE

CATLOW VALLEY

MCDADE CACHE

SQUARE MOUNTAIN

DEADMAN CANYON

CAMP

BASQUE HILLS

ACKLEY

BALD MOUNTAIN

ACTY MOUNTAIN

HAWKS VALLEY

HAWKS MOUNTAIN

LONG

DRAW

LONE JUNIPER

LONE MOUNTAIN

RD

CAMP

ACKLEY

ALVORD PEAK
LONG HOLLOW SUMMIT

PEARL WISE CANYON

FIELDS BASIN

BAILES CANYON

MAHOGANY RIM

HARNEY COUNTY

OREGON

ROBBERS ROOST
BOX CANYON

PUEBLO

DOMINGO PASS

LADYCOMB PEAK

OLEACHEA PASS

SNAKE DEN BUTTE

RINCON

CREEK

WILLOW CREEK

MOUNTAINS

VAN HORN BASIN

ROUGH CANYON

OREGON END TABLE

Fields

HOT SPRINGS

BLACK POINT

LOOKOUT BUTTE

BUCKSKIN MOUNTAIN

FLAGSTAFF BUTTE

RD

WHITEHORSE RANCH

TUM TUM LAKE

PUEBLO

RED POINT

COTTONWOOD

TABLE MOUNTAIN

WINDY POINT

ALS CANYON

LONG CANYON

CROW CREEK

TROUT

CREEK

FIELDS-DENIO

DENIO BASIN

POOR FARM

140

WARNER CO

HWY

LAKE

WASHOE CO

CHARLES

SHELDON

ANTELOPE

WASHOE COUNTY

CATNIP CANYON

SOUTH CATNIP CREEK

CATNIP MOUNTAIN

FISH CREEK

HORSE CANYON

CEDARVILLE

ECHO CANYON

RD

HELL MOUNTAIN

FISH CREEK

BADGER CREEK

HARNEY CO
HUMBOLDT CO

BIG SPRING BUTTE

BIG SPRING RESERVOIR

BIG SPRING CREEK

FLAT TOP BUTTE

140

THOUSAND

VIRGIN VALLEY RANCH RD

REFUGE

SAGEBRUSH

VIRGIN

CREEK

OREGON
NEVADA

BIG SPRING TABLE

LONG DRAW

CREEK

LONG DRAW

RINCON CREEK

LONG

BOG HOT RESERVOIR

BOG HOT VALLEY

HUMBOLDT COUNTY

NEVADA

KNOTT CREEK

GRIDLEY LAKE

LITTLE IDAHO CANYON

KNOTT CREEK

CRANE

Denio

292

CONTINENTAL LAKE

PUEBLO

BLACK MOUNTAIN

LONE MOUNTAIN

RD

MAHOGANY MOUNTAIN

ANTELOPE

LITTLE ALDER CANYON

ALDER

PINE FOREST RANGE

CHERRY CREEK

LITTLE SAGE

ALTA

GRANITE

ONION VALLEY RESERVOIR

LITTLE ONION RESERVOIR

BLUE LAKE

KNOTT CREEK RESERVOIR

PUEBLO VALLEY

MAGGIE CREEK

NORTH BRANCH

SOUTH BRANCH

LITTLE WILDER CREEK

WILDER

GRANITE MOUNTAINS

CREEK

MUD

SAGE

WOO CANYON

SHYSTER BUTTE

SHYSTER CREEK

RATTLESNAKE CREEK

140

BLACK BUTTE

NORTH FORK

BIG

DEEP CREEK

CREEK

0 2.5 5 7.5 10
miles 1 in. = 7.5 mi.

154

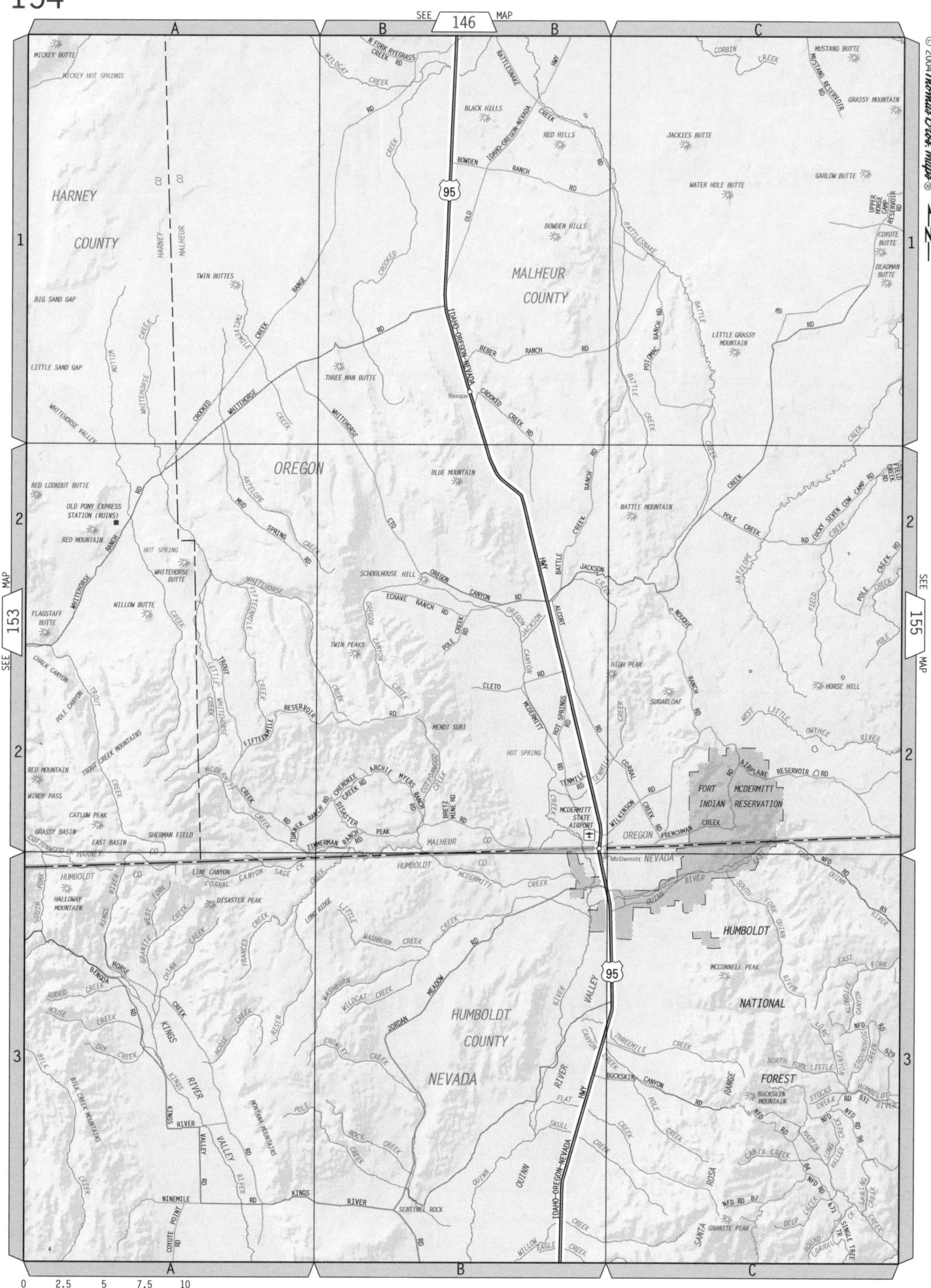

A — B — B — C

HARNEY COUNTY

MICKEY BUTTE

MICKEY HOT SPRINGS

BIG SAND GAP

LITTLE SAND GAP

TWIN BUTTES

N FORK RYEGRASS CREEK RD

WILDCAT CREEK RD

RATTLESNAKE

BLACK HILLS

IDAHO-OREGON-NEVADA CREEK

RED HILLS

BOWDEN RANCH RD

95

MALHEUR COUNTY

BOWDEN HILLS

JACKIES BUTTE

WATER HOLE BUTTE

GARLOW BUTTE

CORBIN CREEK

MUSTANG BUTTE

MUSTANG RESERVOIR RD

GRASSY MOUNTAIN

UPPER HORSE CAMP RESERVOIR RD

COYOTE BUTTE

DEADMAN BUTTE

1

HARNEY CO

MALHEUR CO

NOTTIN

WHITEHORSE CREEK

THACKERVILLE RANGE

CROOKED

WHITEHORSE CREEK

THREE MAN BUTTE

WHITEHORSE

IDAHO-OREGON-NEVADA HWY

Basque

CROOKED CREEK RD

BEBER RANCH

BLUE MOUNTAIN

BATTLE CREEK

RATTLESNAKE

POTOMAC RANCH RD

BATTLE CREEK

LITTLE GRASSY MOUNTAIN

FIELD CREEK RD

OREGON

WHITEHORSE VALLEY

RED LOOKOUT BUTTE

OLD PONY EXPRESS STATION (RUINS)

RED MOUNTAIN RANCH

HOT SPRING

WHITEHORSE BUTTE

MUD SPRING CREEK RD

ANTELOPE

CTO

OREGON CANYON

SCHOOLHOUSE HILL

BATTLE MOUNTAIN

JACKSON

HWY

POLE CREEK

ANTELOPE

FIELD

POLE CREEK RD

IVORY SEVEN COM CAMP RD

2

SEE 153 MAP

HWY

SEE 155 MAP

FLAGSTAFF BUTTE

WHITEHORSE

WILLOW BUTTE

FIFTEENMILE CREEK

WHITEHORSE CREEK

ECHAVE RANCH RD

OREGON CANYON CREEK

POLE CREEK RD

OREGON CANYON RD

JACKSON CANYON

ALCORT

HIGH PEAK

SUGARLOAF

NOUQUE

HORSE HILL

WEST LITTLE OWYHEE RIVER

CHALK CANYON

POLE CANYON

TROUT CREEK MOUNTAINS

LITTLE WHITEHORSE CREEK

FIFTEENMILE

RESERVOIR

TWIN PEAKS

CLETO

MENDI SURI

MCDERMITT

HOT SPRINGS RD

RANCH

CREEK

FORT MCDERMITT INDIAN RESERVATION

AIRPLANE RESERVOIR RD

2

RED MOUNTAIN

WINDY PASS

CATLOW PEAK

GRASSY BASIN

TROUT CREEK

MCDERMITT CREEK RD

TURNER RANCH RD

CHEROKEE CREEK RD

ARCHIE MYERS RANCH RD

COTTONWOOD CREEK

BRETT MINE RD

HOT SPRING

TENMILE

TENMILE

WILKINSON CREEK RD

CORRAL CREEK RD

FRENCHMAN CREEK

EAST BASIN

SHERMAN FIELD

DISASTER PEAK

TIMMERMAN RANCH RD

MALHEUR CO

MCDERMITT STATE AIRPORT

OREGON

NEVADA

COTTONWOOD CK

HARNEY CO

SOUTH FORK

HALLOWAY MOUNTAIN

LINE CANYON

CORRAL CANYON

SAGE CK

CANYON CREEK

HUMBOLDT

MCDERMITT CREEK

McDermitt

QUINN RIVER

HUMBOLDT

NFD RD

QUINN RIVER

83

KINGS RIVER

WEST FORK

DISASTER PEAK

LONG RIDGE

LITTLE WASHBURN CREEK

McCONNELL PEAK

SOUTH FORK QUINN RIVER

EAST FORK

NATIONAL

GRANITE CREEK

CHIMM CREEK

FRANCES CREEK

RISER CREEK

WASHBURN CREEK

MEADOW CREEK

RIVER

QUINN RIVER VALLEY

THREEMILE CREEK

GROUNDHOG CANYON

NFD RD 529

3

HORSE

BONDIA

RODEO

HOUSE CREEK

HORSE CREEK RD

DRY CREEK

KINGS CREEK

HORSE CREEK

JORDAN CREEK

CROWLEY CREEK

WASHBURN

WILDCAT CREEK

95

HUMBOLDT COUNTY NEVADA

BUCKSKIN CANYON RD

POLE CREEK

NORTH FORK LITTLE

BUCKSKIN MOUNTAIN

SANTA ROSA RANGE

STOCKS CREEK

LONG VALLEY

HUMBOLDT RIVER

NFD RD 531

NFD RD 96

FOREST

BILK CREEK

BILK CREEK MOUNTAINS

KINGS RIVER

KINGS RIVER VALLEY

MONTANA MOUNTAINS

POLE CREEK

ROCK CREEK

QUINN

QUINN RIVER

SKULL CREEK

FLAT

BUCKSKIN CANYON RD

CABIN CREEK

NFD RD

NFD RD 87

GRANITE PEAK

DEEP CREEK

ROUND CORRAL CK

SINGLE TREE STR

SPRING CREEK

NFD RD 471

3

NINEMILE RD

COYOTE POINT RD

KINGS RIVER

SENTINEL ROCK

IDAHO-OREGON-NEVADA HWY

WILLOW CREEK

EAGLE CREEK

A — B — B — C

0 2.5 5 7.5 10

miles 1 in. = 7.5 mi.

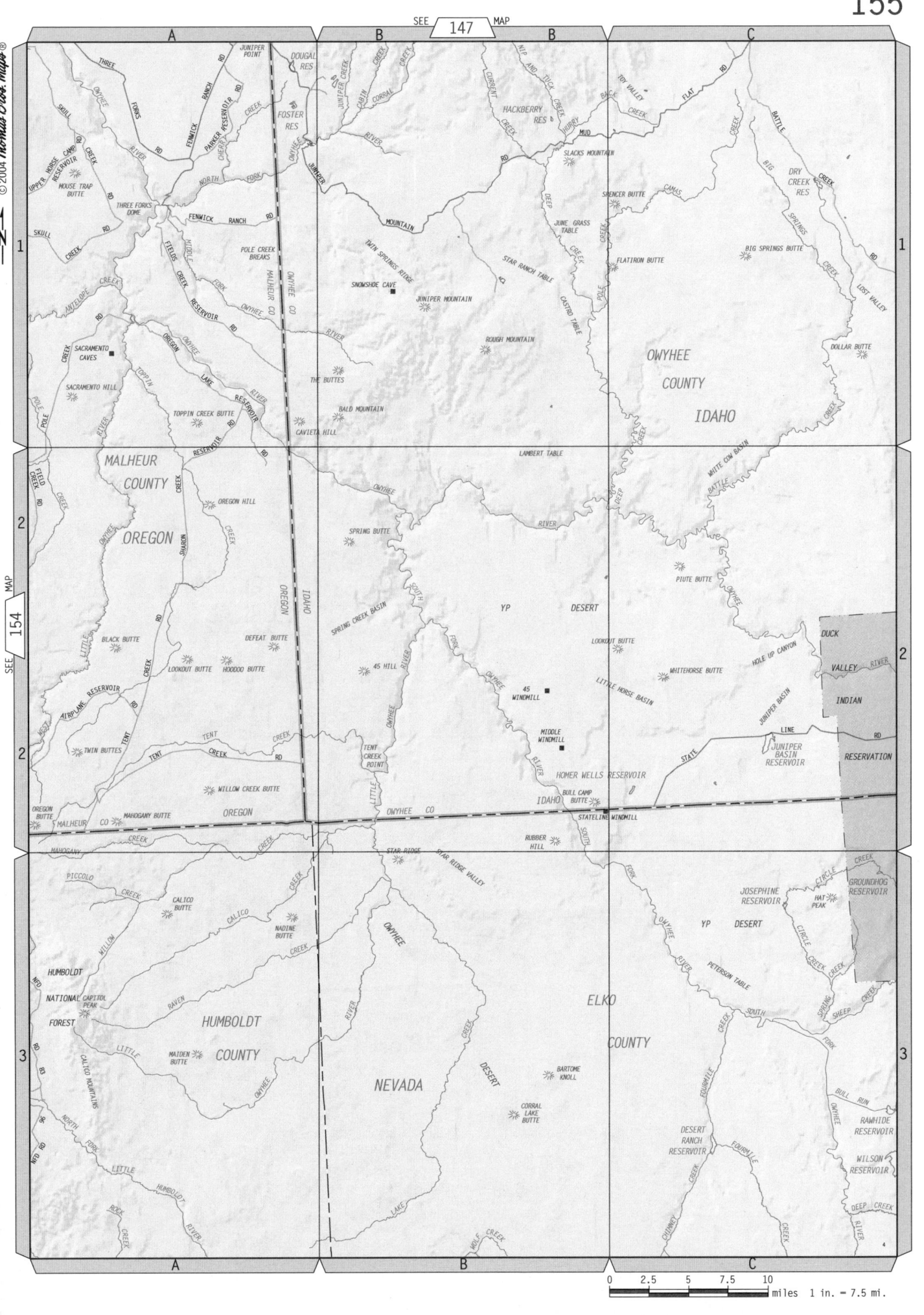

HWY

SEE 154 MAP

0 2.5 5 7.5 10 miles 1 in. = 7.5 mi.

SEE 93 MAP

A B C D

1

CYPRESS

DISTRICT OF WEST VANCOUVER

LYNN

HEADWATERS

MOUNT SEYMOUR

FISH HATCHERY

DISTRICT OF NORTH VANCOUVER

2

FERRY

MARINE DR

Horseshoe Bay

PROVINCIAL PARK

CYPRESS BOWL

CAPILANO LAKE

BALLANTREE PARK

REGIONAL PARK

PROVINCIAL PARK

SEYMOUR RIVER

LARSEN BAY

NELSON CANYON PARK

CYPRESS FALLS PARK

CYPRESS BOWL RD

FYREMOUNT RD

Eagle Harbour

MARINE

BEACON LN

LIGHTHOUSE PARK

Caulfeild

TRANS CANADA HWY

QUEENS

MATHERS

21ST

15TH

KEITH

Hollyburn

CEDARDALE

22ND

23RD

MONTROYAL BLVD

CAPILANO FISH HATCHERY

EDGEMONT BLVD

HIGHLAND BLVD

MELBOURNE AV

QUEENS RD

29TH

BRAEMAR

DEMPSEY

MONAIR

MOUNT SEYMOUR PKWY

SEYMOUR RIVER

INDIAN RIVER DR

INDIAN ARM

3

Point Atkinson

Dundarave

MARINE DR

Norgate

WELCH

13TH ST

1ST ST

KEITH RD

Lower Lonsdale

CITY OF NORTH VANCOUVER

19TH ST

GRAND BLVD

LONSDALE

Keith Lynn

255

Lynn Valley

LYNN CREEK

MOUNTAIN HWY

LYNN VALLEY RD

BERKELEY

Seymour

MOUNT SEYMOUR PKWY

DOLLARTON HWY

Dollarton

Deep Cove

BEDWELL BAY RD

CATES PARK

ADMIRALTY PARK

BELCARRA

4

UNIVERSITY ENDOWMENT LANDS

MUSEUM OF ANTHROPOLOGY

UNIV OF BRITISH COLUMBIA

MARINE DR

CHANCELLOR BLVD

NW MARINE DR

Point Grey

ENGLISH BAY

ROBSON ST

DAVIE ST

PACIFIC

NELSON ST

SEYMOUR

POWELL

ST

MAIN ST

PRIOR ST

PANDORA PARK

7A

DUNDAS ST

VANCOUVER HARBOR

SECOND NARROWS

BURRARD INLET

DISTRICT OF BURNABY

HASTINGS ST

CURTIS

PARKER

GILMORE

BOUNDARY RD

Lochdale

HOLDOM

SPERLING

DUTHIE

UNIVERSITY DR

SIMON FRASER UNIV

PORT MOODY

5

Wreck Beach

PACIFIC SPIRIT REGIONAL PARK

MARINE DR

SHAUGHNESSY GOLF COURSE

IONA ISLAND

WESTBROOK MALL

EAST MALL

WEST MALL

UNIVERSITY BLVD

BLANCA ST

16TH AV

10TH AV

UNIVERSITY GOLF COURSE

4TH AV

CORNWALL

BROADWAY

16TH AV

33RD

41ST

49TH AV

57TH

70TH AV

BLENHEIM

QUILCHENA

MACDONALD

ARBUTUS

BURRARD

GRANVILLE ST

OAK ST

CAMBIE ST

MAIN ST

FRASER ST

KNIGHT ST

VICTORIA DR

KINGSWAY

NANAIMO ST

RENFREW ST

BROADWAY

12TH AV

16TH

EDWARD

29TH

33RD

41ST

49TH AV

57TH

MARINE

Kerrisdale

Marpole

Fraser

Cedar Cottage

Sunset

Killarney

54TH AV

Fraserview

GRANDVIEW HWY

TROUT LAKE

Central Park

CASCADE HEIGHTS

MOSCROP

Garden

DEER LAKE PARK

BURNABY LAKE PARK

Museum

BURRIS

ROYAL OAK

IMPERIAL

MARINE

LOUGHEED HWY

GAGLARDI WY

CARIBOO

NEW WESTMINSTER

COLUMBIA ST

6

VANCOUVER INTERNATIONAL AIRPORT

SEA ISLAND

GRANT McCONACHIE WY

SWISHWASH ISLAND

STURGEON BANK

WESTMINSTER

GRANVILLE

Thompson

BLUNDELL

FRANCIS

Brighouse

CAMBIE

ALDERBRIDGE WY

SHELL

GARDEN

Broadmoor

RICHMOND FRWY

WESTMINSTER HWY

RICHMOND

LULU ISLAND

FRASER RIVER

FRASER RIVER PARK

Queen Borough

South Westminster

DOUGLAS COLLEGE

96TH AV

Annieville

92ND

88TH AV

84TH AV

80TH

CLIVEDEN

ANNACIS ISLAND

ANNACIS

NORDEL WY

112

116

120

7

STRAIT OF GEORGIA

GARY POINT

REIFEL WILDLIFE SANCTUARY

GULF OF GEORGIA CANNERY NATIONAL HISTORIC SITE

STEVESTON MUSEUM

Steveston

MONCTON ST

GILBERT

RAILWAY

WILLIAMS

FINN RD

NO 3 RD

STEVESTON HWY

MYLORA GOLF COURSE

KIRKLAND ISLAND

WOODWARD ISLAND

DEAS ISLAND REGIONAL RIVER PARK

TILBURY ISLAND

GRAVESEND REACH

DISTRICT OF DELTA

SUNSHINE HILLS GOLF COURSE

72ND AV

KITTSON PKWY

64TH AV

WESTVIEW DR

104

A B C D

SEE 101 MAP

METRO

SEE 93 MAP

SEE 157 MAP

0 1 2 3 4 miles   1 in. – 2.5 mi.

© 2004 Thomas Bros. Maps

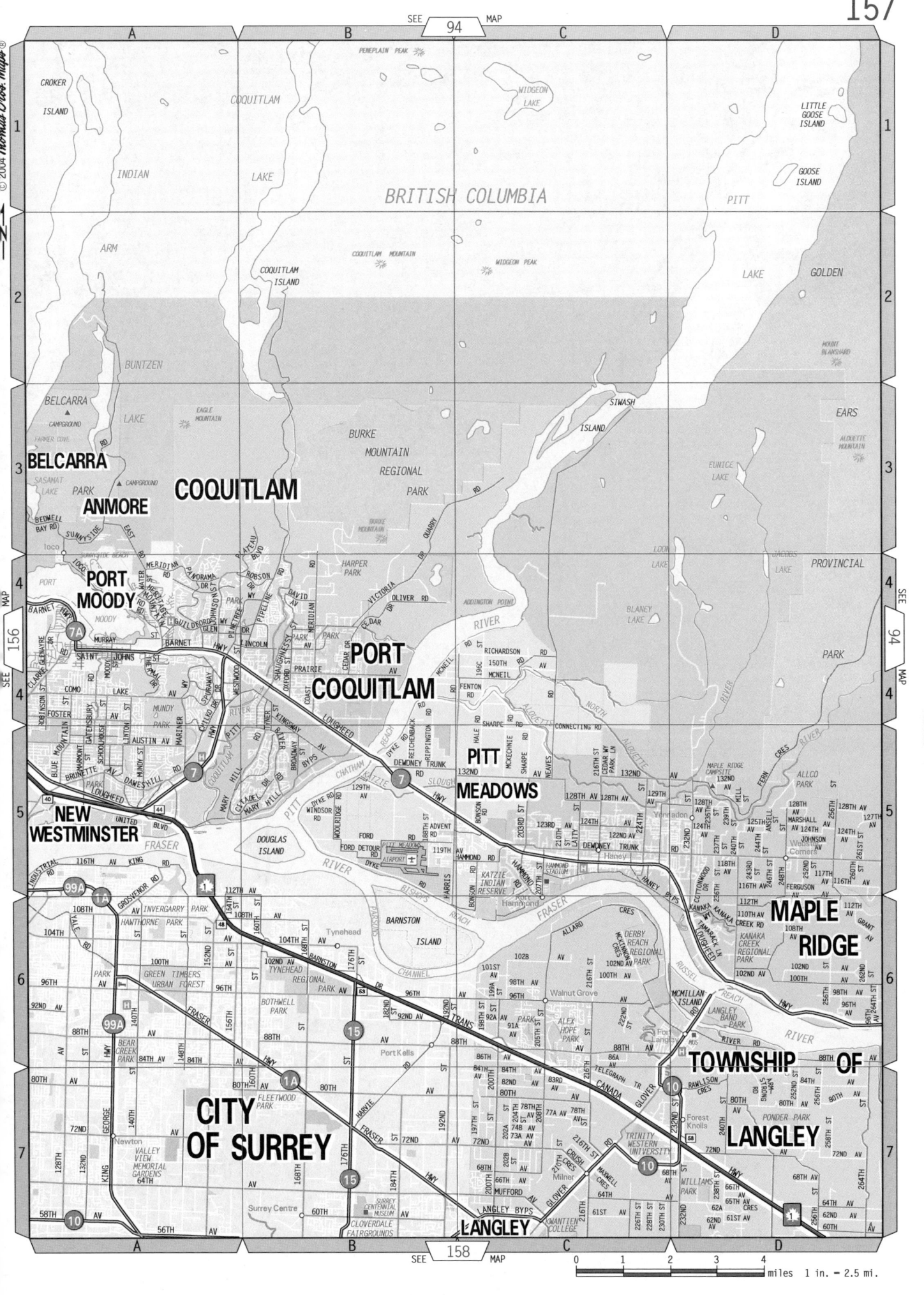

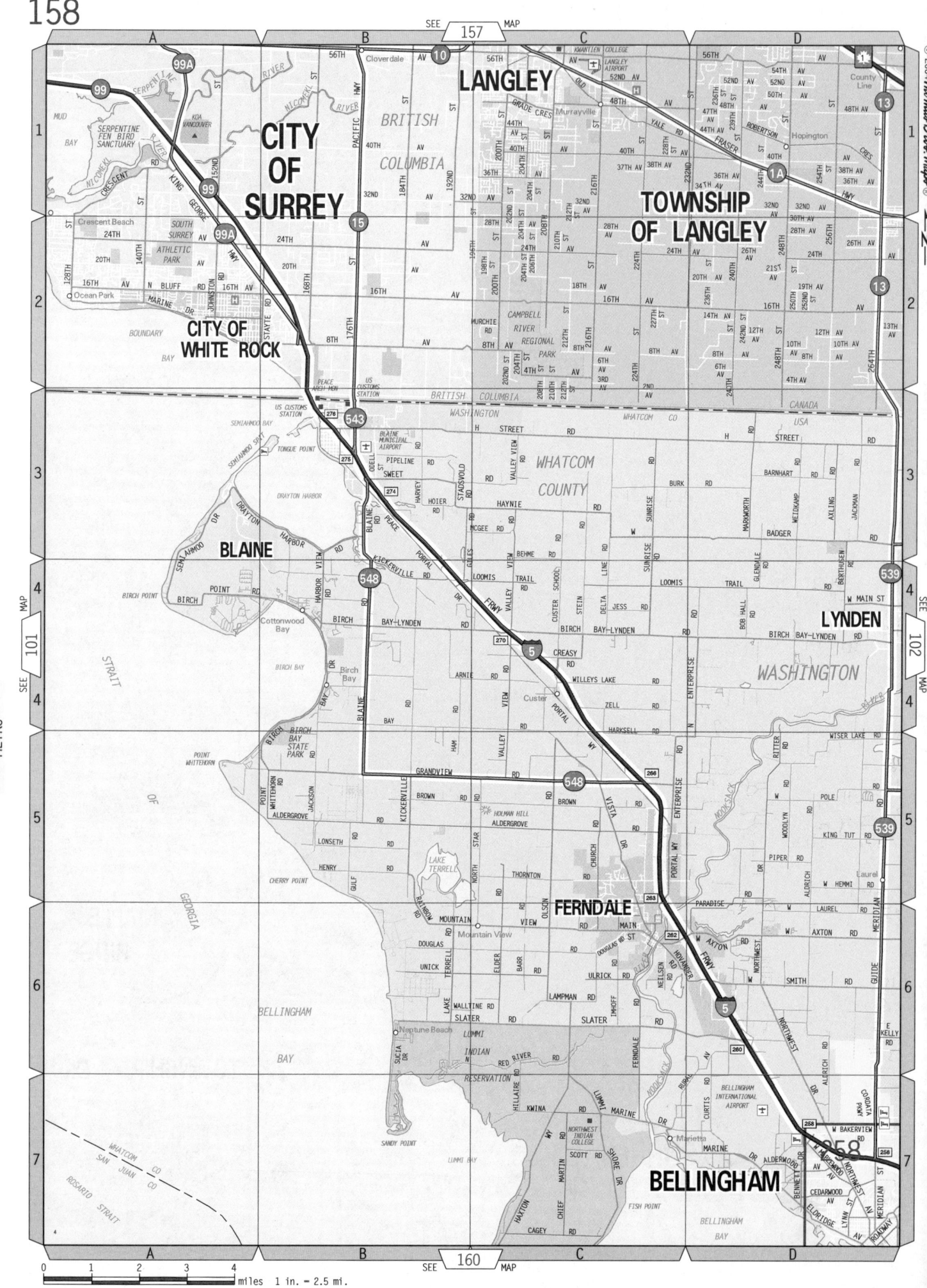

158

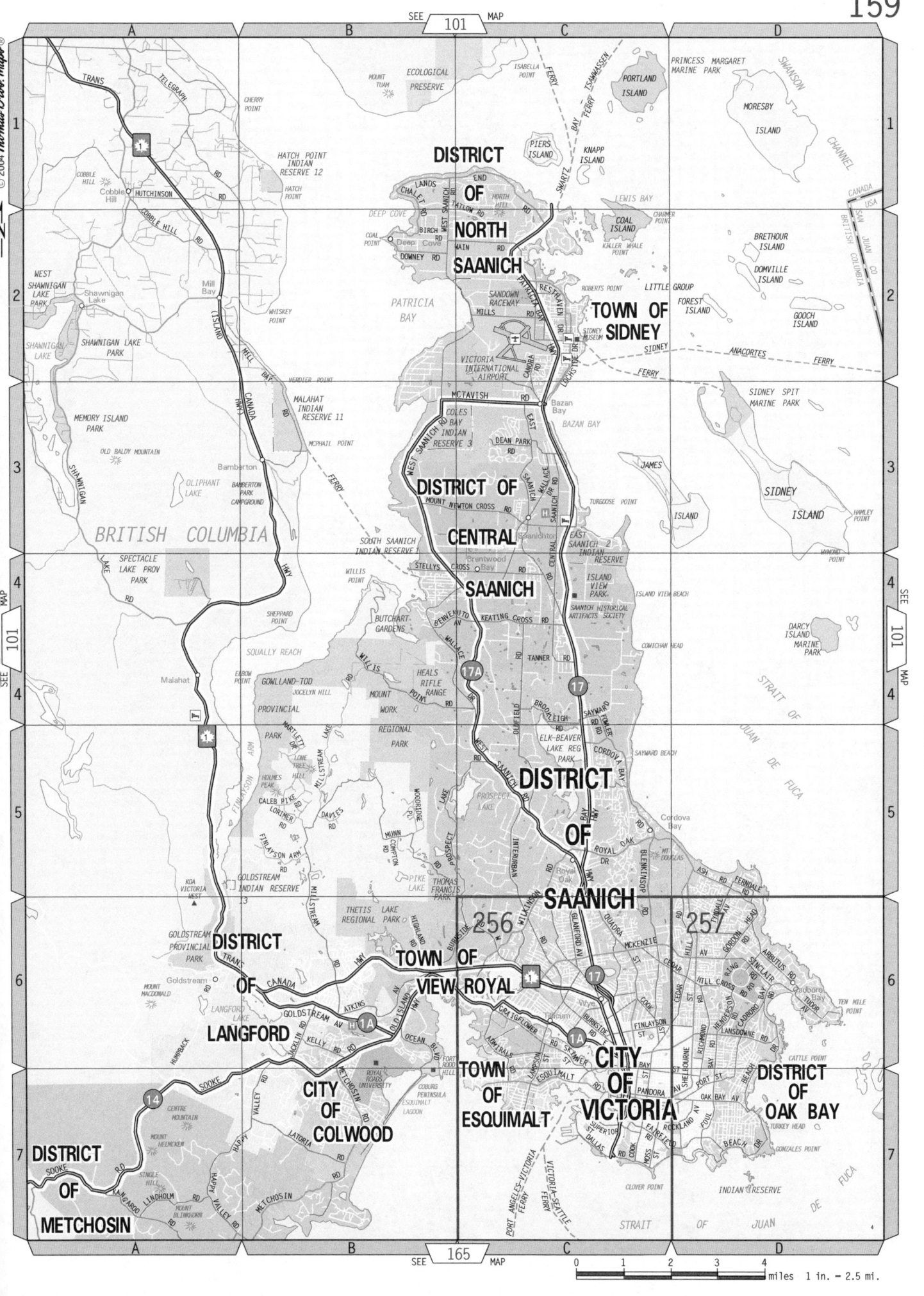

METRO

| A | B | C | D |

TRANS

TELEGRAPH

© 2004 Thomas Bros. Maps ®

COBBLE HILL

Cobble Hill

Hutchinson

COBBLE HILL RD

CHERRY POINT

MOUNT TUAM

ECOLOGICAL PRESERVE

ISABELLA POINT

SWARTZ BAY FERRY TSAWWASSEN

PORTLAND ISLAND

PRINCESS MARGARET MARINE PARK

SWANSON CHANNEL

MORESBY ISLAND

1

HATCH POINT INDIAN RESERVE 12

HATCH POINT

DISTRICT

OF

NORTH

DEEP COVE

LANDS END RD

CHALET RD

WEST SAANICH RD

TATLOW RD

NORTH HILL

PIERS ISLAND

KNAPP ISLAND

LEWIS BAY

COAL ISLAND

CHARMER POINT

CANADA USA

BRITISH COLUMBIA SAN JUAN CO

WEST SHAWNIGAN LAKE PARK

Shawnigan Lake

Mill Bay

COAL POINT

Deep Cove

BIRCH RD

MAIN RD

DOWNEY RD

SAANICH

KILLER WHALE POINT

ROBERTS POINT

LITTLE GROUP

FOREST ISLAND

BRETHOUR ISLAND

DOMVILLE ISLAND

GOOCH ISLAND

2

SHAWNIGAN LAKE PARK

WHISKEY POINT

PATRICIA BAY

SANDOWN RACEWAY

MILLS

PATRICIA BAY

RESTHAVEN DR

SIDNEY MUSEUM

TOWN OF

SIDNEY

SIDNEY

ANACORTES FERRY

SHAWNIGAN LAKE

ISLAND HWY

MILL BAY

CANADA HWY

VERDIER POINT

VICTORIA INTERNATIONAL AIRPORT

CAMOSUN

LOCHSIDE DR

3

MEMORY ISLAND PARK

OLD BALDY MOUNTAIN

MALAHAT INDIAN RESERVE 11

MCPHAIL POINT

FERRY

MCTAVISH RD

COLES BAY INDIAN RESERVE 3

DEAN PARK RD

EAST SAANICH RD

WALLACE DR

Bazan Bay

BAZAN BAY

TURGOOSE POINT

JAMES ISLAND

SIDNEY SPIT MARINE PARK

SIDNEY

ISLAND

HAMLEY POINT

3

BRITISH COLUMBIA

BAMBERTON

BAMBERTON PARK CAMPGROUND

OLIPHANT LAKE

DISTRICT OF

MOUNT NEWTON CROSS RD

CENTRAL

Saanichton

CENTRAL SAANICH RD

EAST SAANICH INDIAN RESERVE

HYMOND POINT

SHANNIGAN

SPECTACLE LAKE PROV PARK

LAKE RD

SOUTH SAANICH INDIAN RESERVE 1

WILLIS POINT

SAANICH

STELLYS CROSS RD

Brentwood Bay

ISLAND VIEW PARK

ISLAND VIEW BEACH

SAANICH HISTORICAL ARTIFACTS SOCIETY

COWICHAN HEAD

DARCY ISLAND MARINE PARK

SEE 101 MAP

4

SEE 101 MAP

Malahat

ELBOW POINT

SQUALLY REACH

BUTCHART GARDENS

WILLIS POINT RD

WALLACE DR

KEATING CROSS RD

BENVENUTO AV

HEALS RIFLE RANGE

17A

TANNER RD

DUFFIELD RD

17

STRAIT OF JUAN DE FUCA

4

GOWLLAND-TOD

JOCELYN HILL

MOUNT WORK

PROVINCIAL

MARTLETT DR

LONE TREE HILL

MILLSTREAM LAKE

REGIONAL

PARK

WEST SAANICH RD

BROADMEAD

SAYWARD RD

ELK-BEAVER LAKE REG PARK

CORDOVA BAY

SAYWARD BEACH

5

HOLMES PEAK

CALEB PIKE

LORIMER RD

DAVIES RD

FINLAYSON ARM

MUNN RD

COMPTON RD

PROSPECT LAKE

PIKE LAKE

WEST SAANICH RD

INTERURBAN RD

PROSPECT LAKE RD

DISTRICT

OF

ROYAL OAK

Royal Oak

ROYAL OAK DR

Cordova Bay

MT DOUGLAS

BLENKINSOP RD

ASH RD FERNDALE RD

5

FINLAYSON ARM RD

KOA VICTORIA WEST

GOLDSTREAM INDIAN RESERVE

MILLSTREAM RD

THETIS LAKE REGIONAL PARK

THOMAS FRANCIS PARK

HIGHLAND RD

SAANICH

256

WILKINSON RD

BAY HWY

GLANFORD AV

QUADRA ST

MCKENZIE AV

CEDAR HILL CROSS RD

257

TIMBELL

GORDON HEAD RD

ARBUTUS RD

SINCLAIR RD

Cadboro Bay

TUDOR

TEN MILE POINT

6

GOLDSTREAM PROVINCIAL PARK

Goldstream

MOUNT MACDONALD

DISTRICT

OF

LANGFORD

TRANS CANADA HWY

GOLDSTREAM AV

TOWN OF

VIEW ROYAL

1

17

Wye

BURNSIDE RD

TILLICUM RD

CRAIGFLOWER RD

COOK ST

FINLAYSON ST

CEDAR HILL RD

RICHMOND RD

LANSDOWNE

HENDERSON RD

CADBORO BAY RD

BEACH DR

CATTLE POINT

6

LANGFORD LAKE

Langford

JOCELYN HILL RD

GOLDSTREAM AV

ATKINS AV

KELLY RD

OLD ISLAND HWY

OCEAN BLVD

FORT RODD HILL

1A

ADMIRALS RD

LAMPSON ST

ESQUIMALT RD

1A

SKINNER ST

BAY ST

CRAIGFLOWER RD

CITY OF

VICTORIA

SHELBOURNE ST

RICHMOND AV

FOUL BAY RD

PORT ST

DISTRICT

OF

OAK BAY

TURKEY HEAD

7

HUMPBACK RD

SOOKE RD

14

CENTRE MOUNTAIN

MOUNT HELMCKEN

HAPPY VALLEY RD

LATORIA RD

VALLEY RD

METCHOSIN RD

CITY

OF

COLWOOD

ROYAL ROADS UNIVERSITY

COBURG PENINSULA ESQUIMALT LAGOON

TOWN

OF

ESQUIMALT

PORT ANGELES-VICTORIA FERRY

VICTORIA-SEATTLE FERRY

SUPERIOR ST

DALLAS RD

COOK ST

MOSS ST

FAIRFIELD RD

ROCKLAND AV

BEACH DR

GONZALES POINT

7

DISTRICT

OF

METCHOSIN

SOOKE RD

KANGAROO RD

LINDHOLM RD

SINGLE HILLS

MOUNT BLINKHORN

MOUNT HELMCKEN

HAPPY VALLEY RD

METCHOSIN RD

CLOVER POINT

INDIAN RESERVE

STRAIT OF JUAN DE FUCA

| A | B | C | D |

0 1 2 3 4 miles 1 in. = 2.5 mi.

258

BELLINGHAM

© 2004 Thomas Bros. Maps ®

EAGLE POINT
ROLFE COVE
MATIA ISLAND
MATIA ISLAND STATE PARK

ROSARIO STRAIT

SAN JUAN CO
WHATCOM CO

POINT MIGLEY
WEST BEACH
LUMMI POINT
LANE SPIT
FISHERMANS COVE
FERN POINT
BLIZZARD RD
LEGOE
LEGOE BAY
LOVERS BLUFF
Lummi Island
BAY RD
PORTAGE POINT
SUNRISE
SUNRISE COVE
ECHO POINT
SEACREST
PASSAGE

SMOKEHOUSE RD
LUMMI INDIAN
SHORE
RESERVATION
LUMMI VIEW DR
BRANT ISLAND
HERMOSA BEACH
BRANT POINT
NEONTAMMITA BEACH
BUNSTEAD SPIT
PORTAGE BAY

PORTAGE ISLAND

BELLINGHAM

S HIGHLAND DR
HOLLY ST
COLLEGE PKWY
32ND ST
S STATE ST
FREELESTONE
OLD SAMISH RD
South Bellingham
HARRIS AVE
VALLEY PKWY
5
250
Chuckanut Village

CLARK ISLAND
CLARK ISLAND STATE MARINE PARK
LONE TREE ISLAND
LITTLE SISTER
BARNES ISLAND

BUCK MOUNTAIN
RACCOON POINT
SAN JUAN
MOUNT CONSTITUTION
COUNTY
MORAN
MOUNT PICKETT
STATE
HIDDEN RIDGE
LITTLE SUMMIT
MOUNTAIN LAKE
ORCAS ISLAND
SEA ACRES RD
KANGAROO POINT
LAWRENCE POINT

WHATCOM COUNTY

SMUGGLERS COVE
INATI BAY
LUMMI PEAK
REIL HARBOR
LUMMI ISLAND

CHUCKANUT ISLAND
GOVERNORS POINT
PLEASANT BAY
LARRABEE STATE PARK
CHUCKANUT BAY
CHUCKANUT DR
11

ORCAS TO OLGA RD
RUSTIC FALLS
CASCADE LAKE
ENTRANCE MOUNTAIN
LAWRENCE RD
SHORE RD
OLGA TO PT
Olga
OBSTRUCTION PASS RD
PARK
BOND MILL RD
HOMESTEAD RD
DOE BAY
DOE ISLAND
DOE ISLAND STATE MARINE PARK
NORTH PEAPOD
PEAPOD ROCKS
SOUTH PEAPOD

THREE ROCKS
ELIZA ISLAND
WILDCAT COVE
CARTER POINT

BUCK BAY
DIAMOND POINT
EAST SOUND
BROWN ROCK
DEER POINT

SAN JUAN CO
SKAGIT CO

SINCLAIR ISLAND
TOWHEAD ISLAND
SINCLAIR ISLAND LIGHT
VITI ROCKS
VENDOVI ISLAND

WHATCOM CO
SKAGIT CO

SAMISH BAY

OBSTRUCTION ISLAND
EAGLE CLIFF
CONE ISLANDS
CONE ISLANDS STATE PARK
CLARK POINT
WILLIAM POINT

HORSESHOE LAKE
BLAKELY PEAK
TIDE POINT
EAGLE HARBOR
CYPRESS
JACK ISLAND
GUEMES ISLAND
Indian Village
SHORE DR
Samish Island
HALLORAN RD
FISH POINT
SCOTTS POINT

SEE MAP 101

SEE MAP 161

BLAKELY ISLAND
BALD BLUFF
SPENCER LAKE
STRAWBERRY ISLAND
STRAWBERRY BAY
CYPRESS ISLAND LIGHT
CYPRESS ISLAND
DEEPWATER BAY
SECRET HARBOR
GUEMES ISLAND
SHORE DR
SAMISH ISLAND

METRO

LED REEF LIGHT
THATCHER RD
Thatcher ISLAND
BLACK ROCK
OLIVINE HILL
REEF POINT
EDENS RD
SHORE DR
OSUMES ISLAND RD
HOLIDAY
Guemes S
SHORE
CHANNEL VIEW BLVD
BOAT HARBOR
DEADMAN BAY
COOKS COVE
SOUTHEAST POINT
HUCKLEBERRY ISLAND
SADDLEBAG ISLAND
SADDLEBAG ISLAND STATE PARK
DOT ISLAND
PADILLA
EDISON RD

FROST ISLAND
LOPEZ ISLAND
THATCHER PASS
FAUNTLEROY POINT
STATE
TOLL
KELLYS POINT
SKAGIT COUNTY
CHANNEL
HAT ISLAND
MARCH POINT LIGHT
BAY

SYLVAN COVE
THATCHER PASS RD
SAN ELMO
DECATUR ISLAND
DAVIS BAY
JAMES ISLAND STATE PARK
DECATUR HEAD
Decatur
BOWERS BLVD
ARMITAGE
SUNSET BEACH
BELLE ROCK LIGHT
FERRY
259
SHIP HARBOR
GUEMES
CAP SANTE
20

BRIGANTINE BAY
TRUMP ISLAND
READS BAY
WHITE CLIFF
GREEN POINT
WASHINGTON PARK
OAKS AV
ANACORTES
COMMERCIAL AV
Cranberry Lake
FIDALGO
MARCH POINT
N TEXAS RD
PERSONS RD
20
JOSH WILSON RD
Bay View

CENTER ISLAND
LOPEZ PASS
SPERRY POINT
BIRD ROCKS
SHORT BAY
FIDALGO HEAD
FLOUNDER BAY
BURROWS ISLAND LIGHTHOUSE
BURROWS ISLAND
ALICE BIGHT
Alexander Beach
41ST ST
MARINE DR
HAVEKOST RD
HEART LAKE
FIDALGO
20
MARCH POINT RD
Whitmarsh
MEMORIAL HWY

JASPER BAY
HUNTER BAY
SHOAL BIGHT
PEARTREE BAY
YOUNG ISLAND
BURROWS
ALLEN ISLAND
BAY
EDITH POINT
LAKE ERIE
MOUNT ERIE PARK
ANACORTES
MOUNT ERIE
ISLAND
WHISTLE LAKE
CHRISTIANSON RD
STEVENSON RD
SWINOMISH
20
SATTERLEE RD
TURNERS BAY
RESERVATION
SNEE-OOSH RD

SPERRY RD
ELIZA DR
CAPE SAINT MARY
WILLIAMSON ROCKS
BIZ POINT
BIZ POINT RD
ROSARIO RD
SHARPE RD
CAMPBELL LAKE RD
GINNETT HILL
CAMPBELL LAKE
Similk Beach
GIBRALTER RD
SIMILK BAY
SWINOMISH
INDIAN
FLAGSTAFF LN
DOWNEY RD

LOPEZ ISLAND
MUD BAY RD
COLE RD
ALECK BAY RD
CHADWICK HILL
WATMOUGH HEAD
ALECK ROCKS
POINT COLVILLE
WASHINGTON
GINNETT
Rosario Beach
Rosario
DECEPTION PASS STATE PARK
Dewey
CAMPBELL LAKE RD
4TH ST
SIMILK
SNEE-OOSH RD
INDIAN
RESERVATION
Snee Oosh
Swinomish Village

COLVILLE ISLAND
DAVIDSON ROCK LIGHT
SKAGIT CO
ISLAND CO
NORTHWEST ISLAND
BOWMAN BAY
PASS ISLAND
DECEPTION ISLAND
MACS COVE
GOOSE ROCK
BEN URE ISLAND
DECEPTION PASS STATE PARK
YOKEKO
YOKEKO POINT
YOKEKO DR
HOYPUS POINT
HOYPUS HILL
SKAGIT ISLAND
KIKET ISLAND
KIKET BAY
LANG BAY
SKAGIT BAY
WHITNEY RD
LA CONNER RD

0 1 2 3 4 miles 1 in. = 2.5 mi.

A B C D

© 2004 Thomas Bros. Maps ®

758

OHIO ST
IOWA ST
LAKEWAY
253
252
5
YEW ST
ELECTRIC AVE
NORTH SHORE DR
Geneva
WHATCOM LAKE
WHATCOM
LAKE
DUTCH HARBOR
SOUTH BAY
STEWART MOUNTAIN
HARD SCRABBLE FALLS
STRAND RD
HOMESTEADER RD
BLUE MOUN TAIN RD
LAKE BLUE MOUNTAIN RD

BELLINGHAM

Happy Valley
YEW WY
SAMISH WY
TOWER RD
SAMISH
NORTH RD
Y RD
STRAWBERRY POINT
LAKE
SHORE DR
REVEILLE ISLAND
LAKE LOUISE
LOUISE RD
BLEND
WHATCOM COUNTY
TURKINGTON RD
FORK
DIKE RD
MOSQUITO

Acme
BLUE MOUNTAIN

LAKE PADDEN
OLD SAMISH HWY
5
246
LOOKOUT MOUNTAIN
SOUTH BAY
Park
PARK RD
TR
VALLEY
9
EDDYS MOUNTAIN

CHUCKANUT MOUNTAIN
ROY RD
SAMISH LAKE
IOWA HEIGHTS RD
SOUTH BAY RD
2ND
WICKERSHAM TRUCK
EINNIS CREEK
DORAN RD
BOWMAN RD
SAXON RD

LARRABEE
LAKE SAMISH DR
SUMERLAND RD
LAKE SAMISH OLD HWY
CAIN LAKE
CAIN
CAMP 2
Wickersham
WHATCOM CO
SKAGIT CO

STATE
243
240 RD
CAIN LAKE RD
RIVER
FORK

PARK
DOGFISH POINT
BARRELL SPRINGS RD
Alger
BUTLER CREEK RD
KILBY HILL LOGGING
ANDERSON MOUNTAIN
Prairie
LYMAN HILL
LYMAN PASS

PIGEON POINT
CHICKANUT
WINDY POINT
WOOD RD
COLONY RD
N
PARSON CREEK RD
HUMPHREY HILL
PRAIRIE RD
RIVER
UPPER SAMISH RD
Thornwood
SKAGIT COUNTY

SAMISH BAY
Blanchard
COLONY MOUNTAIN RD
FRIDAY CREEK
FRWY

Edison
Edison Station
Bow
HILL
236
SKAGIT VALLEY CASINO
DOUBLE CREEK LN
PARK RIDGE LN
Hoogdal
OLD NORTHERN STATE HOSPITAL RD

BAY VIEW
EDISON RD
BOW HILL RD
CHUCKANUT DR
NORLINE RD
ERSHIG RD
SAMISH HTS
HOBSON RD
SAMISH
GRIPP RD
BUTLER HILL
BRIDGEWATER RD
MOSIER RD
9
HELMICK RD
STATE HWY
BACUS RD
BACUS HILL

SULLIVAN RD
BOW RD
SAMISH FIELD
11
5
BURLINGTON-ALGER RD
KELLEHER RD
KOA BURLINGTON
AND
GRADE RD
BASSET RD
GRIPP RD
SAPP RD
TOWNSHIP RD
FRUITDALE RD
MCGARIGLE RD
H
MINKLER RD
Cookedale
20
LYMAN HAMILTON RD

DARCY RD
MARKET RD
ALLEN
WEST
THOMAS RD
BENSON RD
BRADLEY RD
SAM BELL RD
COOK
232
GREEN RD
LINE RD
COOK RD
MOORE ST
BD
BURMASTER RD
HOEHN RD
WALBERG RD

BAY VIEW RIDGE
231
260
BURLINGTON-ALGER RD
230
PULVER RD
DISTRICT LINE RD
COLLINS RD
20
3RD ST
STATE ST
JAMESON ST
FRUITDALE
RIVER
SEDRO-WOOLLEY
SKAGIT HWY
S HWY

MARIHUGH RD
BAYVIEW RD
WATER TANK
PETERSON RD
AVON-ALLEN RD
WILSON RD
JOSH RD
Sterling
LAFAYETTE RD
CASCADE
GARDNER RD
9
Clear Lake
CLEAR LAKE
MORFORD RD
DAY RD
SKAGIT HWY

ELBRES KALSO
OVENELL RD
SKAGIT REGIONAL BAY VIEW AIRPORT
HIGGINS AIRPORT WY
CUT-OFF
AVON
20
BURLINGTON
BURLINGTON BLVD
S ANACORTES ST
FRANCIS RD
MUD LAKE RD
SWAN RD
BARNEY LAKE
LAKE
AUSTIN RD
BEAVER LAKE
BEAVER LAKE RD
WASHINGTON
HAYSTACK MOUNTAIN

Fredonia
MEMORIAL HWY
20
536
MEMORIAL HWY
Avon
AVON-ALLEN RD
RIVER BEND RD
GEORGE HOPPER RD
HOAG RD
MARTIN RD
BIG ROCK
GUNDERSON RD
BAKER HEIGHTS RD
GUNGESEN RD
LANGE RD
CULTUS MOUNTAIN

BEST RD
BRADSHAW RD
MCLEAN RD
DONNELLY RD
DUNBAR RD
MARSH RD
JUNGQUIST RD
PENN RD
227
FREEWAY DR
5
COLLEGE WY
FIR ST
538
9

226
DIVISION ST
BROAD ST
BLACKBURN ST
2ND ST
18TH ST
34TH ST
MOUNT VERNON-BIG LAKE RD
DIGBY
MOUNT VERNON

SEE 160 MAP
SEE 102 MAP

0 1 2 3 4 miles   1 in. = 2.5 mi.

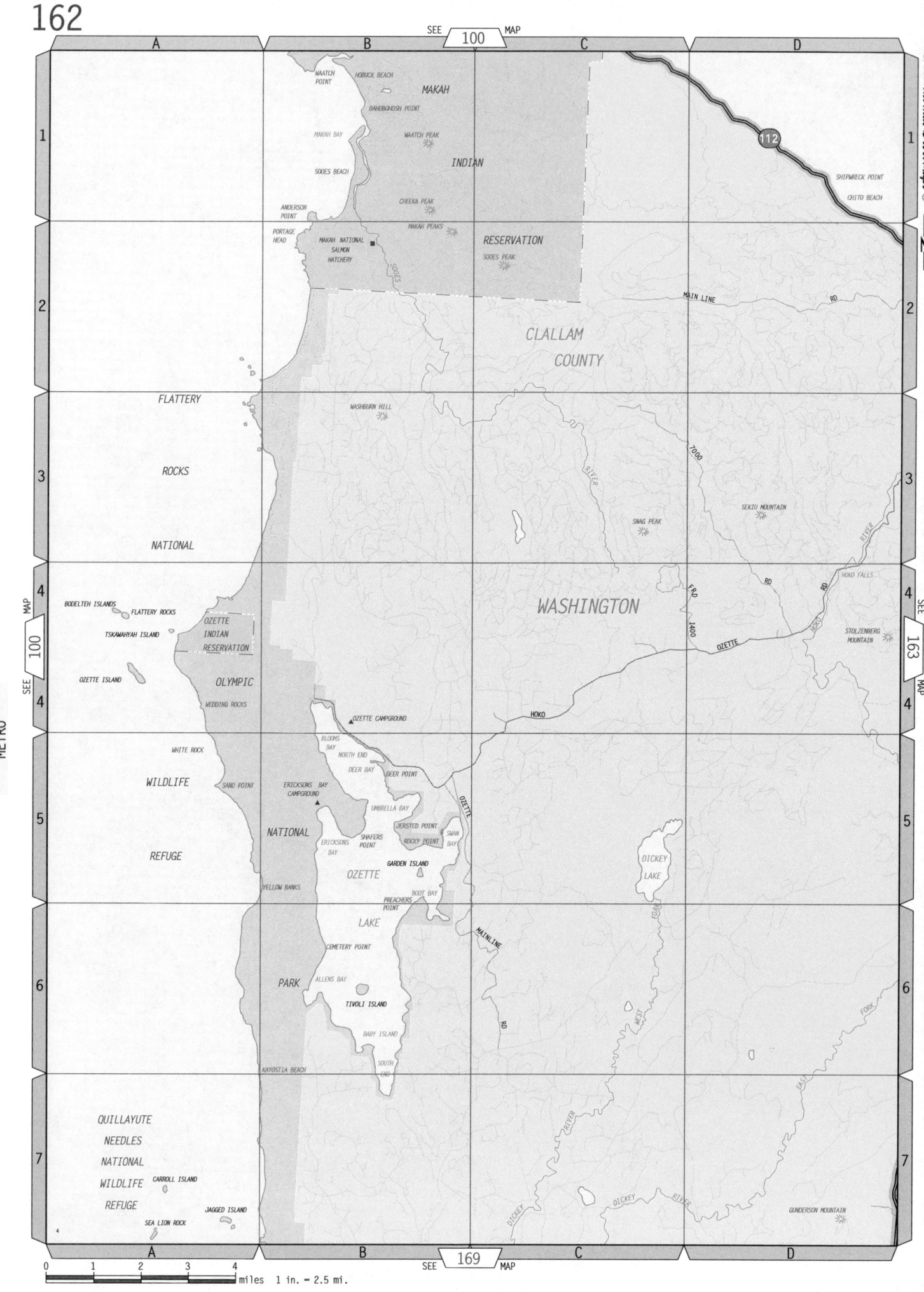

METRO

A   B   C   D

© 2004 Thomas Bros. Maps ®

—N—

1

WAATCH POINT
HOBUCK BEACH
MAKAH
BAHOBOHOSH POINT
MAKAH BAY
WAATCH PEAK
INDIAN
SOOES BEACH
ANDERSON POINT
CHEEKA PEAK
112
SHIPWRECK POINT
CHITO BEACH

2

PORTAGE HEAD
MAKAH PEAKS
RESERVATION
SOOES
MAKAH NATIONAL SALMON HATCHERY
SOOES PEAK
MAIN LINE
RD
CLALLAM COUNTY

3

FLATTERY
WASHBURN HILL
ROCKS
RIVER
7000
SEKIU MOUNTAIN
NATIONAL
SNAG PEAK
RIVER

4

BODELTEH ISLANDS
FLATTERY ROCKS
TSKAWAHYAH ISLAND
OZETTE INDIAN RESERVATION
WASHINGTON
RD
HOKO FALLS
OZETTE ISLAND
OLYMPIC
F RD
1400
OZETTE
RD
RD
STOLZENBERG MOUNTAIN
WEDDING ROCKS
HICKEY

SEE [100] MAP   SEE [163] MAP

HOKO

5

WHITE ROCK
BLOOMS BAY
NORTH END
DEER BAY
DEER POINT
WILDLIFE
SAND POINT
ERICKSONS BAY CAMPGROUND
UMBRELLA BAY
OZETTE
NATIONAL
SHAFERS POINT
JERSTED POINT
SWAN BAY
REFUGE
ERICKSONS BAY
ROCKY POINT
DICKEY LAKE
OZETTE
GARDEN ISLAND
YELLOW BANKS
BOOT BAY

6

LAKE
PREACHERS POINT
MAINLINE
PARK
CEMETERY POINT
ALLENS BAY
TIVOLI ISLAND
RD
WEST
FORK
BABY ISLAND
KAYOSTIA BEACH
SOUTH END

7

QUILLAYUTE
NEEDLES
NATIONAL
RIVER
WILDLIFE
CARROLL ISLAND
REFUGE
JAGGED ISLAND
DICKEY
DICKEY
RIVER
GUNDERSON MOUNTAIN
SEA LION ROCK
4

A   B   C   D

0   1   2   3   4
miles   1 in. = 2.5 mi.

SEE 100 MAP

A   B   C   D

1

BRITISH COLUMBIA

BRITISH COLUMBIA
CLALLAM CO
WASHINGTON
CANADA
USA

2

EAGLE POINT

Hoko

SEKIU
AIRPORT

112

Sekiu

SLIP POINT
SLIP POINT LIGHTHOUSE

CLALLAM BAY
MIDDLE POINT

Clallam Bay

STRAIT OF JUAN DE FUCA

RIVER   RD

HOKO

3

HOKO OZETTE

BLUE CANYON

CLALLAM COUNTY

CLALLAM RIVER CAMPGROUND

PILLAR POINT

WASHINGTON

SEE 162 MAP

4

112

BUTLER COVE

112

HERMAN FALLS

ELLIS
MOUNTAIN

GIBSON FARM

SEE 164 MAP

RD

BURNT
MOUNTAIN

NFD RD 3117

113

BEAR CREEK FALLS

NFD RD 3116

NFD RD 3031

NFD RD 3029

5

NELSON
HILL

HOKO

RIVER

MOUNTAIN

OLYMPIC

NFD RD 3016

NFD RD 3031

NFD RD 3028

DICKEY HOKO SUMMIT

DEADMANS HILL

NFD RD 30

NFD RD 3067

3040

TYEE HILL

BEAVER FALLS

BURNT

DICKEY
EAST
RIVER
FORK

BEAVER HILL

NFD RD 3007

NATIONAL

NFD RD 3040

NFD
RD

6

BOAT
LAUNCH

LAKE PLEASANT RD

Sappho

BEAR CREEK
CAMPGROUND

NFD RD
3041

KLAHOWA CAMPGROUND

NFD RD 3069

W LAKE PLEASANT RD

LAKE
PLEASANT

CLARK

RD

101

Beaver

E LAKE PLEASANT RD

PAVEL

SOL DUC
SALMON
HATCHERY
EAGLE POINT

RD

RD

RIVER

SOL   DUC

SOL   DUC

RIVER

101

WHEELER RD

2902

SOL DUC

VALLEY

EAGLE CREEK RANCH

RD

FOREST

NFD RD 2929

NFD RD 2938

RD

NFD RD 29

NFD RD 2929

7

NFD RD
2933

2903

BIGLER MOUNTAIN

NFD RD 2912

NFD
RD

CALAWAH RIDGE

NFD
RD

NFD RD 2937

NFD RD 2923

2978

SOL DUC VALLEY

29

NFD RD

A   B   C   D

SEE 108 MAP

0   1   2   3   4
miles   1 in. = 2.5 mi.

METRO

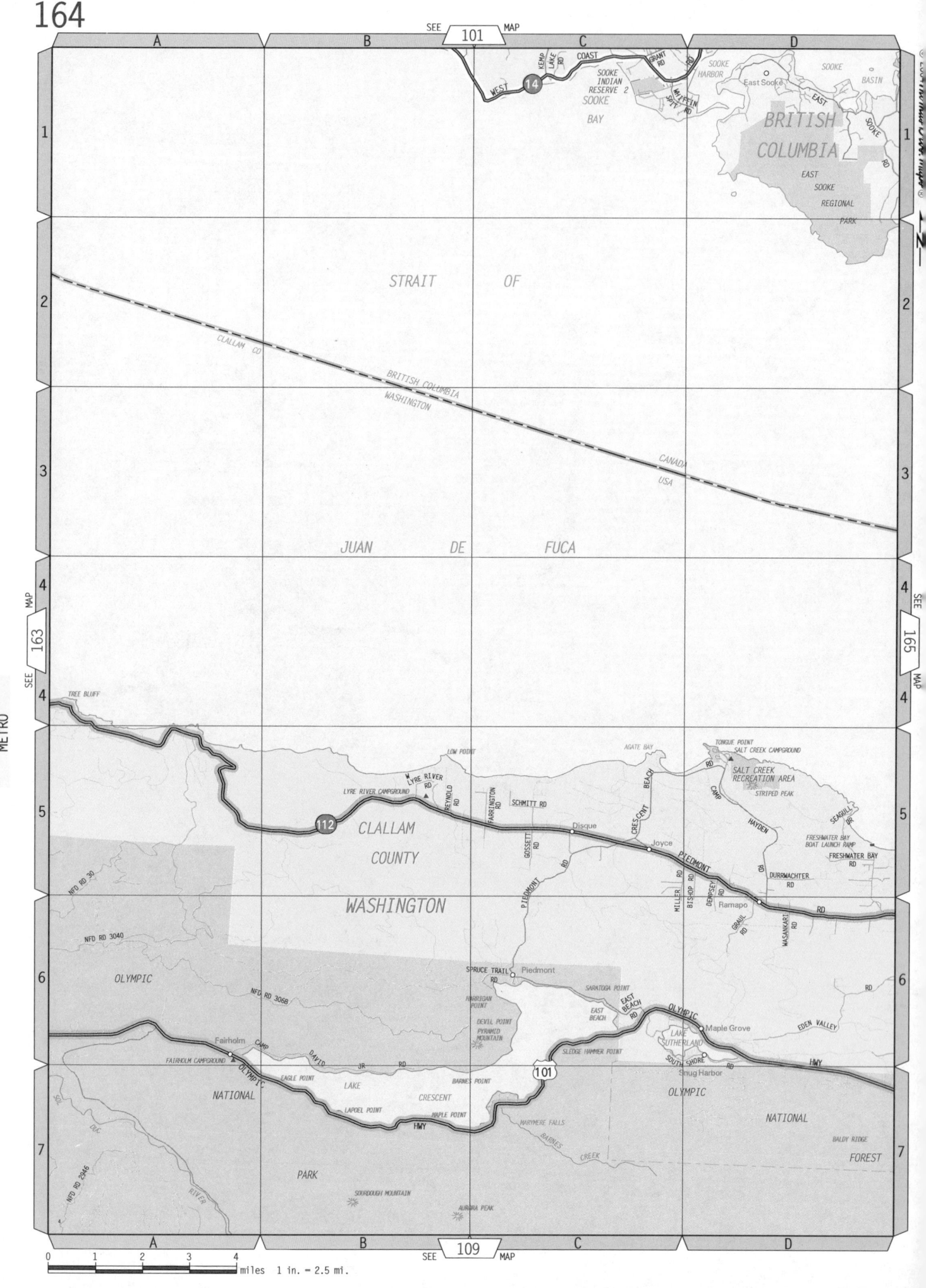

METRO

A   B   C   D

1

SOOKE
INDIAN
RESERVE 2
SOOKE
BAY

KEMP LAKE RD
WEST COAST
14
GRANT RD
WIFFIN SPIT RD
SOOKE HARBOR
East Sooke
SOOKE BASIN

EAST
SOOKE

BRITISH
COLUMBIA

EAST
SOOKE
REGIONAL
PARK

SOOKE RD

STRAIT   OF

2

CLALLAM CO

BRITISH COLUMBIA
WASHINGTON

CANADA
USA

3

JUAN   DE   FUCA

4

TREE BLUFF

LOW POINT
AGATE BAY
TONGUE POINT
SALT CREEK CAMPGROUND

W LYRE RIVER RD
LYRE RIVER CAMPGROUND
REYNOLD RD
FARRINGTON RD
SCHMITT RD
CRESCENT BEACH RD
CAMP RD
SALT CREEK
RECREATION AREA
STRIPED PEAK
SEAGULL DR

5

112

CLALLAM
COUNTY

GOSSETT RD
Disque
RD
Joyce
PIEDMONT
HAYDEN
FRESHWATER BAY
BOAT LAUNCH RAMP
FRESHWATER BAY RD

WASHINGTON

NFD RD 30

NFD RD 3040

PIEDMONT RD
MILLER RD
BISHOP RD
DEMPSEY RD
Ramapo
GRAUL RD
WASANKART RD
DURRWACHTER RD

RD

6

OLYMPIC

NFD RD 3068

SPRUCE TRAIL RD
Piedmont
HURRICAN POINT
DEVIL POINT
PYRAMID MOUNTAIN
SARATOGA POINT
EAST BEACH
EAST BEACH RD
OLYMPIC
Maple Grove
LAKE
SUTHERLAND
SOUTH SHORE RD
EDEN VALLEY
HWY

Fairholm
FAIRHOLM CAMPGROUND
OLYMPIC
CAMP DAVID JR RD
EAGLE POINT
LAKE
LAPOEL POINT
CRESCENT
BARNES POINT
MAPLE POINT
SLEDGE HAMMER POINT
101
Snug Harbor

NATIONAL

NATIONAL

NFD RD 2946

PARK
SOL DUC RIVER
SOURDOUGH MOUNTAIN
AURORA PEAK
HARYMERE FALLS
BARNES CREEK
BALDY RIDGE
FOREST

7

A   B   C   D

0 1 2 3 4
miles 1 in. = 2.5 mi.

SEE 159 MAP

A   B   C   D

DISTRICT OF METCHOSIN

ROCHE COVE REGIONAL PARK

MATHESON LAKE REGIONAL PARK

Metchosin

ROCKY POINT

WILLIAM HEAD RD

MOUNT MATHESON RD

MATHESON RD

BECHER BAY INDIAN RESERVE 1

SOOKE RD

EAST

DEPARTMENT OF NATIONAL DEFENSE

BRITISH

COLUMBIA

BECHER BAY INDIAN RESERVE 2

ROCKY POINT NAVAL ESTABLISHMENT

1

STRAIT   OF

VICTORIA SEATTLE FERRY

2

BRITISH COLUMBIA
WASHINGTON

CANADA
USA

VICTORIA FERRY

PORT ANGELES FERRY

CLALLAM CO

3

SEE 164 MAP

MAP

JUAN   DE   FUCA

SEE 166 MAP

METRO

4

ANGELES POINT

FRESHWATER BAY

PORT ANGELES

EDIZ HOOK

US COAST GUARD STATION

PORT ANGELES HARBOR

261

5

OXENFORD

ST CHARLES

STRATTON

PLACE

HUNT RD

LOWER ELWHA

LONER ELWHA

LOWER ELWHA INDIAN RES

PETERS RD

RANGER RD

PIEDMONT RD

112

ELWHA PLACE

ELWHA RIVER

RIFE

WILLIAM R FAIRCHILD INTERNATIONAL AIRPORT

EDGEWOOD

DR

W LAURIDSEN BLVD

C ST

TUMWATER ACCESS RD

101

8TH ST

LINCOLN ST

RACE ST

117

GREEN POINT

FINN HALL RD

OLYMPIC

EDEN VALLEY

DAN KELLY RD

LAKE ALDWELL

OLYMPIC HWY

Crane

LEMON RD

OLYMPIC HWY

HULSE RD

SUTER RD

OBRIEN RD

OLD OLYMPIC HWY

LEWIS RD

SHORE RD

GUNN RD

Agnew

101

6

101

CLALLAM COUNTY

STATE FOREST

LAKE ADWELL BOAT LAUNCH RAMP

BLACK DIAMOND RD

MOUNT ANGELES RD

KOA PORT ANGELES/SEQUIM

DEER PARK RD

OBRIEN RD

EMERY RD

BLUE MOUNTAIN RD

BARR RD

OLYMPIC

LITTLE RIVER

ELWHA HOT SPRINGS RD

NFD RD 3030

McDONALD MOUNTAIN

LITTLE RIVER RD

WASHINGTON

HEART OF THE HILLS CAMPGROUND

OBRIEN RD

TOWNSHIP LINE RD

Little Oklahoma

GELLOR RD

7

OLYMPIC   NATIONAL   FOREST

OLYMPIC   NATIONAL   PARK

A   B   C   D

SEE 109 MAP

0   1   2   3   4   miles   1 in. = 2.5 mi.

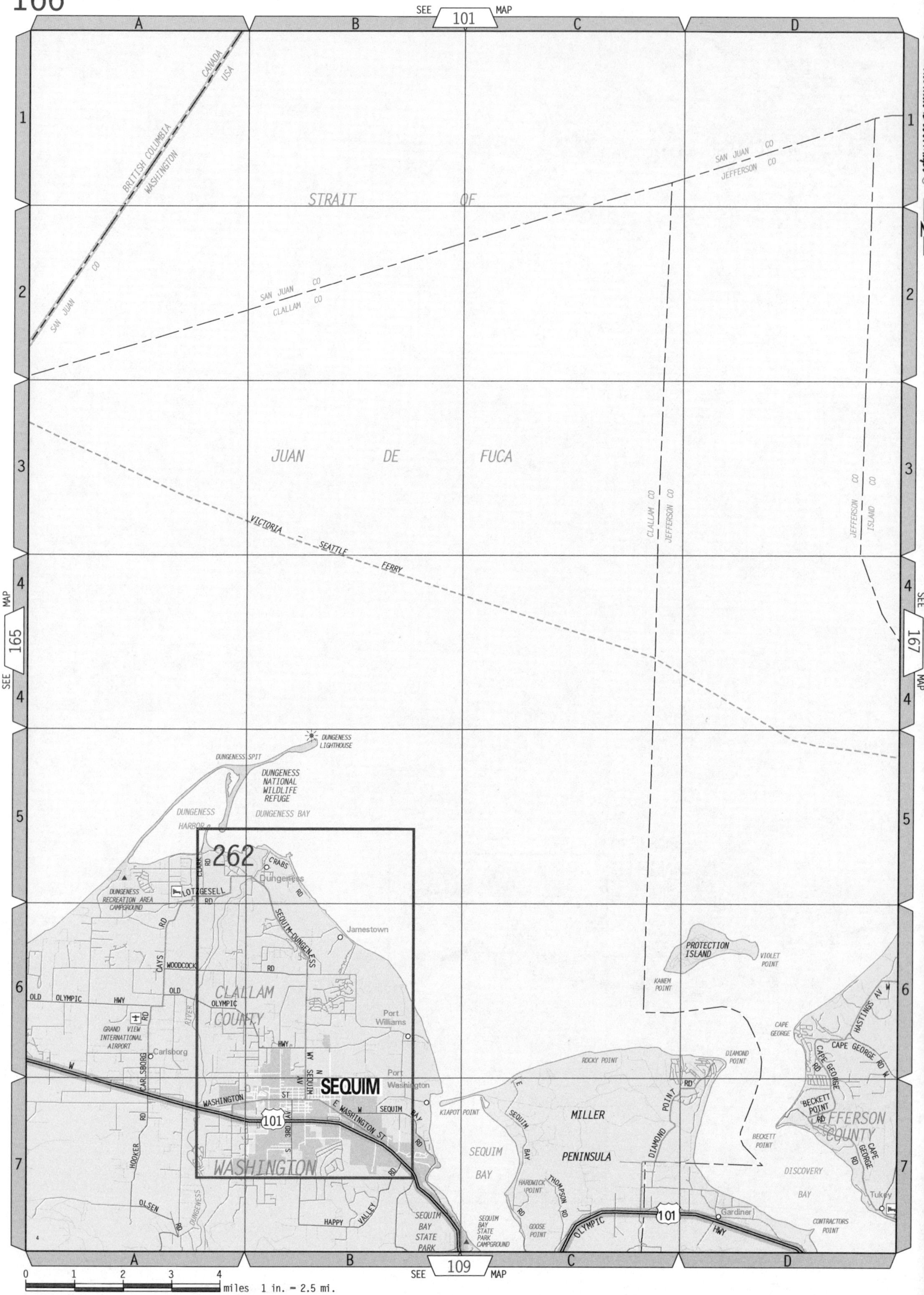

METRO

SEE 101 MAP

A B C D

1

BRITISH COLUMBIA
WASHINGTON
CANADA
USA

STRAIT OF

SAN JUAN CO
JEFFERSON CO

2

SAN JUAN CO

SAN JUAN CO
CLALLAM CO

JUAN DE FUCA

3

VICTORIA — SEATTLE FERRY

CLALLAM CO
JEFFERSON CO

JEFFERSON CO
ISLAND

SEE 165 MAP

4

SEE 167 MAP

DUNGENESS
LIGHTHOUSE

DUNGENESS SPIT

DUNGENESS
NATIONAL
WILDLIFE
REFUGE

DUNGENESS
HARBOR

DUNGENESS BAY

5

262

CRABS

Dungeness

DUNGENESS
RECREATION AREA
CAMPGROUND

TIGESELL
RD

PROTECTION
ISLAND

VIOLET
POINT

KANEM
POINT

6

OLD OLYMPIC HWY

CAYS

WOODCOCK

OLD

CLALLAM
COUNTY

OLYMPIC

SEQUIM-DUNGENESS

RD

Jamestown

Port
Williams

CAPE
GEORGE

DIAMOND
POINT

CAPE GEORGE RD W

HASTINGS AV W

GRAND VIEW
INTERNATIONAL
AIRPORT

CARLSBORG RD

Carlsborg

HWY

Port
Washington

ROCKY POINT

DIAMOND
POINT RD

CAPE GEORGE

BECKETT
POINT
RD

7

WASHINGTON

SEQUIM

SEQUIM
AV
S

E WASHINGTON ST

SEQUIM
BAY
RD

KIAPOT POINT

SEQUIM
BAY

MILLER
PENINSULA

BECKETT
POINT

JEFFERSON
COUNTY

DISCOVERY
BAY

Tukey

HOOKER RD

WASHINGTON

SEQUIM DUNGENESS

HAPPY VALLEY

SEQUIM
BAY
STATE
PARK

SEQUIM
BAY
STATE PARK
CAMPGROUND

GOOSE
POINT

HARDWICK
POINT

THOMPSON RD

DIAMOND POINT RD

OLYMPIC HWY

CAPE GEORGE RD

CONTRACTORS
POINT

Gardiner

OLSEN

SEE 109 MAP

A B C D

0 1 2 3 4 miles 1 in. = 2.5 mi.

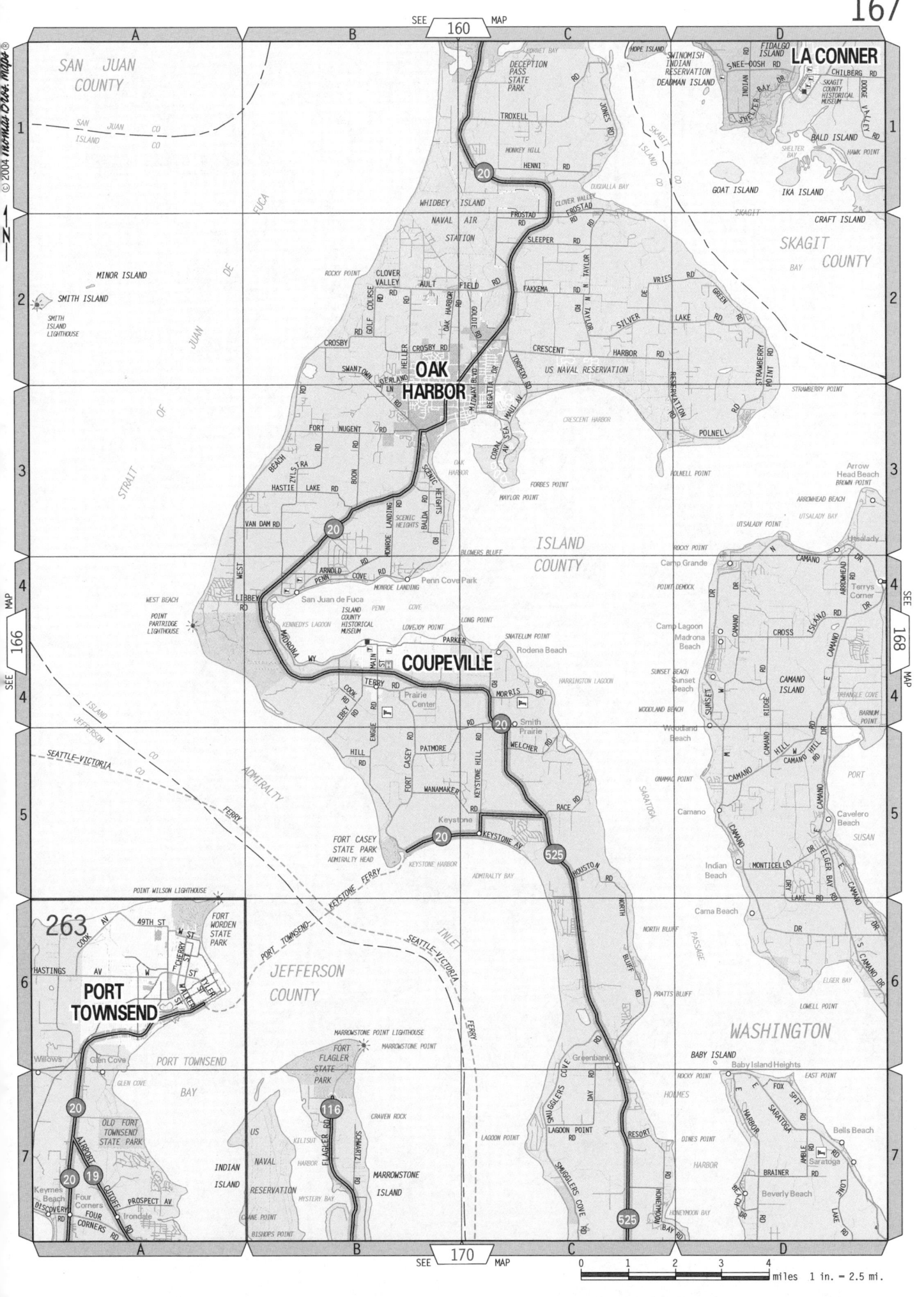

LA CONNER

SAN JUAN COUNTY

SKAGIT COUNTY

OAK HARBOR

ISLAND COUNTY

COUPEVILLE

CAMANO ISLAND

SEE 166 MAP

SEE 168 MAP

METRO

263

PORT TOWNSEND

JEFFERSON COUNTY

WASHINGTON

0 1 2 3 4 miles 1 in. = 2.5 mi.

SEE 161 MAP

© 2004 Thomas Bros. Maps ®

←—N—→

A | B | C | D

MOUNT VERNON

SKAGIT COUNTY

SPLIT ROCK

TABLE MOUNTAIN

LITTLE MOUNTAIN

Big Lake

Montborne

Cedardale

Skagit City

Scott Mountain

DEVILS MOUNTAIN

Devils Mountain

534

9

PILCHUCK BRIDGE CAMPGROUND

Conway

221

Milltown

McMurray

Lake McMurray

STIMSON HILL

SKAGIT CO
SNOHOMISH CO

218

Monson Corner

Corner

Brandstrom

Pilchuck

Cedarhome

STANWOOD

215

212

532

9

Bryant

Stanwood-Bryant RD

ARMSTRONG LAKE

Florence

PRESTLIENS BLUFF

532

530

210

Norman

Silvana

Island School Crossing

ARLINGTON

208

SNOHOMISH

COUNTY

530

531

Lakewood

531

Arlington Airport

Smokey Point

Edgecomb

ISLAND COUNTY

Mountain View Beach

Cornell

CAMANO ISLAND

KAYAK POINT COUNTY PARK

KAYAK POINT

WENBERG CAMPGROUND

Crossing

Sisco

Sisco Heights

Getchell Hill

9

531

Sunny Shore Acres

Sunny Shores

WASHINGTON

Warm Beach

LAKE GOODWIN

Kruse

Mabana

Dallman

Tulare Beach

TULALIP

Getchell Hill

Getchell

MARYSVILLE

Tyee Beach

Spee-bi-dah

Tulalip Shores

Tulalip Shores

INDIAN

202

Pebble Beach

Hermosa Point

Tulalip

TULALIP MARINA

RESERVATION

200

Tulalip Casino

Camano Head

POSSESSION SOUND

SKIOU POINT

5

PASSAGE

SEE 171 MAP

SEE 167 MAP

SEE 102 MAP

METRO

LIVINGSTON BAY

SKAGIT BAY

FIR ISLAND

0 1 2 3 4 miles 1 in. = 2.5 mi.

SEE 162 MAP

A | B | C | D

N

1

OLYMPIC

CHILEAN MEMORIAL MONUMENT

CLALLAM COUNTY

NATIONAL

OLYMPIC

NFD RD 2924

NFD RD 2932

NATIONAL

KLAHANIE CAMPGROUND

HOLE-IN-THE-WALL

DAHDAYLA ISLAND

DICKEY RD

QUILLAYUTE STATE AIRPORT

RIVER

MINA SMITH RD

WENTWORTH RD

RD

MORIARTY RD

QUILLAYUTE

RD

SOL DUC

LA PUSH

RIVER

110

CALAWAH

RD

MERCHANTS RD

CALAWAH WY

ELK CREEK RIDGE

TILLICUM PARK

PENINSULA COLLEGE

FORKS

FOREST

2

LITTLE JAMES ISLAND

RIALTO BEACH

MORA

MORA CAMPGROUND

MORA RD

JAMES

La Push

JAMES ISLAND

FIRST BEACH

QUATEATA

KILMER RD

SOL

DUC

GOODMAN MAIN LINE RD

WASHINGTON

ANDERSON RIDGE

CALAWAH

BOGACHIEL

GARBAGE DUMP RD

BOGACHIEL

FORKS MUNICIPAL AIRPORT

WY

H

FORKS TIMBER MUSEUM

GRADER CREEK HILL

BOGACHIEL STATE PARK

QUILLAYUTE INDIAN RESERVATION

LA PUSH RD

101

RIVER

Bogachiel

UMTEE RD

READE HILL

3

CRYING LADY ROCK

THREE D BEACH

CLALLAM CO

JEFFERSON CO

LAGITOS HILL

DOWANS CREEK RD

TEAHWHIT HEAD

STRAWBERRY BAY

TAYLOR POINT

SCOTTS BLUFF

QUILLAYUTE

GIANTS GRAVEYARD

STRAWBERRY POINT

JEFFERSON COUNTY

PACIFIC

4

NEEDLES

ROUNDED ISLAND

OLYMPIC

TOLEAK POINT

NATIONAL

NATIONAL

PARK

BOULDER BEACH

ALEXANDER ISLAND

SEE 108 MAP

5

OCEAN

WILDLIFE

HOH HEAD

JEFFERSON COVE

DIAMOND ROCK

OIL CITY RD

OIL CITY RIVER

COTTONWOOD CAMPGROUND

RD

6

REFUGE

OIL

CITY

LOWER HOH

HOH INDIAN RES

HOH RD

101

ABBEY ISLAND

RUBY BEACH

7

DESTRUCTION ISLAND VIEWPOINT

DESTRUCTION ISLAND

DESTRUCTION ISLAND LIGHTHOUSE

KALALOCH RIDGE

SEE 172 MAP

A | B | C | D

METRO

0 1 2 3 4 miles   1 in. = 2.5 mi.

SEE MAP 167

METRO

SEE MAP 109

SEE MAP 171

© 2004 Thomas Bros. Maps ®

— N —

A   B   C   D

QUIMPER PENINSULA

ANDERSON LAKE STATE PARK

20
19
Irondale
Irondale Rd
NESS CORNER
NESS RD
CHIMACUM
JORGENSEN HILL
Hadlock
Anderson Lake

INDIAN ISLAND US NAVAL RESERVATION

FLAGLER RD
116
E MARROWSTONE RD
MARROWSTONE ISLAND
NODULE POINT
LIPLIP POINT

BUSH POINT LIGHT
SMUGGLERS COVE
WHIDBEY ISLAND
BUSH POINT
HONEYMOON BAY
525
BERCOT RD
SCENIC DR
Freeland
Newman

HOLMES HARBOR
GOSS LAKE RD
GOSS LAKE
LONE LAKE RD

ISLAND COUNTY

Woodmans
ANDERSON LAKE
Chimacum
BEAVER VALLEY RD
OAK BAY
OAK BAY RD

PUGET

ADMIRALTY INLET

JEFFERSON ISLAND CO

SEATTLE-VICTORIA

MILLMAN RD
Bayview

LANCASTER RD
Austin
MUTINY BAY
DOUBLE BLUFF RD
DEER LAGOON
Sunlight Beach
USELESS BAY
EWING RD
BAYVIEW
SILLS RD

GIBBS LAKE
GIBBS LAKE RD
WEST VALLEY RD
CENTER RD
EGG AND I RD
19
OLELE POINT
MATS MATS BAY
BASALT POINT
BURNER POINT

EAGLEMOUNT RD
VAN TROJAN RD

COLVOS ROCKS LIGHT

DOUBLE BLUFF
DOUBLE BLUFF LIGHT

SOUND

ISLAND CO
KITSAP CO

Center
LARSON LAKE
SWANSONVILLE RD
OLYMPUS BLVD
Swansonville
Port Ludlow
TALA POINT

FOULWEATHER BLUFF
Foulweather Bluff
NE TWIN SPITS RD
SKUNK BAY LIGHT
Hansville
NORWEGIAN POINT
POINT NO POINT LIGHT

JEFFERSON COUNTY

SANDY SHORE LAKE RD
CENTER RD
104
PARADISE BAY RD
OAK BAY
BULLS HEAD
LUDLOW BAY RD
E LUDLOW RIDGE
TALA SHORE DR
WATSON RD
WHITE ROCK
POINT HANNON LIGHT
HOOD HEAD

HOOD CANAL DR NE
HANSVILLE RD NE
NE 360TH ST
PILOT POINT
NE EGLON RD
Eglon
HOFFMAN RD NE

104
TEAL LAKE RD
S POINT RD
Shine
TERMINATION POINT
BYWATER BAY

LITTLE BOSTON
HANSVILLE
PORT GAMBLE INDIAN RESERVATION

DABOB
DABOB POST OFFICE
COYLE RD
THORNTON
Dabob

SQUAMISH HARBOR

PORT GAMBLE HISTORIC MUSEUM
OF SEA AND SHORE MUSEUM
Port Gamble
NE BABCOCK ST
3
KITSAP COUNTY
NE 288TH ST
GAMBLE BAY RD NE
PARCELL RD NE
SANDY BEACH LN NE
APPLE COVE POINT LIGHT
Apple Cove Point

TARBOO BAY
TOANDOS RD
Camp Discovery
CAMP DISCOVERY RD
THORNDYKE RD
THORNDYKE BAY

JEFFERSON CANAL CO
KITSAP CO

Four Corners
104
PORT GAMBLE RD NE
NE SHORTY CAMPBELL RD
104
Kingston
W KINGSTON RD NE
EDMONDS-KINGSTON FERRY

WASHINGTON

HOOD

LINDSAYS BEACH
THORNDYKE RD
Lofall
F
Breidablick
307
Striebels Corner
NE CRAWFORD DR
APPLETREE COVE

LEMONDS RD
TOANDOS PENINSULA
HOOD CANAL LIGHT
BROWN POINT

Vinland
PIONEER HILL RD NW
BIG VALLEY RD NE
NE SAWDUST HILL RD
NE ROVA RD
Kemper Brewery
NE IVERSON RD
GAMBLE RD NE
GUNDERSON RD NE
HANSVILLE RD NE
S KINGSTON RD NE
TULIN RD NE
PRESIDENT POINT

AMBERJACK AV
DARTER RD
RHODODENDRON LN NW
FINN HILL RD NW
NW RUDE RD
LINCOLN RD NE
STOTTLEMYER RD
MILLER BAY RD NE
PORT MADISON INDIAN RESERVATION
MILLER BAY

TABOOK POINT
EASTERN BOUNDARY RD
SEALION ST
BULLHEAD ST
US NAVAL RESERVATION
FRONT ST
305
NE HOSTMARK ST
Marine Science Center
F
NE MESFORD ST
SUQUAMISH WY NE
AUGUSTA AV NE
Suquamish
Indianola

POULSBO

ARCHERFISH ST
ELLER RD
SEAHAWK ST
3
3RD AV NE
NE COLUMBIA
PORT MADISON
AGATE POINT
CLEARWATER CASINO

Bangor
ESCOLAR ST
STURGEON ST
TRIGGER AV
LIBERTY INLET
NOLL RD NE
TOTTEN RD NE
DIVISION AV NE
Suquamish
AGATE PASS
BLOEDEL RESERVE

PUGET

COYLE RD
HAZEL POINT RD
Olympic View
OLYMPIC VIEW LOOP RD
RESERVATION
CLEAR CREEK RD
VIKING WY NW
LUOTO RD
SILVERDALE WY NW
Virginia
Lemolo
SHORE DR NE
Naval Undersea Museum
Keyport
308
NE
POINT BOLIN
305
Seabold
SUNRISE DR NE
Port Madison
POINT MONROE LIGHT

ZELATCHED POINT RD
HAZEL POINT
FISHERMAN HARBOR
THRESHER AV
RABAAL
WIDME RD
SHORE DR
NAVAL UNDERSEA MUSEUM
SUQUAMISH MUSEUM

SOUND
KITSAP CO
KING CO

0 1 2 3 4 miles   1 in. = 2.5 mi.

SEE MAP 174

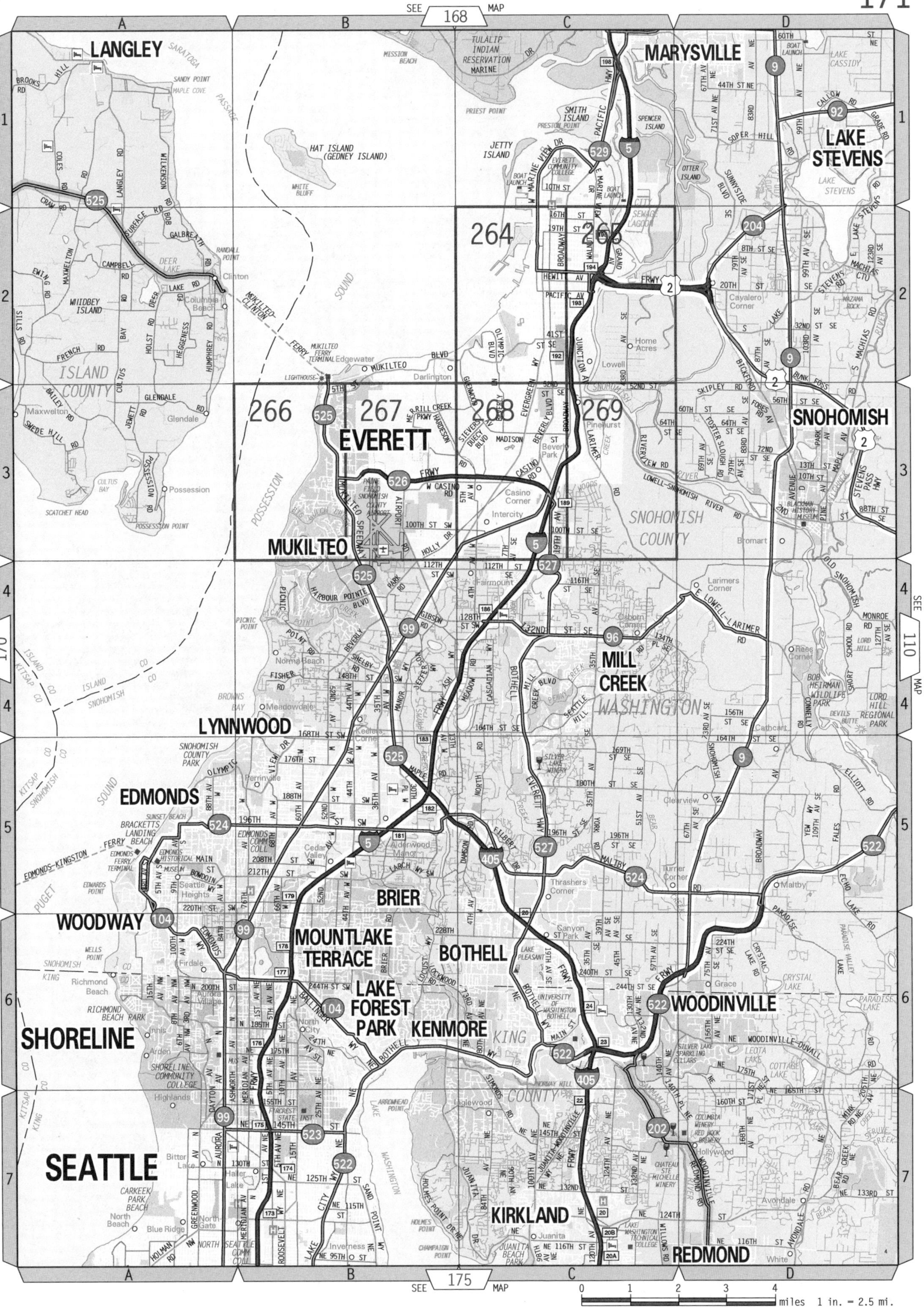

SEE MAP 168

LANGLEY

MARYSVILLE

LAKE STEVENS

264   267   265

266   267   268   269

EVERETT

SNOHOMISH

MUKILTEO

SNOHOMISH COUNTY

WASHINGTON

MILL CREEK

LYNNWOOD

EDMONDS

WOODWAY

BRIER

MOUNTLAKE TERRACE

BOTHELL

WOODINVILLE

LAKE FOREST PARK

KENMORE

SHORELINE

KING COUNTY

SEATTLE

KIRKLAND

REDMOND

SEE MAP 175

0 1 2 3 4 miles   1 in. = 2.5 mi.

METRO

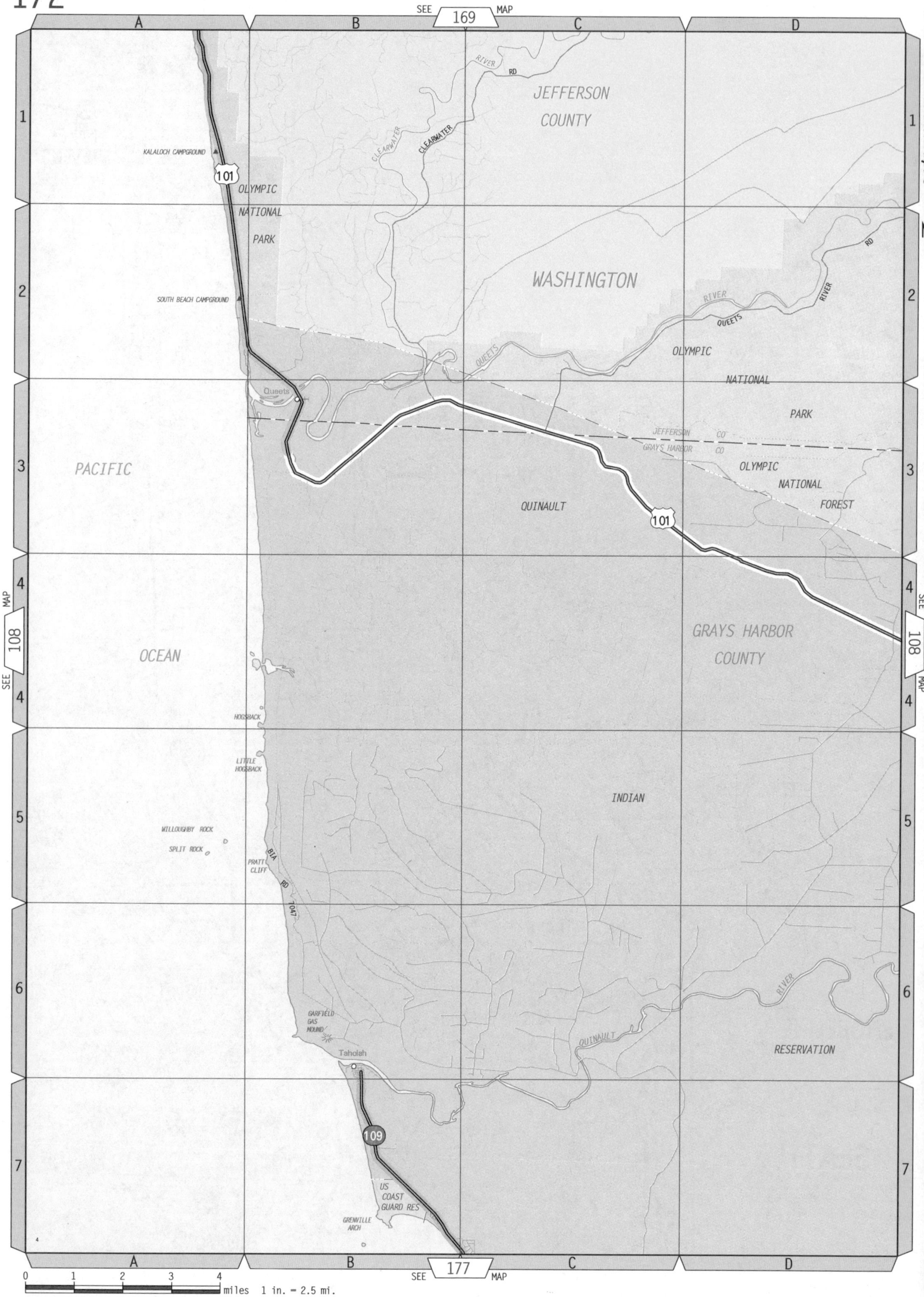

172

A   B   C   D

1   1

JEFFERSON
COUNTY

CLEARWATER RIVER RD

CLEARWATER

CLEARWATER

KALALOCH CAMPGROUND

101

OLYMPIC

NATIONAL

PARK

WASHINGTON

2   2

SOUTH BEACH CAMPGROUND

RIVER

QUEETS

RIVER RD

OLYMPIC

NATIONAL

QUEETS

PARK

Queets

PACIFIC

3   3

SEE 108 MAP

QUINAULT

JEFFERSON CO
GRAYS HARBOR CO

OLYMPIC

NATIONAL

FOREST

101

OCEAN

4   4

GRAYS HARBOR
COUNTY

SEE 108 MAP

HOGSBACK

LITTLE
HOGSBACK

INDIAN

5   5

WILLOUGHBY ROCK

SPLIT ROCK

PRATT
CLIFF

BIA RD 7047

6   6

RIVER

GARFIELD
GAS
MOUND

Taholah

QUINAULT

RESERVATION

7   7

109

US
COAST
GUARD RES

GRENVILLE
ARCH

A   B   C   D

METRO

0   1   2   3   4   miles 1 in. = 2.5 mi.

METRO

A B C D

1

OLYMPIC NATIONAL PARK

OLYMPIC NATIONAL FOREST

JEFFERSON COUNTY

SAINT PETERS DOME

TRAP PASS

NFD RD 2530
NFD RD 2540

NORTH ROCK

NFD RD 2546

NFD RD 2510

NFD RD 2515

DUCKABUSH RIVER

NFD RD 2510

MOUNT JUPITER

DUCKABUSH RD

BLACK POINT
Duckabush

PLEASANT HARBOR

QUATSAP POINT

JEFFERSON CO
KITSAP CO

MISERY POINT
MIAMI BEACH

MAPLE BEACH

MISERY POINT LOOP NW

Seabeck

2

LENA LAKE CAMPGROUND

WEST ROCK
EAST ROCK

NFD RD 25-24

NFD RD 240.3

WEBB MOUNTAIN

JEFFERSON CO
MASON CO

FT SEACOUNT DR

McDONALD COVE

TRITON COVE

TRITON HEAD

HOOD POINT

STAVIS BAY RD NW

LARSON LN NW

KITSAP COUNTY

HITE CENTER

SEABECK-HOLLY RD NW

25
LENA CREEK CAMPGROUND

HAMMA HAMMA CAMPGROUND

NFD RD 2421

NFD RD 2472

HAMMA HAMMA RD

NFD RD 2510

TEKIU POINT

Nellita

NELLITA RD NW

HITE CENTER NW

NW FOUR WHEEL DR

NW HOLLY RD

Camp Union

TAHUYA LAKE RD NW

OLYMPIC

JEFFERSON RIDGE

3

NFD RD 2401

NATIONAL

FOREST

NFD RD 2420

NFD RD 2470

NFD RD 2480

2469

RIVER

Eldon

CUMMINGS POINT

SEABECK RD

Holly

HOLLY RD

WASHINGTON

W WINTERGREEN LN

Morgan Marsh

PETER HAGEN RD NW

Crosby

HINTZVILLE RD NW

LEWIS RD NW

McCaslin Marsh

NORTH MISSION RD

GOLD CREEK RD

4

NFD RD 2464

WASHINGTON PASS

24

AYOCK POINT

CAPSTAN ROCK

DEWATTO RD

CHINOM POINT

KITSAP CO
MASON CO

W BEAR CREEK RD

BEAR CREEK

DEWATTO RD

LOST HWY

PANTHER LAKE RD

SCARIFICATION RD

SAND HILL

DEWATTO RD

OLD BELFAIR HWY

SEE MAP 109

SEE MAP 174

LILLIWAUP CREEK CAMPGROUND

SADDLE MOUNTAIN

HOLLY RD

TOONERVILLE RD

5

LILLIWAUP FALLS

Lilliwaup

LILLIWAUP BAY

101

HOOD CANAL

Dewatto

DEWATTO BAY

LONG POINT

DEWATTO

DEWATTO RD

TAHUYA BLACKSMITH RD

BELFAIR-TAHUYA

ELFENDAHL PASS

PLANTATION RD

NORTH SHORE RD

3

300

Belfair

LYNCH COVE

PLUM POINT

DOW MOUNTAIN

6

HOODSPORT TRAIL STATE PARK

HOODSPORT WINERY

RED BLUFF

NORTH SHORE RD

TAHUYA RIVER

TAHUYA RIVER

BELFAIR-TAHUYA RD

TAHUYA RIVER

NORTH SHORE RD

Sunset Beach

HOOD CANAL

OLD BELFAIR HWY

3

302

LAKE CUSHMAN RD

119

101

Hoodsport

MUSQUETI POINT

Allyn

7

POTLATCH STATE PARK CAMPGROUND

ANNAS BAY

Potlatch

AYRES POINT

NORTH SHORE RD

Tahuya

SISTERS POINTS

106

Forest Beach

TWANOH STATE PARK

MASON LAKE DR W

MASON LAKE

MASON LAKE RD

NORTH BAY

ROCKY POINT

3

REACH ISLAND

SKOKOMISH INDIAN RES

SKOKOMISH VALLEY

101 106

Union

McREAVY RD

DALBY RD

McREAVY RD

Grahamsville

Fernwood

MASON LAKE RD

MASON-BENSON RD

NORTH SHORE TRAILS DR

Allyn-Grapeview

GRAPEVIEW LOOP RD

MASON COUNTY

A B C D

0 1 2 3 4 miles   1 in. = 2.5 mi.

© 2004 Thomas Bros. Maps

SEE 170 MAP

A   B   C   D

METRO

SEE 173 MAP

SEE 175 MAP

SEE 181 MAP

© 2007 Thomas Bros. Maps ®

1

2

3

4

4

5

6

7

270   **271**

BREMERTON

PORT ORCHARD

GIG HARBOR

JEFFERSON CO
KITSAP CO

HOOD CANAL

OAK HEAD
LONE ROCK
SEABECK HWY
PIONEER RD
MANLEY RD NW
ANDERSON HILL RD
SESAME ST NW
DICKEY RD
NW NEWBERRY HILL RD
KLAHOWYA TR
LARSON RD
NW GROSS RD
CAMP WESLEY HARRIS NAVAL RESERVATION
Wildcat Lake
NW HOLLY RD
WILDCAT LAKE
Wildcat Lake
UNION RIVER RESERVOIR
GREAT PENINSULA
BELFAIR VALLEY RD
Bremerton Junction
KITSAP COUNTY AIRPORT
MINARD RD
OLD BELFAIR RD
OLD BARNEY WHITE
KITSAP CO
MASON CO
FERN Lake
WYE Lake
ALTA VISTA DR
CARNEY LAKE
Carney Lake
STANSBERRY LAKE
MINTERWOOD LAKE
PIERCE COUNTY
ROCKY POINT
ROCKY BAY
WINDY BLUFF
CASE INLET
VAUGHN
VAUGHN BAY
OLSON
BAYVIEW
GLENCOVE HOTEL
KEY PEN HWY
WRIGHT-BLISS RD
BLISS-COCHRANE RD
118TH ST KPN
128TH ST KPN
144TH ST KPN
ELGIN
CLIFTON
Elgin
302
HENDERSON BAY
126TH AV KPN
CRESTVIEW DR
WAUNA
144TH ST NW
SEHMEL RD
THOMAS RD
ALLEN POINT
Rosedale
GIG HARBOR PENINSULA HISTORICAL MUSEUM
BURNHAM DR
96TH ST NW
SUNRISE BEACH COUNTY PK
HALLSTROM
CRESCENT VALLEY
PEACOCK HILL AV
Maplewood
BURLEY LAGOON
BURLEY
OLYMPIC DR
STEVENS
BETHEL-BURLEY RD
Burley
HORSESHOE LAKE
WEST OAK RD
PINE RD
SPRUCE
MADRONA DR
WEST BROOK
WINTERBROOK
GLENWOOD RD
SIDNEY RD
WILDWOOD RD
Lake Helena
OAKRIDGE DR SW
Lake Flora
LAKE FLORA RD
J M DICKENSON RD
WASHINGTON
KITSAP COUNTY
Long Lake
PHILLIPS RD
MULLENIK RD
OLALLA VALLEY RD
SE VIEWPARK RD
FRAGARIA
COMMAND POINT
OLALLA
COLVOS PASSAGE
PUGET SOUND
PIERCE CO
KING CO
VASHON ISLAND
VASHON MUNICIPAL AIRPORT
KING COUNTY
WESTSIDE HWY SW
Cedarhurst
BEALS POINT
PETER POINT
FERN COVE
Colvos
Glen Acres
Dilworth
Vashon
Cove
SUNRISE
SW BANK RD
Sunset Beach
Vashon Center
204TH ST
111TH AV SW
Lisabeula
220TH ST SW
Cross
SANFORD
CHRISTIANSON COVE
Portage
Burton
QUARTERMASTER HARBOR
Magnolia Beach
DOCKTON
MAURY ISLAND
PUBLIC BOAT LAUNCH
LOST LAKE PARK
99TH AV SW
Rosehilla
Manzanita
Northilla
PINER PT
EAST PASSAGE
TACOMA YACHT CLUB
CAMP SEALTH RECREATION AREA
Spring Beach
Camp Sealth
TRAMP HARBOR
ST Ellisport
MONUMENT RD

SILVERDALE
CLEAR CREEK RD
WAAGA WAY
BUCKLIN HILL RD
NE BUCKLIN HILL RD
OLD FRONTIER RD
RIDGETOP BLVD
SILVERDALE WAY
KITSAP COUNTY MUSEUM
DYES INLET
Chico
CHICO WAY
Tracyton
Erlands Point
Rocky Point
MARINE DRIVE
SHORE DRIVE
ROCKY POINT RD
KITSAP WAY
Kitsap Lake
HARLOW WY
PRICE RD
WEST PARK
WerCharleston
15TH ST
6TH ST
1ST ST
NAVY YARD CITY
SINCLAIR INLET
310
304
303
166
Central Valley
NE WILLIAMS RD
NE MCWILLIAMS RD
Meadowdale
STAMPEDE BLVD NW
FAIRGROUNDS RD
PERRY AV
WHEATON WY
TRENTON AV
SYLVAN WY
Sheridan Park
East Bremerton
NE RIDDELL RD
NE SYLVAN AV
PINE RD NE
ILLAHEE RD NE
GILBERTON-ILLAHEE RD
Gilberton
Illahee
Fairview
Manette
OLD MILITARY RD
VALLEY RD NE
OLD NE MADISON
CENTRAL VALLEY RD NE
COLE RD NE
PORT ORCHARD
ORCHARD
BATTLE POINT
BATTLE POINT LIGHT
Venice
Manzanita
ARROW POINT
MANZANITA RD NE
HIDDEN COVE RD NE
DAY RD NE
DAY RD NE
WARDWELL RD NE
LOVGREN RD NE
SUNRISE DR NE
Rollingbay
SKIFF POINT
Manitou Beach
BAINBRIDGE ISLAND
SPORTSMAN CLUB RD NE
SPRINGRIDGE RD NE
FLETCHER BAY RD NE
MILLER RD NE
New Brooklyn
NEW BROOKLYN RD NE
NE HIGH SCHOOL RD
Fletcher Bay
BAKER HILL RD
Lynwood Center
Point White
PLEASANT BEACH
Eagledale
Winslow
BAINBRIDGE ISLAND VINEYARDS & WINERY
BLAKELY AV NE
Blakely Rock
BLAKELY HARBOR
BLAKELY ROCK LIGHT
COUNTRY CLUB RD NE
RESTORATION POINT
EAGLE HARBOR
PUGET SOUND
WHITE POINT LIGHT
SEATTLE-VICTORIA FERRY
SEATTLE FERRY
SEATTLE-BREMERTON FERRY
JOE JAM HILL RD NE
EAGLE HARBOR DR NE
South Beach
305
WESTWOOD DR NE
Manchester
MANCHESTER STATE PARK
NAVAL RESERVATION
Waterman
POINT WHITE DR
Wautauga Beach
Waterman Point
Enetai
COLLINS RD
ALASKA AV SE
COLCHESTER DR SE
Colchester
South Colby
Harper
Yukon Harbor
Annapolis
Parkwood
ORCHARD HEIGHTS
SE MILE HILL DR
GARFIELD
E COLLINS RD
MITCHELL
PORT ORCHARD BLVD
SIDNEY AV
BETHEL RD
SEDGWICK RD
BANNER RD SE
LOCKER RD
ARVICK RD SE
SE LUND AV
SALMONBERRY RD
SE BAKER RD
OVERRA RD
BIELMEIR RD
LIDER RD
BLACK RD
OLALLA VALLEY
VALLEY RD
ORCHARD
ANDERSON POINT
160
Southworth
SOUTHWORTH FERRY TERMINAL
SEATTLE-VASHON PASSENGER ONLY FERRY
SEATTLE-SOUTHWORTH FERRY
VASHON FERRY TERMINAL
VASHON POINT
DOLPHIN POINT
Vashon Heights
Biloxi
SYLVAN BEACH
OLD HWY 160
OLD OLYMPIC DR
Blake Island
BLAKE ISLAND STATE PARK
SEABECK
16
3
BLAINE

HULL ST
TREMONT ST
JACKSON AV
LOTTERY
CLIFTON
ANDERSON HILL
VICTORY DR
SUNNYSLOPE
FEIGLEY RD
GORST
SW BERRY RD
Fernwood
BEAR LAKE
WAVA LN
HUNTER
PARADISE LN
FAIRVIEW LAKE RD
CARNEY
KITSAP CO
DAISY ST
BANDIX RD
WILLOCK RD
GEODUCK
BOAT LAUNCH
NORTH RD
34TH AV NW
70TH AV NW
86TH AV NW
94TH ST NW
Tardy

0 1 2 3 4 miles   1 in. = 2.5 mi.

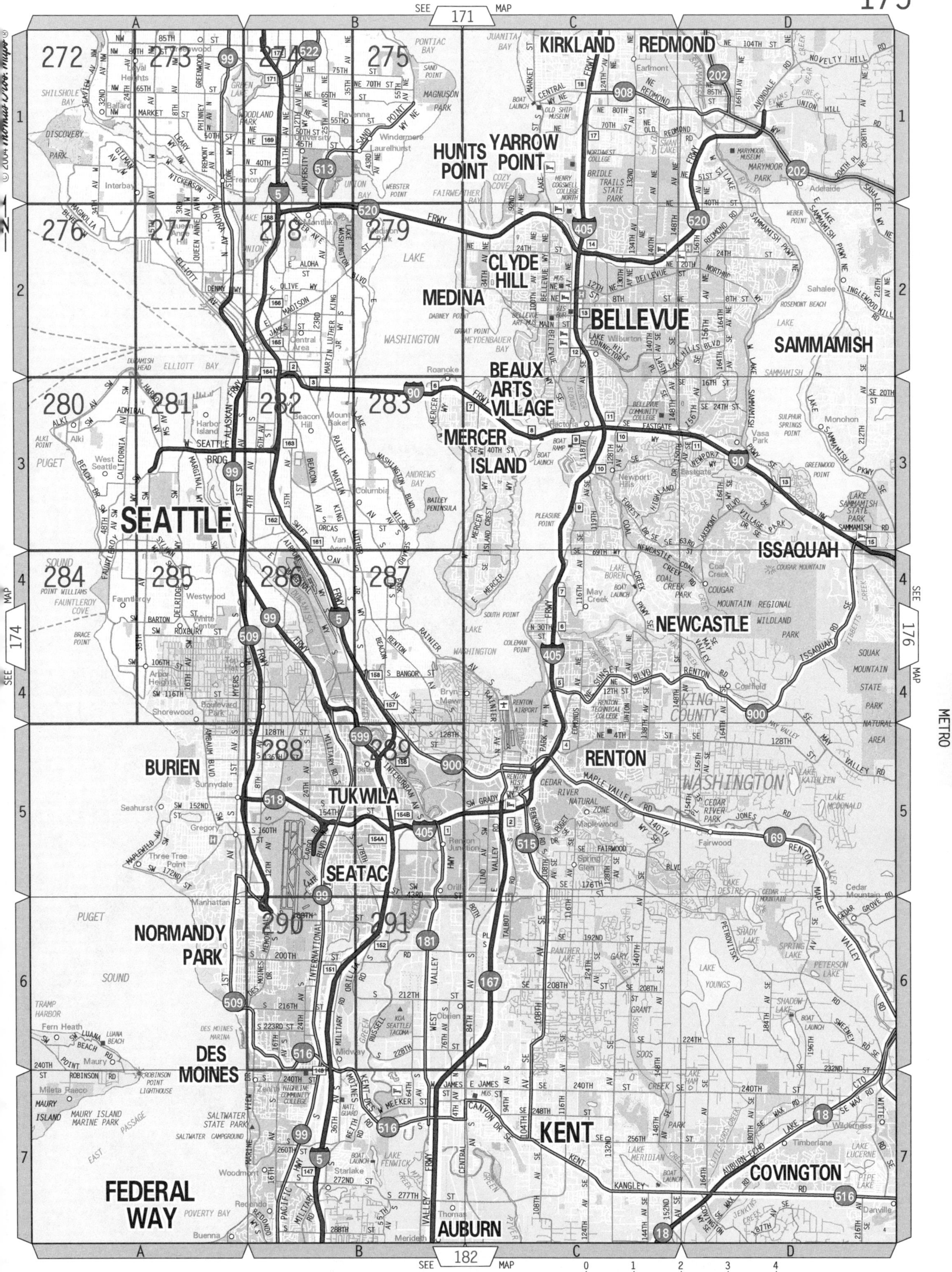

SEE 171 MAP

METRO

© 2004 Thomas Bros. Maps®

KIRKLAND **REDMOND**

HUNTS POINT **YARROW POINT**

CLYDE HILL

MEDINA

BELLEVUE

SAMMAMISH

BEAUX ARTS VILLAGE

MERCER ISLAND

SEATTLE

ISSAQUAH

NEWCASTLE

BURIEN

TUKWILA

RENTON

WASHINGTON

KING COUNTY

SEATAC

NORMANDY PARK

DES MOINES

KENT

COVINGTON

FEDERAL WAY

AUBURN

272 273 274 275
276 277 278 279
280 281 282 283
284 285 286 287
288 289
290 291

SEE 174 MAP
SEE 176 MAP
SEE 182 MAP

0 1 2 3 4 miles   1 in. = 2.5 mi.

A B C D
1 2 3 4 5 6 7

A   B   SEE 110 MAP   C   D

1

2

3

4

5

6

7

METRO

SEE 175 MAP

SEE 111 MAP

NOVELTY HILL RD

CARNATION-DUVALL

STILLWATER PARK

Stillwater

LAKE MARGARET

LAKE JOY

SOUTH FORK

TOLT RIVER

TOLT RIVER RESERVOIR

SIKES LAKE

PETERSON POND

UNION HILL

AMES LAKE

NE CARNATION FARM RD

CARNATION FARM

HORSESHOE LAKE

TOLT HILL

TOLT RIVER HIGHLANDS AREA

CARNATION

BLACK LAKE

RIVER RD

REDMOND FALL CITY RD

MACDONALD MEMORIAL PARK

TOLT

LANGLOIS LAKE

SAMMAMISH

228TH AV NE

244TH AV NE

NE 8TH ST

AMES LAKE RD

FALL CITY

203

PLATT POND

HANS LAKE

KING COUNTY

BRIDGES LAKE

METCALF MARSH

NORTH FORK COUNTY

SNOQUALMIE

202

BEAVER LAKE

SE 32ND ST

DUTHIE HILL RD

REDMOND FALL CITY RD

SNOQUALMIE

GRIFFIN CREEK

RUTHERFORD SLOUGH

WASHINGTON

FULLER MOUNTAIN

KLAUS LAKE

TEN CREEK

CALLIGAN LAKE

228TH AV SE

ISSAQUAH PINE LAKE RD

SE 43RD WY

TRINITY LUTHERAN COLLEGE

SNOQUALMIE BLVD

FALL CITY RD

324TH AV SE

Fall City

FALL CITY-SNOQUALMIE

TOKUL

LAKE HANCOCK

88TH ST SE

NORTH FORK

56TH ST

ISSAQUAH

GRAND RIDGE

SNOQUALMIE FALLS

RIVER

BORST LAKE

THREE FORKS PARK REINIG

Ernies Grove

MOON VALLEY RD

17

18

90

FRONT ST

ISSAQUAH STATE SALMON HATCHERY

High Point

EAST

SE HIGH POINT WY

20

TRADITION LAKE

TIGER MOUNTAIN

Preston

22

PRESTON-FALL CITY RD

TEATERS BLUFF

LAKE ALICE

OUR LAKE

NORTHWEST RAILWAY MUSEUM

RAILROAD AV SE

NORTH BEND

202

GREEN MOUNTAIN

ISSAQUAH

SQUAK/TIGER MOUNTAIN CORRIDOR

25

FRWY

27

90

ECHO LAKE

H

428TH AV SE

NORTH BEND WY

SQUAK MOUNTAIN STATE PARK NATURAL AREA

MAY VALLEY RD

SE TIGER MOUNTAIN RD

Mirrormont

FOREST

STATE

Upper Preston

LAKE CREEK

RAGING RIVER

18

CANYON CREEK

CEDAR FALLS RD SE

RATTLESNAKE MOUNTAIN SCENIC AREA

RATTLESNAKE MOUNTAIN

Tanner

31

MUSEUM

BEND

LITTLE SI

32

436TH AV SE

SNOQUALMIE

34

GROUSE RIDGE

ISSAQUAH HOBART RD

SE 156TH ST

GROVE RD

Four Lakes

SOUTH TIGER MOUNTAIN

DEEP CREEK

Taylor Mountain

BREW HILL

Edgewick

RATTLESNAKE LEDGE

CEDAR BUTTE

90

FRWY

38

WEBSTER LAKE

FRANCIS LAKE

LAKE 196TH ST

SE 200TH ST

AUBURN-ECHO LAKE RD

CEDAR GROVE RD

WEBSTER CREEK

HOTEL CREEK

WILLIAM CREEK

RATTLESNAKE LAKE

Cedar Falls

LOOKOUT MOUNTAIN

CEDAR LAKE

GRANGE CREEK

HULL CREEK

MAPLE VALLEY

169

Wilderness

LANDSBURG RD

276TH AV SE

WALSH LAKE

DIVERSION DITCH

CEDAR RIVER

DUCK CREEK

ROCK CREEK

Bagley Jct

Barneston

MOUNT BAKER-SNOQUALMIE

CHESTER MORSE LAKE

NFD RD 50

Summit

516

KENT

SE SUMMIT

Landsburg

Georgetown

KANGLEY RD

Kangley

RAVENSDALE LAKE

Ravensdale

LAKE RETREAT

Trude

Selleck

Sugarloaf Mountain

NATIONAL FOREST

0 1 2 3 4 miles 1 in. = 2.5 mi.

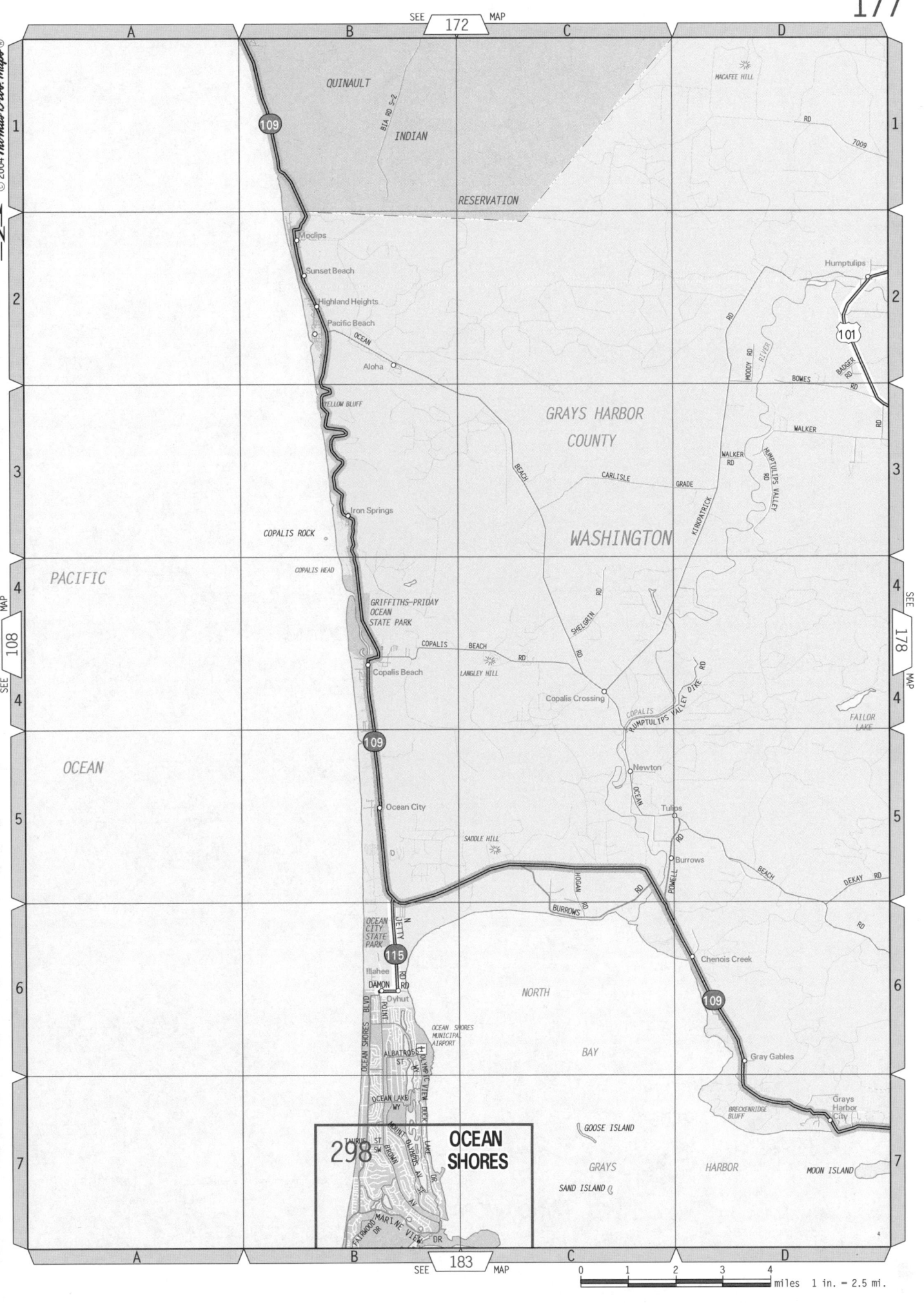

© 2004 Thomas Bros. Maps®

N

QUINAULT

BIA RD S-2

INDIAN

RESERVATION

MACAFEE HILL

RD

7009

109

Moclips

Sunset Beach

Highland Heights

Pacific Beach

OCEAN

Aloha

YELLOW BLUFF

COPALIS ROCK

Iron Springs

COPALIS HEAD

PACIFIC

GRIFFITHS-PRIDAY
OCEAN
STATE PARK

COPALIS   BEACH

COPALIS   BEACH   RD

Copalis Beach

LANGLEY HILL

OCEAN

Copalis Crossing

GRAYS HARBOR

COUNTY

CARLISLE   GRADE

WASHINGTON

BEACH

SHELGRIN   RD

RD

WALKER
RD

KIRKPATRICK

HUMPTULIPS VALLEY

Humptulips

101

MOODY RD

RIVER

BOWES

RD

WALKER

BOWES
RD

RD

COPALIS

HUMPTULIPS VALLEY DYKE RD

RD

FAILOR
LAKE

SEE 108 MAP

SEE 178 MAP

METRO

109

Newton

OCEAN

Ocean City

SADDLE HILL

Tulips

RD

Burrows

HOGAN RD

BURROWS

POWELL RD

BEACH

DEKAY RD

RD

OCEAN
CITY
STATE
PARK

Illahee

DAMON

Dyhut

N JETTY RD RD

115

OCEAN SHORES BLVD

POINT

ALBATROSS
ST

OCEAN LAKE
WY

OCEAN SHORES
MUNICIPAL
AIRPORT

OLYMPIC VIEW DUCK

NORTH

BAY

Chenois Creek

109

Gray Gables

BRECKENRIDGE
BLUFF

Grays
Harbor
City

298

TAURUS ST SW

ST SW

MT BROWN

LAKE

MOUNT OLYMPUS AV

OCEAN
SHORES

GOOSE ISLAND

GRAYS   HARBOR

MOON ISLAND

SAND ISLAND

FAIRWOOD DR

MARINE VIEW DR

0   1   2   3   4
miles   1 in. = 2.5 mi.

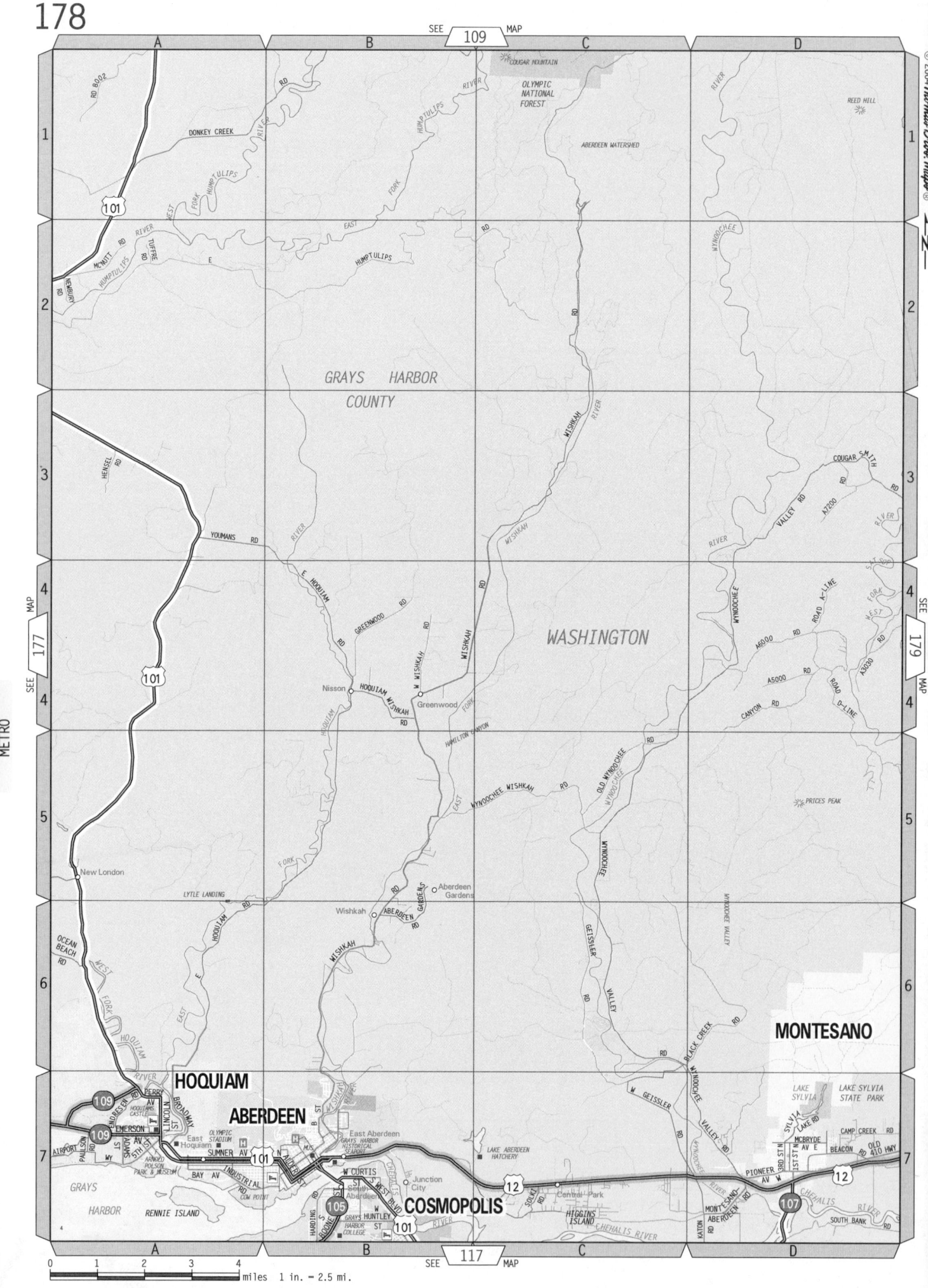

METRO

SEE 109 MAP

© 2004 Thomas Bros. Maps ®

—N—

SEE 177 MAP

SEE 179 MAP

A   B   C   D

1
2
3
4
4
5
6
7

RD 8002

DONKEY CREEK

101

WEST FORK HUMPTULIPS RIVER

HUMPTULIPS RIVER

EAST FORK

COUGAR MOUNTAIN

OLYMPIC
NATIONAL
FOREST

ABERDEEN WATERSHED

REED HILL

RIVER

WYNOOCHEE RIVER

MCNUTT RD
HUMPTULIPS RD
TUFFRE RD
NEWBURY RD

HUMPTULIPS

RD

GRAYS HARBOR
COUNTY

WISHKAH RIVER

COUGAR SMITH RD

HENSEL RD

YOUMANS RD

RIVER

WASHINGTON

E HOQUIAM RD

GREENWOOD RD

W WISHKAH RD

WISHKAH RD

RIVER

VALLEY RD
A7200 RD

RIVER

WEST FORK

WYNOOCHEE E RD

A6000 RD

ROAD A-LINE

A5000 RD

ROAD D-LINE

A3030

Nisson

HOQUIAM WISHKAH RD

Greenwood

EAST FORK

HAMILTON CANYON

CANYON RD

HOQUIAM RIVER

WYNOOCHEE WISHKAH RD

OLD WYNOOCHEE RD

WYNOOCHEE RD

PRICES PEAK

New London

LYTLE LANDING

FORK

HOQUIAM RD

Wishkah

ABERDEEN RD

GARDEN RD

Aberdeen
Gardens

WYNOOCHEE

GEISSLER VALLEY RD

WYNOOCHEE VALLEY RD

OCEAN
BEACH
RD

WEST FORK

EAST FORK HOQUIAM

WISHKAH RD

BLACK CREEK RD

MONTESANO

HOQUIAM
ABERDEEN

109
109

PERRY AV
HOQUIAM'S CASTLE
BROADWAY
LINCOLN ST

EMERSON

AIRPORT WY
PAULSON RD
SUMNER AV
5TH WY
SUMNER AV

OLYMPIC
STADIUM

East Hoquiam

ARNOLD POLSON PARK & MUSEUM

B ST
WISHKAH ST
East Aberdeen
GRAYS HARBOR HISTORICAL SEAPORT

W GEISSLER RD

RD

W GEISSLER RD

WYNOOCHEE VALLEY RD

LAKE
SYLVIA

LAKE SYLVIA
STATE PARK

SYLVIA LAKE RD

CAMP CREEK RD

MCBRYDE AV
BEACON
3RD ST N
1ST ST N

OLD 410 HWY

101

BAY AV

INDUSTRIAL

COW POINT

W CURTIS ST

South Aberdeen

Junction
City

Central Park

12

107

PIONEER AV W

MONTESANO
ABERDEEN RD

KAMON RD

GRAYS
HARBOR

RENNIE ISLAND

105

HARDING S
BOONE S
GRAYS HARBOR COLLEGE
HUNTLEY ST

COSMOPOLIS

101

CHEHALIS RIVER

SO RD

HIGGINS
ISLAND

CHEHALIS RIVER

SOUTH BANK RD

CHEHALIS RIVER

Lake Aberdeen
Hatchery

SEE 117 MAP

0   1   2   3   4
miles   1 in. = 2.5 mi.

SEE 109 MAP

METRO

A | B | C | D

WASHINGTON

NFD RD 21.53

NFD RD 2199
NFD RD 2399
NFD RD 2255
CREEK
NFD RD 3RD
2341
NFD RD 2199

SOUTH MOUNTAIN

SKOKOMISH RIVER
SKOKOMISH VALLEY
RD
Mohrweis
SHELTON TROUT HATCHERY

KELLY HALL RD
BEEVILLE LOOP RD
ANDERSON RD
FORD RD

NFD RD 1700

NAHWATZEL LAKE
SHELTON-MATLOCK

DAYTON-AIRPORT
102
WASHINGTON CORRECTIONS CENTER

Matlock

Frisken Wye
DECKERVILLE RD
Deckerville

Dayton

WEST FORK SATSOP RIVER
CANYON
KELLY RD

MASON COUNTY

WARDEN
BINGHAM
DELL
ADAMS RD

LITTLE EGYPT VALLEY EGYPT
LITTLE RD
RD

MARY M KNIGHT RD

CONGAR SMITH RD
MIDDLE SATSOP
SATSOP FORK
DRY CREEK
FIRE

DAYTON PEAK

FISH HATCHERY RD
FORD LOOP RD

HIGHLAND
GALLAGHER RD
CLOQUALLUM RD

STAR LAKE
SNAG HILL
LOST LAKE
LOST LAKE
WHITE STAR

SEE 178 MAP
SEE 180 MAP

MIDDLE SATSOP RD
RD B-LINE
RD A-LINE

SIMPSON STATE SALMON HATCHERY

RIVER
CS30
CLOQUALLUM RD
Cloquallum

A2000 RD
DECKER
PLUG MILL RD
BEERBOWER
SATSOP
CLOQUALLUM RD

G-LINE
A-LINE
A1000 RD

SCHAFER STATE PARK
MASON CO
GRAYS HARBOR CO

CLOQUALLUM CREEK
CREEK

108
TORNQUIST RD

MASON CO
THURSTON CO

G1100
G100 RD
SATSOP RD
EAST SATSOP

GRAYS HARBOR COUNTY

HICKLIN
SUMMIT RD
Hillgrove
ELMA-MCCLEARY RD
MCCLEARY
HICKLIN HILL

8

MIDDLE SATSOP RD

A900 RD
FALLS CREEK RD
BUSH RD
POWER CREEK

Garden City
ELMA-

McKNIGHT RD
S LINE RD

BO-X CREEK
GRAYS HARBOR CO
THURSTON CO

MONTESANO

W RIVER
STEPHEN RD
SATSOP

Whites
OLD 410 HWY
LOST LAKE RD

FOREMAN RD

8

Satsop
MOORE RD
ONEILL RD
HURD RD
NEWMAN CREEK RD
STAMPER

R
SOUTH UNION RD

OLD SAND CREEK RD

A4000 RD

CAPITOL STATE FOREST

410
OLD
KEYES RD
BRADY LOOP RD
HENRY FOSTER RD

Brady
12

WAKEFIELD RD
W MARTIN ST
W MAIN ST
ELMA
BUSHWELL RD

MOX-CHEHALIS RD

RD A-LINE

BUCK RIDGE

ELMA MUNICIPAL AIRPORT

12

NOX-CHEHALIS RD

RD B-1000
RD C-LINE

WENZEL SLOUGH RD
CHEHALIS RIVER
South Elma
Damon
SOUTH BANK RD
WORKMAN CREEK RD

Malone

PORTER CREEK RD

SEE 117 MAP

A | B | C | D

0 1 2 3 4 miles 1 in. = 2.5 mi.

METRO

SEE MAP 173

SEE MAP 179

SEE MAP 181

SEE MAP 184

miles 1 in. = 2.5 mi.

MASON COUNTY

PIERCE COUNTY

SKOKOMISH INDIAN RES

WEBB HILL

GEORGE ADAMS SALMON HATCHERY

PURDY CUTOFF

BROCKDALE RD

CRANBERRY LAKE

LAKE LIMERICK

MCREAVY RD

MCEWAN PRAIRIE RD

MASON LAKE RD W

MASON LAKE RD

MASON LAKE

Little Hoquiam

LAKE DR W

MASON BENSON RD

GRAPEVIEW LOOP

MCLANE COVE

DOUGALL POINT

INDIAN COVE

STRETCH ISLAND

HERRON BAY

HERRON ISLAND

Herron

DAYTON AIRPORT RD

SANDERSON FIELD AIRPORT

SHELTON

Bayshore

JOHNS PRAIRIE RD

MASON LAKE RD W

SPENCER LAKE

SPENCER LAKE RD

PICKERING RD

PHILLIPS LAKE

Graham Point

Hartstene

MASON ISLAND DR

NORTH ISLAND DR

YATES RD

HARTSTENE ISLAND

MCMICKEN ISLAND

PIERCE CO

MASON CO

SUN POINT

JARRELL COVE

BALLOW RD

FUDGE POINT

JOEMMA BEACH CAMPGROUND

WHITMAN COVE

CASE INLET

Oakland

Oakland Bay

CHAPMAN COVE

DANIELS RD

AGATE RD

CRESTVIEW DR

AGATE RD

CHURCH POINT

Cape Cod

HUNGERFORD POINT

ARCADIA POINT

SQUAXIN ISLAND INDIAN RES

PATTLATCH POINT

HARTSTENE

LANSKY DR

ISLAND SHORE RD

WILSON POINT

JARED RD

BURGUNDY RD

SLIVA RD

THURSTON CO

PIERCE CO

MASON COUNTY MUSEUM

RAILROAD

SHELTON VALLEY RD

DEEGAN RD

ISABELLA LAKE

OLYMPIC HWY

COLE RD

EAGLE POINT

MILLER POINT

HAMMERSLEY INLET

ARCADIA

Arcadia

HOPE ISLAND

BELSPEW POINT

WASHINGTON

JOHNSON POINT

SHELTON-MATLOCK RD

CLOQUALLUM RD

MAINLINE

ISABELLA VALLEY

2900

LYNCH

KAMILCHE POINT

DEER HARBOR

MUD-CAT POINT

QUARTERS POINT

SLOCUM RIDGE

DEEPWATER POINT

BLOOMFIELD RD

LITTLE SKOOKUM INLET

LYNCH CO

WINDY POINT CO

TOTTEN INLET

HUNTER POINT

MASON

THURSTON

MINTER POINT

SALTY POINT

90TH AV NW

85TH AV NW

81ST

78TH AV NW

79TH AV NW

GALLAGHER COVE

SANDERSON HARBOR

JEAL POINT

DOVER POINT

LIGHTHOUSE

Boston Harbor

3RD AV WY

ZANGLE

81ST AV NE

77TH AV NE

78TH AV NE

TUCKSEL POINT

BRISCO POINT

DANA PASSAGE

BIG FISHTRAP

FISHTRAP LP

CLIFF POINT

HENDERSON INLET

BAIRD COVE

PONCIN COVE

BAIRD RD NE

Kamilche

LITTLE SKOOKUM INLET

KAMILCHE POINT

COUGAR POINT

HUDSON COVE

69TH AV NW

YOUNG

ELD INLET

66TH AV NW

64TH AV NW

WOODARD BAY

WHITHAM RD

CHAPMAN BAY

WOODARD BAY NE

POINT

KAMILCHE VALLEY

LITTLE SKOOKUM VALLEY

New Kamilche

HURLEY-WALDRIP RD

OYSTER BAY

SHELLRIDGE RD NW

BURNS POINT

BURNS COVE

SCOTT RD NW

54TH AV NW

HOFFMAN RD NW

FRYE COVE

YOUNG COVE

61ST AV NW

57TH WY NW

BIG TYKLE COVE

GULL HARBOR

North Olympia

46TH AV NE

HEIGHTS LN NE

SHINCKE RD NE

61ST AV NE

63RD AV NE

PUGET

JOHNSON

KAMILCHE VALLEY

108

HOLIDAY VALLEY DR NW

42ND AV NW

GRAVELLY BEACH

KEATING RD

STEAMBOAT ISLAND RD

SUNRISE BEACH RD NW

GREEN COVE

SNYDER COVE

BISCAY ST NW

COOPER POINT

46TH AV NW

43RD AV NW

LITTLE TYKLE COVE

46TH AV NE

GULL HARBOR RD NE

LIBBY RD NE

LEMMON RD NE

SHINCKE RD NE

KINNEY RD NE

41ST AV NE

HAWKS PRAIRIE

MASON CO / THURSTON CO

SCHNEIDERS PRAIRIE

FRANZ STEAMBOAT

36TH AV NW

BUTLER COVE

BOSTON HARBOR RD NE

36TH AV NE

South Bay

SOUTH BAY RD NE

THURSTON COUNTY

WHITTAKER RD

ROCKY POINT

BREWER

SIMMONS RD

SP WALL

MUD BAY

THE EVERGREEN STATE COLLEGE DRIFTWOOD RD

296

28TH AV NW

14TH AV NW

DIVISION ST NW

ELLIS COVE

26TH AV NE

26TH AV NE

15TH AV NE

297

SUMMIT LAKE SHORE RD NW

SUMMIT LAKE

WILSON RD NW

SUMMIT LAKE RD NW

WILSON RD NW

8

OLD HWY

OLYMPIC SW

RANDALL

MCKENZIE

101

EVERGREEN PKWY

THE COLLEGE PKWY

11TH AV NW

KAISER RD

HARRISON AV

MUD BAY HWY

COOPER PT RD

BAY DR

EAST BAY

WEST BAY

PINE AV NE

12TH AV NE

STATE AV

MARTIN WY

LILLY RD NE

SLEATER

15TH AV SE

5

109

108

107

LACEY

FIVE FORKS RD SW

PORTER PASS RD

POWERLINE RD SW

CAPITOL

STATE

FOREST

ROCK CANDY MOUNTAIN

LARCH MOUNTAIN

CAPITOL PEAK

BORDEAUX CAMPGROUND

CEDAR FLATS

MAPLE VALLEY RD SW

BAKER RD SW

MINSON DR SW

ALPINE DR SW

BROWN RD SW

DELPHI RD SW

62ND AV SW

BLACK LAKE BLVD SW

PERCIVAL CREEK

SAPP RD

BLACK LAKE

TUMWATER

49TH AV SW

54TH AV SW

66TH AV SW

70TH AV SW

ISRAEL RD

LITTLEROCK RD

CAPITOL FERRY

104

103

102

5

101

OLYMPIA

NORTH ST SE

CLEVELAND AV

22ND AV

FONES RD

BOULEVARD RD SE

HOFFMAN RD SE

CARPENTER

37TH AV

HIGH ST SE

YELM HWY

COLLEGE ST SE

RUDDELL RD SE

RAINIER

DESCHUTES RIVER

105

106

102

101

103

108

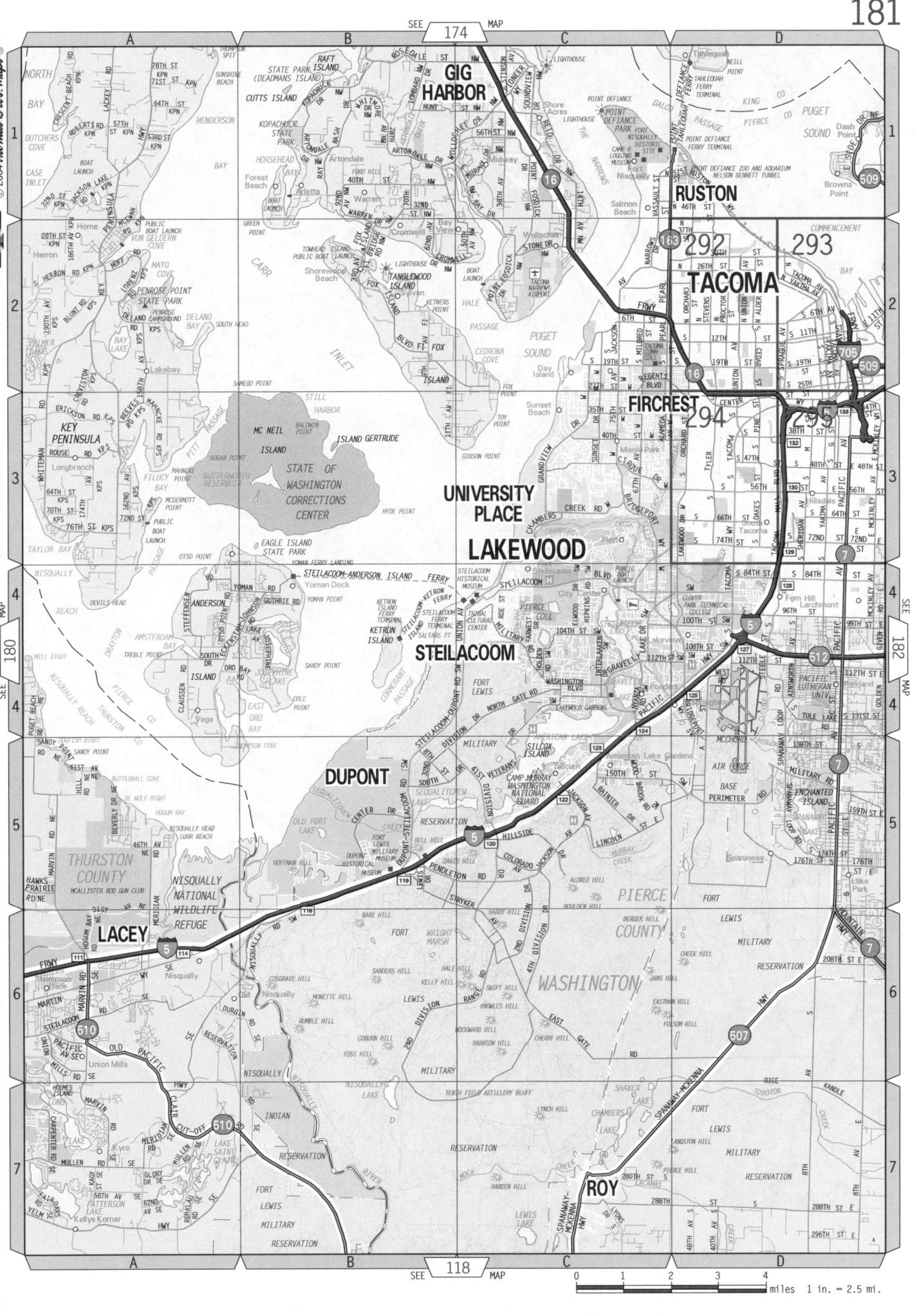

METRO

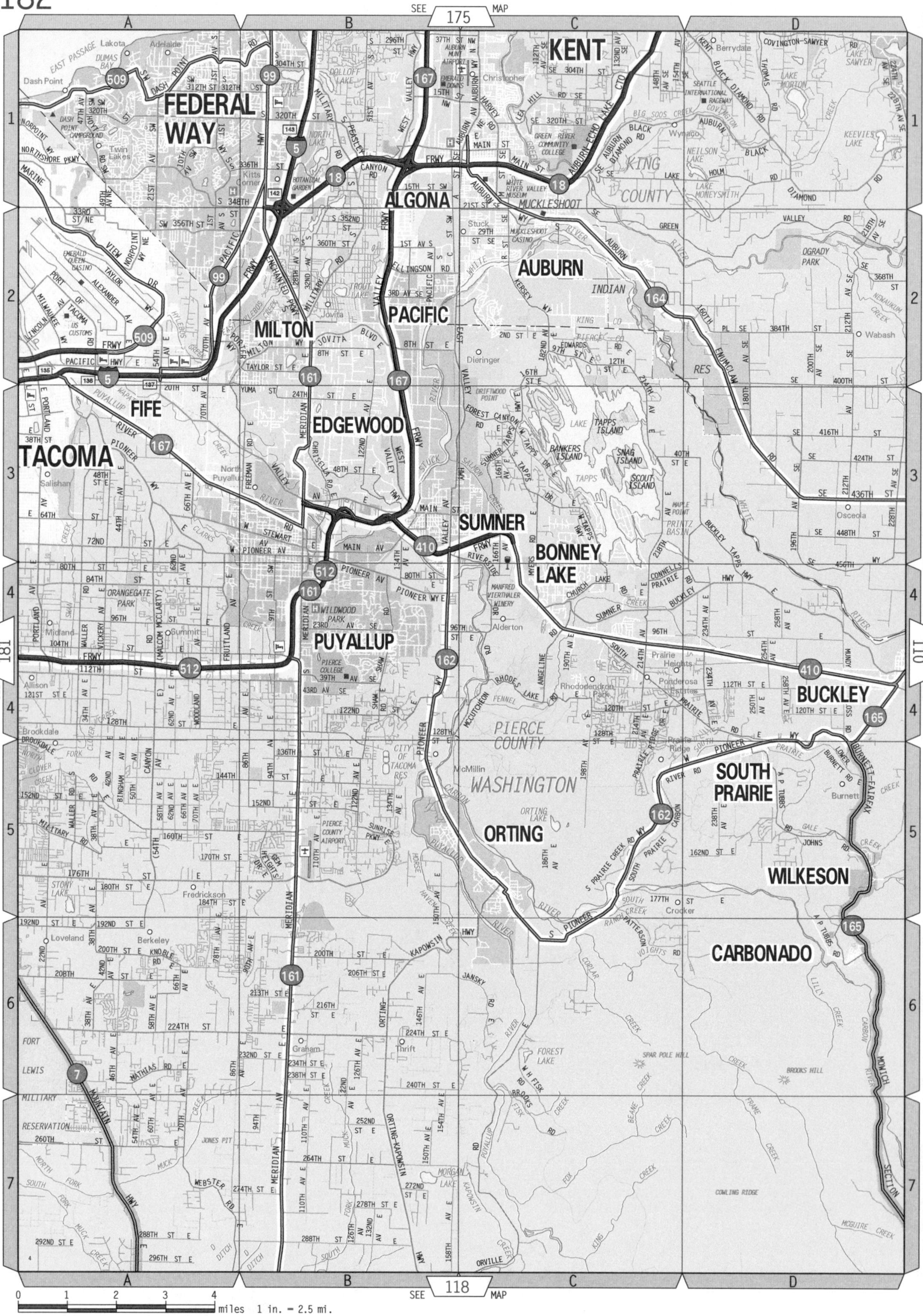

SEE 175 MAP
SEE 118 MAP
SEE 181 MAP
SEE 110 MAP
METRO
A
B
C
D
1
2
3
4
5
6
7
FEDERAL WAY
KENT
ALGONA
AUBURN
MILTON
PACIFIC
FIFE
TACOMA
EDGEWOOD
SUMNER
BONNEY LAKE
PUYALLUP
BUCKLEY
SOUTH PRAIRIE
ORTING
WILKESON
CARBONADO
KING COUNTY
PIERCE COUNTY
WASHINGTON
FORT LEWIS MILITARY RESERVATION
PORT OF TACOMA
Dash Point
Lakota
Adelaide
Twin Lakes
Kitts Corner
Berrydale
Wynaco
Stuck
Christopher
Jovita
Dieringer
North Puyallup
Salishan
Midland
Summit
Alderton
Allison
Brookdale
McMillin
Fredrickson
Loveland
Berkeley
Graham
Thrift
Prairie Heights
Ponderosa Estates
Rhododendron Park
Prairie Ridge
Burnett
Crocker
Osceola
Wabash
LAKE TAPPS
TAPPS ISLAND
BANKERS ISLAND
SNAG ISLAND
SCOUT ISLAND
ORTING LAKE
FOREST LAKE
MORGAN LAKE
STONY LAKE
LAKE SAWYER
LAKE MORTON
KEEVIES LAKE
NEILSON LAKE
LAKE MONEYSMITH
PIERCE COLLEGE
PIERCE COUNTY AIRPORT
GREEN RIVER COMMUNITY COLLEGE
WHITE RIVER VALLEY MUSEUM
MUCKLESHOOT CASINO
EMERALD QUEEN CASINO
SEATTLE INTERNATIONAL RACEWAY
WILDWOOD PARK
ORANGEGATE PARK
OGRADY PARK
SPAR POLE HILL
BROOKS HILL
COWLING RIDGE
0 1 2 3 4
miles 1 in. = 2.5 mi.

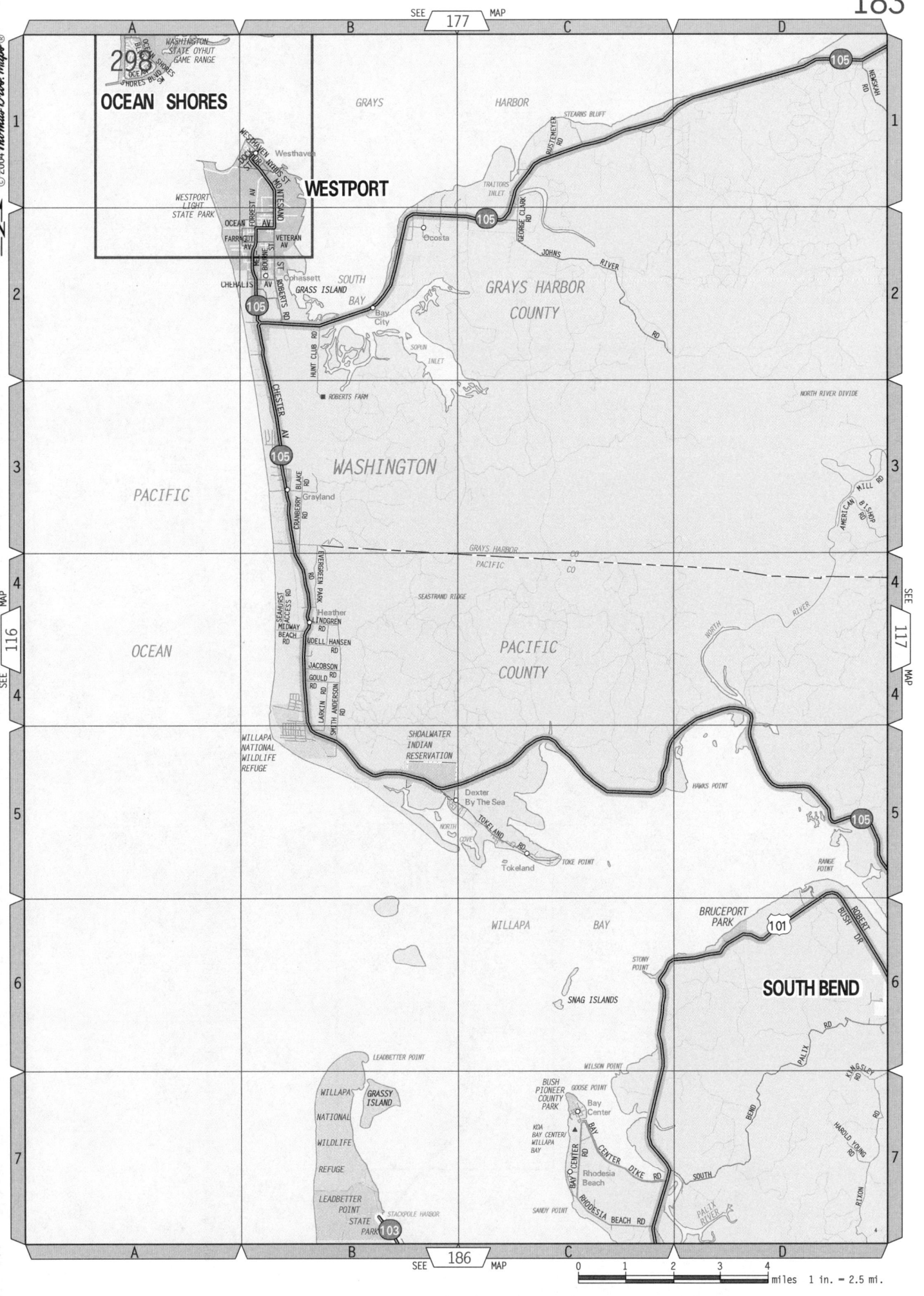

A B C D

1

2

3

4

5

6

7

OCEAN SHORES

298

WESTPORT

Washington State Oyhut Game Range

Westhaven

Westport Light State Park

GRAYS HARBOR

STEARNS BLUFF

KRUSTEMEYER RD

105

TRAITORS INLET

OCEAN AV

FARRAGUT AV

VETERAN AV

GEORGE CLARK RD

JOHNS RIVER

CHEHALIS

Cohassett

GRASS ISLAND

SOUTH BAY

Bay City

105

HUNT CLUB RD

SOPUN INLET

GRAYS HARBOR COUNTY

RD

NORTH RIVER DIVIDE

CHESTER AV

Roberts Farm

WASHINGTON

PACIFIC

105

CRANBERRY RD

BLAKE RD

Grayland

AMERICAN MILL RD

BISHOP RD

GRAYS HARBOR CO

PACIFIC CO

EVERGREEN PARK DR

SEASTRAND RIDGE

SEE 116 MAP

SEAHURST ACCESS RD

MIDWAY BEACH RD

Heather

Lindgren

UDELL RD

HANSEN RD

JACOBSON RD

GOULD RD

LARKIN RD

SMITH ANDERSON RD

OCEAN

PACIFIC COUNTY

NORTH RIVER

SEE 117 MAP

METRO

WILLAPA NATIONAL WILDLIFE REFUGE

SHOALWATER INDIAN RESERVATION

HAWKS POINT

Dexter By The Sea

TOKELAND RD

NORTH COVE

Tokeland

TOKE POINT

105

RANGE POINT

WILLAPA BAY

STONY POINT

BRUCEPORT PARK

101

BUSH DR

ROBERT DR

SOUTH BEND

SNAG ISLANDS

LEADBETTER POINT

WILSON POINT

PALIX RD

KINGSLEY RD

WILLAPA

GRASSY ISLAND

NATIONAL

WILDLIFE

REFUGE

LEADBETTER POINT STATE PARK

BUSH PIONEER COUNTY PARK

GOOSE POINT

Bay Center

KOA BAY CENTER/ WILLAPA BAY

BAY CENTER RD

BAY CENTER DIKE RD

Rhodesia Beach

RHODESIA BEACH RD

SANDY POINT

SOUTH BEND RD

BEND RD

HAROLD YOUNG RD

RIXON RD

PALIX RIVER

STACKPOLE HARBOR

103

0 1 2 3 4 miles 1 in. = 2.5 mi.

METRO

SEE 180 MAP

SEE 117 MAP

SEE 118 MAP

SEE 187 MAP

A B C D

1 2 3 4 5 6 7

CAPITOL STATE FOREST

Little Larch Mountain
Fall Creek Campground
Fuzzy Top
Mount Molly Campground
Yew Tree Campground
Middle Waddel Campground
Margaret McKenny Campground
Mina Falls Trailhead Campground
Sherman Valley Campground
Sherman Valley
Lost Valley

GRAYS HARBOR CO
THURSTON CO

Delphi
Bordeaux
Littlerock
Mima
Mumby
Gate
Rochester
CHEHALIS INDIAN RESERVATION
Helsing Junction
Michigan Hill
Prather
Meadows
Grand Mound
Galvin

Olympia Airport
South Union
MILLER-SYLVANIA STATE PARK
Maytown
Chain Hill
Tenino Junction
Oregon Trail Monument
TENINO
TENINO DEPOT MUSEUM
Blumauer Hill
Northcraft Mountain
Sunnydale
East Olympia
Fir Tree Dr
FORT LEWIS MILITARY RESERVATION
Offutt Lake

THURSTON COUNTY
BUCODA
Zenkner Valley
Wabash
LEWIS COUNTY
Mendota
Nulls Crossing
Kopiah

CENTRALIA
299
CHEHALIS
STAN HEDWALL PARK
Chehalis Junction
Claquato
Littell
Milburn
Adna
Ocean
Newaukum
Logan Hill
Rogerson Rd
Alpha

WASHINGTON

THURSTON CO
LEWIS CO

0 1 2 3 4 miles   1 in. = 2.5 mi.

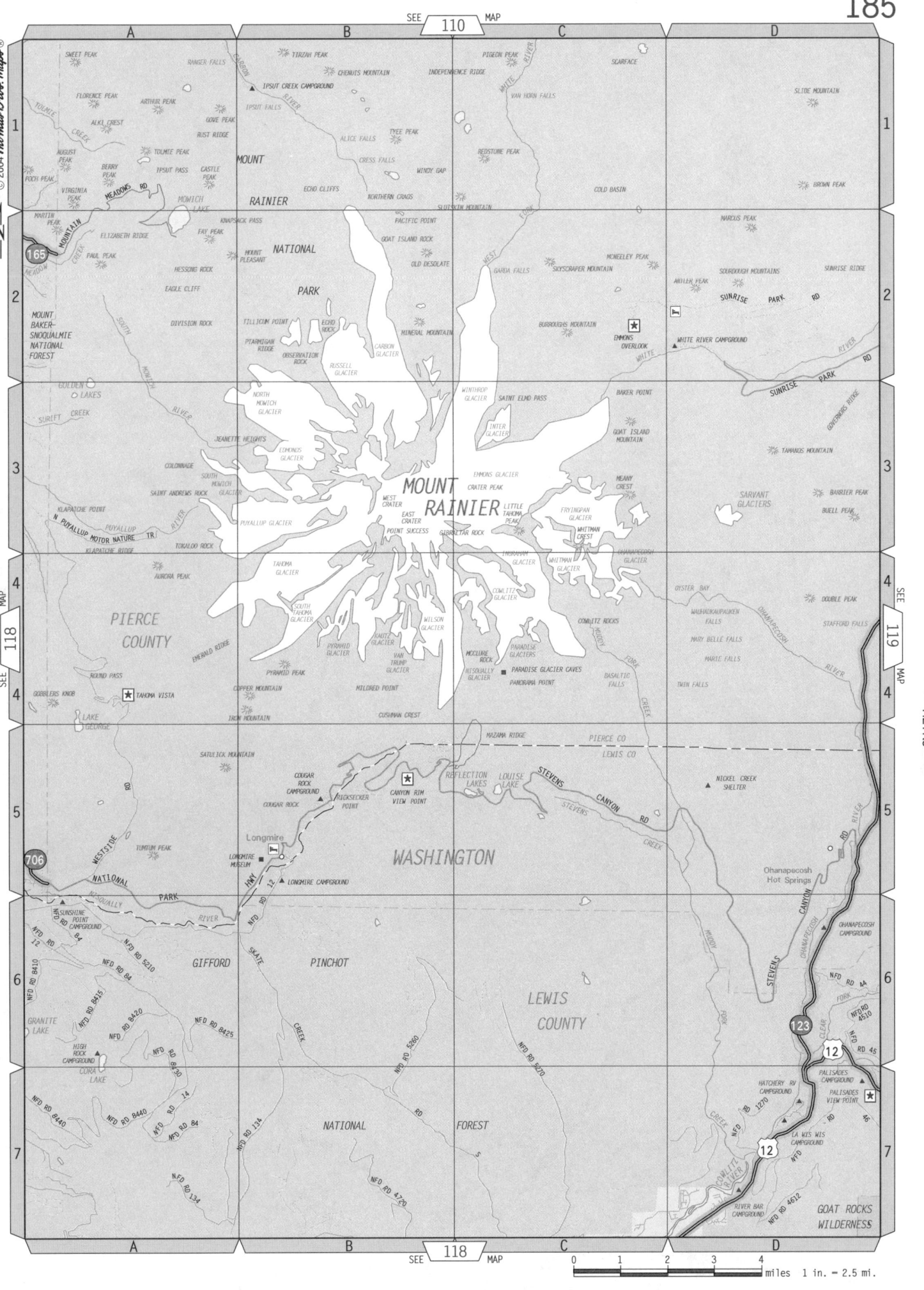

METRO

© 2004 THOMAS BROS. MAPS®

N

SEE 165

SEE 118 MAP

SEE 119 MAP

MOUNT
RAINIER
NATIONAL
PARK

MOUNT
BAKER-
SNOQUALMIE
NATIONAL
FOREST

MOUNT
RAINIER

PIERCE
COUNTY

WASHINGTON

LONGMIRE

GIFFORD   PINCHOT

LEWIS
COUNTY

NATIONAL   FOREST

GOAT ROCKS
WILDERNESS

0   1   2   3   4
miles 1 in. = 2.5 mi.

←N→

SEE 183 MAP

A   B   C   D

1

WILLAPA

RAMSEY POINT

101

BAY

NORTH

STACKPOLE RD

BEACH
103
Oysterville
OYSTERVILLE
RD
ESPY
PL
DOUGLAS DR

PENINSULA

2

JOE JOHNS RD

Nahcotta

BAY AV

LYNN POINT

NEEDLE POINT

Ocean Park

245 ST

Klipsan Beach
227
Y ST
PL
RD

DIAMOND POINT

SUNSHINE POINT

PACIFIC

3

JENSEN POINT

WILLAPA

LONG ISLAND

NATIONAL

PARADISE POINT

CHETLO

STANLEY PENINSULA

HARBOR

101

208 PL
BIRCH
198 PL

OCEAN

WILDLIFE

REFUGE

SMOKY HOLLOW

HIGH POINT

SEE 116 MAP

4

177TH ST

ST

Oceanside
BIRCH
Pacific Beach
CRANBERRY RD
Y PL
SANDRIDGE

SHOALWATER BAY

ROUND ISLAND

OMEARA POINT

PORTER POINT

PAR PALA

SEE 117 MAP

4

101

103
Breakers
101 PL
PIONEER RD
SPRUCE ST
113 ST

LONG BEACH

WILLAPA

PL

NATIONAL

4

NASELLE STATE SALMON HATCHERY

LONGFELLOW HILL

RD

5

WORLD KITE MUSEUM AND HALL OF FAME

WASHINGTON AV S

WOODGATE RD
67TH

Moores Corner
TARLATT RD
55 ST
JIM ST

WILDLIFE

REFUGE

SELDNESS RD

PACIFIC COUNTY

Naselle

4

SALMON CREEK RD

Seaview

41 PL

BEAR RIVER RIDGE

RD

5

METRO

Holman

101

ALT 101

101

WASHINGTON

6

NORTH HEAD LIGHT-HOUSE
100
BEARDS HOLLOW
NORTH HEAD LIGHTHOUSE RD
HEAD RD
NORTH HEAD RD

KOA ILWACO
STRINGTOWN RD

ILWACO
Ilwaco Heritage Museum

CHINOOK

BEAR RIVER RD

BEAR RIVER RD

SHOALWATER BAY

VALLEY

RD

NASELLE RIDGE

FERRY

401

BALD RIDGE

BRIX BAY

6

MCKENZIE HEAD

ROBERT GRAY DR

US NAVAL RESERVATION

BAKER BAY

101

BEAR MOUNTAIN

KINAPTON

ROCKY POINT LIGHT

FORT CANBY STATE PARK

CAPE DISAPPOINTMENT LIGHTHOUSE

2ND ST

SAND ISLAND

PACIFIC CO
CLATSOP CO

COLUMBIA

Lingenfelter RD

Chinook
HOUTCHEN ST

FORT COLUMBIA STATE PARK

SCARBORO HILL

CLIFF POINT

GRAYS POINT

GRAYS POINT LIGHT

GRAYS BAY LIGHT

GRAYS BAY

7

WASHINGTON
OREGON

REAR ENTRANCE RANGE LIGHTHOUSE

SAND ISLAND DIKE MIDDLE LIGHT

SAND ISLAND DIKE LIGHT

RIVER

CHINOOK POINT

HUNGRY HARBOR

COLUMBIA

RIVER

PACIFIC CO
CLATSOP CO

7

CLATSOP COUNTY

CHINOOK DIKE LIGHT

FORT STEVENS STATE PARK

A   B   C   D

SEE 188 MAP

0   1   2   3   4   miles   1 in. = 2.5 mi.

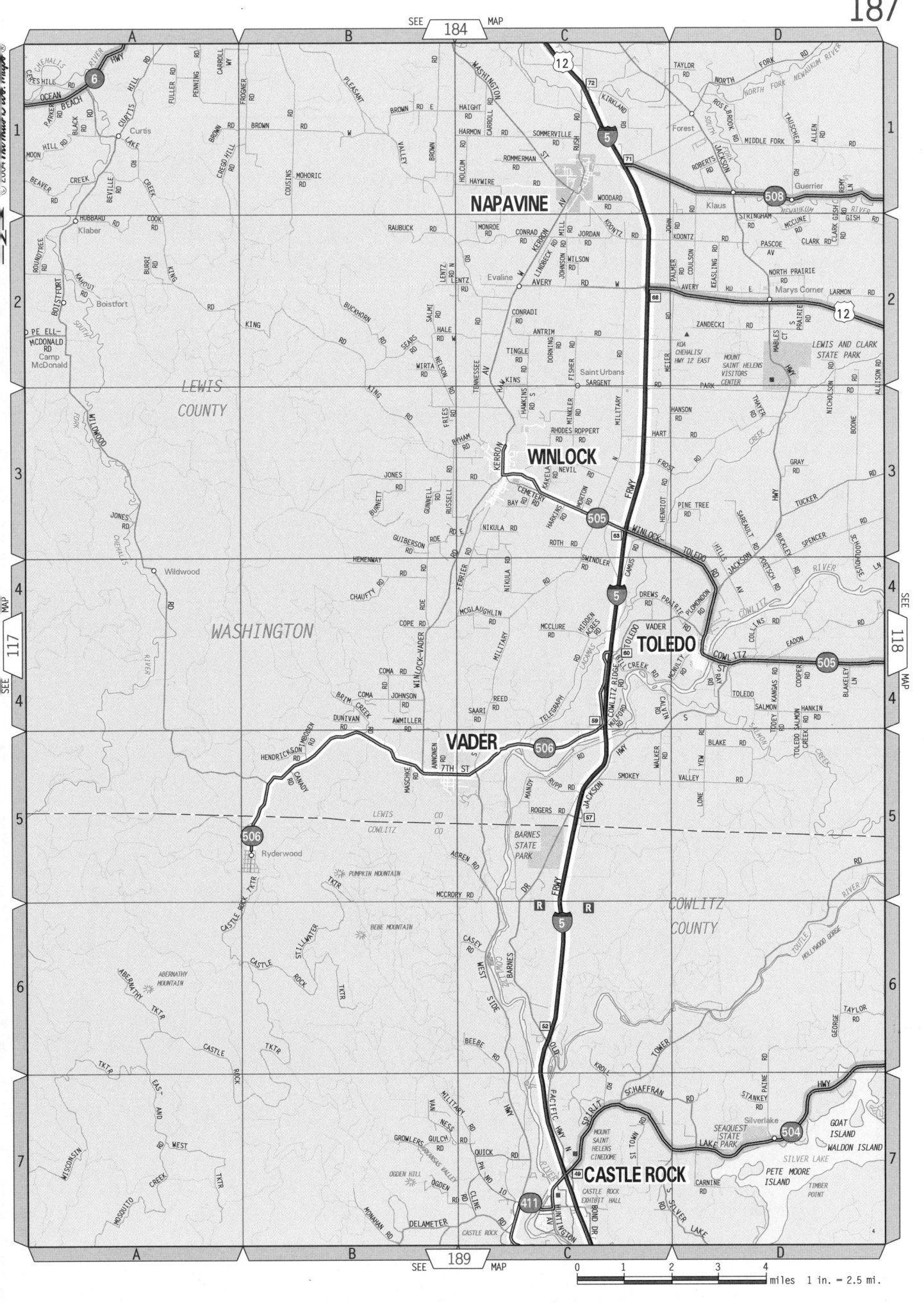

METRO

SEE 117 MAP

SEE 118 MAP

NAPAVINE

WINLOCK

TOLEDO

VADER

CASTLE ROCK

LEWIS COUNTY

WASHINGTON

COWLITZ COUNTY

LEWIS AND CLARK STATE PARK

BARNES STATE PARK

SEAQUEST STATE PARK

SILVER LAKE

0 1 2 3 4 miles   1 in. = 2.5 mi.

A B SEE 186 MAP C D

SEE 116 MAP
SEE 117 MAP

METRO

1

CLATSOP SPIT

COLUMBIA

RIVER

REAR RANGE LIGHT
FRONT RANGE LIGHT

101
COAST HWY

300

GENERAL ANCHORAGE
TONGUE POINT LIGHTHOUSE
TONGUE POINT NAVAL BASE (HISTORICAL)
Tongue Point Village
MOTT ISLAND
WEST LIGHT
LOIS ISLAND

POINT ADAMS
Fort Stevens
Hammond
POINT ADAMS
Coast Guard Station
LOWER SANDS LIGHTHOUSE

JETTY RD

FORT STEVENS STATE PARK

KOA
ASTORIA/SEASIDE

LAKE DR
PACIFIC HWY
NW WARRENTON DR

SKIPANON WATERWAY LIGHTHOUSE

YOUNGS BAY ENTRANCE LIGHT

101
26

30 AV
IRVING
LEXINGTON AV
NIAGARA AV
ALAMEDA AV
7TH ST

ASTORIA

COLUMBIA

EMERALD HEIGHTS

Fern Hill

2

WARRENTON

COLUMBIA BEACH

WARRENTON
SCHOOL RD
E HARBOR ST
SE 7TH ST
SW MAIN

PORT OF ASTORIA AIRPORT

101 BUS
WARRENTON

202
NEHALEM HWY
YOUNGS BAY
Jeffers Garden
Miles Crossing

YOUNGS
CLATSOP STATE FOREST

WALLUSKI LOOP

HWY

CAMP RILEA

OCEANVIEW
CEMETERY RD
FORT STEVENS HWY
COAST HWY
OREGON

101

26

FORT CLATSOP NATIONAL MEMORIAL

CLARK AND
YOUNGS RIVER
FRY ISLAND
GRANT ISLAND
HAVEN ISLAND

NEHALEM
LABISKE RD
PALMER RD

3

PACIFIC

Clatsop Station
PERKINS RD

OREGON NATIONAL

GUARD

Glenwood

SOUTH POST RD

SUNSET BEACH
Sunset Beach
LEWIS AV
MANTON
CULLABY LAKE RD
Carnahan

SUNSET BEACH

DELLMOOR LP
West Lake

CULLABY LAKE COUNTY PARK

CULLABY LAKE

FORT CLATSOP RD
CLATSOP RIDGE
TUCKER CREEK
LEWIS AND
LOGAN RD

PETER JOHNSON LOOP

LONE RIDGE
Melville

YOUNGS RIVER FALLS

Olney
LILLENAS RD

GREEN MOUNTAIN RD

KLASKANINE FISH HATCHERY

4

OCEAN

301

SURF PINES RD

OCEAN DR
COAST HWY

GEARHART LOOP RD
Butterfield

GEARHART

MARION AV
PACIFIC WY
COTTAGE AV
G ST

WADSWORTH RD

CLARK AND

LEWIS AND

CLATSOP COUNTY

YOUNGS

CLATSOP STATE FOREST

GREEN MOUNTAIN RD

CLATSOP STATE FOREST

5

Neawanna Station
N HOLLADAY DR
BROADWAY
WAHANNA RD

SEASIDE

Sister Green Mountain
EELS RIDGE

GREEN MOUNTAIN

6

ECOLA STATE PARK

TILLAMOOK HEAD
TILLAMOOK ROCK
BALD MOUNTAIN
BIRD POINT

TILLAMOOK HEAD COVE
SUNSET BEACH
WEST POINT
RIPPET
RIPPET RD
RIPPET MOUNTAIN

101
26
COAST HWY

Cannon Beach Junction

TWIN PEAKS

DAVIS POINT

OREGON

SADDLE MOUNTAIN
SADDLE MOUNTAIN STATE PARK
RD

HUMBUG MOUNTAIN

7

INDIAN BEACH
SUBMARINE ROCK
SEA LION ROCK ARCH
CRESCENT BEACH
BIRD ROCKS
CHAPMAN BEACH

101
N HEMLOCK ST

KLOOTCHIE CREEK CAMPGROUND

SUNSET HWY
NECANICUM
Necanicum Junction

26

SADDLE MOUNTAIN RD
SUNSET HWY

RIVER

CANNON BEACH

HAYSTACK ROCK
SUNSET BLVD

CLATSOP STATE FOREST

BAILEY POINT

53
Hamlet

A B SEE 191 MAP C D

0 1 2 3 4 miles   1 in. = 2.5 mi.

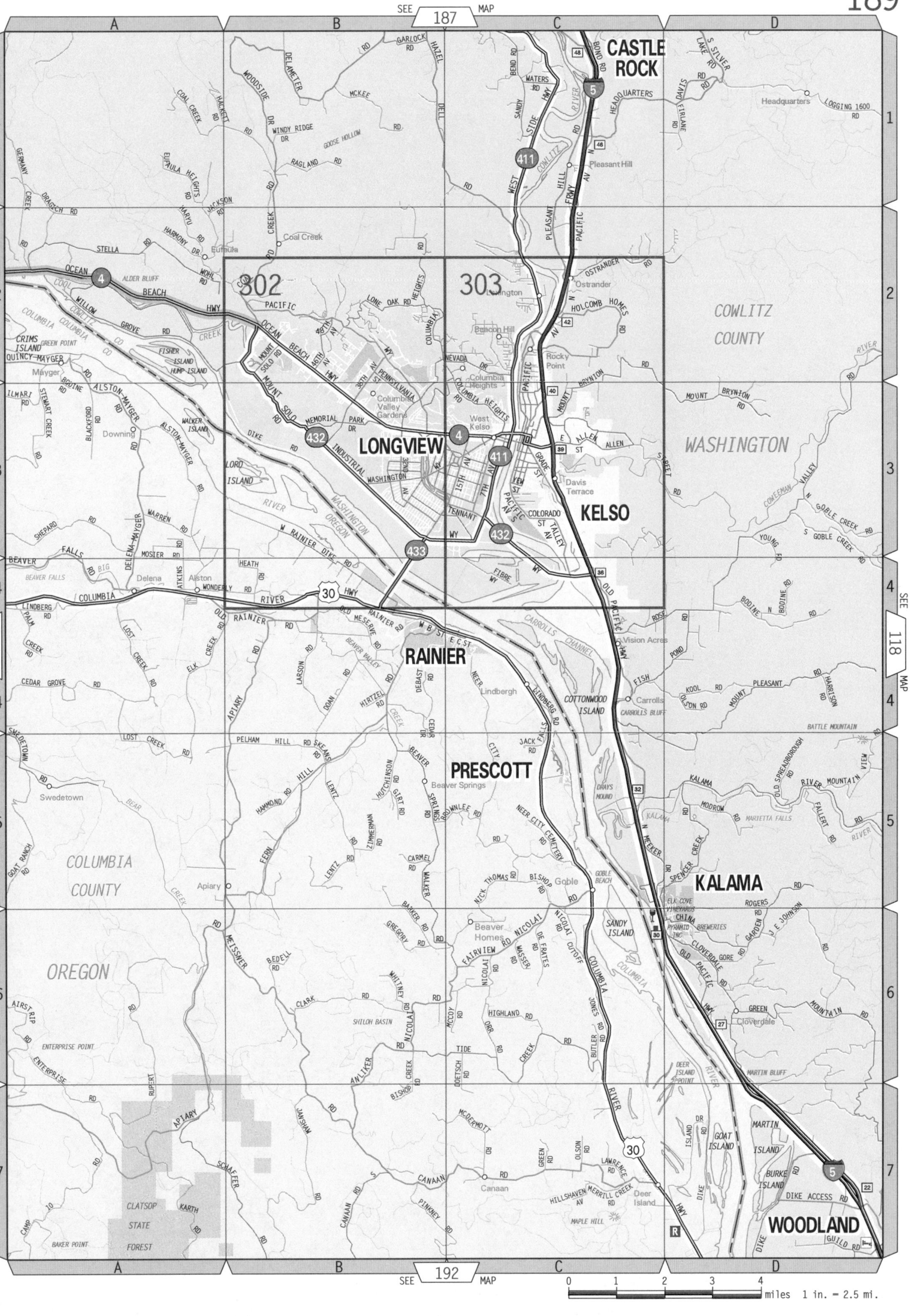

SEE 187 MAP
SEE 192 MAP
SEE 117 MAP
SEE 118 MAP
A
B
C
D
1
2
3
4
5
6
7
CASTLE ROCK
LONGVIEW
KELSO
RAINIER
PRESCOTT
KALAMA
WOODLAND
302
303
COWLITZ COUNTY
WASHINGTON
COLUMBIA COUNTY
OREGON
CLATSOP STATE FOREST
Coal Creek
Eufaula
Mayger
Downing
Delena
Alston
Swedetown
Apiary
Lexington
Ostrander
Beacon Hill
Rocky Point
Columbia Heights
Columbia Valley Gardens
West Kelso
Davis Terrace
Pleasant Hill
Headquarters
Vision Acres
Carrolls
Lindbergh
Beaver Springs
Goble
Beaver Homes
Cloverdale
Canaan
Deer Island
CRIMS ISLAND
LORD ISLAND
COTTONWOOD ISLAND
SANDY ISLAND
GOAT ISLAND
MARTIN ISLAND
BURKE ISLAND
COLUMBIA RIVER
COWLITZ RIVER
OCEAN BEACH HWY
PACIFIC HWY
0 1 2 3 4
miles 1 in. = 2.5 mi.

METRO

SEE 118 MAP

A B C D

METRO

SEE 118 MAP

1

SPUD MOUNTAIN

SPOTTED BUCK MOUNTAIN

CASTLE PEAK

CASTLE CREEK MARSH

MOUNT

NORTH FORK TOUTLE RIVER

JOHNSTON RIDGE

504

HARRYS RIDGE

SPIRIT LAKE

DUCK BAY

★ HARMONY VIEW POINT
★ CEDAR CREEK VIEW POINT

NFD RD 2560

NFD RD 2560

NFD RD 94

NFD RD 9403

★ DENNY BROOK VIEW POINT

MOUNT SAINT HELENS

NATIONAL VOLCANIC

MONUMENT

STUDEBAKER RIDGE

WINDY RIDGE VIEW POINT ★

NFD RD 99

★ SMITH CREEK VIEW POINT

COWLITZ COUNTY SAINT

SOUTH FORK

TOUTLE

MOUNT SAINT HELENS

2

RIVER

HELENS

SHEEP CANYON

★ SHEEP CANYON VIEW POINT

WISHBONE GLACIER

TOUTLE GLACIER

TALUS GLACIER

CRESCENT RIDGE

DRYER GLACIER

TIMBERLINE CAMPGROUND

ALPINE BUTTE

NELSON GLACIER

APE GLACIER

1980 CRATER

SHOESTRING GLACIER

SWIFT GLACIER

MONITOR RIDGE

APE CANYON

PUMICE BUTTE

PINE

RIVER

NFD RD 270

NFD RD 380

CLEARWATER

NFD RD 83

NFD RD 700

RIVER RD

GIFFORD

PINCHOT

NATIONAL

FOREST

GOAT MOUNTAIN

NFD RD 81

COWLITZ CO
SKAMANIA CO

VOLCANIC

MONUMENT

NFD RD 8123

NFD RD 81

BEDROCK PASS

BUTTE CAMP DOME

NFD RD 81

RIVER

NFD RD 30

KALAMA

SWIFT CREEK FLOW

WORM FLOWS

NFD RD 83

JACKPINE SHELTER ★

KADIN RIVER RIDGE

LAHAR VIEW POINT ★

NFD RD 810

NFD RD 8320

NFD RD 2588

LAVA CANYON

NFD RD 2586

GIFFORD

3

KALAMA FALLS

NFD RD 81

CINNAMON PEAK

MERRILL LAKE CAMPGROUND

MERRILL LAKE

NFD RD 8303

APE CAVE MUSEUM

GREEN MOUNTAIN

MARBLE MOUNTAIN

NFD RD 9015

PINCHOT

NATIONAL

FOREST

MUDDY RIVER VIEW POINT ★

LEWIS

SEE 118 MAP

4

SWIFT DAM OVERLOOK ★

WASHINGTON

COUGAR

BEAVER BAY CAMPGROUND

CHRISTMAS CANYON

503

LEWIS RIVER

LEWIS

RIVER

COONEY POINT

RIVER RD

SKAMANIA COUNTY

NFD RD 9015

RIVER

SWIFT CREEK RESERVOIR

SWIFT FOREST CAMPGROUND

NFD RD 90

MCCLELLAN MOUNTAIN

5

SPEELYAI STATE HATCHERY

SPEELYAI HILL VIEW POINT ★

503

WILLIAMS RD

YALE LAKE

CLARK COUNTY

CLARK CO
SKAMANIA CO

GIFFORD

NFD RD 6403

NFD RD 207

NFD RD 64

PARADISE VALLEY

NFD RD 3105

6

HAM RD

SADDLE DAM CAMPGROUND

FRAZIER RD

COWLITZ CO
CLARK CO

PRIVATE

503

PINCHOT

NFD RD 64

NFD RD 64

TIMBERED PEAK

NFD RD 6403

NATIONAL

FOREST

NFD RD 203

7

HEALY

RD

TUMUM MOUNTAIN

NFD RD 5701

NFD RD 54

CALAMITY PEAK

NFD RD 320

RD

HORSESHOE RIDGE

NFD RD 317

NFD RD 6406

SISTER ROCKS

OBSERVATION BERRYFIELD CAMPGROUND

A B C D

0 1 2 3 4 miles   1 in. = 2.5 mi.

SEE 193 MAP

© 2004 Thomas Bros. Maps ®

A   B   C   D

CANNON BEACH

CANNON BEACH
Tolovana Park

CLATSOP STATE FOREST

SILVER POINT
JOCKEY CAP
Double Peak

101

HUMBUG POINT
ARCADIA BEACH
HUG POINT
HUG POINT STATE PARK
ADAIR POINT

CLATSOP STATE FOREST

CLATSOP COUNTY

SUGARLOAF MOUNTAIN

SOUTH SUGARLOAF

HAMLET

53

CLATSOP

COLE MOUNTAIN

NEHALEM DR

AUSTIN POINT

OCEAN

Arch Cape
CASTLE ROCK
ARCH CAPE
GULL ROCK
COVE BEACH

OREGON COAST HWY

ONION PEAK

CLATSOP STATE FOREST

OREGON

BLACK BUTTE

NORTH HWY

COLE MOUNTAIN

COUNTY LINE

STATE

NORTH FORK FALLS

FORIS RD

FOREST

ANGORA PEAK

CLATSOP CO
TILLAMOOK CO

SHORT SAND CROSS OVER

TIDE AV

OSWALD WEST STATE PARK

ARMSTEAD MEMORIAL
FALCON ROCK
SMUGGLER COVE
DEVILS CAULDRON

TILLAMOOK STATE FOREST
ROCK MOUNTAIN

RD

TILLAMOOK STATE FOREST

Aldervale

RD

GODS VALLEY

VALLEY

SECTOR RIDGE

NEAHKAHNIE MOUNTAIN

CLASSIC RIDGE

NEHALEM QUARRY

MASON ANDERSON RD

NECANICUM

RIVER

RD

FOSS RD

Neahkahnie Beach

NORTH FORK RD

GATEWAY RD

MCDONALD RD

NEHALEM RIVER

NEHALEM FALLS

MANZANITA

NEHALEM

NEHALEM RD
OCEAN RD
3RD AV
LANEDA
CAREY

SHOLLMEYER
ORANGE
B ST
1 ST

Bayside Gardens

MCKIMMENS RD

TIDELAN

53

Mohler

SHIFFMAN RD

FOSS

FOSS RD

Batterson

COOK RD

VENNE BEACH

NEHALEM BAY STATE AIRPORT

NEHALEM BAY

DEAN POINT

3RD ST

SHIFFMAN RD

CREEK RD

SUNSET BEACH
FISHERY POINT

HWY

Wheeler Heights

WHEELER

MIAMI RIVER

SHIFFMAN RD

TILLAMOOK

PACIFIC

NEHALEM BAY STATE PARK
NEHALEM BEACH

Brighton

OREGON COAST HWY

NEHALEM FISH HATCHERY

CRAB ROCK

CRAIG MOUNTAIN

Nedonna Beach

101

Barnesdale

CRANE RD

FRANK RD

Manhattan Beach

ROCKAWAY BEACH

N 3RD AV
S 2ND AV
S QUADRANT
EASY ST

TILLAMOOK COUNTY

RIVER RD

MIAMI RIVER

STATE

TWIN ROCKS
PAINTED ROCK
Twin Rocks

CAPTAIN GRAY MOUNTAIN

GRAYS MOUNTAIN

Watseco

MIAMI RIVER

Barview
GREEN HILL

TILLAMOOK

MOSS CREEK RD

FOREST

GARIBALDI

CRAB ROCK

GARIBALDI AV

MIAMI COVE

EKROTH RD

STATE

BAYOCEAN DIKE

TILLAMOOK BAY COAST GUARD STATION
CRAB HARBOR
HOBSONVILLE POINT

Hobsonville

HOBSONVILLE POINT DR

HIGH ST

FOREST

BAYOCEAN PENINSULA

TILLAMOOK BAY

Bayocean

LARSON COVE
SANDSTONE POINT

BAY CITY

KILCHIS RIVER RD

0 1 2 3 4 miles   1 in. = 2.5 mi.

METRO

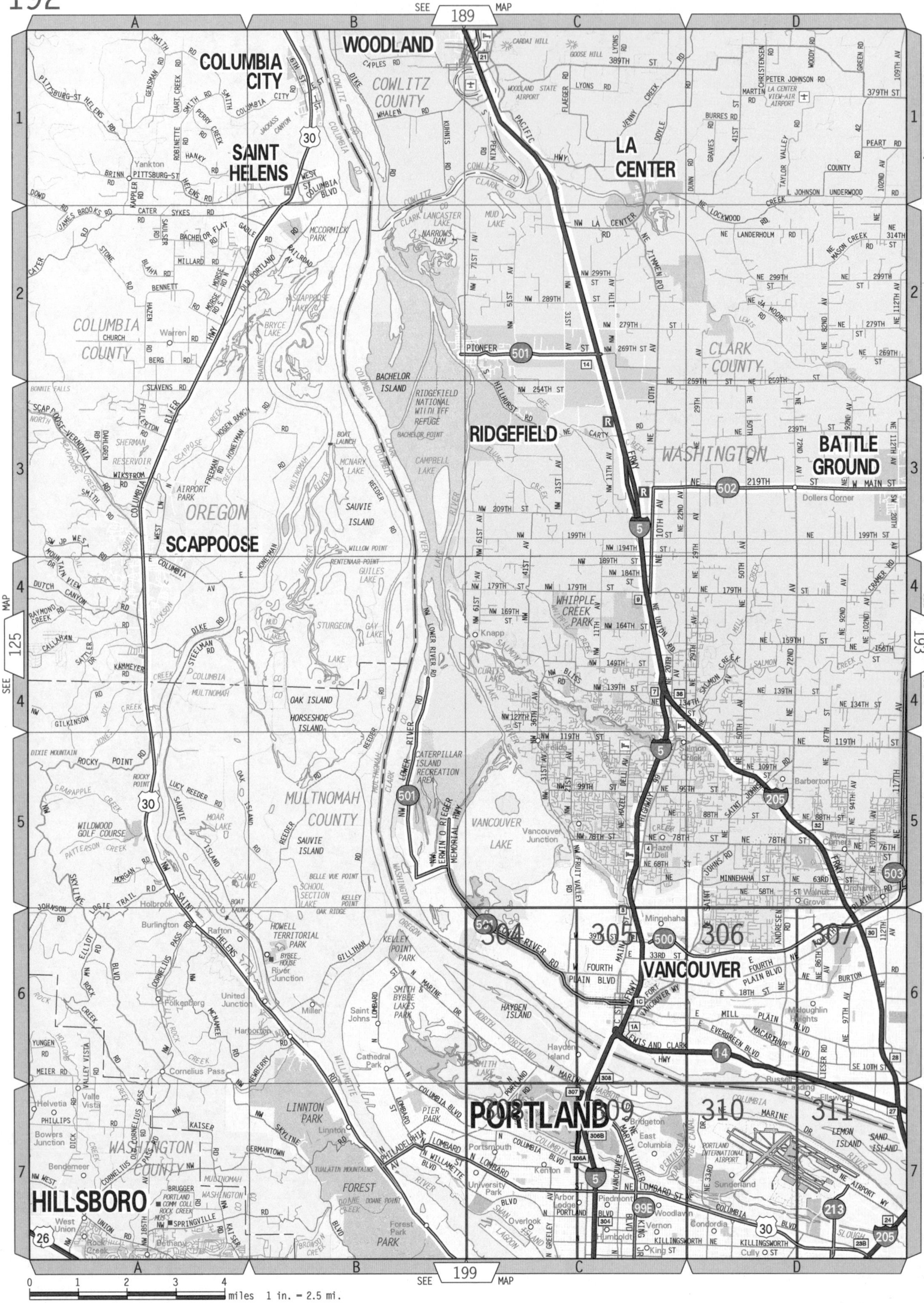

SEE 189 MAP

WOODLAND

COLUMBIA CITY

SAINT HELENS

COWLITZ COUNTY

LA CENTER

RIDGEFIELD

WASHINGTON

BATTLE GROUND

COLUMBIA COUNTY

CHURCH

SCAPPOOSE

OREGON

SAUVIE ISLAND

RIDGEFIELD NATIONAL WILDLIFE REFUGE

BACHELOR ISLAND

CLARK COUNTY

MULTNOMAH COUNTY

CATERPILLAR ISLAND RECREATION AREA

VANCOUVER LAKE

VANCOUVER

ERWIN O RIEGER MEMORIAL HWY

304 305 500 306 307

WILDWOOD GOLF COURSE

HOWELL TERRITORIAL PARK

BYBEE HOUSE

SMITH & BYBEE LAKES PARK

HAYDEN ISLAND

PORTLAND

309 310 311

LINNTON PARK

FOREST PARK

PORTLAND INTERNATIONAL AIRPORT

HILLSBORO

WASHINGTON COUNTY

SEE 199 MAP

SEE 125 MAP

SEE 193 MAP

METRO

0 1 2 3 4 miles   1 in. = 2.5 mi.

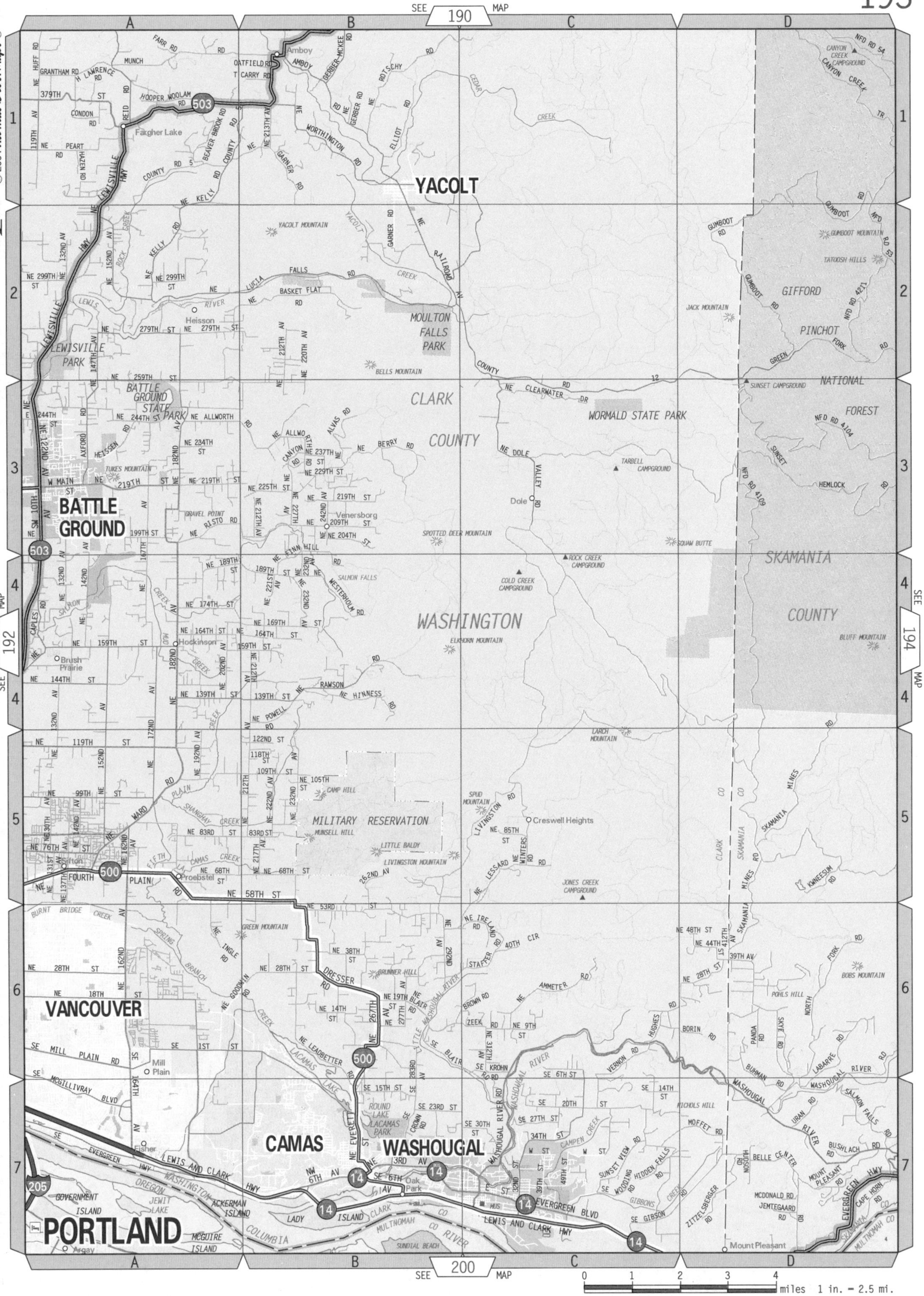

© 2004 THOMAS BROS. MAPS®

SEE 190 MAP

YACOLT

CLARK COUNTY

WASHINGTON

GIFFORD PINCHOT NATIONAL FOREST

SKAMANIA COUNTY

BATTLE GROUND

WORMALD STATE PARK

MILITARY RESERVATION

VANCOUVER

CAMAS

WASHOUGAL

PORTLAND

COLUMBIA RIVER

METRO

SEE 192 MAP

SEE 194 MAP

SEE 200 MAP

0 1 2 3 4 miles   1 in. = 2.5 mi.

SEE 190 MAP

A B C D

—N—

METRO

1

CALAMITY
CALAMITY PEAK
PEAK
NFD RD 5B
CANYON
NFD RD 58
NFD RD 54
CREEK
NFD RD 527
TWIN ROCKS TR

OBSERVATION PEAK
BARE MOUNTAIN
RIDGE TR

GIFFORD

HOME RIDGE

MIDDLE BUTTE
NFD RD 64
CREEK
3062
SOUTH BUTTE
NFD RD

PINCHOT

MINERAL SPRINGS RD
MEADOW RD
NFD RD
CARSON RD
GILER
NFD RD 65
NFD RD 6053
NFD RD 65
2509

NATIONAL

2

SATURDAY ROCK
GREEN LOOKOUT MOUNTAIN
NFD RD 42
RIDGE
WEST CRATER
SODA PEAK
SODA PEAKS
NFD RD 42
COUGAR ROCK
FORK RD
GREEN
TR
NFD RD 4306
SODA PEAK
NFD RD 413
TROUT CREEK HILL
WIND RIVER
NFD RD 43
CARSON RD
LITTLE SODA SPRINGS
CARSON NATIONAL FISH HATCHERY
LITTLE SODA SPRINGS CAMPGROUND
NFD RD 3050
BEAVER CAMPGROUND
NFD RD 417
WARREN GAP
NFD RD 6517
PANTHER CREEK CAMPGROUND

FOREST

PANTHER CREEK
GOBBLERS KNOB
EXPERIMENTAL FOREST
WEIGLE HILL

3

SUNSET
RIDGE
MCKINLEY RIDGE
LITTLE LOOKOUT MOUNTAIN
HEMLOCK
SKAMANIA COUNTY
RD
SNAG RD
CREEK
PACIFIC
EXPERIMENTAL FOREST
SUNSET
CREST
HEMLOCK RD
GREEN KNOB
STEVENSON
NFD RD 43
NFD RD 417
HEMLOCK RD
FOSTER RD
BLACKLEDGE RD
PANTHER CREEK RD
Stabler
WIND RIVER
PILOT KNOB

4

SEE 193 MAP

RIVER
WASHINGTON
TR
SNAG CREEK
TR
CREEK
RIDGE
TR
ROCK CREEK BUTTE
SKAAR RD
BEAR CREEK RD

CARSON

Carson River Valley
STEVENSON RIDGE TR
HOT SPRINGS AV

SEE 195 MAP

5

WASHOUGAL RIVER RD
DOUGAN CREEK CAMPGROUND
GREENLEAF PEAK
GREENLEAF BASIN
TABLE MOUNTAIN
HOT SPRINGS
KALLYK RD
RYAN-ALLEN RD
LOOP RD
AALVIK TR
KANAKA CREEK RD
LOOP
CASCADE-LOCKS HWY
SKAMANIA CO
HOOD RIVER CO
COLUMBIA RIVER
ANDERSON POINT
GOVERNMENT COVE
HERMAN CREEK RD
14
STEVENSON
ROCK COVE
ASH LAKE
AGA LAKE RD
BOW FISH HATCHERY
47
HWY

6

WASHOUGAL MINES
WASHOUGAL STATE SALMON HATCHERY
MCCLOSKEY CREEK RD
CEDAR RD
SWAMP RD
SCOTT RD
MCDONALD CREEK RD
KUEFFLER RD
BEACON ROCK STATE PARK
HAMILTON MOUNTAIN
HARDY FALLS
EAGLE CREEK CAMPGROUND
NORTH BONNEVILLE
Fort Rains
EVERGREEN HWY
COLUMBIA
14
CASCADE SALMON HATCHERY
MARINE PARK AND CAMPGROUND
CASCADE LOCKS
CASCADE LOCKS-STEVENSON STATE AIRPORT
HOOD RIVER COUNTY
PACIFIC
MABEE CREEK RD
DIMRILL DALE RD
DUNCAN CREEK RD
COUNTRY QUARRY RD
BEACON ROCK
Skamania
PIERCE ISLAND
84
30
40
Bonneville
TOOTH ROCK TUNNEL
WAUNA POINT
MUNRA POINT
DEVILLE RD
CREST
WETLAND FALLS
BENSON PLATEAU
PUNCH BOWL FALLS

7

MCCLOSKEY RD
RYAN-TAVELLI RD
SNEIDER-BANKS RD
ARCHER MOUNTAIN
FRANZ RD
14
Cruzatt
EVERGREEN HWY
Pringle
SKAMANIA CO
MULTNOMAH CO
SKAMANIA ISLAND
WASHINGTON
OREGON
35
TUMALT CREEK RD
COLUMBIA RIVER
HWY 30
Dodson
HWY 87
ELOWAH FALLS
WAUNEKA POINT
MOFFETT FALLS
MOUNT HOOD
NESMITH POINT
TANNER CREEK RD
MULTNOMAH CO
HOOD RIVER CO
COLUMBIA
WILDERNESS
LOOWIT FALLS
WY'EAST CAMPSITE
BLUE GROUSE CAMPSITE
TUNNEL FALLS
MULTNOMAH COUNTY
OREGON
NATIONAL FOREST
TALAPUS RIDGE
CROWN POINT
MIST FALLS
DALTON POINT
WAHKEENA FALLS
HORSETAIL FALLS
ONEONTA FALLS
WAHSPE POINT
YEON MOUNTAIN
NE SMITH POINT RD
PALMER PEAK
SEVEN-AND-A-HALF MILE CAMPSITE
31

SEE 201 MAP

0 1 2 3 4 miles   1 in. = 2.5 mi.

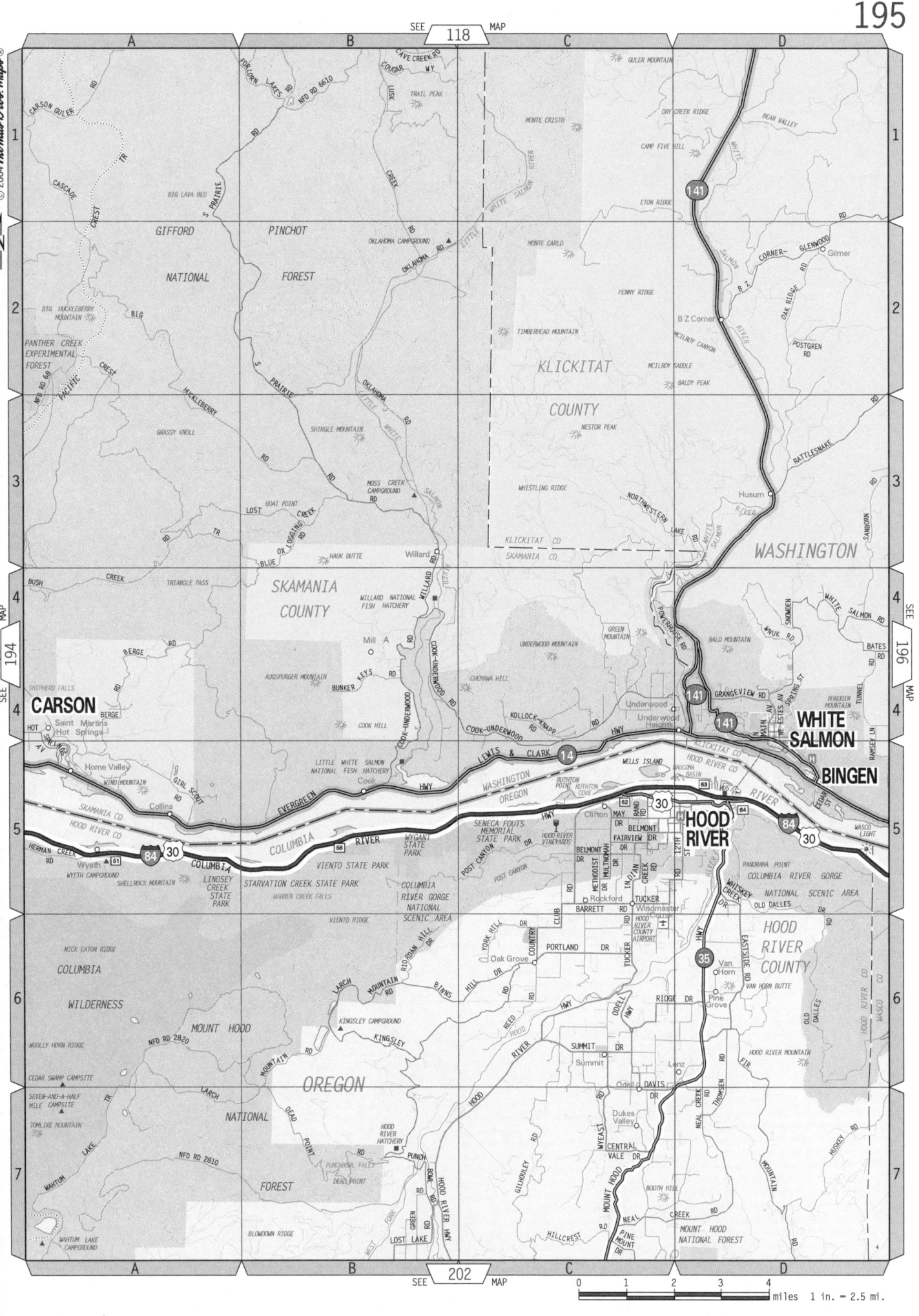

METRO

SEE MAP 194

SEE MAP 196

0 1 2 3 4 miles 1 in. = 2.5 mi.

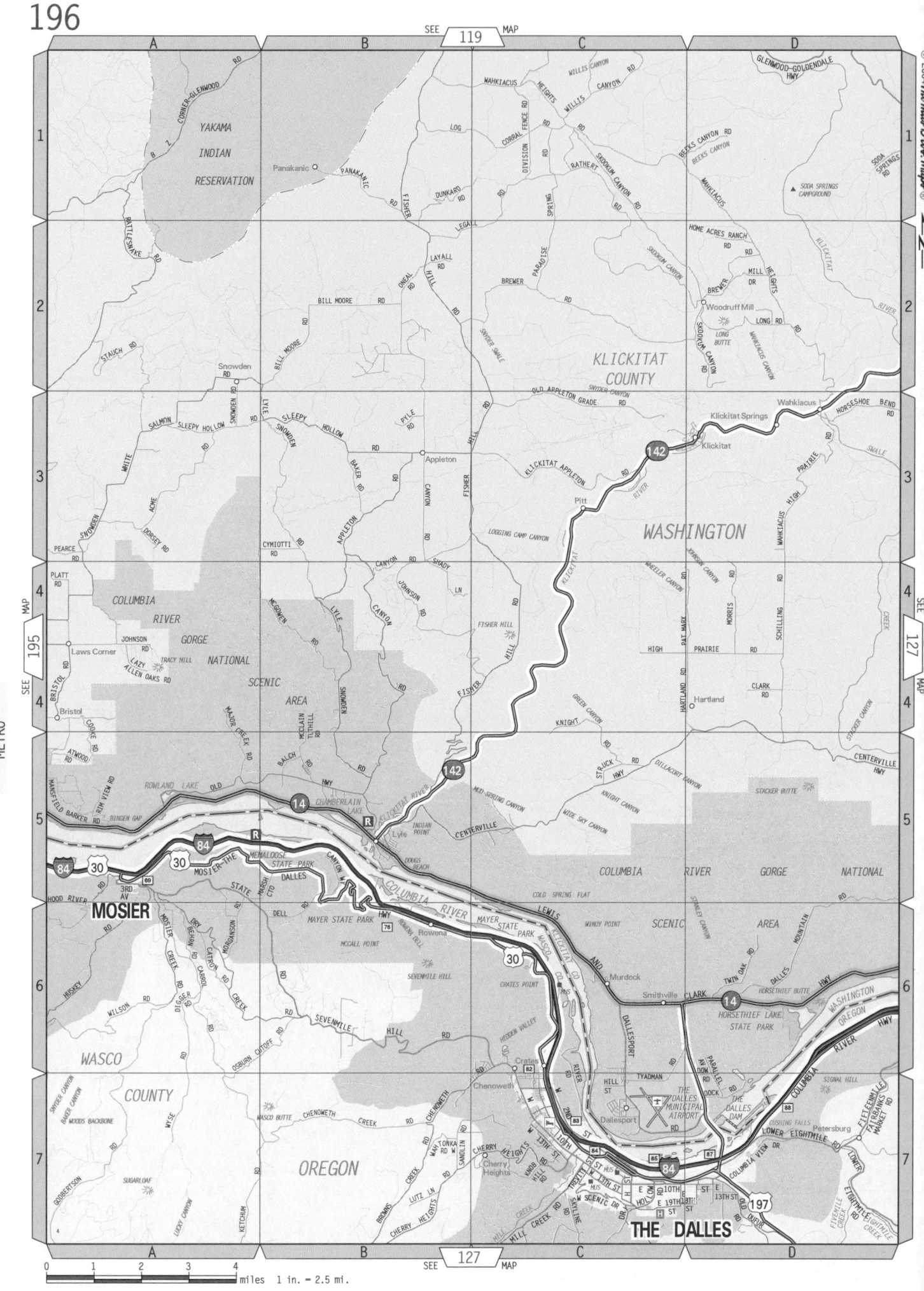

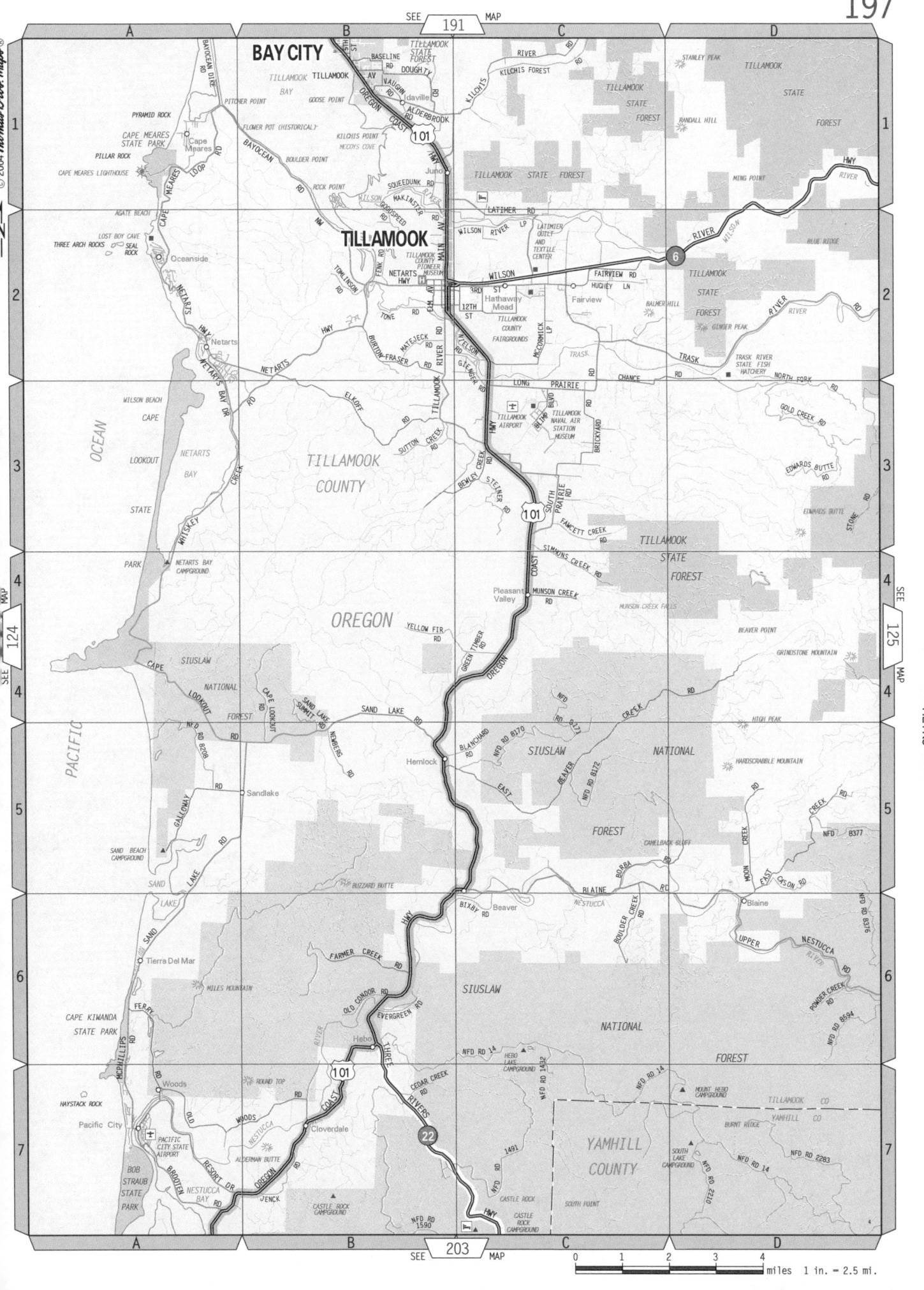

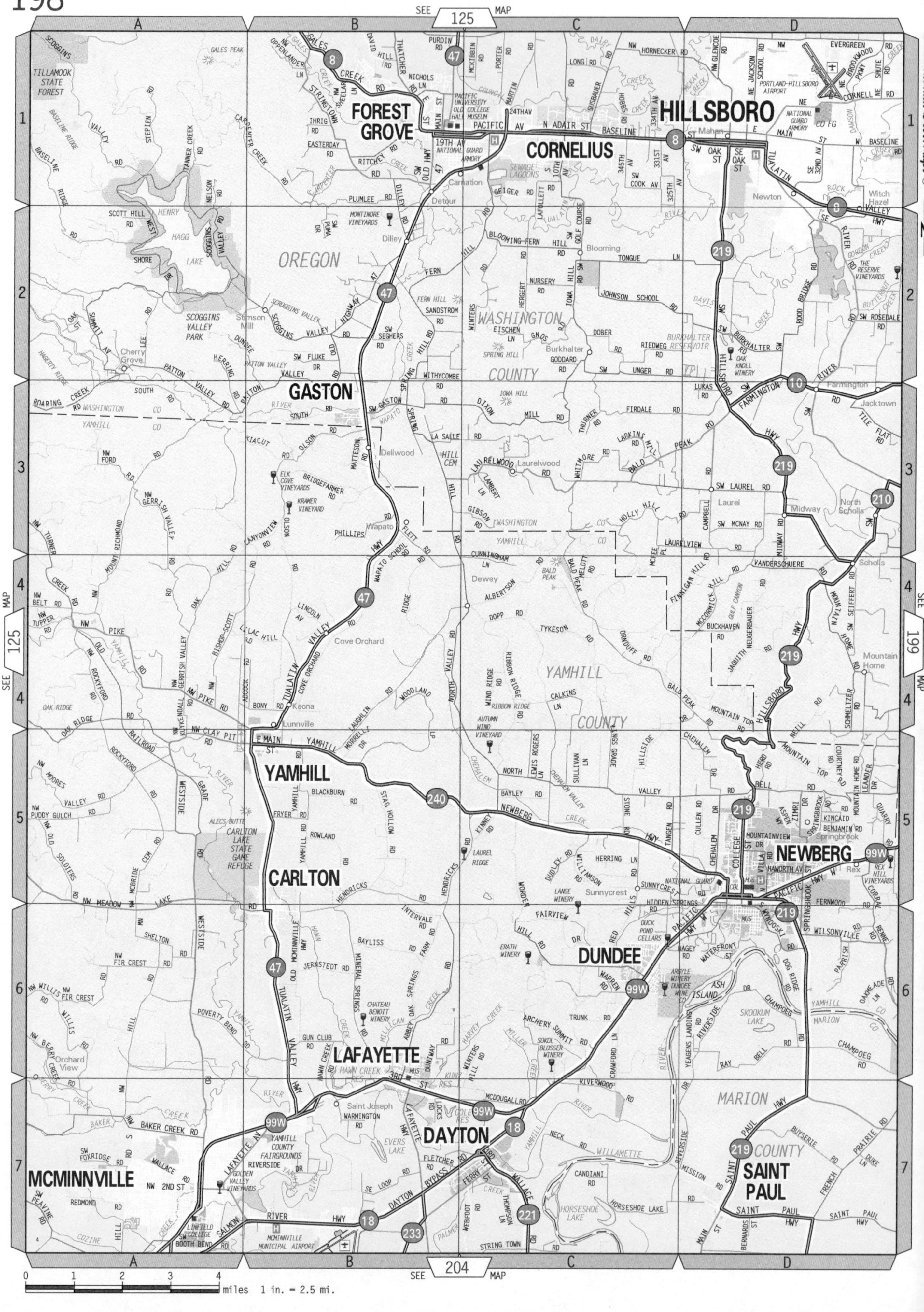

METRO

A | B | C | D

1

TILLAMOOK STATE FOREST

FOREST GROVE

CORNELIUS

HILLSBORO

PACIFIC UNIVERSITY OLD COLLEGE HALL MUSEUM

PORTLAND-HILLSBORO AIRPORT

NATIONAL GUARD ARMORY

OREGON

2

WASHINGTON COUNTY

The Reserve Vineyards

Montinore Vineyards

Dilley

3

GASTON

Elk Cove Vineyards

Kramer Vineyard

Dellwood

Wapato

Laurelwood

Laurel

Midway

North Scholls

4

Cove Orchard

Keona

Lunnville

Dewey

YAMHILL COUNTY

Bald Peak

Mountain Home

5

YAMHILL

CARLTON

240

NEWBERG

Laurel Ridge

Sunnycrest

6

Chateau Benoit Winery

DUNDEE

Erath Winery

Duck Pond Cellars

Argyle Winery

Dundee Wine Island

Sokol Blosser Winery

Skookum Lake

MARION COUNTY

7

MCMINNVILLE

LAFAYETTE

DAYTON

Saint Joseph

Warmington

Yamhill County Fairgrounds

Golden Valley Vineyards

Linfield College

McMinnville Municipal Airport

SAINT PAUL

Horseshoe Lake

Willamette River

99W | 18 | 221 | 233 | 219 | 47 | 8 | 10 | 210

0 1 2 3 4 miles 1 in. = 2.5 mi.

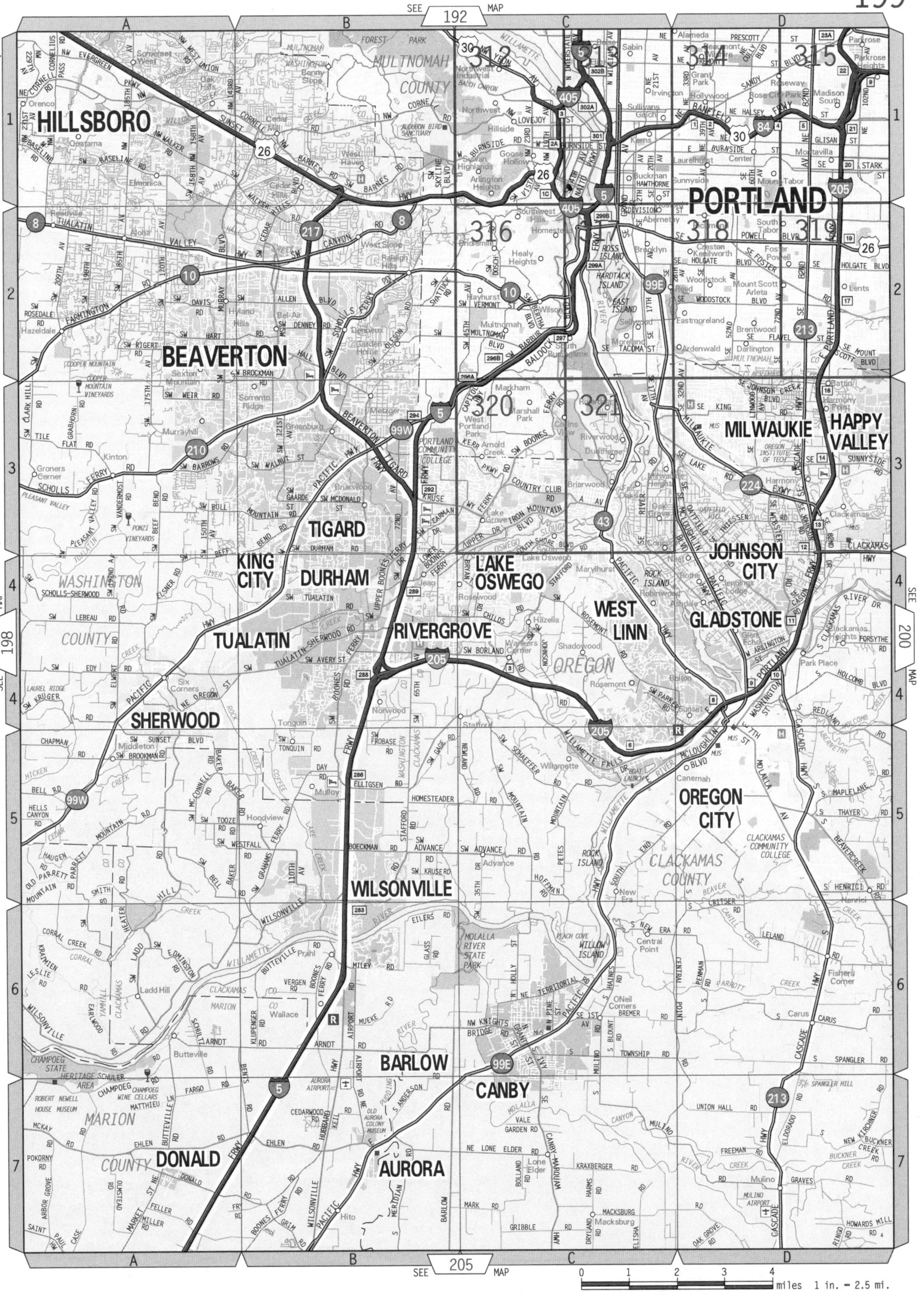

HILLSBORO

PORTLAND

BEAVERTON

MILWAUKIE

HAPPY VALLEY

TIGARD

KING CITY

DURHAM

LAKE OSWEGO

JOHNSON CITY

TUALATIN

RIVERGROVE

WEST LINN

GLADSTONE

SHERWOOD

WILSONVILLE

OREGON CITY

BARLOW

CANBY

DONALD

AURORA

MULTNOMAH COUNTY

WASHINGTON COUNTY

CLACKAMAS COUNTY

MARION COUNTY

OREGON

312 313 314 315

316 318 319

320 321

FOREST PARK

CHAMPOEG STATE HERITAGE AREA

MOLALLA RIVER STATE PARK

PORTLAND COMMUNITY COLLEGE

CLACKAMAS COMMUNITY COLLEGE

SEE MAP 192
SEE MAP 205
SEE MAP 198
SEE MAP 200

METRO

0 1 2 3 4 miles   1 in. = 2.5 mi.

© 2004 Thomas Bros. Maps®

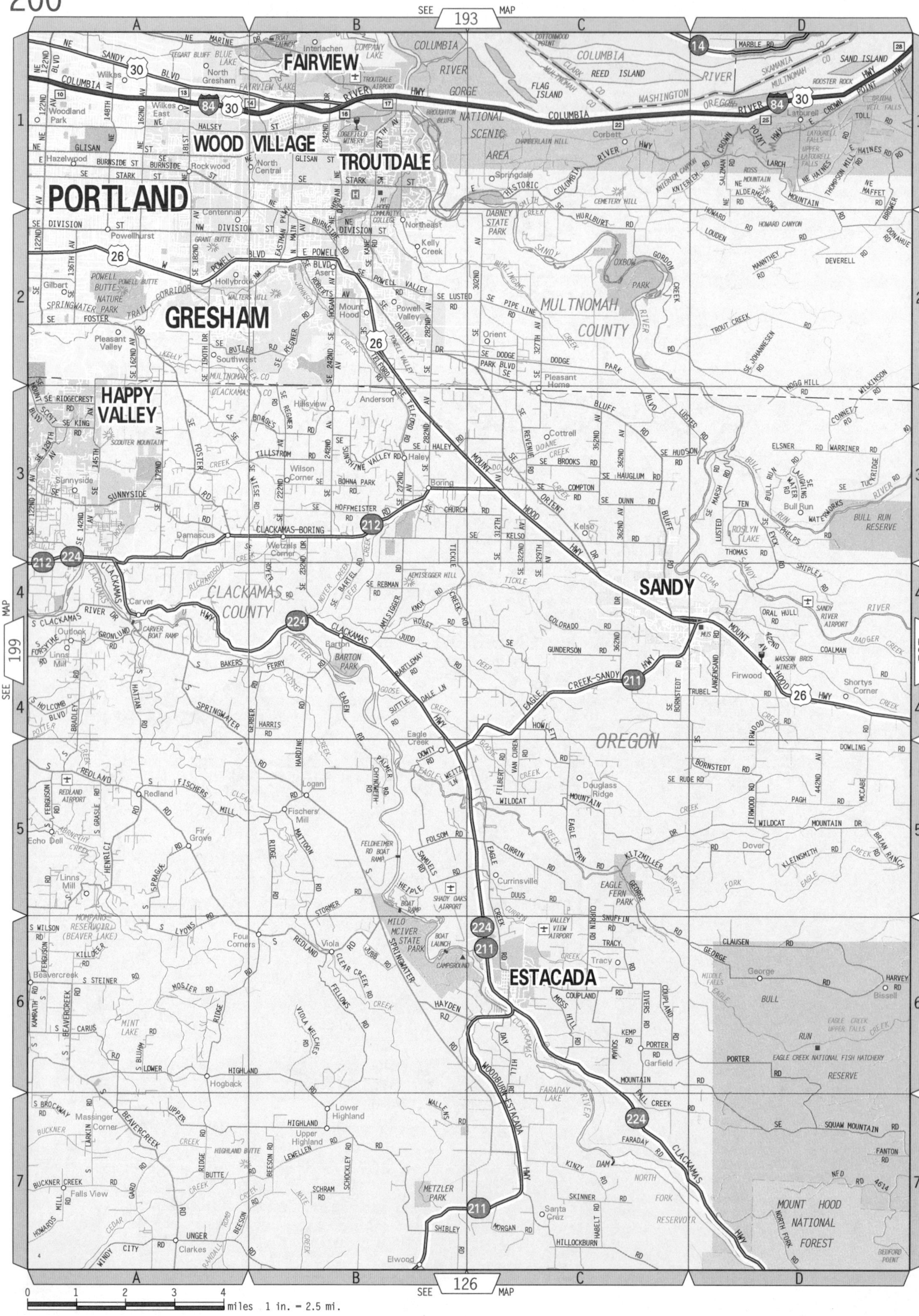

SEE 193 MAP
SEE 126 MAP
SEE 199 MAP
SEE 201 MAP
METRO
A
B
C
D
1
2
3
4
5
6
7
PORTLAND
GRESHAM
FAIRVIEW
WOOD VILLAGE
TROUTDALE
HAPPY VALLEY
SANDY
ESTACADA
CLACKAMAS COUNTY
MULTNOMAH COUNTY
OREGON
WASHINGTON
COLUMBIA RIVER
COLUMBIA RIVER GORGE NATIONAL SCENIC AREA
REED ISLAND
FLAG ISLAND
BLUE LAKE
FAIRVIEW LAKE
COMPANY LAKE
Interlachen
North Gresham
Wilkes
Wilkes East
Woodland Park
Hazelwood
Rockwood
North Central
Centennial
Powellhurst
Gilbert
Hollybrook
Pleasant Valley
Southwest
Springdale
Corbett
Latourell
Northeast
Kelly Creek
Powell Valley
Mount Hood
Asert
Orient
Pleasant Home
Anderson
Hillsview
Haley
Wilson Corner
Boring
Cottrell
Kelso
Damascus
Wetzels Corner
Sunnyside
Carver
Outlook
Linns Mill
Barton
BARTON PARK
Firwood
Shortys Corner
Eagle Creek
Redland
Logan
Fischers Mill
Fir Grove
Echo Dell
Douglass Ridge
Dover
Currinsville
EAGLE FERN PARK
MILO MCIVER STATE PARK
Four Corners
Viola
Beavercreek
Tracy
George
Bissell
Garfield
Hogback
Lower Highland
Upper Highland
Massinger Corner
Falls View
Clarkes
Elwood
Santa Cruz
METZLER PARK
DABNEY STATE PARK
OXBOW PARK
POWELL BUTTE NATURE PARK
BULL RUN RESERVE
ROSLYN LAKE
Bull Run
Ten Eyck
SANDY RIVER AIRPORT
REDLAND AIRPORT
SHADY OAKS AIRPORT
VALLEY VIEW AIRPORT
TROUTDALE AIRPORT
MOUNT HOOD NATIONAL FOREST
BULL RUN
EAGLE CREEK NATIONAL FISH HATCHERY
FARADAY LAKE
NORTH FORK RESERVOIR
MINT LAKE
MOMPANO RESERVOIR (BEAVER LAKE)
MT HOOD COMMUNITY COLLEGE
EDGEFIELD WINERY
WASSON BROS WINERY
CARVER BOAT RAMP
CAMPGROUND
84
30
26
14
212
224
211
0 1 2 3 4 miles 1 in. = 2.5 mi.

MAP

SEE 194 MAP

METRO

A B C D

1

Angels Rest
SHEPPERDS DELL STATE PARK
Bridal Veil
PILLARS OF HERCULES
DEVILS REST
MOUNT HOOD
NATIONAL
FOREST
COLUMBIA RIVER GORGE NATIONAL SCENIC AREA
GEORGE SMITH RD
PALMER MILL RD
BROWER RD
MULTNOMAH BASIN
LARCH MOUNTAIN RD
NE SMITH POINT
ONEONTA GORGE
TALAPUS RIDGE RD
TALAPUS MOUNTAIN
COLUMBIA
TANNER BUTTE
WILDERNESS
HOOD RIVER
COUNTY
INDIAN SPRINGS CAMPGROUND
EAGLE CREEK TR
PACIFIC CREST TR
INDIAN MOUNTAIN
MOUNT HOOD
NATIONAL
SUNSHINE ROCK
PEPPER MOUNTAIN
LARCH MOUNTAIN RD
SHERRARD POINT
LARCH MOUNTAIN
NFD RD 20

2

DONAHUE RD
NFD RD 1509
NFD RD 1010
NFD RD 1008
LOOKOUT POINT
WALKER PEAK
NFD RD 10
NFD RD 20
BULL RUN RIVER
NFD RD 10
MULTNOMAH COUNTY
BIG BEND MOUNTAIN
BULL RUN RESERVE
BULL RUN RESERVOIR NO 1
EAGLE BUTTE
MULTNOMAH RIVER
HOOD RIVER
TABLE MOUNTAIN
WAHTUM
BUCK PEAK
SAWTOOTH MOUNTAIN
BAKER POINT
LOST LAKE CAMPGROUND
NFD RD 13
LOST LAKE
LO CO HO CO
LAKE BRANCH
FOREST
DEVILS PULPIT
PREACHERS PEAK

3

NFD RD 10
BULL RUN RESERVOIR NO 2
NFD RD 12
NFD RD 14
NFD RD 410
NFD RD 201
NFD RD 201
NFD RD 1210
NFD RD 1210
NFD RD 1210
NFD RD 1414
NFD RD 1217
NFD RD 12
NFD RD 1027
MULTNOMAH CO
CLACKAMAS CO
THIMBLE MOUNTAIN
DEER MEADOWS
ASCHOFF
ASCHOFF BUTTES
ASCHOFF RD
THUNDER ROCK
BLAZED ALDER BUTTE
HALFWAY HILL
BURNT PEAK
NFD RD 10
1027
NFD RD 10
SENTINEL PEAK
BULL RUN LAKE
BULL RUN NATURAL AREA
HIYU MOUNTAIN

4

DEVILS BACKBONE
MARMOT
BIG SANDY RD
SANDY
BATY
BADGER
COALMAN RD
CHERRYVILLE
26
MOUNT HOOD NATIONAL FOREST
MARMOT
GOODFELLOW LAKES RD
CLACKAMAS COUNTY
NORTH BOULDER CREEK
BARLOW TRAIL RD
BRIGHTWOOD
BRIGHTWOOD LOOP
MOUNT HOOD HWY
SANDY RIVER
SALMON
WILDCAT
ALDER CREEK
ALDER CREEK
TERRA FERN DR
WEBER RD
NFD RD 1228
NORTH MOUNTAIN
NORTH MOUNTAIN RD
ASCHOFF
BARLOW TRAIL RD
MOUNT HOOD NATIONAL FOREST
HICKMAN BUTTE
CLEAR FORK BUTTE
SUGARLOAF MOUNTAIN
LOLO PASS
NFD RD 1828
LAST CHANCE MOUNTAIN
NFD RD 1825
FRED MCNEIL CAMPGROUND
NFD RD 382
SANDY RIVER
CRUTCHER BENCH
LOLO PASS RD

5

LENHART BUTTE
WILDCAT MOUNTAIN
TROUT CREEK
NORTH FORK
EAGLE CREEK
CEDAR CREEK
ALDER CREEK
MCINTYRE RIDGE
SALMON RIVER
BLM
FAIRWAY AV
WEMME
ZIGZAG
WELCHES
FAUBION
WELCHES
MOUNTAIN VIEW DR
SALMON RIVER
BARLOW TRAIL RD
LOLO PASS
SANDY RIVER
MOUNT HOOD WILDERNESS AREA
WEST ZIGZAG LOOKOUT
RHODODENDRON
HENRY CREEK
ENOLA HILL
ZIGZAG MOUNTAIN
HORSESHOE RIDGE
ZIGZAG RIVER
DEVILS MEADOW CAMPGROUND
DEVIL CANYON
26

6

BULL RUN NATIONAL FOREST
NFD RD 255
EAGLE CREEK
MOUNT HOOD NATIONAL FOREST
HUCKLEBERRY MOUNTAIN
WILDCAT MOUNTAIN
SALMON HUCKLEBERRY WILDERNESS
BOULDER CREEK
SALMON MOUNTAIN
HUNCHBACK MOUNTAIN
GREEN CANYON CAMPGROUND
NFD RD 2618
OREGON
ZIGZAG RIVER
FLAG MOUNTAIN
CAMP CREEK
CAMP CREEK CAMPGROUND
NFD RD 2612
TWIN BRIDGES CAMPGROUND
TWIN BRIDGES RD
ZIGZAG RIVER
MOUNT HOOD HWY
BARLOW CAMPGROUND
BRUIN RUN CAMPGROUND
LAUREL HILL
STILL CREEK
WIND CREEK BASIN
MOUNT HOOD NATIONAL FOREST
STILL CREEK

7

RESERVE
SQUAW MOUNTAIN
NFD RD 4615
NFD RD 4613
GITHERS MOUNTAIN
SHEEPSHEAD ROCK
SQUAW MOUNTAIN
ABBOTT RD
SALMON BUTTE
OLD BALDY
BIGHORN CAMPGROUND
MOUNT HOOD NATIONAL FOREST
SALMON BUTTE
SOUTH FORK CAMPGROUND
FINAL FALLS
FRUSTRATION FALLS
LITTLE NIAGARA FALLS
VANISHING FALLS
SPLIT FALLS
HIDEAWAY FALLS
STEIN FALLS
LINNEY CREEK CAMPGROUND
DEVILS PEAK
ROLLING RIFFLE CAMPGROUND
KINZEL LAKE CAMPGROUND
KINZEL CREEK
WOLF CAMP BUTTE
SALMON RIVER
LINNEY CREEK RD
WOLF CAMP RD

SEE 126 MAP

SEE 200 MAP

SEE 202 MAP

0 1 2 3 4 miles 1 in. = 2.5 mi.

© 2004 Thomas Bros. Maps ®

© 2004 Thomas Bros. Maps ®

—N—

METRO

	A	B	C	D

1

INDIANHEAD ROCK
NFD RD 1310
LOST
NFD
LAKE
BRANCH 13
13
WEST FORK LAKE
LOST LAKE
TONY CREEK RD
TROUT CREEK
HOOD RIVER RD
WEST FORK RD
WOODWORTH
HWY
PINE MOUNT DR
Mount Hood
DR
BALD BUTTE
BOOTH HILL
NFD RD 1710
FIR MOUNTAIN
FIR MOUNTAIN
NFD RD 1711

2

NFD RD
FORK
WEST
PASS
NFD RD 16
NFD RD 1640
BLUE RIDGE
MOUNT
NFD
RED
HILL RD
RED RD
1610
NFD RD 1611
NFD RD 1610
HOOD
NATIONAL
FOREST
MIDDLE FORK
Parkdale
BASE LINE
CULBERTSON DR
MCINTOSH RD
CLEAR CREEK RD
COOPER SPUR RD
HUTSON DR
LONDON DR
MOUNT
SURVEYORS RIDGE
RIM ROCK
170
CO
NORTH
JOHNS MILL
MILL RIDGE
MILL CREEK LOOKOUT
HILLARY GRADE
HILLARY GRADE

3

BUTCHER PEAK
LOLO
NFD RD 16
NFD RD 1670
NFD RD 1650
NFD RD 1810
LADD CREEK CAMPGROUND
RED HILL
NFD RD 1611
RESERVOIR CAMPGROUND
LAURANCE LAKE DR
KINNIKINNICK CAMPGROUND
NFD RD 2840
OREGON
COOPER SPUR
WEYGANDT CANYON
ROUTSON COUNTY PARK CAMPGROUND
MOUNT HWY
35
SHELLROCK MOUNTAIN
NFD RD
SOUTH FORK HOOD RIVER
WASCO
HOOD RIVER COUNTY
MILL CREEK BUTTES
BROOKS MEADOW
FIVEMILE
FIVEMILE RD
NFD RD 1720

4

BALD MOUNTAIN SHELTER
BALD MOUNTAIN
MOUNT HOOD
LOLO PASS
NFD RD 1810
VISTA RIDGE
INSPIRATION POINT
NFD RD 3512
CATHEDRAL RIDGE
CAIRN BASIN
ELK COVE
STRANAHAN RIDGE
LADD GLACIER
BARRETT SPUR
CLOUD CAP SADDLE CAMPGROUND
LANGILLE CRAGS
MCNEIL POINT
COE GLACIER
YOCUM RIDGE
LANGILLE GLACIER
ELIOT GLACIER
COOPER SPUR SKI AREA
SAND CANYON
TAMANAWAS FALLS
POLALLIE CAMPGROUND
CLINGER CAMPGROUND
44
SHERWOOD CAMPGROUND
NFD RD 4410
PERRY POINT
44
KNEBAL SPRING CAMPGROUND
LOWER EIGHTMILE CAMPGROUND
HOLLOW RD
RAIL
BALDWIN
EIGHTMILE
PEBBLE FORD CAMPGROUND
FIVEMILE BUTTE
NFD RD 4450
NFD RD 4450
MOUNT HOOD NATIONAL FOREST

MOUNT HOOD WILDERNESS AREA
SANDY RIVER
RAMONA FALLS
SANDY GLACIER
REID GLACIER
SLIDE MOUNTAIN
PACIFIC
CREST
LEUTHOLD COULOIR
ZIGZAG GLACIER
MISSISSIPPI HEAD
PALMER GLACIER
MOUNT HOOD
STEEL CLIFF
NEWTON CLARK GLACIER
LAMBERSON BUTTE
GNARL RIDGE
SILCOX WARMING HUT
TRIANGLE MORAINE
STEEL CLIFF GLACIER
WHITE RIVER GLACIER
BLUEGRASS RIDGE
NOTTINGHAM CAMPGROUND
ROBINHOOD CAMPGROUND
MOUNT HOOD HWY
EAST FORK
BULO POINT
COLD SPRINGS
MARION POINT
NATIONAL
FOREST
FIFTEENMILE
4420
GUMJUWAC SADDLE
FIFTEEN MILE CAMPGROUND
COLD SPRINGS
COLD POINT
LOOKOUT MOUNTAIN
FLAG POINT
JORDAN CREEK
NFD RD 2720
JORDAN

5

CLACKAMAS
COUNTY
ZIGZAG CANYON
LITTLE ZIGZAG CANYON
ZIGZAG RIVER
SAND CANYON
LEG
PHLOX POINT CAMPGROUND
ALPINE CAMPGROUND
MOUNT HOOD MEADOW SKI AREA
UMBRELLA FALLS
SAHALE FALLS
SWITCHBACK FALLS
WHITE RIVER
ELK MOUNTAIN
3550
GUNSIGHT BUTTE
3540
NFD RD
BADGER
BADGER CREEK WILDERNESS AREA
GORDON BUTTE

6

YOCUM FALLS
Government Camp
26
SKI BOWL AND MULTORPOR WINTER SPORTS AREA
TOM DICK AND HARRY MOUNTAIN
MULTORPOR MOUNTAIN
STILL CREEK CAMPGROUND
TIMBERLINE
NANITCH CAMPGROUND
TIMBERLINE LODGE
TIMBERLINE HWY
SUMMIT MEADOW RD
MOUNT HOOD HWY
WEST
CLACKAMAS CO
HOOD RIVER
EASTLEG
WHITE RIVER PARK CAMPGROUND
RD 48
BARLOW BUTTE
BENNETT PASS
35
BADGER LAKE CAMPGROUND
BADGER BUTTE
NFD RD 4860
TYGH BURN RD
FLAG POINT
NFD RD 4811
WILDERNESS
AREA

7

STILL CREEK RD
EUREKA PEAK
VEDA BUTTE
KINZEL CREEK
TRILLIUM LAKE
TRILLIUM LAKE CAMPGROUND
WARM SPRINGS RIVER
26
SALMON HUCKLEBERRY WILDERNESS
MUD CREEK RIDGE
SALMON RIVER MEADOWS
SALMON RIVER
BUZZARD POINT
DEVILS HALF ACRE MEADOW CAMPGROUND
BARLOW RD
BARLOW RIDGE
BIRD BUTTE
LOWER TWIN CAMPGROUND
WAPINITIA PASS
FROG LAKE CAMPGROUND
FROG LAKE RD
FROG LAKE BUTTES
WASCO COUNTY
BONNEY MEADOWS CAMPGROUND
ECHO POINT
BONNEY BUTTE
BUCK DRAW
TR
GRASSHOPPER POINT
THREEMILE CREEK
ROCKY BUTTE
WAMIC MILL RD
ROCKY BUTTE RD
BOULDER RIDGE RD
GATE CREEK
NFD RD 4820
BONNEY MEADOWS RD
NFD RD 4860
NFD RD 4870
NFD RD 48

0 1 2 3 4 miles   1 in. = 2.5 mi.

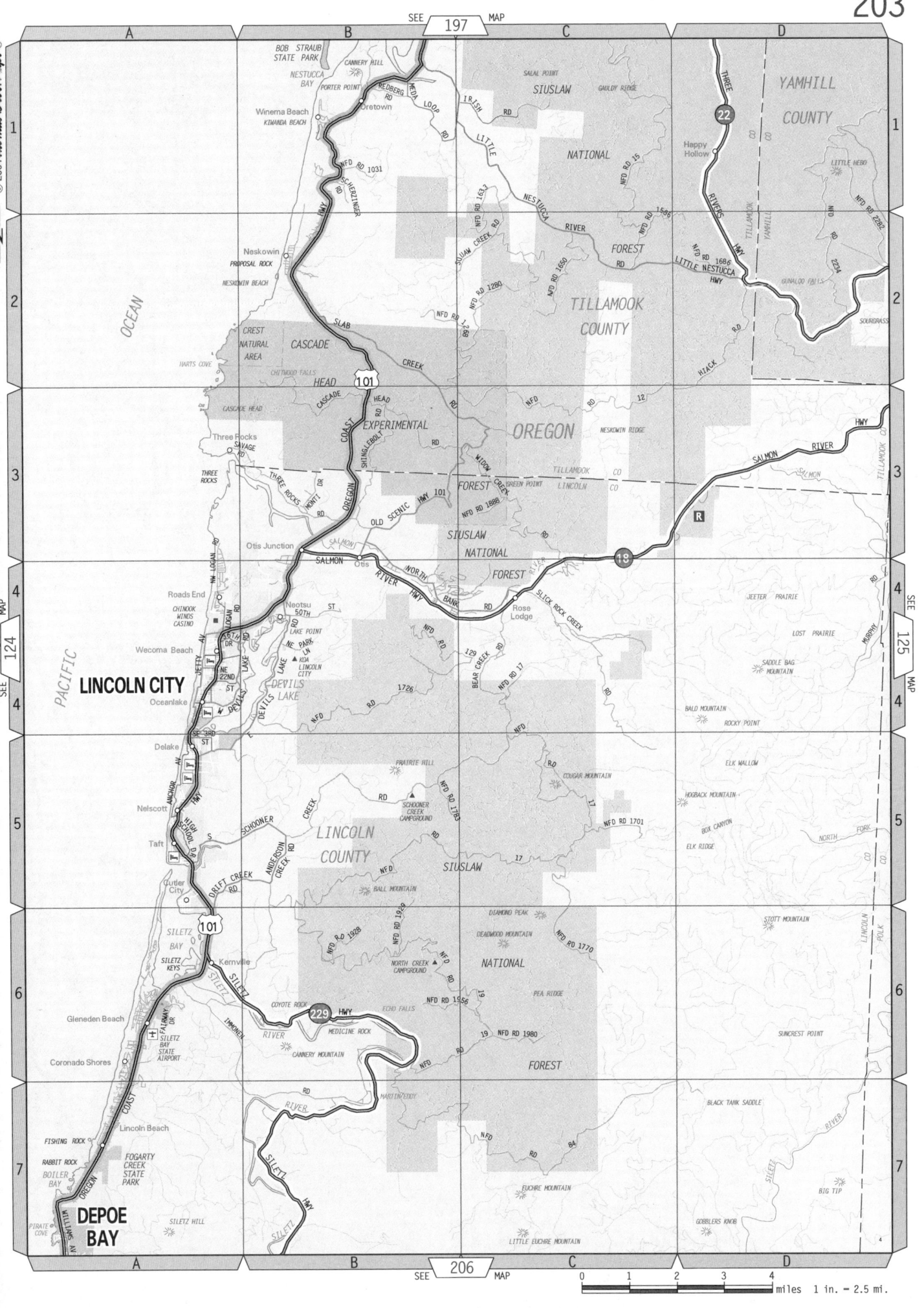

METRO

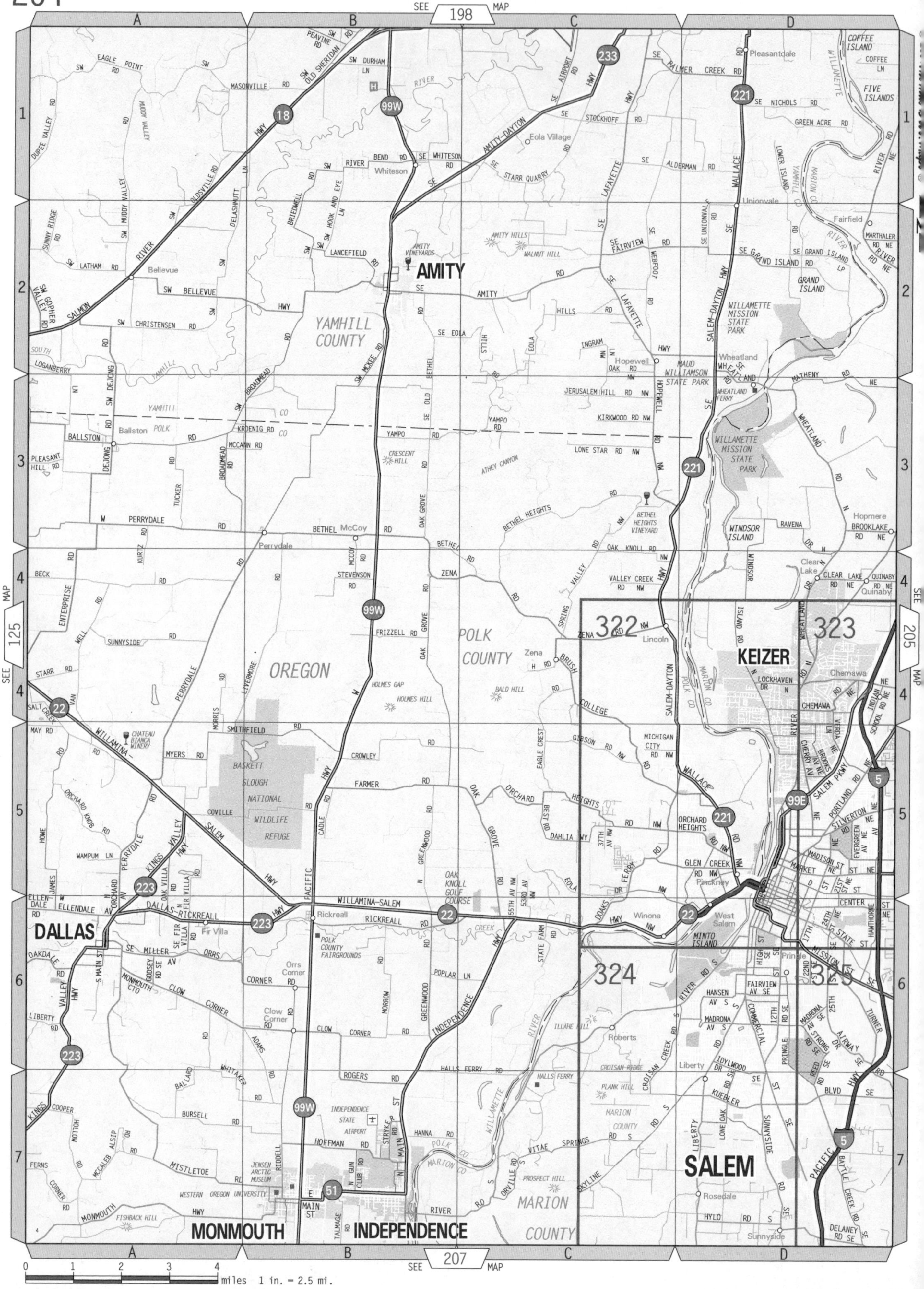

SEE 198 MAP
SEE 207 MAP
SEE METRO 125 MAP
SEE 205 MAP
A
B
C
D
1
2
3
4
5
6
7
AMITY
YAMHILL COUNTY
POLK COUNTY
OREGON
MARION COUNTY
KEIZER
SALEM
DALLAS
MONMOUTH
INDEPENDENCE
322
323
324
325
Pleasantdale
Eola Village
Whiteson
Unionvale
Fairfield
Bellevue
Hopewell
Wheatland
Ballston
McCoy
Perrydale
Lincoln
Zena
Clear Lake
Quinaby
Hopmere
Chemawa
Pinckney
Winona
West Salem
MINTO ISLAND
Rickreall
Fir Villa
Orrs Corner
Clow Corner
Roberts
Liberty
Rosedale
Sunnyside
Pringle
COFFEE ISLAND
FIVE ISLANDS
GRAND ISLAND
WINDSOR ISLAND
WILLAMETTE MISSION STATE PARK
MAUD WILLIAMSON STATE PARK
BASKETT SLOUGH NATIONAL WILDLIFE REFUGE
OAK KNOLL GOLF COURSE
POLK COUNTY FAIRGROUNDS
INDEPENDENCE STATE AIRPORT
JENSEN ARCTIC MUSEUM
WESTERN OREGON UNIVERSITY
AMITY VINEYARDS
BETHEL HEIGHTS VINEYARD
CHATEAU BIANCA WINERY
AMITY HILLS
CRESCENT HILL
HOLMES GAP
HOLMES HILL
BALD HILL
ILLAHE HILL
CROISAN RIDGE
PLANK HILL
PROSPECT HILL
FISHBACK HILL
HALLS FERRY
WHEATLAND FERRY
ATHEY CANYON
WALNUT HILL
WILLAMETTE RIVER
YAMHILL RIVER
SOUTH YAMHILL
99W
18
233
221
22
223
99E
5
51
SW PEAVINE RD
SW OLD SHERIDAN RD
SW DURHAM LN
EAGLE POINT RD
MASONVILLE RD
SALMON RIVER HWY
AMITY-DAYTON HWY
SE AIRPORT RD
SE STOCKHOFF RD
SE PALMER CREEK RD
SE NICHOLS RD
GREEN ACRE RD
SE WHITESON RD
SW RIVER BEND RD
SE STARR QUARRY RD
SE LAFAYETTE HWY
SE ALDERMAN RD
WALLACE RD NE
SALEM-DAYTON HWY
SE UNIONVALE RD
LOWER ISLAND RD
SE FAIRVIEW RD
SE WEBFOOT RD
SE GRAND ISLAND LP
MARTHALER RD NE
RIVER RD NE
SW LANCEFIELD RD
SW HOOK AND EYE LN
BRIEDWELL RD
SW LATHAM RD
SW BELLEVUE HWY
SE AMITY RD
SE EOLA HILLS RD
SE HILLS RD
SW CHRISTENSEN RD
LOGANBERRY LN
SW DEJONG RD
SW BROADMEAD RD
SW MCKEE RD
SE OLD BETHEL RD
INGRAM LN NW
OAK RD NW
JERUSALEM HILL RD NW
KIRKWOOD RD NW
LONE STAR RD NW
HOPEWELL RD NW
MATHENY RD NE
WHEATLAND RD NE
KROENIG RD
MCCANN RD
YAMPO RD
BALLSTON RD
PLEASANT HILL RD
TUCKER RD
OAK GROVE RD
BETHEL HEIGHTS RD
W PERRYDALE RD
BETHEL RD
RAVENA DR
BROOKLAKE RD NE
OAK KNOLL RD NW
VALLEY CREEK RD NW
SPRING VALLEY RD NW
CLEAR LAKE RD NE
QUINABY RD NE
BECK RD
ENTERPRISE RD
KURTZ RD
MCCOY RD
STEVENSON RD
ZENA RD NW
FRIZZELL RD
SUNNYSIDE RD
WELL RD
STARR RD
VAN WELL RD
LIVERMORE RD
PERRYDALE RD
BRUSH COLLEGE RD
LOCKHAVEN DR N
CHEMAWA RD NE
SALT CREEK RD
MAY RD
WILLAMINA-SALEM HWY
MORRIS RD
SMITHFIELD RD
MYERS RD
CROWLEY RD
GIBSON RD NW
MICHIGAN CITY RD NW
EAGLE CREST RD
FARMER RD
ORCHARD KNOB RD
COVILLE RD
CADLE RD
PACIFIC HWY W
OAK GROVE RD
ORCHARD HEIGHTS RD
BEST RD
DAHLIA WY
37TH AV NW
GLEN CREEK RD NW
FERRY DR
DOAKS FERRY RD NW
CHERRY AV NE
PORTLAND RD NE
SILVERTON RD NE
SALEM PKWY
VERDA LN NE
INDIAN SCHOOL RD NE
EVERGREEN AV NE
MADISON ST NE
MARKET ST NE
CENTER ST NE
HAWTHORNE AV NE
STATE ST
MISSION ST SE
HOWE RD
WAMPUM LN
JAMES RD
KINGS VALLEY HWY
OAK VILLA RD
FIR VILLA RD
ELLENDALE AV
DALLAS-RICKREALL HWY
RICKREALL RD
55TH AV NW
53RD AV NW
STATE FARM RD
OAKDALE RD
VALLEY HWY
S MAIN ST
SE MILLER AV
GODSEY RD SE
ORRS CORNER RD
MONMOUTH CTO
CLOW CORNER RD
POPLAR LN
GREENWOOD RD
MORROW RD
INDEPENDENCE HWY
LIBERTY RD
ADAMS RD
RIVER RD S
HANSEN AV S
MADRONA AV S
FAIRVIEW AV SE
COMMERCIAL ST
12TH ST SE
22ND ST SE
25TH ST SE
STRONG RD SE
TURNER RD SE
AIRWAY DR
PRINGLE RD SE
REED RD SE
HALLS FERRY RD
CROISAN CREEK RD S
IDYLWOOD DR
ROGERS RD
WHITAKER RD
BALLARD RD
BURSELL RD
KINGS VALLEY HWY
COOPER HOLLOW RD
KUEBLER BLVD SE
LONE OAK RD
SUNNYSIDE RD SE
HANNA RD
STRYKER RD
HOFFMAN RD
MAIN ST
GUN CLUB RD
RIDDELL RD
ALSIP RD
MCCALEB RD
MISTLETOE RD
FERNS CORNER RD
MONMOUTH HWY
VITAE SPRINGS RD
ORVILLE RD
SKYLINE RD
MARION COUNTY RD
HYLO RD S
PACIFIC HWY
BATTLE CREEK RD
DELANEY RD SE
TALMAGE RD
RIVER RD
0 1 2 3 4
miles 1 in. = 2.5 mi.

SEE 199 MAP

A   B   C   D

HUBBARD

WOODBURN

GERVAIS

MOUNT ANGEL

SCOTTS MILLS

SILVERTON

SALEM

TURNER   AUMSVILLE

CLACKAMAS COUNTY

MARION COUNTY

OREGON

SILVER FALLS STATE PARK

METRO

SEE 204 MAP   SEE 126 MAP

SEE 133 MAP

323   325

0 1 2 3 4 miles   1 in. = 2.5 mi.

© 2004 Thomas Bros. Maps

OREGON STATE FISH HATCHERY FEASTERS ROCKS

Silver Falls City

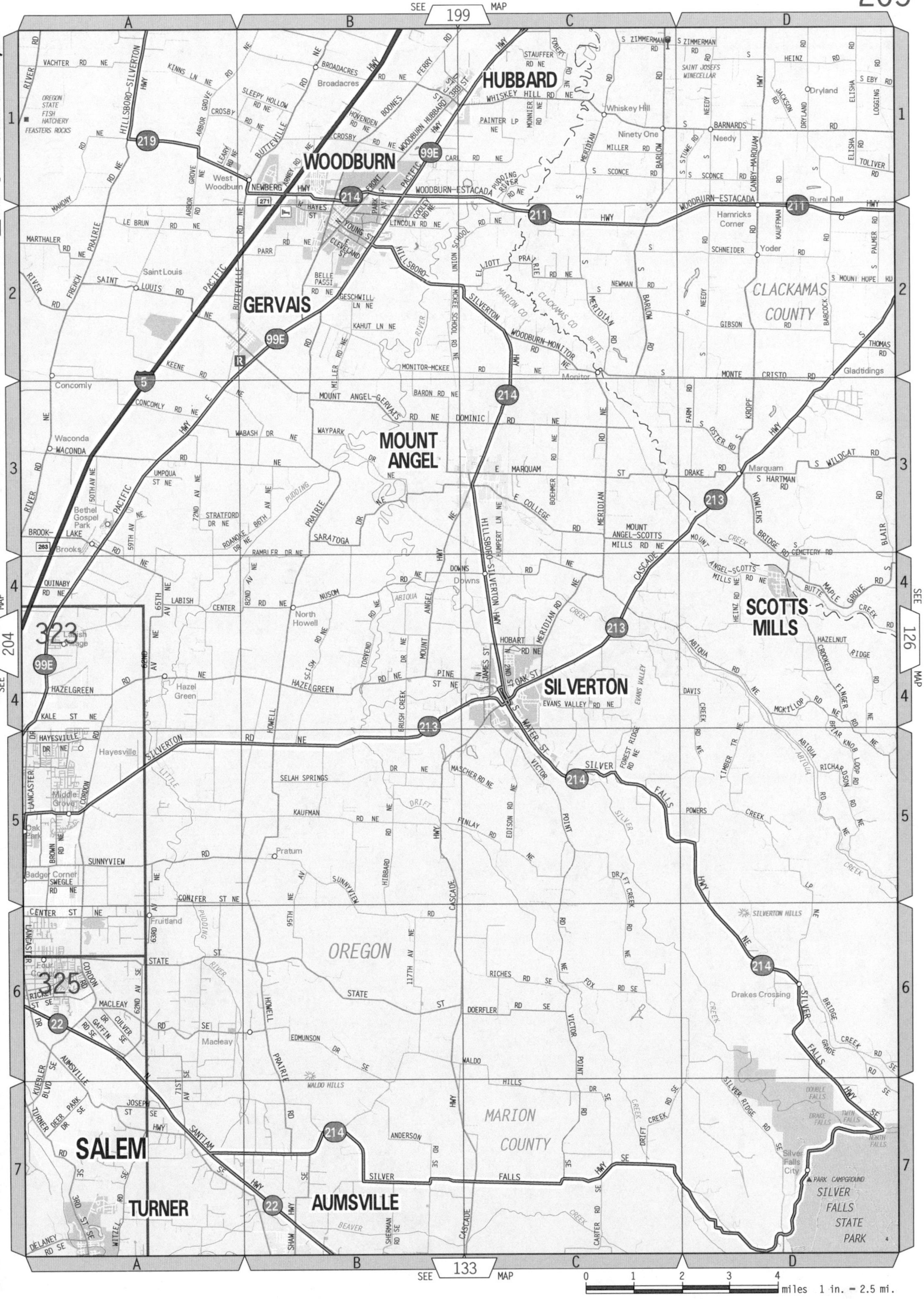

METRO

SEE MAP 203
SEE MAP 132
SEE MAP 133
SEE MAP 209

A   B   C   D

1   2   3   4   5   6   7

DEPOE BAY

SILETZ

NEWPORT

TOLEDO

OREGON

LINCOLN COUNTY

PACIFIC

OCEAN

DEPOE BAY AQUARIUM
DEPOE BAY
WINCHELL ST
AINSLEE DR
WHALE COVE
HWY COAST DR
1 01

BUTTERFIELD RIFFLE
SILETZ HWY
229
LAMBERT POINT
LOWER GORGE
MOONSHINE PARK
THE MAPLES
KOSYDAR
MILLER RD
SILETZ
OJALLA RD
HUHTALA RD
RD
Upper Farm
RD
RIVER

OTTER CREST
GULL ROCK
FINGER ROCK
DEVILS PUNCH BOWL STATE PARK
Otter Rock
OTTER ROCK
COAST
BEVERLY BEACH STATE PARK
Beverly Beach
DEWEY
CREEK
SILETZ
SILETZ AIRPORT
OLD SILETZ INDIAN RESERVATION
GOVERNMENT HILL
GAITHER
SWAN AV
MADE RD
HAMER RD
LOBSDEN
RIVER
RD

100TH
WY
NEWTON HILL
Camp Twelve
CAMP TWELVE LP
SILETZ
CREEK
RD

MOOLACK BEACH
SCHOONER POINT
IRON MOUNTAIN
MARTIN FALLS
STARFISH COVE
LIGHTHOUSE
YAQUINA HEAD
Agate Beach
HARNEY NE
BIG CREEK RD
PIONEER SUMMIT
PIONEER MOUNTAIN
20
HIGHWAY 20
HIGHWAY
RIVER
COOKS RD
SAMS
THORNTON
CREEK
JACOBSON RD
ELK CITY RD
DEVILS WELL
TRAP CREEK RD

OCEAN VIEW DR
JUMPOFF JOE
NW 12TH ST
BEACH NYE
W OLIVE ST
12TH ST
NE EADS ST
NE
Newport Heights
NE
YAQUINA HEIGHTS DR
LINCOLN COUNTY FAIRGROUNDS
Buford Hill
FRUITVALE
HIGHWAY 20
CHRISTIANSEN
BUS 20
ARCADIA DR
SKYLINE DR
SLOPE
STURDAVENT
20
YAQUINA RIVER
Elk City
HARLAN RD
UPDIKE
ELK RD

ELIZABETH ST
Oregon Coast History Center
SE
UNDERSEA GARDENS
HATFIELD MARINE SCIENCE CENTER
BAY
MARINE BLVD
BENSON ST
Yaquina
Oregon State University Marine Science Center
Oregon Coast Aquarium
South Beach
YAQUINA BAY
YAQUINA
BAY
TOLEDO STATE AIRPORT
CITY
SUNNYRIDGE
MILL CREEK
Strawberry Mountain

YAQUINA BAY LIGHTHOUSE
SOUTH BEACH STATE PARK
Yaquina
Coquille Point
VALLEY RD
WIDDEN
BOONE ISLAND
YAQUINA
BAY RD
SOUTHBAY
ELK CITY RD
SUNNYRIDGE
TOLEDO RESERVOIR
PALMER MOUNTAIN
ERROL RIDGE
RD
CREEK

NEWPORT MUNICIPAL AIRPORT
WEISER POINT
ONEATTA POINT
Winant
BONE SLOUGH
Oysterville
YAQUINA RIVER
SOUTH BAY
Craigie Point
Grassy Point
PETERSON RIDGE
MILL CREEK DIVIDE
BEAVER
CAPE HORN RIDGE

Holliday Beach
Egrstar
LOST CREEK STATE RECREATION SITE
1 01
MCCAFFREY ISLAND
WRIGHT
CREEK
RD
MOLKAV
CREEK
SIUSLAW
BEAVER
NFD RD
GOPHER RIDGE
3120

ONA BEACH
COAST
BEAVER CREEK
N BEAVER VALLEY DR
ELKHORN CREEK RD
Ona
NFD RD 50
NATIONAL
NFD 5087
FIVEMILE SHELTER
NFD RD 1030
NFD RD 1014

ELEPHANT ROCK
Seal Rock
BEAVER
HOME CANYON
DRIFT CREEK WILDERNESS
FOREST
NFD RD 52
NFD RD 1000
TABLE MOUNTAIN
PEAVINE RIDGE

HOLLY BEACH
OREGON
DRIFT CREEK

0 1 2 3 4 miles   1 in. = 2.5 mi.

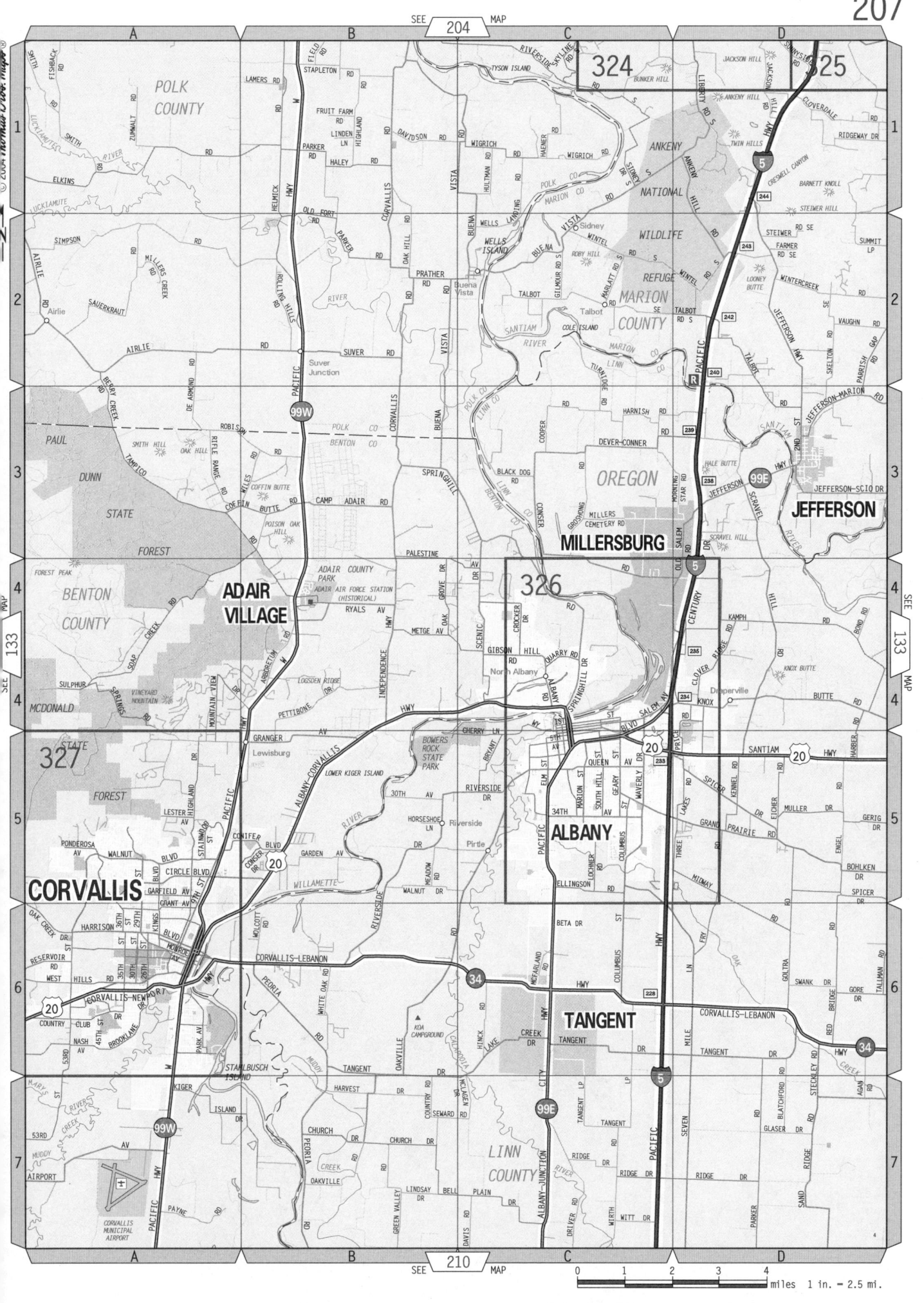

METRO

SEE 127 MAP

METRO

A B C D

WASCO COUNTY

KLAHHOP BUTTE

HELIGATE

Kahneeta Hot Springs

WARM SPRINGS RIVER

South Junction

SOUTH JUNCTION RD

GATE SPRING CANYON

1

EAGLE BUTTE

WARM SPRINGS INDIAN RESERVATION

WEBSTER FLAT RD

STIMMASHO HOT SPRINGS RD

TEE WEES BUTTE

WASCO CO
JEFFERSON CO

NE COLEMAN

COLEMAN POINT

BAKER CANYON

COLEMAN RD

TROUT CREEK

2

WARM SPRINGS HWY 26

WOLFORD CANYON RD

DRY CREEK TRAIL

UPPER DRY CREEK RD

DRY CREEK RD

AGENCY-HOT SPRINGS

THE MUSEUM AT WARM SPRINGS

MILLER HEIGHTS

DRY CREEK CAMPGROUND

MECCA GRADE

DESCHUTES

FROG SPRINGS CANYON

NE MARKET ST

NE GATEWAY GRADE

NE CLEMENS DR

Gateway

NE MCFARLAND LN

NE COOK LN

OREGON

CREEK

97

OLD HWY

2

WEST HILLS

Warm Springs

ELLIOT HEIGHTS

NW TENINO RD

TRAIL RD

NW JUNIPER LN

NE JUNIPER LN

NEFF

BUCKLEY

NE EMERSON DR

IVY LN

QUAALE LN

DALLES-CALIFORNIA

HWY 97

3

DESCHUTES DR

COLUMBIA DR

NW IVY LN

NW HICKORY LN

ADAMS DR

BOISE DR

MUD SPRINGS DR

CLARK DR

NE FERN LN

HEREFORD LN

3

DRY HOLLOW RD

JACKSON LN

RD P-110

NW RIMROCK RD 26 WARM

JEFFERSON COUNTY

NEGRO BROWN CANYON

NW GUMWOOD

NE BARNES DR

SPRINGS

NW FIR LN

MUD SPRINGS VALLEY LN

NE EMERSON

THE

EMERSON LN

CROOKED

4

DRY HOLLOW RD

SEEKSEEQUA

LUNA BUTTE

JACKSON BUTTES

DESCHUTES DR

ELBE DR

NW ELM LN

NE DOGWOOD

ADAMS DR

NE ELM LN

4

SEE 135 MAP

SEEKSEEQUA CREEK RD

Seekseequa Junction

WILLOW CREEK RD

CLACKAMAS DR

NW DOGWOOD LN

MADRAS CITY-COUNTY AIRPORT

NE CHERRY

COLEMAN CANYON

RIVER

DAVIS CANYON

HAY CREEK

4

METOLIUS BENCH RD

BOX CANYON TRAIL

JACKSON TRAIL

HARPERS CANYON

WILLOW CREEK CANYON

BIRCH

Madras Station

NE LOUCKS RD

LOUCKS LN

RED SIDED CANYON

ASHWOOD RD

5

SW ALMA LN

ALMA LN

ELK DR

DESCHUTES DR

SW ASHWOOD

NE H B ST ASHWOOD

HENDERSON DR

NFD RD 1176

NATIONAL

5

LOWER BEND RD

SW BELMONT

DRY CANYON

ELBE LN

MADRAS

SE BUFF ST

SE J ST

GRIZZLY RD

BUCK BUTTE

BALDWIN HILLS

6

RIVERVIEW RD OBSERVATORY

CROOKED RIVER NATIONAL GRASSLAND

THE COVE PALISADES STATE PARK

CANADIAN BENCH

ROUND BUTTE DR

MOUNTAIN VIEW

METOLIUS

SW DOVER

SW GALLOWAY LN

JEFFERSON AV

9TH ST

BUTTE AV

BEAR DR

CULVER HWY

JEFFERSON COUNTY FAIRGROUNDS

MADRAS-PRINEVILLE HWY

SE BALDWIN DR

DOVER

SE DIXON DR

WAGONBLAST CANYON

MUD SPRINGS

6

JUNIPER CANYON

CROOKED RIVER

CROOKED RIVER NATIONAL GRASSLAND

SW EUREKA LN

SW COLUMBIA DR

Crooked River Gorge

EUREKA LN

97

FRANKLIN

FALCON LN

BEAR FORD LN

ADAMS DR

26 FRANKLIN LN

FOSTER LN

MADRAS-PRINEVILLE HWY

JASPER

GRASSLAND

FRANK FOREST RD

7

SW GLOVER RD

NATIONAL GRASSLAND

ROUND BUTTE DR

FEATHER

GEM LN

SW PECK RD

SW FRAZIER

361

DALLES-CALIFORNIA HWY

HIGHLAND

BEAR LN

COLUMBIA DR

ADAMS DR

HOLLY

SE GRIZZLY

7

LAKE BILLY CHINOOK STATE AIRPORT

SW JORDAN

SW GREEN DR

CULVER

HUBER LN

1ST AV

6TH ST

VIEWPOINT DR

SW IRIS

SW IRVING LN

IMBLER LN

A B C D

SEE 212 MAP

0 1 2 3 4 miles 1 in. = 2.5 mi.

SEE 206 MAP

DRIFT CREEK WILDERNESS

328

PACIFIC

OCEAN

WALDPORT

Wakonda Beach

San Marine

SW WAKONDA BEACH RD

BAYVIEW

BEAVER CREEK RD

Bayview

BAYVIEW

DRIFT CREEK RD

Eckman Lake

ALSEA BAY

ALSEA

DRIFT CREEK HWY

Drift Creek

ALSEA RIVER

Tidewater

SIUSLAW

NATIONAL

FOREST

DRIFT CREEK SHELTER

WEST RIDGE

TENMILE SHELTER

BOULDER RIDGE

RD

KLICKITAT SHELTER

HEATH RIDGE

THREEMILE SHELTER

SURVEYORS BENCHES

MIDDLE RIDGE

BUTLER PEAK

RISLEY

CREEK

34

ALSEA

TIDEWATER RD

SCOTT CREEK RD

HELLION CANYON

HELLION HWY

Little Albany

CANAL

CREEK

RD

SLIDE CAMPGROUND

HELLION RIDGE

HELLION RAPIDS

SCOTT MOUNTAIN

STONEY MOUNTAIN

BLACKBERRY CAMPGROUND

STONEY POINT

RIVER EDGE CAMPGROUND

BEAR

CREEK

RD

BURNT TIMBER MOUNTAIN

ECKMAN

CREEK

ECKMAN MOUNTAIN

DESOLATION SADDLE

CANAL CREEK CAMPGROUND

LINCOLN COUNTY

PITCHFORK RIDGE

CANNIBAL MOUNTAIN

DENZER BRIDGE

LOBSTER VALLEY

FLEECE RIDGE

LINCOLN CO

BENTON CO

LOBSTER CREEK RD

BENTON COUNTY

101

OREGON

COAST

BLODGETT

BLODGETT PEAK

DICKS RIDGE

ECKMAN CREEK RD

YACHATS MOUNTAIN

KERBY MOUNTAIN

VINGIE CREEK

STARR

KERBY RIDGE

GREEN MOUNTAIN

SIUSLAW

CANNIBAL MOUNTAIN RD

CASCADE

RIVERS

CASCADE FALLS

FOREST

DENZER RIDGE

YACHATS

YACHATS

OCEAN VIEW DR

KING ST

YACHATS RIVER

NATIONAL

YACHATS RIDGE

YACHATS MOUNTAIN

SITZ

RIDGE

SITZ

FIVE

WILSON CREEK RD

AGATE POINT

DEVILS CHURN

OVERLOOK RD

CUMMINS

COOKS CHASM

CAPE PERPETUA CAMPGROUND

FOURMILE CAMPGROUND

PEAK

CREEK

RD

AXTEL

RD

NORTH FORK YACHATS RD

HOWELL RIDGE

RIVER

YACHATS RD

KELLER CREEK CAMPGROUND

LINCOLN CO

LANE CO

Fisher

UPPER DEADWOOD RD

E CRAB RD

SEE 132 MAP

SEE 133 MAP

METRO

CUMMINS

CREEK

RD

CAPE RIDGE

NEPTUNE STATE PARK

RD

BUCK CREEK

MALCOLM RIDGE

SIUSLAW

GREEN RIVER

GWYNN KNOLL

CUMMINS CREEK WILDERNESS

CUMMINS RIDGE

KLICKITAT RIDGE

KLICKITAT MOUNTAIN

OREGON

BRAY POINT

Searose Beach

CUMMINS PEAK

TENMILE RIDGE

KLICKITAT

TRAIL

RD

NFD

NATIONAL

2160

NFD RD 32

TENMILE

LANE COUNTY

CREEK

GRIZZLY RIDGE

RD

58

INDIAN

CREEK

58

MANN RD

NFD

FOREST

FAIRVIEW

FAIRVIEW MOUNTAIN

MOUNTAIN

SADDLE MOUNTAIN

RD

NFD

RD

RD

ROCK

CREEK

WILDERNESS

ROCKY KNOLL

ROOSEVELT BEACH

FORMANDLR RIDGE

NFD

RD

TAYLOR RIDGE

NFD RD

BIG

CREEK

NFD

RD

CARL G WASHBURNE MEMORIAL PARK

52

UPPER NORTH FORK

WEST FORK INDIAN CREEK

101

BLUE RIDGE RD

THREE BUTTES

NORTH FORK

TRAIL CREEK NFD

25

INDIAN CREEK

FATOR RIDGE

DEVILS ELBOW PARK

CAPE CREEK

DEVILS ELBOW

SEA LION CAVES

NFD

52

NFD RD 5842

HERMAN PEAK

CLOVER RIDGE

NFD

DREW RIDGE

UPPER NORTH FORK RD

NFD

25

THOMPSON CREEK

INDIAN CREEK R

GREEN CREEK

SEE 214 MAP

0 1 2 3 4 miles 1 in. = 2.5 mi.

METRO

SEE 207 MAP
SEE 215 MAP
SEE 133 MAP
SEE 133 MAP

A   B   C   D

BROWNSVILLE

HALSEY

HARRISBURG

JUNCTION CITY

COBURG

LINN COUNTY

LANE COUNTY

OREGON

99E · 99W · 5 · 228 · 216 · 209 · 36 · 99 · 99

PLAINVIEW · Plainview

Peoria · ABRAHAM · HOACUM ISLAND

Shedd · BOSTON

Fayetteville

THE LIVING ROCK MUSEUM

LINN COUNTY HISTORICAL MUSEUM

KIRK AV

American · Lancaster · Wilkins · Marcola

BENTON CO / LANE CO

LINN CO / LANE CO

Selected roads: BRATTAIN DR, GREENBACK RD, GREEN VALLEY RD, FAYETTEVILLE DR, PECKENPAUGH RD, MUDDY DR, PEORIA RD, HARMONY, OAK, PLAIN DR, CREEK BEND, DANNEN DR, AMERICAN DR, NICEWOOD DR, POTTER RD, LINN WEST, CALAPOOIA, ROBERTS RD, SHEDD CEMETERY RD, MILL DR, WARD BUTTE, MORGAN DR, MANNING LN, SEVEN MILE LN, ROCK RIDGE, SAND RIDGE, ROCK HILL, TY VALLEY RD, MIDDLE RIDGE, OAK, LONE PINE BUTTE, WASHBURN BUTTE, BROWNSVILLE, COCHRAN CREEK, CEDAR BUTTE, ROBE HILL, SNAKE HILL, KIRK DR, HOME, HARRISON DR, POWELL HILLS, HALSEY-SWEET, OAKVIEW, NORTHERN, MOUNTAIN DR, SEEFELD DR, WEBER, CREEK DR, COURTNEY CREEK RD, COURTNEY CREEK, RIVER, CROOK DR, POWERLINE RD, ALBANY-JUNCTION CITY RD, LAKE CREEK, FALK CREEK, BRANDON RD, SCHOOL RD, DIMIDDIE VALLEY, TIMBER RD, LITTLE VALLEY LN, NIXON DR, OREGON, TWIN BUTTES W DR, WAGGENER RD, CENTER RD, TWIN BUTTES, INDIAN HEAD, GAP, HORSE ROCK, CARTNEY DR, WILLAMETTE, RICKARD, SUBSTATION, ISOM DR, TANDY LN, BOND BUTTE DR, ROWLAND, BELTS, MUDDY, NORTHERNWOOD DR, DIAMOND HILL, COUGAR RIDGE, JAGER LN, MCMULLEN, NORATEN RD, HOWARD LN, LINGO LN, DIAMOND, TALBOTT RD, TERRITORIAL ST, HARRIS DR, HILL DR, GAP RD, BALD MOUNTAIN, PACIFIC, TOFTDAHL RD N, LINK HWY, PRICEBORO DR, WEATHERFORD, STRODA DR, COBURG, CURTIS, DALE DR, BOWERS DR, DANE LN, WYATT DR, WILLAMETTE, CROOKED CREEK RD, 15-1-31, 15-2-26-1, RD 15-2-25, 15-1-31, 15-2-25-1, ROUND MOUNTAIN, EL RIO, BUSH GARDEN DR, MOUNT TOM DR, TOM MOUNT, WEST POINT HILL, 16-2-10-2, BUCK MOUNTAIN, 16-2-10, 16-2-16-1, 16-2-7-1, PITNEY LN, CULVER RD, HAYES, HARPER RD, MARSHALL ISLAND E CROSSROAD, HERMAN LN, LANES TURN LN, COMPTON LN, 16-2-17-1, 16-2-18, JONES ACRES, PARSONS, PITCH, ROSE RD, MEADOWVIEW RD, MILLIRON RD, MORGAN LN, SOVERN, MAPLE DR, COUNTRY LN, CENTENNIAL BUTTE, WILKINS RD, LENON HILL, TRIPLE OAK, MOUNT TOM RD, 16-3-13, 16-2-27, 16-2-18, 16-2-29, MCGOWAN CREEK, MARCOLA, MOHAWK HILL RD, SUNDIAL, CALONE RD, MOHAWK VALLEY, MOHAWK RIVER, GREEN PACIFIC, HEATHER OAK DR, MONTMORENCE DR, BISHOP LN, VICTORY RD, LASSEN LN, GREEN ISLAND RD, W BEACON DR, PRAIRIE, PEARL ST, FUNKE RD, COBURG BOTTOM LOOP RD, VAN DUYN, OAK CREST RD, HERFERD RD

Scale: 0 1 2 3 4 miles · 1 in. = 2.5 mi.

© 2004 Thomas Bros. Maps®

METRO

A   **B**   **C**   **D**

PORCUPINE PEAK TR.

MOUNT

THREE FINGERED JACK

JEFFERSON

*JEFFERSON
COUNTY*

JACK LAKE CAMPGROUND

WHISKEY LAKE   JACK   JACK

CANYON CREEK RD   SW JACK CREEK

JACK CREEK RD

WARM SPRINGS

CANYON CREEK CAMPGROUNDS

RIVER

BEAR SPURS   PRAIRIE FARM CTO

THORN LP   SPRING RD

BEAR SPURS

BIG SQUAWBACK RIDGE

LITTLE SQUAWBACK

DESCHUTES

JACK CREEK RD

NFD

JACK CREEK RD 280

400   010 04N

N FIRST CREEK RD

ROUND   LAKE

JACK LAKE NFD RD 1425

RANKIN

METOLIUS

STRIEBEL

Camp Sherman

ALLINGHAM

SANTIAM

RANGE   *PACIFIC*   *LINN*   *JEFFERSON*

HOGG ROCK

CORBETT SNO-PARK

WILDERNESS

AREA

SW FIRST CREEK CTO

ROUND LAKE LP

NFD RD 12

SUTTLE-SHERMAN

NATIONAL

SHERMAN

CAMP

NFD RD 130 CTO

WHISKEY SPRINGS RD

GREEN RIDGE

SUMMIT

SW LITTLE SQUAWBACK

LITTLE

FOREST

SANTIAM HWY

SANTIAM SNO-PARK

ELLIOTT R CORBETT II MEMORIAL STATE PARK

SUTTLE LAKE LP

SUTTLE LAKE

SCOUT LAKE RD

NFD RD 2066

NFD RD 600   SCOTT LAKE RD

TOLL STATION

SUTTLE LAKE

NFD RD 1110   BLACK BUTTE RD

BLACK BUTTE

ALLINGHAM CTO

BLACK CUTOFF RD

RAY BENSON SNO-PARK

NFD RD 2076

CLAYPOOL BUTTE

NFD RD 2068

STATION

SCOTT LAKE

2066

BLACK BUTTE

JEFFERSON CO

DESCHUTES CO

GARRISON RIDGE

BUTTE

GREEN RIDGE RD

GARRISON BUTTE

CINDER BUTTE

BRANDENBURG BUTTE

CACHE MOUNTAIN

OLD SANTIAM

WAGON   LITTLE CACHE MOUNTAIN

800 TOLL RD

NFD RD 2061

OLD   SANTIAM WAGON

2061

CREEK

Black Butte Ranch

20   **126**

SANTIAM

BROOKS-SCANLON LOG

GREEN SPRINGS RD

SUNDOWN

SPRING

*WILLAMETTE
NATIONAL
FOREST*

CACHE RD

SIDE HILL RD

NFD RD 2060

FIVEMILE BUTTE

2060

INDIAN FORD

BROOKS-SCANLON

LOG HWY

LUNDGREN

STEVENS CANYON RD

SEE 212 MAP

DRY CREEK

NFD SKYLIGHT CAVE

SIXMILE BUTTE

SUICIDE GULCH

NFD RD 160

Camp Polk

*MOUNT
WASHINGTON
WILDERNESS*

MOUNT WASHINGTON

DESCHUTES

DUGOUT LAKE

BLUEGRASS BUTTE

GRAHAM BUTTE

1028

FOURMILE BUTTE

MCKENZIE

NFD RD 400

Camp Polk Rd

SISTERS EAGLE AIR AIRPORT

POLK RD   RIDGE

AREA

CREST TR.

DUGOUT BUTTE

LITTLE BUTTE   FOURMILE BUTTE

BUTTE RD

COLD SPRINGS RD

NFD RD 406

THUMPER RD   BLUEGRASS LN

NFD RD 1510

LUNDY RD

POLK RD

CAMP RD   BARCLAY

BAY   CHESTNUT DR

*LINN
COUNTY*

BELKNAP CRATER

LITTLE BELKNAP

DEE WRIGHT OBSERVATORY

242 HWY

WINDY POINT

BLACK CRATER

*DESCHUTES
COUNTY*

NATIONAL

COM RD

BURSH DRAW RD

SISTERS STATE PARK

SISTERS

ELM ST

CASCADE

BROOKS-SCANLON

126

MCKENZIE HWY

MCKENZIE-BEND

20 HWY

LINN CO   MCKENZIE PASS

LANE CO

MCKENZIE PASS

MCKENZIE

NFD RD 150

MILLICAN CRATER

SCOTT PASS

HUCKLEBERRY BUTTE

NFD RD 1024

TROUT

NFD RD 1028

TROUT CREEK BUTTE

FOREST

NFD RD 1514

NFD RD 1522

NFD RD 800

BURN

PETERSON RIDGE RD

NFD RD 100

NFD RD 1608

*LANE
COUNTY*

THREE

YAPOAH CRATER

FOUR IN ONE CONE

SCOTT PASS

DESCHUTES   *LANE CO*

PACIFIC

NFD RD 1018

POLE RD

SQUAW CREEK RD

NFD RD 1514

NFD RD 1516

PETERSON CREEK RD

SHATTUCK RD

SISTERS

*WILDERNESS
AREA*

COLLIER CONE

COLLIER GLACIER VIEW ★

OBSIDIAN CLIFFS

COLLIER GLACIER

OBSIDIAN FALLS

RENFREW GLACIER

LANE PLATEAU

LINN GLACIER

VILLARD GLACIER

NORTH SISTER

THAYER GLACIER

NFD RD 600

1526 RD

NFD RD 1514

1516

THREE

LOWER THREE CREEK SNO-PARK

MELVIN BUTTE

UPPER THREE CREEK SNO-PARK

NFD RD 1628

NFD RD 1610

NFD RD 1620

PARTON RD

LIVESAY RD

1610

0 1 2 3 4 miles   1 in. = 2.5 mi.

SEE 208 MAP

A | B | C | D

© 2004 Thomas Bros. Maps ®

METRO

—N—

1

DESCHUTES

NATIONAL

SQUAWBACK RIDGE

1179

SW SQUAW GULCH RD

LOWER LOOP RD

DESERT

SW SQUAW FLAT RD

CROOKED

SQUAW FLAT RD

GREEN MOUNTAIN

NFD RD 1399

GENEVA OVERLOOK

POTTER CANYON

TRAHAN CANYON

DESCHUTES CANYON

CROOKED CANYON

SW PENINSULA

SW PIKE

SW KENT LN

SW KING

SW WOODWARD

SW FEATHER DR

JERICHO

CULVER HWY

361 97

KOA MADRAS/CULVER

HAYSTACK RESERVOIR

SMITH LN

KING LN

SW HAYSTACK

KING LN

2

FOREST

GRANDVIEW

JEFFERSON COUNTY

CUTOFF RD

NFD RD

BLACK BUTTE

FLAT

BLACK BUTTE RD

NFD RD 2050

SQUAW SW SQUAW CREEK RD

1993

NFD RD

CREEK

LOWER BRIDGE RD

SQUAM FLAT CANYON

SQUAW CREEK CANYON

NATIONAL

GRASSLAND

RIVER

PENINSULA DR

CRATER LP

CHIPMUNK

GOLDEN MANTEL

HORNY HOLLOW TR

SHAD RD

SWALLOW DR

RIM RD

CHICKADEE DR

ROBIN DR

MEADOWLARK DR

PERCH RD

STEELHEAD RD

SPARROW DR

RAINBOW DR

STEELHEAD FALLS

DESCHUTES

STEELHEAD

ERMINE DR

DINGO

COUGAR RD

BLACKTAIL DR

SW KEENEY LN

SW GREEN RD

MONROE LN

ELBE DR

GORGINE CANYON

THE DALLES-CALIFORNIA

OPAL CITY

OPAL LN

PARK LN

NORRIS

SHERWOOD DR

JUNIPER BUTTE

HAYSTACK BUTTE

97

3

STEVENS CANYON

FREMONT CANYON

WILT VIEW RD

DESCHUTES COUNTY

JEFFERSON CO

DESCHUTES CO

LOWER

FALLS

RIVER

BIG FALLS

GALENA DR

PARKEY DR

NW RAINBOW DR

FLUME

WIMP

NW 43RD ST RANCH RD

NW 27TH ST

P S OGDEN RD

10TH ST

COYOTE BUTTE

DONEY RD

SMITH ROCK STATE PARK

NE EBY

NE 9TH

NE 13TH AV

4

WILT RD

BUFFALO DR

HENKLE BUTTE

SQUAW

MOUNTAIN

CANYON CREST DR

HOLMES RD

MCKENZIE CANYON

BUCKHORN CANYON

W LAMBERT RD

BRIDGE RD

LAFOLLETTE BUTTE

BESSIE BUTTE

THEATER AV

HUNT RD

JAEGER RD

TERREBONNE-LOWER BRIDGE

NW SEDGEWICK

NW KNICKERBOCKER AV

HL99

HL109

NW 31ST ST

NW 19TH ST

NW ODEM

NW COYNER AV

NW 10TH ST

TERREBONNE

NE WILCOX AV

NE 11TH

NE 5TH DI RD

NE 1ST ST

OB AV

SMITH ROCK

NE 17TH

SEE 213 MAP

SEE 211 MAP

5

NASHUA LN

GREEN RIDGE LN

SQUAW CREEK LN

HENKLE BUTTE DR

EDMUNDSON RD

FADJUR

HOLMES RD

GOODRICH RD

HURTLEY RANCH RD

DEER CANYON

HUNT RD

MCKENZIE

CLOVERDALE

POLK RD

CAMP RD

126 HWY

BUCKHORN RD

NW 91ST ST

NW 74TH ST

8380 ST

ODIN FALLS

NW COYER AV

YUCCA AV

NW KACHINA

NW 101 LN

QUINCE LN

REASON CT

CASHMUR CT

OAK RD

NW ATKINSON AV

NW SPRUCE AV

HOMESTEAD ST

ATKINSON AV

POPLAR DR

TULLAR RD

FETHEROW

LARCH

TULLAR RD

RIVER

FRANK

EAGLE DR

BARR RD

CLINE FALLS

NW HELMHOLTZ

UPAS AV

NW SPRUCE

35TH

NW MAPLE AV

NW HEMLOCK AV

NW ANTLER AV

NE KING

NE 13TH ST

NE MAPLE

NE HEMLOCK

126 MCKENZIE HWY

CANAL

REDMOND-POWELL BUTTE RD

BLVD

NE YUCCA AV

UPAS AV

VEGIS RD

PERSHALL WY

ONEILL

PRINEVILLE JUNCTION

6

TROUT RD

HARRINGTON LP

VARCO RD

20

KOA SISTERS/BEND

IVY LN

CLOVERDALE RD

FORKED HORN

FRYREAR BUTTE

A J WARRIN RD

FRYREAR RD

KENT RD

GEO CYPRUS RD

JORDAN RD

CASCADE ESTATES DR

PLAINVIEW

WEST ST

CENTRAL

THIRD

2ND AV

1ST ST

OREGON

DRY CANYON

BARR RD

CLINE BUTTES

HWY

FALLS RD

NEWCOMB RD

OCHOCO HWY

CLINE FALLS STATE PARK

SW LAVA

OBSIDIAN

58TH

YEW AV

ZENITH

SW COYOTE

SW 35TH

WICKIUP AV

SALMON AV

SW 27TH

SE AIRPORT WY

DESCHUTES REDMOND CAVE CO FAIRGROUNDS

REDMOND MUNICIPAL AIRPORT

REDMOND

97

7

DESCHUTES

NATIONAL

FOREST

BROOKS

SMALL LN

KONFIELD RD

SNOW CREEK RD

BARBARA WY

DELICIOUS ST

SISEMORE RD

COLLINS RD

ALLEN RD

COUCH MARKET RD

SMOKY BUTTE RD

RUDI

DAYTON RD

GERKING MARKET

CLINE

BRANDYWINE

INNES

MCKENZIE-BEND

DUSTY LP

OLSON RD

WHITE ROCK LOOP RD

MARSH RD

SW BROWN RD

CONNARN RD

SWALLEY RD

HARPER RD

KRIEGER RD

PETERSON-PLEASANT MARKET

GIFT AV

ARID RD

GIFT RD

AMBERY FALLS

LIMESTONE AV

STURGEON RD

TUMALO-DESCHUTES HWY

REDMOND-PLEASANT RIDGE MARKET RD

THE DALLES-CALIFORNIA

HORNER RD

MORRILL

0 1 2 3 4 miles 1 in. = 2.5 mi.

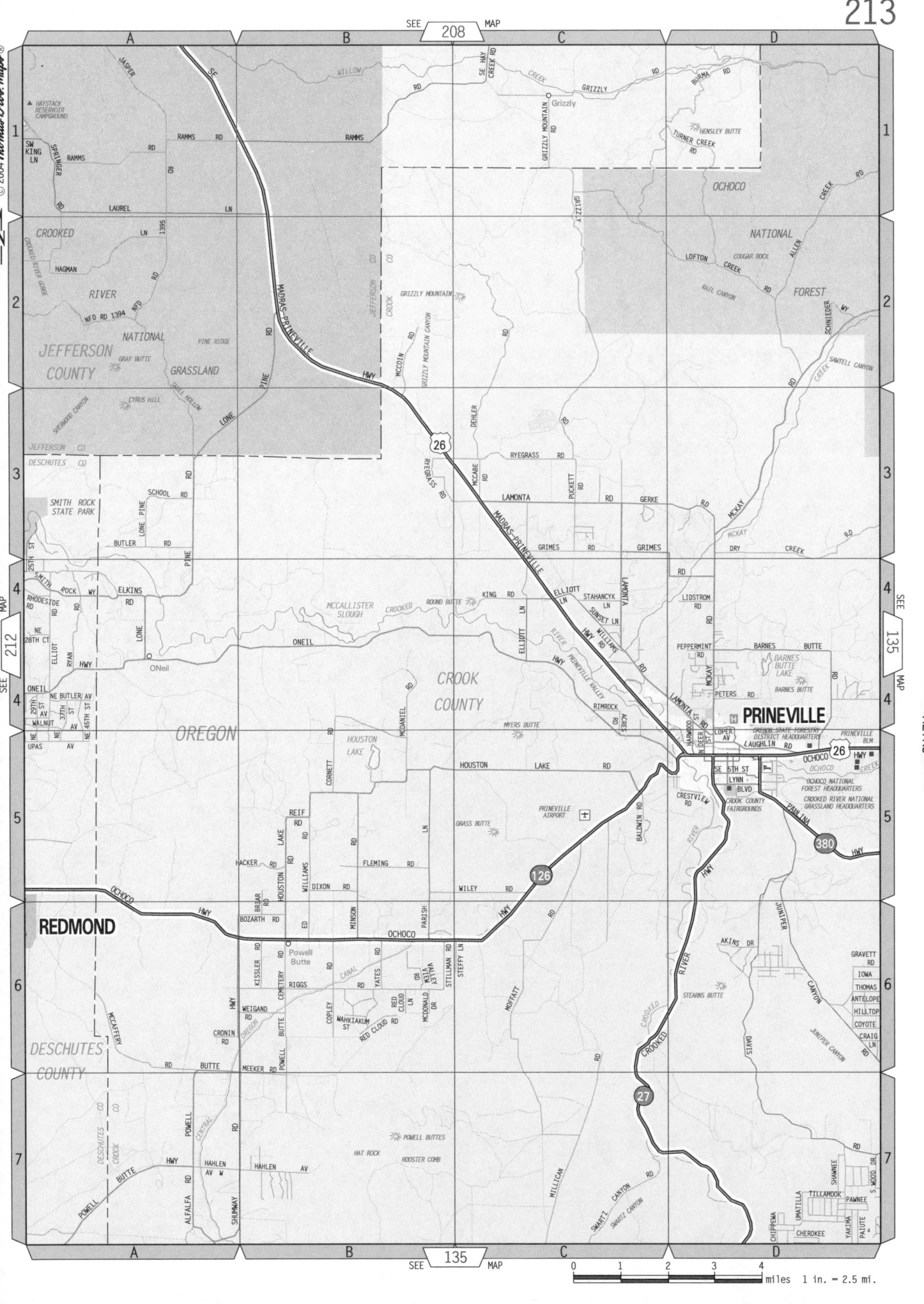

A | B | C | D

METRO

0 1 2 3 4 miles   1 in. = 2.5 mi.

A   B   C   D

© 2004 Thomas Bros. Maps ®

METRO

SEE 132 MAP

SEE 132 MAP

SEE 218 MAP

FLORENCE

DUNES CITY

OREGON

SIUSLAW NATIONAL FOREST

Cape Mountain

5842

ENCHANTED VALLEY

North Fork Siuslaw Campground

UPPER NORTH FORK RD

Minerva

NORTH FORK SIUSLAW

Stout Canyon

David Ridge   719

Thompson Creek RD

Davis Rapids

36

Rainrock
ROCK CANYON
Brickerville

MAPLETON JUNCTION

E MAPLETON RD

BALD MOUNTAIN

2610   NFD RD 719

BELLSTROM CANYON

HANSON RIDGE

NEELY MOUNTAIN

MISERY RIDGE

Mapleton

FLORENCE-EUGENE HWY

Tiernan

2610

Point Terrace

SIUSLAW NATIONAL FOREST

LANE COUNTY

Sutton Lake
Ben Bunch Lake
Mercer Lake
Sutton Lake Campground
Sutton Creek Campground
Sutton Beach RD

MERCER
COAST HWY

Heceta Beach
HECETA BEACH RD
RHODODENDRON RD
Heceta Junction

COLLARD LAKE

CLEAR LAKE

THE PORTAGE

101

35TH ST
DOLLY VARDENS
LANE COMMUNITY COLLEGE
9TH ST
MUNSEL LAKE
MUNSEL LAKE RD
DOLLY VARDEN MUS

BENDER LANDING

WENDSON CANYON

Wendson

126

Cushman

BERNHARDT RD
KAMINSKY CREEK RD

BULL ISLAND

SKUNK HOLLOW
COX ISLAND

SIUSLAW RIVER

OREGON

SIUSLAW VISTA

Glenada

SIUSLAW PIONEER MUSEUM

SOUTH INLET
SOUTH SLOUGH

JESSIE M HONEYMAN MEMORIAL STATE PARK

DUNES

NATIONAL

RECREATION

AREA

CANARY RD

Canary   UPPER

MAPLE CREEK RD

HENDERSON CREEK RD

HENDERSON CREEK

MOUNT PETER

SWEET CREEK
SWEET CREEK FALLS
BEAVER CREEK FALLS
SWEET CREEK RD
ROCKY POINT
GOODWIN PEAK

SUNSET MOUNTAIN   2480

4830

RD 49

958   4811

FIDDLE CREEK RIDGE

MOUNT GRAYBACK

WOAHINK LAKE
CLEAR LAKE

North Beach

DRIFTWOOD CAMPGROUND
DRIFTWOOD II CAMPGROUND
LAGOON CAMPGROUND
TYEE CAMPGROUND
Westlake
MAXMYRTLE CAMPGROUND
LODGEPOLE CAMPGROUND

NORTH BEACH BAY

SILTCOOS LAKE

BOOTH ISLAND

Siltcoos
SILTCOOS STATION

CANARY RD S

Ada   FIDDLE

MILES CANYON

HENDERSON CANYON

OREGON

4820

ROBINSON RIDGE

CARTER LAKE CAMPGROUND
EAST CARTER BOAT RAMP
EAST CARTER CAMPGROUND
COUNTY LINE RD

REED ISLAND
ADA
HARMONY BAY

SMITH CREEK
MILES CANYON

LANE CO
DOUGLAS CO

SILTCOOS RD

59

BOOTH RIDGE

SULPHUR RIDGE

4811

101
OREGON DUNES OVERLOOK
CROWN ZELLERBACK CAMPGROUND
BOOTH RD
LOST LAKE CAMPGROUND

CATFISH HOLE

4811

NFD RD 23

NORTH FORK

BLM RD 2-3
BLM RD 33-0
LITTLE BURMA RD
BLM RD 24
SPENCER CREEK

CLAY POINT

TAHKENITCH LAKE

HALFWAY POINT
SNARE POINT

HENDERSON PEAK

BUZZARDS BUTTE

North Fork
Sulphur Springs

BLM RD 36-0

SMITH RIVER

WASSON RIDGE

TAHKENITCH LANDING
TAHKENITCH CAMPGROUND
ELBOW LAKE CAMPGROUND

OREGON

DUNES

NATIONAL

RECREATION

AREA

HOME POINT
GARDINER LANDING
CLEAR LAKE RD
FOURMILE LIGHT
THREEMILE LIGHT
SPARROW PARK RD

MIDDLE POINT
FIVEMILE

DOUGLAS COUNTY

LOWER SMITH RIVER

UMPQUA RIVER

0   1   2   3   4 miles   1 in. = 2.5 mi.

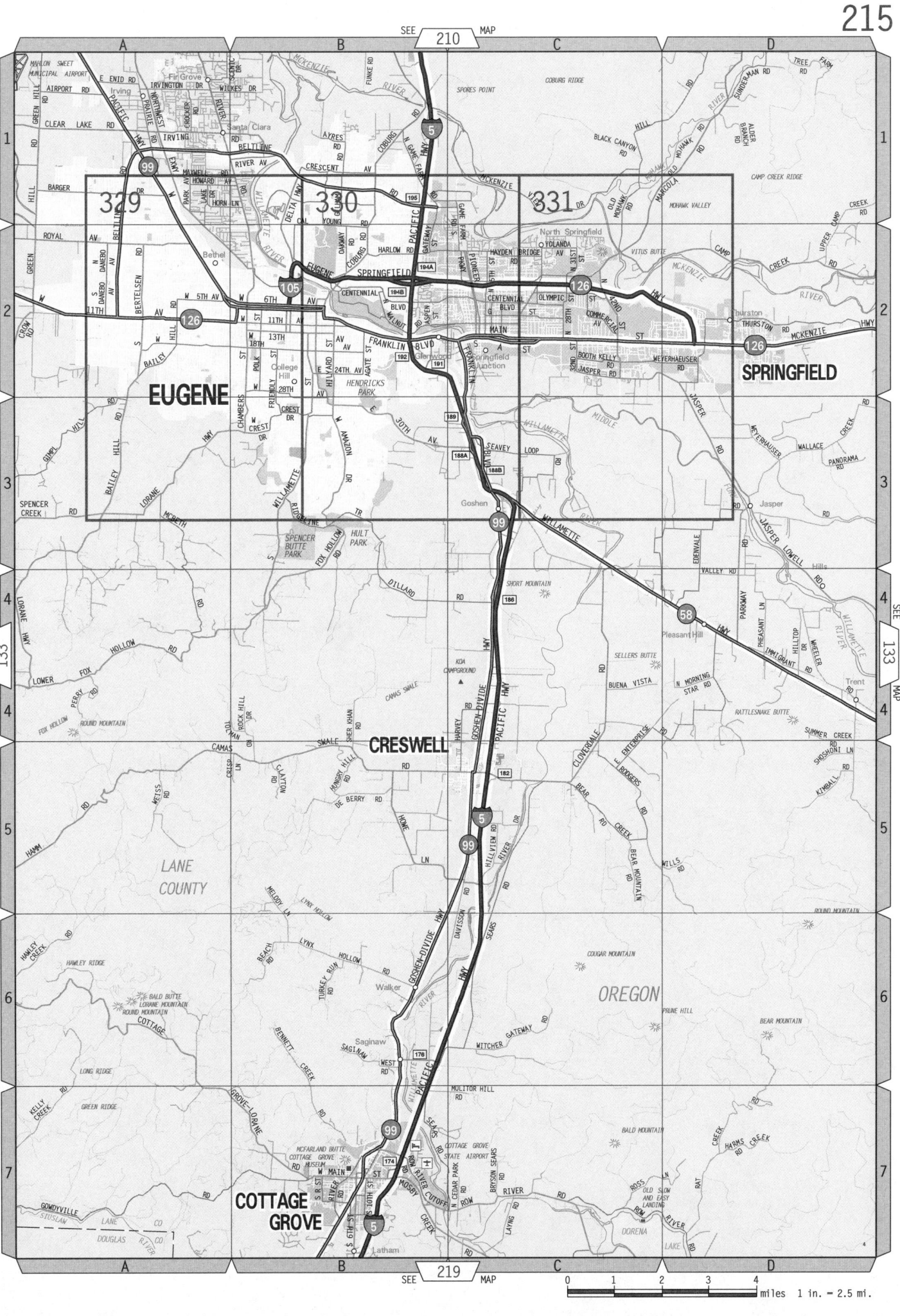

© 2004 THOMAS BROS. MAPS®

N

A   B   C   D

329   330   331

EUGENE

SPRINGFIELD

1

2

CRESWELL

LANE COUNTY

OREGON

3

SEE MAP 133

4

5

6

COTTAGE GROVE

7

METRO

0   1   2   3   4   miles   1 in. = 2.5 mi.

SEE 211 MAP

© 2004 Thomas Bros. Maps ®

← N →

A **B** **C** **D**

1

MIDDLE SISTER
HAYDEN GLACIER
DILLER GLACIER
CREEK
SQUAW CREEK FALLS
IRVING GLACIER
SQUAW
CARVER GLACIER
SKINNER GLACIER
LANE COUNTY
EUGENE GLACIER
PROUTY GLACIER
LOST CREEK GLACIER
SOUTH SISTER

THREE CREEK BUTTE
NFD RD 1628
THREE CREEK
RD
THREE CREEK MEADOW CAMPGROUND
NFD RD 370
DRIFTWOOD CAMPGROUND

SNOW CREEK RD

2

JAMES CREEK SHELTER
CLARK GLACIER
RIDGE CREST
LEWIS GLACIER
THREE
SISTERS
WILDERNESS
AREA

BEND GLACIER
BROKEN TOP
CROOK GLACIER
BROKEN HAND
BALL BUTTE
CAYUSE CRATER

IAN McARTHUR RIM
THREE CREEK LAKE CAMPGROUND
HAPPY VALLEY

TRIANGLE HILL
BEAR WALLOW
BEARWALLOW BUTTE
BEARWALLOWS
BUTTE
TUMALO LOOP

ROCK MESA
LE CONTE CRATER
LAVE 03 TR
DESCHUTES 03

3

RED HILL
KALEETAN BUTTE
DEVILS HILL
CASCADE
LAKES
KOKOSTICK BUTTE
KOOSAH MOUNTAIN
TALAPUS BUTTE
KATSUK BUTTE
TODD LAKE CAMPGROUND
SPARKS LAKE
HWY

NFD RD
370
RD

PACIFIC CREST

TUMALO MOUNTAIN
SWAMPY LAKES SHELTER

NFD RD 4601
TUMALO FALLS
TUMALO FALLS SHELTER
CREEK
TUMALO
SWEDE RIDGE SHELTER
SWEDE RIDGE RD
NFD RD 4615
BIG SPRING BURN
NFD RD 4612

4

NFD RD 450
ELK LAKE
MOOLACK BUTTE
DESCHUTES
ELK LAKE CAMPGROUND
ELK LAKE
HOSMER LAKE
LITTLE FAWN CAMPGROUND
ELK MOUNTAIN
POINT CAMPGROUND
SOUTH CAMPGROUND
BEACH CAMPGROUND
MALLARD MARSH CAMPGROUND
MUD LAKE RD
RED CRATER

POMA SKI TOW
BACHELOR SKI LIFT
CENTURY

TOT MOUNTAIN
NATIONAL
OREGON
KWOLH BUTTE

KAPKA BUTTE
372
DRIVE
SWAMPY LAKES SNOPARK
WANOGA SNOWMOBILE SNOPARK
VIRGINIA MEISSNER SNOPARK
HWY
BIG SPRING RD
KATALO BUTTE
NFD RD 4613
KIWA BUTTE

SEE 134 MAP

SEE 217 MAP

5

WILLIAMSON MOUNTAIN
LAVA LAKE
FOREST
LAVA LAKE CAMPGROUND
LITTLE LAVA LAKE
LAVA LAKE RD
LITTLE LAVA LAKE CAMPGROUND
SHERIDAN MOUNTAIN

DESCHUTES COUNTY
EDISON BUTTE
EDISON SNO-PARK
ICE
EDISON ICE CAVE
KAPKA BUTTE
WANOGA LOOKOUT RD
KUAMAKSI BUTTE
EDISON
NFD RD 400
PITSUA BUTTE
NFD RD 4180
TELEPHONE

6

WILLIAMSON MOUNTAIN RD
UPPER CAMPGROUND
MILE CAMPGROUND
SIAH BUTTE
LOLO BUTTE
KLAK BUTTE
K'LAK
LOLO BUTTE
EDISON ICE CAVE RD
BUTTE RD
PRATER
PITSUA BUTTE
NFD RD 160
DESCHUTES
ANNIS BUTTE
NFD RD 4220

7

MARK BUTTE RD
BENCH MARK BUTTE
CULTUS LAKE
CULTUS LAKE CAMPGROUND
CENTURY
BENCH
LAKE
4630
LOOKOUT
MOUNTAIN
LOLAH BUTTE
LOLAL BUTTE
LOOKOUT RD
LUNKUM BUTTE
DRY BUTTE
THREE
WAKE BUTTE
TRAPPER
UPPER
NFD
CLTN RD
4635
NFD
LAVA
CRANE PRAIRIE RESERVOIR
COW CAMP CAMPGROUND
CRANE PRAIRIE CAMPGROUND
LOOKOUT MOUNTAIN
PRINGLE FALLS EXPERIMENTAL FOREST ADDITION
DR N
MOUNTAIN R
UPPER DESCHUTES
INDIAN CREEK RD
PISTOL BUTTE RD
SITKUM BUTTE
PISTOL BUTTE
LLOYD
CENTURY DR
BIG RIVER CAMPGROUND
BATES BUTTE

A **B** **C** **D**

METRO

SEE 142 MAP

0 1 2 3 4 miles   1 in. = 2.5 mi.

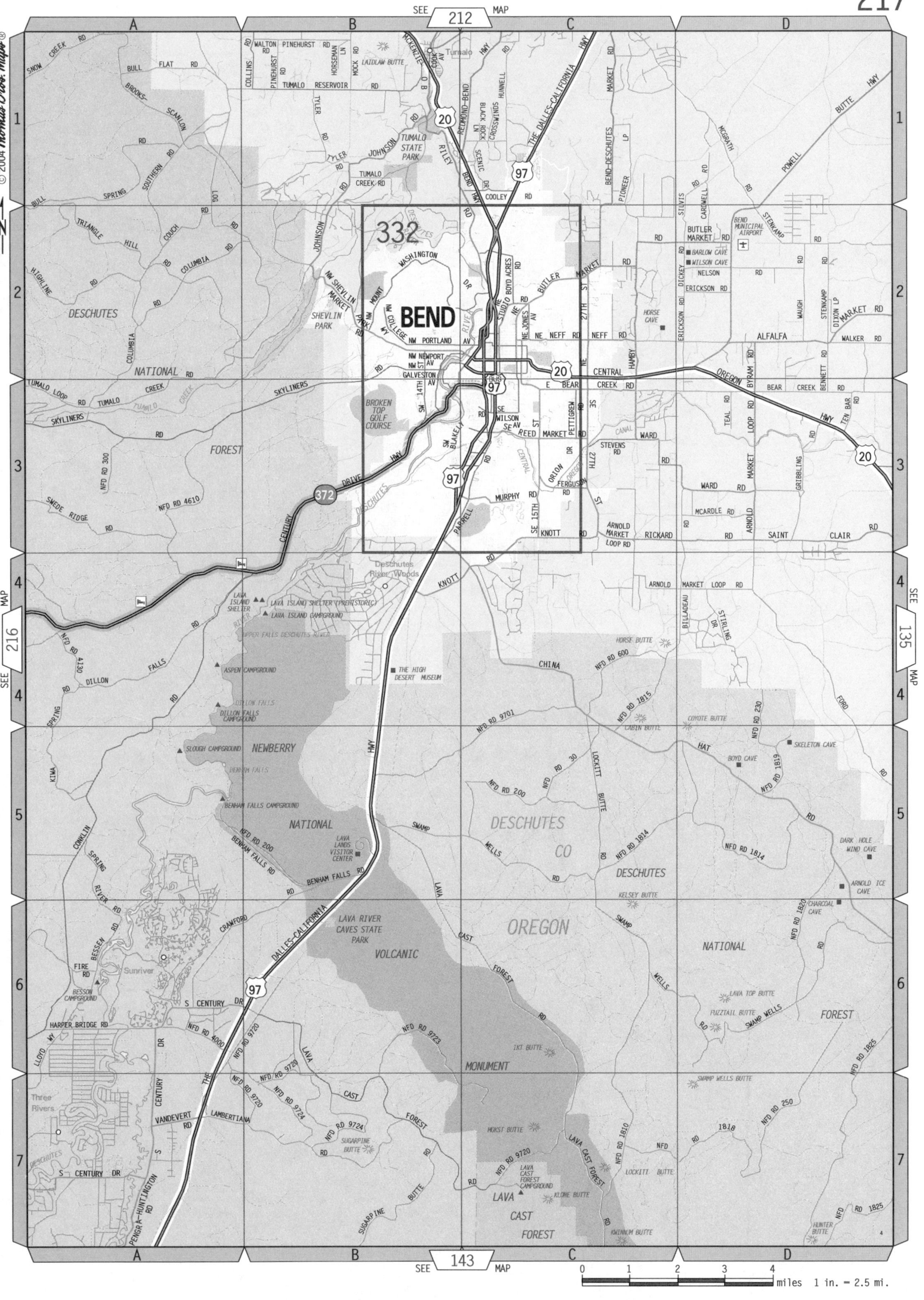

© 2004 Thomas Bros. Maps®

METRO

BEND

332

N

Selected labels (north/top area):

SNOW CREEK RD · BULL FLAT RD · BROOKS SCANLON RD · SOUTHERN RD · SPRING RD · BULL SPRING RD · COLLINS · WALTON RD · PINEHURST RD · PINEHURST · TUMALO RESERVOIR RD · MOCK RD · LAIDLAW BUTTE · MCKENZIE B · TUMALO · REDMOND-BEND HWY · HUNNELL RD · SONSMOSSCROSS · BLACK ROCK LN · SCENIC DR · THE DALLES-CALIFORNIA HWY · MARKET RD · MCGRATH RD · POWELL RD · BUTTE HWY

TRIANGLE HILL RD · COUCH RD · COLUMBIA RD · HIGHLINE RD · JOHNSON RD · TYLER RD · TUMALO CREEK RD · JOHNSON RD · TUMALO STATE PARK · RILEY RD · COOLEY RD · BEND-DESCHUTES · PIONEER · SILVIS RD · CARWELL RD · STENKAMP RD · BEND MUNICIPAL AIRPORT

DESCHUTES · NW SHEVLIN MARKET RD · SHEVLIN PARK · WASHINGTON · NW MONT · NW COLLEGE WY · NW PORTLAND AV · BUTLER MARKET RD · BARLOW CAVE · WILSON CAVE · NELSON · ERICKSON RD · DICKEY RD · STENKAMP · DIXON LP · WAUGH · MARKET RD

NATIONAL · COLUMBIA RD · CREEK RD · NW NEWPORT AV · NW ST · GALVESTON AV · 14TH ST · NE JONES AV · NE NEFF AV · BUTLER · 27TH ST · NEFF · HORSE CAVE · ALFALFA · WALKER RD

TUMALO LOOP RD · TUMALO RD · SKYLINERS RD · SKYLINERS · NFD RD 300 · SWEDE RIDGE RD · NFD RD 4610 · FOREST · BROKEN TOP GOLF COURSE · SW BLAKELY RD · SE WILSON AV · REED MARKET RD · CENTRAL DR · PETTIGREW · STEVENS RD · CANAL · WARD RD · TEAL RD · MARKET RD · E BEAR CREEK RD · OREGON · BYRAM RD · BEAR CREEK RD · BENNETT · TEN BAR · HWY

CENTURY DRIVE · DESCHUTES · 372 · 97 · MURPHY RD · DARREL RD · SE 15TH ST · ORION · FERGUSON · 27TH ST · KNOTT · WARD RD · MCARDLE RD · ARNOLD RD · SAINT · CLAIR RD · ARNOLD MARKET LOOP RD · RICKARD · 20

Central / lower area:

DESCHUTES RIVER WOODS · LAVA ISLAND SHELTER · LAVA ISLAND SHELTER (PREHISTORIC) · LAVA ISLAND CAMPGROUND · UPPER FALLS DESCHUTES RIVER · NFD RD 4130 · DILLON FALLS RD · DILLON FALLS · ASPEN CAMPGROUND · DILLON FALLS · DILLON FALLS CAMPGROUND · KNOTT · CHINA · THE HIGH DESERT MUSEUM · ARNOLD MARKET LOOP RD · BILLADEAU DR · STIRLING DR · HORSE BUTTE · NFD RD 600 · NFD RD 230 · FORD · NFD RD 1815 · CABIN BUTTE · COYOTE BUTTE · SKELETON CAVE · HAT · BOYD CAVE · NFD RD 1819

SLOUGH CAMPGROUND · NEWBERRY · BENHAM FALLS · KIWA · NFD RD 200 · BENHAM FALLS CAMPGROUND · NATIONAL · NFD RD 200 · LAVA LANDS VISITOR CENTER · BENHAM FALLS RD · SWAMP · WELLS · NFD RD 9701 · NFD RD 30 · LOCKITT BUTTE · DESCHUTES CO · DESCHUTES · NFD RD 1814 · NFD RD 1814 · DARK HOLE WIND CAVE · ARNOLD ICE CAVE · KELSEY BUTTE · CHARCOAL CAVE · NFD RD 1820

CONKLIN RD · SPRING RIVER RD · BESSEN RD · FIRE RD · SUNRIVER · BESSEN CAMPGROUND · HARPER BRIDGE RD · LLOYD WY · CRAMFORD RD · NFD RD 200 · LAVA RIVER CAVES STATE PARK · VOLCANIC · THE DALLES-CALIFORNIA · 97 · S CENTURY DR · NFD RD 4000 · BENHAM FALLS RD · LAVA · CAST · FOREST · SWAMP · OREGON · WELLS · NATIONAL · FOREST · LAVA TOP BUTTE · FUZZTAIL BUTTE · SWAMP WELLS · NFD RD 1825

THREE RIVERS · S CENTURY DR · VANDEVERT RD · LAMBERTIANA · CENTURY DR · THE · NFD RD 9720 · NFD RD 9729 · NFD RD 9720 · NFD RD 9724 · SUGARPINE BUTTE · LAVA · CAST · FOREST · MONUMENT · IKT BUTTE · SWAMP WELLS BUTTE · NFD RD 250 · NFD 1818

DESCHUTES · S CENTURY DR · PENGRA-HUNTINGTON RD · NFD RD 9724 · NFD RD 9720 · SUGARPINE BUTTE · LAVA CAST FOREST · LAVA CAST FOREST CAMPGROUND · KLONE BUTTE · MOKST BUTTE · NFD RD 9720 · NFD RD 1810 · LOCKITTI BUTTE · NFD · NFD RD 1825 · KWINNUM BUTTE · HUNTER BUTTE · LAVA CAST FOREST

0 1 2 3 4 miles   1 in. = 2.5 mi.

METRO

A   **B**   **C**   **D**

SEE 214 MAP

— N —

1

STEAMBOAT ISLAND

BARRETTS LANDING

BRUSHY HILL

HENDERSON COVE

OREGON DUNES NATIONAL RECREATION AREA

DOUBLE COVE POINT

LEEDS ISLAND

HUNT COVE

ARMY HILL

MACEY COVE

RANCH

RIDGEWAY DR

JERDEN COVE

BOLON ISLAND STATE PARK

Gardiner

East Gardiner

SMITH RIVER RD

SOUTH SIDE RD

OTTER SLOUGH

BUTLER

LOWER SMITH

SMITH RIVER LIGHT

CREEK

SIUSLAW NATIONAL FOREST

1

2

CORNWALL POINT

Winchester Bay

UMPQUA DR

COAST

REEDSPORT

BOWMAN RD

LONGWOOD

UMPQUA DISCOVER CENTER

DOUGLAS COUNTY

SCHOLFIELD RD

UMPQUA RIVER

UMPQUA HWY 38

DEAN MOUNTAIN RD

SCHOLFIELD RIDGE RD

2

UMPQUA LIGHTHOUSE

UMPQUA LIGHTHOUSE STATE PARK

SALMON HARBOR DR

OREGON

Lake Marie Campground

CLEAR LAKE

LAKE EDNA

WILLIAM M TUGMAN STATE PARK

EEL LAKE

SCHOLFIELD RD

DOUGLAS CO

COOS CO

BLACKS ARM

CARSON ARM

TWIN SISTERS

ELLIOTT

3

OCEAN

OREGON DUNES NATIONAL RECREATION AREA

HWY

NORTH TENMILE LAKE

BIG CREEK RD

NOBLE CREEK RD

BIG CREEK RD

3

SEE 140 MAP

NORTH EEL CAMPGROUND

MIDDLE EEL CAMPGROUND

EEL CREEK CAMPGROUND

SOUTH EEL CREEK CAMPGROUND

SPINREEL CAMPGROUND

Tenmile

LAKESIDE

BIG CREEK ARM

LINDROS ARM

BIG CREEK ARM

NORTH LAKE

STATE

4

COAST RD

OREGON DUNES NATIONAL RECREATION AREA

OREGON HWY

Saunders Lake

DEVORE ARM

WILLOW POINT

SCHOOL LAND BAY

COLEMAN ARM

SHUTTER ARM

TENMILE LAKE

TEMPLETON ARM

SHUTTERS LANDING

Templeton

TEMPLETON RD

BENSON CREEK

ROBERT CREEK RD

FOREST

4

SEE 140 MAP

PACIFIC

STAGE RD

Hauser

MILLWOOD DR

NORTH ZARA DR

COOS COUNTY

OREGON

TENMILE BUTTE

TRAIL BUTTE

5

KOA OREGON DUNES

101

NORTH RIDGE DR

HAYNES WY

WY

LARSON

BALDY BUTTE

BUTTE RD

WEST FORK MILLICOMA

WEST FORK MILLICOMA RIVER

HENRYS FALLS

ESTELL FALLS

PIDGEON FALLS

5

6

HORSEFALL BEACH

BLUEBILL LAKE CAMPGROUND

TRANS PACIFIC PKWY

Shorewood

HAYNES INLET

NORTH BAY DR

MEADOW LN

LARSON WY

DEAN MOUNTAIN

RETTMAN CREEK

WEST FORK

DEVILS ELBOW

6

7

JORDAN COVE

COOS BAY

333

COOS

COLORADO AV

NORTH BEND

FENWICK ST

VIRGINIA AV

SHERMAN AV

TREMONT ST

EAST BAY DR

KENTUCK INLET

Glasgow

Cooston

Kentuck

NOAH BUTTE

KENTUCK WY

WILLANCH WY

COOS RD

Allegany

EAST FORK MILLICOMA RIVER

ELK HWY

MCKEEVER MOUNTAIN

7

COOS BAY

CAPE ARAGO HWY

EMPIRE COOS BAY HWY

NEWMARK ST

SHERMAN AV

COOS BAY

A   **B**   **C**   **D**

SEE 220 MAP

0 1 2 3 4 miles   1 in. = 2.5 mi.

PACIFIC

A   B   C   D

METRO

SEE 141 MAP

DRAIN

YONCALLA

OAKLAND

LANE COUNTY

DOUGLAS COUNTY

OREGON

Kimwood
Divide
GOSHEN-DIVIDE HWY
Comstock
Curtin
Anlauf
Safley
Leona
Krewson
LAUREL HILLS RD
GREEN MOUNTAIN
Boswell
BOSWELL MINERAL SPRINGS
JESSIE APPLEGATE HISTORICAL MARKER
DODGE CANYON
CHARLES APPLEGATE HOUSE
YONCALLA VALLEY
HALO
ELKHEAD
AMBROSE HILL
WILSON
RED HILL
DEVORE MOUNTAIN
Skelley
SKULL MOUNTAIN
SWEET POINT
FIVE POINT CANYON
PANTHER CANYON
RICE HILL
BLACKBERRY CANYON
CHURCHILL CANYON
RACCOON DR
Isadore
TURKEY HILL
INDIAN CREEK DR
EAGLE POINT
WHEELER CANYON
METZ HILL RD
CORNWALL HISTORICAL MARKER
Old Town
GREEN VALLEY RD
STEARNS LN

LOOKOUT MOUNTAIN
WINDY GAP
UPPER SMITH RIVER RD
S FORK SMITH RIVER RD
SAND CREEK RD
CHURCHILL RD
NELSON RD
TERRITORIAL RD
OLD SAND CREEK RD
ROCK CREEK RD
RIVER RD
HAYHURST RD
BEAR HILL
SHEEP HILL
HAYHURST VALLEY
COUGAR PASS
SKELLEY RD
HAYHURST RD
ANDREWS RD
APPLEGATE AV
1ST ST
DRAIN-YONCALLA RD
VALLEY RD
UPPER RIDGE RD
PLEASANT VALLEY RD
RED HILL RD
OAKWOOD DR
RICE VALLEY RD
GOODRICH RD
EVANS BUTTE
HOGAN
BLM RD 23-5-191
BLM RD 24-5-10
TRUITT RD
OAK ST
LOCUST ST
5TH ST
HALO TRAIL RD
PLEASANT VALLEY RD
ADAMS CREEK RD
DICKINSON MOUNTAIN
MEDLEYS RD
BEN MORE MOUNTAIN
ENGLISH SETTLEMENT
BEN MORE RD
DRIVER VALLEY RD
FAIROAKS RD
ELKHEAD VALLEY RD
HALL RIDGE
CALAPOOYA
DRIVER CREEK

Curtin
BUCK CREEK RD
LEES CREEK
THIEF CREEK
COX CREEK RD
COX
SCOTTS VALLEY
YONCALLA-ELKHEAD RD
MILLTOWN HILL
SHOESTRING VALLEY
Elkhead
ELKHEAD RD
ROMIE RD
BLM RD 23-4-26
BLM RD 23-4-90
BLM RD 23-4-28-0
HOWARD RD
SCOTTS VALLEY RD
OLDHAM CREEK RD
HANEY RIDGE
ROBINSON RIDGE
DRIVER VALLEY
LONG VALLEY RD
NONPAREIL RD
GASSY CREEK RD
JEFFERS CREEK RD
CALAPOOYA CREEK

WARDS BUTTE
WARDS
BEAR CREEK RD
N CREEK
REDFORD BUTTE
CEDAR CREEK
KELLY'S BUTTE
CHAPMAN BUTTE
CUTTOCK BUTTE
SLITER BUTTE
DOOLITTLE BUTTE
INDIAN BUTTE
SPIKE BUCK BUTTE
SCOTTS VALLEY
HOBART BUTTE
FIRECLAY RD
ALTON HILL
BLACK BUTTE
LITTLE BALDY
BIG BALDY
SCORPION BUTTE
KNOB HILL
CINNABAR MOUNTAIN
HORNET BUTTE
MURRY HILL
HARNESS MOUNTAIN
SEVENMILE HILL
TIMOTHY RIDGE
THE BUTTES
GOBBLERS KNOB
TAYLOR RIDGE
HINKLE CREEK
BLM RD 24-3-31-2
BLM RD 23-4-31-2

MARTIN CREEK RD
WILLIAMS CREEK RD
KENNEDY LN
NICHOLS LN
LONDON RD
WHITES CREEK RD
ROY PAYNE RD
TAYLOR BUTTE
SHORTRIDGE BUTTE
YOUNGS BUTTE
COTTAGE GROVE LAKE
COTTAGE GROVE RESERVOIR
PINE MEADOWS CAMPGROUND
PRIMITIVE CAMPGROUND
TWIN PRAIRIE BUTTES
RAISOR RD
COUGAR MOUNTAIN
LONDON RD
London
WHITE ROCK RIDGE
AKERSON BUTTE
WITT BUTTE
COUGAR BEND
BIG BEND
STENNETT BUTTE
SHOESTRING RD
LONDON HILL RD
METZKER RD
6TH ST
Gap
WHITES CREEK

HARDSCRABBLE RD
UMPQUA HWY
SIDE RD
S
DRAIN VALLEY RD
EAGLE VALLEY RD
INLO VALLEY
DRAIN HILL
HAYMURST VALLEY

PACIFIC HWY
99
5
38
162
163
160
159
154
150
148
146
142
138
170

LANE CO
DOUGLAS CO

miles   1 in. = 2.5 mi.
0   1   2   3   4

METRO

SEE 218 MAP

A   B   C   D

1

2

3

4

5

6

7

333

COOS BAY

EMPIRE COOS BAY
Englewood
Eastside
COOS RIVER
Bay Park
McCormac
Libby
Millington
Cleo

SQUAW ISLAND
Arago Light
SUNSET BAY
SUNSET BAY STATE PARK
BASTENDORFF BEACH
YOAKAM POINT
YOAKAM COUNTY PARK
Charleston
COOS HEAD US NAVAL FACILITY
OREGON INST OF MARINE BIOLOGY
Barview
CAPE ARAGO
COOS BAY
UPPER PONY CREEK RES.

SHELL ISLAND
NORTH COVE
CAPE ARAGO STATE PARK
SHORE ACRES STATE PARK
SEA LION VIEW POINT
CAPE ARAGO
SOUTH COVE
DRAKE POINT
COLLVER POINT
YOUNKER POINT
Crown Point
CROWN POINT
JOE NEY-DAVIS
SOUTH SLOUGH NATIONAL ESTUARY
LONG ISLAND POINT
YOAKAM HILL
THE BUTTES
OLIVE-BARBER RD
ROSS INLET RD
EASTSIDE-SUMNER RD
CITY-SUMNER RD

OCEAN

AGATE BEACH
SEVEN DEVILS RD
BEAVER HILL RD
FINCH RD
COOS CANYON
COAL CANYON
COOS COUNTY FOREST
COOS COUNTY
OREGON
DELMAR RD
42
UPPER LOOP
TIMBER WY
GREEN ACRES RD
Green Acres
BOONE CREEK RD
Overland
OVERLAND RD
BEAVER CREEK
Coaledo

FIVEMILE POINT
WHISKEY RUN RD
E HUMPHREYS RD
DEVILS
W HUMPHREYS RD
101
BEAVER HILL RD
OLD BEAVER HILL RD
Leneve
BANK RD
COQUILLE
Chrome
COOS GARDEN VALLEY RD
BAY-ROSEBURG HWY
BUDD MOUNTAIN
COQUILLE-FAIRVIEW RD
140

SEE 140 MAP

PACIFIC

BULLARDS BEACH STATE PARK
SEVEN MILE RD
BANK RD
ROCKY POINT
PARKERSBURG-PROSPER
JUNCTION RD
Parkersburg
Prosper
SPRUCE HOLLOW
TOM SMITH RD
BEAR CREEK RD
Winterville
COQUILLE RIVER
HATCHET SLOUGH RD
BANK RD
Riverton
BAKER RD
COQUILLE-FAT ELK RD
42S
COQUILLE
W CENTRAL BLVD
Cedar Point
E 2ND ST
E 1ST ST
SHELLEY RD
DUTCH JOHN RAVINE
FISHTRAP RD
RUNK CREEK RD
COQUILLE-FAT ELK RD
GLEN AIKEN CREEK RD
Johnson
42
BAY-ROSEBURG HWY

FIVE FOOT ROCK
COQUILLE POINT
BANDON BEACH
CAT AND KITTENS ROCK
1ST ST
RIVERSIDE DR
2ND ST SE
8TH ST SW
SEA BIRD DR
BANDON
BANDON STATE AIRPORT
HAYSTACK ROCK
BEACH LOOP RD
WINDHURST RD
MORRISON RD
BARNEKUFF RD
ROSA RD
COQUILLE-BANDON
MYRTLE RD
LAMPA RD
LAMPA VALLEY RD
POINT-LAMPA
Lampa Mountain
MYRTLE RD
Arago
ARAGO LN
LOWER NORWAY RD
Norway
POINT-LAMPA
PLEASANT VALLEY

BANDON STATE PARK
BEACH RD
BOAT RD
DEW VALLEY RD
Twomile
TWOMILE RD
DEW VALLEY RD
101
Laurel Grove
HALL CREEK RD
WARD CREEK RD
GRIGSBY ROCK
HORSE HOLLOW RD
MATHENY CREEK RD
WEST SIDE RD
PLEASANT VALLEY RD
CATCHING CREEK RD

SEE 224 MAP

0 1 2 3 4 miles   1 in. = 2.5 mi.

SEE 219 MAP

A B C D

METRO

WAPITI LN
TYEE RD
CHURCHILL RAPIDS
UMPQUA
COLES VALLEY
HUBBARD CREEK RD
UMPQUA ESTATE WINERY
IVERSON RD
JOELSON RD
WOODRUFF MOUNTAIN
CROW RAPIDS
MELQUA
GARDEN VALLEY
HEYDON RD
Cleveland
LEATHERWOOD RAPIDS
CLEVELAND RAPIDS
BEAR RIDGE
PONDEROSA DR
BIG BEND
MILLWOOD
UPPER CLEVELAND RAPIDS
RED HILL
KLAHOWYA LN
MELQUA
CLEVELAND HILL
WILBUR-GARDEN VALLEY
TWIN RIVERS CAMPGROUND
COYOTE HILL
ELGAROSE
BECKER
DONGUSS DR
CLEVELAND HILL RD
WOODRUFF RD
Elgarose
ELGAROSE RD
NORTH
ORCHARD LN
CURRY
Riversdale RD
FISHER
MOOREA DR
DOERNER RD
DOERNER CTO
MELROSE
Melrose
FLOURNOY VALLEY RD
CHAMPAGNE CREEK VALLEY
TANGLEWOOD LN
OLD MELROSE RD
GARDEN VALLEY BLVD
Edenbower
NW STEWART PKWY
NW TROOST ST
W HARVARD BLVD
SUNRISE LN
WHITE TAIL RIDGE
COLONIAL
MULFF LN
LOOKINGGLASS
MTBBOR LN
LOOKINGGLASS HILL
LOOKINGGLASS RD
BAY-WAGON
COOS
Lookingglass
LOOKINGGLASS VALLEY
MORGAN HILL
CRITESER RD
LARSON
LOOKINGGLASS CREEK
INDIAN NOSE
HAPPY
VALLEY
STRICKLAND
BROCKWAY
SWAN HILL
PORTER CREEK RD
OLALLA
HOOVER HILL
MCNABB
QUALLA
HOOVER HILL
SQUAW CREEK RD
FOOS BAY-WD
BEND AV
BROSI ORCHARD RD
DARRELL AV
THOMPSON AV
BROCKWAY
Dillard
RICE CREEK RD
DILLARD
RAINBOW HOLLOW
WILLIS CREEK RD
KENT CREEK RD
WINSTON
WILDLIFE SAFARI
Roseburg
ROBERTS CREEK RD
Great
Glengary
ROBERTS MOUNTAIN
GLENGARY RD
ROBERTS MOUNTAIN
PACIFIC HWY
Round Prairie
SOUTH UMPQUA RIVER RD
CLARKS BRANCH
RICHARDSON
GOBBLERS KNOB
BORG MOUNTAIN

SUTHERLIN
OLD HWY
WILCOX RD
COLE RD
Stephens
FORT McKAY
STEARNS LN
Union Gap
ELKTON-SUTHERLIN HWY
PARK PL N
DUKE LN
GROSS LN
CALAPOOYA ST
COMSTOCK
SUTHERLIN MUNICIPAL AIRPORT
RICHARDS BUTTE
6TH AV
NE CENTRAL AV
NORTH SIDE RD
VALLEY VIEW RD
SOUTH SIDE RD
SUTHERLIN-NONPAREIL RD
FAIROAKS RD
Fairoaks
CALAPOOYA CREEK
CAMAS SWALE
COPPER CREEK RD
FRASER CANYON
BLM RD 25-4-13-0
SMITH CANYON

SUTHERLIN-UMPQUA
WILBUR-UMPQUA
DAVIS HILL RD
PIPELINE RD
HENRY RD
EDENBOWER RD
TURKEY CREEK LN
BROZIO RD
WESTVIEW DR
WILBUR RD
CLEARVIEW DR
WILBUR-UMPQUA RD
ROGERS RD
SHADY RD
Wilbur
HALFMILE RD
PACIFIC HWY
Deady
DEADY CROSSING RD
DEADY CAVES
ROUND TIMBER
DOUGLAS COUNTY

NORTH RD
RIO WES RD
SOUTH BANK UMPQUA RD
NORTH UMPQUA
WILD FERN DR
ECHO BUTTE
SUNSHINE RD
OREGON
WHISTLERS BEND PARK RD
WHISTLERS LN
OAK CREEK VALLEY
ROUND TOP
BLACK MUD SUMMIT
NORTH UMPQUA HWY

OAKLAND
Winchester
WINCHESTER BALDY
UMPQUA COMMUNITY COLLEGE
PAGE
BROZIO WINCHESTER RD
NW BROAD ST
ROSEBURG
NE STEPHENS ST
NEWTON CREEK
NE DIAMOND LAKE BLVD
NE DOUGLAS AV
BUCKHORN RD
Dixonville
BUCKHORN RD
DIXONVILLE RD
MOUNT NEBO
PACIFIC HWY
OAKLAND SHADY HWY
Oaks
Shady
S DEER CREEK
HOOT N HOLLER LN
ROBERTS CREEK RD
ROBERTS CREEK
BELGER CREEK RD
RIGHT FORK CREEK
FROZEN CREEK RD
BIG LICK CREEK
BRUSHY BUTTE
BLM RD 28-4-29-0
NORTH MYRTLE PARK

334

SEE 225 MAP

0 1 2 3 4 miles   1 in. = 2.5 mi.

SEE 141 MAP

METRO

SEE 142 MAP

A B C D

1

NFD RD 3817
NFD RD 100
GRANDDAD BUTTE
REYNOLDS BUTTE
BULLDOG RD
REYNOLDS RIDGE
BULLDOG ROCK
LOST PRAIRIE ROCK
STALEY RIDGE
FISH LAKE
COAL CREEK
WILLAMETTE
NATIONAL
FOREST
REYNOLDS SHELTER
RD
CREEK
REYNOLDS CREEK
WABASH
CREEK

2

STEAMBOAT
STEAMBOAT FALLS CAMPGROUND
STEAMBOAT
SINGLE CREEK RD
LITTLE FALLS
QUARTZ POINT
WILD ROSE POINT
HARDING BUTTE
DEVILS STAIRWAY
SPRING MOUNTAIN
BEAR POINT
ILLAHEE ROCK
BOULDER
CREEK
WILDERNESS
SILVER ROCK
BALM MOUNTAIN
UMPQUA
NFD RD 34
NFD RD 500
NFD RD 200
DOG MOUNTAIN
RAGGED RIDGE
RAGGED BUTTE
BARTRUMS ROCK
DOUGLAS COUNTY
BOULDER CREEK
PERRY BUTTE
THORN MOUNTAIN
NATIONAL

3

JACK FALLS
JACK POINT
LIMPY ROCK
INDIAN CAVE
BRADLEY RIDGE
UMPQUA
138
RIVER
NORTH
PANTHER LEAP
REYNOLDS RIDGE
EAGLE RIDGE
PINE POINT
RATTLESNAKE RIDGE
RATTLESNAKE ROCK
EAGLE ROCK
PINE BENCH
BOULDER FLAT CAMPGROUND
OLD MAN ROCK
PINE BENCH
CAMEL HUMP
OREGON
FOREST
WEEPING ROCK CAMPGROUND
EAGLE ROCK CAMPGROUND
NORTH UMPQUA
HWY
LEMOLO TWO FOREBAY CAMPGROUND
UMPQUA RD
HORSESHOE BEND CAMPGROUND
CHARCOAL POINT
BIG
FLATIRON POINT
TOKETEE LAKE CAMPGROUND

4

CALF RIDGE
CREEK
CAMAS CREEK RD
SNUFF SHELTER
RD
TOKETEE FALLS
TOKETEE RESERVOIR
138
CLEARWATER
CLEARWATER RIVER
NFD RD 75
WATSON FALLS RD
BRINK RD
FAIRY SHELTER
BACHELOR BUTTE
LIMPY MOUNTAIN
COLDWATER CAMPGROUND
OAK BUTTE
BIG TWIN LAKES CAMPGROUND
TWIN LAKES
UMPQUA
BIG
CAMAS
CAMAS CREEK CAMPGROUND
FISH CREEK CAMPGROUND
FISH CREEK DESERT
NFD RD 35
FISH CREEK RD

SEE 141 MAP

SEE 223 MAP

5

LITTLE RIVER RD
HEMLOCK FALLS
QUARTZ
HEMLOCK LAKE CAMPGROUND
HEMLOCK MEADOW CAMPGROUND
MOUNTAIN
SNOWBIRD SHELTER
RIVER
CALF
TWIN LAKES MOUNTAIN
DOEHEAD MOUNTAIN
COPELAND
SNOWBIRD MOUNTAIN
RAVEN ROCK
BUCKHEAD MOUNTAIN
SNOWBIRD
BEAR WALLOW
NATIONAL
RHODODENDRON RIDGE
RD
MUD LAKE MOUNTAIN
RD
NFD RD

6

QUARTZ MOUNTAIN
RD
BUCKHEAD MOUNTAIN CAMPGROUND
BLACK ROCK RD
FOREST
BLACK ROCK FORK
ROLLING GROUNDS CAMP
BEAVER SHELTER
RD
BOZE SHELTER
DEER LICK FALLS
QUARTZ CANYON

7

MOUNTAIN
FLAGSTONE PEAK
QUARTZ CREEK RD
BLACK
FISH LAKE
RIVER
LAKE CREEK RD
CASTLE
BLACK ROCK FORK
ROGUE-UMPQUA
DIVIDE
RATTLESNAKE MOUNTAIN
WINDY GAP
FISH CREEK VALLEY
FISH CREEK SHELTER
BUCKNECK MOUNTAIN
TILLER-SOUTH UMPQUA CAMP RD
EMERSON RD
SOUTH UMPQUA
BEAVER SWAMP CAMPGROUND
ROCKY RIDGE
CASTLE ROCK
WILDERNESS
DEVILS SLIDE
WILEY CAMP
FISH LAKE CAMPGROUND
SKIMMERHORN CAMPGROUND
FISH LAKE
ROGUE RIVER NATIONAL FOREST
BUCK CANYON
QUARTZ

SEE 226 MAP

A B C D

0 1 2 3 4 miles 1 in. = 2.5 mi.

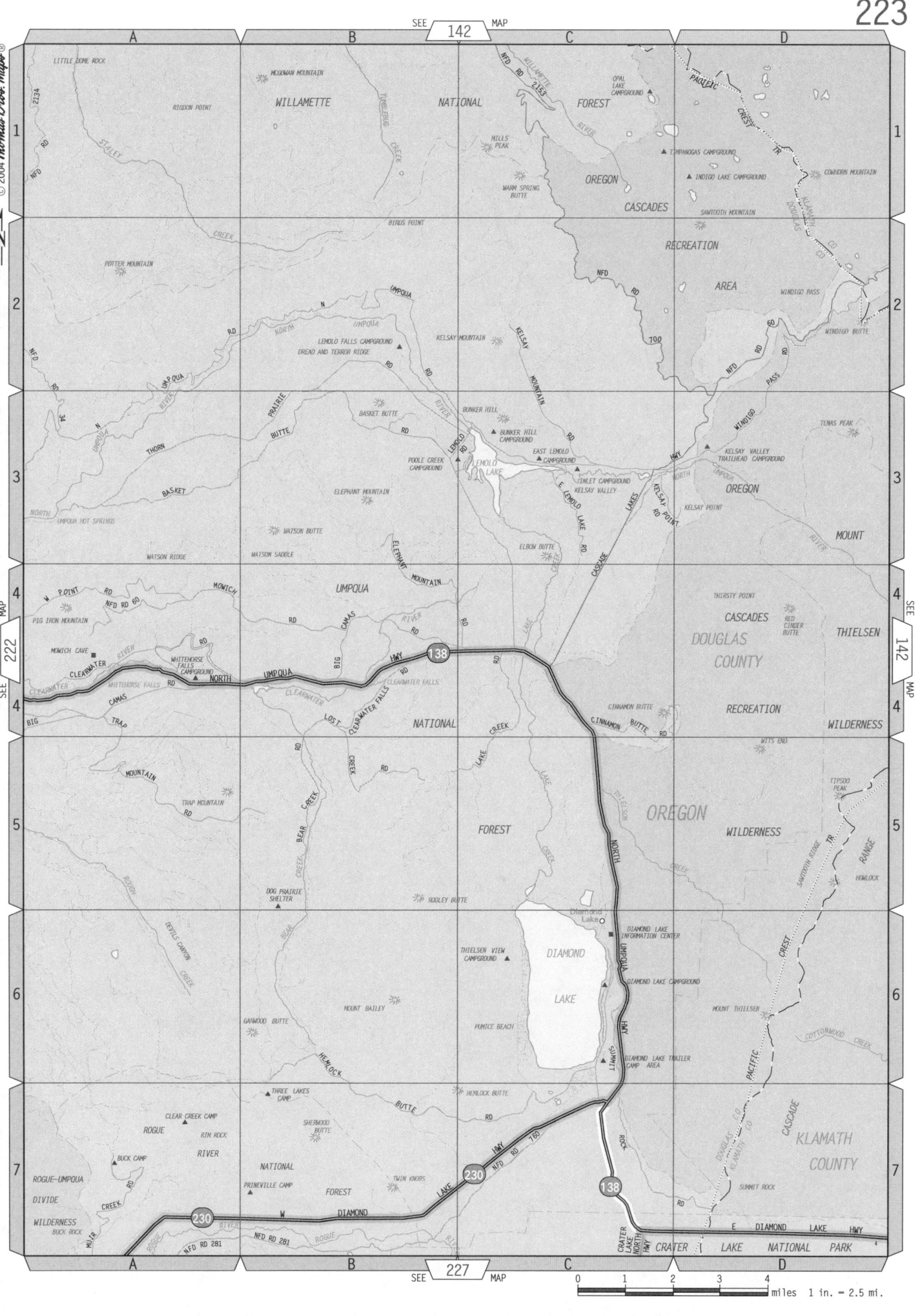

METRO

miles   1 in. = 2.5 mi.

METRO

SEE 220 MAP

A | B | C | D

1

STEWART RD

LOWER FOURMILE RD
Fourmile

NEW RIVER PARK

COOS COUNTY

NORTH FOURMILE RD

BLIZZARD BUTTE

CROFT LAKE RD

101

SYDNAM RD

2

COOS CO
CURRY CO

NEW LAKE RD

MORTON BUTTE

COTTON BUTTE

BENNETT BUTTE

OCEAN

PACIFIC

HWY

LANGLOIS

ROUND TOP MOUNTAIN LN

RD

WATCHES BUTTE

Langlois

3

FLORAS CREEK

LOOP RD

FLORAS

CALF RANCH MOUNTAIN

FLORAS LAKE RD

FLORAS LAKE

PACIFIC VW

GROUSE LN
FERN RIDGE RD

CREEK

RD

BANDON-PORT ORFORD

Denmark

WHITE MOUNTAIN

TOWER ROCK

FLORAS LAKE

COAST

STONE BUTTE

SUMMIT MOUNTAIN

BLACKLOCK POINT

4

CASTLE ROCK

CAPE BLANCO STATE AIRPORT

GULL ROCK

SIXES BEACH

AIRPORT RD

OREGON

EIGHTMILE PRAIRIE MOUNTAIN

CURRY COUNTY

OREGON

SUGARLOAF MOUNTAIN

CAPE BLANCO

MADDEN BUTTE

RD

CAPE BLANCO LIGHTHOUSE

CAPE BLANCO STATE PARK

CAPE BLANCO

SIXES

CRYSTAL CREEK

SQUAW BLUFF

HEREFORD RD

SADDLE ROCK

RIVER

HWY

Sixes

SIXES

RIVER

RIVER

RD

5

MCKENZIE RD

GRASSY KNOB

SISKIYOU

POVERTY RIDGE

RD

MOON MOUNTAIN

GRASSY

CHINA PEAK

RUSTY BUTTE

SILVER BUTTE

ELK

NATIONAL

FOREST

ELK RIVER

KNOB

WILDERNESS

6

AGATE BEACH

PORT ORFORD

OREGON ST

PORT ORFORD HWY

SISKIYOU

NATIONAL

ANVIL MOUNTAIN

KLOOQUEH ROCK

FORT POINT

OREGON

CHINA MOUNTAIN

ELK RIVER STATE FISH HATCHERY

FOREST

BUTLER BAR CAMPGROUND

NELLIES COVE
NELLIES POINT

101

TICHENOR ROCK

ROCKY POINT

CHINA MOUNTAIN

7

COAST

COAL POINT

NFD RD 20

MCGRIBBLE CAMPGROUND

PANTHER CREEK CAMPGROUND

MILBURY MOUNTAIN

HUMBUG MOUNTAIN

NFD RD 5400

HUMBUG MOUNTAIN STATE PARK

HWY

HUMBUG MOUNTAIN CAMPGROUND

FATHER MOUNTAIN

RD

HUMBUG MOUNTAIN

A | B | C | D

SEE 228 MAP

SEE 140 MAP

0 1 2 3 4 miles   1 in. = 2.5 mi.

SEE 221 MAP

A B C D

© 2004 Thomas Bros. Maps ®

MYRTLE CREEK

RIDDLE

CANYONVILLE

GLENDALE

DOUGLAS COUNTY

OREGON

OREGON STATE FOREST

JOSEPHINE COUNTY

JACKSON COUNTY

DOUGLAS CO
JOSEPHINE CO

DOUGLAS CO
JACKSON CO

METRO

SEE 141 MAP

SEE 141 MAP

SEE 229 MAP

Labels and roads:

BLM 30-70-50, BLM RD 29-7-25-1, RICE CREEK RD, WILLIS CREEK RD, EAST FORK RD, DOLE, SPRING BROOK, MYRTLE CREEK RD, BLM RD 29-4-20, SCHOOL HOLLOW, MYRTLE CREEK RD

99, 110 RD, PACIFIC, HWY, LILLIAN ST, RICE ST, DIVISION ST S, NEAL LN, RIVERSIDE DR, DAYS, 108, 5, 106, CEDAR HOLLOW CREEK, SOUTH MYRTLE CREEK

BIG BALDY, BOOMER HILL, SHEEP HILL, RED RIDGE, CHADWICK CANYON, Weaver, MYRTLE CREEK MUNICIPAL AIRPORT, 99

BOOMER HILL, MOUNT RAMBLER, WEAVER, SOUTH, OLD, PACIFIC, LIMPQUA, Tri-City, GAZLEY RD NORTH, River Hwy, Days Creek, SHIVELY CREEK RD

NICKEL MOUNTAIN, BOYER RD, BOYER, MOUNT ISAAC, RIDDLE BYPS, 5TH AV, PRUNER RD, GAZLEY, PACIFIC HWY, STANTON PARK, 103, 102, GAZLEY RD, 227, Gazley

COW CREEK RD, DOE CREEK RD, NICKEL, NICKEL MINE RD, CREEK, 1ST AV, LP, GLENBROOK, SHOESTRING, YOKUM, 101, DRY CREEK CANYON RD, 99, SEVEN FEATHERS CASINO, GAZLEY, SOUTH, TILLER-TRAIL, BEALS CREEK RD, BEALS MOUNTAIN, HYDE RIDGE

CANYONVILLE-RIDDLE, ASH CREEK RD, 98, CANYON CREEK RD, 1ST ST, MAIN ST

TELLURIUM PEAK, CANYON MOUNTAIN, 95, RD, BATES, HWY, BLM RD 31-4-35-0

SILVER BUTTE, MIDDLE CREEK RD, BUCKHORN MOUNTAIN, CANYON CREEK PASS, PATRICK MOUNTAIN, COW CREEK RD, BLM RD 32-4-9

WOODS CREEK RD, PACIFIC, OLD PACIFIC HWY, 88, Azalea, CREEK, STARVEOUT CREEK, ROGUM CREEK RD, WHITEHORSE CREEK RD, BURMA RD

PANTHER BUTTE, McCULLOUGH CREEK RD, FERNWALE, Glendale Junction, 83, Fortune Branch, COW, RANCHERO, Quines Creek, 86, QUINES CREEK RD, MURPHY RD, BULL RUN RD

REUBEN RD, MOUNT REUBEN RD, N REUBEN RD, PACIFIC AV, OLD GLENDALE RD, VALLEY RD, TUNNEL RD, 80, BARTON, BUCKHORN, GREEN MOUNTAIN RD, QUARTZMILL PEAK, WAGGONER GAP, LAST CHANCE CREEK

5, 99, 78, SPEAKER RD, HOLE IN THE GROUND

0 1 2 3 4 miles 1 in. = 2.5 mi.

METRO

© 2004 Thomas Bros. Maps ®

N

A **B** **C** **D**

1

TILLER-SOUTH
SOUTH UMPQUA
SOUTH UMPQUA FALLS
UMPQUA CAMP RD
UMPQUA RIVER
ACKER ROCK
TWINBUCK SHELTER
BUCKEYE CREEK RD
BUCKEYE CREEK
DOUGLAS COUNTY
UMPQUA
BUCKEYE LAKE CAMPGROUND
ROGUE-UMPQUA
DIVIDE
GRASSHOPPER MOUNTAIN
HIGHROCK MOUNTAIN
JACKASS MOUNTAIN
WEAVER MOUNTAIN
FISH MOUNTAIN
ALKALI CAMP
HOLE IN THE GROUND
LEWIS CAMP
ROGUE
RIVER
FOSTER CREEK RD
HERSHBERGER MOUNTAIN
HERSHBERGER

2

TALLOW BUTTE
FIVESTICKS RD
JACKSON
JACKSON CREEK RD
NATIONAL
CLIFF LAKE CAMPGROUND
WILDERNESS
CREEK
ANDERSON MOUNTAIN
RABBIT EARS
RD
PRAIRIE CREEK RD
NATIONAL
DIAMOND LAKE HWY
230
COPELAND CREEK

3

COW HORN ARCH
COUGAR BUTTE
CREEK
CREEK
SQUAW CREEK
ABBOTT BUTTE
WINDY GAP
NFD RD 950
FOREST
FALCON BUTTE
ELEPHANT HEAD
ABBOTT CREEK
ABBOTT
OREGON
CREEK NATURAL
RESEARCH AREA
DOUGLAS CO
JACKSON CO
WOLF PEAK
MOUNT STELLA RD
MOUNT STELLA
FOREST
BYBEE CREEK RD
OLD BYBEE CREEK
DEER CREEK
CASTLE CREEK
CASTLE CREEK
WHISKEY CREEK
CRATER LAKE HWY
62

4

HUCKLEBERRY GAP
NEAL SPRINGS CAMPGROUND
HUCKLEBERRY LAKE CAMPGROUND
WHALEBACK
QUARTZ MOUNTAIN
COLD SPRT
GREY ROCK
CAMP RD
TRIPOD
OLD
BUTLER BUTTE
SUGARPINE SHELTER
TUCKER GAP
ABBOTT CREEK RD
SUNSHINE CREEK RD
ABBOTT CREEK CAMPGROUND
RIVER
CREEK
WOODRUFF
KNOB HILL
NATURAL BRIDGE
UNION CREEK CAMPGROUND
UNION CREEK
ROGUE GORGE VIEW POINT
62
NATURAL BRIDGE VIEW POINT
WEST HWY
RD
UNION CREEK
HUCKLEBERRY RD
JACKSON COUNTY
SEE 141 MAP
SEE 227 MAP

5

GOODVIEW POINT
GREY
BUZZARD MINE
GRUB BOX GAP
BUCK BASIN
ROUND TOP
NEEDLE ROCKS
JIM CREEK SPUR
HOG CREEK RD
BUZZARD MINE RD
NEEDLE RIDGE
NEEDLE ROCK RD
NEEDLE CREEK
GRAVEL BUTTE
LICK ROCK
ABBOTT CREEK RD
TAKELMA GORGE
MILL LOOP RD
LAKE RD
NATIONAL
GINKGO
ELK CREEK
MILL CREEK
UPPER INJUN CREEK
ELK CREEK RD
ELK CREEK
GINKGO
MILL CREEK RIDGE

6

TIMBER CREEK RD
ELKHORN RIDGE RD
MILLER MOUNTAIN
SUGAR PINE RD
MULE HILL
GREY RD
ELK CREEK RD
HIBBARD POINT
SANDOZ GAP
HALLS POINT
BALD MOUNTAIN
LARSON CREEK RD
GRAHAM CREEK RD
RIVER BRIDGE CAMPGROUND
KITER CREEK
KITER CREEK SPUR
ROGUE RIVER
MILL CREEK CAMPGROUND
FOREST
RED BLANKET MOUNTAIN RD
RED BLANKET CREEK

7

ELK CREEK
BURNT PEAK
BAILEY BUTTE
DODES CREEK RD
WILLITS RIDGE
ULRICH RD
CASCADE GORGE
FLOUNCE ROCK
TATOUCHE PEAK
WHETSTONE POINT
WHITE POINT
SCHOOLMARM SPUR
MILL CREEK DR
RED BLANKET
Prospect
CRATER LAKE
MILL CREEK
MILL CREEK FALLS
BESSIE CREEK
RED BLANKET RD
BESSIE CREEK
MIDDLE FORK ROGUE RIVER
BUTTE FALLS PROSPECT RD
PARKER MEADOWS RD
62

0 1 2 3 4 miles 1 in. = 2.5 mi.

METRO

A | B | C | D

DOUGLAS COUNTY

230

MUIR CREEK RD
HAMAKER RD
MUIR CREEK FALLS
HAMAKER CAMPGROUND
HAMAKER BUTTE
ROGUE RIVER
LAKE
DIAMOND
HURRYON CAMP
OLD NATIONAL
STREAM
DOUGLAS CO
JACKSON CO
CRATER CREEK RD
CRATER LAKE NATIONAL PARK
CRATER CREEK MTWY

HAMAKER BLUFF
DOUGLAS CO
KLAMATH CO
CRATER
LAKE
CRESCENT RIDGE
BALD CRATER
OASIS BUTTE
NATIONAL
PARK

ROGUE RIVER
DESERT RIDGE
GAYWAS PEAK
KLAMATH RIDGE
DESERT CONE
PUMICE DESERT
TIMBER CRATER
RED CONE
GROUSE HILL
RUGGED CREST
PACIFIC CREST TR
NORTH
LAKE

KLAMATH COUNTY

BYBEE CREEK
BYBEE CREEK RD
DEER BRANCH
BYBEE RD
COPELAND CREEK
ROCK CREEK RD
CASTLE CREEK
WHISKEY CREEK
CASTLE CREEK RD

WILLIAMS CRATER
THE WATCHMAN
HILLMAN PEAK
DEVILS BACKBONE
RIM
DR
DISCOVERY POINT
EAGLE COVE
SINNOTT MEMORIAL OVERLOOK

LLAO ROCK
STEEL BAY
PUMICE POINT
CLEETWOOD COVE
PALISADE POINT
RIM OF THE CRATER
LIDO BAY
MERRIAM POINT
PALISADES
ROUNDTOP
DR
WINEGLASS
GROTTO COVE
SKELL HEAD
SCOTT BLUFFS
REDCLOUD CLIFF
CLOUDCAP
CRATER LAKE
WIZARD ISLAND
FUMAROLE BAY
GOVERNORS BAY
CHASKI BAY
DANGER BAY
CLOUDCAP BAY
PUMICE CASTLE
CASTLE ROCK
MOUNT SCOTT
VICTOR VIEW
PHANTOM SHIP
DUTTON CLIFF
PHANTOM SHIP OVERLOOK
DUTTON RIDGE
PINNACLE VALLEY

OREGON
HUCKLEBERRY
ELEPHANTS BACK
CASTLE CREEK
NATIONAL
62
LLAOS HALLWAY
PARK
WHITEHORSE BLUFF
THOUSAND SPRINGS RD
UNION CREEK RD
CASTLE POINT
CASCADE DIVIDE
CRATER
MAZAMA CAMPGROUND
DUWEE FALLS
GODFREY GLEN
CRATER LAKE NATIONAL PARK HEADQUARTERS
GARFIELD PEAK
EAGLE CRAGS
APPLEGATE PEAK
MUNSON RIDGE
MUNSON POINT
MUNSON VALLEY
VIDAE RIDGE
TUTUTNI PASS
GRAYBACK RIDGE
MAKLAKS PASS

NORTH GINKGO SPUR
HUCKLEBERRY MOUNTAIN
ALDER SPRING RD
ROCKTOP BUTTE
ARANT POINT
COLD SPRINGS CAMPGROUND
HWY
CRATER PEAK
SUN
ANNIE
MAKLAKS CRATER

DEAD SOLDIER CREEK
GINKGO RD
RED BLANKET MOUNTAIN
BLANKET RD
RED MOUNTAIN
UNION PEAK
BALD TOP
SCORIA CONE
RANGE
ANNIE FALLS
RED BLANKET CREEK
STUART FALLS
RED BLANKET FALLS
GOOSE NEST
WINEMA

SKY
BESSIE ROCK
JERRY MOUNTAIN
TOM MOUNTAIN
CINNAMON PEAK
LAKES
BESSIE CREEK
BESSIE SHELTER
MUDJEKEEWIS MOUNTAIN
KERBY CREEK RD
KERBY HILL
JACKSON CO
KLAMATH CO
WILDERNESS
PACIFIC
OREGON DESERT
ROGUE WATERSHED
GOOSE EGG
CASCADE
NATIONAL
FOREST
CRATER LAKE HWY
62
MIDDLE FORK ROGUE RIVER
LONE WOLF
RUTH MOUNTAIN

0 1 2 3 4 miles   1 in. = 2.5 mi.

SEE 224 MAP

METRO

A   **B**   **C**   **D**

1

OREGON COAST HWY

ELK RIVER RD

NFD RD 150

ROCKY PEAK

SISKIYOU

PANTHER MOUNTAIN

3402

SUNSHINE CREEK CAMPGROUND

CHISMORE BUTTE

MCCURDY CAMPGROUND

OPHIR MOUNTAIN

ELK RIVER RD

NFD RD 3310

RD 110

LOOKOUT ROCK

NATIONAL

FOREST

2

FRANKPORT

SISTERS ROCKS

COLEBROOK BUTTE

PREHISTORIC GARDENS

DEVILS BACKBONE

COFFEE BUTTE

NFD

FALL MOUNTAIN

LAKE OF THE WOODS MOUNTAIN

CREEK RD

NFD RD

3340

PACIFIC

EUCHRE

Ophir

CURRY COUNTY

CREEK

SOLDIER CAMP MOUNTAIN

3

OPHIR RD

R

ULMER MOUNTAIN

SQUAW RD

BRUSHY BALD MOUNTAIN

FIRST PRAIRIE MOUNTAIN

SECOND PRAIRIE MOUNTAIN

POTATO ILLAHE MOUNTAIN

ROGUE RIVER

AGNESS RD

OCEAN

LOBSTER CREEK

LOBSTER HILL

4

NORTH ROCK

Nesika Beach

VONDERGREEN HILL

VALLEY RD

NFD RD

3533

QUOSATANA CAMPGROUND

ROGUE

AGNESS

SEE 148 MAP

WAKEMAN BEACH

NESIKA RD

EDSON CREEK

CANFIELD HILL

ROGUE RIVER RD

LOBSTER CREEK CAMPGROUND

AGNESS RD

3313

AGATE BEACH

HUBBARD MOUND

RUMLEY HILL

NORTH BANK FLAT

KIMBALL HILL

SISKIYOU

SKOOKUMHOUSE BUTTE

OTTER POINT

JERRYS RD

RD

5

BARLEY BEACH

RACETRACK HILL

NORTH BANK ROGUE RIVER

SAUNDERS CREEK RD

NFD RD 150

WILDHORSE CAMPGROUND

101

Wedderburn

ROGUE RIVER

JERRYS FLAT RD

NATIONAL

DOYLE POINT

GOLD BEACH

INDIAN CREEK CAMPGROUND

OREGON

NFD RD

TOMCAT HILL

SIGNAL BUTTES

QUOSATANA BUTTE

GOLD BEACH MUNICIPAL AIRPORT

H

CURRY COUNTY FAIRGROUNDS

6

GRIZZLY MOUNTAIN

SUGARLOAF MOUNTAIN

FOREST

SADDLE MOUNTAIN

Hunter Creek

BUENA VISTA OCEAN WAYSIDE STATE PARK

3680

KALMIOPSIS

OREGON HUNTER CREEK

FAIRVIEW MOUNTAIN

WILDERNESS

NFD RD

PISTOL RIVER

COLLIER BUTTE

7

COAST HWY

CAPE SEBASTIAN FRONTAGE HWY

FAIRVIEW CAMPGROUND

JACOBY BUTTE

CAPE SEBASTIAN STATE PARK

SNOW CAMP MOUNTAIN

SEE 232 MAP

A   **B**   **C**   **D**

SEE 148 MAP

0   1   2   3   4   miles   1 in. = 2.5 mi.

SEE MAP 225

METRO

A B C D

GRANTS PASS

ROGUE RIVER

JOSEPHINE COUNTY

JACKSON COUNTY

OREGON

335

Wolf Creek
Bridge
Wolf Creek
Coyote Creek
Sugarloaf
Malone Peak
London Peak
Smith Hill Summit
Post Mountain
King Mountain
Saint Peter Mountain
Saint Paul Mountain
Black Canyon
Brushy Gulch
Lower Grave Creek Rd
Leland
Flume Gulch
Grave
Brimstone
Sunnyglen
KOA Grants Pass/Sunny Valley
Sunny Valley
Placer
King
Greenback Mine
Placer
Daisy Mine Rd
Pleasant Creek
Copper Queen
Sexton Mountain Pass
Sexton Mountain
Short Horn Gulch
Carrie
Daisy
Mine
Ditch Creek
Toad
China Gap
Hugo
Tunnel Creek Rd
Tunnel Loop
Quartz Creek
Three Pines
Monument
Jump-Off Joe Creek
Jack Creek
Agee Dr
Roberts Mountain
Winona
Jump-Off Joe Rd
Coker Gap
Pleasant Valley
Russell
Boyer Rd
Red Mountain
Merlin-Galice
Crow
Hugo
Merlin
Robertson Bridge Rd
Josephine County Airport
Pleasant Valley
Walker Mountain
Sportsman Park
Elk Mountain
Pleasant Valley
Wimer
Queens Branch Rd
Evans Valley
Fairbanks
Everton Riffle
Ewe Creek Rd
Azalea
Highland Av
Colonial Dr
Granite Hill Rd
Granite Hill
Old Baldy
Starvation Heights
Donaldson Rd
Granite Hill
Evans Creek
Fielder Creek Rd
Griffin Park
Boat Launch
Ferry Rd
Rogue River
Pinecrest
Stewart
Ashbrook Ln
Barbara Dr
NW Highland Av
NE 10th St
NE Beacon Dr
Redwood Hwy
Savage Creek Rd
Valley of the Rogue State Park
Foothills Blvd
Main St
Pine St
E Main St
Upper River
Gunnell Riffle
Whitehorse Riffle
Riverbanks Rd
Leonard
Rounds
Redwood
Lower River
Rogue River
E D St
SE M St
Redwood Hwy
Rogue River
N River Rd
Schieffelin Gulch Rd
Marcy Lp
Daily Ln
Sloan Mountain
Applegate
Jerome Prairie
Rogue Community College
Grandview Av
Fruitdale
Harbeck-Fruitdale
Bald Mountain
Grants Pass Peak
Owl Hollow Creek Rd
Birdseye Creek Rd
Wilderville
Rail Canyon
Fish Hatchery Park
Wetherbee
Woodland Park
Jerome Prairie
Laurel Av
Demaray
Sleepy Hollow Lp
Stringer Gap
Elk
Jaynes
Cloverlawn Dr
Pickett Mountain
Luther Divide
Board Shanty
Little Bald Spot
Right Fork Foots Creek
Cheney Creek
Marble Mountain Rd
Bull Creek
Bolt Mountain
Fish Hatchery Park
New Hope
Murphy
South Side Rd

1 in. = 2.5 mi.

METRO

SEE 141 MAP

A   B   C   D

1

WEST FORK

WHITE ROCK MOUNTAIN

COLD SPRING CREEK RD

ROCK CREEK RD

CREEK RD

PEAVINE RIDGE

ROUND TOP RD

ROUND TOP

MISTY

HORSE MOUNTAIN

CLEVELAND RIDGE RD

EAST FORK EVANS CREEK

CREEK

ROMINE CREEK RD

TILLER-TRAIL HWY

WILLY ROCK

WILLY MOUNTAIN

227

2

BATTLE MOUNTAIN

LITTLE BATTLE MOUNTAIN

BATTLE CREEK

FRY PEAK

MAYS RD

BLACK BUTTE

BEAR WALLOW

CREEK

SPIGNET BUTTE

MILL HOLLOW

EVANS CREEK

POMEROY

BOSWELL MOUNTAIN

BOARD MOUNTAIN

ROGUE

RIVER

NATIONAL

FOREST

OLD TRAIL CREEK RD

SAWYER RD

SHADY COVE

Trail

Trail

3

SNAKE CREEK

FAWN CREEK RD

FALSE FACE MOUNTAIN

NEATHAMMER GULCH RD

EVANS CREEK

BALD MOUNTAIN

MAPLE GULCH RD

RAMSEY CANYON

HULL MOUNTAIN

RAMSEY-CANYON

OREGON

LUCKY HOLLOW CREEK

EVANS

RIVER RD

E EVANS CREEK RD

CINNABAR MOUNTAIN

MEADOWS

ANTIOCH

JACKSON COUNTY

RIVER RD

RIVER

LAKE

DR

62

4

SEE 229 MAP

EVANS CREEK RD

LOVER PEAK

MURPHY GULCH RD

MCCONVILLE PEAK

HILLIS PEAK

SARDINE MOUNTAIN

SARDINE

WILCOX PEAK

SARDINE CREEK

BRATON HOLLOW

ELKHORN BUTTE

RIGHT FORK

SALT CREEK

CREEK RD

SARDINE RD

RAMSEY RD

TURTLE ROCK

NEIL ROCK

CHIMNEY ROCK BUTTE

EAGLE DR

BEAGLE

DODGE RD

JONES RD

NEW JONES RD

SHILOH RD

DEBENGER GAP

IRONWOOD DR

LEAFWOOD DR

ROGUE RD

ROGUE

HAMMELL RD

CRATER

MOSSER MOUNTAIN

BUTTE FALLS

BALL RD

SEE 149 MAP

5

LEFT FORK

FORK RD

BOYD CREEK RD

SARDINE CREEK RD

LYMAN MOUNTAIN

THE OREGON VORTEX & HOUSE OF MYSTERY

SARDINE CREEK RD

SAMS VALLEY

RAMSEY

VALLEY

DILLON FALLS

SAMS VALLEY

JOHN DAY DR

SAMS VALLEY

OLD SAMS VALLEY

TRESHAM LN

TABLE ROCK TRAIL RD

WHEELER RD

UPPER TABLE ROCK

PERRY RD

ANTIOCH RD

RATTLESNAKE RAPIDS

RIVER

HWY

234 GLASS LN

LONG MOUNTAIN

HWY

REESE RD

W LINN

EAGLE POINT

S SHASTA AV N

ROYAL AV

6

WARDS

RIVER RD

GOLD HILL

99

234

4TH AV

OLD STAGE RD

GOLD HILL

BLACKWELL

KOA MEDFORD GOLD HILL

PACIFIC

40

BLACKWELL HILL

UPPER RIVER RD

ROGUE RIVER

HARDY RIFFLE

GOLD RAY RD

KIRTLAND

LOWER TABLE ROCK

TABLE RD

Table Rock

AGATE DESERT

TOU VELLE STATE PARK

ANTELOPE RD

NEWLAND RD

MODOC RD

TOWELLE RD

AGATE RD

NICK YOUNG RD

White City

ALTA VISTA

62

BIGHAM BROWN RD

LAKE OF THE WOODS HWY

140

45

46

GALLS CREEK RD

OLD STAGE RD

5 HWY

35

BEAR CREEK

ANTELOPE RD

E GREGORY RD

KERSHAW RD

7

FOOTS CREEK RD

LEFT FORK FOOTS CREEK RD

MIDDLE FORK FOOTS CREEK RD

ROUGH & RUGGED RD

KANE CREEK RD

OLD STAGE RD

SCENIC AV

CRATER ROCK MUSEUM

Seven Oaks

MILLPOND CAMPGROUND OLD STAGE

CENTRAL POINT

99

W PINE ST

N HAVEN RD

ROGUE VALLEY

FREEMAN RD

UPTON RD

GIBBON RD

336

HAMRICK RD

Midway

TABLE ROCK RD

BIDDLE RD

Four Corners

VILAS RD

COKER BUTTE

MCLAUGHLIN RD

FOOTHILL RD

TAYLOR RD

BEALL LN

93

LAKE

MEDFORD

62

DELTA WATERS RD

SEE 234 MAP

0 1 2 3 4 miles   1 in. = 2.5 mi.

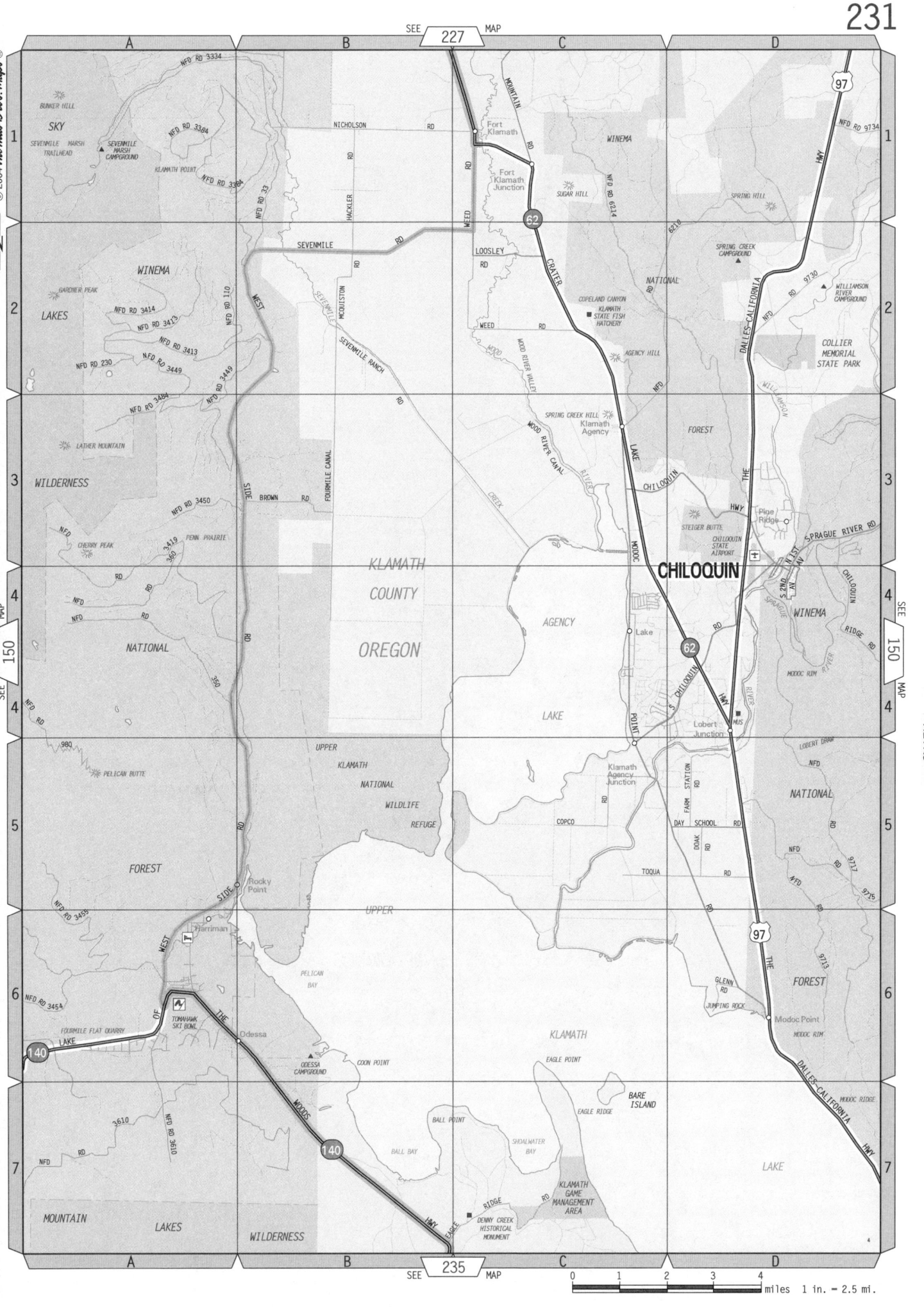

METRO

SEE 227 MAP

SEE MAP 150

SEE 150 MAP

SEE 235 MAP

CHILOQUIN

KLAMATH
COUNTY
OREGON

0 1 2 3 4 miles   1 in. = 2.5 mi.

METRO

SEE MAP 228

A | B | C | D

SISKIYOU

CAVE ROCK
MYERS
HENRY ROCK
CREEK RD

PISTOL RIVER

SUNDOWN MOUNTAIN

PINE POINT

NATIONAL

NFD RD 230

STACK YARDS

Pistol River

NORTH BANK PISTOL RIVER

PISTOL RIVER STATE PARK

RED ROCK

FOREST

THREE TREES CAMP (HISTORICAL)
THREE TREES

SADDLE ROCK
MACK POINT

HOG MOUNTAIN

NFD RD 130
BUZZARD ROOST
NFD RD 1846

MACK ARCH COVE

101
OREGON

RIDGE KNOB

S FORK PISTOL RIVER
Carpenterville
BURNT HILL SUMMIT

PISTOL RD

BOSLEY BUTTE

YELLOW ROCK
ARCH ROCK
WINDY POINT
BLACK ROCK
LEANING ROCK

COAST

CARPENTERVILLE

FITZPATRICK RIDGE

COLEGROVE BUTTE
INDIAN ROCK
CASSIDAY BUTTE

HAZEL CAMP

PACIFIC

SEAL COVE

NATURAL BRIDGES

FRONTAGE

CASHNER BUTTE

RD

THOMAS POINT
SAMUEL H BOARDMAN STATE PARK

HWY

THOMAS HILL

CURRY COUNTY

SMITH HILL

BUSH MOUND

RIDGE

WHALEHEAD
GREENHILL
SHORE PINE RD
MARTIN RANCH RD

WHALEHEAD ISLAND

MORTON BUTTE

ALFRED A LOEB STATE PARK

SUNDOWN RD

SUN RAY
CAPE FERRELO RD

RD

PALMER BUTTE

GARDNER

OREGON

RED MOUND

SAND HILL

BARNACLE ROCK
HOUSE ROCK

OCEAN

DULEY CREEK RD

101
COAST

LONE RANCH BEACH

BLACK POINT

RAINBOW ROCK RD

GARDNER RIDGE

BLACK MOUND

RD

CHETCO RIVER

TWIN ROCKS

WHITE ROCK

HARRIS BUTTE

BROOKINGS STATE AIRPORT

HARRIS BEACH STATE PARK CAMPGROUND

TIDE ROCK

NORTH BANK

SOUTH BANK

CHETCO RIVER

GOAT ISLAND

ARCH ROCK
HARRIS BEACH STATE PARK
FOUNTAIN ROCK

HWY

HARRIS BEACH

EASY ST AZALEA PK
CHETCO AV

Harbor

BROOKINGS

DIVER ROCK
CHETCO POINT

CHETCO COVE

OREGON COAST

RED POINT

OCEAN VIEW

HWY

TWIN COUSINS

DR
WINCHUCK RIVER
NFD RD 1101

CAMEL ROCK

CURRY CO
DEL NORTE CO
OCEAN VIEW

CALIFORNIA

CALIFORNIA COASTAL NATIONAL MONUMENT

REDWOOD HWY

D5

GILBERT CREEK

DR

SEE MAP 148

SEE MAP 148

A | B | C | D

0 1 2 3 4 miles   1 in. = 2.5 mi.

A B C D

METRO

SEE 148 MAP

SEE 149 MAP

1

SQUAW MOUNTAIN

67 RD

NFD

4705 RD

NFD

NFD RD 16

SWEDE BASIN

HAYES HILL RD

HAYES HILL

DRAPER VALLEY

INDIAN CREEK RD

DAVIS CREEK RD

DRAPER VALLEY RD

MOUNTAIN

MOONEY

MOONEY MOUNTAIN

CROOKS CREEK RD

MARBLE MOUNTAIN

BULL CREEK RD

EAGLE MOUNTAIN

RD

2

ILLINOIS RIVER

ILLINOIS RIVER RD

POCKETT KNOLL

EIGHT DOLLAR MOUNTAIN

ILLINOIS RIVER RD

Selma

LAKESHORE

DEER CREEK

LAKE SELMAC CAMPGROUND

LAKE SELMAC PARK

LAKE SELMAC

McMULLIN CREEK

DR

THOMPSON CREEK

DRYDEN RD

DRYDEN OVERLOOK

DEER CREEK

ROUNDTOP MOUNTAIN

MURPHY MOUNTAIN

CROOKS CREEK RD

3

SISKIYOU

EIGHT DOLLAR MOUNTAIN

4201 RD

LITTLE ILLINOIS RIVER FALLS

REEVES RD

CREEK RD

KERBY MAINLINE

E. McMULLIN CREEK RD

McMULLIN CREEK RD

FOREST CREEK RD

WHITE CREEK RD

E. WHITE CREEK

JOSEPHINE COUNTY

KERBY PEAK

LITTLE GRAYBACK PEAK

BLM RD 39-6-9

RD 37-6-36

BLM

TENNESSEE MOUNTAIN

FREE AND EASY PASS

TENNESSEE PASS

FINCH RD

Kerby

JOSEPHINE COUNTY KERBYVILLE MUSEUM

ILLINOIS VALLEY GOLF CLUB

39-7-24

BLM RD 39-7-16

HOLCOMB PEAK

4

NATIONAL

RD

WOODCOCK MOUNTAIN

RIVER

LAUREL ST

OLD STAGE RD

CAVE JUNCTION

ILLINOIS VALLEY PARK RD

BRIDGEVIEW VINEYARD AND WINERY

CAVES

Oregon 46

WHITE SCHOOL HOUSE

GARNER RD

SISKIYOU VINEYARDS

ROBINSON RD

HOLLAND

HWY

CREEK

BEAR

BLM RD

LITTLE GRAYBACK

NFD 4609

LP

LP

SQUAW MOUNTAIN

LOST CANYON

GRAYBACK RD

SEE 149 MAP

5

FOREST

ILLINOIS RIVER STATE PARK

WEST SIDE RD

PILLER PL

MYRNA LN

CASCADE DR

FERNWOOD DR

KRAUSS RD

Illinois Valley

BUCK CANYON RD

AIRPORT DR

HWY

MARTIN RD

HOLLAND

RIVER

PINECONE DR

POWER LINE EASEMENT RD

Bridgeview

BRIDGEVIEW-TAKILMA

DICK GEORGE RD

HOLLAND

PULLEN LN

KIRKHAM LN

JACKADEL LN

SUCKER

ALTHOUSE

LP

Holland

FORIS VINEYARD WINERY

TARTAR GULCH RD

ALTHOUSE CREEK

FRENCH

MOUNTAIN

SUCKER CREEK RD

NFD RD

OREGON

OREGON CAVES HWY

NFD 4613

RD

SISKIYOU

OREGON CAVES NATIONAL MONUMENT

6

LONE MOUNTAIN RD

REDWOOD HWY

NFD RD 11

OBRIEN

WALDO

OBrien

GENE BROWN RD

ROCKYDALE RD

ILLINOIS RIVER

EAST FORK

HAPPY CAMP RD

HAPPY

Takilma

HORSE MOUNTAIN

NUMBER EIGHT PEAK

NATIONAL

NFD RD 80

NFD RD 4612

NFD RD 472

7

199

SISKIYOU NATIONAL FOREST

NFD RD 4803

NFD RD 9938

BRIDGEVIEW-TAKILMA RD

PAGE CREEK RD

LUCKY 4808 RD

CAMP

NFD RD 15

NFD RD 85

NFD RD 17

MESTON MOUNTAIN

BOLAN LAKE RD

BOLAN LAKE CAMPGROUND

EAST FORK RIDGE

NFD RD 4703

NFD RD 41

NFD RD 98

FOREST

TANNEN MOUNTAIN

Elk Valley

JOSEPHINE CO. DEL NORTE CO.

ILLINOIS VALLEY

OREGON CALIFORNIA

DEL NORTE CO. SISKIYOU CO.

DEL NORTE COUNTY

JOSEPHINE CO. SISKIYOU CO.

SISKIYOU COUNTY

CALIFORNIA

A B C D

0 1 2 3 4 miles 1 in. = 2.5 mi.

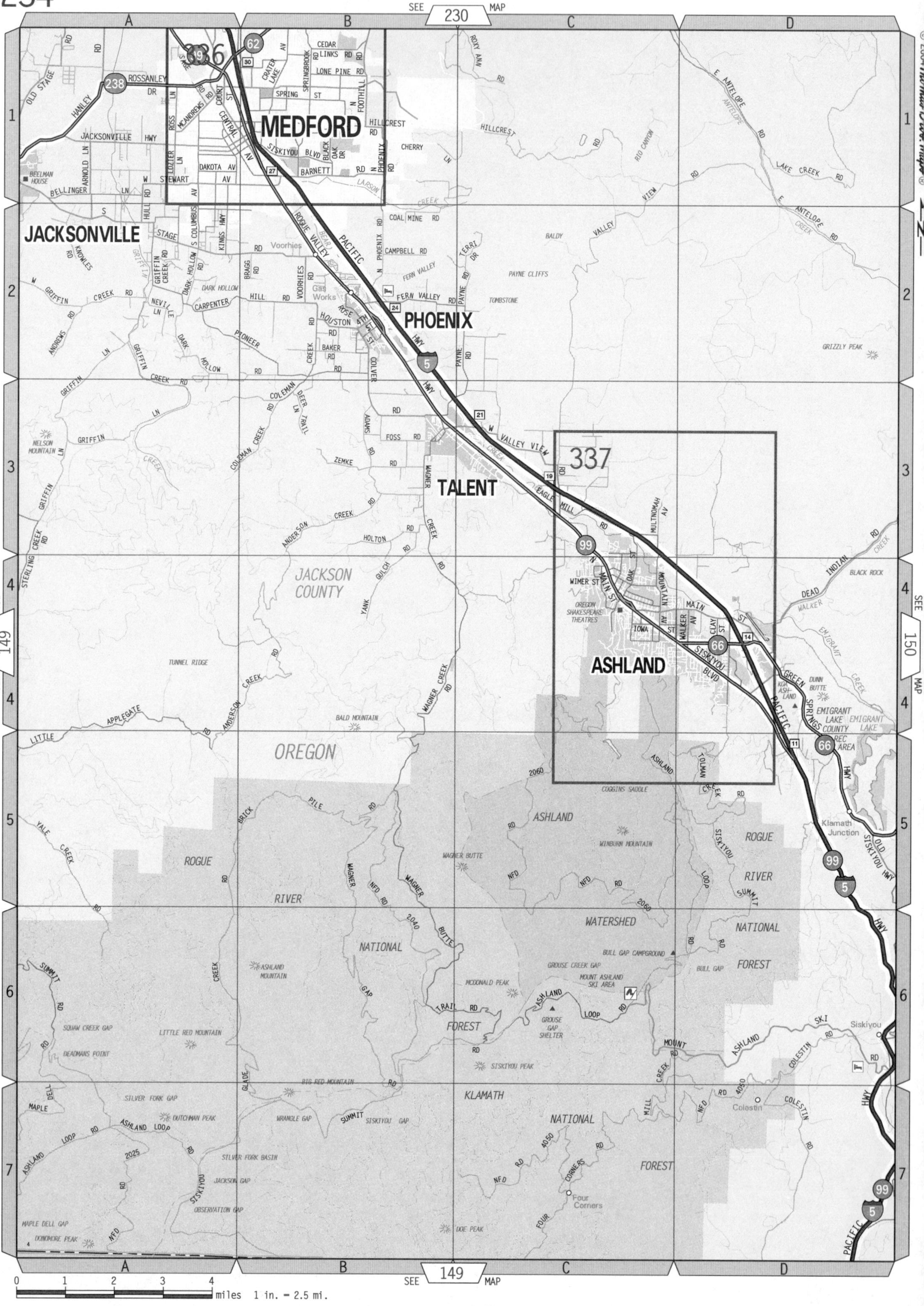

SEE 230 MAP
SEE 149 MAP
SEE 150 MAP
SEE 149 MAP
METRO
A
B
C
D
1
2
3
4
5
6
7
336
337
MEDFORD
JACKSONVILLE
PHOENIX
TALENT
ASHLAND
JACKSON COUNTY
OREGON
ROGUE RIVER NATIONAL FOREST
ROGUE RIVER NATIONAL FOREST
ASHLAND WATERSHED
KLAMATH NATIONAL FOREST
5
62
238
99
66
30
27
24
21
19
14
11
2060
2040
2025
4050
ROSSANLEY DR
OLD STAGE RD
HANLEY RD
JACKSONVILLE HWY
ARNOLD LN
BEELMAN HOUSE
BELLINGER LN
STEWART AV
HULL RD
ROSS LN
LOZIER LN
MCANDREWS RD
CENTRAL AV
COURT ST
DAKOTA AV
CEDAR LINKS RD
LONE PINE RD
CRATER LAKE AV
SPRINGBROOK RD
SPRING ST
FOOTHILL RD
HILLCREST RD
SISKIYOU BLVD
BLACK OAK DR
BARNETT RD
N PHOENIX RD
CHERRY LN
LARSON CREEK
ROXY ANN RD
RIO CANYON RD
E ANTELOPE RD
ANTELOPE CREEK
LAKE CREEK RD
VALLEY VIEW RD
COAL MINE RD
S STAGE RD
S COLUMBUS AV
KINGS HWY
KNOWLES RD
GRIFFIN CREEK RD
DARK HOLLOW RD
BRAGG RD
VOORHIES RD
Voorhies
ROGUE VALLEY
PACIFIC HWY
BEAR CREEK
CAMPBELL RD
TERRI DR
BALDY
PAYNE CLIFFS
TOMBSTONE
FERN VALLEY RD
PAYNE RD
W GRIFFIN CREEK RD
NEVILLE LN
CARPENTER HILL RD
Gas Works
HOUSTON RD
ROSE ST
4TH ST
BAKER RD
PIONEER RD
CREEK RD
COLVER RD
GRIZZLY PEAK
GRIFFIN LN
COLEMAN CREEK RD
DEER TRAIL LN
ADAMS RD
FOSS RD
NELSON MOUNTAIN
ZEMKE RD
W VALLEY VIEW RD
WAGNER CREEK RD
EAGLE MILL RD
ANDERSON CREEK RD
HOLTON RD
GULCH RD
MULTNOMAH AV
STERLING CREEK RD
YANK GULCH
WIMER ST
N MAIN ST
OAK ST
MOUNTAIN AV
OREGON SHAKESPEARE THEATRES
IOWA ST
WALKER AV
CLAY ST
E MAIN ST
SISKIYOU BLVD
INDIAN CREEK RD
BLACK ROCK
DEAD INDIAN
WALKER CREEK
EMIGRANT CREEK
DUNN BUTTE
KOA ASHLAND
GREEN SPRINGS HWY
EMIGRANT LAKE COUNTY REC AREA
EMIGRANT LAKE
TUNNEL RIDGE
BALD MOUNTAIN
LITTLE APPLEGATE RD
ASHLAND CREEK
TOLMAN CREEK
COGGINS SADDLE
Klamath Junction
OLD SISKIYOU HWY
BRICK PILE RD
YALE CREEK RD
WAGNER BUTTE
WINBURN MOUNTAIN
NFD RD
WAGNER GAP RD
WAGNER BUTTE RD
SISKIYOU LOOP RD
SUMMIT RD
BULL GAP CAMPGROUND
BULL GAP
GROUSE CREEK GAP
MOUNT ASHLAND SKI AREA
MCDONALD PEAK
ASHLAND MOUNTAIN
SQUAW CREEK GAP
LITTLE RED MOUNTAIN
DEADMANS POINT
ASHLAND LOOP RD
TRAIL RD
GROUSE GAP SHELTER
SISKIYOU PEAK
MOUNT ASHLAND SKI RD
Siskiyou
COLESTIN RD
Colestin
BIG RED MOUNTAIN
GLADE CREEK
MAPLE DELL
SILVER FORK GAP
DUTCHMAN PEAK
WRANGLE GAP
SUMMIT
SISKIYOU GAP
MILL CREEK
SILVER FORK BASIN
JACKSON GAP
OBSERVATION GAP
FOUR CORNERS RD
Four Corners
MAPLE DELL GAP
DONOMORE PEAK
DOE PEAK
0
1
2
3
4
miles 1 in. = 2.5 mi.

METRO

A | B | C | D

1

Spence Mountain
Doak Mountain
KLAMATH GAME MANAGEMENT AREA
WOCUS
LAKE
UPPER
KLAMATH
SQUAW POINT
ALGOMA INCLINE
PLUM VALLEY
HERLIHY CANYON
NAYLOX MOUNTAIN
WHITELINE
WHITELINE RESERVOIR
SWAN LAKE
ANTELOPE VALLEY
TWOMILE RIDGE
TWOMILE VALLEY
EDGEWOOD LN
ALGOMA RD
ALGOMA
97
THE SHADY PINE RD
SIMPSON CANYON
PLUM VALLEY
FORT
OLD
RD
HOLCOMB SPRING RD
COLEMAN RD
WHITELINE RD

140
ASPEN
LANE RD

2

BAY
LAKE
OF
THE
WOODS
SKILLET HANDLE
BUCK ISLAND
PAYNE CANYON
BENNETT POINT
GOVERNMENT HILL
COVE POINT
UPPER KLAMATH NATIONAL WILDLIFE REFUGE
SHADY PINE
BALD HILL
PLUM HILLS
KLAMATH COUNTY OREGON
DALLES-CALIFORNIA WOODS HWY
SWAN LAKE RD
ROUND LAKE RD
BEAR WALLOW

3

ROUND LAKE HILL
PORTER BUTTE
LONG
LAKE
LONG LAKE VALLEY
LAKESHORE DR
140
WOCUS
PELICAN CITY
97
KLAMATH FALLS-MALIN
OLD FORT KLAMATH
338
339

KLAMATH FALLS

4

SEE 150 MAP
BUCK
LAKE RD
BALSAM DR
BALSAM
INDIAN SPRING RIDGE
ROUND LAKE
BUCK LAKE RD
HWY
ORINDALE RD
RD
DR
140
97
S KLAMATH FALLS HWY
BIS 97
39
39
ALTAMONT
WASHBURN WY
ALTAMONT DR
SIMMERS LN
HARLAN RD
MADISON ST
PATTERSON
KLAMATH
140 FALLS-LAKEVIEW HWY
140
39

5

GREEN
CLOVER
CREEK
RD
66
RIVER
SPRINGS
KERN SWAMP RD
MILLER ISLAND RD
WEST KLAMATH
JOE
WRIGHT RD
MIDLAND
MIDLAND HWY
DELFATTI LN
TINGLEY
WASHBURN WY
MILLER HILL
SPRING LAKE
KLAMATH FALLS INTERNATIONAL AIRPORT
SPRING LAKE RD
LOMBARDY LN
GEM
HOMEDALE RD
HOMEDALE
AIRWAY DR
HENLEY RD
HENLEY
SHORT RD
REEDER RD
CRYSTAL SPRINGS RD
HILL RD
KLAMATH

6

CHASE MOUNTAIN
BEAR
VALLEY
NATIONAL
KENO RD
KENO
DALLES CALIFORNIA
KLAMATH
MIDLAND
OLD MIDLAND RD
BIG HOT SPRING
CROSS
GRAY RIDGE
JORY CANYON
MANN RD
FALCON HEIGHTS
SPRING LAKE
SPRING LAKE VALLEY
OCONNOR RD
HOMEDALE RD
SPRING LAKE
MANNING RIDGE
FALLS-MALIN
MATNEY
MATNEY WY
39
DEHLINGER
DEHLINGER LN
LOST
HILL
CHEYNE RD

7

HAMAKER MOUNTAIN
WILDLIFE
REFUGE
BEAR VALLEY RD
WORDEN RD
GORR ISLAND
WILD HORSE BUTTE
97
WORDEN
THE
TOWNSHIP RD
TULANA FARMS
CAPTAIN JACK
KLAMATH HILLS
LOWER KLAMATH LAKE
RD
LOWER KLAMATH NATIONAL WILDLIFE REFUGE
HOSLEY
HWY
CHIN RD
BUESING
RIVER
7

A | B | C | D

0 1 2 3 4 miles   1 in. = 2.5 mi.

METRO

SEE 112 MAP
SEE 112 MAP
SEE 239 MAP

A B C D

1
2
3
4
5
6
7

RAMONA PARK CAMPGROUND
8410
WENATCHEE
Hollywood Beach
SLIDE RIDGE
Shrine Beach
SLIDE PEAK
NATIONAL
FIRST CREEK RD
NFD RD
LAKESHORE
LOWER JOE RD
JOE CREEK
GRAVE RD
UPPER JOE CREEK
IVAN MORSE RD
WAPATO LAKE
ROSES LAKE
GREEN
DRY LAKE
WASHINGTON ST
GREEN AV
MANSON BLVD
WILLOW POINT
WAPATO LAKE RD
WAPATO
Manson
WAPATO POINT
CHELAN-STEHEKIN FERRY
150 WY
NORTHSHORE RD
WINESAP AV
COOLEY
BOYD RD
SWANSON GULCH
COOPER MOUNTAIN
NFD RD 8020
ECHO VALLEY SKI AREA
WENATCHEE NATIONAL FOREST
PURTEMAN GULCH
UNION VALLEY LOOP RD
UNION VALLEY
ROGERS AND HOBSON LOOP
UNION VALLEY LOOP RD
CHELAN COUNTY
CHELAN CO
ANTOINE CREEK
HIGHLAND BENCH
BROMFIELD CANYON
BIGELOW CANYON
APPLE ACRES
HOWARD FLAT RD
CHELAN MUNICIPAL AIRPORT
DEER MOUNTAIN
97
CHELAN
150
FOREST MOUNTAIN
WASHINGTON
NATIONAL FOREST
NFD RD 8500
COULEE
LAKESHORE RD
BEAR MOUNTAIN
NEAR BEAR MOUNTAIN
MOWRY RD
LAKE CHELAN
MINNEAPOLIS BEACH
971
SPADERS BAY
GIBSON ST
WOODIN AV
Lakeside
GORGE
150
ALT 97
MILLWORTH RD
97
McNEIL CANYON RD
Beebe
DOUGLAS CO
971
NAVARRE COULEE
KNAPP COULEE
DOWNEY GULCH RD
8550
ALT 97
STAYMAN RD
CHELAN BUTTE RD
CHELAN BUTTE
DOWNEY GULCH
HOMESTEAD CANYON
CHELAN BUTTE
CHELAN BUTTE
DAYBREAK CANYON
CHELAN STATE FISH HATCHERY
Chelan Falls
WASHINGTON AV
GREENS CANYON
FARNHAM CANYON
JACKSON CANYON
HIGH RIM RD
ROCKY
CHELAN HILL
OLMSTEAD RD NW
8410
5300
NFD RD
GOMAN PEAK
OKLAHOMA GULCH
PALMETO CANYON
SNETOBACK CANYON
BYRD CANYON
FISHER CANYON
CHELAN CO
DOUGLAS CO
COLUMBIA RIVER
BIG BENCH
97
10
NW
RIVERS CANYON
McKINSTRY CANYON
BARBER RD NW
8 RD NW
7 3/4 RD NW
7 1/2 RD NW
BRAYS NW
BRAYS
HIGGINS LOOP RD
BROWNS CANYON
BROWNS
CANYON RD
DOUGLAS COUNTY
LAMOINE
8 1/2 RD NW
7 1/2 RD NW
7 RD NW
JOHN LONG RD
9 RD
LUDEMAN
GIBSON
PIERCE
7 RD NW
RIBBON MESA
97
EARTHQUAKE POINT
CRUM CANYON
DICK MESA
HAAN CANYON
PORTER RD
NELS NELSON RD NW
PORTER
HARDIN
JONES RD
5 RD NW
ROCK
SLUSSER RD
CARLOCK
ENTIAT
ENTIAT RIVER
SAUNDERS CANYON
ENTIAT RIVER
McELROY CANYON
MOODY CANYON
3 RD NW
U 1/2 RD NW
2 1/4 RD NW
1 1/2 RD NW
Orondo
PINE CANYON
CLOSE
NORTH
BARNES RD
WATERVILLE
DOUGLAS COUNTY HISTORICAL MUSEUM
STANDPIPE HILL
GOLL
TOLER
MILLS
KEYSTONE POINT
PETERS POINT
WENATCHEE NATIONAL FOREST
SPENCER CANYON
SPENCER LAKE
ALT 97
97
CORBALEY CANYON
McGLOTHLIN CANYON
2
PLEATZ
BASELINE
2
BALLARD
Douglas

miles 1 in. = 2.5 mi.
0 1 2 3 4

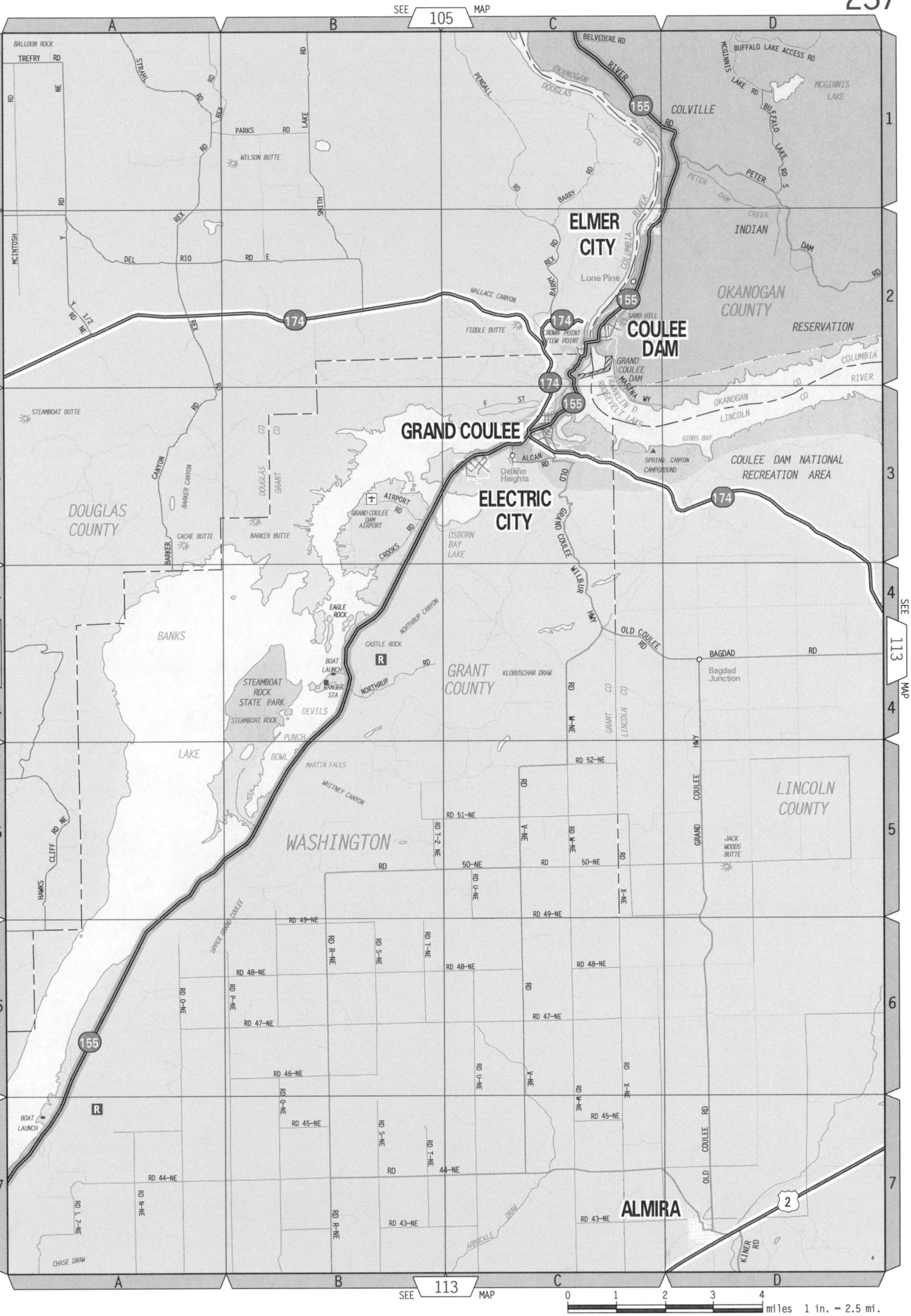

A B C D

ELMER CITY

COULEE DAM

GRAND COULEE

ELECTRIC CITY

ALMIRA

BALLOON ROCK
TREFRY RD
STRAHL RD
RD NE
REX
PARKS RD
WILSON BUTTE
LAKE
MCINTOSH
DEL RIO
Y RD NE
RD E
RD
174
WALLACE CANYON
FIDDLE BUTTE
STEAMBOAT BUTTE
CANYON
BARKER CANYON
DOUGLAS CO
GRANT CO
CACHE BUTTE
BARKER BUTTE
BARKER
CROOKS
AIRPORT RD
GRAND COULEE DAM AIRPORT
DELANO HEIGHTS
ALCAN
OSBORN BAY LAKE

BELVEDERE RD
OKANOGAN RIVER
DOUGLAS
COLUMBIA RIVER
155
COLVILLE
MCGINNIS LAKE
BUFFALO LAKE ACCESS RD
MCGINNIS LAKE
BUFFALO LAKE RD S
PETER DAM CREEK
PETER
RD
INDIAN
OKANOGAN COUNTY
RESERVATION
Lone Pine
BARRY
REX
BARRY
155
SAND HILL
CROWN POINT VIEW POINT
GRAND COULEE DAM
FRANKLIN D ROOSEVELT LAKE
GRAND COULEE MARINA WY
F ST
155
174
OKANOGAN CO
LINCOLN CO
COLUMBIA RIVER
GIBBS BAY
SPRING CANYON CAMPGROUND
COULEE DAM NATIONAL RECREATION AREA
174

DOUGLAS COUNTY

BANKS

WASHINGTON

STEAMBOAT ROCK STATE PARK
STEAMBOAT ROCK
DEVILS
PUNCH BOWL
LAKE
EAGLE ROCK
CASTLE ROCK
BOAT LAUNCH
RANGER STA
R
NORTHRUP
NORTHRUP CANYON
MARTIN FALLS
WHITNEY CANYON
UPPER BANKS COULEE

GRANT COUNTY
KLOBUSCHAR DRAW

OLD GRAND COULEE HWY
WILBUR HWY
OLD COULEE RD
BAGDAD RD
BAGDAD JUNCTION
GRANT CO
LINCOLN CO
GRAND COULEE HWY
JACK WOODS BUTTE
LINCOLN COUNTY

RD 52-NE
RD 51-NE
RD T-2 NE
50-NE
RD U-NE
RD 49-NE
RD 49-NE
RD 48-NE
RD 48-NE
RD 47-NE
RD 47-NE
RD 46-NE
RD 45-NE
RD 44-NE
RD 43-NE
RD 43-NE

RD R-NE
RD S-NE
RD T-NE
RD Q-NE
RD P-NE
RD O-NE
RD N-NE
RD T-NE
RD S-NE
RD R-NE

V-NE
W-NE
X-NE
RD
RD
RD
RD
RD

155
R
BOAT LAUNCH
HAWKS CLIFF RD NE
CHASE DRAW

ALMIRA
2
KLINER RD
ARBUCKLE DRAW

miles 1 in. = 2.5 mi.
0 1 2 3 4

SEE 113 MAP

METRO

METRO

SEE 111 MAP SEE 241 MAP

A | B | C | D

LEAVENWORTH
SKI HILL RD
PINE ST
KOA LEAVENWORTH/WENATCHEE
WENATCHEE RIVER
ICICLE RD
WILSON SHORE
PROWELL ST
E LEAVENWORTH RD
MOUNTAIN HOME RD
PETERS AV
LEAVENWORTH NATIONAL FISH HATCHERY
ICICLE RD
MUNDUN CANYON RD
PESHASTIN
BEACHER HILL RD
SAUNDERS RD
ANDERSON CANYON
ANDERSON CANYON RD
WILLIAMS CANYON
WILLIAMS CANYON RD
JUDGE CANYON RD
7400
BLAG MOUNTAIN

DEAD MAN RD
DRYDEN
NORTH RD
OLLALA
N. DRYDEN RD
STINEHILL RD

BOUNDARY BUTTE
NFD RD 7300
NFD RD 400
NFD RD 510
NFD RD 7202
NFD RD 200
NFD 7200
NFD RD
PENDLETON CANYON
CAMAS CREEK
BRONZER CANYON
SHY MEADOW
TRIPP CANYON
POTSON CANYON
MISSION CREEK
SHERMAN CANYON
YAKSUM CANYON
FAIRVIEW CANYON

OLLALA CANYON
OLLALA CANYON RD
TIBBETS MOUNTAIN
TIBBETTS MOUNTAIN
SPRING CANYON
NFD
WENATCHEE
NATIONAL
FOREST
CHELAN COUNTY
WARNEM CANYON
WARNER CANYON RD
EAGLE ROCK
WARNER CANYON
MAIN SPRINGS CANYON
MAIN MOUNTAIN RD
BURCH MOUNTAIN
NFD RD 7412
NFD RD 7413
NFD RD 5215
SWAKANE
BURCH CANYON

FRWY NAHAHUM CANYON
WILLIS CAREY HISTORICAL MUSEUM
CASHMERE
SUNSET HWY
PIONEER DR
TIGNER
SUNSET DR
EELS RD
HUGHES RD
ZAGER RD
KELLY RD
MONITOR
E MAIN ST
AMERICAN FRUIT RD
CRESTVIEW DR
FIRST ST
SCHOOL ST
SUNNYSLOPE
SLEEPY HOLLOW
EASY ST
LOWER SUNNYSLOPE RD
PETERS ST
FRWY
EUCLID AV
COLUMBIA ST
WENATCHEE RIVER
97
2
285

WENATCHEE
WEST WENATCHEE
WENATCHEE VALLEY JUNIOR COLLEGE
MAPLE ST
SPRINGWATER AV
NINTH ST
FIFTH ST
ORCHARD AV
WESTERN
WASHINGTON ST
CASTLEROCK AV
CHERRY ST
SKYLINE
RED APPLE RD
MILLER ST
OKANOGAN AV
CRAWFORD ST

WENATCHEE
WASHINGTON
TIPTOP
WINDMILL POINT
NATIONAL
CEDAR GROVE CAMPGROUND
97
SHEEP MOUNTAIN
BLEWETT
NFD 200
SCOTTY CREEK CAMPGROUND
NFD 7320 RD
7324
NFD RD
FOREST
RED HILL
BONANZA CAMPGROUND
TRONSEN RIDGE
STUMP CAMPGROUND
PINE CAMPGROUND
MISSION RIDGE
HORSE LAKE MOUNTAIN
SHEEP ROCK
NFD 7100
PENDLETON CANYON
PEAVINE CANYON
OLD BUTTE
ROOSTER COMB
PITCHER CANYON RD
PITCHER CANYON
SQUILCHUCK RD
METHOW ST
WENATCHEE HEIGHTS RD

NFD RD 9715
NFD RD 9714
PARK CAMPGROUND
SWAUK PASS SNO-PARK
SWAUK CAMPGROUND
MOUNTAIN HOME
BLEWETT PASS
TRONSEN CAMPGROUND
NFD RD 9711
NFD RD 9705
NFD RD 116
NFD RD 9716
NFD RD 9712
HANEY MEADOW CAMPGROUND
ALPHINE CAMPGROUND
MEADOW CAMPGROUND
SPRING CAMPGROUND
BEEHIVE MOUNTAIN
BEEHIVE SPRING CAMPGROUND
WHEELER HILL
STEMILT LOOP

SWAUK RIDGE
NFD RD 9718
NFD RD 118
NFD RD 9712
NFD RD 115
NFD RD 35
NFD RD 36
NANEUM RD 3530
NANEUM
MEAGHERSVILLE
KITTITAS
SNOWSHOE RIDGE
NFD RD 125
COUNTY
CHELAN CO
KITTITAS CO
CREEK
MISSION PEAK
WENATCHEE MOUNTAIN
NANEUM POINT
MISSION RIDGE WINTER SPORTS AREA

SEE 239 MAP

0 1 2 3 4 miles 1 in. = 2.5 mi.

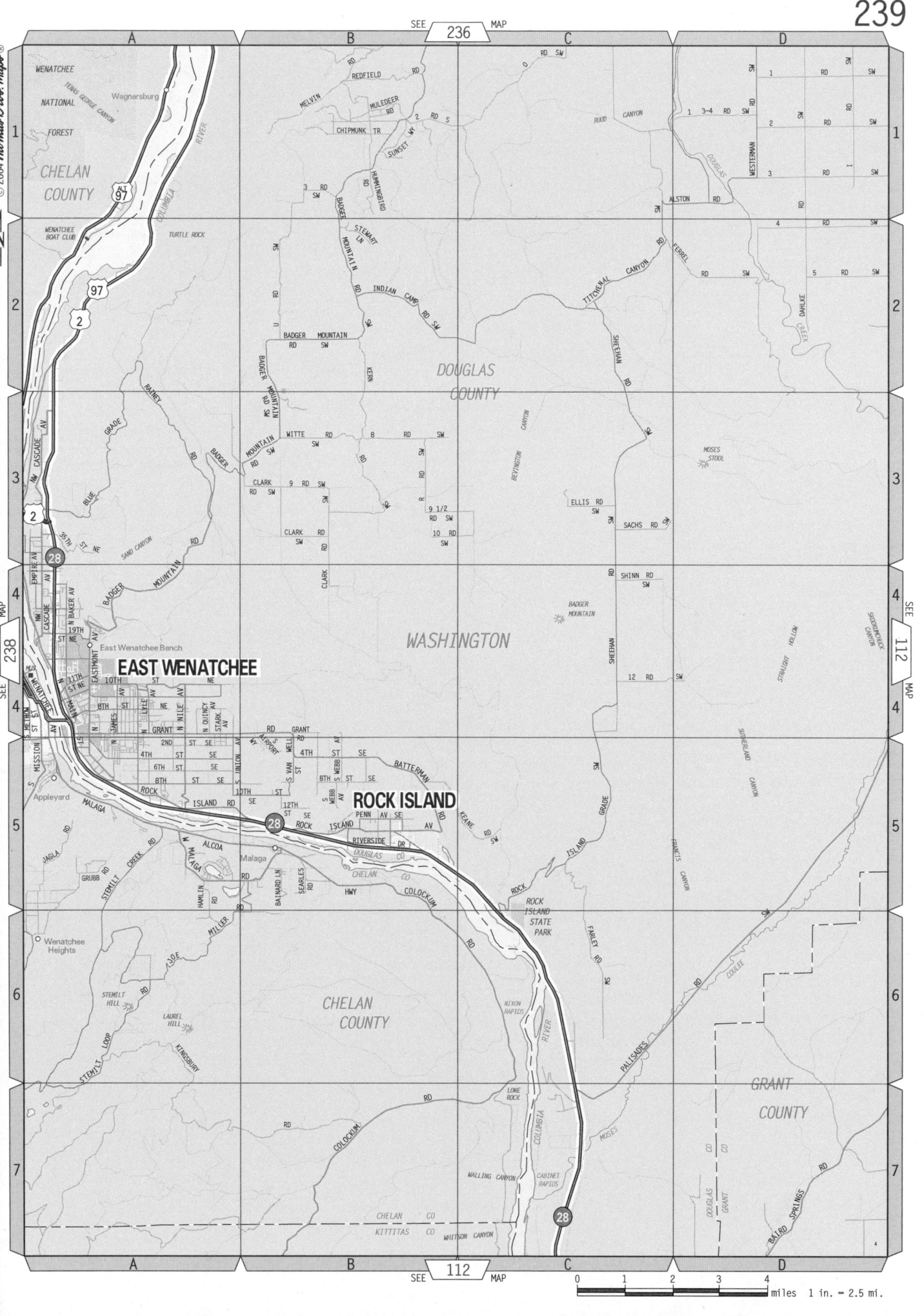

METRO

© 2004 Thomas Bros. Maps ®

| A | B | C | D |

CHELAN COUNTY

WENATCHEE

TEXAS GEORGE CANYON

Wagnersburg

NATIONAL

FOREST

COLUMBIA RIVER

ALT 97

97

2

Wenatchee Boat Club

TURTLE ROCK

WENATCHEE

REDFIELD RD

MELVIN

MULEDEER RD S

CHIPMUNK TR

SUNSET HWY

HUMMINGBIRD RD SW

STEWART LN

BADGER MOUNTAIN RD

INDIAN CAMP RD SW

FLUID CANYON

DOUGLAS

ALSTON RD

STERMAN

RD SW

1 3-4 RD SW

1

2

RD SW

RD SW

RD SW

TITCHENAL CANYON

FERREL RD SW

DAHLKE CREEK

RD SW

DOUGLAS COUNTY

BADGER MOUNTAIN RD SW

RANEY

GRADE RD

BLUE GRADE

BADGER

SAND CANYON

MOUNTAIN RD SW

KERN

WITTE RD

8 RD SW

CLARK 9 RD SW

CLARK RD SW

9 1/2 RD SW

10 RD SW

CLARK SW

SHEEHAN RD

BEVINGTON CANYON

ELLIS RD SW

SACHS RD SW

SHINN RD SW

MOSES STOOL

WASHINGTON

BADGER MOUNTAIN

SHEEHAN

12 RD SW

GRADE

STRAIGHT HOLLOW

SUTHERLAND CANYON

SKADOOWACK CANYON

2

28

EMPIRE AV

N CASCADE AV

35TH ST NE

CASCADE AV

N BAKER AV

BADGER MOUNTAIN

19TH ST NE

EASTMONT AV

EAST WENATCHEE

East Wenatchee Bench

10TH ST NE

11TH ST NE

8TH ST NE

N NILE

N QUINCY AV

STARK AV

GRANT

2ND ST SE

4TH ST SE

6TH ST SE

8TH ST SE

10TH ST

12TH ST

JAMES ST

LYLE ST

S METHOW

MISSION ST

S WENATCHEE

MUR

N JAMES ST

GRANT RD

AIRPORT

WELLS

S VAN WELL

4TH ST SE

8TH ST

WEBB ST

S WEBB

ROCK ISLAND

PENN AV SE

RIVERSIDE DR

BATTERMAN

KEANE RD SW

ROCK ISLAND GRADE

FRANCIS CANYON

S METHOW

ROCK ISLAND RD

28

Appleyard

MALAGA

ROCK ISLAND RD

ALCOA

Malaga

MALAGA RD

BAINARD LN

SEARLES RD

HAMLIN RD

DOUGLAS CO

CHELAN CO

HWY

COLOCKUM RD

ROCK ISLAND STATE PARK

FARLEY RD SW

NIXON RAPIDS

COLUMBIA RIVER

PALISADES RD

COULEE SW

SKADOOWACK CANYON

JAGLA RD

GRUBB

STEMILT CREEK RD

MILLER

30 E

Wenatchee Heights

STEMILT HILL

LAUREL HILL

KINGSBURY

STEMILT LOOP

CHELAN COUNTY

RD

COLOCKUM RD

LONE ROCK

MOSES

WALLING CANYON

CABINET RAPIDS

COLUMBIA RIVER

28

GRANT COUNTY

DOUGLAS CO

GRANT CO

BAIRD SPRINGS RD

CHELAN CO

KITTITAS CO

WHITSON CANYON

| A | B | C | D |

SEE 238 MAP

SEE 112 MAP

0 1 2 3 4 miles   1 in. = 2.5 mi.

METRO

ROSLYN

CLE ELUM

SOUTH
CLE ELUM

SEE 111 MAP
SEE 111 MAP
SEE 119 MAP
SEE 241 MAP

Ronald

ROSLYN
MUSEUM

903

CLE ELUM TELEPHONE MUSEUM

Nelson

78

80

90

AIRPORT RD

MASTERSON RD

970

970

97

Virden

Liberty

WENATCHEE

NATIONAL

FOREST

TEANAWAY

TEANAWAY RD

MASON CREEK RD

CLE ELUM RIDGE

YAKIMA

RIVER

Teanaway

E MASTERSON RD

W BALLARD DR

LEY RD

HARTMAN RD

SWAUK PRAIRIE

LAMBERT RD

HART RD

HIDDEN VALLEY

HIDDEN VALLEY RD

HORSE CANYON

BETTAS RD

LOWER PEOH POINT RD

UPPER PEOH POINT RD

INDIAN JOHN HILL

THORP PRAIRIE

Bristol

LOOKOUT MOUNTAIN

R

R

CLE ELUM POINT

SOUTH CLE
ELUM RIDGE

TANEUM POINT

NORTH FORK TANEUM

CREEK

CREEK

WENATCHEE

TANEUM RIDGE

TANEUM

MOON LIGHT CANYON

MORRISON CANYON

93

Horlick

TANEUM CAMPGROUND

SWAUK

RIVER

Kountze

10

HORLICK RD

BRUKETTA RD

Dudley

DUDLEY RD

DYKMAN RD

HAMMAN RD

NATIONAL

MOLE MOUNTAIN

SOUTH FORK

FROST MOUNTAIN

QUARTZ MOUNTAIN RD

TANEUM RD

LEWIS AND CLARK TRAIL STATE PARK

TANEUM CANYON

TANEUM RD

90

TANEUM RD

EBWY

TAMARACK SPRING CAMPGROUND

WYNNE CANYON

RATTLESNAKE CANYON

WATT CANYON

WATT CANYON

WATT CANYON RD

WINEGAR CANYON

WAGNER CANYON

KITTITAS

COUNTY

PAGE CANYON

ROBINSON CANYON

FOREST

FORK

SHELL

ROCK RD

KLOSS RD

WESKY CANYON

AINSLEY CANYON

COLEMAN CANYON

NORTH RIDGES CANYON

NFD RD 1708

BALD MOUNTAIN

NFD RD

MANASTASH

MANASTASH

CREEK

SOUTH RIDGES CANYON

Cliffdell

1703

NFD RD

1720

721

1701

NFD RD

HOG

WENAS

RANCH RD

CREEK

WASHINGTON

410

NACHES RIVER

COTTONWOOD CAMPGROUND

MOUNT BAKER-SNOQUALMIE NATIONAL FOREST

YAKIMA COUNTY

KITTITAS CO

YAKIMA CO

WENAS RD

0 1 2 3 4 miles   1 in. = 2.5 mi.

SEE 238 MAP

A   B   C   D

© 2004 Thomas Bros. Maps ®

WENATCHEE NATIONAL FOREST

LION ROCK
LION ROCK SPRING CAMPGROUND
TABLE MOUNTAIN

KITTITAS COUNTY

MANEUM RIDGE
JUMPOFF RIDGE RD

LIBERTY RD
NFD RD 35.07
NFD RD 9726
NFD RD 213
NFD RD 9726
NFD RD 114
NFD RD 3506

WENATCHEE
NATIONAL
FOREST

RD 114
NFD RD 107
REECER CREEK RD
NFD RB 111
NFD RD 3521
NFD RD 113
NFD RD 112
NFD RD 115
NFD RD 114
NFD RD 116
NFD RD 3517

NANEUM BASIN

TEANAWAY WILSON STOCK TR.
WILSON CREEK
CURRIER CANYON

WASHINGTON

REECER CREEK RD
GREEN CANYON RD
HABBERMAN RD
UPPER GREEN CANYON RD

SWIG CANYON
LILLARD HILL

CAVE CANYON
CANYON
NANEUM CANYON
SCHNEBLY CANYON
CHARLTON CANYON
COLEMAN CANYON
COLOCKUM CANYON

SMITHSON
PUMP RD
RD
SMITHSON
ROBBINS RD
CHARLTON RD

LOWER GREEN CANYON
DITCH
WILSON CREEK
THOMAS RD
LEWIS LN
THOMAS
NANEUM
BAR 14 RD
PUMP RD
CREEK RD
GAGE RD
SCHNEBLY CANYON RD
COOKE RD
EGLEMAN CREEK
COOKE RD

97

THORP
GOODWIN
THORP
PASSMORE RD
CLARKE RD
CANAL
REECER CREEK RD
KERR RD
ALFORD RD
TIPTON RD
RADER
LESTER RD
COOKE RD
COLOCKUM
BRICK
SCHNEBLY DITCH
MILL

10

CASCADE YAKIMA CREEK
HOWARD RD
MCMANAMY RD

HUNTER RD
KILLMORE RD
ROBINSON CANYON RD
MILLER RD

101

90

97

FAUST RD
DRY CREEK RD
HUNGRY JUNCTION
Waldale
BENDER RD
AIRPORT RD
WILLOWDALE
BRICK RD
MILL RD
COLEMAN CREEK
FAIRVIEW
LYONS
GILBERT
GRINROD
VENTURE
BRICK
MILL
LYONS
81
SNODGRASS RD
CARIBOU CREEK
CHRISTENSEN RD
NUMBER
LAKHOMA FOX
YAKIMA FARM LN
PARK

ELLENSBURG
E 14TH AV
W 15TH AV
NICHOLSON PAVILION
CENTRAL WASHINGTON UNIVERSITY
FAIRGROUNDS
Regal
GAME FARM RD
WATSON
VANTAGE
NANEUM
WILSON FIELDS RD

WEAVER RD
ELLENSBURG
106
DOLARWAY
CLYMER MUSEUM
KITTITAS COUNTY HISTORICAL MUSEUM
MOUNTAIN
VIEW AV
KITTITAS HWY
110
KITTITAS
OLMSTEAD PLACE STATE PARK
FRWY
4TH AV
KITTITAS
MAIN ST
HWY
CARIBOU

90
East Kittitas

HANSON RD
COVE
RICHARDS RD
MANASTASH
SUSAN RD
MANASTASH
SOUTH FORK MANASTASH CREEK
BARNES RD
BRONDT RD
DAMMAN RD
RIVER RD
Holmes
NANEUM CREEK
COLEMAN CREEK
CLEMAN RD
CANAL
PUMP

STONE QUARRY CANYON
MCNEIL RD
LONG TOM CANYON
SHUSHUSKIN CANYON
BADGER CANYON
UMPTANUM
DURR RD
BUTTE
YAKIMA RIVER
CANYON
THRALL RD
THRALL RD
CASCADE
BADGER POCKET
DITCH

HANSON RD
KITTITAS CO
YAKIMA CO
WENAS RD
THRALL
Thrall
821
82
97

SEE 240 MAP
SEE 112 MAP
SEE 243 MAP

METRO

0 1 2 3 4 miles 1 in. = 2.5 mi.

A   B   C   D

SEE 112 MAP

A   B   C   D

METRO

© 2004 Thomas Bros. Maps ®

← N —

CANAL W-20

RD 10-NE   RD 10-NE   RD 10-NE   RD 0-NE   RD 0-NE

RD 9-NW

1

DRUMHELLER

NEPPEL   RD   17

RD 8-NW

LAKE VISTA DR   8-10-NE   RD

STONECREST RD

MCCONIHE

MCCONIHE

STRATFORD

GRANT COUNTY INTERNATIONAL AIRPORT

CRAB   CREEK

RD 1-NE

RD 9-NE

RD H-NE

RD 8-NE   RD 8-NE

EAST

2

7-NW

8-NW   RD

A-NW   RD   A-NE   RD

WESTSHORE DR

CHANUTE ST   PATTON BLVD

22ND AV

RANDOLPH

RANDOLPH   ST

TYNDALL   RD

7-NE

RD   I-NE

GRANT COUNTY

RD 5-NE

ROCKY COULEE

RD 6-NE

RD H-NE

RD 0-NE

5-NW   RD   5-NE

4-NW   RD   4-NE   D-NE   E-NE   F-NE   4-NE

DICK   DR

MAPLE   DR

PARK   KINDER

PARK ORCHARD DR

RD 4-NE

RD H-NE

MOSES LAKE MUNICIPAL AIRPORT

3

DIVISION

3-NW   RD   3-NE   D-NE   E-NE   3-NE

HIAWATHA   MAE

VALLEY

2-NW   2-NE

WESTSHORE DR

OTTMAR

CASCADE VALLEY

LEWIS

VALLEY   RD

GRANT COUNTY FAIRGROUNDS

VALLEY   CENTRAL DR

ATWAY DR

KINDER

AV

MOSES LAKE

17

171

3-NE   RD

RD   L-NE

NELSON   RD

RD 0-NE

MOSES   LAKE

HANSEN DR   MOSES LAKE COMMUNITY PARK

CREST ISLAND

MARSHA DR   BROADWAY

PELICAN HORN   MARSH ISLAND

DIVISION ST

HILL

PIONEER WY

E   AV

N   FRONTAGE   90   N   FRONTAGE   RD   SAGE   RD   175   90   FRWY

FRONTAGE   RD   169   FRONTAGE   RD   179   RD 1-NE   182

SEE 112 MAP
SEE 113 MAP

4

S DIVISION   A-SE   C-SE   RD

1-SW   RD

W PENINSULA   GOAT ISLAND

POTATO HILL   RD   BASELINE   RD E

BASELINE .5   RD   SE

RD K-SE

N-SE   3S-0   RD

17

GAILEYS ISLAND

WASHINGTON

RD 3-SE

WINCHESTER   WASTEWAY

SAND   DUNES

RD   RD 4-SE   M-SE

5

THE   POTHOLES   RESERVOIR

RD K-SE

3S-0

L-SE   RD 5-SE

RD 5-SE

RD 6-SE

LIND COULEE

OSULLIVAN   DAM   RD

6

POTHOLES STATE PARK

262

CORRAL LAKE

COLUMBIA

SODA LAKE

7-SW   RD   OSULLIVAN   DAM   RD   SE

NATIONAL

WILDLIFE

A-SE   FRENCHMAN HILLS   10 5 SE   BIG GOOSE LAKE   REFUGE

7

11-SW   RD   B-SE   262   KULM   H   MCMANNON   GRANT   CO   CRAB   ADAMS COUNTY

13-SW   12-SE   13-SE   PHILLIPS   MAY RD   COLUMBIA NATIONAL WILDLIFE REFUGE   MORGAN RD

SEE 120 MAP

0 1 2 3 4   miles 1 in. = 2.5 mi.

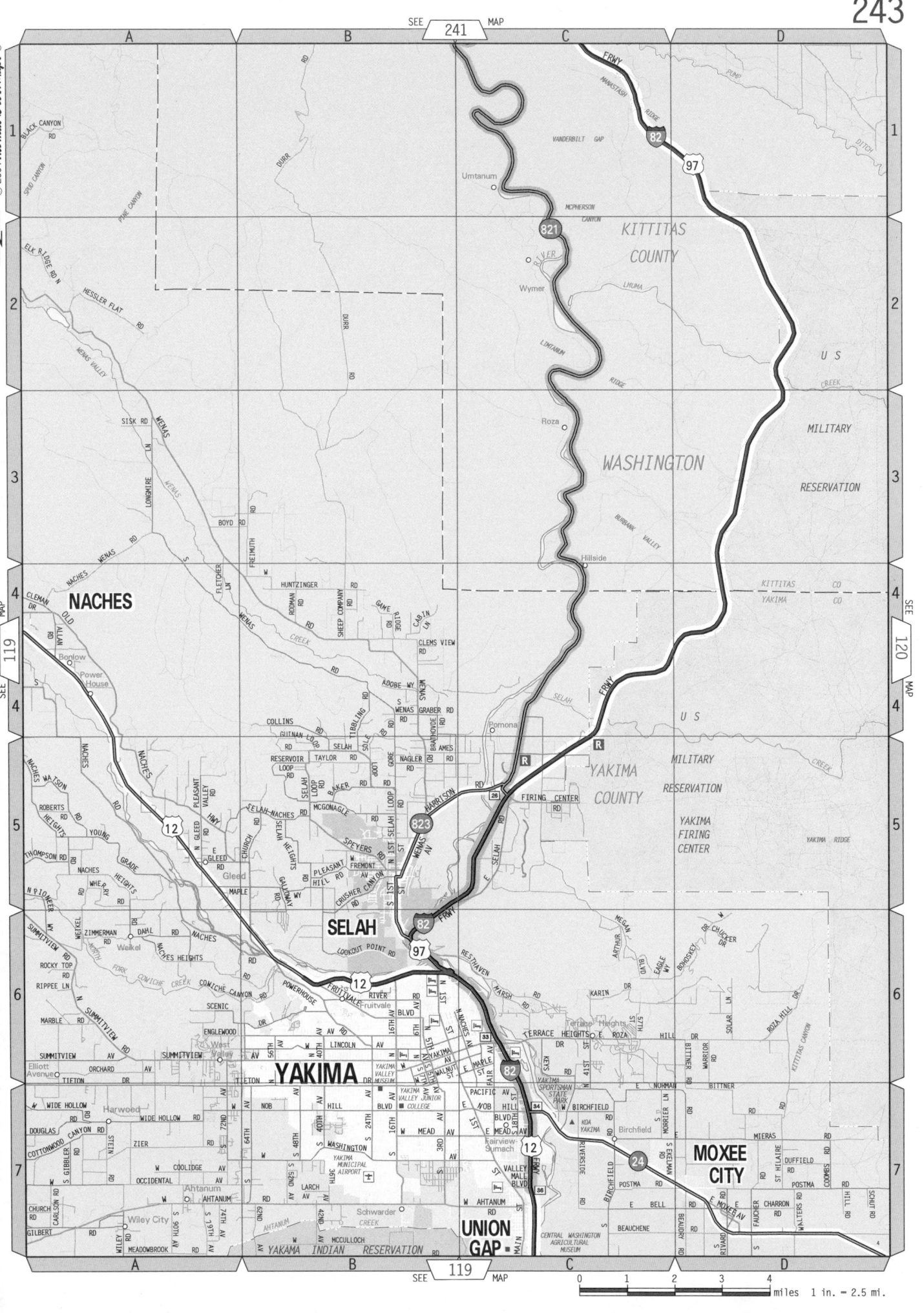

METRO

NACHES

KITTITAS COUNTY

WASHINGTON

YAKIMA COUNTY

US MILITARY RESERVATION

US MILITARY RESERVATION

YAKIMA FIRING CENTER

SELAH

YAKIMA

MOXEE CITY

UNION GAP

YAKAMA INDIAN RESERVATION

0 1 2 3 4 miles   1 in. = 2.5 mi.

A   B   C   D

HIDDEN VALLEY RD
SCHWEITZER BASIN RD
95
2
E BRONX RD
N KOOTENAI RD
W KOOTENAI RD
W SHINGLE MILL RD
E SHINGLE MILL RD
SHINGLE MILL
HICKEY RD
COLBURN CULVER RD
LOWER PACK RIVER RD
PACK RIVER RD
TROUT CREEK
TROUT PEAK
TRESTLE PEAK

1

KANIKSU

GRIEF MOUNTAIN

KOOTENAI
1ST AV
WHISKEY JACK RD
200
SUNNYSIDE RD
KOOTENAI CTO
PONDER POINT
KOOTENAI BAY
KOOTENAI POINT
ODEN BAY
SUNNYSIDE MOUNTAIN
SUNNYSIDE RD
TRESTLE CREEK
TRESTLE CREEK
NATIONAL
COCHRAN DRAW
ROUND TOP MOUNTAIN
NFD 489
AUXOR BASIN

PONDERAY
MOUNTAIN VIEW DR
MOUNTAIN VIEW DR
BALDY MOUNTAIN RD
BOYER AV
DIVISION ST
FISHERMAN ISLAND
HAWKINS POINT
PACK RIVER BOAT RAMP
TRESTLE CREEK BOAT RAMP

2

SANDPOINT
LARCH ST
PINE ST
DIVISION ST
PRINGLE BOAT LAUNCH
HOPE
DAVID THOMPSON HISTORICAL MONUMENT
FOREST
COUGAR PEAK

ONTARIO ST
2
CONTEST POINT
SOURDOUGH POINT
BOTTLE BAY RD
YUANCY LAKE
BOTTLE BAY POINT
ANDERSON POINT
SUNRISE BAY
WARREN ISLAND
EAST HOPE

DOVER
PEND OREILLE RIVER
ROCKY POINT
LAKESHORE DR
SPADES
MURPHY BAY
OSPREY NESTS VIEWPOINT
BOTTLE BAY
GOLD HILL
GOLD HILL CTR
BOTTLE BAY
BOTTLE BAY RD
GLENGARY BAY RD
MARTIN BAY
COTTAGE ISLAND
PEARL ISLAND
ELLISPORT BAY
RED FIR RD
HOPE PENINSULA
N SPRING CREEK RD

3

SPRING POINT CAMPGROUND
SANDPOINT FISH HATCHERY
LIGNITE
GOLD MOUNTAIN
GOLD MOUNTAIN
GLENGARY BAY RD
GLENGARY BAY
GOLD MOUNTAIN RD
CAMP BAY RD
PICARD POINT
ELLIOT BAY
MEMALOOSE ISLAND
OWENS BAY
SHEEPHERDER POINT
HOWE MOUNTAIN

GUN CLUB RD
Sagle
GARFIELD BAY ACCESS AREA
GARFIELD BAY CTO
GREEN BAY RD
CAMP BAY
PETROGLYPHS
200

4

95
REED HILL
TALACHE
SHEPHERD LAKE ACCESS AREA
ALGOMA SPUR
S SAGLE RD
GARFIELD BAY
GARFIELD BAY
BONNER COUNTY
GROUSE MOUNTAIN
GREEN BAY
MINERAL POINT
LONG POINT
LAKE PEND
DERR ISLAND

HEATH LAKE RD
DUFORT RD
MIRROR LAKE ACCESS
GROUSE MOUNTAIN POINT
PONDEROSA RD
NFD RD 2233

4

BEEKS RD
COCOLALLA LAKE ACCESS AREA
WESTMOND RD
Talache
BIMETALLIC RIDGE
OREILLE
JAKES MOUNTAIN
JOHNSON POINT VISTA
NFD RD 278

5

Westmond
KANIKSU
BUTLER MOUNTAIN
BLACKTAIL MOUNTAIN
KILROY BAY
INDIAN POINT
WINDY POINT
DEADMAN POINT
GREEN MONARCH MOUNTAIN
IDAHO
GREEN MONARCH RIDGE
JOHNSON PEAK
BUTLER CREEK RD
PINE COVE
SCHAFER PEAK
NFD RD

UPPER COCOLALLA CREEK
MAIDEN ROCK
ECHO ROCK
GRANITE POINT
SHERMAN RIDGE
WHITE QUARTZ RIDGE
RD 278

6

COCOLALLA CREEK
LITTLE BLACKTAIL MOUNTAIN
NATIONAL
NFD RD
FLEMING POINT
TOMS RIDGE
RD
NFD 1066
MINERVA PEAK
MINERVA RIDGE
NFD 1088
PEEP A DAY RIDGE
JOHNSON SADDLE
NFD RD 332

LITTLE BLACKTAIL MOUNTAIN
KANIKSU
WHISKEY ROCK BAY
WHISKEY ROCK
NFD RD
NATIONAL
CO RD
SHOSHONE
COEUR D'ALENE

7

THREE SISTERS PEAKS
FOREST
SUNSET RD
NFD RD 22
BARTON HUMP
PACKSADDLE MOUNTAIN
FOREST
NFD 1060 RD
NFD RD 332
BONNER
SHOSHONE
COEUR
D'ALENE RIVER
D'ALENE
NATIONAL
NFD RD 306
LARCH MOUNTAIN
FOREST
POWER MOUNTAIN
SHOSHONE COUNTY

METRO

0 1 2 3 4 miles   1 in. = 2.5 mi.

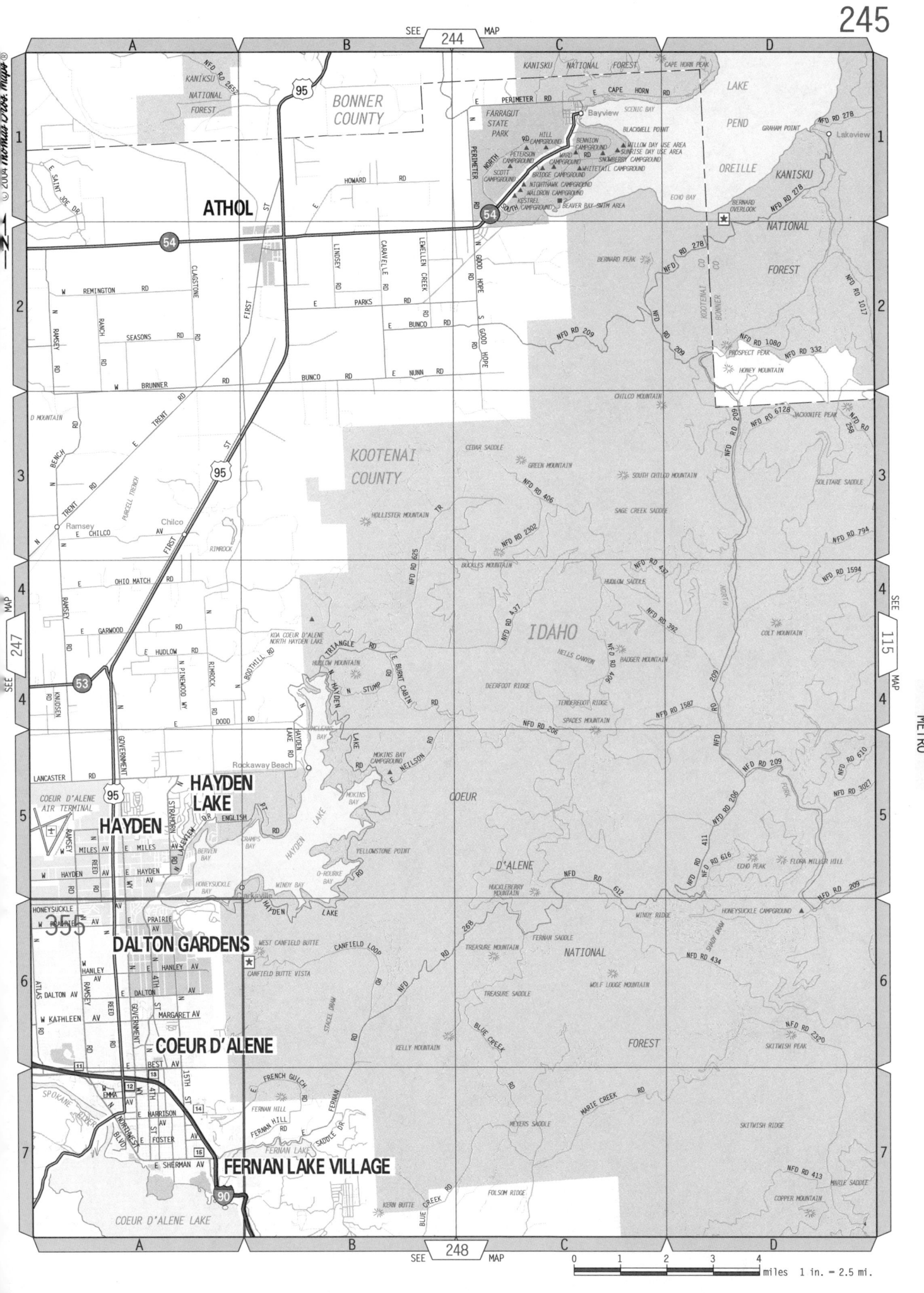

METRO

miles 1 in. = 2.5 mi.

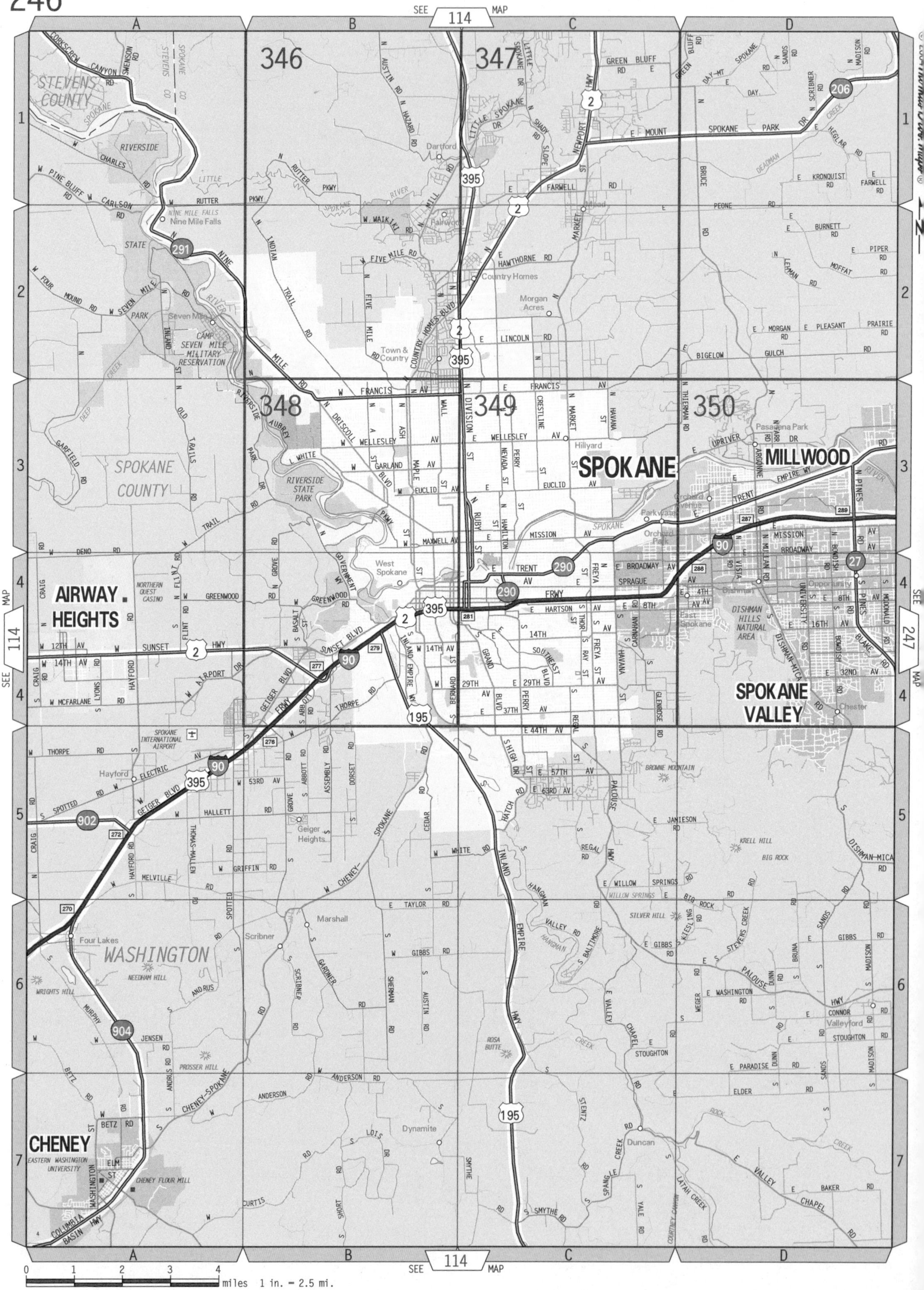

246

SEE 114 MAP

346 347

© Thomas Bros. Maps ®

N

STEVENS COUNTY
RIVERSIDE
Nine Mile Falls

291

348 349 350

SPOKANE COUNTY

SPOKANE MILLWOOD

Riverside State Park

AIRWAY HEIGHTS

West Spokane

90 395 2

Spokane International Airport

Hayford

902 272

270

904

Four Lakes

WASHINGTON

CHENEY
Eastern Washington University
Cheney Flour Mill

195

METRO

SEE 114 MAP

SEE 247 MAP

SEE 114 MAP

0 1 2 3 4 miles 1 in. = 2.5 mi.

SPOKANE VALLEY

DISHMAN HILLS NATURAL AREA

206

27

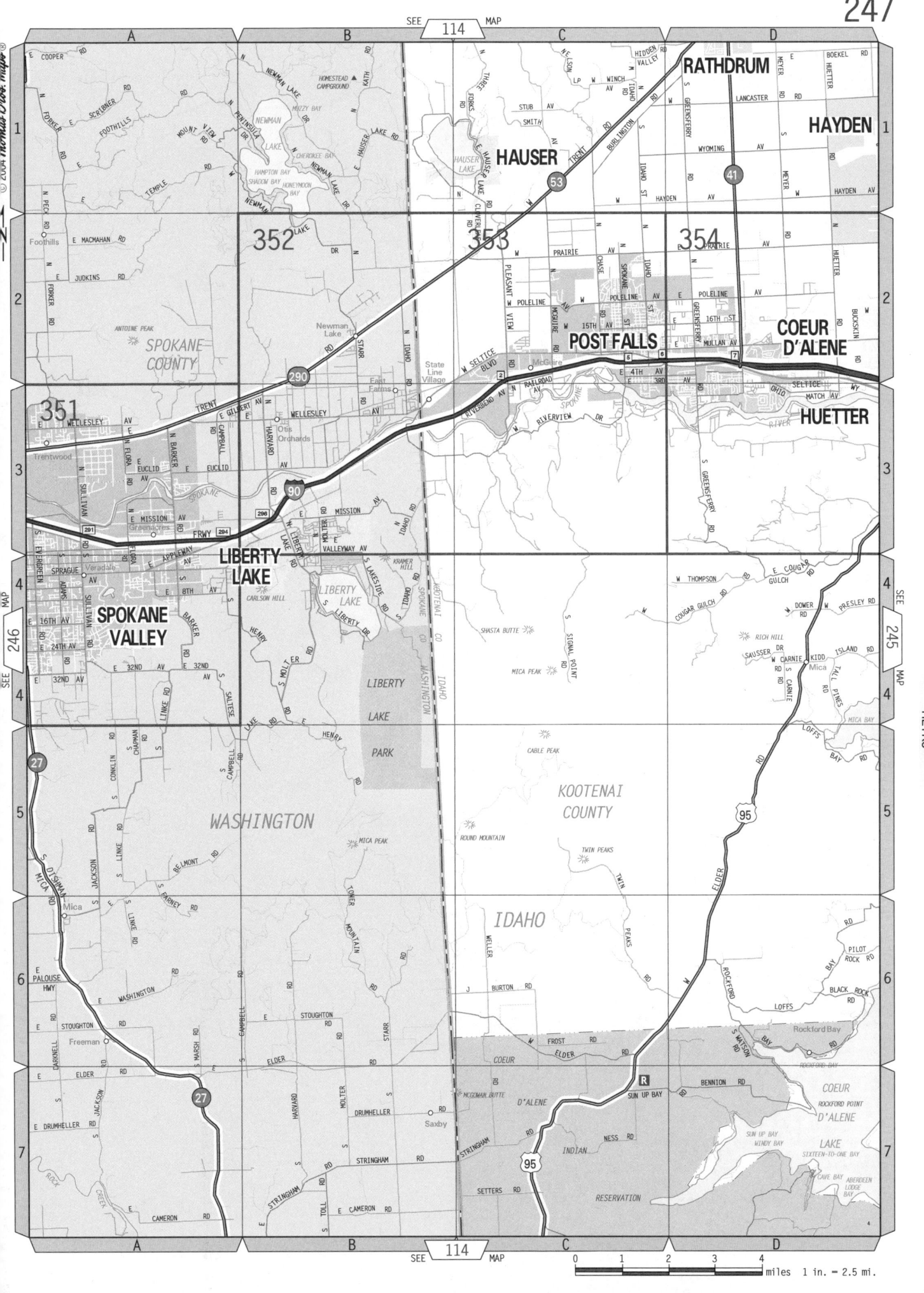

RATHDRUM

HAYDEN

HAUSER

352   353   354

POST FALLS

COEUR D'ALENE

351

HUETTER

SPOKANE COUNTY

LIBERTY LAKE

SPOKANE VALLEY

WASHINGTON

LIBERTY LAKE PARK

KOOTENAI COUNTY

IDAHO

COEUR D'ALENE

COEUR D'ALENE LAKE

SEE MAP 246

SEE MAP 245

METRO

0 1 2 3 4 miles   1 in. = 2.5 mi.

METRO

SEE 245 MAP

A   B   C   D

1

KID ISLAND BAY
KID ISLAND
W PRESLEY HILL RD
MENGER RD
KIDD ISLAND
Twin Beaches
ARROW POINT
SQUAW BAY
EDDYVILLE
BENNETT BAY
E YELLOWSTONE TR
BLUE CREEK BAY
Wolf Lodge
ALDER CREEK RD
FOURTH OF JULY SUMMIT
90
22
28
KOA COEUR D'ALENE
BLUE POINT PUBLIC BOAT RAMP
MOSCOW BAY
MINERAL RIDGE BOAT RAMP
BEAUTY CREEK
BEAUTY CREEK CAMPGROUND
ELK MOUNTAIN
KILLARNEY MOUNTAIN
BIGLE DRAW
RAINEY DRAW
90

W VALHALLA RD
Eddyville
ECHO BAY
GOZIER RD
EVERWELL BAY

2

COEUR
GOTHAM BAY
GOTHAM BAY RD
BURMA RD
97
CARLIN BAY RD
COEUR
D'ALENE
NATIONAL
KOOTENAI COUNTY
GOTHAM BAY RD
JAGSHAW DRAW
LAKES DIVIDE RD
WARD RIDGE RD
BEAUTY SADDLE
NFD RD 438
RED HORSE MOUNTAIN
FOREST
WARD RIDGE
ROSE LAKE ACCESS AREA RD
OLD ROSE CREEK RD
DOYLE
ROSE LAKE
Rose Lake
LOFFS BAY
DELCARDO BAY
HAPPY COVE
TURNER BAY
GAND BAY
LOFFS BAY
D'ALENE
TURNER PEAK

3

CRESCENT BAY
PILOT ROCK RD
LAKE
MARTIN BAY
BLACK BAY
CARLIN BAY
ROUND BAY RD
DEER DR
CARLIN CREEK
ASBURY
HALF
HALF ROUND BAY
POWDERHORN BAY
BLACK ROCK BAY
NFD
CARILL PEAK
808
COTTONWOOD PEAK
NFD RD 810
CHATFIELD SADDLE
POPCORN ISLAND
SWAN SADDLE
KILLARNEY LAKE
HOGBACK RIDGE
SWAN PEAK
IDAHO
COEUR
D'ALENE RIVER
Lane Cemetery
CANARY CREEK
BLACK ROCK RD
INITIAL PEAK

4

MAP 247
SEE 115 MAP

THOMPSON LAKE RD
THOMPSON LAKE
SPRINGSTON RD
Springston
BLUE LAKE
COEUR D'ALENE RIVER
LAMB RD
LAMB CANYON
LAMB PEAK
EAST POINT RD
BELL BAY CAMPGROUND
ANDERSON LAKE
LAKE AV
HARLOW POINT
SIRAN LAKE
CAVE LAKE
MEDIMONT
Medimont
MEDICINE MOUNTAIN
RAINY HILL CAMPGROUND
EVANS CREEK
EAGLE PEAK
PETIT PEAK
EAGLE PEAK
BLACKROCK RIDGE
3
HARRISON
HARRISON BOAT LANDING
COEUR
D'ALENE
LITTLE COTTONWOOD BAY
HARLOW POINT
BELL BAY
VAN OUSEN RD
SMITH RIDGE
BUTLER CREEK

5

COTTONWOOD BAY
COTTONWOOD
ATOR HILL
ZEHM HILL
TALBOT HILL
CEMETERY
INDIAN
CLELAN BAY
LOWMEISTER BAY
FULLERS BAY
BLOOMSBURG BAY
LAKE
BROWNS BAY
SHINGLE BAY
CAREY BAY
SQUAW BAY RD
HARRISON RD
SUNRISE DR
SUNSET DR
COEUR
D'ALENE
SOLCIA PEAK
KOOTENAI CO
BENEWAH CO
GRASSY MOUNTAIN
ROUND TOP
BENEWAH COUNTY

6

CONKLING PARK
LITTLE
CONKLING PARK RD
SHOEFFLER BUTTE
SUNNY SLOPE
CHATCOLET
O-GARA BAY
Conkling Park
BEEDLE POINT
INDIAN MOUNTAIN RD
INDIAN MOUNTAIN
CHATCOLET LAKE
PLUMMER PENINSULA
Rocky Point
ROUND LAKE
3
INDIAN
HOLLY GULCH RD
HELLS GULCH RD
RESERVATION
HELLS GULCH
SHARP TOP
CEDAR DRAW
JOE

7

ELLIS LN
MINALOOSA
MINALOOSA
MINALOOSA RD
CEDAR ST
HEYBURN STATE PARK
CEDAR ST
5
BENEWAH LAKE
NEGRO BROWN HILL
SHAY HILL
SHAY HILL RD
HELLS GULCH RD
5
SAINT MARIES MUNICIPAL AIRPORT
SAINT JOE RIVER
SAINT
COON CREEK RD
BENEWAH CREEK
CHERRY CREEK
KINGS PEAK
SAINT MARIES
SAINT MARIES RIVER ACCESS AREA
JACOT
SAINT MARIES RIVER
3

SEE 115 MAP

0 1 2 3 4 miles   1 in. = 2.5 mi.

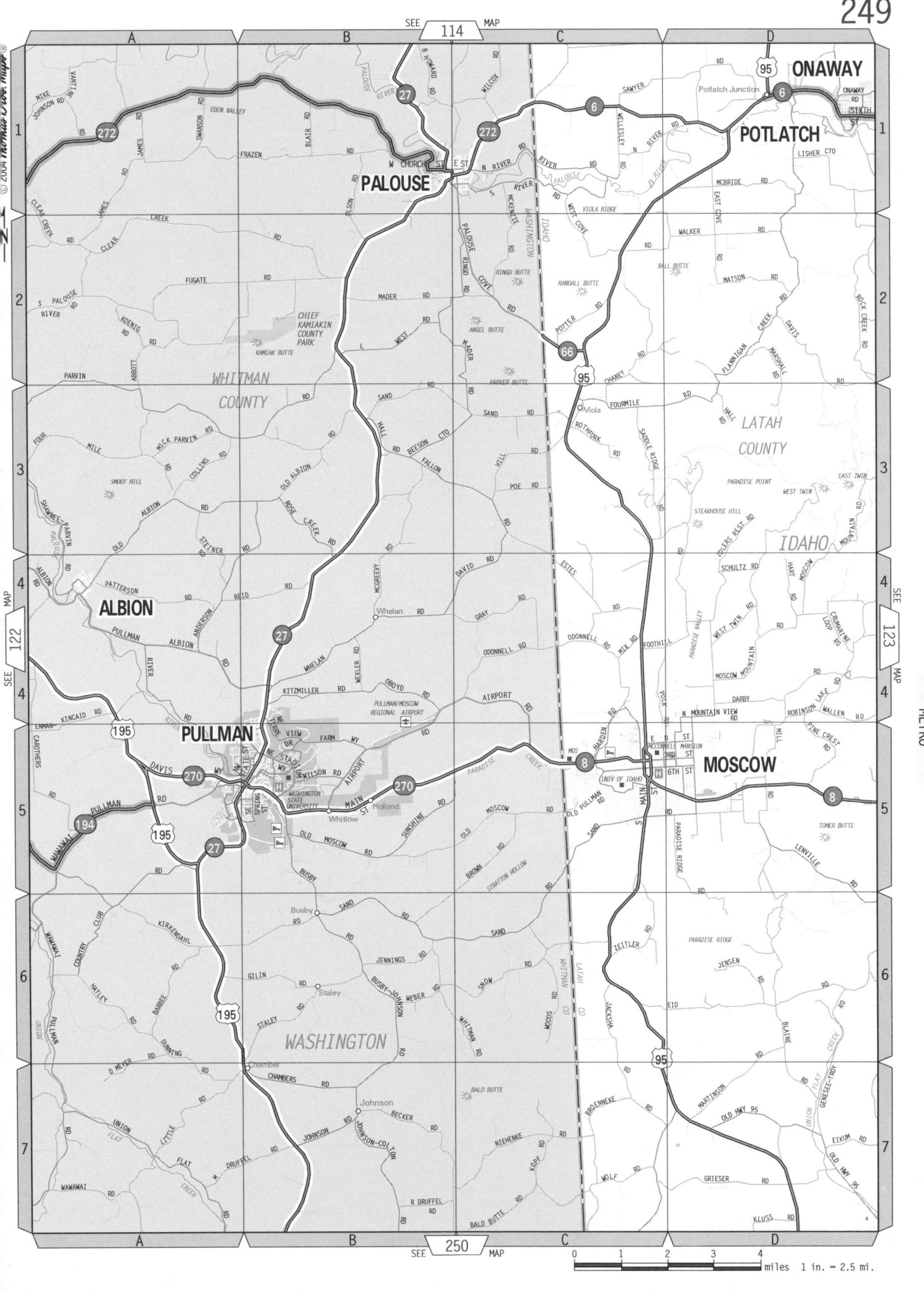

METRO

ONAWAY

POTLATCH

PALOUSE

WHITMAN
COUNTY

LATAH
COUNTY

IDAHO

ALBION

PULLMAN

MOSCOW

WASHINGTON

miles 1 in. = 2.5 mi.

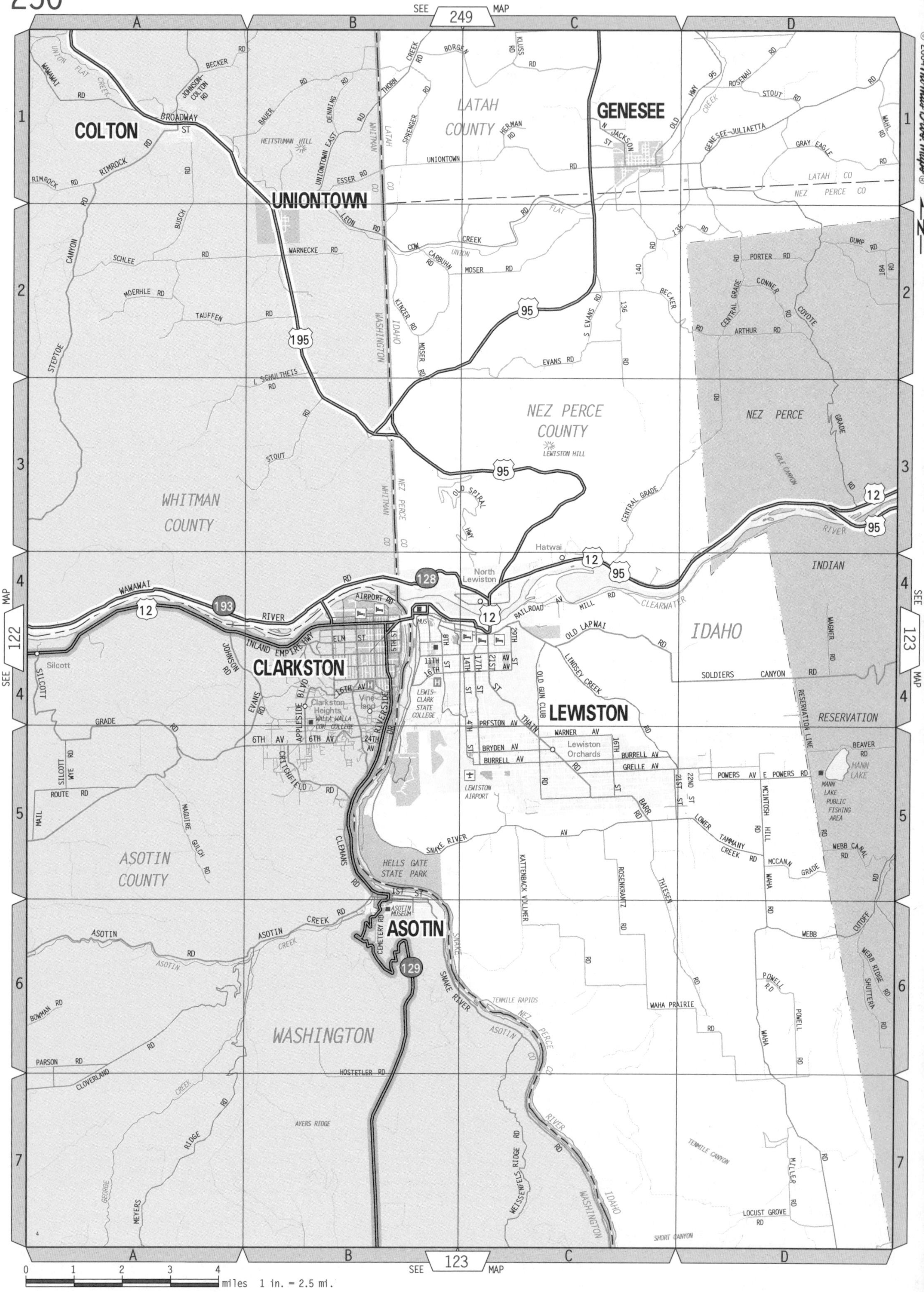

SEE 249 MAP

METRO

COLTON

UNIONTOWN

GENESEE

LATAH COUNTY

UNIONTOWN

N JACKSON ST

GENESEE-JULIAETTA

GRAY EAGLE

LATAH CO
NEZ PERCE CO

HEITSTUMAN HILL

WARNECKE RD

PORTER RD

CENTRAL GRADE

CONNER

COYOTE

ARTHUR

DUMP RD

195

95

EVANS RD

NEZ PERCE
COUNTY

NEZ PERCE

LEWISTON HILL

WHITMAN
COUNTY

STOUT

OLD SPIRAL HWY

95

128

North
Lewiston

12

Hatwai

12

95

INDIAN

12
95

RIVER

SEE 122 MAP

SEE 123 MAP

WAWAWAI

12

193

RIVER

INLAND EMPIRE HWY

CLARKSTON

ELM ST

Clarkston
Heights

WALLA WALLA
COM COLLEGE

6TH AV

LEWIS-
CLARK STATE
COLLEGE

RAILROAD AV

MILL

OLD LAPWAI

IDAHO

SOLDIERS CANYON RD

RESERVATION LINE

LEWISTON

LINDSEY CREEK

OLD GIN CLUB

WARNER AV

PRESTON AV

BRYDEN AV

BURRELL AV

Lewiston
Orchards

GRELLE AV

RESERVATION

BEAVER RD

MANN
LAKE

POWERS AV

E POWERS RD

MANN
LAKE
PUBLIC
FISHING
AREA

McINTOSH HILL

WEBB CANAL

LEWISTON
AIRPORT

BARR RD

22ND ST

21ST ST

ASOTIN COUNTY

SILCOTT

JOHNSON RD

EVANS RD

CRITCHFIELD

CLEMANS

HELLS GATE
STATE PARK

SNAKE RIVER

KATTENBACK VILMER

ROSENKRANTZ

THIESEN

LOWER
TAMMANY
CREEK RD

McCANN

WAHA
GRADE

WEBB RIDGE

SHUTTERA

CEMETERY RD

ASOTIN
MUSEUM

ASOTIN

129

ASOTIN CREEK

POWELL RD

POWELL RD

WAHA

CUTOFF

WEBB RD

WASHINGTON

BOWMAN RD

PARSON RD

CLOVERLAND RD

AYERS RIDGE

HOSTETLER RD

TENMILE RAPIDS

WAHA PRAIRIE

SNAKE RIVER

TENMILE CANYON

MILLER RD

LOCUST GROVE RD

WEISSENFELS RIDGE

IDAHO
WASHINGTON

SHORT CANYON

SEE 123 MAP

0 1 2 3 4 miles 1 in. = 2.5 mi.

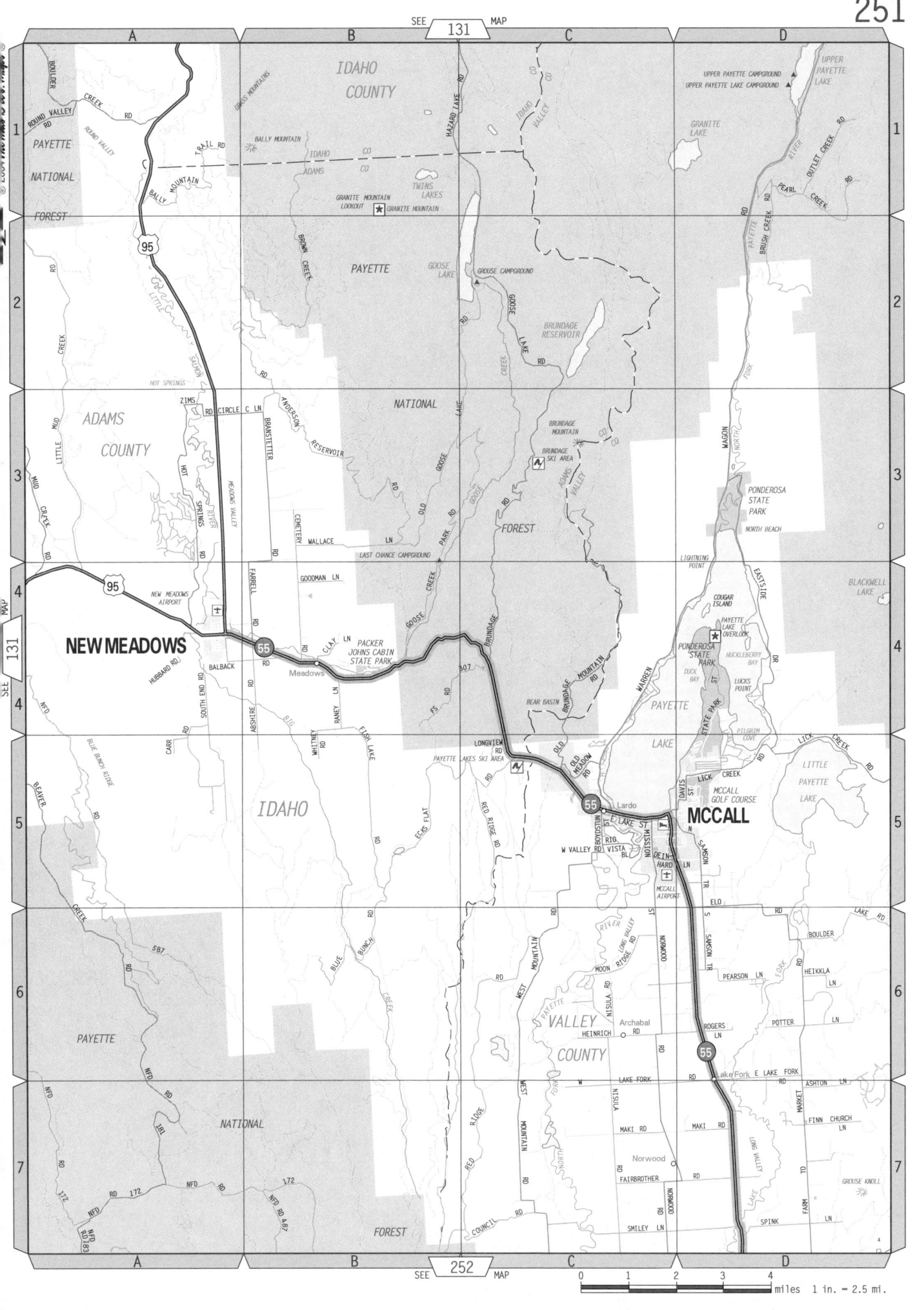

METRO

A | B | C | D

1

2

3

4

IDAHO COUNTY

PAYETTE

NATIONAL

ADAMS COUNTY

PAYETTE

NATIONAL

FOREST

BOULDER CREEK RD

ROUND VALLEY RD

ROUND VALLEY

PAYETTE

NATIONAL

FOREST

TRAIL RD

BALLY MOUNTAIN

BALLY MOUNTAIN

95

LITTLE SALMON RIVER

HOT SPRINGS

ZIMS RD CIRCLE C LN

MUD CREEK RD

HOT SPRINGS RD

MEADOWS VALLEY

BRANSTETTER

ANDERSON RESERVOIR

CEMETERY RD

WALLACE LN

FARRELL RD

GRASS MOUNTAINS

IDAHO CO
ADAMS CO

GRANITE MOUNTAIN LOOKOUT ★ GRANITE MOUNTAIN

TWINS LAKES

BROWN CREEK

GOOSE LAKE

GOOSE LAKE RD

GROUSE CAMPGROUND

BRUNDAGE RESERVOIR

BRUNDAGE MOUNTAIN

BRUNDAGE SKI AREA

ADAMS CO
VALLEY CO

OLD GOOSE LAKE PARK RD

LAST CHANCE CAMPGROUND

HAZARD LAKE

IDAHO VALLEY

UPPER PAYETTE CAMPGROUND
UPPER PAYETTE LAKE CAMPGROUND ▲

UPPER PAYETTE LAKE

GRANITE LAKE

PAYETTE RIVER

BRUSH CREEK RD

PEARL CREEK RD

OUTLET CREEK RD

NORTH FORK

WAGON RD

PONDEROSA STATE PARK

NORTH BEACH

EASTSIDE

BLACKWELL LAKE

5

6

7

95

NEW MEADOWS

NEW MEADOWS AIRPORT

HUBBARD RD

BALBACK RD

SOUTH END RD

ASHLEY RD

BIG RD

55

GOODMAN LN

CLAY LN

PACKER JOHNS CABIN STATE PARK

Meadows

RANEY LN

WHITNEY RD

FISH LAKE RD

CARR RD

IDAHO

BEAVER CREEK

BLUE BUNCH RIDGE

NFD

PAYETTE

NFD 181

NFD RD 172

NFD RD 172

NFD 172

NFD RD

NATIONAL

FOREST

FS RD

307

GOOSE CREEK RD

BRUNDAGE RD

BRUNDAGE MOUNTAIN RD

BEAR BASIN

LONGVIEW RD

PAYETTE LAKES SKI AREA

OLD MEADOW RD

OLD RD

RED RIDGE RD

EGGS FLAT RD

BLUE BUNCH CREEK RD

BLUE BUNCH RD

WEST MOUNTAIN RD

RED RIDGE RD

NORTH FORK PAYETTE RIVER

55

55

Lardo

LIGHTNING POINT

COUGAR ISLAND

PAYETTE LAKE OVERLOOK ★

PONDEROSA STATE PARK

DUCK BAY

HUCKLEBERRY BAY

LUCKS POINT

PILGRIM COVE

PAYETTE LAKE

WARREN RD

STATE PARK

DAVIS ST

LICK CREEK

MCCALL GOLF COURSE

MCCALL

E LAKE ST

MISSION ST

BOYDSTUN ST

RIO VISTA BL

W VALLEY RD

DEIN-HARD LN

MCCALL AIRPORT

SAMSON TR

ELO

LICK CREEK RD

LITTLE PAYETTE LAKE

BOULDER RD

HEIKKLA LN

LAKE RD

PEARSON LN

POTTER LN

LOG VALLEY RD

MOON RIDGE RD

LONG VALLEY RD

WEST MOUNTAIN RD

NISULA RD

ARCHABAL RD

HEINRICH RD

NORWOOD RD

ROGERS LN

Archabal

55

Lake Fork E LAKE FORK

W LAKE FORK RD

ASHTON LN

MARKET RD

FINN CHURCH LN

MAKI RD

MAKI RD

NISULA RD

Norwood

FAIRBROTHER RD

SMILEY LN

COUNCIL RD

NORWOOD RD

LONG VALLEY RD

SPINK LN

TO FARM RD

GROUSE KNOLL

VALLEY COUNTY

0 1 2 3 4 miles 1 in. = 2.5 mi.

SEE MAP 131

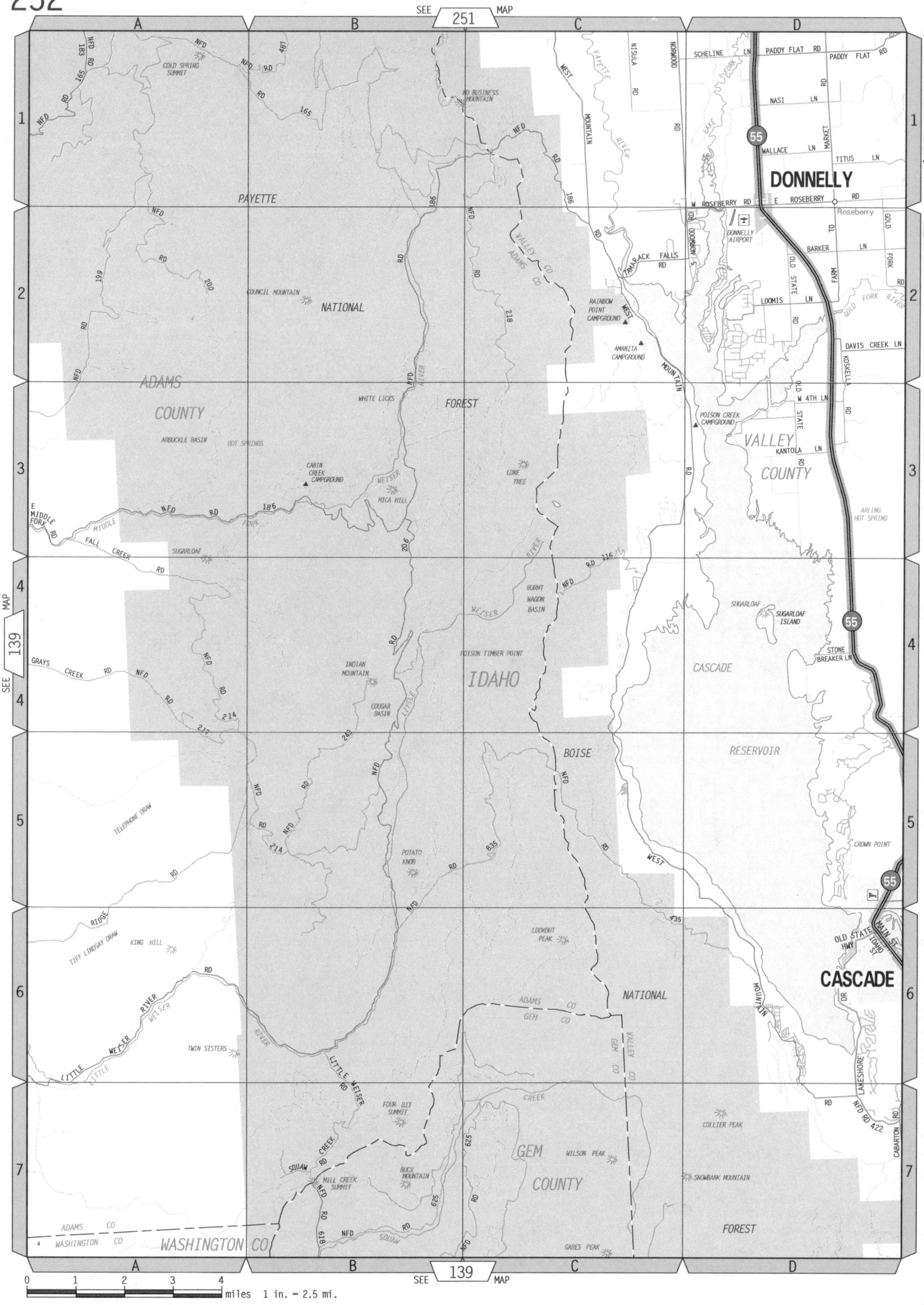

252

METRO

SEE 139 MAP

A | B | C | D

DONNELLY

CASCADE

PAYETTE

NATIONAL

FOREST

ADAMS

COUNTY

IDAHO

VALLEY

COUNTY

CASCADE

RESERVOIR

BOISE

NATIONAL

GEM

COUNTY

FOREST

COLD SPRING SUMMIT

NFD 183 RD

NFD 165 RD

NFD 487

NFD RD 165

NO BUSINESS MOUNTAIN

NFD 186

WEST MOUNTAIN

PAYETTE RIVER

NISULA RD

NORWOOD

SCHELINE LN

PADDY FLAT RD

PADDY FLAT RD

NASI LN

MARKET

LAKE FORK

55

WALLACE LN

TITUS LN

W ROSEBERRY RD

E ROSEBERRY RD

Roseberry

GOLD FORK

GOLD FORK RIVER

TAMARACK FALLS

DONNELLY AIRPORT

BARKER LN

LOOMIS LN

DAVIS CREEK LN

OOONOMY S

WEST MOUNTAIN

RAINBOW POINT CAMPGROUND

AMANITA CAMPGROUND

POISON CREEK CAMPGROUND

KOSKELL RD

W OLD STATE RD

W 4TH LN

OLD STATE

KANTOLA RD

ARLING HOT SPRING

COUNCIL MOUNTAIN

NFD 199 RD

NFD 200 RD

NFD RD

NATIONAL

ADAMS CO

VALLEY CO

NFD 218 RD

WHITE LICKS

WEISER RIVER

LONE TREE

ARBUCKLE BASIN HOT SPRINGS

CABIN CREEK CAMPGROUND

MICA HILL

E MIDDLE FORK RD

NFD RD 186

MIDDLE FORK

FALL CREEK RD

SUGARLOAF

NFD 206 RD

WEISER RIVER

NFD RD 116

BURNT WAGON BASIN

SUGARLOAF

SUGARLOAF ISLAND

STONE BREAKER LN

55

GRAYS CREEK RD

NFD RD

NFD RD 214

NFD RD 217

INDIAN MOUNTAIN

COUGAR BASIN

LITTLE

NFD 248 RD

POISON TIMBER POINT

WEISER RIVER

NFD RD

CROWN POINT

TELEPHONE DRAW

NFD 214 RD

NFD RD

POTATO KNOB

NFD 835 RD

NFD RD

WEST

55

RIDGE

TIFF LINDSAY DRAW

KING HILL

RD

WEISER RIVER

LITTLE WEISER RIVER

TWIN SISTERS

LITTLE WEISER RD

LOOKOUT PEAK

NFD 835

ADAMS CO

GEM CO

VALLEY CO

GEM CO

MOUNTAIN

OLD STATE HWY

MAIN ST

IDAHO

LAKESHORE DR

FOUR-BIT SUMMIT

BUCK MOUNTAIN

SQUAW CREEK

CREEK

WILSON PEAK

COLLIER PEAK

SQUAW

MILL CREEK SUMMIT

NFD RD

NFD 625 RD

GABES PEAK

SNOWBANK MOUNTAIN

LAKESHORE RD

CABARTON RD

NFD RD 422

ADAMS CO

WASHINGTON CO

WASHINGTON CO.

NFD 618 RD

SQUAW

0 1 2 3 4 miles   1 in. = 2.5 mi.

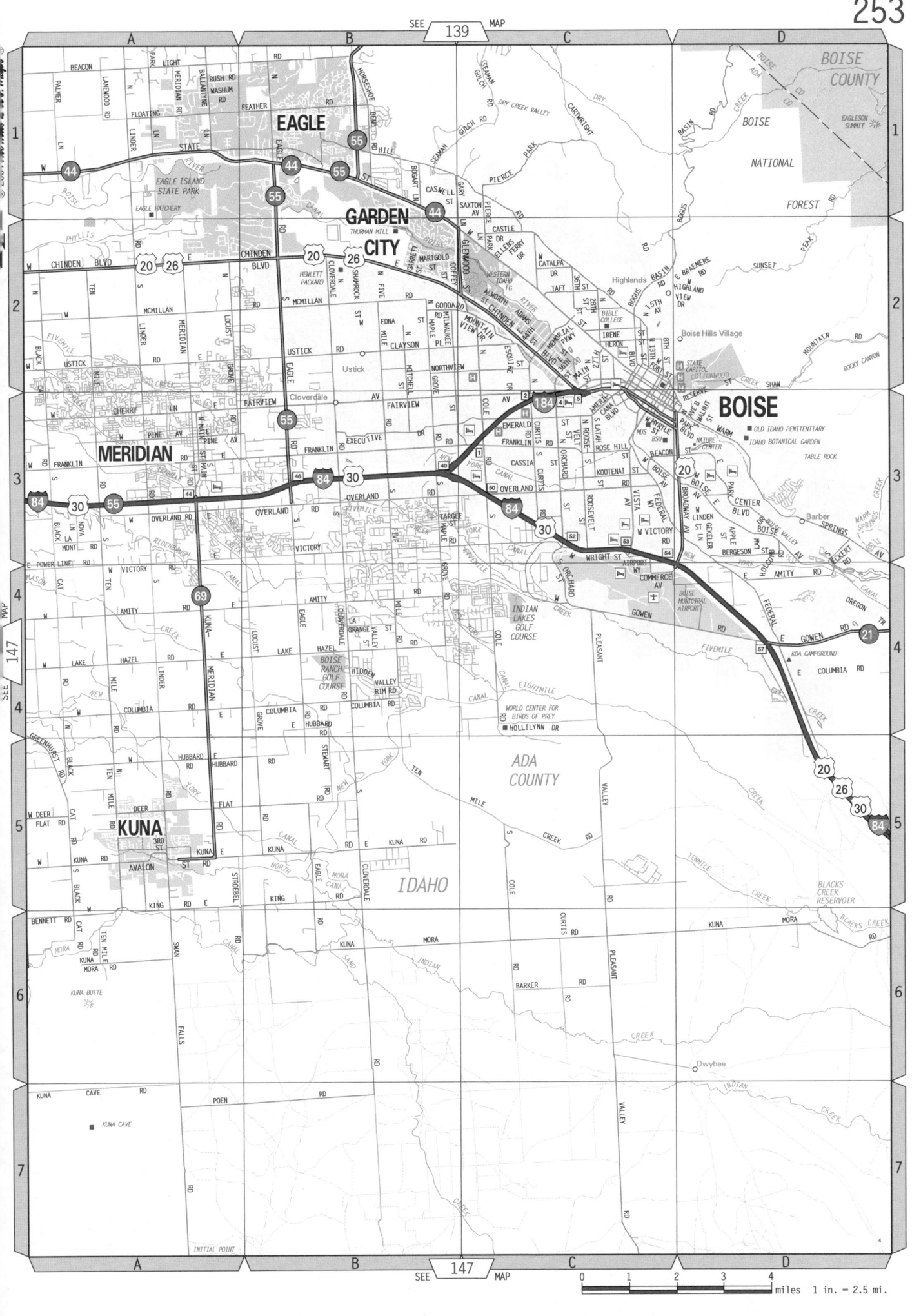

METRO

0 1 2 3 4 miles 1 in. = 2.5 mi.

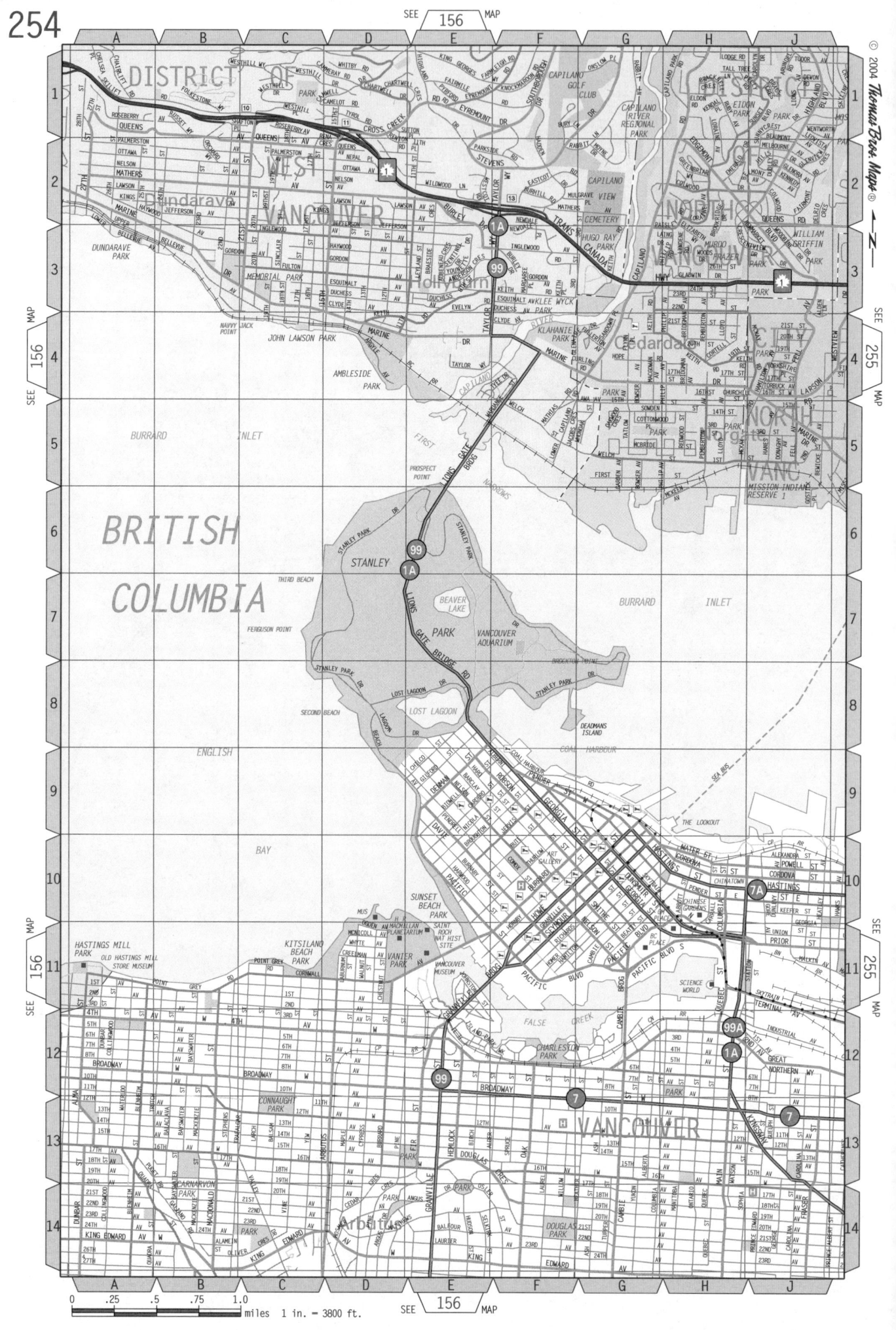

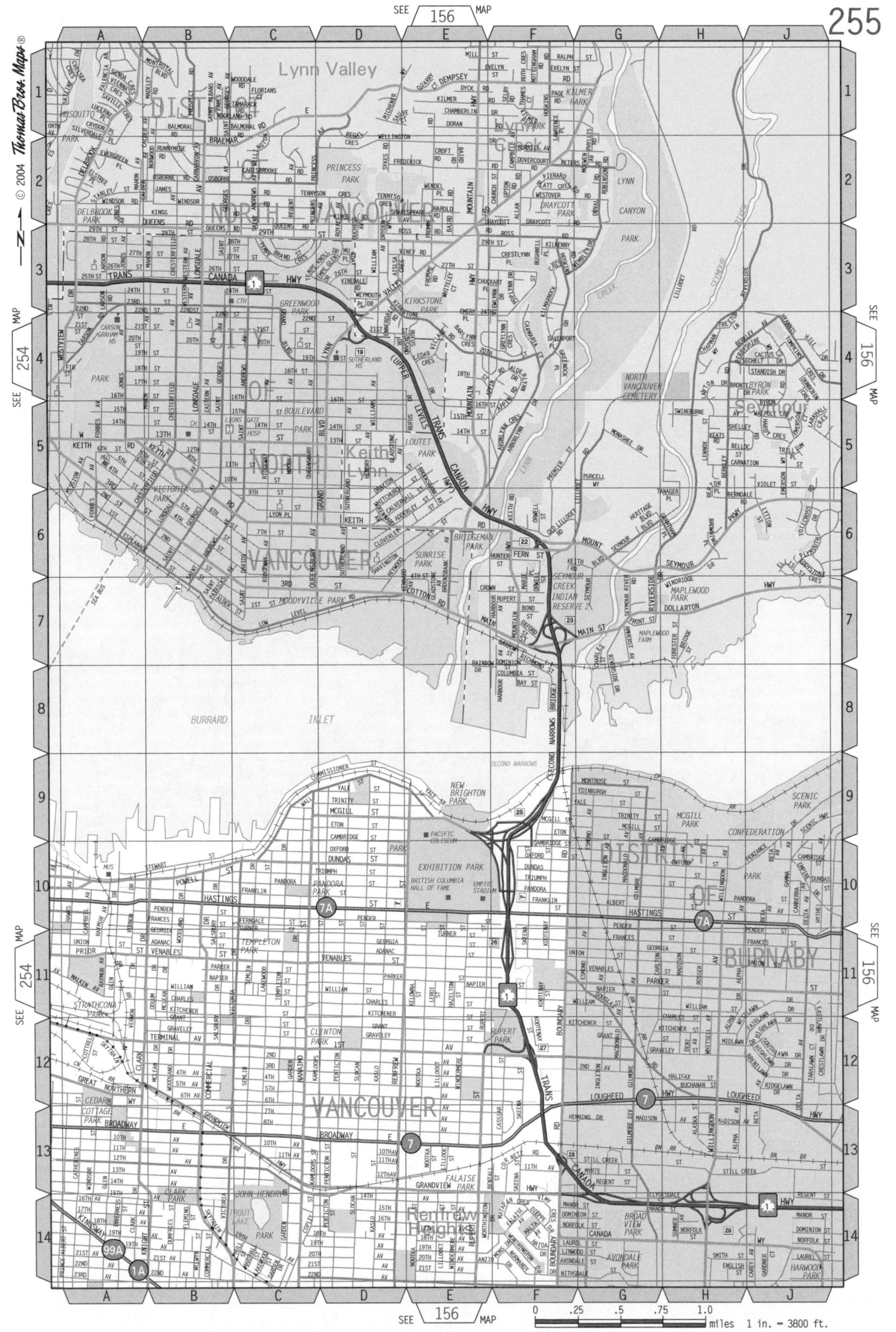

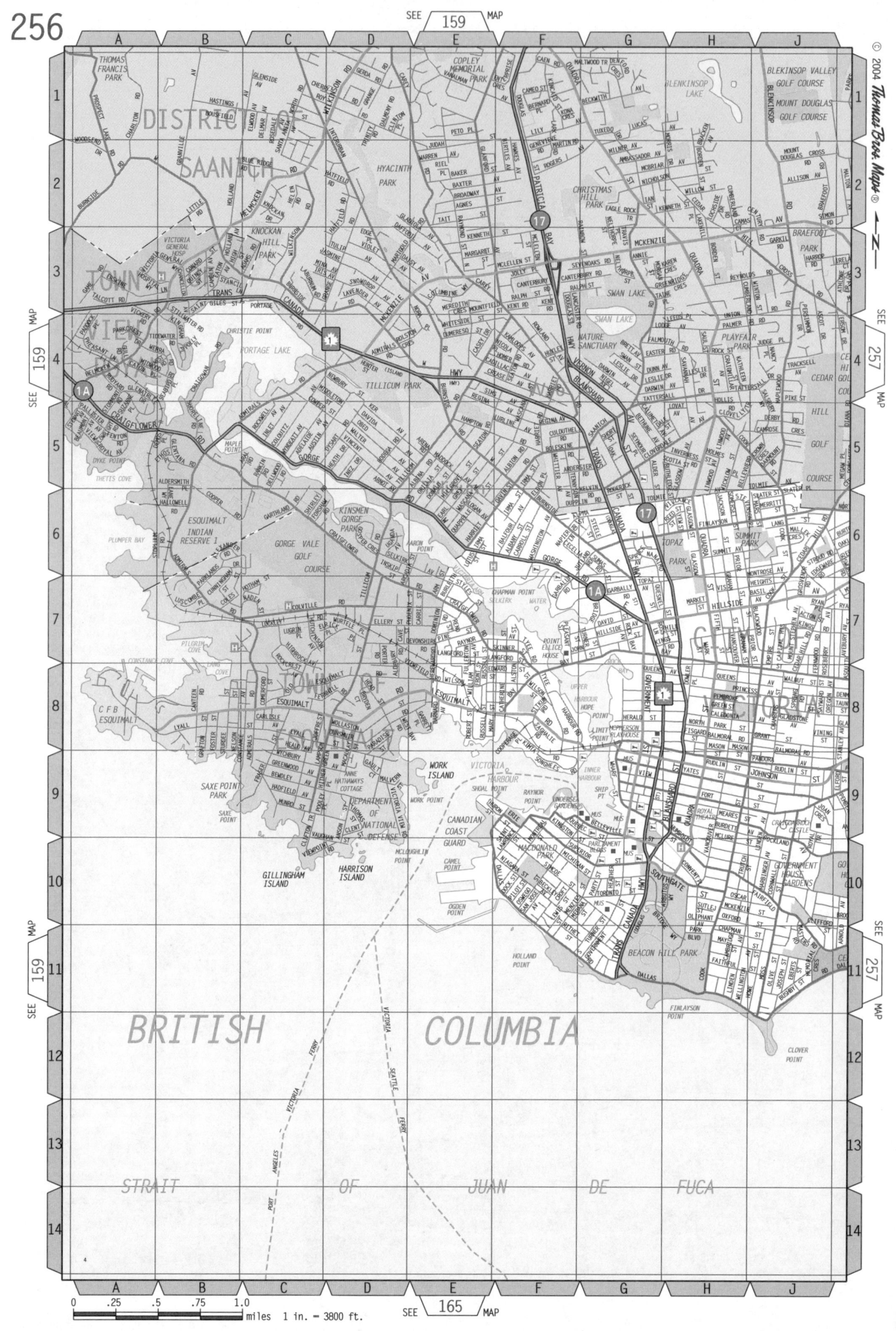

DISTRICT

OF

SAANICH

UNIVERSITY
OF
VICTORIA

Cadboro Bay

CEDAR HILL
GOLF
COURSE

MOUNT TOLMIE

MT TOLMIE
PARK

HENDERSON
PARK

UPLANDS
GOLF
CLUB

CADBORO GYRO
PARK

CADBORO
BAY

FLAMBOROUGH HEAD

TEN MILE POINT

CADBORO POINT

STAINES
ISLAND

SHEEP
ISLAND

FLOWER
ISLAND

SKEGNESS POINT

SPOON
BAY

FANNEL COVE
CATTLE POINT

BAYNES

CHANNEL

UPLANDS
PARK

DISTRICT
OF
OAK BAY

OAK BAY

WILLOWS BEACH

BRITISH

COLUMBIA

MARY
TOD
ISLAND

OAK BAY
MARINA

TURKEY HEAD

GREAT CHAIN
ISLAND

DISCOVERY ISLAND
MARINE PARK

VICTORIA

GOLF

COURSE

VICTORIA BAY

GOVERNMENT
HOUSE
GARDENS

ANDERSON
HILL
PARK

GONZALES POINT

MCMICKING POINT

MCNEILL BAY

CEMETERY

GONZALES BAY

TRAFALGAR
PARK

HARLING POINT

ENTERPRISE   CHANNEL

INDIAN
RESERVE

TRIAL
ISLANDS

OF

JUAN

DE

FUCA

STRAIT

0   .25   .5   .75   1.0
miles 1 in. = 3800 ft.

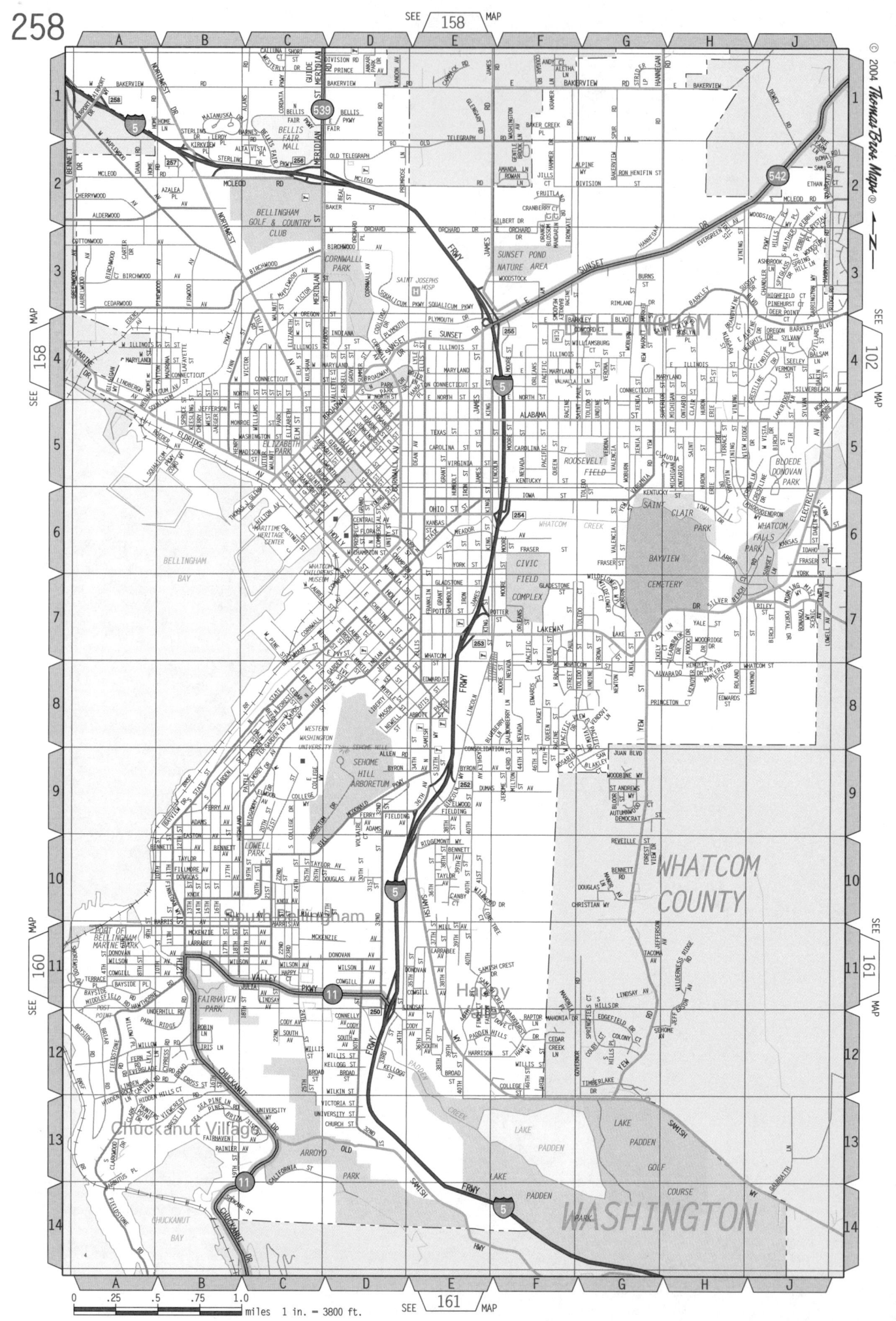

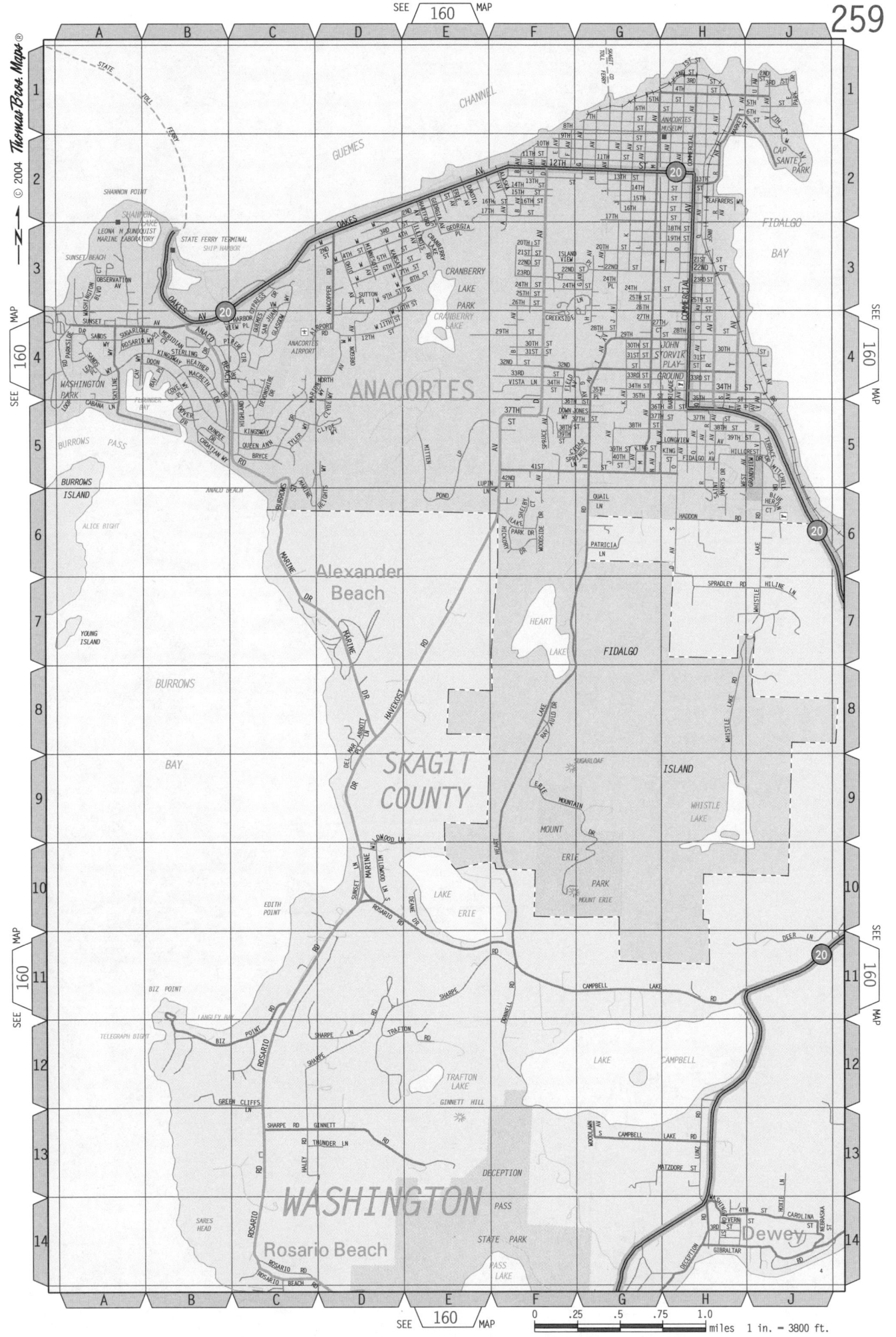

GUEMES CHANNEL

SHANNON POINT

SHANNON LAKE

LEONA M SUNDQUIST MARINE LABORATORY

STATE FERRY TERMINAL SHIP HARBOR

SUNSET BEACH

OBSERVATION AV

WASHINGTON PARK

BURROWS PASS

ANACO BEACH

BURROWS ISLAND

ALICE BIGHT

YOUNG ISLAND

ANACORTES

CRANBERRY LAKE PARK

CRANBERRY LAKE

ANACORTES AIRPORT

ANACORTES MUSEUM

CAP SANTE PARK

FIDALGO BAY

SEAFARERS WY

JOHN STORVIK PLAYGROUND

CREEKSIDE

Alexander Beach

MARINE DR

HEART LAKE

FIDALGO

QUAIL LN

PATRICIA LN

HADDON

BURROWS BAY

SKAGIT COUNTY

SUGARLOAF

ISLAND

ERIE MOUNTAIN

MOUNT ERIE PARK

MOUNT ERIE

WHISTLE LAKE

LAKE ERIE

EDITH POINT

BIZ POINT

LANGLEY BAY

TELEGRAPH BIGHT

BIZ POINT

ROSARIO

SHARPE

TRAFTON

TRAFTON LAKE

GINNETT HILL

CAMPBELL LAKE

LAKE CAMPBELL

WASHINGTON

GREEN CLIFFS

SHARPE RD GINNETT

HALEY RD THUNDER LN

DECEPTION PASS STATE PARK

Rosario Beach

ROSARIO BEACH

SARES HEAD

PASS LAKE

DEER LN

DECEPTION

Dewey

0 .25 .5 .75 1.0   miles 1 in. = 3800 ft.

© 2004 Thomas Bros. Maps®

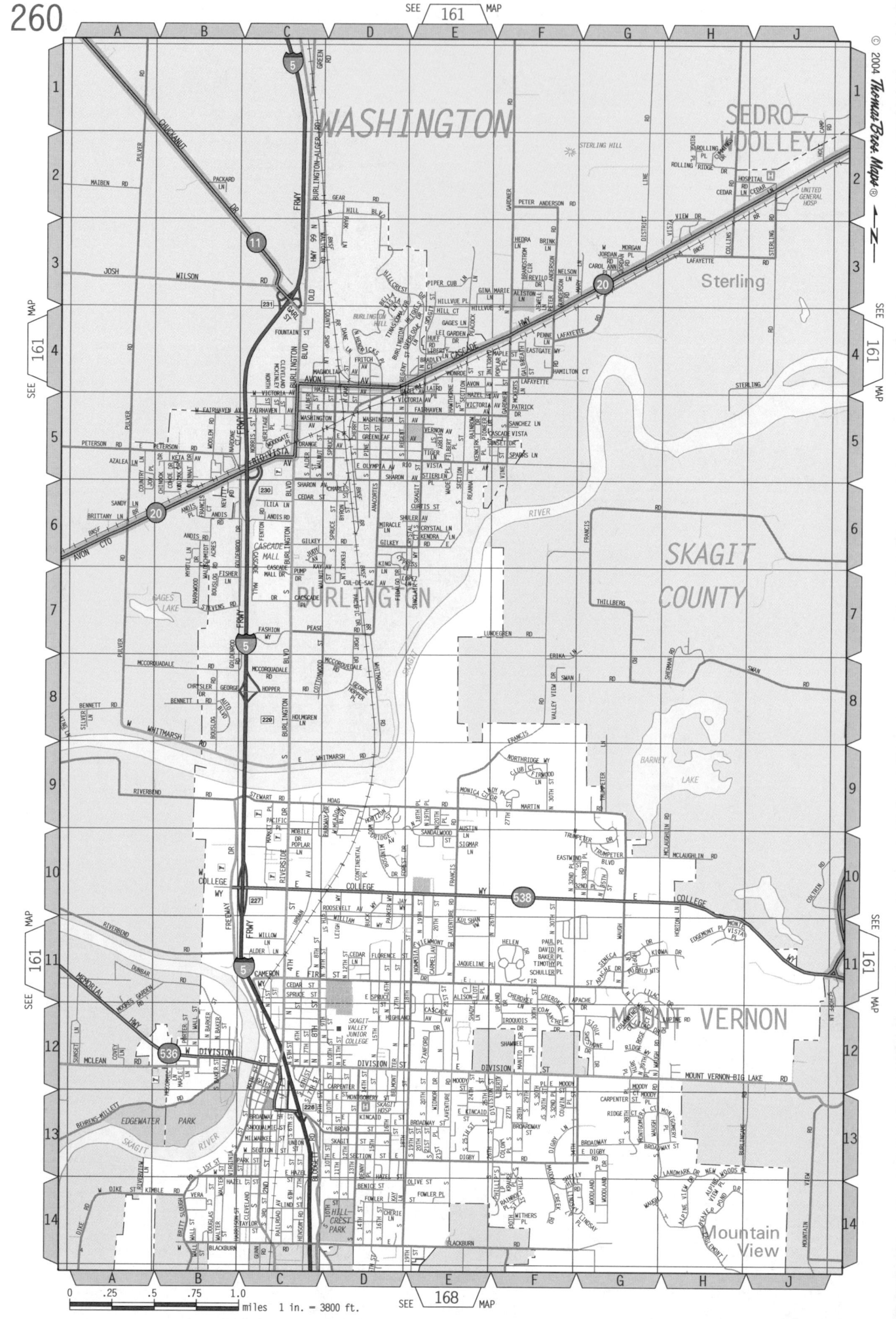

SEE 161 MAP

WASHINGTON

SEDRO-WOOLLEY

Sterling

SKAGIT

COUNTY

BURLINGTON

MOUNT VERNON

Mountain
View

SEE 168 MAP

0   .25   .5   .75   1.0
miles   1 in. = 3800 ft.

© 2004 Thomas Bros. Maps ®   ←N→

DETAIL

DETAIL

SEE 165 MAP

SEE 165 MAP

SEE 165 MAP

SEE 165 MAP

SEE 165 MAP

PORT ANGELES

PORT ANGELES HARBOR

US COAST GUARD STATION

Lighthouse

Port Angeles Victoria Ferry

WASHINGTON

OLYMPIC NATIONAL PARK

CLALLAM COUNTY

0   .25   .5   .75   1.0   miles   1 in. = 3800 ft.

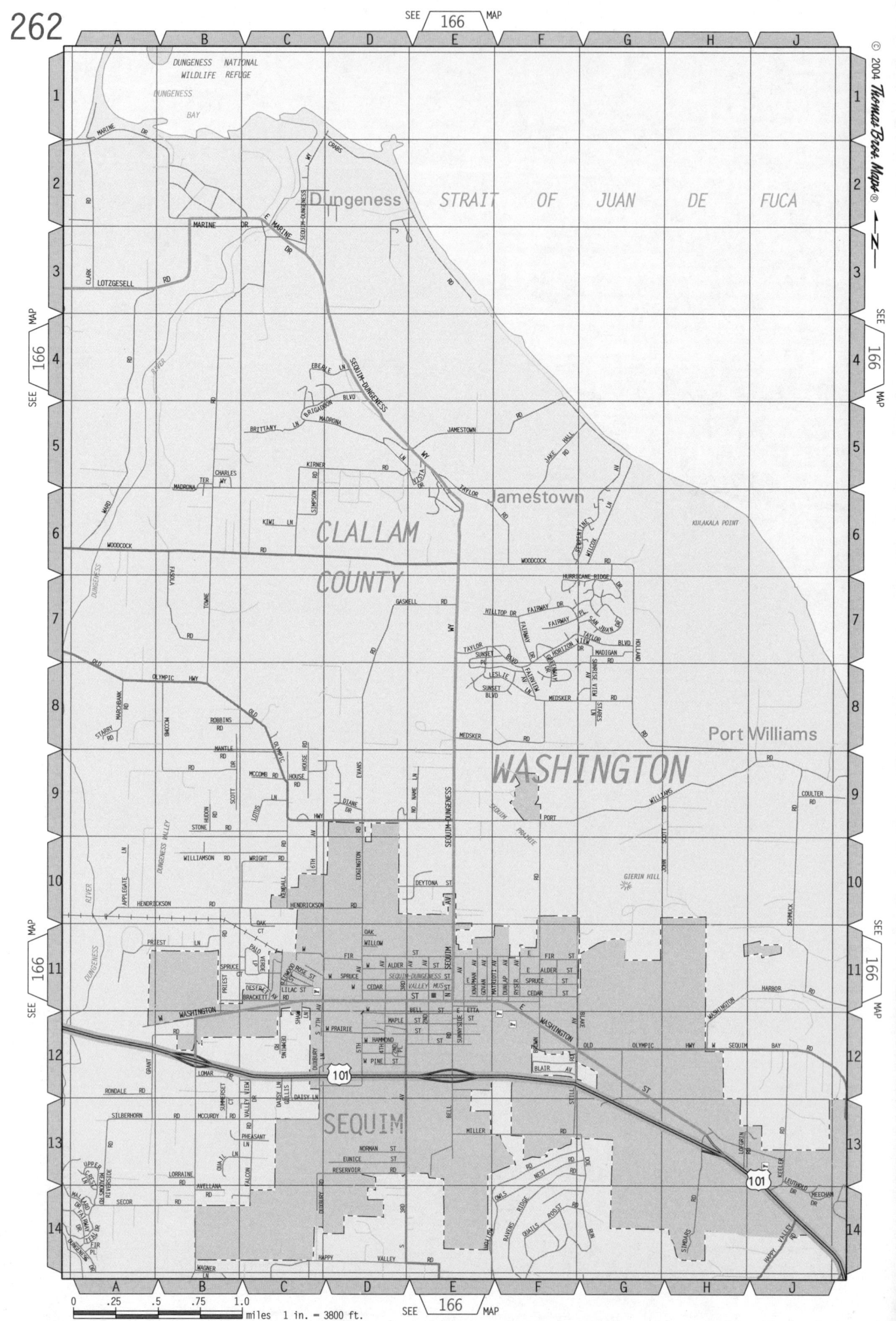

SEE 166 MAP

SEE 166 MAP

SEE 166 MAP

SEE 166 MAP

SEE 166 MAP

DETAIL

DUNGENESS NATIONAL WILDLIFE REFUGE

DUNGENESS BAY

Dungeness STRAIT OF JUAN DE FUCA

CLALLAM COUNTY

WASHINGTON

Jamestown

KULAKALA POINT

Port Williams

GIERIN HILL

SEQUIM

miles 1 in. = 3800 ft.

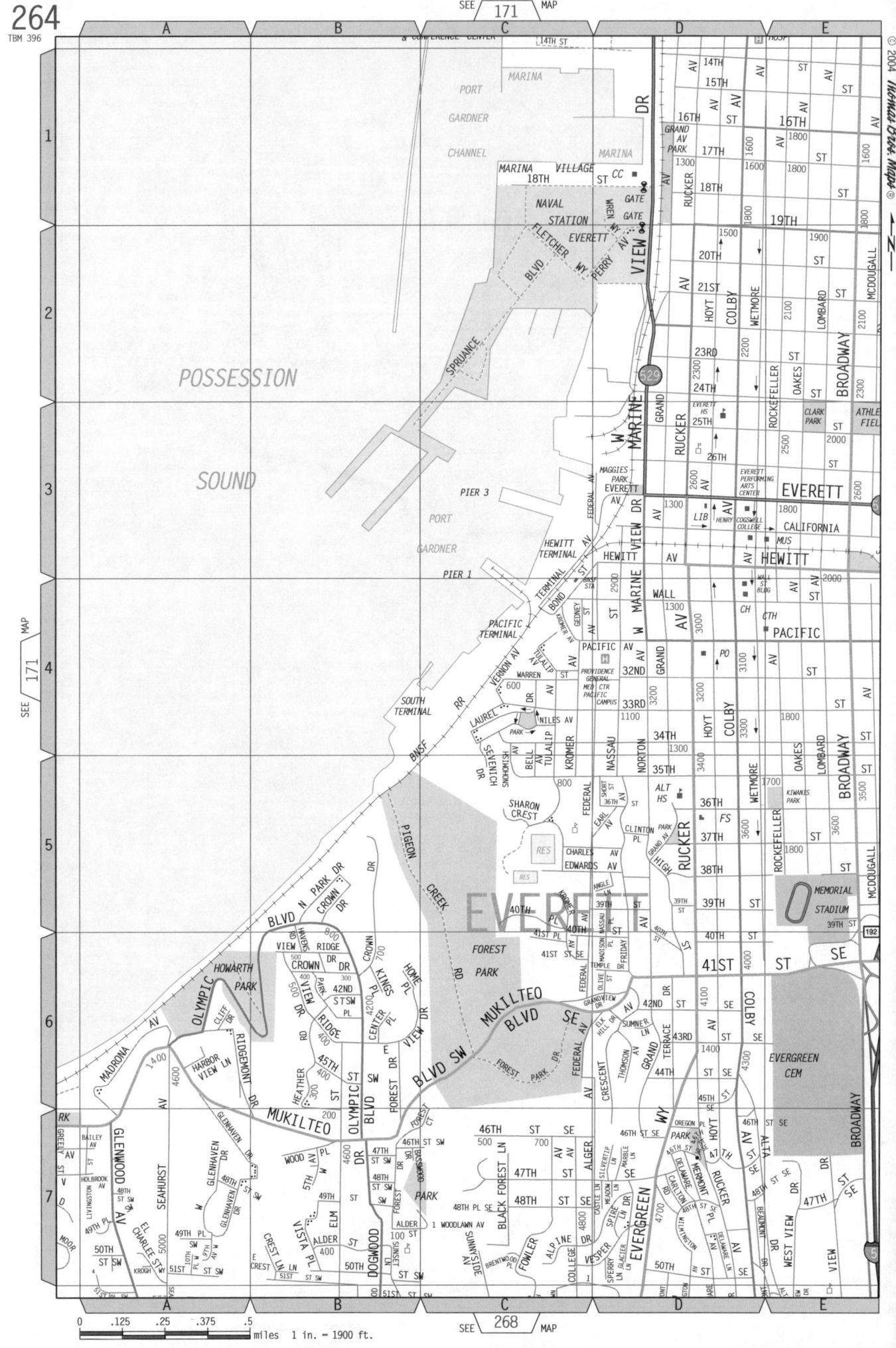

DETAIL

SEE 171 MAP

SEE 171 MAP

© 2004 Thomas Bros. Maps ® —N→

POSSESSION

SOUND

PORT GARDNER CHANNEL

MARINA

PORT GARDNER CHANNEL

MARINA

MARINA VILLAGE

NAVAL STATION EVERETT

PIER 3

PORT GARDNER

PIER 1

PACIFIC TERMINAL

SOUTH TERMINAL

HEWITT TERMINAL

SHARON CREST

HOWARTH PARK

PIGEON CREEK

OLYMPIC

EVERETT

FOREST PARK

MUKILTEO BLVD SE

MEMORIAL STADIUM

EVERGREEN CEM

FOREST PARK

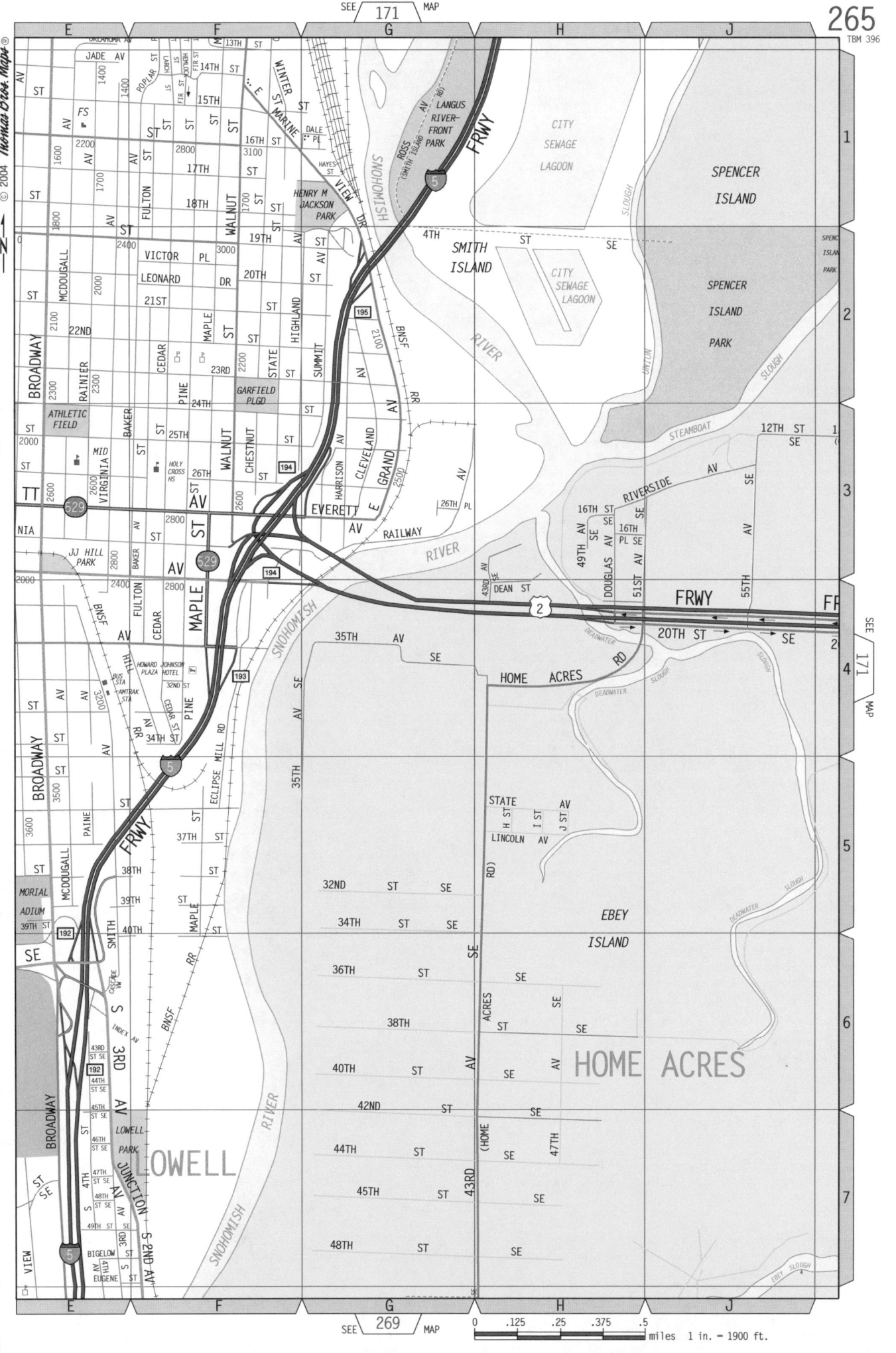

© 2004 *Thomas Bros. Maps* ®

DETAIL

0   .125   .25   .375   .5
miles 1 in. = 1900 ft.

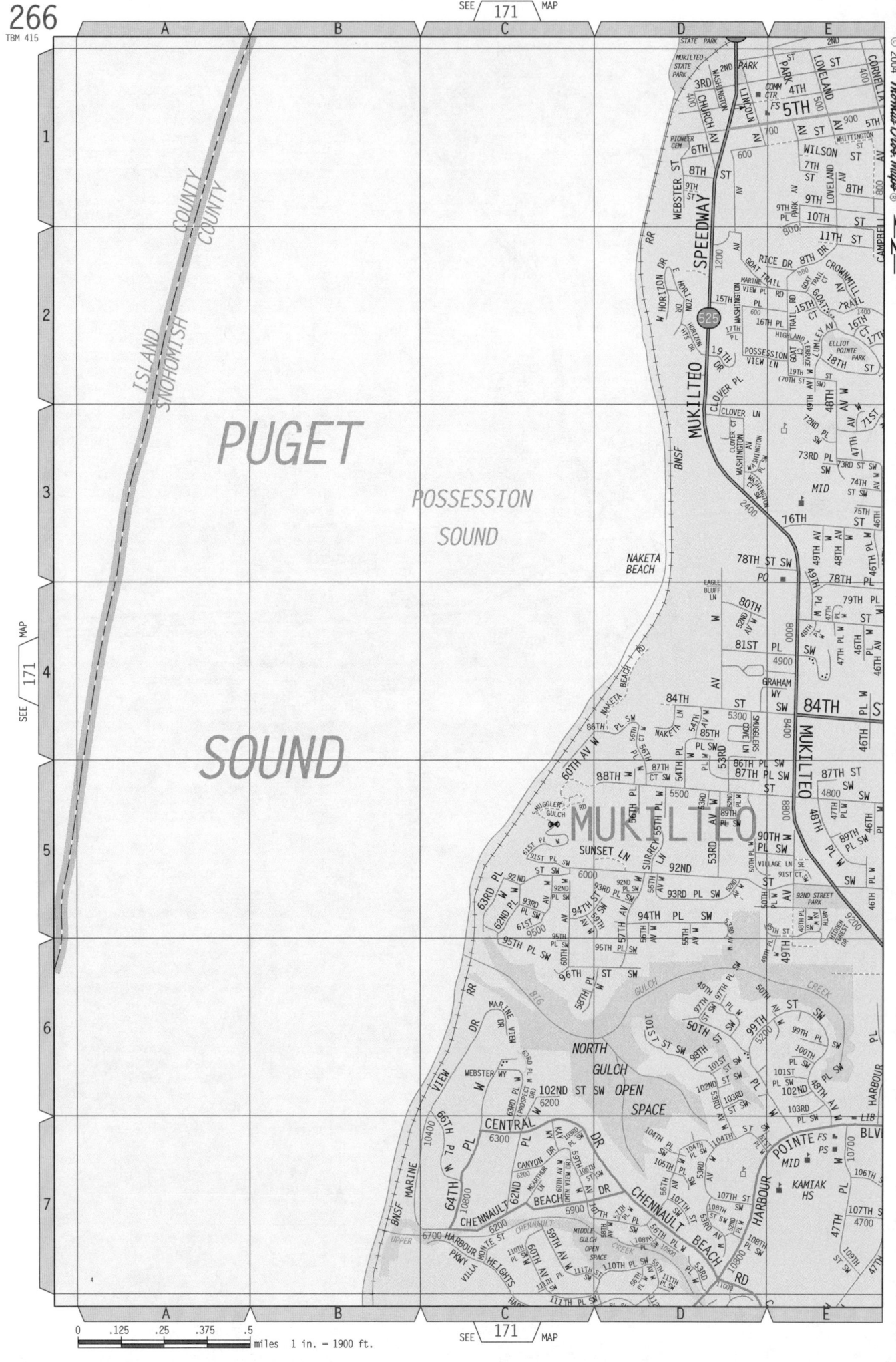

SEE 171 MAP

PUGET

POSSESSION

SOUND

SOUND

MUKILTEO

0 .125 .25 .375 .5 miles   1 in. = 1900 ft.

DETAIL

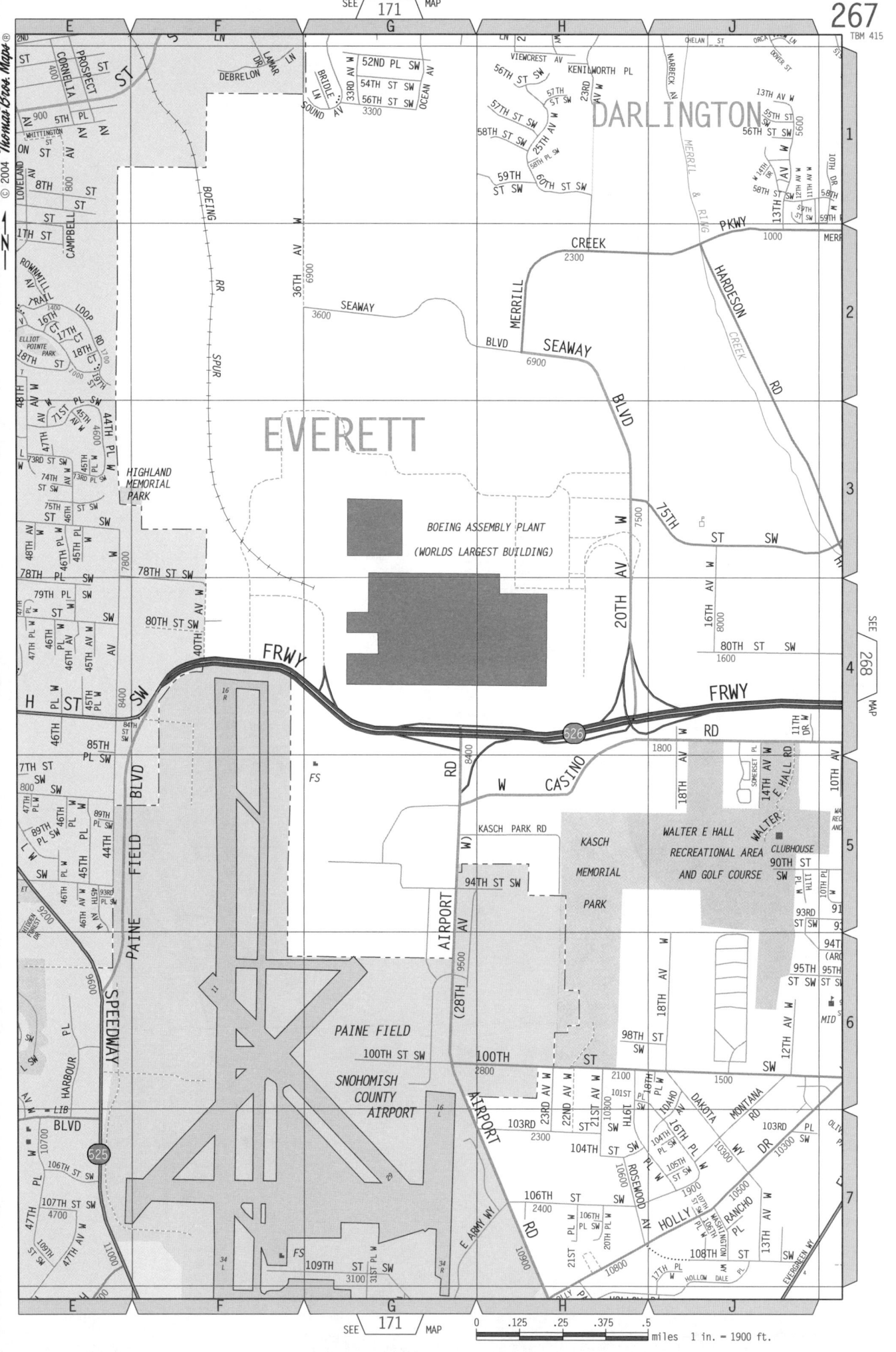

© 2004 Thomas Bros. Maps ®

—N—

DARLINGTON

EVERETT

BOEING ASSEMBLY PLANT
(WORLDS LARGEST BUILDING)

HIGHLAND
MEMORIAL
PARK

MERRILL CREEK

SEAWAY

SEAWAY BLVD

HARDESON RD

MERRILL & RING PKWY

CASINO RD

KASCH PARK RD

KASCH
MEMORIAL
PARK

WALTER E HALL
RECREATIONAL AREA
AND GOLF COURSE

CLUBHOUSE

PAINE FIELD

SNOHOMISH
COUNTY
AIRPORT

100TH ST SW

PAINE FIELD BLVD

SPEEDWAY BLVD

HARBOUR

E ARMY WY

AIRPORT RD

ELLIOT
POINTE
PARK

DETAIL

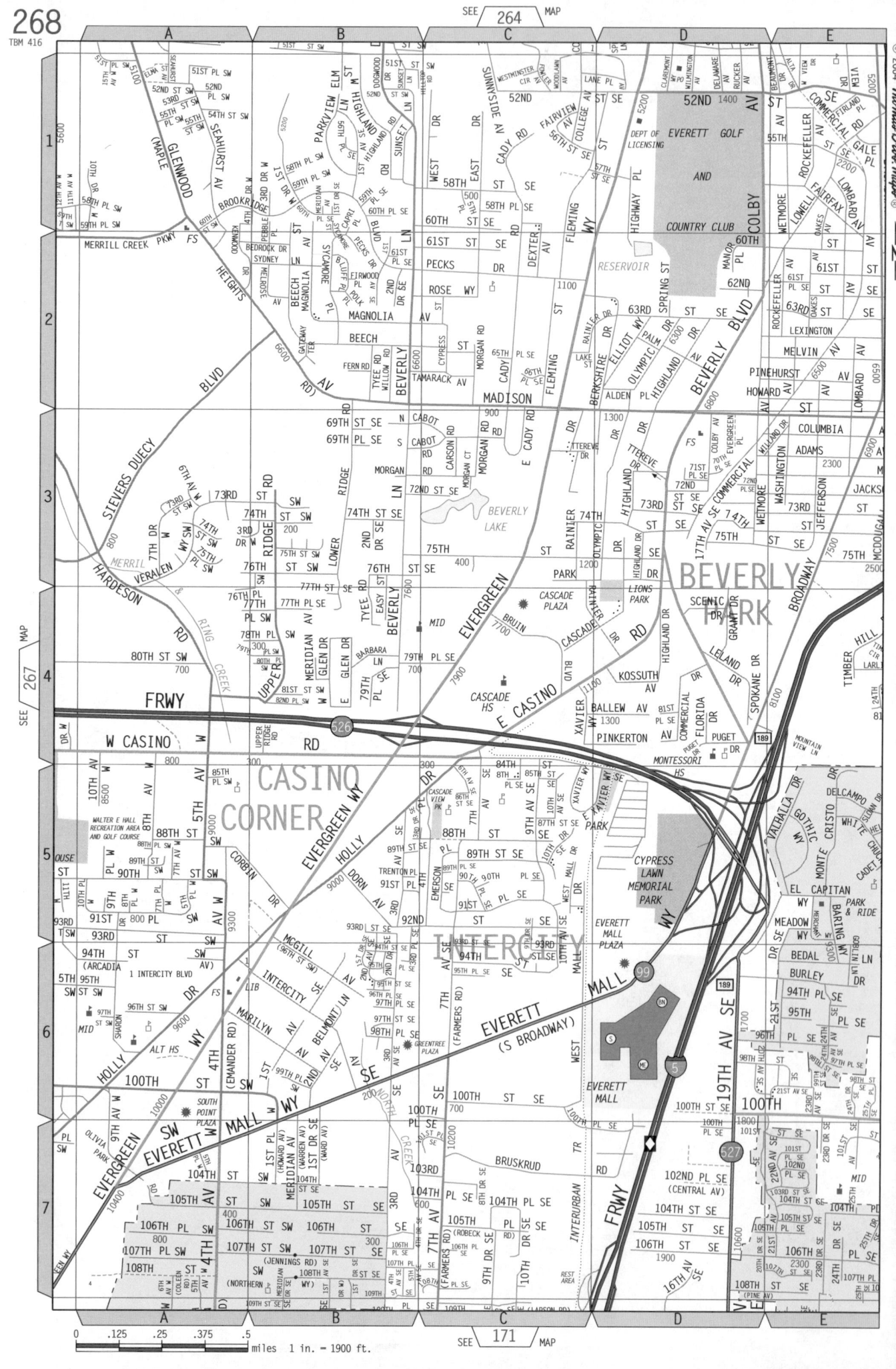

SEE 264 MAP

© 2004 Thomas Bros. Maps ®

—N—

0   .125   .25   .375   .5
miles   1 in. = 1900 ft.

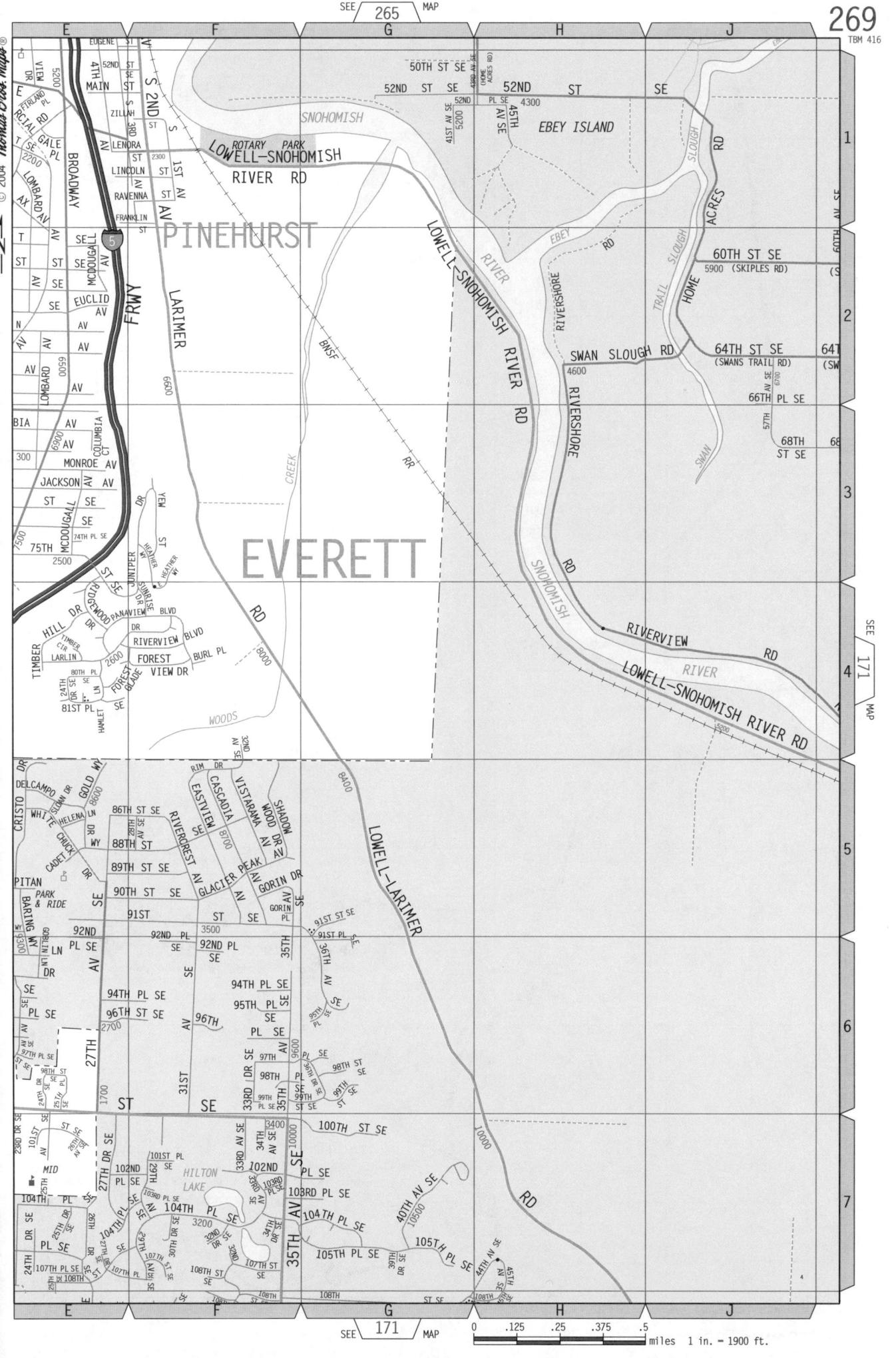

© 2004 Thomas Bros. Maps®

E   F   G   H   J

EUGENE ST
50TH ST SE
52ND   ST   SE

4TH   MAIN
52ND ST
52ND ST SE
SNOHOMISH
52ND   ST   SE
PL SE 4300
45TH AV SE

S 2ND
ZILLAH   ST
ROTARY   PARK
LOWELL-SNOHOMISH
EBEY ISLAND

3RD   ST
LENORA   ST   2300
RIVER RD
41ST AV SE
5200

LINCOLN   ST
1ST AV   S

RAVENNA   ST

FRANKLIN   ST

5   PINEHURST

LARIMER

RIVER

LOWELL-SNOHOMISH RIVER RD

1

SEL
EBEY   RD
RIVERSHORE

EUCLID   AV

60TH ST SE
5900 (SKIPLES RD)

2

LOMBARD
6500
BNSF
SWAN SLOUGH RD
4600
64TH ST SE
(SWANS TRAIL RD)

BIA   AV
COLUMBIA CT
6900

RIVERSHORE   RD

66TH PL SE

MONROE AV
300
CREEK

JACKSON   AV   AV

ST   SE

68TH
ST SE

3

McDOUGALL
7500
24TH PL SE
75TH
2500

EVERETT

SNOHOMISH

JUNIPER DR
YEW   ST

HEATHER

RR
RD
8000

RIVERVIEW   RD

LOWELL-SNOHOMISH RIVER RD
RIVER
5200

4

TIMBER HILL DR
SUNRISE
EDGEWOOD DR
PANAVIEW BLVD
RIVERVIEW BLVD

LARLIN
2600
FOREST   GLADE
BURL PL
FOREST VIEW DR

80TH PL

24TH DR SE

81ST PL   HAMLET

WOODS

RD
8400

LOWELL-LARIMER

5

CRISTO DR
DELCAMPO
GOLD WY
8600

86TH ST SE
RIM DR
CASCADIA
VISTARAMA AV
WOOD DR AV
SHADOW

WHITE
HELENA
LN DR WY
EASTVIEW
8700

88TH ST SE
RIVERCREST AV
GLACIER PEAK   AV
GORIN DR

CADET DR
89TH ST SE

PITAN
PARK & RIDE
90TH ST   SE
GORIN PL
35TH

BARING WY
9300
91ST
91ST ST SE

92ND
PL SE
92ND PL   SE
3500
91ST PL SE
36TH   AV   SE

6

94TH PL SE
94TH PL SE
95TH PL SE
95TH PL SE

96TH ST SE
96TH
PL SE
96TH AV

27TH
2700

97TH PL SE
97TH   AV
9600
98TH ST SE

33RD / DR SE
98TH
98TH ST SE

31ST   SE
1700
99TH PL SE   35TH
99TH ST SE

7

23RD DR SE
101ST   ST SE
100TH   ST SE

MID
27TH DR SE
101ST PL
102ND AV SE
34TH AV SE
3400
102ND
PL SE

104TH   PL
HILTON   LAKE
102ND PL SE
103RD PL SE

104TH PL SE
3200
103RD PL SE
104TH PL SE
40TH AV SE
10500

107TH PL SE
108TH
105TH PL SE
105TH PL SE
44TH AV SE
45TH
108TH ST SE

E   F   G   H   J

0   .125   .25   .375   .5   miles   1 in. = 1900 ft.

SEE 171 MAP

DETAIL

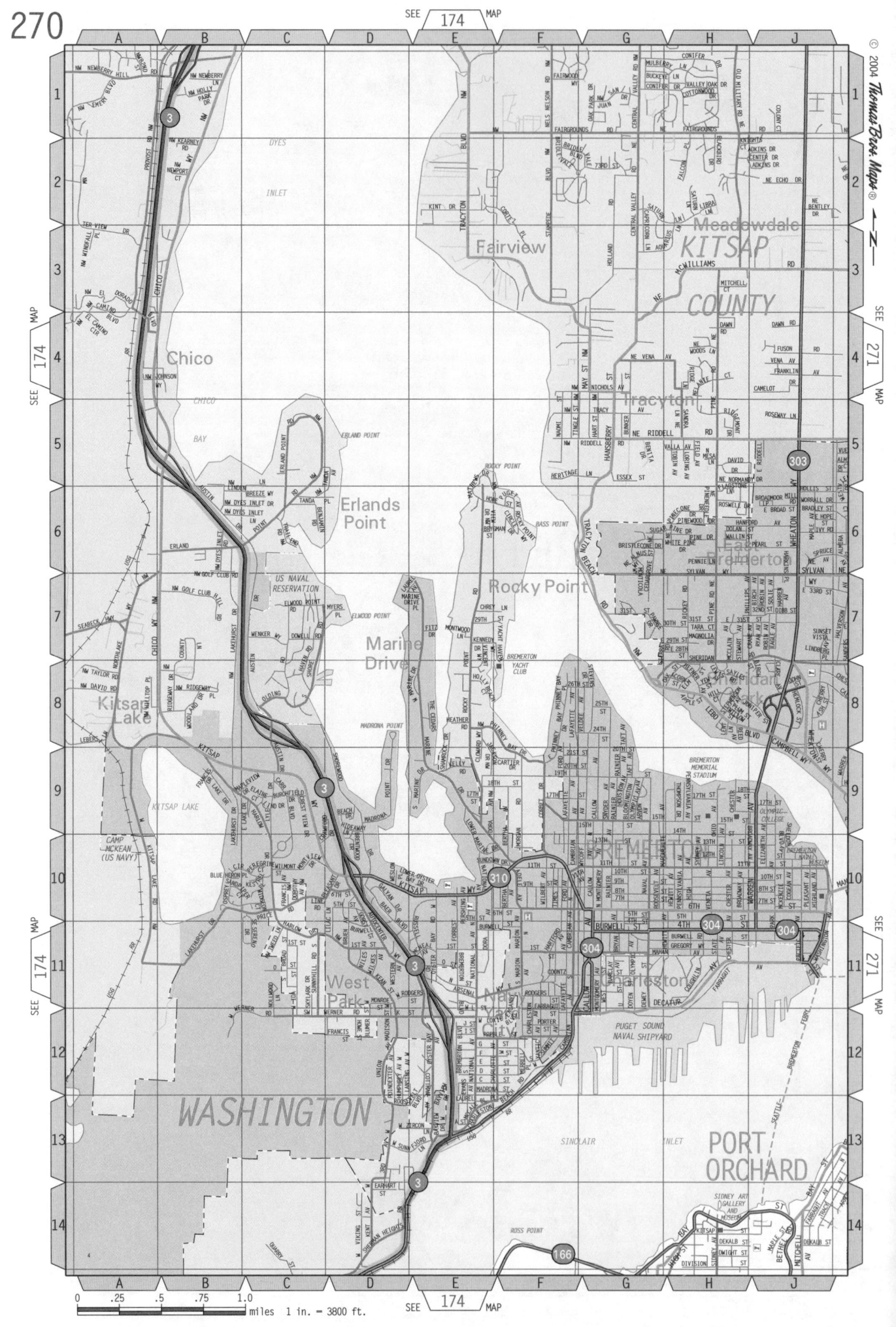

© 2004 Thomas Bros. Maps®

N

SEE 270 MAP

SEE 270 MAP

SEE 174 MAP

SEE 174 MAP

DETAIL

Gilberton

UNIVERSITY POINT

PORT

ORCHARD

BAINBRIDGE ISLAND

Winslow

EAGLE HARBOR

GAZZAM LAKE

KITSAP

COUNTY

WASHINGTON

Illahee

Crystal Springs

Lynwood Center

Point White

West Blakely

Waterman Point

Wautauga Beach

BREMERTON

Enetai

Waterman

MANCHESTER STATE PARK

MIDDLE POINT

CLAM BAY

Manette

ORCHARD POINT

NAVAL RESERVATION

SINCLAIR INLET

SEATTLE

Manchester

Annapolis

MITCHELL POINT

PORT ORCHARD

Colchester

0   .25   .5   .75   1.0

miles 1 in. = 3800 ft.

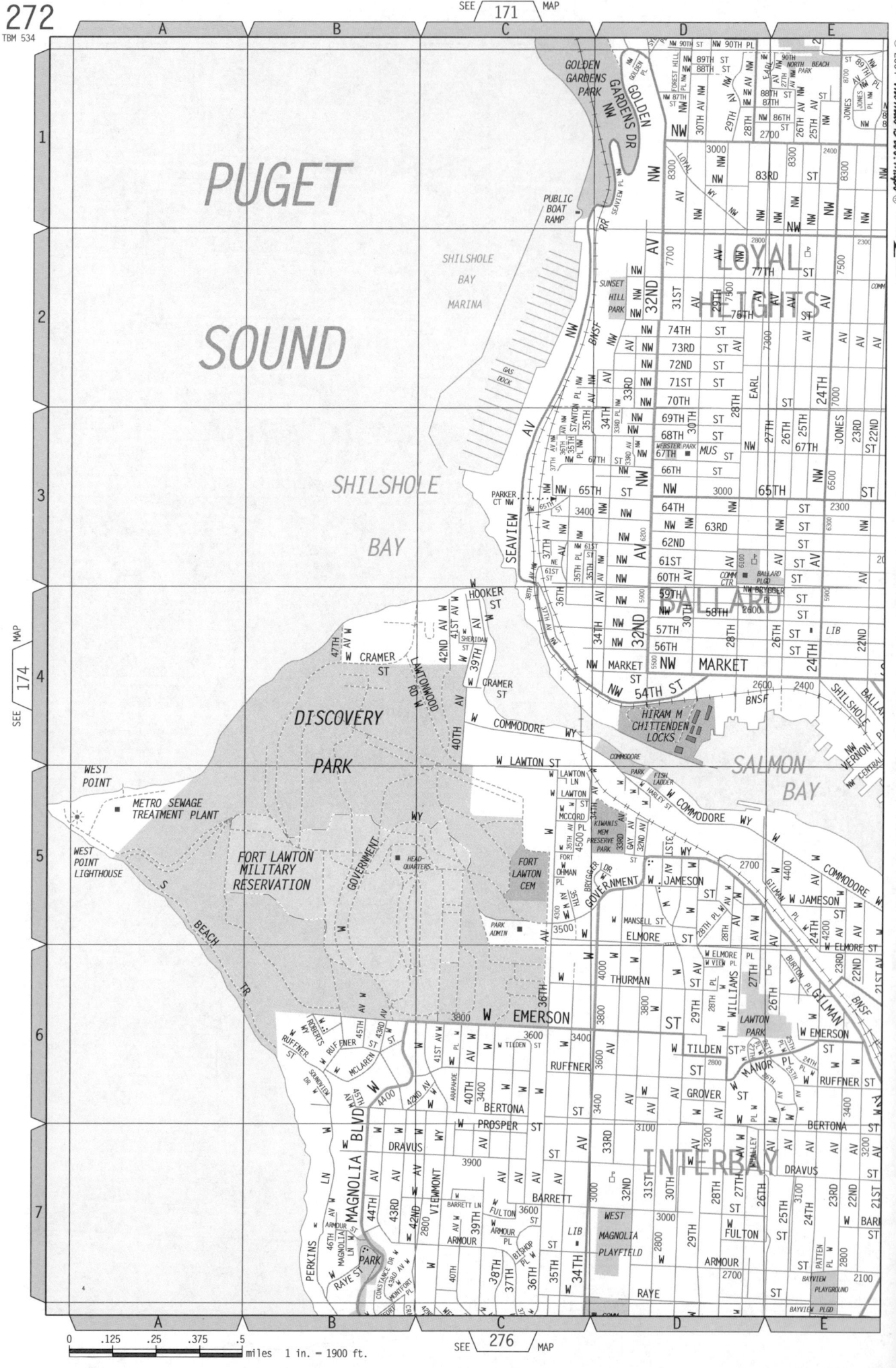

SEE 171 MAP

PUGET

SOUND

SHILSHOLE

BAY

GOLDEN
GARDENS
PARK

GOLDEN GARDENS DR NW

PUBLIC
BOAT
RAMP

SHILSHOLE
BAY
MARINA

GAS
DOCK

LOYAL HEIGHTS

SUNSET
HILL PARK

BALLARD

SEAVIEW AV

HOOKER ST

CRAMER ST

DISCOVERY

PARK

LAWTONWOOD RD W

CRAMER ST

COMMODORE WY

W LAWTON ST

COMMODORE WY

HIRAM M
CHITTENDEN
LOCKS

SALMON
BAY

WEST
POINT

METRO SEWAGE
TREATMENT PLANT

FORT LAWTON
MILITARY
RESERVATION

HEAD-
QUARTERS

FORT
LAWTON
CEM

KIWANIS
MEM
PRESERVE
PARK

W COMMODORE WY

W JAMESON

W JAMESON

WEST
POINT
LIGHTHOUSE

S BEACH TR

GOVERNMENT WY

PARK
ADMIN

ELMORE

W

THURMAN ST

LAWTON
PARK

W EMERSON

SEE 174 MAP

W EMERSON

MAGNOLIA BLVD W

RUFFNER ST

McLAREN

RUFFNER
ST

RUFFNER ST

BERTONA

W TILDEN ST

TILDEN ST

GROVER ST

MANOR PL

RUFFNER ST

PROSPER ST

DRAVUS

MAGNOLIA BLVD

DRAVUS

BERTONA

ST

BARRETT LN

BARRETT

VIEWMONT

INTERBAY

WEST
MAGNOLIA
PLAYFIELD

ARMOUR

FULTON

FULTON

MAGNOLIA
PARK

RAYE ST

ARMOUR

RAYE

BAYVIEW
PLAYGROUND

PERKINS LN

0   .125   .25   .375   .5   miles   1 in. = 1900 ft.

SEE 276 MAP

DETAIL

© 2004 Thomas Bros. Maps®

GREENWOOD

CROWN HILL

SEATTLE

CROWN HILL CEMETERY

BAKER PARK ON CROWN HILL

COMM CTR LOYAL HEIGHTS PLAYFIELD

CANOE SALMON BAY PARK SLOOP

BALLARD HS PLGD

SWEDISH HEALTH SERVICES BALLARD

GILMAN PLGD

GREEN LAKE

GREEN LAKE PARK

GREEN LAKE GOLF COURSE

WOODLAND PARK

WOODLAND PARK ZOO

ROSE GARDEN

ROSS PLGD

BRIGHT

BOAT LAUNCH

FISHERMANS TERMINAL

B F DAY PLGD

BOWDOIN PL

MENFORD PLGD

WALLINGFORD PLGD

NICKERSON ST

W EWING ST

WEST EWING PK

FREMONT CANAL PARK

ROYAL BROUGHAM PAVILION

SEATTLE PACIFIC UNIV

LAKE WASHINGTON SHIP CANAL

N CANAL ST

FREMONT

NORTHLAKE WY

LAKE UNION

BURKE

INTERBAY ATHLETIC FIELD

MT PLEASANT CEM

HILLS OF ETERNITY CEM

ARMOUR

NEWELL

QUEEN ANNE BOWL PLFD

DAVID RODGERS PARK

DETAIL

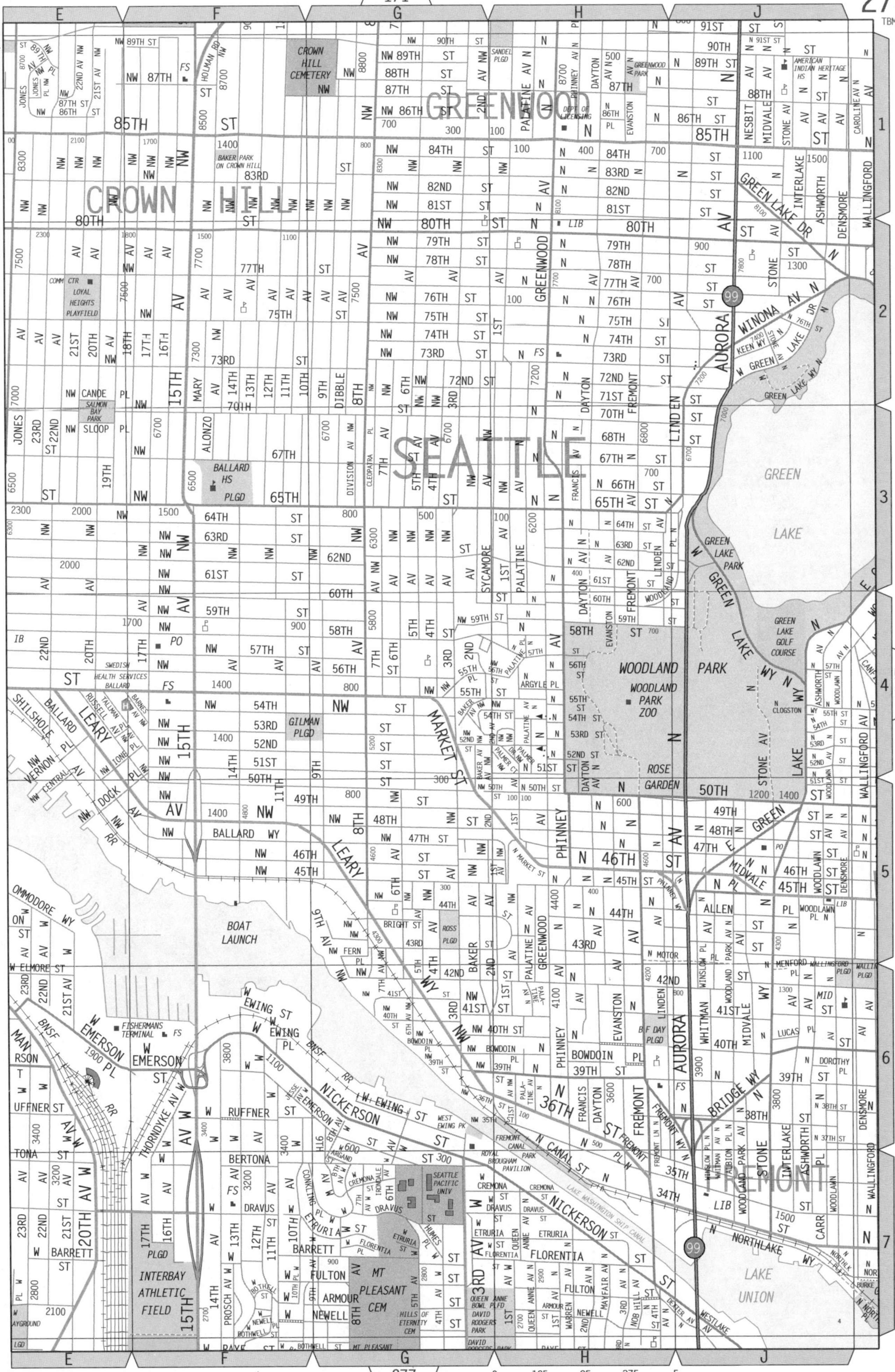

SEE 274 MAP

SEE 277 MAP

0 .125 .25 .375 .5 miles   1 in. = 1900 ft.

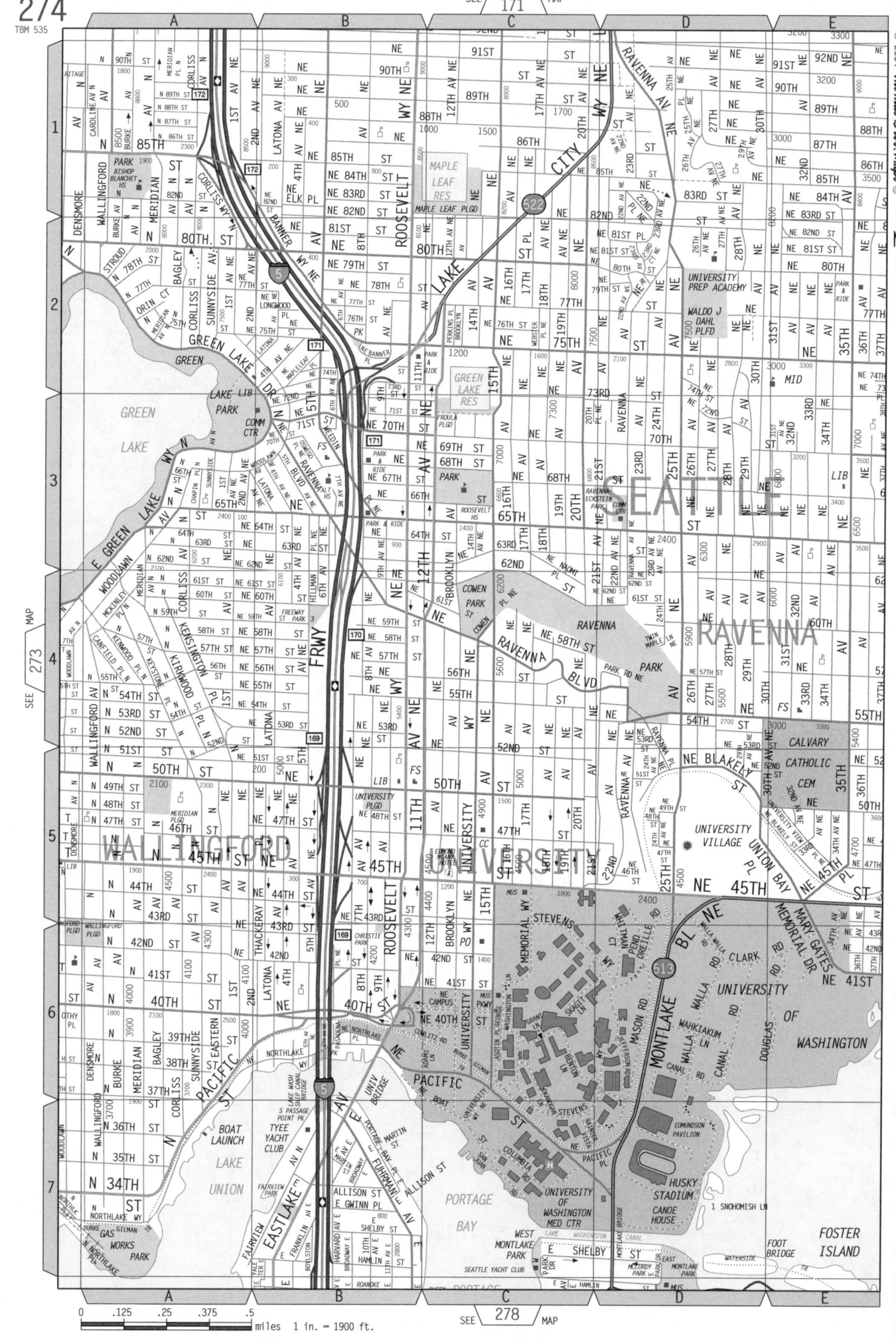

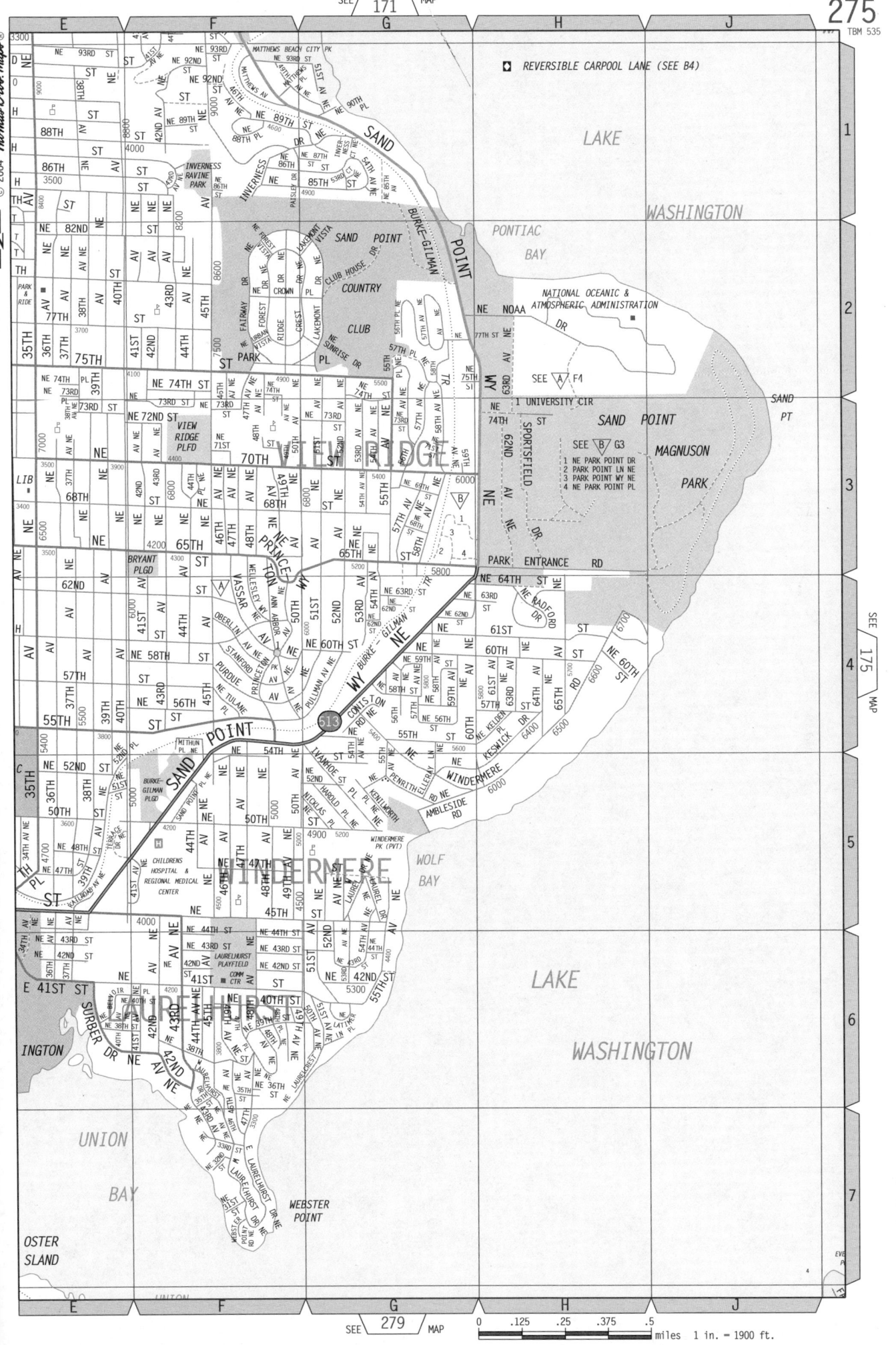

© 2004 Thomas Bros. Maps®

REVERSIBLE CARPOOL LANE (SEE B4)

LAKE

WASHINGTON

PONTIAC BAY

NATIONAL OCEANIC & ATMOSPHERIC ADMINISTRATION

SAND POINT

MAGNUSON PARK

SEE A F4

1 UNIVERSITY CIR

SEE B G3
1 NE PARK POINT DR
2 PARK POINT LN NE
3 PARK POINT WY NE
4 NE PARK POINT PL

SAND PT

VIEW RIDGE

VIEW RIDGE PLFD

PARK ENTRANCE RD

SAND POINT COUNTRY CLUB PARK

BRYANT PLGD

513

SAND POINT

WINDERMERE

WOLF BAY

CHILDRENS HOSPITAL & REGIONAL MEDICAL CENTER

WINDERMERE PK (PVT)

LAURELHURST PLAYFIELD

COMM CTR

LAURELHURST

SURBER DR NE

LAKE

WASHINGTON

UNION

BAY

OSTER SLAND

WEBSTER POINT

DETAIL

SEE 175 MAP

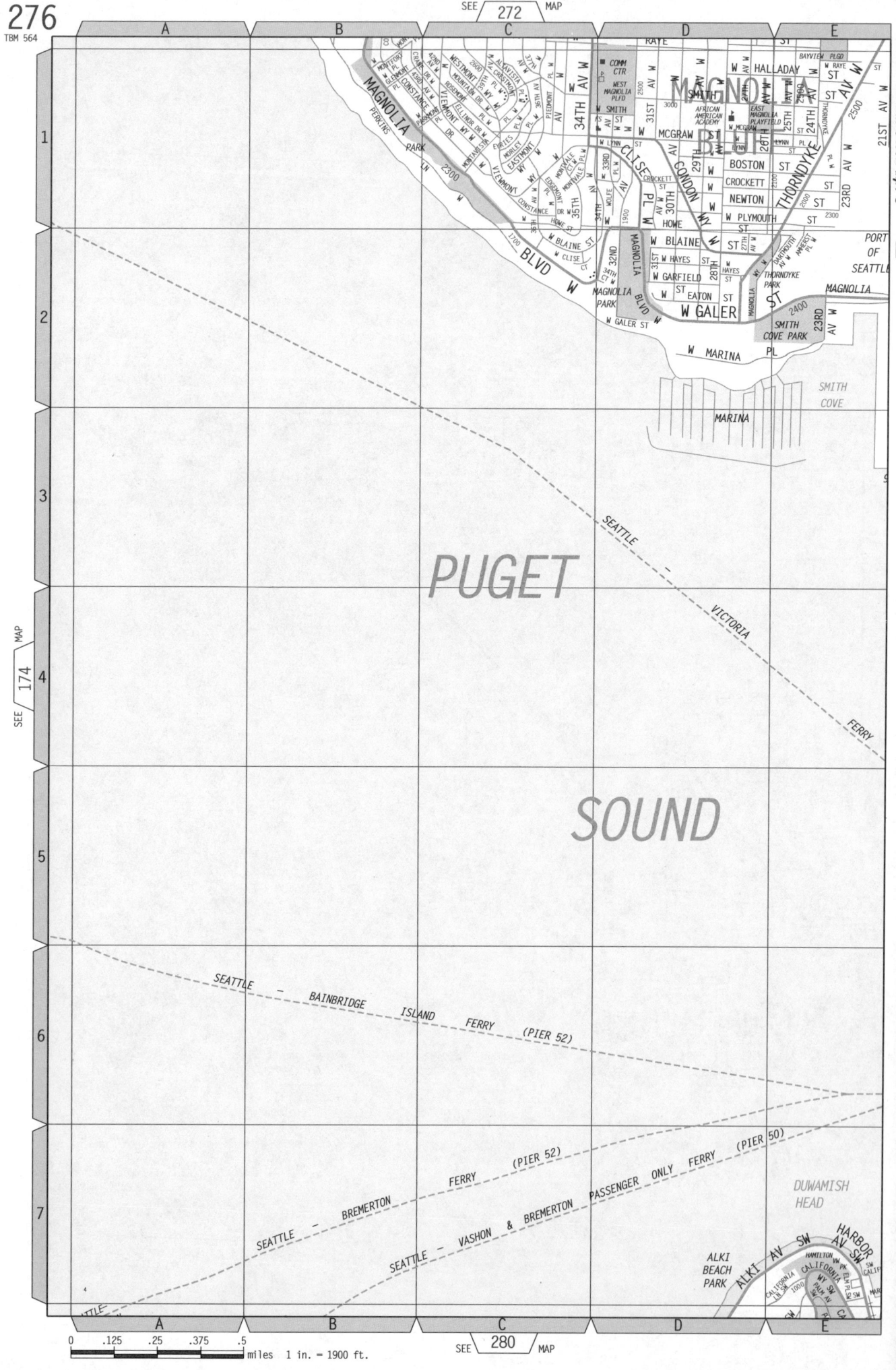

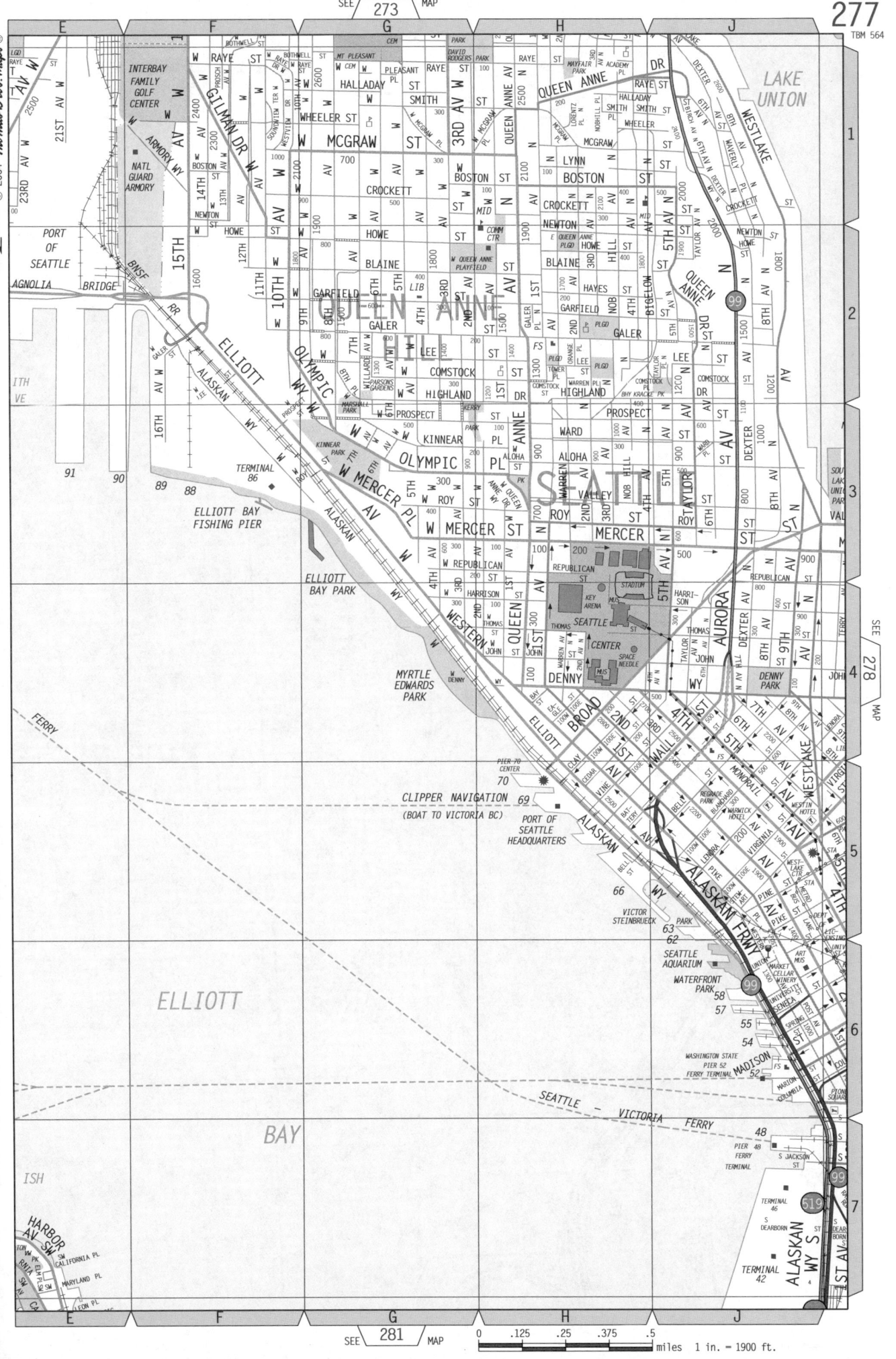

© 2004 Thomas Bros. Maps®

—N—1

LAKE
UNION

PORT
OF
SEATTLE

AGNOLIA   BRIDGE

ITH
VE

91   90   89   88

TERMINAL
86

ELLIOTT BAY
FISHING PIER

ELLIOTT
BAY PARK

MYRTLE
EDWARDS
PARK

INTERBAY
FAMILY
GOLF
CENTER

NATL
GUARD
ARMORY

QUEEN ANNE

SEATTLE

QUEEN ANNE HILL

KEY ARENA

SEATTLE
CENTER

SPACE
NEEDLE

DENNY
PARK

FERRY

ELLIOTT

BAY

ISH

PIER 70
CENTER
70

CLIPPER NAVIGATION
69
(BOAT TO VICTORIA BC)

PORT OF
SEATTLE
HEADQUARTERS

66

VICTOR
STEINBRUECK
PARK

63
62

SEATTLE
AQUARIUM

WATERFRONT
PARK   58

57

55
54

WASHINGTON STATE
PIER 52
FERRY TERMINAL
52

SEATTLE – VICTORIA   FERRY

48
PIER 48
FERRY
TERMINAL

TERMINAL
46

TERMINAL
42

HARBOR
AV SW

CALIFORNIA PL

MARYLAND PL

LEON PL

ALASKAN FRWY

DEARBORN

99

519

DETAIL

0   .125   .25   .375   .5
miles 1 in. = 1900 ft.

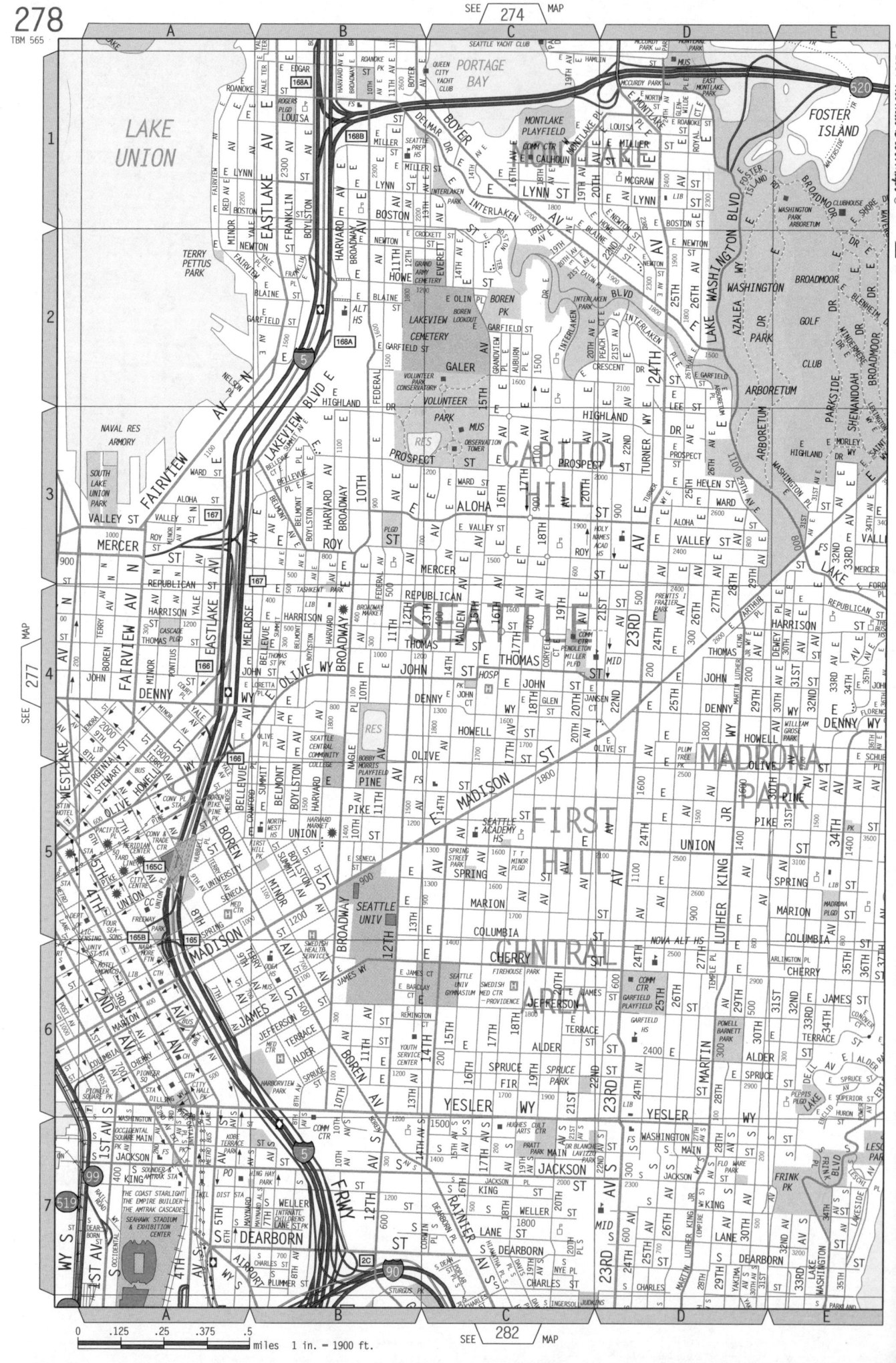

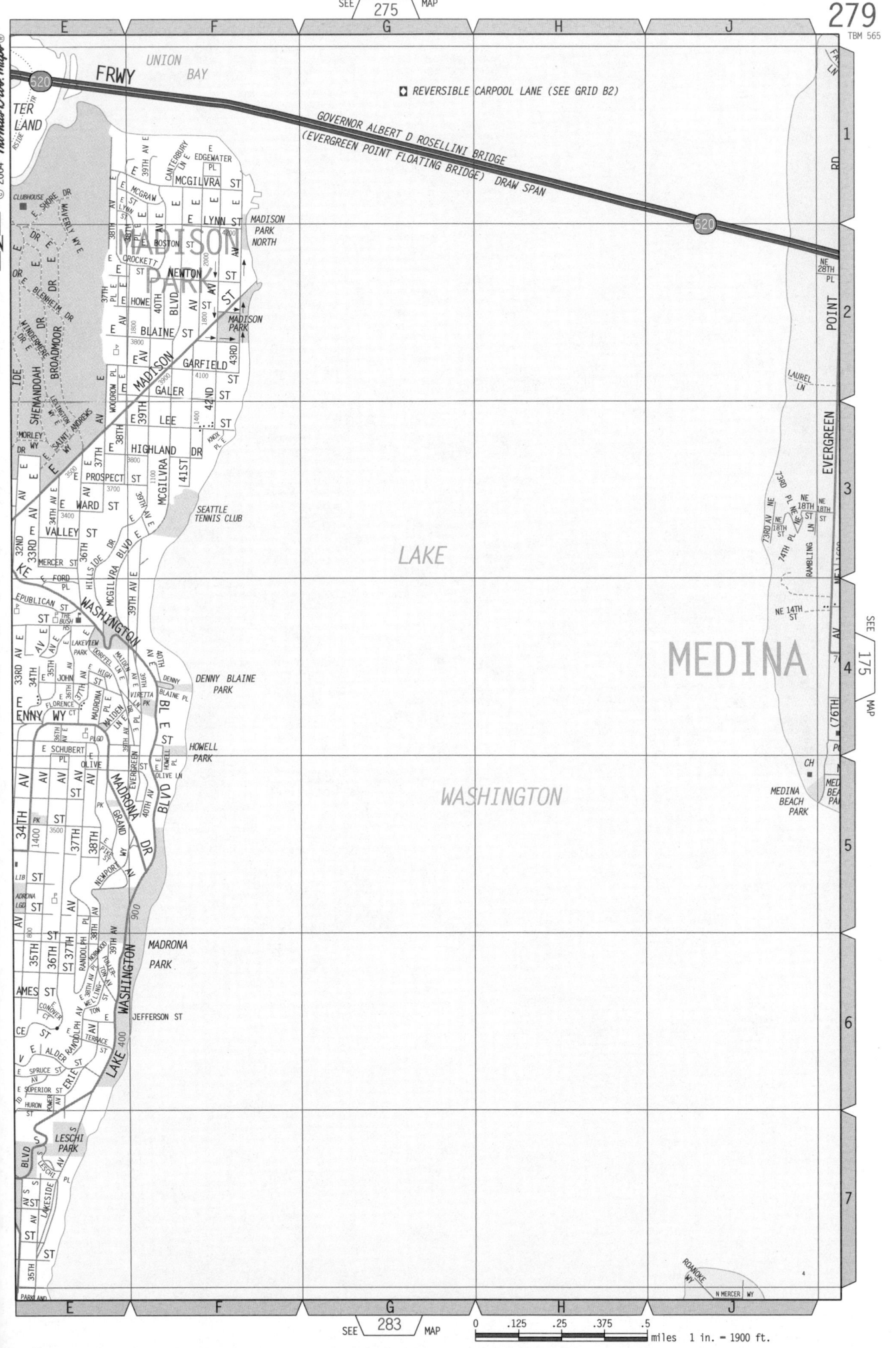

© 2004 *Thomas Bros. Maps* ®

0   .125   .25   .375   .5
miles   1 in. = 1900 ft.

DETAIL

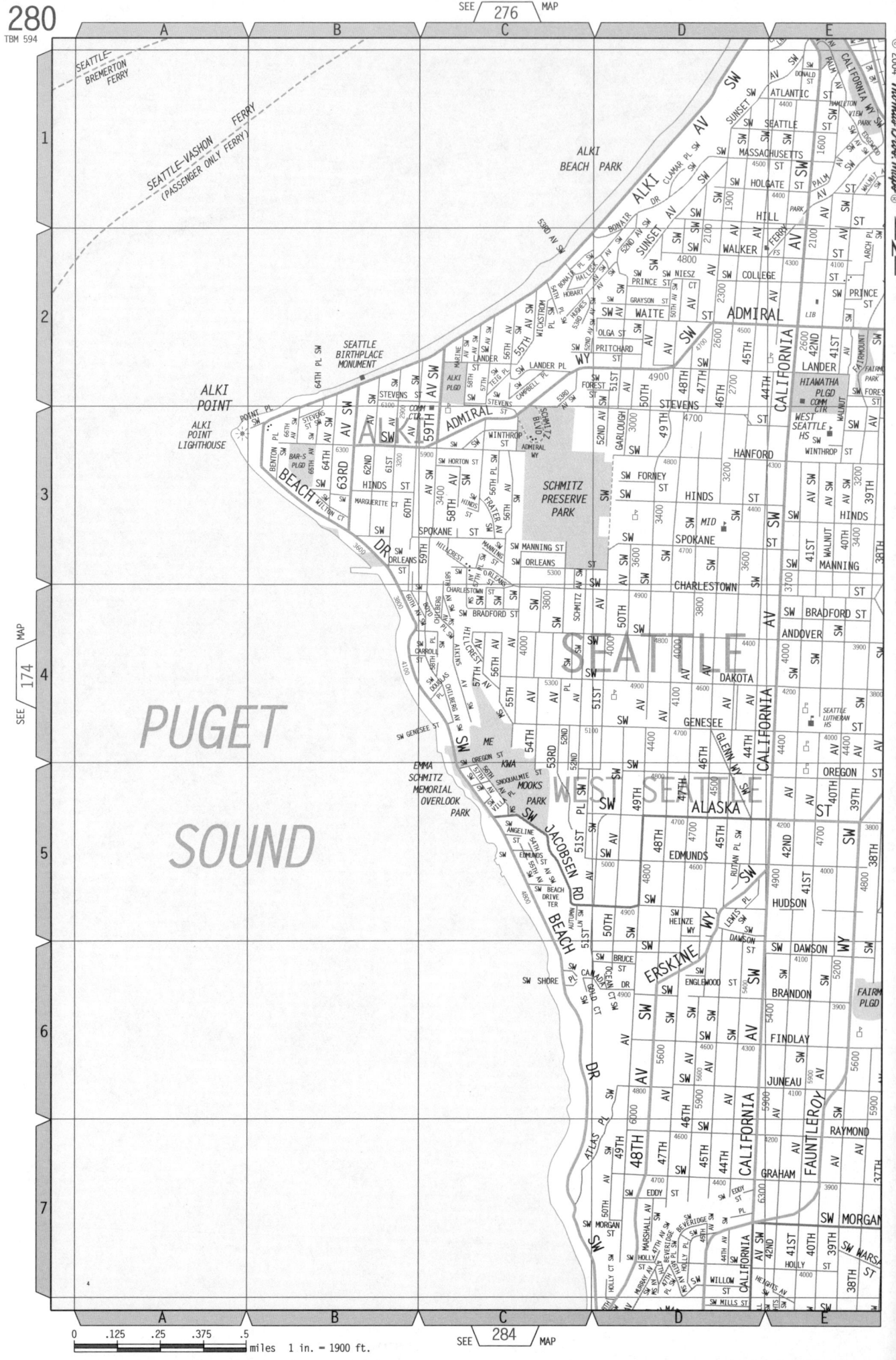

© 2004 Thomas Bros. Maps® —N—

PUGET

SOUND

SEATTLE

WEST SEATTLE

ALKI
BEACH PARK

ALKI
POINT

ALKI
POINT
LIGHTHOUSE

SEATTLE
BIRTHPLACE
MONUMENT

SCHMITZ
PRESERVE
PARK

EMMA
SCHMITZ
MEMORIAL
OVERLOOK
PARK

0 .125 .25 .375 .5 miles   1 in. = 1900 ft.

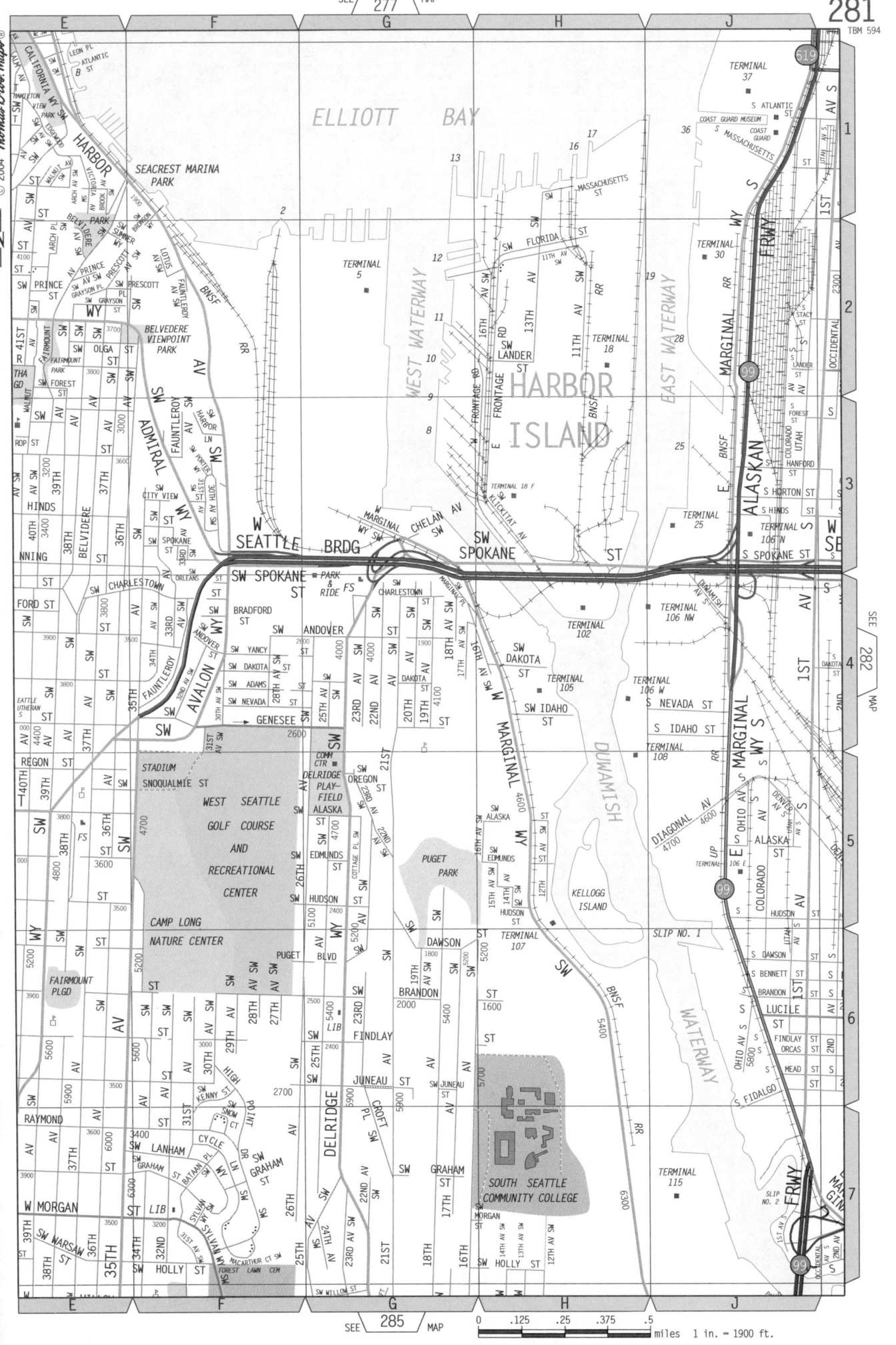

ELLIOTT BAY

HARBOR ISLAND

WEST WATERWAY

EAST WATERWAY

SEACREST MARINA PARK

BELVEDERE VIEWPOINT PARK

TERMINAL 37

COAST GUARD MUSEUM

TERMINAL 30

TERMINAL 18

TERMINAL 25

TERMINAL 106 NW

TERMINAL 102

TERMINAL 105

TERMINAL 106 W

TERMINAL 108

W SEATTLE BRDG

SW SPOKANE ST

PARK & RIDE

DUWAMISH

WEST SEATTLE GOLF COURSE AND RECREATIONAL CENTER

CAMP LONG NATURE CENTER

FAIRMOUNT PLGD

PUGET PARK

KELLOGG ISLAND

TERMINAL 106 E

ALASKA ST

SLIP NO. 1

TERMINAL 107

WATERWAY

SOUTH SEATTLE COMMUNITY COLLEGE

TERMINAL 115

FOREST LAWN CEM

SLIP NO. 2

DETAIL

0 .125 .25 .375 .5 miles 1 in. = 1900 ft.

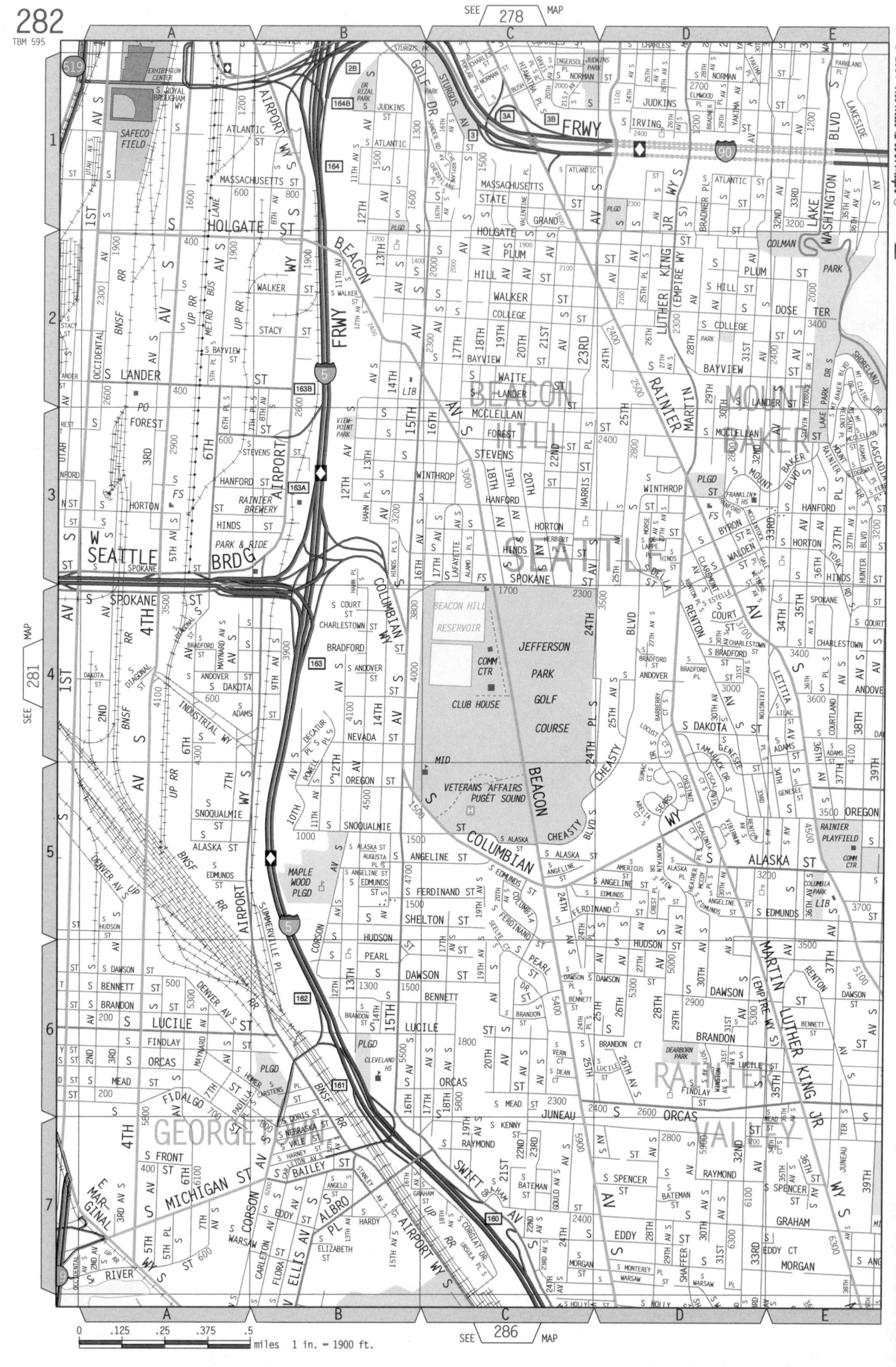

SEE 278 MAP

© 2004 Thomas Bros. Maps® —N—

DETAIL

0 .125 .25 .375 .5 miles   1 in. = 1900 ft.

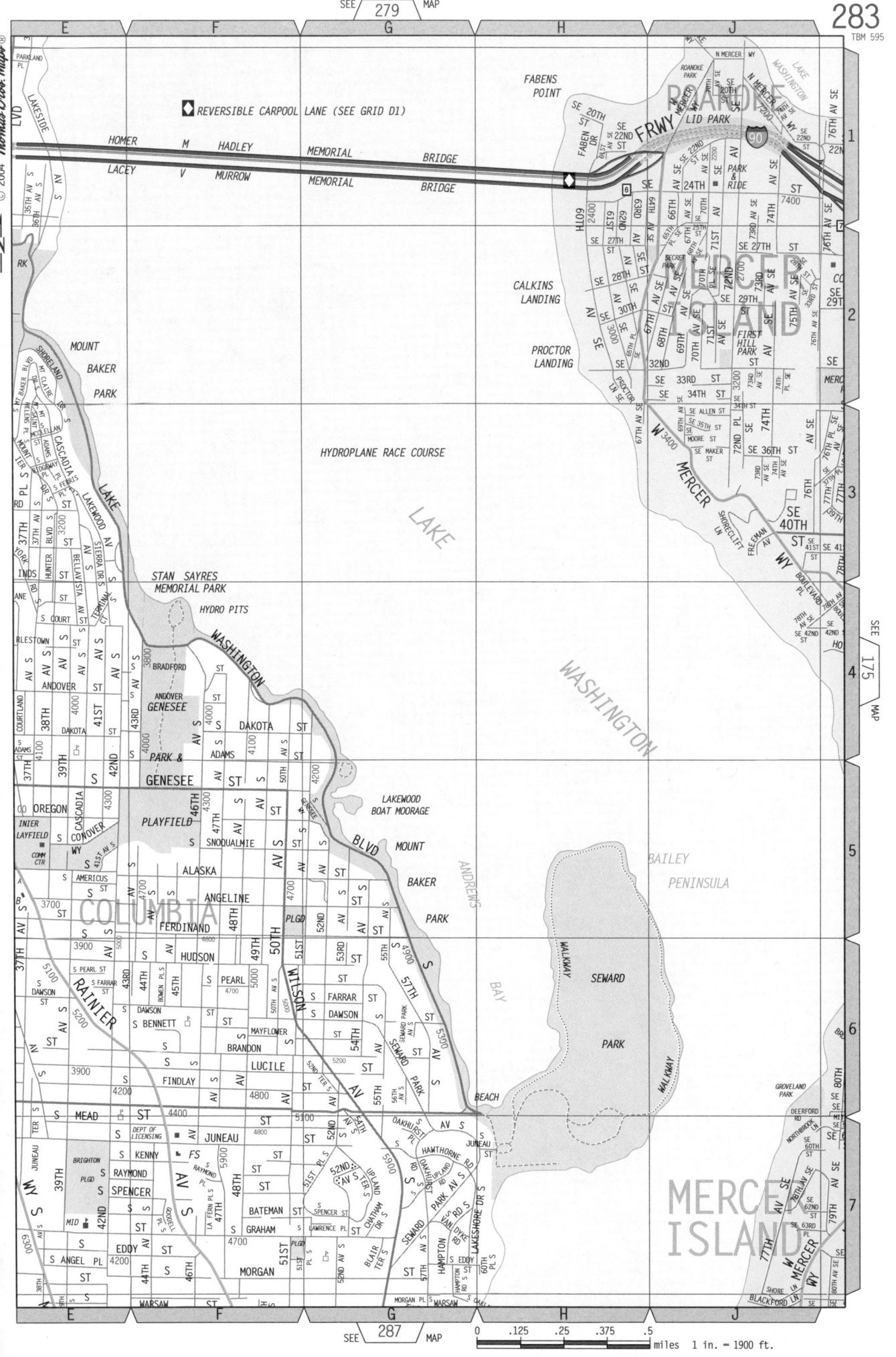

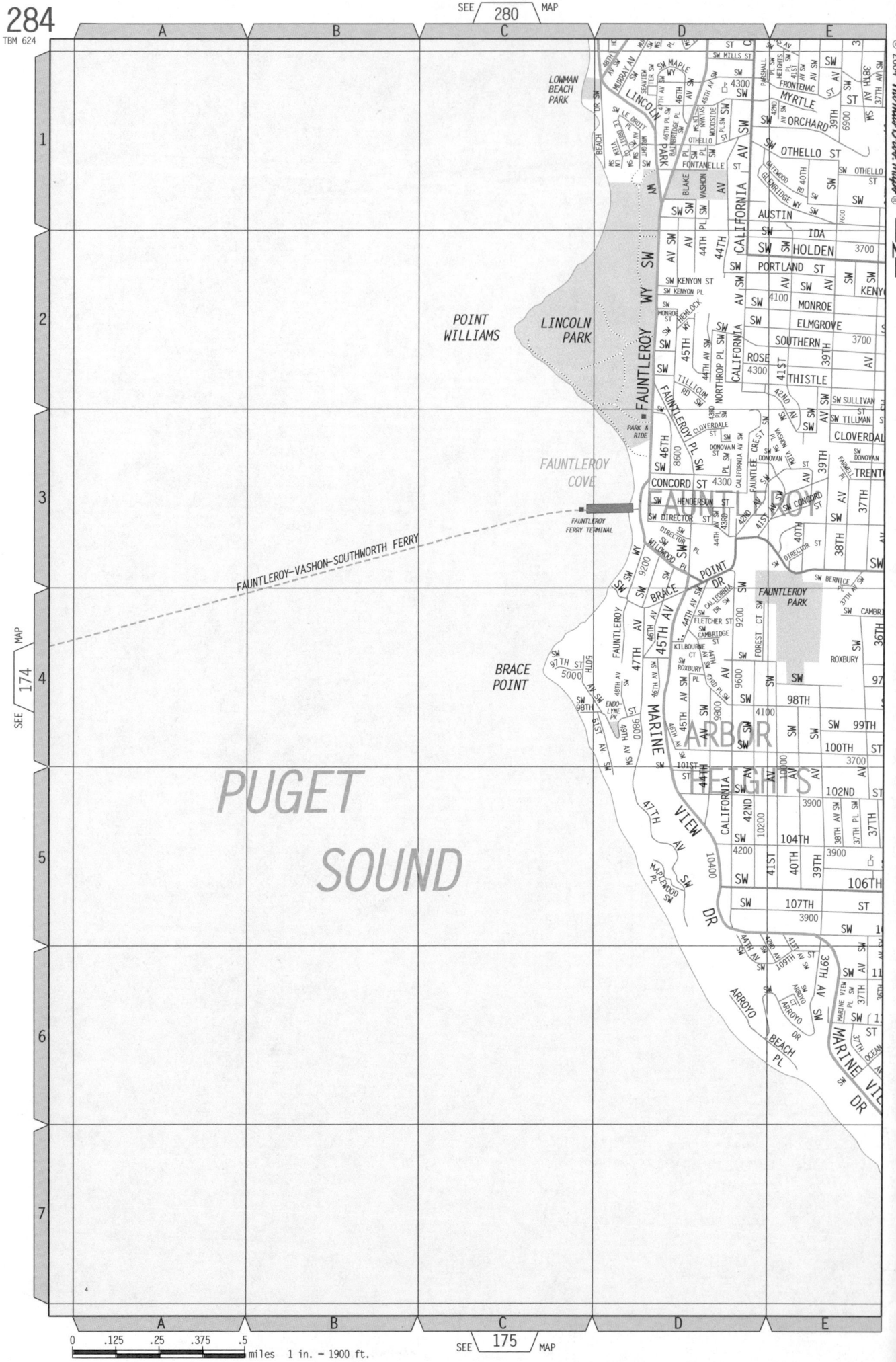

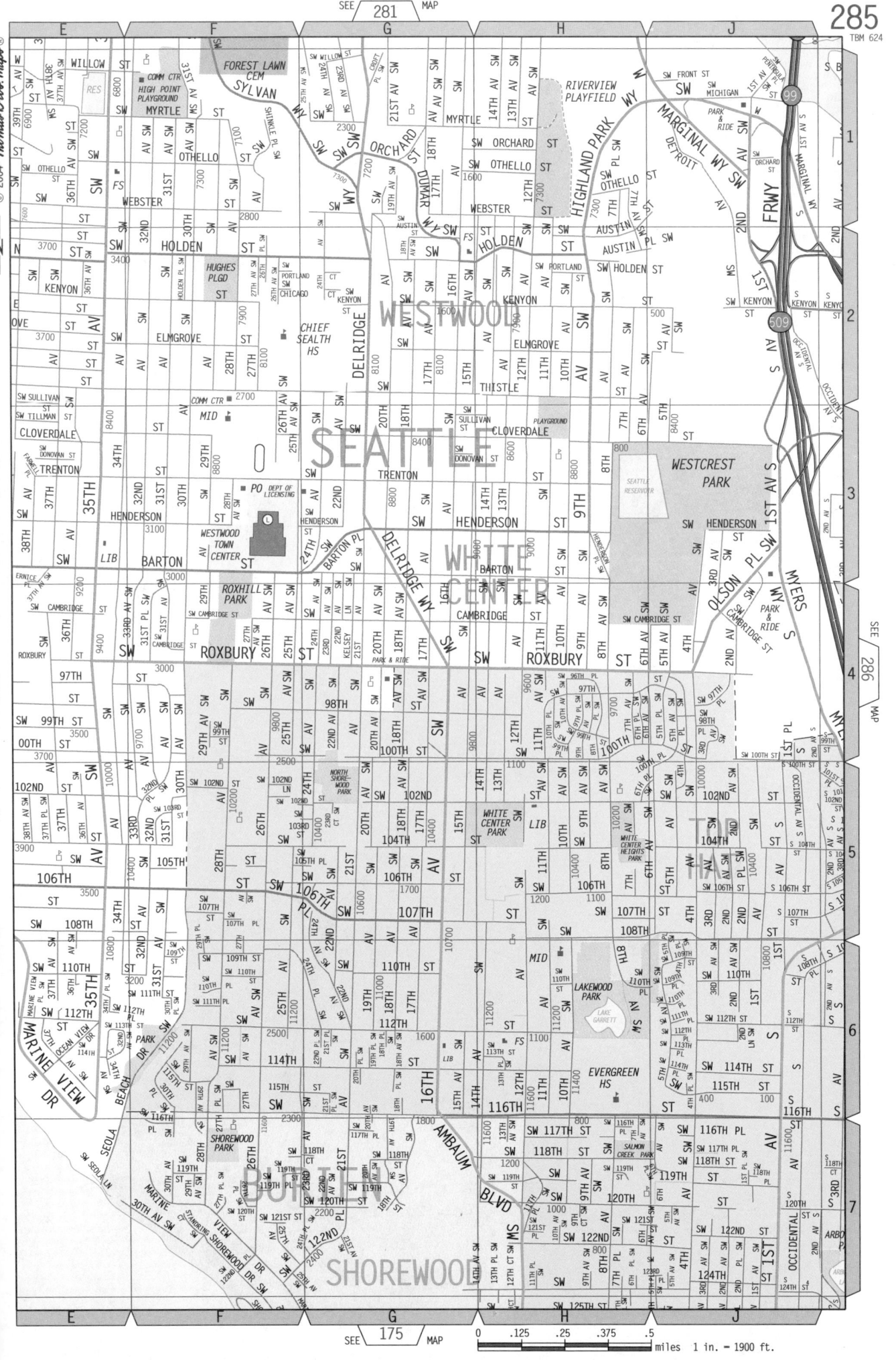

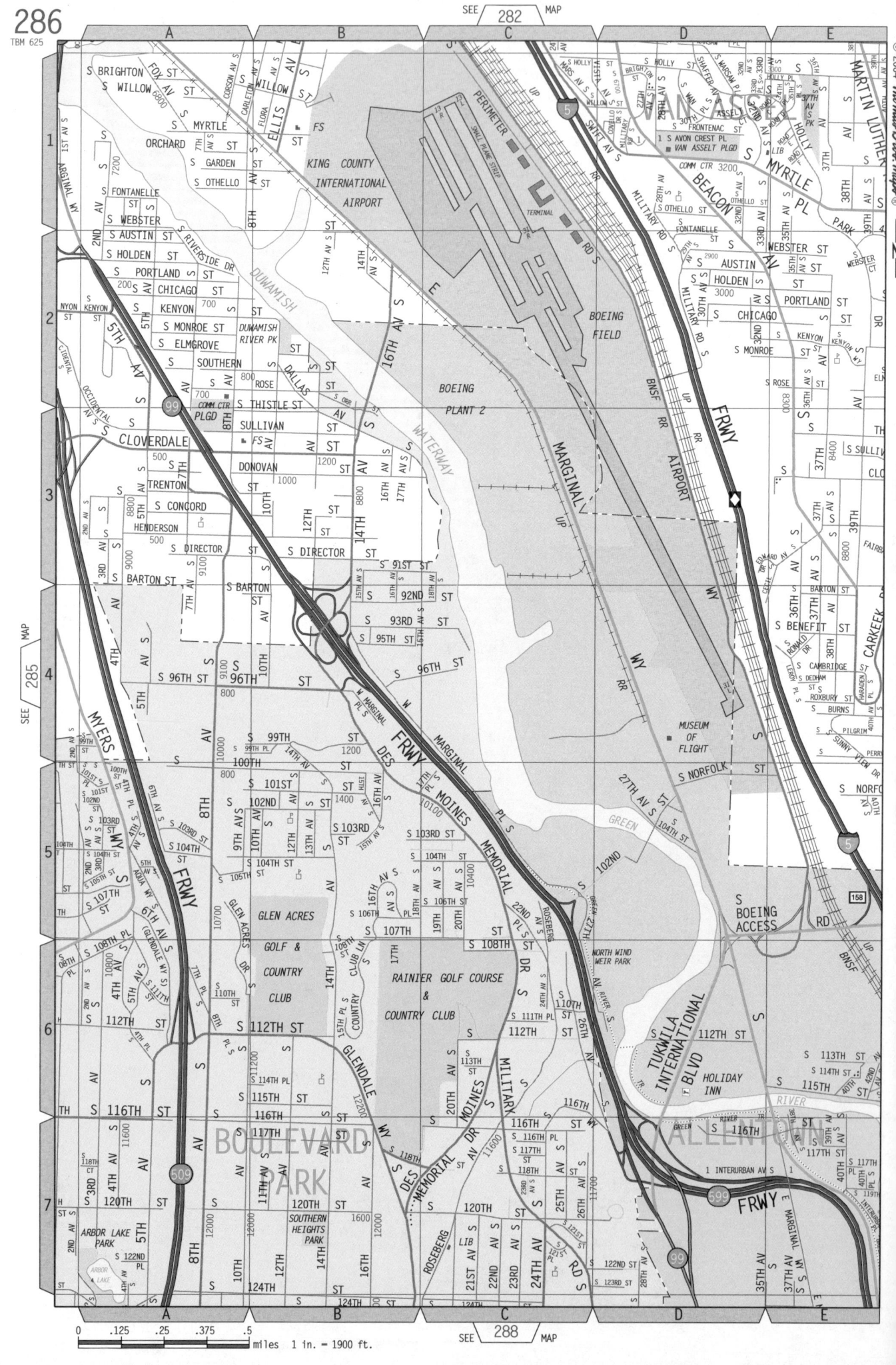

© 2004 Thomas Bros. Maps®

SEE 282 MAP

SEE 285 MAP

DETAIL

0 .125 .25 .375 .5 miles   1 in. = 1900 ft.

SEE 288 MAP

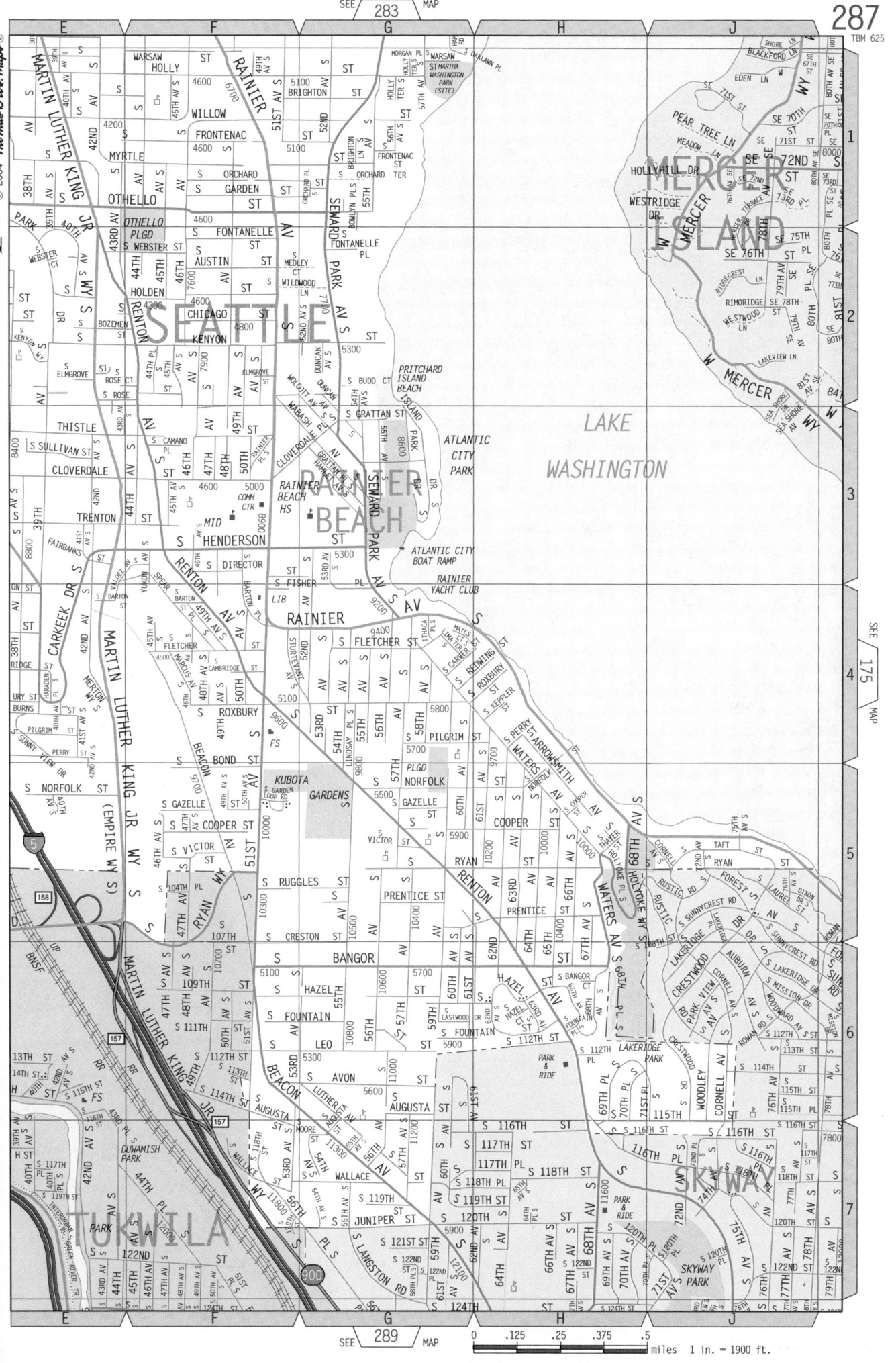

DETAIL

SEE 175 MAP

0 .125 .25 .375 .5
miles 1 in. = 1900 ft.

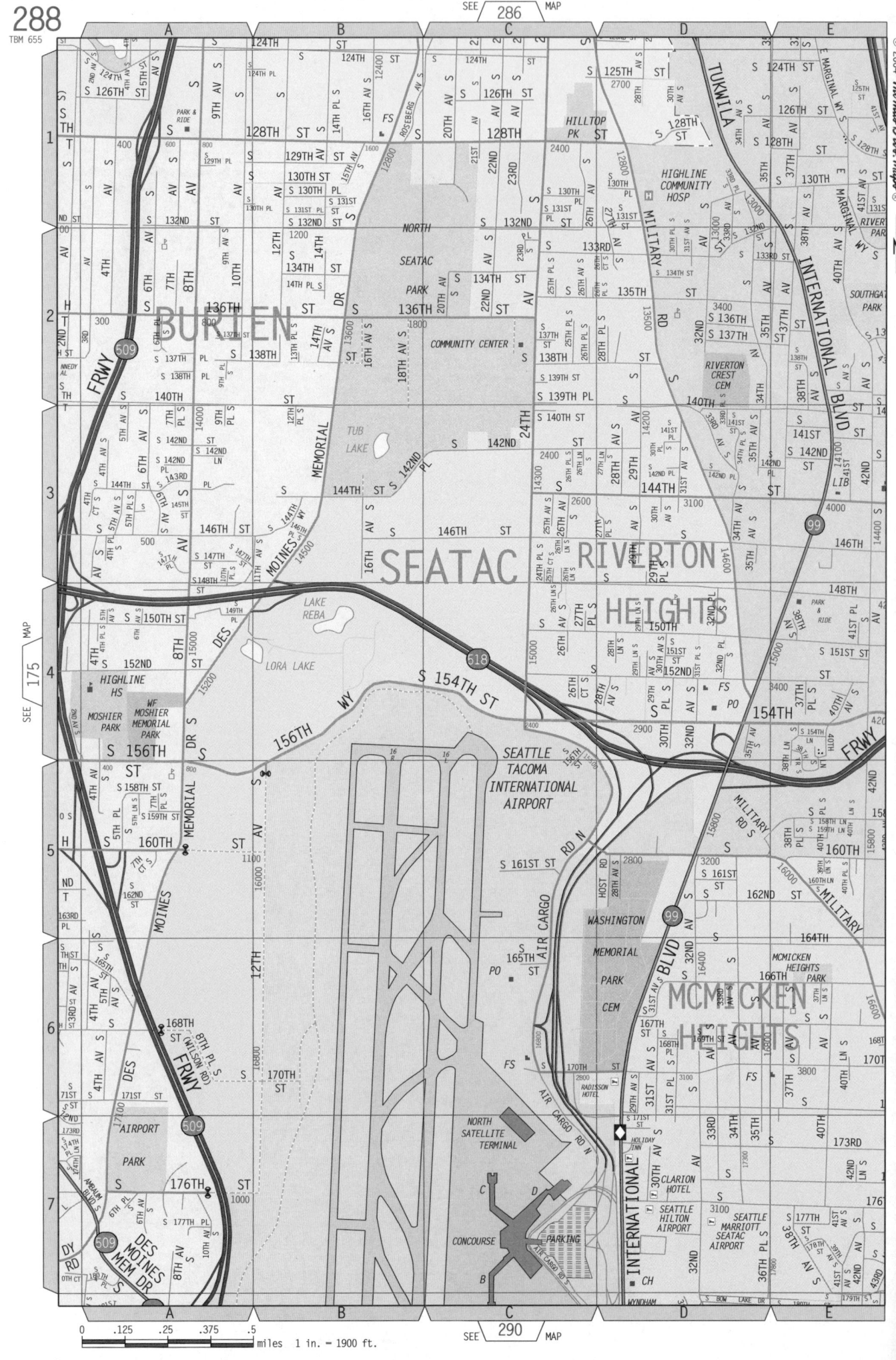

© 2004 Thomas Bros. Maps ®

—N—

SEE / 286 \ MAP

SEE / 175 \ MAP

DETAIL

BURIEN

NORTH SEATAC PARK

SEATAC

RIVERTON HEIGHTS

MCMICKEN HEIGHTS

TUKWILA

HILLTOP PK

HIGHLINE COMMUNITY HOSP

RIVERTON CREST CEM

SOUTHGATE PARK

RIVER PARK

COMMUNITY CENTER

TUB LAKE

LAKE REBA

LORA LAKE

HIGHLINE HS

MOSHIER PARK

WF MOSHIER MEMORIAL PARK

AIRPORT PARK

SEATTLE TACOMA INTERNATIONAL AIRPORT

WASHINGTON MEMORIAL PARK CEM

NORTH SATELLITE TERMINAL

RADISSON HOTEL

HOLIDAY INN

CLARION HOTEL

SEATTLE HILTON AIRPORT

SEATTLE MARRIOTT SEATAC AIRPORT

CONCOURSE

PARKING

WYNDHAM

SEE / 290 \ MAP

0 .125 .25 .375 .5

miles 1 in. = 1900 ft.

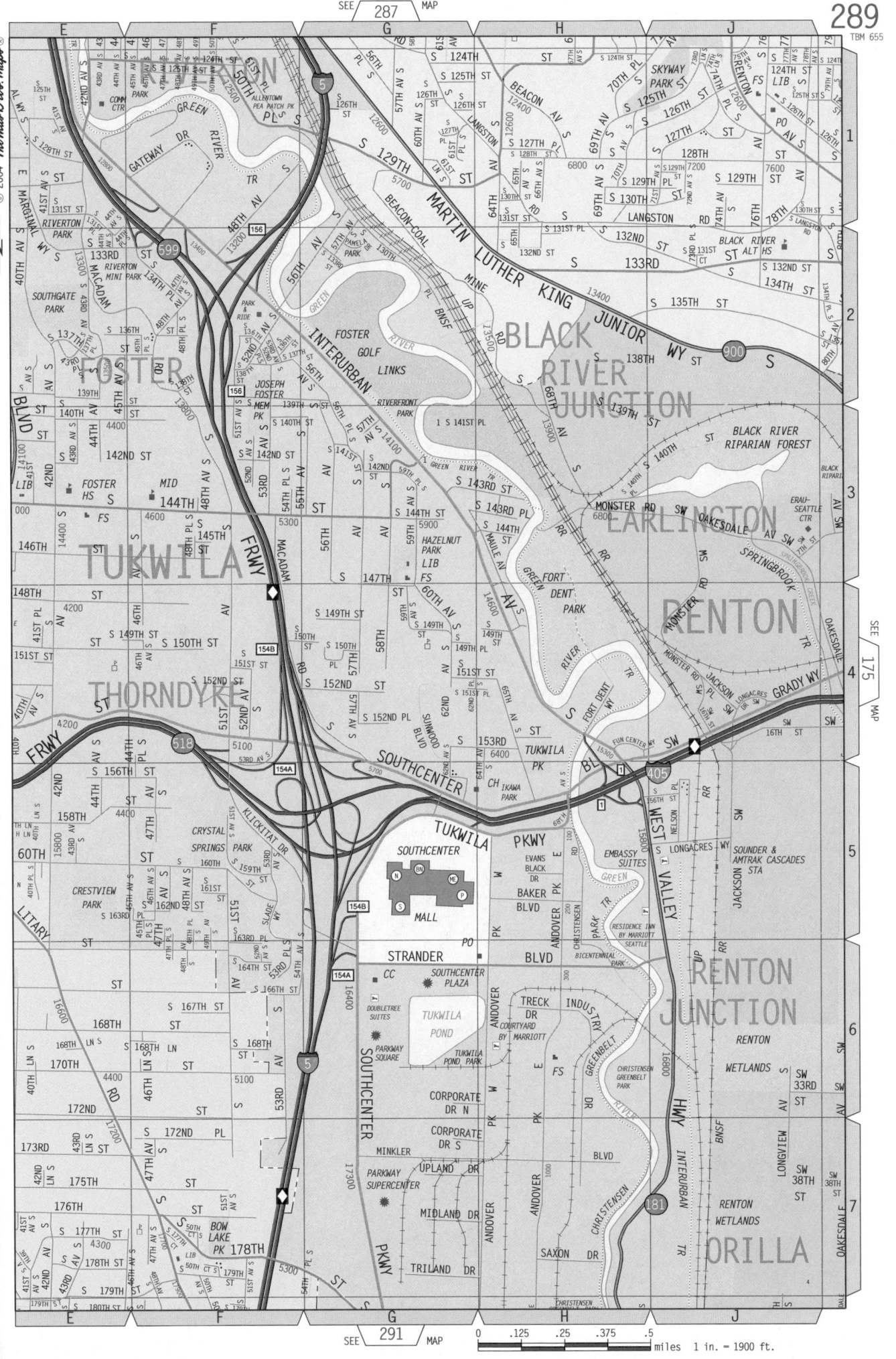

© 2004 Thomas Bros. Maps®

N

SEE 175 MAP

DETAIL

0   .125   .25   .375   .5
miles 1 in. = 1900 ft.

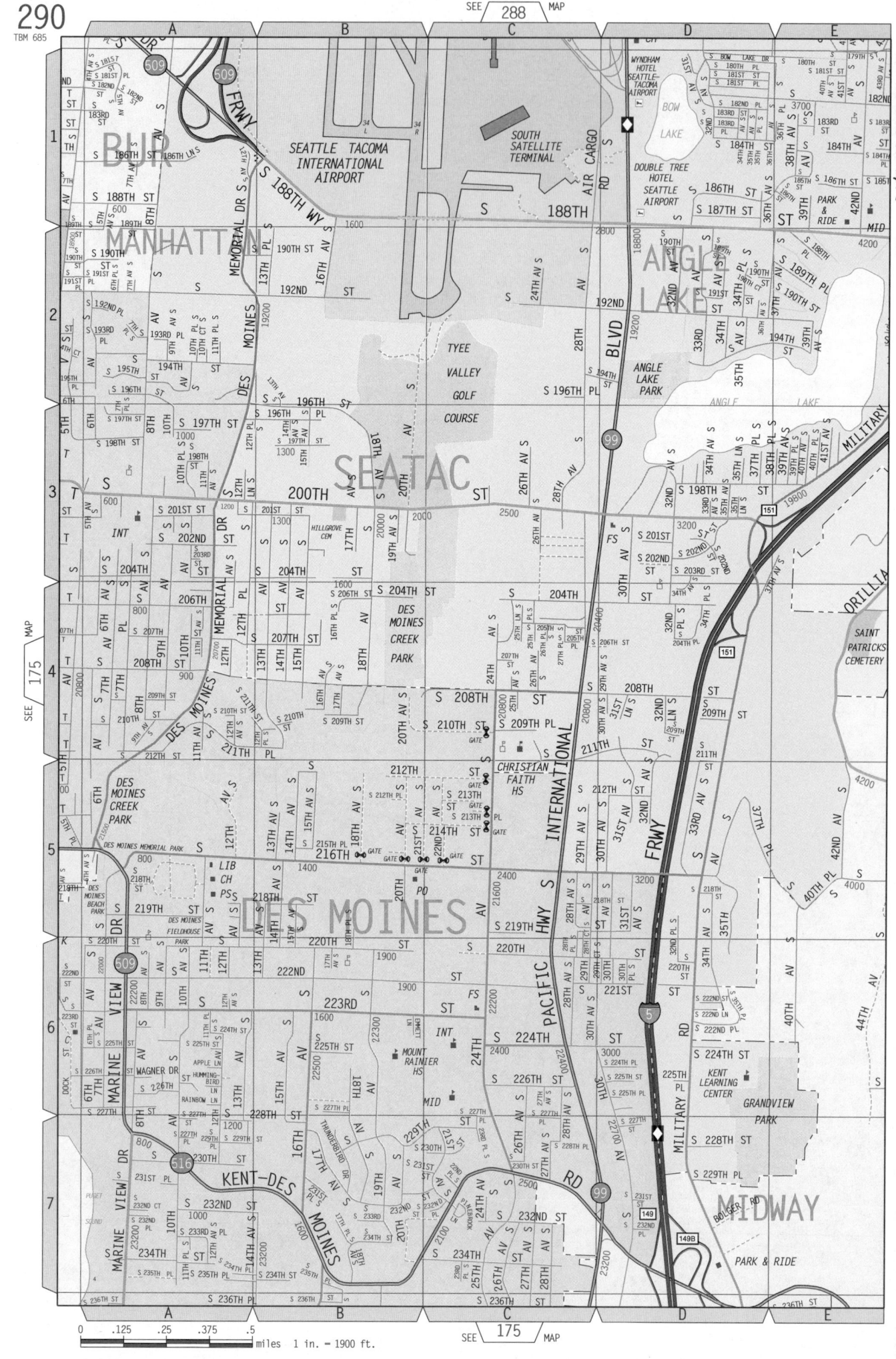

SEE 288 MAP

© 2004 Thomas Bros. Maps ®

—N—

BUR

MANHATTAN

SEATTLE TACOMA
INTERNATIONAL
AIRPORT

SOUTH
SATELLITE
TERMINAL

WYNDHAM
HOTEL
SEATTLE-
TACOMA
AIRPORT

BOW
LAKE

DOUBLE TREE
HOTEL
SEATTLE
AIRPORT

PARK
&
RIDE

MID

ANGLE
LAKE

ANGLE LAKE

TYEE
VALLEY
GOLF
COURSE

ANGLE LAKE PARK

SEATAC

MILITARY

ORILLIA

SAINT
PATRICKS
CEMETERY

DES
MOINES
CREEK
PARK

HILLGROVE CEM

INT

SEE 175 MAP

DES MOINES
CREEK
PARK

DES MOINES MEMORIAL PARK

CHRISTIAN
FAITH
HS

DES MOINES BEACH PARK

DES MOINES FIELDHOUSE PARK

LIB
CH
PS

DES MOINES

INT

MOUNT
RAINIER
HS

KENT
LEARNING
CENTER

GRANDVIEW
PARK

MARINE VIEW DR

WAGNER DR

APPLE LN
HUMMINGBIRD LN
RAINBOW LN

KENT-DES MOINES

THUNDERBIRD DR

PUGET SOUND

MIDWAY

PARK & RIDE

DETAIL

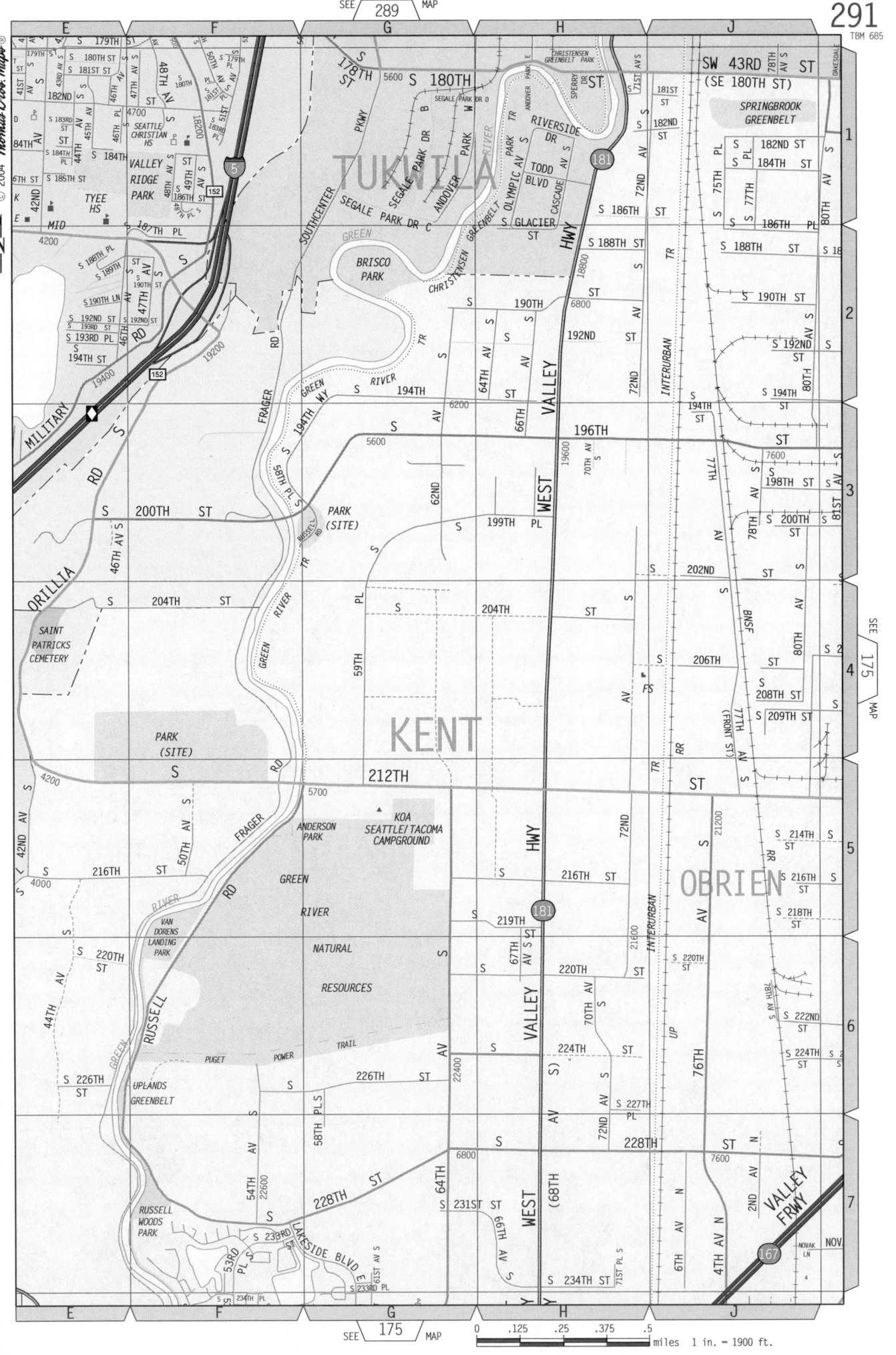

© 2004 *Thomas Bros. Maps*®

—N—

E F G H J

179TH
S 179TH ST
41ST
AV
43RD
41ST
AV
S 180TH ST
48TH AV
S
S 181ST ST
50TH
179TH
182ND
ST
46TH AV
47TH AV
PL
4700
48TH
180TH
PL
43RD
179TH
PL
ST
4800
S 5600 S 180TH
178TH
ST
178TH ST
SEGALE PARK DR B
SEGALE PARK DR D
RIVER
ANDOVER PARK E
CHRISTENSEN GREENBELT PARK
SPERRY DR
ST
71ST AVS
SW 43RD ST
(SE 180TH ST)
181ST
ST
182ND

SEATTLE CHRISTIAN HS
S 183RD ST
45TH AV PL
46TH PL
184TH
184TH ST
ST
49TH
AV
TUKWILA
RIVERSIDE DR
TODD BLVD
CASCADE
S GLACIER ST
181
72ND AV
S
S 186TH
75TH PL
77TH
PL
182ND ST
184TH ST

84TH AV
6TH ST
42ND AV
K
E
TYEE HS
MID
4200
VALLEY RIDGE PARK
48TH AV S
49TH AV
S 185TH ST
186TH ST
S 186TH PL
187TH PL
SEGALE PARK DR C
OLYMPIC AV S
ANDOVER PARK W
CHRISTENSEN GREENBELT
S
S 188TH ST
18800
S
71ST TR
S 188TH ST
80TH AV
S 18

5
152
S 188TH PL
S 189TH
ST
47TH
AV
ST
S
S 190TH LN
S 192ND ST
46TH RD S
192ND ST
S 193RD PL
194TH ST
19200
19400
152
S 190TH
ST
ST
64TH AV
S
66TH
S
194TH
6200
S
ST
S
190TH
192ND
72ND AV
S
INTERURBAN
S 190TH ST
S 192ND
AV
80TH
S 194TH
ST

MILITARY
RD
S
FRAGER RD
GREEN
58TH PL S
194TH WY
RIVER
5600
196TH
WEST
19600
70TH AV
S
196TH
ST
194TH
ST
77TH
AV
7600
198TH ST
81ST
S
ST
SEE 175 MAP

ORILLIA
200TH ST
46TH AV S
PARK (SITE)
RUSSELL RD
TR
62ND
S
199TH PL
S
202ND
78TH
AV
ST
S 200TH ST
81ST
S

SAINT PATRICKS CEMETERY
204TH ST
59TH
PL
S
204TH
ST
S
ST
206TH
BNSF
80TH
ST
S 2
208TH ST
S
209TH ST
77TH (FRONT ST)

PARK (SITE)
4200
S
RD
212TH
5700
KENT
KOA SEATTLE/TACOMA CAMPGROUND
212TH
ST
TR
RR
AV

42ND AV
S
S
216TH
ST
4000
50TH AV
S
FRAGER RD
ANDERSON PARK
GREEN RIVER
NATURAL
216TH
HWY
181
219TH
72ND
AV
S
21200
RR
S
OBRIEN
S 214TH
ST
S 216TH
ST
S 218TH
ST
78TH AV S

44TH AV
S 220TH
ST
RIVER
VAN DORENS LANDING PARK
RESOURCES
67TH
AV S
220TH
ST
21600
INTERURBAN
76TH
AV
S 220TH
ST
S 222ND
ST

58TH PL S
226TH
ST
FRAGER RD
PUGET POWER TRAIL
226TH
ST
64TH AV
22400
70TH AV
S
224TH
ST
S 227TH
PL
21200
UP
S 224TH
ST

S 226TH
ST
UPLANDS GREENBELT
58TH
ST
22600
54TH AV
S
72ND AV
S
228TH
6800
228TH
ST
7600
2ND AV
N
VALLEY FRWY

RUSSELL WOODS PARK
53RD
PL
23RD
LAKESIDE BLVD E
228TH
ST
64TH
S
231ST
WEST
(68TH)
169TH
AV
71ST PL S
6TH
4TH AV
167
NOVAK LN
NOV

E F G H J

DETAIL

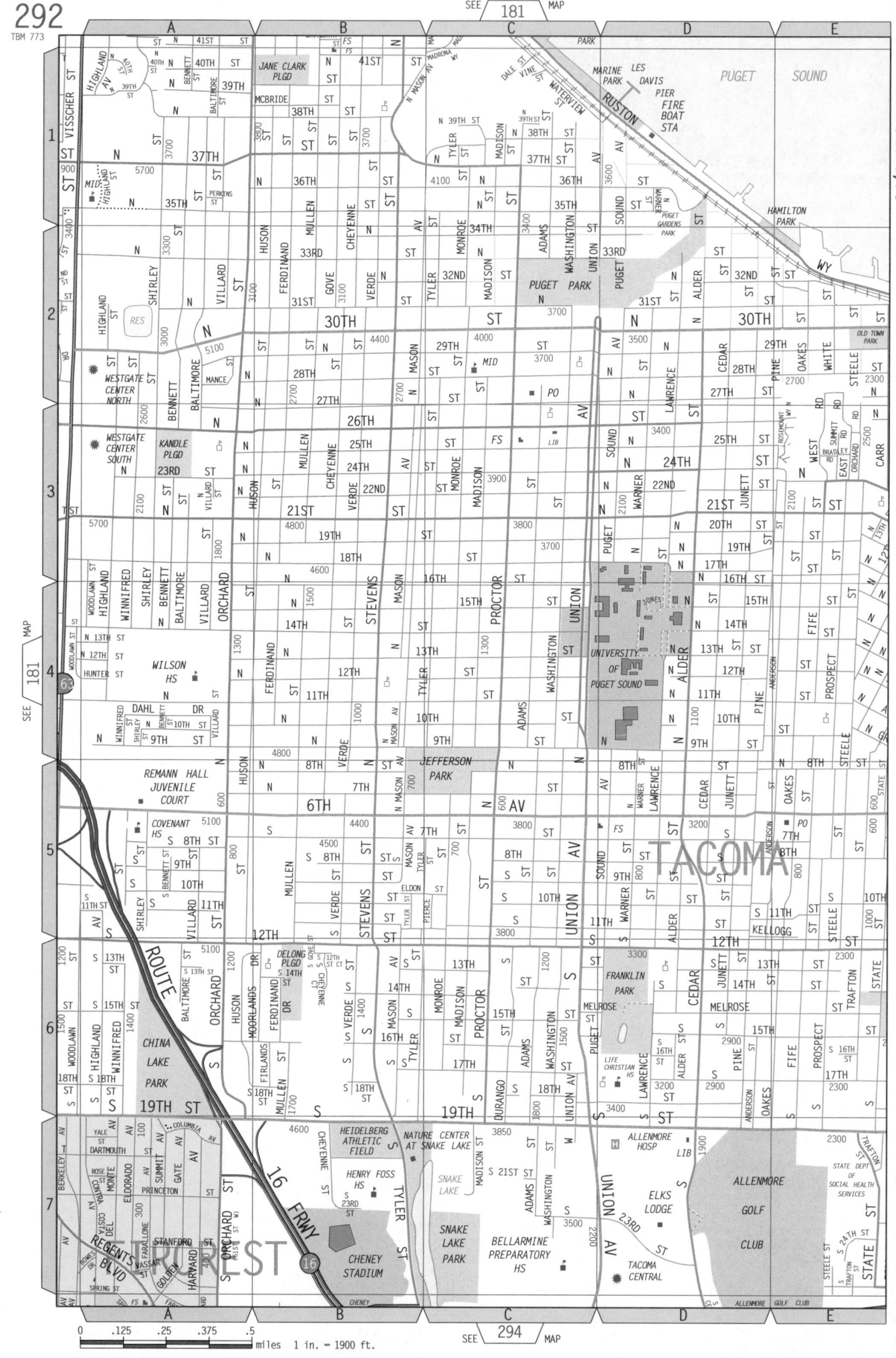

292

TBM 773

PUGET SOUND

TACOMA

FIRCREST

0   .125   .25   .375   .5
miles   1 in. = 1900 ft.

DETAIL

SEE 181 MAP

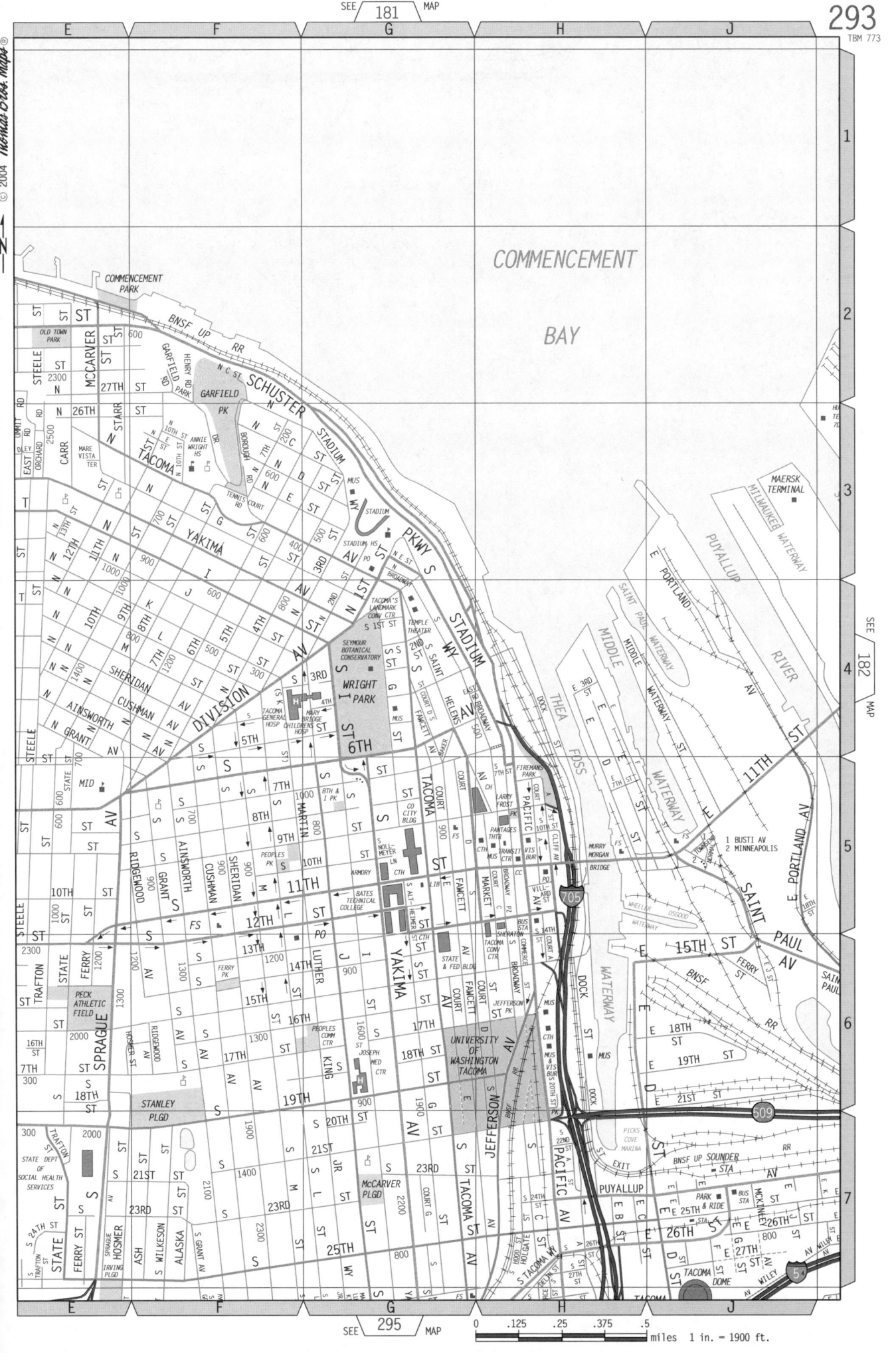

© 2004 Thomas Bros. Maps ®

COMMENCEMENT

BAY

0   .125   .25   .375   .5

miles   1 in. = 1900 ft.

DETAIL

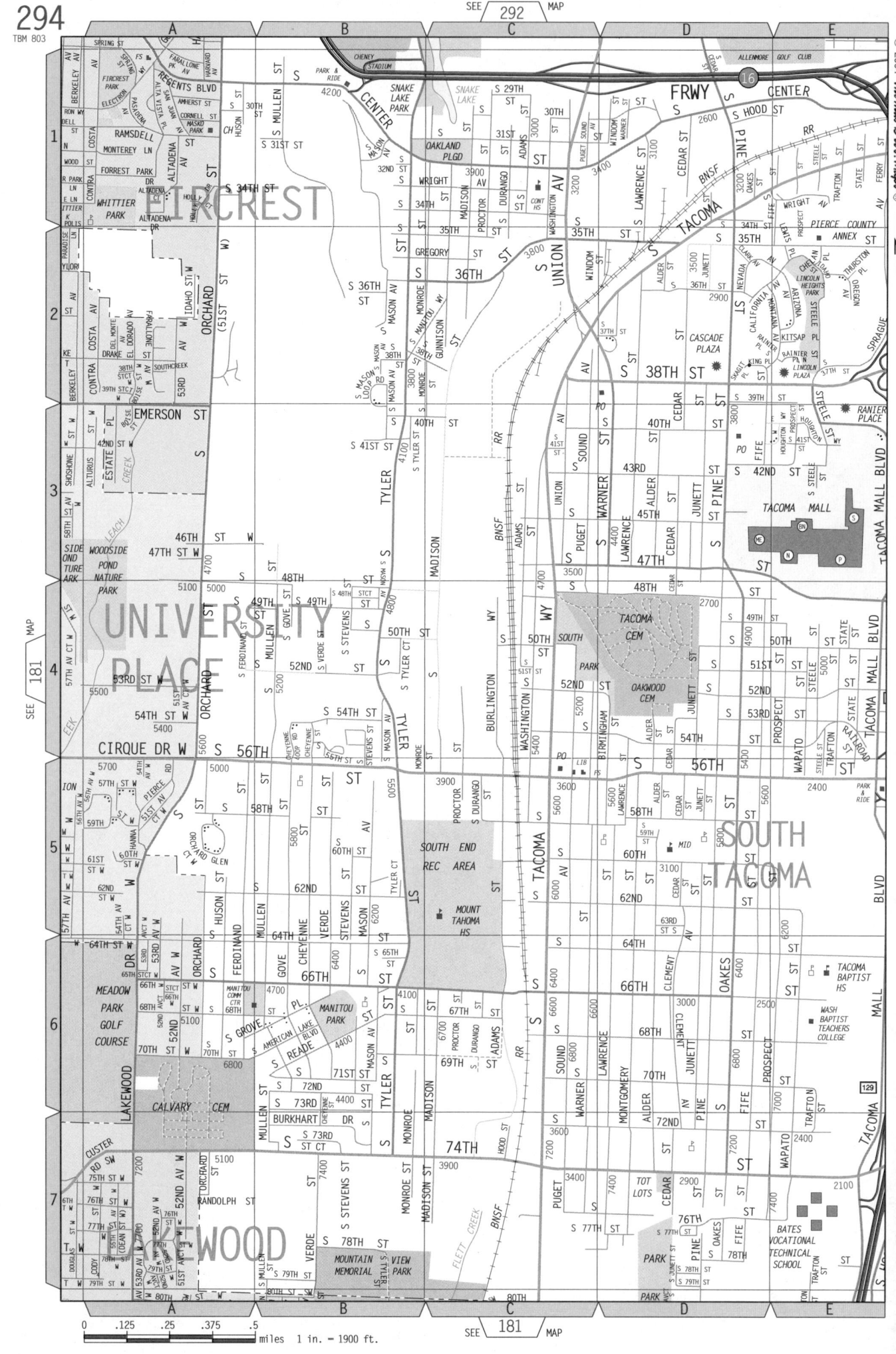

© 2004 Thomas Bros. Maps®

DETAIL

TACOMA

HILLDALE

Lincoln Park
Lincoln HS
Puget Sound Hosp
Tacoma Dome
McKinley Park
Upper Park
Sawyer Park
Ranier Place
Irving Plgd
CE County Annex
Tacoma Mall Blvd
Tacoma Baptist HS
Tacoma Place
Tacoma South Center
Wapato Lake Park
Wapato Lake
Alling Park
Stewart Heights Playfield
Park & Ride
Dept of Licensing

FRWY 5
705
133
132
130
129
182
7

Streets (partial): Hosmer, Ash, Wilkeson, Alaska, Asotin, Ainsworth, Cushman, Sheridan, Thompson, Yakima, Fawcett, Tacoma, Pacific, Bell, McKinley, Spokane, Winnetka, Golden Given Rd

28TH ST, 27TH ST, 29TH ST, 30TH ST, 32ND ST, 34TH ST, 35TH ST, 36TH ST, 37TH ST, 38TH ST, 39TH, 40TH, 41ST, 42ND, 43RD, 44TH, 45TH, 46TH, 47TH, 48TH, 49TH, 50TH, 51ST, 52ND, 53RD, 54TH, 55TH, 56TH ST, 57TH, 58TH, 59TH, 60TH, 61ST, 62ND, 63RD, 64TH, 65TH, 66TH, 67TH, 68TH, 69TH, 70TH, 72ND ST, 73RD, 74TH, 75TH, 76TH, 77TH, 78TH

0   .125   .25   .375   .5
miles   1 in. = 1900 ft.

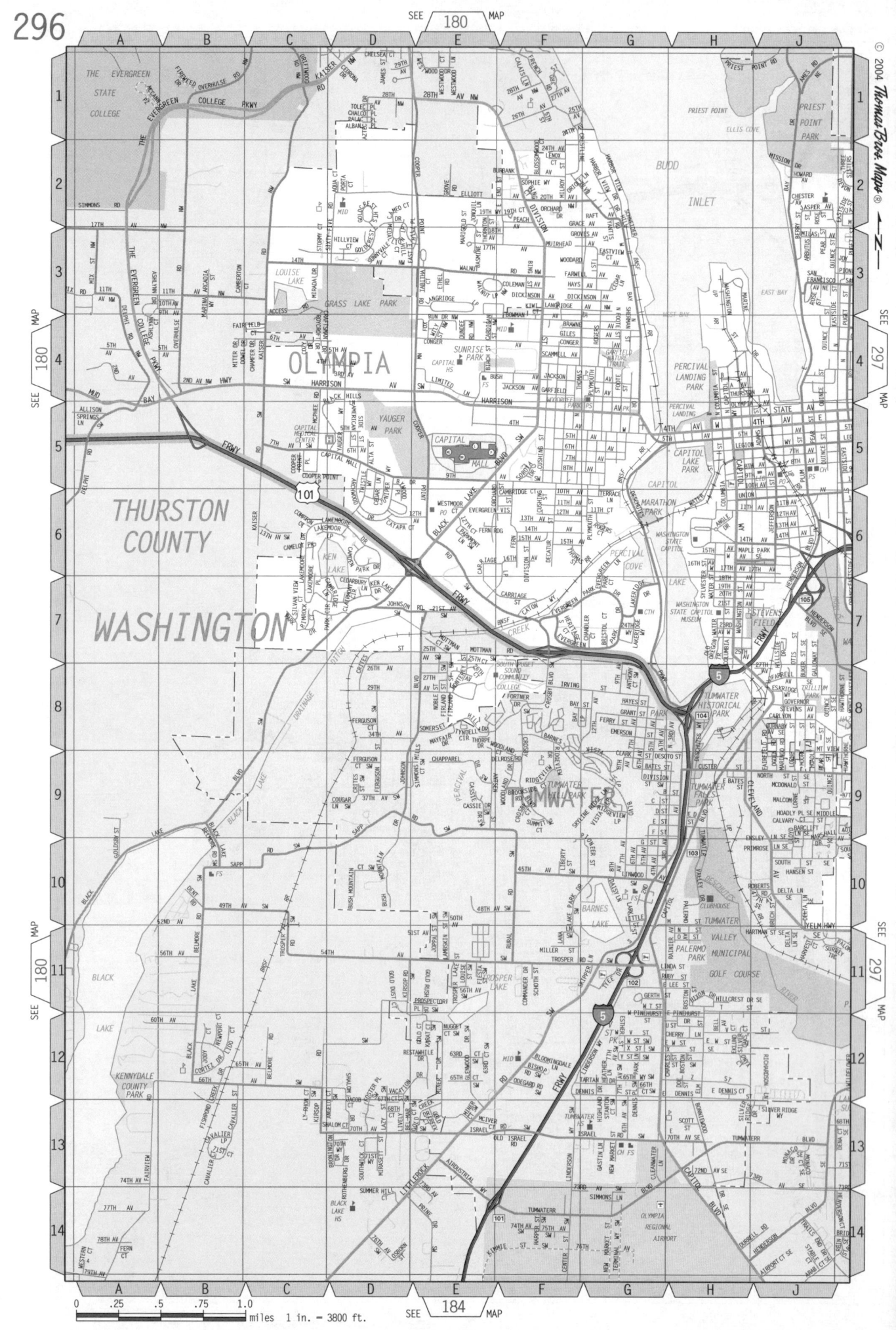

SEE 180 MAP

SEE 180 MAP

SEE 297 MAP

SEE 180 MAP

SEE 297 MAP

SEE 184 MAP

DETAIL

THE EVERGREEN STATE COLLEGE

OLYMPIA

THURSTON COUNTY

WASHINGTON

TUMWATER

BUDD INLET

PRIEST POINT PARK

0   .25   .5   .75   1.0

miles   1 in. = 3800 ft.

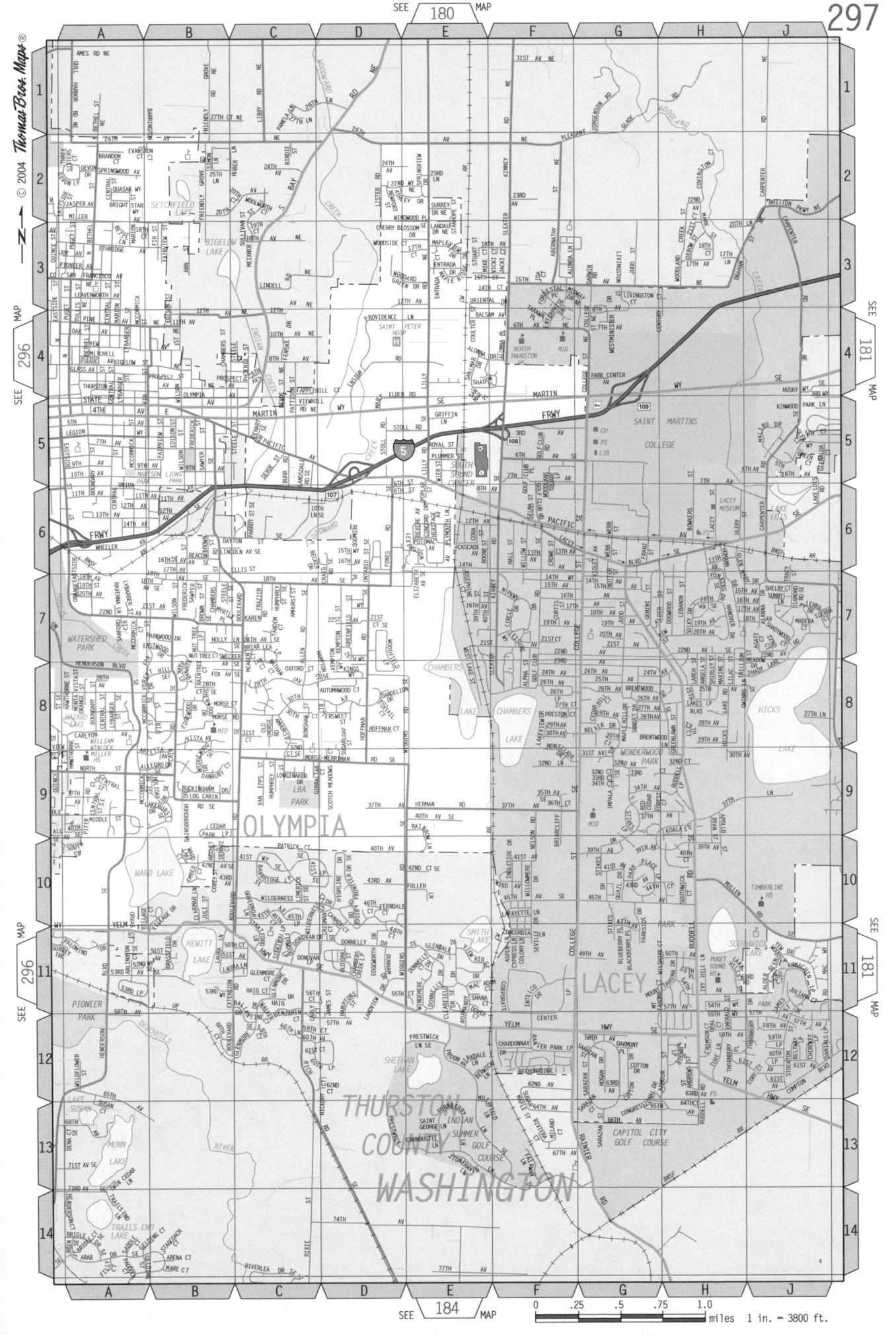

0   .25   .5   .75   1.0
miles   1 in. = 3800 ft.

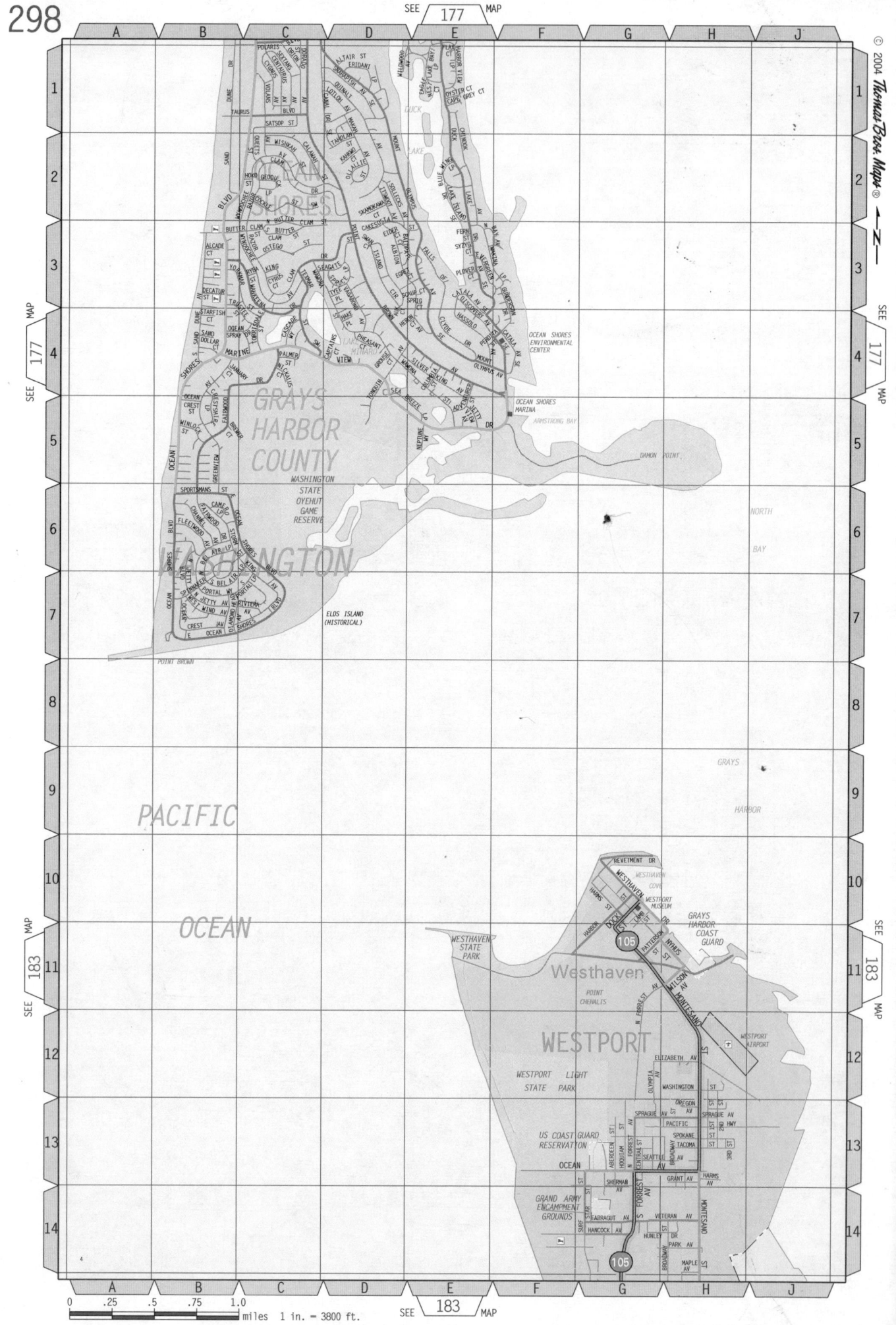

© 2004 Thomas Bros. Maps ® ——N——

GRAYS
HARBOR
COUNTY

WASHINGTON
STATE
OYEHUT
GAME
RESERVE

WASHINGTON

OCEAN SHORES
ENVIRONMENTAL
CENTER

OCEAN SHORES
MARINA

ARMSTRONG BAY

DAMON POINT

NORTH
BAY

ELDS ISLAND
(HISTORICAL)

POINT BROWN

PACIFIC

OCEAN

GRAYS

HARBOR

DETAIL

REVETMENT DR

WESTHAVEN
COVE

WESTPORT
MUSEUM

GRAYS
HARBOR
COAST
GUARD

WESTHAVEN
STATE
PARK

Westhaven

POINT
CHEHALIS

WESTPORT

WESTPORT
AIRPORT

WESTPORT LIGHT
STATE PARK

US COAST GUARD
RESERVATION

GRAND ARMY
ENCAMPMENT
GROUNDS

0   .25   .5   .75   1.0
miles 1 in. = 3800 ft.

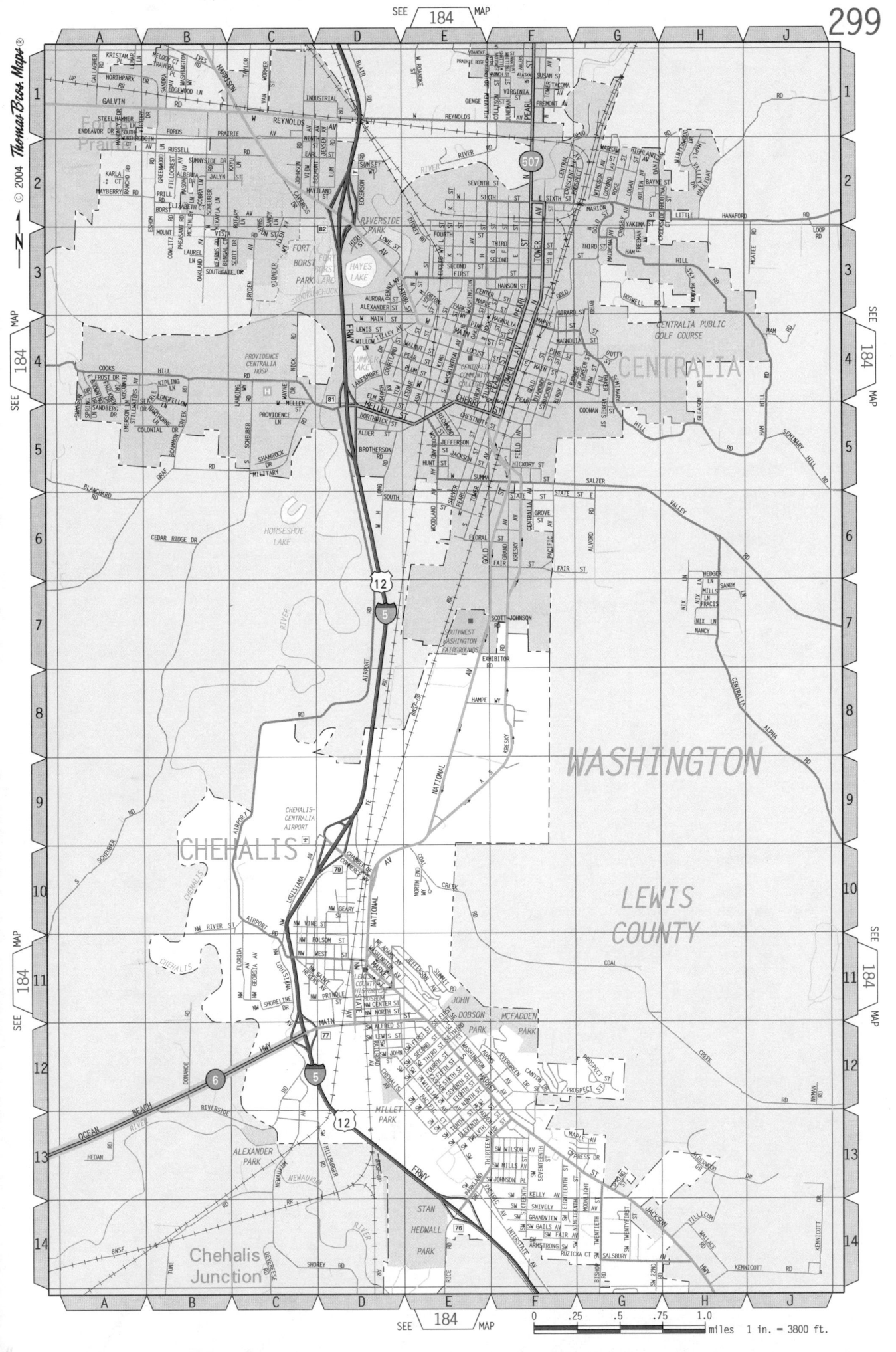

DETAIL

294

CENTRALIA

WASHINGTON

LEWIS
COUNTY

CHEHALIS

Chehalis
Junction

0   .25   .5   .75   1.0
miles   1 in. = 3800 ft.

© 2004 Thomas Bros. Maps®

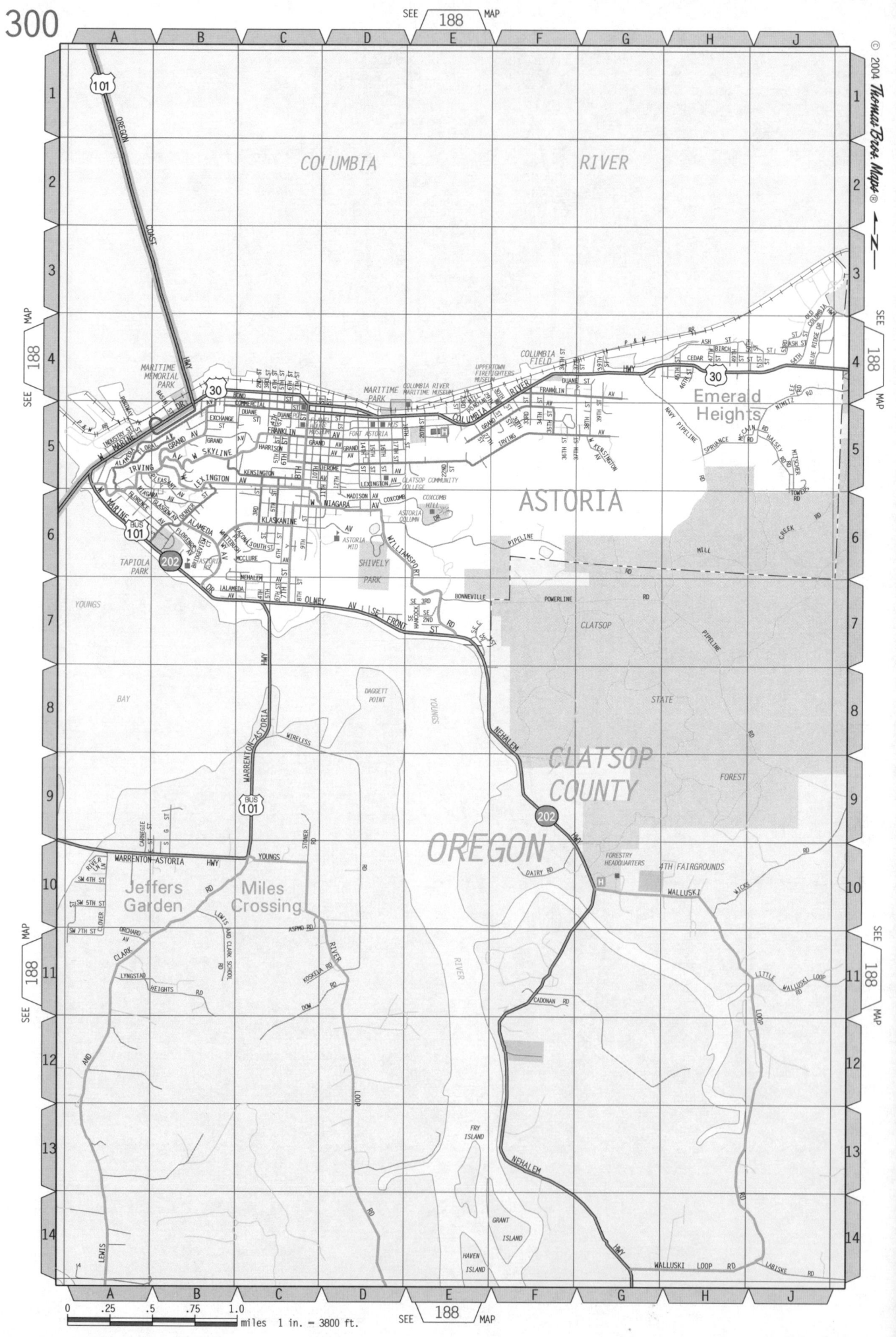

© 2004 *Thomas Bros. Maps* ®

DETAIL

SEE 188 MAP

SEE 188 MAP

SEE 188 MAP

SEE 188 MAP

COLUMBIA   RIVER

ASTORIA

Emerald
Heights

CLATSOP
COUNTY

OREGON

YOUNGS

BAY

Jeffers
Garden

Miles
Crossing

STATE

FOREST

0   .25   .5   .75   1.0
miles   1 in. = 3800 ft.

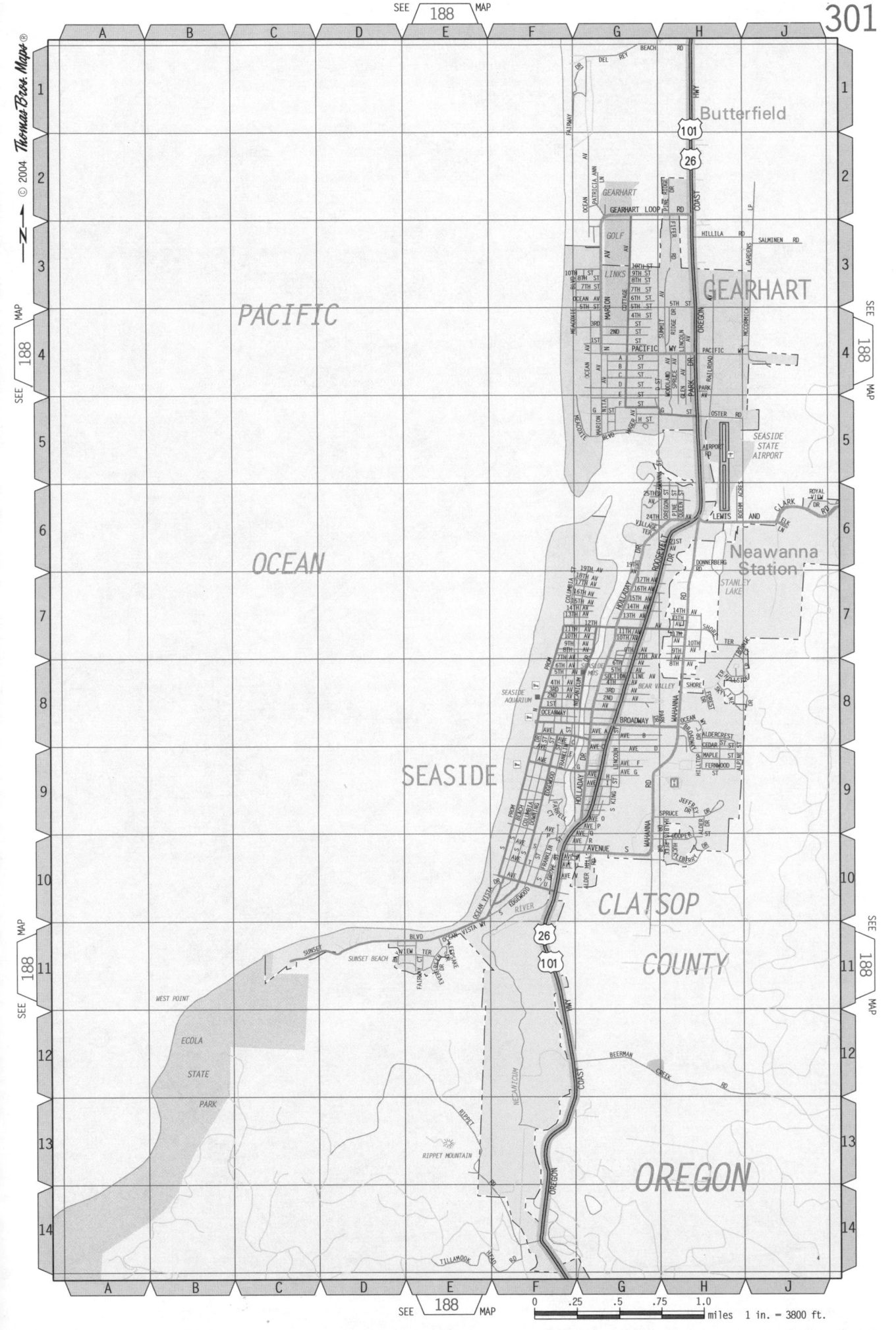

—N—→

SEE 188 MAP

SEE 188 MAP

SEE 188 MAP

Butterfield

101

26

GEARHART

GOLF

LINKS

PACIFIC

OCEAN

Neawanna
Station

STANLEY
LAKE

SEASIDE
AQUARIUM

SEASIDE
STATE
AIRPORT

SEASIDE

CLATSOP

COUNTY

SUNSET BEACH

WEST POINT

ECOLA

STATE

PARK

RIPPET MOUNTAIN

NECANICUM

OREGON

DETAIL

SEE 188 MAP

SEE 188 MAP

SEE 188 MAP

0   .25   .5   .75   1.0
miles   1 in. = 3800 ft.

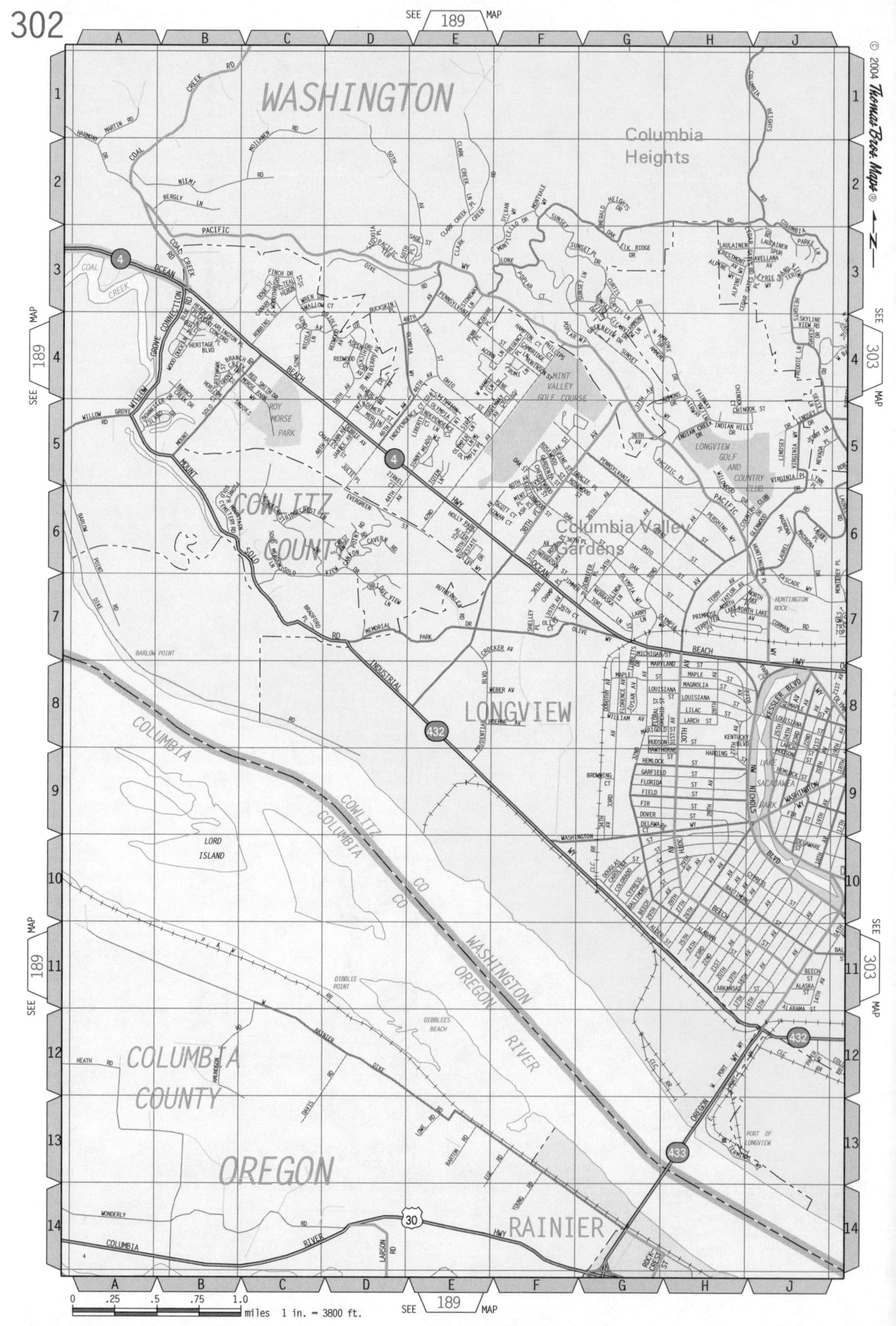

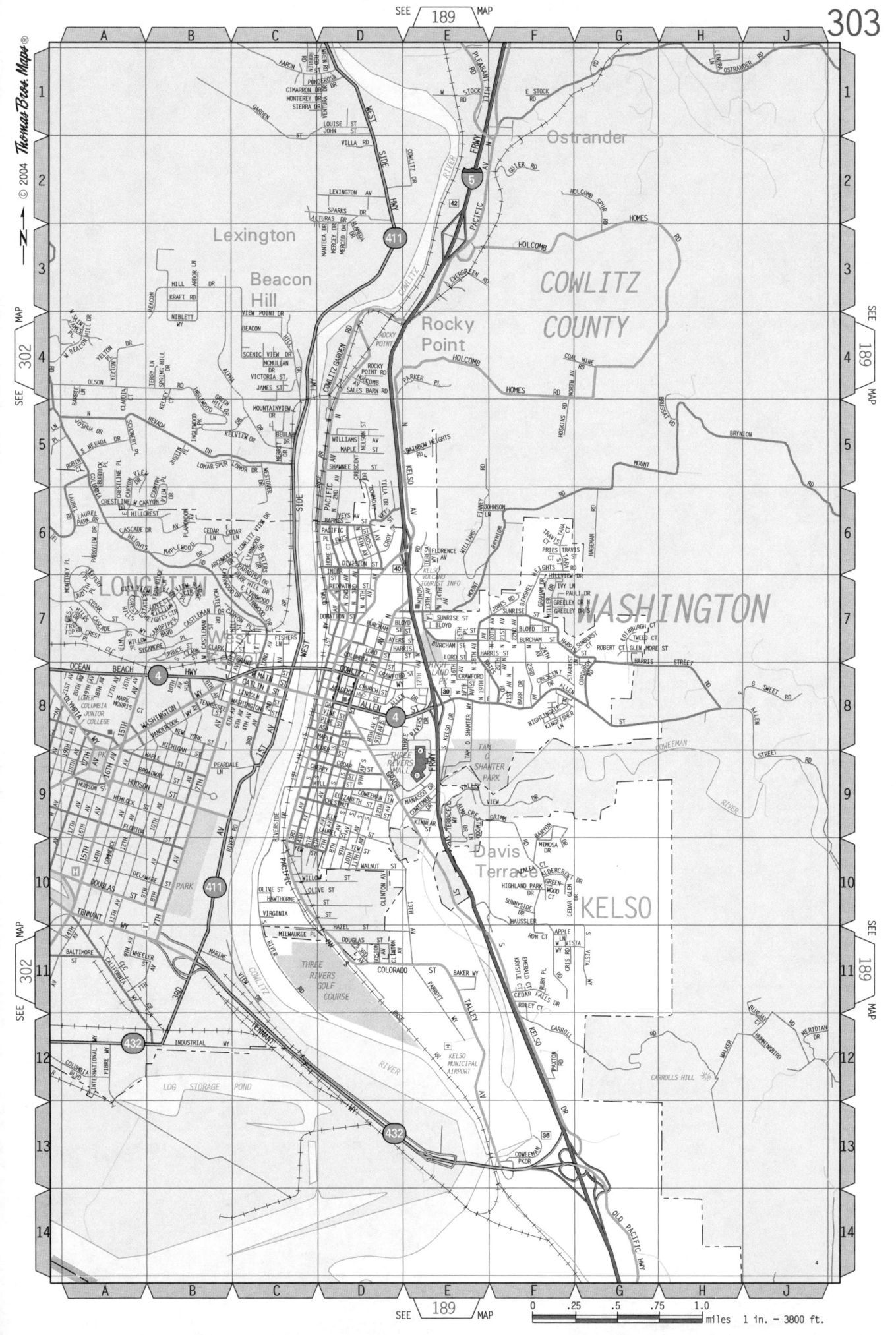

DETAIL

N

SEE 189 MAP

SEE 302 MAP

SEE 189 MAP

SEE 189 MAP

SEE 302 MAP

SEE 189 MAP

Ostrander

COWLITZ
COUNTY

Lexington

Beacon
Hill

Rocky Point

Rocky
Point

WASHINGTON

LONGVIEW

West
Kelso

Davis
Terrace

KELSO

THREE
RIVERS
MALL

TAM O
SHANTER
PARK

THREE
RIVERS
GOLF
COURSE

KELSO
MUNICIPAL
AIRPORT

CARROLLS HILL

LOG STORAGE POND

KELSO
VOLCANO
TOURIST
INFO

0   .25   .5   .75   1.0
miles 1 in. = 3800 ft.

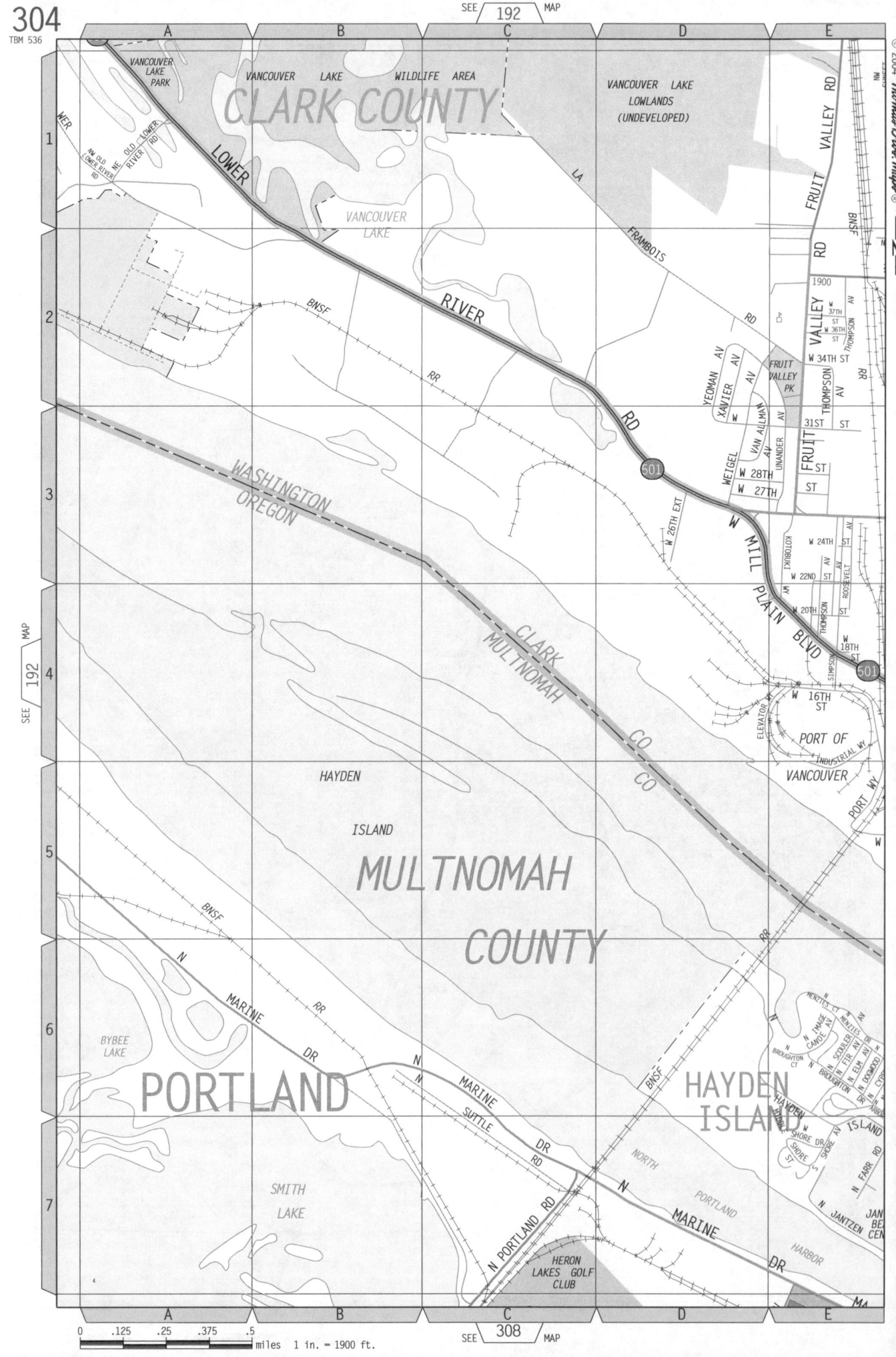

© 2004 Thomas Bros. Maps ® —N—

SEE 192 MAP

A   B   C   D   E

CLARK COUNTY

VANCOUVER LAKE PARK

VANCOUVER   LAKE   WILDLIFE   AREA

VANCOUVER LAKE LOWLANDS (UNDEVELOPED)

FRUIT VALLEY RD

BNSF

1

NW OLD NE OLD LOWER
LOWER RIVER RD
RIVER RD

WER

LOWER

VANCOUVER LAKE

LA

FRAMBOIS

RD

1900

VALLEY

W 37TH ST
W 36TH ST

THOMPSON AV

RR

2

BNSF

RIVER

RD

W 34TH ST

YEOMAN AV
XAVIER AV
VAN AILLMAN AV
UNANDER AV

FRUIT VALLEY PK

31ST ST

FRUIT

WASHINGTON
OREGON

501

WEIGEL AV
W 28TH
W 27TH

ST

3

RR

W 26TH EXT

W 24TH ST
KOTOBIRW

W 22ND
W 20TH

ROOSEVELT AV

W MILL PLAIN BLVD

W 18TH ST

SIMPSON

CLARK
MULTNOMAH

501

4

SEE 192 MAP

CO
CO

ELEVATOR

W 16TH ST

INDUSTRIAL WY

PORT OF
VANCOUVER

PORT WY

W

HAYDEN

ISLAND

MULTNOMAH

5

DETAIL

BNSF

RR

COUNTY

N

RR

HAYDEN
ISLAND

MENZIES CT
MENZIES CT
N CANOE

MARINE

N IMAGE
CANOE

N SOULIER AV
N FIR AV
N ELM AV
N KOWOOD

6

BYBEE LAKE

DR

N BROUGHTON CT
N BROUGHTON CT

BNSF

HAYDEN ISLAND DR
N CYPRESS

PORTLAND

N MARINE

SUTTLE

DR

N

SHORE DR
SHORE AV
SHORE ST

ISLAND

N FARR RD

JAN
BEN
CEN

N PORTLAND

SMITH LAKE

7

RD

N PORTLAND RD

HERON LAKES GOLF CLUB

N MARINE

DR

HARBOR

JANTZEN AV

NORTH

PORTLAND

M

A   B   C   D   E

0   .125   .25   .375   .5
miles 1 in. = 1900 ft.

© 2004 Thomas Bros. Maps®

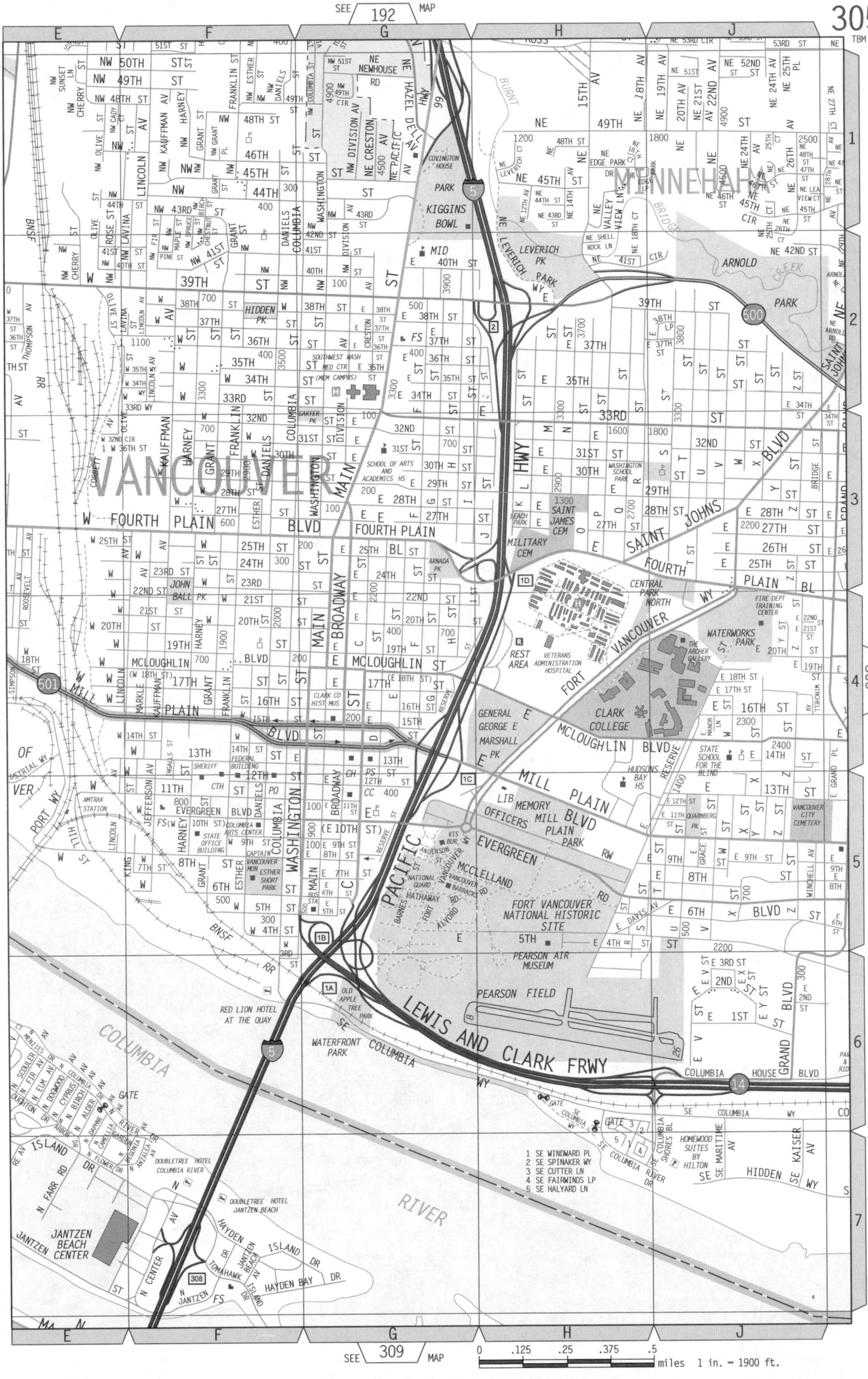

N↑

VANCOUVER

MENNEHAHA

BURNT BRIDGE CREEK

ARNOLD PARK

KIGGINS BOWL

COVINGTON HOUSE PARK

SOUTHWEST WASH MED CTR (MEM CAMPUS)

SCHOOL OF ARTS AND ACADEMICS HS

W FOURTH PLAIN BLVD — FOURTH PLAIN — FOURTH PLAIN BL

JOHN BALL PK

MCLOUGHLIN ST (E 18TH ST)

CENTRAL PARK NORTH

WATERWORKS PARK

FIRE DEPT TRAINING CENTER

VETERANS ADMINISTRATION HOSPITAL

REST AREA

CLARK COLLEGE

FORT VANCOUVER

MCLOUGHLIN BLVD

THE ARCHER GALLERY

STATE SCHOOL FOR THE BLIND

GENERAL GEORGE E MARSHALL PK

HUDSONS BAY HS

MILL PLAIN BLVD

MEMORY PLAIN PARK

OFFICERS ROW

VANCOUVER CITY CEMETERY

PACIFIC

MCCLELLAND

EVERGREEN

FORT VANCOUVER NATIONAL HISTORIC SITE

VANCOUVER BARRACKS

NATIONAL GUARD

PEARSON AIR MUSEUM

PEARSON FIELD

RED LION HOTEL AT THE QUAY

OLD APPLE TREE PARK

WATERFRONT COLUMBIA PARK

LEWIS AND CLARK FRWY

COLUMBIA WY

COLUMBIA HOUSE BLVD

HOMEWOOD SUITES BY HILTON

SE COLUMBIA SHORES BL

GATE 3

SE HIDDEN WY

COLUMBIA RIVER

COLUMBIA GATE

DOUBLETREE HOTEL COLUMBIA RIVER

DOUBLETREE HOTEL JANTZEN BEACH

JANTZEN BEACH CENTER

JANTZEN ISLAND DR

HAYDEN BAY DR

RIVER

1 SE WINDWARD PL
2 SE SPINAKER WY
3 SE CUTTER LN
4 SE FAIRWINDS LP
5 SE HALYARD LN

DETAIL

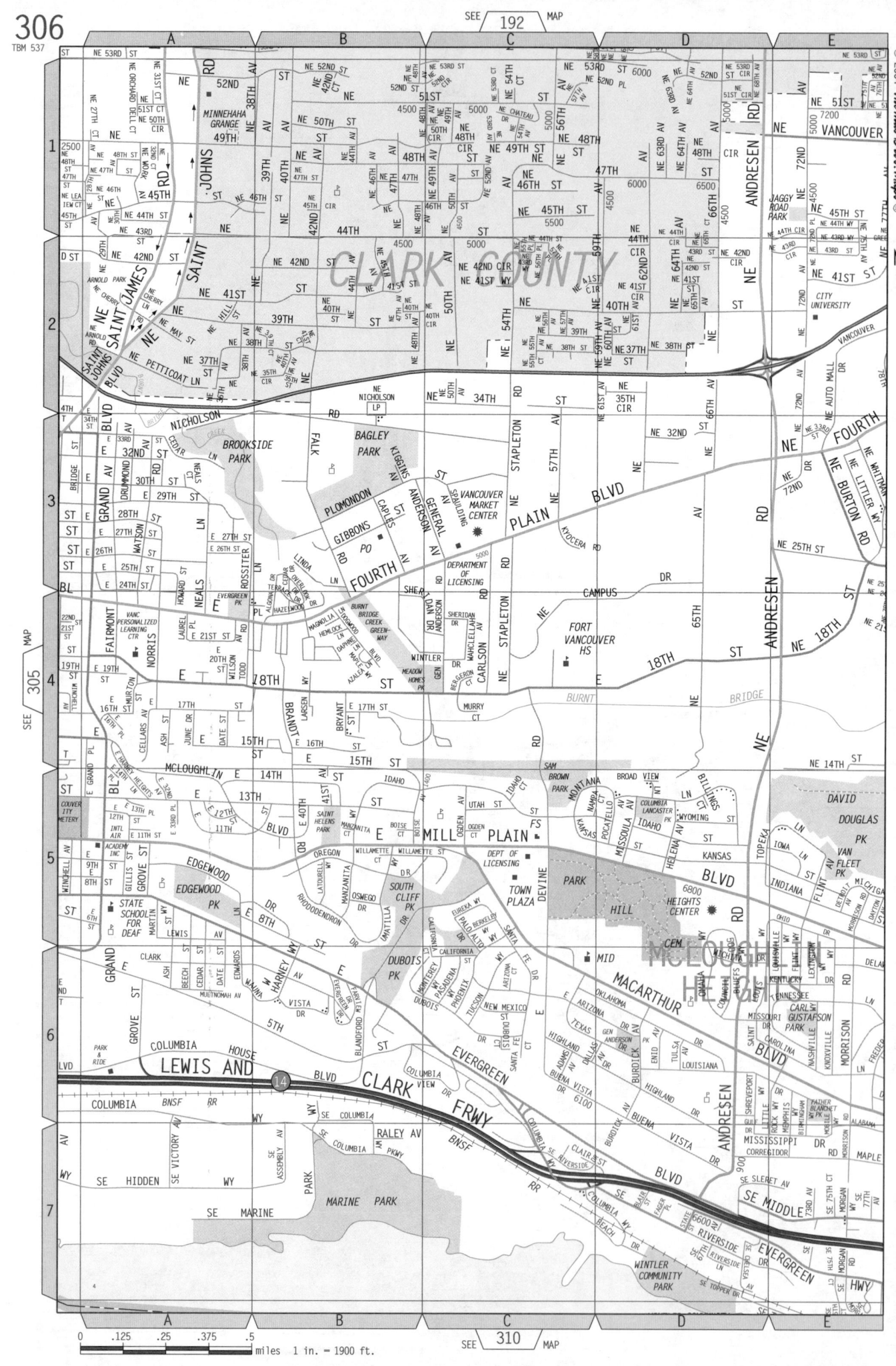

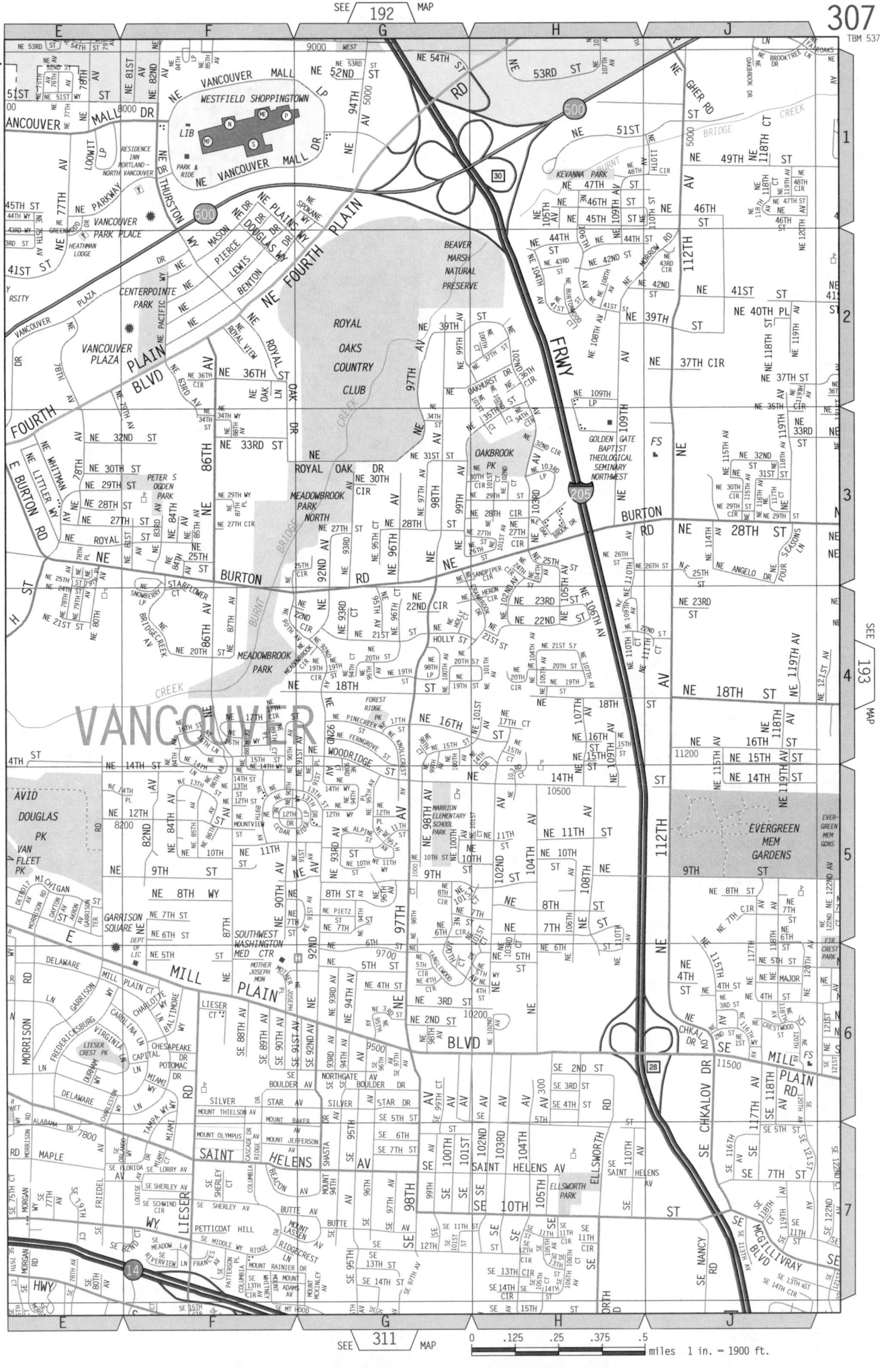

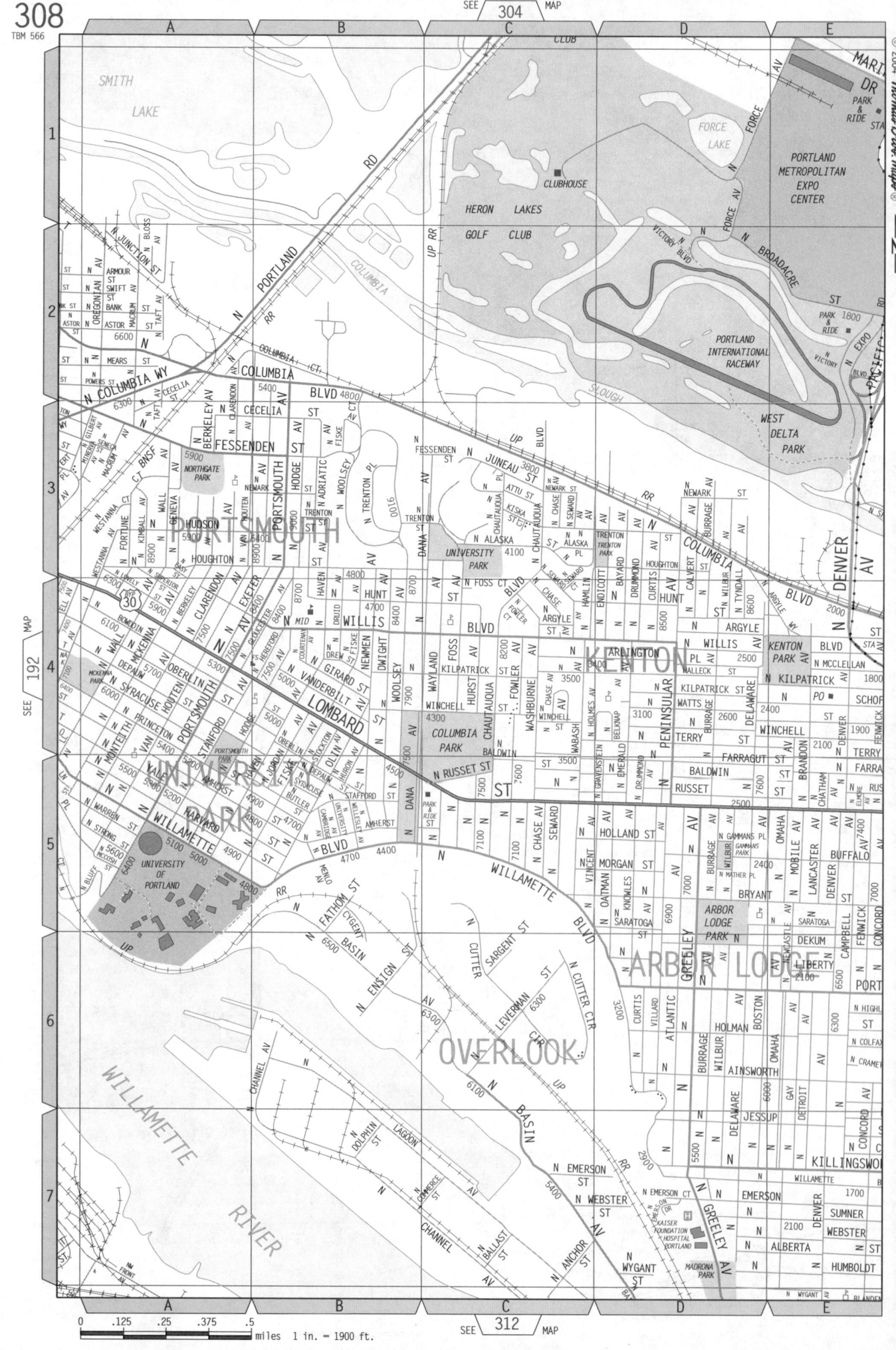

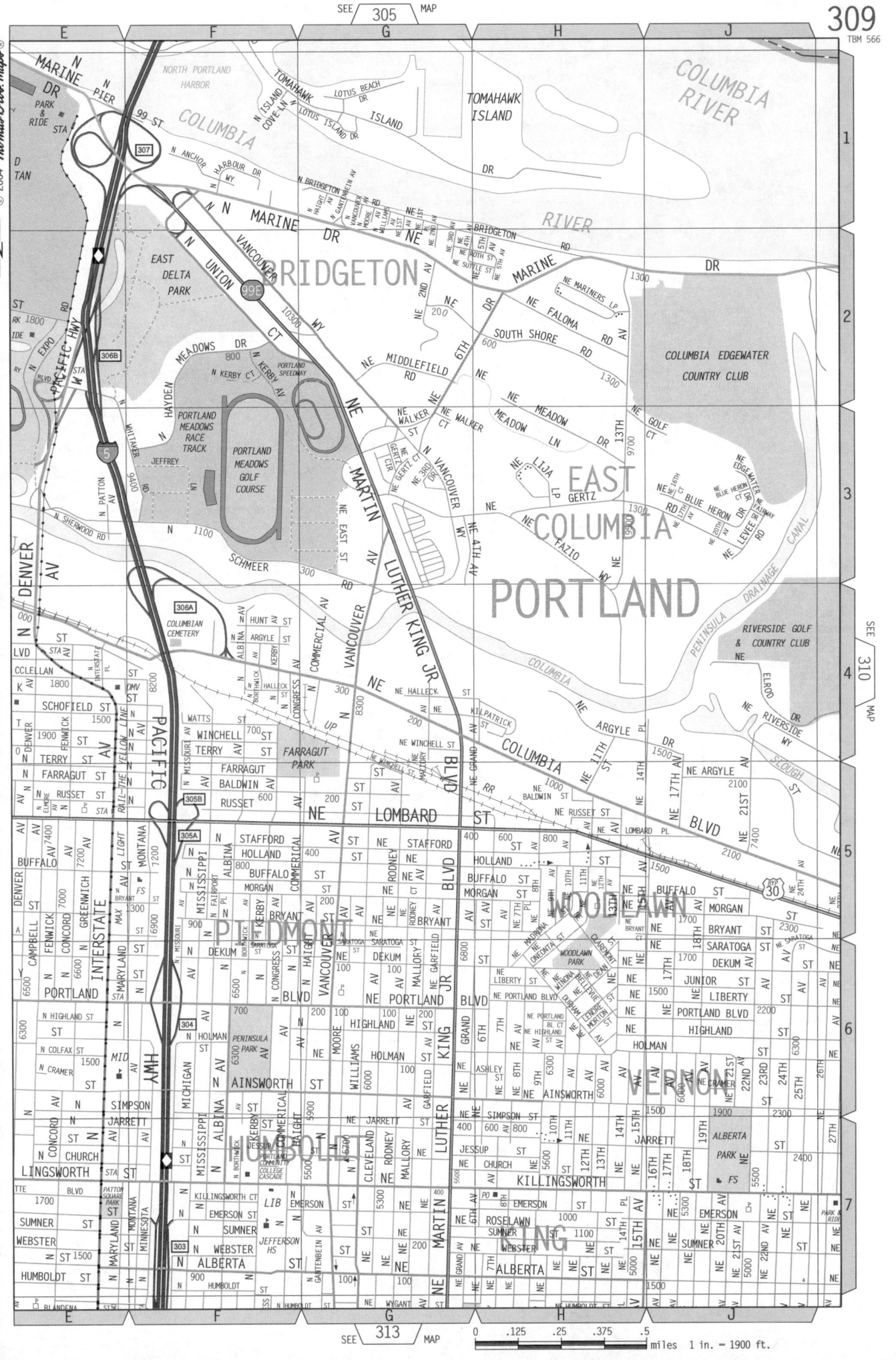

SEE 305 MAP

© 2004 Thomas Bros. Maps®

COLUMBIA RIVER

NORTH PORTLAND HARBOR

TOMAHAWK ISLAND

LOTUS BEACH

COLUMBIA RIVER

MARINE DR

BRIDGETON

EAST DELTA PARK

PORTLAND MEADOWS RACE TRACK

PORTLAND MEADOWS GOLF COURSE

COLUMBIA EDGEWATER COUNTRY CLUB

EAST COLUMBIA

PORTLAND

PENINSULA DRAINAGE CANAL

RIVERSIDE GOLF & COUNTRY CLUB

SEE 310 MAP

COLUMBIA

NE LOMBARD ST

NE LOMBARD BLVD

PIEDMONT

WOODLAWN

WOODLAWN PARK

VERNON

HUMBOLDT

PORTLAND COMMUNITY COLLEGE CASCADE

KING

ALBERTA PARK

SEE 313 MAP

0 .125 .25 .375 .5   miles   1 in. = 1900 ft.

DETAIL

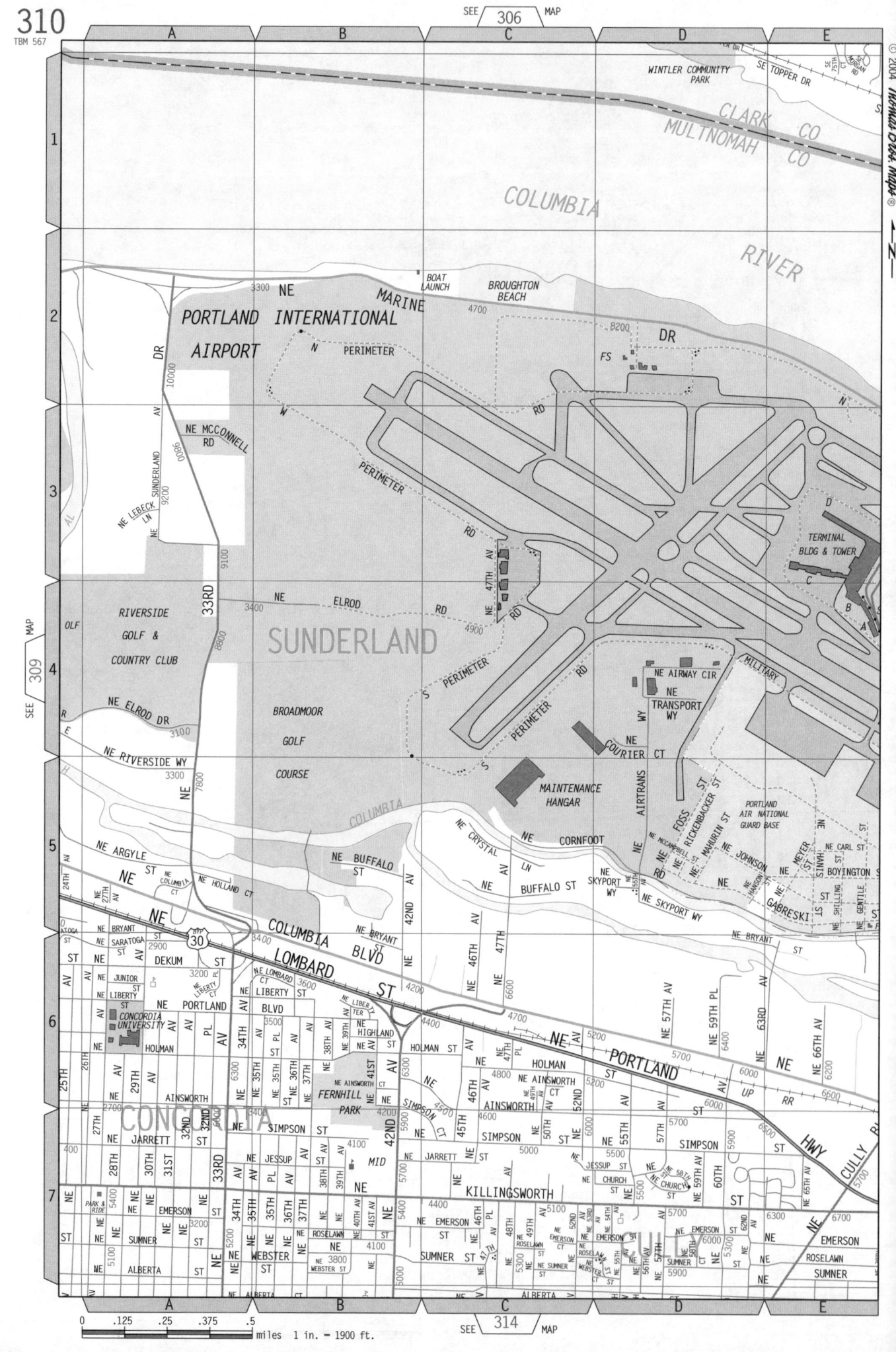

© 2004 Thomas Bros. Maps® ←N—

SEE 306 MAP

WINTLER COMMUNITY PARK

SE TOPPER DR

CLARK CO

MULTNOMAH CO

COLUMBIA

RIVER

1

BOAT LAUNCH

BROUGHTON BEACH

3300 NE MARINE

DR

4700

8200

DR

2

PORTLAND INTERNATIONAL

AIRPORT

N PERIMETER

FS

10000

NE McCONNELL RD

9000

PERIMETER

NE SUNDERLAND

AL

NE LEBECK LN

9200

RD

3

9100

47TH AV

TERMINAL BLDG & TOWER

D

33RD

NE ELROD RD

3400

4900

C

SEE 309 MAP

OLF

RIVERSIDE GOLF & COUNTRY CLUB

8800

SUNDERLAND

S PERIMETER

RD

NE AIRWAY CIR

MILITARY

B

A

4

R E

NE ELROD DR

3100

BROADMOOR

GOLF

PERIMETER

NE TRANSPORT WY

NE RIVERSIDE WY

3300

7800

COURSE

NE COURIER CT

S PERIMETER

AIRTRANS ST

FOSS ST

RICKENBACKER ST

MAHURIN ST

PORTLAND AIR NATIONAL GUARD BASE

COLUMBIA

MAINTENANCE HANGAR

NE JOHNSON

NE CARL ST

ST

5

NE ARGYLE ST

NE CRYSTAL LN

NE CORNFOOT

NE McCAMPBELL

NE HINIS

MEYER ST

24TH AV

NE COLUMBIA CT

NE HOLLAND CT

NE BUFFALO ST

42ND AV

NE BUFFALO ST

NE SKYPORT WY

555TH RD

NE JOHNSON

SHILLING ST

GENTILE ST

BOYINGTON

GABRESKI ST

27TH

NE BRYANT

NE BRYANT ST

NE SKYPORT WY

NE BRYANT

ST

ATOGA

NE BRYANT

2900

NE 30

COLUMBIA

3400

BLVD

46TH AV

47TH

57TH AV

59TH PL

63RD

66TH AV

DEKUM

ST

LOMBARD

ST

4200

4700

NE

6600

5200

5700

6000

6200

6

NE JUNIOR ST

3200

NE LOMBARD CT

3600

NE LIBERTY ST

NE HIGHLAND ST

NE PORTLAND

UP RR

6600

NE LIBERTY ST

NE LIBERTY CT

NE PORTLAND BLVD

34TH

3500

NE 38TH AV

39TH

HOLMAN ST

NE HOLMAN ST

NE 47TH PL

CONCORDIA UNIVERSITY

29TH

32ND AV

PL AV

AV

41ST AV

NE AINSWORTH CT

6300

46TH

4800

NE AINSWORTH CT

50TH

5200

55TH

57TH

60TH

HWY

HOLMAN ST

25TH

26TH

NE

ST

34TH

35TH

35TH

36TH

37TH

FERNHILL PARK

4200

5900

SIMPSON CT

45TH AV

4600

AINSWORTH

6000

5700

SIMPSON

CULLY

27TH

28TH

NE JARRETT

30TH

31ST

33RD AV

32ND PL AV

38TH PL

39TH

42ND

MID

NE SIMPSON ST

4100

NE JARRETT

5000

NE JESSUP

5500

NE CHURCH

59TH PL

6600

2700

3400

400

5400

KILLINGSWORTH

4400

5100

5700

7

NE EMERSON

PARK & RIDE

34TH

35TH

36TH

37TH

40TH

41ST AV

47TH

48TH

49TH

52ND

58TH

60TH

63RD

NE EMERSON

6700

NE SUMNER

3200

NE ROSELAWN

4100

SUMNER ST

5300

5000

5900

NE EMERSON

NE ROSELAWN SUMNER

5100

NE ALBERTA

5200

NE WEBSTER

3800

WEBSTER ST

5000

NE ALBERTA

NE SUMNER

SEE 314 MAP

DETAIL

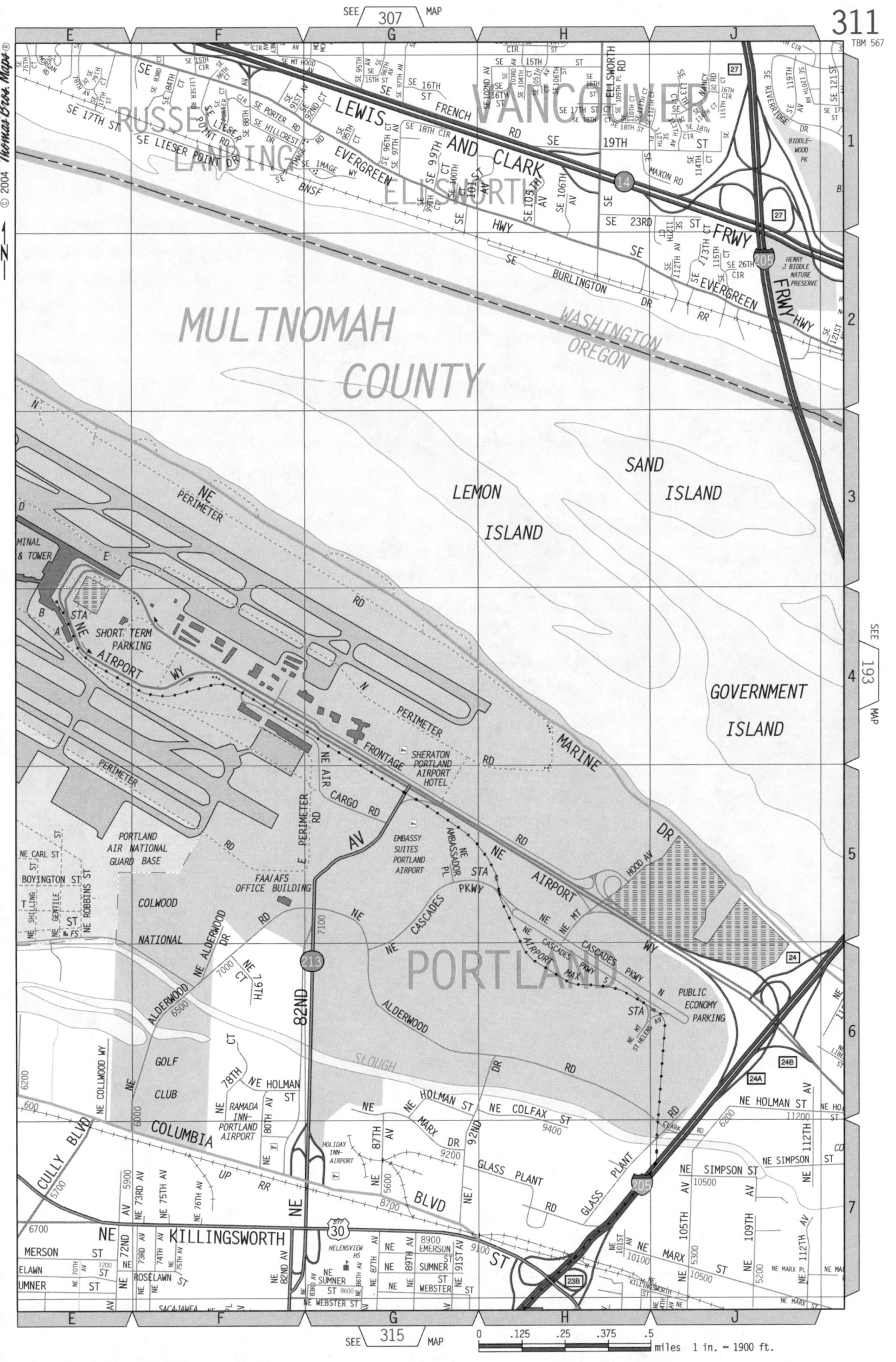

© 2004 Thomas Bros. Maps ®

MULTNOMAH

COUNTY

VANCOUVER

WASHINGTON
OREGON

RUSSELL
LANDING

LEMON
ISLAND

SAND
ISLAND

GOVERNMENT
ISLAND

SEE 193 MAP

SHORT TERM
PARKING

AIRPORT

SHERATON
PORTLAND
AIRPORT
HOTEL

EMBASSY
SUITES
PORTLAND
AIRPORT

PORTLAND
AIR NATIONAL
GUARD BASE

FAA/AFS
OFFICE BUILLDING

COLWOOD

NATIONAL

PORTLAND

PUBLIC
ECONOMY
PARKING

GOLF

CLUB

SLOUGH

RAMADA
INN-
PORTLAND
AIRPORT

HOLIDAY
INN-
AIRPORT

GLASS PLANT

DETAIL

0   .125   .25   .375   .5
miles 1 in. = 1900 ft.

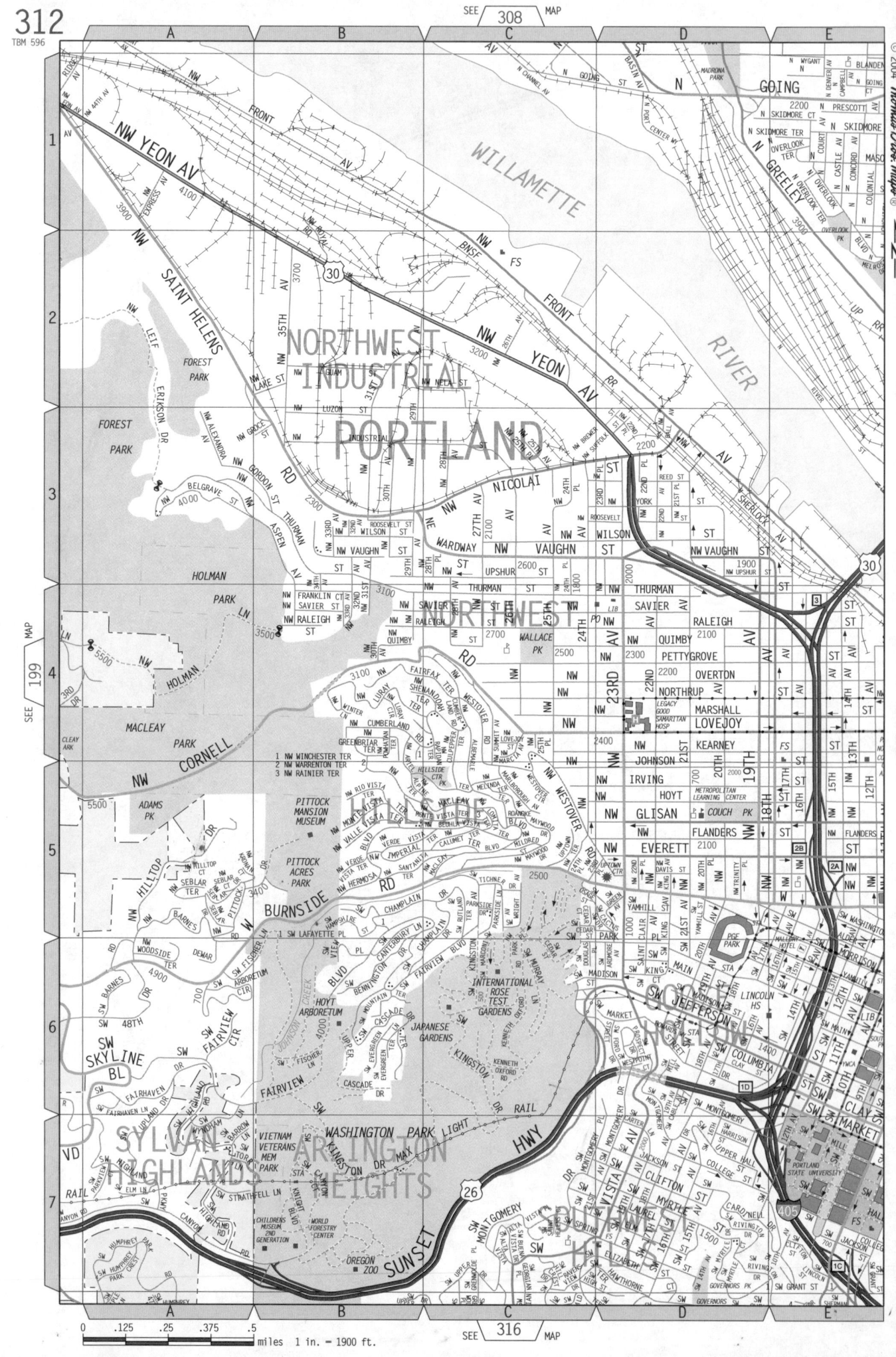

© 2004 Thomas Bros. Maps ®

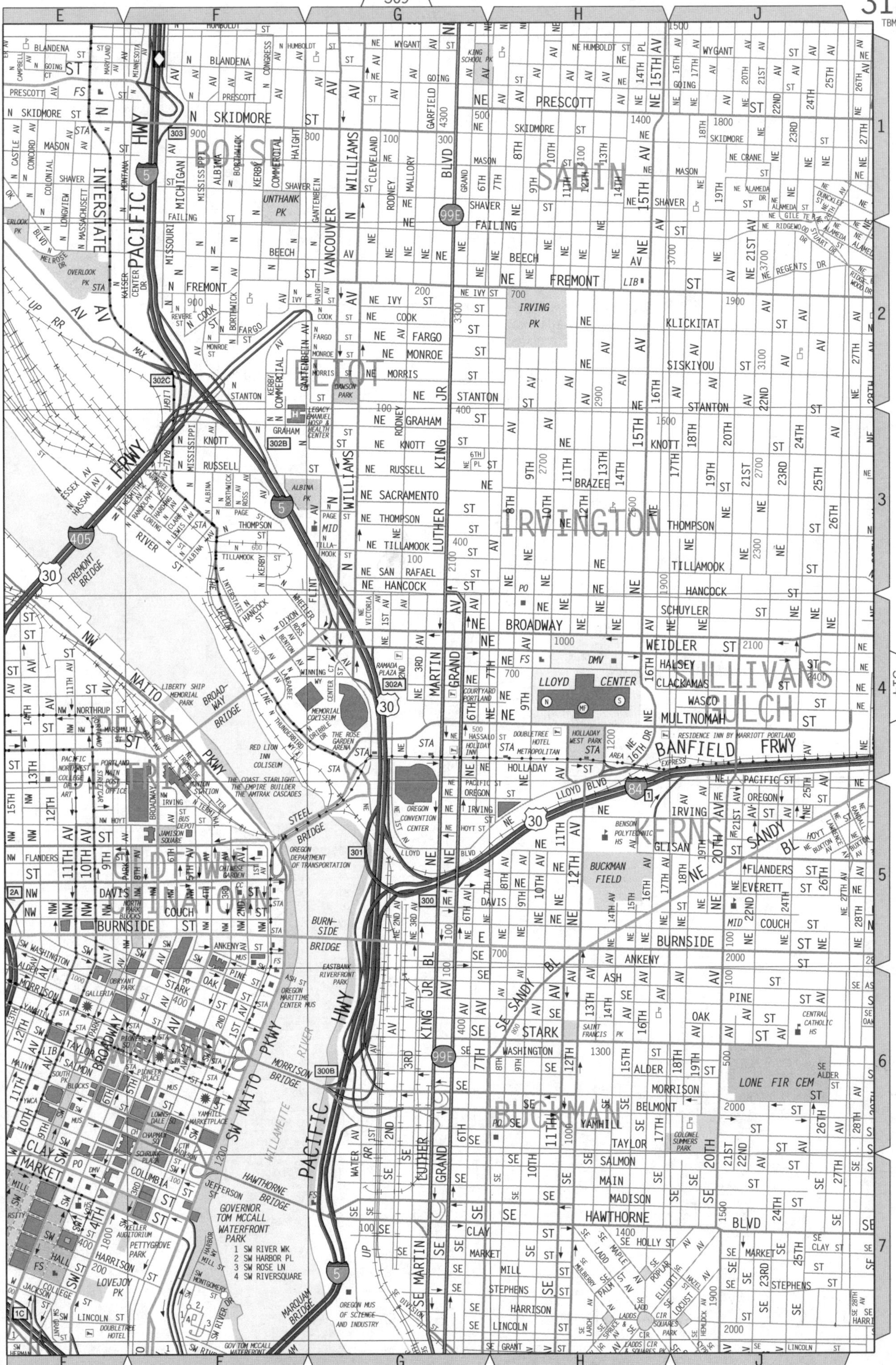

0   .125   .25   .375   .5
miles   1 in. = 1900 ft.

DETAIL

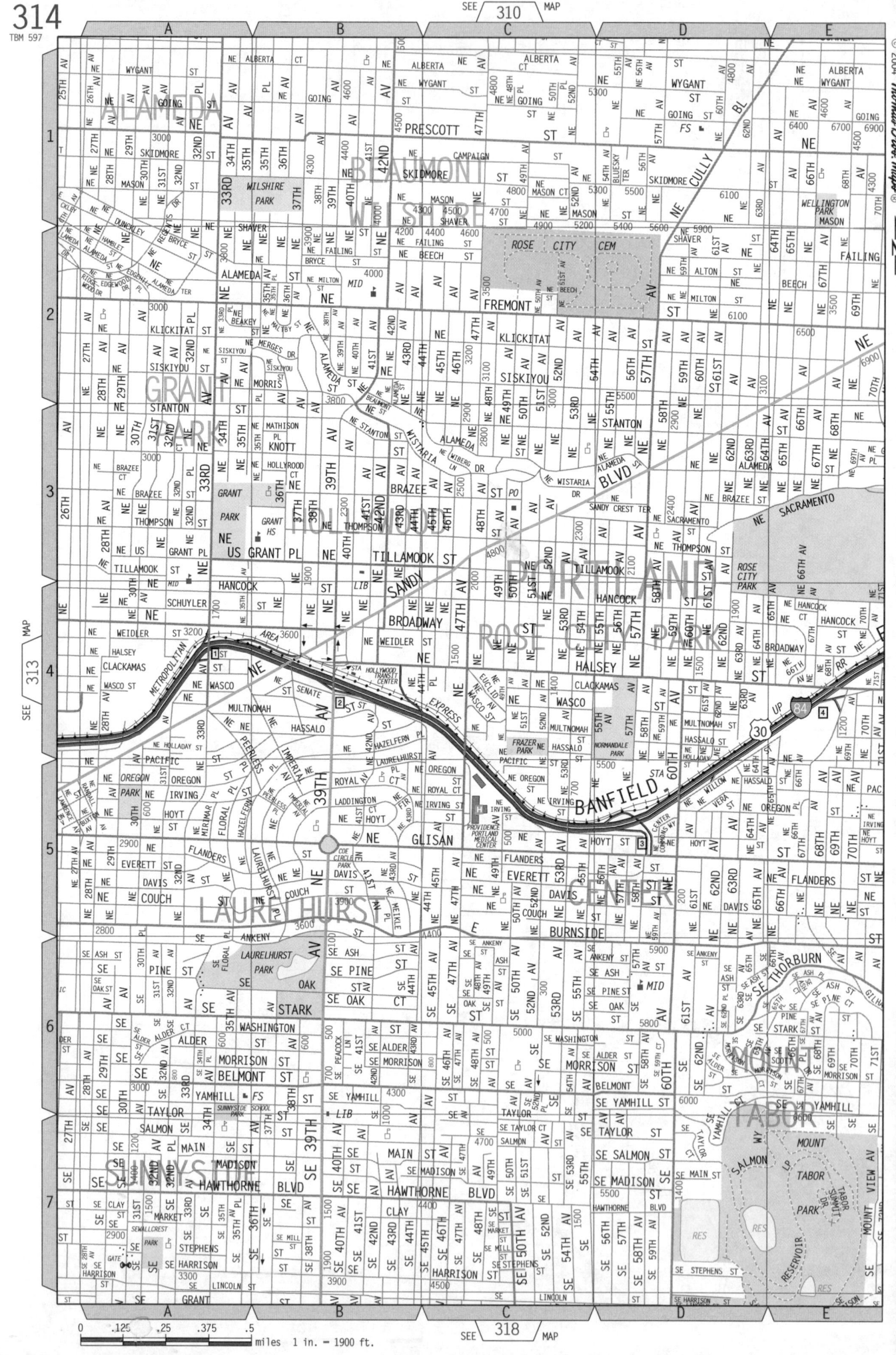

© 2004 Thomas Bros. Maps ®

—N—

SEE 200 MAP

DETAIL

Major labels:

SANDY BLVD

PARKROSE

MAYWOOD PARK

PARKROSE HEIGHTS

ROSEWAY

THE GROTTO

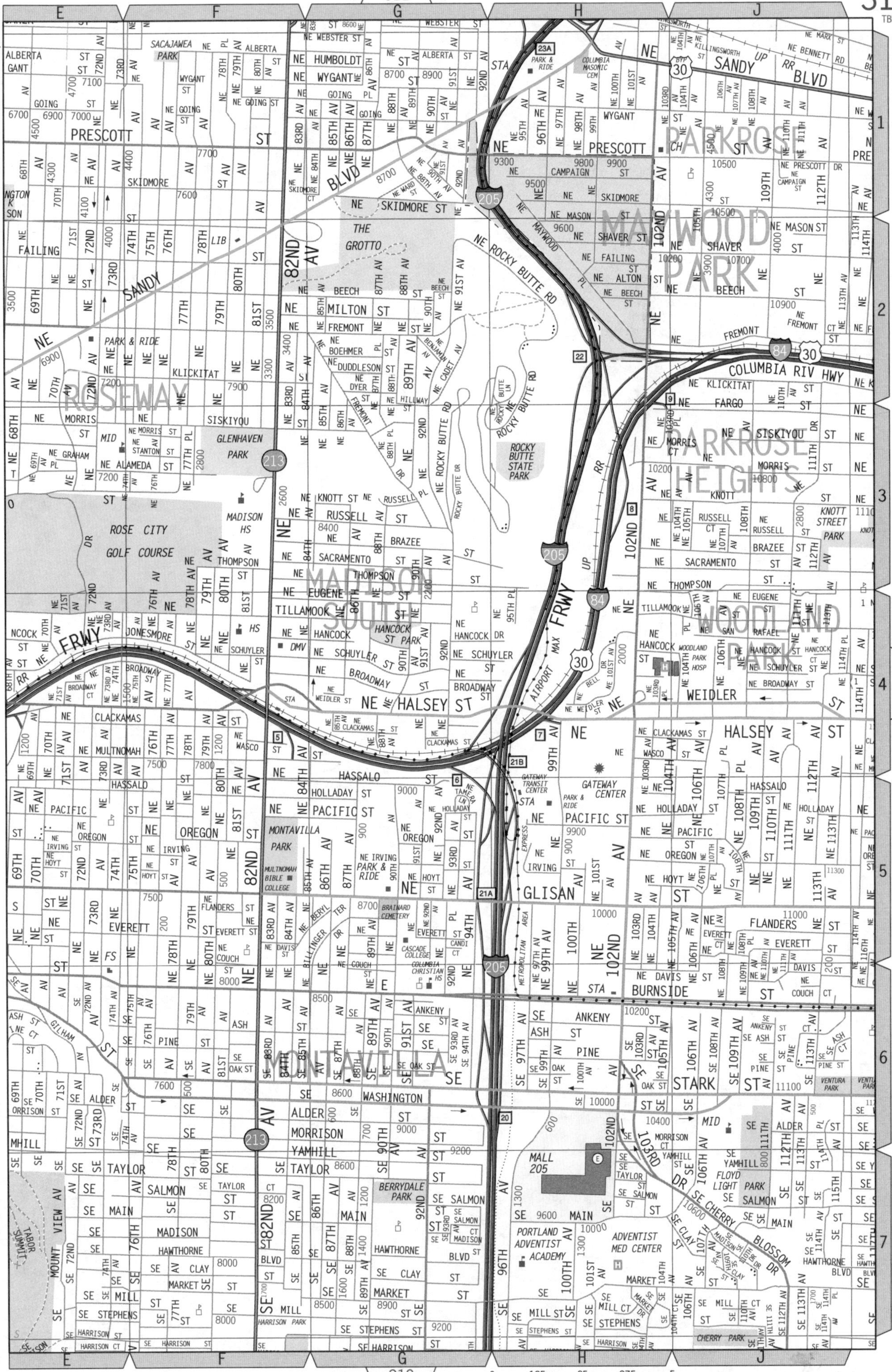

ROCKY BUTTE STATE PARK

GLENHAVEN PARK

ROSE CITY GOLF COURSE

MADISON HS

MADISON SOUTH

WOODLAND PARK

HANCOCK ST PARK

GATEWAY TRANSIT CENTER

GATEWAY CENTER

MONTAVILLA PARK

MULTNOMAH BIBLE COLLEGE

COLUMBIA CHRISTIAN HS

CASCADE COLLEGE

BRAINARD CEMETERY

METROPOLITAN AREA

MALL 205

BERRYDALE PARK

PORTLAND ADVENTIST ACADEMY

ADVENTIST MED CENTER

FLOYD LIGHT PARK

VENTURA PARK

CHERRY PARK

COLUMBIA RIV HWY

AIRPORT WAY

82ND AV

102ND AV

NE HALSEY ST

BURNSIDE

STARK ST

E STARK ST

GLISAN

PACIFIC ST

NE BROADWAY

WEIDLER

PRESCOTT ST

SKIDMORE ST

FAILING

KLICKITAT

SISKIYOU

FREMONT

KNOTT ST

RUSSELL

SACRAMENTO

THOMPSON

TILLAMOOK

HANCOCK

SCHUYLER

CLACKAMAS

MULTNOMAH

WASCO

HASSALO

HOLLADAY

OREGON

IRVING

HOYT

EVERETT

FLANDERS

COUCH

DAVIS

ANKENY

ASH ST

PINE

OAK ST

WASHINGTON

ALDER

MORRISON

YAMHILL

TAYLOR

SALMON

MAIN

MADISON

HAWTHORNE BLVD

CLAY

MARKET

MILL ST

STEPHENS

HARRISON

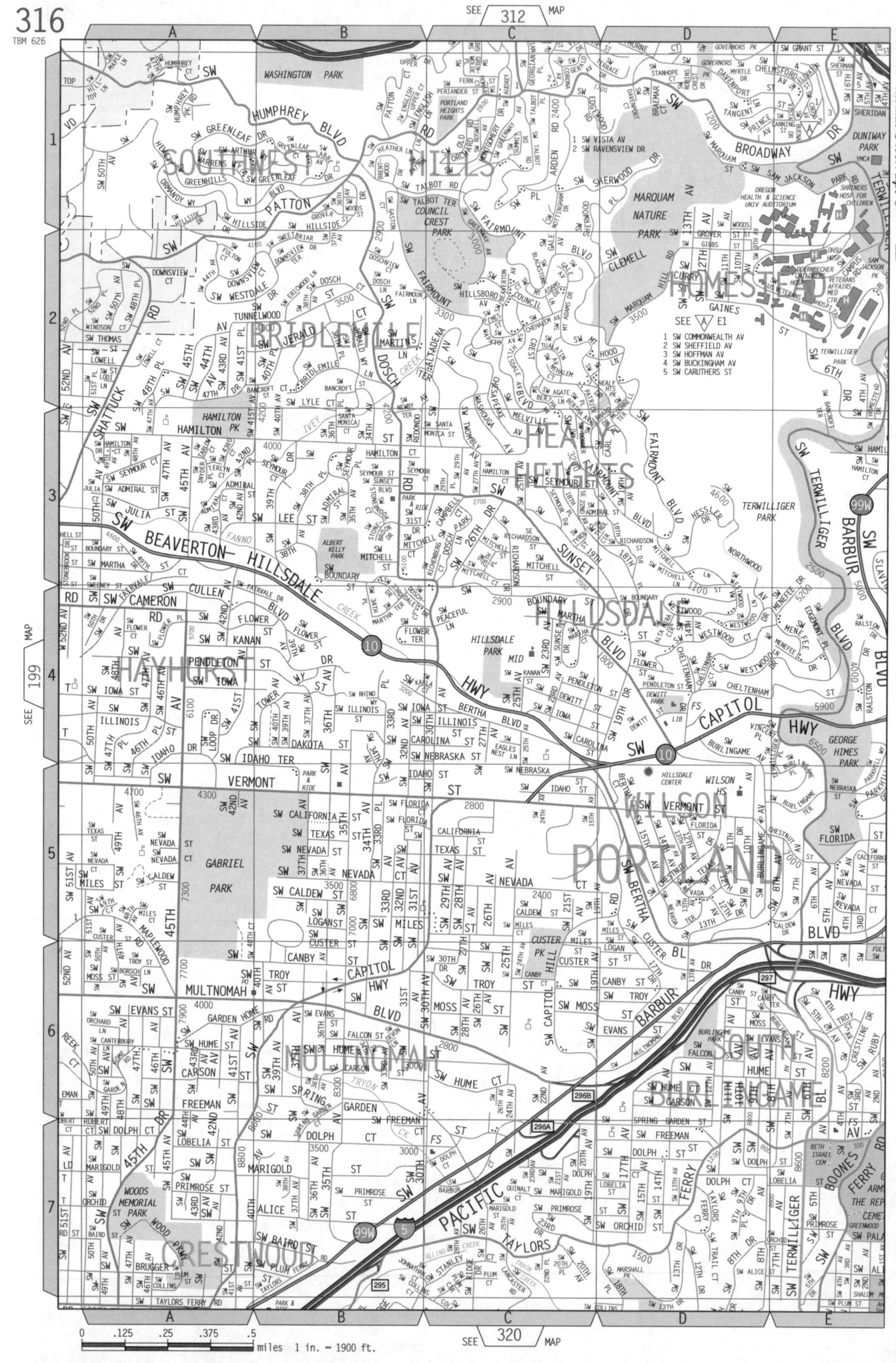

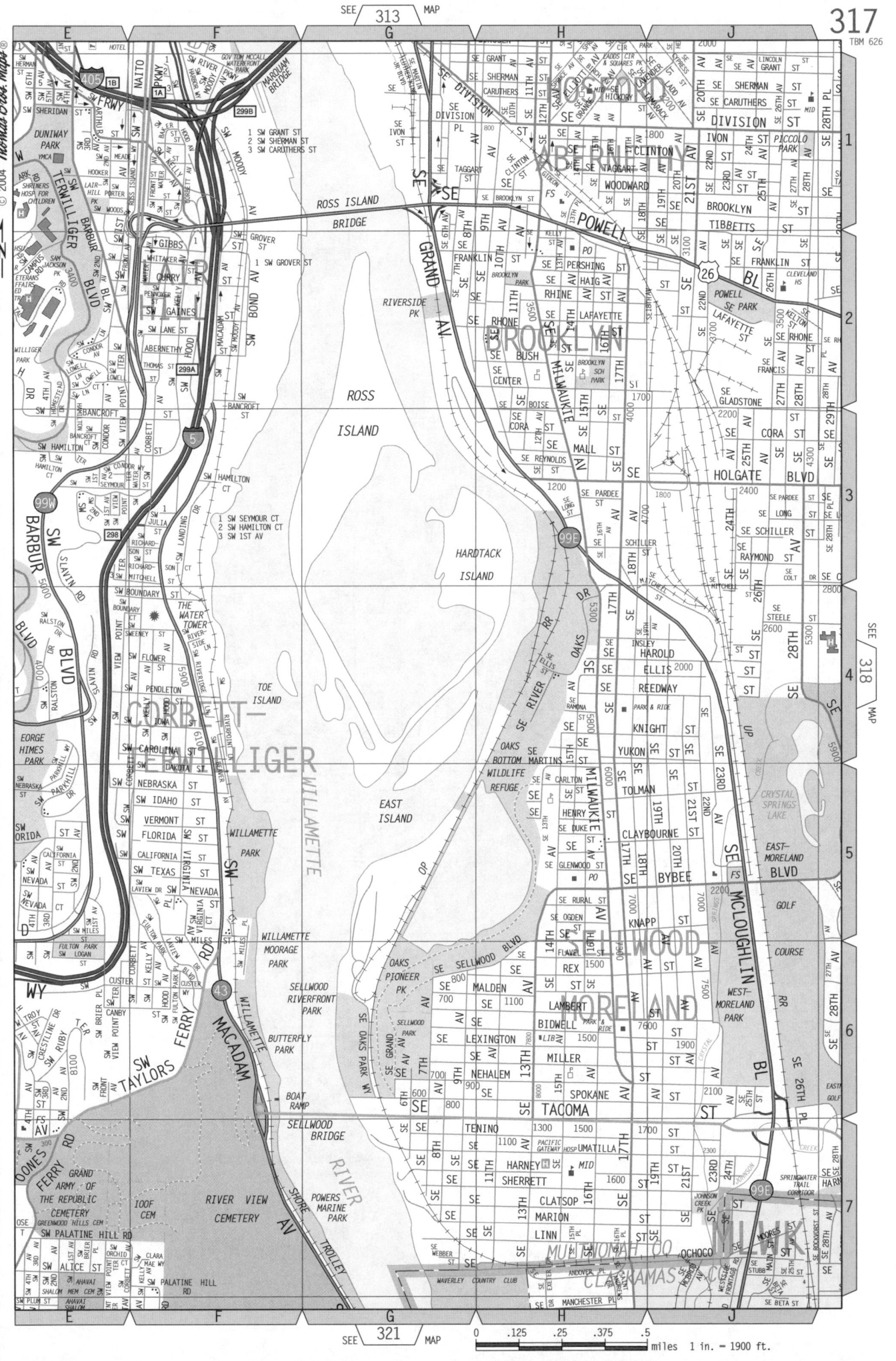

© 2004 Thomas Bros. Maps®

—N—

DETAIL

0 .125 .25 .375 .5
miles 1 in. = 1900 ft.

SEE 318 MAP

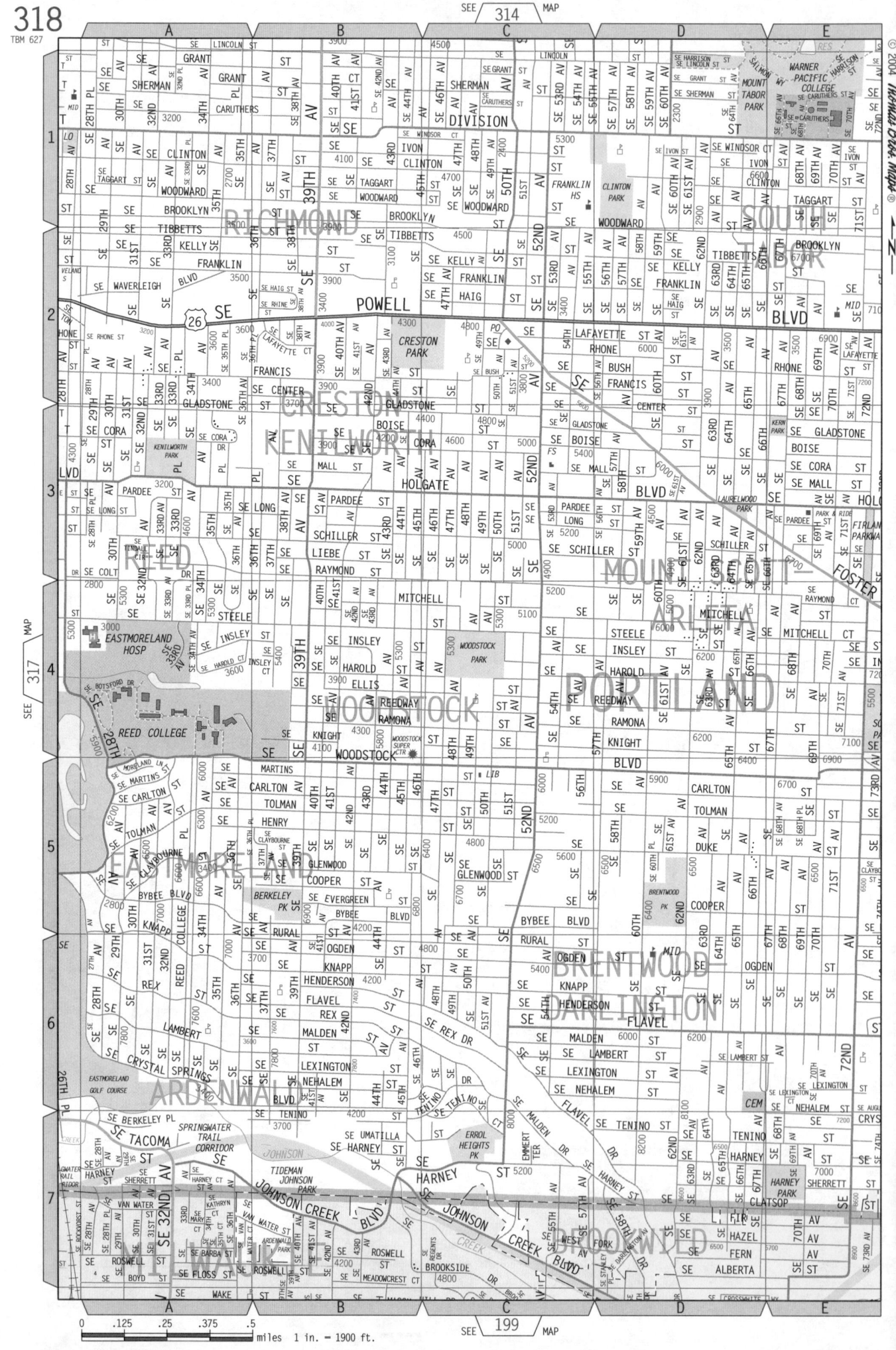

MULTNOMAH COUNTY

KELLY BUTTE PARK

LENTS PARK

EASTPORT PLAZA

MARSHALL HS

ED BENEDICT PARK

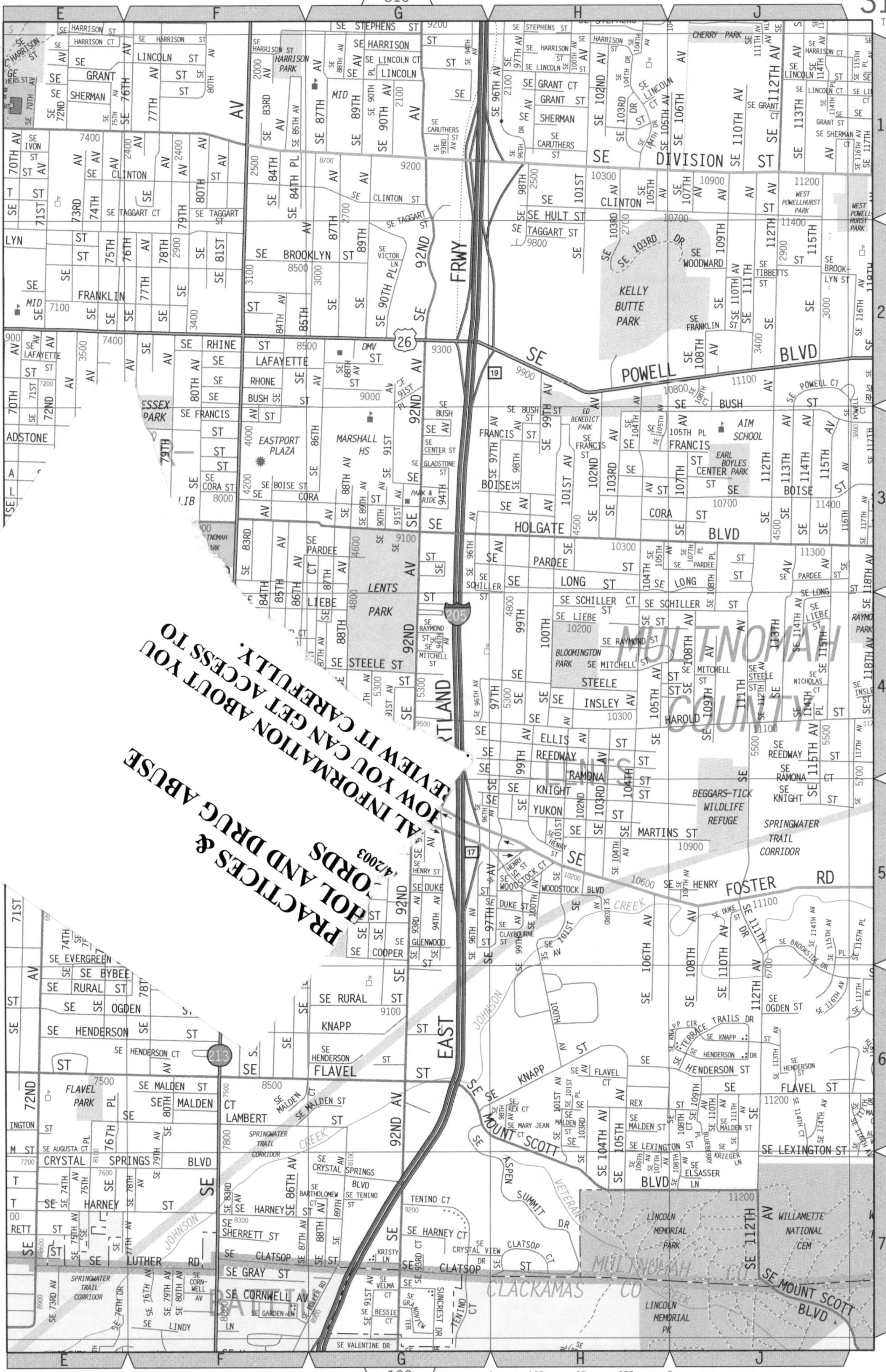

AIM SCHOOL

EARL BOYLES CENTER PARK

BLOOMINGTON PARK

BEGGARS-TICK WILDLIFE REFUGE

SPRINGWATER TRAIL CORRIDOR

LINCOLN MEMORIAL PARK

WILLAMETTE NATIONAL CEM

LINCOLN MEMORIAL PK

MULTNOMAH CO. CLACKAMAS CO.

FLAVEL PARK

SPRINGWATER TRAIL CORRIDOR

SE POWELL BLVD

SE DIVISION ST

SE HOLGATE BLVD

SE FOSTER RD

SE MOUNT SCOTT BLVD

92ND AV

FRWY

205

DETAIL

Overlaid text block (rotated):
PRACTICES & ... DRUG ABUSE ...ORDS '42003 ...AL INFORMATION ABOUT YOU HOW YOU CAN GET ACCESS TO REVIEW IT CAREFULLY.

© 2004 Thomas Bros. Maps®

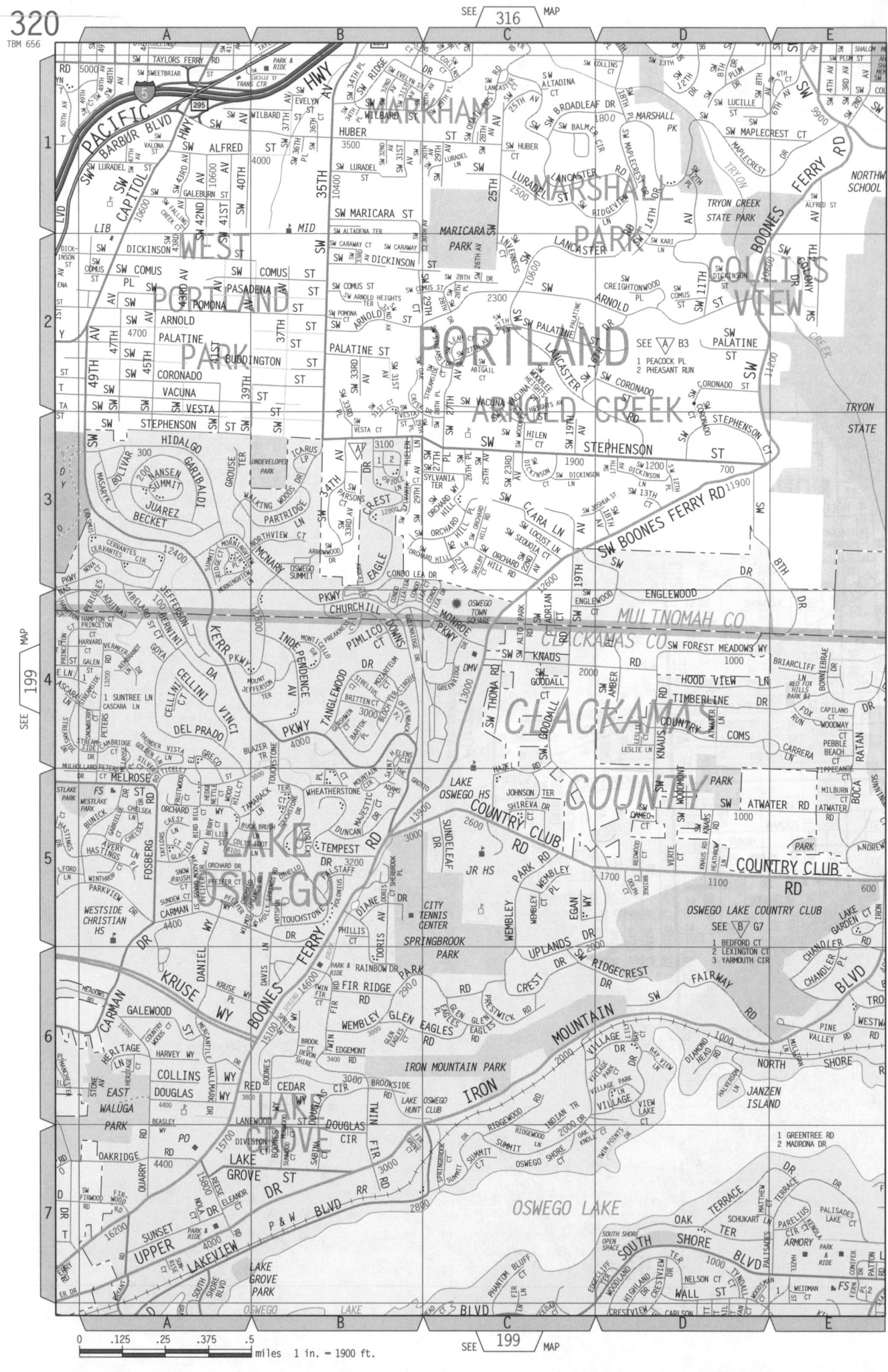

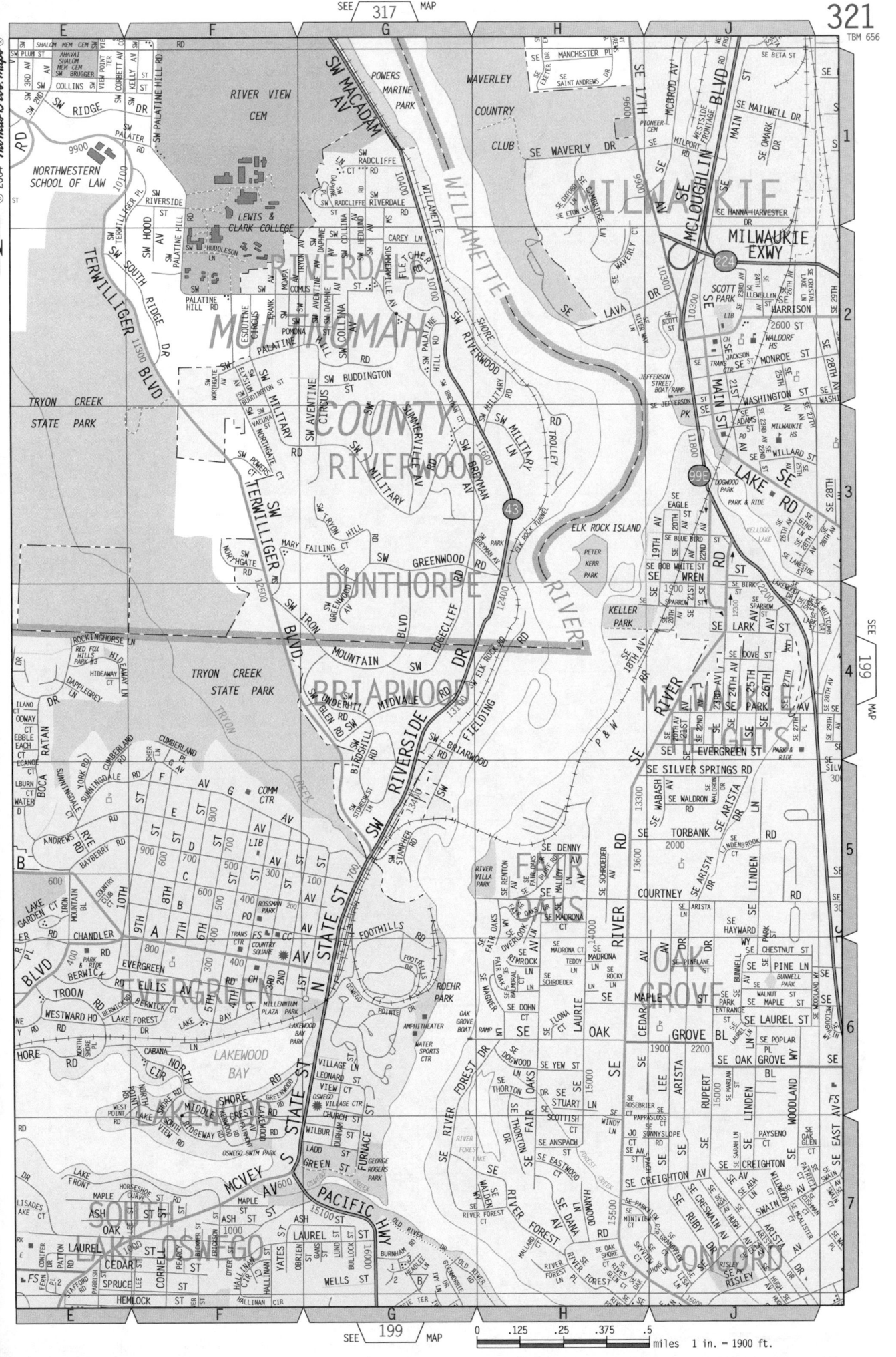

© 2004 Thomas Bros. Maps ®

0 .125 .25 .375 .5
miles 1 in. = 1900 ft.

DETAIL

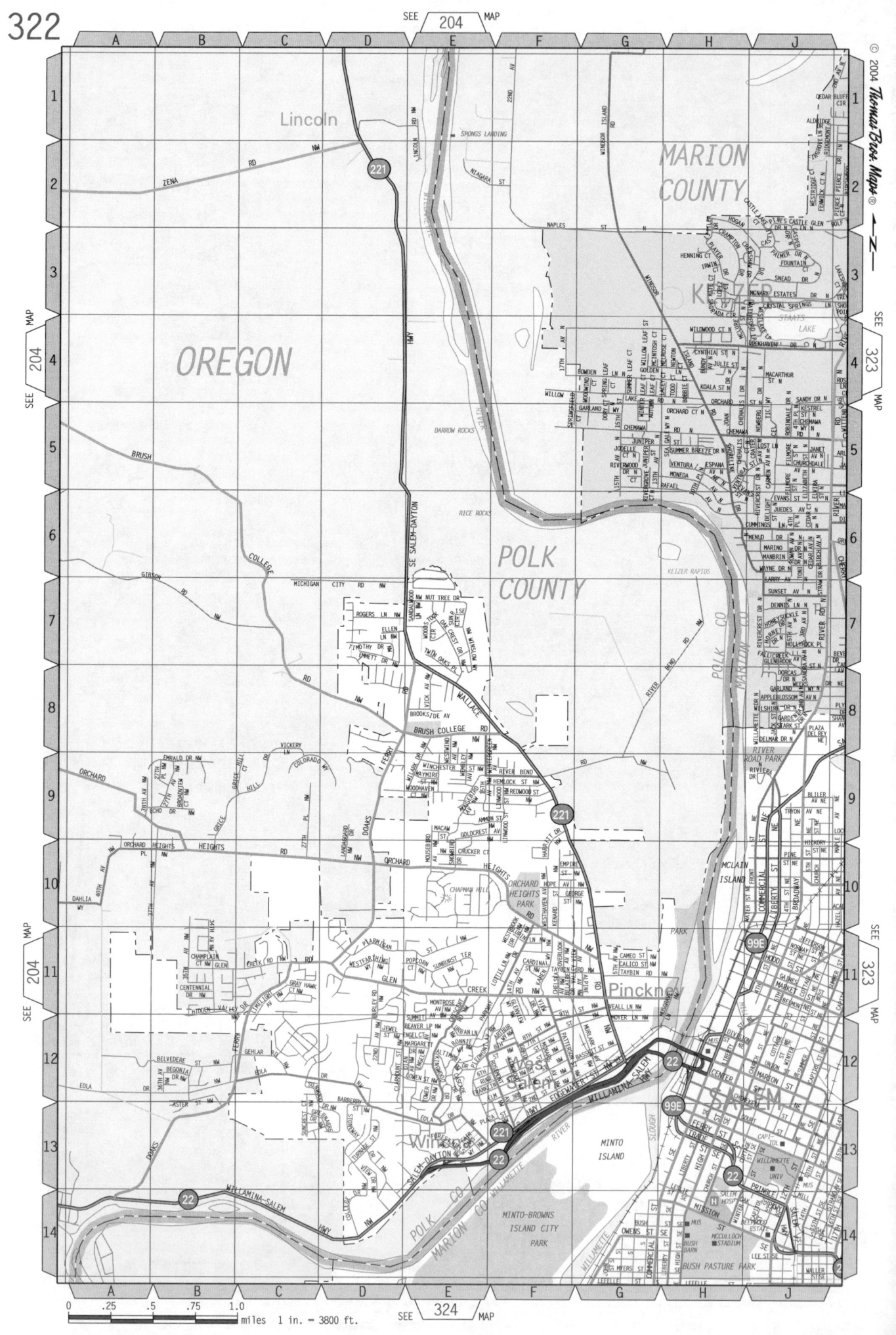

© 2004 Thomas Bros. Maps ® —N—

SEE 204 MAP

Lincoln

OREGON

MARION COUNTY

KEIZER

POLK COUNTY

SEE 204 MAP

SEE 323 MAP

West Salem

Pinckner

SALEM

Winsor

SEE 204 MAP

SEE 323 MAP

MINTO ISLAND

MINTO-BROWNS ISLAND CITY PARK

BUSH PASTURE PARK

0   .25   .5   .75   1.0
miles   1 in. = 3800 ft.

SEE 324 MAP

DETAIL

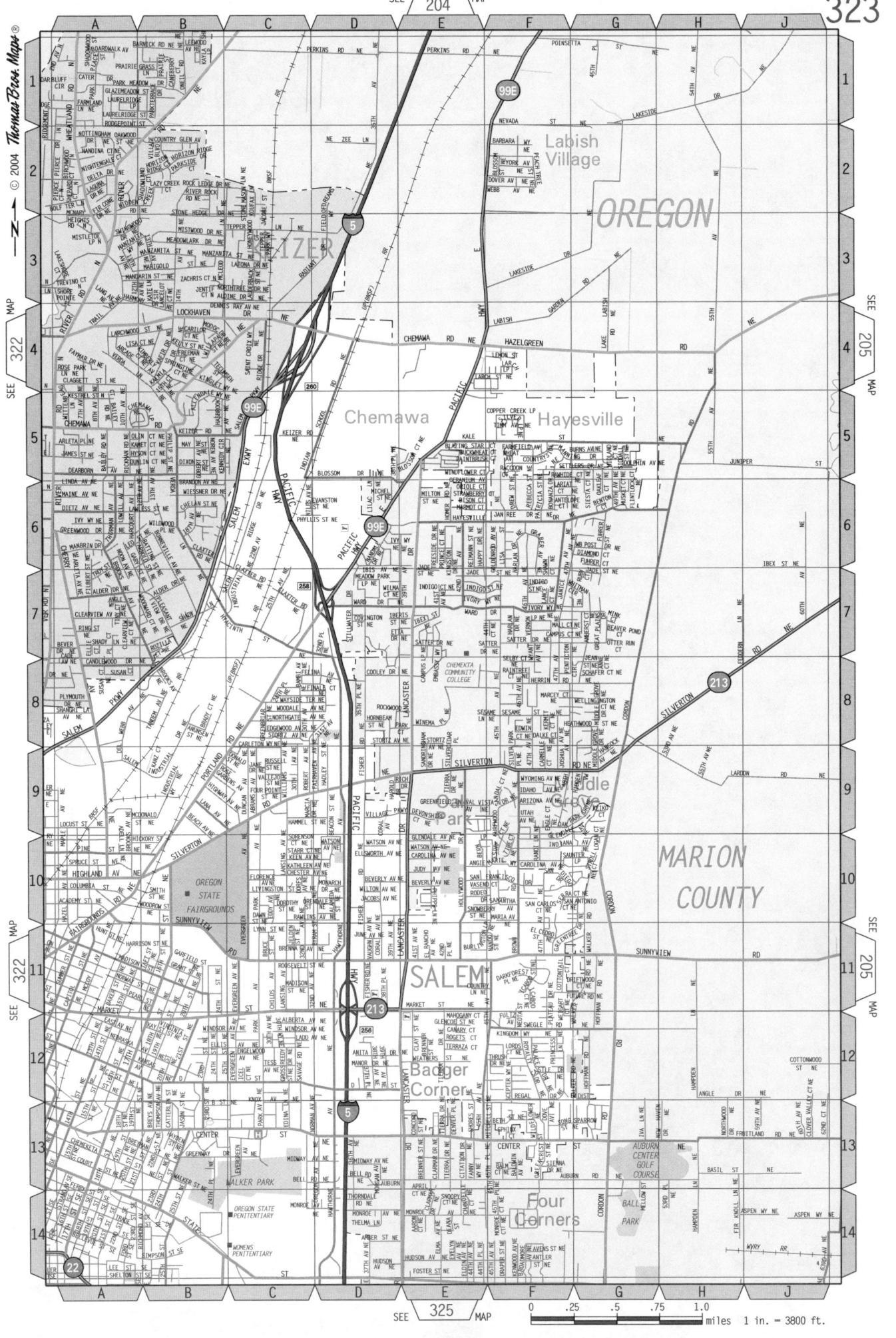

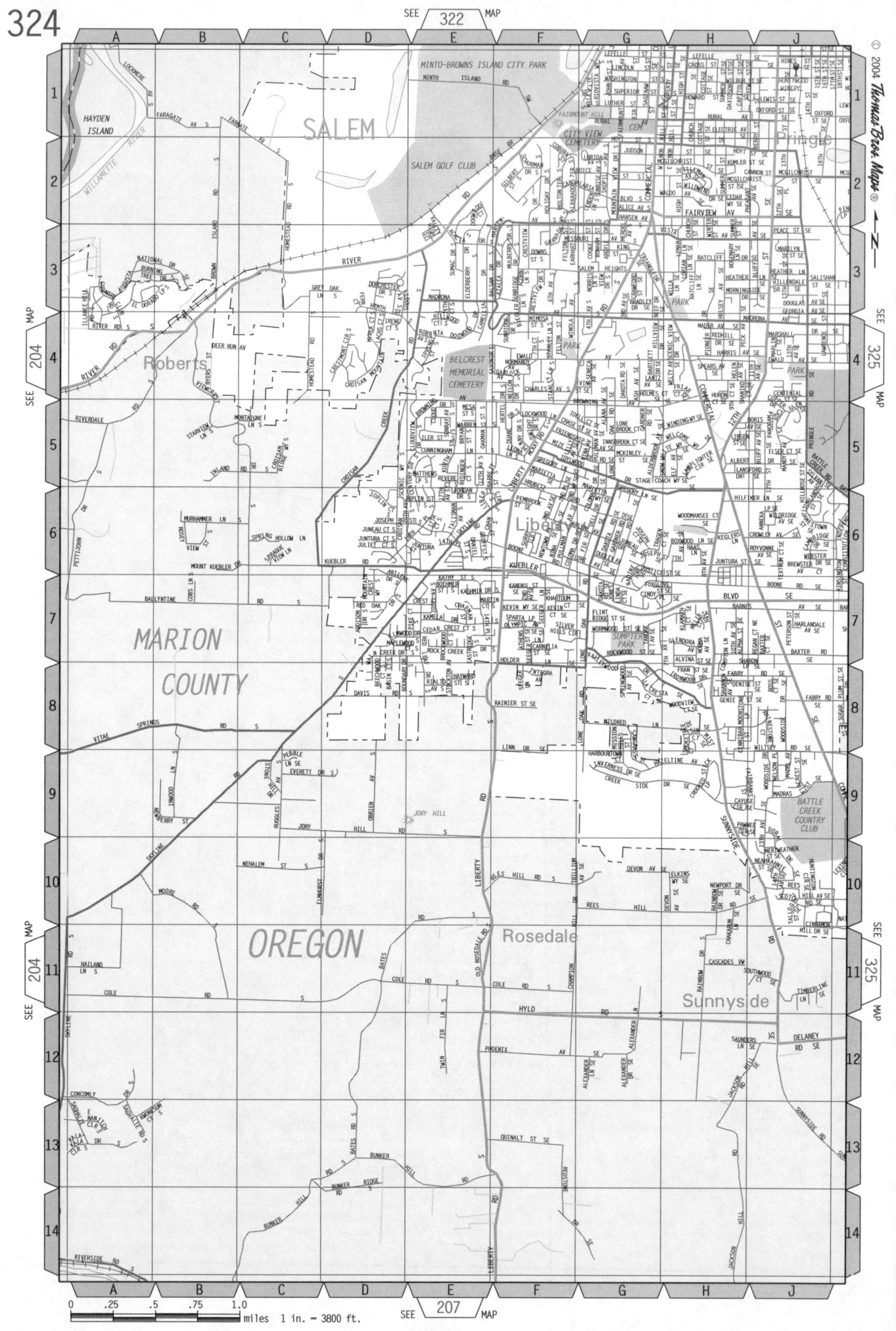

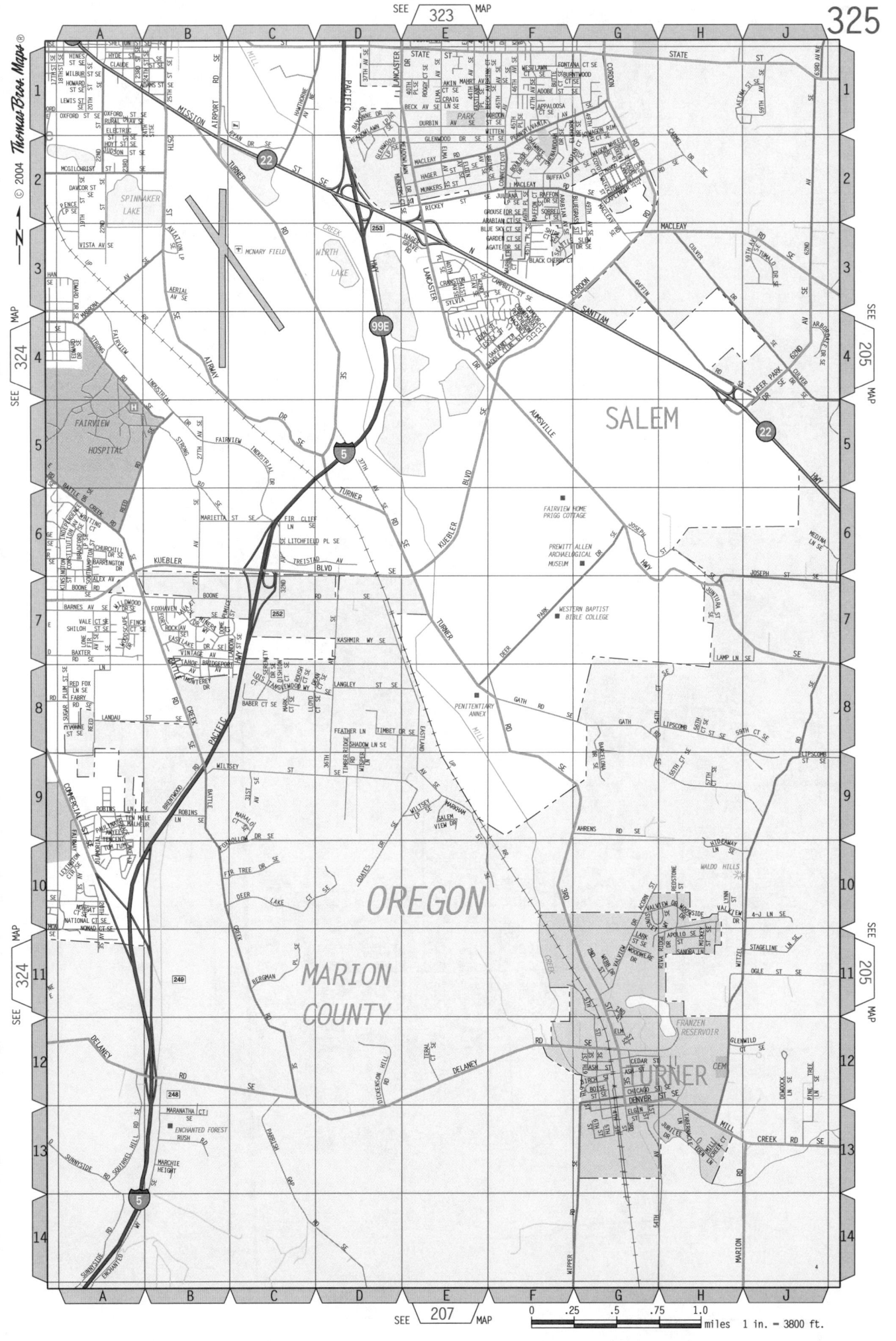

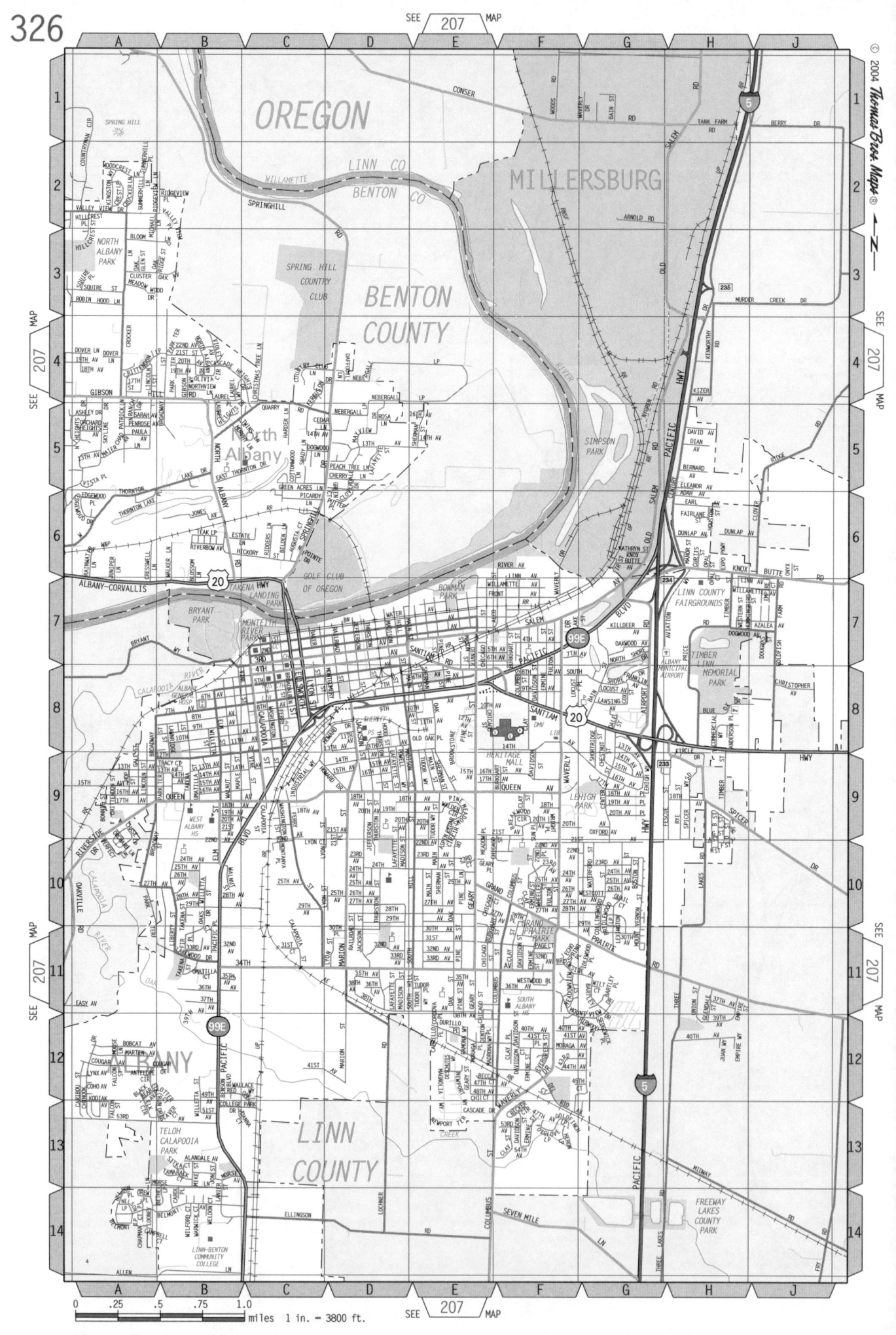

© 2004 Thomas Bros. Maps®

OREGON

MILLERSBURG

BENTON
COUNTY

North
Albany

ALBANY

LINN
COUNTY

SEE 207 MAP

SEE 207 MAP

miles 1 in. = 3800 ft.

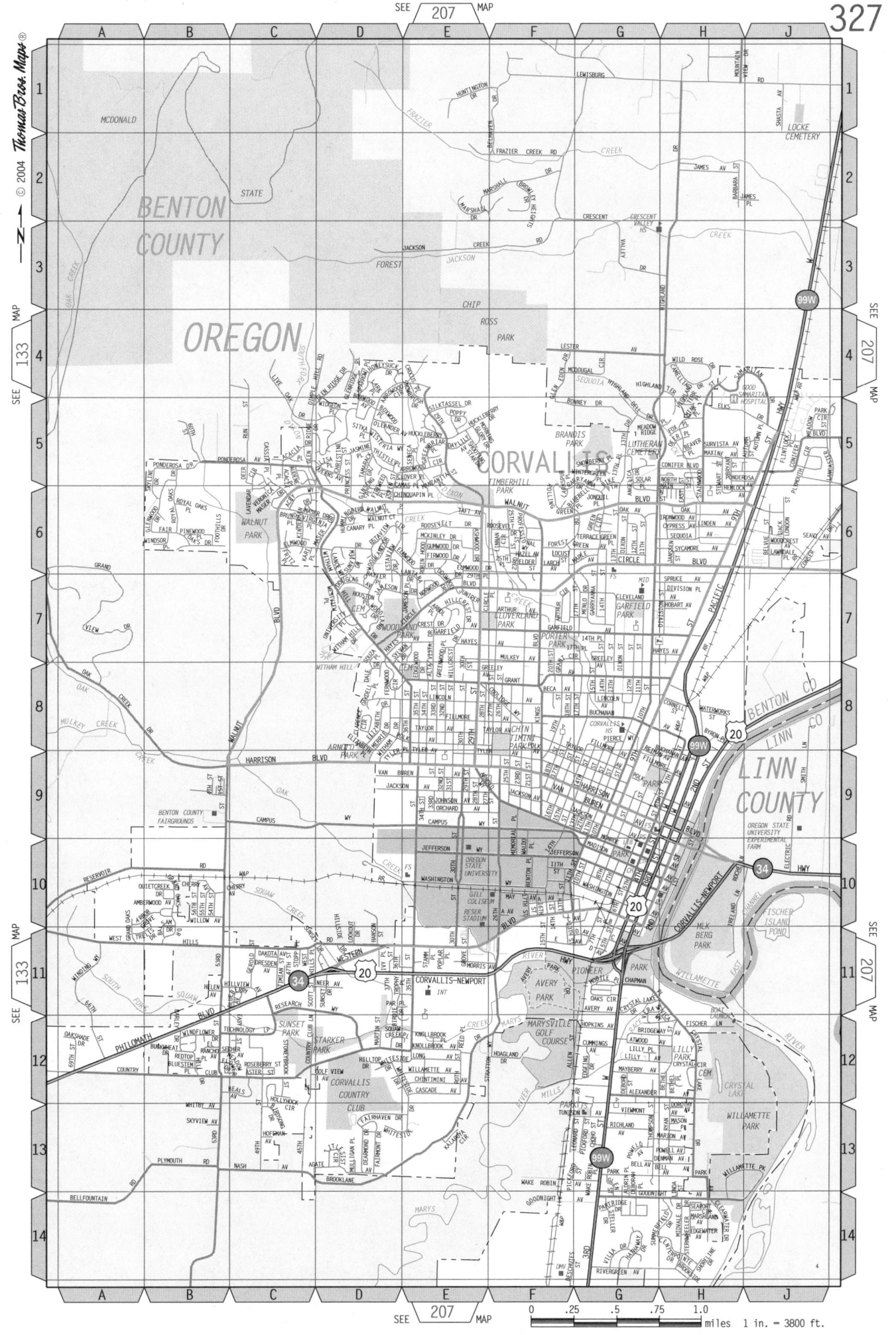

SEE 207 MAP

A B C D E F G H J

SEE MAP 133

SEE 207 MAP

DETAIL

MCDONALD

BENTON COUNTY

STATE

OREGON

FOREST

CHIP ROSS PARK

CORVALLIS

BRANDIS PARK

LUTHERAN CEMETERY

GOOD SAMARITAN HOSPITAL

LOCKE CEMETERY

WALNUT PARK

TIMBERHILL PARK

GARFIELD PARK

CLOVERLAND PARK

PORTER PARK

BENTON CO

LINN CO

LINN COUNTY

BENTON COUNTY FAIRGROUNDS

OREGON STATE UNIVERSITY

OREGON STATE UNIVERSITY EXPERIMENTAL FARM

GILL COLISEUM

RESER STADIUM

MLK JR BERG PARK

FISCHER ISLAND POND

SUNSET PARK

STARKER PARK

PIONEER PARK

AVERY PARK

MARYSVILLE GOLF COURSE

LILLY PARK

CRYSTAL LAKE

WILLAMETTE PARK

CORVALLIS COUNTRY CLUB

WILLAMETTE RIVER

SEE 207 MAP

SEE MAP 133

SEE 207 MAP

A B C D E F G H J

SEE 207 MAP

0 .25 .5 .75 1.0
miles   1 in. = 3800 ft.

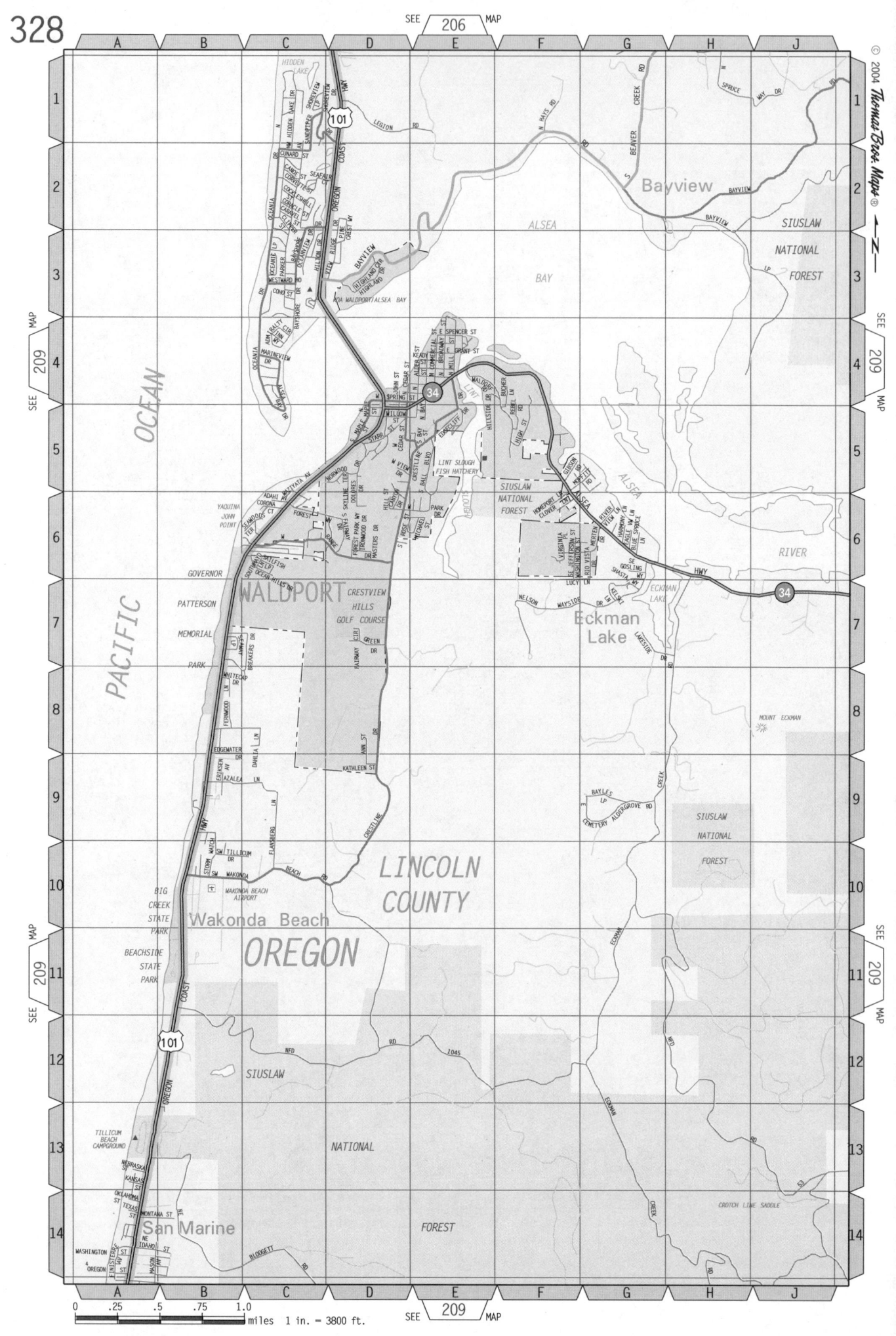

SEE 206 MAP

SEE 209 MAP

SEE 209 MAP

DETAIL

PACIFIC OCEAN

ALSEA BAY

NOA WALDPORT/ALSEA BAY

Bayview

SIUSLAW NATIONAL FOREST

WALDPORT

YAQUINA JOHN POINT

GOVERNOR PATTERSON MEMORIAL PARK

CRESTVIEW HILLS GOLF COURSE

LINT SLOUGH FISH HATCHERY

SIUSLAW NATIONAL FOREST

ALSEA RIVER

Eckman Lake

MOUNT ECKMAN

SIUSLAW NATIONAL FOREST

LINCOLN COUNTY

OREGON

Wakonda Beach

BIG CREEK STATE PARK

BEACHSIDE STATE PARK

Wakonda Beach Airport

SIUSLAW

NATIONAL

FOREST

TILLICUM BEACH CAMPGROUND

CROTCH LINE SADDLE

San Marine

SEE 209 MAP

SEE 209 MAP

0   .25   .5   .75   1.0
miles   1 in. = 3800 ft.

SEE 209 MAP

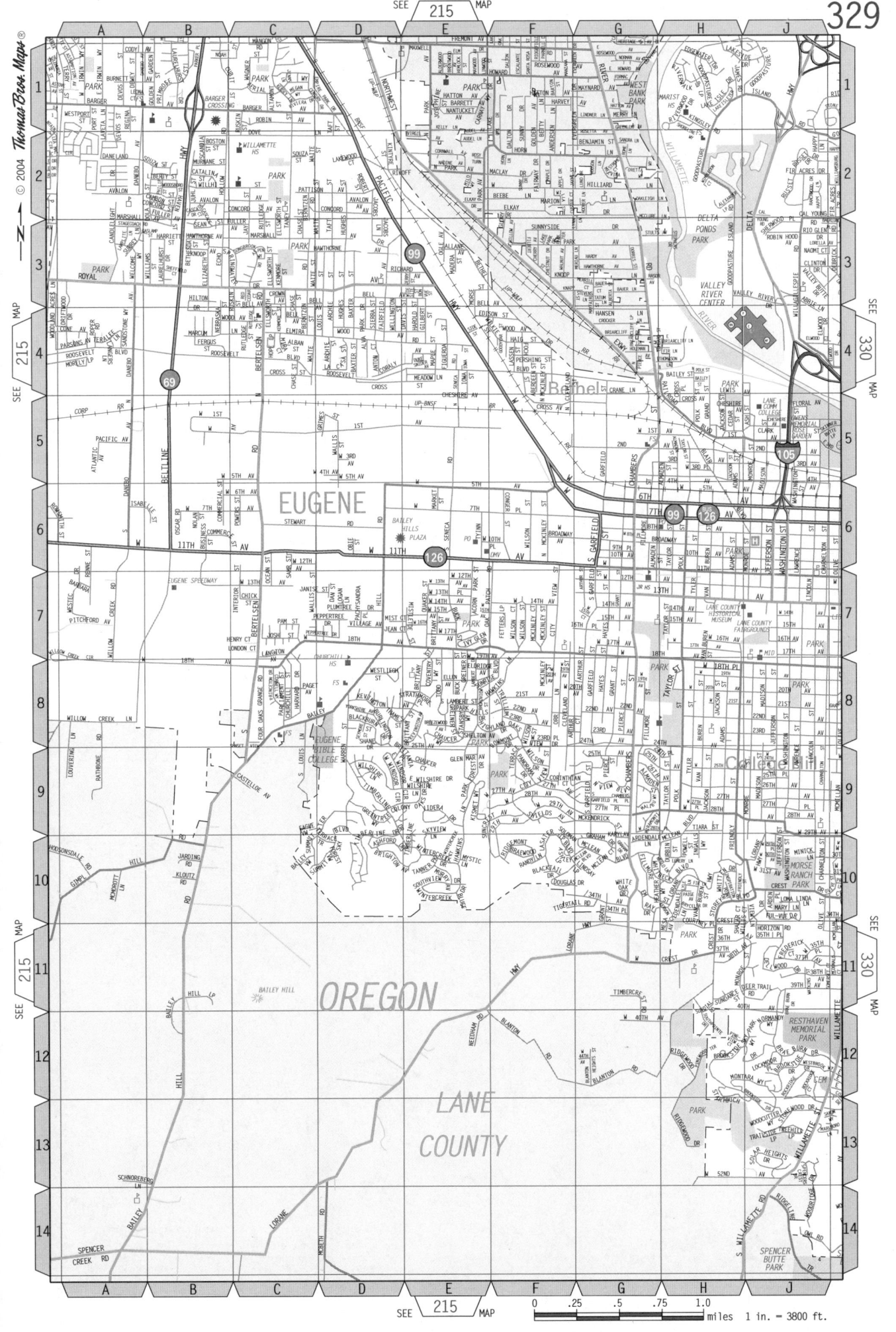

DETAIL

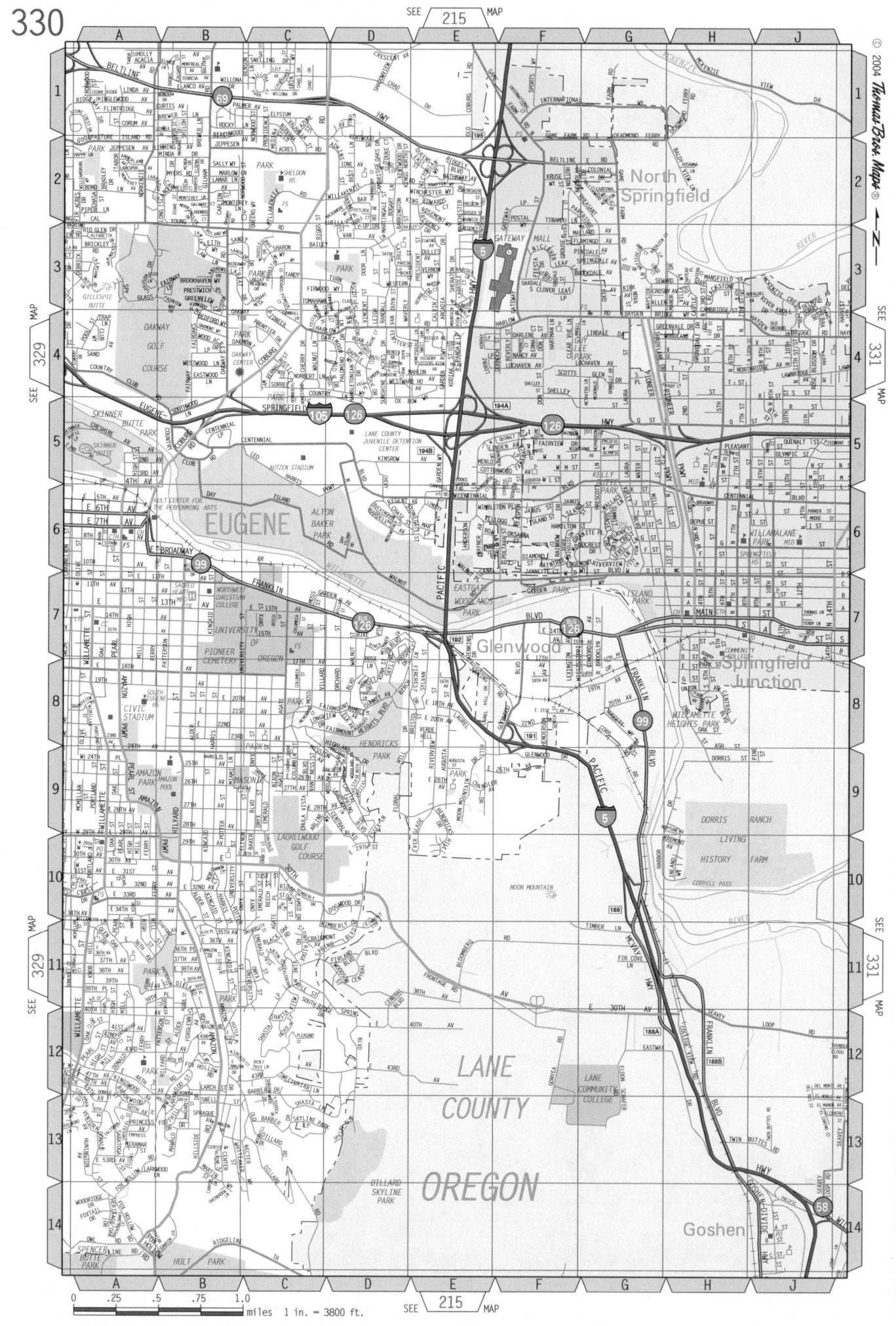

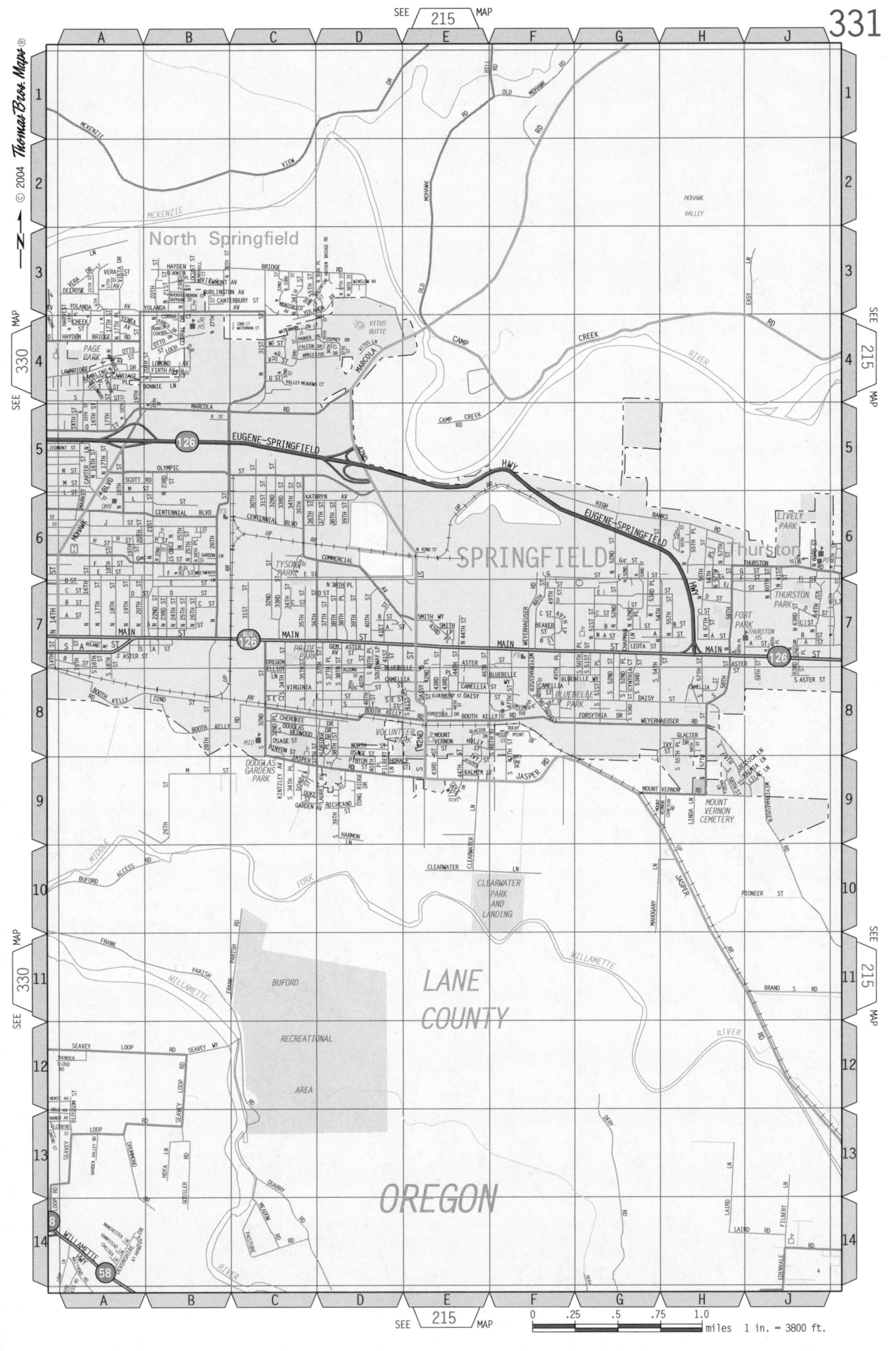

SEE 215 MAP

© 2004 Thomas Bros. Maps®

North Springfield

MCKENZIE

MOHAWK VALLEY

SEE 330 MAP

SEE 215 MAP

Vitus Butte

Camp Creek

River

126 EUGENE-SPRINGFIELD HWY

Lively Park

SPRINGFIELD

Thurston

Thurston Park

Fort Park

126

Tysons Park

MAIN ST

BUS 126 MAIN ST

MAIN

Pride Park

Volunteer Park

Mount Vernon Cemetery

Douglas Gardens Park

Clearwater Park and Landing

SEE 330 MAP

BUFORD RECREATIONAL AREA

LANE COUNTY

WILLAMETTE

OREGON

SEE 215 MAP

River

8

58

DETAIL

0 .25 .5 .75 1.0
miles 1 in. = 3800 ft.

SEE 215 MAP

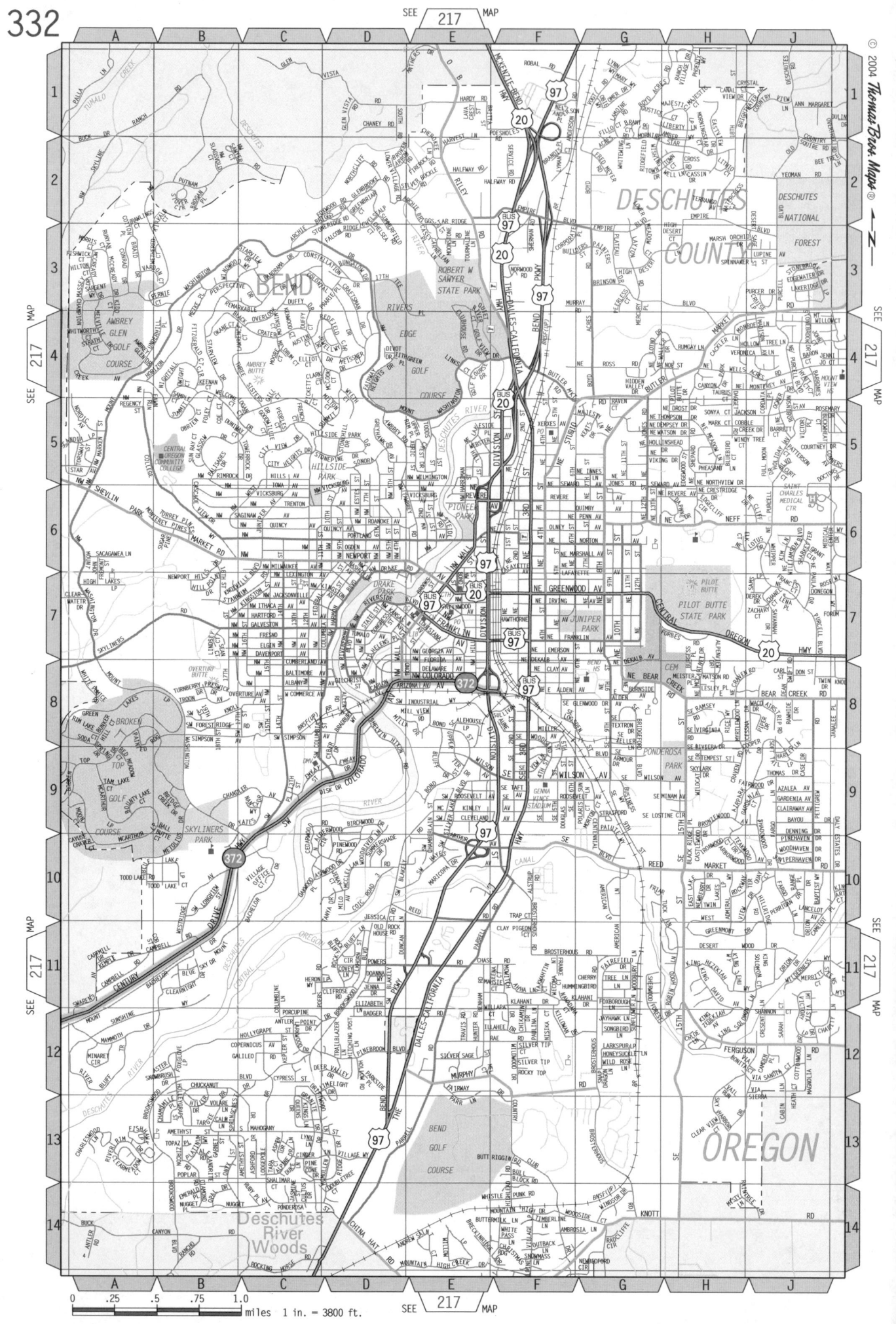

DETAIL

miles   1 in. = 3800 ft.

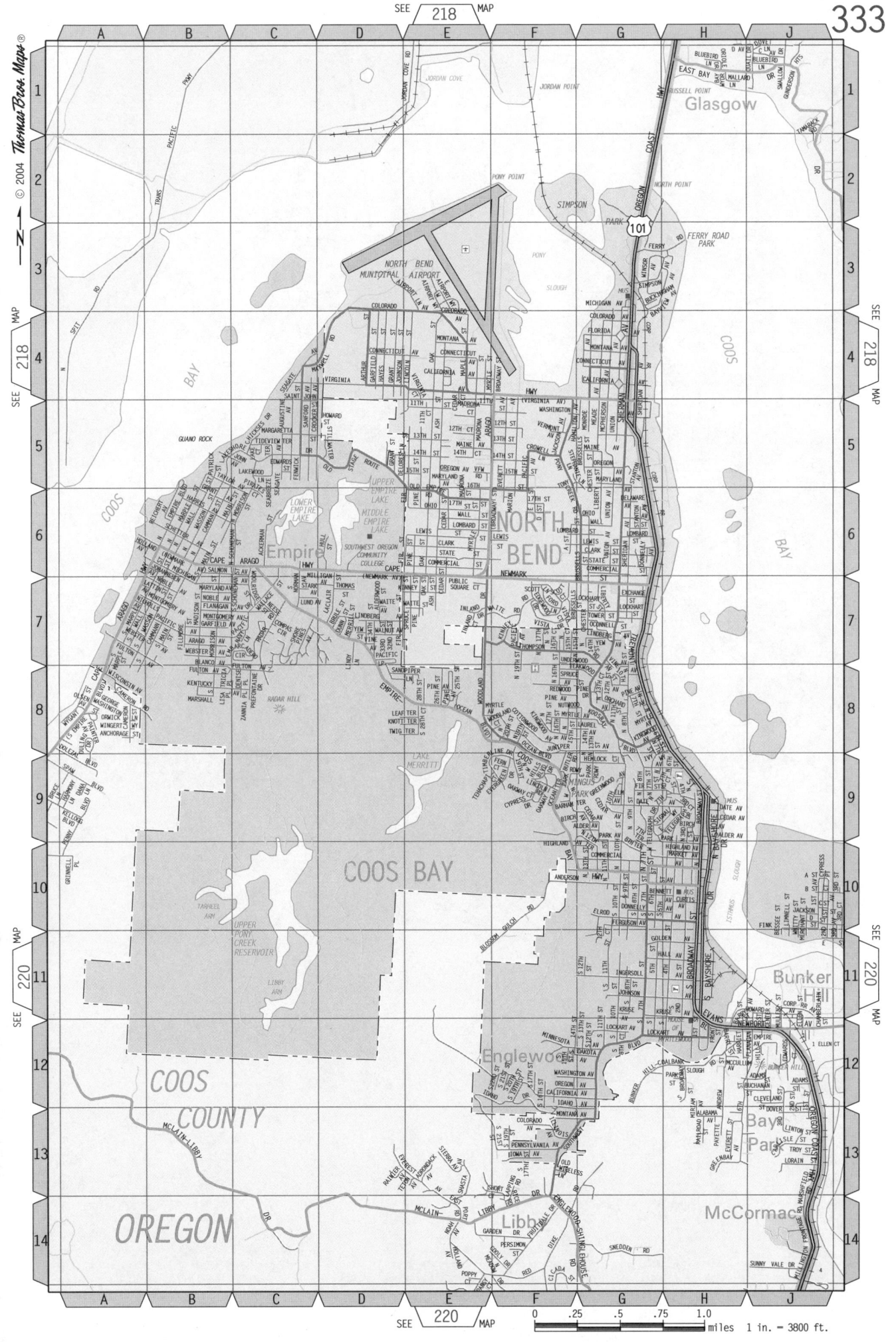

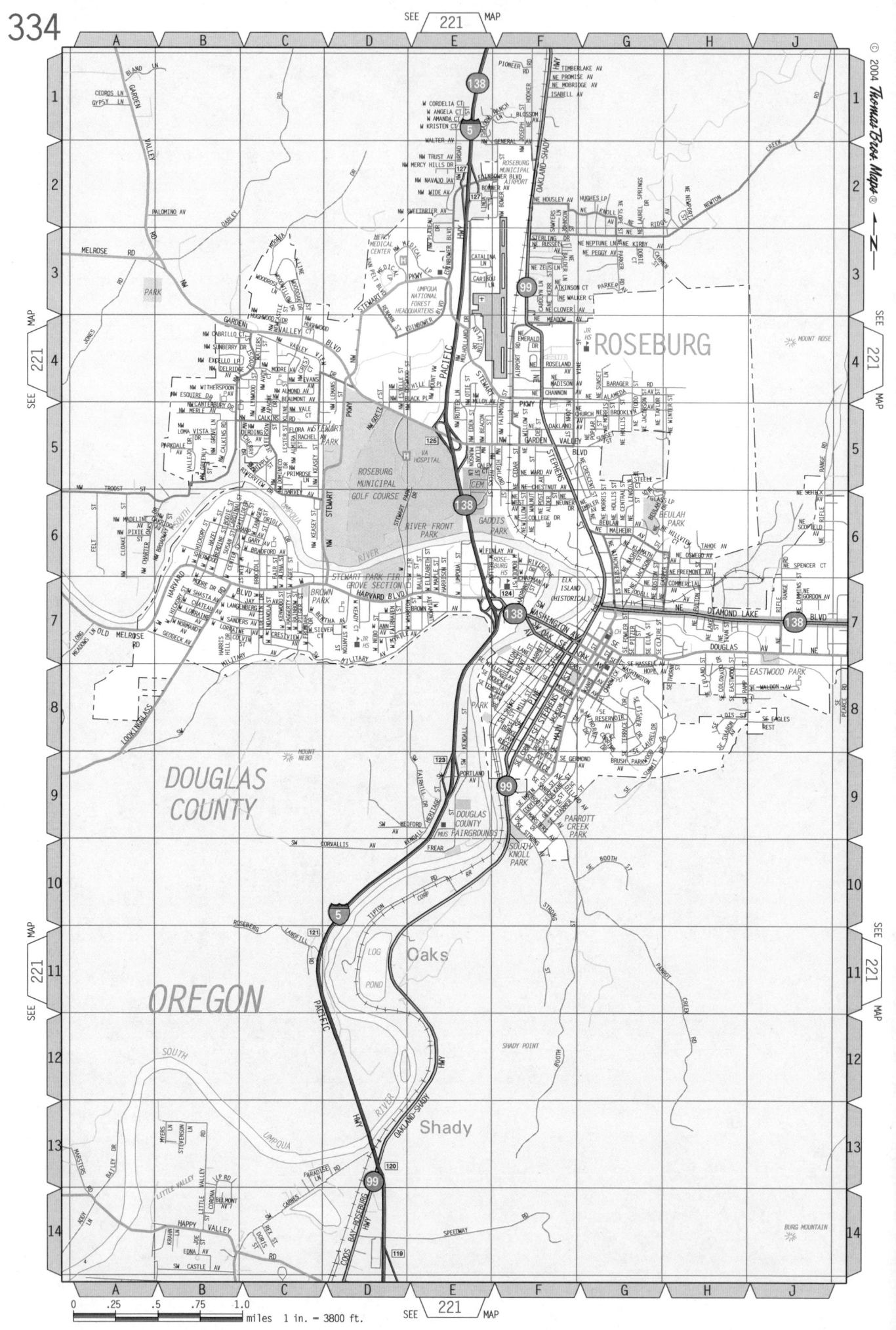

334

© 2004 Thomas Bros. Maps ®   —N—

ROSEBURG

DOUGLAS COUNTY

OREGON

Oaks

Shady

DETAIL

0   .25   .5   .75   1.0
miles 1 in. = 3800 ft.

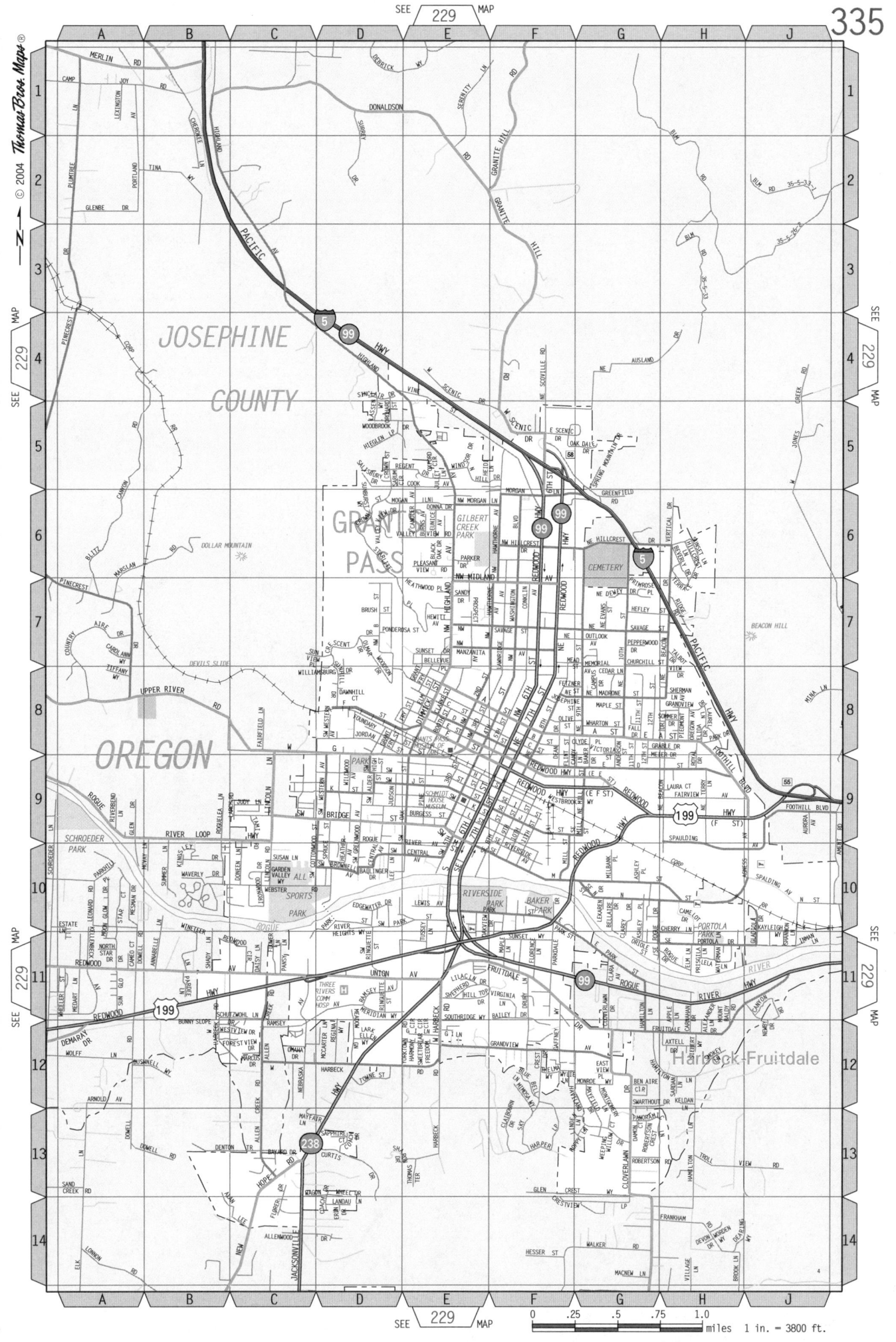

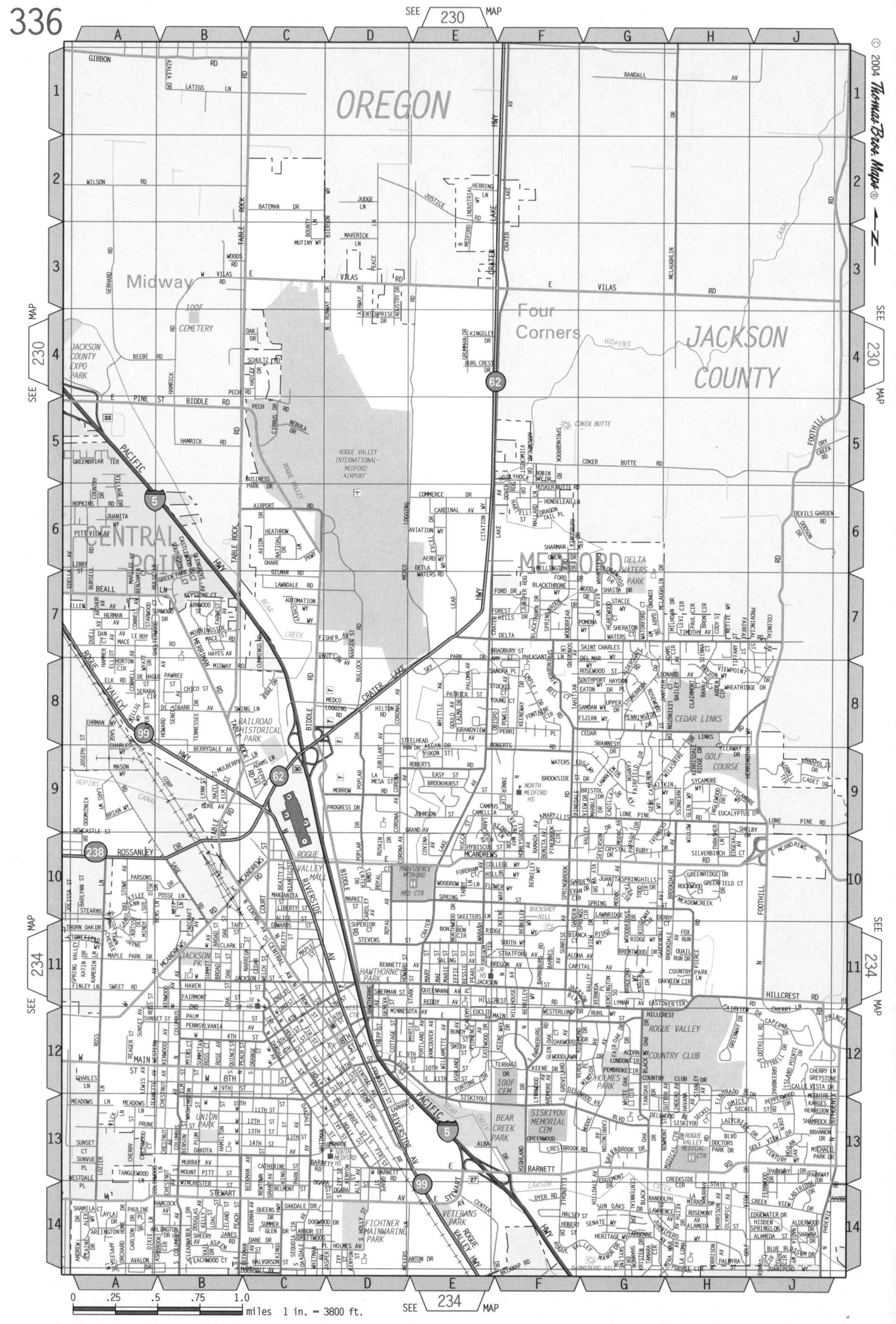

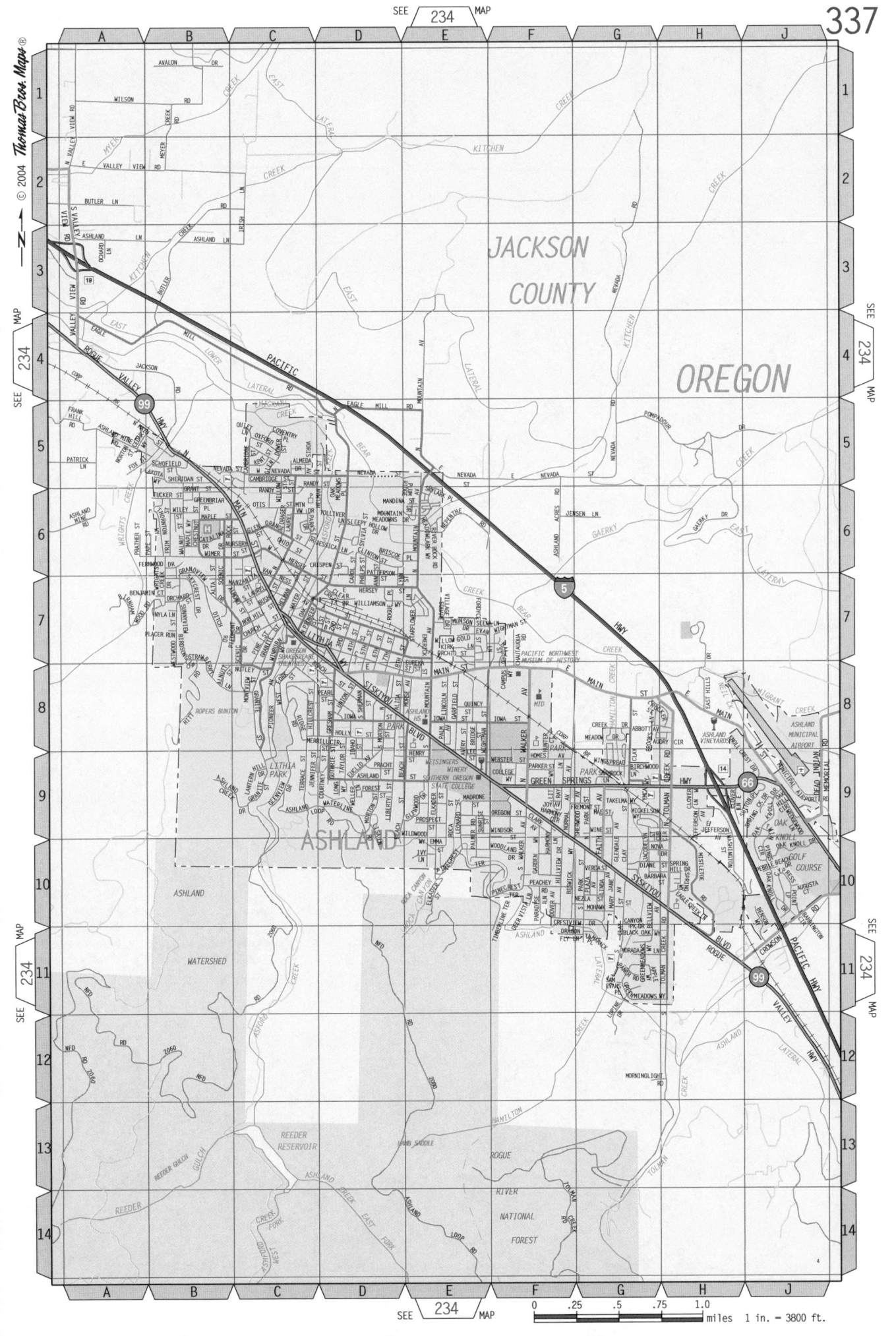

JACKSON

COUNTY

OREGON

ASHLAND

ASHLAND

WATERSHED

REEDER
RESERVOIR

ROGUE

RIVER

NATIONAL

FOREST

DETAIL

0   .25   .5   .75   1.0
miles 1 in. = 3800 ft.

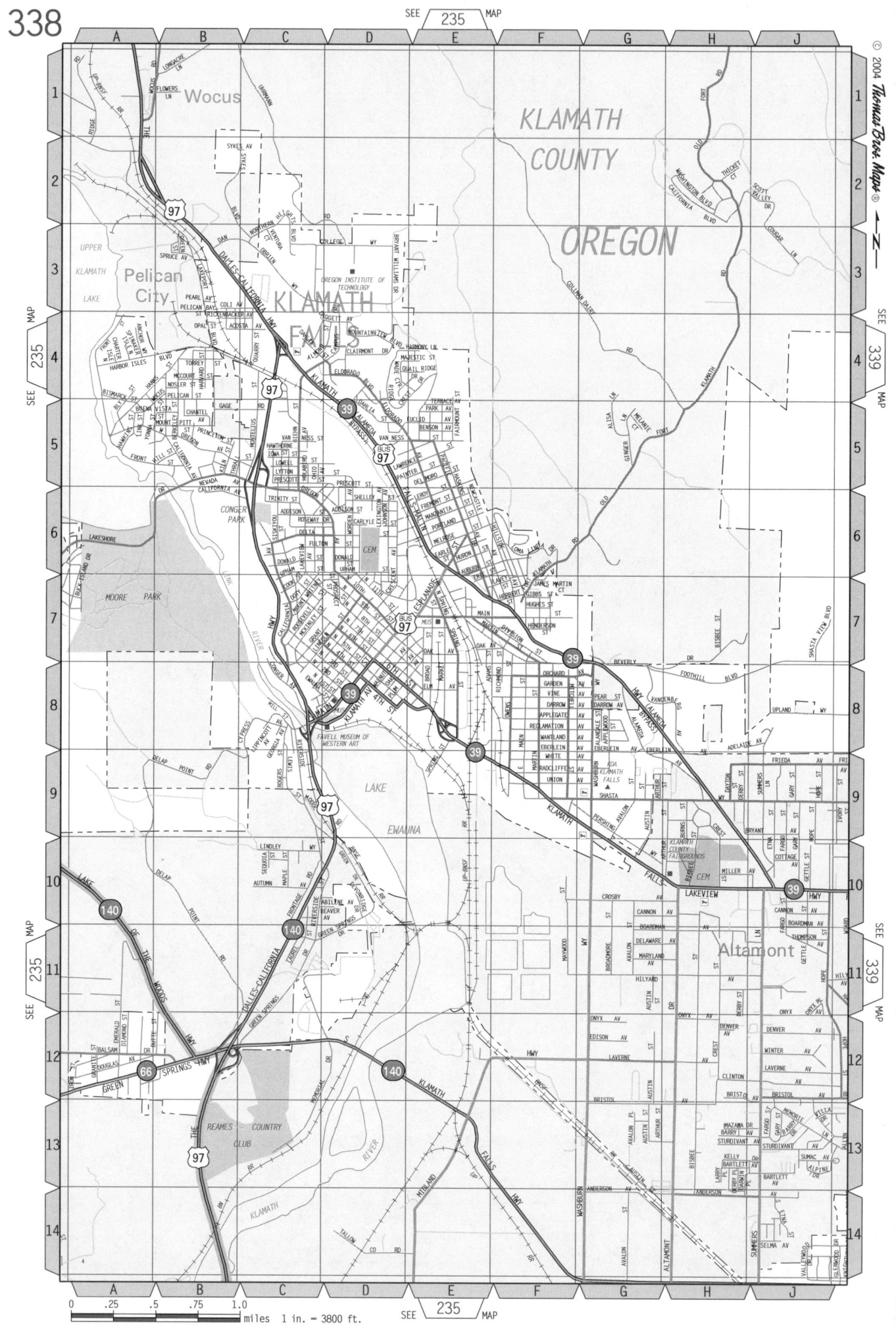

SEE 235 MAP

© 2004 Thomas Bros. Maps ®

KLAMATH
COUNTY

OREGON

Wocus

KLAMATH
FALLS

Pelican
City

UPPER
KLAMATH
LAKE

Conger
Park

MOORE PARK

Favell Museum of
Western Art

LAKE
EWAUNA

NOAA
KLAMATH
FALLS

KLAMATH COUNTY
FAIRGROUNDS

Altamont

Lakeview

REAMES
COUNTRY
CLUB

SEE 235 MAP

SEE 339 MAP

SEE 339 MAP

SEE 235 MAP

DETAIL

0   .25   .5   .75   1.0
miles   1 in. = 3800 ft.

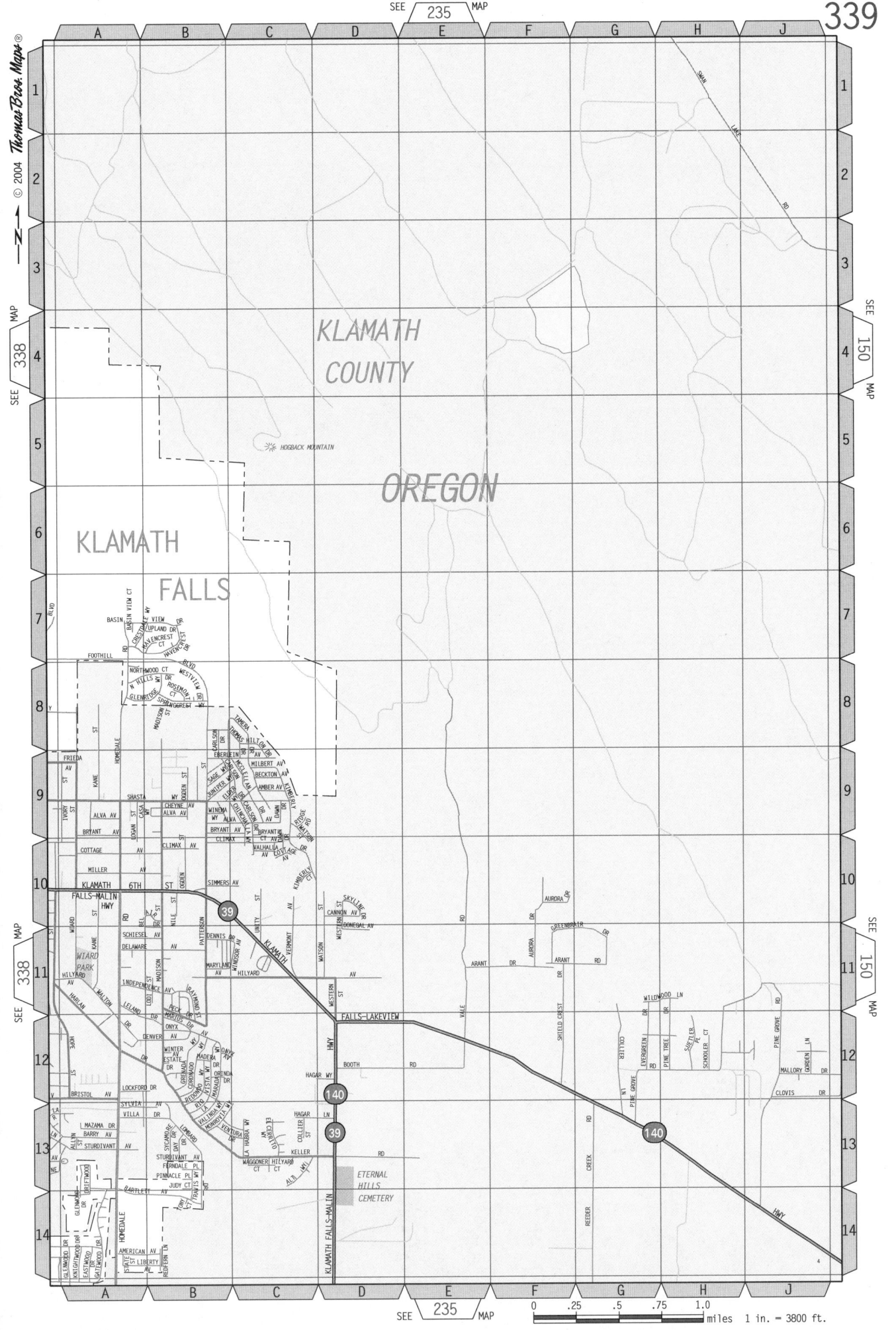

SEE 235 MAP

© 2004

Thomas Bros. Maps®

DETAIL

KLAMATH
COUNTY

OREGON

KLAMATH

FALLS

HOGBACK MOUNTAIN

KLAMATH
FALLS-MALIN
HWY

WIARD
PARK

ETERNAL
HILLS
CEMETERY

SEE 338 MAP

SEE 150 MAP

SEE 338 MAP

SEE 150 MAP

SEE 235 MAP

0   .25   .5   .75   1.0
miles 1 in. = 3800 ft.

SEE 121 MAP

SEE 121 MAP

SEE 121 MAP

SEE 121 MAP

SEE 121 MAP

FRANKLIN COUNTY

BENTON COUNTY

US DEPARTMENT

OF ENERGY

HANFORD SITE

JOHNSON ISLAND

HOODED ISLAND

BARB ISLAND

MCNARY NATIONAL WILDLIFE REFUGE

WASHINGTON

RICHLAND

WEST RICHLAND

WEST RICHLAND GOLF COURSE

YAKIMA RIVER

RICHLAND AIRPORT

NORTH RICHLAND WELL FIELD PARK

LESLIE GROVES PARK

SEAGULL ISLAND

NELSON ISLAND

W E JOHNSON PARK

BY-PASS SHELTERBELT

DETAIL

0 .25 .5 .75 1.0

miles 1 in. = 3800 ft.

SEE 341 MAP

SEE 121 MAP

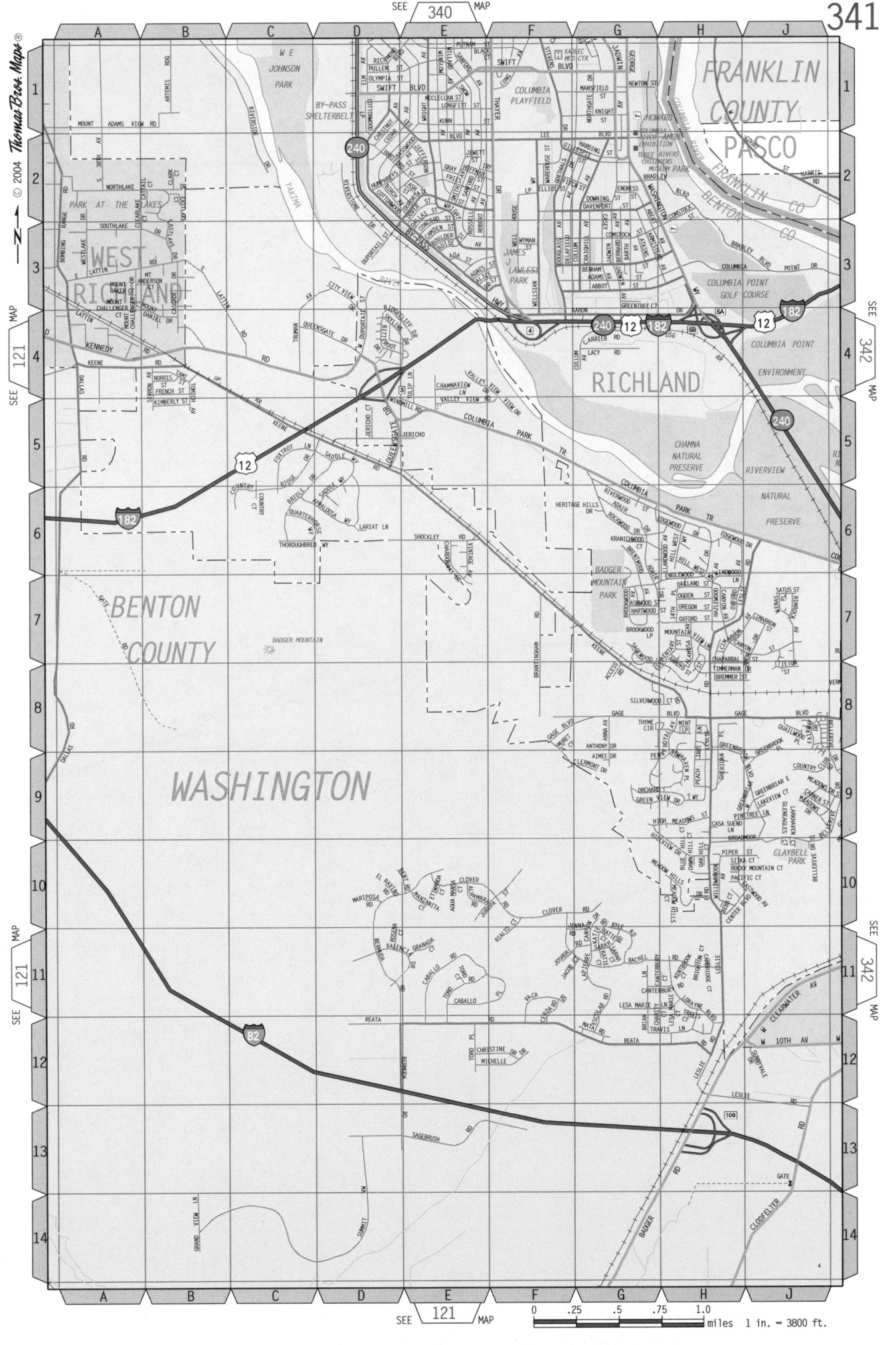

FRANKLIN
COUNTY
PASCO

WEST
RICHLAND

RICHLAND

BENTON
COUNTY

WASHINGTON

© 2004 Thomas Bros. Maps®

DETAIL

0   .25   .5   .75   1.0
miles   1 in. = 3800 ft.

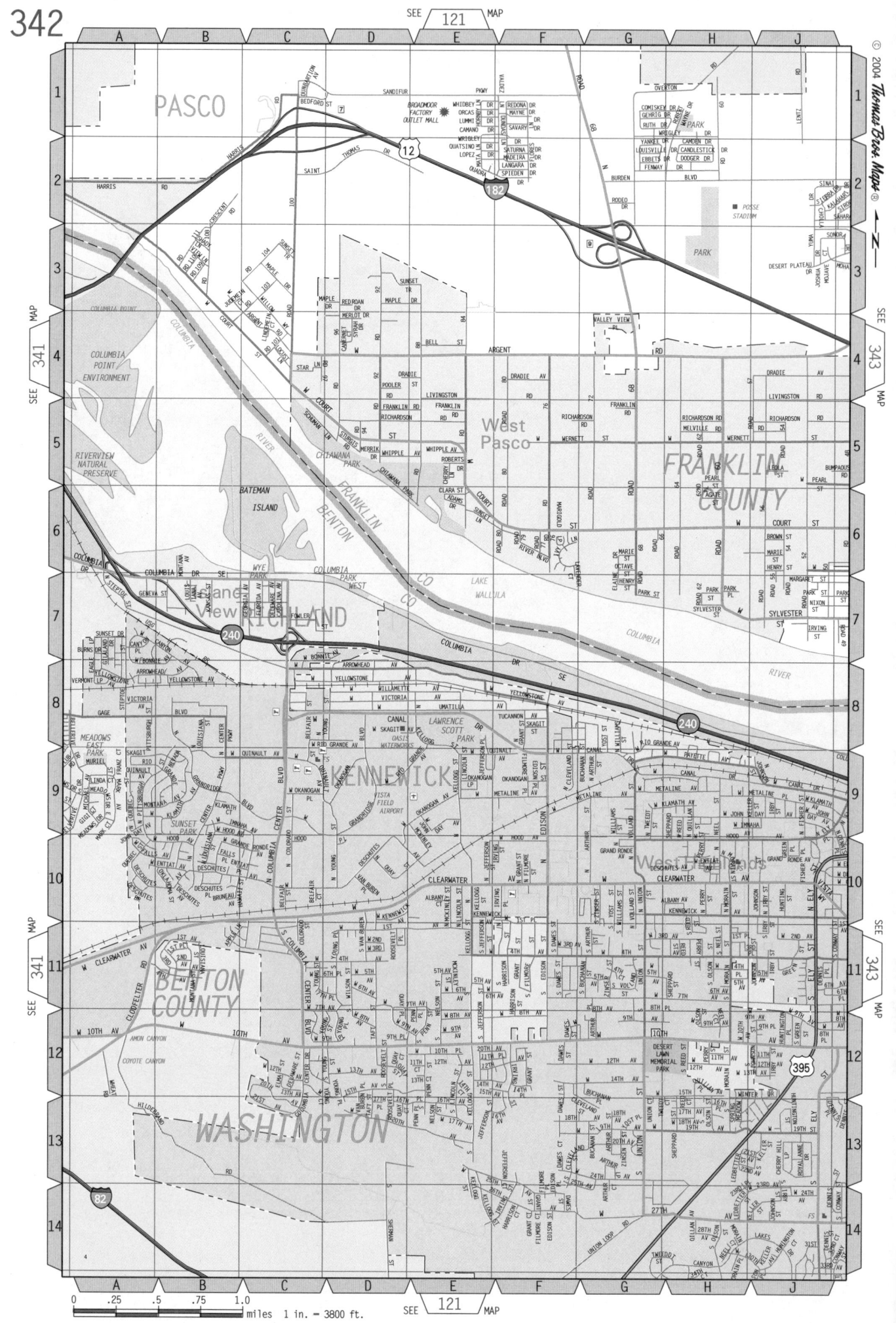

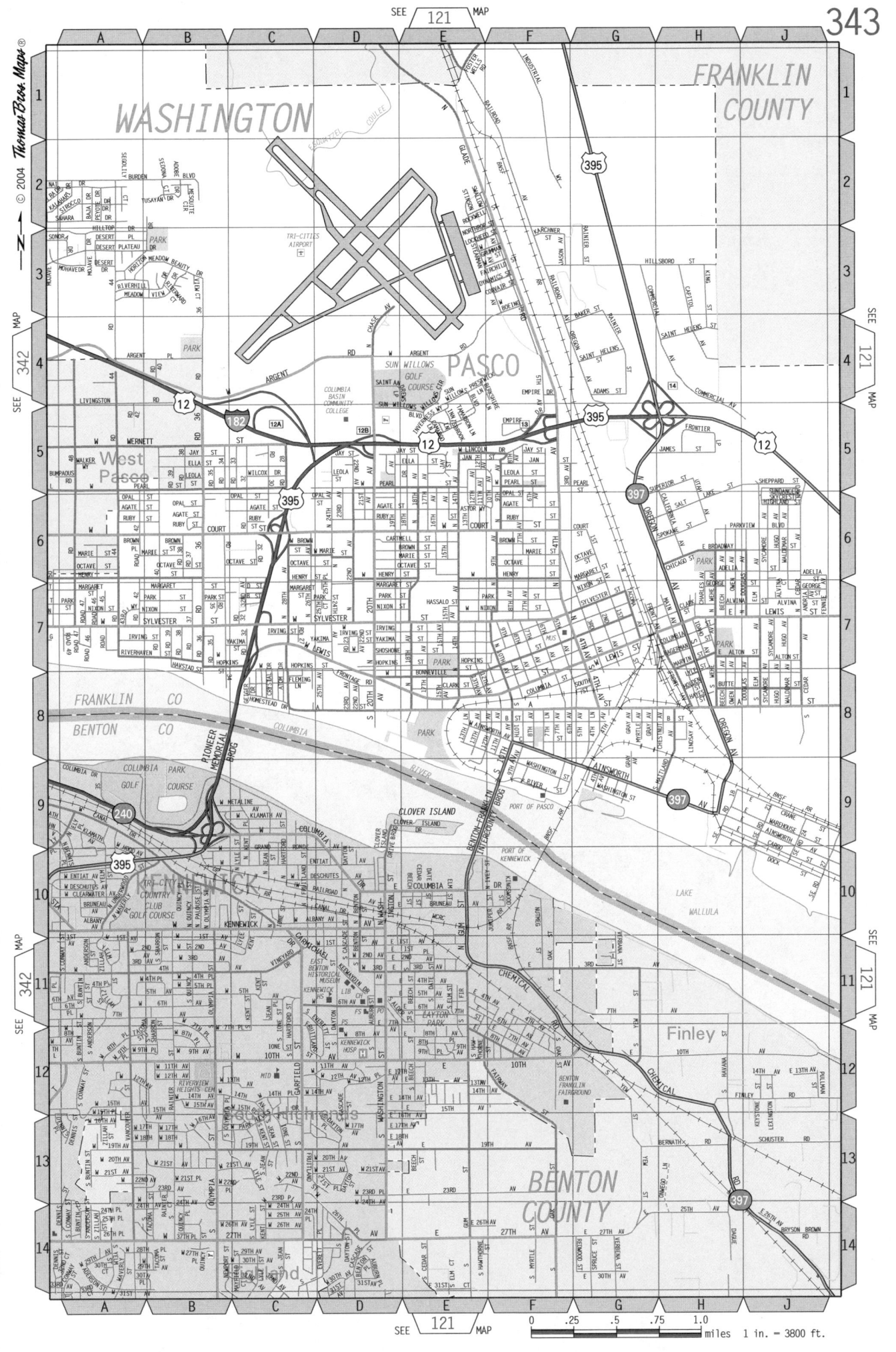

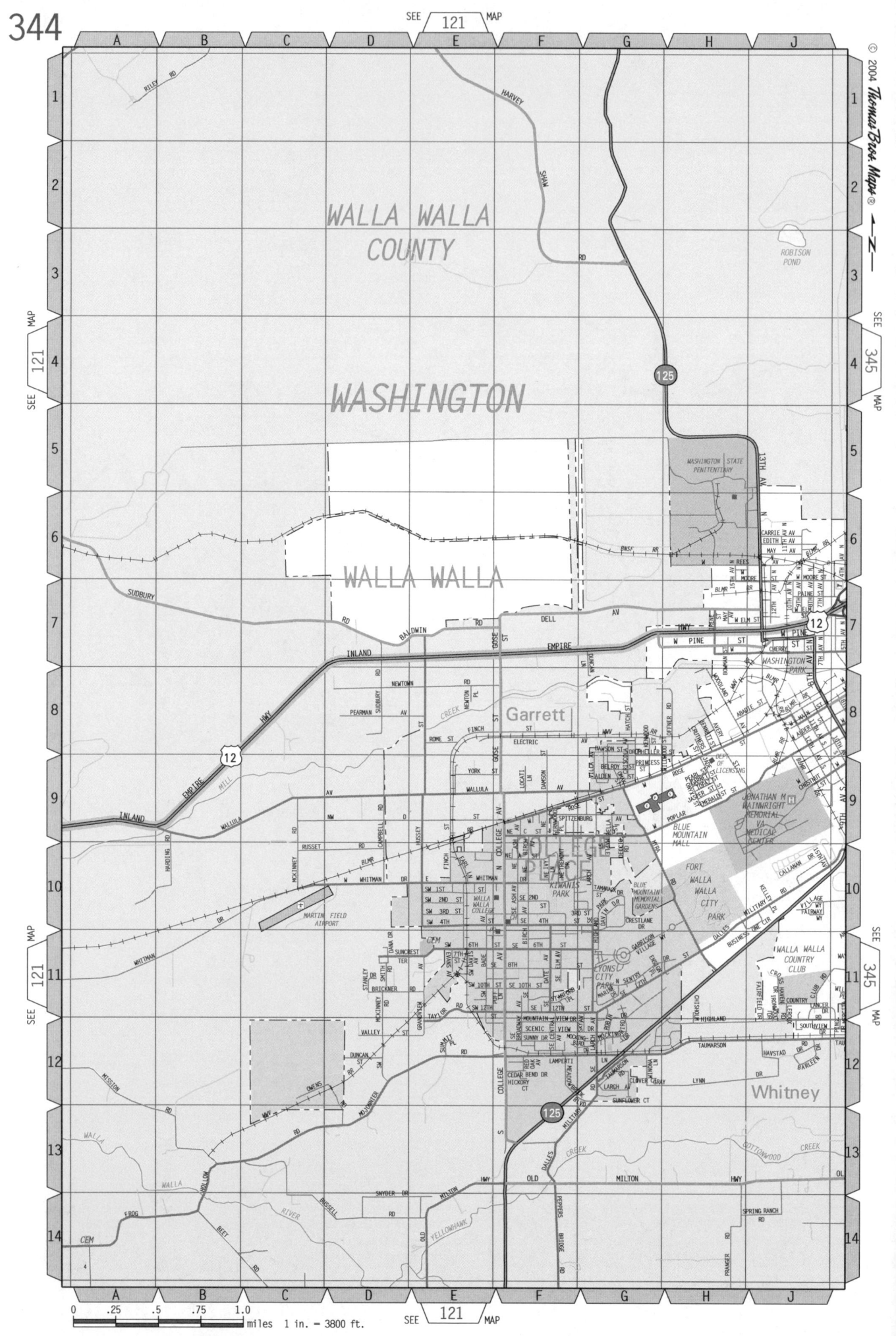

© 2004 *Thomas Bros. Maps* ® ←N→

SEE 121 MAP

SEE 121 MAP

SEE 345 MAP

SEE 345 MAP

SEE 121 MAP

SEE 121 MAP

DETAIL

WALLA WALLA COUNTY

WASHINGTON

WALLA WALLA

ROBISON POND

WASHINGTON STATE PENITENTIARY

Garrett

COLLEGE PLACE

WALLA WALLA COLLEGE

MARTIN FIELD AIRPORT

BLUE MOUNTAIN MALL

JONATHAN M WAINWRIGHT MEMORIAL VA MEDICAL CENTER

FORT WALLA WALLA CITY PARK

WALLA WALLA COUNTRY CLUB

Whitney

0 .25 .5 .75 1.0
miles 1 in. = 3800 ft.

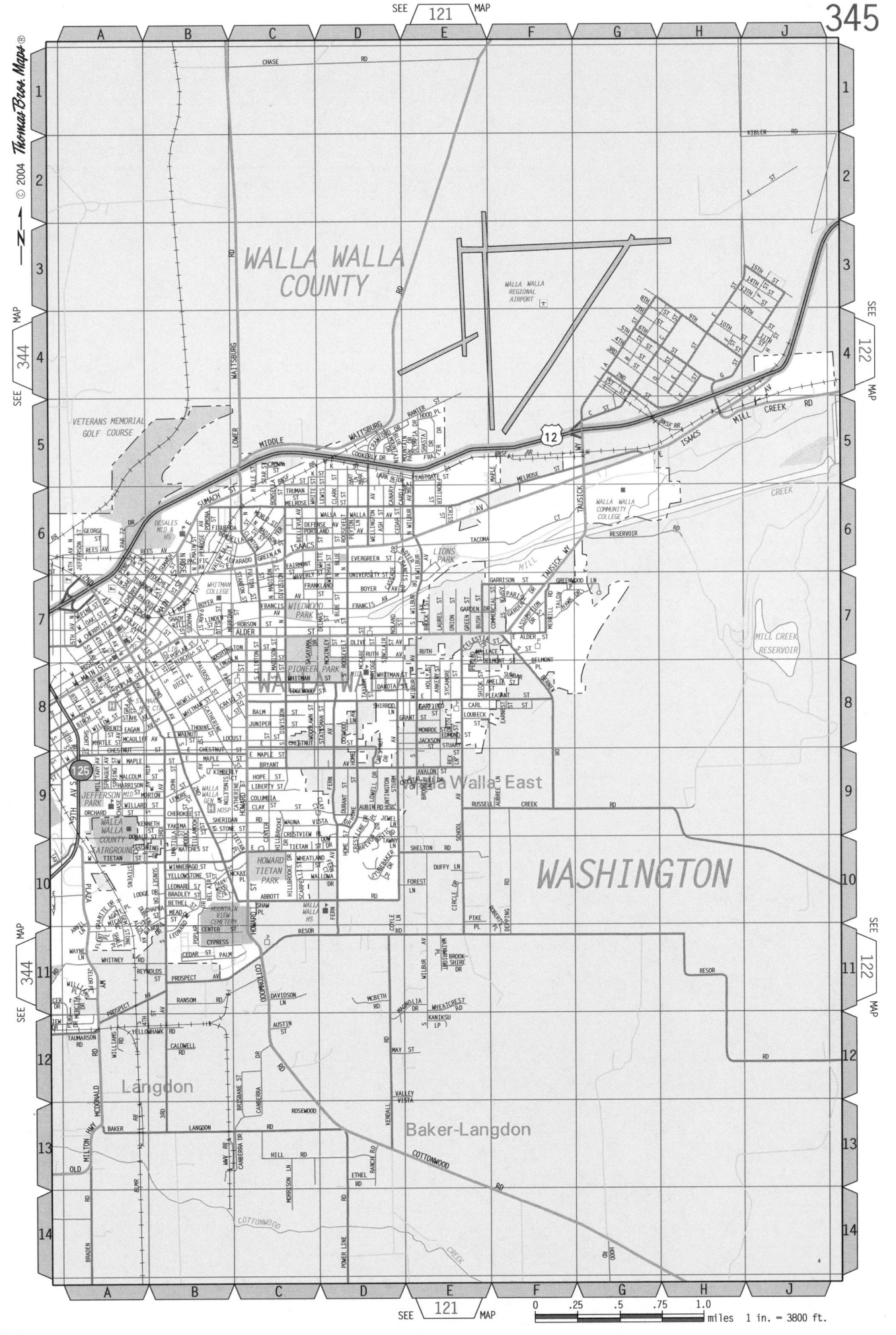

SEE 121 MAP

A B C D E F G H J

1

2

KIBLER RD

E ST

3

WALLA WALLA
COUNTY

WALLA WALLA
REGIONAL
AIRPORT

SEE 344 MAP

SEE 122 MAP

15TH ST
14TH ST
13TH ST
12TH ST

4

VETERANS MEMORIAL
GOLF COURSE

CHASE RD

5

US 12

MILL CREEK RD

ISAACS

CREEK

6

WALLA WALLA
COMMUNITY
COLLEGE

RESERVOIR

7

WHITMAN COLLEGE

LIONS
PARK

WILDWOOD
PARK

MILL CREEK
RESERVOIR

8

PIONEER PARK

WALLA WA
Walla Walla East

9

125

JEFFERSON
PARK

WALLA WALLA
HOSP

WASHINGTON

10

WALLA WALLA
COUNTY
FAIRGROUNDS

HOWARD
TIETAN
PARK

WALLA
WALLA HS

SEE 344 MAP

MOUNTAIN
VIEW
CEMETERY

SEE 122 MAP

11

12

Langdon

13

Baker-Langdon

COTTONWOOD

14

A B C D E F G H J

SEE 121 MAP

0 .25 .5 .75 1.0
miles 1 in. = 3800 ft.

DETAIL

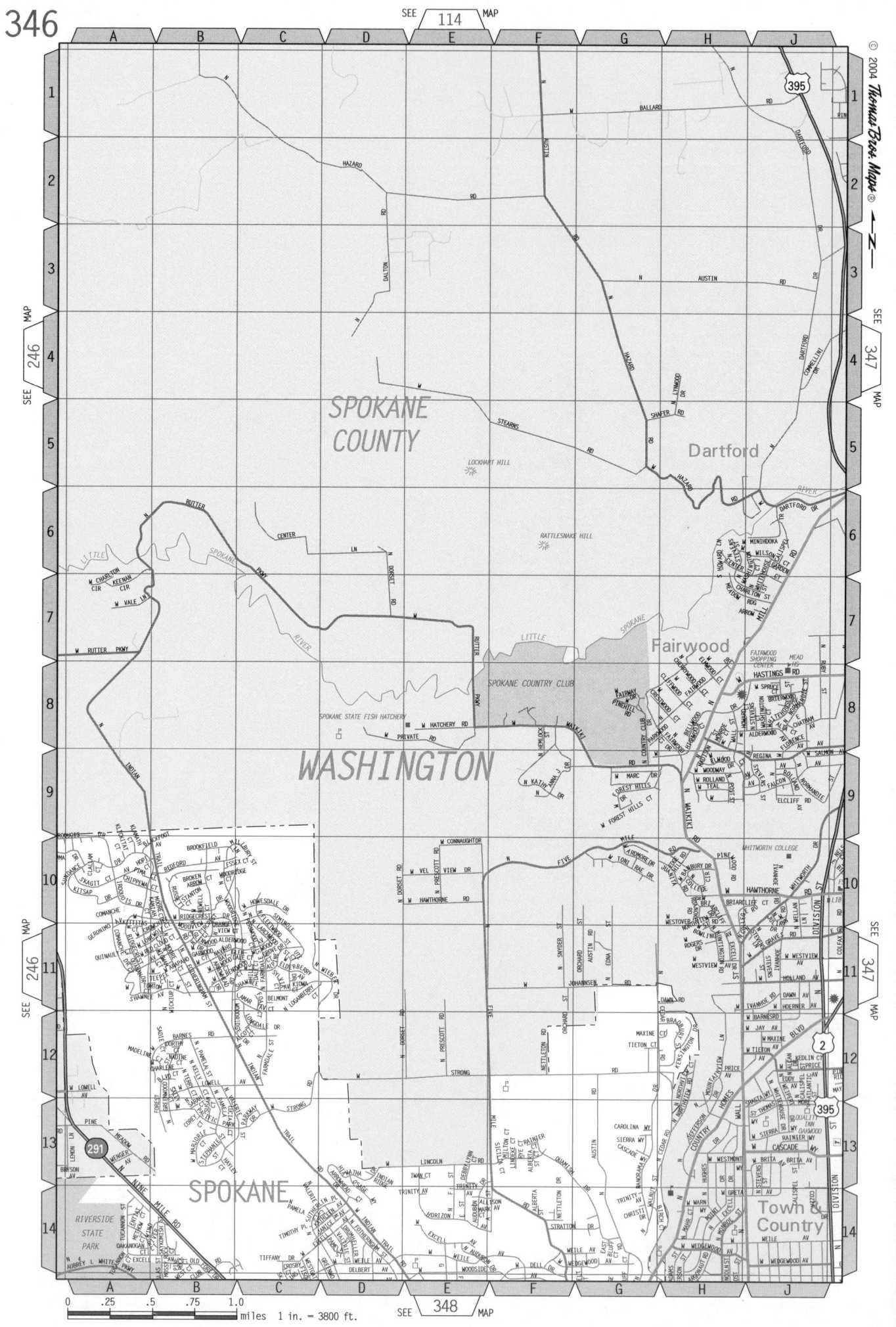

SEE 114 MAP

© 2004 Thomas Bros. Maps®

DETAIL

SEE 346 MAP

SEE 246 MAP

SEE 349 MAP

SEE 346 MAP

SEE 246 MAP

SPOKANE COUNTY

WASHINGTON

Country Homes

Morgan Acres

SPOKANE

Mead

Fairwood Camelot Park

Wandermere Lake Golf Course

Lake Wandermere

0   .25   .5   .75   1.0   miles   1 in. = 3800 ft.

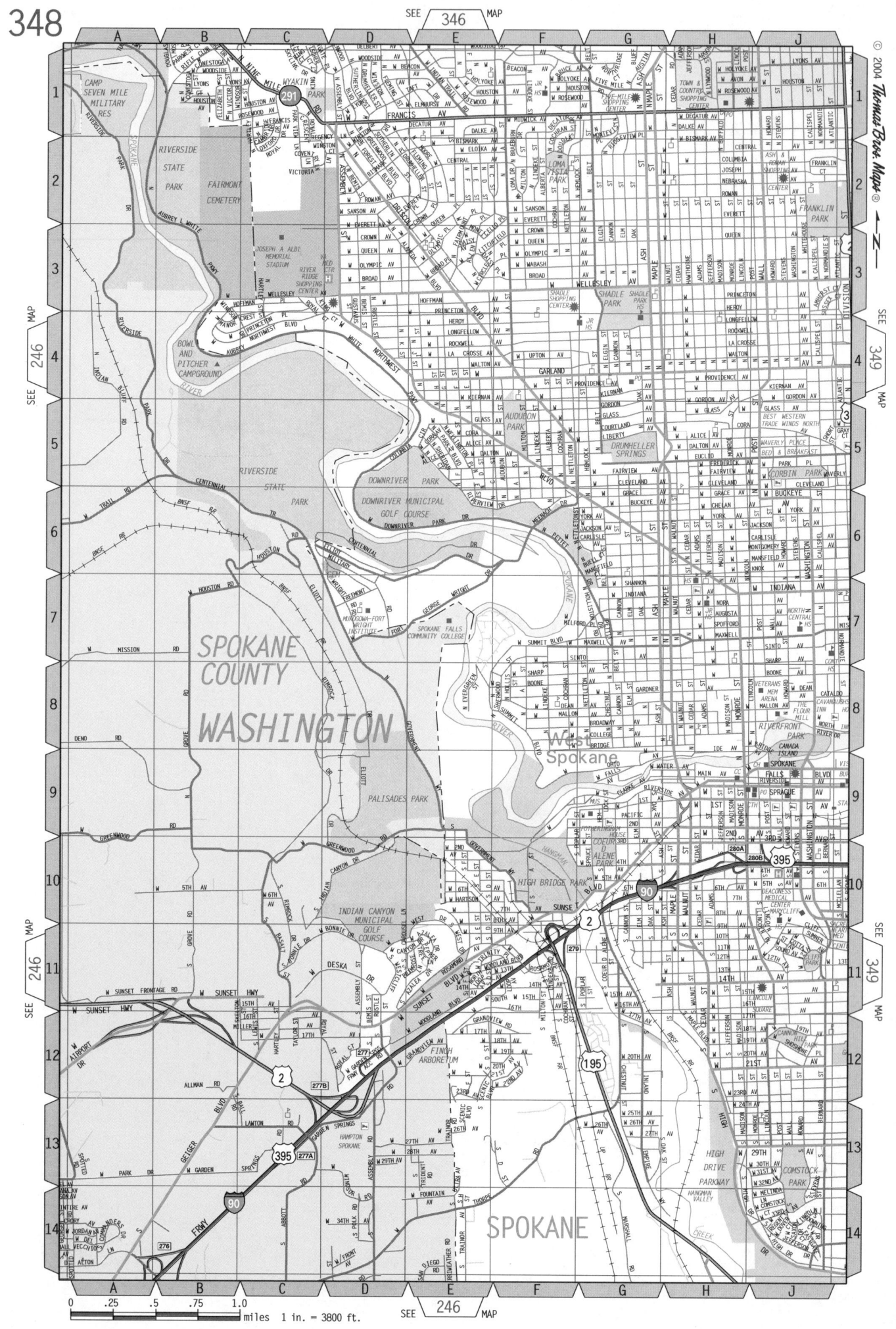

SPOKANE COUNTY

WASHINGTON

SPOKANE

0   .25   .5   .75   1.0
miles   1 in. = 3800 ft.

SEE 246 MAP

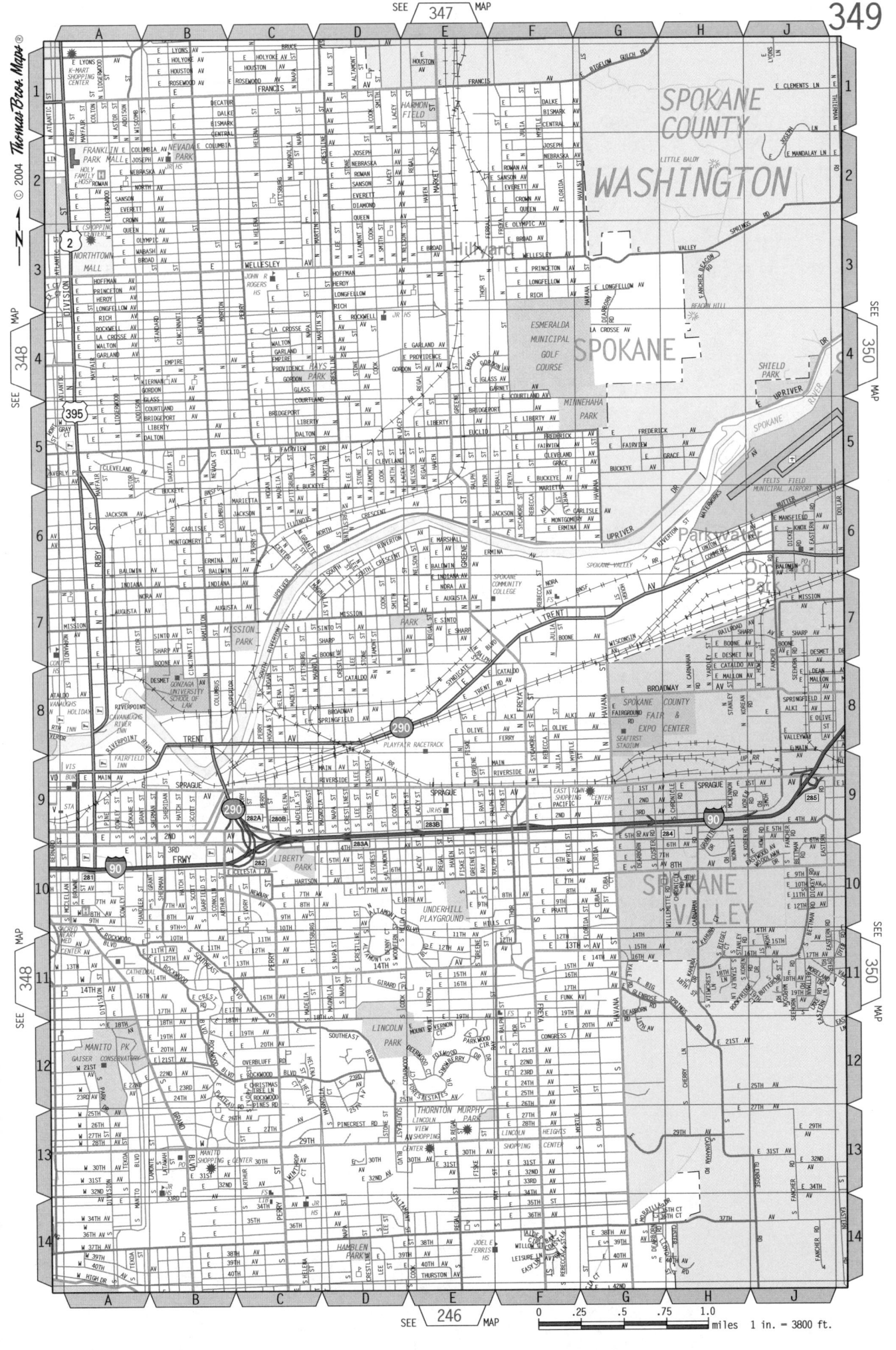

SPOKANE
COUNTY
WASHINGTON

SPOKANE

SPOKANE
VALLEY

© 2004 Thomas Bros. Maps®

DETAIL

0 .25 .5 .75 1.0
miles 1 in. = 3800 ft.

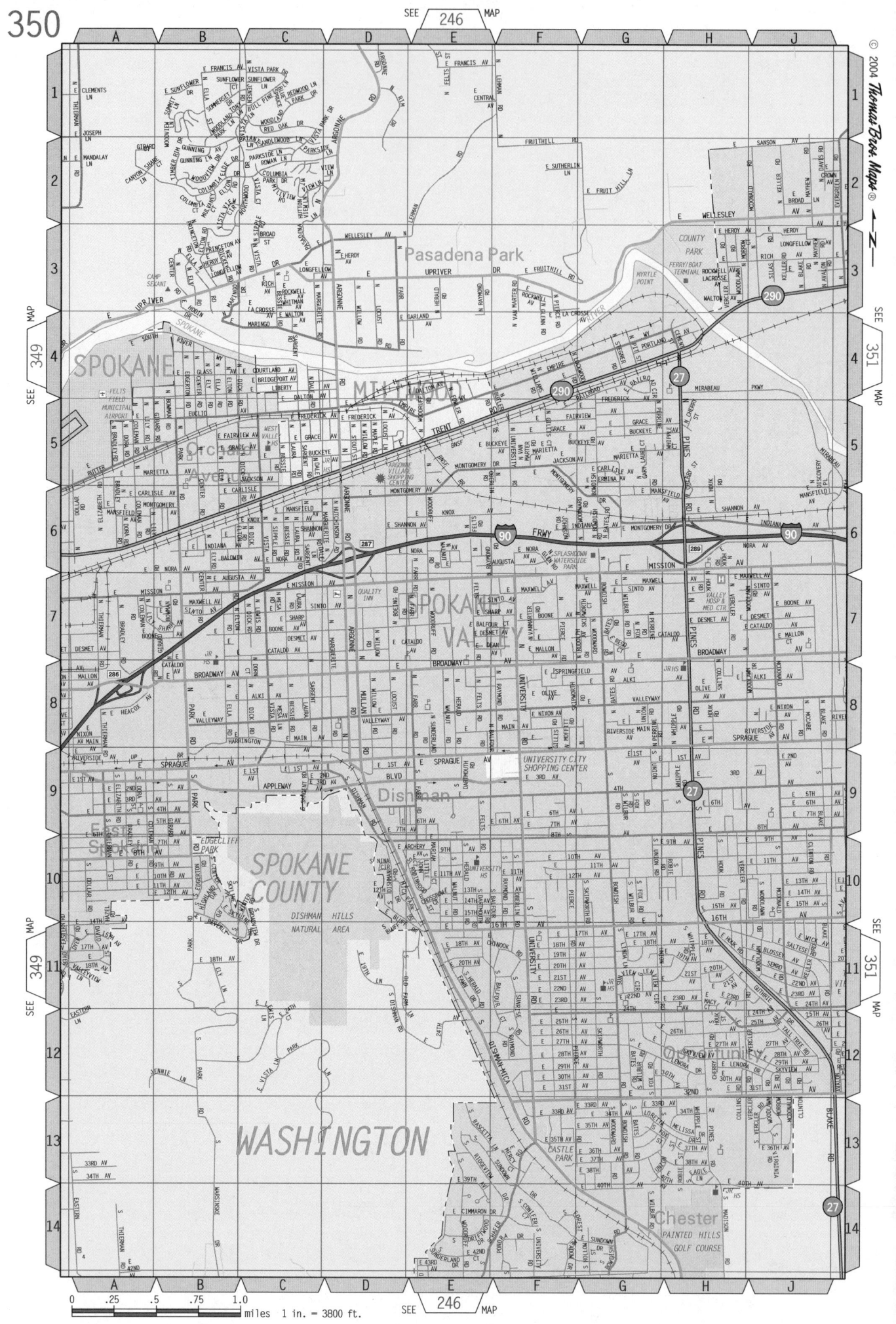

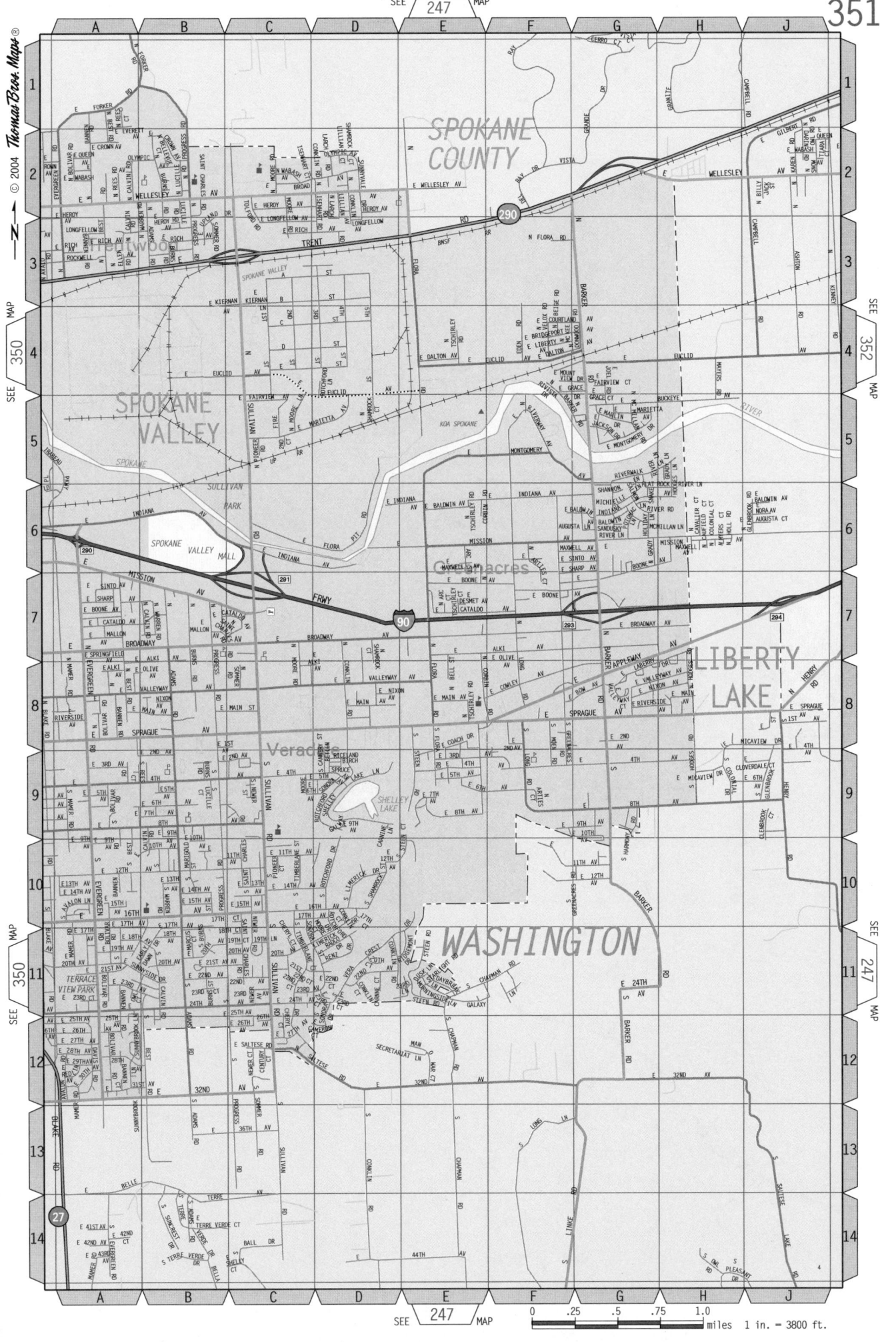

© 2004 Thomas Bros. Maps®

SEE 350 MAP

SEE 352 MAP

SEE 350 MAP

SEE 247 MAP

DETAIL

SPOKANE COUNTY

SPOKANE VALLEY

LIBERTY LAKE

WASHINGTON

Veradale

Terrace View Park

0   .25   .5   .75   1.0
miles   1 in. = 3800 ft.

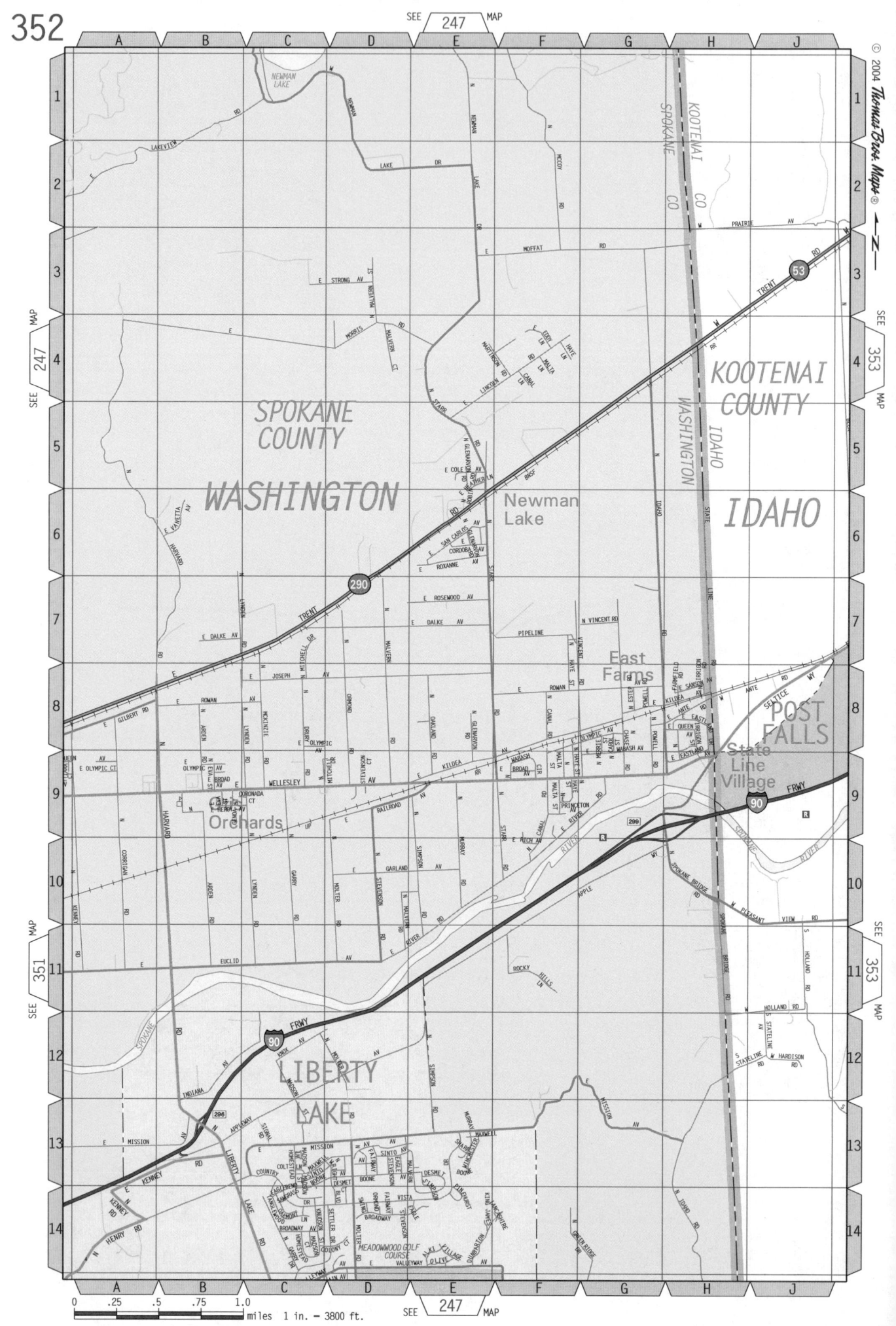

SEE 247 MAP

© 2004 Thomas Bros. Maps® —N—

NEWMAN
LAKE

SEE 247 MAP

SEE 353 MAP

SPOKANE
COUNTY

WASHINGTON

KOOTENAI
COUNTY

IDAHO

Newman
Lake

290

TRENT

53

POST
FALLS

State
Line
Village

East
Farms

Orchards

90

299

R

R

SEE 351 MAP

SEE 353 MAP

90 FRWY

296

LIBERTY

LAKE

MEADOWWOOD GOLF COURSE

DETAIL

0   .25   .5   .75   1.0
miles 1 in. = 3800 ft.

SEE 247 MAP

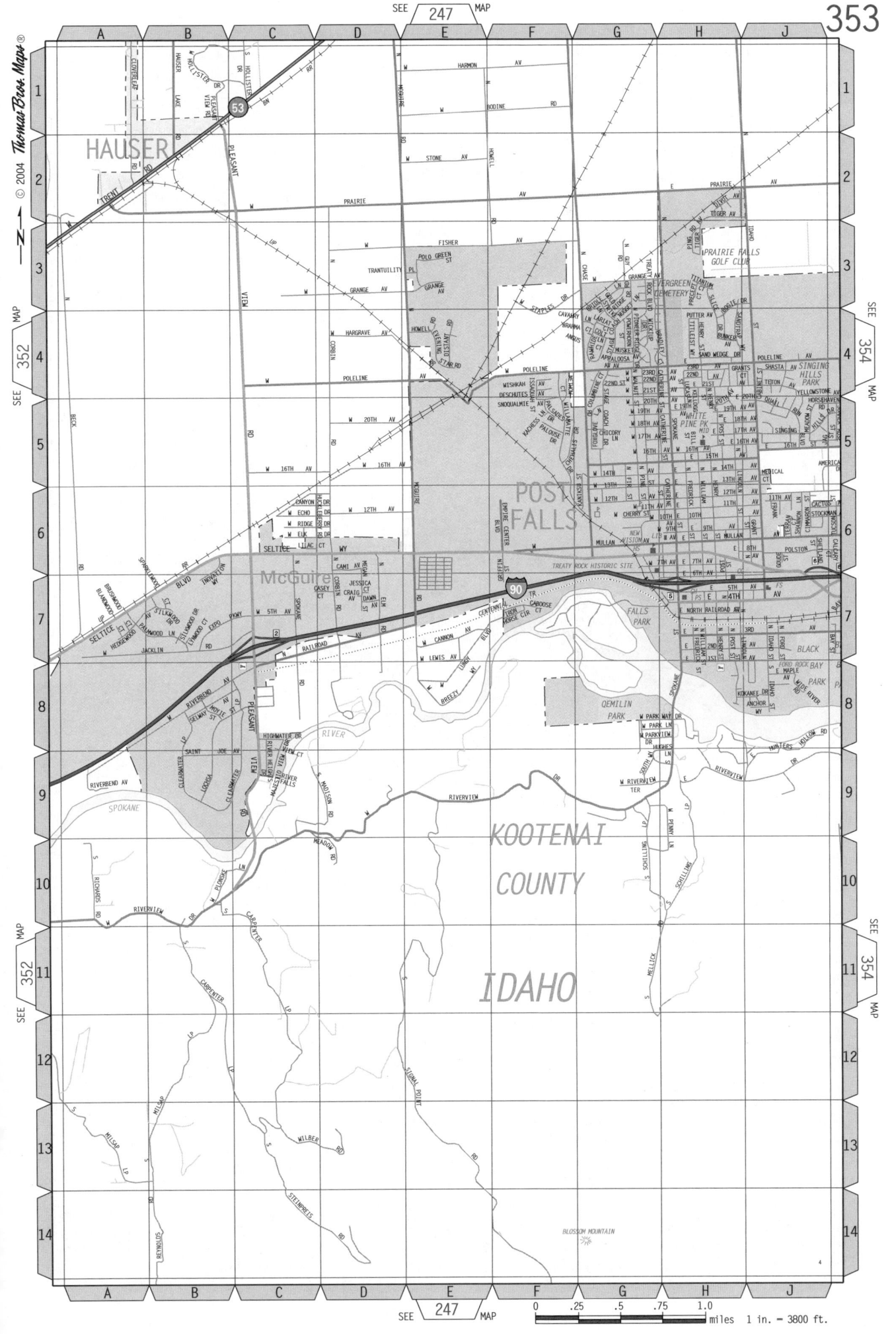

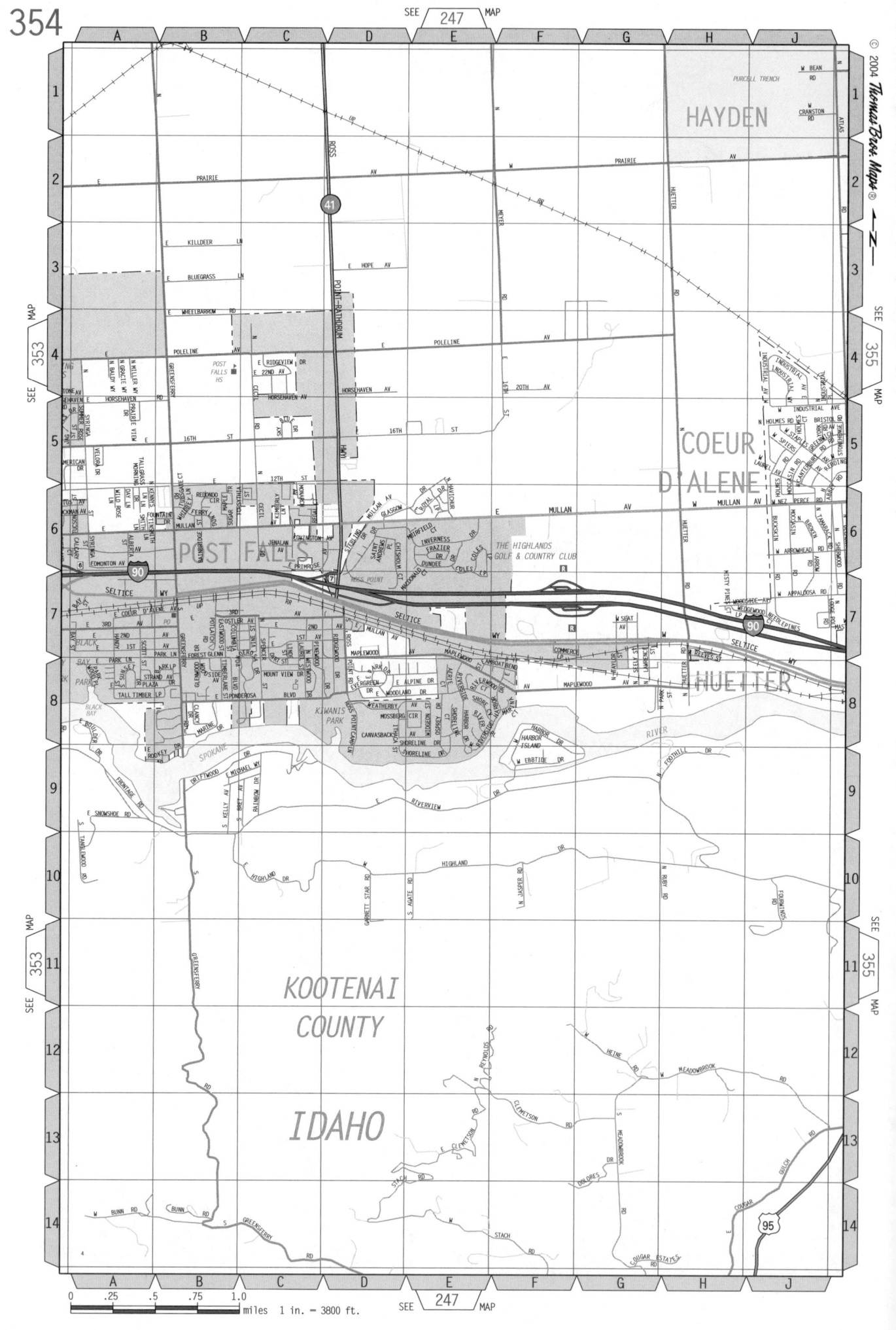

354

—N—

SEE 247 MAP

A B C D E F G H J

HAYDEN

PURCELL TRENCH

W BEAN RD

W CRANSTON RD

ATLAS RD

PRAIRIE AV

41

KILLDEER LN

BLUEGRASS LN

WHEELBARROW RD

HOPE AV

POLELINE

POLELINE

POST FALLS HS

RIDGEVIEW DR

E 22ND AV

HORSEHAVEN AV

HORSEHAVEN AV

16TH

20TH AV

16TH ST

16TH ST

COEUR D'ALENE

INDUSTRIAL

HOLMES RD

SPIERS

MULLAN AV

MULLAN AV

MULLAN AV

POST FALLS

THE HIGHLANDS GOLF & COUNTRY CLUB

HUETTER

90

SELTICE WY

SELTICE WY

E COEUR D'ALENE AV

90

SELTICE WY

KIWANIS PARK

MAPLEWOOD

MAPLEWOOD AV

HUETTER

BLACK BAY

SPOKANE

RIVER

RIVERVIEW

HIGHLAND

HIGHLAND DR

KOOTENAI COUNTY

IDAHO

95

W BUNN RD

BUNN RD

GREENSFERRY

STACH RD

COUGAR ESTATES RD

SEE 247 MAP

0 .25 .5 .75 1.0
miles 1 in. = 3800 ft.

DETAIL

SEE 353 MAP

SEE 355 MAP

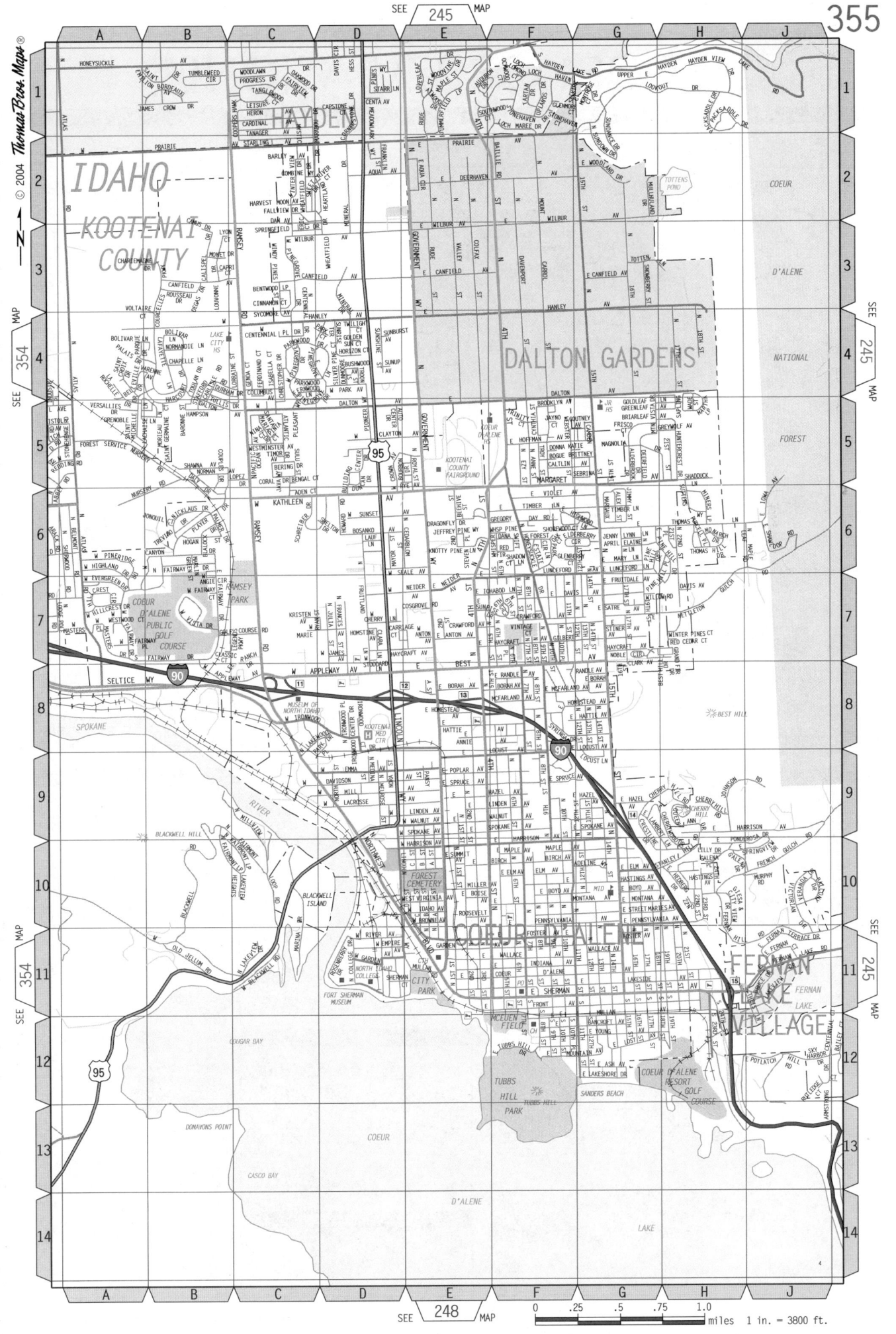

IDAHO

KOOTENAI
COUNTY

HAYDEN

DALTON GARDENS

COEUR D'ALENE

COEUR D'ALENE

COEUR D'ALENE

NATIONAL

FOREST

SPOKANE

RIVER

Blackwell Hill

Blackwell
Island

FORT SHERMAN
MUSEUM

COUGAR BAY

FORESTCEMETERY

TUBBS
HILL
PARK

SANDERS BEACH

FERNAN
LAKE
VILLAGE

COEUR D'ALENE RESORT
GOLF COURSE

COEUR

D'ALENE

LAKE

CASCO BAY

DONAVONS POINT

DETAIL

0 .25 .5 .75 1.0
miles 1 in. = 3800 ft.

LIST OF ABBREVIATIONS

PREFIXES AND SUFFIXES

AL	ALLEY	DR	DRIVE	RDSP	ROAD SPUR
ARC	ARCADE	DRAV	DRIVE AVENUE	RDWY	ROAD WAY
AV,AVE	AVENUE	DRCT	DRIVE COURT	RR	RAILROAD
AVCT	AVENUE COURT	DRLP	DRIVE LOOP	RUE	RUE
AVD	AVENIDA	DVDR	DIVISION DR	RUE D	RUE D
AVD D LA	AVENIDA DE LA	EXAV	EXTENSION AVENUE	RW	ROW
AVD D LOS	AVENIDA DE LOS	EXBL	EXTENSION BOULEVARD	RY	RAILWAY
AVD DE	AVENIDA DE	EXRD	EXTENSION ROAD	SKWY	SKYWAY
AVD DE LAS	AVENIDA DE LAS	EXST	EXTENSION STREET	SQ	SQUARE
AVD DEL	AVENIDA DEL	EXT	EXTENSION	ST	STREET
AVDR	AVENUE DRIVE	EXWY	EXPRESSWAY	STAV	STREET AVENUE
AVEX	AVENUE EXTENSION	FOREST RT	FOREST ROUTE	STCT	STREET COURT
AV OF	AVENUE OF	FRWY	FREEWAY	STDR	STREET DRIVE
AV OF THE	AVENUE OF THE	FRY	FERRY	STEX	STREET EXTENSION
AVPL	AVENUE PLACE	GDNS	GARDENS	STLN	STREET LANE
BAY	BAY	GN, GLN	GLEN	STLP	STREET LOOP
BEND	BEND	GRN	GREEN	ST OF	STREET OF
BL, BLVD	BOULEVARD	GRV	GROVE	ST OF THE	STREET OF THE
BLCT	BOULEVARD COURT	HTS	HEIGHTS	STOV	STREET OVERPASS
BLEX	BOULEVARD EXTENSION	HWY	HIGHWAY	STPL	STREET PLACE
BRCH	BRANCH	ISL	ISLE	STPM	STREET PROMENADE
BRDG	BRIDGE	JCT	JUNCTION	STWY	STREET WAY
BYPS	BYPASS	LN	LANE	STXP	STREET EXPRESSWAY
BYWY	BYWAY	LNCR	LANE CIRCLE	TER	TERRACE
CIDR	CIRCLE DRIVE	LNDG	LANDING	TFWY	TRAFFICWAY
CIR	CIRCLE	LNDR	LAND DRIVE	THWY	THROUGHWAY
CL	CALLE	LNLP	LANE LOOP	TKTR	TRUCK TRAIL
CL DE	CALLE DE	LP	LOOP	TPKE	TURNPIKE
CL DL	CALLE DEL	MNR	MANOR	TRC	TRACE
CL D LA	CALLE DE LA	MT	MOUNT	TRCT	TERRACE COURT
CL D LAS	CALLE DE LAS	MTWY	MOTORWAY	TR, TRL	TRAIL
CL D LOS	CALLE DE LOS	MWCR	MEWS COURT	TRWY	TRAIL WAY
CL EL	CALLE EL	MWLN	MEWS LANE	TTSP	TRUCK TRAIL SPUR
CLJ	CALLEJON	NFD	NAT'L FOREST DEV	TUN	TUNNEL
CL LA	CALLE LA	NK	NOOK	UNPS	UNDERPASS
CL LAS	CALLE LAS	OH	OUTER HIGHWAY	VIA D	VIA DE
CL LOS	CALLE LOS	OVL	OVAL	VIA DL	VIA DEL
CLTR	CLUSTER	OVLK	OVERLOOK	VIA D LA	VIA DE LA
CM	CAMINO	OVPS	OVERPASS	VIA D LAS	VIA DE LAS
CM D	CAMINO DE	PAS	PASEO	VIA D LOS	VIA DE LOS
CM DL	CAMINO DEL	PAS DE	PASEO DE	VIA LA	VIA LA
CM D LA	CAMINO DE LA	PAS DE LA	PASEO DE LA	VW	VIEW
CM D LAS	CAMINO DE LAS	PAS DE LAS	PASEO DE LAS	VWY	VIEW WAY
CM D LOS	CAMINO DE LOS	PAS DE LOS	PASEO DE LOS	VIS	VISTA
CMTO	CAMINITO	PAS DL	PASEO DEL	VIS D	VISTA DE
CMTO DEL	CAMINITO DEL	PASG	PASSAGE	VIS D L	VISTA DE LA
CMTO D LA	CAMINITO DE LA	PAS LA	PASEO LA	VIS D LAS	VISTA DE LAS
CMTO D LAS	CAMINITO DE LAS	PAS LOS	PASEO LOS	VIS DEL	VISTA DEL
CMTO D LOS	CAMINITO DE LOS	PASS	PASS	WK	WALK
CNDR	CENTER DRIVE	PIKE	PIKE	WY	WAY
COM	COMMON	PK	PARK	WYCR	WAY CIRCLE
COMS	COMMONS	PKDR	PARK DRIVE	WYDR	WAY DRIVE
CORR	CORRIDOR	PKWY, PKY	PARKWAY	WYLN	WAY LANE
CRES	CRESCENT	PL	PLACE	WYPL	WAY PLACE
CRLO	CIRCULO	PLWY	PLACE WAY		
CRSG	CROSSING	PLZ, PZ	PLAZA		
CST	CIRCLE STREET	PT	POINT		
CSWY	CAUSEWAY	PTAV	POINT AVENUE		
CT	COURT	PTH	PATH		
CTAV	COURT AVENUE	PZ DE	PLAZA DE		
CTE	CORTE	PZ DEL	PLAZA DEL		
CTE D	CORTE DE	PZ D LA	PLAZA DE LA		
CTE DEL	CORTE DEL	PZ D LAS	PLAZA DE LAS		
CTE D LAS	CORTE DE LAS	PZWY	PLAZA WAY		
CTO	CUT OFF	RAMP	RAMP		
CTR	CENTER	RD	ROAD		
CTST	COURT STREET	RDAV	ROAD AVENUE		
CUR	CURVE	RDBP	ROAD BYPASS		
CV	COVE	RDCT	ROAD COURT		
DE	DE	RDEX	ROAD EXTENSION		
DIAG	DIAGONAL	RDG	RIDGE		

DIRECTIONS

E	EAST
KPN	KEY PENINSULA NORTH
KPS	KEY PENINSULA SOUTH
N	NORTH
NE	NORTHEAST
NW	NORTHWEST
S	SOUTH
SE	SOUTHEAST
SW	SOUTHWEST
W	WEST

DEPARTMENT STORES

BD	BLOOMINGDALES
BN	THE BON MARCHE
D	DIAMONDS
DL	DILLARDS
G	GOLDWATERS
GT	GOTTSCHALKS
H	HARRIS
IM	I MAGNIN
MA	MACY'S
ME	MERVYN'S
MF	MEIER & FRANK
N	NORDSTROM
NM	NEIMAN-MARCUS
P	J C PENNEY
RM	ROBINSONS MAY
S	SEARS
SF	SAKS FIFTH AVENUE

BUILDINGS

CC	CHAMBER OF COMMERCE
CH	CITY HALL
CHP	CALIFORNIA HIGHWAY PATROL
COMM CTR	COMMUNITY CENTER
CON CTR	CONVENTION CENTER
CONT HS	CONTINUATION HIGH SCHOOL
CTH	COURT HOUSE
DMV	DEPT OF MOTOR VEHICLES
FAA	FEDERAL AVIATION ADMIN
FS	FIRE STATION
HOSP	HOSPITAL
HS	HIGH SCHOOL
INT	INTERMEDIATE SCHOOL
JR HS	JUNIOR HIGH SCHOOL
LIB	LIBRARY
MID	MIDDLE SCHOOL
MUS	MUSEUM
PO	POST OFFICE
PS	POLICE STATION
SR CIT CTR	SENIOR CITIZENS CENTER
STA	STATION
THTR	THEATER
VIS BUR	VISITORS BUREAU

OTHER ABBREVIATIONS

BCH	BEACH
BLDG	BUILDING
CEM	CEMETERY
CK	CREEK
CO	COUNTY
COMM	COMMUNITY
CTR	CENTER
EST	ESTATE
HIST	HISTORIC
HTS	HEIGHTS
LK	LAKE
MDW	MEADOW
MED	MEDICAL
MEM	MEMORIAL
MHP	MOBILE HOME PARK
MT	MOUNT
MTN	MOUNTAIN
NATL	NATIONAL
PKG	PARKING
PLGD	PLAYGROUND
RCH	RANCH
RCHO	RANCHO
REC	RECREATION
RES	RESERVOIR
RIV	RIVER
RR	RAILROAD
SPG	SPRING
STA	SANTA
VLG	VILLAGE
VLY	VALLEY
VW	VIEW

STREET — City State — Page-Grid

A

A U.S.-95
COTTONWOOD ID ... 123-C3
GRANGEVILLE ID ... 123-C3
IDAHO CO ID ... 123-B3
A AV
ANACORTES WA ... 259-F6
LAKE OSWEGO OR ... 321-F5
A RD SW
DOUGLAS CO WA ... 112-B2
A ST
ASHLAND OR ... 337-D7
GRANTS PASS OR ... 335-E8
PIERCE CO WA ... 181-D5
TACOMA WA ... 293-H5
WALLA WALLA CO WA ... 345-G4
A ST Rt#-38
DOUGLAS CO WA ... 141-A1
ELKTON OR ... 141-A1
A ST Rt#-411
CASTLE ROCK WA ... 187-C7
E A ST
GRANTS PASS OR ... 335-G8
PASCO WA ... 121-A3
PASCO WA ... 343-H8
N A ST
ELLENSBURG WA ... 241-B5
SPOKANE WA ... 348-F2
S A ST
SPOKANE WA ... 348-F10
S A ST Rt#-126 Bus
LANE CO OR ... 330-J7
SPRINGFIELD OR ... 330-J7
SPRINGFIELD OR ... 331-A7
W A ST
PASCO WA ... 343-D8
A ST E U.S.-20
VALE OR ... 139-A3
A ST SE
AUBURN WA ... 182-B1
EPHRATA WA ... 112-C3
GRANT CO WA ... 112-C3
A ST W
MALHEUR CO OR ... 138-C3
VALE OR ... 138-C3
A ST W U.S.-20
VALE OR ... 139-A3
A900 RD
GRAYS HARBOR CO WA ... 179-B6
A 1000 RD
GRAYS HARBOR CO WA ... 179-A5
A2000 RD
GRAYS HARBOR CO WA ... 179-A5
A3030 RD
JACKSON CO OR ... 230-D6
MASON CO WA ... 180-B3
A4000 RD
GRAYS HARBOR CO WA ... 179-D7
A5000 RD
GRAYS HARBOR CO WA ... 178-D4
A6000 RD
GRAYS HARBOR CO WA ... 178-D4
A7200 RD
GRAYS HARBOR CO WA ... 178-D3
AALVIK RD
SKAMANIA CO WA ... 194-C5
AARON DR
RICHLAND WA ... 341-F4
ABBEY RD
YAMHILL CO OR ... 198-B6
ABBOT ST
RICHLAND WA ... 341-G3
ABBOTSFORD-MISSION HWY Rt#-11
DISTRICT OF ABBOTSFORD BC ... 102-B1
DISTRICT OF MATSQUI BC ... 94-B3
DISTRICT OF MATSQUI BC ... 102-B1
ABBOTT RD
CLACKAMAS CO OR ... 126-C3
CLACKAMAS CO OR ... 201-A7
WALLA WALLA WA ... 345-C10
WALLA WALLA WA ... 122-A3
Walla Walla East WA ... 345-D10
WHITMAN CO WA ... 249-A2
S ABBOTT RD
SPOKANE CO WA ... 246-B5
SPOKANE CO WA ... 348-C13
ABBOTT CREEK RD
JACKSON CO OR ... 226-C4
ABERDEEN GARDENS RD
GRAYS HARBOR CO WA ... 178-B6
ABERNATHY ST NE
LACEY WA ... 297-F3
THURSTON CO WA ... 297-F3
ABERNATHY TKTR
COWLITZ CO WA ... 187-A6
ABIQUA RD NE
MARION CO OR ... 205-D4
ABRAHAM DR
LINN CO OR ... 210-A1
ABSHIRE RD
ADAMS CO ID ... 251-B4
ACADEMY ST
KELSO WA ... 303-D8
LEBANON OR ... 133-C1
ACADIA RD
UNIV ENDOWMENT LANDS BC ... 156-A4
ACCESS RD
SISKIYOU CO CA ... 149-C3
ACKLEY CAMP RD
HARNEY CO OR ... 153-A2
ACME RD
KLICKITAT CO WA ... 196-A3
ADA RD
DOUGLAS CO OR ... 214-B5
N ADAIR ST Rt#-8
CORNELIUS OR ... 198-C1
FOREST GROVE OR ... 198-C1
ADAMS AV U.S.-30
LA GRANDE OR ... 130-A2
ADAMS DR
MADRAS OR ... 208-C5
N ADAMS DR
BENTON CO OR ... 208-C3
S ADAMS DR
MADRAS OR ... 208-C5
ADAMS RD
JACKSON CO OR ... 234-B3
POLK CO OR ... 204-B6
N ADAMS RD
SPOKANE VALLEY WA ... 351-B8
S ADAMS RD
SPOKANE CO WA ... 351-B11
SPOKANE VALLEY WA ... 351-B11
ADAMS ST
HOQUIAM WA ... 178-A7
OLYMPIA WA ... 296-J5

E ADAMS ST
GARDEN CITY ID ... 253-C2
N ADAMS ST
SPOKANE WA ... 348-H9
N ADAMS ST Rt#-42
COQUILLE OR ... 220-D5
NE ADAMS ST Rt#-14B
CAMAS WA ... 193-B7
NW ADAMS ST Rt#-99W
MCMINNVILLE OR ... 198-A7
SW ADAMS ST Rt#-99W
MCMINNVILLE OR ... 198-A7
W ADAMS ST
GARDEN CITY ID ... 253-C2
ADAMS CREEK RD
DOUGLAS CO OR ... 219-B4
ADCOCK RD
YAMHILL CO OR ... 198-B4
E ADDISON DR
SPOKANE WA ... 349-A1
N ADDISON ST
SPOKANE WA ... 349-A1
ADDY-GIFFORD RD
STEVENS CO WA ... 106-A3
ADELE AV
BREMERTON WA ... 270-F10
ADKISSON MARKET RD
WASCO CO OR ... 127-B2
ADLER RD
FRANKLIN CO WA ... 121-A2
SW ADMIRAL WY
SEATTLE WA ... 280-D2
SEATTLE WA ... 281-F3
ADMIRALS RD
BRITISH COLUMBIA BC ... 256-B6
DISTRICT OF SAANICH BC ... 256-C5
TOWN OF ESQUIMALT BC ... 256-B6
TOWN OF VIEW ROYAL BC ... 256-C5
ADMIRALTY AV
PORT TOWNSEND WA ... 263-F2
ADOBE WY
YAKIMA CO WA ... 243-B4
ADRIAN BLVD Rt#-201
NYSSA OR ... 139-A3
SW ADVANCE RD
CLACKAMAS CO OR ... 199-B5
WILSONVILLE OR ... 199-B5
ADVENT RD
PITT MEADOWS BC ... 157-B5
AENEAS VALLEY RD
OKANOGAN CO WA ... 105-A2
AGAN RD
LINN CO OR ... 207-D7
AGATE RD
JACKSON CO OR ... 230-D6
MASON CO WA ... 180-B3
AGATE ST
ASTORIA OR ... 300-A5
EUGENE OR ... 330-C8
AGATE POINT RD NE
KITSAP CO WA ... 170-C7
AGEE DR
JOSEPHINE CO OR ... 229-C3
AGENCY-HOT SPRINGS RD
JEFFERSON CO OR ... 208-A2
Warm Springs OR ... 208-A2
AGER RD
MONTAGUE CA ... 150-A3
SISKIYOU CO CA ... 150-A3
AGER BESWICK RD
SISKIYOU CO CA ... 150-A3
NE AGNESS AV
GRANTS PASS OR ... 335-J9
AGNESS RD
CURRY CO OR ... 148-B1
CURRY CO OR ... 228-C4
AGNESS-ILLAHE RD
CURRY CO OR ... 148-B1
AGREN RD
COWLITZ CO WA ... 187-B5
AHSAHKA RD Rt#-7
OROFINO ID ... 123-C2
AHTANUM RD
UNION GAP WA ... 243-A7
YAKIMA CO WA ... 119-C2
YAKIMA CO WA ... 243-A7
W AHTANUM RD
UNION GAP WA ... 243-C7
AINSLEE AV
DEPOE BAY OR ... 206-B1
E AINSWORTH AV Rt#-397
PASCO WA ... 343-G9
W AINSWORTH AV Rt#-397
PASCO WA ... 343-F8
AINSWORTH AV S
PIERCE CO WA ... 181-D4
N AINSWORTH ST
PORTLAND OR ... 309-G6
NE AINSWORTH ST
PORTLAND OR ... 309-G6
AIR CARGO RD N
SEATAC WA ... 288-C4
AIRDUSTRIAL WY
TUMWATER WA ... 296-E13
AIRLIE RD
POLK CO OR ... 133-B1
POLK CO OR ... 207-A4
AIRPLANE RESERVOIR RD
MALHEUR CO OR ... 154-C2
MALHEUR CO OR ... 155-A2
AIRPORT AV
BENTON CO OR ... 133-B1
BENTON CO OR ... 207-B5
AIRPORT DR
BELLINGHAM WA ... 258-A1
JOSEPHINE CO OR ... 233-A5
LEBANON OR ... 133-C1
LINN CO OR ... 133-C1
WHATCOM CO WA ... 158-D7
WHATCOM CO WA ... 258-A1
W AIRPORT DR
SPOKANE CO WA ... 246-A4
SPOKANE CO WA ... 348-B11
AIRPORT RD
ALBANY OR ... 326-G8
BENTON CO OR ... 133-B1
CANYON CO ID ... 147-C1
CENTRALIA WA ... 299-D8
CHEHALIS WA ... 299-C9
CLALLAM CO WA ... 261-A4
CLARKSTON WA ... 250-B4
CURRY CO OR ... 224-A4
EUGENE OR ... 215-A1
EVERETT WA ... 171-B4
EVERETT WA ... 267-G6
GRANT CO WA ... 237-B3
HARNEY CO OR ... 145-B1
KITTITAS CO WA ... 240-C2
KITTITAS CO WA ... 241-B5

AIRPORT RD
LEWIS CO WA ... 299-D8
MALHEUR CO OR ... 138-C3
MEDFORD OR ... 336-C6
OKANOGAN WA ... 104-C3
OKANOGAN CO WA ... 104-C3
PORT ANGELES WA ... 261-A4
PULLMAN WA ... 249-C4
SNOHOMISH CO WA ... 171-B4
SNOHOMISH CO WA ... 267-G6
WHITMAN CO WA ... 249-C4
NE AIRPORT RD
CLACKAMAS CO OR ... 199-B6
ROSEBURG OR ... 334-F4
SE AIRPORT RD
YAMHILL CO OR ... 204-C1
W AIRPORT RD
BAKER CO OR ... 130-B3
BAKER CO OR ... 138-B1
AIRPORT RD NE
MARION CO OR ... 199-B6
AIRPORT RD SE
SALEM OR ... 323-B14
SALEM OR ... 325-B1
AIRPORT WY
BELLINGHAM WA ... 258-A1
HOQUIAM WA ... 178-A7
LAKESIDE OR ... 218-B4
SNOHOMISH WA ... 171-D3
TILLAMOOK CO OR ... 197-A7
NE AIRPORT WY
PORTLAND OR ... 311-E4
S AIRPORT WY
DOUGLAS CO OR ... 239-B5
SE AIRPORT WY
REDMOND OR ... 212-D6
W AIRPORT WY
BOISE ID ... 253-C4
AIRPORT WY S
SEATTLE WA ... 278-A7
SEATTLE WA ... 282-B1
SEATTLE WA ... 286-D3
TUKWILA WA ... 286-D3
AIRPORT CUTOFF RD Rt#-19
Irondale WA ... 263-B11
JEFFERSON CO WA ... 263-B11
AIRSTRIP RD
COLUMBIA CO WA ... 189-A6
MALHEUR CO OR ... 146-B3
AIRWAY DR
GRANT CO WA ... 242-C2
KLAMATH CO OR ... 235-D5
MOSES LAKE WA ... 242-C2
AIRWAY DR SE
SALEM OR ... 325-B4
A J WARRIN RD
DESCHUTES CO OR ... 212-A5
AKINS DR
CROOK CO OR ... 213-D6
ALABAMA ST
BELLINGHAM WA ... 258-F5
LONGVIEW WA ... 302-G10
ALAMEDA AV
ASTORIA OR ... 300-A5
FIRCREST WA ... 181-C3
NE ALAMEDA AV
ROSEBURG OR ... 334-F4
ALAMO LN
CANYON CO ID ... 147-B1
ALASKA AV E
Colby WA ... 271-G14
S ALASKA ST
SEATTLE WA ... 282-D5
SW ALASKA ST
SEATTLE WA ... 280-D5
SEATTLE WA ... 281-E5
ALASKA ST SE
Colby WA ... 271-G14
ALASKAN FRWY Rt#-99
SEATTLE WA ... 277-J5
SEATTLE WA ... 278-A6
SEATTLE WA ... 281-J3
SEATTLE WA ... 282-A1
ALASKAN WY
SEATTLE WA ... 277-H5
ALASKAN WY S Rt#-519
SEATTLE WA ... 277-J7
SEATTLE WA ... 278-A7
SEATTLE WA ... 281-J1
ALASKAN WY W
SEATTLE WA ... 277-H5
ALBANY RD U.S.-2
BONNER CO ID ... 107-A3
PRIEST RIVER ID ... 107-A3
ALBANY ST Rt#-82
ELGIN OR ... 130-A1
ALBANY ST SW
Rochester WA ... 184-A3
THURSTON CO WA ... 184-A3
ALBANY-CORVALLIS HWY U.S.-20
ALBANY OR ... 207-B5
ALBANY OR ... 326-A1
BENTON CO OR ... 207-B5
BENTON CO OR ... 326-A7
CORVALLIS OR ... 207-B5
CORVALLIS OR ... 327-J8
ALBANY-JCT CITY HWY Rt#-9E
ALBANY OR ... 207-C7
ALBANY OR ... 326-C14
HALSEY OR ... 210-B3
HARRISBURG OR ... 210-A5
JUNCTION CITY OR ... 210-A5
LANE CO OR ... 210-A5
LINN CO OR ... 207-C7
LINN CO OR ... 210-B3
TANGENT OR ... 210-A5
ALBANY-LYONS HWY Rt#-226
LINN CO OR ... 133-C1
LINN CO OR ... 134-A1
SCIO OR ... 133-C1
ALBATROSS ST
OCEAN SHORES WA ... 177-B6
ALBERT ST
NANAIMO BC ... 93-A3
N ALBERTA ST
PORTLAND OR ... 309-F7
NE ALBERTA ST
PORTLAND OR ... 309-H7
SE ALBERTA ST
CLACKAMAS CO OR ... 318-E7
ALBERTSON RD
YAMHILL CO OR ... 198-C4
N ALBINA AV
PORTLAND OR ... 309-F7
ALBION RD
ALBION WA ... 249-A4

ALBION RD
WHITMAN CO WA ... 122-C1
WHITMAN CO WA ... 249-A4
S ALBRO PL
SEATTLE WA ... 282-B7
ALCAN RD
GRAND COULEE WA ... 237-C3
ALCORT RD
MALHEUR CO OR ... 154-B2
ALDER
PIERCE CO WA ... 182-A4
ALDER AV
SUMNER WA ... 182-B3
N ALDER AV
GRANITE FALLS WA ... 102-C3
S ALDER AV
GRANITE FALLS WA ... 102-C3
ALDER DR NE
KEIZER OR ... 323-A7
ALDER RD
FRANKLIN CO WA ... 121-C2
ALDER ST
CATHLAMET WA ... 117-B3
LA GRANDE OR ... 130-A2
MOSES LAKE WA ... 242-C3
ALDER ST Rt#-507
CENTRALIA WA ... 299-E4
E ALDER ST
WALLA WALLA WA ... 345-C7
Walla Walla East WA ... 345-F7
N ALDER ST
TACOMA WA ... 292-D4
N ALDER ST U.S.-101
ABERDEEN WA ... 178-B7
S ALDER ST Rt#-21
ODESSA WA ... 113-B3
S ALDER ST U.S.-101
ABERDEEN WA ... 178-B7
SW ALDER ST
GRANTS PASS OR ... 335-D9
PORTLAND OR ... 313-F6
ALDER BRANCH RD
BENTON CO OR ... 133-A1
ALDERBRIDGE WY
CITY OF RICHMOND BC ... 156-B6
ALDERBROOK RD
BAY CITY OR ... 197-B1
TILLAMOOK CO OR ... 197-B1
ALDER CREEK LN
CLACKAMAS CO OR ... 201-A4
ALDER CREEK RD
BAKER CO OR ... 138-B1
KOOTENAI CO ID ... 248-C1
WHEELER CO OR ... 128-B3
WHEELER CO OR ... 136-B1
ALDER CUTOFF RD
EATONVILLE WA ... 118-B1
PIERCE CO WA ... 118-B1
ALDERDALE RD
KLICKITAT CO WA ... 120-B3
KLICKITAT CO WA ... 128-B1
YAKIMA CO WA ... 120-B3
ALDERDALE WYE
YAKIMA CO WA ... 120-B3
ALDERGROVE RD
Birch Bay WA ... 158-B5
WHATCOM CO WA ... 158-C5
SE ALDERMAN RD
YAMHILL CO OR ... 204-C1
NE ALDERMEADOWS RD
MULTNOMAH CO OR ... 200-D1
ALDER SPRING RD
GRANT CO WA ... 227-A5
ALDERWOOD AV
BELLINGHAM WA ... 258-A2
WHATCOM CO WA ... 158-D7
WHATCOM CO WA ... 258-A2
ALDERWOOD MALL PKWY
LYNNWOOD WA ... 171-B5
SNOHOMISH CO WA ... 171-B4
ALDRICH RD
WHATCOM CO WA ... 158-D5
ALECK BAY RD
SAN JUAN CO WA ... 160-A7
ALEXANDER AV
BENTON CO OR ... 327-G12
CORVALLIS OR ... 327-G12
TACOMA WA ... 182-A2
ALEXANDER RD
SUNNYSIDE WA ... 120-B2
YAKIMA CO WA ... 120-B2
ALEXANDER RD Rt#-241
SUNNYSIDE WA ... 120-B2
YAKIMA CO WA ... 120-B2
ALFALFA RD
CROOK CO OR ... 135-B3
CROOK CO OR ... 213-A7
ALFALFA-GRANGER RD Rt#-223
YAKIMA CO WA ... 120-A2
ALFALFA MARKET RD
DESCHUTES CO OR ... 135-B3
DESCHUTES CO OR ... 217-D2
ALFORD RD
KITTITAS CO WA ... 241-B4
ALFRED JOHNSON RD
SKAGIT CO WA ... 168-B1
SKAGIT CO WA ... 260-C14
ALGER HILL LOGGING TR
SKAGIT CO WA ... 161-B3
ALGOMA RD
KLAMATH CO OR ... 235-B1
ALGOMA SPUR RD
BONNER CO ID ... 244-A4
ALICE AV S
SALEM OR ... 324-G2
ALKALI GULCH RD
MALHEUR CO OR ... 139-A2
ALKI AV SW
SEATTLE WA ... 276-D7
SEATTLE WA ... 280-D1
ALLAN RD
YAKIMA CO WA ... 243-A4
ALLARD CRES
TOWNSHIP OF LANGLEY BC ... 157-C6
SW ALLEN BLVD
BEAVERTON OR ... 199-B2
ALLEN RD
DESCHUTES CO OR ... 212-B7
LEWIS CO WA ... 187-D1
SUNNYSIDE WA ... 120-B2
YAKIMA CO WA ... 120-B2
ALLEN ST
KELSO WA ... 303-C8
ALLEN ST Rt#-4
KELSO WA ... 303-D8
E ALLEN ST
COWLITZ CO WA ... 303-F8
KELSO WA ... 303-F8

ALLEN CREEK RD
CROOK CO OR ... 213-D2
GRANTS PASS OR ... 335-C12
JOSEPHINE CO OR ... 335-C12
ALLEN WEST RD
SKAGIT CO WA ... 161-A5
ALLINGHAM CTO
JEFFERSON CO OR ... 211-C1
ALLISON RD
LEWIS CO WA ... 187-D3
NE ALLWORTH RD
CLARK CO WA ... 193-A3
ALMA LN
JEFFERSON CO OR ... 208-B5
SW ALMA LN
JEFFERSON CO OR ... 208-A5
ALMA ST
UNIV ENDOWMENT LANDS BC ... 254-A13
VANCOUVER BC ... 254-A13
NW ALMETER WY
DESCHUTES CO OR ... 212-D4
ALMIRA RD S
LINCOLN CO WA ... 113-B2
ALM LANE RD
STEVENS CO WA ... 106-B3
ALMOTA RD
WHITMAN CO WA ... 122-C1
ALMOTA RD Rt#-194
WHITMAN CO WA ... 122-B1
ALMOTA ST Rt#-27
PALOUSE WA ... 249-B1
ALMOTA FERRY RD
GARFIELD CO WA ... 122-B1
E ALOHA ST
SEATTLE WA ... 278-C3
ALPINE DR SW
THURSTON CO WA ... 180-B7
ALPINE RD
BENTON CO OR ... 133-B2
SE ALPINE RD
KITSAP CO WA ... 174-C6
ALSEA HWY Rt#-34
BENTON CO OR ... 133-A1
LINCOLN CO OR ... 133-A1
LINCOLN CO OR ... 209-D2
LINCOLN CO OR ... 328-F6
WALDPORT OR ... 328-F6
ALSEA BAY DR
LINCOLN CO OR ... 328-C4
ALSEA-DEADWOOD HWY
BENTON CO OR ... 133-A2
ALSIP RD
POLK CO OR ... 204-A7
ALSTON RD W
DOUGLAS CO WA ... 239-D1
ALSTON-MAYGER RD
COLUMBIA CO OR ... 189-A3
ALTA LAKE RD
BRITISH COLUMBIA BC ... 93-C1
WHISTLER BC ... 93-C1
ALTAMONT DR
Altamont OR ... 235-C5
Altamont OR ... 338-H14
KLAMATH FALLS OR ... 338-H14
SW ALTA VISTA DR
KITSAP CO WA ... 174-A6
ALTA VISTA RD
EAGLE POINT OR ... 230-D6
JACKSON CO OR ... 230-D6
S ALTHEIMER ST
VANCOUVER WA ... 306-D1
ALTHOUSE CREEK RD
JOSEPHINE CO OR ... 233-C5
SE ALTMAN RD
CLACKAMAS CO OR ... 200-C3
MULTNOMAH CO OR ... 200-C2
ALTNOW-BEULAH RD
HARNEY CO OR ... 138-A3
ALTO RD
COLUMBIA CO WA ... 122-A2
E ALTON ST
PASCO WA ... 343-H7
ALTOONA PILLAR ROCK RD
WAHKIAKUM CO WA ... 117-A2
ALVADORE RD
LANE CO OR ... 133-B2
ALVADORE RD S
LANE CO OR ... 133-B3
NE ALVAS RD
CLARK CO WA ... 193-B3
ALVILLE LN
GILLIAM CO OR ... 128-A2
ALWARD COUNTY RD
PIERCE CO WA ... 182-C5
W ALWORTH ST
GARDEN CITY ID ... 253-C2
W AMAZON DR
EUGENE OR ... 330-B12
AMAZON PKWY
EUGENE OR ... 330-A8
AMBAUM BLVD S
BURIEN WA ... 175-A5
AMBAUM BLVD S Rt#-509
BURIEN WA ... 175-A5
BURIEN WA ... 288-A7
AMBAUM BLVD SW
BURIEN WA ... 175-A5
BURIEN WA ... 285-G7
KING CO WA ... 175-A5
KING CO WA ... 285-G7
AMBERJACK AV
KITSAP CO WA ... 170-B6
AMBLE RD
ISLAND CO WA ... 167-D7
AMBOY Rt#-503
CLARK CO WA ... 193-B1
AMBOY RD
CLARK CO WA ... 193-B1
AMERICAN DR
HALSEY OR ... 210-A2
HALSEY OR ... 210-A2
N AMERICANA BLVD
BOISE ID ... 253-C3
AMERICAN FRUIT RD
Sunnyslope WA ... 238-D3
AMERICAN LAKE AV
PIERCE CO WA ... 181-C5
AMERICAN MILL RD
GRAYS HARBOR CO WA ... 183-D3
AMES RD
YAKIMA CO WA ... 243-B5
AMES RD NE
OLYMPIA WA ... 296-J1
THURSTON CO WA ... 296-J1
THURSTON CO WA ... 297-A1
NE AMES LAKE RD
KING CO WA ... 176-A1
AMES LAKE CARNATION RD NE
KING CO WA ... 176-A1

AMICK RD
SKAGIT CO WA ... 168-C1
AMISIGGER RD
CLACKAMAS CO OR ... 200-B4
E AMITY RD
ADA CO ID ... 253-B4
BOISE ID ... 253-D4
SE AMITY RD
AMITY OR ... 204-C2
YAMHILL CO OR ... 204-C2
W AMITY RD
ADA CO ID ... 253-A4
AMITY DAYTON HWY
DAYTON OR ... 198-C7
YAMHILL CO OR ... 198-B7
AMITY DAYTON HWY Rt#-233
YAMHILL CO OR ... 198-B7
YAMHILL CO OR ... 204-C1
SE AMITY-DAYTON HWY Rt#-233
YAMHILL CO OR ... 204-C1
ANACO BEACH RD
ANACORTES WA ... 259-B4
ANACOPPER RD
ANACORTES WA ... 259-D3
N ANACORTES AV
BURLINGTON WA ... 260-D4
S ANACORTES ST
BURLINGTON WA ... 260-D6
SW ANCHOR AV
LINCOLN CITY OR ... 203-A5
ANDERSON AV
Altamont OR ... 338-H14
COOS BAY OR ... 333-G10
ANDERSON RD
GRAYS HARBOR CO WA ... 184-A3
LEWIS CO WA ... 184-D6
MASON CO WA ... 179-B2
THURSTON CO WA ... 184-A3
WHITMAN CO WA ... 249-A4
S ANDERSON RD
CLACKAMAS CO OR ... 199-B7
W ANDERSON RD
SPOKANE CO WA ... 246-B7
ANDERSON RD SE
MARION CO OR ... 205-B7
ANDERSON RD SE Rt#-214
MARION CO OR ... 205-B7
ANDERSON CANYON RD
CHELAN CO WA ... 238-A1
ANDERSON CREEK RD
JACKSON CO OR ... 234-B3
LINCOLN CO OR ... 203-B5
NW ANDERSON HILL RD
KITSAP CO WA ... 174-A1
ANDERSON HILL RD SW
KITSAP CO WA ... 174-B4
ANDERSON LAKE RD
JACKSON CO OR ... 170-A1
ANDERSON RESERVOIR RD
ADAMS CO ID ... 251-B3
ANDERSON VALLEY RD
HARNEY CO OR ... 145-C2
ANDRAIN
PIERCE CO WA ... 182-A6
ANDRESEN RD
VANCOUVER WA ... 306-D7
NE ANDRESEN RD
CLARK CO WA ... 192-D5
CLARK CO WA ... 306-D1
CLARK CO WA ... 306-D1
ANDREWS RD
DOUGLAS CO OR ... 219-A4
JACKSON CO OR ... 234-A2
S ANDRUS RD
SPOKANE CO WA ... 246-A6
ANGELINE RD
BONNEY LAKE WA ... 182-C4
PIERCE CO WA ... 182-C4
ANGUS DR
THURSTON CO WA ... 184-D2
ANKENY HILL RD
MARION CO OR ... 207-D1
ANKENY HILL RD SE
MARION CO OR ... 207-D2
ANKERTON RD
SHERMAN CO OR ... 127-C2
ANLIKER RD
COLUMBIA CO OR ... 189-B6
ANNACIS HWY Rt#-91
CITY OF RICHMOND BC ... 156-D6
DISTRICT OF DELTA BC ... 101-C1
DISTRICT OF DELTA BC ... 156-D6
NEW WESTMINSTER BC ... 156-D6
ANNACIS HWY Rt#-91A
CITY OF RICHMOND BC ... 156-D6
ANNASIS HWY
DISTRICT OF DELTA BC ... 101-C1
ANNAWALT RD
MALHEUR CO OR ... 146-C3
ANNEX RD
MALHEUR CO OR ... 139-A2
ANNONEN RD
LEWIS CO WA ... 187-B5
ANSELL ST
MAPLE RIDGE BC ... 157-D5
ANTELOPE
CROOK CO OR ... 213-D6
ANTELOPE HWY Rt#-293
JEFFERSON CO OR ... 135-C1
WASCO CO OR ... 127-C3
WASCO CO OR ... 135-C1
ANTELOPE RD
JACKSON CO OR ... 230-C6
White City OR ... 230-D6
E ANTELOPE RD
JACKSON CO OR ... 149-C1
JACKSON CO OR ... 234-D1
ANTELOPE CANAL RD
MALHEUR CO OR ... 147-A3
ANTELOPE FLAT RD
MALHEUR CO OR ... 146-B2
ANTELOPE SPRINGS RD
OWYHEE CO ID ... 147-C3
ANT FLAT RD
ENTERPRISE OR ... 130-C2
WALLOWA CO OR ... 130-C2
ANTHONY LAKES HWY
BAKER CO OR ... 130-A3
HAINES OR ... 130-A3
ANTHONY LAKES RD
BAKER CO OR ... 130-A3
ANTIOCH RD
JACKSON CO OR ... 230-C5
W ANTLER AV
DESCHUTES CO OR ... 212-D5
REDMOND OR ... 212-D5
ANTLES RD
UNION CO OR ... 130-B2

358 ANTOINE CREEK RD — STREET INDEX — BASE LINE DR

STREET
City State Page-Grid

ANTOINE CREEK RD
CHELAN CO WA 236-D1
ANTRIM RD
LEWIS CO WA 187-C2
A-P-A RD
WHATCOM CO WA 101-C1
APEL DR
PORT COQUITLAM BC 157-B4
APIARY RD
COLUMBIA CO OR 117-B3
COLUMBIA CO OR 189-B4
S APPLE ST
BOISE ID 253-D3
APPLE ACRES RD
CHELAN CO WA 112-B1
CHELAN CO WA 236-D2
APPLEFORD RD
ASOTIN CO WA 123-A3
APPLEGATE AV
DOUGLAS CO OR 219-A4
JOSEPHINE CO OR 229-A6
APPLEGATE RD
JACKSON CO OR 149-B2
N APPLEGATE RD
JACKSON CO OR 149-B2
JOSEPHINE CO OR 149-B2
APPLEGATE ST
JACKSON CO OR 149-B2
JACKSONVILLE OR 149-B2
APPLESIDE BLVD
ASOTIN CO WA 250-B5
Vineland WA 250-B5
APPLETON RD
KLICKITAT CO WA 196-B3
APPLE VALLEY RD
CANYON CO ID 139-A3
E APPLEWAY AV
LIBERTY LAKE WA 351-G8
SPOKANE CO WA 351-G8
SPOKANE VALLEY WA 351-G8
W APPLEWAY AV
COEUR D'ALENE ID 355-C8
APPLEWAY BLVD
SPOKANE VALLEY WA 350-C9
A P TUBBS RD
CARBONADO WA 182-D5
PIERCE CO WA 182-D5
ARAGO LN
COOS CO OR 220-D6
ARAGO-ARAGO JCT
COOS CO OR 220-D6
ARAGO CROSS RD
COOS CO OR 220-D6
ARBORETUM RD
BENTON CO OR 207-B4
ARBOR GROVE RD
MARION CO OR 199-A7
MARION CO OR 205-B1
ARBOR GROVE RD NE
MARION CO OR 205-A1
ARBORLYNN DR
DIST OF NORTH VANCOUVER BC 255-F5
ARBUTUS RD
DISTRICT OF SAANICH BC 257-D2
ARBUTUS ST
VANCOUVER BC 156-B5
VANCOUVER BC 254-D13
E ARCADIA AV
MASON CO WA 180-A3
SHELTON WA 180-A3
ARCADIA DR NE
LINCOLN CO OR 206-C4
ARCADIA RD
MASON CO WA 180-B3
ARCHERFISH RD
KITSAP CO WA 170-B7
ARCHER MOUNTAIN RD
SKAMANIA CO WA 194-B6
ARCHIE MYERS RANCH RD
MALHEUR CO OR 154-B2
ARDENA RD
FIFE WA 182-A2
ARDMORE DR
LAKEWOOD WA 181-C4
W ARGENT RD
FRANKLIN CO WA 342-E4
FRANKLIN CO WA 343-C4
PASCO WA 342-E4
PASCO WA 343-C4
N ARGONNE RD
MILLWOOD WA 350-D3
SPOKANE CO WA 246-D2
SPOKANE CO WA 350-D2
SPOKANE VALLEY WA 350-D6
ARGYLE DR
VANCOUVER BC 156-C5
ARGYLE DR S
SALEM OR 324-G3
ARGYLE ST
VANCOUVER BC 156-C5
ARID AV
DESCHUTES CO OR 212-C7
W ARLINGTON ST
GLADSTONE OR 199-D4
ARLINGTON HEIGHTS RD
SNOHOMISH CO WA 168-D4
ARMAR RD
ARLINGTON WA 168-C7
MARYSVILLE WA 168-C7
SNOHOMISH CO WA 168-C7
ARMITAGE RD
SAN JUAN CO WA 160-A5
ARMSTRONG RD
TOWNSHIP OF LANGLEY BC 157-D7
ARMSTRONG ST
PACIFIC CO WA 117-A1
ARMSWORTHY ST
WASCO OR 127-C1
ARMSWORTHY ST Rt#-206
WASCO OR 127-C1
ARNDT RD
CLACKAMAS CO OR 199-B6
MARION CO OR 199-A6
ARNEY RD NE
MARION CO OR 205-B1
ARNIE RD
WHATCOM CO WA 158-B4
ARNOLD LN
JACKSON CO OR 234-A1
ARNOLD RD
ISLAND CO WA 167-B4
ARNOLD WY
CORVALLIS OR 327-E9
ARNOLD MARKET LOOP RD
DESCHUTES CO OR 217-C3
ARNOT RD
SNOHOMISH CO WA 168-D4
AROCK RD
MALHEUR CO OR 146-C3

ARRAH WANNA BLVD
CLACKAMAS CO OR 201-C5
ARRITOLA PLACE RD
MALHEUR CO OR 146-C3
MALHEUR CO OR 147-A3
ARROW AV U.S.-12
NEZ PERCE CO ID 123-A2
W ARROWHEAD AV
BENTON CO WA 342-D8
KENNEWICK WA 342-D8
ARROWHEAD RD
ISLAND CO WA 167-D4
ARSENAL WY E
BREMERTON WA 270-E11
Navy Yard City WA 270-E11
ART DALZELL RD
MORROW CO OR 128-B2
ARTHUR AV
BEND OR 332-E10
ARTHUR BLVD
YAKIMA CO WA 243-C6
ARTHUR DR
DISTRICT OF DELTA BC 101-C1
ARTHUR RD
NEZ PERCE CO ID 250-D2
ARTHUR ST
NORTH BEND OR 333-D4
S ARTHUR ST
SPOKANE WA 349-B10
SW ARTHUR ST
PORTLAND OR 317-E1
ARTHUR LAING BRDG
CITY OF RICHMOND BC 156-B5
ARTHUR V GOLTZ
PIERCE CO WA 182-B5
ARTONDALE DR NW
PIERCE CO WA 181-B1
ARVICK RD SE
KITSAP CO WA 174-C4
ARVID NELSON RD
CROOK CO OR 136-A2
ASBURY RD
KOOTENAI CO ID 248-A3
ASCHOFF RD
CLACKAMAS CO OR 201-B3
N ASH AV
WARDEN WA 121-A1
S ASH AV
WARDEN WA 121-A1
ASH RD
DISTRICT OF SAANICH BC 159-D5
ASH ST
BROWNSVILLE OR 210-C2
KELSO WA 303-D8
SODAVILLE OR 133-C2
N ASH ST
SPOKANE WA 346-G14
SPOKANE WA 348-G1
NE ASH ST
PULLMAN WA 249-B5
ASH ST N
OMAK WA 104-C2
ASH ST S
OMAK WA 104-C3
ASH WY
SNOHOMISH CO WA 171-B4
ASHBROOK LN
JOSEPHINE CO OR 229-A5
ASH CREEK RD
DOUGLAS CO OR 225-C3
ASH LAKE RD
SKAMANIA CO WA 194-C5
ASHLAND ST
ASHLAND OR 337-D9
ASHLAND LOOP RD
JACKSON CO OR 234-C6
ASHTON LN
VALLEY CO ID 251-D7
SW ASHWOOD LN
JEFFERSON CO OR 208-B5
ASHWOOD RD
JEFFERSON CO OR 208-C5
ASHWORTH AV N
SHORELINE WA 171-A7
A S KRESKY RD
CHEHALIS WA 299-E9
LEWIS CO WA 299-E9
ASOTIN RD
ASOTIN CO WA 122-C2
ASOTIN CO WA 250-A6
ASOTIN CREEK RD
ASOTIN WA 250-B6
ASOTIN CO WA 250-B6
ASPEN ST
LANE CO OR 330-F7
SPRINGFIELD OR 330-F7
N ASPEN ST Rt#-231
LINCOLN CO WA 114-A2
REARDAN WA 114-A2
ASPEN WY
NEWBERG OR 198-D5
YAMHILL CO OR 198-D5
ASPEN LAKE RD
KLAMATH CO OR 235-A1
ASPENWALL RD
THURSTON CO WA 180-B6
S ASSEMBLY RD
SPOKANE CO WA 246-B5
SPOKANE CO WA 348-D13
N ASSEMBLY ST
SPOKANE WA 348-D2
ATHENA-HOLDMAN HWY
ATHENA OR 129-C1
UMATILLA CO OR 129-B1
E ATHENA-HOLDMAN HWY
ATHENA OR 129-C1
ATKINS AV
DISTRICT OF LANGFORD BC 159-B6
TOWN OF VIEW ROYAL BC 159-B6
ATKINS RD
COLUMBIA CO OR 189-A4
ATKINSON AV
DESCHUTES CO OR 212-C4
NW ATKINSON AV
DESCHUTES CO OR 212-C4
N ATLAS RD
COEUR D'ALENE ID 355-A4
HAYDEN ID 355-A1
KOOTENAI CO ID 355-A6
ATOR HILL RD
KOOTENAI CO ID 248-A5
ATWOOD RD
KLICKITAT CO WA 196-A5
AUBREY L WHITE PKWY
SPOKANE WA 348-B4
SPOKANE CO WA 348-B4
N AUBREY L WHITE PKWY
SPOKANE WA 346-A14
SPOKANE WA 348-B2

N AUBREY L WHITE PKWY
SPOKANE CO WA 348-B2
AUBURN AV
AUBURN WA 182-B2
BAKER CITY OR 138-B1
AUBURN AV U.S.-30
BAKER CITY OR 138-B1
AUBURN AV E
AUBURN WA 182-C1
AUBURN ST
KLAMATH FALLS OR 338-E6
AUBURN WY N
AUBURN WA 175-C7
AUBURN WA 182-C1
AUBURN WY N Rt#-164
AUBURN WA 182-C1
AUBURN WY S Rt#-164
AUBURN WA 182-C1
AUBURN BLACK DIAMOND RD
AUBURN WA 182-D1
BLACK DIAMOND WA 110-C3
KING CO WA 110-C3
KING CO WA 182-D1
SE AUBURN BLACK DIAMOND RD
KING CO WA 182-C1
AUBURN-ECHO LAKE CTO Rt#-18
AUBURN WA 182-C1
COVINGTON WA 175-D7
KENT WA 175-D7
KING CO WA 175-D7
KING CO WA 176-A6
KING CO WA 182-C1
MAPLE VALLEY WA 175-D7
AUBURN-ECHO LAKE CTO SE Rt#-18
KING CO WA 176-A6
AUBURN ENUMCLAW RD Rt#-164
AUBURN WA 182-C2
KING CO WA 182-C2
S AUDUBON ST
SPOKANE WA 348-F10
AUFDERHEIDE SCENIC BYWY
LANE CO OR 134-A3
LANE CO OR 142-A1
WESTFIR OR 142-A1
W AUGUSTA AV
SPOKANE WA 348-J7
AUGUSTA AV NE
Suquamish WA 170-C7
AULT FIELD RD
Ault Field WA 167-B2
ISLAND CO WA 167-B2
AUMSVILLE HWY SE
AUMSVILLE OR 133-C1
AUMSVILLE OR 205-B7
MARION CO OR 205-A7
MARION CO OR 325-F5
SALEM OR 325-F5
AUNE HALL RD
WHITMAN CO WA 122-A1
AURORA AV N Rt#-99
SEATTLE WA 171-A7
SEATTLE WA 273-J2
SEATTLE WA 277-J4
SHORELINE WA 171-A7
AUSTIN AV
COQUITLAM BC 157-A5
DISTRICT OF COQUITLAM BC 156-D5
AUSTIN DR
BREMERTON WA 270-C8
AUSTIN RD
DISTRICT OF BURNABY BC 156-D5
DISTRICT OF COQUITLAM BC 156-D5
SKAGIT CO WA 161-C7
N AUSTIN RD
SPOKANE CO WA 346-F2
S AUSTIN RD
SPOKANE CO WA 246-B6
AUTOCENTER WY
BREMERTON WA 270-D10
AVALON ST Rt#-69
ADA CO ID 253-A5
KUNA ID 253-A5
W AVALON ST
KUNA ID 253-A5
SW AVALON WY
SEATTLE WA 281-F4
AVENUE A
SEASIDE OR 301-F8
AVENUE B
GRANDVIEW WA 120-B3
SEASIDE OR 301-G8
N AVENUE B
BOISE ID 253-D3
GRANDVIEW WA 120-B3
AVENUE D
SNOHOMISH WA 171-D3
SNOHOMISH CO WA 171-D3
AVENUE G
SEASIDE OR 301-G9
AVENUE S
SEASIDE OR 301-G10
CLATSOP CO OR 301-F10
AVENUE U
CLATSOP CO OR 301-F10
SEASIDE OR 301-F10
AVERY RD E
LEWIS CO WA 187-D2
AVERY RD W
LEWIS CO WA 187-C2
SW AVERY ST
TUALATIN OR 199-B4
AVON AV Rt#-20
BURLINGTON WA 260-C4
AVON CTO Rt#-20
SKAGIT CO WA 161-A6
SKAGIT CO WA 260-A6
AVON-ALLEN RD
SKAGIT CO WA 161-A6
AVONDALE PL NE
KING CO WA 171-D7
AVONDALE RD NE
KING CO WA 171-D7
KING CO WA 175-D1
REDMOND WA 171-D7
REDMOND WA 175-D1
AVONDALE WY NE
REDMOND WA 175-D1
AWMILLER RD
LEWIS CO WA 187-B4
AXFORD RD
BATTLE GROUND WA 193-A3
CLARK CO WA 193-A3
AXLING RD
WHATCOM CO WA 158-D3

AXTEL CREEK RD
LINCOLN CO OR 209-B4
E AXTON RD
WHATCOM CO WA 102-B1
WHATCOM CO WA 158-D6
W AXTON RD
FERNDALE WA 158-D6
WHATCOM CO WA 158-D6
AYER RD
WALLA WALLA CO WA 121-C2
AZALEA DR
JOSEPHINE CO OR 229-A5

B

B AV
DESCHUTES CO OR 212-D4
Terrebonne OR 212-D4
W B AV Rt#-99
DRAIN OR 219-A3
B ST
ABERDEEN WA 178-B7
ASHLAND OR 337-D7
TILLAMOOK CO OR 191-B4
B ST Rt#-82
ISLAND CITY OR 130-A2
E B ST U.S.-30
RAINIER OR 189-C4
NE B ST
MADRAS OR 208-C5
S B ST
ISLAND CITY OR 130-A2
W B ST
RAINIER OR 189-B4
W B ST U.S.-30
RAINIER OR 189-C4
B ST E
PIERCE CO WA 181-D5
B 1/2-NE RD
GRANT CO WA 112-C3
B 5-NE
GRANT CO WA 112-C2
E BABB RD
SPOKANE CO WA 114-C3
BABCOCK RD
WALLA WALLA CO WA 121-C2
S BABCOCK RD
CLACKAMAS CO OR 205-D2
NE BABCOCK ST
KITSAP CO WA 170-C4
B A BENSON RD
SKAGIT CO WA 161-A5
BABY DOLL RD E
KITSAP CO WA 271-D14
BABY DOLL RD SE
KITSAP CO WA 271-D14
BACHELOR DR
LINCOLN CO WA 113-C1
BACHELOR FLAT RD
COLUMBIA CO OR 192-A2
SAINT HELENS OR 192-A2
BACONA RD
WASHINGTON CO OR 125-C1
BACON CAMP RD
HARNEY CO OR 144-B3
BACUS RD
SKAGIT CO WA 161-D5
BADGER RD
BENTON CO WA 120-C3
BENTON CO WA 121-A3
BENTON CO WA 341-G14
GRAYS HARBOR CO WA 177-D2
KENNEWICK WA 341-G14
E BADGER RD Rt#-546
WHATCOM CO WA 102-B1
WHATCOM CO WA 158-D3
E BADGER RD Rt#-547
WHATCOM CO WA 102-B1
W BADGER RD
WHATCOM CO WA 158-D3
BADGER CANYON RD
BENTON CO WA 120-C3
BADGER CREEK RD
CROOK CO OR 136-A2
WASCO CO OR 127-A3
WHEELER CO OR 136-B2
BADGER MOUNTAIN RD
DOUGLAS CO WA 239-A4
BADGER MOUNTAIN RD SW
DOUGLAS CO WA 239-B2
BADGER POCKET RD
KITTITAS WA 241-C6
KITTITAS CO WA 241-C6
BAGBY RD
CLACKAMAS CO OR 126-B3
BAGDAD RD
LINCOLN CO WA 113-B1
LINCOLN CO WA 237-D4
BAILER HILL RD
SAN JUAN CO WA 101-C2
BAILEY RD
CITY OF CHILLIWACK BC 94-C3
ISLAND CO WA 171-A3
S BAILEY ST
SEATTLE WA 282-B7
BAILEY HILL RD
EUGENE OR 329-C8
LANE CO OR 329-A14
BAINARD LN
CHELAN CO WA 239-B5
BAINBRIDGE IS-SEATTLE FERRY
KING CO WA 174-D2
BAIRD RD NE
THURSTON CO WA 180-D4
BAIRD SPRINGS RD
GRANT CO WA 112-C3
GRANT CO WA 239-D7
BAKEOVEN RD
MAUPIN OR 127-B3
WASCO CO OR 127-B3
BAKEOVEN MARKET RD
WASCO CO OR 127-B3
N BAKER AV
East Wenatchee Bench WA 239-A4
BAKER RD
CLACKAMAS CO OR 199-A5
COOS CO OR 220-C5
JACKSON CO OR 234-B2
KLICKITAT CO WA 196-B3
MORROW CO OR 128-B1
YAKIMA CO WA 243-B5
E BAKER RD
SPOKANE CO WA 246-D7
SE BAKER RD
KITSAP CO WA 174-C4
BAKER RD SW
THURSTON CO WA 180-B6

NE BAKER ST
MCMINNVILLE OR 198-A7
NE BAKER ST Rt#-99W
MCMINNVILLE OR 198-A7
SE BAKER ST Rt#-99W
MCMINNVILLE OR 198-A7
BAKER-COPPERFIELD HWY Rt#-86
BAKER CO OR 130-B3
BAKER CO OR 131-A3
BAKER CO OR 138-C1
BAKER CO OR 139-A1
RICHLAND OR 139-A1
NW BAKER CREEK RD
MCMINNVILLE OR 198-A7
YAMHILL CO OR 198-A7
BAKER HEIGHTS RD
SKAGIT CO WA 161-C7
NE BAKER HILL RD
KITSAP CO WA 271-G5
BAKER LAKE HWY
WHATCOM CO WA 102-C2
BAKER LAKE RD
SKAGIT CO WA 102-C2
BAKER LANGDON RD
WALLA WALLA CO WA 345-A13
S BAKERS FERRY RD
CLACKAMAS CO OR 200-A4
E BAKERVIEW RD
BELLINGHAM WA 258-F1
WHATCOM CO WA 258-F1
BALBACK RD
ADAMS CO ID 251-A4
BALCH RD
KLICKITAT CO WA 196-B5
BALDA RD
ISLAND CO WA 167-B3
BALD BUTTE RD
WHITMAN CO WA 249-C7
BALD HILLS RD SE
THURSTON CO WA 118-A1
BALD PEAK RD
WASHINGTON CO OR 198-C3
YAMHILL CO OR 198-C4
BALD RIDGE RD N
LINCOLN CO WA 114-A1
SE BALDWIN DR
JEFFERSON CO OR 208-C6
BALDWIN RD
CROOK CO OR 213-C5
Garrett WA 344-D7
HOOD RIVER CO OR 202-D4
WALLA WALLA WA 344-D7
WASCO CO OR 127-A2
WASCO CO OR 202-D4
BALDY MOUNTAIN RD
BONNER CO ID 107-A3
BONNER CO ID 244-A2
BALL RD
JACKSON CO OR 230-D4
BALL ST
MOUNT VERNON WA 260-B12
N BALLANTYNE LN
ADA CO ID 253-A1
EAGLE ID 253-A1
W BALLARD DR
KITTITAS CO WA 240-D2
BALLARD RD
POLK CO OR 204-A7
BALLARD RD NW
DOUGLAS CO WA 236-D7
BALLINGER DR
GRANTS PASS OR 335-D10
BALLINGER WY NE Rt#-104
LAKE FOREST PARK WA 171-B6
SHORELINE WA 171-B6
BALL MOUNTAIN LITTLE SHASTA RD
MONTAGUE CA 150-A3
SISKIYOU CO CA 150-A3
SISKIYOU CO CA 150-A3
BALLOW RD
MASON CO WA 180-D2
BALLSTON RD
POLK CO OR 204-A3
YAMHILL CO OR 204-A3
SW BALLSTON RD
YAMHILL CO OR 125-B3
YAMHILL CO OR 204-A3
BALLY MOUNTAIN TRAIL RD
ADAMS CO ID 251-A1
BALM FORK RD
MORROW CO OR 128-C2
BALSAM DR
KLAMATH CO OR 235-A4
KLAMATH CO OR 338-A12
KLAMATH FALLS OR 338-A12
BALSAM DR S
SALEM OR 324-F3
S BALTIMORE RD
SPOKANE CO WA 246-C6
BALTIMORE ST
LONGVIEW WA 302-H10
LONGVIEW WA 303-A11
BANDIX RD SE
KITSAP CO WA 174-C6
BANDY RD
BONNER CO ID 107-A3
BANFIELD FRWY I-84
PORTLAND OR 313-H4
PORTLAND OR 314-C5
PORTLAND OR 315-J2
S BANGOR ST
SEATTLE WA 287-G6
N BANK RD
COOS CO OR 220-C4
S BANK RD
GRAYS HARBOR CO WA 117-B1
S BANK RD Rt#-107
GRAYS HARBOR CO WA 117-A1
SW BANK RD
KING CO WA 174-D5
NE BANNER PL
SEATTLE WA 274-B2
N BANNER RD
KITSAP CO WA 174-C4
BANNER RD SE
KITSAP CO WA 174-C5
BANNER WY NE
SEATTLE WA 274-B2
BANNISTER RD
UMATILLA CO OR 129-C1
WESTON OR 129-C1
BANTA RD
BAKER CO OR 130-B3
BAPTIST CHURCH DR
LINN CO OR 133-C1
BAR 14 RD
KITTITAS CO WA 241-C4

BARBARA DR
JOSEPHINE CO OR 229-A5
BARBARA WY
DESCHUTES CO OR 212-A7
BARBEE RD
WHITMAN CO WA 249-A6
BARBER RD NW
DOUGLAS CO WA 236-B5
SW BARBUR BLVD
PORTLAND OR 317-E1
SW BARBUR BLVD Rt#-99W
PORTLAND OR 199-B3
PORTLAND OR 316-E3
PORTLAND OR 317-E2
PORTLAND OR 320-A1
TIGARD OR 199-B3
BARCLAY DR
DESCHUTES CO OR 211-D5
BARGER AV
EUGENE OR 329-A1
BARKER LN
VALLEY CO ID 252-D2
BARKER RD
COLUMBIA CO OR 189-B5
LANE CO OR 133-B3
N BARKER RD
SPOKANE VALLEY WA 351-G3
S BARKER RD
SPOKANE CO WA 351-G10
SPOKANE VALLEY WA 351-G8
W BARKER RD
ADA CO ID 253-C6
BARKER CANYON RD
DOUGLAS CO WA 237-A3
BARKES RD
HARRAH WA 119-C2
BARKLEY BLVD
BELLINGHAM WA 258-J4
E BARKLEY BLVD
BELLINGHAM WA 258-H3
BARLOW RD
BARLOW OR 199-B7
CLACKAMAS CO OR 199-B7
CLACKAMAS CO OR 205-C1
HOOD RIVER CO OR 202-B7
S BARLOW RD
CLACKAMAS CO OR 205-C1
S BARLOW MONTE CRISTO RD
CLACKAMAS CO OR 205-C2
MARION CO OR 205-C2
BARLOW TRAIL RD
CLACKAMAS CO OR 201-B4
BARNARDS RD
CLACKAMAS CO OR 126-A3
CLACKAMAS CO OR 205-D1
S BARNARDS RD
CLACKAMAS CO OR 205-D1
S BARNEBURG RD
MEDFORD OR 336-F12
BARNEKOFF RD
COOS CO OR 220-B7
BARNES AV U.S.-395
SENECA OR 137-B3
BARNES DR
COWLITZ CO WA 187-C6
LEWIS CO WA 187-C6
NE BARNES DR
JEFFERSON CO OR 208-C3
BARNES RD
KITTITAS CO WA 241-B6
NW BARNES RD
WASHINGTON CO OR 199-B1
SW BARNES RD
WASHINGTON CO OR 199-B1
BARNES RD NW
DOUGLAS CO WA 236-D7
BARNES ST
KELSO WA 303-D6
BARNES BUTTE RD
CROOK CO OR 213-D4
BARNET HWY Rt#-7A
COQUITLAM BC 157-A4
DISTRICT OF BURNABY BC 156-D4
PORT MOODY BC 157-A4
BARNETT RD
GILLIAM CO OR 128-A2
E BARNETT RD
MEDFORD OR 234-B1
MEDFORD OR 336-F13
W BARNETT RD
MEDFORD OR 336-D13
BARNHART RD
WHATCOM CO WA 158-D3
YAKIMA CO WA 120-A2
BARNSTON DR E
CITY OF SURREY BC 157-B6
BARNSTON DR W
CITY OF SURREY BC 157-B6
BARON RD NE
MARION CO OR 205-B3
BARR RD
CLALLAM CO WA 165-D6
DESCHUTES CO OR 212-B5
LEWISTON ID 250-C5
NEZ PERCE CO ID 250-C5
WHATCOM CO WA 158-C6
BARR-ALEX RD Rt#-219
WASHINGTON CO OR 198-D3
BARRELL SPRINGS RD
SKAGIT CO WA 161-B3
BARRETT RD
HOOD RIVER CO OR 195-C5
SW BARROWS RD
BEAVERTON OR 199-A3
WASHINGTON CO OR 199-A3
BARRY RD
DOUGLAS CO WA 237-C1
BARRY REX RD
DOUGLAS CO WA 237-C2
BARSTOW-PIERRE LAKE RD
STEVENS CO WA 105-C1
SE BARTEL RD
CLACKAMAS CO OR 200-B4
BARTLEMAY RD
CLACKAMAS CO OR 200-B4
BARTLETTE RD
PEND OREILLE CO WA 106-B3
SW BARTON PL
SEATTLE WA 285-G3
BARTON RD
DOUGLAS CO OR 225-C6
SW BARTON ST
SEATTLE WA 284-D3
SEATTLE WA 285-F3
S BASALT ST
SPOKANE CO WA 348-C11
BASE LINE DR
HOOD RIVER CO OR 202-C2

INDEX

BASE LINE RD STREET INDEX BIG VALLEY RD NE 359

STREET City State Page-Grid

BASE LINE RD
GILLIAM CO OR 128-A2
BASELINE RD
BAY CITY OR 197-B1
DOUGLAS CO WA 236-C7
GRANT CO WA 112-B3
W BASELINE RD
HILLSBORO OR 198-D1
HILLSBORO OR 199-A1
WASHINGTON CO OR 198-D1
WASHINGTON CO OR 199-A1
BASELINE RD E
GRANT CO WA 242-C4
BASELINE ST Rt#-8
CORNELIUS OR 198-C1
SE BASELINE ST Rt#-8
HILLSBORO OR 198-D1
SW BASELINE ST Rt#-8
HILLSBORO OR 198-D1
BASELINE .5 RD SE
GRANT CO WA 242-D4
BASELINE RIDGE RD
WASHINGTON CO OR 198-A1
BASEY CANYON RD
MORROW CO OR 128-C2
N BASIN AV
PORTLAND OR 308-C7
PORTLAND OR 312-D1
W BASIN RD
DESCHUTES CO OR 135-B3
BASIN ST N Rt#-28
EPHRATA WA 112-C3
GRANT CO WA 112-C3
BASIN ST NW Rt#-28
EPHRATA WA 112-C3
GRANT CO WA 112-C3
BASIN ST S Rt#-28
EPHRATA WA 112-C3
GRANT CO WA 112-C3
BASKET BUTTE RD
DOUGLAS CO OR 223-A3
NE BASKET FLAT RD
CLARK CO WA 193-B2
BASL HILL RD
MARION CO OR 134-A1
BASSET RD
SKAGIT CO WA 161-C5
BATES RD
COOS CO OR 220-B6
DOUGLAS CO OR 225-C4
KELSO WA 303-E8
KLICKITAT CO WA 195-D4
BATES RD E
LINCOLN CO WA 113-B3
BATH
PIERCE CO WA 182-B6
BATTELLE BLVD
RICHLAND WA 340-F6
BATTERMAN RD
DOUGLAS CO WA 239-B5
BATTERY ST
SEATTLE WA 277-J4
BATTLE CREEK RD
JACKSON CO OR 230-A2
OWYHEE CO ID 155-C1
BATTLE CREEK RD SE
MARION CO OR 325-B9
SALEM OR 324-J5
SALEM OR 325-A5
BATTLE CREEK RANCH RD
MALHEUR CO OR 154-B2
BATTLE POINT RD NE
KITSAP CO WA 174-C1
BATUM RD
ADAMS CO WA 113-B3
LINCOLN CO WA 113-B3
BATY RD
CLACKAMAS CO OR 201-A4
BAUER RD
WHITMAN CO WA 250-B1
BAUMAN RD
ADAMS CO WA 113-C3
ADAMS CO WA 121-C1
RITZVILLE WA 113-C3
BAUMEISTER DR
ASOTIN WA 250-B5
BAY AV
HOQUIAM WA 178-A7
BAY AV Rt#-103
Ocean Park WA 186-A2
SE BAY BLVD
NEWPORT OR 206-B4
SW BAY BLVD
NEWPORT OR 206-B4
E BAY DR
OLYMPIA WA 296-J2
W BAY DR
OLYMPIA WA 296-G3
E BAY DR NW
PIERCE CO WA 181-C1
S BAY LP NE
THURSTON CO WA 180-D5
BAY PL
DESCHUTES CO OR 211-D5
BAY RD
Birch Bay WA 158-B4
LEWIS CO WA 187-C3
S BAY RD NE
OLYMPIA WA 297-C2
THURSTON CO WA 180-D5
THURSTON CO WA 297-C2
BAY ST
CITY OF VICTORIA BC 256-H7
CITY OF VICTORIA BC 257-A8
PORT ORCHARD WA 270-J14
PORT ORCHARD WA 271-A13
BAY ST Rt#-166
PORT ORCHARD WA 174-B4
PORT ORCHARD WA 270-H14
BAY ST Rt#-167
TACOMA WA 182-A2
S BAY ST
WALDPORT OR 328-E5
SW BAY ST
NEWPORT OR 206-B4
BAYARD ST Rt#-206
CONDON OR 128-A2
E BAYARD ST Rt#-206
CONDON OR 128-A2
BAY CENTER RD
PACIFIC CO WA 183-C7
BAY CENTER DIKE RD
PACIFIC CO WA 183-C7
BAYLEY RD
YAMHILL CO OR 198-C5
BAYLISS RD
YAMHILL CO OR 198-B6
BAYNES RD
DISTRICT OF SAANICH BC 257-G5
BAYOCEAN RD NW
TILLAMOOK CO OR 197-B1
BAYOCEAN DIKE RD
TILLAMOOK CO OR 191-A7
TILLAMOOK CO OR 197-A1
BAYSHORE DR
LINCOLN CO OR 328-C3
N BAYSHORE DR
COOS BAY OR 333-H9
S BAYSHORE DR
COOS BAY OR 333-H11
BAYVIEW DR
WHATCOM CO WA 101-C1
BAYVIEW DR W
BREMERTON WA 270-E13
Navy Yard City WA 270-E13
BAYVIEW RD
ISLAND CO WA 170-D2
LINCOLN CO OR 328-H2
SKAGIT CO WA 161-A6
WALDPORT OR 328-D3
BAYVIEW RD KPN
PIERCE CO WA 174-A7
BAY VIEW EDISON RD
SKAGIT CO WA 160-D5
SKAGIT CO WA 161-A5
B D MINKLER RD
SKAGIT CO WA 161-C5
BEACH DR
DISTRICT OF OAK BAY BC 257-E5
ISLAND CO WA 167-D7
S BEACH DR
KITSAP CO WA 271-J8
SEASIDE OR 301-F10
BEACH DR E
Colby WA 271-F9
KITSAP CO WA 271-F9
PORT ORCHARD WA 271-C12
BEACH DR NE
KITSAP CO WA 170-B5
BEACH DR SW
SEATTLE WA 280-B3
SEATTLE WA 284-D1
BEACH RD
LANE CO OR 215-B6
BEACH ST
ASHLAND OR 337-E9
BEACHER HILL RD
CHELAN CO WA 238-A1
BEACH LOOP DR SW
BANDON OR 220-A6
BEACH LOOP RD
BANDON OR 220-A7
COOS CO OR 220-A7
BEACON AV S
KING CO WA 287-F6
KING CO WA 289-H1
SEATTLE WA 282-B2
SEATTLE WA 286-D1
SEATTLE WA 287-F6
E BEACON DR
LANE CO OR 210-A7
Santa Clara OR 210-A7
NE BEACON DR
GRANTS PASS OR 335-H7
W BEACON DR
LANE CO OR 210-A7
BEACON LN
DISTRICT OF W VANCOUVER BC 156-A3
BEACON RD
GRAYS HARBOR CO WA 178-D7
WHITMAN CO WA 122-A1
W BEACON ST
BOISE ID 253-C3
E BEACON LIGHT RD
ADA CO ID 253-B1
EAGLE ID 253-B1
W BEACON LIGHT RD
ADA CO ID 253-A1
BEAGLE RD
JACKSON CO OR 230-C4
E BEAKMAN ST Rt#-203
UNION OR 130-B2
BEALL LN
CENTRAL POINT OR 230-C7
CENTRAL POINT OR 336-A7
JACKSON CO OR 230-C7
MEDFORD OR 230-C7
MEDFORD OR 336-A7
BEALL RD SW
KING CO WA 174-D6
BEALS CREEK RD
DOUGLAS CO OR 225-D3
BEAM RD
YAKIMA CO WA 120-A2
BEAR AV
CITY OF HARRISON HOT SPGS BC 94-C3
BEAR DR
JEFFERSON CO OR 208-B7
SW BEAR DR
JEFFERSON CO OR 208-B6
BEAR CREEK RD
COOS CO OR 220-B6
CROOK CO OR 136-A1
DESCHUTES CO OR 217-D3
DOUGLAS CO OR 219-C1
DOUGLAS CO OR 223-B5
GRANT CO OR 137-B2
JOSEPHINE CO OR 233-C4
LANE CO OR 215-C5
LINCOLN CO OR 203-C4
LINCOLN CO OR 209-B2
SKAMANIA CO WA 194-D4
WALLOWA CO OR 130-B2
E BEAR CREEK RD
BEND OR 217-C3
BEND OR 332-J8
DESCHUTES CO OR 217-C3
N BEAR CREEK RD
DOUGLAS CO OR 219-C1
NE BEAR CREEK RD
BEND OR 332-G8
W BEAR CREEK RD
KITSAP CO WA 173-C4
MASON CO WA 173-C4
BEAR CREEK RD NE
KING CO WA 171-D7
BEAR CREEK DEWATTO RD
KITSAP CO WA 173-C4
MASON CO WA 173-C4
BEAR CREEK-FIFE RD
CROOK CO OR 135-C3
CROOK CO OR 136-A3
CROOK CO OR 144-B1
BEAR CREST DR Rt#-99
JACKSON CO OR 234-B2
PHOENIX OR 234-B2
BEAR FLAT RD
KLAMATH CO OR 143-A2
BEAR FLAT RD
LAKE CO OR 143-A2
BEAR LAKE RD
KITSAP CO WA 174-A5
BEAR MOUNTAIN RD
CHELAN CO WA 236-B3
LANE CO OR 215-C5
BEAR RIVER RD
PACIFIC CO WA 186-B6
BEAR SPURS LP
JEFFERSON CO OR 211-D1
BEAR SPURS RD
JEFFERSON CO OR 211-D1
BEAR WALLOW BUTTE RD
DESCHUTES CO OR 216-D1
BEATYS BUTTE RD
LAKE CO OR 152-C2
E BEAUCHENE RD
YAKIMA CO WA 243-C7
S BEAUDRY RD
YAKIMA CO WA 243-D7
BEAUTY CREEK RD
KOOTENAI CO ID 248-B1
BEAVER RD
DISTRICT OF N VANCOUVER BC 255-B1
NEZ PERCE CO ID 250-D5
BEAVERBROOK DR
DISTRICT OF BURNABY BC 156-D4
NE BEAVER BROOK RD
CLARK CO WA 193-A1
BEAVER BUTTE RD
WASCO CO OR 127-A3
BEAVER CREEK RD
ADAMS CO ID 131-C3
ADAMS CO ID 251-A5
COOS CO OR 220-D3
CROOK CO OR 136-B3
LEWIS CO WA 187-A1
LINCOLN CO OR 206-B6
WAHKIAKUM CO WA 117-B3
E BEAVER CREEK RD
Colby WA 271-F10
KITSAP CO WA 271-F10
N BEAVER CREEK RD
LINCOLN CO OR 206-B6
S BEAVER CREEK RD
LINCOLN CO OR 206-B7
LINCOLN CO OR 328-G2
S BEAVERCREEK RD
CLACKAMAS CO OR 126-A3
CLACKAMAS CO OR 199-D5
CLACKAMAS CO OR 200-A6
OREGON CITY OR 199-D5
BEAVER FALLS RD
CLATSKANIE OR 117-B3
COLUMBIA CO OR 117-B3
COLUMBIA CO OR 189-A4
E BEAVER HILL RD
COOS CO OR 220-C4
W BEAVER HILL RD
COOS CO OR 220-B3
BEAVER LAKE RD
SKAGIT CO WA 161-C7
BEAVER MARSH RD
SKAGIT CO WA 168-A1
BEAVER SPRINGS RD
COLUMBIA CO OR 189-B5
SW BEAVRTN-HLLSDLE HWY Rt#-10
BEAVERTON OR 199-B2
PORTLAND OR 199-B2
PORTLAND OR 316-A3
WASHINGTON CO OR 199-B2
BEAVERTON-TIGRD FRWY Rt#-217
BEAVERTON OR 199-B3
LAKE OSWEGO OR 199-B3
TIGARD OR 199-B3
WASHINGTON CO OR 199-B3
BEAVERTON VALLEY RD
SAN JUAN CO WA 101-C2
N BEAVER VALLEY DR
LINCOLN CO OR 206-B7
BEAVER VALLEY RD Rt#-19
JEFFERSON CO WA 170-A1
BEBER RANCH RD
MALHEUR CO OR 154-B1
BECK RD
BENTON CO WA 121-A3
POLK CO OR 204-A4
STEVENS CO WA 106-A3
NE BECK RD
KITSAP CO WA 271-H6
BECKER RD
DOUGLAS CO OR 221-A3
NEZ PERCE CO ID 250-C2
WHITMAN CO WA 249-B7
WHITMAN CO WA 250-A1
BECKETT POINT RD
JEFFERSON CO WA 166-D7
BECKLEY RD
ADAMS CO WA 122-A1
BEDELL RD
COLUMBIA CO OR 189-B6
BED ROCK FLAT RD
WASHINGTON CO ID 139-B1
BEDWELL BAY RD
ANMORE BC 157-A3
BELCARRA BC 157-A3
CITY OF PORT MOODY BC 156-D3
MAPLE RIDGE BC 157-A3
VILLAGE OF BELCARRA BC 156-D3
BEEBE RD
COWLITZ CO WA 187-C6
BEECH ST
ARLINGTON OR 128-A1
LONGVIEW WA 302-H10
E BEECH CREEK RD
GRANT CO OR 137-B1
SW BEEF BEND RD
KING CITY OR 199-A4
WASHINGTON CO OR 199-A4
BEEKS RD
BONNER CO ID 244-A5
BEEKS CANYON RD
KLICKITAT CO WA 196-C1
BEE MILL RD
JEFFERSON CO WA 109-C1
BEERBOWER RD
MASON CO WA 179-A5
BEESON CTO
WHITMAN CO WA 249-B3
BEESON RD
CLACKAMAS CO OR 200-A7
BEET RD
CANYON CO ID 147-B1
BEEVILLE LOOP RD
MASON CO WA 179-B2
BEGBIE ST
CITY OF VICTORIA BC 256-J9
CITY OF VICTORIA BC 257-A9
BEHME RD
WHATCOM CO WA 158-C3
BEHRENS LN
UNION CO OR 130-A2
BEHRENS-MILLETT RD
MOUNT VERNON WA 260-A13
SKAGIT CO WA 260-A13
BEHRN RD
WASCO CO OR 196-A6
BEIRMAN RD
ADAMS CO WA 113-C3
BEITEY RD
STEVENS CO WA 106-B3
BELFAIR-TAHUYA RD
MASON CO WA 173-C5
BELKNAP SPRINGS HWY Rt#-126
LANE CO OR 134-B2
LINN CO OR 134-B2
SE BELL AV
CLACKAMAS CO OR 318-E7
BELL RD
WASHINGTON CO OR 199-A5
YAMHILL CO OR 198-D5
E BELL RD
YAKIMA CO WA 243-C7
SW BELL RD
CLACKAMAS CO OR 199-A5
BELL ST
DISTRICT OF MISSION BC 94-B3
BELLE CENTER RD
SKAMANIA CO WA 193-D7
BELLE PASSI RD NE
MARION CO OR 205-B2
BELLEVILLE ST
CITY OF VICTORIA BC 256-G9
BELLEVUE HWY
AMITY OR 204-B2
YAMHILL CO OR 204-B2
SW BELLEVUE HWY
YAMHILL CO OR 204-A2
BELLEVUE WY NE
BELLEVUE WA 175-C2
BELLEVUE WY SE
BELLEVUE WA 175-C2
NE BELLEVUE REDMOND RD
BELLEVUE WA 175-C2
REDMOND WA 175-C2
BELLFOUNTAIN RD
BENTON CO OR 133-B2
BENTON CO OR 327-A14
BELLINGER LN
JACKSON CO OR 234-A1
BELLINGER SCALE RD
LINN CO OR 133-C1
BELL PLAIN DR
LINN CO OR 207-B7
BELL PLAIN RD
GARFIELD CO WA 122-B2
N BELLWOOD ST
UNION OR 130-B2
S BELLWOOD ST
UNION OR 130-B2
BELMONT AV E
SEATTLE WA 278-B3
BELMONT DR
HOOD RIVER CO OR 195-C5
SW BELMONT LN
JEFFERSON CO OR 208-B5
MADRAS OR 208-B5
BELMONT RD
HOOD RIVER OR 195-C5
HOOD RIVER CO OR 195-C5
E BELMONT RD
SPOKANE CO WA 247-A5
SE BELMONT ST
PORTLAND OR 313-G6
PORTLAND OR 314-A6
BELMONT-FARMINGTON RD
FARMINGTON WA 115-A3
NW BELT RD
YAMHILL CO OR 198-A4
N BELT ST
SPOKANE WA 348-G2
BELTLINE HWY
EUGENE OR 215-B1
EUGENE OR 329-B2
LANE CO OR 215-B1
Santa Clara OR 215-B1
BELTLINE HWY Rt#-69
EUGENE OR 329-B5
EUGENE OR 330-A1
SPRINGFIELD OR 330-A1
BELTLINE E RD
North Springfield OR 330-F2
SPRINGFIELD OR 330-F2
BELTS DR
LINN CO OR 210-B4
BELVEDERE RD
OKANOGAN CO WA 237-C1
BEN BUNCH RD
LANE CO OR 214-B1
S BEN BURR BLVD
SPOKANE WA 349-F11
N BENCH RD
KOOTENAI CO ID 245-A3
W BENCH RD
ADAMS CO WA 121-A1
BENCH MARK BUTTE RD
DESCHUTES CO OR 216-A7
BEND AV
WINSTON OR 221-B6
BEND PKWY U.S.-97
BEND OR 332-F3
DESCHUTES CO OR 332-F3
BEN DAY GULCH RD
GARFIELD CO WA 122-B2
BEND-DESCHUTES MARKET RD
BEND OR 217-C1
DESCHUTES CO OR 212-C7
DESCHUTES CO OR 217-C1
BENDER RD
KITTITAS CO WA 241-B5
LYNDEN WA 102-B1
WHATCOM CO WA 102-B1
BENDIGO BLVD N Rt#-202
NORTH BEND WA 176-C4
SNOQUALMIE WA 176-C4
BENDIGO BLVD S Rt#-202
NORTH BEND WA 176-C5
BENDIRE RD
MALHEUR CO OR 138-A3
BEND ON RD N
OKANOGAN CO WA 104-C3
BENEKE RD
CLATSOP CO OR 117-B3
BENEWAH RD
BENEWAH CO ID 115-A3
BENEWAH CO ID 248-B7
S BEN GARNETT WY
SPOKANE WA 348-J10
BENGE WASHTUCNA RD
ADAMS CO WA 122-A1
BENGE-WASHTUCNA RD
ADAMS CO WA 121-C1
BENGE WINONA RD
ADAMS CO WA 122-A1
BENGOA RD
HUMBOLDT CO NV 154-A3
BENHAM ST
RICHLAND WA 341-G3
BENHAM FALLS RD
DESCHUTES CO OR 217-A5
BEN HOWARD RD
SNOHOMISH CO WA 110-C1
BENJAMIN RD
YAMHILL CO OR 198-D5
BEN MORE RD
DOUGLAS CO OR 219-B6
BENNETT DR
WHATCOM CO WA 158-D7
WHATCOM CO WA 258-A1
BENNETT RD
CANYON CO ID 147-C1
COLUMBIA CO OR 192-A2
DESCHUTES CO OR 217-D3
PEND OREILLE CO WA 106-C3
WASCO CO OR 127-C3
BENNETT CREEK RD
LANE CO OR 215-B6
BENNION RD
KOOTENAI CO ID 247-D7
BENSON RD Rt#-515
KENT WA 175-C6
KING CO WA 175-C6
SE BENSON RD
LINCOLN CO OR 206-B4
NEWPORT OR 206-B4
BENSON RD S
KING CO WA 175-C5
RENTON WA 175-C5
BENSON RD SE Rt#-515
KING CO WA 175-C6
BENSON CREEK RD
COOS CO OR 218-D4
OKANOGAN CO WA 104-B3
BENSTON CORNER CLEAR LAKE
PIERCE CO WA 118-B1
BENSTON-KAPOWSIN
PIERCE CO WA 182-A7
BENTON ST
PORT TOWNSEND WA 263-G5
N BENTON ST
KENNEWICK WA 343-D10
S BENTON ST
KENNEWICK WA 343-D11
BENTON-FRANKLIN INTERCOUNTY BR
KENNEWICK WA 343-E10
PASCO WA 343-F9
BENTS RD
MARION CO OR 199-B6
BENVENUTO AV
DIST OF CENTRAL SAANICH BC 159-B4
BERCOT RD
Freeland WA 170-D1
BERG RD
COLUMBIA CO OR 192-A2
DOUGLAS CO WA 112-C2
BERGE RD
SKAMANIA CO WA 195-A4
BERGER-FEELEY RD
HARNEY CO OR 136-C3
E BERGESON ST
BOISE ID 253-D3
BERKELEY AV SW
LAKEWOOD WA 181-C5
PIERCE CO WA 181-C5
BERKLEY AV
DIST OF N VANCOUVER BC 255-H4
BERKLEY RD
DIST OF N VANCOUVER BC 255-H5
BERLIN RD
CRESWELL OR 133-C1
LEBANON OR 133-C1
LINN CO OR 133-C1
LOWELL OR 133-C1
BERMUDA RD
BENTON CO WA 341-D12
S BERNARD ST
SPOKANE WA 348-J13
BERNARDS ST
MARION CO OR 198-D7
S BERNEY DR
WALLA WALLA WA 345-F8
WALLA WALLA CO WA 345-F8
Walla Walla East WA 345-F8
BERNHARDT CREEK RD
LANE CO OR 214-C3
BERRY DR
LINN CO OR 326-J1
NE BERRY RD
CLARK CO WA 193-B3
BERRY CREEK RD
POLK CO OR 207-A2
NW BERRY CREEK RD
YAMHILL CO OR 198-A6
SW BERRY LAKE RD
KITSAP CO WA 174-B4
N BERTELSEN RD
EUGENE OR 329-C4
S BERTELSEN RD
EUGENE OR 329-C7
LANE CO OR 329-C7
SW BERTHA BLVD
PORTLAND OR 316-D5
BERTHUSEN RD
WHATCOM CO WA 158-D4
BERT JAMES RD
BENTON CO WA 120-C3
BESSEN RD
DESCHUTES CO OR 217-A6
BESSIE CREEK RD
JACKSON CO OR 226-C7
JACKSON CO OR 227-A7
E BEST AV
COEUR D'ALENE ID 355-E8
BEST RD
POLK CO OR 204-C5
SKAGIT CO WA 161-A7
SKAGIT CO WA 168-A1
BETA DR
ALBANY OR 207-C6
BETHANY RD
YAKIMA CO WA 120-B2
BETHANY-ALEXANDER WYE
YAKIMA CO WA 120-B2
BETHEL RD
East Port Orchard WA 174-B4
KITSAP CO WA 174-B4
POLK CO OR 204-B3
BETHEL RD Rt#-166
PORT ORCHARD WA 174-B4
PORT ORCHARD WA 270-J14
N BETHEL ST
OLYMPIA WA 297-A3
BETHEL BURLEY RD SE
KITSAP CO WA 174-B5
BETHEL-BURLEY RD SE
KITSAP CO WA 174-B5
BETHEL HEIGHTS RD
POLK CO OR 204-C3
BETTAS RD
KITTITAS CO WA 240-D2
S BETTMAN RD
SPOKANE VALLEY WA 349-J11
W BETZ RD
CHENEY WA 246-A7
SPOKANE CO WA 246-A6
BEULAH RD
MALHEUR CO OR 138-A3
MALHEUR CO OR 146-A1
BEVERLY BLVD
EVERETT WA 268-D2
BEVERLY DR NE
THURSTON CO WA 181-A5
BEVERLY LN
EVERETT WA 268-B2
BEVERLY BURKE RD
GRANT CO WA 120-B1
BEVERLY PARK RD
EVERETT WA 171-B4
MUKILTEO WA 171-B4
SNOHOMISH CO WA 171-B4
BEVILLE RD
LEWIS CO WA 187-A1
BEWLEY CREEK RD
TILLAMOOK CO OR 197-C3
BEWLEYS ST
BAY CITY OR 197-B1
B HOWARD RD
WHITMAN CO WA 249-B1
BIA RD 10
OKANOGAN CO WA 105-A3
BIA RD 33
JEFFERSON CO OR 134-C1
JEFFERSON CO OR 135-A1
BIA RD 108
YAKIMA CO WA 119-A2
BIA RD 140
YAKIMA CO WA 119-B3
BIA RD 255
YAKIMA CO WA 119-A3
BIA RD 7047
GRAYS HARBOR CO WA 172-B5
BIA RD S-2
GRAYS HARBOR CO WA 177-B1
BIBLE CREEK RD
TILLAMOOK CO OR 125-A2
SW BIBLE CREEK RD
TILLAMOOK CO OR 125-A2
YAMHILL CO OR 125-A2
BICKFORD AV
SNOHOMISH WA 171-D2
SNOHOMISH CO WA 171-D2
BIDDLE RD
JACKSON CO OR 336-B5
MEDFORD OR 336-C8
BIEHN ST
KLAMATH FALLS OR 338-C5
SE BIELMEIR RD
KITSAP CO WA 174-B5
BIG ALKALI RD
WHITMAN CO WA 122-A1
BIG BENCH RD
DOUGLAS CO WA 236-D4
BIG BEND RD
DOUGLAS CO OR 221-A3
BIG BUTTER CREEK RD
MORROW CO OR 128-C1
MORROW CO OR 129-A2
BIG CAMAS RD
DOUGLAS CO OR 222-C3
DOUGLAS CO OR 223-B4
BIG CREEK RD
BONNER CO ID 107-A3
COOS CO OR 218-D3
LANE CO OR 209-A6
SHOSHONE CO ID 115-C2
NE BIG CREEK RD
LINCOLN CO OR 206-B3
BIG ELK RD
JACKSON CO OR 150-A2
BIGELOW ST NE
OLYMPIA WA 297-B4
E BIGELOW GULCH RD
SPOKANE CO WA 246-D2
SPOKANE CO WA 347-H14
SPOKANE CO WA 349-G1
BIG FALL CREEK RD
LANE CO OR 133-C3
LANE CO OR 134-A3
BIG FLAT RD
BAKER CO OR 138-A1
WASHINGTON CO ID 139-C2
BIGHAM BROWN RD
JACKSON CO OR 230-D6
BIG HANAFORD RD
LEWIS CO WA 184-C5
BIG HUCKLEBERRY RD
SKAMANIA CO WA 195-A2
W BIG LAKE BLVD
SKAGIT CO WA 168-C1
BIG LICK LN
DOUGLAS CO OR 221-D7
E BIG MEADOWS RD
SPOKANE CO WA 114-C1
E BIG ROCK RD
SPOKANE CO WA 246-D5
BIG SANDY RD
CLACKAMAS CO OR 201-A4
BIG SPRING RD
DESCHUTES CO OR 216-D4
BIG SPRING BURN RD
DESCHUTES CO OR 216-D3
E BIG SPRINGS RD
SPOKANE CO WA 349-G11
BIG SQUAWBACK RD
JEFFERSON CO OR 211-D1
BIG STICK RD
HARNEY CO OR 144-C2
HARNEY CO OR 145-A2
BIG VALLEY RD NE
KITSAP CO WA 170-B6

INDEX

INDEX

STREET — City State Page-Grid

BIG WILLOW RD
PAYETTE CO ID ... 139-B3
BILGER CREEK RD
DOUGLAS CO OR ... 221-D7
BILLADEAU RD
DESCHUTES CO OR ... 217-D4
BILL CREEK RD
LEWIS CO WA ... 187-C4
BILL MCDONALD PKWY
BELLINGHAM WA ... 258-C10
BILL MOORE RD
KLICKITAT CO WA ... 196-B2
BILYEU CREEK RD
LINN CO WA ... 134-A1
BINGHAM AV E
PIERCE CO WA ... 182-A5
BINGHAM RD
UMATILLA CO OR ... 129-C1
BINGHAMPTON ST Rt#-507
RAINIER WA ... 118-A1
THURSTON CO WA ... 118-A1
BINNS HILL DR
HOOD RIVER CO OR ... 195-B6
BIRCH AV
HARRAH WA ... 119-C2
LAPWAI ID ... 123-A2
NW BIRCH LN
JEFFERSON CO OR ... 208-B5
BIRCH PL
PACIFIC CO WA ... 186-A3
BIRCH RD
DISTRICT OF NORTH SAANICH BC ... 159-B2
FRANKLIN CO WA ... 121-A2
BIRCH ST
BAKER CITY OR ... 138-B1
JUNCTION CITY OR ... 210-A6
PACIFIC CO WA ... 186-A4
N BIRCH ST Rt#-42S
COQUILLE OR ... 220-D5
BIRCH BAY DR
Birch Bay WA ... 158-B5
BIRCH BAY-LYNDEN RD
Birch Bay WA ... 158-B4
LYNDEN WA ... 158-D4
WHATCOM CO WA ... 158-C4
BIRCH CREEK RD
MALHEUR CO OR ... 146-C2
UMATILLA CO OR ... 121-C3
E BIRCH CREEK RD
PILOT ROCK OR ... 129-B2
UMATILLA CO OR ... 129-B2
S BIRCHFIELD RD
YAKIMA WA ... 243-C7
W BIRCHFIELD RD
YAKIMA WA ... 243-C7
YAKIMA CO WA ... 243-C7
BIRCH POINT RD
Birch Bay WA ... 158-A4
BIRCHWOOD AV
BELLINGHAM WA ... 258-C3
S BIRD RD
CLACKAMAS CO OR ... 126-A3
BIRDSEYE CREEK RD
JACKSON CO OR ... 229-D7
BISCAY ST NW
THURSTON CO WA ... 180-C5
BISCUIT BUTTE RD
MALHEUR CO OR ... 146-C2
BISHOP LN
LANE CO WA ... 210-A7
BISHOP RD
CLALLAM CO WA ... 164-D6
COLUMBIA CO OR ... 189-C5
GRAYS HARBOR CO WA ... 183-D3
BISHOP CREEK RD
COLUMBIA CO OR ... 189-B7
NW BISHOP-SCOTT RD
YAMHILL CO OR ... 198-A4
BISSELL RD
STEVENS CO WA ... 105-C3
BISSINGER RD
UMATILLA CO OR ... 129-B1
BITTERS RD
KOOTENAI CO ID ... 115-A2
BITTNER RD
YAKIMA CO WA ... 243-D6
E BITTNER RD
YAKIMA CO WA ... 243-D7
BIXBY RD
TILLAMOOK CO OR ... 197-C6
BIZ POINT RD
SKAGIT CO WA ... 259-B12
BJORN RD
SNOHOMISH CO WA ... 168-C5
BJORNDAHL RD
SNOHOMISH CO WA ... 168-C3
BLACK RD
LEWIS CO WA ... 187-A1
N BLACK RD
SPOKANE CO WA ... 347-F4
SE BLACK RD
KITSAP CO WA ... 174-C5
W BLACK RD
COUPEVILLE WA ... 167-B4
ISLAND CO WA ... 167-B4
BLACK BRIDGE RD
PAYETTE CO ID ... 139-B3
BLACKBURN RD
CITY OF CHILLIWACK BC ... 102-C1
YAMHILL CO OR ... 198-B5
E BLACKBURN RD
MOUNT VERNON WA ... 260-E14
SKAGIT CO WA ... 260-E14
W BLACKBURN RD
MOUNT VERNON WA ... 260-B14
SKAGIT CO WA ... 260-B14
BLACK BUTTE LN
WHEELER CO OR ... 128-A3
BLACK BUTTE RD
JEFFERSON CO OR ... 211-C2
JEFFERSON CO OR ... 212-A2
E BLACK CANYON HWY Rt#-52
GEM CO ID ... 139-C3
W BLACK CANYON HWY
GEM CO ID ... 139-B3
BLACK CANYON RD
LANE CO WA ... 215-C1
YAKIMA CO WA ... 243-A1
N BLACK CAT RD
ADA CO ID ... 253-A2
MERIDIAN ID ... 253-A2
S BLACK CAT RD
ADA CO ID ... 253-A3
BLACK CREEK RD
GRAYS HARBOR CO WA ... 178-D6
BLACK DIAMOND RD
CLALLAM CO WA ... 261-C7
BLACK DOG RD
LINN CO WA ... 207-C3

BLACKFORD RD
COLUMBIA CO OR ... 189-A3
BLACK LAKE BLVD SW
OLYMPIA WA ... 296-E6
THURSTON CO WA ... 296-A10
TUMWATER WA ... 296-E6
BLACK LAKE BELMORE RD SW
THURSTON CO WA ... 296-B9.
BLACKLEDGE RD
SKAMANIA CO WA ... 194-C3
BLACK MOUNTAIN RD
BAKER OR ... 138-A1
BLACK OAK DR
MEDFORD OR ... 336-G12
BLACK ROCK LN
DESCHUTES CO OR ... 217-C1
BLACK ROCK RD
DOUGLAS CO OR ... 222-B7
KOOTENAI CO ID ... 247-D6
KOOTENAI CO ID ... 248-D3
BLACKTAIL DR
JEFFERSON CO OR ... 212-C3
BLACKWELL RD
JACKSON CO OR ... 230-B6
BLAHA RDEX
COLUMBIA CO OR ... 192-A2
BLAINE RD
LATAH CO ID ... 249-D6
PAYETTE CO ID ... 139-B3
TILLAMOOK CO OR ... 197-C6
WHATCOM CO WA ... 158-B3
BLAINE RD Rt#-548
Birch Bay WA ... 158-B4
BLAINE WA ... 158-B4
WHATCOM CO WA ... 158-B3
BLAINE ST
PORT TOWNSEND WA ... 263-G4
BLAINE ST U.S.-30
CALDWELL ID ... 147-B1
W BLAINE ST
SEATTLE WA ... 276-D2
BLAIR RD
WHITMAN CO WA ... 249-B1
NE BLAIR RD
CLARK CO WA ... 193-B6
S BLAIR RD
CLACKAMAS CO OR ... 205-D3
SE BLAIR RD
CLARK CO WA ... 193-B6
BLAKE RD
GRAYS HARBOR CO WA ... 183-B3
LEWIS CO WA ... 187-D5
BLAKE RD Rt#-27
SPOKANE CO WA ... 351-A12
SPOKANE VALLEY WA ... 350-H10
SPOKANE VALLEY WA ... 351-A12
BLAKELEY LN
LEWIS CO WA ... 187-D4
BLAKELY AV NE
KITSAP CO WA ... 174-D2
KITSAP CO WA ... 271-H4
W BLAKELY AV NE
KITSAP CO WA ... 271-J6
NE BLAKELY ST
SEATTLE WA ... 274-D5
BLALOCK CANYON RD
GILLIAM CO OR ... 128-A1
BLANCA ST
UNIV ENDOWMENT LANDS ... 156-A4
BLANCHARD RD
TILLAMOOK CO OR ... 197-C5
E BLANCHARD RD
SPOKANE CO WA ... 114-C1
BLANK RD
WHITMAN CO WA ... 114-C3
BLANSHARD ST
CITY OF VICTORIA BC ... 256-M9
DISTRICT OF SAANICH BC ... 256-F4
BLANSHARD ST Rt#-17
CITY OF VICTORIA BC ... 256-G6
DISTRICT OF SAANICH BC ... 256-G5
BLANTON RD
FRANKLIN CO WA ... 121-B2
BLANTON RD Rt#-260
FRANKLIN CO WA ... 121-B1
BLATCHFORD RD
LINN CO OR ... 207-D7
BLENHEIM ST
VANCOUVER BC ... 156-B5
VANCOUVER BC ... 254-A13
BLENKINSOP RD
DISTRICT OF SAANICH BC ... 159-C5
DISTRICT OF SAANICH BC ... 256-J1
BLIMP BLVD
TILLAMOOK CO OR ... 197-C3
NW BLISS RD
CLARK CO WA ... 192-C4
N BLISS ST
PORTLAND OR ... 192-B7
BLISS-COCHRANE RD KPN
PIERCE CO WA ... 174-A7
BLIZZARD RD
WHATCOM CO WA ... 160-B1
BLM ACCESS RD
MAUPIN OR ... 127-B3
BLM RD 2-3
DOUGLAS CO OR ... 214-D6
BLM RD 23-4-26
DOUGLAS CO OR ... 219-C5
BLM RD 23-4-28-0
JOSEPHINE CO OR ... 229-C7
BLM RD 23-4-90
DOUGLAS CO OR ... 219-B5
BLM RD 23-5-191
Clinton WA ... 171-A2
BLM RD 24-1
WHATCOM CO WA ... 158-D4
BLM RD 24-3-31-2
COLUMBIA CO OR ... 189-A3
COWLITZ CO WA ... 189-D4
BLM RD 24-5-10
COWLITZ CO WA ... 189-D4
BLM RD 25-4-13-0
DOUGLAS CO OR ... 221-D1
BLM RD 25-7-5-1
DOUGLAS CO OR ... 141-A1
BLM RD 28-4-29-0
DOUGLAS CO OR ... 221-D6
BLM RD 29-4-20
DOUGLAS CO OR ... 225-D1
BLM RD 29-7-25-1
DOUGLAS CO OR ... 225-A1
BLM RD 30-70-50
DOUGLAS CO OR ... 225-A1
BLM RD 31-4-35-0
DOUGLAS CO OR ... 225-D4
BLM RD 32-4-9
DOUGLAS CO OR ... 225-D5
BLM RD 32-9-3
COOS CO OR ... 140-C3

BLM RD 33-0
DOUGLAS CO OR ... 214-D6
BLM RD 33-5-18
JOSEPHINE CO OR ... 229-C1
BLM RD 33-5-26
JOSEPHINE CO OR ... 229-C1
BLM RD 33-5-27
JOSEPHINE CO OR ... 229-C1
BLM RD 33-5-35-1
JOSEPHINE CO OR ... 229-C1
BLM RD 33-7-22
JOSEPHINE CO OR ... 229-A1
BLM RD 34-4-5
JOSEPHINE CO OR ... 229-C1
BLM RD 34-5-1
JOSEPHINE CO OR ... 229-C1
BLM RD 34-5-32
JOSEPHINE CO OR ... 229-C3
BLM RD 34-5-9
JOSEPHINE CO OR ... 229-C2
BLM RD 34-6-12
JOSEPHINE CO OR ... 229-B3
BLM RD 34-6-13
JOSEPHINE CO OR ... 229-B2
BLM RD 34-8-1
JOSEPHINE CO OR ... 141-A3
BLM RD 36-0
DOUGLAS CO OR ... 214-C7
BLM RD 37-6-36
JOSEPHINE CO OR ... 233-D3
BLM RD 39-6-9
JOSEPHINE CO OR ... 233-D3
BLM RD 39-7-16
JOSEPHINE CO OR ... 233-C4
BLM RD 61064
LAKE CO OR ... 152-C2
BLODGETT RD
LINCOLN CO OR ... 209-A3
MOUNT VERNON WA ... 260-C13
SKAGIT CO WA ... 168-B1
SKAGIT CO WA ... 260-C13
BLOMBERG RD SW
THURSTON CO WA ... 184-C1
BLOODGOOD RD
KLICKITAT CO WA ... 127-C1
BLOOMFIELD RD
MASON CO WA ... 180-B5
BLOOMING-FERN HILL RD
WASHINGTON CO OR ... 198-C2
BLOSSOM DR NE
Hayesville OR ... 323-D5
SALEM OR ... 323-D5
S BLOUNT RD
CLACKAMAS CO OR ... 199-C6
BLOWOUT RESERVOIR RD
MALHEUR CO OR ... 146-C2
MALHEUR CO OR ... 147-A2
BLUE BUNCH RD
JOSEPHINE CO OR ... 251-B6
BLUE CREEK RD
KOOTENAI CO ID ... 245-C6
BLUE CREEK RD W
STEVENS CO WA ... 106-A3
BLUE CREEK WEST RD
STEVENS CO WA ... 106-A3
BLUE GRADE
DOUGLAS CO OR ... 239-A3
BLUEGRASS LN
DESCHUTES CO OR ... 211-C5
BLUE LAKE RD
OKANOGAN CO WA ... 104-C1
BLUE MOUNTAIN RD
CLALLAM CO WA ... 165-D7
WHATCOM CO WA ... 161-D1
BLUE MOUNTAIN ST
COQUITLAM BC ... 157-A5
BLUE MOUNTAIN LOGGING RD
WHATCOM CO WA ... 161-C1
BLUE OX LOGGING RD
SKAMANIA CO WA ... 195-B3
BLUESTEM RD
LINCOLN CO WA ... 114-A2
BLUFF RD
CLACKAMAS CO OR ... 200-C3
PAYETTE CO ID ... 139-B3
SANDY OR ... 200-C3
N BLUFF RD
CITY OF SURREY BC ... 158-A2
CITY OF WHITE ROCK BC ... 158-A2
SE BLUFF RD
CLACKAMAS CO OR ... 200-C3
MULTNOMAH CO OR ... 200-C3
BLUFF ST
WINTHROP WA ... 104-A2
S BLUHM RD
CLACKAMAS CO OR ... 200-A6
BLUMAUER RD SE
THURSTON CO WA ... 184-D3
BLUNDELL RD
CITY OF RICHMOND BC ... 156-B6
BLUNT RD KPS
PIERCE CO WA ... 181-A2
BLY MOUNTAIN CTO
KLAMATH CO OR ... 151-A2
BOARDMAN IRRIGON RD
MORROW CO OR ... 128-C1
BOARDMAN-IRRIGON RD
MORROW CO OR ... 128-C1
BOARD SHANTY RD
JOSEPHINE CO OR ... 229-C7
BOAT RD
COOS CO OR ... 220-A7
BOB GALBREATH RD
Clinton WA ... 171-A2
BOB HALL RD
WHATCOM CO WA ... 158-D4
BODINE RD
COLUMBIA CO OR ... 189-A3
COWLITZ CO WA ... 189-D4
N BODINE RD
COWLITZ CO WA ... 189-D4
BOE RD
SNOHOMISH CO WA ... 168-A4
SW BOECKMAN RD
WILSONVILLE OR ... 199-B5
BOEHMER RD NE
MARION CO OR ... 205-C3
S BOEING ACCESS RD
TUKWILA WA ... 286-D5
TUKWILA WA ... 287-E5
E BOEKEL RD
KOOTENAI CO ID ... 247-D1
BOGACHIEL WY
CLALLAM CO WA ... 169-C2
N BOGART LN
CLARK CO WA ... 253-B1
BOG CREEK RD
BOUNDARY CO ID ... 106-C1
BOUNDARY CO ID ... 107-A1

N BOGUS BASIN RD
ADA CO ID ... 253-D2
BOISE ID ... 253-C2
BOGUS RANCH RD
MALHEUR CO OR ... 146-C3
BOHLKEN DR
LINN CO WA ... 133-C1
LINN CO OR ... 207-D5
BOH MOUNTAIN RD
JOSEPHINE CO OR ... 229-B3
SE BOHNA PARK RD
CLACKAMAS CO OR ... 200-B3
BOHOSKEY DR W
YAKIMA CO WA ... 243-D6
BOISE AV
BENTON CO OR ... 133-B2
E BOISE AV
ADA CO ID ... 253-D3
BOISE ID ... 253-D3
W BOISE AV
ADA CO ID ... 253-C3
NW BOISE DR
JEFFERSON CO OR ... 208-B3
BOISE ST
KOOTENAI ID ... 244-A1
BOISTFORT RD
LEWIS CO WA ... 187-A2
BOLAN LAKE RD
JOSEPHINE CO OR ... 233-C7
BOLEN RD
CLARK CO WA ... 192-C1
LA CENTER WA ... 192-C1
BOLESKINE RD
DISTRICT OF SAANICH BC ... 256-F5
BOLLAND RD
CLACKAMAS CO OR ... 199-C7
N BOLLENBAUGH HILL RD
SNOHOMISH CO WA ... 110-C1
BOLTON HILL RD
LANE CO WA ... 133-B3
VENETA OR ... 133-B3
BOMBING RANGE RD
MORROW CO OR ... 128-C2
WEST RICHLAND WA ... 341-A3
BONAPARTE RD
OKANOGAN CO WA ... 105-A1
BONAPARTE LAKE RD
OKANOGAN CO WA ... 105-A2
BOND DR
COWLITZ CO WA ... 187-C7
BOND RD
COWLITZ CO WA ... 189-C1
LINN CO OR ... 207-D4
BOND RD NE
POULSBO WA ... 170-B6
BOND RD NE Rt#-307
KITSAP CO WA ... 170-C6
POULSBO WA ... 170-C6
BOND ST
ASTORIA OR ... 300-C4
COWLITZ OR ... 187-C7
DISTRICT OF BURNABY BC ... 156-C5
NW BOND ST
BEND OR ... 332-E6
W BOND ST
ASTORIA OR ... 300-B4
BOND BUTTE DR
LINN CO OR ... 210-B4
BOND CREEK RD
SHOSHONE CO ID ... 115-B2
BOND MILL RD
SAN JUAN CO WA ... 160-A3
BONITA RD
WHATCOM CO WA ... 138-B3
W BONNEVILLE ST
PASCO WA ... 343-E8
BONNEY MEADOWS TR
WASCO CO OR ... 202-C7
BONNIEWOOD DR SE
TUMWATER WA ... 296-H13
BONSON RD
BRITISH COLUMBIA ... 157-C6
PITT MEADOWS BC ... 157-C5
BONY RD
YAMHILL CO OR ... 198-B4
BOOKER RD
ADAMS CO WA ... 121-A1
BOOMER HILL RD
DOUGLAS CO OR ... 225-B1
BOON RD
ISLAND CO WA ... 167-B3
BOONE RD
LEWIS CO WA ... 187-D3
N BOONE ST Rt#-105
ABERDEEN WA ... 178-B7
S BOONE ST Rt#-105
ABERDEEN WA ... 117-A1
ABERDEEN WA ... 178-B7
GRAYS HARBOR CO WA ... 117-A1
BOONE CREEK RD
COOS CO OR ... 220-D3
BOONES FERRY RD
CLACKAMAS CO OR ... 199-B6
CLACKAMAS CO OR ... 320-B6
LAKE OSWEGO OR ... 199-B6
LAKE OSWEGO OR ... 320-B6
LAKE OSWEGO OR ... 320-B6
MARION CO OR ... 205-B1
MULTNOMAH CO OR ... 320-B6
PORTLAND OR ... 320-B6
SW BOONES FERRY RD
DURHAM OR ... 199-B4
PORTLAND OR ... 316-E7
PORTLAND OR ... 317-E7
PORTLAND OR ... 320-D2
TUALATIN OR ... 199-B4
TUALATIN OR ... 199-B4
WASHINGTON CO OR ... 199-B4
WILSONVILLE OR ... 199-B4
BOONES FERRY RD NE
MARION CO OR ... 199-B7
MARION CO OR ... 205-B1
WOODBURN OR ... 205-B1
BOOTH LN
UNION CO OR ... 130-A2
BOOTH RD
DOUGLAS CO OR ... 214-A6
SW BOOTH BEND RD
MCMINNVILLE OR ... 198-A7
BOOTH HILL RD
HOOD RIVER CO OR ... 202-D1
N BOOTHILL RD
KOOTENAI CO ID ... 245-B4
BOOTH KELLY RD
SPRINGFIELD OR ... 331-D8
W BORAH ST
BOISE ID ... 253-C2

BORBA RD
TILLAMOOK CO OR ... 197-C5
BORDEAUX RD SW
THURSTON CO WA ... 184-A2
BOREN AV
SEATTLE WA ... 278-A5
BOREN AV S
SEATTLE WA ... 278-B6
BORGEN RD
LATAH CO ID ... 250-B1
WALLA WALLA CO WA ... 121-C3
SE BORGES RD
CLACKAMAS CO OR ... 200-B3
NE BORIN RD
CLARK CO WA ... 193-D6
SE BORING RD
GRESHAM OR ... 200-B2
SW BORLAND RD
CLACKAMAS CO OR ... 199-C4
TUALATIN OR ... 199-C4
WEST LINN OR ... 199-C4
SE BORNSTEDT RD
CLACKAMAS CO OR ... 200-C4
N BORSETH ST Rt#-9
SEDRO-WOOLLEY WA ... 161-C5
BOSK RD
SNOHOMISH CO WA ... 168-B3
BOSSBURG RD
STEVENS CO WA ... 106-A1
BOSTIAN RD
SNOHOMISH CO WA ... 171-D6
BOSTON ST
SEATTLE WA ... 277-H1
BOSTON HARBOR RD NE
THURSTON CO WA ... 180-C5
BOSTON MILL DR
LINN CO OR ... 210-B1
BOSWELL RD
DOUGLAS CO OR ... 219-B3
NE BOTHELL WY Rt#-522
BOTHELL WA ... 171-B6
KENMORE WA ... 171-B6
KING CO WA ... 171-B6
LAKE FOREST PARK WA ... 171-B6
BOTHELL WY NE Rt#-522
BOTHELL WA ... 171-C6
LAKE FOREST PARK WA ... 171-B7
SHORELINE WA ... 171-B7
BOTHELL WY NE Rt#-527
BOTHELL WA ... 171-C6
BOTHELL WA ... 171-C6
BOTHELL EVERETT HWY Rt#-527
BOTHELL WA ... 171-C4
MILL CREEK WA ... 171-C4
SNOHOMISH CO WA ... 171-C4
BOTTLE BAY RD
BONNER CO ID ... 244-A3
BOULDER CREEK RD
ADAMS CO ID ... 131-C3
TILLAMOOK CO OR ... 251-A1
TILLAMOOK CO OR ... 197-C6
BOULDER LAKE RD
VALLEY CO ID ... 251-D6
BOULDER RIDGE RD
WASCO CO OR ... 202-C7
BOULEVARD PL
MERCER ISLAND WA ... 283-J3
BOULEVARD RD SE
OLYMPIA WA ... 297-C7
THURSTON CO WA ... 297-C10
BOUNDARY HWY Rt#-22A
NORTHPORT WA ... 106-B1
STEVENS CO WA ... 106-B1
BOUNDARY RD
CITY OF CHILLIWACK BC ... 102-C1
DISTRICT OF BURNABY BC ... 156-C5
DISTRICT OF BURNABY BC ... 255-F12
JACKSON CO OR ... 150-A1
PEND OREILLE CO WA ... 106-B1
VANCOUVER BC ... 156-C5
VANCOUVER BC ... 255-F12
W BOUNDARY RD
KLAMATH CO OR ... 142-C3
LANE CO OR ... 134-A3
BOUNDARY RD S
DISTRICT OF BURNABY BC ... 156-C5
VANCOUVER BC ... 156-C5
BOUNDARY BAY RD
DISTRICT OF DELTA BC ... 101-C1
WHATCOM CO WA ... 101-C1
BOUNDARY CREEK RD
BOUNDARY CO ID ... 107-A1
BOURBON RD
SHERMAN CO OR ... 127-C2
BOW RD
SKAGIT CO WA ... 161-A5
N BOWDISH RD
SPOKANE VALLEY WA ... 350-G7
S BOWDISH RD
SPOKANE VALLEY WA ... 350-G10
BOWDOIN WY
EDMONDS WA ... 171-A5
BOWE LN SE
KITSAP CO WA ... 174-C5
BOWEN RD
NANAIMO BC ... 93-A3
BOWERS BLVD
SAN JUAN CO WA ... 160-A5
BOWERS DR
LINN CO OR ... 210-B5
BOWES RD
GRAYS HARBOR CO WA ... 177-D2
BOW HILL RD
SKAGIT CO WA ... 161-A4
BOWLES RD
Finley WA ... 121-A3
BOWMAN RD
COLUMBIA CO WA ... 122-A2
BOWMAN HILL RD
COLUMBIA CO WA ... 122-A2
BOWMONT AV
KELSO WA ... 303-D6
BOWMONT RD
CANYON CO ID ... 147-B1
BOX CANYON-LE CLERC RD
PEND OREILLE CO WA ... 106-B1
BOYD RD
CHELAN CO WA ... 236-C2
CHELAN CO WA ... 236-C2
JACKSON CO OR ... 230-A5
YAKIMA CO WA ... 243-A3
BOYD ST
NEW WESTMINSTER BC ... 156-D6

BOYD ACRES RD
BEND OR ... 332-G4
BOYD LOOP RD
DUFUR OR ... 127-B2
WASCO CO OR ... 127-B2
BOYDSTUN ST
VALLEY CO ID ... 251-C5
N BOYER AV
SANDPOINT ID ... 244-A2
BOYER AV E
SEATTLE WA ... 274-B7
SEATTLE WA ... 278-B1
BOYER RD
DOUGLAS CO OR ... 225-B2
JOSEPHINE CO OR ... 229-B3
BOYLSTON AV E
SEATTLE WA ... 278-B2
BOZARTH RD
CROOK CO OR ... 213-B6
BOZY CREEK RD
GRAYS HARBOR CO WA ... 179-D6
SW BRACE POINT DR
SEATTLE WA ... 284-D3
BRADEN RD
WALLA WALLA CO WA ... 345-A14
BRADLEY RD
SKAGIT CO WA ... 161-A5
S BRADLEY RD
CLACKAMAS CO OR ... 200-A4
BRADNER RD
DISTRICT OF MATSQUI BC ... 102-A1
BRADSHAW RD
SKAGIT CO WA ... 161-A7
SKAGIT CO WA ... 168-A1
E BRADSHAW RD
SPOKANE CO WA ... 114-C2
BRADY LOOP RD
GRAYS HARBOR CO WA ... 179-A7
BRAEMAR DR N
DIST OF NORTH VANCOUVER BC ... 255-B2
E BRAEMERE RD
BOISE ID ... 253-D2
BRAGG RD
JACKSON CO OR ... 234-B2
BRAID ST
NEW WESTMINSTER BC ... 156-D5
NEW WESTMINSTER BC ... 157-A5
BRAINER RD
ISLAND CO WA ... 167-D7
BRAMHALL RD
COLUMBIA CO WA ... 122-A2
BRANCH RD
HARRAH WA ... 119-C2
YAKIMA WA ... 119-C2
YAKIMA CO WA ... 119-C2
YAKIMA CO WA ... 120-A2
BRANDON RD
LINN CO OR ... 210-B3
BRANDSTROM RD
SNOHOMISH CO WA ... 168-B3
BRANDYWINE RD
DESCHUTES CO OR ... 212-A7
BRANSTETTER RD
ADAMS CO ID ... 251-B3
BRATHOVDE RD
YAKIMA CO WA ... 243-B5
BRATTAIN DR
LINN CO OR ... 210-A1
BRAYS RD NW
DOUGLAS CO WA ... 236-A3
BRECHIN RD
NANAIMO BC ... 93-A3
BREITENBUSH RD
DETROIT OR ... 134-B1
MARION CO OR ... 134-B1
S BREMER RD
CLACKAMAS CO OR ... 199-C6
BRENNER RD NW
THURSTON CO WA ... 180-B6
BRENNER CANYON RD
MORROW CO OR ... 128-B2
BRETZ MINE RD
MALHEUR CO OR ... 154-B2
BREWER RD
KLICKITAT CO WA ... 196-C2
BREWERY GRADE ST
THE DALLES OR ... 196-C7
BREWSTER RD
LEBANON OR ... 133-C1
LINN CO OR ... 133-C1
BREYMAN ORCHARDS RD
YAMHILL CO OR ... 198-C2
BRIAN RANCH RD
CLACKAMAS CO OR ... 200-D3
BRIAR RD
CROOK CO OR ... 213-B6
BRIAR KNOB LOOP RD
MARION CO OR ... 205-D4
BRICE CREEK RD
LANE CO OR ... 141-C1
BRICKEL CREEK RD
KOOTENAI CO ID ... 115-A1
BRICK MILL RD
KITTITAS CO WA ... 241-B5
BRICK PILE RD
JACKSON CO OR ... 234-B5
BRICKYARD RD
TILLAMOOK CO OR ... 197-C5
NW BRIDGE AV U.S.-30
PORTLAND OR ... 192-B7
BRIDGE LN
JOSEPHINE CO OR ... 229-B3
BRIDGE RD
UMATILLA CO OR ... 129-A1
BRIDGE ST
FALLS CITY OR ... 125-B3
MIDVALE ID ... 139-B1
UKIAH OR ... 129-B3
UMATILLA CO OR ... 129-B3
WINTHROP WA ... 104-A2
BRIDGE ST U.S.-12
CLARKSTON WA ... 250-A6
LEWISTON ID ... 250-B4
BRIDGE ST U.S.-30
BAKER CITY OR ... 138-B1
E BRIDGE ST Rt#-47
VERNONIA OR ... 125-B1
N BRIDGE ST Rt#-27
PALOUSE WA ... 249-B1
S BRIDGE ST
SHERIDAN OR ... 125-B3
YAMHILL CO OR ... 125-B3
S BRIDGE ST Rt#-27
PALOUSE WA ... 249-B1
SW BRIDGE ST
GRANTS PASS OR ... 335-D9
PRAIRIE CITY OR ... 137-B2
BRIDGE ST N Rt#-173
BREWSTER WA ... 104-B3

BRIDGE ST S Rt#-173 STREET INDEX CALIFORNIA AV 361

STREET City State Page-Grid

BRIDGE ST S Rt#-173
BREWSTER WA 104-B3
BRIDGE ST SW Rt#-162
ORTING WA 182-C5
BRIDGE WY N
SEATTLE WA 273-J6
BRIDGE CREEK RD
FERRY CO WA 105-B3
Inchelium WA 105-B3
LAKE CO OR 143-B3
WHEELER CO OR 136-A1
BRIDGE CREEK RD SE
MARION CO OR 205-D6
BRIDGEFARMER RD
YAMHILL CO OR 198-B3
BRIDGEPORT HWY Rt#-174
GRAND COULEE WA 237-C3
BRIDGEPORT RD
BAKER CO OR 138-B1
CITY OF RICHMOND BC 156-B6
MALHEUR CO OR 138-B2
POLK CO OR 125-B3
SW BRIDGEPORT RD
TUALATIN OR 199-B4
TUALATIN OR 199-B4
BRIDGEPORT WY
LAKEWOOD WA 181-C4
BRIDGEPORT WY SW
LAKEWOOD WA 181-D4
PIERCE CO WA 181-D4
BRIDGEPORT WY W
LAKEWOOD WA 181-C3
TACOMA WA 181-C3
UNIVERSITY PLACE WA 181-C3
BRIDGEPORT HILL RD NE
DOUGLAS CO WA 112-C1
BRIDGEVIEW-TAKILMA RD
JOSEPHINE CO OR 233-B5
BRIDGEWATER RD
SKAGIT CO WA 161-C5
SW BRIEDWELL RD
YAMHILL CO OR 204-B2
BRIER RD
BRIER WA 171-B6
BRIGHTWOOD LOOP RD
CLACKAMAS CO OR 201-B4
BRIM CREEK RD
LEWIS CO WA 187-B4
BRIMSTONE RD
JOSEPHINE CO OR 229-A2
BRINES RD
COLUMBIA CO WA 122-A2
BRINK RD
DOUGLAS CO OR 222-D4
WHITMAN CO WA 122-B1
BRINN RD
COLUMBIA CO OR 192-A1
BRISTOL AV
Altamont OR 338-J12
Altamont OR 339-A12
BRISTOL RD
KLICKITAT CO WA 196-A4
BRITTON PKWY NE
LACEY WA 297-J2
THURSTON CO WA 297-J2
BRITT SLOUGH RD
MOUNT VERNON WA 260-B14
SKAGIT CO WA 260-B14
BROAD ST
BUTTE FALLS OR 150-A1
MOUNT VERNON WA 260-D13
SEATTLE WA 277-H4
BROADACRES RD NE
MARION CO OR 205-B1
BROADMEAD RD
POLK CO OR 204-A3
SW BROADMEAD RD
YAMHILL CO OR 204-B3
BROADWAY
BELLINGHAM WA 258-D5
DISTRICT OF BURNABY BC 156-D4
EVERETT WA 171-C1
EVERETT WA 264-E3
EVERETT WA 265-E7
EVERETT WA 268-E4
EVERETT WA 269-E1
HOQUIAM WA 178-A7
SEASIDE OR 301-G8
SEATTLE WA 278-B4
VANCOUVER WA 305-G4
BROADWAY Rt#-99
EVERETT WA 268-D5
BROADWAY Rt#-529
EVERETT WA 171-C1
E BROADWAY Rt#-99
EUGENE OR 330-B6
E BROADWAY Rt#-142
GOLDENDALE WA 127-C1
KLICKITAT CO WA 127-C1
NE BROADWAY
PORTLAND OR 313-H4
PORTLAND OR 314-B4
NW BROADWAY
PORTLAND OR 313-F5
S BROADWAY Rt#-99
EVERETT WA 268-C6
SW BROADWAY
PORTLAND OR 312-E7
PORTLAND OR 313-E6
SW BROADWAY Rt#-8
BEAVERTON OR 199-B2
W BROADWAY
MILTON-FREEWATER OR 121-C3
W BROADWAY Rt#-142
GOLDENDALE WA 127-C1
KLICKITAT CO WA 127-C1
BROADWAY E
SEATTLE WA 278-B4
BROADWAY E Rt#-7
VANCOUVER BC 254-H13
VANCOUVER BC 255-A13
BROADWAY NE
SALEM OR 322-J10
BROADWAY W
VANCOUVER BC 254-A12
BROADWAY W Rt#-7
VANCOUVER BC 254-E12
BROADWAY AV
MALDEN WA 114-B3
SNOHOMISH CO WA 171-D5
BROADWAY AV Rt#-171
GRANT CO WA 242-C3
MOSES LAKE WA 242-C3
BROADWAY AV U.S.-20
ADA CO ID 253-D3
BOISE ID 253-D3
E BROADWAY AV
SPOKANE VALLEY WA 349-G8
SPOKANE VALLEY WA 350-H7
E BROADWAY AV
SPOKANE VALLEY WA 351-A7
N BROADWAY AV
BOISE ID 253-D3
N BROADWAY AV U.S.-20
BURNS OR 145-B1
S BROADWAY AV Rt#-24
ADAMS CO WA 121-A1
OTHELLO WA 121-A1
S BROADWAY AV U.S.-20
BOISE ID 253-D3
SW BROADWAY DR
PORTLAND OR 312-E7
PORTLAND OR 316-D1
BROADWAY ST
ALBANY OR 326-A9
LINN CO OR 326-A9
MALIN OR 151-A3
NORTH BEND OR 333-F6
PORT COQUITLAM BC 157-B5
BROADWAY ST U.S.-30
BAKER CITY OR 138-B1
BROADWAY ST U.S.-195
COLTON WA 250-A1
E BROADWAY ST
MILTON-FREEWATER OR 121-C3
PASCO WA 343-H6
UMATILLA CO OR 121-C3
E BROADWAY ST U.S.-2
REARDAN WA 114-A2
N BROADWAY ST U.S.-101
COOS BAY OR 333-H9
NE BROADWAY ST
PORTLAND OR 314-B4
S BROADWAY ST U.S.-101
COOS BAY OR 333-H11
W BROADWAY ST U.S.-2
REARDAN WA 114-A2
BROCKDALE RD
MASON CO WA 180-A1
SW BROCKMAN ST
BEAVERTON OR 199-B2
BROCKWAY RD
DOUGLAS CO OR 221-A6
S BROCKWAY RD
CLACKAMAS CO OR 200-A7
BROENNEKE RD
LATAH CO ID 249-C7
BRONDT RD
KITTITAS CO WA 241-B6
BRONSON WY N Rt#-900
RENTON WA 175-C5
E BRONX RD
BONNER CO ID 244-A1
BROOKDALE AV
MEDFORD OR 336-H10
BROOKDALE RD E
PIERCE CO WA 182-A5
BROOKLAKE RD NE
MARION CO OR 204-D3
MARION CO OR 205-A3
BROOKLANE DR
BENTON CO OR 327-D13
CORVALLIS OR 327-D13
BROOKLEIGH RD
DISTRICT OF SAANICH BC 159-C4
SW BROOKMAN RD
WASHINGTON CO OR 199-A5
BROOKS AV NE
KEIZER OR 323-A6
MARION CO OR 323-A6
SALEM OR 323-A6
BROOKS LN SE
THURSTON CO WA 184-D1
BROOKS RD
PIERCE CO WA 182-C6
S BROOKS RD
MEDICAL LAKE WA 114-B2
SPOKANE CO WA 114-B2
SE BROOKS RD
CLACKAMAS CO OR 200-C3
W BROOKS RD
MEDICAL LAKE WA 114-B2
N BROOKS ST
MEDICAL LAKE WA 114-B2
BROOKSBANK AV
CITY OF NORTH VANCOUVER BC 255-E7
DIST OF N VANCOUVER BC 255-E7
BROOKS HILL RD
ISLAND CO WA 171-A1
LANGLEY WA 171-A1
BROOKSIDE BLVD
JOSEPHINE CO OR 229-B4
BROOKS MEADOW RD
HOOD RIVER CO OR 202-D3
WASCO CO OR 202-D3
BROOKS-SCANLON LOG RD
DESCHUTES CO OR 211-C3
DESCHUTES CO OR 212-A7
DESCHUTES CO OR 217-A1
NE BROOKWOOD PKWY
HILLSBORO OR 198-D1
BROOTEN RD
TILLAMOOK CO OR 197-A7
BROSI ORCHARD RD
WINSTON OR 221-B6
BROSTERHOUS RD
BEND OR 332-F10
BROWER RD
MULTNOMAH CO OR 200-D2
MULTNOMAH CO OR 201-A1
BROWN RD
CLACKAMAS CO OR 199-B5
DOUGLAS CO OR 225-A7
GLENDALE OR 225-A7
KITTITAS CO WA 241-B6
KLAMATH CO OR 231-B3
WHATCOM CO WA 158-B5
WHITMAN CO WA 249-C5
WILSONVILLE OR 199-B5
NE BROWN RD
CLARK CO WA 193-C6
SW BROWN RD
DESCHUTES CO OR 212-B7
BROWN RD E
LEWIS CO WA 187-B1
BROWN RD NE
Hayesville OR 323-F11
SALEM OR 323-F11
BROWN RD SW
THURSTON CO WA 180-B7
BROWN RD W
LEWIS CO WA 187-A1
W BROWN ST
PASCO WA 343-C6
BROWN CREEK RD
ADAMS CO ID 251-B2
GILLIAM CO OR 128-B3
LONEROCK OR 128-B3
N BROWNE ST U.S.-2
SPOKANE WA 349-A9
S BROWNE ST U.S.-2
SPOKANE WA 349-A10
SW BROWNELL AV
GRANTS PASS OR 335-D10
BROWNLEE RD
COLUMBIA CO OR 189-C5
BROWNSBORO EAGLE POINT HWY
JACKSON CO OR 149-C1
JACKSON CO OR 230-D5
BROWNS CANYON RD NW
DOUGLAS CO WA 236-B5
BROWNS CREEK RD
WASCO CO OR 196-B7
BROWNS POINT BLVD NE
TACOMA WA 181-D1
TACOMA WA 182-A1
BROWNSTOWN RD
HARRAH WA 119-C2
YAKIMA CO WA 119-C2
BROWNSVILLE RD
BROWNSVILLE OR 210-C1
LINN CO OR 210-C1
BROZIO RD
DOUGLAS CO OR 221-B2
BRUCE AV
NANAIMO BC 93-A3
BRUCE AV SW
BREWSTER WA 104-B3
N BRUCE RD
SPOKANE CO WA 246-D1
NW BRUGGER RD
WASHINGTON CO OR 192-A7
BRUKETTA RD
KITTITAS CO WA 240-D3
S BRUNA RD
SPOKANE CO WA 246-D6
BRUNDAGE RD
ADAMS CO ID 251-C4
BRUNETTE AV
COQUITLAM BC 157-A5
NEW WESTMINSTER BC 156-D5
NEW WESTMINSTER BC 157-A5
BRUNNER RD Rt#-500
CLARK CO WA 193-B6
W BRUNNER RD
KOOTENAI CO ID 245-A2
BRUSH COLLEGE RD NW
POLK CO OR 204-C4
POLK CO OR 322-A5
SALEM OR 322-E8
BRUSH CREEK DR NE
MARION CO OR 205-B4
BRUSH CREEK RD
LANE CO OR 133-C2
LINN CO OR 133-C2
VALLEY CO ID 251-D2
BRUSHY GULCH RD
JOSEPHINE CO OR 229-A1
BRUSSELLS ST
NORTH BEND OR 333-G7
BRYANT AV
WALLA WALLA WA 345-C9
Walla Walla East WA 345-C9
BRYANT RD
CLACKAMAS CO OR 320-A7
LAKE OSWEGO OR 199-C4
LAKE OSWEGO OR 320-A7
BRYANT WY
ALBANY OR 326-A7
LINN CO OR 207-C5
LINN CO OR 326-A7
BRYDEN AV
LEWISTON ID 250-C5
BRYNION ST
KELSO WA 303-E7
BRYSON SEARS RD
LANE CO OR 215-C7
BUCHANAN AV
CORVALLIS OR 327-G8
BUCHANAN LN
LA GRANDE OR 130-A2
UNION CO OR 130-A2
BUCKAROO PASS RD
HARNEY CO OR 153-A2
BUCKAROO SPRING RD
MALHEUR CO OR 138-B3
BUCK CANYON RD
JOSEPHINE CO OR 233-A5
BUCK CREEK RD
CROOK CO OR 144-B1
DOUGLAS CO OR 219-C2
LANE CO OR 209-C4
W BUCKEYE AV
SPOKANE WA 348-J6
BUCKEYE ST
WOODLAND WA 192-B1
BUCKEYE CREEK RD
DOUGLAS CO OR 226-B1
SW BUCKHAVEN RD
WASHINGTON CO OR 198-D4
YAMHILL CO OR 198-D4
BUCK HOLLOW RD
CROOK CO OR 136-B2
WHEELER CO OR 136-B2
BUCKHORN LN
GILLIAM CO OR 128-A3
BUCKHORN RD
DESCHUTES CO OR 212-B5
DOUGLAS CO OR 141-B2
DOUGLAS CO OR 221-C4
LEWIS CO WA 187-B2
WALLOWA CO OR 131-A1
BUCK LAKE RD
KLAMATH CO OR 235-A4
BUCKLEY BLVD
PIERCE CO WA 182-D4
BUCKLEY LN
JEFFERSON CO OR 208-C3
BUCKLEY RD
LEWIS CO WA 187-D3
BUCKLEY TAPPS HWY
PIERCE CO WA 182-D3
NE BUCKLIN HILL RD Rt#-303
KITSAP CO WA 174-B1
NW BUCKLIN HILL RD
Silverdale WA 174-B1
NW BUCKLIN HILL RD Rt#-303
KITSAP CO WA 174-B1
Silverdale WA 174-B1
BUCKLIN HILL RD NE
KITSAP CO WA 271-H3
BUCKNER CREEK RD
CLACKAMAS CO OR 199-D7
CLACKAMAS CO OR 200-A7
BUCK POINT RD
WHEELER CO OR 136-B2
BUCKSKIN CANYON RD
HUMBOLDT CO NV 154-B3
BUCODA HWY Rt#-507
LEWIS CO WA 184-C5
BUENA RD Rt#-22
YAKIMA CO WA 120-A2
BUENA WY Rt#-22
TOPPENISH WA 120-A2
BUENA VISTA
LANE CO OR 215-C4
BUENA VISTA RD
BENTON CO OR 207-B3
POLK CO OR 207-C2
BUENA VISTA RD S
MARION CO OR 207-C2
BUESING RD
KLAMATH CO OR 235-D7
SE BUFF ST
MADRAS OR 208-C5
BUFFALO DR
DESCHUTES CO OR 212-A4
BUFFALO LAKE RD S
OKANOGAN CO WA 105-A3
OKANOGAN CO WA 237-D1
BUFFALO LAKE ACCESS RD
OKANOGAN CO WA 237-D1
BUHMAN RD
SKAMANIA CO WA 193-D6
BULLARD RD
PACIFIC CO WA 117-A1
BULLARDS-PROSPER JUNCTION RD
COOS CO OR 220-B5
BULL CREEK RD
JOSEPHINE CO OR 229-A7
JOSEPHINE CO OR 233-D1
BULLDOG RD
DOUGLAS CO OR 222-B1
BULL FLAT RD
DESCHUTES CO OR 217-A1
BULLHEAD RD
KITSAP CO WA 170-B7
BULL LAKE RD Rt#-56
LINCOLN CO MT 107-C3
SANDERS CO MT 107-C3
SW BULL MOUNTAIN RD
TIGARD OR 199-A3
WASHINGTON CO OR 199-A3
BULL RUN RD
DOUGLAS CO OR 225-C6
SE BULL RUN RD
CLACKAMAS CO OR 200-D3
BULL RUN TO BAKER RD
GRANITE OR 137-C1
GRANT CO OR 137-C1
GRANT CO OR 138-A1
BULL SPRING RD
CROOK CO OR 136-B2
DESCHUTES CO OR 217-A1
WHEELER CO OR 136-B2
BULLY CREEK RD
MALHEUR CO OR 138-B3
BULSON RD
SKAGIT CO WA 168-B2
BUNCH RD
OKANOGAN CO WA 105-A1
BUNCO RD
KOOTENAI CO ID 245-B2
E BUNCO RD
KOOTENAI CO ID 245-B2
BUNKER CREEK RD
LEWIS CO WA 117-B1
LEWIS CO WA 184-A6
BUNKER KEYS RD
SKAMANIA CO WA 195-B4
BUNK FOSS RD
SNOHOMISH CO WA 171-D2
BURBEE HILL RD
CONCRETE WA 102-C2
SKAGIT CO WA 102-C2
BURCHAM ST
KELSO WA 303-E7
BURCH MOUNTAIN RD
CHELAN CO WA 238-D2
Sunnyslope WA 238-D2
BURDETT WY
WALLA WALLA CO WA 121-B3
N BURGARD ST
PORTLAND OR 192-B6
BURGDORF RD
KLAMATH CO OR 151-A2
BURGESS RD
DESCHUTES CO OR 143-A1
BURGUNDY RD
MASON CO WA 180-D3
BURK RD
WHATCOM CO WA 158-C3
BURKE RD Rt#-4
SHOSHONE CO ID 115-C2
WALLACE ID 115-C2
BURKE ST
DISTRICT OF BURNABY BC 156-C5
BURKE-CANYON CREEK RD Rt#-4
SHOSHONE CO ID 115-C2
SW BURKHALTER RD
WASHINGTON CO OR 198-D2
BURKHART ST
ALBANY OR 326-F8
BURKLAND RD
SKAGIT CO WA 168-B1
BURLEY DR
DIST OF WEST VANCOUVER BC 254-E2
SE BURLEY OLALLA RD
KITSAP CO WA 174-C6
BURLINGTON BLVD
BURLINGTON WA 260-C4
BURLINGTON BLVD Rt#-20
BURLINGTON WA 260-C4
S BURLINGTON BLVD
BURLINGTON WA 260-C8
S BURLINGTON BLVD Rt#-20
BURLINGTON WA 260-C6
BURLINGTON RD
KOOTENAI CO ID 247-C1
BURLINGTON-ALGER RD
BURLINGTON WA 260-C2
SKAGIT CO WA 161-B5
SKAGIT CO WA 260-C2
BURMA RD
DOUGLAS CO OR 225-D6
JEFFERSON CO OR 213-D1
KOOTENAI CO ID 248-A2
OKANOGAN CO WA 104-B3
BURMASTER RD
SKAGIT CO WA 161-C5
BURN RD
ARLINGTON WA 168-D5
GRANITE FALLS WA 102-C3
SNOHOMISH CO WA 102-C3
SNOHOMISH CO WA 168-D5
BURNETT RD
LEWIS CO WA 187-B3
E BURNETT RD
SPOKANE CO WA 246-D2
BURNETT-FAIRFAX Rt#-165
BUCKLEY WA 182-D5
CARBONADO WA 182-D5
PIERCE CO WA 182-D5
WILKESON WA 182-D5
BURNHAM DR NW
GIG HARBOR WA 174-C7
PIERCE CO WA 174-C7
NE BURNSIDE RD
GRESHAM OR 200-B2
W BURNSIDE RD
PORTLAND OR 199-B1
PORTLAND OR 199-B1
PORTLAND OR 312-B5
WASHINGTON CO OR 199-B1
BURNSIDE RD E
CITY OF VICTORIA BC 256-F6
BURNSIDE RD W
DISTRICT OF SAANICH BC 256-A2
TOWN OF VIEW ROYAL BC 256-C3
E BURNSIDE ST
PORTLAND OR 200-A1
PORTLAND OR 313-H5
PORTLAND OR 314-C5
PORTLAND OR 315-H6
SE BURNSIDE ST
GRESHAM OR 200-A1
W BURNSIDE ST
PORTLAND OR 312-C5
PORTLAND OR 313-E5
E BURNT CABIN RD
KOOTENAI CO ID 245-B4
BURNT MOUNTAIN RD Rt#-113
CLALLAM CO WA 163-B6
BURNT MOUNTAIN ACCESS RD
COOS CO OR 140-C2
BURNT RIVER CANYON RD
BAKER CO OR 138-B1
BURNT WOODS-HARLAN RD
LINCOLN CO OR 133-A1
BURRARD ST
VANCOUVER BC 254-F10
BURR CANYON RD Rt#-263
FRANKLIN CO WA 121-C2
BURRELL AV
LEWISTON ID 250-C5
BURRES RD
CLARK CO WA 192-D1
BURRI RD
LEWIS CO WA 187-A2
BURRIS ST
DISTRICT OF BURNABY BC 156-D5
BURROWS RD
GRAYS HARBOR CO WA 177-C6
WALLA WALLA CO WA 121-C3
BURROWS ST
ANACORTES WA 259-C6
BURSELL RD
POLK CO OR 204-A7
BURTON LN
WASHINGTON CO ID 139-B1
NE BURTON RD
VANCOUVER WA 306-E3
VANCOUVER WA 307-F3
BURTON-FRASER RD
TILLAMOOK CO OR 197-B2
BURWELL ST Rt#-304
BREMERTON WA 270-G11
BUSBY RD
WHITMAN CO WA 249-B5
BUSBY-JOHNSON RD
WHITMAN CO WA 249-B6
BUSCH RD
WHITMAN CO WA 250-A2
BUSH ST
Walla Walla East WA 345-E7
BUSH CREEK RD
GRAYS HARBOR CO WA 179-C6
SKAMANIA CO WA 195-A4
BUSH GARDEN DR
LINN CO OR 210-B6
BUSHLACH RD
SKAMANIA CO WA 193-D7
BUSH POINT RD
Freeland WA 170-C1
ISLAND CO WA 170-C1
BUSH RANCH TO COUNTY LINE RD
GRANT CO OR 136-C3
BUSHWELL RD
GRAYS HARBOR CO WA 179-B7
NE BUTLER AV
DESCHUTES CO OR 213-A4
BUTLER BLVD
MALHEUR CO OR 139-A3
BUTLER RD
COLUMBIA CO OR 189-C6
CROOK CO OR 213-A3
SW BUTLER RD
GRESHAM OR 200-A2
BUTLER BRIDGE RD SE
LINCOLN CO OR 206-C5
TOLEDO OR 206-C4
BUTLER CREEK RD
BONNER CO ID 244-A5
DOUGLAS CO OR 218-D1
KOOTENAI CO ID 248-D4
SKAGIT CO WA 161-B3
BUTLER GRADE RD
UMATILLA CO OR 121-B3
BUTLER MARKET RD
DESCHUTES CO OR 217-D2
NE BUTLER MARKET RD
BEND OR 217-C2
BEND OR 332-G4
DESCHUTES CO OR 217-C2
BUTLER MKT RD
BEND OR 332-F4
BUTTE AV
JEFFERSON CO OR 208-B6
BUTTE CT
WEST RICHLAND WA 340-A12
BUTTE RD
CANYON CO ID 147-C2
CLACKAMAS CO OR 200-A7
BUTTE ST U.S.-97
DORRIS CA 150-B3
E BUTTE ST
PASCO WA 343-H8
BUTTE CREEK RD
CLACKAMAS CO OR 205-D4
WHEELER CO OR 128-A3
BUTTE FALLS RD
BUTTE FALLS OR 150-A1
JACKSON CO OR 149-C1
JACKSON CO OR 150-A1
JACKSON CO OR 230-D4
BUTTE FALLS-FISH LAKE RD
JACKSON CO OR 150-A1
BUTTE FALLS-PROSPECT RD
BUTTE FALLS OR 150-A1
JACKSON CO OR 150-A1
JACKSON CO OR 226-C7
BUTTER CREEK RD
MORROW CO OR 128-C1
MORROW CO OR 129-A2
UMATILLA CO OR 128-C1
UMATILLA CO OR 129-A2
BUTTER CREEK RD Rt#-207
HERMISTON OR 129-A1
UMATILLA CO OR 129-A1
BUTTERMILK CANYON RD
GILLIAM CO OR 128-B3
MORROW CO OR 128-B3
BUTTEVILLE RD
CLACKAMAS CO OR 199-B6
MARION CO OR 199-A7
MARION CO OR 205-B1
BUTTEVILLE RD NE
GERVAIS OR 205-B2
MARION CO OR 205-B1
BUTTEVILLE RD NE Rt#-219
MARION CO OR 205-B1
BUTTON
PIERCE CO WA 182-B6
BUTTON BRIDGE RD U.S.-30
HOOD RIVER CO OR 195-D5
BUYSERIE RD
MARION CO OR 198-D7
BUZZARD MINE RD
JACKSON CO OR 226-B5
SE BYBEE BLVD
PORTLAND OR 317-J5
PORTLAND OR 318-A5
BYBEE CREEK RD
JACKSON CO OR 226-D3
BYBEE CREEK BRANCH RD
JACKSON CO OR 227-A3
SE BYERS AV
PENDLETON OR 129-B1
NW BYHAM RD
LEWIS CO WA 187-C3
BY-PASS HWY
RICHLAND WA 340-F11
BY-PASS HWY Rt#-240
RICHLAND WA 340-E12
RICHLAND WA 341-E3
BYRAM RD
DESCHUTES CO OR 217-D3
BYRNES RD
WALLA WALLA CO WA 121-B3
B Z CORNER-GLENWOOD RD
KLICKITAT CO WA 119-A3
KLICKITAT CO WA 195-D2
KLICKITAT CO WA 196-A1

C

C AV
LA GRANDE OR 130-A2
C RD NW Rt#-172
DOUGLAS CO WA 112-B1
C ST
CULVER OR 208-B7
NESPELEM WA 105-A3
PORT ANGELES WA 261-C4
VANCOUVER WA 305-G4
WALLA WALLA CO WA 345-H4
C ST Rt#-214
SILVERTON OR 205-C4
E C ST
RAINIER OR 189-C4
NE C ST
COLLEGE PLACE WA 344-F9
WALLA WALLA CO WA 344-F9
C ST NW
EPHRATA WA 112-C3
C ST S
PIERCE CO WA 181-D4
C ST SE
QUINCY WA 112-B3
C ST SW
AUBURN WA 182-B2
EPHRATA WA 112-C3
QUINCY WA 112-B3
CABIN LN
YAKIMA CO WA 243-B4
CABIN LAKE RD
LAKE CO OR 143-B2
CACHE CREEK RD
FERRY CO WA 105-B3
NESPELEM WA 105-B3
OKANOGAN CO WA 105-B3
CADBORO BAY RD
DISTRICT OF OAK BAY BC 257-D6
DISTRICT OF SAANICH BC 257-E5
CADLE RD
POLK CO OR 204-B5
CADY RD
JACKSON CO OR 149-B2
CAGEY RD
WHATCOM CO WA 158-C7
S CAHILL RD
SPOKANE CO WA 114-C2
CAIN RD SE
OLYMPIA WA 297-B9
CAIN LAKE RD
SKAGIT CO WA 161-B3
WHATCOM CO WA 161-B3
CALAMITY PEAK RD
SKAMANIA CO WA 190-C7
SKAMANIA CO WA 194-A1
CALAPOOIA ST
ALBANY OR 326-C8
CALAPOOYA ST Rt#-99
DOUGLAS CO OR 221-C1
SUTHERLIN OR 221-C1
CALAWAH WY
CLALLAM CO WA 169-D1
CALDWELL BLVD U.S.-30
CANYON CO ID 147-B1
NAMPA ID 147-B1
CALEB PIKE RD
BRITISH COLUMBIA BC 159-B5
CALHOUN RD
SKAGIT CO WA 168-A1
CALIFORNIA AV
KLAMATH FALLS OR 338-C7

INDEX

STREET — City State Page-Grid

CALIFORNIA AV E
Colby WA ... 271-G13
CALIFORNIA AV SE
Colby WA ... 271-G14
CALIFORNIA AV SW
SEATTLE WA ... 276-E7
SEATTLE WA ... 280-E2
SEATTLE WA ... 284-D2
CALIFORNIA ST Rt#-238
JACKSONVILLE OR ... 149-B2
E CALIFORNIA ST
JACKSONVILLE OR ... 149-B2
E CALIFORNIA ST Rt#-238
JACKSONVILLE OR ... 149-B2
W CALIFORNIA ST Rt#-238
JACKSONVILLE OR ... 149-B2
CALIFORNIA WY
LONGVIEW WA ... 303-A11
CALIFORNIA WY SW
SEATTLE WA ... 276-E7
SEATTLE WA ... 280-E1
SEATTLE WA ... 281-E1
N CALIMUS RD
KLAMATH CO OR ... 151-A1
S CALISPELL AV
NEWPORT WA ... 106-C3
CALISTOGA AV
ORTING WA ... 182-C5
PIERCE CO WA ... 182-C5
CALISTOGA ST W
ORTING WA ... 182-C5
PIERCE CO WA ... 182-C5
CALKINS LN
YAMHILL CO OR ... 198-C4
NW CALKINS RD
ROSEBURG OR ... 334-C5
CALLAHAN RD
CLACKAMAS CO OR ... 126-A3
COLUMBIA CO OR ... 192-A4
S CALLAHAN RD
CLACKAMAS CO OR ... 126-A3
CALLIGAN AV
MAPLE RIDGE BC ... 157-C5
CALLOW AV N Rt#-304
BREMERTON WA ... 270-G10
CALLOW AV S Rt#-304
BREMERTON WA ... 270-G11
CALLOW RD
SNOHOMISH CO WA ... 171-D1
CALLOWAY RD
ADAMS CO WA ... 121-B1
CALONE RD
LANE CO OR ... 210-D7
CALVERT DR
DISTRICT OF DELTA BC ... 101-C1
DISTRICT OF DELTA BC ... 156-C7
CALVIN RD
LEWIS CO WA ... 187-C4
CAL YOUNG RD
EUGENE OR ... 329-J2
EUGENE OR ... 330-A2
CAMANO AV
ISLAND CO WA ... 171-A1
LANGLEY WA ... 171-A1
E CAMANO DR
ISLAND CO WA ... 167-D4
ISLAND CO WA ... 168-A7
N CAMANO DR
ISLAND CO WA ... 167-D4
S CAMANO DR
ISLAND CO WA ... 167-D6
ISLAND CO WA ... 168-A7
W CAMANO DR
ISLAND CO WA ... 167-D4
ISLAND CO WA ... 168-A6
CAMANO ST
STANWOOD WA ... 168-A4
CAMANO HILL RD
ISLAND CO WA ... 167-D5
ISLAND CO WA ... 168-A4
W CAMANO HILL RD
ISLAND CO WA ... 167-D5
CAMANO RIDGE RD
ISLAND CO WA ... 167-D5
CAMAS RD
LEWIS CO ID ... 123-B2
CAMAS ST
UKIAH OR ... 129-B3
WINCHESTER ID ... 123-B2
CAMAS CREEK RD
CHELAN CO WA ... 238-B3
CAMAS PRAIRIE RD
MORROW CO OR ... 128-C3
WASCO CO OR ... 127-A3
CAMAS SWALE RD
CRESWELL OR ... 215-A5
LANE CO OR ... 215-A5
CAMBIE BRDG
VANCOUVER BC ... 254-G12
CAMBIE RD
CITY OF RICHMOND BC ... 156-B6
CAMBIE ST
VANCOUVER BC ... 156-B5
VANCOUVER BC ... 254-G14
CAMBRIAN AV N
BREMERTON WA ... 270-F11
CAMBRIAN AV S
BREMERTON WA ... 270-F11
CAMBRIAN AV S Rt#-304
BREMERTON WA ... 270-F12
E CAMERON RD
SPOKANE CO WA ... 247-A7
SW CAMERON RD
PORTLAND OR ... 316-A4
CAMERON ST
DISTRICT OF BURNABY BC ... 156-D5
DISTRICT OF COQUITLAM BC ... 156-D5
CAMERON WY
MOUNT VERNON WA ... 260-C11
CAMP RD
WHITMAN CO WA ... 122-A1
CAMP 2 RD
WHATCOM CO WA ... 161-B3
CAMP 10 RD
COLUMBIA CO OR ... 189-A7
CAMP 12 RD
CHELAN CO WA ... 111-C1
CAMP 12 RIVERSIDE LN
LINCOLN CO OR ... 206-C2
CAMP ADAIR RD
BENTON CO OR ... 207-B3
CAMP BAY RD
BONNER CO ID ... 244-C3
CAMPBELL RD
ISLAND CO WA ... 171-A2
JACKSON CO OR ... 234-B2
KLAMATH CO OR ... 151-B1
Otis Orchards WA ... 351-J3
SPOKANE CO WA ... 351-J3

CAMPBELL RD
YAKIMA CO WA ... 120-A2
S CAMPBELL RD
SPOKANE CO WA ... 247-A5
SW CAMPBELL RD
WASHINGTON CO OR ... 198-D3
CAMPBELL ST
BAKER CITY OR ... 138-B1
CAMPBELL ST Rt#-7
BAKER CITY OR ... 138-B1
CAMPBELL WY
BREMERTON WA ... 270-J8
CAMPBELL LAKE RD
SKAGIT CO WA ... 259-G11
S CAMPBELL LAKE RD
SKAGIT CO WA ... 259-G13
CAMP CREEK RD
BAKER CO OR ... 137-C1
CROOK CO OR ... 136-A3
DOUGLAS CO OR ... 140-C1
GRAYS HARBOR CO WA ... 178-D7
LANE CO WA ... 133-C3
LANE CO OR ... 215-D2
LANE CO OR ... 331-E4
E CAMP CREEK RD
BAKER CO OR ... 138-A2
CAMP DAVID JR RD
CLALLAM CO WA ... 164-A6
CAMP DISCOVERY RD
JEFFERSON CO WA ... 170-A5
CAMP HARMONY RD
JEFFERSON CO WA ... 170-A6
CAMP HAYDEN RD
CLALLAM CO WA ... 164-D5
CAMP KETTLE CREEK RD
MALHEUR CO OR ... 147-A1
CAMP MORRISON DR
LINN CO OR ... 134-A1
CAMP POLK RD
DESCHUTES CO OR ... 211-D4
DESCHUTES CO OR ... 212-A4
SISTERS OR ... 211-D5
CAMP SHERMAN RD
DESCHUTES CO OR ... 211-C2
JEFFERSON CO OR ... 211-C2
CAMP TWELVE LP
LINCOLN CO OR ... 206-C3
CAMPUS DR
KLAMATH FALLS OR ... 338-D6
SW CAMPUS DR
FEDERAL WAY WA ... 182-A1
CAMPUS WY
BENTON CO OR ... 327-C9
CORVALLIS OR ... 327-E9
CAMUS RD
LEWIS CO WA ... 187-C4
CAMWELL DR
DISTRICT OF WEST VANCOUVE BC ... 254-C1
CANAAN RD
COLUMBIA CO OR ... 189-B7
CANADA WY
DISTRICT OF BURNABY BC ... 156-D5
DISTRICT OF BURNABY BC ... 255-G14
CANADY RD
LEWIS CO WA ... 187-B5
CANAL BLVD
DESCHUTES CO OR ... 212-D6
N CANAL BLVD
DESCHUTES CO OR ... 212-D5
REDMOND OR ... 212-D5
S CANAL BLVD
DESCHUTES CO OR ... 212-D6
REDMOND OR ... 212-D6
W CANAL DR
KENNEWICK WA ... 342-D8
KENNEWICK WA ... 343-A9
CANAL RD
UMATILLA CO OR ... 129-A1
CANAL CREEK RD
LINCOLN CO OR ... 209-C2
CANAL W-20
GRANT CO WA ... 242-A1
CANARY RD
DUNES CITY OR ... 214-B4
LANE CO OR ... 214-B4
CANARY RD S
LANE CO OR ... 214-B4
CANARY CREEK RD
KOOTENAI CO ID ... 248-D3
CANBY-MARQUAM HWY
CLACKAMAS CO OR ... 205-D1
SE CANBY-MARQUAM HWY
CANBY OR ... 199-C7
CLACKAMAS CO OR ... 199-C7
CLACKAMAS CO OR ... 205-D1
CANDIANI RD
MARION CO OR ... 198-C7
CANDLEWOOD DR NE
KEIZER OR ... 323-A8
MARION CO OR ... 323-A8
SALEM OR ... 323-A8
CANFIELD LOOP RD
KOOTENAI CO ID ... 245-B6
CANNA ST N
SOAP LAKE WA ... 112-C2
CANNA ST S
SOAP LAKE WA ... 112-C2
CANNIBAL MOUNTAIN RD
LINCOLN CO OR ... 209-C3
CANORA RD
DISTRICT OF NORTH SAANICH BC ... 159-C2
TOWN OF SIDNEY BC ... 159-C2
CANTON CREEK RD
DOUGLAS CO OR ... 141-C1
S CANYON BLVD U.S.-395
JOHN DAY OR ... 137-B2
CANYON DR
DESCHUTES CO OR ... 212-C7
CANYON DR SE Rt#-516
KENT WA ... 175-C7
CANYON RD
ELLENSBURG WA ... 241-B6
GRAYS HARBOR CO WA ... 178-D4
KITTITAS CO WA ... 241-B6
KLICKITAT CO WA ... 196-B3
LANE CO WA ... 134-B3
WHITMAN CO WA ... 122-A1
NE CANYON RD
CLARK CO WA ... 193-B3
SW CANYON RD
JEFFERSON CO OR ... 208-B5
SW CANYON RD Rt#-8
BEAVERTON OR ... 199-B2
WASHINGTON CO OR ... 199-B2
CANYON RD E
PIERCE CO WA ... 182-A5
E CANYON ST Rt#-272
COLFAX WA ... 122-C1
WHITMAN CO WA ... 122-C1

CANYON WY
WASCO CO OR ... 196-B5
CANYON CITY EAST RD
CANYON CITY OR ... 137-B2
GRANT CO OR ... 137-B2
CANYON CREEK RD
CROOK CO OR ... 136-A2
DOUGLAS CO OR ... 225-C3
GRANT CO OR ... 137-B2
CANYON CREEK TR
SKAMANIA CO WA ... 193-D1
SKAMANIA CO WA ... 194-A1
CANYON CREST DR
DESCHUTES CO OR ... 212-A4
CANYONVIEW RD
YAMHILL CO OR ... 198-B3
CANYONVILLE-RIDDLE RD
CANYONVILLE OR ... 225-C3
DOUGLAS CO OR ... 225-C3
CAPE ARAGO HWY
Barview OR ... 220-C1
COOS BAY OR ... 333-B6
COOS CO OR ... 220-B2
COOS CO OR ... 333-A8
NORTH BEND OR ... 333-D6
CAPE BLANCO HWY
CURRY CO OR ... 224-A4
CAPE CREEK RD
LANE CO OR ... 209-A7
CAPE FERRELO RD
CURRY CO OR ... 232-C4
CAPE GEORGE RD
JEFFERSON CO WA ... 166-D6
JEFFERSON CO WA ... 263-A7
CAPE GEORGE RD W
JEFFERSON CO WA ... 166-D6
CAPE HORN RD
SKAMANIA CO WA ... 193-D7
E CAPE HORN RD
KOOTENAI CO ID ... 245-C1
CAPE KIWANDA DR
TILLAMOOK CO OR ... 197-A7
CAPE LOOKOUT RD
TILLAMOOK CO OR ... 197-A4
CAPE MEARES LOOP RD
TILLAMOOK CO OR ... 197-A2
CAPE SAINT MARY RD
SAN JUAN CO WA ... 160-A7
CAPE SEBASTIAN FRONTAGE RD
CURRY CO OR ... 228-A7
CAPILANO RD
DIST OF NORTH VANCOUVER BC ... 254-G3
CAPITAL MALL DR
OLYMPIA WA ... 296-C5
CAPITOL BLVD
OLYMPIA WA ... 296-H7
THURSTON CO WA ... 296-H13
TUMWATER WA ... 296-H10
S CAPITOL BLVD
BOISE ID ... 253-C3
SW CAPITOL HWY
PORTLAND OR ... 316-B6
PORTLAND OR ... 320-A1
SW CAPITOL HWY Rt#-10
PORTLAND OR ... 316-D4
PORTLAND OR ... 317-E4
CAPITOL ST NE
SALEM OR ... 322-J12
SALEM OR ... 323-A11
CAPITOL WY
OLYMPIA WA ... 296-H5
N CAPITOL WY
OLYMPIA WA ... 296-H5
CAPITOL HILL RD
MASON CO WA ... 180-B3
CAPLES RD
COWLITZ CO WA ... 192-B1
NE CAPLES RD
CLARK CO WA ... 193-A4
CAPLINGER RD SE
MARION CO OR ... 325-G2
SALEM OR ... 325-G2
CARAVELLE RD
KOOTENAI CO ID ... 245-B2
CARBERRY RD
JACKSON CO OR ... 149-B2
JOSEPHINE CO OR ... 149-B2
CARBUHN RD
NEZ PERCE CO ID ... 250-B2
NW CARDEN AV
PENDLETON OR ... 129-B1
CARDWELL RD
DESCHUTES CO OR ... 217-D2
CAREY RD
DISTRICT OF SAANICH BC ... 256-D1
CAREY ST
MANZANITA OR ... 191-B4
TILLAMOOK CO OR ... 191-B4
CARIBOO RD
DISTRICT OF BURNABY BC ... 156-D5
NEW WESTMINSTER BC ... 156-D5
CARIBOU RD
KITTITAS CO WA ... 241-D6
CARICO HILLS RD
ADAMS CO WA ... 114-A3
CARKEEK DR S
SEATTLE WA ... 287-E4
CARL RD NE
MARION CO OR ... 205-B1
CARLIN BAY RD
KOOTENAI CO ID ... 248-A2
CARLIN CREEK RD
KOOTENAI CO ID ... 248-A3
CARLISLE AV
LEWIS CO WA ... 118-A2
CARLOCK RD NW
DOUGLAS CO WA ... 236-C6
NW CARLON AV
BEND OR ... 332-D8
CARLON RD
LAKE CO OR ... 143-C3
CARLSBORG RD
CLALLAM CO WA ... 166-A7
CARLSON RD
LINCOLN CO WA ... 113-C2
S CARLSON RD
YAKIMA CO WA ... 243-A7
W CARLSON RD
SPOKANE CO WA ... 246-A1
CARLYLE HALL RD NW
SHORELINE WA ... 171-A6
CARMAN DR
CLACKAMAS CO OR ... 199-B3
CLACKAMAS CO OR ... 320-A6
LAKE OSWEGO OR ... 199-B3
LAKE OSWEGO OR ... 320-A6
CARMARIA CT
DIST OF NORTH VANCOUVER ... 255-F4

CARMEL RD
COLUMBIA CO OR ... 189-B5
CARMICHAEL DR
KENNEWICK WA ... 343-C11
S CARNAHAN RD
SPOKANE CO WA ... 349-H11
SPOKANE VALLEY WA ... 349-H11
CARNATION-DUVALL RD NE Rt#-203
DUVALL WA ... 110-C1
KING CO WA ... 110-C1
KING CO WA ... 176-A1
NE CARNATION FARM RD
KING CO WA ... 176-B1
SW CARNES RD
DOUGLAS CO OR ... 221-B6
DOUGLAS CO OR ... 223-C4
CARNEY LAKE RD SW
KITSAP CO WA ... 174-A6
S CARNIE RD
KOOTENAI CO ID ... 247-D4
W CARNIE RD
KOOTENAI CO ID ... 247-D4
CARNINE RD
COWLITZ CO WA ... 187-D7
CAROLINA ST
SKAGIT CO WA ... 259-J14
WALLA WALLA CO WA ... 121-C2
CAROLINA ST U.S.-20
LEBANON OR ... 133-C1
CAROLYN DR
DISTRICT OF NORTH VANCOUV BC ... 254-J1
CAROTHERS RD
WHITMAN CO WA ... 249-A5
CARPENTER RD NE
LACEY WA ... 297-J3
THURSTON CO WA ... 297-J3
CARPENTER RD SE
LACEY WA ... 181-A7
LACEY WA ... 297-J6
THURSTON CO WA ... 181-A7
THURSTON CO WA ... 297-J6
CARPENTER CREEK RD
WASHINGTON CO OR ... 198-A1
CARPENTER HILL RD
JACKSON CO OR ... 234-A2
CARPENTERVILLE FRONTAGE RD
CURRY CO OR ... 232-C2
CARPER ST SW
THURSTON CO WA ... 184-B4
CARR RD
ADAMS CO ID ... 251-A5
KING CO WA ... 175-C6
RENTON WA ... 175-C6
S CARR RD
KING CO WA ... 175-C6
RENTON WA ... 175-C6
SE CARR RD
KING CO WA ... 175-C5
RENTON WA ... 175-C5
CARRALL ST
VANCOUVER BC ... 254-H10
CARRIE ST
JOSEPHINE CO OR ... 229-C2
CARROL RD
WASCO CO OR ... 196-A6
CARROLL AV
BONANZA OR ... 151-A2
KLAMATH CO OR ... 151-A2
CARROLL RD
LEWIS CO WA ... 187-C1
CARROLL WY
LEWIS CO WA ... 187-A1
CARRS INLET WOLLOCHET
PIERCE CO WA ... 181-B1
CARSON GULER RD
SKAMANIA CO WA ... 194-D1
SKAMANIA CO WA ... 195-A1
CARTER RD SE
MARION CO OR ... 205-C7
CARTNEY DR
LINN CO OR ... 210-A3
N CARTWRIGHT RD
ADA CO ID ... 253-C1
BOISE ID ... 253-C1
NW CARTY RD
CLARK CO WA ... 192-C3
S CARUS RD
CLACKAMAS CO OR ... 199-D6
CLACKAMAS CO OR ... 200-A6
SW CARUTHERS ST
PORTLAND OR ... 317-E1
SE CARVER HWY Rt#-212
CLACKAMAS CO OR ... 200-A3
CASCADE AV
LANGLEY WA ... 171-A1
CASCADE AV U.S.-30
HOOD RIVER OR ... 195-C5
HOOD RIVER OR ... 195-C5
NE CASCADE AV
CHEHALIS WA ... 299-D11
NW CASCADE AV
DOUGLAS CO WA ... 239-A3
East Wenatchee Bench WA ... 239-A3
CASCADE DR
JOSEPHINE CO OR ... 233-A5
CASCADE HWY
BURLINGTON WA ... 260-D4
MARION CO OR ... 205-B6
SILVERTON OR ... 205-B6
CASCADE HWY Rt#-9
SEDRO-WOOLLEY WA ... 161-C6
CASCADE HWY Rt#-20
BURLINGTON WA ... 260-E4
SEDRO-WOOLLEY WA ... 161-C6
SEDRO-WOOLLEY WA ... 260-E4
SKAGIT CO WA ... 260-E4
CASCADE HWY Rt#-213
CLACKAMAS CO OR ... 205-C4
SE CASCADE HWY Rt#-213
CLACKAMAS CO OR ... 199-D3
CASCADE HWY S Rt#-213
CLACKAMAS CO OR ... 126-A3
CLACKAMAS CO OR ... 199-D4
CLACKAMAS CO OR ... 205-D3
MARION CO OR ... 205-D3
MOLALLA OR ... 126-A3
OREGON CITY OR ... 199-D4
CASCADE HWY SE
MARION CO OR ... 133-C1
MARION CO OR ... 205-C7
SUBLIMITY OR ... 133-C1
CASCADE RD
GEM CO ID ... 139-B3
SKAGIT CO WA ... 103-A2
CASCADE ST U.S.-20
SISTERS OR ... 211-D5

CASCADE VW
EVERETT WA ... 265-E6
W CASCADE WY
Town and Country WA ... 346-J13
Town and Country WA ... 347-A13
CASCADE CREEK RD
LINCOLN CO OR ... 209-C3
CASCADE CREST TR
SKAMANIA CO WA ... 195-A1
CASCADE ESTATES DR
DESCHUTES CO OR ... 212-A6
CASCADE HEAD RD
TILLAMOOK CO OR ... 203-B3
CASCADE LAKES HWY
DESCHUTES CO OR ... 216-B3
DOUGLAS CO OR ... 223-C4
CASCADE LOCKS HWY U.S.-30
CASCADE LOCKS OR ... 194-D5
CASCADIA WY
SNOHOMISH CO WA ... 171-C4
CASE RD
MARION CO OR ... 199-A7
CASE RD SW
THURSTON CO WA ... 184-C1
CASEY RD
COWLITZ CO WA ... 187-C6
CASEY CREEK RD
GARFIELD CO WA ... 122-B1
CASHMUR CT
DESCHUTES CO OR ... 212-C5
CASHUP NORTH RD
WHITMAN CO WA ... 114-C3
E CASINO RD
EVERETT WA ... 268-C4
W CASINO RD
EVERETT WA ... 267-H5
EVERETT WA ... 268-A4
CASON RD
TILLAMOOK CO OR ... 197-D5
SE CASON RD
CLACKAMAS CO OR ... 199-D4
GLADSTONE OR ... 199-D4
NE CASPER ST
ROSEBURG OR ... 334-H7
CASPERS ST Rt#-524
EDMONDS WA ... 171-A5
SE CASS AV
ROSEBURG OR ... 334-F8
W CASSIA ST
BOISE ID ... 253-C3
W CASTLE DR
BOISE ID ... 253-C2
CASTLE CREEK RD
JACKSON CO OR ... 226-D3
JACKSON CO OR ... 227-A3
OWYHEE CO ID ... 147-C3
CASTLEMAN RD
CITY OF CHILLIWACK BC ... 94-C3
CASTLEROCK AV
WENATCHEE WA ... 238-D4
CASTLE ROCK RD
MALHEUR CO OR ... 138-A3
CASTLE ROCK TKTR
COWLITZ CO WA ... 187-A6
W CASWELL ST
ADA CO ID ... 253-B1
BOISE ID ... 253-B1
CATALA AV SE
OCEAN SHORES WA ... 298-F4
W CATALPA DR
BOISE ID ... 253-C2
CATCHING CREEK RD
COOS CO OR ... 140-B3
COOS CO OR ... 220-D7
E CATCHING SLOUGH RD
COOS CO OR ... 140-B2
COOS CO OR ... 220-D1
CATER RD
COLUMBIA CO OR ... 192-A2
CATHERINE ST
CITY OF VICTORIA BC ... 256-F8
CATHERINE CREEK LN
UNION CO OR ... 130-B3
CATLIN ST
KELSO WA ... 303-C8
CATLOW VALLEY RD
HARNEY CO OR ... 153-B2
CATLOW VALLEY RD Rt#-205
HARNEY CO OR ... 153-B1
CATRON RD
WASCO CO OR ... 196-A6
CATTLE POINT RD
SAN JUAN CO WA ... 101-C2
CAVALERO RD
SNOHOMISH CO WA ... 171-D2
CAVE CREEK RD
SKAMANIA CO WA ... 195-B1
CAVENDISH RD
CLEARWATER CO ID ... 123-B2
CAVITT CREEK RD
DOUGLAS CO OR ... 141-B2
CAYS RD
CLALLAM CO WA ... 166-A6
CAYUSE RD
Mission OR ... 129-C1
UMATILLA CO OR ... 129-C1
CC ST
WOODLAND WA ... 192-B1
CECIL RD
MORROW CO OR ... 128-B1
CEDAR AV
PIERCE CO WA ... 182-A6
S CEDAR AV
PASCO WA ... 343-J8
CEDAR DR
COLUMBIA CO OR ... 189-B4
COQUITLAM BC ... 157-B4
PORT COQUITLAM BC ... 157-B4
W CEDAR DR
WALDPORT OR ... 328-D5
N CEDAR RD
SPOKANE CO WA ... 114-B1
CEDAR ST
BAKER CITY OR ... 138-B1
BAKER CO OR ... 138-B1
BINGEN WA ... 195-D5
DISTRICT OF MISSION BC ... 94-B3
KELSO WA ... 303-D9
SANDPOINT ID ... 244-A2
CEDAR ST Rt#-5
BENEWAH CO ID ... 115-A2
BENEWAH CO ID ... 248-A1
PLUMMER ID ... 115-A2
CEDAR ST Rt#-231
STEVENS CO WA ... 106-B3
CEDAR ST U.S.-95
SANDPOINT ID ... 244-A2

E CEDAR ST
MCCLEARY WA ... 179-D6
N CEDAR ST
COLFAX WA ... 122-C1
WALDPORT OR ... 328-D4
N CEDAR ST Rt#-99
DRAIN OR ... 219-A3
NE CEDAR ST
ROSEBURG OR ... 334-F5
S CEDAR ST
SPOKANE WA ... 348-H12
TACOMA WA ... 292-D6
TACOMA WA ... 294-D1
WALDPORT OR ... 328-D5
S CEDAR ST Rt#-99
DRAIN OR ... 219-A3
CEDAR WY
MAPLE RIDGE BC ... 157-C5
CEDAR BURN RD
WASCO CO OR ... 126-C3
CEDAR CREEK RD
CLARK CO WA ... 118-A3
LANE CO OR ... 219-C2
LATAH CO ID ... 123-B1
CEDARDALE RD
MOUNT VERNON WA ... 168-B2
MOUNT VERNON WA ... 260-C14
SKAGIT CO WA ... 168-B2
SKAGIT CO WA ... 260-C14
CEDAR FALLS RD SE
KING CO WA ... 176-C6
CEDAR FLAT RD
JOSEPHINE CO OR ... 149-A2
CEDAR FLATS RD SW
THURSTON CO WA ... 180-B6
CEDAR GROVE RD
COLUMBIA CO OR ... 189-A4
KING CO WA ... 175-D6
KING CO WA ... 176-A5
CEDAR HILL RD
CITY OF VICTORIA BC ... 256-J6
DISTRICT OF SAANICH BC ... 159-D5
DISTRICT OF SAANICH BC ... 256-J6
DISTRICT OF SAANICH BC ... 257-A1
CEDAR HILL CROSS RD
DISTRICT OF OAK BAY BC ... 257-B4
DISTRICT OF SAANICH BC ... 256-H2
DISTRICT OF SAANICH BC ... 257-B4
SW CEDAR HILLS BLVD
BEAVERTON OR ... 199-B2
CEDARHOME RD
SNOHOMISH CO WA ... 168-B3
CEDAR LINKS RD
JACKSON CO OR ... 336-G8
MEDFORD OR ... 336-G8
N CEDAR PARK RD
LANE CO OR ... 215-C7
CEDAR RIVER PIPELINE RD
KING CO WA ... 176-A7
MAPLE VALLEY WA ... 176-A7
CEDAR SPRINGS RD
GILLIAM CO OR ... 128-C3
CEDAR SWAMP RD
SKAMANIA CO WA ... 194-B6
N CEDARVALE LOOP RD
SNOHOMISH CO WA ... 168-D3
CEDARVILLE RD
HUMBOLDT CO NV ... 153-A3
WASHOE CO NV ... 153-A3
CEDARWOOD AV
BELLINGHAM WA ... 258-A3
WHATCOM CO WA ... 258-A3
CEDARWOOD RD NE
MARION CO OR ... 199-B7
CEDONIA-ADDY Y RD
STEVENS CO WA ... 105-C3
STEVENS CO WA ... 106-A3
E CELESTA AV
SPOKANE WA ... 349-C10
CELILO-WASCO HWY Rt#-206
SHERMAN CO OR ... 127-C1
N CEMENT ST
SPOKANE VALLEY WA ... 350-H4
CEMETERY RD
ADAMS CO ID ... 251-B3
ASOTIN CO WA ... 250-B6
CANYON CO ID ... 147-B1
KLICKITAT CO WA ... 119-A3
LANE CO OR ... 215-B7
SNOHOMISH CO WA ... 168-C3
WINLOCK WA ... 187-C3
CEMETERY RD Rt#-55
MARSING ID ... 147-B1
OWYHEE CO ID ... 147-B1
CEMETERY RD U.S.-95
OWYHEE CO ID ... 147-B1
S CEMETERY RD
CLACKAMAS CO OR ... 205-D4
SW CEMETERY RD
KING CO WA ... 174-D6
CEMETERY HILL RD
COLUMBIA CO WA ... 122-A2
CENTENNIAL BLVD
EUGENE OR ... 330-C5
SPRINGFIELD OR ... 330-H6
SPRINGFIELD OR ... 331-B6
W CENTENNIAL BLVD
LANE CO OR ... 330-C5
LANE CO OR ... 330-E6
E CENTENNIAL ST
CALDWELL ID ... 147-B1
CENTENNIAL TR
SPOKANE CO WA ... 348-B5
CENTENNIAL WY U.S.-30
CALDWELL ID ... 147-B1
CENTER AV Rt#-25
NORTHPORT WA ... 106-A1
STEVENS CO WA ... 106-A1
E CENTER AV
PAYETTE ID ... 139-C2
CENTER DR
DUPONT WA ... 181-B5
N CENTER PKWY
KENNEWICK WA ... 342-E6
CENTER RD
JEFFERSON CO WA ... 109-C1
JEFFERSON CO WA ... 170-A2
CENTER ST
SUBLIMITY OR ... 133-C1
N CENTER ST
SPOKANE WA ... 349-C6
S CENTER ST
TACOMA WA ... 294-B1
TACOMA WA ... 295-E1
CENTER ST E
EATONVILLE WA ... 118-B1
CENTER ST NE
Four Corners OR ... 204-D6
Four Corners OR ... 323-F13

INDEX

STREET City State	Page-Grid
CENTER ST NE	
MARION CO OR	323-F13
SALEM OR	322-H12
SALEM OR	323-B13
CENTER ST NE Rt#-22	
SALEM OR	322-H12
CENTER ST W	
EATONVILLE WA	118-B1
CENTER RIDGE MARKET RD	
WASCO CO OR	127-B2
CENTER SCHOOL RD	
LINN CO OR	210-C3
CENTER ST BRDG Rt#-22	
SALEM OR	322-H12
CENTER ST BRDG NE Rt#-22	
SALEM OR	322-H12
CENTERVILLE HWY	
KLICKITAT CO WA	196-D5
CENTRAL	
DESCHUTES CO OR	212-A6
CENTRAL AV	
COOS BAY OR	333-G10
GRANTS PASS OR	335-D10
E CENTRAL AV	
DOUGLAS CO OR	221-C1
SUTHERLIN OR	221-C1
N CENTRAL AV	
JACKSON CO OR	336-B10
MEDFORD OR	336-C10
S CENTRAL AV	
WATERVILLE WA	236-C7
S CENTRAL AV U.S.-2	
WATERVILLE WA	236-C7
SW CENTRAL AV	
GRANTS PASS OR	335-E10
CENTRAL AV N	
KENT WA	175-C6
CENTRAL AV N Rt#-516	
KENT WA	175-C7
CENTRAL AV S	
AUBURN WA	175-B7
GRANT CO WA	112-B3
KENT WA	175-B7
KING CO WA	175-B7
QUINCY WA	112-B3
CENTRAL AV S Rt#-281	
GRANT CO WA	112-B3
QUINCY WA	112-B3
CENTRAL AV S Rt#-516	
KENT WA	175-C7
CENTRAL AV W	
OROVILLE WA	104-C1
CENTRAL BLVD U.S.-95	
CAMBRIDGE ID	139-B1
WASHINGTON CO ID	139-B1
N CENTRAL BLVD Rt#-42	
COQUILLE OR	220-D4
W CENTRAL BLVD Rt#-42	
COQUILLE OR	220-D4
CENTRAL DR	
MOSES LAKE WA	242-C3
MUKILTEO WA	266-C7
CENTRAL RD	
LANE CO OR	133-B3
CENTRAL WY	
KIRKLAND WA	175-C1
CENTRAL FERRY CANYON RD	
DOUGLAS CO OR	112-B1
CENTRAL GRADE RD	
NEZ PERCE CO ID	250-C3
CENTRALIA ALPHA RD	
LEWIS CO WA	118-A1
LEWIS CO WA	184-C6
LEWIS CO WA	299-H8
CENTRAL OREGON HWY U.S.-20	
BEND OR	217-C2
BEND OR	332-G7
BURNS OR	145-A1
DESCHUTES CO OR	135-B3
DESCHUTES CO OR	143-C1
DESCHUTES CO OR	144-A1
DESCHUTES CO OR	217-C2
HARNEY CO OR	138-A3
HARNEY CO OR	144-B1
HARNEY CO OR	145-A1
HARNEY CO OR	146-A1
HINES OR	145-A1
LAKE CO OR	144-A1
MALHEUR CO OR	138-C3
MALHEUR CO OR	139-A3
MALHEUR CO OR	146-A1
NYSSA OR	139-A3
VALE OR	138-C3
VALE OR	139-A3
S CENTRAL POINT RD	
CLACKAMAS CO OR	199-C6
CENTRAL RIDGE RD	
LEWIS CO ID	123-C2
NEZ PERCE CO ID	123-C2
PECK ID	123-C2
CENTRAL SAANICH RD	
DISTRICT OF CENTRAL SAANI BC	159-C4
CENTRAL VALE DR	
HOOD RIVER CO OR	195-C7
CENTRAL VALLEY RD NE	
KITSAP CO WA	174-B1
KITSAP CO WA	270-G3
Tracyton WA	270-G3
CENTRAL VALLEY RD NW	
KITSAP CO WA	270-G1
CENTURY DR	
ALBANY OR	326-H6
LINN CO OR	326-H6
S CENTURY DR	
DESCHUTES CO OR	143-A1
DESCHUTES CO OR	216-D7
DESCHUTES CO OR	217-A6
Three Rivers OR	216-D7
Three Rivers OR	217-A7
CENTURY LN	
WALLOWA CO OR	130-C2
CENTURY DRIVE HWY Rt#-372	
BEND OR	217-B3
BEND OR	332-A11
DESCHUTES CO OR	216-C4
DESCHUTES CO OR	217-A6
DESCHUTES CO OR	332-A11
CERES HILL RD	
LEWIS CO WA	184-A7
LEWIS CO WA	187-A1
SE CHADWICK ST	
ROSEBURG OR	334-G8
CHAIN LAKE RD	
SNOHOMISH CO WA	110-C1
CHALET RD	
DISTRICT OF NORTH SAANICH BC	159-B1
CHALK BUTTE RD	
MALHEUR CO OR	139-A3

STREET City State	Page-Grid
CHALK HILLS RD NE	
DOUGLAS CO WA	112-C1
CHAMBER OF COMMERCE WY	
CHEHALIS WA	299-D10
CHAMBERS LN W	
UNIVERSITY PLACE WA	181-C3
CHAMBERS RD	
WHITMAN CO WA	249-B7
CHAMBERS ST	
EUGENE OR	329-G6
LANE CO OR	329-G9
CHAMBERS CREEK RD	
PIERCE CO WA	181-C3
STEILACOOM WA	181-C3
UNIVERSITY PLACE WA	181-C3
CHAMBERS CREEK RD W	
UNIVERSITY PLACE WA	181-C3
CHAMPOEG RD	
MARION CO OR	198-D6
MARION CO OR	199-A7
CHANCE RD	
TILLAMOOK CO OR	197-C3
CHANCELLOR BLVD	
UNIV ENDOWMENT LANDS BC	156-A4
CHANDLER LN	
BAKER CO OR	130-B3
CHANDLER RD	
LAKE OSWEGO OR	321-E5
CHANEY RD	
LATAH CO ID	249-C2
CHANNEL DR	
SKAGIT CO WA	160-D7
CHANNEL VIEW DR	
SKAGIT CO WA	160-C5
CHANUTE ST	
GRANT CO WA	242-C2
CHAPEL DR	
BENTON CO OR	133-B1
PHILOMATH OR	133-B1
W CHAPIN AV	
ADA CO ID	253-B4
CHAPMAN PL	
CORVALLIS OR	327-G11
CHAPMAN RD	
WASHINGTON CO OR	199-A7
S CHAPMAN RD	
LATAH CO ID	114-C3
SPOKANE CO WA	114-C3
SPOKANE CO WA	247-A5
CHARLES RD	
CLALLAM CO WA	165-A5
CHARLES RD	
SPOKANE CO WA	246-A1
CHARLES ST	
PORT MOODY BC	157-A4
CHARLESTON BEACH RD W	
Navy Yard City WA	270-E13
CHARLOTTE AV W	
Navy Yard City WA	270-F12
CHARLTON RD	
KITTITAS CO WA	241-C3
CHAROLAIS RD	
WALLOWA CO OR	130-C1
E CHARRON RD	
YAKIMA CO WA	243-D7
CHARTWELL DR	
DIST OF WEST VANCOUVER BC	254-D1
N CHASE AV	
PASCO WA	343-D4
N CHASE RD	
KOOTENAI CO ID	353-A3
POST FALLS ID	353-A3
CHASE MOUNTAIN RD	
KLAMATH CO OR	235-A6
CHATCOLET RD	
KOOTENAI CO ID	115-A2
CHATHAM DR	
CITY OF NORTH VANCOUVER BC	255-B5
CHATHAM HILL DR	
Sunnyslope WA	238-D3
CHAUFTY RD	
LEWIS CO WA	187-B4
CHEAM AV Rt#-9	
DISTRICT OF KENT BC	94-C3
CHEESE FACTORY RD	
KLAMATH CO OR	151-A2
CHEHALEM DR	
NEWBERG OR	198-D5
YAMHILL CO OR	198-D5
CHEHALIS AV	
GRAYS HARBOR CO WA	183-A2
N CHELAN AV	
DOUGLAS CO WA	236-C7
WATERVILLE WA	236-C7
N CHELAN AV Rt#-285	
WENATCHEE WA	238-D4
N CHELAN AV U.S.-2	
WATERVILLE WA	236-C7
S CHELAN AV	
WATERVILLE WA	236-C7
S CHELAN AV Rt#-285	
WENATCHEE WA	238-D4
WENATCHEE WA	239-A4
S CHELAN ST	
RITZVILLE WA	113-C3
CHELAN BUTTE RD	
CHELAN CO WA	236-C3
CHELAN FALLS RD	
CHELAN CO WA	236-D3
CHELAN FALLS RD Rt#-150	
CHELAN CO WA	236-D3
CHELAN FALLS RD U.S.-97	
CHELAN CO WA	236-D3
CHELAN-OKANOGAN HWY U.S.-97	
Sunnyslope WA	238-D3
CHELAN-STEHEKIN FERRY	
CHELAN CO WA	236-B2
CHELAN CO WA	236-B2
CHEMAWA RD N	
KEIZER OR	322-H5
KEIZER OR	323-A5
CHEMAWA RD NE	
KEIZER OR	323-A5
MARION CO OR	204-D4
MARION CO OR	323-E4
SALEM OR	204-D4
SALEM OR	323-E4
CHEMEKETA ST NE	
SALEM OR	322-H12
CHEMICAL RD Rt#-397	
Finley WA	121-A3
Finley WA	343-G12
KENNEWICK WA	343-F11
CHENEY CREEK RD	
JOSEPHINE CO OR	229-A7
CHENEY-PLAZA RD	
SPOKANE CO WA	114-B2
S CHENEY-PLAZA RD	
CHENEY WA	246-A7
SPOKANE CO WA	114-B3

STREET City State	Page-Grid
S CHENEY-PLAZA RD	
	246-A7
W CHENEY-SPANGLE RD	
CHENEY WA	246-A7
SPOKANE CO WA	114-B2
SPOKANE CO WA	246-A7
S CHENEY-SPOKANE RD	
SPOKANE WA	246-A7
SPOKANE WA	348-H14
SPOKANE CO WA	246-A7
W CHENEY-SPOKANE RD	
SPOKANE WA	246-B5
SPOKANE CO WA	246-B5
CHENNAULT BEACH DR	
MUKILTEO WA	266-C7
CHENNAULT BEACH RD	
MUKILTEO WA	266-D7
MUKILTEO WA	267-E7
CHENOWETH RD	
WASCO CO OR	196-B7
CHENOWETH CREEK RD	
THE DALLES OR	196-B7
WASCO CO OR	196-B7
CHEROKEE	
CROOK CO OR	213-D7
CHEROKEE RD	
GRANT CO WA	242-D2
CHEROKEE CREEK RD	
GRANT CO WA	154-B2
CHERRY AV NE	
KEIZER OR	322-J6
KEIZER OR	323-A6
SALEM OR	323-A6
CHERRY LN	
CANYON CO ID	147-B1
LINN CO OR	207-C5
MEDFORD OR	234-B1
E CHERRY LN	
CANYON CO ID	147-C1
NE CHERRY LN	
JEFFERSON CO OR	208-C4
W CHERRY LN	
ADA CO ID	253-A3
MERIDIAN ID	253-A3
CHERRY ST	
PORT TOWNSEND WA	263-G4
WENATCHEE WA	238-D4
E CHERRY ST	
SEATTLE WA	278-C6
WALLA WALLA WA	345-A5
W CHERRY ST	
WALLA WALLA WA	344-J7
WALLA WALLA WA	345-A7
W CHERRY ST Rt#-507	
CENTRALIA WA	299-E4
SE CHERRY BLOSSOM DR	
PORTLAND OR	315-J7
CHERRY CREEK RD	
BENEWAH CO ID	248-C7
WHITMAN CO WA	114-B3
CHERRY HEIGHTS RD	
THE DALLES OR	196-C7
WASCO CO OR	196-B7
CHERRY HILL RD	
GRANGER WA	120-A2
CHERRY LANE RD	
NEZ PERCE CO ID	123-B2
CHESNIMNUS LN	
WALLOWA CO OR	131-A1
CHESTER AV	
GRAYS HARBOR CO WA	183-B3
E CHESTER RD	
Colby WA	271-F13
KITSAP CO WA	271-F13
CHESTERFIELD AV	
CITY OF NORTH VANCOUVER BC	255-B5
E CHESTNUT AV	
GENESEE ID	250-C1
W CHESTNUT AV	
ROSEBURG OR	334-F5
E CHESTNUT ST	
GENESEE ID	250-C1
LATAH CO ID	250-C1
CHESTNUT DR	
DESCHUTES CO OR	211-D5
WALLA WALLA WA	345-A9
Walla Walla East WA	345-A9
CHESTNUT ST	
ASHLAND OR	337-B6
ASOTIN CO WA	250-B4
CLARKSTON WA	250-B4
KELSO WA	303-C9
E CHESTNUT ST	
WALLA WALLA WA	345-C8
Walla Walla East WA	345-C8
S CHESTNUT ST	
SPOKANE WA	348-G12
W CHESTNUT ST	
WALLA WALLA WA	344-J9
WALLA WALLA WA	345-A9
CHETCO AV U.S.-101	
BROOKINGS OR	232-C6
W CHEWACK RD	
OKANOGAN CO WA	104-A2
CHEWILIKEN RD	
OKANOGAN CO WA	105-A2
CHEWILIKEN VALLEY RD	
OKANOGAN CO WA	104-C2
E CHEWUCH RD	
OKANOGAN CO WA	104-A2
CHEYNE RD	
KLAMATH CO OR	235-D7
CHICAGO ST	
PASCO WA	343-H6
CHICAGO ST SE	
TURNER OR	325-G12
CHICKADEE DR	
JEFFERSON CO OR	212-C2
CHICKAHOMINY RD	
LANE CO OR	133-A3
CHICKEN DINNER RD	
CANYON CO ID	147-B1
CHICO WY NW	
BREMERTON WA	270-A7
KITSAP CO WA	270-B3
Silverdale WA	270-B3
Tracyton WA	270-A7
CHIEF MARTIN RD	
WHATCOM CO WA	158-C7
CHILBERG RD	
LA CONNER WA	167-D1
SKAGIT CO WA	167-D1
E CHILCO RD	
KOOTENAI CO ID	245-A3
SW CHILDS RD	
CLACKAMAS CO OR	199-C4
CHILKO DR	
COQUITLAM BC	157-A5

STREET City State	Page-Grid
CHILLIWACK LAKE RD	
BRITISH COLUMBIA BC	102-C1
BRITISH COLUMBIA BC	103-A1
CITY OF CHILLIWACK BC	102-C1
CHILOQUIN HWY	
CHILOQUIN OR	231-C3
KLAMATH CO OR	231-C3
S CHILOQUIN RD	
CHILOQUIN OR	231-D4
KLAMATH CO OR	231-D4
CHILOQUIN CAMP RD	
KLAMATH CO OR	142-C3
CHILOQUIN RIDGE RD	
KLAMATH CO OR	231-D4
CHILVERS RD	
LEWIS CO WA	184-A7
CHIMACUM RD	
Hadlock-Irondale WA	170-A1
JEFFERSON CO WA	170-A1
CHIMNEY CREEK RD	
MALHEUR CO OR	138-A3
MALHEUR CO OR	146-A1
CHIN RD	
KLAMATH CO OR	235-D7
CHINA CREEK RD	
DOUGLAS CO OR	105-A3
CHINA GARDEN RD	
KALAMA WA	189-D6
CHINA GRADE RD	
SISKIYOU CO CA	149-A3
CHINA HAT RD	
BEND OR	217-C4
BEND OR	332-D14
DESCHUTES CO OR	135-B3
DESCHUTES CO OR	143-B1
DESCHUTES CO OR	217-C4
DESCHUTES CO OR	332-D14
CHINA MOUNTAIN RD	
CURRY CO OR	224-B6
CHINA PEAK LOOKOUT RD	
SISKIYOU CO CA	149-B3
CHINDEN BLVD U.S.-20	
ADA CO ID	147-C1
E CHINDEN BLVD U.S.-20	
ADA CO ID	253-B2
BOISE ID	253-B2
EAGLE ID	253-B2
W CHINDEN BLVD U.S.-20	
ADA CO ID	147-C1
ADA CO ID	253-A2
BOISE ID	253-B2
CANYON CO ID	147-C1
EAGLE ID	253-B2
GARDEN CITY ID	253-C2
CHINOOK PASS HWY Rt#-410	
PIERCE CO WA	111-A3
CHINOOK VALLEY RD	
PACIFIC CO WA	186-B6
CHIPMUNK	
JEFFERSON CO OR	212-C2
CHIPMUNK TR	
DOUGLAS CO OR	239-B1
CHIPPEWA	
CROOK CO OR	213-D7
CHIWALA LP	
CHELAN CO WA	111-C1
CHIWAWA RIVER RD	
CHELAN CO WA	103-C3
CHELAN CO WA	111-C1
NE CHKALOV DR	
VANCOUVER WA	307-J6
SE CHKALOV DR	
VANCOUVER WA	307-J7
E CHOCKTOOT ST	
CHILOQUIN OR	231-D4
N CHOCKTOOT ST	
CHILOQUIN OR	231-D4
W CHOCKTOOT ST	
CHILOQUIN OR	231-D3
E CHRIS CT	
SPOKANE CO WA	347-F5
CHRISELLA RD E	
EDGEWOOD WA	182-B3
CHRISTENSEN RD	
CLARK CO WA	192-D1
KITTITAS CO WA	241-D5
SW CHRISTENSEN RD	
YAMHILL CO OR	204-A2
CHRISTIANSEN RD	
LINCOLN CO WA	206-C4
CHRISTIANSON RD	
SKAGIT CO WA	160-C3
CHRISTIE RD	
BENTON CO WA	120-C3
BENTON CO WA	121-A3
BENTON CO WA	128-C1
CHRISTMAS VALLEY-WAGONTIRE RD	
LAKE CO OR	143-B2
LAKE CO OR	144-A2
CHROME RIDGE RD	
JOSEPHINE CO OR	148-C2
CHUCKANUT DR Rt#-11	
BELLINGHAM WA	258-B12
SKAGIT CO WA	160-D2
SKAGIT CO WA	161-A3
SKAGIT CO WA	260-B1
WHATCOM CO WA	160-D2
WHATCOM CO WA	258-B14
CHUCKER DR	
YAKIMA CO WA	243-D6
CHURCH AV Rt#-219	
MARION CO OR	198-D7
SAINT PAUL OR	198-D7
CHURCH DR	
LINN CO OR	207-B7
CHURCH RD	
COLUMBIA CO WA	192-A2
WHATCOM CO WA	158-C5
YAKIMA CO WA	243-B5
SW CHURCH RD	
PORTLAND OR	312-E6
PORTLAND OR	313-E7
SE CHURCH RD	
CLACKAMAS CO OR	200-B3
W CHURCH RD	
MARION CO OR	205-B1
MOUNT ANGEL OR	205-B3
Silverdale WA	270-B3
YAKIMA CO WA	243-A7
CHURCH ST Rt#-165	
WILKESON WA	182-D5
CHURCH ST Rt#-216	
GRASS VALLEY OR	127-C2
W CHURCH ST	
MONMOUTH OR	204-B7
W CHURCH ST Rt#-272	
PALOUSE WA	249-B1
WHITMAN CO WA	249-A1
CHURCH ST NE	
SALEM OR	322-J12
Olympic View WA	170-B7
Silverdale WA	174-B1
CHURCH ST SE	
SALEM OR	322-H13

STREET City State	Page-Grid
CHURCH HILL RD	
WHITMAN CO WA	122-B1
CHURCHILL RD	
DOUGLAS CO OR	219-A1
CHURCHILL RD SE	
THURSTON CO WA	184-D3
CHURCH LAKE RD E	
BONNEY LAKE WA	182-C4
PIERCE CO WA	182-C4
CHYNOWETH RD	
DOUGLAS CO OR	200-B5
CINDER BUTTE RD	
DESCHUTES CO OR	211-D3
CINDER HILL RD	
DESCHUTES CO OR	135-B3
DESCHUTES CO OR	143-B1
CINEBAR RD	
LEWIS CO WA	118-A2
CINNAMON BUTTE RD	
DOUGLAS CO OR	223-C4
CIRCLE BLVD	
BENTON CO OR	207-B5
BENTON CO OR	327-G6
CORVALLIS OR	207-B5
CORVALLIS OR	327-G6
CIRCLE C LN	
ADAMS CO ID	251-A3
CIRQUE DR W	
TACOMA WA	294-A4
UNIVERSITY PLACE WA	181-C3
UNIVERSITY PLACE WA	294-A4
CISPUS RD Rt#-131	
LEWIS CO WA	118-C2
CITADEL RD	
PORT COQUITLAM BC	157-A5
NW CLACKAMAS DR	
JEFFERSON CO OR	208-B4
CLACKAMAS HWY Rt#-211	
CLACKAMAS CO OR	200-B4
ESTACADA OR	200-C5
CLACKAMAS HWY Rt#-212	
CLACKAMAS CO OR	199-D3
CLACKAMAS CO OR	200-A4
CLACKAMAS HWY Rt#-224	
CLACKAMAS CO OR	126-B3
CLACKAMAS CO OR	200-B4
ESTACADA OR	200-C7
CLACKAMAS-BORING RD Rt#-212	
CLACKAMAS CO OR	200-B3
S CLACKAMAS RIVER DR	
CLACKAMAS CO OR	199-D4
CLACKAMAS CO OR	200-A4
OREGON CITY OR	199-D4
CLACKAMAS RIVER RD	
CLACKAMAS CO OR	126-B3
MARION CO OR	126-C3
CLAGSTONE RD	
KOOTENAI CO ID	245-A2
CLAIR CUT-OFF RD Rt#-510	
THURSTON CO WA	181-A7
CLAREMONT DR	
JEFFERSON CO OR	208-C5
MADRAS OR	208-C5
CLARK BLVD	
MALHEUR CO OR	139-A3
CLARK DR	
VANCOUVER BC	255-A12
NE CLARK DR	
JEFFERSON CO OR	208-C3
CLARK LN	
HARNEY CO OR	137-C3
CLARK RD	
CLALLAM CO WA	163-B6
COLUMBIA CO WA	189-B6
FRANKLIN CO WA	121-A2
KLICKITAT CO WA	196-D4
LEWIS CO WA	187-D2
CLARK RD SW	
DOUGLAS CO WA	239-B3
CLARK ST	
BAKER CITY OR	138-B1
SHERMAN CO OR	127-C1
WASCO OR	127-C1
CLARK ST U.S.-95	
LEWIS CO WA	123-B2
WINCHESTER ID	123-B2
E CLARK ST	
CONNELL WA	121-B1
W CLARK ST	
CONNELL WA	121-B1
FRANKLIN CO WA	121-B1
CLARK CREEK RD	
PIERCE CO WA	182-A3
UNION CO OR	130-B1
CLARKE RD	
COQUITLAM BC	157-A4
DISTRICT OF COQUITLAM BC	156-D4
KITTITAS CO WA	241-A4
PORT MOODY BC	157-A4
SW CLARK HILL RD	
WASHINGTON CO OR	199-A3
CLARKS BRANCH RD	
DOUGLAS CO OR	221-C7
CLARKS CANYON RD	
MORROW CO OR	128-C2
CLARKS CREEK RD	
BAKER CO OR	138-B1
CLAUSSEN RD	
PIERCE CO WA	181-A4
CLAY LN	
ADAMS CO WA	251-B4
CLAY ST	
ASHLAND OR	337-G9
DISTRICT OF MISSION BC	94-B3
JACKSON CO OR	337-G9
CLAYBURN RD	
DISTRICT OF MATSQUI BC	102-B1
NW CLAY PIT RD	
YAMHILL CO OR	198-A5
CLAYTON RD	
LANE CO OR	215-B5
CLEARBROOK RD	
DISTRICT OF MATSQUI BC	102-B1
CLEAR CREEK RD	
CLACKAMAS CO OR	126-B3
HOOD RIVER CO OR	202-C2
WHITMAN CO WA	249-A1
CLEAR CREEK RD NW	
KITSAP CO WA	170-B7
KITSAP CO WA	174-B1

STREET City State	Page-Grid
CLEAR LAKE RD	
DOUGLAS CO OR	214-A7
DUNES CITY OR	214-B4
LANE CO OR	133-B3
LANE CO OR	215-A1
MODOC CO CA	151-A3
CLEAR LAKE RD NE	
KEIZER OR	204-D4
CLEARVIEW DR	
DOUGLAS CO OR	221-B3
W CLEARWATER AV	
BENTON CO WA	341-J12
KENNEWICK WA	341-J12
KENNEWICK WA	342-E10
NE CLEARWATER DR	
CLARK CO WA	193-C3
CLEARWATER RD	
DOUGLAS CO OR	222-D4
DOUGLAS CO OR	223-A4
JEFFERSON CO WA	108-C1
JEFFERSON CO WA	172-B1
CLEARWATER FALLS RD	
DOUGLAS CO OR	223-D4
CLEMAN RD	
KITTITAS CO WA	241-C7
CLEMANS RD	
ASOTIN CO WA	250-B5
ASOTIN CO WA	250-B5
NE CLEMENS DR	
JEFFERSON CO OR	208-C2
CLEMENTS RD	
TILLAMOOK CO OR	197-C3
CLEMS VIEW RD	
YAKIMA CO WA	243-B4
CLETO RD	
MALHEUR CO OR	154-B2
CLEVELAND AV	
TUMWATER WA	296-H9
CLEVELAND BLVD U.S.-30	
CALDWELL ID	147-B1
CANYON CO ID	147-B1
NAMPA ID	147-B1
CLEVELAND ST Rt#-202	
REDMOND WA	175-D1
E CLEVELAND ST	
WOODBURN OR	205-B4
CLEVELAND HILL RD	
DOUGLAS CO OR	221-A3
CLEVELAND RIDGE RD	
JACKSON CO OR	230-C1
CLIFFRIDGE AV	
DIST OF NORTH VANCOUVER BC	156-B2
CLIFTON RD	
CLATSOP CO OR	117-B3
CLIFTON RD SW	
KITSAP CO WA	174-B4
PORT ORCHARD WA	174-B4
CLINE RD	
COWLITZ CO WA	187-C7
CLINE FALLS HWY	
DESCHUTES CO OR	212-B7
DESCHUTES CO OR	217-B1
CLINTON RD	
LEWIS CO WA	184-A7
N CLINTON ST	
WALLA WALLA WA	345-C6
S CLINTON ST	
WALLA WALLA WA	345-C8
CLINTON FERRY	
MUKILTEO WA	171-B2
SNOHOMISH CO WA	171-B2
CLISE PL W	
SEATTLE WA	276-D1
CLIVEDEN AV	
DISTRICT OF DELTA BC	156-D6
CLODFELTER RD	
BENTON CO WA	121-A3
BENTON CO WA	341-J14
BENTON CO WA	342-A12
KENNEWICK WA	341-J14
KENNEWICK WA	342-A12
CLOQUALLUM RD	
MASON CO WA	179-D4
MASON CO WA	180-A4
CLOQUALLUM LOST LAKE RD	
GRAYS HARBOR CO WA	179-B5
CLOSE RD NW	
DOUGLAS CO WA	236-C7
WATERVILLE WA	236-C7
CLOVER BLOSSOM LN NE	
KITSAP CO WA	271-A3
CLOVER CREEK RD	
KLAMATH CO OR	150-B2
KLAMATH CO OR	235-A4
CLOVERDALE AV	
DISTRICT OF SAANICH BC	256-G5
CLOVERDALE BYP Rt#-15	
CITY OF SURREY BC	157-B7
CLOVERDALE RD	
COWLITZ CO WA	189-D6
CRESWELL OR	215-C5
DESCHUTES CO OR	212-B5
LANE CO OR	215-C5
LINCOLN CO WA	114-A2
MARION CO OR	207-D1
N CLOVERDALE RD	
BOISE ID	253-B2
S CLOVERDALE RD	
ADA CO ID	253-B4
BOISE ID	253-B4
COWLITZ CO WA	189-D6
S CLOVERDALE ST	
SEATTLE WA	285-J3
SEATTLE WA	286-A3
CLOVER ISLAND DR	
KENNEWICK WA	343-D9
CLOVER ISLAND DRIVE BRDG	
KENNEWICK WA	343-D9
CLOVERLAND RD	
ASOTIN CO WA	122-C2
ASOTIN CO WA	250-A7
CLOVERLAWN DR	
GRANTS PASS OR	335-G13
JOSEPHINE CO OR	229-B7
JOSEPHINE CO OR	335-G13
N CLOVERLEAF RD	
HAUSER ID	247-C1
KOOTENAI CO ID	247-C1
CLOVER RIDGE RD	
ALBANY OR	326-J6
LINN CO OR	326-J6
CLOVER VALLEY RD	
Ault Field WA	167-B2
ISLAND CO WA	167-B2
CLOW CORNER RD	
POLK CO OR	204-A6
E CLUB CT	
SPOKANE WA	246-C5

STREET City State Page-Grid	STREET City State Page-Grid	STREET City State Page-Grid	STREET City State Page-Grid	STREET City State Page-Grid	STREET City State Page-Grid
CLUGSTON CREEK-ONION CREEK RD	**S COLLEGE AV**	**COLUMBIA BASIN HWY I-90**	**E COMMERCIAL ST**	**COOPER HOLLOW RD**	**CORVALLIS-LEBANON HWY**
STEVENS CO WA 106-A2	WALLA WALLA CO WA 344-F12	ADAMS CO WA 113-C3	WEISER ID 139-A2	POLK CO OR 204-A7	Rt#-34
COAL CREEK PKWY SE	**E COLLEGE ST**	**COLUMBIA BASIN HWY**	**W COMMERCIAL ST**	**COOPER MOUNTAIN RD**	LEBANON OR 133-C1
BELLEVUE WA 175-C3	MARION CO OR 205-C3	Rt#-904	ASTORIA OR 300-B5	CHELAN CO WA 236-C2	LINN CO OR 133-C1
KING CO WA 175-C3	MOUNT ANGEL OR 205-C3	CHENEY WA 246-A7	WEISER ID 139-A2	**COOPER POINT RD NW**	LINN CO OR 207-B6
NEWCASTLE WA 175-C3	**COLLEGE ST Rt#-219**	SPOKANE CO WA 246-A7	**COMMERCIAL ST NE**	OLYMPIA WA 296-E2	TANGENT OR 207-B6
COAL CREEK RD	NEWBERG OR 198-D5	**N COLUMBIA CENTER BLVD**	SALEM OR 322-J9	THURSTON CO WA 180-C5	**CORVALLIS-NEWPORT HWY**
COWLITZ CO WA 189-A1	YAMHILL CO OR 198-D5	KENNEWICK WA 342-C10	**COMMERCIAL ST NE Rt#-99E**	THURSTON CO WA 296-E2	Rt#-34
COWLITZ CO WA 302-B3	**N COLLEGE ST Rt#-219**	RICHLAND WA 342-C7	SALEM OR 322-J10	**COOPER POINT RD SW**	CORVALLIS OR 327-H11
LONGVIEW WA 302-B3	NEWBERG OR 198-D5	**S COLUMBIA CENTER BLVD**	**COMMERCIAL ST SE**	OLYMPIA WA 296-E5	LINN CO OR 207-B6
COALMAN RD	**S COLLEGE ST**	KENNEWICK WA 342-C11	SALEM OR 322-H13	**COOPER SPUR RD**	LINN CO OR 327-H11
CLACKAMAS CO OR 200-D4	NEWBERG OR 198-D5	**COLUMBIA HEIGHTS RD**	SALEM OR 324-G2	HOOD RIVER CO OR 202-C2	**CORVALLIS-NEWPORT HWY**
CLACKAMAS CO OR 201-A4	**SW COLLEGE ST**	COWLITZ CO WA 189-B2	SALEM OR 325-A9	**COOS BAY-ROSEBURG HWY**	U.S.-20
COAL MINE RD	MILTON-FREEWATER OR 121-C3	COWLITZ CO WA 302-H1	**COMO LAKE AV**	Rt#-42	BENTON CO OR 133-A1
JACKSON CO OR 234-B2	**COLLEGE ST NE**	COWLITZ CO WA 303-A5	COQUITLAM BC 157-A4	COOS CO OR 140-C2	CORVALLIS OR 133-A1
COAL MINE HILL RD	LACEY WA 297-G4	KELSO WA 303-A5	DISTRICT OF COQUITLAM BC .. 156-D4	COOS CO OR 220-D4	CORVALLIS OR 327-E11
MORROW CO OR 129-A3	**COLLEGE ST SE**	LONGVIEW WA 303-A5	**COMOX RD**	COQUILLE OR 220-D4	PHILOMATH OR 133-A1
COAST DR	LACEY WA 297-G7	**COLUMBIA HOUSE BLVD**	NANAIMO BC 93-A3	DOUGLAS CO OR 140-C3	**COTTAGE AV**
DEPOE BAY OR 206-B1	THURSTON CO WA 297-F11	VANCOUVER WA 305-J6	**COMPTON LN**	DOUGLAS CO OR 141-A2	CASHMERE WA 238-C2
SW COAST CREEK RD	**COLLEGE WY**	**S COLUMBIAN WY**	LANE CO OR 210-A6	DOUGLAS CO OR 221-A6	CLATSOP CO OR 301-G3
YAMHILL CO OR 125-A3	FOREST GROVE OR 198-B1	SEATTLE WA 282-B4	**COMPTON RD**	MYRTLE POINT OR 140-C2	GEARHART OR 301-G3
COAST MERIDIAN RD	**COLLEGE WY Rt#-538**	**COLUMBIA PARK TR**	BRITISH COLUMBIA BC 159-B5	WINSTON OR 221-B6	**COTTAGE ST**
COQUITLAM BC 157-B4	MOUNT VERNON WA 260-J11	BENTON CO WA 341-E5	**SE COMPTON RD**	**COOS BAY-ROSEBURG HWY**	MEDFORD OR 336-D12
PORT COQUITLAM BC 157-B4	SKAGIT CO WA 161-C7	RICHLAND WA 341-G5	CLACKAMAS CO OR 200-C3	Rt#-99	**E COTTAGE GROVE CONN**
COBBLE HILL RD	SKAGIT CO WA 260-J11	**COLUMBIA RIVER HWY I-84**	**COMSTOCK RD**	DOUGLAS CO OR 221-B6	COTTAGE GROVE OR 215-B7
BRITISH COLUMBIA BC 159-A2	**E COLLEGE WY Rt#-538**	ARLINGTON OR 128-A1	SUTHERLIN OR 221-C1	DOUGLAS CO OR 334-D14	**COTTAGE GROVE-LORANE RD**
COBURG RD	MOUNT VERNON WA 260-D10	BOARDMAN OR 128-A1	WINSTON OR 221-B6	DOUGLAS CO OR 221-B6	COTTAGE GROVE OR 215-A6
COBURG OR 210-B7	SKAGIT CO WA 260-H10	CASCADE LOCKS OR 194-C6	**CONCOMLY RD NE**	**COOS BAY-WAGON RD**	LANE CO OR 133-B3
EUGENE OR 215-B1	**NW COLLEGE WY**	FAIRVIEW OR 200-A1	MARION CO OR 205-A5	DOUGLAS CO OR 141-A2	LANE CO OR 215-A6
LANE CO OR 330-C4	BEND OR 332-A5	GILLIAM CO OR 127-C1	**CONCONULLY RD**	DOUGLAS CO OR 221-A5	**COTTAGE GROVE RESERVOIR**
LANE CO OR 210-B6	**W COLLEGE WY Rt#-538**	GILLIAM CO OR 128-A1	OKANOGAN CO WA 104-B2	**COOS CITY-SUMNER RD**	RD
LINN CO OR 210-A5	MOUNT VERNON WA 260-B10	GRESHAM OR 200-A1	OKANOGAN CO WA 104-B2	COOS CO OR 140-B2	LANE CO OR 219-D2
COBURG RD Rt#-99	**E COLLINS DR**	HOOD RIVER CO OR 195-A5	**CONCRETE SAUK VALLEY RD**	COOS CO OR 220-D2	**COTTON RD**
EUGENE OR 330-A6	KLICKITAT CO WA 127-C1	HOOD RIVER CO OR 194-C6	CONCRETE WA 102-C2	**COOS RIVER HWY**	CITY OF NORTH VANCOUVER BC 255-E7
N COBURG RD	**E COLLINS RD**	HOOD RIVER CO OR 195-A5	SKAGIT CO WA 102-C2	COOS BAY OR 220-D1	DISTRICT OF NORTH VANCOUV BC 255-E7
COBURG OR 210-B7	DESCHUTES CO OR 212-B7	MORROW CO OR 128-B1	SKAGIT CO WA 103-A2	COOS CO OR 140-B2	**COTTONWOOD BAY**
LANE CO OR 210-B7	DESCHUTES CO OR 217-B1	MOSIER OR 196-D7	**CONDON RD**	COOS CO OR 218-D7	KOOTENAI CO ID 115-A2
LEWIS CO WA 187-D4	LEWIS CO WA 187-D4	MULTNOMAH CO OR 194-B7	CLARK CO WA 193-A1	COOS CO OR 220-D1	KOOTENAI CO ID 248-A5
SEDRO-WOOLLEY WA 260-H1	SEDRO-WOOLLEY WA 260-H1	MULTNOMAH CO OR 200-C1	**CONDON WY W**	COOS CO OR 220-D2	**COTTONWOOD DR**
SKAGIT CO WA 161-B5	SKAGIT CO WA 161-B5	MULTNOMAH CO OR 201-A1	SEATTLE WA 276-D1	**S COOS RIVER RD**	Birch Bay WA 158-B4
SKAGIT CO WA 260-H3	UNION CO OR 130-B3	PORTLAND OR 200-A1	**CONGER CREEK RD**	COOS CO OR 140-C2	MAPLE RIDGE BC 157-D6
UNION CO OR 130-B3	WHITMAN CO WA 249-A3	PORTLAND OR 315-J2	OKANOGAN CO WA 104-B2	**COPALIS BEACH RD**	RICHLAND WA 341-D2
COBURG BOTTOM LOOP RD	YAKIMA CO WA 243-B4	RUFUS OR 127-C1	**CONIFER BLVD**	GRAYS HARBOR CO WA 177-B4	**COTTONWOOD RD**
LANE CO OR 210-B7	**E COLLINS RD**	SHERMAN CO OR 127-C1	CORVALLIS OR 207-B5	**COPALIS CROSSING RD**	ADAMS CO ID 139-C1
N COCHRAN ST	KITSAP CO WA 271-E13	THE DALLES OR 196-D7	CORVALLIS OR 327-J5	GRAYS HARBOR CO WA 177-D2	STEVENS CO WA 114-A1
SPOKANE WA 348-F5	**COLOCKUM RD**	TROUTDALE OR 200-A1	**CONIFER ST NE**	**COPCO RD**	WALLA WALLA CO WA 121-C3
COCHRAN CREEK DR	CHELAN CO WA 239-B5	WASCO CO OR 127-C1	MARION CO OR 205-A5	KLAMATH CO OR 231-C5	WALLA WALLA CO WA 122-A3
LINN CO OR 210-C2	KITTITAS CO WA 112-A3	WASCO CO OR 196-D7	**S CONKLIN RD**	SISKIYOU CO CA 150-A3	WALLA WALLA CO WA 345-C11
COCOLALLA CREEK RD	KITTITAS CO WA 239-B7	WASCO CO OR 195-A5	SPOKANE CO WA 247-A5	**COPE RD**	**COTTONWOOD ST Rt#-19**
BONNER CO ID 244-A6	KITTITAS CO WA 241-D3	WOOD VILLAGE OR 200-A1	**CONKLING PARK RD**	LEWIS CO WA 187-B4	ARLINGTON OR 128-A1
W COE AV	**COLONIAL DR**	**COLUMBIA RIVER HWY**	KOOTENAI CO ID 115-A2	**COPELAND CREEK RD**	**SW COTTONWOOD ST**
STANFIELD OR 129-A1	JOSEPHINE CO OR 229-B4	Rt#-730	KOOTENAI CO ID 248-A5	DOUGLAS CO OR 222-C4	GRANTS PASS OR 335-C10
E COEUR D'ALENE AV Rt#-97	**COLONIAL RD**	UMATILLA CO OR 121-A3	**CONNARN RD**	**COPLEY RD**	**COTTONWOOD BUTTE RD**
HARRISON ID 248-A4	DOUGLAS CO OR 221-A5	WALLA WALLA CO WA 121-A3	DESCHUTES CO OR 212-B7	CROOK CO OR 213-B6	IDAHO CO ID 123-B3
KOOTENAI CO ID 248-A4	**COLONY RD**	**COLUMBIA RIVER HWY**	**CONNECTICUT AV**	**COPPEI AV U.S.-12**	**COTTONWOOD CANYON RD**
E COEUR D'ALENE AV	SKAGIT CO WA 161-B4	U.S.-30	NORTH BEND OR 333-G4	WAITSBURG WA 122-A2	YAKIMA CO WA 119-C2
U.S.-95	**COLONY MOUNTAIN RD**	ASTORIA OR 188-D1	**CONNECTICUT AV SE**	**COPPER QUEEN RD**	YAKIMA CO WA 243-A4
BENEWAH CO ID 115-A3	SKAGIT CO WA 161-A4	ASTORIA OR 300-E5	Four Corners OR 325-F2	JOSEPHINE CO OR 229-B2	**COTTONWOOD CREEK RD**
TENSED ID 115-A3	**COLORADO AV**	CLATSKANIE OR 117-A3	SALEM OR 325-F2	**COQUILLE-BANDON HWY**	NEZ PERCE CO ID 123-B2
COFFEE LN NE	NORTH BEND OR 333-D3	CLATSOP CO OR 117-A3	**W CONNECTICUT ST**	Rt#-42S	STEVENS CO WA 106-A3
MARION CO OR 204-D1	PIERCE CO WA 181-C5	CLATSOP CO OR 188-D1	BELLINGHAM WA 258-C4	BANDON OR 220-C6	**COUCH RD**
COFFEEPOT RD	**NW COLORADO AV Rt#-372**	COLUMBIA CITY OR 192-A3	**CONNECTING RD**	COOS CO OR 220-C6	DESCHUTES CO OR 217-B4
LINCOLN CO WA 113-B2	BEND OR 332-E8	COLUMBIA CO OR 117-B3	MAPLE RIDGE BC 157-C5	COQUILLE OR 220-C6	**COUCH MARKET RD**
COFFEY RD	**SW COLORADO AV Rt#-372**	COLUMBIA CO OR 189-A4	PITT MEADOWS BC 157-C5	**COQUILLE-FAIRVIEW RD**	DESCHUTES CO OR 212-B7
BAKER CO OR 130-B3	BEND OR 332-D9	COLUMBIA CO OR 192-A3	**CONNELL HILL RD**	COOS CO OR 140-C2	**COUGAR RD**
N COFFEY ST	**COLORADO RD**	COLUMBIA CO OR 302-A14	GARFIELD CO WA 122-C2	COOS CO OR 220-D4	CROOK CO OR 135-C1
ADA CO ID 253-B2	CLACKAMAS CO OR 200-C4	RAINIER OR 189-A4	**CONNELLS PRAIRIE RD**	COQUILLE OR 220-D4	JEFFERSON CO OR 212-C3
GARDEN CITY ID 253-B2	**COLORADO ST**	SAINT HELENS OR 192-A3	PIERCE CO WA 182-C4	**COQUILLE-FAT ELK RD**	**COUGAR WY**
COFFIN RD	KELSO WA 303-D11	SCAPPOOSE OR 192-A3	**CONNELLY RD**	COOS CO OR 220-D5	SKAMANIA CO WA 195-B1
BENTON CO WA 121-A3	**NE COLORADO ST**	**COLUMBIA RIVER HWY**	SNOHOMISH CO WA 171-D4	**CORAL SEA AV**	**COUGAR BEND RD**
COFFIN BUTTE RD	PULLMAN WA 249-B5	U.S.-730	**CONNER RD**	OAK HARBOR WA 167-C3	LANE CO OR 219-D4
BENTON CO OR 207-A3	**COLTON RD**	IRRIGON OR 128-C1	NEZ PERCE CO ID 250-D2	**CORBET DR**	**COUGAR CREEK RD**
COGLAN BUTTE RD	BAKER CO OR 130-B3	MORROW CO OR 128-C1	**CONNER RD SE**	BREMERTON WA 270-F9	ASOTIN CO WA 122-C3
LAKE CO OR 144-A3	**N COLTON ST**	UMATILLA CO OR 129-A1	THURSTON CO WA 184-C4	KITSAP CO WA 270-F9	**E COUGAR GULCH RD**
LAKE CO OR 151-C1	SPOKANE WA 347-A13	UMATILLA CO OR 128-C1	**CONNETT RD**	**SW CORBETT AV**	KOOTENAI CO ID 247-D4
LAKE CO OR 152-A1	**COLUMBIA AV**	UMATILLA CO OR 129-A1	CLACKAMAS CO OR 200-D3	PORTLAND OR 317-F1	KOOTENAI CO ID 354-J13
COLBURN CULVER RD	BRIDGEPORT WA 112-C1	**COLUMBIA RIVER RD**	**E CONNOR RD**	**CORDATA PKWY**	KOOTENAI CO ID 355-A13
BONNER CO ID 107-B2	DOUGLAS CO WA 112-C1	FRANKLIN CO WA 121-A2	SPOKANE CO WA 246-D6	BELLINGHAM WA 158-D7	**W COUGAR GULCH RD**
BONNER CO ID 244-B1	**COLUMBIA AV Rt#-155**	FRANKLIN CO WA 340-H1	**CONRAD RD**	**CORDON RD**	KOOTENAI CO ID 247-D4
COLBURN-MCCUTCHEON RD	COULEE DAM WA 237-C2	**COLUMBIA SCHOOL RD**	LEWIS CO WA 187-C2	Four Corners OR 323-G14	**COUGAR MOUNTAIN RD**
PIERCE CO WA 182-B4	**COLUMBIA AV Rt#-173**	Burbank WA 121-A3	**CONRADI RD**	Four Corners OR 325-G1	LANE CO OR 219-D3
COLBY AV	BRIDGEPORT WA 112-C1	**COLUMBIA TIE RD**	LEWIS CO WA 187-C2	Hayesville OR 323-G8	**COUGAR SMITH RD**
EVERETT WA 264-D2	**E COLUMBIA AV**	CLARK CO WA 118-A3	**CONSER DR**	MARION CO OR 323-G10	GRAYS HARBOR CO WA 178-D3
EVERETT WA 268-D1	COLUMBIA CO OR 192-A4	**COLUMBIA VIEW DR**	CORVALLIS OR 207-B5	MARION CO OR 323-G8	GRAYS HARBOR CO WA 179-A3
COLCHESTER DR E	**COLUMBIA BLVD**	THE DALLES OR 196-D7	MARION CO OR 207-B5	SALEM OR 323-G10	**COUGHANOUR LN**
Colby WA 271-H13	SAINT HELENS OR 192-B1	**N COLUMBIA AV**	**CONSER RD**	SALEM OR 325-G2	UNION CO OR 130-A3
COLCHESTER DR SE	**N COLUMBIA BLVD**	GOLDENDALE WA 127-C1	LINN CO OR 207-C3	**CORDOVA ST**	**COULEE BLVD Rt#-155**
Colby WA 174-C4	PORTLAND OR 192-B7	MEDFORD OR 336-B12	LINN CO OR 326-E1	VANCOUVER BC 254-H10	ELECTRIC CITY WA 237-C2
Colby WA 271-H13	PORTLAND OR 308-D3	**S COLUMBIA AV**	MILLERSBURG OR 326-E1	VANCOUVER BC 255-A10	GRANT CO WA 237-C2
COLD CAMP RD	PORTLAND OR 309-E4	GOLDENDALE WA 127-C1	**CONSER RD**	**CORDOVA BAY RD**	**COULSON RD**
WASCO CO OR 135-C1	**NE COLUMBIA BLVD**	JACKSON CO OR 234-A2	LINN CO OR 207-C3	DISTRICT OF SAANICH BC 159-C5	LEWIS CO WA 187-B2
COLD SPRING RD	PORTLAND OR 309-H4	KLICKITAT CO WA 127-C1	**CONWAY RD**	**CORDUROY RD**	**COUNCIL RD**
JACKSON CO OR 226-B4	PORTLAND OR 310-B5	MEDFORD OR 234-A2	SKAGIT CO WA 168-B2	KELSO WA 303-G8	ADAMS CO ID 139-C1
JACKSON CO OR 230-B1	PORTLAND OR 311-F7	MEDFORD OR 336-B13	**COOK AV**	**COREY RD**	VALLEY CO ID 251-C2
COLD SPRINGS RD	**COLUMBIA DR**	**S COLUMBUS AV Rt#-238**	DESCHUTES CO OR 217-B1	JACKSON CO OR 230-D6	**COUNCIL ST**
DESCHUTES CO OR 211-C4	JEFFERSON CO OR 208-B7	MEDFORD OR 336-B12	JEFFERSON CO WA 263-B3	**CORKSCREW CANYON RD**	FOREST GROVE OR 198-B1
LANE CO OR 214-B1	**E COLUMBIA DR**	**COLUMBUS ST**	PORT TOWNSEND WA 263-B3	STEVENS CO WA 114-A1	**COUNTRY LN**
LEWIS CO ID 123-B2	KENNEWICK WA 343-E10	ALBANY OR 326-F11	**NE COOK LN**	**CORKSCREW CANYON RD**	LANE CO OR 210-B7
WASCO CO OR 202-D4	**NW COLUMBIA DR**	LINN CO OR 207-C6	JEFFERSON CO OR 208-C7	Rt#-291	**COUNTRY RD**
S COLD SPRINGS RD	JEFFERSON CO OR 208-B3	LINN CO OR 326-E14	**COOK RD**	STEVENS CO WA 114-B1	LINN CO OR 207-B7
UMATILLA CO OR 129-B1	**SW COLUMBIA DR**	**COLVER RD**	BAKER CO OR 130-C3	STEVENS CO WA 246-A1	**COUNTRY CLUB DR**
COLE RD	JEFFERSON CO OR 208-B6	JACKSON CO OR 234-B2	ISLAND CO WA 167-B4	**CORLISS WY N**	BENTON CO OR 327-A12
DOUGLAS CO OR 221-B1	**W COLUMBIA DR**	PHOENIX OR 234-B2	LEWIS CO WA 187-A2	SEATTLE WA 274-A1	CORVALLIS OR 327-A12
MASON CO WA 180-B3	KENNEWICK WA 343-C9	TALENT OR 234-B2	SEDRO-WOOLLEY WA 161-B5	**NW CORNELIUS PASS RD**	**COUNTRY CLUB RD**
SAN JUAN CO WA 160-A7	**COLUMBIA DR SE**	**COLVILLE RD**	SKAGIT CO WA 161-B5	HILLSBORO OR 199-A1	CLACKAMAS CO OR 320-D5
N COLE RD	RICHLAND WA 341-H6	TOWN OF ESQUIMALT BC 256-C7	YAKIMA CO WA 120-A2	MULTNOMAH CO OR 192-A7	EUGENE OR 329-J4
BOISE ID 253-C3	RICHLAND WA 342-A6	**COLVILLE-ALADDIN-**	**SW COOK RD**	WASHINGTON CO OR 192-A7	EUGENE OR 330-A4
S COLE RD	**COLUMBIA RD**	**NORTHPORT RD**	WASHINGTON CO OR 198-C1	WASHINGTON CO OR 199-A1	HOOD RIVER CO OR 195-C6
ADA CO ID 253-C4	DESCHUTES CO OR 217-A2	NORTHPORT WA 106-B1	**COOK ST**	**CORNELIUS-SCHEFFLIN RD**	LAKE OSWEGO OR 320-C5
BOISE ID 253-C4	**E COLUMBIA RD**	STEVENS CO WA 106-B1	CITY OF VICTORIA BC 256-J6	WASHINGTON CO OR 198-C1	LAKE OSWEGO OR 321-E6
COLE ST	ADA CO ID 253-D4	**COLVILLE-TIGER RD Rt#-20**	DISTRICT OF SAANICH BC 256-H5	**NE CORNELL RD**	WHITMAN CO WA 249-A6
HAINES OR 130-A3	BOISE ID 253-D4	STEVENS CO WA 106-A2	**COOK CREEK RD**	HILLSBORO OR 198-D1	**COUNTRY CLUB RD NE**
COLE ST Rt#-410	**W COLUMBIA RD**	**COLWOOD DR**	TILLAMOOK CO OR 191-D4	HILLSBORO OR 199-A1	KITSAP CO WA 174-C2
ENUMCLAW WA 110-C3	ADA CO ID 253-A4	DISTRICT OF NORTH VANCOUV BC 254-H2	**COOKE RD**	**NW CORNELL RD**	**N COUNTRY HOMES BLVD**
COLEMAN RD	**COLUMBIA ST**	**COMA RD**	KLICKITAT CO WA 196-A4	BEAVERTON OR 199-B1	Country Homes WA 346-H13
KLAMATH CO OR 235-D1	CATHLAMET WA 117-B3	LEWIS CO WA 187-B4	**COOKE CANYON RD**	HILLSBORO OR 199-B1	SPOKANE WA 346-H13
MALHEUR CO OR 138-C3	DOUGLAS CO WA 112-B2	**COMMERCE AV**	KITTITAS CO WA 241-D4	MULTNOMAH CO OR 199-B1	SPOKANE WA 347-A12
NE COLEMAN RD	MESA WA 121-A2	LONGVIEW WA 303-A8	**COOKS RD**	PORTLAND OR 199-B1	Town and Country WA 346-H13
JEFFERSON CO OR 208-C7	NEW WESTMINSTER BC 156-D6	**W COMMERCE AV**	LINCOLN CO OR 206-D3	PORTLAND OR 312-A5	**COUNTRY QUARRY RD**
COLEMAN CREEK RD	POMEROY WA 122-B2	BOISE ID 253-C4	**COOKS HILL RD**	WASHINGTON CO OR 199-B1	SKAMANIA CO WA 194-B6
JACKSON CO OR 234-B3	VANCOUVER BC 254-H11	**S COMMERCE ST**	CENTRALIA WA 299-A4	**CORNETT RD**	**COUNTRYSIDE RD**
KITTITAS CO WA 241-D4	**COLUMBIA ST Rt#-150**	TACOMA WA 293-H4	LEWIS CO WA 299-A4	CROOK CO OR 213-B5	CLACKAMAS CO OR 199-D5
COLEMAN VALLEY RD	CHELAN WA 236-D3	**COMMERCIAL AV**	**COOK-UNDERWOOD RD**	**CORNWALL AV**	**COUNTY RD Rt#-27**
LAKE CO OR 152-B2	**COLUMBIA ST Rt#-544**	ANACORTES WA 259-H2	SKAMANIA CO WA 195-B4	BELLINGHAM WA 258-D5	WHITMAN CO WA 114-C2
COLE MOUNTAIN RD	NOOKSACK WA 102-B1	COOS BAY OR 333-G10	**COOLEY RD**	VANCOUVER BC 254-C11	**COUNTY 1 RD**
CLATSOP CO OR 191-D2	**NE COLUMBIA ST**	SPRINGFIELD OR 331-D6	BEND OR 217-C1	**CORONA AV**	LA CENTER WA 192-C1
COLES RD	KITSAP CO WA 170-C6	**COMMERCIAL AV Rt#-20**	DESCHUTES CO OR 217-C1	MEDFORD OR 336-D9	**COUNTY LINE RD**
ISLAND CO WA 171-A1	Suquamish WA 170-C6	ANACORTES WA 259-H4	**COOLEY RD NE**	**CORRAL CREEK RD**	BENTON CO WA 120-B3
COLESTIN RD	**NW COLUMBIA ST**	**COMMERCIAL DR**	MARION CO OR 205-B2	MALHEUR CO OR 147-B1	CLATSOP CO OR 191-D2
JACKSON CO OR 234-D6	BEND OR 332-D7	VANCOUVER BC 156-C5	WOODBURN OR 205-B2	YAMHILL CO OR 198-D5	DOUGLAS CO WA 214-A3
COLINWOOD RD	**SW COLUMBIA ST**	VANCOUVER BC 255-B12	**W COOLIDGE AV**	YAMHILL CO OR 199-A6	GEM CO ID 139-B3
TOWN OF SIDNEY BC 159-C2	BEND OR 332-C9	**COMMERCIAL ST**	YAKIMA CO WA 243-A7	**CORSON AV S**	SKAGIT CO WA 168-B3
COLLAWASH RIVER RD	PORTLAND OR 312-D6	ASTORIA OR 300-C5	**COOMBS RD**	SEATTLE WA 282-B7	WASCO CO OR 135-A1
CLACKAMAS CO OR 126-B3	**COLUMBIA WY**	HARNEY CO OR 137-C3	YAKIMA CO WA 243-D7	**CORVALLIS RD**	**COUNTY RD 5**
COLLEGE AV Rt#-5	VANCOUVER BC 306-C7	SPOKANE CO WA 246-A7	**COOMBS CANYON RD**	INDEPENDENCE OR 204-B7	CLARK CO WA 193-A1
SAINT MARIES ID 248-D7	WALLA WALLA CO WA 121-B3	WAVERLY WA 114-C2	UMATILLA CO OR 129-B1	LINN CO OR 207-C3	**COUNTY RD 12**
N COLLEGE AV	**N COLUMBIA WY**	**COMMERCIAL ST U.S.-30**	**COOPER RD**	POLK CO OR 204-B7	CLARK CO WA 193-C2
COLLEGE PLACE WA 344-F10	PORTLAND OR 308-A3	ASTORIA OR 300-C5	LEWIS CO WA 187-D4	POLK CO OR 207-B2	**COUNTY RD 722**
Garrett WA 344-F9			LINN CO OR 207-C3	**COOPER CREEK RD**	UMATILLA CO OR 129-C1
S COLLEGE AV			**COOPER CREEK RD**	DOUGLAS CO OR 221-C1	
COLLEGE PLACE WA 344-F12			DOUGLAS CO OR 221-C1		

INDEX

STREET — City State — Page-Grid

COUNTY RD 725
UMATILLA CO OR — 129-C1
COUNTY RD 802
UMATILLA CO OR — 129-B1
COUNTY RD 821
UMATILLA CO OR — 129-B1
COUNTY RD 900
Mission OR — 129-B1
UMATILLA CO OR — 129-B1
COUNTY RD 900 U.S.-30
PENDLETON OR — 129-B1
UMATILLA CO OR — 129-B1
COUNTY RD 1046
UMATILLA CO OR — 129-C2
COUNTY WELL RD
BENTON CO WA — 120-C3
COUPLAND RD
CLACKAMAS CO OR — 200-C6
ESTACADA OR — 200-C6
N COURT AV U.S.-20
BURNS OR — 145-B1
NW COURT AV
PENDLETON OR — 129-B1
NW COURT AV U.S.-30
PENDLETON OR — 129-B1
SE COURT AV U.S.-30
PENDLETON OR — 129-B1
SW COURT AV U.S.-30
PENDLETON OR — 129-B1
SE COURT PL
PENDLETON OR — 129-B1
SW COURT PL
PENDLETON OR — 129-B1
SW COURT PL Rt#-37
PENDLETON OR — 129-B1
COURT ST
DUFUR OR — 127-B2
MEDFORD OR — 336-C10
COURT ST Rt#-74
HEPPNER OR — 128-C2
E COURT ST
GOLDENDALE WA — 127-C1
NE COURT ST
DUFUR OR — 127-B2
W COURT ST
FRANKLIN CO WA — 340-H14
FRANKLIN CO WA — 341-J2
FRANKLIN CO WA — 342-C5
FRANKLIN CO WA — 343-B6
GOLDENDALE WA — 127-C1
PASCO WA — 341-J2
PASCO WA — 342-B4
PASCO WA — 343-B6
COURT ST NE
SALEM OR — 322-H13
COURTNEY RD
WASHINGTON CO OR — 198-D5
YAMHILL CO OR — 198-D5
COURTNEY CREEK DR
LINN CO OR — 210-D3
COURTNEY CREEK RD
LINN CO OR — 210-D3
COUSE CREEK RD
ASOTIN CO WA — 123-A3
COUSINS RD
LEWIS CO WA — 187-B1
COVE HWY Rt#-237
COVE OR — 130-A2
UNION OR — 130-A2
UNION OR — 130-A2
E COVE HWY Rt#-237
UNION OR — 130-B2
COVE RD
KITTITAS CO WA — 241-A6
WASHINGTON CO ID — 139-B2
SW COVE RD
KING CO WA — 174-D5
COVE ORCHARD RD
YAMHILL CO OR — 198-B4
COVERED BRIDGE RD
WAHKIAKUM CO WA — 117-A2
COVILLE RD
POLK CO OR — 204-A5
COVINGTON WY SE
COVINGTON WA — 175-D7
COVINGTON-SAWYER RD
KING CO WA — 182-D1
COW CAMP RD
DESCHUTES CO OR — 211-C5
WASHINGTON CO ID — 139-A1
COW CREEK RD
DOUGLAS CO OR — 141-A3
DOUGLAS CO OR — 225-A3
NEZ PERCE CO ID — 250-B2
RIDDLE OR — 225-A3
WASHINGTON CO ID — 139-B1
W COW CREEK RD
MALHEUR CO OR — 146-C3
COWEN PL NE
SEATTLE WA — 274-C4
COW HOLLOW RD
MALHEUR CO OR — 139-C1
N COWICHE RD
YAKIMA CO WA — 119-C1
W COWICHE CANYON RD
YAKIMA CO WA — 243-A6
COWICHE MILL RD
YAKIMA CO WA — 119-C1
COWICHE-TIETON RD
TIETON WA — 119-C1
YAKIMA CO WA — 119-C1
COWLITZ AV
CASTLE ROCK WA — 187-C7
COWLITZ CO WA — 187-C7
E COWLITZ
CASTLE ROCK WA — 187-C7
COWLITZ ST Rt#-505
LEWIS CO WA — 187-D4
TOLEDO WA — 187-D4
COWLITZ WY
KELSO WA — 303-D8
COWLITZ WY Rt#-4
KELSO WA — 303-D8
COWLITZ GARDEN RD
COWLITZ CO WA — 303-D4
COWLITZ LOOP RD
LEWIS CO WA — 187-C4
COWLITZ RIDGE RD
LEWIS CO WA — 187-C4
COX RD
DOUGLAS CO OR — 219-B3
COX CREEK RD
DOUGLAS CO OR — 219-C3
NW COYER AV
DESCHUTES CO OR — 212-C4
COYLE RD
JEFFERSON CO WA — 170-A4
NW COYNER AV
DESCHUTES CO OR — 212-D4

NW COYNER AV
Terrebonne OR — 212-D4
COYOTE
CROOK CO OR — 213-D6
SW COYOTE
DESCHUTES CO OR — 212-C6
COYOTE CREEK RD
JOSEPHINE CO OR — 229-B1
COYOTE GRADE RD
NEZ PERCE CO ID — 250-D2
COYOTE POINT RD
HUMBOLDT CO NV — 154-A3
E COZZA DR U.S.-2
SPOKANE WA — 347-A14
CRAB CREEK RD
GRANT CO WA — 120-C1
E CRAB CREEK RD
LINCOLN CO WA — 209-D4
CRACKER CREEK RD
BAKER CO OR — 138-A1
CRAIG LN
CROOK CO OR — 213-D6
N CRAIG RD
SPOKANE WA — 246-A4
S CRAIG RD
SPOKANE WA — 246-A4
CRAIGFLOWER RD
BRITISH COLUMBIA BC — 256-D6
CITY OF VICTORIA BC — 256-E7
TOWN OF ESQUIMALT BC — 256-D6
TOWN OF VIEW ROYAL BC — 256-D6
CRAIGFLOWER RD Rt#-1A
TOWN OF VIEW ROYAL BC — 256-A5
CRAIG JUNCTION RD
LEWIS CO ID — 123-B2
CRAMER RD
CLARK CO WA — 192-D4
CRAMER RD KPN
PIERCE CO WA — 174-A7
CRANBERRY RD
GRAYS HARBOR CO WA — 183-B3
PACIFIC CO WA — 186-A4
N CRANE RD
WASHINGTON CO ID — 139-C2
CRANE-BUCHANAN RD
HARNEY CO OR — 145-C1
CRANE CREEK RD
WASHINGTON CO ID — 139-B2
CRANE CREEK RESERVOIR RD
WASHINGTON CO ID — 139-B2
CRANE ORCHARD
DOUGLAS CO WA — 112-B1
CRANE ORCHARD RD
DOUGLAS CO WA — 104-B3
CRANES RD NW
DOUGLAS CO WA — 104-B3
CRANE-VENATOR RD
HARNEY CO OR — 145-C2
HARNEY CO OR — 146-A2
HARNEY CO OR — 146-A2
CRANLEY DR
CITY OF SURREY BC — 158-A2
CRATER LP
JEFFERSON CO OR — 212-C2
CRATER CREEK MTWY
JACKSON CO OR — 227-A2
CRATER CREEK RD
KLAMATH CO OR — 227-C5
CRATER LAKE AV
JACKSON CO OR — 336-F3
MEDFORD OR — 336-E11
CRATER LAKE HWY Rt#-62
EAGLE POINT OR — 230-D4
JACKSON CO OR — 149-C1
JACKSON CO OR — 150-A1
JACKSON CO OR — 226-C7
JACKSON CO OR — 227-D7
JACKSON CO OR — 227-D7
JACKSON CO OR — 336-F3
KLAMATH CO OR — 227-D7
KLAMATH CO OR — 231-C2
MEDFORD OR — 336-F3
SHADY COVE OR — 230-D4
White City OR — 230-D6
CRATER LAKE RD
MALHEUR CO OR — 146-C2
CRATER LAKE NORTH HWY
DOUGLAS CO OR — 223-C7
DOUGLAS CO OR — 227-C2
KLAMATH CO OR — 227-C2
CRATER RD
ISLAND CO WA — 171-A1
NE CRAWFORD DR
KITSAP CO WA — 170-C5
CRAWFORD LN
YAMHILL CO OR — 198-C6
CRAWFORD RD
DESCHUTES CO OR — 217-A6
CRAWFORD ST
WENATCHEE WA — 238-D5
WENATCHEE WA — 239-A5
E CRAWFORD ST
DEER PARK WA — 114-B1
W CRAWFORD ST
DEER PARK WA — 114-B1
CREASY RD
WHATCOM CO WA — 158-C4
CREEK DR
LINN CO OR — 210-A2
CREEK RD
HARNEY CO OR — 137-B3
E CREEK RD
TILLAMOOK CO OR — 197-D5
CREEK BEND RD
LINN CO OR — 210-A2
CREGO HILL RD
LEWIS CO WA — 187-A1
CRESCENT AV
EUGENE OR — 215-B1
CRESCENT RD
CITY OF SURREY BC — 158-A1
CITY OF VICTORIA BC — 257-B11
DISTRICT OF OAK BAY BC — 257-B11
LINCOLN CO OR — 114-A1
CRESCENT RD NW
SALEM OR — 322-E12
CRESCENT BEACH RD
CLALLAM CO WA — 164-C5
CRESCENT BEACH RD KPN
PIERCE CO WA — 181-A1
CRESCENT CUT-OFF RD
KLAMATH CO OR — 142-C1
CRESCENT HARBOR RD
ISLAND CO WA — 167-C2
OAK HARBOR WA — 167-C2
CRESCENT LAKE HWY
KLAMATH CO OR — 142-B1
CRESCENT VALLEY DR NW
PIERCE CO WA — 174-C7

CRESCENT VALLEY RD SE
KITSAP CO WA — 174-C6
CREST DR
EUGENE OR — 329-J10
EUGENE OR — 330-A10
LANE CO OR — 329-H11
W CREST DR
EUGENE OR — 329-H11
LANE CO OR — 329-H11
CRESTLINE BLVD NW
OLYMPIA WA — 296-G2
CRESTLINE DR
LINCOLN CO OR — 328-D9
WALDPORT OR — 328-E5
S CRESTLINE DR
WALDPORT OR — 328-E5
N CRESTLINE ST
SPOKANE WA — 347-D13
SPOKANE WA — 349-D2
SPOKANE WA — 347-D13
CRESTVIEW DR
MASON CO WA — 180-B3
CRESTVIEW LN
SKAGIT CO WA — 161-A6
CRESTVIEW RD
CROOK CO OR — 213-D5
Sunnyslope WA — 238-D3
CRESWELL RD
SNOHOMISH CO WA — 110-C1
CREVISTON DR NW
PIERCE CO WA — 174-A7
CREVISTON RD KPS
PIERCE CO WA — 181-A3
CRISP LN
LANE CO OR — 215-B5
CRITCHFIELD RD
ASOTIN CO WA — 250-B5
Vineland WA — 250-B5
CRITES RD
SHERMAN CO OR — 127-C2
CRITESER RD
DOUGLAS CO OR — 221-A5
S CRITSER RD
CLACKAMAS CO OR — 199-D6
CROCKER LN
ALBANY OR — 326-A4
CROCKER RD
Santa Clara OR — 215-A1
CROFT AV U.S.-2
GOLD BAR WA — 110-C1
SNOHOMISH CO WA — 110-C1
CROFT RD
COOS CO OR — 224-B1
CROFT LAKE RD
COOS CO OR — 224-B1
CROISAN CREEK RD S
MARION CO OR — 324-D5
SALEM OR — 324-D5
CROMWELL DR NW
PIERCE CO WA — 181-B2
CRONIN RD
CROOK CO OR — 213-A6
CROOK DR
LINN CO OR — 210-A3
CROOKED CREEK RD
LANE CO OR — 210-D5
MALHEUR CO OR — 146-B3
MALHEUR CO OR — 154-B1
CROOKED CREEK RANGE RD
MALHEUR CO OR — 154-A1
CROOKED FINGER RD
MARION CO OR — 205-D4
CROOKED FINGER RD NE
MARION CO OR — 126-A3
CROOKED RIVER HWY Rt#-27
CROOK CO OR — 135-C3
CROOK CO OR — 213-C6
DESCHUTES CO OR — 135-C3
PRINEVILLE OR — 213-C6
CROOKS RD
GRANT CO WA — 237-B3
CROOKS CREEK RD
JOSEPHINE CO OR — 233-C1
CROSBY RD
Ault Field WA — 167-B2
BENTON CO WA — 120-C2
ISLAND CO WA — 167-B2
CROSBY RD NE
MARION CO OR — 205-A1
CROSBY RD Rt#-27
TEKOA WA — 114-C3
CROSS RD
KLAMATH CO OR — 235-C6
CROSS CREEK RD
DISTRICT OF WEST VANCOUVER BC — 254-D1
CROSS ISLAND RD
ISLAND CO WA — 167-D4
E CROSSROAD LN
LANE CO OR — 210-A6
N CROSS STATE HWY Rt#-20
SEDRO-WOOLLEY WA — 161-C5
SKAGIT CO WA — 161-C5
CROSSWINDS
DESCHUTES CO OR — 217-C1
CROW RD
JOSEPHINE CO OR — 229-A4
LANE CO OR — 133-B3
LANE CO OR — 215-A2
CROW CREEK RD
WALLOWA CO OR — 130-C2
WALLOWA CO OR — 131-A1
CROWELL LN
NORTH BEND OR — 333-F5
CROWFOOT RD
JACKSON CO OR — 149-C1
CROWLEY RD
MALHEUR CO OR — 138-B3
MALHEUR CO OR — 146-B1
POLK CO OR — 204-B5
CROWLEY-RIVERSIDE RD
MALHEUR CO OR — 146-A1
SE CROWN RD
CLACKAMAS CO OR — 193-B7
CROWN ST
VANCOUVER BC — 156-C1
CROWN POINT HWY
MULTNOMAH CO OR — 194-A7
MULTNOMAH CO OR — 200-D1
MULTNOMAH CO OR — 201-A1
E CROWN POINT HWY
MULTNOMAH CO OR — 200-D1
MULTNOMAH CO OR — 201-A1
CROWN POINT RD Rt#-174
DOUGLAS CO WA — 237-C2
CROWN PT RD
COOS CO OR — 220-C2
CROWSNEST HWY Rt#-3
BRITISH COLUMBIA BC — 103-C1
CROWSON RD
JACKSON CO OR — 234-D4
JACKSON CO OR — 337-J11

CYPRESS BOWL RD
DISTRICT OF WEST VANCOUVE BC — 156-A2

D

D AV
ANACORTES WA — 259-F4
D ST
BAKER CITY OR — 138-B1
CULVER OR — 208-B7
GRANTS PASS OR — 335-E8
HUBBARD OR — 205-B1
SALEM OR — 322-J12
SALEM OR — 323-B12
SPRINGFIELD OR — 330-H7
D ST Rt#-14
WASHOUGAL WA — 193-C7
D ST Rt#-14B
WASHOUGAL WA — 193-C7
D ST Rt#-218
SHANIKO OR — 127-C3
D ST Rt#-507
TENINO WA — 184-D3
D ST U.S.-12
LEWISTON ID — 250-B4
E D ST
GRANTS PASS OR — 335-G9
MOSCOW ID — 249-D5
TACOMA WA — 293-H6
TACOMA WA — 295-J1
SW D ST Rt#-361
MADRAS OR — 208-C5
W D ST
LANE CO OR — 330-F7
SPRINGFIELD OR — 330-G7
DABOB RD
JEFFERSON CO WA — 170-A3
DABOB POST OFFICE RD
JEFFERSON CO WA — 170-A4
DAHL RD
YAKIMA CO WA — 243-A6
DAHLGREN RD
COLUMBIA CO OR — 192-A3
DAHLIA WY
POLK CO OR — 204-C5
POLK CO OR — 322-A10
DAHLKE RD SW
DOUGLAS CO WA — 239-D2
DAILY LN
JOSEPHINE CO OR — 229-A6
DAIRY-BONANZA HWY Rt#-70
BONANZA OR — 151-A2
KLAMATH CO OR — 151-A2
SW DAISY ST
KITSAP CO WA — 174-A6
DAISY ST N Rt#-17
GRANT CO WA — 112-C2
SOAP LAKE WA — 112-C2
DAISY ST S Rt#-17
SOAP LAKE WA — 112-C2
DAISY MINE RD
JACKSON CO OR — 229-D2
JOSEPHINE CO OR — 229-C2
STEVENS CO WA — 105-C3
STEVENS CO WA — 106-A3
DAKIN ST
BELLINGHAM WA — 258-J4
DAKOTA AV
MEDFORD OR — 336-B13
DALBY RD
MASON CO WA — 173-B7
DALE DR
LINN CO OR — 210-B5
DALE LN
CLACKAMAS CO OR — 200-B4
DALE RD
BRITISH COLUMBIA BC — 94-B3
DALE ST
WOODLAND OR — 192-C1
DALLAS RD
BENTON CO WA — 341-A4
CITY OF VICTORIA BC — 256-F10
CITY OF VICTORIA BC — 257-A11
RICHLAND WA — 341-A4
WEST RICHLAND WA — 341-A4
NE DALLAS ST Rt#-500
CAMAS WA — 193-B7
DALLAS-RICKREALL HWY Rt#-223
DALLAS OR — 204-A6
POLK CO OR — 204-A6
DALLES MILITARY RD
COLLEGE PLACE WA — 344-H11
WALLA WALLA WA — 344-H11
WALLA WALLA CO WA — 345-A10
WALLA WALLA CO WA — 344-F13
DALLES MOUNTAIN RD
KLICKITAT CO WA — 127-B1
KLICKITAT CO WA — 196-D6
DALLESPORT RD
KLICKITAT CO WA — 196-C6
DALLMAN RD
ISLAND CO WA — 168-A7
E DALTON AV
COEUR D'ALENE ID — 355-F4
DALTON GARDENS ID — 355-F4
KOOTENAI CO ID — 355-F4
W DALTON AV
COEUR D'ALENE ID — 355-D5
DALY CREEK RD
BAKER CO OR — 139-A1
DAMMAN RD
KITTITAS CO WA — 241-B6
DAMON RD
ADAMS CO WA — 113-B3
ADAMS CO WA — 121-B1
DAMON RD Rt#-115
GRAYS HARBOR CO WA — 177-B6
OCEAN SHORES WA — 177-B6
DAMSON RD
SNOHOMISH CO WA — 171-D1
DANBY DR SW
THURSTON CO WA — 184-C3
DANE LN
LANE CO OR — 210-A6
N DANEBO AV
EUGENE OR — 210-A6
S DANEBO AV
EUGENE OR — 329-A6
DANEKAS RD
ADAMS CO WA — 113-C3
ADAMS CO WA — 114-A3
RITZVILLE WA — 113-C3
DANIELS RD
MASON CO WA — 180-B2
DAN KELLY RD
CLALLAM CO WA — 165-A6
DANNEN RD
LINN CO OR — 210-B2

DANNER LP
MALHEUR CO OR — 147-A3
DANNER RD
MALHEUR CO OR — 146-C3
MALHEUR CO OR — 147-A3
SNOHOMISH CO WA — 168-C5
DARBY RD
LATAH CO ID — 249-D4
DARK HOLLOW RD
JACKSON CO OR — 234-A2
S DARKNELL RD
SPOKANE CO WA — 247-A6
E DARLAND ST
GOLDENDALE WA — 127-C1
DARLEY RD
MARION CO OR — 133-C1
DARRELL AV
WINSTON OR — 221-B6
DARRNGTN BENTTS STR RD Rt#-530
DARRINGTON WA — 103-A3
SKAGIT CO WA — 103-A3
SNOHOMISH CO WA — 103-A3
DARRINGTON CLEAR CREEK RD
DARRINGTON WA — 103-A3
SNOHOMISH CO WA — 103-A3
DART CREEK RD
COLUMBIA CO OR — 192-A1
DARTER RD
KITSAP CO WA — 170-B6
W DARTFORD DR
Fairwood OR — 346-J6
Fairwood WA — 347-A6
SPOKANE CO WA — 346-J6
DARTMOUTH ST U.S.-95
ADAMS CO ID — 139-C1
COUNCIL ID — 139-C1
S DASH POINT RD Rt#-509
FEDERAL WAY WA — 182-B1
SW DASH POINT RD Rt#-509
FEDERAL WAY WA — 182-A1
SE DATE AV
COLLEGE PLACE WA — 344-F11
DAVENPORT ST
RICHLAND WA — 341-G2
DAVID AV
COQUITLAM BC — 157-B4
DAVID RD
WHITMAN CO WA — 249-C4
DAVID HILL RD
WASHINGTON CO OR — 198-B1
DAVIDSON AV
COWLITZ CO WA — 192-B1
WOODLAND WA — 192-B1
DAVIDSON RD
POLK CO OR — 207-B1
DAVIE ST
VANCOUVER BC — 254-E9
DAVIES RD
PIERCE CO WA — 182-B7
DAVIES RD
BRITISH COLUMBIA BC — 159-B5
N DAVIES RD
SNOHOMISH CO WA — 171-D1
S DAVIES RD
SNOHOMISH CO WA — 171-D2
DAVIS DR
HOOD RIVER CO OR — 195-C6
DAVIS RD
ADAMS CO WA — 113-B3
ASOTIN CO WA — 123-A3
COWLITZ CO WA — 189-D1
CROOK CO OR — 213-D6
LATAH CO ID — 249-D2
LINCOLN CO WA — 113-B3
LINN CO OR — 207-C7
LINN CO OR — 150-C3
SW DAVIS RD
BEAVERTON OR — 199-A2
DAVIS ST
MCCALL ID — 251-D6
DAVIS WY Rt#-270
PULLMAN WA — 249-A5
WHITMAN CO WA — 249-A5
DAVIS CREEK LN
VALLEY CO ID — 252-D2
DAVIS CREEK RD
JOSEPHINE CO OR — 233-B1
DAVIS CREEK RD NE
MARION CO OR — 205-D4
DAVIS PEAK RD
COWLITZ CO WA — 118-A3
DAVISSON RD
LANE CO OR — 215-C6
S DAVIS SPUR RD
COWLITZ CO WA — 189-D1
DAWES HILL RD
COQUITLAM BC — 157-A5
DAWSON RD
BENTON CO WA — 133-B2
DAY RD
IDAHO CO ID — 123-C3
ISLAND CO WA — 167-C7
WASHINGTON CO OR — 199-B5
WILSONVILLE OR — 199-B5
E DAY RD
SPOKANE CO WA — 246-D1
NE DAY RD E
KITSAP CO WA — 174-D1
NE DAY RD W
KITSAP CO WA — 174-C1
DAY HILL RD
CLACKAMAS CO OR — 200-C6
DAY ISLAND RD
EUGENE OR — 330-B6
DAY-MT SPOKANE RD
SPOKANE CO WA — 246-D1
SPOKANE CO WA — 347-J3
DAY SCHOOL RD
KLAMATH CO OR — 231-D5
DAYS CREEK RD
DOUGLAS CO OR — 141-B3
DAYS CREEK CUTOFF RD
DOUGLAS CO OR — 225-C1
E DAYTON AV
DAYTON WA — 122-A2
W DAYTON AV
DAYTON WA — 122-A2
DAYTON AV N
SHORELINE WA — 171-A7
DAYTON CO OR
DESCHUTES CO OR — 212-B7
DAYTON ST
Altamont OR — 338-H9
S DAYTON ST
KENNEWICK WA — 343-D14
DAYTON-AIRPORT RD
MASON CO WA — 179-D2

STREET | City State | Page-Grid

DAYTON-AIRPORT RD Rt#-102
- MASON CO WA — 179-D2
- MASON CO WA — 180-A2

SE DAYTON BYPASS RD Rt#-18
- DAYTON OR — 198-B7
- YAMHILL CO OR — 198-B7

DEAD INDIAN RD
- JACKSON CO OR — 150-A2
- JACKSON CO OR — 234-D4
- KLAMATH CO OR — 150-B2

DEAD INDIAN MEMORIAL RD
- ASHLAND OR — 337-J9
- JACKSON CO OR — 234-D4
- JACKSON CO OR — 337-J9

DEAD MAN RD
- CHELAN CO WA — 238-B2

N DEADMAN RD
- GARFIELD CO WA — 122-B2

DEADMAN CREEK RD
- DOUGLAS CO OR — 141-C3

DEADMAN GULCH RD
- MALHEUR CO OR — 146-C1

DEADMOND FERRY RD
- LANE CO OR — 330-G2
- North Springfield OR — 330-G2
- SPRINGFIELD OR — 330-G2

DEAD POINT RD
- HOOD RIVER CO OR — 195-B7

DEADY CROSSING RD
- DOUGLAS CO OR — 221-C2

DEAL RD
- ADAMS CO WA — 113-B3
- ADAMS CO WA — 121-B1

DEAN MOUNTAIN RD
- COOS CO OR — 218-C6
- DOUGLAS CO OR — 218-D2

DEAN PARK RD
- DISTRICT OF NORTH SAANICH BC — 159-C3

DEARBORN AV NE
- KEIZER OR — 322-J5
- KEIZER OR — 323-A5

S DEARBORN ST
- SEATTLE WA — 278-A7

DE ARMOND RD
- POLK CO OR — 207-A3

DEBAST RD
- COLUMBIA CO OR — 189-B4

DE BERRY RD
- LANE CO OR — 215-B5

DECATUR AV
- BREMERTON WA — 270-G11

DECEPTION RD
- SKAGIT CO WA — 160-C7
- SKAGIT CO WA — 259-H14

DECKER RD
- BENTON CO WA — 133-B2

DECKERVILLE RD
- MASON CO WA — 179-B2

DEEGAN RD W
- MASON CO WA — 180-A3

DEEP CREEK RD
- CLACKAMAS CO OR — 200-B3
- LEWIS CO WA — 184-A7

DEEP LAKE BOUNDARY RD
- STEVENS CO WA — 106-B1

DEEP RIVER VALLEY RD
- WAHKIAKUM CO WA — 117-A2

DEER DR
- KOOTENAI CO ID — 248-A3

DEER RD
- WHEELER CO OR — 136-B2

N DEER ST
- PRINEVILLE OR — 213-D5

DEER CREEK RD
- JACKSON CO OR — 226-D3
- JOSEPHINE CO OR — 233-B2
- KLAMATH CO OR — 227-A3
- STEVENS CO WA — 106-A3

S DEER CREEK RD
- DOUGLAS CO OR — 221-D5

DEER CREEK-BOULDER CREEK RD
- FERRY CO WA — 105-B1

DEER FLAT RD
- CANYON CO ID — 147-B1

E DEER FLAT RD
- ADA CO ID — 253-A5
- KUNA ID — 253-A5

W DEER FLAT RD
- ADA CO ID — 253-A5

DEERHORN RD
- LANE CO OR — 133-C3

DEER LAKE AV
- DISTRICT OF BURNABY BC — 156-D5

DEER LAKE PL
- DISTRICT OF BURNABY BC — 156-D5

DEER LAKE RD
- Clinton WA — 171-A2

DEER LAKE LOOP RD
- STEVENS CO WA — 106-B3

DEER PARK DR SE
- MARION CO OR — 325-J5
- SALEM OR — 325-J5

DEER PARK RD
- CLALLAM CO WA — 165-C7

DEER PARK-MILAN RD
- DEER PARK WA — 114-B1
- SPOKANE CO WA — 114-B1

E DEER PARK-MILAN RD
- SPOKANE CO WA — 114-B1

W DEER PARK-MILAN RD
- SPOKANE CO WA — 114-B1

DEER RIDGE RD
- DESCHUTES CO OR — 211-D4

DEER TRAIL LN
- JACKSON CO OR — 234-B3

DEER VALLEY RD
- NEWPORT WA — 106-C3
- PEND OREILLE CO WA — 106-C3

DE FRATES RD
- COLUMBIA CO OR — 189-C6

DEGGLER RD
- LEWIS CO WA — 118-A2

SW DEHAVEN ST
- MILTON-FREEWATER OR — 121-C3

DEHLER RD
- CROOK CO OR — 213-C3

DEHLINGER LN
- KLAMATH CO OR — 235-D6

DEINHARD LN
- MCCALL ID — 251-C5

DEJEE RD N
- LINCOLN CO WA — 113-B2

DEJONG RD
- POLK CO OR — 204-A3
- YAMHILL CO OR — 204-A3

SW DEJONG RD
- YAMHILL CO OR — 204-A2

DEKAY RD
- GRAYS HARBOR CO WA — 177-D5

DEKKER RD
- YAKIMA CO WA — 120-A2

DELAMETER RD
- COWLITZ CO WA — 187-B7
- COWLITZ CO WA — 189-B1

DELANEY RD
- FRANKLIN CO WA — 121-B2

DELANEY RD SE
- MARION CO OR — 207-D1
- MARION CO OR — 324-J12
- MARION CO OR — 325-A12
- TURNER OR — 325-E12

DELANO RD KPS
- PIERCE CO WA — 181-A2

SW DELASHMUTT LN
- YAMHILL CO OR — 204-A2

DELBROOK RD
- DIST OF NORTH VANCOUVER BC — 255-A7

DELENA-MAYGER RD
- COLUMBIA CO OR — 189-A4

DELEZENNE RD
- GRAYS HARBOR CO WA — 117-B1

DELFATTI LN
- KLAMATH CO OR — 235-C5

DELICIOUS ST
- DESCHUTES CO OR — 212-A7

DELINTMENT LAKE RD
- HARNEY CO OR — 136-C1

DELL AV
- Garrett WA — 344-F7
- WALLA WALLA WA — 344-F7

DELL RD W
- WASCO CO OR — 196-B6

DELL ADAMS RD
- MASON CO WA — 179-C3

DELLMOOR LP
- CLATSOP CO OR — 188-B4

DELMAR DR E
- SEATTLE WA — 278-B1

DELMAR RD
- COOS CO OR — 220-D3

DELPHI RD NW
- THURSTON CO WA — 296-A3

DELPHI RD SW
- THURSTON CO WA — 180-B7
- THURSTON CO WA — 184-B1
- THURSTON CO WA — 296-A6

DELRIDGE WY SW
- KING CO WA — 285-G3
- SEATTLE WA — 281-G7
- SEATTLE WA — 285-G2

DEL RIO RD
- DOUGLAS CO WA — 113-A1

DEL RIO RD E
- DOUGLAS CO WA — 237-C2

DEL RIO COULEE CITY RD
- DOUGLAS CO WA — 113-A1

DELTA AV
- DISTRICT OF BURNABY BC — 255-J13

DELTA HWY
- EUGENE OR — 329-J3

DELTA ST
- KLAMATH FALLS OR — 338-C6

DELTA LINE RD
- WHATCOM CO WA — 158-C4

DELTAPORT WY
- DISTRICT OF DELTA BC — 101-C1

DELTA WATERS RD
- JACKSON CO OR — 336-F7
- MEDFORD OR — 336-F7

DEMARAY DR
- JOSEPHINE CO OR — 229-A7
- JOSEPHINE CO OR — 335-A12

DEMPSEY RD
- CLALLAM CO WA — 164-D6
- DIST OF NORTH VANCOUVER BC — 255-E1

DENBROOK RD
- CLACKAMAS CO OR — 199-B6

E DENISON-CHATTAROY RD
- SPOKANE CO WA — 114-C1

W DENISON-CHATTAROY RD
- SPOKANE CO WA — 114-B1

DENMAN ST
- VANCOUVER BC — 254-E9

DENMARK ST SW
- THURSTON CO WA — 184-B1

SW DENNEY RD
- BEAVERTON OR — 199-B2

DENNIS RD
- BENTON CO WA — 120-C3

DENNY WY
- SEATTLE WA — 277-H4
- SEATTLE WA — 278-A4

E DENNY WY
- SEATTLE WA — 278-A4
- SEATTLE WA — 279-E4

W DENNY WY
- SEATTLE WA — 277-H4

W DENNY WY
- SEATTLE WA — 277-H4

DENNY SCHOOL RD
- LINN CO OR — 133-C1

W DENO RD
- SPOKANE CO WA — 246-A2

DENT RD
- FRANKLIN CO WA — 340-J14

N DENVER AV
- PORTLAND OR — 308-E4

DENVER RD
- IDAHO CO ID — 123-C3

S DENVER ST
- ASTORIA OR — 300-B6

DENVER ST SE
- TURNER OR — 325-G12

DEPARTURE BAY RD
- NANAIMO BC — 93-A3

DERRICK CAVES RD
- LAKE CO OR — 143-B2

DESCHUTES AV U.S.-197
- MAUPIN OR — 127-B3

DESCHUTES DR
- JEFFERSON CO OR — 208-B3

NW DESCHUTES DR
- JEFFERSON CO OR — 208-B3

DESCHUTES PKWY
- OLYMPIA WA — 296-G6
- OLYMPIA WA — 296-G6

E DESCHUTES RD
- DESCHUTES CO OR — 142-C1

DESCHUTES ST
- WASCO CO OR — 127-C1

DESCHUTES WY
- TUMWATER WA — 296-H9

DESCHUTES-PLEASANT RIDGE MKT RD
- DESCHUTES CO OR — 212-C7

DESCHUTES RIVER RD
- MAUPIN OR — 127-B3
- WASCO CO OR — 127-B3

DESERT RD
- GEM CO ID — 139-B3

W DESKA DR
- SPOKANE CO WA — 348-C11

DES MOINES MEMORIAL DR S
- BURIEN WA — 288-A4
- DES MOINES WA — 290-A2
- KING CO WA — 286-B4
- KING CO WA — 288-A4
- SEATAC WA — 288-A4
- SEATAC WA — 290-A2

DES MOINES MEM DR S Rt#-509
- BURIEN WA — 288-A7
- BURIEN WA — 290-A1
- SEATAC WA — 290-A1

NW DESPAIN AV
- PENDLETON OR — 129-B1

DESPAIN GULCH RD
- UMATILLA CO OR — 129-A1

DETHMAN RIDGE DR
- HOOD RIVER CO OR — 195-C6

DETROIT BLVD
- AUBURN WA — 182-B1

DETROIT BLVD S
- PACIFIC WA — 182-B2

DETTLING RD
- SNOHOMISH CO WA — 168-B3

DEVER-CONNER RD
- LINN CO OR — 207-C3

DEVERELL RD
- MULTNOMAH CO OR — 200-D2

DEVILLE RD
- SKAMANIA CO WA — 194-A6

DEVILS CANYON RD Rt#-263
- FRANKLIN CO WA — 121-C1
- KAHLOTUS WA — 121-C1

DEVILS GAP RD
- LINCOLN CO WA — 114-A1

E DEVILS LAKE RD
- LINCOLN CITY OR — 203-B4
- LINCOLN CO OR — 203-B4

W DEVILS LAKE RD
- LINCOLN CITY OR — 203-A4
- LINCOLN CO OR — 203-A4

DEVILS MTN RD
- SKAGIT CO WA — 168-B1

DEVILS WELL RD
- LINCOLN CO WA — 206-D4

DEVINE RIDGE RD
- HARNEY CO OR — 137-B3

DE VRIES RD
- ISLAND CO WA — 167-C2

DEWATO RD W
- KITSAP CO WA — 173-C3

DEWATTO RD
- KITSAP CO WA — 173-D4
- MASON CO WA — 173-D4
- MASON CO WA — 174-A4

DEWATTO-HOLLY RD
- MASON CO WA — 173-B5

DEWDNEY TRUNK RD
- DISTRICT OF MISSION BC — 94-B3
- MAPLE RIDGE BC — 94-B3
- MAPLE RIDGE BC — 157-C5
- PITT MEADOWS BC — 157-B5

DEWEY AV Rt#-7
- BAKER CITY OR — 138-B1

DEWEY ST
- BREMERTON WA — 270-G11

DEWEY CREEK LP
- LINCOLN CO OR — 206-C2

DEW VALLEY RD
- COOS CO OR — 220-A7

S DHOOGHE RD
- CLACKAMAS CO OR — 126-A3

DIAGONAL ST Rt#-129
- CLARKSTON WA — 250-B4

DIAL LN
- UNION CO OR — 130-A2

DIAMOND LN
- HARNEY CO OR — 145-B3

DIAMOND HILL DR
- LINN CO OR — 210-A4

DIAMOND HILL RD
- HARRISBURG OR — 210-A5
- LINN CO OR — 210-A5

NE DIAMOND LAKE BLVD Rt#-138
- ROSEBURG OR — 221-C4
- ROSEBURG OR — 334-H7

E DIAMOND LAKE HWY Rt#-138
- DOUGLAS CO OR — 223-D7
- KLAMATH CO OR — 142-B2
- KLAMATH CO OR — 223-D7

W DIAMOND LAKE HWY Rt#-230
- DOUGLAS CO OR — 223-B7
- DOUGLAS CO OR — 226-D3
- DOUGLAS CO OR — 227-A1
- JACKSON CO OR — 226-D3
- KLAMATH CO OR — 332-D12

DIAMOND MATCH CAMP RD
- CLEARWATER CO ID — 123-C1

DIAMOND POINT RD
- CLALLAM CO WA — 166-C7
- JEFFERSON CO WA — 166-C7

DICK RD
- GRANT CO WA — 242-C2

NW DICK RD
- WASHINGTON CO OR — 192-A7

DICKENSHEET RD
- BONNER CO ID — 107-A2

DICKENSON RD
- BRITISH COLUMBIA BC — 93-A3
- NANAIMO BC — 93-A3

DICKEY RD
- DESCHUTES CO OR — 217-D2

S DICKEY RD
- SPOKANE VALLEY WA — 349-J10

DICKEY RD NW
- KITSAP CO WA — 174-A1

DICKEY PRAIRIE RD
- CLACKAMAS CO OR — 126-A3

DICK GEORGE RD
- JOSEPHINE CO OR — 233-B5

DIETZ AV NE
- KEIZER OR — 322-J6
- KEIZER OR — 323-A6

E DIGBY RD
- MOUNT VERNON WA — 260-E13

DIGGER RD
- WASCO CO OR — 196-A6

DIKE BYPS U.S.-12
- LEWISTON ID — 250-B4

DIKE RD
- COLUMBIA CO OR — 189-D7
- COLUMBIA CO WA — 192-A4

DIKE RD
- COWLITZ CO WA — 189-D7
- COWLITZ CO WA — 192-B1
- SKAGIT CO WA — 168-B1
- SKAGIT CO WA — 260-A14
- SNOHOMISH CO WA — 168-D5
- WHATCOM CO WA — 161-D1

DIKE ACCESS RD
- COWLITZ CO WA — 189-D7
- WOODLAND WA — 189-D7

DILLARD HWY Rt#-99
- DOUGLAS CO OR — 221-B7
- WINSTON OR — 221-B7

DILLARD RD
- LANE CO OR — 215-B4

SW DILLEY RD
- WASHINGTON CO OR — 198-B1

DILLON FALLS RD
- DESCHUTES CO OR — 217-A4

NW DIMMICK ST
- GRANTS PASS OR — 335-E8

SW DIMMICK ST
- GRANTS PASS OR — 335-E8

DIMRILL DALE RD
- SKAMANIA CO WA — 194-A6

DINGO
- JEFFERSON CO OR — 212-C3

DINSMORE BRDG
- CITY OF RICHMOND BC — 156-B6

DINWITTY LN
- MALHEUR CO OR — 147-A3

DISASTER PEAK RD
- MALHEUR CO OR — 154-B2

DISCOVERY AV SE
- OCEAN SHORES WA — 298-F4

DISCOVERY RD
- JEFFERSON CO WA — 166-D7
- JEFFERSON CO WA — 263-A9
- PORT TOWNSEND WA — 263-F4

S DISHMAN RD
- SPOKANE VALLEY WA — 350-D9

E DISHMAN-MICA RD
- SPOKANE CO WA — 246-D5
- SPOKANE CO WA — 247-A5

S DISHMAN-MICA RD
- SPOKANE CO WA — 246-D5
- SPOKANE VALLEY WA — 246-D5
- SPOKANE VALLEY WA — 350-E12

S DISHMAN-MICA RD Rt#-27
- SPOKANE CO WA — 247-A5

DISTRICT LINE RD
- BENTON CO WA — 120-C3

DITCH RD
- DESCHUTES CO OR — 212-D4

DITCH CREEK RD
- JACKSON CO OR — 229-D3

DIVERS RD
- CLACKAMAS CO OR — 200-C3

NE DIVIDE RD
- JEFFERSON CO OR — 135-C1

DIVISION AV
- EPHRATA WA — 112-C3
- TACOMA WA — 293-F4

S DIVISION AV Rt#-225
- BENTON CITY WA — 120-C3

DIVISION AV E
- EPHRATA WA — 112-C3

DIVISION AV NE
- Suquamish WA — 170-C7

DIVISION AV W
- EPHRATA WA — 112-C3

E DIVISION LN
- TACOMA WA — 295-J2

N DIVISION RD
- DOUGLAS CO WA — 112-B2
- GRANT CO WA — 242-A3

S DIVISION RD
- DOUGLAS CO WA — 112-B2
- GRANT CO WA — 242-A4

DIVISION ST
- BEND OR — 332-F9
- CASHMERE WA — 238-C2
- DOUGLAS CO OR — 225-C1
- GRANT CO WA — 242-C3
- KELSO WA — 303-D6
- MOSES LAKE WA — 242-C3
- MYRTLE CREEK OR — 225-C1
- OLYMPIA WA — 296-F2
- PORT ORCHARD WA — 270-H14
- THURSTON CO WA — 296-F2

DIVISION ST Rt#-20
- TWISP WA — 104-A3

DIVISION ST Rt#-204
- ELGIN OR — 130-A1
- UNION CO OR — 130-A1

DIVISION ST U.S.-20
- BEND OR — 332-F5

DIVISION ST U.S.-97
- BEND OR — 332-F9

E DIVISION ST
- MOUNT VERNON WA — 260-D12

N DIVISION ST
- CASHMERE WA — 238-C2
- CHELAN CO WA — 238-C2
- RITZVILLE WA — 113-C3
- SANDPOINT ID — 244-A2
- WALLA WALLA WA — 345-C7

N DIVISION ST Rt#-21
- ODESSA WA — 113-B3

N DIVISION ST Rt#-27
- PALOUSE WA — 249-B1

N DIVISION ST U.S.-2
- SPOKANE WA — 346-J12
- SPOKANE WA — 347-A14
- SPOKANE WA — 349-A3

N DIVISION ST U.S.-395
- Country Homes WA — 346-J11
- Country Homes WA — 347-A8
- Fairwood WA — 347-A8
- SPOKANE WA — 346-J11
- Town and Country WA — 346-J11

NE DIVISION ST
- BEND OR — 332-F4
- CHEHALIS WA — 299-D11
- GRESHAM OR — 200-B2

NW DIVISION ST
- GRESHAM OR — 200-A2
- MYRTLE CREEK OR — 225-C1

S DIVISION ST
- ADAMS CO WA — 113-C3
- CASHMERE WA — 238-C2
- MOSES LAKE WA — 242-C3

S DIVISION ST
- RITZVILLE WA — 113-C3
- SANDPOINT ID — 244-A2
- WALLA WALLA WA — 345-C8
- Walla Walla East WA — 345-C8

S DIVISION ST Rt#-225
- BENTON CITY WA — 120-C3

S DIVISION ST U.S.-2
- SPOKANE WA — 349-A9

SE DIVISION ST
- GRESHAM OR — 200-A2
- PORTLAND OR — 200-A2
- PORTLAND OR — 313-G7
- PORTLAND OR — 317-G1
- PORTLAND OR — 318-C1
- PORTLAND OR — 319-H1

W DIVISION ST Rt#-536
- MOUNT VERNON WA — 260-B12

DIVISION ST E
- QUINCY WA — 112-B3

DIVISION ST N
- SOAP LAKE WA — 112-C2

DIVISION ST NE
- SALEM OR — 322-H12

DIVISION ST S
- GRANT CO WA — 112-C2
- KELLOGG ID — 115-C2
- SOAP LAKE WA — 112-C2

DIVISION FENCE RD
- KLICKITAT CO WA — 196-C1

DIXIE CREEK RD
- BAKER CO OR — 138-C2
- GRANT CO OR — 137-B2

DIXIE MOUNTAIN RD
- WASHINGTON CO OR — 125-C1

SE DIXON DR
- JEFFERSON CO OR — 208-C6

DIXON LP
- DESCHUTES CO OR — 217-D2

DIXON RD
- CROOK CO OR — 213-B5

DIXON MILL RD
- WASHINGTON CO OR — 198-C3

DIXONVILLE RD
- DOUGLAS CO OR — 221-D5

D MEYER RD
- WHITMAN CO WA — 249-A7

DOAK RD
- KLAMATH CO OR — 231-D5

DOAKS FERRY RD
- POLK CO OR — 322-D9
- SALEM OR — 322-D9

DOAN RD
- COLUMBIA CO OR — 189-B4

E DOBBIE POINT LN
- SHERMAN CO OR — 127-C3

DOBBIN RD
- WALLOWA CO OR — 130-C2

DOBER RD
- WASHINGTON CO OR — 198-C2

DOCK RD
- KLICKITAT CO WA — 196-D7

DOCK ST Rt#-105
- WESTPORT WA — 298-G11

E DODD RD
- KOOTENAI CO ID — 245-A4

DODDS RD
- DESCHUTES CO OR — 135-B3

DODES CREEK RD
- JACKSON CO OR — 226-A7

DODGE RD
- DOUGLAS CO OR — 230-C4

SE DODGE PARK BLVD
- MULTNOMAH CO OR — 200-C2

DODGE VALLEY RD
- SKAGIT CO WA — 167-D1

DODSON RD
- EPHRATA WA — 112-B2
- GRANT CO WA — 112-C3

DOE CREEK RD
- DOUGLAS CO OR — 225-A3

DOERFLER RD SE
- MARION CO OR — 205-C6

DOERNER CTO
- DOUGLAS CO OR — 221-A4

DOERNER RD
- DOUGLAS CO OR — 221-A4

DOETSCH RD
- COLUMBIA CO OR — 189-C6

DOG RD
- GRANT CO OR — 137-B2

DOG LAKE RD
- LAKE CO OR — 151-C2
- LAKE CO OR — 152-A2

DOG RIDGE RD
- NEWBERG OR — 198-D6
- YAMHILL CO OR — 198-D6

DOGWOOD AV
- ALBANY OR — 326-H7

DOGWOOD DR
- EVERETT WA — 264-B7
- EVERETT WA — 268-B1

DOGWOOD LN
- JEFFERSON CO OR — 208-B4

NE DOGWOOD LN
- JEFFERSON CO OR — 208-C4

E DOGWOOD RD
- FRANKLIN CO WA — 121-A2

W DOLARWAY RD
- ELLENSBURG WA — 241-B5

DOLE RD
- DOUGLAS CO OR — 221-B7
- DOUGLAS CO OR — 225-C1
- MYRTLE CREEK OR — 225-C1

NE DOLE VALLEY RD
- CLARK CO WA — 193-C3

DOLLARHIDE RD
- WHEELER CO OR — 136-B1

DOLLARTON HWY
- DIST OF NORTH VANCOUVER BC — 156-D3
- DIST OF NORTH VANCOUVER BC — 255-H7

DOMINIC RD
- MARION CO OR — 205-C3

DONAHUE RD
- MULTNOMAH CO OR — 200-D2

DONALD RD
- MARION CO OR — 199-A7
- WAPATO WA — 120-A2
- YAKIMA CO WA — 120-A2

DONALDSON RD
- MYRTLE CREEK OR — 225-C1

DONALD-WAPATO RD
- YAKIMA CO WA — 120-A2

DONELLY RD
- HARNEY CO OR — 136-C3

DONELLY RD
- HARNEY CO OR — 144-C1
- HARNEY CO OR — 145-A1

DONEY RD
- DESCHUTES CO OR — 212-D3
- JEFFERSON CO OR — 212-D3

DONKEY CREEK RD
- GRAYS HARBOR CO WA — 109-C3
- GRAYS HARBOR CO WA — 178-A1

DONNELLY RD
- SKAGIT CO WA — 161-A7

DONOVAN AV
- BELLINGHAM WA — 258-D11

DONRUSS DR
- DOUGLAS CO OR — 221-A3

DOOLEY MOUNTAIN HWY Rt#-245
- BAKER CO OR — 138-A1

DOPP RD
- YAMHILL CO OR — 198-C4

DORAN RD
- WHATCOM CO WA — 161-C2

SE DORION AV U.S.-30
- PENDLETON OR — 129-B1

SW DORION AV U.S.-30
- PENDLETON OR — 129-B1

DORMAIER RD
- SHERMAN CO OR — 127-C1

DORNING RD
- LEWIS CO WA — 187-C2

DORRANCE MEADOW RD
- DESCHUTES CO OR — 143-A1

DORRIS BROWNELL RD
- SISKIYOU CO CA — 150-C3

S DORSET RD
- SPOKANE CO WA — 246-B5

DORSEY RD
- KLICKITAT CO WA — 196-A3

SW DOSCH RD
- PORTLAND OR — 316-B2

DOSEWALLIPS RD
- JEFFERSON CO WA — 109-C1

DOT RD
- KLICKITAT CO WA — 120-A3
- KLICKITAT CO WA — 128-A1

DOUBLE BLUFF RD
- ISLAND CO WA — 170-D2

DOUBLE CREEK LN
- SKAGIT CO WA — 161-B4

DOUBLEDAY RD
- JACKSON CO OR — 150-A1

DOUBLE O RD
- HARNEY CO OR — 145-A2

DOUGHERTY DR
- CASTLE ROCK WA — 187-C2
- COWLITZ CO WA — 187-C2

DOUGHTY RD
- BAY CITY OR — 197-B1
- TILLAMOOK CO OR — 197-B1

DOUGLAS AV
- GERVAIS OR — 205-A2
- MARION CO OR — 205-A2
- SNOHOMISH CO WA — 265-H4

N DOUGLAS AV
- PASCO WA — 343-J7

NE DOUGLAS AV
- DOUGLAS CO OR — 221-C5
- ROSEBURG OR — 221-C5
- ROSEBURG OR — 334-H7

SE DOUGLAS AV
- ROSEBURG OR — 334-H7

N DOUGLAS BLVD Rt#-99
- WINSTON OR — 221-B6

W DOUGLAS BLVD Rt#-42
- WINSTON OR — 221-B6

DOUGLAS CRES
- LANGLEY BC — 158-C1
- VANCOUVER BC — 254-E13

DOUGLAS DR
- PACIFIC CO WA — 186-A2

DOUGLAS RD
- DISTRICT OF BURNABY BC — 156-D4
- DISTRICT OF BURNABY BC — 255-G11
- FERNDALE WA — 158-C5
- WHATCOM CO WA — 158-B6
- YAKIMA CO WA — 243-A7

DOUGLAS ST
- LONGVIEW WA — 302-E13
- LONGVIEW WA — 303-A13

DOUGLAS ST Rt#-1
- CITY OF VICTORIA BC — 256-G6
- DISTRICT OF SAANICH BC — 256-G6

DOUGLAS FALLS RD
- STEVENS CO WA — 106-A2

SE DOVER LN
- JEFFERSON CO OR — 208-C7

SW DOVER LN
- JEFFERSON CO OR — 208-B6

S DOVER RD
- SPOKANE CO WA — 114-B2

DOVER ST
- DISTRICT OF BURNABY BC — 156-C5

DOW RD
- KLICKITAT CO WA — 196-C6

DOWANS CREEK RD
- JEFFERSON CO OR — 169-B3

DOWD RD
- COLUMBIA CO OR — 192-A3

W DOWD RD
- KOOTENAI CO ID — 247-C6

SE DOWLING RD
- CLACKAMAS CO OR — 200-D5

DOWNES RD
- DISTRICT OF MATSQUI BC — 102-B1

DOWNEY RD
- DISTRICT OF NORTH SAANICH BC — 159-B2
- SKAGIT CO WA — 160-D3

DOWNEY GULCH RD
- CHELAN CO WA — 236-C3

S DOWNING DR
- SEASIDE OR — 301-F10

E DOWNING RD Rt#-507
- CENTRALIA WA — 184-C5
- LEWIS CO WA — 184-C5

S DOWNING ST
- SEASIDE OR — 301-F10

DOWN RIVER RD Rt#-128
- LEWISTON ID — 250-B4

W DOWNRIVER PARK DR
- SPOKANE WA — 348-A9

DOWNS RD NE
- MARION CO OR — 205-B4

SE DOWTY RD
- CLACKAMAS CO OR — 200-B5

DOYLE RD
- CLARK CO WA — 192-C3

N DOYLE RD
- KOOTENAI CO ID — 248-D2

STREET — City State Page-Grid

DRAGICH RD
COWLITZ CO WA 189-A1
DRAHAM ST NE
THURSTON CO WA 297-H3
DRAIN RD
DOUGLAS CO OR 219-A3
DRAIN 10 RD
MODOC CO CA 151-A3
DRAIN-YONCALLA HWY Rt#-99
DOUGLAS CO OR 219-A3
DRAIN OR 219-A3
YONCALLA OR 219-A3
DRAKE RD
CLACKAMAS CO OR 205-D3
NW DRAKE RD
BEND OR 332-D6
DRAKE RD NE
CLACKAMAS CO OR 205-C3
MARION CO OR 205-C3
DRAPER SPRINGS RD
KLICKITAT CO WA 119-A3
DRAPER VALLEY RD
JOSEPHINE CO OR 233-B1
W DRAVUS ST
SEATTLE WA 273-E7
DRAYTON ST
LYNDEN WA 102-B1
DRAYTON HARBOR RD
Birch Bay WA 158-A3
BLAINE WA 158-A3
WHATCOM CO WA 158-A3
DRAZIL RD
KLAMATH CO OR 151-A2
DREGER RD E
LINCOLN CO WA 113-B1
DRESSER RD Rt#-500
CLARK CO WA 193-B6
DREWS RD
KLAMATH CO OR 151-A1
DREWSEY RD
HARNEY CO OR 137-C3
HARNEY CO OR 145-C1
DREWSEY MARKET RD
HARNEY CO OR 137-C3
DREWS PRAIRIE RD
LEWIS CO WA 187-C4
D REX RD
DOUGLAS CO WA 105-A3
DRIFT CREEK RD
LINCOLN CO OR 203-A5
LINCOLN CO OR 209-B1
DRIFT CREEK RD NE
MARION CO OR 205-C5
DRIFT CREEK RD SE
MARION CO OR 205-C5
DRIFTWOOD RD NW
THURSTON CO WA 180-C5
THURSTON CO WA 296-C1
N DRISCOLL BLVD
SPOKANE WA 348-D2
DRIVER RD
LINN CO OR 207-C7
DRIVER VALLEY RD
DOUGLAS CO OR 219-B7
DRUMHELLAR RD
GRANT CO WA 242-A1
DRUMHELLER RD
SPOKANE CO WA 247-B7
E DRUMHELLER RD
SPOKANE CO WA 247-A7
DRY COULEE RD
GRANT CO WA 112-C2
DRY CREEK CTO
MALHEUR CO OR 146-B1
DRY CREEK LN
UNION CO OR 130-A2
DRY CREEK RD
CROOK CO OR 213-D3
IDAHO CO ID 131-B1
JEFFERSON CO OR 208-B2
KITTITAS CO WA 241-B5
MALHEUR CO OR 146-C1
PAYETTE CO ID 139-B2
Warm Springs OR 208-B2
WASCO CO OR 196-A6
WHITMAN CO WA 114-C3
DRY CREEK RD U.S.-97
KITTITAS CO WA 241-A4
DRY CREEK CANYON RD
DOUGLAS CO OR 225-C3
DRY CREEK TRAIL RD
Warm Springs OR 208-A2
DRYDEN RD
JOSEPHINE CO OR 233-C2
N DRYDEN RD
CHELAN CO WA 238-B2
DRYDEN OVERLOOK RD
JOSEPHINE CO OR 233-C2
DRY HOLLOW RD
JEFFERSON CO OR 208-A4
THE DALLES OR 196-C7
WASCO CO OR 196-C7
WHEELER CO OR 136-A1
DRY LAKE RD
CHELAN CO WA 236-B1
ISLAND CO WA 167-D5
MALHEUR CO OR 146-B2
DRYLAND RD
CLACKAMAS CO OR 199-C7
S DRYLAND RD
CLACKAMAS CO OR 205-D1
DRY SLOUGH RD
SKAGIT CO WA 168-A2
DRY VALLEY HWY
HARNEY CO OR 144-B2
DRY VALLEY RD
HARNEY CO OR 144-C2
N DUBOIS RD
COWLITZ CO WA 118-A3
DUBUQUE RD
SNOHOMISH CO WA 110-C1
SNOHOMISH CO WA 171-D2
DUCKABUSH RD
JEFFERSON CO WA 173-C1
DUCK LAKE DR
OCEAN SHORES WA 177-B7
DUCK LAKE DR SE
OCEAN SHORES WA 298-E1
DUCK LAKE RD
LINCOLN CO WA 113-B2
DUDLEY RD
KITTITAS CO WA 240-D3
KOOTENAI CO ID 115-B2
YAMHILL CO OR 198-C5
E DUFFIELD RD
YAKIMA CO WA 243-D7

DUFORT RD
BONNER CO ID 107-A3
E DUFORT RD
BONNER CO ID 244-A4
DUFUR BYPASS RD
WASCO CO OR 127-B2
DUFUR GAP RD
WASCO CO OR 127-B2
DUFUR VALLEY RD
WASCO CO OR 127-B2
DUGOUT LAKE RD
DESCHUTES CO OR 211-B4
DUKE LN
MARION CO OR 198-D7
W DUKE RD
DOUGLAS CO OR 221-C1
DUKE POINT HWY Rt#-19
BRITISH COLUMBIA BC 93-A3
NANAIMO BC 93-A3
DULEY CREEK RD
CURRY CO OR 232-C5
DUMAR WY SW
SEATTLE WA 285-G1
DUMP RD
NEZ PERCE CO ID 250-D2
DUNBAR RD
SKAGIT CO WA 161-A2
DUNBAR ST
UNIV ENDOWMENT LANDS BC ... 156-A5
VANCOUVER BC 156-A5
VANCOUVER BC 254-A14
DUNBAR DIV
VANCOUVER BC 254-A13
DUNCAN CREEK RD
SKAMANIA CO WA 194-B6
DUNDAS ST
VANCOUVER BC 255-D10
SW DUNDEE RD
WASHINGTON CO OR 198-A2
DUNIVAN RD
LEWIS CO WA 187-B4
DUNIWAY RD
YAMHILL CO OR 198-B6
DUNKARD RD
KLICKITAT CO WA 196-B1
DUNLAP RD SW
THURSTON CO WA 184-C4
DUNN RD
CLARK CO WA 192-D1
S DUNN RD
SPOKANE CO WA 246-D6
SE DUNN RD
CLACKAMAS CO OR 200-C3
DUNNING RD
WHITMAN CO WA 249-A6
DUNSMUIR ST
VANCOUVER BC 254-G10
DUPONT ST
BELLINGHAM WA 258-C5
DUPONT-STEILACOOM RD SW
DUPONT WA 181-B5
PIERCE CO WA 181-B5
DUPORTAIL ST
RICHLAND WA 341-E2
DURBIN CREEK RD
BAKER CO OR 138-C2
SW DURHAM LN
YAMHILL CO OR 204-B1
SW DURHAM RD
TIGARD OR 199-B3
DURR RD
KITTITAS CO WA 241-B5
KITTITAS CO WA 243-B1
YAKIMA CO WA 243-B2
DURRWACHTER RD
CLALLAM CO WA 164-D5
DURY RD
ADAMS CO WA 113-C3
DUSTY LP
DESCHUTES CO OR 212-B4
DUTCH CANYON RD
COLUMBIA CO OR 125-C1
COLUMBIA CO OR 192-A4
DUTCH HENRY RD
DOUGLAS CO OR 141-A3
DUTCHY CREEK RD
JOSEPHINE CO OR 148-C1
DUTHIE AV
DISTRICT OF BURNABY BC ... 156-D4
SE DUTHIE HILL RD
KING CO WA 176-A3
SAMMAMISH WA 176-A3
DUTTON RD
UNION CO OR 130-B2
DUUS RD
CLACKAMAS CO OR 200-C5
DUVAL RD
DIST OF NORTH VANCOUVER BC ... 255-G2
DUVAL AV NE
KING CO WA 175-C4
RENTON WA 175-C4
DUVALL-MONROE RD Rt#-203
KING CO WA 110-C1
SNOHOMISH CO WA 110-C1
DUVALL-MONROE RD NE Rt#-203
DUVALL WA 110-C1
KING CO WA 110-C1
DWIGHT HALSEY RD
ASOTIN CO WA 123-A3
DYKE RD
CITY OF RICHMOND BC 156-B7
PITT MEADOWS BC 157-B5

E

E RD
COTTONWOOD ID 123-C3
IDAHO CO ID 123-C3
E RD SE
DOUGLAS CO WA 112-C2
E ST
COLUMBIA CITY OR 192-B1
CULVER OR 208-B7
ENDICOTT WA 122-B1
GRANTS PASS OR 335-E8
NESPELEM WA 105-A3
NORTH POWDER OR 130-B3
SISKIYOU CO OR 151-A3
TULELAKE CA 151-A3
WALLA WALLA CO WA 345-H4
WHITMAN CO WA 122-B1
E ST Rt#-8
FOREST GROVE OR 198-B1
E ST Rt#-14B
WASHOUGAL WA 193-C7
E ST Rt#-207
LEXINGTON OR 128-C2

E ST Rt#-272
PALOUSE WA 249-C1
E ST U.S.-97
SHANIKO OR 127-C3
E E ST
GRANTS PASS OR 335-G9
N E ST
TACOMA WA 293-G3
N E ST Rt#-272
PALOUSE WA 249-C1
S E ST
ABERDEEN WA 178-B7
E ST NE
GRANT CO WA 112-C2
EADEN RD
CLACKAMAS CO OR 200-B4
EADON RD
LEWIS CO WA 187-D4
NE EADS ST
NEWPORT OR 206-B4
EAGAR RD
COLUMBIA CO WA 122-A2
EAGLE DR
DESCHUTES CO OR 212-C5
JACKSON CO OR 230-C4
EAGLE LN
JEFFERSON CO OR 208-C2
E EAGLE RD
BAKER CO OR 130-C3
N EAGLE RD
EAGLE ID 253-B1
S EAGLE RD
ADA CO ID 253-B4
MERIDIAN ID 253-B4
S EAGLE RD Rt#-55
ADA CO ID 253-B2
BOISE ID 253-B2
EAGLE ID 253-B2
MERIDIAN ID 253-B2
EAGLE WY
YAKIMA CO WA 243-C6
EAGLE CREEK DR
BAKER CO OR 130-C3
EAGLE CREEK LN
UNION CO OR 130-B3
EAGLE CREEK RD
CHELAN CO WA 111-C2
CLACKAMAS CO OR 200-C5
EAGLE CREEK RANCH RD
CLALLAM CO WA 163-C7
EAGLE CREEK-SANDY HWY Rt#-211
CLACKAMAS CO OR 200-C4
SANDY OR 200-C4
EAGLE CREST RD
POLK CO OR 204-C5
EAGLE FERN RD
CLACKAMAS CO OR 200-C5
NE EAGLE HARBOR DR
KITSAP CO WA 174-D2
KITSAP CO WA 271-J3
EAGLE MILL RD
JACKSON CO OR 337-A4
N EAGLE MILL RD
JACKSON CO OR 337-D5
EAGLEMOUNT RD
JEFFERSON CO WA 170-A2
EAGLE PEAK RD
KOOTENAI CO ID 248-D4
SW EAGLE POINT RD
YAMHILL CO OR 204-A1
EAGLE RIDGE RD
KLAMATH CO OR 231-B7
EAGLE ROCK RD
CLACKAMAS CO OR 211-D5
EAGLE SPRINGS RD E
LINCOLN CO WA 113-B2
EAGLE VALLEY RD Rt#-99
DOUGLAS CO OR 219-A3
EARLES ST
VANCOUVER BC 156-C5
EARLWOOD RD
CLACKAMAS CO OR 199-A6
YAMHILL CO OR 199-A6
EAST BLVD NE
KITSAP CO WA 271-C3
EAST MALL
UNIV ENDOWMENT LANDS BC ... 156-A4
EAST RD
ANMORE BC 157-A3
KLICKITAT CO WA 128-A3
KLICKITAT CO WA 128-A1
EAST AND WEST TKTR
COWLITZ CO WA 187-A7
EAST BAY DR
COOS BAY OR 220-D1
COOS CO OR 140-B2
COOS CO OR 218-B7
COOS CO OR 220-D1
COOS CO OR 333-H1
EAST BEACH RD
CLALLAM CO WA 164-C6
EAST BEAVER CREEK RD
TILLAMOOK CO OR 197-C5
EAST COVE RD
LATAH CO ID 249-D1
EASTERDAY RD
WASHINGTON CO OR 198-B1
EASTERN BOUNDARY RD
KITSAP CO WA 170-B6
EAST FORK RD
DOUGLAS CO OR 225-B1
JOSEPHINE CO OR 149-B2
EAST FORK EVANS CREEK RD
JACKSON CO OR 230-C1
EAST FORK GLENN CREEK RD
COOS CO OR 140-C1
EAST FORK PINE CREEK RD
SHOSHONE CO ID 115-C2
EAST GATE RD
PIERCE CO WA 181-C6
WASCO CO OR 126-C3
WASCO CO OR 127-A3
SE EASTGATE WY
BELLEVUE WA 175-C3
EASTLAKE AV E
SEATTLE WA 274-B7
SEATTLE WA 278-B1
EASTLAKE DR
DISTRICT OF BURNABY BC ... 156-D4
NW EASTMAN PKWY
GRESHAM OR 200-B2
N EASTMONT AV
DOUGLAS CO WA 239-A4
EAST WENATCHEE WA 239-A4
East Wenatchee Bench WA ... 239-A4
EASTON CANYON RD
WASCO CO OR 127-B2

EAST POINT RD
KOOTENAI CO ID 248-A4
EAST PORTLAND FRWY I-205
CLACKAMAS CO OR 199-D4
CLACKAMAS CO OR 319-G6
GLADSTONE OR 199-D4
OREGON CITY OR 199-D4
PORTLAND OR 319-G6
TUALATIN OR 199-D4
WASHINGTON CO OR 199-D4
WEST LINN OR 199-D4
EAST RIVERSIDE RD
OKANOGAN CO WA 104-C2
EAST SAANICH RD
DISTRICT OF NORTH SAANICH BC . 159-C3
EAST SHORE RD
BONNER CO ID 107-A1
EASTSIDE DR
VALLEY CO ID 251-D6
EASTSIDE DR NE Rt#-509
PIERCE CO WA 181-B5
PIERCE CO WA 182-A1
EAST SIDE RD
UMATILLA CO OR 121-C3
EASTSIDE RD
BONNER CO ID 107-A2
HOOD RIVER CO OR 195-D6
EASTSIDE ST
OLYMPIA WA 297-A5
N EASTSIDE ST
OLYMPIA WA 296-J5
OLYMPIA WA 297-A5
EASTSIDE ACCESS RD
OKANOGAN CO WA 104-C3
EASTSIDE CHEWACK RD
OKANOGAN CO WA 104-A3
WINTHROP WA 104-A2
EASTSIDE OROVILLE RD
OKANOGAN CO WA 104-C1
EASTSIDE OSOYOOS RD
OKANOGAN CO WA 104-C1
EASTSIDE-SUMNER RD
COOS CO OR 140-D2
COOS CO OR 220-D2
EAST SOOKE RD
BRITISH COLUMBIA BC 164-D1
BRITISH COLUMBIA BC 165-A1
DISTRICT OF METCHOSIN BC ... 165-A1
EAST TWISP-WINTHROP RD
OKANOGAN CO WA 104-A3
TWISP WA 104-A2
EAST VALLEY HWY
AUBURN WA 182-B2
AUBURN WA 182-B2
PACIFIC WA 182-B2
SUMNER WA 182-B2
EAST WEST RD
SISKIYOU CO CA 150-C3
SISKIYOU CO CA 151-A3
EASY ST
BROOKINGS OR 232-C6
SISKIYOU CO OR 149-C3
Sunnyslope WA 238-D3
S EASY ST
ROCKAWAY BEACH OR ... 191-B6
EATON RD
CLARK CO WA 118-A3
CLARK CO WA 193-B1
EATONVILLE HWY
EATONVILLE WA 118-B1
PIERCE CO WA 118-B1
EATONVILLE CUT-OFF RD
PIERCE CO WA 118-B1
EATONVILLE CUT-OFF RD Rt#-161
EATONVILLE WA 118-B1
PIERCE CO WA 118-B1
EATONVILLE-LA GRANDE Rt#-161
EATONVILLE WA 118-B1
PIERCE CO WA 118-B1
EBELL CREEK RD
BAKER CO OR 138-B1
EBEY RD
ISLAND CO WA 167-B4
NE EBY AV
DESCHUTES CO OR 212-D3
Terrebonne OR 212-D3
S EBY RD
CLACKAMAS CO OR 205-D1
ECHAVE RANCH RD
MALHEUR CO OR 154-B2
ECHO LAKE CTO SE Rt#-18
KING CO WA 176-B5
ECHO LAKE RD
SNOHOMISH CO WA 171-C4
ECHO LAKE-SNOQUALMIE CTO SE
KING CO WA 176-B4
ECKENSTAM-JOHNSON RD
PIERCE CO WA 181-A4
S ECKERT RD
ADA CO ID 253-D3
BOISE ID 253-D3
ECKLER MOUNTAIN RD
COLUMBIA CO WA 122-B2
ECKMAN CREEK RD
LINCOLN CO OR 209-B3
ECKS FLAT RD
ADAMS CO WA 251-B5
EDDYVILLE RD
KOOTENAI CO ID 248-B1
EDDYVILLE BLODGETT HWY
BENTON CO OR 133-A1
LINCOLN CO OR 133-A1
EDENBOWER MILLWOOD RD
DOUGLAS CO OR 221-B2
EDENS RD
SKAGIT CO WA 160-C5
EDENVALE RD
LANE CO OR 215-D3
LANE CO OR 331-J14
EDEN VALLEY RD
CLALLAM CO WA 164-D6
CLALLAM CO WA 165-A6
WAHKIAKUM CO WA 117-A2
EDER RD
OKANOGAN CO WA 104-C1
EDGEMONT BLVD
DIST OF NORTH VANCOUVER BC ... 254-H2
EDGEWATER ST NW Rt#-221
SALEM OR 322-F12
EDGEWOOD DR
CLALLAM CO WA 165-A6
CLALLAM CO WA 261-A5
PORT ANGELES WA 165-A6
PORT ANGELES WA 261-A5
EDGEWOOD LN
KLAMATH CO OR 235-D1

EDINBOWER BLVD
DOUGLAS CO OR 334-E2
ROSEBURG OR 334-E3
EDISON AV SW
BANDON OR 220-B6
N EDISON ST
BENTON CO WA 342-F9
KENNEWICK WA 342-F9
S EDISON ST
BENTON CO WA 342-F11
KENNEWICK WA 342-F11
EDISON ICE CAVE RD
DESCHUTES CO OR 216-C5
EDLER RD
KLAMATH CO OR 151-B1
SW EDMINSTON RD
CLACKAMAS CO OR 199-A6
EDMONDS AV NE
RENTON WA 175-C5
EDMONDS RD
DISTRICT OF BURNABY BC ... 156-D5
EDMONDS WY Rt#-104
EDMONDS WA 171-A6
SNOHOMISH CO WA 171-A6
WOODWAY WA 171-A6
EDMONDS-KINGSTON FERRY
EDMONDS WA 171-A5
Kingston WA 170-D5
EDMONDSON RD
DESCHUTES CO OR 212-A4
EDMUNSON DR SE
MARION CO OR 205-B6
W EDNA ST
BOISE ID 253-B2
EDSON CREEK RD
CURRY CO OR 228-A4
EDWARDS DR
WHATCOM CO WA 101-C1
EDWARDS RD E
PIERCE CO WA 182-C2
EDWARDS BUTTE RD
TILLAMOOK CO OR 197-D3
SW EDY RD
WASHINGTON CO OR 199-A4
EELLS ST
TACOMA WA 182-A2
EELS RD
CHELAN CO WA 238-C2
S EGAN AV
BURNS OR 145-B1
HARNEY CO OR 145-B1
EGAN SPRINGS RD
KLAMATH CO OR 142-C3
EGBERS KALSO RD
SKAGIT CO WA 161-A6
EGG AND I RD
JEFFERSON CO WA 170-A2
NE EGLON RD
KITSAP CO WA 170-D4
EGYPT CANYON RD
HARNEY CO OR 144-C1
EHLEN RD
AURORA OR 199-B7
MARION CO OR 199-A7
N EHORN LN
CHEWELAH WA 106-B3
EICHER RD
LINN CO OR 207-D5
EID RD
LATAH CO ID 249-D6
EIGHT DOLLAR MOUNTAIN RD
JOSEPHINE CO OR 233-A2
EILERS RD
CLACKAMAS CO OR 199-B6
SW EISCHEN DR
WASHINGTON CO OR 198-C2
S EKELMAN RD
YAKIMA CO WA 243-C7
EKROTH RD
TILLAMOOK CO OR 191-B7
ELBE DR
JEFFERSON CO OR 212-D2
NW ELBE DR
JEFFERSON CO OR 208-B4
SW ELBE DR
JEFFERSON CO OR 208-B7
ELDER RD
WHATCOM CO WA 158-C6
E ELDER RD
SPOKANE CO WA 246-D7
W ELDER RD
SPOKANE CO WA 247-A7
W ELDER RD U.S.-95
KOOTENAI CO ID 247-C6
ELDORADO AV
KLAMATH FALLS OR 338-D5
ELDORADO BLVD
KLAMATH FALLS OR 338-D4
NW EL DORADO BLVD
KITSAP CO WA 270-A3
ELDORADO RD
CLACKAMAS CO OR 199-D7
ELDRIDGE AV
BELLINGHAM WA 258-B5
ELDRIDGE-FRAZIER RD
PIERCE CO WA 182-C4
ELECTRIC AV
BELLINGHAM WA 258-J6
W ELECTRIC AV
SPOKANE CO WA 246-A5
ELEPHANT MOUNTAIN RD
DOUGLAS CO OR 223-B3
ELFENDAHL PASS RD
MASON CO WA 173-C5
ELGAROSE LOOP RD
DOUGLAS CO OR 221-A3
ELGER BAY RD
ISLAND CO WA 167-D5
ELGIN AV U.S.-20
CANYON CO ID 147-B1
NOTUS ID 147-B1
ELGIN RD
CITY OF SURREY BC 158-A1
PAYETTE CO ID 139-B3
ELGIN-CLIFTON Rt#-302
OKANOGAN CO WA 174-A7
ELIJAH RD
STEVENS CO WA 114-A1
ELISHA RD
CLACKAMAS CO OR 205-C2
CLACKAMAS CO OR 205-D1
ELIZA DR
SAN JUAN CO WA 160-A6
ELIZABETH ST Rt#-27
TEKOA WA 114-C3

NE ELIZABETH ST
MILTON-FREEWATER OR ... 121-C3
SW ELIZABETH ST
NEWPORT OR 206-A4
NW ELK DR
JEFFERSON CO OR 208-B5
SW ELK DR
JEFFERSON CO OR 208-B5
ELK RD
JACKSON CO OR 226-C5
ELK BUTTE RD
CLEARWATER CO ID 123-C1
N ELK- CHATTAROY RD
SPOKANE CO WA 114-C1
ELK CITY RD
LINCOLN CO OR 206-D4
ELK CREEK RD
COLUMBIA CO WA 189-A4
JACKSON CO OR 226-B6
ELK CREEK RIDGE RD
CLALLAM CO WA 169-D1
ELKHEAD RD
DOUGLAS CO OR 219-B4
ELKHORN CREEK RD
LINCOLN CO OR 206-B6
ELKHORN RIDGE RD
JACKSON CO OR 226-A5
ELKINS RD
CROOK CO OR 213-A4
POLK CO OR 207-A1
ELK LAKE RD
IDAHO CO ID 131-C2
ELK MOUNTAIN RD
COOS CO OR 218-D7
ELKOFF RD
TILLAMOOK CO OR 197-B3
ELK PRAIRIE RD
PACIFIC CO WA 117-A2
ELK RIDGE RD N
YAKIMA CO WA 243-A2
ELK RIVER RD
CLEARWATER CO ID 123-C1
CURRY CO OR 140-B3
CURRY CO OR 224-B6
CURRY CO OR 228-C1
ELK RIVER RD Rt#-3
LATAH CO ID 123-B1
ELKTON-SUTHERLIN HWY Rt#-138
DOUGLAS CO OR 141-A1
DOUGLAS CO OR 221-C1
ELKTON OR 141-A1
SUTHERLIN OR 221-C1
E ELKTON-SUTHERLIN HWY Rt#-99
SUTHERLIN OR 221-C1
W ELKTON-SUTHERLIN HWY Rt#-138
DOUGLAS CO OR 221-C1
SUTHERLIN OR 221-C1
ELK VALLEY RD Rt#-D2
CRESCENT CITY CA 148-B3
DEL NORTE CO CA 148-B3
ELK VALLEY CROSS RD Rt#-D2
DEL NORTE CO CA 148-B3
ELK VIEW RD
CITY OF CHILLIWACK BC .. 102-C1
ELLA RD
MORROW CO OR 128-B2
E ELLENDALE AV Rt#-223
DALLAS OR 204-A6
W ELLENDALE AV
DALLAS OR 204-A6
ELLENDALE RD
DALLAS OR 204-A6
POLK CO OR 125-B3
POLK CO OR 204-A6
W ELLENDALE RD
POLK CO OR 125-B3
W ELLENS FERRY DR
BOISE ID 253-C2
ELLIGSEN RD
WASHINGTON CO OR 199-B5
WILSONVILLE OR 199-B5
ELLINGSON RD
ALBANY OR 326-C14
ALGONA WA 182-B2
AUBURN WA 182-B2
KING CO WA 182-B2
LINN CO OR 326-C14
PACIFIC WA 182-B2
ELLIOT DR
SPOKANE WA 348-D6
ELLIOT RD
CLARK CO WA 193-B1
DESCHUTES CO OR 213-A4
MULTNOMAH CO OR 192-A6
ELLIOT ST
DISTRICT OF DELTA BC ... 101-C1
ELLIOTT AV
SEATTLE WA 277-H4
ELLIOTT AV W
SEATTLE WA 277-F2
ELLIOTT LN
CROOK CO OR 213-C4
ELLIOTT RD
SNOHOMISH CO WA 171-D5
ELLIOTT PRAIRIE RD NE
MARION CO OR 205-C2
ELLIS AV S
SEATTLE WA 282-B7
SEATTLE WA 286-B1
ELLIS LN
BENEWAH CO ID 248-A7
ELLIS RD
BAKER CO OR 130-A3
UNION CO OR 130-A3
ELLIS RD SW
DOUGLAS CO WA 239-C3
ELLIS ST
BELLINGHAM WA 258-E4
SE ELLSWORTH RD
VANCOUVER WA 307-H7
VANCOUVER WA 311-H1
ELLSWORTH ST U.S.-20
ALBANY OR 326-C8
ELM AV
TILLAMOOK CO OR 197-B2
E ELM AV
COEUR D'ALENE ID 355-G10
HERMISTON OR 129-A1
UMATILLA CO OR 129-A1
S ELM AV
PASCO WA 343-J8
W ELM AV
HERMISTON OR 129-A1
ELM LN
CANYON CO ID 147-C1

STREET City State Page-Grid

NE ELM LN
JEFFERSON CO OR ... 208-C4
NW ELM LN
JEFFERSON CO OR ... 208-B4
ELM ST
ALBANY OR ... 326-B8
ASOTIN CO WA ... 250-B4
BELLINGHAM WA ... 258-C5
CANNON BEACH OR ... 188-B7
CHENEY WA ... 246-A4
CLARKSTON WA ... 250-B4
SISTERS OR ... 211-D5
SUMNER WA ... 182-B3
WHATCOM CO WA ... 101-C1
ELM ST U.S.-30
BAKER CITY OR ... 138-B1
E ELM ST
DOUGLAS CO WA ... 236-C7
WATERVILLE WA ... 236-C7
S ELM ST Rt#-22
TOPPENISH WA ... 120-A2
ELMA-GATE RD
GRAYS HARBOR CO WA ... 117-B1
ELMA-HICKLIN RD
GRAYS HARBOR CO WA ... 179-C6
ELMA-MCCLEARY RD
GRAYS HARBOR CO WA ... 179-C6
ELMA-MCCLEARY RD Rt#-108
GRAYS HARBOR CO WA ... 179-C6
MCCLEARY WA ... 179-C6
ELMORE RD
PAYETTE CO ID ... 139-A3
ELMWAY Rt#-20
OKANOGAN WA ... 104-C3
OKANOGAN CO WA ... 104-C3
OMAK WA ... 104-C3
ELO RD
VALLEY CO ID ... 251-D5
EL RIO LN
LANE CO OR ... 210-A6
ELROD AV
COOS BAY OR ... 333-G10
ELSNER RD
CLACKAMAS CO OR ... 200-D3
SW ELSNER RD
WASHINGTON CO OR ... 199-A4
ELTOPIA WEST RD
FRANKLIN CO WA ... 121-A2
ELTOPIA WEST RD W
FRANKLIN CO WA ... 121-A2
SW ELWERT RD
WASHINGTON CO OR ... 199-A4
ELWHA RIVER RD
CLALLAM CO WA ... 165-A6
ELWOOD DR SW
LAKEWOOD WA ... 181-C4
N ELY PL
KENNEWICK WA ... 342-J9
KENNEWICK WA ... 343-A9
N ELY ST U.S.-395
KENNEWICK WA ... 342-J10
S ELY ST
KENNEWICK WA ... 342-J13
KENNEWICK WA ... 343-A12
S ELY ST U.S.-395
KENNEWICK WA ... 342-J11
EMANDER RD
EVERETT WA ... 268-A6
SNOHOMISH CO WA ... 268-A6
EMENS AV
DARRINGTON WA ... 103-A3
EMENS AV Rt#-530
DARRINGTON WA ... 103-A3
EMERALD RD
GRANGER WA ... 120-B2
YAKIMA CO WA ... 120-B2
W EMERALD ST
BOISE ID ... 253-C3
EMERSON AV Rt#-109
HOQUIAM WA ... 178-A7
NE EMERSON DR
JEFFERSON CO OR ... 208-D3
EMERSON LN
JEFFERSON CO OR ... 208-D4
W EMERSON PL
SEATTLE WA ... 272-E6
SEATTLE WA ... 273-E6
EMERSON RD
DOUGLAS CO OR ... 222-B7
EMERSON ST
FIRCREST WA ... 294-A3
UNIVERSITY PLACE WA ... 294-A3
W EMERSON ST
SEATTLE WA ... 272-C6
SEATTLE WA ... 273-C6
EMERSON LOOP RD
WASCO CO OR ... 127-B2
WASCO CO OR ... 196-D7
EMERY RD
CLALLAM CO WA ... 165-D7
SE EMIGRANT AV Rt#-37
PENDLETON OR ... 129-B1
SW EMIGRANT AV Rt#-37
PENDLETON OR ... 129-B1
EMIGRANT CREEK RD
HARNEY CO OR ... 136-C3
HARNEY CO OR ... 137-A3
EMIGRANTS RD
UMATILLA CO OR ... 129-B1
EMIGRANT SPRINGS RD
SHERMAN CO OR ... 127-C1
W EMMA AV
COEUR D'ALENE ID ... 355-D9
EMMA ST Rt#-278
ROCKFORD WA ... 114-C2
N EMMETT HWY Rt#-16
ADA CO ID ... 139-C3
ADA CO ID ... 147-C1
EMMETT RD
ADAMS CO ID ... 139-C3
CANYON CO ID ... 147-B1
NW EMPIRE WY
East Wenatchee Bench WA ... 239-A4
EMPIRE BLVD
BEND OR ... 332-F2
S EMPIRE BLVD
COOS BAY OR ... 333-A8
COOS CO OR ... 220-C1
COOS CO OR ... 333-A8
E EMPIRE WY
MILLWOOD WA ... 350-D5
SPOKANE VALLEY WA ... 350-F4
EMPIRE WY S
SEATTLE WA ... 278-D2
SEATTLE WA ... 282-D2
SEATTLE WA ... 283-E7

EMPIRE WY S
SEATTLE WA ... 287-E5
TUKWILA WA ... 287-E5
EMPIRE CENTER BLVD
POST FALLS ID ... 353-F6
EMPIRE-COOS BAY HWY
COOS BAY OR ... 333-D8
ENCHANTED PKWY Rt#-161
FEDERAL WAY WA ... 182-B1
ENCHANTED PKWY S Rt#-161
EDGEWOOD WA ... 182-B2
FEDERAL WAY WA ... 182-B2
FEDERAL WAY WA ... 182-B2
MILTON WA ... 182-B2
S ENDICOTT RD
ENDICOTT WA ... 122-B1
WHITMAN CO WA ... 122-B1
ENDICOTT RD E
WHITMAN CO WA ... 122-B1
ENDICOTT RD SW
THURSTON CO WA ... 184-B2
ENDICOTT RD W
ENDICOTT WA ... 122-A1
WHITMAN CO WA ... 122-A1
ENDICOTT-SAINT JOHN RD
ENDICOTT WA ... 122-B1
WHITMAN CO WA ... 114-B3
WHITMAN CO WA ... 122-B1
ENDICOTT-ST JOHN RD
WHITMAN CO WA ... 114-B3
ENDICOTT-ST JOHN RD Rt#-23
SAINT JOHN WA ... 114-B3
WHITMAN CO WA ... 114-B3
ENDRESEN RD
HOQUIAM WA ... 178-A7
ENGEL RD
LINN CO OR ... 207-D5
ENGLE RD
ISLAND CO WA ... 167-B5
ENGLEWOOD AV
YAKIMA WA ... 243-A6
YAKIMA CO WA ... 243-A6
ENGLEWOOD-SHINGLEHOUSE RD
COOS CO OR ... 220-D2
COOS CO OR ... 333-F14
ENGLISH RD
SKAGIT CO WA ... 168-B2
ENGLISH BLUFF RD
DISTRICT OF DELTA BC ... 101-C1
ENGLISH GRADE RD
SNOHOMISH CO WA ... 168-B3
ENGLISH PT RD
KOOTENAI CO ID ... 245-A5
E ENID RD
LANE CO OR ... 215-A1
ENMAN-KINCAID RD
JEFFERSON CO OR ... 249-A5
ENNIS CREEK RD
WHATCOM CO WA ... 161-C3
W ENOCH RD
SPOKANE CO WA ... 114-B1
ENTERPRISE AV
MALHEUR CO OR ... 139-A3
ENTERPRISE RD
COLUMBIA CO OR ... 189-A6
FERNDALE WA ... 158-C5
POLK CO OR ... 125-B3
POLK CO OR ... 204-A4
WHATCOM CO WA ... 158-C5
E ENTERPRISE RD
LANE CO OR ... 215-C5
N ENTERPRISE RD
WHATCOM CO WA ... 158-D4
ENTERPRISE-LEWISTON HWY Rt#-3
WALLOWA CO OR ... 122-C3
WALLOWA CO OR ... 130-C1
ENTIAT RIVER RD
CHELAN CO WA ... 112-A1
CHELAN CO WA ... 236-A6
ENTRANCE MOUNTAIN RD
SAN JUAN CO WA ... 160-A3
ENUMCLAW BLK DIM RD SE Rt#-169
BLACK DIAMOND WA ... 110-C3
KING CO WA ... 110-C3
ENUMCLAW BUCKLEY RD Rt#-410
ENUMCLAW WA ... 110-C3
KING CO WA ... 110-C3
ENUMCLAW CHNOOK PSS RD Rt#-410
ENUMCLAW WA ... 110-C3
KING CO WA ... 110-C3
SE ENMCLAW CHNK PSS RD Rt#-410
KING CO WA ... 110-C3
PIERCE CO WA ... 110-C3
PIERCE CO WA ... 111-A3
EOLA DR NW
POLK CO OR ... 322-C12
SALEM OR ... 322-E13
SE EOLA HILLS RD
YAMHILL CO OR ... 204-B2
ERICKSON RD
DESCHUTES CO OR ... 217-D2
ERICKSON RD KPS
PIERCE CO WA ... 181-A3
ERIE ST
CITY OF VICTORIA BC ... 256-F9
ERLAND POINT RD NW
Tracyton WA ... 270-C5
ERMINE DR
JEFFERSON CO OR ... 212-C3
ERNEST S BRAZILL ST
TACOMA WA ... 293-F6
ERSHING RD
SKAGIT CO WA ... 161-A5
ERSKINE RD SW
THURSTON CO WA ... 184-B2
ERSKINE WY SW
SEATTLE WA ... 280-D6
NW ERWIN O RIEGER MEMORIAL HWY
VANCOUVER WA ... 192-B5
ESCOLAR RD
KITSAP CO WA ... 170-A7
ESPANOLA RD
MEDICAL LAKE WA ... 114-B2
SPOKANE CO WA ... 114-B2
S ESPANOLA RD
SPOKANE CO WA ... 114-B2
ESPLANADE AV
CITY OF HARRISON HOT SPRG BC ... 94-C3
ESPLANADE ST
CITY OF NORTH VANCOUVER BC ... 255-A6
KLAMATH FALLS OR ... 338-E6

ESPLANADE ST U.S.-97 Bus
KLAMATH FALLS OR ... 338-E7
ESPY DR
PACIFIC WA ... 186-A1
ESQUIMALT RD
CITY OF VICTORIA BC ... 256-E8
TOWN OF ESQUIMALT BC ... 256-C8
N ESQUIRE DR
BOISE ID ... 253-C2
ESSER RD
WHITMAN CO WA ... 250-B1
NE ESTES AV
WHITE SALMON WA ... 195-D4
ESTES RD
LATAH CO ID ... 249-C4
EUCHRE CREEK RD
CURRY CO OR ... 228-B3
EUCLID AV
GRANDVIEW WA ... 120-B3
Sunnyslope WA ... 238-D3
YAKIMA CO WA ... 120-B3
E EUCLID AV
Otis Orchards WA ... 352-B11
SPOKANE WA ... 349-A5
SPOKANE CO WA ... 351-F4
SPOKANE CO WA ... 352-A11
SPOKANE VALLEY WA ... 350-B5
SPOKANE VALLEY WA ... 351-C4
W EUCLID AV
SPOKANE WA ... 348-H5
SPOKANE WA ... 349-A5
EUCLID RD
GRANDVIEW WA ... 120-B3
MABTON WA ... 120-B3
YAKIMA CO WA ... 120-B3
E EUCLID RD
YAKIMA CO WA ... 120-B3
N EUCLID RD
GRANDVIEW WA ... 120-B3
S EUCLID RD
YAKIMA CO WA ... 120-B3
EUFAULA HEIGHTS RD
COWLITZ CO WA ... 189-A1
EUGENE ST
HOOD RIVER CO OR ... 195-D5
EUGENE-SPRINGFIELD HWY I-105
EUGENE OR ... 329-J4
EUGENE OR ... 330-A5
SPRINGFIELD OR ... 330-A5
EUGENE-SPRINGFIELD HWY Rt#-126
EUGENE OR ... 330-E5
LANE CO OR ... 331-G6
SPRINGFIELD OR ... 330-E5
SPRINGFIELD OR ... 331-C5
SW EUREKA LN
JEFFERSON CO OR ... 208-B6
EUREKA RD N
WALLA WALLA CO WA ... 121-C2
EVANS BLVD U.S.-101
COOS BAY OR ... 333-H11
EVANS RD
ASOTIN CO WA ... 250-B4
HARRAH WA ... 119-C2
KLAMATH CO OR ... 151-A3
YAKIMA CO WA ... 119-C2
S EVANS RD
NEZ PERCE CO ID ... 250-C2
EVANS CREEK RD
JACKSON CO OR ... 229-D4
JACKSON CO OR ... 230-C1
KOOTENAI CO ID ... 248-C4
E EVANS CREEK RD
JACKSON CO OR ... 229-D5
JACKSON CO OR ... 230-C3
ROGUE RIVER OR ... 229-D5
W EVANS CREEK RD
JACKSON CO OR ... 229-D4
EVANS HILL CUTOFF RD
CHELAN CO WA ... 106-A2
EVANS-LEAP RD
WALLOWA CO OR ... 130-C2
EVANS VALLEY LP
MARION CO OR ... 205-C4
EVANS VALLEY RD NE
MARION CO OR ... 205-C4
EVERETT AV
EVERETT WA ... 265-G3
EVERETT AV Rt#-529
EVERETT WA ... 264-E3
EVERETT WA ... 265-E3
SE EVERETT RD Rt#-500
CLARK CO WA ... 193-B6
NE EVERETT ST
PORTLAND OR ... 313-F5
NE EVERETT ST Rt#-500
CAMAS WA ... 193-B7
CLARK CO WA ... 193-B7
NW EVERETT ST
PORTLAND OR ... 312-D5
PORTLAND OR ... 313-F5
EVERETT MALL WY Rt#-99
EVERETT WA ... 268-D5
SE EVERETT MALL WY Rt#-99
EVERETT WA ... 268-C6
SW EVERETT MALL WY Rt#-99
EVERETT WA ... 268-A7
SE EVERGREEN AV Rt#-126
REDMOND OR ... 212-D5
EVERGREEN AV NE
SALEM OR ... 323-C11
E EVERGREEN BLVD
VANCOUVER WA ... 305-G5
VANCOUVER WA ... 306-D7
SE EVERGREEN BLVD Rt#-14B
CLARK CO WA ... 193-C7
WASHOUGAL WA ... 193-C7
W EVERGREEN BLVD
VANCOUVER WA ... 305-G5
EVERGREEN DR Rt#-9
DISTRICT OF KENT BC ... 94-C3
EVERGREEN HWY
VANCOUVER WA ... 306-D7
EVERGREEN HWY Rt#-14
CARSON WA ... 194-C6
CARSON WA ... 195-A3
CLARK CO WA ... 193-D7
NORTH BONNEVILLE WA ... 194-C6
SKAMANIA CO WA ... 194-A7
SKAMANIA CO WA ... 195-B5
SKAMANIA CO WA ... 200-D1
STEVENSON WA ... 194-C6
EVERGREEN HWY Rt#-22
TOPPENISH WA ... 120-A2
YAKIMA CO WA ... 120-A2

EVERGREEN HWY U.S.-97
TOPPENISH WA ... 120-A2
YAKIMA CO WA ... 120-A2
SE EVERGREEN HWY
VANCOUVER WA ... 193-A7
VANCOUVER WA ... 306-E7
VANCOUVER WA ... 307-E7
VANCOUVER WA ... 311-G1
EVERGREEN LN
SKAGIT CO WA ... 160-C5
NW EVERGREEN PKWY
HILLSBORO OR ... 199-A1
EVERGREEN RD
TILLAMOOK CO OR ... 197-B6
N EVERGREEN RD
SPOKANE VALLEY WA ... 351-A2
NW EVERGREEN RD
WASHINGTON CO OR ... 198-D1
S EVERGREEN RD
SPOKANE VALLEY WA ... 351-A12
SPOKANE VALLEY WA ... 351-A10
EVERGREEN WY
EVERETT WA ... 264-C7
EVERETT WA ... 268-C4
EVERGREEN WY Rt#-14B
WASHOUGAL WA ... 193-C7
EVERGREEN WY Rt#-99
EVERETT WA ... 171-B4
EVERETT WA ... 267-J7
EVERETT WA ... 268-A7
SNOHOMISH CO WA ... 171-B4
EVERGREEN PARK DR
OLYMPIA WA ... 296-F7
S EVERGREEN PARK DR
OLYMPIA WA ... 296-F7
EVERGREEN PARK RD
PACIFIC CO WA ... 183-B4
EVERSON AV Rt#-544
EVERSON WA ... 102-B1
NOOKSACK WA ... 102-B1
EVERSON GOSHEN RD
WHATCOM CO WA ... 102-B1
EVERSON GOSHEN RD Rt#-544
EVERSON WA ... 102-B1
WHATCOM CO WA ... 102-B1
EWARTSVILLE RD
WHITMAN CO WA ... 122-C1
WHITMAN CO WA ... 249-A6
EWE CREEK RD
JOSEPHINE CO OR ... 229-A5
EWING RD
ISLAND CO WA ... 170-D2
ISLAND CO WA ... 171-A2
NE EXCHANGE DR
ROSEBURG OR ... 334-F4
W EXECUTIVE DR
BOISE ID ... 253-B3
EXTENSION RD
BRITISH COLUMBIA BC ... 93-A3
NANAIMO BC ... 93-A3
EXTROM RD
CITY OF CHILLIWACK BC ... 102-C1
EYREMOUNT DR
DIST OF WEST VANCOUVER BC ... 254-E1
EYREMOUNT RD
DIST OF WEST VANCOUVER BC ... 156-B2
DIST OF WEST VANCOUVER BC ... 254-E1

F

F ST
BELLINGHAM WA ... 258-D5
CHENEY WA ... 246-A4
GEARHART OR ... 301-G5
GRANT CO WA ... 237-C3
GRANTS PASS OR ... 335-D8
PORT TOWNSEND WA ... 263-F4
WALLA WALLA CO WA ... 345-H5
F ST U.S.-95
WORLEY ID ... 115-A2
F ST U.S.-199
GRANTS PASS OR ... 335-H9
JOSEPHINE CO OR ... 335-H9
E F ST
TACOMA WA ... 293-J5
E F ST U.S.-199
GRANTS PASS OR ... 335-G9
N F ST
ELMA WA ... 179-B7
F ST N U.S.-395
LAKEVIEW OR ... 152-A2
F ST S U.S.-395
LAKE CO OR ... 152-A2
LAKEVIEW OR ... 152-A2
F ST SE Rt#-28
GRANT CO WA ... 112-B3
QUINCY WA ... 112-B3
F ST SW Rt#-28
GRANT CO WA ... 112-B3
QUINCY WA ... 112-B3
FACTORIA BLVD SE
BELLEVUE WA ... 175-C3
FACTORY RD
YAKIMA CO WA ... 120-B2
FADJUR LN
DESCHUTES CO OR ... 212-A4
FAGAN RD
SKAGIT CO WA ... 168-B3
FAGERUD RD SE
KITSAP CO WA ... 174-C6
FAIL RD
SNOHOMISH CO WA ... 171-D3
FAIR AV
YAKIMA WA ... 243-C6
YAKIMA CO WA ... 243-C6
FAIRBANKS RD
WHITMAN CO WA ... 114-C3
FAIRBANKS-SEABURY RD
WHITMAN CO WA ... 114-C3
FAIRBROTHER RD
VALLEY CO ID ... 251-C7
FAIRFIELD RD
CITY OF VICTORIA BC ... 256-J10
CITY OF VICTORIA BC ... 257-A11
DISTRICT OF OAK BAY BC ... 257-A11
NE FAIRGROUNDS RD
KITSAP CO WA ... 270-H1
NW FAIRGROUNDS RD
KITSAP CO WA ... 270-F1
FAIRGROUNDS RD NE
SALEM OR ... 322-J11
SALEM OR ... 323-A11
E FAIRHAVEN AV
BURLINGTON WA ... 260-E5
SKAGIT CO WA ... 260-E5
FAIROAKS RD
DOUGLAS CO WA ... 219-B7
DOUGLAS CO WA ... 221-D1

FAIROAKS RD SE
THURSTON CO WA ... 181-A7
FAIRVIEW RD
PAYETTE CO ID ... 139-A3
E FAIRVIEW AV
ADA CO ID ... 253-B3
BOISE ID ... 253-B3
MERIDIAN ID ... 253-B3
N FAIRVIEW AV
BOISE ID ... 253-B3
SW FAIRVIEW AV Rt#-223
DALLAS OR ... 204-A6
W FAIRVIEW AV
ADA CO ID ... 253-B3
BOISE ID ... 253-B3
GARDEN CITY ID ... 253-B3
FAIRVIEW AV N
SEATTLE WA ... 278-A5
FAIRVIEW AV SE
SALEM OR ... 324-H2
FAIRVIEW DR
HOOD RIVER CO OR ... 195-C5
SNOHOMISH CO WA ... 171-D2
YAMHILL CO OR ... 198-C6
FAIRVIEW LN
GILLIAM CO OR ... 128-B1
FAIRVIEW RD
COLUMBIA CO OR ... 189-C6
KITTITAS CO WA ... 241-C5
LINN CO OR ... 133-C2
TILLAMOOK CO OR ... 197-C2
SE FAIRVIEW RD
YAMHILL CO OR ... 204-C2
FAIRVIEW RD SW
THURSTON CO WA ... 184-B1
N FAIRVIEW ST
PRINEVILLE OR ... 213-D5
S FAIRVIEW ST
CROOK CO OR ... 213-D5
PRINEVILLE OR ... 213-D5
FAIRVIEW CANYON RD
CHELAN CO WA ... 238-C3
FAIRVIEW LAKE RD SW
KITSAP CO WA ... 174-A4
FAIRVIEW-MCKINLEY RD
COOS CO OR ... 140-C2
FAIRVIEW MOUNTAIN RD
LANE CO OR ... 209-A5
E FAIRWAY AV
CLACKAMAS CO OR ... 201-C5
FAIRWAY DR
LINCOLN CO OR ... 203-A6
FAIRWAY ST
Finley WA ... 343-F12
WALLA WALLA CO WA ... 343-F12
SE FAIRWOOD BLVD
KING CO WA ... 175-C5
FAIRWOOD DR
OCEAN SHORES WA ... 298-B5
FAITH AV
ASHLAND OR ... 337-G10
FAKKEMA RD
ISLAND CO WA ... 167-C2
FALCON LN
JEFFERSON CO OR ... 208-B7
FALES RD
SNOHOMISH CO WA ... 171-D5
FALK RD
LINN CO OR ... 210-B3
FALL CITY-CRNTN RD NE Rt#-203
CARNATION WA ... 176-B2
KING CO WA ... 176-B2
FALL CITY-CRNTN RD SE Rt#-203
KING CO WA ... 176-B3
FALL CITY-DUVALL RD
KING CO WA ... 176-B3
FALL CITY-SNOQUALM RD Rt#-203
KING CO WA ... 176-B3
SNOQUALMIE WA ... 176-B3
FALL CREEK RD
ADAMS CO ID ... 252-A3
CLACKAMAS CO OR ... 200-C7
LINCOLN CO OR ... 133-C2
FALLERT RD
COWLITZ CO WA ... 189-D5
FALLON DR
WEST RICHLAND WA ... 340-A12
FALLON RD
WHITMAN CO WA ... 249-B3
FALLS CITY HWY
MONMOUTH OR ... 204-B7
POLK CO OR ... 204-B7
FALLS CITY RD
FALLS CITY OR ... 125-B3
POLK CO OR ... 125-B3
FALLS CREEK RD
GRAYS HARBOR CO WA ... 179-B6
N FANCHER RD
SPOKANE WA ... 349-J8
SPOKANE VALLEY WA ... 349-J8
S FANCHER RD
SPOKANE VALLEY WA ... 349-J9
FANDANGO PASS RD
MODOC CO CA ... 152-A3
F AND S GRADE RD
SEDRO-WOOLLEY WA ... 161-B5
SKAGIT CO WA ... 161-B5
FANTON RD
CLACKAMAS CO OR ... 200-D7
FARADAY RD
CLACKAMAS CO OR ... 200-C7
FARGO RD
MARION CO OR ... 199-A7
FARLEY RD SW
DOUGLAS CO WA ... 239-C6
FARM RD
CLACKAMAS CO OR ... 205-D3
FARM WY
WHITMAN CO WA ... 249-B5
FARMER RD
POLK CO OR ... 204-B5
FARMER RD SE
MARION CO OR ... 207-D2
FARMER CREEK RD
TILLAMOOK CO OR ... 197-B6
FARMERS RD
EVERETT WA ... 268-C6
SW FARMINGTON RD Rt#-10
BEAVERTON OR ... 199-A2
WASHINGTON CO OR ... 198-D3
WASHINGTON CO OR ... 199-A2
FARMS RD
BRITISH COLUMBIA BC ... 94-B3
FARM STATION RD
KLAMATH CO OR ... 231-D5

FARM TO MARKET RD
VALLEY CO ID ... 251-D7
VALLEY CO ID ... 252-D2
WASHINGTON CO ID ... 139-B2
FARM TO MARKET LOOP RD
STEVENS CO WA ... 106-A3
FARMWAY RD
CANYON CO ID ... 147-B1
S FARNEY RD
SPOKANE VALLEY WA ... 247-A6
FARR RD
CLARK CO WA ... 193-A1
N FARR RD
SPOKANE WA ... 350-D3
SPOKANE VALLEY WA ... 350-E8
S FARR RD
SPOKANE VALLEY WA ... 350-E9
FARRAGUT AV
BREMERTON WA ... 270-H11
WESTPORT WA ... 298-G14
FARRAGUT ST Rt#-304
BREMERTON WA ... 270-F12
FARRELL RD
ADAMS CO ID ... 251-B4
FARRINGTON RD
CLALLAM CO WA ... 164-C5
E FARWELL RD
Fairwood WA ... 347-C7
SPOKANE CO WA ... 246-D1
SPOKANE CO WA ... 347-C7
FARWEST DR SW
LAKEWOOD WA ... 181-C4
S FAUCHER RD
YAKIMA CO WA ... 243-D7
FAUNTLEROY WY SW
SEATTLE WA ... 280-E7
SEATTLE WA ... 281-F4
SEATTLE WA ... 284-D2
FAUST RD
KITTITAS CO WA ... 241-B5
FAUST RD U.S.-97
KITTITAS CO WA ... 241-B5
FAWCETT CREEK RD
TILLAMOOK CO OR ... 197-C3
FAWN CREEK RD
JACKSON CO OR ... 230-A3
FAYETTEVILLE DR
LINN CO OR ... 210-A1
SW FEATHER DR
JEFFERSON CO OR ... 208-B7
JEFFERSON CO OR ... 212-D1
S FEDERAL WY
ADA CO ID ... 253-D4
BOISE ID ... 253-C3
FEEDVILLE RD
UMATILLA CO OR ... 129-A1
FEIGLEY RD W
KITSAP CO WA ... 174-B4
FELL AV
CITY OF NORTH VANCOUVER BC ... 254-J4
DIST OF NORTH VANCOUVER BC ... 254-J4
FELLER RD
MARION CO OR ... 199-A7
FELLOWS RD
CLACKAMAS CO OR ... 200-B6
FELTHAM RD
DISTRICT OF SAANICH BC ... 257-B2
FENK RD
TILLAMOOK CO OR ... 197-B2
FENTON LN
KLICKITAT CO WA ... 127-C1
FENTON RD
PITT MEADOWS BC ... 157-C4
FENWICK ST
COOS BAY OR ... 333-G11
FENWICK RANCH RD
MALHEUR CO OR ... 155-A1
FERGIE RD
UMATILLA CO OR ... 121-B3
UMATILLA CO OR ... 129-B1
FERGUSON HALE
PIERCE CO WA ... 181-B1
FERGUSON
PIERCE CO WA ... 182-D4
FERGUSON AV
MAPLE RIDGE BC ... 157-D5
FERGUSON RD
BEND OR ... 217-C3
DESCHUTES CO OR ... 332-H12
DESCHUTES CO OR ... 217-C3
KLICKITAT CO WA ... 120-A3
S FERGUSON RD
CLACKAMAS CO OR ... 200-A5
FERGUSON DIV
CITY OF SURREY BC ... 157-A6
FERN AV
WALLA WALLA WA ... 345-D9
Walla Walla East WA ... 345-D9
FERN CRES
MAPLE RIDGE BC ... 157-D5
NE FERN LN
JEFFERSON CO OR ... 208-B7
FERN RD
BENTON CO OR ... 133-B1
FERN ST
DIST OF NORTH VANCOUVER BC ... 255-A6
E FERNAN RD
KOOTENAI CO ID ... 245-B1
FERNAN HILL RD
KOOTENAI CO ID ... 245-B1
E FERNAN LAKE RD
COEUR D'ALENE ID ... 355-J11
FERNAN LAKE VILLAGE ID ... 355-J11
KOOTENAI CO ID ... 355-J11
FERNCLIFF AV NE
KITSAP CO WA ... 174-C2
FERNDALE AV
DISTRICT OF MISSION BC ... 94-B3
FERNDALE RD
DISTRICT OF SAANICH BC ... 159-D5
DISTRICT OF SAANICH BC ... 257-D1
WHATCOM CO WA ... 158-C5
FERN HILL RD
COLUMBIA CO OR ... 189-B5
RAINIER OR ... 189-B5
SW FERN HILL RD
WASHINGTON CO OR ... 198-B2
FERN HILL RD W
RAINIER OR ... 189-B4
FERN RIDGE RD
CURRY CO OR ... 224-B3
MARION CO OR ... 134-C1
FERN RIDGE RD SE
MARION CO OR ... 133-C1
STAYTON OR ... 133-C1
FERNS CORNER RD
POLK CO OR ... 204-A7

STREET City State Page-Grid

FERNVALE RD
DOUGLAS CO OR 225-B6
FERN VALLEY RD
JACKSON CO OR 234-B2
PHOENIX OR 234-B2
FERNWOOD DR
JOSEPHINE CO OR 233-A5
FERNWOOD RD
YAMHILL CO OR 198-D5
FERRALL RD
COLUMBIA CO OR 122-A2
S FERRALL ST
SPOKANE WA 349-F11
FERREL RD SW
DOUGLAS CO WA 239-C2
FERRIER RD
LEWIS CO WA 187-C4
FERRY
BRITISH COLUMBIA BC 101-A1
BRITISH COLUMBIA BC 159-C1
DIST OF CENTRAL SAANICH BC 159-B3
TOWN OF SIDNEY BC 159-C2
FERRY RD
JOSEPHINE CO OR 229-A5
TILLAMOOK CO OR 197-A6
FERRY ST
ALBANY OR 326-C8
DAYTON OR 198-C7
WENATCHEE OR 238-D4
WENATCHEE WA 239-A4
WENATCHEE WA 198-C7
FERRY ST SE Rt#-22
SALEM OR 322-H13
FERRY CANYON RD
GILLIAM CO OR 128-A2
FERTILE VALLEY RD
POND OREILLE CO WA 106-C3
N FESSENDEN ST
PORTLAND OR 308-A3
FIDDLE CREEK RD
LANE CO OR 214-B5
FIELD RD
POLK CO OR 207-B1
SKAGIT CO WA 161-A5
FIELD ST
LONGVIEW WA 302-G9
FIELD CREEK RD
GRANT CO OR 137-A2
MALHEUR CO OR 154-C2
MALHEUR CO OR 155-A2
FIELDER CREEK RD
JACKSON CO OR 229-D5
FIELDING AV
BELLINGHAM WA 258-D9
FIELDS RD
KITTITAS CO WA 241-C5
FIELDS CREEK RESERVOIR RD
MALHEUR CO OR 155-A1
FIELDS-DENIO RD
HARNEY CO OR 145-C3
HARNEY CO OR 146-A3
HARNEY CO OR 153-C1
FIELDS GULCH RD
COLUMBIA CO OR 122-A2
FIELDSTONE RD
BELLINGHAM WA 160-D2
BELLINGHAM WA 258-A12
FIFE ST
TACOMA WA 292-E3
FIFTEENMILE BOULE RD
WASCO CO OR 127-B2
FIFTEENMILE FAIRBNKS MKT RD
WASCO CO OR 127-B2
WASCO CO OR 196-D7
FIFTEENMILE RESERVOIR RD
MALHEUR CO OR 154-A2
FIFTH AV
DOUGLAS CO OR 225-B2
YAKIMA CO WA 120-A2
FIFTH AV Rt#-172
DOUGLAS CO OR 112-C1
MANSFIELD WA 112-C1
FIFTH ST
Burbank WA 121-A3
TOWN OF SIDNEY BC 159-C2
WALLA WALLA CO WA 121-A3
WALLACE ID 115-C2
WENATCHEE WA 238-D4
West Wenatchee WA 238-D4
FILBERT DR
SNOHOMISH CO WA 171-C5
FILBERT RD
CLACKAMAS CO OR 200-C2
FILBERT RD Rt#-524
BOTHELL WA 171-C5
LYNNWOOD WA 171-B5
SNOHOMISH CO WA 171-C5
FILLMORE DR NW
PIERCE CO WA 181-C1
FINCH PL
TOWN OF SIDNEY BC 159-C2
FINCH RD
JOSEPHINE CO OR 233-A3
WHITMAN CO WA 114-C3
FINCH RD NE
KITSAP CO WA 271-J2
FINK RD E
LINCOLN CO OR 113-B3
FINLAY RD NE
MARION CO OR 205-B5
FINLAYSON ST
CITY OF VICTORIA BC 256-H6
FINLAYSON ARM RD
BRITISH COLUMBIA BC 159-B5
FINLEY RD
BENTON CO OR 121-A3
FINLEY BUTTE RD
DESCHUTES CO OR 143-B1
FINN RD
CITY OF RICHMOND BC 156-B7
FINN CHURCH LN
VALLEY CO ID 251-D7
FINNEGAN RD
SHERMAN CO OR 127-C2
FINNEGAN WY
BELLINGHAM WA 258-B10
FINNERTY RD
DISTRICT OF SAANICH BC 257-D3
FINNEY ST
CULDESAC ID 123-B2
FINN HALL RD
CLALLAM CO WA 165-D6
NE FINN HILL RD
CLARK CO WA 193-B4
NW FINN HILL RD
KITSAP CO WA 170-B6
SW FINNIGAN HILL RD
WASHINGTON CO OR 198-C4

STREET City State Page-Grid

FINN SETTLEMENT RD
SNOHOMISH CO WA 168-C3
NW FIR LN
JEFFERSON CO OR 208-C4
FIR LP Rt#-109
Taholah WA 172-B6
FIR RD
COOS CO OR 220-B4
FIR ST
COULEE DAM WA 237-C2
LEAVENWORTH WA 238-A1
NORTHPORT WA 106-A1
OLYMPIA WA 297-B5
PORT TOWNSEND WA 263-G4
STEVENS CO WA 106-A1
VANCOUVER BC 254-E13
E FIR ST
MOUNT VERNON WA 260-C11
FIR ST SE
TOLEDO OR 206-C5
NW FIR CREST RD
YAMHILL CO OR 198-A6
FIRDALE RD
WASHINGTON CO OR 198-C3
FIRE RD
DESCHUTES CO OR 217-A6
FIRECLAY RD
LANE CO OR 219-D4
FIRE TRAIL RD
SNOHOMISH CO WA 168-B6
FIRE WARDEN RD
MASON CO WA 179-B3
FIREWOOD RD
CLACKAMAS CO OR 126-A3
FIR GROVE LN SE
MARION CO OR 133-C1
FIRING CENTER RD
YAKIMA CO WA 243-C5
FIR ISLAND RD
SKAGIT CO WA 168-A2
FIRLANE RD
COWLITZ CO WA 189-D1
FIR MOUNTAIN RD
HOOD RIVER CO OR 195-D6
HOOD RIVER CO OR 202-D1
FIRST AV
ZILLAH WA 120-A2
FIRST ST
ATHOL ID 245-B2
ELK RIVER ID 123-C1
KOOTENAI CO ID 245-B2
WALLA WALLA CO WA 121-B3
FIRST ST Rt#-8
ELK RIVER ID 123-C1
FIRST ST Rt#-27
FAIRFIELD WA 114-C2
FIRST ST Rt#-904
CHENEY WA 246-A7
FIRST ST U.S.-97
DORRIS CA 150-B3
FIRST ST U.S.-101
COSMOPOLIS WA 178-B7
E FIRST ST Rt#-903
CLE ELUM WA 240-B2
E FIRST ST U.S.-101
COSMOPOLIS WA 117-A1
N FIRST ST Rt#-903
ROSLYN WA 240-A1
S FIRST ST Rt#-903
ROSLYN WA 240-A1
W FIRST ST
CENTRALIA WA 299-E3
WAPATO WA 120-A2
YAKIMA CO WA 120-A2
N FIRST ST Rt#-21
LIND WA 121-B1
W FIRST ST Rt#-903
CLE ELUM WA 240-B2
W FIRST ST Rt#-904
CHENEY WA 246-A7
SW FIRST CREEK CTO
JEFFERSON CO OR 211-B2
FIRST CREEK RD
CHELAN WA 236-A2
N FIRST CREEK RD
JEFFERSON CO OR 211-B1
FIR TREE DR SE
THURSTON CO WA 184-D1
N FIR VILLA RD
POLK CO OR 204-A6
SE FIR VILLA RD
DALLAS OR 204-A6
POLK CO OR 204-A6
FIRWOOD RD
CLACKAMAS CO OR 200-D5
FISCHER PL NE Rt#-522
SEATTLE WA 171-B7
S FISCHERS MILL RD
CLACKAMAS CO OR 200-A5
FISH RD
Freeland WA 170-D1
S FISH RD
Freeland WA 170-D1
FISHBACK RD
POLK CO OR 207-A1
FISH CREEK RD
DOUGLAS CO OR 222-D5
FISHER RD
DOUGLAS CO OR 221-B3
LEWIS CO ID 123-B2
LEWIS CO WA 187-C2
SNOHOMISH CO WA 171-B4
FISHER HILL RD
KLICKITAT CO WA 196-B4
FISHERMAN RD
MALHEUR CO OR 147-A1
FISH HATCHERY DR
LINN CO OR 133-C1
FISH HATCHERY RD
ENTERPRISE OR 130-C2
JOSEPHINE CO OR 229-A7
MASON CO WA 179-B3
WALLOWA CO OR 130-C2
FISHHAWK RD
COLUMBIA CO OR 117-B3
FISHHAWK FALLS HWY
CLATSOP CO OR 117-A3
CLATSOP CO OR 125-A1
FISH HOOK RD
WALLA WALLA CO WA 121-B2
FISH LAKE RD
ADAMS CO ID 251-B4
HARNEY CO OR 145-B3
OKANOGAN CO WA 104-C3
FISH LAKE CREEK RD
DOUGLAS CO OR 222-B7
FISHOOK ELGIN RD
FRANKLIN CO WA 121-B2

STREET City State Page-Grid

FISH POND RD
COWLITZ CO WA 189-C4
FISHTRAP RD
COOS CO OR 220-D5
FISHTRAP LANDING RD
COOS CO OR 220-D6
FIVE CORNERS RD
LAKE CO OR 152-A2
FIVE FORKS RD SW
THURSTON CO WA 180-A6
FIVE MILE RD
WALLA WALLA CO WA 122-A3
FIVEMILE RD
BAKER CO OR 138-C1
WASCO CO OR 127-B2
WASCO CO OR 202-D3
N FIVE MILE RD
ADA CO ID 253-B2
BOISE ID 253-B2
Country Homes WA 346-F10
SPOKANE WA 346-F11
SPOKANE CO WA 346-F11
S FIVE MILE RD
ADA CO ID 253-B4
BOISE ID 253-B4
W FIVE MILE RD
SPOKANE WA 346-F14
SPOKANE WA 348-G1
FIVE RIVERS RD
LINCOLN CO OR 209-D3
FIVESTICKS RD
DOUGLAS CO OR 226-B2
FJORD DR NE
KITSAP CO WA 170-B7
FLAEGER RD
CLARK CO WA 192-C1
FLAGLER RD Rt#-116
Hadlock-Irondale WA 170-B1
JEFFERSON CO WA 167-B7
JEFFERSON CO WA 170-B1
FLAG POINT RD
WASCO CO OR 202-D5
FLAGSTAFF LN
SKAGIT CO WA 160-D7
FLAGSTAFF LAKE RD
LAKE CO OR 152-B1
FLANNIGAN CREEK RD
LATAH CO ID 249-D2
SE FLAVEL ST
PORTLAND OR 318-D6
PORTLAND OR 319-G6
FLEMING RD
CROOK CO OR 213-B5
WHITMAN CO WA 122-A1
FLESHMAN WY
ASOTIN CO WA 250-B4
FLETCHER LN
YAKIMA CO WA 243-A4
FLETCHER RD
COLUMBIA CO WA 122-A2
LEWIS CO ID 123-B2
SE FLETCHER RD
YAMHILL CO OR 198-B7
FLETCHER BAY RD NE
KITSAP CO WA 174-C1
KITSAP CO WA 271-G2
FLETT RD
YAMHILL CO OR 198-B3
FLIER RD
KITSAP CO WA 170-B7
FLINT RD
OWYHEE CO ID 147-B3
N FLINT RD
SPOKANE WA 246-A4
W FLOATING FEATHER RD
ADA CO OR 253-A1
EAGLE ID 253-A1
FLORA LN
WALLOWA CO OR 122-C3
N FLORA RD
SPOKANE CO WA 351-E3
SPOKANE VALLEY WA 351-E3
FLORA ST
BELLINGHAM WA 258-D6
FLORAL AV
ASTORIA OR 300-A5
FLORAS CREEK RD
CURRY CO OR 224-B3
FLORAS LAKE RD
CURRY CO OR 224-B3
FLORAS LAKE LOOP RD
CURRY CO OR 224-B3
FLORENCE AV
ASTORIA OR 300-A5
FLORENCE ACRES RD
SNOHOMISH CO WA 110-C1
FLORENCE-EUGENE HWY
LANE CO OR 133-A3
FLORENCE-EUGENE HWY Rt#-126
FLORENCE OR 214-C2
LANE CO OR 132-C3
LANE CO OR 133-A3
LANE CO OR 214-C2
LANE CO OR 215-A2
VENETA OR 133-A3
FLORIDA ST
LONGVIEW WA 302-J9
LONGVIEW WA 303-A9
FLOURNOY VALLEY RD
DOUGLAS CO OR 141-A2
DOUGLAS CO OR 221-A4
N FORREST AV
WESTPORT WA 298-G13
S FORREST AV Rt#-105
WESTPORT WA 298-G14
FLOWERY TRAIL RD
STEVENS CO WA 106-B3
SW FLUKE DR
WASHINGTON CO OR 198-B2
FLUME GULCH RD
JOSEPHINE CO OR 229-A4
FLUME RANCH RD
DESCHUTES CO OR 212-D3
FLYNN ST
BELLINGHAM WA 258-J6
FOBERT RD
MARION CO OR 205-C1
FOBERT RD NE
MARION CO OR 205-C1
FOBES AV
SNOHOMISH CO WA 171-D3
SNOHOMISH CO WA 171-D3
FOLEY DR
HARNEY CO OR 145-B1
N FOLEY DR
BURNS OR 145-B1
HARNEY CO OR 145-B1
FOLEY RD
ADAMS CO WA 121-A1
FOLLY FARM CTO
MALHEUR CO OR 146-A3

STREET City State Page-Grid

FOLLY FARM RD
MALHEUR CO OR 146-A3
FOLSOM RD
CLACKAMAS CO OR 200-B5
FONES RD SE
OLYMPIA WA 297-D6
FOOT PTH
POLK CO OR 105-B1
FOOT TR
POLK CO OR 204-A7
FORT KLAMATH RD
KLAMATH CO OR 338-F7
KLAMATH FALLS OR 338-F7
FORT MCKAY RD
DOUGLAS CO OR 221-B1
SUTHERLIN OR 221-B1
FORT NUGENT RD
ISLAND CO WA 167-B3
FORT ROCK RD
LAKE CO OR 143-B2
FORT STEVENS HWY
CLATSOP CO OR 188-B2
WARRENTON WA 188-B2
FORT VANCOUVER WY
VANCOUVER WA 305-H4
FORTY FIVE RD
SNOHOMISH CO WA 168-C6
FOSBERG RD
LAKE OSWEGO OR 320-A5
FOSS RD
JACKSON CO OR 234-B3
TILLAMOOK CO OR 125-A1
TILLAMOOK CO OR 191-C4
FOSSIL ST Rt#-218
ANTELOPE OR 127-C2
FOSTER AV
COQUITLAM BC 157-A4
COTTONWOOD BC 123-C3
DISTRICT OF COQUITLAM BC 156-D4
E FOSTER AV
COEUR D'ALENE ID 355-F11
FOSTER LN
JEFFERSON CO OR 208-C7
FOSTER RD
SKAMANIA CO WA 194-C3
SE FOSTER RD
CLACKAMAS CO OR 200-A3
MULTNOMAH CO OR 200-A2
PORTLAND OR 200-A2
PORTLAND OR 318-E3
PORTLAND OR 319-J5
FOSTER CREEK AV Rt#-173
BRIDGEPORT WA 112-C1
FOSTER CREEK RD
DOUGLAS CO OR 226-D1
FOSTER SLOUGH RD
SNOHOMISH CO WA 171-D3
FOSTER WELLS RD
PASCO WA 343-E1
FOUL BAY RD
CITY OF VICTORIA BC 257-B8
DISTRICT OF OAK BAY BC 257-C6
DISTRICT OF SAANICH BC 257-B7
FOULKES RD
ADAMS CO WA 121-B1
FOUR CORNERS RD
JACKSON CO OR 234-C7
JEFFERSON CO WA 263-B13
FOUR MILE RD
WASHINGTON CO ID 139-B2
WHITMAN CO WA 249-A3
FOURMILE RD
GILLIAM CO OR 128-A1
LATAH CO ID 249-C3
N FORK AHTANUM RD
YAKIMA CO WA 119-B2
S FORK AHTANUM RD
YAKIMA CO WA 119-B2
FORKED HORN RD
DESCHUTES CO OR 212-A5
E FORKER RD
SPOKANE CO WA 351-A1
N FORKER RD
SPOKANE CO WA 247-A1
SPOKANE CO WA 351-A1
N FORK JOHN DAY RD
GRANT CO OR 129-A3
UMATILLA CO OR 129-A3
S FORK PISTOL RIVER RD
CURRY CO OR 232-C2
N FORK RYEGRASS CREEK RD
MALHEUR CO OR 146-A3
MALHEUR CO OR 154-B1
FORKS AV N U.S.-101
VANCOUVER WA 305-J3
FORKS AV S U.S.-101
VANCOUVER WA 306-B3
S FORK SMITH RIVER RD
DOUGLAS CO OR 219-A1
W FORK SMITH RIVER RD
DOUGLAS CO OR 133-A3
N FORK TEANAWAY RD
KITTITAS CO WA 111-C3
N FORK TOUCHET RIVER RD
COLUMBIA CO WA 122-A2
FORLORN LAKES RD
SKAMANIA CO WA 195-B1
E FORREST AV
SPOKANE VALLEY WA 350-J11

STREET City State Page-Grid

W FORT GEORGE WRIGHT DR
SPOKANE WA 348-D7
SPOKANE WA 348-D7
FORT HILL RD
POLK CO OR 125-A3
YAMHILL CO OR 125-A3
SW FORT HILL RD
YAMHILL CO OR 125-A3
FORT RD
HARRAH WA 119-C2
YAKIMA CO WA 120-A2
FORT RD Rt#-220
HARRAH WA 119-C2
YAKIMA CO WA 119-C2
YAKIMA CO WA 120-A2
FORT ST
CITY OF VICTORIA BC 256-H9
CITY OF VICTORIA BC 257-A9
W FORT ST
BOISE ID 253-C2
FORT CANBY RD Rt#-100
PACIFIC CO WA 186-A7
FORT CASEY RD
ISLAND CO WA 167-B5
FORT CLATSOP RD
CLATSOP CO OR 188-C3
FORT CLATSOP LOOP RD
CLATSOP CO OR 188-C2
FOX-ROUND BASIN RD
GRANT CO OR 137-A1
FOX SPIT RD
KITSAP CO WA 167-D7
FR 613
BENEWAH CO ID 115-B2
SE FRAGARIA RD
KITSAP CO WA 174-C5
E FRANCIS AV
SPOKANE CO WA 349-C1
SPOKANE CO WA 349-E1
W FRANCIS AV Rt#-291
SPOKANE WA 348-D1
SPOKANE WA 349-A1
Town and Country WA 348-D1
Town and Country WA 349-A1
FRANCIS RD
CITY OF RICHMOND BC 156-B6
MOUNT VERNON WA 260-E10
SKAGIT CO WA 161-C6
SKAGIT CO WA 260-G6
FRANK RD
DESCHUTES CO OR 212-C5
FRANK CRANE RD
TILLAMOOK CO OR 191-C6
SE FRANK FOREST RD
JEFFERSON CO OR 208-D7
FRANKLIN AV
ASTORIA OR 300-F4
FRANKLIN AV U.S.-26
DAYVILLE OR 136-C2
GRANT CO OR 136-C2
NE FRANKLIN AV
BEND OR 332-F7
NE FRANKLIN AV U.S.-97
BEND OR 332-F7
NW FRANKLIN AV U.S.-97
BEND OR 332-E7
FRANKLIN BLVD Rt#-99
EUGENE OR 330-C2
LANE CO OR 330-G8
FRANKLIN BLVD Rt#-126 Bus
LANE CO OR 330-F7
FRANKLIN LN
JEFFERSON CO OR 208-B6
FRANKLIN RD U.S.-20
CALDWELL ID 147-B1
CANYON CO ID 147-B1
E FRANKLIN RD
ADA CO ID 253-B3
BOISE ID 253-B3
MERIDIAN ID 253-B3
W FRANKLIN RD
ADA CO ID 253-A3
BOISE ID 253-C3
FRANKS CREEK RD
DAYVILLE OR 136-C1
GRANT CO OR 136-C1
FRANK SMITH RD
COWLITZ CO WA 118-A2
FRANKTON RD
HOOD RIVER CO OR 195-C5
FRANK WATERS RD
SNOHOMISH CO WA 168-B5
FRANZ RD
SKAMANIA CO WA 194-B7
FRASER HWY Rt#-1A
CITY OF SURREY BC 157-A6
DISTRICT OF MATSQUI BC 102-B1
LANGLEY BC 157-B7
LANGLEY BC 158-D1
TOWNSHIP OF LANGLEY BC 102-B1
TOWNSHIP OF LANGLEY BC 158-D1
FRASER ST
VANCOUVER BC 156-B5
VANCOUVER BC 254-J14
FRAZEE-FREDERICK BUTTE RD
LAKE CO OR 143-C2
LAKE CO OR 144-A1
FRAZEN RD
WHITMAN CO WA 249-B1
SE FRAZER AV Rt#-37
PENDLETON OR 129-B1
SW FRAZER AV Rt#-37
PENDLETON OR 129-B1
SW FRAZIER DR
JEFFERSON CO OR 208-A7
FRAZIER RD
COWLITZ CO WA 190-A7
FRD 1400
CLALLAM CO WA 162-D4
FRED D HAIGHT DR Rt#-D4
DEL NORTE CO CA 148-B3
FREDERICK BUTTE RD
DESCHUTES CO OR 144-A1
FREDRICKSON INDUSTRIAL PARK RD
PIERCE CO WA 182-A5
FREEBORN RD
SNOHOMISH CO WA 168-C3
FREEMAN RD
CENTRAL POINT OR 230-C7
CLACKAMAS CO OR 199-D7
COLUMBIA CO OR 192-A3
FREEMAN RD E
EDGEWOOD WA 182-B3
FIFE WA 182-B3
FREEWATER HWY
MILTON-FREEWATER OR 121-C3
UMATILLA CO OR 121-C3
WALLA WALLA CO WA 121-C3
FRWY
BOISE ID 253-B3
FRWY I-5
ARLINGTON WA 168-C5
BELLINGHAM WA 161-A2
BELLINGHAM WA 258-A11
BLAINE WA 158-B3
BURLINGTON WA 260-C3
CASTLE ROCK WA 187-C7
CENTRALIA WA 299-D1
CHEHALIS WA 299-D8
COWLITZ CO WA 187-C5
COWLITZ CO WA 189-C1
COWLITZ CO WA 303-F1
DES MOINES WA 290-C7
DUPONT WA 181-C5
EVERETT WA 171-C1
EVERETT WA 265-H1
EVERETT WA 268-E4
EVERETT WA 269-E1
FEDERAL WAY WA 175-B7
FEDERAL WAY WA 182-B1
FERNDALE WA 158-C5
FIFE WA 182-B3
Grand Mound WA 184-B3
KELSO WA 189-C4
KELSO WA 303-D5

INDEX

FRWY I-5
KENT WA ... 175-B7
KENT WA ... 290-D7
KING CO WA ... 289-G1
LACEY WA ... 181-A6
LACEY WA ... 297-J3
LAKEWOOD WA ... 181-D4
LEWIS CO WA ... 184-B5
LEWIS CO WA ... 187-C1
LEWIS CO WA ... 299-D1
LYNNWOOD WA ... 171-B5
MARYSVILLE WA ... 168-C6
MARYSVILLE WA ... 171-C1
MILTON WA ... 182-A2
MOUNT VERNON WA ... 260-C9
MOUNTLAKE TERRACE WA ... 171-B5
OLYMPIA WA ... 296-J6
OLYMPIA WA ... 297-G5
PIERCE CO WA ... 181-D4
PIERCE CO WA ... 182-A2
PORTLAND OR ... 313-G7
SEATAC WA ... 289-F7
SEATAC WA ... 290-E3
SEATAC WA ... 291-F1
SEATTLE WA ... 171-B7
SEATTLE WA ... 274-A1
SEATTLE WA ... 278-B1
SEATTLE WA ... 282-B1
SEATTLE WA ... 286-C1
SEATTLE WA ... 287-E5
SHORELINE WA ... 171-B6
SISKIYOU CO CA ... 149-C3
SISKIYOU CO CA ... 150-A3
SKAGIT CO WA ... 161-B3
SKAGIT CO WA ... 168-B1
SKAGIT CO WA ... 260-C1
SNOHOMISH CO WA ... 168-B3
SNOHOMISH CO WA ... 171-C1
TACOMA WA ... 181-D4
TACOMA WA ... 182-A2
TACOMA WA ... 293-J7
TACOMA WA ... 295-H1
THURSTON CO WA ... 181-A6
THURSTON CO WA ... 184-C1
THURSTON CO WA ... 296-E14
THURSTON CO WA ... 297-C6
TUKWILA WA ... 287-E5
TUKWILA WA ... 289-G1
TUKWILA WA ... 291-F1
TUMWATER WA ... 184-C1
TUMWATER WA ... 296-H8
WHATCOM CO WA ... 158-B3
WHATCOM CO WA ... 161-A2
WHATCOM CO WA ... 258-A1
WOODLAND WA ... 189-D7
YREKA CA ... 149-C3

FRWY I-82
BENTON CO WA ... 120-C3
BENTON CO WA ... 121-A3
BENTON CO WA ... 341-A9
BENTON CO WA ... 342-A13
GRANDVIEW WA ... 120-B3
GRANGER WA ... 120-A2
KENNEWICK WA ... 341-H13
KITTITAS CO WA ... 241-B6
KITTITAS CO WA ... 243-C1
PROSSER WA ... 120-C3
SUNNYSIDE WA ... 120-B2
UNION GAP WA ... 243-C7
UNION GAP WA ... 243-B6
YAKIMA WA ... 243-B6
YAKIMA WA ... 120-A2
YAKIMA WA ... 243-D4
ZILLAH WA ... 120-A2

FRWY I-84
ADA CO ID ... 147-C1
ADA CO ID ... 253-B3
BOISE ID ... 253-B3
CALDWELL ID ... 147-B1
CANYON CO ID ... 139-B3
CANYON CO ID ... 147-B1
MERIDIAN ID ... 253-B3
NAMPA ID ... 147-B1
PAYETTE CO ID ... 139-A3

FRWY I-90
ADAMS CO WA ... 113-C3
ADAMS CO WA ... 114-A3
BELLEVUE WA ... 175-C3
CLE ELUM WA ... 240-B2
COEUR D'ALENE ID ... 354-H7
COEUR D'ALENE ID ... 355-A7
ELLENSBURG WA ... 241-B5
FERNAN LAKE VILLAGE ID ... 355-H11
GRANT CO WA ... 112-C3
GRANT CO WA ... 113-A3
GRANT CO WA ... 120-B1
GRANT CO WA ... 242-C3
ISSAQUAH WA ... 175-D3
ISSAQUAH WA ... 176-A4
KELLOGG ID ... 115-C2
KING CO WA ... 111-A2
KING CO WA ... 175-C3
KING CO WA ... 176-A4
KITTITAS CO WA ... 111-A2
KITTITAS CO WA ... 120-A1
KITTITAS CO WA ... 240-A1
KITTITAS CO WA ... 241-A4
KOOTENAI CO ID ... 115-B2
KOOTENAI CO ID ... 245-B7
KOOTENAI CO ID ... 248-B1
KOOTENAI CO ID ... 352-J9
KOOTENAI CO ID ... 353-A8
KOOTENAI CO ID ... 354-C7
KOOTENAI CO ID ... 355-A7
LIBERTY LAKE WA ... 351-J7
LIBERTY LAKE WA ... 352-D11
LINCOLN CO WA ... 114-A2
MERCER ISLAND WA ... 175-C3
MERCER ISLAND WA ... 283-J1
MOSES LAKE WA ... 242-C3
NORTH BEND WA ... 176-C5
OSBURN ID ... 115-C2
PINEHURST ID ... 115-C2
POST FALLS ID ... 352-J9
POST FALLS ID ... 353-G6
POST FALLS ID ... 354-B7
SEATTLE WA ... 278-B1
SEATTLE WA ... 282-B1
SEATTLE WA ... 283-J1
SHOSHONE CO ID ... 115-C2
SNOQUALMIE WA ... 176-C4
SPOKANE I-5 ... 348-J10
SPOKANE WA ... 349-G9
SPOKANE WA ... 114-B2
SPOKANE CO WA ... 246-B5
SPOKANE CO WA ... 348-E12
SPOKANE CO WA ... 351-J2
SPOKANE CO WA ... 352-H9
SPOKANE VALLEY WA ... 349-J8

FRWY I-90
SPOKANE VALLEY WA ... 350-J6
SPOKANE VALLEY WA ... 351-A6
SPRAGUE WA ... 114-A3
WALLACE ID ... 115-C2

FRWY I-99
CITY OF SURREY BC ... 101-C1
DISTRICT OF DELTA BC ... 101-C1

FRWY I-182
BENTON CO WA ... 121-A3
BENTON CO WA ... 341-E4
FRANKLIN CO WA ... 342-B2
FRANKLIN CO WA ... 343-A4
PASCO WA ... 342-C1
PASCO WA ... 343-A4
RICHLAND WA ... 341-J3
RICHLAND WA ... 342-A3

FRWY I-205
CLARK CO WA ... 192-C4
MAYWOOD PARK OR ... 315-G1
PORTLAND OR ... 193-A7
PORTLAND OR ... 311-J2
PORTLAND OR ... 315-H1
PORTLAND OR ... 319-G1
VANCOUVER WA ... 192-D5
VANCOUVER WA ... 307-G1
VANCOUVER WA ... 311-J1

FRWY I-405
BELLEVUE WA ... 175-C2
BOTHELL WA ... 171-C5
BOTHELL WA ... 171-C6
KING CO WA ... 171-C7
KING CO WA ... 175-C3
KIRKLAND WA ... 171-C7
KIRKLAND WA ... 175-C1
NEWCASTLE WA ... 175-C3
PORTLAND OR ... 312-E3
PORTLAND OR ... 313-F3
PORTLAND OR ... 317-E1
RENTON WA ... 175-C4
RENTON WA ... 289-J4
SNOHOMISH CO WA ... 171-B5
SNOHOMISH CO WA ... 289-J4

FRWY I-705
TACOMA WA ... 293-H4
TACOMA WA ... 295-H1

FRWY Rt#-3
BREMERTON WA ... 174-B4
BREMERTON WA ... 270-C6
KITSAP CO WA ... 170-B6
KITSAP CO WA ... 174-B1
KITSAP CO WA ... 270-B1
Navy Yard City WA ... 270-E11
PORT ORCHARD WA ... 174-B4
Silverdale WA ... 174-B1
Silverdale WA ... 270-B1
Tracyton WA ... 270-A4

FRWY Rt#-7
TACOMA WA ... 295-H1

FRWY Rt#-16
GIG HARBOR WA ... 174-B7
GIG HARBOR WA ... 181-C1
PIERCE CO WA ... 174-B6
PIERCE CO WA ... 181-C1
PORT ORCHARD WA ... 174-B4
TACOMA WA ... 181-C2

FRWY Rt#-18
AUBURN WA ... 182-B1
FEDERAL WAY WA ... 182-B1
KING CO WA ... 182-B1

FRWY Rt#-26
GRANT CO WA ... 120-B1

FRWY Rt#-91
CITY OF RICHMOND BC ... 156-B6

FRWY Rt#-99
CITY OF RICHMOND BC ... 156-B6
CITY OF SURREY BC ... 158-A1
DISTRICT OF DELTA BC ... 156-C7
KING CO WA ... 286-B4
SEATTLE WA ... 281-J7
SEATTLE WA ... 285-J1
SEATTLE WA ... 286-A2
TUKWILA WA ... 286-C5
WHATCOM CO WA ... 158-B3

FRWY Rt#-167
PACIFIC WA ... 182-B2
PIERCE CO WA ... 182-B2
PUYALLUP WA ... 182-B2
SUMNER WA ... 182-B2

FRWY Rt#-240
KENNEWICK WA ... 342-D7
KENNEWICK WA ... 343-A9
RICHLAND WA ... 341-H4
RICHLAND WA ... 342-A6

FRWY Rt#-410
PIERCE CO WA ... 182-C3

FRWY Rt#-509
BURIEN WA ... 175-A5
BURIEN WA ... 288-A1
BURIEN WA ... 290-A1
KING CO WA ... 286-A4
KING CO WA ... 288-A1
SEATAC WA ... 288-A6
SEATAC WA ... 290-A1
SEATTLE WA ... 285-J1
SEATTLE WA ... 286-A3
TACOMA WA ... 182-A2
TACOMA WA ... 293-J6

FRWY Rt#-512
LAKEWOOD WA ... 181-D4
PIERCE CO WA ... 181-D4
PIERCE CO WA ... 182-B3
PUYALLUP WA ... 182-B3

FRWY Rt#-518
BURIEN WA ... 175-A5
BURIEN WA ... 288-B4
SEATAC WA ... 288-B4
TUKWILA WA ... 288-D5
TUKWILA WA ... 289-F4

FRWY Rt#-520
BELLEVUE WA ... 175-C2
CLYDE HILL WA ... 175-C2
HUNTS POINT WA ... 175-C2
KING CO WA ... 175-D1
MEDINA WA ... 175-C2
MEDINA WA ... 279-J2
REDMOND WA ... 175-D1
SEATTLE WA ... 278-D1
SEATTLE WA ... 279-E1
YARROW POINT WA ... 175-C2

FRWY Rt#-522
BOTHELL WA ... 171-J7
SNOHOMISH CO WA ... 171-D5
WOODINVILLE WA ... 171-C6

FRWY Rt#-525
SNOHOMISH CO WA ... 171-B4

FRWY Rt#-526
EVERETT WA ... 267-F4
EVERETT WA ... 268-A1
MUKILTEO WA ... 267-F4
SNOHOMISH CO WA ... 267-F4

FRWY Rt#-599
TUKWILA WA ... 286-D7
TUKWILA WA ... 287-E7
TUKWILA WA ... 289-E1

FRWY U.S.-2
CASHMERE WA ... 238-C2
CHELAN CO WA ... 238-A3
DOUGLAS CO WA ... 239-A3
East Wenatchee Bench WA ... 238-D3
East Wenatchee Bench WA ... 239-A3
EVERETT WA ... 265-G3

FRWY U.S.-12
PASCO WA ... 343-H5
YAKIMA WA ... 243-B6
YAKIMA CO WA ... 243-B6

FRWY U.S.-101
MASON CO WA ... 180-A3
OLYMPIA WA ... 296-D6
THURSTON CO WA ... 180-D5
THURSTON CO WA ... 296-B5
TUMWATER WA ... 296-G7

FRWY U.S.-395
BENTON CO WA ... 121-A3
Finley WA ... 121-A3
KENNEWICK WA ... 343-B9
LEWISTON ID ... 121-A3
PASCO WA ... 343-D5
UMATILLA CO OR ... 121-A3

FREEWAY DR
MOUNT VERNON WA ... 260-B11

FREIMUTH RD
YAKIMA CO WA ... 243-B4

E FREMONT AV
SELAH WA ... 243-B5

W FREMONT AV
SELAH WA ... 243-B5

FREMONT AV N
SEATTLE WA ... 273-H5

FREMONT HWY Rt#-31
DESCHUTES CO OR ... 143-A1
KLAMATH CO OR ... 143-A1
LAKE CO OR ... 143-B2
LAKE CO OR ... 151-A1
LAKE CO OR ... 152-A1
PAISLEY OR ... 151-C1

FREMONT HWY U.S.-395
LAKE CO OR ... 152-A2
LAKEVIEW OR ... 152-A2
MODOC CO CA ... 152-A2

FREMONT PL N
SEATTLE WA ... 273-H6

N FREMONT ST
PORTLAND OR ... 313-G2

NE FREMONT ST
PORTLAND OR ... 313-H2
PORTLAND OR ... 314-C2
PORTLAND OR ... 315-E2

FREMONT ST E
THE DALLES OR ... 196-D7

FREMONT WY N
SEATTLE WA ... 273-H6

FRENCH RD
ISLAND CO WA ... 171-A2

FRENCHGLEN HWY Rt#-205
HARNEY CO OR ... 145-B6

FRENCHGLEN RD
LAKE CO OR ... 152-C1
LAKE CO OR ... 153-A1

E FRENCH GULCH RD
KOOTENAI CO ID ... 245-B7

FRENCHMAN CREEK RD
MALHEUR CO OR ... 154-C2

FRENCHMAN HILL RD
GRANT CO WA ... 112-B3
GRANT CO WA ... 120-B1

FRENCH MOUNTAIN RD
JOSEPHINE CO OR ... 233-C5

FRENCH PRAIRIE RD
MARION CO OR ... 205-A1

FRENCH PRAIRIE RD Rt#-219
MARION CO OR ... 198-D7
MARION CO OR ... 205-A1

FRENCH PRAIRIE RD NE
MARION CO OR ... 205-A2

FRESHWATER BAY RD
CLALLAM CO WA ... 164-D5

N FREYA ST
SPOKANE WA ... 349-F8

S FREYA ST
SPOKANE WA ... 246-C5
SPOKANE WA ... 349-F11
SPOKANE CO WA ... 246-C5

FRIDAY CREEK RD
SKAGIT CO WA ... 161-B4

FRIEDA AV
Altamont OR ... 338-J9
Altamont OR ... 339-A9

FRIEND RD
WASCO CO OR ... 127-A2

FRIENDLY ST
EUGENE OR ... 329-H10

FRIENDS RD
CANYON CO ID ... 147-B1

FRIES RD
LINN CO OR ... 207-D6

FRIZZELL RD
POLK CO OR ... 204-B4

SW FROBASE RD
WASHINGTON CO OR ... 199-B5

FROG CREEK RD
WASCO CO OR ... 202-B7

FROG HOLLOW RD
WALLA WALLA CO WA ... 121-C3

FROG LAKE BUTTE RD
WASCO CO OR ... 202-B7

FROGNER RD
LEWIS CO WA ... 187-B1

NW FRONT AV
PORTLAND OR ... 312-C2

S FRONT AV
PASCO WA ... 343-H8

SW FRONT AV U.S.-26
PORTLAND OR ... 317-F1

W FRONT AV Rt#-21
LINCOLN CO WA ... 113-B1
WILBUR WA ... 113-B1

FRONT ST
COOS BAY OR ... 333-H12

FRONT ST
IDAHO CO ID ... 123-B3
JOSEPHINE CO OR ... 229-B1
LYNDEN WA ... 102-B1
LYNDEN WA ... 158-D4
MARION CO OR ... 205-B1
POULSBO WA ... 170-B6
SHOSHONE CO ID ... 115-C2
WALLACE ID ... 115-C2
WOODBURN OR ... 205-B1

FRONT ST Rt#-23
SAINT JOHN WA ... 114-B3

FRONT ST Rt#-47
GASTON OR ... 198-B3

FRONT ST Rt#-99
YONCALLA OR ... 219-B4

FRONT ST Rt#-409
CATHLAMET WA ... 117-B3
CLATSOP CO OR ... 117-B3

FRONT ST Rt#-507
BUCODA WA ... 184-D4
THURSTON CO WA ... 184-D4

FRONT ST Rt#-547
SUMAS WA ... 102-B1
WHATCOM CO WA ... 102-B1

FRONT ST U.S.-26
GRANT CO WA ... 137-B2
PRAIRIE CITY OR ... 137-B2

FRONT ST U.S.-30
HOOD RIVER OR ... 195-D5

E FRONT ST
ALBION WA ... 249-A4

E FRONT ST Rt#-39
MERRILL OR ... 150-C2

E FRONT ST U.S.-101
PORT ANGELES WA ... 261-G5

N FRONT ST Rt#-99
CENTRAL POINT OR ... 230-C7

NW FRONT ST
CHEHALIS WA ... 299-D11

S FRONT ST Rt#-99
CENTRAL POINT OR ... 230-C7
OAKLAND OR ... 219-A7

SE FRONT ST Rt#-202
ASTORIA OR ... 300-C7
CLATSOP CO OR ... 300-C7

W FRONT ST
ALBION WA ... 249-A4
BOISE ID ... 253-C2

W FRONT ST Rt#-39
MERRILL OR ... 150-C2

FRONT ST N
ISSAQUAH WA ... 176-A4

FRONT ST NE
SALEM OR ... 322-J10

FRONT ST NE Rt#-22
SALEM OR ... 322-H12

FRONT ST NE Rt#-99E
SALEM OR ... 322-H12

FRONT ST S
ISSAQUAH WA ... 176-A4

FRONT ST SE Rt#-22
SALEM OR ... 322-H13

FRONTAGE RD
CURRY CO OR ... 232-B1
GRANT CO OR ... 242-A3
MORROW CO OR ... 128-C1

N FRONTAGE RD
GRANT CO WA ... 112-C3
GRANT CO WA ... 242-A3
JOSEPHINE CO OR ... 225-B7

N FRONTAGE RD Rt#-509
TACOMA WA ... 182-A2

S FRONTAGE RD Rt#-509
TACOMA WA ... 182-A2

W FRONTAGE RD
BAKER CO OR ... 130-B3

FROST RD
KOOTENAI CO ID ... 247-C6
LEWIS CO WA ... 187-C1

FROSTAD RD
ISLAND CO WA ... 167-C2

FROSTY CREEK RD
OKANOGAN CO WA ... 105-A2

FROZEN CREEK RD
DOUGLAS CO OR ... 221-D7

FRUITDALE DR
GRANTS PASS OR ... 335-F11
JOSEPHINE CO OR ... 335-G12

FRUITDALE LN
ISLAND CITY OR ... 130-A2
UNION CO OR ... 130-A2

FRUITDALE RD
SEDRO-WOOLLEY WA ... 161-C6
SKAGIT CO WA ... 161-C5

FRUIT FARM RD
POLK CO OR ... 207-B2

FRUITLAND AV E
PIERCE CO WA ... 182-A4
PUYALLUP WA ... 182-A4

FRUITLAND RD NE
MARION CO OR ... 323-H13

FRUITVALE BLVD
YAKIMA WA ... 243-B6

W FRUITVALE BLVD
YAKIMA WA ... 243-B6

FRUITVALE RD
ADAMS CO ID ... 131-C3
LINCOLN CO OR ... 206-B4

FRUIT VALLEY RD
VANCOUVER WA ... 192-C5
VANCOUVER WA ... 304-E1

FRY LN
HARNEY CO OR ... 145-B2

FRY RD
LINN CO OR ... 207-D6
LINN CO OR ... 326-J14
MARION CO OR ... 199-A7

FRYER RD
YAMHILL CO OR ... 198-B5

FRYREAR RD
DESCHUTES CO OR ... 212-A5

FS RD 307
ADAMS CO ID ... 251-D4

FUGATE RD
WHITMAN CO WA ... 249-A2

FUHRMAN AV E
SEATTLE WA ... 274-B7

FULLER RD
LEWIS CO WA ... 187-A1

FULLER CANYON RD
MORROW CO OR ... 128-C2

FULLERTON RD
COLUMBIA CO OR ... 192-A3

FULTON AV
DISTRICT OF WEST VANCOUVE BC ... 254-C1

FULTON RD
UMATILLA CO OR ... 129-B7

FUNKE RD
LANE CO OR ... 210-B7
LANE CO OR ... 215-B1

G

G ST
GEARHART OR ... 301-H5
LEWISTON ID ... 250-C4
SPRINGFIELD OR ... 330-H6
SPRINGFIELD OR ... 331-B1
WALLA WALLA CO OR ... 345-H4

E G ST
TACOMA WA ... 293-J7

N G ST
ABERDEEN WA ... 178-B7

S G ST
ABERDEEN WA ... 178-B7
TACOMA WA ... 295-G2

S G ST U.S.-101
ABERDEEN WA ... 178-B7

W G ST
GRANTS PASS OR ... 335-D8
JOSEPHINE CO OR ... 335-D8

G ST N U.S.-395
LAKEVIEW OR ... 152-A2

G 100 RD
GRAYS HARBOR CO WA ... 179-A6

G 1100 RD
GRAYS HARBOR CO WA ... 179-A5

SW GAARDE ST
TIGARD OR ... 199-B3

GABLE RD
COLUMBIA CO OR ... 192-A2
SAINT HELENS OR ... 192-A2

GAFFIN RD SE
MARION CO OR ... 325-G3
SALEM OR ... 325-G3

GAGE BLVD
KENNEWICK WA ... 342-A8
RICHLAND WA ... 341-H8
RICHLAND WA ... 342-A8

GAGE RD
KITTITAS CO WA ... 241-D4
POLK CO OR ... 133-A1

SW GAGE RD
CLACKAMAS CO OR ... 199-B5

GAGLARDI WY
DISTRICT OF BURNABY BC ... 156-D4

GAITHER ST Rt#-229
LINCOLN CO OR ... 206-C2
SILETZ OR ... 206-C2

GALE RD
KLAMATH CO OR ... 151-A2

GALENA DR
DESCHUTES CO OR ... 212-C3

W GALER ST
SEATTLE WA ... 276-D2
SEATTLE WA ... 277-F2

GALES CREEK RD Rt#-8
FOREST GROVE OR ... 125-B1
WASHINGTON CO OR ... 125-B1
WASHINGTON CO OR ... 198-B1

GALICE RD
JOSEPHINE CO OR ... 148-C1
JOSEPHINE CO OR ... 149-A1

GALLAGHER RD
MASON CO WA ... 179-D3

GALLAHER RD
DOUGLAS CO WA ... 112-B1

GALLOWAY DR
JEFFERSON CO OR ... 208-B6

GALLOWAY RD
TILLAMOOK CO OR ... 197-A5
YAKIMA CO WA ... 243-B5

GALLS CREEK RD
JACKSON CO OR ... 230-A6

NW GALVESTON AV
BEND OR ... 332-C7

GALVIN RD
CENTRALIA WA ... 184-B5
CENTRALIA WA ... 299-A1
LEWIS CO WA ... 184-B5
LEWIS CO WA ... 299-A1

GAMBLE PL NE
KITSAP CO WA ... 170-C5

S GAMBLE BAY RD NE
KITSAP CO WA ... 170-C5

GAME FARM RD
EUGENE OR ... 330-E1
KITTITAS CO WA ... 241-C5
LANE CO OR ... 330-E1
SPRINGFIELD OR ... 330-F1

N GAME FARM RD
LANE CO OR ... 215-B1

GAME FARM RD E
LANE CO OR ... 330-F2
SPRINGFIELD OR ... 330-F2

GAME FARM RD N
SPRINGFIELD OR ... 330-E1

GAME FARM RD S
North Springfield OR ... 330-G2
SPRINGFIELD OR ... 330-G2

GAME RIDGE RD
YAKIMA CO WA ... 243-B4

GANON ST SE
MARION CO OR ... 325-J5

GAP RD
BROWNSVILLE OR ... 210-C4
LINN CO OR ... 210-C4

N GAP RD
BENTON CO WA ... 120-B3

S GAP RD
BENTON CO WA ... 120-B3
PROSSER WA ... 120-B3

GAP RANCH-WAGONTIRE RD
HARNEY CO OR ... 144-B2

GARBAGE DUMP RD
CLALLAM CO WA ... 169-C2

GARD RD
CLACKAMAS CO OR ... 200-A7

GARDEN AV
BENTON CO OR ... 207-B5

W GARDEN AV
COEUR D'ALENE ID ... 355-D11

GARDEN WY
LANE CO OR ... 330-G7
SPRINGFIELD OR ... 330-G7

GARDENA SCHOOL RD
WALLA WALLA CO WA ... 121-B3

GARDEN CITY RD
CITY OF RICHMOND BC ... 156-B6

GARDEN SPRINGS RD
SPOKANE WA ... 348-C13
SPOKANE CO WA ... 348-C13

NE GARDEN VALLEY BLVD
ROSEBURG OR ... 334-F5

NW GARDEN VALLEY BLVD
DOUGLAS CO OR ... 334-E4
ROSEBURG OR ... 334-F5

GARDEN VALLEY RD
COOS CO OR ... 220-D4
DOUGLAS CO OR ... 221-B3
DOUGLAS CO OR ... 334-A1

GARDNER RD
POLK CO OR ... 125-B3

N GARDNER RD
SKAGIT CO WA ... 260-F2

S GARDNER RD
SKAGIT CO WA ... 260-F4
SPOKANE CO WA ... 246-B6

S GARDNER ST
BURLINGTON WA ... 260-F5
SKAGIT CO WA ... 260-F5

GARDNER RIDGE RD
CURRY CO OR ... 232-D4

GARFIELD AV
CORVALLIS OR ... 327-F7

GARFIELD AV SE
KITSAP CO WA ... 174-C4

N GARFIELD RD
SPOKANE CO WA ... 246-A3

NE GARFIELD ST Rt#-500
CAMAS WA ... 193-B7

S GARFIELD ST
KENNEWICK WA ... 343-C13

S GARFIELD ST Rt#-126
EUGENE OR ... 329-G6

GARFIELD BAY CTO
BONNER CO ID ... 244-B4

GARFIELD BAY RD
BONNER CO ID ... 244-B4

GARFIELD-FARMINGTON RD
FARMINGTON WA ... 115-A3
GARFIELD WA ... 114-C3
WHITMAN CO WA ... 114-C3
WHITMAN CO WA ... 115-A3

GARIBALDI AV U.S.-101
GARIBALDI OR ... 191-B7
TILLAMOOK CO OR ... 191-B7

N GARL ST
BURLINGTON WA ... 260-C4

W GARLAND AV
SPOKANE WA ... 348-F4
SPOKANE WA ... 349-A4

GARLOCK RD
COWLITZ CO WA ... 189-B1

GARNER RD
CLARK CO WA ... 193-B2
JOSEPHINE CO OR ... 233-B4
KLICKITAT CO WA ... 127-B1
YACOLT WA ... 193-B2

NE GARNER RD
CLARK CO WA ... 193-B1

GARRARD CREEK RD
GRAYS HARBOR CO WA ... 117-B1
OAKVILLE WA ... 117-B1

N GARRETT RD
GARDEN CITY ID ... 253-B2

GARRISON RD Rt#-547
WHATCOM CO WA ... 102-B1

GARRISON ST
WALLA WALLA WA ... 345-F7
Walla Walla East WA ... 345-F7

GARRISON BUTTE RD
JEFFERSON CO OR ... 211-D3

GARRITY BLVD U.S.-30
CANYON CO ID ... 147-C1
NAMPA ID ... 147-C1

S GARRY RD
SPOKANE CO WA ... 247-B5

E GARWOOD RD
KOOTENAI CO ID ... 245-A4

N GARY LN
ADA CO ID ... 253-C1
BOISE ID ... 253-C1

GASSY CREEK RD
DOUGLAS CO OR ... 219-C2

SW GASTON RD
GASTON OR ... 198-B3
WASHINGTON CO OR ... 198-B3

GATE CREEK RD
WASCO CO OR ... 202-D7

GATE MIMA RD
THURSTON CO WA ... 184-C4

GATENSBURY RD
COQUITLAM BC ... 157-A5
PORT MOODY BC ... 157-A5

GATENSBURY ST
COQUITLAM BC ... 157-A4

GATEWAY DR
COOS CO OR ... 220-C4

GATEWAY RD
COOS CO OR ... 220-C4

GATEWAY ST
SPRINGFIELD OR ... 330-F4

NE GATEWAY GRADE
JEFFERSON CO OR ... 208-C2

GATFIELD
GEM CO ID ... 139-C3

GAZLEY RD
DOUGLAS CO OR ... 225-C3

GAZLEY BRIDGE RD
DOUGLAS CO OR ... 225-C3

GAZLEY NORTH RD
DOUGLAS CO OR ... 225-C2

GAZLEY PACIFIC HWY
DOUGLAS CO OR ... 225-C3

GEARHART LOOP RD
CLATSOP CO OR ... 301-G2
GEARHART OR ... 301-G2

GEARY ST
ALBANY OR ... 326-E10

GEHRING RD
PIERCE CO WA ... 182-A3

S GEIGER BLVD
SPOKANE CO WA ... 246-B5
SPOKANE CO WA ... 348-B13

W GEIGER BLVD
SPOKANE WA ... 246-A5
SPOKANE WA ... 348-C11

SW GEIGER BLVD
FOREST GROVE OR ... 198-C1

GEISSLER RD
GRAYS HARBOR CO WA ... 178-C6

W GEISSLER RD
GRAYS HARBOR CO WA ... 178-C7

GEKELER LN
LA GRANDE OR ... 130-B2
UNION CO OR ... 130-B2

S GEKELER LN
BOISE ID ... 253-C1

GELLOR RD
CLALLAM CO WA ... 165-D7

STREET — City State	Page-Grid
GEM AV	
MALHEUR CO OR	139-A3
SW GEM LN	
JEFFERSON CO OR	208-B7
GEM HEIGHTS DR E	
PIERCE CO WA	182-B5
GENE BROWN RD	
JOSEPHINE CO OR	233-A6
S GENESEE ST	
SEATTLE WA	282-E5
SEATTLE WA	283-F5
SW GENESEE ST	
SEATTLE WA	281-F4
GENESEE-JULIAETTA RD	
LATAH CO ID	250-D1
GENESEE-TROY RD	
LATAH CO ID	249-D7
GENSMAN RD	
COLUMBIA CO OR	192-A1
GENZER RD	
WASHINGTON CO OR	125-B1
GEO CYPRUS RD	
DESCHUTES CO OR	212-A5
GEORGE RD	
CLACKAMAS CO OR	200-C5
GEORGE CLARK RD	
GRAYS HARBOR CO WA	183-C2
GEORGE KNOTT RD	
WHITMAN CO WA	114-A3
GEORGE MASSEY TUN Rt#-99	
CITY OF RICHMOND BC	156-B7
DISTRICT OF DELTA BC	156-C7
GEORGE SMITH RD	
MULTNOMAH CO OR	200-D1
GEORGE TAYLOR RD	
COWLITZ CO WA	187-D6
GEORGE WASHINGTON WY	
BENTON CO WA	340-F4
RICHLAND WA	340-G9
RICHLAND WA	341-G1
GEORGIA ST	
VANCOUVER BC	254-G10
GEORGIA ST Rt#-99	
VANCOUVER BC	254-F9
GERBER RD	
CLACKAMAS CO OR	200-B4
KLAMATH CO OR	151-A2
NE GERBER RD	
CLARK CO WA	193-B1
GERBER-MCKEE RD	
CLARK CO WA	193-B1
GERBER RANCH RD	
KLAMATH CO OR	151-B2
GERIG DR	
LINN CO OR	207-D5
GERKE RD	
CROOK CO OR	213-C3
GERKING MARKET RD	
DESCHUTES CO OR	212-B7
NW GERMANTOWN RD	
MULTNOMAH CO OR	192-B7
WASHINGTON CO OR	192-B7
GERMANY CREEK RD	
COWLITZ CO WA	117-B3
COWLITZ CO WA	189-A1
NW GERRISH VALLEY RD	
YAMHILL CO OR	198-A3
GERTH ST NW	
SALEM OR	322-F12
GERTLER RD	
FRANKLIN CO WA	121-B2
GESCHWILL LN NE	
MARION CO OR	205-B2
GETCHELL RD	
MARYSVILLE WA	168-D7
SNOHOMISH CO WA	102-C3
SNOHOMISH CO WA	168-D7
NE GHER RD	
CLARK CO WA	307-J1
VANCOUVER WA	307-J1
S GIBBER LN	
YAKIMA CO WA	243-A7
GIBBON RD	
JACKSON CO OR	230-C7
JACKSON CO OR	336-A1
E GIBBS RD	
SPOKANE CO WA	246-C6
W GIBBS RD	
SPOKANE CO WA	246-B6
GIBBS LAKE RD	
JEFFERSON CO WA	170-A2
GIBRALTAR RD	
SKAGIT CO WA	259-H14
GIBSON RD	
COWLITZ CO WA	187-D7
SNOHOMISH CO WA	171-B4
WASHINGTON CO OR	198-C3
S GIBSON RD	
CLACKAMAS CO OR	205-D2
SE GIBSON RD	
CLARK CO WA	193-C7
GIBSON RD NW	
DOUGLAS CO WA	236-D5
POLK CO OR	204-C5
GIBSON RD SW	
THURSTON CO WA	184-C3
GIBSON ST	
CHELAN CO WA	236-C3
GIBSON CREEK RD	
CROOK CO OR	135-C3
GIBSON HILL RD	
ALBANY OR	207-C4
ALBANY OR	326-A4
GIBSON PASS RD	
BRITISH COLUMBIA BC	103-B1
GIENGER RD	
TILLAMOOK CO OR	197-C2
GIFFORD RD SW	
THURSTON CO WA	184-B2
GIFFORD LENORE GRADE	
NEZ PERCE CO ID	123-B2
GIFFORD REUBENS RD	
NEZ PERCE CO ID	123-B2
GIFT AV	
DESCHUTES CO OR	212-C2
GIFT RD	
DESCHUTES CO OR	212-C2
KLAMATH CO OR	151-A2
GILBERT AV	
GLENDALE OR	225-A7
GILBERT RD	
CITY OF RICHMOND BC	156-B7
KITTITAS CO WA	241-D5
SNOHOMISH CO WA	168-C4
YAKIMA CO WA	243-A7
E GILBERT RD	
Otis Orchards WA	351-J2
Otis Orchards WA	352-A8

STREET — City State	Page-Grid
GILBERT CREEK RD	
YAMHILL CO OR	125-A2
SW GILBERT CREEK RD	
YAMHILL CO OR	125-A2
GILBERT GRADE Rt#-7	
CLEARWATER CO ID	123-C2
GILBERTSON-ILLAHEE RD NE	
KITSAP CO WA	174-C1
KITSAP CO WA	271-B1
NW GILCHRIST ST	
BEND OR	332-D8
GILES RD	
WHATCOM CO WA	158-C4
GILHAM RD	
EUGENE OR	330-B2
GILHOULEY RD	
HOOD RIVER CO OR	195-C7
GILIN RD	
WHITMAN CO WA	249-B6
GILKEY RD	
LINN CO OR	133-C1
GILKEY RD E	
BURLINGTON WA	260-D6
NW GILKINSON RD	
MULTNOMAH CO OR	192-A4
GILLESPIE RD	
BRITISH COLUMBIA BC	159-A7
BRITISH COLUMBIA BC	164-D1
BRITISH COLUMBIA BC	165-A1
DISTRICT OF METCHOSIN BC	159-A7
GILLESPIE ST	
RICHLAND WA	341-F2
GILLEY AV	
DISTRICT OF BURNABY BC	156-D5
GILLIHAN RD	
MULTNOMAH CO OR	192-B6
W GILLIS RD	
ADAMS CO WA	120-C1
ADAMS CO WA	121-A1
GILMAN AV W	
SEATTLE WA	272-E6
SEATTLE WA	273-E6
NW GILMAN BLVD	
ISSAQUAH WA	175-D4
ISSAQUAH WA	176-A4
GILMAN DR W	
SEATTLE WA	277-F1
GILMORE AV	
DISTRICT OF BURNABY BC	255-G10
GILMORE DIV	
DISTRICT OF BURNABY BC	255-G13
GILMOUR RD S	
MARION CO OR	207-C2
GIMPL HILL RD	
EUGENE OR	329-B10
LANE OR	215-A3
LANE CO OR	329-A10
GINKGO RD	
JACKSON CO OR	226-D6
JACKSON CO OR	227-A5
GINKGO ELK RD	
JACKSON CO OR	226-C5
GINNETT RD	
SKAGIT CO WA	259-C13
GIRL SCOUT RD	
SKAMANIA CO WA	195-A5
GIRT RD	
COLUMBIA CO OR	189-B5
GISH RD	
LEWIS CO WA	187-D2
N GLADE RD	
FRANKLIN CO WA	121-A2
FRANKLIN CO WA	343-D1
PASCO WA	343-E1
GLADE CREEK RD	
JACKSON CO OR	234-B7
GLADIOLA DR	
GRANTS PASS OR	335-J11
JOSEPHINE CO OR	335-J11
GLADWIN RD	
DISTRICT OF MATSQUI BC	102-B1
GLANFORD AV	
DISTRICT OF SAANICH BC	159-C5
DISTRICT OF SAANICH BC	256-E2
GLASER DR	
LINN CO OR	207-D7
GLASS LN	
JACKSON CO OR	230-C5
GLASS RD	
CLACKAMAS CO OR	199-B6
GLASSER HILL RD	
STEVENS CO WA	106-B3
E GLEED RD	
YAKIMA CO WA	243-A5
N GLEED RD	
YAKIMA CO WA	243-A5
GLEN DR	
COQUITLAM BC	157-A4
GLEN ST	
ASHLAND OR	337-C6
GLEN AIKEN CREEK RD	
COOS CO OR	220-D5
GLENAYRE DR	
PORT MOODY BC	157-A4
GLENBROOK LP	
DOUGLAS CO OR	225-B3
GLENBROOK RD	
BENTON CO OR	133-A2
NW GLENCOE RD	
HILLSBORO OR	198-D1
GLEN COVE MILL RD	
JEFFERSON CO OR	263-C6
PORT TOWNSEND WA	263-C6
GLEN CREEK RD NW	
SALEM OR	322-D11
GLENDALE RD	
ISLAND CO WA	171-A3
WHATCOM CO WA	158-D4
GLENDALE WY S	
KING CO WA	286-B6
GLENDALE VALLEY RD	
DOUGLAS CO OR	225-B7
GLENGARY BAY	
BONNER CO ID	244-B3
GLENGARY RD	
DOUGLAS CO OR	221-C6
GLENGARY BAY RD	
BONNER CO ID	244-B3
GLENN ST S	
VALE OR	139-A3
GLEN RIDGE DR	
CORVALLIS OR	327-C5
E GLENROSE RD	
SPOKANE WA	349-G11
SPOKANE CO WA	349-G11
S GLENROSE RD	
SPOKANE WA	246-C5
SPOKANE CO WA	349-J13

STREET — City State	Page-Grid
GLENWAY AV	
PAYETTE CO ID	139-A3
GLENWOOD AV	
EVERETT WA	264-A7
EVERETT WA	268-A1
GLENWOOD BLVD	
EUGENE OR	330-F8
GLENWOOD DR	
LONGVIEW WA	302-J6
GLENWOOD RD SW	
KITSAP CO WA	174-B5
N GLENWOOD ST	
BOISE ID	253-C2
GARDEN CITY ID	253-C2
N GLENWOOD ST Rt#-44	
ADA CO ID	253-C2
GARDEN CITY ID	253-C2
GLENWOOD-GOLDENDALE HWY	
KLICKITAT CO WA	127-B1
KLICKITAT CO WA	196-D1
GLENWOOD-GOLDENDALE RD	
KLICKITAT CO WA	119-A3
G-LINE RD	
GRAYS HARBOR CO WA	179-A5
NE GLISAN ST	
FAIRVIEW OR	200-B1
GRESHAM OR	200-B1
MULTNOMAH CO OR	200-A1
PORTLAND OR	200-A1
PORTLAND OR	313-J5
PORTLAND OR	314-B5
PORTLAND OR	315-H5
NW GLISAN ST	
PORTLAND OR	312-D5
PORTLAND OR	313-E5
GLORY DR SE	
THURSTON CO WA	181-A7
GLOVER RD	
TOWNSHIP OF LANGLEY BC	157-C7
GLOVER RD Rt#-10	
LANGLEY BC	157-C7
TOWNSHIP OF LANGLEY BC	157-C7
SW GLOVER RD	
JEFFERSON CO OR	208-A7
G L WILLIAMS RD	
CLARK CO WA	118-A3
GNAT CREEK RD	
CLATSOP CO OR	117-A3
GNOS RD	
WASHINGTON CO OR	198-C2
GOAT RANCH RD	
COLUMBIA CO OR	189-A5
N GOBLE CREEK RD	
COWLITZ CO OR	189-D3
S GOBLE CREEK RD	
COWLITZ CO OR	189-D3
GODBERTSON RD	
WASCO CO OR	196-A7
SW GODDARD RD	
WASHINGTON CO OR	198-C2
W GODDARD RD	
BOISE ID	253-B2
GODOWA SPRINGS RD	
KLAMATH CO OR	151-A2
SE GODSEY RD	
DALLAS OR	204-A6
GODS VALLEY RD	
TILLAMOOK CO OR	191-C3
GOERIG ST	
WOODLAND WA	118-A3
WOODLAND WA	192-C1
GOERIG ST Rt#-503	
WOODLAND WA	118-A3
WOODLAND WA	192-C1
GOETHALS DR	
RICHLAND WA	341-D2
N GOING ST	
PORTLAND OR	312-D1
PORTLAND OR	313-E1
GOLD ST	
CENTRALIA WA	299-E6
LEWIS CO WA	299-E6
N GOLD ST	
CENTRALIA WA	299-G3
GOLD CREEK RD	
TILLAMOOK CO OR	197-D3
GOLD CREEK RD W	
KITSAP CO WA	173-C3
GOLDENDALE BICKLETON RD	
KLICKITAT CO WA	120-A3
KLICKITAT CO WA	127-C1
KLICKITAT CO WA	128-A1
YAKIMA CO WA	120-A3
GOLDENDALE-CENTERVILLE RD	
KLICKITAT CO WA	127-C1
GOLDENDALE-GLENWOOD HWY	
KLICKITAT CO WA	119-A3
GOLDENDALE GOODNOE HILLS RD	
KLICKITAT CO WA	127-C1
KLICKITAT CO WA	128-A1
GOLDEN GARDENS DR NW	
SEATTLE WA	272-D1
GOLDEN GIVEN RD E	
PIERCE CO WA	181-D4
PIERCE CO WA	295-J7
GOLDEN MANTEL	
JEFFERSON CO OR	212-C2
GOLDFISH FARM RD	
ALBANY OR	326-J7
LINN CO OR	326-J7
GOLD FORK RD	
VALLEY CO ID	252-D2
GOLD HILL CIR	
BONNER CO ID	244-B3
GOLD HILL SPUR Rt#-99	
GOLD HILL OR	230-B6
JACKSON CO OR	230-B6
GOLDIE RD	
ISLAND CO WA	167-C2
GOLD LAKE RD	
OKANOGAN CO WA	105-A3
GOLD MOUNTAIN RD	
BONNER CO ID	244-B3
GOLD RAY RD	
JACKSON CO OR	230-B6
GOLDSTREAM AV Rt#-1A	
CITY OF COLWOOD BC	159-B6
DISTRICT OF LANGFORD BC	159-B6

STREET — City State	Page-Grid
GOLF COURSE RD	
Ault Field WA	167-B2
ISLAND CO WA	167-B2
PACIFIC CO WA	117-A1
WALLOWA CO OR	130-C2
N GOLF COURSE RD U.S.-101	
PORT ANGELES WA	261-H6
SW GOLF COURSE RD	
WASHINGTON CO OR	198-C2
GOLL RD NW	
DOUGLAS CO WA	236-D7
GOLTRA RD	
LINN CO OR	207-D6
GOOD RD	
BENTON CO WA	120-C3
ISLAND CO WA	168-A3
GOODACRE-BENSTON	
	182-A7
GOODFELLOW LAKES RD	
CLACKAMAS CO OR	201-B4
N GOOD HOPE RD	
KOOTENAI CO ID	245-C2
S GOOD HOPE RD	
KOOTENAI CO ID	245-C2
GOODMAN LN	
ADAMS CO WA	251-B4
GOODMAN MAIN LINE RD	
CLACKAMAS CO OR	169-B2
GOODNIGHT AV	
BENTON CO WA	327-G14
CORVALLIS OR	327-G14
GOODNOE STATION RD	
KLICKITAT CO WA	127-C1
KLICKITAT CO WA	128-A1
GOODPASTURE ISLAND RD	
EUGENE OR	329-H2
EUGENE OR	330-A2
GOODRICH DR NW	
PIERCE CO WA	174-B7
GOODRICH HWY	
DOUGLAS CO OR	219-A6
GOODRICH RD	
DESCHUTES CO OR	212-A5
WASHINGTON CO ID	139-B1
GOODRICH CREEK RD	
ADAMS CO ID	139-B1
GOODSPEED RD	
TILLAMOOK CO OR	197-B1
SE GOODWIN AV	
PENDLETON OR	129-B1
SW GOODWIN AV	
PENDLETON OR	129-B1
SW GOODWIN LN	
PENDLETON OR	129-B1
GOODWIN RD	
KITTITAS CO WA	241-A4
NE GOODWIN RD	
CAMAS WA	193-A6
CLARK CO WA	193-A6
GOOSEBERRY RD	
IONE CO WA	128-B2
MORROW CO OR	128-B2
GOOSE CREEK RD Rt#-194	
WHITMAN CO WA	122-C1
GOOSE CREEK PARK RD	
ADAMS CO ID	251-B4
GOOSE LAKE RD	
ADAMS CO ID	251-C2
GOPHER VALLEY RD	
YAMHILL CO OR	125-B3
SW GOPHER VALLEY RD	
YAMHILL CO OR	125-B3
YAMHILL CO OR	204-A2
GORDON CREEK RD	
MULTNOMAH CO OR	200-C2
GORDON HEAD RD	
DISTRICT OF SAANICH BC	257-C3
GORDON RIDGE RD	
SHERMAN CO OR	127-C3
GORE DR	
LINN CO OR	207-D6
GORE RD	
COWLITZ CO WA	189-D6
YAKIMA CO WA	243-B5
GORGE RD	
CHELAN CO WA	236-D3
GORGE RD E Rt#-1A	
CITY OF VICTORIA BC	256-F6
GORGE RD W Rt#-1A	
DISTRICT OF SAANICH BC	256-C5
DISTRICT OF SAANICH BC	256-C5
GOSE ST	
Garrett WA	344-F7
GOSHEN-DIVIDE HWY Rt#-99	
COTTAGE GROVE OR	215-B6
CRESWELL OR	215-C4
LANE CO OR	215-C4
LANE CO OR	219-C1
LANE CO OR	330-J14
N GOSHEN-DIVIDE HWY Rt#-99	
COTTAGE GROVE OR	215-B7
N GOSHEN-DIVIDE ST Rt#-99	
COTTAGE GROVE OR	215-B7
S GOSHEN-DIVIDE ST Rt#-99	
CRESWELL OR	215-C5
GOSNER RD	
JEFFERSON CO OR	136-A1
NE GOSNER RD	
JEFFERSON CO OR	135-C1
GOSSETT RD	
CLALLAM CO WA	164-C5
GOSS LAKE RD	
ISLAND CO WA	170-D1
GOTHAM BAY RD	
KOOTENAI CO ID	248-A2
GOULD	
PIERCE CO WA	182-A6
GOULD RD	
PACIFIC CO WA	183-B4
GOULD CITY-MAYVIEW RD	
GARFIELD CO WA	122-B2
GOVERNMENT RD	
GRANT CO WA	120-B1
LANE CO OR	141-C1
LANE CO OR	215-C7
GOVERNMENT ST	
BRITISH COLUMBIA BC	101-A1
CITY OF VICTORIA BC	256-G8
DISTRICT OF BURNABY BC	156-D5
DUNCAN BC	101-A1
N GOVERNMENT WY	
COEUR D'ALENE ID	355-E5
DALTON GARDENS ID	355-E5
HAYDEN ID	245-A5
HAYDEN ID	355-E5
KOOTENAI CO ID	245-A5
KOOTENAI CO ID	355-E5

STREET — City State	Page-Grid
N GOVERNMENT WY	
SPOKANE WA	348-E8
SPOKANE CO WA	348-E8
S GOVERNMENT WY	
SPOKANE WA	348-E10
SPOKANE CO WA	348-E9
W GOVERNMENT WY	
SEATTLE WA	272-D5
GOWDYVILLE RD	
LANE CO OR	215-A7
E GOWEN RD Rt#-21	
ADA CO ID	253-D4
BOISE ID	253-D4
W GOWEN RD	
ADA CO ID	253-C4
BOISE ID	253-C4
GOZZER RD	
KOOTENAI CO ID	248-A1
GRABER RD	
YAKIMA CO WA	243-B4
GRABHORN RD	
WASHINGTON CO OR	199-A3
GRADE CRES	
LANGLEY BC	158-C1
GRADE RD	
LAKE STEVENS WA	171-D1
GRADE RD SE	
MARION CO OR	205-D6
GRADE ST	
COWLITZ CO WA	303-D9
KELSO WA	303-D9
GRADE ST SE	
THURSTON CO WA	184-C4
GRADE CREEK RD	
THURSTON CO WA	236-B1
S GRADY WY	
RENTON WA	175-C5
S GRADY WY Rt#-515	
RENTON WA	175-C5
SW GRADY WY	
RENTON WA	175-C5
RENTON WA	289-J4
TUKWILA WA	289-J4
GRAHAM BLVD	
MALHEUR CO OR	138-C3
SW GRAHAM RD	
JEFFERSON CO OR	135-A1
GRAHAM CREEK RD	
JACKSON CO OR	226-C6
SW GRAHAMS FERRY RD	
CLACKAMAS CO OR	199-B5
GRAN RD	
SNOHOMISH CO WA	168-D1
GRAND AV	
ASTORIA OR	300-E5
E GRAND AV	
EVERETT WA	265-G3
N GRAND AV Rt#-27	
PULLMAN WA	249-B5
NE GRAND AV Rt#-99E	
PORTLAND OR	313-G4
S GRAND AV Rt#-27	
PULLMAN WA	249-B5
SE GRAND AV Rt#-99E	
PORTLAND OR	313-G7
PORTLAND OR	317-G2
W GRAND AV	
ASTORIA OR	300-B5
GRAND AV NE	
KITSAP CO WA	174-D2
GRAND BLVD	
CITY OF NORTH VANCOUVER BC	255-C4
VANCOUVER WA	305-J6
VANCOUVER WA	306-A3
S GRAND BLVD	
SPOKANE WA	246-C5
SPOKANE WA	349-B13
GRAND COULEE AV Rt#-155	
ELECTRIC CITY WA	237-C3
GRAND COULEE WA	237-C3
GRANT CO WA	237-C3
GRAND COULEE AV E Rt#-174	
GRAND COULEE WA	237-C3
GRANT CO WA	237-C3
GRAND COULEE AV W Rt#-174	
GRAND COULEE WA	237-C3
GRAND COULEE HWY Rt#-155	
GRAND COULEE WA	237-C3
GRANDE RONDE RD	
ASOTIN CO WA	122-C3
WALLOWA CO OR	122-C3
GRANDE RONDE RIVER RD	
UNION CO OR	129-C2
SE GRAND ISLAND LP	
YAMHILL CO OR	204-D2
SE GRAND ISLAND RD	
YAMHILL CO OR	204-D2
GRAND PRAIRIE RD	
ALBANY OR	326-E10
LINN CO OR	207-D5
LINN CO OR	326-G11
GRAND RONDE RD	
POLK CO OR	125-A3
YAMHILL CO OR	125-A3
SW GRAND RONDE RD	
YAMHILL CO OR	125-A3
GRANDSTROM RD	
SKAGIT CO WA	168-C3
GRANDVIEW AV	
GRANTS PASS OR	335-F12
JOSEPHINE CO OR	335-F12
GRANDVIEW DR	
DISTRICT OF SAANICH BC	257-D1
GRANDVIEW DR W	
UNIVERSITY PLACE WA	181-C3
GRANDVIEW HWY	
VANCOUVER BC	255-B13
GRANDVIEW RD	
Birch Bay WA	158-B5
SNOHOMISH CO WA	168-D4
WHATCOM CO WA	158-C5
GRANDVIEW RD Rt#-548	
Birch Bay WA	158-B5
WHATCOM CO WA	158-B5
SW GRANDVIEW LOOP RD	
JEFFERSON CO OR	212-A2
GRANDVIEW PAVEMENT RD	
GRANDVIEW WA	120-B3
YAKIMA CO WA	120-B3
GRANGE RD NE	
DOUGLAS CO WA	104-C2
GRANGE ST	
DISTRICT OF BURNABY BC	156-C5
GRANGEMONT RD	
CLEARWATER CO ID	123-C2
OROFINO ID	123-C2
GRANGER AV	
BENTON CO OR	207-B5

STREET — City State	Page-Grid
GRANGEVIEW RD	
KLICKITAT CO WA	195-D4
GRANITE RD	
GRANITE OR	137-C1
GRANT CO OR	137-C1
GRANITE CREEK RD	
MALHEUR CO OR	146-A1
GRANITE FALLS HWY Rt#-92	
GRANITE FALLS WA	102-C3
SNOHOMISH CO WA	102-C3
SNOHOMISH CO WA	110-C1
GRANITE HILL RD	
BAKER CO OR	138-A1
JOSEPHINE CO OR	229-C4
JOSEPHINE CO OR	335-F2
SUMPTER OR	138-A1
GRANT AV	
CORVALLIS OR	327-F8
MAPLE RIDGE BC	157-D6
GRANT RD	
BRITISH COLUMBIA BC	164-C1
DOUGLAS CO WA	239-B4
EAST WENATCHEE WA	239-A4
East Wenatchee Bench WA	239-A4
GRANT ST	
LEBANON OR	133-C1
LINN CO OR	133-C1
PORT MOODY BC	157-A4
N GRANT ST	
CANBY OR	199-C6
GRANTHAM PL	
DIST OF NORTH VANCOUVER BC	255-G6
GRANTHAM RD	
CLARK CO WA	193-A1
GRANT MCCONACHIE WY	
CITY OF RICHMOND BC	156-B6
GRANVILLE AV	
CITY OF RICHMOND BC	156-B6
GRANVILLE BRDG	
VANCOUVER BC	254-E12
GRANVILLE BRDG Rt#-99	
VANCOUVER BC	254-E12
GRANVILLE ST	
VANCOUVER BC	156-B5
VANCOUVER BC	254-F11
VANCOUVER BC	254-E14
GRANVILLE ST Rt#-99	
VANCOUVER BC	156-B5
VANCOUVER BC	254-E14
GRAPE AV W	
OMAK WA	104-C2
GRAPEVIEW LOOP RD	
MASON CO WA	173-D7
MASON CO WA	180-D1
S GRASLE RD	
CLACKAMAS CO OR	200-A5
GRASS CREEK RD	
BOUNDARY CO ID	107-A1
GRASSHOPPER RD	
WASCO CO OR	202-D7
GRASS MOUNTAIN LP	
MALHEUR CO OR	146-C3
GRASSY KNOB RD	
CURRY CO OR	224-B5
GRAUL RD	
CLALLAM CO WA	164-D6
GRAVE CREEK RD	
IDAHO CO ID	123-C3
JACKSON CO OR	229-D2
GRAVELLY BEACH RD NW	
THURSTON CO WA	180-B5
GRAVELLY LAKE DR SW	
LAKEWOOD WA	181-C4
GRAVES RD	
CLACKAMAS CO OR	199-D7
CLARK CO WA	192-D1
E GRAVES RD	
Country Homes WA	346-J11
Country Homes WA	347-A11
SPOKANE WA	347-A11
W GRAVES RD	
Country Homes WA	346-J11
GRAVETT RD	
CROOK CO OR	213-D6
GRAY RD	
LEWIS CO WA	187-D3
PEND OREILLE CO WA	106-C3
WHITMAN CO WA	249-C4
GRAYBACK RD	
JOSEPHINE CO OR	149-A2
JOSEPHINE CO OR	233-D4
GRAY EAGLE RD	
LATAH CO ID	250-D1
GRAYS CORNER RD	
UNION CO OR	130-A2
GRAYS CREEK RD	
ADAMS CO ID	139-C1
ADAMS CO ID	252-A4
GREASY SPOON RD	
CLATSOP CO OR	117-B3
GREAT NORTHERN RD	
MODOC CO CA	151-A3
GREAT NORTHERN WY	
VANCOUVER BC	254-J12
VANCOUVER BC	255-A12
N GREELEY AV	
PORTLAND OR	308-D6
PORTLAND OR	312-E1
PORTLAND OR	313-E2
GREEN AV	
CHELAN CO WA	236-B2
SW GREEN DR	
JEFFERSON CO OR	208-A7
JEFFERSON CO OR	212-C1
GREEN RD	
CLARK CO WA	192-D1
COLUMBIA CO OR	189-C7
HOOD RIVER CO OR	195-B7
ISLAND CO WA	167-D2
SKAGIT CO WA	161-B5
WHATCOM CO WA	260-C1
GREEN ST	
IONE CO WA	128-B2
SE GREEN ACRE RD	
YAMHILL CO OR	204-D1
GREEN ACRES RD	
COOS CO OR	220-D3
GREENACRES RD	
OKANOGAN CO WA	104-C2
GREENAWAY RD	
OKANOGAN CO WA	104-C3
GREENBACK RD	
LINN CO OR	210-A1
GREENBACK MINE RD	
JOSEPHINE CO OR	229-C2
GREEN BAY RD	
BONNER CO ID	244-B4
GREENBERRY RD	
BENTON CO OR	133-B2

STREET — City State — Page-Grid

GREEN BLUFF RD
SPOKANE CO WA — 347-J2
GREEN BLUFF RD E
SPOKANE CO WA — 347-G2
GREEN BLUFF RD N
SPOKANE CO WA — 347-J1
GREEN CREEK RD
LANE CO OR — 209-D7
GREENCREEK RD
IDAHO CO ID — 123-C3
N GREENE ST
SPOKANE WA — 349-E6
S GREEN FERRY RD
KOOTENAI CO ID — 247-D1
GREEN FORK RD
SKAMANIA CO WA — 193-D2
SKAMANIA CO WA — 194-A2
GREEN HILL RD
EUGENE OR — 215-A2
LANE CO OR — 210-A7
LANE CO OR — 215-A1
GREEN HOLLOW RD
WHITMAN CO WA — 114-C3
WHITMAN CO WA — 122-C1
GREENHORN RD
BAKER CO OR — 137-C1
GREENHOUSE LN
HARNEY CO OR — 145-A1
GREENHURST RD
CANYON CO ID — 147-C1
NAMPA ID — 147-C1
N GREENHURST RD
ADA CO ID — 253-A5
W GREENHURST RD
CANYON CO ID — 147-B1
GREEN ISLAND RD
LANE CO OR — 210-B7
GREEN LAKE DR N
SEATTLE WA — 273-J1
SEATTLE WA — 274-A2
GREEN LAKE DR N Rt#-99
SEATTLE WA — 273-J2
E GREEN LAKE WY N
SEATTLE WA — 273-J5
SEATTLE WA — 274-A3
W GREEN LAKE WY N
SEATTLE WA — 273-J3
W GREEN LAKE WY N Rt#-99
SEATTLE WA — 273-J3
GREEN MOUNTAIN RD
CLATSOP CO OR — 188-D4
COWLITZ CO WA — 189-D6
WASHINGTON CO OR — 125-B1
GREEN RIDGE RD
DESCHUTES CO OR — 211-D3
DESCHUTES CO OR — 212-A4
JEFFERSON CO OR — 211-D2
GREEN RIVER RD
LANE CO OR — 209-D5
N GREENSFERRY RD
KOOTENAI CO ID — 354-B4
POST FALLS ID — 354-B4
S GREENSFERRY RD
KOOTENAI CO ID — 354-B11
POST FALLS ID — 354-B7
GREEN SPRINGS HWY Rt#-66
ASHLAND OR — 337-F9
JACKSON CO OR — 150-A2
JACKSON CO OR — 234-D4
JACKSON CO OR — 337-F9
KLAMATH CO OR — 150-A2
KLAMATH CO OR — 235-A5
KLAMATH CO OR — 338-A12
KLAMATH FALLS OR — 338-A12
GREEN SPRINGS HWY Rt#-140
KLAMATH CO OR — 338-B12
GREEN TIMBER RD
TILLAMOOK CO OR — 197-C4
GREEN VALLEY RD
DOUGLAS CO OR — 141-A1
DOUGLAS CO OR — 219-A7
LINN CO OR — 207-B7
LINN CO OR — 210-A1
SE GREEN VALLEY RD
KING CO WA — 182-C2
GREENVILLE RD
WALLA WALLA CO WA — 121-C2
WASHINGTON CO OR — 125-B1
NE GREENWOOD AV U.S.-20
BEND OR — 332-F7
NW GREENWOOD AV U.S.-20
BEND OR — 332-E7
SW GREENWOOD AV
GRANTS PASS OR — 335-D10
GREENWOOD AV N
SEATTLE WA — 171-A7
SEATTLE WA — 273-H2
GREENWOOD RD
DIST OF WEST VANCOUVER BC — 156-B2
GRAYS HARBOR CO WA — 178-B4
POLK CO OR — 204-B6
N GREENWOOD RD
POLK CO OR — 204-B5
W GREENWOOD RD
SPOKANE WA — 348-E9
SPOKANE CO WA — 246-A4
SPOKANE CO WA — 348-A10
GREGORY RD
COLUMBIA CO WA — 189-B6
E GREGORY RD
JACKSON CO OR — 230-D6
GREINER LN
GILLIAM CO OR — 128-A3
GRELLE AV
LEWISTON ID — 250-C5
GRESHAM ST
ASHLAND OR — 337-D8
GREY BLVD
MALHEUR CO OR — 139-A3
GREY RD
JACKSON CO OR — 226-B3
YAKIMA CO WA — 120-B3
GRIBBLE RD
CLACKAMAS CO OR — 199-C7
GRIBBLING RD
DESCHUTES CO OR — 217-D3
GRIDER RD
SISKIYOU CO CA — 149-B3
GRIESER RD
LATAH CO ID — 249-D7
GRIFFIN AV Rt#-164
ENUMCLAW WA — 110-C3
KING CO WA — 110-C3
GRIFFIN LN
JACKSON CO OR — 234-A3
W GRIFFIN RD
SPOKANE CO WA — 246-A5
GRIFFIN CREEK RD
JACKSON CO OR — 234-A2

W GRIFFIN CREEK RD
JACKSON CO OR — 234-A2
E GRIFFIN CREEK RD NE
KING CO WA — 176-B2
GRIM RD NE
MARION CO OR — 199-B7
GRIMES RD
CROOK CO OR — 213-C3
LEWIS CO OR — 184-C6
GRINDSTONE RD
CROOK CO OR — 136-B3
GRINNEL RD
CLARK CO WA — 118-A3
GRINROD RD
KITTITAS CO WA — 241-D5
GRIPP RD
SKAGIT CO WA — 161-C5
GRIZZLY RD
CROOK CO OR — 213-C1
JEFFERSON CO OR — 213-C1
SE GRIZZLY RD
JEFFERSON CO OR — 208-C5
GRIZZLY MOUNTAIN RD
JEFFERSON CO OR — 213-C1
S GRONLUND RD
CLACKAMAS CO OR — 200-A4
GROSHONG RD
LINN CO OR — 207-C3
S GROSHONG RD
CLACKAMAS CO OR — 126-A3
CLACKAMAS CO OR — 205-D4
GROSS LN
DOUGLAS CO OR — 221-B1
NW GROSS RD
KITSAP CO WA — 174-A2
GROSS ST
WATERLOO OR — 133-C1
GROSVENOR RD
CITY OF SURREY BC — 157-A6
GROUSE LN
CURRY CO OR — 224-B3
GROUSE CREEK RD
STEVENS CO WA — 106-B3
GROUSE FLAT RD
ASOTIN CO WA — 122-C3
N GROVE RD
SPOKANE CO WA — 348-B8
S GROVE RD
SPOKANE CO WA — 246-B5
SPOKANE CO WA — 348-B11
GROVE ST
MARYSVILLE WA — 168-C7
MARYSVILLE WA — 168-C7
E GROVE ST U.S.-95
CANYON CO ID — 139-A3
PARMA ID — 139-A3
S GROVE ST
SPOKANE WA — 348-J11
W GROVE ST U.S.-95
PARMA ID — 139-A3
GROWLERS GULCH RD
COWLITZ CO WA — 187-B7
GRUBB RD
CHELAN CO WA — 239-A5
GRUBSTAKE WY
DESCHUTES CO OR — 212-C4
G STOUFFER RD
LEWIS CO WA — 299-H2
GUARD ST
FRIDAY HARBOR WA — 101-C2
GUEMES ISLAND RD
SKAGIT CO WA — 160-C4
GUERANT RD
UMATILLA CO OR — 129-B1
GUIBERSON RD
LEWIS CO WA — 187-B3
GUIDE MERIDIAN RD Rt#-539
BELLINGHAM WA — 158-D6
BELLINGHAM WA — 258-C1
LYNDEN WA — 158-D6
WHATCOM CO WA — 158-D6
GUILD RD
COWLITZ CO WA — 189-D7
GUILDFORD WY
COQUITLAM BC — 157-A4
GUINAN LOOP RD
YAKIMA CO WA — 243-B5
GULCH PLACE RD
MALHEUR CO OR — 147-A3
GULF RD
WHATCOM CO WA — 158-B5
GULL HARBOR RD NE
OLYMPIA WA — 297-A1
THURSTON CO WA — 180-C5
THURSTON CO WA — 297-A1
GUM ST Rt#-397
KENNEWICK WA — 343-E14
S GUM ST
Finley WA — 343-E14
KENNEWICK WA — 343-E14
GUMBOOT RD
CLARK CO WA — 193-D2
SKAMANIA CO WA — 193-D2
NW GUMWOOD LN
JEFFERSON CO OR — 208-C3
GUN CLUB RD
BONNER CO ID — 244-A3
YAMHILL CO OR — 198-B6
N GUN CLUB RD
INDEPENDENCE OR — 204-B7
POLK CO OR — 204-B7
GUNDERSEN RD
SKAGIT CO WA — 161-C7
GUNDERSON RD
SKAGIT CO WA — 161-C7
SNOHOMISH CO WA — 168-B3
NE GUNDERSON RD
KITSAP CO WA — 170-C6
SE GUNDERSON RD
CLACKAMAS CO OR — 200-C4
GUNN RD
CLALLAM CO WA — 165-D6
GUNNELL RD
JOSEPHINE CO OR — 229-A5
LEWIS CO WA — 187-B3
GUN STONE ST SW
THURSTON CO WA — 184-C2
GUTHRIE RD
PIERCE CO WA — 181-B4
GUTHRIE ST
ASHLAND OR — 337-D9
GWINN RD
BENTON CO OR — 120-C3
COLUMBIA CO WA — 122-B2

H

H AV
ANACORTES WA — 259-G5

E H AV U.S.-30
LA GRANDE OR — 130-A2
H RD
POLK CO OR — 204-C4
H RD NE
DOUGLAS CO WA — 112-C2
H RD SE
DOUGLAS WA — 112-C2
H ST
CENTRALIA WA — 299-E3
CULVER OR — 208-B7
JEFFERSON CO OR — 208-B7
THE DALLES OR — 196-C7
H ST U.S.-101
NEHALEM OR — 191-B4
N H ST
ABERDEEN WA — 178-B7
S H ST
ABERDEEN WA — 178-B7
S H ST U.S.-101
ABERDEEN WA — 178-B7
HAAS RD
WASHINGTON CO ID — 139-A2
HAASE RD
ADAMS CO WA — 121-C1
HABBERMAN RD
KITTITAS CO WA — 241-A2
HABELT RD
CLACKAMAS CO OR — 200-C7
HACKER RD
CROOK CO OR — 213-B5
HACKETT RD
COWLITZ CO WA — 189-A1
HACKLER RD
KLAMATH CO OR — 231-B1
HADEN RD
OKANOGAN CO WA — 105-A2
HAEFER LN
UNION CO OR — 130-B2
HAENER RD
POLK CO OR — 207-C1
HAFER RD
STEVENS CO WA — 106-B3
HAGEN RD
GARFIELD CO WA — 122-B2
HAGEY RD
YAMHILL CO OR — 198-D6
HAGMAN LN
JEFFERSON CO OR — 213-A2
HAHLEN AV
CROOK CO OR — 213-B7
HAHLEN AV W
CROOK CO OR — 213-A7
HAIG HWY Rt#-9
DISTRICT OF KENT BC — 94-C3
HAIGHT RD
NEWBERG OR — 198-D5
SW HAILEY AV
PENDLETON OR — 129-B1
UMATILLA CO OR — 129-B1
E HAINES RD
MULTNOMAH CO OR — 200-D1
NE HAINES RD
MULTNOMAH CO OR — 200-D1
S HAINES RD
CLACKAMAS CO OR — 199-C6
HAINES ST
PORT TOWNSEND WA — 263-F5
HAINES CEMETERY RD
BAKER CO OR — 130-A3
HALE RD
PITT MEADOWS BC — 157-C5
HALE RD W
LEWIS CO WA — 187-B2
HALES PASSAGE RD NW
PIERCE CO WA — 181-B1
HALEY RD
POLK CO OR — 207-B1
SE HALEY RD
CLACKAMAS CO OR — 200-B3
HALFMILE RD
DOUGLAS CO OR — 221-C2
HALF ROUND BAY RD
KOOTENAI CO ID — 248-A3
HALFWAY SPUR
BAKER CO OR — 131-A3
HALFWAY OR — 131-A3
HALFWAY-CORNUCOPIA HWY
BAKER CO OR — 131-A3
HALFWAY OR — 131-A3
SW HALL BLVD
BEAVERTON WA — 199-B2
TIGARD OR — 199-B2
WASHINGTON CO OR — 199-B2
HALL RD
LATAH CO ID — 249-D3
SNOHOMISH CO WA — 168-B3
WHITMAN CO WA — 249-B3
HALL ST
STEVENS CO WA — 106-A3
HALLADAY ST
SEATTLE WA — 277-J1
HALL CREEK RD
COOS CO OR — 220-C7
HALLECK ST
BELLINGHAM WA — 258-D5
W HALLETT RD
SPOKANE CO WA — 246-A5
N HALLETT RD Rt#-902
SPOKANE CO WA — 246-A5
HALLIDAY RD
LEWIS CO WA — 184-C5
HALLMAN RD NW
KITSAP CO WA — 170-B7
HALLORAN RD
SKAGIT CO WA — 160-D4
HALLS FERRY RD
POLK CO OR — 204-B6
NE HALLS RD
KITSAP CO WA — 174-D2
NE HALLS HILL RD
KITSAP CO WA — 174-D2
HALLSTROM DR NW
KITSAP CO WA — 174-C7
HALO TRAIL RD
DOUGLAS CO OR — 219-B4
NE HALSEY ST
GRESHAM OR — 200-A1
PORTLAND OR — 200-A1
PORTLAND OR — 314-C4
PORTLAND OR — 315-G4
HALSEY-SWEET HOME HWY Rt#-228
BROWNSVILLE OR — 210-B2
HALSEY OR — 210-B2
LINN CO OR — 133-C2
LINN CO OR — 210-B2
SWEET HOME OR — 133-C2
HALVERSTICK RD
WHATCOM CO WA — 102-B1

HALVERSTICK RD Rt#-547
SUMAS WA — 102-B1
WHATCOM CO WA — 102-B1
HAM RD
COWLITZ CO WA — 190-A6
WHATCOM CO WA — 158-B5
HAMAKER RD
DOUGLAS CO OR — 227-A1
HAMBY RD
DESCHUTES CO OR — 217-C2
HAMER RD
LINCOLN CO OR — 206-D2
HAM HILL RD
CENTRALIA WA — 299-G3
LEWIS CO WA — 299-J5
HAMILTON LN
JOSEPHINE CO OR — 335-G12
HAMILTON RD
WHITMAN CO WA — 122-B1
S HAMILTON RD
KENT WA — 175-C7
N HAMILTON ST
SPOKANE WA — 349-B7
N HAMILTON ST Rt#-290
SPOKANE WA — 349-B8
HAMILTON CEMETERY RD
SKAGIT CO WA — 102-C2
HAMILTON TO COURTROCK RD
GRANT CO OR — 137-A1
HAMLET RD
CLATSOP CO OR — 191-D1
HAMLIN RD
CHELAN CO WA — 239-A5
HAMM RD
LANE CO OR — 133-B3
LANE CO OR — 215-A5
N HAMMA HAMMA RD
MASON CO WA — 173-B2
HAMMELL RD
JACKSON CO OR — 230-D4
HAMMER GRADE RD
WHITMAN CO WA — 122-A1
HAMMOND RD
COLUMBIA CO OR — 189-B5
MAPLE RIDGE BC — 157-C5
PITT MEADOWS BC — 157-B5
HAMMOND BAY RD
NANAIMO BC — 93-A3
HAMPTON RD
ADAMS CO WA — 121-C1
HANCOCK AV
WESTPORT WA — 298-G14
HANCOCK RD
GEM CO ID — 139-C2
E HANCOCK ST Rt#-99W
NEWBERG OR — 198-D5
W HANCOCK ST Rt#-99W
NEWBERG OR — 198-D5
HANEY BYPS
MAPLE RIDGE BC — 157-C5
HANFORD RD Rt#-24
YAKIMA CO WA — 120-A2
S HANGMAN VALLEY RD
SPOKANE CO WA — 246-C5
HANKEY RD
COLUMBIA CO WA — 192-A1
HANKS RD
BENTON CO WA — 120-B3
HANKS BUTTE RD
PEND OREILLE CO WA — 106-B2
E HANLEY AV
DALTON GARDENS ID — 355-F3
W HANLEY AV
COEUR D'ALENE ID — 355-C4
HANLEY RD
CENTRAL POINT OR — 230-C7
JACKSON CO OR — 230-C7
JACKSON CO OR — 234-A1
HANLEY RD Rt#-238
JACKSON CO OR — 234-A1
HANNA AV
GEM CO ID — 139-B3
HANNA RD
POLK CO OR — 204-B7
HANNEGAN RD
BELLINGHAM WA — 102-B1
BELLINGHAM WA — 258-G1
LYNDEN WA — 102-B1
WHATCOM CO WA — 102-B1
HANSBERRY ST
KITSAP CO WA — 270-G5
Tracyton WA — 270-G5
HANSEN AV S
SALEM OR — 324-F3
HANSEN DR
GRANT CO WA — 242-C3
MOSES LAKE WA — 242-C3
NE HANSEN RD
KITSAP CO WA — 271-E1
HANSON RD
KITTITAS CO WA — 241-A6
LEWIS CO WA — 187-D3
YAKIMA CO WA — 241-A7
HANSON HARBOR RD N
LINCOLN CO WA — 113-B1
HANSON LOOP RD
Burbank WA — 121-B3
WALLA WALLA CO WA — 121-B3
HANSON STATION RD
LINCOLN CO WA — 237-C7
HANSVILLE RD NE
KITSAP CO WA — 170-C4
HAPPY CAMP RD
JOSEPHINE CO OR — 233-B6
HAPPY CAMP DUMP RD
SISKIYOU CO CA — 149-A3
HAPPY HOLLOW RD
SNOHOMISH CO WA — 168-B5
HAPPY VALLEY RD
CLALLAM CO WA — 166-B7
CLALLAM CO WA — 262-J14
DISTRICT OF LANGFORD BC — 159-A7
DISTRICT OF METCHOSIN BC — 159-A7
DOUGLAS CO OR — 221-A5
DOUGLAS CO OR — 334-B14
HARNEY CO OR — 145-C2
SEQUIM WA — 262-J14
SNOHOMISH CO WA — 168-B5
W HARBECK RD
GRANTS PASS OR — 335-E12
JOSEPHINE CO OR — 335-D12
HARBER RD
BELLINGHAM WA — 258-B11
NW HARBOR AV
LINCOLN CITY OR — 203-A4
HARBOR AV SW
SEATTLE WA — 276-E7
SEATTLE WA — 277-E7
SEATTLE WA — 281-E1

E HARBOR RD
Freeland WA — 170-D1
ISLAND CO WA — 167-D7
ISLAND CO WA — 170-D1
HARBOR ST
WESTPORT WA — 298-G11
E HARBOR ST
WARRENTON OR — 188-B2
HARBORVIEW DR
GIG HARBOR WA — 181-C1
HARBOR VIEW RD
Birch Bay WA — 158-B4
HARBOUR POINTE BLVD
MUKILTEO WA — 171-B4
MUKILTEO WA — 266-D7
MUKILTEO WA — 267-E7
E HARDCASTLE AV
MARION CO OR — 205-B2
WOODBURN OR — 205-B2
SW HARDEBECK RD
WASHINGTON CO OR — 198-B3
HARDEN RD
LATAH CO ID — 249-C5
MOSCOW ID — 249-C5
HARDESON RD
EVERETT WA — 267-J2
EVERETT WA — 268-A3
HARDIN RD NW
DOUGLAS CO WA — 236-B6
HARDING RD
ABERDEEN WA — 178-B7
CLACKAMAS CO OR — 200-B5
HARDING RD Rt#-380
CROOK CO OR — 213-D5
HARDING ST
RICHLAND WA — 341-G2
HARDSCRABBLE RD
DOUGLAS CO OR — 219-A2
HAREWOOD RD
NANAIMO BC — 93-A3
HAREWOOD MINES RD
BRITISH COLUMBIA BC — 93-A3
NANAIMO BC — 93-A3
HARKINS RD
LEWIS CO WA — 187-C3
HARKINS ST
BREMERTON WA — 271-A10
HARKSELL RD
WHATCOM CO WA — 158-C5
HARLAN DR
Altamont OR — 338-J11
Altamont OR — 339-A11
HARLAN RD
LINCOLN CO OR — 133-A1
LINCOLN CO OR — 206-D5
HARL BUTTE RD
WALLOWA CO OR — 131-A2
HARLOW DR
BREMERTON WA — 270-C9
KITSAP CO WA — 270-C9
HARLOW DR NW
BREMERTON WA — 270-C11
KITSAP CO WA — 270-C11
HARLOW RD
EUGENE OR — 330-C4
SPRINGFIELD OR — 330-F4
HARLOW POINT RD
KOOTENAI CO ID — 248-A4
HARMAN RD
DESCHUTES CO OR — 144-A1
HARMAN WY S Rt#-162
ORTING WA — 182-C5
PIERCE CO WA — 182-C5
NW HARMON BLVD
BEND OR — 332-D7
HARMON RD
COWLITZ CO WA — 189-A2
COWLITZ CO WA — 302-A2
HARMONY DR
LINN CO OR — 210-A2
POLK CO OR — 125-B3
YAMHILL CO OR — 125-B3
HARMONY RD Rt#-122
LEWIS CO WA — 118-A2
MOSSYROCK WA — 118-A2
SE HARMONY RD
CLACKAMAS CO OR — 199-D3
MILWAUKIE OR — 199-D3
SW HARMONY RD
YAMHILL CO OR — 125-B3
HARMS RD
CLACKAMAS CO OR — 199-C7
HARMS ST
WESTPORT WA — 298-G10
HARMS CREEK RD
LANE CO OR — 215-D7
NE HARNEY DR
NEWPORT OR — 206-B3
N HARNEY RD
HARNEY CO OR — 145-B1
SE HARNEY ST
PORTLAND OR — 318-C7
HARNISH RD
LINN CO OR — 207-C3
HAROLD YOUNG RD
PACIFIC WA — 183-D7
HARPER RD
DESCHUTES CO OR — 212-C7
LANE CO OR — 210-A6
HARPER BRIDGE RD
DESCHUTES CO OR — 217-A6
Three Rivers OR — 217-A6
HARPER-WESTFALL RD
MALHEUR CO OR — 138-B3
HARPOLD RD
KLAMATH CO OR — 151-A2
HARPSTER GRADE RD Rt#-13
IDAHO CO ID — 123-C3
S HARRAH RD
YAKIMA CO WA — 119-C2
HARRIET RD
CITY OF VICTORIA BC — 256-E6
DISTRICT OF SAANICH BC — 256-E6
HARRINGTON LP
DESCHUTES CO OR — 212-A6
HARRINGTON TOKIO RD
HARRINGTON WA — 113-C3
LINCOLN CO WA — 113-C3
HARRIS AV
BELLINGHAM WA — 258-B11
HARRIS DR
LINN CO OR — 210-B4
HARRIS RD
CLACKAMAS CO OR — 200-B4
DISTRICT OF MATSQUI BC — 102-B1
FRANKLIN CO WA — 341-J2
FRANKLIN CO WA — 342-A2

HARRIS RD
PASCO WA — 342-B2
PITT MEADOWS BC — 157-B5
RICHLAND WA — 340-H10
HARRIS ST
KELSO WA — 303-F7
HARRISON AV
CENTRALIA WA — 299-B1
LEWIS CO WA — 184-B5
LEWIS CO WA — 299-B1
OLYMPIA WA — 296-E5
E HARRISON AV
COEUR D'ALENE ID — 355-F10
W HARRISON AV
COEUR D'ALENE ID — 355-E10
HARRISON AV SW
OLYMPIA WA — 296-C4
HARRISON BLVD
BENTON CO OR — 327-C9
CORVALLIS OR — 327-C9
HARRISON BLVD Rt#-34
CORVALLIS OR — 327-G9
LINN CO OR — 327-G9
N HARRISON BLVD
BOISE ID — 253-C2
HARRISON RD
COWLITZ CO WA — 189-D4
LINN CO OR — 210-C1
HARRISON RD Rt#-97
KOOTENAI CO ID — 248-B5
HARRISON RD Rt#-823
YAKIMA CO WA — 243-B5
SE HARRISON ST
MILWAUKIE OR — 199-D3
MILWAUKIE OR — 321-J2
HARRIS STREET RD
COWLITZ CO WA — 303-G8
KELSO WA — 303-G8
HARSTINE ISLAND RD N
MASON CO WA — 180-D2
HARSTINE ISLAND RD S
MASON CO WA — 180-D3
HART RD
KITTITAS CO WA — 240-C2
LATAH CO ID — 249-D4
LEWIS CO WA — 187-C3
WALLA WALLA CO WA — 121-C3
SW HART RD
BEAVERTON OR — 199-A2
HART RD SE
THURSTON CO WA — 184-C1
HARTEL RD
UMATILLA CO OR — 121-B3
UMATILLA CO OR — 129-B1
HARTFORD DR
LAKE STEVENS WA — 110-C1
LAKE STEVENS WA — 171-D1
HARTFORD ST
ELGIN OR — 130-A1
HARTLEY RD
BRITISH COLUMBIA BC — 94-B3
HARTMAN RD
KITTITAS CO WA — 240-D1
S HARTMAN RD
CLACKAMAS CO OR — 205-D3
HART MOUNTAIN RD
LAKE CO OR — 152-B1
HARTS LAKE RD S
PIERCE CO WA — 118-A1
HARTS LAKE LOOP RD
PIERCE CO WA — 118-A1
PIERCE CO WA — 181-D7
E HARTSON AV
SPOKANE WA — 349-C10
W HARTSON AV
SPOKANE WA — 348-F10
HARVARD AV E
SEATTLE WA — 278-B2
SW HARVARD BLVD Rt#-138
ROSEBURG OR — 334-B7
W HARVARD BLVD
ROSEBURG OR — 334-B7
W HARVARD BLVD Rt#-138
ROSEBURG OR — 334-E7
N HARVARD RD
LIBERTY LAKE WA — 352-B9
Otis Orchards WA — 352-B9
SPOKANE CO WA — 352-B9
S HARVARD RD
SPOKANE CO WA — 247-B10
HARVEST DR
LINN CO OR — 207-B7
SW HARVEST LN
DESCHUTES CO OR — 212-C6
HARVEY AV
ROSEBURG OR — 334-C6
HARVEY RD
AUBURN WA — 182-C1
CLACKAMAS CO OR — 200-D6
LANE CO OR — 215-C4
WHATCOM CO WA — 158-B3
HARVEY SHAW RD
WALLA WALLA CO WA — 121-C3
WALLA WALLA CO WA — 344-F1
HARVIE RD
CITY OF SURREY BC — 157-B7
HARWOOD ST
PRINEVILLE OR — 213-D5
HARYU RD
COWLITZ CO WA — 189-D4
HASIS DR
JOSEPHINE CO OR — 229-B3
HASKINS RD
KLAMATH CO OR — 151-A2
HASTIE LAKE RD
ISLAND CO WA — 167-B3
HASTINGS AV W
JEFFERSON CO OR — 166-D6
JEFFERSON CO WA — 263-A4
PORT TOWNSEND WA — 263-A4
E HASTINGS RD
Fairwood WA — 346-J8
Fairwood WA — 347-A8
SPOKANE WA — 347-A8
W HASTINGS RD
Fairwood WA — 346-J8
HASTINGS ST
VANCOUVER BC — 254-G10
HASTINGS ST E
DISTRICT OF BURNABY BC — 156-D4
DISTRICT OF BURNABY BC — 255-G10
VANCOUVER BC — 255-F10
HASTINGS ST E Rt#-1
VANCOUVER BC — 255-F10
HASTINGS ST E Rt#-7A
VANCOUVER BC — 254-J10
VANCOUVER BC — 255-B10
HASTINGS HILL RD
GARFIELD CO WA — 122-B1

STREET — City State — Page-Grid

S HATCH RD
- SPOKANE WA — 246-C5
- SPOKANE CO WA — 246-C5

HATCHET SLOUGH RD
- COOS CO OR — 220-C5

HATFIELD HWY Rt#-39
- KLAMATH CO OR — 151-A2
- SISKIYOU CO CA — 151-A3

HATLEY RD
- WHITMAN CO WA — 249-A6

S HATTAN RD
- CLACKAMAS CO OR — 200-A4

W HATTON RD
- ADAMS CO WA — 121-A1

HAUGEN RD
- SKAGIT CO WA — 168-B3
- WASHINGTON CO OR — 199-A5
- YAMHILL CO OR — 199-A5

SE HAUGLUM RD
- CLACKAMAS CO OR — 200-C3

HAUSER LAKE RD
- HAUSER ID — 353-B1
- KOOTENAI CO ID — 353-B1

E HAUSER LAKE RD
- HAUSER ID — 247-C1
- SPOKANE CO WA — 247-B1

N HAVANA ST
- SPOKANE WA — 349-G2
- SPOKANE CO WA — 349-G2
- SPOKANE VALLEY WA — 349-G8

S HAVANA ST
- SPOKANE WA — 246-C5
- SPOKANE CO WA — 349-G12
- SPOKANE CO WA — 246-C5
- SPOKANE CO WA — 349-G12
- SPOKANE VALLEY WA — 349-G12

HAVANA-HELIX HWY
- HELIX OR — 129-B1
- UMATILLA CO OR — 129-B1

HAVEKOST RD
- ANACORTES WA — 259-D8
- SKAGIT CO WA — 259-D8

HAVERLAND KOONTZ RD
- FRANKLIN CO WA — 121-B2

HAVLINA RD Rt#-260
- FRANKLIN CO WA — 121-B1

HAWKINS RD
- LEWIS CO WA — 187-C3

HAWKINS RD S
- LEWIS CO WA — 187-C3

HAWKS CLIFF RD NE
- DOUGLAS CO WA — 113-A1
- DOUGLAS CO WA — 237-A3

HAWKS PRAIRIE RD NE
- LACEY WA — 181-A5
- THURSTON CO WA — 180-D5
- THURSTON CO WA — 181-A5

HAWLEY CREEK RD
- LANE CO OR — 215-A6

HAWN CREEK RD
- YAMHILL CO OR — 198-B6

HAWORTH AV
- NEWBERG OR — 198-D5

HAWTHORNE AV
- MEDFORD OR — 336-D12

NW HAWTHORNE AV
- GRANTS PASS OR — 335-F6

HAWTHORNE AV NE
- SALEM OR — 323-D11
- SALEM OR — 325-C1

SE HAWTHORNE BLVD
- PORTLAND OR — 313-H7
- PORTLAND OR — 314-A7

HAWTHORNE RD
- BELLINGHAM WA — 258-A12

E HAWTHORNE RD
- Country Homes WA — 346-J10
- Country Homes WA — 347-A10
- SPOKANE WA — 347-B10
- SPOKANE WA — 347-C10

W HAWTHORNE RD
- Country Homes WA — 346-J10

S HAWTHORNE ST
- Finley WA — 343-E12
- KENNEWICK WA — 343-E12

HAXTON WY
- WHATCOM CO WA — 158-C7
- WHATCOM CO WA — 160-C1

NE HAY CREEK RD
- JEFFERSON CO OR — 135-B1
- JEFFERSON CO OR — 208-D4

SE HAY CREEK RD
- JEFFERSON CO OR — 135-B1
- JEFFERSON CO OR — 213-C1

E HAYDEN AV
- HAYDEN ID — 245-A5

W HAYDEN AV
- HAYDEN ID — 245-A5
- HAYDEN ID — 247-D1
- KOOTENAI CO ID — 247-C1

HAYDEN RD
- CLACKAMAS CO OR — 200-B6
- LINCOLN CO WA — 113-A1
- LINN CO OR — 133-C1

HAYDEN BRIDGE RD
- North Springfield OR — 330-J4
- North Springfield OR — 331-A4
- SPRINGFIELD OR — 330-J4

HAYDEN BRIDGE WY
- North Springfield OR — 330-G4
- SPRINGFIELD OR — 330-G4

E HAYDEN LAKE RD
- KOOTENAI CO ID — 245-B6

N HAYDEN LAKE RD
- KOOTENAI CO ID — 245-B4

S HAYDEN LAKE RD
- HAYDEN ID — 355-F1
- KOOTENAI CO ID — 355-F1

HAYES LN
- LANE CO OR — 210-A6

HAYES RD
- CLARK CO WA — 118-A3
- CLARK CO WA — 192-C1

S HAYES ST
- MOSCOW ID — 249-D5

W HAYES ST
- WOODBURN OR — 205-B2

HAYES HILL RD
- JOSEPHINE CO OR — 233-B1

HAYESVILLE DR NE
- Hayesville OR — 323-E6
- MARION CO OR — 323-E6
- SALEM OR — 323-E6

S HAYFORD RD
- AIRWAY HEIGHTS WA — 246-A4
- SPOKANE CO WA — 246-A5

HAYHURST RD
- DOUGLAS CO OR — 219-A3

HAY-LA CROSSE RD
- WHITMAN CO WA — 122-A1

HAYNES WY
- COOS CO OR — 218-C6

HAYNIE RD
- WHATCOM CO WA — 158-C3

HAYSTACK DR
- JEFFERSON CO OR — 212-D1

HAYSTACK ROCK RD
- MALHEUR CO OR — 146-C1

HAYWARD RD
- KITTITAS CO WA — 240-D3

HAYWIRE RD
- LEWIS CO WA — 187-C1

N HAZARD RD
- SPOKANE CO WA — 346-G4

W HAZARD RD
- SPOKANE CO WA — 346-H5

HAZARD LAKE RD
- IDAHO CO ID — 251-B1

HAZEL AV
- BENTON CITY WA — 120-C3

W HAZEL ST
- MOUNT VERNON WA — 260-B14

HAZEL CAMP RD
- CURRY CO OR — 232-D3

NE HAZEL DELL AV
- CLARK CO WA — 192-C5
- CLARK CO WA — 305-G1
- VANCOUVER WA — 305-G1

HAZEL DELL RD
- COWLITZ CO WA — 187-B7
- COWLITZ CO WA — 189-B1

HAZELGREEN RD NE
- Hayesville OR — 323-F4
- MARION CO OR — 205-B4
- MARION CO OR — 323-F4
- SALEM OR — 323-F4

HAZELNUT RIDGE RD NE
- MARION CO OR — 205-D4

HAZEL POINT RD
- JEFFERSON CO WA — 170-A7

HAZEN RD
- CLARK CO WA — 193-A1
- COLUMBIA CO OR — 192-A2

HEADQUARTERS RD
- COWLITZ CO WA — 189-C1

HEADQUATERS RD
- COWLITZ CO WA — 189-C1

HEALY RD
- CLARK CO WA — 190-A7

HEART LAKE RD
- ANACORTES WA — 259-F10
- SKAGIT CO WA — 259-F10

HEART OF THE HILLS
- CLALLAM CO WA — 109-B1

HEART OF THE HILLS PKWY
- CLALLAM CO WA — 261-G14

HEATER RD
- CLACKAMAS CO OR — 199-A6
- WASHINGTON CO OR — 199-A6

HEATHER OAK DR
- LANE CO OR — 210-A7

HEATH LAKE RD
- BONNER CO ID — 244-A4

HEBER RD
- UNION CO OR — 130-A3

HECETA BEACH RD
- LANE CO OR — 214-A2

HECKARD RD
- PACIFIC CO WA — 117-A1

E HEDGER AV Rt#-225
- BENTON CITY WA — 120-C3

E HEGLAR RD
- SPOKANE CO WA — 246-D1

HEIGHTS LN NE
- THURSTON CO WA — 180-D5

HEIKKILA LN
- VALLEY CO ID — 251-D6

HEIMER RD
- SNOHOMISH CO WA — 168-D3

HEIMRICH ST
- DUFUR OR — 127-B2
- WASCO CO OR — 127-B2

HEINE RD
- STEVENS CO WA — 106-A3

HEINEMAN RD
- ADAMS CO WA — 113-C3

HEINRICH RD
- VALLEY CO ID — 251-C6

HEINZ BLVD
- MALHEUR CO OR — 139-A3

S HEINZ RD
- CLACKAMAS CO OR — 205-D1

HEINZ RD NE
- MARION CO OR — 205-D4

HEIPLE RD
- CLACKAMAS CO OR — 200-B5

HEISSON RD
- BATTLE GROUND WA — 193-A3
- CLARK CO WA — 193-A3

HELIX-VANCYCLE RD
- HELIX OR — 129-B1
- UMATILLA CO OR — 121-B3
- UMATILLA CO OR — 129-B1

HELLER RD
- Ault Field WA — 167-B2
- ISLAND CO WA — 167-B2
- OAK HARBOR WA — 167-B2

HELLS CANYON RD
- WASHINGTON CO OR — 199-A5

HELLS GULCH RD
- BENEWAH CO ID — 248-C6
- KOOTENAI CO ID — 248-C6

HELM RD
- JOSEPHINE CO OR — 229-A6

HELMAN ST
- ASHLAND OR — 337-C7

HELMCKEN RD
- DISTRICT OF SAANICH BC — 256-C2
- TOWN OF VIEW ROYAL BC — 256-A4

NW HELMHOLTZ WY
- DESCHUTES CO OR — 212-D5

SW HELMHOLTZ WY
- DESCHUTES CO OR — 212-D5

HELMICK RD
- POLK CO OR — 207-B1
- SKAGIT CO WA — 161-C5

NW HELVETIA RD
- WASHINGTON CO OR — 125-C1

HEMENWAY RD
- LEWIS CO WA — 187-B4

NE HEMLOCK AV
- DESCHUTES CO OR — 212-D5
- REDMOND OR — 212-D5

NW HEMLOCK AV
- DESCHUTES CO OR — 212-D5

HEMLOCK RD
- SKAMANIA CO WA — 194-C3

HEMLOCK ST
- LONGVIEW WA — 302-G9
- VANCOUVER WA — 254-E13

N HEMLOCK ST
- CANNON BEACH OR — 188-A7

S HEMLOCK ST
- CANNON BEACH OR — 188-A7
- CANNON BEACH OR — 191-A1

W HEMLOCK ST Rt#-34
- WALDPORT OR — 328-E4

HEMLOCK BUTTE RD
- DOUGLAS CO OR — 223-B6

HEMLOCK VALLEY RD
- BRITISH COLUMBIA BC — 94-C3

HEMMERING RD
- LINCOLN CO WA — 113-B2

W HEMMI RD
- WHATCOM CO WA — 158-D5

HENDERER RD
- DOUGLAS CO OR — 141-A1

HENDERSON BLVD
- OLYMPIA WA — 296-J7

HENDERSON BLVD SE
- OLYMPIA WA — 296-J7
- OLYMPIA WA — 297-A8
- THURSTON CO WA — 296-J7
- THURSTON CO WA — 297-A8
- TUMWATER WA — 297-A8

NE HENDERSON DR
- JEFFERSON CO OR — 208-C3

HENDERSON LN
- OWYHEE CO ID — 147-C2

HENDERSON RD
- DISTRICT OF OAK BAY BC — 257-C5

S HENDERSON ST
- SEATTLE WA — 287-F3

SW HENDERSON ST
- SEATTLE WA — 285-G3

HENDERSON CREEK RD
- LANE CO OR — 214-C2

HENDRICKS RD
- FRANKLIN CO WA — 121-A1
- YAMHILL CO OR — 198-B5

HENDRICKSON RD
- LEWIS CO WA — 187-B5

HENKLE ST Rt#-6
- PACIFIC CO WA — 117-A1
- RAYMOND WA — 117-A1

HENKLE BUTTE DR
- DESCHUTES CO OR — 212-A4

HENLEY RD
- KLAMATH CO OR — 235-C2

HENLEY HORNBROOK RD
- SISKIYOU CO CA — 150-A3

HENNI RD
- ISLAND CO WA — 167-C1

HENRICHS RD
- SHERMAN CO OR — 127-C2

S HENRICI RD
- CLACKAMAS CO OR — 199-D5
- CLACKAMAS CO OR — 200-A5

HENRIOT RD
- LEWIS CO WA — 187-C3

E HENRY RD
- SPOKANE CO WA — 247-B5

N HENRY RD
- LIBERTY LAKE WA — 351-J8
- LIBERTY LAKE WA — 352-A14
- SPOKANE CO WA — 351-J8

S HENRY RD
- SPOKANE CO WA — 287-B4
- SPOKANE CO WA — 351-J9

W HENRY ST
- FRANKLIN CO WA — 342-J6
- PASCO WA — 342-J6
- PASCO WA — 343-D6

HENRY CREEK RD
- WHEELER CO OR — 128-B3

HENRY FOSTER RD
- GRAYS HARBOR CO WA — 179-A7

HENSEL RD
- GRAYS HARBOR CO WA — 178-A3

HENSON RD
- BENTON CO WA — 120-C3

HEPPNER HWY Rt#-74
- GILLIAM CO OR — 128-B1
- HEPPNER OR — 128-C2
- IONE OR — 128-B1
- LEXINGTON OR — 128-C2
- MORROW CO OR — 128-B1
- MORROW CO OR — 129-A2

HEPPNER-SPRAY HWY Rt#-207
- MORROW CO OR — 128-C3
- WHEELER CO OR — 128-C3
- WHEELER CO OR — 136-C1

HERBERT HOOVER HWY Rt#-99W
- NEWBERG OR — 198-D5
- YAMHILL CO OR — 198-D5

HERD RD
- YAMHILL CO OR — 198-D5

NE HEREFORD LN
- JEFFERSON CO OR — 208-D4

HEREFORD RD
- CURRY CO OR — 224-B4

HERFERD RD
- LANE CO OR — 210-C7

SW HERGERT RD
- WASHINGTON CO OR — 198-C2

HERITAGE MOUNTAIN RD
- PORT MOODY BC — 157-A4

HERITAGE MOUNTAIN WY
- PORT MOODY BC — 157-A4

HERMAN RD
- ADAMS CO WA — 121-C1
- LANE CO OR — 210-B6
- LATAH CO ID — 250-C1
- OLYMPIA WA — 297-E9

HERMAN CREEK RD
- HOOD RIVER CO OR — 194-D5
- HOOD RIVER CO OR — 195-A5

W HERMISTON AV Rt#-207
- HERMISTON OR — 129-A1

HERMISTON HWY Rt#-207
- HERMISTON OR — 129-A1
- UMATILLA CO OR — 129-A1

HERMISTON-HINKLE RD
- HERMISTON OR — 129-A1
- UMATILLA CO OR — 129-A1

HERMISTON LOOP RD
- HERMISTON OR — 129-A1
- UMATILLA CO OR — 129-A1

E HERON ST U.S.-101
- ABERDEEN WA — 178-B7

W HERON ST U.S.-101
- ABERDEEN WA — 178-B7

HERRIN RD
- SHERMAN CO OR — 127-C1

HERRING LN
- YAMHILL CO OR — 198-C5

HERRING RD
- WASHINGTON CO OR — 198-A2

S HERRON RD KPN
- PIERCE CO WA — 181-A2

E HERSEY ST
- ASHLAND OR — 337-D7

W HERSEY ST
- ASHLAND OR — 337-C6

HERSHBERGER RD
- DOUGLAS CO OR — 226-C1

HESS RD
- BENTON CO WA — 120-C3

HESSELTINE RD
- STEVENS CO WA — 106-A3

HESSLER FLAT RD
- YAKIMA CO WA — 243-A2

HEWITT AV
- EVERETT WA — 264-E3
- EVERETT WA — 265-F3

E HEWITT AV
- SNOHOMISH CO WA — 171-D2

HEWITT PARK HWY
- BAKER CO OR — 139-A1

HEYBURN RD
- CHATCOLET ID — 248-A6
- KOOTENAI CO ID — 248-A6

HEYDON RD
- DOUGLAS CO OR — 221-A3

HIACK RD
- TILLAMOOK CO OR — 203-D2

HIAWATHA RD NE
- GRANT CO WA — 242-B3

HIBBARD RD NE
- MARION CO OR — 205-B5

HICKEY RD
- BONNER CO ID — 244-B1

NW HICKORY LN
- JEFFERSON CO OR — 208-B3

HICKOX RD
- SKAGIT CO WA — 168-B1

HIDDEN ACRES RD
- LEWIS CO WA — 187-C4

NE HIDDEN COVE LN
- KITSAP CO WA — 174-C1

NE HIDDEN COVE RD
- KITSAP CO WA — 174-C1

HIDDEN FALLS RD
- CLARK CO WA — 193-C7

HIDDEN SPRINGS RD
- YAMHILL CO OR — 198-C5

HIDDEN VALLEY RD
- BONNER CO ID — 244-A1
- KITTITAS CO WA — 240-D2
- LINCOLN CO WA — 206-B5

W HIDDEN VALLEY RD
- KOOTENAI CO ID — 247-C1

HIGGINS AIRPORT WY
- SKAGIT CO WA — 161-A7

HIGGINS LOOP RD NW
- DOUGLAS CO OR — 236-B5

E HIGH DR
- SPOKANE WA — 246-C5

S HIGH DR
- SPOKANE WA — 246-C5
- SPOKANE WA — 348-H13
- SPOKANE CO WA — 246-C5

W HIGH DR
- SPOKANE WA — 246-C5
- SPOKANE WA — 348-H13
- SPOKANE WA — 349-A14

HIGH ST
- BAY CITY OR — 191-B7
- BELLINGHAM WA — 258-C8
- PORT ORCHARD WA — 270-H14
- PRIEST RIVER ID — 107-A3

SW HIGH ST
- GRANTS PASS OR — 335-D9

HIGH ST NE
- SALEM OR — 322-H13

HIGH ST SE
- SALEM OR — 322-H14
- SALEM OR — 324-H1

HIGH BRIDGE RD
- SNOHOMISH CO WA — 110-C1

HIGHGRADE RD
- MODOC CO CA — 152-A3

HIGHLAND AV
- ASOTIN CO WA — 250-B4
- CLARKSTON WA — 250-B4
- GRANTS PASS OR — 335-D4
- JOSEPHINE CO OR — 335-B1

E HIGHLAND AV
- HERMISTON OR — 129-A1

NW HIGHLAND AV
- GRANTS PASS OR — 335-E7

SW HIGHLAND AV Rt#-126
- DESCHUTES CO OR — 212-D5
- REDMOND OR — 212-D5

W HIGHLAND AV
- HERMISTON OR — 129-A1
- UMATILLA CO OR — 129-A1

HIGHLAND AV NE
- SALEM OR — 322-J10
- SALEM OR — 323-A10

HIGHLAND BLVD
- DIST OF NORTH VANCOUVER BC — 156-B2
- DIST OF NORTH VANCOUVER BC — 254-J1

E HIGHLAND BLVD
- SPOKANE WA — 349-B12

HIGHLAND DR
- BELLEVUE WA — 175-C3
- BELLINGHAM WA — 258-C10
- BENTON CO OR — 327-H3
- CORVALLIS OR — 327-H3
- ISLAND CO WA — 168-A6
- MEDFORD OR — 336-F13

E HIGHLAND DR
- ARLINGTON WA — 168-D5

SW HIGHLAND LN
- JEFFERSON CO OR — 208-B7

HIGHLAND RD
- BRITISH COLUMBIA BC — 159-B6
- COLUMBIA CO OR — 189-C6
- COLUMBIA CO OR — 122-B2
- MASON CO WA — 179-D4
- POLK CO OR — 207-B1
- TOWN OF VIEW ROYAL BC — 159-B6

HIGHLAND RD NE
- KITSAP CO WA — 170-C5

HIGHLAND FLATS RD
- BOUNDARY CO ID — 107-B2

HIGHLAND PARK WY SW
- SEATTLE WA — 285-H1

HIGHLAND SCHOOL RD SE
- DOUGLAS CO WA — 112-C2

E HIGHLAND VIEW DR
- BOISE ID — 253-D2

N HIGHLAND VIEW DR
- BOISE ID — 253-C2

S HIGHLINE DR
- EAST WENATCHEE WA — 239-A4
- East Wenatchee Bench WA — 239-A4

HIGHLINE RD
- DESCHUTES CO OR — 217-A2

HIGH PASS RD
- JUNCTION CITY OR — 210-A6
- LANE CO OR — 133-A2
- LANE CO OR — 210-A6

HIGH RIM RD
- DOUGLAS CO OR — 236-D4

HIGH SCHOOL DR
- LINCOLN CITY OR — 203-A5

NE HIGH SCHOOL RD
- KITSAP CO WA — 271-H1
- Winslow WA — 271-H1

HIGH VALLEY RD
- UNION CO OR — 130-B2

HIGHWAY
- BEND OR — 332-D13

HIGHWAY I-18
- BRITISH COLUMBIA BC — 101-A1

HIGHWAY I-82
- YAKIMA CO WA — 120-A2

HIGHWAY Rt#-1
- BOUNDARY CO ID — 107-B1

HIGHWAY Rt#-1A
- CITY OF VICTORIA BC — 256-F6
- DISTRICT OF SAANICH BC — 256-B5
- LANGLEY BC — 158-C1

HIGHWAY Rt#-3
- BENEWAH CO ID — 115-B3
- BENEWAH CO ID — 248-B6
- BREMERTON WA — 174-B4
- BRITISH COLUMBIA BC — 95-C3
- BRITISH COLUMBIA BC — 104-B1
- BRITISH COLUMBIA BC — 105-C1
- BRITISH COLUMBIA BC — 106-C1
- GRAND FORKS BC — 105-C1
- GREENWOOD BC — 105-B1
- HOPE BC — 95-A3
- JULIAETTA ID — 123-B2
- KENDRICK ID — 123-B1
- KITSAP CO WA — 170-C4
- KOOTENAI CO ID — 115-B2
- KOOTENAI CO ID — 248-B2
- LATAH CO ID — 115-B3
- LATAH CO ID — 123-B1
- MASON CO WA — 173-D5
- MASON CO WA — 174-A5
- MASON CO WA — 180-D1
- MONTAGUE CA — 150-A3
- Navy Yard City WA — 270-E14
- NEZ PERCE CO ID — 123-A2
- PRINCETON BC — 95-C3
- SAINT MARIES ID — 248-D7
- SHOSHONE CO ID — 115-B3
- SISKIYOU CO CA — 149-C3
- SISKIYOU CO CA — 150-A3
- YREKA CA — 149-C3

HIGHWAY Rt#-3B
- BRITISH COLUMBIA BC — 106-A1
- MONTROSE BC — 106-B1
- ROSSLAND BC — 106-A1

HIGHWAY Rt#-4
- BRITISH COLUMBIA BC — 92-A3
- CATHLAMET WA — 117-B3
- PACIFIC CO WA — 186-C4
- PORT ALBERNI BC — 92-B3
- SHOSHONE CO ID — 115-C2
- WAHKIAKUM CO WA — 117-A2
- WAHKIAKUM CO WA — 186-D5
- WALLACE ID — 115-C2

HIGHWAY Rt#-5
- BENEWAH CO ID — 248-A7
- BRITISH COLUMBIA BC — 95-C1
- CHATCOLET ID — 248-B6
- HOPE BC — 95-A3
- SAINT MARIES ID — 248-C7

HIGHWAY Rt#-5A
- BRITISH COLUMBIA BC — 95-C1
- PRINCETON BC — 95-C3

HIGHWAY Rt#-6
- BRITISH COLUMBIA BC — 106-C1
- LATAH CO ID — 123-B1
- LATAH CO ID — 249-D1
- LEWIS CO WA — 117-B2
- PACIFIC CO WA — 117-A1
- PE ELL WA — 117-A1
- POTLATCH ID — 249-D1

HIGHWAY Rt#-7
- BRITISH COLUMBIA BC — 95-A3
- CLEARWATER CO ID — 123-C2
- LEWIS CO WA — 118-B1
- OROFINO ID — 123-C2
- PIERCE CO WA — 118-B1

HIGHWAY Rt#-7A
- DISTRICT OF BURNABY BC — 156-D4

HIGHWAY Rt#-8
- BOVILL ID — 123-B1
- BRITISH COLUMBIA BC — 95-C1
- CLEARWATER CO ID — 123-B1
- ELK RIVER ID — 123-C1
- ELMA WA — 179-B7
- GRAYS HARBOR CO WA — 179-A7
- LATAH CO ID — 123-B1
- LATAH CO ID — 249-D5
- MCCLEARY WA — 179-C6
- MOSCOW ID — 249-C5
- THURSTON CO WA — 179-B7
- THURSTON CO WA — 180-B6
- TROY ID — 123-A1
- WASHINGTON CO OR — 199-B1

HIGHWAY Rt#-9
- ARLINGTON WA — 168-D5
- BRITISH COLUMBIA BC — 94-C3
- DISTRICT OF KENT BC — 94-C3
- LATAH CO ID — 123-A1
- MARYSVILLE WA — 168-D7
- MARYSVILLE WA — 171-D1
- SEDRO-WOOLLEY WA — 161-C6
- SKAGIT CO WA — 161-C3
- SKAGIT CO WA — 168-C1
- SNOHOMISH WA — 260-J11
- SNOHOMISH WA — 171-D3
- SNOHOMISH CO WA — 168-C3
- SNOHOMISH CO WA — 171-D1

HIGHWAY Rt#-10
- KITTITAS CO WA — 240-C2
- KITTITAS CO WA — 241-A3
- TOWNSHIP OF LANGLEY BC — 157-D7

HIGHWAY Rt#-11
- BURLINGTON WA — 260-C3
- CLEARWATER CO ID — 123-C2
- SKAGIT CO WA — 161-A5
- SKAGIT CO WA — 260-A1

HIGHWAY Rt#-12
- CLEARWATER CO ID — 123-C2

HIGHWAY Rt#-13
- TOWNSHIP OF LANGLEY BC — 158-D2

HIGHWAY Rt#-14
- BENTON CO WA — 120-C3
- BENTON CO WA — 121-A3
- BENTON CO WA — 128-C1
- BRITISH COLUMBIA BC — 100-C2
- IDAHO CO ID — 123-C3
- KLICKITAT CO WA — 128-B1

HIGHWAY Rt#-16
- BREMERTON WA — 174-B4
- KITSAP CO WA — 139-C3
- KITSAP CO WA — 174-B4

HIGHWAY Rt#-17
- ADAMS CO WA — 121-A1
- BRIDGEPORT WA — 112-C1
- DOUGLAS CO WA — 112-C1
- DOUGLAS CO WA — 113-A2
- FRANKLIN CO WA — 121-A1
- GRANT CO WA — 112-C1
- GRANT CO WA — 113-A2
- GRANT CO WA — 121-A1
- GRANT CO WA — 242-B1
- MESA WA — 121-A2
- MOSES LAKE WA — 242-C2
- OKANOGAN CO WA — 104-C3
- OKANOGAN CO WA — 112-C1
- SOAP LAKE WA — 112-C2

HIGHWAY Rt#-17A
- DISTRICT OF SAANICH BC — 159-C5

HIGHWAY Rt#-18
- BRITISH COLUMBIA BC — 100-C1
- BRITISH COLUMBIA BC — 101-A1
- Lake Cowichan BC — 101-A1

HIGHWAY Rt#-19
- BRITISH COLUMBIA BC — 92-A1
- CAMPBELL RIVER BC — 92-A1
- COURTENAY BC — 92-A2

HIGHWAY Rt#-19A
- BRITISH COLUMBIA BC — 92-A1
- COURTENAY BC — 92-A2
- PARKSVILLE BC — 92-C3

HIGHWAY Rt#-20
- ANACORTES WA — 160-C6
- ANACORTES WA — 259-H5
- Ault Field WA — 167-C2
- BURLINGTON WA — 260-C5
- CONCRETE WA — 102-C2
- COUPEVILLE WA — 167-B4
- CUSICK WA — 106-C3
- FERRY CO WA — 105-B2
- FERRY CO WA — 106-C3
- HAMILTON WA — 102-C2
- ISLAND CO WA — 160-C7
- ISLAND CO WA — 167-C1
- JEFFERSON CO WA — 109-C1
- JEFFERSON CO WA — 170-A1
- JEFFERSON CO WA — 263-C6
- LYMAN WA — 102-C2
- NEWPORT WA — 106-C3
- OAK HARBOR WA — 167-C2
- OKANOGAN WA — 104-C2
- OKANOGAN CO WA — 104-C2
- OKANOGAN CO WA — 105-A2
- PEND OREILLE CO WA — 106-B2
- PORT TOWNSEND WA — 263-C6
- REPUBLIC WA — 105-B2
- SKAGIT CO WA — 102-C2
- SKAGIT CO WA — 160-C6
- SKAGIT CO WA — 161-D5
- SKAGIT CO WA — 259-J6
- SKAGIT CO WA — 260-B6
- WINTHROP WA — 104-A2

HIGHWAY Rt#-21
- ADAMS CO WA — 113-B3
- BOUNDARY CO ID — 107-B1
- BRITISH COLUMBIA BC — 105-C1
- BRITISH COLUMBIA BC — 107-B1
- FERRY CO WA — 105-C1
- FERRY CO WA — 113-B1
- GRAND FORKS BC — 105-C1
- LINCOLN CO WA — 113-B1
- LIND WA — 121-B1
- ODESSA WA — 113-B3
- REPUBLIC WA — 105-B2

HIGHWAY Rt#-22
- BENTON CO WA — 120-B3
- BRITISH COLUMBIA BC — 106-A1
- MABTON WA — 120-B3
- PROSSER WA — 120-B3
- TOPPENISH WA — 120-A2
- YAKIMA CO WA — 120-A2

HIGHWAY Rt#-22A
- BRITISH COLUMBIA BC — 106-B1
- STEVENS CO WA — 106-A1

HIGHWAY Rt#-23
- HARRINGTON WA — 113-C2
- LINCOLN CO WA — 113-C1
- LINCOLN CO WA — 114-A2
- SAINT JOHN WA — 114-B3
- SPRAGUE WA — 114-A3
- WHITMAN CO WA — 114-A3

HIGHWAY Rt#-24
- ADAMS CO WA — 120-C1
- ADAMS CO WA — 121-A1
- BENTON CO WA — 120-C1
- GRANT CO WA — 120-C1
- MOXEE WA — 243-D7
- YAKIMA CO WA — 120-A2
- YAKIMA CO WA — 243-C7

HIGHWAY Rt#-25
- DAVENPORT WA — 114-A2
- LINCOLN CO WA — 113-C1
- LINCOLN CO WA — 114-A1
- MARCUS WA — 106-A1
- NORTHPORT WA — 106-A1
- STEVENS CO WA — 106-A1
- STEVENS CO WA — 106-A1
- STEVENS CO WA — 113-C1

INDEX

STREET | City State | Page-Grid

HIGHWAY Rt#-26
ADAMS CO WA — 120-C1
ADAMS CO WA — 121-A1
ADAMS CO WA — 122-A1
COLFAX WA — 122-C1
GRANT CO WA — 120-B1
OTHELLO WA — 121-A1
ROYAL CITY WA — 120-C1
WASHTUCNA WA — 121-C1
WHITMAN CO WA — 122-C1

HIGHWAY Rt#-27
FAIRFIELD WA — 114-C2
GARFIELD WA — 114-C3
LATAH WA — 114-C3
OAKESDALE WA — 114-C3
PALOUSE WA — 249-B1
PULLMAN WA — 249-B4
SPOKANE CO WA — 114-C2
SPOKANE CO WA — 247-A5
SPOKANE CO WA — 351-A14
TEKOA WA — 114-C3
WHITMAN CO WA — 114-C3
WHITMAN CO WA — 249-B1

HIGHWAY Rt#-28
DAVENPORT WA — 114-A2
DOUGLAS CO WA — 112-B3
DOUGLAS CO WA — 239-A5
EAST WENATCHEE WA — 239-A4
East Wenatchee Bench WA — 239-A3
GRANT CO WA — 112-C2
GRANT CO WA — 113-A2
HARRINGTON WA — 113-C2
LINCOLN CO WA — 113-C2
LINCOLN CO WA — 114-A2
ODESSA WA — 113-B3
ROCK ISLAND WA — 239-B5
SOAP LAKE WA — 112-C2

HIGHWAY Rt#-31
IONE WA — 106-B1
METALINE WA — 106-B1
METALINE FALLS WA — 106-B1
PEND OREILLE CO WA — 106-C1

HIGHWAY Rt#-33
BRITISH COLUMBIA BC — 105-A1

HIGHWAY Rt#-41
BONNER CO ID — 106-C3
BONNER CO ID — 107-A3
BONNER CO ID — 115-A1
KOOTENAI CO ID — 115-A1
KOOTENAI CO ID — 247-D1
NEWPORT ID — 106-C3
NEWPORT ID — 106-C3
RATHDRUM ID — 115-A1
RATHDRUM ID — 247-D1
SPIRIT LAKE ID — 115-A1

HIGHWAY Rt#-42
COOS CO OR — 220-D2
DOUGLAS CO OR — 140-C3
DOUGLAS CO OR — 221-B6

HIGHWAY Rt#-44
CANYON CO ID — 147-B1

HIGHWAY Rt#-47
CARLTON OR — 198-B6
GASTON OR — 198-B3
WASHINGTON CO OR — 198-B2
YAMHILL OR — 198-B4
YAMHILL OR — 198-B3

HIGHWAY Rt#-52
BOISE CO ID — 139-C3
GEM CO ID — 139-C3
HORSESHOE BEND ID — 139-C3
MALHEUR CO OR — 139-A2
PAYETTE ID — 139-A3
PAYETTE CO ID — 139-A3

HIGHWAY Rt#-53
KOOTENAI CO ID — 115-A1
KOOTENAI CO ID — 245-A4
KOOTENAI CO ID — 247-D1
RATHDRUM ID — 115-A1

HIGHWAY Rt#-54
ATHOL ID — 245-B2
KOOTENAI CO ID — 115-A1
KOOTENAI CO ID — 245-C1

HIGHWAY Rt#-55
ADAMS CO ID — 251-A4
CASCADE ID — 252-D5
DONNELLY ID — 252-D1
MCCALL ID — 251-C5
NEW MEADOWS ID — 251-C5
VALLEY CO ID — 251-C5
VALLEY CO ID — 252-D1

HIGHWAY Rt#-56
SANDERS CO MT — 107-C3

HIGHWAY Rt#-57
BONNER CO ID — 106-C2
BONNER CO ID — 107-A2

HIGHWAY Rt#-58
KOOTENAI CO ID — 115-A2

HIGHWAY Rt#-62
CRAIGMONT ID — 123-B2
LEWIS CO ID — 123-C2
NEZPERCE ID — 123-C2

HIGHWAY Rt#-64
KAMIAH ID — 123-C2
LEWIS CO ID — 123-C2
NEZPERCE ID — 123-C2

HIGHWAY Rt#-71
ADAMS CO ID — 131-A3
CAMBRIDGE ID — 139-B1
WASHINGTON CO ID — 131-A3
WASHINGTON CO ID — 139-A1

HIGHWAY Rt#-72
PAYETTE CO ID — 139-B3

HIGHWAY Rt#-91A
NEW WESTMINSTER BC — 156-D6

HIGHWAY Rt#-92
LAKE STEVENS WA — 171-D1
SNOHOMISH CO WA — 110-C1
SNOHOMISH CO WA — 171-D1

HIGHWAY Rt#-95
BRITISH COLUMBIA BC — 107-B1

HIGHWAY Rt#-96
SISKIYOU CO CA — 149-A3
SISKIYOU CO CA — 150-A3

HIGHWAY Rt#-97
BRITISH COLUMBIA BC — 104-C1
HARRISON ID — 248-A4
KOOTENAI CO ID — 248-A1
OSOYOOS BC — 104-C1

HIGHWAY Rt#-97C
BRITISH COLUMBIA BC — 95-C1

HIGHWAY Rt#-99
CITY OF RICHMOND BC — 156-B5
EDMONDS WA — 171-B5
KENDRICK ID — 123-B1
LATAH CO ID — 123-A1
LYNNWOOD WA — 171-B4
MOUNTLAKE TERRACE WA — 171-B5
SEATTLE WA — 286-A2

HIGHWAY Rt#-99
SNOHOMISH CO WA — 171-B4
TROY ID — 123-A1

HIGHWAY Rt#-99A
CITY OF SURREY BC — 156-D5
NEW WESTMINSTER BC — 156-D5

HIGHWAY Rt#-99E
MILWAUKIE OR — 321-J2
SALEM OR — 322-H12

HIGHWAY Rt#-100
ILWACO WA — 186-A6
PACIFIC WA — 186-A6

HIGHWAY Rt#-101
BRITISH COLUMBIA BC — 92-B1
BRITISH COLUMBIA BC — 93-A1
Gibson BC — 93-B3
PACIFIC CO WA — 186-C4
POWELL RIVER BC — 92-C1
Sechelt BC — 93-A2

HIGHWAY Rt#-104
JEFFERSON CO WA — 109-C1
JEFFERSON CO WA — 170-A3
Kingston WA — 170-D5
KITSAP CO WA — 170-C4

HIGHWAY Rt#-105
ABERDEEN WA — 117-A1
GRAYS HARBOR CO WA — 117-A1
GRAYS HARBOR CO WA — 183-D1
PACIFIC CO WA — 117-A1
PACIFIC CO WA — 183-B3
RAYMOND WA — 117-A1
WESTPORT WA — 183-B2
WESTPORT WA — 298-G11

HIGHWAY Rt#-106
MASON CO WA — 173-D5
MASON CO WA — 180-A1

HIGHWAY Rt#-107
GRAYS HARBOR CO WA — 178-D7
MONTESANO WA — 178-D7

HIGHWAY Rt#-108
GRAYS HARBOR CO WA — 179-D5
MASON CO WA — 179-D5
MASON CO WA — 180-A4

HIGHWAY Rt#-109
GRAYS HARBOR CO WA — 172-B7
GRAYS HARBOR CO WA — 177-B1
HOQUIAM WA — 177-D7
HOQUIAM WA — 178-A7
Taholah WA — 172-B7

HIGHWAY Rt#-112
CLALLAM CO WA — 100-B2
CLALLAM CO WA — 162-C1
CLALLAM CO WA — 163-A2
CLALLAM CO WA — 164-A4
CLALLAM CO WA — 165-A6
Neah Bay WA — 100-B2

HIGHWAY Rt#-119
MASON CO WA — 109-B2
MASON CO WA — 173-A6

HIGHWAY Rt#-123
LEWIS CO WA — 185-D5
PIERCE CO WA — 119-A1
PIERCE CO WA — 185-D4

HIGHWAY Rt#-124
PRESCOTT WA — 121-C2
WALLA WALLA CO WA — 121-C2
WALLA WALLA CO WA — 122-A2

HIGHWAY Rt#-125
COLLEGE PLACE WA — 344-H11
WALLA WALLA WA — 344-H5
WALLA WALLA CO WA — 345-A10
WALLA WALLA CO WA — 121-C2
WALLA WALLA CO WA — 344-G1

HIGHWAY Rt#-127
GARFIELD CO WA — 122-B1
WHITMAN CO WA — 122-B1

HIGHWAY Rt#-128
ASOTIN CO WA — 250-B4
CLARKSTON WA — 250-B4
LEWISTON ID — 250-B4
WHITMAN CO WA — 250-B4

HIGHWAY Rt#-129
ASOTIN WA — 250-B5
ASOTIN CO WA — 122-C3
ASOTIN CO WA — 123-A3
ASOTIN CO WA — 250-B5
CLARKSTON WA — 250-B4
Vineland WA — 250-B5

HIGHWAY Rt#-139
MODOC CO CA — 151-A3
SISKIYOU CO CA — 151-A3

HIGHWAY Rt#-141
BINGEN WA — 195-D5
KLICKITAT CO WA — 119-A3
KLICKITAT CO WA — 195-D1
WHITE SALMON WA — 195-D4

HIGHWAY Rt#-142
KLICKITAT CO WA — 127-B1
KLICKITAT CO WA — 196-D2

HIGHWAY Rt#-150
CHELAN WA — 236-C3
CHELAN CO WA — 236-C3

HIGHWAY Rt#-153
OKANOGAN CO WA — 104-B3
OKANOGAN CO WA — 112-B1

HIGHWAY Rt#-155
COULEE DAM WA — 237-C2
GRAND COULEE WA — 237-C3
GRANT CO WA — 113-A1
GRANT CO WA — 237-C2
NESPELEM WA — 105-A3
OKANOGAN CO WA — 104-C3
OKANOGAN CO WA — 105-A3
OMAK WA — 104-C3

HIGHWAY Rt#-160
KITSAP CO WA — 174-D4

HIGHWAY Rt#-161
SISKIYOU CO CA — 150-C3

HIGHWAY Rt#-165
PIERCE CO WA — 118-C1

HIGHWAY Rt#-166
KITSAP CO WA — 174-B4
PORT ORCHARD WA — 174-B4
PORT ORCHARD WA — 270-F14

HIGHWAY Rt#-167
TACOMA WA — 182-A2

HIGHWAY Rt#-173
BREWSTER WA — 104-B3
BRIDGEPORT WA — 112-C1
DOUGLAS CO WA — 104-B3
DOUGLAS CO WA — 112-C1
OKANOGAN CO WA — 104-B3

HIGHWAY Rt#-174
DOUGLAS CO WA — 112-C1
DOUGLAS CO WA — 113-A1
DOUGLAS CO WA — 237-C2
GRAND COULEE WA — 237-C3
GRANT CO WA — 237-C2
LINCOLN CO WA — 113-B1

HIGHWAY Rt#-174
LINCOLN CO WA — 237-C3

HIGHWAY Rt#-200
BONNER CO ID — 107-C3
BONNER CO ID — 244-B1
CLARK FORK ID — 107-C3
EAST HOPE ID — 244-D2
HOPE ID — 244-A1
KOOTENAI ID — 244-A1
PONDERAY ID — 244-A1
SANDERS CO MT — 107-C3

HIGHWAY Rt#-204
SNOHOMISH CO WA — 171-D1

HIGHWAY Rt#-206
SPOKANE CO WA — 114-C1

HIGHWAY Rt#-207
CHELAN WA — 111-C1

HIGHWAY Rt#-211
PEND OREILLE CO WA — 106-C3

HIGHWAY Rt#-221
BENTON CO WA — 120-C3
DAYTON OR — 198-C7
PROSSER WA — 120-C3
YAMHILL CO OR — 198-C7

HIGHWAY Rt#-223
GRANGER WA — 120-A2
YAKIMA CO WA — 120-A2

HIGHWAY Rt#-224
BENTON CO WA — 120-C2
WEST RICHLAND WA — 120-C2

HIGHWAY Rt#-231
LINCOLN CO WA — 114-A1
SPRINGDALE WA — 106-B3
STEVENS CO WA — 106-B3
STEVENS CO WA — 114-B1

HIGHWAY Rt#-240
BENTON CO WA — 120-C2
RICHLAND WA — 120-C2
RICHLAND WA — 121-A2
RICHLAND WA — 340-A7

HIGHWAY Rt#-241
BENTON CO WA — 120-B2
SUNNYSIDE WA — 120-B2
YAKIMA CO WA — 120-B2

HIGHWAY Rt#-243
GRANT CO WA — 120-B1

HIGHWAY Rt#-260
ADAMS CO WA — 121-C1
CONNELL WA — 121-B1
FRANKLIN CO WA — 121-C1
KAHLOTUS WA — 121-C1

HIGHWAY Rt#-261
ADAMS CO WA — 121-C1
COLUMBIA CO WA — 122-A2
FRANKLIN CO WA — 121-C1
FRANKLIN CO WA — 122-A2
STARBUCK WA — 122-A2

HIGHWAY Rt#-263
SISKIYOU CO CA — 149-C3
SISKIYOU CO CA — 150-A3
YREKA CA — 149-C3

HIGHWAY Rt#-270
MOSCOW ID — 249-C5
PULLMAN WA — 249-B5
WHITMAN CO WA — 249-C5

HIGHWAY Rt#-271
OAKESDALE WA — 114-C3
WHITMAN CO WA — 114-C3

HIGHWAY Rt#-272
COLFAX WA — 122-C1
LATAH CO ID — 249-C1
PALOUSE WA — 249-B1
WHITMAN CO WA — 122-C1
WHITMAN CO WA — 249-B1

HIGHWAY Rt#-274
BENEWAH CO ID — 115-A3
TEKOA WA — 114-C3
WHITMAN CO WA — 114-C3
WHITMAN CO WA — 115-A3

HIGHWAY Rt#-281
GRANT CO WA — 112-B3

HIGHWAY Rt#-282
EPHRATA WA — 112-C3
GRANT CO WA — 112-C3

HIGHWAY Rt#-283
GRANT CO WA — 120-B2

HIGHWAY Rt#-285
EAST WENATCHEE WA — 239-A4
Sunnyslope WA — 238-D3
WENATCHEE WA — 238-D3
WENATCHEE WA — 239-A4
West Wenatchee WA — 238-D3

HIGHWAY Rt#-292
SPRINGDALE WA — 106-B3
STEVENS CO WA — 106-B3

HIGHWAY Rt#-300
MASON CO WA — 173-D5

HIGHWAY Rt#-302
MASON CO WA — 173-D6

HIGHWAY Rt#-303
KITSAP CO WA — 174-B1
KITSAP CO WA — 270-J1

HIGHWAY Rt#-304
BREMERTON WA — 270-F12
Navy Yard City WA — 270-F12

HIGHWAY Rt#-305
KITSAP CO WA — 170-B6
KITSAP CO WA — 174-B1
POULSBO WA — 170-B6
Suquamish WA — 170-B6
Winslow WA — 174-D1

HIGHWAY Rt#-308
KITSAP CO WA — 170-B7

HIGHWAY Rt#-395
BRITISH COLUMBIA BC — 105-C1

HIGHWAY Rt#-397
Finley WA — 121-A3

HIGHWAY Rt#-401
PACIFIC CO WA — 186-C5

HIGHWAY Rt#-409
CATHLAMET WA — 117-B3
WAHKIAKUM CO WA — 117-B3

HIGHWAY Rt#-410
BONNEY LAKE WA — 182-C4
BUCKLEY WA — 110-C3
BUCKLEY WA — 182-D4
KING CO WA — 110-C3
PIERCE CO WA — 119-A1
PIERCE CO WA — 111-A3
SUMNER WA — 182-C3
YAKIMA CO WA — 119-B1
YAKIMA CO WA — 240-A6

HIGHWAY Rt#-432
COWLITZ CO WA — 303-C12
KELSO WA — 303-B13
LONGVIEW WA — 303-C12

HIGHWAY Rt#-500
CLARK CO WA — 192-D5
CLARK CO WA — 306-C2
CLARK CO WA — 307-J1
VANCOUVER WA — 192-D5
VANCOUVER WA — 305-H2
VANCOUVER WA — 306-E2
VANCOUVER WA — 307-H1

HIGHWAY Rt#-503
CLARK CO WA — 118-A3
CLARK CO WA — 190-A7
CLARK CO WA — 193-A1
COWLITZ CO WA — 118-A3
COWLITZ CO WA — 190-A6
WOODLAND WA — 192-C1

HIGHWAY Rt#-504
COWLITZ CO WA — 118-A2
SKAMANIA CO WA — 118-B2
SKAMANIA CO WA — 190-B1

HIGHWAY Rt#-505
COWLITZ CO WA — 118-A3
LEWIS CO WA — 118-A2
LEWIS CO WA — 187-C3
TOLEDO WA — 187-D4
WINLOCK WA — 187-C3

HIGHWAY Rt#-506
COWLITZ CO WA — 187-B5
LEWIS CO WA — 187-C2
VADER WA — 187-C5

HIGHWAY Rt#-507
LEWIS CO WA — 184-C5
THURSTON CO WA — 118-A1
THURSTON CO WA — 184-D3

HIGHWAY Rt#-508
LEWIS CO WA — 118-A2
LEWIS CO WA — 187-C1
MORTON WA — 118-B2

HIGHWAY Rt#-510
THURSTON CO WA — 181-A6

HIGHWAY Rt#-515
KING CO WA — 175-C5
RENTON WA — 175-C5

HIGHWAY Rt#-522
MONROE WA — 110-C1
SNOHOMISH CO WA — 110-C1
SNOHOMISH CO WA — 171-D5

HIGHWAY Rt#-525
Clinton WA — 171-A2
Freeland WA — 170-C1
ISLAND CO WA — 167-C5
ISLAND CO WA — 170-C1
ISLAND CO WA — 171-A1
SNOHOMISH CO WA — 171-B4

HIGHWAY Rt#-529
MARYSVILLE WA — 171-C1
SNOHOMISH CO WA — 171-C1

HIGHWAY Rt#-530
ARLINGTON WA — 168-D5
DARRINGTON WA — 103-A3
MARYSVILLE WA — 168-C5
SNOHOMISH CO WA — 102-C3
SNOHOMISH CO WA — 103-A3
SNOHOMISH CO WA — 168-D4

HIGHWAY Rt#-532
SNOHOMISH CO WA — 168-A4
STANWOOD WA — 168-A4

HIGHWAY Rt#-534
SKAGIT CO WA — 168-B2

HIGHWAY Rt#-543
BLAINE WA — 158-B3
WHATCOM CO WA — 158-B3

HIGHWAY Rt#-706
PIERCE CO WA — 185-A5

HIGHWAY Rt#-730
WALLA WALLA CO WA — 121-B3

HIGHWAY Rt#-821
KITTITAS CO WA — 241-B7
KITTITAS CO WA — 243-B1
YAKIMA CO WA — 243-C4

HIGHWAY Rt#-823
YAKIMA CO WA — 243-B6

HIGHWAY Rt#-902
MEDICAL LAKE WA — 114-B2
SPOKANE CO WA — 114-B2
SPOKANE CO WA — 246-A5

HIGHWAY Rt#-903
CLE ELUM WA — 240-B2
KITTITAS CO WA — 240-A1
ROSLYN WA — 240-A1

HIGHWAY Rt#-904
CHENEY WA — 246-A7
SPOKANE CO WA — 114-B2
SPOKANE CO WA — 246-A6

HIGHWAY Rt#-906
KING CO WA — 111-A2
KITTITAS CO WA — 111-A2

HIGHWAY Rt#-970
KITTITAS CO WA — 240-D1

HIGHWAY U.S.-2
ALMIRA WA — 237-D7
BONNER CO ID — 106-C3
BONNER CO ID — 107-A3
BONNER CO ID — 244-A2
BOUNDARY CO ID — 107-B1
CHELAN CO WA — 111-C1
CHELAN CO WA — 238-C1
COULEE CITY WA — 113-A2
Country Homes WA — 347-A10
CRESTON WA — 113-C1
DAVENPORT WA — 114-A2
DOUGLAS CO WA — 112-C2
DOUGLAS CO WA — 113-A2
DOUGLAS CO WA — 236-B6
DOUGLAS CO WA — 239-A1
DOVER ID — 107-A3
DOVER ID — 244-A2
Fairchild Air Force Base WA — 114-B2
Fairwood WA — 347-C7
GRANT CO WA — 113-A2
LEAVENWORTH WA — 238-A1
LINCOLN CO MT — 107-C2
LINCOLN CO WA — 113-C1
LINCOLN CO WA — 114-A2
LINCOLN CO WA — 237-D7
MOYIE SPRINGS ID — 107-B1
NEWPORT ID — 106-C3
NEWPORT WA — 106-C3
PEND OREILLE CO WA — 106-C3
SANDPOINT ID — 244-A2
SPOKANE WA — 346-J12
SPOKANE WA — 347-A11
SPOKANE CO WA — 106-C3
SPOKANE CO WA — 114-C1
SPOKANE CO WA — 246-A4
SPOKANE CO WA — 347-F1
SPOKANE CO WA — 348-A11
TROY MT — 107-C2
WATERVILLE WA — 236-C7
WILBUR WA — 113-B1

HIGHWAY U.S.-11
CLEARWATER CO ID — 123-C2
LEWIS CO ID — 123-C2

HIGHWAY U.S.-12
ASOTIN CO WA — 122-C2
ASOTIN CO WA — 250-A4
Burbank WA — 121-A3
Central Park WA — 178-C7
CLEARWATER CO ID — 123-B2
COLUMBIA CO WA — 122-A2
DAYTON WA — 122-A2
ELMA WA — 179-B7
FRANKLIN CO WA — 121-A3
GARFIELD CO WA — 122-A2
Garrett WA — 344-G2
Grand Mound WA — 184-B4
GRAYS HARBOR CO WA — 117-B1
GRAYS HARBOR CO WA — 178-B7
GRAYS HARBOR CO WA — 179-B7
GRAYS HARBOR CO WA — 184-A3
IDAHO CO ID — 123-C2
KAMIAH ID — 123-C2
LEWIS CO ID — 123-C2
LEWIS CO ID — 118-C2
LEWIS CO WA — 119-A1
LEWIS CO WA — 185-D6
LEWIS CO WA — 187-C2
LEWISTON ID — 250-C4
MONTESANO WA — 118-D7
MORTON WA — 118-B2
MOSSYROCK WA — 118-B2
NACHES WA — 119-C1
NEZ PERCE CO ID — 123-B2
NEZ PERCE CO ID — 250-D3
OAKVILLE WA — 117-B1
OROFINO ID — 123-C2
PASCO WA — 121-A3
PASCO WA — 343-H5
POMEROY WA — 122-B2
Rochester WA — 184-A3
THURSTON CO WA — 184-A3
WAITSBURG WA — 122-A2
WALLA WALLA WA — 344-J7
WALLA WALLA WA — 345-J4
WALLA WALLA CO WA — 121-A3
WALLA WALLA CO WA — 345-J3
YAKIMA WA — 243-B6
YAKIMA CO WA — 119-C1
YAKIMA CO WA — 243-A4

HIGHWAY U.S.-20
CALDWELL ID — 147-B1
CANYON CO ID — 139-A3
CANYON CO ID — 147-B1
LINCOLN CO OR — 206-C4
MALHEUR CO OR — 139-A3
TOLEDO OR — 206-C4
VALE OR — 139-A3

HIGHWAY U.S.-26
PORTLAND OR — 317-F1

HIGHWAY U.S.-30
HOOD RIVER OR — 195-D5
HOOD RIVER CO OR — 195-C5
MALHEUR CO OR — 139-A3
NEW PLYMOUTH ID — 139-B3
PAYETTE CO ID — 139-B3

HIGHWAY U.S.-95
ADAMS CO ID — 131-C2
ADAMS CO ID — 251-A1
ATHOL ID — 245-B2
BENEWAH CO ID — 115-A2
BONNER CO ID — 107-B2
BONNER CO ID — 244-A1
BONNERS FERRY ID — 107-B1
BOUNDARY CO ID — 107-B1
CANYON CO ID — 139-A3
CANYON CO ID — 147-A1
COEUR D'ALENE ID — 355-D2
COUNCIL ID — 139-C1
CRAIGMONT ID — 123-B2
CULDESAC ID — 123-B2
FRUITLAND ID — 139-A3
GRANGEVILLE ID — 123-B2
HAYDEN ID — 245-A5
HAYDEN ID — 355-D1
IDAHO CO ID — 123-B3
IDAHO CO ID — 131-C1
IDAHO CO ID — 251-A1
KOOTENAI CO ID — 115-A2
KOOTENAI CO ID — 247-D4
KOOTENAI CO ID — 354-J13
KOOTENAI CO ID — 355-D2
LAPWAI ID — 123-B2
LATAH CO ID — 115-A3
LATAH CO ID — 249-D1
LEWIS CO ID — 250-C1
LEWISTON ID — 250-C4
MALHEUR CO OR — 139-A2
MIDVALE ID — 139-B1
MOSCOW ID — 249-C5
NEZ PERCE CO ID — 123-A2
NEZ PERCE CO ID — 250-C1
OWYHEE CO ID — 147-A1
PAYETTE ID — 139-A3
PAYETTE CO ID — 139-A2
PLUMMER ID — 115-A2
PONDERAY ID — 244-A1
RIGGINS ID — 131-C2
SANDPOINT ID — 244-A2
WASHINGTON CO ID — 139-B1
WEISER ID — 139-A2
WILDER ID — 147-A1
WINCHESTER ID — 123-B2
WORLEY ID — 115-A2

HIGHWAY U.S.-97
BREWSTER WA — 104-B3
CHELAN WA — 236-C3
CHELAN CO WA — 111-C1
CHELAN CO WA — 112-B1
CHELAN CO WA — 236-D2
CHELAN CO WA — 238-B1
CHELAN CO WA — 239-A1
DORRIS CA — 150-B3
DOUGLAS CO WA — 236-D3
ELLENSBURG WA — 241-B5
ENTIAT WA — 236-B6
GOLDENDALE WA — 127-C1
KITTITAS CO WA — 111-C3
KITTITAS CO WA — 238-D1
KITTITAS CO WA — 240-D1
KITTITAS CO WA — 241-B5
KLAMATH CO OR — 150-C3
KLAMATH FALLS OR — 338-C4

HIGHWAY U.S.-97
KLICKITAT CO WA — 119-C3
KLICKITAT CO WA — 127-C1
OKANOGAN CO WA — 104-C3
OKANOGAN CO WA — 104-C1
OKANOGAN CO WA — 112-B1
OMAK WA — 104-C2
OROVILLE WA — 104-C1
PATEROS WA — 104-B3
PATEROS WA — 112-B1
RIVERSIDE WA — 104-C2
SHERMAN CO OR — 127-C1
SISKIYOU CO CA — 150-C3
Sunnyslope WA — 238-D3
TONASKET WA — 104-C2
TOPPENISH WA — 120-A2
WAPATO WA — 120-A2
YAKIMA WA — 243-B6
YAKIMA CO WA — 119-C3
YAKIMA CO WA — 120-A2

HIGHWAY U.S.-101
CLALLAM CO WA — 109-C1
CLALLAM CO WA — 162-D7
CLALLAM CO WA — 163-B6
CLALLAM CO WA — 164-A6
CLALLAM CO WA — 165-A6
CLALLAM CO WA — 166-A7
CLALLAM CO WA — 169-C1
CLALLAM CO WA — 262-A12
COSMOPOLIS WA — 117-A1
FORKS WA — 169-C1
GRAYS HARBOR CO WA — 108-C2
GRAYS HARBOR CO WA — 109-A2
GRAYS HARBOR CO WA — 117-A1
GRAYS HARBOR CO WA — 172-B3
GRAYS HARBOR CO WA — 177-D2
GRAYS HARBOR CO WA — 178-A1
HOQUIAM WA — 178-A6
ILWACO WA — 186-A6
JEFFERSON CO WA — 108-C1
JEFFERSON CO WA — 109-C1
JEFFERSON CO WA — 169-D3
JEFFERSON CO WA — 172-A1
JEFFERSON CO WA — 173-D1
MASON CO WA — 173-C2
MASON CO WA — 180-A1
PACIFIC CO WA — 117-A1
PACIFIC CO WA — 183-C6
PACIFIC CO WA — 186-B1
PACIFIC CO WA — 188-C1
RAYMOND WA — 117-A1
SEQUIM WA — 166-B7
SEQUIM WA — 262-E12
SHELTON WA — 180-A2
SOUTH BEND WA — 117-A1

HIGHWAY U.S.-195
COLFAX WA — 122-C1
COLTON WA — 250-A1
NEZ PERCE CO ID — 250-B3
SPOKANE WA — 348-F11
SPOKANE CO WA — 114-C2
SPOKANE CO WA — 246-C6
UNIONTOWN WA — 250-B1
WHITMAN CO WA — 114-C3
WHITMAN CO WA — 122-C1
WHITMAN CO WA — 249-A4
WHITMAN CO WA — 250-A1

HIGHWAY U.S.-197
DEL NORTE CO CA — 148-B3
KLICKITAT CO WA — 196-C6

HIGHWAY U.S.-395
ADAMS CO WA — 113-C3
ADAMS CO WA — 121-C1
BENTON CO WA — 121-A3
COLVILLE WA — 106-A2
CONNELL WA — 121-B1
DEER PARK WA — 114-B1
Fairwood WA — 347-A6
FERRY CO WA — 105-C1
FERRY CO WA — 106-A1
Finley WA — 121-A3
FRANKLIN CO WA — 121-B1
FRANKLIN CO WA — 343-F1
KENNEWICK WA — 121-A3
KENNEWICK WA — 342-J10
KENNEWICK WA — 343-B10
KETTLE FALLS WA — 106-A2
MESA WA — 121-B2
MODOC CO CA — 152-A3
PASCO WA — 121-A2
PASCO WA — 343-G1
SPOKANE CO WA — 114-B1
SPOKANE CO WA — 346-J1
SPOKANE CO WA — 347-A2
STEVENS CO WA — 106-A2
STEVENS CO WA — 114-B1

HIGHWAY ADRIAN RD
CANYON CO ID — 139-A3

HILDERBRAND LN
SHERMAN CO OR — 127-C1

HILL AV
MOSES LAKE WA — 242-C3

E HILL AV
MOSES LAKE WA — 242-C3

HILL RD
ISLAND CO WA — 167-B5
KLAMATH CO OR — 235-D5
LANE CO OR — 215-C1
LANE CO OR — 331-F1
MODOC CO CA — 151-A3
OWYHEE CO ID — 147-A1
SISKIYOU CO CA — 150-C3
SISKIYOU CO CA — 151-A3
WASHINGTON CO ID — 139-A2
WHITMAN CO WA — 249-C3
YAKIMA CO WA — 243-D7

N HILL RD
YAMHILL CO OR — 198-A6

NW HILL RD
YAMHILL CO OR — 198-A6

SW HILL RD
YAMHILL CO OR — 198-A7

W HILL RD
ADA CO ID — 253-B1
BOISE ID — 253-B1

HILL RD NE
THURSTON CO WA — 181-A5

HILL ST
ALBANY OR — 326-C2
KLICKITAT CO WA — 196-C7

HILL ST Rt#-162
KAMIAH ID — 123-C2

HILLAIRE RD
WHATCOM CO WA — 158-C7

HILLARY GRADE
WASCO CO OR — 202-D2

E HILLCREST DR
KITSAP CO WA — 271-D11

NE HILLCREST DR
GRANTS PASS OR — 335-G6

STREET — City State — Page-Grid

NE HILLCREST DR
JOSEPHINE CO OR ... 335-G6
NW HILLCREST DR
GRANTS PASS OR ... 335-F6
HILLCREST RD
HOOD RIVER CO OR ... 195-C7
JACKSON CO OR ... 234-C1
JACKSON CO OR ... 336-J11
MEDFORD OR ... 234-C1
MEDFORD OR ... 336-G12
HILLCREST LOOP RD
CLATSOP CO OR ... 117-A3
HILLDALE RD E
KITSAP CO WA ... 271-E9
S HILLHURST RD
RIDGEFIELD WA ... 192-C3
HILL LOOP RD
STEVENS CO WA ... 106-A1
HILLOCKBURN RD
CLACKAMAS CO OR ... 200-C7
HILL PASSAGE
PIERCE CO WA ... 181-B1
HILLS AV
LEWIS CO WA ... 187-D3
S HILLS DR
WENATCHEE WA ... 238-D4
West Wenatchee WA ... 238-D4
HILLS RD
ADAMS CO WA ... 113-C3
HILLSBORO HWY Rt#-219
NEWBERG OR ... 198-D5
WASHINGTON CO OR ... 198-D5
YAMHILL CO OR ... 198-D5
SW HILLSBORO HWY Rt#-219
HILLSBORO OR ... 198-D2
WASHINGTON CO OR ... 198-D2
HILLSBORO-SLVERTON HWY Rt#-219
MARION CO OR ... 205-B1
MARION CO OR ... 205-B2
MOUNT ANGEL OR ... 205-C3
SILVERTON OR ... 205-C3
WOODBURN OR ... 205-B2
HLLSBORO-SLVRTN HWY NE Rt#-219
MARION CO OR ... 205-A1
HILLSHAVEN AV
COLUMBIA WA ... 189-C7
HILLSIDE DR
CITY OF VICTORIA BC ... 256-H7
CITY OF VICTORIA BC ... 257-A6
HILLSIDE DR
PIERCE CO WA ... 181-C5
YAMHILL CO OR ... 198-C5
HILLSIDE RD
WASHINGTON CO OR ... 125-B1
HILLTOP
CROOK CO OR ... 213-D6
HILLTOP DR
LANE CO OR ... 215-D4
HILLVIEW RD
GEM CO OR ... 139-B3
LANE CO OR ... 215-C5
HILYARD AV
Altamont OR ... 339-C11
HILYARD ST
EUGENE OR ... 330-B9
HINCH RD
COOS CO OR ... 220-C3
HINCK RD
LINN CO OR ... 207-C6
HINES ST SE
SALEM OR ... 324-J1
SALEM OR ... 325-A1
HINES LOGGING RD
HARNEY CO OR ... 137-A3
HARNEY CO OR ... 145-A1
HINKLE CREEK RD
DOUGLAS CO OR ... 219-D7
NE HINNESS RD
CLARK CO WA ... 193-B4
HINTON RD
WASCO CO OR ... 127-C3
HINTZVILLE RD NW
KITSAP CO WA ... 173-D3
HIPKINS RD SW
LAKEWOOD WA ... 181-C4
HIRTZEL RD
COLUMBIA WA ... 189-B4
HISTORIC COLUMBIA RIVER HWY
TROUTDALE OR ... 200-B1
E HISTORIC COLUMBIA RIVER HWY
MULTNOMAH CO OR ... 200-C1
TROUTDALE OR ... 200-C1
NW HITE CENTER RD
KITSAP CO WA ... 173-D2
H LAWRENCE RD
CLARK CO WA ... 193-A1
HOAG RD
MOUNT VERNON WA ... 260-D9
HOBART RD NE
MARION CO OR ... 205-C4
SILVERTON OR ... 205-C4
NW HOBBS RD
CORNELIUS OR ... 198-C1
WASHINGTON CO OR ... 198-C1
HOBO PASS RD
SHOSHONE CO ID ... 115-C3
HOBSON RD
SKAGIT CO WA ... 161-B5
HOBSON RD SW
THURSTON CO WA ... 184-B4
HOBSONVILLE POINT DR
BAY CITY OR ... 191-B7
TILLAMOOK CO OR ... 191-B7
HODGEN RD
UMATILLA CO OR ... 121-C3
NW HODGEN RD
MILTON-FREEWATER OR ... 121-C3
HOEHN RD
SKAGIT CO WA ... 161-D6
HOERSTER LN
JACKSON CO OR ... 229-D4
HOFF RD
PIERCE CO WA ... 181-A2
HOFFMAN RD
CLACKAMAS CO OR ... 199-C5
INDEPENDENCE OR ... 204-B7
POLK CO OR ... 204-B7
WASHINGTON CO OR ... 125-B1
HOFFMAN RD NE
KITSAP CO WA ... 170-D4
HOFFMAN RD NW
THURSTON CO WA ... 180-C5
HOFFMAN RD SE
OLYMPIA WA ... 297-D8

STREET — City State — Page-Grid

HOFFMAN ST
WOODLAND WA ... 192-C1
SE HOFFMEISTER RD
CLACKAMAS CO OR ... 200-B3
NE HOGAN DR
GRESHAM OR ... 200-B1
HOGAN RD
CLACKAMAS CO OR ... 200-B3
DOUGLAS CO OR ... 219-A6
GRAYS HARBOR CO WA ... 177-C5
SE HOGAN RD
GRESHAM OR ... 200-B2
HOGAN RANCH RD
COLUMBIA CO OR ... 192-B3
HOGBACK RD
LAKE CO OR ... 144-B3
LAKE CO OR ... 152-B1
HOG CREEK RD
WASHINGTON CO OR ... 139-B1
HOGG HILL RD
MULTNOMAH CO OR ... 200-D3
HOG RANCH RD
KITTITAS CO WA ... 240-B6
HOGUM BAY RD NE
LACEY WA ... 181-A6
HOGUM CREEK RD
DOUGLAS CO OR ... 225-D6
HOIER RD
WHATCOM CO WA ... 158-B3
HOKO OZETTE RD
CLALLAM CO WA ... 162-C4
CLALLAM CO WA ... 163-A3
HOLBROOK RD
COLUMBIA CO OR ... 189-C6
S HOLCOMB BLVD
CLACKAMAS CO OR ... 199-D4
CLACKAMAS CO OR ... 200-A4
S HOLCOMB RD
ADA CO ID ... 253-D3
BOISE ID ... 253-D3
HOLCOMB HOMES RD
COWLITZ CO WA ... 303-F3
HOLCOMB SPRING RD
KLAMATH CO OR ... 235-D2
HOLCUM RD
LEWIS CO WA ... 187-C1
HOLDEN RD SW
LAKEWOOD WA ... 181-C4
SW HOLDEN ST
SEATTLE WA ... 284-E2
SEATTLE WA ... 285-F2
HOLDER LN SE
MARION CO OR ... 324-F7
SALEM OR ... 324-F7
HOLDMAN RD
HELIX OR ... 129-B1
UMATILLA CO OR ... 129-B1
SE HOLGATE BLVD
PORTLAND OR ... 317-J3
PORTLAND OR ... 318-B3
PORTLAND OR ... 319-E3
S HOLGATE ST
SEATTLE WA ... 282-A2
HOLIDAY BLVD
SKAGIT CO WA ... 160-C5
HOLIDAY VALLEY DR NW
THURSTON CO WA ... 180-B5
N HOLLADAY DR
SEASIDE OR ... 301-G7
S HOLLADAY DR
SEASIDE OR ... 301-G9
E HOLLAND AV
SPOKANE WA ... 346-J11
SPOKANE WA ... 347-A11
W HOLLAND AV
Country Homes WA ... 346-J11
HOLLAND LP
JOSEPHINE CO OR ... 233-B4
W HOLLILYNN DR
ADA CO ID ... 253-C4
HOLLY LN
EVERETT WA ... 267-J7
EVERETT WA ... 268-B5
SE HOLLY LN
JEFFERSON CO OR ... 208-C7
HOLLY RD
MALHEUR CO OR ... 139-A2
NW HOLLY RD
KITSAP CO WA ... 173-D2
KITSAP CO WA ... 174-A2
HOLLY ST
MAPLE RIDGE BC ... 157-C5
E HOLLY ST
BELLINGHAM WA ... 258-D7
N HOLLY ST
CLACKAMAS CO OR ... 199-C6
MEDFORD OR ... 336-C12
S HOLLY ST
MEDFORD OR ... 336-C12
W HOLLY ST
BELLINGHAM WA ... 258-D6
HOLLY GULCH RD
BENEWAH CO ID ... 248-C6
HOLLY HILL RD
WASHINGTON CO OR ... 198-C3
HOLLYWOOD CRES
CITY OF VICTORIA BC ... 257-A11
HOLLYWOOD DR NE
Hayesville OR ... 323-E9
SALEM OR ... 323-E10
HOLM RD SW
THURSTON CO WA ... 184-A3
HOLMAN RD NW
SEATTLE WA ... 171-A7
SEATTLE WA ... 273-F1
HOLMES RD
DESCHUTES CO OR ... 212-B4
HOLMES POINT DR NE
KING CO WA ... 171-B7
HOLST RD
CLACKAMAS CO OR ... 200-B4
CLACKAMAS CO OR ... 171-A2
HOLTON RD
JACKSON CO OR ... 234-B3
HOLYOKE PL S
SEATTLE WA ... 287-H5
HOLYOKE WY S
SEATTLE WA ... 287-H5
HOME AV
WALLA WALLA WA ... 345-D9
Walla Walla East WA ... 345-D9
HOME ST
WALLA WALLA WA ... 345-D9
Walla Walla East WA ... 345-D9
HOME ACRES RD
SNOHOMISH CO WA ... 265-H4
SNOHOMISH CO WA ... 269-H1

STREET — City State — Page-Grid

HOME ACRES RANCH RD
KLICKITAT CO WA ... 196-D2
HOMEDALE RD
Altamont OR ... 235-D5
Altamont OR ... 339-A14
CANYON CO ID ... 147-B1
KLAMATH CO OR ... 235-D6
KLAMATH CO OR ... 339-A14
KLAMATH FALLS OR ... 339-A14
W HOMER LN
ADA CO ID ... 139-C3
HOMESTEAD RD
MORROW CO OR ... 128-C1
SAN JUAN CO WA ... 160-A3
HOMESTEAD WY
DESCHUTES CO OR ... 212-C4
HOMESTEADER RD
CLACKAMAS CO OR ... 199-B5
WASHINGTON CO OR ... 199-B5
WHATCOM CO WA ... 161-C1
E HONEYMAN RD
COLUMBIA CO OR ... 192-B4
N HONEYMAN RD
COLUMBIA CO OR ... 192-A3
SCAPPOOSE OR ... 192-A3
HONEYMOON BAY RD
Freeland WA ... 170-C1
ISLAND CO WA ... 167-C7
HONEYSUCKLE AV
HAYDEN ID ... 355-A1
KOOTENAI CO ID ... 355-A1
N HONEYSUCKLE DR
COEUR D'ALENE ID ... 355-F6
W HOOD AV
KENNEWICK WA ... 342-H10
HOOD ST NE
SALEM OR ... 322-J11
HOOD CANAL DR NE
KITSAP CO WA ... 170-C3
HOOD RIVER HWY
HOOD RIVER CO OR ... 195-B7
HOOD RIVER CO OR ... 202-C1
HOOD RIVER RD
MOSIER OR ... 196-A5
WASCO CO OR ... 196-A5
HOOGDAL RD
SKAGIT CO WA ... 161-C5
SW HOOK AND EYE LN
YAMHILL CO OR ... 204-B2
HOOKER RD
CLALLAM CO WA ... 166-A7
HOOPER WOOLAM RD
CLARK CO WA ... 193-A1
HOOT N HOLLER LN
DOUGLAS CO OR ... 221-D5
HOOVER CREEK LN
WHEELER CO OR ... 128-A3
HOOVER HILL RD
DOUGLAS CO OR ... 221-A7
HOP CREEK RD
JACKSON CO OR ... 226-B5
HOPE ST
Altamont OR ... 338-J11
Altamont OR ... 339-A12
HOPE PENINSULA RD
BONNER CO ID ... 244-D3
HOPEWELL RD Rt#-9
WHATCOM CO WA ... 102-B1
HOPEWELL RD NW
POLK CO OR ... 204-C3
POLK CO OR ... 204-C3
W HOPKINS ST
PASCO WA ... 343-B7
HOPP RD N
LINCOLN CO WA ... 113-B3
HOPPER AV Rt#-71
CAMBRIDGE WA ... 139-B1
WASHINGTON CO ID ... 139-B1
E HOQUIAM RD
GRAYS HARBOR CO WA ... 178-A6
HOQUIAM WA ... 178-A6
HOQUIAM WISHKAH RD
GRAYS HARBOR CO WA ... 178-B4
HORLICK RD
KITTITAS CO WA ... 240-D3
HORN LN
EUGENE OR ... 329-F2
LANE CO OR ... 329-F2
HORN RD Rt#-225
BENTON CITY WA ... 120-C2
BENTON CO WA ... 120-C2
HORNBROOK RD
SISKIYOU CO CA ... 150-A3
NW HORNECKER RD
WASHINGTON CO OR ... 198-C1
HORNER RD
DESCHUTES CO OR ... 212-D7
N HORNET CREEK RD
ADAMS CO ID ... 131-B3
ADAMS CO ID ... 139-B1
WASHINGTON CO ID ... 131-B3
HORNY HOLLOW TR
JEFFERSON CO OR ... 212-C2
NW HOYT ST
PORTLAND OR ... 313-E5
HOYT ST S
SALEM OR ... 324-G2
HOYT ST SE
SALEM OR ... 324-H2
H STREET RD
BLAINE WA ... 158-C3
WHATCOM CO WA ... 158-D3
HUBBARD RD
ADAMS CO ID ... 251-A4
LEWIS CO WA ... 187-A2
E HUBBARD RD
ADA CO ID ... 253-B4
N HUBBARD ST
COEUR D'ALENE ID ... 355-D11
HUBBARD CREEK RD
DOUGLAS CO OR ... 221-A1
HUBBARD GULCH RD
NEZ PERCE CO ID ... 123-B2
HUBER LN
JEFFERSON CO OR ... 208-B7
HUBER RD
PACIFIC CO WA ... 117-B2
HUCKELBERRY LN
COOS CO OR ... 220-B4
HUCKLEBERRY RD
JACKSON CO OR ... 226-D5
JACKSON CO OR ... 227-A4
HUDDLESTON RD
WHEELER CO OR ... 128-B3
E HUDLOW RD
KOOTENAI CO ID ... 245-A4
HUDSON RD
LANE CO OR ... 133-A2
SKAMANIA CO WA ... 193-D7
SE HUDSON RD
CLACKAMAS CO OR ... 200-C3

STREET — City State — Page-Grid

SE HORTSMAN RD
KITSAP CO WA ... 271-C14
PORT ORCHARD WA ... 271-B14
HOSKINS RD
DIST OF NORTH VANCOUVER ... 255-F1
HOSKINS-SUMMIT RD
BENTON CO OR ... 133-A1
S HOSMER ST
PIERCE CO WA ... 181-D4
TACOMA WA ... 181-D4
TACOMA WA ... 295-E7
HOSPITAL WY
BREWSTER WA ... 104-B3
HOSTETLER RD
ASOTIN CO WA ... 250-B7
HOSTETLER ST W
THE DALLES OR ... 196-C7
WASCO CO OR ... 196-C7
NE HOSTMARK ST
POULSBO WA ... 170-B7
HOTCHKISS LN
HARNEY CO OR ... 145-A1
HOT SPRINGS AV
CARSON WA ... 194-D4
CARSON WA ... 195-A4
HOT SPRINGS RD
ADAMS CO ID ... 251-A3
MALHEUR CO OR ... 154-B2
HOT SPRINGS RD Rt#-9
CITY OF HARRISON HOT SPRG BC ... 94-C3
DISTRICT OF KENT BC ... 94-C3
HOUSER WY S Rt#-900
RENTON WA ... 175-C5
NE HOUSLEY AV
DOUGLAS CO OR ... 334-F2
ROSEBURG OR ... 334-F2
HOUSTON RD
ISLAND CO WA ... 167-C5
JACKSON CO OR ... 234-B2
LEWIS CO ID ... 123-B3
N HOUSTON RD
SPOKANE CO WA ... 348-C6
W HOUSTON RD
SPOKANE CO WA ... 348-B6
HOUSTON LAKE RD
CROOK CO OR ... 213-C5
HOUTCHEN ST
PACIFIC CO WA ... 186-B7
HOVANDER RD
FERNDALE WA ... 158-C6
HOVENDEN RD NE
MARION CO OR ... 205-B1
HOWARD AV
EUGENE OR ... 329-F1
LANE CO OR ... 329-F1
HOWARD LN
LANE CO OR ... 210-A5
HOWARD RD
KITTITAS CO WA ... 241-A4
E HOWARD RD
KOOTENAI CO ID ... 245-B1
SE HOWARD RD
MULTNOMAH CO OR ... 200-D2
HOWARD ST
WALLA WALLA WA ... 345-C9
Walla Walla East WA ... 345-C9
S HOWARD ST
WALLA WALLA WA ... 345-C11
HOWARD CREEK RD
CROOK CO OR ... 136-A2
HOWARD FLAT RD
CHELAN CO WA ... 236-D2
HOWARDS MILL RD
CLACKAMAS CO OR ... 199-D7
CLACKAMAS CO OR ... 200-A7
HOWE
PIERCE CO WA ... 182-B6
HOWE LN
LANE CO OR ... 215-B5
HOWE ST
VANCOUVER BC ... 254-G9
HOWE ST Rt#-99
VANCOUVER BC ... 254-F10
W HOWE ST
SEATTLE WA ... 276-D1
SEATTLE WA ... 277-F2
HOWELL ST
SEATTLE WA ... 278-A5
HOWELL GRADE RD
GARFIELD CO WA ... 122-C2
HOWELL PRAIRIE RD
MARION CO OR ... 205-B4
HOWLETT RD
CLACKAMAS CO OR ... 200-C4
E HOXIE RD
SPOKANE CO WA ... 115-A2
E HOXIE RD Rt#-278
ROCKFORD WA ... 114-C2
SPOKANE CO WA ... 114-C2
HOYT RD SW
FEDERAL WAY WA ... 182-A1
HUDSON ST
CITY OF RICHMOND BC ... 156-B5
LONGVIEW WA ... 303-A9
VANCOUVER BC ... 156-B5
SW HUDSON ST
SEATTLE WA ... 280-C5
HUETTNER RD
HAYDEN ID ... 354-H2
KOOTENAI CO ID ... 354-H2
N HUETTER RD
KOOTENAI CO ID ... 354-H6
NE HUFF RD
CLARK CO WA ... 193-A1
NE HUGHES RD
CLARK CO WA ... 193-C3
HUGHES AV
CHELAN CO WA ... 238-C2
HUGHEY LN
TILLAMOOK CO OR ... 197-C2
HUGO RD
JOSEPHINE CO OR ... 229-A4
HUHTALA RD
LINCOLN CO OR ... 206-C2
HULL RD
JACKSON CO OR ... 234-A2
HULL ST
PORT ORCHARD WA ... 174-B4
PORT ORCHARD WA ... 270-G14
HULSE RD
CLALLAM CO WA ... 165-D6
HULTMAN RD
POLK CO OR ... 207-C1
HUMBOLDT ST
CITY OF VICTORIA BC ... 256-H9
HUME RD
WHITMAN CO WA ... 114-C3
HUMMINGBIRD RD
DOUGLAS CO WA ... 239-B1
HUMORIST RD
Burbank WA ... 121-B3
WALLA WALLA CO WA ... 121-B3
HUMPBACK RD
BRITISH COLUMBIA BC ... 159-A6
DISTRICT OF LANGFORD BC ... 159-A6
HUMPERT LN NE
MARION CO OR ... 205-C3
SW HUMPHREY BLVD
MULTNOMAH CO OR ... 316-B1
PORTLAND OR ... 316-B1
HUMPHREY RD
ISLAND CO WA ... 171-A2
HUMPHREY HILL RD
SKAGIT CO WA ... 161-B4
E HUMPHREYS RD
COOS CO OR ... 220-B4
W HUMPHREYS RD
COOS CO OR ... 220-B4
E HUMPTULIPS RD
GRAYS HARBOR CO WA ... 178-B2
HUMPTULIPS VALLEY RD
GRAYS HARBOR CO WA ... 177-D3
HUNGRY HILL RD
LANE CO OR ... 215-B5
HUNGRY JUNCTION RD
KITTITAS CO WA ... 241-B5
HUNNELL RD
DESCHUTES CO OR ... 217-C1
HUNT LN
JOSEPHINE CO OR ... 229-A6
HUNT RD
CLALLAM CO WA ... 165-A5
DESCHUTES CO OR ... 212-B4
HUNT ST NW
GIG HARBOR WA ... 181-B1
PIERCE CO WA ... 181-B1
HUNT CLUB RD
GRAYS HARBOR CO WA ... 183-B2
HUNTER RD
ISLAND CITY OR ... 130-A2
KITTITAS CO WA ... 241-A5
UNION CO OR ... 130-A2
SW HUNTER RD
KITSAP CO WA ... 174-B6
HUNTER RD SW
THURSTON CO WA ... 184-A3
HUNTER CREEK LP
CURRY CO OR ... 228-A6
HUNTER CREEK RD
CURRY CO OR ... 228-A6
HUNTER POINT RD NW
THURSTON CO WA ... 180-C4
HUNTINGDON RD
DISTRICT OF ABBOTSFORD BC ... 102-B1
DISTRICT OF MATSQUI BC ... 102-B1
HUNTINGTON AV
CASTLE ROCK WA ... 187-C7
CASTLE ROCK WA ... 189-C1
COWLITZ CO WA ... 189-C1
HUNTINGTON AV Rt#-411
CASTLE ROCK WA ... 187-C7
COWLITZ CO WA ... 187-C7
HUNTINGTON HWY U.S.-30
BAKER CO OR ... 138-C2
BAKER CO OR ... 139-A2
HUNTINGTON OR ... 139-A2
MALHEUR CO OR ... 139-A2
HUNTINGTON PL
LONGVIEW WA ... 302-J6
HUNTINGTON RD
MALHEUR CO OR ... 138-C2
W HUNTLEY RD
ABERDEEN WA ... 178-B7
COSMOPOLIS WA ... 178-B7
W HUNTZINGER RD
YAKIMA CO WA ... 243-B4
HURD RD
GRAYS HARBOR CO WA ... 179-B7
SE HURLBURT RD
MULTNOMAH CO OR ... 200-C2
HURLEY-WALDRIP RD
MASON CO WA ... 180-A5
HURRICANE CREEK RD
ENTERPRISE OR ... 130-C2
JOSEPH OR ... 130-C2
WALLOWA CO OR ... 130-C2
HURTLEY RANCH RD
DESCHUTES CO OR ... 212-A5
HUSKEY RD
HOOD RIVER CO OR ... 195-D7
WASCO CO OR ... 196-A6
HUSSEY ST
COLLEGE PLACE WA ... 344-E9
Garrett WA ... 344-E9
WALLA WALLA CO WA ... 344-E9
HUTCHENS HILL RD
GARFIELD CO WA ... 122-B2

STREET — City State — Page-Grid

HUTCHINSON RD
BRITISH COLUMBIA BC ... 159-A1
COLUMBIA CO OR ... 189-B5
HUTSON DR
HOOD RIVER CO OR ... 202-C2
HYACINTH ST NE
SALEM OR ... 323-B7
HYANNIS DR
DIST OF NORTH VANCOUVER ... 255-J4
HYATT RD SE
THURSTON CO WA ... 184-D2
HYATT PRAIRIE RD
JACKSON CO OR ... 150-A2
HYLINE RD
MALHEUR CO OR ... 139-A2
HYLO RD S
MARION CO OR ... 324-F11

I

I AV
ANACORTES WA ... 259-G4
I RD SW
DOUGLAS CO WA ... 239-D1
I ST
COLUMBIA CITY OR ... 192-B1
NEHALEM OR ... 191-B4
N I ST
LIND WA ... 121-B1
TACOMA WA ... 293-F3
S I ST
TACOMA WA ... 293-G4
SW I ST
GRANTS PASS OR ... 335-D9
ICE HARBOR DR
WALLA WALLA CO WA ... 121-B3
ICE HARBOR DR Rt#-124
WALLA WALLA CO WA ... 121-B3
ICICLE RD
CHELAN CO WA ... 238-A1
IDAHO AV U.S.-30
ONTARIO OR ... 139-A3
E IDAHO AV U.S.-95
HOMEDALE OR ... 147-A1
W IDAHO AV
ONTARIO OR ... 139-A3
W IDAHO AV Rt#-19
HOMEDALE OR ... 147-A1
W IDAHO BLVD
GEM CO OR ... 139-B3
N IDAHO RD
KOOTENAI CO ID ... 247-C1
Otis Orchards WA ... 352-G6
SPOKANE CO WA ... 352-G6
S IDAHO RD
SPOKANE CO WA ... 247-B4
IDAHO ST
CASCADE ID ... 252-D6
E IDAHO ST
BOISE ID ... 253-C3
N IDAHO ST
KOOTENAI CO ID ... 353-J3
POST FALLS ID ... 353-J3
S IDAHO ST
KOOTENAI CO ID ... 247-C1
W IDAHO ST
BOISE ID ... 253-C2
W IDAHO ST U.S.-95
WEISER ID ... 139-A2
IDAHO-OREGON-NEVADA HY U.S.-95
HUMBOLDT CO NV ... 154-B3
JORDAN VALLEY OR ... 147-A3
MALHEUR CO OR ... 146-B3
MALHEUR CO OR ... 147-A2
MALHEUR CO OR ... 154-B1
OWYHEE CO ID ... 147-A2
IDAHO POWER RD
BAKER CO OR ... 131-A3
IDLERS REST RD
LATAH CO ID ... 249-D4
IDYLWOOD DR SE
SALEM OR ... 324-F5
IGO RD
GILLIAM CO OR ... 128-C2
IHRIG RD
WASHINGTON CO OR ... 198-B1
S ILER ST
MOXEE WA ... 243-D7
ILLAHEE RD NE
KITSAP CO WA ... 174-C1
KITSAP CO WA ... 271-C6
ILLINOIS AV U.S.-95
COUNCIL ID ... 139-C1
S ILLINOIS AV
PASCO WA ... 343-E8
ILLINOIS RIVER RD
JOSEPHINE CO OR ... 233-A1
ILLINOIS VALLEY RD
DEL NORTE CO CA ... 233-B7
ILLINOIS VALLEY PARK RD
CAVE JUNCTION OR ... 233-B4
JOSEPHINE CO OR ... 233-B4
ILMARI RD
COLUMBIA CO OR ... 189-A3
IMBLER LN
JEFFERSON CO OR ... 208-C7
IMBODEN RD
LEWIS CO WA ... 187-B5
IMHOFF RD
WHATCOM CO WA ... 158-C6
IMMIGRANT RD
LANE CO OR ... 215-D4
S IMMONEN RD
LINCOLN CO OR ... 203-A6
IMPERIAL RD
DISTRICT OF BURNABY BC ... 156-C5
INCHELIUM-KETTLE FALLS RD
FERRY CO WA ... 105-C2
Inchelium WA ... 105-C2
INDEPENDENCE HWY
BENTON CO OR ... 207-B4
INDEPENDENCE HWY Rt#-51
POLK CO OR ... 204-B6
INDEPENDENCE RD
YAKIMA CO WA ... 120-B2
INDEPENDENCE RD SW
LEWIS CO WA ... 117-B1
INDEX-GALENA RD
SNOHOMISH CO WA ... 111-A1
INDIAN RD
Shelter Bay WA ... 167-D1
SKAGIT CO WA ... 160-D7
SKAGIT CO WA ... 167-D1
INDIAN ST
BELLINGHAM WA ... 258-D8
E INDIANA AV
SPOKANE WA ... 349-A7
SPOKANE VALLEY WA ... 350-J6

376 E INDIANA AV — STREET INDEX — NE JUANITA DR

STREET
City State Page-Grid

E INDIANA AV
SPOKANE VALLEY WA 351-A6
S INDIANA AV
CALDWELL ID 147-B1
CANYON CO ID 147-B1
W INDIANA AV
SPOKANE WA 348-J7
SPOKANE WA 349-A7
INDIAN CAMP RD SW
DOUGLAS CO WA 239-B2
INDIAN CEMETERY RD
KOOTENAI CO ID 248-A5
INDIAN CHURCH RD
GRANGER WA 120-A2
YAKIMA CO WA 120-A2
INDIAN CREEK DR
DOUGLAS CO OR 219-A6
INDIAN CREEK RD
DESCHUTES CO OR 216-C7
GRANT CO OR 137-B2
HOOD RIVER CO OR 195-C5
JOSEPHINE CO OR 233-B1
LANE CO OR 209-D7
SISKIYOU CO CA 149-A3
INDIAN FORD RD
DESCHUTES CO OR 211-C4
INDIAN FORT CREEK RD
MALHEUR CO OR 146-C3
INDIAN GULCH RD
MALHEUR CO OR 138-B2
INDIAN HEAD RD
WASHINGTON CO ID 139-A2
INDIAN MOUNTAIN RD
KOOTENAI CO ID 248-B6
INDIANOLA RD NE
Indianola WA 170-C6
INDIAN RIVER DR
DIST OF NORTH VANCOUVER BC 156-D3
INDIAN SCHOOL RD NE
SALEM OR 323-C5
N INDIAN TRAIL RD
SPOKANE WA 346-C12
SPOKANE CO WA 346-A9
W INDIAN TRAIL RD
SPOKANE WA 346-D14
SPOKANE WA 348-E1
INDIAN VALLEY RD
ADAMS CO ID 139-C1
INDUSTRIAL RD
ABERDEEN WA 178-A7
CITY OF SURREY BC 157-A5
HOQUIAM WA 178-A7
INDUSTRIAL WY Rt#-432
COWLITZ CO WA 302-D8
LONGVIEW WA 302-D8
LONGVIEW WA 303-A12
INGALLS LN
JOSEPHINE CO OR 229-A7
INGALLS RD
LEWIS CO WA 117-B1
WAHKIAKUM CO WA 117-B2
INGLE CREEK RD
GRANT CO OR 137-A2
INGLEWOOD AV
DIST OF WEST VANCOUVER BC 254-C3
INGLEWOOD HILL RD
SAMMAMISH WA 175-D2
INGRAM LN NW
YAMHILL CO OR 204-C2
INGRAM ISLAND RD
BENTON CO OR 133-B2
INITIAL PEAK RD
KOOTENAI CO ID 248-D3
INLAND ST U.S.-195
WHITMAN CO WA 114-C3
N INLAND ST
SPOKANE CO WA 246-A2
INLAND EMPIRE HWY
GRANDVIEW WA 120-B3
SUNNYSIDE WA 120-B2
YAKIMA CO WA 120-B2
INLAND EMPIRE HWY U.S.-12
ASOTIN CO WA 250-B4
Garrett WA 344-D7
WALLA WALLA CO WA 344-D7
S INLAND EMPIRE HWY U.S.-195
SPOKANE WA 246-C5
SPOKANE CO WA 246-C5
N INLAND EMPIRE RD
GRANDVIEW WA 120-B3
S INLAND EMPIRE WY
SPOKANE WA 348-G12
INLAND ISLAND HWY Rt#-19
BRITISH COLUMBIA BC 92-A1
NW INLET AV
LINCOLN CITY OR 203-A4
INLET DR Rt#-7A
DISTRICT OF BURNABY BC 156-D4
INNES RD
DESCHUTES CO OR 212-B7
INTERLAAKEN DR SW
LAKEWOOD WA 181-C4
INTERNATIONAL BLVD Rt#-99
DES MOINES WA 290-C5
SEATAC WA 288-D7
SEATAC WA 290-C5
TUKWILA WA 288-D7
INTERNATIONAL WY
LANE CO OR 330-F1
SPRINGFIELD OR 330-F1
INTER-PROVINCIAL HWY
DISTRICT OF ABBOTSFORD BC 94-B3
DISTRICT OF ABBOTSFORD BC 102-B1
DISTRICT OF MATSQUI BC 102-B1
N INTERSTATE AV
PORTLAND OR 308-E4
PORTLAND OR 309-E6
PORTLAND OR 313-E1
INTERURBAN AV S
TUKWILA WA 286-D7
TUKWILA WA 287-E7
TUKWILA WA 289-G2
INTERURBAN RD
DISTRICT OF SAANICH BC 256-D1
INTERVALE RD
YAMHILL CO OR 198-B6
IOCO RD
PORT MOODY BC 157-A4
IOLANDA PL
WHATCOM CO WA 101-C1
IONE RD
FRANKLIN CO WA 121-A2
N IONE ST
KENNEWICK WA 343-C10
IONE-BOARDMAN RD
MORROW CO OR 128-B2
IONE-GOOSEBERRY RD
MORROW CO OR 128-B2

IOWA
CROOK CO OR 213-D6
S IOWA AV
East Wenatchee Bench WA 239-A5
PAYETTE ID 139-A3
PAYETTE CO ID 139-A3
IOWA AV N
PAYETTE ID 139-A3
PAYETTE CO ID 139-A3
IOWA ST
ASHLAND OR 337-D8
BELLINGHAM WA 258-F6
IOWA HEIGHTS RD
WHATCOM CO WA 161-B2
IOWA HILL RD
WASHINGTON CO OR 198-C2
IRBY RD
LINCOLN CO WA 113-B2
IRBY RD N
LINCOLN CO WA 113-B2
IRELAND RD
WALLA WALLA CO WA 121-C3
NE IRELAND RD
CLARK CO WA 193-C6
IRENE ST
WALLA WALLA WA 344-H7
W IRENE ST
BOISE ID 253-C2
SW IRIS LN
CULVER OR 208-B7
JEFFERSON CO OR 208-A7
IRISH RD
TILLAMOOK CO OR 203-C1
IRISH BEND LP
LINN CO OR 210-A3
IRONDALE RD
Hadlock-Irondale WA 170-A1
Irondale WA 263-E14
IRON MOUNTAIN BLVD
LAKE OSWEGO OR 320-C6
LAKE OSWEGO OR 321-E6
IRON MOUNTAIN RD
MALHEUR CO OR 146-A3
IRONWOOD DR
JACKSON CO OR 230-D4
W IRONWOOD DR
COEUR D'ALENE ID 355-C8
IRVING AV
ASTORIA OR 300-F5
W IRVING AV
ASTORIA OR 300-B5
SW IRVING LN
JEFFERSON CO OR 208-B7
IRVING RD
EUGENE OR 215-A1
LANE CO OR 215-A1
Santa Clara OR 215-A1
IRVINGTON DR
Santa Clara OR 215-A1
SE ISAAC AV
PENDLETON OR 129-B1
SW ISAAC AV
PENDLETON OR 129-B1
E ISAACS AV
WALLA WALLA WA 345-C6
WALLA WALLA CO WA 345-H5
ISLAND DR
COLUMBIA CO OR 189-D7
N ISLAND DR
MASON CO WA 180-C2
S ISLAND DR
MASON CO WA 180-C2
ISLAND HWY Rt#-1
BRITISH COLUMBIA BC 101-A1
BRITISH COLUMBIA BC 159-B6
DISTRICT OF LANGFORD BC 159-B6
DISTRICT OF SAANICH BC 256-D4
DUNCAN BC 101-A1
TOWN OF VIEW ROYAL BC 159-B6
TOWN OF VIEW ROYAL BC 256-D4
ISLAND HWY N Rt#-19
BRITISH COLUMBIA BC 93-A3
NANAIMO BC 93-A3
ISLAND HWY N Rt#-19A
BRITISH COLUMBIA BC 93-A3
NANAIMO BC 93-A3
SE ISLAND CREST WY
MERCER ISLAND WA 175-C3
ISLAND SHORE RD
MASON CO WA 180-D3
ISOM RD
LINN CO OR 210-A4
ISRAEL RD SW
TUMWATER WA 296-E13
SE ISSAQUAH FALL CITY RD
KING CO WA 176-A3
ISSAQUAH HOBART RD
ISSAQUAH WA 176-A5
KING CO WA 176-A5
ISSAQUAH PINE LAKE RD SE
KING CO WA 176-A3
SAMMAMISH WA 176-A3
IVANHOE AV
MALHEUR CO OR 139-A3
N IVANHOE ST U.S.-30
PORTLAND OR 192-B7
IVAN MORSE RD
CHELAN CO WA 236-B1
IVERSON RD
DOUGLAS CO OR 221-A2
ISLAND CO WA 168-A4
SNOHOMISH CO WA 110-C1
YAKIMA CO WA 120-A2
NE IVERSON RD
KITSAP CO WA 170-C6
IVORY PINE RD
KLAMATH CO OR 151-B1
IVY AV
GERVAIS OR 205-B2
IVY LN
DESCHUTES CO OR 212-A6
JEFFERSON CO OR 208-D3
NW IVY LN
JEFFERSON CO OR 208-B3
IVY ST Rt#-99
JUNCTION CITY OR 210-A5
N IVY ST
CANBY OR 199-C6
S IVY ST
CANBY OR 199-C6
IZEE-OFFICER RANCH RD
GRANT CO OR 137-A3
IZEE RD TO BUSH RANCH RD
GRANT CO OR 137-A3

J

J ST
COSMOPOLIS WA 178-B7
HUBBARD OR 205-B1
MARION CO OR 205-B1
E J ST
HUBBARD OR 205-C1
S J ST
TACOMA WA 293-G6
TACOMA WA 295-G1
SE J ST
GRANTS PASS OR 335-F9
MADRAS OR 208-C5
SW J ST
GRANTS PASS OR 335-E9
MADRAS OR 208-C5
J ST SE
QUINCY WA 112-B3
J ST SW
QUINCY WA 112-B3
JACKADEL LN
JOSEPHINE CO OR 233-B5
JACK CREEK RD
JEFFERSON CO OR 211-B1
JOSEPHINE CO OR 229-C3
S JACK CREEK RD
JEFFERSON CO OR 211-B1
SW JACK CREEK LOOP RD
JEFFERSON CO OR 211-B1
JACK FALLS RD
COLUMBIA CO OR 189-C5
JACK LAKE RD
JEFFERSON CO OR 211-B1
JACKLIN RD
DISTRICT OF LANGFORD BC 159-B6
JACKMAN RD
WHATCOM CO WA 158-D3
JACK MOUNTAIN RD
HARNEY CO OR 145-B3
JACK MOUNTAIN SPUR
HARNEY CO OR 145-B2
JACKSHA RD
LATAH CO ID 249-C6
JACKSON AV
KITSAP CO WA 174-C4
PIERCE CO WA 181-C5
TACOMA WA 181-C5
S JACKSON AV
TACOMA WA 181-C2
E JACKSON BLVD
MEDFORD OR 336-F11
JACKSON HWY
CHEHALIS WA 299-G14
LEWIS CO WA 184-C7
LEWIS CO WA 187-D1
LEWIS CO WA 299-G14
JACKSON HWY S
LEWIS CO WA 187-C5
JACKSON RD
Birch Bay WA 158-B5
COWLITZ CO WA 189-A2
WASHINGTON CO ID 139-A2
E JACKSON RD
SPOKANE CO WA 247-A5
S JACKSON RD
CLACKAMAS CO OR 205-D1
SPOKANE CO WA 114-C2
SPOKANE CO WA 247-A5
JACKSON ST
ALBANY OR 326-D8
PORT TOWNSEND WA 263-H3
E JACKSON ST
MEDFORD OR 336-E11
N JACKSON ST
GENESEE ID 250-C1
N JACKSON ST U.S.-95
MOSCOW ID 249-C5
NE JACKSON ST
ROSEBURG OR 334-G7
S JACKSON ST
SEATTLE WA 277-J7
SEATTLE WA 278-A7
S JACKSON ST U.S.-95
MOSCOW ID 249-C5
SE JACKSON ST
ROSEBURG OR 334-F8
W JACKSON ST
MEDFORD OR 336-B11
JACKSON CANYON RD
DOUGLAS CO WA 236-D4
JACKSON CREEK RD
DOUGLAS CO OR 141-C3
DOUGLAS CO OR 226-A2
MALHEUR CO OR 154-B2
JACKSON HILL RD
MARION CO OR 207-D1
JACKSON LAKE RD KPN
PIERCE CO WA 181-A1
NE JACKSON SCHOOL RD
HILLSBORO OR 198-D1
NW JACKSON SCHOOL RD
WASHINGTON CO OR 125-C1
JACKSON TRAIL RD
JEFFERSON CO OR 208-A5
JACKSONVILLE HWY
JACKSON CO OR 234-A1
JACKSONVILLE HWY Rt#-238
GRANTS PASS OR 229-B7
GRANTS PASS OR 335-C14
JACKSON CO OR 149-B2
JACKSON CO OR 234-A1
JACKSONVILLE OR 149-B2
JACKSONVILLE OR 234-A1
JOSEPHINE CO OR 149-B2
JOSEPHINE CO OR 229-B7
JOSEPHINE CO OR 335-C14
JACK VAUGHN RD
GRANT CO OR 137-A1
SW JACOBSEN RD
SEATTLE WA 280-C5
JACOBSON BLVD
BREMERTON WA 271-B10
KITSAP CO WA 271-B9
JACOBSON RD
PACIFIC CO WA 183-B4
JACOMBS RD
CITY OF RICHMOND BC 156-C6
JACOT RD
BENEWAH CO ID 248-D7
JADWIN AV
RICHLAND WA 340-F12
RICHLAND WA 341-G1
JAEGER RD
DESCHUTES CO OR 212-B4
JAGER LN
LANE CO OR 210-A5
JAGLA RD
CHELAN CO WA 239-A5
N JAMES AV
East Wenatchee Bench WA 239-A4

JAMES RD
BELLINGHAM WA 258-E3
CLALLAM CO WA 169-A2
WHATCOM CO WA 258-E3
WHITMAN CO WA 249-A1
JAMES RD SW
THURSTON CO WA 184-A4
JAMES ST
BELLINGHAM WA 258-E5
SEATTLE WA 278-A6
E JAMES ST
KENT WA 175-C7
E JAMES ST U.S.-195
COLFAX WA 122-C1
N JAMES ST
MARION CO OR 205-C4
SILVERTON OR 205-C4
S JAMES ST
SILVERTON OR 205-C4
W JAMES ST
KENT WA 175-B7
E JAMES WY
SEATTLE WA 278-B6
JAMES BROOKS RD
COLUMBIA CO OR 192-A2
JAMES HOWE RD
POLK CO OR 204-A5
JAMESON ST
SEDRO-WOOLLEY WA 161-C6
JAMESON LAKE RD
DOUGLAS CO WA 112-C2
JAMESON LAKE EAST ACCESS RD NE
DOUGLAS CO WA 112-C2
JAMES SCHOOLHOUSE LN
BAKER CO OR 138-B1
JAMESTOWN AV
BENTON CO OR 133-B2
E JAMIESON RD
SPOKANE CO WA 246-C5
NE JA MOORE RD
CLARK CO WA 192-D2
JANETA AV
MALHEUR CO OR 139-A3
JANICE AV NE
Hayesville OR 323-F7
JANICKI RD
SKAGIT CO WA 161-C7
JANIS-OROVILLE WESTSIDE RD
OKANOGAN CO WA 104-C1
OROVILLE WA 104-C1
JANSHAW RD
COLUMBIA CO OR 189-B7
JANSKY RD E
PIERCE CO WA 182-C6
JANTZ RD
ADAMS CO WA 121-B1
JAPANESE HOLLOW RD
WASCO CO OR 127-B2
JAQUITH RD
WASHINGTON CO OR 198-D4
YAMHILL CO OR 198-D4
JARE ST SW
Grand Mound WA 184-B4
THURSTON CO WA 184-B4
JARED RD
MASON CO WA 180-D3
JASPER RD
JEFFERSON CO OR 208-C7
JEFFERSON CO OR 213-A1
LANE CO OR 215-D3
LANE CO OR 331-F9
SPRINGFIELD OR 331-C9
JASPER-LOWELL RD
LANE CO OR 133-C3
LANE CO OR 215-D3
LOWELL OR 133-C3
JAYNES DR
JOSEPHINE CO OR 229-B7
J BURTON RD
KOOTENAI CO ID 247-C6
JEFFERS CREEK RD
DOUGLAS CO OR 219-C7
JEFFERSON AV
CORVALLIS OR 327-G10
JEFFERSON AV Rt#-361
JEFFERSON CO OR 208-B6
METOLIUS OR 208-B6
S JEFFERSON AV
TACOMA WA 293-H7
TACOMA WA 295-G1
JEFFERSON DR
MALHEUR CO OR 139-A3
JEFFERSON HWY
JEFFERSON OR 207-D2
LINN CO OR 207-D2
MARION CO OR 207-D2
JEFFERSON HWY Rt#-99E
LINN CO OR 207-D3
JEFFERSON ST
EUGENE OR 329-J7
OLYMPIA WA 296-J6
PORT TOWNSEND WA 263-G5
E JEFFERSON ST
STAYTON OR 133-C1
N JEFFERSON ST
BENTON CO WA 342-E8
NW JEFFERSON ST
ROSEBURG OR 334-C5
SE JEFFERSON ST Rt#-223
DALLAS OR 204-A6
SW JEFFERSON ST
PORTLAND OR 312-D6
JEFFERSON WY
CORVALLIS OR 327-E10
SNOHOMISH CO WA 171-B4
JEFFERSON-MARION RD
JEFFERSON OR 207-D3
MARION CO OR 133-C1
MARION CO OR 207-D3
JEFFERSON-SCIO DR
JEFFERSON OR 207-D3
LINN CO OR 133-C1
MARION CO OR 133-C1
MARION CO OR 207-D3
SCIO OR 133-C1
JEFFRIES RD
LEWIS CO WA 184-A7
J E JOHNSON RD
COWLITZ CO WA 189-D6
JELDNESS RD
PACIFIC CO WA 186-B5
JEMTEGAARD RD
SKAMANIA CO WA 193-D7
JENCK RD
TILLAMOOK CO OR 197-B7
JENKINS CREEK RD
WASHINGTON CO ID 139-A2

JENNINGS RD
WHITMAN CO WA 249-B6
JENNY CREEK RD
CLARK CO WA 192-C1
JENSEN RD
LATAH CO ID 249-D6
SNOHOMISH CO WA 168-B4
W JENSEN RD
SPOKANE CO WA 246-A6
JENTGES RD
IDAHO CO ID 123-C3
JEPPESEN ACRES RD
EUGENE OR 330-B2
JERICHO LN
JEFFERSON CO OR 212-D1
JERNSTEDT RD
YAMHILL CO OR 198-B6
JEROME PRAIRIE RD
JOSEPHINE CO OR 229-A7
JERRYS FLAT RD
CURRY CO OR 228-A5
GOLD BEACH OR 228-A5
JERUSALEM HILL RD NW
YAMHILL CO OR 204-C3
JERVIS ST
VANCOUVER BC 254-F9
JESS RD
WHATCOM CO WA 158-C4
JESSUP RD
IDAHO CO ID 123-C3
NE JESSUP ST
PORTLAND OR 309-G7
JETTY AV
LINCOLN CITY OR 203-A4
JETTY RD
CLATSOP CO OR 188-A1
N JETTY RD Rt#-115
GRAYS HARBOR CO WA 177-B6
JEWELL RD
SNOHOMISH CO WA 171-C5
E JEWETT BLVD Rt#-141
WHITE SALMON WA 195-D4
W JEWETT BLVD Rt#-141
KLICKITAT CO WA 195-D4
WHITE SALMON WA 195-D4
JEWETT RD
ISLAND CO WA 171-A3
JIM ST
PACIFIC CO WA 186-A5
JIM CREEK RD
SNOHOMISH CO WA 102-C3
JIM CREEK SPUR
JACKSON CO OR 226-B5
JIM DAVIS RD
WHITMAN CO WA 114-B3
JIM TOWN LN
LOSTINE OR 130-C1
WALLOWA CO OR 130-C1
JINGLE POT RD
BRITISH COLUMBIA BC 93-A3
NANAIMO BC 93-A3
J LINE RD
GRAYS HARBOR CO WA 117-B1
J M DICKENSON RD SW
KITSAP CO WA 174-A5
JOE JOHNS RD
Ocean Park WA 186-A2
PACIFIC CO WA 186-A2
JOELSON RD
DOUGLAS CO OR 221-A2
JOE MILLER RD
CHELAN CO WA 239-A6
JOE NEY-DAVIS SL RD
COOS CO OR 220-C2
JOE SHERWOOD RD
STEVENS CO WA 114-A1
JOE WRIGHT RD
KLAMATH CO OR 235-C5
SE JOHANNESEN RD
MULTNOMAH CO OR 200-D2
JOHN RD
DISTRICT OF NORTH SAANICH BC 159-C2
LEWIS CO WA 187-D2
E JOHN ST
SEATTLE WA 278-B4
JOHN DAY DR
JACKSON CO OR 230-B5
JOHN DAY HWY Rt#-19
ARLINGTON OR 128-A2
CONDON OR 128-A2
FOSSIL OR 128-A3
GILLIAM CO OR 128-A2
GRANT CO OR 136-B1
SPRAY OR 136-B1
WHEELER CO OR 128-A3
WHEELER CO OR 136-B1
JOHN DAY HWY U.S.-26
BAKER CO OR 137-C2
BAKER CO OR 138-A2
DAYVILLE OR 136-C1
GRANT CO OR 136-C1
GRANT CO OR 137-C2
JOHN DAY OR 137-C2
MALHEUR CO OR 138-B2
MALHEUR CO OR 139-A3
MOUNT VERNON OR 137-C2
UNITY OR 138-A2
VALE OR 139-A3
JOHN DAY HWY U.S.-395
GRANT CO OR 137-A2
JOHN DAY OR 137-A2
MOUNT VERNON OR 137-A2
JOHN DAY-BURNS HWY U.S.-395
CANYON CITY OR 137-B2
GRANT CO OR 137-B2
HARNEY CO OR 137-B3
HARNEY CO OR 145-B1
JOHN DAY OR 137-B2
SENECA OR 137-B3
JOHN DAY RD TO COUNTY LINE RD
GRANT CO OR 137-A3
JOHN HENLEY RD
WHITMAN CO WA 122-A1
JOHN JUMP RD
SNOHOMISH CO WA 171-D3
JOHN LONG RD NW
DOUGLAS CO WA 236-C5
JOHN MEEKER
TACOMA WA 182-A2
JOHNS RD
PIERCE CO WA 182-D5
JOHNS MILL RD
WASCO CO OR 202-D2
JOHNSON AV
MAPLE RIDGE BC 157-D5
JOHNSON BLVD
OLYMPIA WA 296-D9
TUMWATER WA 296-D9
JOHNSON RD
ASOTIN CO WA 122-C3
ASOTIN CO WA 250-A4
BENTON CO WA 120-B3
DESCHUTES CO OR 217-B2
KLAMATH CO OR 151-A2
KLICKITAT CO WA 196-A4
LEWIS CO WA 187-C2
WHITMAN CO WA 249-B7
NW JOHNSON RD
MULTNOMAH CO OR 192-A6
SE JOHNSON RD
CLACKAMAS CO OR 199-D3
SW JOHNSON RD
CLACKAMAS CO OR 199-C4
W JOHNSON RD
SKAGIT CO WA 168-B1
JOHNSON RD SW
OLYMPIA WA 296-D7
TUMWATER WA 296-D7
JOHNSON ST
BENTON CO OR 133-B2
CITY OF VICTORIA BC 256-J9
CITY OF VICTORIA BC 257-A9
COQUITLAM BC 157-A4
N JOHNSON ST
KENNEWICK WA 342-J9
NE JOHNSON ST
DOUGLAS CO OR 334-F3
MCMINNVILLE OR 198-A7
SW JOHNSON ST
STANFIELD OR 129-A1
UMATILLA CO OR 129-A1
JOHNSON-COLTON RD
WHITMAN CO WA 249-B7
WHITMAN CO WA 250-A1
SE JOHNSON CREEK BLVD
CLACKAMAS CO OR 199-D3
CLACKAMAS CO OR 318-B7
MILWAUKIE OR 318-B7
PORTLAND OR 318-B7
PORTLAND OR 318-B7
JOHNSON GRADE RD
MORROW CO OR 128-B2
STEVENS CO WA 106-A1
JOHNSON MARKET RD
DESCHUTES CO OR 135-B3
JOHNSON POINT RD NE
THURSTON CO WA 180-D5
JOHNSON SCHOOL RD
WASHINGTON CO OR 198-C2
JOHNS PRAIRIE RD
MASON CO WA 180-B2
JOHNS RIVER RD
GRAYS HARBOR CO WA 183-C2
JOHNSTON RD
CITY OF SURREY BC 158-A2
CITY OF WHITE ROCK BC 158-A2
JOHNSTONE RD
OWYHEE CO ID 147-A1
JOHN WAYNE TR
ADAMS CO WA 114-A3
ADAMS CO WA 121-C1
JOHN WIDMAN RD
BAKER CO OR 138-C1
JOLLIFF RD
STEVENS CO WA 106-B2
JONATHAN RD
WASHINGTON CO ID 139-A2
JONATHAN ST
TONASKET WA 104-C2
JONES AV
CITY OF NORTH VANCOUVER BC 255-A4
JONES RD
COLUMBIA CO OR 189-C6
ISLAND CO WA 167-C1
JACKSON CO OR 230-C4
KING CO WA 175-D5
LEWIS CO WA 184-D6
LEWIS CO WA 187-A3
WHITMAN CO WA 114-B3
NE JONES RD
BEND OR 332-G5
JONES RD NW
DOUGLAS CO WA 236-C6
JONES RD SW
THURSTON CO WA 184-C1
JONES ACRES RD
LANE CO OR 210-D7
JORDAN RD
DESCHUTES CO OR 212-A5
GRANITE FALLS WA 102-C3
LEWIS CO WA 187-C2
SNOHOMISH CO WA 102-C3
SNOHOMISH CO WA 168-D5
SW JORDAN RD
JEFFERSON CO OR 135-A1
JEFFERSON CO OR 208-A7
JORDAN ST SW
Rochester WA 184-A3
THURSTON CO WA 184-A4
JORDAN CRATERS RD
MALHEUR CO OR 147-A2
JORDAN CREEK RD
WASCO CO OR 202-D5
JORDAN MEADOW RD
HUMBOLDT CO NV 154-B3
JOSELYN SW
THURSTON CO WA 184-B4
JOSEPH AV U.S.-95
WINCHESTER ID 123-B2
JOSEPH ST SE
MARION CO OR 205-A7
MARION CO OR 325-J7
JOSEPH CREEK RD
ASOTIN CO WA 123-A3
NE JOSEPHINE ST
GRANTS PASS OR 335-F8
JOSEPH-WALLOWA LAKE HWY Rt#-82
WALLOWA CO OR 130-C2
JOSH WILSON RD
SKAGIT CO WA 160-D6
SKAGIT CO WA 161-A6
SKAGIT CO WA 260-A3
JOVITA BLVD E
EDGEWOOD WA 182-B2
PACIFIC WA 182-B2
PIERCE CO WA 182-B2
JOYCE ST
VANCOUVER BC 156-C5
SW JP WEST RD
COLUMBIA CO OR 192-A3
NE JUANITA DR
KING CO WA 171-C7
KIRKLAND WA 171-C7

STREET / City State / Page-Grid

JUANITA DR NE
KENMORE WA — 171-B6
KING CO WA — 171-B7
JUANITA-WOODINVILLE WY NE
KING CO WA — 171-C7
JUBB RD
CLACKAMAS CO OR — 200-B6
JUDD RD
CLACKAMAS CO OR — 200-B4
E JUDKINS RD
SPOKANE CO WA — 247-A4
E JUMPOFF RD
STEVENS CO WA — 106-B3
JUMP-OFF JOE RD
JOSEPHINE CO OR — 229-C3
JUMP-OFF JOE CREEK RD
JOSEPHINE CO OR — 229-B3
JUMPOFF RIDGE RD
KITTITAS CO WA — 241-D1
JUNCTION AV
EVERETT WA — 265-E7
JUNCTION RD
DOUGLAS CO OR — 225-B6
JUNGQUIST RD
SKAGIT CO WA — 161-A7
NE JUNIPER LN
JEFFERSON CO OR — 208-C2
NW JUNIPER LN
JEFFERSON CO OR — 208-B2
JUNIPER RD
MORROW CO OR — 128-C1
JUNIPER BEACH RD
ISLAND CO WA — 168-A4
JUNIPER CANYON RD
CROOK CO OR — 135-C3
CROOK CO OR — 213-D6
N JUNIPER CANYON RD
UMATILLA CO OR — 121-B3
S JUNIPER CANYON RD
UMATILLA CO OR — 129-B1
JUNIPER MOUNTAIN RD
OWYHEE CO ID — 155-A1
JUNTURA CUTOFF RD
HARNEY CO OR — 138-A3
JUNTURA-RIVERSIDE RD
MALHEUR CO OR — 146-A1
JUSTICE RANCH WEST RD
GRANT CO OR — 137-A1

K

K AV
LA GRANDE OR — 130-A2
K ST
BREMERTON WA — 270-D12
Navy Yard City WA — 270-D12
SW K ST
GRANTS PASS OR — 335-D9
K 4-10-NE
GRANT CO WA — 242-C1
KACHESS LAKE RD
KITTITAS CO WA — 111-A3
NW KACHINA AV
DESCHUTES CO OR — 212-C5
KACKMAN RD
SNOHOMISH CO WA — 168-C4
WHITMAN CO WA — 114-B3
WHITMAN CO WA — 122-B1
KAGY ST SE
THURSTON CO WA — 181-A7
KAHLER BASIN RD
WHEELER CO OR — 128-B3
WHEELER CO OR — 136-B1
KAHOUT RD
LEWIS CO WA — 187-A2
KAHUT LN NE
MARION CO OR — 205-B2
NW KAISER RD
MULTNOMAH CO OR — 192-A7
WASHINGTON CO OR — 192-A7
KAISER RD NW
OLYMPIA WA — 296-C1
THURSTON CO WA — 180-C5
THURSTON CO WA — 296-C1
KAISER RD SW
THURSTON CO WA — 296-C6
KAKELA RD
LEWIS CO WA — 187-C3
KALAMA RIVER RD
COWLITZ CO WA — 118-A3
COWLITZ CO WA — 189-D5
KALE ST Rt#-544
EVERSON WA — 102-B1
KALE ST NE
Hayesville OR — 323-E5
MARION CO OR — 323-E5
SALEM OR — 323-E5
KAMB RD
SKAGIT CO WA — 168-A1
NE KAMIAKEN ST
PULLMAN WA — 249-B5
NE KAMIAKEN ST Rt#-270
PULLMAN WA — 249-B5
KAMILCHE POINT RD
MASON CO WA — 180-B4
KAMMEYER RD
COLUMBIA CO OR — 192-A4
KAMPH RD
LINN CO OR — 207-D4
S KAMRATH RD
CLACKAMAS CO OR — 200-A6
KANAKA WY
MAPLE RIDGE BC — 157-D6
KANAKA CREEK RD
MAPLE RIDGE BC — 157-D6
SKAMANIA CO WA — 194-D5
KANASKAT KANGLEY RD SE
KING CO WA — 110-C3
KING CO WA — 176-B7
SE KANE DR
GRESHAM OR — 200-B2
SE KANE ST
ROSEBURG OR — 334-G8
KANE CREEK RD
JACKSON CO OR — 230-B7
KANGAROO RD
DISTRICT OF METCHOSIN BC — 159-A7
KANGAS RD
LEWIS CO WA — 187-D4
KANNIWAI CREEK RD
GRANT CO WA — 113-A2
KANSAS CITY RD
COLUMBIA CO OR — 125-B1
KANTOLA LN
VALLEY CO ID — 252-D3
KAPKA BUTTE RD
DESCHUTES CO OR — 216-D5
KAPOWSIN HWY
PIERCE CO WA — 118-B1

KAPOWSIN HWY
PIERCE CO WA — 182-C7
KAPOWSIN-EATONVILLE-LA GRANDE
EATONVILLE WA — 118-B1
PIERCE CO WA — 118-B1
W KAPPLER RD
COLUMBIA CO OR — 192-C1
KARCHER RD Rt#-55
CANYON CO ID — 147-B1
NAMPA ID — 147-B1
KARIN DR
YAKIMA CO WA — 243-C6
KARNOWSKY CREEK RD
LANE CO OR — 214-C2
KARTH RD
COLUMBIA CO OR — 189-A7
N KATH RD
SPOKANE CO WA — 247-A4
W KATHLEEN AV
COEUR D'ALENE ID — 355-C6
KOOTENAI CO ID — 355-C6
KATON RD
GRAYS HARBOR CO WA — 178-D7
KATTENBACK VOLLMER RD
NEZ PERCE CO ID — 250-C5
KAUFFMAN RD
CLACKAMAS CO OR — 205-D2
KAUFMAN RD NE
MARION CO OR — 205-B5
KAYAK POINT RD
SNOHOMISH CO WA — 168-B6
KEAN ST
BREMERTON WA — 270-D11
KEANE RD SW
DOUGLAS CO WA — 239-C5
KEASEY RD
COLUMBIA CO OR — 125-B1
NW KEASEY ST
ROSEBURG OR — 334-C5
KEASLING RD
LEWIS CO WA — 187-D2
KEATING RD NW
THURSTON CO WA — 180-B5
KEATING CROSS RD
DISTRICT OF CENTRAL SAANI BC — 159-C4
KEATING CUTOFF RD
BAKER CO OR — 130-B3
BAKER CO OR — 138-B1
KEATING GRANGE HALL RD
BAKER CO OR — 130-C3
KEEFER RD
CLACKAMAS CO OR — 142-C1
KEENE RD
BENTON CO WA — 341-A4
RICHLAND WA — 341-C5
KEENE RD NE
MARION CO OR — 205-A2
SW KEENEY LN
JEFFERSON CO OR — 212-C2
KEENEY FORKS RD
GRANT CO OR — 137-B1
LONG CREEK OR — 137-B1
E KEEVEY RD
SPOKANE CO WA — 114-C2
KEIL RD NE
MARION CO OR — 199-B7
KEITH RD
CITY OF NORTH VANCOUVER BC — 255-B5
DIST OF NORTH VANCOUVER BC — 254-G4
DIST OF NORTH VANCOUVER BC — 255-D6
DIST OF WEST VANCOUVER BC — 254-D4
W KEITH RD
CITY OF NORTH VANCOUVER BC — 254-J5
CITY OF NORTH VANCOUVER BC — 255-A5
KEITHLY CREEK RD
WASHINGTON CO ID — 139-B1
KEITH WILSON RD
CITY OF CHILLIWACK BC — 102-C1
KEIZER RD NE
KEIZER OR — 323-B5
KELLEHER RD
SKAGIT CO WA — 161-B5
KELLER RD
Altamont OR — 339-C13
N KELLOGG ST
KENNEWICK WA — 342-E10
S KELLOGG ST
KENNEWICK WA — 342-E11
SW KELLY AV
PORTLAND OR — 317-F1
KELLY RD
CHELAN CO WA — 238-C3
CITY OF COLWOOD BC — 159-B6
DISTRICT OF LANGFORD BC — 159-B6
GRAYS HARBOR CO WA — 179-A1
LINN CO OR — 133-C1
NE KELLY RD
CLARK CO WA — 193-A1
KELLY CREEK RD
LANE CO OR — 215-A7
KELLY CUTOFF RD
WASCO CO OR — 127-C1
KELLY HALL RD
MASON CO WA — 179-B1
KELSAY MOUNTAIN RD
DOUGLAS CO OR — 223-C2
KELSAY POINT RD
DOUGLAS CO OR — 223-C2
N KELSO AV
COWLITZ CO WA — 303-E5
KELSO WA — 303-E5
S KELSO DR
KELSO WA — 303-F13
SE KELSO RD
CLACKAMAS CO OR — 200-C3
KEMP RD
CLACKAMAS CO OR — 200-C6
KEMP LAKE RD
BRITISH COLUMBIA BC — 101-A2
BRITISH COLUMBIA BC — 164-C1
KENDALL RD
WALLA WALLA CO WA — 345-D13
Walla Walla East WA — 345-D13
KENDALL RD Rt#-547
WHATCOM CO WA — 102-B1
KENNEDY LN
LANE CO OR — 219-C1
KENNEDY RD
BENTON CO WA — 120-C3
BENTON CO WA — 121-A3
BENTON CO WA — 341-A4
RICHLAND WA — 341-A4
WEST RICHLAND WA — 121-A3
WEST RICHLAND WA — 341-A4
KENNEDY RD Rt#-224
BENTON CO WA — 120-C3
KENNEL RD
LINN CO OR — 207-D5

W KENNEWICK AV
KENNEWICK WA — 342-H10
KENNEWICK WA — 343-B10
E KENNEY RD
LIBERTY LAKE WA — 352-A13
N KENNEY RD
LIBERTY LAKE WA — 352-A14
KENO WORDEN RD
KLAMATH CO OR — 235-A6
KENSINGTON AV
ASTORIA OR — 300-C5
DISTRICT OF BURNABY BC — 156-D4
W KENSINGTON AV
ASTORIA OR — 300-B5
KENT AV W
KITSAP CO WA — 270-D14
Navy Yard City WA — 270-D14
SW KENT LN
JEFFERSON CO OR — 212-C1
KENT RD
DESCHUTES CO OR — 212-A6
KENT BLACK DIAMOND RD
KING CO WA — 175-C7
KING CO WA — 182-D1
KENT CREEK RD
DOUGLAS CO OR — 221-A7
KENT-DES MOINES RD Rt#-516
DES MOINES WA — 290-A7
KENT WA — 175-B7
KENT WA — 290-A7
KENT-DES MOINES RD S Rt#-516
KENT WA — 175-B7
KENT WA — 290-E7
KING CO WA — 290-E7
KING CO WA — 290-E7
KENT-GRASS VALLEY RD
SHERMAN CO OR — 127-C2
KENT KANGLEY RD
KENT WA — 176-A7
KING CO WA — 176-A7
MAPLE VALLEY WA — 176-A7
KENT KANGLEY RD Rt#-516
COVINGTON WA — 175-C7
KENT WA — 175-C7
KING CO WA — 175-C7
KING CO WA — 176-A7
MAPLE VALLEY WA — 175-C7
MAPLE VALLEY WA — 176-A7
KENTUCK WY
COOS CO OR — 218-C7
N KENTUCKY AV
East Wenatchee Bench WA — 239-A4
KENWORTHY RD
LINN CO OR — 326-H4
S KENYON ST
SEATTLE WA — 285-J2
SEATTLE WA — 286-A2
KERBY CREEK RD
JACKSON CO OR — 227-A7
KERBY MAINLINE RD
JOSEPHINE CO OR — 233-B3
KERN RD SW
DOUGLAS CO OR — 239-B2
KERN SWAMP RD
KLAMATH CO OR — 235-B6
KERR PKWY
LAKE OSWEGO OR — 320-A4
LAKE OSWEGO OR — 320-A4
PORTLAND OR — 320-A4
KERR RD
KITTITAS CO WA — 241-B5
KERR ST
VANCOUVER BC — 156-C5
KERRON AV
LEWIS CO WA — 187-C3
WINLOCK WA — 187-C3
KERRON AV Rt#-505
WINLOCK WA — 187-C3
W KERRON AV
LEWIS CO WA — 187-C2
NAPAVINE WA — 187-C2
KERRY RD
COLUMBIA CO OR — 117-B3
KERSEY WY
AUBURN WA — 182-C2
KERSHAW RD
JACKSON CO OR — 230-D6
KESSLER BLVD
LONGVIEW WA — 302-J8
LONGVIEW WA — 303-A10
W KETTLE RIVER RD
FERRY CO WA — 105-B1
KEY RD
UMATILLA CO OR — 129-C1
WESTON OR — 129-C1
KEYES RD
GRAYS HARBOR CO WA — 179-A1
KEY PENINSULA HWY
PIERCE CO WA — 174-A7
PIERCE CO WA — 181-A2
KEY PENINSULA HWY Rt#-302
PIERCE CO WA — 174-B6
KEYS RD
YAKIMA CO WA — 243-B6
KEYSTONE AV
DISTRICT OF MISSION BC — 94-B3
ISLAND CO WA — 167-C5
KEYSTONE RD
OKANOGAN CO WA — 104-C2
KEYSTONE HILL RD
ISLAND CO WA — 167-C5
KEYSTONE RANCH RD
CROOK CO OR — 135-C2
KIACUT RD
YAMHILL CO OR — 198-B3
KICKERVILLE RD
Birch Bay WA — 158-B4
WHATCOM CO WA — 158-B4
KIDD ISLAND RD
KOOTENAI CO ID — 247-D4
KOOTENAI CO ID — 248-A1
S KIESLING RD
SPOKANE CO WA — 246-C3
KIGER RD
MALHEUR CO OR — 146-B3
KIGER ISLAND DR
BENTON CO OR — 207-A7
KILCHIS FOREST RD
TILLAMOOK CO OR — 197-C1
KILCHIS RIVER RD
TILLAMOOK CO OR — 191-C7
TILLAMOOK CO OR — 197-C1
KILLDEER RD
CLACKAMAS CO OR — 200-A6
KILLEBREW DR
PAYETTE CO ID — 139-A3

N KILLINGSWORTH ST
PORTLAND OR — 308-E7
PORTLAND OR — 309-F7
NE KILLINGSWORTH ST
PORTLAND OR — 309-H7
PORTLAND OR — 310-C7
PORTLAND OR — 311-E7
NE KILLINGSWORTH ST U.S.-30
PORTLAND OR — 311-F7
KILLMORE RD
KITTITAS CO WA — 241-A5
KILMER RD
CLALLAM CO WA — 169-B2
KIMBALL DR
GIG HARBOR WA — 181-C1
KIMBALL RD
LANE CO OR — 215-D5
KIMBERLY-LONG CREEK HWY
GRANT CO OR — 136-C1
GRANT CO OR — 137-A1
LONG CREEK OR — 137-A1
MONUMENT OR — 136-C1
KIMBLE RD
MOUNT VERNON OR — 260-A14
SKAGIT CO WA — 260-A14
KINCAID RD
JOSEPHINE CO OR — 149-A2
YAMHILL CO OR — 198-D5
KINCAID ST Rt#-536
MOUNT VERNON OR — 260-C13
KINDER DR
GRANT CO WA — 242-C2
KINER RD
LINCOLN CO WA — 113-B2
LINCOLN CO WA — 237-D7
KING LN
JEFFERSON CO OR — 212-D1
SW KING LN
JEFFERSON CO OR — 212-C1
JEFFERSON CO OR — 213-A1
KING RD
CITY OF SURREY BC — 157-A5
CROOK CO OR — 213-C4
DISTRICT OF MATSQUI BC — 102-B1
LEWIS CO WA — 187-B2
E KING RD
ADA CO ID — 253-B5
SE KING RD
CLACKAMAS CO OR — 199-D3
HAPPY VALLEY OR — 200-A3
KITSAP CO WA — 174-C4
MILWAUKIE OR — 199-D3
W KING RD
ADA CO ID — 147-C1
ADA CO ID — 253-A5
CANYON CO ID — 147-C1
KING ST
COTTONWOOD ID — 123-C3
IDAHO CO ID — 123-C3
YACHATS OR — 209-A3
N KING ST
GOLDENDALE WA — 127-C1
NE KING WY
DESCHUTES CO OR — 212-D5
REDMOND OR — 212-D5
KING EDWARD AV E
VANCOUVER BC — 156-B5
KING EDWARD AV W
VANCOUVER BC — 156-B5
VANCOUVER BC — 254-A14
KINGFISHER DR
BRITISH COLUMBIA BC — 104-C1
OSOYOOS BC — 104-C1
KING GEORGE HWY Rt#-99A
CITY OF SURREY BC — 156-D5
CITY OF SURREY BC — 157-A7
CITY OF SURREY BC — 158-A1
KING GEORGE TR
DISTRICT OF OAK BAY BC — 257-C11
KING GRADE RD
COLUMBIA CO WA — 122-B2
KING MOUNTAIN RD
JOSEPHINE CO OR — 229-C2
KINGS BLVD
CORVALLIS OR — 327-F8
KINGS HWY
JACKSON CO OR — 234-A2
MEDFORD OR — 336-C14
KINGSBURY RD
CHELAN CO WA — 239-A6
KINGS CORNER RD
YAMHILL CO OR — 129-B1
KINGS GRADE
YAMHILL CO OR — 198-C5
KINGSLEY RD
HOOD RIVER CO OR — 195-B6
PACIFIC CO WA — 183-D7
KINGSLEY-FRIEND MARKET RD
WASCO CO OR — 127-B2
KINGS RIVER RD Rt#-293
HUMBOLDT CO NV — 154-A3
KINGS RIVER VALLEY RD
HUMBOLDT CO NV — 154-A3
S KINGSTON RD NE
Indianola WA — 170-D6
KITSAP CO WA — 170-D6
W KINGSTON RD NE
KITSAP CO WA — 170-C5
KINGSTON ST
CITY OF VICTORIA BC — 256-F9
KINGSTON-JORDAN DR
LINN CO OR — 133-C1
KINGSTON-JORDAN RD
LINN CO OR — 133-C1
LINN CO OR — 134-A1
KINGS VALLEY HWY Rt#-223
BENTON CO OR — 133-A1
DALLAS OR — 204-A5
POLK CO OR — 125-B3
POLK CO OR — 204-A5
POLK CO OR — 204-A5
KINGSWAY
VANCOUVER BC — 254-J13
KINGSWAY Rt#-1A
VANCOUVER BC — 156-C5
VANCOUVER BC — 255-A14
KINGSWAY Rt#-99A
DISTRICT OF BURNABY BC — 156-C5
NEW WESTMINSTER BC — 156-C5
KINGSWAY AV
PORT COQUITLAM BC — 157-B4
KING-THOMPSON RD
SNOHOMISH CO WA — 168-C5
KING TULL RD
KLICKITAT CO WA — 120-B3
E KING TULL RD
BENTON CO WA — 120-B3

W KING TUT RD
WHATCOM CO WA — 158-D5
KINGWOOD AV
MILL CITY OR — 134-A1
KINGWOOD DR NW
SALEM OR — 322-E12
KINNEY RD
YAMHILL CO OR — 198-C5
KINNS LN NE
MARION CO OR — 205-A1
KINSMAN RD
PIERCE CO WA — 181-D7
KINZEL CREEK RD
CLACKAMAS CO OR — 201-D7
CLACKAMAS CO OR — 202-A7
KINZER RD
NEZ PERCE CO ID — 250-B2
KINZUA LN
WHEELER CO OR — 128-A3
KINZUA RD
MORROW CO OR — 128-C3
WHEELER CO OR — 128-B3
KINZY RD
CLACKAMAS CO OR — 200-C7
KIPLING RD
OKANOGAN CO WA — 105-A1
KIRBY MAYVIEW RD
GARFIELD CO WA — 122-C2
KIRK AV
BROWNSVILLE OR — 210-C2
LINN CO OR — 210-C2
KIRK DR
LINN CO OR — 210-D2
KIRK RD
BENTON CO WA — 121-A3
KIRKENDAHL RD
WHITMAN CO WA — 249-A6
KIRKHAM RD
JOSEPHINE CO OR — 233-B5
KIRKLAND RD
LEWIS CO WA — 187-C1
KIRKSTONE RD
DIST OF NORTH VANCOUVER BC — 255-D3
KIRKWOOD RD NW
YAMHILL CO OR — 204-C3
KIRSOP RD SW
THURSTON CO WA — 296-C13
KIRTLAND RD
JACKSON CO OR — 230-C6
KISSLER RD
CROOK CO OR — 213-B6
KITER CREEK RD
JACKSON CO OR — 226-B6
KITER CREEK SPUR
JACKSON CO OR — 226-C6
KITSAP CT NW
Silverdale WA — 174-B1
KITSAP WY
BREMERTON WA — 270-B9
KITSAP WY Rt#-310
BREMERTON WA — 270-D10
W KITSAP LAKE RD NW
BREMERTON WA — 270-A9
Erlands Point-Kitsap Lake WA — 270-A10
KITSILANO DIV
VANCOUVER BC — 254-B12
KITSON SPRINGS RD
LANE CO OR — 142-A1
KITTITAS HWY
ELLENSBURG WA — 241-B6
KITTITAS CO WA — 241-C6
KITTITAS CO WA — 241-B6
KITTSON PKWY
CITY OF SURREY BC — 156-D7
DISTRICT OF DELTA BC — 156-D7
KITZMILLER RD
CLACKAMAS CO OR — 200-C5
WHITMAN CO WA — 249-B4
KIWA SPRING RD
DESCHUTES CO OR — 217-A5
KIZER AV
LINN CO OR — 326-H4
SE KLAHANIE BLVD
KING CO WA — 176-A3
KLAHOWYA LN
DOUGLAS CO OR — 221-B3
NW KLAHOWYA TR
KITSAP CO WA — 174-A2
KLAK BUTTE RD
DESCHUTES CO OR — 216-C2
KLAMATH AV Rt#-39
KLAMATH FALLS OR — 338-D8
S KLAMATH FALLS HWY Rt#-140
Altamont OR — 235-D5
KLAMATH CO OR — 235-C5
KLAMATH CO OR — 338-D12
KLAMATH CO OR — 235-C5
KLAMATH FALLS OR — 338-C12
KLAMATH FLLS-LKEVW HWY Rt#-39
Altamont OR — 338-F9
Altamont OR — 339-C11
KLAMATH CO OR — 339-E12
KLAMATH FALLS OR — 338-F9
LAKE CO OR — 151-C2
LAKE CO OR — 152-A2
KLAMATH FALLS-MALIN HWY Rt#-39
Altamont OR — 338-C4
KLAMATH CO OR — 338-C4
KLAMATH CO OR — 338-C4
MALIN OR — 151-A3
KLAMATH FALLS-MALIN HWY Rt#-39
Altamont OR — 338-C4
KLAMATH FALLS OR — 338-C4
MERRILL OR — 150-C2
KLAMATH FALLS-MALIN HY Rt#-140
Altamont OR — 339-D14
KLAMATH CO OR — 235-D5
KLAMATH CO OR — 339-D14
KLASKANINE AV
ASTORIA OR — 300-C6
KLEIN RD
ADAMS CO WA — 113-C3
KLEINSMITH RD
CLACKAMAS CO OR — 200-D5
KLEMGARD RD
WHITMAN CO WA — 249-A6
KLICKITAT APPLETON RD
KLICKITAT CO WA — 196-C3

KLICKITAT TRAIL RD
LANE CO OR — 209-B5
KLONDIKE RD
FERRY CO WA — 105-B2
SHERMAN CO OR — 127-C2
N KLONDIKE RD
SHERMAN CO OR — 127-C1
KLOOCHMAN CREEK RD
CROOK CO OR — 136-A3
KLUPENGER RD
MARION CO OR — 199-B6
KLUSS RD
LATAH CO ID — 250-C1
KNAPPA RD
CLATSOP CO OR — 117-A3
KNAPPTON FERRY RD Rt#-401
PACIFIC CO WA — 186-C7
NW KNICKERBOCKER AV
DESCHUTES CO OR — 212-D4
KNIERIEM RD
MULTNOMAH CO OR — 200-C1
KNIGHT RD
KLICKITAT CO WA — 127-C1
KLICKITAT CO WA — 196-C4
KNIGHT ST
CITY OF RICHMOND BC — 156-C5
VANCOUVER BC — 156-C5
VANCOUVER BC — 255-A14
KNIGHTS BRIDGE RD
CANBY OR — 199-C6
CLACKAMAS CO OR — 199-C6
NW KNIGHTS BRIDGE RD
CANBY OR — 199-C6
KNOB HILL RD
WASCO CO OR — 196-C7
KNOB HILL-TROUT CREEK RD
FERRY CO WA — 105-B2
KNOBLE RD E
PIERCE CO WA — 182-A6
NE KNOLL AV
DOUGLAS CO OR — 334-G2
KNOTGRASS RIDGE RD
ASOTIN CO WA — 122-C2
KNOTT RD
BEND OR — 217-B4
BEND OR — 332-G14
DESCHUTES CO OR — 217-B4
DESCHUTES CO OR — 332-G14
KNOTT CREEK RD
HUMBOLDT CO NV — 153-B3
KNOWLES RD
JACKSON CO OR — 234-A2
KNOWLES RD SE
THURSTON CO WA — 184-D3
KNOX AV
BELLINGHAM WA — 258-B10
KNOX RD
CLACKAMAS CO OR — 200-B4
KNOX BUTTE RD
ALBANY OR — 207-D4
ALBANY OR — 326-J7
LINN CO OR — 133-C1
LINN CO OR — 207-D4
LINN CO OR — 326-J7
KNUDSEN RD
KOOTENAI CO ID — 245-A4
KOCH RD
ADAMS CO WA — 113-B3
KOENIG RD
WHITMAN CO WA — 249-A2
KOHFIELD RD
DESCHUTES CO OR — 212-A7
KOLLOCK-KNAPP RD
SKAMANIA CO WA — 195-C4
KONKOLVILLE RD
CLEARWATER CO ID — 123-C2
IDAHO CO ID — 123-C2
KOOL RD
COWLITZ CO WA — 189-D4
KOONTZ RD
LINN CO OR — 187-C2
KOOSBAY BLVD
COOS CO OR — 333-G8
NORTH BEND OR — 333-G8
KOOTENAI CTO
PONDERAY ID — 244-A1
N KOOTENAI RD
BONNER CO ID — 244-A1
KOOTENAI RD
BONNERS FERRY ID — 107-B2
KOOTENAI ST
BOISE ID — 253-C3
KOPACHUCK DR NW
PIERCE CO WA — 181-B1
KOPF RD
WHITMAN CO WA — 249-C7
KOSKELLA RD
VALLEY CO ID — 252-D2
KOSYDAR RD
LINCOLN CO WA — 206-C1
KOWITZ RD
LINN CO OR — 133-C1
KRAEMIEN RD
SNOHOMISH CO WA — 168-D5
KRAIMIEN RD
YAMHILL CO OR — 199-A6
KRAIN WABASH RD
KING CO WA — 182-D2
KRAUSS RD
JOSEPHINE CO OR — 233-A5
KRAXBERGER RD
CLACKAMAS CO OR — 199-C7
KRESKY AV
CENTRALIA WA — 299-F6
LEWIS CO WA — 299-F6
KRIEGER RD
DESCHUTES CO OR — 212-C7
KROENIG RD
POLK CO OR — 204-A3
SE KROHN RD
CLARK CO WA — 193-C6
KROLL RD
COWLITZ CO WA — 187-C6
KRONQUIST RD
JACKSON CO OR — 182-A7
E KRONQUIST RD
JACKSON CO OR — 246-D1
S KROPF RD
CLACKAMAS CO OR — 205-D3
SW KRUGER RD
WASHINGTON CO OR — 199-A4
SW KRUSE RD
CLACKAMAS CO OR — 199-B5
KRUSE WY
CLACKAMAS CO OR — 199-B3
CLACKAMAS CO OR — 320-A6
LAKE OSWEGO OR — 199-B3
LAKE OSWEGO OR — 320-A6

INDEX

STREET INDEX

STREET / City State	Page-Grid
KUEBLER BLVD SE	
MARION CO OR	325-B6
SALEM OR	204-D7
SALEM OR	324-F6
SALEM OR	325-B6
KUEBLER RD	
MARION CO OR	324-D6
SALEM OR	324-D6
KUEFFLER RD	
SKAMANIA CO WA	194-B6
KUEHNE RD	
YAMHILL CO OR	198-C5
KUHNHAUSEN RD	
SNOHOMISH CO WA	168-C3
KUHNIS RD	
COWLITZ CO WA	192-B1
KULM RD	
GRANT CO WA	242-C7
E KUNA RD	
ADA CO ID	253-B5
W KUNA RD	
ADA CO ID	253-A5
W KUNA CAVE RD	
ADA CO ID	253-A7
KUNA-MERIDIAN RD Rt#-69	
ADA CO ID	253-A4
MERIDIAN ID	253-A4
E KUNA-MORA RD	
ADA CO ID	253-B6
W KUNA-MORA RD	
ADA CO ID	147-C1
ADA CO ID	253-A6
CANYON CO ID	147-C1
KUNZE RD	
MORROW CO OR	128-B1
KUNZE RD SW	
BOARDMAN OR	128-C1
MORROW CO OR	128-C1
KURTZ RD	
POLK CO OR	204-A4
NW KUYKENDALL RD	
YAMHILL CO OR	198-A5
KWINA RD	
WHATCOM CO WA	158-C7
KWNEESUM RD	
SKAMANIA CO WA	193-D5

L

STREET / City State	Page-Grid
L RD NE	
DOUGLAS CO WA	112-C1
L RD NW	
DOUGLAS CO WA	236-D5
L RD SE	
DOUGLAS CO WA	112-C2
L ST U.S.-101	
CRESCENT CITY CA	148-B3
E L ST	
TACOMA WA	182-A3
N L ST	
TOPPENISH WA	120-A2
YAKIMA CO WA	120-A2
S L ST	
TOPPENISH WA	120-A2
YAKIMA CO WA	120-A2
L 1/2-SW RD	
GRANT CO WA	112-B3
LABARRE RD	
SKAMANIA CO WA	193-D6
LABIEUX RD	
NANAIMO BC	93-A3
LABISH CENTER RD NE	
MARION CO OR	205-A4
LABISKE RD	
CLATSOP CO OR	188-D3
LABOR CAMP	
CANYON CO ID	147-B1
NW LA CENTER RD	
CLARK CO WA	192-C2
LA CENTER WA	192-C2
LACEY BLVD SE	
LACEY WA	297-F6
LACKEY RD	
PIERCE CO WA	181-A1
LACOMB DR	
LINN CO OR	133-C1
LA CROSSE AIRPORT RD	
LA CROSSE WA	122-A1
WHITMAN CO WA	122-A1
LADD CREEK RD	
UNION CO OR	130-A3
SW LADD HILL RD	
CLACKAMAS CO OR	199-A6
SHERWOOD OR	199-A6
WASHINGTON CO OR	199-A6
LADNER TRUNK RD	
DISTRICT OF DELTA BC	101-C1
LADNER TRUNK RD Rt#-10	
DISTRICT OF DELTA BC	101-C1
DISTRICT OF DELTA BC	156-D7
LAEL-FLAT CREEK RD	
STEVENS CO WA	106-A1
NE LAFAYETTE AV	
MCMINNVILLE OR	198-A7
LAFAYETTE HWY	
YAMHILL CO OR	204-C1
SE LAFAYETTE HWY	
LAFAYETTE OR	198-B7
YAMHILL CO OR	198-B7
YAMHILL CO OR	204-B7
SE LAFAYETTE HWY Rt#-233	
YAMHILL CO OR	198-B7
LAFAYETTE RD	
SKAGIT CO WA	260-H3
LAFAYETTE ST	
STEILACOOM WA	181-C4
LAFOLLETT RD	
WASHINGTON CO OR	198-C2
LAGOON DR	
MALHEUR CO OR	139-A3
VALE OR	139-A3
LAGOON POINT RD	
ISLAND CO WA	167-C7

STREET / City State	Page-Grid
LA GRANDE-BAKER HWY U.S.-30	
BAKER CO OR	130-A3
BAKER CO OR	138-B1
HAINES OR	130-A3
LA GRANDE OR	130-A3
UNION CO OR	130-A3
W LA GRANGE ST	
ADA CO ID	253-B4
LAIRD RD	
CLALLAM CO WA	165-A6
LAITY ST	
MAPLE RIDGE BC	157-C5
LAKE AV	
CANYON CO ID	147-B1
LAKE AV Rt#-97	
HARRISON ID	248-A4
LAKE DR	
DESCHUTES CO OR	212-A4
EUGENE OR	329-F1
LANE CO OR	329-F1
WARRENTON OR	188-B1
N LAKE RD	
WALLA WALLA CO WA	121-B3
S LAKE RD	
Burbank WA	121-B3
WALLA WALLA CO WA	121-B3
SE LAKE RD	
CLACKAMAS CO OR	199-D3
MILWAUKIE OR	199-D3
MILWAUKIE OR	321-J3
W LAKE RD	
YAMHILL CO OR	198-A5
E LAKE ST Rt#-55	
MCCALL ID	251-C6
LAKE ST S	
KIRKLAND WA	175-C1
LAKE BALLINGER WY Rt#-104	
EDMONDS WA	171-B6
MOUNTLAKE TERRACE WA	171-B6
SHORELINE WA	171-B6
LAKE CAVANAUGH RD	
SKAGIT CO WA	168-C2
LAKE CITY WY NE	
SEATTLE WA	274-C5
LAKE CITY WY NE Rt#-522	
SEATTLE WA	171-B7
SEATTLE WA	274-C2
LAKE CREEK DR	
LINN CO OR	207-C6
LINN CO OR	210-A3
TANGENT OR	207-C6
LAKE CREEK RD	
DOUGLAS CO OR	223-C5
JACKSON CO OR	234-D1
LEWIS CO WA	187-A1
LAKE CUSHMAN RD Rt#-119	
MASON CO WA	109-B2
MASON CO WA	173-A6
LAKE EARL DR Rt#-D3	
DEL NORTE CO CA	148-B3
SW LAKE FLORA RD	
KITSAP CO WA	174-A7
E LAKE FOREST DR	
BOISE ID	253-D4
E LAKE FORK RD	
VALLEY CO ID	251-D6
W LAKE FORK RD	
VALLEY CO ID	251-C7
LAKE FRANCIS RD SE	
KING CO WA	176-A6
E LAKE GOODWIN RD Rt#-531	
SNOHOMISH CO WA	168-B5
W LAKE GOODWIN RD	
SNOHOMISH CO WA	168-B6
LAKE GROVE ST	
LAKE OSWEGO WA	320-A7
E LAKE HAZEL RD	
ADA CO ID	253-B4
W LAKE HAZEL RD	
ADA CO ID	253-A4
SW LAKE HELENA RD	
KITSAP CO WA	174-A5
LAKE HILLS BLVD	
BELLEVUE WA	175-C2
LAKE HILLS CONNECTOR	
BELLEVUE WA	175-C2
SE LAKE HOLM RD	
KING CO WA	182-C1
LAKEHURST DR	
BREMERTON WA	270-B11
LAKE JOSEPHINE BLVD	
PIERCE CO WA	181-B4
LAKE LOMA DR	
SNOHOMISH CO WA	168-C6
LAKE LOUISE RD	
Sudden Valley WA	161-A1
WHATCOM CO WA	161-A1
LAKEMONT BLVD SE	
BELLEVUE WA	175-D3
ISSAQUAH WA	175-D3
LAKE OF THE WOODS HWY Rt#-99	
CENTRAL POINT OR	230-C7
JACKSON CO OR	230-C7
MEDFORD OR	230-C7
LAKE OF THE WOODS HWY Rt#-140	
JACKSON CO OR	149-C1
JACKSON CO OR	150-A1
JACKSON CO OR	230-D6
KLAMATH CO OR	150-B1
KLAMATH CO OR	231-A6
KLAMATH CO OR	235-A1
KLAMATH CO OR	338-A10
KLAMATH FALLS OR	235-A1
KLAMATH FALLS OR	338-B12
White City OR	230-D6
E LAKE PLEASANT RD	
CLALLAM CO WA	163-A6
W LAKE PLEASANT RD	
CLALLAM CO WA	163-A6
LAKERIDGE DR	
OLYMPIA WA	296-G7
N LAKE ROESIGER RD	
SNOHOMISH CO WA	110-C1
S LAKE ROESIGER RD	
SNOHOMISH CO WA	110-C1
LAKE SAMISH DR	
WHATCOM CO WA	161-A2
LAKE SAMISH RD	
SKAGIT CO WA	161-B3
WHATCOM CO WA	161-B3

STREET / City State	Page-Grid
E LAKE SAMMAMISH PKWY NE	
REDMOND WA	175-D2
SAMMAMISH WA	175-D2
W LAKE SAMMAMISH PKWY NE	
BELLEVUE WA	175-D1
KING CO WA	175-D1
REDMOND WA	175-D1
E LAKE SAMMAMISH PKWY SE	
ISSAQUAH WA	175-D3
ISSAQUAH WA	176-A3
KING CO WA	175-D3
SAMMAMISH WA	175-D3
W LAKE SAMMAMISH PKWY SE	
BELLEVUE WA	175-D2
LAKES DIVIDE RD	
KOOTENAI CO ID	248-C2
LAKE SHORE DR	
CANYON CO ID	147-B1
LAKESHORE DR	
BONNER CO ID	107-A3
BONNER CO ID	244-A3
CASCADE ID	252-D7
CLARK CO WA	192-C1
COOS BAY OR	333-B5
COWLITZ CO WA	192-C1
JOSEPHINE CO OR	233-B2
KLAMATH CO OR	235-B3
KLAMATH CO OR	338-A6
KLAMATH FALLS OR	338-A6
VALLEY CO ID	252-D7
WOODLAND WA	192-C1
E LAKESHORE DR	
LAKE STEVENS WA	171-D1
S LAKESHORE RD Rt#-971	
CHELAN CO WA	236-B3
LAKESIDE RD	
KLICKITAT CO WA	119-A3
S LAKESIDE RD	
LIBERTY LAKE WA	352-F14
SPOKANE CO WA	247-B4
E LAKE STEVENS RD	
LAKE STEVENS WA	171-D2
SNOHOMISH CO WA	171-D2
S LAKE STEVENS RD	
SNOHOMISH CO WA	171-D2
LAKE TAPPS PKWY E	
AUBURN WA	182-B2
PIERCE CO WA	182-C2
SUMNER WA	182-C2
LAKE TERRELL RD	
WHATCOM CO WA	158-B6
LAKEVIEW BLVD	
LAKE OSWEGO OR	320-A7
LAKEVIEW BLVD E	
SEATTLE WA	278-B3
LAKE VIEW DR	
LAKE STEVENS WA	171-D1
SNOHOMISH CO WA	171-D1
LAKEVIEW DR	
HAYDEN LAKE ID	245-A5
LAKEVIEW-BURNS HWY U.S.-395	
HARNEY CO OR	144-C2
LAKE CO OR	144-B3
LAKE CO OR	152-A1
LAKE VISTA DR	
GRANT CO WA	242-B1
LAKE WASHINGTON BLVD	
SEATTLE WA	279-E6
LAKE WASHINGTON BLVD E	
SEATTLE WA	278-D2
SEATTLE WA	279-F4
LAKE WASHINGTON BLVD N	
RENTON WA	175-C4
LAKE WASHINGTON BLVD NE	
BELLEVUE WA	175-C2
KIRKLAND WA	175-C1
LAKE WASHINGTON BLVD S	
SEATTLE WA	278-E7
SEATTLE WA	282-E1
SEATTLE WA	283-E3
LAKE WASHINGTON BLVD SE	
BELLEVUE WA	175-C3
NEWCASTLE WA	175-C4
RENTON WA	175-C4
LAKEWAY DR	
BELLINGHAM WA	258-F7
BONNEY LAKE WA	182-C4
PIERCE CO WA	182-C4
WHATCOM CO WA	161-A1
WHATCOM CO WA	258-F7
LAKE WHATCOM BLVD	
Sudden Valley WA	161-A1
WHATCOM CO WA	161-A1
LAKEWOOD DR	
ALBANY OR	326-B11
LAKEWOOD DR W	
LAKEWOOD WA	294-A7
LAKEWOOD WA	294-A7
TACOMA WA	294-A7
UNIVERSITY PLACE WA	294-A7
LAKEWOOD RD	
SNOHOMISH CO WA	168-B5
LAKEWOOD RD Rt#-531	
SNOHOMISH CO WA	168-B5
SE LAKE YOUNGS WY	
KING CO WA	175-C6
LAMAR RD	
WALLA WALLA CO WA	121-C2
LAMB RD	
KOOTENAI CO ID	248-B4
UMATILLA CO OR	128-C1
UMATILLA CO OR	129-A1
LAMBERSON RD	
GILLIAM CO OR	128-A2
SW LAMBERT LN	
WASHINGTON CO OR	198-C3
LAMBERT RD	
KLAMATH CO OR	240-C2
W LAMBERT RD	
KLAMATH FALLS OR	212-B3
LAMBERTIANA RD	
DESCHUTES CO OR	217-A7
LAMERS RD	
POLK CO OR	207-B1
LAMOINE RD NW	
DOUGLAS CO WA	112-A1
DOUGLAS CO WA	236-C5
LAMONT RD	
WHITMAN CO WA	114-A3
W LAMONT RD	
ADA CO ID	253-A3
LAMONTA RD	
CROOK CO OR	213-C3
LAMPA VALLEY RD	
COOS CO OR	220-C6
LAMPERTI LN	
COLLEGE PLACE WA	344-F12

STREET / City State	Page-Grid
LAMPMAN RD	
WHATCOM CO WA	158-C6
LAMPSON ST	
TOWN OF ESQUIMALT BC	256-C9
LANA AV NE	
SALEM OR	323-B9
LANCASTER DR	
Four Corners OR	323-E12
Four Corners OR	325-D1
Hayesville OR	323-E8
SALEM OR	204-D5
SALEM OR	323-E12
SALEM OR	325-E3
LANCASTER DR Rt#-213	
Hayesville OR	323-E11
SALEM OR	204-D5
SALEM OR	323-E11
LANCASTER RD	
Freeland WA	170-D2
KOOTENAI CO ID	245-A5
SAINT JOHN WA	114-B3
WHITMAN CO WA	114-B3
WHITMAN CO WA	122-B1
W LANCASTER RD	
HAYDEN ID	247-D1
KOOTENAI CO ID	247-D1
SW LANCEFIELD RD	
YAMHILL CO OR	204-B2
S LANDER ST	
SEATTLE WA	282-A1
NE LANDERHOLM RD	
CLARK CO WA	192-D2
LANDES ST	
PORT TOWNSEND WA	263-F5
LANDING RD	
COOS CO OR	220-D6
SKAGIT CO WA	168-A1
LANDRITH RD	
COOS CO OR	140-C2
LANDSBURG RD SE	
KING CO WA	176-A7
LANDS END RD	
DISTRICT OF NORTH SAANICH BC	159-B1
LANE AV	
ROSEBURG OR	334-F7
LANEDA AV	
MANZANITA OR	191-A4
E LANE PARK RD	
SPOKANE CO WA	347-E4
LANES TURN RD	
LANE CO OR	210-A6
LANEY RD	
LINCOLN CO OR	113-C3
LANEY BROTHERS RD	
LINCOLN CO OR	113-C3
LANGE RD	
SKAGIT CO WA	161-C7
LANGE GATEWAY RD	
SNOHOMISH CO WA	191-B4
E LANGELL VALLEY RD	
BONANZA OR	151-A2
KLAMATH CO OR	151-A2
W LANGELL VALLEY RD	
KLAMATH CO OR	151-A2
LANGENSAND RD	
CLACKAMAS CO OR	200-D4
SANDY OR	200-D4
LANGFORD RD	
FRANKLIN CO WA	121-A2
LANGLEY BYPS	
LANGLEY BC	158-C1
LANGLEY BYPS Rt#-10	
CITY OF SURREY BC	157-C7
CITY OF SURREY BC	158-B3
LANGLEY BC	157-C7
LANGLEY RD	
ISLAND CO WA	171-A1
LANGLEY WA	171-A1
LANGLOIS MOUNTAIN RD	
CURRY CO OR	224-B2
LANGWORTHY RD SW	
THURSTON CO WA	184-A2
LANSDOWNE RD	
DISTRICT OF OAK BAY BC	257-C6
DISTRICT OF SAANICH BC	257-B6
LANSKY RD	
MASON CO WA	180-D3
LANTZ LN	
UNION CO OR	130-B2
LA PUSH RD	
CLALLAM CO WA	169-A2
LA PUSH RD Rt#-110	
CLALLAM CO WA	169-C1
FORKS WA	169-C1
SE LARCH AV	
COLLEGE PLACE WA	344-G12
W LARCH AV	
YAKIMA CO WA	243-B7
LARCH DR	
DESCHUTES CO OR	212-C5
LARCH ST	
LONGVIEW WA	303-A9
SANDPOINT ID	244-A2
VANCOUVER BC	156-B5
LARCH WY SW	
SNOHOMISH CO WA	171-B5
LARCH MOUNTAIN RD	
HOOD RIVER CO OR	195-B6
MULTNOMAH CO OR	200-D1
MULTNOMAH CO OR	201-A1
LARGENT RD	
FRANKLIN CO WA	121-B2
LARIMER RD	
EVERETT WA	269-F2
SNOHOMISH CO WA	269-F2
LARKIN RD	
PACIFIC CO WA	183-B4
S LARKIN RD	
KLAMATH CO OR	200-A7
SW LARKINS MILL RD	
WASHINGTON CO OR	198-C3
LARMON RD	
LEWIS CO WA	187-D2
LARSON LN NW	
KITSAP CO WA	173-D2
LARSON RD	
CITY OF NORTH VANCOUVER BC	254-A1
CITY OF NORTH VANCOUVER BC	255-A4
COLUMBIA CO OR	189-B4
COLUMBIA CO OR	302-D14
DOUGLAS CO OR	221-A5
KITSAP CO WA	174-A2
SNOHOMISH CO WA	168-B4
LARSON ST Rt#-161	
EATONVILLE WA	118-B1
LARSON WY	
JACKSON CO OR	218-C6
LARSON BEACH SHORE ACC RD	
STEVENS CO WA	106-B3

STREET / City State	Page-Grid
LARSON CREEK RD	
JACKSON CO OR	226-C6
LARSON LAKE RD	
JEFFERSON CO OR	170-A3
SW LA SALLE LN	
JEFFERSON CO OR	212-C1
LA SALLE RD	
WASHINGTON CO OR	198-B3
LA SALLE ST	
HARRISBURG OR	210-A5
LASSEN LN	
LANE CO OR	210-A7
LAST CHANCE CREEK RD	
JACKSON CO OR	225-D7
S LATAH ST	
BOISE ID	253-C3
S LATAH CREEK RD	
SPOKANE CO WA	246-D7
SW LATHAM RD	
YAMHILL CO OR	204-A2
LATIMER RD	
TILLAMOOK CO OR	197-C2
WHITMAN CO WA	122-B1
LATORIA RD	
CITY OF COLWOOD BC	159-B7
DISTRICT OF LANGFORD BC	159-B7
LAUCK RD	
SNOHOMISH CO WA	168-D7
LAUER CROSSING RD U.S.-95	
IDAHO CO ID	123-B3
LAUFERS RD	
LEWIS CO ID	123-B3
SE LAUGHING WATER RD	
CLACKAMAS CO OR	200-D3
LAUGHLIN RD	
PRINEVILLE OR	213-D5
YAMHILL CO OR	198-B4
LAURA ST	
COOS CO OR	218-B3
LAURANCE LAKE DR	
HOOD RIVER CO OR	202-B3
LAUREL AV	
Navy Yard City WA	270-E13
LAUREL RD	
CAVE JUNCTION OR	233-B4
JOSEPHINE CO OR	233-B4
LONGVIEW WA	302-J6
LONGVIEW WA	303-A6
N LAUREL ST	
ASHLAND OR	337-C6
LAUREL HILLS RD	
DOUGLAS CO OR	219-A2
LAURELVIEW RD	
WASHINGTON CO OR	198-C3
LAURELWOOD RD	
WASHINGTON CO OR	198-C3
W LAURIDSEN BLVD	
CLALLAM CO WA	261-A4
PORT ANGELES WA	261-A4
SW LAVA AV	
DESCHUTES CO OR	212-C5
LAVA BEDS RD	
HARNEY CO OR	145-B2
LAVA BEDS NATIONAL MONUMENT RD	
MODOC CO CA	151-A3
LAVA CAST FOREST RD	
DESCHUTES CO OR	217-B6
LAVA LAKE RD	
DESCHUTES CO OR	142-C1
DESCHUTES CO OR	216-A5
LAVA-ODELL RD	
KLAMATH CO OR	142-B1
LA VENTURE RD	
MOUNT VERNON WA	260-E11
LAVERNE AV	
Altamont OR	338-G12
LAVERNE PARK NORTH RD	
COOS CO OR	140-C2
S LAW DR	
BOISE ID	253-D3
LAWEN LN	
HARNEY CO OR	145-B2
LAWEN-HARNEY RD	
HARNEY CO OR	145-B1
LAWRENCE RD	
COLUMBIA CO OR	189-C7
LANE CO OR	133-B2
LEWIS CO WA	299-D5
LAWRENCE RD Rt#-9	
WHATCOM CO WA	102-B1
LAWRENCE ST	
PORT TOWNSEND WA	263-G5
LAWTON RD	
SPOKANE CO WA	348-C13
LAWYERS CANYON RD Rt#-162	
IDAHO CO ID	123-C3
LEWIS CO ID	123-C3
NEZPERCE ID	123-C3
LAYALL RD	
KLICKITAT CO WA	196-B2
LAYNG RD	
LANE CO OR	215-C7
LAZY ALLEN OAKS RD	
KLICKITAT CO WA	196-A4
NE LEADBETTER RD	
CLARK CO WA	193-B6
LEAFWOOD DR	
JACKSON CO OR	230-D4
LEA HILL RD SE	
AUBURN WA	182-C1
KING CO WA	182-C1
LEAHY RD N	
DOUGLAS CO WA	112-C1
LEAHY RD S Rt#-17	
DOUGLAS CO WA	112-C1
LEAHY-MANSFIELD-MAYFIELD RD NE	
DOUGLAS CO WA	112-C1
LEANDER DR	
YAMHILL CO OR	198-D5
LEAP LN	
WALLOWA CO OR	130-C1
LEARY AV NW	
SEATTLE WA	273-E4
LEARY RD NE	
MARION CO OR	205-A1
LEARY WY NW	
SEATTLE WA	273-G5

STREET / City State	Page-Grid
E LEAVENWORTH RD	
CHELAN CO WA	238-A1
LEBANON ST	
ARLINGTON WA	168-D5
SW LEBEAU RD	
WASHINGTON CO OR	199-A4
LEBO BLVD	
BREMERTON WA	270-H8
LE BRUN RD NE	
MARION CO OR	205-A3
LE CLERC CREEK RD	
PEND OREILLE CO WA	106-C3
LEDGERWOOD SPUR RD	
GARFIELD CO WA	122-C2
LEE BLVD	
RICHLAND WA	341-E1
LEE RD	
WASHINGTON CO OR	198-A2
LEE MCKINLEY RD	
COOS CO OR	140-C2
LEES CREEK RD	
DOUGLAS CO OR	219-B3
LEFEUVRE RD	
DISTRICT OF MATSQUI BC	102-B1
LEFEVRE ST Rt#-902	
MEDICAL LAKE WA	114-B2
LEFFEL RD	
UNION CO OR	130-A2
LEFT FORK FOOTS CREEK RD	
JACKSON CO OR	230-A7
LEFT FORK SARDINE CREEK RD	
JACKSON CO OR	230-A5
LEGALL RD	
KLICKITAT CO WA	196-B2
LEGION WY	
OLYMPIA WA	296-H5
OLYMPIA WA	297-A5
LEGOE BAY RD	
WHATCOM CO WA	160-B1
N LEHMAN RD	
SPOKANE CO WA	246-D2
LEISLE RD	
ADAMS CO WA	113-B3
LEITNER RD SW	
THURSTON CO WA	184-B3
LELAND RD	
JOSEPHINE CO OR	229-A1
S LELAND RD	
CLACKAMAS CO OR	199-D6
S LE MAIRE ST	
MOXEE WA	243-D7
LEMLEY RD	
BENTON CO WA	120-B3
LEMMON RD NE	
THURSTON CO WA	180-D5
LEMOLO RD	
DOUGLAS CO OR	223-B8
E LEMOLO LAKE RD	
DOUGLAS CO OR	223-C8
LEMOLO SHORE DR NE	
KITSAP CO WA	170-B7
Suquamish WA	170-B7
LEMON RD	
CLALLAM CO WA	165-D6
LEMONDS RD	
JEFFERSON CO OR	170-A6
W LEMP ST	
BOISE ID	253-C2
LENORA ST	
EVERETT WA	269-F1
LENTZ RD	
COLUMBIA CO OR	189-B5
LEWIS CO WA	187-B2
LENTZ RD E	
LINCOLN CO WA	113-C2
LENTZ RD N	
LEWIS CO WA	187-B2
LENVILLE RD	
LATAH CO ID	123-A3
LATAH CO ID	249-D5
LEON RD	
WHITMAN CO WA	250-B2
LEONARD RD	
JOSEPHINE CO OR	229-A6
LEWIS CO WA	118-A2
LESLIE AV	
LA CROSSE WA	122-A1
WHITMAN CO WA	122-A1
LESLIE RD	
BENTON CO WA	341-H12
RICHLAND WA	341-H7
YAMHILL CO OR	199-A6
LESLIE GULCH RD	
MALHEUR CO OR	146-C2
MALHEUR CO OR	147-A2
NE LESSARD RD	
CLARK CO WA	193-C5
LESSIG SOUTH FORK RD	
STEVENS CO WA	106-A3
LESTER AV	
BENTON CO WA	327-F4
LESTER RD	
KITTITAS CO WA	241-D5
LESTER CAMP RD	
WHITMAN CO WA	122-B1
LEVEE	
KLAMATH CO OR	231-C3
LEVEE ST U.S.-101	
HOQUIAM WA	178-A7
LEVEL RD N	
LINCOLN CO WA	114-A1
LEWELLEN RD	
CLACKAMAS CO OR	200-B7
LEWELLEN CREEK RD	
KOOTENAI CO ID	245-B2
LEWIS AV	
CLATSOP CO OR	188-B3
LEWIS DR	
PIERCE CO WA	181-B3
LEWIS LN	
CANYON CO ID	147-C3
KITTITAS CO WA	241-C4
W LEWIS LN	
CANYON CO ID	147-B1
LEWIS RD	
CLALLAM CO WA	165-B3
GARFIELD CO WA	122-B2
WALLOWA CO OR	131-A1
LEWIS RD W	
KITSAP CO WA	173-D3
LEWIS ST Rt#-214	
SILVERTON OR	205-C4
E LEWIS ST	
PASCO WA	121-A3
PASCO WA	343-J7
N LEWIS ST Rt#-203	
MONROE WA	110-C1

STREET / City State / Page-Grid

S LEWIS ST Rt#-203
MONROE WA — 110-C1
SNOHOMISH CO WA — 110-C1
W LEWIS ST
PASCO WA — 343-D7
LEWIS AND CLARK FRWY Rt#-14
VANCOUVER WA — 193-A7
VANCOUVER WA — 305-G6
VANCOUVER WA — 306-A6
VANCOUVER WA — 307-E7
VANCOUVER WA — 311-G1
LEWIS AND CLARK HWY Rt#-14
BINGEN WA — 195-C5
CAMAS WA — 193-A7
CLARK CO WA — 193-A7
KLICKITAT CO WA — 127-B1
KLICKITAT CO WA — 195-C5
KLICKITAT CO WA — 196-C6
SKAMANIA CO WA — 195-C5
VANCOUVER WA — 193-A7
WASHOUGAL WA — 193-C7
WHITE SALMON WA — 195-C5
LEWIS AND CLARK RD
CLATSOP CO OR — 188-C3
CLATSOP CO OR — 300-A14
CLATSOP CO OR — 301-H6
SEASIDE OR — 188-C5
SEASIDE OR — 301-H6
LEWIS GULCH RD
COLUMBIA CO WA — 122-B2
LEWIS RIVER DR Rt#-503
COWLITZ CO WA — 118-A3
COWLITZ CO WA — 190-A6
WOODLAND WA — 118-A3
LEWIS RIVER RD
SKAMANIA CO WA — 118-C2
SKAMANIA CO WA — 190-B4
LEWIS RIVER RD Rt#-503
COWLITZ CO WA — 190-A6
LEWIS ROGERS LN
YAMHILL CO OR — 198-C5
LEWISTON RD
WALLA WALLA CO WA — 122-A3
NE LEWISVILLE HWY Rt#-503
CLARK CO WA — 193-A1
LEY RD
KITTITAS CO WA — 240-D1
LIBBEY RD
ISLAND CO WA — 167-A4
LIBBY RD NE
THURSTON CO WA — 180-D4
THURSTON CO WA — 297-C1
LIBBY CREEK RD
OKANOGAN CO WA — 104-A3
S LIBERTY DR
SPOKANE CO WA — 247-B4
LIBERTY RD
KITTITAS CO WA — 241-A1
POLK CO OR — 204-A6
SHERMAN CO OR — 127-C2
LIBERTY RD S
MARION CO OR — 207-D1
MARION CO OR — 324-C1
SALEM OR — 324-F6
LIBERTY ST
ALBANY OR — 326-B11
N LIBERTY ST
BOISE ID — 253-C2
LIBERTY ST NE
AURORA OR — 199-B7
SALEM OR — 322-H12
LIBERTY ST NE Rt#-99E
SALEM OR — 322-J10
LIBERTY ST SE
SALEM OR — 322-H13
SALEM OR — 324-H1
N LIBERTY LAKE RD
LIBERTY LAKE WA — 247-B4
LIBERTY LAKE WA — 352-B13
S LIBERTY LAKE RD
LIBERTY LAKE WA — 247-B4
SPOKANE CO WA — 247-B4
LIBERTY PARK PL
SPOKANE WA — 349-C9
LICK CREEK RD
MCCALL ID — 251-D5
VALLEY CO ID — 251-D5
LICKFORK RD
ASOTIN CO WA — 122-C2
LICKMAN RD
CITY OF CHILLIWACK BC — 94-C3
CITY OF CHILLIWACK BC — 102-C1
SE LIDER RD
KITSAP CO WA — 174-B5
LIDFORD
PIERCE CO WA — 182-A3
LIDSTROM RD
CROOK CO OR — 213-D4
LIDSTROM RD E
KITSAP CO WA — 271-C14
E LIDSTROM HILL RD
KITSAP CO WA — 271-B13
LIESER RD
VANCOUVER WA — 307-F7
LIGHTNING CREEK RD Rt#-200
CLARK FORK ID — 107-C3
LIGNITE RD
BONNER CO ID — 244-A3
LILAC HILL RD
YAMHILL CO OR — 198-A4
LILENAS RD
CLATSOP CO OR — 188-D3
LILLIAN ST
DOUGLAS CO OR — 225-C4
MYRTLE CREEK OR — 225-C1
LILLOOET AV
CITY OF HARRISON HOT SPRG BC — 94-C3
LILLOOET RD
DIST OF NORTH VANCOUVER BC — 156-C2
DIST OF NORTH VANCOUVER BC — 255-G6
LILLY RD NE
OLYMPIA WA — 297-E4

LILLY RD NE
THURSTON CO WA — 297-E4
LILLY RD SE
OLYMPIA WA — 297-E5
LILLY WHEATON RD
PACIFIC WA — 117-A1
LIMBERT RD
DISTRICT OF KENT BC — 94-C3
LIME KILN RD
WALLOWA CO OR — 130-C2
LIMESTONE AV
DESCHUTES CO OR — 212-C7
LINCOLN AV
COQUITLAM BC — 157-A5
KENT WA — 175-B7
PORT COQUITLAM BC — 157-B4
SNOHOMISH WA — 171-D3
SNOHOMISH CO WA — 171-D3
TACOMA WA — 182-A2
YAMHILL CO OR — 198-B4
E LINCOLN AV
SUNNYSIDE WA — 120-B2
W LINCOLN AV
CHEWELAH WA — 106-B3
YAKIMA WA — 243-B6
LINCOLN AV SE
East Port Orchard WA — 174-B4
NE LINCOLN DR
POULSBO WA — 170-C6
W LINCOLN DR
PASCO WA — 343-E5
LINCOLN LN
JOSEPHINE CO OR — 335-C9
LINCOLN RD
BENTON CO WA — 120-B3
GRANTS PASS OR — 335-C9
E LINCOLN RD
PIERCE CO WA — 181-C5
SPOKANE WA — 347-C13
SPOKANE CO WA — 347-C13
Town and Country WA — 347-C13
LINCOLN RD NE
MARION CO OR — 205-B2
LINCOLN ST
ASTORIA OR — 300-B5
KLAMATH FALLS OR — 338-C7
PIERCE CO WA — 181-C5
LINCOLN ST U.S.-101
HOQUIAM WA — 178-A7
N LINCOLN ST U.S.-101
PORT ANGELES WA — 261-H7
S LINCOLN ST
SPOKANE WA — 348-J13
S LINCOLN ST U.S.-101
PORT ANGELES WA — 261-E5
LINCOLN WY U.S.-95
COEUR D'ALENE ID — 355-C8
N LINCOLN WY
COEUR D'ALENE ID — 355-D10
KOOTENAI CO ID — 355-D10
LINCOLN CREEK RD
LEWIS CO WA — 117-B1
LEWIS CO WA — 184-B5
LINCOLN MOUNTAIN RD
UMATILLA CO OR — 129-C1
UMATILLA CO OR — 130-A1
LINCOLN PARK WY
SEATTLE WA — 284-D1
LINCOLN-ZENA RD
POLK CO OR — 204-C4
LIND AV SW
RENTON WA — 175-C5
LIND RD
FRANKLIN CO WA — 121-B1
LINDBECK RD
LEWIS CO WA — 187-C2
LINDBERG
PIERCE CO WA — 182-A7
LINDBERG RD
COLUMBIA CO OR — 189-A4
LINDEN AV N
SEATTLE WA — 273-J3
LINDEN LN
POLK CO OR — 207-B1
LINDEN ST
MILTON-FREEWATER OR — 121-C3
E LINDEN ST
BOISE ID — 253-D3
W LINDEN WY Rt#-74
HEPPNER OR — 128-C2
N LINDER RD
ADA CO ID — 253-A1
S LINDER RD
ADA CO ID — 253-A4
LINDGREN RD
PACIFIC WA — 183-B4
LIND-HATTON RD
ADAMS CO WA — 121-B1
LINDHOLM RD
DISTRICT OF METCHOSIN BC — 159-A7
LIND-KAHLOTUS RD Rt#-21
ADAMS CO WA — 121-C1
FRANKLIN CO WA — 121-C1
KAHLOTUS WA — 121-C1
LINDSAY DR
LINN CO OR — 207-B7
LINDSEY DR
COWLITZ CO WA — 302-J5
LINDSEY RD
KOOTENAI CO ID — 245-B2
LINDSEY CREEK RD
NEZ PERCE CO ID — 250-C4
LINDSTROM RD
STANWOOD WA — 168-B4
LIND-WARDEN RD
ADAMS CO WA — 121-B1
LINE RD
MARYSVILLE WA — 171-D1
SNOHOMISH CO WA — 171-D1
LINGENFELTER RD
PACIFIC CO WA — 186-B7
LINGER LONGER RD
JEFFERSON CO WA — 109-C1
LINGO LN
LANE CO OR — 210-A5
LINK LN
LANE CO OR — 210-A5
S LINKE RD
SPOKANE CO WA — 247-A5
SPOKANE CO WA — 351-F14
W LINN RD
JACKSON CO OR — 230-D5
LINN WY
BROWNSVILLE OR — 210-C2
LINNEY CREEK RD
CLACKAMAS CO OR — 201-D7
LINN WEST DR
LINN CO OR — 210-B2

LINTON ST
COQUITLAM BC — 157-A5
LINVILLE GULCH RD
GARFIELD CO WA — 122-B2
LINVILLE RIDGE RD
GARFIELD CO WA — 122-B2
SE LINWOOD AV
CLACKAMAS CO OR — 199-D3
MILWAUKIE OR — 199-D3
LINWOOD AV SW
TUMWATER WA — 296-G10
SE LION LAKE RD
REDMOND OR — 212-D5
LIONS GATE BRDG Rt#-99
DIST OF WEST VANCOUVER BC — 254-E5
VANCOUVER BC — 254-E5
LIONS GATE BRIDGE RD Rt#-99
DIST OF WEST VANCOUVER BC — 254-E7
VANCOUVER BC — 254-E7
LIPPMAN RD
HOOD RIVER CO OR — 195-C6
LISHER CTO
LATAH CO ID — 249-D1
LITHIA WY
ASHLAND OR — 337-C7
LITHIA WY Rt#-99
ASHLAND OR — 337-C7
LITTLE RD
WHITMAN CO WA — 249-A7
LITTLE ALKALI RD
WHITMAN CO WA — 122-B1
LITTLE APPLEGATE RD
JACKSON CO OR — 234-A5
LITTLE BEAR CREEK RD
CROOK CO OR — 135-C3
LITTLE BLACKTAIL MOUNTAIN RD
BONNER CO ID — 244-A6
LITTLE BOSTON RD NE
KITSAP CO WA — 170-C4
LITTLE BURMA RD
DOUGLAS CO OR — 214-D6
LITTLE BUTTER CREEK RD
MORROW CO OR — 129-A2
LITTLE EGYPT RD
MASON CO WA — 179-D3
LITTLE FALLS RD
LINCOLN CO WA — 114-A1
LITTLE FALLS CHAMOKANA RD
STEVENS CO WA — 114-A1
LITTLE FALLS LONGLAKE RD
STEVENS CO WA — 114-A1
LITTLE GOOSE DAM RD
COLUMBIA CO WA — 122-A2
LITTLE GRAYBACK RD
JOSEPHINE CO OR — 233-C4
LITTLE HANAFORD RD
CENTRALIA WA — 299-H2
LEWIS CO WA — 184-H2
LEWIS CO WA — 299-H2
LITTLE JUNIPER RD
HARNEY CO OR — 144-B3
LITTLE KALAMA RIVER RD
COWLITZ CO WA — 118-A3
LITTLE MCKAY RD
CROOK CO OR — 135-C2
LITTLE MOUNTAIN RD
KLICKITAT CO WA — 119-A3
SKAGIT CO WA — 168-B1
SKAGIT CO WA — 260-F14
LITTLE MUD CREEK RD
ADAMS CO ID — 251-A3
LITTLE NESTUCCA HWY
TILLAMOOK CO OR — 203-D2
LITTLE NESTUCCA RIVER RD
TILLAMOOK CO OR — 203-C1
LITTLE RIVER RD
CLALLAM CO OR — 165-A7
DOUGLAS CO OR — 141-B2
DOUGLAS CO OR — 222-A5
LITTLE RIV - POWELL RIV FERRY
BRITISH COLUMBIA BC — 92-B1
LITTLEROCK RD SW
Rochester WA — 184-A3
THURSTON CO WA — 184-B1
THURSTON CO WA — 296-D14
TUMWATER WA — 296-D14
LITTLE SHEEP CREEK HWY
JOSEPH OR — 130-C2
WALLOWA CO OR — 130-C2
WALLOWA CO OR — 131-A2
LITTLE SHEEP CREEK RD Rt#-25
STEVENS CO WA — 106-A1
LITTLE SPOKANE DR
SPOKANE CO WA — 347-C1
SW LITTLE SQUAWBACK RD
JEFFERSON CO OR — 211-D2
LITTLE SQUAW BAY RD
KOOTENAI CO ID — 248-A6
LITTLE VALLEY LN
LINN CO OR — 210-D4
LITTLE WEISER RD
ADAMS CO ID — 252-B6
LITTLE WEISER RD U.S.-95
ADAMS CO ID — 139-B1
LITTLE WEISER RIVER RD
ADAMS CO ID — 252-A6
LITTLE WILLOW RD
PAYETTE CO ID — 139-B3
LIVERMORE RD
POLK CO OR — 204-B4
LIVESAY RD
DESCHUTES CO OR — 211-D7
LIVINGSTON RD
CLARK CO WA — 193-C5
LIZARD CREEK RD
DESCHUTES CO OR — 144-A1
L JOHNSON RD
CLARK CO WA — 192-D1
LLEWELLYN RD
BENTON CO OR — 133-B2
NE LLOYD BLVD
PORTLAND OR — 313-H5
LLOYD ST
JOSEPHINE CO OR — 229-B4
LLOYD WY
DESCHUTES CO OR — 216-D7
DESCHUTES CO OR — 217-A6
Three Rivers OR — 217-A6
LOBSTER CREEK RD
CURRY CO OR — 228-B3
LINCOLN CO OR — 209-D3
LOBSTER VALLEY RD
BENTON CO OR — 133-A2
BENTON CO OR — 209-D3

LOCARNO CRES
UNIV ENDOWMENT LANDS BC — 156-A4
LOCHNER RD
ALBANY OR — 326-D14
LINN CO OR — 326-D14
LOCHSIDE DR
DIST OF NORTH SAANICH BC — 159-C3
TOWN OF SIDNEY BC — 159-C3
LOCKART AV
COOS BAY OR — 333-G12
LOCKER RD SE
KITSAP CO WA — 174-C4
LOCKETT RD
MALHEUR CO OR — 139-A2
NE LOCKWOOD CREEK RD
CLARK CO WA — 192-D2
LOCKWOOD RD
SNOHOMISH CO WA — 171-B6
LOCKHAVEN DR N
KEIZER OR — 322-J4
KEIZER OR — 323-A4
LOCKHAVEN DR NE
KEIZER OR — 323-B4
LOCKITT BUTTE RD
DESCHUTES CO OR — 217-C5
SE LOCKS RD
YAMHILL CO OR — 198-B7
LOCUST AV
BROWNSVILLE OR — 210-C2
E LOCUST AV
COEUR D'ALENE ID — 355-E9
E LOCUST LN
CANYON CO ID — 147-C1
LOCUST ST
ALMIRA WA — 237-D7
OAKLAND OR — 219-A7
SISTERS OR — 211-D5
LOCUST ST Rt#-19
ARLINGTON OR — 128-A1
N LOCUST ST Rt#-19
ARLINGTON OR — 128-A1
GILLIAM CO OR — 128-A1
S LOCUST ST Rt#-19
ARLINGTON OR — 128-A1
LOCUST WY
SNOHOMISH CO WA — 171-B6
LOCUST GROVE RD
BENTON CO WA — 121-A3
NEZ PERCE CO ID — 250-D7
N LOCUST GROVE RD
MERIDIAN ID — 253-B4
S LOCUST GROVE RD
ADA CO ID — 253-B4
MERIDIAN ID — 253-B4
LODGEPOLE RD
JACKSON CO OR — 150-A1
LOERLAND LN
ISLAND CO WA — 167-B2
LOFFS BAY RD
KOOTENAI CO ID — 247-D6
KOOTENAI CO ID — 248-A2
LOFTON CREEK RD
CROOK CO OR — 213-D2
LOGAN RD
CLATSOP CO OR — 188-C3
NE LOGAN RD
LINCOLN CO OR — 203-A4
NW LOGAN RD
LINCOLN CO OR — 203-A4
SW LOGANBERRY LN
SHERIDAN OR — 125-B3
YAMHILL CO OR — 125-B3
YAMHILL CO OR — 204-A2
LOGAN HILL RD
LEWIS CO WA — 184-D7
LOGAN VALLEY RD
GRANT CO OR — 137-B3
SENECA OR — 137-B3
LOG CABIN RD SE
OLYMPIA WA — 297-B9
LOG CORRAL RD
KLICKITAT CO WA — 196-B1
LOGEN RD
SNOHOMISH CO WA — 168-A3
LOGGING 1600 RD
COWLITZ CO WA — 118-A3
COWLITZ CO WA — 189-D1
LOGIE TRAIL RD
MULTNOMAH CO OR — 192-A6
LOGSDEN RD
LINCOLN CO OR — 133-A1
LINCOLN CO OR — 206-D2
SILETZ OR — 206-D2
S LOIS DR
SPOKANE CO WA — 246-B7
W LOLAH BUTTE RD
DESCHUTES CO OR — 216-B7
LOLO BUTTE RD
DESCHUTES CO OR — 216-C6
LOLO PASS RD
BENEWAH CO ID — 115-A3
CLACKAMAS CO OR — 201-D4
HOOD RIVER CO OR — 202-A3
LOMBARD DR NW
PIERCE CO WA — 181-B1
N LOMBARD ST
PORTLAND OR — 192-B6
N LOMBARD ST U.S.-30
PORTLAND OR — 192-B7
PORTLAND OR — 308-B4
PORTLAND OR — 309-E5
NE LOMBARD ST U.S.-30
PORTLAND OR — 309-G5
PORTLAND OR — 310-B6
LOMBARDY LN
KLAMATH CO OR — 235-C5
LONDON DR
HOOD RIVER CO OR — 202-C2
LONDON RD
LANE CO OR — 219-D1
LONDON HILL RD
DOUGLAS CO OR — 219-C4
S LONE ELDER RD
CLACKAMAS CO OR — 199-C7
LONE FIR RD
BAKER CO OR — 131-A3
LONE LAKE RD
ISLAND CO WA — 167-D7
ISLAND CO WA — 170-D1
LONE MOUNTAIN RD
JOSEPHINE CO OR — 233-A6
LONE OAK RD
COWLITZ CO WA — 302-F3
LONGVIEW WA — 302-F3
LONE OAK RD SE
SALEM OR — 324-G7
LONE PINE DR
LANE CO OR — 210-A7

LONE PINE RD
CROOK CO OR — 213-A4
JACKSON CO OR — 336-G9
JEFFERSON CO OR — 213-A3
MEDFORD OR — 336-G9
LONE PINE-DORA RD
COOS CO OR — 140-C2
LONE PINE SCHOOL RD
CROOK CO OR — 213-A3
LONE ROCK RD
MORO OR — 127-C2
SHERMAN CO OR — 127-C2
LONEROCK RD
GILLIAM CO OR — 128-B3
WHEELER CO OR — 128-B3
LONE STAR RD NW
POLK CO OR — 204-C3
LONE YEW RD
LEWIS CO WA — 187-D5
LONG AV
KELSO WA — 303-C8
LONG RD
KLICKITAT CO WA — 196-D2
NW LONG RD
WASHINGTON CO OR — 198-C1
S LONG RD
SPOKANE VALLEY WA — 351-F9
LONG CREEK RD
GRANT CO OR — 129-A3
GRANT CO OR — 137-A1
LONG HOLLOW RD
WHITMAN CO WA — 122-A1
LONG HOLLOW MARKET RD
WASCO CO OR — 127-B2
LONG JOHN MORASCH RD
WHITMAN CO WA — 122-B1
LONG LAKE RD
KLAMATH CO OR — 235-A3
LINCOLN CO WA — 114-A1
W LONG LAKE RD
SPOKANE CO WA — 114-B1
LONG LAKE RD SE
KITSAP CO WA — 174-C4
LONGMIRE LN
YAKIMA CO WA — 243-A3
LONG PRAIRIE RD
STEVENS CO WA — 106-B3
TILLAMOOK CO OR — 197-C3
LONG RIDGE RD
DOUGLAS CO OR — 141-A2
LONG VALLEY RD
DOUGLAS CO OR — 219-C7
LONGVIEW RD
ADAMS CO ID — 251-C5
LONGWOOD DR
REEDSPORT OR — 218-C2
LONSDALE AV
CITY OF NORTH VANCOUVER BC — 255-B3
DIST OF NORTH VANCOUVER BC — 255-B3
LONSETH RD
WHATCOM CO WA — 158-B5
LOOK RD
KITTITAS CO WA — 241-B5
LOOKINGGLASS RD
DOUGLAS CO OR — 334-A8
ROSEBURG OR — 334-A8
WINSTON OR — 221-A5
NW LOOKINGGLASS RD
WINSTON OR — 221-B6
LOOKINGGLASS-BROCKWAY RD
DOUGLAS CO OR — 221-A5
LOOKOUT RD
KLAMATH CO OR — 151-A1
N LOOKOUT RD
DESCHUTES CO OR — 216-B7
LOOKOUT MOUNTAIN RD
DESCHUTES CO OR — 216-B7
MARION CO OR — 134-A1
UNION CO OR — 130-B1
LOOKOUT POINT RD
SELAH WA — 243-B6
LOOMIS LN
VALLEY CO ID — 252-D2
LOOMIS-OROVILLE RD
OKANOGAN CO WA — 104-C1
LOOMIS TRAIL RD
WHATCOM CO WA — 158-C4
LOON LAKE RD
DOUGLAS CO OR — 140-C1
LOON LAKE-MCVAY PIT RD
STEVENS CO WA — 106-B3
LOON LAKE SOUTHSIDE RD
STEVENS CO WA — 106-B3
STEVENS CO WA — 114-B1
LOOP RD
JACKSON CO OR — 226-C5
SKAMANIA CO WA — 194-D4
STEVENS CO WA — 114-A1
N LOOP RD
BENEWAH CO ID — 129-A1
SE LOOP RD
YAMHILL CO OR — 198-B7
LOOSLEY RD
KLAMATH CO OR — 231-C2
LOPER AV
PRINEVILLE OR — 213-D5
LORAINE AV
DIST OF NORTH VANCOUVER BC — 254-H2
LORANE HWY
EUGENE OR — 329-C14
LANE CO OR — 133-B3
LANE CO OR — 215-A4
LANE CO OR — 329-C14
LORD ST
KELSO WA — 303-D7
LORDS LAKE LOOP RD
JEFFERSON CO WA — 109-C1
LORENZ RD KPS
PIERCE CO WA — 181-A2
LORIMER RD
BRITISH COLUMBIA BC — 159-B5
LOST HWY W
KITSAP CO WA — 173-D4
LOST CREEK RD
COLUMBIA CO OR — 189-A4
DOUGLAS CO OR — 223-B4
SKAMANIA CO WA — 193-B3
LOSTINE RIVER RD
WALLOWA CO OR — 130-C2
LOST LAKE RD
HOOD RIVER CO OR — 195-B7
HOOD RIVER CO OR — 202-A1
MASON CO WA — 179-D6
MASON CO WA — 180-A3
SHELTON WA — 180-A3
LOST MTN RD
CLALLAM CO OR — 109-C1

LOST PRAIRIE RD
WALLOWA CO OR — 122-C3
LOST RIVER RD
OKANOGAN CO WA — 104-A2
LOST VALLEY RD
WHEELER CO OR — 128-B3
LOTZGESELL RD
CLALLAM CO WA — 166-A5
CLALLAM CO WA — 262-A3
NE LOUCKS RD
JEFFERSON CO OR — 208-C1
LOUDEN RD
MULTNOMAH CO OR — 200-D2
LOUGHEED HWY Rt#-7
BRITISH COLUMBIA BC — 94-B3
COQUITLAM BC — 157-A5
DISTRICT OF BURNABY BC — 156-D4
DISTRICT OF BURNABY BC — 255-G12
DISTRICT OF COQUITLAM BC — 156-D4
DISTRICT OF KENT BC — 94-B3
DISTRICT OF MISSION BC — 94-B3
MAPLE RIDGE BC — 94-B3
MAPLE RIDGE BC — 157-D6
PITT MEADOWS BC — 157-B4
PORT COQUITLAM BC — 157-B4
LOUIE FAVE RD
WASHINGTON CO ID — 139-B1
LOUISIANA ST
LONGVIEW WA — 303-A8
NW LOVEJOY ST
PORTLAND OR — 312-D4
PORTLAND OR — 313-F4
LOVE LAKE RD
LANE CO OR — 210-A5
LOVELL VALLEY RD
BENEWAH CO ID — 115-A3
LOVE RESERVOIR RD
BAKER CO OR — 138-C1
LOVES AV
WOODLAND WA — 192-B1
NE LOVGREN RD E
KITSAP CO WA — 174-D1
NE LOVGREN RD W
KITSAP CO WA — 174-C1
LOWDEN GARDENA RD
WALLA WALLA CO WA — 121-C3
W LOWELL AV
SPOKANE CO WA — 246-A2
SPOKANE CO WA — 346-A12
LOWELL LARIMER RD
SNOHOMISH CO WA — 269-G5
LOWELL-LARIMER RD
SNOHOMISH CO WA — 171-C4
SNOHOMISH CO WA — 269-H7
E LOWELL-LARIMER RD Rt#-96
SNOHOMISH CO WA — 171-D4
LOWELL-SNOHOMISH RIVER RD
EVERETT WA — 269-F1
SNOHOMISH CO WA — 171-D3
SNOHOMISH CO WA — 269-H4
LOWER ANTELOPE RD Rt#-293
ANTELOPE OR — 127-C3
WASCO CO OR — 127-C3
LOWER BENCH RD
GEM CO ID — 139-B3
SW LOWER BEND RD
JEFFERSON CO OR — 208-A5
LOWER BOONES FERRY RD
LAKE OSWEGO OR — 199-B4
TUALATIN OR — 199-B4
SW LOWER BOONES FERRY RD
DURHAM OR — 199-B4
TUALATIN OR — 199-B4
LOWER BRIDGE RD
DESCHUTES CO OR — 212-B3
SW LOWER BRIDGE RD
JEFFERSON CO OR — 212-B2
LOWER BURNETT RD E
PIERCE CO WA — 182-D5
LOWER COVE RD
UNION CO OR — 130-B2
LOWER COW CREEK RD
MALHEUR CO OR — 146-C2
MALHEUR CO OR — 147-A3
LOWER CRAB CREEK RD
GRANT CO WA — 120-B1
LOWER DEADMAN RD
GARFIELD CO WA — 122-B1
LOWER DEADWOOD CREEK RD
LANE CO OR — 133-A2
LOWER DIAMOND RD
WALLOWA CO OR — 130-B1
LOWER DRY CREEK RD
WALLA WALLA CO WA — 121-C3
LOWER EIGHTMILE RD
THE DALLES OR — 196-D7
WASCO CO OR — 127-B2
WASCO CO OR — 196-D7
LOWER ELWHA RD
CLALLAM CO WA — 165-A2
LOWER FORDS CREEK RD
CLEARWATER CO ID — 123-C2
LOWER FOURMILE RD
COOS CO OR — 224-B1
LOWER FOX HOLLOW RD
LANE CO OR — 215-A4
LOWER GRAVE CREEK RD
JOSEPHINE CO OR — 149-A1
JOSEPHINE CO OR — 229-A1
LOWER GREEN CANYON RD
KITTITAS CO OR — 241-A4
LOWER HIGHLAND RD
CLACKAMAS CO OR — 200-A6
LOWER HOGEYE RD
COLUMBIA CO OR — 122-A2
LOWER HOH RD
JEFFERSON CO WA — 169-C5
SE LOWER ISLAND RD
YAMHILL CO OR — 204-D1
LOWER JOE CREEK RD
CHELAN CO WA — 236-B1
LOWER KEITH RD
CITY OF NORTH VANCOUVER BC — 255-B5
LOWER KLAMATH RD
SISKIYOU CO CA — 150-C3
LOWER KLAMATH LAKE RD
KLAMATH CO OR — 150-C3
KLAMATH CO OR — 235-C7
LOWER LITTLE SHASTA RD
SISKIYOU CO CA — 150-A3
LOWER MONITOR RD
Sunnyslope WA — 238-D3
LOWER MONUMENTAL RD
WALLA WALLA CO WA — 121-C2
LOWER NEHALEM RD
CLATSOP CO OR — 125-A1
LOWER NORWAY RD
COOS CO OR — 220-D6

STREET — City State Page-Grid

LOWER PACK RIVER RD
BONNER CO ID 244-B1
LOWER PEOH POINT RD
KITTITAS CO WA 240-C2
LOWER PLEASANT RIDGE RD
CANYON CO ID 147-B1
LOWER RIVER RD Rt#-501
CLARK CO WA 304-A1
VANCOUVER WA 304-A1
NW LOWER RIVER RD
CLARK CO WA 192-B4
NW LOWER RIVER RD Rt#-501
CLARK CO WA 192-B5
CLARK CO WA 304-A1
KITTITAS CO WA 241-C5
VANCOUVER WA 192-B5
VANCOUVER WA 304-A1
LOWER SMITH RIVER RD
DOUGLAS CO OR 214-B7
DOUGLAS CO OR 218-D1
LOWER SUMAS MOUNTAIN RD
DISTRICT OF ABBOTSFORD BC .. 102-B1
LOWER SUNNYSLOPE RD
Sunnyslope WA 238-D3
LOWER TAMMANY CREEK RD
NEZ PERCE CO ID 250-D5
LOWER WAITSBURG RD
WALLA WALLA CO WA 345-C5
WALLA WALLA CO WA 121-C1
WALLA WALLA CO WA 345-C5
LOWER WAITSBURG RD Rt#-124
WALLA WALLA CO WA 122-A2
LOWER WHETSTONE RD
COLUMBIA CO WA 122-A2
LOWER WOLF CREEK RD
JOSEPHINE CO OR 229-A1
LOW LEVEL RD
CITY OF NORTH VANCOUVER BC .. 255-C7
LOYAL AV NW
SEATTLE WA 272-D1
LOZIER LN
JACKSON CO OR 336-A13
MEDFORD OR 336-A13
L SCHULTHEIS RD
WHITMAN CO WA 250-B3
SW LUANA BEACH RD
KING CO WA 175-A6
NE LUCIA FALLS RD
CLARK CO WA 193-B2
S LUCILE ST
SEATTLE WA 281-J6
SEATTLE WA 282-A6
LUCKENBILL RD
WALLA WALLA CO WA 121-B1
LUCKIAMUTE RD
BENTON CO OR 133-A1
LUCKY SEVEN COW CAMP RD
MALHEUR CO OR 154-C2
LUCKY STRIKE RD
JOSEPHINE CO OR 233-B7
LUCY REEDER RD
MULTNOMAH CO OR 192-A5
LUDEMAN RD NW
DOUGLAS CO WA 236-D5
LUDLOW BAY RD
JEFFERSON CO WA 170-B3
LUDLOW PARADISE RD
JEFFERSON CO WA 170-B3
E LUDLOW RIDGE RD
JEFFERSON CO WA 170-B3
LUFT RD
WHITMAN CO WA 122-B1
SW LUKAS RD
WASHINGTON CO OR 198-D3
LUMMI SHORE DR
WHATCOM CO WA 158-C7
LUMMI SHORE RD
WHATCOM CO WA 158-C7
WHATCOM CO WA 160-C1
LUMMI VIEW DR
WHATCOM CO WA 160-C1
LUNBLAD
PIERCE CO WA 182-B4
E LUNCEFORD AV
COEUR D'ALENE ID 355-F6
SE LUND AV
East Port Orchard WA 174-B4
LUND RD
SNOHOMISH CO WA 168-B3
LUNDEEN RD SW
THURSTON CO WA 184-A4
LUNDGREN MILL RD
DESCHUTES CO OR 211-D4
LUNDY RD
DESCHUTES CO OR 211-D4
NW LUOTO RD Rt#-308
KITSAP CO WA 170-B7
LUSK CREEK RD
SKAMANIA CO WA 195-B1
LUSTED RD
CLACKAMAS CO OR 200-C3
SE LUSTED RD
GRESHAM OR 200-B2
MULTNOMAH CO OR 200-B2
LUTZ LN
WASCO CO OR 196-B7
L WEST RD
WHITMAN CO WA 249-B2
N LYLE AV
East Wenatchee Bench WA 239-A4
LYLE GOLDENDALE RD
KLICKITAT CO WA 127-B1
LYLE SNOWDEN RD
KLICKITAT CO WA 196-B3
LYMAN HAMILTON RD
SKAGIT CO WA 161-D5
LYMAN LAKE-MOSES MOUNTAIN RD
OKANOGAN CO WA 105-A3
LYNCH RD
MASON CO WA 180-B4
LYNN BLVD
CROOK CO OR 213-D5
PRINEVILLE OR 213-D5
LYNN ST
BELLINGHAM WA 258-B4
E LYNN ST
SEATTLE WA 278-C1
W LYNN ST
SEATTLE WA 276-C1
LYNN VALLEY RD
CITY OF NORTH VANCOUVER BC .. 255-D4
DIST OF NORTH VANCOUVER BC .. 255-D4
LYNWOOD RD
CANYON CO ID 147-B1
LYNWOOD CENTER RD NE
KITSAP CO WA 271-H4
LYNX HOLLOW RD
LANE CO OR 215-B6

LYON ST U.S.-20
ALBANY OR 326-C8
E LYONS AV
SPOKANE WA 349-A1
Town and Country WA 349-A1
W LYONS AV
Town and Country WA 348-J1
Town and Country WA 349-A1
LYONS DR S
PIERCE CO WA 181-C7
LYONS RD
CLARK CO WA 118-A3
CLARK CO WA 192-C1
KITTITAS CO WA 241-C5
S LYONS RD
AIRWAY HEIGHTS WA 246-A4
CLACKAMAS CO OR 200-A6
LYONS FERRY RD
WALLA WALLA CO WA 121-C2
LYONS-MILL CITY DR
LINN CO OR 134-A1
W LYRE RIVER RD
CLALLAM CO WA 164-B5
LYTLE BLVD
MALHEUR CO OR 139-A3

M

M AV
ANACORTES WA 259-G2
M ST U.S.-101
CRESCENT CITY CA 148-B3
S M ST
TACOMA WA 295-F2
SE M ST
GRANTS PASS OR 335-F10
SW M ST
GRANTS PASS OR 335-E9
M ST NE
AUBURN WA 182-C1
M ST SE
AUBURN WA 182-C1
MABEE MINES RD
SKAMANIA CO WA 194-A6
MABLES CT
LEWIS CO WA 187-D2
MABTON-BICKLETON RD
MABTON WA 120-B3
YAKIMA CO WA 120-A3
MABTON-SUNNYSIDE RD
SUNNYSIDE WA 120-B2
YAKIMA CO WA 120-B2
MABTON-SUNNYSIDE RD Rt#-241
SUNNYSIDE WA 120-B3
YAKIMA CO WA 120-B3
SW MACADAM AV Rt#-43
MULTNOMAH CO OR 321-G1
PORTLAND OR 317-F6
PORTLAND OR 321-G1
MACARTHUR BLVD
VANCOUVER WA 306-D6
VANCOUVER WA 307-E6
MACDONALD ST
VANCOUVER BC 254-B14
N MACHIAS RD
LAKE STEVENS WA 110-C1
SNOHOMISH CO WA 110-C1
S MACHIAS RD
SNOHOMISH CO WA 171-D2
SNOHOMISH CO WA 110-C1
SNOHOMISH CO WA 171-D2
MACHIAS CUTOFF
SNOHOMISH CO WA 110-C1
SNOHOMISH CO WA 171-D2
MAC HOKE RD
UMATILLA CO OR 129-A1
MACK RD
ADAMS CO WA 122-A1
MACKENZIE ST
VANCOUVER BC 156-B5
VANCOUVER BC 254-B14
MACKSBURG RD
CLACKAMAS CO OR 199-C7
MACLEAY RD SE
Four Corners WA 325-E2
MARION CO OR 205-A6
MARION CO OR 325-H3
SALEM OR 325-F2
MACLURE RD
DISTRICT OF MATSQUI BC 102-B1
E MACMAHAN RD
SPOKANE CO WA 247-A2
S MADELIA ST
SPOKANE WA 349-C9
MADER RD
WHITMAN CO WA 122-B1
WHITMAN CO WA 249-B2
MADISON AV
CORVALLIS OR 327-G10
MADISON AV NE
KITSAP CO WA 174-D1
Winslow WA 174-D1
N MADISON RD
SPOKANE CO WA 246-D1
NE MADISON RD
KITSAP CO WA 174-B1
S MADISON RD
OKANOGAN CO WA 104-B3
MADISON ST
Altamont OR 339-B11
EVERETT WA 268-C2
EVERETT WA 269-E3
LAFAYETTE OR 198-B7
SEATTLE WA 277-J6
SEATTLE WA 278-A6
E MADISON ST
CALDWELL ID 147-B1
SEATTLE WA 278-C5
SEATTLE WA 279-F2
N MADISON ST Rt#-82
WALLOWA OR 130-B1
SE MADISON ST
PORTLAND OR 313-H7
SW MADISON ST
PORTLAND OR 313-E6
MADISON ST NE
SALEM OR 322-J10
SALEM OR 323-A11
MADRAS-PRINEVILLE HWY U.S.-26
CROOK CO OR 213-C3
JEFFERSON CO OR 213-C3
PRINEVILLE OR 213-C3
SE MADRAS-PRNEVLLE HWY U.S.-26
JEFFERSON CO OR 208-C7
JEFFERSON CO OR 213-B2

SW MADRAS-PRNEVLLE HWY U.S.-26
JEFFERSON CO OR 208-C6
MADRONA AV S
SALEM OR 324-E3
MADRONA AV SE
SALEM OR 324-H4
SALEM OR 325-A4
NE MADRONA BLVD
KITSAP CO WA 170-C2
MADRONA DR
DISTRICT OF NORTH SAANICH BC . 159-B2
SEATTLE WA 279-E5
MADRONA RD SW
KITSAP CO WA 174-B6
MADRONA WY
Colby WA 167-B4
NE MADRONE AV
Colby WA 271-G12
NE MADRONE ST
GRANTS PASS OR 335-G8
MAE VALLEY RD
GRANT CO WA 242-A3
NE MAFFET RD
MULTNOMAH CO OR 200-D1
E MAGNESIUM RD
SPOKANE WA 346-J12
SPOKANE WA 347-B12
SPOKANE WA 347-B12
Town and Country WA 346-J12
MAGNOLIA BLVD W
SEATTLE WA 272-B7
SEATTLE WA 276-B1
MAGNOLIA BRDG
SEATTLE WA 276-E2
SEATTLE WA 277-E2
MAGNOLIA WY W
SEATTLE WA 276-E2
MAGNUS-LARSON
PIERCE CO WA 182-A4
MAGPIE GRADE
NEZ PERCE CO ID 123-B2
MAGUIRE GULCH RD
ASOTIN CO WA 250-A5
MAHNCKE RD KPS
PIERCE CO WA 181-A3
MAHOGANY RD
MALHEUR CO OR 146-C2
MAHOGANY GAP RD
MALHEUR CO OR 147-A2
MAHONY RD NE
MARION CO OR 205-A2
MAIDEN LN
WENATCHEE WA 238-D4
MAIL ROUTE RD
ASOTIN CO WA 250-A5
MAIN AV
LA CROSSE WA 122-A1
PINEHURST ID 115-C2
SHOSHONE CO ID 115-C2
SUMNER WA 182-B3
WHITMAN CO WA 122-A1
MAIN AV Rt#-5
SAINT MARIES ID 248-C7
MAIN AV Rt#-508
MORTON WA 118-B2
MAIN AV U.S.-101
TILLAMOOK OR 197-B2
TILLAMOOK OR 197-B2
E MAIN AV
BREWSTER WA 104-B3
CHEWELAH WA 106-B3
PIERCE CO WA 182-B3
PUYALLUP WA 182-B3
SUMNER WA 182-B3
E MAIN AV U.S.-2
LINCOLN CO WA 113-B1
WILBUR WA 113-B1
N MAIN AV
GRESHAM OR 200-B2
KLICKITAT CO WA 195-D4
WARRENTON OR 188-B2
WHITE SALMON WA 195-D4
S MAIN AV
MORROW CO OR 128-C1
WARRENTON OR 188-B2
W MAIN AV
BREWSTER WA 104-B3
OKANOGAN CO WA 104-B3
W MAIN AV U.S.-2
WILBUR WA 113-B1
MAIN AV E
SOAP LAKE WA 112-C2
MAIN AV E U.S.-730
IRRIGON OR 128-C1
S MAIN AV E
IRRIGON OR 128-C1
MAIN AV S Rt#-515
RENTON WA 175-C5
MAIN AV W
GRANT CO WA 112-C2
SOAP LAKE WA 112-C2
S MAIN AV W
IRRIGON OR 128-C1
MORROW CO OR 128-C1
MAIN RD
BREWSTER WA 104-B3
LEBANON OR 133-C1
OKANOGAN CO WA 104-B3
W MAIN RD
COTTAGE GROVE OR 215-B7
LANE CO OR 215-B7
MAIN ST
ALBANY OR 326-D7
AUMSVILLE OR 133-C1
BAKER CITY OR 138-B1
BELLEVUE OR 175-C2
BONNERS FERRY ID 107-B2
BOTHELL WA 171-C6
BROWNSVILLE OR 210-C2
CANYON CITY OR 137-B2
CHEHALIS WA 299-D12
CHELAN CO WA 238-C3
CONCONULLY WA 104-B2
COTTONWOOD ID 123-B2
CRAIGMONT ID 123-C1
Crowfoot OR 133-C1
CULDESAC ID 123-B2
DIST OF NORTH VANCOUVER BC .. 255-E7
DOUGLAS CO OR 225-B3
DUFUR OR 127-C2
ECHO OR 129-A1
EDMONDS WA 171-A5
ELLENSBURG WA 241-B6
FERNDALE WA 158-C6
FOREST GROVE OR 198-B1
Freeland WA 170-D1
GRANGER WA 120-A2
HALFWAY OR 131-A3

MAIN ST
IONE OR 128-B2
KITTITAS CO WA 241-C6
KLAMATH FALLS OR 338-E7
KLICKITAT CO WA 119-A3
LAKE STEVENS WA 171-A5
LAPWAI ID 123-B2
LEWISTON ID 250-B4
LINN CO OR 133-C1
LYNDEN WA 102-B1
MABTON WA 120-B3
MALIN OR 151-A3
MARION CO OR 205-C3
MILTON-FREEWATER OR 121-C3
MONROE WA 110-C1
MOUNT VERNON WA 260-C12
NEZ PERCE CO ID 123-B2
PACIFIC CO WA 117-A1
PECK ID 123-B2
PIERCE CO WA 182-B4
POLK CO OR 207-C2
RIDDLE OR 225-B2
RUFUS OR 127-C1
SAINT PAUL OR 198-D7
SCIO OR 133-C1
SODAVILLE OR 133-C2
STEVENS CO WA 106-A3
SUMNER WA 182-B3
TROY ID 123-B2
UNION GAP WA 120-A2
UNION GAP WA 243-C7
VANCOUVER BC 156-B5
VANCOUVER BC 254-H13
VANCOUVER BC 305-G3
WAITSBURG WA 122-A2
WARDNER ID 115-C2
WINTHROP WA 104-A2
YAKIMA CO WA 120-A2
MAIN ST Rt#-3
BRITISH COLUMBIA BC 104-C1
JULIAETTA ID 123-B1
KENDRICK ID 123-B1
OSOYOOS BC 104-C1
MAIN ST Rt#-5
SAINT MARIES ID 248-D7
MAIN ST Rt#-6
PE ELL WA 117-B2
MAIN ST Rt#-7
BAKER CITY OR 138-B1
MAIN ST Rt#-8
TROY ID 123-A1
MAIN ST Rt#-9
SKAGIT CO WA 168-C2
MAIN ST Rt#-19
CANYON CO ID 147-B1
GREENLEAF ID 147-B1
MAIN ST Rt#-31
PAISLEY OR 151-C1
MAIN ST Rt#-39
KLAMATH FALLS OR 338-C8
MAIN ST Rt#-44
CANYON CO ID 147-B1
MAIN ST Rt#-55
CASCADE ID 252-D6
MARSING ID 147-B1
OWYHEE CO ID 147-B1
MAIN ST Rt#-62
CRAIGMONT ID 123-B2
MAIN ST Rt#-74
HEPPNER OR 128-C2
LEXINGTON OR 128-C2
MAIN ST Rt#-86
RICHLAND OR 139-A1
MAIN ST Rt#-99
CANYONVILLE OR 225-C3
DOUGLAS CO OR 225-C3
PHOENIX OR 234-B2
MAIN ST Rt#-124
WAITSBURG WA 122-A2
MAIN ST Rt#-126
LANE CO OR 330-H7
MAIN ST Rt#-203
DUVALL WA 110-C1
MAIN ST Rt#-206
HEPPNER OR 128-C2
MAIN ST Rt#-212
OREGON CITY OR 199-D4
MAIN ST Rt#-214
MOUNT ANGEL OR 205-C3
MAIN ST Rt#-219
SAINT PAUL OR 198-D7
MAIN ST Rt#-226
LINN CO OR 133-C1
LYONS OR 134-A1
SCIO OR 133-C1
MAIN ST Rt#-231
LINCOLN CO WA 114-A2
MAIN ST Rt#-237
COVE OR 130-B2
UNION CO OR 130-B2
MAIN ST Rt#-260
WASHTUCNA WA 121-C1
MAIN ST Rt#-261
WASHTUCNA WA 121-C1
MAIN ST Rt#-409
CATHLAMET WA 117-B3
MAIN ST Rt#-524
EDMONDS WA 171-A5
MAIN ST Rt#-544
NOOKSACK WA 102-B1
MAIN ST U.S.-12
DAYTON WA 122-B2
LEWISTON ID 250-C4
POMEROY WA 122-B2
MAIN ST U.S.-20
BENTON CO OR 133-B1
LEBANON OR 133-C1
LINN CO OR 133-C1
MALHEUR CO OR 139-A3
NYSSA OR 139-A3
PHILOMATH OR 133-B1
SWEET HOME OR 133-C1
MAIN ST U.S.-30
BAKER CITY OR 138-B1
MAIN ST U.S.-95
BONNERS FERRY ID 107-B2
FERDINAND ID 123-B3
HOMEDALE ID 147-A1
IDAHO CO ID 123-B3
MAIN ST U.S.-97
DORRIS CA 150-B3
MORO OR 127-C2
OKANOGAN CO WA 104-C1
OROVILLE WA 104-C1
E MAIN ST
ALMIRA WA 237-D7

E MAIN ST
ASHLAND OR 337-E8
AUBURN WA 182-C1
BATTLE GROUND WA 193-A3
CANYON CITY OR 137-B2
CHELAN WA 238-D3
Colby WA 271-H12
COTTAGE GROVE OR 215-B7
ELMA WA 179-B7
FERNDALE WA 158-A6
GRANDVIEW WA 120-B3
HERMISTON OR 129-A1
HILLSBORO OR 198-D1
JACKSON CO OR 337-G8
LEWISTON ID 250-C4
LINCOLN CO OR 237-D7
LONG CREEK OR 137-A1
LYNDEN WA 102-B1
LYNDEN WA 158-D4
MEDFORD OR 336-F12
MONMOUTH OR 204-B7
MONROE WA 110-C1
PULLMAN WA 249-B5
ROGUE RIVER OR 229-D6
Sunnyslope WA 238-D3
WALLA WALLA WA 345-B7
YAKIMA CO WA 120-B3
YAMHILL OR 198-D1
E MAIN ST Rt#-13
GRANGEVILLE ID 123-C3
IDAHO CO ID 123-C3
E MAIN ST Rt#-18
SHERIDAN OR 125-B3
WILLAMINA OR 125-A3
E MAIN ST Rt#-23
HARRINGTON WA 113-C2
E MAIN ST Rt#-27
GARFIELD WA 114-C3
E MAIN ST Rt#-51
MONMOUTH OR 204-B7
E MAIN ST Rt#-211
MOLALLA OR 126-A3
E MAIN ST Rt#-238
MEDFORD OR 336-D12
E MAIN ST Rt#-240
YAMHILL OR 198-B5
E MAIN ST Rt#-270
PULLMAN WA 249-B5
E MAIN ST Rt#-272
PALOUSE WA 249-C1
E MAIN ST U.S.-12
COLUMBIA CO WA 122-A2
DAYTON WA 122-A2
LEWISTON ID 250-C4
E MAIN ST U.S.-26
CANYON CO ID 147-B1
GREENLEAF ID 147-B1
GRANT CO OR 137-B2
JOHN DAY OR 137-B2
E MAIN ST U.S.-95
WEISER ID 139-A2
E MAIN ST U.S.-395
MOUNT VERNON OR 137-A2
N MAIN ST
BOARDMAN OR 128-C1
EAST WENATCHEE WA 239-A4
East Wenatchee Bench WA 239-A4
FALLS CITY OR 125-B3
MABTON WA 120-B3
MERIDIAN ID 253-A3
MILTON-FREEWATER OR 121-C3
MOSCOW ID 249-C5
PENDLETON OR 129-B1
PRINEVILLE OR 213-D4
SPANGLE WA 114-C2
TOLEDO OR 206-C4
N MAIN ST Rt#-47
BANKS OR 125-B1
N MAIN ST Rt#-51
INDEPENDENCE OR 204-B7
POLK CO OR 204-B7
N MAIN ST Rt#-82
JOSEPH OR 130-C2
WALLOWA CO OR 130-C2
N MAIN ST Rt#-99
ASHLAND OR 337-C6
CANYONVILLE OR 225-C3
JACKSON CO OR 337-C6
PHOENIX OR 234-B2
N MAIN ST Rt#-203
UNION OR 130-B2
N MAIN ST Rt#-214
MOUNT ANGEL OR 205-C3
N MAIN ST Rt#-231
SPRINGDALE WA 106-B3
N MAIN ST Rt#-240
NEWBERG OR 198-D5
N MAIN ST U.S.-95
LATAH CO ID 249-C4
MOSCOW ID 249-C5
N MAIN ST U.S.-195
COLFAX WA 122-C1
N MAIN ST U.S.-395
COLVILLE WA 106-A2
NW MAIN ST
SHERWOOD OR 199-A4
S MAIN ST
BOARDMAN OR 128-C1
DALLAS OR 204-A6
FALLS CITY OR 125-B3
INDEPENDENCE OR 204-A6
JEFFERSON OR 207-D3
KLAMATH CO OR 150-C3
MARION CO OR 205-C3
MARION CO OR 207-D3
MERIDIAN ID 253-A3
MERRILL OR 150-C2
MILTON-FREEWATER OR 121-C3
MOUNT ANGEL OR 205-C3
TOLEDO OR 206-C4
S MAIN ST Rt#-11
MILTON-FREEWATER OR 121-C3
S MAIN ST Rt#-18
WILLAMINA OR 125-A3
S MAIN ST Rt#-19
CONDON OR 128-A2
S MAIN ST Rt#-47
BANKS OR 125-B1
WASHINGTON CO OR 125-B1
S MAIN ST Rt#-51
INDEPENDENCE OR 204-B7
S MAIN ST Rt#-82
JOSEPH OR 130-C2
S MAIN ST Rt#-99
CANYONVILLE OR 225-C3
S MAIN ST Rt#-223
DALLAS OR 204-A6

S MAIN ST Rt#-237
UNION OR 130-B2
S MAIN ST U.S.-95
BONNERS FERRY ID 107-B2
S MAIN ST U.S.-195
COLFAX WA 122-C1
S MAIN ST U.S.-395
COLVILLE WA 106-A2
SE MAIN ST
MILWAUKIE OR 321-J2
ROSEBURG OR 334-F8
SW MAIN ST
PORTLAND OR 313-E6
W MAIN ST
ALMIRA WA 237-D7
AUBURN WA 182-B1
BATTLE GROUND WA 193-A3
BOISE ID 253-C2
CENTRALIA WA 299-E4
COTTAGE GROVE OR 215-B7
ELMA WA 179-B7
GRANDVIEW WA 120-B3
JACKSON CO OR 234-A1
JACKSON CO OR 336-A12
KELSO WA 303-C8
LANE CO OR 215-B7
LONG CREEK OR 137-A1
LYNDEN WA 158-D4
MARION CO OR 205-C4
MEDFORD OR 234-A1
MEDFORD OR 336-C12
MONMOUTH OR 204-B7
MONROE WA 110-C1
PULLMAN WA 249-B5
ROGUE RIVER OR 229-D6
SANDPOINT ID 244-A2
SILVERTON OR 205-C4
SNOHOMISH CO WA 110-C1
WALLA WALLA WA 344-J8
WALLA WALLA WA 345-A8
WHATCOM CO WA 158-D4
WHITMAN CO WA 249-A5
WILLAMINA OR 125-A3
W MAIN ST Rt#-13
GRANGEVILLE ID 123-C3
IDAHO CO ID 123-C3
W MAIN ST Rt#-18
SHERIDAN OR 125-B3
W MAIN ST Rt#-27
GARFIELD WA 114-C3
W MAIN ST Rt#-44
CANYON CO ID 147-B1
MIDDLETON ID 147-B1
W MAIN ST Rt#-47
CARLTON OR 198-B6
W MAIN ST Rt#-99
CANYONVILLE OR 225-C3
W MAIN ST Rt#-211
CLACKAMAS CO OR 126-A3
MOLALLA OR 126-A3
W MAIN ST Rt#-213
SILVERTON OR 205-C4
W MAIN ST Rt#-502
BATTLE GROUND WA 192-D3
BATTLE GROUND WA 193-A3
W MAIN ST U.S.-12
DAYTON WA 122-A2
W MAIN ST U.S.-26
MOUNT VERNON OR 137-A2
W MAIN ST U.S.-95
WEISER ID 139-A2
W MAIN ST U.S.-395
GRANT CO OR 137-B2
JOHN DAY OR 137-B2
MAIN ST E
SUMNER WA 182-B3
MAIN ST N
COUPEVILLE WA 167-B4
MAIN ST S
MONTESANO WA 178-D7
MAIN ST S Rt#-20
OMAK WA 104-C3
MAIN EAST WEST RD
MODOC CO CA 151-A3
MAIN LINE RD
CLALLAM CO WA 162-C2
MAINLINE RD
MASON CO WA 180-A2
S MAITLAND AV
PASCO WA 343-H9
MAJOR CREEK RD
KLICKITAT CO WA 196-C4
MAKI RD
VALLEY CO ID 251-C7
MAKINSTER RD
TILLAMOOK CO OR 197-B2
W MALAGA RD
CHELAN CO WA 239-A5
MALAGA ALCOA HWY
Appleyard WA 239-A5
CHELAN CO WA 239-A5
MALAVIEW ST
TOWN OF SIDNEY BC 159-C2
MALCOM MCCLARTY
PIERCE CO WA 182-A4
MALDEN RD
MALDEN WA 114-C3
WHITMAN CO WA 114-C3
NE MALHEUR AV
ROSEBURG OR 334-G6
MALHEUR CAVE RD
HARNEY CO OR 146-A2
MALHEUR LINE RD
BAKER CO OR 138-C2
MALHEUR RESERVOIR RD
BAKER CO OR 138-B2
MALHEUR CO OR 138-B2
MALIN LP
KLAMATH CO OR 151-A2
N MALIN RD
KLAMATH CO OR 151-A2
MALLIS LANDING RD
PACIFIC CO WA 117-A1
MALONEY MOUNTAIN RD
COLUMBIA CO WA 122-B2
MALPASS RD
LINN CO OR 210-A4
MALTBY RD Rt#-524
BOTHELL WA 171-C5
SNOHOMISH CO WA 171-C5
MANASTASH RD
KITTITAS CO WA 240-C2
KITTITAS CO WA 241-A6
MANDY RD
LEWIS CO WA 187-C5
MANETTE BRDG
BREMERTON WA 270-J10
BREMERTON WA 271-A10

STREET — City State Page-Grid

MANILA CREEK RD
FERRY CO WA 113-B1
MANION RD
CLATSOP CO OR 188-B4
NE MANITOU BEACH DR
KITSAP CO WA 174-D1
MANLEY RD
WHATCOM CO WA 161-B2
MANLEY RD NW
KITSAP CO WA 174-A1
MANN RD
KLAMATH CO OR 235-C6
LANE CO OR 209-D6
SKAGIT CO WA 168-A2
SNOHOMISH CO WA 110-C1
UMATILLA CO OR 129-C1
MANN CREEK RD
WASHINGTON CO ID 139-B2
MANNERS RD
LEWIS CO WA 117-B1
LEWIS CO WA 184-A4
THURSTON CO WA 184-A4
MANNERS RD SW
LEWIS CO WA 117-B1
MANNING DR
LINN CO OR 210-C1
MANNING BASIN RD
BAKER CO OR 138-C1
MANNTHEY RD
MULTNOMAH CO OR 200-D2
W MANOR PL
SEATTLE WA 272-D6
MANOR WY
SNOHOMISH CO WA 171-B4
MANSFIELD RD NE
DOUGLAS CO WA 112-C1
MANSFIELD BARKER RD
KLICKITAT CO WA 196-A5
MANSON BLVD
CHELAN CO WA 236-B2
MANSON RD
DISTRICT OF MISSION BC 94-B3
NW MANZANITA AV
GRANTS PASS OR 335-E7
MANZANITA RD NE
KITSAP CO WA 174-C1
MANZER ST
DISTRICT OF MISSION BC 94-B3
MAPLE AV
LA CONNER WA 167-D1
SNOHOMISH WA 171-D3
NE MAPLE AV
DESCHUTES CO OR 212-D5
REDMOND OR 212-D5
NW MAPLE AV
DESCHUTES CO OR 212-D5
REDMOND OR 212-D5
MAPLE AV E
PORT ORCHARD WA 271-A14
MAPLE CRES
MAPLE RIDGE BC 157-C5
MAPLE DR
GRANT CO WA 242-C2
LANE CO OR 210-A7
MAPLE RD
SNOHOMISH CO WA 171-B5
MAPLE ST
ASHLAND OR 337-B6
LONGVIEW WA 302-J8
LONGVIEW WA 303-B9
NORTH BEND OR 333-E4
SODAVILLE OR 133-C2
WENATCHEE WA 238-D4
West Wenatchee WA 238-D4
MAPLE ST Rt#-173
BRIDGEPORT WA 112-C1
DOUGLAS CO WA 112-C1
MAPLE ST Rt#-529
EVERETT WA 265-F4
E MAPLE ST
BELLINGHAM WA 258-D7
CENTRALIA WA 299-F4
YAKIMA WA 243-C6
N MAPLE ST
SPOKANE WA 348-G1
WALDPORT OR 328-D5
N MAPLE ST Rt#-47
YAMHILL CO OR 198-B4
NE MAPLE ST
PULLMAN WA 249-B5
S MAPLE ST
SPOKANE WA 348-H10
WALDPORT OR 328-D5
S MAPLE ST Rt#-47
YAMHILL OR 198-B5
MAPLE WY
YAKIMA CO WA 243-A5
MAPLE DELL RD
JACKSON CO OR 234-A7
MAPLE GROVE RD
CLACKAMAS CO OR 205-D3
POLK CO OR 133-B1
N MAPLE GROVE RD
BOISE ID 253-B2
S MAPLE GROVE RD
ADA CO ID 253-B3
BOISE ID 253-B3
CLACKAMAS CO OR 126-A3
MAPLE GULCH RD
JACKSON CO OR 230-B3
MAPLE HEIGHTS RD
EVERETT WA 268-A1
S MAPLELANE RD
CLACKAMAS CO OR 199-D5
OREGON CITY OR 199-D5
MAPLE PARK AV SE
OLYMPIA WA 296-H6
E MAPLETON RD
LANE CO OR 214-D2
MAPLETON-JCT CITY HWY
Rt#-36
LANE CO OR 132-C3
LANE CO OR 133-B2
LANE CO OR 210-A6
LANE CO OR 214-D2
MAPLE VALLEY HWY Rt#-169
LANE CO OR 175-C5
RENTON WA 175-C5
MAPLE VALLEY RD SW
THURSTON CO WA 180-B6
MAPLE VLY BLCK DIAMND RD
BLACK DIAMOND WA 110-C3
KING CO WA 110-C3
MAPLE VLY BLCK DMND RD
Rt#-169
MAPLE VALLEY WA 110-C3
MAPLE VALLEY WA 175-D7
MAPLE VALLEY WA 176-A7

MAPLEWILD AV SW
BURIEN WA 175-A5
MAPLEWOOD AV
KOOTENAI CO ID 354-D7
POST FALLS ID 354-E7
W MAPLEWOOD AV
BELLINGHAM WA 258-A2
WHATCOM CO WA 158-D7
WHATCOM CO WA 258-A2
MAPLEWOOD RD
DISTRICT OF SAANICH BC 256-J4
MAP ROCK RD
CANYON CO ID 147-B1
MARBLE RD
SKAMANIA CO WA 200-D1
W MARBLE RD
YAKIMA CO WA 243-A6
MARBLE CREEK RD
SHOSHONE CO ID 115-C3
MARBLE FRONT RD
CALDWELL ID 147-B1
MARBLE MOUNTAIN RD
JOSEPHINE CO OR 229-A7
MARBLE VALLEY SOUTH
BASIN RD
STEVENS CO WA 106-A2
MARCELLUS RD
ADAMS CO WA 113-C3
ADAMS CO WA 121-C1
RITZVILLE WA 113-C3
MARCH POINT RD
SKAGIT CO WA 160-C6
E MARCH POINT RD
SKAGIT CO WA 160-D6
S MARCH POINT RD
ANACORTES WA 160-D6
SKAGIT CO WA 160-D6
W MARCH POINT RD
ANACORTES WA 160-C6
MARCOLA RD
LANE CO OR 133-C2
LANE CO OR 210-D7
LANE CO OR 215-D1
LANE CO OR 331-D4
SPRINGFIELD OR 331-D4
MARCY LP
JOSEPHINE CO OR 229-A6
MARGARET AV
COEUR D'ALENE ID 355-F5
KOOTENAI CO ID 355-F5
MARGIN ST
ENDICOTT WA 122-B1
E MARGINAL WY S
SEATTLE WA 281-J2
SEATTLE WA 282-A7
SEATTLE WA 286-C3
TUKWILA WA 286-C3
E MARGINAL WY S Rt#-99
SEATTLE WA 281-J5
W MARGINAL WY S
SEATTLE WA 285-J1
W MARGINAL WY SW
SEATTLE WA 281-H4
SEATTLE WA 285-J1
S MARGUERITE RD
SPOKANE VALLEY WA 350-D9
W MARIE ST
PASCO WA 343-D6
MARIE CREEK RD
KOOTENAI CO ID 245-C7
W MARIGOLD ST
GARDEN CITY ID 253-B2
MARIHUGH RD
SKAGIT CO WA 161-A6
MARINA DR
WHATCOM CO WA 101-C1
W MARINA DR
MOSES LAKE WA 242-C3
MARINE DR
ANACORTES WA 259-C6
BELLINGHAM WA 258-A4
BREMERTON WA 270-E8
CITY OF NORTH VANCOUVER BC 254-J5
CITY OF SURREY BC 158-A2
CITY OF WHITE ROCK BC 158-A2
CLALLAM CO WA 262-B3
DISTRICT OF BURNABY BC 156-D5
DIST OF NORTH VANCOUVER BC 254-F4
DIST OF WEST VANCOUVER BC 156-A2
DIST OF WEST VANCOUVER BC 254-A2
NEW WESTMINSTER BC 156-C5
PORT ANGELES WA 261-E3
SKAGIT CO WA 259-C6
SNOHOMISH CO WA 168-B4
SNOHOMISH CO WA 171-C1
WHATCOM CO WA 101-C1
WHATCOM CO WA 158-C2
WHATCOM CO WA 258-A4
MARINE DR Rt#-99
DISTRICT OF WEST VANCOUVER BC 254-E4
MARINE DR U.S.-30
ASTORIA OR 300-C5
E MARINE DR
CLALLAM CO WA 262-C3
N MARINE DR
PORTLAND OR 192-B6
PORTLAND OR 304-A6
PORTLAND OR 308-E1
PORTLAND OR 309-F1
N MARINE DR Rt#-99E
PORTLAND OR 309-E1
NE MARINE DR
FAIRVIEW OR 200-A1
GRESHAM OR 200-A1
PORTLAND OR 193-A7
PORTLAND OR 200-A1
PORTLAND OR 309-H2
PORTLAND OR 310-B2
PORTLAND OR 311-H4
NW MARINE DR
TROUTDALE OR 200-B1
UNIV ENDOWMENT LANDS BC 156-A4
SE MARINE DR
VANCOUVER BC 156-C5
SW MARINE DR
UNIV ENDOWMENT LANDS BC 156-A5
VANCOUVER BC 156-B5
W MARINE DR Rt#-202
ASTORIA OR 300-A6
W MARINE DR U.S.-30
ASTORIA OR 300-B4
W MARINE DR U.S.-101
ASTORIA OR 300-A5
MARINE DR NE
SNOHOMISH CO WA 168-C7
SNOHOMISH CO WA 171-C1
MARINE WY
DISTRICT OF BURNABY BC 156-C5
NEW WESTMINSTER BC 156-C5

MARINE WY
VANCOUVER BC 156-C5
MARINER WY
COQUITLAM BC 157-A5
MARINE VIEW DR
DES MOINES WA 290-A7
OCEAN SHORES WA 298-B4
SEATTLE WA 284-D4
SEATTLE WA 285-E6
MARINEVIEW DR
LINCOLN CO OR 328-C4
MARINE VIEW DR Rt#-509
DES MOINES WA 290-A6
TACOMA WA 181-D1
TACOMA WA 182-A1
E MARINE VIEW DR
EVERETT WA 171-C1
EVERETT WA 265-F1
E MARINE VIEW DR Rt#-529
EVERETT WA 171-C1
W MARINE VIEW DR
EVERETT WA 264-D4
W MARINE VIEW DR Rt#-529
EVERETT WA 171-C1
EVERETT WA 264-D3
MARINE VIEW DR S
DES MOINES WA 175-B7
DES MOINES WA 290-A7
N MARINGO DR
SPOKANE WA 350-B3
E MARINGO RD
SPOKANE CO WA 350-C4
MARION AV
CLATSOP CO OR 301-G4
GEARHART OR 301-G4
S MARION AV
BREMERTON WA 270-F11
MARION AV N
BREMERTON WA 270-F10
MARION RD
DISTRICT OF ABBOTSFORD BC 102-B1
MARION CO OR 133-C1
MARION CO OR 325-H14
MARION ST
ALBANY OR 326-D11
CENTRALIA WA 299-G2
SALEM OR 322-J12
SALEM OR 323-A13
SEATTLE WA 277-J6
SEATTLE WA 278-A6
MARION ST Rt#-22
SALEM OR 322-H12
YAKIMA CO WA 120-A2
MARION DRAIN RD
YAKIMA CO WA 120-A2
MARION ST BRDG Rt#-22
SALEM OR 322-H12
MARK RD
CLACKAMAS CO OR 199-C7
N MARKET EXT
SPOKANE WA 349-E5
MARKET LN
UNION CO OR 130-A2
MARKET RD
SHERMAN CO OR 127-C3
E MARKET RD
OWYHEE CO ID 147-B1
MARKET ST
ANACORTES WA 259-H1
BONANZA OR 151-A2
CHEHALIS WA 299-D11
KIRKLAND WA 175-C1
KLAMATH CO OR 151-A2
KLICKITAT CO WA 120-A3
MALIN OR 151-A3
MARKET ST Rt#-27
LATAH CO WA 114-C3
N MARKET ST
ABERDEEN WA 178-B7
SEATTLE WA 273-H5
SPOKANE WA 349-E2
SPOKANE CO WA 347-E6
SPOKANE CO WA 349-E2
NE MARKET ST
JEFFERSON CO OR 208-C2
NW MARKET ST
SEATTLE WA 272-D4
SEATTLE WA 273-G4
S MARKET ST
TACOMA WA 293-H5
SW MARKET ST
PORTLAND OR 312-E7
PORTLAND OR 313-E7
MARKET ST NE
DONALD OR 199-A7
SALEM OR 322-J11
SALEM OR 323-A11
MARKET ST NE Rt#-213
SALEM OR 323-D11
MARKSMAN ST SW
THURSTON CO WA 184-B2
MARKWORTH RD
WHATCOM CO WA 158-D3
MARLATT RD S
MARION CO OR 207-C2
MARMONT ST
COQUITLAM BC 157-A5
MARMOT RD
CLACKAMAS CO OR 201-A4
E MARQUAM ST
MARION CO OR 205-C3
MOUNT ANGEL OR 205-C3
W MARQUAM ST
MARION CO OR 205-B3
MALHEUR CO OR 205-B3
E MARROWSTONE RD
JEFFERSON CO WA 170-B1
MARSH CTO
WASCO CO OR 196-B5
MARSH RD
DESCHUTES CO OR 212-B7
YAKIMA CO WA 243-C6
S MARSH RD
SPOKANE CO WA 114-C2
SPOKANE CO WA 247-A6
SE MARSH RD
CLACKAMAS CO OR 200-D3
MARSHALL AV
LINCOLN CO OR 157-D5
SW MARSHALL AV
PENDLETON OR 129-B1
MARSHALL RD
CHENEY WA 246-A5
DISTRICT OF ABBOTSFORD BC 102-B1
DISTRICT OF MATSQUI BC 102-B1
LATAH CO ID 249-D2
SPOKANE CO WA 246-A7
NW MARSHALL ST
PORTLAND OR 312-D4

MARSING RD
CANYON CO ID 147-B1
MARSING-MURPHY RD Rt#-78
MARSING ID 147-B1
OWYHEE CO ID 147-B1
MARTHA BOARDMAN RD
STEVENS CO WA 114-A1
MARTHALER RD NE
MARION CO OR 204-D2
MARION CO OR 205-A2
MARTIN RD
CLARK CO WA 192-D1
JOSEPHINE CO OR 233-B4
MOUNT VERNON WA 260-F9
SHERMAN CO OR 127-C2
SKAGIT CO WA 260-F9
WASHINGTON CO ID 198-C1
W MARTIN RD
SPOKANE CO WA 114-B3
MARTIN ST
KLAMATH FALLS OR 338-E7
W MARTIN ST
ELMA WA 179-B7
MARTIN WY SE
LACEY WA 181-A6
LACEY WA 297-F5
OLYMPIA WA 297-C5
THURSTON CO WA 181-A6
THURSTON CO WA 297-F5
MARTIN CREEK RD
LANE CO OR 219-D1
NE MARTIN LUTHER KING JR
BLVD
PORTLAND OR 309-G3
PORTLAND OR 313-G4
SE MARTIN LUTHER KING JR
BLVD
PORTLAND OR 313-G7
PORTLAND OR 317-G1
MARTIN LUTHER KING JR WY
SEATTLE WA 278-D6
MARTIN LUTHER KING JR WY
E
SEATTLE WA 278-D4
MARTIN LUTHER KING JR WY
S
SEATTLE WA 278-D2
SEATTLE WA 282-D3
SEATTLE WA 283-E7
SEATTLE WA 287-E4
SEATTLE WA 287-E4
MARTIN L KING JR WY S
Rt#-900
KING CO WA 175-C5
KING CO WA 287-E6
KING CO WA 289-G1
RENTON WA 175-C5
RENTON WA 289-G1
SEATTLE WA 287-E6
TUKWILA WA 287-E6
TUKWILA WA 289-G1
MARTIN RANCH RD
CURRY CO OR 232-C4
MARTINSON RD
LATAH CO OR 249-D7
MARTLETT DR
BRITISH COLUMBIA BC 159-B5
MARVIN RD NE
LACEY WA 181-A5
THURSTON CO WA 181-A5
MARVIN RD NE Rt#-510
LACEY WA 181-A6
MARVIN RD SE
THURSTON CO WA 181-A7
MARVIN RD SE Rt#-510
LACEY WA 181-A6
THURSTON CO WA 181-A6
E MARVIN ST
ABERDEEN WA 343-H7
MARX ST U.S.-95
IDAHO CO ID 131-C2
RIGGINS ID 131-C2
MARY GATES MEMORIAL DR
SEATTLE WA 274-E5
MARY HILL BYPS
PORT COQUITLAM BC 157-B5
MARYHILL DR
EVERETT WA 171-B4
SNOHOMISH CO WA 171-B4
MARY HILL RD
PORT COQUITLAM BC 157-A5
MARYLAND AV Rt#-42
MYRTLE POINT OR 140-B2
MARY M KNIGHT RD
MASON CO WA 179-B3
MARYS PEAK RD
BENTON CO OR 133-A1
MARYS RIVER RD
BENTON CO OR 133-A1
MASCHER RD NE
MARION CO OR 205-B5
MASCHKE RD
LEWIS CO WA 187-B5
MASHELL AV S Rt#-161
EATONVILLE WA 118-B1
E MASON AV
BUCKLEY WA 110-C3
BUCKLEY WA 182-D4
W MASON AV
BUCKLEY WA 182-D4
MASON DR
CROOK CO OR 213-D5
PRINEVILLE OR 213-D5
MASON RD
WASCO CO OR 127-B2
MASON ANDERSON RD
TILLAMOOK CO OR 191-B3
MASON BENSON RD
MASON CO WA 173-C7
MASON CO WA 180-C1
MASON CREEK RD
KITTITAS CO WA 240-C1
NE MASON CREEK RD
CLARK CO WA 192-D2
MASON LAKE DR W
MASON CO WA 173-C7
MASON LAKE RD
MASON CO WA 173-C7
MASON CO WA 180-C1
MASON LAKE RD W
MASON CO WA 180-B1
SW MASONVILLE RD
YAMHILL CO OR 204-A1
E MASTERSON RD
KITTITAS CO WA 240-C2
W MASTERSON RD
KITTITAS CO WA 240-C2

MATEJECK RD
TILLAMOOK CO OR 197-B2
MATHENY RD N
MARION CO OR 204-D3
YAMHILL CO OR 204-D3
MATHENY RD NE
MARION CO OR 204-D3
MATHENY CREEK RD
COOS CO OR 220-D7
MATHER MEMORIAL PKWY
Rt#-410
PIERCE CO WA 119-A1
MATHERS AV
DIST of WEST VANCOUVER BC 254-A2
MATHIAS RD E
PIERCE CO WA 182-A6
MATLOCK-BRADY RD
MASON CO WA 179-A4
MATNEY RD
KLAMATH CO OR 235-D6
MATNEY WY
KLAMATH CO OR 235-D6
MATSEN RD
KLICKITAT CO WA 120-A3
MATSON RD
LATAH CO ID 249-D2
MATTESON RD
YAMHILL CO OR 198-B3
MATTHIEU LN
MARION CO OR 199-A7
MATTOON RD
CLACKAMAS CO OR 200-B5
MATTSON RD
LEWIS CO WA 184-B5
MAUI AV
OAK HARBOR WA 167-C3
MAUPIN RD
DOUGLAS CO OR 141-A1
SKAGIT CO WA 168-A2
MAXFIELD CREEK RD
BENTON CO OR 133-B1
POLK CO OR 133-B1
POLK CO OR 207-A2
MAX HARDER RD
LINCOLN CO WA 114-A3
W MAXWELL AV
SPOKANE WA 348-G7
MAXWELL CRES
TOWNSHIP OF LANGLEY BC 157-C7
MAXWELL RD
COOS CO OR 333-C4
EUGENE OR 329-E1
LANE CO OR 329-E1
NORTH BEND OR 333-C4
MAXWELL ST
COOS BAY OR 333-C4
MAXWELTON RD
ISLAND CO WA 171-A2
MAY AV
HOOD RIVER OR 195-D5
W MAY AV Rt#-21
ODESSA WA 113-B3
MAY DR
HOOD RIVER OR 195-C5
HOOD RIVER CO OR 195-C5
MAY RD
POLK CO OR 204-A5
S MAY RD
ADAMS CO WA 242-C7
E MAY ST Rt#-74
HEPPNER OR 128-C2
MAY ST NW
Tracyton WA 270-G4
MAYFIELD RD NE
DOUGLAS CO WA 112-C1
MAYS CREEK RD
JACKSON CO OR 230-A2
MAYTOWN RD SW
THURSTON CO WA 184-B2
MAYTOWN RD SW Rt#-121
THURSTON CO WA 184-C2
SE MAY VALLEY RD
KING CO WA 175-D4
KING CO WA 176-A5
MAZAMA RD
OKANOGAN CO WA 104-A2
MCADAMS CREEK RD
SISKIYOU CO CA 149-C3
MCALISTER RD
ISLAND CITY OR 130-A2
UNION CO OR 130-A2
E MCANDREWS RD
JACKSON CO OR 234-B1
MEDFORD OR 234-B1
MEDFORD OR 336-C10
W MCANDREWS RD
MEDFORD OR 336-B11
MEDFORD OR 336-B11
MCARDLE RD
DESCHUTES CO OR 217-D3
MCBEE RD
BENTON CO WA 120-C3
MCBETH RD
LANE CO OR 215-A3
LANE CO OR 329-D14
MCBRIDE BLVD
NEW WESTMINSTER BC 156-D5
MCBRIDE BLVD Rt#-99A
NEW WESTMINSTER BC 156-D5
MCBRIDE DR
CITY OF SURREY BC 157-A5
MCBRIDE RD
LATAH CO ID 249-D1
MALHEUR CO OR 147-A2
NW MCBRIDE CEM RD
YAMHILL CO OR 198-A5
MCBRYDE AV E
MONTESANO WA 178-D7
MCCABE RD
CLACKAMAS CO OR 200-D5
MCCAFFERY RD
CROOK CO OR 213-A6
MCCALEB RD
POLK CO OR 204-A7
MCCALL BLVD
Navy Yard City WA 270-E13
MCCALLAN RD
CITY OF RICHMOND BC 156-B6
MCCALLUM RD
DISTRICT OF ABBOTSFORD BC 102-B1
DISTRICT OF KENT BC 94-C3
DISTRICT OF MATSQUI BC 102-B1
MCCANLIES RD
HARNEY CO OR 144-C1
MCCANN RD
LEWIS CO OR 123-B3
POLK CO OR 204-A3

MCCANN GRADE
NEZ PERCE CO ID 250-D5
MCCANSE RD
UNION CO OR 130-A3
MCCARVER ST
TACOMA WA 293-E2
MCCLAINE ST Rt#-213
MARION CO OR 205-C4
SILVERTON OR 205-C4
MCCLAIN TUTHILL RD
KLICKITAT CO WA 196-B5
S MCCLELLAN ST
SPOKANE WA 349-A10
MCCLENNY RD
FRANKLIN CO WA 121-B2
MCCLOSKEY CREEK RD
SKAMANIA CO WA 194-A6
MCCLURE RD
LEWIS CO WA 187-C4
MCCOIN RD
CROOK CO OR 213-B2
MCCONIHE RD
GRANT CO WA 242-B2
SW MCCONNELL RD
CLACKAMAS CO OR 199-A5
MCCORKLE RD SE
THURSTON CO WA 184-D1
MCCORMICK LP
TILLAMOOK CO OR 197-C2
MCCORMICK HILL RD
WASHINGTON CO OR 198-D4
MCCOY RD
COLUMBIA CO OR 189-C6
POLK CO OR 204-B4
MCCRORY RD
COWLITZ CO WA 187-B5
MCCROSKEY RD
WHITMAN CO WA 114-C3
W MCCULLOCH RD
YAKIMA CO WA 243-B7
MCCULLOUGH CREEK RD
DOUGLAS CO OR 225-A6
MCCUNE RD
LEWIS CO WA 187-D2
MCCUTCHEON RD
PIERCE CO WA 182-C4
MCDANIEL RD
CROOK CO OR 213-B5
MCDERMITT RD
MALHEUR CO OR 154-B2
MCDERMOTT RD
COLUMBIA CO OR 189-C7
N MCDERMOTT RD
CANYON CO ID 147-C1
S MCDERMOTT RD
ADA CO ID 147-C1
CANYON CO ID 147-C1
MCDONALD DR
CROOK CO OR 213-B6
MCDONALD RD
COLUMBIA CO OR 125-B1
PIERCE CO WA 182-B7
SKAMANIA CO WA 193-D7
TILLAMOOK CO OR 191-B3
WALLA WALLA CO WA 121-C3
WALLA WALLA CO WA 345-A13
N MCDONALD RD
SPOKANE VALLEY WA 350-J8
S MCDONALD RD
SPOKANE VALLEY WA 350-J10
MCDONALD RDG
SKAMANIA CO WA 119-A3
SW MCDONALD ST
TIGARD OR 199-B3
MCDOUGALL RD
YAMHILL CO OR 198-C7
MCDOWELL CREEK DR
LINN CO OR 133-C2
LINN CO OR 134-A2
MCDUFF RD SE
THURSTON CO WA 184-D3
MCELLIGOTT RD
MORROW CO OR 128-C3
MCELROY RD
SNOHOMISH CO WA 168-D6
N MC ENTEE ST
COULEE CITY WA 113-A2
S MC ENTEE ST
COULEE CITY WA 113-A2
GRANT CO WA 113-A2
MCEWAN RD KPN
PIERCE CO WA 181-A2
MCEWAN PRAIRIE RD
MASON CO WA 180-A2
MCEWEN RD
MALHEUR CO OR 146-A1
W MCFARLAND LN
JEFFERSON CO OR 208-C2
MCFARLAND RD
TANGENT OR 207-C6
W MCFARLANE RD
AIRWAY HEIGHTS WA 246-A3
SPOKANE CO WA 114-B2
SPOKANE CO WA 246-A4
SW MCFEE PL
WASHINGTON CO OR 198-C4
MCFEELY RD
WALLA WALLA CO WA 121-C2
MCGARIGLE RD
SEDRO-WOOLLEY WA 161-C5
SKAGIT CO WA 161-C5
MCGEE RD
WHATCOM CO WA 158-C3
MCGILCHRIST ST SE
SALEM OR 324-J2
SALEM OR 325-A2
MCGILL ST
VANCOUVER BC 255-D9
SE MCGILLIVRAY BLVD
VANCOUVER WA 193-A7
VANCOUVER WA 307-J7
MCGINNIS LAKE RD
OKANOGAN CO WA 237-D1
MCGLAUGHLIN RD
LEWIS CO WA 187-C4
MCGONAGLE RD
LANE CO OR 210-D7
MCGOWAN CREEK RD
LANE CO OR 210-D7
MCGOWEN RD
KLICKITAT CO WA 196-B4
MCGRADY RD
WHITMAN CO WA 114-C3
MCGRATH RD
DESCHUTES CO OR 217-D1
W MCGRAW ST
SEATTLE WA 276-C1
SEATTLE WA 277-G1

STREET City State	Page-Grid
MCGREEVY RD	
WHITMAN CO WA	249-B4
MCGREGOR RD	
WHITMAN CO WA	122-A1
MCGUIRE RD	
CITY OF CHILLIWACK BC	94-C3
N MCGUIRE RD	
KOOTENAI CO ID	353-D1
POST FALLS ID	353-E5
MCINTOSH RD	
DOUGLAS CO WA	237-A2
HOOD RIVER CO OR	202-C2
WHITMAN CO WA	122-A1
MCINTOSH HILL RD	
NEZ PERCE CO ID	250-D5
MCINTYRE SPRING RD	
MALHEUR CO OR	147-A1
MCKAY DR	
UMATILLA CO OR	129-B1
MCKAY RD	
CITY OF NORTH VANCOUVER BC	254-J4
CROOK CO OR	213-D3
DIST OF NORTH VANCOUVER BC	254-J4
MARION CO OR	198-D7
MARION CO OR	199-A7
PRINEVILLE OR	213-D4
WALLA WALLA CO WA	121-B3
MCKAY CREEK RD	
CROOK CO OR	135-C2
CROOK CO OR	213-D2
UMATILLA CO OR	129-B2
MCKECHNIE RD	
PITT MEADOWS BC	157-C5
MCKEE RD	
COWLITZ CO WA	189-B1
SW MCKEE RD	
YAMHILL CO OR	204-B2
MCKEE SCHOOL RD NE	
MARION CO OR	205-B2
MCKENNA TANWAX Rt#-702	
PIERCE CO WA	118-A1
MCKENNA-YELM HWY Rt#-507	
PIERCE CO WA	118-A1
THURSTON CO WA	118-A1
YELM WA	118-A1
MCKENZIE AV	
DISTRICT OF SAANICH BC	256-G3
DISTRICT OF SAANICH BC	257-A3
MCKENZIE HWY Rt#-126	
DESCHUTES CO OR	211-D5
DESCHUTES CO OR	212-A5
LANE CO OR	133-C3
LANE CO OR	134-B2
LANE CO OR	215-D2
LINN CO OR	134-B2
REDMOND OR	212-D5
SISTERS OR	211-D5
SPRINGFIELD OR	215-D2
MCKENZIE HWY Rt#-242	
DESCHUTES CO OR	211-C4
LANE CO OR	134-C2
LANE CO OR	211-A6
LINN CO OR	211-A6
SISTERS OR	211-C4
MCKENZIE LN	
SUMMERVILLE OR	130-A2
UNION CO OR	130-A2
MCKENZIE RD	
CURRY CO OR	224-A5
WHITMAN CO WA	249-C1
MCKENZIE RD SW	
THURSTON CO WA	180-B6
MCKENZIE-BEND HWY U.S.-20	
BEND OR	332-F1
DESCHUTES CO OR	211-D5
DESCHUTES CO OR	212-A6
DESCHUTES CO OR	217-C1
DESCHUTES CO OR	332-F1
SISTERS OR	211-D5
MCKENZIE CANYON RD	
DESCHUTES CO OR	212-B4
MCKENZIE VIEW DR	
LANE CO OR	215-C1
LANE CO OR	330-H1
LANE CO OR	331-A1
MCKERN-SCOTT RD	
STEVENS CO WA	106-A3
MCKIBBIN RD	
WASHINGTON CO OR	198-C1
MCKILLOP RD NE	
MARION CO OR	205-D4
MCKIMMENS RD	
TILLAMOOK CO OR	191-B4
MCKINLEY AV	
PIERCE CO WA	181-D4
TACOMA WA	181-D4
E MCKINLEY AV	
PIERCE CO WA	295-J7
TACOMA WA	295-J5
MCKINLEY AV W	
KELLOGG ID	115-C2
SHOSHONE CO ID	115-C2
W MCKINLEY RD	
SMELTERVILLE ID	115-C2
MCKINLEY ST	
COLTON WA	250-A1
E MCKINLEY WY	
TACOMA WA	295-J1
MCKINLEY SPRINGS RD	
BENTON CO WA	120-B3
MCKINNEY RD	
ADAMS CO WA	121-A1
MCKINNON CRES	
TOWNSHIP OF LANGLEY BC	157-C6
MCKNIGHT RD	
GRAYS HARBOR CO WA	179-C6
MCLAGEN RD	
LINN CO OR	207-C7
MCLAIN-LIBBY DR	
Barview OR	220-C1
COOS CO OR	220-C1
COOS CO OR	333-B13
MCLAUGHLIN DR	
JACKSON CO OR	336-H3
MCLEAN AV	
PORT COQUITLAM BC	157-B5
MCLEAN RD	
MOUNT VERNON WA	260-A12
SKAGIT CO WA	160-D7
SKAGIT CO WA	161-A7
SKAGIT CO WA	260-A12
UMATILLA CO OR	129-C1
MCLEOD RD	
BELLINGHAM WA	258-B2
E MCLEOD RD	
BELLINGHAM WA	258-J2
WHATCOM CO WA	258-J2
E MCLOUGHLIN BLVD	
VANCOUVER WA	305-H4

STREET City State	Page-Grid
E MCLOUGHLIN BLVD	
VANCOUVER WA	306-A4
SE MCLOUGHLIN BLVD Rt#-99E	
CLACKAMAS CO OR	199-D3
CLACKAMAS CO OR	321-J2
GLADSTONE OR	199-D3
MILWAUKIE OR	317-J5
MILWAUKIE OR	321-J2
OREGON CITY OR	199-D3
PORTLAND OR	317-J5
W MCLOUGHLIN BLVD	
VANCOUVER WA	305-G4
MCLOUGHLIN BLVD E Rt#-99E	
CLACKAMAS CO OR	199-D5
OREGON CITY OR	199-D5
E MCLOUGHLIN ST	
VANCOUVER WA	305-G4
MCMANAMY RD	
KITTITAS CO WA	241-A4
MCMANOMON RD	
ADAMS CO WA	121-A1
ADAMS CO WA	242-C7
E MCMILLAN RD	
ADA CO ID	253-A2
BOISE ID	253-B2
W MCMILLAN RD	
ADA CO ID	253-A2
MCMULLEN LN	
LANE CO WA	210-A5
MCMULLIN CREEK RD	
JOSEPHINE CO OR	233-C2
E MCMULLIN CREEK RD	
JOSEPHINE CO OR	233-C2
MCMURRAY RD	
TACOMA WA	182-A2
MCMURRAY ST	
RICHLAND WA	340-F12
MCNABB CREEK RD	
DOUGLAS CO WA	221-A7
MCNAIR DR	
DISTRICT OF NORTH VANCOUV BC	156-C2
NW MCNAMEE RD	
MULTNOMAH CO OR	192-A6
MCNARY HWY I-82	
UMATILLA CO OR	129-A1
UMATILLA CO OR	129-A1
MCNARY HWY U.S.-395	
UMATILLA CO OR	129-A1
UMATILLA CO OR	129-A1
MCNAUGHT ST Rt#-507	
ROY WA	181-C7
SW MCNAY RD	
WASHINGTON CO OR	198-D3
MCNEALY WY	
COOS CO OR	220-D6
MCNEIL RD	
KITTITAS CO WA	241-A6
PITT MEADOWS BC	157-B4
MCNEIL CANYON RD NW	
DOUGLAS CO WA	112-B1
DOUGLAS CO WA	236-D3
MCNEILLY RD	
WHITMAN CO WA	122-B1
MCNULTY RD	
LEWIS CO WA	187-D4
MCNUTT RD	
GRAYS HARBOR CO WA	178-A2
MCPHILLIPS RD	
TILLAMOOK CO OR	197-A7
MCQUISTON RD	
KLAMATH CO OR	231-B2
MCRAE RD NE	
SNOHOMISH CO WA	168-C6
MCREAVY RD	
MASON CO WA	173-A7
MASON CO WA	180-A1
MCSWEEN RD	
CITY OF CHILLIWACK BC	94-C3
MCTAVISH RD Rt#-17A	
DISTRICT OF NORTH SAANICH BC	159-C3
MCVAY HWY Rt#-99	
LANE CO OR	330-G11
MCVEY AV	
LAKE OSWEGO OR	321-F7
NE MCWILLIAMS RD	
KITSAP CO WA	270-H3
KITSAP CO WA	271-A3
Tracyton WA	270-H3
M DRUFFEL RD	
WHITMAN CO WA	249-A7
E MEAD AV	
YAKIMA CO WA	243-C7
W MEAD AV	
YAKIMA WA	243-B7
MEAD RD	
COLUMBIA CO WA	122-A2
NE MEADOW AV	
DOUGLAS CO OR	334-F4
ROSEBURG OR	334-F4
MEADOW LN	
COOS CO OR	218-B6
MEADOW RD	
LINN CO OR	207-B5
SNOHOMISH CO WA	171-C4
W MEADOWBROOK RD	
YAKIMA CO WA	243-A7
MEADOW CREEK RD	
BOUNDARY CO ID	107-B1
GARFIELD CO WA	122-B2
PEND OREILLE CO WA	106-B2
SKAMANIA CO WA	118-C3
SKAMANIA CO WA	194-C1
STEVENS CO WA	106-B1
MEADOW CREEK RD U.S.-95	
IDAHO CO ID	123-B3
NW MEADOW LAKE RD	
YAMHILL CO OR	125-B2
YAMHILL CO OR	198-A6
MEADOWLARK DR	
JEFFERSON CO OR	212-C2
MEADOWS RD	
JACKSON CO OR	230-C3
MEALS RD	
BENTON CO WA	121-A3
MEDA LOOP RD	
TILLAMOOK CO OR	203-B1
MEDCO HAUL RD	
MEDFORD OR	336-D8
MEDICAL LAKE RD Rt#-902	
MEDICAL LAKE WA	114-B2
SPOKANE CO WA	114-B2
S MEDICAL LK TYLER RD Rt#-902	
MEDICAL LAKE WA	114-B2
MEDICAL SPRINGS HWY Rt#-203	
BAKER CO OR	130-B3
UNION OR	130-B2

STREET City State	Page-Grid
MEDICAL SPRINGS HWY Rt#-203	
UNION CO OR	130-B2
E MEDICAL SPRINGS HWY Rt#-203	
UNION OR	130-B2
MEDIMONT RD	
KOOTENAI CO ID	248-C4
MEDLEYS ELKHEAD RD	
DOUGLAS CO OR	219-B5
MEDOHILL RD	
COOS CO OR	220-B4
MEEKER RD	
COWLITZ CO WA	189-C4
N MEEKER DR	
COWLITZ CO WA	189-C5
MEEKER RD	
CROOK CO OR	213-B6
W MEEKER ST	
KENT WA	175-B7
MEENACH DR	
SPOKANE WA	348-F6
MEGAN BLVD	
YAKIMA CO WA	243-C6
MEHL CREEK RD	
DOUGLAS CO OR	141-A1
MEIER RD	
LEWIS CO WA	187-C2
NW MEIER RD	
WASHINGTON CO OR	192-A6
MEINIG AV Rt#-211	
SANDY OR	200-D4
MEISS LAKE RD	
SISKIYOU CO CA	150-B3
MEISS LAKE SAMS NECK RD	
SISKIYOU CO CA	150-B3
MEISSNER RD	
COLUMBIA CO OR	189-B6
MELBA RD	
CANYON CO ID	147-B1
MELBOURNE ST	
COLUMBIA CO OR	189-B4
WESTPORT WA	183-B2
MELLEN ST	
CENTRALIA WA	299-D5
MELLEN ST Rt#-507	
CENTRALIA WA	299-D5
MELMONT RD	
CANYON CO ID	147-B1
MELODY LN	
LANE CO OR	215-B5
MELOTT RD	
YAMHILL CO OR	198-C4
MELQUA RD	
DOUGLAS CO OR	221-A2
MELROSE RD	
DOUGLAS CO OR	221-A4
DOUGLAS CO OR	334-A3
MELROSE ST	
LAKE OSWEGO OR	320-A5
WALLA WALLA WA	345-C6
WALLA WALLA WA	345-F5
W MELVILLE RD	
SPOKANE CO WA	246-A5
MELVILLE ST	
VANCOUVER WA	254-F9
MELVILLE ST SE	
THURSTON CO WA	184-C3
MELVIN RD	
DOUGLAS CO WA	239-B1
MEMORIAL HWY Rt#-20	
SKAGIT CO WA	160-D6
SKAGIT CO WA	161-A7
MEMORIAL HWY Rt#-536	
MOUNT VERNON WA	260-A11
SKAGIT CO WA	161-A7
SKAGIT CO WA	260-A11
MEMORIAL PARK DR	
COWLITZ CO WA	302-D7
LONGVIEW WA	302-D7
MENLO SOUTH FORK RD	
PACIFIC CO WA	117-A1
MENZEL LAKE RD	
GRANITE FALLS WA	102-C3
SNOHOMISH CO WA	102-C3
SNOHOMISH CO WA	110-C1
MENZIE RD SE	
KITSAP CO WA	174-C4
W MERCER PL	
SEATTLE WA	277-G3
MERCER ST	
SEATTLE WA	277-H3
SEATTLE WA	278-A3
W MERCER ST	
SEATTLE WA	277-G3
E MERCER WY	
MERCER ISLAND WA	175-C4
W MERCER WY	
MERCER ISLAND WA	175-C3
MERCER ISLAND WA	283-J3
MERCER ISLAND WA	287-J2
MERCER LAKE RD	
LANE CO OR	214-B2
MERCHANTS RD	
CLALLAM CO WA	169-D1
N MERIDIAN	
PUYALLUP WA	182-B3
N MERIDIAN Rt#-161	
PUYALLUP WA	182-B3
S MERIDIAN	
PUYALLUP WA	182-B4
S MERIDIAN Rt#-161	
PUYALLUP WA	182-B4
MERIDIAN E Rt#-161	
EDGEWOOD WA	182-B3
MILTON WA	182-B3
PIERCE CO WA	118-B1
PIERCE CO WA	182-B3
YAMHILL CO OR	182-B3
MERIDIAN AV E Rt#-161	
EATONVILLE WA	118-B1
PIERCE CO WA	118-B1
PIERCE CO WA	182-B7
MERIDIAN AV N	
SEATTLE WA	171-B7
SHORELINE WA	171-B7
MERIDIAN RD	
ANMORE BC	157-A3
COQUITLAM BC	157-A4
LINN CO OR	133-C1
MARION CO OR	205-C4
PORT MOODY BC	157-A4
SILVERTON OR	205-C4
N MERIDIAN RD	
ADA CO ID	253-A1
EAGLE ID	253-A1
MERIDIAN ID	253-A2
S MERIDIAN RD	
CLACKAMAS CO OR	199-B7
CLACKAMAS CO OR	205-C2

STREET City State	Page-Grid
MERIDIAN RD NE	
LACEY WA	181-A6
MARION CO OR	205-C3
MERIDIAN RD SE	
THURSTON CO WA	181-A7
MERIDIAN ST	
BELLINGHAM WA	258-C3
MERIDIAN ST Rt#-539	
BELLINGHAM WA	258-C2
S MERIDIAN ST	
MERIDIAN ID	253-A3
E MERLENE AV	
SPOKANE CO WA	347-F4
MERLIN RD	
JOSEPHINE CO OR	229-A4
JOSEPHINE CO OR	335-A1
MERLIN-GALICE RD	
JOSEPHINE CO OR	149-A1
JOSEPHINE CO OR	229-A4
MERRILL RD	
DESCHUTES CO OR	136-A3
WALLA WALLA WA	345-F7
S MERRILL RD	
KLAMATH CO OR	150-C3
SISKIYOU CO OR	150-C3
MERRILL CREEK PKWY	
EVERETT WA	267-H2
EVERETT WA	268-A2
MERRILL CREEK RD	
COLUMBIA CO OR	189-C7
MERRIMAN RD	
CENTRAL POINT OR	336-B7
MEDFORD OR	336-B7
MERRITT LN	
UNION CO OR	130-B1
MERRY CREEK RD	
SHOSHONE CO ID	115-C3
MESA KAHLOTUS RD	
FRANKLIN CO WA	121-B2
MESERVE RD	
COLUMBIA CO OR	189-B4
NE MESFORD RD	
STEVENS CO WA	106-A3
MESKILL RD	
LEWIS CO WA	184-A7
MESSNER RD	
COLUMBIA CO WA	122-A2
METCHOSIN RD	
CITY OF COLWOOD BC	159-B7
DISTRICT OF METCHOSIN BC	159-B7
DISTRICT OF METCHOSIN BC	165-B1
METGE AV	
BENTON CO OR	207-B4
METHODIST DR	
HOOD RIVER CO OR	195-C5
METHOW ST	
CHELAN CO WA	238-D5
CHELAN CO WA	239-A5
S METHOW ST	
WENATCHEE WA	239-A4
E METHOW VALLEY HWY Rt#-20	
OKANOGAN CO WA	104-B3
TWISP WA	104-A3
METOLIUS BENCH RD	
JEFFERSON CO OR	208-A5
METOLIUS RIVER RD	
JEFFERSON CO OR	211-C1
METTMAN CREEK RD	
COOS CO OR	218-C7
METZ HILL RD	
DOUGLAS CO OR	219-A7
METZLER PARK RD	
CLACKAMAS CO OR	200-C7
N MEYER RD	
KOOTENAI CO ID	354-F2
S MEYER RD	
KOOTENAI CO ID	247-D1
MEYERS W	
PIERCE CO WA	182-A6
MEYERS ST	
KETTLE FALLS WA	106-A7
MEYERS RIDGE RD	
ASOTIN CO WA	122-C3
MIAMI RIVER RD	
TILLAMOOK CO OR	191-B5
MICHIGAN AV	
OROFINO OR	123-C2
E MICHIGAN AV	
CLEARWATER CO ID	123-C2
OROFINO ID	123-C2
MICHIGAN ST U.S.-95	
COUNCIL ID	139-C1
S MICHIGAN ST	
SEATTLE WA	282-A7
MICHIGAN HILL RD SW	
THURSTON CO WA	184-A4
MICK PARVIN RD	
WHITMAN CO WA	249-A7
MIDDLE RD	
KLICKITAT CO WA	128-A1
SE MIDDLE WY	
VANCOUVER WA	306-E7
VANCOUVER WA	307-E7
MIDDLE CREEK RD	
DOUGLAS CO OR	225-A5
MIDDLE CREEK ACCESS RD	
COOS CO OR	140-C2
MIDDLE CREEK RANCH RD	
SISKIYOU CO OR	149-B3
MIDDLE FORK RD	
LEWIS CO WA	118-A2
LEWIS CO WA	187-D1
MIDDLEFORK RD	
CLACKAMAS CO OR	126-A3
E MIDDLE FORK RD	
ADAMS CO ID	139-C1
ADAMS CO ID	252-A3
MIDDLE FORK FOOTS CREEK RD	
JACKSON CO OR	230-A7
MIDDLE FORK MILL CREEK RD	
STEVENS CO WA	106-B2
MIDDLE RIDGE DR	
LINN CO OR	210-D1
MIDDLE SATSOP RD	
GRAYS HARBOR CO WA	179-A3
MIDDLE WAITSBURG RD	
WALLA WALLA WA	345-C5
WALLA WALLA WA	121-C3
WALLA WALLA WA	122-A3
WALLA WALLA CO WA	345-C5
NW MIDLAND AV	
GRANTS PASS OR	335-E7
MIDLAND BLVD	
CANYON CO ID	147-B1
MIDLAND HWY	
KLAMATH CO OR	235-C5
KLAMATH FALLS OR	338-E14

STREET City State	Page-Grid
MIDLAND HWY	
KLAMATH FALLS OR	235-C5
KLAMATH FALLS OR	338-E14
N MIDVALE PL	
SEATTLE WA	273-J5
MIDVALE RD	
SUNNYSIDE WA	120-B3
YAKIMA CO WA	120-B3
MIDWAY AV	
JOSEPHINE CO OR	229-A6
MIDWAY BLVD	
OAK HARBOR WA	167-C3
MIDWAY RD	
CANYON CO ID	147-B1
LINN CO OR	207-D5
LINN CO OR	326-H13
WASHINGTON CO OR	198-D3
MIDWAY BEACH RD	
PACIFIC CO WA	183-B4
E MIERAS RD	
YAKIMA CO WA	243-D7
MIKE JOHNSON RD	
WHITMAN CO WA	249-A1
MIKKALO RD	
GILLIAM CO OR	128-A2
MILAN-ELK RD	
SPOKANE CO WA	114-C1
S MILDRED ST	
TACOMA WA	181-C2
SE MILE HILL DR	
Colby WA	174-C4
KITSAP CO WA	174-C4
SE MILE HILL DR Rt#-166	
East Port Orchard WA	174-C4
KITSAP CO WA	174-C4
PORT ORCHARD WA	174-B4
E MILES AV	
HAYDEN ID	245-A5
W MILES AV	
HAYDEN ID	245-A5
MILES RD	
STEVENS CO WA	106-A3
MILES BRIDGE RD	
BAKER CO OR	130-B3
MILES CRESTON RD	
LINCOLN CO WA	113-C1
MILEY RD	
WILSONVILLE OR	199-B6
MILITARY RD	
COWLITZ CO WA	187-B7
FEDERAL WAY WA	175-B7
FEDERAL WAY WA	182-A5
KING CO WA	182-B1
KING CO WA	182-B2
LAKEWOOD WA	181-C4
N MILITARY RD	
LEWIS CO WA	187-C3
S MILITARY RD	
LEWIS CO WA	187-C4
MILITARY RD E	
PIERCE CO WA	182-A5
MILITARY RD S	
FEDERAL WAY WA	175-B7
KENT WA	175-B7
KING CO WA	175-B7
KING CO WA	286-C6
KING CO WA	288-D1
MILTON WA	182-B2
PIERCE CO WA	181-D5
SEATAC WA	288-E5
SEATAC WA	289-E6
SEATAC WA	290-E3
SEATAC WA	291-F1
TUKWILA WA	288-D1
MILITARY CROSSING RD	
KLAMATH CO OR	142-C3
MILL AV S Rt#-900	
RENTON WA	175-C5
MILL DR	
KLICKITAT CO WA	196-D2
MILL RD	
ASOTIN CO WA	122-C3
LATAH CO ID	249-D5
LEWIS CO WA	187-C2
NEZ PERCE CO ID	250-C4
WASHINGTON CO OR	139-B1
N MILL RD	
Fairwood WA	346-J7
Fairwood WA	347-A6
SPOKANE CO WA	347-A6
MILL ST	
CHENEY WA	246-A7
CLEARWATER CO ID	123-C1
ELK RIVER ID	123-C1
GRANTS PASS OR	335-F10
KELSO WA	303-C9
MAPLE RIDGE BC	157-D5
SPOKANE CO WA	246-A7
NE MILL ST	
KLICKITAT CO WA	128-A1
SE MILL ST	
DALLAS OR	204-A6
GRANTS PASS OR	335-G9
SW MILL ST	
SHERIDAN OR	125-B3
YAMHILL CO OR	125-B3
MILLARD RD	
COLUMBIA CO OR	192-A2
MILL BAY RD	
BRITISH COLUMBIA BC	159-B2
MILL CREEK BLVD	
MILL CREEK WA	171-C4
MILL CREEK DR	
JACKSON CO OR	226-C7
MILL CREEK RD	
ADAMS CO ID	139-C1
AUMSVILLE OR	133-C1
COWLITZ CO WA	117-B3
MARION CO OR	133-C1
MARION CO OR	325-H13
PACIFIC CO WA	117-A1
POLK CO WA	125-B3
THE DALLES OR	196-C7
TURNER OR	325-H13
UNION CO OR	130-B2
WALLA WALLA WA	122-A3
WALLA WALLA WA	345-H5
WALLA WALLA CO WA	122-A3
WASCO CO OR	196-C7
MILL CREEK LOOKOUT RD	
WASCO CO OR	202-D2

STREET City State	Page-Grid
MILL CREEK RIDGE RD	
JACKSON CO OR	226-C5
SE MILLER AV	
DALLAS OR	204-A6
POLK CO OR	204-A6
MILLER RD	
CLACKAMAS CO OR	205-C1
CLALLAM CO WA	164-C6
JEFFERSON CO OR	263-B7
KITTITAS CO WA	241-A5
LINCOLN CO OR	206-C1
MARION CO OR	199-A7
NEZ PERCE CO ID	250-D7
SNOHOMISH CO WA	168-B4
S MILLER RD	
JEFFERSON CO WA	263-B6
MILLER RD NE	
KITSAP CO WA	174-C1
MARION CO OR	205-B3
MILLER RD NW	
KITSAP CO WA	174-C1
N MILLER ST	
WENATCHEE WA	238-D4
N MILLER ST Rt#-285	
WENATCHEE WA	238-D4
S MILLER ST	
WENATCHEE WA	238-D4
MILLER BAY RD NE	
KITSAP CO WA	170-C6
Suquamish WA	170-C6
MILLER CANYON RD	
HARNEY CO OR	144-C1
MILLER CEMETERY RD	
LINN CO OR	133-C1
MILLER ISLAND RD	
KLAMATH CO OR	235-B5
MILLERS CEMETERY RD	
LINN CO OR	207-C3
MILLERS CREEK RD	
POLK CO OR	207-A2
MILLICAN RD	
CROOK CO OR	135-B3
CROOK CO OR	213-C7
LAKE CO OR	143-C1
W MILLIRON RD	
LANE CO OR	210-A7
MILLMAN RD	
ISLAND CO WA	170-D1
MILL PLAIN BLVD Rt#-501	
VANCOUVER WA	305-G4
E MILL PLAIN BLVD	
VANCOUVER WA	305-H5
VANCOUVER WA	306-C5
VANCOUVER WA	307-F6
W MILL PLAIN BLVD Rt#-501	
VANCOUVER WA	304-D3
VANCOUVER WA	305-E4
SE MILL PLAIN RD	
VANCOUVER WA	193-A6
VANCOUVER WA	307-J6
MILL RIDGE RD	
WASCO CO OR	202-D2
MILLS RD	
DISTRICT OF NORTH SAANICH BC	159-C2
TOWN OF SIDNEY BC	159-C2
MILLS CANYON RD	
CHELAN CO WA	236-C4
MILLSTREAM RD	
DISTRICT OF LANGFORD BC	159-B5
MILLSTREAM LAKE RD	
BRITISH COLUMBIA BC	159-B5
MILLTOWN RD	
SKAGIT CO WA	168-B2
MILTON WY	
MILTON WA	182-B2
MILTON CEMETERY RD	
MILTON-FREEWATER OR	121-C3
UMATILLA CO OR	121-C3
MILWAUKEE DR	
COEUR D'ALENE ID	355-E10
N MILWAUKEE ST	
BOISE ID	253-B2
MILWAUKEE WY	
TACOMA WA	182-A2
SE MILWAUKIE AV	
PORTLAND OR	317-H2
MILWAUKIE EXWY Rt#-224	
CLACKAMAS CO OR	199-D3
MILWAUKIE OR	199-D3
MILWAUKIE OR	321-J2
MILWAUKIE-FOSTER RD	
CLACKAMAS CO OR	199-D3
MIMA ACRES RD SE	
THURSTON CO WA	184-D3
MINALOOSA RD	
BENEWAH CO ID	248-A7
MINARD RD W	
KITSAP CO WA	174-A4
MINA SMITH RD	
CLALLAM CO WA	169-B1
MINERAL RD	
WASHINGTON CO ID	139-A1
MINERAL SPRINGS RD	
SKAMANIA CO WA	194-C1
YAMHILL CO OR	198-B6
MINK RD	
CANYON CO ID	147-B1
MINK RD NE	
KING CO WA	171-D7
MINKLER RD	
LEWIS CO WA	187-C2
NE MINNEHAHA ST	
CLARK CO WA	192-D5
MINNESOTA AV	
RAINIER WA	118-A1
MINOR AV	
KELSO WA	303-E7
MINSON RD	
CROOK CO OR	213-B6
SW MINTERBROOK RD	
KITSAP CO WA	174-A6
MIRROR LN	
COOS CO OR	221-A6
MISERY POINT LOOP RD NW	
KITSAP CO WA	173-D4
MISSIMER RD	
CANYON CO ID	120-B2
E MISSION AV	
LIBERTY LAKE WA	352-C13
SPOKANE WA	349-D7
SPOKANE WA	352-G3
SPOKANE VALLEY WA	349-J7
SPOKANE VALLEY WA	350-G6
SPOKANE VALLEY WA	351-A7
W MISSION AV	
SPOKANE WA	348-J7
SPOKANE WA	349-A7
MISSION RD	
MARION CO OR	198-D7

MISSION RD STREET INDEX MYRTLE PARK RD 383

STREET INDEX

STREET City State Page-Grid

MISSION RD
SAINT PAUL OR 198-D7
MISSION ST
MCCALL ID 251-C5
N MISSION ST Rt#-285
WENATCHEE WA 238-D4
S MISSION ST
Appleyard WA 239-A5
WENATCHEE WA 239-A5
S MISSION ST Rt#-285
WENATCHEE WA 238-D4
WENATCHEE WA 239-A4
MISSION ST SE
SALEM OR 322-H14
MISSION ST SE Rt#-22
SALEM OR 322-J14
SALEM OR 323-A14
SALEM OR 325-B1
MISSION CREEK RD
CHELAN CO WA 238-C3
MISSOULA AV U.S.-2
LINCOLN CO MT 107-C2
TROY MT 107-C2
E MISSOULA AV U.S.-2
TROY MT 107-C2
MISSOURI AV
CANYON CO ID 147-B1
MIST DR Rt#-47
COLUMBIA CO OR 125-B1
VERNONIA OR 125-B1
MIST-CLATSKANIE HWY Rt#-47
CLATSKANIE OR 117-B3
COLUMBIA CO OR 117-B3
MISTLETOE RD
ASHLAND OR 337-H10
DALLAS OR 204-A7
MONMOUTH OR 204-A7
POLK CO OR 204-A7
MISTY CREEK RD
JACKSON CO OR 230-B1
MITCHELL AV
PORT ORCHARD WA 174-B4
PORT ORCHARD WA 270-J14
MITCHELL RD
PIERCE CO WA 181-D6
MITCHELL RD SE
East Port Orchard WA 174-B4
PORT ORCHARD WA 174-B4
MITCHELL ST
KLAMATH FALLS OR 338-F8
N MITCHELL ST
BOISE ID 253-B2
MITCHELL BUTTE RD
MALHEUR CO OR 139-A3
MALHEUR CO OR 146-C1
MIX RD
LATAH CO ID 249-C4
MIX ST NW
THURSTON CO WA 296-A3
MOCK RD
DESCHUTES CO OR 217-B1
MOCLIPS HWY
GRAYS HARBOR CO WA 108-C2
GRAYS HARBOR CO WA 109-A2
MOCTILEME RD Rt#-60
BENEWAH CO ID 115-A3
MODOC RD
JACKSON CO OR 230-C6
MODOC POINT RD
KLAMATH CO OR 231-C3
MODROW RD
COWLITZ CO WA 189-D5
MOE RD NE
DOUGLAS CO WA 104-C3
MOELLERING RD
LINCOLN CO WA 113-C2
MOERHLE RD
WHITMAN CO WA 250-A2
E MOFFAT RD
SPOKANE CO WA 246-D2
MOFFATT RD
CROOK CO OR 213-C6
SE MOFFET RD
CLARK CO WA 193-D7
MOHAWK BLVD
SPRINGFIELD OR 330-J6
SPRINGFIELD OR 331-A6
MOHAWK HILL RD
LANE CO OR 210-D7
MOHLER RD
LINCOLN CO WA 113-C2
LINCOLN CO WA 114-A2
MOHLER CHEESE FACTORY RD
TILLAMOOK CO OR 191-B7
MOHORIC RD
LEWIS CO WA 187-B1
MOJONNIER RD
COLLEGE PLACE WA 344-D13
WALLA WALLA CO WA 344-D13
MOLALLA AV
CLACKAMAS CO OR 126-A3
OREGON CITY OR 199-D5
N MOLALLA AV
MOLALLA OR 126-A3
S MOLALLA AV
CLACKAMAS CO OR 126-A3
MOLALLA OR 126-A3
MOLALLA FOREST RD
CANBY OR 199-C6
CLACKAMAS CO OR 199-C6
MOLITOR HILL RD
LANE CO OR 215-C7
MOLSON RD
OKANOGAN CO WA 105-A1
N MOLTER RD
LIBERTY LAKE WA 352-D14
S MOLTER RD
SPOKANE CO WA 247-B4
MONAHAN RD
COWLITZ CO WA 187-B7
MONCTON ST
CITY OF RICHMOND BC 156-B7
NE MONEY CREEK RD
KING CO WA 111-A2
MONITOR-MCKEE RD NE
MARION CO OR 205-B2
MONKLAND RD
SHERMAN CO OR 127-C2
N MONMOUTH AV
MONMOUTH OR 204-B7
MONMOUTH CTO
DALLAS OR 204-A6
POLK CO OR 204-A6
MONMOUTH HWY
POLK CO OR 125-B3
POLK CO OR 133-B1
POLK CO OR 204-A7
POLK CO OR 207-A1
MONMOUTH ST Rt#-51
INDEPENDENCE OR 204-B7
MONMOUTH-INDPNDNCE HWY Rt#-51
INDEPENDENCE OR 204-B7
MONMOUTH OR 204-B7
POLK CO OR 204-B7
MONNIER RD NE
MARION CO OR 205-C1
MONROE AV
CORVALLIS OR 327-G10
LA GRANDE OR 130-A2
NORTH BEND OR 333-G4
SW MONROE LN
JEFFERSON CO OR 212-C1
MONROE RD
LEWIS CO WA 187-C2
N MONROE RD
SPOKANE CO WA 114-B1
W MONROE RD
DEER PARK WA 114-B1
SPOKANE CO WA 114-B1
MONROE ST
PORT TOWNSEND WA 263-H4
E MONROE ST Rt#-78
BURNS OR 145-B1
HARNEY CO OR 145-B1
N MONROE ST
SPOKANE WA 348-H8
Town and Country WA 346-H14
Town and Country WA 348-H8
S MONROE ST
SPOKANE WA 348-H9
W MONROE ST U.S.-20
BURNS OR 145-B1
MONROE CREEK RD
WASHINGTON CO ID 139-A2
MONROE LANDING RD
ISLAND CO WA 167-B3
MONSE SOUTH RD
OKANOGAN CO WA 104-C3
MONSON RD
LINCOLN CO WA 113-B2
MONSOR RD Rt#-21
LINCOLN CO WA 113-B2
MONTAGUE GRENADA RD
MONTAGUE CA 150-A3
SISKIYOU CO CA 150-A3
MONTE CRISTO RD
SNOHOMISH CO WA 111-A1
S MONTE CRISTO RD
CLACKAMAS CO OR 205-D2
SW MONTEE DR
PENDLETON OR 129-B1
UMATILLA CO OR 129-B1
MONTERAY AV
DIST OF NORTH VANCOUVER BC 255-B1
MONTEREY DR NE
RENTON WA 175-C5
MONTESANO ST
GRAYS HARBOR CO WA 183-B2
WESTPORT WA 183-B2
WESTPORT WA 298-H14
MONTESANO ST Rt#-105
WESTPORT WA 298-H11
MONTESANO-ABERDEEN RD
GRAYS HARBOR CO WA 178-D7
E MONTGOMERY AV
SPOKANE VALLEY WA 350-D6
SPOKANE VALLEY WA 351-F5
E MONTGOMERY DR
SPOKANE VALLEY WA 350-E5
MONTGOMERY RD
DESCHUTES CO OR 136-A3
DESCHUTES CO OR 144-A1
JEFFERSON CO OR 135-A1
MONTGOMERY RIDGE RD
ASOTIN CO WA 123-A3
MONTI DR
LINCOLN CO OR 203-B3
MONTICELLO DR
ISLAND CO WA 167-D5
MONTLAKE BLVD NE Rt#-513
SEATTLE WA 274-D6
SEATTLE WA 278-D1
E MONTLAKE PL E
SEATTLE WA 278-D1
W MONTLAKE PL E
SEATTLE WA 278-C1
MONTMORENCE DR
LANE CO OR 210-A7
MONTOUR RD
GEM CO ID 139-C3
MONTREAL ST
CITY OF VICTORIA BC 256-F9
MONTROSE ST
DISTRICT OF BURNABY BC 255-G9
MONTROYAL BLVD
DIST OF NORTH VANCOUVER BC 156-B2
DIST OF NORTH VANCOUVER BC 255-A1
MONUMENT DR
JOSEPHINE CO OR 229-B3
JOSEPHINE CO OR 335-B1
MONUMENT RD
GRANT CO OR 136-C1
GRANT CO OR 112-B3
MONUMENT RD SW
KING CO WA 174-D6
MONUMENT TO COUNTY LINE
GRANT CO OR 128-C3
GRANT CO OR 136-C1
MONUMENT TO COURTROCK RD
GRANT CO OR 136-C1
GRANT CO OR 137-A1
MOODY RD
GRAYS HARBOR CO WA 177-D2
MOODY ST
PORT MOODY BC 157-A4
MOON RD SW
THURSTON CO WA 184-A3
MOON CREEK RD
TILLAMOOK CO OR 197-D5
MOONEY MOUNTAIN RD
JOSEPHINE CO OR 233-C1
MOON HILL RD
LEWIS CO WA 187-A1
MOON RIDGE RD
VALLEY CO ID 251-C6
MOONSHINE PARK RD
LINCOLN CO OR 206-D1
MOON VALLEY RD
KING CO WA 176-D4
MOORE LN
SHERMAN CO OR 127-C2
MOORE RD
GRAYS HARBOR CO WA 179-A7
SKAGIT CO WA 168-A1
MOORE ST Rt#-9
SEDRO-WOOLLEY WA 161-C5
MOOREA DR
DOUGLAS CO OR 221-B3
MOOREHOUSE RD
UMATILLA CO OR 129-A1
MOORES HOLLOW RD
MALHEUR CO OR 139-A2
NW MOORES VALLEY RD
YAMHILL CO OR 198-A5
MORA RD
CLALLAM CO WA 169-A2
MORA RD Rt#-110
CLALLAM CO WA 169-B2
N MORAIN ST
KENNEWICK WA 342-H10
S MORAIN ST
BENTON CO WA 342-H11
KENNEWICK WA 342-H11
MORAY BRDG
CITY OF RICHMOND BC 156-B6
MORCOM RD
MALHEUR CO OR 146-C2
MORELAND AV
MALDEN WA 114-B3
MORFORD RD
SKAGIT CO WA 161-C6
MORGAN AV
MALHEUR CO OR 139-A3
MORGAN DR
Birch Bay WA 158-B4
LINN CO OR 210-C1
MORGAN LN
LANE CO OR 210-A6
NE MORGAN LN
GRANTS PASS OR 335-F6
NW MORGAN LN
GRANTS PASS OR 335-E6
MORGAN RD
CLACKAMAS CO OR 200-C7
MORROW CO OR 128-B2
MULTNOMAH CO OR 192-A5
E MORGAN RD
SPOKANE CO WA 246-D2
MORGAN ST U.S.-2
DAVENPORT WA 114-A2
LINCOLN CO WA 114-A2
SW MORGAN ST
SEATTLE WA 280-E7
SEATTLE WA 281-F7
MORGAN LAKE RD
ADAMS CO WA 242-D7
MORGANSON RD
WASCO CO OR 196-A6
MORIARTY RD
CLALLAM CO WA 169-B2
MORMON BASIN RD
MALHEUR CO OR 138-B2
MORMON BASIN CUTOFF RD
MALHEUR CO OR 138-B2
MORNING STAR RD
LINN CO OR 207-D3
N MORNING-STAR RD
LANE CO OR 215-D4
MORRELLI DR
YAMHILL CO OR 198-B5
MORRILL RD
DESCHUTES CO OR 212-D7
MORRIS RD
ISLAND CO WA 167-C4
KLICKITAT CO WA 196-D4
POLK CO OR 204-A5
MORRIS ST
LA CONNER WA 167-D1
MORRISON RD
COOS CO OR 220-B6
SE MORRISON ST
PORTLAND OR 313-G6
MORRIS VALLEY RD
BRITISH COLUMBIA BC 94-C3
MORROW RD
MEDFORD OR 336-D9
POLK CO OR 204-B6
MORSE RD N
COLUMBIA CO OR 192-A2
MORSE RD S
COLUMBIA CO OR 192-A2
MORSE ST
COWLITZ CO WA 187-B5
MORSE-MERRIMAN RD SE
OLYMPIA WA 297-C9
MORTON RD
LEWIS CO WA 187-C3
MORTON RD Rt#-7
LEWIS CO WA 118-B2
MORTON WA 118-B2
MORTON ST Rt#-34
LEBANON OR 133-C1
N MORTON ST
COLFAX WA 122-C1
MORTON-BEAR CANYON RD Rt#-508
LEWIS CO WA 118-B2
MORTON WA 118-B2
MOSBY CREEK RD
COTTAGE GROVE OR 215-B7
LANE CO OR 141-C1
LANE CO OR 215-B7
MOSCOW RD Rt#-27
PALOUSE WA 249-B1
MOSCOW MOUNTAIN RD
LATAH CO ID 249-D4
MOSCROP ST
DISTRICT OF BURNABY BC 156-C5
MOSER RD
NEZ PERCE CO ID 250-B2
MOSES RD
OKANOGAN CO WA 105-B3
SNOHOMISH CO WA 168-D4
MOSES COULEE RD SE
DOUGLAS CO WA 112-C2
MOSES CREEK LN
UNION CO OR 130-A1
SE MOSHER AV
ROSEBURG OR 334-F8
MOSIER RD
CLACKAMAS CO OR 200-A6
COLUMBIA CO OR 189-A3
SKAGIT CO WA 161-C5
MOSIER CREEK RD
WASCO CO OR 196-A6
MOSIER-THE DALLES HWY U.S.-30
MOSIER OR 196-A5
THE DALLES OR 196-A5
WASCO CO OR 196-A5
MOSQUITO CREEK RD
COWLITZ CO WA 187-A7
MOSQUITO LAKE RD
WHATCOM CO WA 102-B1
WHATCOM CO WA 161-D1
MOSS ST
CITY OF VICTORIA BC 256-J11
MOSS CREEK RD
TILLAMOOK CO OR 191-B7
MOSS HILL RD
CLACKAMAS CO OR 200-C6
MOUNT ADAMS RD
KLICKITAT CO WA 119-A3
MOUNT ADAMS ST
HARRAH WA 119-C2
YAKIMA CO WA 119-C2
MOUNT ADAMS RECREATION AREA RD
KLICKITAT CO WA 119-A3
YAKIMA CO WA 119-A3
N MOUNTAIN AV
ASHLAND OR 337-E6
JACKSON CO OR 337-E6
S MOUNTAIN AV
ASHLAND OR 337-E8
MOUNTAIN BLVD U.S.-395
MOUNT VERNON OR 137-A2
MOUNTAIN HWY
DIST OF NORTH VANCOUVER BC 255-E2
MOUNTAIN HWY E Rt#-7
PIERCE CO WA 118-B1
PIERCE CO WA 181-D6
PIERCE CO WA 182-A7
MOUNTAIN HWY E Rt#-706
PIERCE CO WA 118-B1
PIERCE CO WA 185-A5
MOUNTAIN RD
ASOTIN CO WA 122-C3
GARFIELD CO WA 122-B2
KLAMATH CO OR 231-C1
SW MOUNTAIN RD
CLACKAMAS CO OR 199-C5
MOUNTAIN HOME DR
LINN CO OR 210-D2
MOUNTAIN HOME RD
CHELAN CO WA 238-A1
WASHINGTON CO OR 198-D4
YAMHILL CO OR 198-D5
MOUNTAIN LOOP HWY
DARRINGTON WA 103-A3
GRANITE FALLS WA 102-C3
SNOHOMISH CO WA 102-C3
SNOHOMISH CO WA 103-A3
SNOHOMISH CO WA 111-A1
MOUNTAIN MEADOWS RD
PIERCE CO WA 185-A2
MOUNTAIN MEADOWS RD Rt#-165
PIERCE CO WA 118-C1
PIERCE CO WA 185-A2
MOUNTAIN TOP RD
YAMHILL CO OR 198-D4
E MOUNTAIN VIEW AV
ELLENSBURG WA 241-B6
KITTITAS CO WA 241-B6
W MOUNTAIN VIEW AV
ELLENSBURG WA 241-B6
MOUNTAIN VIEW DR
BENTON CO OR 207-A4
BENTON CO OR 327-H1
BONNER CO ID 244-A2
CLACKAMAS CO OR 201-C5
MOUNTAINVIEW DR
NEWBERG OR 198-D5
YAMHILL CO OR 198-D5
N MOUNTAIN VIEW DR
BOISE ID 253-C2
SW MOUNTAIN VIEW DR
JEFFERSON CO OR 208-A6
W MOUNTAIN VIEW DR
BOISE ID 253-C2
MOUNTAIN VIEW DR E
KITSAP CO WA 271-D12
MOUNTAIN VIEW DR S
SALEM OR 324-G2
MOUNTAIN VIEW RD
COLUMBIA CO OR 192-A3
COWLITZ CO WA 189-D5
DESCHUTES CO OR 212-A4
FERNDALE WA 158-B6
SKAGIT CO WA 260-J14
WHATCOM CO WA 158-B6
N MOUNTAIN VIEW RD
LATAH CO ID 249-D4
MOUNT ANGEL HWY NE
MARION CO OR 205-B4
MOUNT ANGELES RD
CLALLAM CO WA 261-G8
PORT ANGELES WA 261-G8
MOUNT ANGEL-GERVAIS RD NE
MARION CO OR 205-B3
MOUNT ANGEL-SCOTTS MILLS RD NE
MARION CO OR 205-C3
MOUNT ASHLAND SKI RD
JACKSON CO OR 234-D6
MOUNT BAKER HWY Rt#-542
WHATCOM CO WA 102-B1
WHATCOM CO WA 103-A1
MOUNT BALDY LOOKOUT RD
SISKIYOU CO CA 149-A3
MOUNT BRYNION RD
COWLITZ CO WA 189-D3
COWLITZ CO WA 303-H5
KELSO WA 303-F6
N MOUNT CARROL ST
DALTON GARDENS ID 355-F2
MOUNT GLEN RD
UNION CO OR 130-A2
MOUNT HOOD AV Rt#-214
MARION CO OR 205-B1
WOODBURN OR 205-B1
MOUNT HOOD HWY Rt#-35
CLACKAMAS CO OR 202-C5
HOOD RIVER CO OR 195-C7
HOOD RIVER CO OR 202-C1
MOUNT HOOD HWY U.S.-26
CLACKAMAS CO OR 200-C3
CLACKAMAS CO OR 201-B4
CLACKAMAS CO OR 202-A6
GRESHAM OR 200-C3
MULTNOMAH CO OR 200-C3
SANDY OR 200-C3
SE MOUNT HOOD HWY U.S.-26
MULTNOMAH CO OR 200-A2
PORTLAND OR 200-A2
MOUNT HOOD ST
THE DALLES OR 196-C7
S MOUNT HOPE RD
CLACKAMAS CO OR 205-D2
MOUNT HOREB RD SE
MARION CO OR 134-A1
MOUNT JUPITER RD
JEFFERSON CO WA 173-C1
MOUNT LEHMAN RD
DISTRICT OF MATSQUI BC 102-B1
MOUNT MATHESON RD
BRITISH COLUMBIA BC 165-A1
DISTRICT OF METCHOSIN BC 165-A1
MOUNT NEWTON CROSS RD
DISTRICT OF CENTRAL SAANI BC 159-B3
MOUNT OLYMPUS AV
OCEAN SHORES WA 298-E4
MOUNT OLYMPUS AV SE
OCEAN SHORES WA 298-D2
MOUNT PLEASANT RD
COWLITZ CO WA 189-D4
SKAMANIA CO WA 193-D7
MOUNT REUBEN RD
DOUGLAS CO OR 225-A7
NW MOUNT RICHMOND RD
YAMHILL CO OR 198-A4
SE MOUNT SCOTT BLVD
CLACKAMAS CO OR 200-A3
CLACKAMAS CO OR 319-J7
HAPPY VALLEY OR 200-A3
MULTNOMAH CO OR 319-H6
PORTLAND OR 200-A3
PORTLAND OR 319-H6
PORTLAND OR 319-J7
MOUNT SEYMOUR PKWY
DIST OF NORTH VANCOUVER BC 156-D3
DIST OF NORTH VANCOUVER BC 255-H6
MOUNT SEYMOUR RD
DIST OF NORTH VANCOUVER BC 156-D3
MOUNT SHASTA DR
VANCOUVER WA 307-G7
MOUNT SOLO RD
COWLITZ CO WA 302-B5
LONGVIEW WA 302-B5
MOUNT SOLO RD Rt#-432
COWLITZ CO WA 302-C6
LONGVIEW WA 302-C6
E MOUNT SPOKANE PARK DR Rt#-20
SPOKANE CO WA 114-C1
SPOKANE CO WA 246-D1
SPOKANE CO WA 247-A1
SPOKANE CO WA 347-H5
N MOUNT SPOKANE PARK DR Rt#-20
SPOKANE CO WA 114-C1
MOUNT STELLA RD
JACKSON CO OR 226-D3
MOUNT TOM DR
LINN CO OR 210-B6
MOUNT TOM RD
LANE CO OR 210-C7
MOUNT VERNON RD
LANE CO OR 331-H9
SPRINGFIELD OR 331-H9
MOUNT VERNON RD S
SKAGIT CO WA 168-B1
MOUNT VERNON-BIG LAKE RD
MOUNT VERNON WA 260-H12
SKAGIT CO WA 161-C7
SKAGIT CO WA 260-H12
MOUNT VIEW RD
SPOKANE CO WA 247-A1
NW MOUNT WASHINGTON DR
BEND OR 332-B3
MOWICH RD
DOUGLAS CO OR 223-A4
MOWICH SECTION Rt#-165
CARBONADO WA 182-D6
PIERCE CO WA 110-C3
PIERCE CO WA 118-C1
PIERCE CO WA 182-D6
MOWREY RD
CHELAN CO WA 236-B3
MOX-CHEHALIS RD
GRAYS HARBOR CO WA 117-B1
GRAYS HARBOR CO WA 179-C7
E MOXEE AV
MOXEE WA 243-D7
YAKIMA CO WA 243-D7
MOYIE RIVER RD
BOUNDARY CO ID 107-B1
MUCK-KAPOWSIN
PIERCE CO WA 182-A6
MUD BAY HWY SW
OLYMPIA WA 296-A4
THURSTON CO WA 180-B6
THURSTON CO WA 296-A4
MUD BAY RD
SAN JUAN CO WA 160-A7
MUD CREEK RD
ADAMS CO ID 251-A3
MUDDY RD
WASCO CO OR 135-C1
MUDDY CREEK RD
BAKER CO OR 130-A3
SW MUDDY VALLEY RD
YAMHILL CO OR 204-A2
MUD FLAT RD
MALHEUR CO OR 146-C2
OWYHEE CO ID 147-C3
OWYHEE CO ID 155-B1
WHITMAN CO WA 122-B1
MUD LAKE RD
DESCHUTES CO OR 216-A4
SKAGIT CO WA 161-C6
MUD SPRING RD
MALHEUR CO OR 154-A2
MUD SPRINGS RD NE
DOUGLAS CO WA 112-C1
MUD SPRINGS RD NW
DOUGLAS CO WA 112-B1
MUEKE RD
CLACKAMAS CO OR 199-B6
MUELLER RD
UMATILLA CO OR 121-C3
MUFFORD AV
LANGLEY BC 157-C7
TOWNSHIP OF LANGLEY BC 157-C7
MUIR CREEK RD
DOUGLAS CO OR 223-A7
DOUGLAS CO OR 227-A1
MUKILTEO BLVD
EVERETT WA 171-B2
EVERETT WA 264-A7
MUKILTEO WA 171-B2
MUKILTEO BLVD SE
EVERETT WA 264-C6
MUKILTEO BLVD SW
EVERETT WA 264-B7
MUKILTEO SPEEDWAY Rt#-525
MUKILTEO WA 171-B2
MUKILTEO WA 266-D3
MUKILTEO WA 267-E5
SNOHOMISH CO WA 171-B4
SNOHOMISH CO WA 267-E6
MULEDEER RD
DOUGLAS CO WA 239-B1
MULE SPRING RD
HARNEY CO OR 144-C3
MULFORD RD
LEWIS CO WA 187-C4
NW MULHOLLAND DR
ROSEBURG OR 334-E4
MULINO RD
CLACKAMAS CO OR 199-C7
S MULINO RD
CANBY OR 199-C6
CLACKAMAS CO OR 199-C6
MULKEY RD
WHITMAN CO WA 114-B3
E MULLAN AV
KOOTENAI CO ID 353-H6
KOOTENAI CO ID 354-F6
OSBURN ID 115-C2
POST FALLS ID 353-H6
POST FALLS ID 354-B6
W MULLAN AV
KOOTENAI CO ID 354-H6
POST FALLS ID 353-G6
MULLAN RD
ADAMS CO WA 122-A1
N MULLAN RD
SPOKANE VALLEY WA 350-D8
MULLEN RD SE
LACEY WA 297-H10
THURSTON CO WA 181-A7
THURSTON CO WA 297-J11
SE MULLENIX RD
KITSAP CO WA 174-C5
MULLER DR
LINN CO OR 207-D5
S MULLINIX RD
SPOKANE CO WA 114-B2
SW MULTNOMAH BLVD
PORTLAND OR 199-B2
PORTLAND OR 316-A6
MULTNOMAH DR
HOOD RIVER CO OR 195-C5
NE MULTNOMAH ST
PORTLAND OR 313-H4
PORTLAND OR 314-A4
MULTNOMAH BASIN RD
MULTNOMAH CO OR 201-A1
MUNCH RD
CLARK CO WA 193-A1
MUNDUN CANYON RD
CHELAN CO WA 238-A2
MUNDY ST
COQUITLAM BC 157-A5
MUNDY LOSS RD
PIERCE CO WA 182-D4
MUNN RD
BRITISH COLUMBIA BC 159-B5
DISTRICT OF SAANICH BC 256-A1
MUNSEL LAKE RD
FLORENCE OR 214-B2
LANE CO OR 214-B2
MUNSON DR SW
THURSTON CO WA 180-B6
MUNSON CREEK RD
TILLAMOOK CO OR 197-C4
MURCHIE RD
TOWNSHIP OF LANGLEY BC 158-C2
MURDER CREEK DR
LINN CO OR 326-H3
MURPHY DR NW
PIERCE CO WA 181-C1
MURPHY RD
BEND OR 332-E12
DOUGLAS CO OR 225-C7
FRANKLIN CO WA 121-B2
LINCOLN CO OR 203-D4
S MURPHY RD
SPOKANE CO WA 246-A6
MURPHY CREEK RD
JOSEPHINE CO OR 149-A2
MURPHY-GRANDVIEW RD Rt#-78
OWYHEE CO ID 147-C2
MURPHY GULCH RD
JACKSON CO OR 230-A4
NW MURRAY BLVD
WASHINGTON CO OR 199-B1
SW MURRAY BLVD
BEAVERTON OR 199-A2
WASHINGTON CO OR 199-A2
MURRAY RD SW
LAKEWOOD WA 181-C5
PIERCE CO WA 181-C5
MURRAY ST
PORT MOODY BC 157-A4
MUSTANG RESERVOIR RD
MALHEUR CO OR 154-C1
MUTINY BAY RD
Clinton WA 171-A2
Freeland WA 170-C1
MYERS RD
POLK CO OR 204-A5
TOPPENISH WA 120-A2
YAKIMA CO WA 120-A2
MYERS RD E
BONNEY LAKE WA 182-C4
MYERS WY S
KING CO WA 285-J3
KING CO WA 286-A4
SEATTLE WA 285-J3
SEATTLE WA 286-A4
MYERS CREEK RD
CURRY CO OR 232-B1
MYRA RD
COLLEGE PLACE WA 344-G9
WALLA WALLA WA 344-G9
WALLA WALLA CO WA 344-G9
MYRNA LN
JOSEPHINE CO OR 233-A4
S MYRTLE PL
SEATTLE WA 286-D1
E MYRTLE ST
BOISE ID 253-C3
S MYRTLE ST
SEATTLE WA 286-D1
W MYRTLE ST
BOISE ID 253-C3
MYRTLE CREEK RD
COOS CO OR 140-C3
N MYRTLE CREEK RD
DOUGLAS CO OR 141-B2
DOUGLAS CO OR 221-D7
DOUGLAS CO OR 225-D1
S MYRTLE CREEK RD
DOUGLAS CO OR 225-D1
MYRTLE PARK RD
HARNEY CO OR 137-A3

INDEX

STREET / City State	Page-Grid
MYRTLE POINT-COOPER BRIDGE RD	
COOS OR	140-B2
MYRTLE POINT OR	140-B2
MYRTLE POINT-LAMPA RD	
COOS CO OR	140-B2
COOS CO OR	220-C6
MYRTLE POINT OR	140-B2
MYRTLE POINT-SITKUM RD	
COOS CO OR	140-C2

N

STREET / City State	Page-Grid
N ST	
GRANTS PASS OR	335-G10
JOSEPHINE CO OR	335-H10
SE N ST	
GRANTS PASS OR	335-G10
NACHES AV	
TIETON WA	119-C1
E NACHES AV Rt#-823	
SELAH WA	243-B5
S NACHES AV	
YAKIMA WA	243-C6
S NACHES RD	
NACHES WA	119-C1
YAKIMA WA	119-C1
YAKIMA CO WA	243-A5
S NACHES WY	
YAKIMA WA	119-C1
W NACHES WY	
YAKIMA WA	119-C1
NACHES HEIGHTS RD	
YAKIMA CO WA	243-A5
NACHES-TIETON RD	
TIETON WA	119-C1
YAKIMA CO WA	119-C1
NACHES WENAS RD	
YAKIMA CO WA	243-A4
NAGLER RD	
YAKIMA CO WA	243-B5
NAHAHUM CANYON RD	
CHELAN CO WA	238-C2
NW NAITO PKWY	
PORTLAND OR	312-E3
PORTLAND OR	313-F4
SW NAITO PKWY	
PORTLAND OR	313-F6
PORTLAND OR	317-F1
SW NAITO PKWY Rt#-99W	
PORTLAND OR	317-F1
NAMPA BLVD Rt#-55	
NAMPA ID	147-B1
NANAIMO PKWY Rt#-19	
NANAIMO BC	93-A3
NANAIMO ST	
VANCOUVER BC	156-C5
VANCOUVER BC	255-C12
NANAIMO-HORSESHOE FERRY	
BRITISH COLUMBIA BC	93-A3
NANAIMO LAKES RD	
NANAIMO BC	93-A3
NANAIMO-TSAWWASSEN FERRY	
BRITISH COLUMBIA BC	93-A3
BRITISH COLUMBIA BC	101-B1
NANAIMO BC	93-A3
NANCY GREENE WY	
DIST OF NORTH VANCOUVER BC	156-B2
NANEUM RD	
KITTITAS CO WA	241-C4
NANEUM RIDGE RD	
KITTITAS CO WA	241-D1
NAPOLEON-BARSTOW RD	
STEVENS CO WA	106-A1
NARROWS DR	
TACOMA WA	181-C2
NARROWS-PRINCETON RD	
HARNEY CO OR	145-B2
NASH AV	
BENTON CO OR	327-C13
NASH LN	
CANYON CO ID	147-B1
NASHUA LN	
DESCHUTES CO OR	212-A4
NW NASHVILLE AV	
BEND OR	332-D6
NASI LN	
VALLEY CO ID	252-D1
NASTY FLAT RD	
HARNEY CO OR	144-B3
SW NATERLIN DR	
NEWPORT OR	206-B4
NATIONAL AV	
CHEHALIS WA	299-E9
LEWIS CO WA	299-E9
S NATIONAL AV	
Navy Yard City WA	270-E12
NATIONAL AV N	
BREMERTON WA	270-E11
Navy Yard City WA	270-E11
NATIONAL PARK HWY	
LEWIS CO WA	185-A5
PIERCE CO WA	185-A5
NATIONAL PARK HWY Rt#-62	
KLAMATH CO OR	227-B4
NATIONAL PARK HWY U.S.-12	
LEWIS CO WA	118-B2
MORTON WA	118-B2
NAVAL AV	
BREMERTON WA	270-G10
NAVARRE ST	
CHELAN WA	236-D3
NAVARRE COULEE RD Rt#-971	
CHELAN CO WA	236-B3
NEACOXIE DR	
GEARHART OR	301-G5
NEAH BAY RD	
CLALLAM WA	100-B2
Neah Bay WA	100-B2
NEAH BAY RD Rt#-112	
CLALLAM CO WA	100-B2
Neah Bay WA	100-B2
NEAL LN	
DOUGLAS CO OR	225-C1
NEAL CREEK RD	
HOOD RIVER CO OR	195-C7
NEALEY RD	
OKANOGAN CO WA	105-A1
NEATHAMMER GULCH RD	
JACKSON CO OR	230-A3
NEAVES RD	
PITT MEADOWS BC	157-C5
NEBRASKA ST	
SKAGIT CO WA	259-J14
NECANICUM DR	
SEASIDE OR	301-G8
NECANICUM HWY Rt#-53	
CLATSOP CO OR	188-D7
CLATSOP CO OR	191-C3
NECANICUM HWY Rt#-53	
TILLAMOOK CO OR	191-C3
NECK RD	
YAMHILL CO OR	198-C7
NEEDLE CREEK RD	
JACKSON CO OR	226-C5
NEEDLE RIDGE RD	
JACKSON CO OR	226-C5
NEEDLE ROCK RD	
JACKSON CO OR	226-B5
S NEEDY RD	
CLACKAMAS CO OR	205-D1
NEER CITY RD	
COLUMBIA CO OR	189-C4
NEER CITY CEMETERY RD	
COLUMBIA CO OR	189-C5
NEERGAARD RD	
ADAMS CO WA	113-B3
NEFF RD	
BEND OR	217-C2
DESCHUTES CO OR	217-C2
JEFFERSON CO OR	208-C3
NE NEFF RD	
BEND OR	217-C2
BEND OR	332-H6
NEGUS WY	
DESCHUTES CO OR	212-D5
NEHALEM DR	
CLATSOP CO OR	191-D1
NEHALEM HWY Rt#-47	
COLUMBIA CO OR	117-B3
COLUMBIA CO OR	125-B1
WASHINGTON CO OR	125-B1
NEHALEM HWY Rt#-202	
CLATSOP CO OR	117-B3
CLATSOP CO OR	188-D3
CLATSOP CO OR	300-F8
COLUMBIA CO OR	117-B3
NEHALEM RD	
TILLAMOOK CO OR	191-A4
NEHALEM ST	
CLATSKANIE OR	117-B3
NEHALEM QUARRY RD	
TILLAMOOK CO OR	191-B3
E NEIDER AV	
COEUR D'ALENE ID	355-E7
NEILL RD	
WASHINGTON CO OR	198-D5
NEILSEN RD	
WHATCOM CO WA	158-C6
E NEILSON RD	
KOOTENAI CO ID	245-B5
NELLITA RD NW	
KITSAP CO WA	173-C2
NELS NELSON RD NW	
DOUGLAS CO WA	236-B6
KITSAP CO WA	174-B1
KITSAP CO WA	270-F1
Silverdale WA	174-B1
NELSON AV	
DISTRICT OF BURNABY BC	156-C5
NELSON LP	
KOOTENAI CO ID	247-C5
NELSON RD	
DESCHUTES CO OR	217-D2
DOUGLAS CO OR	219-B1
LEWIS CO WA	187-B2
WALLA WALLA CO WA	121-B3
WASHINGTON CO OR	198-A1
E NELSON RD	
GRANT CO WA	242-D3
SE NELSON RD	
KITSAP CO WA	174-C6
NELSON ST	
VANCOUVER BC	254-E9
NELSON SIDING RD	
KITTITAS CO WA	111-B3
NEPPEL RD	
ADAMS CO WA	242-B1
NESIKA RD	
CURRY CO OR	228-A4
NESS RD	
KOOTENAI CO ID	247-C7
NESS RD Rt#-116	
Hadlock-Irondale WA	170-A1
JEFFERSON CO WA	170-A1
NESS CORNER RD Rt#-116	
Hadlock-Irondale WA	170-A1
NESTUCCA RIVER RD	
TILLAMOOK CO OR	125-B2
YAMHILL CO OR	125-B2
NW NESTUCCA RIVER RD	
YAMHILL CO OR	125-B2
NETARTS HWY	
TILLAMOOK OR	197-B2
TILLAMOOK CO OR	197-A2
NETARTS BAY DR	
TILLAMOOK OR	197-A2
N NETTLETON ST	
SPOKANE WA	348-F5
SW NEUGEBAUER RD	
WASHINGTON CO OR	198-D4
NEVADA AV	
KLAMATH FALLS OR	338-B5
W NEVADA AV Rt#-903	
ROSLYN WA	240-A1
N NEVADA DR	
COWLITZ CO WA	302-J5
COWLITZ CO WA	303-A5
E NEVADA ST	
ASHLAND OR	337-D5
N NEVADA ST	
SPOKANE WA	347-B11
SPOKANE WA	349-B4
SPOKANE CO WA	347-B12
W NEVADA ST	
ASHLAND OR	337-C5
NEVADA STATE ROUTE Rt#-140	
HARNEY CO OR	153-A3
HUMBOLDT CO NV	153-C3
NEVADA STATE ROUTE Rt#-292	
HUMBOLDT CO NV	153-C3
NEVIL RD	
LEWIS CO WA	187-C3
NEVILLE LN	
JACKSON CO OR	234-A2
NEVIN RD	
CITY OF CHILLIWACK BC	94-C3
E NEWARK AV	
SPOKANE WA	349-C10
NEWBERG HWY Rt#-214	
WOODBURN OR	205-B1
NEWBERG HWY Rt#-219	
MARION CO OR	205-B1
WASHINGTON CO OR	198-D2
WOODBURN OR	205-B1
NEWBERG RD	
TILLAMOOK CO OR	197-B5
NW NEWBERRY RD	
MULTNOMAH CO OR	192-B6
PORTLAND OR	192-B6
NEWBERRY CRATER RD	
DESCHUTES CO OR	143-A1
NW NEWBERRY HILL RD	
KITSAP CO WA	174-A2
Silverdale WA	270-A1
NEW BRIDGE RD	
BAKER CO OR	139-A1
NE NEW BROOKLYN RD	
KITSAP CO WA	174-C1
NEWBURY RD	
GRAYS HARBOR CO WA	178-A2
SE NEWCASTLE COAL CREEK RD	
NEWCASTLE WA	175-C3
NEWCOMB RD	
DESCHUTES CO OR	212-C6
NEW CREEK RD	
MALHEUR CO OR	146-B1
NEW HOPE RD	
GRANTS PASS OR	335-C14
JOSEPHINE CO OR	149-A2
JOSEPHINE CO OR	229-B7
JOSEPHINE CO OR	335-C14
NEW JONES RD	
JACKSON CO OR	230-C4
S NEW KIRCHNER RD	
CLACKAMAS CO OR	199-D7
NEW LAKE RD	
COOS CO OR	224-B2
NEWLAND RD	
CLACKAMAS CO OR	199-C5
CLACKAMAS CO OR	230-C6
NEWMAN RD	
ISLAND CO WA	170-D1
S NEWMAN RD	
CLACKAMAS CO OR	205-C2
NEWMAN CREEK RD	
GRAYS HARBOR CO WA	179-B7
N NEWMAN LAKE DR	
SPOKANE CO WA	247-B1
W NEWMAN LAKE DR	
SPOKANE CO WA	247-B1
SPOKANE CO WA	352-D1
NEWMARK AV	
COOS BAY OR	333-B6
NORTH BEND OR	333-D7
NEWMARK ST	
NORTH BEND OR	333-F6
NEW OMAK LAKE RD	
OKANOGAN CO WA	104-C3
NEWPORT AV	
COOS CO OR	220-D1
COOS BAY OR	333-H12
DISTRICT OF OAK BAY BC	257-D9
NEWPORT AV U.S.-101	
COOS BAY OR	333-H12
KLAMATH CO OR	231-B1
NW NEWPORT AV	
BEND OR	332-D6
N NEWPORT HWY U.S.-2	
Country Homes WA	347-B9
Fairwood WA	347-B9
SPOKANE WA	347-E5
NW NEWPORT WY	
ISSAQUAH WA	175-D4
SE NEWPORT WY	
BELLEVUE WA	175-D3
NEWPORT WY NW	
ISSAQUAH WA	175-D4
ISSAQUAH WA	176-A4
NEWSKAH RD	
GRAYS HARBOR CO WA	183-D1
NEWSOME CREEK RD	
CROOK CO OR	136-A3
NEWTON RD	
STEVENS CO WA	106-B3
NEWTON ST	
CITY OF VICTORIA BC	257-B7
DISTRICT OF SAANICH BC	257-B7
E NEWTON ST	
SEATTLE WA	278-B2
NE NEWTON CREEK RD	
DOUGLAS CO OR	334-H2
ROSEBURG OR	334-G3
NEWTON HILL RD	
LINCOLN CO OR	206-B3
NEZ PERCE AV	
WINCHESTER ID	123-B2
W NEZ PERCE RD	
COEUR D'ALENE ID	354-J6
COEUR D'ALENE ID	355-A6
NEZPERCE-CRAIGMONT RD	
LEWIS CO ID	123-B2
NFD RD 2	
ADAMS CO ID	131-B3
NFD RD 9	
SHOSHONE CO ID	115-C1
WASHINGTON CO ID	139-A1
NFD RD 10	
CLACKAMAS CO OR	201-A3
GRANT CO OR	129-B3
GRANT CO OR	137-B1
MULTNOMAH CO OR	201-B2
NFD RD 11	
SPOKANE CO WA	233-A5
NFD RD 12	
CLACKAMAS CO OR	201-A3
JEFFERSON CO OR	134-C1
LEWIS CO WA	185-A6
LINCOLN CO OR	206-D7
TILLAMOOK CO OR	203-C3
NFD RD 13	
BAKER CO OR	137-C2
GRANT CO OR	137-C3
HOOD RIVER CO OR	201-D2
HOOD RIVER CO OR	202-A1
NFD RD 14	
CLACKAMAS CO OR	201-A3
GRANT CO OR	137-C3
SKAMANIA CO WA	193-D1
SKAMANIA CO WA	194-A1
TILLAMOOK CO OR	197-C6
TILLAMOOK CO OR	197-D7
NFD RD 15	
GRANT CO OR	137-B3
JOSEPHINE CO OR	233-B7
JOSEPHINE CO OR	203-C2
NFD RD 16	
BAKER CO OR	138-A2
GRANT CO OR	137-C2
HOOD RIVER CO OR	202-A2
NFD RD 16	
JOSEPHINE CO OR	233-A1
NFD RD 17	
HOOD RIVER CO OR	202-C3
JOSEPHINE CO OR	233-C7
LINCOLN CO OR	203-C4
NFD RD 18	
LAKE CO OR	143-B1
NFD RD 19	
LINCOLN CO OR	203-B6
NFD RD 20	
CURRY CO OR	224-B7
MULTNOMAH CO OR	201-A1
NFD RD 21	
GRANT CO OR	137-A2
LANE CO OR	142-A1
MORROW CO OR	195-A3
UMATILLA CO OR	129-C3
UNION CO OR	129-C2
NFD RD 22	
BONNER CO ID	244-A7
KLAMATH CO OR	143-A1
LAKE CO OR	143-A1
LANE CO OR	142-A1
NFD RD 23	
CURRY CO OR	148-C1
DOUGLAS CO OR	214-C6
LANE CO OR	142-B1
LANE CO OR	118-C2
MASON CO WA	109-B2
SKAMANIA CO WA	119-A3
NFD RD 24	
GRANT CO OR	136-C2
GRANT CO OR	137-A2
LAKE CO OR	143-A1
LANE CO OR	142-A1
NFD RD 25	
LANE CO OR	209-C6
LEWIS CO WA	118-C2
MASON CO WA	173-A2
SKAMANIA CO WA	118-C2
WASHINGTON CO ID	139-A1
WHEELER CO OR	128-B3
NFD RD 28	
GRANT CO OR	137-A2
LANE CO OR	197-D6
NFD RD 29	
CLALLAM CO OR	163-C7
NFD RD 30	
CLALLAM CO OR	163-C6
CLALLAM CO OR	164-A5
COWLITZ CO WA	190-A3
DESCHUTES CO OR	217-C5
NFD RD 31	
GRANT CO OR	137-A3
UMATILLA CO OR	130-A1
WASHINGTON CO ID	139-B1
NFD RD 32	
LANE CO OR	209-D6
OKANOGAN CO WA	105-A1
UMATILLA CO OR	130-A1
NFD RD 33	
CURRY CO OR	148-B1
KLAMATH CO OR	231-B1
NFD RD 34	
DOUGLAS CO OR	222-D2
DOUGLAS CO OR	223-A2
NFD RD 35	
DOUGLAS CO OR	222-D4
KITTITAS CO WA	238-B7
NFD RD 36	
GRANT CO OR	137-B1
NFD RD 37	
GRANT CO OR	137-A3
NFD RD 38	
LANE CO OR	209-B1
OKANOGAN CO WA	104-B2
NFD RD 40	
GRAYS HARBOR CO WA	190-B7
GARFIELD CO WA	122-B2
NFD RD 41	
JOSEPHINE CO OR	233-D7
NFD RD 42	
JOSEPHINE CO OR	233-C5
SKAMANIA CO WA	194-A2
NFD RD 43	
KLAMATH CO OR	142-C3
SKAMANIA CO WA	194-B3
NFD RD 44	
HOOD RIVER CO OR	202-C4
LEWIS CO WA	185-D6
OKANOGAN CO WA	104-A3
NFD RD 46	
KLAMATH CO OR	151-A1
LEWIS CO WA	185-D7
MARION CO OR	126-C3
MARION CO OR	134-C1
NFD RD 48	
HOOD RIVER CO OR	202-B6
LANE CO OR	214-D4
WASCO CO OR	127-A3
WASCO CO OR	202-C7
NFD RD 48N	
KLAMATH CO OR	151-B3
LAKE CO OR	151-B3
NFD RD 49	
KLAMATH CO OR	143-A3
NFD RD 50	
KING CO WA	176-D7
LINCOLN CO OR	206-C7
SHOSHONE CO ID	115-B2
NFD RD 51	
GRANT CO OR	137-C3
UNION CO OR	129-C3
NFD RD 52	
GRANT CO OR	129-C3
JEFFERSON CO OR	211-C2
LANE CO OR	209-A7
LINCOLN CO OR	206-D7
UMATILLA CO OR	129-B3
NFD RD 53	
MORROW CO OR	129-A3
SKAMANIA CO WA	193-D2
UMATILLA CO OR	129-A3
NFD RD 54	
LANE CO OR	209-C4
SKAMANIA CO WA	193-D1
SKAMANIA CO WA	194-A1
NFD RD 55	
WASHINGTON CO ID	131-B3
NFD RD 58	
CROOK CO OR	136-C2
GRANT CO OR	136-C2
LANE CO OR	209-C5
SKAMANIA CO WA	194-A1
NFD RD 59	
DOUGLAS CO OR	214-B6
NFD RD 60	
DOUGLAS CO OR	223-D2
KLAMATH CO OR	142-B1
NFD RD 62	
UNION CO OR	130-B1
NFD RD 63	
UNION CO OR	130-A1
NFD RD 64	
SKAMANIA CO WA	190-D6
UNION CO OR	130-A1
NFD RD 65	
CHELAN CO WA	111-B1
MULTNOMAH CO OR	194-D1
NFD RD 67	
JOSEPHINE CO OR	233-A1
NFD RD 68	
MORROW CO OR	195-A3
NFD RD 70	
CURRY CO OR	232-C1
UNION CO OR	129-C2
NFD RD 73	
GRANITE OR	137-C1
GRANT CO OR	129-C3
GRANT CO OR	130-A3
GRANT CO OR	137-C1
GRANT CO OR	130-A3
NFD RD 75	
DOUGLAS CO OR	222-D4
NFD RD 77	
CLACKAMAS CO OR	201-A6
BAKER CO OR	130-C3
NFD RD 80	
GRAYS HARBOR CO WA	109-A2
JOSEPHINE CO OR	233-D6
NFD RD 81	
COWLITZ CO WA	190-A3
SKAMANIA CO WA	190-B3
NFD RD 83	
HUMBOLDT CO NV	154-C3
HUMBOLDT CO NV	155-C3
SKAMANIA CO WA	190-D2
NFD RD 84	
HUMBOLDT CO NV	154-C3
LEWIS CO WA	185-A6
LINCOLN CO OR	203-C7
NFD RD 85	
JOSEPHINE CO OR	233-C7
LANE CO OR	125-C3
NFD RD 87	
HUMBOLDT CO NV	154-C3
NFD RD 89	
ADAMS CO	131-C3
NFD RD 90	
SKAMANIA CO WA	118-C3
SKAMANIA CO WA	190-D5
NFD RD 92 Rt#-508	
LINCOLN CO MT	107-C1
NFD RD 94	
SKAMANIA CO WA	190-D1
NFD RD 96	
HUMBOLDT CO NV	154-C3
HUMBOLDT CO NV	155-A3
NFD RD 98	
JOSEPHINE CO OR	233-D7
NFD RD 99	
KLAMATH CO OR	190-C1
NFD RD 100	
DESCHUTES CO OR	211-D6
DOUGLAS CO OR	222-B1
OKANOGAN CO WA	105-B2
NFD RD 105	
ADAMS CO ID	131-B3
NFD RD 110	
CURRY CO OR	228-D1
KLAMATH CO OR	231-A2
NFD RD 111	
KITTITAS CO WA	241-B1
NFD RD 112	
CHELAN CO WA	111-C2
KITTITAS CO WA	241-A2
TILLAMOOK CO OR	125-A2
NFD RD 113	
KITTITAS CO WA	241-B1
NFD RD 114	
KITTITAS CO WA	241-A1
NFD RD 115	
KITTITAS CO WA	238-A7
KITTITAS CO WA	241-B2
NFD RD 116	
KITTITAS CO WA	238-A6
KITTITAS CO WA	241-B2
VALLEY CO OR	252-C4
NFD RD 118	
KITTITAS CO WA	238-A7
NFD RD 128	
ADAMS CO ID	131-B3
NFD RD 129	
LINCOLN CO OR	203-B4
NFD RD 130	
CURRY CO OR	232-D2
JEFFERSON CO OR	211-C2
NFD RD 134	
LEWIS CO WA	185-A7
NFD RD 150	
CURRY CO OR	228-B1
GRANT CO OR	211-A6
NFD RD 151	
SHOSHONE CO ID	115-C1
NFD RD 160	
DESCHUTES CO OR	211-C4
DESCHUTES CO OR	216-D6
NFD RD 165	
ADAMS CO ID	139-C1
ADAMS CO ID	252-A1
NFD RD 172	
ADAMS CO ID	251-A7
NFD RD 181	
ADAMS CO ID	251-A7
NFD RD 183	
ADAMS CO ID	251-A7
ADAMS CO ID	252-A1
NFD RD 186	
ADAMS CO ID	252-A1
VALLEY CO ID	252-C1
NFD RD 199	
ADAMS CO ID	252-A2
NFD RD 200	
ADAMS CO ID	252-A2
CHELAN CO WA	238-C3
NFD RD 203	
SKAMANIA CO WA	194-A1
NFD RD 206	
ADAMS CO ID	252-B4
NFD RD 206	
KOOTENAI CO ID	245-C4
NFD RD 207	
SKAMANIA CO WA	190-D6
NFD RD 208	
SHOSHONE CO ID	115-C1
NFD RD 209	
KOOTENAI CO ID	245-C2
NFD RD 213	
KITTITAS CO WA	241-A1
NFD RD 214	
ADAMS CO ID	252-A4
NFD RD 217	
ADAMS CO ID	252-A4
NFD RD 218	
ADAMS CO ID	252-C2
NFD RD 230	
CURRY CO OR	232-D1
DESCHUTES CO OR	217-D5
NFD RD 231	
KLAMATH CO OR	231-A2
NFD RD 231	
BOUNDARY CO ID	107-A2
NFD RD 243	
ADAMS CO ID	252-B5
NFD RD 250	
DESCHUTES CO OR	217-D7
NFD RD 255	
CLACKAMAS CO OR	201-A6
NFD RD 258	
KOOTENAI CO ID	245-D3
NFD RD 268	
KOOTENAI CO ID	245-B6
NFD RD 270	
SKAMANIA CO WA	190-D2
NFD RD 278	
BONNER CO ID	244-D5
BONNER CO ID	245-D1
KOOTENAI CO ID	245-D2
NFD RD 280	
JEFFERSON CO OR	211-B1
NFD RD 281	
DOUGLAS CO OR	223-A7
NFD RD 288	
KLAMATH CO OR	143-B3
KLAMATH CO OR	151-B1
LAKE CO OR	143-B3
NFD RD 291	
BOUNDARY CO ID	107-B2
NFD RD 294	
BOUNDARY CO ID	107-B2
NFD RD 300	
DESCHUTES CO OR	217-A3
NFD RD 301	
SHOSHONE CO ID	115-C3
NFD RD 302	
BONNER CO ID	106-C2
NFD RD 306	
SHOSHONE CO ID	244-D7
NFD RD 317	
SKAMANIA CO WA	190-D7
NFD RD 320	
SKAMANIA CO WA	190-D7
NFD RD 331	
KLAMATH CO OR	151-B1
NFD RD 332	
BONNER CO ID	244-C7
NFD RD 348	
KLAMATH CO OR	151-B1
LAKE CO OR	151-C1
NFD RD 350	
KLAMATH CO OR	231-A4
NFD RD 360	
KLAMATH CO OR	231-A4
NFD RD 370	
DESCHUTES CO OR	216-C1
NFD RD 375	
KLAMATH CO OR	231-A4
NFD RD 380	
SKAMANIA CO WA	190-D2
NFD RD 381	
KLAMATH CO OR	151-B2
NFD RD 382	
CLACKAMAS CO OR	201-D4
NFD RD 392	
KOOTENAI CO ID	245-C4
NFD RD 400	
CHELAN CO WA	238-A2
DESCHUTES CO OR	211-C5
DESCHUTES CO OR	216-D5
JEFFERSON CO OR	211-B1
SHOSHONE CO ID	115-C1
NFD RD 406	
KOOTENAI CO ID	245-D2
NFD RD 410	
CLACKAMAS CO OR	201-A3
NFD RD 411	
KOOTENAI CO ID	245-D5
NFD RD 413	
KOOTENAI CO ID	245-D7
SKAMANIA CO WA	194-B2
NFD RD 422	
VALLEY CO ID	252-D7
NFD RD 434	
KOOTENAI CO ID	245-D6
NFD RD 435	
VALLEY CO ID	252-C5
NFD RD 437	
KOOTENAI CO ID	245-C4
NFD RD 438	
KOOTENAI CO ID	248-C2
NFD RD 450	
KOOTENAI CO ID	245-C4
NFD RD 456	
DESCHUTES CO OR	216-A3
NFD RD 471	
SHOSHONE CO ID	115-C2
NFD RD 471	
HUMBOLDT CO NV	154-C3
NFD RD 472	
JOSEPHINE CO OR	233-D6
NFD RD 480	
LANE CO OR	142-A1
NFD RD 487	
ADAMS CO ID	251-B7
ADAMS CO ID	252-B1
NFD RD 489	
BONNER CO ID	244-D2
NFD RD 500	
DOUGLAS CO OR	222-B2
NFD RD 503	
SHOSHONE CO ID	115-C1
NFD RD 508 Rt#-508	
LINCOLN CO MT	107-C2
NFD RD 510	
CHELAN CO WA	238-C2
NFD RD 527	
SKAMANIA CO WA	194-A1
NFD RD 529	
HUMBOLDT CO NV	154-C3

INDEX

STREET City State	Page-Grid
NFD RD 531 HUMBOLDT CO NV	154-C3
NFD RD 587 ADAMS CO ID	251-A5
NFD RD 600 DESCHUTES CO OR	211-C7
DESCHUTES CO OR	217-C4
JEFFERSON CO OR	211-B2
NFD RD 610 KOOTENAI CO ID	245-D5
NFD RD 612 KOOTENAI CO ID	245-C5
NFD RD 616 KOOTENAI CO ID	245-D5
NFD RD 618 GEM CO ID	252-B7
NFD RD 625 GEM CO ID	252-B7
KOOTENAI CO ID	245-B4
NFD RD 700 DOUGLAS CO OR	223-C2
LINN CO OR	134-A2
SKAMANIA CO WA	190-D3
NFD RD 719 LANE CO OR	214-C2
NFD RD 760 DOUGLAS CO OR	223-C7
NFD RD 794 KOOTENAI CO ID	245-D3
NFD RD 800 DESCHUTES CO OR	211-B3
NFD RD 808 KOOTENAI CO ID	248-B3
NFD RD 810 KOOTENAI CO ID	248-C2
SKAMANIA CO WA	190-D3
NFD RD 831 LANE CO OR	214-D3
NFD RD 835 ADAMS CO ID	252-B5
NFD RD 855 KLAMATH CO OR	142-C1
NFD RD 950 DOUGLAS CO OR	222-C6
DOUGLAS CO OR	226-B3
NFD RD 953 LANE CO OR	214-B4
NFD RD 958 LANE CO OR	214-D4
NFD RD 980 KLAMATH CO OR	231-A4
NFD RD 1000 LINCOLN CO OR	206-D7
NFD RD 1008 MULTNOMAH CO OR	201-A2
NFD RD 1010 MULTNOMAH CO OR	201-A2
NFD RD 1012 DESCHUTES CO OR	211-C4
NFD RD 1013 BOUNDARY CO ID	106-C1
NFD RD 1014 LINCOLN CO OR	206-D7
NFD RD 1017 BONNER CO ID	245-D2
NFD RD 1018 DESCHUTES CO OR	211-B6
NFD RD 1024 DESCHUTES CO OR	211-B6
NFD RD 1026 DESCHUTES CO OR	211-B6
NFD RD 1027 CLACKAMAS CO OR	201-C3
NFD RD 1028 DESCHUTES CO OR	211-B4
NFD RD 1030 LINCOLN CO OR	206-D7
NFD RD 1031 TILLAMOOK CO OR	203-B1
NFD RD 1050 BONNER CO ID	244-B7
NFD RD 1066 BONNER CO ID	244-D6
NFD RD 1080 BONNER CO ID	245-D2
NFD RD 1088 BONNER CO ID	244-C6
NFD RD 1101 CURRY CO OR	232-D7
NFD RD 1110 JEFFERSON CO OR	211-C2
NFD RD 1176 JEFFERSON CO OR	208-C5
NFD RD 1179 JEFFERSON CO OR	212-A2
NFD RD 1207 YAKIMA CO WA	119-A2
NFD RD 1210 CLACKAMAS CO OR	201-B3
NFD RD 1217 MULTNOMAH CO OR	201-C2
NFD RD 1228 CLACKAMAS CO OR	201-C4
NFD RD 1268 TILLAMOOK CO OR	203-B2
NFD RD 1270 LEWIS CO WA	185-D7
NFD RD 1280 TILLAMOOK CO OR	203-C2
NFD RD 1310 HOOD RIVER CO OR	202-A1
NFD RD 1340 HOOD RIVER CO OR	202-A2
NFD RD 1341 BONNER CO ID	107-A1
NFD RD 1376 CURRY CO OR	148-B2
NFD RD 1393 JEFFERSON CO OR	212-B3
NFD RD 1394 JEFFERSON CO OR	213-A2
NFD RD 1395 JEFFERSON CO OR	213-A2
NFD RD 1399 JEFFERSON CO OR	212-B1
NFD RD 1414 CLACKAMAS CO OR	201-B3
NFD RD 1425 JEFFERSON CO OR	211-C1
NFD RD 1441 CHELAN CO WA	103-C3
NFD RD 1491 TILLAMOOK CO OR	197-C7
NFD RD 1509 MULTNOMAH CO OR	201-A2
NFD RD 1510 DESCHUTES CO OR	211-C5
NFD RD 1514 DESCHUTES CO OR	211-C6

STREET City State	Page-Grid
NFD RD 1516 DESCHUTES CO OR	211-C7
NFD RD 1520 DESCHUTES CO OR	211-C5
NFD RD 1522 DESCHUTES CO OR	211-C6
NFD RD 1526 DESCHUTES CO OR	211-C7
NFD RD 1587 KOOTENAI CO ID	245-C4
NFD RD 1590 TILLAMOOK CO OR	197-B7
NFD RD 1594 KOOTENAI CO ID	245-D4
NFD RD 1608 DESCHUTES CO OR	211-D6
NFD RD 1610 DESCHUTES CO OR	211-D7
HOOD RIVER CO OR	202-B2
NFD RD 1611 HOOD RIVER CO OR	202-B2
NFD RD 1614 IDAHO CO ID	131-C2
NFD RD 1620 DESCHUTES CO OR	211-C7
NFD RD 1628 DESCHUTES CO OR	211-C7
DESCHUTES CO OR	216-C1
NFD RD 1631 HOOD RIVER CO OR	202-B3
NFD RD 1633 TILLAMOOK CO OR	203-C2
NFD RD 1640 HOOD RIVER CO OR	202-A2
NFD RD 1650 HOOD RIVER CO OR	202-A3
TILLAMOOK CO OR	203-C2
NFD RD 1660 HOOD RIVER CO OR	202-A3
NFD RD 1670 HOOD RIVER CO OR	202-A3
NFD RD 1686 TILLAMOOK CO OR	203-D2
NFD RD 1700 MASON CO WA	179-B2
NFD RD 1701 LINCOLN CO OR	203-C5
YAKIMA CO WA	240-B7
NFD RD 1703 KITTITAS CO WA	240-A7
NFD RD 1708 KITTITAS CO WA	240-A6
NFD RD 1710 HOOD RIVER CO OR	202-D1
NFD RD 1711 HOOD RIVER CO OR	202-D1
NFD RD 1720 HOOD RIVER CO OR	202-D3
KITTITAS CO WA	240-B7
NFD RD 1721 KITTITAS CO WA	240-A7
NFD RD 1726 LINCOLN CO OR	203-B4
NFD RD 1770 LINCOLN CO OR	203-C6
NFD RD 1783 LINCOLN CO OR	203-B5
NFD RD 1800 YAKIMA CO WA	119-B1
NFD RD 1810 DESCHUTES CO OR	217-C7
HOOD RIVER CO OR	202-A3
NFD RD 1814 DESCHUTES CO OR	217-C5
NFD RD 1815 DESCHUTES CO OR	217-C4
NFD RD 1818 DESCHUTES CO OR	217-D7
NFD RD 1819 DESCHUTES CO OR	217-D5
NFD RD 1820 DESCHUTES CO OR	217-D6
NFD RD 1825 CLACKAMAS CO OR	201-D4
DESCHUTES CO OR	217-D6
NFD RD 1828 CLACKAMAS CO OR	201-D4
NFD RD 1846 CURRY CO OR	232-D7
NFD RD 1888 LINCOLN CO OR	203-C3
Rose Lodge OR	203-C3
NFD RD 1928 LINCOLN CO OR	203-B6
NFD RD 1929 LINCOLN CO OR	203-B6
NFD RD 1956 LINCOLN CO OR	203-B6
NFD RD 1980 LINCOLN CO OR	203-C6
NFD RD 2022 LINN CO OR	134-A2
NFD RD 2025 JACKSON CO OR	234-A7
NFD RD 2026 LINN CO OR	134-A2
NFD RD 2040 JACKSON CO OR	234-B5
NFD RD 2050 JEFFERSON CO OR	212-A3
NFD RD 2060 DESCHUTES CO OR	211-B4
DESCHUTES CO OR	234-C5
NFD RD 2061 DESCHUTES CO OR	211-B3
NFD RD 2066 JEFFERSON CO OR	211-B2
NFD RD 2068 JEFFERSON CO OR	211-B3
NFD RD 2076 JEFFERSON CO OR	211-A3
NFD RD 2134 DOUGLAS CO OR	223-A1
LANE CO OR	142-A1
NFD RD 2153 DOUGLAS CO OR	223-C1
GRAYS HARBOR CO WA	179-A1
NFD RD 2160 DESCHUTES CO OR	209-D6
NFD RD 2199 MASON CO WA	179-C1
NFD RD 2207 MARION CO OR	134-A1
NFD RD 2210 YAMHILL CO OR	197-D7
NFD RD 2233 BONNER CO ID	244-B4
NFD RD 2234 YAMHILL CO OR	203-D2

STREET City State	Page-Grid
NFD RD 2255 MASON CO WA	179-B1
NFD RD 2260 GRAYS HARBOR CO WA	109-B2
NFD RD 2282 YAMHILL CO OR	203-D1
NFD RD 2283 YAMHILL CO OR	197-D7
NFD RD 2302 GRAYS HARBOR CO WA	109-A2
KOOTENAI CO ID	245-C3
NFD RD 2308 CURRY CO OR	148-C1
NFD RD 2312 GRAYS HARBOR CO WA	109-B2
NFD RD 2320 KOOTENAI CO ID	245-D6
NFD RD 2341 MASON CO WA	179-B1
NFD RD 2399 MASON CO WA	179-B1
NFD RD 2401 JEFFERSON CO WA	173-A3
NFD RD 2403 JEFFERSON CO WA	173-B2
NFD RD 2420 MASON CO WA	173-A3
NFD RD 2421 MASON CO WA	173-A2
NFD RD 2464 MASON CO WA	173-A4
NFD RD 2469 MASON CO WA	173-A3
NFD RD 2470 MASON CO WA	173-A3
NFD RD 2472 MASON CO WA	173-B2
NFD RD 2480 LANE CO OR	214-D4
MASON CO WA	173-B3
NFD RD 2510 JEFFERSON CO WA	109-C1
JEFFERSON CO WA	173-B1
NFD RD 2512 BONNER CO ID	107-A2
NFD RD 2515 JEFFERSON CO WA	173-C1
NFD RD 2516 KLAMATH CO OR	143-A2
LAKE CO OR	143-A2
NFD RD 2524 JEFFERSON CO WA	173-B2
NFD RD 2530 JEFFERSON CO WA	173-B1
NFD RD 2540 JEFFERSON CO WA	173-B1
NFD RD 2546 JEFFERSON CO WA	173-B1
NFD RD 2550 BONNER CO ID	107-A3
NFD RD 2560 SKAMANIA CO WA	190-D1
NFD RD 2586 SKAMANIA CO WA	190-D3
NFD RD 2588 SKAMANIA CO WA	190-D3
NFD RD 2605 BOUNDARY CO ID	107-A2
NFD RD 2610 LANE CO OR	214-C2
NFD RD 2612 CLACKAMAS CO OR	201-C6
NFD RD 2618 CLACKAMAS CO OR	201-C6
NFD RD 2652 BONNER CO ID	245-A1
NFD RD 2654 LINN CO OR	134-B2
NFD RD 2720 WASCO CO OR	202-D5
NFD RD 2820 HOOD RIVER CO OR	195-A6
NFD RD 2823 LAKE CO OR	151-C1
NFD RD 2840 HOOD RIVER CO OR	202-B3
NFD RD 2902 CLALLAM CO WA	163-B7
CLALLAM CO WA	169-D1
NFD RD 2903 CLALLAM CO WA	163-B7
NFD RD 2918 CLALLAM CO WA	109-A1
NFD RD 2922 CLALLAM CO WA	163-C7
NFD RD 2923 CLALLAM CO WA	163-C7
NFD RD 2924 CLALLAM CO WA	169-D1
NFD RD 2929 CLALLAM CO WA	163-D7
NFD RD 2933 CLALLAM CO WA	163-A7
NFD RD 2937 CLALLAM CO WA	163-C7
NFD RD 2938 CLALLAM CO WA	163-A7
NFD RD 2946 CLALLAM CO WA	164-A7
NFD RD 2978 CLALLAM CO WA	163-D7
NFD RD 3006 CLALLAM CO WA	163-B5
NFD RD 3007 CLALLAM CO WA	163-B6
NFD RD 3010 OKANOGAN CO WA	105-A2
NFD RD 3027 KOOTENAI CO ID	245-D5
NFD RD 3028 CLALLAM CO WA	163-D5
NFD RD 3029 CLALLAM CO WA	163-D5
NFD RD 3030 CLALLAM CO WA	165-A7
NFD RD 3031 CLALLAM CO WA	163-C5
NFD RD 3040 CLALLAM CO WA	163-C6
CLALLAM CO WA	164-A6
NFD RD 3041 CLALLAM CO WA	163-C6
NFD RD 3062 SKAMANIA CO WA	194-C1
NFD RD 3067 CLALLAM CO WA	163-D6
NFD RD 3068 CLALLAM CO WA	164-A6

STREET City State	Page-Grid
NFD RD 3069 CLALLAM CO WA	163-D6
NFD RD 3080 SKAMANIA CO WA	194-C2
NFD RD 3105 SKAMANIA CO WA	190-D6
NFD RD 3116 CLALLAM CO WA	163-B5
NFD RD 3117 CLALLAM CO WA	163-B5
NFD RD 3120 LINCOLN CO OR	206-D6
NFD RD 3142 LAKE CO OR	143-B3
NFD RD 3230 DOUGLAS CO OR	141-C3
NFD RD 3310 CURRY CO OR	228-D1
NFD RD 3312 KLAMATH CO OR	151-B1
NFD RD 3313 CURRY CO OR	228-C5
NFD RD 3334 KLAMATH CO OR	231-A1
NFD RD 3340 CURRY CO OR	228-D3
NFD RD 3348 COOS CO OR	140-C3
NFD RD 3384 KLAMATH CO OR	231-A1
NFD RD 3402 CURRY CO OR	228-B1
NFD RD 3413 KLAMATH CO OR	231-A2
NFD RD 3414 KLAMATH CO OR	231-A2
NFD RD 3419 KLAMATH CO OR	231-A4
NFD RD 3449 KLAMATH CO OR	231-A2
NFD RD 3450 KLAMATH CO OR	231-A3
NFD RD 3454 KLAMATH CO OR	231-A6
NFD RD 3455 KLAMATH CO OR	231-A5
NFD RD 3484 KLAMATH CO OR	231-A3
NFD RD 3506 KITTITAS CO WA	241-A2
NFD RD 3507 KITTITAS CO WA	241-A1
NFD RD 3512 HOOD RIVER CO OR	202-B3
NFD RD 3517 KITTITAS CO WA	241-B2
NFD RD 3521 KITTITAS CO WA	241-B1
NFD RD 3530 KITTITAS CO WA	238-B7
NFD RD 3533 CURRY CO OR	228-C4
NFD RD 3540 LANE CO OR	209-A7
HOOD RIVER CO OR	202-C6
NFD RD 3550 HOOD RIVER CO OR	202-C6
NFD RD 3610 KLAMATH CO OR	231-A7
NFD RD 3640 GRANT CO OR	137-B1
NFD RD 3660 GRANT CO OR	137-B1
NFD RD 3670 GRANT CO OR	137-B1
NFD RD 3680 CURRY CO OR	228-B6
NFD RD 3817 DOUGLAS CO OR	222-B1
NFD RD 4000 DESCHUTES CO OR	217-A6
NFD RD 4017 LAKE CO OR	151-C3
NFD RD 4050 JACKSON CO OR	234-C7
NFD RD 4104 SKAMANIA CO WA	193-D3
NFD RD 4105 JOSEPHINE CO OR	233-A1
NFD RD 4109 CLARK CO WA	193-D3
NFD RD 4130 DESCHUTES CO OR	217-A4
NFD RD 4180 DESCHUTES CO OR	216-D5
NFD RD 4201 JOSEPHINE CO OR	233-A2
NFD RD 4211 SKAMANIA CO WA	193-D2
NFD RD 4220 DESCHUTES CO OR	216-D6
NFD RD 4235 CROOK CO OR	136-A2
NFD RD 4240 WALLOWA CO OR	131-B2
NFD RD 4260 WALLOWA CO OR	131-B1
NFD RD 4273 DESCHUTES CO OR	142-C1
NFD RD 4305 UNION CO OR	129-C3
NFD RD 4306 SKAMANIA CO WA	194-B2
NFD RD 4410 HOOD RIVER CO OR	202-C4
NFD RD 4420 HOOD RIVER CO OR	202-D5
NFD RD 4430 WASCO CO OR	202-D3
NFD RD 4450 WASCO CO OR	202-D4
NFD RD 4510 LEWIS CO WA	185-D6
NFD RD 4601 DESCHUTES CO OR	216-D3
NFD RD 4609 JOSEPHINE CO OR	233-D4
NFD RD 4610 DESCHUTES CO OR	217-A3
NFD RD 4612 DESCHUTES CO OR	216-D3
JOSEPHINE CO OR	233-D6
NFD RD 4613 CLACKAMAS CO OR	201-A7
DESCHUTES CO OR	216-D4
DESCHUTES CO OR	233-D5
NFD RD 4614 CLACKAMAS CO OR	200-D7

STREET City State	Page-Grid
NFD RD 4615 CLACKAMAS CO OR	201-A7
DESCHUTES CO OR	216-D3
NFD RD 4630 DESCHUTES CO OR	216-A7
NFD RD 4635 DESCHUTES CO OR	216-A7
NFD RD 4650 DESCHUTES CO OR	142-C1
NFD RD 4703 JOSEPHINE CO OR	233-C7
NFD RD 4720 LEWIS CO WA	185-B7
NFD RD 4803 JOSEPHINE CO OR	233-A7
NFD RD 4808 JOSEPHINE CO OR	233-B7
NFD RD 4811 DOUGLAS CO OR	214-D5
HOOD RIVER CO OR	202-C6
WASCO CO OR	202-D7
NFD RD 4814 WASCO CO OR	202-D7
NFD RD 4820 DOUGLAS CO OR	214-D5
WASCO CO OR	202-D7
NFD RD 4830 LANE CO OR	214-C4
NFD RD 4860 HOOD RIVER CO OR	202-C6
NFD RD 4870 WASCO CO OR	202-C7
NFD RD 4880 HOOD RIVER CO OR	202-C6
WASCO CO OR	202-C7
NFD RD 5087 LINCOLN CO OR	206-C7
NFD RD 5125 UNION CO OR	129-C3
UNION CO OR	130-A3
NFD RD 5130 OKANOGAN CO WA	104-A2
NFD RD 5185 BAKER CO OR	130-A3
GRANT CO OR	130-A3
UNION CO OR	130-A3
NFD RD 5210 LEWIS CO WA	185-A6
NFD RD 5215 CHELAN CO WA	238-D1
NFD RD 5260 LEWIS CO WA	185-B7
NFD RD 5270 LEWIS CO WA	185-C6
NFD RD 5300 CHELAN CO WA	236-A4
NFD RD 5400 CURRY CO OR	224-B7
OKANOGAN CO WA	103-C2
NFD RD 5701 SKAMANIA CO WA	190-B7
NFD RD 5842 LANE CO OR	209-A7
LANE CO OR	214-B1
NFD RD 5850 LANE CO OR	142-A1
NFD RD 5875 LANE CO OR	142-A1
NFD RD 5900 CHELAN CO WA	112-A4
NFD RD 6020 KLAMATH CO OR	142-C2
NFD RD 6052 SKAMANIA CO WA	194-D3
NFD RD 6210 KLAMATH CO OR	231-C2
NFD RD 6214 KLAMATH CO OR	231-C1
NFD RD 6231 UNION CO OR	130-B1
NFD RD 6401 SKAMANIA CO WA	190-D7
NFD RD 6403 SKAMANIA CO WA	190-D6
NFD RD 6406 SKAMANIA CO WA	190-D7
NFD RD 6517 SKAMANIA CO WA	194-D3
NFD RD 6728 COLUMBIA CO OR	189-C5
NFD RD 6750 KOOTENAI CO ID	245-D3
NFD RD 7100 CHELAN CO WA	111-C1
NFD RD 7184 Rt#-410 PIERCE CO WA	111-A3
NFD RD 7200 CHELAN CO WA	238-B3
NFD RD 7202 CHELAN CO WA	238-B3
NFD RD 7300 CHELAN CO WA	238-A5
NFD RD 7320 CHELAN CO WA	238-A5
NFD RD 7324 CHELAN CO WA	238-A5
NFD RD 7400 CHELAN CO WA	238-B1
NFD RD 7412 CHELAN CO WA	238-C1
NFD RD 7412 Rt#-109 CHELAN CO WA	238-C1
NFD RD 7413 CHELAN CO WA	238-D1
NFD RD 7601 CHELAN CO WA	111-C2
NFD RD 7755 BAKER CO OR	130-C1
NFD RD 8020 CHELAN CO WA	236-C1
NFD RD 8123 COWLITZ CO WA	190-B3
NFD RD 8170 TILLAMOOK CO OR	197-C5
NFD RD 8171 TILLAMOOK CO OR	197-C4
NFD RD 8172 TILLAMOOK CO OR	197-C5
NFD RD 8208 TILLAMOOK CO OR	197-A5
NFD RD 8303 SKAMANIA CO WA	190-B4
NFD RD 8320 SKAMANIA CO WA	190-D3
NFD RD 8376 TILLAMOOK CO OR	197-D6
NFD RD 8410 CHELAN CO WA	236-A1

STREET City State	Page-Grid
NFD RD 8415 LEWIS CO WA	185-A6
NFD RD 8420 LEWIS CO WA	185-A6
NFD RD 8425 LEWIS CO WA	185-A6
NFD RD 8430 LEWIS CO WA	185-A6
NFD RD 8440 LEWIS CO WA	185-A7
NFD RD 8500 CHELAN CO WA	236-A3
NFD RD 8550 CHELAN CO WA	236-B3
NFD RD 8594 TILLAMOOK CO OR	197-D6
NFD RD 9015 SKAMANIA CO WA	190-C4
NFD RD 9403 SKAMANIA CO WA	190-D1
NFD RD 9701 DESCHUTES CO OR	217-C5
NFD RD 9705 KITTITAS CO WA	238-A6
NFD RD 9711 KITTITAS CO WA	238-A6
NFD RD 9712 KITTITAS CO WA	238-A7
NFD RD 9713 KLAMATH CO OR	231-D5
NFD RD 9714 KITTITAS CO WA	238-A6
NFD RD 9715 KITTITAS CO WA	238-A6
KLAMATH CO OR	231-D5
NFD RD 9716 KITTITAS CO WA	238-A6
NFD RD 9717 KLAMATH CO OR	231-D5
NFD RD 9718 KITTITAS CO WA	238-A7
NFD RD 9720 DESCHUTES CO OR	217-A6
NFD RD 9723 DESCHUTES CO OR	217-B6
NFD RD 9724 DESCHUTES CO OR	217-B7
NFD RD 9726 KITTITAS CO WA	241-A1
NFD RD 9730 KLAMATH CO OR	231-D2
NFD RD 9734 KLAMATH CO OR	231-D1
NFD RD 9938 JOSEPHINE CO OR	233-A7
NFH 50 BENEWAH CO ID	115-B2
NF HWY 50 SHOSHONE CO ID	115-C3
NHS 11 Rt#-60 BENEWAH CO ID	115-A3
W NIAGARA AV ASTORIA OR	300-D6
NICE RD	130-A3
NICEWOOD DR LINN CO OR	210-A2
NICEWOOD LN LINN CO OR	210-A3
NW NICHOLS AV Tracyton WA	270-G4
NW NICHOLS BLVD LONGVIEW WA	302-J9
LONGVIEW WA	303-A10
NICHOLS LN FOREST GROVE OR	198-B1
LANE CO OR	219-D1
WASHINGTON CO OR	198-B1
SE NICHOLS RD YAMHILL CO OR	204-D1
NICHOLSON RD KLAMATH CO OR	231-B1
LEWIS CO WA	187-D3
NICKEL MINE RD DOUGLAS CO OR	225-B3
NICKERSON ST SEATTLE WA	273-H7
W NICKERSON ST SEATTLE WA	273-G6
NICK THOMAS RD COLUMBIA CO OR	189-C5
NICK YOUNG RD EAGLE POINT OR	230-D5
JACKSON CO OR	230-D5
NICOLAI RD COLUMBIA CO OR	189-C6
NW NICOLAI ST PORTLAND OR	312-C3
NICOLAI CUTOFF RD COLUMBIA CO OR	189-C6
NIEHENKE RD WHITMAN CO WA	249-C7
NIELSON RD TILLAMOOK CO OR	197-C2
NIKULA RD LEWIS CO WA	187-C3
N NILE AV DOUGLAS CO WA	239-A4
S NILE AV DOUGLAS CO WA	239-A4
NILLES RD DOUGLAS CO WA	112-C1
NINE CANYON RD BENTON CO WA	121-A3
NINEMILE RD HUMBOLDT CO NV	154-A3
N NINE MILE RD Rt#-291 SPOKANE WA	246-A2
SPOKANE WA	346-A14
SPOKANE WA	348-B1
SPOKANE WA	246-A2
SPOKANE WA	346-A13
NINTH ST WENATCHEE WA	238-D4
NISQUALLY RD SW PIERCE CO WA	181-B6
NISULA RD VALLEY CO ID	251-C6
VALLEY CO ID	252-C1
NIXON DR LINN CO OR	210-A3
W NIXON ST PASCO WA	343-E7
NO 1 RD CITY OF RICHMOND BC	156-A7
DISTRICT OF ABBOTSFORD BC	94-B3
NO 2 RD CITY OF RICHMOND BC	156-B7

INDEX

STREET — City State Page-Grid

NO 3 RD
CITY OF RICHMOND BC 156-B7
DISTRICT OF ABBOTSFORD BC 102-B1
NO 4 RD
CITY OF RICHMOND BC 156-B7
NO 5 RD
CITY OF RICHMOND BC 156-B6
NO 6 RD
CITY OF RICHMOND BC 156-C6
NO 7 RD
CITY OF RICHMOND BC 156-C6
N NOAMI LN
ADA CO ID 253-A2
E NOB HILL BLVD
YAKIMA WA 243-C7
YAKIMA WA 243-C7
W NOB HILL BLVD
YAKIMA WA 243-B7
NOBLE CREEK RD
COOS CO OR 218-D4
NOLL RD NE
KITSAP CO WA 170-C7
NONPAREIL RD
DOUGLAS CO OR 219-C7
NOOKSACK AV Rt#-9
NOOKSACK WA 102-B1
NOOKSACK RD Rt#-9
NOOKSACK WA 102-B1
WHATCOM CO WA 102-B1
NORATEN RD
LANE CO OR 210-A5
NORDEL WY
DISTRICT OF DELTA BC 156-D6
NORKENZIE RD
EUGENE OR 330-A2
NORMA BEACH RD
SNOHOMISH CO WA 171-B4
NORMAN RD
SNOHOMISH CO WA 168-B4
E NORMAN RD
YAKIMA CO WA 243-C7
S NORMANDY RD
BURIEN WA 288-A7
NORPOINT WY NE
TACOMA WA 182-A2
NORRIS AV Rt#-55
NEW MEADOWS ID 251-A4
NORRIS AV U.S.-95
ADAMS CO ID 251-A4
NEW MEADOWS ID 251-A4
NORRIS LN
JEFFERSON CO OR 212-D2
NORTH AV
JEFFERSON OR 207-D3
NORTH RD
CHELAN CO WA 238-B2
DISTRICT OF COQUITLAM BC 156-D5
KOOTENAI CO ID 245-C1
NEW WESTMINSTER CO WA 156-D5
SNOHOMISH CO WA 171-C5
NORTH RD NW
DOUGLAS CO WA 236-C6
NORTH SPUR
JACKSON CO OR 227-A5
NORTH ST Rt#-26
WASHTUCNA WA 121-C1
E NORTH ST
ENTERPRISE OR 130-C2
W NORTH ST Rt#-82
ENTERPRISE OR 130-C2
NORTH ST SE
OLYMPIA WA 296-J9
OLYMPIA WA 297-A9
TUMWATER WA 296-J9
TUMWATER WA 297-A9
NORTH WY
COOS CO OR 218-B5
NORTH ALBANY RD
ALBANY OR 326-B5
NORTH BANK RD
DOUGLAS CO OR 141-B2
DOUGLAS CO OR 221-C2
LINCOLN CO OR 203-B4
Rose Lodge OR 203-B4
NORTH BANK CHETCO RIVER RD
CURRY CO OR 232-D5
NORTH BANK PISTOL RIVER RD
CURRY CO OR 232-C1
NORTH BANK ROGUE RIVER RD
CURRY CO OR 228-B4
NORTH BAY DR
COOS CO OR 218-B6
E NORTH BEND WY
KING CO WA 176-C5
NORTH BEND WA 176-C5
SE NORTH BEND WY
KING CO WA 176-C4
SNOQUALMIE WA 176-C4
W NORTH BEND WY
NORTH BEND WA 176-C4
NORTH BLUFF RD
ISLAND CO WA 167-C6
NORTH CASCADES HWY Rt#-20
CHELAN CO WA 103-C2
OKANOGAN CO WA 103-C2
SKAGIT CO WA 103-A2
WHATCOM CO WA 103-A2
N NORTHCLIFF RD
SHELTON WA 180-A2
NORTHCRAFT RD SE
THURSTON CO WA 184-D3
NORTHCREST DR Rt#-D3
CRESCENT CITY CA 148-B3
DEL NORTE CO CA 148-B3
NORTH DAIRY RD
CITY OF VICTORIA BC 257-A6
DISTRICT OF SAANICH BC 257-A6
NORTH END OMAK LAKE RD
OKANOGAN CO WA 104-C3
NORTHERN DR
LINN CO OR 210-C2
NORTHERNWOOD DR
LINN CO OR 210-C4
NORTH FORK RD
CLACKAMAS CO OR 200-D7
DOUGLAS CO OR 214-C6
LANE CO OR 134-A3
LANE CO OR 142-A1
LEWIS CO WA 184-D7
LEWIS CO WA 187-D1
MARION CO OR 134-A1
NEHALEM OR 191-B4
SKAMANIA CO WA 193-D6
TILLAMOOK CO OR 191-B4
TILLAMOOK CO OR 197-D2
WESTFIR OR 142-A1

NORTH FORK BURNT RIVER RD
BAKER CO OR 138-A1
NORTH FORK COUNTY RD
KING CO WA 176-D3
NORTH FORK SIUSLAW RD
FLORENCE OR 214-B3
LANE CO OR 214-B3
NORTH FORK SIUSLAW RD Rt#-5
LANE CO OR 214-C1
NORTH FORK YACHATS RD
LINCOLN CO OR 209-B3
NORTH FOURMILE RD
COOS CO OR 224-C1
NORTH GATE RD
PIERCE CO WA 181-C4
N NORTHGATE WY
SEATTLE WA 171-B7
NE NORTHGATE WY
SEATTLE WA 171-B7
NORTH HEAD RD Rt#-100
ILWACO WA 186-A6
PACIFIC CO WA 186-A6
NORTH HEAD LIGHTHOUSE RD
PACIFIC CO WA 186-A6
NORTH LAKE RD
COOS CO OR 218-C4
NORTHLAKE WY NW
BREMERTON WA 270-A8
Tracyton WA 270-A8
NORTH MISSION RD W
KITSAP CO WA 173-D3
NORTH MOUNTAIN RD
CLACKAMAS CO OR 201-C4
NORTH PINE CREEK RD
BAKER CO OR 131-B4
NORTHPORT-FLAT CREEK RD
STEVENS CO WA 106-A1
NORTH POWDER-LADD CANYON RD
NORTH POWDER OR 130-A3
UNION CO OR 130-A3
NORTH POWDER RIVER LN
UNION CO OR 130-A3
NORTH POWDER RIVER RD
NORTH POWDER OR 130-A3
UNION CO OR 130-A3
NORTH PRAIRIE RD
LEWIS CO WA 187-D2
NORTH RAILWAY AV Rt#-7
DISTRICT OF MISSION BC 94-B3
NORTH RIVER DR
LINN CO OR 134-A2
NORTH RIVER RD
GRAYS HARBOR CO WA 117-A1
IDAHO CO ID 123-C3
NORTH RIVER VALLEY RD
PACIFIC CO WA 117-B1
NORTHRUP RD
GRANT CO WA 237-B4
NORTH SHORE DR
BELLINGHAM WA 102-B1
BELLINGHAM WA 161-A1
BELLINGHAM WA 258-J5
LOWELL OR 133-C3
WHATCOM CO WA 102-B1
WHATCOM CO WA 161-A1
NORTHSHORE PKWY
TACOMA WA 182-A1
NORTH SHORE RD
MASON CO WA 173-A6
NORTHSHORE RD Rt#-150
CHELAN CO WA 236-C2
NORTH SHORE RD Rt#-300
MASON CO WA 173-D6
NORTH SIDE DR
LINN CO OR 133-C2
NORTH SIDE RD
DOUGLAS CO OR 221-B1
SHOSHONE CO ID 115-C3
NORTHSIDE RD
CANYON CO ID 147-B1
NORTH STAR RD
WHATCOM CO WA 158-C5
NORTH UMPQUA HWY Rt#-138
DOUGLAS CO OR 141-C2
DOUGLAS CO OR 221-D4
DOUGLAS CO OR 222-B3
DOUGLAS CO OR 223-A4
ROSEBURG OR 221-D4
NORTHUP WY
BELLEVUE WA 175-D2
NORTH VALLEY RD
YAMHILL CO OR 198-C5
W NORTHVIEW ST
BOISE ID 253-B2
NORTHWEST AV
BELLINGHAM WA 258-B2
N NORTHWEST BLVD
COEUR D'ALENE ID 355-D9
KOOTENAI CO ID 355-D10
W NORTHWEST BLVD
SPOKANE WA 348-A4
NORTHWEST DR
BELLINGHAM WA 158-B2
BELLINGHAM WA 258-A1
WHATCOM CO WA 158-D6
NORTHWEST EXWY
EUGENE OR 215-A1
EUGENE OR 329-D1
LANE CO OR 215-A1
LANE CO OR 329-D1
Santa Clara OR 215-A1
NORTHWEST WY
DESCHUTES CO OR 212-D4
Terrebonne OR 212-D4
NORTHWESTERN LAKE RD
KLICKITAT CO WA 195-C3
NE NORTH WOODINVILLE WY
WOODINVILLE WA 171-C6
NE NORTON AV
BEND OR 332-G6
NORWAY-LEE-FAIRVIEW RD
COOS CO OR 140-B2
NORWELL DR
NANAIMO BC 93-A3
NORWOOD RD
VALLEY CO ID 251-C7
VALLEY CO ID 252-C1
S NORWOOD RD
VALLEY CO ID 252-D2
NOUQUE RANCH RD
MALHEUR CO OR 154-C2
S NOVA LN
ADA CO ID 253-A3
NOVELTY HILL RD
KING CO WA 110-C1
KING CO WA 175-D1
KING CO WA 176-A1

NOVELTY HILL RD
REDMOND WA 175-D1
NOWLENS BRIDGE RD
CLACKAMAS CO OR 205-D3
SCOTTS MILLS OR 205-D3
NUGENT RD
WHATCOM CO WA 160-B1
N NUGENT RD
WHATCOM CO WA 160-B1
S NUGENT RD
WHATCOM CO WA 160-B1
NULLE RD
SKAGIT CO WA 161-A3
WHATCOM CO WA 161-B3
NUMBER 4 RD
KITTITAS CO WA 127-C1
NUMBER 81 RD
KITTITAS CO WA 241-C5
NUMBER TWO CANYON RD
WENATCHEE WA 238-D4
E NUNN RD
KOOTENAI CO ID 245-B2
NURSERY AV
AMITY OR 204-B2
SW NURSERY RD
WASHINGTON CO OR 198-C2
NUSOM RD NE
MARION CO OR 205-B4
NUTLEY ST
ASHLAND OR 337-C8
NUTMEG ST SW
Grand Mound WA 184-B4
NYANZA RD SW
LAKEWOOD WA 181-C4
SW NYBERG ST
TUALATIN OR 199-B4
SE NYE AV
PENDLETON OR 129-B1
SW NYE AV
PENDLETON OR 129-B1
NW NYE ST
NEWPORT OR 206-B4
NYHUS ST
WESTPORT WA 298-H11

O

O RD NW
DOUGLAS CO WA 236-C7
O RD SW
DOUGLAS CO WA 239-C1
OAK AV
LAKE CO OR 152-A2
GLADSTONE OR 199-D4
SE OAK AV
ROSEBURG OR 334-G7
SE OAK AV Rt#-138
ROSEBURG OR 334-F7
SW OAK AV Rt#-138
ROSEBURG OR 334-F7
OAK RD
DESCHUTES CO OR 212-C5
SW OAK RD
BEND OR 332-E1
OAK RD NW
YAMHILL CO OR 204-C2
OAK ST
ASHLAND OR 337-C7
JACKSON CO OR 337-C7
LEBANON OR 133-C1
LINN CO OR 133-C1
MILTON WA 182-B2
OKANOGAN WA 104-C3
OKANOGAN CO WA 104-C3
VANCOUVER BC 156-B5
VANCOUVER BC 254-F13
WASHINGTON CO OR 198-A2
OAK ST Rt#-99
CITY OF RICHMOND BC 156-B5
VANCOUVER BC 156-B5
OAK ST Rt#-141
BINGEN WA 195-D5
OAK ST Rt#-162
NEZPERCE ID 123-C2
OAK ST Rt#-213
MARION CO OR 205-C4
SILVERTON OR 205-C4
OAK ST U.S.-30
HOOD RIVER OR 195-C5
S OAK ST
Finley WA 121-A3
Finley WA 343-F14
SE OAK ST Rt#-8
HILLSBORO OR 198-D1
SW OAK ST
GRANTS PASS OR 335-E9
SW OAK ST Rt#-8
HILLSBORO OR 198-D1
OAK AV
MANZANITA OR 191-B4
WESTPORT WA 298-G13
OAK BAY AV
CITY OF VICTORIA BC 257-B9
DISTRICT OF OAK BAY BC 257-B9
OAK BAY RD
JEFFERSON CO WA 170-B1
OAK BAY RD Rt#-116
Hadlock-Irondale WA 170-A1
JEFFERSON CO WA 170-A1
OAK CREEK DR
BENTON CO OR 327-A8
OAK CREST RD
LANE CO OR 210-C7
N OAKDALE AV
MEDFORD OR 336-C12
S OAKDALE AV
MEDFORD OR 336-C13
SW OAKDALE AV
DALLAS OR 204-A6
OAKDALE RD
POLK CO OR 125-B3
POLK CO OR 204-A6
OAK GROVE FORK RD
CLACKAMAS CO OR 126-B3
OAK HARBOR RD
ISLAND CO WA 167-B2
OAK HILL RD
POLK CO OR 207-B2
YAMHILL CO OR 198-A3

NW OAK HILL RD
YAMHILL CO OR 198-A4
OAKHURST RD
ELMA WA 179-B7
OAK ISLAND RD
MULTNOMAH CO OR 192-A5
OAK KNOLL RD NW
.... 204-C3
OAKLAND ST
DISTRICT OF BURNABY BC 156-D5
OAKLAND-SHADY HWY Rt#-99
DOUGLAS CO OR 219-A7
DOUGLAS CO OR 221-C3
DOUGLAS CO OR 334-F2
OAKLAND OR 219-A7
ROSEBURG OR 334-F2
SUTHERLIN OR 221-C3
OAKLEA DR
LANE CO OR 210-A5
OAKMEADE LN
YAMHILL CO OR 198-D6
OAK PLAIN RD
LINN CO OR 210-A2
OAKRIDGE DR SW
HOOD RIVER CO OR 195-C6
OAK RIDGE RD
DESCHUTES CO OR 142-C1
NW OAK RIDGE RD
YAMHILL CO OR 198-A5
OAK SPRINGS FARM RD
YAMHILL CO OR 198-B6
OAKVIEW DR
LINN CO OR 210-C2
OAK VILLA RD
POLK CO OR 204-A6
OAKVILLE RD
GRAYS HARBOR CO WA 117-B1
LINN CO OR 207-B6
SAN CO WA 326-A10
OAKVILLE CEMETERY RD
GRAYS HARBOR CO WA 117-B1
OAKWAY RD
EUGENE OR 330-B4
OAKWOOD DR
DOUGLAS CO OR 219-A6
OASIS RD
CANYON CO ID 139-B3
GEM CO ID 139-B3
PAYETTE CO ID 139-B3
OATFIELD RD
CLACKAMAS CO OR 199-D4
CLARK CO WA 193-A1
SE OATFIELD RD
CLACKAMAS CO OR 199-D3
MILWAUKIE OR 199-D3
OBOYD RD
WHITMAN CO WA 249-B4
OBRIEN RD
CLALLAM CO WA 165-D7
JOSEPHINE CO OR 233-A6
O B RILEY RD
BEND OR 332-E1
DESCHUTES CO OR 217-B1
DESCHUTES CO OR 332-E1
SW OBSIDIAN AV
DESCHUTES CO OR 212-C5
W OCCIDENTAL AV
YAKIMA CO WA 243-A7
OCEAN AV
MANZANITA OR 191-B4
WESTPORT WA 298-G13
OCEAN AV Rt#-105
WESTPORT WA 298-F13
OCEAN AV U.S.-101
RAYMOND WA 117-A1
OCEAN BLVD
CITY OF COLWOOD BC 159-B6
COOS BAY OR 333-E8
OCEAN BLVD SW
BANDON OR 220-A6
OCEAN DR
CLATSOP CO OR 188-B4
OCEAN RD
MANZANITA OR 191-B4
TILLAMOOK CO OR 191-B4
OCEAN BEACH HWY Rt#-4
CATHLAMET WA 117-B3
COWLITZ CO WA 117-B3
COWLITZ CO WA 189-C4
COWLITZ CO WA 302-B3
LONGVIEW WA 302-F6
LONGVIEW WA 303-A8
WAHKIAKUM CO WA 117-B3
OCEAN BEACH HWY Rt#-6
CHEHALIS WA 299-A13
LEWIS CO WA 117-B1
LEWIS CO WA 184-B7
LEWIS CO WA 187-A1
LEWIS CO WA 299-A13
PE ELL WA 117-B2
OCEAN BEACH HWY Rt#-103
LONG BEACH WA 186-A5
PACIFIC CO WA 186-A5
OCEAN BEACH RD
KLICKITAT CO WA 196-C3
OCEANIA DR
LINCOLN CO OR 328-C4
OCEANIA DR N
LINCOLN CO OR 328-C2
OCEAN LAKE WY
OCEAN SHORES WA 177-B7
OCEAN SHORES BLVD
OCEAN SHORES WA 177-B6
OCEAN SHORES WA 298-B5
NE OCEAN SHORES BLVD
OCEAN SHORES WA 177-B6
E OCEAN SHORES BLVD
OCEAN SHORES WA 298-B6
OCEAN SHORES BLVD SW
OCEAN SHORES WA 177-B7
OCEAN VIEW BLVD NE
KITSAP CO WA 271-C4
OCEAN VIEW DR
CURRY CO OR 232-D6
Harbor OR 232-D6
NEWPORT OR 206-B4
YACHATS OR 209-A3
OCEAN VIEW DR Rt#-D5
DEL NORTE CO CA 148-B3
DEL NORTE CO CA 232-D7
OCEANVIEW CEMETERY RD
CLATSOP CO OR 188-B2
WARRENTON OR 188-B2
OCEAN VISTA WY
SEASIDE OR 301-E11
OCHOCO HWY Rt#-126
CROOK CO OR 213-A5

OCHOCO HWY Rt#-126
DESCHUTES CO OR 212-D5
DESCHUTES CO OR 213-A5
PRINEVILLE OR 213-B6
REDMOND OR 212-D5
REDMOND OR 213-A5
OCHOCO HWY U.S.-26
CROOK CO OR 135-C2
CROOK CO OR 136-B1
CROOK CO OR 213-D5
GRANT CO OR 136-B1
MITCHELL OR 136-B1
PRINEVILLE OR 213-D5
WHEELER CO OR 136-B1
OCHOCO CREEK RD
CROOK CO OR 135-C2
CROOK CO OR 136-A2
OCONNER RD SE
THURSTON CO WA 184-C4
OCONNOR RD
KLAMATH CO OR 235-C6
NE ODDFELLOW RD
KITSAP CO WA 271-J6
ODELL HWY
HOOD RIVER CO OR 195-C6
ODELL ST
BLAINE WA 158-B3
WHATCOM CO WA 158-B3
NW ODEM AV
DESCHUTES CO OR 212-D4
Terrebonne OR 212-D4
ODENS
PIERCE CO WA 182-B4
ODEY
PIERCE CO WA 182-B6
ODONNELL RD
LATAH CO ID 249-C4
WHITMAN CO WA 249-C4
OENNING RD
WHITMAN CO WA 250-B1
OFFUTT LAKE RD SE
THURSTON CO WA 184-D2
O-GARA RD
KOOTENAI CO ID 248-B5
OGDEN RD
COWLITZ CO WA 187-B7
OGLE RD NE
KITSAP CO WA 174-C1
OHARA RD
UMATILLA CO OR 129-C1
WESTON OR 129-C1
OHIO ST
BELLINGHAM WA 258-E6
E OHIO MATCH RD
KOOTENAI CO ID 245-A4
OHOP VALLEY RD E
PIERCE CO WA 118-B1
OIL CITY RD
CLALLAM CO WA 169-C5
OJALLA RD
LINCOLN CO OR 206-C2
S OKANOGAN AV
WENATCHEE WA 238-D4
OKLAHOMA RD
SKAMANIA CO WA 195-B2
OKLAHOMA GULCH RD
CHELAN CO WA 236-A4
OK MILL RD
SNOHOMISH CO WA 110-C1
OKMA DR Rt#-20
OKANOGAN CO WA 104-C3
OMAK WA 104-C3
OLA HWY
GEM CO ID 139-C3
OLALLA RD
DOUGLAS CO OR 141-A2
DOUGLAS CO OR 221-A7
LINCOLN CO OR 206-C4
SE OLALLA VALLEY RD
KITSAP CO WA 174-C6
OLALLA VALLEY RD SE
KITSAP CO WA 174-C5
OLANDER RD
LEWIS CO ID 123-B3
OLD HWY
DOUGLAS CO OR 221-B1
KLICKITAT CO WA 196-C5
OLD 26 RD
ADAMS CO WA 122-A1
OLD 99 HWY
SISKIYOU CO CA 149-C3
SISKIYOU CO CA 150-A3
OLD 302 Rt#-302
MASON CO WA 173-D6
OLD 410 HWY
ELMA WA 179-A7
GRAYS HARBOR CO WA 178-D7
GRAYS HARBOR CO WA 179-C6
OLD ALBION RD
WHITMAN CO WA 249-A3
OLD ALTURAS HWY
KLAMATH CO OR 151-A3
MODOC CO CA 151-A3
OLD APPLETON GRADE RD
KLICKITAT CO WA 196-C3
SW OLD BARNEY WHITE LN
KITSAP CO WA 174-A4
OLD BEAVER HILL RD
COOS CO OR 220-C4
OLD BELFAIR HWY
MASON CO WA 173-D5
MASON CO WA 174-A4
OLD BELFAIR HWY Rt#-300
MASON CO WA 173-D5
NE OLD BELFAIR HWY
MASON CO WA 174-A4
W OLD BELFAIR VALLEY RD
BREMERTON WA 174-A4
KITSAP CO WA 174-A4
SE OLD BETHEL RD
YAMHILL CO OR 204-B2
OLD BRIDGE DR
LINN CO OR 133-C1
OLD BRUNDAGE MOUNTAIN RD
MCCALL ID 251-C6
OLD BUZZARD MINE RD
JACKSON CO OR 226-B4
SW OLD CLIFTON RD
KITSAP CO WA 174-A4
OLD CONDOR RD N
TILLAMOOK CO OR 197-B6
NW OLD CORNELIUS PASS RD
WASHINGTON CO OR 192-A7
OLD COULEE RD
ALMIRA WA 237-D7
GRANT CO WA 237-D7
OLD MEADOW RD
LINCOLN CO OR 237-C4

OLD CRATER LAKE HWY
EAGLE POINT OR 230-D5
JACKSON CO OR 230-D5
OLD DALLES DR
HOOD RIVER CO OR 195-D5
OLD DALLES RD
HOOD RIVER CO OR 195-D6
OLD DAY CREEK RD
SKAGIT CO WA 161-C6
OLD DIAMOND LAKE RD
DOUGLAS CO OR 227-A2
JACKSON CO OR 226-D3
OLD DUFUR RD
THE DALLES OR 196-D7
WASCO CO OR 196-D7
OLD EASTSIDE RD
BONNER CO ID 107-A3
OLD EMIGRANT HILL SCENIC FRNTG
UNION CO OR 129-C2
OLD EMPIRE RD
NORTH BEND OR 333-E6
OLD EXPERIMENT RD
HARNEY CO OR 145-B1
OLD FAIRHAVEN PKWY Rt#-11
BELLINGHAM WA 258-B11
OLDFIELD RD
DIST OF CENTRAL SAANICH BC 159-C5
DISTRICT OF SAANICH BC 159-C5
OLD FORT RD
KLAMATH CO OR 235-C1
KLAMATH CO OR 338-H2
POLK CO OR 207-B1
OLD FORT HARNEY RD
HARNEY CO OR 145-B1
OLD FORT KLAMATH RD
KLAMATH CO OR 338-G6
OLD FRONTIER RD NW
KITSAP CO WA 174-B1
OLD GED BROWN
PIERCE CO WA 182-A6
OLD GOOSE LAKE RD
ADAMS CO ID 251-B3
OLD GRAND COULEE WILBUR HWY
GRANT CO WA 237-C3
OLD GUN CLUB RD
LEWISTON ID 250-C4
NEZ PERCE CO ID 250-C4
OLDHAM CREEK RD
DOUGLAS CO OR 219-C7
OLD HIGHWAY RD
WASHINGTON CO ID 139-D3
OLD HWY RD
MIDVALE ID 139-D3
WASHINGTON CO ID 139-B1
OLD HIGHWAY 22 CUTOFF RD
STEVENS CO WA 113-C1
OLD HWY 30 E
BAKER CITY OR 138-B1
BAKER CO OR 138-B1
OLD HIGHWAY 47
WASHINGTON CO OR 198-B2
SW OLD HIGHWAY 47
FOREST GROVE OR 198-B1
WASHINGTON CO OR 198-B1
SW OLD HIGHWAY 47 Rt#-8
FOREST GROVE OR 198-B1
OLD HWY 95
LATAH CO ID 249-D7
OLD HWY 97
BREWSTER WA 104-C3
JEFFERSON CO OR 208-D3
OKANOGAN CO WA 104-C3
OLD HWY 99
SKAGIT CO WA 168-B3
SNOHOMISH CO WA 168-B3
THURSTON CO WA 184-D1
OLD HWY 99 N
BURLINGTON WA 260-C5
SKAGIT CO WA 161-B3
SKAGIT CO WA 168-B2
WHATCOM CO WA 161-B3
OLD HWY 99 SE
THURSTON CO WA 296-H14
OLD HWY 99 SW
Grand Mound WA 184-B4
THURSTON CO WA 184-D1
OLD HWY 101
CANNON BEACH OR 188-B7
CLATSOP CO OR 188-B7
OLD HWY 160
KITSAP CO WA 174-D4
OLD HWY 195
WHITMAN CO WA 114-C3
OLD HWY EAST SPRINGDALE RD
STEVENS CO WA 106-B3
OLD HWY NORTHPORT RD
STEVENS CO WA 106-A1
OLD HWY-NW CHEWELAH RD
CHEWELAH WA 106-B3
OLD IDAHO-OREGON-NEVADA HWY
MALHEUR CO OR 146-B3
MALHEUR CO OR 154-B1
OLD IMNAHA RD
WALLOWA CO OR 131-C2
OLDING RD
BREMERTON WA 270-C4
OLD INLAND EMPIRE HWY
BENTON CITY WA 120-C3
BENTON CO WA 120-C3
OLD ISLAND HWY
CITY OF COLWOOD BC 159-B6
OLD ISLAND HWY Rt#-1A
CITY OF COLWOOD BC 159-B6
DISTRICT OF SAANICH BC 256-B5
TOWN OF ESQUIMALT BC 256-B5
TOWN OF VIEW ROYAL BC 159-B6
TOWN OF VIEW ROYAL BC 256-A4
OLD KETTLE RD
STEVENS CO WA 106-A2
W OLD KETTLE RD
KETTLE FALLS WA 106-A2
STEVENS CO WA 106-A2
OLD LAKE RD
LAKE CO OR 143-C2
OLD LAPWAI RD
LEWISTON ID 250-C4
NEZ PERCE CO ID 250-C4
OLD LORANE RD
LANE CO OR 133-B3
OLD MARINE DR
WHATCOM CO WA 158-D7
OLD MCMINNVILLE HWY
YAMHILL CO OR 198-B6
OLD MEADOW RD
MCCALL ID 251-C5

STREET — City State Page-Grid

OLD MEHAMA RD SE
MARION CO OR 133-C1
STAYTON OR 133-C1
OLD MELROSE RD
DOUGLAS CO OR 221-B4
DOUGLAS CO OR 334-A7
ROSEBURG OR 334-A7
OLD MIDLAND RD
KLAMATH CO OR 235-C5
OLD MILITARY RD
FEDERAL WAY WA 175-B7
OLD MILITARY RD NE
KITSAP CO WA 174-B1
KITSAP CO WA 270-H1
OLD MILITARY RD SE
THURSTON CO WA 184-D3
NE OLD MILL RD
KITSAP CO WA 271-J4
OLD MILL RD SW
KING CO WA 174-D7
OLD MILL SCHOOLIE RD
WASCO CO OR 127-A3
OLD MILTON HWY
WALLA WALLA CO WA 344-F13
WALLA WALLA CO WA 345-A13
OLD MOHAWK RD
LANE CO OR 215-D1
LANE CO OR 331-E3
OLD MONITOR RD
CASHMERE WA 238-C2
CHELAN CO WA 238-C2
OLD MOSCOW RD
WHITMAN CO WA 249-B5
OLD NACHES HWY
NACHES WA 119-C1
YAKIMA CO WA 119-C1
YAKIMA CO WA 243-A4
OLD NORTHERN STATE HOSPITAL RD
SKAGIT CO WA 161-C4
OLD NORTHPORT HWY
STEVENS CO WA 106-A1
OLD OCHOCO HWY
CROOK CO OR 136-A2
OLD OLYMPIC HWY
CLALLAM CO WA 165-D6
CLALLAM CO WA 166-A6
CLALLAM CO WA 262-A8
MASON CO WA 180-A4
OLD OLYMPIC HWY Rt#-3
MASON CO WA 180-A3
SHELTON WA 180-A3
OLD OLYMPIC HWY SW
THURSTON CO WA 180-B6
OLD OREGON TRAIL HWY I-84
BAKER CITY OR 138-B1
BAKER CO OR 130-C3
BAKER CO OR 138-B1
LA GRANDE OR 130-A2
MALHEUR CO OR 138-B1
MALHEUR CO OR 139-A2
MORROW CO OR 128-C1
NORTH POWDER OR 130-A3
ONTARIO OR 139-A2
PAYETTE CO ID 139-A2
PENDLETON OR 129-A1
UMATILLA CO OR 128-C1
UMATILLA CO OR 129-A1
UNION CO OR 129-C2
UNION CO OR 130-A2
OLD OWEN RD
MONROE WA 110-C1
SNOHOMISH CO WA 110-C1
OLD PACIFIC HWY
COWLITZ CO WA 118-A3
COWLITZ CO WA 187-C6
COWLITZ CO WA 189-C4
DOUGLAS CO OR 225-C5
KELSO WA 189-C4
KELSO WA 303-G14
SNOHOMISH CO WA 168-A4
WOODLAND WA 118-A3
WOODLAND WA 189-D7
OLD PACIFIC HWY Rt#-99
DOUGLAS CO OR 225-C2
MYRTLE CREEK OR 225-C2
Tri-City OR 225-C2
OLD PACIFIC HWY Rt#-432
KELSO WA 303-F13
OLD PACIFIC HWY N
CASTLE ROCK WA 187-C7
COWLITZ CO WA 187-C6
OLD PACIFIC HWY S
COWLITZ CO WA 189-D6
OLD PACIFIC HWY SE
THURSTON CO WA 181-A6
OLD PARRETT MOUNTAIN RD
YAMHILL CO OR 199-A5
OLD PENDLETON RIVER RD
ECHO OR 129-A1
UMATILLA CO OR 129-A1
OLD PENGRA RD
LANE CO OR 133-C3
LOWELL OR 133-C3
OLD PORTLAND RD
COLUMBIA CO OR 192-A2
SAINT HELENS OR 192-A2
OLD PULLMAN RD
MOSCOW ID 249-C5
OLD RAINIER RD
COLUMBIA CO OR 189-A4
NE OLD REDMOND RD
KING CO WA 175-C1
REDMOND WA 175-C1
OLD REDWOOD HWY
JOSEPHINE CO OR 229-A7
OLD RIVER RD
BENTON CO OR 133-B2
BENTON CO OR 210-A4
LINCOLN CO OR 206-C2
OLD ROSE CREEK RD
KOOTENAI CO ID 248-D2
OLD RR GRADE
YAMHILL CO OR 198-A4
NW OLD RR GRADE
YAMHILL CO OR 198-A5
OLD SAMISH RD
MILLERSBURG OR 207-D3
MILLERSBURG OR 326-H3
OLD SAMISH HWY
BELLINGHAM WA 258-D13
WHATCOM CO WA 161-A2
WHATCOM CO WA 258-D13
OLD SAMS VALLEY RD
JACKSON CO OR 230-B5
OLD SAND CREEK RD
DOUGLAS CO OR 219-B2
GRAYS HARBOR CO WA 179-C6

STREET — City State Page-Grid

OLD SANDERS RD
BENEWAH CO ID 115-A3
OLD SANTIAM WAGON RD
DESCHUTES CO OR 211-A3
OLD SCENIC HWY 101
LINCOLN CO OR 203-B3
Rose Lodge OR 203-B3
OLD SEEKSEEQUA RD
JEFFERSON CO OR 208-A4
OLDS FERRY RD
WASHINGTON CO ID 139-A2
OLDS FERRY-ONTARIO HWY Rt#-201
MALHEUR CO OR 139-A2
ONTARIO OR 139-A2
OLDS FERRY-ONTARIO HWY U.S.-30
MALHEUR CO OR 139-A3
ONTARIO OR 139-A3
SW OLD SHERIDAN RD
MCMINNVILLE OR 204-B1
YAMHILL CO OR 204-B1
OLD SHERMAN HWY
SHERMAN CO OR 127-C1
OLD SISKIYOU HWY
JACKSON CO OR 234-D5
OLD SNOHOMISH MONROE RD
SNOHOMISH CO WA 110-C1
SNOHOMISH CO WA 171-D4
NW OLD SOLDIERS RD
YAMHILL CO OR 198-A5
OLD SOLDIERS GRADE
LAPWAI ID 123-A2
NEZ PERCE CO ID 123-A2
NEZ PERCE CO ID 250-D4
OLD SOUTH RD
CLEARWATER CO ID 123-B2
OLD SPIRAL HWY
NEZ PERCE CO ID 250-B3
OLD SPIRAL HWY Rt#-128
LEWISTON ID 250-B4
OLD SPREADBOROUGH RD
COWLITZ CO WA 189-D5
OLD SR 195
SPOKANE CO WA 114-C2
OLD STAGE RD
CAVE JUNCTION OR 233-B4
JACKSON CO OR 149-B2
JACKSON CO OR 230-B6
JACKSON CO OR 234-A1
JOSEPHINE CO OR 233-B4
OLD STAGE RD Rt#-99
JACKSON CO OR 230-B6
OLD STAGE ROUTE
COOS BAY OR 333-D5
COOS CO OR 333-D5
NORTH BEND OR 333-D5
OLD STATE HWY
CASCADE ID 252-D6
SISKIYOU CO CA 150-B3
WHITMAN CO WA 114-C3
OLD STATE RD
VALLEY CO ID 252-D2
OLD STITES STAGE RD
IDAHO CO ID 123-C3
SW OLDSVILLE RD
YAMHILL CO OR 204-A1
OLD THORNTON HWY
WHITMAN CO WA 114-C3
N OLD TRAIL RD
SPOKANE CO WA 246-A3
OLD TRAIL CREEK RD
JACKSON CO OR 230-D2
OLD TYGH MARKET RD
WASCO CO OR 127-B2
OLD US HWY 2
BOUNDARY CO ID 107-B1
MOYIE SPRINGS ID 107-B1
OLD US HWY 30
CLATSOP CO OR 117-A3
OLD WAPINITIA RD
WASCO CO OR 127-A3
OLD WILLAMETTE HWY
LANE CO OR 142-A1
OLD WILLAPA
PACIFIC CO WA 117-A1
OLD WOODS RD
TILLAMOOK CO OR 197-A3
OLD WYNOOCHEE RD
GRAYS HARBOR CO WA 178-C5
OLD YALE RD
CITY OF SURREY BC 157-A3
DISTRICT OF ABBOTSFORD BC 102-B1
DISTRICT OF MATSQUI BC 102-B1
TOWNSHIP OF LANGLEY BC 158-C1
SW OLESON RD
PORTLAND OR 199-B2
WASHINGTON CO OR 199-B2
OLEX-MCNAB RD
MORROW CO OR 128-B2
OLGA TO PT LAWRENCE RD
SAN JUAN CO WA 160-A3
E OLIPHANT RD
COLUMBIA CO WA 122-B2
GARFIELD CO WA 122-B2
OLIVE ST
LINCOLN CO OR 206-B4
NEWPORT OR 206-B4
OLIVE ST U.S.-20
NEWPORT OR 206-B4
E OLIVE ST U.S.-20
NEWPORT OR 206-B4
W OLIVE ST
NEWPORT OR 206-A4
OLIVE WY
LONGVIEW WA 302-F7
SEATTLE WA 277-J5
SEATTLE WA 278-A5
E OLIVE WY
SEATTLE WA 278-B4
OLIVE BARBER RD
COOS CO OR 220-D2
OLIVER RD
COQUITLAM BC 157-B4
OLLALA CANYON RD
CHELAN CO WA 238-B2
OLMSTEAD RD
MARION CO OR 199-A7
OLMSTEAD RD NW
DOUGLAS CO WA 236-D4
OLNEY AV Rt#-202
ASTORIA OR 300-C7
NE OLNEY AV
BEND OR 332-F6
OLNEY AV SE
KITSAP CO WA 271-A14
OLNEY AV SE
KITSAP CO WA 271-A14
PORT ORCHARD WA 271-A14
OLNEY CUTOFF RD
CLATSOP CO OR 188-D3

STREET — City State Page-Grid

OLSEN RD
CLALLAM CO WA 166-A7
SNOHOMISH CO WA 168-B4
TILLAMOOK CO OR 197-C2
SE OLSEN ST Rt#-270
PULLMAN WA 249-B5
OLSON DR KPN
PIERCE CO WA 174-A7
OLSON PL SW
SEATTLE WA 285-J4
OLSON RD
COLUMBIA CO OR 189-C7
COWLITZ CO WA 189-C7
DESCHUTES CO OR 212-B7
WHATCOM CO WA 158-C6
WHITMAN CO WA 249-B1
NW OLSON RD
YAMHILL CO OR 198-B3
S OLYMPIA ST
KENNEWICK WA 121-A3
KENNEWICK WA 343-B11
OLYMPIA WY
COWLITZ CO WA 302-D4
LONGVIEW WA 302-J8
LONGVIEW WA 303-A8
SE OLYMPIAD DR
KITSAP CO WA 174-D4
OLYMPIA TENINO HWY N
TENINO WA 184-D3
OLYMPIA-YELM HWY Rt#-510
THURSTON CO WA 118-A1
THURSTON CO WA 181-B7
YELM WA 118-A1
N OLYMPIC AV
ARLINGTON WA 168-D5
S OLYMPIC AV
ARLINGTON WA 168-D5
OLYMPIC BLVD
EVERETT WA 264-A6
OLYMPIC DR NW
GIG HARBOR WA 181-C1
OLYMPIC DR SE
KITSAP CO WA 174-B6
OLYMPIC HWY U.S.-101
CLALLAM CO WA 164-C6
CLALLAM CO WA 165-B6
CLALLAM CO WA 166-C7
CLALLAM CO WA 261-A6
JEFFERSON CO WA 109-C1
JEFFERSON CO WA 166-C7
PORT ANGELES WA 261-A6
OLYMPIC PL
ARLINGTON WA 168-D5
W OLYMPIC PL
SEATTLE WA 277-G3
OLYMPIC ST
SPRINGFIELD OR 331-B5
OLYMPIC WK NE
SHORELINE WA 171-B6
OLYMPIC WY SE Rt#-305
Winslow WA 174-D2
OLYMPIC WAY W
SEATTLE WA 277-F2
OLYMPIC HOT SPRINGS RD
CLALLAM CO WA 109-A1
CLALLAM CO WA 165-A7
OLYMPIC VIEW DR
EDMONDS WA 171-A5
LYNNWOOD WA 171-A5
SNOHOMISH CO WA 171-A5
OLYMPIC VIEW RD NW
KITSAP CO WA 174-A1
OLYMPIC VIEW WY
OCEAN SHORES WA 177-B6
OLYMPIC VIEW LOOP RD NW
KITSAP CO WA 170-A7
OLYMPUS BLVD
JEFFERSON CO WA 170-B2
OLYMPUS DR
BREMERTON WA 271-A7
KITSAP CO WA 271-A7
OMAK AV E Rt#-155
OKANOGAN CO WA 104-C3
OMAK WA 104-C3
OMAK LAKE RD
OKANOGAN CO WA 104-C3
OMAK LAKE COLUMBIA RIVER RD
OKANOGAN CO WA 105-A3
ONAWAY RD
LATAH CO ID 249-D1
ONEAL RD
KLICKITAT CO WA 196-B2
ONEIL HWY
CROOK CO OR 213-B4
DESCHUTES CO OR 212-D4
DESCHUTES CO OR 213-A4
ONEILL RD
GRAYS HARBOR CO WA 179-A4
ONTARIO ST
SANDPOINT ID 244-A2
VANCOUVER BC 156-B5
OPAL LN
JEFFERSON CO OR 212-D2
OPHIR RD
CURRY CO OR 228-A3
NW OPPENLANDER LN
WASHINGTON CO OR 198-B1
ORAL HULL RD
CLACKAMAS CO OR 200-D4
ORANGE ST
ASHLAND OR 337-C6
S ORCAS ST
SEATTLE WA 282-D6
SEATTLE WA 283-E6
ORCAS TO OLGA RD
SAN JUAN CO WA 101-C2
SAN JUAN CO WA 160-A2
ORCHARD RD
CANYON CO ID 147-B1
KLAMATH CO OR 338-F8
KLAMATH FALLS OR 338-F8
WENATCHEE WA 238-D4
YAKIMA CO WA 243-A6
N ORCHARD AV
DALLAS OR 204-A6
POLK CO OR 204-A6
ORCHARD AV SE
KITSAP CO WA 174-C6
ORCHARD LN
DOUGLAS CO OR 221-A4
N ORCHARD ST
BOISE ID 253-C2
GARDEN CITY ID 253-C2
TACOMA WA 292-A4
S ORCHARD ST
BOISE ID 253-C3

STREET — City State Page-Grid

S ORCHARD ST
FIRCREST WA 292-A7
FIRCREST WA 294-A2
TACOMA WA 292-A6
TACOMA WA 294-A2
UNIVERSITY PLACE WA 294-A2
SW ORCHARD ST
SEATTLE WA 285-G1
ORCHARD GRADE
OKANOGAN CO WA 104-C3
ORCHARD HEIGHTS PL NW
POLK CO OR 322-A10
ORCHARD HEIGHTS RD NW
POLK CO OR 204-C5
POLK CO OR 322-A9
SALEM OR 322-D10
ORCHARD KNOB RD
POLK CO OR 204-A5
ORCUTT RD
SNOHOMISH CO WA 168-B5
OREANA RD
OWYHEE CO ID 147-C2
OREGON AV
KLAMATH FALLS OR 338-C6
E OREGON AV
CRESWELL OR 215-C5
N OREGON AV Rt#-397
PASCO WA 343-G6
S OREGON AV Rt#-397
PASCO WA 343-H8
W OREGON AV
CRESWELL OR 215-C5
OREGON RD
SISKIYOU CO CA 150-A3
OREGON ST
ASTORIA OR 300-A5
BENTON CO WA 120-C2
FRANKLIN CO WA 343-E1
PASCO WA 343-E1
OREGON ST Rt#-231
LINCOLN CO WA 114-A2
OREGON ST U.S.-30
MALHEUR CO OR 139-A3
ONTARIO OR 139-A3
OREGON ST U.S.-101
PORT ORFORD OR 224-A6
N OREGON ST
JACKSON CO OR 149-B2
JACKSONVILLE OR 149-B2
N OREGON ST U.S.-30
ONTARIO OR 139-A3
NE OREGON ST
PORTLAND OR 313-G5
SHERWOOD OR 199-A4
S OREGON ST
ONTARIO OR 139-A3
OREGON WY
LONGVIEW WA 302-H13
LONGVIEW WA 303-A10
OREGON WY Rt#-433
COLUMBIA CO WA 189-B4
COWLITZ CO WA 302-H13
LONGVIEW WA 302-J12
RAINIER OR 189-B4
RAINIER OR 302-H13
OREGON CANYON RD
MALHEUR CO OR 154-B2
OREGON CAVES HWY Rt#-46
CAVE JUNCTION OR 233-B4
JOSEPHINE CO OR 233-B4
OREGON CENTRAL HWY U.S.-20
CANYON CO ID 139-A3
SNOHOMISH CO WA 168-D6
OREGON COAST HWY
CLATSOP CO OR 188-B6
OREGON COAST HWY U.S.-101
ASTORIA OR 188-C1
ASTORIA OR 300-A1
BANDON OR 220-C4
BAY CITY OR 191-B5
BAY CITY OR 197-B1
BROOKINGS OR 232-C5
CANNON BEACH OR 188-B7
CANNON BEACH OR 191-A2
CLATSOP CO OR 188-C1
CLATSOP CO OR 191-A2
CLATSOP CO OR 300-A1
CLATSOP CO OR 301-F14
COOS CO OR 218-B5
COOS CO OR 220-C4
COOS CO OR 224-B4
COOS CO OR 333-J13
CURRY CO OR 224-B4
CURRY CO OR 228-A1
CURRY CO OR 232-B2
DEPOE BAY OR 203-A7
DEPOE BAY OR 206-B3
DOUGLAS CO OR 214-A7
DOUGLAS CO OR 218-B2
DUNES CITY OR 214-B4
FLORENCE OR 214-B4
GARIBALDI OR 191-B5
GEARHART OR 301-H4
GOLD BEACH OR 228-A6
Harbor OR 232-D6
LAKESIDE OR 218-B2
LANE CO OR 132-B2
LANE CO OR 209-A6
LANE CO OR 214-B4
Lincoln Beach OR 203-A7
LINCOLN CITY OR 203-B3
LINCOLN CO OR 203-B3
LINCOLN CO OR 206-B3
LINCOLN CO OR 209-A3
LINCOLN CO OR 328-D2
MANZANITA OR 191-B5
NEWPORT OR 206-B3
NORTH BEND OR 333-G2
PORT ORFORD OR 224-B6
REEDSPORT OR 218-B2
ROCKAWAY BEACH OR 191-B5
SEASIDE OR 188-B7
SEASIDE OR 301-H4
TILLAMOOK OR 191-B5
TILLAMOOK CO OR 197-C4
TILLAMOOK CO OR 203-B3
WALDPORT OR 328-D2
WARRENTON OR 188-B2
WHEELER OR 191-B5
YACHATS OR 209-A3
OREGON LAKE RESERVOIR RD
MALHEUR CO OR 155-A1
OREGON SKYLINE RD
CLACKAMAS CO OR 126-C3
WASCO CO OR 126-C3
OREGON TRAIL RD
UNION CO OR 130-A3

STREET — City State Page-Grid

OREGON-WASHINGTON HWY Rt#-11
ADAMS OR 129-B1
ATHENA OR 129-B1
MILTON-FREEWATER OR 121-C3
PENDLETON OR 129-B1
UMATILLA CO OR 121-C3
UMATILLA CO OR 129-B1
WALLA WALLA CO WA 121-C3
SE ORIENT DR
CLACKAMAS CO OR 200-C3
GRESHAM OR 200-B2
MULTNOMAH OR 200-B2
ORILLIA RD S
KENT WA 290-E4
KING CO WA 290-E4
KING CO WA 291-F2
SEATAC WA 290-E4
SEATAC WA 291-F2
ORINDALE RD
KLAMATH CO OR 235-B4
ORNDUFF RD
YAMHILL CO OR 198-C4
ORO BAY RD
PIERCE CO WA 181-A4
ORONDO AV
WENATCHEE WA 238-D4
WENATCHEE WA 239-A4
E ORONDO AV
WENATCHEE WA 239-A4
S ORONDO AV
WENATCHEE WA 238-D4
OROVILLE-TORODA CREEK RD
OKANOGAN CO WA 104-C1
OKANOGAN CO WA 105-A1
OROVILLE WA 104-C1
ORR RD
COLUMBIA CO OR 189-C6
ORRS CORNER RD
POLK CO OR 204-A6
ORTING-KAPOWSIN HWY
PIERCE CO WA 118-B1
PIERCE CO WA 182-B6
ORVILLE RD
EATONVILLE WA 118-B1
PIERCE CO WA 118-B1
ORVILLE RD E
PIERCE CO WA 182-C7
ORVILLE RD S
MARION CO OR 204-C7
OSBORNE RD
DIST OF NORTH VANCOUVER BC 255-B2
MODOC CO CA 151-A3
SISKIYOU CO CA 151-A3
OSBURN CUTOFF RD
WASCO CO OR 196-A6
S OSTER RD
CLACKAMAS CO OR 205-D3
OSTRANDER RD
COWLITZ CO WA 303-H1
OSULLIVAN DAM RD Rt#-262
GRANT CO WA 121-A1
GRANT CO WA 242-B6
S OTHELLO ST
SEATTLE WA 286-E1
SEATTLE WA 287-E1
OTIS VALLEY RD
HARNEY CO OR 137-C3
HARNEY CO OR 138-A3
OTSO POINT RD
PIERCE CO WA 181-A4
OTTER RD
BRITISH COLUMBIA BC 101-A2
OTTER POINT RD
DOUGLAS CO OR 218-D1
OTTER SLOUGH RD
GRANT CO WA 242-C3
OTTMAR RD
VANCOUVER BC 254-F11
OUTLET CREEK RD
VALLEY CO ID 251-D1
OUTLOOK RD
SUNNYSIDE WA 120-B2
YAKIMA CO WA 120-B2
N OUTLOOK RD
YAKIMA CO WA 120-B2
OUTLOOK RD W
YAKIMA CO WA 120-B2
OVENELL RD
SKAGIT CO WA 161-A6
OVERHULSE RD NW
THURSTON CO WA 296-B1
OVERLAND RD
COOS CO OR 220-D3
E OVERLAND RD
ADA CO ID 253-B3
MERIDIAN ID 253-B3
W OVERLAND RD
ADA CO ID 147-C1
ADA CO ID 253-B3
BOISE ID 253-B3
OVERLOOK RD
LINCOLN CO OR 209-A4
SE OVERRA RD
KITSAP CO WA 174-C4
OVERSTREET RD
MALHEUR CO OR 139-A3
OWENS RD
BENTON CO WA 120-B2
COLUMBIA CO WA 122-B2
Finley WA 121-A3
OWENS ST
KLAMATH FALLS OR 338-F8
OWENS ST S
SALEM OR 322-G14
OWHI LAKE RD
OKANOGAN CO WA 105-B3
OWHI LOOP RD
FERRY CO WA 105-B3
OWL CAMP RD
TILLAMOOK CO OR 125-B1
OWL CREEK RD
JEFFERSON CO WA 108-C1
OWSLEY CANYON RD
UNION CO OR 130-A2
OWSLEY GRADE RD
GARFIELD CO WA 122-B2
OWSLEY GRADE RD Rt#-126
GARFIELD CO WA 122-B2
OWYHEE AV
MALHEUR CO OR 139-A3
OWYHEE BLVD Rt#-19
OWYHEE CO ID 147-A1
OWYHEE LAKE RD
MALHEUR CO OR 139-A3
MALHEUR CO OR 147-A1
OWYHEE TUNNEL RD
MALHEUR CO OR 147-A1

STREET — City State Page-Grid

OXENFORD RD
CLALLAM CO WA 165-A5
OXFORD ST
COQUITLAM BC 157-B4
PORT COQUITLAM BC 157-B4
OYSTER BAY AV
BREMERTON WA 270-E12
Navy Yard City WA 270-E12
OYSTER BAY RD NW
THURSTON CO WA 180-B5
OYSTERVILLE RD
PACIFIC CO WA 186-A1
OZETTE MAINLINE RD
CLALLAM CO WA 162-B5

P

P RD NW
DOUGLAS CO WA 236-C7
P ST
PORT TOWNSEND WA 263-G3
PACIFIC AV
BREMERTON WA 270-J11
EVERETT WA 264-D4
EVERETT WA 265-E4
GLENDALE OR 225-A7
NORTH BEND OR 333-F5
OLYMPIA WA 297-C5
PIERCE CO WA 182-B3
SUMNER WA 182-B3
TACOMA WA 293-H5
TACOMA WA 295-H1
THURSTON CO WA 297-C5
TILLAMOOK CO OR 197-A3
WOODLAND WA 189-D7
WOODLAND WA 192-B1
YAKIMA WA 243-C7
PACIFIC AV Rt#-7
PIERCE CO WA 181-D4
TACOMA WA 181-D4
TACOMA WA 295-H3
PACIFIC AV Rt#-8
CORNELIUS OR 198-C1
FOREST GROVE OR 198-C1
PACIFIC AV Rt#-529
EVERETT WA 265-F4
PACIFIC AV U.S.-101
TILLAMOOK OR 197-B2
TILLAMOOK CO OR 197-B2
N PACIFIC AV Rt#-99W
MONMOUTH OR 204-B7
POLK CO OR 204-B7
NW PACIFIC AV
CHEHALIS WA 299-D11
S PACIFIC AV Rt#-99W
MONMOUTH OR 204-B7
PACIFIC AV N
COWLITZ CO WA 189-C2
COWLITZ CO WA 303-E3
KELSO WA 303-D6
PACIFIC AV S
ALGONA WA 182-B2
AUBURN WA 182-B2
COWLITZ CO WA 303-C10
KELSO WA 303-C10
PACIFIC AV S Rt#-7
PIERCE CO WA 181-D5
PACIFIC AV SE
LACEY WA 297-F6
OLYMPIA WA 297-F6
THURSTON CO WA 181-A6
THURSTON CO WA 297-F6
PACIFIC AV SE Rt#-510
THURSTON CO WA 181-A6
PACIFIC BLVD
VANCOUVER BC 254-F11
PACIFIC BLVD Rt#-99E
ALBANY OR 326-F7
LINN CO OR 326-F7
MILLERSBURG OR 326-F7
PACIFIC BLVD N
VANCOUVER BC 254-G11
PACIFIC BLVD S
VANCOUVER BC 254-G11
PACIFIC BLVD SE
THURSTON CO WA 184-C1
PACIFIC HWY
CLARK CO WA 192-C1
SKAGIT CO WA 168-B2
WARRENTON OR 188-B1
PACIFIC HWY I-5
ALBANY OR 326-H5
ASHLAND OR 337-C4
CANYONVILLE OR 225-C1
CENTRAL POINT OR 230-B6
CENTRAL POINT OR 336-A5
CLACKAMAS CO OR 199-B3
CLARK CO WA 192-C1
COBURG OR 210-B6
COBURG OR 215-B7
COTTAGE GROVE OR 215-B7
COWLITZ CO WA 192-C1
CRESWELL OR 215-C5
DOUGLAS CO OR 219-C1
DOUGLAS CO OR 221-C2
DOUGLAS CO OR 225-C1
DOUGLAS CO OR 334-C11
EUGENE OR 330-E7
Four Corners OR 323-D9
Four Corners OR 325-D1
GRANTS PASS OR 335-H7
Hayesville OR 323-D9
JACKSON CO OR 149-C3
JACKSON CO OR 150-A2
JACKSON CO OR 229-B4
JACKSON CO OR 230-B6
JACKSON CO OR 234-B2
JACKSON CO OR 336-A5
JACKSON CO OR 337-C4
JOSEPHINE CO OR 225-C5
JOSEPHINE CO OR 229-B1
JOSEPHINE CO OR 335-C3
KEIZER OR 323-C5
LAKE OSWEGO OR 199-B3
LANE CO OR 210-B6
LANE CO OR 215-C5
LANE CO OR 219-C1
LANE CO OR 330-G9
LINN CO OR 210-B6
LINN CO OR 326-G14
MARION CO OR 199-B6
MARION CO OR 205-A2
MARION CO OR 207-D2
MARION CO OR 323-C5
MARION CO OR 325-B8
MARYSVILLE WA 168-C7
MARYSVILLE WA 171-C1
MEDFORD OR 234-B2

STREET — City State Page-Grid

PACIFIC HWY I-5
MEDFORD OR ... 336-E13
MILLERSBURG OR ... 326-H5
PHOENIX OR ... 234-B2
PORTLAND OR ... 199-B3
PORTLAND OR ... 305-G5
PORTLAND OR ... 309-F4
PORTLAND OR ... 313-F2
PORTLAND OR ... 316-C7
PORTLAND OR ... 317-F1
PORTLAND OR ... 320-A1
RIDGEFIELD WA ... 192-C2
ROGUE RIVER OR ... 229-B4
ROSEBURG OR ... 334-E4
SALEM OR ... 323-C5
SALEM OR ... 325-D1
SNOHOMISH CO WA ... 168-C7
SNOHOMISH CO WA ... 171-C1
SPRINGFIELD OR ... 330-E7
SUTHERLIN OR ... 221-C2
TIGARD OR ... 199-B3
Tri-City OR ... 225-C1
TUALATIN OR ... 199-B4
VANCOUVER WA ... 192-C5
VANCOUVER WA ... 305-G5
WASHINGTON CO OR ... 199-B4
WILSONVILLE OR ... 199-B5
WOODBURN OR ... 205-A2
WOODLAND WA ... 192-B1
PACIFIC HWY Rt#-15
CITY OF SURREY BC ... 158-B1
PACIFIC HWY Rt#-43
LAKE OSWEGO OR ... 199-C4
LAKE OSWEGO OR ... 321-G7
WEST LINN OR ... 199-C4
PACIFIC HWY Rt#-99
FEDERAL WAY WA ... 182-B1
PACIFIC HWY Rt#-99E
MARION CO OR ... 205-B2
WOODBURN OR ... 205-B1
PACIFIC HWY Rt#-103
Ocean Park WA ... 186-A2
PACIFIC CO WA ... 186-A3
PACIFIC HWY Rt#-529
EVERETT WA ... 171-C1
MARYSVILLE WA ... 171-C1
SNOHOMISH CO WA ... 171-C1
PACIFIC HWY E
FIFE WA ... 182-A2
PACIFIC HWY E Rt#-99
FEDERAL WAY WA ... 182-A2
FIFE WA ... 182-A2
MILTON WA ... 182-A2
PIERCE CO WA ... 182-A2
PACIFIC HWY E Rt#-99E
AURORA OR ... 199-B7
BARLOW OR ... 199-C6
CANBY OR ... 199-C6
CLACKAMAS CO OR ... 199-D4
GERVAIS OR ... 205-B1
GLADSTONE OR ... 199-D4
Hayesville OR ... 204-D5
Hayesville OR ... 323-E5
HUBBARD OR ... 205-B1
MARION CO OR ... 199-B7
MARION CO OR ... 205-A3
MARION CO OR ... 323-E5
OREGON CITY OR ... 199-D4
SALEM OR ... 323-E5
WOODBURN OR ... 205-B1
PACIFIC HWY N
KELSO WA ... 303-E6
PACIFIC HWY S Rt#-99
DES MOINES WA ... 175-B7
DES MOINES WA ... 290-C6
FEDERAL WAY WA ... 175-B7
FEDERAL WAY WA ... 182-A2
KENT WA ... 175-B7
KENT WA ... 290-C6
KING CO WA ... 175-B7
PACIFIC HWY S Rt#-103
LONG BEACH WA ... 186-A5
PACIFIC HWY SE
TENINO WA ... 184-C3
THURSTON CO WA ... 184-C3
PACIFIC HWY SE Rt#-510
THURSTON CO WA ... 181-A6
PACIFIC HWY SW
Grand Mound WA ... 184-B4
LAKEWOOD WA ... 181-C4
THURSTON CO WA ... 184-B4
PACIFIC HWY W
PORTLAND OR ... 308-E3
PORTLAND OR ... 309-E2
PACIFIC HWY W Rt#-99
EUGENE OR ... 215-A1
EUGENE OR ... 329-D2
JUNCTION CITY OR ... 210-A7
LANE CO OR ... 210-A7
LANE CO OR ... 215-A1
PACIFIC HWY W Rt#-99W
ADAIR VILLAGE OR ... 207-B3
AMITY OR ... 204-B3
BENTON CO OR ... 133-B2
BENTON CO OR ... 207-B3
BENTON CO OR ... 327-H7
CORVALLIS OR ... 133-B2
CORVALLIS OR ... 327-H7
JUNCTION CITY OR ... 210-A5
KING CITY OR ... 199-B3
LANE CO OR ... 133-B2
LANE CO OR ... 210-A5
MONMOUTH OR ... 204-B5
MONROE OR ... 133-B2
NEWBERG OR ... 198-C6
POLK CO OR ... 204-B5
POLK CO OR ... 207-B3
SHERWOOD OR ... 199-A4
TIGARD OR ... 199-B3
TUALATIN OR ... 199-B3
WASHINGTON CO OR ... 199-B3
YAMHILL CO OR ... 198-C6
YAMHILL CO OR ... 204-B5
PACIFIC HWY W Rt#-103
LONG BEACH WA ... 186-A5
NE PACIFIC PL
SEATTLE WA ... 274-C7
PACIFIC ST
VANCOUVER BC ... 254-E10
WOODLAND WA ... 189-D7
N PACIFIC ST
SEATTLE WA ... 274-A6
NE PACIFIC ST
SEATTLE WA ... 274-B6
PACIFIC TER
KLAMATH FALLS OR ... 338-E5
PACIFIC VW
CURRY CO OR ... 224-B3

PACIFIC WY
COWLITZ CO WA ... 302-B3
GEARHART OR ... 301-G4
LONGVIEW WA ... 302-H6
PACIFIC CREST TR
CASCADE LOCKS OR ... 194-D6
CLACKAMAS CO OR ... 126-C3
CLACKAMAS CO OR ... 202-A5
DESCHUTES CO OR ... 134-B3
HOOD RIVER CO OR ... 194-D6
HOOD RIVER CO OR ... 201-D2
JACKSON CO OR ... 150-A2
KLAMATH CO OR ... 150-A2
KLAMATH CO OR ... 142-B1
KLAMATH CO OR ... 150-A2
KLAMATH CO OR ... 223-D1
KLAMATH CO OR ... 227-B7
LEWIS CO WA ... 119-A2
OKANOGAN CO WA ... 103-C1
PIERCE CO WA ... 119-A2
SKAMANIA CO WA ... 118-C3
RAYMOND WA ... 117-A1
SKAMANIA CO WA ... 194-B4
SKAMANIA CO WA ... 195-A3
PACK RIVER RD
BONNER CO ID ... 107-B2
PADDEN PKWY
CLARK CO WA ... 192-D5
NE PADDEN PKWY
CLARK CO WA ... 192-D5
CLARK CO WA ... 193-A5
PADDY FLAT RD
VALLEY CO ID ... 252-D1
PAGE RD
DISTRICT OF MATSQUI BC ... 94-B3
DOUGLAS CO OR ... 221-C3
PAGE CREEK RD
JOSEPHINE CO OR ... 233-B7
PAGE PLACE RD
MALHEUR CO OR ... 146-C2
PAGH RD
CLACKAMAS CO OR ... 200-D5
PAHA PACKARD RD
ADAMS CO WA ... 113-C3
PAINE RD
COWLITZ CO WA ... 187-D7
PAINE FIELD BLVD Rt#-525
MUKILTEO WA ... 267-F6
SNOHOMISH CO WA ... 267-F6
PAINTER LP NE
MARION CO OR ... 205-C1
E PAINTER RD
SPOKANE CO WA ... 114-C2
PAISLEY RD
DIST OF NORTH VANCOUVER BC ... 254-G3
PAIUTE
CROOK CO OR ... 213-D7
PALERMO DR SW
THURSTON CO WA ... 184-B1
PALESTINE AV
BENTON CO OR ... 207-B3
PALISADES RD SW
DOUGLAS CO WA ... 112-B2
DOUGLAS CO WA ... 239-C6
S PALIX RD
PACIFIC CO WA ... 186-B1
PALM CREEK RD
COLUMBIA CO OR ... 189-A4
PALMER AV
OKANOGAN CO WA ... 104-C1
N PALMER LN
ADA CO ID ... 253-A1
PALMER RD
CLACKAMAS CO OR ... 200-B5
CLATSOP CO OR ... 188-D3
LEWIS CO WA ... 187-D2
TEKOA WA ... 114-C3
WOODLAND WA ... 192-C1
S PALMER RD
CLACKAMAS CO OR ... 205-B2
SE PALMER CREEK RD
YAMHILL CO OR ... 204-C1
PALMER JUNCTION RD
ELGIN OR ... 130-A1
UNION CO OR ... 130-A1
PALMER MILL RD
MULTNOMAH CO OR ... 201-A1
PALO ALTO RD
CLALLAM CO WA ... 109-C1
PALOUSE HWY
SPOKANE CO WA ... 114-C2
WAVERLY WA ... 114-C2
E PALOUSE HWY
SPOKANE CO WA ... 246-C5
SPOKANE CO WA ... 247-A6
S PALOUSE HWY
SPOKANE CO WA ... 246-C5
N PALOUSE HWY
COLFAX WA ... 122-C1
WHITMAN CO WA ... 122-C1
PALOUSE ST
ENDICOTT WA ... 122-B1
PALOUSE COVE RD
PALOUSE WA ... 249-C2
WHITMAN CO WA ... 249-C2
PALOUSE COVE RD Rt#-66
LATAH CO ID ... 249-C2
S PALOUSE RIVER RD
WHITMAN CO WA ... 249-C2
PANAKANIC RD
KLICKITAT CO WA ... 196-B1
PANDA RD
SKAMANIA CO WA ... 193-D6
PANDORA AV
CITY OF VICTORIA BC ... 256-J9
CITY OF VICTORIA BC ... 257-A9
PANDORA RD
ROSALIA WA ... 114-C3
WHITMAN CO WA ... 114-C3
PANORAMA DR
COQUITLAM BC ... 157-A4
PANORAMA RD
LANE CO OR ... 215-D2
PANTHER CREEK RD
SKAMANIA CO WA ... 194-D3
PANTHER LAKE RD W
KITSAP CO WA ... 173-D4
PARADISE DR
WALLA WALLA CO WA ... 121-B3
SW PARADISE LN
WALLA WALLA CO WA ... 174-A6
PARADISE LP
WALLA WALLA CO WA ... 121-B3
PARADISE RD
WHATCOM CO WA ... 158-D3
E PARADISE RD
SPOKANE CO WA ... 246-D6
PARADISE WY
COOS CO OR ... 220-D6
PARADISE BAY RD
JEFFERSON CO WA ... 170-B3
PARADISE CREEK RD
DOUGLAS CO OR ... 141-A1

PARADISE HILL RD
OKANOGAN CO WA ... 104-B3
PARADISE LAKE RD
SNOHOMISH CO WA ... 171-D5
PARADISE LAKE RD Rt#-524
SNOHOMISH CO WA ... 171-D5
PARADISE RIDGE RD
LATAH CO ID ... 249-D5
PARADISE SPRING RD
KLICKITAT CO WA ... 196-C2
PARALLEL AV
KLICKITAT CO WA ... 196-D6
PARCELL RD NE
MARION CO OR ... 205-B2
KITSAP CO WA ... 170-D5
PARISH LN
CROOK CO OR ... 213-B6
PARK AV
BENTON CO OR ... 327-H13
MALHEUR CO OR ... 139-A3
PACIFIC CO WA ... 117-A1
RAYMOND WA ... 117-A1
SNOHOMISH WA ... 171-D3
WINTHROP WA ... 104-A2
WOODBURN OR ... 205-B2
PARK AV Rt#-3
BOVILL ID ... 123-B1
LATAH CO ID ... 123-B1
PARK AV Rt#-105
RAYMOND WA ... 117-A1
N PARK AV
EUGENE OR ... 329-E1
EUGENE OR ... 329-E2
PARK AV N
RENTON WA ... 175-C5
PARK BLVD
ONTARIO OR ... 139-A3
E PARK BLVD
BOISE ID ... 253-D3
SW PARK BLVD
ONTARIO OR ... 139-A3
PARK DR
VANCOUVER BC ... 156-B5
PARK DR U.S.-101
GEARHART OR ... 301-H4
N PARK DR
RENTON WA ... 175-C4
N PARK DR Rt#-900
RENTON WA ... 175-C4
NE PARK DR Rt#-900
RENTON WA ... 175-C4
W PARK DR
SPOKANE CO WA ... 348-A13
PARK LN
JEFFERSON CO OR ... 212-D2
MAPLE RIDGE BC ... 157-C5
N PARK LN
ADA CO ID ... 253-A1
NE PARK LN
LINCOLN CO OR ... 203-B4
PARK RD
BANDON OR ... 220-B5
DISTRICT OF DELTA BC ... 156-D6
LEWIS CO WA ... 187-D3
WHATCOM CO WA ... 161-C2
PARK RD Rt#-150
CHELAN WA ... 236-C3
PARK RD SE
SPOKANE VALLEY WA ... 350-B5
S PARK RD
SPOKANE VALLEY WA ... 350-B9
PARK ST
GRANTS PASS OR ... 335-E10
POLK CO OR ... 207-C2
TEKOA WA ... 114-C3
WOODLAND WA ... 192-C1
PARK ST U.S.-20
LEBANON OR ... 133-C1
E PARK ST
GRANTS PASS OR ... 335-F10
JOSEPHINE CO OR ... 335-G11
WEISER ID ... 139-A2
N PARK ST U.S.-101
ABERDEEN WA ... 178-B7
N PARK ST U.S.-395
CHEWELAH WA ... 106-B3
STEVENS CO WA ... 106-B3
NW PARK ST
CHEHALIS WA ... 299-D11
S PARK ST U.S.-101
ABERDEEN WA ... 178-B7
S PARK ST U.S.-395
CHEWELAH WA ... 106-B3
STEVENS CO WA ... 106-B3
W PARK ST Rt#-27
TEKOA WA ... 114-C3
PARKATO RD
YAKIMA CO WA ... 120-A2
E PARKCENTER BLVD
BOISE ID ... 253-D3
PARK CITY LOOP RD
OKANOGAN CO WA ... 105-A3
PARK CREEK RD
KITTITAS CO WA ... 241-D5
PARKER RD
ISLAND CO WA ... 167-B4
LEWIS CO WA ... 187-A1
LINN CO OR ... 207-B7
POLK CO OR ... 207-B1
SW PARKER RD
WEST LINN OR ... 199-C4
PARKER ST
DISTRICT OF BURNABY BC ... 156-D4
DISTRICT OF BURNABY BC ... 255-G11
PARKER BRIDGE RD
YAKIMA CO WA ... 120-A2
PARKERBURG-PROSPER JUNCTION RD
COOS CO OR ... 220-B5
PARKER MEADOWS RD
JACKSON CO OR ... 226-D7
PARKER RESERVOIR RD
MALHEUR CO OR ... 155-A1
PARKEY DR
DESCHUTES CO OR ... 212-C3
PARK HILL LN
DOUGLAS CO OR ... 221-C1
SUTHERLIN OR ... 221-C1
SW PARKLAND DR
CHEHALIS WA ... 299-E13
PARK ORCHARD DR
GRANT CO WA ... 242-C2
PARK RIDGE LN
SKAGIT CO WA ... 161-B4
PARKS RD
DOUGLAS CO WA ... 237-B1
E PARKS RD
KOOTENAI CO ID ... 245-B2

PARKSVILLE - LASQUETI FERRY
BRITISH COLUMBIA BC ... 92-C2
PARKWAY DR NW
SALEM OR ... 322-E12
PARKWAY RD
LANE CO OR ... 215-D4
PARPALA RD
SPOKANE CO WA ... 186-C4
PARR RD NE
MARION CO OR ... 205-B2
PARRELL RD
BEND OR ... 332-E11
DESCHUTES CO OR ... 332-D13
SW PARRETT MOUNTAIN RD
CLACKAMAS CO OR ... 199-A5
WASHINGTON CO OR ... 199-A5
YAMHILL CO OR ... 199-A5
PARRISH RD
YAMHILL CO OR ... 198-D6
PARRISH CREEK RD
SPRAY OR ... 136-B1
WHEELER CO OR ... 136-B1
PARRISH GAP RD
MARION CO OR ... 133-C1
MARION CO OR ... 207-D2
PARSON RD
ASOTIN CO WA ... 122-C3
ASOTIN CO WA ... 250-A6
PARSON CREEK RD
SKAGIT CO WA ... 161-B4
PARSONS CREEK RD
LANE CO OR ... 210-D6
PARTON RD
DESCHUTES CO OR ... 211-D7
PARVIN RD
WHITMAN CO WA ... 122-C1
WHITMAN CO WA ... 249-A2
PASCOE AV
LEWIS CO WA ... 187-D2
Vineland WA ... 250-B5
PASCO-KAHLOTUS RD
FRANKLIN CO WA ... 121-B2
PASCO WA ... 121-B2
PASSAGE RD (W PASSAGE RD)
GIG HARBOR WA ... 174-C7
PASSMORE RD
KITTITAS CO WA ... 241-A4
PATAHA CREEK RD
GARFIELD CO WA ... 122-B2
PATEROS FERRY RD
DOUGLAS CO WA ... 112-B1
PATERSON RD
PROSSER WA ... 120-C3
PATIT RD
COLUMBIA CO WA ... 122-A2
PAT MARX RD
KLICKITAT CO WA ... 196-D4
PATMORE RD
ISLAND CO WA ... 167-B5
PATRICIA BAY HWY Rt#-17
DISTRICT OF CENTRAL SAANICH BC ... 159-C2
DISTRICT OF NORTH SAANICH BC ... 159-C2
DISTRICT OF SAANICH BC ... 159-C2
DISTRICT OF SAANICH BC ... 256-F2
TOWN OF SIDNEY BC ... 159-C2
PATRICK AV
KITTITAS WA ... 241-C6
PATSY DR SE
THURSTON CO WA ... 184-D2
PATTEE RD
LEWIS CO WA ... 184-D7
PATTERSON AV
DISTRICT OF BURNABY BC ... 156-C5
PATTERSON RD
PIERCE CO WA ... 182-C6
WHITMAN CO WA ... 249-A4
PATTERSON ST
Altamont OR ... 339-B11
WESTPORT WA ... 298-G11
PATTERSON ST NW
SALEM OR ... 322-F12
PATTERSON FERRY RD
MORROW CO OR ... 128-C1
PATTERSON LAKE RD
OKANOGAN CO WA ... 104-A2
PATTON BLVD
GRANT CO WA ... 242-C2
SW PATTON RD
MULTNOMAH CO OR ... 316-B1
PORTLAND OR ... 316-B1
SW PATTON VALLEY RD
WASHINGTON CO OR ... 198-A2
PATTULLO BRDG Rt#-99A
CITY OF SURREY BC ... 156-D5
PATTY RD
ASOTIN CO WA ... 122-C3
PAULINA HWY Rt#-380
CROOK CO OR ... 135-C2
CROOK CO OR ... 136-A3
CROOK CO OR ... 213-D5
PRINEVILLE OR ... 213-D5
PAULINA-EAST LAKE RD
DESCHUTES CO OR ... 143-A1
PAULINA SUPLEE RD
CROOK CO OR ... 136-B3
PAULINA SUPLEE RD Rt#-380
CROOK CO OR ... 136-B3
MOUNT VERNON OR ... 137-A1
PAULSON RD
HOQUIAM WA ... 178-A7
PAVEL RD
CLALLAM CO WA ... 163-A6
PAWNEE
CROOK CO OR ... 213-D7
W PAYETTE AV
BENTON CO OR ... 342-H9
KENNEWICK WA ... 342-H9
PAYETTE RIVER SCENIC RT Rt#-55
BOISE CO ID ... 139-C2
PAYNE RD
BENTON CO OR ... 207-A7
JACKSON CO OR ... 234-C2
PEACE PORTAL DR
WHATCOM CO WA ... 158-B3
S PEACH ST
JACKSON CO OR ... 336-C14
MEDFORD OR ... 336-C14
W PEACH ST
YAKIMA WA ... 243-B7
PEACHEY ST Rt#-285
WENATCHEE WA ... 239-A4
PEACOCK WK
CROOK CO OR ... 213-C4
PEACOCK HILL AV NW
PIERCE CO WA ... 174-C7
PEARCE RD
KLICKITAT CO WA ... 196-A3
PEARDALE LN Rt#-411
LONGVIEW WA ... 303-C9

PEARDONVILLE RD
DISTRICT OF MATSQUI BC ... 102-B1
PEARL RD
CANYON CO ID ... 139-A3
PAYETTE CO ID ... 139-A3
PEARL ST
COBURG OR ... 210-B7
EUGENE OR ... 330-A7
LANE CO OR ... 210-B7
PEARL ST Rt#-163
RUSTON WA ... 181-C2
TACOMA WA ... 181-C2
N PEARL ST Rt#-507
CENTRALIA WA ... 184-C5
CENTRALIA WA ... 299-F1
LEWIS CO WA ... 184-C5
S PEARL ST
TACOMA WA ... 181-C2
S PEARL ST Rt#-507
CENTRALIA WA ... 299-F4
W PEARL ST
FRANKLIN CO WA ... 342-J5
FRANKLIN CO WA ... 343-A5
PASCO WA ... 343-A5
PEARL CREEK RD
VALLEY CO ID ... 251-D1
PEARL HILL RD
DOUGLAS CO WA ... 112-C1
PEARSON LN
VALLEY CO ID ... 251-D6
PEARSON CREEK RD
UMATILLA CO OR ... 129-B2
PEART RD
CLARK CO WA ... 192-D1
NE PEART RD
CLARK CO WA ... 193-A1
PEASE RD
BURLINGTON WA ... 260-C7
PEASLEE AV
ASOTIN CO WA ... 250-B5
S PEASLEY CANYON RD
AUBURN WA ... 182-B1
KING CO WA ... 182-B1
SW PEAVINE RD
YAMHILL CO OR ... 198-A7
YAMHILL CO OR ... 204-B1
PEAVINE VALLEY RD
JOSEPHINE CO OR ... 148-C1
PEBBLE CREEK RD
COLUMBIA CO OR ... 125-B1
PECK DR
Altamont OR ... 339-B11
N PECK RD
SPOKANE CO WA ... 247-A1
SW PECK RD
JEFFERSON CO OR ... 208-A7
PECKENPAUGH RD
LINN CO OR ... 210-A1
PECK RIDGE RD
LEWIS CO WA ... 123-B2
E PE ELL AV
LEWIS CO WA ... 117-B2
PE ELL-MCDONALD RD
LEWIS CO WA ... 117-B2
LEWIS CO WA ... 187-A2
LEWIS CO WA ... 117-B2
PEER-HOPE RD
BAKER CO OR ... 131-A3
S PEKIN RD
COWLITZ CO WA ... 192-C1
PELHAM HILL RD
COLUMBIA CO OR ... 189-B5
PEMBERTON AV
DIST OF NORTH VANCOUVER BC ... 254-H5
PENAWAWA RD
WHITMAN CO WA ... 122-B1
PENDALL RD
DOUGLAS CO WA ... 237-C1
PENDER ST E
VANCOUVER BC ... 254-H10
VANCOUVER BC ... 255-A10
PENDER ST W
VANCOUVER BC ... 254-F9
PENDLETON CTO
ECHO OR ... 129-A1
UMATILLA CO OR ... 129-A1
PENDLETON HWY U.S.-30
UMATILLA CO OR ... 129-B1
NW PENDLETON HWY U.S.-30
PENDLETON OR ... 129-B1
UMATILLA CO OR ... 129-B1
PENDLETON RD
PIERCE CO WA ... 181-B5
PENDLETON ST SW
Rochester WA ... 184-A3
PENDLETON-COLD SPGS HWY Rt#-37
PENDLETON OR ... 129-A1
UMATILLA CO OR ... 129-A1
PENDLETON-JOHN DAY HWY U.S.-39
GRANT CO OR ... 129-B3
GRANT CO OR ... 137-A1
LONG CREEK OR ... 137-A1
MOUNT VERNON OR ... 137-A1
PENDLETON OR ... 129-B2
PILOT ROCK OR ... 129-B2
UMATILLA CO OR ... 129-B2
PENDLETON RIVER RD
PENDLETON OR ... 129-B1
UMATILLA CO OR ... 129-B1
PENGRA-HUNTINGTON RD
DESCHUTES CO OR ... 143-A1
DESCHUTES CO OR ... 217-A2
Three Rivers OR ... 143-A1
Three Rivers OR ... 217-A7
PENINSULA DR
JEFFERSON CO OR ... 212-C2
N PENINSULA DR
KING CO WA ... 175-D6
W PENINSULA DR
MOSES LAKE WA ... 242-C4
PENINSULA RD
BONNER CO ID ... 107-A3
SW PENINSULA RD
JEFFERSON CO OR ... 212-C1
N PENINSULAR AV
PORTLAND OR ... 308-D4
S PENMAN RD
CLACKAMAS CO OR ... 199-D6
PENN AV SE
DOUGLAS CO WA ... 239-B5
PENN RD
SKAGIT CO WA ... 161-A7
PENN COVE RD
ISLAND CO WA ... 167-B4
PENNING RD
LEWIS CO WA ... 187-A1

PENNSYLVANIA AV U.S.-95
PAYETTE CO ID ... 139-A3
E PENNSYLVANIA AV
COEUR D'ALENE ID ... 355-G10
S PENNSYLVANIA AV U.S.-95
FRUITLAND ID ... 139-A3
PAYETTE CO ID ... 139-A3
PENNSYLVANIA AV SE
Four Corners OR ... 325-F2
PENNSYLVANIA ST
LONGVIEW WA ... 302-G5
PENNY CREEK RD
JEFFERSON CO WA ... 109-C1
E PEONE RD
SPOKANE CO WA ... 246-D2
PEORIA RD
HARRISBURG OR ... 210-A2
LINN CO OR ... 207-B6
LINN CO OR ... 210-A2
PEPIOT RD
FRANKLIN CO WA ... 121-B2
MESA WA ... 121-B2
PEPPERMINT RD
CROOK CO OR ... 213-D4
PEPPERS BRIDGE RD
WALLA WALLA CO WA ... 344-F14
PERCH RD
JEFFERSON CO OR ... 212-C2
PERDITA ST
OCEAN SHORES WA ... 298-E4
PERIMETER RD
PIERCE CO WA ... 181-D5
E PERIMETER RD
KOOTENAI CO ID ... 245-C1
N PERIMETER RD
KOOTENAI CO ID ... 245-C1
PERKINS RD
CLATSOP CO OR ... 188-B3
PERKINS ST NE
MARION CO OR ... 205-A4
PERRY AV U.S.-101
HOQUIAM WA ... 178-A7
PERRY AV NE
BREMERTON WA ... 271-A8
KITSAP CO WA ... 271-A8
PERRY RD
JACKSON CO OR ... 230-C5
LANE CO OR ... 215-A4
N PERRY RD
SPOKANE CO WA ... 114-C1
PERRY ST
WINTHROP WA ... 104-A2
N PERRY ST
SPOKANE WA ... 349-C4
S PERRY ST
SPOKANE CO WA ... 246-C5
SPOKANE CO WA ... 349-C9
SPOKANE CO WA ... 246-C5
PERRY CREEK RD
COLUMBIA CO OR ... 192-A1
PERRYDALE RD
DALLAS OR ... 204-A5
POLK CO OR ... 204-A4
W PERRYDALE RD
POLK CO OR ... 204-A3
N PERRY NB CONNECTION ST
SPOKANE WA ... 349-C6
E PERSHALL RD
OWYHEE CO ID ... 147-B1
NW PERSHALL WY
DESCHUTES CO OR ... 212-D4
Terrebonne OR ... 212-D4
PETER ANDERSON RD
SKAGIT CO WA ... 260-F2
PETER BURNS RD
SKAGIT CO WA ... 168-C1
PETER DAM RD
OKANOGAN CO WA ... 113-B1
OKANOGAN CO WA ... 237-D1
PETER HAGEN RD NW
KITSAP CO WA ... 173-D7
PETER JOHNSON RD
CLATSOP CO OR ... 192-D1
CLATSOP CO OR ... 188-C3
PETERS AV
CHELAN CO WA ... 238-A2
PETERS RD
CLALLAM CO WA ... 165-A6
CROOK CO OR ... 213-D4
DIST OF NORTH VANCOUVER BC ... 255-F2
PETERS ST
Sunnyslope WA ... 238-D3
PETERSON RD
DESCHUTES CO OR ... 212-C7
JEFFERSON CO OR ... 109-C1
KLICKITAT CO WA ... 120-B3
KLICKITAT CO WA ... 128-B1
SKAGIT CO WA ... 161-A6
SKAGIT CO WA ... 260-B5
E PETERSON RD
BURLINGTON WA ... 260-B5
SKAGIT CO WA ... 260-B5
PETERSON BURN RD
DESCHUTES CO OR ... 211-D6
PETERSON CREEK RD
CROOK CO OR ... 136-A2
PETERSON HAWK
PIERCE CO WA ... 118-A1
PIERCE CO WA ... 181-B1
PETERSON RIDGE RD
DESCHUTES CO OR ... 211-D6
PETERS PASTURE RD
JEFFERSON CO OR ... 135-A1
PETERSVILLE RD NE
BREMERTON WA ... 271-A6
KITSAP CO WA ... 271-A6
SW PETES MOUNTAIN RD
CLACKAMAS CO OR ... 199-C5
PETROVITSKY RD
KING CO WA ... 175-D6
N PETTET DR
SPOKANE WA ... 348-F6
PETTIBONE DR
BENTON CO OR ... 207-B4
PETTIGREW RD
BEND OR ... 332-J9
PETTYJOHN RD
WALLA WALLA CO WA ... 121-C3
PETZOLD RD
LANE CO OR ... 133-B3
PFEIFER RD
LINCOLN CO WA ... 113-C2
PFEIFER RD E
LINCOLN CO WA ... 113-B2
PH 15
FRANKLIN CO WA ... 121-B2
PHARR RD
OKANOGAN CO WA ... 104-C2

STREET — City State — Page-Grid

PHEASANT LN
LANE CO OR ... 215-D4
PHELPS RD
CLACKAMAS CO OR ... 200-D3
PHELPS RD NE
KITSAP CO WA ... 174-C1
N PHILADELPHIA AV U.S.-30
PORTLAND OR ... 192-B7
PHILLIPS RD
YAMHILL CO OR ... 198-B3
NW PHILLIPS RD
WASHINGTON CO OR ... 192-A7
W PHILLIPS RD
ADAMS CO WA ... 242-C7
PHILLIPS RD SE
KITSAP CO WA ... 174-C5
PHILOMATH BLVD U.S.-20
BENTON CO OR ... 133-B1
BENTON CO OR ... 327-A12
CORVALLIS OR ... 133-B1
CORVALLIS OR ... 327-A12
PHILOMATH RD
BENTON CO OR ... 133-B1
PHINNEY AV N
SEATTLE WA ... 273-H5
N PHINNEY WY
SEATTLE WA ... 273-H5
NW PHINNEY BAY DR
BREMERTON WA ... 270-E8
KITSAP CO WA ... 270-E8
PH NO 10
COWLITZ CO WA ... 187-C7
PH NO 10 Rt#-411
CASTLE ROCK WA ... 187-C7
COWLITZ CO WA ... 187-C7
N PHOENIX RD
JACKSON CO OR ... 234-B2
JACKSON CO OR ... 336-J14
MEDFORD OR ... 234-B2
MEDFORD OR ... 336-J14
UNION CO OR ... 130-B2
PHYS POINT RD
UNION CO OR ... 130-B2
PICARD RD
SISKIYOU CO CA ... 150-B3
PICKERING RD
MASON CO WA ... 180-C2
PICKETT RD
KLAMATH CO OR ... 151-A2
PICNIC POINT RD
SNOHOMISH CO WA ... 171-B4
PICTURE LN
LAKE CO OR ... 143-B2
PIEDMONT RD
CLALLAM CO WA ... 164-C6
PIEDMONT RD Rt#-112
CLALLAM CO WA ... 164-C5
CLALLAM CO WA ... 165-A6
PIERCE RD
MEDFORD OR ... 336-H11
UNION CO OR ... 130-A2
PIERCE RD NW
DOUGLAS CO WA ... 236-D5
N PIERCE PARK LN
ADA CO ID ... 253-C1
BOISE ID ... 253-C1
PIERSON RD
WHITMAN CO WA ... 114-B3
PIKE RD
YAMHILL CO OR ... 198-B4
YAMHILL CO OR ... 198-A4
NW PIKE RD
YAMHILL CO OR ... 198-A4
SW PIKE RD
JEFFERSON CO OR ... 212-C1
PILLER PL
JOSEPHINE CO OR ... 233-A4
PILOT ROCK RD
KOOTENAI CO ID ... 247-D6
PINCUS
PIERCE CO WA ... 181-D7
N PINE
LA GRANDE OR ... 130-A2
PINE AV
SNOHOMISH WA ... 171-D3
E PINE AV
ADA CO ID ... 253-A3
MERIDIAN ID ... 253-A3
W PINE AV
ADA CO ID ... 253-A3
PINE AV NE
OLYMPIA WA ... 297-A4
THURSTON CO WA ... 297-A4
PINE LN
COOS CO OR ... 220-B4
SE PINE RD
KITSAP CO WA ... 174-B6
SW PINE RD
KITSAP CO WA ... 174-B6
PINE RD NE
BREMERTON WA ... 270-H7
KITSAP CO WA ... 270-H5
Tracyton WA ... 270-H5
PINE ST
CHELAN CO WA ... 238-A1
LEAVENWORTH WA ... 238-A1
MARION CO OR ... 205-C4
NORTHPORT WA ... 106-A1
ROGUE RIVER OR ... 229-D6
SANDPOINT ID ... 244-A2
SILVERTON OR ... 205-C4
PINE ST Rt#-524
EDMONDS WA ... 171-A5
PINE ST U.S.-2
SANDPOINT ID ... 244-A2
PINE ST U.S.-12
OAKVILLE WA ... 117-B1
PINE ST U.S.-95
SANDPOINT ID ... 244-A2
E PINE ST
CENTRAL POINT OR ... 230-C7
JACKSON CO OR ... 230-C7
JACKSON CO OR ... 336-A5
E PINE ST Rt#-3
MASON CO WA ... 180-A3
SHELTON WA ... 180-A3
N PINE ST
CANBY OR ... 199-C6
S PINE ST
TACOMA WA ... 294-D1
SE PINE ST Rt#-99
ROSEBURG OR ... 334-F8
SE PINE ST Rt#-138
ROSEBURG OR ... 334-G7
W PINE ST
CENTRAL POINT OR ... 230-C7
WALLA WALLA WA ... 344-H7
W PINE ST Rt#-125
WALLA WALLA WA ... 344-J7

PINE ST NE
MARION CO OR ... 205-B4
SALEM OR ... 322-J10
SALEM OR ... 323-A10
SILVERTON OR ... 205-B4
W PINE BLUFF RD
SPOKANE CO WA ... 114-B1
SPOKANE CO WA ... 246-A1
N PINE BLUFF WYE RD
SPOKANE CO WA ... 114-B1
PINE CITY RD
MALDEN WA ... 114-B3
WHITMAN CO WA ... 114-B3
PINECONE DR
JOSEPHINE CO OR ... 233-B5
PINE CREEK HWY
BAKER CO OR ... 131-A3
HALFWAY OR ... 131-A3
PINE CREEK RD
GRANT CO OR ... 137-B2
HARNEY CO OR ... 137-C3
HARNEY CO OR ... 145-C1
OKANOGAN CO WA ... 104-C2
SHOSHONE CO ID ... 115-C2
UMATILLA CO OR ... 129-C1
WALLOWA CO OR ... 131-A1
E PINE CREEK RD
BAKER CO OR ... 131-A3
N PINE CREEK RD
OKANOGAN CO WA ... 104-C2
PINECREST DR
JOSEPHINE CO OR ... 229-B5
JOSEPHINE CO OR ... 335-A7
LA GRANDE OR ... 130-A2
PINE CREST RD
LATAH CO ID ... 249-D5
PINE GROVE RD
LANE CO OR ... 133-B3
PINEHURST RD
DESCHUTES CO OR ... 217-B1
PINEHURST WY NE
SEATTLE WA ... 171-B7
PINE MOUNT DR
HOOD RIVER CO OR ... 195-C7
HOOD RIVER CO OR ... 202-C1
N PINES RD Rt#-27
SPOKANE VALLEY WA ... 350-H5
S PINES RD Rt#-27
SPOKANE VALLEY WA ... 350-H10
S PINE SPRING RD
SPOKANE CO WA ... 114-B2
S PINE SPRINGS RD
SPOKANE CO WA ... 114-B2
PINE TOWN RD
BAKER CO OR ... 131-A3
PINE TREE RD
LEWIS CO WA ... 187-D3
PINETREE WY
COQUITLAM BC ... 157-A4
N PINEWOOD WY
KOOTENAI CO ID ... 245-A4
PING GULCH RD
GARFIELD CO WA ... 122-B1
PINKNEY RD
COLUMBIA CO OR ... 189-B7
PINTO RIDGE RD
GRANT CO WA ... 113-A2
PIOCH LN
LANE CO OR ... 210-D7
PIONEER AV
CASHMERE WA ... 238-C2
E PIONEER AV
PUYALLUP WA ... 182-B4
W PIONEER AV
PUYALLUP WA ... 182-B4
PIONEER AV E
GRAYS HARBOR CO WA ... 178-D7
MONTESANO WA ... 178-D7
PIONEER AV W
GRAYS HARBOR CO WA ... 178-D7
MONTESANO WA ... 178-D7
PIONEER BLVD U.S.-26
SANDY OR ... 200-C4
PIONEER DR
CASHMERE WA ... 238-B2
CHELAN CO WA ... 238-B2
PIONEER HWY
SKAGIT CO WA ... 168-B2
SNOHOMISH CO WA ... 168-B4
STANWOOD WA ... 168-B2
PIONEER HWY Rt#-530
SKAGIT CO WA ... 168-B2
PIONEER HWY E
SNOHOMISH CO WA ... 168-C5
PIONEER LP
DESCHUTES CO OR ... 217-C1
PIONEER PKWY
SKAGIT CO WA ... 160-D7
Swinomish Village WA ... 167-D1
PIONEER PKWY E
North Springfield OR ... 330-G4
SPRINGFIELD OR ... 330-G4
PIONEER PKWY W
North Springfield OR ... 330-G4
SPRINGFIELD OR ... 330-G4
PIONEER RD
JACKSON CO OR ... 234-A2
LONG BEACH WA ... 186-A5
OWYHEE CO ID ... 147-A1
PACIFIC CO WA ... 186-A5
S PIONEER RD
PIERCE CO WA ... 182-C5
PIONEER RD NW
KITSAP CO WA ... 174-A1
PIONEER ST
LANE CO OR ... 133-C3
LOWELL OR ... 133-C3
PIONEER ST Rt#-501
RIDGEFIELD WA ... 192-C2
PIONEER WY
CHELAN CO WA ... 238-C3
GIG HARBOR WA ... 181-C1
MOSES LAKE WA ... 242-C3
PIONEER WY Rt#-20
OAK HARBOR WA ... 167-B3
PIONEER WY Rt#-162
ORTING WA ... 182-B5
PIERCE CO WA ... 182-B5
SOUTH PRAIRIE WA ... 182-B5
SUMNER WA ... 182-B5
N PIONEER WY
YAKIMA CO WA ... 243-A5
S PIONEER WY
SHELTON WA ... 180-A3
S PIONEER WY Rt#-162
PIERCE CO WA ... 182-C6
W PIONEER WY Rt#-162
PIERCE CO WA ... 182-D5

PIONEER WY E
PIERCE CO WA ... 182-A3
PUYALLUP WA ... 182-B4
TACOMA WA ... 182-A3
PIONEER WY NW
KITSAP CO WA ... 170-B6
NW PIONEER HILL RD
KITSAP CO WA ... 170-B6
PIONEER MEMORIAL BRDG U.S.-395
KENNEWICK WA ... 343-B8
PASCO WA ... 343-B8
PIONEER PARKWAY RD
LA CONNER WA ... 167-D1
Shelter Bay WA ... 167-D1
SKAGIT CO WA ... 167-D1
Swinomish Village WA ... 167-D1
PIPELINE RD
COQUITLAM BC ... 157-B4
DOUGLAS CO OR ... 221-B2
WHATCOM CO WA ... 158-B3
SE PIPE LINE RD
MULTNOMAH CO OR ... 200-C2
PIPER RD
WHATCOM CO WA ... 158-D5
E PIPER RD
SPOKANE CO WA ... 246-D2
PIPER CANYON RD
WALLA WALLA CO WA ... 121-C2
PISCALE LOOKOUT RD
CROOK CO OR ... 136-A2
PISTOL BUTTE RD
MARION CO OR ... 216-D7
PISTOL RIVER LP
CURRY CO OR ... 232-B1
PITCHER CANYON RD
CHELAN CO WA ... 238-D5
PITNEY LN
LANE CO OR ... 210-A6
PITSUA BUTTE RD
DESCHUTES CO OR ... 216-D5
PITT AV
BREMERTON WA ... 271-A10
PITT RIVER RD
COQUITLAM BC ... 157-A5
PORT COQUITLAM BC ... 157-A5
PITTSBURG RD
COLUMBIA CO OR ... 192-A1
PLACE RD
CLALLAM CO WA ... 165-A5
LANE CO OR ... 133-C3
PLACER RD
JOSEPHINE CO OR ... 229-B2
PLAINVIEW DR
LINN CO OR ... 210-C1
PLANETZ RD NW
DOUGLAS CO WA ... 236-C7
PLANK RD
YAKIMA CO WA ... 120-A3
PLATEAU BLVD
COQUITLAM BC ... 157-B4
PLAT I RD
DOUGLAS CO WA ... 221-D1
PLAT K RD
DOUGLAS CO WA ... 221-D1
PLAT M RD
DOUGLAS CO WA ... 221-D1
PLATT RD
KLICKITAT CO WA ... 196-A4
PLAZA WY
WALLA WALLA WA ... 345-A10
WALLA WALLA WA ... 345-A11
PLEASANT DR
BREMERTON WA ... 270-D10
E PLEASANT ST
WALLA WALLA WA ... 345-E8
Walla Walla East WA ... 345-E8
PLEASANT BEACH DR NE
KITSAP CO WA ... 271-H6
PLEASANT CREEK RD
JACKSON CO OR ... 229-D2
PLEASANT HILL RD
COWLITZ CO WA ... 189-C2
COWLITZ CO WA ... 303-E1
GRANT CO OR ... 137-A2
POLK CO OR ... 204-A3
YAKIMA CO WA ... 243-B5
E PLEASANT PRAIRIE RD
SPOKANE CO WA ... 246-D2
PLEASANT RIDGE RD
WASCO CO OR ... 127-B2
PLEASANT VALLEY RD
COOS CO OR ... 220-D7
DOUGLAS CO OR ... 219-B5
JOSEPHINE CO OR ... 229-A4
LEWIS CO WA ... 187-B1
LINN CO OR ... 133-C2
YAKIMA CO WA ... 243-A5
S PLEASANT VALLEY RD
ADA CO ID ... 253-C4
BOISE ID ... 253-C4
SW PLEASANT VALLEY RD
WASHINGTON CO OR ... 199-A3
PLEASANT VIEW RD
KOOTENAI CO ID ... 353-B1
POST FALLS ID ... 353-C8
E PLEASANT VIEW RD
SPOKANE CO WA ... 352-H10
W PLEASANT VIEW RD
KOOTENAI CO ID ... 352-H10
PLOMONDON RD
LEWIS CO WA ... 187-D4
PLUG MILL RD
MASON CO WA ... 179-B5
PLUM ST
OLYMPIA WA ... 296-J5
PLUMLEE RD
WASHINGTON CO OR ... 198-B1
PLUMTREE LN
JOSEPHINE CO OR ... 335-A2
PLUSH CUTOFF RD
LAKE CO OR ... 152-B2
PLYMOUTH AV U.S.-30
NEW PLYMOUTH ID ... 139-B3
PLYMOUTH RD
BENTON CO OR ... 327-B13
BENTON CO OR ... 121-A3
PLYMPTON CREEK RD Rt#-409
CLATSOP CO OR ... 117-B3
POCAHONTAS RD
BAKER CITY OR ... 138-A1
BAKER CO OR ... 130-A3
BAKER CO OR ... 138-A1
POE RD
WHITMAN CO WA ... 249-C3
POEN RD
ADA CO ID ... 253-A7
POETSCH RD
LEWIS CO WA ... 187-D4

N POE VALLEY RD
KLAMATH CO OR ... 151-A2
S POE VALLEY RD
KLAMATH CO OR ... 150-C2
KLAMATH CO OR ... 151-A2
POINT DR NE
KITSAP CO WA ... 271-H5
S POINT RD
JEFFERSON CO WA ... 170-B4
W POINT RD
DOUGLAS CO OR ... 223-A4
POINT BROWN AV
OCEAN SHORES WA ... 177-B6
OCEAN SHORES WA ... 298-D3
POINT DEFIANCE TAHLEQUAH FERRY
KING CO WA ... 181-D1
POINT FOSDICK DR NW
PIERCE CO WA ... 181-C2
POINT GREY RD
VANCOUVER BC ... 254-B11
POINT ROBERTS RD
DISTRICT OF DELTA BC ... 101-C1
SW POINT ROBINSON RD
KING CO WA ... 175-A6
POINT WHITEHORN RD
Birch Bay WA ... 158-B5
POINT WILSON RD
MASON CO WA ... 180-D3
POISON CREEK CTO
OWYHEE CO ID ... 147-C3
POKORNY RD
MARION CO OR ... 199-A7
E POLE RD Rt#-544
EVERSON WA ... 102-B1
WHATCOM CO WA ... 102-B1
W POLE RD
WHATCOM CO WA ... 158-D5
POLE CREEK RD
DESCHUTES CO OR ... 211-C6
MALHEUR CO OR ... 138-B3
MALHEUR CO OR ... 154-B2
MALHEUR CO OR ... 155-A1
POLEHN RD SW
THURSTON CO WA ... 184-B3
E POLELINE AV
KOOTENAI CO ID ... 354-B4
POST FALLS ID ... 353-J4
POST FALLS ID ... 354-B4
W POLELINE AV
KOOTENAI CO ID ... 353-D4
POST FALLS ID ... 353-F4
POLE LINE RD
BAKER CO OR ... 130-A3
MORROW CO OR ... 128-C1
POLK RD
LATAH CO ID ... 249-C4
POLK ST
EUGENE OR ... 329-H6
INDEPENDENCE OR ... 204-B7
POLLMAN RD
LEWIS CO WA ... 184-D7
POLNELL RD
ISLAND CO WA ... 167-D3
POLSON RD
SKAGIT CO WA ... 168-A1
POMEROY RD
JACKSON CO OR ... 230-C2
PONDEROSA AV
BENTON CO OR ... 327-B5
CORVALLIS OR ... 327-B5
E PONDEROSA BLVD
KOOTENAI CO ID ... 354-B8
POST FALLS ID ... 354-B8
PONDEROSA DR
DOUGLAS CO OR ... 221-A3
PONDEROSA RD
BONNER CO ID ... 244-B5
PONY BUTTE RD
JEFFERSON CO OR ... 135-B1
PONY CREEK RD
NORTH BEND OR ... 333-F5
POODLE CREEK RD
LANE CO OR ... 133-A3
POPLAR AV
DISTRICT OF SAANICH BC ... 257-B4
POPLAR DR
DESCHUTES CO OR ... 212-C5
MEDFORD OR ... 336-D9
POPLAR LN
POLK CO OR ... 204-B6
POPLAR ST
POWERS OR ... 140-B3
E POPLAR ST U.S.-2
DOUGLAS CO WA ... 236-C7
WATERVILLE WA ... 236-C7
NW POPLAR ST
MILTON-FREEWATER OR ... 121-C3
W POPLAR ST
WALLA WALLA WA ... 344-H9
WALLA WALLA WA ... 345-A8
POPULAR ST Rt#-27
TEKOA WA ... 114-C3
POPULAR ST Rt#-274
TEKOA WA ... 114-C3
PORCUPINE BAY RD
LINCOLN CO WA ... 114-A1
PORCUPINE RIDGE RD
MORROW CO OR ... 129-A3
PORTAL WY
FERNDALE WA ... 158-C5
WHATCOM CO WA ... 158-C4
PORT ANGELES-VICTORIA FERRY
BRITISH COLUMBIA BC ... 165-C3
PORTER RD
CLACKAMAS CO OR ... 200-C6
NEZ PERCE CO ID ... 250-D2
WASHINGTON CO OR ... 198-C1
PORTER RD NW
DOUGLAS CO WA ... 236-B6
PORTER ST Rt#-169
ENUMCLAW WA ... 110-C3
KING CO WA ... 110-C3
PORTER WY
MILTON WA ... 182-B5
PORTER CREEK RD
DOUGLAS CO OR ... 221-A6
GRAYS HARBOR CO WA ... 117-B1
GRAYS HARBOR CO WA ... 179-C7
PORT GAMBLE RD NE
KITSAP CO WA ... 170-C5
PORT INDUSTRIAL RD
ABERDEEN WA ... 178-B7
PORTLAND AV
FAIRFIELD WA ... 114-C2
SPOKANE CO WA ... 114-C2

E PORTLAND AV
TACOMA WA ... 182-A3
TACOMA WA ... 293-J5
NW PORTLAND AV
BEND OR ... 332-D6
PORTLAND AV E
PIERCE CO WA ... 182-A4
TACOMA WA ... 182-A4
N PORTLAND BLVD
PORTLAND OR ... 308-D6
PORTLAND OR ... 309-G6
NE PORTLAND BLVD
PORTLAND OR ... 309-G6
PORTLAND DR
HOOD RIVER CO OR ... 195-C6
E PORTLAND FRWY I-205
CLACKAMAS CO OR ... 319-G7
NE PORTLAND HWY U.S.-30
PORTLAND OR ... 310-D6
PORTLAND OR ... 311-E7
PORTLAND AV Rt#-99W
NEWBERG OR ... 198-D5
WASHINGTON CO OR ... 199-A5
YAMHILL CO OR ... 198-D5
YAMHILL CO OR ... 199-A5
N PORTLAND RD
PORTLAND OR ... 304-C7
PORTLAND OR ... 308-B2
PORTLAND RD NE
SALEM OR ... 323-B9
PORTLAND ST
WILBUR WA ... 113-B1
PORTLAND HUBBARD HWY
CLACKAMAS CO OR ... 199-B6
W PORT MADISON RD
KITSAP CO WA ... 170-C7
PORT OF TACOMA RD
FIFE WA ... 182-A2
TACOMA WA ... 182-A2
SE PORTOLA DR
GRANTS PASS OR ... 335-H11
JOSEPHINE CO OR ... 335-H11
PORT ORCHARD BLVD
PORT ORCHARD WA ... 174-B4
PORT ORCHARD WA ... 270-H14
PORT ORFORD HWY
CURRY CO OR ... 224-A6
PORT ORFORD OR ... 224-A6
N PORTSMOUTH AV
PORTLAND OR ... 308-B3
PORT TOWNSEND-KEYSTONE FRY
ISLAND CO WA ... 167-B5
POSSESSION RD
ISLAND CO WA ... 171-A3
N POST ST
SPOKANE WA ... 348-J5
POST CANYON DR
HOOD RIVER CO OR ... 195-C5
POSTGREN RD
KLICKITAT CO WA ... 195-D2
POSTMA RD
YAKIMA CO WA ... 243-D7
E POSTMA RD
YAKIMA CO WA ... 243-C7
POTATO HILL RD
WALLOWA CO OR ... 130-C2
POTOMAC RANCH RD
MALHEUR CO OR ... 154-C1
POTTER LN
VALLEY CO ID ... 251-D6
POTTER RD
LATAH CO ID ... 249-C2
LINN CO OR ... 210-A2
POTTERY AV
PORT ORCHARD WA ... 174-B4
POTTS RD
WHITMAN CO WA ... 114-A3
POVERTY BEND RD
YAMHILL CO OR ... 198-A6
POWDER CREEK RD
TILLAMOOK CO OR ... 197-D6
E POWELL BLVD
GRESHAM OR ... 200-B2
E POWELL BLVD U.S.-26
GRESHAM OR ... 200-B2
SE POWELL BLVD U.S.-26
GRESHAM OR ... 200-A2
PORTLAND OR ... 200-A2
PORTLAND OR ... 317-H1
PORTLAND OR ... 318-B2
PORTLAND OR ... 319-H2
W POWELL BLVD U.S.-26
GRESHAM OR ... 200-A2
POWELL RD
COWLITZ CO WA ... 187-C7
GRAYS HARBOR CO WA ... 177-C5
NEZ PERCE CO ID ... 250-D6
NE POWELL RD
CLARK CO WA ... 193-B4
POWELL ST
VANCOUVER BC ... 254-J10
VANCOUVER BC ... 255-B10
POWELL BUTTE HWY
CROOK CO OR ... 213-A7
DESCHUTES CO OR ... 135-A3
DESCHUTES CO OR ... 213-A7
DESCHUTES CO OR ... 217-D1
POWELL BUTTE CEMETERY RD
CROOK CO OR ... 213-B6
SE POWELL VALLEY RD
GRESHAM OR ... 200-B2
POWER RD
MALHEUR CO OR ... 139-A2
POWER CREEK RD
GRAYS HARBOR CO WA ... 179-C6
POWERHOUSE RD
KLICKITAT CO WA ... 195-C4
YAKIMA CO WA ... 243-B6
YAKIMA CO WA ... 243-B6
POWER LINE RD
UMATILLA CO OR ... 121-C3
WALLA WALLA CO WA ... 345-D14
POWERLINE RD
IDAHO CO ID ... 123-C3
LANE CO OR ... 210-B6
LEWIS CO OR ... 123-C2
LINN CO OR ... 210-B3
POWERLINE RD SW
THURSTON CO WA ... 180-A7
POWER LINE EASEMENT RD
JOSEPHINE CO OR ... 233-B5
POWERS AV
NEZ PERCE CO ID ... 250-D5
POWERS HWY
COOS CO OR ... 140-B3
POWERS RD
BEND OR ... 332-D11
COLUMBIA CO OR ... 122-A2

E POWERS RD
NEZ PERCE CO ID ... 250-D5
POWERS CREEK LP NE
MARION CO OR ... 205-D5
POWERS SOUTH RD
COOS CO OR ... 140-B3
CURRY CO OR ... 140-B3
POWERS OR ... 140-B3
POW WAH KEE RD
GARFIELD CO WA ... 122-C2
PRAIRIE AV
LEWIS CO WA ... 184-B5
PORT COQUITLAM BC ... 157-B4
PRAIRIE AV U.S.-95
CRAIGMONT ID ... 123-B2
E PRAIRIE AV
DALTON GARDENS ID ... 355-E2
KOOTENAI CO ID ... 353-H2
KOOTENAI CO ID ... 354-B2
KOOTENAI CO ID ... 355-E2
W PRAIRIE AV
COEUR D'ALENE ID ... 355-B2
DALTON GARDENS ID ... 354-G2
HAYDEN ID ... 355-B2
HAYDEN ID ... 355-B2
KOOTENAI CO ID ... 353-D2
KOOTENAI CO ID ... 354-G2
KOOTENAI CO ID ... 355-B2
PRAIRIE RD
JUNCTION CITY OR ... 210-A3
LANE CO OR ... 210-A7
LANE CO OR ... 215-A1
SKAGIT CO WA ... 161-B4
S PRAIRIE RD
LEWIS CO WA ... 187-D2
SKAMANIA CO WA ... 195-A1
PRAIRIE CTY S SDE OF RV RD
GRANT CO OR ... 137-C2
PRAIRIE CITY OR ... 137-C2
PRAIRIE CREEK RD
DOUGLAS CO OR ... 226-D2
S PRAIRIE CREEK RD
PIERCE CO WA ... 182-C5
PRAIRIE FARM CTO
JEFFERSON CO OR ... 211-D1
PRAIRIE FARM RD
JEFFERSON CO OR ... 135-A1
PRAIRIE PKWY LN SW
THURSTON CO WA ... 184-B2
PRAIRIE RIDGE DR E
PIERCE CO WA ... 182-C5
PRAIRIE ROAD CONN
LANE CO OR ... 210-A6
PRAIRIE ROAD CONN Rt#-36
LANE CO OR ... 210-A6
S PRAIRIE VIEW RD
SPOKANE WA ... 114-C2
PRATER RD
DESCHUTES CO OR ... 216-C6
PRATHER RD
POLK CO OR ... 207-B2
PRATHER RD SW
THURSTON CO WA ... 184-A4
PRATT RD
WALLOWA CO OR ... 130-C2
PREACHER CREEK RD
LANE CO OR ... 133-A2
PREBLE ST
BREMERTON WA ... 270-E12
Navy Yard City WA ... 270-E12
NE PRESCOTT ST
MAYWOOD PARK OR ... 315-H1
PORTLAND OR ... 313-H1
PORTLAND OR ... 314-B1
PORTLAND OR ... 315-E1
PRESLEY
PIERCE CO WA ... 182-B6
W PRESLEY RD
KOOTENAI CO ID ... 247-D4
KOOTENAI CO ID ... 248-A1
PRESTON AV
LEWISTON ID ... 250-C5
PRESTON AV U.S.-12
WAITSBURG WA ... 122-A2
PRESTON-FALL CITY RD SE
KING CO WA ... 176-B4
W PREWETT RD
SPOKANE CO WA ... 114-B1
W PRICE AV
Town and Country WA ... 346-J12
PRICE RD
ALBANY OR ... 326-H7
BREMERTON WA ... 270-C10
KITSAP CO WA ... 270-C10
LINN CO OR ... 326-H7
YAKIMA CO WA ... 120-B2
N PRICE RD
LINN CO OR ... 120-B2
PRICEBORO DR
LINN CO OR ... 210-A5
PRICE-TWELVEMILE RD
CROOK CO OR ... 136-B3
PRIEST RAPIDS RD
BENTON CO WA ... 120-B2
YAKIMA CO WA ... 120-B2
PRINCESS AV
DIST OF NORTH VANCOUVER BC ... 255-C2
PRINCETON AV NE
SEATTLE WA ... 275-F4
NE PRINCETON WY
SEATTLE WA ... 275-F3
PRINGLE PKWY SE Rt#-22
SALEM OR ... 322-J13
PRINGLE RD
WASHINGTON CO ID ... 139-A2
PRINGLE RD SE
SALEM OR ... 324-J5
PRINGLE FALLS LP
DESCHUTES CO OR ... 142-C1
DESCHUTES CO OR ... 143-A1
PRINGLE FLAT RD
DESCHUTES CO OR ... 136-A3
PRIOR ST
VANCOUVER BC ... 254-J11
VANCOUVER BC ... 255-A11
PRIVATE RD
CLARK CO WA ... 190-A7
PROCTOR BLVD U.S.-26
SANDY OR ... 200-C4
N PROCTOR ST
TACOMA WA ... 292-C4
S PROCTOR ST
TACOMA WA ... 292-C6
PROFFITT RD
LEWIS CO OR ... 184-D6
N PROGRESS RD
SPOKANE CO WA ... 351-B2
SPOKANE VALLEY WA ... 351-B2

390 W PROGRESS RD
STREET INDEX
RIDGE RD

STREET City State Page-Grid

W PROGRESS RD
UMATILLA CO OR 129-A1
PROGRESSIVE RD
HARRAH WA 119-C2
N PROM
SEASIDE OR 301-F8
S PROM
SEASIDE OR 301-F9
PROMISE RD
WALLOWA CO OR 130-B1
PROMONTORY RD
CITY OF CHILLIWACK BC 102-C1
PROSPECT AV
Irondale WA 263-D13
WALLA WALLA WA 345-B11
WALLA WALLA CO WA 345-B11
PROSPECT DR
BENTON CITY WA 120-C3
PROSPECT RD
DIST OF NORTH VANCOUVER BC 255-B1
PROSPECT ST
BELLINGHAM WA 258-D6
PROSPECT LAKE RD
DISTRICT OF SAANICH BC 159-B5
DISTRICT OF SAANICH BC 256-A1
PROVIDENCE RD
ADAMS CO WA 121-C1
PROVIDENCE RD Rt#-261
ADAMS CO WA 121-C1
PROVOST RD NW
KITSAP CO WA 270-A2
Silverdale WA 270-A2
PROWELL ST
CHELAN CO WA 238-A1
PRUNEDALE RD
UMATILLA CO OR 121-C3
PRUNER RD
DOUGLAS CO OR 225-B2
RIDDLE OR 225-B2
P S OGDEN RD
DESCHUTES CO OR 212-D3
SW PUCKER HUDDLE RD Rt#-141
KLICKITAT CO WA 195-D4
PUCKETT RD
CROOK CO OR 213-C3
PUDDING RIVER RD NE
MARION CO OR 205-C1
NW PUDDY GULCH RD
YAMHILL CO OR 198-A5
PUGET DR
VANCOUVER BC 254-B14
PUGET DR Rt#-524
EDMONDS WA 171-A5
PUGET DR E
Colby WA 271-G14
PUGET DR SE
Colby WA 271-G14
RENTON WA 175-C5
PUGET RD NE
THURSTON CO WA 180-D5
N PUGET ST
OLYMPIA WA 297-A4
PUGET BEACH RD NE
THURSTON CO WA 181-A4
PUGH RD NE
KITSAP CO WA 170-C6
PUITT RD
CROOK CO OR 136-B2
PULLEN LN
JOSEPHINE CO OR 233-B5
PULLMAN ALBION RD
ALBION WA 249-A4
WHITMAN CO WA 249-A4
PULVER RD
BURLINGTON WA 260-A5
SKAGIT CO WA 260-A2
SW PUMA DR
WASHINGTON CO OR 198-B2
PUMP RD
CANYON CO ID 147-B1
NW PUMPKIN RIDGE RD
WASHINGTON CO OR 125-C1
PUNCH BOWL RD
HOOD RIVER CO OR 195-B7
PUNKIN CENTER RD
UMATILLA CO OR 129-A1
NW PURDIN RD
WASHINGTON CO OR 198-B1
PURDY DR Rt#-302
KITSAP CO WA 174-B6
PIERCE CO WA 174-B6
PURDY CRESCENT
PIERCE CO WA 174-C6
PURDY CUTOFF RD
MASON CO WA 180-A1
PURDY KITSAP RD
PIERCE CO WA 174-C6
PURTTEMAN GULCH RD
CHELAN CO WA 236-C2
PUYALLUP AV
TACOMA WA 182-A2
TACOMA WA 293-H7
PUYALLUP ST
STEILACOOM WA 181-C4
N PUYALLUP MOTOR NATURE TR
PIERCE CO WA 185-A3
PYLE RD
KLICKITAT CO WA 196-B3

Q

Q RD NW
DOUGLAS CO WA 236-C7
Q ST
PORT TOWNSEND WA 263-H3
SPRINGFIELD OR 330-G5
SPRINGFIELD OR 331-A5
NE QUAALE RD
JEFFERSON CO OR 208-D3
QUADRA ST
CITY OF VICTORIA BC 256-H6
DISTRICT OF SAANICH BC 159-C5
DISTRICT OF SAANICH BC 256-F1
VANCOUVER BC 254-A13
S QUADRANT ST
ROCKAWAY BEACH OR 191-B6
QUARRY RD
ALBANY OR 326-C5
COQUITLAM BC 157-B3
YAMHILL CO OR 198-D5
QUARTZ CREEK RD
DOUGLAS CO OR 222-B7
JOSEPHINE CO OR 229-A3
QUARTZ MOUNTAIN RD
DOUGLAS CO OR 222-A5
KITTITAS CO WA 240-C4
QUARTZVILLE DR
LINN CO OR 134-A1
QUEBEC ST
CITY OF VICTORIA BC 256-F9
VANCOUVER BC 254-H11
QUEEN AV
ALBANY OR 326-B9
LINN CO OR 326-B9
S QUEEN ANN BLVD
YAKIMA WA 243-B7
QUEEN ANNE AV N
SEATTLE WA 277-H1
QUEEN ANNE DR
SEATTLE WA 277-H1
W QUEEN ANNE DR WY
SEATTLE WA 277-H3
QUEEN MARY BLVD
CITY OF SURREY BC 157-A6
QUEENS AV
DIST OF WEST VANCOUVER BC 254-A1
QUEENS RD
DIST OF NORTH VANCOUVER BC 254-J2
DIST OF NORTH VANCOUVER BC 255-B3
QUEENSBOROUGH BRDG Rt#-91A
CITY OF RICHMOND BC 156-D6
NEW WESTMINSTER BC 156-D6
QUEENS BRANCH RD
JACKSON CO OR 229-D4
QUEENSBURY AV
CITY OF NORTH VANCOUVER BC 255-C7
QUEENSGATE DR
BENTON CO WA 341-D5
RICHLAND WA 341-D5
QUEETS RIVER RD
JEFFERSON CO WA 172-D2
QUESNEL DR
VANCOUVER BC 254-B14
QUICK RD
COWLITZ CO WA 187-C7
QUILCEDA RD
SNOHOMISH CO WA 168-C7
E QUILCENE RD
JEFFERSON CO WA 109-C1
QUILLAYUTE RD
CLALLAM CO WA 169-B2
QUINABY RD NE
MARION CO OR 204-D4
MARION CO OR 205-A4
W QUINAULT AV
KENNEWICK WA 342-C9
QUINCE AV
DESCHUTES CO OR 212-C5
QUINCE ST Rt#-47
FOREST GROVE OR 198-C1
WASHINGTON CO OR 198-C1
N QUINCY AV
DOUGLAS CO WA 239-A4
QUINCY ST
PORT TOWNSEND WA 263-H4
QUINCY-MAYGER RD
COLUMBIA CO OR 117-B3
COLUMBIA CO OR 189-A2
QUINES CREEK RD
DOUGLAS CO OR 225-C6
QUINN RD
GILLIAM CO OR 128-A3
QUIRK RD E
LINCOLN CO WA 113-B2

R

R AV
ANACORTES WA 259-H2
R RD NE Rt#-17
DOUGLAS CO WA 112-C1
R RD SW
DOUGLAS CO WA 239-B3
S R ST
COTTAGE GROVE OR 215-B7
R ST SE
AUBURN WA 182-C2
NW RABAUL DR
KITSAP CO WA 170-B7
RABBIT CAMP RD
LINN CO OR 134-B2
RABY LN
PAYETTE CO ID 139-A3
RACCOON DR
DOUGLAS CO OR 219-A5
RACE RD
EPHRATA WA 112-C3
GRANT CO WA 112-C3
ISLAND CO WA 167-C5
RACE ST
PORT ANGELES WA 261-G5
RADAR RD
HARNEY CO OR 145-A1
RADAR HILL RD
ADAMS CO WA 121-A1
FRANKLIN CO WA 121-A1
RADER RD
KITTITAS CO WA 241-C4
RAFT AV
OLYMPIA WA 296-G2
RAGER RD
CROOK CO OR 136-B2
RAGLAND RD
COWLITZ CO WA 189-B1
RAIL HOLLOW RD
HOOD RIVER CO OR 202-D4
WASCO CO OR 127-B2
WASCO CO OR 202-D4
RAILROAD AV
DEL NORTE CO CA 148-B3
JOSEPHINE CO OR 225-B7
JOSEPHINE CO OR 229-B1
KITTITAS WA 241-C6
LEWISTON ID 250-C4
MOUNT ANGEL OR 205-C3
POWERS OR 140-B3
RAILROAD AV Rt#-200
KOOTENAI ID 244-A1
E RAILROAD AV
Otis Orchards WA 352-D9
N RAILROAD AV
COOS CO OR 140-B3
KOOTENAI CO ID 353-C7
POST FALLS ID 353-C7
POWERS OR 140-B3
SAINT HELENS OR 192-B2
NE RAILROAD AV
CLARK CO WA 193-B2
W RAILROAD AV
MASON CO WA 180-A3
SHELTON WA 180-A3
RAILROAD AV SE Rt#-202
KING CO WA 176-C4
SNOQUALMIE WA 176-C4
RAILROAD BLVD
EUGENE OR 329-H4
RAILROAD ST Rt#-27
ROCKFORD WA 114-C2
SPOKANE CO WA 114-C2
RAILROAD ST U.S.-95
MIDVALE ID 139-B1
SW RAILROAD ST
SHERIDAN OR 125-B3
SHERWOOD OR 199-A4
RAILWAY AV
CITY OF RICHMOND BC 156-B7
RAINBOW DR
JEFFERSON CO OR 212-C2
NW RAINBOW DR
DESCHUTES CO OR 212-C3
RAINBOW RD
WHATCOM CO WA 158-B5
RAINBOW ROCK RD
CURRY CO OR 232-C5
RAINEY RD
DOUGLAS CO WA 239-A2
RAINIER AV N
KING CO WA 175-C5
RENTON WA 175-C5
RAINIER AV S
KING CO WA 175-C4
KING CO WA 287-F4
RENTON WA 175-C4
SEATTLE WA 278-C7
SEATTLE WA 282-D2
SEATTLE WA 283-E6
SEATTLE WA 287-F1
RAINIER AV S Rt#-167
RENTON WA 175-C5
RAINIER DR
PIERCE CO WA 181-C5
RAINIER RD
LACEY WA 297-G13
THURSTON CO WA 297-G13
RAINIER RD SE
RAINIER WA 118-A1
THURSTON CO WA 118-A1
THURSTON CO WA 184-D1
THURSTON CO WA 297-G14
RAINIER ST
STEILACOOM WA 181-C4
RAINIER DIKE RD
RAINIER OR 302-G14
W RAINIER DIKE RD
COLUMBIA CO OR 302-C12
RAINIER OR 302-C12
RAINIER-YELM HWY Rt#-507
THURSTON CO WA 118-A1
YELM WA 118-A1
RAISOR RD
LANE CO OR 219-D3
RALSTON-BENGE RD
ADAMS CO WA 121-C1
ADAMS CO WA 122-A1
RAMBLER DR NE
MARION CO OR 205-B4
N RAMBO RD
SPOKANE CO WA 114-B2
RAMMS RD
JEFFERSON CO OR 213-A1
S RAMSBY RD
CLACKAMAS CO OR 126-A3
RAMSEY LN
KLICKITAT CO WA 195-D5
RAMSEY RD
COEUR D'ALENE ID 355-C3
HAYDEN ID 245-A5
HAYDEN ID 355-C3
JACKSON CO OR 230-B4
KOOTENAI CO ID 245-A5
KOOTENAI CO ID 355-C3
N RAMSEY RD
COEUR D'ALENE ID 355-C6
KOOTENAI CO ID 245-A2
RAMSEY RD E
LINCOLN CO WA 113-B1
S RAMSEY ST Rt#-27
TEKOA WA 114-C3
RAMSEY-CANYON RD
JACKSON CO OR 230-B3
RANCH RD
DESCHUTES CO OR 144-B1
DOUGLAS CO OR 218-C1
KOOTENAI CO ID 245-A2
RANCHERIA CIRCLE RD
SISKIYOU CO CA 150-A3
RANCHERO RD
DOUGLAS CO OR 225-C6
RAND RD
HOOD RIVER OR 195-C5
RANDAL RD
COOS CO OR 220-B6
RANDALL RD SW
THURSTON CO WA 180-B6
RANDOLPH RD
GRANT CO WA 242-C2
RANEY LN
ADAMS CO ID 251-B4
W RANGE DR
LINCOLN CO OR 328-D6
WALDPORT OR 328-D6
RANGER RD
CLALLAM CO WA 165-A5
RANKIN RD
JEFFERSON CO OR 211-C1
RANKIN HILL RD
Vineland WA 250-B5
RAT CREEK RD
LANE CO OR 215-D7
RATHERT RD
KLICKITAT CO WA 196-C1
RATTLESNAKE RD
HARNEY CO OR 145-B1
KLICKITAT CO WA 195-D3
KLICKITAT CO WA 196-A2
RATTLESNAKE CREEK RD
MALHEUR CO OR 154-B1
RAUBUCK RD
LEWIS CO WA 187-B2
RAVENA DR N
MARION CO OR 204-D3
RAVENNA AV NE
SEATTLE WA 274-D1
NE RAVENNA BLVD
SEATTLE WA 274-B3
RAWLINS RD
SKAGIT CO WA 168-A1
RAWLISON CRES
TOWNSHIP OF LANGLEY BC 157-D7
RAWLISON CRES Rt#-10
TOWNSHIP OF LANGLEY BC 157-C7
NE RAWSON RD
CLARK CO WA 193-B4
RAY RD
LEWIS CO WA 187-D4
S RAY ST
SPOKANE WA 349-F12
RAY BELL RD
MARION CO OR 198-D6
RAYE ST
SEATTLE WA 277-H1
RAYMOND CREEK RD
COLUMBIA CO OR 192-A4
RAY NASH DR NW
PIERCE CO WA 181-B1
RAZOR CLAM DR
OCEAN SHORES WA 298-C3
R DRUFFEL RD
WHITMAN CO WA 249-B7
REASON CT
DESCHUTES CO OR 212-C5
REATA RD
BENTON CO WA 341-D12
REAVIS LN
WALLOWA CO OR 130-C2
SE REBMAN RD
CLACKAMAS CO OR 200-B4
RECORD ST
BAKER CO OR 131-A3
HALFWAY OR 131-A3
RECREATIONAL CORR
GRANT CO WA 121-A1
RED APPLE RD
WENATCHEE WA 238-D4
REDBERG RD
TILLAMOOK CO OR 203-B1
RED BLANKET RD
JACKSON CO OR 226-C7
S RED BLANKET RD
JACKSON CO OR 226-D7
RED BLANKET MOUNTAIN RD
JACKSON CO OR 226-D6
JACKSON CO OR 227-A6
RED BRIDGE RD
LINN CO OR 207-D6
RED CLOUD LN
CROOK CO OR 213-B6
RED CLOUD RD
CROOK CO OR 213-B6
REDDING RD
MORROW CO OR 128-B2
REDFIELD RD
DOUGLAS CO WA 239-B1
RED FIR RD
BONNER CO ID 244-D3
KLAMATH CO OR 151-B1
RED HILL RD
DOUGLAS CO OR 219-B5
HOOD RIVER CO OR 202-B2
WALLOWA CO OR 131-A1
RED HILLS RD
YAMHILL CO OR 198-C6
RED HOUSE RD
LAKE CO OR 152-A1
S REDLAND RD
CLACKAMAS CO OR 199-D4
CLACKAMAS CO OR 200-A5
OREGON CITY OR 199-D4
RED MARBLE RD
STEVENS CO WA 106-A3
NE REDMOND WY Rt#-202
REDMOND WA 175-D1
NE REDMOND WY Rt#-908
REDMOND WA 175-C1
REDMOND-BEND HWY
DESCHUTES CO OR 212-C7
DESCHUTES CO OR 217-C1
REDMOND FALL CITY RD Rt#-202
KING CO WA 175-D1
KING CO WA 176-A1
REDMOND WA 175-D1
SAMMAMISH WA 175-D1
SE REDMND FALL CITY RD Rt#-203
KING CO WA 176-B3
REDMND FALL CITY RD NE Rt#-203
KING CO WA 176-A2
REDMND FALL CITY RD SE Rt#-203
KING CO WA 176-A2
REDMOND GRADE RD
WALLOWA CO OR 122-C3
SW REDMOND HILL RD
MCMINNVILLE OR 198-A7
YAMHILL CO OR 198-A7
REDMOND-POWELL BUTTE RD
DESCHUTES CO OR 212-D5
REDONDO WY S
DES MOINES WA 175-B7
FEDERAL WAY WA 175-B7
RED RIDGE RD
ADAMS CO ID 251-C5
VALLEY CO ID 251-C7
N RED RIVER RD
WHATCOM CO WA 158-C6
RED ROCK RD
SISKIYOU CO CA 150-B3
REDWOOD AV
GRANTS PASS OR 335-A11
JOSEPHINE CO OR 229-B6
JOSEPHINE CO OR 335-A11
REDWOOD HWY
GRANTS PASS OR 335-F9
REDWOOD HWY Rt#-99
GRANTS PASS OR 335-F6
REDWOOD HWY U.S.-101
CRESCENT CITY CA 148-B3
DEL NORTE CO CA 148-B3
DEL NORTE CO CA 232-D7
REDWOOD HWY U.S.-199
CAVE JUNCTION OR 233-B3
DEL NORTE CO CA 148-C3
DEL NORTE CO CA 233-A6
GRANTS PASS OR 335-F9
JOSEPHINE CO OR 149-A1
JOSEPHINE CO OR 229-A7
JOSEPHINE CO OR 233-B3
JOSEPHINE CO OR 335-A12
NE REDWOOD HWY Rt#-99
GRANTS PASS OR 335-F7
REECER CREEK RD
KITTITAS CO WA 241-B2
REED RD
BEND OR 332-E10
HOOD RIVER CO OR 195-C6
LEWIS CO WA 187-C4
N REED RD
HAYDEN ID 245-A5
HAYDEN ID 355-D1
REED RD SE
SALEM OR 325-A6
REEDER RD
COLUMBIA CO OR 192-B3
KLAMATH CO OR 235-D5
MULTNOMAH CO OR 192-B5
REEDER RD SW
THURSTON CO WA 184-C2
SE REED MARKET RD
BEND OR 217-C3
BEND OR 332-G10
REESE RD
LAKE OSWEGO OR 320-A7
REESE CREEK RD
JACKSON CO OR 230-D5
REESE HILL RD Rt#-547
WHATCOM CO WA 102-B1
REEVES RD KPS
PIERCE CO WA 181-A3
REEVES CREEK RD
JOSEPHINE CO OR 233-B3
S REGAL RD
SPOKANE CO WA 246-C5
S REGAL ST
SPOKANE WA 349-E14
REGATTA DR
OAK HARBOR WA 167-C3
REGENTS BLVD
FIRCREST WA 181-C2
FIRCREST WA 292-A7
FIRCREST WA 294-A1
E REGINA AV
Fairwood WA 346-J8
Fairwood WA 347-A8
W REGINA AV
Fairwood WA 346-J9
SE REGNER RD
GRESHAM OR 200-B2
MULTNOMAH CO OR 200-B2
REHKLAU RD SE
THURSTON CO WA 181-A7
REHN RD
ADAMS CO WA 113-C3
REICHENBACK RD
PITT MEADOWS BC 157-B5
REID DR NW
GIG HARBOR WA 181-C1
PIERCE CO WA 181-C1
REID RD
CLARK CO WA 193-A1
WHITMAN CO WA 249-A4
REIF RD
CROOK CO OR 213-B5
REIMANN ST NE
Hayesville OR 323-E6
SE REINIG RD
KING CO WA 176-C4
REITER RD
SNOHOMISH CO WA 111-A1
REITH RD
KENT WA 175-B7
REKDAL RD
ISLAND CO WA 168-A4
W REMINGTON RD
KOOTENAI CO ID 245-A2
REMY LN
LEWIS CO WA 187-D1
RENANN ST
ROSEBURG OR 334-D3
RENFREW ST
VANCOUVER BC 255-D12
RENFRO CREEK RD
BENEWAH CO ID 115-B3
RENNE RD
YAMHILL CO OR 198-D6
RENTON AV S
KING CO WA 287-G5
KING CO WA 289-J1
SEATTLE WA 287-F2
SE RENTON ISSAQUAH RD Rt#-900
KING CO WA 175-D4
RENTON WA 175-D4
RENTON ISSAQUAH RD SE
ISSAQUAH WA 175-D4
RENTON ISSAQUAH RD SE Rt#-900
ISSAQUAH WA 175-D4
KING CO WA 175-D4
RENTON MAPLE VALLEY RD Rt#-169
KING CO WA 175-D5
KING CO WA 176-A6
MAPLE VALLEY WA 175-D5
RESEARCH WY
CORVALLIS OR 327-C11
RESERVATION RD
ANACORTES WA 160-D7
ISLAND CO WA 167-C2
OAK HARBOR WA 167-C2
SKAGIT CO WA 160-D7
WASCO CO OR 127-A3
RESERVATION RD Rt#-241
YAKIMA CO WA 120-B3
W RESERVATION RD Rt#-241
YAKIMA CO WA 120-B3
RESERVATION RD SE
THURSTON CO WA 181-A6
RESERVATION LINE RD
IDAHO CO ID 123-C3
NEZ PERCE CO ID 250-D4
E RESERVE ST
BOISE ID 253-D3
RESERVOIR RD
BENTON CO OR 327-A10
CORVALLIS OR 327-A10
CROOK CO OR 135-B3
MALHEUR CO OR 138-C3
MALHEUR CO OR 146-A1
RESERVOIR LOOP RD
YAKIMA CO WA 243-B5
RESOR RD
WALLA WALLA CO WA 345-H11
Walla Walla East WA 345-C11
RESORT DR
TILLAMOOK CO OR 197-A7
RESTHAVEN DR
TOWN OF SIDNEY BC 159-C2
RESTON RD
DOUGLAS CO OR 141-A2
RETREAT KANASKAT RD
KING CO WA 110-C3
RETSIL RD SE
PORT ORCHARD WA 271-A14
REUBEN RD
DOUGLAS CO OR 225-A7
N REUBEN RD
DOUGLAS CO OR 225-A6
REUBENS RD
LEWIS CO ID 123-B2
REUBENS GRADE
NEZ PERCE CO ID 123-B2
SE REVENUE RD
CLACKAMAS CO OR 200-C3
NE REVERE AV
BEND OR 332-F6
NE REVERE AV U.S.-20
BEND OR 332-F6
NW REVERE AV
BEND OR 332-E6
REVETMENT DR
WESTPORT WA 298-G10
REX RD
DOUGLAS CO WA 237-B1
REYNOLD RD
CLALLAM CO WA 164-B5
W REYNOLDS AV
CENTRALIA WA 299-C1
LEWIS CO WA 299-E1
REYNOLDS RD
FRANKLIN CO WA 121-B2
REYNOLDS CREEK RD
DOUGLAS CO OR 222-B1
REYNOLDS CREEK STAGE RD
OWYHEE CO ID 147-B2
REYNOLDS RIDGE RD
DOUGLAS CO OR 222-B3
RHEA RD
GILLIAM CO OR 128-A1
RHEA CREEK RD
MORROW CO OR 128-B2
RHINEHART RD
UNION CO OR 130-A2
RHODES RD
LEWIS CO WA 187-C3
RHODESIA BEACH RD
PACIFIC CO WA 183-C7
RHODESIDE RD
DESCHUTES CO OR 213-A4
RHODES LAKE RD E
PIERCE CO WA 182-C4
RHODODENDRON DR
FLORENCE OR 214-A2
LANE CO OR 214-A2
RHODODENDRON LN NW
KITSAP CO WA 170-B6
RHODODENDRON RD
DOUGLAS CO OR 222-C5
RHODY DR Rt#-19
Hadlock-Irondale WA 170-A1
Irondale WA 263-E14
JEFFERSON CO WA 170-A1
JEFFERSON CO WA 263-E14
RIBBON RIDGE RD
YAMHILL CO OR 198-C4
SE RICE AV
ROSEBURG OR 334-F9
RICE RD
BAKER CO OR 138-A1
RICE ST
MYRTLE CREEK OR 225-C1
RICE CREEK RD
DOUGLAS CO OR 221-B7
DOUGLAS CO OR 225-A1
RICE KANDLE
PIERCE CO WA 181-D7
RICE-ORIN RD
STEVENS CO WA 105-C2
STEVENS CO WA 106-A2
RICE VALLEY RD
DOUGLAS CO OR 219-A5
RICH RD SE
THURSTON CO WA 184-D1
THURSTON CO WA 297-C12
RICHARDS RD
BELLEVUE WA 175-C2
KITTITAS CO WA 241-A6
RICHARDSON RD
DOUGLAS CO OR 221-C7
LINCOLN CO WA 113-C2
PITT MEADOWS BC 157-C4
SISKIYOU CO CA 150-B3
RICHARDSON RD NE
MARION CO OR 205-D5
RICHARDSONS GAP RD
LINN CO OR 133-C1
RICHES RD SE
MARION CO OR 205-C6
RICHMOND AV
CITY OF VICTORIA BC 257-B8
DISTRICT OF SAANICH BC 257-B8
N RICHMOND AV U.S.-30
PORTLAND OR 192-B7
RICHMOND FRWY Rt#-91
CITY OF RICHMOND BC 156-C6
RICHMOND RD
DISTRICT OF SAANICH BC 257-B4
GILLIAM CO OR 128-A2
N RICHMOND BEACH RD
SHORELINE WA 171-A6
NW RICHMOND BEACH RD
SHORELINE WA 171-A6
RICHMOND SIXSHOOTER RD
WHEELER CO OR 136-B1
RICKARD RD
BENTON CO OR 210-A4
DESCHUTES CO OR 217-C3
RICKEY ST SE
SALEM OR 325-E2
RICKREALL RD
POLK CO OR 204-B6
RIDDELL RD
POLK CO OR 204-B7
NE RIDDELL RD
BREMERTON WA 270-G5
KITSAP CO WA 270-G5
KITSAP CO WA 271-A5
Tracyton WA 270-G5
NW RIDDELL RD
KITSAP CO WA 270-G5
RIDDLE BYPS
DOUGLAS CO OR 225-B2
RIDDLE OR 225-B2
Tri-City OR 225-B2
RIDGE DR
ASTORIA OR 300-C6
HOOD RIVER CO OR 195-C6
LINN CO OR 207-C7
OROVILLE WA 104-C1
RIDGE DR NE
KEIZER OR 323-C4
RIDGE RD
ADAMS CO ID 252-A6
CLACKAMAS CO OR 200-B5
COOS CO OR 218-B6
GILLIAM CO OR 128-B2
HARNEY CO OR 137-B3

INDEX

STREET City State	Page-Grid
RIDGE RD	
MORROW CO OR	128-B2
WARRENTON OR	188-B2
YAMHILL CO OR	198-B4
RIDGE TR	
SKAMANIA CO WA	194-B1
SE RIDGECREST RD	
CLACKAMAS CO OR	200-A3
HAPPY VALLEY OR	200-A3
RIDGELINE TR	
EUGENE OR	329-J14
EUGENE OR	330-B14
LANE CO OR	215-B3
LANE CO OR	329-J14
RIDGETOP BLVD	
Silverdale WA	174-B1
RIDGEVIEW DR NE	
KITSAP CO WA	271-C7
RIDGEWAY DR	
REEDSPORT OR	218-C1
RIDGEWAY DR SE	
MARION CO OR	207-D1
SW RIEDWEG RD	
WASHINGTON CO OR	198-C2
RIETH RD	
UMATILLA CO OR	129-A1
RIFE RD	
CLALLAM CO WA	165-A6
RIFLE RANGE RD	
BENTON CO OR	207-A3
NE RIFLE RANGE RD	
ROSEBURG OR	334-J7
RIGDON RD	
LANE CO OR	142-A1
SW RIGERT RD	
WASHINGTON CO OR	199-A2
RIGGS RD	
CROOK CO OR	213-B6
WALLA WALLA CO WA	121-B3
RIGHT FORK RD	
DOUGLAS CO OR	221-D6
RIGHT FORK FOOTS CREEK RD	
JACKSON CO OR	229-D7
RIGHT FORK SARDINE CREEK RD	
JACKSON CO OR	230-B4
RIM DR	
KLAMATH CO OR	227-C2
RIM RD	
CANYON CO ID	147-B1
JEFFERSON CO OR	212-C2
MODOC CO CA	151-A3
RIMROCK RD	
COLTON WA	250-A1
WHITMAN CO WA	250-A1
N RIMROCK RD	
KOOTENAI CO ID	245-A4
NW RIMROCK RD	
JEFFERSON CO OR	208-B3
RIMROCK RD E	
LINCOLN CO WA	113-B2
RIMROCK ACRES RD	
CROOK CO OR	213-C4
RIM VIEW RD	
KLICKITAT CO WA	196-A5
RINEHART RD	
MALHEUR CO OR	146-C2
RINEHART RANCH RD	
MALHEUR CO OR	146-B2
RINGO RD	
CLACKAMAS CO OR	199-D7
WHITMAN CO WA	249-C2
RINGOLD RD	
FRANKLIN CO WA	121-A2
RINK CREEK RD	
COOS CO OR	220-D5
RIO NES LN	
DOUGLAS CO OR	221-C3
RIORDAN HILL DR	
HOOD RIVER CO OR	195-B6
RIO VISTA AV	
BURLINGTON WA	260-D5
SKAGIT CO WA	260-D5
RIO VISTA AV Rt#-20	
BURLINGTON WA	260-C5
RIO VISTA BLVD	
VALLEY CO ID	251-C5
RIPON AV	
LEWISTON ID	250-C5
RIPPEE LN	
YAKIMA CO WA	243-A6
RIPPINGTON RD	
PITT MEADOWS BC	157-B5
RISLEY CREEK RD	
LINCOLN CO OR	209-C1
NE RISTO RD	
CLARK CO WA	193-A3
RITCHEY RD	
WASHINGTON CO OR	198-B1
RITTER RD	
WHATCOM CO WA	158-D5
RITTER SPRINGS RD	
GRANT CO OR	129-A3
S RIVARD RD	
YAKIMA CO WA	243-D7
RIVER AV	
EUGENE OR	215-B1
TILLAMOOK CO OR	197-A7
RIVER DR	
LANE CO OR	215-C5
RIVER DR Rt#-155	
COULEE DAM WA	237-C2
OKANOGAN CO WA	237-C2
N RIVER DR	
LINN CO OR	133-C2
RIVER RD	
CITY OF RICHMOND BC	156-B6
CITY OF SURREY BC	156-D6
CLALLAM CO WA	262-B12
DISTRICT OF DELTA BC	156-C7
EUGENE OR	215-A1
EUGENE OR	329-G1
JACKSON CO OR	150-A1
JACKSON CO OR	226-C6
JUNCTION CITY OR	210-A6
KOOTENAI CO ID	151-C1
LAKE CO OR	151-C1
LANE CO OR	210-A6
LANE CO OR	215-A1
LANE CO OR	329-G1
LINN CO OR	134-B2
MARION CO OR	198-D7
MARION CO OR	205-A1
Santa Clara OR	210-A7
Santa Clara OR	215-A1
SEQUIM WA	262-B12
SKAGIT CO WA	161-C6
TOWNSHIP OF LANGLEY BC	157-D6
RIVER RD	
UMATILLA OR	129-A1
UMATILLA OR	129-A1
WASCO CO OR	196-C6
WHITMAN CO WA	249-A4
YAKIMA WA	243-B6
RIVER RD Rt#-155	
ELMER CITY WA	237-C1
OKANOGAN CO WA	237-C1
RIVER RD Rt#-167	
PIERCE CO WA	182-A3
PUYALLUP WA	182-A3
TACOMA WA	182-A3
E RIVER RD	
PUYALLUP WA	182-B3
N RIVER RD	
JACKSON CO OR	229-D6
JACKSON CO OR	230-A6
LATAH CO ID	249-C1
ROGUE RIVER OR	229-D6
WHITMAN CO WA	249-C1
S RIVER RD	
COTTAGE GROVE OR	215-B7
WHITMAN CO WA	249-C1
SE RIVER RD	
CLACKAMAS CO OR	199-C4
CLACKAMAS CO OR	321-J4
GLADSTONE OR	199-D4
HILLSBORO OR	198-D2
MILWAUKIE OR	321-J4
WASHINGTON CO OR	198-D2
SW RIVER RD	
HILLSBORO OR	198-D2
WASHINGTON CO OR	198-D2
RIVER RD N	
KEIZER OR	322-J7
KEIZER OR	323-A4
SALEM OR	322-J7
RIVER RD NE	
KEIZER OR	323-A2
MARION CO OR	204-D1
MARION CO OR	205-A1
MARION CO OR	323-A2
RIVER RD S	
MARION CO OR	204-B7
MARION CO OR	324-D3
SALEM OR	322-G14
SALEM OR	324-D3
S RIVER RD S	
INDEPENDENCE OR	204-B7
RIVER RD W	
DISTRICT OF DELTA BC	101-C1
RIVER ST	
CAVE JUNCTION OR	233-B4
JOSEPHINE CO OR	233-B4
LEBANON OR	133-C1
N RIVER ST Rt#-82	
ENTERPRISE OR	130-C2
N RIVER ST Rt#-99W	
NEWBERG OR	198-D5
S RIVER ST Rt#-82	
ENTERPRISE OR	130-C2
W RIVER ST	
CAVE JUNCTION OR	233-A4
RIVERBANKS RD	
JOSEPHINE CO OR	149-A1
JOSEPHINE CO OR	229-A5
RIVER BEND RD	
SALEM OR	322-F9
RIVERBEND RD	
MOUNT VERNON WA	260-A9
SKAGIT CO WA	161-A7
SKAGIT CO WA	260-A9
SW RIVER BEND RD	
YAMHILL CO OR	204-B1
RIVER BOTTOM RD	
KITTITAS CO WA	241-B6
RIVERCREST DR N	
KEIZER OR	322-J6
NW RIVERFRONT BLVD	
BEND OR	332-D7
RIVERFRONT RD	
COLUMBIA CO OR	117-B3
RIVERHAVEN ST	
PASCO WA	343-A7
RIVERIA RD	
COLUMBIA CO OR	122-A2
RIVERSHORE RD	
SNOHOMISH CO WA	269-H2
RIVERSIDE AV Rt#-7	
OROFINO ID	123-C2
RIVERSIDE AV Rt#-20	
OKANOGAN CO WA	104-A2
WINTHROP WA	104-A2
RIVERSIDE AV U.S.-101	
HOQUIAM WA	178-A7
N RIVERSIDE AV Rt#-99	
MEDFORD OR	336-C10
S RIVERSIDE AV Rt#-99	
MEDFORD OR	336-D13
W RIVERSIDE AV	
SPOKANE WA	348-H9
NW RIVERSIDE BLVD	
BEND OR	332-D7
RIVERSIDE DR	
BANDON OR	220-B5
BURLINGTON WA	260-C9
COOS CO OR	220-B5
DIST OF NORTH VANCOUVER BC	255-J3
DOUGLAS CO OR	225-C1
DOUGLAS CO OR	239-B5
LINN CO OR	207-C5
LINN CO OR	326-A10
LINN CO OR	207-C5
MARION CO OR	198-D6
MOUNT VERNON WA	260-C10
MYRTLE CREEK OR	225-C1
PIERCE CO WA	182-C3
RIVERSIDE DR Rt#-20	
OKANOGAN CO WA	104-C2
OMAK WA	104-C2
RIVERSIDE DR Rt#-129	
ASOTIN CO WA	250-B5
Vineland WA	250-B5
RIVERSIDE DR U.S.-101	
NEHALEM OR	191-B4
NE RIVERSIDE DR	
MCMINNVILLE OR	198-B7
SE RIVERSIDE DR	
VANCOUVER WA	306-C7
SW RIVERSIDE DR Rt#-43	
CLACKAMAS CO OR	321-G5
LAKE OSWEGO OR	321-G5
MULTNOMAH CO OR	321-G5
RIVERSIDE DR NE	
BANDON OR	220-B6
S RIVERSIDE RD	
YAKIMA WA	243-C7
RIVERSIDE RD S	
MARION CO OR	207-C1
RIVERSIDE RD S	
MARION CO OR	324-A14
RIVERSIDE ST	
BONNERS FERRY ID	107-B2
BOUNDARY CO ID	107-B2
RIVERSIDE CUTOFF RD	
OKANOGAN CO WA	104-C2
RIVERSIDE WA	104-C2
RIVERSIDE PARK DR	
SPOKANE CO WA	348-A1
RIVERVIEW BLVD	
CLARKSTON WA	250-B4
RIVERVIEW DR	
DESCHUTES CO OR	143-A1
LANE CO OR	210-A7
ROSEBURG OR	334-C5
W RIVERVIEW DR	
KOOTENAI CO ID	353-E9
RIVERVIEW RD	
JEFFERSON CO OR	208-A6
SNOHOMISH CO WA	171-D3
SNOHOMISH CO WA	171-D3
SNOHOMISH CO WA	269-H4
SE RIVERWOOD RD	
YAMHILL CO OR	198-C7
RIXIE DR SE	
THURSTON CO WA	184-D1
RIXON RD	
PACIFIC CO WA	183-D7
ROAD 1-NE	
GRANT CO WA	242-D3
ROAD 1-NW	
GRANT CO WA	112-B3
ROAD 1-SW	
GRANT CO WA	112-B3
GRANT CO WA	242-A4
ROAD 2-NE	
GRANT CO WA	242-A3
ROAD 2-NW	
GRANT CO WA	112-B3
GRANT CO WA	242-A3
ROAD 3-NE	
GRANT CO WA	113-A2
GRANT CO WA	242-A3
ROAD 3-NW	
GRANT CO WA	112-B3
GRANT CO WA	242-A3
MOSES LAKE WA	242-D3
ROAD 3-SE	
GRANT CO WA	113-A2
GRANT CO WA	242-D4
ROAD 3-SW	
GRANT CO WA	112-B3
ROAD 4-NE	
GRANT CO WA	242-B2
ROAD 4-NW	
GRANT CO WA	112-C3
GRANT CO WA	242-A2
ROAD 4-SE	
GRANT CO WA	242-D5
ROAD 4-SW	
GRANT CO WA	112-C3
ROAD 5-NE	
GRANT CO WA	242-A2
ROAD 5-NW	
GRANT CO WA	112-C3
ROAD 5-SE	
GRANT CO WA	242-C5
ROAD 5-SW	
GRANT CO WA	112-B3
ROAD 6-NE	
GRANT CO WA	242-D2
ROAD 6-NW	
GRANT CO WA	112-B3
ROAD 6-SE	
GRANT CO WA	242-D5
ROAD 6-SW	
GRANT CO WA	112-B3
ROAD 7-NE	
GRANT CO WA	113-A3
GRANT CO WA	242-D2
ROAD 7-NW	
GRANT CO WA	112-C3
GRANT CO WA	242-A2
ROAD 7-SW	
GRANT CO WA	120-B1
ROAD 8-NE	
GRANT CO WA	242-D1
ROAD 8-NW	
GRANT CO WA	242-A1
ROAD 8-SE Rt#-170	
WARDEN WA	121-A1
ROAD 9-NE	
GRANT CO WA	113-A3
GRANT CO WA	242-D1
ROAD 9-NW	
GRANT CO WA	112-C3
GRANT CO WA	242-A1
ROAD 10-NE	
GRANT CO WA	242-C1
ROAD 10-NW Rt#-28	
GRANT CO WA	112-B3
ROAD 10-NW Rt#-281	
GRANT CO WA	112-B3
ROAD 11-NW Rt#-28	
GRANT CO WA	112-C3
ROAD 11-SW	
GRANT CO WA	120-B1
GRANT CO WA	242-A7
ROAD 12 SE	
ADAMS CO WA	121-A2
GRANT CO WA	242-C7
ROAD 12-NE	
GRANT CO WA	113-A3
ROAD 12-NW	
GRANT CO WA	112-C3
ROAD 12-SE	
GRANT CO WA	242-B7
ROAD 13-SE	
GRANT CO WA	242-B7
ROAD 13-SW	
GRANT CO WA	242-A7
ROAD 13-SW Rt#-26	
GRANT CO WA	120-B1
ROAD 15-NE	
GRANT CO WA	113-A3
ROAD 15-1-31	
LANE CO OR	210-D5
LANE CO OR	210-D5
ROAD 15-2-25	
LANE CO OR	210-D5
ROAD 15-2-25-1	
LANE CO OR	210-D6
ROAD 15-2-26-1	
LINN CO OR	210-D5
ROAD 16-NE	
GRANT CO WA	113-A3
ROAD 16-2-10	
LANE CO OR	210-D6
ROAD 16-2-10-2	
LANE CO OR	210-D6
ROAD 16-2-17-1	
LANE CO OR	210-C6
ROAD 16-2-18	
LANE CO OR	210-D7
ROAD 16-2-18-1	
LANE CO OR	210-C6
ROAD 16-2-27	
LANE CO OR	210-C7
ROAD 16-2-28	
LANE CO OR	210-D7
ROAD 16-2-29	
LANE CO OR	210-C7
ROAD 16-2-7-1	
LANE CO OR	210-C6
ROAD 16-3-13-2	
LANE CO OR	210-C7
ROAD 19-NE	
GRANT CO WA	112-C2
ROAD 19-NW	
GRANT CO WA	112-C2
ROAD 20-NE	
GRANT CO WA	112-C2
GRANT CO WA	113-A2
ROAD 20-NW	
GRANT CO WA	112-C2
ROAD 21 1/2-NE	
GRANT CO WA	113-A2
ROAD 22-NE	
GRANT CO WA	113-A2
ROAD 23 SW	
GRANT CO WA	120-B1
ROAD 23-NE	
GRANT CO WA	112-C2
GRANT CO WA	113-A2
ROAD 24-NW	
GRANT CO WA	112-B2
ROAD 24-SW	
GRANT CO WA	120-B1
MATTAWA WA	120-B1
ROAD 25-NE	
GRANT CO WA	112-C2
ROAD 27-SW	
GRANT CO WA	120-B1
ROAD 28	
PASCO WA	343-C5
ROAD 29-NE	
GRANT CO WA	112-C2
ROAD 31-NE	
GRANT CO WA	113-A2
ROAD 36	
FRANKLIN CO WA	343-B6
PASCO WA	343-B6
ROAD 36-NE	
GRANT CO WA	113-A2
ROAD 42-NE	
GRANT CO WA	113-A2
ROAD 43-NE	
GRANT CO WA	237-B7
ROAD 44	
FRANKLIN CO WA	343-A4
PASCO WA	343-A4
ROAD 44-NE	
GRANT CO WA	237-A7
ROAD 45-NE	
GRANT CO WA	237-B7
ROAD 46-NE	
GRANT CO WA	237-B6
ROAD 47-NE	
GRANT CO WA	237-B6
ROAD 48	
FRANKLIN CO WA	343-A5
PASCO WA	343-A5
ROAD 48-NE	
GRANT CO WA	237-B6
ROAD 49-NE	
GRANT CO WA	237-C5
ROAD 50-NE	
GRANT CO WA	237-C5
ROAD 51-NE	
GRANT CO WA	237-C5
ROAD 52-NE	
GRANT CO WA	237-C5
ROAD 60	
FRANKLIN CO WA	342-H5
ROAD 68	
FRANKLIN CO WA	342-G4
PASCO WA	342-G4
ROAD 68 N	
FRANKLIN CO WA	121-A2
PASCO WA	342-G1
ROAD 76	
FRANKLIN CO WA	342-F5
PASCO WA	342-F5
ROAD 84	
FRANKLIN CO WA	342-E4
ROAD 92	
FRANKLIN CO WA	342-D4
ROAD 100	
FRANKLIN CO WA	342-C2
PASCO WA	342-C2
ROAD 170	
WASCO CO OR	127-B3
2900 RD	
MASON CO WA	180-A4
ROAD 4370	
LINCOLN CO WA	113-B1
WILBUR WA	113-B1
ROAD 7009	
GRAYS HARBOR CO WA	177-D1
ROAD 8002	
GRAYS HARBOR CO WA	178-A1
ROAD A-LINE	
GRAYS HARBOR CO WA	117-B1
GRAYS HARBOR CO WA	178-D4
GRAYS HARBOR CO WA	179-A4
ROAD A-NE	
GRANT CO WA	112-C2
GRANT CO WA	242-A2
ROAD A-NW	
GRANT CO WA	242-A1
ROAD A-SE	
GRANT CO WA	113-A2
GRANT CO WA	242-A4
ROAD A-SE Rt#-262	
GRANT CO WA	120-C1
GRANT CO WA	242-A7
ROAD B-210	
GRANT CO WA	135-A1
ROAD B-1000	
GRAYS HARBOR CO WA	179-D7
ROAD B-LINE	
GRAYS HARBOR CO WA	179-A4
ROAD B-NE	
GRANT CO WA	112-C2
ROAD B-NW	
GRANT CO WA	112-C2
GRANT CO WA	242-A2
ROAD B-SE	
GRANT CO WA	120-C1
GRANT CO WA	242-B7
ROAD C-LINE RD	
GRAYS HARBOR CO WA	179-D7
ROAD C-NW	
EPHRATA WA	112-C3
GRANT CO WA	112-C3
ROAD CS30	
MASON CO WA	179-B4
ROAD C-SE	
GRANT CO WA	242-B4
ROAD D-LINE	
GRAYS HARBOR CO WA	178-D4
ROAD D-NE	
GRANT CO WA	112-C2
GRANT CO WA	242-B3
ROAD D-SE	
GRANT CO WA	120-C1
ROAD E-NE	
GRANT CO WA	242-B3
ROAD E-NW	
GRANT CO WA	112-C3
ROAD E-SW	
GRANT CO WA	120-C1
ROAD F-NE	
GRANT CO WA	112-C2
GRANT CO WA	242-B2
ROAD H SE	
GRANT CO WA	242-C7
ROAD I-NE	
GRANT CO WA	242-C2
ROAD J-NE	
GRANT CO WA	113-A2
ROAD K-NE	
GRANT CO WA	242-D2
ROAD K-NW	
GRANT CO WA	112-C3
ROAD K-SE	
GRANT CO WA	242-D4
ROAD K-SW	
GRANT CO WA	112-C3
ROAD L-5-SW	
GRANT CO WA	112-B3
GRANT CO WA	120-B1
ROAD L 7-NE	
GRANT CO WA	237-A7
ROAD L-NE	
GRANT CO WA	113-A2
GRANT CO WA	242-D1
ROAD L-SE	
GRANT CO WA	242-D5
ROAD L-SW	
GRANT CO WA	120-B1
ROAD M-110	
JEFFERSON CO OR	208-A6
ROAD M-NW	
GRANT CO WA	112-B3
ROAD M-SE	
GRANT CO WA	242-D5
ROAD M-SW	
GRANT CO WA	112-B3
GRANT CO WA	120-B1
ROAD N-NE	
GRANT CO WA	242-D1
ROAD N-SE	
GRANT CO WA	242-D4
ROAD O-NE	
GRANT CO WA	237-A6
GRANT CO WA	242-D1
ROAD O-SE	
GRANT CO WA	242-D4
ROAD O-SW	
GRANT CO WA	120-B1
ROAD P-110	
JEFFERSON CO OR	208-A4
ROAD P-NE	
GRANT CO WA	113-A2
GRANT CO WA	237-B6
ROAD P-NW	
GRANT CO WA	112-B3
ROAD Q-NE	
GRANT CO WA	113-A3
GRANT CO WA	237-B6
ROAD Q-SE	
GRANT CO WA	113-A3
ROAD Q-SW	
GEORGE WA	112-B3
GRANT CO WA	112-B3
GRANT CO WA	120-B1
ROAD R-NE	
GRANT CO WA	113-A2
GRANT CO WA	237-B6
ROAD R-NW	
GRANT CO WA	112-B3
ROAD R-SW	
GRANT CO WA	112-B3
GRANT CO WA	120-B1
ROAD S-322	
WASCO CO OR	127-B3
ROAD S-NE	
GRANT CO WA	113-A3
GRANT CO WA	237-B6
ROAD S-NW	
GRANT CO WA	112-B3
ROAD T-2 NE	
GRANT CO WA	237-B5
ROAD T-NE	
GRANT CO WA	237-B6
ROAD U-NE	
GRANT CO WA	113-A3
WARDEN WA	121-A1
ROAD U-SE	
GRANT CO WA	113-A3
WARDEN WA	121-A1
ROAD U-SW	
GRANT CO WA	112-B3
GRANT CO WA	120-B1
ROAD V-NE	
GRANT CO WA	237-C5
ROAD WA-NA-PA	
CASCADE LOCKS OR	194-D6
ROAD W-NE	
GRANT CO WA	113-A2
GRANT CO WA	237-C4
LINCOLN CO WA	113-A2
MARLIN WA	113-A2
ROAD W-SE	
GRANT CO WA	121-A1
ROAD X-NE	
GRANT CO WA	237-C5
LINCOLN CO WA	237-C5
ROANOKE DR NE	
MARION CO OR	205-A3
E ROANOKE ST	
SEATTLE WA	278-B1
ROARING CREEK RD	
WASHINGTON CO OR	198-A3
ROBBINS RD	
KITTITAS CO WA	241-B4
ROBERTA AV	
LAKE CO OR	152-A2
ROBERT BUSH DR U.S.-101	
PACIFIC CO WA	183-D6
SOUTH BEND WA	117-A1
SOUTH BEND WA	183-D6
ROBERT CREEK RD	
COOS CO OR	218-D4
ROBERT GRAY DR Rt#-100	
PACIFIC CO WA	186-A6
SE ROBERTS AV	
GRESHAM OR	200-B2
ROBERTS DR	
BLACK DIAMOND WA	110-C3
ROBERTS RD	
CROOK CO OR	135-C2
CROOK CO OR	136-A3
GRAYS HARBOR CO WA	183-B2
LEWIS CO WA	187-D1
LINN CO OR	210-B1
MEDFORD OR	336-E9
YAKIMA CO WA	243-A5
ROBERTS RD KPN	
PIERCE CO WA	181-A1
ROBERTS BANK SUPERPORT CSWY	
DISTRICT OF DELTA BC	101-C1
ROBERTS BUTTE RD	
WALLOWA CO OR	130-C1
ROBERTS CREEK RD	
DOUGLAS CO OR	221-B6
ROBERTS MOUNTAIN RD	
DOUGLAS CO OR	221-B6
ROBERTSON CRES	
TOWNSHIP OF LANGLEY BC	158-D1
ROBERTSON ST	
CITY OF VICTORIA BC	257-A11
ROBERTSON BRIDGE RD	
JOSEPHINE CO OR	229-A4
ROBIN DR	
JEFFERSON CO OR	212-C2
ROBINETTE RD	
COLUMBIA CO OR	192-A1
ROBINSON RD	
JOSEPHINE CO OR	233-C4
SNOHOMISH CO WA	168-C7
ROBINSON ST	
COQUITLAM BC	157-A4
ROBINSON CANYON RD	
KITTITAS CO WA	241-A5
ROBINSON LAKE RD	
LATAH CO ID	249-D4
ROBINSON PARK RD	
LATAH CO ID	249-D4
ROBISON RD	
BENTON CO OR	207-A3
POLK CO OR	207-A3
ROBSON DR	
COQUITLAM BC	157-B4
ROBSON ST	
VANCOUVER BC	254-F9
ROCHAT RD	
KOOTENAI CO ID	115-B2
ROCHAT DIVIDE RD	
BENEWAH CO ID	115-B2
ROCHE HARBOR RD	
FRIDAY HARBOR WA	101-C2
SAN JUAN CO WA	101-C2
ROCK RD Rt#-547	
WHATCOM CO WA	102-B1
ROCK RD NW	
DOUGLAS CO WA	236-C6
ROCKAWAY BEACH RD	
KITSAP CO WA	174-D2
ROCK CANDY MOUNTAIN RD SW	
THURSTON CO WA	180-A7
ROCK CANYON RD	
MALHEUR CO OR	146-C1
ROCK CREEK RD	
COLUMBIA CO OR	125-B1
COOS CO OR	140-C3
DOUGLAS CO OR	141-C2
DOUGLAS CO OR	219-B2
HARNEY CO OR	145-A3
HARNEY CO OR	153-A1
JACKSON CO OR	227-A3
JACKSON CO OR	230-B1
KLICKITAT CO WA	128-A1
LINCOLN CO OR	133-A1
MALHEUR CO OR	146-C3
WASHINGTON CO ID	139-A2
NW ROCK CREEK RD	
MULTNOMAH CO OR	192-A6
S ROCK CREEK RD	
BAKER CO OR	130-A3
ROCK CREEK DAM RD	
WASCO CO OR	127-A3
ROCKCREST ST	
COLUMBIA CO OR	189-B4
RAINIER OR	189-B4
RAINIER OR	302-G14
ROCK CUT RD	
STEVENS CO WA	105-C1
ROCKFORD BAY RD	
KOOTENAI CO ID	247-D6
ROCK HILL DR	
Crowfoot OR	133-C1
LANE CO OR	215-B4
LINN CO OR	133-C1
LINN CO OR	210-C1
ROCK ISLAND AV	
DOUGLAS CO WA	239-B5
ROCK ISLAND WA	239-B5
ROCK ISLAND RD	
DOUGLAS CO WA	239-A5
East Wenatchee Bench WA	239-A5
ROCK ISLAND GRADE SW	
DOUGLAS CO WA	239-C5
S ROCK LAKE RD	
SPOKANE CO WA	114-B3
ROCK LAKE RD	
WHITMAN CO WA	114-B3
ROCKLAND AV	
CITY OF VICTORIA BC	256-J10
CITY OF VICTORIA BC	257-A10
W ROCKLAND RD	
DIST OF NORTH VANCOUVER BC	255-B1

392 ROCKLYN RD
STREET INDEX
E SANTIAM ST

STREET City State Page-Grid

ROCKLYN RD
LINCOLN CO WA 113-C2
ROCKPORT CASCADE RD
SKAGIT CO WA 103-A2
ROCK SPRINGS RD
JEFFERSON CO OR 211-D3
WHITMAN CO WA 122-A1
ROCKWELL DR
CITY OF HARRISON HOT SPRG BC 94-C3
DISTRICT OF KENT BC 94-C3
E ROCKWOOD BLVD
SPOKANE WA 349-A11
S ROCKWOOD BLVD
SPOKANE WA 349-B12
ROCKY RD
DOUGLAS CO WA 236-D4
ROCKY BAY PT Rt#-302
MASON CO WA 173-D7
ROCKY BAY POINT DR Rt#-302
MASON CO WA 174-A7
ROCKY BAY POINT DR KPN Rt#-302
MASON CO WA 174-A7
PIERCE CO WA 174-A7
ROCKY BUTTE RD
WASCO CO OR 202-D7
ROCKY CANYON RD
IDAHO CO ID 123-B3
IDAHO CO ID 131-C1
ROCKY CREEK RD KPN
PIERCE CO WA 174-A6
ROCKYDALE RD
JOSEPHINE CO OR 233-B6
ROCKY FORD RD
LINCOLN CO WA 113-C2
YAKIMA CO WA 120-A2
NW ROCKYFORD RD
YAMHILL CO OR 198-A4
ROCKY POINT RD
BREMERTON WA 270-E8
DISTRICT OF METCHOSIN BC 159-A7
DISTRICT OF METCHOSIN BC 165-A1
KITSAP CO WA 270-E8
MULTNOMAH CO OR 125-C1
MULTNOMAH CO OR 192-A5
ROCKY TOP RD
YAKIMA CO WA 243-A6
RODGERS RD
LANE CO OR 215-C5
RODMAN RD
YAKIMA CO WA 243-B4
ROE RD
LEWIS CO WA 187-B4
ROE RD E
LEWIS CO WA 187-B3
ROE ST
STEILACOOM WA 181-C4
ROGERS LN
VALLEY CO ID 251-D6
ROGERS RD
COWLITZ CO WA 189-D5
DOUGLAS CO OR 221-C2
LEWIS CO WA 187-C5
POLK CO OR 204-B7
ROGERS AND HOBSON RD
CHELAN CO WA 236-D2
ROGERSON RD
LEWIS CO WA 184-D7
SE ROGUE DR
GRANTS PASS OR 335-G11
ROGUE RIVER DR
JACKSON CO OR 230-D4
SHADY COVE OR 230-D4
ROGUE RIVER HWY Rt#-99
GRANTS PASS OR 335-J11
JACKSON CO OR 229-C6
JACKSON CO OR 230-A6
JOSEPHINE CO OR 229-C6
JOSEPHINE CO OR 335-J11
ROGUE RIVER OR 229-C6
ROGUE RIVER LOOP HWY
GRANTS PASS OR 335-A9
JOSEPHINE CO OR 149-A1
JOSEPHINE CO OR 229-A4
JOSEPHINE CO OR 335-A9
ROGUE VALLEY HWY
MEDFORD OR 336-C9
ROGUE VALLEY HWY Rt#-99
ASHLAND OR 337-A4
CENTRAL POINT OR 230-C7
JACKSON CO OR 230-C7
JACKSON CO OR 234-B2
JACKSON CO OR 337-A4
MEDFORD OR 230-C7
MEDFORD OR 234-B2
MEDFORD OR 336-A7
PHOENIX OR 234-B2
TALENT OR 234-B3
ROITZ RD
STEVENS CO WA 106-B3
ROLLING HILLS RD
POLK CO OR 207-B2
ROLOFF RD
ADAMS CO WA 113-C3
ROME RD
MALHEUR CO OR 146-C3
ROMIE HOWARD RD
DOUGLAS CO OR 219-C5
ROMINE CREEK RD
JACKSON CO OR 230-C1
ROMMERMAN RD
LEWIS CO WA 187-C1
RONDO RD
PIERCE CO WA 181-C7
SW ROOD BRIDGE RD
WASHINGTON CO OR 198-D2
ROOSEVELT AV Rt#-410
ENUMCLAW WA 110-C3
W ROOSEVELT AV
CANYON CO ID 147-B1
ROOSEVELT AV E Rt#-410
ENUMCLAW WA 110-C3
KING CO WA 110-C3
ROOSEVELT DR U.S.-101
SEASIDE OR 301-G6
S ROOSEVELT DR U.S.-101
CLATSOP CO OR 301-F10
SEASIDE OR 301-G8
ROOSEVELT ST
ABERDEEN WA 178-B7
N ROOSEVELT ST
WALLA WALLA WA 345-D6
S ROOSEVELT ST
BOISE ID 253-C3
WALLA WALLA WA 345-D8
ROOSEVELT WY
WHATCOM CO WA 101-C1

ROOSEVELT WY NE
SEATTLE WA 171-B7
SEATTLE WA 274-B2
ROOSEVELT GRADE RD
KLICKITAT CO WA 128-A1
ROPPERT RD
LEWIS CO WA 187-C3
ROSA RD
COOS CO OR 220-B7
ROSALYNN SUMNERS BLVD
EDMONDS WA 171-A5
ROSARIO RD
SKAGIT CO WA 160-C7
SKAGIT CO WA 259-D10
ROSARIO BEACH RD
SKAGIT CO WA 259-C14
ROSE AV Rt#-47
COLUMBIA CO OR 125-B1
VERNONIA OR 125-B1
ROSE RD
LANE CO OR 210-D6
SNOHOMISH CO WA 168-C4
ROSE ST
PHOENIX OR 234-B2
N ROSE ST
WALLA WALLA WA 345-B6
W ROSE ST
COLLEGE PLACE WA 344-F9
WALLA WALLA WA 344-H9
ROSEBERG ST SW
THURSTON CO WA 184-A4
E ROSEBERRY RD
DONNELLY ID 252-D1
VALLEY CO ID 252-D1
W ROSEBERRY RD
VALLEY CO ID 252-D1
ROSEBROOK RD
LEWIS CO WA 187-D1
ROSE CREEK RD
MALHEUR CO OR 138-A2
WHITMAN CO WA 249-B3
ROSEDALE RD
CATHLAMET WA 117-B3
WAHKIAKUM CO WA 117-B3
SW ROSEDALE RD
WASHINGTON CO OR 198-D2
WASHINGTON CO OR 199-A2
ROSEDALE ST NW
GIG HARBOR WA 181-B1
PIERCE CO WA 181-B1
ROSEDALE BAY
PIERCE CO WA 181-B1
ROSEDALE PURDY
PIERCE CO WA 174-B7
W ROSE HILL ST
BOISE ID 253-C3
ROSEMONT AV NW
SALEM OR 322-F12
ROSEMONT RD
CLACKAMAS CO OR 199-C4
ROSENAU RD
LATAH CO ID 250-D1
ROSENKRANTZ RD
NEZ PERCE CO ID 250-C5
ROSENOFF RD
ADAMS CO WA 113-B3
RITZVILLE WA 113-B3
ROSENOFF RD Rt#-21
ADAMS CO WA 113-B3
ROSE VALLEY RD
COWLITZ CO WA 118-A3
COWLITZ CO WA 189-C4
ROSS LN
JACKSON CO OR 234-A1
JACKSON CO OR 336-A12
LANE CO OR 215-C7
MEDFORD OR 336-A12
ROSS LN Rt#-238
MEDFORD OR 336-A12
ROSS RD
DISTRICT OF MATSQUI BC 102-B1
DIST OF NORTH VANCOUVER BC 255-F3
ROSSANLEY DR Rt#-238
JACKSON CO OR 234-A1
JACKSON CO OR 336-B10
MEDFORD OR 336-A10
ROSS INLET RD
COOS CO OR 220-D2
S ROSS POINT RD
KOOTENAI CO ID 354-D7
POST FALLS ID 354-D7
ROSS POINT-RATHDRUM HWY Rt#-41
KOOTENAI CO ID 247-D1
KOOTENAI CO ID 354-D2
POST FALLS ID 354-D2
ROSWELL RD
MALHEUR CO OR 147-A1
ROTH RD
LEWIS CO WA 187-C3
ROTHFORK RD
LATAH CO ID 249-C3
ROTHROCK RD
BENTON CO WA 120-C2
NE ROTSCHY RD
CLARK CO WA 193-B1
ROUGH & RUGGED RD
JACKSON CO OR 230-B7
SW ROUND BUTTE DR
JEFFERSON CO OR 208-A6
ROUND BUTTE LOOP RD
KLAMATH CO OR 142-C3
ROUND LAKE RD
JEFFERSON CO OR 211-B1
KLAMATH CO OR 235-A2
ROUNDS AV
JOSEPHINE CO OR 229-A6
ROUND TOP RD
JACKSON CO OR 230-B1
ROUNDTREE RD
LEWIS CO WA 187-A2
ROUND VALLEY RD
ADAMS CO ID 131-C3
ADAMS CO ID 251-A1
ROUPE RD
ASOTIN CO WA 122-C2
ROUSE RD KPS
PIERCE CO WA 181-A3
NE ROVA RD
KITSAP CO WA 170-C6
ROWDY CREEK RD
DEL NORTE CO CA 148-B3
ROWE CREEK RD
WHEELER CO OR 128-A3
WHEELER CO OR 136-A1
ROWLAND RD
LINN CO OR 210-B4
YAMHILL CO OR 198-B5

ROW RIVER RD
COTTAGE GROVE OR 215-C7
LANE CO OR 141-C1
LANE CO OR 215-C7
ROW RIVER CUTOFF RD
COTTAGE GROVE OR 215-B7
SW ROXBURY ST
KING CO WA 285-F4
SEATTLE WA 285-F4
ROXY ANN RD
JACKSON CO OR 234-C1
ROY RD
WHATCOM CO WA 161-A2
NW ROY RD
WASHINGTON CO OR 125-C1
ROY ST
SEATTLE WA 277-H3
E ROY ST
SEATTLE WA 278-B3
ROYAL AV
EUGENE OR 215-A2
EUGENE OR 329-A3
LANE CO OR 215-A2
MEDFORD OR 336-D11
NEW WESTMINSTER BC 156-D5
ROYAL AV N
EAGLE POINT OR 230-D5
JACKSON CO OR 230-D5
ROYAL AV S
EAGLE POINT OR 230-D5
S ROYAL BROUGHAM WY Rt#-519
SEATTLE WA 281-J1
SEATTLE WA 282-A1
ROYAL OAK AV
DISTRICT OF BURNABY BC 156-C5
ROYAL OAK DR
DISTRICT OF SAANICH BC 159-C5
ROY CHRISTIE
PIERCE CO WA 118-B1
SE ROYER RD
CLACKAMAS CO OR 200-B4
ROY PAYNE RD
LANE CO OR 219-D1
ROY PETTIT
PIERCE CO WA 181-D7
SW ROY ROGERS RD
WASHINGTON CO OR 199-A3
ROZA HILL DR
YAKIMA CO WA 243-D6
E ROZA HILL DR
YAKIMA CO WA 243-C6
N RUBY ST U.S.-2
SPOKANE WA 349-A6
RUCKEL RD
UNION CO OR 130-A1
RUCKER AV
EVERETT WA 264-D3
RUCKMAN AV Rt#-82
IMBLER OR 130-A2
RUDDELL RD SE
LACEY WA 297-H11
THURSTON CO WA 297-H11
NW RUDE RD
KITSAP CO WA 170-B6
SE RUDE RD
CLACKAMAS CO OR 200-C5
RUDI RD
DESCHUTES CO OR 212-B7
RUE CREEK RD
PACIFIC CO WA 117-A1
RUEPPELL ST
TILLAMOOK CO OR 197-A7
RUMBLE ST
DISTRICT OF BURNABY BC 156-C5
SE RUPERT DR
CLACKAMAS CO OR 321-J6
RUPERT RD
COLUMBIA CO OR 189-A7
RUPERT ST
VANCOUVER BC 156-C5
VANCOUVER BC 255-E14
RUPP RD
LEWIS CO WA 187-C5
RUPPERT RD
BENTON CO WA 120-C2
RURAL AV
WHATCOM CO WA 158-C7
RURAL AV SE
SALEM OR 324-H1
RURAL RD SW
TUMWATER WA 296-F11
RURAL S ST
HARNEY CO OR 145-B2
RUSH AV
KLAMATH CO OR 151-A3
MALIN OR 151-A3
RUSH RD
LEWIS CO WA 187-C1
W RUSH RD
EAGLE ID 253-A1
RUSH CREEK RD
WASHINGTON CO ID 139-B1
RUSS BAKER WY
CITY OF RICHMOND BC 156-B6
RUSSEL RD
JOSEPHINE CO OR 229-B3
RUSSELL LN
JOSEPH OR 130-C2
WALLOWA CO OR 130-C2
RUSSELL RD
KENT WA 291-F6
LEWIS CO WA 187-B3
MALHEUR CO OR 138-C3
RUSSELL ST
WENATCHEE WA 238-D4
RUSSELL CREEK RD
WALLA WALLA CO WA 345-E9
Walla Walla East WA 345-E9
RUSSELL RIDGE RD
LEWIS CO ID 123-C2
RUSSELL RIDGE RD Rt#-7
CLEARWATER CO ID 123-C2
RUSTEMEYER RD
GRAYS HARBOR CO WA 183-C1
RUSTIC LN
LANE CO OR 214-B1
S RUSTLE ST
SPOKANE WA 348-D12
RUSTON WY
TACOMA WA 181-D1
TACOMA WA 292-D1
TACOMA WA 293-E2
RUTLEDGE LN
SHERMAN CO OR 127-C2
RUTLEDGE RD
SHERMAN CO OR 127-C2
E RUTTER AV
SPOKANE WA 349-J6

E RUTTER AV
SPOKANE WA 350-A5
SPOKANE VALLEY WA 349-J6
SPOKANE VALLEY WA 350-A5
N RUTTER PKWY
SPOKANE CO WA 346-B6
W RUTTER PKWY
Fairwood WA 346-E8
SPOKANE CO WA 246-A1
SPOKANE CO WA 346-B6
RUX RD E
LINCOLN CO WA 113-B1
RYALS AV
BENTON CO OR 207-B4
RYAN RD
DESCHUTES CO OR 213-A4
S RYAN WY
SEATTLE WA 287-F5
TUKWILA WA 287-F5
RYAN-ALLEN RD
SKAMANIA CO WA 194-C5
RYAN-TAVELLI RD
SKAMANIA CO WA 194-A7
RYE GRASS LN
HARNEY CO OR 145-B1
RYEGRASS RD
CROOK CO OR 213-B3
RYE VALLEY-MORMON BASIN RD
BAKER CO OR 138-C2

S

SAANICH RD
DISTRICT OF SAANICH BC 256-G5
SAARI RD
LEWIS CO WA 187-C4
SACHS RD SW
DOUGLAS CO WA 239-C3
SADDLE DR
KOOTENAI CO ID 245-B7
SADDLE BUTTE RD
HARNEY CO OR 145-C2
SADDLE MOUNTAIN RD
CLATSOP CO OR 188-D4
SADDLE RIDGE RD
LATAH CO ID 249-C3
SAGE RD
GRANT CO WA 242-C3
JACKSON CO OR 336-B10
MALHEUR CO OR 139-A3
OWYHEE CO ID 147-A1
SAGEBRUSH FLAT RD
EPHRATA WA 112-C2
GRANT CO WA 112-C2
SAGEHILL RD
FRANKLIN CO WA 121-A1
W SAGEMOOR RD
FRANKLIN CO WA 121-A2
FRANKLIN CO WA 340-J2
SAGINAW EAST RD
LANE CO OR 215-B6
SAGINAW WEST RD
LANE CO OR 215-B6
S SAGLE RD
BONNER CO ID 244-A4
SAHALEE WY NE
KING CO WA 175-D1
SAMMAMISH WA 175-D1
SAMMAMISH WA 176-A2
SAINT ST
RICHLAND WA 340-F11
SAINT ANDREWS AV
CITY OF NORTH VANCOUVER BC 255-C5
SAINT ANDREWS RD E
DOUGLAS CO WA 112-C2
SAINT ANDREWS RD S
DOUGLAS CO WA 112-C2
SAINT ANDREWS RD W
DOUGLAS CO WA 112-C2
SAINT CHARLES ST
CITY OF VICTORIA BC 257-A9
SAINT CLAIR RD
DESCHUTES CO OR 135-B3
DESCHUTES CO OR 217-D3
SAINT GEORGES AV
CITY OF NORTH VANCOUVER BC 255-B5
SAINT HELENS AV
CHEHALIS WA 299-C11
SAINT HELENS AV
CHEHALIS WA 299-C11
VANCOUVER WA 307-F7
S SAINT HELENS AV
TACOMA WA 293-G4
NW SAINT HELENS RD
PORTLAND OR 199-B1
PORTLAND OR 312-A2
NW SAINT HELENS RD U.S.-30
MULTNOMAH CO OR 192-A5
PORTLAND OR 192-A5
PORTLAND OR 199-B1
SAINT HELENS ST
SAINT HELENS OR 192-B1
SAINT HILAIRE RD
YAKIMA CO WA 243-D7
NE SAINT JAMES RD
VANCOUVER WA 192-D5
VANCOUVER WA 306-A2
E SAINT JOE DR
KOOTENAI CO ID 245-A1
SAINT JOE RD
BENEWAH CO ID 248-D7
SAINT JOHN RD
WHITMAN CO WA 114-C3
SAINT JOHNS BLVD
CLARK CO WA 306-A2
VANCOUVER WA 305-H3
VANCOUVER WA 306-A2
NE SAINT JOHNS RD
CLARK CO WA 192-D5
CLARK CO WA 306-A2
VANCOUVER WA 192-D5
VANCOUVER WA 306-A2
SAINT JOHNS ST Rt#-7A
CITY OF PORT MOODY BC 156-D4
DISTRICT OF BURNABY BC 156-D4
PORT MOODY BC 157-A4
SAINT LAWRENCE ST
CITY OF VICTORIA BC 256-F9
SAINT LOUIS RD NE
MARION CO OR 205-A2
SAINT PAUL AV
TACOMA WA 182-A2
TACOMA WA 293-J5
SAINT PAUL HWY
MARION CO OR 198-D7
MARION CO OR 199-A7

SAINT PAUL HWY Rt#-219
MARION CO OR 198-D7
NEWBERG OR 198-D7
SAINT PAUL OR 198-D7
YAMHILL CO OR 198-D7
SALAL LN
COOS CO OR 220-C2
SALEM AV
ALBANY OR 326-F7
LINN CO OR 326-F7
MILLERSBURG OR 326-F7
SALEM EXWY Rt#-99E
KEIZER OR 323-C6
SALEM OR 323-C6
SALEM HWY Rt#-22
SALEM OR 322-J14
SALEM PKWY
KEIZER OR 323-C5
SALEM PKWY Rt#-99E
KEIZER OR 323-A8
MARION CO OR 323-A8
SALEM OR 322-J8
SALEM OR 323-A8
SE SALEM-DAYTON HWY Rt#-221
POLK CO OR 204-D2
POLK CO OR 322-E6
YAMHILL CO OR 204-D2
SALEM-DAYTON HWY NW Rt#-221
SALEM OR 322-E13
SALMI RD
LEWIS CO WA 187-B2
SW SALMON AV
REDMOND OR 212-D6
SE SALMONBERRY RD
East Port Orchard WA 174-B4
SALMON BUTTE RD
CLACKAMAS CO OR 201-C7
NE SALMON CREEK AV
CLARK CO WA 192-D4
SALMON CREEK RD
LANE CO OR 142-A1
OKANOGAN CO WA 104-C3
WAHKIAKUM CO WA 117-A2
WAHKIAKUM CO WA 186-D5
SALMON FALLS RD
SKAMANIA CO WA 193-D7
SALMON HARBOR DR
DOUGLAS CO OR 218-B2
SALMON LA SAC RD
KITTITAS CO WA 111-B3
SALMON LA SAC RD Rt#-903
KITTITAS CO WA 111-B3
KITTITAS CO WA 240-A1
SALMON RIVER HWY Rt#-18
LINCOLN CO OR 203-B4
MCMINNVILLE OR 198-A7
MCMINNVILLE OR 204-A2
POLK CO OR 125-A3
Rose Lodge OR 203-D3
SHERIDAN OR 125-B3
TILLAMOOK CO OR 125-A3
TILLAMOOK CO OR 203-D3
YAMHILL CO OR 125-B3
YAMHILL CO OR 198-A7
YAMHILL CO OR 204-A2
NE SALMON RIVER HWY Rt#-18
YAMHILL CO OR 198-B7
SE SALMON RIVER HWY Rt#-18
MCMINNVILLE OR 198-A7
YAMHILL CO OR 198-B7
SALMON RIVER RD
CLACKAMAS CO OR 201-C5
W SALNAVE RD
SPOKANE CO WA 114-B2
SPOKANE CO WA 246-A7
W SALNAVE RD Rt#-902
MEDICAL LAKE WA 114-B2
SPOKANE CO WA 114-B2
W SALNAVE MEDICAL LAKE RD
CHENEY WA 246-A7
SPOKANE CO WA 246-A7
SALSBURY AV
CHEHALIS WA 299-G14
LEWIS CO WA 299-G14
SALT CREEK RD
CROOK CO OR 135-C3
JACKSON CO OR 230-B1
N SALTESE RD
SPOKANE CO WA 351-C12
SPOKANE VALLEY WA 351-C12
S SALTESE LAKE RD
SPOKANE CO WA 351-J13
SALTY DR NW
THURSTON CO WA 180-C4
NW SALTZMAN RD
WASHINGTON CO OR 199-B1
SALZER VALLEY RD
LEWIS CO WA 184-C6
LEWIS CO WA 299-G5
NE SALZMAN RD
MULTNOMAH CO OR 200-D1
SAMARITAN DR
CORVALLIS OR 327-H4
SAM BELL RD
SKAGIT CO WA 161-A5
SAMISH WY
BELLINGHAM WA 258-E10
WHATCOM CO WA 161-A2
WHATCOM CO WA 258-H13
N SAMISH WY
BELLINGHAM WA 258-E8
SAMISH ISLAND RD
SKAGIT CO WA 160-D4
SAMISH POINT RD
SKAGIT CO WA 160-D4
NW SAMMAMISH RD
ISSAQUAH WA 175-D3
KING CO WA 175-D3
SAMS CREEK RD
LINCOLN CO OR 206-D3
N SAMSON TR
MCCALL ID 251-D5
VALLEY CO ID 251-D5
S SAMSON TR
VALLEY CO ID 251-D6
SAMS VALLEY AV Rt#-234
GOLD HILL OR 230-B6
JACKSON CO OR 230-B6
SAMS VALLEY HWY Rt#-99
GOLD HILL OR 230-A6
JACKSON CO OR 230-A6
SAMS VALLEY HWY Rt#-234
JACKSON CO OR 230-B6
SAMUELS RD
CLACKAMAS CO OR 200-B5

SANBORN RD
KLICKITAT CO WA 195-D3
SAND RD
LATAH CO ID 249-C5
WHITMAN CO WA 249-B3
SAND CANYON RD
CHEWELAH WA 106-B3
STEVENS CO WA 106-B3
SAND CREEK RD
DOUGLAS CO OR 219-B1
KLAMATH CO OR 142-C3
STEVENS CO WA 105-C1
SAND DUNES RD
GRANT CO WA 242-C4
SANDERS RD
BENEWAH CO ID 115-A3
SANDERS ST U.S.-97
CHELAN WA 236-D3
SAND FLATS-ICE CAVE RD
DESCHUTES CO OR 143-A1
SAND HILL RD
MASON CO WA 173-D4
SAND HILL RD U.S.-2
BOUNDARY CO ID 107-B1
SAND HOLLOW RD
ADAMS OR 129-C1
MALHEUR CO OR 138-C3
PAYETTE CO ID 139-B3
UMATILLA CO OR 129-C1
SAND LAKE RD
TILLAMOOK CO OR 197-B4
SAND LAKE SUMMIT RD
TILLAMOOK CO OR 197-B4
SANDLIN RD
WASCO CO OR 196-B7
SANDNER DR
LINN CO OR 133-C1
SANDPIPER DR
LINCOLN CO OR 328-C1
SAND PIT RD
WALLA WALLA CO WA 121-B3
SAND POINT WY NE
SEATTLE WA 171-B7
SEATTLE WA 275-G1
SAND POINT WY NE Rt#-513
SEATTLE WA 275-F5
SANDRA LN NE
KITSAP CO WA 270-H5
Tracyton WA 270-H5
SAND RIDGE RD
KLICKITAT CO WA 120-B3
KLICKITAT CO WA 128-B1
LINN CO OR 133-C1
LINN CO OR 207-D7
LINN CO OR 210-C1
SANDRIDGE RD
ILWACO WA 186-A5
Ocean Park WA 186-A5
PACIFIC CO WA 186-A5
SANDRIDGE RD Rt#-103
Ocean Park WA 186-A2
PACIFIC CO WA 186-A1
N SANDS RD
SPOKANE CO WA 246-D1
S SANDS RD
SPOKANE CO WA 246-D6
SAND SPRINGS RD
DESCHUTES CO OR 135-B3
DESCHUTES CO OR 143-B1
SW SANDSTROM RD
WASHINGTON CO OR 198-B2
NE SANDY BLVD
PORTLAND OR 313-J5
PORTLAND OR 314-B4
PORTLAND OR 315-F2
NE SANDY BLVD U.S.-30
FAIRVIEW OR 200-A1
GRESHAM OR 200-A1
PORTLAND OR 200-A1
PORTLAND OR 315-J1
WOOD VILLAGE OR 200-A1
SE SANDY BLVD
PORTLAND OR 313-H6
SANDY BEACH LN NE
KITSAP CO WA 170-D5
SANDY BEND RD
COWLITZ CO WA 189-C1
SANDY CREEK RD
COOS CO OR 140-C3
SANDY POINT RD NE
THURSTON CO WA 181-A5
SANDY SHORE LAKE RD
JEFFERSON CO WA 170-A3
SANFORD CANYON RD
MORROW CO OR 128-C2
SAN FRANCISCO AV NE
OLYMPIA WA 296-J3
OLYMPIA WA 297-A3
SANGSTER RD
ASOTIN CO WA 122-C3
SAN JUAN AV
PORT TOWNSEND WA 263-F4
SAN SALVADOR RD
MEDICAL LAKE WA 114-B2
SANTIAM HWY U.S.-20
ALBANY OR 326-F8
Crowfoot OR 133-C1
DESCHUTES CO OR 211-C3
JEFFERSON CO OR 211-A2
LEBANON OR 133-C1
LINN CO OR 133-C1
LINN CO OR 134-A2
LINN CO OR 207-D5
LINN CO OR 211-A2
LINN CO OR 326-F8
SISTERS OR 211-C3
SWEET HOME OR 133-C1
SWEET HOME OR 134-A2
N SANTIAM HWY Rt#-22
AUMSVILLE OR 205-A7
DETROIT OR 134-A1
GATES OR 134-A1
IDANHA OR 134-A1
LINN CO OR 134-C1
MARION CO OR 133-C1
MARION CO OR 134-A1
MARION CO OR 205-A7
MARION CO OR 325-G3
MILL CITY OR 134-A1
SALEM OR 204-D6
SALEM OR 325-G3
STAYTON OR 133-C1
SUBLIMITY OR 133-C1
SANTIAM RD
ALBANY OR 326-D7
E SANTIAM ST
MARION CO OR 133-C1
STAYTON OR 133-C1

INDEX

STREET
City State Page-Grid

SAPP RD
SEDRO-WOOLLEY WA 161-C5
SAPP RD SW
THURSTON CO WA 296-B10
TUMWATER WA 296-D9
E SARATOGA AV
ISLAND CO WA 167-D7
SARATOGA DR NE
MARION CO OR 205-B3
SARATOGA RD
ISLAND CO WA 171-A1
LANGLEY WA 171-A1
E SARATOGA RD
ISLAND CO WA 167-D7
ISLAND CO WA 168-A7
ISLAND CO WA 171-A1
SARDINE CREEK RD
BAKER CO OR 138-C1
JACKSON CO OR 230-A5
SAREAULT RD
LEWIS CO WA 187-D3
SARGENT RD
LEWIS CO WA 187-C2
SARGENT RD SW
THURSTON CO WA 184-B3
E SATSOP RD
GRAYS HARBOR CO WA 179-A6
W SATSOP RD
GRAYS HARBOR CO WA 179-A5
SATSOP- CLOQUALLUM RD
MASON CO WA 179-B5
SATTERLEE RD
SKAGIT CO WA 160-C7
SATTLER DR
COLUMBIA CO OR 192-A4
N SATUS RD
YAKIMA CO WA 120-A2
W SATUS RD
YAKIMA CO WA 120-A3
SAUERKRAUT RD
POLK CO OR 207-A2
SAUK VALLEY RD Rt#-530
SKAGIT CO WA 103-A2
SAULSER RD
COLUMBIA CO OR 192-A2
SAUNDERS RD
CHELAN CO WA 238-B1
SAUNDERS ST
DOUGLAS CO WA 239-B5
ROCK ISLAND WA 239-B5
SAUNDERS CREEK RD
CURRY CO OR 228-B5
SAUSSER DR
KOOTENAI CO ID 247-D4
SAUVIE ISLAND RD
MULTNOMAH CO OR 192-A5
SAVAGE RD
TILLAMOOK CO OR 203-A3
NE SAVAGE ST
GRANTS PASS OR 335-G7
NW SAVAGE ST
GRANTS PASS OR 335-F7
SAVAGE CREEK RD
JACKSON CO OR 229-D6
NE SAWDUST HILL RD
KITSAP CO WA 170-C6
SAWMILL CREEK RD
HARNEY CO OR 144-C1
SAWMILL CUTOFF RD
BAKER CO OR 131-A3
SAWTELL RD
CLACKAMAS CO OR 126-A3
S SAWTELL RD
CLACKAMAS CO OR 126-A3
SAWYER RD
JACKSON CO OR 230-D2
LATAH CO ID 249-C1
SAWYER CREEK RD
DOUGLAS CO OR 141-A1
SAXON RD
WHATCOM CO WA 161-C2
W SAXTON AV
BOISE ID 253-C1
SAYWARD RD
DISTRICT OF SAANICH BC 159-C4
SCAPPOOSE-VERNONIA RD
COLUMBIA CO OR 125-C1
COLUMBIA CO OR 192-A3
SCAPPOOSE OR 192-A3
SCARIFICATION RD
MASON CO WA 173-D4
SCENIC AV
JACKSON CO OR 230-B7
SCENIC DR
ALBANY OR 207-C4
ASHLAND OR 337-B7
BENTON CO OR 207-C4
DESCHUTES CO OR 217-C1
Freeland WA 170-D1
Santa Clara OR 215-B1
YAKIMA CO WA 243-A6
W SCENIC DR
GRANTS PASS OR 335-F5
JOSEPHINE CO OR 335-F5
THE DALLES OR 196-C7
SCENIC WY
ASOTIN CO WA 250-B4
Vineland WA 250-B4
SCENIC HEIGHTS RD
ISLAND CO WA 167-B3
SCHAD RD
DOUGLAS CO OR 141-A1
SCHAEFFER RD
UMATILLA CO OR 129-B1
SW SCHAEFFER RD
CLACKAMAS CO OR 199-C5
S SCHAFER RD
SPOKANE VALLEY WA 350-E14
SCHAFER PARK RD
MASON CO WA 179-A5
SCHAFFER RD
COLUMBIA CO OR 189-A7
SCHAFFRAN RD
COWLITZ CO WA 187-C7
SCHARPENBERG HILL RD
LA CROSSE WA 122-A1
WHITMAN CO WA 122-A1
SCHELINE LN
VALLEY CO ID 252-D1
SCHERZINGER RD
TILLAMOOK CO OR 203-B1
SCHIEFFELIN GULCH RD
JACKSON CO OR 229-D6
SCHILLING RD
KLICKITAT CO WA 196-D4
SCHLARB RD KPN
PIERCE CO WA 181-A1
SCHLEE RD
WHITMAN CO WA 250-A2
SCHLIMMER RD E
LINCOLN CO WA 113-B2
SCHMELTZER RD
WASHINGTON CO OR 198-D4
SCHMIDLEKOFER RD
CHEWELAH WA 106-B3
STEVENS CO WA 106-B3
SCHMITT RD
CLALLAM CO WA 164-C5
SCHNEBLY RD
KITTITAS CO WA 241-C4
S SCHNEIDER RD
CLACKAMAS CO OR 205-C2
SCHNEIDER HILL RD
OLYMPIA WA 296-G2
SCHNIEDER WY
CROOK CO OR 213-D2
SCHOCKLEY RD
CLACKAMAS CO OR 200-B7
SCHOESSLER RD
ADAMS CO WA 113-B3
SCHOLFIELD RD
DOUGLAS CO OR 218-D2
SCHOLFIELD RIDGE RD
DOUGLAS CO OR 218-D2
SW SCHOLLS FERRY RD
PORTLAND OR 199-B1
SW SCHOLLS FERRY RD Rt#-210
BEAVERTON OR 199-B2
TIGARD OR 199-B2
WASHINGTON CO OR 198-D3
WASHINGTON CO OR 199-B2
SW SCHOLLS-SHERWOOD RD
WASHINGTON CO OR 199-A4
SCHOOL AV
WALLA WALLA WA 345-E7
Walla Walla East WA 345-E10
SCHOOL DR
KLICKITAT CO WA 196-D3
SCHOOL ST
Sunnyslope WA 238-D3
SCHOOL FLAT LN
WALLOWA CO OR 130-C2
SCHOOLHOUSE LN
LEWIS CO WA 187-D3
SCHOOL HOUSE RD
SISKIYOU CO CA 150-B3
SCHOOLHOUSE ST
COQUITLAM BC 157-A5
SCHOOLHOUSE LOOP RD
NESPELEM WA 105-A3
OKANOGAN CO WA 105-A3
SCHOOLIE MOUNT WILSON RD
WASCO CO OR 126-C3
SCHOOL LAND RD SW
THURSTON CO WA 184-A3
SCHOOLMARM SPUR
JACKSON CO OR 226-C7
S SCHOONER CREEK RD
LINCOLN CITY OR 203-A5
LINCOLN CO OR 203-A5
SCHOONOVER RD
LINCOLN CO WA 113-B3
SCHRAEDER RD
DESCHUTES CO OR 144-B1
SCHRAG RD
ADAMS CO WA 113-B3
SCHRAM RD
CLACKAMAS CO OR 200-B7
SCHULER RD
MARION CO OR 199-A6
SCHULTZ RD
LATAH CO ID 249-D4
MARION CO OR 199-A6
SCHUSTER PKWY
TACOMA WA 293-F2
SCHUSTER RD E
LINCOLN CO WA 113-B2
SCHUT RD
YAKIMA CO WA 243-D7
SCHWARTZ RD
JEFFERSON CO WA 167-B7
SCHWEITZER CTO
PONDERAY ID 244-A1
SANDPOINT ID 244-A1
SCHWEITZER BASIN RD
BONNER CO ID 244-A1
SCISM RD NE
MARION CO OR 205-B4
SW SCOGGINS VALLEY RD
WASHINGTON CO OR 198-B2
S SCONCE RD
CLACKAMAS CO OR 205-C1
SCOTIA RD
PEND OREILLE CO WA 106-C3
E SCOTT AV
WOODLAND WA 118-A3
SCOTT RD
CITY OF SURREY BC 156-D6
CITY OF SURREY BC 157-A5
DISTRICT OF DELTA BC 156-D7
SKAMANIA CO WA 194-B6
WHATCOM CO WA 158-C7
WHITMAN CO WA 122-A1
SCOTT RD NW
THURSTON CO WA 180-B5
SCOTT ST
CITY OF VICTORIA BC 257-A6
NE SCOTT ST
BEND OR 332-F8
SE SCOTT ST
BEND OR 332-F8
SCOTT CAMP RD
CROOK CO OR 136-B2
SCOTT CANYON RD
RUFUS OR 127-C1
SHERMAN CO OR 127-C1
SCOTT CREEK RD
LINCOLN CO OR 209-D2
SCOTT HILL RD
WASHINGTON CO OR 198-A2
SCOTT RIVER RD
SISKIYOU CO CA 149-B3
SCOTTS VALLEY RD
DOUGLAS CO OR 219-C5
SCOUT LAKE RD
JEFFERSON CO OR 211-B2
NE SCOVILLE RD
GRANTS PASS OR 335-F4
SCRAVEL HILL RD
LINN CO OR 207-D3
E SCRIBNER RD
SPOKANE CO WA 247-A1
N SCRIBNER RD
SPOKANE CO WA 246-D1
S SCRIBNER RD
SPOKANE CO WA 246-B6
SEA ACRES RD
SAN JUAN CO WA 160-B2
SEABECK HWY
KITSAP CO WA 270-A7
Tracyton WA 270-A7
SEABECK HWY NW
KITSAP CO WA 174-A1
SEABECK HOLLY RD NW
KITSAP CO WA 173-C3
SEA BIRD DR
BANDON OR 220-A6
COOS CO OR 220-A6
SEACREST DR
WHATCOM CO WA 160-B1
SEAGULL DR
CLALLAM CO WA 164-D5
SEAHURST ACCESS RD
PACIFIC CO WA 183-B4
SEA ISLAND WY
CITY OF RICHMOND BC 156-B6
SEALION RD
KITSAP CO WA 170-A7
N SEAMAN GULCH RD
ADA CO ID 253-B1
N SEAMANS GULCH RD
ADA CO ID 253-C1
SEAMOUNT DR
JEFFERSON CO WA 173-C1
SEARLES RD
CHELAN CO WA 239-B5
SEARS RD
LANE CO OR 215-B7
LEWIS CO WA 187-B2
NANAIMO BC 93-A3
SEASONS RD
KOOTENAI CO ID 245-A2
N SEASONS RD
KOOTENAI CO ID 115-A1
E SEATTLE AV
MOXEE WA 243-D7
W SEATTLE AV
MOXEE WA 243-D7
W SEATTLE BRDG
SEATTLE WA 281-F3
SEATTLE WA 282-A3
SEATTLE HILL RD
SNOHOMISH CO WA 171-C4
SEATTLE HILL RD Rt#-96
SNOHOMISH CO WA 171-C4
SEATTLE-VASHON FERRY
KING CO WA 174-D4
SEATTLE-VICTORIA FERRY
ISLAND CO WA 170-C2
KING CO WA 174-D1
KITSAP CO WA 170-C2
SEAVEY LOOP RD
LANE CO OR 330-H12
LANE CO OR 331-A12
SEAVIEW AV NW
SEATTLE WA 272-C3
SEAVIEW PL NW
SEATTLE WA 272-D1
SEAVIEW RD
DISTRICT OF SAANICH BC 257-F4
SEAWAY BLVD
EVERETT WA 267-H2
SEAWOLF RD
KITSAP CO WA 170-B6
SECHELT DR
DIST OF NORTH VANCOUVER BC 255-J4
SECOND AV
YAKIMA CO WA 120-A2
ZILLAH WA 120-A2
SECOND AV Rt#-3
DEARY ID 123-B1
LATAH CO ID 123-B1
SECOND AV Rt#-8
DEARY ID 123-B1
LATAH CO ID 123-B1
S SECOND AV Rt#-31
IONE WA 106-B1
SECOND AV N Rt#-20
OKANOGAN WA 104-C3
SECOND AV NW Rt#-20
OKANOGAN WA 104-C3
SECOND AV SW Rt#-20
OKANOGAN WA 104-C3
W SECOND RD
CHENEY WA 246-A7
SECOND ST
FRIDAY HARBOR WA 101-C2
LANGLEY WA 171-A1
SECOND ST Rt#-124
PRESCOTT WA 121-C2
WALLA WALLA CO WA 121-C2
E SECOND ST
ABERDEEN WA 178-B7
E SECOND ST Rt#-21
LIND WA 121-B1
N SECOND ST Rt#-231
SPRINGDALE WA 106-B3
S SECOND ST
Burbank WA 121-A3
WALLA WALLA CO WA 121-A3
S SECOND ST Rt#-231
SPRINGDALE WA 106-B3
W SECOND ST
ABERDEEN WA 178-B7
W SECOND ST Rt#-903
CLE ELUM WA 240-B2
SECOND ST W Rt#-903
CLE ELUM WA 240-B2
SECOND NARROWS BRDG Rt#-1
DIST OF NORTH VANCOUVER BC 255-F9
VANCOUVER BC 255-F9
NW SEDGEWICK AV
DESCHUTES CO OR 212-D4
SE SEDGWICK RD Rt#-160
KITSAP CO WA 174-C4
PORT ORCHARD WA 174-B4
SEEFELD DR
LINN CO OR 210-B3
SEEKSEEQUA CREEK RD
JEFFERSON CO OR 208-A4
SEELANDER RD
COOS CO OR 140-B2
SEEMANN ST Rt#-530
DARRINGTON WA 103-A3
SW SEGHERS RD
WASHINGTON CO OR 198-B2
SEHMEL DR NW
PIERCE CO WA 174-B7
SEIDEL RD
KING CO WA 171-D7
SW SEIFFERT RD
WASHINGTON CO OR 198-D4
SELAH RD Rt#-823
YAKIMA CO WA 243-B6
E SELAH RD
YAKIMA CO WA 243-C5
SELAH HEIGHTS RD
YAKIMA CO WA 243-B5
SELAH LOOP RD
SELAH WA 243-B5
YAKIMA CO WA 243-B5
SELAH-NACHES RD
YAKIMA CO WA 243-B5
SELAH SPRINGS DR NE
MARION CO OR 205-B5
SELDON RD
DISTRICT OF MATSQUI BC 102-B1
SELLARDS RD
BENTON CO WA 120-B3
E SELLE RD
BONNER CO ID 107-B2
SELPH LANDING RD
FRANKLIN CO WA 121-A2
FRANKLIN CO WA 340-J9
SELTICE BLVD
KOOTENAI CO ID 353-A7
POST FALLS ID 353-A7
SELTICE WY
COEUR D'ALENE ID 355-A8
KOOTENAI CO ID 352-J8
KOOTENAI CO ID 353-C6
KOOTENAI CO ID 354-D7
KOOTENAI CO ID 355-A8
POST FALLS ID 352-J8
POST FALLS ID 353-C6
POST FALLS ID 354-A7
SEMIAHMOO DR
Birch Bay WA 158-A4
BLAINE WA 158-A4
WHATCOM CO WA 158-A4
SEMINARY HILL RD
CENTRALIA WA 299-G4
LEWIS CO WA 299-G4
N SEQUIM AV
CLALLAM CO WA 262-E11
SEQUIM WA 262-E11
E SEQUIM BAY RD
CLALLAM CO WA 166-C7
W SEQUIM BAY RD
CLALLAM CO WA 262-H12
SEQUIM WA 262-H12
SEQUIM-DUNGENESS WY
CLALLAM CO WA 262-D4
SERVICE CK-MITCHLL HWY Rt#-207
MITCHELL OR 136-A1
WHEELER CO OR 136-A1
NE SERWOLD RD
POULSBO WA 170-C7
SESAME ST NW
KITSAP CO WA 174-A1
SETHER AV
DOUGLAS CO OR 225-B7
GLENDALE OR 225-A7
SETTERS RD
KOOTENAI CO ID 247-C7
SETTLEMIER AV
MARION CO OR 205-B2
WOODBURN OR 205-B1
SEVEN DEVILS RD
COOS CO OR 220-B2
N SEVEN MILE EXT
SPOKANE CO WA 246-A2
SEVEN MILE LN
BROWNSVILLE OR 210-C2
LINN CO OR 207-D6
LINN CO OR 210-C1
LINN CO OR 326-F14
SEVEN MILE RD
COOS CO OR 220-B5
SEVENMILE RD
KLAMATH CO OR 231-B2
SEVEN MILE RD Rt#-162
IDAHO CO ID 123-C3
KAMIAH ID 123-C3
LEWIS CO ID 123-C3
W SEVEN MILE RD
SPOKANE CO WA 246-A2
SEVENMILE HILL RD
WASCO CO OR 196-B6
SEVENMILE RANCH RD
KLAMATH CO OR 231-B2
SEVEN SPRINGS DAIRY RD E
LINCOLN CO WA 113-C2
SEVENTH ST U.S.-101
HOQUIAM WA 178-A7
E SEVENTH ST
ROSALIA WA 114-C3
N SEVENTH ST Rt#-903
ROSLYN WA 240-A1
SEWARD DR
LINN CO OR 207-B7
SEWARD PARK AV S
SEATTLE WA 283-G7
SEATTLE WA 287-G1
SEYMOUR BLVD
DIST OF NORTH VANCOUVER BC 255-G6
SEYMOUR ST Rt#-99
VANCOUVER BC 254-F11
SHAD RD
JEFFERSON CO OR 212-C2
SHADY LN
KLICKITAT CO WA 196-B4
SHADY PINE RD
KLAMATH CO OR 235-C1
N SHADY SLOPE RD
SPOKANE CO WA 347-D5
SHAFF RD
MARION CO OR 133-C1
SHAFF RD SE
MARION CO OR 133-C1
STAYTON OR 133-C1
W SHAFFER AV Rt#-231
SPRINGDALE WA 106-B3
N SHAMROCK ST
BOISE ID 253-B2
SHANDROW
PIERCE CO WA 182-A7
SHANIKO-FOSSIL HWY Rt#-218
ANTELOPE OR 127-C3
FOSSIL OR 128-A3
SHANIKO OR 127-C3
WASCO CO OR 127-C3
WASCO CO OR 128-A3
WHEELER CO OR 128-A3
SHARON AV
BURLINGTON WA 260-C6
SHARON CREEK RESERVOIR RD
MALHEUR CO OR 155-A2
SHARPE RD
PITT MEADOWS BC 157-C5
SKAGIT CO WA 259-C13
SHARPS CREEK RD
LANE CO OR 141-C1
LANE CO OR 142-A1
S SHASTA AV
EAGLE POINT OR 230-D5
SHASTA WY
Altamont OR 338-G9
Altamont OR 339-A9
KLAMATH CO OR 338-G9
KLAMATH FALLS OR 338-G9
SHATTUCK RD
DESCHUTES CO OR 211-D6
SW SHATTUCK RD
MULTNOMAH CO OR 316-A3
PORTLAND OR 199-B2
PORTLAND OR 316-A3
SHAUGHNESSY ST
COQUITLAM BC 157-B4
PORT COQUITLAM BC 157-B4
SHAW HWY SE
AUMSVILLE OR 205-B7
MARION CO OR 205-B7
SHAW RD
PUYALLUP WA 182-B4
UMATILLA CO OR 129-B2
SHAW RD E
PIERCE CO WA 182-B4
SHAW-HOLMES RD
UMATILLA CO OR 129-B2
E SHAW MOUNTAIN RD
ADA CO ID 253-D2
SHAWNEE
CROOK CO OR 213-D7
SHAWNEE-PARVIN RD
WHITMAN CO WA 249-A3
SHAWNIGAN LAKE RD
BRITISH COLUMBIA BC 159-A3
SHAY LN
DESCHUTES CO OR 143-A1
SHAY HILL RD
BENEWAH CO ID 248-C7
SHEARERS BRIDGE HWY Rt#-216
WASCO CO OR 127-B2
SHEDD CEMETERY RD
LINN CO OR 210-B1
SHEEHAN RD SW
DOUGLAS CO WA 239-C2
NW SHEELAR LN
WASHINGTON CO OR 198-B1
SHEEP CANYON RD
GRANT CO WA 112-C2
SHEEP COMPANY RD
YAKIMA CO WA 243-B4
SHEEP CREEK RD
STEVENS CO WA 106-A1
WASHINGTON CO ID 139-C2
SHEFFIELD RD
FRANKLIN CO WA 121-A2
MESA WA 121-A2
SHEFFLER RD
WALLA WALLA CO WA 121-B2
SHELBOURNE ST
CITY OF VICTORIA BC 257-A7
DISTRICT OF SAANICH BC 159-D5
DISTRICT OF SAANICH BC 257-A1
SHELBURN DR
LINN CO OR 133-C1
SHELBY RD
SNOHOMISH CO WA 171-B4
SHELDON RD SE
THURSTON CO WA 184-D1
SHELDON ST
FALLS CITY OR 125-B3
POLK CO OR 125-B3
SHELGRIN RD
GRAYS HARBOR CO WA 177-C4
SHELL RD
CITY OF RICHMOND BC 156-B6
SHELLER RD
YAKIMA CO WA 120-B2
SHELLEY RD
COOS CO OR 220-D5
SHELLRIDGE RD NW
THURSTON CO WA 180-B5
SHELL ROCK RD
CLACKAMAS CO OR 126-C3
KITTITAS CO WA 240-C6
SHELTER BAY DR
Shelter Bay WA 167-D1
SHELTON RD
Walla Walla East WA 345-E10
NW SHELTON RD
YAMHILL CO OR 198-A6
SHELTON-MATLOCK RD
MASON CO WA 179-C2
MASON CO WA 180-A3
SHELTON VALLEY RD
MASON CO WA 180-A3
SHEPARD RD
COLUMBIA CO OR 189-A3
SHERARS BRIDGE HWY Rt#-216
GRASS VALLEY OR 127-B2
SHERMAN CO OR 127-B2
SHERIDAN AV U.S.-101
NORTH BEND OR 333-G5
S SHERIDAN AV
TACOMA WA 295-F6
SHERIDAN RD
BREMERTON WA 270-H7
BREMERTON WA 271-A8
KITSAP CO WA 271-A8
SHERIDAN ST
PORT TOWNSEND WA 263-E5
SE SHERIDAN ST
SHERIDAN OR 125-B3
SW SHERIDAN ST
PORTLAND OR 317-E1
SHER KHAN RD
LANE CO OR 215-B4
NW SHERLOCK AV
PORTLAND OR 312-B1
E SHERLOCK ST Rt#-23
HARRINGTON WA 113-C2
SHERMAN AV
NORTH BEND OR 333-G5
SHERMAN AV U.S.-101
NORTH BEND OR 333-G5
E SHERMAN AV
COEUR D'ALENE ID 355-F11
KOOTENAI CO ID 355-F11
SHERMAN HWY U.S.-97
GRASS VALLEY OR 127-C2
MORO OR 127-C2
SHANIKO OR 127-C2
SHERMAN CO OR 127-C1
WASCO CO OR 127-B3
SHERMAN RD
ISLAND CO WA 167-B4
S SHERMAN RD
SPOKANE CO WA 246-B6
SHERMAN RD SE
MARION CO OR 205-B7
S SHERMAN ST
ASHLAND OR 337-D8
SPOKANE WA 349-B9
SHERMAN HEIGHTS RD
KITSAP CO WA 270-D14
Navy Yard City WA 270-D14
S SHERWOOD BLVD
SHERWOOD OR 199-A4
SHERWOOD DR
JEFFERSON CO OR 212-D2
SHERWOOD RD
CROOK CO OR 136-A3
NW SHEVLIN PARK MARKET RD
BEND OR 217-B2
BEND OR 332-A6
DESCHUTES CO OR 217-B2
SHIBLEY RD
CLACKAMAS CO OR 200-B7
SHIFFMAN RD
TILLAMOOK CO OR 191-C4
SHILOH RD
JACKSON CO OR 230-C4
SHINCKE RD NE
THURSTON CO WA 180-D5
SHINGLEBOLT RD
TILLAMOOK CO OR 203-B3
E SHINGLE MILL RD
BONNER CO ID 244-B1
W SHINGLE MILL RD
BONNER CO ID 244-B1
SHINN RD SW
DOUGLAS CO WA 239-C4
SHIPLEY RD
CLACKAMAS CO OR 200-D4
SHIRTTAIL CREEK RD
BAKER CO OR 138-C2
SHIVELY CREEK RD
DOUGLAS CO OR 225-D2
SHOALWATER BAY
PACIFIC CO WA 186-B6
SHOEPEG RD
WASHINGTON CO ID 139-B1
SHOESTRING RD
DOUGLAS CO OR 225-B3
LANE CO OR 219-C3
SHOLLMEYER RD
TILLAMOOK CO OR 191-B4
SHORE DR
BREMERTON WA 271-A10
S SHORE DR
SKAGIT CO WA 160-C5
W SHORE DR
SKAGIT CO WA 160-C4
WHATCOM CO WA 160-B1
SHORE RD
CLALLAM CO WA 165-D6
S SHORE RD
BREMERTON WA 270-C8
SKAGIT CO WA 160-C5
SHORE ST
CHELAN CO WA 238-A1
SHORELINE DR N
KEIZER OR 322-H5
SHORE PINE RD
CURRY CO OR 232-C4
SHOREVIEW DR
LINCOLN CO OR 328-C1
SHOREWOOD
SAN JUAN CO WA 160-A3
SHORT RD
KLAMATH CO OR 235-D5
N SHORT RD
SPOKANE CO WA 114-B1
SHORT ST
ASTORIA OR 300-B5
SHORT HORN GULCH RD
JOSEPHINE CO OR 229-B2
SHORT ROAD BEECH CREEK
GRANT CO OR 137-A1
SHORT ROAD IN FOX
GRANT CO OR 137-A1
SHORT SAND CROSS OVER RD
TILLAMOOK CO OR 191-B3
SHORT SCHOOL RD
SNOHOMISH CO WA 171-D4
NE SHORTY CAMPBELL RD
Kingston WA 170-D5
KITSAP CO WA 170-D5
SHOSHONI LN
LANE CO OR 215-D5
SHROPSHIRE RD
WHITMAN CO WA 122-A1
SHUFFIELD RD
LAKE CO OR 143-C3
SHUMAKER RD
ASOTIN CO WA 123-A3
SHUMWAY RD
CROOK CO OR 213-A7
MALHEUR CO OR 146-A1
SHUMWAY CUTOFF RD
MALHEUR CO OR 146-B1
SHUMWAY RANCH RD
MALHEUR CO OR 146-B1
NE SHUTE RD
HILLSBORO OR 198-D1
SHUTTERA RD
NEZ PERCE CO ID 250-D6
SHUTTERS LANDING RD
COOS CO OR 218-C4
SHY MEADOW
CHELAN CO WA 238-B2
SIAH BUTTE RD
DESCHUTES CO OR 216-C6
SIDAWAY RD
CITY OF RICHMOND BC 156-C7
S SIDE RD
DOUGLAS CO OR 219-A3
W SIDE RD
BOUNDARY CO ID 107-B1
SIDE HILL RD
DESCHUTES CO OR 211-B3
SIDNEY AV
PORT ORCHARD WA 174-B4
PORT ORCHARD WA 270-H14
SIDNEY AV SW
PORT ORCHARD WA 174-B4
SIDNEY RD S
MARION CO OR 207-C1
SIDNEY RD SW
KITSAP CO WA 174-B5
PIERCE CO WA 174-B6
PORT ORCHARD WA 174-B5

STREET / City State / Page-Grid

SIDNEY-ANACORTES FERRY
BRITISH COLUMBIA BC 101-C2
BRITISH COLUMBIA BC 159-C2
SAN JUAN CO WA 101-C2
TOWN OF SIDNEY BC 159-C2
SIEVERS DUECY BLVD
EVERETT WA 268-A3
SIGHTLY RD
COWLITZ CO WA 118-A2
SIGNAL PEAK RD
HARRAH WA 119-C2
SIGNAL PEAK RD Rt#-220
HARRAH WA 119-C2
S SIGNAL POINT RD
KOOTENAI CO ID 247-C4
SILCOTT GRADE RD
ASOTIN CO WA 250-A4
SILCOTT WYE RD
ASOTIN CO WA 250-A5
SILETZ HWY Rt#-229
LINCOLN CO OR 203-A6
LINCOLN CO OR 206-C1
SILETZ OR 206-C1
TOLEDO OR 206-C4
SILL RD
SNOHOMISH CO WA 168-C5
SILLS RD
ISLAND CO WA 170-D2
ISLAND CO WA 171-A2
SILTCOOS STATION RD
LANE CO OR 214-B5
SILVER ST
PORT TOWNSEND WA 263-E3
SILVER CITY RD
OWYHEE CO ID 147-B2
SILVER CREEK RD
FERRY CO WA 105-B3
HARNEY CO OR 144-C1
JOSEPHINE CO OR 148-C1
SILVERCREEK RD Rt#-122
LEWIS CO WA 118-A2
SILVER CROWN AV
NORTHPORT WA 106-A1
SILVERDALE WY NW
KITSAP CO WA 170-B7
KITSAP CO WA 174-B1
Silverdale WA 174-B1
Silverdale WA 270-B1
SILVER FALLS HWY Rt#-214
MARION CO OR 205-A7
SILVER FALLS HWY NE
Rt#-214
MARION CO OR 205-C5
SILVERTON OR 205-C5
SILVER FALLS HWY NW
Rt#-214
MARION CO OR 205-B7
SILVER FALLS HWY SE
Rt#-214
MARION CO OR 205-D6
SILVER LAKE RD
ISLAND CO WA 167-C2
KLAMATH CO OR 142-C3
KLAMATH CO OR 143-A3
WHATCOM CO WA 102-C1
S SILVER LAKE RD
COWLITZ CO WA 187-C7
COWLITZ CO WA 189-D1
SILVERNAIL RD
SKAGIT CO WA 168-B3
SILVER RIDGE RD SE
MARION CO OR 205-D7
SILVERTON AV Rt#-214
MARION CO OR 205-B2
WOODBURN OR 205-B2
SILVERTON HWY Rt#-214
WOODBURN OR 205-B2
NE SILVERTON HWY Rt#-213
MARION CO OR 205-B4
SILVERTON RD NE
Hayesville OR 204-D5
Hayesville OR 323-H8
SALEM OR 323-B10
SILVERTON RD NE Rt#-213
Hayesville OR 323-E9
MARION CO OR 205-A5
MARION CO OR 323-E9
SILVER VALLEY RD
SHOSHONE CO ID 115-B2
SILVIES-HOPPER RANCH RD
GRANT CO OR 137-B3
SILVIS RD
DESCHUTES CO OR 217-D2
SIMCOE MOUNTAIN RD
KLICKITAT CO WA 127-B1
SIMILKAMEEN RD
OKANOGAN CO WA 104-C1
SIMMONS RD
KLICKITAT CO WA 195-D4
YAKIMA CO WA 119-C1
SIMMONS RD NW
THURSTON CO WA 180-B6
SIMMONS CREEK RD
TILLAMOOK CO OR 197-C3
SIMMONS RIDGE RD
TILLAMOOK CO OR 197-D3
SIMNASHO RD
WASCO CO OR 127-A3
SIMNASHO HOT SPRINGS RD
WASCO CO OR 127-B3
WASCO CO OR 208-B1
SIMONDS RD NE
KENMORE WA 171-C6
SIMPLOT BLVD Rt#-19
CALDWELL ID 147-B1
CANYON CO ID 147-B1
WILDER ID 147-B1
SIMPSON AV Rt#-108
MCCLEARY WA 179-D6
SIMPSON AV U.S.-101
ABERDEEN WA 178-B7
HOQUIAM WA 178-A7
SIMPSON RD
DISTRICT OF MATSQUI BC 102-B1
POLK CO OR 207-A2
UMATILLA CO OR 129-B1
SIMPSON RD NW
THURSTON CO WA 180-B5
SIMPSON CANYON RD
KLAMATH CO OR 235-C1
SIMS WY Rt#-20
PORT TOWNSEND WA 263-C6
SINCLAIR RD
BAKER CO OR 138-C1
CITY OF CHILLIWACK BC 102-C1
DISTRICT OF SAANICH BC 257-D3
SINE RD
GRAYS HARBOR CO WA 179-D6
MCCLEARY WA 179-D6

SINGLE CREEK RD
DOUGLAS CO OR 222-B2
SINGLE TREE TR
HUMBOLDT CO NV 154-C3
SINK RD
LAKE CO OR 143-C2
SINLAHEKIN RD
OKANOGAN CO WA 104-C2
SISCO HEIGHTS RD
SNOHOMISH CO WA 168-D7
SISCO HEIGHTS RD Rt#-531
ARLINGTON WA 168-D6
SNOHOMISH CO WA 168-D6
SISEMORE RD
DESCHUTES CO OR 212-A7
SISK RD
YAKIMA CO WA 243-A3
SISKIYOU BLVD
MEDFORD OR 336-E13
SISKIYOU BLVD Rt#-99
ASHLAND OR 337-D8
JACKSON CO OR 337-H10
SISKIYOU HWY
JACKSON CO OR 150-A2
SISKIYOU SUMMIT RD
JACKSON CO OR 234-D5
S SISTER RD
DOUGLAS CO OR 133-A3
LANE CO OR 133-A3
SISTERS AV
REDMOND OR 212-D5
SITKUM-COUNTY LINE RD
COOS CO OR 140-C2
COOS CO OR 141-A2
SI TOWN RD
COWLITZ CO WA 187-C7
SITZ RIDGE RD
LINCOLN CO OR 209-C3
SIUSLAW RIVER RD
LANE CO OR 133-C2
SIXES RIVER RD
CURRY CO OR 224-B5
SIX PRONG RD
KLICKITAT CO WA 128-A1
SIXTH ST Rt#-6
POTLATCH ID 249-D1
SIXTH ST Rt#-20
OKANOGAN CO WA 104-C2
TONASKET WA 104-C2
SIXTH ST Rt#-507
TENINO WA 184-D3
SIXTH ST U.S.-101
RAYMOND WA 117-A1
E SIXTH ST
CENTRALIA WA 299-F2
LANGLEY WA 171-A1
E SIXTH ST Rt#-507
CENTRALIA WA 299-F2
W SIXTH ST
CENTRALIA WA 299-F2
SKAAR RD
SKAMANIA CO WA 194-D4
S SKAGIT HWY
SKAGIT CO WA 102-C2
SKAGIT CO WA 161-C6
N SKAGIT ST
BURLINGTON WA 260-E4
S SKAGIT ST
BURLINGTON WA 260-E6
SKAGIT CITY RD
SKAGIT CO WA 168-A1
SKAMANIA MINES RD
SKAMANIA CO WA 193-D5
SKATE CREEK RD N
LEWIS CO WA 118-C1
SKATE CREEK RD S
LEWIS CO WA 185-B6
SKEANS RD
COLUMBIA CO OR 189-B5
SKELLEY RD
DOUGLAS CO OR 219-A4
SKELLEY RD S
DOUGLAS CO OR 219-A4
SKELTON RD SE
MARION CO OR 207-D2
N SKIDMORE ST
PORTLAND OR 313-F1
NE SKIDMORE ST
PORTLAND OR 313-G1
SKI HILL RD
CHELAN CO WA 238-A1
LEAVENWORTH WA 238-A1
SKINNER RD
CLACKAMAS CO OR 200-C2
SKINNER ST
CITY OF VICTORIA BC 256-E7
SKIPLES RD
SNOHOMISH CO WA 269-J2
SKIPLEY RD
SNOHOMISH CO WA 171-D3
SKI RUN RD
WALLOWA CO OR 130-C2
SKOKOMISH VALLEY RD
MASON CO WA 179-D1
SKOOKUM CANYON RD
KLICKITAT CO WA 196-C1
SKOOKUMCHUCK RD SE
THURSTON CO WA 184-D2
SKULL CREEK RD
MALHEUR CO OR 146-C3
MALHEUR CO OR 155-A1
SKYE RD
SKAMANIA CO WA 193-D6
W SKYLINE AV
ASTORIA OR 300-B5
NW SKYLINE BLVD
MULTNOMAH CO OR 192-A5
PORTLAND OR 192-B7
SW SKYLINE BLVD
MULTNOMAH CO OR 199-B1
MULTNOMAH CO OR 312-A6
PORTLAND OR 199-B1
PORTLAND OR 312-A6
SKYLINE DR
COLUMBIA CO OR 122-B3
WENATCHEE WA 238-D4
West Wenatchee WA 238-D4
NW SKYLINE DR
TOLEDO OR 206-C2
SKYLINE RD
BAKER CO OR 138-A1
CANYON CO ID 147-B1
WASCO CO OR 196-C7
SKYLINE RD S
MARION CO OR 207-C1
MARION CO OR 324-D8
SALEM OR 324-E6
SKYLINE WY
ANACORTES WA 259-A4

SKYLINERS RD
BEND OR 332-A7
DESCHUTES CO OR 217-A3
SLAB CREEK RD
TILLAMOOK CO OR 203-B2
SLACK CANYON RD SW
DOUGLAS CO WA 112-B2
SLATE CREEK RD
IDAHO CO ID 131-C1
SLATER RD
FERNDALE WA 158-C6
WHATCOM CO WA 158-B6
SLAVENS WY
COLUMBIA CO OR 192-A3
SLEATER KINNEY RD NE
LACEY WA 297-F3
OLYMPIA WA 297-F3
THURSTON CO WA 297-F3
SLEATER KINNEY RD SE
LACEY WA 297-F8
OLYMPIA WA 297-F8
SLEEPER RD
ISLAND CO WA 167-C2
SLEEPY HOLLOW LP
JOSEPHINE CO OR 229-A7
SLEEPY HOLLOW RD
CHELAN CO WA 238-C3
KLICKITAT CO WA 196-A3
SLEEPY HOLLOW RD NE
MARION CO OR 205-B1
N SLICK ROCK CREEK RD
LINCOLN CO OR 203-C4
SLIDE CREEK RD
COWLITZ CO WA 117-B3
SLIVA LN
MASON CO OR 180-D3
E SLOPE RD
LINCOLN CO OR 206-C4
TOLEDO OR 206-C4
E SLOPE RD SE
TOLEDO OR 206-C4
NE SLOPE ST
BEND OR 334-G2
SLUSSER RD NW
DOUGLAS CO WA 112-B2
DOUGLAS CO WA 236-C6
SMILEY LN
VALLEY CO ID 251-C7
SMITH AV
DISTRICT OF BURNABY BC 156-C5
DISTRICT OF BURNABY BC 255-G14
KOOTENAI CO ID 247-C1
SMITH LN
JEFFERSON CO OR 212-D1
SMITH RD
CLACKAMAS CO OR 199-A5
COLUMBIA CO OR 192-A1
HARRAH WA 119-C2
KLICKITAT CO WA 120-B3
POLK CO OR 207-A1
WALLA WALLA CO WA 121-C3
WALLA WALLA CO WA 122-A3
YAMHILL CO OR 199-A5
E SMITH RD
WHATCOM CO WA 102-B1
WHATCOM CO WA 158-D6
W SMITH RD
FERNDALE WA 158-D6
WHATCOM CO WA 158-D6
SMITH ST
HARRISBURG OR 210-A5
SEATTLE WA 277-H1
E SMITH ST Rt#-516
KENT WA 175-C7
W SMITH ST
KENT WA 175-B7
SMITH ANDERSON RD
PACIFIC WA 183-B5
SMITH CANYON RD
FRANKLIN CO WA 121-B2
SMITH COLUMBIA CITY RD
COLUMBIA CO OR 192-A1
SMITH CREEK RD
PACIFIC WA 117-A1
SMITHE ST
VANCOUVER BC 254-G10
SMITHFIELD RD
POLK CO OR 204-A5
SMITH HOLLOW RD
COLUMBIA CO OR 122-A2
SMITH LAKE RD
DOUGLAS CO OR 237-B2
NE SMITH POINT RD
MULTNOMAH CO OR 194-B7
MULTNOMAH CO OR 201-B1
SMITH RIVER RD
DOUGLAS CO OR 132-C3
DOUGLAS CO OR 133-A3
DOUGLAS CO OR 141-A1
DOUGLAS CO OR 214-D7
SMITH ROCK WY
DESCHUTES CO OR 212-D4
DESCHUTES CO OR 213-A4
SMITHSON RD
KITTITAS CO WA 241-A3
SMITH SPRINGS RD
PRESCOTT WA 121-C2
WALLA WALLA CO WA 121-C2
SMOCK RD
WASCO CO OR 127-A3
SMOKEHOUSE RD
WHATCOM CO WA 160-C1
SMOKEY POINT BLVD
ARLINGTON WA 168-C5
MARYSVILLE WA 168-C5
SNOHOMISH CO WA 168-C5
SMOKEY VALLEY RD
LEWIS CO WA 187-C5
SMOKY BUTTE DR
DESCHUTES CO OR 212-B7
SMOOTHING IRON RD
ASOTIN CO WA 122-C3
SMUGGLERS COVE RD
ISLAND CO WA 167-C7
ISLAND CO WA 170-C1
S SMUGGLERS COVE RD
ISLAND CO WA 167-C7
S SMYTHE RD
SPOKANE CO WA 246-B7
SNAG CREEK TR
SKAMANIA CO WA 194-C4
SNAKE CREEK RD
JACKSON CO OR 230-A3
SNAKE RIVER AV
LEWISTON ID 250-B5
SNAKE RIVER RD
ASOTIN WA 250-B6
ASOTIN WA 123-A3
ASOTIN WA 250-B6

SNAKE RIVER RD
BAKER CO OR 138-C2
BAKER CO OR 139-A1
HUNTINGTON OR 138-C2
N SNAKE RIVER RD
BAKER CO OR 139-A1
RICHLAND OR 139-A1
SNEE-OOSH RD
Shelter Bay WA 167-D1
SKAGIT CO WA 160-D7
SKAGIT CO WA 167-D1
Snee Oosh WA 167-D1
Swinomish Village WA 167-D1
SNEIDER-BARKS RD
SKAMANIA CO WA 194-A7
SNELLSTROM BUSH
PIERCE CO WA 182-A6
SNIPES RD
BENTON CO WA 120-B2
SNIVELY GULCH RD
MALHEUR CO OR 147-A1
SNODGRASS RD
KITTITAS CO WA 241-C5
SNOHOMISH AV
SNOHOMISH CO WA 171-D5
SNOQUALMIE PKWY
KING CO WA 176-B4
SNOQUALMIE WA 176-C4
W SNOQUALMIE VALLEY RD
KING CO WA 110-C1
W SNOQUALMIE VALLEY RD NE
KING CO WA 110-C1
KING CO WA 176-A1
SNOW RD
WHITMAN CO WA 249-C6
SNOWBIRD RD
DOUGLAS CO OR 222-B5
SNOW CREEK RD
DESCHUTES CO OR 212-A7
DESCHUTES CO OR 216-D1
DESCHUTES CO OR 217-A1
DOUGLAS CO OR 141-B3
SNOWDEN RD
KLICKITAT CO WA 196-A3
SNOWDEN HOVEY GULCH RD
SISKIYOU CO CA 150-A3
SNOWDEN WHITE SALMON RD
KLICKITAT CO WA 195-D4
SNUFFIN RD
CLACKAMAS CO OR 200-C6
SOAP CREEK RD
BENTON CO OR 207-A4
SOAP HILL RD
UMATILLA CO OR 129-B3
SODA PEAK TR
SKAMANIA CO WA 194-B1
SODA SPRINGS RD
KLICKITAT CO WA 196-D1
SODAVILLE RD
LINN CO OR 133-C1
SODAVILLE OR 133-C1
SODAVILLE-WATERLOO DR
LINN CO OR 133-C1
SODAVILLE OR 133-C2
SOLAR LN
YAKIMA CO WA 243-D6
SOLDIER CREEK RD
JOSEPHINE CO OR 229-B4
MALHEUR CO OR 147-A3
SOLDIERS CANYON RD
NEZ PERCE CO ID 250-D4
SOLDIERS MEADOW RD
NEZ PERCE CO ID 123-A3
SOL DUC VALLEY RD
CLALLAM CO WA 163-B7
SOLE RD
YAKIMA CO WA 243-B5
SOLKI RD
Central Park WA 178-C7
SOMMER CAMP RD
OWYHEE CO ID 147-B1
SOMMERS RD
WHITMAN CO WA 122-B1
SOMMERVILLE RD
LEWIS CO WA 187-C1
SOOKE RD
CITY OF COLWOOD BC 159-A7
DISTRICT OF LANGFORD BC 159-A7
SOOKE RD Rt#-14
BRITISH COLUMBIA BC 101-A2
BRITISH COLUMBIA BC 159-A7
DISTRICT OF LANGFORD BC 159-A7
DISTRICT OF METCHOSIN BC 159-A7
SOPER HILL RD
SNOHOMISH CO WA 171-D1
SORENSON RD
CLARK CO WA 192-D1
SOUNDVIEW DR
GIG HARBOR WA 181-C1
PIERCE CO WA 181-C1
W SOUTH AV
CHEWELAH WA 106-B3
STEVENS CO WA 106-B3
SOUTH DR
PIERCE CO WA 181-A4
SOUTH RD
KOOTENAI CO ID 245-C1
WASHINGTON CO OR 198-A3
YAMHILL CO OR 198-A3
SOUTH ST Rt#-293
ANTELOPE OR 127-C3
SOUTH BANK RD
DOUGLAS CO OR 221-D3
GRAYS HARBOR CO WA 178-D7
GRAYS HARBOR CO WA 179-B7
SOUTH BANK RD Rt#-107
GRAYS HARBOR CO WA 178-D7
W SOUTH BANK RD
SPOKANE CO WA 114-B1
SOUTH BANK CHETCO RIVER RD
CURRY CO OR 232-D6
SOUTH BANK MAPLETON WEST RD
LANE CO OR 214-D2
SOUTH BAY RD
WHATCOM CO WA 161-B2
SOUTH BAY RD NE
THURSTON CO WA 138-C1
THURSTON CO WA 139-A1
SOUTHBAY RD
LINCOLN CO OR 206-B5
SOUTH BEND PALIX RD
PACIFIC CO WA 183-D7
SOUTHBOROUGH DR
DIST OF WEST VANCOUVER BC 156-B2
DIST OF WEST VANCOUVER BC 254-F1
SOUTHCENTER BLVD
TUKWILA WA 288-D4

SOUTHCENTER BLVD
TUKWILA WA 289-E4
SOUTHCENTER PKWY
TUKWILA WA 289-G6
TUKWILA WA 291-G1
SOUTH CRANE CREEK RD
WASHINGTON CO ID 139-B2
SOUTHEAST AV U.S.-30
NEW PLYMOUTH ID 139-B3
PAYETTE CO ID 139-B3
SOUTHEAST BLVD
EPHRATA WA 112-C3
E SOUTHEAST BLVD
SPOKANE WA 349-D12
S SOUTHEAST BLVD
SPOKANE WA 349-B11
SOUTH END RD
ADAMS CO ID 251-A4
CLACKAMAS CO OR 199-C5
SOUTHERN RD
MALHEUR CO OR 217-A1
SOUTH FORK RD
BENTON CO OR 133-A2
DEL NORTE CO CA 148-B3
GRANT CO OR 136-C2
LANE CO OR 134-B3
TILLAMOOK CO OR 125-A2
SOUTH FORK BURNT RIVER RD
BAKER CO OR 138-A2
SOUTH FORK JOHN DAY RD
GRANT CO OR 136-C2
SOUTH FORK LITTLE BUTTE RD
JACKSON CO OR 150-A1
SOUTH FORK MILL CREEK RD
STEVENS CO WA 106-B2
SOUTH FRASER WY
DISTRICT OF ABBOTSFORD BC 102-B1
DISTRICT OF MATSQUI BC 102-B1
SOUTHGATE PL
PENDLETON OR 129-B1
UMATILLA CO OR 129-B1
SW SOUTHGATE PL
UMATILLA CO OR 129-B1
SOUTHGATE ST
CITY OF VICTORIA BC 256-G10
SOUTH HILL ST
ALBANY OR 326-E11
SOUTH JUNCTION RD
WASCO CO OR 208-C1
SOUTH PASS RD
WHATCOM CO WA 102-B1
SOUTH POST RD
CLATSOP CO OR 188-B3
SOUTH PRAIRIE RD
TILLAMOOK CO OR 197-C3
SOUTH PRAIRIE RD E
BONNEY LAKE WA 182-C4
PIERCE CO WA 182-C4
SOUTH PRAIRIE WA 182-C4
SOUTH PRAIRIE CARBON RIVER RD
PIERCE CO WA 182-C5
SOUTH PRAIRIE-CONNELL RD
PIERCE CO WA 182-D4
SOUTH ROCK CREEK RD
BAKER CO OR 130-A3
SOUTH SHORE BLVD
LAKE OSWEGO OR 199-C4
LAKE OSWEGO OR 320-A7
LAKE OSWEGO OR 321-E7
SOUTH SHORE RD
CLALLAM CO WA 164-C6
GRAYS HARBOR CO WA 109-A2
JEFFERSON CO WA 109-A2
SOUTHSIDE BLVD
CANYON CO ID 147-C1
SOUTH SIDE RD
DOUGLAS CO OR 218-D1
DOUGLAS CO OR 221-C1
JOSEPHINE CO OR 149-A2
JOSEPHINE CO OR 229-B7
SOUTH SLOUGH RD
LANE CO OR 214-B4
SOUTH SUMAS RD
CITY OF CHILLIWACK BC 94-C3
SOUTH TOUTLE RD
COWLITZ CO WA 118-A2
SOUTH UNION RD
GRAYS HARBOR CO WA 179-C7
SOUTH VALLEY RD
WASCO CO OR 127-A2
SOUTHWEST AV
NEW PLYMOUTH ID 139-B3
SOUTHWEST BLVD
COOS BAY OR 333-F13
COOS CO OR 333-F13
SOUTHWOOD LN
EUGENE OR 330-B5
SOVERN LN
LANE CO OR 210-A6
SPADES RD
BONNER CO ID 244-A3
SPANAWAY LOOP RD S
PIERCE CO WA 181-D4
SPANAWAY-MCKENNA HWY Rt#-507
PIERCE CO WA 118-A1
PIERCE CO WA 181-C7
ROY WA 181-C7
W SPANGLE RD
CHENEY WA 246-A7
SPOKANE CO WA 246-A7
S SPANGLE CREEK RD
SPOKANE CO WA 246-C7
S SPANGLER RD
CLACKAMAS CO OR 199-D6
E SPANGLE WAVERLY RD
SPOKANE CO WA 114-C2
SPARROW DR
JEFFERSON CO OR 212-C2
SE SPARROW ST
MILWAUKIE OR 321-J4
SPARROW PARK RD
DOUGLAS CO OR 214-A7
SPARTA RD
BAKER CO OR 138-C1
BAKER CO OR 139-A1
SPAULDING AV
GRANTS PASS OR 335-H9
JOSEPHINE CO OR 335-H9
SPEAKER RD
JOSEPHINE CO OR 225-C7
SPEARE CANYON RD
UMATILLA CO OR 129-A1
SPENCER RD
LEWIS CO WA 187-D3

SPENCER CREEK RD
COWLITZ CO WA 189-C5
DOUGLAS CO WA 214-D6
LANE CO OR 133-B3
LANE CO OR 215-A3
LANE CO OR 329-A14
SPENCER LAKE RD
MASON CO WA 180-B2
SPENCER WELLS RD
DESCHUTES CO OR 135-B3
SPEOS RD
PAYETTE CO ID 139-A3
SPERLING AV
DISTRICT OF BURNABY BC 156-D4
SPERRY RD
SAN JUAN CO WA 160-A6
SPEYERS RD
SELAH WA 243-B5
YAKIMA CO WA 243-B5
SPICER DR
ALBANY OR 326-H9
LINN CO OR 133-C1
LINN CO OR 207-D5
LINN CO OR 326-H9
SPINK LN
VALLEY CO ID 251-D7
SPIRIT LAKE HWY Rt#-504
CASTLE ROCK WA 187-C7
COWLITZ CO WA 118-A2
COWLITZ CO WA 187-C7
SPIRIT LAKE RD
BONNER CO ID 107-A3
KOOTENAI CO ID 115-A1
SPOFFORD RD
UMATILLA CO OR 121-C3
N SPOKANE ST
KOOTENAI CO ID 353-H5
POST FALLS ID 353-H5
S SPOKANE ST
KOOTENAI CO ID 353-H9
POST FALLS ID 353-H8
SEATTLE WA 281-J3
SEATTLE WA 282-A3
SW SPOKANE ST
SEATTLE WA 281-G3
SPOKANE WY
GRAND COULEE WA 237-C3
GRANT CO WA 237-C3
N SPOKANE BRIDGE RD
SPOKANE CO WA 352-H10
W SPOKANE FALLS BLVD
SPOKANE WA 348-J9
SPOKANE WA 349-A9
W SPOKANE FALLS BLVD U.S.-2
SPOKANE WA 349-A9
SPOONER RD
LEWIS CO WA 184-A7
SPORTSMAN CLUB RD NE
KITSAP CO WA 174-B1
KITSAP CO WA 271-J2
SPORTSMANS ST
OCEAN SHORES WA 298-B6
S SPOTTED RD
SPOKANE CO WA 246-A5
SPOKANE CO WA 348-A13
SPOUT CREEK RD
LINCOLN CO OR 133-A1
SPRAGUE AV
WESTPORT WA 298-G13
E SPRAGUE AV
SPOKANE WA 349-B9
SPOKANE VALLEY WA 351-G8
SPOKANE VALLEY WA 349-H9
SPOKANE VALLEY WA 350-H8
SPOKANE VALLEY WA 351-A8
S SPRAGUE AV
TACOMA WA 293-E6
W SPRAGUE AV
SPOKANE WA 348-J9
SPOKANE WA 349-A9
S SPRAGUE RD
CLACKAMAS CO OR 200-A5
SPRAGUE ST
WILSON CREEK WA 113-A2
E SPRAGUE AVE ACCESS 1
SPOKANE WA 349-C9
E SPRAGUE AVE ACCESS 3
SPOKANE WA 349-C9
SPRAGUE RIVER RD
KLAMATH CO OR 150-C1
KLAMATH CO OR 151-A1
KLAMATH CO OR 231-A1
SPRAUER RD NW
DOUGLAS CO WA 112-B1
SPRENGER RD
LATAH CO ID 249-B7
SPRING ST
IONE OR 128-B2
KLAMATH FALLS OR 338-E7
KLICKITAT CO WA 195-D4
MAUPIN OR 127-B3
MEDFORD OR 336-E10
WHITE SALMON WA 195-D4
N SPRING ST
KLAMATH FALLS OR 338-E7
SE SPRING ST
PULLMAN WA 249-B5
W SPRING ST
WALDPORT OR 328-A3
SPRING BROOK RD
DOUGLAS CO OR 225-C1
SPRINGBROOK RD
MEDFORD OR 336-F7
N SPRINGBROOK RD
NEWBERG OR 198-D5
YAMHILL CO OR 198-D5
S SPRINGBROOK RD
NEWBERG OR 198-D6
YAMHILL CO OR 198-D6
SPRING COULEE RD
OKANOGAN CO WA 104-C2
SPRING CREEK RD
UNION CO OR 129-C2
SPRING CREEK RD Rt#-231
LINCOLN CO WA 114-A1
N SPRING CREEK RD
BONNER CO ID 244-D3
SPRINGDALE-HUNTERS RD
SPRINGDALE WA 106-A3
STEVENS CO WA 105-C3
STEVENS CO WA 106-A3
STEVENS CO WA 114-A1
SPRINGER RD
JEFFERSON CO OR 213-A4
SPRINGHILL DR
ALBANY OR 326-C6
SPRINGHILL RD
ALBANY OR 326-C2

STREET City State	Page-Grid
SPRINGHILL RD	
BENTON CO OR	207-B3
BENTON CO OR	326-C2
SW SPRING HILL RD	
WASHINGTON CO OR	198-B3
SPRING HOLLOW RD	
UMATILLA CO OR	129-C1
SPRING LAKE RD	
KLAMATH CO OR	235-C5
SPRINGRIDGE RD NE	
KITSAP CO WA	271-F2
SPRING RIVER RD	
DESCHUTES CO OR	217-A5
SPRINGS RD	
JEFFERSON CO OR	211-D2
SPRINGSTON RD	
KOOTENAI CO ID	248-B4
SPRING VALLEY RD	
WASHINGTON CO OR	114-C3
E SPRING VALLEY RD	
SPOKANE CO WA	114-C3
SPRING VALLEY RD NW	
POLK CO OR	204-C4
NW SPRINGVILLE RD	
WASHINGTON CO OR	192-A7
SPRINGWATER AV	
WENATCHEE WA	238-D4
West Wenatchee WA	238-D4
SPRINGWATER RD	
CLACKAMAS CO OR	200-B6
S SPRINGWATER RD	
CLACKAMAS CO OR	200-A4
SPROTT ST	
DISTRICT OF BURNABY BC	156-D5
SPROUT RD	
RICHLAND WA	340-G8
NW SPRUCE	
DESCHUTES CO OR	212-D5
NW SPRUCE AV	
DESCHUTES CO OR	212-C5
SW SPRUCE RD	
KITSAP CO WA	174-B6
SPRUCE ST	
CANNON BEACH OR	188-B7
MYRTLE POINT OR	140-B2
PACIFIC WA	186-A5
PORT TOWNSEND WA	263-G2
N SPRUCE ST	
BURLINGTON WA	260-D4
LA GRANDE OR	130-A2
S SPRUCE ST	
BURLINGTON WA	260-D5
SPRUCE ST E Rt#-100	
ILWACO WA	186-A6
SPRUCE ST W Rt#-100	
ILWACO WA	186-A6
SPRUCE TRAIL RD	
CLALLAM CO WA	164-B6
SPURAWAY DR	
COQUITLAM BC	157-A4
SQUAW RD	
WHITMAN CO WA	114-B3
SQUAWBACK RIDGE RD	
JEFFERSON CO OR	135-A1
JEFFERSON CO OR	211-D1
SQUAW BUTTE RD	
HARNEY CO OR	144-C1
SQUAW CREEK DR	
DESCHUTES CO OR	212-A4
SQUAW CREEK RD	
ADAMS CO ID	252-B7
DOUGLAS CO OR	221-A7
TILLAMOOK CO OR	203-C2
S SQUAW CREEK RD	
SPOKANE CO WA	114-B3
SW SQUAW CREEK RD	
JEFFERSON CO OR	212-A2
SQUAW FLAT RD	
KLAMATH CO OR	151-A2
SW SQUAW FLAT RD	
JEFFERSON CO OR	212-B1
SW SQUAW GULCH RD	
JEFFERSON CO OR	212-A2
SQUAW MOUNTAIN RD	
CLACKAMAS CO OR	200-C6
CLACKAMAS CO OR	201-A7
SE SQUAW MOUNTAIN RD	
CLACKAMAS CO OR	200-D7
SQUAW VALLEY RD	
CURRY CO OR	228-B3
SQUEEDUNK RD	
TILLAMOOK CO OR	197-B1
SQUILCHUCK RD	
CHELAN CO WA	238-D5
STACKPOLE RD Rt#-103	
PACIFIC WA	183-B7
PACIFIC WA	186-A1
NE STADIUM WY	
PULLMAN WA	249-B5
NW STADIUM WY	
PULLMAN WA	249-B5
S STADIUM WY	
TACOMA WA	293-G3
SE STADIUM WY	
PULLMAN WA	249-B5
STADSVOLD RD	
WHATCOM CO WA	158-B3
STAFFORD AV Rt#-903	
CLE ELUM WA	240-B2
STAFFORD RD	
CLACKAMAS CO OR	199-B5
LAKE OSWEGO OR	199-B5
LAKE OSWEGO OR	321-E7
SW STAFFORD RD	
CLACKAMAS CO OR	199-C4
STAGE RD	
COOS CO OR	218-B5
S STAGE RD	
JACKSON CO OR	234-A2
JACKSONVILLE OR	234-A2
STAGE RD S	
JACKSONVILLE OR	149-B2
JACKSONVILLE OR	234-A1
STAGECOACH RD	
LANE CO OR	133-A3
STAG HOLLOW RD	
YAMHILL CO OR	198-B5
STAHANCYK LN	
CROOK CO OR	213-C4
STAINWOOD ST	
BENTON CO OR	327-H4
CORVALLIS OR	327-H4
STALEY RD	
WHITMAN CO WA	249-B6
W STALEY RD	
SPOKANE CO WA	114-B1
STAMPEDE BLVD NW	
KITSAP CO WA	270-F3

STREET City State	Page-Grid
STAMPER RD	
ELMA WA	179-B7
GRAYS HARBOR CO WA	179-B7
N STANDARD ST	
SPOKANE WA	347-A13
STANDLEY LN	
UNION CO OR	130-A2
STANFIELD MEADOWS RD	
UMATILLA CO OR	129-A1
STANKEY RD	
COWLITZ CO WA	187-D7
STANLEY AV S	
SEATTLE WA	282-B7
E STANLEY ST Rt#-92	
GRANITE FALLS WA	102-C3
W STANLEY ST Rt#-92	
GRANITE FALLS WA	102-C3
STANTON BLVD	
MALHEUR CO OR	139-A3
STANTON PARK RD Rt#-99	
DOUGLAS CO OR	225-C3
STANWOOD-BRYANT RD	
SNOHOMISH CO WA	168-C4
STAPLETON RD	
POLK CO OR	207-B1
STAR BLVD Rt#-44	
CANYON CO ID	147-B1
MIDDLETON ID	147-B1
STARBIRD RD	
SKAGIT CO WA	168-B2
N STARK AV	
DOUGLAS CO WA	239-A4
SE STARK ST	
GRESHAM OR	200-A1
MULTNOMAH CO WA	200-B1
PORTLAND OR	200-A1
PORTLAND OR	313-H6
PORTLAND OR	314-B6
PORTLAND OR	315-J6
TROUTDALE OR	200-B1
SW STARK ST	
PORTLAND OR	313-E5
STAR LAKE RD	
MASON CO OR	179-C4
N STARR RD	
Otis Orchards WA	352-E6
SPOKANE CO WA	352-E5
S STARR RD	
SPOKANE CO WA	247-B6
STARR ST	
MARION CO OR	133-C1
SUBLIMITY OR	133-C1
STAR RANCH RD	
MALHEUR CO OR	146-A2
STARR CREEK RD	
LINCOLN CO OR	209-A3
SE STARR QUARRY RD	
YAMHILL CO OR	204-C1
STARVEOUT CREEK RD	
DOUGLAS CO OR	225-D6
STATE AV	
COLUMBIA CO OR	125-B1
MARYSVILLE WA	168-C7
MARYSVILLE WA	171-C1
OLYMPIA WA	296-J5
OLYMPIA WA	297-A5
SNOHOMISH CO WA	168-C7
VERNONIA OR	125-B1
STATE AV Rt#-529	
MARYSVILLE WA	171-C1
STATE AV U.S.-30	
HOOD RIVER OR	195-D5
HOOD RIVER OR	195-D5
N STATE AV Rt#-41	
NEWPORT ID	106-C3
NW STATE AV	
CHEHALIS WA	299-D11
S STATE AV Rt#-41	
NEWPORT WA	106-C3
NEWPORT WA	106-C3
STATE RD	
WASCO CO OR	127-B2
WASCO CO OR	196-A5
STATE ST	
Four Corners OR	204-D6
Four Corners OR	323-B14
Four Corners OR	325-E1
MARION CO OR	205-A6
MARION CO OR	325-H1
OAKVILLE WA	117-B1
SALEM OR	322-H13
SALEM OR	323-B14
SALEM OR	325-E1
SEDRO-WOOLLEY WA	161-C6
SKAGIT CO WA	161-C6
VANCOUVER WA	306-D7
STATE ST Rt#-82	
LOSTINE OR	130-C2
STATE ST U.S.-95	
WEISER ID	139-A2
E STATE ST	
SEDRO-WOOLLEY WA	161-C6
E STATE ST Rt#-44	
ADA CO ID	253-B1
EAGLE ID	253-B1
N STATE ST	
BELLINGHAM WA	258-E6
N STATE ST Rt#-43	
CLACKAMAS CO OR	321-G6
LAKE OSWEGO OR	321-G6
NE STATE ST Rt#-99	
DOUGLAS CO OR	221-C1
SUTHERLIN OR	221-C1
NW STATE ST	
PULLMAN WA	249-B5
S STATE ST	
BELLINGHAM WA	258-B9
TACOMA WA	293-E7
S STATE ST Rt#-43	
LAKE OSWEGO OR	321-G6
W STATE ST	
BOISE ID	253-C2
GARDEN CITY ID	253-C2
SEDRO-WOOLLEY WA	161-C6
W STATE ST Rt#-44	
ADA CO ID	147-C1
ADA CO ID	253-A1
CANYON CO ID	147-B1
EAGLE ID	253-A1
GARDEN CITY ID	253-A1
STAR ID	147-C1
STATE FARM RD	
POLK CO OR	204-C6
STATE FOREST RD	
CLALLAM CO WA	165-A6

STREET City State	Page-Grid
STATE LINE RD	
CANYON CO ID	147-A1
KLAMATH CO OR	151-A3
MALHEUR CO OR	147-A1
MODOC CO CA	151-A3
OWYHEE CO ID	155-C2
STATE LINE RD Rt#-161	
SISKIYOU CO CA	150-C3
SISKIYOU CO CA	151-A3
STATE PARK ST	
MCCALL ID	251-D4
VALLEY CO ID	251-D4
STATE TOLL FERRY	
SAN JUAN CO WA	160-B5
SKAGIT CO WA	160-B5
STAUCH RD	
KLAMATH CO OR	196-A2
NE STAUFFER RD	
CLARK CO WA	193-C6
STAUFFER RD NE	
MARION CO OR	205-C1
STAVE LAKE RD	
BRITISH COLUMBIA BC	94-B3
STAVE LAKE ST	
DISTRICT OF MISSION BC	94-B3
NW STAVIS BAY RD	
KITSAP CO WA	173-D2
STAYMAN RD	
CHELAN CO WA	236-B4
STAYTE RD	
CITY OF SURREY BC	158-B2
CITY OF WHITE ROCK BC	158-B2
W STAYTON	
MARION CO OR	133-C1
STAYTON RD	
MARION CO OR	133-C1
STAYTON OR	133-C1
W STAYTON RD	
AUMSVILLE OR	133-C1
MARION CO OR	133-C1
STAYTON RD SE	
MARION CO OR	133-C1
STAYTON-SCIO RD	
LINN CO OR	133-C1
MARION CO OR	133-C1
STAYTON OR	133-C1
STEAMBOAT CREEK RD	
DOUGLAS CO OR	142-A1
DOUGLAS CO OR	222-A2
STEAMBOAT ISLAND RD NW	
THURSTON CO WA	180-B5
STEARNS LN	
DOUGLAS CO OR	219-A7
DOUGLAS CO OR	221-C1
STEARNS RD	
CROOK CO OR	135-B3
STECKLEY RD	
LINN CO OR	207-D7
STEDMAN RD SE	
THURSTON CO WA	184-D1
STEELE RD	
WASCO CO OR	127-B2
WASCO CO OR	196-C7
S STEELE ST	
PIERCE CO WA	181-D4
TACOMA WA	181-D4
TACOMA WA	294-E2
STEELE ST S	
LAKEWOOD WA	181-D4
PIERCE CO WA	181-D4
STEELHEAD CT	
JEFFERSON CO OR	212-C2
STEELHEAD RD	
JEFFERSON CO OR	212-C2
SW STEELHEAD FALLS DR	
DESCHUTES CO OR	212-C2
JEFFERSON CO OR	212-C2
STEELMAN RD	
COLUMBIA CO OR	192-A4
STEENS HWY Rt#-78	
HARNEY CO OR	145-B1
HARNEY CO OR	146-A2
MALHEUR CO OR	146-B3
STEENS MOUNTAIN LOOP RD	
HARNEY CO OR	153-B1
STEFFENSEN RD	
PIERCE CO WA	181-A4
STEFFY LN	
CROOK CO OR	213-C6
STEGEMAN RD	
KLICKITAT CO WA	120-A3
STEHEKIN VALLEY RD	
CHELAN CO WA	103-B2
STEILACOOM BLVD	
LAKEWOOD WA	181-C4
STEILACOOM WA	181-C4
STEILACOOM BLVD SW	
LAKEWOOD WA	181-C4
STEILACOOM RD SE	
THURSTON CO WA	181-A6
STEILACOOM-ANDERSON ISLAND FRY	
STEILACOOM WA	181-B4
STEILACOOM-DUPONT RD SW	
PIERCE CO WA	181-B5
STEILACOOM-KETRON ISLAND FERRY	
PIERCE CO WA	181-B4
STEILACOOM WA	181-B4
STEIN RD	
WHATCOM CO WA	158-C4
S STEIN RD	
YAKIMA CO WA	243-A7
STEINER RD	
TILLAMOOK CO OR	197-C3
WHITMAN CO WA	249-A3
S STEINER RD	
CLACKAMAS CO OR	200-A6
STEIWER RD SE	
MARION CO OR	207-D2
STELLA RD	
COWLITZ CO WA	189-A2
STELLYS CROSS RD	
DIST OF CENTRAL SAANICH BC	159-B4
STEMILT CREEK RD	
CHELAN CO WA	239-A5
STEMILT LOOP RD	
CHELAN CO WA	238-D6
CHELAN CO WA	239-A7
STENKAMP RD	
DESCHUTES CO OR	217-D2
S STENTZ RD	
SPOKANE CO WA	246-C7
STEPHEN RD	
GRAYS HARBOR CO WA	179-A6
NE STEPHENS ST Rt#-99	
ROSEBURG OR	334-F5

STREET City State	Page-Grid
SE STEPHENS ST Rt#-99	
ROSEBURG OR	334-G7
SE STEPHENS ST Rt#-138	
ROSEBURG OR	334-F8
SW STEPHENSON ST	
LAKE OSWEGO OR	320-C3
PORTLAND OR	320-C3
STEPIEN RD	
WASHINGTON CO OR	198-A1
STEPTOE AV Rt#-27	
OAKESDALE WA	114-C3
STEPTOE ST	
COLTON WA	250-A1
STEPTOE CANYON RD	
WHITMAN CO WA	122-C2
WHITMAN CO WA	250-A2
STERLING RD	
SEDRO-WOOLLEY WA	260-J3
SKAGIT CO WA	260-J3
STERLING CREEK RD	
JACKSON CO OR	149-B2
JACKSON CO OR	234-A4
STEUBEN ST Rt#-14	
BINGEN WA	195-D5
STEVENS DR	
BENTON CO WA	340-F5
DIST OF WEST VANCOUVER BC	156-B2
DIST OF WEST VANCOUVER BC	254-E2
RICHLAND WA	340-F6
RICHLAND WA	341-F1
STEVENS RD	
BEND OR	217-C3
DESCHUTES CO OR	217-C3
STEVENS RD SE	
KITSAP CO WA	174-B6
STEVENS ST	
CHEWELAH WA	106-B3
MEDFORD OR	336-D11
STEVENS CO WA	106-B3
STEVENS ST Rt#-285	
WENATCHEE WA	239-A4
N STEVENS ST	
TACOMA WA	292-B1
S STEVENS ST	
SPOKANE WA	348-J9
TACOMA WA	292-B5
STEVENS CANYON RD	
DESCHUTES CO OR	211-D4
DESCHUTES CO OR	212-A3
LEWIS CO WA	185-C5
S STEVENS CREEK RD	
DESCHUTES CO OR	246-D6
STEVENSON RD	
ANACORTES WA	160-D6
POLK CO WA	204-B4
SKAGIT CO WA	160-D6
N STEVENSON RD	
Otis Orchards WA	352-D10
STEVENSON RIDGE TR	
CARSON WA	194-D4
SKAMANIA CO WA	194-D4
STEVENS PASS HWY U.S.-2	
GOLD BAR WA	110-C1
KING CO WA	111-B1
MONROE WA	110-C1
SNOHOMISH WA	171-D3
SNOHOMISH CO WA	110-C1
SNOHOMISH CO WA	111-A1
SNOHOMISH CO WA	171-D3
SULTAN WA	110-C1
NE STEVENS PASS HWY U.S.-2	
KING CO WA	111-A1
SKYKOMISH WA	111-A1
SNOHOMISH CO WA	111-A1
STEVENS PASS RD U.S.-2	
SNOHOMISH CO WA	171-D2
STEVESTON HWY	
CITY OF RICHMOND BC	156-B7
STEWARDSON WY	
NEW WESTMINSTER BC	156-D5
STEWART AV	
PIERCE CO WA	182-A3
PUYALLUP WA	182-A3
E STEWART AV	
MEDFORD OR	336-E14
W STEWART AV	
JACKSON CO OR	234-A1
JACKSON CO OR	336-B14
MEDFORD OR	336-B14
PUYALLUP WA	182-B3
STEWART LN	
DOUGLAS CO OR	239-B2
STEWART PKWY	
ROSEBURG OR	334-E4
NE STEWART PKWY	
ROSEBURG OR	334-F5
NW STEWART PKWY	
ROSEBURG OR	334-D3
STEWART RD	
COOS CO OR	224-B1
JOSEPHINE CO OR	229-A5
MOUNT VERNON WA	260-C9
S STEWART RD	
ADA CO ID	253-B5
STEWART RD SE	
PACIFIC WA	181-B5
STEWART RD SW	
INDEPENDENCE OR	204-B7
STEWART ST	
SEATTLE WA	277-J5
SEATTLE WA	278-A4
STEWART CREEK RD	
COLUMBIA CO OR	189-A3
UMATILLA CO OR	129-C2
STIDMAN	
PIERCE CO WA	182-B7
S STILLAGUAMISH AV	
ARLINGTON WA	168-D5
STILL CREEK RD	
CLACKAMAS CO OR	201-D6
CLACKAMAS CO OR	202-A6
STILLMAN RD	
CROOK CO OR	213-B6
STILLWATER TKTR	
COWLITZ CO WA	187-B6
STIMSON RD	
SNOHOMISH CO WA	168-C6
STINEHILL RD	
CHELAN CO WA	238-B2
STINSON AV	
GIG HARBOR WA	181-C1
STIRLING DR	
DESCHUTES CO OR	217-D4
STITZEL RD	
MALHEUR CO OR	146-C1
STOCK DRIVE RD	
LAKE CO OR	152-A2

STREET City State	Page-Grid
SE STOCKHOFF RD	
YAMHILL CO OR	204-C1
STOCKSHOW RD	
EVERETT WA	171-C4
STOCKYARD RD	
KLICKITAT CO WA	127-C1
STOLTE CANYON RD	
NEZ PERCE CO ID	123-B2
STOLTZ HILL RD	
Crowfoot OR	133-C1
LEBANON OR	133-C1
LINN CO OR	133-C1
STONE DR NW	
PIERCE CO WA	181-C2
STONE RD	
COLUMBIA CO OR	192-A2
TILLAMOOK CO OR	197-D3
YAMHILL CO OR	198-C5
STONE WY N	
SEATTLE WA	273-J7
STONE BREAKER LN	
VALLEY CO OR	252-D4
STONE CABIN RD	
WHEELER CO OR	128-A3
STONECIPHER RD	
WALLA WALLA CO WA	122-A3
STONECREST RD	
GRANT CO WA	242-B1
STONER	
PIERCE CO WA	182-B7
STOREY BLVD	
EUGENE OR	329-H10
N STORIE ST	
WALLOWA OR	130-C1
STORMER RD	
CLACKAMAS CO OR	200-B5
STOTTLEMEYER RD NE	
KITSAP CO WA	170-C2
STOTTS RD SW	
DOUGLAS CO OR	112-B2
E STOUGHTON RD	
SPOKANE CO WA	246-C6
SPOKANE CO WA	247-B6
STOUT RD	
LATAH CO ID	250-D1
WHITMAN CO WA	250-B3
E STOVER RD	
YAKIMA CO WA	120-B3
STRAHL RD	
DOUGLAS CO WA	105-A3
DOUGLAS CO WA	237-A1
STRAHL CANYON RD	
DOUGLAS CO WA	105-A3
N STRAHORN RD	
HAYDEN ID	245-A5
HAYDEN ID	355-F1
HAYDEN LAKE ID	245-A5
KOOTENAI CO ID	245-A5
KOOTENAI CO ID	355-F1
STRAND RD	
WHATCOM CO WA	161-C1
STRANDER BLVD	
TUKWILA WA	289-G6
STRATFORD DR NE	
MARION CO OR	205-A3
STRATFORD RD	
GRANT CO WA	113-A2
GRANT CO WA	242-C1
MOSES LAKE WA	242-C1
STRATTON RD	
CLALLAM CO WA	165-A5
STRAWBERRY RD	
GRANT CO OR	137-B2
STRAWBERRY POINT RD	
ISLAND CO WA	167-D2
STRAWN LN SE	
THURSTON CO WA	184-D3
STRICKLAND CANYON RD	
DOUGLAS CO OR	221-A6
STRIEBEL RD	
JEFFERSON CO OR	211-C1
STRIKER LN	
IMBLER OR	130-A2
STRINGER GAP RD	
JOSEPHINE CO OR	229-B7
STRINGHAM RD	
KOOTENAI CO ID	247-C7
LEWIS CO WA	187-D2
E STRINGHAM RD	
ROCKFORD WA	114-C2
SPOKANE CO WA	247-B7
STRINGTOWN RD	
PACIFIC CO WA	186-A6
WASHINGTON CO OR	198-B1
YAMHILL CO OR	198-C7
STRODA DR	
LINN CO OR	210-A5
S STROEBEL RD	
ADA CO ID	253-A5
STROME LN	
LANE CO OR	210-A6
STRONG RD SE	
SALEM OR	325-A4
STRUCK RD	
KLICKITAT CO WA	196-C5
STRYKER AV	
PIERCE CO WA	181-B5
STRYKER RD	
INDEPENDENCE OR	204-B7
STUB AV	
KOOTENAI CO ID	247-C1
STUBB RD	
SNOHOMISH CO WA	168-B4
NE STUDIO RD	
BEND OR	332-F5
N STUMP RD	
KOOTENAI CO ID	245-B4
STURDAVENT RD	
LINCOLN CO OR	206-C4
TOLEDO OR	206-C4
STURGEON RD	
DESCHUTES CO OR	212-C7
STURGEON ST	
KITSAP CO WA	170-A7
STURM RD	
WALLA WALLA CO WA	345-D9
Walla Walla East WA	345-D9
S STUWE RD	
CLACKAMAS CO OR	205-D1
SUBLIMITY RD	
MARION CO OR	133-C1
SUBLIMITY OR	133-C1
SUBSTATION DR	
LINN CO OR	210-A4
SUCCOR CREEK HWY Rt#-201	
ADRIAN OR	147-A1
MALHEUR CO OR	139-A3
MALHEUR CO OR	147-A1
NYSSA OR	139-A3

STREET City State	Page-Grid
SUCCOR CREEK RD	
MALHEUR CO OR	147-A1
SUCIA DR	
WHATCOM CO WA	158-B6
SUCKER CREEK RD	
JOSEPHINE CO OR	233-D5
SUDBURY RD	
WALLA WALLA WA	344-A7
WALLA WALLA CO WA	121-C3
WALLA WALLA CO WA	344-A7
SUGAR PINE RD	
JACKSON CO OR	226-A6
SUGARPINE BUTTE RD	
DESCHUTES CO OR	217-B7
SUICIDE GULCH RD	
DESCHUTES CO OR	211-B4
SULLIVAN LN	
YAMHILL CO OR	198-C5
SULLIVAN RD	
SKAGIT CO WA	161-A5
N SULLIVAN RD	
SPOKANE VALLEY WA	351-C5
S SULLIVAN RD	
SPOKANE VALLEY WA	351-C11
SPOKANE VALLEY WA	351-C9
SULLIVAN CREEK RD	
PEND OREILLE CO WA	106-C1
SULLIVAN LAKE RD	
PEND OREILLE CO WA	106-B1
SULPHUR SPRINGS RD	
SNOHOMISH CO WA	110-C1
SULTAN WA	110-C1
SULTAN BASIN RD	
SNOHOMISH CO WA	110-C1
E SUMACH ST	
WALLA WALLA WA	345-B6
SUMAS Rt#-547	
WHATCOM CO WA	102-B1
SUMAS WY	
DISTRICT OF ABBOTSFORD BC	102-B1
DISTRICT OF MATSQUI BC	102-B1
E SUMMA ST	
CENTRALIA WA	299-F5
LEWIS CO WA	299-F5
W SUMMA ST	
CENTRALIA WA	299-E5
SUMMER ST	
BELLINGHAM WA	258-D4
SUMMER ST NE	
SALEM OR	322-J12
SALEM OR	323-A11
SUMMER CREEK RD	
LANE CO OR	215-D4
SUMMERHURST WK SW	
LAKEWOOD WA	174-D7
SUMMERLAND RD	
WHATCOM CO WA	161-A2
SUMMERS LN	
Altamont OR	235-C5
Altamont OR	338-J14
KLAMATH FALLS OR	235-C5
KLAMATH FALLS OR	338-J14
SUMMERVILLE RD	
IMBLER OR	130-A2
SUMMERVILLE OR	130-A2
UNION CO OR	130-A2
SUMMIT AV	
WASHINGTON CO OR	198-A2
SUMMIT DR	
HOOD RIVER CO OR	195-C6
SUMMIT HWY	
BENTON CO OR	133-A1
SUMMIT LP	
MARION CO OR	207-D2
SUMMIT RD	
JACKSON CO OR	149-B2
JACKSON CO OR	234-A6
JEFFERSON CO OR	211-D2
WHEELER CO OR	136-A2
SUMMIT RD Rt#-108	
GRAYS HARBOR CO WA	179-D6
MCCLEARY WA	179-D6
SUMMIT LAKE RD NW	
THURSTON CO WA	180-A6
SUMMIT LAKE SHORE RD NW	
THURSTON CO WA	180-A6
SE SUMMIT LANDSBURG RD	
KING CO WA	176-A7
E SUMMIT MEADOW RD	
CLACKAMAS CO OR	202-A6
SUMMIT ROCK RD	
DOUGLAS CO OR	223-C6
SUMMIT VALLEY RD	
STEVENS CO WA	106-A3
SUMMITVIEW AV	
YAKIMA CO WA	243-A6
YAKIMA CO WA	243-A6
W SUMMITVIEW AV	
YAKIMA CO WA	243-A6
SUMMITVIEW RD	
YAKIMA CO WA	119-C1
YAKIMA CO WA	243-A6
N SUMMITVIEW RD	
YAKIMA CO WA	243-A6
SUMNER AV U.S.-101	
HOQUIAM WA	178-A7
SUMNER ST Rt#-507	
BUCODA WA	184-D4
TENINO WA	184-D4
THURSTON CO WA	184-D4
SUMNER ST U.S.-101	
ABERDEEN WA	178-B7
HOQUIAM WA	178-A7
SUMNER-BUCKLEY HWY Rt#-410	
PIERCE CO WA	182-B3
SUMNER WA	182-B3
SUMNER BUCKLEY HWY E	
BONNEY LAKE WA	182-C4
BUCKLEY WA	182-C4
PIERCE CO WA	182-C4
SUMNER-FAIRVIEW RD	
COOS CO OR	140-B2
SUMNER TAPPS HWY	
PIERCE CO WA	182-C3
SUMPTER HWY	
BAKER CO OR	138-A1
SUMPTER OR	138-A1
SE SUN DR	
JEFFERSON CO OR	208-C5
MADRAS OR	208-C5
SUNCREST TER	
WALLA WALLA CO WA	344-D11
NW SUNDE RD	
KITSAP CO WA	174-B1
SUNDERMAN RD	
KITSAP CO WA	210-D7
SUNDOWN RD	
CURRY CO OR	232-C4

396 SUNDOWN RD
STREET INDEX
THORNDYKE AV W

STREET
City State Page-Grid

SUNDOWN RD
DESCHUTES CO OR 211-D3
SUNFLOWER RD
MORROW CO OR 128-C3
SUNFLOWER FLAT RD
MORROW CO OR 128-C3
SUN MOUNTAIN RD
KLAMATH CO OR 142-B3
SUNNY COVE DR SE
KITSAP CO WA 174-C6
SUNNYCREST RD
NEWBERG OR 198-C5
YAMHILL CO OR 198-C5
SUNNY DELL RD
BAKER CO OR 131-A3
SUNNYGLEN WY
JOSEPHINE CO OR 229-B2
SUNNYHILL RD S
BREMERTON WA 270-C11
KITSAP CO WA 270-C11
SUNNY RIDGE RD
YAMHILL CO OR 204-A2
SUNNYRIDGE RD
LINCOLN CO OR 206-C5
SUNNYSIDE AV
GRANGER WA 120-A2
SUNNYSIDE BLVD
MARYSVILLE WA 171-D1
SNOHOMISH CO WA 171-D1
SUNNYSIDE BLVD NE
MARYSVILLE WA 171-D1
SUNNYSIDE RD
ANMORE BC 157-A3
BONNER CO ID 244-B1
LINN CO OR 134-A2
POLK CO OR 204-A4
SE SUNNYSIDE RD
CLACKAMAS CO OR 199-D3
CLACKAMAS CO OR 200-A3
HAPPY VALLEY OR 200-A3
SUNNYSIDE RD SE
MARION CO OR 207-D1
MARION CO OR 324-H9
SALEM OR 324-H9
SUNNYSIDE-UMAPINE HWY
UMATILLA CO OR 121-C3
SUNNY SLOPE LN
BAKER CO OR 130-B3
SUNNYSLOPE LN
BAKER CO OR 138-B1
SUNNY SLOPE RD Rt#-55
CANYON CO ID 147-B1
SUNNYSLOPE RD SW
KITSAP CO WA 174-A4
SUNNY VALLEY LP
JOSEPHINE CO OR 229-B2
SUNNYVIEW RD
MARION CO OR 205-B5
MARION CO OR 323-G11
SALEM OR 204-D5
SALEM OR 323-B10
SUN RAY
CURRY CO OR 232-C4
SUNRISE AV
MEDFORD OR 336-F11
SUNRISE BLVD
PIERCE CO WA 182-B5
N SUNRISE BLVD
ISLAND CO WA 167-D4
SUNRISE BLVD E
PIERCE CO WA 182-B5
SUNRISE DR
KOOTENAI CO ID 248-B5
SUNRISE DR NE
KITSAP CO WA 170-D7
KITSAP CO WA 174-D1
SUNRISE LN
DOUGLAS CO OR 221-A5
SUNRISE PKWY E
PIERCE CO WA 182-B5
SUNRISE RD
WALLOWA CO OR 130-C2
WHATCOM CO WA 158-C3
WHATCOM CO WA 160-B2
SUNRISE ST
KELSO WA 303-F7
SUNRISE BEACH RD NW
THURSTON CO WA 180-B5
SUNRISE PARK RD
PIERCE CO WA 119-A1
PIERCE CO WA 185-D2
SUNSET AV
ANACORTES WA 259-A4
SUNSET AV N
KEIZER OR 322-J7
SUNSET BLVD
CANNON BEACH OR 188-B7
CLATSOP CO OR 301-C11
DIST OF NORTH VANCOUVER BC 254-J1
SEASIDE OR 301-C11
E SUNSET BLVD
CANNON BEACH OR 188-B7
NE SUNSET BLVD Rt#-900
RENTON WA 175-C4
S SUNSET BLVD
SPOKANE WA 348-G10
SW SUNSET BLVD
PORTLAND OR 316-C3
SHERWOOD OR 199-A5
SW SUNSET BLVD Rt#-900
RENTON WA 175-C5
W SUNSET BLVD
SPOKANE WA 348-E11
SPOKANE CO WA 348-E11
SUNSET BLVD N Rt#-900
RENTON WA 175-C5
SUNSET BLVD NE
RENTON WA 175-C4
SUNSET DR
BELLINGHAM WA 258-D4
FOREST GROVE OR 198-B1
ISLAND CO WA 167-D4
KOOTENAI CO ID 248-B5
LA GRANDE OR 130-A2
WALLA WALLA CO WA 121-B3
WASHINGTON CO OR 198-B1
E SUNSET DR
BELLINGHAM WA 258-E4
E SUNSET DR Rt#-542
BELLINGHAM WA 258-G3
WHATCOM CO WA 102-B1
WHATCOM CO WA 258-G3
SUNSET DR W
UNIVERSITY PLACE WA 181-C3
SUNSET FRWY U.S.-2
DOUGLAS CO WA 238-D3
East Wenatchee Bench WA 238-D3
Sunnyslope WA 238-D3

SUNSET HWY
CHELAN CO WA 238-C2
SUNSET HWY Rt#-970
KITTITAS CO WA 240-B2
SUNSET HWY U.S.-26
BEAVERTON OR 199-A1
CLATSOP CO OR 117-A3
CLATSOP CO OR 125-A1
CLATSOP CO OR 188-C7
COLUMBIA CO OR 125-B1
HILLSBORO OR 125-B1
HILLSBORO OR 192-A7
HILLSBORO OR 199-A1
MULTNOMAH CO OR 199-A1
MULTNOMAH CO OR 312-B7
NORTH PLAINS OR 125-B1
PORTLAND OR 199-A1
PORTLAND OR 312-B7
PORTLAND OR 316-B1
TILLAMOOK CO OR 125-B1
WASHINGTON CO OR 125-B1
WASHINGTON CO OR 192-A7
WASHINGTON CO OR 199-A1
W SUNSET HWY
SPOKANE WA 348-B11
SPOKANE CO WA 348-B11
W SUNSET HWY U.S.-2
AIRWAY HEIGHTS WA 246-A4
SPOKANE CO WA 246-A4
SPOKANE CO WA 348-A12
SUNSET LN
CROOK CO OR 213-C4
SUNSET RD
BONNER CO ID 244-A7
SKAGIT CO WA 161-A5
WHITMAN CO WA 114-B3
SUNSET WY
CHELAN CO WA 238-C3
DOUGLAS CO WA 239-B1
E SUNSET WY
ISSAQUAH WA 176-A4
W SUNSET WY
ISSAQUAH WA 176-A4
SUNSET BEACH RD
CLATSOP CO OR 188-B3
SUNSET HEMLOCK RD
SKAMANIA CO WA 193-D3
SKAMANIA CO WA 194-A3
SUNSET HWY RD E
LINCOLN CO WA 114-A2
SE SUNSET VIEW RD
CLARK CO WA 193-C7
WASHOUGAL WA 193-C7
SUNSHINE RD
DOUGLAS CO OR 221-D3
WHITMAN CO WA 249-B5
SUNSHINE CREEK RD
JACKSON CO OR 226-C4
SE SUNSHINE VALLEY RD
CLACKAMAS CO OR 200-B3
SUN UP BAY RD
KOOTENAI CO ID 247-C7
SUPERIOR AV
CONCRETE WA 102-C2
SUPERIOR ST
CITY OF VICTORIA BC 256-F10
SUPERIOR ST U.S.-95
CAMBRIDGE ID 139-B1
SANDPOINT ID 244-A2
S SUPERIOR ST U.S.-95
CAMBRIDGE ID 139-B1
SUQUAMISH WY NE
Suquamish WA 170-C7
SURBER DR NE
SEATTLE WA 275-E6
SURF ST
WESTPORT WA 298-G14
SURFACE RD
Clinton WA 171-A2
ISLAND CO WA 171-A2
SURF PINES RD
CLATSOP CO OR 188-B4
SURPRISE VALLEY RD
LAKE CO OR 152-A3
MODOC CO CA 152-A3
SUSAN RD
KITTITAS CO WA 241-A6
SUSBAUER RD
WASHINGTON CO OR 198-C1
SUSSEX ST Rt#-507
TENINO WA 184-D3
THURSTON CO WA 184-D3
SUTHERLIN-NONPAREIL RD
DOUGLAS CO OR 141-B2
DOUGLAS CO OR 221-D1
SUTHERLIN-UMPQUA RD
DOUGLAS CO OR 221-B1
SUTTER RD
CLALLAM CO WA 165-D6
SUTTLE RD
CLACKAMAS CO OR 200-B4
SUTTLE LAKE LP
JEFFERSON CO OR 211-B2
SUTTLE-SHERMAN RD
JEFFERSON CO OR 211-B2
SUTTON RD
ADAMS CO WA 121-C1
SUTTON BEACH RD
LANE CO OR 214-B1
SUTTON CREEK RD
TILLAMOOK CO OR 197-B3
SUTTON LAKE RD
LANE CO OR 214-B1
SUVER RD
POLK CO OR 207-B2
SWAKANE CANYON RD
CHELAN CO WA 238-C1
SWALLEY RD
DESCHUTES CO OR 212-C7
SWALLOW DR
JEFFERSON CO OR 212-C2
SWALWELL RD
SNOHOMISH CO WA 171-D2
SWAMP CREEK RD
MALHEUR CO OR 146-A1
SWAMP CREEK TO COUNTY LINE RD
GRANT CO OR 136-C3
SWAMP WELLS RD
DESCHUTES CO OR 217-C6
E SWAN AV
SILETZ OR 206-C2
SWAN RD
SKAGIT CO WA 260-J8
S SWAN FALLS RD
ADA CO ID 253-A6
SWAN HILL RD
DOUGLAS CO OR 221-A6

SWANK DR
LINN CO OR 207-D6
SWAN LAKE RD
FERRY CO WA 105-B2
KLAMATH CO OR 235-C1
SWAN SLOUGH RD
SNOHOMISH CO WA 269-H2
SWANSON RD
WHITMAN CO WA 249-A1
SWANSON GULCH RD
CHELAN CO WA 236-C1
SWANSON LAKE RD N
CRESTON WA 113-C1
LINCOLN CO WA 113-C1
SWANSONVILLE RD
JEFFERSON CO WA 170-B2
SWANS TRAIL RD
SNOHOMISH CO WA 171-D3
SNOHOMISH CO WA 269-J2
SWANTOWN RD
ISLAND CO WA 167-B2
OAK HARBOR WA 167-B2
SWARTZ BAY-TSAWWASSEN FERRY
BRITISH COLUMBIA BC 101-B1
BRITISH COLUMBIA BC 159-C1
DIST OF NORTH SAANICH BC 159-C1
SWARTZ CANYON RD
CROOK CO OR 213-C7
SWAUK PRAIRIE RD
KITTITAS CO WA 240-D1
SWAWILLA BASIN RD
FERRY CO WA 113-B1
SWEDE BASIN RD
JOSEPHINE CO OR 148-C1
JOSEPHINE CO OR 233-B1
SWEDE HILL RD
ISLAND CO WA 171-A3
SWEDE RIDGE RD
DESCHUTES CO OR 216-D3
DESCHUTES CO OR 217-A3
SWEDETOWN RD
COLUMBIA CO OR 117-B3
COLUMBIA CO OR 189-A5
SWEENEY RD SE
KING CO WA 175-D6
SWEENEY GULCH RD
GARFIELD CO WA 122-B2
SWEET RD
WHATCOM CO WA 158-B3
SWEET CREEK RD
LANE CO OR 214-D4
SWEGLE RD NE
MARION CO OR 323-F12
SALEM OR 323-F12
SWENSON RD
STEVENS CO WA 114-B1
STEVENS CO WA 246-A1
SWENSON-WILLIAMS VALLEY RD
STEVENS CO WA 114-B1
SWIFT AV S
SEATTLE WA 282-C7
SEATTLE WA 286-C1
SWIFT BLVD
RICHLAND WA 341-D1
SWINDLER RD
LEWIS CO WA 187-C4
SYDNAM RD
COOS CO OR 224-B1
SYKES RD
SAINT HELENS OR 192-A2
NE SYLVAN WY
BREMERTON WA 270-H7
BREMERTON WA 271-B6
KITSAP CO WA 271-B6
SYLVAN WY SW
SEATTLE WA 281-F7
SEATTLE WA 285-F1
SYLVESTER RD
BRITISH COLUMBIA BC 94-B3
W SYLVESTER ST
FRANKLIN CO WA 342-J7
PASCO WA 342-J7
PASCO WA 343-A7
SYLVIA LAKE RD
MONTESANO WA 178-D7
SYMONS ST
RICHLAND WA 340-F14

T

T AV
ANACORTES WA 259-H4
T RD NW
DOUGLAS CO WA 236-B5
T 1-2-SW ST
GRANT CO WA 120-B1
TABLE ROCK RD
JACKSON CO OR 230-C6
JACKSON CO OR 336-C3
MEDFORD OR 336-B8
TABLE ROCK TRAIL RD
JACKSON CO OR 230-C5
N TACOMA AV
PASCO WA 343-G7
TACOMA WA 293-F3
S TACOMA AV
TACOMA WA 293-G5
TACOMA AV S
TACOMA WA 293-G7
TACOMA WA 295-H3
SE TACOMA ST
PORTLAND OR 317-H6
PORTLAND OR 318-A7
S TACOMA WY
LAKEWOOD WA 181-D4
TACOMA WA 181-D4
TACOMA WA 293-H7
TACOMA WA 294-D2
TACOMA WA 295-F1
TACOMA MALL BLVD
TACOMA WA 294-E3
TACOMA WA 295-E3
TACOMA-ORTING-PRAIRIE
PIERCE CO WA 182-A6
TAFT ST Rt#-8
ELK RIVER ID 123-C1
W TAFT ST
BOISE ID 253-C2
TAHUYA BLACKSMITH RD
MASON CO WA 173-B5
TAHUYA LAKE RD NW
KITSAP CO WA 173-D2
TAHUYA RIVER DR
MASON CO WA 173-C6
TAHUYA RIVER RD
MASON CO WA 173-B6

TAKHOMA FARM LN
KITTITAS CO WA 241-D5
TALACHE RD
BONNER CO ID 244-A4
TALAPUS RIDGE RD
MULTNOMAH CO OR 194-C7
MULTNOMAH CO OR 201-C1
TALA SHORE DR
JEFFERSON CO WA 170-B3
TALBOT RD
MARION CO OR 207-D2
TALBOT RD S
KING CO WA 175-C6
MARION CO OR 207-D2
RENTON WA 175-C6
TALBOT RD S Rt#-515
RENTON WA 175-C5
TALBOT RD SE
MARION CO OR 207-C2
TALBOTT LN
LANE CO OR 210-A5
TALLEY AV
KELSO WA 303-E11
TALLEY WY
KELSO WA 303-F13
TALLMAN RD
LINN CO OR 207-D6
PIERCE CO WA 182-B7
TALL PINES RD
KOOTENAI CO ID 247-D4
TALMAGE RD
POLK CO OR 204-B7
TALMAKS RD
LEWIS CO ID 123-B3
TAMARACK LN
MAPLE RIDGE BC 157-D6
TAMARACK FALLS RD
VALLEY CO ID 252-C2
TAMPICO RD
BENTON CO OR 207-A3
TANDY LN
LINN CO OR 210-A4
TANEUM RD
KITTITAS CO WA 240-D4
TANGELWOOD LN
DOUGLAS CO OR 221-A4
TANGEN RD
YAMHILL CO OR 198-C5
TANGENT DR
LINN CO OR 207-B6
TANGENT OR 207-C6
TANGENT LP
LINN CO OR 207-C7
TANGENT ST Rt#-34
LEBANON OR 133-C1
TANKE RD
LINCOLN CO WA 113-C2
TANNER RD
DIST OF CENTRAL SAANICH BC 159-C4
TANNER CREEK RD
MULTNOMAH CO OR 194-C7
WASHINGTON CO OR 198-A1
S TAPPS DR E
PIERCE CO WA 182-C3
W TAPPS DR E
PIERCE CO WA 182-C3
W TAPPS HWY
BONNEY LAKE WA 182-C3
TARBOO LAKE RD
JEFFERSON CO WA 109-C1
W TARGEE ST
ADA CO ID 253-B3
TARLATT RD
PACIFIC CO WA 186-A5
TARTAR GULCH RD
JOSEPHINE CO OR 233-C5
TATLOW RD
DISTRICT OF NORTH SAANICH BC 159-C1
TATTERSALL DR
DISTRICT OF SAANICH BC 256-G4
TAUFFEN RD
WHITMAN CO WA 250-A2
TAUMARSON RD
COLLEGE PLACE WA 344-G12
WALLA WALLA WA 344-H12
WALLA WALLA CO WA 344-H12
WALLA WALLA CO WA 345-A12
TAURUS BLVD
OCEAN SHORES WA 298-B1
TAUSCHER RD
LEWIS CO WA 187-D1
TAUSICK WY
WALLA WALLA WA 345-G6
WALLA WALLA CO WA 345-G6
TAYLOR AV
ASTORIA OR 300-A5
BELLINGHAM WA 258-C10
TAYLOR AV N
SEATTLE WA 277-J2
TAYLOR RD
COLLEGE PLACE WA 344-E12
JACKSON CO OR 230-C7
LEWIS CO WA 187-D1
WALLA WALLA CO WA 344-E12
YAKIMA CO WA 243-B5
E TAYLOR RD
SPOKANE CO WA 246-B6
N TAYLOR RD
ISLAND CO WA 167-C2
TAYLOR ST E
MILTON WA 182-B2
TAYLOR WY
DIST OF WEST VANCOUVER BC 254-F2
TACOMA WA 182-A2
TAYLOR WY Rt#-99
DIST OF WEST VANCOUVER BC 254-E4
TAYLOR FLATS RD
FRANKLIN CO WA 121-A2
TAYLOR RICE
PIERCE CO WA 181-D7
SW TAYLORS FERRY RD
PORTLAND OR 316-B7
PORTLAND OR 317-F6
PORTLAND OR 320-A1
TAYLOR VALLEY RD
CLARK CO WA 192-D1
T CARRY RD
CLARK CO WA 193-A1
TEAGUE RD
THURSTON CO WA 184-A5
TEAL RD
DESCHUTES CO OR 217-D3
TEAL LAKE RD
JEFFERSON CO WA 170-B4
TEANAWAY RD
KITTITAS CO WA 240-C1
TEANAWAY WILSON STOCK TR
KITTITAS CO WA 241-B1

TEATERS RD
CROOK CO OR 136-A3
TECHNOLOGY LP
CORVALLIS OR 327-B12
TECHNOR ROBISON RD
SISKIYOU CO CA 150-C3
TEITZEL RD
LEWIS CO WA 184-C5
TEKOA-FARMINGTON RD
TEKOA WA 114-C3
WHITMAN CO WA 114-C3
WHITMAN CO WA 115-A3
TEKOA OAKSDALE RD Rt#-27
OAKESDALE WA 114-C3
WHITMAN CO WA 114-C3
TELEGRAPH RD
BRITISH COLUMBIA BC 159-A1
LEWIS CO WA 187-C4
TELEGRAPH TR
TOWNSHIP OF LANGLEY BC 157-C7
TELEPHONE RD
DESCHUTES CO OR 216-D5
TELEPHONE POLE RD
UMATILLA CO OR 121-C3
SE TELFORD RD
CLACKAMAS CO OR 200-B3
MULTNOMAH CO OR 200-B2
TELFORD RD N
LINCOLN CO WA 113-C2
TELOCASET LN
UNION CO OR 130-B3
E TEMPLE RD
SPOKANE CO WA 247-A1
TEMPLETON RD
COOS CO OR 218-C4
TEN BAR RD
DESCHUTES CO OR 217-D3
TEN EYCK RD
CLACKAMAS CO OR 200-D3
NW TENINO RD
JEFFERSON CO OR 135-A1
Warm Springs OR 208-A3
TENMILE RD
MALHEUR CO OR 154-B2
N TEN MILE RD
ADA CO ID 253-A2
MERIDIAN ID 253-A2
S TEN MILE RD
ADA CO ID 253-A4
TENMILE CREEK RD
LANE CO OR 209-A5
W TENMILE CREEK RD
ADA CO ID 253-B5
TENNANT WY
LONGVIEW WA 303-A10
TENNANT WY Rt#-432
COWLITZ CO WA 303-C12
LONGVIEW WA 303-C12
TENNESSEE RD
LEWIS CO WA 187-C3
LINN CO OR 133-C1
TENT CREEK RD
MALHEUR CO OR 155-A2
TENTH ST
KETTLE FALLS WA 106-A2
NESPELEM WA 105-A3
TERMINAL AV
VANCOUVER BC 254-J11
VANCOUVER BC 255-B12
SW TERRA DR
JEFFERSON CO OR 212-C1
TERRACE HEIGHTS DR
YAKIMA WA 243-C6
YAKIMA CO WA 243-C6
TERRA FERN DR
CLACKAMAS CO OR 201-A4
TERREBONNE-LOWER BRIDGE WY
DESCHUTES CO OR 212-C3
Terrebonne OR 212-C3
NE TERRE VIEW DR
PULLMAN WA 249-B4
TERRI DR
JACKSON CO OR 234-C2
TERRITORIAL HWY
BENTON CO OR 133-B2
DOUGLAS CO OR 133-B2
LANE CO OR 133-B2
VENETA OR 133-B3
TERRITORIAL RD
COLUMBIA CO WA 122-A2
DOUGLAS CO OR 219-B1
NE TERRITORIAL RD
CANBY OR 199-C6
CLACKAMAS CO OR 199-C6
TERRITORIAL ST
HARRISBURG OR 210-A5
LINN CO OR 210-A5
TERRY RD
COUPEVILLE WA 167-B4
ISLAND CO WA 167-B4
SW TERWILLIGER BLVD
CLACKAMAS CO OR 321-F3
LAKE OSWEGO OR 321-F3
MULTNOMAH CO OR 321-F3
PORTLAND OR 316-E3
PORTLAND OR 317-E1
PORTLAND OR 320-E1
PORTLAND OR 321-E2
TETHEROW RD
DESCHUTES CO OR 212-C5
N TEXAS RD
SKAGIT CO WA 160-C6
TEXAS LAKE RD
WHITMAN CO WA 114-A3
TEXMAR ST SW
OCEAN SHORES WA 298-C3
THAIN RD
LEWISTON ID 250-C4
THATCHER RD
FOREST GROVE OR 198-B1
WASHINGTON CO OR 125-B1
WASHINGTON CO OR 198-B1
THATCHER PASS RD
SAN JUAN CO WA 160-A5
THAYER DR
RICHLAND WA 340-F13
RICHLAND WA 341-F1
THAYER RD
LEWIS CO WA 187-D3
S THAYER RD
CLACKAMAS CO OR 199-D5
NW THEATER AV
DESCHUTES CO OR 212-C4
THE CRESCENT TR
INDEX WA 111-A1
THE DALLES-CALIF HWY U.S.-97
BEND OR 217-C1

THE DALLES-CALIF HWY U.S.-97
BEND OR 332-D13
BEND OR 332-F1
BEND OR 332-F3
CHILOQUIN OR 231-D3
DESCHUTES CO OR 143-A1
DESCHUTES CO OR 212-C7
DESCHUTES CO OR 217-C1
DESCHUTES CO OR 332-D14
DESCHUTES CO OR 332-F3
Deschutes River Woods OR 217-C1
Deschutes River Woods OR 332-D14
DUFUR OR 127-B2
JEFFERSON CO OR 135-B1
JEFFERSON CO OR 208-C4
JEFFERSON CO OR 208-C6
JEFFERSON CO OR 212-D3
KLAMATH CO OR 142-C2
KLAMATH CO OR 143-A1
KLAMATH CO OR 150-C1
KLAMATH CO OR 231-D3
KLAMATH CO OR 235-C1
KLAMATH CO OR 338-A1
KLAMATH FALLS OR 338-A1
MADRAS OR 208-C4
MADRAS OR 208-C5
MAUPIN OR 127-B3
REDMOND OR 212-D3
Terrebonne OR 212-D3
THE DALLES OR 196-D7
WASCO CO OR 127-B2
WASCO CO OR 127-B3
WASCO CO OR 135-B1
WASCO CO OR 196-D7
THE EVERGREEN COLLEGE PKWY
THURSTON CO WA 296-A2
THERMAL DR
COQUITLAM BC 157-A4
THIEF CREEK RD
DOUGLAS CO OR 219-B3
THIELSON ST
ECHO OR 129-A1
UMATILLA CO OR 129-A1
N THIERMAN RD
SPOKANE CO WA 350-A1
S THIERMAN ST
SPOKANE VALLEY WA 350-A10
THIESEN RD
NEZ PERCE CO ID 250-C5
SE THIESSEN RD
CLACKAMAS CO OR 199-D3
THILLBERG RD
SKAGIT CO WA 260-G7
THIRD
DESCHUTES CO OR 212-A6
THIRD AV
FERNDALE WA 158-C6
E THIRD AV
PORT ORCHARD WA 271-A14
THIRD AV NW
OKANOGAN WA 104-C3
THIRD AV SW
OKANOGAN WA 104-C3
THIRD ST
FARMINGTON WA 115-A3
LINCOLN CO WA 114-A2
WHITMAN CO WA 115-A3
THIRD ST Rt#-507
TENINO WA 184-D3
THIRD FORK RD
GEM CO ID 139-C2
SW THIRTEENTH ST
CHEHALIS WA 299-E13
THOMAS
CROOK CO OR 213-D6
THOMAS RD
CLACKAMAS CO OR 126-A3
CLACKAMAS CO OR 205-D2
KING CO WA 182-D1
KITTITAS CO WA 241-C4
SKAGIT CO WA 161-A5
STEVENS CO WA 105-C3
STEVENS CO WA 106-A3
SE THOMAS RD
CLACKAMAS CO OR 200-D3
THOMAS RD KPN
PIERCE CO WA 174-A7
E THOMAS ST
SEATTLE WA 278-C4
THOMAS CREEK DR
LINN CO OR 134-A1
THOMAS CREEK RD
LAKE CO OR 152-A2
S THOMAS-MALLEN RD
SPOKANE CO WA 246-A6
THOMLE RD
SNOHOMISH CO WA 168-A4
THOMPSON AV
DOUGLAS CO OR 221-B6
WINSTON OR 221-B6
S THOMPSON AV
TACOMA WA 295-G1
THOMPSON LN
YAMHILL CO OR 198-D7
THOMPSON RD
CLALLAM CO WA 166-C7
COOS BAY OR 333-F7
YAKIMA CO WA 243-A5
W THOMPSON RD
KOOTENAI CO ID 247-D4
THOMPSON ST
SUMNER WA 182-B3
THOMPSON CREEK RD
JACKSON CO OR 149-B2
JOSEPHINE CO OR 149-B2
JOSEPHINE CO OR 233-C2
LANE CO OR 209-C7
LANE CO OR 214-D1
THOMPSON LAKE RD
KOOTENAI CO ID 248-B4
THOMPSON MILL RD
MULTNOMAH CO OR 200-D1
THOMSEN RD
HOOD RIVER CO OR 195-D7
S THOR ST
SPOKANE WA 349-F10
SE THORBURN ST
PORTLAND OR 314-E6
PORTLAND OR 315-E6
THORMAN AV NE
KEIZER OR 323-A6
THORN CREEK RD
WHITMAN CO WA 114-B3
THORNDYKE AV W
SEATTLE WA 273-E7
SEATTLE WA 276-E1
SEATTLE WA 277-E1

INDEX

THORNDYKE RD STREET INDEX UNGER RD 397

STREET INDEX

STREET — City State Page-Grid

THORNDYKE RD
JEFFERSON CO WA 170-B5
N THORNE LN SW
LAKEWOOD WA 181-C5
THORN HOLLOW RD
COLUMBIA CO WA 122-A2
THORN PRAIRIE RD
DOUGLAS CO OR 223-A3
THORN SPRING RD
JEFFERSON CO OR 211-D1
THORNTON RD
WHATCOM CO WA 158-C5
THORNTON CREEK RD
LINCOLN CO OR 206-D3
W THORNTON LAKE DR
ALBANY OR 326-A6
THORP HWY
KITTITAS CO WA 241-A4
S THORPE RD
SPOKANE WA 348-G12
W THORPE RD
SPOKANE WA 348-E14
SPOKANE CO WA 114-B2
SPOKANE CO WA 246-A5
SPOKANE CO WA 348-E14
THORP PRAIRIE RD
KITTITAS CO WA 240-C2
THOUSAND SPRINGS RD
JACKSON CO OR 227-A4
THRALL RD
KITTITAS CO WA 241-C7
THRALL RD Rt#-821
KITTITAS CO WA 241-B7
THREE CREEK RD
DESCHUTES CO OR 211-D5
DESCHUTES CO OR 216-C1
SISTERS OR 211-D5
THREE DEVILS GRADE RD SW
DOUGLAS CO WA 112-B2
THREE FORKS RD
MALHEUR CO OR 146-C3
MALHEUR CO OR 147-A3
MALHEUR CO OR 155-A1
N THREE FORKS RD
KOOTENAI CO ID 247-C1
THREE FORKS RESERVOIR RD
MALHEUR CO OR 146-A3
THREE LAKES RD
ALBANY OR 326-H11
LINN CO OR 326-H11
SNOHOMISH CO WA 110-C1
SNOHOMISH CO WA 171-D3
NE THREE MILE LN
MCMINNVILLE OR 198-A7
YAMHILL CO OR 198-A7
SE THREE MILE LN
MCMINNVILLE OR 198-A7
YAMHILL CO OR 198-A7
THREEMILE RD
WASCO CO OR 127-A2
WASCO CO OR 196-C7
THREE MILE LN HWY Rt#-18
MCMINNVILLE OR 198-B7
YAMHILL CO OR 198-B7
THREE PINES RD
JOSEPHINE CO OR 229-B3
THREE RIVERS HWY Rt#-22
POLK CO OR 125-A3
TILLAMOOK CO OR 197-B6
TILLAMOOK CO OR 203-D1
YAMHILL CO OR 125-A3
YAMHILL CO OR 203-D1
THREE ROCKS RD
LINCOLN CO OR 203-B3
THREE TRAPPER RD
DESCHUTES CO OR 216-C7
THRESHER AV
Olympic View WA 170-B7
THRIFT
PIERCE CO WA 182-B6
THUMPER RD
DESCHUTES CO OR 211-C5
NW THURMAN ST
PORTLAND OR 312-E4
THURSTON RD
LANE CO OR 215-D2
SPRINGFIELD OR 215-D2
SPRINGFIELD OR 331-J6
NE THURSTON WY
VANCOUVER WA 307-F1
TIBBETS MOUNTAIN RD
CHELAN CO WA 238-C1
TIBBLING RD
YAKIMA CO WA 243-B4
TICKLE CREEK RD
CLACKAMAS CO OR 200-B3
TICKNER RD
SISKIYOU CO CA 151-A3
TIDE AV
TILLAMOOK CO OR 191-A3
TIDE CREEK RD
COLUMBIA CO OR 189-C6
TIDELAND RD
TILLAMOOK CO OR 191-B4
TIDEWATER RD
LINCOLN CO OR 209-D2
TIEDMAN RD KPS
PIERCE CO WA 180-D2
E TIETAN ST
WALLA WALLA WA 345-C10
W TIETAN ST
WALLA WALLA WA 345-A10
WALLA WALLA CO WA 345-A10
W TIETON AV
Country Homes WA 346-J12
TIETON DR
YAKIMA WA 243-A6
YAKIMA CO WA 243-A7
TIETON RESERVOIR RD
YAKIMA CO WA 119-B2
SE TIGER MOUNTAIN RD
KING CO WA 176-A5
TIGNER RD
CHELAN CO WA 238-C2
W TILDEN ST
SEATTLE WA 272-D6
TILE FLAT RD
WASHINGTON CO OR 198-D3
WASHINGTON CO OR 199-A3
TILLAMOOK
CROOK CO OR 213-D7
TILLAMOOK AV
BAY CITY OR 197-B1
NE TILLAMOOK ST
PORTLAND OR 314-B3
TILLAMOOK RIVER RD
TILLAMOOK OR 197-B3
TILLAMOOK CO OR 197-B3
TILLER-SOUTH UMPQUA CAMP RD
DOUGLAS CO OR 141-C3
DOUGLAS CO OR 222-A7
DOUGLAS CO OR 226-A1
TILLER-TRAIL HWY Rt#-227
CANYONVILLE OR 225-D3
DOUGLAS CO OR 141-B3
DOUGLAS CO OR 225-D3
JACKSON CO OR 141-C3
JACKSON CO OR 230-D1
TILLEY RD SW
THURSTON CO WA 184-C3
TILLEY RD SW Rt#-121
THURSTON CO WA 184-C2
TILLICUM RD
DISTRICT OF SAANICH BC 256-D5
TOWN OF ESQUIMALT BC 256-D7
SE TILLSTROM RD
CLACKAMAS CO OR 200-B3
TIMBER RD
COLUMBIA CO OR 125-B1
LINN CO OR 210-D3
WASHINGTON CO OR 125-B1
TIMBER ST
ALBANY OR 326-H7
TIMBER TR NE
MARION CO OR 205-D5
TIMBER WY
COOS CO OR 220-D3
TIMBER CREEK RD
JACKSON CO OR 226-A6
TIMBERLINE HWY
CLACKAMAS CO OR 202-A6
TIMBERLINE EAST LEG
CLACKAMAS CO OR 202-A6
TIMBERLINE WEST LEG
CLACKAMAS CO OR 202-A6
NE TIMMEN RD
CLARK CO WA 192-C2
NW TIMMEN RD
CLARK CO WA 192-C2
TIMOTHY LAKE RD
CLACKAMAS CO OR 126-C3
TINGLE RD
LEWIS CO WA 187-C2
TINGLEY LN
KLAMATH CO OR 235-C5
TIPTON RD
KITTITAS CO WA 241-B4
TISCH
PIERCE CO WA 118-A1
TITCHENAL CANYON RD SW
DOUGLAS CO WA 239-C2
TITUS LN
VALLEY CO ID 252-D1
TOAD RD
JACKSON CO OR 229-D3
TOANDOS RD
JEFFERSON CO WA 170-A5
TODEY RD
LEWIS CO WA 187-D5
TOE JAM HILL RD NE
KITSAP CO WA 174-D3
TOFTDAHL RD N
LANE CO OR 210-A5
TOKELAND RD
PACIFIC CO WA 183-C5
TOKIO RD
ADAMS CO WA 113-B3
LINCOLN CO WA 113-C3
TOLEDO SALMON CREEK RD
LEWIS CO WA 187-D5
TOLEDO SALMON HANKIN RD
LEWIS CO WA 187-D4
TOLEDO VADER RD
LEWIS CO WA 187-C4
TOLEDO WA 187-C4
TOLER RD NW
DOUGLAS CO WA 236-D7
TOLIVER RD
CLACKAMAS CO OR 205-D1
TOLL RD
MULTNOMAH CO OR 200-D1
S TOLL RD
SPOKANE CO WA 247-B7
TOLL STATION RD
DESCHUTES CO OR 211-B3
JEFFERSON CO OR 211-B2
TOLMAN RD
LANE CO OR 215-A4
SE TOLMAN ST
PORTLAND OR 318-A5
TOLMAN CREEK RD
JACKSON CO OR 234-D5
N TOLMAN CREEK RD
ASHLAND OR 337-H9
JACKSON CO OR 337-H9
S TOLMAN CREEK RD
ASHLAND OR 337-H11
TOLMIE RD
DISTRICT OF ABBOTSFORD BC 102-B1
TOLO RD
JACKSON CO OR 230-B7
TOLONEN RD E
LINCOLN CO WA 113-B2
TOLT AV Rt#-203
CARNATION WA 176-B2
KING CO WA 176-B2
NE TOLT HILL RD
KING CO WA 176-A2
TOMLINSON RD
TILLAMOOK CO OR 197-B2
TOM SMITH RD
COOS CO OR 220-B5
TOM WRIGHT
PIERCE CO WA 182-A6
TONASKET-HAVILLAH RD
OKANOGAN CO WA 104-C2
OKANOGAN CO WA 105-A1
TONASKET WA 104-C2
TONE RD
TILLAMOOK CO OR 197-B2
SW TONGUE LN
WASHINGTON CO OR 198-C2
TONO RD SE
THURSTON CO WA 184-D4
SW TONQUIN RD
WASHINGTON CO OR 199-B5
TONY CREEK RD
HOOD RIVER CO OR 202-B1
TOONERVILLE DR
MASON CO WA 173-D4
SW TOOZE RD
CLACKAMAS CO OR 199-A5
TOPE RD
WALLOWA CO OR 130-C1
E TOPPENISH AV
TOPPENISH WA 120-A2
S TOPPENISH AV
TOPPENISH WA 120-A2
TOPPENISH-ZILLAH RD
YAKIMA CO WA 120-A2
ZILLAH WA 120-A2
TOQUA RD
KLAMATH CO OR 231-C5
TORNQUIST RD
GRAYS HARBOR CO WA 179-D5
TORODA BRIDGE CUSTOMS RD
FERRY CO WA 105-B1
TORODA CREEK RD
FERRY CO WA 105-B1
OKANOGAN CO WA 105-A2
TORPEDO RD
ISLAND CO WA 167-C2
OAK HARBOR WA 167-C2
TORVEND RD NE
MARION CO OR 205-B4
TOTTEN RD NE
Suquamish WA 170-C7
TOUCHET RD
WALLA WALLA CO WA 121-B3
S TOUCHET RD
COLUMBIA CO WA 122-A3
TOUCHET-GARDENA RD
WALLA WALLA CO WA 121-B3
TOUVELLE RD
JACKSON CO OR 230-C5
N TOWER AV Rt#-507
CENTRALIA WA 299-F3
S TOWER AV Rt#-507
CENTRALIA WA 299-F4
TOWER RD
COWLITZ CO WA 118-A2
COWLITZ CO WA 187-C6
MORROW CO OR 128-B1
WHATCOM CO WA 161-A1
TOWER MOUNTAIN RD
SPOKANE CO WA 247-B5
TOWN RD
CITY OF CHILLIWACK BC 102-B1
DISTRICT OF ABBOTSFORD BC 102-B1
TOWNSEND-SACKMAN RD
STEVENS CO WA 106-A2
TOWNSHIP RD
KLAMATH CO OR 235-B7
TOWNSHIP RD Rt#-9
SEDRO-WOOLLEY WA 161-C5
SKAGIT CO WA 161-C5
S TOWNSHIP RD
CLACKAMAS CO OR 199-C6
TOWNSHIP LINE RD
CLALLAM CO WA 165-D7
N TRACK RD
WAPATO WA 120-A2
YAKIMA CO WA 120-A2
TRACY RD
CLACKAMAS CO OR 200-C6
TRACYTON BLVD NW
KITSAP CO WA 270-E3
Silverdale WA 174-B1
Silverdale WA 270-E3
Tracyton WA 270-E3
TRACYTON BEACH RD NW
BREMERTON WA 270-G6
KITSAP CO WA 270-G6
Tracyton WA 270-G6
TRADE ST SE Rt#-22
SALEM OR 322-H13
S TRAFTON ST
TACOMA WA 293-E7
W TRAIL RD
SPOKANE CO WA 246-A3
SPOKANE CO WA 348-A6
TRAIL BUTTE RD
COOS CO OR 218-D6
TRAIL CREEK RD
JACKSON CO OR 230-D1
LANE CO OR 209-C7
TRAIL FORK RD
GILLIAM CO OR 128-A3
TRAILS RD
MASON CO WA 173-C7
TRAM RD
IDAHO CO ID 123-C3
TRAM RD Rt#-162
IDAHO CO ID 123-C3
TRAMWAY RD
GARFIELD CO WA 122-C1
TRANS CANADA HWY Rt#-1
BRITISH COLUMBIA BC 93-C1
BRITISH COLUMBIA BC 94-C3
BRITISH COLUMBIA BC 95-A1
BRITISH COLUMBIA BC 101-A1
BRITISH COLUMBIA BC 102-B1
BRITISH COLUMBIA BC 156-A2
BRITISH COLUMBIA BC 159-A1
CITY OF CHILLIWACK BC 94-C3
CITY OF NORTH VANCOUVER BC 255-A3
CITY OF SURREY BC 157-B6
CITY OF VICTORIA BC 256-G11
COQUITLAM BC 157-B6
DISTRICT OF ABBOTSFORD BC 94-C3
DISTRICT OF ABBOTSFORD BC 102-B1
DISTRICT OF BURNABY BC 156-D4
DISTRICT OF BURNABY BC 255-F12
DISTRICT OF COQUITLAM BC 156-D4
DISTRICT OF LANGFORD BC 159-A6
DISTRICT OF MATSQUI BC 102-B1
DIST OF NORTH VANCOUVER BC 254-F2
DIST OF NORTH VANCOUVER BC 255-A3
DISTRICT OF SAANICH BC 256-G5
DIST OF WEST VANCOUVER BC 156-A2
DIST OF WEST VANCOUVER BC 254-F2
DUNCAN BC 101-A1
HOPE BC 95-A3
NANAIMO BC 93-A3
SQUAMISH BC 93-C1
TOWN OF VIEW ROYAL BC 159-A6
TOWN OF VIEW ROYAL BC 256-B3
TOWNSHIP OF LANGLEY BC 102-B1
TOWNSHIP OF LANGLEY BC 157-B6
TOWNSHIP OF LANGLEY BC 158-D1
VANCOUVER BC 255-F12
WHISTLER BC 93-C1
TRANSFORMER RD
KLAMATH CO OR 151-A2
TRANS PACIFIC PKWY
COOS CO OR 218-A6
TRAP CREEK RD
LINCOLN CO OR 206-D4
TRAP MOUNTAIN RD
DOUGLAS CO OR 223-A4
TRASK RIVER RD
TILLAMOOK CO OR 125-A2
TILLAMOOK CO OR 197-D2
TRAVIS RD
BENTON CO WA 120-C3
TREADWELL RD
LANE CO OR 215-C5
TREE FARM RD
LANE CO OR 215-D1
TREFRY RD
DOUGLAS CO WA 237-A1
TREMONT ST
COOS BAY OR 333-H9
TREMONT ST U.S.-101
COOS BAY OR 333-G7
NORTH BEND OR 333-G7
TREMONT ST W
PORT ORCHARD WA 174-B4
E TRENT AV Rt#-290
MILLWOOD WA 350-C5
SPOKANE WA 349-F7
SPOKANE VALLEY WA 349-F7
SPOKANE VALLEY WA 350-C6
TRENT RD Rt#-53
KOOTENAI CO ID 247-C1
E TRENT RD
KOOTENAI CO ID 245-A3
E TRENT RD Rt#-290
MILLWOOD WA 350-E5
Otis Orchards WA 351-C3
Otis Orchards WA 352-C7
SPOKANE CO WA 351-C3
SPOKANE CO WA 352-C7
SPOKANE VALLEY WA 350-E5
SPOKANE VALLEY WA 351-C3
N TRENT RD
KOOTENAI CO ID 115-A1
W TRENT RD Rt#-53
KOOTENAI CO ID 247-C1
KOOTENAI CO ID 352-J3
KOOTENAI CO ID 353-A2
TRENTON AV
BREMERTON WA 271-B10
KITSAP CO WA 271-B8
S TRENTON ST
SEATTLE WA 286-A3
TRESHAM LN
JACKSON CO OR 230-C5
TRESTLE RD
KLAMATH CO OR 235-C1
TRESTLE CREEK RD
BONNER CO ID 244-C2
TREVITT ST
THE DALLES OR 196-C7
TRIANGLE RD
KOOTENAI CO ID 245-B4
OWYHEE CO ID 147-B3
TRIANGLE HILL RD
DESCHUTES CO OR 217-A2
TRIGGER AV
KITSAP CO WA 170-A7
Olympic View WA 170-A7
TRILLIUM LAKE RD
CLACKAMAS CO OR 202-A7
TRIPLE OAK DR
LANE CO OR 210-C7
TRIPOD CAMP RD
JACKSON CO OR 226-B4
TRONSON RD
SNOHOMISH CO WA 168-C4
NW TROOST ST
DOUGLAS CO OR 334-A6
ROSEBURG OR 334-C4
TROSPER RD SW
THURSTON CO WA 296-C11
TUMWATER WA 296-F11
TROUT LN
DESCHUTES CO OR 212-A6
TROUT CREEK RD
BONNER CO ID 244-C1
CROOK CO OR 135-C1
HOOD RIVER CO OR 202-B1
MALHEUR CO OR 154-A2
NE TROUT CREEK RD
JEFFERSON CO OR 135-C1
SE TROUT CREEK RD
JEFFERSON CO OR 135-C1
MULTNOMAH CO OR 200-D2
TROUT CREEK BUTTE RD
DESCHUTES CO OR 211-B6
TROUT LAKE HWY
KLICKITAT CO WA 119-A3
TROUT LAKE GREENWOOD RD
KLICKITAT CO WA 119-A3
TROUT LODGE RD
GRANT CO WA 112-C3
TROXELL RD
ISLAND CO WA 167-C1
TROY RD
WALLOWA CO OR 122-C3
WALLOWA CO OR 130-C1
TRUAX RD
SPOKANE CO WA 114-C2
TRUBEL RD
CLACKAMAS CO OR 200-D4
NW TRUE ST
PULLMAN WA 249-B5
TRUITT RD
DOUGLAS CO OR 219-A7
TRUNK RD
DUNCAN BC 101-A1
YAMHILL CO OR 198-C6
N TRUNK RD
SNOHOMISH CO WA 171-A6
TSAWWASSEN FERRY CSWY Rt#-17
DISTRICT OF DELTA BC 101-C1
SW TUALATIN RD
TUALATIN OR 199-B4
SW TUALATIN-SHERWOOD RD
SHERWOOD OR 199-B4
TUALATIN OR 199-B4
WASHINGTON CO OR 199-B4
TUALATIN VALLEY HWY Rt#-8
CORNELIUS OR 198-C1
HILLSBORO OR 198-D1
WASHINGTON CO OR 198-C1
SE TUALATIN VALLEY HWY Rt#-8
HILLSBORO OR 198-D1
HILLSBORO OR 199-A2
WASHINGTON CO OR 199-A2
SW TUALATIN VALLEY HWY Rt#-8
BEAVERTON OR 199-A2
HILLSBORO OR 199-A2
WASHINGTON CO OR 199-A2
TUB SPRINGS RD
MALHEUR CO OR 146-B3
WASCO CO OR 135-C1
TUCANNON RD
COLUMBIA CO WA 122-A2
TUCKER AV
FRIDAY HARBOR WA 101-C2
TUCKER RD
CLACKAMAS CO OR 200-C7
HOOD RIVER CO OR 195-C5
LEWIS CO WA 118-A2
LEWIS CO WA 187-D3
POLK CO OR 204-A3
TUCKER CREEK CTO
CLATSOP CO OR 188-C3
TUCKNESS RD
MALHEUR CO OR 146-C3
SE TUCKRIDGE RD
CLACKAMAS CO OR 200-D3
TUDOR AV
DISTRICT OF SAANICH BC 257-F5
TUFFRE RD
GRAYS HARBOR CO WA 178-A2
TUKWILA PKWY
TUKWILA WA 289-G5
TUKWILA INTERNATIONL BLVD
KING CO WA 286-D6
TUKWILA WA 286-D6
TUKWILA INTRNATIONL BL Rt#-99
SEATAC WA 288-D1
TUKWILA WA 286-D7
TUKWILA WA 288-D1
TULALIP RD
SNOHOMISH CO WA 168-A6
SNOHOMISH CO WA 171-C1
TULE LAKE RD S
PIERCE CO WA 181-D4
TULIN RD NE
KITSAP CO WA 170-D6
TULL RD
COLUMBIA CO WA 122-A2
NW TUMALO AV
BEND OR 332-D7
TUMALO CREEK RD
DESCHUTES CO OR 217-B1
TUMALO-DESCHUTES HWY
DESCHUTES CO OR 212-C7
DESCHUTES CO OR 217-C1
TUMALO FALLS RD
DESCHUTES CO OR 216-D3
TUMALO LOOP RD
DESCHUTES CO OR 216-D2
DESCHUTES CO OR 217-A3
TUMALO RESERVOIR RD
DESCHUTES CO OR 217-B1
TUM-A-LUM RD
UMATILLA CO OR 121-C3
TUM TUM RD
BENTON CO OR 133-A1
TUMWATER ACCESS RD Rt#-117
CLALLAM CO WA 261-C5
PORT ANGELES WA 261-C5
TUMWATERR BLVD SE
THURSTON CO WA 296-H13
TUMWATER WA 296-H13
TUMWIT RD
MULTNOMAH CO OR 194-B7
TUNK CREEK RD
OKANOGAN CO WA 104-C2
OKANOGAN CO WA 105-A2
TUNNEL RD
DOUGLAS CO OR 225-B7
KLICKITAT CO WA 195-D4
TUNNEL CREEK RD
JOSEPHINE CO OR 229-A3
TUNNEL HILL RD
LAKE CO OR 152-A2
TUNNEL LOOP RD
JOSEPHINE CO OR 229-A3
TUPPER RD
MORROW CO OR 128-C3
NW TUPPER RD
YAMHILL CO OR 198-A4
TURK DR
SNOHOMISH CO WA 168-B7
TURKEY CRICK LN
DOUGLAS CO OR 221-B2
TURKEY RANCH RD
WALLA WALLA CO WA 121-C3
TURKEY RUN RD
LANE CO OR 215-B6
TURKINGTON RD
WHATCOM CO WA 161-C1
TURNER RD
COLUMBIA CO WA 122-B2
TURNER RD SE
MARION CO OR 325-E7
SALEM OR 204-D7
SALEM OR 325-C2
TURNER CREEK RD
JEFFERSON CO OR 213-D1
NW TURNER CREEK RD
YAMHILL CO OR 198-A3
TURNER RANCH RD
MALHEUR CO OR 154-A2
TURNERS CUTOFF RD
OKANOGAN CO WA 105-A1
TURNIDGE RD
LINN CO OR 207-C2
TUTTLE LN
WHATCOM CO WA 160-B1
SW TUTUILLA CREEK RD
PENDLETON OR 129-B1
UMATILLA CO OR 129-B1
TVEIT RD
SNOHOMISH CO WA 168-D5
TWEED RD
DESCHUTES CO OR 212-B7
TWELFTH ST Rt#-28
DAVENPORT WA 114-A2
TWELVE MILE RD
STEVENS CO WA 106-A2
SW TWENTIETH ST
CHEHALIS WA 299-G14
TWENTYMILE RD
LAKE CO OR 152-B3
N TWICKENHAM RD
WHEELER CO OR 136-A1
S TWICKENHAM RD
WHEELER CO OR 136-A1
TWIN BRIDGE RD
FERRY CO WA 106-A2
TWIN BRIDGES RD
CLACKAMAS CO OR 201-D6
TWIN BUTTES W DR
LINN CO OR 210-B3
TWIN HOUSE RD
IDAHO CO ID 123-C3
TWIN LAKES RD
FERRY CO WA 105-C3
N TWIN LAKES RD
DESCHUTES CO OR 142-C1
TWIN OAK RD
KLICKITAT CO WA 196-D6
TWIN PEAKS RD
KOOTENAI CO ID 247-C5
NE TWIN SPITS RD
KITSAP CO WA 170-C3
TWIN SPRINGS RD
MALHEUR CO OR 146-C1
TWISP-CARLTON RD
OKANOGAN CO WA 104-B3
TWISP RIVER RD
OKANOGAN CO WA 104-A3
TWISP-WINTHROP EAST RD
WINTHROP WA 104-A2
TWOMILE RD
COOS CO OR 220-B7
T W WALTERS RD Rt#-26
COLFAX WA 122-C1
TYADMAN RD
KLICKITAT CO WA 196-C7
TYEE DR
WHATCOM CO WA 101-C1
TYEE RD
DOUGLAS CO OR 141-A1
DOUGLAS CO OR 221-A1
TYGH BURN RD
WASCO CO OR 202-D5
TYGH RIDGE MARKET RD
WASCO CO OR 127-B2
TYKESON RD
YAMHILL CO OR 198-C4
TYLER RD
DESCHUTES CO OR 217-B1
TYLER ST
PORT TOWNSEND WA 263-H4
S TYLER ST
TACOMA WA 292-B7
TACOMA WA 294-B3
TYNDALL AV
DISTRICT OF SAANICH BC 257-C2
TYNDALL RD
GRANT CO WA 242-C1
TYNE ST
VANCOUVER BC 156-C5
TYNER ST
PORT COQUITLAM BC 157-B5
TYRELL RD
BENTON CO WA 120-C3
TYRELL RD SE
THURSTON CO WA 184-D4
TY VALLEY RD
LINN CO OR 210-D1
TZOUHALEM RD
BRITISH COLUMBIA BC 101-A1
DUNCAN BC 101-A1

U

U RD NE
DOUGLAS CO WA 113-A1
U RD SW
DOUGLAS CO WA 239-B2
U ST
PORT TOWNSEND WA 263-G2
U 1/2 RD NW
DOUGLAS CO WA 236-B7
UDELL RD
SNOHOMISH CO WA 168-D3
UDELL HANSEN RD
PACIFIC CO WA 183-B4
SE UGLOW AV
DALLAS OR 204-A6
POLK CO OR 204-A6
UKIAH-ALBEE RD
UKIAH OR 129-B3
UMATILLA CO OR 129-B3
UKIAH-HILGARD HWY Rt#-244
UKIAH OR 129-B3
UMATILLA CO OR 129-B3
UNION CO OR 129-C3
UNION CO OR 130-A2
ULRICH RD
JACKSON CO OR 226-B7
ULRICK RD
WHATCOM CO WA 158-C6
UMAPINE RD
UMATILLA CO OR 121-C3
UMAPINE-BEAUCHAMP RD
UMATILLA CO OR 121-C3
UMATILLA
CROOK CO OR 213-D7
UMATILLA AV
PORT TOWNSEND WA 263-E3
UMATILLA MISSION HWY
Mission OR 129-B1
UMATILLA CO OR 129-B1
UMATILLA RIVER RD
HERMISTON OR 129-A1
UMATILLA CO OR 129-A1
UMATILLA-STANFIELD HWY U.S.-39
HERMISTON OR 129-A1
STANFIELD OR 129-A1
UMATILLA OR 129-A1
UMATILLA CO OR 129-A1
UMIKER RD
COWLITZ CO WA 118-A2
UMPQUA AV Rt#-38
REEDSPORT OR 218-C1
UMPQUA HWY Rt#-38
DOUGLAS CO OR 140-C1
DOUGLAS CO OR 141-A1
DOUGLAS CO OR 218-D2
DOUGLAS CO OR 219-A3
DRAIN OR 219-A3
ELKTON OR 141-A1
REEDSPORT OR 218-D2
UMPQUA HWY Rt#-99
DOUGLAS CO OR 219-A2
DRAIN OR 219-A2
N UMPQUA RD
DOUGLAS CO OR 222-D3
DOUGLAS CO OR 223-B2
UMPQUA ST NE
MARION CO OR 205-A3
UMPTANUM RD
KITTITAS CO WA 241-B7
UNDERHILL AV
DISTRICT OF BURNABY BC 156-D4
UNDERPASS RD
DOUGLAS CO OR 219-A7
DOUGLAS CO OR 221-C1
UNDERWOOD RD
CLARK CO WA 192-D1
N UNDERWOOD ST
KENNEWICK WA 343-A10
UNDIE RD
CLALLAM CO WA 169-D3
UNGER RD
CLACKAMAS CO OR 200-A7

INDEX

398 SW UNGER RD — STREET INDEX — E WALNUT ST Rt#-505

STREET — City State Page-Grid

SW UNGER RD
WASHINGTON CO OR 198-C2
UNICK RD
WHATCOM CO WA 158-B6
UNION AV
BREMERTON WA 270-D12
GRANTS PASS OR 335-D11
Navy Yard City WA 270-D12
OLYMPIA WA 296-H6
OLYMPIA WA 297-A6
PIERCE CO WA 181-C4
STEILACOOM WA 181-C4
N UNION AV
TACOMA WA 292-C4
S UNION AV
DOUGLAS CO WA 239-B5
TACOMA WA 292-C5
TACOMA WA 294-C2
W UNION AV
PALOUSE WA 249-B1
UNION AV NE
RENTON WA 175-C4
N UNION CT
PORTLAND OR 309-F2
NE UNION RD
CLARK CO WA 192-C4
E UNION ST
SEATTLE WA 278-D5
N UNION ST
KENNEWICK WA 342-G10
S UNION ST
KENNEWICK WA 342-G11
SE UNION ST Rt#-500
CAMAS WA 193-B7
UNION ST NE
SALEM OR 322-J12
UNION BAY PL
SEATTLE WA 274-D5
UNION CREEK RD
JACKSON CO OR 226-D4
JACKSON CO OR 227-A4
UNION FLAT RD
WHITMAN CO WA 122-C1
WHITMAN CO WA 249-A7
UNION FLAT CREEK RD
WHITMAN CO WA 122-B1
UNION HALL RD
CLACKAMAS CO OR 199-D7
NE UNION HILL RD
KING CO WA 175-D1
KING CO WA 176-A1
UNION MILLS RD
CLACKAMAS CO OR 126-A3
UNION MILLS RD SE
THURSTON CO WA 181-A6
UNION SCHOOL RD NE
MARION CO OR 205-B2
UNIONTOWN RD
LATAH CO ID 250-B1
UNIONTOWN EAST RD
WHITMAN CO WA 250-B1
SE UNIONVALE RD
YAMHILL CO OR 204-D2
UNION VALLEY LOOP RD
CHELAN CO WA 236-C2
UNITED BLVD
COQUITLAM BC 157-A5
UNIVERSITY AV
FOREST GROVE OR 198-B1
UNIVERSITY BLVD
UNIV ENDOWMENT LANDS BC 156-A4
UNIVERSITY DR
DISTRICT OF BURNABY BC 156-D4
N UNIVERSITY RD
SPOKANE VALLEY WA 350-F8
S UNIVERSITY RD
SPOKANE VALLEY WA 350-F11
UNIVERSITY WY
KITTITAS CO WA 241-B5
UNIVERSITY WY NE
SEATTLE WA 274-C5
UP RR
PONDERAY ID 244-A1
UPAS AV
DESCHUTES CO OR 212-D5
DESCHUTES CO OR 213-A5
UPDIKE RD
LINCOLN CO OR 206-D5
UPPER AV
GEM CO ID 139-B3
UPPER DR
CLACKAMAS CO OR 199-B3
CLACKAMAS CO OR 320-A7
LAKE OSWEGO OR 199-B4
LAKE OSWEGO OR 320-A7
SW UPPER BOONES FERRY RD
DURHAM OR 199-B4
TIGARD OR 199-B4
TUALATIN OR 199-B4
UPPER CALAPOOIA DR
LINN CO OR 133-C2
LINN CO OR 134-A2
UPPER CLEVELAND RAPIDS RD
DOUGLAS CO OR 221-B3
UPPER COCOLALLA CREEK RD
BONNER CO ID 244-A5
UPPER COW CREEK RD
DOUGLAS CO OR 225-D5
UPPER CROSSING RD
JEFFERSON CO OR 135-A1
UPPER DEADWOOD CREEK RD
LINCOLN CO OR 209-D4
UPPER DESCHUTES RD
DESCHUTES CO OR 216-C7
UPPER DIAMOND RD
WALLOWA CO OR 130-B1
UPPER DRY CREEK RD
WALLA WALLA CO WA 122-A3
Warm Springs OR 208-A2
UPPER EIGHTMILE RD
WASCO CO OR 127-A2
UPPER FERRY LN
UNION CO OR 130-A2
UPPER FORDS CREEK RD
CLEARWATER CO ID 123-C2
UPPER GREEN CANYON RD
KITTITAS CO WA 241-A2
UPPER HAYDEN LAKE RD
KOOTENAI CO ID 355-G1
UPPER HIGHLAND RD
CLACKAMAS CO OR 200-A7
UPPER HOH RD
JEFFERSON CO WA 108-C1
JEFFERSON CO WA 109-A1
UPPER HORSE CAMP RESERVOIR RD
MALHEUR CO OR 154-C1
MALHEUR CO OR 155-A1
UPPER IMNAHA RD
WALLOWA CO OR 131-A2
UPPER INJUN CREEK RD
JACKSON CO OR 226-D5
UPPER JOE CREEK RD
CHELAN CO WA 236-B1
UPPER KEITH RD
CITY OF NORTH VANCOUVER BC 255-B5
UPPER LEVELS HWY Rt#-1
CITY OF NORTH VANCOUVER BC 255-D4
DIST OF NORTH VANCOUVER BC 254-H3
DIST OF NORTH VANCOUVER BC 255-D4
DIST OF WEST VANCOUVER BC 156-A2
DIST OF WEST VANCOUVER BC 254-A1
UPPER LOOP RD
COOS CO OR 220-D3
UPPER MAPLE CREEK RD
LANE CO OR 214-C4
UPPER MIDDLE FORK RD
GRANT CO OR 137-B1
UPPER MOUNTAIN RD
WALLOWA CO OR 131-A3
UPPER NESTUCCA RD
TILLAMOOK CO OR 197-D6
UPPER NORTH FORK RD
LANE CO OR 209-C7
LANE CO OR 214-C1
UPPER OLALLA RD
DOUGLAS CO OR 141-A3
UPPER PEOH POINT RD
KITTITAS CO WA 240-C2
UPPER REYNOLDS CREEK RD
OWYHEE CO ID 147-B2
UPPER RHEA CREEK RD
MORROW CO OR 128-C2
UPPER RIDGE RD
DOUGLAS CO OR 219-A5
EVERETT WA 268-B4
UPPER RIVER RD
JACKSON CO OR 230-B6
JOSEPHINE CO OR 229-B5
JOSEPHINE CO OR 335-A8
UPPER ROCK CREEK RD
GILLIAM CO OR 128-A2
UPPER SAMISH RD
SKAGIT CO WA 161-C4
UPPER SMITH RIVER RD
DOUGLAS CO OR 133-A3
DOUGLAS CO OR 219-A1
UPPER SUMAS MOUNTAIN RD
DISTRICT OF ABBOTSFORD BC 102-B1
S UPPER TERRACE RD
SPOKANE WA 349-B11
UPPER WHETSTONE RD
COLUMBIA CO WA 122-A2
E UPRIVER DR
SPOKANE WA 349-C7
SPOKANE WA 350-A3
SPOKANE CO WA 349-G6
SPOKANE CO WA 350-A3
UPTON RD
CENTRAL POINT OR 230-C7
JACKSON CO OR 230-C7
URAN RD
SKAMANIA CO WA 193-D7
URQUHART RD
ADAMS CO WA 113-B3
NE U S GRANT PL
PORTLAND OR 314-B3
US RESERVATION RD
BENTON CO WA 120-C2
US RESERVATION RD Rt#-225
BENTON CO WA 120-C2
USTICK RD
CALDWELL ID 147-B1
CANYON CO ID 147-B1
E USTICK RD
ADA CO ID 253-B2
BOISE ID 253-B2
MERIDIAN ID 253-B2
W USTICK RD
ADA CO ID 253-A2
BOISE ID 253-A2
MERIDIAN ID 253-A2
UTSALADY RD
ISLAND CO WA 168-A3

V

V PL
PACIFIC CO WA 186-A1
V ST
PACIFIC CO WA 186-A3
VACHTER RD NE
MARION CO OR 205-A1
VAIL RD SE
THURSTON CO WA 118-A1
VAIL LOOP RD SE
THURSTON CO WA 118-A1
VALBY RD
MORROW CO OR 128-B2
VALDE RD
SNOHOMISH CO WA 168-B4
VALE GARDEN RD
CLACKAMAS CO OR 199-C7
VALENTINE RD
SKAGIT CO WA 168-A1
VALENTINE RIDGE RD
GARFIELD CO WA 122-C2
VALE WEST HWY
MALHEUR CO OR 138-C3
VALE-WEST HWY U.S.-20
VALE OR 139-A3
W VALHALLA RD
KOOTENAI CO ID 248-A1
VALLEY AV
SUMNER WA 182-B3
VALLEY AV Rt#-162
PIERCE CO WA 182-B3
SUMNER WA 182-B3
VALLEY AV E
EDGEWOOD WA 182-B3
FIFE WA 182-B3
PIERCE CO WA 182-B3
PUYALLUP WA 182-B3
SUMNER WA 182-B3
VALLEY FRWY Rt#-167
ALGONA WA 182-B2
AUBURN WA 175-B7
AUBURN WA 182-B2
KENT WA 175-B7
KENT WA 291-J7
KING CO WA 175-B7
PACIFIC WA 182-B2
RENTON WA 175-B7
VALLEY HWY Rt#-9
WHATCOM CO WA 102-B1
WHATCOM CO WA 161-C2
E VALLEY HWY
KENT WA 175-C6
W VALLEY HWY Rt#-18
SHERIDAN OR 125-B3
WILLAMINA OR 125-B3
YAMHILL CO OR 125-B3
VALLEY PKWY Rt#-11
BELLINGHAM WA 258-C11
VALLEY RD
DOUGLAS CO OR 221-A4
GRANT CO WA 242-C3
LANE CO OR 215-D4
MOSES LAKE WA 242-C3
E VALLEY RD
KENT WA 175-C5
RENTON WA 175-C5
NE VALLEY RD
KITSAP CO WA 174-D1
VALLEY ST
SEATTLE WA 277-J3
SEATTLE WA 278-A3
S VALLEY ST
ADA CO ID 253-B4
E VALLEY CHAPEL RD
SPOKANE CO WA 114-C2
SPOKANE CO WA 246-C6
VALLEY CREEK RD NW
POLK CO OR 204-C4
VALLEY GROVE RD
WALLA WALLA CO WA 121-C3
VALLEY MALL BLVD
UNION GAP WA 243-C7
E VALLEY SPRINGS RD
SPOKANE WA 349-H3
SPOKANE CO WA 349-H3
SPOKANE CO WA 350-A2
VALLEY VIEW DR
ALBANY OR 326-A2
MEDFORD OR 336-G11
NW VALLEY VIEW DR
ROSEBURG OR 334-C4
VALLEY VIEW RD
CROOK CO OR 213-B6
DOUGLAS CO OR 221-D1
JACKSON CO OR 234-C2
JACKSON CO OR 337-A4
WHATCOM CO WA 158-C3
S VALLEY VIEW RD
JACKSON CO OR 337-A2
W VALLEY VIEW RD
JACKSON CO OR 234-C3
JACKSON CO OR 337-A2
TALENT OR 234-C3
NW VALLEY VISTA RD
WASHINGTON CO OR 192-A7
E VALLEYWAY AV
LIBERTY LAKE WA 352-D14
SPOKANE VALLEY WA 350-B8
SPOKANE VALLEY WA 351-A8
VALLEY-WESTSIDE RD
STEVENS CO WA 106-A2
VALLEYWOOD DR SE
SALEM OR 324-G7
VAN BELLE RD
YAKIMA CO WA 120-B2
VAN BELLE RD Rt#-223
GRANGER WA 120-A2
YAKIMA CO WA 120-A2
VAN BUREN AV
CORVALLIS OR 327-F9
VAN BUREN AV Rt#-34
CORVALLIS OR 327-F9
LINN CO OR 327-F9
N VANCOUVER AV
PORTLAND OR 309-G4
PORTLAND OR 313-G2
S VANCOUVER ST
BENTON CO WA 343-A13
KENNEWICK WA 343-A13
N VANCOUVER WY
PORTLAND OR 309-F2
NE VANCOUVER MALL DR
VANCOUVER WA 306-E1
VANCOUVER WA 307-F1
VAN CUREN RD
CLACKAMAS CO OR 200-C5
VAN DAM RD
ISLAND CO WA 167-B3
SW VANDERMOST RD
WASHINGTON CO OR 199-A3
VANDERSCHUERE RD
WASHINGTON CO OR 198-D4
VAN DEUSEN RD
GEM CO ID 139-C3
VANDEVERT RD
DESCHUTES CO OR 217-A7
VAN-DREWSEY RD
HARNEY CO OR 137-C3
VAN DUSEN RD
KOOTENAI CO ID 248-B5
VAN DUYN RD
LANE CO OR 210-B7
N VAN DUYN RD
OKANOGAN WA 104-C3
OKANOGAN CO WA 104-C3
VAN DUYN ST
COBURG OR 210-B7
VAN DYKE RD SW
THURSTON CO WA 184-A4
VAN GIESEN ST
RICHLAND WA 340-E13
VAN GIESEN ST Rt#-224
RICHLAND WA 340-B12
WEST RICHLAND WA 120-C2
W VAN GIESEN ST Rt#-224
BENTON CO WA 340-A12
RICHLAND WA 340-A12
WEST RICHLAND WA 121-A2
WEST RICHLAND WA 340-A12
VAN GILDER RD
SHERMAN CO OR 127-C2
VAN LAKE RD
DESCHUTES CO OR 144-A1
VAN NESS RD
COWLITZ CO WA 187-B7
VAN NESS ST
KLAMATH FALLS OR 338-D5
VAN NESS WY
SNOHOMISH CO WA 168-C7
VAN OGLES FORD SUMNER
PIERCE CO WA 182-C4
VANTAGE HWY
KITTITAS CO WA 120-A1
KITTITAS CO WA 241-C5
VANTINE RD
WHITMAN CO WA 249-A1
VANTINE RD SE
THURSTON CO WA 184-D3
VAN TROJAN RD
JEFFERSON CO WA 170-A1
VAN WELL RD
POLK CO OR 204-A4
S VAN WELL ST
DOUGLAS CO WA 239-B5
VARCO RD
DESCHUTES CO OR 212-A6
VASHON HWY SW
KING CO WA 174-D7
KING CO WA 181-D1
VASSAULT ST
TACOMA WA 181-C1
VAUGHN RD
MARION CO OR 207-D2
TILLAMOOK CO OR 197-B1
S VAUGHN RD KPN
PIERCE CO WA 174-A7
NW VAUGHN ST
PORTLAND OR 312-C3
VAY EDGEMERE RD
BONNER CO ID 107-A3
VEAZIE-CUMBERLAND RD
KING CO WA 110-C3
VEDDER RD
CITY OF CHILLIWACK BC 94-C3
CITY OF CHILLIWACK BC 102-C1
VEDDER RD Rt#-1A
CITY OF CHILLIWACK BC 94-C3
VEDDER MOUNTAIN RD
BRITISH COLUMBIA BC 102-C1
CITY OF CHILLIWACK BC 102-C1
NE VENA AV
Tracyton WA 270-G4
NW VENA AV
Tracyton WA 270-G4
VENABLES ST
VANCOUVER BC 255-B11
VENTURA CRES
DIST OF NORTH VANCOUVER BC 255-B1
VENTURE RD
KITTITAS CO WA 241-D5
VERA CRUZ ST
SISKIYOU CO CA 150-B3
VERDA LN NE
KEIZER OR 323-B5
SALEM OR 323-B5
N VERDE DR
MALHEUR CO OR 139-A3
ONTARIO OR 139-A3
NW VERDE DR
ONTARIO OR 139-A3
SW VERDE DR
ONTARIO OR 139-A3
VERGEN RD
CLACKAMAS CO OR 199-B6
SW VERMONT ST
PORTLAND OR 316-A5
VERNON AV
DISTRICT OF SAANICH BC 256-F4
VERNON RD
SNOHOMISH CO WA 171-D1
SE VERNON RD
CLARK CO WA 193-C6
VERNONIA RD
WASHINGTON CO OR 125-B1
VETERAN AV
WESTPORT WA 298-G14
VETERANS DR SW
PIERCE CO WA 181-C4
N VETERANS MEMORIAL PKWY
BOISE ID 253-C2
VEYS DR
COWLITZ CO WA 303-D6
KELSO WA 303-D6
VEYS ST
COWLITZ CO WA 303-D6
KELSO WA 303-D6
VICKERY AV E
PIERCE CO WA 182-A4
VICTOR RD
WASCO CO OR 127-A3
VICTORIA DR
COQUITLAM BC 157-B4
VANCOUVER BC 156-C5
VICTORIA DR S
VANCOUVER BC 255-C11
VICTORIA-SEATTLE FERRY
BRITISH COLUMBIA BC 165-C1
CLALLAM CO WA 166-B3
ISLAND CO WA 167-A5
JEFFERSON CO WA 166-B3
JEFFERSON CO WA 167-A5
VICTOR POINT RD NE
MARION CO OR 205-C5
VICTOR POINT RD SE
MARION CO OR 205-C6
VICTORY DR SW
KITSAP CO WA 174-A4
VICTORY RD
LANE CO OR 210-A7
W VICTORY RD
ADA CO ID 253-B3
BOISE ID 253-C3
SE VIEWPARK RD
KITSAP CO WA 174-C5
VIEWPOINT DR
CULVER OR 208-B7
VIEW POINT RD
CLEARWATER CO ID 123-C2
VIKING WY NW
KITSAP CO WA 170-B7
POULSBO WA 170-B7
E VILAS RD
JACKSON CO OR 230-D7
JACKSON CO OR 336-D3
MEDFORD OR 336-D3
N VILLA RD
NEWBERG OR 198-D5
VILLAGE RD
SNOHOMISH CO WA 168-B3
VILLAGE PARK DR SE
BELLEVUE WA 175-D3
NE VINE ST
ROSEBURG OR 334-G4
VINEYARD DR
KENNEWICK WA 343-C11
VINGIE CREEK RD
LINCOLN CO OR 209-A3
VIOLA WELCHES RD
CLACKAMAS CO OR 200-B6
VIOLET AV Rt#-21
KAHLOTUS WA 121-C1
VIRGINIA AV
NORTH BEND OR 333-D4
VIRGINIA RD
BELLINGHAM WA 258-G6
VIRGINIA ST
MOUNT VERNON WA 260-B13
SEATTLE WA 277-J5
SEATTLE WA 278-A5
VIRGINIA ST Rt#-55
NEW MEADOWS ID 251-A4
VIRGINIA ST U.S.-95
ADAMS CO ID 251-A4
NEW MEADOWS ID 251-A4
VIRGINIA WY
COWLITZ CO WA 302-J5
LONGVIEW WA 302-J5
VIRGINIA VALLEY RD
HARNEY CO OR 145-C2
VIRGIN VALLEY RANCH RD
HUMBOLDT CO NV 153-B3
S VISTA AV
BOISE ID 253-C3
SW VISTA AV
PORTLAND OR 312-D7
PORTLAND OR 316-C1
W VISTA AV
BOISE ID 253-C3
VISTA AV SE
SALEM OR 324-H3
VISTA DR
FERNDALE WA 158-C5
WHATCOM CO WA 158-C5
N VISTA RD
SPOKANE VALLEY WA 350-C6
VISTA WY
KENNEWICK WA 342-J10
KENNEWICK WA 343-A10
VISTA RAMA DR E
KITSAP CO WA 271-C13
VITAE SPRINGS RD S
MARION CO OR 204-C7
MARION CO OR 324-A8
N VOLLAND ST
KENNEWICK WA 342-G9
VOORHIES RD
JACKSON CO OR 234-B2
VULCAN WY
CITY OF RICHMOND BC 156-B6
VYE RD
DISTRICT OF ABBOTSFORD BC 102-B1

W

W AV
RICHLAND WA 340-F7
W ST
CLARK CO WA 193-C7
PORT TOWNSEND WA 263-G2
WASHOUGAL WA 193-C7
WAAGA WY Rt#-303
KITSAP CO WA 174-B1
Silverdale WA 174-B1
WABASH AV
MEDFORD OR 336-E11
WABASH DR NE
MARION CO OR 205-A3
WABASH RD
DOUGLAS CO OR 222-B1
WACONDA RD NE
MARION CO OR 205-A3
WADDELL CREEK RD SW
THURSTON CO WA 184-B1
WADE RD
LINCOLN CO OR 206-C2
SNOHOMISH CO WA 168-D6
WADSWORTH RD
CLATSOP CO OR 188-C4
WAGGENER RD
LINN CO OR 210-B4
WAGHORN RD NW
KITSAP CO WA 170-B6
WAGNER RD
CANYON CO ID 147-B1
NEZ PERCE CO ID 250-D4
SNOHOMISH CO WA 110-C1
WALLA WALLA CO WA 121-B3
WHITMAN CO WA 114-A3
WAGNER ST
TWISP WA 104-A3
WAGNER BUTTE TRAIL RD
JACKSON CO OR 234-B5
WAGNER CREEK RD
JACKSON CO OR 234-B3
WAGNER GAP RD
JACKSON CO OR 234-B5
WAGON RD NE
MARION CO OR 205-C3
WAHA RD
NEZ PERCE CO ID 250-D5
WAHANNA RD
CLATSOP CO OR 301-H8
SEASIDE OR 301-H8
WAHA PRAIRIE RD
NEZ PERCE CO ID 250-C6
WAHKEENA DR
OCEAN SHORES WA 298-C3
WAHKIACUS HEIGHTS RD
KLICKITAT CO WA 196-C1
WAHKIACUS HIGH PRAIRIE RD
KLICKITAT CO WA 196-D3
WAHKIAKUM ST
CROOK CO OR 213-B6
WAHL RD
ADAMS CO WA 113-B3
ADAMS CO WA 121-B1
ISLAND CO WA 170-D2
LATAH CO ID 250-D1
WAHLUKE SLOPE RD
GRANT CO WA 120-C1
WAHTONKA RD W
WASCO CO OR 196-B7
WAHTUM LAKE TR
HOOD RIVER CO OR 195-A7
HOOD RIVER CO OR 201-D2
N WAIKIKI RD
Country Homes WA 346-H9
Fairwood WA 346-H9
W WAIKIKI RD
Fairwood WA 346-F8
SPOKANE CO WA 346-F8
WAIN RD
DIST OF NORTH SAANICH BC 159-C2
WAKEFIELD RD
GRAYS HARBOR CO WA 179-B7
S WAKEFIELD RD
ELMA WA 179-B7
GRAYS HARBOR CO WA 179-B7
WAKEFIELD CAMERON LAKE RD
OKANOGAN CO WA 104-C3
WAKLY LN
THURSTON CO WA 184-B3
WAKONDA BEACH RD
LINCOLN CO OR 328-B10
SW WAKONDA BEACH RD
LINCOLN CO OR 328-B10
WALBERG RD
SKAGIT CO WA 161-D6
WALDO RD
JOSEPHINE CO OR 233-A6
WALDO HILLS DR SE
MARION CO OR 205-C6
WALDRICK RD SE
THURSTON CO WA 184-D2
N WALKER AV
ASHLAND OR 337-F9
WALKER RD
COLUMBIA CO OR 189-B5
DESCHUTES CO OR 217-D2
GRAYS HARBOR CO WA 177-D3
LEWIS CO WA 187-C5
UMATILLA CO OR 129-A1
WALLA WALLA CO WA 122-A3
E WALKER RD
LATAH CO ID 249-D2
NW WALKER RD
BEAVERTON OR 199-A1
SW WALKER RD
WASHINGTON CO OR 199-B1
WALKER ST
PORT TOWNSEND WA 263-G5
WALKER VALLEY RD
SKAGIT CO WA 168-C1
WALKING WOODS DR
PORTLAND OR 320-B1
WALL ST
SEATTLE WA 277-J4
VANCOUVER BC 255-C9
N WALL ST
Country Homes WA 346-H13
SPOKANE WA 348-J3
Town and Country WA 346-H13
Town and Country WA 348-J3
NW WALL ST
BEND OR 332-D7
NW WALL ST U.S.-20
BEND OR 332-E6
S WALL ST
MOUNT VERNON WA 260-B12
WALLACE DR
DIST OF CENTRAL SAANICH BC 159-C3
DISTRICT OF SAANICH BC 159-C3
WALLACE LN
ADAMS CO ID 251-B3
VALLEY CO ID 252-D1
WALLACE RD Rt#-221
DAYTON OR 198-C7
YAMHILL CO OR 198-C7
YAMHILL CO OR 204-D1
NW WALLACE RD
MCMINNVILLE OR 198-A7
SE WALLACE RD Rt#-221
YAMHILL CO OR 204-D1
WALLACE RD NW Rt#-221
POLK CO OR 322-E8
SALEM OR 322-E8
WALLACE CREEK RD
LANE CO OR 215-D3
WALLA WALLA RIVER RD
UMATILLA CO OR 129-C1
WALLEN RD
LATAH CO ID 249-D4
WALLENS RD
CLACKAMAS CO OR 200-B7
WALLER RD
PIERCE CO WA 182-A4
WALLER RD E
PIERCE CO WA 182-A5
WALLINGFORD AV N
SEATTLE WA 274-A1
WALLOWA AV
JOSEPH OR 130-C2
WALLOWA LAKE HWY Rt#-82
ELGIN OR 130-B1
ENTERPRISE OR 130-C2
IMBLER OR 130-A2
ISLAND CITY OR 130-A2
LA GRANDE OR 130-A2
LOSTINE OR 130-C2
UNION CO OR 130-B1
WALLOWA OR 130-B1
WALLOWA CO OR 130-B1
WALLOWA MOUNTAIN LP
BAKER CO OR 131-A3
WALLOWA CO OR 131-A3
WALLOWA MOUNTAIN RD
WALLOWA CO OR 131-A2
WALLTINE RD
WHATCOM CO WA 158-B6
WALLULA AV
COLLEGE PLACE WA 344-E9
Garrett WA 344-E9
WALLA WALLA CO WA 344-B9
WALLUPA RD
WALLOWA CO OR 122-C3
WALLOWA CO OR 130-B1
WALLUSKI LOOP RD
CLATSOP CO OR 300-H10
WALNUT AV
BROWNSVILLE OR 210-C2
DESCHUTES CO OR 213-A4
W WALNUT AV
COEUR D'ALENE ID 355-E9
WALNUT BLVD
BENTON CO OR 327-C8
CORVALLIS OR 327-F6
WALNUT DR
LINN CO OR 207-B5
S WALNUT PL
SPOKANE WA 348-H11
N WALNUT RD
EUGENE OR 330-D7
LANE CO OR 330-D7
SPRINGFIELD OR 330-D7
WALNUT RD NW
OLYMPIA WA 296-E3
WALNUT ST
EVERETT WA 171-C1
EVERETT WA 265-F2
PORT TOWNSEND WA 263-H3
WALLA WALLA CO WA 121-B3
WALNUT ST U.S.-2
NEWPORT ID 106-C3
NEWPORT WA 106-C3
E WALNUT ST
COULEE CITY WA 113-A2
GRANT CO WA 113-A2
YAKIMA WA 243-C6
E WALNUT ST Rt#-19
CONDON OR 128-A2
E WALNUT ST Rt#-505
WINLOCK WA 187-C3

INDEX

N WALNUT ST — STREET INDEX — WHATCOM RD 399

STREET / City State Page-Grid

N WALNUT ST
BOISE ID 253-D3
S WALNUT ST
SPOKANE WA 348-H10
SW WALNUT ST
TIGARD OR 199-B3
W WALNUT ST
COULEE CITY WA 113-A2
YAKIMA WA 243-B6
W WALNUT ST Rt#-206
CONDON OR 128-A2
GILLIAM CO OR 128-A2
WALTERS RD
YAKIMA CO WA 243-D7
WALTERS RD S
TACOMA WA 181-C2
WALTON RD
DESCHUTES CO OR 217-B1
WAMIC MARKET RD
WASCO CO OR 127-A2
WAMIC MILL RD
WASCO CO OR 202-D7
WAMPUM LN
POLK CO OR 204-A5
WAMSTAD RD
CANYON CO ID 139-A3
WANAMAKER RD
ISLAND CO WA 167-B5
WANETA RD
SUNNYSIDE WA 120-B3
YAKIMA CO WA 120-B3
WANETA RD Rt#-241
SUNNYSIDE WA 120-B2
YAKIMA CO WA 120-B2
WANNACUT LAKE RD
OKANOGAN CO WA 104-C1
WANOGA LOOKOUT RD
DESCHUTES CO OR 216-D5
W WAPATO RD
YAKIMA CO WA 119-C2
YAKIMA CO WA 120-A2
WAPATO WY Rt#-150
CHELAN CO WA 236-B2
WAPATO LAKE RD
CHELAN CO WA 236-B2
WAPATO SCHOOL RD
YAMHILL CO OR 198-B4
WAPENISH RD
TOPPENISH WA 120-A2
WAPATO WA 120-A2
YAKIMA CO WA 120-A2
WAPENISH RD Rt#-22
YAKIMA CO WA 120-A2
WAPINITIA HWY Rt#-216
WASCO CO OR 127-A3
WAPINITIA RD
WASCO CO OR 127-A3
WAPINITIA MARKET RD
WASCO CO OR 127-A3
WAPITI LN
DOUGLAS CO OR 221-A1
NE WARD AV
CLARK CO WA 193-A5
WARD DR NE
Hayesville OR 323-D7
SALEM OR 323-D7
WARD RD
DESCHUTES CO OR 217-C3
WASCO CO OR 127-B2
NE WARD RD
CLARK CO WA 193-A5
WARD CREEK RD
COOS CO OR 220-C7
PACIFIC CO WA 117-A1
WARD GAP RD
BENTON CO WA 120-B3
WARD RIDGE RD
KOOTENAI CO ID 248-C2
WARDS BUTTE RD
DOUGLAS CO OR 219-C1
WARDS CREEK RD
JACKSON CO OR 230-A6
NE WARDWAY ST
PORTLAND OR 312-C3
WARMINGTON RD
YAMHILL CO OR 198-B7
WARM LAKE RD
CASCADE ID 252-D5
VALLEY CO ID 252-D5
WARM SPRING RD
WASCO CO OR 208-B1
E WARM SPRINGS AV
BOISE ID 253-D3
WARM SPRINGS HWY U.S.-26
CLACKAMAS CO OR 202-A7
JEFFERSON CO OR 135-A1
JEFFERSON CO OR 208-B3
MADRAS OR 208-B3
Warm Springs OR 135-A1
Warm Springs OR 208-A2
WASCO CO OR 126-C3
WASCO CO OR 127-A3
WASCO CO OR 135-A1
WASCO CO OR 202-A7
WARM SPRINGS RD
HARNEY CO OR 145-C1
HARNEY CO OR 146-A1
JEFFERSON CO OR 211-C1
WARNECKE RD
WHITMAN CO WA 250-B2
WARNER AV
KING CO WA 110-C3
NEZ PERCE CO ID 250-C5
WARNER DR SE
MARION CO OR 205-B6
WARNER HWY Rt#-140
HARNEY CO OR 153-A3
LAKE CO OR 152-A2
LAKE CO OR 153-A3
S WARNER ST
TACOMA WA 294-D3
WARNER CANYON RD
CHELAN CO WA 238-C2
WARNOCK RD
WALLOWA CO OR 130-C1
WARREN AV Rt#-303
BREMERTON WA 270-J10
N WARREN AV
NEWPORT WA 106-C3
S WARREN AV
NEWPORT WA 106-C3
WARREN DR NW
PIERCE CO WA 181-B1
WARREN RD
COLUMBIA CO OR 189-A3
YAMHILL CO OR 198-C6
WARRENS SPUR
CANYON CO ID 147-C2

NW WARRENTON DR
WARRENTON OR 188-B1
WARRENTON-ASTORIA HWY U.S.-101
ASTORIA OR 300-C9
CLATSOP CO OR 188-B2
CLATSOP CO OR 300-C9
WARRENTON OR 188-B2
WARRENTON DUMP SCHOOL RD
WARRENTON OR 188-B2
WARREN WAGON RD
MCCALL ID 251-C4
VALLEY CO ID 251-C4
WARRINER RD
CLACKAMAS CO OR 200-D3
S WARRIOR RD
YAKIMA CO WA 243-D6
WASANKARI RD
CLALLAM CO WA 164-D6
WASCO-HEPPNER HWY
SHERMAN CO OR 127-C1
WASCO OR 127-C1
WASCO-HEPPNER HWY Rt#-206
CONDON OR 128-A2
GILLIAM CO OR 128-A2
HEPPNER OR 128-B2
MORROW CO OR 128-B2
SHERMAN CO OR 127-C2
SHERMAN CO OR 128-A2
WASCO OR 127-C2
WASCO RUFUS RD
SHERMAN CO OR 127-C1
WASCO OR 127-C1
W WASHAM RD
EAGLE ID 253-A1
WASHBOARD RD
GARFIELD CO WA 122-B1
WASHBURN ST
BROWNSVILLE OR 210-C2
WASHBURN WY
Altamont OR 235-C5
Altamont OR 338-G9
KLAMATH CO OR 235-C5
KLAMATH CO OR 338-G14
KLAMATH FALLS OR 338-G9
WASHINGTON AV
BREMERTON WA 270-J10
CHELAN CO WA 236-D4
LA GRANDE OR 130-A2
WASHINGTON AV Rt#-169
ENUMCLAW WA 110-C3
WASHINGTON AV Rt#-304
BREMERTON WA 270-J11
N WASHINGTON AV
CENTRALIA WA 299-E3
N WASHINGTON AV Rt#-52
GEM CO ID 139-C3
N WASHINGTON AV U.S.-2
NEWPORT WA 106-C3
NE WASHINGTON AV
CHEHALIS WA 299-D11
S WASHINGTON AV
CENTRALIA WA 299-E4
S WASHINGTON AV Rt#-52
EMMETT ID 139-C3
GEM CO ID 139-C3
S WASHINGTON AV U.S.-2
NEWPORT WA 106-C3
SE WASHINGTON AV
ROSEBURG OR 334-G8
SW WASHINGTON AV Rt#-138
ROSEBURG OR 334-F7
W WASHINGTON AV
YAKIMA WA 243-B7
WASHINGTON AV N Rt#-161
EATONVILLE WA 118-B1
PIERCE CO WA 118-B1
WASHINGTON AV N Rt#-162
ORTING WA 182-C5
WASHINGTON AV N Rt#-181
KENT WA 175-B7
WASHINGTON AV S
KENT WA 175-B7
KING CO WA 175-B7
LONG BEACH WA 186-A5
WASHINGTON AV S Rt#-161
EATONVILLE WA 118-B1
WASHINGTON AV S Rt#-162
ORTING WA 182-C5
WASHINGTON AV S Rt#-181
KENT WA 175-B7
WASHINGTON BLVD
LAKEWOOD WA 181-C4
WASHINGTON BLVD Rt#-D1
CRESCENT CITY CA 148-B3
DEL NORTE CO CA 148-B3
E WASHINGTON BLVD Rt#-D1
DEL NORTE CO CA 148-B3
NW WASHINGTON BLVD
GRANTS PASS OR 335-F7
E WASHINGTON RD
SPOKANE CO WA 246-D6
SPOKANE CO WA 247-A6
WASHINGTON ST
ASTORIA OR 300-B4
CHELAN CO WA 236-B1
CHENEY WA 246-A7
EUGENE OR 329-J7
FERNDALE WA 158-C6
LEWIS CO WA 187-C1
MABTON WA 120-B3
MORROW CO OR 128-C1
NAPAVINE WA 187-C1
OREGON CITY OR 199-D4
PORT TOWNSEND WA 263-G5
SEDRO-WOOLLEY WA 161-C5
SKAGIT CO WA 259-H14
SODAVILLE OR 133-C2
SPOKANE CO WA 246-A7
VANCOUVER WA 305-F5
WENATCHEE WA 238-D4
WOODLAND WA 192-C1
WASHINGTON ST Rt#-26
ADAMS CO WA 121-A1
OTHELLO WA 121-A1
WASHINGTON ST Rt#-129
ASOTIN WA 250-B5
WASHINGTON ST Rt#-218
FOSSIL OR 128-A3
E WASHINGTON ST
SEQUIM WA 262-E11
STAYTON OR 133-C1
N WASHINGTON ST
KENNEWICK WA 343-D10
SPOKANE WA 348-J6
N WASHINGTON ST Rt#-19
CONDON OR 128-A2
S WASHINGTON ST
Finley WA 343-D13

S WASHINGTON ST
KENNEWICK WA 343-D13
SPOKANE WA 348-J10
S WASHINGTON ST Rt#-19
CONDON OR 128-A2
S WASHINGTON ST U.S.-95
MOSCOW ID 249-C5
SE WASHINGTON ST
PORTLAND OR 315-G6
SE WASHINGTON ST Rt#-223
DALLAS OR 204-A6
SW WASHINGTON ST
PORTLAND OR 313-F6
SW WASHINGTON ST Rt#-223
DALLAS OR 204-A6
W WASHINGTON ST
CLALLAM CO WA 262-B12
SEQUIM WA 262-B12
STAYTON OR 133-C1
W WASHINGTON ST U.S.-101
CLALLAM CO WA 165-D6
CLALLAM CO WA 166-A6
WASHINGTON ST E
HUNTINGTON OR 138-C2
WASHINGTON ST E U.S.-20
VALE OR 139-A3
WASHINGTON ST E U.S.-30
HUNTINGTON OR 138-C2
WASHINGTON ST W U.S.-20
VALE OR 139-A3
WASHINGTON ST W U.S.-30
HUNTINGTON OR 138-C2
WASHINGTON WY
COLUMBIA CO OR 189-B4
GEORGE WA 112-B3
GRANT CO WA 112-B3
LONGVIEW WA 302-J9
LONGVIEW WA 303-B8
RAINIER OR 189-B4
WASHOUGAL RIVER RD
CLARK CO WA 193-D7
SKAMANIA CO WA 193-D7
SKAMANIA CO WA 194-A6
SE WASHOUGAL RIVER RD
CLARK CO WA 193-C7
WASHOUGAL WA 193-C7
WASSER RD
COLUMBIA CO OR 189-C6
WATER ST
PORT MOODY BC 157-A4
PORT TOWNSEND WA 263-J4
VANCOUVER BC 254-H10
WATER ST Rt#-20
PORT TOWNSEND WA 263-H5
WATER ST Rt#-27
TEKOA WA 114-C3
WHITMAN CO WA 114-C3
WATER ST Rt#-82
LOSTINE OR 130-C2
N WATER ST
OLYMPIA WA 296-H5
SILVERTON OR 205-C4
WESTON OR 129-C1
N WATER ST Rt#-214
SILVERTON OR 205-C4
S WATER ST
WESTON OR 129-C1
S WATER ST Rt#-214
SILVERTON OR 205-C4
WATERFRONT ST
YAMHILL CO OR 198-D6
WATER GAP RD
JOSEPHINE CO OR 149-B2
WATER GULCH RD
BAKER CO OR 138-A1
WATERLOO RD
LINN CO OR 133-C1
WATERLOO OR 133-C1
WATERMAN RD
WHITMAN CO WA 114-C3
WATERS AV S
SEATTLE WA 287-H5
WATERS RD
COWLITZ CO WA 189-C1
WATER TANK RD
SKAGIT CO WA 161-A6
WATER WHEEL RD
GEM CO ID 139-C3
WATERWORKS RD
CLACKAMAS CO OR 200-D3
SNOHOMISH CO WA 168-B7
SW WATSON AV
BEAVERTON OR 199-B2
WATSON RD
JEFFERSON CO WA 170-B3
KITTITAS CO WA 241-C5
WALLA WALLA CO WA 121-B3
YAKIMA CO WA 243-A5
S WATSON RD
KOOTENAI CO ID 247-D6
WATSON ST U.S.-2
CRESTON WA 113-C1
WATT CANYON RD
KITTITAS CO WA 240-D4
WAUGH RD
DESCHUTES CO OR 217-D2
N WAUGH RD
MOUNT VERNON WA 260-G11
WAUKON RD
LINCOLN CO WA 114-A2
WAUNA VISTA DR
WALLA WALLA WA 345-C9
WAUNCHER GULCH RD
LATAH CO ID 123-B1
NEZ PERCE CO ID 123-B1
SW WAVA LN
KITSAP CO WA 174-A6
WAVERLY DR
ALBANY OR 326-F9
E WAVERLY RD
SPOKANE CO WA 114-C2
WAVERLY WA 114-C2
WAWAWAI RD
WHITMAN CO WA 249-A7
WHITMAN CO WA 250-A1
WAWAWAI GRADE RD
WHITMAN CO WA 122-C1
WAWAWAI-PULLMAN RD
PULLMAN WA 249-A6
WHITMAN CO WA 249-A6
WAWAWAI-PULLMAN RD Rt#-194
WHITMAN CO WA 249-A5
WAWAWAI RIVER RD
WHITMAN CO WA 122-C2
WHITMAN CO WA 250-B4
WAWAWAI RIVER RD Rt#-128
WHITMAN CO WA 250-B4

WAWAWAI RIVER RD Rt#-193
WHITMAN CO WA 122-C2
WHITMAN CO WA 250-A4
SE WAX RD
COVINGTON WA 175-D7
KING CO WA 175-D7
MAPLE VALLEY WA 175-D7
WAX ORCHARD RD SW
KING CO WA 174-D7
WAYNE DR N
KEIZER OR 322-J6
WAYNITA WY NE
BOTHELL WA 171-C7
WAYPARK DR NE
MARION CO OR 205-B3
WEATHERFORD RD
LINN CO OR 210-B5
WEAVER RD
DOUGLAS CO OR 225-C2
KITTITAS CO WA 241-A5
WEAVER RD N
KITSAP CO WA 271-J2
S WEBB AV
DOUGLAS CO WA 239-B5
WEBB ST Rt#-3
MONTAGUE CA 150-A3
WEBB CANAL RD
NEZ PERCE CO ID 250-D5
WEBB CUTOFF RD
NEZ PERCE CO ID 250-D6
WEBB DISTRICT RD
COLUMBIA CO OR 117-B3
WEBBER ST
THE DALLES OR 196-C7
WEBBER CANYON RD
BENTON CO WA 120-C3
WEBBER CANYON RD Rt#-224
BENTON CO WA 120-C3
WEBBER CANYON RD Rt#-225
BENTON CO WA 120-C3
WEBB HILL RD
MASON CO WA 180-A1
WEBB RIDGE RD
NEZ PERCE CO ID 250-D6
WEBER RD
ADAMS CO WA 113-C3
CLACKAMAS CO OR 201-A5
LINCOLN CO WA 113-C3
LINN CO OR 210-C3
WHITMAN CO WA 249-B6
S WEBER COULEE RD
ADAMS CO WA 113-B3
WEBERG RD
CROOK CO OR 136-C3
WEBFOOT RD
DAYTON OR 198-C7
YAMHILL CO OR 198-C7
SE WEBFOOT RD
YAMHILL CO OR 204-C2
WEBSTER AV
CHELAN WA 236-D3
WEBSTER AV U.S.-97
CHELAN WA 236-D3
N WEBSTER AV
CHEWELAH WA 106-B3
WEBSTER EXT
PIERCE CO WA 182-A6
WEBSTER RD
GLADSTONE OR 199-D4
PIERCE CO WA 118-B1
SE WEBSTER RD
CLACKAMAS CO OR 199-D3
GLADSTONE OR 199-D3
WEBSTER RD E
PIERCE CO WA 182-A7
WEBSTER FLAT RD
JEFFERSON CO OR 208-B1
W WEDGEWOOD AV
Town and Country WA 346-H14
Town and Country WA 347-A14
WEED RD
KLAMATH CO OR 231-C2
WEEDIN PL NE
SEATTLE WA 274-B3
S WEGER RD
SPOKANE CO WA 246-D6
N WEHE AV
PASCO WA 343-H7
S WEHE AV
PASCO WA 343-H8
WEHRLI CANYON RD
GILLIAM CO OR 128-A3
WEIDKAMP RD
WHATCOM CO WA 158-D3
NE WEIDLER ST
PORTLAND OR 313-H4
PORTLAND OR 315-J4
WEIGAND RD
CROOK CO OR 213-B6
WEIKEL RD
YAKIMA CO WA 243-A6
N WEIPERT DR
Country Homes WA 346-J12
Town and Country WA 346-J12
SW WEIR RD
BEAVERTON OR 199-A3
WEISER SPUR U.S.-95
MALHEUR CO OR 139-A2
WEISER RIVER RD
WASHINGTON CO ID 139-A2
WEISER ID 139-A2
WEISS RD
LANE CO OR 215-A5
WEISSENFELS RIDGE RD
ASOTIN CO WA 123-A3
ASOTIN CO WA 250-C7
WEITZ LN
CLACKAMAS CO OR 200-B5
WEITZ RD
CANYON CO ID 147-B1
WELCH ST
DIST OF NORTH VANCOUVER BC 254-G5
WELCH CREEK RD
LINCOLN CO WA 113-C1
WELCHER RD
ISLAND CO WA 167-C5
WELCHES RD
CLACKAMAS CO OR 201-C5
WELLER RD
KOOTENAI CO ID 247-C6
E WELLESLEY AV
Otis Orchards WA 351-H2
Otis Orchards WA 352-C9
SPOKANE WA 349-C3
SPOKANE CO WA 350-H2
SPOKANE CO WA 351-H2
SPOKANE VALLEY WA 350-H2
SPOKANE VALLEY WA 351-B2

W WELLESLEY AV
SPOKANE WA 348-F3
SPOKANE WA 349-A3
WELLESLEY RD
LATAH CO ID 249-C1
WELLINGTON AV
WALLA WALLA WA 345-D6
E WELLINGTON RD
NANAIMO BC 93-A3
WELLPINIT-LITTLE FALLS RD
STEVENS CO WA 114-A1
WELLPINIT-MCCOY LAKE RD
STEVENS CO WA 113-C1
STEVENS CO WA 114-A1
WELLS RD
DOUGLAS CO OR 141-A1
S WELLS RD
SPOKANE CO WA 114-B2
WELLSANDT RD
ADAMS CO WA 113-C3
ADAMS CO WA 114-A3
RITZVILLE WA 113-C3
WELLS BENCH RD
CLEARWATER CO ID 123-C2
WELLSIAN WY
RICHLAND WA 341-F3
WELLS LANDING RD
POLK CO OR 207-C2
WELLS LINE
DISTRICT OF ABBOTSFORD BC 102-B1
WELLS STATION RD
UMATILLA CO OR 129-A1
WEMBLEY DR
DIST OF NORTH VANCOUVER BC 255-G3
WENAS AV Rt#-823
SELAH WA 243-B5
YAKIMA CO WA 243-B5
WENAS RD
YAKIMA CO WA 119-C1
YAKIMA CO WA 240-D7
YAKIMA CO WA 241-A7
YAKIMA CO WA 243-A3
S WENAS RD
YAKIMA CO WA 243-B4
WENATCHEE AV
WENATCHEE WA 238-D4
WENATCHEE WA 239-A4
WENATCHEE AV Rt#-285
WENATCHEE WA 239-A4
N WENATCHEE AV Rt#-285
WENATCHEE WA 238-D4
West Wenatchee WA 238-D4
S WENATCHEE AV
Appleyard WA 239-A5
WENATCHEE WA 239-A4
S WENATCHEE AV Rt#-285
WENATCHEE WA 239-A4
WENATCHEE HEIGHTS RD
CHELAN CO WA 238-D6
WENIGER HILL RD
KOOTENAI CO ID 248-A1
WENTWORTH RD
CLALLAM CO WA 169-B1
WENTWORTH ST
NANAIMO BC 93-A3
WENZEL SLOUGH RD
GRAYS HARBOR CO WA 179-A7
SW WERNER RD
BREMERTON WA 270-D12
KITSAP CO WA 270-D12
W WERNETT ST
FRANKLIN CO WA 342-F5
FRANKLIN CO WA 343-A5
PASCO WA 343-A5
WERRON RD
PIERCE CO WA 182-D4
WESGATE PL
PENDLETON OR 129-B1
UMATILLA CO OR 129-B1
WESLEY RD
HARRAH WA 119-C2
WEST AV
ARLINGTON WA 168-D5
WEST BLVD
VANCOUVER BC 156-B5
S WEST BLVD U.S.-101
ABERDEEN WA 178-B7
COSMOPOLIS WA 178-B7
WEST LN
COLUMBIA CO OR 192-A3
WEST MALL
UNIV ENDOWMENT LANDS BC 156-A4
WEST RD
PIERCE CO WA 181-D4
WEST SPUR
JACKSON CO OR 226-C4
WEST ST
DESCHUTES CO OR 212-A6
LINCOLN CO WA 114-A2
SAINT HELENS OR 192-B1
NW WEST ST
CHEHALIS WA 299-C11
S WEST ST Rt#-21
WILBUR WA 113-B1
WEST BEACH RD
Ault Field WA 167-A4
ISLAND CO WA 167-A4
WESTBROOK DR SW
KITSAP CO WA 174-B6
WESTBROOK MALL
UNIV ENDOWMENT LANDS BC 156-A4
WEST COAST RD Rt#-14
BRITISH COLUMBIA BC 101-A2
BRITISH COLUMBIA BC 164-C1
WEST COVE RD
LATAH CO ID 249-C1
NE WESTERHOLM RD
CLARK CO WA 193-B4
WESTERMAN RD SW
DOUGLAS CO WA 239-D1
WESTERN AV
SEATTLE WA 277-G4
WENATCHEE WA 238-D4
West Wenatchee WA 238-D4
SW WESTERN AV
GRANTS PASS OR 335-D9
WESTERN BLVD
BENTON CO OR 327-D11
CORVALLIS OR 327-D11
WESTERN ST
Altamont OR 339-D11
WESTERN ROUTE RD
MORROW CO OR 128-C3
SW WESTFALL RD
CLACKAMAS CO OR 199-A5
WESTFIR RD
LANE CO OR 142-A1
WESTFIR OR 142-A1

WEST FORK RD
OKANOGAN CO WA 104-B2
WEST FORK EVANS CREEK RD
JACKSON CO OR 230-A1
WEST FORK INDIAN CREEK RD
LANE CO OR 209-C7
WEST FORK-MILLICOMA RD
COOS CO OR 218-D6
WESTGATE AV U.S.-30
PENDLETON OR 129-B1
WESTHAVEN DR
WESTPORT WA 298-G10
WEST HILLS RD
BENTON CO OR 133-B1
BENTON CO OR 327-A11
CORVALLIS OR 327-A11
WESTLAKE AV
SEATTLE WA 273-J7
SEATTLE WA 277-J1
WESTLAKE AV N
SEATTLE WA 277-J5
WESTLAKE RD
LEWIS CO ID 123-B2
WESTLAND RD
UMATILLA CO OR 129-A1
WESTMINSTER HWY
CITY OF RICHMOND BC 156-A6
WESTMINSTER HWY S
CITY OF RICHMOND BC 156-C6
WESTMINSTER WY N
SHORELINE WA 171-A7
WESTMOND RD
BONNER CO ID 244-A5
WEST MOUNTAIN RD
VALLEY CO ID 251-C5
VALLEY CO ID 252-C1
WESTON-ELGIN HWY Rt#-204
UMATILLA CO OR 129-C1
UMATILLA CO OR 130-A1
UNION CO OR 130-A1
WESTPORT RD Rt#-105
GRAYS HARBOR CO WA 117-A1
WESTPORT DOCK RD Rt#-409
CLATSOP CO OR 117-B3
WEST SAANICH RD
DIST OF NORTH SAANICH BC 159-B2
WEST SAANICH RD Rt#-17A
DIST OF CENTRAL SAANICH BC 159-B3
DIST OF NORTH SAANICH BC 159-B3
DIST OF SAANICH BC 159-C5
WEST SHORE DR
WASHINGTON CO OR 198-A2
WESTSHORE DR
GRANT CO WA 242-C2
MOSES LAKE WA 242-C3
WEST SIDE HWY
COWLITZ CO WA 187-C6
LEWIS CO WA 187-C6
VADER WA 187-C6
WEST SIDE HWY Rt#-411
COWLITZ CO WA 187-C7
COWLITZ CO WA 189-C1
COWLITZ CO WA 303-C7
KELSO WA 303-C7
LONGVIEW WA 303-C7
WESTSIDE HWY SW
KING CO WA 174-D5
WEST SIDE RD
COOS CO OR 140-B3
COOS CO OR 220-D7
JOSEPHINE CO OR 233-A4
KLAMATH CO OR 231-B2
LAKE CO OR 151-C3
LAKE CO OR 152-A2
MODOC CO CA 151-C3
MODOC CO CA 152-A3
MYRTLE POINT OR 140-B3
WESTSIDE RD
PIERCE CO WA 185-A5
YAMHILL CO OR 198-A5
NE WESTSIDE RD
MCMINNVILLE OR 198-A7
YAMHILL CO OR 198-A6
WEST SIDE WOLLOCHET BAY
PIERCE CO WA 181-C2
WEST TWIN RD
LATAH CO ID 249-D4
NW WEST UNION RD
WASHINGTON CO OR 125-C1
WASHINGTON CO OR 192-A7
WASHINGTON CO OR 199-A1
WEST VALLEY HWY
AUBURN WA 175-B7
AUBURN WA 182-B1
EDGEWOOD WA 182-B1
KENT WA 175-B7
KING CO WA 175-B7
PACIFIC WA 182-B1
PACIFIC WA 182-B1
PIERCE CO WA 182-B1
SUMNER WA 182-B3
WEST VALLEY HWY Rt#-181
KENT WA 291-H2
TUKWILA WA 289-J5
TUKWILA WA 291-H2
WEST VALLEY HWY N
ALGONA WA 182-B1
WEST VALLEY HWY S
ALGONA WA 182-B2
KING CO WA 182-B2
PACIFIC WA 182-B2
WEST VALLEY RD
JEFFERSON CO WA 170-A2
WESTVIEW DR
CITY OF NORTH VANCOUVER BC 255-A4
DISTRICT OF DELTA BC 156-D7
DIST OF NORTH VANCOUVER BC 255-A4
DOUGLAS CO OR 221-B2
WESTWARD HO
LINCOLN CO OR 328-C3
WESTWICK RD
SNOHOMISH CO WA 110-C1
WESTWOOD ST
PORT COQUITLAM BC 157-A4
WETHERBEE RD
JOSEPHINE CO OR 229-A7
WEXLER RD
WHITMAN CO WA 249-B4
WEYERHAEUSER RD
SPRINGFIELD OR 331-G8
WEYERHAUSER RD
LANE CO OR 219-D1
WHALEN RD
COWLITZ CO WA 192-B1
WHARF ST
CITY OF VICTORIA BC 256-G9
WHATCOM RD
DISTRICT OF ABBOTSFORD BC 102-B1

INDEX

STREET City State Page-Grid	STREET City State Page-Grid	STREET City State Page-Grid	STREET City State Page-Grid	STREET City State Page-Grid	STREET City State Page-Grid
SE WHEATLAND RD	**W WHITMARSH RD**	**WILLAMETTE HWY Rt#-58**	**WILLOW GROVE CONN RD**	**WINONA RD**	**WOODBURN HUBBARD HWY**
YAMHILL CO OR 204-D2	SKAGIT CO WA 260-A8	KLAMATH CO OR 142-C2	**Rt#-432**	JOSEPHINE CO OR 229-C3	HUBBARD OR 205-B1
WHEATLAND RD N	**WHITMORE DR NW**	LANE CO OR 133-C3	COWLITZ CO WA 302-A5	**WINONA SOUTH RD**	MARION CO OR 205-B1
KEIZER OR 204-D3	PIERCE CO WA 181-B1	LANE CO OR 134-A3	LONGVIEW WA 302-A5	WHITMAN CO WA 122-A1	**WOODBURN-MONITOR RD NE**
KEIZER OR 323-A2	**WHITMORE RD**	LANE CO OR 142-B1	**WILLOWLAKE RD**	**WINSLOW RD**	MARION CO OR 205-C2
MARION CO OR 204-D3	WASHINGTON CO OR 198-C3	LANE CO OR 215-C3	GRANT CO OR 112-C2	WASCO CO OR 127-B2	**WOODCOCK RD**
WHEATON WY	**WHITNEY HWY Rt#-7**	LANE CO OR 330-J14	**WILLOWS RD**	**WINSTON RD**	CLALLAM CO WA 262-A6
BREMERTON WA 270-J8	BAKER CITY OR 138-B1	LANE CO OR 331-A14	ILWACO WA 186-A6	DOUGLAS CO OR 221-B6	**WOODELL LN**
BREMERTON WA 271-A9	BAKER CO OR 137-C1	OAKRIDGE OR 142-B1	PACIFIC CO WA 186-A6	WINSTON OR 221-B6	UNION CO OR 130-A2
WHEATON WY Rt#-303	BAKER CO OR 138-A1	**S WILLAMETTE RD**	REDMOND WA 171-C7	**WINSTON ST**	**WOODGATE RD**
BREMERTON WA 270-J6	GRANT CO OR 137-C1	LANE CO OR 215-B3	**E WILLOW SPRINGS RD**	DISTRICT OF BURNABY BC 156-D4	PACIFIC CO WA 186-A5
KITSAP CO WA 270-J6	**WHITNEY RD**	LANE CO OR 329-J14	SPOKANE CO WA 246-C5	**WINTEL RD S**	**WOODIN AV**
WHEELER RD	ADAMS CO ID 251-B5	**WILLAMETTE ST**	**WILLOW VALLEY RD**	MARION CO OR 207-C2	CHELAN WA 236-D3
CLALLAM CO WA 163-A7	COLUMBIA CO OR 189-B6	COBURG OR 210-B7	KLAMATH CO OR 151-B2	**WINTER ST SE**	CHELAN WA 236-C3
GRANT CO OR 242-D3	COOS CO OR 140-B3	EUGENE OR 329-J13	MODOC CO CA 151-B2	SALEM OR 322-H14	**WOODIN AV Rt#-150**
JACKSON CO OR 230-C5	**E WHITNEY HILL RD**	EUGENE OR 330-A8	**WILLOW VALLEY RD**	**WINTERCREEK RD**	CHELAN WA 236-D3
LANE CO OR 215-D4	KING CO WA 110-C3	LANE CO OR 210-B7	KLAMATH CO OR 151-B2	MARION CO OR 207-D2	**WOODIN AV U.S.-97**
MOSES LAKE WA 242-D3	KING CO WA 182-D2	LANE CO OR 329-H14	**WILLS RD**	**WINTERGREEN AV NW**	CHELAN WA 236-D3
E WHEELER RD	**WHITNEY-LA CONNER RD**	SAINT HELENS OR 192-B1	LANE CO OR 215-D5	SALEM OR 322-F9	CHELAN WA 236-C3
MOSES LAKE WA 242-C3	SKAGIT CO WA 160-D7	**WILLAMETTE FALLS DR**	**WILLWORTH RD Rt#-150**	**W WINTERGREEN LN**	**SE WOODING RD**
S WHEELER RD	SKAGIT CO WA 167-D1	WEST LINN OR 199-C5	CHELAN CO WA 236-D3	KITSAP CO WA 173-C3	CLARK CO WA 193-C7
SPOKANE CO WA 114-C3	**WHITTAKER RD NW**	**WILLAMETTE FERRY ST**	**WILSON AV**	**WINTERS RD**	**WOODINVILLE DR Rt#-522**
WHELAN RD	THURSTON CO WA 180-B5	MARION CO OR 207-C2	BEND OR 332-E9	WASHINGTON CO OR 198-C2	BOTHELL WA 171-C6
WHITMAN CO WA 249-B4	**WHITTEMORE RD**	POLK CO OR 207-C2	WESTPORT WA 298-H11	**NE WINTERS RD**	**NE WOODINVILLE-DUVALL RD**
WHERRY RD	DESCHUTES CO OR 212-C6	**WILLAMETTE-MERIDIAN RD**	**SE WILSON AV**	DUVALL WA 110-C1	DUVALL WA 110-C1
YAKIMA CO WA 243-A5	**N WHITWORTH DR**	KITSAP CO WA 174-A1	BEND OR 332-F9	KING CO WA 110-C1	KING CO WA 110-C1
WHETSTONE RD	COUNTRY HOMES WA 346-J10	**SW WILLAMINA CREEK RD**	**WILSON AV S**	KING CO WA 171-D6	KING CO WA 171-D6
COLUMBIA CO WA 122-A2	FAIRWOOD WA 346-J9	WILLAMINA OR 125-A3	SEATTLE WA 283-F6	WOODINVILLE WA 171-D6	WOODINVILLE WA 171-D6
WHIFFIN SPIT RD	FAIRWOOD WA 347-A9	YAMHILL CO OR 125-A3	**WILSON HWY**	**WINTERS HILL RD**	**WOODINVILLE REDMOND RD**
BRITISH COLUMBIA BC 164-C1	**WHOOPEMUP RD**	**WILLAMINA-SALEM HWY**	YAKIMA CO WA 120-B2	YAMHILL CO OR 198-C6	**Rt#-202**
WHISKEY CREEK DR	COLUMBIA CO WA 122-A2	**Rt#-22**	**WILSON LN**	**WIPPER RD SE**	REDMOND WA 171-D7
HOOD RIVER CO OR 195-D5	**WIARD ST**	POLK CO OR 125-B3	SKAGIT CO WA 161-A6	MARION CO OR 325-F14	REDMOND WA 171-D7
WHISKEY CREEK RD	ALTAMONT OR 339-A9	POLK CO OR 204-A5	**WILSON RD**	TURNER OR 325-F14	WOODINVILLE WA 171-D7
COLUMBIA CO WA 122-A3	**WICKERSHAM TRUCK TR**	POLK CO OR 322-G12	BOARDMAN OR 128-C1	**WIRTA RD**	**WOODINVLLE RDMND RD NE**
JACKSON CO OR 226-D3	WHATCOM CO WA 161-C2	SALEM OR 322-G12	CLACKAMAS CO OR 126-C3	LEWIS CO WA 187-B2	**Rt#-202**
MALHEUR CO OR 146-A1	**WICKIEUP RD Rt#-1**	**WILLAMINA-SALEM HWY NW**	DOUGLAS CO OR 219-B4	**WIRTH RD**	REDMOND WA 171-D7
TILLAMOOK CO OR 197-A3	BRITISH COLUMBIA BC 101-B1	**Rt#-22**	GRANDVIEW WA 120-B3	LINN CO OR 207-C7	REDMOND WA 175-D1
WALLOWA CO OR 130-C1	BRITISH COLUMBIA BC 159-A1	POLK CO OR 204-B6	LEWIS CO ID 123-C2	**WISCONSIN ST**	**WOODINVILLE SNOHOMISH RD**
WALLOWA CO OR 130-C1	DISTRICT OF LANGFORD BC 159-A5	POLK CO OR 322-B14	LEWIS CO WA 187-B2	PRIEST RIVER ID 107-A3	SNOHOMISH CO WA 171-D6
E WHISKEY CREEK RD	**SW WICKIUP AV**	SALEM OR 322-B14	MORROW CO OR 128-C1	**WISCONSIN TKTR**	WOODINVILLE WA 171-C6
WALLOWA CO OR 130-C1	DESCHUTES CO OR 212-D6	**WILLAMINA-SHERIDAN HWY**	WASCO CO OR 127-C3	COWLITZ CO WA 117-B2	**NE WOODINVILLE SNOHOMISH RD**
S WHISKEY HILL RD	**WICKIUP RD**	**Rt#-18**	WASCO CO OR 196-A6	COWLITZ CO WA 187-A7	**Rt#-9**
CLACKAMAS CO OR 205-C1	DESCHUTES CO OR 142-C1	POLK CO OR 125-A3	WHITMAN CO WA 249-B5	**W WISER LAKE RD**	SNOHOMISH CO WA 171-D6
WHISKEY HILL RD NE	**W WIDE HOLLOW RD**	WILLAMINA OR 125-A3	YAKIMA CO WA 120-B3	WHATCOM CO WA 158-D5	**WOODINVLLE SNOHOMSH RD**
HUBBARD OR 205-C1	YAKIMA CO WA 243-A7	**WILLANCH WY**	YONCALLA OR 219-B4	**WISHKAH RD**	**Rt#-202**
MARION CO OR 205-C1	**WIDME RD NE**	COOS CO OR 218-C7	**S WILSON RD**	ABERDEEN WA 178-B6	WOODINVILLE WA 171-C6
WHISKEY JACK RD	SUQUAMISH WA 170-C7	**WILLAPA RD**	CLACKAMAS CO OR 200-A6	GRAYS HARBOR CO WA 178-C3	**WOODLAND AV**
BONNER CO ID 244-A1	**WIDOW CREEK RD**	PACIFIC CO WA 117-A1	**WILSON RD NW**	GRAYS HARBOR CO WA 178-B4	CENTRALIA WA 299-E5
JEFFERSON CO OR 211-B1	LINCOLN CO OR 203-C3	**WILLAPA-MONOHAN LANDING**	THURSTON CO WA 180-A6	**W WISHKAH RD**	**WOODLAND AV E**
WHISKEY RUN RD	ROSE LODGE OR 203-C3	**RD**	**WILSON ST**	GRAYS HARBOR CO WA 178-B4	PIERCE CO WA 182-A4
COOS CO OR 220-B4	**SE WIESE RD**	PACIFIC CO WA 117-A1	ASOTIN WA 250-B5	**WISHKAH ST**	**WOODLAND DR**
WHISKEY SPRING CREEK RD	CLACKAMAS CO OR 200-B3	RAYMOND WA 117-A1	CHELAN WA 238-A1	ABERDEEN WA 178-B7	COOS BAY OR 333-E8
CROOK CO OR 135-C2	**WIGGINS RD SE**	**WILLARD RD**	DISTRICT OF MISSION BC 94-B3	**WISHKAH ST U.S.-12**	NORTH BEND OR 333-E8
WHISKEY SPRINGS RD	OLYMPIA WA 297-D11	DESCHUTES CO OR 135-B3	MAPLE RIDGE BC 94-B3	ABERDEEN WA 178-B7	**WOODLAND LP**
JEFFERSON CO OR 211-D2	THURSTON CO WA 297-D11	SKAMANIA CO WA 195-B4	THURSTON CO WA 297-B5	GRAYS HARBOR CO WA 178-B7	YAMHILL CO OR 198-B4
WHISTLE CREEK RD	**WIGHTMAN ST**	**WILLEYS LAKE RD**	**N WILSON ST**	**WISHKAH ST U.S.-101**	**WOODLAND RD**
HARNEY CO OR 136-C3	ASHLAND OR 337-E9	WHATCOM CO WA 158-C4	POST FALLS ID 353-F6	ABERDEEN WA 178-B7	IDAHO CO ID 123-C2
WHISTLERS LN	**WIGRICH RD**	**WILLIAM H BUNDY BLVD**	**WILSON CREEK RD**	**E WISHKAH ST U.S.-101**	SNOHOMISH CO WA 168-B4
DOUGLAS CO OR 221-D3	POLK CO OR 207-C1	**U.S.-95**	KITTITAS CO WA 241-B2	ABERDEEN WA 178-B7	**WOODLAND GRADE RD**
WHISTLERS BEND PARK RD	**WIKSTROM RD**	LAPWAI ID 123-A2	LINCOLN CO WA 209-C4	**W WISHKAH ST U.S.-101**	IDAHO CO ID 123-C2
DOUGLAS CO OR 221-D3	COLUMBIA CO WA 192-A3	NEZ PERCE CO ID 123-A2	**WILSON RIVER HWY Rt#-6**	ABERDEEN WA 178-B7	**WOODLAND PARK RD**
WHITAKER RD	**N WILBUR AV**	**WILLIAM HEAD RD**	BANKS OR 125-B1	**NE WISTARIA DR**	JOSEPHINE CO OR 229-A7
POLK CO OR 204-A7	WALLA WALLA WA 345-E6	DISTRICT OF METCHOSIN BC 165-A1	TILLAMOOK OR 197-C2	PORTLAND OR 314-B2	**WOODLAWN AV**
WHITCOMB AV U.S.-97	**S WILBUR AV**	**N WILLIAMS AV**	TILLAMOOK CO OR 125-B1	**WITCHER GATEWAY RD**	SKAGIT CO WA 259-G13
OKANOGAN CO WA 104-C2	WALLA WALLA WA 345-E7	PORTLAND OR 309-G7	TILLAMOOK CO OR 197-C2	LANE CO OR 215-C6	**WOODLAWN AV N**
TONASKET WA 104-C2	WALLA WALLA EAST WA 345-E7	PORTLAND OR 313-G1	WASHINGTON CO OR 125-B1	**WITHAM HILL DR**	SEATTLE WA 274-A3
WHITE RD	**WILBUR RD**	**WILLIAMS RD**	**WILSON RIVER LP**	CORVALLIS OR 327-D6	**WOODLYN RD**
WALLA WALLA CO WA 121-B3	DOUGLAS CO OR 221-B2	ADAMS CO WA 121-B1	TILLAMOOK CO OR 197-C2	**WITHROW RD NW**	WHATCOM CO WA 158-D5
W WHITE RD	BENTON CO OR 133-B1	BENTON CO OR 133-B1	**WILSONVILLE RD**	DOUGLAS CO WA 112-B2	**WOODMONT DR S**
SPOKANE CO WA 246-B5	**WILBUR-GARDEN VALLEY RD**	CITY OF RICHMOND BC 156-B7	CLACKAMAS CO OR 199-B6	**SW WITHYCOMBE RD**	DES MOINES WA 175-B7
E WHITEAKER AV	DOUGLAS CO OR 221-B3	COWLITZ CO WA 190-A6	NEWBERG OR 198-D6	WASHINGTON CO OR 198-B2	**WOODRIDGE PL**
COTTAGE GROVE OR 215-B7	**WILBUR GULCH RD Rt#-194**	CROOK CO OR 213-C4	WILSONVILLE OR 199-B6	**WITT DR**	BRITISH COLUMBIA BC 159-B5
WHITE CREEK RD	WHITMAN CO WA 122-C1	LINCOLN CO WA 113-B1	YAMHILL CO OR 198-D6	LINN CO OR 207-C7	**WOOD RIVER CANAL**
JOSEPHINE CO OR 233-D3	WHITMAN CO WA 249-A5	**WILLIAMS CANYON RD**	YAMHILL CO OR 199-A6	**WITTE RD SE**	KLAMATH CO OR 231-C3
E WHITE CREEK RD	**WILBUR-UMPQUA RD**	CHELAN CO WA 238-B1	**WILSONVILLE HUBBARD HWY**	KING CO WA 175-D7	**WOODRUFF RD**
JOSEPHINE CO OR 233-D3	DOUGLAS CO OR 221-B1	**WILLIAMS CREEK RD**	MARION CO OR 199-B7	MAPLE VALLEY WA 175-D7	DOUGLAS CO OR 221-A3
WHITEHALL RD SE	**WILCO RD**	GRAYS HARBOR CO WA 117-B1	MARION CO OR 205-C1	**WITTE RD SW**	**WOODRUFF CREEK RD**
DOUGLAS CO OR 112-C2	MARION CO OR 133-C1	LANE CO OR 219-D2	**WILT RD**	DOUGLAS CO OR 239-B3	JACKSON CO OR 226-C4
WHITEHORSE CTO	STAYTON OR 133-C1	**WILLIAMS LAKE RD**	DESCHUTES CO OR 211-D4	**WITTIG RD NE**	**WOODS RD**
MALHEUR CO OR 154-B1	**NE WILCOX AV**	LINCOLN CO WA 114-A3	DESCHUTES CO OR 212-A4	DOUGLAS CO WA 112-C1	WHITMAN CO WA 249-C6
WHITEHORSE RD	DESCHUTES CO OR 212-D4	STEVENS CO WA 106-A1	**WIMER RD**	**WITZEL RD SE**	**E WOODS RD**
MALHEUR CO OR 154-A1	**WILCOX RD**	**W WILLIAMS LAKE RD**	JOSEPHINE CO OR 148-C2	MARION CO OR 325-H11	KITSAP CO WA 271-E9
WHITEHORSE CREEK RD	DOUGLAS CO OR 221-B1	SPOKANE CO WA 114-B2	**WIMER ST**	TURNER OR 325-H11	**WOODS RD E**
DOUGLAS CO OR 225-D6	WHITMAN CO WA 122-B1	**WILLIAMSON RD**	ASHLAND OR 337-B6	**NE W KINGSON RD**	KITSAP CO WA 271-E10
WHITEHORSE RANCH RD	WHITMAN CO WA 249-C1	YAMHILL CO OR 198-C5	**NW WIMP WY**	KITSAP CO WA 170-C5	**WOODS RD NE**
HARNEY CO OR 153-C2	**WILDCAT RD**	**WILLIAMSON MOUNTAIN RD**	DESCHUTES CO OR 212-D3	**WNUK RD**	DOUGLAS CO WA 112-C2
HARNEY CO OR 154-A2	MALHEUR CO OR 146-A3	DESCHUTES CO OR 216-A6	**WINBURN WY**	KLICKITAT CO WA 195-D4	**WOODS RD SE**
WHITELINE RD	**S WILDCAT RD**	**WILLIAMSON RIVER RD**	ASHLAND OR 337-C7	**WOCUS RD**	KITSAP CO WA 271-F14
KLAMATH CO OR 235-D1	CLACKAMAS CO OR 126-A3	KLAMATH CO OR 143-A3	**W WINCH AV**	KLAMATH CO OR 235-C2	**WOODS CREEK RD**
WHITEMAN RD KPS	CLACKAMAS CO OR 205-D3	KLAMATH CO OR 150-C1	KOOTENAI CO ID 247-C1	KLAMATH CO OR 338-A1	DOUGLAS CO OR 225-B6
PIERCE CO WA 181-A3	**NW WILDCAT LAKE RD**	KLAMATH CO OR 151-A1	**WINCHELL ST**	**WOHL RD**	MONROE WA 110-C1
WHITE OAK RD	KITSAP CO WA 174-A2	**WILLIAMSPORT RD**	DEPOE BAY OR 206-B1	COWLITZ CO WA 189-A2	SNOHOMISH CO WA 110-C1
LINN CO OR 207-B6	**WILDCAT MOUNTAIN DR**	ASTORIA OR 300-D6	**WINCHESTER AV**	**WOLCOTT AV S**	**WOODS CREEK RD Rt#-131**
WHITE PINE DR Rt#-6	CLACKAMAS CO OR 200-C5	**WILLIAMS VALLEY RD**	REEDSPORT OR 218-D1	SEATTLE WA 287-G3	LEWIS CO WA 118-C2
BENEWAH CO ID 115-B3	CLACKAMAS CO OR 201-A5	STEVENS CO WA 114-B1	**WINCHESTER AV U.S.-101**	**WOLCOTT RD**	**WOODSIDE DR**
LATAH CO ID 115-B3	**WILD FERN DR**	**WILLIMINA CREEK RD**	REEDSPORT OR 218-C1	LINN CO OR 207-B6	COWLITZ CO WA 189-B1
WHITE RIVER RD	DOUGLAS CO OR 221-C3	YAMHILL CO OR 125-A3	**WINCHESTER RD**	**WOLF RD**	**WOODS LAKE RD**
CHELAN CO WA 111-C1	**WILDHORSE RD**	**WILLINGDON AV**	DOUGLAS CO OR 221-B3	LATAH CO ID 249-C7	SNOHOMISH CO WA 110-C1
WASCO CO WA 127-A3	UMATILLA CO OR 129-C1	DISTRICT OF BURNABY BC 156-C5	LEWIS CO ID 123-C2	**WOLF CREEK LN**	**SE WOODSTOCK BLVD**
WHITE ROCK LOOP RD	**WILDWOOD DR**	DISTRICT OF BURNABY BC 255-H13	**NE WINCHESTER ST**	UNION CO OR 130-A3	PORTLAND OR 318-B5
DESCHUTES CO OR 212-B7	COOS CO OR 218-B5	**N WILLIS BLVD**	ROSEBURG OR 334-G6	**WOLF CREEK RD**	PORTLAND OR 319-F5
WHITE SCHOOL HOUSE RD	**SW WILDWOOD PL**	PORTLAND OR 308-B4	**WINCHUCK RIVER RD**	LANE CO OR 133-A3	**WOODWARD RD**
JOSEPHINE CO OR 233-B4	SEATTLE WA 284-D3	**E WILLIS RD**	CURRY CO OR 232-D7	**WOLFE RD**	FREELAND WA 170-C2
WHITES CREEK RD	**WILDWOOD RD**	CANYON CO ID 147-B1	**WINDHURST RD**	CITY OF CHILLIWACK BC 94-C3	**SW WOODWARD RD**
LANE CO OR 219-D1	LEWIS CO WA 187-A3	**NW WILLIS RD**	COOS CO OR 220-B6	**WOLF HOLLOW LN**	JEFFERSON CO OR 212-C2
SE WHITESON RD	**SW WILDWOOD RD**	YAMHILL CO OR 198-A6	**WINDIGO PASS RD**	GILLIAM CO OR 128-B2	**WOODWARD CREEK RD**
YAMHILL CO OR 204-B1	KITSAP CO WA 174-B5	**W WILLIS ST Rt#-516**	DOUGLAS CO OR 223-D3	**WOLFORD CANYON RD**	SKAMANIA CO WA 194-B3
N WHITE SWAN RD	**WILES RD**	KENT WA 175-C7	KLAMATH CO OR 142-B2	JEFFERSON CO OR 208-A2	**WOODWORTH DR**
HARRAH WA 119-C2	BENTON CO OR 207-B1	**WILLIS CANYON RD**	**WIND MOUNTAIN RD**	**N WOLKAV RD**	HOOD RIVER CO OR 202-C4
W WHITE SWAN RD Rt#-220	**WILEY RD**	KLICKITAT CO WA 196-C1	SKAMANIA CO WA 195-A5	LINCOLN CO OR 206-B6	**WOODY RD**
HARRAH WA 119-C2	CROOK CO OR 213-C5	**WILLIS CREEK RD**	**WIND RIDGE RD**	**WOLLOCHET DR NW**	CLARK CO WA 192-D1
WHITHAM RD NE	**W WILEY RD**	DOUGLAS CO OR 221-B7	YAMHILL CO OR 198-C4	GIG HARBOR WA 181-B1	**E WOOLARD RD**
THURSTON CO WA 180-D4	YAKIMA CO WA 243-A7	DOUGLAS CO OR 225-B1	**WIND RIVER RD**	PIERCE CO WA 181-B1	SPOKANE CO WA 114-C1
WHITING WY	**WILEY CREEK DR**	**WILLIS POINT RD**	CARSON WA 194-D3	**WOLLOCHET-GIG HARBOR**	**WOOLRIDGE RD**
DISTRICT OF COQUITLAM BC 156-D5	LINN CO OR 134-A2	DISTRICT OF SAANICH BC 159-B4	SKAMANIA CO WA 194-D3	GIG HARBOR WA 181-C1	PITT MEADOWS BC 157-B5
WHITLEY DR U.S.-95	**WILHOIT RD**	**WILLOW AV Rt#-39**	**WINDSOR RD**	PIERCE CO WA 181-C1	**NE WORDEN HILL RD**
FRUITLAND ID 139-A3	CLACKAMAS CO OR 126-A3	KLAMATH FALLS OR 338-D8	DISTRICT OF OAK BAY BC 257-D9	**N WOLVERTON CT**	YAMHILL CO OR 198-C5
N WHITLEY DR U.S.-95	**WILKENSON RD**	**WILLOW RD SE**	PITT MEADOWS BC 157-B5	SPOKANE WA 349-B5	**WORLINE RD**
FRUITLAND ID 139-A3	ISLAND CO WA 171-A1	KITSAP CO WA 174-B6	**WINDSOR ISLAND RD**	**WONDERLY RD**	SKAGIT CO WA 161-A5
PAYETTE CO ID 139-A3	**WILKES DR**	PIERCE CO WA 174-B6	KEIZER OR 322-G3	COLUMBIA CO WA 302-D14	**NE WORTHINGTON RD**
E WHITMAN DR	SANTA CLARA OR 215-A1	**N WILLOW ST**	MARION CO OR 204-D3	**S WOOD DR**	CLARK CO WA 193-C7
COLLEGE PLACE WA 344-F10	**WILKINS RD**	LA GRANDE OR 130-A2	MARION CO OR 322-G2	CROOK CO OR 213-D7	**WREN ST**
W WHITMAN DR	LANE CO OR 210-B7	**WILLOW CREEK RD**	**WINDY RIDGE DR**	**WOOD RD**	DISTRICT OF MISSION BC 94-B1
COLLEGE PLACE WA 344-E10	**WILKINSON RD**	COLUMBIA CO WA 122-A2	COWLITZ CO WA 189-B1	SKAGIT CO WA 161-A4	**WRENTHAM MARKET RD**
WALLA WALLA CO WA 344-D10	DISTRICT OF SAANICH BC 159-C5	JEFFERSON CO OR 208-B4	**WINESAP AV**	**WOODARD RD**	WASCO CO OR 127-B2
WHITMAN RD	DISTRICT OF SAANICH BC 256-D1	MALHEUR CO OR 138-B2	CHELAN CO WA 236-C2	LEWIS CO WA 187-C1	**WRIGHT AV**
WHITMAN CO WA 249-C6	MALHEUR CO OR 154-C2	MORROW CO OR 129-A2	**WINGVILLE RD**	**WOODARD BAY RD NE**	RICHLAND WA 340-E13
E WHITMAN RD	MULTNOMAH CO OR 200-D3	MORROW CO OR 129-A2	BAKER CO OR 130-A3	THURSTON CO WA 180-D5	RICHLAND WA 341-E1
SPOKANE CO WA 114-C3	**WILLAGILLESPIE RD**	**WILLOW CREEK RED ROCK RD**	BAKER CO OR 138-A1	**WOODBROOK RD SW**	**WRIGHT RD SE**
WHITMAN ST	EUGENE OR 329-J4	SISKIYOU CO CA 150-C3	**WINLOCK LN**	LAKEWOOD WA 181-C2	THURSTON CO WA 184-C3
WALLA WALLA WA 345-C8	**WILLAMETTE AV**	**WILLOWDALE RD**	WHEELER CO OR 128-B3	**WOODBROOK COUNTY PARK RD**	**W WRIGHT ST**
S WHITMAN ST	MEDFORD OR 336-E12	KITTITAS CO WA 241-B5	**WINLOCK-TOLEDO RD Rt#-505**	COWLITZ CO WA 303-J1	BOISE ID 253-C3
MONMOUTH OR 204-B7	**N WILLAMETTE BLVD**	**WILLOW GROVE RD**	LEWIS CO WA 187-C3	**WOODBURN-ESTACADA HWY**	**WRIGHT-BLISS RD KPN**
ROSALIA WA 114-C3	PORTLAND OR 192-B7	COWLITZ CO WA 189-A2	**WINLOCK-VADER RD**	**Rt#-211**	PIERCE CO WA 174-A7
WHITMAN CO WA 114-C3	PORTLAND OR 308-A5	COWLITZ CO WA 302-A5	LEWIS CO WA 187-B4	CLACKAMAS CO OR 126-A3	**WRIGHT CREEK RD**
W WHITMAN ST	**WILLAMETTE DR**	**WILLOW GROVE RD Rt#-432**	WINLOCK WA 187-B4	CLACKAMAS CO OR 200-C6	LINCOLN CO OR 206-B4
ROSALIA WA 114-C3	LANE CO OR 210-A6	COWLITZ CO WA 302-A5	**WINONA AV N**	CLACKAMAS CO OR 205-D2	**WTC 8000 RD**
W WHITMARSH RD	**WILLAMETTE DR Rt#-43**	LONGVIEW WA 302-A5	SEATTLE WA 273-J2	ESTACADA OR 200-C6	DOUGLAS CO OR 140-C2
BURLINGTON WA 260-A8	LAKE OSWEGO OR 199-C4			MARION CO OR 205-B1	
	WEST LINN OR 199-C4			MOLALLA OR 126-A3	
				WOODBURN OR 205-B1	

INDEX

WULFF LN
STREET INDEX
S 3RD ST U.S.-95 401

STREET
City State Page-Grid

WULFF LN
DOUGLAS CO OR 221-A4
WYATT DR
LINN CO OR 210-A6
NE WYATT WY
KITSAP CO WA 271-J2
Winslow WA 271-J2
WYATT WY NW
KITSAP CO WA 271-J2
Winslow WA 271-J2
WYEAST RD
HOOD RIVER CO OR 195-C7
WYNOOCHEE VALLEY RD
GRAYS HARBOR CO WA 178-D4
WYNOOCHEE WISHKAH RD
GRAYS HARBOR CO WA 178-C5
S WYNOOSKI ST
NEWBERG OR 198-D6
YAMHILL CO OR 198-D6
WYOMING AV
HAYDEN ID 245-A5
KOOTENAI CO ID 245-A5
KOOTENAI CO ID 247-D1
WYOMING ST Rt#-3
DEARY ID 123-B1
LATAH CO ID 123-B1
WYSE RD
WASCO CO OR 196-A7

X

XL RANCH RD
LAKE CO OR 144-A3

Y

Y AV
LA GRANDE OR 130-A2
Y PL
PACIFIC CO WA 186-A4
Y RD
WHATCOM CO WA 102-B1
WHATCOM CO WA 161-B1
Y RD NE
DOUGLAS CO WA 237-A2
Y 1/2 RD NE
DOUGLAS CO WA 237-A2
YACHATS OCEAN RD
YACHATS OR 209-A3
YACHATS RIVER RD
LINCOLN CO OR 209-A3
YACHATS OR 209-A3
YAKIMA
CROOK CO OR 213-D7
E YAKIMA AV
YAKIMA WA 243-C6
N YAKIMA AV
TACOMA WA 292-E3
TACOMA WA 293-F3
S YAKIMA AV
TACOMA WA 293-G6
TACOMA WA 295-G1
W YAKIMA AV
YAKIMA WA 243-B6
YAKIMA VALLEY HWY
GRANGER WA 120-A2
SUNNYSIDE WA 120-A2
YAKIMA CO WA 120-A2
YAKSUM CANYON RD
CHELAN CO WA 238-C3
YALE RD E Rt#-1A
BRITISH COLUMBIA BC 94-C3
CITY OF CHILLIWACK BC 94-C3
YALE RD W Rt#-1A
CITY OF CHILLIWACK BC 94-C3
N YALE ST
SPOKANE CO WA 347-F5
YALE CREEK RD
JACKSON CO OR 234-A5
YAMHILL HWY Rt#-240
NEWBERG OR 198-B5
YAMHILL CO OR 198-B5
YAMHILL RD
YAMHILL CO OR 198-B5
N YAMHILL ST Rt#-47
CARLTON OR 198-B5
YAMPO RD
POLK CO OR 204-B3
YAMHILL CO OR 204-C3
YANK GULCH RD
JACKSON CO OR 234-B4
YAQUINA BAY RD
LINCOLN CO OR 206-B4
NEWPORT OR 206-B4
TOLEDO OR 206-B4
NE YAQUINA HEIGHTS DR
LINCOLN CO OR 206-B4
YARRINGTON RD
UNION CO OR 130-B1
YARROW CENTRAL RD
CITY OF CHILLIWACK BC 102-C1
YARROW POINT RD
YARROW POINT WA 175-C2
YATES RD
CROOK CO OR 213-B6
LEWIS CO WA 184-D7
MASON CO WA 180-D2
YATES ST
CITY OF VICTORIA BC 256-H9
YEAGENS LANDING RD
MARION CO OR 198-D6
YEAZELL RD KPS
PIERCE CO WA 181-A3
YELLOW FIR RD
TILLAMOOK CO OR 197-B4
YELLOW JACKET RD
UMATILLA CO OR 129-B2
YELLOWSTONE AV
OSBURN ID 115-C2
W YELLOWSTONE AV
BENTON CO WA 342-F8
E YELLOWSTONE TR
KOOTENAI CO ID 248-B1
YELM AV Rt#-507
YELM WA 118-A1
YELM AV Rt#-510
THURSTON CO WA 118-A1
YELM WA 118-A1
YELM HWY SE
LACEY WA 297-F12
OLYMPIA WA 296-J11
OLYMPIA WA 297-A11
THURSTON CO WA 181-A7
THURSTON CO WA 297-A11
TUMWATER WA 296-J11
NW YEON AV U.S.-30
PORTLAND OR 199-B1
PORTLAND OR 312-A1
YERGEN RD
MARION CO OR 199-A7
YESLER WY
SEATTLE WA 277-J6
SEATTLE WA 278-C6
YEW AV
OLYMPIA WA 297-B4
SW YEW AV
DESCHUTES CO OR 212-C6
YEW RD
WHATCOM CO WA 258-G12
YEW ST
BELLINGHAM WA 258-G5
KELSO WA 303-C10
WHATCOM CO WA 258-G8
S YEW ST
Finley WA 343-G12
YEW WY
SNOHOMISH CO WA 171-D5
YEW WY Rt#-524
SNOHOMISH CO WA 171-D5
YOAKUM GRADE RD
UMATILLA CO OR 129-B1
YOKEKO DR
SKAGIT CO WA 160-C7
YOKUM RD
DOUGLAS CO OR 225-C3
RIDDLE OR 225-C3
YOLANDA AV
North Springfield OR 331-B3
SPRINGFIELD OR 331-B3
YOMAN RD
PIERCE CO WA 181-A4
YONCALLA-ELKHEAD RD
DOUGLAS CO OR 219-B4
YORK RD
SISKIYOU CO CA 150-A3
SNOHOMISH CO WA 171-C5
UMATILLA CO OR 129-C1
WALLA WALLA CO WA 121-C3
YORK ST
BELLINGHAM WA 258-D6
YORK HILL DR
HOOD RIVER CO OR 195-C6
YOST RD
HARRAH WA 119-C2
YAKIMA CO WA 119-C2
YAKIMA CO WA 120-A2
YOUMANS RD
GRAYS HARBOR CO WA 178-A3
YOUNG RD
CITY OF CHILLIWACK BC 94-C3
COWLITZ CO WA 189-D3
YOUNG RD NW
THURSTON CO WA 180-C5
YOUNG ST
ABERDEEN WA 178-B7
WOODBURN OR 205-B2
E YOUNG ST
ELMA WA 179-B7
YOUNG GRADE
YAKIMA CO WA 243-A5
YOUNGS RIVER LOOP RD
CLATSOP CO OR 188-C3
CLATSOP CO OR 300-C10
YTURRI BLVD
MALHEUR CO OR 147-A3
YUANCY LAKE RD
BONNER CO ID 244-B2
YUCCA AV
DESCHUTES CO OR 212-C4
NE YUCCA AV
DESCHUTES CO OR 212-D4
DESCHUTES CO OR 213-A4
YUMA ST
EDGEWOOD WA 182-B3
MILTON WA 182-B3
NW YUNGEN RD
WASHINGTON CO OR 192-A6

Z

ZAGER RD
CHELAN CO WA 238-C3
ZANDECKI RD
LEWIS CO WA 187-D2
ZANGLE RD NE
THURSTON CO WA 180-D4
ZARA DR
COOS CO OR 218-B5
ZAZA RD
NEZ PERCE CO ID 123-A3
ZEEK RD
CLARK CO WA 193-C6
ZEITLER RD
LATAH CO ID 249-C6
ZELATCHED POINT RD
JEFFERSON CO WA 170-A7
ZELL RD
WHATCOM CO WA 158-C4
ZEMKE RD
JACKSON CO OR 234-B3
ZENA RD
POLK CO OR 204-B4
ZENA RD NW
POLK CO OR 204-C4
POLK CO OR 322-B2
SW ZENITH
DESCHUTES CO OR 212-C6
ZENKER RD SW
THURSTON CO WA 184-C4
ZIAK-GNAT CREEK RD
CLATSOP CO OR 117-A3
W ZIER RD
YAKIMA CO WA 243-A7
ZIGZAG MOUNTAIN RD
CLACKAMAS CO OR 201-D5
E ZILLAH DR
YAKIMA CO WA 120-A2
ZILLIG RD
COWLITZ CO WA 118-A3
ZIMMER RD
STEVENS CO WA 106-A3
ZIMMERMAN RD
COLUMBIA CO OR 189-B5
YAKIMA CO WA 243-A6
S ZIMMERMAN RD
CLACKAMAS CO OR 205-C1
ZIMMERMAN RANCH RD
MALHEUR CO OR 154-A2
ZIMRI DR
NEWBERG OR 198-D5
YAMHILL CO OR 198-D5
ZIMS RD
ADAMS CO ID 251-A3
SE ZITZELSBERGER RD
CLARK CO WA 193-D7
SKAMANIA CO WA 193-D7
ZUMWALT RD
POLK CO OR 207-A1
WALLOWA CO OR 131-A2
ZYLSTRA RD
ISLAND CO WA 167-B3

#

1/2-NE RD
GRANT CO WA 112-C2
SOAP LAKE WA 112-C2
1-2-SE RD
GRANT CO WA 121-A1
1 AV
DISTRICT OF DELTA BC 101-C1
1ST AV
ALBANY OR 326-C7
ALGONA WA 182-B2
BONNER CO ID 244-A1
DISTRICT OF BURNABY BC 255-D12
KOOTENAI ID 244-A1
POWERS OR 140-B3
RIDDLE OR 225-B3
SEASIDE OR 301-F8
SEATTLE WA 277-H4
SEATTLE WA 278-A6
SHOSHONE CO ID 115-C2
SMELTERVILLE ID 115-C2
VANCOUVER BC 255-D12
1ST AV Rt#-3
BOVILL ID 123-B1
1ST AV Rt#-7
DISTRICT OF MISSION BC 94-B3
1ST AV Rt#-226
SCIO OR 133-C1
1ST AV Rt#-241
MABTON WA 120-B3
YAKIMA CO WA 120-B3
1ST AV Rt#-361
CULVER OR 208-B7
1ST AV Rt#-411
KELSO WA 303-C9
LONGVIEW WA 303-C9
E 1ST AV
JUNCTION CITY OR 210-A6
LANE CO OR 210-A6
RITZVILLE WA 113-C3
E 1ST AV Rt#-28
ODESSA WA 113-B3
N 1ST AV
CHILOQUIN OR 231-D3
KLAMATH CO OR 231-D3
STAYTON OR 133-C1
N 1ST AV Rt#-99
DRAIN OR 219-A3
N 1ST AV U.S.-95
SANDPOINT ID 244-A2
NW 1ST AV
CANBY OR 199-C6
MILTON-FREEWATER OR 121-C3
PAYETTE CO ID 139-B3
S 1ST AV
STAYTON OR 133-C1
S 1ST AV U.S.-95
SANDPOINT ID 244-A2
SE 1ST AV
CANBY OR 199-C6
CLACKAMAS CO OR 199-C6
SW 1ST AV
NEW PLYMOUTH ID 139-B3
PAYETTE CO ID 139-B3
PORTLAND OR 317-F1
W 1ST AV
ADAMS CO WA 113-C3
EUGENE OR 329-H5
JUNCTION CITY OR 210-A6
LANE CO OR 210-A6
RITZVILLE WA 113-C3
SPOKANE WA 348-H9
TOPPENISH WA 120-A2
YAKIMA CO WA 120-A2
W 1ST AV Rt#-21
ODESSA WA 113-B3
W 1ST AV Rt#-28
ODESSA WA 113-B3
1ST AV N
KELSO WA 303-D7
SEATTLE WA 277-H4
1ST AV N U.S.-101
ILWACO WA 186-A6
PACIFIC CO WA 186-A6
1ST AV NE
SEATTLE WA 171-B7
SHORELINE WA 171-B6
1ST AV NW
EPHRATA WA 112-C3
GRANT CO WA 112-C3
1ST AV NW Rt#-411
KELSO WA 303-C7
1ST AV S
BURIEN WA 175-A5
FEDERAL WAY WA 182-A1
KELSO WA 303-D8
KING CO WA 175-A5
KING CO WA 285-J6
NORMANDY PARK WA 175-A5
SEATTLE WA 278-A7
SEATTLE WA 281-J4
SEATTLE WA 282-A1
SEATTLE WA 285-J2
1ST AV S Rt#-509
BURIEN WA 175-A6
DES MOINES WA 175-A6
NORMANDY PARK WA 175-A6
1ST AV SW
QUINCY WA 112-B3
1ST PL
HERMISTON OR 129-A1
1ST PL W
EVERETT WA 268-B6
1ST RD
POWERS OR 140-B3
1 RD NE
DOUGLAS CO WA 112-C2
1 RD SE U.S.-2
DOUGLAS CO WA 112-C2
1 RD SW
DOUGLAS CO WA 239-D1
1ST ST
ASOTIN WA 250-B5
BANDON OR 220-B6
BREMERTON WA 270-D11
CANYONVILLE OR 225-C3
CITY OF NORTH VANCOUVER BC 254-H5
CLARKSTON WA 250-B5
DESCHUTES CO OR 212-A6
DIST OF NORTH VANCOUVER BC 254-H5
HERMISTON OR 129-A1
LINN CO OR 133-C1
1ST ST
LYNDEN WA 102-B1
MORO OR 127-C2
NEWPORT WA 106-C3
OAKLAND OR 219-A7
RICHLAND OR 139-A1
RICHLAND WA 340-F8
RUFUS OR 127-C1
WATERLOO OR 133-C1
WILSON CREEK WA 113-A2
YONCALLA OR 219-A4
1ST ST Rt#-4
SHOSHONE CO ID 115-C2
1ST ST Rt#-6
TILLAMOOK OR 197-B2
1ST ST Rt#-27
OAKESDALE WA 114-C3
1ST ST Rt#-82
ISLAND CITY OR 130-A2
1ST ST Rt#-129
ASOTIN WA 250-B5
1ST ST Rt#-214
SILVERTON OR 205-C4
1ST ST Rt#-237
ISLAND CITY OR 130-A2
UNION CO OR 130-A2
1ST ST Rt#-304
BREMERTON WA 270-J11
1ST ST U.S.-12
LEWISTON ID 250-B4
E 1ST ST
COLFAX WA 122-C1
COQUILLE OR 220-D5
PORT ANGELES WA 261-F4
WEISER ID 139-A2
E 1ST ST Rt#-82
WALLOWA OR 130-C1
E 1ST ST Rt#-99W
NEWBERG OR 198-D5
E 1ST ST Rt#-170
GRANT CO WA 121-A1
WARDEN WA 121-A1
E 1ST ST Rt#-219
NEWBERG OR 198-D5
YAMHILL CO OR 198-D5
E 1ST ST U.S.-101
PORT ANGELES WA 261-F4
N 1ST ST
AUMSVILLE OR 133-C1
AUMSVILLE OR 205-B7
MARION CO OR 205-B7
MOUNT VERNON WA 260-C12
SELAH WA 243-B5
TACOMA WA 293-G4
YAKIMA WA 243-B6
YAKIMA CO WA 243-B5
N 1ST ST Rt#-99
OAKLAND OR 219-A7
N 1ST ST Rt#-21
ODESSA WA 113-B3
N 1ST ST Rt#-214
SILVERTON OR 205-C4
N 1ST ST U.S.-395
HERMISTON OR 129-A1
NE 1ST ST
BELLEVUE WA 175-C2
DESCHUTES CO OR 212-D4
MEDINA WA 175-C2
NW 1ST ST Rt#-3
ENTERPRISE OR 130-C2
WALLOWA CO OR 130-C2
S 1ST ST
MOUNT VERNON WA 260-C13
SHELTON WA 180-A3
SUNNYSIDE WA 120-B2
UNION GAP WA 243-C7
YAKIMA WA 243-C7
S 1ST ST Rt#-823
SELAH WA 243-B5
YAKIMA CO WA 243-B5
SE 1ST ST
CLARK CO WA 193-A6
PENDLETON OR 129-B1
VANCOUVER WA 193-A6
SW 1ST ST
MADRAS OR 208-C5
ONTARIO OR 139-A3
PENDLETON OR 129-B1
W 1ST ST
MEDFORD OR 336-C11
NEWPORT WA 106-C3
PEND OREILLE CO WA 106-C3
PORT ANGELES WA 261-E4
WALLOWA OR 130-B1
WALLOWA CO OR 130-B1
W 1ST ST Rt#-82
WALLOWA OR 130-B1
W 1ST ST Rt#-170
WARDEN WA 121-A1
W 1ST ST Rt#-219
NEWBERG OR 198-D5
1ST ST N
MONTESANO WA 178-D7
1ST ST SW
BANDON OR 220-B6
1ST WY S
FEDERAL WAY WA 182-A1
1 1/2 RD NW
DOUGLAS CO WA 236-A7
1 3-4 RD SW
DOUGLAS CO WA 239-D1
2ND AV
ALBANY OR 326-C7
ASTORIA OR 300-C5
DESCHUTES CO OR 212-A6
SEATTLE WA 277-H4
SEATTLE WA 278-A6
TOWNSHIP OF LANGLEY BC 158-C3
VANCOUVER BC 254-J12
2ND AV Rt#-7
MORTON WA 118-B2
2ND AV Rt#-99
GOLD HILL OR 230-A6
2ND AV Rt#-903
KITTITAS CO WA 240-A1
E 2ND AV
SPOKANE WA 349-B9
NW 2ND AV
MYRTLE CREEK OR 225-C1
S 2ND AV
CHILOQUIN OR 231-D4
EVERETT WA 265-F7
EVERETT WA 269-F1
ROCKAWAY BEACH OR 191-B6
TUMWATER WA 296-G10
W 2ND AV
SPOKANE WA 348-H9
SPOKANE WA 349-A9
2ND AV N
WALLA WALLA WA 345-A7
2ND AV S
WALLA WALLA WA 345-B8
2ND AV S Rt#-52
PAYETTE ID 139-A3
2ND AV SE
SOAP LAKE WA 112-C2
2ND AV SW
SEATTLE WA 285-J2
SOAP LAKE WA 112-C2
2ND AVEX S
SEATTLE WA 278-A6
NW 2ND DR
LINCOLN CITY OR 203-A4
2ND EXT
PIERCE CO WA 182-B6
2 RD NW
DOUGLAS CO WA 236-B7
WATERVILLE WA 236-B7
2 RD S
DOUGLAS CO WA 239-B1
2 RD SE
DOUGLAS CO WA 112-C2
2 RD SW
DOUGLAS CO WA 239-D1
2ND ST
ASOTIN WA 250-B5
CLARKSTON WA 250-B4
CORVALLIS OR 327-G10
HARRAH WA 119-C2
JEFFERSON OR 207-D3
LA GRANDE OR 130-A2
LEBANON OR 133-C1
MARION CO OR 207-D3
NACHES WA 119-C1
NEW WESTMINSTER BC 156-D5
SHERMAN CO OR 127-C3
SNOHOMISH WA 171-D3
WALLA WALLA CO WA 345-G4
YAKIMA CO WA 119-C1
2ND ST Rt#-30
NORTH POWDER OR 130-B3
2ND ST Rt#-34
LEBANON OR 133-C1
2ND ST Rt#-42S
COQUILLE OR 220-D5
2ND ST Rt#-99E
HALSEY OR 210-B2
2ND ST Rt#-100
ILWACO WA 186-A6
PACIFIC CO WA 186-A6
2ND ST Rt#-237
NORTH POWDER OR 130-B3
2ND ST U.S.-20
BENTON CO OR 327-H9
CORVALLIS OR 327-H9
E 2ND ST
COQUILLE OR 220-D5
WARDEN WA 121-A1
N 2ND ST
CENTRAL POINT OR 230-C7
LA GRANDE OR 130-A2
REEDSPORT OR 218-D1
SILVERTON OR 205-C4
NE 2ND ST
BEND OR 332-F6
NW 2ND ST
GRANTS PASS OR 335-E8
MCMINNVILLE OR 198-A7
S 2ND ST
MOUNT VERNON WA 260-C14
SKAGIT CO WA 260-C14
S 2ND ST Rt#-900
RENTON WA 175-C5
SE 2ND ST
BEND OR 332-F8
W 2ND ST
THE DALLES OR 196-C7
WARDEN WA 121-A1
WASCO CO OR 196-C7
W 2ND ST Rt#-124
WAITSBURG WA 122-A2
WALLA WALLA CO WA 122-A2
2ND ST E
PIERCE CO WA 182-C2
2ND ST NE
PUYALLUP WA 182-B3
2ND ST S
CANYON CO ID 147-B1
NAMPA ID 147-B1
2ND ST S U.S.-30
NAMPA ID 147-B1
2ND ST SE
DOUGLAS CO WA 239-A5
SNOHOMISH CO WA 110-C1
SNOHOMISH CO WA 171-D2
2ND ST SE U.S.-101
BANDON OR 220-B6
N 2ND ST W
CHEWELAH WA 106-B3
S 2ND ST W
CHEWELAH WA 106-B3
STEVENS CO WA 106-B3
2ND DIVISION DR
PIERCE CO WA 181-C6
2ND DIVISION RANGE RD
PIERCE CO WA 181-B6
2 1/4 RD NW
DOUGLAS CO WA 236-B7
2 1/2 RD NW U.S.-2
DOUGLAS CO WA 236-C7
WATERVILLE WA 236-C7
3 AV
DISTRICT OF DELTA BC 101-C1
3RD AV
ALBANY OR 326-C7
BREWSTER WA 104-B3
KELSO WA 303-C8
LONGVIEW WA 303-C8
MOSIER OR 196-A5
TOWNSHIP OF LANGLEY BC 158-C2
WASCO CO OR 196-A5
3RD AV Rt#-169
BLACK DIAMOND WA 110-C3
3RD AV Rt#-411
LONGVIEW WA 303-C9
3RD AV Rt#-432
LONGVIEW WA 303-B11
E 3RD AV
Finley WA 343-G11
KENNEWICK WA 343-E11
POST FALLS ID 353-J7
POST FALLS ID 354-A7
SPOKANE WA 349-B10
E 3RD AV Rt#-20
COLVILLE WA 106-A2
STEVENS CO WA 106-A2
N 3RD AV
ROCKAWAY BEACH OR 191-B6
STAYTON OR 133-C1
NE 3RD AV
GOLDENDALE WA 127-C1
KLICKITAT CO WA 127-C1
NE 3RD AV Rt#-14B
CAMAS WA 193-B7
CLARK CO WA 193-B7
WASHOUGAL WA 193-B7
NW 3RD AV
KELSO WA 303-C8
S 3RD AV
CLALLAM CO WA 262-D14
EVERETT WA 265-E6
SEQUIM WA 262-D14
UNION GAP WA 243-B7
YAKIMA WA 243-B7
YAKIMA CO WA 243-B7
SW 3RD AV
KELSO WA 303-C8
PAYETTE CO ID 139-A3
W 3RD AV
KENNEWICK WA 343-D11
SPOKANE WA 348-J10
SPOKANE WA 349-A10
3RD AV FI
PIERCE CO WA 181-B2
3RD AV N
KELSO WA 303-D7
PAYETTE ID 139-A3
3RD AV N Rt#-4
KELSO WA 303-D8
3RD AV N Rt#-524
EDMONDS WA 171-A5
3RD AV NE
SNOHOMISH CO WA 168-C5
S 3RD AV NE
POULSBO WA 170-B7
3RD AV NW
SHORELINE WA 171-A6
3RD AV S
KELSO WA 303-C9
WALLA WALLA WA 345-B9
WALLA WALLA CO WA 345-B13
3RD AV S Rt#-524
EDMONDS WA 171-A5
3RD AV SE
QUINCY WA 112-B3
3RD AV SW
EPHRATA WA 112-C3
PACIFIC WA 182-B2
3RD AV W
BREMERTON WA 270-D13
Navy Yard City WA 270-D13
SEATTLE WA 273-G7
SEATTLE WA 277-G1
SE 3RD DR
PENDLETON OR 129-B1
3RD PL
THE DALLES OR 196-C7
3 RD NE
DOUGLAS CO WA 112-C2
3 RD NW
DOUGLAS CO WA 236-B7
3 RD SW
DOUGLAS CO WA 239-B1
3RD ST
ASOTIN CO WA 250-B4
ASTORIA OR 300-C6
CANNON BEACH OR 188-B7
CITY OF NORTH VANCOUVER BC 254-J5
CITY OF NORTH VANCOUVER BC 255-A5
CLARKSTON WA 250-B4
HAINES OR 130-A3
HUBBARD OR 205-B1
LEAVENWORTH WA 238-A1
MANZANITA OR 191-B4
MARYSVILLE WA 171-C1
MCCLEARY WA 179-D6
NACHES WA 119-C1
NEWPORT WA 106-C3
OAKESDALE WA 114-C3
SEDRO-WOOLLEY WA 161-C6
THE DALLES OR 196-C7
TILLAMOOK OR 197-C2
TILLAMOOK CO OR 197-C2
WHEELER OR 191-B4
WHITMAN CO WA 114-C3
YAKIMA CO WA 119-C1
3RD ST Rt#-6
TILLAMOOK OR 197-C2
3RD ST Rt#-42
COQUILLE OR 220-D5
3RD ST Rt#-99E
HARRISBURG OR 210-A5
3RD ST Rt#-99W
LAFAYETTE OR 198-B6
3RD ST Rt#-112
Neah Bay WA 100-B2
3RD ST Rt#-221
DAYTON OR 198-C7
YAMHILL CO OR 198-C7
E 3RD ST
MOSCOW ID 249-D5
E 3RD ST Rt#-8
MOSCOW ID 249-C5
N 3RD ST
ALMIRA WA 237-D7
CENTRAL POINT OR 230-C7
DAYTON WA 122-A2
DUFUR OR 127-B2
JACKSON CO OR 230-C7
OSBURN ID 115-C2
WASCO CO OR 127-B2
NE 3RD ST
MALHEUR CO OR 139-A3
MCMINNVILLE OR 198-A7
ONTARIO OR 139-A3
RENTON WA 175-C5
NE 3RD ST Rt#-500
CLARK CO WA 193-B6
NE 3RD ST U.S.-20
BEND OR 332-F4
NE 3RD ST U.S.-97 Bus
BEND OR 332-F9
NW 3RD ST
GRANTS PASS OR 335-F8
S 3RD ST
ELMA WA 179-B7
S 3RD ST Rt#-23
HARRINGTON WA 113-C2
S 3RD ST Rt#-536
MOUNT VERNON WA 260-C12
S 3RD ST Rt#-900
RENTON WA 175-C5
S 3RD ST U.S.-95
FRUITLAND ID 139-A3

INDEX

INDEX

STREET / City State	Page-Grid
SE 3RD ST	
LINCOLN CITY OR	203-A5
ONTARIO OR	139-A3
PENDLETON OR	129-B1
SE 3RD ST U.S.-97 Bus	
BEND OR	332-F10
W 3RD ST	
KUNA ID	253-A5
W 3RD ST Rt#-8	
MOSCOW ID	249-C5
W 3RD ST Rt#-126	
CROOK CO OR	213-D5
PRINEVILLE OR	213-D5
3RD ST N	
MONTESANO WA	178-D7
3RD ST S	
NAMPA ID	147-B1
3RD ST S U.S.-30	
NAMPA ID	147-B1
3RD ST SE	
MARION CO OR	325-F10
PUYALLUP WA	182-B3
TURNER OR	325-F10
3RD ST SW	
AUBURN WA	182-B1
3RD ST W Rt#-99W	
CORVALLIS OR	207-A7
CORVALLIS OR	327-G14
3RD ST W U.S.-20	
CORVALLIS OR	327-G10
4TH AV	
ALBANY OR	326-C8
GOLD HILL OR	230-A6
KITTITAS WA	241-C6
SCIO OR	133-C1
SEATTLE WA	277-J4
SEATTLE WA	278-A5
TOWNSHIP OF LANGLEY BC	158-C2
UNIV ENDOWMENT LANDS BC	156-A4
4TH AV Rt#-234	
GOLD HILL OR	230-B6
E 4TH AV	
EUGENE OR	330-A5
POST FALLS ID	353-H7
POST FALLS ID	354-A7
SPOKANE WA	349-D10
SPOKANE VALLEY WA	349-J9
SPOKANE VALLEY WA	350-B9
SPOKANE VALLEY WA	351-B9
N 4TH AV	
PASCO WA	343-F6
NW 4TH AV	
ONTARIO OR	139-A3
S 4TH AV	
PASCO WA	343-G7
YAKIMA WA	243-B7
SE 4TH AV	
PAYETTE CO ID	139-B3
SW 4TH AV	
PORTLAND OR	313-E7
PORTLAND OR	317-E1
SW 4TH AV Rt#-201	
ONTARIO OR	139-A3
W 4TH AV	
BENTON CO WA	342-F11
KENNEWICK WA	342-G11
KENNEWICK WA	343-B11
SPOKANE WA	348-H10
4TH AV E	
OLYMPIA WA	296-J5
OLYMPIA WA	297-A5
4TH AV N	
KELSO WA	303-D7
KENT WA	175-B7
KENT WA	291-J7
4TH AV NW	
SNOHOMISH CO WA	168-C4
4TH AV S	
SEATTLE WA	278-A7
SEATTLE WA	282-A4
4TH AV S Rt#-519	
SEATTLE WA	278-A7
SEATTLE WA	282-A1
4TH AV W	
BOTHELL WA	171-C6
EVERETT WA	268-A6
OLYMPIA WA	296-G5
SNOHOMISH CO WA	171-C4
SNOHOMISH CO WA	268-A6
UNIV ENDOWMENT LANDS BC	156-A4
VANCOUVER BC	156-A4
VANCOUVER BC	254-A12
W 4TH LN	
VALLEY CO ID	252-D3
4 RD SW	
DOUGLAS CO WA	239-D2
4TH ST	
ANACORTES WA	259-H1
GERVAIS OR	205-B2
GRANTS PASS OR	335-E8
HAINES OR	130-A3
LA GRANDE OR	130-A2
LEWISTON ID	250-C4
NANAIMO BC	93-A3
NORTHPORT WA	106-A1
PHOENIX OR	234-B2
SKAGIT CO WA	259-H14
SNOHOMISH CO WA	171-C1
SUMMERVILLE OR	130-A2
4TH ST Rt#-5	
SAINT MARIES ID	248-D7
4TH ST Rt#-27	
GARFIELD WA	114-C3
4TH ST Rt#-39	
KLAMATH FALLS OR	338-D8
4TH ST Rt#-234	
GOLD HILL OR	230-B6
4TH ST Rt#-304	
BREMERTON WA	270-H11
4TH ST Rt#-528	
MARYSVILLE WA	171-C1
SNOHOMISH CO WA	171-C1
4TH ST U.S.-97	
GRASS VALLEY OR	127-C2
SHANIKO OR	127-C3
WASCO CO OR	127-C3
E 4TH ST	
MEDFORD OR	336-C11
NEWBERG OR	198-D6
THE DALLES OR	196-C7
N 4TH ST	
ALMIRA WA	237-D7
COEUR D'ALENE ID	355-E6
COULEE CITY WA	113-A2
DALTON GARDENS WA	355-F4
HAYDEN ID	355-E1
KLAMATH FALLS OR	338-D7
KOOTENAI CO ID	355-E1
MOUNT VERNON WA	260-C11
NE 4TH ST	
BELLEVUE WA	175-C5
BEND OR	332-F6
ENTERPRISE OR	130-C2
RENTON WA	175-C5
NW 4TH ST U.S.-26	
MADRAS OR	208-C5
S 4TH ST	
COLUMBIA CO WA	122-A2
DAYTON WA	122-A2
SE 4TH ST	
COLLEGE PLACE WA	344-F10
SW 4TH ST	
COLLEGE PLACE WA	344-F10
MALHEUR CO OR	139-A3
ONTARIO OR	139-A3
PENDLETON OR	129-B1
SW 4TH ST U.S.-26	
MADRAS OR	208-C5
W 4TH ST	
MEDFORD OR	336-B12
THE DALLES OR	196-C7
4TH ST N Rt#-140	
LAKE CO OR	152-A2
LAKEVIEW OR	152-A2
4TH ST NE	
SNOHOMISH CO WA	171-D2
4TH ST NW	
BREWSTER WA	104-B3
OKANOGAN CO WA	104-B3
4TH ST SE	
DOUGLAS CO WA	239-B5
East Wenatchee Bench WA	239-A5
4TH ST SW	
BANDON OR	220-A6
BREWSTER WA	104-B3
OKANOGAN CO WA	104-B3
4TH ST W Rt#-99W	
CORVALLIS OR	327-H9
4TH ST W U.S.-20	
CORVALLIS OR	327-H9
4TH DIVISION DR	
PIERCE CO WA	181-C6
4TH ST GRADE	
THE DALLES OR	196-C7
4 1/2 RD NW	
DOUGLAS CO WA	112-B2
5TH AV	
ALBANY OR	326-C8
BENTON CO OR	133-B2
MONROE WA	133-B2
OLYMPIA WA	296-G5
RIDDLE OR	225-B3
SEATTLE WA	277-J4
SEATTLE WA	278-A5
5TH AV Rt#-41	
SPIRIT LAKE ID	115-A1
5TH AV Rt#-99W	
MONROE WA	133-B2
5TH AV Rt#-109	
Taholah WA	172-B6
5TH AV U.S.-95	
SANDPOINT ID	244-A2
N 5TH AV	
YAKIMA WA	243-B6
N 5TH AV U.S.-95	
SANDPOINT ID	244-A2
S 5TH AV	
YAKIMA WA	243-B6
SW 5TH AV	
ONTARIO OR	139-A3
PORTLAND OR	312-E7
PORTLAND OR	316-E1
PORTLAND OR	317-E1
W 5TH AV	
EUGENE OR	329-E6
W 5TH AV U.S.-395	
COLVILLE WA	106-A2
5TH AV N	
KELSO WA	303-D7
SEATTLE WA	277-J2
5TH AV N Rt#-4	
KELSO WA	303-D8
5TH AV NE	
SEATTLE WA	171-B7
SEATTLE WA	274-B3
SHORELINE WA	171-B6
5TH AV NW	
KELSO WA	303-C8
5TH AV S	
EDMONDS WA	171-A5
KELSO WA	303-C10
KING CO WA	286-A2
SEATTLE WA	278-A7
SEATTLE WA	286-A2
5TH AV W	
EVERETT WA	268-A5
5 RD NE	
DOUGLAS CO WA	112-C2
5 RD NW	
DOUGLAS CO WA	236-C6
5 RD SW	
DOUGLAS CO WA	112-B2
DOUGLAS CO WA	239-D2
5TH ST	
ASTORIA OR	300-C6
BAY CITY OR	197-B1
CLARKSTON WA	250-B4
CORVALLIS OR	327-H9
HOQUIAM WA	178-A7
LEWISTON ID	250-B4
MUKILTEO WA	171-B2
MUKILTEO WA	266-E1
MUKILTEO WA	267-E1
OAKLAND OR	219-A7
YAKIMA WA	120-B3
5TH ST Rt#-39	
KLAMATH FALLS OR	338-E8
5TH ST Rt#-129	
ASOTIN WA	250-B4
CLARKSTON WA	250-B4
5TH ST Rt#-162	
KAMIAH ID	123-C2
5TH ST Rt#-226	
LYONS OR	134-A1
MARION CO OR	134-A1
5TH ST U.S.-12	
LEWISTON ID	250-B4
5TH ST U.S.-26	
MADRAS OR	208-C5
5TH ST U.S.-95	
CANYON CO ID	147-A1
WILDER ID	147-A1
N 5TH ST	
DUFUR OR	127-B2
North Springfield OR	330-H5
N 5TH ST	
SPRINGFIELD OR	330-H5
N 5TH ST Rt#-238	
JACKSONVILLE OR	149-B2
N 5TH ST Rt#-505	
LEWIS CO WA	187-D4
TOLEDO WA	187-D4
NE 5TH ST	
CLATSKANIE OR	117-B3
DESCHUTES CO OR	212-D4
NW 5TH ST	
CLATSKANIE OR	117-B3
COLUMBIA CO OR	117-B3
NW 5TH ST U.S.-97	
REDMOND OR	212-D5
S 5TH ST	
POMEROY WA	122-B2
SPRINGFIELD OR	330-H7
S 5TH ST Rt#-39	
KLAMATH FALLS OR	338-D8
SE 5TH ST	
PRINEVILLE OR	213-D5
SW 5TH ST	
GRANTS PASS OR	335-E10
SW 5TH ST Rt#-99	
CANYONVILLE OR	225-C3
SW 5TH ST U.S.-97	
REDMOND OR	212-D5
W 5TH ST	
GRANDVIEW WA	120-B3
WALLOWA WA	130-C1
YAKIMA CO WA	120-B3
5TH ST NE	
East Wenatchee Bench WA	239-A4
SALEM OR	322-J11
6TH AV	
ASOTIN CO WA	250-B5
NEW WESTMINSTER BC	156-D5
SEATTLE WA	278-A6
TACOMA WA	181-C2
TACOMA WA	292-B5
TACOMA WA	293-E5
TOWNSHIP OF LANGLEY BC	158-C2
VANCOUVER BC	254-G12
Vineland WA	250-B5
E 6TH AV	
JUNCTION CITY OR	210-A6
E 6TH AV Rt#-21	
ODESSA WA	113-B3
E 6TH AV Rt#-99	
EUGENE OR	330-A6
N 6TH AV	
RIDDLE OR	225-B3
YAKIMA WA	243-B6
NE 6TH AV	
SUTHERLIN OR	221-C1
NW 6TH AV	
SUTHERLIN OR	221-C1
NW 6TH AV Rt#-14B	
CAMAS WA	193-B7
S 6TH AV	
TACOMA WA	293-G4
SE 6TH AV Rt#-500	
CAMAS WA	193-B7
SW 6TH AV	
PORTLAND OR	312-E7
PORTLAND OR	316-E1
W 6TH AV	
JUNCTION CITY OR	210-A6
KENNEWICK WA	343-D11
LANE CO OR	210-A6
W 6TH AV Rt#-99	
EUGENE OR	329-G6
EUGENE OR	330-A6
6TH AV N	
SEATTLE WA	277-J1
6TH AV NE	
LACEY WA	297-F4
6TH AV S	
SEATTLE WA	282-A3
6TH AV SW	
GRANT CO WA	112-C2
LACEY WA	297-F5
SOAP LAKE WA	112-C2
GRANT CO WA	112-C2
SOAP LAKE WA	112-C2
NE 6TH DR	
PORTLAND OR	309-G2
6 RD SE	
DOUGLAS CO WA	112-C2
6TH ST	
ANACORTES WA	259-J1
ASTORIA OR	300-C5
BREMERTON WA	270-D10
COLUMBIA CITY OR	192-B1
DESCHUTES CO OR	143-A1
HARRISBURG OR	210-A5
HOOD RIVER OR	195-D5
LANE CO OR	219-D1
NEW WESTMINSTER BC	156-D5
THE DALLES OR	196-C7
WALLA WALLA CO WA	345-G4
6TH ST Rt#-39	
KLAMATH FALLS OR	338-D8
6TH ST Rt#-129	
CLARKSTON WA	250-B4
6TH ST Rt#-226	
LINN CO OR	134-A1
LYONS OR	134-A1
6TH ST Rt#-310	
BREMERTON WA	270-G10
6TH ST U.S.-2	
NEWPORT WA	106-C3
6TH ST U.S.-730	
UMATILLA OR	129-A1
UMATILLA CO OR	129-A1
E 6TH ST	
COLFAX WA	122-C1
MOSCOW ID	249-D5
N 6TH ST	
GRANTS PASS OR	335-F6
KLAMATH FALLS OR	338-D7
SAINT HELENS OR	192-B1
N 6TH ST Rt#-52	
PAYETTE ID	139-A3
NW 6TH ST U.S.-97	
REDMOND OR	212-D5
S 6TH ST	
COTTAGE GROVE OR	215-B7
LANE CO OR	215-B7
SUNNYSIDE WA	120-B2
S 6TH ST Rt#-39	
KLAMATH FALLS OR	338-E8
SE 6TH ST	
COLLEGE PLACE WA	344-F11
SW 6TH ST	
COLLEGE PLACE WA	344-E11
WALLA WALLA CO WA	344-E11
SW 6TH ST U.S.-97	
REDMOND OR	212-D5
W 6TH ST	
MOSCOW ID	249-C5
W 6TH ST Rt#-20	
REPUBLIC WA	105-B2
6TH ST N	
NAMPA ID	147-B1
6TH ST SE	
DOUGLAS CO WA	239-A5
East Wenatchee Bench WA	239-A5
7TH AV	
CITY OF RICHMOND BC	326-B8
CITY OF RICHMOND BC	156-A7
DISTRICT OF MISSION BC	94-B3
KELSO WA	303-B9
LONGVIEW WA	303-B9
E 7TH AV	
SPOKANE WA	349-C10
E 7TH AV Rt#-99	
EUGENE OR	330-A6
N 7TH AV	
YAKIMA WA	243-B6
S 7TH AV	
YAKIMA WA	243-B6
SE 7TH AV	
PORTLAND OR	313-G6
PORTLAND OR	317-G1
W 7TH AV	
SPOKANE WA	348-F10
W 7TH AV Rt#-99	
EUGENE OR	329-G6
EUGENE OR	330-A6
7TH AV N	
KELSO WA	303-D8
PAYETTE ID	139-A3
PAYETTE CO ID	139-A3
SEATTLE WA	277-J4
7TH AV S	
DES MOINES WA	290-A5
KELSO WA	303-D10
SEATTLE WA	286-A3
7TH AV SE	
EVERETT WA	268-C7
7TH AV SW	
KELSO WA	303-C8
OLYMPIA WA	296-C5
THURSTON CO WA	296-C5
7 RD NE	
DOUGLAS CO WA	112-C1
7 RD NW	
DOUGLAS CO WA	236-C5
7TH ST	
ASTORIA OR	300-C7
GOLD HILL OR	230-B6
HARRISBURG OR	210-A5
NEHALEM OR	191-B4
OREGON CITY OR	199-D5
PROSSER WA	120-B3
7TH ST Rt#-43	
OREGON CITY OR	199-D4
WEST LINN OR	199-D4
7TH ST Rt#-506	
VADER WA	187-B5
7TH ST U.S.-101	
NEHALEM OR	191-B4
7TH ST U.S.-95	
WEISER ID	139-A2
E 7TH ST	
PRINEVILLE OR	213-D5
E 7TH ST Rt#-19	
FOSSIL OR	128-A3
E 7TH ST U.S.-95	
WEISER ID	139-A2
N 7TH ST	
BREWSTER WA	104-B3
COEUR D'ALENE ID	355-F8
COOS BAY OR	333-G10
SPRINGFIELD OR	330-H6
N 7TH ST Rt#-52	
PAYETTE ID	139-A3
S 7TH ST	
COOS BAY OR	333-G10
SPRINGFIELD OR	330-H7
TACOMA WA	293-H5
S 7TH ST Rt#-52	
PAYETTE ID	139-A3
S 7TH ST U.S.-95	
PAYETTE ID	139-A3
SE 7TH ST	
WARRENTON OR	188-B2
7TH ST SW	
BANDON OR	220-A6
7TH ST W	
RAINIER OR	189-B4
7 1/2 RD NW	
DOUGLAS CO WA	236-C5
7 3/4 RD NW	
DOUGLAS CO WA	236-C5
8TH AV	
CITY OF SURREY BC	158-B2
CITY OF WHITE ROCK BC	158-B2
LONGVIEW WA	303-B10
NEW WESTMINSTER BC	156-D5
TOWNSHIP OF LANGLEY BC	158-C2
8TH AV Rt#-162	
NEZPERCE ID	123-C2
E 8TH AV	
KENNEWICK WA	343-F12
SPOKANE WA	349-G10
SPOKANE CO WA	351-G9
SPOKANE VALLEY WA	349-H10
SPOKANE VALLEY WA	350-J9
SPOKANE VALLEY WA	351-B9
N 8TH AV Rt#-82	
MILTON-FREEWATER OR	121-C3
NE 8TH AV	
MILTON-FREEWATER OR	121-C3
NW 8TH AV	
MILTON-FREEWATER OR	121-C3
ONTARIO OR	139-A3
S 8TH AV Rt#-82	
ELGIN OR	130-A1
UNION CO OR	130-A1
SW 8TH AV	
MILTON-FREEWATER OR	121-C3
W 8TH AV	
SPOKANE WA	348-J10
SPOKANE WA	349-A10
8TH AV E	
NEW WESTMINSTER BC	156-D5
PIERCE CO WA	118-A1
PIERCE CO WA	181-D7
8TH AV N Rt#-125	
WALLA WALLA WA	344-J8
8TH AV NW	
SEATTLE WA	273-G2
SHORELINE WA	171-A6
8TH AV S	
BURIEN WA	288-A2
KING CO WA	286-A5
KING CO WA	288-A2
PIERCE CO WA	118-A1
SEATAC WA	288-A4
SEATTLE WA	286-A5
8 RD NW	
DOUGLAS CO WA	236-B5
8 RD SE	
DOUGLAS CO WA	112-C2
8 RD SW	
DOUGLAS CO WA	239-B3
8TH ST	
ASHLAND OR	337-D8
ASTORIA OR	300-C5
LEWISTON ID	250-B4
NEW WESTMINSTER BC	156-D5
PIERCE CO WA	181-B5
8TH ST Rt#-42	
MYRTLE POINT OR	140-B2
8TH ST U.S.-30	
ASTORIA OR	300-C5
E 8TH ST	
MEDFORD OR	336-D12
PORT ANGELES WA	261-E5
E 8TH ST Rt#-82	
JOSEPH OR	130-C2
WALLOWA CO OR	130-C2
N 8TH ST	
BOISE ID	253-C2
MOUNT VERNON WA	260-C12
PAYETTE ID	139-A3
NE 8TH ST	
BELLEVUE WA	175-C2
BEND OR	332-G6
GRANTS PASS OR	335-F8
SAMMAMISH WA	176-A2
S 8TH ST	
AUMSVILLE OR	133-C1
BOISE ID	253-C3
JEFFERSON CO WA	263-C7
PAYETTE ID	139-A3
SE 8TH ST	
PENDLETON OR	129-B1
W 8TH ST	
MEDFORD OR	336-B12
PORT ANGELES WA	261-D4
8TH ST E	
AUBURN WA	182-B2
EDGEWOOD WA	182-B2
PACIFIC WA	182-B2
PIERCE CO WA	182-B2
SUMNER WA	182-B2
8TH ST N	
East Wenatchee Bench WA	239-A4
8TH ST NW	
SALEM OR	322-F12
8TH ST SE	
DOUGLAS CO WA	239-B5
East Wenatchee Bench WA	239-A5
SNOHOMISH CO WA	171-D2
8TH ST SW	
BANDON OR	220-A6
8 1/2 RD NW	
DOUGLAS CO WA	236-C5
8-10-NE RD	
GRANT CO WA	242-B1
9TH AV	
ALBANY OR	326-D8
LONGVIEW WA	303-B8
SEATTLE WA	277-J4
N 9TH AV	
PASCO WA	343-F6
E 9TH AV	
MILTON-FREEWATER OR	121-C3
W 9TH AV	
SPOKANE WA	348-J10
SPOKANE WA	349-A10
9TH AV FI	
PIERCE CO WA	181-B2
9TH AV N	
SEATTLE WA	277-J4
9TH AV N Rt#-524	
EDMONDS WA	171-A5
9TH AV S	
EDMONDS WA	171-A5
9TH AV S Rt#-125	
WALLA WALLA WA	344-J8
WALLA WALLA WA	345-A9
9TH ST	
CORVALLIS OR	327-H6
FLORENCE OR	214-B3
HARRISBURG OR	210-A5
HOOD RIVER OR	195-D5
JEFFERSON CO OR	208-B6
ONTARIO OR	139-A3
PORT ORFORD OR	224-A6
WALLA WALLA CO WA	345-H4
9TH ST Rt#-57	
BONNER CO ID	107-A3
PRIEST RIVER ID	107-A3
9TH ST Rt#-225	
BENTON CITY WA	120-C3
BENTON CO WA	120-C3
E 9TH ST	
THE DALLES OR	196-C7
N 9TH ST	
BOISE ID	253-C3
COEUR D'ALENE ID	355-F9
TACOMA WA	181-C2
NE 9TH ST	
BEND OR	332-G8
CLARK CO WA	193-C6
DESCHUTES CO OR	212-D5
GRANTS PASS OR	335-G8
JOSEPHINE CO OR	335-G8
S 9TH ST	
BOISE ID	253-C3
SE 9TH ST	
BEND OR	332-G8
9TH ST E	
PIERCE CO WA	182-C2
9TH ST NE	
East Wenatchee WA	239-A4
9TH ST NW	
SALEM OR	322-F12
9TH ST S	
LAKE CO OR	152-A2
LAKEVIEW OR	152-A2
9TH ST SW	
PUYALLUP WA	182-B4
9 1-2 RD SW	
DOUGLAS CO WA	239-B3
10TH AV	
DISTRICT OF BURNABY BC	156-A4
NEW WESTMINSTER BC	156-A4
TOWNSHIP OF LANGLEY BC	158-C2
VANCOUVER BC	156-A4
VANCOUVER BC	254-A12
10TH AV Rt#-99A	
DISTRICT OF BURNABY BC	156-D5
NEW WESTMINSTER BC	156-D5
E 10TH AV	
Finley WA	343-F12
KENNEWICK WA	343-F12
SPOKANE WA	349-B11
N 10TH AV	
ELGIN OR	130-A1
PASCO WA	343-F7
STAYTON OR	133-C1
NE 10TH AV	
CLARK CO WA	192-C3
PAYETTE ID	139-A3
PAYETTE CO ID	139-A3
RIDGEFIELD WA	192-C3
NE 10TH AV Rt#-502	
CLARK CO WA	192-C3
NW 10TH AV	
PORTLAND OR	313-E5
NW 10TH AV Rt#-503	
BATTLE GROUND WA	193-A3
S 10TH AV	
CALDWELL ID	147-B1
CANYON CO ID	147-B1
CORNELIUS OR	198-C1
PASCO WA	343-F8
S 10TH AV Rt#-397	
PASCO WA	343-F9
SE 10TH AV	
HILLSBORO OR	198-D1
SE 10TH AV Rt#-8	
HILLSBORO OR	198-D1
SW 10TH AV	
PORTLAND OR	312-E6
PORTLAND OR	313-E5
SW 10TH AV Rt#-503	
BATTLE GROUND WA	193-A3
CLARK CO WA	193-A3
W 10TH AV	
BENTON CO WA	341-J12
BENTON CO WA	342-B12
KENNEWICK WA	341-J12
KENNEWICK WA	342-A12
KENNEWICK WA	343-C12
10TH AV E	
DISTRICT OF BURNABY BC	156-D5
NEW WESTMINSTER BC	156-D5
SEATTLE WA	278-A5
10TH AV NE	
SHORELINE WA	171-B7
10TH AV SW	
FEDERAL WAY WA	182-A1
QUINCY WA	112-B3
10TH AV W	
SEATTLE WA	277-F2
10 RD NW	
DOUGLAS CO WA	236-C5
10 RD SW	
DOUGLAS CO WA	239-B3
10TH ST	
CORVALLIS OR	327-G8
EVERETT WA	171-C1
NANAIMO BC	93-A3
SNOHOMISH CO WA	171-D3
10TH ST Rt#-173	
BRIDGEPORT WA	112-C2
10TH ST U.S.-30	
BAKER CITY OR	138-C7
E 10TH ST	
MEDFORD OR	336-D12
THE DALLES OR	196-C7
N 10TH ST	
CENTRAL POINT OR	230-C7
KLAMATH FALLS OR	338-D7
SPRINGFIELD OR	330-H6
NE 10TH ST	
BEND OR	332-G8
GRANTS PASS OR	335-F8
JOSEPHINE CO OR	335-G7
NW 10TH ST	
DESCHUTES CO OR	212-D3
PENDLETON OR	129-B1
Terrebonne OR	212-D4
NW 10TH ST U.S.-97	
Terrebonne OR	212-D3
S 10TH ST	
COTTAGE GROVE OR	215-B7
SPRINGFIELD OR	330-J7
SE 10TH ST	
PENDLETON OR	129-B1
VANCOUVER WA	307-H7
SE 10TH ST Rt#-37	
PENDLETON OR	129-B1
SW 10TH ST	
PENDLETON OR	129-B1
W 10TH ST	
MEDFORD OR	336-D12
PRINEVILLE OR	213-D5
THE DALLES OR	196-C7
WASCO CO OR	196-C7
10TH ST NE	
DOUGLAS CO WA	239-A4
EAST WENATCHEE WA	239-A4
East Wenatchee Bench WA	239-A4
10TH ST SE	
DOUGLAS CO WA	239-B5
10 5 SE RD	
GRANT CO WA	242-C7
11TH AV	
BREMERTON WA	270-F10
LEWISTON ID	250-B4
11TH AV Rt#-11	
DISTRICT OF MISSION BC	94-B3
11TH AV Rt#-30	
NAMPA ID	147-B1
E 11TH AV	
EUGENE OR	330-A7
NE 11TH AV	
PORTLAND OR	313-H4
NW 11TH AV	
CLARK CO WA	192-C2
PORTLAND OR	313-E5
RIDGEFIELD WA	192-C2
SE 11TH AV	
PORTLAND OR	313-H6

STREET — City State	Page-Grid
SE 11TH AV	
PORTLAND OR	317-H1
SW 11TH AV	
PORTLAND OR	312-E6
PORTLAND OR	313-E6
W 11TH AV	
EUGENE OR	329-H7
EUGENE OR	330-A7
W 11TH AV Rt#-126	
EUGENE OR	215-A2
EUGENE OR	329-B6
LANE CO OR	215-A2
11TH AV FI	
PIERCE CO WA	181-B3
11TH AV N U.S.-30	
NAMPA ID	147-B1
11TH AV NE	
SEATTLE WA	274-B5
SNOHOMISH CO WA	168-C6
THURSTON CO WA	297-B4
11TH AV NW	
OLYMPIA WA	296-B3
OLYMPIA WA	296-A3
11TH ST	
BELLINGHAM WA	258-B10
BREMERTON WA	270-G10
CORVALLIS OR	327-F10
DIST OF WEST VANCOUVER BC	254-D4
MONTAGUE CA	150-A3
E 11TH ST	
BREMERTON WA	271-A10
TACOMA WA	182-A2
TACOMA WA	293-J5
N 11TH ST	
AUMSVILLE OR	133-C1
COEUR D'ALENE ID	355-G11
NE 11TH ST	
DESCHUTES CO OR	212-D4
NW 11TH ST Rt#-207	
HERMISTON OR	129-A1
S 11TH ST	
COEUR D'ALENE ID	355-G12
TACOMA WA	293-F5
SW 11TH ST Rt#-207	
HERMISTON OR	129-A1
UMATILLA CO OR	129-A1
W 11TH ST	
KETTLE FALLS WA	106-A2
STEVENS CO WA	106-A2
WARDEN WA	121-A1
11TH ST NE	
EAST WENATCHEE WA	239-A4
12 AV	
DISTRICT OF DELTA BC	101-C1
12TH AV	
ALBANY OR	326-B9
CLATSOP CO OR	301-G7
SEASIDE OR	301-G7
SEATTLE WA	278-B6
TOWNSHIP OF LANGLEY BC	158-D2
VANCOUVER BC	254-J13
VANCOUVER BC	255-A13
E 12TH AV	
SPOKANE WA	349-F11
NE 12TH AV	
PORTLAND OR	313-H5
SE 12TH AV	
PORTLAND OR	313-H6
PORTLAND OR	317-H1
SW 12TH AV	
PORTLAND OR	312-E6
W 12TH AV	
AIRWAY HEIGHTS WA	246-A4
12TH AV E	
SEATTLE WA	278-B4
VANCOUVER BC	254-H13
12TH AV NE	
SEATTLE WA	274-C4
THURSTON CO WA	297-B4
12TH AV S	
SEATAC WA	288-B6
SEATTLE WA	278-B7
WALLA WALLA WA	344-J8
12TH AV S Rt#-45	
NAMPA ID	147-B1
12TH AV W	
VANCOUVER BC	254-C13
12 RD NE	
DOUGLAS CO WA	112-C2
12 RD NE U.S.-2	
DOUGLAS CO WA	112-C2
12 RD SW	
DOUGLAS CO WA	239-C4
12TH ST	
BELLINGHAM WA	258-B10
HOOD RIVER OR	195-D5
LEBANON OR	133-C1
LINN CO OR	133-C1
NEW WESTMINSTER BC	156-D5
TILLAMOOK OR	197-C2
TILLAMOOK CO OR	197-C2
12TH ST Rt#-11	
BELLINGHAM WA	258-B11
12TH ST Rt#-20	
ANACORTES WA	259-F2
E 12TH ST	
MEDFORD OR	336-D12
NE 12TH ST	
BELLEVUE WA	175-C2
BEND OR	332-G6
CLYDE HILL WA	175-C2
MEDINA WA	175-C2
NEWPORT OR	206-B4
RENTON WA	175-C4
NW 12TH ST	
LINCOLN CITY OR	203-A4
NEWPORT OR	206-A4
S 12TH ST	
TACOMA WA	292-A6
TACOMA WA	293-E6
SE 12TH ST	
COLLEGE PLACE WA	344-F11
PENDLETON OR	129-B1
WALLA WALLA CO WA	344-G11
SW 12TH ST	
COLLEGE PLACE WA	344-E11
WALLA WALLA CO WA	344-E11
12TH ST E	
PIERCE CO WA	182-C2
12TH ST N U.S.-26	
MALHEUR CO OR	139-A3
VALE OR	139-A3
12TH ST NE	
SALEM OR	322-J12
12TH ST SE	
DOUGLAS CO WA	239-B5
SALEM OR	322-J14
SALEM OR	324-H5

STREET — City State	Page-Grid
12TH ST SE Rt#-22	
SALEM OR	322-J14
12TH AVENUE RD Rt#-45	
CANYON CO ID	147-B1
NAMPA ID	147-B1
OWYHEE CO ID	147-B1
13TH AV	
TOWNSHIP OF LANGLEY BC	158-D2
E 13TH AV	
EUGENE OR	330-A7
SPOKANE WA	349-F11
NE 13TH AV	
PORTLAND OR	313-H4
SE 13TH AV	
PORTLAND OR	317-H6
SW 13TH AV	
PORTLAND OR	312-E6
W 13TH AV	
EUGENE OR	329-G7
EUGENE OR	330-B7
13TH AV N Rt#-125	
WALLA WALLA WA	344-J5
WALLA WALLA CO WA	344-J5
13TH AV S	
SEATTLE WA	282-B2
13TH AV W	
SNOHOMISH CO WA	171-B5
13 RD NE	
DOUGLAS CO WA	113-A1
13TH ST	
ANACORTES WA	259-H2
ASOTIN CO WA	250-B4
CITY OF NORTH VANCOUVER BC	255-B5
CLARKSTON WA	250-B4
DESCHUTES CO OR	212-D3
HOOD RIVER CO OR	195-D5
SNOHOMISH WA	171-D3
Vineland WA	250-B5
E 13TH ST	
WASCO CO OR	196-D7
N 13TH ST	
BOISE ID	253-C2
NE 13TH ST	
DESCHUTES CO OR	212-D5
S 13TH ST	
MOUNT VERNON WA	260-D13
TACOMA WA	293-G5
SW 13TH ST	
PENDLETON OR	129-B1
W 13TH ST	
THE DALLES OR	196-C7
WASCO CO OR	196-C7
13TH ST NE	
SALEM OR	322-J13
SALEM OR	323-A13
14TH AV	
OLYMPIA WA	296-H6
SEATTLE WA	278-C6
TOWNSHIP OF LANGLEY BC	158-D2
E 14TH AV	
ELLENSBURG WA	241-B5
SPOKANE WA	349-D11
N 14TH AV	
PASCO WA	343-E6
NE 14TH AV Rt#-500	
CAMAS WA	193-B7
NW 14TH AV	
PORTLAND OR	312-E4
W 14TH AV	
SPOKANE WA	348-H11
SPOKANE WA	349-A11
W 14TH AV U.S.-2	
AIRWAY HEIGHTS WA	246-A4
SPOKANE WA	246-A4
14TH AV NW	
OLYMPIA WA	296-C3
PIERCE CO WA	174-C7
PIERCE CO WA	181-C1
THURSTON CO WA	296-C3
14TH AV S	
KING CO WA	286-B3
SEATTLE WA	278-C7
SEATTLE WA	286-B3
14 RD NE	
DOUGLAS CO WA	112-C1
14 RD NE Rt#-172	
DOUGLAS CO WA	112-C1
14 RD NW Rt#-172	
DOUGLAS CO WA	112-B1
14TH ST	
LEWISTON ID	250-C4
PORT TOWNSEND WA	263-D5
REEDSPORT OR	218-C1
E 14TH ST	
BREMERTON WA	271-A10
N 14TH ST	
SPRINGFIELD OR	330-J7
NE 14TH ST	
CLARK CO WA	193-B6
NW 14TH ST	
BEND OR	332-C7
PENDLETON OR	129-B1
SE 14TH ST	
CLARK CO WA	193-C7
SW 14TH ST	
BEND OR	332-C8
14TH ST NE	
SALEM OR	322-J13
SALEM OR	323-A13
14TH ST SE	
SALEM OR	322-J14
SALEM OR	324-J1
15TH AV	
LONGVIEW WA	303-A8
E 15TH AV	
POST FALLS ID	353-H5
NE 15TH AV	
PORTLAND OR	309-H7
PORTLAND OR	313-H1
W 15TH AV	
ELLENSBURG WA	241-B5
KITTITAS WA	241-B5
POST FALLS ID	353-H5
15TH AV E	
SEATTLE WA	278-C4
15TH AV NE	
LACEY WA	297-F3
LAKE FOREST PARK WA	171-B7
SEATTLE WA	171-B7
SEATTLE WA	274-C2
SHORELINE WA	171-B7
SNOHOMISH CO WA	168-C4
THURSTON CO WA	297-F3
15TH AV NW	
SEATTLE WA	273-F2
SHORELINE WA	171-A6
15TH AV S	
SEATTLE WA	282-B3

STREET — City State	Page-Grid
15TH AV SW	
EPHRATA WA	112-C3
15TH AV W	
SEATTLE WA	273-F7
SEATTLE WA	277-F2
15 RD NE	
DOUGLAS CO WA	112-C1
15TH ST	
ASOTIN CO WA	250-B4
BREMERTON WA	270-G9
CLARKSTON WA	250-B4
DIST OF WEST VANCOUVER BC	254-D3
OROVILLE WA	104-C1
WALLA WALLA CO WA	345-J3
WASHOUGAL WA	193-C7
E 15TH ST	
TACOMA WA	293-J6
N 15TH ST	
BOISE ID	253-C2
COEUR D'ALENE ID	355-G8
DALTON GARDENS ID	355-G2
KOOTENAI CO ID	355-G2
S 15TH ST	
BOISE ID	253-C2
POMEROY WA	122-B2
SE 15TH ST	
BEND OR	332-H10
CLARK CO WA	193-B7
DESCHUTES CO OR	332-H12
SW 15TH ST	
PENDLETON OR	129-B1
W 15TH ST Rt#-501	
VANCOUVER WA	305-F4
15TH ST NE	
AUBURN WA	182-C1
15TH ST NW	
AUBURN WA	182-B1
East Wenatchee Bench WA	239-A4
15TH ST NW U.S.-2	
East Wenatchee Bench WA	239-A4
15TH ST SW	
AUBURN WA	182-B1
16TH AV	
ASOTIN CO WA	250-B4
CITY OF SURREY BC	158-A2
CITY OF WHITE ROCK BC	158-A2
LEWISTON ID	250-B4
LONGVIEW WA	303-A9
TOWNSHIP OF LANGLEY BC	102-B1
TOWNSHIP OF LANGLEY BC	158-C2
E 16TH AV	
SPOKANE VALLEY WA	349-H11
SPOKANE VALLEY WA	350-H10
SPOKANE VALLEY WA	351-A10
N 16TH AV	
YAKIMA WA	243-B6
NE 16TH AV	
PORTLAND OR	313-H4
S 16TH AV	
YAKIMA WA	243-B7
YAKIMA WA	243-B7
W 16TH AV	
SPOKANE VALLEY WA	349-H11
16TH AV NW	
SNOHOMISH CO WA	168-C6
16TH AV S	
DES MOINES WA	175-B7
DES MOINES WA	290-B7
KING CO WA	175-B7
KING CO WA	286-B2
SEATTLE WA	286-B3
TUKWILA WA	286-B2
16TH AV S Rt#-99	
FEDERAL WAY WA	182-B1
16TH AV S Rt#-161	
FEDERAL WAY WA	182-B1
16TH AV SW	
KING CO WA	285-G6
SEATTLE WA	285-G6
16TH AV W	
UNIV ENDOWMENT LANDS BC	156-A4
VANCOUVER BC	254-A13
NE 16TH DR	
PORTLAND OR	313-H4
E 16TH PL	
THE DALLES OR	196-C7
WASCO CO OR	196-C7
16 RD NE	
DOUGLAS CO WA	112-C1
16TH ST	
ASTORIA OR	300-D6
EVERETT WA	264-E1
EVERETT WA	265-F1
HOQUIAM WA	178-A7
LEWISTON ID	250-C5
NORTH BEND OR	333-E5
E 16TH ST	
KOOTENAI CO ID	353-J5
KOOTENAI CO ID	354-B5
POST FALLS ID	353-J5
POST FALLS ID	354-B5
N 16TH ST	
BOISE ID	253-C2
N 16TH ST U.S.-95	
PAYETTE ID	139-A3
NE 16TH ST	
FRUITLAND ID	139-A3
PAYETTE ID	139-A3
NE 16TH ST Rt#-30	
FRUITLAND ID	139-A3
PAYETTE CO ID	139-A3
S 16TH ST	
BOISE ID	253-C2
MOUNT VERNON WA	260-D13
SUNNYSIDE WA	120-B2
S 16TH ST U.S.-95	
PAYETTE ID	139-A3
SE 16TH ST	
BELLEVUE WA	175-D3
SW 16TH ST	
RENTON WA	175-C5
16TH ST E	
PIERCE CO WA	182-C2
16TH ST W	
CITY OF NORTH VANCOUVER BC	254-J4
17TH AV	
LONGVIEW WA	303-A9
SE 17TH AV	
CLACKAMAS CO OR	321-H11
MILWAUKIE OR	317-H7
MILWAUKIE OR	321-H1
PORTLAND OR	317-H2
PORTLAND OR	317-H1
PORTLAND OR	321-H1
17TH AV NW	
THURSTON CO WA	296-A3
17TH AV NW Rt#-900	
ISSAQUAH WA	175-D3

STREET — City State	Page-Grid
17TH ST	
ASOTIN CO WA	250-C4
BAKER CITY OR	138-B1
LEWISTON ID	250-C4
NORTH BEND WA	333-E6
WASHOUGAL WA	193-C7
17TH ST Rt#-173	
BRIDGEPORT WA	112-C1
NE 17TH ST	
DESCHUTES CO OR	212-D4
SE 17TH ST	
PENDLETON OR	129-B1
SW 17TH ST Rt#-37	
PENDLETON OR	129-B1
17TH ST NE	
SALEM OR	323-A12
17TH ST SE	
SALEM OR	323-A14
N 18 AV	
PASCO WA	343-E6
18TH AV	
LONGVIEW WA	302-J10
LONGVIEW WA	303-A9
TOWNSHIP OF LANGLEY BC	158-C2
E 18TH AV	
EUGENE OR	330-B8
SPOKANE WA	349-B12
N 18TH AV	
PASCO WA	343-E6
NW 18TH AV	
PORTLAND OR	312-E5
SW 18TH AV	
MALHEUR CO OR	139-A3
W 18TH AV	
EUGENE OR	329-D7
EUGENE OR	330-A8
JUNCTION CITY OR	210-A5
LANE CO OR	210-A5
18TH AV SE	
KELSO WA	303-E7
18TH AV SE	
OLYMPIA WA	297-C7
18TH AV S	
LEWISTON ID	250-C4
18TH AV S U.S.-12	
LEWISTON ID	250-C4
18TH ST	
THE DALLES OR	196-C7
VANCOUVER WA	305-G4
VANCOUVER WA	306-B4
N 18TH ST	
MOUNT VERNON WA	260-E11
SPRINGFIELD OR	331-A6
NE 18TH ST	
VANCOUVER WA	193-A6
VANCOUVER WA	306-E4
VANCOUVER WA	307-J4
S 18TH ST	
MOUNT VERNON WA	260-E13
POMEROY WA	122-B2
YAKIMA WA	243-C7
S 18TH ST Rt#-52	
PAYETTE ID	139-A3
W 18TH ST	
VANCOUVER WA	305-G4
19TH AV	
TOWNSHIP OF LANGLEY BC	158-D2
19TH AV Rt#-8	
FOREST GROVE OR	198-B1
E 19TH AV	
Finley WA	343-E13
KENNEWICK WA	343-E13
NW 19TH AV	
PORTLAND OR	312-D5
W 19TH AV	
KENNEWICK WA	342-H13
KENNEWICK WA	343-C13
19TH AV W	
SEATTLE WA	278-C1
19TH AV WE	
SNOHOMISH CO WA	168-C4
19TH AV SE Rt#-527	
BOTHELL WA	171-C6
19TH AV SE Rt#-527	
EVERETT WA	171-C4
EVERETT WA	268-D6
HOOD RIVER OR	195-C5
HOOD RIVER CO OR	195-C5
SNOHOMISH CO WA	171-C4
16TH ST	
BENTON CO OR	133-B1
CITY OF NORTH VANCOUVER BC	254-H4
CITY OF NORTH VANCOUVER BC	255-C4
DISTRICT OF BURNABY BC	156-D5
DIST OF NORTH VANCOUVER BC	254-H4
EVERETT WA	264-E2
EVERETT WA	265-E2
NORTH SPRINGFIELD OR	331-A5
PHILOMATH OR	133-B1
PORT TOWNSEND WA	263-F5
SPRINGFIELD OR	331-A5
E 19TH ST	
THE DALLES OR	196-C7
NE 19TH ST	
CLARK CO WA	193-B6
NW 19TH ST	
DESCHUTES CO OR	212-D5
REDMOND OR	212-D5
Terrebonne OR	212-D4
S 19TH ST	
FIRCREST WA	181-C2
FIRCREST WA	292-A6
TACOMA WA	181-C2
TACOMA WA	292-A6
UNIVERSITY PLACE WA	181-C2
SW 19TH ST	
REDMOND OR	212-D5
W 19TH ST	
KENNEWICK WA	342-J13
19TH ST NE	
East Wenatchee Bench WA	239-A4
19TH ST NW	
East Wenatchee Bench WA	239-A4
19TH WY Rt#-8	
FOREST GROVE OR	198-C1
19-20 ST DIV	
DISTRICT OF BURNABY BC	156-D5
20TH AV	
CITY OF SURREY BC	158-A2
TOWNSHIP OF LANGLEY BC	158-D2
N 20TH AV	
PASCO WA	343-D7
NE 20TH AV	
CLARK CO WA	192-C4
PORTLAND OR	313-J5
NW 20TH AV	
MALHEUR CO OR	139-A3
S 20TH AV	
PASCO WA	343-D8

STREET — City State	Page-Grid
SE 20TH AV	
PORTLAND OR	313-J7
PORTLAND OR	317-J1
SW 20TH AV	
BATTLE GROUND WA	192-D3
CLARK CO WA	192-D3
20TH AV NE	
SEATTLE WA	274-C1
20TH AV NW	
OLYMPIA WA	296-F2
20TH AV W	
EVERETT WA	267-H4
SEATTLE WA	273-E7
S 20TH ST	
BELLINGHAM WA	258-C10
DIST OF NORTH VANCOUVER BC	255-E4
LA GRANDE OR	130-A2
NEW WESTMINSTER BC	156-D5
NE 20TH ST	
BELLEVUE WA	175-D3
SE 20TH ST	
CLARK CO WA	193-C7
SAMMAMISH WA	175-D3
SW 20TH ST	
PENDLETON OR	129-B1
20TH ST E	
FIFE WA	182-A3
20TH ST KPN	
PIERCE CO WA	181-A2
20TH ST NE	
LAKE STEVENS WA	110-C1
LAKE STEVENS WA	171-D1
20TH ST SE	
SNOHOMISH CO WA	171-D2
SNOHOMISH CO WA	265-J4
21ST AV	
LONGVIEW WA	302-J8
LONGVIEW WA	303-A8
TOWNSHIP OF LANGLEY BC	158-D2
E 21ST AV	
SPOKANE WA	349-B12
NE 21ST AV	
PORTLAND OR	313-J4
NW 21ST AV	
VANCOUVER WA	192-C5
SE 21ST AV	
PORTLAND OR	317-J1
W 21ST AV	
SPOKANE WA	348-J12
21ST AV SW	
FEDERAL WAY WA	182-A1
E 21 HWY	
ADA CO ID	253-D3
BOISE ID	253-D3
21ST ST	
BELLINGHAM WA	258-C10
DIST OF WEST VANCOUVER BC	254-C3
LEWISTON ID	250-C4
N 21ST ST	
TACOMA WA	292-B3
TACOMA WA	293-E3
NW 21ST ST	
LINCOLN CITY OR	203-A4
21ST ST NE	
SALEM OR	323-B12
21ST ST SE	
AUBURN WA	182-C2
22ND AV	
GRANT CO WA	242-C2
OLYMPIA WA	297-A7
VANCOUVER BC	255-C14
N 22ND AV	
PASCO WA	343-D6
NE 22ND AV	
CLARK CO WA	192-C3
SE 22ND AV	
MILWAUKIE OR	321-J3
22ND AV E	
PIERCE CO WA	182-A6
SEATTLE WA	278-D1
22ND ST	
ANACORTES WA	259-H3
DIST OF NORTH VANCOUVER BC	254-H3
EVERETT WA	264-D2
HOOD RIVER OR	195-C5
HOOD RIVER CO OR	195-C5
HOQUIAM WA	178-A7
LEWISTON ID	250-D5
NEZ PERCE CO ID	250-D5
NE 22ND ST	
LINCOLN CITY OR	203-A4
S 22ND ST	
REEDSPORT OR	218-C1
22ND ST SE	
SALEM OR	325-A2
23RD AV	
LONGVIEW WA	302-J8
SEATTLE WA	278-D6
NW 23RD AV	
PORTLAND OR	312-D4
23RD AV E	
SEATTLE WA	278-D4
23RD AV NE	
SNOHOMISH CO WA	168-C5
23RD AV S	
SEATTLE WA	278-D7
SEATTLE WA	282-D1
23RD AV SE	
PUYALLUP WA	182-B4
23RD ST	
CITY OF NORTH VANCOUVER BC	255-A3
S 23RD ST	
COEUR D'ALENE ID	355-H12
KOOTENAI CO ID	355-H12
SE 23RD ST	
CLARK CO WA	193-B7
SW 23RD ST	
REDMOND OR	212-D5
23RD ST NE	
SALEM OR	323-B13
24TH AV	
ALBANY OR	326-B10
ASOTIN CO WA	250-B5
CITY OF SURREY BC	158-A2
FOREST GROVE OR	198-B1
LONGVIEW WA	302-J8
SEASIDE OR	301-G6
TOWNSHIP OF LANGLEY BC	158-C2
WASHINGTON CO OR	198-C1
E 24TH AV	
EUGENE OR	330-A9
SPOKANE CO WA	351-G11
SPOKANE VALLEY WA	350-J11
SPOKANE VALLEY WA	351-B11
N 24TH AV	
PASCO WA	343-D6

STREET — City State	Page-Grid
NE 24TH AV	
PORTLAND OR	313-J4
S 24TH AV	
YAKIMA WA	243-B7
24TH AV E	
SEATTLE WA	278-D2
24TH AV NE	
SHORELINE WA	171-B6
24TH AV NW	
SEATTLE WA	272-E2
24TH AV S	
DES MOINES WA	290-C4
KING CO WA	286-C7
KING CO WA	288-C3
NAMPA ID	147-C1
SEATAC WA	288-C3
SEATAC WA	290-C4
24TH PL S	
DES MOINES WA	290-C6
24 RD NW	
DOUGLAS CO WA	112-B2
GRANT CO WA	112-B2
N 24TH ST	
TACOMA WA	292-D3
NE 24TH ST	
CLYDE HILL WA	175-C2
REDMOND WA	175-D2
SE 24TH ST	
BELLEVUE WA	175-D3
24TH ST E	
EDGEWOOD WA	182-B3
24TH ST NE	
SALEM OR	323-B14
E 25TH AV	
SPOKANE VALLEY WA	350-J12
25TH AV NE	
SEATTLE WA	274-D3
SHORELINE WA	171-B7
25TH ST	
DESCHUTES CO OR	213-A4
N 25TH ST	
TACOMA WA	293-J7
S 25TH ST	
TACOMA WA	293-G7
25TH ST SE	
SALEM OR	323-B14
SALEM OR	325-B1
26TH AV	
LONGVIEW WA	302-H10
TOWNSHIP OF LANGLEY BC	158-D2
N 26TH AV	
PASCO WA	343-C7
NE 26TH AV	
OLYMPIA WA	297-A2
THURSTON CO WA	297-D1
W 26TH PL	
KENNEWICK WA	343-D14
26TH ST	
CORVALLIS OR	327-F10
E 26TH ST	
TACOMA WA	293-J7
N 26TH ST	
TACOMA WA	181-C2
TACOMA WA	292-B3
S 26TH ST	
TACOMA WA	293-H7
27TH AV	
ALBANY OR	326-A10
LINN CO OR	326-A10
E 27TH AV	
FINLEY WA	343-F14
KENNEWICK WA	343-F14
W 27TH AV	
BENTON CO WA	343-B14
Finley WA	343-B14
KENNEWICK WA	342-G14
KENNEWICK WA	343-B14
27TH AV NE	
SNOHOMISH CO WA	168-C4
27TH AV SE	
SNOHOMISH CO WA	269-E6
27TH ST	
DIST OF WEST VANCOUVER BC	254-A2
N 27TH ST	
BOISE ID	253-C2
NE 27TH ST	
DESCHUTES CO OR	217-C2
DESCHUTES CO OR	217-C2
NW 27TH ST	
DESCHUTES CO OR	212-D3
SE 27TH ST	
BEND OR	217-C3
CLARK CO WA	193-C7
DESCHUTES CO OR	217-C3
SW 27TH ST	
REDMOND OR	212-D6
27TH ST W	
UNIVERSITY PLACE WA	181-C2
28 AV	
DISTRICT OF DELTA BC	101-C1
28 AV	
DISTRICT OF DELTA BC	101-C1
28TH AV	
TOWNSHIP OF LANGLEY BC	158-C2
N 28TH AV	
PASCO WA	343-C7
SE 28TH AV	
PORTLAND OR	317-J3
PORTLAND OR	318-A4
W 28TH AV	
EUGENE OR	329-H9
28TH AV NW	
SNOHOMISH CO WA	168-B4
THURSTON CO WA	296-E1
28TH AV S	
KING CO WA	288-B2
28TH AV W	
EVERETT WA	267-G6
LYNNWOOD WA	171-B5
SNOHOMISH CO WA	272-D6
SNOHOMISH CO WA	171-B4
SNOHOMISH CO WA	267-G6
NE 28TH CT	
DESCHUTES CO OR	213-A4
N 28TH ST	
BOISE ID	253-C2
SPRINGFIELD OR	331-B6
NE 28TH ST	
CLARK CO WA	193-B6
VANCOUVER WA	193-A6
VANCOUVER WA	307-J3
S 28TH ST	
LAKE STEVENS WA	110-C1
LAKE STEVENS WA	110-C1
29TH AV	
VANCOUVER BC	156-B5
E 29TH AV	
EUGENE OR	330-A10

STREET / City State / Page-Grid

E 29TH AV
SPOKANE WA 349-H13
SPOKANE WA 349-H13
NE 29TH AV
CLARK CO WA 192-D3
W 29TH AV
EUGENE OR 329-J10
EUGENE OR 330-A10
SPOKANE WA 348-J13
SPOKANE WA 349-C13
29TH AV W
SEATTLE WA 276-D2
29TH ST
ANACORTES WA 259-G4
CORVALLIS OR 327-E8
LEWISTON ID 250-C4
MANZANITA OR 191-B4
NE 29TH ST
DESCHUTES CO OR 213-A4
29TH ST E
DIST OF N VANCOUVER BC 255-C3
29TH ST NE
FEDERAL WAY WA 182-A2
TACOMA WA 182-A2
29TH ST SE
AUBURN WA 182-C2
30TH AV
LINN CO WA 207-B5
LONGVIEW WA 302-H8
TOWNSHIP OF LANGLEY BC 158-D2
E 30TH AV
EUGENE OR 330-C10
LANE CO OR 330-G12
30TH AV NE
SEATTLE WA 274-D5
30TH AV W
SEATTLE WA 272-D6
30TH ST
BELLINGHAM WA 258-D12
CORVALLIS OR 327-E10
E 30TH ST
KITSAP CO WA 271-B7
N 30TH ST
RENTON WA 175-C4
TACOMA WA 181-C2
TACOMA WA 292-B2
TACOMA WA 293-E2
NE 30TH ST
KITSAP CO WA 271-C7
SE 30TH ST
CLARK CO WA 193-C7
SW 30TH ST
PENDLETON OR 129-B1
NW 31ST AV
CLARK CO WA 192-C2
RIDGEFIELD WA 192-C2
31ST AV NE
LACEY WA 181-A6
31ST AV SW Rt#-161
PUYALLUP WA 182-B4
N 31ST ST
North Springfield OR 331-C4
SPRINGFIELD OR 331-C4
NW 31ST ST
DESCHUTES CO OR 212-D4
31ST ST NE
TACOMA WA 182-A2
32ND AV
CITY OF SURREY BC 158-B1
LONGVIEW WA 302-G9
TOWNSHIP OF LANGLEY BC 158-C1
E 32ND AV
SPOKANE CO WA 350-H12
SPOKANE CO WA 351-B12
SPOKANE VALLEY WA 350-H12
NE 32ND AV
PORTLAND OR 314-A2
SE 32ND AV
HILLSBORO OR 198-D1
MILWAUKIE OR 199-D3
MILWAUKIE OR 318-A7
PORTLAND OR 318-A7
32ND AV NW
SEATTLE WA 272-D2
32ND AV S
FEDERAL WAY WA 175-B7
KENT WA 175-B7
KING CO WA 175-B7
KING CO WA 182-B2
32ND ST
ANACORTES WA 259-F4
BELLINGHAM WA 258-D11
WASHOUGAL WA 193-C7
S 32ND ST
LANE CO WA 331-C8
SPRINGFIELD OR 331-C8
SE 32ND ST
KING CO WA 176-A3
SAMMAMISH WA 176-A3
32ND ST KPN
PIERCE CO WA 181-A1
32ND ST NW
PIERCE CO WA 181-B1
32ND ST SE
SNOHOMISH CO WA 171-D2
32ND DIVISION DR
PIERCE CO WA 181-B5
33A AV
DISTRICT OF DELTA BC 101-C1
33RD AV
VANCOUVER BC 156-B5
E 33RD AV
EUGENE OR 330-A10
NE 33RD AV
PORTLAND OR 310-A7
PORTLAND OR 314-A1
NE 33RD DR
PORTLAND OR 310-A4
33RD ST
ASTORIA OR 300-F5
E 33RD ST
VANCOUVER BC 305-H3
VANCOUVER BC 306-A3
33RD ST NE
TACOMA WA 182-A2
34TH AV
ALBANY OR 326-B11
SEATTLE WA 278-E5
SEATTLE WA 279-E4
TOWNSHIP OF LANGLEY BC 158-D1
34TH AV E
PIERCE CO WA 182-A4
34TH AV W
SEATTLE WA 272-C7
SEATTLE WA 276-C1
34TH ST
ANACORTES WA 259-H4
CLARK CO WA 193-C7
MOUNT VERNON WA 260-G13

34TH ST
WASHOUGAL WA 193-C7
E 34TH ST
TACOMA WA 295-J1
N 34TH ST
SEATTLE WA 273-H7
SEATTLE WA 274-A7
S 34TH ST
TACOMA WA 295-H1
SW 34TH ST
PORTLAND OR 316-B7
PORTLAND OR 320-B1
35TH AV
SEATTLE WA 276-D2
35TH AV NE
CLARK CO WA 193-D6
35TH AV SE
BOTHELL WA 171-C6
MILL CREEK WA 171-C4
SNOHOMISH CO WA 171-C5
SNOHOMISH CO WA 269-F7
35TH AV SW
SEATTLE WA 281-E7
SEATTLE WA 285-E3
35TH AV W
SNOHOMISH CO WA 171-B4
SW 35TH DR
CLACKAMAS CO OR 199-C5
35TH ST
ASTORIA OR 300-F5
BENTON CO OR 327-E11
CORVALLIS OR 327-E11
FLORENCE OR 214-B2
SPRINGFIELD OR 331-C6
NW 35TH ST
DESCHUTES CO OR 212-D5
S 35TH ST
TACOMA WA 294-C2
SW 35TH ST
REDMOND WA 212-D5
35TH ST NE
DOUGLAS CO WA 239-A3
35TH ST W
UNIVERSITY PLACE WA 181-C3
36 AV
DISTRICT OF DELTA BC 101-C1
36TH AV
BELLINGHAM WA 258-E9
TOWNSHIP OF LANGLEY BC 158-C1
NW 36TH AV
CLARK CO WA 192-C4
S 36TH AV
YAKIMA CO WA 243-B7
YAKIMA CO WA 243-B7
36TH AV NE
THURSTON CO WA 180-D5
36TH AV NW
SNOHOMISH CO WA 168-B4
THURSTON CO WA 180-C5
36TH AV NW Rt#-531
SNOHOMISH CO WA 168-B6
36TH AV S
KENT WA 175-B7
KING CO WA 175-B7
36TH AV W
LYNNWOOD WA 171-B5
SNOHOMISH CO WA 171-B5
NE 36TH DR
LINCOLN CITY OR 203-A4
36TH ST
CORVALLIS OR 327-E8
E 36TH ST
GARDEN CITY ID 253-C2
N 36TH ST
BOISE ID 253-C2
SEATTLE WA 273-H6
NW 36TH ST
SEATTLE WA 273-H6
S 36TH ST
TACOMA WA 294-C2
W 36TH ST
GARDEN CITY ID 253-C2
36TH ST SE
LACEY WA 297-F9
TOWNSHIP OF LANGLEY BC 158-C1
E 37TH AV
SPOKANE WA 349-H14
SPOKANE WA 349-H14
W 37TH AV
SPOKANE WA 348-J14
SPOKANE WA 349-A14
37TH ST
ANACORTES WA 259-F5
N 37TH ST
TACOMA WA 292-A1
NE 37TH ST
DESCHUTES CO OR 213-A4
SW 37TH ST
PENDLETON OR 129-B1
UMATILLA CO OR 129-B1
37TH ST NE
AUBURN WA 182-C1
37TH ST NW
AUBURN WA 182-B1
38TH AV
COWLITZ CO WA 302-F6
LONGVIEW WA 302-F6
TOWNSHIP OF LANGLEY BC 158-C1
S 38TH AV
WEST RICHLAND WA 340-A13
38TH AV E
PIERCE CO WA 182-A5
38TH AV NW
GIG HARBOR WA 181-C1
PIERCE CO WA 181-C1
NE 38TH PL
KIRKLAND WA 175-C1
38TH ST
EVERETT WA 265-E5
E 38TH ST
TACOMA WA 182-A3
TACOMA WA 295-J2
E 38TH ST Rt#-7
TACOMA WA 295-H2
N 38TH ST
SEATTLE WA 273-H6
NE 38TH ST
CLARK CO WA 193-B6
S 38TH ST
TACOMA WA 294-D2
TACOMA WA 295-G2
39TH AV
SKAMANIA CO WA 193-D6
NE 39TH AV
PORTLAND OR 314-B5
SE 39TH AV
PORTLAND OR 314-B7
PORTLAND OR 318-B1
39TH AV S
SEATTLE WA 287-E4

39TH AV SE
PUYALLUP WA 182-B4
SNOHOMISH CO WA 171-C6
39TH AV SW
PUYALLUP WA 182-B4
39TH ST
WASHOUGAL WA 193-C7
E 39TH ST
VANCOUVER WA 305-G2
N 39TH ST
SEATTLE WA 273-H6
NE 39TH ST
CLARK CO WA 193-D6
NW 39TH ST
SEATTLE WA 273-H6
W 39TH ST
VANCOUVER WA 304-E2
VANCOUVER WA 305-F2
40TH AV
CITY OF SURREY BC 158-B1
TOWNSHIP OF LANGLEY BC 158-C1
N 40TH AV
YAKIMA WA 243-B6
S 40TH AV
YAKIMA WA 243-B7
40TH AV NE
SEATTLE WA 274-B2
40TH AV NW
POLK CO WA 322-A10
SNOHOMISH CO WA 168-B3
40TH AV S
PIERCE CO WA 118-A1
SEATTLE WA 181-D7
NE 40TH CIR
CLARK CO WA 193-C6
N 40TH ST
SEATTLE WA 273-J6
SEATTLE WA 274-A6
NE 40TH ST
REDMOND WA 175-D2
SEATTLE WA 274-B6
NW 40TH ST
SEATTLE WA 273-A4
SE 40TH ST
MERCER ISLAND WA 175-C3
MERCER ISLAND WA 283-J3
40TH ST E
PIERCE CO WA 182-C3
40TH ST NW
PIERCE CO WA 181-B1
40TH ST W
UNIVERSITY PLACE WA 181-C3
41ST AV
UNIV ENDOWMENT LANDS BC 156-B5
VANCOUVER BC 156-B5
NE 41ST AV
PORTLAND OR 314-B2
NW 41ST AV
CLARK CO WA 192-C4
41ST AV NE
THURSTON CO WA 180-D5
41 PL
PACIFIC CO WA 186-A6
41ST ST
ANACORTES WA 259-F5
CLARK CO WA 192-D1
N 41ST ST
YAKIMA CO WA 243-C6
NE 41ST ST
SEATTLE WA 274-E6
SEATTLE WA 275-E6
41ST ST SE
AUBURN WA 182-B2
EVERETT WA 264-D6
EVERETT WA 265-E5
41ST DIVISION DR
PIERCE CO WA 181-C5
41B ST
DISTRICT OF DELTA BC 101-C1
NE 42ND AV
PORTLAND OR 310-B7
PORTLAND OR 314-B1
S 42ND AV
YAKIMA CO WA 243-B7
42ND AV E
PIERCE CO WA 182-A5
42ND AV NE
Hayesville OR 323-E7
SEATTLE WA 275-F6
42ND AV NW
THURSTON CO WA 180-B5
42ND AV S
TUKWILA WA 289-E1
42ND ST
SPRINGFIELD OR 331-D5
S 42ND ST
LANE CO WA 331-E8
SPRINGFIELD OR 331-E8
E 43RD AV
SPOKANE WA 246-C5
43RD AV NE
SEATTLE WA 275-F6
43RD AV NW
THURSTON CO WA 180-C5
43RD AV SE
PUYALLUP WA 182-B4
SNOHOMISH CO WA 265-G7
SNOHOMISH CO WA 269-H1
E 43RD ST
TACOMA WA 295-J3
NW 43RD ST
DESCHUTES CO OR 212-D3
S 43RD ST
RENTON WA 175-C6
SW 43RD ST
KENT WA 175-C6
KENT WA 291-J1
RENTON WA 175-C6
RENTON WA 291-J1
TUKWILA WA 291-J1
SE 43RD WY
KING CO WA 175-D3
KING CO WA 176-A3
SAMMAMISH WA 175-D3
SAMMAMISH WA 176-A3
44TH AV
TOWNSHIP OF LANGLEY BC 158-D1
E 44TH AV
SPOKANE WA 246-C5
44TH AV E
PIERCE CO WA 182-A3
44TH AV NW
MOUNTLAKE TERRACE WA 171-B6
44TH AV W
LYNNWOOD WA 171-B4
MOUNTLAKE TERRACE WA 171-B4
E 44TH ST
ADA CO ID 253-C2

E 44TH ST
GARDEN CITY ID 253-C2
NE 44TH ST
RENTON WA 175-C4
NE 44TH ST Rt#-500
CLARK CO WA 193-B6
44TH ST NE
MARYSVILLE WA 171-D1
SNOHOMISH CO WA 171-D1
45TH AV
VANCOUVER BC 156-C5
E 45TH AV
Finley WA 121-A3
SW 45TH AV
PORTLAND OR 316-A5
W 45TH AV
Finley WA 121-A3
KENNEWICK WA 121-A3
45TH AV NE
Four Corners OR 323-E13
SALEM OR 323-F12
45TH AV SE
SNOHOMISH CO WA 171-C6
45TH AV SW
SEATTLE WA 284-D4
TUMWATER WA 296-F10
SW 45TH DR
PORTLAND OR 316-A7
NE 45TH PL
SEATTLE WA 274-E5
N 45TH ST
SEATTLE WA 273-J5
SEATTLE WA 274-A5
NE 45TH ST
DESCHUTES CO OR 213-A4
SEATTLE WA 274-B5
NE 45TH ST Rt#-513
SEATTLE WA 274-D5
SEATTLE WA 275-E5
46TH AV
LONGVIEW WA 302-D5
46TH AV E
PIERCE CO WA 182-A6
46TH AV NE
THURSTON CO WA 180-D5
THURSTON CO WA 181-A5
46TH AV NW
THURSTON CO WA 180-C5
N 46TH ST
SEATTLE WA 273-H5
TACOMA WA 181-D1
47A AV
DISTRICT OF DELTA BC 101-C1
47TH AV
ARLINGTON WA 168-D5
SNOHOMISH CO WA 168-D5
TOWNSHIP OF LANGLEY BC 158-D1
NE 47TH AV
PORTLAND OR 314-C4
47TH AV NE
MARYSVILLE WA 168-C7
47TH AV SW
FEDERAL WAY WA 182-A1
S 47TH ST
TACOMA WA 294-D3
TACOMA WA 295-E4
48TH AV
COWLITZ CO WA 302-D4
LANGLEY BC 158-C1
TOWNSHIP OF LANGLEY BC 158-C1
S 48TH AV
YAKIMA WA 243-B7
SW 48TH AV
PORTLAND OR 316-A7
PORTLAND OR 320-A1
48TH AV NW
SNOHOMISH CO WA 168-B5
48TH AV S
PIERCE CO WA 181-D7
SEATTLE WA 280-D7
SEATTLE WA 284-D1
48 ST
DISTRICT OF DELTA BC 101-C1
E 48TH ST
TACOMA WA 295-J4
NE 48TH ST
CLARK CO WA 193-D6
S 48TH ST
TACOMA WA 295-F4
48TH ST E
EDGEWOOD WA 182-B3
PIERCE CO WA 182-A3
SW 49TH AV
LAKE OSWEGO OR 320-A2
PORTLAND OR 320-A2
49TH AV E
VANCOUVER BC 156-B5
49TH AV NE
TACOMA WA 182-A1
49TH AV SW
SEATTLE WA 280-D5
THURSTON CO WA 296-B10
49TH AV W
VANCOUVER BC 156-B5
49TH ST
CLARK CO WA 193-C7
PORT TOWNSEND WA 263-E2
WASHOUGAL WA 193-C7
TOWNSHIP OF LANGLEY BC 158-D1
NE 50TH AV
CLARK CO WA 192-D3
SE 50TH AV
PORTLAND OR 314-C7
PORTLAND OR 318-C1
50TH AV E
PIERCE CO WA 182-A5
50TH AV NE
MARION CO OR 205-A3
50TH AV NW
SNOHOMISH CO WA 168-B5
50TH AV S
SEATTLE WA 283-F6
50TH PL S
KING CO WA 289-F1
TUKWILA WA 289-F1
N 50TH ST
SEATTLE WA 273-J5
SEATTLE WA 274-A5
NE 50TH ST
LINCOLN CO OR 203-B4
SEATTLE WA 274-D5
NW 51ST AV
CLARK CO WA 192-C2
RIDGEFIELD WA 192-C2

51ST AV NE
MARYSVILLE WA 168-C7
SNOHOMISH CO WA 168-C7
51ST AV S
KING CO WA 182-B1
SEATTLE WA 287-F5
TUKWILA WA 287-F5
51ST AV SE
SNOHOMISH CO WA 171-C5
SNOHOMISH CO WA 265-H4
51ST AV SW
LAKEWOOD WA 181-D4
N 51ST ST
RUSTON WA 181-D1
NE 51ST ST
REDMOND WA 175-D1
SE 51ST ST
LINCOLN CITY OR 203-A5
SW 51ST ST
DESCHUTES CO OR 212-C6
51ST ST W
FIRCREST WA 292-A7
FIRCREST WA 294-A2
TACOMA WA 292-A7
UNIVERSITY PLACE WA 294-A2
52ND AV
TOWNSHIP OF LANGLEY BC 158-C1
S 52ND AV
YAKIMA CO WA 243-B7
SE 52ND AV
PORTLAND OR 318-C2
52ND AV NW
SNOHOMISH CO WA 168-B5
52ND AV W
LYNNWOOD WA 171-B5
SNOHOMISH CO WA 171-B4
52ND ST NE
AUBURN WA 175-C7
KING CO WA 175-D7
52ND ST SE
EVERETT WA 268-D1
EVERETT WA 269-H1
SNOHOMISH CO WA 269-H1
W 53RD AV
SPOKANE WA 246-B5
53RD AV NE
TACOMA WA 182-A2
53RD AV NW
POLK CO WA 204-C6
53RD ST
BENTON CO OR 207-A7
BENTON CO OR 327-B11
CORVALLIS OR 327-B11
NE 53RD ST
CLARK CO WA 193-B6
53RD ST KPN
PIERCE CO WA 181-A1
54TH AV
TOWNSHIP OF LANGLEY BC 158-D1
VANCOUVER BC 156-C5
54TH AV E
FIFE WA 182-A2
PIERCE CO WA 182-A5
54TH AV E Rt#-99
FIFE WA 182-A2
54TH AV NW
PIERCE CO WA 174-C7
THURSTON CO WA 180-B5
54TH AV SW
THURSTON CO WA 296-C11
YAKIMA WA 296-C11
NE 54TH ST Rt#-500
CLARK CO WA 193-B6
NW 54TH ST
SEATTLE WA 272-D4
55TH AV NE
MARION CO OR 323-H5
MARION CO OR 275-G3
SNOHOMISH CO WA 168-D4
55TH AV NW
POLK CO WA 204-C6
55TH AV S
KING CO WA 175-B7
SW 55TH PL
DESCHUTES CO OR 212-C5
55 ST
PACIFIC CO WA 186-A5
NE 55TH ST
SEATTLE WA 274-D4
SEATTLE WA 275-F4
SW 55TH ST
DESCHUTES CO OR 212-C5
56TH AV
CITY OF SURREY BC 158-C1
LANGLEY BC 158-C1
TOWNSHIP OF LANGLEY BC 102-B3
56TH AV Rt#-10
CITY OF SURREY BC 157-A7
CITY OF SURREY BC 158-B1
N 56TH AV
YAKIMA WA 243-B6
56TH AV NW
SNOHOMISH CO WA 168-B4
56 ST
DISTRICT OF DELTA BC 101-C1
E 56TH ST
TACOMA WA 295-J5
S 56TH ST
TACOMA WA 294-D5
TACOMA WA 295-G5
56TH ST NW
GIG HARBOR WA 181-C1
PIERCE CO WA 181-C1
56TH ST SE
SNOHOMISH CO WA 171-D3
57TH AV
VANCOUVER BC 156-B5
E 57TH AV
SPOKANE WA 246-C5
SPOKANE WA 246-C5
NE 57TH AV
PORTLAND OR 314-D2
57TH AV SE
SNOHOMISH CO WA 171-D3
N 57TH ST
YAKIMA CO WA 243-C6
S 57TH ST
LANE CO WA 331-H9
SPRINGFIELD OR 331-H9
57TH ST KPN
PIERCE CO WA 181-A1
57TH ST NE
TACOMA WA 182-A1
57TH WY NW
THURSTON CO WA 180-C5

58TH AV Rt#-10
CITY OF SURREY BC 156-D7
CITY OF SURREY BC 157-A7
DISTRICT OF DELTA BC 156-D7
58TH AV E
PIERCE CO WA 182-A5
58TH AV S
TUKWILA WA 289-G3
58TH AV SE
THURSTON CO WA 181-A7
58TH ST
SPRINGFIELD OR 331-H7
N 58TH ST
CLARK CO WA 192-D5
NE 58TH ST Rt#-500
CLARK CO WA 193-B5
S 58TH ST
SPRINGFIELD OR 331-H8
SW 58TH ST
DESCHUTES CO OR 212-C6
59TH AV NE
ARLINGTON WA 168-D5
MARION CO OR 205-A4
SNOHOMISH CO WA 168-D4
59TH AV SW
SEATTLE WA 280-C3
NW 59TH ST
DESCHUTES CO OR 212-C5
60TH AV
CITY OF SURREY BC 157-B7
TOWNSHIP OF LANGLEY BC 157-D7
NE 60TH AV
PORTLAND OR 314-D6
SE 60TH AV
PORTLAND OR 318-D1
60TH AV E
PIERCE CO WA 182-A7
60TH AV W
LYNNWOOD WA 171-B5
60 ST Rt#-17
DISTRICT OF DELTA BC 101-C1
60TH ST Rt#-17
DISTRICT OF DELTA BC 156-C7
NE 60TH ST
SEATTLE WA 274-B4
NW 60TH ST
DESCHUTES CO OR 212-C4
60TH ST NE
SNOHOMISH CO WA 171-D1
60TH ST SE
SNOHOMISH CO WA 171-D3
BENTON CO OR 327-B11
BENTON CO OR 269-J2
61ST AV
TOWNSHIP OF LANGLEY BC 157-C7
NW 61ST AV
CLARK CO WA 192-C3
61ST AV NE
THURSTON CO WA 180-D5
THURSTON CO WA 181-A5
61ST AV NW
THURSTON CO WA 180-C5
61ST AV SW
LAKEWOOD WA 181-C3
61ST ST NE
MARYSVILLE WA 171-C1
62ND AV
TOWNSHIP OF LANGLEY BC 157-D7
S 62ND AV
YAKIMA CO WA 243-B7
62ND AV E
PIERCE CO WA 182-A4
62ND AV NE
MARION CO OR 205-A4
62ND AV NW
PIERCE CO WA 181-B2
62ND AV SE
MARION CO OR 325-J3
THURSTON CO WA 181-A4
62ND AV SW
THURSTON CO WA 180-B7
62A CRES
TOWNSHIP OF LANGLEY BC 157-D7
62B ST
DISTRICT OF DELTA BC 156-C7
E 63RD AV
SPOKANE WA 246-C5
63RD AV NE
MARION CO OR 205-A6
MARION CO OR 323-J14
MARION CO OR 325-J1
THURSTON CO WA 180-D5
63RD AV SW
SEATTLE WA 280-B3
NE 63RD ST
CLARK CO WA 192-D5
SE 63RD ST
BELLEVUE WA 175-D3
64TH AV
CITY OF SURREY BC 156-D7
CITY OF SURREY BC 157-A7
DISTRICT OF DELTA BC 156-D7
TOWNSHIP OF LANGLEY BC 157-D7
S 64TH AV
YAKIMA CO WA 243-B7
64TH AV NW
THURSTON CO WA 180-C5
64TH AV S
KENT WA 175-B7
KING CO WA 291-G2
KING CO WA 289-H1
64TH PL W
MUKILTEO WA 266-C7
E 64TH ST
TACOMA WA 182-A3
TACOMA WA 295-J6
N 64TH ST
SEATTLE WA 274-A4
S 64TH ST
TACOMA WA 295-G6
64TH ST E
PIERCE CO WA 182-C3
SUMNER WA 182-C3
64TH ST KPN
PIERCE CO WA 181-A1
64TH ST KPS
PIERCE CO WA 181-A3
64TH ST NE Rt#-528
MARYSVILLE WA 168-D7
MARYSVILLE WA 171-C1
SNOHOMISH CO WA 168-D7
SNOHOMISH CO WA 171-D1
64TH ST NW
PIERCE CO WA 181-C1
64TH ST SE
SNOHOMISH CO WA 171-D3
SNOHOMISH CO WA 269-J2

64TH ST W — STREET INDEX — 128TH ST SW 405

STREET / City State / Page-Grid

64TH ST W
UNIVERSITY PLACE WA 181-C3
65TH AV
TOWNSHIP OF LANGLEY BC 157-D7
SW 65TH AV
CLACKAMAS CO OR 199-B4
TUALATIN OR 199-B4
WASHINGTON CO OR 199-B4
65TH AV NE
MARION CO OR 205-A4
N 65TH ST
SEATTLE WA 273-H3
SEATTLE WA 274-A3
NE 65TH ST
SEATTLE WA 274-C3
SEATTLE WA 275-F3
NW 65TH ST
SEATTLE WA 272-D3
SEATTLE WA 273-F3
66TH AV
TOWNSHIP OF LANGLEY BC 157-C7
66TH AV E
PIERCE CO WA 182-A3
66TH AV NE
MARION CO OR 205-A4
66TH AV NW
SNOHOMISH CO WA 168-B6
THURSTON CO WA 180-C4
66TH AV SW
THURSTON CO WA 296-B12
66TH AV W
MOUNTLAKE TERRACE WA 171-B5
NW 66TH ST
DESCHUTES CO OR 212-C4
S 66TH ST
TACOMA WA 294-B6
66TH ST W
PIERCE CO WA 294-A6
67TH AV NE
ARLINGTON WA 168-D7
MARYSVILLE WA 168-D7
MARYSVILLE WA 171-D1
SNOHOMISH CO WA 168-D7
67TH AV SE
SNOHOMISH CO WA 171-D5
67TH AV W
UNIVERSITY PLACE WA 181-C3
67TH PL
PACIFIC CO WA 186-A5
68TH AV
TOWNSHIP OF LANGLEY BC 157-C7
68TH AV NE
KENMORE WA 171-B6
68TH AV NW
SNOHOMISH CO WA 168-B3
68TH AV S
KING CO WA 287-H7
KING CO WA 289-H5
SEATTLE WA 287-H5
TUKWILA WA 289-H5
68TH AV S Rt#-181
KENT WA 175-B7
KENT WA 291-H5
68TH AV SW
LAKEWOOD WA 181-C4
68TH AV W
LYNNWOOD WA 171-B5
NE 68TH ST
CLARK CO WA 192-C5
CLARK CO WA 193-A5
SE 68TH ST
BELLEVUE WA 175-C4
NEWCASTLE WA 175-C4
69TH AV NW
THURSTON CO WA 180-B4
69TH AV SE
SNOHOMISH CO WA 171-D3
SE 69TH WY
BELLEVUE WA 175-C4
NEWCASTLE WA 175-C4
70TH AV
VANCOUVER BC 156-B5
70TH AV Rt#-99
VANCOUVER BC 156-B5
70TH AV E
FIFE WA 182-A3
MILTON WA 182-A2
PIERCE CO WA 182-A2
70TH AV NW
PIERCE CO WA 174-B7
PIERCE CO WA 181-B1
SNOHOMISH CO WA 168-B6
70TH AV S
TUKWILA WA 289-H6
70TH AV SE
MARION CO OR 133-C1
TUMWATER WA 296-H13
70TH AV SW
THURSTON CO WA 296-D13
TUMWATER WA 296-D13
NE 70TH ST
KIRKLAND WA 175-C1
SEATTLE WA 274-B3
SEATTLE WA 275-F3
70TH ST KPS
PIERCE CO WA 181-A3
NW 71ST AV
CLARK CO WA 192-C2
71ST AV NE
MARYSVILLE WA 171-D1
SNOHOMISH CO WA 171-D1
71ST AV SE
MARION CO OR 205-A7
NE 71ST ST
SEATTLE WA 274-B3
71ST ST KPN
PIERCE CO WA 181-A1
72ND AV
CITY OF SURREY BC 156-D7
CITY OF SURREY BC 157-A7
DISTRICT OF DELTA BC 156-D7
TOWNSHIP OF LANGLEY BC 157-C7
NE 72ND AV
CLARK CO WA 192-D3
S 72ND AV
YAKIMA CO WA 243-A7
SE 72ND AV
CLACKAMAS CO OR 318-E6
PORTLAND OR 318-E6
PORTLAND OR 319-E6
SW 72ND AV
TIGARD OR 199-B3
72ND AV NE
MARION CO OR 205-A3
72ND AV NW
STANWOOD WA 168-B4
72 ST
DISTRICT OF DELTA BC 101-C1
E 72ND ST
PIERCE CO WA 182-A3
PIERCE CO WA 295-H7
TACOMA WA 182-A3
TACOMA WA 295-H7
S 72ND ST
TACOMA WA 295-G7
SE 72ND ST
MERCER ISLAND WA 287-J1
72ND ST E
PIERCE CO WA 182-A3
72ND ST KPS
PIERCE CO WA 181-A3
72ND ST SE
SNOHOMISH CO WA 171-D3
73RD AV NE
KENMORE WA 171-C6
73RD AV SE
SNOHOMISH CO WA 171-D4
73RD WY NE
THURSTON CO WA 180-D4
73A AV
TOWNSHIP OF LANGLEY BC 157-C7
S 74TH AV
YAKIMA CO WA 243-A7
NW 74TH ST
DESCHUTES CO OR 212-C4
S 74TH ST
LAKEWOOD WA 294-C7
TACOMA WA 294-C7
TACOMA WA 295-E7
74B AV
TOWNSHIP OF LANGLEY BC 157-C7
75TH AV SE
SNOHOMISH CO WA 171-D6
75TH AV W
UNIVERSITY PLACE WA 181-C3
NE 75TH ST
SEATTLE WA 274-C2
SEATTLE WA 275-E2
75TH ST SW
EVERETT WA 267-J3
EVERETT WA 268-A3
76TH AV NW
SNOHOMISH CO WA 168-B3
76TH AV S
KENT WA 291-J6
76TH AV W
EDMONDS WA 171-B5
LYNNWOOD WA 171-B5
NE 76TH ST
CLARK CO WA 192-D5
CLARK CO WA 193-A5
76TH ST KPS
PIERCE CO WA 181-A3
77TH AV NE
SNOHOMISH CO WA 168-D6
THURSTON CO WA 180-D4
77A AV
TOWNSHIP OF LANGLEY BC 157-C7
78TH AV
TOWNSHIP OF LANGLEY BC 157-C7
78TH AV E
PIERCE CO WA 182-A6
78TH AV NE
THURSTON CO WA 180-D4
78TH AV NW
THURSTON CO WA 180-B4
78TH ST
DESCHUTES CO OR 212-C7
NE 78TH ST
CLARK CO WA 192-C5
NW 78TH ST
CLARK CO WA 192-C5
78TH ST KPN
PIERCE CO WA 181-A1
S 79TH AV
YAKIMA CO WA 243-A7
79TH AV NW
THURSTON CO WA 180-C4
79TH AV SE
SNOHOMISH CO WA 171-D2
80TH AV
CITY OF SURREY BC 156-D7
CITY OF SURREY BC 157-A7
DISTRICT OF DELTA BC 156-D7
TOWNSHIP OF LANGLEY BC 157-C7
80TH AV NE
KENMORE WA 171-C6
80TH AV NW
SNOHOMISH CO WA 168-B4
80TH PL S
KENT WA 175-C6
N 80TH ST
SEATTLE WA 273-H2
SEATTLE WA 274-A2
NE 80TH ST
KIRKLAND WA 175-C1
SEATTLE WA 274-B2
NW 80TH ST
SEATTLE WA 272-D2
SEATTLE WA 273-E2
80TH ST E
PIERCE CO WA 182-A4
80TH ST NE
MARYSVILLE WA 168-C7
81ST AV NE
THURSTON CO WA 180-D4
81ST AV NW
THURSTON CO WA 180-C4
81ST AV SW
THURSTON CO WA 184-C1
82ND AV
TOWNSHIP OF LANGLEY BC 157-C7
NE 82ND AV
CLARK CO WA 192-D2
NE 82ND AV Rt#-213
PORTLAND OR 311-G6
PORTLAND OR 315-F2
SE 82ND AV Rt#-213
CLACKAMAS CO OR 199-D3
CLACKAMAS CO OR 319-F6
MULTNOMAH CO OR 319-F6
PORTLAND OR 315-F7
PORTLAND OR 319-F3
82ND AV NE
MARION CO OR 205-B4
SE 82ND DR
CLACKAMAS CO OR 199-D3
SE 82ND ST
KING CO WA 176-B4
83RD AV
TOWNSHIP OF LANGLEY BC 157-C7
83RD AV NE
MARYSVILLE WA 168-D7
SNOHOMISH CO WA 168-D7
SNOHOMISH CO WA 171-D1
83RD AV SE
SNOHOMISH CO WA 171-D3
83RD AV SW
THURSTON CO WA 184-C1
TUMWATER WA 184-C1
NE 83RD ST
CLARK CO WA 193-A5
NW 83RD ST
DESCHUTES CO OR 212-C4
84TH AV
CITY OF SURREY BC 157-A6
DISTRICT OF DELTA BC 156-D6
TOWNSHIP OF LANGLEY BC 157-C7
84TH AV NE
CLYDE HILL WA 175-C2
KING CO WA 171-C7
MEDINA WA 175-C2
84TH AV NW
SNOHOMISH CO WA 168-B4
STANWOOD WA 168-B4
84TH AV S
KENT WA 175-C6
84TH AV W
SNOHOMISH CO WA 171-A6
E 84TH ST
TACOMA WA 181-D4
S 84TH ST
PIERCE CO WA 181-D4
TACOMA WA 181-D4
84TH ST E
PIERCE CO WA 182-A4
84TH ST NE
MARYSVILLE WA 168-C7
SNOHOMISH CO WA 102-C3
SNOHOMISH CO WA 168-C7
84TH ST S
LAKEWOOD WA 181-D4
84TH ST SW Rt#-526
MUKILTEO WA 266-E4
MUKILTEO WA 267-F4
85TH AV NW
THURSTON CO WA 180-C4
85TH ST
DESCHUTES CO OR 212-C7
N 85TH ST
SEATTLE WA 273-J1
SEATTLE WA 274-A1
NE 85TH ST
CLARK CO WA 193-C5
KIRKLAND WA 175-D1
REDMOND WA 175-D1
NE 85TH ST Rt#-908
KIRKLAND WA 175-C1
NW 85TH ST
SEATTLE WA 272-D1
SEATTLE WA 273-F1
85TH ST E
PIERCE CO WA 181-D4
PIERCE CO WA 182-A4
86TH AV
TOWNSHIP OF LANGLEY BC 157-C6
NE 86TH AV
VANCOUVER WA 307-F3
86TH AV E
PIERCE CO WA 182-A6
86TH AV NE
MARION CO OR 205-B3
86TH AV NW
PIERCE CO WA 174-B7
86TH ST NW
SNOHOMISH CO WA 168-B7
86A AV
TOWNSHIP OF LANGLEY BC 157-C6
NE 87TH AV
CLARK CO WA 192-D5
87TH AV SE
SNOHOMISH CO WA 171-D2
88TH AV
CITY OF SURREY BC 156-D6
CITY OF SURREY BC 157-A6
DISTRICT OF DELTA BC 156-D6
TOWNSHIP OF LANGLEY BC 157-C6
SE 88TH AV
VANCOUVER WA 311-F1
88TH AV NW
SNOHOMISH CO WA 168-B4
STANWOOD WA 168-B4
88TH AV SW
THURSTON CO WA 184-C1
TUMWATER WA 184-C1
88TH AV W
EDMONDS WA 171-A5
NE 88TH ST
CLARK CO WA 192-D5
SE 88TH ST
KING CO WA 176-D3
88TH ST NE
MARYSVILLE WA 168-C7
SNOHOMISH CO WA 168-C7
88TH ST SE
SNOHOMISH CO WA 171-D3
88TH ST SW
LAKEWOOD WA 181-C4
89TH AV SE
THURSTON CO WA 184-D1
89TH ST
BRITISH COLUMBIA BC 104-C1
89TH ST SW
LAKEWOOD WA 181-D4
90TH AV
DISTRICT OF DELTA BC 156-D6
S 90TH AV
YAKIMA CO WA 243-A7
90TH AV E
PIERCE CO WA 182-B6
90TH AV NE
KING CO WA 171-C7
90TH AV NW
THURSTON CO WA 180-C4
90TH ST SW
EVERETT WA 268-A5
91A AV
TOWNSHIP OF LANGLEY BC 157-C6
91ST AV NE
SNOHOMISH CO WA 168-D6
NW 91ST ST
DESCHUTES CO OR 212-C4
92ND AV
CITY OF SURREY BC 157-A6
DISTRICT OF DELTA BC 156-D6
NE 92ND AV
CLARK CO WA 192-D3
SE 92ND AV
CLACKAMAS CO OR 319-G6
PORTLAND OR 315-G7
PORTLAND OR 319-G2
PORTLAND OR 319-G6
VANCOUVER WA 307-G6
92ND AV NE
SNOHOMISH CO WA 171-D1
YARROW POINT WA 175-C2
92ND AV NW
PIERCE CO WA 181-B1
SNOHOMISH CO WA 168-A5
92ND ST KPN
PIERCE CO WA 174-A7
92ND ST NW
SNOHOMISH CO WA 168-C7
92ND ST SE
SNOHOMISH WA 171-D3
SNOHOMISH CO WA 171-D3
92A AV
TOWNSHIP OF LANGLEY BC 157-C6
93RD AV SE
THURSTON CO WA 184-C1
93RD AV SW
THURSTON CO WA 184-C1
93RD AV SW Rt#-121
THURSTON CO WA 184-C1
TUMWATER WA 184-C1
93RD ST
DESCHUTES CO OR 212-C7
93RD ST SW
LAKEWOOD WA 181-C4
94TH AV
CLARK CO WA 192-D1
NE 94TH AV
CLARK CO WA 192-D5
94TH AV E
PIERCE CO WA 182-B7
94TH AV S
KENT WA 175-C7
94TH ST
DESCHUTES CO OR 212-C7
95TH AV NE
MARION CO OR 205-B6
NE 95TH ST
SEATTLE WA 171-B7
96TH AV
CITY OF SURREY BC 156-D6
CITY OF SURREY BC 157-A6
DISTRICT OF DELTA BC 156-D6
MAPLE RIDGE BC 157-D6
TOWNSHIP OF LANGLEY BC 157-C6
96TH AV NE
BOTHELL WA 171-C6
96TH DR SE
SNOHOMISH WA 171-D3
SNOHOMISH CO WA 171-D3
S 96TH ST
KING CO WA 286-B4
PIERCE CO WA 181-D4
TACOMA WA 181-D4
96TH ST E
PIERCE CO WA 182-A4
96TH ST NW
GIG HARBOR WA 174-C7
NE 97TH AV
VANCOUVER WA 307-G5
98TH AV
MAPLE RIDGE BC 157-D6
TOWNSHIP OF LANGLEY BC 157-C6
NE 98TH AV
VANCOUVER WA 307-G3
SE 98TH AV
VANCOUVER WA 307-G7
98TH AV NE
KIRKLAND WA 171-C7
KIRKLAND WA 175-C1
99TH AV NE
SNOHOMISH CO WA 168-D4
SNOHOMISH CO WA 171-D1
99TH AV SE
SNOHOMISH CO WA 171-D2
99TH AV SW
KING CO WA 174-D7
LAKEWOOD WA 181-C4
NE 99TH ST
CLARK CO WA 192-C5
CLARK CO WA 193-A5
NW 99TH ST
CLARK CO WA 192-C5
99TH ST E
PIERCE CO WA 181-D4
100TH AV
CITY OF SURREY BC 157-A6
MAPLE RIDGE BC 157-D6
TOWNSHIP OF LANGLEY BC 157-C6
100TH AV NE
BELLEVUE WA 175-C2
BOTHELL WA 171-C7
KING CO WA 171-C7
KIRKLAND WA 171-C7
100TH AV SE
THURSTON CO WA 184-C1
100TH AV W
EDMONDS WA 171-A6
SW 100TH ST U.S.-101
NEWPORT OR 206-A5
100TH ST NE
GRANITE FALLS WA 102-C3
SNOHOMISH CO WA 102-C3
SNOHOMISH CO WA 168-C7
100TH ST SE
EVERETT WA 268-D6
EVERETT WA 269-G7
SNOHOMISH CO WA 268-D6
SNOHOMISH CO WA 269-G7
100TH ST SW
EVERETT WA 267-H6
EVERETT WA 268-A6
LAKEWOOD WA 181-D4
SNOHOMISH CO WA 267-H6
100TH WY
LINCOLN CO OR 206-B3
101ST AV
TOWNSHIP OF LANGLEY BC 157-C6
101ST AV SW
THURSTON CO WA 184-B1
NW 101 LN
DESCHUTES CO OR 212-C5
101 PL
PACIFIC CO WA 186-A5
102ND AV
CITY OF SURREY BC 157-B6
MAPLE RIDGE BC 157-D6
TOWNSHIP OF LANGLEY BC 157-C6
NE 102ND AV
CLARK CO WA 192-D1
MAYWOOD PARK OR 315-H2
PORTLAND OR 315-H2
SE 102ND AV
PORTLAND OR 315-H6
102ND AV NW
STANWOOD WA 168-A4
102B AV
TOWNSHIP OF LANGLEY BC 157-C6
103RD AV SE
SNOHOMISH CO WA 171-D2
THURSTON CO WA 184-D1
103RD AV SW
THURSTON CO WA 184-B1
SE 103RD DR
PORTLAND OR 315-H6
104 AV
CITY OF SURREY BC 156-D6
104TH AV
CITY OF SURREY BC 157-A6
104TH AV SE Rt#-515
KENT WA 175-C7
104TH AV SW
KING CO WA 174-D5
THURSTON CO WA 184-C1
104 ST
DISTRICT OF DELTA BC 156-D7
NE 104TH ST
REDMOND WA 175-D1
104TH ST E
PIERCE CO WA 182-A4
104TH ST NW
PIERCE CO WA 174-B7
104TH ST SW
LAKEWOOD WA 181-C4
N 105TH ST
SEATTLE WA 171-A7
NE 105TH ST
CLARK CO WA 193-B5
106TH AV SW
KING CO WA 174-D4
SW 106TH PL
KING CO WA 285-G5
SW 106TH ST
KING CO WA 285-E5
SEATTLE WA 284-D5
SEATTLE WA 285-E5
NE 107TH AV
CLARK CO WA 192-D5
107TH AV SW
THURSTON CO WA 184-C1
SW 107TH ST
KING CO WA 285-G5
108TH AV
CITY OF SURREY BC 157-A6
MAPLE RIDGE BC 157-D6
108TH AV SE
KENT WA 175-C7
108TH AV SE Rt#-515
KENT WA 175-C6
KING CO WA 175-C6
SW 108TH ST
SEATTLE WA 284-E5
108TH ST NE
SNOHOMISH CO WA 168-D7
108TH ST SW
LAKEWOOD WA 181-D4
109TH AV
CLARK CO WA 192-D1
109TH AV SE
SNOHOMISH CO WA 171-D5
NE 109TH ST
CLARK CO WA 192-D5
CLARK CO WA 193-B5
110TH AV
CLACKAMAS CO OR 199-B5
MAPLE RIDGE BC 157-D6
WILSONVILLE OR 199-B5
110TH AV E
PIERCE CO WA 182-B5
110TH AV SW
THURSTON CO WA 184-B1
111TH AV SW
KING CO WA 174-D6
112TH AV
CITY OF SURREY BC 157-A5
MAPLE RIDGE BC 157-D6
NE 112TH AV
BATTLE GROUND WA 192-D3
CLARK CO WA 192-D2
VANCOUVER WA 307-J2
SE 112TH AV
MULTNOMAH CO OR 319-J7
PORTLAND OR 315-J7
PORTLAND OR 319-J1
112TH AV NE
BELLEVUE WA 175-C2
112TH AV SE
BELLEVUE WA 175-C2
KING CO WA 182-C1
112 ST
DISTRICT OF DELTA BC 156-D7
S 112TH ST
KING CO WA 286-A6
112TH ST E
PIERCE CO WA 181-D4
PIERCE CO WA 182-A4
PUYALLUP WA 182-A4
112TH ST S
PIERCE CO WA 181-D4
112TH ST SE
EVERETT WA 171-C4
SNOHOMISH CO WA 171-C4
112TH ST SW
EVERETT WA 171-B4
LAKEWOOD WA 181-C4
SNOHOMISH CO WA 171-B4
113TH AV SW
THURSTON CO WA 184-B1
113 ST
PACIFIC CO WA 186-A5
114TH AV NE
MARION CO OR 205-B3
114TH ST NE
SNOHOMISH CO WA 168-C7
115TH AV NE
SNOHOMISH CO WA 168-D7
NE 115TH ST
SEATTLE WA 171-B7
116TH AV
CITY OF SURREY BC 157-A5
MAPLE RIDGE BC 157-D5
116TH AV NE
BELLEVUE WA 175-C2
116TH AV SE
BELLEVUE WA 175-C4
KENT WA 175-C7
KING CO WA 175-C6
NEWCASTLE WA 175-C4
116 ST
DISTRICT OF DELTA BC 156-D7
NE 116TH ST
KIRKLAND WA 171-C7
REDMOND WA 171-D7
S 116TH ST
KING CO WA 285-J6
KING CO WA 286-A6
SW 116TH ST
BURIEN WA 285-H6
KING CO WA 285-H6
116TH ST NE
MARYSVILLE WA 168-C7
SNOHOMISH CO WA 102-C3
SNOHOMISH CO WA 168-C7
116TH ST S
PIERCE CO WA 181-D4
116TH ST SE
SNOHOMISH CO WA 171-C4
117TH AV
MAPLE RIDGE BC 157-D5
NE 117TH AV Rt#-503
CLARK CO WA 192-D5
CLARK CO WA 193-A4
117TH AV NE
MARION CO OR 205-B6
118TH AV
MAPLE RIDGE BC 157-D5
118TH AV NW
PIERCE CO WA 174-B7
118TH AV SE
BELLEVUE WA 175-C3
S 118TH ST
KING CO WA 286-B7
118TH ST KPN
PIERCE CO WA 174-A7
118TH ST NE
SNOHOMISH CO WA 168-C7
119TH AV
CLARK CO WA 193-A1
PITT MEADOWS BC 157-B5
119TH AV SE
BELLEVUE WA 175-C3
NE 119TH ST
CLARK CO WA 192-D5
CLARK CO WA 193-A5
NW 119TH ST
CLARK CO WA 192-C5
120TH AV NE
KIRKLAND WA 171-C7
NE 120TH PL
KIRKLAND WA 171-C7
120 ST
CITY OF SURREY BC 156-D7
DISTRICT OF DELTA BC 156-D7
120TH ST E
PIERCE CO WA 182-C4
SW 121ST AV
TIGARD OR 199-B3
121ST ST E
PIERCE CO WA 182-A4
122ND AV
MAPLE RIDGE BC 157-C5
NE 122ND AV
PORTLAND OR 200-A1
NE 122ND AV Rt#-503
BATTLE GROUND WA 193-A3
CLARK CO WA 193-A3
SE 122ND AV
CLACKAMAS CO OR 200-A3
PORTLAND OR 200-A2
122ND AV E
EDGEWOOD WA 182-B3
PIERCE CO WA 182-B5
NE 122ND BLVD
PORTLAND OR 193-A7
PORTLAND OR 200-A1
NE 122ND ST
CLARK CO WA 193-B5
122ND ST E
PIERCE CO WA 182-B4
123RD AV
MAPLE RIDGE BC 157-C5
123RD AV NE
SNOHOMISH CO WA 168-D5
123RD AV SE
SNOHOMISH CO WA 171-D2
124TH AV
MAPLE RIDGE BC 157-C5
124TH AV NE
KING CO WA 171-C7
KIRKLAND WA 175-C1
WOODINVILLE WA 171-C7
124TH AV SE
KING CO WA 175-C6
NE 124TH ST
KING CO WA 171-C7
KIRKLAND WA 171-C7
REDMOND WA 171-C7
S 124TH ST
KING CO WA 289-H1
TUKWILA WA 289-H1
NE 124TH WY
KING CO WA 171-D7
125TH AV
MAPLE RIDGE BC 157-D5
NE 125TH ST
SEATTLE WA 171-B7
126TH AV E
PIERCE CO WA 182-B6
126TH AV KPN
PIERCE CO WA 174-B7
126TH ST NW
SNOHOMISH CO WA 168-B6
127TH AV
MAPLE RIDGE BC 157-D5
127TH AV SE
SNOHOMISH CO WA 171-D4
127TH PL SE
BELLEVUE WA 175-C2
NW 127TH ST
CLARK CO WA 192-C4
128TH AV
MAPLE RIDGE BC 157-C5
128TH AV SE
BELLEVUE WA 175-C5
KING CO WA 175-C5
128TH ST
CITY OF SURREY BC 157-A7
CITY OF SURREY BC 158-A2
NE 128TH ST
KING CO WA 171-D7
S 128TH ST
BURIEN WA 288-B1
KING CO WA 288-B1
SEATAC WA 288-B1
SE 128TH ST
KING CO WA 175-D5
RENTON WA 175-D5
128TH ST E
PIERCE CO WA 182-A4
128TH ST KPN
PIERCE CO WA 174-A7
128TH ST NE
SNOHOMISH CO WA 168-C6
128TH ST SE Rt#-96
SNOHOMISH CO WA 171-C4
128TH ST SW
SNOHOMISH CO WA 171-C4

INDEX

STREET — City State Page-Grid

128TH ST SW Rt#-96
SNOHOMISH CO WA 171-C4
SE 128TH WY
KING CO WA 175-D5
129TH AV
MAPLE RIDGE BC 157-C5
PITT MEADOWS BC 157-B5
SE 129TH AV
CLACKAMAS CO OR 200-A3
HAPPY VALLEY OR 200-A3
129TH PL SE
BELLEVUE WA 175-C3
S 129TH ST
KING CO WA 289-G1
NE 130TH AV
CLARK CO WA 193-A5
130TH AV NE
BELLEVUE WA 175-C2
BOTHELL WA 171-C6
KING CO WA 171-C6
WOODINVILLE WA 171-C6
N 130TH ST
SEATTLE WA 171-A7
NE 130TH ST
KING CO WA 171-D7
SEATTLE WA 171-B7
NE 131ST AV
CLARK CO WA 193-A5
131ST AV NE
LAKE STEVENS WA 110-C1
SNOHOMISH CO WA 110-C1
131ST AV NE Rt#-202
BOTHELL WA 171-C6
WOODINVILLE WA 171-C6
131ST AV NE Rt#-92
SNOHOMISH CO WA 110-C1
131ST AV SE
THURSTON CO WA 184-C2
131ST ST E
PIERCE CO WA 181-D4
131ST ST NW
SNOHOMISH CO WA 168-C6
132ND AV
MAPLE RIDGE BC 157-C5
PITT MEADOWS BC 157-C5
NE 132ND AV
CLARK CO WA 193-A2
132ND AV E
PIERCE CO WA 182-B7
132ND AV NE
BOTHELL WA 171-C6
KING CO WA 171-C7
KIRKLAND WA 175-C1
REDMOND WA 175-C1
WOODINVILLE WA 171-C6
132ND AV SE
BELLEVUE WA 175-C7
KENT WA 175-C7
KING CO WA 175-C7
KING CO WA 182-C1
WOODINVILLE WA 171-C6
132ND ST
CITY OF SURREY BC 157-A7
NE 132ND ST
KING CO WA 171-C7
KIRKLAND WA 171-C7
S 132ND ST
KING CO WA 289-J2
132ND ST SE
SNOHOMISH CO WA 168-D6
132ND ST SE Rt#-96
MILL CREEK WA 171-C4
SNOHOMISH CO WA 171-C4
133RD AV SE
NEWCASTLE WA 175-C4
133RD AV SW
THURSTON CO WA 184-B2
NE 133RD ST
KING CO WA 171-D7
S 133RD ST
KING CO WA 289-H2
TUKWILA WA 289-H2
134TH AV E
PIERCE CO WA 182-B5
134TH AV NE
BELLEVUE WA 175-C2
134TH PL SE
SNOHOMISH CO WA 171-C4
NE 134TH ST
CLARK CO WA 192-C4
135 RD
NEZ PERCE CO ID 250-C2
SE 136TH AV
PORTLAND OR 200-A2
136 RD
NEZ PERCE CO ID 250-C2
S 136TH ST
BURIEN WA 288-A2
SEATAC WA 288-B2
136TH ST E
PIERCE CO WA 182-B5
136TH ST NE
MARYSVILLE WA 168-C6
SNOHOMISH CO WA 168-C6
NE 137TH AV
CLARK CO WA 193-A5
138TH AV SE
KING CO WA 175-C4
138TH ST S
PIERCE CO WA 181-D5
NE 139TH ST
CLARK CO WA 192-D4
CLARK CO WA 193-A4
NW 139TH ST
CLARK CO WA 192-C4
140TH AV NE
BELLEVUE WA 175-D2
WOODINVILLE WA 171-C6
140TH AV SE
BELLEVUE WA 175-C2
KING CO WA 175-C6
140TH AV SW
THURSTON CO WA 184-B2
140TH PL NE
KING CO WA 171-C6
WOODINVILLE WA 171-C6
140 RD
NEZ PERCE CO ID 250-C2
140TH ST
CITY OF SURREY BC 157-A6
CITY OF SURREY BC 157-A6
CITY OF WHITE ROCK BC 158-A2
140TH ST NE
SNOHOMISH CO WA 168-C6
140TH ST NW
SNOHOMISH CO WA 168-B6
140TH WY SE
KING CO WA 175-C5

NE 142ND AV
CLARK CO WA 193-A4
SE 142ND AV
CLACKAMAS CO OR 200-A1
NW 143RD AV
WASHINGTON CO OR 199-A1
143RD AV SE
THURSTON CO WA 184-C2
143RD AV SW
THURSTON CO WA 184-C2
144TH AV SE
KENT WA 175-C7
144TH AV
CITY OF SURREY BC 158-A1
NE 144TH ST
CLARK CO WA 193-A4
S 144TH ST
SEATAC WA 288-D3
TUKWILA WA 288-D3
TUKWILA WA 289-F3
144TH ST E
PIERCE CO WA 182-A5
144TH ST KPN
PIERCE CO WA 174-A6
144TH ST NW
PIERCE CO WA 174-C6
SE 145TH AV
HAPPY VALLEY OR 200-A3
145TH PL SE
BELLEVUE WA 175-C2
N 145TH ST
SEATTLE WA 171-A7
SEATTLE WA 171-A7
N 145TH ST Rt#-523
SEATTLE WA 171-A7
SHORELINE WA 171-A7
NE 145TH ST
KING CO WA 171-C7
NE 145TH ST Rt#-202
KING CO WA 171-D7
WOODINVILLE WA 171-C7
NE 145TH ST Rt#-523
SEATTLE WA 171-B7
SHORELINE WA 171-B7
146TH AV E
PIERCE CO WA 182-B6
NE 147TH AV
CLARK CO WA 193-A2
NE 148TH AV
PORTLAND OR 200-A1
148TH AV NE
BELLEVUE WA 175-C2
REDMOND WA 175-C2
148TH AV SE
BELLEVUE WA 175-C3
COVINGTON WA 175-C7
KENT WA 175-C7
KING CO WA 175-D4
KING CO WA 182-C1
148TH ST
CITY OF SURREY BC 157-A6
SW 148TH ST
BURIEN WA 175-A5
148TH ST SW
SNOHOMISH CO WA 171-B4
NW 149TH ST
CLARK CO WA 192-C4
150TH AV
PITT MEADOWS BC 157-C4
SW 150TH AV
WASHINGTON CO OR 199-A3
150TH AV E
PIERCE CO WA 182-B7
150TH AV SE
BELLEVUE WA 175-D3
KING CO WA 175-D3
150 WY ST
OAK HARBOR WA 167-B2
150TH ST SW
LAKEWOOD WA 181-C5
PIERCE CO WA 181-C5
NE 152ND AV
CLARK CO WA 193-A2
152ND AV SE
COVINGTON WA 175-C7
KENT WA 175-C7
KING CO WA 175-C7
152ND AV SW
THURSTON CO WA 184-B3
152ND ST
CITY OF SURREY BC 157-A6
CITY OF SURREY BC 158-A1
SW 152ND ST
BURIEN WA 175-A5
152ND ST E
PIERCE CO WA 182-A5
152ND ST NE
MARYSVILLE WA 168-C6
154TH AV E
PIERCE CO WA 182-B7
154TH AV SE
KING CO WA 182-C1
154TH PL SE
KING CO WA 175-D5
154TH ST
CITY OF SURREY BC 157-A6
S 154TH ST
SEATAC WA 288-C4
N 155TH ST
SHORELINE WA 171-B7
155TH ST SW
LAKEWOOD WA 181-C5
PIERCE CO WA 181-C5
156TH AV NE
BELLEVUE WA 175-D2
REDMOND WA 175-D2
WOODINVILLE WA 171-D6
156TH AV NE Rt#-202
KING CO WA 171-D7
REDMOND WA 171-D7
WOODINVILLE WA 171-D7
156TH AV SE
BELLEVUE WA 175-D3
KING CO WA 175-D5
156TH ST
CITY OF SURREY BC 157-A6
NE 156TH ST
CLARK CO WA 192-D4
S 156TH ST
BURIEN WA 175-A5
BURIEN WA 288-A4
SE 156TH ST
BURIEN WA 175-A5
156TH ST NE
SNOHOMISH CO WA 168-C6
156TH ST SE
SNOHOMISH CO WA 171-D4

S 156TH WY
SEATAC WA 288-B4
157TH ST
CITY OF SURREY BC 158-A2
NW 158TH AV
BEAVERTON OR 199-A1
158TH AV E
PIERCE CO WA 182-B7
158TH AV KPS
PIERCE CO WA 181-A3
159TH AV NE
SNOHOMISH CO WA 102-C3
NE 159TH ST
CLARK CO WA 192-D4
CLARK CO WA 193-A4
159TH ST E
PIERCE CO WA 181-D5
160TH AV E
SUMNER WA 182-C3
160TH PL SE
KING CO WA 182-D2
160TH ST
CITY OF SURREY BC 157-B6
S 160TH ST
KING CO WA 171-D7
S 160TH ST
BURIEN WA 288-A5
SEATAC WA 288-A5
TUKWILA WA 288-A5
160TH ST E
PIERCE CO WA 181-D5
PIERCE CO WA 182-A5
NE 162ND AV
CLARK CO WA 193-A5
GRESHAM OR 200-A1
PORTLAND OR 200-A1
VANCOUVER WA 193-A6
SE 162ND AV
MULTNOMAH CO OR 200-A2
PORTLAND OR 200-A2
162ND AV KPS
PIERCE CO WA 181-A3
162ND ST E
PIERCE CO WA 182-D5
163RD AV NE
SNOHOMISH CO WA 102-C3
163RD AV SW
THURSTON CO WA 184-C3
SE 164TH AV
VANCOUVER WA 193-A7
164TH AV NE
BELLEVUE WA 175-D2
164TH AV NE Rt#-202
REDMOND WA 175-D1
164TH AV SE
BELLEVUE WA 175-D2
COVINGTON WA 175-D7
KING CO WA 175-D5
NE 164TH ST
CLARK CO WA 193-A4
NW 164TH ST
CLARK CO WA 192-C4
164TH ST NE
SNOHOMISH CO WA 168-D6
164TH ST SE
MILL CREEK WA 171-C4
SNOHOMISH CO WA 171-C4
164TH ST SW
LYNNWOOD WA 171-B4
LYNNWOOD WA 171-B4
NE 165TH ST
KING CO WA 171-D7
166TH AV E
PIERCE CO WA 182-C3
166TH AV NE
REDMOND WA 175-D1
NE 167TH AV
CLARK CO WA 193-A4
168TH AV NE
KING CO WA 175-D1
168TH ST
CITY OF SURREY BC 157-B6
CITY OF SURREY BC 158-B2
168TH ST SW
LYNNWOOD WA 171-B5
169TH AV SW
THURSTON CO WA 184-B3
NE 169TH ST
CLARK CO WA 193-B4
NW 169TH ST
CLARK CO WA 192-C4
169TH ST SE
SNOHOMISH CO WA 171-C5
SW 170TH ST
WASHINGTON CO OR 199-A2
S 170TH ST
SEATAC WA 288-C6
170TH ST E
PIERCE CO WA 182-A5
171ST AV SE
KING CO WA 110-C1
171ST PL NE
KING CO WA 171-D7
171ST ST NE
ARLINGTON WA 168-C6
NE 172ND AV
CLARK CO WA 193-A5
SE 172ND AV
HAPPY VALLEY OR 200-A3
NE 172ND ST
CLARK CO WA 171-D6
SW 172ND ST
BURIEN WA 175-A5
172ND ST NE Rt#-531
ARLINGTON WA 168-C6
SNOHOMISH CO WA 168-C6
173RD AV SW
ROCHESTER WA 184-A3
THURSTON CO WA 184-A3
174TH AV KPS
PIERCE CO WA 181-A3
S 174TH ST Rt#-509
KING CO WA 175-A5
174TH ST S
KING CO WA 181-D5
SW 175TH AV
WASHINGTON CO OR 199-A3
175TH AV SW
THURSTON CO WA 184-A3
NE 175TH ST
CLARK CO WA 171-D6
SHORELINE WA 171-B6
WOODINVILLE WA 171-B6
NE 176TH AV
CLARK CO WA 193-A3

176TH AV SW
THURSTON CO WA 184-A3
176TH ST
CITY OF SURREY BC 157-B6
176TH ST Rt#-15
CITY OF SURREY BC 157-B7
CITY OF SURREY BC 158-B2
WHATCOM CO WA 158-B2
S 176TH ST
BURIEN WA 288-A7
SEATAC WA 288-A7
SEATAC WA 289-F7
SE 176TH ST
KING CO WA 175-C5
176TH ST E
PIERCE CO WA 181-D5
PIERCE CO WA 182-A5
176TH ST NW
SNOHOMISH CO WA 168-A6
176TH ST S
PIERCE CO WA 175-D6
KING CO WA 182-D3
176TH ST SW
LYNNWOOD WA 171-B5
177TH ST
PACIFIC CO WA 186-A4
177TH ST E
BONNEY LAKE WA 182-C3
178TH AV E
BONNEY LAKE WA 182-C3
S 178TH ST
SEATAC WA 289-F7
TUKWILA WA 289-F7
TUKWILA WA 291-G1
NE 179TH ST
CLARK CO WA 192-D4
NW 179TH ST
CLARK CO WA 192-C4
180TH AV SE
COVINGTON WA 175-D7
KING CO WA 175-D7
KING CO WA 182-D2
S 180TH ST
TUKWILA WA 291-G1
SE 180TH ST
KENT WA 175-C6
180TH ST E
PIERCE CO WA 182-A5
180TH ST SE
SNOHOMISH CO WA 171-C5
180TH WY SW
THURSTON CO WA 184-B3
NE 181ST AV
GRESHAM OR 200-A1
NE 182ND AV
CLARK CO WA 193-A3
SE 182ND AV
DAMASCUS OR 200-A2
182ND AV E
PIERCE CO WA 182-C2
182ND ST
CITY OF SURREY BC 157-B6
183RD AV SW
THURSTON CO WA 184-A3
183RD AV SW U.S.-12
ROCHESTER WA 184-A3
THURSTON CO WA 184-A3
E 184 I-84
BOISE ID 253-C2
W 184 I-84
BOISE ID 253-C2
184 RD
NEZ PERCE CO ID 250-D2
184TH AV SE
KING CO WA 175-D6
184TH ST
CITY OF SURREY BC 157-B7
CITY OF SURREY BC 158-B1
NW 184TH ST
CLARK CO WA 192-C4
184TH ST E
PIERCE CO WA 182-A6
NW 185TH AV
HILLSBORO OR 199-A1
WASHINGTON CO OR 192-A7
WASHINGTON CO OR 199-A1
SW 185TH AV
WASHINGTON CO OR 199-A2
N 185TH ST
SHORELINE WA 171-B6
NE 185TH ST
SHORELINE WA 171-B6
186TH AV E
PIERCE CO WA 182-C5
186TH AV KPN
PIERCE CO WA 174-A7
PIERCE CO WA 181-A7
186TH ST NE
ARLINGTON WA 168-D5
SNOHOMISH CO WA 168-D5
187TH AV SE
KING CO WA 175-D7
187TH AV SW
THURSTON CO WA 184-B4
188TH AV SW
THURSTON CO WA 184-A4
188TH ST
PITT MEADOWS BC 157-B5
S 188TH ST
SEATAC WA 290-C1
SEATAC WA 291-E2
188TH ST NE
ARLINGTON WA 168-C5
SNOHOMISH CO WA 168-C5
188TH ST NW
SNOHOMISH CO WA 168-B5
188TH ST SW
LYNNWOOD WA 171-B5
S 188TH WY
SEATAC WA 290-B1
NW 189TH ST
CLARK CO WA 192-C4
190TH AV E
PIERCE CO WA 182-C4
190TH AV KPS
PIERCE CO WA 181-A2
SE 190TH DR
MULTNOMAH CO OR 200-A2
191ST AV SW
THURSTON CO WA 184-A3
NE 192ND AV
CLARK CO WA 193-A5
SE 192ND AV
CLARK CO WA 193-A6
VANCOUVER WA 193-A6

SW 192ND AV
WASHINGTON CO OR 199-A4
192ND AV SE
KING CO WA 182-D1
192ND PL SE
KING CO WA 182-D3
192ND ST
CITY OF SURREY BC 157-B6
CITY OF SURREY BC 158-B1
SE 192ND ST
KING CO WA 175-C6
192ND ST E
PIERCE CO WA 182-A6
NW 194TH ST
CLARK CO WA 192-C3
195TH AV SW
THURSTON CO WA 184-B4
NW 195TH ST
SHORELINE WA 171-A6
196TH AV SE
KING CO WA 175-D6
KING CO WA 182-D3
196TH AV
CITY OF SURREY BC 158-C2
S 196TH ST
KENT WA 291-H3
SE 196TH ST
KING CO WA 176-A6
196TH ST NW
SNOHOMISH CO WA 168-B5
196TH ST SE
SNOHOMISH CO WA 171-C5
196TH ST SW Rt#-524
EDMONDS WA 171-B5
LYNNWOOD WA 171-B5
SNOHOMISH CO WA 171-B5
196C ST
PITT MEADOWS BC 157-C4
197TH ST
TOWNSHIP OF LANGLEY BC 157-C7
SW 198TH ST
WASHINGTON CO OR 199-A2
198TH AV E
PIERCE CO WA 182-C5
198 PL
PACIFIC CO WA 186-A3
198TH ST
TOWNSHIP OF LANGLEY BC 157-C6
CITY OF SURREY BC 158-C2
NE 199TH AV
CLARK CO WA 193-A6
NE 199TH ST
CLARK CO WA 193-A3
NW 199TH ST
CLARK CO WA 192-C3
S 199TH ST
DES MOINES WA 175-A6
NE 202ND AV
DES MOINES WA 290-A3
199A ST
TOWNSHIP OF LANGLEY BC 157-C6
200TH AV SE
KING CO WA 182-D2
200TH ST
LANGLEY BC 157-C7
LANGLEY BC 158-C1
TOWNSHIP OF LANGLEY BC 157-C7
TOWNSHIP OF LANGLEY BC 158-C1
N 200TH ST
SHORELINE WA 171-A6
S 200TH ST
DES MOINES WA 290-B3
KENT WA 291-F3
KING CO WA 291-F3
SEATAC WA 290-B3
SE 200TH ST
KING CO WA 176-A6
200TH ST E
PIERCE CO WA 182-A6
200TH ST NE
SNOHOMISH CO WA 168-C5
NE 202ND AV
CLARK CO WA 193-A4
202ND ST
TOWNSHIP OF LANGLEY BC 158-C2
202A ST
TOWNSHIP OF LANGLEY BC 157-C7
202B ST
TOWNSHIP OF LANGLEY BC 157-C7
203RD ST
MAPLE RIDGE BC 157-C5
PITT MEADOWS BC 157-C5
204TH AV NE
KING CO WA 171-D6
204TH PL NE
KING CO WA 175-D1
204TH ST
TOWNSHIP OF LANGLEY BC 157-C7
TOWNSHIP OF LANGLEY BC 158-C1
NE 204TH ST
CLARK CO WA 193-B3
SNOHOMISH CO WA 168-D5
SW 204TH ST
ARLINGTON WA 168-D5
SNOHOMISH CO WA 168-D5
SE 204TH WY
KING CO WA 175-C6
205TH AV KPS
PIERCE CO WA 180-D2
205TH ST
TOWNSHIP OF LANGLEY BC 157-C6
NE 205TH ST
MOUNTLAKE TERRACE WA 171-B6
SHORELINE WA 171-B6
NE 205TH ST Rt#-104
EDMONDS WA 171-B6
MOUNTLAKE TERRACE WA 171-B6
SHORELINE WA 171-B6
206TH ST
TOWNSHIP OF LANGLEY BC 158-C2
207TH ST
MAPLE RIDGE BC 157-C5
207TH ST NE
ARLINGTON WA 168-D5
208 PL
PACIFIC CO WA 186-A3
208TH AV NE
KING CO WA 175-D1
208TH AV SE
KING CO WA 175-D7
208TH ST
LANGLEY BC 158-C2
TOWNSHIP OF LANGLEY BC 157-C7
TOWNSHIP OF LANGLEY BC 158-C2
S 208TH ST
SEATAC WA 290-C4

SE 208TH ST
KENT WA 175-C6
KING CO WA 175-C6
208TH ST E
PIERCE CO WA 181-D6
PIERCE CO WA 182-A6
208TH ST SE Rt#-524
BOTHELL WA 171-C5
SNOHOMISH CO WA 171-C5
208TH ST SW
LYNNWOOD WA 171-B5
SW 209TH AV
WASHINGTON CO OR 199-A2
NE 209TH ST
CLARK CO WA 193-B3
NW 209TH ST
CLARK CO WA 192-C3
210TH AV E
PIERCE CO WA 182-C2
210TH AV SW
THURSTON CO WA 184-B4
210TH ST
MAPLE RIDGE BC 157-C5
TOWNSHIP OF LANGLEY BC 157-C7
TOWNSHIP OF LANGLEY BC 158-C2
211TH PL NE
ARLINGTON WA 168-D5
SNOHOMISH CO WA 168-D5
NE 212TH AV
CLARK CO WA 193-B2
212TH AV SE
KING CO WA 182-D2
SAMMAMISH WA 175-D3
212TH ST
TOWNSHIP OF LANGLEY BC 158-C2
S 212TH ST
KENT WA 175-C6
KENT WA 290-E4
KENT WA 291-G5
212TH ST NW
SNOHOMISH CO WA 168-C5
212TH ST SW
EDMONDS WA 171-B5
LYNNWOOD WA 171-B5
MOUNTLAKE TERRACE WA 171-B5
SNOHOMISH CO WA 171-B5
S 212TH WY
KENT WA 175-C6
KING CO WA 175-C6
213TH AV SW
THURSTON CO WA 184-B4
213TH ST E
PIERCE CO WA 182-B6
214TH AV E
BONNEY LAKE WA 182-C4
PIERCE CO WA 182-C4
215 RD
CLEARWATER CO ID 123-B1
NEZ PERCE CO ID 123-B1
NE 216TH AV
CLARK CO WA 193-B2
216TH AV NE
SAMMAMISH WA 175-D2
216TH AV SE
MAPLE VALLEY WA 175-D7
216TH AV SW
THURSTON CO WA 184-B4
216TH ST
LANGLEY BC 158-C1
MAPLE RIDGE BC 157-C5
TOWNSHIP OF LANGLEY BC 157-C6
TOWNSHIP OF LANGLEY BC 158-C1
S 216TH ST
DES MOINES WA 290-B5
SEATAC WA 290-B5
S 216TH ST Rt#-509
DES MOINES WA 175-A6
DES MOINES WA 290-A5
NORMANDY PARK WA 175-A6
NORMANDY PARK WA 290-A5
SE 216TH ST
KING CO WA 176-A6
216TH ST E
PIERCE CO WA 182-B6
NE 217TH AV
CLARK CO WA 193-B5
218TH AV E
PIERCE CO WA 182-C3
218TH AV SE
KING CO WA 182-D2
219TH AV SW
THURSTON CO WA 184-B4
NE 219TH ST
BATTLE GROUND WA 193-A3
CLARK CO WA 193-A3
NE 219TH ST Rt#-502
BATTLE GROUND WA 192-D3
CLARK CO WA 192-D3
NE 220TH AV
CLARK CO WA 193-B2
SW 220TH ST
KING CO WA 174-D6
220TH ST NW
SNOHOMISH CO WA 168-B5
220TH ST SW
EDMONDS WA 171-A5
NE 222ND AV
CLARK CO WA 193-B5
SE 222ND AV
CLACKAMAS CO OR 200-A3
222ND ST
TOWNSHIP OF LANGLEY BC 157-C6
SE 223RD DR
KING CO WA 175-C6
223RD PL SE
MAPLE VALLEY WA 175-D7
S 223RD ST
DES MOINES WA 290-B6
224TH AV SE
BLACK DIAMOND WA 182-D1
KING CO WA 182-D1
224TH ST
MAPLE RIDGE BC 157-C5
TOWNSHIP OF LANGLEY BC 158-C2
S 224TH ST
DES MOINES WA 290-C6
KENT WA 291-F6
SE 224TH ST
KING CO WA 175-D6
KING CO WA 176-A6
224TH ST E
PIERCE CO WA 182-A6
224TH ST SE
SNOHOMISH CO WA 171-D6
NE 225TH ST
CLARK CO WA 193-B3
226TH ST
TOWNSHIP OF LANGLEY BC 157-C7

STREET City State	Page-Grid
NE 227TH AV	
CLARK CO WA	193-B3
227 PL	
PACIFIC CO WA	186-A3
227TH ST	
TOWNSHIP OF LANGLEY BC	158-C2
228TH AV NE	
SAMMAMISH WA	176-A2
228TH AV SE	
BLACK DIAMOND WA	182-D1
KING CO WA	176-A3
KING CO WA	182-D1
SAMMAMISH WA	176-A2
228 ST	
TOWNSHIP OF LANGLEY BC	157-C7
TOWNSHIP OF LANGLEY BC	158-C1
S 228TH ST	
KENT WA	291-G7
228TH ST NE	
SNOHOMISH CO WA	168-D4
228TH ST SE	
BOTHELL WA	171-C6
SNOHOMISH CO WA	171-C6
228TH ST SW	
BOTHELL WA	171-B6
SNOHOMISH CO WA	171-B6
NW 229TH AV	
HILLSBORO OR	199-A1
NE 229TH ST	
CLARK CO WA	193-B3
230TH AV SE	
ISSAQUAH WA	176-A3
230TH ST	
TOWNSHIP OF LANGLEY BC	157-C7
NW 231ST AV	
HILLSBORO OR	199-A1
WASHINGTON CO OR	199-A1
NE 232ND AV	
CLARK CO WA	193-B4
NE 232ND AV Rt#-500	
CLARK CO WA	193-B5
SE 232ND DR	
CLACKAMAS CO OR	200-B4
232ND ST	
MAPLE RIDGE BC	157-D5
TOWNSHIP OF LANGLEY BC	157-D5
TOWNSHIP OF LANGLEY BC	158-D1
232ND ST Rt#-10	
TOWNSHIP OF LANGLEY BC	157-D7
SE 232ND ST	
KING CO WA	175-D7
232ND ST E	
PIERCE CO WA	182-B6
234TH AV E	
PIERCE CO WA	182-D4
NE 234TH ST	
CLARK CO WA	193-A3
234TH ST E	
PIERCE CO WA	182-B6
235TH ST	
MAPLE RIDGE BC	157-D5
236TH AV NE	
KING CO WA	176-A2
236TH AV SE	
KING CO WA	110-C3
236TH ST	
MAPLE RIDGE BC	157-D6
TOWNSHIP OF LANGLEY BC	158-D1
236TH ST NE	
SNOHOMISH CO WA	168-C4
NE 237TH AV Rt#-500	
CLARK CO WA	193-B6
237TH ST	
MAPLE RIDGE BC	157-D5
NE 237TH ST	
CLARK CO WA	193-B3
NE 238TH AV Rt#-500	
CLARK CO WA	193-B6
238TH AV E	
PIERCE CO WA	182-D5
238TH AV NE	
KING CO WA	176-A1
238TH ST	
TOWNSHIP OF LANGLEY BC	157-D7
238TH ST E	
PIERCE CO WA	182-B6
239TH ST	
MAPLE RIDGE BC	157-D5
TOWNSHIP OF LANGLEY BC	158-D1
NE 239TH ST	
CLARK CO WA	192-D3
240TH ST	
MAPLE RIDGE BC	157-D5
TOWNSHIP OF LANGLEY BC	157-D7
TOWNSHIP OF LANGLEY BC	158-D2
S 240TH ST	
DES MOINES WA	175-B7
SE 240TH ST	
COVINGTON WA	175-C7
KENT WA	175-C7
KING CO WA	175-C7
SW 240TH ST	
KING CO WA	175-A6
240TH ST E	
PIERCE CO WA	182-B6
240TH ST SE	
BOTHELL WA	171-C6
SNOHOMISH CO WA	171-C6
NE 242ND AV	
CLARK CO WA	193-B3
NE 242ND AV Rt#-500	
CLARK CO WA	193-B6
SE 242ND AV	
CLACKAMAS CO OR	200-B3
MULTNOMAH CO OR	200-B2
NE 242ND DR	
TROUTDALE OR	200-B1
WOOD VILLAGE OR	200-B1
242ND ST	
TOWNSHIP OF LANGLEY BC	158-D2
243RD ST	
MAPLE RIDGE BC	157-D5
244TH AV	
CLARK CO WA	118-A3
CLARK CO WA	193-B1
244TH AV NE	
KING CO WA	176-A2
SAMMAMISH WA	176-A2
244TH AV SE	
KING CO WA	176-A6
244TH ST	
MAPLE RIDGE BC	157-D5
TOWNSHIP OF LANGLEY BC	158-D1
NE 244TH ST	
CLARK CO WA	193-A3
SE 244TH ST	
COVINGTON WA	175-C7
KING CO WA	175-C7

STREET City State	Page-Grid
244TH ST SW	
MOUNTLAKE TERRACE WA	171-B6
SHORELINE WA	171-B6
244TH ST SW Rt#-104	
MOUNTLAKE TERRACE WA	171-B6
SHORELINE WA	171-B6
245 ST	
Ocean Park WA	186-A3
PACIFIC CO WA	186-A3
246TH ST	
MAPLE RIDGE BC	157-D5
248TH ST	
MAPLE RIDGE BC	157-D5
TOWNSHIP OF LANGLEY BC	157-D5
TOWNSHIP OF LANGLEY BC	158-D2
SE 248TH ST	
KENT WA	175-C7
250TH AV E	
PIERCE CO WA	182-D4
250TH ST	
TOWNSHIP OF LANGLEY BC	158-D2
252ND ST	
MAPLE RIDGE BC	157-D5
TOWNSHIP OF LANGLEY BC	157-D7
TOWNSHIP OF LANGLEY BC	158-D2
252ND ST E	
PIERCE CO WA	182-B7
252ND ST NE	
SNOHOMISH CO WA	168-C4
254TH AV E	
PIERCE CO WA	182-D4
254TH ST	
TOWNSHIP OF LANGLEY BC	158-D1
NW 254TH ST	
CLARK CO WA	192-C3
256TH ST	
MAPLE RIDGE BC	157-D5
TOWNSHIP OF LANGLEY BC	157-D7
TOWNSHIP OF LANGLEY BC	158-D2
SE 256TH ST	
KING CO WA	175-C7
SE 256TH ST Rt#-516	
KENT WA	175-C7
SW 257TH AV	
TROUTDALE OR	200-B1
258TH AV E	
PIERCE CO WA	182-D4
258TH ST	
TOWNSHIP OF LANGLEY BC	157-D7
NE 259TH ST	
CLARK CO WA	192-D3
CLARK CO WA	193-A2
260TH ST	
MAPLE RIDGE BC	157-D5
S 260TH ST	
DES MOINES WA	175-B7
260TH ST E	
PIERCE CO WA	182-A7
261ST ST	
MAPLE RIDGE BC	157-D5
NE 262ND AV	
CLARK CO WA	193-B5
262ND ST	
MAPLE RIDGE BC	157-D6
264TH AV SE Rt#-169	
KING CO WA	110-C3
264TH ST	
MAPLE RIDGE BC	157-D6
TOWNSHIP OF LANGLEY BC	157-D7
TOWNSHIP OF LANGLEY BC	158-D1
264TH ST Rt#-13	
TOWNSHIP OF LANGLEY BC	158-D2
264TH ST E	
PIERCE CO WA	182-B7
S 265TH PL	
DES MOINES WA	175-B7
NE 267TH AV Rt#-500	
CLARK CO WA	193-B6
267TH ST NW	
SNOHOMISH CO WA	168-B4
268TH ST NW	
SNOHOMISH CO WA	168-B4
STANWOOD WA	168-B4
268TH ST NW Rt#-532	
ISLAND CO WA	167-D4
ISLAND CO WA	168-A4
STANWOOD WA	168-A4
NE 269TH ST	
CLARK CO WA	192-D2
271ST ST NW	
STANWOOD WA	168-A4
SE 272ND AV	
CLACKAMAS CO OR	200-B3
272ND AV E	
PIERCE CO WA	182-D5
272ND ST	
MAPLE RIDGE BC	94-B3
TOWNSHIP OF LANGLEY BC	102-B1
TOWNSHIP OF LANGLEY BC	158-D1
S 272ND ST	
DES MOINES WA	175-B7
FEDERAL WAY WA	175-B7
KENT WA	175-B7
KING CO WA	175-B7
SE 272ND ST Rt#-516	
COVINGTON WA	175-D7
KENT WA	175-C7
MAPLE VALLEY WA	175-D7
272ND ST E	
PIERCE CO WA	182-B7
S 272ND WY	
KING CO WA	175-B7
SE 274TH ST	
KENT WA	175-C7
274TH ST E	
PIERCE CO WA	182-A7
276TH AV SE	
KING CO WA	176-A7
276TH ST NW	
SNOHOMISH CO WA	168-B4
NE 277TH AV	
CLARK CO WA	193-B6
S 277TH ST	
AUBURN WA	175-B7
KENT WA	175-B7
KING CO WA	175-C7
278TH ST E	
PIERCE CO WA	182-B7
NE 279TH ST	
CLARK CO WA	192-D2
CLARK CO WA	193-A2
NW 279TH ST	
RIDGEFIELD WA	192-C2
280TH ST NW	
SNOHOMISH CO WA	168-B4
280TH ST S	
PIERCE CO WA	181-C7

STREET City State	Page-Grid
SE 282ND AV	
CLACKAMAS CO OR	200-B3
GRESHAM OR	200-B2
282ND ST NE	
KING CO WA	168-C4
SE 283RD AV	
CLACKAMAS CO OR	193-B7
284TH ST NE	
SNOHOMISH CO WA	168-C4
284TH ST NW	
SNOHOMISH CO WA	168-B3
NE 288TH ST	
KITSAP CO WA	170-C5
S 288TH ST	
FEDERAL WAY WA	175-B7
KING CO WA	175-B7
288TH ST E	
PIERCE CO WA	181-D7
PIERCE CO WA	182-A7
288TH ST NE	
SNOHOMISH CO WA	168-C3
288TH ST NW	
SNOHOMISH CO WA	168-C3
288TH ST S	
PIERCE CO WA	181-C7
NW 289TH ST	
CLARK CO WA	192-C2
NE 292ND AV	
CLARK CO WA	193-B6
292ND ST E	
PIERCE CO WA	182-A7
292ND ST NW	
SNOHOMISH CO WA	168-A3
S 296TH ST	
FEDERAL WAY WA	182-B1
296TH ST E	
PIERCE CO WA	182-A7
296TH ST S	
PIERCE CO WA	181-D7
299TH AV SE	
SNOHOMISH CO WA	110-C1
SULTAN WA	110-C1
NE 299TH ST	
CLARK CO WA	192-D2
NW 299TH ST	
CLARK CO WA	192-C2
300TH ST NE	
SNOHOMISH CO WA	168-C3
300TH ST NW	
SNOHOMISH CO WA	168-B3
SE 302ND AV	
MULTNOMAH CO OR	200-C2
S 304TH ST	
FEDERAL WAY WA	182-B1
SE 304TH ST	
KING CO WA	182-C1
304TH ST E	
PIERCE CO WA	118-A1
311TH AV SE	
SNOHOMISH CO WA	110-C1
SULTAN WA	110-C1
NE 312TH AV	
CLARK CO WA	193-C6
SE 312TH AV	
CLACKAMAS CO OR	200-C3
S 312TH ST	
FEDERAL WAY WA	182-A1
SE 312TH ST	
KING CO WA	110-C3
SW 312TH ST	
FEDERAL WAY WA	182-A1
NE 314TH ST	
CLARK CO WA	192-D2
316TH ST NW	
SNOHOMISH CO WA	168-C3
S 320TH ST	
FEDERAL WAY WA	182-B1
KING CO WA	182-B1
SE 320TH ST	
AUBURN WA	182-C1
SW 320TH ST	
FEDERAL WAY WA	182-A1
320TH ST E	
PIERCE CO WA	118-B1
SE 322ND AV	
CLACKAMAS CO OR	200-C3
323RD AV SE	
SNOHOMISH CO WA	110-C1
SULTAN WA	110-C1
324TH AV SE	
KING CO WA	176-B3
324TH ST NW	
SNOHOMISH CO WA	168-B3
SW 325TH ST	
WASHINGTON CO OR	198-C1
SW 327TH AV	
WASHINGTON CO OR	198-C1
SE 329TH AV	
CLACKAMAS CO OR	200-C4
SW 331ST AV	
WASHINGTON CO OR	198-C1
332ND ST NW	
SKAGIT CO WA	168-B3
NW 334TH AV	
WASHINGTON CO OR	198-C1
S 336TH ST	
FEDERAL WAY WA	182-B1
SW 336TH ST	
FEDERAL WAY WA	182-A1
336TH ST S	
PIERCE CO WA	118-A1
SW 345TH AV	
WASHINGTON CO OR	198-C1
S 348TH ST	
FEDERAL WAY WA	291-F1
349TH ST	
CLARK CO WA	192-D1
352ND AV	
CLACKAMAS CO OR	200-C3
S 352ND ST	
KING CO WA	182-B2
352ND ST E	
PIERCE CO WA	118-B1
S 356TH ST	
FEDERAL WAY WA	182-A2
SW 356TH ST	
FEDERAL WAY WA	182-A2
NE 360TH ST	
KITSAP CO WA	170-D4
S 360TH ST	
KING CO WA	182-B2
SE 362ND AV	
CLACKAMAS CO OR	200-C3
SE 362ND DR	
CLACKAMAS CO OR	200-C4
SE 368TH ST	
KING CO WA	110-C3
KING CO WA	182-D2

STREET City State	Page-Grid
379TH ST	
CLARK CO WA	192-D1
CLARK CO WA	193-A1
SE 384TH ST	
KING CO WA	182-D2
389TH ST	
CLARK CO WA	192-C1
SE 400TH ST	
SNOHOMISH CO WA	168-C4
284TH ST NW	
SNOHOMISH CO WA	168-B3
412TH AV	
CLARK CO WA	193-D6
SKAMANIA CO WA	193-D6
SE 416TH ST	
KING CO WA	182-D3
422ND AV	
CLACKAMAS CO OR	200-D4
SANDY OR	200-D4
SE 424TH ST	
KING CO WA	110-C3
KING CO WA	182-D3
428TH AV SE	
KING CO WA	176-C4
436TH AV SE	
KING CO WA	176-C5
SE 436TH ST Rt#-164	
KING CO WA	110-C3
KING CO WA	182-D3
SE 436TH WY Rt#-164	
ENUMCLAW WA	110-C3
KING CO WA	110-C3
442ND AV	
CLACKAMAS CO OR	200-D5
SE 448TH ST	
KING CO WA	182-D3
SE 456TH WY	
KING CO WA	182-D4
468TH AV SE	
KING CO WA	176-D5
2900 RD	
MASON CO WA	180-A4
7000 RD	
CLALLAM CO WA	162-D3
I-5 FRWY	
ARLINGTON WA	168-C5
BELLINGHAM WA	161-A2
BELLINGHAM WA	258-A1
BLAINE WA	158-B3
BURLINGTON WA	260-C3
CASTLE ROCK WA	187-C7
CENTRALIA WA	299-D1
CHEHALIS WA	299-D8
SNOHOMISH CO WA	168-C7
SNOHOMISH CO WA	171-C1
SPRINGFIELD OR	330-E7
COWLITZ CO WA	187-D6
COWLITZ CO WA	189-C1
COWLITZ CO WA	303-F1
DES MOINES WA	290-D5
DUPONT WA	181-B5
EVERETT WA	171-C1
EVERETT WA	265-H1
EVERETT WA	268-E4
EVERETT WA	269-E1
FEDERAL WAY WA	175-B7
FEDERAL WAY WA	182-B1
FERNDALE WA	158-C5
FIFE WA	182-A2
Grand Mound WA	184-B3
KALAMA WA	189-C4
KELSO WA	189-C4
KELSO WA	303-D5
KENT WA	175-B7
KENT WA	290-D7
KING CO WA	289-G1
LACEY WA	181-A6
LACEY WA	297-J3
LAKEWOOD WA	181-D4
LEWIS CO WA	184-B5
LEWIS CO WA	187-C1
LEWIS CO WA	299-D1
LYNNWOOD WA	171-B5
MARYSVILLE WA	168-C6
MARYSVILLE WA	171-C1
MILTON WA	182-A2
MOUNT VERNON WA	260-C9
MOUNTLAKE TERRACE WA	171-B5
OLYMPIA WA	296-J6
OLYMPIA WA	297-G5
PIERCE CO WA	181-D4
PIERCE CO WA	182-A2
PORTLAND OR	313-G7
SEATAC WA	289-F7
SEATAC WA	290-E3
SEATTLE WA	171-B7
SEATTLE WA	274-A1
SEATTLE WA	278-B1
SEATTLE WA	282-B1
SEATTLE WA	286-C1
SEATTLE WA	287-E5
SHORELINE WA	171-B6
SISKIYOU CO CA	149-C3
SISKIYOU CO CA	150-A3
SKAGIT CO WA	161-B3
SKAGIT CO WA	168-B1
SKAGIT CO WA	260-C1
SNOHOMISH CO WA	168-B3
SNOHOMISH CO WA	171-C1
TACOMA WA	181-D4
TACOMA WA	182-A2
TACOMA WA	293-J7
TACOMA WA	295-J1
THURSTON CO WA	181-A6
THURSTON CO WA	184-C1
THURSTON CO WA	296-E14
THURSTON CO WA	297-C6
TUKWILA WA	287-E5
TUKWILA WA	289-G1
TUKWILA WA	291-F1
TUMWATER WA	184-C1
TUMWATER WA	296-H8
WHATCOM CO WA	158-B3
WHATCOM CO WA	161-A2
WHATCOM CO WA	258-A1
WOODLAND WA	189-D7
YREKA WA	149-C3
I-5 PACIFIC HWY	
ALBANY OR	326-H5
ASHLAND OR	337-C4
CANYONVILLE OR	225-D1
CENTRAL POINT OR	230-B6
CENTRAL POINT OR	336-A5
CLACKAMAS CO OR	199-B3
CLARK CO WA	192-C1
COBURG OR	210-B6
COBURG OR	215-C5
COTTAGE GROVE OR	215-C5
CRESWELL OR	215-C5
DOUGLAS CO OR	219-C1
DOUGLAS CO OR	221-C2
DOUGLAS CO OR	225-C1

STREET City State	Page-Grid
I-5 PACIFIC HWY	
DOUGLAS CO OR	334-C11
EUGENE OR	330-E7
Four Corners OR	323-D9
Four Corners OR	325-C1
GRANTS PASS OR	335-H7
Hayesville OR	323-D9
JACKSON CO OR	149-C3
JACKSON CO OR	150-A2
JACKSON CO OR	229-B4
JACKSON CO OR	230-B6
JACKSON CO OR	234-B2
JACKSON CO OR	336-A5
JACKSON CO OR	337-C4
JOSEPHINE CO OR	229-B1
JOSEPHINE CO OR	335-D5
KEIZER OR	323-C5
LAKE OSWEGO OR	199-B3
LANE CO OR	210-B6
LANE CO OR	215-C5
LANE CO OR	219-C1
LANE CO OR	330-G9
LINN CO OR	207-C7
LINN CO OR	210-B6
LINN CO OR	326-G14
MARION CO OR	199-B6
MARION CO OR	205-A2
MARION CO OR	207-D2
MARION CO OR	323-C5
MARION CO OR	325-B8
MARYSVILLE WA	168-C2
MARYSVILLE WA	171-C1
MEDFORD OR	234-B2
MEDFORD OR	336-E13
MILLERSBURG OR	326-H5
PHOENIX OR	234-B2
PORTLAND OR	199-B3
PORTLAND OR	305-G5
PORTLAND OR	309-F4
PORTLAND OR	313-F2
PORTLAND OR	316-C7
PORTLAND OR	317-F1
PORTLAND OR	320-A1
RIDGEFIELD WA	192-C2
ROGUE RIVER OR	229-B4
ROSEBURG OR	334-E4
SALEM OR	323-C5
SALEM OR	325-D1
SNOHOMISH CO WA	168-C7
SNOHOMISH CO WA	171-C1
SPRINGFIELD OR	330-E7
SUTHERLIN OR	221-C2
TIGARD OR	199-B3
Tri-City OR	225-C1
TUALATIN OR	199-B4
VANCOUVER WA	192-C5
VANCOUVER WA	305-G5
WASHINGTON CO OR	199-B4
WILSONVILLE OR	199-B5
WOODBURN OR	205-A2
WOODLAND WA	192-B1
I-18 HIGHWAY	
BRITISH COLUMBIA BC	101-A1
I-82 FRWY	
BENTON CO WA	120-C3
BENTON CO WA	121-A3
BENTON CO WA	341-A9
BENTON CO WA	343-A13
GRANDVIEW WA	120-B3
GRANGER WA	120-A2
KENNEWICK WA	341-H13
KITTITAS CO WA	241-B6
PROSSER WA	120-C3
SUNNYSIDE WA	120-B2
UNION GAP WA	120-A2
UNION GAP WA	243-C7
YAKIMA CO WA	120-A2
YAKIMA CO WA	243-B6
ZILLAH WA	120-A2
I-82 HIGHWAY	
YAKIMA CO WA	120-A2
I-82 MCNARY HWY	
UMATILLA OR	129-A1
UMATILLA CO OR	129-A1
I-84 E 184	
BOISE ID	253-C2
I-84 W 184	
BOISE ID	253-C2
I-84 BANFIELD FRWY	
PORTLAND OR	313-H4
PORTLAND OR	314-C5
PORTLAND OR	315-J2
I-84 COLUMBIA RIVER HWY	
ARLINGTON OR	128-A1
BOARDMAN OR	128-B1
CASCADE LOCKS OR	194-C6
FAIRVIEW OR	200-A1
GILLIAM CO OR	127-C1
GILLIAM CO OR	128-A1
GRESHAM OR	200-A1
HOOD RIVER OR	195-A5
HOOD RIVER OR	194-C6
HOOD RIVER OR	195-A5
MORROW CO OR	128-B1
MOSIER OR	196-D7
MULTNOMAH CO OR	200-C1
MULTNOMAH CO OR	201-A1
PORTLAND OR	200-A1
PORTLAND OR	315-J2
RUFUS OR	127-C1
SHERMAN CO OR	127-C1
THE DALLES OR	196-D7
TROUTDALE OR	200-A1
WASCO CO OR	127-B1
WASCO CO OR	195-A5
WASCO CO OR	196-D7
WOOD VILLAGE OR	200-A1
I-84 FRWY	
ADA CO ID	147-C1
ADA CO ID	253-B3
BOISE ID	253-B3
BOISE ID	253-B3
CALDWELL ID	147-B1
CANYON CO ID	147-B1
CANYON CO ID	147-B1
MERIDIAN ID	253-B3
NAMPA ID	147-B1
PAYETTE CO ID	139-A3
I-84 OLD OREGON TRAIL HWY	
BAKER CITY OR	138-B1
BAKER CO OR	130-A3
BAKER CO OR	138-B1
LA GRANDE OR	130-A2
MALHEUR CO OR	138-B1
MALHEUR CO OR	139-A2
MORROW CO OR	128-C1

STREET City State	Page-Grid
I-84 OLD OREGON TRAIL HWY	
NORTH POWDER OR	130-A3
PAYETTE CO ID	139-A2
PAYETTE CO ID	139-A2
PENDLETON OR	129-A1
UMATILLA CO OR	128-C1
UMATILLA CO OR	129-A1
UNION CO OR	129-C2
UNION OR	130-A2
I-90 COLUMBIA BASIN HWY	
ADAMS CO WA	113-C3
I-90 FRWY	
ADAMS CO WA	113-C3
ADAMS CO WA	114-A3
BELLEVUE WA	175-C3
CLE ELUM WA	240-B2
COEUR D'ALENE ID	354-H17
COEUR D'ALENE ID	355-A7
ELLENSBURG WA	241-B5
FERNAN LAKE VILLAGE ID	355-H11
GRANT CO WA	112-C3
GRANT CO WA	113-A3
GRANT CO WA	120-B1
GRANT CO WA	242-C3
ISSAQUAH WA	175-D3
ISSAQUAH WA	176-A4
KELLOGG ID	115-C2
KING CO WA	175-C3
KING CO WA	176-A4
KITTITAS CO WA	111-A2
KITTITAS CO WA	120-A1
KITTITAS CO WA	240-A1
KITTITAS CO WA	241-A4
KOOTENAI CO ID	115-B2
KOOTENAI CO ID	245-B7
KOOTENAI CO ID	248-B1
KOOTENAI CO ID	352-J9
KOOTENAI CO ID	353-A8
KOOTENAI CO ID	354-C7
KOOTENAI CO ID	355-A7
LIBERTY LAKE WA	351-J7
LINCOLN CO WA	114-A2
MERCER ISLAND WA	175-C3
MERCER ISLAND WA	283-J1
MOSES LAKE WA	242-C3
NORTH BEND WA	176-C5
OSBURN ID	115-C2
PINEHURST ID	115-C2
POST FALLS ID	352-J9
POST FALLS ID	353-G6
POST FALLS ID	354-B7
SEATTLE WA	278-B7
SEATTLE WA	282-B1
SEATTLE WA	283-E1
SHOSHONE CO ID	115-C2
SNOQUALMIE WA	176-C4
SPOKANE WA	348-J10
SPOKANE WA	349-G9
SPOKANE CO WA	114-B2
SPOKANE CO WA	246-B5
SPOKANE CO WA	348-E12
SPOKANE CO WA	351-J7
SPOKANE WA	352-H9
SPOKANE VALLEY WA	349-J8
SPOKANE VALLEY WA	350-J6
SPOKANE VALLEY WA	351-A6
SPRAGUE WA	114-A3
WALLACE ID	115-C2
I-99 FRWY	
CITY OF SURREY BC	101-C1
DISTRICT OF DELTA BC	101-C1
I-105 EUGENE-SPRINGFIELD HWY	
EUGENE OR	329-J4
EUGENE OR	330-A5
SPRINGFIELD OR	330-A5
I-182 FRWY	
BENTON CO WA	121-A3
BENTON CO WA	341-E4
FRANKLIN CO WA	342-B2
FRANKLIN CO WA	343-A4
PASCO WA	342-C1
PASCO WA	343-A4
RICHLAND WA	341-J3
RICHLAND WA	342-A3
I-184 184	
BOISE ID	253-C3
I-205 EAST PORTLAND FRWY	
CLACKAMAS CO OR	199-D5
CLACKAMAS CO OR	319-G6
GLADSTONE OR	199-D4
OREGON CITY OR	199-D4
PORTLAND OR	319-G6
TUALATIN OR	199-D4
WASHINGTON CO OR	199-D4
WEST LINN OR	199-D4
I-205 FRWY	
CLARK CO WA	192-C4
CLARK CO WA	307-G1
MAYWOOD PARK OR	315-G1
PORTLAND OR	193-A7
PORTLAND OR	311-J2
PORTLAND OR	315-H1
PORTLAND OR	319-G1
VANCOUVER WA	192-D5
VANCOUVER WA	307-G1
VANCOUVER WA	311-J1
I-405 FRWY	
BELLEVUE WA	175-C2
BOTHELL WA	171-C5
KING CO WA	171-C7
KING CO WA	175-C2
KIRKLAND WA	171-C6
KIRKLAND WA	175-C1
NEWCASTLE WA	175-C3
PORTLAND OR	312-E3
PORTLAND OR	313-F3
PORTLAND OR	317-E1
RENTON WA	175-C4
RENTON WA	289-J4
SNOHOMISH CO WA	171-B5
TUKWILA WA	289-J4
I-705 FRWY	
TACOMA WA	293-H4
TACOMA WA	295-H1
Rt#-D1 E WASHINGTON BLVD	
DEL NORTE CO CA	148-B3
Rt#-D1 WASHINGTON BLVD	
CRESCENT CITY CA	148-B3
Rt#-D2 ELK VALLEY CROSS RD	
DEL NORTE CO CA	148-B3
Rt#-D2 ELK VALLEY RD	
CRESCENT CITY CA	148-B3
DEL NORTE CO CA	148-B3

INDEX

408 Rt#-D3 LAKE EARL DR — STREET INDEX — Rt#-19 JOHN DAY HWY

STREET City State Page-Grid

Rt#-D3 LAKE EARL DR
DEL NORTE CO CA 148-B3
Rt#-D3 NORTHCREST DR
CRESCENT CITY CA 148-B3
DEL NORTE CO CA 148-B3
Rt#-D4 FRED D HAIGHT DR
DEL NORTE CO CA 148-B3
Rt#-D5 OCEAN VIEW DR
DEL NORTE CO CA 148-B3
DEL NORTE CO CA 232-D7
Rt#-1 DOUGLAS ST
CITY OF VICTORIA BC 256-G6
DISTRICT OF SAANICH BC 256-G6
Rt#-1 HASTINGS ST E
VANCOUVER BC 255-F10
Rt#-1 HIGHWAY
BOUNDARY CO ID 107-B1
Rt#-1 ISLAND HWY
BRITISH COLUMBIA BC 101-A1
BRITISH COLUMBIA BC 159-B6
DISTRICT OF LANGFORD BC 159-B6
DISTRICT OF SAANICH BC 256-D4
DUNCAN BC 101-A1
TOWN OF VIEW ROYAL BC 159-B6
TOWN OF VIEW ROYAL BC 256-D4
Rt#-1 SECOND NARROWS BRDG
DIST OF NORTH VANCOUVER BC 255-F9
VANCOUVER BC 255-F9
Rt#-1 TRANS CANADA HWY
BRITISH COLUMBIA BC 93-C1
BRITISH COLUMBIA BC 94-C3
BRITISH COLUMBIA BC 95-A1
BRITISH COLUMBIA BC 101-A1
BRITISH COLUMBIA BC 102-B1
BRITISH COLUMBIA BC 156-A2
BRITISH COLUMBIA BC 159-A1
CITY OF CHILLIWACK BC 94-C3
CITY OF NORTH VANCOUVER BC 255-A3
CITY OF SURREY BC 157-B6
CITY OF VICTORIA BC 256-G11
COQUITLAM BC 157-B6
DISTRICT OF ABBOTSFORD BC 94-C3
DISTRICT OF ABBOTSFORD BC 102-B1
DISTRICT OF BURNABY BC 156-D4
DISTRICT OF BURNABY BC 255-F12
DISTRICT OF COQUITLAM BC 156-D4
DISTRICT OF LANGFORD BC 159-A6
DISTRICT OF MATSQUI BC 102-B1
DIST OF NORTH VANCOUVER BC 254-F2
DIST OF NORTH VANCOUVER BC 255-A3
DISTRICT OF SAANICH BC 256-G5
DIST OF WEST VANCOUVER BC 156-A2
DIST OF WEST VANCOUVER BC 254-F2
DUNCAN BC 101-A1
HOPE BC 95-A3
NANAIMO BC 93-A3
SQUAMISH BC 93-C1
TOWN OF VIEW ROYAL BC 159-A6
TOWN OF VIEW ROYAL BC 256-B3
TOWNSHIP OF LANGLEY BC 102-B1
TOWNSHIP OF LANGLEY BC 157-B6
TOWNSHIP OF LANGLEY BC 158-D1
VANCOUVER BC 255-F12
WHISTLER BC 93-C1
Rt#-1 UPPER LEVELS HWY
CITY OF NORTH VANCOUVER BC 255-D4
DIST OF NORTH VANCOUVER BC 254-H3
DIST OF NORTH VANCOUVER BC 255-D4
DIST OF WEST VANCOUVER BC 156-A2
DIST OF WEST VANCOUVER BC 254-A1
Rt#-1 WICKIEUP RD
BRITISH COLUMBIA BC 101-B1
BRITISH COLUMBIA BC 159-A1
DISTRICT OF LANGFORD BC 159-A5
Rt#-1A CRAIGFLOWER RD
TOWN OF VIEW ROYAL BC 256-A5
Rt#-1A FRASER HWY
CITY OF SURREY BC 157-A6
DISTRICT OF MATSQUI BC 102-B1
LANGLEY BC 157-B7
LANGLEY BC 158-D1
TOWNSHIP OF LANGLEY BC 102-B1
TOWNSHIP OF LANGLEY BC 158-D1
Rt#-1A GOLDSTREAM AV
CITY OF COLWOOD BC 159-B6
DISTRICT OF LANGFORD BC 159-B6
Rt#-1A GORGE RD E
CITY OF VICTORIA BC 256-F6
Rt#-1A GORGE RD W
CITY OF VICTORIA BC 256-C5
DISTRICT OF SAANICH BC 256-C5
Rt#-1A HIGHWAY
CITY OF VICTORIA BC 256-F6
DISTRICT OF SAANICH BC 256-B5
LANGLEY BC 158-C1
Rt#-1A KINGSWAY
VANCOUVER BC 156-C5
VANCOUVER BC 254-J13
VANCOUVER BC 255-A14
Rt#-1A OLD ISLAND HWY
CITY OF COLWOOD BC 159-B6
DISTRICT OF SAANICH BC 256-B5
TOWN OF ESQUIMALT BC 256-B5
TOWN OF VIEW ROYAL BC 159-B6
TOWN OF VIEW ROYAL BC 256-A4
Rt#-1A VEDDER RD
CITY OF CHILLIWACK BC 94-C3
Rt#-1A YALE RD E
BRITISH COLUMBIA BC 94-C3
CITY OF CHILLIWACK BC 94-C3
Rt#-1A YALE RD W
CITY OF CHILLIWACK BC 94-C3
Rt#-3 1ST AV
BOVILL ID 123-B1
Rt#-3 NW 1ST ST
ENTERPRISE OR 130-C2
WALLOWA CO OR 130-C2
Rt#-3 BALL MTN LTLE SHASTA RD
MONTAGUE CA 150-A3
SISKIYOU CO CA 150-A3
Rt#-3 CROWSNEST HWY
BRITISH COLUMBIA BC 103-C1
Rt#-3 ELK RIVER RD
LATAH CO ID 123-B1
Rt#-3 ENTERPRISE-LEWISTON HWY
WALLOWA CO OR 122-C3
WALLOWA CO OR 130-C1
Rt#-3 FRWY
BREMERTON WA 174-B4
BREMERTON WA 270-C6
KITSAP CO WA 170-B6
KITSAP CO WA 174-B1
KITSAP CO WA 270-B1
Navy Yard City WA 270-E11
PORT ORCHARD WA 174-B4
Silverdale WA 174-B1
Silverdale WA 270-B1

Rt#-3 FRWY
Tracyton WA 270-A4
Rt#-3 HIGHWAY
BENEWAH CO ID 115-B3
BENEWAH CO ID 248-B6
BREMERTON WA 174-B4
BRITISH COLUMBIA BC 95-C3
BRITISH COLUMBIA BC 104-B1
BRITISH COLUMBIA BC 105-C1
BRITISH COLUMBIA BC 106-C1
GRAND FORKS BC 105-C1
GREENWOOD BC 105-B1
HOPE BC 95-A3
JULIAETTA ID 123-B2
KENDRICK ID 123-B1
KITSAP CO WA 170-C4
KITSAP CO WA 174-B4
KITSAP CO WA 270-D14
KOOTENAI CO ID 115-B2
KOOTENAI CO ID 248-D2
LATAH CO ID 115-B3
LATAH CO ID 123-B1
MASON CO WA 173-D5
MASON CO WA 174-A5
MASON CO WA 180-D1
MONTAGUE CA 150-A3
Navy Yard City WA 270-E14
NEZ PERCE CO ID 123-A2
PRINCETON BC 95-C3
SAINT MARIES ID 248-D7
SHOSHONE CO ID 115-B3
SISKIYOU CO CA 149-C3
SISKIYOU CO CA 150-A3
YREKA CA 149-C3
Rt#-3 MAIN ST
BRITISH COLUMBIA BC 104-C1
JULIAETTA ID 123-B1
KENDRICK ID 123-B1
OSOYOOS BC 104-C1
Rt#-3 OLD OLYMPIC HWY
MASON CO WA 180-A3
SHELTON WA 180-A3
Rt#-3 PARK AV
BOVILL ID 123-B1
LATAH CO ID 123-B1
Rt#-3 E PINE ST
MASON CO WA 180-A3
SHELTON WA 180-A3
Rt#-3 SECOND AV
DEARY ID 123-B1
LATAH CO ID 123-B1
Rt#-3 WEBB ST
MONTAGUE CA 150-A3
Rt#-3 WYOMING ST
DEARY ID 123-B1
LATAH CO ID 123-B1
Rt#-3B HIGHWAY
BRITISH COLUMBIA BC 106-A1
MONTROSE BC 106-B1
ROSSLAND BC 106-A1
Rt#-4 1ST ST
SHOSHONE CO ID 115-C2
Rt#-4 3RD AV N
KELSO WA 303-D8
Rt#-4 5TH AV N
KELSO WA 303-D8
Rt#-4 ALLEN ST
KELSO WA 303-D8
Rt#-4 BURKE RD
SHOSHONE CO ID 115-C2
WALLACE ID 115-C2
Rt#-4 BURKE-CANYON CREEK RD
SHOSHONE CO ID 115-C2
Rt#-4 COWLITZ WY
KELSO WA 303-D8
Rt#-4 HIGHWAY
BRITISH COLUMBIA BC 92-A3
CATHLAMET WA 117-B3
PACIFIC CO WA 186-C4
PORT ALBERNI BC 92-B3
SHOSHONE CO ID 115-C2
WAHKIAKUM CO WA 117-A2
WAHKIAKUM CO WA 186-D5
WALLACE ID 115-C2
Rt#-4 OCEAN BEACH HWY
CATHLAMET WA 117-B3
COWLITZ CO WA 117-B3
COWLITZ CO WA 189-A2
COWLITZ CO WA 302-B3
LONGVIEW WA 302-F6
LONGVIEW WA 303-A8
WAHKIAKUM CO WA 117-B3
Rt#-5 4TH ST
SAINT MARIES ID 248-D7
Rt#-5 CEDAR ST
BENEWAH CO ID 115-A2
BENEWAH CO ID 248-A7
PLUMMER ID 115-A2
Rt#-5 COLLEGE AV
SAINT MARIES ID 248-D7
Rt#-5 HIGHWAY
BENEWAH CO ID 248-A7
BRITISH COLUMBIA BC 95-C1
CHATCOLET ID 248-B6
HOPE BC 95-A3
SAINT MARIES ID 248-C7
Rt#-5 MAIN AV
SAINT MARIES ID 248-C7
Rt#-5 MAIN ST
SAINT MARIES ID 248-D7
Rt#-5 NORTH FORK SIUSLAW RD
LANE CO OR 214-C1
Rt#-5A HIGHWAY
BRITISH COLUMBIA BC 95-C1
PRINCETON BC 95-C3
Rt#-6 1ST ST
TILLAMOOK OR 197-B2
Rt#-6 3RD ST
TILLAMOOK OR 197-C2
Rt#-6 W FOURTH AV
PE ELL WA 117-B2
Rt#-6 HENKLE ST
PACIFIC CO WA 117-A1
RAYMOND WA 117-A1
Rt#-6 HIGHWAY
BRITISH COLUMBIA BC 106-C1
LATAH CO ID 123-B1
LATAH CO ID 249-D1
LEWIS CO WA 117-B2
PACIFIC CO WA 117-A1
PE ELL WA 117-B2
POTLATCH ID 249-D1
Rt#-6 MAIN ST
PE ELL WA 117-B2
Rt#-6 OCEAN BEACH HWY
CHEHALIS WA 299-A13
LEWIS CO WA 117-B1

Rt#-6 OCEAN BEACH HWY
LEWIS CO WA 184-B7
LEWIS CO WA 187-A1
LEWIS CO WA 299-A13
PE ELL WA 117-B2
Rt#-6 SIXTH ST
POTLATCH ID 249-D1
Rt#-6 WHITE PINE DR
BENEWAH CO ID 115-B3
LATAH CO ID 115-B3
Rt#-6 WILSON RIVER HWY
BANKS OR 125-B1
TILLAMOOK OR 197-C2
TILLAMOOK CO OR 125-B1
TILLAMOOK CO OR 197-C2
WASHINGTON CO OR 125-B1
Rt#-7 1ST AV
DISTRICT OF MISSION BC 94-B3
Rt#-7 2ND AV
MORTON WA 118-B2
Rt#-7 E 38TH ST
TACOMA WA 295-H2
Rt#-7 AHSAHKA RD
OROFINO ID 123-C2
Rt#-7 BROADWAY E
VANCOUVER BC 254-H13
VANCOUVER BC 255-A13
Rt#-7 BROADWAY W
VANCOUVER BC 254-E12
Rt#-7 CAMPBELL ST
BAKER CITY OR 138-B1
Rt#-7 DEWEY AV
BAKER CITY OR 138-B1
Rt#-7 FRWY
TACOMA WA 295-H1
Rt#-7 GILBERT GRADE
CLEARWATER CO ID 123-C2
Rt#-7 HIGHWAY
BRITISH COLUMBIA BC 95-A3
CLEARWATER CO ID 123-C2
LEWIS CO WA 118-B1
OROFINO ID 123-C2
PIERCE CO WA 118-B1
Rt#-7 LOUGHEED HWY
BRITISH COLUMBIA BC 94-B3
COQUITLAM BC 157-A5
DISTRICT OF BURNABY BC 156-D4
DISTRICT OF BURNABY BC 255-G12
DISTRICT OF COQUITLAM BC 156-D4
DISTRICT OF KENT BC 94-B3
DISTRICT OF MISSION BC 94-B3
MAPLE RIDGE BC 94-B3
MAPLE RIDGE BC 157-D6
PITT MEADOWS BC 157-B4
PORT COQUITLAM BC 157-B4
Rt#-7 MAIN ST
BAKER CITY OR 138-B1
Rt#-7 MORTON RD
LEWIS CO WA 118-B2
MORTON WA 118-B2
Rt#-7 MOUNTAIN HWY E
PIERCE CO WA 118-B1
PIERCE CO WA 181-D6
PIERCE CO WA 182-A7
Rt#-7 NORTH RAILWAY AV
DISTRICT OF MISSION BC 94-B3
Rt#-7 PACIFIC AV
PIERCE CO WA 181-D4
TACOMA WA 181-D4
TACOMA WA 295-H3
Rt#-7 PACIFIC AV S
PIERCE CO WA 181-D5
Rt#-7 RIVERSIDE AV
OROFINO ID 123-C2
Rt#-7 RUSSELL RIDGE RD
CLEARWATER CO ID 123-C2
Rt#-7 WHITNEY HWY
BAKER CITY OR 138-B1
BAKER CO OR 137-C1
BAKER CO OR 138-A1
GRANT CO OR 137-C1
Rt#-7A BARNET HWY
COQUITLAM BC 157-A4
DISTRICT OF BURNABY BC 156-D4
PORT MOODY BC 157-A4
Rt#-7A HASTINGS ST
DISTRICT OF BURNABY BC 156-D4
DISTRICT OF BURNABY BC 255-G10
VANCOUVER BC 255-F10
Rt#-7A HASTINGS ST E
VANCOUVER BC 254-J10
VANCOUVER BC 255-B10
Rt#-7A HIGHWAY
DISTRICT OF BURNABY BC 156-D4
Rt#-7A INLET DR
DISTRICT OF BURNABY BC 156-D4
Rt#-7A SAINT JOHNS ST
CITY OF PORT MOODY BC 156-D4
DISTRICT OF BURNABY BC 156-D4
PORT MOODY BC 157-A4
Rt#-8 E 3RD ST
MOSCOW ID 249-C5
Rt#-8 W 3RD ST
MOSCOW ID 249-C5
Rt#-8 SE 10TH AV
HILLSBORO OR 198-D1
Rt#-8 19TH AV
FOREST GROVE OR 198-B1
Rt#-8 19TH WY
FOREST GROVE OR 198-C1
Rt#-8 N ADAIR ST
CORNELIUS OR 198-C1
FOREST GROVE OR 198-C1
Rt#-8 BASELINE ST
CORNELIUS OR 198-C1
Rt#-8 SE BASELINE ST
HILLSBORO OR 198-D1
Rt#-8 SW BASELINE ST
HILLSBORO OR 198-D1
Rt#-8 SW BROADWAY
BEAVERTON OR 199-B2
Rt#-8 SW CANYON RD
BEAVERTON OR 199-B2
WASHINGTON CO OR 199-B2
Rt#-8 E ST
FOREST GROVE OR 198-B1
Rt#-8 FIRST ST
ELK RIVER ID 123-C1
Rt#-8 GALES CREEK RD
FOREST GROVE OR 198-B1
WASHINGTON CO OR 125-B1
WASHINGTON CO OR 198-B1
Rt#-8 HIGHWAY
BOVILL ID 123-B1
BRITISH COLUMBIA BC 95-C1
CLEARWATER CO ID 123-B1
ELK RIVER ID 123-C1
ELMA WA 179-B7
GRAYS HARBOR CO WA 179-C6

Rt#-8 HIGHWAY
LATAH CO ID 123-B1
LATAH CO ID 249-D5
MCCLEARY WA 179-C6
MOSCOW ID 249-C5
THURSTON CO WA 179-D6
THURSTON CO WA 180-B6
TROY ID 123-A1
WASHINGTON CO OR 199-B1
Rt#-8 MAIN ST
TROY ID 123-A1
Rt#-8 SE OAK ST
HILLSBORO OR 198-D1
Rt#-8 SW OAK ST
HILLSBORO OR 198-D1
Rt#-8 SW OLD HIGHWAY 47
FOREST GROVE OR 198-B1
Rt#-8 PACIFIC AV
CORNELIUS OR 198-C1
FOREST GROVE OR 198-C1
Rt#-8 SECOND AV
DEARY ID 123-B1
LATAH CO ID 123-B1
Rt#-8 TAFT ST
ELK RIVER ID 123-C1
Rt#-8 TUALATIN VALLEY HWY
CORNELIUS OR 198-C1
HILLSBORO OR 198-D1
WASHINGTON CO OR 198-C1
Rt#-8 SE TUALATIN VALLEY HWY
HILLSBORO OR 198-D1
HILLSBORO OR 199-A2
WASHINGTON CO OR 199-A2
Rt#-8 SW TUALATIN VALLEY HWY
BEAVERTON OR 199-A2
HILLSBORO OR 199-A2
WASHINGTON CO OR 199-A2
Rt#-9 N BORSETH ST
SEDRO-WOOLLEY WA 161-C5
Rt#-9 CASCADE HWY
SEDRO-WOOLLEY WA 161-C6
Rt#-9 CHEAM AV
DISTRICT OF KENT BC 94-C3
Rt#-9 EVERGREEN DR
DISTRICT OF KENT BC 94-C3
Rt#-9 HAIG HWY
DISTRICT OF KENT BC 94-C3
Rt#-9 HIGHWAY
ARLINGTON WA 168-D5
BRITISH COLUMBIA BC 94-C3
DISTRICT OF KENT BC 94-C3
LATAH CO ID 123-A1
MARYSVILLE WA 168-D7
MARYSVILLE WA 171-D1
SEDRO-WOOLLEY WA 161-C6
SKAGIT CO WA 161-C3
SKAGIT CO WA 168-C1
SKAGIT CO WA 260-J11
SNOHOMISH WA 171-D3
SNOHOMISH CO WA 168-C3
SNOHOMISH CO WA 171-D1
Rt#-9 HOPEWELL RD
WHATCOM CO WA 102-B1
Rt#-9 HOT SPRINGS RD
CITY OF HARRISON HOT SPRG BC 94-C3
DISTRICT OF KENT BC 94-C3
Rt#-9 LAWRENCE RD
WHATCOM CO WA 102-B1
Rt#-9 MAIN ST
SKAGIT CO WA 168-C2
Rt#-9 MOORE ST
SEDRO-WOOLLEY WA 161-C5
Rt#-9 NOOKSACK AV
NOOKSACK WA 102-B1
Rt#-9 NOOKSACK RD
NOOKSACK WA 102-B1
WHATCOM CO WA 102-B1
Rt#-9 TOWNSHIP RD
SEDRO-WOOLLEY WA 161-C5
SKAGIT CO WA 161-C5
Rt#-9 VALLEY HWY
WHATCOM CO WA 102-B1
WHATCOM CO WA 161-C2
Rt#-9 WOODINVLLE SNOHOMISH RD
SNOHOMISH CO WA 171-D6
Rt#-10 56TH AV
CITY OF SURREY BC 157-A7
CITY OF SURREY BC 158-B1
Rt#-10 58TH AV
CITY OF SURREY BC 156-D7
CITY OF SURREY BC 157-A7
DISTRICT OF DELTA BC 156-D7
Rt#-10 232ND ST
TOWNSHIP OF LANGLEY BC 157-D7
Rt#-10 SW BEAVRTN-HLLSDLE HWY
BEAVERTON OR 199-B2
PORTLAND OR 199-B2
PORTLAND OR 199-B2
PORTLAND OR 316-A3
WASHINGTON CO OR 199-B2
Rt#-10 SW CAPITOL HWY
PORTLAND OR 316-D4
PORTLAND OR 317-E4
Rt#-10 SW FARMINGTON RD
BEAVERTON OR 199-A2
WASHINGTON CO OR 198-D3
WASHINGTON CO OR 199-A2
Rt#-10 GLOVER RD
LANGLEY BC 157-C7
TOWNSHIP OF LANGLEY BC 157-C7
Rt#-10 HIGHWAY
KITTITAS CO WA 240-C2
KITTITAS CO WA 241-A3
TOWNSHIP OF LANGLEY BC 157-D7
Rt#-10 LADNER TRUNK RD
DISTRICT OF DELTA BC 101-C1
DISTRICT OF DELTA BC 156-D7
Rt#-10 LANGLEY BYPS
CITY OF SURREY BC 157-C7
CITY OF SURREY BC 158-B1
LANGLEY BC 157-C7
Rt#-10 RAWLISON CRES
TOWNSHIP OF LANGLEY BC 157-C7
Rt#-11 11TH AV
DISTRICT OF MISSION BC 94-B3
Rt#-11 12TH ST
BELLINGHAM WA 258-B11
Rt#-11 ABBOTSFORD-MISSION HWY
DISTRICT OF ABBOTSFORD BC 102-B1
DISTRICT OF MATSQUI BC 94-B3
DISTRICT OF MATSQUI BC 102-B1
Rt#-11 CHUCKANUT DR
BELLINGHAM WA 258-B12
SKAGIT CO WA 160-D2

Rt#-11 CHUCKANUT DR
SKAGIT CO WA 161-A3
SKAGIT CO WA 260-B1
WHATCOM CO WA 160-D2
WHATCOM CO WA 258-B14
Rt#-11 HIGHWAY
BURLINGTON WA 260-C3
CLEARWATER CO ID 123-C2
SKAGIT CO WA 161-A5
SKAGIT CO WA 260-A1
Rt#-11 S MAIN ST
MILTON-FREEWATER OR 121-C3
Rt#-11 OLD FAIRHAVEN PKWY
BELLINGHAM WA 258-B11
Rt#-11 OREGON-WASHINGTON HWY
ADAMS OR 129-B1
ATHENA OR 129-B1
MILTON-FREEWATER OR 121-C3
PENDLETON OR 129-B1
UMATILLA CO OR 121-C3
UMATILLA CO OR 129-B1
WALLA WALLA CO WA 121-C3
Rt#-11 VALLEY PKWY
BELLINGHAM WA 258-C11
Rt#-12 HIGHWAY
CLEARWATER CO ID 123-C2
Rt#-13 264TH ST
TOWNSHIP OF LANGLEY BC 158-D2
Rt#-13 HARPSTER GRADE RD
IDAHO CO ID 123-C3
Rt#-13 HIGHWAY
TOWNSHIP OF LANGLEY BC 158-D2
Rt#-13 E MAIN ST
GRANGEVILLE ID 123-C3
IDAHO CO ID 123-C3
Rt#-13 W MAIN ST
GRANGEVILLE ID 123-C3
IDAHO CO ID 123-C3
Rt#-14 D ST
WASHOUGAL WA 193-C7
Rt#-14 EVERGREEN HWY
CARSON WA 194-C6
CARSON WA 195-B5
CLARK CO WA 193-D7
CLARK CO WA 200-C1
NORTH BONNEVILLE WA 194-C6
SKAMANIA CO WA 193-D7
SKAMANIA CO WA 194-A7
SKAMANIA CO WA 195-B5
SKAMANIA CO WA 200-D1
STEVENSON WA 194-C6
Rt#-14 HIGHWAY
BENTON CO WA 120-C3
BENTON CO WA 121-A3
BENTON CO WA 128-C1
BRITISH COLUMBIA BC 100-C2
IDAHO CO ID 123-C3
KLICKITAT CO WA 128-B1
Rt#-14 LEWIS AND CLARK FRWY
VANCOUVER WA 193-A7
VANCOUVER WA 305-G6
VANCOUVER WA 306-A6
VANCOUVER WA 307-E7
VANCOUVER WA 311-G1
Rt#-14 LEWIS AND CLARK HWY
BINGEN WA 195-C5
CAMAS WA 193-B7
CLARK CO WA 193-A7
KLICKITAT CO WA 127-B1
KLICKITAT CO WA 195-C5
KLICKITAT CO WA 196-C6
SKAMANIA CO WA 195-C5
VANCOUVER WA 193-A7
WASHOUGAL WA 193-C7
WHITE SALMON WA 195-C5
Rt#-14 SOOKE RD
BRITISH COLUMBIA BC 101-A2
BRITISH COLUMBIA BC 159-A7
DISTRICT OF LANGFORD BC 159-A7
DISTRICT OF METCHOSIN BC 159-A7
Rt#-14 STEUBEN ST
BINGEN WA 195-D5
Rt#-14 WEST COAST RD
BRITISH COLUMBIA BC 101-A2
BRITISH COLUMBIA BC 164-C1
Rt#-14B NE 3RD AV
CAMAS WA 193-B7
CLARK CO WA 193-B7
WASHOUGAL WA 193-B7
Rt#-14B NW 6TH AV
CAMAS WA 193-B7
Rt#-14B NE ADAMS ST
CAMAS WA 193-B7
Rt#-14B D ST
WASHOUGAL WA 193-C7
Rt#-14B E ST
WASHOUGAL WA 193-C7
Rt#-14B EVERGREEN WY
WASHOUGAL WA 193-C7
Rt#-14B SE EVERGREEN BLVD
CLARK CO WA 193-C7
WASHOUGAL WA 193-C7
Rt#-15 176TH ST
CITY OF SURREY BC 157-B7
CITY OF SURREY BC 158-B2
WHATCOM CO WA 158-B2
Rt#-15 CLOVERDALE BYPS
CITY OF SURREY BC 157-B7
Rt#-15 PACIFIC HWY
CITY OF SURREY BC 158-B1
Rt#-16 EMMETT HWY
ADA CO ID 139-C3
GEM CO ID 139-C3
Rt#-16 N EMMETT HWY
ADA CO ID 139-C3
ADA CO ID 147-C1
Rt#-16 FRWY
GIG HARBOR WA 174-B7
GIG HARBOR WA 181-C1
KITSAP CO WA 174-B4
PIERCE CO WA 174-B6
PIERCE CO WA 181-C1
PORT ORCHARD WA 174-B4
TACOMA WA 181-C2
TACOMA WA 292-A5
TACOMA WA 294-E1
TACOMA WA 295-E1
Rt#-16 HIGHWAY
BREMERTON WA 174-B4
GEM CO ID 139-C3
KITSAP CO WA 174-B4
Rt#-17 60 ST
DISTRICT OF DELTA BC 101-C1
Rt#-17 60TH ST
DISTRICT OF DELTA BC 156-C7

Rt#-17 BLANSHARD ST
CITY OF VICTORIA BC 256-G6
DISTRICT OF SAANICH BC 256-G5
Rt#-17 DAISY ST N
GRANT CO WA 112-C2
SOAP LAKE WA 112-C2
Rt#-17 DAISY ST S
SOAP LAKE WA 112-C2
Rt#-17 HIGHWAY
ADAMS CO WA 121-A1
BRIDGEPORT WA 112-C1
DOUGLAS CO WA 112-C1
DOUGLAS CO WA 113-A2
FRANKLIN CO WA 121-A1
GRANT CO WA 112-C2
GRANT CO WA 113-A2
GRANT CO WA 121-A1
GRANT CO WA 242-B1
MESA WA 121-A2
MOSES LAKE WA 242-C2
OKANOGAN CO WA 104-C3
OKANOGAN CO WA 112-C1
SOAP LAKE WA 112-C2
Rt#-17 LEAHY RD S
DOUGLAS CO WA 112-C1
Rt#-17 PATRICIA BAY HWY
DIST OF CENTRAL SAANICH BC 159-C2
DIST OF NORTH SAANICH BC 159-C2
DISTRICT OF SAANICH BC 159-C2
DISTRICT OF SAANICH BC 256-F2
TOWN OF SIDNEY BC 159-C2
Rt#-17 R RD NE
DOUGLAS CO WA 112-C1
Rt#-17 TSAWWASSEN FERRY CSWY
DISTRICT OF DELTA BC 101-C1
Rt#-17A HIGHWAY
DISTRICT OF SAANICH BC 159-C5
Rt#-17A MCTAVISH RD
DIST OF NORTH SAANICH BC 159-C3
Rt#-17A WEST SAANICH RD
DIST OF CENTRAL SAANICH BC 159-B3
DIST OF NORTH SAANICH BC 159-B3
DISTRICT OF SAANICH BC 159-C5
Rt#-18 AUBURN-ECHO LAKE CTO
AUBURN WA 182-C1
COVINGTON WA 175-D7
KENT WA 175-D7
KING CO WA 175-D7
KING CO WA 176-A6
KING CO WA 182-C1
MAPLE VALLEY WA 175-D7
Rt#-18 AUBURN-ECHO LAKE CTO S
KING CO WA 176-A6
Rt#-18 SE DAYTON BYPASS RD
DAYTON OR 198-B7
YAMHILL CO OR 198-B7
Rt#-18 ECHO LAKE CTO SE
KING CO WA 176-B5
Rt#-18 FRWY
AUBURN WA 182-B1
FEDERAL WAY WA 182-B1
KING CO WA 182-B1
Rt#-18 HIGHWAY
BRITISH COLUMBIA BC 100-C1
BRITISH COLUMBIA BC 101-A1
Lake Cowichan BC 100-C1
Rt#-18 HIGHWAY 99 S
YAMHILL CO OR 204-B1
Rt#-18 E MAIN ST
SHERIDAN OR 125-B3
WILLAMINA OR 125-A3
Rt#-18 S MAIN ST
WILLAMINA OR 125-A3
Rt#-18 W MAIN ST
SHERIDAN OR 125-B3
Rt#-18 SALMON RIVER HWY
LINCOLN CO OR 203-B4
MCMINNVILLE OR 198-A7
MCMINNVILLE OR 204-A2
POLK CO OR 125-A3
Rose Lodge OR 203-D3
SHERIDAN OR 125-B3
TILLAMOOK CO OR 125-A3
TILLAMOOK CO OR 203-D3
YAMHILL CO OR 125-B3
YAMHILL CO OR 198-A7
YAMHILL CO OR 204-A2
Rt#-18 NE SALMON RIVER HWY
YAMHILL CO OR 198-B7
Rt#-18 SE SALMON RIVER HWY
MCMINNVILLE OR 198-A7
YAMHILL CO OR 198-B7
Rt#-18 THREE MILE LN HWY
MCMINNVILLE OR 198-B7
YAMHILL CO OR 198-B7
Rt#-18 W VALLEY HWY
SHERIDAN OR 125-B3
WILLAMINA OR 125-B3
YAMHILL CO OR 125-B3
Rt#-18 WILLAMINA-SHERIDAN HWY
POLK CO OR 125-A3
WILLAMINA OR 125-A3
Rt#-19 E 7TH ST
FOSSIL OR 128-A3
Rt#-19 AIRPORT CUTOFF RD
Irondale WA 263-B11
JEFFERSON CO WA 263-B11
Rt#-19 BEAVER VALLEY RD
JEFFERSON CO WA 170-A1
Rt#-19 COTTONWOOD ST
ARLINGTON OR 128-A1
Rt#-19 DUKE POINT HWY
BRITISH COLUMBIA BC 93-A3
NANAIMO BC 93-A3
Rt#-19 HIGHWAY
BRITISH COLUMBIA BC 92-A1
CAMPBELL RIVER BC 92-A1
COURTENAY BC 92-A2
Rt#-19 W IDAHO AV
HOMEDALE ID 147-A1
Rt#-19 INLAND ISLAND HWY
BRITISH COLUMBIA BC 92-A1
Rt#-19 ISLAND HWY N
BRITISH COLUMBIA BC 93-A3
NANAIMO BC 93-A3
Rt#-19 JOHN DAY HWY
ARLINGTON OR 128-A2
CONDON OR 128-A2
FOSSIL OR 128-A3
GILLIAM CO OR 128-A2
GRANT CO OR 136-B1
SPRAY OR 136-B1

INDEX

STREET / City State / Page-Grid

Rt#-19 JOHN DAY HWY
WHEELER CO OR ... 128-A3
WHEELER CO OR ... 136-B1
Rt#-19 LOCUST ST
ARLINGTON OR ... 128-A1
Rt#-19 N LOCUST ST
ARLINGTON OR ... 128-A1
GILLIAM CO OR ... 128-A1
Rt#-19 S LOCUST ST
ARLINGTON OR ... 128-A1
Rt#-19 MAIN ST
CANYON CO ID ... 147-B1
GREENLEAF ID ... 147-B1
Rt#-19 S MAIN ST
CONDON OR ... 128-A2
Rt#-19 NANAIMO PKWY
NANAIMO BC ... 93-A3
Rt#-19 OWYHEE BLVD
OWYHEE CO ID ... 147-A1
Rt#-19 RHODY DR
Hadlock-Irondale WA ... 170-A1
Irondale WA ... 263-E14
JEFFERSON CO WA ... 170-A1
JEFFERSON CO WA ... 263-E14
Rt#-19 SIMPLOT BLVD
CALDWELL ID ... 147-B1
CANYON CO ID ... 147-B1
WILDER ID ... 147-B1
Rt#-19 E WALNUT ST
CONDON OR ... 128-A2
Rt#-19 N WASHINGTON ST
CONDON OR ... 128-A2
Rt#-19 S WASHINGTON ST
CONDON OR ... 128-A2
Rt#-19A HIGHWAY
BRITISH COLUMBIA BC ... 92-A1
COURTENAY BC ... 92-A2
PARKSVILLE BC ... 92-C3
Rt#-19A ISLAND HWY N
BRITISH COLUMBIA BC ... 93-A3
NANAIMO BC ... 93-A3
Rt#-20 E 3RD AV
COLVILLE WA ... 106-A2
STEVENS CO WA ... 106-A2
Rt#-20 W 6TH ST
REPUBLIC WA ... 105-B2
Rt#-20 12TH ST
ANACORTES WA ... 259-F2
Rt#-20 AVON AV
BURLINGTON WA ... 260-C4
Rt#-20 AVON CTO
SKAGIT CO WA ... 161-A6
SKAGIT CO WA ... 260-A6
Rt#-20 AVON CUT-OFF
SKAGIT CO WA ... 161-A7
Rt#-20 BURLINGTON BLVD
BURLINGTON WA ... 260-C4
Rt#-20 S BURLINGTON BLVD
BURLINGTON WA ... 260-C6
Rt#-20 CASCADE HWY
BURLINGTON WA ... 260-E4
SEDRO-WOOLLEY WA ... 161-C6
SEDRO-WOOLLEY WA ... 260-E4
SKAGIT CO WA ... 260-E4
Rt#-20 S CLARK AV
REPUBLIC WA ... 105-B2
Rt#-20 COLVILLE-TIGER RD
STEVENS CO WA ... 106-A2
Rt#-20 COMMERCIAL AV
ANACORTES WA ... 259-H4
Rt#-20 N CROSS STATE HWY
SEDRO-WOOLLEY WA ... 161-C5
SKAGIT CO WA ... 161-C5
Rt#-20 DIVISION ST
TWISP WA ... 104-A3
Rt#-20 ELMWAY
OKANOGAN WA ... 104-C3
OKANOGAN CO WA ... 104-C3
OMAK WA ... 104-C3
Rt#-20 FOURTH AV W
OMAK WA ... 104-C3
Rt#-20 HIGHWAY
ANACORTES WA ... 160-C6
ANACORTES WA ... 259-H5
Ault Field WA ... 167-C2
BURLINGTON WA ... 260-C5
CONCRETE WA ... 102-C2
COUPEVILLE WA ... 167-B4
CUSICK WA ... 106-C3
FERRY CO WA ... 105-B2
FERRY CO WA ... 106-A2
HAMILTON WA ... 102-C2
ISLAND CO WA ... 160-C7
ISLAND CO WA ... 167-C1
JEFFERSON CO WA ... 109-C1
JEFFERSON CO WA ... 170-A1
JEFFERSON CO WA ... 263-C6
LYMAN WA ... 102-C2
NEWPORT WA ... 106-C3
OAK HARBOR WA ... 167-C2
OKANOGAN WA ... 104-C3
OKANOGAN CO WA ... 104-C2
OKANOGAN CO WA ... 105-A2
PEND OREILLE CO WA ... 106-B2
PORT TOWNSEND WA ... 263-C6
REPUBLIC WA ... 105-B2
SKAGIT CO WA ... 102-C2
SKAGIT CO WA ... 160-C6
SKAGIT CO WA ... 161-D5
SKAGIT CO WA ... 259-J6
SKAGIT CO WA ... 260-B6
WINTHROP WA ... 104-A2
Rt#-20 MAIN ST S
OMAK WA ... 104-C3
Rt#-20 MEMORIAL HWY
SKAGIT CO WA ... 160-D6
SKAGIT CO WA ... 161-A7
Rt#-20 E METHOW VALLEY HWY
OKANOGAN CO WA ... 104-B3
TWISP WA ... 104-A3
Rt#-20 NORTH CASCADES HWY
CHELAN CO WA ... 103-C3
OKANOGAN CO WA ... 103-C3
OKANOGAN CO WA ... 104-A2
WHATCOM CO WA ... 103-C3
Rt#-20 OAKES AV
ANACORTES WA ... 259-B3
Rt#-20 OKOMA DR
OKANOGAN CO WA ... 104-C3
OMAK WA ... 104-C3
Rt#-20 PIONEER WY
OAK HARBOR WA ... 167-B3
Rt#-20 RIO VISTA AV
BURLINGTON WA ... 260-C5
Rt#-20 RIVERSIDE AV
OKANOGAN CO WA ... 104-A2
WINTHROP WA ... 104-A2

Rt#-20 RIVERSIDE DR
OKANOGAN CO WA ... 104-C2
OMAK WA ... 104-C2
Rt#-20 SECOND AV N
OKANOGAN WA ... 104-C3
Rt#-20 SECOND AV NW
OKANOGAN WA ... 104-C3
Rt#-20 SECOND AV SW
OKANOGAN WA ... 104-C3
Rt#-20 SIMS WY
PORT TOWNSEND WA ... 263-C6
Rt#-20 SIXTH ST
OKANOGAN CO WA ... 104-C2
TONASKET WA ... 104-C2
Rt#-20 WATER ST
PORT TOWNSEND WA ... 263-H5
Rt#-21 N 1ST ST
ODESSA WA ... 113-B3
Rt#-21 W 1ST AV
ODESSA WA ... 113-B3
Rt#-21 E 6TH AV
ODESSA WA ... 113-B3
Rt#-21 S ALDER ST
ODESSA WA ... 113-B3
Rt#-21 N DIVISION ST
ODESSA WA ... 113-B3
Rt#-21 W FIRST ST
LIND WA ... 121-B1
Rt#-21 W FRONT AV
LINCOLN CO WA ... 113-B1
WILBUR WA ... 113-B1
Rt#-21 E GOWEN RD
ADA CO ID ... 253-D4
BOISE ID ... 253-D4
Rt#-21 HIGHWAY
ADAMS CO WA ... 113-B3
ADAMS CO WA ... 121-B1
BOUNDARY CO ID ... 107-B1
BRITISH COLUMBIA BC ... 105-C1
BRITISH COLUMBIA BC ... 107-B1
FERRY CO WA ... 105-C1
FERRY CO WA ... 113-B1
GRAND FORKS BC ... 105-C1
LINCOLN CO WA ... 113-B1
LIND WA ... 121-B1
ODESSA WA ... 113-B3
REPUBLIC WA ... 105-B2
Rt#-21 LIND-KAHLOTUS RD
FRANKLIN CO WA ... 121-C1
KAHLOTUS WA ... 121-C1
Rt#-21 W MAY AV
ODESSA WA ... 113-B3
Rt#-21 MONSOR RD
LINCOLN CO WA ... 113-B2
Rt#-21 ROSENOFF RD
ADAMS CO WA ... 113-B3
Rt#-21 E SECOND ST
LIND WA ... 121-B1
Rt#-21 VIOLET AV
KAHLOTUS WA ... 121-C1
Rt#-21 S WEST ST
WILBUR WA ... 113-B1
Rt#-22 12TH ST SE
SALEM OR ... 322-J14
Rt#-22 BUENA RD
YAKIMA CO WA ... 120-A2
Rt#-22 BUENA WY
TOPPENISH WA ... 120-A2
Rt#-22 CENTER ST BRDG
SALEM OR ... 322-H12
Rt#-22 CENTER ST BRDG NE
SALEM OR ... 322-H12
Rt#-22 CENTER ST NE
SALEM OR ... 322-H12
Rt#-22 S ELM ST
TOPPENISH WA ... 120-A2
Rt#-22 EVERGREEN HWY
TOPPENISH WA ... 120-A2
YAKIMA CO WA ... 120-A2
Rt#-22 FERRY ST SE
SALEM OR ... 322-H13
Rt#-22 FRONT ST NE
SALEM OR ... 322-H12
Rt#-22 FRONT ST SE
SALEM OR ... 322-H13
Rt#-22 HIGHWAY
BENTON CO OR ... 120-B3
BRITISH COLUMBIA BC ... 106-A1
MABTON WA ... 120-B3
PROSSER WA ... 120-C3
TOPPENISH WA ... 120-A2
Rt#-22 MARION ST
SALEM OR ... 322-H12
Rt#-22 MARION ST BRDG
SALEM OR ... 322-H12
Rt#-22 MISSION ST SE
SALEM OR ... 322-J14
SALEM OR ... 323-A14
SALEM OR ... 325-B1
Rt#-22 PRINGLE PKWY SE
SALEM OR ... 322-J13
Rt#-22 SALEM HWY
POLK CO OR ... 322-H12
Rt#-22 N SANTIAM HWY
AUMSVILLE OR ... 205-A7
DETROIT OR ... 134-A1
GATES OR ... 134-A1
IDANHA OR ... 134-A1
LINN CO OR ... 134-C1
MARION CO OR ... 133-C1
MARION CO OR ... 134-A1
MARION CO OR ... 205-A7
MILL CITY OR ... 134-A1
SALEM OR ... 204-D6
SALEM OR ... 325-G3
STAYTON OR ... 133-C1
SUBLIMITY OR ... 133-C1
Rt#-22 THREE RIVERS HWY
POLK CO OR ... 125-A3
TILLAMOOK CO OR ... 197-B6
TILLAMOOK CO OR ... 203-D1
YAMHILL CO OR ... 125-A3
YAMHILL CO OR ... 203-D1
Rt#-22 TRADE ST SE
SALEM OR ... 322-H13
Rt#-22 WAPENISH RD
YAKIMA CO WA ... 120-A2
Rt#-22 WILLAMINA-SALEM HWY NW
POLK CO OR ... 204-B6

Rt#-22 WILLAMINA-SALEM HWY NW
POLK CO OR ... 322-B14
SALEM OR ... 322-B14
Rt#-22A BOUNDARY HWY
NORTHPORT WA ... 106-B1
STEVENS CO WA ... 106-B1
Rt#-22A HIGHWAY
BRITISH COLUMBIA BC ... 106-B1
STEVENS CO WA ... 106-A1
Rt#-23 S 3RD ST
HARRINGTON WA ... 113-C2
Rt#-23 ENDICOTT-ST JOHN RD
SAINT JOHN WA ... 114-B3
WHITMAN CO WA ... 114-B3
Rt#-23 FRONT ST
SAINT JOHN WA ... 114-B3
Rt#-23 HIGHWAY
HARRINGTON WA ... 113-C2
LINCOLN CO WA ... 114-A2
SAINT JOHN WA ... 114-B3
SPRAGUE WA ... 114-A3
WHITMAN CO WA ... 114-A3
Rt#-23 E MAIN ST
HARRINGTON WA ... 113-C2
Rt#-23 E SHERLOCK ST
HARRINGTON WA ... 113-C2
Rt#-24 S BROADWAY AV
ADAMS CO WA ... 121-A1
OTHELLO WA ... 121-A1
Rt#-24 HANFORD RD
YAKIMA CO WA ... 120-A2
Rt#-24 HIGHWAY
ADAMS CO WA ... 120-C1
ADAMS CO WA ... 121-A1
BENTON CO WA ... 120-C1
GRANT CO WA ... 120-C1
MOXEE WA ... 243-D7
YAKIMA CO WA ... 120-A2
YAKIMA CO WA ... 243-C7
Rt#-25 CENTER AV
NORTHPORT WA ... 106-A1
STEVENS CO WA ... 106-A1
Rt#-25 HIGHWAY
DAVENPORT WA ... 114-A2
LINCOLN CO WA ... 113-C1
LINCOLN CO WA ... 114-A1
MARCUS WA ... 106-A2
NORTHPORT WA ... 106-A1
STEVENS CO WA ... 105-C2
STEVENS CO WA ... 106-A1
STEVENS CO WA ... 113-C1
Rt#-25 LITTLE SHEEP CREEK RD
STEVENS CO WA ... 106-A1
Rt#-26 FRWY
GRANT CO WA ... 120-B1
Rt#-26 HIGHWAY
ADAMS CO WA ... 120-C1
ADAMS CO WA ... 121-A1
ADAMS CO WA ... 122-A1
COLFAX WA ... 122-C1
GRANT CO WA ... 120-B1
OTHELLO WA ... 121-A1
ROYAL CITY WA ... 120-C1
WASHTUCNA WA ... 121-C1
WHITMAN CO WA ... 122-C1
Rt#-26 NORTH ST
WASHTUCNA WA ... 121-C1
Rt#-26 ROAD 13-SW
GRANT CO WA ... 120-B1
Rt#-26 T W WALTERS RD
COLFAX WA ... 122-C1
Rt#-26 WASHINGTON ST
ADAMS CO WA ... 121-A1
OTHELLO WA ... 121-A1
Rt#-27 1ST ST
OAKESDALE WA ... 114-C3
Rt#-27 4TH ST
GARFIELD WA ... 114-C3
Rt#-27 ALMOTA ST
PALOUSE WA ... 249-C1
Rt#-27 BLAKE RD
SPOKANE WA ... 351-A13
SPOKANE VALLEY WA ... 350-H10
SPOKANE VALLEY WA ... 351-A12
Rt#-27 N BRIDGE ST
PALOUSE WA ... 249-B1
Rt#-27 S BRIDGE ST
PALOUSE WA ... 249-B1
Rt#-27 COUNTY RD
WHITMAN CO WA ... 114-C3
Rt#-27 CROOKED RIVER HWY
CROOK CO OR ... 135-C3
CROOK CO OR ... 213-C6
DESCHUTES CO OR ... 135-C3
PRINEVILLE OR ... 213-C6
Rt#-27 CROSBY ST
TEKOA WA ... 114-C3
Rt#-27 S DISHMAN-MICA RD
SPOKANE CO WA ... 247-A5
Rt#-27 N DIVISION ST
PALOUSE WA ... 249-B1
Rt#-27 ELIZABETH ST
TEKOA WA ... 114-C3
Rt#-27 FIRST ST
FAIRFIELD WA ... 114-C3
Rt#-27 N GRAND AV
PULLMAN WA ... 249-B5
Rt#-27 S GRAND AV
PULLMAN WA ... 249-B5
Rt#-27 HIGHWAY
FAIRFIELD WA ... 114-C3
GARFIELD WA ... 114-C3
LATAH WA ... 114-C3
OAKESDALE WA ... 114-C3
PALOUSE WA ... 249-B1
PULLMAN WA ... 249-B4
SPOKANE CO WA ... 114-C2
SPOKANE CO WA ... 247-A5
SPOKANE CO WA ... 351-A14
TEKOA WA ... 114-C3
WHITMAN CO WA ... 114-C3
WHITMAN CO WA ... 249-B1
Rt#-27 E MAIN ST
GARFIELD WA ... 114-C3
Rt#-27 W MAIN ST
GARFIELD WA ... 114-C3
Rt#-27 MARKET ST
LATAH WA ... 114-C3
Rt#-27 MOSCOW RD
PALOUSE WA ... 249-B1
Rt#-27 W PARK ST
TEKOA WA ... 114-C3
Rt#-27 N PINES RD
SPOKANE VALLEY WA ... 350-H5

Rt#-27 S PINES RD
SPOKANE VALLEY WA ... 350-H10
Rt#-27 POPULAR ST
TEKOA WA ... 114-C3
Rt#-27 RAILROAD ST
ROCKFORD WA ... 114-C2
TEKOA WA ... 114-C3
Rt#-27 S RAMSEY ST
TEKOA WA ... 114-C3
Rt#-27 STEPTOE AV
OAKESDALE WA ... 114-C3
Rt#-27 TEKOA OAKSDALE RD
OAKESDALE WA ... 114-C3
WHITMAN CO WA ... 114-C3
Rt#-27 WATER ST
TEKOA WA ... 114-C3
WHITMAN CO WA ... 114-C3
Rt#-28 E 1ST AV
ODESSA WA ... 113-B3
Rt#-28 W 1ST AV
ODESSA WA ... 113-B3
Rt#-28 BASIN ST N
EPHRATA WA ... 112-C3
GRANT CO WA ... 112-C3
Rt#-28 BASIN ST NW
EPHRATA WA ... 112-C3
GRANT CO WA ... 112-C3
Rt#-28 BASIN ST S
EPHRATA WA ... 112-C3
GRANT CO WA ... 112-C3
Rt#-28 F ST SE
GRANT CO WA ... 112-B3
Rt#-28 F ST SW
QUINCY WA ... 112-B3
Rt#-28 F ST SW
QUINCY WA ... 112-B3
GRANT CO WA ... 112-B3
Rt#-28 HIGHWAY
DAVENPORT WA ... 114-A2
DOUGLAS CO WA ... 112-B3
DOUGLAS CO WA ... 239-A5
EAST WENATCHEE WA ... 239-A4
East Wenatchee Bench WA ... 239-A3
GRANT CO WA ... 112-C2
GRANT CO WA ... 113-A2
HARRINGTON WA ... 113-C2
LINCOLN CO WA ... 113-C2
LINCOLN CO WA ... 114-A2
ODESSA WA ... 113-B3
ROCK ISLAND WA ... 239-B5
SOAP LAKE WA ... 112-C2
Rt#-28 ROAD 10-NW
GRANT CO WA ... 112-B3
Rt#-28 ROAD 11-NW
GRANT CO WA ... 112-C3
Rt#-28 TWELFTH ST
DAVENPORT WA ... 114-A2
Rt#-30 2ND ST
NORTH POWDER OR ... 130-B3
Rt#-30 NE 16TH ST
FRUITLAND ID ... 139-A3
PAYETTE CO ID ... 139-A3
Rt#-30 LA GRANDE-BAKER HWY
NORTH POWDER OR ... 130-B3
UNION CO OR ... 130-B3
Rt#-31 FREMONT HWY
DESCHUTES CO OR ... 143-A1
KLAMATH CO OR ... 143-A1
LAKE CO OR ... 143-B2
LAKE CO OR ... 151-C1
LAKE CO OR ... 152-A1
PAISLEY OR ... 151-C1
Rt#-31 HIGHWAY
IONE WA ... 106-B1
METALINE WA ... 106-B1
METALINE FALLS WA ... 106-B1
PEND OREILLE CO WA ... 106-B1
Rt#-31 MAIN ST
PAISLEY OR ... 151-C1
Rt#-31 S SECOND AV
IONE WA ... 106-B1
Rt#-33 HIGHWAY
BRITISH COLUMBIA BC ... 105-A1
Rt#-34 2ND ST
LEBANON OR ... 133-C1
Rt#-34 ALSEA HWY
BENTON CO OR ... 133-A1
LINCOLN CO OR ... 133-A2
LINCOLN CO OR ... 209-D2
WALDPORT OR ... 328-F6
Rt#-34 CORVALLIS-LEBANON HWY
LEBANON OR ... 133-C1
LINN CO OR ... 133-C1
LINN CO OR ... 207-B6
TANGENT OR ... 207-B6
Rt#-34 CORVALLIS-NEWPORT HWY
CORVALLIS OR ... 327-H11
LINN CO OR ... 207-B6
LINN CO OR ... 327-H11
Rt#-34 HARRISON BLVD
CORVALLIS OR ... 327-G9
CORVALLIS OR ... 327-G9
Rt#-34 W HEMLOCK ST
WALDPORT OR ... 328-E4
Rt#-34 MORTON ST
LEBANON OR ... 133-C1
Rt#-34 TANGENT ST
LEBANON OR ... 133-C1
Rt#-34 VAN BUREN AV
CORVALLIS OR ... 327-F9
LINN CO OR ... 327-F9
Rt#-35 MOUNT HOOD HWY
CLACKAMAS CO OR ... 202-C5
HOOD RIVER OR ... 195-C7
HOOD RIVER CO OR ... 202-C1
Rt#-36 MAPLETON-JCT CITY HWY
LANE CO OR ... 132-C3
LANE CO OR ... 133-B2
LANE CO OR ... 210-A6
LANE CO OR ... 214-D2
Rt#-36 PRAIRIE ROAD CONN
LANE CO OR ... 210-A6
Rt#-37 SE 10TH ST
PENDLETON OR ... 129-B1
Rt#-37 SW 17TH ST
PENDLETON OR ... 129-B1
Rt#-37 SW COURT PL
PENDLETON OR ... 129-B1
Rt#-37 SW EMIGRANT AV
PENDLETON OR ... 129-B1
Rt#-37 SE EMIGRANT AV
PENDLETON OR ... 129-B1
Rt#-37 SW FRAZER AV
PENDLETON OR ... 129-B1

Rt#-37 SE FRAZER AV
PENDLETON OR ... 129-B1
Rt#-37 PENDLTN-CLD SPRNGS HWY
PENDLETON OR ... 129-A1
UMATILLA CO OR ... 129-A1
Rt#-38 A ST
DOUGLAS CO OR ... 141-A1
ELKTON OR ... 141-A1
Rt#-38 UMPQUA AV
REEDSPORT OR ... 218-C1
Rt#-38 UMPQUA HWY
DOUGLAS CO OR ... 140-C1
DOUGLAS CO OR ... 141-A1
DOUGLAS CO OR ... 218-D2
DOUGLAS CO OR ... 219-A3
DRAIN OR ... 219-A3
ELKTON OR ... 141-A1
REEDSPORT OR ... 218-D2
Rt#-39 4TH ST
KLAMATH FALLS OR ... 338-D8
Rt#-39 5TH ST
KLAMATH FALLS OR ... 338-E8
Rt#-39 S 5TH ST
KLAMATH FALLS OR ... 338-D8
Rt#-39 6TH ST
KLAMATH FALLS OR ... 338-D8
Rt#-39 S 6TH ST
KLAMATH FALLS OR ... 338-E8
Rt#-39 E FRONT ST
MERRILL OR ... 150-C2
Rt#-39 W FRONT ST
MERRILL OR ... 150-C2
Rt#-39 HATFIELD HWY
KLAMATH CO OR ... 151-A2
SISKIYOU CO CA ... 151-A3
Rt#-39 KLAMATH AV
KLAMATH FALLS OR ... 338-D8
Rt#-39 KLAMATH FLLS-LKVIEW HW
Altamont OR ... 338-F9
Altamont OR ... 339-C11
KLAMATH FALLS OR ... 338-F9
Rt#-39 KLAMATH FLLS-MALIN HWY
Altamont OR ... 338-C4
Altamont OR ... 339-A10
KLAMATH CO OR ... 150-C2
KLAMATH CO OR ... 235-D5
KLAMATH CO OR ... 338-C4
KLAMATH CO OR ... 338-C4
MERRILL OR ... 150-C2
Rt#-39 MAIN ST
KLAMATH FALLS OR ... 338-C8
Rt#-39 WILLOW AV
KLAMATH FALLS OR ... 338-D8
Rt#-41 5TH AV
SPIRIT LAKE ID ... 115-A1
Rt#-41 HIGHWAY
BONNER CO ID ... 106-C3
BONNER CO ID ... 107-A3
BONNER CO ID ... 115-A1
KOOTENAI CO ID ... 115-A1
KOOTENAI CO ID ... 247-D1
NEWPORT OR ... 106-C3
NEWPORT WA ... 106-C3
RATHDRUM ID ... 115-A1
RATHDRUM ID ... 247-D1
SPIRIT LAKE ID ... 115-A1
Rt#-41 ROSS PNT-RATHDRUM HWY
KOOTENAI CO ID ... 247-D1
KOOTENAI CO ID ... 354-D2
POST FALLS ID ... 354-D2
Rt#-41 N STATE AV
NEWPORT WA ... 106-C3
Rt#-41 S STATE AV
NEWPORT WA ... 106-C3
PEND OREILLE CO WA ... 106-C3
Rt#-42 3RD ST
COQUILLE OR ... 220-D5
Rt#-42 8TH ST
MYRTLE POINT OR ... 140-B2
Rt#-42 N ADAMS ST
COQUILLE OR ... 220-D5
Rt#-42 N CENTRAL BLVD
COQUILLE OR ... 220-D4
Rt#-42 W CENTRAL BLVD
COQUILLE OR ... 220-D4
Rt#-42 COOS BAY-ROSEBURG HWY
COOS CO OR ... 140-C2
COOS CO OR ... 220-D4
DOUGLAS CO OR ... 140-C3
DOUGLAS CO OR ... 141-A2
DOUGLAS CO OR ... 221-A6
MYRTLE POINT OR ... 140-C2
WINSTON OR ... 221-B6
Rt#-42 W DOUGLAS BLVD
WINSTON OR ... 221-B6
Rt#-42 HIGHWAY
COOS CO OR ... 220-D2
DOUGLAS CO OR ... 140-C3
DOUGLAS CO OR ... 221-B6
Rt#-42 MARYLAND AV
MYRTLE POINT OR ... 140-B2
Rt#-42S 2ND ST
COQUILLE OR ... 220-D5
Rt#-42S N BIRCH ST
COQUILLE OR ... 220-D5
Rt#-42S COQUILLE-BANDON HWY
BANDON OR ... 220-C6
COOS CO OR ... 220-C6
COQUILLE OR ... 220-C6
Rt#-43 7TH ST
OREGON CITY OR ... 199-D4
WEST LINN OR ... 199-D4
Rt#-43 N STATE ST
CLACKAMAS CO OR ... 321-G5
CLACKAMAS CO OR ... 321-G5
Rt#-43 S STATE ST
LAKE OSWEGO OR ... 321-G6
Rt#-43 SW MACADAM AV
MULTNOMAH CO OR ... 321-G1
PORTLAND OR ... 317-F6
PORTLAND OR ... 321-G1
Rt#-43 PACIFIC HWY
LAKE OSWEGO OR ... 199-C4
LAKE OSWEGO OR ... 321-G7
LAKE OSWEGO OR ... 199-C4
Rt#-43 SW RIVERSIDE DR
CLACKAMAS CO OR ... 321-G5
LAKE OSWEGO OR ... 321-G5
MULTNOMAH CO OR ... 321-G5
Rt#-43 S STATE ST
LAKE OSWEGO OR ... 321-G6
Rt#-43 WILLAMETTE DR
LAKE OSWEGO OR ... 199-C4
WEST LINN OR ... 199-C4

Rt#-44 N GLENWOOD ST
ADA CO ID ... 253-C2
GARDEN CITY ID ... 253-C2
Rt#-44 HIGHWAY
CANYON CO ID ... 147-B1
Rt#-44 MAIN ST
CANYON CO ID ... 147-B1
Rt#-44 W MAIN ST
CANYON CO ID ... 147-B1
MIDDLETON ID ... 147-B1
Rt#-44 STAR BLVD
CANYON CO ID ... 147-B1
MIDDLETON ID ... 147-B1
Rt#-44 E STATE ST
ADA CO ID ... 253-B1
EAGLE ID ... 253-B1
Rt#-44 W STATE ST
ADA CO ID ... 147-B1
ADA CO ID ... 253-A1
EAGLE ID ... 253-A1
GARDEN CITY ID ... 253-A1
STAR ID ... 147-C1
Rt#-45 12TH AV S
NAMPA ID ... 147-B1
Rt#-45 12TH AVENUE RD
CANYON CO ID ... 147-B1
NAMPA ID ... 147-B1
OWYHEE CO ID ... 147-B1
Rt#-46 OREGON CAVES HWY
CAVE JUNCTION OR ... 233-B4
JOSEPHINE CO OR ... 233-B4
Rt#-47 E BRIDGE ST
VERNONIA OR ... 125-B1
Rt#-47 FRONT ST
GASTON OR ... 198-B3
Rt#-47 HIGHWAY
CARLTON OR ... 198-B6
GASTON OR ... 198-B3
WASHINGTON CO OR ... 198-B3
YAMHILL OR ... 198-B4
Rt#-47 NW HIGHWAY 47
FOREST GROVE OR ... 125-B1
WASHINGTON CO OR ... 125-B1
WASHINGTON CO OR ... 198-B1
Rt#-47 SW HIGHWAY 47
FOREST GROVE OR ... 198-C1
WASHINGTON CO OR ... 198-B1
Rt#-47 N MAIN ST
BANKS OR ... 125-B1
Rt#-47 S MAIN ST
BANKS OR ... 125-B1
WASHINGTON CO OR ... 125-B1
Rt#-47 W MAIN ST
CARLTON OR ... 198-B6
Rt#-47 N MAPLE ST
YAMHILL OR ... 198-B4
Rt#-47 S MAPLE ST
YAMHILL OR ... 198-B5
Rt#-47 MIST DR
COLUMBIA CO OR ... 125-B1
VERNONIA OR ... 125-B1
Rt#-47 MIST-CLATSKANIE HWY
CLATSKANIE OR ... 117-B3
COLUMBIA CO OR ... 117-B3
Rt#-47 NEHALEM HWY
COLUMBIA CO OR ... 125-B1
WASHINGTON CO OR ... 125-B1
Rt#-47 QUINCE ST
FOREST GROVE OR ... 198-C1
WASHINGTON CO OR ... 198-C1
Rt#-47 ROSE AV
VERNONIA OR ... 125-B1
Rt#-47 N YAMHILL ST
CARLTON OR ... 198-B5
Rt#-51 INDEPENDENCE HWY
POLK CO OR ... 204-B6
Rt#-51 E MAIN ST
MONMOUTH OR ... 204-B7
Rt#-51 N MAIN ST
INDEPENDENCE OR ... 204-B7
POLK CO OR ... 204-B7
Rt#-51 S MAIN ST
INDEPENDENCE OR ... 204-B7
Rt#-51 MONMOUTH ST
INDEPENDENCE OR ... 204-B7
Rt#-51 MONMOUTH-INDPNDNCE HWY
INDEPENDENCE OR ... 204-B7
MONMOUTH OR ... 204-B7
POLK CO OR ... 204-B7
Rt#-52 2ND AV S
PAYETTE ID ... 139-A3
Rt#-52 N 6TH ST
PAYETTE ID ... 139-A3
Rt#-52 N 7TH ST
PAYETTE ID ... 139-A3
Rt#-52 S 7TH ST
PAYETTE ID ... 139-A3
Rt#-52 S 18TH ST
PAYETTE ID ... 139-A3
Rt#-52 E BLACK CANYON RD
GEM CO ID ... 139-C3
Rt#-52 HIGHWAY
BOISE CO ID ... 139-C3
GEM CO ID ... 139-C3
HORSESHOE BEND ID ... 139-C3
MALHEUR CO ID ... 139-A3
PAYETTE ID ... 139-A3
PAYETTE CO ID ... 139-A3
Rt#-52 N WASHINGTON AV
GEM CO ID ... 139-C3
Rt#-52 S WASHINGTON AV
EMMETT ID ... 139-C3
GEM CO ID ... 139-C3
Rt#-53 HIGHWAY
KOOTENAI CO ID ... 115-A1
KOOTENAI CO ID ... 245-A4
KOOTENAI CO ID ... 247-D1
RATHDRUM ID ... 115-A1
Rt#-53 NECANICUM HWY
CLATSOP CO OR ... 188-D7
CLATSOP CO OR ... 191-C3
CLATSOP CO OR ... 191-C3
Rt#-53 TRENT RD
KOOTENAI CO ID ... 247-C1
Rt#-53 W TRENT RD
KOOTENAI CO ID ... 247-C1
KOOTENAI CO ID ... 352-J3
KOOTENAI CO ID ... 353-A2
Rt#-54 HIGHWAY
ATHOL ID ... 245-B2
KOOTENAI CO ID ... 115-A1
KOOTENAI CO ID ... 245-C1
Rt#-55 CEMETERY RD
MARSING ID ... 147-B1

INDEX

410 Rt#-55 CEMETERY RD STREET INDEX Rt#-105 HIGHWAY

STREET City State Page-Grid

Rt#-55 CEMETERY RD
OWYHEE CO ID 147-B1
Rt#-55 S EAGLE RD
ADA CO ID 253-B2
BOISE ID 253-B2
EAGLE ID 253-B2
MERIDIAN ID 253-B2
Rt#-55 HIGHWAY
ADAMS CO ID 251-A4
CASCADE ID 252-D5
DONNELLY ID 252-D1
MCCALL ID 251-C5
NEW MEADOWS ID 251-A4
VALLEY CO ID 251-C5
VALLEY CO ID 252-D1
Rt#-55 N HIGHWAY 55
ADA CO ID 253-B1
Rt#-55 HORSESHOE BEND RD
BOISE CO ID 139-C3
HORSESHOE BEND ID 139-C3
Rt#-55 N HORSESHOE BEND RD
ADA CO ID 139-C3
ADA CO ID 253-B1
BOISE CO ID 139-C3
EAGLE ID 253-B1
Rt#-55 KARCHER RD
CANYON CO ID 147-B1
NAMPA ID 147-B1
Rt#-55 E LAKE ST
MCCALL ID 251-C5
Rt#-55 MAIN ST
CASCADE ID 252-D6
MARSING ID 147-B1
OWYHEE CO ID 147-B1
Rt#-55 NAMPA BLVD
NAMPA ID 147-B1
Rt#-55 NORRIS AV
NEW MEADOWS ID 251-A4
Rt#-55 PAYETTE RVR SCENIC RTE
BOISE CO ID 139-C3
Rt#-55 SUNNY SLOPE RD
CANYON CO ID 147-B1
Rt#-55 VIRGINIA ST
NEW MEADOWS ID 251-A4
Rt#-56 BULL LAKE RD
LINCOLN CO MT 107-C3
SANDERS CO MT 107-C3
Rt#-56 HIGHWAY
SANDERS CO MT 107-C3
Rt#-57 9TH ST
BONNER CO ID 107-A3
PRIEST RIVER ID 107-A3
Rt#-57 HIGHWAY
BONNER CO ID 106-C2
BONNER CO ID 107-A2
Rt#-58 HIGHWAY
KOOTENAI CO ID 115-A2
Rt#-58 WILLAMETTE HWY
KLAMATH CO OR 142-C2
LANE CO OR 133-C3
LANE CO OR 134-A3
LANE CO OR 142-B1
LANE CO OR 215-C3
LANE CO OR 330-J14
LANE CO OR 331-A14
OAKRIDGE OR 142-B1
Rt#-60 MOCTILEME RD
BENEWAH CO ID 115-A3
Rt#-60 NHS 11
BENEWAH CO ID 115-A3
Rt#-62 CRATER LAKE HWY
EAGLE POINT OR 230-D4
JACKSON CO OR 149-C1
JACKSON CO OR 150-A1
JACKSON CO OR 226-C7
JACKSON CO OR 227-D7
JACKSON CO OR 230-D4
JACKSON CO OR 336-F3
KLAMATH CO OR 227-D7
KLAMATH CO OR 231-C2
MEDFORD OR 336-F3
SHADY COVE OR 230-D4
White City OR 230-D6
Rt#-62 HIGHWAY
CRAIGMONT ID 123-B2
LEWIS CO ID 123-C2
NEZPERCE ID 123-C2
Rt#-62 MAIN ST
CRAIGMONT ID 123-B2
Rt#-62 NATIONAL PARK HWY
KLAMATH CO OR 227-B4
Rt#-64 HIGHWAY
KAMIAH ID 123-C2
LEWIS CO ID 123-C2
NEZPERCE ID 123-C2
Rt#-66 GREEN SPRINGS HWY
ASHLAND OR 337-F9
JACKSON CO OR 150-A2
JACKSON CO OR 234-D4
JACKSON CO OR 337-F9
KLAMATH CO OR 150-A2
KLAMATH CO OR 235-A5
KLAMATH CO OR 338-A12
KLAMATH FALLS OR 338-A12
Rt#-66 PALOUSE COVE RD
LATAH CO ID 249-C2
Rt#-69 AVALON ST
ADA CO ID 253-A5
KUNA ID 253-A5
Rt#-69 BELTLINE HWY
EUGENE OR 329-B5
EUGENE OR 330-A1
SPRINGFIELD OR 330-A1
Rt#-69 KUNA-MERIDIAN RD
ADA CO ID 253-A4
MERIDIAN ID 253-A4
Rt#-70 DAIRY-BONANZA HWY
BONANZA OR 151-A2
KLAMATH CO OR 151-A2
Rt#-71 HIGHWAY
ADAMS CO ID 131-A3
CAMBRIDGE ID 139-B1
WASHINGTON CO ID 131-A3
WASHINGTON CO ID 139-A1
Rt#-71 HOPPER AV
CAMBRIDGE ID 139-B1
WASHINGTON CO ID 139-B1
Rt#-72 HIGHWAY
PAYETTE CO ID 139-B3
Rt#-74 COURT ST
HEPPNER OR 128-C2
Rt#-74 HEPPNER HWY
GILLIAM CO OR 128-B1
HEPPNER OR 128-C2
IONE OR 128-B1
LEXINGTON OR 128-C2
MORROW CO OR 128-B1
Rt#-74 HEPPNER HWY
MORROW CO OR 129-A2
UMATILLA CO OR 129-A2
Rt#-74 W LINDEN WY
HEPPNER OR 128-C2
Rt#-74 MAIN ST
HEPPNER OR 128-C2
LEXINGTON OR 128-C2
Rt#-74 E MAY ST
HEPPNER OR 128-C2
Rt#-78 MARSING-MURPHY RD
MARSING ID 147-B1
OWYHEE CO ID 147-B1
Rt#-78 E MONROE ST
BURNS OR 145-B1
HARNEY CO OR 145-B1
Rt#-78 MURPHY-GRANDVIEW RD
OWYHEE CO ID 147-C2
Rt#-78 STEENS HWY
HARNEY CO OR 145-B1
HARNEY CO OR 146-A2
MALHEUR CO OR 146-B3
Rt#-82 1ST ST
ISLAND CITY OR 130-A2
Rt#-82 E 1ST ST
WALLOWA OR 130-C1
Rt#-82 W 1ST ST
WALLOWA OR 130-B1
Rt#-82 E 8TH ST
JOSEPH OR 130-C2
WALLOWA CO OR 130-C2
Rt#-82 N 8TH AV
ELGIN OR 130-A1
Rt#-82 S 8TH AV
ELGIN OR 130-A1
UNION CO OR 130-A1
Rt#-82 ALBANY ST
ELGIN OR 130-A1
Rt#-82 B ST
ISLAND CITY OR 130-A2
Rt#-82 JOSEPH-WALLOWA LKE HWY
WALLOWA CO OR 130-C2
Rt#-82 N MADISON ST
WALLOWA OR 130-B1
Rt#-82 N MAIN ST
JOSEPH OR 130-C2
WALLOWA CO OR 130-C2
Rt#-82 S MAIN ST
JOSEPH OR 130-C2
Rt#-82 W NORTH ST
ENTERPRISE OR 130-C2
Rt#-82 N RIVER ST
ENTERPRISE OR 130-C2
Rt#-82 RUCKMAN AV
IMBLER OR 130-A2
Rt#-82 STATE ST
LOSTINE OR 130-C2
Rt#-82 WALLOWA LAKE HWY
ELGIN OR 130-B1
ENTERPRISE OR 130-C2
IMBLER OR 130-A2
ISLAND CITY OR 130-A2
LA GRANDE OR 130-A2
LOSTINE OR 130-C2
UNION CO OR 130-B1
WALLOWA OR 130-B1
WALLOWA CO OR 130-B1
Rt#-82 WATER ST
LOSTINE OR 130-C2
Rt#-86 BAKER-COPPERFIELD HWY
BAKER CO OR 130-B3
BAKER CO OR 131-A3
BAKER CO OR 138-C1
BAKER CO OR 139-A1
RICHLAND OR 139-A1
Rt#-86 MAIN ST
RICHLAND OR 139-A1
Rt#-91 ANNACIS HWY
CITY OF RICHMOND BC 156-D6
DISTRICT OF DELTA BC 101-C1
DISTRICT OF DELTA BC 156-D6
NEW WESTMINSTER BC 156-D6
Rt#-91 FRWY
CITY OF RICHMOND BC 156-B6
Rt#-91 RICHMOND FRWY
CITY OF RICHMOND BC 156-C6
Rt#-91A ANNACIS HWY
CITY OF RICHMOND BC 156-D6
Rt#-91A HIGHWAY
NEW WESTMINSTER BC 156-D6
Rt#-91A QUEENSBOROUGH BRDG
CITY OF RICHMOND BC 156-D6
NEW WESTMINSTER BC 156-D6
Rt#-92 131ST AV NE
SNOHOMISH CO WA 110-C1
Rt#-92 GRANITE FALLS HWY
GRANITE FALLS WA 102-C3
SNOHOMISH CO WA 102-C3
SNOHOMISH CO WA 110-C1
Rt#-92 HIGHWAY
LAKE STEVENS WA 171-D1
SNOHOMISH CO WA 110-C1
SNOHOMISH CO WA 171-D1
Rt#-92 E STANLEY ST
GRANITE FALLS WA 102-C3
Rt#-92 W STANLEY ST
GRANITE FALLS WA 102-C3
Rt#-95 HIGHWAY
BRITISH COLUMBIA BC 107-B1
Rt#-96 128TH ST SE
SNOHOMISH CO WA 171-C4
Rt#-96 128TH ST SW
SNOHOMISH CO WA 171-C4
Rt#-96 132ND ST SE
MILL CREEK WA 171-C4
SNOHOMISH CO WA 171-C4
Rt#-96 HIGHWAY
SISKIYOU CO CA 149-A3
SISKIYOU CO CA 150-A3
Rt#-96 E LOWELL-LARIMER RD
SNOHOMISH CO WA 171-D4
Rt#-96 SEATTLE HILL RD
SNOHOMISH CO WA 171-C4
Rt#-97 E COEUR D'ALENE AV
HARRISON ID 248-A4
KOOTENAI CO ID 248-A4
Rt#-97 HARRISON RD
KOOTENAI CO ID 248-B5
Rt#-97 HIGHWAY
BRITISH COLUMBIA BC 104-C1
HARRISON ID 248-A4
KOOTENAI CO ID 248-A1
OSOYOOS BC 104-C1
Rt#-97 LAKE AV
HARRISON ID 248-A4
Rt#-97C HIGHWAY
BRITISH COLUMBIA BC 95-C1
Rt#-99 N 1ST AV
DRAIN OR 219-A3
Rt#-99 N 1ST ST
OAKLA 219-A7
Rt#-99 2ND AV
GOLD HILL OR 230-A6
Rt#-99 SW 5TH ST
CANYONVILLE OR 225-C3
Rt#-99 E 6TH AV
EUGENE OR 330-A6
Rt#-99 W 6TH AV
EUGENE OR 329-G6
EUGENE OR 330-A6
Rt#-99 E 7TH AV
EUGENE OR 330-A6
Rt#-99 W 7TH AV
EUGENE OR 329-G6
EUGENE OR 330-A6
Rt#-99 16TH AV S
FEDERAL WAY WA 182-B1
Rt#-99 54TH AV E
FIFE WA 182-A2
Rt#-99 70TH AV
VANCOUVER BC 156-B5
Rt#-99 ALASKAN FRWY
SEATTLE WA 277-J5
SEATTLE WA 278-A6
SEATTLE WA 281-J3
SEATTLE WA 282-A1
Rt#-99 AURORA AV N
SEATTLE WA 171-A7
SEATTLE WA 273-J2
SEATTLE WA 277-J4
SHORELINE WA 171-A7
Rt#-99 W B AV
DRAIN OR 219-A3
Rt#-99 BEAR CREST DR
JACKSON CO OR 234-B2
PHOENIX OR 234-B2
Rt#-99 BROADWAY
EVERETT WA 268-D5
Rt#-99 E BROADWAY
EUGENE OR 330-B6
Rt#-99 S BROADWAY
EVERETT WA 268-C6
Rt#-99 CALAPOOYA ST
DOUGLAS CO OR 221-C1
SUTHERLIN OR 221-C1
Rt#-99 N CEDAR ST
DRAIN OR 219-A3
Rt#-99 S CEDAR ST
DRAIN OR 219-A3
Rt#-99 COBURG RD
EUGENE OR 330-A6
Rt#-99 COOS BAY-ROSEBURG HWY
DOUGLAS CO OR 221-B6
DOUGLAS CO OR 334-D14
WINSTON OR 221-B6
Rt#-99 DILLARD HWY
DOUGLAS CO OR 221-B7
WINSTON OR 221-B7
Rt#-99 N DOUGLAS BLVD
WINSTON OR 221-B6
Rt#-99 DRAIN-YONCALLA HWY
DOUGLAS CO OR 219-A3
DRAIN OR 219-A3
YONCALLA OR 219-A3
Rt#-99 EAGLE VALLEY RD
DOUGLAS CO OR 219-A3
Rt#-99 E ELKTON-SUTHERLIN HWY
SUTHERLIN OR 221-C1
Rt#-99 EVERETT MALL WY
EVERETT WA 268-D5
Rt#-99 SE EVERETT MALL WY
EVERETT WA 268-C6
Rt#-99 SW EVERETT MALL WY
EVERETT WA 268-A7
Rt#-99 EVERGREEN WY
EVERETT WA 171-B4
EVERETT WA 267-J7
EVERETT WA 268-A7
SNOHOMISH CO WA 171-B4
Rt#-99 FRANKLIN BLVD
EUGENE OR 330-C7
LANE CO OR 330-G8
Rt#-99 FRONT ST
YONCALLA OR 219-B4
Rt#-99 N FRONT ST
CENTRAL POINT OR 230-C7
Rt#-99 S FRONT ST
CENTRAL POINT OR 230-C7
OAKLAND OR 219-A7
Rt#-99 FRWY
CITY OF RICHMOND BC 156-B6
CITY OF SURREY BC 158-A1
DISTRICT OF DELTA BC 156-C7
KING CO WA 286-B4
SEATTLE WA 281-J7
SEATTLE WA 285-J1
SEATTLE WA 286-A2
TUKWILA WA 286-C5
WHATCOM CO WA 158-B3
Rt#-99 GEORGE MASSEY TUN
CITY OF RICHMOND BC 156-B7
DISTRICT OF DELTA BC 156-C7
Rt#-99 GEORGIA ST
VANCOUVER BC 254-F9
Rt#-99 GOLD HILL SPUR
GOLD HILL OR 230-B6
JACKSON CO OR 230-B6
Rt#-99 GOSHEN-DIVIDE HWY
COTTAGE GROVE OR 215-B6
CRESWELL OR 215-C4
LANE CO OR 215-C4
LANE CO OR 219-C1
LANE CO OR 330-J14
Rt#-99 N GOSHEN-DIVIDE HWY
COTTAGE GROVE OR 215-B7
Rt#-99 N GOSHEN-DIVIDE ST
COTTAGE GROVE OR 215-B7
Rt#-99 S GOSHEN-DIVIDE ST
CRESWELL OR 215-C5
Rt#-99 GRANVILLE BRDG
VANCOUVER BC 254-E12
Rt#-99 GRANVILLE ST
VANCOUVER BC 156-B5
VANCOUVER BC 254-E14
Rt#-99 GREEN LAKE DR N
SEATTLE WA 273-J2
Rt#-99 W GREEN LAKE WY N
SEATTLE WA 273-J3
Rt#-99 HIGHWAY
CITY OF RICHMOND BC 156-B5
EDMONDS WA 171-B5
KENDRICK ID 123-B1
LATAH CO ID 123-A1
LYNNWOOD WA 171-B4
MOUNTLAKE TERRACE WA 171-B5
SEATTLE WA 286-A2
SNOHOMISH CO WA 171-B4
TROY ID 123-A1
Rt#-99 HOWE ST
VANCOUVER BC 254-F10
Rt#-99 INTERNATIONAL BLVD
DES MOINES WA 290-C5
SEATAC WA 288-D7
SEATAC WA 290-C5
TUKWILA WA 288-D7
Rt#-99 IVY ST
JUNCTION CITY OR 210-A5
Rt#-99 LAKE OF THE WOODS HWY
CENTRAL POINT OR 230-C7
JACKSON CO OR 230-C7
MEDFORD OR 230-C7
Rt#-99 LIONS GATE BRDG
DIST OF WEST VANCOUVER BC 254-E5
VANCOUVER BC 254-E5
Rt#-99 LIONS GATE BRIDGE RD
DIST OF WEST VANCOUVER BC 254-E7
VANCOUVER BC 254-E7
Rt#-99 LITHIA WY
ASHLAND OR 337-C7
Rt#-99 MAIN ST
CANYONVILLE OR 225-C3
DOUGLAS CO OR 225-C3
PHOENIX OR 234-B2
Rt#-99 N MAIN ST
ASHLAND OR 337-C6
CANYONVILLE OR 225-C3
JACKSON CO OR 337-C6
PHOENIX OR 234-B2
Rt#-99 S MAIN ST
CANYONVILLE OR 225-C3
Rt#-99 W MAIN ST
CANYONVILLE OR 225-C3
Rt#-99 E MARGINAL WY S
SEATTLE WA 281-J5
Rt#-99 MARINE DR
DIST OF WEST VANCOUVER BC 254-E4
Rt#-99 MCVAY HWY
LANE CO OR 330-G11
Rt#-99 OAK ST
CITY OF RICHMOND BC 156-B5
VANCOUVER BC 156-B5
Rt#-99 OAKLAND-SHADY HWY
DOUGLAS CO OR 219-A7
DOUGLAS CO OR 221-C3
DOUGLAS CO OR 334-F2
OAKLAND OR 219-A7
ROSEBURG OR 334-F2
SUTHERLIN OR 221-C3
Rt#-99 OLD PACIFIC HWY
DOUGLAS CO OR 225-C2
MYRTLE CREEK OR 225-C2
Tri-City OR 225-C2
Rt#-99 OLD STAGE RD
JACKSON CO OR 230-B6
Rt#-99 PACIFIC HWY
FEDERAL WAY WA 182-B1
Rt#-99 PACIFIC HWY E
FEDERAL WAY WA 182-A2
FIFE WA 182-A2
MILTON WA 182-A2
PIERCE CO WA 182-A2
Rt#-99 PACIFIC HWY S
DES MOINES WA 175-B7
DES MOINES WA 290-C6
FEDERAL WAY WA 175-B7
FEDERAL WAY WA 182-A2
KENT WA 175-B7
KENT WA 290-C6
KING CO WA 175-B7
Rt#-99 PACIFIC HWY W
EUGENE OR 215-A1
EUGENE OR 329-D2
JUNCTION CITY OR 210-A7
LANE CO OR 210-A7
LANE CO OR 215-A1
Rt#-99 SE PINE ST
ROSEBURG OR 334-F8
Rt#-99 REDWOOD HWY
GRANTS PASS OR 335-F6
Rt#-99 NE REDWOOD HWY
GRANTS PASS OR 335-F7
Rt#-99 N RIVERSIDE AV
MEDFORD OR 336-C10
Rt#-99 S RIVERSIDE AV
MEDFORD OR 336-D13
Rt#-99 ROGUE RIVER HWY
GRANTS PASS OR 335-J11
JACKSON CO OR 229-C6
JACKSON CO OR 230-A6
JOSEPHINE CO OR 229-C6
JOSEPHINE CO OR 335-J11
ROGUE RIVER OR 229-C6
Rt#-99 ROGUE VALLEY HWY
ASHLAND OR 337-A4
CENTRAL POINT OR 230-C7
JACKSON CO OR 230-C7
JACKSON CO OR 234-B2
JACKSON CO OR 337-A4
MEDFORD OR 230-C7
MEDFORD OR 234-B2
MEDFORD OR 336-A7
PHOENIX OR 234-B2
TALENT OR 234-B3
Rt#-99 SAMS VALLEY HWY
GOLD HILL OR 230-A6
JACKSON CO OR 230-A6
Rt#-99 SEYMOUR ST
VANCOUVER BC 254-F11
Rt#-99 SISKIYOU BLVD
ASHLAND OR 337-D8
JACKSON CO OR 337-H10
Rt#-99 STANTON PARK RD
DOUGLAS CO OR 225-C3
Rt#-99 NE STATE ST
DOUGLAS CO OR 221-C1
SUTHERLIN OR 221-C1
Rt#-99 NE STEPHENS ST
ROSEBURG OR 334-F5
Rt#-99 SE STEPHENS ST
ROSEBURG OR 334-G7
Rt#-99 TAYLOR WY
DIST OF WEST VANCOUVER BC 254-E4
Rt#-99 TUKWILA INTL BLVD
SEATAC WA 288-D1
TUKWILA WA 286-D7
Rt#-99 TUKWILA INTL BLVD
TUKWILA WA 288-D1
Rt#-99 UMPQUA HWY
DOUGLAS CO OR 219-A2
DRAIN OR 219-A2
Rt#-99A 10TH AV
DISTRICT OF BURNABY BC 156-D5
NEW WESTMINSTER BC 156-D5
Rt#-99A HIGHWAY
CITY OF SURREY BC 156-D5
NEW WESTMINSTER BC 156-D5
Rt#-99A KING GEORGE HWY
CITY OF SURREY BC 156-D5
CITY OF SURREY BC 157-A7
CITY OF SURREY BC 158-A1
Rt#-99A KINGSWAY
DISTRICT OF BURNABY BC 156-C5
NEW WESTMINSTER BC 156-C5
Rt#-99A MCBRIDE BLVD
NEW WESTMINSTER BC 156-D5
Rt#-99A PATTULLO BRDG
CITY OF SURREY BC 156-D5
Rt#-99E 2ND ST
HALSEY OR 210-B2
Rt#-99E 3RD ST
HARRISBURG OR 210-A5
Rt#-99E ALBANY-JCT CITY HWY
ALBANY OR 207-C7
ALBANY OR 326-C14
HALSEY OR 210-B3
HARRISBURG OR 210-A5
JUNCTION CITY OR 210-A5
LANE CO OR 210-A5
LINN CO OR 207-C7
LINN CO OR 210-B3
TANGENT OR 207-C7
Rt#-99E COMMERCIAL ST NE
SALEM OR 322-J10
Rt#-99E FRONT ST NE
SALEM OR 322-H12
Rt#-99E NE GRAND AV
PORTLAND OR 313-G4
Rt#-99E SE GRAND AV
PORTLAND OR 313-G7
PORTLAND OR 317-G2
Rt#-99E HIGHWAY
MILWAUKIE OR 321-J2
SALEM OR 322-H12
Rt#-99E HIGHWAY 99
CLARK CO WA 192-C5
VANCOUVER WA 192-C5
VANCOUVER WA 305-G1
Rt#-99E JEFFERSON HWY
LINN CO OR 207-D3
Rt#-99E LIBERTY ST NE
SALEM OR 322-J10
Rt#-99E N MARINE DR
PORTLAND OR 309-E1
Rt#-99E NE MLK JR BLVD
PORTLAND OR 309-G3
PORTLAND OR 313-G4
Rt#-99E SE MLK JR BLVD
PORTLAND OR 313-G7
PORTLAND OR 317-G1
Rt#-99E MCLOUGHLIN BLVD E
CLACKAMAS CO OR 199-D5
OREGON CITY OR 199-D5
Rt#-99E SE MCLOUGHLIN BLVD
CLACKAMAS CO OR 199-D3
CLACKAMAS CO OR 321-J2
GLADSTONE OR 199-D3
MILWAUKIE OR 317-J5
MILWAUKIE OR 321-J2
OREGON CITY OR 199-D3
PORTLAND OR 317-J5
Rt#-99E PACIFIC BLVD
ALBANY OR 326-F7
LINN CO OR 326-F7
MILLERSBURG OR 326-F7
Rt#-99E PACIFIC HWY
MARION CO OR 205-B2
WOODBURN OR 205-B1
Rt#-99E PACIFIC HWY E
AURORA OR 199-B7
BARLOW OR 199-C6
CANBY OR 199-C6
CLACKAMAS CO OR 199-D4
GERVAIS OR 205-B1
GLADSTONE OR 199-D4
Hayesville OR 204-D5
Hayesville OR 323-E5
HUBBARD OR 205-B1
MARION CO OR 199-B7
MARION CO OR 205-A3
MARION CO OR 323-E5
OREGON CITY OR 199-D4
SALEM OR 323-E5
WOODBURN OR 205-B1
Rt#-99E SALEM EXWY
KEIZER OR 323-C6
SALEM OR 323-C6
Rt#-99E SALEM PKWY
KEIZER OR 323-A8
MARION CO OR 323-A8
SALEM OR 322-J8
SALEM OR 323-A8
Rt#-99W E 1ST ST
NEWBERG OR 198-D5
Rt#-99W 3RD ST
LAFAYETTE OR 198-B6
Rt#-99W 3RD ST W
CORVALLIS OR 207-A7
CORVALLIS OR 327-G14
Rt#-99W 4TH ST W
CORVALLIS OR 327-H9
Rt#-99W 5TH AV
MONROE OR 133-B2
Rt#-99W NW ADAMS ST
MCMINNVILLE OR 198-A7
Rt#-99W SW ADAMS ST
MCMINNVILLE OR 198-A7
Rt#-99W NE BAKER ST
MCMINNVILLE OR 198-A7
Rt#-99W SE BAKER ST
MCMINNVILLE OR 198-A7
Rt#-99W SW BARBUR BLVD
PORTLAND OR 199-B3
PORTLAND OR 316-E3
PORTLAND OR 317-E2
PORTLAND OR 320-A1
TIGARD OR 199-B3
Rt#-99W E HANCOCK ST
NEWBERG OR 198-D5
Rt#-99W W HANCOCK ST
NEWBERG OR 198-D5
Rt#-99W HERBERT HOOVER HWY
NEWBERG OR 198-D5
YAMHILL CO OR 198-D5
Rt#-99W N HIGHWAY 99 W
DUNDEE OR 198-C6
YAMHILL CO OR 198-D6
Rt#-99W NE HIGHWAY 99 W
MCMINNVILLE OR 198-B7
YAMHILL CO OR 198-B7
Rt#-99W SW HIGHWAY 99 W
MCMINNVILLE OR 198-A7
MCMINNVILLE OR 204-B1
YAMHILL CO OR 198-A7
YAMHILL CO OR 204-B1
Rt#-99W SW NAITO PKWY
PORTLAND OR 317-F1
Rt#-99W N PACIFIC AV
MONMOUTH OR 204-B7
POLK CO OR 204-B7
Rt#-99W S PACIFIC AV
MONMOUTH OR 204-B7
Rt#-99W PACIFIC HWY W
ADAIR VILLAGE OR 207-B3
AMITY OR 204-B5
BENTON CO OR 133-B2
BENTON CO OR 207-B3
BENTON CO OR 327-H7
CORVALLIS OR 207-B3
CORVALLIS OR 327-H7
JUNCTION CITY OR 210-A5
KING CITY OR 199-B3
LANE CO OR 133-B2
LANE CO OR 210-A5
MONMOUTH OR 204-B5
MONROE OR 133-B2
NEWBERG OR 198-C6
POLK CO OR 204-B5
POLK CO OR 207-B3
SHERWOOD OR 199-A4
TIGARD OR 199-B3
TUALATIN OR 199-B3
WASHINGTON CO OR 199-B3
YAMHILL CO OR 198-C6
YAMHILL CO OR 204-B5
Rt#-99W PORTLAND RD
NEWBERG OR 198-D5
WASHINGTON CO OR 199-A5
YAMHILL CO OR 198-D5
YAMHILL CO OR 199-A5
Rt#-99W N RIVER ST
NEWBERG OR 198-D5
Rt#-100 2ND ST
ILWACO WA 186-A6
PACIFIC CO WA 186-A6
Rt#-100 FORT CANBY RD
PACIFIC CO WA 186-A7
Rt#-100 HIGHWAY
ILWACO WA 186-A6
PACIFIC CO WA 186-A6
Rt#-100 NORTH HEAD RD
ILWACO WA 186-A6
PACIFIC CO WA 186-A6
Rt#-100 ROBERT GRAY DR
PACIFIC CO WA 186-A6
Rt#-100 SPRUCE ST E
ILWACO WA 186-A6
Rt#-100 SPRUCE ST W
ILWACO WA 186-A6
Rt#-101 HIGHWAY
BRITISH COLUMBIA BC 92-B1
BRITISH COLUMBIA BC 93-A1
Gibson BC 93-B3
PACIFIC CO WA 186-C4
POWELL RIVER BC 92-C1
Sechelt BC 93-A2
Rt#-102 DAYTON-AIRPORT RD
MASON CO WA 179-D2
MASON CO WA 180-A2
Rt#-103 BAY AV
Ocean Park WA 186-A2
Rt#-103 OCEAN BEACH HWY
LONG BEACH WA 186-A5
PACIFIC CO WA 186-A5
Rt#-103 PACIFIC HWY
Ocean Park WA 186-A2
PACIFIC CO WA 186-A3
Rt#-103 PACIFIC HWY S
LONG BEACH WA 186-A5
Rt#-103 PACIFIC HWY W
LONG BEACH WA 186-A5
Rt#-103 SANDRIDGE RD
Ocean Park WA 186-A2
PACIFIC CO WA 186-A1
Rt#-103 STACKPOLE RD
PACIFIC CO WA 183-B7
PACIFIC CO WA 186-A1
Rt#-104 NE 205TH ST
EDMONDS WA 171-B6
MOUNTLAKE TERRACE WA 171-B6
SHORELINE WA 171-B6
Rt#-104 244TH ST SW
MOUNTLAKE TERRACE WA 171-B6
SHORELINE WA 171-B6
Rt#-104 BALLINGER WY NE
LAKE FOREST PARK WA 171-B6
SHORELINE WA 171-B6
Rt#-104 EDMONDS WY
EDMONDS WA 171-A6
SNOHOMISH CO WA 171-A6
WOODWAY WA 171-A6
Rt#-104 HIGHWAY
JEFFERSON CO WA 109-C1
JEFFERSON CO WA 170-A3
Kingston WA 170-D5
KITSAP CO WA 170-C4
Rt#-104 LAKE BALLINGER WY
EDMONDS WA 171-B6
MOUNTLAKE TERRACE WA 171-B6
SHORELINE WA 171-B6
Rt#-105 N BOONE ST
ABERDEEN WA 178-B7
Rt#-105 S BOONE ST
ABERDEEN WA 117-A1
ABERDEEN WA 178-B7
GRAYS HARBOR CO WA 117-A1
Rt#-105 DOCK ST
WESTPORT WA 298-G11
Rt#-105 S FORREST AV
WESTPORT WA 298-G14
Rt#-105 HIGHWAY
ABERDEEN WA 117-A1
GRAYS HARBOR CO WA 117-A1
GRAYS HARBOR CO WA 183-D1
PACIFIC CO WA 117-A1
PACIFIC CO WA 183-B3
RAYMOND WA 117-A1
WESTPORT WA 183-B2
WESTPORT WA 298-G11

INDEX

Rt#-105 MONTESANO ST
STREET INDEX
Rt#-205 CATLOW VALLEY RD 411

STREET
City State Page-Grid

Rt#-105 MONTESANO ST
WESTPORT WA 298-H11
Rt#-105 OCEAN AV
WESTPORT WA 298-F13
Rt#-105 PARK AV
RAYMOND WA 117-A1
Rt#-105 WESTPORT RD
GRAYS HARBOR CO WA 117-A1
Rt#-106 HIGHWAY
MASON CO WA 173-D5
MASON CO WA 180-A1
Rt#-107 S BANK RD
GRAYS HARBOR CO WA 117-A1
Rt#-107 HIGHWAY
GRAYS HARBOR CO WA 178-D7
MONTESANO WA 178-D7
Rt#-107 SOUTH BANK RD
GRAYS HARBOR CO WA 178-D7
Rt#-108 ELMA-MCCLEARY RD
GRAYS HARBOR CO WA 179-C6
MCCLEARY WA 179-C6
Rt#-108 HIGHWAY
GRAYS HARBOR CO WA 179-D5
MASON CO WA 179-D5
MASON CO WA 180-A4
Rt#-108 SIMPSON AV
MCCLEARY WA 179-D6
Rt#-108 SUMMIT RD
GRAYS HARBOR CO WA 179-D6
MCCLEARY WA 179-D6
Rt#-109 5TH AV
Taholah WA 172-B6
Rt#-109 EMERSON AV
HOQUIAM WA 178-A7
Rt#-109 FIR LP
Taholah WA 172-B6
Rt#-109 HIGHWAY
GRAYS HARBOR CO WA 172-B7
GRAYS HARBOR CO WA 177-B1
HOQUIAM WA 177-D7
HOQUIAM WA 178-A7
Taholah WA 172-B7
Rt#-109 NFD RD 7412
CHELAN CO WA 238-C1
Rt#-110 LA PUSH RD
CLALLAM CO WA 169-C1
FORKS WA 169-C1
Rt#-110 MORA RD
CLALLAM CO WA 169-B2
Rt#-112 3RD ST
Neah Bay WA 100-B2
Rt#-112 HIGHWAY
CLALLAM CO WA 100-B2
CLALLAM CO WA 162-C1
CLALLAM CO WA 163-A2
CLALLAM CO WA 164-A4
CLALLAM CO WA 165-A6
Neah Bay WA 100-B2
Rt#-112 NEAH BAY RD
CLALLAM CO WA 100-B2
Neah Bay WA 100-B2
Rt#-112 PIEDMONT RD
CLALLAM CO WA 164-C5
CLALLAM CO WA 165-A6
Rt#-113 BURNT MOUNTAIN RD
CLALLAM CO WA 163-B6
Rt#-115 DAMON RD
GRAYS HARBOR CO WA 177-B6
OCEAN SHORES WA 177-B6
Rt#-115 N JETTY RD
GRAYS HARBOR CO WA 177-B6
Rt#-116 FLAGLER RD
Hadlock-Irondale WA 170-B1
JEFFERSON CO WA 167-B7
JEFFERSON CO WA 170-B1
Rt#-116 NESS CORNER RD
Hadlock-Irondale WA 170-A1
Rt#-116 NESS RD
Hadlock-Irondale WA 170-A1
JEFFERSON CO WA 170-A1
Rt#-116 OAK BAY RD
Hadlock-Irondale WA 170-A1
JEFFERSON CO WA 170-A1
Rt#-117 TUMWATER ACCESS RD
CLALLAM CO WA 261-C5
PORT ANGELES WA 261-C5
Rt#-119 HIGHWAY
MASON CO WA 109-B2
MASON CO WA 173-A6
Rt#-119 LAKE CUSHMAN RD
MASON CO WA 109-B2
MASON CO WA 173-A6
Rt#-121 93RD AV SW
THURSTON CO WA 184-C1
TUMWATER WA 184-C1
Rt#-121 MAYTOWN RD SW
THURSTON CO WA 184-C2
Rt#-121 TILLEY RD SW
THURSTON CO WA 184-C2
Rt#-122 HARMONY RD
LEWIS CO WA 118-A2
MOSSYROCK WA 118-A2
Rt#-122 SILVERCREEK RD
LEWIS CO WA 118-A2
Rt#-123 HIGHWAY
LEWIS CO WA 185-D5
PIERCE CO WA 119-A1
PIERCE CO WA 185-D4
Rt#-124 W 2ND ST
WAITSBURG WA 122-A2
WALLA WALLA CO WA 122-A2
Rt#-124 HIGHWAY
PRESCOTT WA 121-C2
WALLA WALLA CO WA 121-C2
WALLA WALLA CO WA 122-A2
Rt#-124 ICE HARBOR DR
WALLA WALLA CO WA 121-B3
Rt#-124 LOWER WAITSBURG RD
WALLA WALLA CO WA 122-A2
Rt#-124 MAIN ST
WAITSBURG WA 122-A2
Rt#-124 SECOND ST
PRESCOTT WA 121-C2
WALLA WALLA CO WA 121-C2
Rt#-125 13TH AV N
WALLA WALLA WA 344-J5
WALLA WALLA CO WA 344-J5
Rt#-125 8TH AV N
WALLA WALLA WA 344-J8
Rt#-125 9TH AV S
WALLA WALLA WA 344-J8
WALLA WALLA WA 345-A9
Rt#-125 HIGHWAY
COLLEGE PLACE WA 344-H11
WALLA WALLA WA 344-H5
WALLA WALLA WA 345-A10
WALLA WALLA CO WA 121-C2
Rt#-125 HIGHWAY
WALLA WALLA CO WA 344-G1
Rt#-125 W PINE ST
WALLA WALLA WA 344-J7
Rt#-126 W 3RD ST
CROOK CO OR 213-D5
PRINEVILLE OR 213-D5
Rt#-126 W 11TH AV
EUGENE OR 215-A2
EUGENE OR 329-B6
LANE CO OR 215-A2
Rt#-126 Bus S A ST
LANE CO OR 330-J7
SPRINGFIELD OR 330-J7
SPRINGFIELD OR 331-A7
Rt#-126 BELKNAP SPRINGS HWY
LANE CO OR 134-B2
LINN CO OR 134-B2
Rt#-126 Bus FRANKLIN BLVD
LANE CO OR 330-F7
Rt#-126 EUGENE-SPRNGFIELD HWY
EUGENE OR 330-E5
LANE CO OR 331-G6
SPRINGFIELD OR 330-E5
SPRINGFIELD OR 331-C5
Rt#-126 SE EVERGREEN AV
REDMOND OR 212-D5
Rt#-126 FLORENCE-EUGENE HWY
FLORENCE OR 214-C2
LANE CO OR 132-C3
LANE CO OR 133-A3
LANE CO OR 214-C2
LANE CO OR 215-A2
VENETA OR 133-A3
Rt#-126 S GARFIELD ST
EUGENE OR 329-G6
Rt#-126 SW HIGHLAND AV
DESCHUTES CO OR 212-D5
REDMOND OR 212-D5
Rt#-126 MAIN ST
LANE CO OR 330-H7
SPRINGFIELD OR 215-D2
SPRINGFIELD OR 330-H7
SPRINGFIELD OR 331-A7
Rt#-126 MCKENZIE HWY
DESCHUTES CO OR 211-D5
DESCHUTES CO OR 212-A5
LANE CO OR 133-C3
LANE CO OR 134-B2
LANE CO OR 215-D2
LINN CO OR 134-B2
REDMOND OR 212-D5
SISTERS OR 211-D5
SPRINGFIELD OR 215-D2
Rt#-126 OCHOCO HWY
CROOK CO OR 213-A5
DESCHUTES CO OR 212-D5
DESCHUTES CO OR 213-A5
PRINEVILLE OR 213-B6
REDMOND OR 212-D5
REDMOND OR 213-A5
Rt#-126 OWSLEY GRADE RD
GARFIELD CO WA 122-B2
Rt#-127 HIGHWAY
GARFIELD CO WA 122-B1
WHITMAN CO WA 122-B1
Rt#-128 DOWN RIVER RD
LEWISTON ID 250-B4
Rt#-128 HIGHWAY
ASOTIN CO WA 250-B4
CLARKSTON WA 250-B4
LEWISTON ID 250-B4
WHITMAN CO WA 250-B4
Rt#-128 OLD SPIRAL HWY
LEWISTON ID 250-B4
Rt#-128 WAWAWAI RIVER RD
WHITMAN CO WA 250-B4
Rt#-129 1ST ST
ASOTIN WA 250-B5
Rt#-129 5TH ST
ASOTIN CO WA 250-B4
CLARKSTON WA 250-B4
Rt#-129 6TH ST
CLARKSTON WA 250-B4
Rt#-129 DIAGONAL ST
CLARKSTON WA 250-B4
Rt#-129 HIGHWAY
ASOTIN WA 250-B5
ASOTIN CO WA 122-C3
ASOTIN CO WA 123-A3
ASOTIN CO WA 250-B5
CLARKSTON WA 250-B4
Vineland WA 250-B5
Rt#-129 RIVERSIDE DR
ASOTIN CO WA 250-B5
Vineland WA 250-B5
Rt#-129 WASHINGTON ST
ASOTIN WA 250-B5
Rt#-131 CISPUS RD
LEWIS CO WA 118-C2
Rt#-131 WOODS CREEK RD
LEWIS CO WA 118-C2
Rt#-138 E DIAMOND LAKE HWY
DOUGLAS CO OR 223-D7
KLAMATH CO OR 142-B2
KLAMATH CO OR 223-D7
Rt#-138 NE DIAMOND LAKE BLVD
ROSEBURG OR 221-C4
ROSEBURG OR 334-H7
Rt#-138 ELKTON-SUTHERLIN HWY
DOUGLAS CO OR 141-A1
DOUGLAS CO OR 221-C1
ELKTON OR 141-A1
SUTHERLIN OR 221-C1
Rt#-138 W ELKTN-SUTHERLIN HWY
DOUGLAS CO OR 221-C1
SUTHERLIN OR 221-C1
Rt#-138 SW HARVARD BLVD
ROSEBURG OR 334-F7
Rt#-138 W HARVARD BLVD
ROSEBURG OR 334-E7
Rt#-138 NORTH UMPQUA HWY
DOUGLAS CO OR 141-C2
DOUGLAS CO OR 221-D4
DOUGLAS CO OR 222-B3
DOUGLAS CO OR 223-A4
ROSEBURG OR 221-D4
Rt#-138 SE OAK AV
ROSEBURG OR 334-F7
Rt#-138 SW OAK AV
ROSEBURG OR 334-F7
Rt#-138 SE PINE ST
ROSEBURG OR 334-G7
Rt#-138 SE STEPHENS ST
ROSEBURG OR 334-F8
Rt#-138 SW WASHINGTON AV
ROSEBURG OR 334-F7
Rt#-139 HIGHWAY
MODOC CO CA 151-A3
SISKIYOU CO CA 151-A3
Rt#-140 4TH ST N
LAKE CO OR 152-A2
LAKEVIEW OR 152-A2
Rt#-140 GREEN SPRINGS HWY
KLAMATH CO OR 338-B12
Rt#-140 KLAMATH FLLS-LKVW HWY
Altamont OR 339-C11
KLAMATH CO OR 150-C2
KLAMATH CO OR 151-A1
KLAMATH CO OR 339-E12
LAKE CO OR 151-C2
LAKE CO OR 152-A2
Rt#-140 KLAMATH FLLS-MALN HWY
Altamont OR 339-D14
KLAMATH CO OR 235-D5
KLAMATH CO OR 339-D14
Rt#-140 S KLAMATH FALLS HWY
Altamont OR 235-D5
KLAMATH CO OR 235-C5
KLAMATH CO OR 338-D12
KLAMATH FALLS OR 235-C5
KLAMATH FALLS OR 338-C12
Rt#-140 LAKE OF THE WOODS HWY
JACKSON CO OR 149-C1
JACKSON CO OR 150-A1
JACKSON CO OR 230-D6
KLAMATH CO OR 150-B1
KLAMATH CO OR 231-A6
KLAMATH CO OR 235-A1
KLAMATH CO OR 338-A10
KLAMATH FALLS OR 235-A1
KLAMATH FALLS OR 338-B12
White City OR 230-D6
Rt#-140 NEVADA STATE ROUTE
HARNEY CO OR 153-A3
HUMBOLDT CO NV 153-C3
Rt#-140 WARNER HWY
HARNEY CO OR 153-A3
LAKE CO OR 152-A2
LAKE CO OR 153-A3
Rt#-141 E JEWETT BLVD
WHITE SALMON WA 195-D4
Rt#-141 W JEWETT BLVD
KLICKITAT CO WA 195-D4
WHITE SALMON WA 195-D4
Rt#-141 HIGHWAY
BINGEN WA 195-D5
KLICKITAT CO WA 119-A3
KLICKITAT CO WA 195-D1
WHITE SALMON WA 195-D4
Rt#-141 OAK ST
BINGEN WA 195-D5
Rt#-141 SW PUCKER HUDDLE RD
KLICKITAT CO WA 195-D4
Rt#-142 E BROADWAY
GOLDENDALE WA 127-C1
KLICKITAT CO WA 127-C1
Rt#-142 W BROADWAY
GOLDENDALE WA 127-C1
KLICKITAT CO WA 127-C1
Rt#-142 HIGHWAY
KLICKITAT CO WA 127-B1
KLICKITAT CO WA 196-D2
Rt#-150 CHELAN FALLS RD
CHELAN CO WA 236-D3
Rt#-150 COLUMBIA ST
CHELAN WA 236-D3
Rt#-150 HIGHWAY
CHELAN WA 236-C3
CHELAN CO WA 236-C3
Rt#-150 NORTHSHORE RD
CHELAN CO WA 236-C2
Rt#-150 PARK RD
CHELAN WA 236-C3
Rt#-150 WAPATO WY
CHELAN CO WA 236-B2
Rt#-150 WILLWORTH RD
CHELAN CO WA 236-D3
Rt#-150 WOODIN AV
CHELAN WA 236-D3
Rt#-153 HIGHWAY
OKANOGAN CO WA 104-B3
OKANOGAN CO WA 112-B1
Rt#-155 COLUMBIA AV
COULEE DAM WA 237-C2
Rt#-155 COULEE BLVD
ELECTRIC CITY WA 237-C3
GRANT CO WA 237-C3
Rt#-155 GRAND COULEE AV
ELECTRIC CITY WA 237-C3
GRAND COULEE WA 237-C3
GRANT CO WA 237-C3
Rt#-155 GRAND COULEE HWY
GRAND COULEE WA 237-C3
Rt#-155 HIGHWAY
COULEE DAM WA 237-C2
GRAND COULEE WA 237-C3
GRANT CO WA 113-A1
GRANT CO WA 237-C2
NESPELEM WA 105-A3
OKANOGAN CO WA 104-C3
OKANOGAN CO WA 105-A3
OMAK WA 104-C3
Rt#-155 OMAK AV E
OKANOGAN CO WA 104-C3
OMAK WA 104-C3
Rt#-155 RIVER DR
COULEE DAM WA 237-C2
OKANOGAN CO WA 237-C2
Rt#-155 RIVER RD
ELMER CITY WA 237-C1
OKANOGAN CO WA 237-C1
Rt#-160 HIGHWAY
KITSAP CO WA 174-D4
Rt#-160 SE SEDGWICK RD
KITSAP CO WA 174-C4
PORT ORCHARD WA 174-B4
Rt#-161 16TH AV S
FEDERAL WAY WA 182-B1
Rt#-161 31ST AV SW
PUYALLUP WA 182-B4
Rt#-161 EATONVILLE CUT-OFF RD
EATONVILLE WA 118-B1
Rt#-161 EATONVILLE CUT-OFF RD
PIERCE CO WA 118-B1
Rt#-161 EATONVILLE-LA GRANDE
EATONVILLE WA 118-B1
PIERCE CO WA 118-B1
Rt#-161 ENCHANTED PKWY
FEDERAL WAY WA 182-B1
Rt#-161 ENCHANTED PKWY S
EDGEWOOD WA 182-B2
FEDERAL WAY WA 182-B2
KING CO WA 182-B2
MILTON WA 182-B2
Rt#-161 HIGHWAY
SISKIYOU CO CA 150-C3
Rt#-161 LARSON ST
EATONVILLE WA 118-B1
Rt#-161 MASHELL AV S
EATONVILLE WA 118-B1
Rt#-161 MERIDIAN AV E
EATONVILLE WA 118-B1
PIERCE CO WA 118-B1
PIERCE CO WA 182-B7
Rt#-161 MERIDIAN E
EDGEWOOD WA 182-B3
MILTON WA 182-B3
PIERCE CO WA 118-B1
PIERCE CO WA 182-B6
PUYALLUP WA 182-B3
Rt#-161 N MERIDIAN
PUYALLUP WA 182-B3
Rt#-161 S MERIDIAN
PUYALLUP WA 182-B4
Rt#-161 STATE LINE RD
SISKIYOU CO CA 150-C3
SISKIYOU CO CA 151-A3
Rt#-161 WASHINGTON AV N
EATONVILLE WA 118-B1
PIERCE CO WA 118-B1
Rt#-161 WASHINGTON AV S
EATONVILLE WA 118-B1
Rt#-162 5TH ST
KAMIAH ID 123-C2
Rt#-162 8TH AV
NEZPERCE ID 123-C2
Rt#-162 BRIDGE ST SW
ORTING WA 182-C5
Rt#-162 HARMAN WY S
ORTING WA 182-C5
PIERCE CO WA 182-C5
Rt#-162 HIGHWAY 162ND E
SOUTH PRAIRIE WA 182-D4
Rt#-162 HIGHWAY 162ND W
SOUTH PRAIRIE WA 182-D5
Rt#-162 HILL ST
KAMIAH ID 123-C2
Rt#-162 LAWYERS CANYON RD
IDAHO CO ID 123-C3
LEWIS CO ID 123-C3
NEZPERCE ID 123-C3
Rt#-162 OAK ST
NEZPERCE ID 123-C2
Rt#-162 PIONEER WY
ORTING WA 182-B5
PIERCE CO WA 182-B5
SOUTH PRAIRIE WA 182-B5
SUMNER WA 182-B5
Rt#-162 S PIONEER WY
PIERCE CO WA 182-C6
Rt#-162 W PIONEER WY
PIERCE CO WA 182-D5
Rt#-162 SEVEN MILE RD
IDAHO CO ID 123-C3
KAMIAH ID 123-C3
LEWIS CO ID 123-C3
Rt#-162 TRAM RD
IDAHO CO ID 123-C3
Rt#-162 VALLEY AV
PIERCE CO WA 182-B3
SUMNER WA 182-B3
Rt#-162 WASHINGTON AV N
ORTING WA 182-C5
Rt#-162 WASHINGTON AV S
ORTING WA 182-C5
Rt#-163 PEARL ST
RUSTON WA 181-C2
TACOMA WA 181-C2
Rt#-164 SE 436TH ST
KING CO WA 110-C3
KING CO WA 182-D3
Rt#-164 SE 436TH WY
ENUMCLAW WA 110-C3
KING CO WA 110-C3
Rt#-164 AUBURN ENUMCLAW RD
AUBURN WA 182-C2
KING CO WA 182-C2
Rt#-164 AUBURN WY N
AUBURN WA 182-C1
Rt#-164 AUBURN WY S
AUBURN WA 182-C1
Rt#-164 GRIFFIN AV
ENUMCLAW WA 110-C3
KING CO WA 110-C3
Rt#-165 BURNETT-FAIRFAX
BUCKLEY WA 182-D5
CARBONADO WA 182-D5
PIERCE CO WA 182-D5
WILKESON WA 182-D5
Rt#-165 CHURCH ST
WILKESON WA 182-D5
Rt#-165 HIGHWAY
PIERCE CO WA 118-C1
Rt#-165 MOUNTAIN MEADOWS RD
PIERCE CO WA 118-C1
PIERCE CO WA 185-A2
Rt#-165 MOWICH SECTION
CARBONADO WA 182-D6
PIERCE CO WA 110-C3
PIERCE CO WA 118-C1
PIERCE CO WA 182-D6
Rt#-166 BAY ST
PORT ORCHARD WA 174-B4
PORT ORCHARD WA 270-H14
Rt#-166 BETHEL RD
PORT ORCHARD WA 174-B4
PORT ORCHARD WA 270-J14
Rt#-166 HIGHWAY
KITSAP CO WA 174-B4
PORT ORCHARD WA 174-B4
PORT ORCHARD WA 270-F14
Rt#-166 SE MILE HILL DR
East Port Orchard WA 174-C4
KITSAP CO WA 174-C4
PORT ORCHARD WA 174-B4
Rt#-167 BAY ST
TACOMA WA 182-A2
Rt#-167 FRWY
PACIFIC WA 182-B2
PIERCE CO WA 182-B2
PUYALLUP WA 182-B3
SUMNER WA 182-B2
Rt#-167 HIGHWAY
TACOMA WA 182-A2
Rt#-167 RAINIER AV S
RENTON WA 175-C5
Rt#-167 RIVER RD
PIERCE CO WA 182-A3
PUYALLUP WA 182-A3
TACOMA WA 182-A3
Rt#-167 VALLEY FRWY
ALGONA WA 182-B2
AUBURN WA 175-B7
AUBURN WA 182-B2
KENT WA 175-B7
KENT WA 291-J7
KING CO WA 175-B7
PACIFIC WA 182-B2
RENTON WA 175-B7
Rt#-169 3RD AV
BLACK DIAMOND WA 110-C3
Rt#-169 264TH AV SE
KING CO WA 110-C3
Rt#-169 ENUMCLW BLK DMND RD
BLACK DIAMOND WA 110-C3
KING CO WA 110-C3
Rt#-169 MAPLE VLY BLK DMND RD
BLACK DIAMOND WA 110-C3
KING CO WA 110-C3
MAPLE VALLEY WA 110-C3
MAPLE VALLEY WA 175-D7
MAPLE VALLEY WA 176-A7
Rt#-169 MAPLE VALLEY HWY
KING CO WA 175-C5
RENTON WA 175-C5
Rt#-169 PORTER ST
ENUMCLAW WA 110-C3
KING CO WA 110-C3
Rt#-169 RENTON MAPLE VLY RD
KING CO WA 175-D5
KING CO WA 176-A6
MAPLE VALLEY WA 175-D5
Rt#-169 WASHINGTON AV
ENUMCLAW WA 110-C3
Rt#-170 E 1ST ST
GRANT CO WA 121-A1
WARDEN WA 121-A1
Rt#-170 W 1ST ST
WARDEN WA 121-A1
Rt#-170 ROAD 8-SE
GRANT CO WA 121-A1
WARDEN WA 121-A1
Rt#-171 BROADWAY AV
GRANT CO WA 242-C3
MOSES LAKE WA 242-C3
Rt#-172 14 RD NE
DOUGLAS CO WA 112-C1
Rt#-172 14 RD NW
DOUGLAS CO WA 112-B1
Rt#-172 C RD NW
DOUGLAS CO WA 112-B1
Rt#-172 FIFTH AV
DOUGLAS CO WA 112-C1
MANSFIELD WA 112-C1
Rt#-173 10TH ST
BRIDGEPORT WA 112-C1
Rt#-173 17TH ST
BRIDGEPORT WA 112-C1
Rt#-173 BRIDGE ST N
BREWSTER WA 104-B3
Rt#-173 BRIDGE ST S
BREWSTER WA 104-B3
Rt#-173 COLUMBIA AV
BRIDGEPORT WA 112-C1
Rt#-173 FOSTER CREEK AV
BRIDGEPORT WA 112-C1
Rt#-173 HIGHWAY
BREWSTER WA 104-B3
BRIDGEPORT WA 112-C1
DOUGLAS CO WA 104-B3
DOUGLAS CO WA 112-C1
OKANOGAN CO WA 104-B3
Rt#-173 MAPLE ST
BRIDGEPORT WA 112-C1
DOUGLAS CO WA 112-C1
Rt#-174 BRIDGEPORT HWY
GRAND COULEE WA 237-C3
Rt#-174 CROWN POINT RD
DOUGLAS CO WA 237-C2
Rt#-174 GRAND COULEE AV E
GRAND COULEE WA 237-C3
GRANT CO WA 237-C3
Rt#-174 GRAND COULEE AV W
GRAND COULEE WA 237-C3
Rt#-174 HIGHWAY
DOUGLAS CO WA 112-C1
DOUGLAS CO WA 113-A1
DOUGLAS CO WA 237-C2
GRAND COULEE WA 237-C3
GRANT CO WA 237-C2
LINCOLN CO WA 113-B1
LINCOLN CO WA 237-C3
Rt#-181 68TH AV S
KENT WA 175-B7
KENT WA 291-H5
Rt#-181 WASHINGTON AV N
KENT WA 175-B7
Rt#-181 WASHINGTON AV S
KENT WA 175-B7
Rt#-181 WEST VALLEY HWY
KENT WA 291-H2
TUKWILA WA 289-J5
TUKWILA WA 291-H2
Rt#-193 WAWAWAI RIVER RD
WHITMAN CO WA 122-C2
WHITMAN CO WA 250-A4
Rt#-194 ALMOTA RD
WHITMAN CO WA 122-B1
Rt#-194 GOOSE CREEK RD
WHITMAN CO WA 122-C1
Rt#-194 WAWAWAI-PULLMAN RD
WHITMAN CO WA 249-A5
Rt#-194 WILBUR GULCH RD
WHITMAN CO WA 122-C1
WHITMAN CO WA 249-A5
Rt#-200 HIGHWAY
BONNER CO ID 107-C3
BONNER CO ID 244-B1
CLARK FORK ID 107-C3
EAST HOPE ID 244-D2
HOPE ID 244-C2
KOOTENAI ID 244-A1
Rt#-200 HIGHWAY
PONDERAY ID 244-A1
SANDERS CO MT 107-C3
Rt#-200 LIGHTNING CREEK RD
CLARK FORK ID 107-C3
Rt#-200 RAILROAD AV
KOOTENAI ID 244-A1
Rt#-201 SW 4TH AV
ONTARIO OR 139-A3
Rt#-201 ADRIAN BLVD
NYSSA OR 139-A3
Rt#-201 OLDS FRRY-ONTARIO HWY
MALHEUR CO OR 139-A2
ONTARIO OR 139-A2
Rt#-201 SUCCOR CREEK HWY
ADRIAN OR 147-A1
MALHEUR CO OR 139-A3
MALHEUR CO OR 147-A1
NYSSA OR 139-A3
Rt#-202 131ST AV NE
BOTHELL WA 171-C6
WOODINVILLE WA 171-C6
Rt#-202 NE 145TH ST
KING CO WA 171-D7
WOODINVILLE WA 171-C7
Rt#-202 156TH AV NE
KING CO WA 171-D7
REDMOND WA 171-D7
WOODINVILLE WA 171-D7
Rt#-202 164TH AV NE
REDMOND WA 175-D1
Rt#-202 BENDIGO BLVD N
NORTH BEND WA 176-C4
SNOQUALMIE WA 176-C4
Rt#-202 BENDIGO BLVD S
NORTH BEND WA 176-C5
Rt#-202 CLEVELAND ST
REDMOND WA 175-D1
Rt#-202 FALL CTY-SNQUALMIE RD
KING CO WA 176-B3
SNOQUALMIE WA 176-B3
Rt#-202 SE FRONT ST
ASTORIA OR 300-D7
CLATSOP CO OR 300-D7
Rt#-202 W MARINE DR
ASTORIA OR 300-A6
Rt#-202 NEHALEM HWY
CLATSOP CO OR 117-B3
CLATSOP CO OR 188-D3
CLATSOP CO OR 300-F8
COLUMBIA CO OR 117-B3
Rt#-202 OLNEY AV
ASTORIA OR 300-C7
Rt#-202 RAILROAD AV SE
KING CO WA 176-C4
SNOQUALMIE WA 176-C4
Rt#-202 REDMOND FALL CITY RD
KING CO WA 175-D1
KING CO WA 176-A1
REDMOND WA 175-D1
SAMMAMISH WA 175-D1
KING CO WA 176-A2
KING CO WA 176-A2
Rt#-202 SE REDMND FLL CTY RD
KING CO WA 176-B3
Rt#-202 NE REDMOND WY
REDMOND WA 175-D1
Rt#-202 WDINVLLE REDMOND RD
KING CO WA 171-D7
REDMOND WA 171-D7
WOODINVILLE WA 171-D7
REDMOND WA 171-D7
Rt#-202 WOODINVILLE RDMOND RD
REDMOND WA 175-D1
Rt#-202 WOODINVILLE SNHMSH RD
WOODINVILLE WA 171-C6
Rt#-203 E BEAKMAN ST
UNION OR 130-B2
Rt#-203 CARNATION-DUVALL RD N
DUVALL WA 110-C1
KING CO WA 110-C1
KING CO WA 176-A1
Rt#-203 DUVALL-MONROE RD
KING CO WA 110-C1
SNOHOMISH CO WA 110-C1
Rt#-203 DUVALL-MONROE RD NE
DUVALL WA 110-C1
KING CO WA 110-C1
Rt#-203 FALL CTY-CARNATION RD
CARNATION WA 176-B2
KING CO WA 176-B2
KING CO WA 176-B3
Rt#-203 LA GRANDE-BAKER HWY
UNION OR 130-A2
UNION CO OR 130-A2
Rt#-203 N LEWIS ST
MONROE WA 110-C1
Rt#-203 S LEWIS ST
MONROE WA 110-C1
SNOHOMISH CO WA 110-C1
Rt#-203 MAIN ST
DUVALL WA 110-C1
Rt#-203 N MAIN ST
UNION OR 130-B2
Rt#-203 MEDICAL SPRINGS HWY
BAKER CO OR 130-B3
UNION OR 130-B2
UNION CO OR 130-B2
Rt#-203 E MEDICAL SPRINGS HWY
UNION OR 130-B2
Rt#-203 TOLT AV
CARNATION WA 176-B2
KING CO WA 176-B2
Rt#-204 DIVISION ST
ELGIN OR 130-A1
UNION CO OR 130-A1
Rt#-204 HIGHWAY
SNOHOMISH CO WA 171-D1
Rt#-204 WESTON-ELGIN HWY
UMATILLA CO OR 129-C1
UMATILLA CO OR 130-A1
UNION CO OR 130-A1
Rt#-205 CATLOW VALLEY RD
HARNEY CO OR 153-B1

INDEX

STREET
City   State   Page-Grid

Rt#-205 FRENCHGLEN HWY
HARNEY CO OR 145-B1
Rt#-206 ARMSWORTHY ST
WASCO CO OR 127-C1
Rt#-206 BAYARD ST
CONDON OR 128-A2
Rt#-206 E BAYARD ST
CONDON OR 128-A2
Rt#-206 CELILO-WASCO HWY
SHERMAN CO OR 127-C1
Rt#-206 E MT SPOKANE PRK DR
SPOKANE CO WA 114-C1
SPOKANE CO WA 246-D1
SPOKANE CO WA 247-A1
SPOKANE CO WA 347-H5
Rt#-206 N MT SPOKANE PRK DR
SPOKANE CO WA 114-C1
Rt#-206 HIGHWAY
SPOKANE CO WA 114-C1
Rt#-206 MAIN ST
HEPPNER OR 128-C2
Rt#-206 W WALNUT ST
CONDON OR 128-A2
GILLIAM CO OR 128-A2
Rt#-206 WASCO-HEPPNER HWY
CONDON OR 128-A2
GILLIAM CO OR 128-A2
HEPPNER OR 128-B2
MORROW CO OR 128-B2
SHERMAN CO OR 127-C2
SHERMAN CO OR 128-A2
WASCO CO OR 127-C2
Rt#-207 NW 11TH ST
HERMISTON OR 129-A1
Rt#-207 SW 11TH ST
HERMISTON OR 129-A1
UMATILLA CO OR 129-A1
Rt#-207 BUTTER CREEK RD
HERMISTON OR 129-A1
UMATILLA CO OR 129-A1
Rt#-207 E ST
LEXINGTON OR 128-C2
Rt#-207 HEPPNER-SPRAY HWY
MORROW CO OR 128-C3
WHEELER CO OR 128-C3
WHEELER CO OR 136-C1
Rt#-207 HERMISTON HWY
HERMISTON OR 129-A1
UMATILLA CO OR 129-A1
Rt#-207 W HERMISTON AV
HERMISTON OR 129-A1
Rt#-207 HIGHWAY
CHELAN CO WA 111-C1
Rt#-207 LEXINGTON-ECHO HWY
LEXINGTON OR 128-C2
MORROW CO OR 128-C2
UMATILLA CO OR 128-C2
UMATILLA CO OR 129-A1
Rt#-207 SW LEXINGTON-ECHO HWY
UMATILLA CO OR 128-C1
UMATILLA CO OR 129-A1
Rt#-207 SERVICE CK-MTCHEL HWY
MITCHELL WA 136-A1
WHEELER CO OR 136-A1
Rt#-210 SW SCHOLLS FERRY RD
BEAVERTON OR 199-B2
TIGARD OR 199-B2
WASHINGTON CO OR 198-D3
WASHINGTON CO OR 199-B2
Rt#-211 CLACKAMAS HWY
CLACKAMAS CO OR 200-B4
ESTACADA OR 200-C5
Rt#-211 EAGLE CREEK-SANDY HWY
CLACKAMAS CO OR 200-C4
SANDY OR 200-C4
Rt#-211 HIGHWAY
PEND OREILLE CO WA 106-C3
Rt#-211 MEINIG AV
SANDY OR 200-D4
Rt#-211 E MAIN ST
MOLALLA OR 126-A3
Rt#-211 W MAIN ST
CLACKAMAS CO OR 126-A3
MOLALLA OR 126-A3
Rt#-211 WOODBURN-ESTACADA HWY
CLACKAMAS CO OR 126-A3
CLACKAMAS CO OR 200-C6
CLACKAMAS CO OR 205-D2
ESTACADA OR 200-C6
MARION CO OR 205-B1
MOLALLA OR 126-A3
WOODBURN OR 205-B1
Rt#-212 SE CARVER HWY
CLACKAMAS CO OR 200-A3
Rt#-212 CLACKAMAS HWY
CLACKAMAS CO OR 199-D3
CLACKAMAS CO OR 200-A3
Rt#-212 CLACKAMAS-BORING RD
CLACKAMAS CO OR 200-B3
Rt#-212 MAIN ST
OREGON CITY OR 199-D4
Rt#-213 NE 82ND AV
PORTLAND OR 311-G6
PORTLAND OR 315-F2
Rt#-213 SE 82ND AV
CLACKAMAS CO OR 319-D3
CLACKAMAS CO OR 319-F6
MULTNOMAH CO OR 319-F6
PORTLAND OR 315-F7
PORTLAND OR 319-F3
Rt#-213 CASCADE HWY
MARION CO OR 205-C4
Rt#-213 CASCADE HWY S
CLACKAMAS CO OR 126-A3
CLACKAMAS CO OR 199-D4
CLACKAMAS CO OR 205-D3
MARION CO OR 205-D3
MOLALLA OR 126-A3
OREGON CITY OR 199-D4
Rt#-213 SE CASCADE HWY
CLACKAMAS CO OR 199-D3
Rt#-213 LANCASTER DR
Haysville OR 323-E11
SALEM OR 204-D5
SALEM OR 323-E11
Rt#-213 W MAIN ST
SILVERTON OR 205-C4
Rt#-213 MARKET ST NE
SALEM OR 323-D11

Rt#-213 MCCLAINE ST
MARION CO OR 205-C4
SILVERTON OR 205-C4
Rt#-213 OAK ST
MARION CO OR 205-C4
SILVERTON OR 205-C4
Rt#-213 SILVERTON RD NE
Haysville OR 323-E9
MARION CO OR 205-A5
MARION CO OR 323-E9
Rt#-213 NE SILVERTON HWY
MARION CO OR 205-B4
Rt#-214 1ST ST
SILVERTON OR 205-C4
Rt#-214 N 1ST ST
SILVERTON OR 205-C4
Rt#-214 ANDERSON RD SE
MARION CO OR 205-B7
Rt#-214 C ST
SILVERTON OR 205-C4
Rt#-214 HLLSBORO-SLVERTON HWY
MARION CO OR 205-B2
MOUNT ANGEL OR 205-C3
SILVERTON OR 205-C3
WOODBURN OR 205-B2
Rt#-214 LEWIS ST
SILVERTON OR 205-C4
Rt#-214 MAIN ST
MOUNT ANGEL OR 205-C3
Rt#-214 N MAIN ST
MOUNT ANGEL OR 205-C3
Rt#-214 MOUNT HOOD AV
MARION CO OR 205-B1
WOODBURN OR 205-B1
Rt#-214 NEWBERG HWY
WOODBURN OR 205-B1
Rt#-214 SILVER FALLS HWY
MARION CO OR 205-A7
Rt#-214 SILVER FALLS HWY NE
MARION CO OR 205-C5
SILVERTON OR 205-C5
Rt#-214 SILVER FALLS HWY NW
MARION CO OR 205-B7
Rt#-214 SILVER FALLS HWY SE
MARION CO OR 205-D6
Rt#-214 SILVERTON AV
MARION CO OR 205-B2
WOODBURN OR 205-B2
Rt#-214 SILVERTON HWY
MARION CO OR 205-B2
WOODBURN OR 205-B2
Rt#-214 N WATER ST
SILVERTON OR 205-C4
Rt#-214 S WATER ST
SILVERTON OR 205-C4
Rt#-216 CHURCH ST
GRASS VALLEY OR 127-C2
Rt#-216 SHERARS BRIDGE HWY
GRASS VALLEY OR 127-B2
SHERMAN CO OR 127-B2
Rt#-216 WAPINITIA HWY
WASCO CO OR 127-A3
Rt#-217 BEAVERTON-TIGARD FRWY
BEAVERTON OR 199-B3
LAKE OSWEGO OR 199-B3
TIGARD OR 199-B3
WASHINGTON CO OR 199-B3
Rt#-218 D ST
SHANIKO OR 127-C3
Rt#-218 FOSSIL ST
ANTELOPE OR 127-C3
Rt#-218 SHANIKO-FOSSIL HWY
ANTELOPE OR 127-C3
FOSSIL OR 128-A3
SHANIKO OR 127-C3
WASCO CO OR 127-C3
WASCO CO OR 128-A3
WHEELER CO OR 128-A3
Rt#-218 WASHINGTON ST
FOSSIL OR 128-A3
Rt#-218 E 1ST ST
NEWBERG OR 198-D5
YAMHILL CO OR 198-D5
Rt#-219 W 1ST ST
NEWBERG OR 198-D5
Rt#-219 BARR-ALEX RD
WASHINGTON CO OR 198-D3
Rt#-219 BUTTEVILLE RD NE
MARION CO OR 205-B1
Rt#-219 CHURCH AV
MARION CO OR 198-D7
SAINT PAUL OR 198-D7
Rt#-219 COLLEGE ST
NEWBERG OR 198-D5
YAMHILL CO OR 198-D5
Rt#-219 N COLLEGE ST
NEWBERG OR 198-D5
Rt#-219 FRENCH PRAIRIE RD
MARION CO OR 198-D7
MARION CO OR 205-A1
Rt#-219 HILLSBORO HWY
NEWBERG OR 198-D5
WASHINGTON CO OR 198-D5
YAMHILL CO OR 198-D5
Rt#-219 SW HILLSBORO HWY
HILLSBORO OR 198-D2
WASHINGTON CO OR 198-D2
Rt#-219 HLLSBORO-SLVERTON HWY
MARION CO OR 205-B1
MARION CO OR 205-A1
Rt#-219 MAIN ST
SAINT PAUL OR 198-D7
Rt#-219 NEWBERG HWY
MARION CO OR 198-D5
WASHINGTON CO OR 198-D2
WOODBURN OR 205-B1
Rt#-219 SAINT PAUL HWY
MARION CO OR 198-D7
NEWBERG OR 198-D5
SAINT PAUL OR 198-D7
YAMHILL CO OR 198-D5
Rt#-220 FORT RD
HARRAH WA 119-C2
YAKIMA CO WA 119-C2
YAKIMA CO WA 120-C1
Rt#-220 SIGNAL PEAK RD
HARRAH WA 119-C2
Rt#-220 W WHITE SWAN RD
HARRAH WA 119-C2
Rt#-221 3RD ST
DAYTON OR 198-C7
YAMHILL CO OR 198-C7

Rt#-221 EDGEWATER ST NW
SALEM OR 322-F12
Rt#-221 HIGHWAY
BENTON CO WA 120-C3
DAYTON OR 198-C7
PROSSER WA 120-C3
YAMHILL CO OR 198-C7
Rt#-221 SALEM-DAYTON HWY NW
SALEM OR 322-E13
Rt#-221 SE SALEM-DAYTON HWY
POLK CO OR 204-D2
POLK CO OR 322-E6
YAMHILL CO OR 204-D2
Rt#-221 WALLACE RD
DAYTON OR 198-C7
YAMHILL CO OR 198-C7
YAMHILL CO OR 204-D1
Rt#-221 WALLACE RD NW
POLK CO OR 322-E8
SALEM OR 322-E8
Rt#-221 SE WALLACE RD
YAMHILL CO OR 204-D1
Rt#-223 ALFALFA-GRANGER RD
YAKIMA CO WA 120-A2
Rt#-223 DALLAS-RICKREALL HWY
DALLAS OR 204-A6
POLK CO OR 204-A6
Rt#-223 E ELLENDALE AV
DALLAS OR 204-A6
Rt#-223 SW FAIRVIEW AV
DALLAS OR 204-A6
Rt#-223 HIGHWAY
GRANGER WA 120-A2
YAKIMA CO WA 120-A2
Rt#-223 SE JEFFERSON ST
DALLAS OR 204-A6
Rt#-223 KINGS VALLEY HWY
BENTON CO WA 133-A1
DALLAS OR 204-A6
POLK CO OR 125-B3
POLK CO OR 133-B1
POLK CO OR 204-A5
Rt#-223 S MAIN ST
DALLAS OR 204-A6
Rt#-223 VAN BELLE RD
GRANGER WA 120-A2
YAKIMA CO WA 120-A2
Rt#-223 SE WASHINGTON ST
DALLAS OR 204-A6
Rt#-223 SW WASHINGTON ST
DALLAS OR 204-A6
Rt#-224 CLACKAMAS HWY
CLACKAMAS CO OR 126-B3
CLACKAMAS CO OR 200-B4
ESTACADA OR 200-C7
Rt#-224 HIGHWAY
BENTON CO WA 120-C2
WEST RICHLAND WA 120-C2
Rt#-224 KENNEDY RD
BENTON CO WA 120-C3
Rt#-224 MILWAUKIE EXWY
CLACKAMAS CO OR 199-D3
MILWAUKIE OR 199-D3
MILWAUKIE OR 321-J2
Rt#-224 VAN GIESEN ST
RICHLAND WA 340-B12
WEST RICHLAND WA 120-C2
Rt#-224 W VAN GIESEN ST
BENTON CO WA 340-A12
RICHLAND WA 340-A12
WEST RICHLAND WA 121-A2
WEST RICHLAND WA 340-A12
Rt#-224 WEBBER CANYON RD
BENTON CO WA 120-C3
Rt#-225 9TH ST
BENTON CITY WA 120-C3
Rt#-225 S DIVISION AV
BENTON CITY WA 120-C3
Rt#-225 S DIVISION ST
BENTON CITY WA 120-C3
Rt#-225 E HEDGER AV
BENTON CITY WA 120-C3
Rt#-225 HORN RD
BENTON CITY WA 120-C2
Rt#-225 US RESERVATION RD
BENTON CITY WA 120-C2
Rt#-225 WEBBER CANYON RD
BENTON CO WA 120-C3
Rt#-226 1ST AV
SCIO OR 133-C1
Rt#-226 5TH ST
LYONS OR 134-A1
MARION CO OR 134-A1
Rt#-226 6TH ST
LINN CO OR 134-A1
LYONS OR 134-A1
Rt#-226 ALBANY-LYONS HWY
LINN CO OR 133-C1
LINN CO OR 134-A1
SCIO OR 133-C1
Rt#-226 MAIN ST
LINN CO OR 133-C1
LYONS OR 134-A1
SCIO OR 133-C1
Rt#-227 TILLER-TRAIL HWY
CANYONVILLE OR 225-D3
DOUGLAS CO OR 141-B3
DOUGLAS CO OR 225-D3
JACKSON CO OR 141-C3
JACKSON CO OR 230-D1
Rt#-228 HALSEY-SWEET HOME HWY
BROWNSVILLE OR 210-B2
HALSEY OR 210-B2
LINN CO OR 133-C2
LINN CO OR 210-B2
SWEET HOME OR 133-C2
Rt#-229 GAITHER ST
LINCOLN CO OR 206-C2
SILETZ OR 206-C2
Rt#-229 SILETZ HWY
LINCOLN CO OR 203-A6
LINCOLN CO OR 206-C1
SILETZ OR 206-C1
TOLEDO OR 206-C4
Rt#-230 W DIAMOND LAKE HWY
DOUGLAS CO OR 223-B7
DOUGLAS CO OR 226-D3
DOUGLAS CO OR 227-A1
JACKSON CO OR 226-D3
KLAMATH CO OR 142-C3

Rt#-231 N ASPEN ST
LINCOLN CO WA 114-A2
REARDAN WA 114-A2
Rt#-231 CEDAR ST
STEVENS CO WA 106-B3
Rt#-231 FOURTH AV
STEVENS CO WA 106-B3
Rt#-231 HIGHWAY
LINCOLN CO WA 114-A1
LINCOLN CO WA 106-B3
SPRINGDALE WA 106-B3
STEVENS CO WA 106-B3
STEVENS CO WA 114-B1
Rt#-231 MAIN ST
LINCOLN CO WA 114-A2
Rt#-231 N MAIN ST
SPRINGDALE WA 106-B3
Rt#-231 OREGON ST
LINCOLN CO WA 114-A2
Rt#-231 N SECOND ST
SPRINGDALE WA 106-B3
Rt#-231 S SECOND ST
SPRINGDALE WA 106-B3
Rt#-231 W SHAFFER AV
SPRINGDALE WA 106-B3
Rt#-231 SPRING CREEK RD
LINCOLN CO WA 114-A1
Rt#-233 AMITY DAYTON HWY
YAMHILL CO OR 198-B7
YAMHILL CO OR 204-C1
Rt#-233 SE AMITY-DAYTON HWY
YAMHILL CO OR 204-C1
Rt#-233 SE LAFAYETTE HWY
YAMHILL CO OR 198-B7
Rt#-234 4TH AV
GOLD HILL OR 230-B6
Rt#-234 4TH ST
GOLD HILL OR 230-B6
Rt#-234 SAMS VALLEY AV
GOLD HILL OR 230-B6
JACKSON CO OR 230-B6
Rt#-234 SAMS VALLEY HWY
JACKSON CO OR 230-B6
Rt#-237 1ST ST
ISLAND CITY OR 130-A2
UNION CO OR 130-A2
Rt#-237 2ND ST
NORTH POWDER OR 130-B3
Rt#-237 COVE HWY
COVE OR 130-A2
UNION CO OR 130-A2
Rt#-237 E COVE HWY
UNION OR 130-B2
Rt#-237 LA GRANDE-BAKER HWY
NORTH POWDER OR 130-B3
UNION CO OR 130-B3
UNION CO OR 138-B3
Rt#-237 MAIN ST
COVE OR 130-B2
UNION OR 130-B2
Rt#-237 S MAIN ST
UNION OR 130-B2
Rt#-238 N 5TH ST
JACKSONVILLE OR 149-B2
Rt#-238 CALIFORNIA ST
JACKSONVILLE OR 149-B2
Rt#-238 W CALIFORNIA ST
JACKSONVILLE OR 149-B2
Rt#-238 E CALIFORNIA ST
JACKSONVILLE OR 149-B2
Rt#-238 S COLUMBUS AV
MEDFORD OR 336-B12
Rt#-238 HANLEY RD
JACKSON CO OR 234-A1
Rt#-238 JACKSONVILLE HWY
GRANTS PASS OR 229-B7
GRANTS PASS OR 335-C14
JACKSON CO OR 149-B2
JACKSON CO OR 234-A1
JACKSONVILLE OR 149-B2
JACKSONVILLE OR 234-A1
JOSEPHINE CO OR 149-B2
JOSEPHINE CO OR 229-B7
JOSEPHINE CO OR 335-C14
Rt#-238 E MAIN ST
MEDFORD OR 336-D12
Rt#-238 ROSS LN
MEDFORD OR 336-A12
Rt#-238 ROSSANLEY DR
JACKSON CO OR 234-A1
JACKSON CO OR 336-B10
MEDFORD OR 336-A10
Rt#-240 BY-PASS HWY
RICHLAND WA 340-E12
Rt#-240 FRWY
KENNEWICK WA 342-D7
KENNEWICK WA 343-A9
RICHLAND WA 341-H4
RICHLAND WA 342-A6
Rt#-240 HIGHWAY
BENTON CO WA 120-C2
RICHLAND WA 120-C2
RICHLAND WA 121-A2
RICHLAND WA 340-A7
Rt#-240 E MAIN ST
YAMHILL CO OR 198-B5
Rt#-240 N MAIN ST
NEWBERG OR 198-D5
Rt#-240 YAMHILL HWY
NEWBERG OR 198-B5
YAMHILL CO OR 198-B5
Rt#-241 1ST AV
MABTON WA 120-B3
YAKIMA CO WA 120-B3
Rt#-241 ALEXANDER RD
SUNNYSIDE WA 120-B2
YAKIMA CO WA 120-B2
Rt#-241 HIGHWAY
BENTON CO WA 120-B2
SUNNYSIDE WA 120-B2
YAKIMA CO WA 120-B2
Rt#-241 MABTON-SUNNYSIDE RD
SUNNYSIDE WA 120-B2
YAKIMA CO WA 120-B3
Rt#-241 RESERVATION RD
YAKIMA CO WA 120-B3
Rt#-241 W RESERVATION RD
YAKIMA CO WA 120-B3
Rt#-241 WANETA RD
SUNNYSIDE WA 120-B2
YAKIMA CO WA 120-B2
Rt#-242 MCKENZIE HWY
DESCHUTES CO OR 211-C4
LANE CO OR 134-C2
LANE CO OR 211-A6

Rt#-242 MCKENZIE HWY
LINN CO OR 211-A6
SISTERS OR 211-C4
Rt#-243 HIGHWAY
GRANT CO WA 120-B1
Rt#-244 UKIAH-HILGARD HWY
UKIAH OR 129-B3
UMATILLA CO OR 129-B3
UNION CO OR 129-C3
UNION CO OR 130-A2
Rt#-245 DOOLEY MOUNTAIN HWY
BAKER CO OR 138-A1
Rt#-260 BLANTON RD
FRANKLIN CO WA 121-B1
Rt#-260 HAVLINA RD
FRANKLIN CO WA 121-B1
Rt#-260 HIGHWAY
ADAMS CO WA 121-C1
CONNELL WA 121-B1
FRANKLIN CO WA 121-C1
KAHLOTUS WA 121-C1
Rt#-260 MAIN ST
WASHTUCNA WA 121-C1
Rt#-261 HIGHWAY
ADAMS CO WA 113-C3
ADAMS CO WA 121-C1
COLUMBIA CO WA 122-A2
FRANKLIN CO WA 121-C1
FRANKLIN CO WA 122-A2
STARBUCK WA 122-A2
Rt#-261 MAIN ST
WASHTUCNA WA 121-C1
Rt#-261 PROVIDENCE RD
ADAMS CO WA 121-C1
Rt#-262 OSULLIVAN DAM RD
GRANT CO WA 121-A1
GRANT CO WA 242-B6
Rt#-262 ROAD A-SE
GRANT CO WA 120-C1
GRANT CO WA 242-A7
Rt#-263 BURR CANYON RD
FRANKLIN CO WA 121-C2
Rt#-263 DEVILS CANYON RD
FRANKLIN CO WA 121-C1
KAHLOTUS WA 121-C1
Rt#-263 HIGHWAY
SISKIYOU CO CA 149-C3
SISKIYOU CO CA 150-A3
YREKA CA 149-C3
Rt#-270 DAVIS WY
PULLMAN WA 249-A5
WHITMAN CO WA 249-A5
Rt#-270 HIGHWAY
MOSCOW ID 249-C5
PULLMAN WA 249-B5
WHITMAN CO WA 249-C5
Rt#-270 NE KAMIAKEN ST
PULLMAN WA 249-B5
Rt#-270 E MAIN ST
PULLMAN WA 249-B5
UNION CO OR 130-B2
Rt#-270 SE OLSEN ST
PULLMAN WA 249-B5
Rt#-271 HIGHWAY
OAKESDALE WA 114-C3
WHITMAN CO WA 114-C3
Rt#-272 E CANYON ST
COLFAX WA 122-C1
WHITMAN CO WA 122-C1
Rt#-272 W CHURCH ST
PALOUSE WA 249-B1
WHITMAN CO WA 249-B1
Rt#-272 E ST
PALOUSE WA 249-C1
Rt#-272 N E ST
PALOUSE WA 249-C1
Rt#-272 HIGHWAY
COLFAX WA 122-C1
LATAH CO ID 249-C1
PALOUSE WA 249-C1
WHITMAN CO WA 122-C1
WHITMAN CO WA 249-B1
Rt#-272 E MAIN ST
PALOUSE WA 249-C1
Rt#-274 HIGHWAY
BENEWAH CO ID 115-A3
TEKOA WA 114-C3
WHITMAN CO WA 114-C3
WHITMAN CO WA 115-A3
Rt#-278 EMMA ST
ROCKFORD WA 114-C2
Rt#-278 E HOXIE RD
ROCKFORD WA 114-C2
SPOKANE CO WA 114-C2
Rt#-281 CENTRAL AV S
GRANT CO WA 112-B3
QUINCY WA 112-B3
Rt#-281 HIGHWAY
GRANT CO WA 112-B3
Rt#-281 ROAD 10-NW
GRANT CO WA 112-B3
Rt#-282 HIGHWAY
EPHRATA WA 112-C3
GRANT CO WA 112-C3
Rt#-283 HIGHWAY
GRANT CO WA 112-C3
Rt#-285 N CHELAN AV
WENATCHEE WA 238-D4
Rt#-285 S CHELAN AV
WENATCHEE WA 238-D4
Rt#-285 HIGHWAY
EAST WENATCHEE WA 239-A4
Sunnyslope WA 238-D3
WENATCHEE WA 238-D3
WENATCHEE WA 238-D4
WENATCHEE WA 239-A4
West Wenatchee WA 238-D3
Rt#-285 N MILLER ST
WENATCHEE WA 238-D4
Rt#-285 N MISSION ST
WENATCHEE WA 238-D4
Rt#-285 S MISSION ST
WENATCHEE WA 239-A4
WENATCHEE WA 239-A4
Rt#-285 PEACHEY ST
WENATCHEE WA 238-D4
Rt#-285 STEVENS ST
WENATCHEE WA 239-A4
Rt#-285 N WENATCHEE AV
WENATCHEE WA 238-D4
West Wenatchee WA 238-D4
Rt#-285 S WENATCHEE AV
WENATCHEE WA 239-A4
Rt#-285 WENATCHEE AV
WENATCHEE WA 239-A4
Rt#-290 N HAMILTON ST
SPOKANE WA 349-B8

Rt#-290 E TRENT AV
MILLWOOD WA 350-C5
SPOKANE WA 349-F7
SPOKANE VALLEY WA 349-F7
SPOKANE VALLEY WA 350-C5
Rt#-290 E TRENT RD
MILLWOOD WA 350-E5
Otis Orchards WA 351-C3
Otis Orchards WA 352-C7
SPOKANE CO WA 351-C3
SPOKANE CO WA 352-C7
SPOKANE VALLEY WA 350-E5
SPOKANE VALLEY WA 351-C3
Rt#-291 CORKSCREW CANYON RD
STEVENS CO WA 114-B1
STEVENS CO WA 246-A1
Rt#-291 W FRANCIS AV
SPOKANE WA 348-D1
SPOKANE WA 349-A1
Town and Country WA 348-D1
Town and Country WA 349-A1
Rt#-291 N NINE MILE RD
SPOKANE WA 246-A2
SPOKANE WA 346-A14
SPOKANE WA 348-B1
SPOKANE CO WA 246-A2
SPOKANE CO WA 346-A13
Rt#-292 HIGHWAY
SPRINGDALE WA 106-B3
STEVENS CO WA 106-B3
Rt#-292 NEVADA STATE ROUTE
HUMBOLDT CO NV 153-C3
Rt#-293 ANTELOPE HWY
JEFFERSON CO OR 135-C1
WASCO CO OR 127-C3
WASCO CO OR 135-C1
Rt#-293 KINGS RIVER RD
HUMBOLDT CO NV 154-A3
Rt#-293 LOWER ANTELOPE RD
ANTELOPE OR 127-C3
WASCO CO OR 127-C3
Rt#-293 SOUTH ST
ANTELOPE OR 127-C3
Rt#-300 HIGHWAY
MASON CO WA 173-D5
Rt#-300 NORTH SHORE RD
MASON CO WA 173-D6
Rt#-300 OLD BELFAIR HWY
MASON CO WA 173-D5
Rt#-302 ELGIN-CLIFTON
PIERCE CO WA 174-A7
Rt#-302 HIGHWAY
MASON CO WA 173-D6
Rt#-302 KEY PENINSULA HWY
PIERCE CO WA 174-A6
Rt#-302 OLD 302
MASON CO WA 173-D6
Rt#-302 PURDY DR
KITSAP CO WA 174-B6
PIERCE CO WA 174-B6
Rt#-302 ROCKY BAY POINT DR
MASON CO WA 174-A7
Rt#-302 ROCKY BAY PNT DR KPN
MASON CO WA 174-A7
PIERCE CO WA 174-A6
Rt#-302 ROCKY BAY PT
MASON CO WA 173-D7
Rt#-303 NE BUCKLIN HILL RD
KITSAP CO WA 174-B1
Rt#-303 NW BUCKLIN HILL RD
KITSAP CO WA 174-B1
Silverdale WA 174-B1
Rt#-303 HIGHWAY
KITSAP CO WA 174-B1
KITSAP CO WA 270-J1
Rt#-303 WAAGA WY
KITSAP CO WA 174-B1
Silverdale WA 174-B1
Rt#-303 WARREN AV
BREMERTON WA 270-J10
Rt#-303 WHEATON WY
BREMERTON WA 270-J6
KITSAP CO WA 270-J6
Rt#-304 1ST ST
BREMERTON WA 270-J6
Rt#-304 4TH ST
BREMERTON WA 270-H11
Rt#-304 BURWELL ST
BREMERTON WA 270-G11
Rt#-304 CALLOW AV N
BREMERTON WA 270-G10
Rt#-304 CALLOW AV S
BREMERTON WA 270-G11
Rt#-304 CAMBRIAN AV S
BREMERTON WA 270-F12
Rt#-304 FARRAGUT ST
BREMERTON WA 270-F12
Rt#-304 HIGHWAY
BREMERTON WA 270-F12
Navy Yard City WA 270-F12
Rt#-304 WASHINGTON AV
BREMERTON WA 270-J11
Rt#-305 HIGHWAY
KITSAP CO WA 170-B6
KITSAP CO WA 174-C1
POULSBO WA 170-B6
Suquamish WA 170-C7
Winslow WA 174-D1
Rt#-305 OLYMPIC WY SE
Winslow WA 174-D2
Rt#-307 BOND RD NE
KITSAP CO WA 170-C6
POULSBO WA 170-C6
Rt#-308 HIGHWAY
KITSAP CO WA 170-B7
Rt#-308 NW LUOTO RD
KITSAP CO WA 170-B7
Rt#-310 6TH ST
BREMERTON WA 270-G10
Rt#-310 KITSAP WY
BREMERTON WA 270-D10
Rt#-361 1ST AV
CULVER OR 208-B7
Rt#-361 CULVER HWY
CULVER OR 208-B7
JEFFERSON CO OR 208-B7
MADRAS OR 212-D1
MADRAS OR 208-B6
METOLIUS OR 208-B6
Rt#-361 SW D ST
MADRAS OR 208-C5
Rt#-361 JEFFERSON AV
JEFFERSON CO OR 208-B6

STREET City State	Page-Grid

Rt#-361 JEFFERSON AV
METOLIUS OR — 208-B6
Rt#-372 CENTURY DRIVE HWY
BEND OR — 217-B3
BEND OR — 332-A11
DESCHUTES CO OR — 216-C4
DESCHUTES CO OR — 217-B3
DESCHUTES CO OR — 332-A11
Rt#-372 NW COLORADO AV
BEND OR — 332-E8
Rt#-372 SW COLORADO AV
BEND OR — 332-D9
Rt#-380 HARDING RD
CROOK CO OR — 213-D5
Rt#-380 PAULINA HWY
CROOK CO OR — 135-C2
CROOK CO OR — 136-A3
CROOK CO OR — 213-D5
PRINEVILLE OR — 213-D5
Rt#-380 PAULINA SUPLEE RD
CROOK CO OR — 136-B3
Rt#-395 HIGHWAY
BRITISH COLUMBIA BC — 105-C1
Rt#-397 S 10TH AV
PASCO WA — 343-F9
Rt#-397 E AINSWORTH AV
PASCO WA — 343-G9
Rt#-397 W AINSWORTH AV
PASCO WA — 343-F8
Rt#-397 BNTN-FRNKLN INTCO BRD
KENNEWICK WA — 343-E10
PASCO WA — 343-F9
Rt#-397 CHEMICAL RD
Finley WA — 121-A3
KENNEWICK WA — 343-G12
KENNEWICK WA — 343-F11
Rt#-397 N GUM ST
KENNEWICK WA — 343-E10
Rt#-397 HIGHWAY
Finley WA — 121-A3
Rt#-397 N OREGON AV
PASCO WA — 343-G6
Rt#-397 S OREGON AV
PASCO WA — 343-H8
Rt#-401 HIGHWAY
PACIFIC CO WA — 186-C5
Rt#-401 KNAPPTON FERRY RD
PACIFIC CO WA — 186-C7
Rt#-409 FRONT ST
CATHLAMET WA — 117-B3
CLATSOP CO OR — 117-B3
Rt#-409 HIGHWAY
CATHLAMET WA — 117-B3
WAHKIAKUM CO WA — 117-B3
Rt#-409 MAIN ST
CATHLAMET WA — 117-B3
Rt#-409 PLYMPTON CREEK
CLATSOP CO OR — 117-B3
Rt#-409 WESTPORT DOCK RD
CLATSOP CO OR — 117-B3
Rt#-410 CHINOOK PASS HWY
PIERCE CO WA — 111-A3
Rt#-410 COLE ST
ENUMCLAW WA — 110-C3
Rt#-410 ENUMCLAW BUCKLEY RD
ENUMCLAW WA — 110-C3
KING CO WA — 110-C3
Rt#-410 ENMCLW CHNK PASS RD
ENUMCLAW WA — 110-C3
Rt#-410 SE ENMCLW CHNK PSS RD
KING CO WA — 110-C3
PIERCE CO WA — 110-C3
PIERCE CO WA — 111-A3
Rt#-410 FRWY
PIERCE CO WA — 182-C3
Rt#-410 HIGHWAY
BONNEY LAKE WA — 182-C4
BUCKLEY WA — 110-C3
BUCKLEY WA — 182-D4
KING CO WA — 110-C3
PIERCE CO WA — 111-A3
PIERCE CO WA — 119-A1
PIERCE CO WA — 182-C3
SUMNER WA — 182-C3
YAKIMA CO WA — 119-B1
YAKIMA CO WA — 240-A6
Rt#-410 MATHER MEMORIAL PKWY
PIERCE CO WA — 119-A1
Rt#-410 NFD RD 7184
PIERCE CO WA — 111-A3
Rt#-410 ROOSEVELT AV
ENUMCLAW WA — 110-C3
Rt#-410 ROOSEVELT AV E
ENUMCLAW WA — 110-C3
KING CO WA — 110-C3
Rt#-410 SUMNER-BUCKLEY HWY
PIERCE CO WA — 182-B3
SUMNER WA — 182-B3
Rt#-411 1ST AV
KELSO WA — 303-C9
LONGVIEW WA — 303-C9
Rt#-411 1ST AV NW
KELSO WA — 303-C7
Rt#-411 3RD AV
LONGVIEW WA — 303-C9
Rt#-411 A ST
CASTLE ROCK WA — 187-C7
Rt#-411 HUNTINGTON AV
CASTLE ROCK WA — 187-C7
COWLITZ CO WA — 187-C7
Rt#-411 PEARDALE LN
LONGVIEW WA — 303-C9
Rt#-411 PH NO 10
CASTLE ROCK WA — 187-C7
COWLITZ CO WA — 187-C7
Rt#-411 WEST SIDE HWY
CASTLE ROCK WA — 187-C7
COWLITZ CO WA — 189-C1
COWLITZ CO WA — 303-C7
KELSO WA — 303-C7
LONGVIEW WA — 303-C9
Rt#-432 3RD AV
LONGVIEW WA — 303-B11
Rt#-432 HIGHWAY
COWLITZ CO WA — 303-C12
KELSO WA — 303-E13
LONGVIEW WA — 303-C12
Rt#-432 INDUSTRIAL WY
COWLITZ CO WA — 302-D8
LONGVIEW WA — 302-D8
LONGVIEW WA — 303-A12

Rt#-432 MOUNT SOLO RD
COWLITZ CO WA — 302-C6
LONGVIEW WA — 302-C6
Rt#-432 OLD PACIFIC HWY
KELSO WA — 303-F13
Rt#-432 TENNANT WY
COWLITZ CO WA — 303-C12
LONGVIEW WA — 303-C12
Rt#-432 WILLOW GROVE CONN RD
COWLITZ CO WA — 302-A5
LONGVIEW WA — 302-A5
Rt#-432 WILLOW GROVE RD
COWLITZ CO WA — 302-A5
LONGVIEW WA — 302-A5
Rt#-433 OREGON WY
COLUMBIA CO OR — 189-B4
COWLITZ CO WA — 302-H13
LONGVIEW WA — 302-J12
RAINIER OR — 189-B4
RAINIER OR — 302-H13
Rt#-500 NE 3RD ST
CLARK CO WA — 193-B6
Rt#-500 SE 6TH AV
CAMAS WA — 193-B7
Rt#-500 NE 14TH AV
CAMAS WA — 193-B7
Rt#-500 NE 44TH ST
CLARK CO WA — 193-B6
Rt#-500 NE 54TH ST
CLARK CO WA — 193-B6
Rt#-500 NE 58TH ST
CLARK CO WA — 193-B6
Rt#-500 NE 232ND AV
CLARK CO WA — 193-B5
Rt#-500 NE 237TH AV
CLARK CO WA — 193-B6
Rt#-500 NE 238TH AV
CLARK CO WA — 193-B6
Rt#-500 NE 242ND AV
CLARK CO WA — 193-B6
Rt#-500 NE 267TH AV
CLARK CO WA — 193-B6
Rt#-500 BRUNNER RD
RIDGEFIELD WA — 192-B5
Rt#-500 NE DALLAS ST
CAMAS WA — 193-B7
Rt#-500 DRESSER RD
CLARK CO WA — 193-B7
THURSTON CO WA — 184-D3
Rt#-500 NE EVERETT ST
CAMAS WA — 193-B7
CLARK CO WA — 193-B7
Rt#-500 SE EVERETT RD
CLARK CO WA — 193-B6
Rt#-500 NE FOURTH PLAIN RD
CLARK CO WA — 192-D5
CLARK CO WA — 193-A5
VANCOUVER WA — 192-D5
VANCOUVER WA — 193-A5
Rt#-500 NE GARFIELD ST
CAMAS WA — 193-B7
Rt#-500 HIGHWAY
CLARK CO WA — 192-D5
CLARK CO WA — 306-C2
CLARK CO WA — 307-J1
VANCOUVER WA — 192-D5
VANCOUVER WA — 305-H2
VANCOUVER WA — 306-E2
VANCOUVER WA — 307-H1
Rt#-500 SE UNION ST
CAMAS WA — 193-B7
Rt#-501 W 15TH ST
VANCOUVER WA — 305-F4
Rt#-501 NW ERWIN O RIEGER MEM
VANCOUVER WA — 192-B5
Rt#-501 W FOURTH PLAIN BLVD
VANCOUVER WA — 304-D3
Rt#-501 LOWER RIVER RD
CLARK CO WA — 304-A1
CLARK CO WA — 304-A1
Rt#-501 NW LOWER RIVER RD
CLARK CO WA — 192-B5
CLARK CO WA — 304-A1
VANCOUVER WA — 192-B5
VANCOUVER WA — 304-A1
Rt#-501 MILL PLAIN BLVD
VANCOUVER WA — 305-G4
Rt#-501 W MILL PLAIN BLVD
VANCOUVER WA — 304-D3
VANCOUVER WA — 305-E4
Rt#-501 PIONEER ST
RIDGEFIELD WA — 192-C2
Rt#-502 NE 10TH AV
CLARK CO WA — 192-D3
Rt#-502 NE 219TH ST
BATTLE GROUND WA — 192-D3
CLARK CO WA — 192-D3
Rt#-502 W MAIN ST
BATTLE GROUND WA — 192-D3
BATTLE GROUND WA — 193-A3
Rt#-503 NW 10TH AV
BATTLE GROUND WA — 193-A3
Rt#-503 SW 10TH AV
BATTLE GROUND WA — 193-A3
CLARK CO WA — 193-A3
Rt#-503 NE 117TH AV
CLARK CO WA — 192-D5
CLARK CO WA — 193-A4
Rt#-503 NE 122ND AV
BATTLE GROUND WA — 193-A3
CLARK CO WA — 193-A3
Rt#-503 AMBOY
CLARK CO WA — 193-B1
Rt#-503 GOERIG ST
WOODLAND WA — 118-A3
WOODLAND WA — 192-C1
Rt#-503 HIGHWAY
CLARK CO WA — 118-A3
CLARK CO WA — 190-A7
CLARK CO WA — 193-A1
COWLITZ CO WA — 118-A3
WOODLAND WA — 192-C1
Rt#-503 LEWIS RIVER DR
COWLITZ CO WA — 118-A3
COWLITZ CO WA — 190-A6
WOODLAND WA — 118-A3
Rt#-503 LEWIS RIVER RD
COWLITZ CO WA — 190-A6
Rt#-503 NE LEWISVILLE HWY
CLARK CO WA — 193-A1
Rt#-504 HIGHWAY
COWLITZ CO WA — 118-A2
SKAMANIA CO WA — 118-B2
SKAMANIA CO WA — 190-B1

Rt#-504 SPIRIT LAKE HWY
CASTLE ROCK WA — 187-C7
COWLITZ CO WA — 118-A2
COWLITZ CO WA — 187-C7
Rt#-505 N 5TH ST
LEWIS CO WA — 187-D4
TOLEDO WA — 187-D4
Rt#-505 COWLITZ ST
LEWIS CO WA — 187-D4
TOLEDO WA — 187-D4
Rt#-505 HIGHWAY
COWLITZ CO WA — 118-A2
LEWIS CO WA — 118-A2
LEWIS CO WA — 187-C3
WINLOCK WA — 187-C3
Rt#-505 KERRON AV
LEWIS CO WA — 187-C3
Rt#-505 E WALNUT ST
LEWIS CO WA — 187-C3
Rt#-505 WINLOCK-TOLEDO RD
LEWIS CO WA — 187-C3
Rt#-506 7TH ST
VADER WA — 187-B5
Rt#-506 HIGHWAY
COWLITZ CO WA — 187-B5
LEWIS CO WA — 187-C4
VADER WA — 187-B5
Rt#-507 ALDER ST
CENTRALIA WA — 299-E4
Rt#-507 BINGHAMPTON ST
RAINIER WA — 118-A1
THURSTON CO WA — 118-A1
Rt#-507 BUCODA HWY
LEWIS CO WA — 184-C5
Rt#-507 W CHERRY ST
CENTRALIA WA — 299-E4
Rt#-507 D ST
TENINO WA — 184-D3
Rt#-507 E DOWNING RD
CENTRALIA WA — 184-C5
LEWIS CO WA — 184-C5
Rt#-507 FRONT ST
BUCODA WA — 184-D4
THURSTON CO WA — 184-D4
Rt#-507 HIGHWAY
LEWIS CO WA — 184-C5
THURSTON CO WA — 118-A1
THURSTON CO WA — 184-D3
Rt#-507 MCKENNA-YELM HWY
PIERCE CO WA — 118-A1
THURSTON CO WA — 118-A1
YELM WA — 118-A1
Rt#-507 MCNAUGHT ST
ROY WA — 181-C7
Rt#-507 MELLEN ST
CENTRALIA WA — 299-D5
Rt#-507 N PEARL ST
CENTRALIA WA — 184-C5
CENTRALIA WA — 299-F1
LEWIS CO WA — 184-C5
Rt#-507 S PEARL ST
CENTRALIA WA — 299-F4
Rt#-507 RAINIER-YELM HWY
THURSTON CO WA — 118-A1
YELM WA — 118-A1
Rt#-507 SIXTH ST
TENINO WA — 184-D3
Rt#-507 E SIXTH ST
CENTRALIA WA — 299-F2
Rt#-507 SPANAWAY-MCKENNA HWY
PIERCE CO WA — 118-A1
PIERCE CO WA — 181-C7
ROY WA — 181-C7
Rt#-507 SUMNER ST
BUCODA WA — 184-D4
TENINO WA — 184-D4
THURSTON CO WA — 184-D4
Rt#-507 SUSSEX AV
TENINO WA — 184-D3
THURSTON CO WA — 184-D3
Rt#-507 THIRD ST
TENINO WA — 184-D3
Rt#-507 N TOWER AV
CENTRALIA WA — 299-F3
Rt#-507 S TOWER AV
CENTRALIA WA — 299-F4
Rt#-507 YELM AV
YELM WA — 118-A1
Rt#-508 HIGHWAY
LEWIS CO WA — 118-A2
LEWIS CO WA — 187-C1
MORTON WA — 118-B2
Rt#-508 MAIN ST
MORTON WA — 118-B2
Rt#-508 MORTON-BEAR CANYON RD
LEWIS CO WA — 118-B2
MORTON WA — 118-B2
Rt#-508 NFD RD 508
LINCOLN CO MT — 107-C2
Rt#-508 NFD RD 92
LINCOLN CO MT — 107-C1
Rt#-509 1ST AV S
BURIEN WA — 175-A6
DES MOINES WA — 175-A6
NORMANDY PARK WA — 175-A6
Rt#-509 S 174TH ST
BURIEN WA — 175-A5
Rt#-509 S 216TH ST
DES MOINES WA — 175-A6
DES MOINES WA — 290-A6
NORMANDY PARK WA — 175-A6
NORMANDY PARK WA — 290-A6
Rt#-509 AMBAUM BLVD S
BURIEN WA — 175-A5
BURIEN WA — 288-A7
Rt#-509 S DASH POINT RD
FEDERAL WAY WA — 182-A1
Rt#-509 SW DASH POINT RD
FEDERAL WAY WA — 182-A1
Rt#-509 DES MOINES MEM DR
BURIEN WA — 288-A7
BURIEN WA — 290-A1
SEATAC WA — 290-A1
Rt#-509 EASTSIDE DR NE
PIERCE CO WA — 181-D1
PIERCE CO WA — 182-A1
Rt#-509 N FRONTAGE RD
TACOMA WA — 182-A2
Rt#-509 S FRONTAGE RD
TACOMA WA — 182-A2
Rt#-509 FRWY
BURIEN WA — 175-A5
BURIEN WA — 288-A1
BURIEN WA — 290-A1
KING CO WA — 286-A4
KING CO WA — 288-A1

Rt#-509 FRWY
SEATAC WA — 288-A6
SEATAC WA — 290-A1
SEATTLE WA — 285-J1
SEATTLE WA — 286-A3
TACOMA WA — 182-A2
TACOMA WA — 293-J6
Rt#-509 MARINE VIEW DR
DES MOINES WA — 290-A6
TACOMA WA — 181-D1
Rt#-510 CLAIR CUT-OFF RD
THURSTON CO WA — 181-A7
Rt#-510 HIGHWAY
THURSTON CO WA — 181-A6
Rt#-510 MARVIN RD NE
LACEY WA — 181-A6
Rt#-510 MARVIN RD SE
LACEY WA — 181-A6
THURSTON CO WA — 181-A6
Rt#-510 OLYMPIA-YELM HWY
THURSTON CO WA — 118-A1
THURSTON CO WA — 181-B7
YELM WA — 118-A1
Rt#-510 PACIFIC AV SE
THURSTON CO WA — 181-A6
Rt#-510 PACIFIC HWY SE
SNOHOMISH CO WA — 181-A6
Rt#-510 YELM AV
THURSTON CO WA — 118-A1
YELM WA — 118-A1
Rt#-512 FRWY
LAKEWOOD WA — 181-D4
PIERCE CO WA — 181-D4
PIERCE CO WA — 182-B3
PUYALLUP WA — 182-B3
Rt#-513 NE 45TH ST
SEATTLE WA — 274-D5
SEATTLE WA — 275-E5
Rt#-513 MONTLAKE BLVD NE
SEATTLE WA — 274-D6
SEATTLE WA — 278-D1
Rt#-513 SAND POINT WY NE
SEATTLE WA — 275-F5
Rt#-515 104TH AV SE
KENT WA — 175-C7
Rt#-515 108TH AV SE
KENT WA — 175-C6
KENT WA — 175-C6
Rt#-515 BENSON RD
KING CO WA — 175-C5
RENTON WA — 175-C5
Rt#-515 BENSON RD SE
KING CO WA — 175-C5
Rt#-515 S GRADY WY
RENTON WA — 175-C5
Rt#-515 HIGHWAY
KING CO WA — 175-C5
RENTON WA — 175-C5
RENTON WA — 175-B4
Rt#-515 MAIN AV S
RENTON WA — 175-C5
Rt#-515 TALBOT RD S
RENTON WA — 175-C5
Rt#-516 SE 256TH ST
COVINGTON WA — 175-C7
KENT WA — 175-C7
Rt#-516 SE 272ND ST
MAPLE VALLEY WA — 175-D7
Rt#-516 CANYON DR SE
KENT WA — 175-C7
Rt#-516 CENTRAL AV N
KENT WA — 175-C7
Rt#-516 CENTRAL AV S
KENT WA — 175-C7
Rt#-516 KENT-DES MOINES RD
DES MOINES WA — 290-A7
KENT WA — 175-B7
KENT WA — 290-A7
Rt#-516 KENT-DES MOINES RD S
DES MOINES WA — 175-B7
KENT WA — 290-E7
KING CO WA — 175-B7
KING CO WA — 290-E7
Rt#-516 KENT KANGLEY RD
COVINGTON WA — 175-C7
KENT WA — 175-C7
KING CO WA — 175-C7
KING CO WA — 176-A7
MAPLE VALLEY WA — 176-A7
MAPLE VALLEY WA — 176-A7
Rt#-516 E SMITH ST
KENT WA — 175-C7
Rt#-516 W WILLIS ST
KENT WA — 175-C7
Rt#-518 FRWY
BURIEN WA — 175-A5
BURIEN WA — 288-B4
SEATAC WA — 288-B4
TUKWILA WA — 288-D5
TUKWILA WA — 289-F4
Rt#-519 4TH AV S
SEATTLE WA — 278-A7
SEATTLE WA — 282-A1
Rt#-519 ALASKAN WY S
SEATTLE WA — 277-J7
SEATTLE WA — 278-A7
SEATTLE WA — 282-A1
Rt#-519 S ROYAL BROUGHAM WY
SEATTLE WA — 281-J1
SEATTLE WA — 282-A1
Rt#-520 FRWY
BELLEVUE WA — 175-C2
CLYDE HILL WA — 175-C2
HUNTS POINT WA — 175-C2
KING CO WA — 175-D1
MEDINA WA — 175-C2
MEDINA WA — 279-J2
REDMOND WA — 175-D1
SEATTLE WA — 278-D1
SEATTLE WA — 279-E1
YARROW POINT WA — 175-C2
Rt#-522 NE BOTHELL WY
BOTHELL WA — 171-B6
KENMORE WA — 171-B6
KING CO WA — 171-B6
SNOHOMISH CO WA — 171-B6
Rt#-522 FISCHER PL NE
BOTHELL WA — 171-B7
Rt#-522 FRWY
BOTHELL WA — 171-C6

Rt#-522 FRWY
SNOHOMISH CO WA — 171-D5
WOODINVILLE WA — 171-C6
Rt#-522 HIGHWAY
MONROE WA — 110-C1
SNOHOMISH CO WA — 110-C1
Rt#-522 LAKE CITY WY NE
SEATTLE WA — 171-B7
SEATTLE WA — 274-C2
Rt#-522 WOODINVILLE DR
BOTHELL WA — 171-C6
Rt#-523 N 145TH ST
SEATTLE WA — 171-A7
SHORELINE WA — 171-A7
Rt#-523 NE 145TH ST
SEATTLE WA — 171-B7
SHORELINE WA — 171-B7
Rt#-524 3RD AV N
EDMONDS WA — 171-A5
Rt#-524 3RD AV S
EDMONDS WA — 171-A5
Rt#-524 9TH AV N
EDMONDS WA — 171-A5
Rt#-524 196TH ST SW
EDMONDS WA — 171-B5
LYNNWOOD WA — 171-B5
SNOHOMISH CO WA — 171-B5
Rt#-524 208TH ST SE
BOTHELL WA — 171-C5
SKAGIT CO WA — 161-A7
SNOHOMISH CO WA — 171-C5
Rt#-524 CASPERS ST
EDMONDS WA — 171-A5
Rt#-524 FILBERT RD
BOTHELL WA — 171-C5
LYNNWOOD WA — 171-B5
SNOHOMISH CO WA — 171-C5
Rt#-524 MAIN ST
EDMONDS WA — 171-A5
Rt#-524 MALTBY RD
BOTHELL WA — 171-C5
SNOHOMISH CO WA — 171-C5
Rt#-524 PARADISE LAKE RD
SNOHOMISH CO WA — 171-D5
Rt#-524 PINE ST
EDMONDS WA — 171-A5
Rt#-524 PUGET DR
EDMONDS WA — 171-A5
Rt#-524 YEW WY
SNOHOMISH CO WA — 171-D5
Rt#-525 FRWY
SNOHOMISH CO WA — 171-B4
Rt#-525 HIGHWAY
Clinton WA — 171-A2
Freeland WA — 170-C1
ISLAND CO WA — 167-C5
ISLAND CO WA — 170-C1
ISLAND CO WA — 171-A1
SNOHOMISH CO WA — 171-B4
Rt#-525 MUKILTEO SPEEDWAY
MUKILTEO WA — 171-B2
MUKILTEO WA — 266-D3
MUKILTEO WA — 267-E5
SNOHOMISH CO WA — 171-B4
SNOHOMISH CO WA — 267-E6
Rt#-525 PAINE FIELD BLVD
MUKILTEO WA — 267-F6
SNOHOMISH CO WA — 267-F6
Rt#-526 84TH ST SW
EVERETT WA — 266-E4
SNOHOMISH CO WA — 267-F4
Rt#-526 FRWY
EVERETT WA — 267-F4
EVERETT WA — 268-A4
MUKILTEO WA — 267-F4
SNOHOMISH CO WA — 267-F4
Rt#-527 19TH AV SE
EVERETT WA — 171-C4
EVERETT WA — 268-D6
SNOHOMISH CO WA — 171-C4
Rt#-527 BOTHELL EVERETT HWY
BOTHELL WA — 171-C4
MILL CREEK WA — 171-C4
SNOHOMISH CO WA — 171-C4
Rt#-527 BOTHELL WY NE
BOTHELL WA — 171-C6
BOTHELL WA — 171-C6
Rt#-528 4TH ST
MARYSVILLE WA — 171-C1
SNOHOMISH CO WA — 171-C1
Rt#-528 64TH ST NE
MARYSVILLE WA — 168-D7
MARYSVILLE WA — 171-C1
SNOHOMISH CO WA — 168-D7
SNOHOMISH CO WA — 171-D1
Rt#-529 BROADWAY
EVERETT WA — 171-C1
Rt#-529 EVERETT AV
EVERETT WA — 264-E3
EVERETT WA — 265-E3
Rt#-529 HIGHWAY
MARYSVILLE WA — 171-C1
SNOHOMISH CO WA — 171-C1
Rt#-529 MAPLE ST
EVERETT WA — 265-F4
Rt#-529 E MARINE VIEW DR
EVERETT WA — 171-C1
Rt#-529 PACIFIC AV
EVERETT WA — 265-F4
Rt#-529 PACIFIC HWY
EVERETT WA — 171-C1
MARYSVILLE WA — 171-C1
SNOHOMISH CO WA — 171-C1
Rt#-529 STATE AV
MARYSVILLE WA — 171-C1
Rt#-529 W MARINE VIEW DR
EVERETT WA — 264-D3
Rt#-530 DARRNGTN BNTTS STR RD
DARRINGTON WA — 103-A3
SKAGIT CO WA — 103-A3
SNOHOMISH CO WA — 103-A3
Rt#-530 EMENS AV
DARRINGTON WA — 103-A3
Rt#-530 HIGHWAY
ARLINGTON WA — 168-D5
DARRINGTON WA — 103-A3
MARYSVILLE WA — 168-C5
SNOHOMISH CO WA — 102-C3
SNOHOMISH CO WA — 103-A3
SNOHOMISH CO WA — 168-D4
Rt#-530 PIONEER HWY
SKAGIT CO WA — 168-B2
Rt#-530 SAUK VALLEY RD
SKAGIT CO WA — 103-A2
Rt#-530 SEEMANN ST
DARRINGTON WA — 103-A3

Rt#-531 36TH AV NW
SNOHOMISH CO WA — 168-B6
Rt#-531 172ND ST NE
ARLINGTON WA — 168-C6
SNOHOMISH CO WA — 168-C6
Rt#-531 E LAKE GOODWIN RD
SNOHOMISH CO WA — 168-B5
Rt#-531 LAKEWOOD RD
SNOHOMISH CO WA — 168-B5
Rt#-531 SISCO HEIGHTS RD
ARLINGTON WA — 168-D6
SNOHOMISH CO WA — 168-D6
Rt#-532 268TH ST NW
ISLAND CO WA — 167-D4
ISLAND CO WA — 168-A4
SNOHOMISH CO WA — 168-A4
STANWOOD WA — 168-A4
Rt#-532 HIGHWAY
SNOHOMISH CO WA — 168-A4
STANWOOD WA — 168-A4
Rt#-534 HIGHWAY
SKAGIT CO WA — 168-B2
Rt#-536 S 3RD ST
MOUNT VERNON WA — 260-C12
Rt#-536 W DIVISION ST
MOUNT VERNON WA — 260-B12
Rt#-536 KINCAID ST
MOUNT VERNON WA — 260-C13
Rt#-536 MEMORIAL HWY
MOUNT VERNON WA — 260-A11
SKAGIT CO WA — 161-A7
SKAGIT CO WA — 260-A11
Rt#-538 COLLEGE WY
MOUNT VERNON WA — 260-J11
SKAGIT CO WA — 161-C7
SKAGIT CO WA — 260-J11
Rt#-538 E COLLEGE WY
MOUNT VERNON WA — 260-D10
SKAGIT CO WA — 260-H10
Rt#-538 W COLLEGE WY
MOUNT VERNON WA — 260-B10
Rt#-539 GUIDE MERIDIAN RD
BELLINGHAM WA — 158-D6
BELLINGHAM WA — 258-C1
LYNDEN WA — 158-D6
WHATCOM CO WA — 158-D6
Rt#-539 MERIDIAN ST
BELLINGHAM WA — 258-C2
Rt#-542 MOUNT BAKER HWY
WHATCOM CO WA — 102-B1
WHATCOM CO WA — 103-A1
Rt#-542 E SUNSET DR
BELLINGHAM WA — 258-G3
WHATCOM CO WA — 102-B1
WHATCOM CO WA — 258-G3
Rt#-543 HIGHWAY
BLAINE WA — 158-B3
WHATCOM CO WA — 158-B3
Rt#-544 COLUMBIA ST
NOOKSACK WA — 102-B1
Rt#-544 EVERSON AV
EVERSON WA — 102-B1
NOOKSACK WA — 102-B1
Rt#-544 EVERSON GOSHEN RD
EVERSON WA — 102-B1
WHATCOM CO WA — 102-B1
Rt#-544 KALE ST
EVERSON WA — 102-B1
Rt#-544 E POLE RD
EVERSON WA — 102-B1
WHATCOM CO WA — 102-B1
WHATCOM CO WA — 158-D5
Rt#-544 MAIN ST
EVERSON WA — 102-B1
NOOKSACK WA — 102-B1
Rt#-546 E BADGER RD
WHATCOM CO WA — 102-B1
Rt#-547 E BADGER RD
WHATCOM CO WA — 102-B1
Rt#-547 FRONT ST
SUMAS WA — 102-B1
WHATCOM CO WA — 102-B1
Rt#-547 GARRISON RD
WHATCOM CO WA — 102-B1
Rt#-547 HALVERSTICK RD
SUMAS WA — 102-B1
WHATCOM CO WA — 102-B1
Rt#-547 KENDALL RD
WHATCOM CO WA — 102-B1
Rt#-547 REESE HILL RD
WHATCOM CO WA — 102-B1
Rt#-547 ROCK RD
WHATCOM CO WA — 102-B1
Rt#-547 SUMAS RD
WHATCOM CO WA — 102-B1
Rt#-548 BLAINE RD
Birch Bay WA — 158-B4
BLAINE WA — 158-B3
WHATCOM CO WA — 158-B5
Rt#-548 GRANDVIEW RD
Birch Bay WA — 158-B5
WHATCOM CO WA — 158-B5
Rt#-599 FRWY
TUKWILA WA — 286-D7
TUKWILA WA — 287-E7
TUKWILA WA — 289-E1
Rt#-702 MCKENNA TANWAX
PIERCE CO WA — 118-A1
Rt#-706 HIGHWAY
PIERCE CO WA — 185-A5
Rt#-706 MOUNTAIN HWY E
PIERCE CO WA — 118-B1
PIERCE CO WA — 185-A5
Rt#-730 COLUMBIA RIVER HWY
UMATILLA CO OR — 121-A3
WALLA WALLA CO WA — 121-A3
Rt#-730 HIGHWAY
WALLA WALLA CO WA — 121-B3
Rt#-821 HIGHWAY
KITTITAS CO WA — 241-B7
KITTITAS CO WA — 243-B1
YAKIMA CO WA — 243-C4
Rt#-821 THRALL RD
KITTITAS CO WA — 241-B7
Rt#-823 S 1ST ST
YAKIMA CO WA — 243-B5
Rt#-823 HARRISON RD
YAKIMA CO WA — 243-B5
Rt#-823 HIGHWAY
YAKIMA CO WA — 243-B6
Rt#-823 E NACHES AV
SELAH WA — 243-B5
Rt#-823 SELAH RD
YAKIMA CO WA — 243-B6
Rt#-823 WENAS AV
SELAH WA — 243-B5
YAKIMA CO WA — 243-B5

INDEX

STREET
City State   Page-Grid

Rt#-900 S 2ND ST
RENTON WA 175-C5
Rt#-900 S 3RD ST
RENTON WA 175-C5
Rt#-900 17TH AV NW
ISSAQUAH WA 175-D3
Rt#-900 BRONSON WY N
RENTON WA 175-C5
Rt#-900 HOUSER WY S
RENTON WA 175-C5
Rt#-900 MARTIN LUTHER
KING JR
KING CO WA 175-C5
KING CO WA 287-E6
KING CO WA 289-G1
RENTON WA 175-C5
SEATTLE WA 287-E6
TUKWILA WA 287-E6
TUKWILA WA 289-G1
Rt#-900 MILL AV S
RENTON WA 175-C5
Rt#-900 N PARK DR
RENTON WA 175-C4
Rt#-900 NE PARK DR
RENTON WA 175-C4
Rt#-900 RENTON ISSAQUAH
RD SE
ISSAQUAH WA 175-D4
KING CO WA 175-D4
Rt#-900 SE RENTON
ISSAQUAH RD
KING CO WA 175-D4
RENTON WA 175-D4
Rt#-900 SUNSET BLVD N
RENTON WA 175-C5
Rt#-900 NE SUNSET BLVD
RENTON WA 175-C4
Rt#-900 SW SUNSET BLVD
RENTON WA 175-C5
Rt#-902 W HALLETT RD
SPOKANE CO WA 246-A5
Rt#-902 HIGHWAY
MEDICAL LAKE WA 114-B2
SPOKANE CO WA 114-B2
SPOKANE CO WA 246-A5
Rt#-902 LEFEVRE ST
MEDICAL LAKE WA 114-B2
Rt#-902 MEDICAL LAKE RD
MEDICAL LAKE WA 114-B2
SPOKANE CO WA 114-B2
Rt#-902 S MEDICAL LK
TYLER RD
MEDICAL LAKE WA 114-B2
Rt#-902 W SALNAVE RD
MEDICAL LAKE WA 114-B2
SPOKANE CO WA 114-B2
Rt#-903 2ND AV
KITTITAS CO WA 240-A1
Rt#-903 E FIRST ST
CLE ELUM WA 240-B2
Rt#-903 N FIRST ST
ROSLYN WA 240-A1
Rt#-903 S FIRST ST
ROSLYN WA 240-A1
Rt#-903 W FIRST ST
CLE ELUM WA 240-B2
ROSLYN WA 240-A1
Rt#-903 HIGHWAY
CLE ELUM WA 240-B2
KITTITAS CO WA 240-A1
ROSLYN WA 240-A1
Rt#-903 W NEVADA AV
ROSLYN WA 240-A1
Rt#-903 SALMON LA SAC RD
KITTITAS CO WA 111-B3
KITTITAS CO WA 240-A1
Rt#-903 W SECOND ST
CLE ELUM WA 240-B2
Rt#-903 SECOND ST W
CLE ELUM WA 240-B2
Rt#-903 N SEVENTH ST
ROSLYN WA 240-A1
Rt#-903 STAFFORD AV
CLE ELUM WA 240-B2
Rt#-904 COLUMBIA BASIN
HWY
CHENEY WA 246-A7
SPOKANE CO WA 246-A7
Rt#-904 FIRST ST
CHENEY WA 246-A7
Rt#-904 W FIRST ST
CHENEY WA 246-A7
Rt#-904 HIGHWAY
CHENEY WA 246-A7
SPOKANE CO WA 114-B2
SPOKANE CO WA 246-A6
Rt#-906 HIGHWAY
KING CO WA 111-A2
KITTITAS CO WA 111-A2
Rt#-908 NE 85TH ST
KIRKLAND WA 175-C1
Rt#-908 NE REDMOND WY
REDMOND WA 175-C1
Rt#-970 HIGHWAY
KITTITAS CO WA 240-D1
Rt#-970 SUNSET HWY
KITTITAS CO WA 240-B2
Rt#-971 S LAKESHORE RD
CHELAN CO WA 236-B3
Rt#-971 NAVARRE COULEE RD
CHELAN CO WA 236-B3
U.S.-2 1 RD SE
DOUGLAS CO WA 112-C2
U.S.-2 2 1/2 RD NW
DOUGLAS CO WA 236-C7
WATERVILLE WA 236-C7
U.S.-2 6TH ST
NEWPORT WA 106-C3
U.S.-2 12 RD NE
DOUGLAS CO WA 112-C2
U.S.-2 W 14TH AV
AIRWAY HEIGHTS WA 246-A4
SPOKANE CO WA 246-A4
U.S.-2 15TH ST NW
East Wenatchee Bench WA . 239-A4
U.S.-2 ALBANY RD
BONNER CO ID 107-A3
PRIEST RIVER ID 107-A3
U.S.-2 E BROADWAY ST
REARDAN WA 114-A2
U.S.-2 W BROADWAY ST
REARDAN WA 114-A2
U.S.-2 N BROWNE ST
SPOKANE WA 349-A9
U.S.-2 S BROWNE ST
SPOKANE WA 349-A10
U.S.-2 S CENTRAL AV
WATERVILLE WA 236-C7

STREET
City State   Page-Grid

U.S.-2 N CHELAN AV
WATERVILLE WA 236-C7
U.S.-2 E COZZA DR
SPOKANE WA 347-A14
U.S.-2 CROFT AV
GOLD BAR WA 110-C1
SNOHOMISH CO WA 110-C1
U.S.-2 N DIVISION ST
SPOKANE WA 346-J12
SPOKANE WA 347-A14
SPOKANE WA 349-A3
Town and Country WA 346-J12
Town and Country WA 347-A14
Town and Country WA 349-A3
U.S.-2 S DIVISION ST
SPOKANE WA 349-A9
U.S.-2 FRWY
CASHMERE WA 238-C2
CHELAN CO WA 239-A3
DOUGLAS CO WA 238-D3
East Wenatchee Bench WA . 238-D3
East Wenatchee Bench WA . 239-A3
EVERETT WA 265-G3
SNOHOMISH CO WA 171-D2
SNOHOMISH CO WA 265-G3
Sunnyslope WA 238-D3
U.S.-2 HIGHWAY
ALMIRA WA 237-D7
BONNER CO ID 106-C3
BONNER CO ID 107-A3
BONNER CO ID 244-A2
BOUNDARY CO ID 107-B1
CHELAN CO WA 111-C1
CHELAN CO WA 238-A1
COULEE CITY WA 113-A2
Country Homes WA 347-A10
CRESTON WA 113-C1
DAVENPORT WA 114-A2
DOUGLAS CO WA 112-C2
DOUGLAS CO WA 113-A2
DOUGLAS CO WA 236-B6
DOUGLAS CO WA 239-A1
DOVER ID 107-A3
DOVER ID 244-A2
Fairchild Air Force Base WA 114-B2
Fairwood WA 347-C7
GRANT CO WA 113-A2
LEAVENWORTH WA 238-A1
LINCOLN CO MT 107-C2
LINCOLN CO WA 113-C1
LINCOLN CO WA 114-A2
LINCOLN CO WA 237-D7
MOYIE SPRINGS ID 107-B1
NEWPORT WA 106-C3
PEND OREILLE CO WA 106-C3
SANDPOINT ID 244-A2
SPOKANE WA 346-J12
SPOKANE WA 347-A11
SPOKANE WA 106-C3
SPOKANE WA 114-C1
SPOKANE WA 246-A4
SPOKANE WA 347-F1
SPOKANE CO WA 348-A11
TROY MT 107-C2
WATERVILLE WA 236-C7
WILBUR WA 113-B1
U.S.-2 E MAIN AV
LINCOLN CO WA 113-B1
WILBUR WA 113-B1
U.S.-2 W MAIN AV
WALLA WALLA CO WA 113-B1
U.S.-2 MISSOULA AV
LINCOLN CO MT 107-C2
TROY MT 107-C2
U.S.-2 E MISSOULA AV
TROY MT 107-C2
U.S.-2 MORGAN ST
DAVENPORT WA 114-A2
LINCOLN CO WA 114-A2
U.S.-2 N NEWPORT HWY
Country Homes WA 347-B9
Fairwood WA 347-B9
SPOKANE CO WA 347-E5
U.S.-2 PINE ST
SANDPOINT ID 244-A2
U.S.-2 E POPLAR ST
DOUGLAS CO WA 236-C7
WATERVILLE WA 236-C7
U.S.-2 N RUBY ST
SPOKANE WA 349-A6
U.S.-2 SAND HILL RD
BOUNDARY CO ID 107-B1
U.S.-2 W SPOKANE FALLS
BLVD
SPOKANE WA 349-A9
U.S.-2 STEVENS PASS HWY
GOLD BAR WA 110-C1
KING CO WA 111-B1
MONROE WA 110-C1
SNOHOMISH CO WA 110-C1
SNOHOMISH CO WA 111-A1
SNOHOMISH CO WA 171-D3
SULTAN WA 110-C1
U.S.-2 NE STEVENS PASS
HWY
KING CO WA 111-A1
SKYKOMISH WA 111-A1
SNOHOMISH CO WA 111-A1
U.S.-2 STEVENS PASS RD
SNOHOMISH CO WA 171-D2
U.S.-2 SUNSET FRWY
DOUGLAS CO WA 238-D3
East Wenatchee Bench WA . 238-D3
Sunnyslope WA 238-D3
U.S.-2 W SUNSET HWY
AIRWAY HEIGHTS WA 246-A4
SPOKANE CO WA 246-A4
SPOKANE CO WA 348-A12
U.S.-2 WALNUT ST
NEWPORT ID 106-C3
NEWPORT WA 106-C3
U.S.-2 N WASHINGTON AV
NEWPORT WA 106-C3
U.S.-2 S WASHINGTON AV
NEWPORT WA 106-C3
U.S.-2 WATSON ST
CRESTON WA 113-C1
U.S.-11 HIGHWAY
CLEARWATER CO ID 123-C2
LEWIS CO ID 123-C2
U.S.-12 1ST ST
LEWISTON ID 250-B4
U.S.-12 5TH ST
LEWISTON ID 250-B4
U.S.-12 18TH ST
LEWISTON ID 250-C4
U.S.-12 183RD AV SW
Rochester WA 184-A3

STREET
City State   Page-Grid

U.S.-12 183RD AV SW
THURSTON WA 184-A3
U.S.-12 ARROW AV
NEZ PERCE CO ID 123-A2
U.S.-12 BRIDGE ST
CLARKSTON WA 250-B4
LEWISTON ID 250-B4
U.S.-12 COPPEI AV
WAITSBURG WA 122-A2
U.S.-12 D ST
LEWISTON ID 250-B4
U.S.-12 DIKE BYPS
LEWISTON ID 250-B4
U.S.-12 FRWY
PASCO WA 343-H5
YAKIMA WA 243-B6
YAKIMA CO WA 243-B6
U.S.-12 HIGHWAY
ASOTIN WA 122-C2
ASOTIN CO WA 250-A4
Burbank WA 121-A3
Central Park WA 178-C7
CLEARWATER CO ID 123-A2
COLUMBIA WA 122-A2
DAYTON WA 122-A2
ELMA WA 179-B7
FRANKLIN CO WA 121-A3
GARFIELD CO WA 122-A2
Garrett WA 344-G7
Grand Mound WA 184-B4
GRAYS HARBOR CO WA 117-B1
GRAYS HARBOR CO WA 178-B7
GRAYS HARBOR CO WA 179-B7
GRAYS HARBOR CO WA 184-A3
IDAHO CO ID 123-C2
KAMIAH ID 123-C2
LEWIS CO ID 123-C2
LEWIS CO ID 118-C2
LEWIS CO WA 119-A1
LEWIS CO WA 185-D6
LEWISTON ID 250-C4
MONTESANO WA 178-D7
MORTON WA 118-B2
MOSSYROCK WA 118-B2
NACHES WA 119-C1
NACHES CO WA 243-A4
NEZ PERCE CO ID 123-B2
NEZ PERCE CO ID 250-D3
OAKVILLE WA 117-B1
OROFINO ID 123-C2
PASCO WA 121-A3
PASCO WA 343-H5
POMEROY WA 122-B2
Rochester WA 184-A3
THURSTON WA 184-A3
WAITSBURG WA 122-A2
WALLA WALLA WA 344-J7
WALLA WALLA WA 345-J4
WALLA WALLA CO WA 121-A3
WALLA WALLA CO WA 122-A2
WALLA WALLA CO WA 344-A9
WALLA WALLA CO WA 345-J3
YAKIMA WA 243-B6
YAKIMA CO WA 119-C1
YAKIMA CO WA 243-A4
U.S.-12 INLAND EMPIRE HWY
ASOTIN WA 250-B4
Garrett WA 344-D7
WALLA WALLA CO WA 344-D7
U.S.-12 MAIN ST
DAYTON WA 122-B2
LEWISTON ID 250-C4
POMEROY WA 122-B2
U.S.-12 E MAIN ST
COLUMBIA WA 122-A2
DAYTON WA 122-A2
LEWISTON ID 250-C4
U.S.-12 W MAIN ST
DAYTON WA 122-A2
U.S.-12 NATIONAL PARK RD
LEWIS CO WA 118-B2
MORTON WA 118-B2
U.S.-12 PINE ST
OAKVILLE WA 117-B1
U.S.-12 PRESTON AV
WAITSBURG WA 122-A2
U.S.-12 WISHKAH ST
ABERDEEN WA 178-B7
GRAYS HARBOR CO WA 178-B7
U.S.-20 2ND ST
BENTON CO OR 327-H9
CORVALLIS OR 327-H9
U.S.-20 NE 3RD ST
BEND OR 332-F4
U.S.-20 3RD ST W
CORVALLIS OR 327-G10
U.S.-20 4TH ST W
CORVALLIS OR 327-H9
U.S.-20 A ST E
VALE OR 139-A3
U.S.-20 A ST W
VALE OR 139-A3
U.S.-20 ALBANY-CORVALLIS
HWY
ALBANY OR 207-B5
ALBANY OR 326-A7
BENTON CO OR 207-B5
BENTON CO OR 326-A7
CORVALLIS OR 207-B5
CORVALLIS OR 327-J8
U.S.-20 N BROADWAY AV
BURNS OR 145-B1
U.S.-20 S BROADWAY AV
BOISE ID 253-D3
U.S.-20 CAROLINA ST
LEBANON OR 133-C1
U.S.-20 CASCADE ST
SISTERS OR 211-D5
U.S.-20 CENTRAL OREGON
HWY
BEND OR 217-C2
BURNS OR 145-A1
DESCHUTES CO OR 135-B3
DESCHUTES CO OR 143-C1
DESCHUTES CO OR 144-A1
DESCHUTES CO OR 217-C2
HARNEY CO OR 138-A3
HARNEY CO OR 144-B1
HARNEY CO OR 145-A1
HARNEY CO OR 146-A1
HINES OR 145-A1
LAKE CO OR 144-A1
MALHEUR CO OR 138-C3

STREET
City State   Page-Grid

U.S.-20 CENTRAL OREGON
HWY
MALHEUR CO OR 139-A3
MALHEUR CO OR 146-A1
NYSSA OR 139-A3
VALE OR 138-C3
VALE OR 139-A3
U.S.-20 CHINDEN BLVD
CANYON CO ID 147-C1
U.S.-20 E CHINDEN BLVD
ADA CO ID 253-B2
BOISE ID 253-B2
EAGLE ID 253-B2
U.S.-20 W CHINDEN BLVD
ADA CO ID 147-C1
ADA CO ID 253-A2
BOISE ID 253-B2
CANYON CO ID 147-C1
CANYON CO ID 253-A2
EAGLE ID 253-B2
GARDEN CITY ID 253-C2
U.S.-20
CORVALLIS-NEWPORT HWY
BENTON CO OR 133-A1
CORVALLIS OR 133-A1
CORVALLIS OR 327-E11
PHILOMATH OR 133-A1
U.S.-20 N COURT AV
BURNS OR 145-B1
U.S.-20 DIVISION ST
BEND OR 332-F5
U.S.-20 ELGIN AV
CANYON CO ID 147-B1
NOTUS ID 147-B1
U.S.-20 ELLSWORTH ST
ALBANY OR 326-C8
U.S.-20 FRANKLIN RD
CALDWELL ID 147-B1
CANYON CO ID 147-B1
U.S.-20 NE GREENWOOD AV
BEND OR 332-F7
U.S.-20 NW GREENWOOD AV
BEND OR 332-E7
U.S.-20 HIGHWAY
CALDWELL ID 147-B1
CANYON CO ID 139-A3
CANYON CO ID 147-B1
LINCOLN CO OR 206-C4
MALHEUR CO OR 139-A3
TOLEDO OR 206-C4
VALE OR 139-A3
U.S.-20 HIGHWAY 20
LINCOLN CO OR 133-A1
LINCOLN CO OR 206-C3
NEWPORT OR 206-B4
TOLEDO OR 206-C3
U.S.-20 LYON ST
ALBANY OR 326-C8
U.S.-20 MAIN ST
BENTON CO OR 133-B1
LEBANON OR 133-C1
LINN CO OR 133-C1
MALHEUR CO OR 139-A3
NYSSA OR 139-A3
PHILOMATH OR 133-B1
SWEET HOME OR 133-C2
U.S.-20 MCKENZIE-BEND HWY
BEND OR 332-F1
DESCHUTES CO OR 211-D5
DESCHUTES CO OR 212-A6
DESCHUTES CO OR 217-C1
DESCHUTES CO OR 332-F1
SISTERS OR 211-D5
U.S.-20 W MONROE ST
BURNS OR 145-B1
U.S.-20 OLIVE ST
NEWPORT OR 206-B4
U.S.-20 E OLIVE ST
NEWPORT OR 206-B4
U.S.-20 OREGON CENTRAL
HWY
CANYON CO OR 139-A3
U.S.-20 PARK ST
LEBANON OR 133-C1
U.S.-20 PHILOMATH BLVD
BENTON CO OR 133-B1
BENTON CO OR 327-A12
CORVALLIS OR 133-B1
CORVALLIS OR 327-A12
U.S.-20 NE REVERE AV
BEND OR 332-F6
U.S.-20 SANTIAM HWY
ALBANY OR 326-F8
Crowfoot OR 133-C1
DESCHUTES CO OR 211-C3
JEFFERSON CO OR 211-A2
LEBANON OR 133-C1
LINN CO OR 133-C1
LINN CO OR 134-A2
LINN CO OR 207-D5
LINN CO OR 211-A2
LINN CO OR 326-F8
SISTERS OR 211-C3
SWEET HOME OR 133-C1
SWEET HOME OR 134-A2
U.S.-20 THE DALLES-CALIF
HWY
BEND OR 332-F3
DESCHUTES CO OR 332-F3
VALE OR 139-A3
U.S.-20 NW WALL ST
BEND OR 332-E6
U.S.-20 WASHINGTON ST E
VALE OR 139-A3
U.S.-20 WASHINGTON ST W
VALE OR 139-A3
U.S.-20 SW 4TH ST
MADRAS OR 208-C5
U.S.-20 NW 4TH ST
MADRAS OR 208-C5
U.S.-20 5TH ST
MADRAS OR 208-C5
U.S.-20 12TH ST N
MALHEUR CO OR 139-A3
U.S.-26 FRANKLIN AV
DAYVILLE OR 136-C2
GRANT CO OR 136-C2
U.S.-26 FRONT ST
GRANT CO OR 137-B2
PRAIRIE CITY OR 137-B2
U.S.-26 SW FRONT ST
PORTLAND OR 317-F1
U.S.-26 HIGHWAY
PORTLAND OR 317-F1
U.S.-26 JOHN DAY HWY
CANYON CO OR 137-C2
BAKER CO OR 138-A3
MALHEUR CO OR 138-C3

STREET
City State   Page-Grid

U.S.-26 JOHN DAY HWY
GRANT CO OR 136-C1
GRANT CO OR 137-C2
JOHN DAY OR 137-C2
MALHEUR CO OR 138-B2
MALHEUR CO OR 139-A3
MOUNT VERNON OR 137-C2
UNITY OR 138-A2
VALE OR 139-A3
U.S.-26
MADRAS-PRINEVILLE HWY
CROOK CO OR 213-C3
JEFFERSON CO OR 213-C3
PRINEVILLE OR 213-C3
U.S.-26 SE
MADRAS-PRNVLLE HWY
JEFFERSON CO OR 208-C7
U.S.-26 SW
MADRAS-PRNVLLE HWY
JEFFERSON CO OR 208-C6
U.S.-26 E MAIN ST
GRANT CO OR 137-B2
JOHN DAY OR 137-B2
U.S.-26 W MAIN ST
MOUNT VERNON OR 137-A2
U.S.-26 MOUNT HOOD HWY
CLACKAMAS CO OR 200-C3
CLACKAMAS CO OR 201-B4
CLACKAMAS CO OR 202-A6
GRESHAM OR 200-C3
MULTNOMAH CO OR 200-C3
SANDY OR 200-C3
U.S.-26 SE MOUNT HOOD HWY
MULTNOMAH CO OR 200-A2
PORTLAND OR 200-A2
U.S.-26 OCHOCO HWY
CROOK CO OR 135-C2
CROOK CO OR 136-A2
CROOK CO OR 213-D5
GRANT CO OR 136-B1
MITCHELL OR 136-B1
PRINEVILLE OR 213-D5
WHEELER CO OR 136-B1
U.S.-26 PIONEER BLVD
SANDY OR 200-C4
U.S.-26 E POWELL BLVD
GRESHAM OR 200-B2
U.S.-26 SE POWELL BLVD
GRESHAM OR 200-A2
PORTLAND OR 200-A2
PORTLAND OR 317-H1
PORTLAND OR 318-B2
PORTLAND OR 319-H2
U.S.-26 W POWELL BLVD
GRESHAM OR 200-A2
U.S.-26 PROCTOR BLVD
SANDY OR 200-C4
U.S.-26 SUNSET HWY
BEAVERTON OR 199-A1
CLATSOP CO OR 117-A3
CLATSOP CO OR 188-C7
COLUMBIA CO OR 125-B1
HILLSBORO OR 125-B1
HILLSBORO OR 192-A7
HILLSBORO OR 199-A1
MULTNOMAH CO OR 199-A1
MULTNOMAH CO OR 312-B7
NORTH PLAINS OR 125-B1
PORTLAND OR 199-A1
PORTLAND OR 312-B7
PORTLAND OR 316-B1
TILLAMOOK CO OR 125-B1
WASHINGTON CO OR 125-B1
WASHINGTON CO OR 192-A7
WASHINGTON CO OR 199-A1
U.S.-26 THE DALLES-CALIF
HWY
JEFFERSON CO OR 208-C6
MADRAS OR 208-C5
U.S.-26 WARM SPRINGS HWY
CLACKAMAS CO OR 202-A7
JEFFERSON CO OR 135-A1
JEFFERSON CO OR 208-B3
MADRAS OR 208-B3
Warm Springs OR 135-A1
Warm Springs OR 208-A2
WASCO CO OR 126-C3
WASCO CO OR 127-A3
WASCO CO OR 135-A1
WASCO CO OR 202-A7
U.S.-30 2ND ST S
NAMPA ID 147-B1
U.S.-30 3RD ST S
NAMPA ID 147-B1
U.S.-30 8TH ST
ASTORIA OR 300-C5
U.S.-30 10TH ST
BAKER CITY OR 138-B1
U.S.-30 11TH AV
NAMPA ID 147-B1
U.S.-30 11TH AV N
NAMPA ID 147-B1
U.S.-30 ADAMS AV
LA GRANDE OR 130-A2
U.S.-30 AUBURN AV
BAKER CITY OR 138-B1
U.S.-30 E B ST
RAINIER OR 189-C4
U.S.-30 N W B ST
RAINIER OR 189-C4
U.S.-30 BLAINE ST
CALDWELL ID 147-B1
U.S.-30 BRIDGE ST
BAKER CITY OR 138-B1
U.S.-30 NW BRIDGE AV
PORTLAND OR 192-B7
U.S.-30 BROADWAY ST
BAKER CITY OR 138-B1
U.S.-30 BUTTON BRIDGE RD
HOOD RIVER OR 195-D5
U.S.-30 CALDWELL BLVD
CANYON CO ID 147-B1
NAMPA ID 147-B1
U.S.-30 CASCADE AV
HOOD RIVER OR 195-D5
HOOD RIVER CO OR 195-C5
U.S.-30 CASCADE LOCKS HWY
CASCADE LOCKS OR 194-D5
U.S.-30 CENTENNIAL WY
CALDWELL ID 147-B1
U.S.-30 CLEVELAND BLVD
CALDWELL ID 147-B1
CANYON CO ID 147-B1
NAMPA ID 147-B1
U.S.-30 COLUMBIA RIVER
HWY
ASTORIA OR 188-D1

STREET
City State   Page-Grid

U.S.-30 COLUMBIA RIVER
HWY
ASTORIA OR 300-E5
CLATSKANIE OR 117-B3
CLATSOP CO OR 117-A3
CLATSOP CO OR 188-D1
COLUMBIA CITY OR 192-A3
COLUMBIA CO OR 117-B3
COLUMBIA CO OR 189-A4
COLUMBIA CO OR 192-A3
COLUMBIA CO OR 302-A14
RAINIER OR 189-A4
SAINT HELENS OR 192-A3
SCAPPOOSE OR 192-A3
U.S.-30 COMMERCIAL ST
ASTORIA OR 300-C5
U.S.-30 COUNTY RD 900
PENDLETON OR 129-B1
UMATILLA CO OR 129-B1
U.S.-30 NW COURT AV
PENDLETON OR 129-B1
U.S.-30 SE COURT AV
PENDLETON OR 129-B1
U.S.-30 SW DORION AV
PENDLETON OR 129-B1
U.S.-30 ELM ST
BAKER CITY OR 138-B1
U.S.-30 FRONT ST
HOOD RIVER OR 195-D5
U.S.-30 GARRITY BLVD
CANYON CO ID 147-C1
NAMPA ID 147-C1
U.S.-30 E H AV
LA GRANDE OR 130-A2
U.S.-30 HIGHWAY
HOOD RIVER OR 195-D5
HOOD RIVER CO OR 195-C5
MALHEUR CO OR 139-A3
NEW PLYMOUTH ID 139-B3
PAYETTE CO ID 139-B3
U.S.-30 HUNTINGTON HWY
BAKER CO OR 138-C2
BAKER CO OR 139-A2
HUNTINGTON OR 138-C2
MALHEUR CO OR 139-A2
U.S.-30 IDAHO AV
ONTARIO OR 139-A3
U.S.-30 N IVANHOE ST
PORTLAND OR 192-B7
U.S.-30 NE KILLINGSWORTH
ST
PORTLAND OR 311-F7
U.S.-30 LA GRANDE-BAKER
HWY
BAKER CITY OR 138-B1
BAKER CO OR 130-A3
HAINES OR 130-A3
LA GRANDE OR 130-A3
UNION CO OR 130-A3
U.S.-30 N LOMBARD ST
PORTLAND OR 192-B7
PORTLAND OR 308-B4
PORTLAND OR 309-E5
U.S.-30 NE LOMBARD ST
PORTLAND OR 309-G5
PORTLAND OR 310-B6
U.S.-30 MAIN ST
BAKER CITY OR 138-B1
U.S.-30 MARINE DR
ASTORIA OR 300-C5
U.S.-30 W MARINE DR
ASTORIA OR 300-A5
U.S.-30 MOSIER-THE
DALLES HWY
MOSIER OR 196-A5
THE DALLES OR 196-A5
WASCO CO OR 196-A5
U.S.-30 OAK ST
HOOD RIVER OR 195-C5
U.S.-30 OLDS
FRRY-ONTARIO HWY
MALHEUR CO OR 139-A3
ONTARIO OR 139-A3
U.S.-30 OREGON ST
MALHEUR CO OR 139-A3
ONTARIO OR 139-A3
U.S.-30 N OREGON ST
ONTARIO OR 139-A3
U.S.-30 PENDLETON HWY
UMATILLA CO OR 129-B1
U.S.-30 NW PENDLETON HWY
PENDLETON OR 129-B1
UMATILLA CO OR 129-B1
U.S.-30 N PHILADELPHIA AV
PORTLAND OR 192-B7
U.S.-30 PLYMOUTH AV
NEW PLYMOUTH ID 139-B3
U.S.-30 NE PORTLAND HWY
PORTLAND OR 310-D6
PORTLAND OR 311-E7
U.S.-30 N RICHMOND AV
PORTLAND OR 192-B7
U.S.-30 NE SANDY BLVD
FAIRVIEW OR 200-A1
GRESHAM OR 200-A1
PORTLAND OR 200-A1
PORTLAND OR 315-J1
WOOD VILLAGE OR 200-A1
U.S.-30 NW SAINT HELENS
RD
MULTNOMAH CO OR 192-A5
PORTLAND OR 192-A5
PORTLAND OR 199-B1
U.S.-30 SOUTHEAST AV
NEW PLYMOUTH ID 139-B3
PAYETTE CO ID 139-B3
U.S.-30 STATE AV
HOOD RIVER OR 195-D5
HOOD RIVER CO OR 195-D5
U.S.-30 WASHINGTON ST E
HUNTINGTON OR 138-C2
U.S.-30 WASHINGTON ST W
HUNTINGTON OR 138-C2
U.S.-30 WESTGATE AV
PENDLETON OR 129-B1
U.S.-30 NW YEON AV
PORTLAND OR 199-B1
PORTLAND OR 312-A1
U.S.-95 N 1ST AV
SANDPOINT ID 244-A4
U.S.-95 S 1ST AV
SANDPOINT ID 244-A4
U.S.-95 S 3RD ST
FRUITLAND ID 139-A3
U.S.-95 5TH AV
SANDPOINT ID 244-A4
U.S.-95 N 5TH AV
SANDPOINT ID 244-A4

INDEX

STREET City State Page-Grid

U.S.-95 5TH ST
CANYON CO ID 147-A1
WILDER ID 147-A1
U.S.-95 7TH ST
WEISER ID 139-A2
U.S.-95 S 7TH ST
PAYETTE ID 139-A3
U.S.-95 E 7TH ST
WEISER ID 139-A2
U.S.-95 N 16TH ST
PAYETTE ID 139-A3
U.S.-95 S 16TH ST
PAYETTE ID 139-A3
U.S.-95 A
COTTONWOOD ID 123-C3
GRANGEVILLE ID 123-C3
IDAHO CO ID 123-B3
U.S.-95 CEDAR ST
SANDPOINT ID 244-A2
U.S.-95 CEMETERY RD
OWYHEE CO ID 147-B1
U.S.-95 CENTRAL BLVD
CAMBRIDGE ID 139-B1
WASHINGTON CO ID 139-B1
U.S.-95 CLARK ST
LEWIS CO ID 123-B2
WINCHESTER ID 123-B2
U.S.-95 E COEUR D'ALENE AV
BENEWAH CO ID 115-A3
TENSED ID 115-A3
U.S.-95 DARTMOUTH ST
ADAMS CO ID 139-C1
COUNCIL ID 139-C1
U.S.-95 W ELDER RD
KOOTENAI CO ID 247-D5
U.S.-95 F ST
WORLEY ID 115-A2
U.S.-95 E GROVE ST
CANYON CO ID 139-A3
PARMA ID 139-A3
U.S.-95 W GROVE ST
PARMA ID 139-A3
U.S.-95 HIGHWAY
ADAMS CO ID 131-C2
ADAMS CO ID 139-C1
ADAMS CO ID 251-A4
ATHOL ID 245-B2
BENEWAH CO ID 115-A2
BONNER CO ID 107-B2
BONNER CO ID 244-A1
BONNER CO ID 245-B1
BONNERS FERRY ID 107-B1
BOUNDARY CO ID 107-B1
CANYON CO ID 139-A3
CANYON CO ID 147-A1
COEUR D'ALENE ID 355-D2
COUNCIL ID 139-C1
CRAIGMONT ID 123-B2
CULDESAC ID 123-B2
FRUITLAND ID 139-A3
GRANGEVILLE ID 123-C3
HAYDEN ID 245-A5
HAYDEN ID 355-D1
HOMEDALE ID 147-A1
IDAHO CO ID 123-B3
IDAHO CO ID 131-C1
IDAHO CO ID 251-A1
KOOTENAI CO ID 115-A2
KOOTENAI CO ID 245-B1
KOOTENAI CO ID 247-D4
KOOTENAI CO ID 354-J13
KOOTENAI CO ID 355-D2
LAPWAI ID 123-A2
LATAH CO ID 115-A3
LATAH CO ID 249-D1
LATAH CO ID 250-C1
LEWIS CO ID 123-B2
LEWISTON ID 250-C4
MALHEUR CO OR 139-A2
MIDVALE ID 139-B1
MOSCOW ID 249-C5
NEZ PERCE CO ID 123-A2
NEZ PERCE CO ID 250-C1
OWYHEE CO ID 147-A1
PAYETTE ID 139-A3
PAYETTE ID 139-A3
PLUMMER ID 115-A2
PONDERAY ID 244-A1
RIGGINS ID 131-C2
SANDPOINT ID 244-A2
WASHINGTON CO ID 139-B1
WEISER ID 139-A2
WILDER ID 147-A1
WINCHESTER ID 123-B2
WORLEY ID 115-A2
U.S.-95 E IDAHO AV
HOMEDALE ID 147-A1
U.S.-95 IDAHO-OREGON-NEV HWY
HUMBOLDT CO NV 154-B2
JORDAN VALLEY OR 147-A3
MALHEUR CO OR 146-B3
MALHEUR CO OR 147-A2
MALHEUR CO OR 154-B1
OWYHEE CO ID 147-A2
U.S.-95 W IDAHO ST
WEISER ID 139-A2
U.S.-95 ILLINOIS AV
COUNCIL ID 139-C1
U.S.-95 N JACKSON ST
MOSCOW ID 249-C5
U.S.-95 S JACKSON ST
MOSCOW ID 249-C5
U.S.-95 JOSEPH AV
WINCHESTER ID 123-B2
U.S.-95 LAUER CROSSING RD
IDAHO CO ID 123-B3
U.S.-95 LINCOLN WY
COEUR D'ALENE ID 355-D8
U.S.-95 LITTLE WEISER RD
ADAMS CO ID 139-B1
U.S.-95 MAIN ST
BONNERS FERRY ID 107-B2
FERDINAND ID 123-B3
HOMEDALE ID 147-A1
IDAHO CO ID 123-B3
U.S.-95 E MAIN ST
WEISER ID 139-A2
U.S.-95 N MAIN ST
LATAH CO ID 249-C4
MOSCOW ID 249-C5
U.S.-95 S MAIN ST
BONNERS FERRY ID 107-B2
MOSCOW ID 249-C5
U.S.-95 W MAIN ST
WEISER ID 139-A2
U.S.-95 MARX ST
IDAHO CO ID 131-C2

U.S.-95 MARX ST
RIGGINS ID 131-C2
U.S.-95 MEADOW CREEK RD
IDAHO CO ID 123-B3
U.S.-95 MICHIGAN ST
COUNCIL ID 139-C1
U.S.-95 NORRIS AV
ADAMS CO ID 251-A4
NEW MEADOWS ID 251-A4
U.S.-95 PENNSYLVANIA AV
PAYETTE CO ID 139-A3
U.S.-95 S PENNSYLVANIA AV
FRUITLAND ID 139-A3
PAYETTE ID 139-A3
U.S.-95 PINE ST
SANDPOINT ID 244-A2
U.S.-95 PRAIRIE AV
CRAIGMONT ID 123-B2
U.S.-95 RAILROAD ST
MIDVALE ID 139-B1
U.S.-95 STATE ST
WEISER ID 139-A2
U.S.-95 SUPERIOR ST
CAMBRIDGE ID 139-B1
SANDPOINT ID 244-A2
U.S.-95 S SUPERIOR ST
CAMBRIDGE ID 139-B1
U.S.-95 VIRGINIA ST
ADAMS CO ID 251-A4
NEW MEADOWS ID 251-A4
U.S.-95 S WASHINGTON ST
MOSCOW ID 249-C5
U.S.-95 WEISER SPUR
MALHEUR CO OR 139-A2
U.S.-95 WHITLEY DR
FRUITLAND ID 139-A3
U.S.-95 N WHITLEY DR
FRUITLAND ID 139-A3
PAYETTE CO ID 139-A3
U.S.-95 WILLIAM H BUNDY BLVD
LAPWAI ID 123-A2
NEZ PERCE CO ID 123-A2
U.S.-97 Bus NE 3RD ST
BEND OR 332-F9
U.S.-97 Bus SE 3RD ST
BEND OR 332-F10
U.S.-97 4TH ST
GRASS VALLEY OR 127-C2
SHANIKO OR 127-C3
WASCO CO OR 127-C3
U.S.-97 NW 5TH ST
REDMOND OR 212-D5
U.S.-97 SW 5TH ST
REDMOND OR 212-D5
U.S.-97 NW 6TH ST
REDMOND OR 212-D5
U.S.-97 SW 6TH ST
REDMOND OR 212-D5
U.S.-97 NW 10TH ST
Terrebonne OR 212-D3
U.S.-97 BEND PKWY
BEND OR 332-F3
DESCHUTES CO OR 332-F3
U.S.-97 BUTTE ST
DORRIS CA 150-B3
U.S.-97 CHELAN FALLS RD
CHELAN CO OR 236-D3
U.S.-97 CHELAN-OKANOGAN HWY
Sunnyslope OR 238-D3
U.S.-97 DIVISION ST
BEND OR 332-F9
DESCHUTES CO OR 332-D12
U.S.-97 DRY CREEK RD
KITTITAS CO OR 241-A4
U.S.-97 E ST
SHANIKO OR 127-C3
U.S.-97 Bus ESPLANADE ST
KLAMATH FALLS OR 338-E7
U.S.-97 EVERGREEN HWY
TOPPENISH OR 120-A2
YAKIMA CO WA 120-A2
U.S.-97 FAUST RD
KITTITAS CO OR 241-B5
U.S.-97 FIRST ST
DORRIS CA 150-B3
U.S.-97 FOURTH ST
DORRIS CA 150-B3
U.S.-97 NE FRANKLIN AV
BEND OR 332-F7
U.S.-97 NW FRANKLIN AV
BEND OR 332-E7
U.S.-97 HIGHWAY
BREWSTER WA 104-B3
CHELAN WA 236-C3
CHELAN CO WA 112-B1
CHELAN CO WA 236-D2
CHELAN CO WA 238-B3
CHELAN CO WA 239-A1
DORRIS CA 150-B3
DOUGLAS CO WA 236-D3
ELLENSBURG WA 241-B5
ENTIAT WA 236-B6
GOLDENDALE WA 127-C1
KITTITAS CO WA 111-C3
KITTITAS CO WA 238-B6
KITTITAS CO WA 240-D1
KITTITAS CO WA 241-A1
KLAMATH CO OR 150-C3
KLAMATH FALLS OR 338-C4
KLICKITAT CO WA 119-C3
KLICKITAT CO WA 127-C1
OKANOGAN WA 104-C3
OKANOGAN CO WA 112-B1
OMAK WA 104-C3
OROVILLE WA 104-C1
PATEROS WA 104-B3
PATEROS WA 112-B1
RIVERSIDE WA 104-C2
SHERMAN CO OR 127-C1
SISKIYOU CA CA 150-C3
Sunnyslope WA 238-D3
TONASKET WA 104-C2
TOPPENISH WA 120-A2
WAPATO WA 120-A2
YAKIMA CO WA 119-C3
YAKIMA CO WA 120-A2
U.S.-97 MARX ST
DORRIS CA 150-B3
MORO OR 127-C2
OKANOGAN CO WA 104-C1
OROVILLE WA 104-C1
U.S.-97 SANDERS ST
CHELAN WA 236-D3
U.S.-97 SHERMAN HWY
GRASS VALLEY OR 127-C2
MORO OR 127-C2

U.S.-97 SHERMAN HWY
SHANIKO OR 127-C2
SHERMAN CO OR 127-C1
WASCO CO OR 127-B3
U.S.-97 THE DALLES-CALIF HWY
BEND OR 217-C1
BEND OR 332-F1
CHILOQUIN OR 231-D3
DESCHUTES CO OR 143-A1
DESCHUTES CO OR 212-C7
DESCHUTES CO OR 217-C1
Deschutes River Woods OR 332-D14
Deschutes River Woods OR 332-D14
JEFFERSON CO OR 135-B1
JEFFERSON CO OR 208-C4
JEFFERSON CO OR 212-D3
KLAMATH CO OR 142-C2
KLAMATH CO OR 143-A1
KLAMATH CO OR 150-C1
KLAMATH CO OR 231-D3
KLAMATH CO OR 235-C1
KLAMATH CO OR 338-A1
KLAMATH FALLS OR 338-A1
MADRAS OR 208-C4
REDMOND OR 212-D3
Terrebonne OR 212-D3
WASCO CO OR 127-B3
WASCO CO OR 135-B1
U.S.-97 Bus THE DLS-CALIF HWY
BEND OR 332-D13
U.S.-97 WEBSTER AV
CHELAN WA 236-D3
U.S.-97 WHITCOMB AV
OKANOGAN CO WA 104-C2
TONASKET WA 104-C2
U.S.-97 WOODIN AV
CHELAN WA 236-C3
CHELAN CO WA 236-C3
U.S.-101 1ST AV N
ILWACO WA 186-A6
PACIFIC CO WA 186-A6
U.S.-101 E 1ST ST
PORT ANGELES WA 261-F4
U.S.-101 2ND ST SE
BANDON OR 220-B6
U.S.-101 7TH ST
NEHALEM OR 191-B4
U.S.-101 SW 100TH ST
NEWPORT OR 206-A5
U.S.-101 N ALDER ST
ABERDEEN WA 178-B7
U.S.-101 S ALDER ST
ABERDEEN WA 178-B7
U.S.-101 N BROADWAY ST
COOS BAY OR 333-H9
U.S.-101 S BROADWAY ST
COOS BAY OR 333-H11
U.S.-101 CHETCO AV
BROOKINGS OR 232-C6
U.S.-101 W CURTIS ST
ABERDEEN WA 178-B7
U.S.-101 EVANS BLVD
COOS BAY OR 333-H11
U.S.-101 FIRST ST
COSMOPOLIS WA 178-B7
U.S.-101 E FIRST ST
COSMOPOLIS WA 117-A1
U.S.-101 E FRONT ST
PORT ANGELES WA 261-G5
U.S.-101 FORKS AV N
FORKS WA 169-D1
U.S.-101 FORKS AV S
FORKS WA 169-D1
U.S.-101 FRWY
MASON CO WA 180-A3
OLYMPIA WA 296-D6
THURSTON CO WA 180-B5
THURSTON CO WA 296-B5
TUMWATER WA 296-G7
U.S.-101 S G ST
ABERDEEN WA 178-B7
U.S.-101 GARIBALDI AV
GARIBALDI OR 191-B7
TILLAMOOK CO OR 191-B7
U.S.-101 N GOLF COURSE RD
PORT ANGELES WA 261-H6
U.S.-101 H ST
NEHALEM OR 191-B4
U.S.-101 S H ST
ABERDEEN WA 178-B7
U.S.-101 E HERON ST
ABERDEEN WA 178-B7
U.S.-101 W HERON ST
ABERDEEN WA 178-B7
U.S.-101 HIGHWAY
CLALLAM CO WA 109-C1
CLALLAM CO WA 162-D7
CLALLAM CO WA 163-B6
CLALLAM CO WA 164-A6
CLALLAM CO WA 165-A6
CLALLAM CO WA 166-A7
CLALLAM CO WA 169-C1
CLALLAM CO WA 262-A12
COSMOPOLIS WA 117-A1
FORKS WA 169-C1
GRAYS HARBOR CO WA 108-C2
GRAYS HARBOR CO WA 109-A2
GRAYS HARBOR CO WA 117-A1
GRAYS HARBOR CO WA 172-B3
GRAYS HARBOR CO WA 177-D2
GRAYS HARBOR CO WA 178-A1
GRAYS HARBOR CO WA 178-A6
HOQUIAM WA 178-A6
ILWACO WA 186-A6
JEFFERSON CO WA 108-C1
JEFFERSON CO WA 109-C1
JEFFERSON CO WA 169-D3
JEFFERSON CO WA 172-A1
JEFFERSON CO WA 173-D1
MASON CO WA 173-C2
MASON CO WA 180-A1
PACIFIC CO WA 117-A1
PACIFIC CO WA 183-C6
PACIFIC CO WA 186-B1
PACIFIC CO WA 188-C1
RAYMOND WA 117-A1
SEQUIM WA 166-B7
SEQUIM WA 262-E12
SHELTON WA 180-A2
SOUTH BEND WA 117-A1
U.S.-101 L ST
CRESCENT CITY CA 148-B3
U.S.-101 LEVEE ST
HOQUIAM WA 178-A7
U.S.-101 LINCOLN ST
HOQUIAM WA 178-A7

U.S.-101 N LINCOLN ST
PORT ANGELES WA 261-F4
U.S.-101 S LINCOLN ST
PORT ANGELES WA 261-E5
U.S.-101 M ST
CRESCENT CITY CA 148-B3
U.S.-101 MAIN AV
TILLAMOOK OR 197-B2
TILLAMOOK CO OR 197-B2
U.S.-101 W MARINE DR
ASTORIA OR 300-A5
U.S.-101 NEWPORT AV
COOS BAY OR 333-H12
COOS CO OR 333-H12
U.S.-101 OCEAN AV
RAYMOND WA 117-A1
U.S.-101 OLYMPIC HWY
CLALLAM CO WA 164-C6
CLALLAM CO WA 165-B6
CLALLAM CO WA 166-C7
CLALLAM CO WA 261-A6
JEFFERSON CO WA 109-C1
JEFFERSON CO WA 166-C7
PORT ANGELES WA 261-A6
U.S.-101 OREGON COAST HWY
ASTORIA OR 188-C1
ASTORIA OR 300-A1
BANDON OR 220-C4
BAY CITY OR 191-B5
BAY CITY OR 197-B1
BROOKINGS OR 232-C5
CANNON BEACH OR 188-B7
CANNON BEACH OR 191-A4
CLATSOP CO OR 188-C1
CLATSOP CO OR 191-A2
CLATSOP CO OR 300-A1
COOS CO OR 218-B5
COOS CO OR 220-C4
COOS CO OR 224-B4
COOS CO OR 333-J13
CURRY CO OR 224-B4
CURRY CO OR 228-A1
CURRY CO OR 232-B2
DEPOE BAY OR 203-A7
DEPOE BAY OR 206-B3
DOUGLAS CO OR 214-A7
DOUGLAS CO OR 218-B2
DUNES CITY OR 214-B4
FLORENCE OR 214-B4
GARIBALDI OR 191-B5
GEARHART OR 301-H4
GOLD BEACH OR 228-A6
Harbor OR 232-D6
LAKESIDE OR 218-B2
LANE CO OR 132-B2
LANE CO OR 209-A6
LANE CO OR 214-B4
Lincoln Beach OR 203-A7
LINCOLN CITY OR 203-B3
LINCOLN CO OR 203-B3
LINCOLN CO OR 206-B3
LINCOLN CO OR 209-A3
LINCOLN CO OR 328-D2
MANZANITA OR 191-B5
NEWPORT OR 206-B3
NORTH BEND OR 333-G2
PORT ORFORD OR 224-B6
REEDSPORT OR 218-B2
ROCKAWAY BEACH OR 191-B5
SEASIDE OR 188-B7
SEASIDE OR 301-H4
TILLAMOOK OR 191-B5
TILLAMOOK CO OR 197-C4
TILLAMOOK CO OR 203-B3
WALDPORT OR 328-D2
WARRENTON OR 188-B2
WHEELER OR 191-B5
YACHATS OR 209-A3
U.S.-101 OREGON ST
PORT ORFORD OR 224-A6
U.S.-101 PACIFIC AV
TILLAMOOK OR 197-B2
TILLAMOOK CO OR 197-B2
U.S.-101 PARK DR
GEARHART OR 301-H4
U.S.-101 N PARK ST
ABERDEEN WA 178-B7
U.S.-101 S PARK ST
ABERDEEN WA 178-B7
U.S.-101 PERRY AV
HOQUIAM WA 178-A7
U.S.-101 REDWOOD HWY
CRESCENT CITY CA 148-B3
DEL NORTE CO CA 148-B3
DEL NORTE CO CA 232-D7
U.S.-101 RIVERSIDE AV
HOQUIAM WA 178-A7
U.S.-101 RIVERSIDE DR
NEHALEM OR 191-B4
U.S.-101 ROBERT BUSH DR
PACIFIC CO WA 183-D6
SOUTH BEND WA 117-A1
SOUTH BEND WA 183-D6
U.S.-101 ROOSEVELT DR
SEASIDE OR 301-G6
U.S.-101 S ROOSEVELT DR
CLATSOP CO OR 301-F10
SEASIDE OR 301-G8
U.S.-101 SEVENTH ST
HOQUIAM WA 178-A7
U.S.-101 SHERIDAN AV
NORTH BEND OR 333-G5
U.S.-101 SHERMAN AV
NORTH BEND OR 333-G5
U.S.-101 SIMPSON AV
ABERDEEN WA 178-A7
HOQUIAM WA 178-A7
U.S.-101 SIXTH ST
RAYMOND WA 117-A1
U.S.-101 SUMNER AV
HOQUIAM WA 178-A7
U.S.-101 SUMNER ST
ABERDEEN WA 178-B7
HOQUIAM WA 178-A7
U.S.-101 TREMONT ST
COOS BAY OR 333-G7
NORTH BEND OR 333-G7
U.S.-101 W WASHINGTON ST
CLALLAM CO WA 165-D6
CLALLAM CO WA 166-A6
U.S.-101 S WEST BLVD
ABERDEEN WA 178-B7
COSMOPOLIS WA 178-B7
U.S.-101 WARRNTON-ASTORIA HWY
ASTORIA OR 300-C9
CLATSOP CO OR 188-B2
CLATSOP CO OR 300-C9

U.S.-101 WARRNTON-ASTORIA HWY
WARRENTON OR 188-B2
REEDSPORT OR 218-C1
U.S.-101 WINCHESTER AV
REEDSPORT OR 218-C1
U.S.-101 WISHKAH ST
ABERDEEN WA 178-B7
U.S.-101 E WISHKAH ST
ABERDEEN WA 178-B7
U.S.-101 W WISHKAH ST
ABERDEEN WA 178-B7
U.S.-195 BROADWAY ST
COLTON WA 250-A1
U.S.-195 HIGHWAY
COLFAX WA 122-C1
COLTON WA 250-A1
NEZ PERCE CO ID 250-B3
SPOKANE WA 348-F11
SPOKANE WA 114-C2
SPOKANE WA 246-C6
UNIONTOWN WA 250-B1
WHITMAN CO WA 114-C3
WHITMAN CO WA 122-C1
WHITMAN CO WA 249-A4
WHITMAN CO WA 250-A1
U.S.-195 S INLAND EMPIRE HWY
SPOKANE WA 246-C5
SPOKANE CO WA 246-C5
U.S.-195 INLAND HWY
WHITMAN CO WA 114-C3
U.S.-195 E JAMES ST
COLFAX WA 122-C1
U.S.-195 N MAIN ST
COLFAX WA 122-C1
U.S.-195 S MAIN ST
COLFAX WA 122-C1
U.S.-197 DESCHUTES AV
MAUPIN OR 127-B3
U.S.-197 HIGHWAY
DEL NORTE CO CA 148-B3
KLICKITAT CO WA 196-C6
U.S.-197 THE DALLES-CALIF HWY
DUFUR OR 127-B2
MAUPIN OR 127-B3
THE DALLES OR 196-D7
WASCO CO OR 127-B2
WASCO CO OR 196-D7
U.S.-199 E F ST
GRANTS PASS OR 335-G9
U.S.-199 F ST
GRANTS PASS OR 335-H9
JOSEPHINE CO OR 335-H9
U.S.-199 REDWOOD HWY
CAVE JUNCTION OR 233-B3
DEL NORTE CO CA 148-C3
DEL NORTE CO CA 233-A6
GRANTS PASS OR 335-F9
JOSEPHINE CO OR 149-A1
JOSEPHINE CO OR 229-A7
JOSEPHINE CO OR 233-B3
JOSEPHINE CO OR 335-A12
U.S.-395 N 1ST ST
HERMISTON OR 129-A1
U.S.-395 W 5TH AV
COLVILLE WA 106-A2
U.S.-395 BARNES AV
SENECA OR 137-B3
U.S.-395 S CANYON BLVD
JOHN DAY OR 137-B2
U.S.-395 N DIVISION ST
Country Homes WA 346-J11
Country Homes WA 347-A8
Fairwood WA 347-A8
SPOKANE WA 346-J11
Town and Country WA 346-J11
U.S.-395 N ELY ST
KENNEWICK WA 342-J10
U.S.-395 S ELY ST
KENNEWICK WA 342-J11
U.S.-395 F ST N
LAKEVIEW OR 152-A2
U.S.-395 F ST S
LAKE CO OR 152-A2
LAKEVIEW OR 152-A2
U.S.-395 FREMONT HWY
LAKE CO OR 152-A2
LAKEVIEW OR 152-A2
MODOC CO CA 152-A2
U.S.-395 FRWY
BENTON CO WA 121-A3
Finley WA 121-A3
KENNEWICK WA 343-B9
LEWISTON OR 121-A3
PASCO WA 343-D5
UMATILLA CO WA 121-A3
U.S.-395 G ST N
LAKEVIEW OR 152-A2
U.S.-395 HIGHWAY
ADAMS CO WA 113-C3
ADAMS CO WA 121-C1
BENTON CO WA 121-A3
COLVILLE WA 106-A2
CONNELL WA 121-B1
DEER PARK WA 114-B1
Fairwood WA 347-A6
FERRY CO WA 105-C1
FERRY CO WA 106-A1
Finley WA 121-A3
FRANKLIN CO WA 121-B1
FRANKLIN CO WA 343-F1
KENNEWICK WA 121-A3
KENNEWICK WA 342-J10
KENNEWICK WA 343-B10
KETTLE FALLS WA 106-A2
MESA WA 121-B2
MODOC CO CA 152-A3
PASCO WA 121-A2
PASCO WA 343-G1
SPOKANE CO WA 114-B1
SPOKANE CO WA 346-J1
SPOKANE CO WA 347-A2
STEVENS CO WA 106-A2
STEVENS CO WA 114-B1
U.S.-395 JOHN DAY HWY
GRANT CO OR 137-A2
JOHN DAY OR 137-A2
MOUNT VERNON OR 137-A2
U.S.-395 JOHN DAY-BURNS HWY
CANYON CITY OR 137-B2
GRANT CO OR 137-B2
HARNEY CO OR 137-B3
JOHN DAY OR 137-B2
SENECA OR 137-B3

U.S.-395 LAKEVIEW-BURNS HWY
HARNEY CO OR 144-C2
LAKE CO OR 144-B3
LAKE CO OR 152-A1
U.S.-395 E MAIN ST
MOUNT VERNON OR 137-A2
U.S.-395 N MAIN ST
COLVILLE WA 106-A2
U.S.-395 S MAIN ST
COLVILLE WA 106-A2
U.S.-395 W MAIN ST
GRANT CO OR 137-B2
JOHN DAY OR 137-B2
U.S.-395 MCNARY HWY
UMATILLA OR 129-A1
UMATILLA CO OR 129-A1
U.S.-395 MOUNTAIN BLVD
MOUNT VERNON OR 137-A2
U.S.-395 N PARK ST
CHEWELAH WA 106-B3
STEVENS CO WA 106-B3
U.S.-395 S PARK ST
CHEWELAH WA 106-B3
STEVENS CO WA 106-B3
U.S.-395 PENDLTN-JOHN DAY HWY
GRANT CO OR 129-B3
GRANT CO OR 137-A1
LONG CREEK OR 137-A1
MOUNT VERNON OR 137-A1
PENDLETON OR 129-B2
PILOT ROCK OR 129-B2
UMATILLA CO OR 129-B2
U.S.-395 PIONEER MEM BRDG
KENNEWICK WA 343-B8
PASCO WA 343-B8
U.S.-395 UMATILLA-STANFLD HWY
HERMISTON OR 129-A1
STANFIELD OR 129-A1
UMATILLA OR 129-A1
UMATILLA CO OR 129-A1
U.S.-730 6TH ST
UMATILLA OR 129-A1
UMATILLA CO OR 129-A1
U.S.-730 COLUMBIA RIVER HWY
IRRIGON OR 128-C1
MORROW CO OR 128-C1
UMATILLA CO OR 128-C1
UMATILLA CO OR 129-A1
U.S.-730 MAIN AV E
IRRIGON OR 128-C1

FEATURE NAME / City State — Page-Grid

AIRPORTS

ALBANY MUNICIPAL — 326 - H7
PRICE RD, ALBANY OR

ALKALI LAKE STATE — 144 - B3
LAKEVIEW-BURNS HWY, LAKE CO OR

ANACORTES — 259 - C4
OFF ANACOPER RD, ANACORTES WA

ARLINGTON — 168 - D5
59TH AV NE, ARLINGTON WA

ARLINGTON MUNICIPAL — 128 - A1
AIRPORT RD, ARLINGTON OR

ASHLAND MUNICIPAL — 337 - J8
DEAD INDIAN RD&MUN AIRPRT RD, ASHLAND OR

AUBURN MUNICIPAL — 182 - C1
23RD ST NE & D ST NE, AUBURN WA

AURORA — 199 - B7
AIRPORT RD NE, MARION CO OR

AVEY FIELD STATE — 105 - C1
HWY 395, FERRY CO WA

BANDERA STATE — 111 - A2
BANDERA, KING CO WA

BANDON STATE — 220 - B6
OREGON COAST HWY, COOS CO OR

BEAVER MARSH STATE — 142 - C2
THE DALLES-CALIFORNIA HWY, KLAMATH CO OR

BELLINGHAM INTL — 158 - D7
W BAKERVIEW RD, WHATCOM CO WA

BEND MUNICIPAL — 217 - D2
PWLL BUTTE HY & MRKT RD, DESCHUTES CO OR

BLAINE MUNICIPAL — 158 - B3
PIPELINE RD, BLAINE WA

BOISE MUNICIPAL — 253 - C4
W WRIGHT ST, BOISE ID

BOUNDARY BAY — 101 - C1
OFF 72 ST, DISTRICT OF DELTA BC

BOUNDARY COUNTY — 107 - B1
HWY 2 & HWY 95, BOUNDARY CO ID

BROOKINGS STATE — 232 - C5
OFF OREGON COAST HWY, CURRY CO OR

BURNS MUNICIPAL — 145 - B1
AIRPORT RD, HARNEY CO OR

CAPE BLANCO STATE — 224 - A4
AIRPORT RD, CURRY CO OR

CASCADE LOCKS-STEVENSON STATE — 194 - D6
BONNEVILLE HWY, HOOD RIVER CO OR

CHEHALIS-CENTRALIA — 299 - C9
NW LOUISIANA AV, CHEHALIS WA

CHELAN MUNICIPAL — 236 - D2
APPLE ACRES RD & HWY 97, CHELAN CO WA

CHILOQUIN STATE — 231 - D3
THE DALLES-CALIFORNIA HWY, CHILOQUIN OR

COEUR D'ALENE AIR TERMINAL — 245 - A5
HAYDEN, KOOTENAI CO ID

COLVILLE MUNICIPAL — 106 - A2
COLVILLE, COLVILLE WA

COMOX — 92 - B2
HWY 19, BRITISH COLUMBIA BC

CONCRETE MUNICIPAL — 102 - C2
OFF HWY 20, SKAGIT CO WA

CONDON STATE — 128 - A2
JOHN DAY HWY, GILLIAM CO OR

CONNELL CITY — 121 - B1
US HWY 395, FRANKLIN CO WA

CORVALLIS MUNICIPAL — 207 - A7
AIRPORT AV & PACIFIC HWY W, BENTON CO OR

COTTAGE GROVE STATE — 215 - C7
SEARS RD, LANE CO OR

COTTONWOOD MUNICIPAL — 123 - C3
OFF HWY 95, IDAHO CO ID

COUNCIL MUNICIPAL — 139 - C1
LITTLE WEISER RD, ADAMS CO ID

CRAIGMONT MUNICIPAL — 123 - B2
COLD SPRINGS RD, CRAIGMONT ID

CRESCENT LAKE STATE — 142 - B1
HWY 58, KLAMATH CO OR

CURLEW — 105 - B1
CURLEW, FERRY CO WA

DALLES MUNICIPAL , THE — 196 - C7
DALLESPORT RD, KLICKITAT CO WA

DAVIS — 134 - A1
N SANTIAM HWY, LINN CO OR

DAY, JOHN STATE — 137 - B2
AIRPORT RD, GRANT CO OR

DEER PK MUNICIPAL — 114 - B1
E DEER PARK-MILAN RD, DEER PARK WA

DONNELLY — 252 - D2
MAIN ST & W ROSEBERRY RD, VALLEY CO ID

EASTON STATE — 111 - B3
KACHESS LAKE, KITTITAS CO WA

ECKHART INTL — 107 - B1
HWY 1, BOUNDARY CO ID

ELMA MUNICIPAL — 179 - B7
WENZEL SLOUGH RD, GRAYS HARBOR CO WA

EMMETT MUNICIPAL — 139 - C3
SOUTHSLOPE RD, GEM CO ID

ENTERPRISE MUNICIPAL — 130 - C2
ANT FLAT RD, WALLOWA CO OR

EPHRATA MUNICIPAL — 112 - C3
DIVISION AV & AIRPORT ST, EPHRATA WA

FAIRCHILD, WILLIAM R INTL — 165 - B6
W LAURIDSEN BLVD, PORT ANGELES WA

FELTS FIELD MUNICIPAL — 349 - J5
E RUTTER AV, SPOKANE WA

FERRY COUNTY — 105 - B2
HWY 21, FERRY CO WA

FLORENCE MUNICIPAL — 214 - B3
HWY 101 & 9TH ST, FLORENCE OR

FORKS MUNICIPAL — 169 - C2
OFF HWY 101, FORKS WA

GOLD BEACH MUNICIPAL — 228 - A6
AIRPORT WY, GOLD BEACH OR

GRAND COULEE DAM — 237 - B3
HWY 155 & AIRPORT RD, GRANT CO WA

GRAND VIEW INTL — 166 - A6
CARLSBORG RD, CLALLAM CO WA

GRANT COUNTY INTL — 242 - C1
7810 ANDREWS ST NE, GRANT CO WA

HAMPTON STATE — 144 - A1
OFF CENTRAL OREGON HWY, DESCHUTES CO OR

HERMISTON MUNICIPAL — 129 - A1
UMATILLA-STANFIELD HWY, HERMISTON OR

HOOD RIVER COUNTY — 195 - C6
TUCKER RD, HOOD RIVER CO OR

IDAHO COUNTY — 123 - C3
OFF HWY 95, IDAHO CO ID

INDEPENDENCE STATE — 204 - B7
OFF HOFFMAN RD, POLK CO OR

IONE MUNICIPAL — 106 - B2
IONE, PEND OREILLE CO WA

JEFFERSON COUNTY INTL — 263 - B12
AIRPORT RD, JEFFERSON CO WA

JOSEPHINE COUNTY — 229 - B4
1441 BROOKSIDE BLVD, JOSEPHINE CO OR

JOSEPH STATE — 130 - C2
RUSSEL LN, WALLOWA CO OR

KAMIAH MUNICIPAL — 123 - C3
OFF HWY 12, IDAHO CO ID

KELSO MUNICIPAL — 303 - E12
TALLEY AV, KELSO WA

KING COUNTY INTL — 286 - B1
AIRPORT WAY, SEATTLE WA

KITSAP COUNTY — 174 - A4
OFF HWY 3, KITSAP CO WA

KLAMATH FALLS INTL — 235 - C5
6775 ARNOLD AV, KLAMATH FALLS OR

LA CENTER VIEW-AIR — 192 - D1
ARIEL, CLARK CO WA

LA CROSSE — 122 - A1
LA CROSSE AIRPORT RD, WHITMAN CO WA

LA GRANDE/UNION COUNTY — 130 - A2
OFF PIERCE RD, UNION CO OR

LAKE BILLY CHINOOK STATE — 208 - A7
SW JORDAN RD, JEFFERSON CO OR

LAKE COUNTY — 152 - A2
OFF STOCK DRIVE RD, LAKE CO OR

LAKE WENATCHEE STATE — 111 - C1
PLAIN, CHELAN CO WA

LANGLEY — 158 - C1
56TH AV & 216TH ST, LANGLEY BC

LEBANON STATE — 133 - C1
AIRPORT DR, LEBANON OR

LEWISTON — 250 - C5
4TH ST & BURRELL AV, LEWISTON ID

LEXINGTON — 128 - C2
AIRPORT RD, MORROW CO OR

LIND — 121 - C1
US HWY 395, ADAMS CO WA

LYNDEN — 102 - B1
OFF HWY 546, LYNDEN WA

MADRAS CITY-COUNTY — 208 - B4
OFF WARM SPRINGS HWY, JEFFERSON CO OR

MCCALL — 251 - C5
MISSION ST, MCCALL ID

MCDERMITT STATE — 154 - B2
IDAHO-OREGON-NEVADA HWY, MALHEUR CO OR

MCKENZIE BRIDGE STATE — 134 - B2
MCKENZIE HWY, LANE CO OR

MCMINNVILLE MUNICIPAL — 198 - B7
SALMON RVR HWY & SE ARPRT, MCMINNVILLE OR

MCNAMARA, JACK FIELD — 148 - B3
PEBBLE BEACH DR & WASHINGTON, DEL NORTE CO

METHOW VALLEY STATE — 104 - A3
HWY 20, OKANOGAN CO WA

MILLICAN — 135 - B3
CENTRAL OREGON HWY, DESCHUTES CO OR

MONTAGUE — 150 - A3
HWY 3 & AIRPORT RD, MONTAGUE CA

MOSES LAKE MUNICIPAL — 242 - D3
CHEROKEE RD & RD L-NE, MOSES LAKE WA

MULINO — 199 - D7
MULINO RD & AIRPORT RD, CLACKAMAS CO OR

MYRTLE CREEK MUNICIPAL — 225 - C2
PACIFIC HWY & WEAVER RD, DOUGLAS CO OR

NAMPA MUNICIPAL — 147 - C1
AIRPORT RD, CANYON CO ID

NEHALEM BAY STATE — 191 - B4
CAREY ST, TILLAMOOK CO OR

NEW MEADOWS — 251 - A4
US HWY 95, ADAMS CO ID

NEWPORT MUNICIPAL — 206 - B5
84TH ST, NEWPORT OR

NEZ PERCE COUNTY — 123 - C2
POWERLINE RD, LEWIS CO ID

NORTH BEND MUNICIPAL — 333 - D3
AIRPORT AV, NORTH BEND OR

OAKRIDGE STATE — 142 - A1
HWY 58, LANE CO OR

OCEAN SHORES MUNICIPAL — 177 - B6
ALBATROSS & OLYMPIC VW, OCEAN SHORES WA

ODESSA MUNICIPAL — 113 - B2
DUCK LAKE RD, LINCOLN CO WA

OLYMPIA — 184 - C1
PACIFIC HWY, TUMWATER WA

OLYMPIA REGL — 296 - G14
CAPITOL BLVD, TUMWATER WA

ONTARIO MUNICIPAL — 139 - A3
OLDS FERRY-ONTARIO HWY, ONTARIO OR

OROFINO MUNICIPAL — 123 - C2
OFF HWY 12, CLEARWATER CO ID

OTHELLO MUNICIPAL — 121 - A1
W BENCH RD, ADAMS CO WA

OWYHEE RESERVOIR STATE — 146 - C1
DEADMAN GULCH RD, MALHEUR CO OR

PACIFIC CITY STATE — 197 - A7
OFF BROOTEN RD, TILLAMOOK CO OR

PARMA — 139 - A3
SAND RD, CANYON CO ID

PAYETTE MUNICIPAL — 139 - A2
IOWA AV N & AIRPORT RD, PAYETTE ID

PENDLETON MUNICIPAL — 129 - B1
STAGE GULCH RD, PENDLETON OR

PIERCE COUNTY — 182 - B5
MERIDIAN E, PIERCE CO WA

PINEHURST STATE — 150 - A2
GREEN SPRINGS HWY, JACKSON CO OR

PITT MEADOWS — 157 - B5
FORD RD & BAYNES RD, PITT MEADOWS BC

PORTLAND-HILLSBORO — 198 - D1
NE CORNELL RD, HILLSBORO OR

PORTLAND INTL — 310 - A2
7000 NE AIRPORT WY, PORTLAND OR

PORT OF ASTORIA — 188 - B2
AIRPORT RD, WARRENTON OR

POWERS STATE — 140 - B3
OFF COQUILLE RIVER RD, COOS CO OR

PRIEST RIVER MUNICIPAL — 107 - A3
HWY 57, PRIEST RIVER ID

PRINEVILLE — 213 - C5
OCHOCO HWY, CROOK CO OR

PULLMAN/MOSCOW REGL — 249 - B4
AIRPORT RD, WHITMAN CO WA

QUILLAYUTE STATE — 169 - B2
QUILLAYUTE RD, CLALLAM CO WA

QUINCY MUNICIPAL — 112 - B3
RD 9-NW & RD P-NW, GRANT CO WA

RANGER CREEK STATE — 111 - A3
SUN TOP, PIERCE CO WA

REDLAND (PRIVATE) — 200 - A5
S REDLAND RD, CLACKAMAS CO OR

REDMOND MUNICIPAL — 212 - D6
SE AIRPORT WY, REDMOND OR

RENTON MUNICIPAL — 175 - C4
N AIRPORT WY, RENTON WA

RICHLAND — 340 - D11
OFF OF AIRPORT WY, RICHLAND WA

RITZVILLE MUNICIPAL — 113 - C3
VAN VLEET RD & WEBER RD, ADAMS CO WA

RIVER BEND — 106 - C2
JAMESON LAKE SW, PEND OREILLE CO WA

ROBERTS YOUNG — 101 - C1
MARINE DR, WHATCOM CO WA

ROGUE VALLEY INTL-MEDFORD — 336 - D6
BIDDLE RD & AIRPORT RD, MEDFORD OR

ROME STATE — 146 - A3
IDAHO-OREGON-NEVADA HWY, MALHEUR CO OR

ROSALIA MUNICIPAL — 114 - C3
MALDEN RD, WHITMAN CO WA

ROSEBURG MUNICIPAL — 334 - E3
AIRPORT RD & STEWART PKWY, ROSEBURG OR

SAINT MARIES MUNICIPAL — 248 - C7
SAINT MARIES, BENEWAH CO ID

SANDERSON FIELD — 180 - A2
HWY 101, MASON CO WA

SANDPOINT — 244 - A1
N BOYER AV, SANDPOINT ID

SANDY RIVER — 200 - D4
SHIPLEY RD, CLACKAMAS CO OR

SANTIAM JUNCTION STATE — 134 - B2
SANTIAM HWY, LINN CO OR

SEASIDE STATE — 301 - H5
AIRPORT RD, CLATSOP CO OR

SEKIU — 163 - A2
HWY 112, CLALLAM CO WA

SHADY OAKS — 200 - B5
HEIPLE RD, CLACKAMAS CO OR

SILETZ — 206 - C2
SILETZ HWY, LINCOLN CO OR

SILETZ BAY STATE — 203 - A6
OREGON COAST HWY, LINCOLN CO OR

SISKIYOU COUNTY — 150 - A3
AIRPORT RD & SHELLEY RD, SISKIYOU CO CA

SISTERS EAGLE AIR — 211 - D4
CAMP POLK RD, DESCHUTES CO OR

SKAGIT REGL BAY VIEW — 161 - A6
HIGGINS AIRPORT WY, SKAGIT CO WA

SNOHOMISH COUNTY-PAINE FIELD — 267 - G7
3220 100TH ST SW, SNOHOMISH CO WA

SPOKANE INTL — 246 - A5
W AIRPORT DR, SPOKANE CO WA

STAR JUMP WEST — 147 - C1
CANYON CO ID

SUNNYSIDE MUNICIPAL — 120 - B2
E EDISON AV, SUNNYSIDE WA

SUTHERLIN MUNICIPAL — 221 - C1
COMSTOCK RD&ELKTN-SUTHERLIN, SUTHERLIN OR

TACOMA NARROWS — 181 - C2
STONE DR NW, PIERCE CO WA

TIETON STATE — 119 - B2
TIETON BASIN, YAKIMA CO WA

TILLAMOOK — 197 - C3
LONG PRAIRIE RD, TILLAMOOK CO OR

TOLEDO STATE — 206 - C5
SOUTHBAY RD, LINCOLN CO OR

TRI-CITIES — 343 - C3
GLADE RD, PASCO WA

TROUTDALE — 200 - B1
NE MARINE DR, TROUTDALE OR

TULELAKE MUNICIPAL — 151 - A3
N OF SR 139, NEAR NEWELL, MODOC CO CA

TWISP MUNICIPAL — 104 - A3
TWISP EAST, OKANOGAN CO WA

VALLEY VIEW — 200 - C6
DUUS RD, CLACKAMAS CO OR

VANCOUVER INTL — 156 - B5
GRANT MCCONACHIE WY, CITY OF RICHMOND BC

VASHON MUNICIPAL — 174 - D5
115TH AV SW & SW 160TH ST, KING CO WA

VICTORIA INTL — 159 - C2
HWY 17, DISTRICT OF NORTH SAANICH BC

VISTA FIELD — 342 - D9
N KELLOGG ST, KENNEWICK WA

WAKONDA BEACH — 328 - B10
SW WAKONDA BEACH RD, LINCOLN CO OR

WALLA WALLA REGL — 345 - F3
MIDDLE WAITSBURG RD, WALLA WALLA CO WA

WALLOWA STATE — 130 - B2
SHERROD RD, WALLOWA CO OR

WARDEN MUNICIPAL — 121 - A1
RD 8-SE, WARDEN WA

WASCO STATE — 127 - C2
WASCO-HEPPNER HWY, SHERMAN CO OR

WEISER MUNICIPAL — 139 - A2
AIRPORT RD, WASHINGTON CO ID

WESTPORT — 298 - H12
MONTESANO ST, WESTPORT WA

WILLAPA HARBOR MUNICIPAL — 117 - A1
HWY 105, PACIFIC CO WA

WOODLAND STATE — 192 - C1
WOODLAND, CLARK CO WA

YAKIMA MUNICIPAL — 243 - B7
W WASHINGTON AV, YAKIMA WA

BEACHES, HARBORS & WATER REC

ALKI BEACH PK — 276 - D7
ALKI AV SW, SEATTLE WA

ANTELOPE RESERVOIR — 147 - A3
ANTELOPE CANAL RD, MALHEUR CO OR

BASS LAKE ACCESS — 107 - B1
OFF HWY 1, BOUNDARY CO ID

BEAVER BAY SWIM AREA — 245 - C1
BAYVIEW, KOOTENAI CO ID

BEULAH RESERVOIR — 138 - A3
BEULAH RD, MALHEUR CO OR

BLACK CANYON RESERVOIR — 139 - C3
OFF HWY 52, GEM CO ID

BONNER LAKE ACCESS AREA — 107 - C1
OFF HWY 2, BOUNDARY CO ID

BRACKETTS LANDING BEACH — 171 - A5
MAIN ST & RAILROAD AV N, EDMONDS WA

BROUGHTON BEACH — 310 - C2
NE MARINE DR, PORTLAND OR

BROWNLEE RESERVOIR — 139 - A1
SNAKE RIVER RD, BAKER CO OR

BULLY CREEK RESERVOIR — 138 - C3
BULLY CREEK RD, MALHEUR CO OR

BUMPING LAKE — 119 - A1
NFD RD 1800, YAKIMA CO WA

CARKEEK PK BEACH — 171 - A7
NW CARKEEK PARK RD, SEATTLE WA

CASCADE RESERVOIR — 252 - D4
WEST MOUNTAIN RD, VALLEY CO ID

CHASE LAKE ACCESS AREA — 107 - A2
EASTSIDE RD, BONNER CO ID

CITY OF BELLEVUE MARINA — 175 - C2
SE BELLEVUE PL, BELLEVUE WA

CLE ELUM LAKE — 111 - B3
SALMON LA SAC RD, KITTITAS CO WA

COCOLALLA LAKE ACCESS AREA — 244 - A5
OFF HWY 95, BONNER CO ID

COLD SPRINGS RESERVOIR — 129 - A1
LOOP RD, UMATILLA CO OR

FEATURE NAME City State	Page-Grid
COLLINS BEACH	192 - B3
REEDER RD & ELLIS FARM RD, COLUMBIA CO OR	
COLUMBIA BEACH	188 - A2
BURMA RD, WARRENTON OR	
COPCO LAKE	150 - A3
COPCO RD, E OF COPCO, SISKIYOU CO CA	
COTTAGE GROVE LAKE	219 - D2
COTTAGE GROVE RESERVOIR RD, LANE CO OR	
COTTONWOOD BEACH	200 - C1
HWY 14 & S 32ND ST, CLARK CO WA	
CRANE CREEK RESERVOIR	139 - B2
CRANE CK RESERVOIR RD, WASHINGTON CO ID	
CRANE PRAIRIE RESERVOIR	142 - C1
LAVA LAKE RD, DESCHUTES CO OR	
CRATER LAKE	227 - C3
OFF NATIONAL PARK HWY, KLAMATH CO OR	
CRESCENT LAKE	142 - B1
CRESCENT LAKE HWY, KLAMATH CO OR	
CRUMP LAKE	152 - B2
HOGBACK RD, LAKE CO OR	
DAVIS LAKE	142 - C1
ODELL RD, DESCHUTES CO OR	
DAWSON LAKE ACCESS AREA	107 - B1
OFF HWY 95, BOUNDARY CO ID	
DEEP CREEK ACCESS AREA	107 - B2
OLD US HWY 2, BOUNDARY CO ID	
DETROIT LAKE	134 - B1
N SANTIAM HWY, MARION CO OR	
DEVILS LAKE	203 - B4
DEVILS LAKE RD, LINCOLN CO OR	
DIAMOND LAKE	223 - C6
DIAMOND LAKE HWY, DOUGLAS CO OR	
DREWS RESERVOIR	151 - C2
KLAMATH FALLS-LAKEVIEW HWY, LAKE CO OR	
EAST LAKE	143 - B1
NEWBERRY CRATER RD, DESCHUTES CO OR	
EDMONDS UNDERWATER PARK	171 - A5
MAIN ST, EDMONDS WA	
FLAGSTAFF LAKE	152 - B1
FLAGSTAFF LAKE RD, LAKE CO OR	
FOSTER LAKE	134 - A2
SANTIAM HWY, LINN CO OR	
GARFIELD BAY ACCESS AREA	244 - B3
GARFIELD BAY CTO, BONNER CO ID	
GERBER RESERVOIR	151 - B2
GERBER RD, KLAMATH CO OR	
GOOSE LAKE	251 - C2
GOOSE LAKE RD, ADAMS CO ID	
GOOSE LAKE	152 - A3
HWY 395, MODOC CO CA	
GRANITE LAKE	251 - D1
OFF WARREN WAGON RD, VALLEY CO ID	
GRANITE LAKE ACCESS	107 - A3
OFF GRANITE-KELSO RD, BONNER CO ID	
GREEN PETER LAKE	134 - A2
QUARTZVILLE DR, LINN CO OR	
HART LAKE	152 - B1
HART MOUNTAIN RD, LAKE CO OR	
HELLS CANYON RESERVOIR	131 - B2
NFD RD 454, ADAMS CO ID	
HILLS CREEK LAKE	142 - A1
RIGDON RD, LANE CO OR	
IRON GATE RESERVOIR & COPCO LAKE	150 - A3
N OF LAKE VIEW RD, SISKIYOU CO CA	
JEWEL LAKE ACCESS AREA	107 - A3
JEWEL LAKE RD, BONNER CO ID	
JUANITA BEACH PK	171 - C7
NE JUANITA DR & 97TH AV NE, KIRKLAND WA	
KELSO LAKE ACCESS	107 - A3
OFF GRANITE-KELSO RD, BONNER CO ID	
LAKE ABERT	152 - A1
LAKEVIEW-BURNS HWY, LAKE CO OR	
LAKE CHELAN	236 - C3
HWY 97 & HWY 150, CHELAN CO WA	
LAKE LOVELY	93 - C2
OFF TRANS CANADA HWY, BRITISH COLUMBIA BC	
LAKE LOWELL	147 - B1
RIVERSIDE RD, CANYON CO ID	
LAKE OWYHEE	147 - A1
OWYHEE LAKE RD, MALHEUR CO OR	
LAKE WENATCHEE	111 - C1
WHITE RIVER RD, CHELAN CO WA	
LITTLE GRASSY RESERVOIR	146 - C3
THREE FORKS RD, MALHEUR CO OR	
LITTLE PAYETTE LAKE	251 - D5
LICK CREEK RD, VALLEY CO ID	
LOST VALLEY RESERVOIR	131 - B3
NFD RD 89, ADAMS CO ID	
LUANA BEACH	175 - A6
SW LUANA BEACH RD, KING CO WA	
MALHEUR LAKE	145 - B2
NARROWS-PRINCETON RD, HARNEY CO OR	
MALHEUR RESERVOIR	138 - B2
WILLOW CREEK RD, MALHEUR CO OR	
MANN CREEK RESERVOIR	139 - A2
JACKSON RD, WASHINGTON CO ID	
MANN LAKE PUB FISHING AREA	250 - D5
RESERVATION LINE RD, NEZ PERCE CO ID	
MATTHEWS BEACH CITY PARK	275 - F1
49TH AV NE & NE 93RD ST, SEATTLE WA	
MCARTHUR LAKE ACCESS	107 - B2
OFF HWY 2, BOUNDARY CO ID	
MCKAY RESERVOIR	129 - B1
SHAW-HOLMES RD, UMATILLA CO OR	
MIRROR LAKE ACCESS AREA	244 - B4
NFD RD 2233, BONNER CO ID	
MORTON SLOUGH ACCESS	107 - A3
DUFORT RD, BONNER CO ID	
MOYIE RIVER ACCESS AREA	107 - C1
MOYIE RIVER RD, BOUNDARY CO ID	
MOYIE RIVER SPORTSMANS ACCESS	107 - C1
HWY 95, BOUNDARY CO ID	
NAKETA BEACH	266 - D3
NAKETA BEACH RD, MUKILTEO WA	
NORTH UNIT BEACH	192 - B2
SAUVIE ISLAND, COLUMBIA CO OR	
ODELL LAKE	142 - B1
WILLAMETTE HWY, KLAMATH CO OR	
OWYHEE LAKE	143 - A1
LESLIE GULCH RD, MALHEUR CO OR	
PAULINA LAKE	143 - B1
NEWBERRY CRATER RD, DESCHUTES CO OR	
PAYETTE LAKE	251 - D4
WARREN WAGON RD, VALLEY CO ID	
PHILLIPS LAKE	138 - A1
WHITNEY HWY, BAKER CO OR	
PRIEST LAKE MARINA	107 - A2
OFF HWY 57, BONNER CO ID	
PRINEVILLE RESERVOIR	135 - C3
SALT CREEK RD, CROOK CO OR	
PRITCHARD ISLAND BEACH	287 - G2
GRATTAN ST & 55TH AV S, SEATTLE WA	
RICHMOND BEACH PARK	171 - A6
RICHMOND BEACH DR NW, SHORELINE WA	

FEATURE NAME City State	Page-Grid
SHEPHERD LAKE ACCESS AREA	244 - A4
OFF TALACHE RD, BONNER CO ID	
SILTCOOS LAKE	214 - B5
SILTCOOS STATION RD, LANE CO OR	
SPIRIT LAKE	190 - C1
OFF NFD RD 99, SKAMANIA CO WA	
SPRING VALLEY RESERVOIR PUB FISHING	123 - A1
OFF HWY 8, LATAH CO ID	
STAR LANE POND PUB FISHING AREA	139 - B3
STAR LN, GEM CO ID	
SUMMER LAKE	143 - C3
FREMONT HWY, LAKE CO OR	
SWIFT CREEK RESERVOIR	190 - C5
NFD RD 91013, SKAMANIA CO WA	
TAHKENITCH LAKE	214 - A6
OREGON COAST HWY, DOUGLAS CO OR	
THOMPSON RESERVOIR	143 - B3
NFD RD 3142, LAKE CO OR	
UPPER COW LAKE	146 - C2
LOWER COW CREEK RD, MALHEUR CO OR	
UPPER PAYETTE LAKE	251 - D1
WARREN WAGON RD, VALLEY CO ID	
WALDO LAKE	142 - B1
HWY 58, LANE CO OR	
WALLOWA LAKE	130 - C2
JOSEPH-WALLOWA LAKE HWY, WALLOWA CO OR	
WALTON BEACH	192 - B3
COLUMBIA CO OR	
WARM SPRINGS RESERVOIR	146 - A1
WARM SPRINGS RD, HARNEY CO OR	
WICKIUP RESERVOIR	142 - C1
WICKIUP RD, DESCHUTES CO OR	
WINCHESTER LAKE PUB FISHING AREA	123 - B2
OFF CAMAS RD, LEWIS CO ID	
YALE LAKE	190 - A6
LEWIS RIVER RD, COWLITZ CO WA	

BUILDINGS

FEATURE NAME City State	Page-Grid
COUCH MANSION	126 - A3
ELK PRAIRIE, CLACKAMAS CO OR	
FAIRVIEW HOME PRIGG COTTAGE	325 - F6
AUMSVILLE HWY SE, SALEM OR	
FERNWELL BLDG	348 - J9
SPOKANE NW, SPOKANE WA	
FOUNTAIN PLAZA	313 - F7
1414 SW 3RD AV, PORTLAND OR	
GEORGIA PACIFIC PAPER COMPANY	193 - B7
NW 6TH AV & NE ADAMS ST, CAMAS WA	
HATFIELD MARINE SCIENCE CTR	206 - B4
MARINE SCIENCE DR, NEWPORT OR	
HEWLETT PACKARD	253 - B2
11311 E CHINDEN BLVD, BOISE ID	
HUTTON BLDG	348 - J9
SPOKANE NW, SPOKANE WA	
IDAHO CTR	147 - C1
GARRITY BLVD & STAMPEDE DR, NAMPA ID	
KIRK, PETER BLDG	175 - C1
MARKET ST & 7TH AV, KIRKLAND WA	
KOIN BLDG	313 - F7
222 W COLUMBIA ST, PORTLAND OR	
LAKEWOOD TACOMA INDUSTRIAL PK	181 - D4
47TH AV SW, LAKEWOOD WA	
MCCHORD AIR FORCE BASE	181 - D4
112TH ST S, PIERCE CO WA	
MED RESEARCH FOUNDATION OF OREGON	199 - A1
505 NW 185TH AV, HILLSBORO OR	
MIKADO BLDG	313 - F6
117 SW TAYLOR ST, PORTLAND OR	
MINNEHAHA GRANGE	306 - A1
NE ST JOHNS RD & NE 52ND ST, CLARK CO WA	
NICHOLSON PAVILION	241 - B5
ELLENSBURG NORTH, ELLENSBURG WA	
PACWEST BANK TOWER	313 - E6
SW MADISON ST & SW 5TH AV, PORTLAND OR	
PITTOCK BLOCK	313 - E6
921 SW WASHINGTON ST, PORTLAND OR	
PORTLAND BLDG	313 - F6
SW MAIN ST & SW 5TH AV, PORTLAND OR	
PORTLAND PLAZA	313 - E7
SW CLAY ST & SW 5TH AV, PORTLAND OR	
ROYAL BROUGHAM PAVILION	273 - G7
3RD AV W & W NICKERSON ST, SEATTLE WA	
SHERWOOD BLDG	349 - A9
SPOKANE NW, SPOKANE WA	
SPOKESMAN REVIEW BLDG	348 - J9
SPOKANE NW, SPOKANE WA	
STANDARD INSURANCE CTR	313 - F6
900 SW 5TH AV, PORTLAND OR	
SUGAR FACTORY	147 - B1
NORTHSIDE BLVD & KARCHER RD, NAMPA ID	
SUNDQUIST, LEONA M MARINE LABORATORY	259 - A3
OFF OAKES AV, ANACORTES WA	
TOWN PLAZA	306 - C5
5411 E MILL PLAIN BLVD, VANCOUVER WA	
US BANCORP TOWER	313 - F5
111 SW 5TH AV, PORTLAND OR	
US BANK BLDG	313 - F6
309 SW 6TH AV, PORTLAND OR	
WALL ST BLDG	264 - D4
COLBY AV & WALL ST, EVERETT WA	
WASHINGTON CORRECTIONS CTR	179 - D2
DAYTON-AIRPORT RD, MASON CO WA	
WELLS FARGO BANK TOWER	313 - E7
1300 SW 5TH AV, PORTLAND OR	
WORLD TRADE CTR	313 - F6
121 SW SALMON ST, PORTLAND OR	
WORLD TRADE CTR	182 - A2
PORT OF TACOMA RD, TACOMA WA	

BUILDINGS - GOVERNMENTAL

FEATURE NAME City State	Page-Grid
ARMY RESERVE TRAINING CTR	182 - A3
5119 E PORTLAND AV, TACOMA WA	
COUNTY/ CITY BLDG	293 - G5
S 11TH ST & S TACOMA AV, TACOMA WA	
FAA/AFS OFFICE BLDG	311 - F5
PORTLAND INTL AIRPORT, PORTLAND OR	
FEDERAL BLDG	305 - F4
500 W 12TH ST, VANCOUVER WA	
FIRCREST STATE INSTITUTE	171 - B7
15230 15TH AV NE, SHORELINE WA	
FIRE DEPARTMENT TRAINING CTR	305 - J4
E RESERVE ST, VANCOUVER WA	
GREEN WYATT FEDERAL BLDG	313 - F7
1220 SW 3RD AV, PORTLAND OR	
IDAHO STATE CAPITOL	253 - C2
W STATE ST, BOISE ID	
KING COUNTY REGL JUSTICE CTR	175 - B7
620 W JAMES ST, KENT WA	
NATL OCEANIC & ATMOSPHERIC ADMIN	275 - H2
SAND POINT WY NE, SEATTLE WA	
NIGHTHAWK CUSTOMS	104 - C1
LOOMIS-OROVILLE RD, OKANOGAN CO WA	

FEATURE NAME City State	Page-Grid
OREGON DEPARTMENT OF TRANSPORTATION	313 - F5
NW 1ST AV & NW GLISAN ST, PORTLAND OR	
OREGON STATE CAPITOL	322 - J13
COURT ST NE, SALEM OR	
PIERCE COUNTY ANNEX	294 - E2
S 35TH ST, TACOMA WA	
POLICE HEADQUARTERS	313 - F6
1120 SW 3RD AV, PORTLAND OR	
PUBLIC SERVICE BLDG	313 - E6
920 SW 6TH AV, PORTLAND OR	
REMANN HALL JUVENILE COURT	292 - A5
6TH AV & SHIRLEY ST, TACOMA WA	
STATE AND FEDERAL OFFICES	293 - G6
S 13TH ST & S TACOMA AV, TACOMA WA	
STATE BLDG	313 - E7
1400 SW 5TH AV, PORTLAND OR	
STATE BLDG	313 - H5
800 NE OREGON ST, PORTLAND OR	
STATE DEPT OF SOCIAL HEALTH SERVICES	293 - E7
S 19TH ST & S SPRAGUE AV, TACOMA WA	
STATE OFFICE BLDG	305 - F5
907 HARNEY ST, VANCOUVER WA	
US CUSTOMS	104 - C1
HWY 3, OKANOGAN CO WA	
US CUSTOMS STA	158 - B2
HWY 543, BLAINE WA	
US CUSTOMS STA	158 - B3
INTERSTATE 5, BLAINE WA	
US FEDERAL BLDG	313 - F5
511 NW BROADWAY, PORTLAND OR	
UNITED STATES WEATHER BUREAU STA	129 - C2
OLD OREGON TRAIL HWY, UMATILLA CO OR	
WASHINGTON STATE CAPITOL	296 - G6
14TH AV, OLYMPIA WA	
WASHINGTON STATE PENITENTIARY	344 - H5
13TH AV N, WALLA WALLA WA	

CAMPGROUNDS

FEATURE NAME City State	Page-Grid
ABBOT CREEK CAMPGROUND	134 - C1
NFD RD 12, JEFFERSON CO OR	
ABBOTT CREEK CAMPGROUND	226 - C4
ABBOTT BUTTE, JACKSON CO OR	
ADAMS FORK CAMPGROUND	118 - C2
EAST CANYON RIDGE, SKAMANIA CO WA	
ADELL CAMPGROUND	142 - B2
MILLER LAKE, KLAMATH CO OR	
AHTANUM MEADOW CAMPGROUND	119 - B2
FOUNDATION RIDGE, YAKIMA CO WA	
ALBENI COVE CAMPGROUND	106 - C3
ALBENI COVE RD, BONNER CO ID	
ALDER CAMPGROUND	104 - B2
CONCONULLY WEST, OKANOGAN CO WA	
ALDER SWAMP SHELTER	126 - B3
BULL OF THE WOODS, CLACKAMAS CO OR	
ALDER THICKET CAMPGROUND	122 - B2
ROSE SPRINGS, GARFIELD CO WA	
ALICE LAKE CAMPGROUND	93 - C2
HWY 99, BRITISH COLUMBIA BC	
ALKALI CAMP	226 - D1
FISH MOUNTAIN, DOUGLAS CO OR	
ALLAN SPRINGS CAMPGROUND	134 - C1
METOLIUS RIVER RD, JEFFERSON CO OR	
ALLEN CREEK CAMPGROUND	136 - A2
OFF SCOTT CAMP RD, CROOK CO OR	
ALLISON CREEK CAMPGROUND	131 - C2
NFD RD 1614, IDAHO CO ID	
ALLISON LAKE CAMPGROUND	95 - C2
HWY 5A, BRITISH COLUMBIA BC	
ALPHINE CAMPGROUND	238 - C6
OFF NFD RD 9712, CHELAN CO WA	
ALPINE CAMPGROUND	202 - A5
MOUNT HOOD SOUTH, CLACKAMAS CO OR	
ALPINE MEADOWS CAMPGROUND	111 - C1
TRINITY, CHELAN CO WA	
ALTA CAMPGROUND	150 - B1
DEVILS PEAK, KLAMATH CO OR	
AMANITA CAMPGROUND	252 - C2
MOUNTAIN RD, VALLEY CO ID	
AMERICANA CAMPGROUND	253 - C3
AMERICANA TER & AMERICANA BLVD, BOISE ID	
AMERICAN ADVENTURE CAMPGROUND	112 - C2
GRANT CO WA	
AMERICAN CAMPSITE	101 - C2
CATTLE POINT RD, SAN JUAN CO WA	
AMERICAN FORKS CAMPGROUND	119 - B1
OLD SCAB MOUNTAIN, YAKIMA CO WA	
ANDREWS CREEK CAMPGROUND	104 - A1
COLEMAN PEAK, OKANOGAN CO WA	
ANTELOPE CAMPGROUND	139 - C2
OFF HANCOCK RD, GEM CO ID	
ANTHONY LAKES CAMPGROUND	130 - A3
ANTHONY LAKES RD, BAKER CO OR	
ANTILON LAKE CAMPGROUND	112 - A1
GRADE CK RD & LONG JIM RES, CHELAN CO WA	
ARCHIE KNOWLES CAMPGROUND	132 - C3
FLORENCE-EUGENE & MAPLETON RD, LANE CO OR	
ASH SWALE SHELTER	133 - A3
LOST CREEK RD, LANE CO OR	
ASPEN CAMPGROUND	217 - A4
BENHAM FALLS, DESCHUTES CO OR	
ASPEN POINT CAMPGROUND	150 - B1
LAKE OF THE WOODS NORTH, KLAMATH CO OR	
ASPERKAHA CAMPGROUND	150 - A2
HYATT RESERVOIR, JACKSON CO OR	
ATKINSON FLAT CAMPGROUND	111 - C1
MOUNT DAVID, TRINITY, CHELAN CO WA	
BADGER LAKE CAMPGROUND	202 - C6
BADGER LAKE, HOOD RIVER CO OR	
BAGBY HOT SPRINGS CAMPGROUND	126 - B3
BAGBY HOT SPRINGS, CLACKAMAS CO OR	
BAKER CREEK CAMPGROUND	111 - C3
LIBERTY, KITTITAS CO WA	
BALD MTN SHELTER	202 - A4
BULL RUN LAKE, HOOD RIVER CO OR	
BALLARD CAMPGROUND	104 - A2
MCLEOD MOUNTAIN, OKANOGAN CO WA	
BALLARD CAMPGROUND	103 - C2
ROBINSON MOUNTAIN, OKANOGAN CO WA	
BAMBERTON PARK CAMPGROUND	159 - B3
TRANS CANADA HWY, BRITISH COLUMBIA BC	
BARK SHANTY SHELTER	109 - C1
MOUNT WALKER, JEFFERSON CO WA	
BARLOW CAMPGROUND	201 - D6
GOVERNMENT CAMP, CLACKAMAS CO OR	
BARNHOUSE CAMPGROUND	136 - B2
BUCK POINT RD, WHEELER CO OR	
BARTOO CAMPGROUND	107 - A2
PRIEST LAKE SW, BONNER CO ID	
BATTLE CREEK SHELTER	134 - B1
OFF BREITENBUSH RD, MARION CO OR	
BEACH CAMPGROUND	216 - A4
CASCADE LAKES HWY, DESCHUTES CO OR	
BEAR CAMPGROUND	131 - B3
NFD RD 105, ADAMS CO ID	

FEATURE NAME	Page-Grid
City State	
BEAR CANYON CAMPGROUND	130 - B1
OFF NFD RD 62, WALLOWA CO OR	
BEAR CREEK CAMPGROUND	140 - C3
BONE MOUNTAIN, DOUGLAS CO OR	
BEAR CREEK CAMPGROUND	163 - B6
DEADMANS HILL, CLALLAM CO WA	
BEAR CREEK SHELTER	103 - A1
COPPER MOUNTAIN, WHATCOM CO WA	
BEAR LAKE CAMPGROUND	119 - B1
TIETON BASIN, YAKIMA CO WA	
BEAR SKULL SHELTER	103 - B1
JACK MOUNTAIN, WHATCOM CO WA	
BEAR WALLOW CREEK CAMPGROUND	129 - B3
UKIAH-HILGARD HWY, UMATILLA CO OR	
BEAR WALLOW SPRING CAMPGROUND	129 - B2
NFD RD 54, UMATILLA CO OR	
BEAUTY CREEK CAMPGROUND	248 - B1
MOUNT COEUR D-ALENE, KOOTENAI CO ID	
BEAVER BAY CAMPGROUND	190 - B5
COUGAR, COWLITZ CO WA	
BEAVER CAMPGROUND	104 - B2
BLUE BUCK MOUNTAIN, OKANOGAN CO WA	
BEAVER CAMPGROUND	194 - C2
STABLER, SKAMANIA CO WA	
BEAVER DAM CAMPGROUND	150 - A2
BROWN MOUNTAIN, JACKSON CO OR	
BEAVER LAKE CAMPGROUND	105 - A1
BODIE, OKANOGAN CO WA	
BEAVER PASS SHELTER	103 - B1
MOUNT PROPHET, WHATCOM CO WA	
BEAVER SHELTER	222 - D6
FISH CREEK DESERT, DOUGLAS CO OR	
BEAVER SWAMP CAMPGROUND	222 - C7
BUCKEYE LAKE, DOUGLAS CO OR	
BEDAL CAMPGROUND	103 - A3
BEDAL, SNOHOMISH CO WA	
BEDROCK CAMPGROUND	134 - A3
BIG FALL CREEK RD, LANE CO OR	
BEECH CREEK CAMPGROUND	137 - A1
PENDLETON-JOHN DAY HWY, GRANT CO OR	
BEEHIVE SPRING CAMPGROUND	238 - C6
NFD RD 9712, CHELAN CO WA	
BELL BAY CAMPGROUND	248 - A4
HARRISON, KOOTENAI CO ID	
BENHAM FALLS CAMPGROUND	217 - A5
BENHAM FALLS, DESCHUTES CO OR	
BENNION CAMPGROUND	245 - C1
BAYVIEW, KOOTENAI CO ID	
BESSIE SHELTER	227 - A7
RED BLANKET MOUNTAIN, JACKSON CO OR	
BESSON CAMPGROUND	217 - A6
BENHAM FALLS, DESCHUTES CO OR	
BETH LAKE CAMPGROUND	105 - A1
BODIE, OKANOGAN CO WA	
BEVERLY CAMPGROUND	111 - B2
MOUNT STUART, KITTITAS CO WA	
BIG BEAR CAMPGROUND	103 - B1
PUMPKIN MOUNTAIN, WHATCOM CO WA	
BIG BEN CAMPGROUND	150 - A1
IMNAHA CREEK, JACKSON CO OR	
BIG CREEK CAMPGROUND	112 - A1
LAKE CHELAN, CHELAN CO WA	
BIG CREEK CAMPGROUND	115 - C2
MARBLE CREEK, SHOSHONE CO ID	
BIG CREEK CAMPGROUND	137 - C2
NFD RD 16, GRANT CO OR	
BIG CREEK CAMPGROUND	118 - C1
SAWTOOTH RIDGE, LEWIS CO WA	
BIG EDDY CAMPGROUND	123 - B2
AHSAHKA, CLEARWATER CO ID	
BIG ELK CAMPGROUND	133 - A1
BIG ELK CREEK RD, LINCOLN CO OR	
BIG FLAT SHELTER	109 - A1
OWL MOUNTAIN, JEFFERSON CO WA	
BIG HANK CAMPGROUND	115 - C1
POND PEAK, SHOSHONE CO ID	
BIG HILL CAMPGROUND	112 - A1
NFD RD 112, CHELAN CO WA	
BIGHORN CAMPGROUND	201 - C6
RHODODENDRON, CLACKAMAS CO OR	
BIG LAKE CAMPGROUND	134 - C2
OFF OLD SANTIAM WAGON RD, LINN CO OR	
BIG MEADOWS CAMPGROUND	134 - B2
OFF SANTIAM HWY, LINN CO OR	
BIG POOL CAMPGROUND	134 - A3
BIG FALL CREEK RD, LANE CO OR	
BIG RIVER CAMPGROUND	216 - D7
ANNS BUTTE, DESCHUTES CO OR	
BIG SLIDE CAMPGROUND	149 - A1
GOLDEN, JOSEPHINE CO OR	
BIG SPRING CAMPGROUND	122 - B3
STENTZ SPRING, GARFIELD CO WA	
BIG SPRINGS CAMPGROUND	136 - B2
OFF BUCK HOLLOW RD, CROOK CO OR	
BIG SPRINGS CAMPGROUND	134 - B1
OFF SANTIAM HWY, MARION CO OR	
BIG TREE CAMPGROUND	140 - C3
CHINA FLAT, COOS CO OR	
BIG TWIN LAKES CAMPGROUND	222 - B4
TWIN LAKES MOUNTAIN, DOUGLAS CO OR	
BIG WINDY CREEK CAMPGROUND	148 - C1
GOLDEN, JOSEPHINE CO OR	
BINGHAM PRAIRIE CAMPGROUND	135 - C2
OPAL MOUNTAIN, CROOK CO OR	
BINGHAMS SHELTER	142 - B1
DIAMOND PEAK, LANE CO OR	
BIRD CREEK CAMPGROUND	119 - A3
GLENWOOD, YAKIMA CO WA	
BLACKBERRY CAMPGROUND	209 - D2
ALSEA HWY, LINCOLN CO OR	
BLACKHORSE CAMPGROUND	131 - A2
WALLOWA MOUNTAIN LP, WALLOWA CO OR	
BLACK LAKE CAMPGROUND	131 - B2
HELLS CANYON RECREATION AREA, ADAMS CO ID	
BLACK PINE CAMPGROUND	111 - B2
JACK RIDGE, CHELAN CO WA	
BLACK PINE CAMPGROUND	123 - A3
WAHA, NEZ PERCE CO ID	
BLACKPINE LAKE CAMPGROUND	104 - A3
HOODOO PEAK, OKANOGAN CO WA	
BLAIR LAKE CAMPGROUND	134 - B3
OFF CANYON RD, LANE CO OR	
BLUEBILL LAKE CAMPGROUND	218 - A6
EMPIRE, COOS CO OR	
BLUE CREEK CAMPGROUND	111 - C1
SILVER FALLS, CHELAN CO WA	
BLUE GROUSE CAMPSITE	194 - D7
WAHTUM LAKE, HOOD RIVER CO OR	
BLUE JAY CAMPGROUND	119 - A3
GLENWOOD, YAKIMA CO WA	
BLUE LAKE CREEK CAMPGROUND	118 - C2
BLUE LAKE, LEWIS CO WA	
BOAT LANDING CAMPGROUND	119 - A1
BUMPING LAKE, YAKIMA CO WA	

FEATURE NAME	Page-Grid
City State	
BOB CREEK SHELTER	109 - A1
BOB CREEK, JEFFERSON CO WA	
BOGACHIEL SHELTER	108 - C1
INDIAN PASS, CLALLAM CO WA	
BOGUS CREEK CAMPGROUND	141 - C2
MACE MOUNTAIN, DOUGLAS CO OR	
BOLAN LAKE CAMPGROUND	233 - D7
BOLAN LAKE RD, JOSEPHINE CO OR	
BOLT SHELTER	118 - C3
BURNT PEAK, SKAMANIA CO WA	
BONA FIDA SHELTER	141 - C1
CHILCOOT MOUNTAIN, LANE CO OR	
BONANZA SHELTER	238 - B5
TIPTOP, CHELAN CO WA	
BONAPARTE CAMPGROUND	105 - A1
MOUNT BONAPARTE, OKANOGAN CO WA	
BONE SPRING CAMPGROUND	130 - A1
NORTH OF NFD RD 63, WALLOWA CO OR	
BONNEY MEADOWS CAMPGROUND	202 - C6
BADGER LAKE, HOOD RIVER CO OR	
BORDEAUX CAMPGROUND	180 - A7
LITTLEROCK, THURSTON CO WA	
BOULDER CREEK CAMPGROUND	141 - C2
DUMONT CREEK, DOUGLAS CO OR	
BOULDER CREEK CAMPGROUND	109 - A1
MOUNT CARRIE, CLALLAM CO WA	
BOULDER CREEK CAMPGROUND	102 - C2
WELKER PEAK, WHATCOM CO WA	
BOULDER FLAT CAMPGROUND	222 - C3
AVD DE UMPQUA HWY, DOUGLAS CO OR	
BOULDER LAKE SHELTER	109 - A1
MOUNT CARRIE, CLALLAM CO WA	
BOULDER PARK CAMPGROUND	130 - C3
NFD RD 7755, BAKER CO OR	
BOULDER SHELTER	109 - C1
MOUNT DECEPTION, JEFFERSON CO WA	
BOUNDARY CAMPGROUND	140 - B3
CHINA FLAT, COOS CO OR	
BOUNDARY CAMPGROUND	130 - B2
END OF BEAR CREEK RD, WALLOWA CO OR	
BOUNDARY CAMPGROUND	123 - C3
GRANGEVILLE EAST, IDAHO CO ID	
BOUNDARY SPRINGS CAMPGROUND	142 - C2
CRESCENT, KLAMATH CO OR	
BOWL AND PITCHER CAMPGROUND	348 - B4
SPOKANE NW, SPOKANE CO WA	
BOZE SHELTER	222 - B6
TWIN LAKES MOUNTAIN, DOUGLAS CO OR	
BRADBURY CAMPGROUND	106 - A2
BANGS MOUNTAIN, STEVENS CO WA	
BRANDYWINE FALLS CAMPGROUND	93 - C1
HWY 99, WHISTLER BC	
BREAKWATER CAMPGROUND	115 - B2
BUMBLEBEE PEAK, KOOTENAI CO ID	
BREITENBUSH CAMPGROUND	134 - B1
BREITENBUSH RD, MARION CO OR	
BRIDGE CAMPGROUND	245 - C1
BAYVIEW, KOOTENAI CO ID	
BRIDGE CREEK CAMPGROUND	111 - C2
CASHMERE MOUNTAIN, CHELAN CO WA	
BRIDGE CREEK CAMPGROUND	103 - C2
MCGREGOR MOUNTAIN, CHELAN CO WA	
BRIGGS CREEK CAMPGROUND	148 - C1
GOLDEN, JOSEPHINE CO OR	
BRIGGS VALLEY CAMPGROUND	149 - A1
GOLDEN, JOSEPHINE CO OR	
BROWN CREEK CAMPGROUND	109 - B2
LIGHTNING PEAK, MASON CO WA	
BROWNS CREEK CAMPGROUND	142 - C1
DAVIS MOUNTAIN, DESCHUTES CO OR	
BROWNS LAKE CAMPGROUND	106 - C2
BROWNS LAKE, PEND OREILLE CO WA	
BRUCES EDDY CAMPGROUND	123 - C2
AHSAHKA, CLEARWATER CO ID	
BRUIN RUN CAMPGROUND	201 - D6
GOVERNMENT CAMP, CLACKAMAS CO OR	
BRUSH LAKE CAMPGROUND	107 - B1
HALL MOUNTAIN, BOUNDARY CO ID	
BRUSHY BAR CAMPGROUND	148 - C1
MARIAL, CURRY CO OR	
BUCK CAMP	223 - A7
HAMAKER BUTTE, DOUGLAS CO OR	
BUCK CREEK CAMPGROUND	103 - A3
HUCKLEBERRY MOUNTAIN, SNOHOMISH CO WA	
BUCK CREEK CAMPGROUND	130 - A1
NFD RD 32, UMATILLA CO OR	
BUCKEYE LAKE CAMPGROUND	226 - C1
BUCKEYE LAKE, DOUGLAS CO OR	
BUCKHEAD MTN CAMPGROUND	222 - B6
TWIN LAKES MOUNTAIN, DOUGLAS CO OR	
BUCKHORN CAMPGROUND	131 - A1
BUCKHORN RD, WALLOWA CO OR	
BUCK LAKE CAMPGROUND	104 - A2
LEWIS BUTTE, OKANOGAN CO WA	
BUCKSKIN CREEK CAMPGROUND	105 - C2
SITDOWN MOUNTAIN, FERRY CO WA	
BUCK SPRING CAMPGROUND	144 - C1
OFF SAWMILL CREEK RD, HARNEY CO OR	
BULL BEND CAMPGROUND	142 - C1
WICKIUP DAM, DESCHUTES CO OR	
BULL GAP CAMPGROUND	234 - C6
MOUNT ASHLAND, JACKSON CO OR	
BULLY CREEK CAMPGROUND	138 - C3
HOPE BUTTE RD, MALHEUR CO OR	
BUMBLEBEE CAMPGROUND	115 - B1
BUMBLEBEE PEAK, SHOSHONE CO ID	
BUMPING DAM CAMPGROUND	119 - A1
BUMPING LAKE, YAKIMA CO WA	
BUNCHGRASS MEADOWS SHELTER	141 - C3
PICKETT BUTTE, DOUGLAS CO OR	
BUNKER HILL CAMPGROUND	223 - C3
LEMOLO LAKE, DOUGLAS CO OR	
BUTLER BAR CAMPGROUND	224 - D6
FATHER MOUNTAIN, CURRY CO OR	
CABIN CREEK CAMPGROUND	252 - B3
NFD RD 186, ADAMS CO ID	
CABIN LAKE CAMPGROUND	143 - B1
NFD RD 18, LAKE CO OR	
CALAWAH SHELTER	108 - C1
INDIAN PASS, CLALLAM CO WA	
CALDWELL CAMPGROUND	147 - B1
EL PASO RD & LEWIS RD, CANYON CO ID	
CAMAS CREEK CAMPGROUND	222 - C5
BIG CAMAS RD, DOUGLAS CO OR	
CAMPBELL LAKE CAMPGROUND	151 - C2
LEE THOMAS CROSSING, LAKE CO OR	
CAMPBELL SHELTER	109 - A2
COLONEL BOB, GRAYS HARBOR CO WA	
CAMPBELL TREE GROVE CAMPGROUND	109 - A2
COLONEL BOB, GRAYS HARBOR CO WA	
CAMP BROWN FOREST PARK	125 - B1
ROARING CREEK, WASHINGTON CO OR	
CAMP CREEK CAMPGROUND	201 - D6
GOVERNMENT CAMP, CLACKAMAS CO OR	

FEATURE NAME	Page-Grid
City State	
CAMPGROUND NUMBER ONE	151 - C2
DOG LAKE, LAKE CO OR	
CAMPGROUND NUMBER TWO	151 - C2
DOG LAKE, LAKE CO OR	
CAMP SEKANI	350 - B3
E UPRIVER DR & N CENTER RD, SPOKANE CO WA	
CANAL CREEK CAMPGROUND	209 - C2
OFF CANAL CREEK RD, LINCOLN CO OR	
CANDLE CREEK CAMPGROUND	134 - C1
OFF METOLIUS RIVER RD, JEFFERSON CO OR	
CANTON CREEK CAMPGROUND	141 - C2
STEAMBOAT, DOUGLAS CO OR	
CANTON SHELTER	141 - C2
SCAREDMAN CREEK, DOUGLAS CO OR	
CANTRALL-BUCKLEY CAMPGROUND	149 - B2
RUCH, JACKSON CO OR	
CANYON CREEK CAMPGROUND	105 - C2
BANGS MOUNTAIN, FERRY CO WA	
CANYON CREEK CAMPGROUND	136 - A2
CANYON CREEK RD, CROOK CO OR	
CANYON CREEK CAMPGROUND	102 - C1
GLACIER, WHATCOM CO WA	
CANYON CREEK CAMPGROUND	193 - D1
SIOUXON PEAK, SKAMANIA CO WA	
CANYON CREEK CAMPGROUNDS	211 - C1
RANKIN RD, JEFFERSON CO OR	
CANYON CREEK SHELTER	109 - A1
BOGACHIEL PEAK, CLALLAM CO WA	
CANYON CREEK SHELTER	103 - B3
GAMMA PEAK, SNOHOMISH CO WA	
CAPE PERPETUA CAMPGROUND	209 - A4
CUMMINS PEAK RD, LINCOLN CO OR	
CARBERRY CAMPGROUND	149 - B2
CARBERRY CREEK, JACKSON CO OR	
CARROL CAMPGROUND	136 - A2
OFF SUMMIT RD, WHEELER CO OR	
CARTER LAKE CAMPGROUND	214 - A5
OREGON COAST HWY, DOUGLAS CO OR	
CASCADE ISLAND CAMPGROUND	103 - A2
MARBLEMOUNT, SKAGIT CO WA	
CASCADE LOCKS KOA	194 - D5
STAR RTE BOX 660, CASCADE LOCKS OR	
CASTLE ROCK CAMPGROUND	197 - C7
HEBO, TILLAMOOK CO OR	
CASTLE ROCK CAMPGROUND	197 - B7
OFF JENCK RD, TILLAMOOK CO OR	
CAT CREEK CAMPGROUND	119 - A2
GREEN MOUNTAIN, SKAMANIA CO WA	
CAT ISLAND CAMPGROUND	103 - B1
HOZOMEEN MOUNTAIN, WHATCOM CO WA	
CAVITT SHELTER	141 - B2
LANE MOUNTAIN, DOUGLAS CO OR	
CAYUSE CAMPGROUND	111 - B2
DAVIS PEAK, KITTITAS CO WA	
CCC CAMPGROUND	115 - C2
MARBLE CREEK, SHOSHONE CO ID	
CEDAR CREEK CAMPGROUND	115 - C3
CLARKIA, SHOSHONE CO ID	
CEDAR GROVE CAMPGROUND	238 - A4
BLEWETT, CHELAN CO WA	
CEDAR SPRINGS CAMPGROUND	119 - B1
OLD SCAB MOUNTAIN, YAKIMA CO WA	
CEDAR SWAMP CAMPSITE	195 - A6
WAHTUM LAKE TR, HOOD RIVER CO OR	
CHAIN OF LAKES CAMPGROUND	119 - A2
GREEN MOUNTAIN, SKAMANIA CO WA	
CHAMBERS LAKE CAMPGROUND	119 - A2
HAMILTON BUTTES, LEWIS CO WA	
CHANCELLOR CAMPGROUND	103 - C2
SHULL MOUNTAIN, WHATCOM CO WA	
CHARLTON LAKE SHELTER	142 - B1
THE TWINS, LANE CO OR	
CHATTER CREEK CAMPGROUND	111 - B2
JACK RIDGE, CHELAN CO WA	
CHEWUCH CAMPGROUND	104 - A2
DOE MOUNTAIN, OKANOGAN CO WA	
CHIEF PAULINA CAMPGROUND	143 - A1
NEWBERRY CRATER RD, DESCHUTES CO OR	
CHIMNEY ROCK CAMPGROUND	135 - C3
STEARNS BUTTE, CROOK CO OR	
CHINA FLAT CAMPGROUND	140 - B3
CHINA FLAT, COOS CO OR	
CHINA HAT CAMPGROUND	143 - B1
CHINA HAT RD, DESCHUTES CO OR	
CHOCWICH CAMPGROUND	103 - A3
BEDAL, SNOHOMISH CO WA	
CHOPAKA LAKE CAMPGROUND	104 - B1
NIGHTHAWK, OKANOGAN CO WA	
CHURCH CREEK SHELTER	109 - B2
MOUNT TEBO, MASON CO WA	
CINDER HILL CAMPGROUND	143 - B1
NEWBERRY CRATER RD, DESCHUTES CO OR	
CITY CREEK SHELTER	142 - A1
REYNOLDS RIDGE, LANE CO OR	
CLACKAMAS LAKE CAMPGROUND	126 - C3
MOUNT WILSON, CLACKAMAS CO OR	
CLALLAM RIVER CAMPGROUND	163 - B3
ELLIS MOUNTAIN, CLALLAM CO WA	
CLEAR CREEK CAMP	223 - A7
HAMAKER BUTTE, DOUGLAS CO OR	
CLEAR CREEK CAMPGROUND	103 - A3
HELENA RIDGE, SNOHOMISH CO WA	
CLEAR CREEK CAMPGROUND	127 - A3
POST POINT, WASCO CO OR	
CLEAR LAKE CAMPGROUND	119 - A2
SPIRAL BUTTE, YAKIMA CO WA	
CLEAR LAKE CAMPGROUND	126 - C3
WAPINITIA PASS, WASCO CO OR	
CLEAR LAKE NORTH CAMPGROUND	119 - A2
SPIRAL BUTTE, YAKIMA CO WA	
CLEAR LAKE SOUTH CAMPGROUND	119 - B2
SPIRAL BUTTE, YAKIMA CO WA	
CLE ELUM RIVER CAMPGROUND	111 - B3
CLE ELUM LAKE, KITTITAS CO WA	
CLIFF LAKE CAMPGROUND	226 - B2
BUCKEYE LAKE, DOUGLAS CO OR	
CLIFF LAKE CAMPGROUND	150 - B1
DEVILS PEAK, KLAMATH CO OR	
CLIFF LAKE SHELTER	134 - C3
THREE SISTERS WILDERNESS AREA, LANE CO OR	
CLINE-CLARK CAMPGROUND	142 - A1
OAKRIDGE, LANE CO OR	
CLINGER CAMPGROUND	202 - C4
DOG RIVER, HOOD RIVER CO OR	
CLOUD CAP SADDLE CAMPGROUND	202 - B4
MOUNT HOOD NORTH, HOOD RIVER CO OR	
CLOVERLEAF BEACH CAMPGROUND	106 - A3
INCHELIUM, STEVENS CO WA	
COAL CREEK CAMPGROUND	140 - C3
CHINA FLAT, COOS CO OR	
COAST CREEK CAMPGROUND	125 - A2
SPRINGER MOUNTAIN, YAMHILL CO OR	
CODWATER CAMPGROUND	222 - A4
TAFT MOUNTAIN, DOUGLAS CO OR	

FEATURE NAME City State	Page-Grid
COHO CAMPGROUND WYNOOCHEE LAKE, GRAYS HARBOR CO WA	109 - A2
COLD CREEK CAMPGROUND DOLE, CLARK CO WA	193 - C4
COLDSPRING CAMPGROUND HWY 3, BRITISH COLUMBIA BC	103 - C1
COLD SPRING CAMPGROUND LONE BUTTE, SKAMANIA CO WA	118 - C3
COLD SPRINGS CAMPGROUND MOUNT ADAMS EAST, YAKIMA CO WA	119 - A3
COLD SPRINGS CAMPGROUND NFD RD 89, ADAMS CO ID	131 - C3
COLD SPRINGS CAMPGROUND UNION PEAK, KLAMATH CO OR	227 - C5
COLE, RAY CAMPGROUND CANYON CREEK RD, GRANT CO OR	137 - B2
COLONIAL CREEK CAMPGROUND ROSS DAM, WHATCOM CO WA	103 - B2
COMMONWEALTH CAMPGROUND SNOQUALMIE PASS, KING CO WA	111 - A2
COMPANY CREEK CAMPGROUND STEHEKIN, CHELAN CO WA	103 - C3
CONTORTA POINT CAMPGROUND COWHORN MOUNTAIN, KLAMATH CO OR	142 - B1
COPPER CREEK CAMPGROUND EASTPORT, BOUNDARY CO ID	107 - C1
COPPERFIELD CAMPGROUND BAKER-COPPERFIELD HWY, BAKER CO OR	131 - A3
COPPER MINE BOTTOM CAMPGROUND CHRISTMAS CREEK, JEFFERSON CO WA	108 - C1
CORRAL CREEK CAMPGROUND GEARHART MOUNTAIN, LAKE CO OR	151 - C1
CORRAL CREEK CAMPGROUND LAKE CHELAN, CHELAN CO WA	112 - A1
CORRIGAL SPRING CAMPGROUND OFF BULL RUN TO BAKER RD, GRANT CO OR	137 - C1
COTTER CAMPGROUND GRANGEVILLE EAST, IDAHO CO ID	123 - C3
COTTONWOOD CAMPGROUND ANDERSON CREEK, JEFFERSON CO WA	169 - D5
COTTONWOOD CAMPGROUND CONCONULLY WEST, OKANOGAN CO WA	104 - B2
COTTONWOOD CAMPGROUND DEER RD, WHEELER CO OR	136 - B2
COTTONWOOD CAMPGROUND OFF HWY 410, YAKIMA CO WA	240 - A7
COTTONWOOD MEADOW CAMPGROUND COUGAR PEAK, LAKE CO OR	151 - C2
COUGAR CREEK CAMPGROUND COUGAR PEAK, LAKE CO OR	151 - C2
COUGAR FLAT CAMPGROUND OLD SCAB MOUNTAIN, YAKIMA CO WA	119 - B1
COUGAR ISLAND CAMPGROUND PUMPKIN MOUNTAIN, WHATCOM CO WA	103 - B2
COUGAR ROCK CAMPGROUND MOUNT RAINIER WEST, PIERCE CO WA	185 - B5
COULEE CITY CAMPGROUND GRANT CO WA	113 - A2
COUNCIL LAKE CAMPGROUND EAST CANYON RIDGE, SKAMANIA CO WA	119 - A3
COVERDALE CAMPGROUND UPPER MOUNTAIN RD, WALLOWA CO OR	131 - A3
COW CAMP CAMPGROUND OFF LOOKOUT MOUNTAIN RD, DESCHUTES CO OR	216 - A7
COWICHAN RIVER CAMPGROUND HWY 18, BRITISH COLUMBIA BC	101 - A1
COYOTE SPRING CAMPGROUND BUCKHORN RD, WALLOWA CO OR	131 - A1
CRANE CREEK CAMPGROUND OFF NFD RD 16, GRANT CO OR	137 - C2
CRANE PRAIRIE CAMPGROUND S CENTURY RD, DESCHUTES CO OR	216 - B7
CRATER CREEK CAMPGROUND HUNGRY MOUNTAIN, OKANOGAN CO WA	104 - A3
CRAWFISH LAKE CAMPGROUND CRAWFISH LAKE, OKANOGAN CO WA	105 - A2
CRAWFISH SHELTER FAIRVIEW PEAK, LANE CO OR	141 - C1
CRESCENT CREEK CAMPGROUNDS ODELL BUTTE, KLAMATH CO OR	142 - C1
CRESCENT LAKE CAMPGROUND BOUNDARY DAM, PEND OREILLE CO WA	106 - C1
CRIPPEN CAMPGROUND BOWEN ISLAND, BRITISH COLUMBIA BC	93 - B3
CROWN ZELLERBACK CAMPGROUND OREGON COAST HWY, DOUGLAS CO OR	214 - A6
CRYSTAL CREEK CAMPGROUND PUGH MOUNTAIN, SNOHOMISH CO WA	103 - A3
CRYSTAL SPRINGS CAMPGROUND STAMPEDE PASS, KITTITAS CO WA	111 - A3
CULTUS CREEK CAMPGROUND LONE BUTTE, SKAMANIA CO WA	118 - C3
CULTUS LAKE CAMPGROUND NFD RD 4635, DESCHUTES CO OR	216 - A7
CURLEW LAKE CAMPGROUND REPUBLIC, FERRY CO WA	105 - B2
CURLY CREEK CAMPGROUND BURNT PEAK, SKAMANIA CO WA	118 - C3
DAIRY CREEK CAMPGROUND COLEMAN POINT, LAKE CO OR	151 - C1
DAIRY CREEK CAMPGROUND LEE THOMAS CROSSING, LAKE CO OR	151 - C1
DAIRY POINT CAMPGROUND COLEMAN POINT, LAKE CO OR	151 - C1
DAISY CAMPGROUND DUNCAN RIDGE, OKANOGAN CO WA	104 - B1
DAM CAMPGROUND ROCK CREEK RESERVOIR, WASCO CO OR	127 - A3
DANA YELVERTON SHELTER OLD SNOWY MOUNTAIN, LEWIS CO WA	119 - A2
DAPHNE GROVE CAMPGROUND ILLAHE, COOS CO OR	140 - B3
DASH POINT CAMPGROUND 5700 SW DASH POINT RD, FEDERAL WAY WA	182 - A1
DAVIS LAKE CAMPGROUND BOYDS, FERRY CO WA	105 - C2
DEADHORSE CAMPGROUND COLEMAN POINT, LAKE CO OR	151 - C1
DEAD HORSE LAKE CAMPGROUND LEE THOMAS CROSSING, LAKE CO OR	151 - C1
DEARINGER CAMPGROUND PRAIRIE MOUNTAIN, SKAGIT CO WA	103 - A3
DECEPTION CREEK CAMPGROUND SCENIC, KING CO WA	111 - B1
DECEPTION FALLS CAMPGROUND SCENIC, KING CO WA	111 - B1
DEEP CREEK CAMPGROUND NAPLES, BOUNDARY CO ID	107 - B2
DEEP CREEK CAMPGROUND NELSON RD, CROOK CO OR	136 - B2
DEEP CREEK CAMPGROUND NFD RD 4015, LAKE CO OR	152 - A2
DEEP CREEK CAMPGROUND PLAIN, CHELAN CO WA	111 - C1

FEATURE NAME City State	Page-Grid
DEER CREEK CAMPGROUND OFF WHITNEY HWY, BAKER CO OR	138 - A1
DEER CREEK SUMMIT CAMPGROUND MOUNT LEONA, FERRY CO WA	105 - C1
DEERHORN CAMPGROUND UPPER MIDDLE FORK RD, GRANT CO OR	137 - C1
DEER LAKE SHELTER BOGACHIEL PEAK, CLALLAM CO WA	109 - A1
DEER PK CAMPGROUND MAIDEN PEAK, CLALLAM CO WA	109 - B1
DEER POINT CAMPGROUND LAKE CHELAN, CHELAN CO WA	112 - A1
DEL NORTE COAST REDWOODS CAMPGROUND E OF US101, S OF HMLTN RD, DL NORTE CO CA	148 - B3
DELP SHELTER BIG FALL CREEK RD, LANE CO OR	134 - A3
DELTA CAMPGROUND MCKENZIE RD, LANE CO OR	134 - B2
DEPRESSION LAKE CAMPGROUND WELKER PEAK, WHATCOM CO WA	102 - C2
DE ROUX CAMPGROUND MOUNT STUART, KITTITAS CO WA	111 - B2
DETILLION CAMPGROUND MCCOY LAKE, LINCOLN CO WA	113 - C1
DEVILS ELBOW CAMPGROUND POND PEAK, SHOSHONE CO ID	115 - C1
DEVILS FLAT CAMPGROUND COW CREEK RD, DOUGLAS CO OR	141 - B3
DEVILS HALF ACRE MEADOW CAMPGROUND BARLOW RD, HOOD RIVER CO OR	202 - B6
DEVILS MEADOW CAMPGROUND GOVERNMENT CAMP, CLACKAMAS CO OR	201 - D5
DIAMOND LAKE CAMPGROUND DIAMOND LAKE, DOUGLAS CO OR	223 - C6
DIAMOND LAKE TRAILER CAMP AREA DIAMOND LAKE, DOUGLAS CO OR	223 - C6
DICKENSHEET CAMPGROUND OUTLET BAY, BONNER CO ID	107 - A2
DICKEY CREEK CAMPGROUND RED TOP MOUNTAIN, KITTITAS CO WA	111 - C3
DICK SPERRY CAMPGROUND SILVERTON, SNOHOMISH CO WA	103 - A3
DIGIT POINT CAMPGROUND MILLER LAKE, KLAMATH CO OR	142 - B2
DILLON FALLS CAMPGROUND BENHAM FALLS, DESCHUTES CO OR	217 - A4
DIRT OVEN CAMPGROUND SHORTY PEAK, BOUNDARY CO ID	107 - A1
DIRTYFACE CAMPGROUND LAKE WENATCHEE, CHELAN CO WA	111 - C1
DIVIDE WELL CAMPGROUND NFD RD 5320, UMATILLA CO OR	129 - A3
DIXIE CAMPGROUND JOHN DAY-BURNS RD, GRANT CO OR	137 - C1
DOE CREEK CAMPGROUND GOLDEN, JOSEPHINE CO OR	149 - A1
DOG LAKE CAMPGROUND DOG LAKE, LAKE CO OR	151 - C2
DOG LAKE CAMPGROUND SPIRAL BUTTE, YAKIMA CO WA	119 - A3
DOG PRAIRIE SHELTER GARWOOD BUTTE, DOUGLAS CO OR	223 - B5
DOLLY VARDEN CAMPGROUND MCGREGOR MOUNTAIN, CHELAN CO WA	103 - C3
DOLLY VARDEN SHELTER BIG FALL CREEK RD, LANE CO OR	134 - A3
DOLLY VISTA SHELTER GAMMA PEAK, SNOHOMISH CO WA	103 - B3
DOMKE FALLS CAMPGROUND LUCERNE, CHELAN CO WA	103 - C3
DOMKE LAKE CAMPGROUND LUCERNE, CHELAN CO WA	103 - C3
DOSEWALLIPS CAMPGROUND THE BROTHERS, JEFFERSON CO WA	109 - A1
DOSEWALLIPS STATE PK CAMPGROUND BRINNON, JEFFERSON CO WA	109 - B1
DOUGAN CREEK CAMPGROUND BOBS MOUNTAIN, SKAMANIA CO WA	194 - A5
DOUGHERTY SPRING CAMPGROUND BUCKHORN RD, WALLOWA CO OR	131 - A1
DOUGLAS FIR CAMPGROUND GLACIER, WHATCOM CO WA	102 - C1
DOVE CREEK CAMPGROUND OFF NFD RD 454, WALLOWA CO OR	131 - B3
DOVRE CAMPGROUND TRASK MOUNTAIN, TILLAMOOK CO OR	125 - A2
DOWNEY CREEK CAMPGROUND DOWNEY MOUNTAIN, SNOHOMISH CO WA	103 - B3
DREWS CREEK CAMPGROUND FITZWATER POINT, LAKE CO OR	151 - C2
DRIFT CAMPGROUND METOLIUS BENCH, JEFFERSON CO OR	135 - A1
DRIFT CREEK SHELTER OFF RISLEY CREEK RD, LINCOLN CO OR	209 - C1
DRIFT FENCE CAMPGROUND NFD RD 52, UMATILLA CO OR	129 - B3
DRIFTWOOD CAMPGROUND OFF OREGON COAST HWY, LANE CO OR	214 - A5
DRIFTWOOD CAMPGROUND THREE CREEKS LAKE RD, DESCHUTES CO OR	216 - C1
DRIFTWOOD II CAMPGROUND OFF OREGON COAST HWY, LANE CO OR	214 - A5
DRY CREEK CAMPGROUND CLE ELUM LAKE, KITTITAS CO WA	111 - B3
DRY CREEK CAMPGROUND DRY CREEK RD, JEFFERSON CO OR	208 - B2
DRY CREEK CAMPGROUND SUN TOP, PIERCE CO WA	111 - A3
DUCKABUSH SHELTER MOUNT STEEL, JEFFERSON CO WA	109 - A1
DUCK LAKE CAMPGROUND OFF DUCK CREEK RD, WALLOWA CO OR	131 - A3
DUNGENESS FORKS CAMPGROUND MOUNT ZION, CLALLAM CO WA	109 - C1
DUNGENESS REC AREA CAMPGROUND WEST OF DUNGENESS, CLALLAM CO WA	166 - A3
DUTCH CREEK SHELTER BULL OF THE WOODS, CLACKAMAS CO OR	126 - B3
EAGLE CREEK CAMPGROUND BONNEVILLE DAM, NORTH BONNEVILLE WA	194 - C6
EAGLE CREEK FOREST CAMPGROUND NFD RD 77, BAKER CO OR	130 - C3
EAGLE FORKS FOREST CAMPGROUND EAGLE CREEK DR, BAKER CO OR	130 - C3
EAGLE ROCK CAMPGROUND AVD DE UMPQUA HWY, DOUGLAS CO OR	222 - B3
EARLY WINTERS CAMPGROUND MAZAMA, OKANOGAN CO WA	104 - A2
EAST CARTER CAMPGROUND OREGON COAST HWY, DOUGLAS CO OR	214 - A5
EAST DAVIS LAKE CAMPGROUND HAMNER BUTTE, KLAMATH CO OR	142 - C1
EAST FORK SHELTER COLONEL BOB, GRAYS HARBOR CO WA	109 - A2

FEATURE NAME City State	Page-Grid
EAST LAKE CAMPGROUND NEWBERRY CRATER RD, DESCHUTES CO OR	143 - B1
EAST LEMOLO CAMPGROUND LEMOLO LAKE, DOUGLAS CO OR	223 - C3
EAST SIDE BUCK CREEK CAMPGROUND HUCKLEBERRY MOUNTAIN, SNOHOMISH CO WA	103 - A3
EASTSIDE CAMPGROUND OFF HANCOCK RD, GEM CO ID	139 - C2
ECHO CAMPGROUND SOUTH FORK RD, LANE CO OR	134 - B3
EDEN VALLEY CAMPGROUND EDEN VALLEY, COOS CO OR	140 - C3
EDGEWATER CAMPGROUND METALINE, PEND OREILLE CO WA	106 - B1
EEL CREEK CAMPGROUND OFF OREGON COAST HWY, COOS CO OR	218 - B4
EIGHTMILE CAMPGROUND CASHMERE MOUNTAIN, CHELAN CO WA	111 - C2
EIGHTMILE LAKE CAMPGROUND CASHMERE MOUNTAIN, CHELAN CO WA	111 - B2
ELBOW LAKE CAMPGROUND LA FLEUR LAKE, FERRY CO WA	105 - C2
ELBOW LAKE CAMPGROUND OREGON COAST HWY, DOUGLAS CO OR	214 - A7
ELDORADO CAMPGROUND E CAMP CREEK RD, BAKER CO OR	138 - A2
ELEPHANT ROCK CAMPGROUND LUCERNE, CHELAN CO WA	103 - C3
ELK CAMPGROUND NFD RD 32, UMATILLA CO OR	130 - A1
ELK CREEK CAMPGROUND CHINA FLAT, COOS CO OR	140 - C3
ELK CREEK CAMPGROUND NFD RD 16, GRANT CO OR	137 - C2
ELK FALLS CREEK CAMPGROUND CHINA FLAT, COOS CO OR	140 - C3
ELK LAKE CAMPGROUND CASCADE LAKES HWY, DESCHUTES CO OR	216 - A4
ELK LAKE CAMPGROUND OFF BREITENBUSH RD, MARION CO OR	134 - B1
EMERALD CREEK CAMPGROUND CLARKIA, SHOSHONE CO ID	115 - B3
EMIGRANT CAMPGROUND EMIGRANT CREEK RD, HARNEY CO OR	137 - A3
EMILE SHELTER TAFT MOUNTAIN, DOUGLAS CO OR	141 - C2
EMORY CREEK CAMPGROUND HWY 1, BRITISH COLUMBIA BC	95 - A2
ENGLISH CAMPSITE SAN JUAN CO WA	101 - C2
ENGLISHMAN FALLS CAMPGROUND OFF HWY 19, BRITISH COLUMBIA BC	93 - A3
ENGLISHMAN RIVER FALLS CAMPGROUND HWY 4, BRITISH COLUMBIA BC	92 - C3
ERICKSONS BAY CAMPGROUND ALLENS BAY, CLALLAM CO WA	162 - B5
ERRIN CAMPGROUND HOLLAND POINT, LANE CO OR	142 - A1
EVANS CAMPGROUND MARCUS, STEVENS CO WA	106 - A2
EVERGREEN CAMPGROUND UPPER MOUNTAIN RD, WALLOWA CO OR	131 - A3
EVERGREEN CAMPGROUND US HWY 95, ADAMS CO ID	131 - C3
FAIRHOLM CAMPGROUND OLYMPIC HWY, CLALLAM CO WA	164 - A6
FAIRVIEW CAMPGROUND COLLIER BUTTE, CURRY CO OR	228 - D7
FAIRY SHELTER STEAMBOAT, DOUGLAS CO OR	222 - A4
FALL CREEK CAMPGROUND CAPITOL PEAK, THURSTON CO WA	184 - A5
FALL CREEK CAMPGROUND MACE MOUNTAIN, DOUGLAS CO OR	141 - C2
FALL RIVER CAMPGROUND PISTOL BUTTE, DESCHUTES CO OR	142 - C1
FALLS CREEK CAMPGROUND DOE MOUNTAIN, OKANOGAN CO WA	104 - C1
FALLS VIEW CAMPGROUND MOUNT TOWNSEND, JEFFERSON CO WA	109 - C1
FAN CREEK CAMPGROUND TRASK MOUNTAIN, TILLAMOOK CO OR	125 - A2
FERRY LAKE CAMPGROUND SWAN LAKE, FERRY CO WA	105 - B2
FIFTEEN MILE CAMPGROUND FLAG POINT, WASCO CO OR	202 - D5
FIFTEENMILE SHELTER HUNGER MOUNTAIN, CLALLAM CO WA	108 - C1
FILLONGLEY CAMPGROUND HWY 19, BRITISH COLUMBIA BC	92 - B2
FINNER CREEK CAMPGROUND SCHAEFER LAKE, CHELAN CO WA	111 - C1
FINNEY CREEK SHELTER FINNEY PEAK, SKAGIT CO WA	102 - C2
FISH CREEK CAMPGROUND BEDFORD POINT, CLACKAMAS CO OR	126 - B3
FISH CREEK CAMPGROUND BIG CAMAS RD, DOUGLAS CO OR	222 - D5
FISH CREEK MEADOW CAMPGROUND GOODWIN MEADOWS, IDAHO CO ID	123 - C3
FISH CREEK SHELTER FISH MOUNTAIN, DOUGLAS CO OR	222 - D7
FISH CREEK SHELTER LUCERNE, CHELAN CO WA	103 - C3
FISH LAKE CAMPGROUND FISH LAKE, DOUGLAS CO OR	222 - C7
FISH LAKE CAMPGROUND FISH LAKE RD, HARNEY CO OR	145 - C3
FISH LAKE CAMPGROUND PEER-HOPE RD, BAKER CO OR	131 - A3
FISH LAKE CAMPGROUND THE CRADLE, KITTITAS CO WA	111 - B2
FISH POND CAMPGROUND PLAIN, CHELAN CO WA	111 - C1
FIVEMILE SHELTER NFD RD 5087, LINCOLN CO OR	206 - C7
FLAPJACK SHELTER HUNGER MOUNTAIN, CLALLAM CO WA	108 - C1
FLAT CAMPGROUND LEWIS BUTTE, OKANOGAN CO WA	104 - A2
FLICK CREEK CAMPGROUND SUN MOUNTAIN, CHELAN CO WA	103 - C3
FLODELLE CAMPGROUND LAKE GILLETTE, STEVENS CO WA	106 - B2
FLUMET FLAT CAMPGROUND SQUAW LAKES, JACKSON CO OR	149 - B2
FOGGY DEW CAMPGROUND HUNGRY MOUNTAIN, OKANOGAN CO WA	104 - A3
FOPIAN CAMPGROUND NFD RD 16, BAKER CO OR	137 - C2
FORLORN LAKES CAMPGROUND GIFFORD PEAK, SKAMANIA CO WA	118 - C3
FOSS RIVER CAMPGROUND SKYKOMISH, KING CO WA	111 - B2

FEATURE NAME City State	Page-Grid
FOSTER BAR CAMPGROUND ILLAHE, CURRY CO OR	148 - B1
FOUR CORNERS CAMPGROUND UKIAH-HILGARD HWY, UMATILLA CO OR	129 - C3
FOURMILE CAMPGROUND CUMMINS PEAK RD, LINCOLN CO OR	209 - A4
FOURMILE LAKE CAMPGROUND LAKE OF THE WOODS NORTH, KLAMATH CO OR	150 - B1
FOX CREEK CAMPGROUND SILVER FALLS, CHELAN CO WA	111 - C1
FRANCIS CREEK CAMPSITE KIMTA PEAK, JEFFERSON CO WA	109 - A2
FRAZIER CAMPGROUND OFF NFD RD 58, GRANT CO OR	136 - C2
FRAZIER CAMPGROUND UKIAH-HILGARD HWY, UMATILLA CO OR	129 - C3
FRAZIER FORK CAMPGROUND HIGH ROCK, CLACKAMAS CO OR	126 - B3
FRAZIER TURNAROUND CAMPGROUND HIGH ROCK, CLACKAMAS CO OR	126 - C3
FREEMAN CREEK CAMPGROUND AHSAHKA, CLEARWATER CO ID	123 - B1
FRENCH BEACH CAMPGROUND BRITISH COLUMBIA BC	101 - A2
FRENCH CREEK CAMPGROUND CHIWAUKUM MOUNTAINS, CHELAN CO WA	111 - B2
FRENCH GULCH CAMPGROUND SQUAW LAKES, JACKSON CO OR	149 - B2
FROG LAKE CAMPGROUND WAPINITIA PASS, WASCO CO OR	202 - A7
GATE CREEK CAMPGROUND MCLEOD MOUNTAIN, OKANOGAN CO WA	104 - A2
GATTON CREEK CAMPGROUND LAKE QUINAULT EAST, GRAYS HARBOR CO WA	109 - A2
GERTRUDE SHELTER BEARBONES MOUNTAIN, LANE CO OR	142 - A1
GLACIER VIEW CAMPGROUND LAKE WENATCHEE, CHELAN CO WA	111 - C1
GODMAN CAMPGROUND GODMAN SPRING, COLUMBIA CO WA	122 - B3
GOLD BASIN CAMPGROUND MALLARDY RIDGE, SNOHOMISH CO WA	102 - C3
GOLD CREEK SHELTER MOUNT ZION, CLALLAM CO WA	109 - C1
GONE CREEK CAMPGROUND TIMOTHY LAKE, CLACKAMAS CO OR	126 - C3
GOODELL CAMPGROUND MOUNT TRIUMPH, WHATCOM CO WA	103 - B2
GOOSE CREEK CAMPGROUND PLAIN, CHELAN CO WA	111 - C1
GOOSE LAKE CAMPGROUND GIFFORD PEAK, SKAMANIA CO WA	118 - C3
GORDON BAY PROVINCIAL CAMPGROUND BRITISH COLUMBIA BC	100 - C1
GORGE CAMPGROUND MOUNT ZION, CLALLAM CO WA	109 - C1
GRAHAM HARBOR CAMPGROUND BIG GOAT MOUNTAIN, CHELAN CO WA	104 - A3
GRANDE RONDE LAKE CAMPGROUND ANTHONY LAKES RD, UNION CO OR	130 - A3
GRANDVIEW CAMPGROUND OFF NFD RD 3120, UNION CO OR	130 - A2
GRASSHOPPER MEADOWS CAMPGROUND MOUNT DAVID, CHELAN CO WA	111 - B1
GRASS LAKE CAMPGROUND DEVILS PEAK, KLAMATH CO OR	150 - B1
GRASS LAKE CAMPGROUND NUMBER 2 DEVILS PEAK, KLAMATH CO OR	150 - B1
GRASSY FLAT CAMPGROUND OFF REDWOOD HWY, DEL NORTE CO CA	148 - C3
GRAVES CREEK CAMPGROUND MOUNT HOQUIAM, JEFFERSON CO WA	109 - B2
GREEN CANYON CAMPGROUND RHODODENDRON, CLACKAMAS CO OR	201 - C6
GREYBALL SHELTER COPPER MOUNTAIN, WHATCOM CO WA	103 - A1
GREY CREEK CAMPGROUND DARLAND MOUNTAIN, YAKIMA CO WA	119 - B2
GROUP CAMPGROUND MOUNT TRIUMPH, WHATCOM CO WA	103 - A2
GROUSE CAMPGROUND OLD GOOSE LAKE RD, ADAMS CO ID	251 - C2
GROUSE CREEK CAMPGROUND CHIKAMIN CREEK, CHELAN CO WA	111 - C1
GROUSE GAP SHELTER MOUNT ASHLAND, JACKSON CO OR	234 - C6
GROUSE MOUNTAIN CAMPGROUND NFD RD 5900, CHELAN CO WA	112 - A1
GULL POINT CAMPGROUND DAVIS MOUNTAIN, DESCHUTES CO OR	142 - C1
HAAG COVE CAMPGROUND BANGS MOUNTAIN, FERRY CO WA	105 - C2
HAGER LAKE SHELTER PACKWOOD LAKE, LEWIS CO WA	119 - A2
HALFWAY FLAT CAMPGROUND CLIFFDELL, YAKIMA CO WA	119 - B1
HALFWAY HOUSE CAMPSITE KIMTA PEAK, JEFFERSON CO WA	109 - A2
HALFWAY SPRING CAMPGROUND SILVER FALLS, CHELAN CO WA	111 - C1
HAMAKER CAMPGROUND HAMAKER BUTTE, DOUGLAS CO OR	227 - A1
HAMBONE SPRINGS CAMPGROUND HIGH ROCK, CLACKAMAS CO OR	126 - C3
HAMMA HAMMA CAMPGROUND HAMMA HAMMA RD, MASON CO WA	173 - A2
HAMPTON CAMPGROUND HWY 3, BRITISH COLUMBIA BC	103 - A1
HAMPTON CAMPGROUND WILLAMETTE HWY, LANE CO OR	134 - A3
HAND LAKE SHELTER MCKENZIE HWY, LANE CO OR	134 - C2
HANDY SPRING CAMPGROUND NFD RD 5900, CHELAN CO WA	112 - A1
HANEY MEADOW CAMPGROUND BLEWETT PASS, KITTITAS CO WA	238 - B6
HANGING TREE CAMPGROUND NILE, YAKIMA CO WA	119 - B1
HANNEGAN CAMPGROUND MOUNT SEFRIT, WHATCOM CO WA	103 - A1
HAPPY FOUR SHELTER MOUNT TOM, JEFFERSON CO WA	109 - A1
HARRIS BEACH STATE PK CAMPGROUND BROOKINGS, BROOKINGS OR	232 - C5
HARRIS PARK CAMPGROUND BIG SADDLE CANYON, UMATILLA CO OR	130 - A1
HATCHERY CAMPGROUND LUCERNE, CHELAN CO WA	103 - C3
HATCHERY RV CAMPGROUND OHANAPECOSH HOT SPRINGS, LEWIS CO WA	185 - D7
HAUSE CREEK CAMPGROUND TIETON BASIN, YAKIMA CO WA	119 - B1
HAYSTACK RESERVOIR CAMPGROUND OPAL CITY, JEFFERSON CO OR	213 - A1

FEATURE NAME City State	Page-Grid
HAZARD CAMPGROUND HAZARD LAKE RD, IDAHO CO ID	131 - C2
HEAD OF THE RIVER CAMPGROUND FUEGO MOUNTAIN, KLAMATH CO OR	151 - A1
HEART LAKE SHELTER MOUNT CARRIE, CLALLAM CO WA	109 - A1
HEART OF THE HILLS CAMPGROUND HEART OF THE HILLS PKWY, CLALLAM CO WA	165 - B7
HEBO LAKE CAMPGROUND HEBO, TILLAMOOK CO OR	197 - C6
HELLIWELL CAMPGROUND BRITISH COLUMBIA BC	92 - B2
HEMLOCK LAKE CAMPGROUND PELICAN BUTTE, KLAMATH CO OR	150 - B1
HEMLOCK LAKE CAMPGROUND QUARTZ MOUNTAIN, DOUGLAS CO OR	222 - A5
HEMLOCK MEADOW CAMPGROUND QUARTZ MOUNTAIN, DOUGLAS CO OR	222 - A5
HEMPLE CREEK CAMPGROUND MALLARDY RIDGE, SNOHOMISH CO WA	102 - C3
HIDDEN BEACH CAMPGROUND MOON MOUNTAIN, FERRY CO WA	105 - C3
HIDDEN CAMPGROUND UPPER MOUNTAIN RD, WALLOWA CO OR	131 - A3
HIDEAWAY LAKE CAMPGROUND MOUNT MITCHELL, CLACKAMAS CO OR	126 - B3
HIGH BRIDGE CAMPGROUND MCGREGOR MOUNTAIN, CHELAN CO WA	103 - C3
HIGH ROCK CAMPGROUND SAWTOOTH RIDGE, LEWIS CO WA	185 - A6
HIGH ROCK SPRING CAMPGROUND HIGH ROCK, CLACKAMAS CO OR	126 - C3
HILL CAMPGROUND BAYVIEW, KOOTENAI CO ID	245 - C1
HOH CAMPGROUND OWL MOUNTAIN, JEFFERSON CO WA	109 - A1
HOH OX BOW CAMPGROUND WINFIELD CREEK, JEFFERSON CO WA	108 - C1
HOLDEN CAMPGROUND HOLDEN, CHELAN CO WA	103 - C3
HOLLYWOOD POINT CAMPGROUND OFF HANCOCK RD, GEM CO ID	139 - C2
HOLMAN CAMPGROUND PASAYTEN PEAK, OKANOGAN CO WA	103 - C1
HOMESTEAD CAMPGROUND NEWMAN LAKE, SPOKANE CO WA	247 - B1
HOME SWEET HOME SHELTER MOUNT STEEL, JEFFERSON CO WA	109 - B2
HONEYMOON CAMPGROUND SWEETGRASS BUTTE, OKANOGAN CO WA	104 - A2
HONEYSUCKLE CAMPGROUND SKITWISH PEAK, KOOTENAI CO ID	245 - D6
HOOD VIEW CAMPGROUND TIMOTHY LAKE, CLACKAMAS CO OR	126 - C3
HOPS HILL CAMPGROUND MONTE CRISTO, SNOHOMISH CO WA	111 - A1
HORNE LAKE CAVES CAMPGROUND HWY 19, BRITISH COLUMBIA BC	92 - B3
HORSESHOE BEND CAMPGROUND STEAMBOAT, DOUGLAS CO OR	222 - B3
HORSESHOE COVE CAMPGROUND WELKER PEAK, WHATCOM CO WA	103 - A2
HOT SPRINGS CAMPGROUND NEWBERRY CRATER RD, DESCHUTES CO OR	143 - B1
HOT SPRINGS CAMPGROUND OFF BLM RD 61064, LAKE CO OR	152 - C1
HOUR CREEK CAMPGROUND DAVIS PEAK, KITTITAS CO WA	111 - B2
HOZOMEEN CAMPGROUND HOZOMEEN MOUNTAIN, WHATCOM CO WA	103 - B1
HUCKLEBERRY CAMPGROUND OFF NFD RD 105, ADAMS CO ID	131 - B3
HUCKLEBERRY FLAT CAMPGROUND MARBLE CREEK, SHOSHONE CO ID	115 - C2
HUCKLEBERRY LAKE CAMPGROUND ABBOTT BUTTE, DOUGLAS CO OR	226 - B4
HUELSDONK CAMPGROUND SPRUCE MOUNTAIN, JEFFERSON CO WA	108 - C1
HUMBUG CAMPGROUND BREITENBUSH RD, MARION CO OR	134 - B1
HUMBUG MOUNTAIN CAMPGROUND PORT ORFORD, CURRY CO OR	224 - B7
HUNTER CAMPGROUND CASTLE ROCK RD, MALHEUR CO OR	138 - A3
HURRYON CAMP HAMAKER BUTTE, DOUGLAS CO OR	227 - A1
HYAK SHELTER SLIDE PEAK, CLALLAM CO WA	109 - A1
HYATT LAKE CAMPGROUND HYATT RESERVOIR, JACKSON CO OR	150 - A2
ICE CAVE CAMPGROUND LITTLE HUCKLEBERRY MOUNTAIN, SKAMANIA CO	118 - C3
ICE CREEK SHELTER SASKA PEAK, CHELAN CO WA	103 - C3
IDA CREEK CAMPGROUND CASHMERE MOUNTAIN, CHELAN CO WA	111 - C2
IDLEWILD CAMPGROUND JOHN DAY-BURNS HWY, HARNEY CO OR	137 - B3
IKE KINSWA CAMPGROUND MAYFIELD LAKE, LEWIS CO WA	118 - A2
ILLAHE CAMPGROUND ILLAHE, CURRY CO OR	148 - B1
INDEPENDENCE CAMPGROUND CATHEDRAL PEAK, SHOSHONE CO ID	115 - C1
INDIAN CREEK CAMPGROUND GOLD BEACH, CURRY CO OR	228 - A5
INDIAN CREEK CAMPGROUND PRIEST LAKE SE, BONNER CO ID	107 - A2
INDIAN CREEK CAMPGROUND RIMROCK LAKE, YAKIMA CO WA	119 - B1
INDIAN CREEK SHELTER COPPER MOUNTAIN, WHATCOM CO WA	103 - A1
INDIAN FLAT CAMPGROUND OLD SCAB MOUNTAIN, YAKIMA CO WA	119 - B1
INDIAN HENRY CAMPGROUND FISH CREEK MOUNTAIN, CLACKAMAS CO OR	126 - B3
INDIAN HOLE CAMPGROUND MORTON, LEWIS CO WA	118 - A2
INDIAN SPRINGS CAMPGROUND OFF NFD RD 16, GRANT CO OR	137 - B2
INDIAN SPRINGS CAMPGROUND WAHTUM LAKE, HOOD RIVER CO OR	201 - D1
INDIGO LAKE CAMPGROUND COWHORN MOUNTAIN, DOUGLAS CO OR	223 - C3
INLET CAMPGROUND LEMOLO LAKE, DOUGLAS CO OR	223 - C3
IPSUT CREEK CAMPGROUND MOWICH LAKE, PIERCE CO WA	185 - B1
IRISH AND TAYLOR CAMPGROUND OFF CANYON RD, LANE CO OR	134 - B3
IRISHMANS CAMPGROUND COX FLAT, LAKE CO OR	151 - C2
IRON CREEK CAMPGROUND GREENHORN BUTTES, LEWIS CO WA	118 - C2

FEATURE NAME City State	Page-Grid
IRON GATE CAMPGROUND HORSESHOE BASIN, OKANOGAN CO WA	104 - B1
ISLAND CAMPGROUND KING MOUNTAIN, YAKIMA CO WA	119 - A3
ISLAND LAKE CAMPGROUND PELICAN BUTTE, KLAMATH CO OR	150 - B1
ISLAND SHELTER STEAMBOAT MOUNTAIN, SKAMANIA CO WA	118 - C3
JACK LAKE CAMPGROUND OFF JACK LAKE RD, JEFFERSON CO OR	211 - A1
JACKMAN PARK CAMPGROUND STEENS MOUNTAIN LOOP RD, HARNEY CO OR	153 - C1
JACKSON CREEK CAMPGROUND WILLIAMSON RIVER RD, KLAMATH CO OR	143 - A3
JAMES CREEK SHELTER THREE SISTERS WILDERNESS AREA, LANE CO OR	216 - A2
JINGLE POT CAMPSITE OFF HWY 19, BRITISH COLUMBIA BC	93 - A3
JOAQUIN MILLER CAMPGROUND JOHN DAY-BURNS HWY, HARNEY CO OR	137 - B3
JOEMMA BEACH CAMPGROUND BAY RD KPS, PIERCE CO WA	180 - D3
JOHNNY CREEK CAMPGROUND CASHMERE MOUNTAIN, CHELAN CO WA	111 - C2
JONES CREEK CAMPGROUND LARCH MOUNTAIN, CLARK CO WA	193 - C5
JORDAN CREEK CAMPGROUND JORDAN CREEK, SHOSHONE CO ID	115 - C1
JUBILEE LAKE CAMPGROUND NFD RD 63, UNION CO OR	130 - A1
JULY CREEK CAMPGROUND LAKE QUINAULT EAST, GRAYS HARBOR CO WA	109 - A2
JUNGLE CREEK CAMPSITE MOUNT CLIFTY, KITTITAS CO WA	111 - B3
JUNIOR POINT CAMPGROUND NFD RD 5900, CHELAN CO WA	112 - A1
JUSTRITE CAMPGROUND NFD RD 9, WASHINGTON CO ID	139 - A1
KACHESS CAMPGROUND KACHESS LAKE, KITTITAS CO WA	111 - A2
KALALOCH CAMPGROUND OFF HIGHWAY 101, JEFFERSON CO WA	172 - A1
KAMLOOPS ISLAND CAMPGROUND MARCUS, FERRY CO WA	106 - A2
KANASKAT-PALMER CAMPGROUND KING CO WA	110 - C3
KANER FLAT CAMPGROUND MOUNT CLIFTY, KITTITAS CO WA	111 - B3
KEENIG CAMPGROUND JORDAN CREEK, TILLAMOOK CO OR	125 - A1
KELLER CREEK CAMPGROUND YACHATS RIVER RD, LINCOLN CO OR	209 - B4
KELLOGG SILVER VALLEY CAMPGROUND KOA BOX 949, SHOSHONE CO ID	115 - C2
KELSAY VALLEY TRAILHEAD CAMPGROUND TOLO MOUNTAIN, DOUGLAS CO OR	223 - D3
KENTUCKY ALLEYNE CAMPGROUND HWY 5A, BRITISH COLUMBIA BC	95 - C1
KERR CAMPGROUND CONCONULLY WEST, OKANOGAN CO WA	104 - B2
KESTREL CAMPGROUND BAYVIEW, KOOTENAI CO ID	245 - C1
KETTLE FALLS CAMPGROUND KETTLE FALLS, STEVENS CO WA	106 - A2
KETTLE RIVER CAMPGROUND MARCUS, FERRY CO WA	106 - A2
KIAHANIE CAMPGROUND CANYON RD, LANE CO OR	134 - B3
KIAWANIS CAMPGROUND NFD RD 9, WASHINGTON CO ID	139 - A1
KILLEN CREEK CAMPGROUND GREEN MOUNTAIN, SKAMANIA CO WA	119 - A2
KIN BEACH CAMPGROUND BRITISH COLUMBIA BC	92 - B2
KINGSLEY CAMPGROUND KINGSLEY RD, HOOD RIVER CO OR	195 - B6
KINNIKINNICK CAMPGROUND MOUNT HOOD NORTH, HOOD RIVER CO OR	202 - B3
KINZEL LAKE CAMPGROUND GOVERNMENT CAMP, CLACKAMAS CO OR	201 - D7
KIRKLAND CAMPGROUND E OF ENTERPRISE-LEWSTN HWY, WALLOWA CO OR	130 - C1
KIT PRICE CAMPGROUND GRIZZLY MOUNTAIN, SHOSHONE CO ID	115 - C1
KLAHANIE CAMPGROUND READE HILL, CLALLAM CO WA	169 - D1
KLAHOWA CAMPGROUND SNIDER PEAK, CLALLAM CO WA	163 - C6
KLICKITAT SHELTER RISLEY CREEK RD, LINCOLN CO OR	209 - D1
KLIPCHUCK CAMPGROUND SILVER STAR MOUNTAIN, OKANOGAN CO WA	103 - C2
KLOOTCHIE CREEK CAMPGROUND TILLAMOOK HEAD, CLATSOP CO OR	188 - B7
KNEBAL SPRING CAMPGROUND FIVEMILE BUTTE, WASCO CO OR	202 - D3
KNUPPENBURG LAKE CAMPGROUND WHITE PASS, LEWIS CO WA	119 - A2
KOA ASHLAND 5310 HWY 66, JACKSON CO OR	234 - D4
KOA ASTORIA/SEASIDE 1100 RIDGE RD, WARRENTON OR	188 - B1
KOA BANDON-PORT ORFORD 46612 HWY 101, CURRY CO OR	224 - B3
KOA BAY CTR WILLAPA BAY BAY CENTER RD, PACIFIC CO WA	183 - C7
KOA BURLINGTON 646 N GREEN RD, SKAGIT CO WA	161 - B5
KOA CAMPGROUND 298 OREGON AV, LANE CO OR	215 - C4
KOA CAMPGROUND 33775 OAKVILLE RD, LINN CO OR	207 - B6
KOA CAMPGROUND FEDERAL WY, BOISE ID	253 - D4
KOA CAMPGROUND HWY 20, OKANOGAN CO WA	104 - A3
KOA CAMPGROUND REDWOOD HWY, DEL NORTE CO CA	148 - B3
KOA CHEHALIS/HWY 12 EAST 118 US HWY 12, LEWIS CO WA	187 - D2
KOA COEUR D'ALENE OFF I-90, KOOTENAI CO ID	248 - C1
KOA COEUR D'ALENE NORTH HAYDEN LAKE HAYDEN, KOOTENAI CO ID	245 - B4
KOA ELLENSBURG TEANAWAY BUTTE, KITTITAS CO WA	241 - A5
KOA GRANTS PASS/REDWOOD HIGHWAY 13370 REDWOOD HWY, JOSEPHINE CO OR	149 - A1
KOA GRANTS PASS/SUNNY VALLEY 140 OLD STAGE RD, JOSEPHINE CO OR	229 - B2
KOA ILWACO HWY 101, ILWACO WA	186 - A6
KOA KLAMATH FALLS 3435 SHASTA WY, KLAMATH FALLS OR	338 - G9

FEATURE NAME City State	Page-Grid
KOA LEAVENWORTH/WENATCHEE OFF HWY 2, CHELAN CO WA	238 - A1
KOA LINCOLN CITY 5298 NE PARK LN, LINCOLN CO OR	203 - B4
KOA LYNDEN E BADGER RD, LYNDEN WA	102 - B1
KOA MADRAS/CULVER 2435 JERICHO LN, JEFFERSON CO OR	212 - D1
KOA MEDFORD/GOLD HILL BLACKWELL RD & HWY 234, JACKSON CO OR	230 - B6
KOA OREGON DUNES 4135 OREGON COAST HWY, COOS CO OR	218 - B5
KOA PORT ANGELES/SEQUIM OBRIEN RD, CLALLAM CO WA	165 - D6
KOA SEATTLE/TACOMA CAMPGROUND 5801 S 212TH ST, KENT WA	291 - G5
KOA SISTERS/BEND 67667 MCKENZIE-BEND HWY, DESCHUTES CO OR	212 - A5
KOA SPOKANE 3025 N BARKER RD, SPOKANE VALLEY WA	351 - E5
KOA SWEET HOME/FOSTER LAKE 6191 SANTIAM HWY, LINN CO OR	134 - A2
KOA VANCOUVER 40TH AV & HWY 99A, CITY OF SURREY BC	158 - A1
KOA VANTAGE VANTAGE HWY, KITTITAS CO WA	120 - B1
KOA VICTORIA WEST TRANS CANADA HWY, BRITISH COLUMBIA BC	159 - A5
KOA WALDPORT/ALSEA BAY OREGON COAST HWY, LINCOLN CO OR	328 - D3
KOA YAKIMA 1500 KEYS RD, YAKIMA CO WA	243 - C7
KULSHAN CAMPGROUND WELKER PEAK, WHATCOM CO WA	102 - C2
KUM BACK SHELTER BURNT PEAK, SKAMANIA CO WA	118 - C3
LADD CREEK CAMPGROUND BULL RUN LAKE, HOOD RIVER CO OR	202 - A3
LAFFERTY CAMPGROUND NFD RD 2, ADAMS CO ID	131 - B3
LAGOON CAMPGROUND OFF OREGON COAST HWY, LANE CO OR	214 - A5
LAKE CREEK CAMPGROUND POE MOUNTAIN, CHELAN CO WA	111 - B1
LAKE CREEK CAMPGROUND SILVER FALLS, CHELAN CO WA	111 - C1
LAKE ELLEN CAMPGROUND BANGS MOUNTAIN, FERRY CO WA	105 - C2
LAKE FORK CAMPGROUND NORTH PINE CREEK RD, BAKER CO OR	131 - A3
LAKE IN THE WOODS CAMPGROUND QUARTZ MOUNTAIN, DOUGLAS CO OR	141 - C2
LAKE LEO CAMPGROUND IONE, PEND OREILLE CO WA	106 - B2
LAKE LOVELY WATER REC AREA CAMPGD OFF TRANS CANADA HWY, BRITISH COLUMBIA BC	93 - C2
LAKE MARIE CAMPGROUND WINCHESTER BAY, DOUGLAS CO OR	218 - C2
LAKE PLEASANT RV PARK 24025 BOTHELL EVERETT HWY, BOTHELL WA	171 - C6
LAKE SELMAC CAMPGROUND LAKESHORE DR, JOSEPHINE CO OR	233 - B2
LAKE THOMAS CAMPGROUND LAKE GILLETTE, STEVENS CO WA	106 - B2
LAKEVIEW PARK CAMPGROUND HIGHWAY 18, BRITISH COLUMBIA BC	100 - C1
LAKE WENATCHEE CAMPGROUND LAKE WENATCHEE, CHELAN CO WA	111 - C1
LANE CREEK CAMPGROUND UKIAH-HILGARD HWY, UMATILLA CO OR	129 - B3
LARCH LAKE CAMPGROUND SASKA PEAK, CHELAN CO WA	103 - C3
LAST CHANCE CAMPGROUND GOOSE CREEK PARK RD, ADAMS CO ID	251 - B3
LATGOWE COVE CAMPGROUND SQUAW LAKES, JACKSON CO OR	149 - B2
LAVA CAMPGROUND HAMNER BUTTE, KLAMATH CO OR	142 - C1
LAVA CAST FOREST CAMPGROUND LAVA CAST FOREST, DESCHUTES CO OR	217 - C7
LAVA FLOW CAMPGROUND HAMNER BUTTE, DESCHUTES CO OR	142 - C1
LAVA ISLAND CAMPGROUND BENHAM FALLS, DESCHUTES CO OR	217 - B4
LAVA ISLAND SHELTER BENHAM FALLS, DESCHUTES CO OR	217 - A4
LAVA ISLAND SHELTER (PREHIST) BENHAM FALLS, DESCHUTES CO OR	217 - B4
LAVA LAKE CAMPGROUND LAVA LAKE RD, DESCHUTES CO OR	216 - B5
LA WIS WIS CAMPGROUND OHANAPECOSH HOT SPRINGS, LEWIS CO WA	185 - D7
LEADER LAKE CAMPGROUND MALOTT, OKANOGAN CO WA	104 - C3
LEE THOMAS CAMPGROUND LEE THOMAS CROSSING, LAKE CO OR	151 - C1
LELAND LAKE CAMPGROUND CENTER, JEFFERSON CO WA	109 - C1
LEMITI CAMPGROUND PINHEAD BUTTES, CLACKAMAS CO OR	126 - C3
LEMOLO FALLS CAMPGROUND LEMOLO LAKE, DOUGLAS CO OR	223 - B2
LEMOLO TWO FOREBAY CAMPGROUND TOKETEE FALLS, DOUGLAS CO OR	222 - D3
LENA CREEK CAMPGROUND NFD RD 25, MASON CO WA	173 - A2
LENA LAKE CAMPGROUND MOUNT WASHINGTON, JEFFERSON CO WA	173 - A2
LEWIS CAMP FISH MOUNTAIN, DOUGLAS CO OR	226 - D1
LEWIS RIVER CAMPGROUND QUARTZ CREEK BUTTE, SKAMANIA CO WA	118 - C3
LICK CREEK CAMPGROUND WALLOWA MOUNTAIN RD, WALLOWA CO OR	131 - A3
LIGHTING CREEK CAMPGROUND HOZOMEEN MOUNTAIN, WHATCOM CO WA	103 - B1
LILLIAN SHELTER HURRICANE HILL, CLALLAM CO WA	109 - B1
LILLIWAUP CREEK CAMPGROUND NFD RD 24, MASON CO WA	173 - A4
LINDSAY CAMPGROUND OLD SCAB MOUNTAIN, YAKIMA CO WA	119 - B1
LINNEY CREEK CAMPGROUND WOLF PEAK, CLACKAMAS CO OR	201 - D7
LION ROCK SPRING CAMPGROUND BLEWETT PASS, KITTITAS CO WA	241 - B1
LITTLE BADGER CAMPGROUND FRIEND, WASCO CO OR	127 - A2
LITTLE BEAVER CAMPGROUND HOZOMEEN MOUNTAIN, WHATCOM CO WA	103 - B1
LITTLE BLANKET SHELTER OFF WINBERRY CREEK RD, LANE CO OR	134 - A3
LITTLE BOULDER CAMPGROUND BOVILL, LATAH CO ID	123 - B1
LITTLE CHILLIWACK SHELTER COPPER MOUNTAIN, WHATCOM CO WA	103 - A1
LITTLE CRANE CAMPGROUND NFD RD 16, GRANT CO OR	137 - C2
LITTLE CRATER CAMPGROUND NEWBERRY CRATER RD, DESCHUTES CO OR	143 - B1
LITTLE CRATER LAKE CAMPGROUND WAPINITIA PASS, CLACKAMAS CO OR	126 - C3
LITTLE CULTUS CAMPGROUND OFF LAVA LAKE RD, DESCHUTES CO OR	134 - C3
LITTLE DESCHUTES CAMPGROUND ODELL BUTTE, KLAMATH CO OR	142 - C2
LITTLE FAN CREEK CAMPGROUND BULL OF THE WOODS, CLACKAMAS CO OR	126 - B3
LITTLE FAWN CAMPGROUND OFF CASCADE LAKES HWY, DESCHUTES CO OR	216 - A4
LITTLE FISH SHELTER SKAGIT PEAK, WHATCOM CO WA	103 - B1
LITTLE GOOSE CAMPGROUND SLEEPING BEAUTY, SKAMANIA CO WA	118 - C3
LITTLE LAVA LAKE CAMPGROUND OFF LAVA LAKE RD, DESCHUTES CO OR	216 - B5
LITTLE NACHES CAMPGROUND CLIFFDELL, YAKIMA CO WA	119 - B1
LITTLE QUALICUM FALL CAMPGROUND HWY 4, BRITISH COLUMBIA BC	92 - B3
LITTLE REDWOOD CAMPGROUND BOSLEY BUTTE, CURRY CO OR	148 - B2
LITTLE SODA SPRINGS CAMPGROUND STABLER, SKAMANIA CO WA	194 - C2
LITTLE SUMMIT CAMPGROUND OFF DEER RD, WHEELER CO OR	136 - B2
LOBSTER CREEK CAMPGROUND QUOSATANA BUTTE, CURRY CO OR	228 - B4
LOCKABY CAMPGROUND BEDFORD POINT, CLACKAMAS CO OR	126 - C3
LODGEPOLE CAMPGROUND NORSE PEAK, YAKIMA CO WA	119 - A1
LODGEPOLE CAMPGROUND OREGON COAST HWY, LANE CO OR	214 - A5
LOFTON RESERVOIR CAMPGROUND QUARTZ VALLEY, LAKE CO OR	151 - C2
LONE FIR CAMPGROUND WASHINGTON PASS, OKANOGAN CO WA	103 - C3
LONE PEAK CAMPGROUND OFF NFD RD 5900, CHELAN CO WA	112 - A1
LONESOME COVE CAMPGROUND RIMROCK LAKE, YAKIMA CO WA	119 - B2
LONESOME SPRING CAMPGROUND OFF PETERSON CREEK RD, CROOK CO OR	136 - B2
LONE WOLF SHELTER WESTFIR WEST, LANE CO OR	142 - A1
LONG CREEK CAMPGROUND OFF NFD RD 16, BAKER CO OR	138 - A2
LONG LAKE CAMPGROUND BALD KNOB, FERRY CO WA	105 - B2
LONGMILE MEADOWS CAMPGROUND MOUNT CLIFTY, KITTITAS CO WA	111 - B3
LONGMIRE CAMPGROUND WAHPENAYO PEAK, LEWIS CO WA	185 - B5
LONG RIDGE CAMPGROUND QUAIL PRAIRIE MOUNTAIN, CURRY CO OR	148 - B2
LONG SWAMP CAMPGROUND CORRAL BUTTE, OKANOGAN CO WA	104 - B1
LOOKOUT SPRINGS CAMPGROUND THREE LYNX, CLACKAMAS CO OR	126 - B3
LOONEY SPRING CAMPGROUND OFF JOHN DAY HWY, GRANT CO OR	137 - C2
LOST LAKE CAMPGROUND BULL RUN LAKE, HOOD RIVER CO OR	201 - D2
LOST LAKE CAMPGROUND MOUNT BONAPARTE, OKANOGAN CO WA	105 - A1
LOST LAKE CAMPGROUND OREGON COAST HWY, DOUGLAS CO OR	214 - A6
LOST LAKE CAMPGROUND SANTIAM HWY, LINN CO OR	134 - C2
LOST LAKE CAMPGROUND TIETON BASIN, YAKIMA CO WA	119 - B1
LOST SPRINGS CAMPGROUND POLAND BUTTE, YAKIMA CO WA	119 - B3
LOUP LOUP CAMPGROUND LOUP LOUP SUMMIT, OKANOGAN CO WA	104 - C3
LOWER BOWMAN CAMPSITE WHITE PINE BUTTES, KLICKITAT CO WA	119 - B3
LOWER BRIDGE CAMPGROUND OFF METOLIUS RIVER RD, JEFFERSON CO OR	134 - C1
LOWER EIGHTMILE CAMPGROUND FIVEMILE BUTTE, WASCO CO OR	202 - D3
LOWER FALLS CAMPGROUND SPENCER BUTTE, SKAMANIA CO WA	118 - C3
LOWER TWIN CAMPGROUND WAPINITIA PASS, WASCO CO OR	202 - B7
LUBY BAY CAMPGROUND PRIEST LAKE SW, BONNER CO ID	107 - A2
LUCERNE CAMPGROUND LUCERNE, CHELAN CO WA	103 - C3
LYNCH CREEK CAMPGROUND OFF NFD RD 454, WALLOWA CO OR	131 - B2
LYRE RIVER CAMPGROUND LYRE RIVER RD, CLALLAM CO WA	164 - B5
MACMILLAN CAMPGROUND HWY 4, BRITISH COLUMBIA BC	92 - B3
MAGONE LAKE CAMPGROUND OFF KEENEY FORKS RD, GRANT CO OR	137 - B1
MAIN EAGLE BRIDGE CAMPGROUND NFD RD 77, BAKER CO OR	130 - C3
MAITLEN METALINE FALLS, PEND OREILLE CO WA	106 - C1
MALLARD MARSH CAMPGROUND OFF MUD LAKE RD, DESCHUTES CO OR	216 - A4
MAMMOTH SPRING CAMPGROUND SOUTH FORK BURNT RIVER RD, BAKER CO OR	137 - C2
MANLY WHAM CAMPGROUND STEHEKIN, CHELAN CO WA	103 - C3
MANSON LANDING CAMPGROUND BRITISH COLUMBIA BC	92 - A1
MAPLE CREEK CAMPGROUND TRINITY, CHELAN CO WA	111 - C1
MAPLE GROVE CAMPGROUND WELKER PEAK, WHATCOM CO WA	103 - A2
MAPLE LEAF CAMPGROUND PURCELL MOUNTAIN, LEWIS CO WA	118 - C2
MAPLE MTN CENTENNIAL CAMPGROUND TRANS CANADA HWY, BRITISH COLUMBIA BC	101 - B1
MAPLE RIDGE CAMPSITE 132ND AV & 236TH ST, MAPLE RIDGE BC	157 - D5
MARBLE CREEK CAMPGROUND BIG DEVIL PEAK, SKAGIT CO WA	103 - B2
MARBLE CREEK CAMPGROUND MARBLE MOUNTAIN, SHOSHONE CO ID	115 - C3
MARCUS ISLAND CAMPGROUND MARCUS, STEVENS CO WA	106 - A2
MARGARET MCKENNY CAMPGROUND LITTLEROCK, THURSTON CO WA	184 - A1
MARIEN CREEK CAMPGROUND SILVERTON, SNOHOMISH CO WA	103 - A3
MARINE PARK AND CAMPGROUND BONNEVILLE DAM, CASCADE LOCKS OR	194 - D6
MARION FORKS CAMPGROUND N SANTIAM HWY, LINN CO OR	134 - C1
MARMES ROCK SHELTER HWY 261, FRANKLIN CO WA	121 - C2
MARMES ROCK SHELTER STARBUCK WEST, FRANKLIN CO WA	122 - A2
MARSTERS SPRING CAMPGROUND MORGAN BUTTE, LAKE CO OR	151 - C1
MARYS PEAK CAMPGROUND MARYS PEAK, BENTON CO OR	133 - A1
MASON DAM CAMPGROUND WHITNEY HWY, BAKER CO OR	138 - A1
MAZAMA CAMPGROUND UNION PEAK, KLAMATH CO OR	227 - C5
MAZAMA CAMPGROUND OFF N SANTIAM HWY, LINN CO OR	134 - C1
MCBRIDE CAMPGROUND EAGLE CREEK DR, BAKER CO OR	130 - C3
MCCORNICK CAMPGROUND OFF HWY 71, ADAMS CO ID	131 - A3
MCCUBBINS GULCH CAMPGROUND FOREMAN POINT, WASCO CO OR	127 - A3
MCCULLY FORKS CAMPGROUND GRANITE HILL RD, BAKER CO OR	138 - A1
MCCURDY CAMPGROUND OPHIR MOUNTAIN, CURRY CO OR	228 - D1
MCGRIBBLE CAMPGROUND PORT ORFORD, CURRY CO OR	224 - B7
MCKENZIE BRIDGE CAMPGROUND MCKENZIE HWY, LANE CO OR	134 - B2
MCNAUGHTON SPRING CAMPGROUND STRAWBERRY RD, GRANT CO OR	137 - B2
MCNEIL, FRED CAMPGROUND BULL RUN LAKE, CLACKAMAS CO OR	201 - D4
MCQUDE CREEK SHELTER OFF QUARTZVILLE DR, LINN CO OR	134 - B1
MEADOW CAMPGROUND OFF NFD RD 9712, CHELAN CO WA	238 - C6
MEADOW CREEK CAMPGROUND GOLDEN, JOSEPHINE CO OR	148 - C2
MEADOW CREEK CAMPGROUND MEADOW CREEK, BOUNDARY CO ID	107 - C1
MEADOW CREEK CAMPGROUND PLAIN, CHELAN CO WA	111 - C1
MEADOW CREEK SHELTER LUCERNE, CHELAN CO WA	103 - C3
MEADOWS CAMPGROUND SLATE PEAK, OKANOGAN CO WA	103 - C2
MEDITATION POINT CAMPGROUND WOLF PEAK, CLACKAMAS CO OR	126 - C3
MEMORIAL CAMPGROUND LEWIS BUTTE, OKANOGAN CO WA	104 - A2
MENEARS BEND CAMPGROUND SANTIAM HWY, LINN CO OR	134 - A2
MERRILL LAKE CAMPGROUND COUGAR, COWLITZ CO WA	190 - A4
MERRYS BAY CAMPGROUND AHSAHKA, CLEARWATER CO ID	123 - C2
MIDDLE EEL CAMPGROUND OFF OREGON COAST HWY, COOS CO OR	218 - B4
MIDDLE FORK CAMPGROUND UPPER MIDDLE FORK RD, GRANT CO OR	137 - B1
MIDDLE WADDEL CAMPGROUND LITTLEROCK, THURSTON CO WA	184 - A1
MILE CAMPGROUND CASCADE LAKES HWY, DESCHUTES CO OR	216 - B6
MILL CREEK CAMPGROUND PROSPECT NORTH, JACKSON CO OR	226 - C6
MILLER RIVER CAMPGROUND GROTTO, KING CO WA	111 - A2
MILL POND CAMPGROUND METALINE FALLS, PEND OREILLE CO WA	106 - C1
MILLPOND CAMPGROUND OFF GRANT RD, JACKSON CO OR	230 - C7
MINA FALLS TRAILHEAD CAMPGROUND LITTLEROCK, THURSTON CO WA	184 - B2
MINERAL CAMPGROUND FAIRVIEW PEAK, LANE CO OR	141 - C1
MINERAL PARK CAMPGROUND SONNY BOY LAKES, SKAGIT CO WA	103 - B2
MINERAL SPRINGS CAMPGROUND LIBERTY, KITTITAS CO WA	111 - C3
MINERS CREEK SHELTER GAMMA PEAK, SNOHOMISH CO WA	103 - B3
MINK LAKE SHELTER THREE SISTERS WILDERNESS AREA, LANE CO OR	134 - C3
MINNIE PETERSON CAMPGROUND WINFIELD CREEK, JEFFERSON CO WA	108 - C1
MISERY SPRING CAMPGROUND SADDLE BUTTE, GARFIELD CO WA	122 - B3
MITCHELL CREEK CAMPGROUND LAKE CHELAN, CHELAN CO WA	112 - A1
MOKINS BAY CAMPGROUND HAYDEN LAKE, KOOTENAI CO ID	245 - B5
MONA CAMPGROUND OFF RABBIT CAMP RD, LANE CO OR	134 - B2
MONCK CAMPGROUND HWY 5A, BRITISH COLUMBIA BC	95 - C1
MONEY CREEK CAMPGROUND NE STEVENS PASS HWY, KING CO WA	111 - A1
MONTAGUE HARBOUR CAMPGROUND BRITISH COLUMBIA BC	101 - B1
MONTE CRISTO CAMPGROUND MONTE CRISTO, SNOHOMISH CO WA	111 - A1
MONTY CAMPGROUND METOLIUS BENCH, JEFFERSON CO OR	135 - A1
MOON LAKE SHELTER WARNER MOUNTAIN, LANE CO OR	142 - A1
MOORE POINT CAMPGROUND LUCERNE, CHELAN CO WA	103 - C3
MORA CAMPGROUND QUILLAYUTE PRAIRIE, CLALLAM CO WA	169 - A2
MORGAN CREEK CAMPGROUND CLE ELUM LAKE, KITTITAS CO WA	111 - B3
MORRISON CREEK CAMPGROUND MOUNT ADAMS WEST, YAKIMA CO WA	119 - A3
MORSE CREEK CAMPGROUND NORSE PEAK, YAKIMA CO WA	119 - A1
MOSS CREEK CAMPGROUND OKLAHOMA RD, SKAMANIA CO WA	195 - B3
MOSS SPRING CAMPGROUND MILL CREEK RD, UNION CO OR	130 - B2
MOTTET CAMPGROUND NORTH OF NFD RD 63, WALLOWA CO OR	130 - A1
MOUNT HEBO CAMPGROUND NIAGARA CREEK, TILLAMOOK CO OR	197 - D7
MOUNT MOLLY CAMPGROUND LITTLEROCK, THURSTON CO WA	184 - A1
MOUNT TOM SHELTER OWL MOUNTAIN, JEFFERSON CO WA	109 - A1

FEATURE NAME City State	Page-Grid
MOWITCH CAMPGROUND WHITNEY HWY, BAKER CO OR	138 - A1
MUD CREEK CAMPGROUND OFF NFD RD 3615, LAKE CO OR	152 - A2
MUD LAKE CAMPGROUND ANTHONY LAKES RD, BAKER CO OR	130 - A3
MUD SPRING CAMPGROUND OFF RAGER RD, CROOK CO OR	136 - C2
MULE DEER CAMPGROUND HWY 3, BRITISH COLUMBIA BC	103 - C1
MULKEY SHELTER LAKE QUINAULT EAST, GRAYS HARBOR CO WA	109 - A2
MULLIGAN BAY CAMPGROUND SQUAW LAKES, JACKSON CO OR	149 - B2
MURRAY CAMPGROUND OFF NFD RD 16, GRANT CO OR	137 - C2
MURRIN PARK CAMPGROUND TRANS CANADA HWY, SQUAMISH BC	93 - C2
MYERS CREEK CAMPGROUND GOLDEN, JOSEPHINE CO OR	149 - A1
MYRTLE GROVE CAMPGROUND CHINA FLAT, COOS CO OR	140 - C3
MYRTLEWOOD CAMPGROUND POWERS, COOS CO OR	140 - C3
MYSTERY CAMPGROUND MIDNIGHT MOUNTAIN, OKANOGAN CO WA	104 - A3
NACHES PASS CAMPSITE MOUNT CLIFTY, KITTITAS CO WA	111 - B3
NANITCH CAMPGROUND MOUNT HOOD SOUTH, CLACKAMAS CO OR	202 - A6
NASON CREEK CAMPGROUND LAKE WENATCHEE, CHELAN CO WA	111 - C1
NAVIGATION CAMPGROUND UPPER PRIEST LAKE, BONNER CO ID	107 - A1
NEAL SPRINGS CAMPGROUND ABBOTT BUTTE, DOUGLAS CO OR	226 - B4
NEBY SHELTER MOUNT TEBO, MASON CO WA	109 - B2
NETARTS BAY CAMPGROUND WHISKEY CREEK RD, TILLAMOOK CO OR	197 - A4
NEWBERRY GROUP CAMPGROUND NEWBERRY CRATER RD, DESCHUTES CO OR	143 - A1
NEWCASTLE ISLAND CAMPGROUND OFF HWY 19, NANAIMO BC	93 - A3
NEWHALEM CAMPGROUND MOUNT TRIUMPH, WHATCOM CO WA	103 - B2
NICE CAMPGROUND DOE MOUNTAIN, OKANOGAN CO WA	104 - A2
NICKEL CREEK SHELTER CHINOOK PASS, LEWIS CO WA	185 - D5
NICOLUM RIVER CAMPGROUND HWY 3, BRITISH COLUMBIA BC	95 - A3
NIGHTHAWK CAMPGROUND BAYVIEW, KOOTENAI CO ID	245 - C1
NINETEENMILE CAMPGROUND TRINITY, CHELAN CO WA	111 - C1
NOISY CREEK CAMPGROUND METALINE FALLS, PEND OREILLE CO WA	106 - C1
NO MAN SHELTER SCAREDMAN CREEK, DOUGLAS CO OR	141 - C1
NO NAME LAKE CAMPGROUND SKOOKUM CREEK, PEND OREILLE CO WA	106 - C3
NOOKSACK CAMPGROUND BEARPAW MOUNTAIN, WHATCOM CO WA	102 - C1
NORDMAN CAMPGROUND PRIEST LAKE NW, BONNER CO ID	107 - A2
NORTH COVE CAMPGROUND NEWBERRY CRATER RD, DESCHUTES CO OR	143 - A1
NORTH COVE CAMPGROUND PRIEST LAKE SW, BONNER CO ID	107 - A2
NORTH CREEK CAMPGROUND CAPITOL PEAK, GRAYS HARBOR CO WA	117 - B1
NORTH CREEK CAMPGROUND LEE THOMAS CROSSING, LAKE CO OR	151 - C1
NORTH CREEK CAMPGROUND NFD RD 19, LINCOLN CO OR	203 - B6
NORTH DAVIS CREEK CAMPGROUND DAVIS MOUNTAIN, DESCHUTES CO OR	142 - C1
NORTH EEL CAMPGROUND OFF OREGON COAST HWY, COOS CO OR	218 - B3
NORTH FORK ANTHONY CAMPGROUND END OF NORTH POWDER RIVER LN, BAKER CO OR	130 - A3
NORTH FORK CAMPGROUND BUNCH LAKE, JEFFERSON CO OR	109 - A2
NORTH FORK CAMPGROUND MOUNT MCLOUGHLIN, JACKSON CO OR	150 - A1
NORTH FORK CAMPGROUND SILVER FALLS, CHELAN CO WA	111 - C1
NORTH FORK CAMPGROUND SLATE CREEK RD, IDAHO CO ID	131 - C1
NORTH FORK CAMPGROUND TOWER ROCK, LEWIS CO WA	118 - C2
NORTH FORK JOHN DAY CAMPGROUND NFD RD 73 & NFD RD 52, GRANT CO OR	129 - C3
NORTH FORK MALHEUR CAMPGROUND NFD RD 16, GRANT CO OR	137 - C2
NORTH FORK NINEMILE CAMPGROUND DUNCAN RIDGE, OKANOGAN CO WA	104 - B1
NORTH FORK SIUSLAW CAMPGROUND UPPER NORTH FORK RD, LANE CO OR	214 - D1
NORTH GORGE CAMPGROUND BOSSBURG, STEVENS CO WA	106 - A1
NORTH PINE CAMPGROUND NORTH PINE CREEK RD, BAKER CO OR	131 - A3
NORTH SKOOKUM CAMPGROUND BROWNS LAKE, PEND OREILLE CO WA	106 - C2
NORTH TWIN LAKE CAMPGROUND DAVIS MOUNTAIN, DESCHUTES CO OR	142 - C1
NORTH WALDO CAMPGROUND WALDO MOUNTAIN, LANE CO OR	142 - B1
NORTH WICKIUP CAMPGROUND DAVIS MOUNTAIN, DESCHUTES CO OR	142 - C1
NOTTINGHAM CAMPGROUND BADGER LAKE, HOOD RIVER CO OR	202 - C5
OAK FORK CAMPGROUND TIMOTHY LAKE, CLACKAMAS CO OR	126 - C3
OBSERVATION BERRYFIELD CAMPGROUND BARE MOUNTAIN, SKAMANIA CO WA	190 - D7
OCHOCO DIVIDE CAMPGROUND OCHOCO HWY, WHEELER CO OR	136 - A2
ODELL CREEK CAMPGROUND ODELL LAKE, KLAMATH CO OR	142 - B1
ODESSA CAMPGROUND PELICAN BAY, KLAMATH CO OR	231 - B6
OGDEN GROUP CAMPGROUND PAULINA-EAST LAKE RD, DESCHUTES CO OR	143 - A1
OHANAPECOSH CAMPGROUND OHANAPECOSH HOT SPRINGS, LEWIS CO WA	185 - D6
OKANOGAN INDIAN CAMPING GROUND 32ND AV, BRITISH COLUMBIA BC	104 - C1
OKEOVER ARM CAMPGROUND HWY 101, BRITISH COLUMBIA BC	92 - B1
OKLAHOMA CAMPGROUND OKLAHOMA RD, SKAMANIA CO WA	195 - B2

FEATURE NAME City State	Page-Grid
OLALLIE LAKE CAMPGROUND GREEN MOUNTAIN, SKAMANIA CO WA	119 - A2
OLALLIE LAKE CAMPGROUND OFF BIA RD 33, JEFFERSON CO OR	134 - C1
OLALLIE PENINSULA CAMPGROUND OFF BIA RD 33, JEFFERSON CO OR	134 - C1
OLLOKOT CAMPGROUND WALLOWA MOUNTAIN LP, WALLOWA CO OR	131 - A3
OPAL LAKE CAMPGROUND COWHORN MOUNTAIN, DOUGLAS CO OR	223 - C1
OREGON CAMPGROUND JOHN DAY-BURNS HWY, BAKER CO OR	137 - C1
ORIENTAL CREEK CAMPGROUND NFD RD 5506, GRANT CO OR	129 - B3
ORIOLE CAMPGROUND CONCONULLY WEST, OKANOGAN CO WA	104 - B2
OSPREY CAMPGROUND PRIEST LAKE SW, BONNER CO ID	107 - A2
OTTER LAKE CAMPGROUND HWY 5A, BRITISH COLUMBIA BC	95 - C2
OUTLET CAMPGROUND OUTLET BAY, BONNER CO ID	107 - A2
OUTLET CREEK CAMPGROUND OUTLET FALLS, KLICKITAT CO WA	119 - B3
OWL CREEK CAMPGROUND PUGH MOUNTAIN, SNOHOMISH CO WA	103 - B3
OZETTE CAMPGROUND OZETTE, CLALLAM CO WA	162 - B4
PACKARD CREEK CAMPGROUND OAKRIDGE, LANE CO OR	142 - A1
PADDOCK CAMP CAMPBELL RESERVOIR, KLAMATH CO OR	151 - B1
PALISADES CAMPGROUND OHANAPECOSH HOT SPRINGS, LEWIS CO WA	185 - D7
PALMER LAKE CAMPGROUND NIGHTHAWK, OKANOGAN CO WA	104 - C1
PANHANDLE CAMPGROUND RUBY, PEND OREILLE CO WA	106 - C2
PANJAB CAMPGROUND PANJAB CREEK, COLUMBIA CO WA	122 - B3
PANORAMA POINT CAMPGROUND WELKER PEAK, WHATCOM CO WA	103 - A2
PANTHER CREEK CAMPGROUND FATHER MOUNTAIN, CURRY CO OR	224 - D7
PANTHER CREEK CAMPGROUND STABLER, SKAMANIA CO WA	194 - D3
PAPOOSE CAMPGROUND SEVEN DEVILS RD, IDAHO CO ID	131 - C2
PARADISE CAMPGROUND NFD RD 9, WASHINGTON CO ID	139 - A1
PARADISE CREEK CAMPGROUND TERMINATION POINT, SKAMANIA CO WA	118 - C3
PARK CAMPGROUND LIBERTY, KITTITAS CO WA	238 - A6
PARK CAMPGROUND STOUT MOUNTAIN, MARION CO OR	205 - D7
PARK CREEK CAMPGROUND GOODE MOUNTAIN, CHELAN CO WA	103 - B2
PARK CREEK CAMPGROUND WELKER PEAK, WHATCOM CO WA	103 - A2
PASS CREEK SHELTER SCAREDMAN CREEK, DOUGLAS CO OR	141 - C1
PATAHA CAMPGROUND ROSE SPRINGS, GARFIELD CO WA	122 - B2
PAULINA CREEK CAMPGROUND NEWBERRY CRATER RD, DESCHUTES CO OR	143 - A1
PAULINA LAKE CAMPGROUND NEWBERRY CRATER RD, DESCHUTES CO OR	143 - A1
PEARSON CAMPGROUND NFD RD 52, UMATILLA CO OR	129 - B3
PEBBLE FORD CAMPGROUND FIVEMILE BUTTE, WASCO CO OR	202 - D4
PELTON CREEK SHELTER BOB CREEK, JEFFERSON CO OR	109 - A1
PENINSULA CAMPGROUND RIMROCK LAKE, YAKIMA CO WA	119 - B1
PENLAND LAKE CAMPGROUND COAL MNE HL RD & NFD RD 210, MORROW CO OR	129 - A3
PENROSE POINT CAMPGROUND 158TH AV KPS, PIERCE CO WA	181 - A2
PERRY CREEK CAMPGROUND SILVERTON, SNOHOMISH CO WA	103 - A3
PERRY CREEK SHELTER MOUNT SPICKARD, WHATCOM CO WA	103 - B1
PERRY SOUTH CAMPGROUND FLY CREEK, JEFFERSON CO OR	135 - A1
PETERSON CAMPGROUND BAYVIEW, KOOTENAI CO ID	245 - C1
PETERSON PRAIRIE CAMPGROUND LITTLE HUCKLEBERRY MTN, SKAMANIA CO WA	118 - C3
PETIT LAKE CAMPGROUND ORWIG HUMP, PEND OREILLE CO WA	106 - C2
PHELPS CREEK CAMPGROUND TRINITY, CHELAN CO WA	103 - C3
PHLOX POINT CAMPGROUND MOUNT HOOD SOUTH, CLACKAMAS CO OR	202 - A5
PIERRE LAKE CAMPGROUND LAURIER, STEVENS CO WA	105 - C1
PILCHUCK BRIDGE CAMPGROUND MCMURRAY, SKAGIT CO WA	168 - D2
PINE CAMPGROUND BLEWETT PASS, CHELAN CO WA	238 - B5
PINE CREEK CAMPGROUND OFF PAULINA HWY, CROOK CO OR	136 - A3
PINE FLAT CAMPGROUND NFD RD 5700, CHELAN CO WA	112 - A1
PINE MEADOWS CAMPGROUND COTTAGE GROVE LAKE, LANE CO OR	219 - D2
PINE NEEDLE CAMPGROUND OLD SCAB MOUNTAIN, YAKIMA CO WA	119 - B1
PINE POINT CAMPGROUND TIMOTHY LAKE, CLACKAMAS CO OR	126 - C3
PINE TREE CAMPGROUND SOUTH FORK RD, GRANT CO OR	136 - C2
PIONEER CAMPGROUND EDEN VALLEY, COOS CO OR	140 - C3
PIONEER FORD CAMPGROUND METOLIUS RIVER RD, JEFFERSON CO OR	134 - C1
PIRATES COVE MARINE CAMPGROUND OFF SHORE ISLAND, BRITISH COLUMBIA BC	93 - A3
PLEASANT VALLEY CAMPGROUND GOOSE PRAIRIE, YAKIMA CO WA	119 - A1
PLOWBOY CAMPGROUND UPPER PRIEST LAKE, BONNER CO ID	107 - A1
POINT CAMPGROUND CASCADE LAKES HWY, DESCHUTES CO OR	216 - A4
POISON CREEK CAMPGROUND OSS PEAK, CHELAN CO WA	104 - A3
POISON CREEK CAMPGROUND WEST MOUNTAIN RD, VALLEY CO ID	252 - D3
POLALLIE CAMPGROUND DOG RIVER, HOOD RIVER CO OR	202 - C4
POLE BRIDGE CAMPGOUND BROWN MOUNTAIN, JACKSON CO OR	150 - A2

FEATURE NAME City State	Page-Grid
POLE PATCH CAMPGROUND FRENCH BUTTE, SKAMANIA CO WA	118 - C2
POOLE CREEK CAMPGROUND LEMOLO LAKE, DOUGLAS CO OR	223 - B3
POPLAR FLAT CAMPGROUND MIDNIGHT MOUNTAIN, OKANOGAN CO WA	104 - A2
PORCUPINE BAY CAMPGROUND MCCOY LAKE, LINCOLN CO WA	113 - C1
PORCUPINE CAMPGROUND CLARK FORK, BONNER CO ID	107 - C3
PORPOISE BAY CAMPGROUND OFF HWY 101, BRITISH COLUMBIA BC	93 - A2
PORTEAU COVE CAMPGROUND TRANS CANADA HWY, BRITISH COLUMBIA BC	93 - C2
POTLATCH STATE PARK CAMPGROUND US 101, MASON CO WA	173 - A7
PRAIRIE CAMPGROUND PAULINA-EAST LAKE RD, DESCHUTES CO OR	143 - A1
PRAIRIE SPRING CAMPGROUND NFD RD 5212, CHELAN CO WA	112 - A2
PRIEST RIVER CAMPGROUND PRIEST RIVER, BONNER CO ID	107 - A3
PRIMITIVE CAMPGROUND COTTAGE GROVE LAKE, LANE CO OR	219 - D2
PRINCE CREEK CAMPGROUND PRINCE CREEK, CHELAN CO WA	104 - A3
PRINEVILLE CAMP HAMAKER BUTTE, DOUGLAS CO OR	223 - B7
PRINGLE FALLS CAMPGROUND CRANE PRAIRIE RESERVOIR, DESCHUTES CO OR	142 - C1
PRIOR CENTENNIAL CAMPGROUND BRITISH COLUMBIA BC	101 - C1
PURPLE POINT CAMPGROUND STEHEKIN, CHELAN CO WA	103 - C3
QUARTZ CREEK BIG TREES CAMPGROUND COWLITZ FALLS, LEWIS CO WA	118 - B2
QUINN RIVER CAMPGROUND CRANE PRAIRIE RESERVOIR, DESCHUTES CO OR	142 - C1
QUOSATANA CAMPGROUND QUOSATANA BUTTE, CURRY CO OR	228 - C4
RAINBOW BAY CAMPGROUND LAKE OF THE WOODS NORTH, KLAMATH CO OR	150 - B1
RAINBOW CAMPGROUND EMIGRANT CREEK RD, HARNEY CO OR	137 - A3
RAINBOW FALLS CAMPGROUND STEHEKIN, CHELAN CO WA	103 - C3
RAINBOW POINT CAMPGROUND MOUNTAIN RD, VALLEY CO ID	252 - C2
RAINBOW POINT CAMPGROUND PUMPKIN MOUNTAIN, WHATCOM CO WA	103 - B1
RAINY HILL CAMPGROUND MEDIMONT, KOOTENAI CO ID	248 - C4
RAMONA PARK CAMPGROUND STORMY MOUNTAIN, CHELAN CO WA	236 - A1
RATHTREVOR BEACH CAMPGROUND HWY 4, BRITISH COLUMBIA BC	92 - C3
RATTLESNAKE CAMPGROUND ROBINSON MOUNTAIN, OKANOGAN CO WA	103 - C2
RED BRIDGE CAMPGROUND MALLARDY RIDGE, SNOHOMISH CO WA	103 - A3
RED LAKE CAMPGROUND PELICAN BUTTE, KLAMATH CO OR	150 - B1
RED MOUNTAIN CAMPGROUND CLE ELUM LAKE, KITTITAS CO WA	111 - B2
REEDER BAY CAMPGROUND OFF HWY 57, BONNER CO ID	107 - A2
REFRIGERATOR CAMPGROUND LUCERNE, CHELAN CO WA	103 - C3
RESERVOIR CAMPGROUND DAVIS MOUNTAIN, DESCHUTES CO OR	142 - C1
RESERVOIR CAMPGROUND MOUNT HOOD NORTH, HOOD RIVER CO OR	202 - B3
REX CREEK SHELTER LUCERNE, CHELAN CO WA	103 - C3
REYNOLDS SHELTER REYNOLDS RIDGE, DOUGLAS CO OR	222 - C1
RHODODENDRON ISLAND CAMPGROUND WALDO LAKE, LANE CO OR	142 - B1
RHODODENDRON RIDGE SHELTER MOUNT LOWE, CLACKAMAS CO OR	126 - C3
RIVER BAR CAMPGROUND MALLARDY RIDGE, SNOHOMISH CO WA	103 - A3
RIVER BAR CAMPGROUND OHANAPECOSH HOT SPRINGS, LEWIS CO WA	185 - D7
RIVERBEND CAMPGROUND SCHAEFER LAKE, CHELAN CO WA	111 - C1
RIVER BEND CAMPGROUND TIETON BASIN, YAKIMA CO WA	119 - B1
RIVER BRIDGE CAMPGROUND PROSPECT NORTH, JACKSON CO OR	226 - C5
RIVER CAMPGROUND CRANE PRAIRIE RESERVOIR, DESCHUTES CO OR	142 - C1
RIVER CAMPGROUND GRANDE RONDE RIVER RD, UNION CO OR	129 - C3
RIVER CAMPGROUND MOUNT ZION, CLALLAM CO OR	109 - C1
RIVER EDGE CAMPGROUND ALSEA HWY, LINCOLN CO OR	209 - D2
RIVERS BEND CAMPGROUND ROBINSON MOUNTAIN, OKANOGAN CO WA	103 - C2
RIVERSIDE CAMPGROUND MOUNT HOWARD, CHELAN CO WA	111 - B1
RIVERSIDE CAMPGROUND N SANTIAM RD, LINN CO OR	134 - C1
ROADS END CAMPGROUND GILBERT, OKANOGAN CO WA	103 - C2
ROARING RIVER CAMPGROUND SOUTH FORK RD, LANE CO OR	134 - B3
ROBERTS CREEK CAMPGROUND 101 HWY, BRITISH COLUMBIA BC	93 - B2
ROBINHOOD CAMPGROUND BADGER LAKE, HOOD RIVER CO OR	202 - C5
ROBINSON LAKE CAMPGROUND EASTPORT, BOUNDARY CO ID	107 - B1
ROCK CAMPGROUND BUCK MOUNTAIN, OKANOGAN CO WA	104 - B3
ROCK CREEK CAMPGROUND CRANE PRAIRIE RESERVOIR, DESCHUTES CO OR	142 - C1
ROCK CREEK CAMPGROUND DOLE, CLARK CO WA	193 - C4
ROCK CREEK CAMPGROUND ILLAHE, COOS CO OR	140 - B3
ROCK CREEK CAMPGROUND SCHAEFER LAKE, CHELAN CO WA	111 - C1
ROCK CREEK RESERVOIR CAMPGROUND ROCK CREEK RESERVOIR, WASCO CO OR	127 - A3
ROCK CREEK SHELTER SNOQUALMIE PASS, KING CO WA	111 - A2
ROCK ISLAND CAMPGROUND JACK RIDGE, CHELAN CO WA	111 - B2
ROCK LAKES CAMPGROUND BUCK MOUNTAIN, OKANOGAN CO WA	104 - B2
ROCK SPRINGS CAMPGROUND SILVIES-HOPPER RANCH RD, GRANT CO OR	137 - B3

FEATURE NAME City State	Page-Grid
ROCKY BEND CAMPGROUND SPRINGER MOUNTAIN, TILLAMOOK CO OR	125 - A2
ROCKY FORD CAMPGROUND ANTHONY LAKES RD, BAKER CO OR	130 - A3
ROCKY POINT CAMPGROUND PRIEST LAKE SW, BONNER CO ID	107 - A2
ROCKY POINT CAMPGROUND TWIN LAKES, FERRY CO WA	105 - C3
ROCKY TOP SHELTER OFF N SANTIAM HWY, MARION CO OR	134 - B1
ROLLING GROUNDS CAMP FISH CREEK DESERT, DOUGLAS CO OR	222 - D6
ROLLING RIFFLE CAMPGROUND RHODODENDRON, CLACKAMAS CO OR	201 - C7
ROSLAND CAMPGROUND BURGESS RD, DESCHUTES CO OR	143 - A1
ROUND LAKE CAMPGROUND MORTON, BONNER CO ID	107 - A3
ROUND LAKE CAMPGROUND MOUNT LOWE, MARION CO OR	126 - B3
ROUND SWAMP CAMPGROUND WICKIUP DAM, DESCHUTES CO OR	142 - C1
ROUTSON COUNTY PARK CAMPGROUND DOG RIVER, HOOD RIVER CO OR	202 - C3
RUCKLE PARK CAMPGROUND BRITISH COLUMBIA BC	101 - B1
RUFFLED GROUSE CAMPGROUND SWEETGRASS BUTTE, OKANOGAN CO WA	104 - A2
RUJADA CAMPGROUND ROSE HILL, LANE CO OR	141 - C1
RUSSIAN CREEK CAMPGROUND GOLDEN, JOSEPHINE CO OR	149 - A1
SACAJAWEA CAMPGROUND NFD RD 4240, WALLOWA CO OR	131 - B2
SACANDAGA CAMPGROUND RIGDON POINT, LANE CO OR	142 - A1
SADDLE CAMPGROUND LONE BUTTE, SKAMANIA CO WA	118 - C3
SADDLE CAMPGROUND RUSTLER PEAK, JACKSON CO OR	150 - A1
SADDLE CREEK CAMPGROUND NFD RD 4240, WALLOWA CO OR	131 - B2
SADDLE DAM CAMPGROUND YALE DAM, COWLITZ CO WA	190 - A6
SAFETY HARBOR CAMPGROUND LAKE CHELAN, CHELAN CO WA	112 - A1
SAFETY HARBOR CREEK CAMPGROUND SOUTH NAVARRE PEAK, CHELAN CO WA	104 - A3
SAGE HEN CAMPGROUND OFF HANCOCK RD, GEM CO ID	139 - C2
SAINT MARYS LAKE CAMPGROUND NORTH END RD, BRITISH COLUMBIA BC	101 - B1
SALMON LA SAC CAMPGROUND DAVIS PEAK, KITTITAS CO WA	111 - B2
SALMON MEADOWS CAMPGROUND COXIT MOUNTAIN, OKANOGAN CO WA	104 - B2
SALT CREEK CAMPGROUND OFF CAMP HAYDEN RD, CLALLAM CO WA	164 - D5
SALT CREEK FALLS CAMPGROUND WILLAMETTE PASS, LANE CO OR	142 - B1
SALTERY BAY CAMPGROUND HWY 101, BRITISH COLUMBIA BC	92 - C1
SALTWATER CAMPGROUND MRINE VW DR S & S 259TH ST, DES MOINES WA	175 - A7
SAND BEACH CAMPGROUND GALLOWAY RD, TILLAMOOK CO OR	197 - A5
SANDHILL CAMPGROUND SANDHILL CROSSING, LAKE CO OR	151 - B1
SAND LAKE SHELTER WHITE PASS, YAKIMA CO WA	119 - A1
SAND PRAIRIE CAMPGROUND WARNER MOUNTAIN, LANE CO OR	142 - A1
SAND SPRING CAMPGROUND SAND SPRINGS RD, DESCHUTES CO OR	143 - C1
SAN JUAN CAMPGROUND BLANCA LAKE, SNOHOMISH CO WA	111 - A1
SAUK RIVER CAMPGROUND MONTE CRISTO, SNOHOMISH CO WA	111 - A1
SAWMILL FLATS CAMPGROUND CLIFFDELL, YAKIMA CO WA	119 - B1
SCATTER CREEK CAMPGROUND THE CRADLE, KITTITAS CO WA	111 - B2
SCHAEFER CREEK CAMPGROUND SCHAEFER LAKE, CHELAN CO WA	111 - C1
SCHNEIDER CAMPGROUND PRIEST LAKE SW, BONNER CO ID	107 - A2
SCHOONER CREEK CAMPGROUND S SCHOONER CREEK RD, LINCOLN CO OR	203 - B5
SCOTT CAMPGROUND BAYVIEW, KOOTENAI CO ID	245 - C1
SCOTT LAKE CAMPGROUND MCKENZIE HWY & NFD RD 260, LANE CO OR	134 - C2
SCOTTS CAMPGROUND SCOTTS CAMP RD, CROOK CO OR	136 - B2
SCOTTY CREEK CAMPGROUND BLEWETT, CHELAN CO WA	238 - A5
SEAL ROCK CAMPGROUND BRINNON, JEFFERSON CO WA	109 - C1
SECRET COVE CAMPGROUND OFF HWY 101, BRITISH COLUMBIA BC	93 - A2
SENATOR CREEK CAMPGROUND CATHEDRAL PEAK, SHOSHONE CO ID	115 - C1
SEQUIM BAY STATE PK CAMPGROUND E WASHINGTON ST, CLALLAM CO WA	166 - C7
SEVEN-AND-A-HALF MILE CAMPSITE WAHTUM LAKE, HOOD RIVER CO OR	194 - D7
SEVEN-AND-A-HALF MILE CAMPSITE WAHTUM LAKE TR, HOOD RIVER CO OR	195 - A7
SEVEN DEVILS CAMPGROUND SEVEN DEVILS RD, IDAHO CO ID	131 - B2
SEVENMILE MARSH CAMPGROUND DEVILS PEAK, KLAMATH CO OR	231 - A1
SEVENMILE SHELTER MOUNT CARRIE, CLALLAM CO WA	109 - A1
SHADOW FALLS CAMPGROUND RED BUTTE, DOUGLAS CO OR	141 - C2
SHADOWY SAINT JOE CAMPGROUND SAINT JOE BALDY, BENEWAH CO ID	115 - B2
SHADY CAMPGROUND MCGREGOR MOUNTAIN, CHELAN CO WA	103 - C3
SHADY COVE CAMPGROUND OFF NFD RD 2207, MARION CO OR	134 - B1
SHADY PASS CAMPGROUND NFD RD 5900, CHELAN CO WA	112 - A1
SHANNON CREEK CAMPGROUND BACON PEAK, WHATCOM CO WA	103 - A2
SHANNON FALLS CAMPGROUND TRANS CANADA HWY, SQUAMISH BC	93 - C2
SHEEP BRIDGE CAMPGROUND DAVIS MOUNTAIN, DESCHUTES CO OR	142 - C1
SHERMAN CREEK CAMPGROUND BANGS MOUNTAIN, FERRY CO WA	106 - A2
SHERMAN PASS CAMPGROUND SHERMAN PEAK, FERRY CO WA	105 - C2

FEATURE NAME City State	Page-Grid
SHERMAN VALLEY CAMPGROUND CAPITOL PEAK, THURSTON CO WA	184 - A2
SHERWOOD CAMPGROUND DOG RIVER, HOOD RIVER CO OR	202 - C4
SHINING LAKE CAMPGROUND THREE LYNX, CLACKAMAS CO OR	126 - B3
SHUKSAN CAMPGROUND MOUNT LARRABEE, WHATCOM CO WA	102 - C1
SILESIA CREEK SHELTER MOUNT SEFRIT, WHATCOM CO WA	103 - A1
SILVER CAMPGROUND PRIEST LAKE SW, BONNER CO ID	107 - A2
SILVER CREEK CAMPGROUND RANDLE, LEWIS CO WA	118 - C2
SILVER CREEK MARSH CAMPGROUND BRIDGE CREEK RD, LAKE CO OR	143 - B3
SILVER CREEK SHELTER MOUNT ZION, CLALLAM CO WA	109 - C1
SILVER FALLS CAMPGROUND SILVER FALLS, CHELAN CO WA	111 - C1
SILVER FIR CAMPGROUND MOUNT LARRABEE, WHATCOM CO WA	102 - C1
SILVER SPRINGS CAMPGROUND WHITE RIVER PARK, PIERCE CO WA	111 - A3
SILVERTIP CAMPGROUND MONTE CRISTO, SNOHOMISH CO WA	111 - A1
SIMAX BEACH CAMPGROUNDS CRESCENT LAKE, KLAMATH CO OR	142 - B1
SISSONS CAMPGROUND GRIZZLY MOUNTAIN, SHOSHONE CO ID	115 - C1
SITKUM SHELTER INDIAN PASS, CLALLAM CO WA	108 - C1
SIXMILE SHELTER DOWNEY MOUNTAIN, SKAGIT CO WA	103 - B3
SKEELTER SHELTER WHITE PASS, LEWIS CO WA	119 - A2
SKIMMERHORN CAMPGROUND BUCKEYE LAKE, DOUGLAS CO OR	222 - C7
SKOOKUMCHUCK CAMPGROUND US HWY 95, IDAHO CO ID	131 - C1
SKOOKUM LAKE CAMPGROUND BAGBY HOT SPRINGS, CLACKAMAS CO OR	126 - B3
SLAUGHTER GULCH CAMPGROUND NFD RD 535, ADAMS CO ID	131 - C3
SLIDE CAMPGROUND ALSEA HWY, LINCOLN CO OR	209 - D2
SLIDE CREEK CAMPGROUND OFF SOUTH FORK RD, LANE CO OR	134 - B3
SLIDE CREEK CAMPGROUND STRAWBERRY RD, GRANT CO OR	137 - B2
SLIM CHANCE CAMPGROUND REYNOLDS RIDGE, LANE CO OR	142 - A1
SLOAN CREEK CAMPGROUND SLOAN PEAK, SNOHOMISH CO WA	111 - A1
SLOUGH CAMPGROUND BENHAM FALLS, DESCHUTES CO OR	217 - A5
SMELT BAY CAMPGROUND BRITISH COLUMBIA BC	92 - A1
SMITH, JEDEDIAH RDWOODS STATE CMPGRD HWY 199 OUTSIDE HIOUCHI, DEL NORTE CO CA	148 - B3
SMITH LAKE CAMPGROUND RITZ, BOUNDARY CO ID	107 - B1
SMITH SPRINGS CAMPGROUND OLD FAIRVIEW, DOUGLAS CO OR	141 - C2
SMOKY CREEK CAMPGROUND SLEEPING BEAUTY, SKAMANIA CO WA	118 - C3
SNAG COVE CAMPGROUND MARCUS, STEVENS CO WA	106 - A2
SNOWBERRY CAMPGROUND BAYVIEW, KOOTENAI CO ID	245 - C1
SNOWBIRD SHELTER QUARTZ MOUNTAIN, DOUGLAS CO OR	222 - A5
SNUFF SHELTER BIG CAMAS RD, DOUGLAS CO OR	222 - C4
SOCHOLIS CAMPGROUND SOCHOLIS CANYON, KLAMATH CO OR	150 - C1
SODA SPRING CAMPGROUND JUNGLE BUTTE, YAKIMA CO WA	119 - A3
SODA SPRINGS CAMPGROUND MOUNT HOWARD, CHELAN CO WA	111 - B1
SODA SPRINGS CAMPGROUND OFF SODA SPRINGS RD, KLICKITAT CO WA	196 - D1
SODA SPRINGS CAMPGROUND OLD SCAB MOUNTAIN, YAKIMA CO WA	119 - B1
SODA SPRINGS CAMPGROUND WHITE PASS, LEWIS CO WA	119 - A1
SOLEDUCK CAMPGROUND BOGACHIEL PEAK, CLALLAM CO WA	109 - A1
SOUTH BEACH CAMPGROUND OFF HIGHWAY 101, JEFFERSON CO WA	172 - A2
SOUTH CAMPGROUND LONE BUTTE, SKAMANIA CO WA	118 - C3
SOUTH CAMPGROUND MUD LAKE RD, DESCHUTES CO OR	216 - A4
SOUTH CREEK CAMPGROUND GILBERT, OKANOGAN CO WA	103 - C2
SOUTH EEL CREEK CAMPGROUND OFF OREGON COAST HWY, COOS CO OR	218 - B4
SOUTH FORK CAMP CREEK CAMPGROUND NFD RD 16, BAKER CO OR	138 - A2
SOUTH FORK CAMPGROUND DARLAND MOUNTAIN, YAKIMA CO WA	119 - B2
SOUTH FORK CAMPGROUND NFD RD 32, UMATILLA CO OR	130 - A1
SOUTH FORK CAMPGROUND RHODODENDRON, CLACKAMAS CO OR	201 - C6
SOUTH FORK CAMPGROUND SOUTH FORK BURNT RIVER RD, BAKER CO OR	138 - A2
SOUTH FORK HOH CAMPGROUND OWL MOUNTAIN, JEFFERSON CO WA	108 - C1
SOUTH FORK JUNCTION CAMPGROUND LOOMIS, OKANOGAN CO WA	104 - C1
SOUTH FORK SHELTER WINBERRY CREEK RD, LANE CO OR	134 - A3
SOUTH ISLAND CAMPGROUND PELICAN BUTTE, KLAMATH CO OR	150 - B1
SOUTH LAKE CAMPGROUND DEVILS PEAK, KLAMATH CO OR	150 - B1
SOUTH LAKE CAMPGROUND NIAGARA CREEK, YAMHILL CO OR	197 - D7
SOUTH NAVARRE CAMPGROUND SOUTH NAVARRE PEAK, CHELAN CO WA	104 - A3
SOUTH SKOOKUM LAKE CAMPGROUND BROWNS LAKE, PEND OREILLE CO WA	106 - C1
SOUTH TWIN LAKE CAMPGROUND DAVIS MOUNTAIN, DESCHUTES CO OR	142 - C1
SOUTH WALDO SHELTER WALDO LAKE, LANE CO OR	142 - B1
SOUTHWEST SHORE CAMPGROUND OFF WHITNEY HWY, BAKER CO OR	138 - A1
SPALDING MILL CAMPGROUND GOLDEN, JOSEPHINE CO OR	148 - C1
SPECTACLE LAKE CAMPGROUND ENTERPRISE, OKANOGAN CO WA	104 - C1

FEATURE NAME City State	Page-Grid
SPIDER LAKE CAMPGROUND HWY 19, BRITISH COLUMBIA BC	92 - B3
SPINREEL CAMPGROUND OFF OREGON COAST HWY, COOS CO OR	218 - B4
SPOOL CART CAMPGROUND GRANDE RONDE RIVER RD, UNION CO OR	129 - C3
SPRING BAR CAMPGROUND NFD RD 1614, IDAHO CO ID	131 - C2
SPRING CAMPGROUND NFD RD 9712, CHELAN CO WA	238 - C6
SPRING CANYON CAMPGROUND LINCOLN CO WA	237 - C3
SPRING CREEK CAMPGROUND FLY CREEK, JEFFERSON CO OR	135 - A1
SPRING CREEK CAMPGROUND FORT KLAMATH, KLAMATH CO OR	231 - D2
SPRING CREEK CAMPGROUND GREEN MOUNTAIN, SKAMANIA CO WA	119 - A2
SPRING CREEK CAMPGROUND NFD RD 9, WASHINGTON CO ID	139 - A1
SPRING POINT CAMPGROUND LAKESHORE RD, BONNER CO ID	244 - A3
SPROAT LAKE CAMPGROUND HWY 4, BRITISH COLUMBIA BC	92 - A3
SPRUCE BAY CAMPGROUND GIBSON PASS RD, BRITISH COLUMBIA BC	103 - C1
SPRUCE BOTTOM SHELTER KLOOCHMAN ROCK, JEFFERSON CO WA	109 - A2
SPRUCE GROVE CAMPGROUND PYRAMID MOUNTAIN, CHELAN CO WA	111 - C1
SPRUCE SPRING CAMPGROUND STENTZ SPRING, GARFIELD CO WA	122 - B3
SQUAW LAKE CAMPGROUND ILLAHE, COOS CO OR	140 - C3
SQUAW LAKES CAMPGROUND SQUAW LAKES, JACKSON CO OR	149 - B2
SQUAW SPRING CAMPGROUND BONE SPRING, WALLOWA CO OR	122 - A3
STAGGER INN CAMPGROUND HELMER MOUNTAIN, PEND OREILLE CO WA	106 - C1
STAG SHELTER OFF HIGH PRAIRIE RD, LANE CO OR	134 - A3
STAIRCASE CAMPGROUND MOUNT SKOKOMISH, MASON CO WA	109 - B2
STAMP FALLS CAMPGROUND HWY 4, BRITISH COLUMBIA BC	92 - A3
STARR CAMPGROUND JOHN DAY-BURNS HWY, GRANT CO OR	137 - B2
STEAMBOAT FALLS CAMPGROUND BENJAMIN LAKE, DOUGLAS CO OR	222 - B2
STEAMBOAT LAKE CAMPGROUND STEAMBOAT MOUNTAIN, SKAMANIA CO WA	118 - C3
STEHEKIN CAMPGROUND STEHEKIN, CHELAN CO WA	103 - C3
STEVENS CREEK CAMPGROUND SOUTH FORK BURNT RIVER RD, BAKER CO OR	137 - C2
STILL CAMPGROUND MOUNT HOOD SOUTH, CLACKAMAS CO OR	202 - A6
STOCKADE SPRING CAMPGROUND ECKLER MOUNTAIN, COLUMBIA CO WA	122 - B3
STOUT CAMPGROUND GLENWOOD, YAKIMA CO WA	119 - A3
STRAWBERRY CAMPGROUND STRAWBERRY RD, GRANT CO OR	137 - C2
STRINGTOWN CAMPGROUND SQUAW LAKES, JACKSON CO OR	149 - B2
STUART CAMPGROUND LUCERNE, CHELAN CO WA	103 - C3
STUMP CAMPGROUND BLEWETT PASS, CHELAN CO WA	238 - B5
SUCKER CREEK SHELTER GOLDEN, JOSEPHINE CO OR	149 - A2
SUGAR CREEK CAMPGROUND RAGER RD, CROOK CO OR	136 - B2
SUGARLOAF CAMPGROUNDS CONCONULLY EAST, OKANOGAN CO WA	104 - C2
SUGAR PINE CAMPGROUND HYATT RESERVOIR, JACKSON CO OR	150 - A2
SUGARPINE SHELTER BUTLER BUTTE, DOUGLAS CO OR	226 - A4
SULLIVAN LAKE CAMPGROUND METALINE FALLS, PEND OREILLE CO WA	106 - C1
SULPHUR CREEK CAMPGROUND LIME MOUNTAIN, SNOHOMISH CO WA	103 - B3
SUMMIT CREEK CAMPGROUND OHANAPECOSH HOT SPRINGS, LEWIS CO WA	119 - A1
SUMMIT LAKE CAMPGROUND EMIGRANT BUTTE, KLAMATH CO OR	142 - B1
SUMMIT LAKE CAMPGROUND TIMOTHY LAKE, CLACKAMAS CO OR	126 - C3
SUNRISE DAY USE AREA BAYVIEW, KOOTENAI CO ID	245 - C1
SUNSET CAMPGROUND GUMBOOT MOUNTAIN, SKAMANIA CO WA	193 - D3
SUNSET COVE CAMPGROUND ODELL LAKE, KLAMATH CO OR	142 - B1
SUNSET SHELTER TAFT MOUNTAIN, DOUGLAS CO OR	141 - C2
SUNSHINE CREEK CAMPGROUND FATHER MOUNTAIN, CURRY CO OR	228 - B1
SUNSHINE POINT CAMPGROUND SAWTOOTH RIDGE, LEWIS CO WA	185 - A6
SUTTON CREEK CAMPGROUND 101 & SUTTON BEACH RD, LANE CO OR	214 - B1
SUTTON LAKE CAMPGROUND 101 & SUTTON BEACH RD, LANE CO OR	214 - B1
SWAMPY LAKES SHELTER OFF CENTURY DRIVE HWY, DESCHUTES CO OR	216 - C3
SWAN LAKE CAMPGROUND SWAN LAKE, FERRY CO WA	105 - B2
SWAUK CAMPGROUND OFF HWY 97, KITTITAS CO WA	238 - A6
SWEAT CREEK CAMPGROUND WAUCONDA SUMMIT, OKANOGAN CO WA	105 - B2
SWEDE RIDGE SHELTER TUMALO FALLS, DESCHUTES CO OR	216 - D3
SWIFT FOREST CAMPGROUND CEDAR FLATS, SKAMANIA CO WA	190 - D5
TAHKENITCH CAMPGROUND OREGON COAST HWY, DOUGLAS CO OR	214 - A6
TALMAKS CAMPGROUND WINCHESTER EAST, LEWIS CO ID	123 - B3
TAMARACK CAMPGROUND NFD RD 77, BAKER CO OR	130 - C3
TAMARACK SPRING CAMPGROUND QUARTZ MOUNTAIN RD, KITTITAS CO WA	240 - B4
TAMARACK SHELTER SOUTH FORK BURNT RIVER RD, BAKER CO OR	138 - A2
TANDY BAY CAMPGROUND COWHORN MOUNTAIN, KLAMATH CO OR	142 - B1
TANEUM CAMPGROUND TANEUM RD, KITTITAS CO WA	240 - C3
TARBELL CAMPGROUND DOLE, CLARK CO WA	193 - C3

INDEX

FEATURE NAME City State	Page-Grid
TARGET MEADOWS CAMPGROUND OFF NFD RD 64, UMATILLA CO OR	130 - A1
TAYLOR ARM CAMPGROUND HWY 4, BRITISH COLUMBIA BC	92 - A3
TENMILE ISLAND CAMPGROUND PUMPKIN MOUNTAIN, WHATCOM CO WA	103 - B1
TENMILE SHELTER MOUNT PROPHET, WHATCOM CO WA	103 - B1
TENMILE SHELTER MOUNT TOWNSEND, JEFFERSON CO WA	109 - C1
TENMILE SHELTER OFF RISLEY CREEK RD, LINCOLN CO OR	209 - D1
TEPEE CAMPGROUND OREGON BUTTE, COLUMBIA CO WA	122 - B3
THESEUS CREEK CAMPGROUND LABYRINTH MOUNTAIN, CHELAN CO WA	111 - B1
THIELSEN VIEW CAMPGROUND DIAMOND LAKE, DOUGLAS CO OR	223 - C6
THIRTEENMILE CAMPGROUND THIRTEENMILE CREEK, FERRY CO WA	105 - B2
THIRTYMILE CAMPGROUND COLEMAN PEAK, OKANOGAN CO WA	104 - B1
THOMAS CREEK CAMPGROUND COX FLAT, LAKE CO OR	151 - C2
THOMPSON RESERVOIR CAMPGROUND BRIDGE CREEK RD, LAKE CO OR	143 - B3
THREE CREEK CAMPGROUND PYRAMID MOUNTAIN, CHELAN CO WA	111 - C1
THREE CREEK LAKE CAMPGROUND OFF THREE CREEKS LAKE RD, DESCHUTES CO OR	216 - C2
THREE CREEK MEADOW CAMPGROUND THREE CREEKS LAKE RD, DESCHUTES CO OR	216 - C1
THREE FORKS SHELTER TYLER PEAK, CLALLAM CO WA	109 - B1
THREEHORN CAMPGROUND RAGSDALE BUTTE, DOUGLAS CO OR	141 - C3
THREE LAKES CAMP GARWOOD BUTTE, DOUGLAS CO OR	223 - B7
THREEMILE SHELTER OFF RISLEY CREEK RD, LINCOLN CO OR	209 - C1
THREE PINES CAMPGROUND PRIEST LAKE SW, BONNER CO ID	107 - A2
THREE TREES CAMP (HIST) COLLIER BUTTE, CURRY CO OR	232 - D1
TIFFANY SPRING CAMPGROUND TIFFANY MOUNTAIN, OKANOGAN CO WA	104 - B2
TILLICUM BEACH CAMPGROUND OFF OREGON COAST HWY, LINCOLN CO OR	328 - A13
TILLICUM CAMPGROUND LONE BUTTE, SKAMANIA CO WA	118 - C3
TIMBERLINE CAMPGROUND MOUNT ADAMS EAST, YAKIMA CO WA	119 - A3
TIMBERLINE CAMPGROUND MOUNT SAINT HELENS, SKAMANIA CO WA	190 - C2
TIME AND A HALF CAMPGROUND GRANDE RONDE RIVER RD, UNION CO OR	129 - C3
TIMOTHY SPRING CAMPGROUND NORTH OF NFD RD 63, WALLOWA CO OR	130 - B1
TIMPANOGAS CAMPGROUND COWHORN MOUNTAIN, DOUGLAS CO OR	223 - C1
TIN CAN CAMPGROUND GOLDEN, JOSEPHINE CO OR	149 - A1
TODD LAKE CAMPGROUND OFF NFD RD 370, DESCHUTES CO OR	216 - B3
TOKETEE LAKE CAMPGROUND TOKETEE FALLS, DOUGLAS CO OR	222 - D3
TOLLBRIDGE CAMPGROUND PENDLETON-JOHN DAY HWY, UMATILLA CO OR	129 - B3
TOMBSTONE PRAIRIE CAMPGROUND SANTIAM HWY, LINN CO OR	134 - B2
TOWER ROCK CAMPGROUND TOWER ROCK, LEWIS CO WA	118 - C2
TRANQUIL COVE CAMPGROUND COWHORN MOUNTAIN, KLAMATH CO OR	142 - B1
TRAPPER SHELTER KIMTA PEAK, JEFFERSON CO WA	109 - A2
TRAPPER SHELTER SCAREDMAN CREEK, DOUGLAS CO OR	141 - C2
TREE PHONES CAMPGROUND PISCOE MEADOW, YAKIMA CO WA	119 - B2
TRIBUNE BAY CAMPGROUND BRITISH COLUMBIA BC	92 - B2
TRILLIUM LAKE CAMPGROUND MOUNT HOOD SOUTH, CLACKAMAS CO OR	202 - A6
TRONSEN CAMPGROUND BLEWETT PASS, CHELAN CO WA	238 - B6
TROUBLESOME CREEK CAMPGROUND MONTE CRISTO, SNOHOMISH CO WA	111 - A1
TROUGH CREEK CAMPGROUND NFD RD 55, UMATILLA CO OR	129 - B3
TROUT LAKE CAMPGROUND BANGS MOUNTAIN, FERRY CO WA	105 - C2
TROUT LAKE CAMPGROUND BIA RD 33, JEFFERSON CO WA	134 - C1
TROUT LAKE CAMPGROUND JACK RIDGE, CHELAN CO WA	111 - B2
TROUT LAKE CREEK CAMPGROUND TROUT LAKE, SKAMANIA CO WA	119 - A3
TUCANNON CAMPGROUND PANJAB CREEK, COLUMBIA CO WA	122 - B3
TUCQUALA MEADOW CAMPGROUND THE CRADLE, KITTITAS CO WA	111 - B2
TUMALO FALLS SHELTER TUMALO FALLS, DESCHUTES CO OR	216 - D3
TUMWATER CAMPGROUND MCGREGOR MOUNTAIN, CHELAN CO WA	103 - C3
TUMWATER CAMPGROUND WINTON, CHELAN CO WA	111 - C2
TUNNEL CREEK SHELTER MOUNT TOWNSEND, JEFFERSON CO WA	109 - C1
TURLO CAMPGROUND MOUNTAIN LOOP HWY, SNOHOMISH CO WA	102 - C3
TWELVE MILE SHELTER MOUNT CHRISTIE, JEFFERSON CO WA	109 - B1
TWENTYNINE PINES CAMPGROUND RED TOP MOUNTAIN, KITTITAS CO WA	111 - C3
TWENTYONE MILE CAMPGROUND THIRTEENMILE CREEK, FERRY CO WA	105 - B3
TWENTYONE MILE SHELTER SLIDE PEAK, CLALLAM CO WA	109 - A1
TWIN BRIDGES CAMPGROUND GOVERNMENT CAMP, CLACKAMAS CO OR	201 - D5
TWINBUCK SHELTER ACKER ROCK, DOUGLAS CO OR	226 - A1
TWIN FALLS CAMPGROUND STEAMBOAT MOUNTAIN, SKAMANIA CO WA	118 - C3
TWIN LAKES CAMPGROUND DUCK CREEK RD, WALLOWA CO OR	131 - A3
TWIN RIVERS CAMPGROUND GARDEN VALLEY, DOUGLAS CO OR	221 - B3
TWIN ROCKS SHELTER FAIRVIEW PEAK, LANE CO OR	141 - C1
TWIN SPRINGS CAMPGROUND OFF BUCK HOLLOW RD, CROOK CO OR	136 - B2
TWIN SPRINGS CAMPGROUND SOUTH FORK RD, LANE CO OR	134 - B3
TWO COLOR CAMPGROUND NFD RD 7755, BAKER CO OR	130 - C3
TWO PAN CAMPGROUND END OF LOSTINE RIVER RD, WALLOWA CO OR	130 - C2
TYE CANYON CAMPGROUND SCENIC, KING CO WA	111 - B2
TYEE CAMPGROUND OREGON COAST HWY, LANE CO OR	214 - A5
UMATILLA FORKS CAMPGROUND NFD RD 32, UMATILLA CO OR	130 - A1
UNION CREEK CAMPGROUND UNION CREEK, JACKSON CO OR	226 - C4
UNION CREEK CAMPGROUND WHITNEY HWY, BAKER CO OR	138 - A1
UPPER ARM CAMPGROUND BREITENBUSH RD, MARION CO OR	134 - B1
UPPER BOWMAN CAMPSITE WHITE PINE BUTTES, KLICKITAT CO WA	119 - B3
UPPER CAMPGROUND CASCADE LAKES HWY, DESCHUTES CO OR	216 - B6
UPPER CLEARWATER CAMPGROUND STEQUALEHO CREEK, JEFFERSON CO WA	108 - C1
UPPER END CAMPGROUND BIG FALL CREEK RD, LANE CO OR	134 - A3
UPPER PAYETTE CAMPGROUND W SIDE OF UPPER PAYETTE LK, VALLEY CO ID	251 - D1
UPPER PAYETTE LAKE CAMPGROUND W SIDE OF UPPER PAYETTE LK, VALLEY CO ID	251 - D1
UPPER SOUTH FORK CMPGRND(ROGUE RIVER) RUSTLER PEAK, JACKSON CO OR	150 - A1
VAN CREEK CAMPGROUND NFD RD 1614, IDAHO CO ID	131 - C2
VERLOT CAMPGROUND MOUNTAIN LOOP HWY, SNOHOMISH CO WA	102 - C3
VERMILLION BAR CAMPGROUND OFF NFD RD 454, WALLOWA CO OR	131 - B3
VIGNE CAMPGROUND CHESNIMNUS LN, WALLOWA CO OR	131 - A1
WAHTUM LAKE CAMPGROUND WAHTUM LAKE, HOOD RIVER CO OR	195 - A7
WALDRON CAMPGROUND BAYVIEW, KOOTENAI CO ID	245 - C1
WALLACE FALLS CAMPGROUND LEY RD, SNOHOMISH CO WA	110 - C1
WALTON LAKE CAMPGROUND HOWARD CREEK RD, CROOK CO OR	136 - A2
WALUPT LAKE CAMPGROUND WALUPT LAKE, LEWIS CO WA	119 - A2
WAMPUS CAMPGROUND WICKIUP DAM, DESCHUTES CO OR	142 - C1
WAR CREEK CAMPGROUND OVAL PEAK, OKANOGAN CO WA	104 - A3
WARD CAMPGROUND BAYVIEW, KOOTENAI CO ID	245 - C1
WARM SPRINGS CAMPGROUND NEWBERRY CRATER RD, DESCHUTES CO OR	143 - A1
WATKINS CAMPGROUND CARBERRY CREEK, JACKSON CO OR	149 - B2
WAXMYRTLE CAMPGROUND OFF OREGON COAST HWY, LANE CO OR	214 - A5
WEAVER POINT CAMPGROUND STEHEKIN, CHELAN CO WA	103 - C3
WEEPING ROCK CAMPGROUND AVD DE UMPQUA HWY, DOUGLAS CO OR	222 - B3
WENBERG CAMPGROUND E LAKE GOODWIN RD, SNOHOMISH CO WA	168 - B6
WEST CULTUS LAKE CAMPGROUND OFF DEER LAKE RD, DESCHUTES CO OR	134 - C3
WEST DAVIS LAKE CAMPGROUND HAMNER BUTTE, KLAMATH CO OR	142 - C1
WEST EAGLE MEADOW CAMPGROUND NFD RD 77, UNION CO OR	130 - C3
WEST FORK CAMPGROUND GROTTO, KING CO WA	111 - A2
WESTVIEW SHELTER WILLAMETTE PASS, LANE CO OR	142 - B1
WETMORE CAMPGROUND JOHN DAY HWY, BAKER CO OR	138 - A1
WHAA-LAA CAMPGROUND PLUMMER, BENEWAH CO ID	115 - A2
WHISKEY CREEK CAMPGROUND GOLDEN, JOSEPHINE CO OR	149 - A1
WHISPERING FALLS CAMPGROUND N SANTIAM HWY, MARION CO OR	134 - B1
WHITE CHUCK CAMPGROUND WHITE CHUCK MOUNTAIN, SNOHOMISH CO WA	103 - A3
WHITE CREEK CAMPGROUND TAFT MOUNTAIN, DOUGLAS CO OR	141 - C2
WHITEHORSE FALLS CAMPGROUND GARWOOD BUTTE, DOUGLAS CO OR	223 - A4
WHITE PASS CAMPGROUND WHITE PASS, YAKIMA CO WA	119 - A1
WHITE PINE CAMPGROUND LAKE OF THE WOODS NORTH, KLAMATH CO OR	150 - B1
WHITE PINE CAMPGROUND LAKE WENATCHEE, CHELAN CO WA	111 - C1
WHITE RIVER CAMPGROUND SUNRISE, PIERCE CO WA	185 - D2
WHITE RIVER FALLS CAMPGROUND MOUNT DAVID, CHELAN CO WA	111 - B1
WHITE RIVER PARK CAMPGROUND MOUNT HOOD SOUTH, HOOD RIVER CO OR	202 - B6
WHITETAIL CAMPGROUND BAYVIEW, KOOTENAI CO ID	245 - C1
WHITEWATER CAMPGROUND N SANTIAM HWY, LINN CO OR	134 - B1
WICKIUP BUTTE CAMPGROUND WICKIUP DAM, DESCHUTES CO OR	142 - C1
WICKIUP CAMPGROUND CANYON CREEK RD, GRANT CO OR	137 - B2
WICKIUP CAMPGROUND PINKHAM BUTTE, GARFIELD CO WA	122 - C3
WICKIUP SHELTER RUSTLER PEAK, KLAMATH CO OR	150 - B1
WICKY CREEK SHELTER TROUT LAKE, SKAMANIA CO WA	119 - A3
WILDCAT CAMPGROUND GOLDEN, JOSEPHINE CO OR	149 - A1
WILDHORSE CAMPGROUND QUOSATANA BUTTE, CURRY CO OR	228 - D5
WILD ROSE CAMPGROUND TIETON BASIN, YAKIMA CO WA	119 - B1
WILDWOOD CAMPGROUND OFF SUMMIT RD, WHEELER CO OR	136 - A2
WILEY CAMP FISH MOUNTAIN, DOUGLAS CO OR	222 - D7
WILEY FLAT CAMPGROUND OFF PAULINA HWY, CROOK CO OR	136 - A3
WILLIAMS CREEK CAMPGROUND MACE MOUNTAIN, DOUGLAS CO OR	141 - C2
WILLIAMSON RIVER CAMPGROUND SOLOMAN BUTTE, KLAMATH CO OR	231 - D2
WILLOUGHBY CREEK CAMPGROUND WINFIELD CREEK, JEFFERSON CO WA	108 - C1
WILLOW CAMPGROUND CHEMULT, KLAMATH CO OR	142 - C2
WILLOW CREEK CAMPGROUND OFF NFD RD 4015, LAKE CO OR	152 - A2
WILLOW DAY USE AREA BAYVIEW, KOOTENAI CO ID	245 - C1
WILLOW POINT CAMPGROUND HYATT RESERVOIR, JACKSON CO OR	150 - A2
WILLOWS CAMPGROUND TIETON BASIN, YAKIMA CO WA	119 - B1
WILLOW VALLEY CAMPGROUND BRADY BUTTE, KLAMATH CO OR	151 - B3
WINBERRY CAMPGROUND WINBERRY CREEK RD, LANE CO OR	134 - A3
WINCHUCK CAMPGROUND FOURTH OF JULY CREEK, CURRY CO OR	148 - B2
WINDY POINT CAMPGROUND WEDDLE CANYON, YAKIMA CO WA	119 - B1
WINDY SADDLE CAMPGROUND SEVEN DEVILS RD, IDAHO CO ID	131 - B2
WINSTON CREEK CAMPGROUND HATCHET MOUNTAIN, LEWIS CO WA	118 - A2
WINTER COVE CAMPGROUND WINTER COVE RD, BRITISH COLUMBIA BC	101 - C1
WISH POOSH CAMPGROUND CLE ELUM LAKE, KITTITAS CO WA	111 - B3
WIZARD FALLS CAMPGROUND OFF METOLIUS RIVER RD, JEFFERSON CO OR	134 - C1
WOLF BAR CAMPSITE MOUNT HOQUIAM, JEFFERSON CO WA	109 - A2
WOLF CREEK CAMPGROUND BULL SPRING RD, CROOK CO OR	136 - B2
WOLF CREEK CAMPGROUND RED BUTTE, DOUGLAS CO OR	141 - C2
WOLF SHELTER GROUNDHOG MOUNTAIN, LANE CO OR	142 - A1
WOODLAND PARK CAMPGROUND WESTON-ELGIN HWY, UNION CO OR	130 - A1
WY EAST CAMPSITE WAHTUM LAKE, HOOD RIVER CO OR	194 - D7
WYETH CAMPGROUND WYETH, HOOD RIVER CO OR	195 - A5
WYNOOCHEE FALLS CAMPGROUND WYNOOCHEE LAKE, GRAYS HARBOR CO WA	109 - B2
WYNOOCHEE SHELTER WYNOOCHEE LAKE, GRAYS HARBOR CO WA	109 - B2
YAHOO LAKE CAMPGROUND STEQUALEHO CREEK, JEFFERSON CO WA	108 - C1
YELLOWJACKET CAMPGROUND OFF HINES LOGGING RD, HARNEY CO OR	137 - A3
YELLOW PINE CAMPGROUND JOHN DAY HWY, BAKER CO OR	138 - A1
YEW TREE CAMPGROUND LITTLEROCK, THURSTON CO WA	184 - A1
YOUNG CREEK SHELTER MUD RIVER, CHELAN CO WA	112 - A1

CASINOS

FEATURE NAME City State	Page-Grid
CHINOOK WINDS CASINO 1777 NW 44TH ST, LINCOLN CITY OR	203 - A4
CLEARWATER CASINO 15347 SUQUAMISH WY NE, SUQUAMISH WA	170 - C7
EMERALD QUEEN CASINO 2102 ALEXANDER AV, TACOMA WA	182 - A2
MUCKLESHOOT CASINO 2402 AUBURN WY, AUBURN WA	182 - C2
NORTHERN QUEST CASINO 100 N HAYFORD RD, AIRWAY HEIGHTS WA	246 - A4
SEVEN FEATHERS CASINO 146 CHIEF MIWALETA LN, DOUGLAS CO OR	225 - C3
SKAGIT VALLEY CASINO 5984 N DARRK LN, SKAGIT CO WA	161 - B4
TULALIP CASINO 6410 33RD AV SE, SNOHOMISH CO WA	168 - C7
WILDHORSE RESORT & CASINO I-84 EXIT 216, UMATILLA CO OR	129 - B1

COLLEGES & UNIVERSITIES

FEATURE NAME City State	Page-Grid
BAKER COLLEGE LA GRANDE-BAKER HWY, BAKER CITY OR	138 - B1
BATES TECHNICAL COLLEGE 1101 YAKIMA AV, TACOMA WA	293 - G5
BATES VOCATIONAL TECHNICAL S 74TH ST & WAPATO ST, TACOMA WA	294 - E7
BELLEVUE COMM COLLEGE 3000 LANDERHOLM CIR SE, BELLEVUE WA	175 - C3
BIBLE COLLEGE IRENE ST, BOISE ID	253 - C2
BLUE MTN COMM COLLEGE COLD SPRINGS HWY, PENDLETON OR	129 - B1
BOISE STATE UNIV MOSS LN & PORTNER RD, NAMPA ID	147 - B1
BOISE STATE UNIV OFF BROADWAY AV, BOISE ID	253 - C3
BRITISH COLUMBIA INST OF TECHNOLOGY WILLINGDON AV, DISTRICT OF BURNABY BC	156 - C5
BUSINESS COMPUTER TRAINING INSTITUTE 204 SE STONE MILL DR, VANCOUVER WA	193 - A6
CASCADE COLLEGE 9101 E BURNSIDE ST, PORTLAND OR	315 - G5
CASCADIA COMM COLLEGE 18345 CAMPUS WY NE, BOTHELL WA	171 - C6
CENTRALIA COMM COLLEGE S WASHINGTON AV & LOCUST ST, CENTRALIA WA	299 - E4
CENTRAL OREGON COMM COLLEGE NW COLLEGE WY, BEND OR	332 - B5
CENTRAL WASHINGTON UNIV ELLENSBURG NORTH, ELLENSBURG WA	241 - B5
CHEMEKTA COMM COLLEGE HAYESVILLE OR	323 - E8
CITY UNIV 3925 NE 72ND AV, VANCOUVER WA	306 - E2
CLACKAMAS COMM COLLEGE 19600 MOLALLA AV, OREGON CITY OR	199 - D5
CLARK COLLEGE 1800 E MCLOUGHLIN BLVD, VANCOUVER WA	305 - H4
CLATSOP COMM COLLEGE JEROME AV, ASTORIA OR	300 - E5
CLOVER PK TECHNICAL COLLEGE 4500 STEILACOOM BLVD SW, LAKEWOOD WA	181 - D4
COGSWELL, HENRY COLLEGE 2802 WETMORE AV, EVERETT WA	264 - D3
COGSWELL, HENRY COLLEGE NORTH 10626 NE 37TH CIR, KIRKLAND WA	175 - C1
COLLEGE OF IDAHO FILLMORE ST & S 20TH AV, CALDWELL ID	147 - B1
COLLEGE OF THE REDWOODS 883 W WASHINGTON BLVD, DEL NORTE CO CA	148 - B3
COLUMBIA BASIN COMM COLLEGE N 20TH AV, PASCO WA	343 - D4

FEATURE NAME City State	Page-Grid
CONCORDIA UNIV	310 - A6
2811 NE HOLMAN ST, PORTLAND OR	
DOUGLAS COLLEGE	156 - D6
8TH ST, NEW WESTMINSTER BC	
EASTERN OREGON COLLEGE	130 - A2
OFF HWY 203, LA GRANDE OR	
EASTERN WASHINGTON UNIV	246 - A7
WASHINGTON ST, CHENEY WA	
EDMONDS COMM COLLEGE	171 - B5
20000 68TH AV W, LYNNWOOD WA	
ERAU FORT LEWIS TEACHING SITE	181 - C5
COLORADO AV & N 9TH ST, PIERCE CO WA	
ERAU - SEATTLE CTR	289 - J3
1300 SW 7TH ST, RENTON WA	
ERAU TACOMA CTR	181 - D5
851 LINCOLN BLVD, PIERCE CO WA	
EUGENE BIBLE COLLEGE	329 - D8
2155 BAILEY HILL, EUGENE OR	
EVERETT COMM COLLEGE	171 - C1
2000 TOWER ST, EVERETT WA	
EVERGREEN STATE COLLEGE, THE	296 - A1
THE EVERGREEN COLLEGE PKY, THURSTON CO WA	
FOX, GEORGE UNIV	198 - D5
414 N MERIDIAN ST, NEWBERG OR	
FOX, GEORGE UNIV PORTLAND CTR	199 - B3
12753 SW 68TH PKWY, TIGARD OR	
FRASER VALLEY COLLEGE	94 - C3
YALE RD E, CITY OF CHILLIWACK BC	
GOLDEN GATE BPTIST THEOLGICAL SEMNRY	307 - H3
3200 NE 109TH AV, VANCOUVER WA	
GONZAGA UNIV	349 - B8
E BOONE AV, SPOKANE WA	
GONZAGA UNIV OF LAW	349 - B8
E BOONE AV, SPOKANE WA	
GRAYS HARBOR COLLEGE	178 - B7
S BOONE ST, ABERDEEN WA	
GREEN RIVER COMM COLLEGE	182 - C1
12401 SE 320TH ST, KING CO WA	
GRUB COLLEGE (SITE)	204 - C1
MCMINNVILLE, YAMHILL CO OR	
HIGHLINE COMM COLLEGE	175 - B7
2400 S 240TH ST, DES MOINES WA	
IDAHO AND HOSP	147 - C1
3100 11TH AV N, NAMPA ID	
INTL AIR ACADEMY INC	306 - A5
2901 E MILL PLAIN BLVD, VANCOUVER WA	
KWANTIEN COLLEGE	158 - C1
56TH AV, LANGLEY BC	
LAKE WASHINGTON TECHNICAL COLLEGE	171 - C7
11605 132ND AV NE, KIRKLAND WA	
LANE COMM COLLEGE	214 - B3
101 & 35TH ST, FLORENCE OR	
LANE COMM COLLEGE	330 - G12
E 30TH AV, LANE CO OR	
LANE COMM COLLEGE	329 - J5
MADISON ST, EUGENE OR	
LEWIS & CLARK COLLEGE	321 - F1
615 SW PALATINE HILL RD, PORTLAND OR	
LEWIS-CLARK STATE COLLEGE	250 - B4
11TH AV, LEWISTON ID	
LINN-BENTON COMM COLLEGE	326 - B14
PACIFIC BLVD & BELMONT AV, ALBANY OR	
LOWER COLUMBIA JUNIOR COLLEGE	303 - A8
MAPLE ST, LONGVIEW WA	
MALASPINA COLLEGE	93 - A3
900 5TH ST, NANAIMO BC	
MARYLHURST UNIV	199 - C4
PACIFIC HWY, LAKE OSWEGO OR	
MOUNT HOOD COMM COLLEGE	200 - B1
26000 SE STARK ST, GRESHAM OR	
MUKOGOWA-FORT WRIGHT INSTITUTE	348 - D7
N WRIGHT RD & OFFUT RD, SPOKANE WA	
MULTNOMAH BIBLE COLLEGE	315 - F5
8435 NE GLISAN ST, PORTLAND OR	
NORTH IDAHO COLLEGE	355 - D11
COLLEGE DR, COEUR D'ALENE ID	
NORTH SEATTLE COMM COLLEGE	171 - A7
9600 COLLEGE WY N, SEATTLE WA	
NORTHWEST CHRISTIAN COLLEGE	330 - B7
KINCAID ST, EUGENE OR	
NORTHWEST COLLEGE	175 - C1
108TH AV NE & NE 53RD ST, KIRKLAND WA	
NORTHWESTERN OF LAW	321 - E1
SW TERWILLIGER BLVD, PORTLAND OR	
NORTHWEST INDIAN COLLEGE	158 - C7
KWINA RD, WHATCOM CO WA	
NORTHWEST NAZARENE COLLEGE	147 - B1
12TH AV RD & LOCUST LN, NAMPA ID	
OLYMPIC COLLEGE	270 - J9
BREMERTON WEST, BREMERTON WA	
OREGON INSTITUTE OF MARINE BIOLOGY	220 - C1
63466 BOAT BASIN DR, COOS CO OR	
OREGON INSTITUTE OF TECHNOLOGY	199 - D3
7726 SE HARMONY RD, CLACKAMAS CO OR	
OREGON INSTITUTE OF TECHNOLOGY	338 - D3
COLLEGE WY, KLAMATH FALLS OR	
OREGON STATE UNIV AGRI EXP STA	129 - C1
OREGON-WASHINGTON HWY, UMATILLA CO OR	
OREGON STATE UNIV	327 - E10
CAMPUS WY, CORVALLIS OR	
OREGON STATE UNIV EXPERIMENT FARM	327 - J9
ELECTRIC RD, LINN CO OR	
OREGON STATE UNIV MARINE SCIENCE	206 - B4
FERRY SLIP RD, NEWPORT OR	
PACIFIC LUTHERAN UNIV	181 - D4
121ST ST S & PARK AV S, PIERCE CO WA	
PACIFIC NORTHWEST COLLEGE OF ART	313 - E4
1241 NW JOHNSON ST, PORTLAND OR	
PACIFIC UNIV	198 - B1
2043 COLLEGE WY, FOREST GROVE OR	
PENINSULA COLLEGE (FORKS CAMPUS)	169 - C1
FORKS AV N, FORKS WA	
PENINSULA JUNIOR COLLEGE	261 - G7
PARK AV, PORT ANGELES WA	
PIERCE COLLEGE	182 - B4
1601 39TH AV SE, PUYALLUP WA	
PIERCE COLLEGE	181 - C4
9401 FARWEST DR SW, LAKEWOOD WA	
PORTLAND COM COLLEGE ROCK CREEK	192 - A7
17705 NW SPRINGVILLE RD, WASHINGTON CO OR	
PORTLAND COMM COLLEGE	320 - A3
12000 SW 49TH AV, PORTLAND OR	
PORTLAND COMM COLLEGE CASCADE CAMP	309 - F7
KERBY AV&NE KILLINGSWORTH ST, PORTLAND OR	
PORTLAND STATE UNIV	312 - E7
724 SW HARRISON ST, PORTLAND OR	
PUGET SOUND CHRISTIAN COLLEGE	171 - B6
7011 226TH PL SW, MOUNTLAKE TERRACE WA	
REED COLLEGE	318 - A4
3203 SE WOODSTOCK BLVD, PORTLAND OR	
RENTON TECHNICAL COLLEGE	175 - C5
3000 NE 4TH ST, RENTON WA	
ROGUE COMM COLLEGE	229 - B6
3345 REDWOOD HWY, JOSEPHINE CO OR	

FEATURE NAME City State	Page-Grid
ROYAL ROADS UNIV	159 - B6
2005 SOOKE RD, CITY OF COLWOOD BC	
SAINT MARTINS COLLEGE	297 - G5
MARTIN WY SE, LACEY WA	
SEATTLE CENTRAL COMM COLLEGE	278 - B4
1701 BROADWAY, SEATTLE WA	
SEATTLE PACIFIC UNIV	273 - G7
3307 3RD AV W, SEATTLE WA	
SEATTLE UNIV	278 - B5
900 BROADWAY, SEATTLE WA	
SEATTLE UNIV GYMNASIUM	278 - C6
E JEFFERSON ST & 15TH AV, SEATTLE WA	
SHORELINE COMM COLLEGE	171 - A6
16101 GREENWOOD AV N, SHORELINE WA	
SIMON FRASER UNIV	156 - D4
UNIVERSITY DR, DISTRICT OF BURNABY BC	
SKAGIT VALLEY JUNIOR COLLEGE	260 - D12
N 9TH ST, MOUNT VERNON WA	
SOUTHERN OREGON STATE COLLEGE	337 - E9
SISKIYOU BLVD, ASHLAND OR	
SOUTH PUGET SOUND COMM COLLEGE	296 - F8
MOTTMAN RD, OLYMPIA WA	
SOUTH SEATTLE COMM COLLEGE	281 - H7
6000 16TH AV SW, SEATTLE WA	
SOUTHWESTERN OREGON COMM COLLEGE	333 - D6
CAPE ARAGO HWY & FIR ST, COOS BAY OR	
SPOKANE COMM COLLEGE	349 - F7
E MISSION AV, SPOKANE WA	
SPOKANE FALLS COMM COLLEGE	348 - E7
3410 W FORT GEO WRIGHT DR, SPOKANE WA	
TACOMA COMM COLLEGE	181 - C2
6501 S 19TH ST, TACOMA WA	
TREASURE VALLEY COMM COLLEGE	139 - A3
SW 4TH ST & SE 5TH AV, ONTARIO OR	
TRINITY LUTHERAN COLLEGE	176 - A3
4221 228TH AV SE, KING CO WA	
TRINITY WESTERN UNIV	157 - C7
7600 GLOVER RD, TOWNSHIP OF LANGLEY BC	
UMPQUA COMM COLLEGE	221 - C3
1140 COLLEGE RD, DOUGLAS CO OR	
UNIV OF BRITISH COLUMBIA	156 - A4
UNIVERSITY BLVD, UNIV ENDOWMENT LANDS BC	
UNIV OF IDAHO	249 - C5
HWY 95 & HWY 8, MOSCOW ID	
UNIV OF IDAHO CLARK FORK FIELD CAMPUS	107 - C3
OFF HWY 200, BONNER CO ID	
UNIV OF OREGON	330 - B7
220 OREGON HALL, EUGENE OR	
UNIV OF PORTLAND	308 - A5
5000 N WILLAMETTE BLVD, PORTLAND OR	
UNIV OF PUGET SOUND	292 - C4
1500 N WARNER ST, TACOMA WA	
UNIV OF VICTORIA	257 - C4
MCKENZIE AVE, DISTRICT OF OAK BAY BC	
UNIV OF WASHINGTON	274 - D6
MONTLAKE BL NE, SEATTLE WA	
UNIV OF WASHINGTON, BOTHELL	171 - C6
18115 CAMPUS WY NE, BOTHELL WA	
UNIV OF WASHINGTON TACOMA	293 - G6
JEFFERSON AV & S 19TH ST, TACOMA WA	
WALLA WALLA COLLEGE	344 - E10
N COLLEGE RD, COLLEGE PLACE WA	
WALLA WALLA COMM COLLEGE	250 - B4
APPLESIDE BLVD, VINELAND WA	
WALLA WALLA COMM COLLEGE	345 - G6
WALLA WALLA WA	
WARNER PACIFIC COLLEGE	318 - E1
2219 SE 68TH AV, PORTLAND OR	
WASH BAPTIST TEACHERS COLLEGE	294 - E6
2402 S 66TH ST, TACOMA WA	
WASHINGTON STATE UNIV (VANCOUVER)	192 - D4
14204 NE SALMON CREEK RD, CLARK CO WA	
WASHINGTON STATE UNIV	249 - B5
STADIUM WY, PULLMAN WA	
WASHINGTON ST TRAINING & CONF CTR	175 - A6
19010 1ST AV S, BURIEN WA	
WENATCHEE VALLEY COLLEGE	238 - D4
FIFTH ST, WENATCHEE WA	
WENATCHEE VALLEY COLLEGE	104 - C2
HWY 215, OMAK WA	
WESTERN BAPTIST BIBLE COLLEGE	325 - F7
DEER PARK DR SE, SALEM OR	
WESTERN BUSINESS COLLEGE	193 - A6
120 NE 136TH AV, VANCOUVER WA	
WESTERN OREGON UNIV	204 - B7
345 N MONMOUTH AV, MONMOUTH OR	
WESTERN STATES CHIROPRACTIC COLLEGE	200 - A1
2900 NE 132ND AV, PORTLAND OR	
WESTERN WASHINGTON UNIV	258 - C8
HIGH ST, BELLINGHAM WA	
WHITMAN COLLEGE	345 - B7
BOYER AV, WALLA WALLA WA	
WHITWORTH COLLEGE	346 - J10
N WHITWORTH DR, COUNTRY HOMES WA	
WILLAMETTE UNIV	322 - J13
STATE ST SE & 12TH ST SE, SALEM OR	
YAKIMA VALLEY JUNIOR COLLEGE	243 - B7
NOB HILL BLVD & S 16TH AV, YAKIMA WA	

ENTERTAINMENT & SPORTS

FEATURE NAME City State	Page-Grid
4TH FAIRGROUNDS	300 - H10
HWY 202 & WALLUSKI LOOP RD, CLATSOP CO OR	
ALBI, JOSEPH A MEM STADIUM	348 - C3
N ASSEMBLY ST, SPOKANE WA	
AUTZEN STADIUM	330 - C5
CENTENNIAL BLVD, EUGENE OR	
BAKER COUNTY FAIRGROUNDS	131 - A3
HALFWAY-CORNUCOPIA HWY, BAKER CO OR	
BAKER COUNTY FAIRGROUNDS	138 - B1
OFF POCAHONTAS RD, BAKER CITY OR	
BENTON COUNTY FAIRGROUNDS	327 - B9
53RD ST & CAMPUS WY, BENTON CO OR	
BENTON FRANKLIN FAIRGROUND	343 - F12
S OAK ST, KENNEWICK WA	
BMX TRACK	126 - A3
OFF MOLALLA FOREST RD, MOLALLA OR	
BREMERTON MEM STADIUM	270 - H9
BREMERTON WEST, BREMERTON WA	
BRITISH COLUMBIA PLACE STADIUM	254 - G11
777 PACIFIC BLVD, VANCOUVER BC	
CHENEY STADIUM	292 - B7
S TYLER ST & FRWY 16, TACOMA WA	
CIVIC STADIUM	330 - A8
2077 WILLAMETTE ST, EUGENE OR	
CLALLAM COUNTY FAIRGROUND	261 - B4
L ST & W LAURIDSEN BLVD, PORT ANGELES WA	
CLOVERDALE FAIRGROUNDS	157 - B7
176TH ST & 60TH AV, CITY OF SURREY BC	
COOS COUNTY FAIRGROUNDS	140 - B2
MYRTLE POINT, MYRTLE POINT OR	
COUNTY FAIRGROUNDS	122 - A3
OFF HWY 12, WALLA WALLA CO WA	
CROOK COUNTY FAIRGROUNDS	213 - D5
CROOKED RIVER HWY & LYNN BL, CROOK CO OR	

FEATURE NAME City State	Page-Grid
CURRY COUNTY FAIRGROUNDS	228 - A6
OREGON COAST HWY, GOLD BEACH OR	
DAYTON & COLUMBIA CO FAIRGROUND	122 - A2
OFF HWY 12, COLUMBIA CO OR	
DEL NORTE COUNTY FAIRGROUNDS	148 - B3
HWY 101 & NORTHCREST DR, CRESCENT CITY CA	
DESCHUTES COUNTY FAIRGROUNDS	212 - D6
THE DALLES-CALIFORNIA HWY, REDMOND OR	
DESERT PK RACE TRCK AND EQSTRIAN CTR	104 - C1
HWY 97, BRITISH COLUMBIA BC	
DOUGLAS COUNTY FAIRGROUNDS	334 - E9
FREAR ST, DOUGLAS CO OR	
DREWSEY RODEO GROUND	137 - C3
DREWSEY RD & OTIS VALLEY RD, HARNEY CO OR	
EMERALD DOWNS	182 - B1
EMERALD DOWNS DR & 29TH ST NW, AUBURN WA	
EMPIRE STADIUM	255 - E10
HASTINGS ST E, VANCOUVER BC	
EUGENE SPEEDWAY	329 - B7
W 11TH AV, EUGENE OR	
EXHIBITION CENTER	282 - A1
800 OCCIDENTAL AV S, SEATTLE WA	
FAIRGROUNDS	241 - B6
7TH AV, ELLENSBURG WA	
GENNA, VINCE STADIUM	332 - F9
401 SE ROOSEVELT AV, BEND OR	
GILL COLISEUM	327 - E10
WASHINGTON WY & 26TH ST, CORVALLIS OR	
GILLIAM COUNTY FAIRGROUNDS	128 - A2
JOHN DAY HWY, GILLIAM CO OR	
GM PLACE	254 - H10
GEORGIA ST & PACIFIC BLVD N, VANCOUVER BC	
GRANT COUNTY FAIRGROUNDS	137 - B2
3RD AV & ELM ST, JOHN DAY OR	
GRANT COUNTY FAIRGROUNDS	242 - C2
AIRWAY DR & VALLEY RD, GRANT CO WA	
HAMMOND STADIUM	157 - C5
207TH ST & RIVER RD W, MAPLE RIDGE BC	
HARNEY COUNTY FAIRGROUNDS	145 - B1
HOTCHKISS LN, HARNEY CO OR	
HEHE MILL RODEO GROUND	127 - A3
WARM SPRINGS HWY, WASCO CO OR	
HUSKY STADIUM	274 - D7
MONTLAKE BL NE, SEATTLE WA	
JEFFERSON COUNTY FAIRGOUNDS	263 - F2
49TH AV & KUHN ST, PORT TOWNSEND WA	
JEFFERSON COUNTY FAIRGROUNDS	208 - B5
SW FAIRGROUNDS AV, MADRAS OR	
KEY ARENA	277 - H4
305 HARRISON ST, SEATTLE WA	
KIGGINS BOWL	305 - G1
800 E 40TH ST, VANCOUVER WA	
KING COUNTY FAIRGROUNDS	110 - C3
SE 456TH ST & 284TH AV SE, KING CO WA	
KLAMATH COUNTY FAIRGROUNDS	338 - H10
CREST ST, ALTAMONT OR	
KOOTENAI COUNTY FAIRGROUND	355 - E5
GOVERNMENT WY MARGARET AV, KOOTENAI CO ID	
LAKE COUNTY FAIRGROUNDS	152 - A2
ROBERTA AV, LAKE CO OR	
LANE COUNTY FAIRGROUNDS	329 - H7
13TH AV, EUGENE OR	
LINCOLN COUNTY FAIRGROUNDS	206 - B4
3RD ST, NEWPORT OR	
LINN COUNTY FAIRGROUNDS	326 - H7
ALBANY OR	
LOGGERS RODEO GROUNDS	110 - C3
HWY 410, BUCKLEY WA	
MALHEUR COUNTY FAIRGROUNDS	139 - A3
NW 8TH AV, ONTARIO OR	
MARINEVIEW RECEPTION & CONFERENCE CTR	171 - C1
13TH ST, EVERETT WA	
MARYMOOR PARK VELODROME	175 - D1
NE MARYMOOR WY, KING CO WA	
MCCULLOCH STADIUM	322 - H14
HIGH ST SE & MISSION ST SE, SALEM OR	
MEMORIAL COLISEUM	313 - G4
1401 N WHEELER AV, PORTLAND OR	
MEMORIAL STADIUM	264 - E5
BROADWAY & 38TH ST, EVERETT WA	
MEYDENBAUER CENTER	175 - C2
NE 6TH ST & 112TH AV NE, BELLEVUE WA	
MORROW COUNTY FAIRGROUNDS	128 - C2
HEPPNER HWY, MORROW CO OR	
MOUNTAIN VIEW ICE ARENA	193 - A6
14313 SE MILL PLAIN BLVD, VANCOUVER WA	
OLYMPIC STADIUM	178 - A7
SUMNER AV, HOQUIAM WA	
OREGON CONVENTION CENTER	313 - G5
777 NE MARTIN L KING JR BL, PORTLAND OR	
OREGON STATE FAIRGROUNDS	323 - B10
SUNNYVIEW RD, SALEM OR	
PACIFIC COLISEUM	255 - E9
MCGILL ST & RENFREW ST, VANCOUVER BC	
PAYETTE COUNTY FAIRGROUNDS	139 - B3
IDAHO ST, PAYETTE CO ID	
PGE PARK	312 - D6
1844 SW MORRISON ST, PORTLAND OR	
PLAYFAIR RACETRACK	349 - D8
OFF E SPRAGUE AV, SPOKANE WA	
POLK COUNTY FAIRGROUNDS	204 - B6
PACIFIC HWY, POLK CO OR	
PORTLAND INTERNATIONAL RACEWAY	308 - D2
N VICTORY AV, PORTLAND OR	
PORTLAND MEADOWS RACE TRACK	309 - F3
N SCHMEER RD, PORTLAND OR	
PORTLAND METROPOLITAN EXPO CTR	309 - E1
N MARINE DR & N FORCE AV, PORTLAND OR	
PORTLAND SPEEDWAY	309 - F2
9727 N M L KING JR BLVD, PORTLAND OR	
POSSE STADIUM	342 - H2
BURDEN BLVD & ROAD 60, PASCO WA	
RENTON MEMORIAL HS STADIUM	175 - C5
N 4TH ST & LOGAN AV N, RENTON WA	
RESER STADIUM	327 - E10
WASHINGTON WY & 26TH ST, CORVALLIS OR	
ROSE GARDEN ARENA, THE	313 - G4
1 CENTER COURT ST, PORTLAND OR	
SAFECO FIELD	282 - A1
1250 1ST AV S, SEATTLE WA	
SAGE ACRES RACETRACK	147 - B1
HOMEDALE RD & WAGNER RD, CANYON CO ID	
SANDOWN RACEWAY	159 - C2
HWY 17, DIST OF NORTH SAANICH BC	
SEAFIRST STADIUM	349 - G8
E FAIRGROUND RD, SPOKANE VALLEY WA	
SEAHAWK STADIUM & EXHIBITION CTR	278 - A7
800 OCCIDENTAL AV S, SEATTLE WA	
SEATTLE CENTER STADIUM	277 - H4
SEATTLE CENTER, SEATTLE WA	
SEATTLE INTERNATIONAL RACEWAY	182 - D1
148TH AV SE, KING CO WA	
SHERMAN COUNTY FAIRGROUNDS	127 - C2
SHERMAN HWY & LONE ROCK RD, SHERMAN CO OR	

FEATURE NAME / City State	Page-Grid
SOUTHWEST WASHINGTON FAIRGROUNDS / NATIONAL AV, LEWIS CO WA	299 - E7
SPOKANE COUNTY FAIR & EXPO CENTER / E BROADWAY AV&N HAVANA ST, SPOKANE VLY WA	349 - G8
SPORTS COMPLEX / NE 28TH AV & NE 25TH AV EXT, HILLSBORO OR	198 - D1
SUNNY-GRAND SPEEDWAY / GRANDVIEW, YAKIMA CO WA	120 - B2
TACOMA CONVENTION CENTER / S 13TH ST & MARKET ST, TACOMA WA	293 - H5
TACOMA DOME / E D ST & E 27TH ST, TACOMA WA	293 - J7
TACOMAS LANDMARK CONVENTION CTR / 47 SAINT HELENS AV, TACOMA WA	293 - G4
TILLAMOOK COUNTY FAIRGROUNDS / TILLAMOOK, TILLAMOOK CO OR	197 - C2
TYGH VALLEY FAIRGROUNDS / FAIRGROUND RD, WASCO CO OR	127 - B2
UMATILLA COUNTY FAIRGROUNDS / W HIGHLAND AV, HERMISTON OR	129 - A1
VETERANS MEMORIAL ARENA / N LINCOLN ST, SPOKANE WA	348 - J8
WALLA WALLA COUNTY FAIRGROUNDS / W TIETAN ST, WALLA WALLA CO WA	345 - A9
WALLOWA COUNTY FAIRGROUNDS / ENTERPRISE-LEWISTON HWY, ENTERPRISE OR	130 - C2
WASHINGTON COUNTY FAIRGROUNDS / 872 NE 28TH AV, HILLSBORO OR	198 - D1
WASHINGTON STATE CONV & TRADE CTR / 800 CONVENTION PL, SEATTLE WA	278 - A5
WENATCHEE SPEEDWAY / WENATCHEE, DOUGLAS CO WA	239 - A4
WESTERN IDAHO FAIRGROUND / OFF GLENWOOD ST, ADA CO ID	253 - C2
WHEELER COUNTY FAIRGROUNDS / JOHN DAY HWY, WHEELER CO OR	128 - A3
YAMHILL COUNTY FAIRGROUNDS / 2070 NE LAFAYETTE AV, MCMINNVILLE OR	198 - B7

GOLF COURSES

FEATURE NAME / City State	Page-Grid
ALLENMORE GC / 2125 S CEDAR ST, TACOMA WA	292 - D7
AUBURN CTR GC / CENTER ST NE, MARION CO OR	323 - G13
AWBREY GLEN GC / NW MT WASHINGTON & NW COLLEGE, BEND OR	332 - A4
BATTLE CREEK GC / COMMERCIAL ST SE & MADRAS ST, SALEM OR	325 - A9
BELLINGHAM GOLF & CC / MCLEOD RD & MERIDUAN ST, BELLINGHAM WA	258 - C2
BEND GC / COUNTRY CLUB DR & HIGHLAND RD, BEND OR	332 - E13
BLENKINSOP VALLEY GC / BLENKINSOP RD, DISTRICT OF SAANICH BC	256 - J1
BOISE RANCH GC / E LAKE HAZEL RD, ADA CO ID	253 - B4
BROADMOOR GC / 2340 BROADMOOR DR E, SEATTLE WA	278 - E2
BROADMOOR GC / 3509 NE COLUMBIA BLVD, PORTLAND OR	310 - B4
BROKEN TOP GC / CENTURY DR HWY & CAMPBELL DR, BEND OR	332 - A8
CAPILANO GC / STEVENS DR, DIST OF WEST VANCOUVER BC	254 - F1
CAPITOL CITY GC / YELM HWY SE, THURSTON CO WA	297 - G13
CEDAR HILL GC / 1400 DERBY RD, DISTRICT OF SAANICH BC	256 - J4
CEDAR LINKS GC / FOOTHILL & CEDAR LINKS RD, MEDFORD OR	336 - H8
CENTRALIA PUB GC / MAGNOLIA ST & BYRD ST, CENTRALIA WA	299 - H4
COEUR D'ALENE PUBLIC GC / E FAIRWAY DR, COEUR D'ALENE ID	355 - A7
COEUR D'ALENE RESORT GC / 115 S 2ND ST, KOOTENAI CO ID	355 - H12
COLUMBIA EDGEWATER CC / 2220 NE MARINE DR, PORTLAND OR	309 - J2
COLUMBIA PARK GC / COLUMBIA DR DR SE, KENNEWICK WA	343 - A9
COLUMBIA POINT GC / 225 COLUMBIA POINT DR, RICHLAND WA	341 - H3
COLWOOD NATIONAL GC / 7313 NE COLUMBIA BLVD, PORTLAND OR	311 - F5
CORVALLIS CC / COUNTRY CLUB DR, CORVALLIS OR	327 - D12
CRESTVIEW HILLS GC / GREEN DR, WALDPORT OR	328 - D7
DOWNRIVER MUNICIPAL GC / W DOWNRIVER PARK DR, SPOKANE WA	348 - D6
EASTMORELAND GC / 2425 SE BYBEE BLVD, PORTLAND OR	317 - J5
ESMERALDA MUNICIPAL GC / N FREYA ST, SPOKANE WA	349 - F4
EVERETT GOLF & CC / 1500 52ND ST SE, EVERETT WA	268 - D1
FOSTER GOLF LINKS / 13500 INTERURBAN AV S, TUKWILA WA	289 - G2
GEARHART GOLF LINKS / 1300 N MARION AV, CLATSOP CO OR	301 - G2
GLEN ACRES GOLF & CC / 1000 S 112TH ST, KING CO WA	286 - B5
GOLF CLUB OF OREGON / 905 NW SPRING HILL DR, BENTON CO OR	326 - C7
GORGE VALE GC / 1005 CRAIGFLOWER RD, TOWN OF ESQUIMALT BC	256 - C6
GREEN LAKE GC / 5701 W GREENLAKE WY N, SEATTLE WA	273 - J4
HALL, WALTER E REC AREA & GC / 1226 W CASINO RD, EVERETT WA	267 - J5
HERON LAKES GC / 3500 N VICTORY BLVD, PORTLAND OR	308 - C1
HIGHLANDS GOLF & CC, THE / 5500 E MULLAN AV, POST FALLS ID	354 - F6
ILLINOIS VALLEY GC / REDWWOD HIGHWAY 199, JOSEPHINE CO OR	233 - B3
INDIAN CANYON MUNICIPAL GC / S INDIAN CANYON DR, SPOKANE WA	348 - D10
INDIAN LAKES GC / OFF S COLE RD, ADA CO ID	253 - C4
INDIAN SUMMER GC / TROON LN SE, THURSTON CO WA	297 - E13
INTERBAY FAMILY GC / 2501 15TH AV W, SEATTLE WA	277 - F1
JEFFERSON PARK GC / 4101 BEACON AV S, SEATTLE WA	282 - C4
LAKE PADDEN GC / SAMISH WY, BELLINGHAM WA	258 - G13
LAURELWOOD GC / EUGENE OR	330 - C10
LONGVIEW GOLF AND CC / PACIFIC WY, LONGVIEW WA	302 - H5
MARYSVILLE GC / ALLEN ST, BENTON CO OR	327 - F12

FEATURE NAME / City State	Page-Grid
MCCALL GC / DAVIS ST & LICK CREEK RD, MCCALL ID	251 - D5
MEADOW PARK GC / 7108 LAKEWOOD DR W, TACOMA WA	294 - A6
MEADOWOOD GC / E VALLEYWAY AV, LIBERTY LAKE WA	352 - E14
MINT VALLEY GC / 42ND, LONGVIEW WA	302 - F4
MOUNT DOUGLAS GC / BLENKINSOP RD, DISTRICT OF SAANICH BC	256 - J1
MYLORA GC / CITY OF RICHMOND BC	156 - B7
OAK KNOLL GC / GREEN SPRINGS HWY & OAK KNOLL, ASHLAND OR	337 - J10
OAK KNOLL GC / WILLAMINA-SALEM HWY, POLK CO OR	204 - B5
OAKWAY GC / OAKWAY RD, EUGENE OR	330 - A4
OSWEGO LAKE CC / 20 IRON MOUNTAIN BLVD, LAKE OSWEGO OR	320 - D5
PAINTED HILLS GC / S DISHMAN-MICA RD, SPOKANE VALLEY WA	350 - H14
PENINSULA GC / GOLF COURSE RD, PORT ANGELES WA	261 - H6
PORTLAND MEADOWS GC / 901 N SCHMEER RD, PORTLAND OR	309 - F3
PORT TOWNSEND GC / 1948 BLANE ST, PORT TOWNSEND WA	263 - F4
PRAIRIE FALLS GC / 3200 N SPOKANE ST, POST FALLS ID	353 - H3
RAINIER GC & CC / 133 DES MOINES MEM DR S, KING CO WA	286 - B6
REAMES CC / 4201 HWY 97 SOUTH, KLAMATH CO OR	338 - B13
RIVERS EDGE GC / NW MT WASHINGTON DR & HWY 97, BEND OR	332 - D3
RIVERSIDE GOLF & CC / 8105 NE 33RD DR, PORTLAND OR	310 - A4
ROGUE VALLEY CC / BLACK OAK DR & CNTRY CLUB DR, MEDFORD OR	336 - H12
ROSEBURG MUNICIPAL GC / NW GARDEN VLY & NW DOGWOOD, ROSEBURG OR	334 - D5
ROSE CITY GC / 2200 NE 71ST AV, PORTLAND OR	314 - E3
ROYAL OAKS CC / 8917 NE FOURTH PLAIN RD, VANCOUVER WA	307 - G2
SALEM GC / RIVER RD S, SALEM OR	324 - E2
SAND POINT CC / 8333 55TH AV NE, SEATTLE WA	275 - G2
SHAUGHNESSY GC / UNIV ENDOWMENT LANDS BC	156 - A5
SPOKANE CC / N COUNTRY CLUB DR, FAIRWOOD WA	346 - F8
SPRING HILL GC / 155 COUNTRY CLUB LN, BENTON CO OR	326 - C3
SUNSHINE HILLS GC / DISTRICT OF DELTA BC	156 - D7
SUN WILLOWS GC / N 20TH AV, PASCO WA	343 - D4
THREE RIVERS GC / S RIVER, KELSO WA	303 - C11
TRI CITY CC GC / W KENNEWICK AV, KENNEWICK WA	343 - B10
TUMWATER VALLEY MUNICIPAL / 4611 TUMWATER VALLEY DR, TUMWATER WA	296 - H10
TYEE VALLEY GC / 2401 S 192ND ST, SEATAC WA	290 - C2
UNIVERSITY GC / UNIV ENDOWMENT LANDS BC	156 - A4
UPLANDS GC / 3300 CADBORO BAY RD, DIST OF OAK BAY BC	257 - D5
VETERANS MEMORIAL GC / US HWY 12, WALLA WALLA WA	345 - A5
VICTORIA GC / 1110 BEACH DR, DISTRICT OF OAK BAY BC	257 - D10
WALLA WALLA CC / COUNTRY CLUB RD, WALLA WALLA WA	344 - J11
WANDERMERE LAKE GC / LITTLE SPOKANE DR & DIVISION S, SPOKANE CO	347 - A5
WAVERLEY CC / 1100 SE WAVERLY DR, CLACKAMAS CO OR	321 - H1
WEST RICHLAND GC / 4000 FALLON DR, WEST RICHLAND WA	340 - A11
WEST SEATTLE GC & REC AREA / 4470 35TH AV SW, SEATTLE WA	281 - F5
WILDWOOD GC / 21881 NW SAINT HELENS RD, MULTNOMAH CO OR	192 - A5

HOSPITALS

FEATURE NAME / City State	Page-Grid
ADVENTIST MED CTR / 10123 SE MARKET ST, PORTLAND OR	315 - H7
ALBANY GENERAL HOSP / 1046 W 6TH AV, ALBANY OR	326 - B8
ALLENMORE HOSP / 1901 S UNION AV, TACOMA WA	292 - D7
ASHLAND COMM HOSP / MAPLE ST & CHESTNUT ST, ASHLAND OR	337 - B6
AUBURN REGL MED CTR / 202 N DIVISION ST, AUBURN WA	182 - C1
BAY AREA HOSP / THOMPSON RD & N 16TH ST, COOS BAY OR	333 - F8
BONNER GENERAL HOSP / US ROUTE 2, SANDPOINT ID	244 - A2
BOUNDARY COMM HOSP / 6640 KINIKSU ST, BOUNDARY CO ID	107 - B1
BRIDGE, MARY CHILDRENS HOSP / 317 MARTIN LUTHER KING JR WY, TACOMA WA	293 - G4
BURNABY GENERAL HOSP / SMITH AV, DISTRICT OF BURNABY BC	156 - C5
CAMPBELL RIVER HOSP / HWY 19, CAMPBELL RIVER BC	92 - A1
CAPITAL MED CTR / 3900 CAPITAL MALL DR SW, OLYMPIA WA	296 - C5
CASCADE COMM HOSP / BUSH ST & 2ND ST, CENTRAL POINT OR	230 - C7
CASCADE VALLEY HOSP / 330 S STILLAGUAMISH AV, ARLINGTON WA	168 - D5
CENTRAL OREGON COMM HOSP / 1253 N CANAL BLVD, REDMOND OR	212 - D5
CENTRAL WASHINGTON HOSP / 1201 S MILLER ST, WENATCHEE WA	238 - D4
CHILDRENS HOSP & REGL MED CTR / 4800 SAND POINT WY NE, SEATTLE WA	275 - F5
CHILLIWACK GENERAL HOSP / 45600 MENHOLM, CITY OF CHILLIWACK BC	94 - C3
CLATSOP COUNTY HOME / NEHALEM HWY, CLATSOP CO OR	300 - G10
COLUMBIA BASIN HOSP / D ST SE & SOUTHEAST BL, EPHRATA WA	112 - C3
COLUMBIA DIST HOSP / 500 COLUMBIA RIVER HWY, SAINT HELENS OR	192 - B1
COLUMBIA MEM HOSP / 22ND ST, ASTORIA OR	300 - E5

FEATURE NAME / City State	Page-Grid
COQUILLE VALLEY HOSP / 5TH ST, COQUILLE OR	220 - D5
CURRY GENERAL HOSP / 94220 E 4TH ST, GOLD BEACH OR	228 - A6
DAYTON GENERAL HOSP / 1012 S 3RD ST, COLUMBIA CO WA	122 - A2
DEACONESS HOSP / CHERRY ST & S OKANOGAN AV, WENATCHEE WA	238 - D4
DEACONESS MED CTR / 800 W 5TH AV, SPOKANE WA	348 - J10
DEER PARK HOSP / 1015 E D ST, DEER PARK WA	114 - B1
DELTA HOSP / 5800 MOUNTAIN VIEW BLVD, DIST OF DELTA BC	101 - C1
DOERNBECHER CHILDRENS HOSP / 3181 SW SAM JACKSON PARK RD, PORTLAND OR	316 - E2
EAGLE RIDGE HOSP / IOCO RD & GUILDFORD WY, PORT MOODY BC	157 - A4
EAST ADAMS RURALHOSP / 903 S ADAMS ST, RITZVILLE WA	113 - C3
EASTERN STATE HOSP / OFF HWY 902, MEDICAL LAKE WA	114 - B2
EASTMORELAND HOSP / 2900 SE STEELE ST, PORTLAND OR	318 - A4
ENUMCLAW COMM HOSP / 1450 BATTERSBY AV, ENUMCLAW WA	110 - C3
EVERGREEN HOSP MED CTR / 12040 NE 128TH ST, KIRKLAND WA	171 - C7
FAIRVIEW HOSP / PRINGLE RD SE, SALEM OR	325 - A5
FORKS COMM HOSP / BOGACHIEL WY, FORKS WA	169 - C2
GEORGE DERBY HOSP / CARIBOO RD, DISTRICT OF BURNABY BC	156 - D5
GOOD SAMARITAN HOSP / 407 14TH AV SE, PUYALLUP WA	182 - B4
GOOD SAMARITAN HOSP CORVALLIS / 3600 NW SAMARITAN DR, CORVALLIS OR	327 - J4
GOOD SHEPHERD MED CTR / 610 NW 11TH ST, HERMISTON OR	129 - A1
GORGE ROAD HOSP / 62 GORGE RD E, CITY OF VICTORIA BC	256 - E6
GRACE HOSP / OAK ST, VANCOUVER BC	156 - B5
GRANDE RONDE HOSP / OFF HWY 203, UNION CO OR	130 - A2
GRAYS HARBOR COMM HOSP / CANNON ST, ABERDEEN WA	178 - A7
GRITMAN MED CTR / HWY 95 & 6TH ST, MOSCOW ID	249 - C5
GROUP HEALTH CO-OP CENTRAL HOSP / 201 16TH AV E, SEATTLE WA	278 - C4
GROUP HEALTH EASTSIDE HOSP / 2700 152ND AV NE, REDMOND WA	175 - D2
HAPPY ACRES MEM HOSP / HWY 99W, YAMHILL CO OR	204 - B1
HARBORVIEW MED CTR / 325 9TH AV, SEATTLE WA	278 - B6
HARRISON MEM HOSP / 2520 CHERRY AV, BREMERTON WA	270 - J8
HIGHLINE COMM HOSP / 16251 SYLVESTER RD SW, BURIEN WA	175 - A5
HIGHLINE COMM HOSP SPECIALTY CTR / 12844 MILITARY RD S, TUKWILA WA	288 - D1
HOLY FAMILY HOSP / 5633 N LIDGERWOOD AV, SPOKANE WA	349 - A2
HOLY FAMILY HOSP / VICTORIA DR, VANCOUVER BC	156 - C5
HOLY ROSARY MED CTR / 351 SW 9TH ST, ONTARIO OR	139 - A3
IDAHO STATE HOSP / 3100 11TH AV N, NAMPA ID	147 - C1
INTERMOUNTAIN HOSP / 303 N ALLUMBAUGH ST, BOISE ID	253 - C3
JEFFERSON GENERAL HOSP / 834 SHERIDAN ST, PORT TOWNSEND WA	263 - E6
KADLEC MED CTR / 888 SWIFT BLVD, RICHLAND WA	341 - F1
KAISER FOUNDATION HOSP PORTLAND / 5055 N GREELEY AV, PORTLAND OR	308 - D7
KAISER SUNNYSIDE MED CTR / 10180 SE SUNNYSIDE RD, CLACKAMAS CO OR	199 - D3
KEIZER MEM HOSP / CAPE ARAGO HWY & UNION AV, NORTH BEND OR	333 - G4
KENNEWICK GENERAL HOSP / W 10TH AV, KENNEWICK WA	343 - D12
KINDRED HOSP SEATTLE / 10560 5TH AV NE, SEATTLE WA	171 - B7
KLICKITAT VALLEY HOSP / 310 S ROOSEVELT AV, GOLDENDALE WA	127 - C1
KOOTENAI MED CTR / 2301 N IRONWOOD PL, COEUR D'ALENE ID	355 - D8
LADNER PRIVATE HOSP / 9321 BURNS DR, DISTRICT OF DELTA BC	101 - C1
LAKE CHELAN COMM HOSP / 503 E HIGHLAND AV, CHELAN WA	236 - D3
LAKE DIST HOSP / 700 S J ST, LAKE CO OR	152 - A2
LANGLY MEM HOSP / 52ND AV, TOWNSHIP OF LANGLEY BC	158 - C1
LANGMACK HOSP / HALSEY-SWEET HOME HWY, LINN CO OR	133 - C2
LEBANON COMM HOSP / SANTIAM HWY, LINN CO OR	133 - C1
LEGACY EMANUEL HOSP & HEALTH CTR / 2801 N GANTENBEIN AV, PORTLAND OR	313 - G3
LEGACY GOOD SAMARITAN HOSP / 1015 NW 22ND AV, PORTLAND OR	312 - D4
LEGACY MERIDIAN PK HOSP / 19300 SW 65TH AV, TUALATIN OR	199 - B4
LEGACY MOUNT HOOD MED CTR / 24800 SE STARK ST, GRESHAM OR	200 - B1
LINCOLN HOSP / 10 NICHOLLS ST, LINCOLN CO WA	114 - A2
LIONS GATE HOSP / 231 E 15TH ST, CITY OF NORTH VANCOUVER BC	255 - B5
LOWER UMPQUA HOSP / RANCH RD, REEDSPORT OR	218 - C1
MADIGAN ARMY MED CTR / 9040 GARDENER LP, PIERCE CO WA	181 - C5
MALHEUR MEM HOSP / OREGON CNTRL HWY & ALBERTA, MALHEUR CO OR	139 - A3
MAPLE RIDGE HOSP / LOUGHEED HWY & LAITY ST, MAPLE RIDGE BC	157 - C5
MASON GENERAL HOSP / 13TH ST, SHELTON WA	180 - A2
MASON, VIRGINIA MED CTR / 1100 9TH AV, SEATTLE WA	278 - A5
MCKENZIE-WILLAMETTE MED CTR / MOHAWK BLVD & N G ST, SPRINGFIELD OR	331 - A6
MERCY MED CTR / 1512 12TH AV RD, NAMPA ID	147 - B1
MERCY MED CTR / 2700 STEWART PKWY, ROSEBURG OR	334 - D3

FEATURE NAME — City State	Page-Grid
MID-COLUMBIA MED CTR — 1700 E 19TH ST, WASCO CO OR	196 - C7
MID VALLEY HOSP — 810 JASMINE, OKANOGAN CO WA	104 - C3
MISSION MEM HOPSITAL — 7324 HURD ST, DISTRICT OF MISSION BC	94 - B3
MOUNTAIN VIEW HOSP — 470 NE A ST, MADRAS OR	208 - C5
MOUNT CARMEL HOSP — 982 E COLUMBIA ST, STEVENS CO WA	106 - A2
MSA HOSP — 2179 MCCALLUM RD, DISTRICT OF MATSQUI BC	102 - B1
NICOLA VALLEY GENERAL HOSP — HWY 5, BRITISH COLUMBIA BC	95 - C1
NORTH VALLEY HOSP — 203 SOUTHWESTERN AV, OKANOGAN CO WA	104 - C2
NORTHVIEW HOSP — 8050 NORTHVIEW ST, BOISE ID	253 - C2
NORTHWEST HOSP — 1550 N 115TH ST, SEATTLE WA	171 - B7
OKANOGAN-DOUGLAS COUNTY HOSP — 507 HOSPITAL WY, OKANOGAN CO WA	104 - B3
OLYMPIC MED CTR — 939 CAROLINE ST, PORT ANGELES WA	261 - H5
OREGON HEALTH & SCIENCE UNIV HOSP — 3181 SW SAM JACKSON PARK RD, PORTLAND OR	316 - E2
OREGON STATE HOSP — 2600 CENTER ST, SALEM OR	323 - C13
OVERLAKE HOSP & MED CTR — 1035 116TH AV NE, BELLEVUE WA	175 - C2
PACIFIC GATEWAY HOSP — 1345 SE HARNEY ST, PORTLAND OR	317 - H7
PEACE ARCH HOSP — 16TH AV, CITY OF WHITE ROCK BC	158 - A2
PIONEER MEM HOSP — 1201 NE ELM ST, CROOK CO OR	213 - D4
PIONEER MEM HOSP — 564 E PIONEER DR, MORROW CO OR	128 - C2
PRINCETON GENERAL HOSP — HWY 3, BRITISH COLUMBIA BC	95 - C3
PROVIDENCE CENTRALIA HOSP — 914 S SCHEUBER RD, CENTRALIA WA	299 - C4
PROVIDENCE EVERETT MED CTR — 1321 COLBY AV, EVERETT WA	171 - C1
PROVIDENCE EVERETT MED CTR-PACIFIC — 916 PACIFIC AV, EVERETT WA	264 - C4
PROVIDENCE HOOD RIVER MEM HOSP — 811 13TH ST, HOOD RIVER OR	195 - D5
PROVIDENCE MEDFORD MED CTR — 1111 CRATER LAKE AV, MEDFORD OR	336 - D10
PROVIDENCE MILWAUKIE HOSP — 10150 SE 32ND AV, MILWAUKIE OR	199 - D3
PROVIDENCE NEWBERG HOSP — 501 N VILLA RD, NEWBERG OR	198 - D5
PROVIDENCE PORTLAND MED CTR — 4805 NE GLISAN ST, PORTLAND OR	314 - C5
PROVIDENCE SAINT VINCENT MED CTR — 9205 SW BARNES RD, WASHINGTON CO OR	199 - B1
PROVIDENCE SEASIDE HOSP — WAHANNA RD, SEASIDE OR	301 - H9
PUGET SOUND HOSP — 215 S 36TH ST, TACOMA WA	295 - H2
PUGET SOUND HOSP — BREMERTON WEST, BREMERTON WA	270 - F10
PULLMAN MEM HOSP — 1125 NE WASHINGTON AV, PULLMAN WA	249 - B5
QUEEN ALEXANDRAS HOSP — ARBUTUS RD, DISTRICT OF SAANICH BC	257 - E3
QUINCY VALLEY MED CTR — 908 10TH AV, GRANT CO WA	112 - B3
REED, MARK HOSP — 322 S BIRCH ST, MCCLEARY WA	179 - D6
RICHMOND GENERAL HOSP — WESTMINSTER HWY, CITY OF RICHMOND BC	156 - B6
RIVERVIEW HOSP — HWY 7, COQUITLAM BC	157 - A5
ROGUE VALLEY MED CTR — 2825 E BARNETT RD, MEDFORD OR	336 - H13
ROSLYN & CLE ELUM HOSP & CLINIC — OFF I-90, CLE ELUM WA	240 - B2
ROYAL COLUMBIAN HOSP — COLUMBIA ST, NEW WESTMINSTER BC	156 - D5
ROYAL JUBILEE HOSP — FORT ST, CITY OF VICTORIA BC	257 - B8
SAANICH PENINSULA HOSP — MT NEWTON CRSS RD, DIST OF CTL SAANCH BC	159 - C3
SACRED HEART MEDICAL CTR — 1255 HILYARD ST, EUGENE OR	330 - B7
SACRED HEART MED CTR — 101 W 8TH AV, SPOKANE WA	349 - A10
SAINT ALPHONSUS REGL MED CTR — 1055 N CURTIS RD, BOISE ID	253 - C3
SAINT ANTHONY HOSP — 1601 SE COURT AV, UMATILLA CO OR	129 - B1
SAINT CHARLES MED CTR — 2500 NE NEFF RD, BEND OR	332 - J6
SAINT CLARE HOSP — 11315 BRIDGEPORT WY SW, LAKEWOOD WA	181 - D4
SAINT FRANCIS HOSP — 34515 9TH AV S, FEDERAL WAY WA	182 - A1
SAINT JOHN MED CTR — 1615 DELAWARE ST, LONGVIEW WA	303 - A10
SAINT JOSEPH HOSP — 16TH AV W, VANCOUVER BC	254 - J14
SAINT JOSEPH HOSP — 2901 SQUALICUM PKWY, BELLINGHAM WA	258 - D3
SAINT JOSEPHS HOSP — 500 E WEBSTER ST, CHEWELAH WA	106 - B3
SAINT JOSEPHS HOSP — N F ST, ABERDEEN WA	178 - B7
SAINT JOSEPH MED CTR — 1717 S J ST, TACOMA WA	293 - G6
SAINT JOSEPH REGL MED CTR — 415 6TH ST, LEWISTON ID	250 - B4
SAINT LUKES REGL MED CTR — 190 E BANNOCK ST, BOISE ID	253 - D3
SAINT MARY MED CTR — 401 W POPLAR ST, WALLA WALLA WA	345 - A8
SAINT MARYS HOSP — 6TH ST, NEW WESTMINSTER BC	156 - D5
SAINT MARYS PRIORY — GOLDSTREAM AV, CITY OF COLWOOD BC	159 - B6
SAINT PAULS HOSP — COMOX ST, VANCOUVER BC	254 - F10
SAINT PETER HOSP — 413 LILLY RD NE, OLYMPIA WA	297 - D4
SAINT VINCENTS HOSP — CAMBIE ST, VANCOUVER BC	156 - B5
SALEM HOSP — 665 WINTER ST SE, SALEM OR	322 - H14
SHAUGHNESSY HOSP — CAMBIE ST, VANCOUVER BC	156 - B5
SHOSHONE MED CTR — 3 JACOBS GULCH, KELLOGG ID	115 - C2

FEATURE NAME — City State	Page-Grid
SHRINERS HOSP FOR CHILDREN — 3101 SW SAM JACKSON PARK RD, PORTLAND OR	316 - E1
SIMPSON HOSP — GLOVER RD & 88TH AV, TOWNSHIP LANGLEY BC	157 - D6
SKAGIT VALLEY HOSP — 13TH ST, MOUNT VERNON WA	260 - D13
SKYLINE HOSP — 211 SKYLINE DR, KLICKITAT CO WA	195 - D5
SNOQUALMIE VALLEY HOSP — 9575 ETHAN WADE WY SE, SNOQUALMIE WA	176 - C4
SOUTHWEST WASHINGTON MED CTR — 400 NE MOTHER JOSEPH PL, VANCOUVER WA	307 - F5
SOUTHWEST WASH MED CTR (MEM CAMPUS) — 3400 MAIN ST, VANCOUVER WA	305 - G2
SQUAMISH HOSP — TRANS CANADA HWY, SQUAMISH BC	93 - C2
STATE HOSP NORTH — 300 HOSPITAL DR, CLEARWATER CO ID	123 - C2
STEVENS HEALTHCARE — 21601 76TH AV W, EDMONDS WA	171 - B5
SURREY MEM HOSP — 9600 KING GEORGE HWY, CITY OF SURREY BC	157 - A6
SUTTER COAST HOSP — 800 E WASHINGTON BLVD, DEL NORTE CO CA	148 - B3
SWEDISH HEALTH SERVICES — 747 BROADWAY, SEATTLE WA	278 - B6
SWEDISH HEALTH SERVICES BALLARD — 5300 TALLMAN AV NW, SEATTLE WA	273 - E4
SWEDISH MED CTR - PROVIDENCE CAMPUS — 500 17TH AV, SEATTLE WA	278 - C6
TACOMA GENERAL HOSP — 315 MARTIN LUTHER KING JR WY, TACOMA WA	293 - F4
THREE RIVERS COMM HOSP — 500 RAMSEY AV, GRANTS PASS OR	335 - D11
TILLAMOOK COUNTY GENERAL HOSP — 1000 3RD ST, TILLAMOOK OR	197 - B2
TRI-STATE MEM HOSP — 1221 HIGHLAND AV, ASOTIN CO WA	250 - B4
TUALITY COMM HOSP — 335 SE 8TH AV, HILLSBORO OR	198 - D1
TUALITY FOREST GROVE HOSP — 1809 MAPLE ST, FOREST GROVE OR	198 - C1
UNITED GENERAL HOSP — 1971 HWY 20, SEDRO-WOOLLEY WA	260 - J2
US VETERANS ADMIN HOSP — STEWART PARK DR, ROSEBURG OR	334 - D5
US VETERANS HOSP — 3710 SW US VERTERANS HOSP, PORTLAND OR	316 - E2
UNIVERSITY HOSP — WESTBROOK MALL, UNIV ENDOWMENT LANDS BC	156 - A4
UNIV OF WASHINGTON MED CTR — 1959 NE PACIFIC ST, SEATTLE WA	274 - C7
VALLEY GENERAL HOSP — 14701 179TH SE, MONROE WA	110 - C1
VALLEY HOSP & MED CTR — 12606 E MISSION AV, SPOKANE VALLEY WA	350 - H7
VALLEY LANE HOSP — MONROE ST, EUGENE OR	329 - J6
VALLEY MED CTR — 2700 THREE MILE LN, MCMINNVILLE OR	198 - B7
VALLEY MED CTR — 400 S 43RD ST, RENTON WA	175 - C6
VANCOUVER GENERAL HOSP — 12TH AV W, VANCOUVER BC	254 - F13
VETERANS ADMIN HOSP — 1601 E FOURTH PLAIN BLVD, VANCOUVER WA	305 - H4
VETERANS AFFAIRS MED CTR — 3710 SW US VETERANS HOSP RD, PORTLAND OR	316 - E2
VETERANS AFFAIRS MED CTR — 4815 N ASSEMBLY ST, SPOKANE WA	348 - D3
VETERANS AFFAIRS MED CTR — 500 W FORT ST, ADA CO ID	253 - D2
VETERANS AFFAIRS MED CTR — VETERANS DR SW, PIERCE CO WA	181 - C4
VETERANS AFFAIRS PUGET SOUND — 1660 S COLUMBIAN WY, SEATTLE WA	282 - C5
VICTORIA GENERAL HOSP — QUADRA ST, CITY OF VICTORIA BC	256 - H10
VICTORIA GENERAL HOSP — VICTORIA GENERAL WY, TOWN OF VW ROYAL BC	256 - B3
WAINWRIGHT, JONATHAN M MEM VA MED — 77 WAINWRIGHT DR, WALLA WALLA WA	344 - J9
WALLA WALLA GENERAL HOSP — 1025 S 2ND AV, WALLA WALLA WA	345 - B9
WESTERN STATE HOSP — 9601 STEILACOOM BLVD SW, LAKEWOOD WA	181 - C4
WEST VALLEY MED CTR — 10TH AVE & LOGAN ST, CALDWELL ID	147 - B1
WHIDBEY GENERAL HOSP — 101 N MAIN ST, COUPEVILLE WA	167 - B4
WHITMAN HOSP & MED CTR — 1200 W FAIRVIEW, WHITMAN CO WA	122 - C1
WILLAMETTE FALLS HOSP — 1500 DIVISION ST, OREGON CITY OR	199 - D5
WOODLAND PK HOSP — 10300 NE HANCOCK ST, PORTLAND OR	315 - H4

HOTELS

FEATURE NAME — City State	Page-Grid
5TH AVENUE SUITES HOTEL — 506 SW WASHINGTON AV, PORTLAND OR	313 - F6
ABENDBLUME PENSION — 12570 RANGER RD, CHELAN CO WA	238 - A1
ABERDEEN MANSION INN B & B — 807 N M ST, ABERDEEN WA	178 - B7
ADOBE MOTEL — 1555 OREGON COAST HWY, LINCOLN CO OR	209 - A3
AERIE RESORT — TRANS CANADA HWY, BRITISH COLUMBIA BC	159 - A4
ALEXANDERS COUNTRY INN — 37515 MOUNTAIN HWY E, PIERCE CO WA	118 - C1
ALEXIS HOTEL — 1007 1ST AV, SEATTLE WA	278 - A6
ALL SEASONS RIVER INN B&B — ICICLE RD, CHELAN CO WA	238 - A2
ALPEN INN — 405 W HWY 2, CHELAN CO WA	111 - C2
AMERITEL INN — 7965 W EMERALD ST, BOISE ID	253 - C3
ANGELICAS MANSION B & B — 1321 W 9TH AV, SPOKANE WA	348 - H10
ANN STARRETT MANSION — 744 CLAY ST, PORT TOWNSEND WA	263 - H4
ASHLEY INN — 3430 OREGON COAST HWY, LINCOLN CITY OR	203 - A4
ATRIUM INN, THE — 2889 HASTINGS ST E, VANCOUVER BC	255 - D10
BARN MOTOR INN — 490 WINE COUNTRY RD, PROSSER WA	120 - C3
BAY CITY MOTOR INN — 116 N SAMISH WY, BELLINGHAM WA	258 - E9
BAYERN ON THE RIVER — 1505 ALPEN SEE STRASSE, LEAVENWORTH WA	238 - A1
BEACHWOOD BED & BREAKFAST — 671 BEACH DR, SEASIDE OR	301 - F9

FEATURE NAME — City State	Page-Grid
BEAR CREEK LODGE — 3492 HWY 55, CASCADE ID	252 - D5
BELLA VISTA RESORT MOTEL — 6904 PONDEROSA DR, BRITISH COLUMBIA BC	104 - C1
BELLEVUE HILTON — 100 112TH AV NE, BELLEVUE WA	175 - C2
BENSON, THE — 309 SW BROADWAY, PORTLAND OR	313 - F5
BEST WESTERN ABERCORN INN — 9260 BRIDGEPORT RD, CITY OF RICHMOND BC	156 - B6
BEST WESTERN EXECUTEL — 20717 INTERNATIONAL BLVD, SEATAC WA	290 - C4
BEST WESTERN MOTOR INN — 2660 AIRPORT WY, BOISE ID	253 - C3
BEST WESTERN ALADDIN MOTOR INN — 310 LONG AV, KELSO WA	303 - C7
BEST WESTERN ALADDIN MOTOR INN — 900 CAPITOL WY, OLYMPIA WA	296 - H5
BEST WESTERN BEACHFRONT INN — OFF OREGON COAST HWY, CURRY CO OR	232 - C6
BEST WESTERN BROOKINGS INN — 1143 CHETCO AV, BROOKINGS OR	232 - C6
BEST WESTERN CAPILANO INN AND SUITES — 1634 CAPILANO RD, DIST OF N VANCOUVER BC	254 - G4
BEST WESTERN CARLTON PLAZA HOTEL — 642 JOHNSON ST, CITY OF VICTORIA BC	256 - G8
BEST WESTERN CHATEAU GRANVILLE — 1100 GRANVILLE ST, VANCOUVER BC	254 - F11
BEST WESTERN COLUMBIA RIVER INN — 735 WANAPA ST, HOOD RIVER OR	194 - D6
BEST WESTERN CONNIES MOTOR INN — 323 W CEDAR ST, SANDPOINT ID	244 - A2
BEST WESTERN COTTON TREE INN — 2300 MARKET PL, MOUNT VERNON WA	260 - C9
BEST WESTERN ELLENSBURG INN — 1700 CANYON RD, KITTITAS CO WA	241 - B6
BEST WESTERN EMERALD MOTOR INN — 2306 BEACON AVE, TOWN OF SIDNEY BC	159 - C2
BEST WESTERN EXHIBITION PARK — 3475 E HASTINGS ST, VANCOUVER BC	255 - F10
BEST WESTERN GRAND MANOR INN — 925 NW GARFIELD AV, CORVALLIS OR	327 - G7
BEST WESTERN HALLMARK INN — 3000 MARINA DR, MOSES LAKE WA	242 - C3
BEST WESTERN HALLMARK RESORT — 744 SW ELIZABETH ST, NEWPORT OR	206 - B4
BEST WESTERN HARBOR PLAZA — 5691 SR 20, ISLAND CO WA	160 - C7
BEST WESTERN HERITAGE INN — 1405 SMITTYS BLVD, ADAMS CO WA	113 - C3
BEST WESTERN HERITAGE INN — 151 E MCLEOD RD, BELLINGHAM WA	258 - D2
BEST WESTERN HERITAGE INN — 1905 N WENATCHEE AV, WEST WENATCHEE WA	238 - D4
BEST WESTERN HOOD RIVER INN — 1108 E MARINA WY, HOOD RIVER OR	195 - D5
BEST WESTERN ICICLE INN — 505 W HWY 2, CHELAN CO WA	111 - C2
BEST WESTERN INN — 251 GOODFELLOW LN, MALHEUR CO OR	139 - A3
BEST WESTERN INN AT THE ROGUE — 8959 ROGUE RIVER HWY, GRANTS PASS OR	335 - E10
BEST WESTERN INNER HARBOR — 412 QUEBEC ST, CITY OF VICTORIA BC	256 - G9
BEST WESTERN INN OF THE BEACHCOMBER — OREGON COAST HWY, CURRY CO OR	228 - A7
BEST WESTERN LAKEWAY INN — 714 LAKEWAY DR, BELLINGHAM WA	258 - E7
BEST WESTERN LINCOLN SANDS — 535 NW INLET AV, LINCOLN CITY OR	203 - A4
BEST WESTERN LISTEL ODOULS HOTEL — 1300 ROBSON ST, VANCOUVER BC	254 - F9
BEST WESTERN MILL CREEK INN — 3125 RYAN DR SE, SALEM OR	325 - C1
BEST WESTERN NEW KINGS INN — 3658 MARKET ST NE, SALEM OR	323 - D11
BEST WESTERN NICOLA INN — 4025 WALTERS ST, BRITISH COLUMBIA BC	95 - C1
BEST WESTERN NORTHPOINTE MINI-SUITE — 9601 N NEWPORT HWY, SPOKANE WA	347 - A10
BEST WESTERN OCEAN VIEW RESORT — 414 N PROM, SEASIDE OR	301 - F8
BEST WESTERN OF PRINEVILLE — 1475 E 3RD ST, CROOK CO OR	213 - D5
BEST WESTERN OLYMPIC INN — 2627 S 6TH ST, KLAMATH FALLS OR	338 - G9
BEST WESTERN OLYMPIC LODGE — 140 DEL GUZZI DR, PORT ANGELES WA	261 - J6
BEST WESTERN PACIFIC HIGHWAY INN — 4646 PORTLAND RD NE, SALEM OR	323 - D6
BEST WESTERN PONDEROSA LODGE — MCKENZIE HWY, SISTERS OR	211 - D5
BEST WESTERN PONY SOLDIER MTR — 2340 CRATER LAKE HWY, MEDFORD OR	336 - D8
BEST WESTERN PONY SOLDIER MTR — HWY 82, UNION CO OR	130 - A2
BEST WESTERN RAMA INN — 1019 S PROGRESS AV, MERIDIAN ID	253 - A3
BEST WESTERN RAMA INN — 2630 SW 17TH PL, REDMOND OR	212 - D6
BEST WESTERN RAMA INN — 4430 OREGON COAST HWY, LINCOLN CITY OR	203 - A5
BEST WESTERN RICHMOND INN AND CONV — 7551 WESTMINSTER, CITY OF RICHMOND BC	156 - B6
BEST WESTERN RIO MIRADA MOTOR INN — 1603 TERRACE HEIGHTS DR, YAKIMA WA	243 - C6
BEST WESTERN RIVERTREE INN — 1257 BRIDGE ST, CLARKSTON WA	250 - B4
BEST WESTERN SAFARI SURF INN — 1070 GROVE ST, BOISE ID	253 - C3
BEST WESTERN SALBASGEON INN — 1400 HWY 101, REEDSPORT OR	218 - C2
BEST WESTERN SANDS — 1755 DAVIE ST, VANCOUVER BC	254 - E9
BEST WESTERN SEQUIM BAY LODGE — 268522 HIGHWAY 101, CLALLAM CO WA	109 - C1
BEST WESTERN SUNRIDGE INN — OLD OREGON TRAIL HWY, BAKER CO OR	138 - B1
BEST WESTERN TEMPLINS RESORT HOTEL — 414 E 1ST AV, POST FALLS ID	353 - H8
BEST WESTERN THUNDERBIRD INN — 120 W 3RD AV, SPOKANE WA	349 - A10
BEST WESTERN TRADE WINDS NORTH — 3033 N DIVISION ST, SPOKANE WA	349 - A5
BEST WESTERN TUMWATER INN — 5188 CAPITOL BLVD, TUMWATER WA	296 - G11
BEST WESTERN UNIVERSITY INN — 1516 W PULLMAN RD, LATAH CO ID	249 - C5
BEST WESTERN VILLAGE GREEN — 725 ROW RIVER RD, COTTAGE GROVE OR	215 - B7
BEST WESTERN VISTA INN — 2645 AIRPORT WY, BOISE ID	253 - C3
BEST WESTRN WALLA WALLA SUITE INN — 7 E OAK ST, WALLA WALLA WA	345 - A7

INDEX

FEATURE NAME City State	Page-Grid
BIG TREE BED & BREAKFAST 4840 FREMONT ST, SUDDEN VALLEY WA	161 - A1
BISHOP VICTORIAN GUEST SUITES 714 WASHINGTON ST, PORT TOWNSEND WA	263 - H4
BLACK BAR LODGE OFF GALICE RD, JOSEPHINE CO OR	148 - C1
BLACKBIRD LODGE 305 8TH ST, LEAVENWORTH WA	238 - A1
BLUE HORIZON HOTEL 1225 ROBSON ST, VANCOUVER BC	254 - F9
BOAT YARD INN 200 WHARF ST, LANGLEY WA	171 - A1
BOISE PARK SUITE HOTEL 424 E PARK CENTER BLVD, BOISE ID	253 - D3
BOSCH GARTEN 9846 DYE RD, CHELAN CO WA	238 - A1
CANTERBURY INN 310 GORGE RD E, CITY OF VICTORIA BC	256 - F6
CANTERBURY INN 643 OCEAN SHORES BLVD, OCEAN SHORES WA	298 - B3
CASTLE ROCK LODGE OFF THREE RIVERS HWY, TILLAMOOK CO OR	197 - C7
CASWELLS ON THE BAY 25204 SANDRIDGE RD, OCEAN PARK WA	186 - A3
CAVANAUGHS AT COLUMBIA CTR 1101 N COLUMBIA CENTER BLVD, KENNEWICK WA	342 - C8
CAVANAUGHS AT YAKIMA CTR 607 W YAKIMA AV, YAKIMA WA	243 - B6
CAVANAUGHS INN AT THE PARK 303 W NORTH RIVER DR, SPOKANE WA	349 - A8
CAVANAUGHS ON FIFTH AVENUE 1415 W 5TH AV, SEATTLE WA	278 - A5
CAVANAUGHS RIVER INN 700 N DIVISION ST, SPOKANE WA	349 - A8
CENTURY PLAZA HOTEL 1015 BARRARD ST, VANCOUVER BC	254 - F10
CHANTICLEER INN 120 GRESHAM ST, ASHLAND OR	337 - D8
CHANTICLEER INN BED & BREAKFAST 1208 FRANKLIN ST, PORT TOWNSEND WA	263 - H4
CHATEAU VICTORIA 740 BURDETT AVE, CITY OF VICTORIA BC	256 - G9
CHATEAU WESTPORT 710 W HANCOCK AV, WESTPORT WA	298 - F14
CHEVY CHASE INN CHEVY CHASE RD, JEFFERSON CO WA	166 - D7
CHICK A DEE INN AT ILWACO 120 WILLIAMS ST, PACIFIC CO WA	186 - A6
CLARION HOTEL 3000 S 176TH ST, SEATAC WA	288 - D7
CLARION HOTEL GRAND PACIFIC 450 QUEBEC ST, CITY OF VICTORIA BC	256 - G9
CLEARWATER INN 5616 W CLEARWATER AV, KENNEWICK WA	342 - F10
CLOUD CAP INN MOUNT HOOD NORTH, HOOD RIVER CO OR	202 - B4
COAST BASTION INN, THE TRANS CANADA HWY, NANAIMO BC	93 - A3
COAST VANCOUVER INN 1041 SW MARINE DR, VANCOUVER BC	156 - B5
COEUR D'ALENE INN 524 E SHERMAN AV, COEUR D'ALENE ID	355 - F11
COEUR D'ALENE RESORT 115 S 2ND AV, COEUR D'ALENE ID	355 - E12
COIT HOUSE B&B 502 N 4TH ST, SANDPOINT ID	244 - A2
COLBURN DAY LODGE OFF HWY 95, BONNER CO ID	107 - A2
COLWELL MOTOR INN 501 W 1ST AV, ADAMS CO WA	113 - C3
COMFORT INN 1100 HILTON RD, MEDFORD OR	336 - D8
COMFORT INN 2526 AIRPORT WY, BOISE ID	253 - C3
COMFORT INN 280 W APPLEWAY AV, COEUR D'ALENE ID	355 - D8
COMFORT INN 520 2ND AV N, WALLA WALLA WA	345 - A7
COMFORT INN 7801 W QUINAULT AV, KENNEWICK WA	342 - C9
COMFORT INN OFF OLD OREGON TRAIL HWY, LA GRANDE OR	130 - A2
COMPASS ROSE 508 S MAIN ST, ISLAND CO WA	167 - B4
COONEY MANSION BED & BREAKFAST 1705 FIFTH ST, COSMOPOLIS WA	178 - B7
COUNTRY WILLOWS INN 1313 CLAY ST, JACKSON CO OR	337 - G11
COUPEVILLE INN 200 COVELAND ST, COUPEVILLE WA	167 - B4
COURTYARD BY MARRIOTT 11550 NE AIRPORT WY, PORTLAND OR	193 - A7
COURTYARD BY MARRIOTT 14615 NE 29TH PL, BELLEVUE WA	175 - C2
COURTYARD BY MARRIOTT 15686 SW SEQUOIA PKWY, TIGARD OR	199 - B3
COURTYARD BY MARRIOTT 3050 NW STUCKI RD, HILLSBORO OR	199 - A1
COURTYARD BY MARRIOTT 400 ANDOVER PARK W, TUKWILA WA	289 - H6
COURTYARD BY MARRIOTT 8500 SW NIMBUS AV, BEAVERTON OR	199 - B2
COURTYARD BY MARRIOTT GATEWAY CENTER BLVD, FEDERAL WAY WA	182 - B1
COURTYARD PORTLAND LLOYD CTR 313 G4
435 NE WASCO ST, PORTLAND OR	313 - G4
CRATER LAKE LODGE RIM DR, KLAMATH CO OR	227 - C4
CROWNE PLAZA 14811 KRUSE OAKS DR, LAKE OSWEGO OR	199 - B3
CROWN PLAZA HOTEL 1113 6TH AV, SEATTLE WA	278 - A5
DAVENPORT HOTEL S POST ST & W 1ST AV, SPOKANE WA	348 - J9
DAYS INN 125 E KELLOGG RD, MOUNT VERNON WA	260 - C10
DAYS INN CITY CENTER 1414 SW 6TH AV, PORTLAND OR	313 - E7
DAYS INN STATE CAPITAL 120 COLLEGE ST SE, LACEY WA	297 - G5
DELTA PACIFIC RESORT AND CONFERENCE CTR 10251 ST EDWARDS DR, CITY OF RICHMOND BC	156 - B6
DELTA VANCOUVER INN 3500 CESSNA DR, CITY OF RICHMOND BC	156 - B6
DER RITTERHOF MOTOR INN 190 HWY 2, CHELAN CO WA	111 - C2
DESERT MOTOR INN 7702 MAIN ST, BRITISH COLUMBIA BC	104 - C1
DOUBLETREE CLUB HOTEL AT PARK CTR 475 W PARK CENTER BLVD, BOISE ID	253 - D3
DOUBLETREE HOTEL BELLEVUE 300 112TH AV SE, BELLEVUE WA	175 - C2
DOUBLETREE HOTEL COLUMBIA RIVER 1401 N HAYDEN ISLAND DR, PORTLAND OR	305 - F7

FEATURE NAME City State	Page-Grid
DOUBLETREE HOTEL-DOWNTOWN 310 SW LINCOLN ST, PORTLAND OR	313 - E7
DOUBLETREE HOTEL-DOWNTOWNER 1800 FAIRVIEW AV, BOISE ID	253 - C2
DOUBLETREE HOTEL JANTZEN BEACH 909 N HAYDEN ISLAND DR, PORTLAND OR	305 - F7
DOUBLETREE HOTEL-LLOYD CTR 1000 NE MULTNOMAH ST, PORTLAND OR	313 - H4
DOUBLE TREE HOTEL SEATTLE 18740 INTERNATIONAL BLVD, SEATAC WA	290 - D1
DOUBLETREE INN / BELLEVUE CTR 818 112TH AV NE, BELLEVUE WA	175 - C2
DOUBLETREE SUITES 16500 SOUTHCENTER PKWY, TUKWILA WA	289 - G6
DRIFTWOOD SHORES RESORT & CONF CTR 88416 1ST AV, LANE CO OR	214 - A2
D-SANDS CONDOMINIUM MOTEL 171 OREGON COAST HWY, LINCOLN CITY OR	203 - A5
DUFFY HOUSE BED & BREAKFAST 685 ARGYLE AV, SAN JUAN CO WA	101 - C2
EAGLES NEST INN 3236 E SARATOGA RD, ISLAND CO WA	167 - D7
ECHO LODGE SURISE RD, WHATCOM CO WA	160 - B2
ECONO LODGE 801 E WASHINGTON ST, SEQUIM WA	262 - F12
EDGEWATER BEACH BED & BREAKFAST 26818 EDGEWATER BLVD, KITSAP CO WA	170 - B5
EDGEWATER INN 275 E JOHNSON AV, COOS BAY OR	333 - H11
ELK LAKE LODGE CASCADE LAKES HWY, DESCHUTES CO OR	216 - A4
EMBASSY INN 520 MENZIES ST, CITY OF VICTORIA BC	256 - G10
EMBASSY SUITES 15920 W VALLEY HWY, TUKWILA WA	289 - H5
EMBASSY SUITES 20610 44TH AV W, LYNNWOOD WA	171 - B5
EMBASSY SUITES 3225 158TH AV SE, BELLEVUE WA	175 - D3
EMBASSY SUITES HOTEL-PRTLND WASHNGTON 9000 SW WASHINGTON SQUARE RD, TIGARD OR	199 - B2
EMBASSY SUITES PORTLAND 7900 NE 82ND AV, PORTLAND OR	311 - G5
EMBASSY SUITES PORTLAND DOWNTOWN 319 SW PINE ST, PORTLAND OR	313 - F5
EMPRESS HOTEL, THE 721 GOVERNMENT ST, CITY OF VICTORIA BC	256 - G9
ENZIAN MOTOR INN 590 HWY 2, CHELAN CO WA	111 - C2
EXECUTIVE HOUSE HOTEL 777 DOUGLAS ST, CITY OF VICTORIA BC	256 - G9
EXECUTIVE INN HOTEL 7211 WESMINSTER HWY, CITY OF RICHMOND BC	156 - B6
FAIRFIELD INN 2303 N 4TH ST, COEUR D'ALENE ID	355 - E8
FAIRFIELD INN BY MARRIOTT 311 N RIVERPOINT BLVD, SPOKANE WA	349 - A9
FAIRFIELD INN BY MARRIOTT 3300 S SHOSHONE ST, BOISE ID	253 - C3
FAIRFIELD INN BY MARRIOTT 7809 W QUINAULT AV, KENNEWICK WA	342 - C9
FALL RIVER LODGE N TWIN LAKES RD, DESCHUTES CO OR	142 - C1
FAR VUE MOTEL 808 E SIMCOE DR, KLICKITAT CO WA	127 - C1
FIDALGO COUNTRY INN 1250 HWY 20, ANACORTES WA	259 - J6
FLAGSHIP INN 4320 KITSAP WY, BREMERTON WA	270 - E10
FOTHERINGHAM HOUSE 2128 W 2ND AV, SPOKANE WA	348 - G9
FOUR SEASONS HOTEL 791 W GEORGIA ST, VANCOUVER BC	254 - G10
FOUR SEASONS OLYMPIC HOTEL 411 UNIVERSITY ST, SEATTLE WA	278 - A5
FRIDAY HARBOR HOUSE 130 WEST ST, FRIDAY HARBOR WA	101 - C2
F W HASTINGS HOUSE OLD CONSULATE 313 WALKER ST, PORT TOWNSEND WA	263 - G5
GALICE RESORT 11744 GALICE RD, JOSEPHINE CO OR	149 - A1
GARDEN ISLE GUEST COTTAGES 207 NW COVELAND ST, COUPEVILLE WA	167 - B4
GEORGIAN COURT HOTEL, THE 773 BEATTY ST, VANCOUVER BC	254 - F11
GOLD BEACH RESORT 29232 S ELLENSBURG AV, GOLD BEACH OR	228 - A6
GOVERNOR HOTEL 611 SW 10TH AV, PORTLAND OR	313 - E6
GREEN GABLES INN 850 BLANSHARD ST, CITY OF VICTORIA BC	256 - G9
GREEN GABLES INN 922 BONSELLA, WALLA WALLA WA	345 - B6
GREGORYS MCFARLAND HOUSE B&B 601 FOSTER AV, COEUR D'ALENE ID	355 - F10
GREY GULL 651 OCEAN SHORES BLVD, OCEAN SHORES WA	298 - B3
GREYWOLF INN 395 KEELER RD, SEQUIM WA	262 - J13
HAMPTON INN 15 NE BUTLER RD, BEND OR	217 - C2
HAMPTON INN 3039 NE 181ST AV, GRESHAM OR	200 - A1
HAMPTON INN 3270 S SHOSHONE ST, BOISE ID	253 - C3
HAMPTON INN 3985 BENNETT DR, WHATCOM CO WA	158 - D7
HAMPTON INN & SUITES SEATTLE NORTH LYNN 19324 ALDERWOOD MALL PKWY, LYNNWOOD WA	171 - B5
HAMPTON SPOKANE 2010 S ASSEMBLY RD, SPOKANE CO WA	348 - D13
HARBORSIDE INN 330 BENEDICT ST, PORT TOWNSEND WA	263 - G5
HARBOUR COURT HWY 14, BRITISH COLUMBIA BC	101 - A2
HARBOUR TOWERS HOTEL 345 QUEBEC ST, CITY OF VICTORIA BC	256 - F9
HARMONY FALLS LODGE SPIRIT LAKE EAST, SKAMANIA CO WA	118 - B2
HARRIMAN LODGE WESTSIDE RD, KLAMATH CO OR	231 - A6
HARRISON HOT SPRINGS HOTEL 100 ESPLANADE AV, DISTRICT OF KENT BC	94 - C3
HEATHMAN HOTEL 1001 SW BROADWAY, PORTLAND OR	313 - E6
HEATHMAN LODGE 7801 NE GREENWOOD DR, VANCOUVER WA	307 - E2
HELMS INN 600 DOUGLAS ST, CITY OF VICTORIA BC	256 - G10
HERON IN LA CONNER 117 MAPLE AV, SKAGIT CO WA	167 - D1
HILTON GARDEN INN SEATTLE-RENTON 1801 E VALLEY RD, RENTON WA	175 - C5

FEATURE NAME City State	Page-Grid
HOLIDAY INN 3300 VISTA AV, BOISE ID	253 - C3
HOLIDAY INN-AIRPORT 8439 NE COLUMBIA BLVD, PORTLAND OR	311 - G7
HOLIDAY INN CROWNE PLAZA 14811 KRUSE OAKS BLVD, LAKE OSWEGO OR	199 - B3
HOLIDAY INN EXPRESS 1095 E WASHINGTON ST, SEQUIM WA	262 - F12
HOLIDAY INN EXPRESS 1100 PRICE RD SE, ALBANY OR	326 - H8
HOLIDAY INN EXPRESS 1121 BAY ST, PORT ORCHARD WA	270 - J14
HOLIDAY INN EXPRESS 1190 SE BISHOP BLVD, PULLMAN WA	249 - B5
HOLIDAY INN EXPRESS 1745 E KITTLESON, GRANT CO WA	242 - D3
HOLIDAY INN EXPRESS 19801 NE 7TH, POULSBO WA	170 - B7
HOLIDAY INN EXPRESS 2209 E SHERMAN AV, COEUR D'ALENE ID	355 - H11
HOLIDAY INN EXPRESS 2475 OREGON COAST HWY, FLORENCE OR	214 - B3
HOLIDAY INN EXPRESS 2613 S VISTA AV, BOISE ID	253 - C3
HOLIDAY INN EXPRESS 4220 W 27TH PL, KENNEWICK WA	343 - B14
HOLIDAY INN EXPRESS 6311 33RD AV NE, SNOHOMISH CO WA	168 - C7
HOLIDAY INN EXPRESS 801 N DIVISION, SPOKANE WA	349 - A8
HOLIDAY INN EXPRESS BELLINGHAM 4160 GUIDE MERIDIAN, BELLINGHAM WA	158 - D7
HOLIDAY INN EXPRESS GRANTS PASS 105 NE AGNESS AV, GRANTS PASS OR	335 - H10
HOLIDAY INN EXPRESS HOTEL 2500 S 6TH ST, KLAMATH FALLS OR	338 - G9
HOLIDAY INN EXPRESS OF LONGVIEW 723 7TH AV, LONGVIEW WA	303 - A11
HOLIDAY INN EXPRESS WOODBURN 2887 NEWBERG HWY, WOODBURN OR	205 - B2
HOLIDAY INN HOTEL & CONF CTR 101 128TH ST SE, SNOHOMISH CO WA	171 - C4
HOLIDAY INN HOTEL AND SUITES 1110 HOWE ST, VANCOUVER BC	254 - F11
HOLIDAY INN ISSAQUAH 1801 12TH AV NW, ISSAQUAH WA	175 - D3
HOLIDAY INN OF YAKIMA 9 N 9TH ST, YAKIMA WA	243 - C6
HOLIDAY INN ONTARIO-OREGON 1249 TAPADERA AV, ONTARIO OR	139 - A3
HOLIDAY INN PORTLAND-DOWNTOWN 1021 NE GRAND AV, PORTLAND OR	313 - G4
HOLIDAY INN PORTLAND-SOUTH 25425 SW 95TH AV, WILSONVILLE OR	199 - B5
HOLIDAY INN SEATAC 17338 INTERNATIONAL BLVD, SEATAC WA	288 - D7
HOLIDAY INN SEATTLE-BOEING FIELD 11244 TUKWILA INTRNATIONL BL, TUKWILA WA	286 - D6
HOLIDAY INN SELECT 2300 S EVERGREEN PARK DR SW, OLYMPIA WA	296 - F7
HOLIDAY INN SELECT SEATTLE-RENTON 1 S GRADY WY, RENTON WA	175 - C5
HOLIDAY INN VICTORIA 3020 BLANSHARD ST, CITY OF VICTORIA BC	256 - G6
HOLLAND HOUSE INN 595 MICHIGAN ST, CITY OF VICTORIA BC	256 - G10
HOLLY HILL HOUSE 611 POLK, PORT TOWNSEND WA	263 - H4
HOMEWOOD SUITES BY HILTON 701 SE COLUMBIA SHORES BLVD, VANCOUVER WA	305 - J7
HOTEL MCCALL 1101 N 3RD ST, MCCALL ID	251 - C5
HOTEL MONACO 1101 4TH AV, SEATTLE WA	278 - A6
HOTEL OLYMPIAN LEGION WY, OLYMPIA WA	296 - H5
HOTEL-PENSION ANNA 926 COMMERCIAL ST, LEAVENWORTH WA	238 - A1
HOTEL PLANTER 715 S FIRST ST, LA CONNER WA	167 - D1
HOTEL RIO VISTA 285 RIVERSIDE AV, OKANOGAN CO WA	104 - A2
HOTEL VANCOUVER 900 W GEORGIA ST, VANCOUVER BC	254 - G10
HOTEL VINTAGE PARK 1100 5TH AV, SEATTLE WA	278 - A6
HOWARD JOHNSON PLAZA HOTEL 3105 PINE ST, EVERETT WA	265 - F4
HYATT REGENCY BELLEVUE 900 BELLEVUE WY NE, BELLEVUE WA	175 - C2
HYATT REGENCY VANCOUVER 655 BURRARD ST, VANCOUVER BC	254 - G10
ILLAHE LODGE OFF NFD RD 33, CURRY CO OR	148 - B1
INN AMERICA 702 21ST ST, LEWISTON ID	250 - C4
INN AT EAGLE CREST 1522 CLINE FALLS RD, DESCHUTES CO OR	212 - C5
INN AT FRIDAY HARBOR SUITES 680 SPRING ST, FRIDAY HARBOR WA	101 - C2
INN AT FRIDAY HARBOR, THE 410 SPRING ST, FRIDAY HARBOR WA	101 - C2
INN AT LAKE STEVENS 1513 MITCHELL RD, LAKE STEVENS WA	171 - D1
INN AT LANGLEY 400 FIRST ST, LANGLEY WA	171 - A1
INN AT PENN COVE 702 N MAIN ST, ISLAND CO WA	167 - B4
INN AT PRIEST LAKE 1 EAST SHORE RD, BONNER CO ID	107 - A2
INN AT SEMI-AH-MOO A WYNDHAM 9565 SEMIAHMOO PKWY, BLAINE WA	158 - B3
INN AT SOAP LAKE 226 E MAIN AV, GRANT CO WA	112 - C2
INN AT SPANISH HEAD 4009 OREGON COAST HWY, LINCOLN CITY OR	203 - A5
INN AT THE MARKET 86 PINE ST, SEATTLE WA	277 - J5
INN OF THE 7TH MTN 18575 CENTURY DRIVE HWY, DESCHUTES CO OR	217 - A4
JACKSONVILLE INN 175 E CALIFORNIA ST, JACKSON CO OR	149 - B2
JAMES HOUSE, THE 1238 WASHINGTON ST, PORT TOWNSEND WA	263 - H5
J J SHAW HOUSE B&B INN 1411 W FRANKLIN ST, BOISE ID	253 - C2
JUAN DE FUCA COTTAGES 182 MARINE DR, CLALLAM CO WA	166 - A5
KENNEWICK SILVER CLOUD INN 7901 W QUINALT AV, KENNEWICK WA	342 - C9
LA CONNER CHANNEL LODGE 205 N 1ST ST, LA CONNER WA	167 - D1
LA CONNER COUNTRY INN 107 S 2ND ST, LA CONNER WA	167 - D1

FEATURE NAME City State	Page-Grid
LANDMARK HOTEL AND CONFERENCE CENTRE 1400 ROBSON ST, VANCOUVER BC	254 - E9
LEAVENWORTH VILLAGE INN 1016 COMMERCIAL ST, LEAVENWORTH WA	238 - A1
LEWIS RIVER INN 1100 LEWIS RIVER RD, CLARK CO WA	192 - C1
LINDERHOF MOTOR INN 690 HWY 2, CHELAN CO WA	111 - C2
LOGANITA LODGE W SHORE DR, WHATCOM CO WA	160 - B1
LONGMIRE HOTEL NATIONAL PARK HWY, PIERCE CO WA	185 - B5
LONSDALE QUAY HOTEL 123 CARRIE CATES CT, CTY OF N VANCOUVR BC	255 - B7
LYTLE HOUSE BED & BREAKFAST 509 CHENAULT, HOQUIAM WA	178 - A7
MADISON-A RENAISSANCE HOTEL, THE 515 MADISON ST, SEATTLE WA	278 - A6
MALLORY HOTEL 729 SW 15TH AV, PORTLAND OR	312 - E6
MANRESA CASTLE 7TH & SHERIDAN, PORT TOWNSEND WA	263 - E6
MARIAL LODGE MARIAL, CURRY CO OR	140 - C3
MARIANNA STOLTZ HOUSE B & B 427 W INDIANA AV, SPOKANE WA	348 - H7
MARINA INN 3300 COMMERCIAL AV, ANACORTES WA	259 - H4
MARKS CREEK LODGE OCHOCO HWY, CROOK CO OR	136 - A2
MARY KAYS WHALEY MANSION 415 3RD ST, CHELAN CO WA	236 - D4
MAYFLOWER PARK HOTEL 405 OLIVE WY, SEATTLE WA	277 - J5
MEANY, EDMOND HOTEL 4507 BROOKLYN AV NE, SEATTLE WA	274 - C5
METROPOLITAN HOTEL 645 HAWE ST, VANCOUVER BC	254 - G10
MIDWAY INN 2909 WHEATON WY, BREMERTON WA	270 - J8
MINAM LODGE OFF MILL CREEK RD, WALLOWA CO OR	130 - B2
MR SANDMAN MOTEL OFF OLD OREGON TRAIL HWY, UNION CO OR	130 - A2
MONARCH HOTEL 12566 SE 93RD AV, CLACKAMAS CO OR	199 - D3
MONET 36 2ND ST, ASHLAND OR	337 - C8
MORICAL HOUSE GARDEN INN 668 N MAIN ST, ASHLAND OR	337 - B5
MOUNT ASHLAND INN 550 MOUNT ASHLAND SKI RD, JACKSON CO OR	234 - D6
MOUNT BAKER LODGE MOUNT BAKER HWY, WHATCOM CO WA	103 - A1
MOUNT HOOD INN 111 NE AGNESS AV, GRANTS PASS OR	335 - J10
MOUNT VERNON 300 W COLLEGE WY, MOUNT VERNON WA	260 - C10
MOUNT VERNON TRAVELODGE 1910 FREEWAY DR, MOUNT VERNON WA	260 - B10
NISQUALLY LODGE 31609 MOUNTAIN HWY E, PIERCE CO WA	118 - C3
NITES INN 1200 S RUBY ST, ELLENSBURG WA	241 - B6
NORTH GARDEN INN 1014 N GARDEN, BELLINGHAM WA	258 - D7
NOTARAS LODGE 14 CANNA ST S, SOAP LAKE WA	112 - C2
OBERTAL MOTOR INN 922 COMMERCIAL ST, LEAVENWORTH WA	238 - A1
OCANADA HOUSE 1114 BARCLAY ST, VANCOUVER BC	254 - F10
OCEAN POINTE RESORT HOTEL AND SPA 45 SONGHEEDS ST, CITY OF VICTORIA BC	256 - G9
OLDE ENGLAND INN 429 LAMPSON ST, TOWN OF ESQUIMALT BC	256 - D9
OLD MORRIS FARM BED & BREAKFAST 105 W MORRIS RD, ISLAND CO WA	167 - C4
OWYHEE PLAZA HOTEL 1109 MAIN ST, BOISE ID	253 - C3
PACIFIC PALISADES HOTEL 1277 ROBSON ST, VANCOUVER BC	254 - F11
PACIFIC PLAZA HOTEL 400 SPRING ST, SEATTLE WA	278 - A6
PALACE HOTEL 1004 WATER ST, PORT TOWNSEND WA	263 - G5
PAN PACIFIC HOTEL VANCOUVER 999 CANADA PL, VANCOUVER BC	254 - G9
PARADISE RANCH RESORT MONUMENT DR&BROOKSIDE BL, JOSEPHINE CO OR	229 - B4
PARKHILL HOTEL 1160 DAVIE ST, VANCOUVER BC	254 - F10
PEAR TREE MOTEL 3730 FERN VALLEY RD, PHOENIX OR	234 - B2
PINE RIDGE INN 1200 CENTURY DRIVE HWY, DESCHUTES CO OR	217 - A4
PIONEER SQUARE HOTEL 77 YESLER WY, SEATTLE WA	278 - A6
PLAZA 500 HOTEL 500 W 12TH AVE, VANCOUVER BC	156 - B5
PLAZA SUITE HOTEL 409 S COLE RD, BOISE ID	253 - C3
POLYNESIAN CONDOMINIUM RESORT 615 OCEAN SHORES BLVD, OCEAN SHORES WA	298 - B3
PONY SOLDIER MOTOR INN 1716 MAIN ST, LEWISTON ID	250 - C4
PONY SOLDIER MOTOR INN 325 E MAIN ST, WALLA WALLA WA	345 - B7
POPLARS MOTEL 6404 67TH ST, BRITISH COLUMBIA BC	104 - C1
PORTLAND HILTON 921 SW 6TH AV, PORTLAND OR	313 - E6
PORTLAND MARRIOTT HOTEL 1401 SW NAITO PKWY, PORTLAND OR	313 - F7
QUALITY INN 350 OLD HOPE PRNCTN HY, BRTSH COLUMBIA BC	95 - A3
QUALITY INN 7001 NE HIGHWAY 99, CLARK CO WA	192 - C4
QUALITY INN 9920 S TACOMA WY, LAKEWOOD WA	181 - D4
QUALITY INN SUITES 2717 VISTA AV, BOISE ID	253 - C3
QUALITY INN BARON SUITES 100 E KELLOGG RD, BELLINGHAM WA	158 - D7
QUALITY INN BREMERTON 4303 KITSAP WY, BREMERTON WA	270 - E10
QUALITY INN CONF CTR 700 PORT DR, CLARKSTON WA	250 - B4
QUALITY INN FLAGSHIP 2520 ASHLAND ST, ASHLAND OR	337 - G9
QUALITY INN HARBOUR VIEW 455 BELLEVILLE ST, CITY OF VICTORIA BC	256 - G9
QUALITY INN OAKWOOD 7919 N DIVISION ST, SPOKANE WA	347 - A13

FEATURE NAME City State	Page-Grid
QUALITY INN PRDS CRK MOTOR INN 1050 SE BISHOP BLVD, PULLMAN WA	249 - B5
QUALITY INN THE DALLES 2114 W 6TH ST, THE DALLES OR	196 - C7
QUALITY INN VALLEY SUITES 8923 E MISSION AV, SPOKANE VALLEY WA	350 - D7
QUALITY INN WADDLING DOG 2476 MT NEWTON RD, CENTRAL SAANICH BC	159 - C3
QUALITY INN-YAKIMA VALLEY 12 E VALLEY MALL BLVD, YAKIMA WA	243 - C7
QUALITY NEW REDMOND HOTEL 521 SW 6TH ST, REDMOND OR	212 - D5
QUEEN VICTORIA INN 655 DOUGLAS ST, CITY OF VICTORIA BC	256 - G9
RADISSON HOTEL 17001 INTERNATIONAL BLVD, SEATAC WA	288 - C6
RADISSON PRESIDENT HOTEL 8181 CAMBIE RD, CITY OF RICHMOND BC	156 - B6
RAINBOW LODGE BAKER CREEK RD, YAMHILL CO OR	125 - B2
RAMADA HUNTINGTON MANOR 330 QUEBEC ST, CITY OF VICTORIA BC	256 - G9
RAMADA INN 2611 E E ST, TACOMA WA	293 - J7
RAMADA INN BELLINGHAM 215 SAMISH WAY, BELLINGHAM WA	258 - E8
RAMADA INN-PORTLAND 6221 NE 82ND AV, PORTLAND OR	311 - F6
RAMADA PLAZA CONVENTION SUITES 621 21ST ST, LEWISTON ID	250 - C4
RAMADA PLAZA HOTEL 1441 NE 2ND AV, PORTLAND OR	313 - G4
RAVENSCROFT 533 QUINCY ST, PORT TOWNSEND WA	263 - H4
RED LION BAYSHORE INN 221 N LINCOLN ST, PORT ANGELES WA	261 - F4
RED LION HOTEL AT THE QUAY 100 COLUMBIA ST, VANCOUVER WA	305 - F6
RED LION HOTEL RIVERSIDE 2900 CHINDEN BLVD, BOISE ID	253 - C3
RED LION INN 1255 N WENATCHEE AV, WENATCHEE WA	238 - D4
RED LION INN 1313 N BAYSHORE DR, COOS BAY OR	333 - H9
RED LION INN 200 N RIVERSIDE AV, MEDFORD WA	336 - D11
RED LION INN 3612 S 6TH ST, ALTAMONT OR	338 - H10
RED LION INN 510 KELSO DR, KELSO WA	303 - E7
RED LION INN 818 N 1ST ST, YAKIMA WA	243 - B6
RED LION INN AT SALMON CREEK 1500 NE 134TH ST, CLARK CO WA	192 - C4
RED LION INN- COLISEUM 1225 N THUNDERBIRD WY, PORTLAND OR	313 - F4
RED LION INN EUGENE-SPRINGFIELD 3280 GATEWAY RD, LANE CO OR	133 - A3
RED LION INN-HANFORD HOUSE 802 GEORGE WASHINGTON WY, RICHLAND WA	341 - G1
RED LION INN INDIAN HILLS 304 SE NYE AV, UMATILLA CO OR	129 - B1
RED LION INN-NORTH 1415 NE 3RD ST, BEND OR	332 - F6
RED LION INN-YAKIMA VALLEY 1507 N 1ST ST, YAKIMA WA	243 - B6
RED LION PASCO 2525 N 20TH AV, PASCO WA	343 - D5
RED LION SPOKANE VALLEY 1100 N SULLIVAN RD, SPOKANE VALLEY WA	351 - C7
REDWOOD OCEANFRONT RESORT A ST & FRONT ST, CRESCENT CITY CA	148 - B3
RESIDENCE INN 15200 SW BANGY RD, LAKE OSWEGO OR	199 - B3
RESIDENCE INN BY MARRIOTT PORTLAND 1710 NE MULTNOMAH ST, PORTLAND OR	313 - J4
RESIDENCE INN BY MARRIOTT SEATTLE 14455 NE 29TH PL, BELLEVUE WA	175 - C2
RESIDENCE INN BY MARRIOTT SEATTLE 16201 WEST VALLEY HWY, TUKWILA WA	289 - H5
RESIDENCE INN BY MARRIOTT SEATTLE 800 FAIRVIEW AV N, SEATTLE WA	278 - A3
RESIDENCE INN BY MARRIOTT-SEATTLE NRTH 18200 ALDERWOOD MALL PKWY, LYNNWOOD WA	171 - B5
RESIDENCE INN PORTLAND - N VANCOUVER 8005 NE PARKWAY DR, VANCOUVER WA	307 - F1
RESORT AT THE MOUNTAIN, THE 68010 E FAIRWAY AV, CLACKAMAS CO OR	201 - C5
RIDDLE LODGE HELLS CANYON RECREATION AREA, IDAHO CO ID	131 - B1
RIDGEWAY BED & BREAKFAST 1292 MCLEAN RD, SKAGIT CO WA	260 - B12
RIDPATH HOTEL 515 W SPRAGUE AVE, SPOKANE WA	348 - J9
RIVERBEND INN 4105 N RIVERBEND AV, POST FALLS ID	353 - C8
RIVERHOUSE MOTOR INN 3075 N HWY 97, BEND OR	332 - F4
RIVERPLACE HOTEL 1510 SW HARBOR WY, PORTLAND OR	313 - F7
RODEWAY INN 3710 MERIDIAN ST, BELLINGHAM WA	258 - C2
ROGUE REGENCY INN 2345 CRATER LAKE HWY, MEDFORD OR	336 - D8
ROMEO INN 295 IDAHO ST, ASHLAND OR	337 - D8
ROOSEVELT HOTEL 1531 7TH AV, SEATTLE WA	278 - A5
ROYAL SCOT INN 425 QUEBEC ST, CITY OF VICTORIA BC	256 - G10
RUN OF THE RIVER 9308 E LEAVENWORTH, CHELAN CO WA	238 - A1
SAHARA COURTYARD INN 6204 67TH ST, BRITISH COLUMBIA BC	104 - C1
SALISH LODGE, THE 6501 RAILROAD AV SE, SNOQUALMIE WA	176 - C4
SCANDINAVIAN GARDENS INN B & B 1610 CALIFORNIA AV S, LONG BEACH WA	186 - A5
SCENIC LODGE RATHDRUM, KOOTENAI CO ID	115 - A1
SCHNAUZER CROSSING 4421 LAKEWAY DR, WHATCOM CO WA	161 - A1
SEASONS MOTEL MORTON RD & HWY 12, LEWIS CO WA	118 - B2
SEATTLE HILTON 1301 6TH AV, SEATTLE WA	278 - A5
SEATTLE HILTON 17620 INTERNATIONAL BLVD, SEATAC WA	288 - D7
SEATTLE MARRIOTT SEATAC 3201 S 176TH ST, SEATAC WA	288 - D7
SEATTLE UNIVERSITY LODGE SUN TOP, PIERCE CO WA	111 - A3
SEQUIM WEST INN 740 W WASHINGTON ST, SEQUIM WA	262 - C11

FEATURE NAME City State	Page-Grid
SHELBURNE INN 4415 PACIFIC HWY, PACIFIC CO WA	186 - A6
SHERATON PORTLAND HOTEL 8235 NE AIRPORT WY, PORTLAND OR	311 - G4
SHERATON SEATTLE HOTEL & TOWERS 1400 6TH AV, SEATTLE WA	278 - A5
SHERATON TACOMA HOTEL 1320 BROADWAY PZ, TACOMA WA	293 - H5
SHILO INN 1609 E HARBOR DR, WARRENTON OR	188 - B2
SHILO INN 1819 E KITTLESON, MOSES LAKE WA	242 - D3
SHILO INN 702 W APPLEWAY, COEUR D'ALENE ID	355 - D7
SHILO INN 923 E 3RD AV, SPOKANE WA	349 - B10
SHILO INN CONF & FAMILY RESORT 707 OCEAN SHORES BLVD, OCEAN SHORES WA	298 - B3
SHILO INN-HAZEL DELL 13206 HWY 99, CLARK CO WA	192 - C5
SHILO INN PORTLAND 11707 NE AIRPORT WY, PORTLAND OR	193 - A7
SHILO INN-RIVERSHORE 50 COMSTOCK ST, RICHLAND WA	341 - H3
SHILO INN SALEM SUITES 3304 MARKET ST NE, SALEM OR	323 - E12
SHILO INN-SEASIDE OCEANFRONT RESORT 30 N PROM, SEASIDE OR	301 - F8
SHILO INN SUITES-BOISE 4111 BROADWAY AV, BOISE ID	253 - D3
SHILO INN SUITES HOTEL 3105 O B RILEY RD, BEND OR	332 - F3
SHILO INN-TILLAMOOK 2515 N MAIN, TILLAMOOK CO OR	197 - C1
SHILO SUITES HOTEL 2500 ALMOND ST, KLAMATH FALLS OR	338 - C4
SILVERDALE HOTEL ON THE BAY 3073 NW BUCKLIN HILL RD, SILVERDALE WA	174 - B1
SORRENTO HOTEL 900 MADISON ST, SEATTLE WA	278 - A6
SPIRIT LAKE LODGE HWY 504, SKAMANIA WA	190 - C1
STATES INN 2039 W VALLEY RD, SAN JUAN CO WA	101 - C2
STAY N SAVE MOTOR INN 10551 ST EDWARDS DR, CITY OF RICHMOND BC	156 - B6
STAY N SAVE MOTOR INN 3233 MAPLE ST, DISTRICT OF SAANICH BC	256 - G5
STEWARD LODGE 805 W FIRST ST, CLE ELUM WA	240 - B2
SUMMITT INN AT SNOQUALMIE PASS SR 906, KITTITAS WA	111 - A2
SUN COUNTRY INN 1700 N 1ST ST, YAKIMA WA	243 - B6
SUN MOUNTAIN LODGE PATTERSON LAKE RD, OKANOGAN CO WA	104 - A2
SUNRISE LODGE SUNRISE PARK RD, PIERCE CO WA	185 - D2
SUNSET INN TRAVEL APARTMENTS 1111 BURNABY ST, VANCOUVER BC	254 - F10
SUPER 8 MOTEL LONG BEACH 500 OCEAN BEACH BLVD, LONG BEACH WA	186 - A5
SURREY INN 9850 KING GEORGE, CITY OF SURREY BC	157 - A6
SUTTON PLACE HOTEL, THE 845 BURRARD ST, VANCOUVER BC	254 - F10
SWANS HOTEL 506 PANDORA AVE, CITY OF VICTORIA BC	256 - G8
SWAUK LODGE OFF HWY 97, KITTITAS CO WA	238 - A6
THREE MEADOWS LODGE OFF VIEW POINT RD, CLEARWATER CO ID	123 - C1
THREE RIVERS INN 210 BALL ST, SEDRO-WOOLLEY WA	161 - C5
TIMBER LODGE MOTEL 301 W FIRST ST, CLE ELUM WA	240 - B2
TOLSTOJ SOKOL LODGE RICHARDSONS GAP RD, LINN CO OR	133 - C1
TOPPENISH INN MOTEL 515 S ELM ST, TOPPENISH WA	120 - A2
TRAVELODGE 101 N SAMISH WY, BELLINGHAM WA	258 - E8
TRAVELODGE CENTRALIA 1049 ECKERSON RD, CENTRALIA WA	299 - D2
TRAVELODGE VANCOUVER 11506 NE 3RD AV, CLARK CO WA	192 - C5
TRAVELODGE VICTORIA 229 GORGE RD E, CITY OF VICTORIA BC	256 - F7
TRAVELODGE WENATCHEE 1004 N WENATCHEE AV, WENATCHEE WA	238 - D4
TROUT LODGE OFF HWY 12, YAKIMA CO WA	119 - B1
TUDOR INN BED & BREAKFAST 1108 S OAK, PORT ANGELES WA	261 - E5
TU TU TUN LODGE 96550 NORTH BANK ROGUE, CURRY CO OR	228 - B4
TWICKENHAM HOUSE INN BED & BREAKFAST 5023 LANGLEY RD, ISLAND CO WA	171 - A2
TYEE LODGE OCEANFRONT B & B 4905 NW FALL ST, NEWPORT OR	206 - B3
UNION CLUB OF BRITISH COLUMBIA 805 GORDON ST, CITY OF VICTORIA BC	256 - G9
UNIV PLAZA HOTEL 400 NE 45TH ST, SEATTLE WA	274 - B5
VAL-U INN 805 LAKEWAY DR, BELLINGHAM WA	258 - E7
VICTORIAN BED & BREAKFAST 602 N MAIN ST, ISLAND CO WA	167 - B4
VICTORIA REGENT HOTEL, THE 1234 WHARF ST, CITY OF VICTORIA BC	256 - G9
VILLAGE INN MOTEL 229 COTTAGE AV, CHELAN CO WA	238 - C2
VILLA ISOLA B&B INN 5489 S COLES RD, ISLAND CO WA	171 - A1
WALL CENTRE GARDEN HOTEL 1088 BURRARD ST, VANCOUVER BC	254 - F10
WALLOWA LAKE LODGE JOSEPH-WALLOWA LAKE HWY, WALLOWA CO OR	130 - C2
WARWICK HOTEL 401 LENORA ST, SEATTLE WA	277 - J5
WATERFRONT CENTRE HOTEL 900 CANADA PLACE WY, VANCOUVER BC	254 - G9
WAUMILLA LODGE OLYMPIC HOT SPRINGS RD, CLALLAM CO WA	109 - B1
WAVERLY PLACE BED & BREAKFAST 709 W WAVERLY PL, SPOKANE WA	348 - J5
WEDGEWOOD HOTEL 845 HORNBY ST, VANCOUVER BC	254 - F10
WEINHARD HOTEL OFF HWY 12, COLUMBIA CO WA	122 - A2
WEST COAST BELLEVUE HOTEL 625 116TH AV NE, BELLEVUE WA	175 - C2
WESTCOAST SEATAC HOTEL 18220 INTERNATIONAL BLVD, SEATAC WA	290 - D2

430 HOTELS

POINTS OF INTEREST

MUSEUMS

FEATURE NAME / City State	Page-Grid
WESTCOAST TYEE HOTEL 500 TYEE DR, TUMWATER WA	296 - G11
WESTCOAST WENATCHEE CTR HOTEL 201 N WENATCHEE AV, WENATCHEE WA	239 - A4
WESTIN BAYSHORE, THE 1601 W GEORGIA ST, VANCOUVER BC	254 - F9
WESTIN HOTEL SEATTLE 1900 5TH AV, SEATTLE WA	277 - J5
WILDHORSE RESORT & CASINO I-84 EXIT 216, UMATILLA CO OR	129 - B1
WILLCOX HOUSE 2390 TEKIU RD NW, KITSAP CO WA	173 - C3
WINDMILL INN OF MEDFORD 1950 BIDDLE RD, MEDFORD OR	336 - D9
WINDMILLS ASHLAND HILLS INN 2525 ASHLAND ST, ASHLAND OR	337 - G9
WOODLANDER INN 1500 ATLANTIC ST, WOODLAND WA	189 - D7
WOODMARK HOTEL ON LAKE WASHINGTON, THE 1200 CARILLON PT, KIRKLAND WA	175 - C1
WOODS HOUSE BED & BREAKFAST INN 333 N MAIN ST, ASHLAND OR	337 - C6
WYNDHAM GARDEN HOTEL BOTHELL 19333 NORTH CREEK PKWY, BOTHELL WA	171 - C6
WYNDHAM HOTEL SEATTLE-TACOMA 18118 INTERNATIONAL BLVD, SEATAC WA	290 - D1

MILITARY INSTALLATIONS

FEATURE NAME / City State	Page-Grid
ARMORY JOHN ADAMS ST, OREGON CITY OR	199 - D5
ARMORY NE 28TH AV, HILLSBORO OR	198 - D1
ARMORY N HARRISON ST, NEWBERG OR	198 - D5
ARMORY S 11TH ST & S YAKIMA AV, TACOMA WA	293 - G5
ARMORY SOUTH SHORE BLVD, LAKE OSWEGO OR	320 - E7
BOARDMAN BOMBING RANGE BOMBING RANGE RD, MORROW CO OR	128 - C1
CAMP BONNEVILLE CLARK CO WA	193 - B5
CAMP CLATSOP MILITARY RESV GEARHART, WARRENTON, CLATSOP CO OR	188 - B3
CAMP MCKEAN (US NAVY) OFF KITSAP LAKE RD, KITSAP CO WA	270 - A10
CAMP MURRAY WASHINGTON NATL GUARD MILITIA DR, PIERCE CO WA	181 - C5
CAMP RILEA (OREGON NATL GUARD) RIDGE LAKE DR, CLATSOP CO OR	188 - B2
CAMP SEVEN MILE MILITARY RESV RIVERSIDE PARK DR, SPOKANE CO WA	348 - A1
CAMP WESLEY HARRIS NAVAL RESV SEABECK HWY NW, KITSAP CO WA	174 - A2
CANADIAN COAST GUARD DALLAS RD & SIMCOE ST, CTY OF VCTRIA BC	256 - E9
CANADIAN FORCES BASE ESQUIMALT ESQUIMALT RD & CANTEEN RD, ESQUIMALT BC	256 - A8
COOS HEAD US NAVAL FACILITY COOS CO OR	220 - C1
DEPARTMENT OF NATL DEFENSE BEWDLEY AV & PETERS ST, ESQUIMLT BC	256 - D9
DEPARTMENT OF NATL DEFENSE WILLIAM HEAD RD, DISTRICT OF METCHOSIN BC	165 - A1
FAIRCHILD AIR FORCE BASE HWY 2 & N RAMBO RD, FAIRCHILD AFB WA	114 - B2
FORT LAWTON MILITARY RESV MAGNOLIA BL W & W EMERSON ST, SEATTLE WA	272 - B5
FORT LEWIS MILITARY RESV STEILACOOM-DUPONT RD SW, PIERCE CO WA	181 - D5
GRAND ARMY ENCAMPMENT GROUNDS FARRAGUT AV, WESTPORT WA	298 - F14
GRAYS HARBOR COAST GUARD NYHUS ST & WILSON AV, WESTPORT WA	298 - H10
MCCHORD AIR FORCE BASE 112TH ST S, PIERCE CO WA	181 - D5
NATL GUARD KINGS RD & PORT ST, NAMPA ID	147 - C1
NATL GUARD ARMORY 1601 W ARMORY WY, SEATTLE WA	277 - F1
NATL GUARD ARMORY KIMBALL AV & PAYNTER AV, CALDWELL ID	147 - B1
NATL GUARD ARMORY N RIVER AV, BUCKLEY WA	110 - C3
NATL GUARD ARMORY TAYLOR WY, FOREST GROVE OR	198 - C1
NAVAL RESERVE BEACH DR E, COLBY WA	271 - G11
NAVAL RES ARMORY VALLEY ST & FAIRVIEW AV N, SEATTLE WA	278 - A3
NAVAL STATION EVERETT W MARINE VIEW DR & 18TH ST, EVERETT WA	264 - C1
PORTLAND AIR NATL GUARD BASE 6801 NE CORNFOOT RD, PORTLAND OR	310 - D5
PUGET SOUND NAVAL SHIPYARD BREMERTON WA	270 - G12
ROCKY POINT NAVAL ESTABLISHMENT EAST SOOKE RD, DISTRICT OF METCHOSIN BC	165 - A1
TILLAMOOK BAY COAST GUARD STA GARIBALDI AV, GARIBALDI OR	191 - B7
TONGUE POINT NAVAL BASE (HIST) OLD COLUMBIA RIVER HWY, ASTORIA OR	300 - J3
US COAST GUARD 1519 ALASKAN HWY S, SEATTLE WA	281 - J1
US COAST GUARD RESERVE OCEAN AV & ABERDEEN ST, WESTPORT WA	298 - F13
US COAST GUARD RESERVE OFF HIGHWAY 109, GRAYS HARBOR CO WA	172 - B7
US COAST GUARD STA EDIZ HOOK RD, PORT ANGELES WA	261 - G1
U S MILITARY RESERVE US 97 & FIRING CENTER RD, YAKIMA CO WA	243 - D4
US NAVAL RESERVE FORT CANBY RD, PACIFIC CO WA	186 - A6
US NAVAL RESERVE OFF CLEAR CREEK RD NW, KITSAP CO WA	170 - B7
US NAVAL RESERVE OFF HWY 116, JEFFERSON CO WA	263 - J13
US NAVAL RESERVE OFF HWY 20, OAK HARBOR WA	167 - C2
US NAVAL RESERVE OFF HWY 3, BREMERTON WA	270 - C7
WASHINGTON NATL GUARD ARMORY 24410 MILITARY RD S, KENT WA	175 - B7
WHIDBEY ISLAND NAVAL AIR STA OFF HWY 20, AULT FIELD WA	167 - B1

MUSEUMS

FEATURE NAME / City State	Page-Grid
ABERDEEN MUS OF HIST 111 E 3RD ST, ABERDEEN WA	178 - B7
ALBANY MUS & LIB 5TH ST & WASHINGTN ST, ALBANY OR	326 - C8
ALPHINSTONE PIONEER MUS OFF HWY 101, BRITISH COLUMBIA BC	93 - B3
AMERICAN ADVERTISING MUS 50 SW 2ND AV, PORTLAND OR	313 - F5
AMERICAN HOP MUS 22 S B ST, TOPPENISH WA	120 - A2
ANACORTES MUS 1305 8TH ST, ANACORTES WA	259 - H1
APE CAVE MUS NFD RAINR RD & RAINIER-YELM, SKAMANIA CO	190 - B4
APPALOOSA HORSE CLUB AND MUS OFF HWY 8, MOSCOW ID	249 - C5
ARCHER GALLERY, THE 1800 E MCLAUGHLIN BLVD, VANCOUVER WA	305 - J4
ASOTIN MUS OFF HWY 129, ASOTIN WA	250 - B6
BALDWIN HOTEL MUS 31 MAIN ST, KLAMATH FALLS OR	338 - D8
BASQUE MUS AND CULTURAL CTR 611 GROVE ST, BOISE ID	253 - C3
BATTERY POINT LIGHTHOUSE MUS A ST BY LIGHTHOUSE, DEL NORTE CO CA	148 - B3
BELLEVUE ART MUS 106TH AV NE & NE 4TH ST, BELLEVUE WA	175 - C2
BENTON CO HIST MUS PATERSON RD, PROSSER WA	120 - B3
BENTON COUNTY HIST MUS 1101 MAIN ST, BENTON CO OR	133 - B1
BERNABY VILLAGE MUS CANADA WY, DISTRICT OF BURNABY BC	156 - D5
BLACK DIAMOND DEPOT MUS RAILROAD AV & BAKER ST, BLACK DIAMOND WA	110 - C3
BLACKMAN HIST MUS 118 AVE B, SNOHOMISH WA	171 - D3
BLEHYL LIBRARY AND POWELL MUS GRANDVIEW, GRANDVIEW WA	120 - B3
BOISE ART MUS 670 S JULIA DAVIS DR, BOISE ID	253 - C3
BREMERTON NAVAL MUS 130 WASHINGTON AV, BREMERTON WA	270 - J10
BRITISH COLUMBIA HALL OF FAME RENFREW ST & HASTINGS ST E, VANCOUVER BC	255 - E10
BRITISH COLUMBIA FRM MACHNRY & AGR MUS 9131 KING ST, TOWNSHIP OF LANGLEY BC	157 - D6
BRITISH COLUMBIA SUGAR MUS ROGER ST, VANCOUVER BC	255 - A10
BRITTANCOURT HOUSE MUS RAINBOW RD, BRITISH COLUMBIA BC	101 - B1
BROUGHER MUS GEORGE FOX UNIVERSITY, NEWBERG OR	198 - D5
BRUCE MEM MUS OFF HWY 124, WALLA WALLA CO WA	122 - A3
BURKE MUS NE 45TH ST & MEMORIAL WY, SEATTLE WA	274 - C5
BUSH BARN HIGH ST SE, SALEM OR	322 - H14
BUSH HOUSE MUS HIGH ST SE, SALEM OR	322 - H14
BUTTERFLY WORLD HWY 4, BRITISH COLUMBIA BC	92 - C3
CAMBRIDGE MUS US 95 & RTE 71, WASHINGTON CO ID	139 - B1
CAMP 6 LOGGING MUS FIVE MILE DR, TACOMA WA	181 - C1
CANADIAN LACROSSE HALL OF FAME MCBRIDE BLVD, NEW WESTMINSTER BC	156 - D5
CENTRAL WASHINGTON AGRICULT MUS 4508 MAIN ST, UNION GAP WA	243 - C7
CHENEY COWLES MUS W RIVERSIDE AV, SPOKANE WA	348 - G9
CHILDRENS MUS PENDLETON-JOHN DAY HWY, GRANT CO OR	137 - A1
CHILDRENS MUS 2ND GENERATION 4015 SW CANYON RD, PORTLAND OR	312 - B7
CHILDRENS MUS OF TACOMA 925 COURT C, TACOMA WA	293 - H5
CHILDRENS MUS, THE 305 HARRISON ST, SEATTLE WA	277 - H4
CHILLIWACK MUS 45820 SPADINA AV, CITY OF CHILLIWACK BC	94 - C3
CLALLAM COUNTY MUS S LINCOLN ST, PORT ANGELES WA	261 - D5
CLARK COUNTY HIST MUS 1511 MAIN ST, VANCOUVER WA	305 - G4
CLATSOP COUNTY HIST SOCIETY HERIT 1618 EXCHANGE ST, ASTORIA OR	300 - D5
CLE ELUM TELEPHONE MUS 221 E FIRST ST, CLE ELUM WA	240 - B2
CLYMER MUS N PEARL ST, ELLENSBURG WA	241 - B6
COAST GUARD MUS PIER 36, SEATTLE WA	281 - J1
COLLIER STATE PARK AND LOGGING MUS THE DALLES-CALIFORNIA HWY, KLAMATH CO OR	231 - D4
COLUMBIA COUNTY HIST MUS 511 E BRIDGE ST, VERNONIA OR	125 - B1
COLUMBIA GORGE DISCOVERY CTR & WASCO 5000 DISCOVERY DR, WASCO CO OR	196 - C6
COLUMBIA RIVER MARITIME MUS 1792 MARINE DR, ASTORIA OR	300 - E4
COOS ART MUS CURTIS AV & 4TH ST, COOS BAY OR	333 - H10
COOS COUNTY HIST SOCIETY MUS SHERMAN AV, NORTH BEND OR	333 - G3
COTTAGE GROVE MUS W MAIN ST, COTTAGE GROVE OR	215 - B7
COWLITZ COUNTY HIST MUS 405 ALLEN ST, KELSO WA	303 - D8
CRAIG HERITAGE MUS 1245 E ISLAND HWY, BRITISH COLUMBIA BC	92 - C3
CRATER ROCK MUS ROGUE VALLEY HWY, JACKSON CO OR	230 - C7
DEL NORTE HIST SOCIETY 577 H ST, CRESCENT CITY CA	148 - B3
DEPOT MUS 888 NE 4TH AV, CANBY OR	199 - C6
DOLLY WARES DOLL MUS 101 & 35TH ST, FLORENCE OR	214 - B3
DOUGLAS COUNTY HIST MUS 124 W WALNUT ST, DOUGLAS CO WA	236 - C7
DOUGLAS COUNTY MUS FREAR ST & SW PRTLND AV, DOUGLAS CO OR	334 - E9
DUPONT HIST MUS 207 BARKSDALE AV, DUPONT WA	181 - B5
EAST BENTON HIST MUS 205 KEEWAYDIN DR, KENNEWICK WA	343 - C11
EASTERN OREGON MUS LA GRANDE-BAKER HWY, BAKER CO OR	130 - A3
EDMONDS HIST MUS 118 5TH AV N, EDMONDS WA	171 - A5
EMILY CARR MUS 207 GOVERNMENT ST, CITY OF VICTORIA BC	256 - G10
FAVELL MUS OF WESTERN ART 125 W MAIN ST, KLAMATH FALLS OR	338 - C8
FLAVEL HOUSE MUS 441 EIGTH ST, ASTORIA OR	300 - C5
FOOTHILLS HIST MUS N RIVER AV & N COTTAGE ST, BUCKLEY WA	110 - C3
FORKS TIMBER MUS HWY 101 & RTE 110, CLALLAM CO WA	169 - D2
FORT DALLES MUS W 13TH ST, THE DALLES OR	196 - C7
FORT LEWIS MILITARY MUS MAIN ST & CONSTITUTION DR, PIERCE CO WA	181 - B5
FORT NISQUALLY MUS 5400 N PEARL ST, TACOMA WA	181 - C1
FORT SHERMAN MUS ROSENBERRY DR DR, COEUR D'ALENE ID	355 - D11
FRANKLIN COUNTY HIST MUS 305 N FOURTH AV, PASCO WA	343 - F7
FRYE ART MUS 704 TERRY AV, SEATTLE WA	278 - B6
GIG HARBOR PENINSULA HIST MUS 4218 HARBORVIEW DR, GIG HARBOR WA	174 - C7
GILBERT HOUSE CHILDRENS MUS 116 MARION ST NE, SALEM OR	322 - H12
GRANT COUNTY HIST MUS 742 N BASIN ST, GRANT CO WA	112 - C2
GRANTS PASS MUS OF ART 229 SW G ST, GRANTS PASS OR	335 - E8
HARNEY COUNTY HIST MUS 18 W D ST, BURNS OR	145 - A1
HENRY ART GALLERY 15TH AV NE & NE 41ST ST, SEATTLE WA	274 - C6
HIGH DESERT MUS, THE 59800 HWY 97, DESCHUTES CO OR	217 - B4
HOOD RIVER COUNTY HIST MUS INT 84 & HWY 35, HOOD RIVER OR	195 - D5
HOOVER-MINTHORN HOUSE MUS 115 S RIVER ST, NEWBERG OR	198 - D5
IDAHO HIST MUS 610 N JULIA DAVIS DR, BOISE ID	253 - C3
IDAHO MUS OF MINING 2455 OLD PENITENTIARY RD, BOISE ID	253 - D3
ILWACO HERITAGE MUS 115 SE LAKE ST, ILWACO WA	186 - A6
ISLAND COUNTY HIST MUS NE PARKER RD, COUPEVILLE WA	167 - B4
JACKSONVILLE MUS OF SOUTHERN OREGON HWY 238 & OLD STAGE RD, JACKSONVILLE OR	149 - B2
JENSEN ARCTIC MUS 590 W CHURCH ST, MONMOUTH OR	204 - B7
JOSEPHINE COUNTY KERBYVILLE MUS US 199 & KIRBY, JOSEPHINE CO OR	233 - B3
KARPELES MANUSCRIPT 407 S G ST, TACOMA WA	293 - G4
KENT HIST SOCIETY MUS JASON AV & E TEMPERANCE ST, KENT WA	175 - C7
KITSAP COUNTY MUS OFF SILVERDALE WY NW, SILVERDALE WA	174 - B1
KITTITAS COUNTY HIST MUS E 3RD ST, ELLENSBURG WA	241 - B6
KLAMATH COUNTY MUS 1451 MAIN ST, KLAMATH FALLS OR	338 - E7
KLAMATH NATL FOREST INTERPRETIVE MUS 1312 FAIRLANE RD, SISKIYOU CO CA	149 - C3
LACEY MUS 829 LACEY ST, LACEY WA	297 - H6
LAKE CHELAN MUS HWY 150 & WOODIN AV, CHELAN WA	236 - D3
LANE COUNTY HIST MUS 740 W 13TH AV, EUGENE OR	329 - H7
LANGLEY CENTENNIAL MUS 9135 KING ST, TOWNSHIP OF LANGLEY BC	157 - D6
LEWIS COUNTY HIST MUS 599 NW FRONT WAY, CHEHALIS WA	299 - D11
LINCOLN COUNTY HIST MUS OFF HWY 2, DAVENPORT WA	114 - A2
LINN COUNTY HIST MUS 101 PARK AV, BROWNSVILLE OR	210 - C2
LIVING ROCK MUS, THE HALSEY-SWEET HOME HWY, LINN CO OR	210 - C2
LONGMIRE MUS NATIONAL PARK HWY, PIERCE CO WA	185 - A5
LOPEZ HIST MUS LOPEZ ISLAND, SAN JUAN CO WA	101 - C2
LUNA HOUSE MUS OFF HWY 12, LEWISTON ID	250 - B4
LYNDEN PIONEER MUS 217 W FRONT ST, LYNDEN WA	102 - B1
MACMILLAN, H R PLANETARIUM 1000 CHESTNUT ST, VANCOUVER BC	254 - D11
MARION COUNTY HIST MUS 260 12TH ST SE, SALEM OR	322 - J13
MARITIME MUS 28 BASTION SQ, CITY OF VICTORIA BC	256 - G9
MARYHILL MUS LEWIS & CLARK HWY, KLICKITAT CO WA	127 - B1
MARYMOOR MUS 6046 W LAKE SAMMAMISH PKWY NE, KING CO WA	175 - D1
MASON COUNTY MUS W RAILROAD AV, SHELTON WA	180 - A3
MILWAUKIE HIST SOCIETY MUS SE RAILROAD AV&SE ADAMS ST, MILWAUKIE OR	199 - D3
MINIATURE WORLD 721 GOVERNMENT ST, CITY OF VICTORIA BC	256 - G9
MINING MUS TRANS CANADA HWY, BRITISH COLUMBIA BC	93 - C2
MISSION MUS 33201 2ND AV, DISTRICT OF MISSION BC	94 - B3
MOLSON MUS MOLSON RD, OKANOGAN CO WA	105 - A1
MUS AT WARM SPRINGS, THE 2189 WARM SPRINGS HWY, WARM SPRINGS OR	208 - A2
MUS OF ANTHROPOLOGY 6393 NW MARINE DR, UNIV ENDWMENT LANDS BC	156 - A4
MUS OF FLIGHT 9404 E MARGINAL WY S, TUKWILA WA	286 - D4
MUS OF GLASS 1801 E DOCK ST, TACOMA WA	293 - H6
MUS OF HIST & INDUSTRY 2700 24TH AV E, SEATTLE WA	278 - D1
MUS OF NORTH IDAHO 115 NORTHWEST BLVD, COEUR D'ALENE ID	355 - C8
MUS OF THE OREGON TERRITORY 211 TUMWATER DR, OREGON CITY OR	199 - D5
NANAIMO MUS TRANS CANADA HWY, NANAIMO BC	93 - A3
NAVAL UNDERSEA MUS OFF HWY 308, KITSAP CO WA	170 - C7
NEWELL HOUSE MUS 8089 CHAMPOEG RD, MARION CO OR	199 - A7
NORDIC HERITAGE MUS 3014 NW 67TH ST, SEATTLE WA	272 - D3
NORTH CENTRAL WASHINGTON MUS 127 S MISSION ST, WENATCHEE WA	239 - A4
NORTHERN PACIFIC RAILROAD MUS 219 SIXTH ST, WALLACE ID	115 - C2

INDEX

FEATURE NAME City State	Page-Grid
NORTH VANCOUVER MUS AND ARCHIVES 4TH ST, CITY OF NORTH VANCOUVER BC	255 - A5
NORTHWEST RAILWAY MUS 38625 SE KING ST, SNOQUALMIE WA	176 - C4
OF SEA AND SHORE MUS OFF HWY 104, KITSAP CO WA	170 - C4
OKANOGAN COUNTY HIST MUS HWY 215, OKANOGAN WA	104 - C3
OLD AURORA COLONY MUS 2ND ST NE & LIBERTY ST NE, AURORA OR	199 - B7
OLD COLLEGE HALL MUS 2043 COLLEGE WY, FOREST GROVE OR	198 - B1
OLD HASTINGS MILL STORE MUS 1575 ALMA RD, UNIV ENDOWMENT LANDS BC	254 - A11
OLD SHIP MUS LAKE ST S & CENTRAL WY NE, KIRKLAND WA	175 - C1
OREGON HIST CTR 1200 SW PARK AV, PORTLAND OR	313 - E6
OREGON MARITIME CTR & MUS 113 SW NAITO PKWY, PORTLAND OR	313 - F6
OREGON MILITARY MUS CAMP WITHYCOMBE, CLACKAMAS CO OR	199 - D3
OREGON MUS OF SCIENCE & INDUSTRY 1945 SE WATER AV, PORTLAND OR	313 - G7
OREGON SPORTS HALL OF FAME 900 SW 4TH AV, PORTLAND OR	313 - F6
OREGON TRAIL REGIONAL MUS OFF HWY 7, BAKER CITY OR	138 - B1
OSOYOOS MUS PARK PL, BRITISH COLUMBIA BC	104 - C1
PACIFIC NORTHWEST MUS OF HIST 1500 E MAIN ST, ASHLAND OR	337 - F7
PACIFIC SCIENCE CTR 200 2ND AV N, SEATTLE WA	277 - H4
PEARSON AIR MUS 1105 E 5TH ST, VANCOUVER WA	305 - H6
PIONEER FARM MUS OHOP VLY RD E & 72ND AVCT E, PIERCE CO WA	118 - B1
PIONEER MEM MUS MOUNT ANGELES RD, PORT ANGELES WA	261 - F6
PITTOCK MANSION 3229 NW PITTOCK DR, PORTLAND OR	312 - B5
POLSON, F ARNOLD PARK AND MUS 1611 RIVERSIDE AV, HOQUIAM WA	178 - A7
PORT GAMBLE HIST MUS OFF HWY 104, KITSAP CO WA	170 - C4
PORTLAND ART MUS 1219 SW PARK ST, PORTLAND OR	313 - E6
PRESBY MUS 127 W BROADWAY, GOLDENDALE WA	127 - C1
PREWITT ALLEN ARCHAEOLOGICAL MUS DEER PARK DR SE, SALEM OR	325 - F6
PRINTING MUS COOS BAY HWY, COOS BAY OR	333 - H9
REDWOOD NATIONAL PARK MUS 1111 2ND ST, CRESCENT CITY CA	148 - B3
RENTON HIST SOCIETY & MUS 235 MILL AV S, RENTON WA	175 - C5
RICHMOND MUS 7700 MINORU GATE, CITY OF RICHMOND BC	156 - B6
ROCKET CITY NEON MUS 1554 NE 3RD AV, CAMAS WA	193 - B7
ROSLYN MUS 203 PENNSYLVANIA AV, ROSLYN WA	240 - A1
ROYAL BC MUS 675 BELLEVILLE ST, CITY OF VICTORIA BC	256 - G10
ROYAL LONDON WAX MUS 470 BELLEVILLE ST, CITY OF VICTORIA BC	256 - G9
SAANICH HIST ARTIFACTS SOCIETY 7321 LOCHSIDE DR, DIST OF CNTRL SAANCH BC	159 - C4
SAMSON V MARITIME MUS MCBRIDE BLVD, NEW WESTMINSTER BC	156 - D5
SANDY HIST MUS 39260 PIONEER BLVD, SANDY OR	200 - D4
SCHMIDT HOUSE MUS 508 SW 5TH ST, GRANTS PASS OR	335 - E9
SCHMINCK MEM MUS OFF HWY 395, LAKEVIEW OR	152 - A2
SCIENCE WORLD 1455 QUEBEC ST, VANCOUVER BC	254 - H11
SEASIDE MUS 570 NECANIUM DR, SEASIDE OR	301 - G8
SEATTLE AQUARIUM 1483 ALASKAN FRWY, PIER 5, SEATTLE WA	277 - J6
SEATTLE ART MUS 100 UNIVERSITY ST, SEATTLE WA	277 - J6
SEATTLE ASIAN ART MUS 1400 E PROSPECT ST, SEATTLE WA	278 - C3
SEQUIM-DUNGENESS VALLEY MUS 175 W CEDAR ST, SEQUIM WA	262 - D11
SHAFER MUS HWY 20, OKANOGAN CO WA	104 - A2
SHORELINE HIST MUS 749 N 175TH ST, SHORELINE WA	171 - A6
SIDNEY ART GALLERY AND MUS 202 SIDNEY AV, PORT ORCHARD WA	270 - H14
SIDNEY MUS 2440 SIDNEY AVE, TOWN OF SIDNEY BC	159 - C2
SISKIYOU COUNTY MUS 910 S MAIN ST, YREKA CA	149 - C3
SIUSLAW PIONEER MUS OREGON COAST HWY, LANE CO OR	214 - B3
SKAGIT COUNTY HIST MUS 501 S 4TH ST, LA CONNER WA	167 - D1
SNOHOMISH COUNTY MUS 2817 ROCKEFELLER AV, EVERETT WA	264 - E3
SNOQUALMIE VALLEY HIST MUS 320 NORTH BEND BLVD S, NORTH BEND WA	176 - C5
SOOKE REGION MUS HWY 14, BRITISH COLUMBIA BC	115 - C2
STAFF HOUSE MUS 820 MC KINLEY AV, KELLOGG ID	181 - C4
STEILACOOM HIST MUS 112 MAIN ST, STEILACOOM WA	181 - C4
STEILACOOM TRIBAL CULTURAL CTR & MUS 1515 LAFAYETTE ST, STEILACOOM WA	181 - C4
STEVENS-CRAWFORD MUS 630 6TH ST, OREGON CITY OR	199 - D5
STEVESTON MUS MONCTON ST, CITY OF RICHMOND BC	156 - A7
SUNNYSIDE MUS 704 S 4TH ST, SUNNYSIDE WA	120 - B2
SUQUAMISH MUS 15838 SANDY HOOK RD, SUQUAMISH WA	170 - C7
SURREY CENTENNIAL MUS 6022 176TH ST, CITY OF SURREY BC	157 - B7
TACOMA ART MUS 1701 PACIFIC AV, TACOMA WA	293 - H6
TAMASTSLIKT CULTURAL INSTITUTE I-84 EXIT 216, UMATILLA CO OR	129 - B1
TENINO DEPOT MUS 339 W PARK ST, TENINO WA	184 - D3
THREE RIVERS CHILDRENS MUS 650 GEORGE WASHINGTON WY, RICHLAND WA	341 - G2

FEATURE NAME City State	Page-Grid
TILLAMOOK COUNTY PIONEER MUS MAIN AV & 1ST ST, TILLAMOOK OR	197 - B2
TILLAMOOK NAVAL AIR STA MUS 6030 HANGAR RD, TILLAMOOK CO OR	197 - B2
TOPPENISH MUS 1 S ELM ST, TOPPENISH WA	120 - A2
TWO RIVERS HERITAGE MUS 1 16TH ST, WASHOUGAL WA	193 - B2
UMATILLA COUNTY HIST MUS 108 SW FRAZER, PENDLETON OR	129 - B1
UNDERSEA GARDENS 490 BELLEVILLE ST, CITY OF VICTORIA BC	256 - F9
UPPERTOWN FIREFIGHTERS MUS 30TH ST, ASTORIA OR	300 - E4
VANCOUVER MARITIME MUS OGDEN AV, VANCOUVER BC	254 - D10
VANCOUVER MUS 1100 CHESTNUT ST, VANCOUVER BC	254 - E11
WAHKIAKUM COUNTY HIST MUS 65 RIVER ST, WAHKIAKUM WA	117 - B3
WALLOWA COUNTY MUS OFF WALLOWA LAKE HWY, WALLOWA CO OR	130 - B1
WANAPUM DAM AND HERITAGE CTR HWY 243, GRANT CO WA	120 - B1
WARHAWK AIR MUS NAMPA ID	147 - C1
WASHINGTON COUNTY HIST MUS 17677 NW SPRINGVILLE RD, WASHINGTON CO OR	192 - A7
WASHINGTON STATE CAPITOL MUS 221 W 21ST AV, OLYMPIA WA	296 - H7
WASHINGTON STATE HIST MUS 1911 PACIFIC AV, TACOMA WA	293 - H6
WASHINGTON STATE HIST SOCIETY 315 N STADIUM WY, TACOMA WA	293 - G3
WESTPORT MUS 2201 WESTHAVEN DR, WESTPORT WA	298 - G10
WHALE MUS 62 FIRST ST N, FRIDAY HARBOR WA	101 - C2
WHATCOM CHILDRENS MUS 227 PROSPECT ST, BELLINGHAM WA	258 - C6
WHATCOM MUS OF HIST 121 PROSPECT ST, BELLINGHAM WA	161 - A1
WHITE RIVER VALLEY MUS 9TH ST SE & N ST SE, AUBURN WA	182 - C1
WHYEL, ROSALIE MUS OF DOLL ART 1116 108TH AV NE, BELLEVUE WA	175 - C2
WILLAMETTE FALLS LOCKS MUS MILL ST & 7TH ST, WEST LINN OR	199 - D4
WILLIAMS, M Y GEOLOGICAL MUS MARINE DR, UNIV ENDOWMENT LANDS BC	156 - A4
WILLIS CAREY HIST MUS RIVERFRONT DR, CASHMERE WA	238 - C2
WONDER WORKS CHILDRENS MUS 419 E 2ND ST, THE DALLES OR	196 - C7
WORLD KITE MUS AND HALL OF FAME PACIFIC HWY, LONG BEACH WA	186 - A5
YAKIMA ELECTRIC RAILWAY MUS 5TH AV AND WALNUT ST, YAKIMA WA	243 - B6
YAKIMA VALLEY MUS 2105 TIETON DR, YAKIMA WA	243 - B6
YAMHILL CO HIST MUS 605 MARKET ST, LAFAYETTE OR	198 - B6

OPEN SPACE PRESERVES

FEATURE NAME City State	Page-Grid
ABBOTT CREEK NATURAL RESEARCH AREA JACKSON CO OR	226 - C3
ALPINE LAKES WILDERNESS KING CO WA	111 - B2
BADGER CREEK WILDERNESS AREA WASCO CO OR	202 - D5
BEAVER MARSH NATURAL PRESERVE NE 98TH AV & NE 39TH ST, VANCOUVER WA	307 - G2
BIDDLE, HENRY J NATURE PRESERVE LEWIS & CLARK HWY, VANCOUVER WA	311 - J2
BLACK CANYON WILDERNESS OCHOCO NATIONAL FOREST, WHEELER CO OR	136 - C2
BOULDER CREEK WILDERNESS NORTH UMPQUA HWY, DOUGLAS CO OR	222 - C2
BOULDER RIVER WILDERNESS OFF HWY 530, SNOHOMISH CO WA	102 - C3
BRIDGE CREEK WILDERNESS OCHOCO NATIONAL FOREST, WHEELER CO OR	136 - A2
BULL OF THE WOODS WILDERNESS BAGBY RD, MARION CO OR	134 - B1
BULL RUN NATURAL AREA CLACKAMAS CO OR	201 - D3
BULL RUN RESERVE CLACKAMAS CO OR	201 - A6
CHAMNA NATURAL PRESERVE RICHLAND WA	341 - H5
COLUMBIA POINT ENVIRONMENT RICHLAND WA	342 - A4
COLUMBIA RIVER GORGE NATL SCENIC AREA COLUMBIA RIVER HWY, WASCO CO OR	195 - B5
CREST NATURAL AREA IN CASCADE HEAD EXP FOREST, TILLAMOOK CO	203 - B2
CUMMINS CREEK WILDERNESS OREGON COAST HWY, LANE CO OR	209 - A5
DRIFT CREEK WILDERNESS LINCOLN CO OR	206 - C7
EAGLE CAP WILDERNESS WALLOWA CO OR	131 - A2
ECOLOGICAL PRESERVE BRITISH COLUMBIA BC	159 - B1
GLACIER PEAK WILDERNESS SNOHOMISH CO WA	103 - B3
GOAT ROCKS WILDERNESS LEWIS CO WA	119 - A2
GRASSY KNOB WILDERNESS CURRY CO OR	224 - C5
GREEN RIVER NATURAL RESOURCES RUSSELL RD & S 212TH ST, KENT WA	291 - F5
JACKSON, HENRY M WILDERNESS SNOHOMISH CO WA	111 - B1
JUNIPER DUNES WILDERNESS PASCO-KAHLOTUS RD, FRANKLIN CO WA	121 - B2
KALMIOPSIS WILDERNESS CURRY CO OR	228 - D6
LAKE CHELAN-SAWTOOTH WILDERNESS OKANOGAN CO WA	104 - A2
MARBLE MOUNTAIN WILDERNESS AREA OFF SCOTT RIVER RD, SISKIYOU CO CA	149 - B3
MENAGERIE WILDERNESS AREA LINN CO OR	134 - B2
MITLENATCH ISLAND NATURE PARK BRITISH COLUMBIA BC	92 - A1
MONUMENT ROCK WILDERNESS BAKER CO OR	137 - C2
MOUNTAIN LAKES WILDERNESS KLAMATH CO OR	231 - A7
MOUNT HOOD WILDERNESS AREA CLACKAMAS CO OR	201 - C5
MOUNT JEFFERSON WILDERNESS AREA JEFFERSON CO OR	134 - C1

FEATURE NAME City State	Page-Grid
MOUNT PASAYTEN WILDERNESS WHATCOM CO WA	103 - C1
MOUNT THIELSEN WILDERNESS KLAMATH CO OR	223 - D3
MOUNT WASHINGTON WILDERNESS AREA DESCHUTES CO OR	211 - A4
NORSE PEAK WILDERNESS PIERCE CO WA	111 - A3
NORTH FORK JOHN DAY WILDERNESS UMATILLA CO OR	129 - C3
NORTH FORK UMATILLA WILDERNESS WESTON-ELGIN HWY, UMATILLA CO OR	130 - A1
OAKS BOTTOM WILDLIFE REFUGE SE BYBEE BLVD & SE 13TH AV, PORTLAND OR	317 - H4
OREGON CASCADES RECREATION WILDERNESS KLAMATH CO OR	142 - B2
PASAYTEN WILDERNESS OKANOGAN CO WA	104 - A1
RENTON WETLANDS LIND AV SW, RENTON WA	289 - J6
RIVERVIEW NATURAL PRESERVE RICHLAND WA	341 - J5
ROCK CREEK WILDERNESS OREGON COAST HWY, LANE CO OR	209 - A6
ROGUE-UMPQUA DIVIDE WILDERNESS DOUGLAS CO OR	226 - C1
SALMON HUCKLEBERRY WILDERNESS MOUNT HOOD HWY, CLACKAMAS CO OR	201 - B6
SALMO-PRIEST WILDERNESS PEND OREILLE CO WA	106 - C1
SERPENTINE FEN BIRD SANCTUARY CITY OF SURREY BC	158 - A1
SKY LAKES WILDERNESS KLAMATH CO OR	231 - A1
SOUTH SLOUGH NATIONAL ESTUARY COOS CO OR	220 - C2
STRAWBERRY MOUNTAIN WILDERNESS GRANT CO OR	137 - B2
TABLE ROCK WILDERNESS MIDDLEFORK RD, CLACKAMAS CO OR	126 - A3
THREE SISTERS WILDERNESS AREA DESCHUTES CO OR	211 - A6
TOLT RIVER HIGHLANDS AREA TOLT HIGHLANDS RD NE, KING CO WA	176 - B1
VANCOUVER LAKE LOWLANDS (UNDEVELOPED) NW FRUIT VALLEY RD, VANCOUVER WA	304 - D1
WALDO LAKE WILDERNESS AREA NFD RD 24, LANE CO OR	142 - B1
WASHINGTON STATE OYEHUT GAME RESERVE OCEAN SHORES, OCEAN SHORES WA	298 - C5
WENAHA-TUCANNON WILDERNESS WALLOWA CO OR	130 - A1
WILDCAT MTN RESEARCH NATURAL AREA LINN CO OR	134 - B2
WILD ROGUE WILDERNESS CURRY CO OR	140 - C3

PARKS & RECREATION

FEATURE NAME City State	Page-Grid
5TH & GRANT PK GRANT ST & 5TH AV, TUMWATER WA	296 - G8
8TH & I PK S 8TH ST & S I ST, TACOMA WA	293 - G5
21ST & IDAHO SOCCER FIELD 21ST AV & IDAHO ST, POST FALLS ID	353 - J4
37TH AV S PK 3551 S HOLLY ST, SEATTLE WA	286 - E1
92ND STREET PK 92ND ST SW & 49TH AV W, MUKILTEO WA	266 - E5
ADAIR COUNTY PK RYALS AV, BENTON CO OR	207 - B4
ADAMS PK NW CORNELL RD, PORTLAND OR	312 - A5
ADMIRALTY PK CITY OF PORT MOODY BC	156 - D3
AGREN MEM PK THORSEN RD SW & SW BANK RD, KING CO WA	174 - D5
ALBERTA PK NE KILLINGSWORTH ST, PORTLAND OR	309 - J7
ALBINA PK N FLINT AV & N RUSSELL ST, PORTLAND OR	313 - F3
ALDERWOOD PK DIST OF N VANCOUVER BC	254 - G5
ALDRICH PK SALEM OR	323 - A14
ALEXANDER PK RIVERSIDE RD, LEWIS CO WA	299 - C13
ALEX HOPE PK 88TH AV & 208TH ST, TWNSHP OF LANGLEY BC	157 - C6
ALKI PLGD 59TH AV SW & LANDER ST, SEATTLE WA	280 - C2
ALLCO PK ALOUETTE RD, MAPLE RIDGE BC	157 - D5
ALLENTOWN PEA PATCH PK 12535 50TH PL S, TUKWILA WA	289 - F1
ALLING PK S SHERIDAN AV & S 61ST ST, TACOMA WA	295 - F5
ALL SPORTS PK LINCOLN RD & WEBSTER RD, GRANTS PASS OR	335 - C10
ALMOND PK VANCOUVER BC	254 - A13
ALTON BAKER PK DAY ISLAND RD, EUGENE OR	330 - C6
AMAZON PK PEARL ST, EUGENE OR	330 - A9
AMBASSADOR PK AMBASSADOR AV, DISTRICT OF SAANICH BC	256 - H2
AMBLESIDE PK DIST OF WEST VANCOUVER BC	254 - D4
AMON, HOWARD PK LEE BLVD, RICHLAND WA	341 - H2
ANDERSON HILL PK BEACH DR, DISTRICT OF OAK BAY BC	257 - D11
ANDERSON LAKE STATE PK OFF ANDERSON LAKE RD, JEFFERSON CO WA	170 - A1
ANDERSON PK RUSSELL RD, KENT WA	291 - F5
ANGLE LAKE PK INTERNATIONAL BL & S 194TH ST, SEATAC WA	290 - D2
ARBOR LAKE PK 124TH ST & 4TH AV S, KING CO WA	286 - A7
ARBOR LODGE PK N BRYANT ST & N GREELEY AV, PORTLAND OR	308 - D5
ARDENWALD PK SE ROSWELL ST, MILWAUKIE OR	318 - B7
ARNADA PK E FOURTH PLAIN BL & F ST, VANCOUVER WA	305 - G3
ARNOLD PK HARRISON BLVD, CORVALLIS OR	327 - D9
ARNOLD PK NE ARNOLD RD, VANCOUVER WA	305 - J2
ARROYO PK CHUCKANUT DR N, BELLINGHAM WA	258 - C13
ATHLETIC FIELD BROADWAY & 24TH ST, EVERETT WA	265 - E3

FEATURE NAME City State	Page-Grid
ATLANTIC CITY PK SEWARD PARK AV S & S HENDERSN, SEATTLE WA	287 - G3
AUDUBON PK N MILTON ST, SPOKANE WA	348 - F5
AVERY PK AVERY PARK DR, CORVALLIS OR	327 - F11
AVONDALE PK AVONDALE ST, DISTRICT OF BURNABY BC	255 - G14
AZALEA PK NORTH BANK CHETCO RIVER RD, BROOKINGS OR	232 - C6
BADGER MTN PK BRENTWOOD AV, RICHLAND WA	341 - G6
BAGLEY PK FALK RD & PLOMONDON ST, VANCOUVER WA	306 - B3
BAKER PK PARK ST & PARKDALE DR, GRANTS PASS OR	335 - F10
BAKER PK ON CROWN HILL MARY AV NE, SEATTLE WA	273 - F1
BALLANTREE PK DISTRICT OF WEST VANCOUVE BC	156 - B2
BALLARD PLGD NW 65TH ST & 14TH AV NW, SEATTLE WA	273 - F3
BALL, JOHN PK KAUFMAN AV & W 23RD ST, VANCOUVER WA	305 - F3
BALL PK MARION CO OR	323 - G14
BANDON STATE PK COOS CO OR	220 - A7
BANFIELD PK CRAIGFLOWER RD, CITY OF VICTORIA BC	256 - E7
BARNARD PK ESQUIMALT RD, CITY OF VICTORIA BC	256 - E8
BARNES STATE PK BARNES DR, COWLITZ CO WA	187 - C5
BAR-S PLGD SW ADMIRAL WY & 65TH AV SW, SEATTLE WA	280 - B3
BARTON PK BARTON PARK RD, CLACKAMAS CO OR	200 - B4
BASTENDORFF BEACH COUNTY PK CAPE ARAGO HWY, COOS CO OR	220 - B1
BATEMAN ISLAND RICHLAND WA	342 - C6
BATTERSBY FIELD HALLECK ST, BELLINGHAM WA	258 - D5
BATTLE GROUND LAKE STATE PK NE 249TH ST, CLARK CO WA	193 - A3
BATTLE MOUNTAIN STATE PK PENDLETON-JOHN DAY HWY, UMATILLA CO OR	129 - B2
BAYVIEW PLGD W ARMOUR ST & 24TH AV W, SEATTLE WA	272 - E7
BEACHSIDE STATE PK OREGON COAST HWY, LINCOLN CO OR	328 - A11
BEACON HILL PK DOUGLAS ST&DALLS RD, CITY OF VICTORIA BC	256 - G11
BEACON ROCK STATE PK EVERGREEN HWY, SKAMANIA CO WA	194 - B6
BEACONSFIELD PK SLOCAN ST, VANCOUVER BC	255 - D14
BEAR CREEK PK 13750 88TH AV, CITY OF SURREY BC	157 - A6
BEAR CREEK PK SISKIYOU BLVD & HIGHLAND DR, MEDFORD OR	336 - F13
BEAVER CREEK PROVINCIAL PK HWY 22A, BRITISH COLUMBIA BC	106 - B1
BEECHER PK EASTLAWN DR, DISTRICT OF BURNABY BC	255 - J12
BELCARRA PK BEDWELL BAY RD, MAPLE RIDGE BC	157 - A3
BELVEDERE VIEWPOINT PK SW ADMIRAL WY & OLGA ST, SEATTLE WA	281 - F2
BENEDICT, ED PK SE 99TH AV & SE POWELL BL, PORTLAND OR	319 - H3
BERKELEY PK SE 39TH AV & SE BYBEE BL, PORTLAND OR	318 - B5
BERRYDALE PK SE 92ND AV & SE TAYLOR ST, PORTLAND OR	315 - G7
BEULAH PK NE LINCOLN ST, ROSEBURG OR	334 - H6
BEVERLY BEACH STATE PK LINCOLN CO OR	206 - B2
B F DAY PLGD N 41ST ST & FREMONT AV N, SEATTLE WA	273 - H6
BHY KRACKE PK 1200 5TH AV N, SEATTLE WA	277 - H2
BICENTENNIAL PK CHRISTENSEN RD & STRANDER BL, TUKWILA WA	289 - H6
BIDDLEWOOD PK SE RIVERRIDGE DR, VANCOUVER WA	311 - J1
BIG CREEK STATE PK OREGON COAST HWY, LINCOLN CO OR	328 - B10
BIGELOW PK OLYMPIA WA	297 - A4
BIRCH BAY STATE PK BIRCH BAY DR, BIRCH BAY WA	158 - B5
BLACK BAY PK POST FALLS ID	353 - J7
BLACK RIVER RIPARIAN FOREST MONSTER RD SW, RENTON WA	289 - J3
BLAINE, DENNY PK LAKE WASHINGTON BL & DENNY BL, SEATTLE WA	279 - F4
BLAKE ISLAND STATE PK BLAKE ISLAND, KITSAP CO WA	174 - D3
BLENKIN MEM PK HWY 19, BRITISH COLUMBIA BC	92 - A1
BLOEDE DONOVAN PK ELECTRIC AV, BELLINGHAM WA	258 - J5
BLOOMINGTON PK SE 100TH AV & SE STEELE ST, PORTLAND OR	319 - H4
BLUEBELLE PK DAISY ST, SPRINGFIELD OR	331 - F8
BLUERIDGE PK BERKLEY AV, DISTRICT OF NORTH VANCOUV BC	255 - J4
BOARDMAN, SAMUEL H STATE PK OREGON COAST HWY, CURRY CO OR	232 - B4
BOGACHIEL STATE PK OFF HWY 101, CLALLAM CO WA	169 - D2
BOISE NATL FOREST BOISE CO ID	253 - D1
BOLON ISLAND STATE PK DOUGLAS CO OR	218 - C1
BOREN PK 15TH AV E & E GARFIELD ST, SEATTLE WA	278 - C2
BOREN-PIKE-PINE PK PINE ST & PIKE ST, SEATTLE WA	278 - A5
BOTHWELL PK 168TH ST & 96TH ST, CITY OF SURREY BC	157 - B6
BOULEVARD PK GRAND BLVD, CITY OF NORTH VANCOUVER BC	255 - C5
BOUNDARY CREEK PROVINCIAL PK HWY 3, BRITISH COLUMBIA BC	105 - B1
BOWERS ROCK STATE PK CHERRY LN, LINN CO OR	207 - B5
BOW LAKE PK 50TH CT S & S 178TH ST, SEATAC WA	289 - F7

FEATURE NAME City State	Page-Grid
BOWL AND PITCHER AUBREY L WHITE PKWY, SPOKANE CO WA	348 - B4
BOWMAN PK FRONT AV, ALBANY OR	326 - E7
BOYLES, EARL PK SE BOISE ST, PORTLAND OR	319 - J3
BRADLEY PK SALEM OR	324 - H3
BRAEFOOT PK MCKENZIE AVE, DISTRICT OF SAANICH BC	256 - J3
BRANDIS PK CORVALLIS OR	327 - F5
BRENTWOOD PK SE 62ND AV & SE COOPER ST, PORTLAND OR	318 - D5
BRENTWOOD PK SOUTHLAWN DR, DISTRICT OF BURNABY BC	255 - J12
BRIDAL VEIL FALLS PROVINCIAL PK BRIDAL FALLS RD, BRITISH COLUMBIA BC	94 - C3
BRIDGEMAN PK KEITH RD, DIST OF NORTH VANCOUVER BC	255 - E6
BRIDLE TRAILS STATE PK 116TH AV NE & N 53RD ST, KING CO WA	175 - C1
BRIGHT ANGEL PK TRANS CANADA HWY, BRITISH COLUMBIA BC	101 - A2
BRIGHTON PLGD S JUNEAU ST & 39TH AV S, SEATTLE WA	283 - E7
BRISCO PK 62ND AV S & S 190TH ST, KENT WA	291 - G2
BROAD VIEW PK CANADA WY, DISTRICT OF BURNABY BC	255 - G14
BROADWAY PK CORNWALL AV, BELLINGHAM WA	258 - D4
BROOKE ST PK BROOKE ST, CITY OF VICTORIA BC	256 - J10
BROOKLYN PK SE 15TH AV & SE BUSH ST, PORTLAND OR	317 - H2
BROOKSBANK PK DRAYTON ST, DISTRICT OF N VANCOUVER BC	255 - E5
BROOKSIDE PK 4100 PLOMONDON ST, VANCOUVER WA	306 - A3
BROOKS MEM STATE PK HWY 97, KLICKITAT CO WA	127 - C1
BROWN PK W HARVARD BLVD, ROSEBURG OR	334 - C7
BROWN, SAM PK E DEVINE RD & IDAHO ST, VANCOUVER WA	306 - C5
BRUCEPORT PK US 101, PACIFIC CO WA	183 - D6
BRUSH COLLEGE PK SALEM OR	322 - D8
BRYANT PK BRYANT WY & CALAPOOIA ST, ALBANY OR	326 - B7
BRYANT PLGD 40TH AV NE & NE 65TH ST, SEATTLE WA	275 - F3
BUCKMAN FIELD NE 12TH AV & NE GLISAN ST, PORTLAND OR	313 - H5
BUENA VISTA OCEAN WAYSIDE STATE PK OREGON COAST HWY, CURRY CO OR	228 - A6
BUFORD REC AREA FRANK PARISH RD, LANE CO OR	331 - C11
BULLARDS BEACH STATE PK PARK RD, COOS CO OR	220 - B5
BULLEN PK ESQUIMALT RD, TOWN OF ESQUIMALT BC	256 - C8
BUNNELL PK SE PARK ST & SE PINE LN, CLACKAMAS CO OR	321 - J6
BURKE-GILMAN PLGD SAND PT WY NE & NE 50TH ST, SEATTLE WA	275 - F5
BURKE MOUNTAIN REGL PK COAST MERIDIAN RD&HARPER RD, COQUITLAM BC	157 - B3
BURLINGAME PK SW 12TH AV & SW FALCON ST, PORTLAND OR	316 - D6
BURNABY HEIGHTS PK TRINITY ST, DISTRICT OF BURNABY BC	255 - G9
BURNABY LAKE PK DISTRICT OF BURNABY BC	156 - D5
BURNT BRIDGE CREEK GREENWAY E FOURTH PLAIN BLVD, VANCOUVER WA	306 - B4
BURRARD VIEW PK TRINITY ST, VANCOUVER BC	255 - D9
BUSH PASTURE PK SALEM OR	324 - H1
BUSH PIONEER COUNTY PK PACIFIC CO WA	183 - C7
BUTCHART GARDENS 800 BENVENUTO AV, DIST OF CTRL SAANICH BC	159 - B4
BUTTERFLY PK 7720 SW MACADAM AV, PORTLAND OR	317 - F6
BY-PASS SHELTERBELT BY-PASS HWY, RICHLAND WA	340 - D14
BYRON PK BYRON RD, DIST OF N VANCOUVER BC	255 - J4
CADBORO GYRO PK CADBORO BAY RD, DIST OF SAANICH BC	257 - E4
CAMPBELL RIVER REGL PK 4TH AV, TOWNSHIP OF LANGLEY BC	158 - C2
CAMP LONG NATURE CTR 5200 35TH AV SW, SEATTLE WA	281 - F5
CAMP SEALTH REC AREA SW CAMP SEALTH RD, KING CO WA	174 - C7
CANNON HILL PK W SHOSHONE PL, SPOKANE WA	348 - J12
CAPE ARGO STATE PK CAPE ARAGO HWY, COOS CO OR	220 - B2
CAPE BLANCO STATE PK CURRY CO OR	224 - A4
CAPE KIWANDA STATE PK MCPHILLIPS RD, TILLAMOOK CO OR	197 - A6
CAPE LOOKOUT STATE PK CAPE LOOKOUT RD, TILLAMOOK CO OR	197 - A3
CAPE MEARES STATE PK CAPE MEARES LOOP RD, TILLAMOOK CO OR	197 - A1
CAPE SEBASTIAN STATE PK OREGON COAST HWY, CURRY CO OR	228 - A7
CAPILANO RIVER REGIONAL PK DIST OF NORTH VANCOUVER BC	254 - G1
CAPITOL LAKE PK WATER ST, OLYMPIA WA	296 - H5
CAP SANTE PK W AV, ANACORTES WA	259 - J2
CARMANAH PACIFIC PROVINCIAL PK BRITISH COLUMBIA BC	100 - B2
CARNARVON PK HENDERSON RD, DISTRICT OF OAK BAY BC	257 - C7
CARNARVON PK VANCOUVER BC	254 - B14
CARTER PK COLUMBIA ST & W 33RD ST, VANCOUVER WA	305 - G3
CASCADE HEAD EXPERIMENTAL FOREST OREGON COAST HWY, TILLAMOOK CO OR	203 - B2
CASCADE PK HARRISON ST & MINOR AV N, SEATTLE WA	278 - A4
CASCADE VIEW PK 88TH ST SE & 4TH PL, EVERETT WA	268 - C5

FEATURE NAME City State	Page-Grid
CASCADIA STATE PK LINN CO OR	134 - A2
CASEY STATE PK CRATER LAKE HWY, JACKSON CO OR	149 - C1
CASTLE PK S UNIVERSITY RD, SPOKANE VALLEY WA	350 - F13
CATERPILLAR ISLAND REC AREA CATERPILLAR ISLAND, CLARK CO WA	192 - B5
CATES PK DIST OF NORTH VANCOUVER BC	156 - D4
CATHEDRAL PROVINCIAL PK BRITISH COLUMBIA BC	104 - A1
CEDAR COTTAGE PK BROADWAY E, VANCOUVER BC	255 - A12
CEDAR RIVER NATURAL ZONE ROYAL HILL DR SE, RENTON WA	175 - C5
CEDAR RIVER PK 1717 MAPLE VALLEY, KING CO WA	175 - D5
CENTENNIAL PK WALLACE DR, DIST OF CENTRAL SAANICH BC	159 - C3
CENTERPOINTE PK NE FOURTH PLAIN BLVD, VANCOUVER WA	307 - F2
CENTRAL PK MADISON AV, CORVALLIS OR	327 - G10
CENTRAL PK QUADRA ST, CITY OF VICTORIA BC	256 - H8
CENTRAL PK NORTH E FOURTH PLAIN BLVD & T ST, VANCOUVER WA	305 - H3
CHAMPOEG STATE HERITAGE AREA 8239 CHAMPOEG RD, MARION CO OR	199 - A6
CHAPMAN SQUARE PK SW MAIN ST & SW 4TH AV, PORTLAND OR	313 - F6
CHARLESTON PK VANCOUVER BC	254 - F12
CHEMAINUS RIVER PROV PK HWY 18, BRITISH COLUMBIA BC	101 - A1
CHERRY PK SE 106TH AV & SE STEPHENS ST, PORTLAND OR	315 - J7
CHETZEMOKA PK JACKSON ST & BLAINE ST, PORT TOWNSEND WA	263 - H3
CHIAWANA PK CHIAWANA PARK & ROAD 88, FRANKLIN CO WA	342 - C5
CHIEF GARRY PK E MISSION AV, SPOKANE WA	349 - E7
CHINA CREEK PK HWY 4, BRITISH COLUMBIA BC	92 - B3
CHINA LAKE PK S 19TH ST & FRWY 16, TACOMA WA	292 - A6
CHIN TIMINI PK TAYLOR AV, CORVALLIS OR	327 - F8
CHIP ROSS PK LESTER AV, BENTON CO OR	327 - E3
CHRISTENSEN GREENBELT PK STRANDER BL & CHRISTENSEN RD, TUKWILA WA	289 - H6
CHRISTIE PK NE 43RD ST & 9TH AV NE, SEATTLE WA	274 - B6
CHRISTINA LAKE PROVINCIAL PK HWY 3 & HWY 395, BRITISH COLUMBIA BC	105 - C1
CHRISTMAS HILL PK RAINBOW ST, DISTRICT OF SAANICH BC	256 - F2
CITY PK COEUR D'ALENE ID	355 - E11
CIVIC FIELD COMPLEX MOORE ST, BELLINGHAM WA	258 - F6
CLAGGET CREEK PK KEIZER OR	323 - B5
CLARK ISLAND STATE MARINE PK CLARK ISLAND, SAN JUAN CO WA	160 - B1
CLARK, JANE PLGD ORCHARD ST & N 39TH ST, TACOMA WA	292 - B1
CLARK PK 15TH AV, VANCOUVER BC	255 - B14
CLARK PK 25TH ST & OAKES AV, EVERETT WA	264 - E3
CLARK-WILSON PK GERMANTOWN RD, PORTLAND OR	192 - B7
CLASSICAL CHINESE GARDEN NW 3RD AV & NW EVERETT ST, PORTLAND OR	313 - F5
CLATSOP ST FOREST CLATSOP CO OR	300 - G7
CLAYBELL PK BOARDMOOR ST & BELLERIVE DR, RICHLAND WA	341 - J10
CLEARWATER PARK AND LANDING CLEARWATER LN, LANE CO OR	331 - E10
CLIFF PK W 12TH AV, SPOKANE WA	348 - J11
CLINE FALLS STATE PK DESCHUTES CO OR	212 - C5
CLINTON PK 1ST AV, VANCOUVER BC	255 - C12
CLINTON PK SE 55TH AV & SE WOODWARD ST, PORTLAND OR	318 - D1
CLOVERLAND PK 29TH ST, CORVALLIS OR	327 - F7
COAL CREEK PK COAL CREEK PKY & SE 60TH ST, NEWCASTLE WA	175 - C4
COE CIRCLE PK NE 39TH AV & NE GLISAN ST, PORTLAND OR	314 - B5
COEUR D'ALENE NATL FOREST KOOTENAI CO ID	355 - J2
COEUR D'ALENE PK W 4TH AV & S CHESTNUT ST, SPOKANE WA	348 - G10
COLLIER MEM STATE PK THE DALLES-CALIFORNIA HWY, KLAMATH CO OR	231 - D2
COLMAN PK LAKE WASHINGTON BLVD S, SEATTLE WA	282 - E2
COLUMBIA LANCASTER PK MISSOULA AV & MONTANA LN, VANCOUVER WA	306 - D5
COLUMBIA PK N LOMBARD ST & N DANA ST, PORTLAND OR	308 - C4
COLUMBIA PK S ALASKA ST & RAINIER AV S, SEATTLE WA	282 - E5
COLUMBIA PK WEST W COLUMBIA DR, RICHLAND WA	342 - C6
COLUMBIA PLAYFIELD SWIFT BLVD & STEVENS DR, RICHLAND WA	341 - F1
COLVILLE NATL FOREST FERRY CO WA	105 - B1
COMMENCEMENT PK MCCARVER ST & RUSTON WY, TACOMA WA	293 - E2
COMMODORE PK W COMMODORE WY & 33RD AV W, SEATTLE WA	272 - D4
COMMONAGE RESERVE HWY 5A, BRITISH COLUMBIA BC	95 - C1
COMSTOCK PK W 29TH AV, SPOKANE WA	348 - J13
CONE ISLANDS STATE PK CONE ISLANDS, SKAGIT CO WA	160 - B4
CONFEDERATION PK PENZANCE DR, DISTRICT OF BURNABY BC	255 - H9
CONGER PK THE DALLES-CALIFORNIA HY, KLAMTH FLLS OR	338 - B6
CONNAUGHT PK VANCOUVER BC	254 - C13

FEATURE NAME City State	Page-Grid
COOS COUNTY FOREST	220 - C3
COOS CO OR	
COPELAND ISLANDS MARINE PK	92 - B1
BRITISH COLUMBIA BC	
COPLEY MEM PK	256 - E1
CAREY RD, DISTRICT OF SAANICH BC	
COQUITLAM RIVER PK	157 - B4
SHAUGHNESSY ST & LINCOLN AV, COQUITLAM BC	
CORBETT, ELLIOTT R II MEM STATE PK	211 - A2
OFF SUTTLE LAKE LP, JEFFERSON CO OR	
CORBIN PK	348 - J5
W WAVERLY PL, SPOKANE WA	
CORNWALLL PK	258 - D3
BIRCHWOOD, BELLINGHAM WA	
COUCH PK	312 - D5
NW 19TH AV & NW GLISAN ST, PORTLAND OR	
COUGAR MOUNTAIN REGL WILDLAND PK	175 - D4
LAKEMONT BLVD SE, KING CO WA	
COULEE DAM NATL REC AREA	114 - A1
ELIJAH RD, STEVENS CO WA	
COUNCIL CREST PK	316 - B1
SW COUNCIL CREST DR, PORTLAND OR	
COUNTY PK	350 - H3
E WELLESLEY AV, SPOKANE CO WA	
COVE PALISADES STATE PARK, THE	208 - A6
JEFFERSON CO OR	
COWEN PK	274 - C4
BROOKLYN AV & NE 62ND ST, SEATTLE WA	
CRAIGHILL PLGD	341 - G3
COMSTOCK ST & CRAIGHILL AVE, RICHLAND WA	
CRANBERRY LAKE PK	259 - E3
CRANBERRY LAKE RD, ANACORTES WA	
CRATER LAKE NATL PK	227 - B1
KLAMATH CO OR	
CRESTON PK	318 - B2
SE 43RD AV & SE POWELL BLVD, PORTLAND OR	
CRESTVIEW PK	289 - E5
S 160TH ST, TUKWILA WA	
CRYSTAL GARDEN	256 - G9
713 DOUGLAS ST, CITY OF VICTORIA BC	
CRYSTAL SPRINGS PK	289 - F5
S 160TH ST & 51ST AV S, TUKWILA WA	
CULLABY LAKE COUNTY PK	188 - B3
OREGON COAST, CLATSOP CO OR	
CUSTER PK	316 - C6
SW CAPITOL HILL RD, PORTLAND OR	
CYPRESS FALLS PK	156 - A2
DIST OF WEST VANCOUVER BC	
CYPRESS PROVINCIAL PK	156 - A1
DIST OF WEST VANCOUVER BC	
DABNEY STATE PK	200 - C2
E HIST COLUMBIA RIV HY, MULTNOMAH CO OR	
DAHL, WALDO J PLAYFIELD	274 - D2
25TH AV NE & NE 80TH ST, SEATTLE WA	
DARCY ISLAND MARINE PK	159 - D4
BRITISH COLUMBIA BC	
DAVID SPENCER PK	257 - A7
SHELBOURNE ST, CITY OF VICTORIA BC	
DAVIS LAKE PROVINCIAL PK	94 - B3
SYLVESTER RD, BRITISH COLUMBIA BC	
DAWSON PK	313 - G2
N WILLIAMS AV & N STANTON ST, PORTLAND OR	
DEADMAN LAKE PROVINCIAL PK	104 - C1
HWY 97, BRITISH COLUMBIA BC	
DEADMANS ISLAND STATE PK	181 - B1
CUTTS ISLAND, PIERCE CO WA	
DEARBORN PK	282 - D6
S BRANDON ST & 29TH S ST, SEATTLE WA	
DEAS ISLAND REGL PK	156 - C7
DISTRICT OF DELTA BC	
DECEPTION PASS STATE PK	259 - E13
OFF HWY 20, SKAGIT CO WA	
DEER CREEK PK	334 - G7
SE JACKSON & NE DIAMOND LAKE, ROSEBURG OR	
DEERFIELD PK	326 - F12
ALBANY OR	
DEER LAKE PK	156 - D5
DISTRICT OF BURNABY BC	
DELBROOK PK	255 - A2
DELBROOK AV, DISTRICT OF NORTH VANCOUV BC	
DEL NORTE COAST REDWOODS STATE PK	148 - B3
DEL NORTE CO CA	
DELONG PLGD	292 - B6
S 12TH & MULLEN ST, TACOMA WA	
DELRIDGE PLAYFIELD	281 - G5
DELRIDGE WY SW&SW GENESEE ST, SEATTLE WA	
DELTA PONDS PK	329 - H3
DELTA HWY, EUGENE OR	
DELTA WATERS PK	336 - G6
SHASTER DR, MEDFORD OR	
DENNY PK	277 - J4
DENNY WY & DEXTER AV, SEATTLE WA	
DERBY REACH REGIONAL PK	157 - C6
ALLARD CR, TOWNSHIP OF LANGLEY BC	
DESCHUTES NATL FOREST	332 - J2
NE BUTLER MKT RD&YEOMAN, DESCHUTES CO OR	
DES MOINES BEACH PK	290 - A5
CLIFF AV S, DES MOINES WA	
DES MOINES CREEK PK	290 - A5
DES MOINES MEMORIAL DR S, DES MOINES WA	
DES MOINES CREEK PK	290 - B4
S 204TH ST, SEATAC WA	
DES MOINES FIELDHOUSE PK	290 - A5
S 219TH ST & 11TH AV S, DES MOINES WA	
DES MOINES MEM PK	290 - A5
SR 509&DES MOINES MEM DR S, DES MOINES WA	
DESOLATION SOUND PROVINCIAL MARINE PK	92 - B1
DESOLATION SOUND, BRITISH COLUMBIA BC	
DETROIT LAKE STATE PK	134 - B1
MARION CO OR	
DEVILS ELBOW PK	209 - A7
OREGON COAST HWY, LANE CO OR	
DEVILS PUNCH BOWL STATE PK	206 - A2
LINCOLN CO OR	
DEWITT PK	316 - D4
SW SUNSET BL & SW DEWITT ST, PORTLAND OR	
DILLARD SKYLINE PK	330 - D14
LANE CO OR	
DIONISIO POINT PROV PK	101 - B1
PORLIER PASS RD, BRITISH COLUMBIA BC	
DISCOVERY ISLAND MARINE PK	257 - J10
OFFSHORE ISLAND, BRITISH COLUMBIA BC	
DISCOVERY PK	272 - B4
36TH AV W & W EMERSON ST, SEATTLE WA	
DOE ISLAND STATE MARINE PK	160 - A3
OFF OLGA TO PT LAWRENCE RD, SN JUAN CO WA	
DOGWOOD PK	321 - J3
SE ADAMS ST & SE MAIN ST, MILWAUKIE OR	
DORAN PK	255 - F1
KILMER PL, DIST OF NORTH VANCOUVER BC	
DOUGLAS, DAVID PK	306 - E5
GARRISON RD, VANCOUVER WA	
DOUGLAS GARDENS PK	331 - C9
REDWOOD DR, SPRINGFIELD OR	

FEATURE NAME City State	Page-Grid
DOUGLAS PK	254 - F14
VANCOUVER BC	
DOWNRIVER PK	348 - D5
W DOWNRIVER PARK DR, SPOKANE WA	
DRAKE PK	332 - D7
NW DRAKE RD & NW NASHVILLE AV, BEND OR	
DRAPER PK	326 - D11
29TH AV, ALBANY OR	
DRAYCOTT PK	255 - F2
DRAYCOTT RD, DIST OF NORTH VANCOUVER BC	
DRUMHELLER SPRINGS	348 - G5
W EUCLID AV, SPOKANE WA	
DUBOIS PK	306 - B6
BLANDFORD DR, VANCOUVER WA	
DUNDARAVE PK	254 - A3
LWR BELLEVUE RD&25TH ST, DIST OF W VAN BC	
DUNIWAY PK	317 - E1
SW 6TH AV & SW SHERIDAN ST, PORTLAND OR	
DUNN, PAUL ST FOREST	207 - A3
TAMPICO RD, BENTON CO OR	
DUWAMISH PK	287 - E7
44TH AV S & 44TH PL S, TUKWILA WA	
DUWAMISH RIVER PK	286 - A2
10TH AV S & S KENYON ST, SEATTLE WA	
EADES PK	326 - F6
FRONT AV, ALBANY OR	
EAGLE FERN PK	200 - C5
EAGLE FERN RD, CLACKAMAS CO OR	
EAGLE ISLAND STATE PK	181 - B3
EAGLE ISLAND, PIERCE CO WA	
EAGLE ISLAND STATE PK	253 - A1
OFF N LINDER RD, ADA CO ID	
EAGLES PK	334 - F8
ROSE ST, ROSEBURG OR	
EASTBANK RIVERFRONT PK	313 - G6
PORTLAND OR	
EAST DELTA PK	309 - F2
PACIFIC HWY WEST & N UNION CT, PORTLND OR	
EASTGATE BASIN PK	323 - D9
SALEM OR	
EASTGATE WOODLANDS PK	330 - E7
WALNUT RD, SPRINGFIELD OR	
EAST MAGNOLIA PLAYFIELD	276 - D1
26TH AV W & W SMITH ST, SEATTLE WA	
EAST MONTLAKE PK	278 - D1
E PARK DR & LAKE WASHINGTN BL, SEATTLE WA	
EAST SOOKE REGL PK	164 - D1
EAST SOOKE RD, BRITISH COLUMBIA BC	
EASTVIEW PK	255 - E4
RUFUS DR, CITY OF NORTH VANCOUVER BC	
EAST WALUGA PK	320 - A6
15522 QUARRY RD, LAKE OSWEGO OR	
EASTWOOD PK	334 - J8
DOUGLAS AV NE, ROSEBURG OR	
ECOLA STATE PK	301 - B12
TILLAMOOK HEAD COVE RD, CLATSOP CO OR	
EDGECLIFF PK	350 - B10
S PARK RD, SPOKANE VALLEY WA	
EDGEWATER PK	260 - A13
BEHRENS-MILLETT RD, SKAGIT CO WA	
EDGEWOOD PK	306 - A5
EDGEWOOD DR, VANCOUVER WA	
EDWARDS, MYRTLE PK	277 - G4
ALASKAN WY W, SEATTLE WA	
EIDON PK	254 - H1
DIST OF NORTH VANCOUVER BC	
ELEANOR PK	326 - E8
FRONT AV, ALBANY OR	
ELIZABETH PK	258 - C5
WASHINGTON ST, BELLINGHAM WA	
ELK-BEAVER LAKE REGL PK	159 - C5
HWY 17, DISTRICT OF SAANICH BC	
ELK FALLS PK	92 - A1
HWY 19, BRITISH COLUMBIA BC	
ELLIOT POINTE PK	267 - E2
LUMLEY AV, MUKILTEO WA	
ELLIOTT BAY PK	277 - G3
ALASKAN WY W, SEATTLE WA	
ELLIOTT ST FOREST	218 - D3
COOS CO OR	
ELLSWORTH PK	307 - H7
SE 10TH ST & SE 105TH AV, VANCOUVER WA	
EMIGRANT LAKE COUNTY REC AREA	234 - D4
OFF EMIGRANT CREEK RD, JACKSON CO OR	
ENDOLYNE PK	284 - D4
SW 98TH ST & 49TH AV SW, SEATTLE WA	
E QUEEN ANNE PLGD	277 - H2
HOWE ST & 2ND AV N, SEATTLE WA	
ERROL HEIGHTS PK	318 - C7
SE 52ND AV & SE TENINO CT, PORTLAND OR	
ESSEX PK	319 - F3
SE 79TH AV & SE CENTER ST, PORTLAND OR	
ESTHER SHORT PK	305 - F5
ESTHER ST & W 8TH ST, VANCOUVER WA	
EVERGREEN PK	306 - A4
ROSSITER LN, VANCOUVER WA	
EXHIBITION PK	255 - E10
HASTINGS ST E, VANCOUVER BC	
FAIRFIELD HILL PK	256 - J11
FAIRFIELD RD, CITY OF VICTORIA BC	
FAIRHAVEN PK	258 - B11
CHUCKANUT DR, BELLINGHAM WA	
FAIRMONT PK	324 - G1
SALEM OR	
FAIRMOUNT PK	281 - E2
FAIRMOUNT AV SW & ADMIRAL WY, SEATTLE WA	
FAIRMOUNT PLGD	281 - E6
FAUNTLEROY WY SW & SW BRANDON, SEATTLE WA	
FAIRVIEW PK	274 - B7
EASTLAKE AVE, SEATTLE WA	
FAIRWOOD CAMELOT PK	347 - A8
N DIVISION ST, FAIRWOOD WA	
FALAISE PK	255 - E13
WORTHINGTON DR, VANCOUVER BC	
FALLS PK	353 - G7
POST FALLS ID	
FARRAGUT PK	309 - F4
N FARRAGUT ST & N KERBY AV, PORTLAND OR	
FARRAGUT STATE PK	245 - C1
KOOTENAI CO ID	
FATHER BLANCHET PK	306 - E6
BIRMINGHAM WY&LOUISIANA DR, VANCOUVER WA	
FAUNTLEROY PK	284 - D4
SW BARTON ST & 40TH AV SW, SEATTLE WA	
FERNHILL PK	310 - B6
NE 37TH AV & NE AINSWORTH ST, PORTLAND OR	
FERRY PK	293 - F6
S 14TH ST & CUSHMAN AV, TACOMA WA	
FERRY ROAD PK	333 - H3
FERRY RD, NORTH BEND OR	
FICHTNER MAINWARING PK	336 - D14
HOMLES AV & HOLLY ST, MEDFORD OR	
FINCH ARBORETUM	348 - E12
W WOODLAND BLVD, SPOKANE WA	

FEATURE NAME City State	Page-Grid
FIRCREST PK	294 - A1
ELECTRON WY & CONTRA CSTA AV, FIRCREST WA	
FIRCREST PK	324 - F4
SALEM OR	
FIREHOUSE PK	278 - C6
E CHERRY ST & 18TH AV, SEATTLE WA	
FIREMANS PK	293 - H5
CLIFF AV & S 9TH ST, TACOMA WA	
FIRLAND PARKWAY	319 - E3
SE 72ND AV & SE FOSTER RD, PORTLAND OR	
FIRST HILL PK	283 - J2
72ND AV SE & SE 32ND ST, MERCER ISLAND WA	
FIRST HILL PK	278 - B5
MINOR AV & UNIVERSITY ST, SEATTLE WA	
FISH CREEK REC AREA	131 - C1
IDAHO CO ID	
FISHERMANS WHARF PK	256 - F9
ERIE ST, CITY OF VICTORIA BC	
FISH HATCHERY PK	229 - A7
FISH HATCHERY RD, JOSEPHINE CO OR	
FLAVEL PK	319 - E6
SE LAMBERT ST & SE 75TH PL, PORTLAND OR	
FLEETWOOD PK	157 - B7
80TH AV & 160TH ST, CITY OF SURREY BC	
FLO WARE PK	278 - D7
S JACKSON ST & 29TH AV S, SEATTLE WA	
FOGARTY CREEK STATE PK	203 - A7
OREGON COAST HWY, LINCOLN CO OR	
FOREST & CEDAR PK	258 - C8
FOREST ST, BELLINGHAM WA	
FOREST PK	312 - A2
NW ST HELENS RD, PORTLAND OR	
FOREST PK	264 - C6
PIGEON CREEK RD, EVERETT WA	
FOREST RIDGE PK	307 - G4
NE PINECREEK ST&NE 17TH ST, VANCOUVER WA	
FORT BORST PK	299 - C3
HARRISON AV & CAVENESS DR, CENTRALIA WA	
FORT CANBY STATE PK	186 - A7
PACIFIC CO WA	
FORT CASEY STATE PK	167 - B5
S ENGLE RD, ISLAND CO WA	
FORT COLUMBIA STATE PK	186 - B7
PACIFIC CO WA	
FORT DENT PK	289 - H3
INTERURBAN AV S&FORT DENT WY, TUKWILA WA	
FORT FLAGLER STATE PK	167 - B6
FLAGLER RD, JEFFERSON CO WA	
FORT PK	331 - H7
N 58TH ST, SPRINGFIELD OR	
FORT SIMCOE HIST STATE PK	119 - C2
FORT SIMCO RD, YAKIMA CO WA	
FORT STEVENS STATE PK	188 - B1
JETTY RD, CLATSOP CO OR	
FORT WALLA WALLA CITY PK	344 - H10
MYRA RD, WALLA WALLA WA	
FORT WORDEN STATE PK	263 - G1
FORT WORDEN WY, PORT TOWNSEND WA	
FOSTER, JOSEPH MEM PK	289 - F2
S 139TH ST & 53RD AV S, TUKWILA WA	
FOUR CORNERS COUNTY PK	325 - E1
FOUR CORNERS OR	
FRANCIS, THOMAS PK	256 - A1
PROSPECT LAKE RD, DISTRICT OF SAANICH BC	
FRANKFORT PLGD	341 - E2
FRANKFORT ST & HARTFORT ST, RICHLAND WA	
FRANKLIN PK	348 - J2
N WHITEHOUSE ST, SPOKANE WA	
FRANKLIN PK	292 - D6
S 12TH ST & PUGENT SOUND AV, TACOMA WA	
FRASER RIVER PK	156 - C6
DISTRICT OF BURNABY BC	
FRAZER PK	314 - C4
NE 52ND AV & NE HASSALO ST, PORTLAND OR	
FRAZIER, PRENTIS I PK	278 - D4
E HARRISON ST & 24TH AV E, SEATTLE WA	
FREEPONS PK	321 - F7
HEMLOCK ST & STANDARD ST, LAKE OSWEGO OR	
FREEWAY LAKES COUNTY PK	326 - H14
THREE LAKES RD, LINN CO OR	
FREEWAY PK	278 - A5
6TH AV & SENECA ST, SEATTLE WA	
FREEWAY PK 3	274 - B4
5TH AV NE & NE 60TH ST, SEATTLE WA	
FREMONT CANAL PK	273 - H6
N CANAL ST & PHINNEY AV, SEATTLE WA	
FREMONT NATL FOREST	143 - A2
LAKE CO OR	
FRIENDSHIP PK	347 - B14
CALKINS DR & STANDARD ST, SPOKANE WA	
FRINK PK	278 - E7
S FRINK PL & LAKE WASHINGTON, SEATTLE WA	
FROST, LARRY PK	293 - H5
PACIFIC AV & S 9TH ST, TACOMA WA	
FROULA PLGD	274 - C3
12TH AV NE & NE 71ST ST, SEATTLE WA	
FRUIT VALLEY PK	304 - E2
FRUIT VALLEY RD, VANCOUVER WA	
FULTON PK	317 - E6
SW BARBUR BL & SW MILES ST, PORTLAND OR	
GABRIEL PK	316 - A5
SW 45TH AV & SW VERMONT ST, PORTLAND OR	
GADDIS PK	334 - E6
NW HICKS ST, ROSEBURG OR	
GAMMANS PK	308 - D5
N BURRAGE AV & N GAMMANS PL, PORTLAND OR	
GARFIELD NATURE TRAIL	296 - G4
ROGERS ST & CONGER AV, OLYMPIA WA	
GARFIELD PK	293 - F3
BOROUGH RD & N STADIUM WY, TACOMA WA	
GARFIELD PK	327 - G7
CLEVELAND AV, CORVALLIS OR	
GARFIELD PLAYFIELD	278 - D6
23RD AV & E JEFFERSON ST, SEATTLE WA	
GARFIELD PLGD	265 - F2
WALNUT ST & 24TH ST, EVERETT WA	
GARIBALDI PROVINCIAL PK	93 - C1
OFF TRANS CANADA HWY, BRITISH COLUMBIA BC	
GAS WORKS PK	274 - A7
N NORTHLAKE WY & MERIDIAN AV, SEATTLE WA	
GEARHART MOUNTAIN WILDERNESS	151 - B1
LAKE CO OR	
GEN ANDERSON PK	306 - D6
BURDICK AV & E ARIZONA DR, VANCOUVER WA	
GENESEE PARK & PLAYFIELD	283 - F4
4316 S GENESEE ST, SEATTLE WA	
GERLINGER, GEORGE T STATE EXP FRST	125 - A3
POLK CO OR	
GIFFORD PINCHOT NATL FOREST	185 - A6
LEWIS CO WA	
GILBERT CREEK PK	335 - E6
HAWTHRNE AV & HLLCRST DR, GRANTS PASS OR	
GILMAN PLGD	273 - F4
NW 54TH ST & 11TH AV NW, SEATTLE WA	

FEATURE NAME City State	Page-Grid
GINKO PETRIFIED FOREST STATE PK	120 - B1
KITTITAS CO WA	
GLANFORD PK	256 - F3
KENNETH ST, DISTRICT OF SAANICH BC	
GLENHAVEN PK	315 - F3
NE 82ND AV & NE SISKIYOU ST, PORTLAND OR	
GLENWOOD PK	319 - G5
SE 87TH AV & SE CLAYBOURNE ST, PORTLND OR	
GOETHALS PLGD	341 - F3
GOETHALS DR, RICHLAND WA	
GOLDEN & SILVER FALLS STATE PK	140 - C1
EAST FORK GLENN CREEK RD, COOS CO OR	
GOLDEN EARS PROVINCIAL PK	94 - A2
FERN CRES, BRITISH COLUMBIA BC	
GOLDEN GARDENS PK	272 - C1
GOLDEN GARDNS DR NW & VIEW AV, SEATTLE WA	
GOLDSTREAM PROVINCIAL PK	159 - A6
TRANS CANADA HWY, DISTRICT OF LANGFORD BC	
GOODLOW MOUNTAIN NATURAL AREA	151 - A2
OFF GERBER RD, KLAMATH CO OR	
GOOSE LAKE REC AREA	152 - A3
OFF FREMONT HWY, LAKE CO OR	
GORDON BAY PROVINCIAL PK	100 - C1
BRITISH COLUMBIA BC	
GORGE PK	256 - E6
GORGE RD W, DISTRICT OF SAANICH BC	
GOVERNMENT HOUSE GARDENS	257 - A10
1401 ROCKLAND AV, CITY OF VICTORIA BC	
GOVERNOR PATTERSON MEM PK	328 - B6
OREGON COAST HWY, LINCOLN CO OR	
GOVERNOR TOM MCCALL WATERFRONT PK	317 - F1
SW NAITO PKWY, PORTLAND OR	
GOVERNORS PK	316 - D1
SW DAVENPORT ST, PORTLAND OR	
GOWLLAND-TOD PROVINCIAL PK	159 - B4
WILLIS POINT RD, BRITISH COLUMBIA BC	
GRAND AV PK	264 - D1
16TH ST & GRAND AV, EVERETT WA	
GRAND PRAIRIE PK	326 - F10
WAVERLY DR, ALBANY OR	
GRANDVIEW PK	290 - D6
MILITARY RD S, SEATAC WA	
GRANT PK	314 - A3
NE US GRANT PL & NE 33RD AV, PORTLAND OR	
GRASS LAKE PK	296 - D3
KAISER & ACCESS RD, OLYMPIA WA	
GREENE, NANCY REC AREA	106 - A1
HWY 22 & HWY 3B, BRITISH COLUMBIA BC	
GREEN LAKE PK	273 - J3
GREEN LAKE DR N, SEATTLE WA	
GREEN PK PLGD	345 - C6
N DIVISION ST, WALLA WALLA WA	
GREEN TIMBERS URBAN FOREST	157 - A6
FRASER HWY & 96TH AV, CITY OF SURREY BC	
GREENWOOD PK	273 - H1
EVANSTON AV N, SEATTLE WA	
GREENWOOD PK	255 - C3
GRAND BLVD, CITY OF NORTH VANCOUVER BC	
GRIFFIN PK	229 - A5
ROGUE RIVER LOOP HWY, JOSEPHINE CO OR	
GRIFFIN, WILLIAM PK	254 - J3
QUEENS RD, DIST OF NORTH VANCOUVER BC	
GRIFFITHS-PRIDAY OCEAN STATE PK	177 - B4
OFF HWY 109, GRAYS HARBOR CO WA	
GROSE, WILLIAM PK	278 - E4
31ST AV & E HOWELL ST, SEATTLE WA	
GROTTO, THE	315 - G2
NE 85TH AV & NE SANDY BLVD, PORTLAND OR	
GROVELAND PK	283 - J6
DEERFORD RD & 80TH AV SE, MERCER ISLND WA	
GROVES, LESLIE PK	340 - H10
HARRIS AV & SNYDER ST, RICHLAND WA	
GUSTAFSON, CARL PK	306 - E6
NASHVILLE WY & TENNESSEE LN, VANCOUVER WA	
GUY LEE PK	330 - F4
HARTMAN LN, SPRINGFIELD OR	
HAINS STREET DIKE PK	340 - G13
HAINS ST & THOMAS ST, RICHLAND WA	
HAMBLEN PK	349 - D14
37TH AV & NAPA ST, SPOKANE WA	
HAMILTON PK	292 - E2
RUSTON WY, TACOMA WA	
HAMILTON PK	316 - A3
SW 45TH AV & SW HAMILTON ST, PORTLAND OR	
HAMILTON VIEW PK	276 - E7
CALIFORNIA WY SW, SEATTLE WA	
HAMPTON PK	256 - E5
TILLICUM RD, DISTRICT OF SAANICH BC	
HANCOCK PK	315 - G4
NE 90TH AV & NE TILLAMOOK ST, PORTLAND OR	
HARBORVIEW PK	278 - B6
JEFFERSON & 8TH, SEATTLE WA	
HARBORVIEW PK	264 - A7
MUKILTEO BL, EVERETT WA	
HARMON FIELD	349 - E1
N MARKET ST, SPOKANE WA	
HARNEY PK	318 - E7
SE 67TH AV & SE HARNEY ST, PORTLAND OR	
HARPER PK	157 - B4
HIGHLAND DR, COQUITLAM BC	
HARRIS BEACH STATE PK	232 - C6
OREGON COAST HWY, BROOKINGS OR	
HARRISON PK	319 - F1
SE 83RD AV & SE HARRISON ST, PORTLAND OR	
HARWOOD PK	255 - J14
LAUREL ST, DISTRICT OF BURNABY BC	
HASTINGS MILL PK	254 - A11
UNIVERSITY ENDOWMENT LAND BC	
HAWTHORNE PK	157 - A6
104TH AV & 148TH ST, CITY OF SURREY BC	
HAWTHORNE PK	336 - D11
JACKSON ST & HAWTHORNE ST, MEDFORD OR	
HAYS PK	349 - C4
N CRESTLINE ST, SPOKANE WA	
HAZELNUT PK	289 - G3
59TH AV S & S 147TH ST, TUKWILA WA	
HAZELWOOD PK	326 - A9
RIVERSIDE DR, ALBANY OR	
HEALS RIFLE RANGE	159 - B4
WILLIS POINT RD, DISTRICT OF SAANICH BC	
HEALY HEIGHTS PK	316 - D2
SW COUNCIL CREST DR, PORTLAND OR	
HEIDELBERG ATHLETIC FIELD	292 - B7
S 19TH ST & S TYLER ST, TACOMA WA	
HEIRMAN, BOB WILDLIFE PK	171 - D4
CONNELLY RD, SNOHOMISH CO WA	
HELLS CANYON NATL REC AREA	131 - B1
NEZ PERCE CO ID	
HELLS GATE STATE PK	250 - B5
SNAKE RIVER AV, NEZ PERCE CO ID	
HELMCKEN PK	256 - B4
HELMCKEN RD, TOWN OF VIEW ROYAL BC	
HENDERSON PK	326 - C8
CALAPOOIA ST, ALBANY OR	

FEATURE NAME City State	Page-Grid
HENDERSON PK	257 - C5
CEDAR HILL CROSS RD, DIST OF OAK BAY BC	
HENDRICKS PK	330 - D8
FAIRMONT HEIGHTS BLVD, EUGENE OR	
HENDRY, JOHN PK	255 - C13
VICTORIA DR S, VANCOUVER BC	
HEYBURN STATE PK	248 - B7
CEDAR ST, CHATCOLET ID	
HIAWATHA PLGD	280 - E2
CALIFORNIA AV SW & LANDER ST, SEATTLE WA	
HIDDEN PK	305 - F2
FRANKLIN ST & W 38TH ST, VANCOUVER WA	
HIGH BRIDGE PK	348 - F10
W SUNSET BLVD, SPOKANE WA	
HIGH DRIVE PARKWAY	348 - H13
S HIGH DR, SPOKANE WA	
HIGHLAND MEM PK	267 - F3
76TH ST SW & 44TH AV W, EVERETT WA	
HIGHLAND PK	303 - E7
BURCHAM ST, KELSO WA	
HIGH POINT PLGD	281 - F7
6920 34TH AV SW, SEATTLE WA	
HIGHROCK PK	256 - D8
LAMPSON ST, TOWN OF ESQUIMALT BC	
HILLCREST PK	260 - D14
E BLACKBURN RD, MOUNT VERNON WA	
HILL, JJ PK	265 - E3
BROADWAY & HEWITT AV, EVERETT WA	
HILLSDALE PK	316 - C4
SW 25TH AV & HILLSDALE HWY, PORTLAND OR	
HILLSIDE CENTER PK	312 - B5
NW ARIEL TER, PORTLAND OR	
HILLSIDE PK	332 - C5
AUBREY BUTTE RD & IOWA AV, BEND OR	
HILLTOP PK	288 - C1
24TH AV S & S 128TH ST, KING CO WA	
HIMES, GEORGE PK	316 - E4
SW TERWILLIGER BLVD, PORTLAND OR	
HING HAY PK	278 - B7
MAYNARD AV S & KING ST, SEATTLE WA	
HOLLADAY WEST PK	313 - H4
NE 11TH AV & NE HOLLADAY ST, PORTLAND OR	
HOLLAND YOUTH PK	323 - G14
MARION CO OR	
HOLLYWOOD PK	257 - A11
FAIRFIELD RD, CITY OF VICTORIA BC	
HOLMAN PK	312 - A3
NW HOLMAN LN IN FOREST PARK, PORTLAND OR	
HOLMES PK	336 - G12
WHITE OAK DR, MEDFORD OR	
HONEYMAN, JESSIE M MEM STATE PK	214 - B4
OREGON COAST HWY, LANE CO OR	
HONEYMOON BAY NATURE PK	100 - C1
BRITISH COLUMBIA BC	
HORNER PK	257 - B4
CEDAR HILL CROSS RD, DIST OF SAANICH BC	
HORSETHIEF LAKE STATE PK	196 - D6
HWY 14, KLICKITAT CO WA	
HOWARD TIETAN PK	345 - C10
E TIETAN ST, WALLA WALLA WA	
HOWARTH PK	264 - A6
OLYMPIC BLVD, EVERETT WA	
HOWELL PK	279 - F4
E HOWELL PL & E HOWELL ST, SEATTLE WA	
HOWELL TERRITORIAL PK	192 - B6
SAUVIE ISLAND RD, MULTNOMAH CO OR	
HUGHES PLGD	285 - F2
SW HOLDEN ST & 28TH AV SW, SEATTLE WA	
HUGO RAY PK	254 - G3
DISTRICT OF WEST VANCOUVE BC	
HUG POINT STATE PK	191 - A2
OREGON COAST HWY, CLATSOP CO OR	
HULT PK	330 - B14
RIDGELINE TR, EUGENE OR	
HUMBOLDT NATL FOREST	154 - C3
HUMBOLDT CO NV	
HUMBUG MOUNTAIN STATE PK	224 - B7
CURRY CO OR	
HYACINTH PK	256 - D2
INTERURBAN RD, DISTRICT OF SAANICH BC	
IKAWA PK	289 - H5
SOUTHCENTER BLVD, TUKWILA WA	
ILLINOIS RIVER STATE PK	233 - A4
REDWOOD HWY, JOSEPHINE CO OR	
INTERBAY ATHLETIC FIELD	273 - F7
15TH AV NW & W DRAVUS ST, SEATTLE WA	
INTERLAKEN PK	278 - C1
E INTERLAKEN BL & DELMAR DR E, SEATTLE WA	
INTL CHILDRENS PK	278 - B7
S LANE ST & 7TH AV S, SEATTLE WA	
INVERGARRY PK	157 - A6
CURRIE DR, CITY OF SURREY BC	
INVERNESS RAVINE PK	275 - F1
45TH AV NE & NE 86TH ST, SEATTLE WA	
IRON MOUNTAIN PK	320 - B6
TWIN FIR RD & BROOKSIDE RD, LK OSWEGO OR	
IRVING PK	256 - G10
MENZIES ST, CITY OF VICTORIA BC	
IRVING PK	313 - H2
NE 7TH AV & NE FREMONT ST, PORTLAND OR	
IRVING PLGD	293 - E7
S 25TH ST & HOSMER ST, TACOMA WA	
ISLAND PK	330 - G7
MAIN ST, SPRINGFIELD OR	
JACKSON COUNTY EXPO PK	336 - A4
PENINGER RD, JACKSON CO OR	
JACKSON, HENRY M PK	265 - E2
E MARINE VIEW DR & SUMMIT DR, EVERETT WA	
JACKSON, MARIA C STATE PK	140 - C2
COOS CO OR	
JACKSON PK	336 - B11
MCANDREWS RD & CLARK ST, MEDFORD OR	
JACKSON, SAM PK	317 - E1
SW TERWILLIGER BLVD, PORTLAND OR	
JAGGY ROAD PK	306 - E1
NE 72ND AV & NE 45TH AV, VANCOUVER WA	
JAMES ISLAND STATE PK	160 - A5
OFF DECATUR ISLAND, SAN JUAN CO WA	
JAMISON SQUARE	313 - F5
NW GLISAN ST & NW 6TH AV, PORTLAND OR	
JEFFERSON PK	345 - A9
MALCOLM ST, WALLA WALLA WA	
JEFFERSON PK	292 - C5
N 9TH ST & MASON AV, TACOMA WA	
JEFFERSON PK	293 - H6
S BROADWAY & S 17TH ST, TACOMA WA	
JOHN DOBSON PK	299 - E11
SE FIRST ST & ADAMS AV, CHEHALIS WA	
JOHNSON CREEK PK	317 - J7
SE 21ST AV & SE CLATSOP ST, PORTLAND OR	
JOHNSON, W E PK	340 - C14
HALL RD, RICHLAND WA	
JOHNSTONE CREEK PROVINCIAL PK	105 - A1
HWY 3, BRITISH COLUMBIA BC	

FEATURE NAME City State	Page-Grid
JOSEPH STEWART STATE PK	149 - C1
CRATER LAKE HWY, JACKSON CO OR	
JUDKINS PK	282 - C1
S CHARLES ST & 23RD AV S, SEATTLE WA	
JUNIPER PK	332 - F7
NE 8TH ST & NE FRANKLIN AV, BEND OR	
KANAKA CREEK REGIONAL PK	157 - D6
256TH ST, MAPLE RIDGE BC	
KANDLE PLGD	292 - A3
N 23RD ST & SHIRLEY ST, TACOMA WA	
KANISKU NATL FOREST	115 - C1
SANDERS CO MT	
KASCH MEM PK	267 - H5
100TH ST SW & 22ND AV W, EVERETT WA	
KAYAK POINT COUNTY PK	168 - A6
140TH ST NW & MARINE DR, SNOHOMISH CO WA	
KEEWAYDIN PK	343 - D11
KEEWAYDIN DR, KENNEWICK WA	
KELLER PK	321 - H4
SE 18TH AV & SE LARK ST, MILWAUKIE OR	
KELLEY POINT PK	192 - B6
N KELLEY POINT PARK RD, PORTLAND OR	
KELLY, ALBERT PK	316 - B3
SW BOUNDARY ST, PORTLAND OR	
KELLY BUTTE PK	319 - H2
SE 103RD AV & SE CLINTON ST, PORTLAND OR	
KELLY BUTTE PK	330 - G5
SUMMIT BLVD, SPRINGFIELD OR	
KENILWORTH PK	318 - A3
SE 34TH AV & SE HOLGATE BL, PORTLAND OR	
KENNYDALE COUNTY PK	296 - A12
FAIRVIEW RD & 66TH AV, THURSTON CO WA	
KENTON PK	308 - E4
N DELAWARE AV & N ARGYLE ST, PORTLAND OR	
KERN PK	318 - E3
SE 67TH AV & SE CENTER ST, PORTLAND OR	
KERR, PETER PK	321 - H3
ELK ROCK ISLAND, MILWAUKIE OR	
KERRY PK	277 - G3
W PROSPECT ST & 3RD AV W, SEATTLE WA	
KETTLE RIVER PROVINCIAL REC AREA	105 - A1
HWY 33, BRITISH COLUMBIA BC	
KEVANNA PK	307 - H1
NE 47TH ST & NE 109TH AV, VANCOUVER WA	
KILMER PK	255 - F1
DEMPSEY RD, DISTRICT OF N VANCOUVER BC	
KIMBALL, JACKSON F STATE PK	142 - C3
SUN MOUNTAIN RD HWY, KLAMATH CO OR	
KING PK	313 - G1
NE GOING ST & NE 6TH AV, PORTLAND OR	
KINNEAR PK	277 - G3
W OLYMPIC PL & 7TH AV W, SEATTLE WA	
KINSMEN GORGE PK	256 - D6
CRAIGFLOWER RD, TOWN OF ESQUIMALT BC	
KIRKSTONE PK	255 - E3
KIRKSTONE RD, DIST OF NORTH VANCOUVER BC	
KITSILANO BEACH PK	254 - C11
VANCOUVER BC	
KIWANIS PK	264 - E5
36TH ST & ROCKEFELLER AV, EVERETT WA	
KIWANIS PK	354 - C8
PONDEROSA BL & ROSS PNT RD, POST FALLS ID	
KIWANIS PK	344 - F10
SE 2ND ST, COLLEGE PLACE WA	
KLAHANIE PK	254 - F4
DISTRICT OF WEST VANCOUVE BC	
KLAMATH NATL FOREST	234 - C7
LAKE OF THE WOODS HWY, JACKSON CO OR	
KLEE WYCK PK	254 - F3
DISTRICT OF WEST VANCOUVE BC	
KNOCKHILL PK	256 - C3
HELMCKEN RD, DISTRICT OF SAANICH BC	
KNOTT STREET PK	315 - J3
NE 117TH AV & NE KNOTT ST, PORTLAND OR	
KOBE TERRACE PK	278 - B7
S MAIN ST & 7TH AV S, SEATTLE WA	
KOKSILAH RIVER PROV PK	101 - A2
BRITISH COLUMBIA BC	
KONUKSON PK	257 - G5
SEA POINT DR, DISTRICT OF SAANICH BC	
KOPACHUCK STATE PK	181 - B1
ARTONDALE DR NW&56TH ST NW, PIERCE CO WA	
KUBOTA GARDENS	287 - F5
RENTON AV S & 55TH AV S, SEATTLE WA	
LACAMAS LAKE PK	193 - B7
2700 SE EVERETT ST, CLARK CO WA	
LADDS CIR & SQUARES PK	313 - H7
SE LADD CIR, PORTLAND OR	
LAFARGE PK	157 - B4
PIPELINE RD & GUILDFORD WY, COQUITLAM BC	
LAIRHILL PK	317 - E1
SW BARBUR BLVD & SW WOODS ST, PORTLAND OR	
LAKE EARL STATE PK	148 - B3
LAKE EARL DR, DEL NORTE CO CA	
LAKE GROVE PK	320 - B7
LAKEVIEW BLVD, LAKE OSWEGO OR	
LAKE LOVELY WATER REC AREA	93 - C2
OFF TRANS CANADA HWY, BRITISH COLUMBIA BC	
LAKE OWYHEE STATE PK	147 - A1
OWYHEE LAKE RD, MALHEUR CO OR	
LAKE PADDEN PK	258 - F13
WILKIN ST, BELLINGHAM WA	
LAKERIDGE PK	287 - H6
HOLYOKE WY S, SEATTLE WA	
LAKE SACAJAWEA PK	302 - J9
KESSLER BLVD & WASHINGTON WY, LONGVIEW WA	
LAKE SAMMAMISH STATE PK	175 - D3
NW SAMMAMISH RD & 17TH AV NW, KING CO WA	
LAKE SELMAC PK	233 - B2
LAKESHORE DR, JOSEPHINE CO OR	
LAKE SYLVIA STATE PK	178 - D7
SYLVIA LAKE RD, MONTESANO WA	
LAKEVIEW PK	279 - E4
LAKE WASHINGTON BL E, SEATTLE WA	
LAKEWOOD BAY PK	321 - F6
STATE ST, LAKE OSWEGO OR	
LAKEWOOD PK	285 - H6
SW 108TH ST & 8TH AV SW, KING CO WA	
LAMBRICK PK	257 - B2
LAMBRICK WY&FELTHAM RD, DIST OF SAANCH BC	
LANGLEY BAND PK	157 - D6
GLOVER RD, TOWNSHIP OF LANGLEY BC	
LANGUS RIVERFRONT PK	265 - G1
ROSS AV, EVERETT WA	
LA PINE STATE REC AREA	143 - A1
LA PINE STATE PARK RD, DESCHUTES CO OR	
LARRABEE STATE PK	160 - D2
HWY 11, WHATCOM CO WA	
LAURELHURST PK	314 - A6
SE 39TH AV & SE STARK ST, PORTLAND OR	
LAURELHURST PLAYFIELD	275 - F6
NE 45TH ST & 48TH AV NE, SEATTLE WA	
LAUREL POINT PK	256 - F9
KINGSTON ST, CITY OF VICTORIA BC	

FEATURE NAME City State	Page-Grid
LAURELWOOD PK SE FOSTER RD & SE HOLGATE BL, PORTLAND OR	318 - D3
LAURELWOOD PK SE STEPHENS ST, ROSEBURG OR	334 - G7
LAVA CAST FOREST NEWBERRY NATL VOLCANIC MON, DESCHUTES CO	217 - C7
LAVA RIVER CAVES STATE PK THE DALLES-CALIFORNIA HY, DESCHUTES CO OR	217 - B6
LAVIZZO, DR BLANCHE PK MAIN ST & 22ND AV S, SEATTLE WA	278 - C7
LAWLESS, JAMES J PK WELLHOUSE LP & WYMAN ST, RICHLAND WA	341 - F3
LAWSON, JOHN PK 16TH ST & ARGYLE AV, DIST OF W VAN BC	254 - C4
LAWTON PK WILLIAMS AV W & W EMERSON ST, SEATTLE WA	272 - D6
LAYTON PK E 6TH AV, KENNEWICK WA	343 - E11
LBA PK OLYMPIA WA	297 - C9
LEACH PK K ST & E 28TH ST, VANCOUVER WA	305 - H3
LEADBETTER POINT STATE PK STACKPOLE RD, PACIFIC CO WA	183 - B7
LEE, JASON PK MCMURRAY AVE & APRIL LOOP, RICHLAND WA	340 - E13
LEE PK SALEM OR	323 - A14
LEHIGH PK WAVERLY DR, ALBANY OR	326 - F9
LENTS PK SE 92ND AV & SE HOLGATE BL, PORTLAND OR	319 - G3
LESCHI PK LAKESIDE AV S, SEATTLE WA	278 - E7
LEVERICH PK NE LEVERICH PARK WY, VANCOUVER WA	305 - H2
LEWIS AND CLARK STATE PK JACKSON HWY, LEWIS CO WA	187 - D2
LEWISVILLE PK NE PARK DR, CLARK CO WA	193 - A2
LEYLAND PK DISTRICT OF WEST VANCOUVE BC	254 - E3
LIBERTY LAKE PK S LIBERTY DR, SPOKANE CO WA	247 - B4
LIBERTY PK E 4TH AV, SPOKANE WA	349 - C10
LIBERTY SHIP MEM PK NW NAITO PKWY, PORTLAND OR	313 - F4
LID PK W MERCER WY & FRWY 90, MERCER ISLAND WA	283 - J1
LIESER CREST PK VIRGINIA LN, VANCOUVER WA	307 - E6
LIGHT, FLOYD PK SE 111TH AV & SE ALDER ST, PORTLAND OR	315 - J7
LIGHTHOUSE PK DISTRICT OF WEST VANCOUVE BC	156 - A3
LILLY PK CORVALLIS OR	327 - H12
LIME BAY PK MILNE ST, CITY OF VICTORIA BC	256 - F8
LINCOLN HEIGHTS PK S 37TH ST & IDAHO ST, TACOMA WA	294 - E2
LINCOLN PK E 17TH AV & S COOK ST, SPOKANE WA	349 - D12
LINCOLN PK FAUNTLEROY WY SW, SEATTLE WA	284 - C2
LINCOLN PK S THOMPSON AV & S 37TH ST, TACOMA WA	295 - G2
LINCOLN PK W LAURIDSEN BLVD, PORT ANGELES WA	261 - A4
LINDSEY CREEK STATE PK COLUMBIA RIVER HWY, HOOD RIVER CO OR	195 - A5
LINNTON PK NW SAINT HELENS RD, PORTLAND OR	192 - B7
LIONS PK PARK DR & CASCADE DR, EVERETT WA	268 - D4
LIONS PK TACOMA CT, WALLA WALLA WA	345 - E6
LIONS PK WILSON ST & 9TH AV, OLYMPIA WA	297 - B5
LITHIA PK PIONEER AV, ASHLAND OR	337 - C9
LIVELY PK THURSTON RD, SPRINGFIELD OR	331 - J6
LIVINGSTON PK SALEM OR	323 - D10
LOEB, ALFRED A STATE PK NORTH BANK CHETCO RIVER RD, CURRY CO OR	232 - D4
LOMA VISTA PK CENTRAL AV & ALBERTA ST, SPOKANE WA	348 - F2
LORD HILL REGIONAL PK 127TH AV SE, SNOHOMISH CO WA	171 - D4
LOSS CREEK PROVINCIAL PK BRITISH COLUMBIA BC	100 - C2
LOST CREEK STATE RECREATION SITE HWY 101, LINCOLN CO OR	206 - A6
LOST FOREST RESEARCH NATURAL AREA OFF CHRISTMAS VLY-WGONTRE LK, LAKE CO OR	144 - A2
LOST LAKE PK SW 266TH LN, KING CO WA	174 - D7
LOUTET PK TRANS CANADA HWY, CITY OF N VANCOUVER BC	255 - E5
LOVEJOY PK SW 4TH AV, PORTLAND OR	313 - E7
LOWELL PK 20TH ST, BELLINGHAM WA	258 - C10
LOWELL PK JUNCTION AV, EVERETT WA	265 - E7
LOWMAN BEACH PK LINCOLN PARK WY SW & BEACH DR, SEATTLE WA	284 - C1
LOWNSDALE SQUARE PK SW SALMON ST & SW 4TH AV, PORTLAND OR	313 - F6
LOYAL HEIGHTS PLAYFIELD 20TH AV NW & NW 75TH ST, SEATTLE WA	273 - E2
LYNN CANYON PK TRANS CANADA HWY, DIST OF N VANCOUVER BC	255 - G2
LYNN HEADWATERS REGL PK BRITISH COLUMBIA BC	156 - C1
LYNN VALLEY PK MOUNTAIN HWY, DIST OF N VANCOUVER BC	255 - E2
LYNNWOOD LOOP PK LYNNWOOD LOOP & REDWOOD LN, RICHLAND WA	340 - G10
LYONS CITY PK SE LARCH AV, COLLEGE PLACE WA	344 - G11
LYONS FERRY STATE PK HWY 261, FRANKLIN CO WA	122 - A2
MACAULAY POINT PK LAMPSON ST, TOWN OF ESQUIMALT BC	256 - C9
MACDONALD MEM PK NE 40TH ST & TOLT AV, KING CO WA	176 - B2
MACDONALD PK NIAGARA ST, CITY OF VICTORIA BC	256 - F10
MACLEAY PK NW CORNELL RD, PORTLAND OR	312 - A4

FEATURE NAME City State	Page-Grid
MADISON PK E MADISON ST & E HOWE ST, SEATTLE WA	279 - F2
MADISON PK NORTH 43RD AV E & E LYNN ST, SEATTLE WA	279 - F1
MADISON SCENIC PK 10TH AV & MCCORMICK, OLYMPIA WA	297 - A5
MADRONA PK N GREELEY AV, PORTLAND OR	308 - D7
MADRONA PK LK WASHINGTON BL & MADRONA DR, SEATTLE WA	279 - F6
MADRONA PLGD MARION ST & 34TH AV, SEATTLE WA	278 - E5
MAGGIES PK EVERETT AV & W MARINE VIEW DR, EVERETT WA	264 - D3
MAGNOLIA PK MAGNOLIA BLVD W &32ND AV W, SEATTLE WA	276 - D2
MALHEUR NATL FOREST GRANT CO OR	136 - C2
MANCHESTER STATE PK BEACH DR E, KITSAP CO WA	271 - G9
MANITO PK S PARK DR, SPOKANE WA	349 - A12
MANITOU COMM CTR 4806 S 66TH ST, TACOMA WA	294 - A6
MANITOU PK S 66TH ST & GROVE ST, TACOMA WA	294 - B6
MANN CREEK STATE REC AREA MONROE CRK RD & JACKSON RD, WSHNGTN CO ID	139 - A2
MANNING PROVINCIAL PK HWY 3, BRITISH COLUMBIA BC	95 - B3
MAPLE LEAF PLGD ROOSEVELT WY NE & NE 82ND ST, SEATTLE WA	274 - B1
MAPLE PK MAPLE PARK AV SE, OLYMPIA WA	296 - J6
MAPLEWOOD PK RIVERSIDE DR, DIST OF N VANCOUVER BC	255 - H7
MAPLE WOOD PLGD CORSON AV S & S SNOQUALMIE ST, SEATTLE WA	282 - B5
MARATHON PK DESCHUTES PKWY, OLYMPIA WA	296 - G6
MARICARA PK SW 30TH AV & SW MARICARA ST, PORTLAND OR	320 - C2
MARINE PK RUSTON WY, TACOMA WA	292 - C1
MARINE PK SE MARINE PARK WY, VANCOUVER WA	306 - B7
MARITIME MEM PK W MARINE DR, ASTORIA OR	300 - A4
MARITIME PK COLUMBIA RIVER HWY, ASTORIA OR	300 - D4
MARQUAM NATURE PK SW MARQUAM HILL RD, PORTLAND OR	316 - D1
MARRION PK NE 14TH ST, VANCOUVER WA	307 - G5
MARSHALL, GEN GEORGE E PK E MCLOUGHLIN BLVD, VANCOUVER WA	305 - H4
MARSHALL PK 8TH PL W & W HIGHLAND DR, SEATTLE WA	277 - G3
MARSHALL PK SW 18TH PL, PORTLAND OR	320 - D1
MARYMOOR PK 6046 W LAKE SAMMAMISH PKWY NE, KING CO WA	175 - D1
MASKO PK S ORCHARD ST & RAMSDELL ST, FIRCREST WA	294 - A1
MATHESON LAKE REGIONAL PK MOUNT MATHESON RD, DIST OF METCHOSIN BC	165 - A1
MATIA ISLAND STATE PK MATIA ISLAND, SAN JUAN CO WA	160 - A1
MAUD WILLIAMSON STATE PK YAMHILL CO OR	204 - D2
MAURY ISLAND MARINE PK SW 244TH ST, KING CO WA	175 - A7
MAYER STATE PK COLUMBIA RIVER HWY, WASCO CO OR	196 - C6
MAYFAIR PK 3RD AV N & NEWELL ST, SEATTLE WA	277 - H1
MAYNARD PK SINCLAIR RD&HOBBIS ST, DIST OF SAANICH BC	257 - E4
MCBRIDE PK VANCOUVER BC	254 - A12
MCCARVER PLGD S J ST & S 23RD ST, TACOMA WA	293 - G7
MCCLUGHAN PK 208TH ST & 91A AV, TOWNSHIP OF LANGLEY BC	157 - C6
MCCORMICK PK OLD PORTLAND RD & S 18TH ST, ST HELENS OR	192 - B2
MCCURDY PK E PARK DR & LK WASHINGTON BL, SEATTLE WA	274 - D7
MCDONALD ST FOREST BENTON CO OR	327 - A1
MCEUEN FIELD COEUR D'ALENE ID	355 - F12
MCFADDEN PK EVERGREEN DR & ADAMS AV, CHEHALIS WA	299 - F11
MCGILL PK MCGILL ST, DISTRICT OF BURNABY BC	255 - H9
MCKAY PK SALEM OR	323 - E10
MCKENNA PK N WALL AV & N PRINCETON ST, PORTLAND OR	308 - A4
MCKINLEY PK E MCKINLEY AV & E 43RD ST, TACOMA WA	295 - J3
MCKINLEY PK UPPER PARK ST & E F ST, TACOMA WA	295 - J1
MCMICKEN HEIGHTS PK S 166TH ST & 40TH AV S, SEATAC WA	288 - E6
MCSPADDEN PK VICTORIA DR S, VANCOUVER BC	255 - B12
MEADOWBROOK PK NE BURTON RD & NE 90TH AV, VANCOUVER WA	307 - F4
MEADOWBROOK PK NORTH NE BURTON RD & NE 86TH AV, VANCOUVER WA	307 - G3
MEADOW HOMES PK E 18TH ST, VANCOUVER WA	306 - B4
MEADOWS EAST PK MURIEL ST & BELLERIVE DR, RICHLAND WA	342 - A8
MEDINA BEACH PK EVERGREEN POINT RD & NE 6TH ST, MEDINA WA	279 - J5
ME KWA MOOKS PK SW JACOBSEN RD & SW BEACH DR, SEATTLE WA	280 - C4
MEMALOOSE STATE PK COLUMBIA RIVER HWY, WASCO CO OR	196 - A5
MEMORIAL PK DIST OF WEST VANCOUVER BC	254 - C3
MEMORY ISLAND PK SHAWNIGAN LAKE RD, BRITISH COLUMBIA BC	159 - A3
MEMORY MILL PLAIN PK E EVERGREEN RD, VANCOUVER WA	305 - H5
MERCERDALE PK SE 32ND ST & 78TH AV SE, MERCER ISLAND WA	283 - J2
MERIDIAN PLGD N 50TH ST & MERIDIAN AV N, SEATTLE WA	274 - A5
METZLER PK METZLER PARK RD, CLACKAMAS CO OR	200 - B7

FEATURE NAME City State	Page-Grid
METZLER PK SE GREEN VALLEY RD, KING CO WA	182 - D2
MICELLI PK SE FLINT ST, ROSEBURG OR	334 - E8
MICHAEL PK DRAYTON ST, DIST OF NORTH VANCOUVER BC	255 - D5
MILLENNIUM PLAZA PK 1ST ST & EVERGREEN RD, LAKE OSWEGO OR	321 - F6
MILLERSYLVANIA STATE PK TILLEY RD SW, THURSTON CO WA	184 - A2
MILLET PK SW CHEHALIS AV, CHEHALIS WA	299 - D13
MILO MCIVER STATE PK SPRINGWATER RD, CLACKAMAS CO OR	200 - B6
MINGUS PK COMMERCIAL AV & N 10TH ST, COOS BAY OR	333 - F9
MINNEHAHA PK E LIBERTY AV, SPOKANE WA	349 - F5
MINOR, T T PLGD E UNION ST & 17TH AV, SEATTLE WA	278 - C5
MINTO-BROWNS ISLAND CITY PK SALEM OR	324 - E1
MISSION PK E MISSION AV, SPOKANE WA	349 - C7
MLK BERG PK LINN CO OR	327 - H11
MODOC NATL FOREST MODOC CO CA	151 - B3
MOLALLA RIVER STATE PK NE 40TH AV, CLACKAMAS CO OR	199 - C6
MONTAVILLA PK NE 82ND AV & NE GLISAN ST, PORTLAND OR	315 - F5
MONTEITH RIVER PK ALBANY OR	326 - C7
MONTLAKE PLAYFIELD E CALHOUN ST & 16TH AV E, SEATTLE WA	278 - C1
MOODYVILLE PK LOW LEVEL RD, CITY OF NORTH VANCOUVER BC	255 - C7
MOORE PK LAKESHORE DR, KLAMATH FALLS OR	338 - A7
MORAN STATE PK ORCAS TO OLGA RD, SAN JUAN CO WA	160 - A2
MORNINGSIDE PK SALEM OR	324 - J4
MORRIS, BOBBY PLAYFIELD E PINE ST & 11TH AV E, SEATTLE WA	278 - B5
MORRIS RANCH PK LINCOLN ST, EUGENE OR	329 - J10
MORSE RANCH PK LINCOLN ST, EUGENE OR	329 - J10
MOSES LAKE COMM PK WESTSHORE DR, MOSES LAKE WA	242 - C3
MOSHIER PK S 156TH ST & 4TH AV S, BURIEN WA	288 - A4
MOSQUITO PK SKYLINE DR, DIST OF NORTH VANCOUVER BC	255 - A1
MOULTON FALLS PK NE LUCIA FALLS RD, CLARK CO WA	193 - B2
MOUNT ARROWSMITH PK HWY 4, BRITISH COLUMBIA BC	92 - B3
MOUNT BAKER PK LAKE WASHINGTON BLVD S, SEATTLE WA	283 - E2
MOUNT BAKER-SNOQUALMIE NATL FOREST SNOHOMISH CO WA	110 - C1
MOUNT DOUGLAS PK CORDOVA BAY RD, DISTRICT OF SAANICH BC	257 - A1
MOUNT ERIE PK ERIE MOUNTAIN DR, ANACORTES WA	259 - F9
MOUNT HOOD NATL FOREST CLACKAMAS HWY, MARION CO OR	134 - C1
MOUNT HOOD NATL FOREST CLACKAMAS HWY, MULTNOMAH CO OR	194 - B7
MOUNT MAXWELL PROV PK SEYMOUR RD, BRITISH COLUMBIA BC	101 - B1
MOUNT RAINIER NATL PK PIERCE CO WA	185 - B1
MOUNT SCOTT PK SE 72ND AV & SE HAROLD ST, PORTLAND OR	319 - E4
MOUNT SEYMOUR PROVINCIAL PK DIST OF N VANCOUVER BC	156 - D1
MOUNT SPOKANE STATE PK SPOKANE CO WA	114 - C1
MOUNT TABOR PK SE SALMON ST E OF 60TH, PORTLAND OR	318 - D1
MOUNT TOLMIE PK CEDAR HILL CROSS RD, DIST OF SAANICH BC	257 - B4
MOUNT WORK REGIONAL PK WILLIS POINT RD, BRITISH COLUMBIA BC	159 - B4
MUKILTEO STATE PK FRONT ST, MUKILTEO WA	266 - D1
MUNDY PK 2200 COMO LAKE AV, COQUITLAM BC	157 - A4
MURDO FRAZER PK DIST OF NORTH VANCOUVER BC	254 - H3
NARAMORE FOUNTAIN PK 6TH AV & SENECA ST, SEATTLE WA	278 - A6
NEHALEM BAY STATE PK OFF CAREY ST, TILLAMOOK CO OR	191 - A5
NELSON CANYON PK DIST OF WEST VANCOUVER BC	156 - A2
NELSON PK VANCOUVER BC	254 - F10
NEPTUNE STATE PK OREGON COAST HWY, LANE CO OR	209 - A4
NEVADA PK JOSEPH AV & CINCINNATI ST, SPOKANE WA	349 - B2
NEW BRIGHTON PK MCGILL ST, VANCOUVER BC	255 - E9
NEW RIVER PK COOS CO OR	224 - B1
NEZ PERCE NATL FOREST IDAHO CO ID	131 - B2
NEZ PERCE NATL HIST PK OFF US HWY 95, IDAHO CO ID	131 - C1
NORGATE PK DIST OF NORTH VANCOUVER BC	254 - G4
NORMANDALE PK NE 57TH AV & NE HALSEY ST, PORTLAND OR	314 - D4
NORTH ALBANY PK ALBANY OR	326 - A3
NORTH BEACH PK EARL AV NW & NW 90TH ST, SEATTLE WA	272 - E1
NORTH CASCADES NATL PK SKAGIT CO WA	103 - B2
NORTHGATE PK N GENEVA AV & N FESSENDEN ST, PORTLAND OR	308 - A3
NORTHGATE PK SALEM OR	323 - D8
NORTH MYRTLE PK N MYRTLE CREEK RD, DOUGLAS CO OR	221 - D7
NORTH PARK BLOCKS NW PARK AV & SW ANKENY ST, PORTLAND OR	313 - F5
NORTH PASSAGE POINT PK NE NORTHLAKE WY & 6TH AV NE, SEATTLE WA	274 - B6
NORTH RICHLAND WELL FIELD PK GEORGE WASHINGTON & SPROUT, RICHLAND WA	340 - G8

FEATURE NAME / City State	Page-Grid
NORTH SEATAC PK / S 136TH ST & DES MOINES MEM DR, SEATAC WA	288 - B2
NORTH SHOREWOOD PK / SW 102ND ST & 21ST AV SW, KING CO WA	285 - G5
NORTH WIND WEIR PK / 27TH AV S, TUKWILA WA	286 - D6
NOTTINGHAM PK / NOTTINGHAM RD, DISTRICT OF OAK BAY BC	257 - D7
OAKBROOK PK / NE 99TH AV & NE 31ST ST, VANCOUVER WA	307 - H3
OAKLAND PLGD / S CENTER ST & S TYLER ST, TACOMA WA	294 - C1
OAKLANDS PK / SHELBOURNE ST, CITY OF VICTORIA BC	257 - A7
OAKS PIONEER PK / SE 7TH AV & SE SELLWOOD BLVD, PORTLAND OR	317 - G6
OBRYANT PK / SW WASHINGTON ST, PORTLAND OR	313 - E6
OCCIDENTAL SQUARE PK / S MAIN ST & OCCIDENTAL AV S, SEATTLE WA	278 - A7
OCEAN CITY STATE PK / OFF HWY 115, GRAYS HARBOR CO WA	177 - B6
OCHOCO NATL FOREST / CROOK CO OR	213 - D1
OGDEN, PETER S PK / NE 27TH ST & NE 81ST AV, VANCOUVER WA	307 - F3
OGRADY PK / SE GREEN VALLEY RD, KING CO WA	182 - D2
OKANOGAN NATL FOREST / OKANOGAN CO WA	104 - A2
OLD APPLE TREE PK / COLUMBIA WY, VANCOUVER WA	305 - G6
OLD FORT TOWNSEND STATE PK / OLD FORT TOWNSEND RD, JEFFERSON CO WA	263 - D10
OLD TOWN PK / N 30TH ST & CARR ST, TACOMA WA	292 - E2
OLMSTEAD PLACE STATE PK / KITTITAS CO WA	241 - C6
OLYMPIC NATL FOREST / CLALLAM CO WA	164 - C7
OLYMPIC NATL FOREST / GRAYS HARBOR CO WA	108 - C2
OLYMPIC NATL PK / CLALLAM CO WA	261 - D14
ORANGEGATE PK / 84TH ST E & 46TH AV E, PIERCE CO WA	182 - A4
ORCHARD HEIGHTS PK / SALEM OR	322 - F10
ORCHARDS PK / NE 58TH ST & NE 102ND AV, CLARK CO WA	307 - G1
ORCHARDS PK WEST / NE 58TH ST & NE 94TH AV, VANCOUVER WA	307 - G1
OREGON DUNES NATL REC AREA / COOS CO OR	218 - B4
OREGON PK / NE 30TH AV & NE OREGON ST, PORTLAND OR	314 - A5
OSWALD PK / KIWANIS CEDAR HLL RD, CITY OF VICTORIA BC	256 - J6
OSWALD WEST STATE PK / OREGON COAST HWY, TILLAMOOK CO OR	191 - A3
OSWEGO SWIM PK / LAKEWOOD AV & RIDGEWAY RD, LAKE OSWEGO OR	321 - F7
OTHELLO PLGD / S OTHELLO ST & 45TH AV S, SEATTLE WA	287 - F1
OVERLOOK PK / N OVERLOOK BL & N MELROSE DR, PORTLAND OR	313 - E2
OXBOW PK / 3010 SE OXBOW PKWY, MULTNOMAH CO OR	200 - C2
PACIFIC RIM NATL PK / BRITISH COLUMBIA BC	100 - A1
PACIFIC SPIRIT REGL PK / UNIV ENDOWMENT LANDS BC	156 - A4
PACKER JOHNS CABIN STATE PK / HWY 55, ADAMS CO ID	251 - B4
PAGE PK / N 15TH ST, NORTH SPRINGFIELD OR	331 - A4
PALERMO PK / PALERMO AV & O ST, TUMWATER WA	296 - H11
PALISADES PK / N GOVERNMENT WY, SPOKANE CO WA	348 - D9
PALMS CIEIA PK / KEIZER OR	322 - H6
PANDORA PK / PANDORA ST, VANCOUVER BC	255 - C10
PANTHER CREEK EXPERIMENTAL FOREST / PANTHER CREEK RD, SKAMANIA CO WA	194 - D2
PARK AT THE LAKES / BOMBING RANGE RD, WEST RICHLAND WA	341 - A2
PARROTT CREEK PK / BOOTH AV & SE STARMER ST, ROSEBURG OR	334 - F9
PARSONS GARDENS / 8TH PL W & W HIGHLAND DR, SEATTLE WA	277 - G2
PATTON SQUARE PK / N INTERSTATE AV&N EMERSON ST, PORTLAND OR	309 - E7
PAYETTE NATL FOREST / ADAMS CO ID	251 - B2
PECK ATHLETIC FIELD / S SPRAGUE AV & S 15TH ST, TACOMA WA	293 - E6
PEMBERTON PK / FOUL BAY RD, CITY OF VICTORIA BC	257 - B10
PENDLETON MILLER PLAYFIELD / 19TH AV E & E HARRISON ST, SEATTLE WA	278 - C4
PENINSULA PK / N ALBINA AV & N AINSWORTH ST, PORTLAND OR	309 - F6
PENROSE POINT STATE PK / 158TH AV KPS, PIERCE CO WA	181 - A2
PEOPLES PK / S L ST & S 10TH ST, TACOMA WA	293 - F5
PEOPLES COMM CTR / M L KING JR WY & S 17TH ST, TACOMA WA	293 - G6
PEPPIS PLGD / LAKE BELL AV E & E SPRUCE ST, SEATTLE WA	278 - E6
PERIWINKLE PK / ERMINE ST, ALBANY OR	326 - F10
PETTUS, TERRY PK / E NEWTON ST & FAIRVIEW AV E, SEATTLE WA	278 - A2
PETTYGROVE PK / SW 1ST AV & SW HARRISON ST, PORTLAND OR	313 - F7
PICCOLO PK / SE 27TH AV & SE DIVISION ST, PORTLAND OR	317 - J1
PIER PK / N SAINT JOHNS AV, PORTLAND OR	192 - B7
PILOT BUTTE STATE PK / CENTRAL OREGON HWY, BEND OR	332 - H7
PINEWAY PK / RAMONA WY, ALBANY OR	326 - E12
PIONEER PK / CORVALLIS-NEWPORT HWY, CORVALLIS OR	327 - G11
PIONEER PK / HENDERSON BLVD, TUMWATER WA	297 - A11
PIONEER PK / NW WALL ST & NW PORTLAND AV, BEND OR	332 - E6
PIONEER PK / WHITMAN ST, WALLA WALLA WA	345 - C8

FEATURE NAME / City State	Page-Grid
PIONEER SQUARE PK / SW YAMHILL ST, PORTLAND OR	313 - E6
PIONEER SQUARE PK / YESLER WY & 1ST AV, SEATTLE WA	278 - A6
PISTOL RIVER STATE PK / OREGON COAST HWY, CURRY CO OR	232 - B1
PITTOCK ACRES PK / NW PITTOCK DR, PORTLAND OR	312 - B5
PLAYFAIR PK / QUADRA ST, DISTRICT OF SAANICH BC	256 - H4
PLUM TREE PK / 26TH AV & E OLIVE ST, SEATTLE WA	278 - D4
POINT DEFIANCE PK / N PARK AV & PEARL ST, TACOMA WA	181 - C1
PONDEROSA PK / SE 15TH ST & SE WILSON AV, BEND OR	332 - G9
PONDEROSA STATE PK / VALLEY CO ID	251 - D3
PONDER PK / 80TH AV, TOWNSHIP OF LANGLEY BC	157 - D7
PORTAGE REGIONAL PK / OLD ISLAND HIGHWAY, TOWN OF VIEW ROYAL BC	256 - A5
PORT COQUITLAM NATURE PK / LNCLN AV&CST MRDN RD PT, PT COQUITLAM BC	157 - B4
PORTER PK / CORVALLIS OR	327 - F7
PORTER, ROBERT J PK / FAIRFIELD RD, CITY OF VICTORIA BC	256 - J10
PORTLAND HEIGHTS PK / SW PATTON RD, PORTLAND OR	316 - C1
PORT OF BELLINGHAM MARINE PK / HARRIS AV, BELLINGHAM WA	258 - A11
PORTOLA PK / PORTOLA DR, GRANTS PASS OR	335 - H10
PORTSMOUTH PK / NE STANFORD AV & N DEPAUW ST, PORTLAND OR	308 - A4
POTHOLES STATE PK / OSULLIVAN DAM RD, GRANT CO WA	242 - C6
POWELL BARNETT PK / E ALDER ST & 29TH AV, SEATTLE WA	278 - D6
POWELL BUTTE NATURE PK / SE 162ND AV & SE POWELL BL, PORTLAND OR	200 - A2
POWELL PK / SE POWELL BLVD & SE 22ND AV, PORTLAND OR	317 - J2
POWERS MARINE PK / SW MACADAM AV, PORTLAND OR	317 - G7
PRATT PK / 18TH AV S & S MAIN ST, SEATTLE WA	278 - C7
PRIDE PK / S 34TH ST, SPRINGFIELD OR	331 - C7
PRIEST POINT PK / E BAY DR, OLYMPIA WA	296 - J1
PRINCESS MARGARET MARINE PK / PORTLAND ISLAND, BRITISH COLUMBIA BC	159 - D1
PRINCESS PK / PRINCESS AV, DIST OF NORTH VANCOUVER BC	255 - D2
PRINGLE FALLS EXPERIMENTAL FOREST ADDIT / DESCHUTES CO OR	216 - B7
PRINGLE PK / SALEM OR	322 - H13
PUGET GARDENS PK / N 36TH ST & N ALDER ST, TACOMA WA	292 - D2
PUGET PK / 18TH AV SW & SW DAWSON ST, SEATTLE WA	281 - G5
PUGET PK / PROCTOR ST & N 31ST ST, TACOMA WA	292 - C2
PUGET POWER TRAIL (UNDEVELOPED) / 64TH AV S & S 224TH ST, KENT WA	291 - F6
PUGNETTI PK / S 21ST ST & PACIFIC AV, TACOMA WA	293 - H7
QEMILIN PK / POST FALLS ID	353 - G8
QUARNBERG PK / E MILL PLAIN BL & U ST, VANCOUVER WA	305 - J5
QUEEN ANNE BOWL PLAYFIELD / 3RD AV W & W FULTON ST, SEATTLE WA	273 - G7
QUINTUS PK / SW CENTER ST, ROSEBURG OR	334 - B6
RAILROAD HIST PK / MEDCO RD, MEDFORD OR	336 - C8
RAINBOW PK / MCKENZIE AVE, DISTRICT OF SAANICH BC	256 - F3
RAINIER PLAYFIELD / 3700 S ALASKA ST, SEATTLE WA	282 - E5
RAMSEY PK / RAMSEY RD, COEUR D'ALENE ID	355 - B7
RAPID RIVER REC AREA / ADAMS CO ID	131 - B2
RATTLESNAKE MOUNTAIN SCENIC AREA / KING CO WA	176 - C5
RAVENNA-ECKSTEIN PK / RAVENNA AVE & NE 65TH ST, SEATTLE WA	274 - C3
RAVENNA PK / NE 62ND AV & 15TH AV NE, SEATTLE WA	274 - C4
RED BRIDGE STATE PK / UKIAH-HILGARD HWY, UNION CO OR	129 - C2
RED FOX HILLS PK #1 / TIMBERLINE DR & FOX RUN, LAKE OSWEGO OR	320 - E4
RED FOX HILLS PK #3 / HIDEAWAY LN, LAKE OSWEGO OR	321 - E4
REGRADE PK / 3RD AV & BELL ST, SEATTLE WA	277 - J5
RENFREW PK / 22ND AV, VANCOUVER BC	255 - D14
REYNOLDS PK / CEDAR HILL CROSS RD, DIST OF SAANICH BC	256 - J3
RISLEY PK / SE SWAIN AV & SE RUBY DR, CLACKAMAS CO OR	321 - J7
RIVERFRONT PK / INTERURBAN AV S, TUKWILA WA	289 - G2
RIVERFRONT PK / MONROE ST AND BRIDGE AV, SPOKANE WA	348 - J8
RIVER FRONT PK / STEWART PARK DR, ROSEBURG OR	334 - E6
RIVER ROAD PK / SALEM OR	322 - J8
RIVERSIDE PK / 7TH ST & PARK ST, GRANTS PASS OR	335 - E10
RIVERSIDE PK / HARRISON AV & LOWE ST, CENTRALIA WA	299 - D2
RIVERSIDE PK / SE GRAND AV, PORTLAND OR	317 - G2
RIVERSIDE PK / SW OAK ST, ROSEBURG OR	334 - F7
RIVERSIDE STATE PK / N AUBREY L WHITE PKWY, SPOKANE CO WA	348 - C5
RIVERTON MINI PK / S 133RD ST & S 134TH PL, TUKWILA WA	289 - E2
RIVERTON PK / 4101 S 131ST ST, TUKWILA WA	289 - E1
RIVERVIEW HEIGHTS PK / ALBANY OR	326 - A4
RIVERVIEW PLAYFIELD / 12TH AV SW & SW WEBSTER ST, SEATTLE WA	285 - H1

FEATURE NAME / City State	Page-Grid
RIVER VILLA PK / SE BLUFF RD, CLACKAMAS CO OR	321 - H5
RIZAL, DR PK / 12TH AV S & S JUDKINS ST, SEATTLE WA	282 - B1
ROANOKE PK / ROANOKE ST & 10TH AV N, SEATTLE WA	278 - B1
ROANOKE PK / W MERCER WY & ROANOKE WY, MERCER ISLND WA	283 - J1
ROBERDEAU PLGD / ROBERDEAU ST & PERKINS AVE, RICHLAND WA	340 - E14
ROBSON PK / 100TH AV, CITY OF SURREY BC	157 - A6
ROCHE COVE REGIONAL PK / MOUNT MATHESON RD, BRITISH COLUMBIA BC	165 - A1
ROCK CREEK PROVINCIAL PK / HWY 3, BRITISH COLUMBIA BC	105 - A1
ROCK ISLAND STATE PK / HWY 28 & ROCK ISLND GRD RD, DOUGLAS CO WA	239 - C5
ROCKY BUTTE STATE PK / NE ROCKY BUTTE RD, PORTLAND OR	315 - H3
RODGERS, DAVID PK / 3RD AV W & W RAYE ST, SEATTLE WA	273 - G7
ROEHR PK / 5065 OSWEGO POINTE DR, LAKE OSWEGO OR	321 - G6
ROGERS, GEORGE PK / STATE ST & LADD ST, LAKE OSWEGO OR	321 - G7
ROGERS PLGD / EASTLAKE AV & ROANOKE ST, SEATTLE WA	278 - B1
ROGUE RIVER NATL FOREST / JACKSON CO OR	337 - F13
ROLLEY LAKE PROVINCIAL PK / BELL RD, DISTRICT OF MISSION BC	94 - B3
ROOSEVELT FIELD / CAROLINA ST, BELLINGHAM WA	258 - F5
ROSE CITY PK / NE 62ND AV & NE TILLAMOOK ST, PORTLAND OR	314 - D3
ROSS LAKE NATL REC AREA / WHATCOM CO WA	103 - B1
ROSSMAN PK / 4TH ST & C AV, LAKE OSWEGO OR	321 - F5
ROSS PLGD / NW 44TH ST & 3RD AV NW, SEATTLE WA	273 - G5
ROTARY PK / LOWELL-SNO RIVER RD, EVERETT WA	269 - F1
ROXHILL PK / SW ROXBURY ST & 28TH AV SW, SEATTLE WA	285 - F4
ROYAL ATHLETIC PK / COOK ST, CITY OF VICTORIA BC	256 - H8
ROYAL OAKS PK / SALEM OR	323 - G12
ROY MORSE PK / MORSE PARK WY, LONGVIEW WA	302 - C5
RUDD PK / BOLESKINE RD, DISTRICT OF SAANICH BC	256 - F5
RUPERT PK / 1ST AV, VANCOUVER BC	255 - F12
RUSSELL WOODS PK / RUSSEL RD & S 228TH ST, KENT WA	291 - F7
SACAJAWEA PK / NE 76TH AV & NE ALBERTA ST, PORTLAND OR	315 - F1
SADDLEBAG ISLAND STATE PK / SADDLEBAG ISLAND, SKAGIT CO WA	160 - D5
SADDLE MOUNTAIN STATE PK / CLATSOP CO OR	188 - D6
SAINT CLAIR PK / SAINT CLAIR ST, BELLINGHAM WA	258 - G6
SAINT FRANCIS PK / SE STARK ST, PORTLAND OR	313 - H6
SAINT HELENS PK / E 13TH ST, VANCOUVER WA	306 - B5
SAINT JOE NATL FOREST / SHOSHONE CO ID	115 - C3
SALMON BAY PK / NW CANOE PL & 19TH AV NW, SEATTLE WA	273 - E2
SALMON CREEK PK / 8TH AV SW & SW 118TH ST, KING CO WA	285 - H7
SALT CREEK REC AREA / OFF CAMP HAYDEN RD, CLALLAM CO WA	164 - D5
SALTWATER STATE PK / MARINE VW DR S&S 257TH ST, DES MOINES WA	175 - A7
SANDEL PLGD / 92ND ST N & 1ST AV NW, SEATTLE WA	273 - H1
SAND POINT MAGNUSON PK / 7400 SAND POINT WY NE, SEATTLE WA	275 - H3
SANDY ISLAND PK / BRITISH COLUMBIA BC	92 - B2
SANTANA COUNTY PK / FOUR CORNERS OR	325 - F2
SANTIAM ST FOREST / S SAWTELL RD, CLACKAMAS CO OR	126 - A3
SASQUATCH PROVINCIAL PK / ROCKWELL DR, DISTRICT OF KENT BC	94 - C3
SATHER PK / FOSTER ST, PORT TOWNSEND WA	263 - G3
SAWYER PK / SAWYER ST, TACOMA WA	295 - F2
SAWYER, ROBERT W STATE PK / O B RILEY RD & HWY 97, BEND OR	332 - E3
SAXE POINT PK / FRASER ST, TOWN OF ESQUIMALT BC	256 - B9
SAYRES, STAN MEM PK / 46TH AV S & LK WASHINGTN BL S, SEATTLE WA	283 - F3
SCENIC PK / PENZANCE DR, DISTRICT OF BURNABY BC	255 - J9
SCHAFER STATE PK / MASON CO WA	179 - B5
SCHMITZ, EMMA MEM OVERLOOK PK / SW BEACH DR & SW OREGON ST, SEATTLE WA	280 - B5
SCHMITZ PRESERVE PK / SCHMITZ BLVD & ADMIRAL WY SW, SEATTLE WA	280 - C3
SCHROEDER PK / SCHROEDER LN, JOSEPHINE CO OR	335 - A9
SCHRUNK PLAZA / SW 4TH AV & MADISON ST, PORTLAND OR	313 - F7
SCOGGINS VALLEY PK / SW SCOGGINS VALLEY RD, WASHINGTON CO OR	198 - A2
SCOTT, LAWRENCE PK / N KELLOGG ST, KENNEWICK WA	342 - E8
SCOTT PK / SE HARRISON ST & SE 23RD AV, MILWAUKIE OR	321 - J2
SEACREST MARINA PK / HARBR AV SW & FAIRMNT AV SW, SEATTLE WA	281 - F1
SEALAND OF THE PUB / BEACH DR, DISTRICT OF OAK BAY BC	257 - D9
SEAQUEST STATE PK / SPIRIT LAKE HWY, COWLITZ WA	187 - D7
SEATTLE TENNIS CLUB / MCGILVRA BLVD E & 39TH AV E, SEATTLE WA	279 - F3
SECOND NARROWS PK / MONTROSE ST, DISTRICT OF BURNABY BC	255 - G9
SECRET PK / W MERCER WY & SE 27TH ST, MERCER ISLND WA	283 - J2
SEHOME HILL ARBORETUM / COLLEGE PKWY, BELLINGHAM WA	258 - D9

INDEX

FEATURE NAME City State	Page-Grid
SELLWOOD PK SE 7TH AV & SE MILLER ST, PORTLAND OR	317 - G6
SELLWOOD RIVERFRONT PK SE OAKS PARK WY, PORTLAND OR	317 - F6
SENECA FOUTS MEM STATE PK COLUMBIA RIVER HWY, HOOD RIVER CO OR	195 - C5
SEVEN OAKS PK BAY DR & HARRISON AV, OLYMPIA WA	296 - G5
SEWALLCREST PK SE 31ST AV & SE MARKET ST, PORTLAND OR	314 - A7
SEWARD PK S JUNEAU ST & WASHINGTON BL S, SEATTLE WA	283 - H6
SEYLYNN PK MOUNTAIN HWY, DIST OF N VANCOUVER BC	255 - F6
SHADLE PK W WELLESLEY AV, SPOKANE WA	348 - G3
SHAWNIGAN LAKE PK SHAWNIGAN LAKE RD, BRITISH COLUMBIA BC	159 - A2
SHEPPERDS DELL STATE PK CROWN POINT HWY, MULTNOMAH CO OR	201 - A1
SHEVLIN PK JACK PINE SPRING RD, DESCHUTES CO OR	217 - B2
SHIELD PK E UPRIVER DR, SPOKANE WA	349 - J4
SHIVELY PK WILLIAMSPORT RD, ASTORIA OR	300 - D6
SHORE ACRES STATE PK CAPE ARAGO HWY, COOS CO OR	220 - B2
SHOREWOOD PK 28TH AV SW, BURIEN WA	285 - F7
SIDNEY SPIT MARINE PK SIDNEY ISLAND, BRITISH COLUMBIA BC	159 - D3
SILVER FALLS STATE PK MARION CO OR	134 - A1
SIMPSON PK OREGON COAST HWY, NORTH BEND OR	333 - F2
SINGING HILLS PK YELLOWSTONE AV & RAINER DR, POST FALLS ID	353 - J4
SISKIYOU NATL FOREST CURRY CO OR	228 - C4
SISTERS STATE PK SISTERS OR	211 - D5
SIUSLAW NATL FOREST LANE CO OR	209 - C1
SKAGIT VALLEY PROVINCIAL PK HWY 3, BRITISH COLUMBIA BC	95 - B3
SKINNER BUTTE PK CHESHIRE AV, EUGENE OR	329 - J5
SKYLINERS PK SW COLORADO AV & SW 14TH ST, BEND OR	332 - B9
SKYWAY PK S 120TH PL & 70TH AV S, KING CO WA	287 - J7
SMITH & BYBEE LAKES PK N COLUMBIA BLVD, PORTLAND OR	308 - A1
SMITH COVE PK W GALER ST & 23RD AV W, SEATTLE WA	276 - E2
SMITH, JEDEDIAH REDWOODS STATE PK DEL NORTE CO CA	148 - B3
SMITH ROCK STATE PK DESCHUTES CO OR	213 - A3
SNAKE LAKE PK S TYLER ST, TACOMA WA	292 - C7
SNOHOMISH COUNTY PK OLYMPIC VIEW DR, EDMONDS WA	171 - A5
SOOKE MOUNTAIN PROV PK HWY 14, BRITISH COLUMBIA BC	101 - A2
SOOS, GARY GRANT CREEK PK SE 204TH WY, KING CO WA	175 - C6
SOUTH BEACH STATE PK NEWPORT OR	206 - A5
SOUTH CLIFF PK UMATILLA WY & OREGON DR, VANCOUVER WA	306 - B5
SOUTH END REC AREA S TYLER ST & S 66TH ST, TACOMA WA	294 - C5
SOUTHERN HEIGHTS PK S 120TH ST & 14TH AV S, KING CO WA	286 - B7
SOUTHGATE PK 40TH ST & TUKWILA, WA	288 - E2
SOUTH KNOLL PK SE MAIN ST & MARSTERS AV, ROSEBURG OR	334 - F10
SOUTH LAKE UNION PK VALLEY ST, SEATTLE WA	278 - A3
SOUTH PK DOUGLAS ST, CITY OF VICTORIA BC	256 - G10
SOUTH PK S TACOMA WY & S 50TH ST, TACOMA WA	294 - C4
SOUTH PARK BLOCKS SW PARK AV & SW JACKSON ST, PORTLAND OR	312 - E7
SOUTH PASSAGE POINT PK FUHRMAN AV E, SEATTLE WA	274 - B7
SOUTH SURREY ATHLETIC PK 24TH AV, CITY OF SURREY BC	158 - A2
SOUTH VILLAGE PK SALEM OR	324 - J4
SPECTACLE LAKE PROVINCIAL PK WILLIS POINT RD, BRITISH COLUMBIA BC	159 - A4
SPENCER BUTTE PK S WILLIAMETTE ST, LANE CO OR	215 - B3
SPENCER ISLAND PK 4TH ST SE, SNOHOMISH CO WA	265 - J2
SPORTSMAN PK E 19TH AV & N WILLIAMS ST, POST FALLS ID	353 - H5
SPORTSMAN PK PACIFIC HWY & HIGHLND AV, JOSEPHINE CO OR	229 - B4
SPRINGBROOK GREENBELT SW 43RD ST, KENT WA	291 - J1
SPRINGBROOK PK DIANE DR, LAKE OSWEGO OR	320 - B5
SPRING STREET PK E SPRING ST & 15TH AV, SEATTLE WA	278 - C5
SPRINGWATER TRAIL CORRIDOR PORTLAND TO BORING, CLACKAMAS CO OR	318 - A7
SPRUCE PK 21ST AV E & E FIR ST, SEATTLE WA	278 - C6
SQUAK MOUNTAIN STATE PK NATURAL AREA SQUAK MOUNTAIN RD, KING CO WA	175 - D4
SQUAK/TIGER MOUNTAIN CORRIDOR ISSAQUAH HOBART RD & SE 113TH, KING CO WA	176 - A4
SQUAW BUTTE EXPERIMENT STA SQUAW BUTTE RD, HARNEY CO OR	144 - C1
STADACONA PK BEGBIE ST, CITY OF VICTORIA BC	257 - A9
STAGLEAP PROVINCIAL PK HWY 3, BRITISH COLUMBIA BC	106 - C1
STAN HEDWALL PK I-5 & RICE RD, CHEHALIS WA	299 - E14
STANLEY PK LIONS GATE BRDG RD&STANLEY, VANCOUVER BC	254 - E7
STANLEY PLGD S 19TH ST & HOSMER ST, TACOMA WA	293 - F6
STARKER PK 45TH ST, CORVALLIS OR	327 - D12
STARKEY EXPERIMENTAL FOREST OFF UKIAH-HILGARD HWY, UNION CO OR	129 - C2

FEATURE NAME City State	Page-Grid
STARVATION CREEK STATE PK COLUMBIA RIVER HWY, HOOD RIVER CO OR	195 - B5
STEAMBOAT ROCK STATE PK GRANT CO WA	237 - B4
STEINBRUECK, VICTOR PK LENORA ST & PIKE PL, SEATTLE WA	277 - H5
STEVENS FIELD WASHINGTON ST & 24TH AV, OLYMPIA WA	296 - J7
STEVENSON, WILLIAM PK PEMBROKE ST, CITY OF VICTORIA BC	256 - J8
STEWART HEIGHTS PLAYFIELD E 60TH ST & E B ST, TACOMA WA	295 - H5
STEWART PK STEWART ST, ROSEBURG OR	334 - C5
STEWART PARK-FIR GROVE SECTION W STEWART PARK DR, ROSEBURG OR	334 - D7
STILLWATER PK CARNATION-DUVALL RD NE, KING CO WA	176 - A1
STORVIK, JOHN PLGD 32ND ST, ANACORTES WA	259 - G4
STRATHCONA PK VENABLES ST, VANCOUVER BC	255 - A11
STRATHCONA PROVINCIAL PK HWY 19, BRITISH COLUMBIA BC	92 - A2
STRAUB, BOB STATE PK MCPHILLIPS RD, TILLAMOOK CO OR	197 - A7
STURGUS PK STURGUS AV S & GOLF DR, SEATTLE WA	282 - C1
SUCCOR CREEK STATE REC AREA SUCCOR CREEK RD, MALHEUR CO OR	147 - A1
SULLIVAN PK N SULLIVAN RD, SPOKANE VALLEY WA	351 - B6
SUMAS MOUNTAIN PROVINCIAL PK TRANS CANADA HWY, BRITISH COLUMBIA BC	94 - B3
SUMMER FALLS STATE PK GRANT CO WA	113 - A2
SUMMERS, COLONEL PK SE TAYLOR ST & SE 20TH AV, PORTLAND OR	313 - J6
SUMMIT PK FINLAYSON ST, CITY OF VICTORIA BC	256 - H6
SUMPTER PK SALEM OR	324 - G7
SUN LAKES STATE PK HWY 17, GRANT CO WA	112 - C2
SUNNYSIDE PK SE 34TH AV & SE TAYLOR ST, PORTLAND OR	314 - A6
SUNRISE BEACH COUNTY PK MOLLER DR NW, PIERCE CO WA	174 - C7
SUNRISE PK BUSH AV, OLYMPIA WA	296 - E4
SUNRISE PK HEYWOOD ST, CITY OF NORTH VANCOUVER BC	255 - E6
SUNRISE PK THURSTON ST, ALBANY OR	326 - D10
SUNSET BAY STATE PK CAPE ARAGO HWY, COOS CO OR	220 - B1
SUNSET BEACH PK PACIFIC ST, VANCOUVER BC	254 - E10
SUNSET HILL PK NW 77TH ST & 34TH AV NW, SEATTLE WA	272 - D2
SUNSET PK N CENTER PKWY, KENNEWICK WA	342 - B9
SUNSET PK RESEARCH WY, CORVALLIS OR	327 - C12
SUNSET POND NATURE AREA JAMES RD, BELLINGHAM WA	258 - F3
SWANSON PK PACIFIC BLVD & MONTGOMERY ST, ALBANY OR	326 - D8
SYLVESTER PK CAPITOL & LEGION WY, OLYMPIA WA	296 - H5
TAKENA LANDING PK ALBANY OR	326 - B7
TAKENA PK LAWNRIDGE ST, ALBANY OR	326 - B8
TAM O SHANTER PK TAM O SHANTER WY, KELSO WA	303 - E9
TAPIOLA PK MARINE DR, ASTORIA OR	300 - A6
TASHKENT PK HARVARD AV E & E MERCER ST, SEATTLE WA	278 - B4
TATLOW PK VANCOUVER BC	254 - B11
TELOH CALAPOOIA PK PACIFIC BLVD & 53RD AV, ALBANY OR	326 - B13
TEMPLETON PK GARDEN DR, VANCOUVER BC	255 - C11
TEMPLIN BEACH PK LANE CO, ROSEBURG OR	334 - F7
TERRACE VIEW PK E 24TH AV, SPOKANE VALLEY WA	351 - A11
TERWILLIGER PK SW TERWILLIGER BLVD, PORTLAND OR	316 - D3
THETIS LAKE REGL PK TRANS CANADA HWY, BRITISH COLUMBIA BC	159 - B6
THOMAS STREET PK THOMAS ST & BELLEVUE AV E, SEATTLE WA	278 - B4
THORNBURY PK THORNBURY DR, LACEY WA	297 - J11
THORNDYKE PK MAGNOLIA WY W & THRNDYKE AV W, SEATTLE WA	276 - D2
THORNTON CREEK NATURAL AREA NE 95TH ST & SAND POINT WY NE, SEATTLE WA	275 - F1
THORNTON MURPHY PK FISKE & 27TH AV, SPOKANE WA	349 - E13
THREE FORKS PK SE REINIG RD, KING CO WA	176 - C4
THUNDERBIRD PK DOUGLAS ST & BELLEVILLE ST, VICTORIA BC	256 - G10
THURSTON PK F ST, SPRINGFIELD OR	331 - J7
TIDEMAN JOHNSON PK SE 37TH AV & SE TENINO ST, PORTLAND OR	318 - B7
TIGER MOUNTAIN ST FOREST KING CO WA	176 - A4
TILLAMOOK ST FOREST TILLAMOOK CO OR	191 - B7
TILLICUM PK OFF HWY 101, FORKS WA	169 - D1
TILLICUM PK TRANS CANADA HWY, DISTRICT OF SAANICH BC	256 - D4
TIMBERHILL PK WALNUT BLVD, CORVALLIS OR	327 - F5
TIMBER LINN MEM PK PRICE RD, ALBANY OR	326 - H7
TOPAZ PK FINLAYSON ST, CITY OF VICTORIA BC	256 - H6
TOT LOTS CEDAR ST & S 74TH ST, TACOMA WA	294 - D7
TOU VELLE STATE PK AGATE RD & TOU VELLE RD, JACKSON CO OR	230 - C6
TRAFALGAR PK KING GEORGE TERR, DISTRICT OF OAK BAY BC	257 - C12
TRENTON PK N HAMLIN AV & N TRENTON ST, PORTLAND OR	308 - D3

FEATURE NAME City State	Page-Grid
TRILLIUM PK HARDY CRES, DIST OF NORTH VANCOUVER BC	255 - J5
TRILLIUM PK HOADLY AV & STEVENS ST, OLYMPIA WA	296 - J8
TRYON CREEK STATE PK 11321 SW TERWILLIGER BLVD, LAKE OSWEGO OR	321 - F4
TUBBS HILL PK 1 TUBBS HILL DR, COEUR D'ALENE ID	355 - F12
TUCANNON GAME RESERVE COLUMBIA CO WA	122 - B2
TUGMAN, WILLIAM M STATE PK COOS CO OR	218 - C3
TUKWILA PK 65TH AV S & S 153RD ST, TUKWILA WA	289 - H4
TUKWILA POND PK ANDOVER PK W, TUKWILA WA	289 - G6
TUMALO STATE PK DESCHUTES CO OR	217 - B1
TUMWATER FALLS PK DESCHUTES WY, TUMWATER WA	296 - H9
TUMWATER HILL PK RIDGEVIEW DR, TUMWATER WA	296 - F9
TUMWATER HIST PK DESCHUTES WY, TUMWATER WA	296 - H8
TUNISON PK CORVALLIS OR	327 - G13
TWANOH STATE PK HWY 106, MASON CO WA	173 - C7
TYNEHEAD REGL PK 176TH AV & 96TH AV, CITY OF SURREY BC	157 - B6
TYSON PK E ST, SPRINGFIELD OR	331 - C6
UMATILLA NATL FOREST UMATILLA CO OR	129 - B2
UMPQUA LIGHTHOUSE STATE PK DOUGLAS CO OR	218 - B2
UMPQUA NATL FOREST LANE CO OR	133 - C3
UMPQUA PK FREAR ST, DOUGLAS CO OR	334 - E10
UNDERHILL PLGD E HARTSON AV, SPOKANE WA	349 - E10
UNION PK PRUNE ST & PLUM ST, MEDFORD OR	336 - B13
UNIVERSITY PK 9009 N FOSS AV, PORTLAND OR	308 - C3
UNIVERSITY PLGD NE 50TH ST & 9TH AV NE, SEATTLE WA	274 - B5
UNTHANK PK 510 N SHAVER ST, PORTLAND OR	313 - F1
UPLANDS GREENBELT FRAGER RD & S 226TH ST, KENT WA	291 - F6
UPLANDS PK LANSDOWNE RD, DISTRICT OF OAK BAY BC	257 - D7
VALLEY OF THE ROGUE STATE PK NORTH RIV RD & PACIFIC HWY, JACKSON CO OR	229 - D6
VALLEY RIDGE PK S 184TH ST & 48TH AV S, SEATAC WA	291 - F1
VAN ASSELT PLGD S MYRTLE PL & BEACON AV S, SEATTLE WA	286 - D1
VANCOUVER LAKE PK HWY 501, CLARK CO WA	304 - A1
VAN DORENS LANDING PK RUSSELL RD, KENT WA	291 - F5
VAN FLEET PK FLINT AV & TOPEKA LN, VANCOUVER WA	306 - E5
VANIER PK CORNWALL AV, VANCOUVER BC	254 - D11
VENTURA PK SE 115TH AV & SE STARK ST, PORTLAND OR	315 - J6
VETERANS PK ROGUE BLVD & STEWART AV, MEDFORD OR	336 - E14
VETS MEMORIAL PK KLAMATH AV, KLAMATH FALLS OR	338 - D8
VICTORIA PK CHARLES ST, VANCOUVER BC	255 - B11
VICTORIA PK KEITH RD, CITY OF NORTH VANCOUVER BC	255 - B6
VICTORIA WEST PK WILSON ST, CITY OF VICTORIA BC	256 - F8
VIENTO STATE PK COLUMBIA RIVER HWY, HOOD RIVER CO OR	195 - B5
VIETNAM VETERANS MEM PK SW KNIGHT BLVD, PORTLAND OR	312 - B7
VIEWLYNN PK VIEWLYNN DR, DIST OF NORTH VANCOUVER BC	255 - F3
VIEWPOINT PK 12TH AV S & S FOREST ST, SEATTLE WA	282 - B3
VIEW RIDGE PLAYFIELD NE 70TH ST & 45TH AV NE, SEATTLE WA	275 - F3
VIRETTA PK EVERGREEN PL & 39TH AV E, SEATTLE WA	279 - F4
VOGEL PK MAIN ST & CENTRAL AV, MEDFORD OR	336 - D12
VOLUNTEER PK 15TH AV E & E PROSPECT ST, SEATTLE WA	278 - C2
VOLUNTEER PK S 42ND ST, LANE CO WA	331 - D8
WALBRAN PK KING GEORGE TERR, DISTRICT OF OAK BAY BC	257 - B11
WALKER PK SALEM OR	323 - C13
WALLACE PK NW 25TH AV & NW RALEIGH ST, PORTLAND OR	312 - C4
WALLINGFORD PLGD WALLINGFORD AV & N 43RD ST, SEATTLE WA	274 - A6
WALLOWA-WHITMAN NATL FOREST WALLOWA CO OR	130 - B2
WALNUT PK WALNUT BLVD, CORVALLIS OR	327 - C6
WAPATO LAKE PK WAPATO LAKE DR, TACOMA WA	295 - F6
WASHBURNE, CARL G MEM PK OREGON COAST HWY, LANE CO OR	209 - A6
WASHINGTON, MARTHA PK (SITE) 57TH AV S & WARSAW ST, SEATTLE WA	287 - G1
WASHINGTON PK FILLMORE AV, CORVALLIS OR	327 - G9
WASHINGTON PK SUNSET AV, ANACORTES WA	259 - A4
WASHINGTON PK SW KINGSTON DR, PORTLAND OR	316 - D3
WASHINGTON PK W CHERRY ST, WALLA WALLA WA	344 - J7
WASHINGTON PK ARBORETUM ARBORETUM DR E, SEATTLE WA	278 - D2
WASHINGTON PK E 31ST & R ST, VANCOUVER WA	305 - H3
WATERFRONT PK ALASKAN WY, SEATTLE WA	277 - J6
WATERFRONT PK COLUMBIA WY, VANCOUVER WA	305 - G6
WATERSHED PK HENDERSON BLVD SE, OLYMPIA WA	297 - A7

INDEX

FEATURE NAME City State	Page-Grid
WATERWORKS PK E RESERVE ST, VANCOUVER WA	305 - J4
WAVERLY PK ALBANY OR	326 - G7
WEAVER CREEK PROVINCIAL PK MORRIS VALLEY RD, BRITISH COLUMBIA BC	94 - C3
WEBSTER PK 2ND ST & EUNICE ST, PORT ANGELES WA	261 - F5
WEBSTER PK NW 68TH ST, SEATTLE WA	272 - D3
WELLINGTON PK NE 66TH AV & NE MASON ST, PORTLAND OR	314 - E1
WENAHA-TUCANNON WILDERNESS AREA COLUMBIA CO WA	122 - B3
WENATCHEE NATL FOREST CHELAN CO WA	238 - C1
WEST BANK PK HILLIARD LN, EUGENE OR	329 - G1
WESTCREST PK SW CLOVERDALE ST, SEATTLE WA	285 - J3
WEST DELTA PK N VICTORY AV, PORTLAND OR	308 - D3
WEST EWING PK W EWING ST & 3RD AV W, SEATTLE WA	273 - G6
WESTHAVEN STATE PK HARBOR AV, WESTPORT WA	298 - E11
WESTHOLM PK WILDWOOD AV & 1ST, GRANTS PASS OR	335 - D9
WESTLAKE PK MELROSE ST, LAKE OSWEGO OR	320 - A5
WEST MAGNOLIA PLAYFIELD 34TH AV W & W BARRET ST, SEATTLE WA	272 - D7
WEST MONTLAKE PK W PARK DR & E SHELBY ST, SEATTLE WA	274 - C7
WESTMORELAND PK SE MCLOUGHLIN BLVD, PORTLAND OR	317 - J6
WESTOVER PK DOVERCOURT RD, DIST OF N VANCOUVER BC	255 - G2
WESTPORT LIGHT STATE PK OCEAN AV, WESTPORT WA	298 - F12
WEST POWELLHURST PK SE DIVISION ST, PORTLAND OR	319 - J1
WEST-SELLS PK FRANCIS ST, DISTRICT OF BURNABY BC	255 - G11
WEST SHAWNIGAN LAKE PK SHAWNIGAN LAKE RD, BRITISH COLUMBIA BC	159 - A2
WEST V ST PK W V ST & ESTHER ST, TUMWATER WA	296 - G12
WHATCOM FALLS PK SILVER BEACH RD, BELLINGHAM WA	258 - J6
WHIPPLE CREEK PK NW 31ST AV & NW 179TH ST, CLARK CO WA	192 - C4
WHITE CENTER HEIGHTS PK 8TH AV SW & SW 102ND ST, KING CO WA	285 - H5
WHITE CENTER PK 15TH AV SW & SW 102ND ST, KING CO WA	285 - H5
WHITE PINE PK POLELINE AV & SPOKANE ST, POST FALLS ID	353 - H5
WHITTIER PK CONTRA COSTA AV&ELM TREE LN, FIRCREST WA	294 - A1
WIARD PK WIARD ST, ALTAMONT OR	339 - A11
WILDWOOD PK 23RD AV SE & 9TH ST SE, PUYALLUP WA	182 - B4
WILDWOOD PK N DIVISION ST, WALLA WALLA WA	345 - C7
WILLAMALANE PK G ST, SPRINGFIELD OR	330 - J6
WILLAMETTE HEIGHTS PK CENTRAL BLVD, SPRINGFIELD OR	330 - H8
WILLAMETTE MISSION STATE PK YAMHILL CO OR	204 - D2
WILLAMETTE MOORAGE PK SW MACADAM AV & SW MILES ST, PORTLAND OR	317 - F6
WILLAMETTE NATL FOREST LINN CO OR	134 - A2
WILLAMETTE PK GOODNIGHT AV, CORVALLIS OR	327 - H13
WILLAMETTE PK SW MACADAM AV & SW NEVADA ST, PORTLAND OR	317 - F5
WILLIAMS PK 64TH AV, TOWNSHIP OF LANGLEY BC	157 - D7
WILLINGDON HEIGHTS PK CARLTON AV, DISTRICT OF BURNABY BC	255 - G12
WILLOWS PK BEACH DR, DISTRICT OF OAK BAY BC	257 - D8
WILSHIRE PK NE 33RD AV & NE SKIDMORE ST, PORTLAND OR	314 - B1
WINDERMERE PK (PRIVATE) NE AMBLESIDE RD & NE PENRITH RD, SEATTLE WA	275 - G5
WINDRIDGE PK LYTTON ST, DISTRICT OF NORTH VANCOUV BC	255 - J6
WIND RIVER EXPERIMENTAL FOREST HEMLOCK RD, SKAMANIA CO WA	194 - C3
WINDSOR PK NEWPORT AVE, DISTRICT OF OAK BAY BC	257 - D9
WINDSOR PK PLYMOUTH DR, DIST OF NORTH VANCOUVER BC	255 - J6
WINEMA NATL FOREST KLAMATH CO OR	227 - C6
WINTLER COMMUNITY PK CHELSEA AV, VANCOUVER WA	306 - D7
WONDERWOOD PK 32ND AV, LACEY WA	297 - G9
WOODLAND PK GREEN LAKE DR N, SEATTLE WA	273 - H4
WOODLAWN PK NE 13TH AV & NE DEKUM ST, PORTLAND OR	309 - H6
WOODMANSEE PK SALEM OR	324 - H6
WOODRUFF PK HARRISON AV & N THOMAS ST, OLYMPIA WA	296 - F5
WOODSIDE POND NATURE PK ALAMEDA AV W & 48TH ST W, UNIV PL WA	294 - A3
WOODS MEM PK SW 45TH DR & SW WOOD PKWY, PORTLAND OR	316 - A7
WOODSTOCK PK SE 47TH AV & SE STEELE ST, PORTLAND OR	318 - C4
WORMALD STATE PK CLARK CO WA	193 - C3
W QUEEN ANNE PLAYFIELD BLAINE ST & 3RD AV W, SEATTLE WA	277 - G2
WRIGHT PK S 6TH AV & S I ST, TACOMA WA	293 - G4
WYAKIN PK SKYLINE DR & ASSEMBLY ST, SPOKANE WA	348 - C1
WYE NEIGHBORHOOD PK W COLUMBIA DR & GEORGIA AVE, RICHLAND WA	342 - C6
YAKIMA SPORTSMAN STATE PK S KEYS RD, YAKIMA CO WA	243 - C7
YAUGER PK COOPER PT RD & CAPITAL MLL DR, OLYMPIA WA	296 - D5

FEATURE NAME City State	Page-Grid
PERFORMING ARTS	
COLUMBIA ARTS CTR 400 W EVERGREEN BLVD, VANCOUVER WA	305 - F5
EVERETT PERF ARTS CTR 2710 WETMORE AV, EVERETT WA	264 - D3
GORGE AMPHITHEATER, THE 754 SILICA RD NW, GRANT CO WA	112 - B3
HUGHES CULT ARTS CTR YESLER WY & 17TH AV S, SEATTLE WA	278 - C7
HULT CTR FOR THE PERF ARTS 6TH AV, EUGENE OR	330 - B6
KELLER AUDITORIUM 1500 SW 3RD AV, PORTLAND OR	313 - F7
MCPHERSON PLAYHOUSE DOUGLAS ST, CITY OF VICTORIA BC	256 - G8
OREGON SHAKESPEARE THEATRES 15 S PIONEER AV, ASHLAND OR	337 - C7
PANTAGES THEATER 901 S BROADWAY, TACOMA WA	293 - H5
PERF ARTS CTR 1111 SW BROADWAY, PORTLAND OR	313 - E6
QUEEN ELIZABETH THEATRE 649 CAMBIE ST, VANCOUVER BC	254 - G10
RIALTO THEATER 310 S 9TH ST, TACOMA WA	293 - H5
ROEHR PARK AMPHITHEATER 5065 OSWEGO POINTE DR, LAKE OSWEGO OR	321 - G6
ROYAL THEATRE 805 BROUGHTON ST, CITY OF VICTORIA BC	256 - H9
SCHNITZER, ARLENE CONCERT HALL 1033 SW BROADWAY, PORTLAND OR	313 - E6
TEMPLE THEATER 47 SAINT HELENS AV, TACOMA WA	293 - G4

FEATURE NAME City State	Page-Grid
POINTS OF INTEREST	
45 WINDMILL OFF SOUTH FORK OWYHEE RIVER, OWYHEE CO ID	155 - B2
1980 CRATER MOUNT SAINT HELENS, SKAMANIA CO WA	190 - C2
ALBRIGHT CAVE OFF CONCONULLY RD, OKANOGAN CO WA	104 - C2
ALKI POINT LIGHTHOUSE POINT PL SW, SEATTLE WA	280 - A3
ALSEA RIVER FISH HATCHERY ALSEA HWY, BENTON CO OR	133 - A2
AMAZON POOL HILYARD ST, EUGENE OR	330 - B9
APPLE COVE POINT LIGHT EDMONDS WEST, KITSAP CO WA	170 - D5
APPLEGATE, CHARLES HOUSE DRAIN-YONCALLA HWY&HALO TR, DOUGLAS CO OR	219 - B4
ARAGO LIGHT CHARLESTON, COOS CO OR	220 - B1
ARMSTEAD MEM OSWALD WEST STATE PARK, TILLAMOOK CO OR	191 - A3
ARNOLD ICE CAVE CHINA HAT RD, DESCHUTES CO OR	217 - D5
ASTORIA COLUMN COXCOMB DR, ASTORIA OR	300 - D6
AUDUBON BIRD SANCTUARY 5151 NW CORNELL RD, MULTNOMAH CO OR	199 - B1
BARLOW CAVE BUTLER MKT RD & DICKEY RD, DESCHUTS CO OR	217 - D2
BATH HOUSE SW SEAHURST PIKE, BURIEN WA	175 - A5
BATTERY POINT LIGHTHOUSE A ST, DEL NORTE CO CA	148 - B3
BATTLE POINT LIGHT SUQUAMISH, KITSAP CO WA	174 - C1
BEAVER CREEK STATE FISH HATCHERY BEAVER CREEK RD, WAHKIAKUM CO WA	117 - B3
BELLE ROCK LIGHT LOPEZ PASS, SAN JUAN CO WA	160 - B6
BENJAMIN CAVES OFF FRAZEE-FREDERICK RD, LAKE CO OR	144 - A1
BENSON, RAY SNO-PARK OFF SANTIAM HWY, LINN CO OR	211 - A3
BIG HOLE FREMONT HWY, LAKE CO OR	143 - A2
BIG QUALICUM RIVER HATCHERY HWY 19, BRITISH COLUMBIA BC	92 - C3
BLAKELY ROCK LIGHT DUWAMISH, KITSAP CO WA	174 - D2
BLITZ-WEINHARD BREWERY 1137 W BURNSIDE ST, PORTLAND OR	313 - E5
BLOEDEL RESERVE 7571 NE DOLPHIN RD, KITSAP CO WA	170 - C7
BOCA CAVE OFF N SANTIAM HWY, MARION CO OR	134 - C1
BOEING ASSEMBLY PLANT 75TH ST SW, EVERETT WA	267 - G3
BOGUS CREEK CAVE OFF BOGUS RANCH RD, MALHEUR CO OR	146 - C3
BONANZA LEAD MILL COLVILLE, STEVENS CO WA	106 - A2
BOULDER CAVE CLIFFDELL, YAKIMA CO WA	119 - B1
BOW FISH HATCHERY CARSON (WA), HOOD RIVER CO OR	194 - D5
BOYD CAVE CHINA HAT RD, DESCHUTES CO OR	217 - D5
BOYER PARK AND MARINA ALMOTA FERRY RD, GARFIELD CO WA	122 - C1
BREMERTON YACHT CLUB BREMERTON WEST, KITSAP CO WA	270 - F7
BURNS CAVE OFF TUB SPRINGS RD, MALHEUR CO OR	146 - B3
BURROWS ISLAND LIGHTHOUSE DECEPTION PASS, SKAGIT CO WA	160 - B6
BUSH POINT LIGHT FREELAND, ISLAND WA	170 - C1
BUTTER CAVE GULER MOUNTAIN, KLICKITAT CO WA	119 - A3
CABINET GORGE HATCHERY HWY 200, BONNER CO ID	107 - C3
CALDWELL PONDS PUB FISHING AREA OFF ELGIN AV, CANYON CO ID	147 - B1
CAMPBELL MILL OFF FREMONT HWY, LAKE CO OR	152 - A1
CAMP IRELAND CUB SCOUT CAMP NW CAMP IRELAND ST, WASHINGTON CO OR	198 - D1
CANNERY LIGHT WAHKIAKUM CO WA	117 - A2
CAPE BLANCO LIGHTHOUSE CAPE BLANCO, CURRY CO OR	224 - A4
CAPE DISAPPOINTMENT LIGHTHOUSE CAPE DISAPPOINTMENT, PACIFIC CO WA	186 - A7
CAPE FLATTERY LIGHTHOUSE CAPE FLATTERY, CLALLAM CO WA	100 - B2
CAPE MEARES LIGHTHOUSE CAPE MEARES LOOP RD, TILLAMOOK CO OR	197 - A1

FEATURE NAME City State	Page-Grid
CAPILANO FISH HATCHERY 4500 CAPILANO PK RD, DIS OF N VANCOUVR BC	156 - B2
CAPTAIN VANCOUVER MONUMENT ESTHER ST & W 6TH ST, VANCOUVER WA	305 - F5
CARNATION FARM 28901 NE CARNATION FARM RD, KING CO WA	176 - B1
CARSON NATL FISH HATCHERY STABLER, TERMINATION PT, SKAMANIA CO WA	194 - C2
CASCADE SALMON HATCHERY BONNEVILLE DAM, MULTNOMAH CO OR	194 - C6
CASCADIA CAVE OFF SANTIAM HWY, LINN CO OR	134 - A2
CATHEDRAL OF SAINT JOHN THE EVANGELIST E 12TH AV & GRAND BLVD, SPOKANE WA	349 - A11
CATTLE POINT LIGHT CATTLE POINT RD, SAN JUAN CO WA	101 - C2
CEDAR CREEK FISH HATCHERY HEBO, TILLAMOOK CO OR	197 - B7
CHARCOAL CAVE CHINA HAT RD, DESCHUTES CO OR	217 - D6
CHEESE CAVE GULER MOUNTAIN, KLICKITAT CO WA	119 - A3
CHEHALIS HATCHERY 16250 MORRIS VALLEY RD, BRITISH COLUMBIA	94 - C3
CHELAN STATE FISH HATCHERY HWY 150, CHELAN CO WA	236 - D3
CHENEY FLOUR MILL OFF HWY 904, CHENEY WA	246 - A7
CHIEF JOSEPH MONUMENT JOSEPH-WALLOWA LAKE HWY, WALLOWA CO OR	130 - C2
CHILEAN MEM MONUMENT OLYMPIC NATIONAL PARK, CLALLAM CO WA	169 - A1
CHINATOWN PENDER ST E, VANCOUVER BC	254 - H10
CHINOOK DIKE LIGHT WARRENTON, CLATSOP CO OR	186 - B7
CHITTENDEN, HIRAM M LOCKS 3015 NW 54TH ST, SEATTLE WA	272 - D4
CHRISTMAS TREE CAVE GULER MOUNTAIN, KLICKITAT CO WA	119 - A3
CLARK FORK FISH HATCHERY HWY 200, BONNER CO ID	107 - C3
COLVOS ROCKS LIGHT PORT LUDLOW, JEFFERSON CO WA	170 - B2
COOS RIVER FISH HATCHERY SOUTH COOS RIVER RD, COOS CO OR	140 - C2
CORBETT SNO-PARK SANTIAM HWY, JEFFERSON CO OR	211 - A2
CORBIN HOUSE S STEVENS ST, SPOKANE WA	348 - J10
COWLITZ TROUT HATCHERY EDEN VALLEY, LEWIS CO WA	118 - A2
COYOTE TRAP CAVE IRON MOUNTAIN RD, MALHEUR CO OR	146 - B3
CROSS RANCH OFF JOHN DAY-BURNS HWY, HARNEY CO OR	137 - B3
CUMBERLAND MILL OFF SILVER CITY RD, OWYHEE CO ID	147 - B3
CYPRESS ISLAND LIGHT CYPRESS ISLAND, SKAGIT CO WA	160 - B4
DAM OBSERVATORY OFF RIVERVIEW RD, JEFFERSON CO OR	208 - A6
DARK HOLE WIND CAVE CHINA HAT RD, DESCHUTES CO OR	217 - D5
DAVIDSON ROCK LIGHT LOPEZ PASS, SAN JUAN CO WA	160 - A7
DAY, JOHN FOSSIL BEDS NATL MONUMENT BRIDGE CREEK RD, WHEELER CO OR	136 - A1
DAY, JOHN FOSSIL BEDS NATL MONUMENT SHANIKO-FOSSIL HWY, WHEELER CO OR	128 - A3
DEADY CAVES DEADY CROSSING RD, DOUGLAS CO OR	221 - C2
DENZER BRIDGE FIVE RIVRS & LOBSTER CK RD, LINCOLN CO OR	209 - D3
DEPOE BAY AQUARIUM DAVENPORT AV, DEPOE BAY OR	206 - A1
DERRICK CAVE NFD RD 2315 & NFD RD 700, LAKE CO OR	143 - C1
DE RUWE FARM AYER RD, WALLA WALLA CO WA	121 - C2
DESTRUCTION ISLAND LIGHTHOUSE DESTRUCTION ISLAND, JEFFERSON CO WA	169 - B7
DEVILS HOLE MILLICAN RD, LAKE CO OR	143 - C1
DEVILS PUNCH BOWL COW CREEK RD, DOUGLAS CO OR	141 - A3
DEVINE MONUMENT JOHN DAY-BURNS HWY, HARNEY CO OR	145 - B1
DIAMOND LAKE INFORMATION CTR N UMPQUA HWY, DOUGLAS CO OR	223 - C6
DOFFLEMYER POINT LIGHTHOUSE BOSTON HARBOR RD NE, THURSTON CO WA	180 - C4
DOUBLE BLUFF LIGHT HANSVILLE, ISLAND CO WA	170 - C2
DUFF LANE POND PUB FISHING AREA DUFF LN & LINDEN RD, CANYON CO ID	147 - B1
DUNGENESS LIGHTHOUSE DUNGENESS BAY, CLALLAM CO WA	166 - B5
DWORSHAK DAM AND VISITOR CENTER VIEW POINT RD, CLEARWATER CO ID	123 - C2
DWORSHAK NATL FISH HATCHERY VIEW POINT RD, CLEARWATER CO ID	123 - C2
EAGLE CREEK NATL FISH HATCHERY 34288 SE RAIBOW RD, CLACKAMAS CO OR	200 - D6
EAGLE HATCHERY OFF N LINDER RD, ADA CO ID	253 - A1
EAST LIGHT CATHLAMET BAY, CLATSOP CO OR	117 - A3
EASTON SNO-PARK KACHESS LAKE, KITTITAS CO WA	111 - B3
EDISON ICE CAVE OFF EDISON ICE CAVE RD, DESCHUTES CO OR	216 - C5
EDISON SNO-PARK EDISON ICE CAVE RD, DESCHUTES CO OR	216 - C5
ELK RIVER DAM PUBLIC FISHING AREA ELK RIVER RD, CLEARWATER CO ID	123 - C1
ELK RIVER STATE FISH HATCHERY ELK RIVER RD, CURRY CO OR	224 - B6
ELKS LODGE 174 1965 S UNION AV, TACOMA WA	292 - D7
ELLINGSON MILL SOUTH FORK JOHN DAY RD, GRANT CO OR	136 - A1
ENGLISH SETTLEMENT ELKHEAD RD & DRIVER VLY RD, DOUGLAS CO OR	219 - B6
ENTIAT FISH HATCHERY ENTIAT RIVER RD, CHELAN CO WA	112 - A2
FAIRGROUNDS BRITISH COLUMBIA BC	101 - A1
FALL CREEK STATE FISH HATCHERY FALL CREEK RD, LINCOLN CO OR	133 - A2
FALL RIVER FISH HATCHERY PISTOL BUTTE, DESCHUTES CO OR	143 - A1
FIRE BOAT STA RUSTON WY, TACOMA WA	292 - D1

FEATURE NAME
City State   **Page-Grid**

FISH HATCHERY — 102 - C3
316TH ST NE, SNOHOMISH CO WA
FISH HATCHERY — 92 - A2
HWY 19, BRITISH COLUMBIA BC
FISH HATCHERY — 156 - D1
OFF LILLOOET RD, BRITISH COLUMBIA BC
FISH HATCHERY — 93 - C1
OFF LILLOOET RD, SQUAMISH BC
FOREST LEARNING CTR MOUNT ST HELENS — 118 - B2
OFF RTE 504, COWLITZ CO WA
FORKS CREEK SALMON HATCHERY — 117 - A2
RTE 6, PACIFIC CO WA
FORT CLATSOP NATIONAL MEMORIAL — 188 - C3
FORT CLATSOP RD, CLATSOP CO OR
FORT NISQUALLY — 181 - C1
5400 N PEARL ST, TACOMA WA
FORT ROCK CAVE — 143 - B2
FORT ROCK RD, LAKE CO OR
FORT ROCK STATE MONUMENT — 143 - B2
OFF CABIN LAKE RD, LAKE CO OR
FORTYMILE CAVE — 146 - B3
OFF IRON MOUNTAIN RD, MALHEUR CO OR
FOUR-H ADVENTURE CLUB — 139 - A3
WILDER, CANYON CO ID
FOURMILE LIGHT — 214 - A7
SPARROW PARK RD, DOUGLAS CO OR
FOX ISLAND FISHING PIER — 181 - C3
END OF 14TH AV FI, PIERCE CO WA
FREEMAN LAKE ACCESS AREA — 106 - C3
NEWPORT, BONNER CO ID
FRONT RANGE LIGHT — 188 - D1
CATHLAMET BAY, CLATSOP CO OR
GABLEHOUSE MILL — 119 - A3
GULER MOUNTAIN, KLICKITAT CO WA
GAISER CONSERVATORY — 349 - A12
S PARK DR, SPOKANE WA
GEORGE ADAMS SALMON HATCHERY — 180 - A1
HWY 101 & PURDY CUTOFF RD, MASON CO WA
GIBSON FARM — 163 - D4
OFF HWY 112, CLALLAM CO WA
GOLDENDALE ASTRONOMICAL OBSERVATORY — 127 - C1
PIPELINE RD, GOLDENDALE WA
GOLDENDALE TROUT HATCHERY — 127 - B1
OFF FISH HATCHERY RD, KLICKITAT CO WA
GOLD LAKE SNO-PARK — 142 - B1
WILLAMETTE PASS, LANE CO OR
GOODWIN TOMB — 138 - A3
OFF CASTLE ROCK RD, MALHEUR CO OR
GRANGE HALL — 192 - C4
NE 154TH ST, CLARK CO WA
GRANGEVILLE HATCHERY — 123 - C3
OFF HWY 95, IDAHO CO ID
GRAYS BAY LIGHT — 186 - D7
GRAYS BAY, PACIFIC CO WA
GRAYS POINT LIGHT — 186 - D7
KNAPPTON FERRY RD, PACIFIC CO WA
GRAYS RIVER STATE FISH HATCHERY — 117 - A2
OFF RTE 4, PACIFIC CO WA
GREEN RIVER SALMON HATCHERY — 118 - A2
SPIRIT LAKE HWY, COWLITZ CO WA
HALLS FERRY — 204 - C7
OFF RIVER RD S, MARION CO OR
H J MONUMENT — 134 - A3
RABBIT CAMP RD, LANE CO OR
HOFFMAN COLUMBIA PLAZA — 313 - E6
1300 SW 6TH AV, PORTLAND OR
HOOD CANAL LIGHT — 170 - A6
QUILCENE, JEFFERSON CO WA
HOOD RIVER HATCHERY — 195 - B7
PUNCH BOWL RD, HOOD RIVER CO OR
HORSE CAVE — 217 - C2
OFF NEFF RD, DESCHUTES CO OR
HOYT ARBORETUM — 312 - B6
4000 SW FAIRVIEW BLVD, PORTLAND OR
HUDSPETH MILL — 136 - A1
OCHOCO HWY, WHEELER CO OR
HYDROPLANE RACE COURSE — 283 - G3
LAKE WASHINGTON, SEATTLE WA
ICE CAVE — 143 - C2
FRAZEE-FREDERICK BUTTE RD, LAKE CO OR
ICE CAVES — 118 - C3
LITTLE HUCKLEBERRY MTN, SKAMANIA CO WA
IDAHO BOTANICAL GARDEN — 253 - D3
2355 OLD PENITENTIARY RD, BOISE ID
IDAHO STATE FISH HATCHERY — 107 - C3
OFF HWY 200, BONNER CO ID
INDIAN CAVE — 222 - B3
OFF NORTH UMPQUA HWY, DOUGLAS CO OR
INDIAN FORT — 146 - C3
INDIAN FORT CREEK RD, MALHEUR CO OR
INTL ROSE TEST GARDENS — 312 - C6
SW MARCONI AV, PORTLAND OR
IRON CREEK INFORMATION CENTER — 118 - C2
GREENHORN BUTTES, LEWIS CO WA
ISLAND WINDMILL — 127 - A3
OFF SIMNASHO RD, WASCO CO OR
ISSAQUAH STATE SALMON HATCHERY — 176 - A4
125 W SUNSET WY, ISSAQUAH WA
JAPANESE GARDENS — 312 - C6
SW KINGSTON DR, PORTLAND OR
JOBS GARDEN — 141 - C2
NORTH UMPQUA HWY, DOUGLAS CO OR
KACHESS SNO-PARK — 111 - B3
STAMPEDE PASS, KITTITAS CO WA
KALAMA FALLS SALMON HATCHERY — 118 - B2
WOOLFORD CREEK, COWLITZ CO WA
KEMPER BREWERY — 170 - B6
22381 FOSS RD NE, KITSAP CO WA
KENT VALLEY ICE CENTRE — 175 - B7
JAMES STREET & LAKESIDE BLVD, KENT WA
KINGS S MINISTRY OF CRISTA — 171 - A6
19303 FREMONT AV N, SHORELINE WA
KLAMATH STATE FISH HATCHERY — 231 - C2
CRATER LAKE HWY, KLAMATH CO OR
KLASKANINE FISH HATCHERY — 188 - D4
NEHALEM HWY, CLATSOP CO OR
KLICKITAT STATE FISH HATCHERY — 119 - B3
OUTLET FALLS, KLICKITAT CO WA
KUNA CAVE — 253 - A7
OFF KUNA CAVE RD, ADA CO ID
LAKE ABERDEEN HATCHERY — 178 - C7
LAKE ABERDEEN, GRAYS HARBOR CO WA
LANGSLET MONUMENT — 152 - C2
WARNER HWY, LAKE CO OR
LAVA BEDS NATL MONUMENT — 151 - A3
30 MILES S OF TULELAKE, SISKIYOU CO CA
LAVA CAVES — 118 - C3
GIFFORD PEAK, SKAMANIA CO WA
LAVACICLE CAVE — 143 - C1
SAND SPRINGS RD, DESCHUTES CO OR
LAVA LANDS VISITOR CENTER — 217 - B5
NEWBRRY NAT VOLCANIC MON, DESCHUTES CO OR
LEAVENWORTH NATL FISH HATCHERY — 238 - A1
LEAVENWORTH, CHELAN CO WA

LEO REEF LIGHT — 160 - A4
BLAKELY ISLAND, SAN JUAN CO WA
LIGHTHOUSE — 206 - A3
LINCOLN CO OR
LIGHTHOUSE — 181 - C1
POINT DEFIANCE PARK, TACOMA WA
LIGHTHOUSE — 261 - J1
PORT ANGELES HARBOR, PORT ANGELES WA
LIGHTHOUSE — 181 - B2
TANGLEWOOD ISLAND, PIERCE CO WA
LIGHTHOUSE — 181 - C1
YOUNGS LANDING RD NW, PIERCE CO WA
LIME KILN LIGHTHOUSE — 101 - C3
WESTSIDE RD N, SAN JUAN CO WA
LINT SLOUGH FISH HATCHERY — 328 - E5
OFF ALSEA HWY, WALDPORT OR
LITTLE WHITE SALMON NATL FISH HATCHERY — 195 - B5
COOK UNDERWOOD RD, SKAMANIA CO WA
LOST BOY CAVE — 197 - A2
CAPE MEARES LOOP RD, TILLAMOOK CO OR
LOWER SANDS LIGHTHOUSE — 188 - B1
WARRENTON, CLATSOP CO OR
LOWER THREE CREEK SNO-PARK — 211 - C7
THREE CREEKS LAKE RD, DESCHUTES CO OR
LUCILE CAVES — 131 - C1
US HWY 95, IDAHO CO ID
MACMILLAN, GORDEN SOUTHAM OBSERVATORY — 254 - D11
1100 CHESTNUT ST, VANCOUVER BC
MAKAH NATL SALMON HATCHERY — 162 - B2
MAKAH BAY, CLALLAM CO WA
MALHEUR CAVE — 146 - A2
MALHEUR CAVE RD, HARNEY CO OR
MAPLES, THE — 206 - C1
OFF KOSYDAR RD, LINCOLN CO OR
MARCH POINT LIGHT — 160 - D5
ANACORTES NORTH, SKAGIT CO WA
MARINE SCIENCE CENTER — 170 - B7
18743 FRONT ST NE, POULSBO WA
MARROWSTONE POINT LIGHTHOUSE — 167 - B6
NORDLAND, JEFFERSON CO WA
MARTINS MILL — 138 - A1
NORTH FORK BURNT RIVER RD, BAKER CO OR
MASONIC TEMPLE — 313 - E6
1119 SW PARK AV, PORTLAND OR
MAYO — 125 - B1
COCHRAN, WASHINGTON CO OR
MCALLISTER ROD GUN CLUB — 181 - A5
NISQUALLY, THURSTON CO WA
MCKENZIE SALMON HATCHERY — 134 - A3
OFF MCKENZIE HWY, LANE CO OR
MCKENZIE TROUT HATCHERY — 134 - A3
MCKENZIE HWY, LANE CO OR
MCNARY DAM FISH LADDER — 121 - A3
UMATILLA, UMATILLA CO OR
MEADOWDALE MARINE — 171 - B4
16111 76TH PL W, EDMONDS WA
MEISSNER, VIRGINIA SNOWPARK — 216 - D4
CENTURY DRIVE HWY, DESCHUTES CO OR
MIDDLE WINDMILL — 155 - B2
OFF SOUTH FORK OWYHEE RIVER, OWYHEE CO ID
MIRROR LAKE ACCESS — 244 - B4
NFD RD 2233, BONNER CO ID
MITCHELL MONUMENT — 151 - B1
NFD RD 348, LAKE CO OR
MORRISON KNUDSEN NATURE CENTER — 253 - D3
600 S WALNUT ST, BOISE ID
MOSSYROCK TROUT HATCHERY — 118 - A2
MAYFIELD LAKE, LEWIS CO WA
MOTHER JOSEPH MONUMENT — 307 - F6
400 NE MOTHER JOSEPH PL, VANCOUVER WA
MOUNT BAKER — 102 - C2
MOUNT BAKER WILDERNESS, WHATCOM CO WA
MOUNT RAINIER — 185 - B3
PIERCE CO WA
MOUNT ST HELENS NATL VOLCANIC MON — 118 - A3
AMBOY, CLARK CO WA
MOUNT ST HELENS NATL VOLCANIC MON — 118 - A3
LEWIS CO WA
MOUNT SAINT HELENS VISITORS CTR — 187 - D2
JACKSON HWY, LEWIS CO WA
MOWICH CAVE — 223 - A4
OFF N UMPQUA HWY, DOUGLAS CO OR
MUKILTEO LIGHTHOUSE — 171 - B2
FRONT ST, MUKILTEO WA
NAMPA HATCHERY — 147 - C1
LOCUST LN, CANYON CO ID
NASELLE STATE SALMON HATCHERY — 186 - C5
RTE 4, PACIFIC CO WA
NATURE CENTER AT SNAKE LAKE — 292 - B7
1919 S TYLER ST, TACOMA WA
NEHALEM FISH HATCHERY — 191 - C5
FOLEY PEAK, TILLAMOOK CO OR
NELSON MONUMENT — 136 - A2
ARVID NELSON RD, CROOK CO OR
NETHERLANDS CENTENNIAL CARILLON, THE — 256 - G10
BLLVLLE ST & GOV ST, VICTORIA BC
NEWBERRY NATL VOLCANIC MONUMENT — 143 - A1
DESCHUTES NATL FOREST, DESCHUTES CO OR
NEWPORT GEOPHYSICAL OBSERVATORY — 106 - C3
LE CLERC RD, PEND OREILLE CO WA
NEZ PERCE INDIAN WAR HIST MONUMENT — 131 - C1
OFF US HWY 95, IDAHO CO OR
NORTH HEAD LIGHTHOUSE — 186 - A6
NORTH HEAD LIGHTHOUSE RD, PACIFIC CO WA
OAKRIDGE FISH HATCHERY — 142 - A1
SALMON CREEK RD, LANE CO OR
OBSERVATION TOWER — 278 - C3
E PROSPECT ST & 14TH AV E, SEATTLE WA
OCEAN SHORES ENVIRONMENTAL CENTER — 298 - F4
1013 CATALA AV SE, OCEAN SHORES WA
OCHOCO DIVIDE RESEARCH AREA — 136 - A2
OCHOCO HWY, WHEELER CO OR
OLD DOLE SMITH HOMESTEAD — 137 - A3
OFF DEVINE RIDGE RD, HARNEY CO OR
OLD IDAHO PENITENTIARY — 253 - D3
2445 OLD PENITENTIARY RD, BOISE ID
OLD KELLY MILL — 136 - A2
OFF SUMMIT RD, WHEELER CO OR
OLD OREGON TRAIL MONUMENT — 128 - A1
BARNETT RD, SHERMAN CO OR
OLD PERPETUAL GEYSER — 152 - A2
OFF HWY 395, LAKE CO OR
OREGON COAST AQUARIUM — 206 - B4
2820 SE FERRY SLIP RD, NEWPORT OR
OREGON COAST HIST CENTERR — 206 - B4
545 SW 9TH ST, NEWPORT OR
OREGONIAN BLDG — 313 - E6
1320 SW BROADWAY, PORTLAND OR
OREGON STATE FISH HATCHERY — 133 - A1
NORTONS, LINCOLN CO OR
OREGON STATE FISH HATCHERY — 205 - A1
RIVER RD, MARION CO OR
OREGON TR INTERPRTVE PK AT BLUE MTN — 129 - C2
I-84 SOUTHEAST OF KAMELA, UNION CO OR

OREGON TRAIL MONUMENT — 138 - B1
LA GRANDE-BAKER HWY, BAKER CO OR
OREGON VORTEX & HOUSE OF MYSTERY, THE — 230 - A5
SARDINE CREEK RD, JACKSON CO OR
OREGON ZOO — 312 - B7
4001 SW CANYON RD, PORTLAND OR
OWYHEE RIVER CAVE — 146 - B3
OFF TUB SPRINGS RD, MALHEUR CO OR
OX BOW SALMON HATCHERY — 194 - D5
CARSON, CASCADE LOCKS OR
PACIFIC BIOLOGICAL STA — 93 - A3
HAMMOND BAY RD, NANAIMO BC
PAPOOSE CAVERN — 131 - B2
SEVEN DEVILS RD, IDAHO CO ID
PARADISE GLACIER CAVES — 185 - C4
STEVENS CANYON RD, PIERCE CO WA
PATAHA RESEARCH NATURAL AREA — 122 - C2
OFF PATAHA CREEK RD, GARFIELD CO WA
PATOS LIGHTHOUSE — 101 - C1
PATOS ISLAND, SAN JUAN CO WA
PEACE ARCH — 158 - B2
USA/CANADA BORDER, CITY OF SURREY BC
PENDLETON UNDERGROUND TOURS — 129 - B1
37 SW EMIGRANT, UMATILLA CO OR
PETROGLYPHS — 244 - D4
OFF HOPE PENINSULA RD, BONNER CO ID
PINE MOUNTAIN OBSERVATORY — 143 - B1
W BASIN RD, DESCHUTES CO OR
PIONEER MONUMENT — 130 - A2
OFF MOUNT GLEN RD, UNION CO OR
POINT DEFIANCE ZOO & AQUARIUM — 181 - C1
540 N PEARL ST, TACOMA WA
POINT HANNON LIGHT — 170 - C4
HANSVILLE, JEFFERSON CO WA
POINT MONROE LIGHT — 170 - D7
SUQUAMISH, KITSAP CO WA
POINT NO POINT LIGHT — 170 - D3
HANSVILLE, KITSAP CO WA
POINT PARTRIDGE LIGHTHOUSE — 167 - A4
PORT TOWNSEND NORTH, ISLAND CO WA
POINT ROBERTS LIGHTHOUSE — 101 - C1
MARINE DR, WHATCOM CO WA
POINT WILSON LIGHTHOUSE — 263 - J1
PORT TOWNSEND NORTH, PORT TOWNSEND WA
POLE PASS LIGHT — 101 - C2
SHAW ISLAND, SAN JUAN CO WA
POOR FARM — 153 - C2
FIELDS-DENIO RD, HARNEY CO OR
PORTAGE, THE — 214 - B2
MERCER LAKE, LANE CO OR
POWELLS BOOKS — 313 - E5
1005 W BURNSIDE ST, PORTLAND OR
PREHIST GARDENS — 228 - A2
OFF HWY 101, CURRY CO OR
PUYALLUP NATL TRIBAL CENTER — 182 - A3
E 32ND ST, TACOMA WA
QUEEN CITY YACHT CLUB — 278 - C1
2608 BOYER AV E, SEATTLE WA
RAINIER BREWERY — 282 - A3
3100 AIRPORT WY S, SEATTLE WA
RAPID RIVER FISH HATCHERY — 131 - C2
RAPID RIVER RD, IDAHO CO ID
RATTLESNAKE CAVE — 146 - C3
IDAHO-OREGON-NEVADA HWY, MALHEUR CO OR
REAR ENTRANCE RANGE LIGHTHOUSE — 186 - A7
CHINOOK, CLATSOP CO WA
REAR RANGE LIGHT — 188 - D1
CATHLAMET BAY, CLATSOP CO OR
REDMOND CAVE — 212 - D6
SE AIRPORT WY, REDMOND OR
RENAISSANCE SQUARE — 156 - D5
DISTRICT OF COQUITLAM BC
RHODODENDRON SPECIES BOTANICAL GARDEN — 182 - B1
OFF HWY 18, FEDERAL WAY WA
RIPLEYS BELIEVE IT OR NOT — 206 - B4
250 SW BAY BLVD, NEWPORT OR
RIVERS, CRATER LAKE M FISH HATCHERY — 149 - C1
CRATER LAKE HWY, JACKSON CO OR
ROARING RIVER STATE FISH HATCHERY — 133 - C1
FISH HATCHERY DR, LINN CO OR
ROBERTS FARM — 183 - B3
HUNT CLUB RD, GRAYS HARBOR CO WA
ROBERTSON FISH HATCHERY — 92 - A3
HWY 4, BRITISH COLUMBIA BC
ROBINSON POINT LIGHTHOUSE — 175 - A7
SW POINT ROBINSON RD, KING CO WA
ROCK CREEK FISH HATCHERY — 141 - C2
ROCK CREEK RD, DOUGLAS CO OR
ROCK CREEK HIDEOUT — 125 - A3
ALVORD AL, POLK CO OR
ROCKY POINT LIGHT — 186 - D7
BRIX BAY, WAHKIAKUM CO WA
ROSE LAKE ACCESS AREA — 248 - D2
ROSE LAKE, KOOTENAI CO ID
ROSS FARM — 121 - C1
SPERRY, FRANKLIN CO WA
ROTARY POND PUB FISHING AREA — 147 - B1
CALDWELL ID
ROUND UP HALL OF FAME — 129 - B1
INTERSTATE 84 & EXIT 207, UMATILLA CO OR
SABIN OCCUPATIONAL SKILL CENTER — 199 - D3
SE JOHNSON RD, CLACKAMAS CO OR
SACRAMENTO CAVES — 155 - A1
OFF POLE CREEK RD, MALHEUR CO OR
SAINT MARIES RIVER ACCESS AREA — 248 - D7
SAINT MARIES, BENEWAH CO ID
SAINT MARYS FARM — 104 - C3
OMAK LAKE RD, OKANOGAN CO WA
SAINT MARYS MISSION — 104 - C3
NORTH END OMAK LAKE RD, OKANOGAN CO WA
SAND ISLAND DIKE LIGHT — 186 - B7
CHINOOK, CLATSOP CO OR
SAND ISLAND DIKE MIDDLE LIGHT — 186 - A7
CHINOOK, CLATSOP CO OR
SANDPOINT FISH HATCHERY — 244 - A3
LAKESHORE DR, BONNER CO ID
SAND STA REC AREA — 129 - A1
COLUMBIA RIVER HWY, UMATILLA CO OR
SANTIAM SNO-PARK — 211 - A2
OFF SANTIAM HWY, LINN CO OR
SAWYERS CAVE — 134 - B2
SANTIAM HWY, LINN CO OR
SCOUTERS MTN BOY SCOUT CAMP — 200 - A3
11300 SE 147TH AV, HAPPY VALLEY OR
SEA LION CAVES — 209 - A7
OFF OREGON COAST HWY, LANE CO OR
SEASIDE AQUARIUM — 301 - F8
N PROM & 2ND AV, SEASIDE OR
SEATTLE BIRTHPLACE MONUMENT — 280 - B2
ALKI AV SW & 63RD AV SW, SEATTLE WA
SEATTLE CENTER — 277 - H4
W THOMAS ST & 5TH AV N, SEATTLE WA
SEATTLE SEAHAWKS HQ — 175 - C1
NE 53RD ST & 112TH AV NE, KIRKLAND WA

FEATURE NAME City State	Page-Grid
SEATTLE YACHT CLUB	274 - C7
E SHELBY ST & W PARK DR, SEATTLE WA	
SEYMOUR BOTANICAL CONSERVATORY	293 - G4
316 S G ST, TACOMA WA	
SHELLFISH RESERVE	93 - A3
HAMMOND BAY RD, NANAIMO BC	
SHELTON TROUT HATCHERY	179 - D1
SATSOP-CLOQUALLUM RD, MASON CO WA	
SHERMAN CRATER	102 - C2
MOUNT BAKER, WHATCOM CO WA	
SILCOX WARMING HUT	202 - A5
MOUNT HOOD SOUTH, CLACKAMAS CO OR	
SIMPSON STATE SALMON HATCHERY	179 - B4
FISH HATCHERY RD, MASON CO WA	
SINCLAIR ISLAND LIGHT	160 - C3
CYPRESS ISLAND, SKAGIT CO WA	
SIX MILE SNOWPARK	143 - A1
PAULINA-EAST LAKE RD, DESCHUTES CO OR	
SKELETON CAVE	217 - D5
CHINA HAT RD, DESCHUTES CO OR	
SKIPANON WATERWAY LIGHTHOUSE	188 - B2
WARRENTON, WARRENTON OR	
SKUNK BAY LIGHT	170 - C3
HANSVILLE, KITSAP CO WA	
SKYLIGHT CAVE	211 - B4
OFF NFD RD 1028, DESCHUTES CO OR	
SLIP POINT LIGHTHOUSE	163 - B2
SLIP POINT, CLALLAM CO WA	
SMELTZER MILL	119 - A3
GULER MOUNTAIN, KLICKITAT CO WA	
SMITH ISLAND LIGHTHOUSE	167 - A2
SMITH ISLAND, ISLAND CO WA	
SMITH RIVER LIGHT	218 - D1
BUTLER CREEK RD, DOUGLAS CO OR	
SNOQUALMIE FALLS	176 - C4
6351 RAILROAD AV SE, SNOQUALMIE WA	
SNOWSHOE CAVE	155 - B1
OFF JUNIPER MOUNTAIN RD, OWYHEE CO ID	
SOL DUC SALMON HATCHERY	163 - A6
LAKE PLEASANT, CLALLAM CO WA	
SPEELYAI STATE HATCHERY	190 - A6
1101 LEWIS RIVER RD, COWLITZ CO WA	
SPLASHDOWN WATERSLIDE PARK	350 - F6
E MISSION AV&N BOWDISH RD, SPOKANE VLY WA	
SPOKANE STATE FISH HATCHERY	346 - D8
W HATCHERY RD, SPOKANE CO WA	
SPOKANE STATE GAME FARM	114 - B1
W STALEY RD, SPOKANE CO WA	
STALEYS JUNCTION	125 - B1
BUXTON, WASHINGTON CO OR	
STATE FISH HATCHERY	110 - C1
STEVENS PASS HWY, SNOHOMISH CO WA	
STATELINE WINDMILL	155 - B2
OFF STATE LINE RD, ELKO CO NV	
STRASSEL	125 - B1
BUXTON, WASHINGTON CO OR	
SUMMIT CRATER	102 - C2
MOUNT BAKER, WHATCOM CO WA	
SUPPAH WINDMILL	127 - A3
OFF HOT SPRINGS RD, WASCO CO OR	
SURVEYORS ICE CAVE	143 - A1
DEVILS HORN RD, DESCHUTES CO OR	
SWAMPY LAKES SNOWPARK	216 - D4
CENTURY DRIVE HWY, DESCHUTES CO OR	
SWAUK PASS SNO-PARK	238 - B6
BLEWETT PASS, KITTITAS CO WA	
SWEETWATER HATCHERY	123 - A3
ZAZA RD, NEZ PERCE CO ID	
TACOMA OUTBOARD ASSOCIATION	181 - C2
646 WILTON RD, TACOMA WA	
TACOMA YACHT CLUB	174 - D7
MANZANITA BEACH RD SW, KING CO WA	
TEN MILE SNOWPARK	143 - A1
PAULINA-EAST LAKE RD, DESCHUTES CO OR	
THOMAS CAIRN	134 - A1
OFF CAMP MORRISON DR, LINN CO OR	
THREEMILE LIGHT	214 - A7
SPARROW PARK RD, DOUGLAS CO OR	
THURMAN MILL	253 - B2
OFF E CHINDEN BLVD, ADA CO ID	
TILLUSQUA FISH HATCHERY	117 - A3
KNAPPA, CLATSOP CO WA	
TIRE TUBE CAVE	146 - B3
OFF IRON MOUNTAIN RD, MALHEUR CO OR	
TITLOW POOL	181 - C2
8355 6TH AV, TACOMA WA	
TONGUE POINT LIGHTHOUSE	188 - D1
ASTORIA, CLATSOP CO OR	
TOUCHET SNO-PARK	122 - B3
N FORK TOUCHET RIVER RD, COLUMBIA CO WA	
TRASK HOUSE	125 - A2
TRASK RIVER RD, TILLAMOOK CO OR	
TRASK RIVER REARING POND	125 - A2
SOUTH FORK RD, TILLAMOOK CO OR	
TRASK RIVER STATE FISH HATCHERY	197 - D2
CHANCE RD, TILLAMOOK CO OR	
TULANE FARMS	235 - B7
TOWNSHIP RD, KLAMATH CO OR	
TULE LAKE NATL WILDLIFE REFUGE	151 - A3
OFF HWY 139, SISKIYOU CO CA	
TURN POINT LIGHTHOUSE	101 - C2
STUART ISLAND, SAN JUAN CO WA	
TURN ROCK LIGHT	101 - C2
SHAW ISLAND, SAN JUAN CO WA	
TYEE YACHT CLUB	274 - B7
FAIRVIEW AV N, SEATTLE WA	
UMPQUA LIGHTHOUSE	218 - B2
SALMON HARBOR DR, DOUGLAS CO OR	
UNDERSEA GARDENS	206 - B4
250 SW BAY BLVD, NEWPORT OR	
UNDERSEA WORLD	148 - B3
304 HWY 101, CRESCENT CITY CA	
US DEPARTMENT OF ENERGY HANFORD SITE	340 - D3
BENTON CO WA	
UNITED STATES FISH HATCHERY	109 - C1
MOUNT WALKER, JEFFERSON CO WA	
UNIV OF IDAHO AGRICULTURE EXPERMNT STA	139 - A3
PARMA, CANYON CO ID	
UPPER PRIEST LAKE SCENIC AREA	107 - A1
OFF EAST SHORE RD, BONNER CO ID	
UPPER THREE CREEK SNO-PARK	211 - C7
THREE CREEKS LAKE RD, DESCHUTES CO OR	
VANCOUVER AQUARIUM	254 - F7
STANLEY PARK DR, VANCOUVER BC	
VANCOUVER HATCHERY	193 - A7
12208 SE EVERGREEN HWY, VANCOUVER WA	
VINCENT MASSEY AUDITORIUM	156 - D5
NEW WESTMINSTER BC	
VOLUNTEER PARK CONSERVATORY	278 - B2
1300 E PROSPECT ST, SEATTLE WA	
WALAN POINT LIGHTHOUSE	263 - H10
INDIAN ISLAND, JEFFERSON CO WA	
WALDO LAKE SNO-PARK	142 - B1
HWY 58, LANE CO OR	

FEATURE NAME City State	Page-Grid
WANOGA SNOWMOBILE SNOWPARK	216 - D4
CENTURY DRIVE HWY, DESCHUTES CO OR	
WASCO LIGHT	195 - D5
COLUMBIA RIVER HWY, HOOD RIVER CO OR	
WASHINGTON PARK ARBORETUM	278 - E1
2300 ARBORETUM DR E, SEATTLE WA	
WASHOUGAL STATE SALMON HATCHERY	194 - A6
WASHOUGAL RIVER RD, SKAMANIA CO WA	
WASP PASSAGE LIGHT	101 - C2
SHAW ISLAND, SAN JUAN CO WA	
WAX WORKS, THE	206 - B4
250 SW BAY BLVD, NEWPORT OR	
WEATHERFORD HIST MONUMENT	128 - A1
JOHN DAY & CEDAR SPRINGS, GILLIAM CO OR	
WEST LIGHT	188 - D1
CATHLAMET BAY, CLATSOP CO OR	
WEST POINT LIGHTHOUSE	272 - A5
SEATTLE WA	
WHEATLAND FERRY	204 - D3
SE WHEATLAND RD, YAMHILL CO OR	
WHITE BIRD BATTLEFIELD	131 - C1
US 95 NORTH OF COPPERVILLE, IDAHO CO ID	
WHITE POINT LIGHT	174 - D1
SEATTLE WA	
WILBURTON HILL BOTANICAL GARDENS	175 - C2
MAIN ST & 124TH AV NE, BELLEVUE WA	
WILLAMETTE FISH HATCHERY	142 - A1
OAKRIDGE, LANE CO OR	
WILLARD NATL FISH HATCHERY	195 - B4
WILLARD RD, SKAMANIA CO WA	
WILSON CAVE	217 - D2
NELSON RD & DICKEY RD, DESCHUTES CO OR	
WINTHROP NATL FISH HATCHERY	104 - A2
OFF HWY 20, OKANOGAN CO WA	
WIZARD FALLS STATE FISH HATCHERY	134 - C1
METOLIUS RIVER RD, JEFFERSON CO OR	
WOODLAND PARK ZOO	273 - H4
5500 PHINNEY AV N, SEATTLE WA	
WOOTEN STATE FISH HATCHERY	122 - B2
TUCANNON RD, COLUMBIA CO WA	
WORLD FORESTRY CENTER	312 - B7
4033 SW CANYON RD, PORTLAND OR	
WORLD TRADE CENTER	313 - F6
SW SALMON ST & SW 1ST AV, PORTLAND OR	
WRIGHT, DEE OBSERVATORY	211 - A5
MCKENZIE HWY, DESCHUTES CO OR	
YAKAMA INDIAN RESV HEADQUARTERS	120 - A2
TOPPENISH, YAKIMA CO WA	
YAQUINA BAY LIGHTHOUSE	206 - A4
GOVERNMENT ST, NEWPORT OR	
YMCA	317 - E1
SW TERWILLIGER BL, PORTLAND OR	
YOUNGS BAY ENTRANCE LIGHT	188 - C1
WARRENTON, ASTORIA OR	
YOUTH SERVICE CENTER	278 - B6
13TH AV & E REMINGTON CT, SEATTLE WA	
YREKA WESTERN RAILROAD	150 - A3
YREKA-AGER RD & HWY 3, SISKIYOU CO CA	
YWCA	312 - E6
1111 SW 10TH AV, PORTLAND OR	
ZOO BOISE	253 - C3
355 JULIA DAVIS DR, BOISE ID	

POINTS OF INTEREST - HISTORIC

FEATURE NAME City State	Page-Grid
ABERT RIM HIST MARKER	152 - A1
LAKEVIEW-BURNS HWY, LAKE CO OR	
ADAIR AIR FORCE STA (HIST)	207 - B4
RYALS AV, ADAIR VILLAGE OR	
ANNE HATHAWAYS COTTAGE	256 - D9
429 LAMPSON ST, TOWN OF ESQUIMALT BC	
APPLEGATE, JESSIE HIST MARKER	219 - B3
DRAIN-YONCALLA HWY&BOSWELL, DOUGLAS CO OR	
ASHFORD MANSION	118 - B1
MT TACOMA CYN RD, PIERCE CO WA	
BEELMAN HOUSE	234 - A1
STAGE RD S, JACKSON CO OR	
BOATMAN-AINSWORTH HOUSE	181 - C4
6000 112TH ST SW, LAKEWOOD WA	
BROTHER JONATHAN CEM	148 - B3
PEBBLE BCH DR & 9TH ST, CRESCENT CITY CA	
BYBEE HOUSE	192 - B6
NW HOWELL PARK RD, MULTNOMAH CO OR	
CASTLE ROCK EXHIBIT HALL	187 - C7
147 FRONT AV NW, CASTLE ROCK WA	
COLUMBIA RIVER EXHIBITION	341 - G2
95 LEE BLVD, RICHLAND WA	
CORNWALL HIST MARKER	219 - A7
PACIFIC HWY & GREEN VALLEY RD, DOUGLAS CO	
COVINGTON HOUSE	305 - G1
4201 MAIN ST, VANCOUVER WA	
COX-WILLIAMS HOUSE	192 - B1
280 S 1ST ST, SAINT HELENS OR	
CRAIGDARROCH CASTLE	256 - J9
1050 JOAN CRESCNT ST, CITY OF VICTORIA BC	
CREEK STATE HIST MONUMENT	146 - B3
IDAHO-OREGON-NEVADA HWY, MALHEUR CO OR	
DEEPWOOD ESTATE	322 - J14
111 MISSION ST SE, SALEM OR	
DENNY CREEK HIST MONUMENT	231 - C7
EAGLE RIDGE RD, KLAMATH CO OR	
DORRIS RANCH LIVING HIST FARM	330 - H9
HARBOR DR, LANE CO OR	
ENCHANTED FOREST	325 - B13
8462 ENCHANTED WY, MARION CO OR	
END OF THE OREGON TRAIL INTERP CTR	199 - D4
1726 WASHINGTON ST, OREGON CITY OR	
FLETT HOUSE	181 - C3
7704 BRIDGEPORT WY W, LAKEWOOD WA	
FORT ASTORIA	300 - D5
15TH ST & EXCHANGE ST, ASTORIA OR	
FORT HARNEY HIST MONUMENT	145 - B1
CENTRAL OREGON HWY, HARNEY CO OR	
FORT LAMERICK (HIST)	140 - C3
KELSEY PEAK, CURRY CO OR	
FORT RODD HILL NATL HIST SITE	159 - B6
HWY 1A, CITY OF COLWOOD BC	
FORT SPOKANE	113 - C1
OFF HWY 25, LINCOLN CO WA	
FORT VANCOUVER NATL HIST SITE	305 - H5
612 E RESERVE ST, VANCOUVER WA	
GLENCOVE HOTEL	174 - A7
VAUGHN-GLENCOVE RD KPN, PIERCE CO WA	
GRAYS HARBOR HIST SEAPORT	178 - B7
813 E HERON ST, ABERDEEN WA	
GREAT BASIN HIST MARKER	145 - C1
CENTRAL OREGON HWY, HARNEY CO OR	
GULF OF GEORGIA CANNERY NATL HIST	156 - A7
12138 4TH AVE, CITY OF RICHMOND BC	
HARLOW HOUSE	200 - B1
726 E HISTORIC COLUMBIA RIV, TROUTDALE OR	
HELLS GATE	95 - A2
HWY 1, BRITISH COLUMBIA BC	
HELMCKEN HOUSE	256 - G10
BELLEVILLE ST & GOV ST, VICTORIA BC	

FEATURE NAME City State	Page-Grid
HIST FLIPPIN CASTLE	117 - B3
620 TICHENOR ST, CLATSKANIE OR	
HIST CENTER	336 - D12
106 S CENTRAL AV, MEDFORD OR	
HOQUIAMS CASTLE	178 - A7
515 CHENAULT AV, HOQUIAM WA	
HOUSE OF MYRTLEWOOD	333 - H12
KRUSE AV & BROADWAY ST, COOS BAY OR	
INDIAN CEREMONIAL GROUND	129 - C1
MISSION, UMATILLA CO OR	
KELLER HISTORIC PARK	106 - A2
700 N WYNNE ST, COLVILLE WA	
KELSO VOLCANO TOURIST INFO	303 - E6
105 MINOR RD, KELSO WA	
KILBY HIST STORE AND FARM	94 - C3
215 KILBY RD, DISTRICT OF KENT BC	
LAKEWOLD GARDENS	181 - C4
12317 GRAVELLY LAKE DR SW, LAKEWOOD WA	
LATIMIER QUILT AND TEXTILE CTR	197 - C2
2105 WILSON RIVER LP, TILLAMOOK CO OR	
MARITIME HERITAGE CENTER	258 - C6
1600 C ST, BELLINGHAM WA	
MCCONNELL MANSION	249 - C5
110 S ADAMS ST, MOSCOW ID	
MCLOUGHLIN HOUSE	199 - D4
713 CENTER ST, OREGON CITY OR	
MEEKER MANSION	182 - B3
321 E PIONEER AV, PUYALLUP WA	
MOUNT SAINT HELENS CINEDOME	187 - C7
1239 MOUNT SAINT HELENS WY, COWLITZ CO WA	
MUNICIPAL ELEVATOR	199 - D4
7TH ST, OREGON CITY OR	
NATL HIST OREGON TRAIL INTERPRE	138 - B1
BAKER-COPPERFIELD HWY, BAKER CO OR	
NEW MARKET VILLAGE	313 - F5
120 SW ANKENY ST, PORTLAND OR	
OASIS WATERWORKS	342 - D8
6321 W CANAL DR, KENNEWICK WA	
OLD CHURCH, THE	312 - E6
1422 SW 11TH AV, PORTLAND OR	
OLD HUMBOLT DIGGINGS	137 - B2
JOHN DAY-BURNS HWY, CANYON CITY OR	
OLD INDIAN VILLAGE AT PEBBLE BEACH	148 - B3
PACIFIC AV&PEBBLE BCH DR, DL NORTE CO CA	
OLD PONY EXPRESS STA (RUINS)	154 - A2
WHITEHORSE RANCH RD, HARNEY CO OR	
OLD SAINT PETERS LANDMARK	196 - C7
4TH ST & LIBERTY ST, THE DALLES OR	
OLD SCOTCH CHURCH	125 - C1
30685 NW SCOTCH CHURCH RD, WSHNGTN CO OR	
OREGON CAVES NATL MONUMENT	233 - D5
OREGON CAVES HWY, JOSEPHINE CO OR	
OWENS MEM ROSE GARDEN	329 - J5
N JEFFERSON ST, EUGENE OR	
PKERSVILLE NATL HIST PARK	193 - B7
24 A ST, WASHOUGAL WA	
PERCIVAL LANDING PARK	296 - H4
WATER ST & 5TH AV, OLYMPIA WA	
PERKINS HOUSE NATL HIST PLACE	122 - C1
OFF HWY 26, COLFAX WA	
PIONEER COURT HOUSE	313 - F6
555 SW YAMHILL ST, PORTLAND OR	
PITTOCK HOUSE	193 - B6
114 NE LEADBETTER RD, CLARK CO WA	
POINT ELLICE HOUSE	256 - F7
2616 PLEASANT ST, CITY OF VICTORIA BC	
PORTLAND MAIN	313 - E4
NW LOVEJOY ST & NW BROADWAY, PORTLAND OR	
POWELL RIVER HIST MUSEUM	92 - B1
HWY 101, BRITISH COLUMBIA BC	
PRAIRIE DIGGINGS	137 - B2
CANYON CITY EAST RD, GRANT CO OR	
PYRAMID BREWERIES INC	189 - D6
110 W MARINE DR, KALAMA WA	
RED HOOK BREWERY	171 - D7
14300 NE 145TH ST, WOODINVILLE WA	
SAINT ROCH NATL HIST SITE	254 - E11
CHESTNUT ST, VANCOUVER BC	
SANDERS HOME	181 - D5
524 160TH ST E, PIERCE CO WA	
SEN, DR SUN CLASSICAL CHINESE GARDENS	254 - H10
578 CARRAL ST, VANCOUVER BC	
SILVER MOUNTAIN GONDOLA	115 - C2
610 BUNKER AV, KELLOGG ID	
SOAMES, NEELY HIST HOUSE	175 - B7
RUSSELL RD & S 237TH PL, KENT WA	
SPACE NEEDLE	277 - H4
5TH AV N & THOMAS ST, SEATTLE WA	
SS EMIDIO	148 - B3
FRONT ST & H ST, CRESCENT CITY CA	
THOMPSON, DAVID HIST MONUMENT	244 - D2
HWY 200, EAST HOPE ID	
THORNEWOOD MANOR HOUSE	181 - C5
8601 N THORNE LN, LAKEWOOD WA	
TREATY ROCK HIST SITE	353 - F6
POST FALLS ID	
UMPQUA DISCOVER CENTER	218 - D1
409 RIVERFRONT WY, REEDSPORT OR	
WHITMAN MISSION NATL HIST SITE	121 - C3
US HWY 12, WALLA WALLA WA	
WINTERS HOUSE	175 - C3
2102 BELLEVUE WY SE, BELLEVUE WA	
WOOLREY-KOEHLER HOP KILN	182 - B5
176TH ST E, PIERCE CO WA	
WORLD CENTER FOR BIRDS OF PREY	253 - C4
5666 W FLYING HAWK LN, ADA CO ID	
YOMAN FERRY LANDING	181 - B4
YOMAN RD & VILLA BEACH RD, PIERCE CO WA	
YREKA NATL HIST DIST	149 - C3
910 S MAIN ST, SISKIYOU CO CA	

SHOPPING - REGIONAL

FEATURE NAME City State	Page-Grid
ALDERWOOD MALL	171 - B5
184TH ST SW & 33RD AV W, LYNNWOOD WA	
BEAVERTON MALL	199 - B2
3205 SW CEDAR HILLS BLVD, BEAVERTON OR	
BELLEVUE SQUARE	175 - C2
NE 8TH ST & BELLEVUE WY, BELLEVUE WA	
BELLIS FAIR MALL	258 - C1
1 BELLIS FAIR PKWY, BELLINGHAM WA	
BLUE MOUNTAIN MALL	344 - H9
1631 W ROSE ST, WALLA WALLA WA	
CAPITAL MALL	296 - E5
BLACK LAKE BL & CAPITAL MALL, OLYMPIA WA	
CASCADE MALL	260 - C6
201 CASCADE MALL DR, BURLINGTON WA	
CLACKAMAS PROMENADE	199 - D3
8974 SE SUNNYSIDE RD, CLACKAMAS CO OR	
CLACKAMAS TOWN CENTER	199 - D3
I-205 & SE SUNNYSIDE RD, CLACKAMAS CO OR	
CROSSROADS	175 - D2
156TH AV NE & NE 8TH ST, BELLEVUE WA	
EVERETT MALL	268 - D6
1402 SE EVERETT MALL WY, EVERETT WA	

FEATURE NAME City State	Page-Grid
FACTORIA MALL 4092 FACTORIA BLVD SE, BELLEVUE WA	175 - C3
FOREST GROVE CTR 2333 PACIFIC AV, FOREST GROVE OR	198 - B1
FRANKLIN PARK MALL DIVISION ST & CENTRAL AV, SPOKANE WA	349 - A2
GATEWAY MALL 3000 GATEWAY ST, SPRINGFIELD OR	330 - F3
GRESHAM TOWN FAIR 400 NW EASTMAN PKWY, GRESHAM OR	200 - B2
HERITAGE MALL 1895 14TH AV, ALBANY OR	326 - E9
JANTZEN BEACH CTR 1700 JANTZEN BEACH CTR, PORTLAND OR	305 - E7
LAKEWOOD TOWNE CTR 10509 GRAVELLY LAKE DR SW, LAKEWOOD WA	181 - C4
LLOYD CTR 825 LLOYD CTR, PORTLAND OR	313 - H4
MALL 205 9900 SE WASHINGTON ST, PORTLAND OR	315 - H7
MARYSVILLE TOWN CTR MALL 4TH ST & STATE AV, MARYSVILLE WA	171 - C1
NORTHGATE MALL NE NORTHGATE WY & 1ST AV NE, SEATTLE WA	171 - B7
NORTHTOWN MALL DIVISION ST & WELLESLEY AV, SPOKANE WA	349 - A3
OREGON CITY SHOPPING CTR 1900 MCLOUGHLIN BLVD, OREGON CITY OR	199 - D4
OVERLAKE FASHION PLAZA 148TH AV NE & NE 24TH ST, REDMOND WA	175 - D2
ROGUE VALLEY MALL 1600 N RIVERSIDE AV, MEDFORD OR	336 - C10
SEATAC MALL S 320TH ST & PACIFIC HWY, FEDERAL WAY WA	182 - B1
SOUTHCENTER MALL TUKWILA PWY & SOUTHCENTER PKWY, TUKWILA WA	289 - G5
SOUTH HILL MALL 9TH ST SW & 39TH AV SW, PUYALLUP WA	182 - B4
SOUTH SOUND CTR SLEATER-KINNEY RD & PACIFIC AV, LACEY WA	297 - E5
SPOKANE VALLEY MALL I-90 & SULLIVAN RD, SPOKANE VALLEY WA	351 - B6
SUNSET ESPLANADE, THE 2525 SE TUALATIN VALLEY HWY, HILLSBORO OR	198 - D1
TACOMA MALL 4502 S STEELE ST, TACOMA WA	294 - D3
THREE RIVERS MALL 351 THREE RIVERS DR, KELSO WA	303 - D9
UNIVERSITY CITY SHOPPING CTR SPRAGUE AV & UNVRSTY RD, SPOKANE VLY WA	350 - F9
VALLEY RIVER CTR 293 VALLEY RIVER CENTER, EUGENE OR	329 - H3
WASHINGTON SQUARE 9585 SW WASHINGTON SQUARE RD, TIGARD OR	199 - B3
WESTFIELD SHOPPINGTOWN 8700 NE VANCOUVER MALL DR, VANCOUVER WA	307 - F1
WESTWOOD TOWN CTR SW BARTON ST & 25TH AV SW, SEATTLE WA	285 - F3

SKI AREAS

ALPENTAL SKI AREA SNOQUALMIE PSS/STAMPEDE PSS, KING CO WA	111 - A2
BACHELOR SKI LIFT OFF CENTURY DRIVE HWY, DESCHUTES CO OR	216 - B4
BLUEWOOD SKI AREA N FORK TOUCHET RIVER RD, COLUMBIA CO WA	122 - B3
BROOKS MEM STATE PK SKI AREA FORT SIMCO RD, KLICKITAT CO WA	119 - C3
BRUNDAGE SKI AREA BRUNDAGE RD, ADAMS CO ID	251 - B5
COOPER SPUR SKI AREA DOG RIVER, HOOD RIVER CO OR	202 - C4
CRATER LAKE SKI BOWL MAKLAKS CRATER, DOUGLAS CO OR	141 - B3
CRYSTAL MOUNTAIN SKI RESORT 33914 CRYSTAL MOUNTAIN BLVD, PIERCE CO WA	119 - A1
DIXIE SKI BOWL JOHN DAY HWY, GRANT CO OR	137 - C1
ECHO VALLEY SKI AREA COOPER MOUNTAIN RD, CHELAN CO WA	236 - C1
ENTIAT VALLEY SKI AREA ENTIAT RIVER RD, CHELAN CO WA	112 - A1
FORTY NINE DEGREES NORTH SKI AREA GODDARDS PEAK, STEVENS CO WA	106 - B3
HEMLOCK SKI AREA MORRIS VALLEY RD, BRITISH COLUMBIA BC	94 - C3
HITT MOUNTAIN SKI AREA COW CAMP RD, WASHINGTON CO ID	139 - A1
HOODOO SKI BOWL SNO-PARK OFF SANTIAM HWY, LINN CO OR	134 - C2
HURRICANE RIDGE SKI LODGE HEART OF THE HILLS RD, CLALLAM CO WA	109 - B1
LOUP LOUP SKI AREA HWY 20, OKANOGAN CO WA	104 - B3
MISSION RIDGE WINTER SPORTS AREA OFF NFD RD 9712, CHELAN CO WA	238 - D7
MOUNT ASHLAND SKI AREA MT ASHLAND SKI RD, JACKSON CO OR	234 - C6
MOUNT BAKER SKI AREA HIGHWAY 542, WHATCOM CO WA	103 - A1
MOUNT HOOD MEADOW SKI AREA MOUNT HOOD HWY, HOOD RIVER CO OR	202 - B5
PAYETTE LAKES SKI AREA HWY 55 & ECKS FLAT RD, ADAMS CO ID	251 - B5
PHOENIX SKI HILL OFF HWY 3, BRITISH COLUMBIA BC	105 - B1
PINE STREET SKI AREA OFF BALDY MOUNTAIN RD, BONNER CO ID	107 - A3
POMA SKI TOW OFF CENTURY DRIVE HWY, DESCHUTES CO OR	216 - B4
RED MOUNTAIN SKI AREA HWY 3, BRITISH COLUMBIA BC	106 - A1
SCHWEITZER BASIN SKI AREA OFF HWY 2, BONNER CO ID	107 - A2
SILVERHORN SKI AREA MASONIA, SHOSHONE CO ID	115 - C2
SKI BOWL MULTORPOR WINTER SPORTS AREA MOUNT HOOD HWY, CLACKAMAS CO OR	202 - A6
SNOW HAVEN SKI AREA OFF HWY 13, IDAHO CO ID	123 - C3
SPOUT SPRINGS SKI AREA WESTON-ELGIN HWY, UNION CO OR	130 - A1
STARR BOWL WINTER SPORTS AREA JOHN DAY-BURNS HWY, GRANT CO OR	137 - A2
STEVENS PASS SKI AREA HIGHWAY 2, KING CO WA	111 - B1
SUMMIT CENTRAL SKI AREA SNOQUALMIE PASS, KITTITAS CO WA	111 - A2
SUMMIT EAST SKI AREA SNOQUALMIE PASS, KITTITAS CO WA	111 - A2
SUMMIT WEST SKI AREA SNOQUALMIE PASS, KITTITAS CO WA	111 - A2
TAMARACK SKI AREA OFF HWY 8, LATAH CO ID	123 - A1

FEATURE NAME City State	Page-Grid
TOMAHAWK SKI BOWL LAKE OF THE WOODS HWY, KLAMATH CO OR	231 - A6
WARNER CANYON SKI AREA WARNER HWY, LAKE CO OR	152 - A2
WHITE PASS SKI AREA WHITE PASS, LEWIS CO WA	119 - A2
WHITE PASS X COUNTRY SKI AREA WHITE PASS, YAKIMA CO WA	119 - A2
WILLAMETTE PASS SKI AREA HWY 58, KLAMATH CO OR	142 - B1
WOOD MOUNTAIN SKI PK HWY 19, BRITISH COLUMBIA BC	92 - A2

TRANSPORTATION

ALBINA/MISSISSIPPI MAX STA N ALBINA AV & N INTRSTATE AV, PORTLAND OR	313 - F3
AMTRAK KING ST STA 303 S JACKSON ST, SEATTLE WA	278 - A7
AMTRAK STA 211 RAILROAD AV S, EDMONDS WA	171 - A5
AMTRAK STA SPOKANE WA	349 - A9
AMTRAK STA W 11TH ST & HILL ST, VANCOUVER WA	305 - E5
AMTRAK TACOMA STA 1001 PUYALLUP AV, TACOMA WA	293 - J7
ANTOINE PLANTE FERRY SITE E WELLESLEY AV, SPOKANE CO WA	350 - H3
BARBUR BLVD TRANSIT CTR 9750 SW BARBUR, PORTLAND OR	320 - A1
BEAVERTON CENTRAL MAX STA SW CEDAR HILLS BLVD, BEAVERTON OR	199 - B2
BEAVERTON CREEK MAX STA SW 153RD DR, BEAVERTON OR	199 - A2
BEAVERTON TRANSIT CTR & MAX STA SW LOMBARD AV & CANYON RD, BEAVERTON OR	199 - B2
BERNARD FERRY GIVENS HOT SPRINGS, CANYON CO ID	147 - B1
BNSF BOND ST, EVERETT WA	264 - C4
CASCADES MAX STA NE CASCADES PY & NE MT ST HE, PORTLAND OR	311 - J6
CLACKAMAS TOWN CTR TRANSIT CENTER SE MONTEREY AV, CLACKAMAS CO OR	199 - D3
CLARKS FERRY CASTLE BUTTE, OWYHEE CO ID	147 - C2
CLEVELAND AV MAX STA NE 8TH ST & NE CLEVELAND AV, GRESHAM OR	200 - B2
CONV CTR MAX STA NE HOLLADAY ST & M L KING BL, PORTLAND OR	313 - G4
CONV PLACE STA PINE ST & 9TH AV, SEATTLE WA	278 - A5
DELTA PARK/VANPORT TC MAX STA N VICTORY BLVD & N EXPO RD, PORTLAND OR	309 - E2
EDMONDS FERRY TERMINAL MAIN ST & RAILROAD AV N, EDMONDS WA	171 - A5
ELMONICA MAX STA SW 170TH AV&SW BASELINE RD, WSHNGTN CO OR	199 - A1
EVERETT AMTRAK STA 3201 SMITH AV, EVERETT WA	265 - E4
EXPO CTR MAX STA N MARINE DR & N EXPO RD, PORTLAND OR	309 - E1
FAIR COMPLEX/HILLSBORO STA NW 34TH AV, HILLSBORO OR	198 - D1
FAUNTLEROY FERRY TERMINAL FAUNTLEROY WY SW, SEATTLE WA	284 - C3
GALLERIA MAX STA SW 10TH AV & MORRISON ST, PORTLAND OR	313 - E6
GATEWAY TRANSIT CTR & MAX STA NE PACIFIC ST & NE 99TH AV, PORTLAND OR	315 - H5
GOOSE HOLLOW MAX STA SW JEFFERSON ST & SW 20TH AV, PORTLAND OR	312 - D6
GRESHAM MAX STA NW EASTMAN PKWY, GRESHAM OR	200 - B2
GRESHAM TRANSIT CTR & MAX STA NE KELLY AV & NE 8TH ST, GRESHAM OR	200 - B2
HATFIELD/GOVERNMENT CTR STA W MAIN ST & SW ADAMS AV, HILLSBORO OR	198 - D1
HAWTHORN FARM MAX STA NE ELAM YOUNG PKWY, HILLSBORO OR	198 - D1
HILLSBORO CENTRAL TRANSIT CTR SE WASHINGTN ST & SE 3RD AV, HILLSBORO OR	198 - D1
HOLLYWOOD TRANSIT CTR & MAX STA NE HALSEY ST & NE 39TH AV, PORTLAND OR	314 - B4
INTL DIST STA 4TH AV S & 2ND AV EXT S, SEATTLE WA	278 - A7
INTERSTATE/ROSE GARDEN MAX STA N INTRSTATE AV & NE MULTNMAH, PORTLAND OR	313 - G4
KENTON/N DENVER AV MAX STA N DENVER AV & N WILLIS BLVD, PORTLAND OR	309 - E4
KETRON ISLAND FERRY TERMINAL MORRIS BLVD, PIERCE CO WA	181 - B4
KINGS HILL MAX STA SW 18TH AV&SW SALMON ST, PORTLAND OR	312 - D6
LLOYD CTR MAX STA NE 11TH AV & NE HOLLADAY ST, PORTLAND OR	313 - H4
LYONS FERRY HWY 261, FRANKLIN CO WA	121 - C2
MALL MONORAIL TERMINAL 4TH AV & PINE ST, SEATTLE WA	277 - J5
MAX PARKROSE/SUMNER STA NE 95TH AV & NE SANDY BLVD, PORTLAND OR	315 - H1
MAX STA NE 102ND AV & E BURNSIDE ST, PORTLAND OR	315 - H6
MAX STA NE 122ND AV & E BURNSIDE ST, PORTLAND OR	200 - A1
MAX STA NE 148TH AV & E BURNSIDE ST, PORTLAND OR	200 - A1
MAX STA NE 162ND AV & SE BURNSIDE ST, GRESHAM OR	200 - A1
MAX STA NE 172ND AV & SE BURNSIDE ST, GRESHAM OR	200 - A1
MAX STA NE 181ST AV & SE BURNSIDE ST, GRESHAM OR	200 - A1
MAX STA NE 60TH AV, PORTLAND OR	314 - D5
MAX STA NE 7TH AV & NE HOLLADAY ST, PORTLAND OR	313 - H4
MAX STA NE 82ND AV & NE HALSEY ST, PORTLAND OR	315 - F4
MAX STA SW 1ST AV & SW OAK ST, PORTLAND OR	313 - F6
MAX STA SW 3RD AV & SW MORRISON ST, PORTLAND OR	313 - F6
MAX STA SW 4TH ST & SW YAMHILL ST, PORTLAND OR	313 - F6
MAX STA SW 5TH AV & SW MORRISON ST, PORTLAND OR	313 - F6
MERLO ROAD MAX STA SW MERLO RD & SW 158TH AV, BEAVERTON OR	199 - A1
MILLIKAN WAY MAX STA SW MILLIKAN WY & SW 141ST AV, WASH CO OR	199 - B2
MILWAUKIE TRANSIT CTR SE MAIN ST & SE JACKSON ST, MILWAUKIE OR	321 - J2

FEATURE NAME City State	Page-Grid
MOUNT HOOD AV MAX STA NE CASCADE PKWY, PORTLAND OR	311 - H5
MUKILTEO FERRY TERMINAL MUKILTEO SPEEDWAY, MUKILTEO WA	171 - B2
OLD TOWN/ CHINATOWN MAX STA NW 1ST AV & NW DAVIS ST, PORTLAND OR	313 - F5
OREGON CITY TRANSIT CTR MAIN ST & 12TH ST, OREGON CITY OR	199 - D4
ORENCO MAX STA NW 231ST AV & NE CAMPUS CT, HILLSBORO OR	199 - A1
OVERLOOK MAX STA N OVERLOOK BLVD & N INTERSTATE, PORTLAND	313 - E2
PGE PK MAX STA SW 18TH AV & SW MORRISON ST, PORTLAND OR	312 - D5
PIER 48 FERRY TERMINAL ALASKAN WY S, SEATTLE WA	277 - J7
PIONEER SQUARE MAX STA NORTH SW MORRISON ST & SW 6TH ST, PORTLAND OR	313 - F6
PIONEER SQUARE MAX STA SOUTH SW YAMHILL ST & SW 6TH ST, PORTLAND OR	313 - E6
PIONEER SQUARE STA JAMES ST & 3RD AV, SEATTLE WA	278 - A6
POINT DEFIANCE FERRY TERMINAL ROUTE 163 & N WATERFRONT DR, TACOMA WA	181 - D1
POLK STA DALLAS, POLK CO OR	204 - A5
PORTLAND INTL MAX STA NE AIRPORT WY, PORTLAND OR	311 - E4
QUATAMA MAX STA NW QUATAMA RD & NW 206TH AV, HILLSBORO OR	199 - A1
QUINTON RAILWAY STA QUINTON, GILLIAM CO OR	127 - C1
QUINTON RAILWAY STA 2ND ST & N OLYMPIC AV, ARLINGTON WA	168 - D5
RAILROAD STA 2ND ST & N OLYMPIC AV, ARLINGTON WA	95 - C3
RAILWAY STA HWY 3, BRITISH COLUMBIA BC	93 - C2
RAILWAY STA TRANS CANADA HWY, BRITISH COLUMBIA BC	200 - A1
ROCKWOOD TRANSIT CTR & MAX STA NE 188TH ST & SE BURNSIDE ST, GRESHAM OR	313 - G4
ROSE QUARTER CTR & MAX STA NE WHEELER AV & MULTNOMAH ST, PORTLAND OR	200 - A1
RUBY JUNCTION MAX STA SE 197TH AV & SE BURNSIDE ST, GRESHAM OR	205 - A2
SAINT LOUIS STA GERVAIS, MARION CO OR	313 - F5
SKIDMORE FOUNTAIN MAX STA N BURNSIDE ST & SW 1ST AV, PORTLAND OR	289 - J5
SOUNDER & AMTRAK CASCADES STA S LONGACRES WY & JACKSON SW, TUKWILA WA	182 - B1
SOUNDER AUBURN STA 23 A ST SW, AUBURN WA	175 - B7
SOUNDER KENT STA 301 RAILROAD AV N, KENT WA	278 - A7
SOUNDER KING ST STA 301 S JACKSON ST, SEATTLE WA	182 - B3
SOUNDER PUYALLUP STA 131 W MAIN AV, PUYALLUP WA	182 - B3
SOUNDER SUMNER STA 810 MAPLE ST, SUMNER WA	293 - J7
SOUNDER TACOMA DOME STA E 25TH ST & E D ST, TACOMA WA	174 - D4
SOUTHWORTH FERRY TERMINAL RTE 160, KITSAP CO WA	259 - B3
STATE FERRY TERMINAL OAKES AV, ANACORTES WA	181 - B4
STEILACOOM FERRY TERMINAL UNION AV & COMMERCIAL ST, STEILACOOM WA	199 - B1
SUNSET TRANSIT CTR AND MAX STA SW BARNES RD & HWY 217, WASHINGTON CO OR	293 - H5
TACOMA STREETCAR S 9TH ST & COMMERCE ST, TACOMA WA	293 - H6
TACOMA STREETCAR S 15TH ST & COMMERCE ST, TACOMA WA	293 - H6
TACOMA STREETCAR S 19TH ST & PACIFIC AV, TACOMA WA	293 - H7
TACOMA STREETCAR S 25TH ST & PACIFIC AV, TACOMA WA	181 - D1
TAHLEQUAH FERRY TERMINAL VASHON HWY SW & TAHLEQUAH RD, KING CO WA	199 - B3
TIGARD TRANSIT CTR SW MAIN ST & SW COMMERCIAL ST, TIGARD OR	293 - H5
TRANSIT CTR 930 COMMERCE ST, TACOMA WA	198 - D1
TUALITY HOSPITAL MAX STA SE WASHINGTON ST&SE 8TH AV, HILLSBORO OR	289 - J5
TUKWILA STA S LONGACRES WY & JACKSON SW, RENTON WA	313 - F5
UNION STA 800 NW 6TH AV, PORTLAND OR	278 - A6
UNIV STREET STA UNIVERSITY ST & 3RD AV, SEATTLE WA	174 - D4
VASHON FERRY TERMINAL VASHON HWY SW & 103RD AV SW, KING CO WA	147 - B1
WARM SPRINGS FERRY GIVENS HOT SPRINGS, OWYHEE CO ID	198 - D1
WASHINGTON MAX STA SE WSHNGTN ST & SE 12TH AV, HILLSBORO OR	312 - B7
WASHINGTON PK MAX STA SW KNIGHT BLVD, PORTLAND OR	277 - J6
WASHINGTON STATE PIER 52 FERRY TERMINAL 801 ALASKAN WY, SEATTLE WA	263 - H5
WATER ST FERRY DOCK HARRISON ST & WATER ST, PORT TOWNSEND WA	278 - A5
WESTLAKE STA 5TH & PINE ST, SEATTLE WA	199 - A1
WILLOW CREEK MAX STA SW 185TH AV & SW SALIX TER, HILLSBORO OR	313 - F6
YAMHILL DIST MAX STA SW YAMHILL ST & SW 1ST ST, PORTLAND OR	

WINERIES

ALPINE VINEYARDS 25904 GREEN PEAK RD, BENTON CO OR	133 - A2
AMITY VINEYARDS 18150 AMITY VINEYRDS RD SE, YAMHILL CO OR	204 - B2
ARGYLE WINERY THE DUNDEE WINE COMPANY 691 HWY 99 W, DUNDEE OR	198 - C6
ASHLAND VINEYARDS 2775 E MAIN ST, JACKSON CO OR	337 - H8
AUTUMN WIND VINEYARD 15225 NE NORTH VALLEY RD, YAMHILL CO OR	198 - C4
BAINBRIDGE ISLAND VINEYARDS OFF FERNCLIFF AVE NE, WINSLOW WA	174 - D2
BETHEL HEIGHTS VINEYARD 6060 BETHEL HEIGHTS, POLK CO OR	204 - C3
BRIDGEVIEW VINEYARD 4210 HOLLAND LOOP RD, JOSEPHINE CO OR	233 - B4
CHAMPOEG WINE CELLARS 10375 CHAMPOEG RD, MARION CO OR	199 - A6
CHATEAU BENOIT 6580 MINERAL SPRINGS RD, YAMHILL CO OR	198 - B6
CHATEAU BIANCA 17485 WILLAMINA-SALEM HWY, POLK CO OR	204 - A5

FEATURE NAME City State	Page-Grid
CHATEAU STE MICHELLE 14111 NE 145TH ST, WOODINVILLE WA	171 - C7
COLUMBIA 14030 NE 145TH ST, WOODINVILLE WA	171 - C7
COOPER MOUNTAIN VINEYARDS 9480 SW GRABHORN RD, WASHINGTON CO OR	199 - A2
DUCK POND CELLARS 23145 HWY 99 W, YAMHILL CO OR	198 - C6
DUNDEE SPRINGS VINEYARD FOX FARM RD & HWY 99W, YAMHILL CO OR	198 - C6
E B FOOTE 127 SW 153RD ST, BURIEN WA	175 - A5
EDGEFIELD 2126 SW HALSEY ST, TROUTDALE OR	200 - B1
ELK COVE VINEYARDS 27751 NW OLSON RD, KALAMA WA	189 - D5
ELK COVE VINEYARDS 27751 NW OLSON RD, YAMHILL CO OR	198 - B3
ERATH VINEYARDS 9409 NE WORDEN HILL RD, YAMHILL CO OR	198 - C6
FORIS VINEYARD 654 KENDALL RD, JOSEPHINE CO OR	233 - C5
GEORGE , THE GRANT CO WA	112 - B3
GOLDEN VALLEY VINEYARDS 980 NE 4TH ST, MCMINNVILLE OR	198 - A7
HEDGES CELLARS 195 NE GILMAN BLVD, ISSAQUAH WA	176 - A4
HINZERLING 1520 SHERIDAN AV, PROSSER WA	120 - B3
HONEYWOOD 1350 HINES ST SE, SALEM OR	324 - J1
HOOD RIVER VINEYARDS 4693 WESTWOOD DR, HOOD RIVER CO OR	195 - C5
HOODSPORT 23501 US 101, MASON CO WA	173 - A6
KRAMER VINEYARD 26830 NW OLSON RD, YAMHILL CO OR	198 - B3
LANGE 18380 NE BUENA VISTA DR, YAMHILL CO OR	198 - C5
LAUREL RIDGE 13301 KUEHNE RD, YAMHILL CO OR	198 - C5
LAUREL RIDGE 46350 NW DAVID HILL RD, WASHINGTON CO OR	125 - B1
MANFRED VIERTHALER 17136 HWY 410 E, PIERCE CO WA	182 - C4
MARKET CELLAR 1432 WESTERN AV, SEATTLE WA	277 - J6
MARQUAM HILL VINEYARDS 35803 S 213 HWY, CLACKAMAS CO OR	126 - A3
MONTINORE VINEYARDS 3663 SW DILLEY RD, WASHINGTON CO OR	198 - B2
MOUNT BAKER VINEYARDS 4298 MOUNT BAKER HWY, WHATCOM CO WA	102 - B1
OAK KNOLL 29700 SW BURKHALTER RD, WASHINGTON CO OR	198 - D2
PONZI VINEYARDS 14665 SW WINERY LN, WASHINGTON CO OR	199 - A3
RESERVE VINEYARDS & GC, THE 4747 SW 229TH AV, WASHINGTON CO OR	198 - D2
REX HILL VINEYARDS 30835 HWY 99 W, YAMHILL CO OR	198 - D5
SAINT JOSEFS WINECELLAR 28836 BARLOW RD, CLACKAMAS CO OR	205 - C1
SAKE ONE CORPORATION 820 ELM ST, FOREST GROVE OR	198 - B1
SHAFER VINEYARD CELLARS 6200 NW GALES CK RD, WASHINGTON CO OR	125 - B1
SILVER LAKE 17616 15TH AV SE, SNOHOMISH CO WA	171 - C5
SILVER LAKE SPARKLING CELLARS 17721 132ND AV NE, WOODINVILLE WA	171 - C6
SISKIYOU VINEYARDS 6220 OREGON CAVES HWY, JOSEPHINE CO OR	233 - C4
SKY RIVER MEADERY 32533 CASCADE VIEW DR, SULTAN WA	110 - C1
SOKOL BLOSSER 5000 NE SOKOL BLOSSER LN, YAMHILL CO OR	198 - C6
STRINGERS ORCHARD HWY 395, MODOC CO CA	152 - A3
TUALATIN VINEYARDS 10850 NW SEAVEY RD, WASHINGTON CO OR	125 - B1
UMPQUA ESTATE HUBBARD CREEK RD, DOUGLAS CO OR	221 - A1
WASSON BROTHERS 41901 MOUNT HOOD HWY, SANDY OR	200 - D4
WEISINGERS WINERY AND TASTING ROOM 3150 SISKIYOU BLVD, ASHLAND OR	337 - E9

FEATURE NAME City State	Page-Grid

FEATURE NAME City State	Page-Grid

INDEX

RAND McNALLY

Thank you for purchasing this Rand McNally Street Guide!
Our goal is to provide you with the information you need.

Please complete the information below so we will be able to serve you better in the future. We value your comments and suggestions for improvements and feedback on corrections. This information can also be e-mailed to: **consumeraffairs@randmcnally.com.** *(This information is for internal use ONLY and will not be distributed or sold to any external third party.)*

Street Guide Title: Pacific Northwest
   Washington • Oregon • Western Idaho • Southwestern British Columbia

ISBN# 0-528-99511-1

2ND FOLD LINE

Today s Date: _____

1. Your Name: _____   Title: _____

2. Address   ☐ Business   ☐ Personal: _____

3. City/State/Zip: _____

4. Phone Number: _____   E-mail address: _____

5. Age Group: ☐ 18 – 24   ☐ 25-31   ☐ 32-40   ☐ 41- 50   ☐ 51+

6. Company name: _____

7. Type of business: _____

8. Where did you purchase this Street Guide? (store name & location) _____

9. How often do you purchase an updated Street Guide?   ☐ Annually   ☐ Every 2 Years   ☐ Other _____

10. How often do you use it?   ☐ Daily   ☐ Weekly   ☐ Monthly   ☐ Other _____

11. What do you use your Street Guide for?

   ☐ Find Address   ☐ Find Unincorporated Areas   ☐ Navigation   ☐ Identifying Routes   ☐ Other _____

12. Do you use it for: ☐ Business   ☐ Personal   ☐ Both

13. If you have used the Digital Edition software:

1st FOLD LINE

   What features do you use? _____

   How often do you use it?   ☐ Daily   ☐ Weekly   ☐ Monthly   ☐ Other _____

14. What information would you add/correct in this Street Guide to better meet your needs?

   Map Page # _____   Grid # _____   Index Page # _____

   ☐ Street Name Missing   ☐ Street Name Misspelled   ☐ Street Information Incorrect

   ☐ Incorrect Location for Point of Interest   ☐ Index Error   ☐ Other

   _____

   _____

15. Please provide any additional comments and suggestions you have: _____

   _____

   _____

16. Would you like to receive information about updated editions and special offers from Rand McNally?   ☐ Yes   ☐ No

SG-PTri

CUT ALONG DOTTED LINE

TAPE SHUT

🌐 RAND McNALLY

**You'll never need to ask for directions again with these
Rand McNally products!**

- EasyFinder® Laminated Maps
- Folded Maps
- Street Guides
- Road Atlas
- Motor Carriers' Road Atlas

get directions at
randmcnally.com